The Grants Register®

2003

Twenty First Edition

palgrave
macmillan

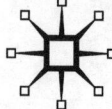
The editor of *The Grants Register* cannot undertake any correspondence in relation to grants listed in this volume.

Editor: Louise Baynes
Editorial assistants: Emma Wilkin, Sarah Maguire, Louise Bussey

This edition published 2002 by
PALGRAVE MACMILLAN
Houndmills, Basingstoke, Hampshire RG21 6XS and
175 Fifth Avenue, New York, N.Y. 10010
Companies and representatives throughout the world.

PALGRAVE MACMILLAN is the global academic imprint of the Palgrave Macmillan division of St. Martin's Press, LLC and of Palgrave Macmillan Ltd. Macmillan™ is a registered trademark in the United States, United Kingdom and other countries. Palgrave is a registered trademark in the European Union and other countries.

ISBN 0–333–96474–8
ISSN 0072–5471

This book is printed on paper suitable for recycling and made from fully managed and sustained forest sources.

A catalogue record for this book is available from the British Library.

A catalog record for this book is available from the Library of Congress

10 9 8 7 6 5 4 3 2 1
11 10 09 08 07 06 05 04 03 02

Printed in Great Britain by
The Bath Press, Bath

LIST OF CONTENTS

PREFACE

The twenty first edition of *The Grants Register* provides a detailed, accurate and comprehensive survey of awards intended for students at or above the postgraduate level, or those who require further professional or advanced vocational training.

Student numbers around the world continue to grow rapidly, and overseas study is now the first choice for many of these students. *The Grants Register* provides comprehensive, up-to-date information about the availability of, and eligibility for, non-refundable postgraduate and professional awards worldwide.

We remain grateful to the institutions which have supplied information for inclusion in this edition, and would also like to thank the International Association of Universities for continued permission to use their subject index within our Subject and Eligibility Guide to Awards.

The Grants Register database is updated continually in order to ensure that the information provided is the most current available. Therefore, if your details have changed or you would like to be included for the first time, please contact the Editor, Louise Baynes, at address below. If you wish to obtain further information relating to specific application procedures, please contact the relevant grant awarding institution, rather than the publisher.

The Grants Register
Paulton House
8 Shepherdess Walk
London
N1 7LB
United Kingdom
Tel: +44 (0)20 7324 2349
Fax: +44 (0)20 7324 2312

Website: http://www.palgrave.com
Email: grants.register@waterlow.com

HOW TO USE THE GRANTS REGISTER

For ease of use, *The Grants Register* 2003 is divided into five sections:

- *The Grants Register*
- Subject and Eligibility Guide to Awards
- Index of Awards
- Index of Discontinued Awards
- Index of Awarding Organisations

The Grants Register

Information in this section is supplied directly by the awarding organisations. Entries are arranged alphabetically by name of organisation, and awards are listed alphabetically within the awarding organisation. This section includes details on subject area, eligibility, purpose, type, numbers offered, frequency, value, length of study, study establishment, country of study, and application procedure. Full contact details appear with each awarding organisation and also appended to individual awards where additional addresses are given.

Subject and Eligibility Guide to Awards

Awards can be located through the Subject and Eligibility Guide to Awards. This section allows the user to find an award within a specific subject area. *The Grants Register* uses a list of subjects endorsed by the International Association of Universities (IAU), the information centre on higher education, located at UNESCO, Paris (please see pp. 787-788 for the complete subject list). It is further subdivided into eligibility by nationality. Thereafter, awards are listed alphabetically within their designated category, along with a page reference where full details of the award can be found.

Index of Awards

All awards are indexed alphabetically with a page reference.

Index of Discontinued Awards

This Index lists awards previously included within *The Grants Register* which are no longer being offered, have been replaced by another programme, or are no longer relevant for inclusion in the publication.

Index of Awarding Organisations

A complete list of all awarding organisations, with country name and page reference.

ACADIA UNIVERSITY

Wolfville, NS, B0P 1X0, Canada
Tel: (1) 902 585 1498
Fax: (1) 902 585 1096
Email: elaine.schofield@acadiau.ca
www: http://www.ace.acadiau.ca/gradstud/gradhome.htm
Contact: Ms Elaine Schofield, Administrator

Acadia University is primarily an undergraduate institution providing a liberal education based on the highest standards. The University provides a scholarly community that aims to ensure a broadening life experience for students, faculty and staff.

Acadia Graduate Teaching Assistantships
Subjects: English, political science, sociology, biology, chemistry, computer science, geology, psychology, education and recreation management.
Purpose: To financially support graduate students.
Eligibility: Open to those registered as full-time graduate students at Acadia University.
Level of Study: Postgraduate.
Type: Teaching assistantship.
Value: Up to canadian $8,000.
Length of Study: One or two years.
Frequency: Annual.

ENGINEERING

GENERAL

Any Country
Alan F Henry/Paul A Greebler Scholarship, 66
Andrew Stratton Scholarship, 705
Arthur Holly Compton Award in Education, 66
Association for Women in Science Educational Foundation Predoctoral Awards, 126
AUC Assistantships, 96
AUC Laboratory Instruction Graduate Fellowships in Engineering and Computer Science, 96
AUC University Fellowships, 97

THE GRANTS REGISTER

A-T CHILDREN'S PROJECT

668 South Military Trail, Deerfield Beach, FL, 33442, United States
of America
Tel: (1) 954 481 6611
Fax: (1) 954 725 1153
Email: info@atcp.org
www: http://www.atcp.org
Contact: Dr Cynthia Rothblum-Oviatt, Science Co-ordinator

The A-T Children's Project is a non-profit organisation that raises
funds to support and co-ordinate biomedical research projects, scientific conferences and a clinical centre aimed at finding a cure for
ataxia-telangiectasia, a lethal genetic disease that attacks children,
causing progressive loss of muscle control, as well as cancer and
immune system problems.

Direct Research on Ataxia-Telangiectasia

Subjects: Research in the area of ATM biology.
Purpose: To accelerate first rate, international scientific research in
the area of ATM biology to help find a cure or life improving treat-
ments for children with ataxia-telangiectasia.
Eligibility: Open to all ages and nationalities.
Level of Study: Research.
Type: Grant.
Value: Up to US$100,000.
Length of Study: One-two years.
Frequency: Annual.
Application Procedure: Applicants must visit the website.
Closing Date: There are no deadlines for submission of grant
proposals.
Funding: Private.

AAUW EDUCATIONAL FOUNDATION

1111 16 Street North West, Washington, DC, 20036, United States
of America
Tel: (1) 202 728 7602
Email: foundation@aauw.org
www: http://www.aauw.org
Contact: Administrative Officer

The AAUW Educational Foundation is composed of three corporations: the Association, a 150,000 member organisation with more
than 1,500 branches nationwide which lobbies and advocates for education and equity; the AAUW Educational Foundation, which funds
pioneering research on girls and education, community action projects, and fellowships and grants for outstanding women around the
globe; and the AAUW Legal Advocacy Fund, which provides funds
and a support system for women seeking judicial redress for sexual
discrimination in higher education.

AAUW Career Development Grants

Subjects: All subjects.
Purpose: To support women who are preparing for a career advancement, career change or to re-enter the work force.
Eligibility: Open to all, yet special consideration is given to AAUW
members, women of colour and women pursuing their advanced de-
gree or credentials in non traditional fields. Applicants must be
United States citizens or permanent residents whose last degree
was received before June 30th 1998. Candidates eligible for another
AAUW Educational Foundation fellowship or grant programme are
not eligible for Career Development Grants.
Level of Study: Graduate, Professional development.
Type: Grant.
Value: US$2,000-8,000.
Frequency: Annual.
Country of Study: United States of America.
No. of awards offered: Approx. 60 in the two categories of aca-
demic grants and professional development institute grants.

Applicati
form, availa
website.
Closing Date:
cation request de
Funding: Private.
No. of awards given
Additional Information
course work towards a Ma
technical or professional fie
a fully accredited two or four y
school that is licensed, accredite
Department of Veterans Affairs. P.
Grants support women's participatio

For further information contact:

c/o Customer Service Center
Department 144
2201 North Dodge Street, Iowa City, IA, 5224
of America
Tel: (1) 319 337 1716 ext. 144

AAUW Community Action Grants

Subjects: All subjects.
Purpose: To provide seed money to individual women, loc
munity-based non-profit organisations, AAUW branches and
state organisations for innovative programmes or non-degree re
search projects that promote education and equity for women and
girls.
Eligibility: Applicants must be women who are United States citizens or permanent residents. Special consideration will be given to
AAUW members and AAUW branch and state applicants who seek
partners for collaborative projects. Collaborators can include local
schools or school districts, businesses and other community-based
organisations. Two year grants are restricted to projects focused on
girls' achievement in mathematics, science or technology. Projects
must involve community and school collaboration. The fund supports
planning and coalition building activities during the first year and implementation and evaluation the following year.
Type: Grant.
Value: US$2,000-7,000 for one year projects and US$5,000-10,000
for two year projects.
Length of Study: One or two years.
Frequency: Annual.
No. of awards offered: Approx. 40.
Application Procedure: Applicants must write for an application
form, which is also available from the website.
Closing Date: January 15th.
Funding: Private.
Additional Information: Two types of grants are available. One
year grants are for short-term projects and topic areas are unrestricted but should have a clearly defined educational activity. Two
year grants are for longer term programmes and are restricted to
projects focused on K-12 girls' achievement in maths, science,
and/or technology. Funds support planning activities and coalition
building during the first year and implementation and evaluation the
following year.

For further information contact:

2201 North Dodge Street, Iowa City, IA, 32243-4030, United States
of America

AAUW Educational Foundation American Fellowships

Subjects: All subjects.
Purpose: To offset a scholar's living expenses while she completes
her final year of dissertation writing, or to increase the number of
women in tenure track faculty positions and promote equality for
women in higher education.
Eligibility: Open to women who are citizens of the United States.
Level of Study: Doctorate, Postdoctorate, Research.
Type: Fellowship.

Private.

information contact:

Dodge Street, Iowa City, IA, 52243-4030, United States
ca

AAUW International Fellowships Program

Subjects: All subjects.
Purpose: To support women studying at the graduate or postgraduate level at a United States Institute of Higher Education.
Eligibility: Open to women who are not United States citizens or permanent residents who hold a United States Bachelor's degree or equivalent. Applicants must be planning to return to their home country upon completion of degree and/or research. English proficiency is required.
Level of Study: Doctorate, Graduate, Postdoctorate, Postgraduate, Predoctorate, Research.
Type: Fellowship.
Value: US$30,000 for the Postdoctoral Fellowship, US$20,000 for the Doctoral Fellowship and US$18,000 for the Master's Fellowship.
Length of Study: One year.
Frequency: Annual.
Study Establishment: Any accredited institution.
Country of Study: United States of America.
No. of awards offered: 46.
Application Procedure: Applicants must complete an application for each year applying. Applications must be obtained from the customer service centre or the AAUW website between August 1st and November 15th. Three letters of recommendation, transcripts and a minimum score of 550 on the Test Of English as a Foreign Language are also required.
Closing Date: Postmarked December 15th. November 15th is the last day applications are available.
Funding: Private.
No. of awards given last year: 47.
No. of applicants last year: 1106.
Additional Information: These awards are non renewable.

For further information contact:

c/o Customer Service Center
2201 North Dodge Street
Department 141, Iowa City, IA, 52243-4030, United States of America

AAUW Selected Professions Fellowships

Subjects: Medicine, law, engineering, business administration, computer science, mathematics, architecture and statistics.
Purpose: To support women in graduate study in designated fields where women's participation has been low, and to support engineering doctoral candidates who are in the final stages of writing their dissertations.
Eligibility: All women are eligible to apply for fellowships in the following degree programmes: architecture (MArch), computer or information sciences (MS), engineering (ME, MS, PhD), and mathematics or statistics (MS). Fellowships for the following degree programmes are restricted to women of colour to increase their participation and access in these historically underrepresented fields: business administration (MBA, EMBA), law (JD) and medicine (MD, DO).
Level of Study: Doctorate, Graduate, MBA.
Type: Fellowship.
Value: The Fellowship Award is US$5,000-12,000 and the Engineering Dissertation Award is US$15,000.
Frequency: Annual.
Country of Study: United States of America.
No. of awards offered: Approx. 40.
Application Procedure: Applicants must write for an application form, which is also available from the website.
Closing Date: Application postmark deadline is January 10th. Engineering Dissertation (only) is November 15th.
Funding: Private.
No. of awards given last year: 40.

AAUW EDUCATIONAL FOUNDA...

Value: US$20,000 for the D...
Postdoctoral Research Le...
search Publication Gra...
Length of Study: On...
Frequency: Annua...
**Country of Stud...
**Application P...
package. Th...
tobiograp...
three l...0, United States
down...
vic...
c...

...olar-in-Residence
...y or distance learning, eco-
...ducational equity.
...dresses an aspect of one of
...nomic security, including work
...y and the computer culture.
...ven to candidates with demonstrated knowl-
...experience with, women's issues in higher education.
...erence will be given to those with three-five years of experience in research and/or information analysis. A Master's or doctorate is required.
Level of Study: Doctorate, Postdoctorate, Research.
Type: Fellowship.
Value: Up to US$45,000 as determined by the nature and duration of the research project proposed. Some benefits may be available.
Length of Study: One year.
Frequency: Every two years.
Country of Study: United States of America.
No. of awards offered: One.
Application Procedure: Proposals will be evaluated on the basis of their relevance to the Foundation's agenda, the qualifications of the researcher, the likely impact of the project, and its potential contribution to knowledge of equity issues in higher education. Application guidelines are available from the Foundation and the website.
Funding: Private.
No. of awards given last year: One.
No. of applicants last year: 50.
Additional Information: The Scholar-in-Residence will be expected to spend some time in Washington DC and to interact with staff and board members, but formal residence in Washington is not required. Contact the Foundation for proposal guidelines and deadlines.

AAUW Eleanor Roosevelt Teacher Fellowships

Subjects: Gender equity.
Purpose: To support professional development for teachers, educational opportunities for girls and the advancement of gender equity in the classroom, school or district.
Eligibility: Open to all public school, K-12 women teachers who are United States citizens or permanent residents. Applicants must be committed to teaching for three years including the fellowship year.
Level of Study: Professional development.
Type: Fellowship.
Value: US$5,000.
No. of awards offered: Approx. 25.
Application Procedure: Applicants must write for an application form, which is also available from the website.
Closing Date: January 10th.

No. of applicants last year: 158.
Additional Information: Applications are no longer available in the two weeks that precede the application deadline.

For further information contact:

c/o Customer Service Center
2201 North Dodge Street, Iowa City, IA, 52243, United States of America
Tel: (1) 319 337 1716

AAUW University Scholar-in-Residence

Subjects: Educational equity for women and girls.
Purpose: To allow a female Scholar to undertake and disseminate research on gender equality for women and girls.
Level of Study: Postdoctorate, Research.
Type: Fellowship.
Value: Not to exceed US$50,000 for a one year project or US$100,000 for a two year project, depending on the nature of the project and cost sharing provided by the institution.
Length of Study: One-two years.
Frequency: Annual.
Country of Study: United States of America.
No. of awards offered: One.
Application Procedure: Institutional applicants must submit a proposal including both activities on gender and educational equity, and dissemination of findings. Successful proposals will be crafted to achieve impact across the institution or among departments or schools, rather than in a single department programme. Proposals must also include confirmation by an authorised institutional official confirming the institution's commitment to the project and cost share provided.
Closing Date: October 15th.
Funding: Private.
No. of awards given last year: One.
No. of applicants last year: 15.
Additional Information: Applicants should contact the Foundation for proposal guidelines.

THE ABBEY ROME AWARDS

43 Carson Road, London, SE21 8HT, England
Tel: (44) 20 8761 7980
Email: janereid@carson43.demon.co.uk
www: http://www.abbey.org.uk
Contact: Ms Jane Reid, Administrator

The Abbey Rome Awards provide opportunities for painters to live and work in Rome.

Abbey Fellowships in Painting

Subjects: Painting.
Purpose: To enable mid-career painters with an established record of achievement to live and work at the British School at Rome.
Eligibility: Open to United Kingdom and United States of America citizens only. There are no age restrictions. Fellowships are for painters only.
Level of Study: Graduate, Professional development.
Type: Fellowship.
Value: All expenses and spending money.
Length of Study: Three months.
Frequency: Annual.
Study Establishment: The British School at Rome.
Country of Study: Italy.
No. of awards offered: Usually three.
Application Procedure: Applicants must write enclosing a stamped addressed envelope, alternatively applicants can download application forms from the website.
Closing Date: Mid January.
Funding: Private.

Contributor: The Incorporated Edwin Austin Abbey Memorial Scholarships.
No. of awards given last year: Four but usually three.
No. of applicants last year: Approx. 70.

Abbey Scholarship in Painting

Subjects: Painting.
Purpose: To enable an exceptionally promising emergent painter to live and work in the British School at Rome.
Eligibility: Open to United Kingdom and United States of America citizens only. There are no age restrictions. Awards are for painters only.
Level of Study: Graduate, Postgraduate.
Type: Scholarship.
Value: All expenses and spending money.
Length of Study: Nine months.
Frequency: Annual.
Study Establishment: The British School at Rome.
Country of Study: Italy.
No. of awards offered: One.
Application Procedure: Applicants must write enclosing a stamped addressed envelope. Alternatively, applicants can download application forms from the website.
Closing Date: Mid January.
Funding: Private.
Contributor: The Incorporated Edwin Austin Memorial Scholarships.
No. of awards given last year: One.
No. of applicants last year: Approx. 60.

THE ABDUS SALAM INTERNATIONAL CENTRE FOR THEORETICAL PHYSICS (ICTP)

Strada Costiera 11, Trieste, I-34014, Italy
Tel: (39) 040 224 0111
Fax: (39) 040 224 163
Email: sci_info@ictp.trieste.it
www: http://www.ictp.trieste.it
Telex: 460392 ICTP I
Contact: Ms Anna Triolo, Public Information Officer

The Abdus Salam International Centre for Theoretical Physics (ICTP) is an institution for research and high level training in physics and mathematics, mainly for scientists from developing countries. It also maintains a network of associate members and federal institutes.

The Abdus Salam ICTP Fellowships

Subjects: Physics and mathematics.
Purpose: To enable qualified applicants to pursue research in the fields of condensed matter physics, mathematics and high energy physics.
Eligibility: Open to qualified applicants of any nationality, who have a PhD in physics or mathematics.
Level of Study: Postdoctorate.
Type: Fellowship.
Value: Monthly stipend, round trip expenses where applicable and allowances according to the length of the visit.
Length of Study: Up to one year.
Frequency: Dependent on funds available.
Study Establishment: ICTP.
Country of Study: Italy.
No. of awards offered: Varies.
Application Procedure: Applicants must request appropriate application forms from the secretariat, or visit the ICTP website.
Closing Date: Applications are accepted at any time.
Funding: Government.
Contributor: The Italian government, IAEA and UNESCO.
No. of awards given last year: 20.

No. of applicants last year: 35.

ACADEMY OF MARKETING SCIENCE FOUNDATION

424 Santa Teresa Street
Stanford University, Stanford, CA, 94305-4015, United States of America
Tel: (1) 650 723 3054
Email: ams.sba@miami.edu
www: http://www.ams-web.org
Contact: Ms Rania Hegazi, Fellowship Administrator

The Academy of Marketing and Science (AMS) was founded in 1971. Under the direction of Dr Harold W Berkman, the Academy of Marketing Science may be considered a full service scholarly professional organisation. The AMS established the Academy of Marketing Science Foundation to provide awards to marketing students, primarily at the graduate level. It is also the intention of the Foundation to provide awards for both the advancement of the teaching of marketing and for research in marketing.

Dr Jagdish N Sheth Best Article Award for the Journal of the Academy of Marketing Science

Subjects: Marketing.
Purpose: To recognise a research contribution to the discipline of marketing.
Eligibility: Open to individuals of any nationality.
Level of Study: Unrestricted.
Value: US$500.
Frequency: Annual.
Country of Study: Any country.
No. of awards offered: One.
Closing Date: December 1st.
Additional Information: The AMS does not fund scholarships or grants towards studies. Awards and cash prizes are presented at the AMS Annual Conference to Academy members that participated in various paper competitions.

Dr M Wayne DeLozier Best Paper Award

Subjects: Marketing.
Purpose: To recognise and reward a research contribution to the discipline of marketing.
Eligibility: Open to individuals of any nationality who are college or university professors and members of the Academy of Marketing Science who participate at the time of annual conference which is usually held in the last week of May.
Level of Study: Professional development.
Type: Competition.
Value: US$250. The maximum cash award is US$500.
Frequency: Annual.
Country of Study: Any country.
No. of awards offered: One.
Closing Date: December 1st.
Additional Information: The Academy of Marketing Science (AMS) does not fund scholarships or grants towards studies. Awards and cash prizes are presented at the AMS Annual Conference to Academy members that participated in various paper competitions.

Mary Kay Doctoral Dissertation Award

Subjects: Areas related to the discipline of marketing, ie. buyer behaviour, channels of distribution, advertising and promotion.
Purpose: To recognise and reward a research contribution to the discipline of marketing.
Eligibility: Open to individuals of any nationality.
Level of Study: Doctorate.
Value: US$500 cash prize and a waiver of the conference registration fee.
Frequency: Annual.

Country of Study: Any country.
No. of awards offered: One.
Closing Date: December 1st.
No. of applicants last year: AMS members who participate.
Additional Information: The Academy of Marketing Science (AMS) does not fund scholarships or grants towards studies. Awards and cash prizes are presented at the AMS Annual Conference to Academy members that participated in various paper competitions.

ACADEMY OF MOTION PICTURE ARTS AND SCIENCES

8949 Wilshire Boulevard, Beverly Hills, CA, 90211-1972, United States of America
Tel: (1) 310 247 3059
Fax: (1) 310 247 2600
Email: nicholl@oscars.org
www: http://www.oscars.org/nicholl
Contact: Mr Greg Beal, Programme Co-ordinator

The Academy of Motion Picture Arts and Sciences annually presents Academy Awards for motion picture artistic achievement. The Academy Film Archive is a leader in preservation and restoration and the Academy's Margaret Herrick Library holds a vast array of film-related materials. The Student Academy Awards honours achievements by talented student film makers.

Don and Gee Nicholl Fellowships in Screenwriting

Subjects: Screenwriting.
Purpose: To foster the development of new writers.
Eligibility: Open to writers in English who have not sold or optioned a screen or teleplay. Those who have not sold or optioned the story for a screen or teleplay are also eligible.
Level of Study: Unrestricted.
Type: Fellowship.
Value: US$30,000.
Length of Study: One year.
Frequency: Annual.
Country of Study: Any country.
No. of awards offered: Up to five.
Application Procedure: Applicants must complete an application form available after January 1st by sending a written request via post or email, or by visiting the website.
Closing Date: May 1st.
Funding: Private.
No. of awards given last year: Five.
No. of applicants last year: 5,489.
Additional Information: The fellowships are not to be used to pursue graduate college degrees. In addition to the Academy Awards or Oscars (no monetary value) and the Nicholl Fellowships, the Academy offers Student Film Awards for films completed by students at an accredited college or university.

ACADEMY OF NATURAL SCIENCES

1900 Benjamin Franklin Parkway, Philadelphia, PA, 19103-1195, United States of America
Tel: (1) 215 299 1000
Fax: (1) 215 299 1028
www: http://www.acnatsci.org/research/jessupinfo.html
Contact: Dr Edward Daeschler, Assistant Curator

The Academy of Natural Sciences, an international museum of natural history operating since 1812, undertakes research and public education that focuses on the environment and its diverse species. The Academy's mission is to expand knowledge of nature through discovery and to inspire stewardship of the environment.

Jessup and McHenry Awards

Subjects: The Jessup award is for zoology and the McHenry award is for botany.
Purpose: To assist predoctoral and postdoctoral students.
Eligibility: Students commuting within the Philadelphia area are ineligible, otherwise eligibility is unrestricted.
Level of Study: Doctorate, Postdoctorate, Postgraduate, Predoctorate.
Type: Grant.
Value: The stipend for subsistence is US$250 per week. This may include round trip travel costs of up to a total of US$500 for North American applicants, including Mexico and the Caribbean, and US$1,000 for applicants from other parts of the world. This is not guaranteed.
Length of Study: 2-12 weeks.
Frequency: Annual.
Study Establishment: The Academy of Natural Sciences.
Country of Study: United States of America.
Application Procedure: Applicants must send queries, requests for information and supporting information to the given address.
Closing Date: March 1st or October 1st.
No. of awards given last year: Three.
Additional Information: The provision of scientific supplies and equipment is the responsibility of the student and the sponsoring curator.

ACADEMY OF SCIENCES OF THE CZECH REPUBLIC

UNESCO-ROSTE Course
Institute of Microbiology
Videnská 1083, Prague, CS-142 20, Czech Republic
Tel: (42) 2 4752 379
Fax: (42) 2 4752 384
Email: nerud@biomed.cas.cz
www: http://www.biomed.cas.cz
Contact: Mr F Nerud, Director of Course

The Institute of Microbiology is one of the major biological institutes of the Academy of Sciences. Main areas of research at the Institute include biogenesis and biotechnology of natural compounds, cell and molecular microbiology, ecology, immunology, gnotobiology and autotrophic micro-organisms.

UNESCO-ROSTE Long-term Postgraduate Training Course

Subjects: Microbiology, biochemistry, biophysics, molecular biology, biotechnology, genetics and ecology.
Purpose: To enable young scientists to obtain a more profound education and prepare for a research career.
Eligibility: Open to young scientists from European countries and a limited number of students from other regions, who hold an MSc, PhD or equivalent degree, and who have two to three years of practical experience in their field. Candidates should be no more than 35 years of age and should possess a good knowledge of English.
Level of Study: Postgraduate.
Type: Training award.
Value: Koruna 5,000 and accommodation.
Length of Study: 11 months.
Frequency: Annual.
Study Establishment: Institutes and laboratories of the Academy of Sciences of the Czech Republic.
Country of Study: Czech Republic.
No. of awards offered: 15.
Application Procedure: Applicants must write for details.
Closing Date: March 31st.
Funding: Government.
Contributor: The Academy of Sciences of the Czech Republic.
No. of awards given last year: 14.

Additional Information: The courses are given in co-operation with the Czech Commission for UNESCO and sponsored by UNESCO-ROSTE and the Academy of Sciences of the Czech Republic.

ACADIA UNIVERSITY

Wolfville, NS, B0P 1X0, Canada
Tel: (1) 902 585 1498
Fax: (1) 902 585 1096
Email: elaine.schofield@acadiau.ca
www: http://www.acadiau.ca
Contact: Ms Elaine Schofield, Administrator

Acadia University is primarily an undergraduate institution providing a liberal education based on the highest standards. The University provides a scholarly community that aims to ensure a broadening life experience for students, faculty and staff.

Acadia Graduate Teaching Assistantships

Subjects: English, political science, sociology, biology, chemistry, computer science, geology, psychology, education and recreation management.
Purpose: To financially support graduate students.
Eligibility: Open to those registered as full-time graduate students at Acadia University.
Level of Study: Postgraduate.
Type: Teaching assistantship.
Value: Up to canadian $8,000.
Length of Study: One or two years.
Frequency: Annual.
Study Establishment: The Division of Research and Graduate Studies at Acadia University.
Country of Study: Canada.
No. of awards offered: Limited.
Application Procedure: Applicants must write for details.
Closing Date: February 1st.
Additional Information: Recipients of a graduate teaching assistantship should expect to undertake certain duties during the academic year (up to a maximum of ten hours per week and to a maximum of 100 hours per semester) as a condition of tenure of the award. The specific duties will be established by agreement at the beginning of each academic year.

ACTION CANCER

1 Marlborough Park, Belfast, BT9 6XS, Northern Ireland
Tel: (44) 28 9080 3344
Fax: (44) 28 9080 3356
Email: info@actioncancer.org
www: http://www.actioncancer.org
Contact: Ms Nicola Nicholls, Director of Development & Policy

Action Cancer is a Northern Ireland cancer charity, funded entirely by voluntary donations. Founded in 1973, it offers awareness and health promotion, free detection clinics for men and women concerned about cancer and a support service for cancer patients and their families. Action Cancer also provides funding for research at local universities and a new cancer genetics programme in Northern Ireland hospitals.

Action Cancer Research Grants

Subjects: Cancer related subjects.
Purpose: To help researchers carry out cancer related projects.
Eligibility: Researchers must be working in Northern Ireland.
Level of Study: Postdoctorate.
Type: Grant.
Value: UK £6,000.
Length of Study: One year.

Frequency: Annual.
Country of Study: United Kingdom.
No. of awards offered: Five.
Application Procedure: Awards are advertised in the local press in March. Applicants must submit an application form and a decision is made by the Scientific and Research Committee.
Closing Date: Early April.
Funding: Private.
Contributor: Voluntary donations.
No. of awards given last year: Five.
No. of applicants last year: Twenty.

Action Cancer Research Studentship

Subjects: An appropriate chemical, biological or biomedical science.
Purpose: To provide an opportunity for an outstanding graduate to work on a cancer related research project and undergo research training with a view to being awarded a PhD from the Queen's University of Belfast or the University of Ulster.
Eligibility: Supervisors must be researchers in Northern Ireland.
Level of Study: Doctorate.
Type: Studentship.
Value: Approx. UK £14,000 per year.
Length of Study: Three years.
Frequency: Annual.
Country of Study: United Kingdom.
No. of awards offered: One.
Application Procedure: Awards are advertised in the local press in December. Applicants' supervisors must submit an application form and on receipt of the award must advertise for an appropriate student.
Closing Date: Early Janurary.
Funding: Private.
Contributor: Voluntary donations.
No. of awards given last year: One.
No. of applicants last year: 10.

ACTION RESEARCH

Vincent House, Horsham, West Sussex, RH12 2DP, England
Tel: (44) 1403 210406
Fax: (44) 1403 210541
Email: research@actionresearch.co.uk
www: http://www.actionresearch.co.uk
Contact: Dr Tracy Swinfield

Action Research is a national research charity dedicated to preventing and treating disabling diseases. The charity supports a broad spectrum of research with the objective of preventing disease and disability, regardless of age group, and alleviating physical handicap, with an emphasis on clinical research, or research at the clinical and basic interface.

Action Research Project Grants

Subjects: With the exception of cancer, cardiovascular, HIV and AIDS research, a broad spectrum of research with the objective of preventing disease and disability (regardless of cause or age group) and alleviating physical handicap is supported. Emphasis is on clinical research or research at the clinical or basic interface.
Purpose: To support one precisely formulated line of research.
Eligibility: Open to researchers based in the United Kingdom only. Grants are not awarded purely for higher education nor to MRC units or to other charities.
Level of Study: Unrestricted.
Type: Grant.
Value: Varies.
Length of Study: Up to three years, assessed annually.
Frequency: Three times each year.
Study Establishment: Hospitals, universities and recognised research establishments.
Country of Study: United Kingdom.

No. of awards offered: Varies.
Application Procedure: Applicants must submit a one page outline of the project before an application form can be issued.
Closing Date: Please contact the organisation.
Contributor: Voluntary income.
No. of awards given last year: 37.
No. of applicants last year: 216.

Action Research Training Fellowship

Subjects: With the exception of cancer, cardiovascular, HIV and AIDS research, a broad spectrum of research with the objective of preventing disease and disability (regardless of cause or age group) and alleviating physical handicap are supported. Emphasis is on clinical research or research at the clinical or basic interface.
Purpose: To enable the training of young medical and non medical graduates in research techniques and methodology in areas of interest to the charity.
Eligibility: Open to medical and non medical graduates preferably between the ages of 23 and 32 years of age, as this is a training position. Although not limited to United Kingdom citizens, those who do not hold United Kingdom citizenship must be able to show that they have all the required statutory documentation (eg. work permits) to cover the period of the research training fellowship. No grants are made purely for higher education.
Level of Study: Doctorate, Postdoctorate, Postgraduate.
Type: Training fellowship.
Value: Varies.
Length of Study: Up to three years.
Frequency: Annual.
Study Establishment: Arranged by the applicant, based in a hospital or university department.
Country of Study: United Kingdom.
No. of awards offered: Varies.
Application Procedure: Applicants must submit the appropriate application.
Closing Date: January 31st.
Contributor: Voluntary income.
No. of awards given last year: Five.
No. of applicants last year: 65.
Additional Information: Fellowships are advertised separately each year in late November.

ACTUARIAL EDUCATION AND RESEARCH FUND (AERF)

475 North Martingale Road
Suite 800, Schaumburg, IL, 60173-2226, United States of America
Tel: (1) 847 706 3573
Fax: (1) 847 706 3599
Email: jyore@soa.org
www: http://www.aerf.org
Contact: Ms Judy Yore, Business Manager

The Actuarial Education and Research Fund (AERF) carries out research and education projects in actuarial science and studies specific projects that could be advanced under this mechanism.

AERF Individual Grants Competition

Subjects: The project may be either theoretical or empirical in nature. A key criteria is that the project should have the potential to contribute significantly to the advancement of knowledge in actuarial science.
Purpose: To produce publications which will advance actuarial science, especially with regard to practical applications.
Eligibility: Proposals are invited from members of the seven sponsoring actuarial organisations (AAA, ASPA, CIA, CAS, CONAC, CCA and SoA), from faculty members of universities or colleges who have teaching and research responsibilities in the actuarial or related field and by others who are qualified by knowledge and experience to contribute to their goals.

Level of Study: Unrestricted.
Type: Cash grant.
Value: Varies, approx. US$10,000.
Length of Study: Projects should generally be of less than one year in duration.
Frequency: Annual.
Country of Study: Any country.
No. of awards offered: Varies.
Application Procedure: Applicants must submit a letter of intent and an application form.
Closing Date: November 30th for the letter of intent.
Funding: Private.
Contributor: The Actuarial Foundation and the Canadian Institute of Actuary and individuals.
No. of awards given last year: Three.
No. of applicants last year: 15.
Additional Information: AERF gives preference to projects relating to current policy issues or having direct applications and those that further the basic or continuing education of actuaries. Proposals for innovative developments in actuarial education are also considered by AERF. More information is available from the website.

THE ADA ENDOWMENT AND ASSISTANCE FUND, INC.

211 East Chicago Avenue, Chicago, IL, 60611-2678, United States of America
Tel: (1) 312 440 2567
Fax: (1) 312 440 2822
www: http://www.ada.org
Contact: Ms Marsha L Mountz, Manager

The purpose of the American Dental Association Endowment and Assistance Fund is to provide a measure of financial assistance to certain groups of individuals who have a financial hardship, whether due to educational needs, chemical dependency, disability or disaster.

The ADA Endowment and Assistance Fund, Inc. Allied Dental Health Scholarship (Dental Hygiene, Dental Assisting, Dental Laboratory Technology)

Subjects: Dental hygiene, dental assisting and dental laboratory technology.
Purpose: To defray study expenses which include tuition, fees, books, supplies and living expenses.
Eligibility: Open to United States citizens only. Applicants must either be entering their first year (Dental Assisting) or final year (Dental Laboratory Technology and Dental Hygiene). Applicants must have a minimum grade point average of 3.0 based on a 4.0 scale and show financial need of at least US$1,000.
Level of Study: Professional development.
Type: Scholarship.
Value: US$1,000.
Frequency: Annual.
Country of Study: United States of America.
No. of awards offered: 15 dental hygiene, 10 dental assisting and five dental laboratory technology.
Application Procedure: Application forms are available from the ADA Health Foundation and are distributed by school officials. Application forms must be original, typed, completed and signed with the assistance of school officials. Applicants must submit a completed application form, including the Academic Achievement Record Form and Financial Needs Assessment Form signed by school officials, two typed reference forms sealed and noted on the back of the envelopes by the referees and a typed biographical sketch.
Closing Date: August 15th for Dental Hygiene and Dental Laboratory Technology or September 15th for Dental Assisting.
Funding: Private.
Contributor: ADA Endowment and Assistance Fund, Inc.
Additional Information: Scholarships are not renewable.

The ADA Endowment and Assistance Fund, Inc. Dental Student Scholarship

Subjects: Dentistry.
Purpose: To defray school expenses which include tuition, fees, books, supplies and living expenses.
Eligibility: Open to United States citizens only. Applicants must be full-time entering second year students enrolled in a dental school accredited by the Commission on Dental Accreditation of the American Dental Association. Applicants must have a minimum grade point average of 3.0 based on a 4.0 scale and show financial need of at least US$2,500.
Level of Study: Postgraduate.
Type: Scholarship.
Value: US$2,500.
Frequency: Annual.
Country of Study: United States of America.
No. of awards offered: 15-25.
Application Procedure: Application forms are available only at dental schools and are distributed by school officials. Forms must be original, typed, completed and signed with the assistance of school officials. Applicants must submit a completed application form, including the Academic Achievement Record Form and Financial Needs Assessment Form signed by school officials, two typed reference forms sealed and noted on the back of the envelopes by the referrers and a typed biographical sketch.
Closing Date: July 31st.
Funding: Private.
Contributor: ADA Endowment and Assistance Fund, Inc. and the ADA Health Foundation.
No. of awards given last year: 25.
No. of applicants last year: 76.
Additional Information: This scholarship is not renewable.

The ADA Endowment and Assistance Fund, Inc. Minority Dental Student Scholarship

Subjects: Dentistry.
Purpose: To defray school expenses which include tuition, fees, books, supplies and living expenses.
Eligibility: Open to United States citizens only. Applicants must be a member of one of the following groups: Black African American, Native American or Hispanic. Applicants must be full-time entering second-year students enrolled in a dental school accredited by the Commission on Dental Accreditation of the American Dental Association. Applicants must have a minimum grade point average of 3.0 based on a 4.0 scale and show financial need of at least US$2,500.
Level of Study: Postgraduate.
Type: Scholarship.
Value: US$2,000.
Frequency: Annual.
Country of Study: United States of America.
No. of awards offered: 15-25.
Application Procedure: Application forms are available only at dental schools and are distributed by school officials. Forms must be original, typed, completed and signed with the assistance of school officials. Applicants must submit a completed application form, including the Academic Achievement Record Form and Financial Needs Assessment Form signed by school officials, two typed reference forms sealed and noted on the back of the envelopes by the referrers and a typed biographical sketch.
Closing Date: July 31st.
Funding: Private.
Contributor: ADA Endowment and Assistance Fund, Inc. and the ADA Health Foundation.
No. of awards given last year: 20.
No. of applicants last year: 37.
Additional Information: This scholarship is not renewable.

ADHA INSTITUTE FOR ORAL HEALTH

Suite 3400
444 North Michigan Avenue, Chicago, IL, 60611, United States of
America
Tel: (1) 312 440 8900
www: http://www.adha.org/institute
Contact: Ms Linda Caradine, Executive Administrator

The ADHA Institute for Oral Health administers scholarship
programmes for full-time dental hygiene students at the certificate-
associate, baccalaureate and graduate levels. ADHA Institute Scholarship awards invest in the future careers of dental hygiene
students.

ADHA Institute Minority Scholarship

Subjects: Dental hygiene.
Purpose: To aid members of minority groups who are currently
underrepresented in dental hygiene programmes.
Eligibility: Eligible applicants include African Americans, Hispanics,
Asians and Native Americans. Open to full-time students at the cer-
tificate, associate, Baccalaureate graduate and doctoral levels.
Scholars must currently be enrolled as full-time students in a dental
hygiene programme in the United States of America, have com-
pleted a minimum of one year with a grade point average of at least
3.0 and be able to demonstrate financial need.
Level of Study: Postgraduate.
Type: Scholarship.
Value: Maximum US$1,250.
Frequency: Dependent on funds available.
Country of Study: United States of America.
No. of awards offered: Two.
Application Procedure: Applicants must write for details or refer to
the website.
Closing Date: June 1st.
Funding: Private.
Additional Information: This is a designated scholarship and is
awarded on the basis of how well the applicant demonstrates the
goal or achievement described.

ADHA Institute Scholarship Program

Subjects: Dental hygiene.
Purpose: To invest in the future careers of dental hygiene students.
Eligibility: Open to full-time students at the certificate or associate,
Baccalaureate graduate and doctoral levels. Scholars must currently
be enrolled as full-time students in a dental hygiene programme in
the United States of America, have completed a minimum of one
year with a grade point average of at least 3.0 and be able to dem-
onstrate financial need. Additional requirements vary depending
upon degree level.
Level of Study: Doctorate, Graduate, Postgraduate.
Type: Scholarship.
Value: Maximum US$1,500.
Length of Study: One year, non renewable.
Frequency: Annual.
Country of Study: United States of America.
No. of awards offered: Approx. 20.
Application Procedure: Applicants must write for details or refer to
the website.
Closing Date: June 1st.
Funding: Private.
Additional Information: Specific areas of this scholarship
programme include the Certificate or Associate Scholarship Pro-
gram, Baccalaureate Scholarship Program and Graduate Scholar-
ship Program.

Colgate 'Bright Smiles, Bright Futures' Minority Scholarships

Subjects: Dental hygiene.
Purpose: To assist members of minority groups currently
underrepresented in dental hygiene programmes.

Eligibility: Open to male African Americans, Hispanics, Asians, and
Native Americans who are full-time students at the certificate, asso-
ciate, Baccalaureate graduate and doctoral levels. Scholars must
currently be enrolled as full-time students in a dental hygiene
programme in the United States of America, have completed a mini-
mum of one year with a grade point average of at least 3.0 and be
able to demonstrate financial need.
Level of Study: Postgraduate.
Type: Scholarship.
Value: Maximum US$1,500.
Frequency: Dependent on funds available.
Country of Study: United States of America.
No. of awards offered: Two.
Application Procedure: Applicants must write for details or refer to
the website.
Closing Date: June 1st.
Funding: Commercial.
Contributor: Colgate Palmolive Company.
Additional Information: This is a designated scholarship and is
awarded on the basis of how well the applicant demonstrates the
goal or achievement described.

Dr Alfred C Fones Scholarship

Subjects: Dental hygiene.
Purpose: To assist an applicant in the baccalaureate or graduate
degree categories who intends to become a dental hygiene teacher
or educator.
Eligibility: Open to full-time students at the certificate, associate,
Baccalaureate graduate and doctoral levels. Scholars must currently
be enrolled as full-time students in a dental hygiene programme in
the United States of America, have completed a minimum of one
year with a grade point average of at least 3.0 and be able to dem-
onstrate financial need. Additional requirements vary depending
upon degree level.
Level of Study: Graduate.
Type: Scholarship.
Value: Maximum US$1,500.
Frequency: Dependent on funds available.
Country of Study: United States of America.
No. of awards offered: One.
Application Procedure: Applicants must write for details or refer to
the website.
Closing Date: June 1st.
Funding: Private.
Additional Information: This is a designated scholarship and is
awarded on the basis of how well the applicant demonstrates the
goal or achievement described.

Dr Harold Hillenbrand Scholarship

Subjects: Dental hygiene.
Purpose: To assist an applicant who demonstrates specific academic excellence and outstanding clinical performance, in addition to
having a minimum dental hygiene cumulative grade point average of
3.5 on a 4.0 scale.
Eligibility: Open to full-time students at the certificate, associate,
Baccalaureate graduate and doctoral levels. Scholars must currently
be enrolled as full-time students in a dental hygiene programme in
the United States of America, have completed a minimum of one
year with a grade point average of at least 3.0 and be able to dem-
onstrate financial need.
Level of Study: Postgraduate.
Type: Scholarship.
Value: Maximum US$1,500.
Frequency: Dependent on funds available.
Country of Study: United States of America.
No. of awards offered: One.
Application Procedure: Applicants must write for details or refer to
the website.
Closing Date: June 1st.
Funding: Private.

Additional Information: This is a designated scholarship and is awarded on the basis of how well the applicant demonstrates the goal or achievement described.

Irene E Newman Scholarship

Subjects: Dental hygiene.
Purpose: To assist an applicant who demonstrates strong potential in public health or community dental health.
Eligibility: Open to full-time students at the certificate, associate, Baccalaureate graduate and doctoral levels. Scholars must currently be enrolled as full-time students in a dental hygiene programme in the United States of America, have completed a minimum of one year with a grade point average of at least 3.0 and be able to demonstrate financial need.
Level of Study: Postgraduate.
Type: Scholarship.
Value: Maximum US$1,500.
Frequency: Dependent on funds available.
Country of Study: United States of America.
No. of awards offered: One.
Application Procedure: Applicants must write for details or refer to the website.
Closing Date: June 1st.
Funding: Private.

Margaret E Swanson Scholarship

Subjects: Dental hygiene.
Purpose: To financially aid an applicant who demonstrates exceptional organisational leadership potential.
Eligibility: Open to full-time students at the certificate, associate, Baccalaureate graduate and doctoral levels. Scholars must currently be enrolled as full-time students in a dental hygiene programme in the United States of America, have completed a minimum of one year with a grade point average of at least 3.0 and be able to demonstrate financial need.
Level of Study: Postgraduate.
Type: Scholarship.
Value: Maximum US$1,500.
Frequency: Dependent on funds available.
Country of Study: United States of America.
No. of awards offered: One.
Application Procedure: Applicants must write for details or refer to the website.
Closing Date: June 1st.
Funding: Private.
Additional Information: This is a designated scholarship and is awarded on the basis of how well the applicant demonstrates the goal or achievement described.

Sigma Phi Alpha Graduate Scholarship

Subjects: Dental hygiene.
Purpose: To aid an outstanding applicant pursuing a degree in dental hygiene or a related field.
Eligibility: Open to full-time students at the graduate and doctoral levels. Scholars must currently be enrolled as full-time students in a dental hygiene programme in the United States of America, have completed a minimum of one year with a grade point average of at least 3.0 and be able to demonstrate financial need.
Level of Study: Graduate.
Type: Scholarship.
Value: Maximum US$1,500.
Frequency: Dependent on funds available.
Country of Study: United States of America.
No. of awards offered: One.
Application Procedure: Applicants must write for details or refer to the website.
Closing Date: June 1st.
Funding: Private.
Contributor: The Sigma Phi Alpha Dental Hygiene Society.

Additional Information: This is a designated scholarship and is awarded on the basis of how well the applicant demonstrates the goal or achievement described.

ADOLPH AND ESTHER GOTTLIEB FOUNDATION, INC.

380 West Broadway, New York, NY, 10012, United States of America
Tel: (1) 212 226 0581
Fax: (1) 212 226 0584
www: http://www.gottliebfoundation.org
Contact: Ms Sheila Ross, Grants Manager

The Adolph and Esther Gottlieb Foundation is a non-profit corporation registered with the state of New York. It was established to award financial aid to mature creative painters, sculptors and printmakers.

Gottlieb Foundation Emergency Assistance Grants

Subjects: Painting, sculpture and printmaking.
Purpose: To provide interim financial assistance to creative visual artists whose need is the result of unforeseen catastrophic events.
Eligibility: Open to painters, sculptors and printmakers who can demonstrate a minimum of 10 years of involvement in a mature phase of their work and who do not have the resources to meet the costs incurred by a catastrophic event eg. fire, flood or emergency medical expenses. The disciplines of film, photography or related forms are not eligible unless the work involves directly, or can be interpreted as, painting or sculpture.
Level of Study: Unrestricted.
Type: Grant.
Value: Up to US$10,000. US$4,000 is typical on a one time basis only.
Frequency: Varies, depending on funds available.
Country of Study: Any country.
No. of awards offered: Varies.
Application Procedure: Applicants must complete and submit an application form with documentation of their situation, such as bills, and professional references.
Closing Date: Please write for details.
Funding: Private.
Contributor: An endowment.
No. of awards given last year: 31.
No. of applicants last year: 150.
Additional Information: 'Maturity' is based on the level of technical, intellectual and creative development of the artist. The programme does not cover general indebtedness, dental work, unemployment, capital improvements, long-term disabilities or project funding.

Gottlieb Foundation Individual Support Grants

Subjects: Painting, sculpture and printmaking.
Purpose: To recognise and support serious, fully committed painters, sculptors and printmakers who are in financial need.
Eligibility: Open to creative painters, sculptors and printmakers who have been in a mature phase of their work for at least 20 years and require financial assistance to continue this work. United States residency is not required.
Level of Study: Unrestricted.
Type: Grant.
Value: Varies.
Length of Study: One year.
Frequency: Annual.
Country of Study: Any country.
No. of awards offered: 10.
Application Procedure: Applicants must submit a written request for an application form, which must then be completed and submitted with slides to document 20 years of mature work, narrative statement and financial information.

Closing Date: December 15th. Awards are distributed the following March.

Funding: Private.

Contributor: An endowment.

No. of awards given last year: 10.

No. of applicants last year: 445.

Additional Information: Artists who have been awarded a grant must allow one year to elapse before reapplication. Only first person written requests for application forms will be honoured.

AFRICAN NETWORK OF SCIENTIFIC AND TECHNOLOGICAL INSTITUTIONS (ANSTI)

PO Box 30592, Nairobi, Kenya

Tel: (254) 2 622 619

Fax: (254) 2 622 750

Email: info@ansti.org

www: http://www.ansti.org

Telex: 22275

Contact: Professor J G M Massaquoi

ANSTI, the African Network of Scientific and Technological Institutions, is an organ of co-operation that embraces institutions engaged in the fields of science and technology. To date it has 87 member institutions in 33 countries in sub-Saharan Africa.

African Network of Scientific and Technological Institutions Postgraduate Fellowships

Subjects: Basic and engineering sciences.

Purpose: To enable students to pursue Master's and PhD courses in the basic and engineering sciences.

Eligibility: Open to African nationals only, who are staff members of ANSTI member institutions. Applicants must possess a good Bachelor's degree and must be below 36 years of age.

Level of Study: Postdoctorate, Postgraduate.

Type: Fellowship.

Value: Varies, approx. US$12,000.

Length of Study: Varies, approx. 18 months.

Frequency: Annual.

Study Establishment: ANSTI member institutions.

Country of Study: African countries outside the applicants' home country.

Application Procedure: Applicants must complete an application form, available by contacting ANSTI by mail, fax or email.

Closing Date: May 31st.

Funding: Government.

Contributor: DAAD/UNESCO.

No. of awards given last year: Seven.

No. of applicants last year: Approx. 50.

Additional Information: The applicant is responsible for gaining admission into the university of his or her choice. Preference is given to graduates with a few years of experience.

AFRO-ASIAN INSTITUTE (AAI) IN VIENNA AND CATHOLIC WOMEN'S LEAGUE OF AUSTRIA

Student Division
Türkenstraße 3, Vienna, A-1090, Austria
Tel: (43) 310 5145
Fax: (43) 310 5145 312
Email: studium@aai-wien.at
www: http://www.aai-wien.at/aai-wien
Contact: Mr Markus Pleschko, Study Advisor

The Afro-Asian Institute (AAI)'s major function is to aid students from developing countries of Africa, Asia and Latin America. Presently the AAI provides services for more than 5,000 students from developing countries and counts as an acknowledged contribution to Austrian development aid.

One World Scholarship Program

Subjects: All subjects.

Purpose: To promote cultural exchange, international development and international co-operation aid.

Eligibility: Open to nationals of developing countries in Africa, Asia and Latin America aged 18 to 35 years who have had adequate previous study or vocational practice in the specific field for which the scholarship is applied. Preference is given to candidates who are able to speak German. Only those in financial need will be considered, and the applicability of the special branch of study or training in the applicant's home country is essential. It is expected that Scholars will return to their home country after studying. Good, and sometimes excellent, study results are also required. Preference is given to applicants from the least developed countries. It is a requirement that applicants have already started their studies in Austria.

Level of Study: Unrestricted.

Type: Scholarship.

Value: Please contact the organisation.

Frequency: Annual.

Study Establishment: Universities.

Country of Study: Austria.

No. of awards offered: Varies.

Application Procedure: Applicants must complete an application form, which is available from the Institute. Only personal applications will be considered. Postal applications from abroad will not be answered.

Closing Date: April 1st-30th, for the following academic year.

Funding: Government, Private.

Contributor: The Catholic Church.

No. of awards given last year: 80.

No. of applicants last year: 160.

Additional Information: It is one of AAI's essential aims to establish a 'partnership' contact between assisted students and the Scholarship donor which continues beyond the termination of studies. Only about 10 per cent of applicants can be accepted.

AGE-IN-ACTION

1st Floor
36-on-Long
Long Street, Cape Town, Western Cape, 8001, South Africa
Tel: (27) 21 426 4280
Fax: (27) 21 426 4290
Email: saca@iafrica.com
www: http://www.age-in-action.co.za
Contact: Mrs Wil Bryan, Chief Executive Officer

Zerilda Steyn Memorial Trust

Subjects: The needs and care of the aged.

Purpose: To advance postgraduate research in South Africa.

Eligibility: Open to researchers in all disciplines caring for the aged.
Level of Study: Postgraduate.
Type: Project grant.
Value: Rand 1,500 per year.
Length of Study: One year, renewable only in exceptional circumstances.
Frequency: Annual.
Study Establishment: Universities.
Country of Study: South Africa.
No. of awards offered: Several grants are made for a variety of small and large projects.
Application Procedure: Applicants must submit an application form to the trustees. A six monthly progress report is required.
Closing Date: January 30th.
Funding: Private.
Contributor: Private trust.
No. of applicants last year: 26.
Additional Information: In exceptional cases a second grant can be awarded, but this would require substantial motivation.

AGRICULTURAL HISTORY SOCIETY

Center for Agricultural History
618 Ross
Iowa State University, Ames, IA, 50011-1202, United States of America
Tel: (1) 515 294 5620
Fax: (1) 515 294 6390
Email: aghist@iastate.edu
www: http://www.iastate.edu/~history_info/aghistry.htm
Contact: Ms Alexandra Kindell, Assistant Editor

The Agricultural History Society recognises the roles of agriculture and agri-business in shaping the political, economic, social and historical profiles of different countries worldwide. Since 1927, the Society's publication Agricultural History has been the international journal for the field and publishes innovative research on agricultural and rural history.

Everett E Edward Awards in Agricultural History
Subjects: Agricultural and rural history.
Purpose: To promote research and publication in the field of agricultural and rural history.
Eligibility: Open to any graduate or doctoral student submitting an article to Agricultural History during the calendar year.
Level of Study: Doctorate, Postgraduate, Predoctorate, Professional development.
Type: Award.
Value: US$200 plus publication in the journal.
Frequency: Annual.
Country of Study: Any country.
No. of awards offered: One.
Application Procedure: Applicants must submit three copies of their manuscript, prepared in accordance with the latest edition of the 'Chicago Manual of Style', to the Editor.
Closing Date: December 31st.
No. of awards given last year: One.
No. of applicants last year: 10-15.
Additional Information: Further information is available on request.

Gilbert C Fite Dissertation Award
Subjects: Agricultural and rural history.
Purpose: To promote research and publication in the field of agricultural and rural history.
Eligibility: Open to any doctoral student who has completed a PhD dissertation.
Level of Study: Doctorate.
Type: Award.
Value: US$300.
Frequency: Annual.

Country of Study: Any country.
No. of awards offered: One.
Application Procedure: Applicants must complete forms and send three copies to the Editor.
Closing Date: Please contact the organisation.
Additional Information: Further information is available on request.

Theodore Saloutos Award
Subjects: Agricultural and rural history in the United States of America.
Purpose: To award the best book published annually in the United States of America on the subject of agricultural history.
Eligibility: Open to nationals of any country.
Level of Study: Unrestricted.
Type: Prize.
Value: US$500.
Frequency: Annual.
Country of Study: Any country.
Application Procedure: Applicants must send four copies of the book to the Editor.
Closing Date: Please contact the organisation.
No. of awards given last year: One.
No. of applicants last year: 15-25.
Additional Information: Further information is available on request.

Vernon Carstenson Award in Agricultural History
Subjects: Agricultural history.
Purpose: To promote research and publication in the field of agricultural and rural history.
Eligibility: Open to any author published in the quarterly journal Agricultural History during the calendar year.
Level of Study: Doctorate, Postdoctorate.
Type: Award.
Value: US$200.
Frequency: Annual.
Country of Study: Any country.
No. of awards offered: One.
Application Procedure: All published articles per issue and year are considered.
Closing Date: The Autumn issue of the journal each year.
No. of awards given last year: One.
Additional Information: Further information is available on request.

AIR FORCE OFFICE OF SCIENTIFIC RESEARCH (AFOSR)

AFOSR/NI
800 North Randolph Street
Room 732, Arlington, VA, 22203-1977, United States of America
Tel: (1) 703 696 7319
Fax: (1) 703 696 7320
www: http://www.afosr.af.mil

The Air Force Office of Scientific Research's mission is to sponsor and sustain basic research, transfer and transition research results and support Air Force goals of control and maximum utilisation of air and space.

NDSEG Fellowship Program
Subjects: Science, engineering and mathematics.
Purpose: To support study and research into areas of interest to the Air Force.
Eligibility: Open to United States citizens who have received their BS degrees.
Level of Study: Doctorate, Postgraduate.
Type: Fellowship.
Value: US$19,000 in the first year, US$20,000 in the second year, and US$21,000 in the third year. In addition to the stipend, the Air Force pays the student's tuition.

Length of Study: Three years.
Frequency: Annual.
Study Establishment: Any approved university.
Country of Study: United States of America.
No. of awards offered: Varies, depending on funds available.
Application Procedure: Applicants must write for details and should visit the website http://www.afosr.sciencewise.com.
Closing Date: January 17th.
Funding: Government.

For further information contact:

NDSEG Program Manager
American Society for Engineering Education
1818 N Street North West
Suite 600, Washington, DC, 20036, United States of America

US Department of Defense/AFOSR Grants and Contracts

Subjects: Sciences of direct interest to strengthening the Air Force operating capabilities such as chemical sciences, mathematical and information sciences, electronics and solid state sciences, aerospace sciences, life sciences, general physics, geophysics and atmospheric sciences.
Purpose: To stimulate high quality scientific research on problems of Air Force interest.
Eligibility: AFOSR principal investigators are predominantly at the postdoctoral level. Awards are not restricted by citizenship.
Level of Study: Postdoctorate.
Value: Varies.
Length of Study: Varies.
Study Establishment: Colleges, universities and industrial or non-profit research laboratories.
Country of Study: Any country.
No. of awards offered: The current research programme consists of approx. 1,125 individual work efforts.
Application Procedure: Prior to formal submission of a proposal, investigators should write for the Proposer's Guide to the AFOSR Research Program. Non United States investigators should contact the European Office of Aerospace Research and Development (EOARD).
Closing Date: Please write for details.
Additional Information: Please see the website http://www.ehis.navy.mil/eoardwebsite2 for details.

For further information contact:

EOARD
223-321 Old Marylebone Road, London, NW1, England
Tel: (44) 20 7514 4950

USAF/NRC Summer Faculty Research Program (SFFP)

Subjects: Science, engineering or mathematics.
Purpose: To provide research opportunities for qualified faculty members of United States colleges and universities at Air Force research facilities within the continental United States.
Eligibility: Applicants must be United States citizens or permanent residents, faculty members of accredited United States of America colleges, universities or technical institutions, and have at least two years of teaching or research experience.
Level of Study: Faculty.
Value: Assistant professors receive US$1,250, associate professors receive US$1,450, and full professors receive US$1,650.
Length of Study: 8-12 weeks.
Frequency: Annual.
Study Establishment: An Air Force facility.
Country of Study: United States of America.
No. of awards offered: Varies.
Application Procedure: Applicants must contact the National Research Council on (1) 202 334 2760.
Closing Date: January 15th.
Funding: Government.
Additional Information: Please see the website http://www.national-academies.org/rap for details.

USAF/NRC-RRA Postdoctoral Research Associateships

Subjects: Scientific and engineering education.
Purpose: To support senior scientists and engineers who are carrying out research in sponsoring Air Force laboratories.
Eligibility: Open to United States citizens and permanent residents who have held doctorates for less than five years at the time of application. A small number of associateships may be available for foreign citizens if laboratory funds are available.
Level of Study: Postdoctorate.
Type: Associateship.
Value: Varies, in the region of US$55,000.
Length of Study: Usually one year, with a possibility of renewal for a second year.
Frequency: Annual.
Study Establishment: An Air Force laboratory.
Country of Study: United States of America.
No. of awards offered: Varies.
Application Procedure: Applicants must contact the National Research Council on (1) 202 334 2760.
Closing Date: Please contact the organisation.
Funding: Government.
Additional Information: Please see the website http://www.national-academies.org/rap for details.

USAF/NRC-RRA Senior Research Associateships

Subjects: Science, engineering and mathematics.
Purpose: To support senior scientists and engineers who are carrying out research at sponsoring Air Force laboratories.
Eligibility: Open to individuals who have held doctorates for more than five years, have significant research experience and are recognised internationally as experts in their specialised fields. United States citizenship is not a requirement.
Level of Study: Postdoctorate.
Type: Associateship.
Value: In the region of US$85,000.
Length of Study: Usually one year, although awards for periods of three months or longer will be considered.
Frequency: Annual.
Study Establishment: An Air Force laboratory.
Country of Study: United States of America.
No. of awards offered: Varies.
Application Procedure: Applicants must contact the National Research Council on (1) 202 334 2760.
Closing Date: Please contact the organisation.
Funding: Government.
Additional Information: Please see the website http://www.national-academies.org/rap for details.

AIREY NEAVE TRUST

40 Charles Street, London, W1X 7PB, England
Tel: (44) 20 7833 4440
Fax: (44) 20 7833 4949
Contact: Mrs Hannah Scott, Administrator

Airey Neave Trust Award

Subjects: Postgraduate education.
Purpose: To help bona fide refugees in the United Kingdom, recognised by the Home Office, to re-qualify or retrain in their professions or trades.
Eligibility: Open to refugees and those given exceptional leave to remain, recognised as such by the Home Office, resident in Britain.
Level of Study: Doctorate, Postdoctorate, Postgraduate, Professional development.
Value: UK £1,000-2,000.
Length of Study: One year, initially.
Frequency: Annual.
Study Establishment: Any college or university.
Country of Study: United Kingdom.
No. of awards offered: 15-20.

Application Procedure: Applicants must submit a completed application form with a letter from the Home Office confirming status. Applications should be addressed to Miss Jeanne Townsend.
Closing Date: May 1st.
Funding: Private.
Contributor: Charitable trusts and fund raising.
No. of awards given last year: 20.
No. of applicants last year: 20.

For further information contact:

Calshott Cottage
Church Street
Sturminster, Newton, Dorset, DT10 1DB, England
Contact: Miss Jeanne Townsend

ALBERT ELLIS INSTITUTE

45 East 65th Street, New York, NY, 10021, United States of America
Tel: (1) 212 535 0822
Fax: (1) 212 249 3582
Email: info@rebt.org
www: http://www.rebt.org
Contact: Fellowships Office

The Albert Ellis Institute is a non-profit training and therapy institute chartered by the regents of the University of the State of New York, specialising in cognitive behaviour therapy and rational emotive behaviour therapy.

Albert Ellis Institute Clinical Fellowship

Subjects: Psychology and counselling.
Purpose: To provide in depth, hands on training in cognitive behavioural therapy and rational emotive behaviour therapy.
Eligibility: Applicants must have a PhD, MSW, MD or RN and be licensed or licence eligible in New York. There are no other restrictions.
Level of Study: Postgraduate.
Type: Fellowship.
Length of Study: Two years.
Frequency: Annual.
Country of Study: United States of America.
No. of awards offered: Varies.
Application Procedure: Applicants must obtain applications and further information by writing the Institute.
Closing Date: March 1st.
Funding: Private.
Additional Information: The programme begins in mid-July.

ALBERTA HERITAGE FOUNDATION FOR MEDICAL RESEARCH (AHFMR)

1500 Bell Tower
10104-103 Avenue, Edmonton, AB, T5J 4A7, Canada
Tel: (1) 780 423 5727
Fax: (1) 780 429 3509
Email: postmaster@ahfmr.ab.ca
www: http://www.ahfmr.ab.ca
Contact: Dr Jacques Magnan, Vice President, Research

The Alberta Heritage Foundation for Medical Research supports a community of researchers who generate knowledge that improves the health and quality of life of Albertans and people throughout the world. The Foundation's long-term commitment is to fund basic patient and health research based on international standards of excellence and carried out by new and established investigators and researchers in training.

Alberta Heritage Clinical Fellowships

Subjects: Medical research.
Purpose: To provide an opportunity for research training to candidates who have completed clinical sub-speciality training requirements.
Eligibility: Open to candidates who hold an MD or DDS and who have received a significant portion of postgraduate training in Alberta.
Level of Study: Postgraduate.
Type: Fellowship.
Value: Canadian $3,000 research allowance plus stipend.
Length of Study: Two years, with a possibility of renewal for a further year.
Frequency: Twice a year.
Study Establishment: An appropriate institution, usually in Alberta.
Country of Study: Canada.
No. of awards offered: Approx. 10.
Application Procedure: Applicants must complete an application form.
Funding: Government.
No. of awards given last year: Seven.
No. of applicants last year: 13.

Alberta Heritage Clinical Investigatorships

Subjects: Medical research.
Purpose: To provide funding for highly qualified clinicians to further their research experience beyond the fellowship level in a setting that provides guidance and supervision by an established scientist.
Eligibility: Open to candidates who hold an MD or DDS, have completed all requirements for clinical speciality recognition and who are eligible to hold a full-time position in a clinical department of the sponsoring institution.
Level of Study: Professional development.
Type: Investigatorship.
Value: A stipend plus an establishment grant. Values are negotiated individually.
Length of Study: Three years, with a possibility of renewal for a further three years.
Frequency: Annual.
Study Establishment: A university, an affiliated hospital or institution in Alberta.
Country of Study: Canada.
No. of awards offered: Varies.
Application Procedure: Applicants must complete an application form.
Closing Date: September 15th.
Funding: Government.
No. of awards given last year: Six.
No. of applicants last year: Nine.

Alberta Heritage Full-Time Fellowships

Subjects: Medical research.
Purpose: To enable doctoral graduates to prepare for careers as independent investigators.
Eligibility: Open to graduates of science programmes relevant to AHFMR objectives or to health professional programmes who have received a PhD not more than five years prior to application. Professional health degrees should not have been received more than 10 years prior to application.
Level of Study: Postdoctorate.
Type: Fellowship.
Value: Canadian $3,000 research allowance plus stipend.
Frequency: Twice a year.
Study Establishment: Usually at an Alberta university.
Country of Study: Canada.
No. of awards offered: Varies, approx. 30.
Application Procedure: Applicants must complete an application form.
Closing Date: March 1st or October 1st.
Funding: Government.
No. of awards given last year: 35.
No. of applicants last year: 113.

Alberta Heritage Full-Time Studentship

Subjects: Research relevant to the objectives of the Foundation.
Purpose: To enable academically superior students to undertake full-time research training in a discipline relevant to the objectives of the Foundation.
Eligibility: Candidates must be sponsored by a faculty supervisor with a record of productive health-orientated research and sufficient competitively acquired research funding to ensure the satisfactory conduct of the student's research during the term of the award. Students must be either engaged in, or accepted into, a full-time university graduate programme in a health related discipline leading to a Master's or doctoral degree, and hold a record of superior academic performance in studies relevant to the proposed training.
Type: Studentship.
Value: Please write for details.
Length of Study: Two years with a possibility of renewal, to a of maximum of five years' support.
Frequency: Annual.
Study Establishment: A university in Alberta.
Country of Study: Canada.
No. of awards offered: Approx. 40-60.
Application Procedure: Applicants must submit the original application and 15 copies to the Foundation's offices by either of the deadlines. They must be completed in full to be entered into the competition.
Closing Date: March 1st or October 1st.
Funding: Government.
No. of awards given last year: 46.
No. of applicants last year: 140.

Alberta Heritage Health Research Studentship

Subjects: Disciplines relevant to the objectives of the Foundation.
Purpose: To enable academically superior students either engaged in, or accepted into, a full-time university programme to undertake full-time research training.
Value: Please write for details.
Length of Study: Two years with a possibility of renewal, to a of maximum of five years' support.
Frequency: Annual.
Study Establishment: A university in Alberta.
Country of Study: Canada.
No. of awards offered: Varies, approx. 10.
Application Procedure: Applicants must submit the original application and 15 complete copies to the Foundation's offices by either of the deadlines. They must be completed in full to be entered into the competition.
Closing Date: March 1st or October 1st.
Funding: Government.
No. of awards given last year: 10.
No. of applicants last year: 35.

Alberta Heritage Medical Scholarships

Subjects: Medical research.
Purpose: To assist in the recruitment and establishment of scientists in Alberta.
Eligibility: Heritage Medical Scholars are investigators who have recently completed their postdoctoral research training and demonstrate the ability to initiate and conduct independent as well as collaborative research. They must exhibit a desire and ability in training future research scientists. Heritage Senior Medical Scholarship candidates must hold a MD, DDS, DVM, PhD or the equivalent, and must have established a record of excellence in independent research over several years as a faculty member. Candidates must also show an interest in training Alberta's future research scientists.
Level of Study: Professional development.
Type: Scholarship.
Value: Stipend plus establishment grant, negotiated individually.
Length of Study: Five years.
Frequency: Annual.
Study Establishment: An Alberta university or affiliate.
Country of Study: Canada.
No. of awards offered: Varies.

Application Procedure: Applicants must complete an application form.
Closing Date: September 15th.
Funding: Government.
No. of awards given last year: 15 to Scholars, 10 to senior Scholars.
No. of applicants last year: 26 for Scholars, 15 for senior Scholars.

Alberta Heritage Medical Scientist Awards

Subjects: Medical research.
Purpose: To assist in the recruitment and establishment of nationally or internationally recognised medical scientists in Alberta.
Eligibility: Open to candidates who hold an MD, DDS, DVM or PhD (or equivalent) in a discipline important to AHFMR objectives and are eligible for a full-time appointment at the sponsoring institution.
Level of Study: Professional development.
Type: Award.
Value: Stipend plus establishment grant, negotiated individually.
Length of Study: Five years, renewable.
Frequency: Annual.
Study Establishment: An Alberta university or affiliate.
Country of Study: Canada.
No. of awards offered: Varies.
Application Procedure: Applicants must complete an application form.
Closing Date: October 1st.
Funding: Government.
No. of awards given last year: 10.
No. of applicants last year: 13.

Alberta Heritage Part-Time Fellowships

Subjects: Medical research.
Purpose: To enable continuing active participation in research during professional education.
Eligibility: Open to graduates holding a PhD in a science relevant to AHFMR objectives or who are registered in a health professional programme in Alberta.
Level of Study: Postdoctorate.
Type: Fellowship.
Value: Pro-rated on full-time fellowship stipend and dependent on the amount of time spent in research.
Length of Study: One year, renewable.
Frequency: Twice a year.
Study Establishment: A university in Alberta.
Country of Study: Canada.
No. of awards offered: Approx. five.
Application Procedure: Applicants must complete an application form.
Closing Date: March 1st or October 1st.
Funding: Government.
No. of awards given last year: Five.
No. of applicants last year: Six.

Alberta Heritage Part-Time Studentship

Subjects: Medical research.
Purpose: To enable full-time degree students to continue research training on a part-time basis.
Eligibility: Open to students enrolled in a full-time professional degree programme who wish to continue research training on a part-time basis during the regular academic year.
Type: Studentship.
Value: Pro-rated on full-time stipend rate of canadian $16,500 and dependent on the amount of time spent in research.
Length of Study: Two years, to a maximum of five years' support.
Frequency: Twice a year.
Study Establishment: A university in Alberta.
Country of Study: Canada.
No. of awards offered: Approx. five.
Application Procedure: Applicants must complete an application form.
Closing Date: March 1st or October 1st.

Funding: Government.
No. of awards given last year: One.
No. of applicants last year: One.

Dr Lionel E Mcleod Health Research Scholarship

Subjects: Health.
Purpose: To enable academically superior students either engaged in, or accepted onto, a full-time university programme to undertake full-time research training.
Eligibility: Open to Canadian citizens or permanent residents at the Universities of Alberta, Calgary or British Columbia for full-time research that is relevant to human health.
Level of Study: Postgraduate.
Type: Scholarship.
Value: Please write for details.
Frequency: Annual.
Country of Study: Canada.
No. of awards offered: One.
Application Procedure: Applicants must write for details.
Funding: Government, Private.

Heritage Health Research Career Renewal Awards

Subjects: Epidemiology, biostatistics, psychosocial sciences or clinical experimental method and design.
Purpose: To enable carefully selected Alberta Faculty members with a demonstrated interest in clinical or health research to obtain training.
Eligibility: Candidates must be proposed and sponsored by an Alberta institution prepared to ensure an adequate environment for the trainee on their return to the province. This environment shall foster the development of a group of scientists capable of independent research and assist others in the design of patient based and population research.
Level of Study: Postdoctorate.
Value: Please write for details.
Frequency: Annual.
Country of Study: Canada.
No. of awards offered: Varies, approx. two.
Application Procedure: Applicants must write for details.
Closing Date: March 1st or October 1st.
Funding: Government.
No. of awards given last year: One.
No. of applicants last year: Three.

Heritage Population Health Investigators

Subjects: Population health.
Purpose: To assist in the recruitment and establishment in Alberta of well trained investigators in population health research.
Eligibility: Open to applicants who have recently completed post MD or PhD research training but have not yet established an independent research record.
Level of Study: Postdoctorate.
Value: Please write for details.
Length of Study: Three years, renewable.
Frequency: Annual.
Country of Study: Canada.
No. of awards offered: Varies, approx. five.
Application Procedure: Applicants must write for details.
Closing Date: September 15th.
Funding: Government.
No. of awards given last year: Three.
No. of applicants last year: Six.

ALCOHOL BEVERAGE MEDICAL RESEARCH FOUNDATION

1122 Kenilworth Drive
Suite 407, Baltimore, MD, 21204, United States of America
Tel: (1) 410 821 7066
Fax: (1) 410 821 7065
Email: info@abmrf.org
www: http://www.abmrf.org
Contact: Dr Albert A Pawlowski, Vice President

The Alcohol Beverage Medical Research Foundation is a non-profit independent research organisation that provides support for scientific studies on the use of alcoholic beverages. It awards grants to study changes in drinking patterns, effects of moderate use of alcohol on health and well being and the mechanisms underlying the behavioural and biomedical effects of alcohol.

Alcohol Beverage Medical Research Foundation Research Project Grant

Subjects: Medical and behavioural sciences.
Purpose: To support new knowledge in order to prevent alcohol related problems.
Eligibility: Open to United States of America and Canadian citizens only.
Level of Study: Doctorate.
Type: Research project grant.
Value: Up to US$40,000 per year.
Length of Study: Up to two years.
Frequency: Twice a year.
Study Establishment: Non-profit universities and research institutions.
Country of Study: United States of America or Canada.
No. of awards offered: 30-40.
Application Procedure: Applicants must complete an application form, available on request or from the website.
Closing Date: February 1st or September 1st.
Funding: Private.
No. of awards given last year: 40.
No. of applicants last year: 150.

ALEXANDER GRAHAM BELL ASSOCIATION FOR THE DEAF AND HARD OF HEARING

3417 Volta Place North West, Washington, DC, 20007, United States of America
Tel: (1) 202 337 5220
Fax: (1) 202 337 8314
Email: info@agbell.org
www: http://www.agbell.org
Contact: Ms Elissa M Brooks, Public Relations

The Alexander Graham Bell Association for the Deaf and Hard of Hearing was established in 1890 to empower hearing-impaired persons to function independently by promoting universal rights and optimal opportunities to learn to use, maintain and improve all aspects of their verbal communications, including their abilities to speak, speech-read, use residual hearing and process both spoken and written language.

Alexander Graham Bell Scholarship Awards

Subjects: All subjects.
Purpose: To encourage severely or profoundly hearing impaired students to attend regular hearing colleges. A G Bell offers financial aid and scholarships through four major programmes which are parent-infant (0-6 years), school age, arts and sciences and college scholarships.

Eligibility: Open to auditory oral students born with profound hearing loss (80 dB loss in the better ear, average), or a severe hearing loss (60 to 80 dB loss), who experienced such a loss before acquiring language. Candidates must use speech and residual hearing and/or speech reading as their preferred customary form of communication and demonstrate a potential for leadership. In addition, applicants must have applied to, or already be enrolled full-time in, a regular college or university programme for hearing students.
Level of Study: Unrestricted.
Type: Scholarship.
Value: US$250-2,000.
Frequency: Annual.
Country of Study: United States of America.
No. of awards offered: Varies.
Application Procedure: Applicants must request an application form in writing by December 1st. Photocopies of applications are not accepted. Applicants may visit the website for up to date information on application procedures and deadlines.
Closing Date: March 15th.
Funding: Private.
Contributor: Members and donors.
No. of awards given last year: 82.
No. of applicants last year: Approx. 250.

ALEXANDER S ONASSIS PUBLIC BENEFIT FOUNDATION

56 Amalias Avenue, Athens, GR-10558, Greece
Tel: (30) 1 371 3000
Fax: (30) 1 037 13013
Email: pubrel@onassis.gr
www: http://www.onassis.gr
Contact: Mr Effie N Tsiotsiou, Deputy Director, Human Resource Manager

The Alexander S Onassis Public Benefit Foundation establishes and supports public benefit projects, offers services and makes contributions to other public benefit institutions for medical care, education, literature, religion, science, research, journalism, art, cultural matters, history, archaeology and sport. It also awards prizes, grants and scholarships to both Greeks and foreigners.

Alexander S Onassis Programme of Research Grants

Subjects: Humanistic and political sciences, architecture, fine arts, law, economics and education.
Purpose: To support non-Greek university professors at all levels, university researchers at PhD level or above, artists and musicians, and translators of Greek literature who wish to conduct research in Greece.
Eligibility: Open to non Greeks from any country. Also open to Scholars of Greek descent or citizenship, provided they have followed a professional career for at least 10 years in a university or research institute outside Greece. There is an age limit of 60 years.
Level of Study: Postdoctorate, Professional development.
Type: Grant.
Value: A monthly allowance plus accommodation in a furnished apartment and a round trip economy airfare.
Length of Study: Up to six months.
Frequency: Annual.
Country of Study: Greece.
No. of awards offered: 15.
Application Procedure: Applicants must complete a formal application and submit this with the required documentation to the Foundation.
Closing Date: January 31st.
Funding: Private.
No. of awards given last year: 20.
No. of applicants last year: 182.

For further information contact:

7 Aeschinou Street, Athens, GR-10558, Greece

Alexander S Onassis Research Grants

Subjects: Humanistic and political sciences, architecture, fine arts, law, economics and education.
Purpose: To support non Greek full members of National Academies and full university professors who wish to conduct research in Greece.
Eligibility: Open to non Greeks from any country. Scholars of Greek citizenship or descent are also eligible provided they have followed a professional academic career for at least 10 years in a university or research institute outside Greece.
Level of Study: Professional development.
Type: Grant.
Value: Please contact the organisation.
Length of Study: One month.
Frequency: Annual.
Country of Study: Greece.
No. of awards offered: 10.
Application Procedure: Applicants must be nominated. The nomination form contains other documentation which has to be submitted to the Foundation.
Closing Date: January 31st.
Funding: Private.
No. of awards given last year: 12.
No. of applicants last year: 111.

For further information contact:

7 Aeschinou Street, Athens, GR-10558, Greece

Onassis Foreigners' Fellowship Programme Educational Scholarships Category B

Subjects: Greek language, Greek literature, Greek history and civilisation.
Purpose: To render possible the acquaintance, collaboration and exchange of information between the scholarship recipients and their Greek colleagues in Greek schools, education or other relevant departments of Greek universities.
Eligibility: Open to active elementary or high school foreign teachers who teach the Greek language (modern or ancient), Greek literature, Greek history and Greek civilisation. Only persons of other than Greek nationality are eligible. However, persons of Greek descent, second generation and on, are also eligible providing they are permanently residing and working abroad or currently studying in foreign universities.
Type: Scholarship.
Value: A monthly allowance plus hotel accommodation and a round trip air ticket.
Length of Study: A maximum of two months.
Frequency: Annual.
Country of Study: Greece.
No. of awards offered: Five.
Application Procedure: Copies of the Announcement and the relevant nomination and application forms are available daily at the Foundation's Secretariat or from the website.
Closing Date: Please contact the Foundation.
Additional Information: The programme presupposes that the scholarship recipients will continue offering their services to their country of origin after they have completed their training in Greece.

Onassis Foreigners' Fellowship Programme Educational Scholarships Category C

Subjects: All subjects.
Purpose: To render possible the acquaintance, collaboration and exchange of information between the scholarship recipients and their Greek colleagues in Greek schools, education or other relevant departments of Greek universities.
Eligibility: Awarded to foreign postgraduate students and PhD candidates up to 40 years of age who pursue studies in universities,

scholarly or research centres or fine art schools either outside Greece or in Greece.

Level of Study: Doctorate, Postgraduate.
Type: Scholarship.
Value: A monthly allowance plus hotel accommodation and a round trip air ticket.
Length of Study: 6-10 months.
Frequency: Annual.
Country of Study: Greece.
No. of awards offered: 17.
Application Procedure: Copies of the Announcement and the relevant nomination and application forms are available daily at the Foundation's Secretariat or from the website.
Closing Date: Please contact the foundation.
Additional Information: The programme presupposes that the scholarship recipients will continue offering their services to their country of origin, after they have completed their training in Greece.

Onassis Foreigners' Fellowships Programme Research Grants Category AI

Subjects: Humanistic sciences eg. philology, literature, translation, linguistics, theology, history, archaeology, philosophy, educational studies, psychology. Political sciences such as sociology, anthropology, public administration, international relations, mass media. Law, economics, architecture and the Arts eg. visual arts, music, dance, theatre, photography and film studies.
Purpose: To enable full members of national academies and full university professors whose scholarly or artistic work has been widely acclaimed and who wish to visit Greece in order to conduct scholarly research or to collaborate with educational institutions, research institutions or organisations.
Eligibility: Only persons of other than Greek nationality are eligible. However, persons of Greek descent, second generation and on, are also eligible providing they are permanently residing and working abroad or currently studying in foreign universities. Applicants must have had a professional academic career of at least 10 years.
Level of Study: Postdoctorate.
Type: Research grant.
Value: A monthly allowance plus a round trip air ticket and A' class hotel accommodation.
Length of Study: One month.
Frequency: Annual.
Country of Study: Greece.
No. of awards offered: Up to 10.
Application Procedure: Copies of the Announcement and the relevant nomination and application forms are available daily at the Foundation's Secretariat or from the website.
Closing Date: Please contact the foundation.
Additional Information: Any person wishing to apply under this programme should specify the category in which they want to be considered in order to receive the relevant nomination and application form. Only one application form for one of the categories can be submitted.

Onassis Foreigners' Fellowships Programme Research Grants Category AII

Subjects: All subjects.
Purpose: To enable university or equivalent institutions' faculty, researchers, PhD holders, artists and musicians, and translators of Greek literature who wish to come to Greece either for scholarly research co-operation with a Greek university, research centre or institute or for their artistic creation or translation.
Eligibility: Only persons of other than Greek nationality are eligible. However, persons of Greek descent, second generation and on, are also eligible providing they are permanently residing and working abroad or currently studying in foreign universities. Applicants must have had a professional academic career of at least 10 years.
Level of Study: Postdoctorate.
Type: Fellowship.
Value: A monthly allowance plus hotel accommodation and a round trip air ticket.
Length of Study: Up to six months.

Frequency: Annual.
Country of Study: Greece.
No. of awards offered: Up to 15.
Application Procedure: Copies of the Announcement and the relevant nomination and application forms are available daily at the Foundation's Secretariat or from the website.
Closing Date: Please contact the foundation.
Additional Information: Any person wishing to apply under this programme should specify the category in which they want to be considered in order to receive the relevant nomination and application form. Only one application form for one of the categories can be submitted.

Onassis Programme of Postgraduate Research Scholarships

Subjects: Humanistic and political sciences, architecture, fine arts, law or economics.
Purpose: To support non Greek postgraduate students studying in or outside Greece who wish to collect material, visit libraries and attend classes in Greek universities. Also to support postgraduate students or PhD candidates who are of Greek descent or citizenship who have obtained a degree abroad, and who have been permanently residing abroad for more than 15 years.
Eligibility: Open to non Greeks from any country or students at the Master's or PhD level who are of Greek descent or citizenship, who have obtained a degree abroad and who have been permanently residing outside Greece for more than 15 years. There is an age limit of 40.
Level of Study: Doctorate, Postgraduate.
Type: Scholarship.
Value: A monthly allowance plus hotel accommodation and a round trip economy airfare.
Length of Study: Up to one year.
Frequency: Annual.
Country of Study: Greece.
No. of awards offered: 15.
Application Procedure: Applicants must complete a formal application and submit this with the required documentation to the Foundation.
Closing Date: January 31st.
Funding: Private.
No. of awards given last year: 18.
No. of applicants last year: 143.

For further information contact:

7 Aeschinou Street, Athens, GR-10558, Greece

Onassis Programme of Scholarships for Post-Educational Training for Teachers of the Greek Language

Subjects: Greek language.
Purpose: To support non Greek teachers of the Greek language at elementary and secondary level who have come to Greece for post educational training.
Eligibility: Open to non Greeks from any country. The award is also open to teachers of Greek language who are of Greek descent or citizenship, who have obtained their degrees outside Greece and who have been permanently residing outside Greece for more than 15 years.
Level of Study: Professional development.
Type: Scholarship.
Value: A monthly allowance plus hotel accommodation and a round trip air ticket (economy class).
Length of Study: Up to two months.
Frequency: Annual.
Country of Study: Greece.
No. of awards offered: Five.
Application Procedure: Applicants must complete a formal application and submit this with the required documentation to the Foundation.
Closing Date: January 31st.

Funding: Private.
No. of awards given last year: Six.
No. of applicants last year: 37.

For further information contact:

7 Aeschinou Street, Athens, GR-10558, Greece

ALEXANDER VON HUMBOLDT FOUNDATION

Jean-Paul Straße 12, Bonn, Bad Godesberg, D-53173, Germany
Tel: (49) 228 833 0
Fax: (49) 228 833 216
Email: post@avh.de
www: http://www.humboldt-foundation.de
Telex: 885 627
Contact: Dr Babara Sheldon

The Alexander von Humboldt Foundation grants research fellowships to foreign scholars who hold doctorates and have not yet reached the age of 40. The Foundation also offers research awards to internationally recognised foreign scholars of any age, enabling them to spend a lengthy period of research in Germany.

Federal Chancellor Scholarship

Subjects: Arts and humanities, business administration and management, fine and applied arts, mass communication and information science, medicine, recreation, welfare, protective services, religion and theology, social, behavioural sciences or law.
Purpose: To maintain and foster a close relationship between the United States of America and Germany by sponsoring individuals who demonstrate the potential of playing a pivotal role in the future development of this relationship.
Eligibility: Open to United States of America citizens only.
Level of Study: Postgraduate.
Type: Scholarship.
Value: Please contact the organisation.
Length of Study: One year.
Frequency: Annual.
Study Establishment: An academic or other research institution.
Country of Study: Germany.
No. of awards offered: 10.
Application Procedure: Applicants must complete an application form.
Closing Date: October 31st for the following academic year.
Funding: Government.
No. of awards given last year: 10.

Feodor Lynen Research Fellowships for German Scholars

Subjects: All academic fields.
Purpose: To enable highly qualified scholars to conduct research of their choice at home institutions of non-German recipients of Humboldt fellowships and prizes.
Eligibility: Open to German nationals or those who have been living and working in Germany for more than five years.
Level of Study: Postdoctorate.
Type: Fellowship.
Value: Please contact the organisation.
Length of Study: One-four years.
Frequency: Annual.
Study Establishment: Research institutions or universities.
Country of Study: Any country except Germany.
No. of awards offered: Up to 150.
Application Procedure: Applicants must complete an application form, available from the Bonn office.
Closing Date: February 15th, June 15th or October 15th.
Funding: Government.

Contributor: The Federal Ministry of Education, Science, Research & Technology.
No. of awards given last year: 136.
No. of applicants last year: 266.

Humboldt Research Award for Foreign Scholars

Subjects: All subjects.
Purpose: To enable internationally recognised foreign scholars to conduct research on a project of their choice in Germany.
Eligibility: Open to all nationalities except Germans.
Level of Study: Research.
Type: Research prize.
Value: Please contact the organisation.
Length of Study: 4-12 months.
Frequency: Annual.
Study Establishment: Universities and research institutions.
Country of Study: Germany.
No. of awards offered: Up to 150.
Application Procedure: Eminent German Scholars propose candidates directly to the Foundation in Bonn. Direct applications are not accepted.
Closing Date: Nominations are accepted throughout the year.
Funding: Government.
No. of awards given last year: 113.
No. of applicants last year: 200.
Additional Information: Selection committee meetings are held twice a year in March and October.

JSPS Research Fellowships

Subjects: All subjects.
Purpose: To enable highly qualified scholars to carry out research projects of their own choice.
Eligibility: Open to German nationals only.
Level of Study: Postdoctorate.
Type: Fellowship.
Value: Yen 270,000 plus travel and housing allowance.
Length of Study: One-two years.
Frequency: Annual.
Study Establishment: A university or other research institution.
Country of Study: Japan.
No. of awards offered: 25.
Application Procedure: Applicants must complete an application form.
Closing Date: February 15th, June 15th or October 15th.
Funding: Government.
Contributor: JSPS.
No. of awards given last year: 12.

Konrad Adenauer Research Award

Subjects: Humanities and social sciences.
Purpose: To promote academic relations between Canada and Germany.
Eligibility: Open to highly qualified Canadian Scholars, whose research work in the humanities or in the social sciences has brought them international recognition and who belong to the group of leading Scholars in their respective area of specialisation. The award will be made regardless of the age, race, religion or sex of the applicants.
Level of Study: Postdoctorate.
Type: Research award or prize.
Value: Please contact the organisation. The Humboldt Foundation will pay the return travel costs once only for award winners and family members (provided the latter stay with them in Germany for more than six months) between Canada and Germany. Medical and accident insurance may be provided for the award winners, and family members, if requested.
Length of Study: One year.
Frequency: Annual.
Study Establishment: German research institutes.
Country of Study: Germany.
No. of awards offered: One.

Application Procedure: Candidates should be nominated by their universities and their dossiers should be sent to the Awards Co-ordinator. Nomination forms and information may also be requested from the Awards Co-ordinator.
Closing Date: December 1st.
Funding: Government.
No. of applicants last year: None.
Additional Information: Nominations will be made jointly by the Royal Society of Canada and the University of Toronto and submitted to the Humboldt Foundation. At least two candidates should be nominated each year.

For further information contact:

Awards Co-ordinator
The Royal Society of Canada
225 Metcalfe Street
Suite 308, Ottawa, ON, K2P 1P9, Canada
Contact: Mrs Kathy Riikonen, Awards Co-ordinator

Max Planck Award for International Co-operation
Subjects: All academic fields.
Purpose: To enable internationally recognised foreign and German scholars to conduct long-term co-operative research.
Eligibility: Open to Scholars of all disciplines and nationalities.
Level of Study: Professional development, Research.
Type: Research prize.
Value: Please contact the organisation.
Length of Study: Three-five years.
Frequency: Annual.
Country of Study: Germany.
No. of awards offered: 12.
Application Procedure: Applicants must be nominated by presidents of German universities, academies of sciences, the Max Planck Society, corporations of large research establishments, the Fraunhofer Society, the German Research Association, former prize holders or selection committee members.
Closing Date: April 15th.
Funding: Government.
Contributor: The Federal Ministry for Education, Science, Research & Technology.
No. of awards given last year: 12.
No. of applicants last year: 70.
Additional Information: Selection occurs once per year.

Postdoctoral Humboldt Research Fellowships
Subjects: Postdoctoral academic research in any subject.
Purpose: To provide opportunities for young, highly qualified scholars to carry out research projects of their own choice in Germany.
Eligibility: Open to persons of any nationality other than German, up to 40 years of age, who have obtained a PhD degree or equivalent, who can furnish proof of independent research and can submit academic publications. Candidates in the arts and humanities should possess sound German language ability. Those in the natural, medical and engineering sciences should possess English language ability (German language courses at the Goethe Institute in Germany for two to four months may be available prior to commencement of the research fellowship). Candidates should already have established relations with a German research institute where the project can be realised.
Level of Study: Postdoctorate.
Type: Research fellowship.
Value: Please contact the organisation.
Length of Study: 6-12 months with the possibility of extension for a limited number of months.
Frequency: Annual.
Study Establishment: Universities or research institutions in Germany.
Country of Study: Germany.
No. of awards offered: Approx. 600.
Application Procedure: Applicants must complete an application form, available from the Bonn office, and submit this to the office five months before the selection committee meeting, during which the decision is to be made.
Closing Date: Applications are accepted at any time.
Funding: Government.
No. of awards given last year: 436.
No. of applicants last year: 1,754.
Additional Information: Applications should be forwarded directly to the Foundation or through diplomatic or consular offices of the Federal Republic of Germany in the candidates' respective countries.

Science and Technology Agency (STA) Research Fellowships
Subjects: All subjects.
Purpose: To enable highly qualified scholars to carry out research projects of their own choice.
Eligibility: Open to German nationals only.
Level of Study: Postdoctorate.
Type: Fellowship.
Value: Yen 270,000 plus travel and housing allowance.
Length of Study: 6-24 months.
Frequency: Annual.
Study Establishment: A non university research institution.
Country of Study: Japan.
No. of awards offered: 10.
Application Procedure: Applicants must complete an application form.
Closing Date: February 15th, June 15th or October 15th.
Funding: Government.
No. of awards given last year: Five.

ALFRED P SLOAN FOUNDATION

Sloan Research Fellowships
Suite 2550
630 Fifth Avenue, New York, NY, 10111, United States of America
Tel: (1) 212 649 1649
Fax: (1) 212 757 5117
www: http://www.sloan.org
Contact: Ms Maureen Gassmann, Programme Administrator

Alfred P Sloan Foundation Research Fellowships
Subjects: Physics, chemistry, computer science, mathematics, economics, neuroscience and certain interdisciplinary fields such as geochemistry or astrophysics.
Purpose: To provide especially promising young scientists with flexible research support at an early stage of their academic careers.
Eligibility: Open to young (no more than six years from completion of PhD) regular faculty members of a university or college in the United States of America or Canada who hold a PhD or equivalent degree in one of the named subjects.
Level of Study: Junior faculty (tenure track).
Type: Fellowship.
Value: Approx. US$40,000, payable in two annual instalments.
Length of Study: Two years, with the possibility of no cost renewal.
Frequency: Annual.
Study Establishment: Recognised universities and colleges.
Country of Study: United States of America or Canada.
No. of awards offered: 104.
Application Procedure: Applicants must write for details.
Closing Date: September 15th.
Funding: Private.
No. of awards given last year: 104.
No. of applicants last year: Approx. 500 per year.
Additional Information: The Fellow's institution is required to report annually on expenditures and the Fellow must submit a brief annual scientific progress report and a final report. Reprints or preprints of scientific papers may be submitted in lieu of such reports. Further information is available on the Foundation's website.

ALICIA PATTERSON FOUNDATION

1730 Pennsylvania Avenue NW
Suite 850, Washington, DC, 20006, United States of America
Tel: (1) 202 393 5995
Fax: (1) 301 951 8512
Email: apfengel@charm.net
www: http://www.aliciapatterson.org
Contact: Ms Margaret Engel, Executive Director

The Alicia Patterson Foundation gives grants to professional print reporters and photo-journalists to investigate a subject of their choice. Their reports are published in a quarterly magazine, the Alicia Patterson Foundation Reporter, and on the Foundation's website.

Alicia Patterson Journalism Fellowships

Subjects: Journalism.
Purpose: To give working print journalists a chance to spend a year researching and writing on a topic of their choosing.
Eligibility: Open to print journalists eg. reporters, editors, photographers with at least five years of full-time professional experience, who are United States citizens.
Level of Study: Professional development.
Type: Fellowship.
Value: US$35,000.
Length of Study: One year.
Frequency: Annual.
Country of Study: Any country.
No. of awards offered: 8-10.
Application Procedure: Applicants must use the APF application and are also required to submit a three page proposal, a two page autobiographical essay, three clips, four letters of reference and a budget.
Closing Date: Postmarked October 1st.
Funding: Private.
No. of awards given last year: Seven.
No. of applicants last year: 261.

ALL SAINTS EDUCATIONAL TRUST

St Katherine Cree Church
86 Leadenhall Street, London, EC3A 3DH, England
Tel: (44) 20 7283 4485
Fax: (44) 20 7621 9758
Email: enquiries@aset.org.uk
www: http://www.aset.org.uk
Contact: Mr Richard C Poulton, Clerk to the Trustees

The funds of the All Saints Educational Trust are dedicated to the formal training, or the better qualification, of teachers and to educational advance by other means eg. research or improvement in communication. There is particular emphasis within the fields of religious education, home economics or related subjects.

All Saints Educational Trust Corporate Awards

Subjects: Research and development of religious education, home economics and kindred subjects, as well as multi-cultural and inter-faith education.
Purpose: To offer assistance to individuals and institutions within certain specified terms of reference.
Type: Award.
Value: Varies, UK £100,000 over four years is the maximum awarded.
Length of Study: Up to five years.
Frequency: Annual.
Country of Study: United Kingdom.
No. of awards offered: Two-six per year.
Application Procedure: Applicants must complete an application form, available on request from the Clerk to the Trust.
Closing Date: January 31st or earlier.

No. of awards given last year: Six.
No. of applicants last year: 19.
Additional Information: The award will normally be used or applied in the United Kingdom. Further information is available on request or from the website.

All Saints Educational Trust Personal Awards

Subjects: Religious education, home economics and multicultural education.
Purpose: To give support to persons who are, or intend to become, teachers or to work in certain capacities associated with education in home economics or kindred subjects and in religious subjects.
Eligibility: Open to individuals over 18 years of age who are, or intend to become, teachers. Grants for research are open to individuals.
Level of Study: Unrestricted.
Type: Grant.
Value: Varies, usually UK £500-7,000, occasionally more.
Length of Study: One-three years.
Frequency: Annual.
Study Establishment: Recognised educational institutions in the United Kingdom.
Country of Study: United Kingdom.
No. of awards offered: Dependent on funds available.
Application Procedure: Applicants must complete an application form, available on request from the Clerk to the Trust or from the website.
Closing Date: December 31st or earlier for overseas students and March 31st for home students.
No. of awards given last year: 58.
No. of applicants last year: 209.
Additional Information: Enquiries should not be delayed until the offer of a place on a course of study has been confirmed. Late applications cannot be considered.

ALZHEIMER'S ASSOCIATION

Medical & Scientific Affairs
919 North Michigan Avenue
Suite 1100, Chicago, IL, 60611-1676, United States of America
Tel: (1) 312 335 5779
Fax: (1) 312 335 4034
Email: grants@alz.org
www: http://www.alz.org
Contact: Grants Co-ordinator

The Alzheimer's Association aims to be a source of information, support and assistance on issues related to Alzheimer's disease. It seeks to provide leadership in attempting to eliminate Alzheimer's disease through the advancement of research, while enhancing care and support services for the individuals concerned and their families. To this end, the Association funds select projects for biomedical, social and behavioural research, as well as promoting, developing and disseminating educational programmes and training guidelines for health and social service professionals.

Alzheimer's Association Investigator-Initiated Research Grants

Subjects: Alzheimer's disease and related disorders.
Purpose: To build on the success of established investigators by providing sustained support for independent research projects.
Eligibility: Investigators from all stages of research career development are encouraged to apply.
Level of Study: Doctorate, Postdoctorate, Postgraduate.
Type: Research grant.
Value: The awards will be limited to US$100,000 per year direct and indirect for up to three years, for a total award of no more than US$240,000 of indirect costs.
Length of Study: Two or three years.
Frequency: Annual.

Country of Study: Any country.

No. of awards offered: Varies.

Application Procedure: Applicants must, before preparing an application for any of the research grant programmes, send a one page letter of intent by email to grantsloi@alz.org. Each letter must include the name and contact information of the principal investigator, institutions involved in the research proposal, the title of the investigation and its specific aims, presented in bullet format. The application will be available upon approval of the letter of intent. Applicants should visit the website for details. It is the responsibility of the applicant to ensure and to verify that the application is received by the Alzheimer's Association prior to the receipt date deadline and that the application is complete and correct prior to submission.

Closing Date: December 3rd. This is subject to change.

Funding: Private.

Additional Information: Multiple submissions of the same research grant application in a single fiscal year will not be accepted. An investigator may not submit more than one application per programme during the research grant competition and each application must be a separate and distinct research proposal with non overlapping aims. Applicants may revise and resubmit applications which were previously submitted which will then be treated as new. Efforts will be made to provide some continuity in reviewers. Animal welfare and human subject protection assurances are not required at the time of submission.

Alzheimer's Association New Investigator Research Grants

Subjects: Alzheimer's disease and related disorders.

Purpose: To stimulate interest by new investigators, to enable new and established investigators to test the feasibility of new ideas on a small scale, and to allow investigators to generate pilot data to support proposals to NIH foundations or the Association for larger grants.

Eligibility: Eligibility is restricted to investigators who have had less than 10 years of research experience, including postdoctoral fellowships or residencies, after receipt of the doctoral degree. This 10 year period is taken from the submission date of the grant application. Applications from graduate and doctoral students for research projects, which will be used for the thesis or dissertation, will be accepted and judged by the usual scientific criteria.

Level of Study: Postgraduate.

Type: Research grant.

Value: US$100,000 per year direct and indirect. Requests in any given year may not exceed US$60,000. Indirect costs are capped at 10 per cent.

Length of Study: Up to two years.

Frequency: Annual.

Country of Study: Any country.

No. of awards offered: Varies.

Application Procedure: Applicants must visit the website for details.

Closing Date: Letters of intent must be received by November 13th.

Additional Information: This award was formally known as the Pilot Research Grant. Annual progress and financial reports are required. Future, non competitive continuation funding is contingent on the timely receipt of scientific and financial reports.

The Alzheimer's Association Pioneer Awards for Alzheimer's Disease Research

Subjects: Alzheimer's disease.

Purpose: To offer investigators the unique opportunity of obtaining substantial research and research support funding. The goal of the award is to support a dual effort in the investigator's laboratory, to work on a focused research project aimed at questions surrounding the interventions for Alzheimer's disease and flexible research support which will allow rapid mid-course adjustments in the ongoing research programme.

Eligibility: Investigators who have made important, ground breaking contributions to Alzheimer's disease are encouraged to apply. It is anticipated that successful applicants will hold senior academic rank, have international recognition of their research contributions, have lengthy records of peer reviewed publications in major scientific journals and have long track records of substantial funding from the National Institutes of Health or other national funding agencies. Investigators who have been Directors of Alzheimer's Disease Centers (P50 and P30), principal investigators on NIH sponsored programme projects grants (P01) or LEAD awardees are eligible, but members of the Medical and Scientific Advisory Council and of the National Board of the Alzheimer's Association are not.

Type: Award.

Value: US$100,000 per year (direct and indirect), for a total award of US$250,000. Indirect costs are capped at 10 per cent.

Length of Study: Investigators may request up to five years of support under this programme and may allocate the funds across the five years as most appropriately supports their research programme.

Frequency: Annual.

No. of awards offered: One.

Application Procedure: Applicants must visit the website for details.

Closing Date: Letters of intent must be received by November 13th.

Funding: Private.

Additional Information: Biannual progress and financial reports are required. Future non competitive continuation funding is contingent on the timely submission of interim scientific and financial reports.

The Senator Mark Hatfield Award for Clinical Research in Alzheimer's Disease

Subjects: Alzheimer's disease and related disorders.

Purpose: To honour Senator Hatfield's long commitment to Alzheimer's disease research in general and clinical research in particular. The award is designed to focus on the Senator's interests in clinical research and support of new investigators.

Eligibility: Open to investigators who received their doctoral degree less than 10 years prior to submission of the application. The Hatfield Award is aimed at those investigators whose goal is to establish research careers focused on clinical issues in Alzheimer's disease.

Type: Award.

Value: The award will be for US$100,000 per year direct and indirect for up to three years, for a total award limited to US$225,000. Indirect costs are capped at 10 per cent.

Length of Study: Up to three years.

Frequency: Annual.

No. of awards offered: One.

Application Procedure: Applicants must visit the website for details.

Closing Date: Letters of intent must be received no later than October 9th. Applications must be received by the close of business on December 18th.

Funding: Private.

Additional Information: Annual progress and financial reports are required. Future non competitive continuation funding is contingent on the timely receipt of scientific progress and financial reports.

Zenith Awards

Subjects: Alzheimer's disease.

Purpose: To provide major support to qualified scientists in basic biomedical research who have already made substantial contributions in the field of Alzheimer's, or have made significant contributions to other areas of science and are now beginning to focus more directly on problems related to Alzheimer's disease and are likely to make substantial contributions to Alzheimer research in the future.

Eligibility: Open to projects that will test new and innovative ideas likely to lead to fundamental findings related to the biology of Alzheimer's disease. The proposed research must be on the cutting edge of basic, biomedical research and therefore may not fit current conventional scientific wisdom or may challenge prevailing orthodoxy. The proposed research should address fundamental problems related to the early detection, aetiology, pathogenesis, treatment and prevention of Alzheimer's disease. Previous recipients of Zenith awards, Alzheimer's Disease Centre directors, Medical and Scientific Advisory Council members and members of the national board of the Alzheimer's Association are ineligible to apply.

Type: Award.
Value: The awards will be for US$150,000 per year direct and indirect for two years, for a total award of US$250,000. Indirect costs are capped at 10 per cent.
Length of Study: Two years, with possible competitive renewal upon review of research progress.
Frequency: Annual.
Country of Study: Any country.
No. of awards offered: Five.
Application Procedure: Applicants must visit the website for details.
Closing Date: The letter of intent must be received by October 23rd. Applications must be received by the close of business on December 4th.
Additional Information: Applications will be evaluated by an expert panel of senior scientists, already well recognised for their own accomplishments in Alzheimer's research. Annual progress and financial reports are required. Future non competitive continuation funding is contingent on the receipt of scientific progress and financial statue reports.

ALZHEIMER'S RESEARCH TRUST

Livanos House
Granham's Road, Cambridge, Cambridgeshire, CB2 5LQ, England
Tel: (44) 1223 843899
Fax: (44) 1223 843325
Email: azt@btinternet.com
Contact: Ms Harriet Millward, Acting Chief Executive

The Alzheimer's Research Trust is the leading national charity funding United Kingdom biomedical research to find a fully effective treatment or prevention for Alzheimer's disease and related dementias.

Alzheimer's Research Trust PhD Studentship
Subjects: Any area of research that promises to further understanding of the basic disease processes in Alzheimer's disease and related dementias that is directed towards identifying risk factors or that offers progress towards more effective early diagnosis and/or treatments.
Purpose: To contribute towards research into Alzheimer's disease and related dementias, and to help ensure that bright young graduates are inducted into this area of research.
Eligibility: Research must take place in the United Kingdom.
Level of Study: Postgraduate.
Type: Scholarship.
Value: UK £63,000 or UK £67,000 in London.
Length of Study: Three years.
Frequency: Annual, if funds are available.
Country of Study: United Kingdom.
No. of awards offered: Three.
Application Procedure: Applications must be submitted by individual or joint prospective supervisors. These should consist of a brief description of the proposed project, a curriculum vitae of proposed supervisor(s), a brief statement on the research and training environment, and confirmation that the application has the approval of the institution. There is no application form.
Closing Date: November prior to commencement in October of the following year.
Contributor: Charitable sources.
No. of awards given last year: Three.

Alzheimer's Research Trust Research Programme Grant
Subjects: Any area of research that promises to further understanding of the basic disease processes in Alzheimer's disease and related dementias that is directed towards identifying risk factors, or that offers progress towards more effective early diagnosis and/or treatments.
Purpose: To contribute towards research into Alzheimer's disease and related dementias.

Eligibility: Research must take place in the United Kingdom.
Level of Study: Research.
Type: Major research programme grant.
Value: Up to UK £1,000,000.
Length of Study: Three-five years.
Frequency: Annual, if funds are available.
Country of Study: United Kingdom.
No. of awards offered: One or more.
Application Procedure: Applicants must submit 14 copies of their preliminary application consisting of a curriculum vitae of each candidate, a research proposal of not more than four sides of A4, a brief statement of the candidate's major achievements in research in the last five years and a brief outline of the host institution. There is no application form.
Closing Date: Preliminary applications are due in November prior to commencement in the following October. Full submissions are due in March prior to commencement in October.
No. of awards given last year: One.

ALZHEIMER'S SOCIETY

Gordon House
10 Greencoat Place, London, SW1P 1PH, England
Tel: (44) 20 7692 1495
Fax: (44) 870 132 0292
Email: qrd@alzheimers.org.uk
www: http://www.alzheimers.org.uk
Contact: Dr Richard Harvey, Director of Research

The Alzheimer's Society is the leading care and research charity for people with all forms of dementia, their families and carers.

Alzheimer's Society Research Grants
Subjects: Research into all forms of dementia, particularly Alzheimer's disease.
Purpose: To support research into the cause, cure and care of dementia.
Eligibility: Awards may only be held by United Kingdom institutions. Non United Kingdom researchers may be sub-contractors.
Level of Study: Postdoctorate, Research.
Type: Project grants, research fellowships and innovation grants.
Value: UK £1,000,000 per year is committed to research. Fellowship grants are approx. UK £250,000, project grants are approx. UK £650,000 and innovation grants are approx. UK £100,000.
Length of Study: Up to five years.
Frequency: Quarterly.
Country of Study: United Kingdom.
No. of awards offered: Varies.
Application Procedure: Applicants must complete an application form, available from the website.
Closing Date: The deadline for fellowship grants is in March and September. There are no deadlines for project grants and innovation grants.
Funding: Commercial, Government, Private.
No. of awards given last year: 15.
No. of applicants last year: 45.
Additional Information: Further information is available on request or from the website.

For further information contact:

Alzheimers Society
Quality Research in Dementia
Box 16
Institute of Neurology
Queen Square, London, WC1N 3BG, England

AMERICA-ISRAEL CULTURAL FOUNDATION (AICF)

32 Allenby Road, Tel Aviv, 63325, Israel
Tel: (972) 3 517 4177
Fax: (972) 3 517 8991
Email: aicf@netvision.net.il
www: http://aicf.webnet.org
Contact: Mr Gideon Paz, Executive Director

The America-Israel Cultural Foundation (AICF) has been promoting and supporting the arts in Israel for over 60 years. While in the past it has supported numerous cultural performing organisations and institutions, it is now focusing its support almost exclusively on the education of artists. Through its Sharett Scholarship Program, the AICF grants hundreds of study scholarships each year to students of the arts, music, dance, the visual arts, film and television, and theatre, mainly for studies in Israel. AICF also provides short-term fellowships to artists and art teachers and financially supports various projects in art schools, workshops, master classes etc.

Sharett Scholarship Program

Subjects: Performing arts, visual arts, design, film or television.
Eligibility: Open to Israeli citizens only.
Level of Study: Unrestricted.
Type: Scholarship.
Value: US$750-2,000.
Length of Study: Varies.
Frequency: Annual.
Country of Study: Any country.
No. of awards offered: Approx. 500 scholarships, fellowships and grants.
Application Procedure: Applicants must complete and submit an application form with recommendations and pre-required repertoire. Application forms are available from February 1st of each year.
Closing Date: March 10th.
Funding: Private.
Contributor: America-Israel Cultural Foundation.
No. of awards given last year: 500.
No. of applicants last year: 1,600.
Additional Information: The programme is revised on an annual basis. For more detailed information please contact the Foundation after February 1st.

AMERICAN ACADEMY OF ARTS AND LETTERS

Richard Rodgers Awards
633 West 155th Street, New York, NY, 10032-7599, United States of America
Tel: (1) 212 368 5900
Fax: (1) 212 491 4615
Contact: Ms Virginia Dajani, Executive Director

Richard Rodgers Awards for the Musical Theater

Subjects: Musical theatre.
Purpose: To encourage the development of musical theatre by subsidising productions and staged readings by a non-profit theatre in the city of New York of works by American composers and writers who are not already established in the field.
Eligibility: Open to United States citizens or permanent residents. Awards are given to professional level works. Musicals being entered should be ready for reading or production by a theatre company in New York.
Level of Study: Professional development.
Type: Award.
Value: Subsidised reading or production of original musical.
Frequency: Annual.
Country of Study: United States of America.

No. of awards offered: Varies.
Application Procedure: Applicants must send a stamped addressed envelope accompanying requests for applications. Applications are available in the Spring. Composers and authors must include tapes and scripts with their applications.
Closing Date: November 1st.
Funding: Private.
Contributor: Richard Rodgers' bequest.
No. of awards given last year: Three.
No. of applicants last year: 140.

AMERICAN ACADEMY OF CHILD AND ADOLESCENT PSYCHIATRY

3615 Wisconsin Avenue North West, Washington, DC, 20016, United States of America
Tel: (1) 202 966 7300
Fax: (1) 202 966 2891
Email: crenner@aacap.org
www: http://www.aacap.org
Contact: Ms Crissie Renner, Deputy Director of Research & Training

The American Academy of Child and Adolescent Psychiatry is a national, professional medical association established in 1953 as a non-profit organisation to support and improve the quality of life for children, adolescents and families affected by mental illnesses.

AACAP/Pfizer Travel Grants

Subjects: Child and adolescent psychiatry.
Purpose: To help defray the cost of attending the AACAP's Annual Meeting in San Francisco, California in October.
Eligibility: Applicants must be child and adolescent psychiatry residents at the time of the AACAP Annual Meeting and all awardees must agree to serve as monitors for one event at this meeting.
Type: Travel grant.
Value: US$800.
Country of Study: United States of America.
No. of awards offered: 50.
Application Procedure: Applicants must submit a copy of their curriculum vitae and a one or two page, double spaced description of why they would like to attend the AACAP Annual Meeting and what they hope to get out of the experience.
Closing Date: August 1st.
Contributor: Pfizer Pharmaceuticals.
Additional Information: Winners will be notified on August 15th.

Jeanne Spurlock Minority Medical Student Clinical Fellowship in Child and Adolescent Psychiatry

Subjects: Psychiatry and mental health.
Purpose: To support work during the Summer with a child and adolescent psychiatrist mentor.
Eligibility: Applications are accepted from African American, Asian American, Native American, Alaskan Native, Mexican American, Hispanic and Pacific Islander students in accredited United States medical schools.
Level of Study: Graduate.
Type: Fellowship.
Value: US$2,500 plus expenses for the AACAP annual meeting.
Frequency: Annual.
Country of Study: United States of America.
No. of awards offered: Five.
Application Procedure: Applicants must submit an application including a two page statement outlining his or her background information, career goals and specific research interests. The student's curriculum vitae and a letter verifying the student's good standing in medical school are also required.
Closing Date: April 1st.
Funding: Government.
No. of awards given last year: Nine.

Jeanne Spurlock Research Fellowship in Drug Abuse and Addiction for Minority Medical Students

Subjects: Psychiatry and mental health.
Purpose: To support work during the Summer with a child and adolescent psychiatrist research mentor.
Eligibility: Applications are accepted from African American, Asian American, Native American, Alaskan Native, Mexican American, Hispanic and Pacific Islander students in accredited United States medical schools. All applications must relate to substance abuse research.
Level of Study: Graduate.
Type: Fellowship.
Value: US$2,500 plus expenses for the AACAP annual meeting.
Frequency: Annual.
Country of Study: United States of America.
No. of awards offered: Five.
Application Procedure: Applicants must submit an application including a two page statement outlining his or her background information, career goals and specific research interests. The student's curriculum vitae and a letter verifying the student's good standing in medical school are also required.
Closing Date: April 1st.
Funding: Government.
No. of awards given last year: Five.

Presidential Scholar Award

Subjects: Child and adolescent psychiatry.
Purpose: To recognise specialised competence among child and adolescent psychiatry residents in research, public policy and innovative service systems.
Eligibility: Nominations must be made by programme and training directors and the nominees must be AACAP resident members.
Level of Study: Research.
Type: Award.
Value: Up to US$2,500 for travel and lodging for one week's tutorial and exchange in the specified area of study. Travel and hotel expenses for participation in the Academy's Annual Meeting are also paid.
Country of Study: United States of America.
Application Procedure: Four copies of the completed nomination pack must be submitted. This must include a statement in support of the nomination, the nominee's curriculum vitae and a statement from the nominee about his or her specific area of interest, plans for the tutorial and exchange and plans for the presentation to the home programme. It should be addressed to Ms Marilyn Benoit, Managing Director, President.
Closing Date: March 15th.
Funding: Private.
Contributor: Bristol-Myers Squibb.

THE AMERICAN ACADEMY OF FACIAL PLASTIC AND RECONSTRUCTIVE SURGERY (AAFPRS) FOUNDATION

310 Henry Street, Alexandria, VA, 22314, United States of America
Tel: (1) 703 299 9291
Fax: (1) 703 299 8898
Email: info@aafprs.org
www: http://www.aafprs.org
Contact: Ms Ann Kent Holton, Development, Research & Humanitarian Program

The American Academy of Facial Plastic and Reconstructive Surgery (AAFPRS) Foundation represents 2,700 facial plastic and reconstructive surgeons throughout the world. Its main mission is to promote the highest quality facial plastic surgery through education, dissemination of professional information and the establishment of professional standards. The AAFPRS was created to address the medical and scientific issues confronting facial plastic surgeons.

AAFPRS Investigator Development Grant

Subjects: Facial plastic surgery, clinical or laboratory research.
Purpose: To support the work of a young faculty member conducting significant clinical or laboratory research, as well as the training of resident surgeons in research.
Eligibility: Open to AAFPRS members.
Level of Study: Postgraduate.
Type: Research grant.
Value: US$15,000.
Length of Study: Two years.
Frequency: Annual.
Study Establishment: The recipient's institution.
Country of Study: United States of America.
No. of awards offered: One.
Application Procedure: Applicants must submit an application form and other documentation including a curriculum vitae and research proposal. Application forms and guidelines are available on request.
Closing Date: December 15th.
Funding: Private.
No. of awards given last year: One.
No. of applicants last year: Two.

AAFPRS Resident Research Grants

Subjects: Facial plastic surgery.
Purpose: To stimulate resident research in projects that are well conceived and scientifically valid.
Eligibility: Open to residents who are AAFPRS members. Residents at any level may apply even if the research work will be done during their fellowship year.
Level of Study: Postgraduate.
Type: Research grant.
Value: US$5,000.
Length of Study: Two years.
Frequency: Annual.
Study Establishment: The recipient's institution.
Country of Study: United States of America.
No. of awards offered: Up to three.
Application Procedure: Applicants must submit an application form and other documentation including a curriculum vitae and research proposal. Application forms and guidelines are available on request.
Closing Date: December 15th.
Funding: Private.
No. of awards given last year: Three.
No. of applicants last year: Eight.
Additional Information: Residents are encouraged to enter early in their training so that their applications may be revised and resubmitted if not accepted the first time.

Bernstein Grant

Subjects: Facial plastic and reconstructive surgery.
Purpose: To encourage original research projects.
Eligibility: Open to AAFPRS members.
Level of Study: Professional development.
Type: Research grant.
Value: US$25,000.
Length of Study: Three years.
Frequency: From time to time.
Study Establishment: The recipient's practice or institution.
Country of Study: United States of America.
No. of awards offered: One.
Application Procedure: Applicants must submit an application form and other documentation including a curriculum vitae and research proposal. Application forms and guidelines are available on request.
Closing Date: December 15th.
Funding: Private.
Contributor: Dr Leslie Bernstein.
No. of awards given last year: One.
No. of applicants last year: Two.

AMERICAN ACADEMY OF FAMILY PHYSICIANS (AAFP)

11400 Tomahawk Creek Parkway
Leawood, Kansas City, MO, 66211, United States of America
Tel: (1) 913 906 6000 ext. 6812
www: http://www.aafp.org
Contact: Ms Debbie Miller, Program Co-ordinator

The American Academy of Family Physicians (AAFP) is a national, non-profit medical association of more than 88,000 members including family physicians, family practice residents and medical students. The AAFP was founded in 1947 to promote and maintain high quality standards for family doctors who are providing continuing comprehensive health care to the public. It has grown to become one of the largest medical organisations in the United States, with chapters in 50 states, as well as international members throughout the world.

American Academy of Family Physicians/Bristol-Myers Squibb Award for Graduate Education in Family Practice
Subjects: Family practice of medicine.
Purpose: To provide financial assistance to outstanding young physicians.
Eligibility: Open to physicians who are second year residents in an approved practice residency programme. They must express the intention to enter the family practice of medicine in the United States of America. Applicants must be resident members of the AAFP.
Level of Study: Postgraduate.
Type: Award.
Value: US$2,000 per year.
Length of Study: One year, non renewable.
Frequency: Annual.
Study Establishment: Hospitals which run training programmes accredited by the Accreditation Council for Graduate Medical Education.
Country of Study: United States of America.
No. of awards offered: 20.
Application Procedure: Applicants must submit a formal application. This must include a curriculum vitae and personal statement, a reference letter and form from the residency programme director, a reference letter and a form from an active member of AAFP.
Closing Date: March 2nd.
Additional Information: Recipients will be guests of honour at an Awards Breakfast hosted by Mead Johnson during the Annual AAFP Meeting.

THE AMERICAN ACADEMY OF FIXED PROSTHODONTICS

Department of Restorative Dentistry
The University of Illinois at Chicago, Chicago, IL, 60612-7212, United States of America
Tel: (1) 312 413 1181
Fax: (1) 312 996 3535
Email: kentk@uic.edu
www: http://www.prosthodontics.org/forum/aafp/index.html
Contact: Dr Kent Knoernschild, Chairman of the Tylman Research Programme

The American Academy of Fixed Prosthodontics consists of over 500 specialists around the world, dedicated to the pursuit of knowledge, truth and competency in research, in teaching, and in the clinical practice of crown and bridge prosthodontics.

Tylman Research Program
Subjects: Dentistry.
Purpose: To promote and support research in the field of fixed prosthodontics by graduate students.
Eligibility: Open to full-time students in the United States and Canada enrolled in any graduate or postgraduate programme who are conducting research pertinent to fixed prosthodontics. Proposals must be endorsed by the programme director of an accredited prosthodontic programme. Priority will be given to students in prosthodontic programmes. Predoctoral dental students are not eligible.
Level of Study: Postgraduate.
Type: Grant.
Value: First place wins US$1,000, a plaque and a trip to the annual AAFP meeting to present research on the programme. Second place wins US$500 and third place US$300.
Frequency: Annual.
Country of Study: United States of America.
No. of awards offered: Six.
Application Procedure: Applicants must submit the protocol of the research project to the Academy Research Committee. The six best protocols are funded. The student must submit progress reports and a final manuscript of the completed project.
Closing Date: March 1st.
Funding: Private.
No. of awards given last year: Five.
No. of applicants last year: 10.

AMERICAN ACCORDION MUSICOLOGICAL SOCIETY

334 South Broadway, Pitman, NJ, 08071, United States of America
Tel: (1) 609 854 6628
Contact: Mr Stanley Darrow, Secretary

The American Accordian Musicological Society sponsors an annual accordion festival in the first weekend in March. It is a festival of workshops, accordion displays, antique accordions, demonstrations, concerts and a flea market of accordions for sale, new and used. The highlight is the Sunday mass accordion band.

American Accordion Musicological Society Music Competition
Subjects: Musical composition.
Purpose: To encourage composers to write classical accordion music.
Eligibility: Open to any composer acquainted with the various types of accordion. There are no restrictions in regard to age or nationality. Applicants competing for the Professional Award should have at least one composition already published.
Level of Study: Professional development.
Type: Contest.
Value: The Amateur Award is US$100 and the Professional Award is US$500, both of which are paid in a lump sum.
Frequency: Annual.
Country of Study: Any country.
No. of awards offered: Four.
Application Procedure: Applicants must write to the American Accordion Musicological Society for details of how to apply.
Closing Date: September 30th.
Funding: Private.
No. of awards given last year: Three.
No. of applicants last year: 50+.
Additional Information: The competition takes place during the first weekend in March every year.

THE AMERICAN ALPINE CLUB (AAC)

710 Tenth Street
Suite 100, Golden, CO, 80401, United States of America
Tel: (1) 303 384 0110
Fax: (1) 303 384 0111
Email: getinfo@americanalpineclub.org
www: http://www.americanalpineclub.org
Contact: Mr Chris Chesak, Corporate Support Co-ordinator

The American Alpine Club (AAC) is a national non-profit organisation that has represented mountaineers and rock climbers for almost a century. Since its inception in 1902, the AAC has been the only national climbers' organisation devoted to the exploration and scientific study of high mountain elevations and polar regions of the world, and the promotion and dissemination of knowledge about the mountains and mountaineering through its meetings, publications and libraries. It is also dedicated to the conservation and preservation of mountain regions and other climbing areas and the representation of the interests and concerns of the American climbing community.

AAC Mountaineering Fellowship Fund Grants

Subjects: Rock climbing.
Purpose: To encourage young American climbers to visit remote areas and seek out climbs more technically demanding than they would normally undertake.
Eligibility: Applicants must be 25 years of age or under, American citizens and experienced climbers. This is not an academic scholarship.
Level of Study: Unrestricted.
Type: Grant, not an academic scholarship.
Value: Usually between US$300 and US$750.
Frequency: Twice a year.
Country of Study: United States of America.
No. of awards offered: 5-16.
Application Procedure: Applicants must write for application forms which are also available from the website.
Closing Date: April 1st or November 1st.
Funding: Private.
No. of awards given last year: 14.
No. of applicants last year: 28.
Additional Information: Grants will be based on the excellence of the proposed project and evidence of mountaineering experience. Membership in the American Alpine Club is not a prerequisite. A report must be written upon project completion. Grants may not be used to fund climbing education or instruction.

AAC Research Grant

Subjects: Scientific research focusing on mountain and polar areas. Recent grants have funded studies of climate change, glaciology, the impact of park designation on indigenous people, avalanche prediction and snow composition.
Purpose: To recognise a specific contribution to scientific endeavour germane to mountain regions and alpine research projects.
Eligibility: There are no restrictions on eligibility, but grants will not be awarded for academic tuition.
Level of Study: Postgraduate.
Type: Research grants, no scholarships.
Value: US$500-2,000.
Frequency: Annual.
Country of Study: Any country.
No. of awards offered: Varies.
Application Procedure: Applicants must write for application forms which are also available from the website.
Closing Date: March 1st.
Funding: Private.
No. of awards given last year: 12.
Additional Information: A report must be submitted upon completion of the project.

AMERICAN ANTIQUARIAN SOCIETY (AAS)

185 Salisbury Street, Worcester, MA, 01609-1634, United States of America
Tel: (1) 508 755 5221
Fax: (1) 508 754 9069
Email: cfs@mwa.org
www: http://www.americanantiquarian.org
Contact: Ms Caroline F Scoat, Director of Scholarly Programmes

The American Antiquarian Society (AAS) is a learned society, founded in 1812 in Worcester, Massachusetts. The Society maintains a research library of American history and culture up to 1876 in order to collect, preserve, and make available for study the printed record of the United States.

The "Drawn to Art" Fellowship

Subjects: American art, visual culture or other projects that will make substantial use of graphic materials as primary sources.
Purpose: To support research.
Eligibility: Applicants are selected on the basis of their scholarly qualifications, the scholarly significance of the project, and the appropriateness of the proposed study to the Society's collections.
Level of Study: Doctorate, Postdoctorate.
Type: Fellowship.
Value: US$1,000.
Length of Study: One month.
Frequency: Annual.
Study Establishment: The Society's Library in Worcester, Massachusetts.
Country of Study: United States of America.
No. of awards offered: One.
Application Procedure: Applicants must request an application packet which provides full details of the fellowships, including certain restrictions that apply for some categories. Applicants must phone or email with any enquiries and requests for application materials. Alternatively applicants must visit the website.
Closing Date: January 15th.
Funding: Private.
Contributor: Diana Korzenik.
No. of awards given last year: One.
Additional Information: Please visit the website.

AAS American Society for Eighteenth-Century Studies Fellowships

Subjects: American eighteenth-century studies.
Eligibility: Open to suitably qualified Scholars. Degree candidates are not eligible. Membership in the American Society for Eighteenth-Century Studies is required upon taking up an award, but not for making an application.
Level of Study: Postdoctorate.
Type: Fellowship.
Value: US$1,000 per month.
Length of Study: One-two months.
Frequency: Annual.
Study Establishment: The Society's Library in Worcester, Massachusetts.
Country of Study: United States of America.
No. of awards offered: One-two.
Application Procedure: Applicants must request an application packet which provides full details of the fellowships, including certain restrictions that apply for some categories. Applicants must phone or email with any enquiries and requests for application materials. Alternatively applicants must visit the website.
Closing Date: January 15th.
Funding: Private.
Contributor: The American Society for Eighteenth-Century Studies and the AAS.
No. of awards given last year: Two.

AAS National Endowment for the Humanities Visiting Fellowships

Subjects: Early American history and culture.
Purpose: To make the Society's research facilities more readily available to qualified Scholars.
Eligibility: Fellowships may not be awarded to degree candidates or for study leading to advanced degrees, nor may they be granted to foreign nationals unless they have been resident in the United States of America for at least three years immediately prior to receiving the award.
Level of Study: Postdoctorate.
Type: Fellowship.
Value: The maximum stipend available is US$30,000.
Length of Study: Either six-twelve months or four-five months.
Frequency: Annual.
Country of Study: United States of America.
No. of awards offered: More than two.
Application Procedure: Applicants must request an application packet which provides full details of the fellowships, including certain restrictions that apply for some categories. Applicants must phone or email with any enquiries and requests for application materials. Alternatively applicants must visit the website.
Closing Date: January 15th.
Funding: Government.
Contributor: The National Endowment for the Humanities.
Additional Information: Fellows may not accept teaching assignments or undertake any other major activities during the tenure of the award. Other major fellowships may be held concurrently.

AAS Northeast Modern Language Association Fellowship

Subjects: American literary studies.
Purpose: To support research.
Eligibility: Applicants are selected on the basis of their scholarly qualifications, the scholarly significance of the project and the appropriateness of the proposed study to the Society's collections.
Level of Study: Doctorate, Postdoctorate.
Type: Fellowship.
Value: US$1,000 per month.
Length of Study: One-three months.
Frequency: Annual.
Study Establishment: The Society's Library in Worcester, Massachusetts.
No. of awards offered: At least two.
Application Procedure: Applicants must request an application packet which provides full details of the fellowships, including certain restrictions that apply for some categories. Applicants must phone or email with any enquiries and requests for application materials. Alternatively applicants must visit the website.
Closing Date: January 15th.
Funding: Private.
Contributor: Jointly funded by the Northeast Modern Language Association and AAS.
No. of awards given last year: One.
Additional Information: Further information is available on request.

ACLS Frederick Burkhardt Fellowship

Subjects: All subjects supported by the AAS library.
Purpose: To support research.
Eligibility: Applicants must be recently tenured humanists selected on the basis of their scholarly qualifications, the scholarly significance of the project, and the appropriateness of the proposed study to the Society's collections.
Level of Study: Postdoctorate.
Type: Fellowship.
Value: Maximum stipend of US$65,000.
Length of Study: One year.
Frequency: Annual.
Study Establishment: The Society's Library in Worcester, Massachusetts.
Country of Study: United States of America.

Application Procedure: Applicants must request an application packet which provides full details of the fellowships, including certain restrictions that apply for some categories. Applicants must phone or email with any enquiries and requests for application materials. Alternatively applicants must visit the website.
Closing Date: October 2nd.
Funding: Private.
Contributor: The Andrew W Mellon Foundation and ACLS.
No. of awards given last year: Eight.

The American Historical Print Collectors Society Fellowship

Subjects: American prints of the eighteenth- and nineteenth-centuries.
Purpose: To support research or projects using prints as primary documentation.
Eligibility: Applicants are selected on the basis of their scholarly qualifications, the scholarly significance of the project and the appropriateness of the proposed study to the Society's collections.
Level of Study: Doctorate, Postdoctorate.
Type: Fellowship.
Value: US$1,000 monthly.
Length of Study: One month.
Frequency: Annual.
Study Establishment: The Society's Library in Worcester, Massachusetts.
Country of Study: United States of America.
Application Procedure: Applicants must request an application packet which provides full details of the fellowships, including certain restrictions that apply for some categories. Applicants must phone or email with any enquiries and requests for application materials. Alternatively applicants must visit the website.
Closing Date: January 15th.
Funding: Private.
Contributor: The American Historical Print Collectors Society and the American Antiquarian Society.

Joyce A Tracy Fellowship

Subjects: Early American history and culture.
Purpose: To support research on newspapers or magazines for projects using these resources as primary documentation.
Eligibility: Applicants are selected on the basis of their scholarly qualifications, the scholarly significance to the project, and the appropriateness of the proposed study to the Society's collections.
Level of Study: Doctorate, Postdoctorate.
Type: Fellowship.
Value: US$1,000 per month.
Length of Study: One-two months.
Frequency: Annual.
Study Establishment: The Society's Library in Worcester, Massachusetts.
Country of Study: United States of America.
No. of awards offered: One.
Application Procedure: Applicants must write for further information or visit the website.
Closing Date: January 15th.
Contributor: An endowment established in memory of Joyce Tracy.
No. of awards given last year: One.
Additional Information: Please visit the website.

Kate B and Hall J Peterson Fellowships

Subjects: Early American history through to 1876.
Purpose: To enable persons, who might not otherwise be able to do so, to travel to the Society in order to make use of its research facilities.
Eligibility: Open to individuals engaged in scholarly research and writing, including foreign nationals and persons at work on doctoral theses.
Level of Study: Doctorate, Postdoctorate.
Type: Fellowship.
Value: US$1,000 per month.

Length of Study: One-three months.
Frequency: Annual.
Study Establishment: The Society's Library in Worcester, Massachusetts.
Country of Study: United States of America.
No. of awards offered: 6-10.
Application Procedure: Applicants must request an application packet which provides full details of the fellowships, including certain restrictions that apply for some categories. Applicants must phone or email with any enquiries and requests for application materials. Alternatively applicants must visit the website.
Closing Date: January 15th.
Funding: Private.
Contributor: The late Hall J Peterson and his wife Kate B Peterson.
No. of awards given last year: 12.
Additional Information: Further information is available on request.

Mellon Postdoctoral Research Fellowships

Subjects: All subjects.
Purpose: To provide support for residence in the Society's library.
Eligibility: Applicants are selected on the basis of their scholarly qualifications, the scholarly significance of the project, and the appropriateness of the proposed study to the Society's collections.
Level of Study: Postdoctorate.
Type: Fellowship.
Value: Maximum stipend US$40,000.
Length of Study: An academic year, 9 or 10 months in residence at the Society's Library.
Frequency: Annual.
Study Establishment: The Society's Library in Worcester, Massachusetts.
Country of Study: United States of America.
Application Procedure: Applicants must request an application packet which provides full details of the fellowships, including certain restrictions that apply for some categories. Applicants must phone or email with any enquiries and requests for application materials. Alternatively applicants must visit the website.
Closing Date: January 15th.
Contributor: The Andrew W Mellon Foundation.
No. of awards given last year: One.

The Reese Fellowship

Subjects: American bibliography and the history of the book in America through to 1876.
Purpose: To support research.
Eligibility: Applicants are selected on the basis of their scholarly qualifications, the scholarly significance of the project and the appropriateness of the proposed study to the Society's collections.
Level of Study: Doctorate, Postdoctorate.
Type: Fellowship.
Value: US$1,000.
Length of Study: One month.
Frequency: Annual.
Study Establishment: The Society's Library in Worcester, Massachusetts.
Country of Study: United States of America.
No. of awards offered: One.
Application Procedure: Applicants must request an application packet which provides full details of the fellowships, including certain restrictions that apply for some categories. Applicants must phone or email with any enquiries and requests for application materials. Alternatively applicants must visit the website.
Closing Date: January 15th.
Contributor: The William Reese Company, New Haven, Connecticut.
No. of awards given last year: One.

The Stephen Botein Fellowship

Subjects: The history of the book in American culture to 1876.
Eligibility: Open to suitably qualified Scholars.
Level of Study: Doctorate, Postdoctorate.

Type: Fellowship.
Value: US$1,000 per month.
Length of Study: Up to two months.
Frequency: Annual.
Study Establishment: The Society's Library in Worcester, Massachusetts.
Country of Study: United States of America.
No. of awards offered: One-two.
Application Procedure: Applicants must request an application packet which provides full details of the fellowships, including certain restrictions that apply for some categories. Applicants must phone or email with any enquiries and requests for application materials. Alternatively applicants must visit the website.
Closing Date: January 15th.
Funding: Private.
Contributor: An endowment established by the family and friends of the late Mr Botein.
No. of awards given last year: Two.

AMERICAN ASSOCIATION FOR CANCER RESEARCH (AACR)

Public Ledger Building
Suite 826
150 South Independence Mall West, Philadelphia, PA, 19106-3483, United States of America
Tel: (1) 215 440 9300
Fax: (1) 215 440 9372
Email: awards@aacr.org
www: http://www.aacr.org
Contact: Ms Sheri Ozard, Program Coordinator

The American Association for Cancer Research (AACR) is a scientific society of over 17,000 laboratory and clinical cancer researchers. It was founded in 1907 to facilitate communication and dissemination of knowledge among scientists and others dedicated to the cancer problem, and to foster research in cancer and related biomedical sciences. It is also dedicated to encouraging the presentation and discussion of new and important observations in the field, fostering public education, science education and training, and advancing the understanding of cancer etiology, prevention, diagnosis and treatment throughout the world.

AACR Career Development Awards in Cancer Research

Subjects: Cancer research.
Purpose: To support research.
Eligibility: Open to scientists in their first or second year of a full-time, tenure tracked faculty appointment, at the level of assistant professor. Candidates must have completed productive postdoctoral research and demonstrated independent, instigator initiated research. Employees of a national government and employees of private industry are not eligible.
Level of Study: Postdoctorate.
Type: Grant.
Value: US$50,000 per year.
Length of Study: Two years.
Frequency: Annual.
Study Establishment: Universities and research institutions.
Country of Study: Any country.
No. of awards offered: Varies.
Application Procedure: Applicants must be nominated by a member of AACR and must be an AACR member or applying for membership by the time the application is submitted. Associate members may not be nominators. Application forms can be downloaded from AACR website.
Closing Date: Varies each year.
Funding: Private.
Contributor: The Cancer Research Foundation of America, the Susan G Komen Breast Cancer Foundation and the California Department of Health Services.

No. of awards given last year: Two.
No. of applicants last year: 40.
Additional Information: For further information, please contact the organisation or refer to the website.

AACR Gertrude B Elion Cancer Research Award

Subjects: Cancer research.
Purpose: To foster meritorious basic, clinical or translational cancer research.
Eligibility: Open to tenure tracked scientists at the level of assistant professor at an institution worldwide, who have completed their post-doctoral studies or clinical research by July 1st of the award year, and ordinarily not more than five years earlier. Candidates must be members of the AACR or apply for membership by the time the applications are submitted.
Level of Study: Postdoctorate.
Type: Research grant.
Value: US$50,000.
Length of Study: One year.
Frequency: Annual.
Study Establishment: Universities or research institution.
Country of Study: Any country.
No. of awards offered: One.
Application Procedure: Applicants must be nominated by a member of the AACR. Application forms can be downloaded from the website.
Closing Date: Varies.
Funding: Private.
Contributor: GlaxoSmithKline.
No. of awards given last year: One.
No. of applicants last year: 35.
Additional Information: For further information please contact the organisation or refer to the website.

AACR HBCU Faculty Award in Cancer Research

Subjects: Medical sciences.
Purpose: To increase the scientific knowledge base of faculty members at historically black colleges and universities (HCBUs), and to encourage them and their students to pursue careers in cancer research.
Eligibility: Open to scientists at the level of assistant professor or above at an HBCU who are engaged in meritorious basic, clinical or translatorial cancer research. Candidates must be citizens of the United States or Canada, or permanent residents of these countries.
Level of Study: Postdoctorate.
Type: Travel grant.
Value: US$1,800.
Length of Study: Varies.
Frequency: Annual.
Study Establishment: AACR conferences.
Country of Study: United States of America.
No. of awards offered: Varies.
Application Procedure: Applicants must submit an application which includes the candidate's curriculum vitae, a list of publications, a statement from the candidate describing the benefit he or she expects to derive from attending the conference and at least one letter of reference.
Closing Date: Varies, please refer to website for details.
Additional Information: For further information about this award programme please contact Ms Robin E Felder, Manager of Membership and Constituency Programs at the AACR office, by telephoning (1) 215 440 9300, faxing (1) 215 440 9412, or emailing constituencies@aacr.org.

AACR Research Fellowships

Subjects: Cancer research.
Purpose: To foster meritorious cancer research.
Eligibility: Candidates must have completed a PhD or other doctoral degree and currently be a postdoctoral or clinical research Fellow. Candidates should have been a Fellow for a minimum of two years and maximum of five years prior to the award. Academic faculty holding the rank of assistant professor or higher, graduates and medical students, medical residents, permanent government employees and employees of private industry are not eligible.
Level of Study: Postdoctorate.
Type: A variable number of fellowships.
Value: US$30,000 per year.
Length of Study: One, two and three year fellowships.
Frequency: Annual.
Study Establishment: Universities or research institutions for cancer research.
Country of Study: Any country.
No. of awards offered: Varies.
Application Procedure: Applicants must be nominated by a member of the AACR or apply for membership by the time the application is submitted. Application forms can be downloaded from AACR website.
Closing Date: Varies each year.
Funding: Private.
Contributor: Amgen, Inc., Astra Zeneca, Bristol-Myers Squibb Oncology, the Cancer Research Foundation of America and the Sidney Kimmel Foundation.
No. of awards given last year: Seven.
No. of applicants last year: 100.
Additional Information: For further information, please contact the organisation or refer to the website.

AACR Scholar-in-Training Awards

Subjects: Cancer research.
Purpose: To allow individuals to attend the AACR Annual Meeting and Special Conferences.
Eligibility: Open to first authors of an abstract submitted for presentation at the AACR Annual Meeting or Special Conference. Eligible candidates are graduate students, medical students and residents, clinical fellows or equivalent and postdoctoral fellows.
Level of Study: Doctorate, Graduate, Postdoctorate, Postgraduate, Predoctorate.
Type: Travel grant.
Value: US$400-2,000.
Frequency: Annual.
No. of awards offered: Varies.
Application Procedure: No application is needed. Qualified persons who want to be considered should follow the instructions included in the abstract submission materials for the AACR Annual Meetings or Special Conference. If a candidate is eligible based on the above criteria, a certification form confirming his or her status will be requested at a later date.
Closing Date: Varies, please contact AACR for details.
Funding: Private.
Contributor: AstraZeneca, Aventis, Bristol-Myers Squibb Oncology, the California Department of Health Services, Genentech, GlaxoSmithKline, ILEX, ITO EN Limited, Janssen Research Foundation, Novartis Pharmaceuticals Corporation, the Pharmacia Corporation and others.
No. of awards given last year: Approx. 400.

Women in Cancer Research Brigid G Leventhal Scholar Awards

Subjects: Cancer research.
Purpose: To allow individuals to attend the AACR Annual Meeting.
Eligibility: Open to medical and graduate students, physicians in training and postdoctorate fellows who have submitted an abstract in the field of cancer or cancer related biomedical research that is highly rated for presentation at the AACR Annual Meeting.
Level of Study: Doctorate, Postgraduate, Predoctorate.
Type: Travel grant.
Value: Travel costs and a subsistence allowance.
Length of Study: Varies.
Frequency: Annual.
Study Establishment: The AACR Annual Meeting.
Country of Study: United States of America.
No. of awards offered: Varies.

Application Procedure: Applicants must have submitted an abstract for presentation at AACR Annual Meeting and must submit the official award application.

Closing Date: November 23rd.

Additional Information: For further information about this award programme, please contact Robin E Felder, Manager of Membership and Constituencies, at the AACR office, extension 124 or via email at felder@aacr.org.

AMERICAN ASSOCIATION FOR DENTAL RESEARCH (AADR)

1619 Duke Street, Alexandria, VA, 22314-3406, United States of America
Tel: (1) 703 548 0066 ext. 14
Fax: (1) 703 548 1883
Email: pat@iadr.com
Contact: Ms Patricia J Reynolds, Executive Secretary

The American Association for Dental Research (AADR) plans and organises research meetings where dentists and dental scientists come together to share cutting edge research. The Association also publishes research journals.

AADR Student Research Fellowships

Subjects: Basic and clinical research related to oral health.

Purpose: To encourage dental students to consider careers in oral health research.

Eligibility: Open to students enrolled in an accredited DDS or DMD or hygiene programme in a dental or health associated institution within the United States of America, who are sponsored by a faculty member at that institution. Students should not have received their degree, nor should they be due to receive their degree in the year of the award. Applicants may have an advanced degree in a basic science subject.

Level of Study: Postgraduate.

Type: Fellowship.

Value: US$2,100 plus US$300 for supplies.

Length of Study: Two years.

Frequency: Annual.

Country of Study: United States of America.

No. of awards offered: Varies.

Application Procedure: Applicants must submit a research proposal. Application guidelines are available on request.

Closing Date: January 15th.

Contributor: Dental product companies, pharmaceutical companies and AADR members.

No. of awards given last year: 24.

No. of applicants last year: 57.

Additional Information: Recipients will present their research at the AADR meeting by submitting abstracts for poster or oral presentations.

AMERICAN ASSOCIATION FOR THE ADVANCEMENT OF SCIENCE (AAAS)

1200 New York Avenue North West, Washington, DC, 20005, United States of America
Tel: (1) 202 326 6760
Fax: (1) 202 371 9849
Email: kmalloy@aaas.org
www: http://www.aaas.org

Founded in 1848, the American Association for the Advancement of Science (AAAS) is a general scientific organisation, with approximately 300 affiliated science and engineering societies and 141,000 individual members. Increasing public understanding of science and technology is one of the principal aims of the AAAS.

AAAS Mass Media Science and Engineering Fellowship

Subjects: Natural and physical sciences, behavioural sciences, mathematics or engineering.

Purpose: To further public understanding of science and technology by promoting more accurate coverage in the news.

Eligibility: Applicants must be students pursuing degrees in the natural sciences and engineering. Students majoring in English, journalism, science journalism or other non technical fields are not eligible. Minorities and persons with disabilities are especially encouraged to apply. Non United States of America citizens must be able to obtain a visa.

Level of Study: Graduate, Postdoctorate, Postgraduate, Predoctorate.

Type: Fellowship.

Value: US$4,500 stipend plus travel expenses.

Length of Study: 10 weeks.

Frequency: Annual.

Study Establishment: Varies.

Country of Study: Any country.

No. of awards offered: 25-30.

Application Procedure: Applicants must submit a completed application form, a curriculum vitae, a brief writing sample, three letters of recommendation and transcripts of undergraduate and graduate work.

Closing Date: January 15th.

Funding: Private.

AMERICAN ASSOCIATION FOR THE HISTORY OF NURSING (AAHN)

PO Box 175, Lanoka Harbor, NJ, 08734, United States of America
Tel: (1) 609 693 7250
Fax: (1) 609 693 1037
Email: aahn@aahn.org
www: http://www.aahn.org
Contact: Executive Secretary

The American Association for the History of Nursing (AAHN) is a professional organisation accessible to everyone interested in the history of nursing. Originally founded in 1978 as a historical methodology group, the Association was briefly named the International History of Nursing Society. The Association's purpose is to foster the importance of history in understanding the present and guiding the future of nursing.

AAHN Student Research Award

Subjects: Nursing historical research.

Purpose: To support research.

Eligibility: Open to students enrolled in an accredited Master's or doctoral programme who are members of the AAHN. Proposals will focus on a significant question in the history of nursing. Selection criteria include the scholarly merit of the proposal, consideration of the student's preparation for this study, the advisor's qualification for guiding the study and the project's potential for contributing to scholarship in the field of nursing history. If the study involves sources requiring approval by an Institutional Review Board protecting human subjects, funds will not be awarded until documentation is received.

Level of Study: Doctorate.

Type: Grant.

Value: US$1,000.

Frequency: Annual.

No. of awards offered: One.

Application Procedure: Applicants must submit four copies of a proposal which should include a title page, narrative, objectives of research, significant background information on the research, primary source availability, methods to be used, facilities to be used and a curriculum vitae. Applicants should visit the website for further details.

Closing Date: May 15th.

Funding: Private.

No. of awards given last year: One.
Additional Information: The address to which applications should be sent changes each year and applicants should check the website for the correct address.

Society for Nursing History Research Award
Subjects: Historical research in nursing.
Purpose: To support postdoctoral study.
Eligibility: Open to students enrolled in an accredited Master's or doctoral programme and who are members of the AAHN. Proposals will focus on a significant question in the history of nursing. Selection criteria include the scholarly merit of the proposal, consideration of the student's preparation for this study, the advisor's qualifications for guiding the study and the project's potential for contributing to scholarship in the field of nursing history. If the study involves sources requiring approval by an Institutional Review Board protecting human subjects, funds will not be awarded until documentation is received.
Level of Study: Postdoctorate.
Value: US$1,000.
Frequency: Annual.
Application Procedure: Applicants must submit four copies of a proposal, of no more than 10 pages, which should include a title page, narrative, objects of research, significant background information on the research, primary source availability, methods to be used, facilities to be used and a curriculum vitae. Applicants should visit the Association website for further details.
Closing Date: May 15th.
Funding: Private.
No. of awards given last year: One.

AMERICAN ASSOCIATION FOR WOMEN RADIOLOGISTS (AAWR)

820 Jorie Boulevard, Oak Brook, IL, 60523, United States of America
Tel: (1) 630 590 7712
Fax: (1) 630 571 7837
Email: admin@aawr.org
www: http://www.aawr.org
Contact: Ms Andrea Perr, AAWR Account Manager

Alice Ettinger Distinguished Achievement Award
Subjects: Radiology.
Purpose: To recognise outstanding residents on the basis of contributions to clinical care, teaching, research or public service.
Eligibility: Nominees must be members of the AAWR as of January 1st of the year the award is presented and must be in an accredited radiology or radiation oncology resident programme.
Level of Study: Unrestricted.
Type: Award.
Value: Per diem expenses to accept award.
Frequency: Annual.
Country of Study: Any country.
No. of awards offered: One.
Application Procedure: Applicants must submit an application including a nominating letter from the residency director, a letter of concurrence from the department chair, a curriculum vitae and a personal statement.
Closing Date: July 1st.
Funding: Private.
Contributor: Membership dues.
No. of awards given last year: One.
No. of applicants last year: 16.

Eleanor Montague Distinguished Resident Award in Radiation Oncology
Subjects: Radiology.

Purpose: To honour a resident radiation oncologist on the basis of outstanding contributions to clinical care, teaching, research and/or public service.
Eligibility: Open to residents in the field of radiation oncology who are members of the AAWR as of January 1st of the year of the award.
Level of Study: Unrestricted.
Value: US$500 and reimbursement of expenses including travel, lodging and per diem.
Frequency: Annual.
Country of Study: Any country.
No. of awards offered: One.
Application Procedure: Applicants must submit an application including a letter of nomination, a letter of concurrence and a curriculum vitae.
Closing Date: July 1st.
Funding: Private.
No. of awards given last year: One.
No. of applicants last year: Two.

Lucy Frank Squire Distinguished Resident Award in Diagnostic Radiology
Subjects: Radiology.
Purpose: To honour a resident diagnostic radiologist on the basis of outstanding contributions to clinical care, teaching, research and/or public service.
Eligibility: Open to residents in the field of diagnostic radiology who are members of the AAWR from January 1st of the year of the award.
Level of Study: Unrestricted.
Value: US$500 and reimbursement of expenses including travel, lodging and per diem.
Frequency: Annual.
Country of Study: Any country.
No. of awards offered: One.
Application Procedure: Applicants must submit an application including a curriculum vitae, a letter of nomination and a letter of concurrence.
Closing Date: July 1st.
Funding: Private.
Contributor: Membership dues.
No. of awards given last year: One.
No. of applicants last year: 14.

Marie Curie Award
Subjects: Radiology.
Purpose: To honour a radiologist, radiation oncologist or other person who has been a mentor, role model or leader in radiology.
Eligibility: Open to practitioners in the field of radiology. There are no nationality restrictions and nominees need not be members of the AAWR.
Level of Study: Unrestricted.
Type: Award.
Value: Reimbursement of expenses including travel, lodging and per diem.
Frequency: Annual.
Country of Study: Any country.
No. of awards offered: One.
Application Procedure: Applicants must submit an application including a letter of nomination, at least one letter of support and a curriculum vitae.
Closing Date: July 1st.
Funding: Private.
Contributor: Membership dues.
No. of awards given last year: One.
No. of applicants last year: Eight.

AMERICAN ASSOCIATION OF CRITICAL-CARE NURSES (AACN)

101 Columbia, Aliso Viejo, CA, 92656-1491, United States of America
Tel: (1) 800 899 2226
Fax: (1) 949 362 2020
Email: rsearch@aacn.org
www: http://www.aacn.org
Contact: Research Department

The American Association of Critical-Care Nurses is the world's largest nursing speciality organisation with approximately 68,000 members worldwide. The AACN is committed to providing the highest quality resources to maximise nurses' contributions to caring and improving the healthcare of critically ill patients and their families.

AACN - Datex Ohmeda Grant

Subjects: Nutritional assessment in the critically ill patient.
Purpose: To provide research support for a study to be conducted by a critical care nurse.
Eligibility: Principal investigators must be nurses holding current AACN membership. Investigators who have received funding from the AACN are ineligible to receive additional funding during the lifetime of their original award. They may apply for a new award when their original award obligations have been met. Research conducted in fulfilment of an academic degree is acceptable.
Type: Grant.
Value: US$5,000.
Application Procedure: Applicants must submit completed application materials and proposals. Details are available directly from the organisation or from the website.
Closing Date: February 1st.

AACN Certification Corporation Research Grant

Subjects: Certified practice including, but not limited to, studies focusing on continued competency, the Synergy Model, the value of certification as it relates to patient care and/or nursing practice, and credentialing concepts.
Purpose: To fund research related to certified practice.
Eligibility: Applicants need not be members of the AACN. The proposed research may be used to met the requirements of an academic degree.
Value: Up to US$10,000.
No. of awards offered: Up to four.
Application Procedure: Applicants must submit completed application materials and proposals. Details are available directly from the organisation or from the website.
Closing Date: February 1st.
Additional Information: For more information regarding AACN Certification Corporation and the Synergy Model, visit the website http://www.certcorp.org.

AACN Clinical Inquiry Grants

Subjects: Clinical research.
Purpose: To provide small awards to qualified individuals carrying out clinical research projects that will directly benefit patients and their families.
Eligibility: Principal investigators must be nurses holding current AACN membership. Investigators who have received funding from the AACN are ineligible to receive additional funding during the lifetime of their original award. They may apply for a new award when their original award obligations have been met. Funds may be awarded for new projects, projects in progress and projects required for an academic degree as long as all other project criteria are met.
Level of Study: Research.
Type: Award.
Value: Up to US$500. Funds may be used to cover direct project expenses such as printed materials, small equipment and supplies including computer software. They may not be used to pay for

salaries, institutional overheads nor to augment funding from formal large grants.
No. of awards offered: Multiple.
Application Procedure: Applicants must submit a completed application form and supporting materials. Details and forms are available directly from the organisation or from the website.
Closing Date: January 15th and July 1st.
Additional Information: Please see the website for further information.

AACN Clinical Practice Grant

Subjects: Research directly related to the AACN clinical research properties.
Purpose: To support research.
Eligibility: Principal investigators must be nurses holding current AACN membership. Investigators who have received funding from the AACN are ineligible to receive additional funding during the lifetime of their original award. They may apply for a new award when their original award obligations have been met. Research conducted in fulfilment of an academic degree is acceptable.
Level of Study: Research.
Type: Grant.
Value: Up to US$6,000.
Frequency: Annual.
No. of awards offered: Varies.
Application Procedure: Applicants must submit completed application materials and proposals. Details are available directly from the organisation or from the website.
Closing Date: October 1st.

AACN Critical Care Grant

Subjects: Critical-care nursing practice.
Purpose: To fund research.
Eligibility: Principal investigators must be nurses holding current AACN membership. Investigators who have received funding from the AACN are ineligible to receive additional funding during the lifetime of their original award. They may apply for a new award when their original award obligations have been met. The proposed research may not be used to meet the requirements of an academic degree.
Level of Study: Research.
Type: Research grant.
Value: Up to US$15,000.
Frequency: Annual.
No. of awards offered: Varies.
Application Procedure: Applicants must submit completed application materials and a proposal. Details and forms are available directly from the organisation or from the website.
Closing Date: February 1st.

AACN Evidence-based Clinical Practice Grant

Subjects: Clinical research.
Purpose: To stimulate the use of patient focused data or previously generated research findings to develop, implement and evaluate changes in acute and critical-care practice.
Eligibility: Principal investigators must be nurses holding current AACN membership. Investigators who have received funding from the AACN are ineligible to receive additional funding during the lifetime of their original award. They may apply for a new award when their original award obligations have been met. Funds may be awarded for new projects, projects in progress and projects required for an academic degree as long as all other project criteria are met. Eligible projects may include research utilisation studies, CQI projects or outcomes evaluation projects. Interdisciplinary and collaborative projects are encouraged and may involve interdisciplinary teams, multiple nursing units, home health, subacute and transitional care, other institutions or community agencies.
Type: Grant.
Value: US$1,000. Funds may be used to cover direct project expenses such as printed materials, small equipment and supplies

including computer software. They may not be used to pay for salaries or institutional overheads.

No. of awards offered: Up to six.

Application Procedure: Applicants must submit a completed application form and supporting materials. Details and forms are available directly from the organisation or from the website.

Closing Date: March 1st or October 1st.

Additional Information: Please see the website for further information.

AACN Mentorship Grant

Subjects: Clinical research.

Purpose: To provide research support for a novice researcher with limited or no research experience working under the direction of a mentor.

Eligibility: Principal investigators must be nurses holding current AACN membership. Investigators who have received funding from the AACN are ineligible to receive additional funding during the lifetime of their original award. They may apply for a new award when their original award obligations have been met. The novice researcher may be conducting the research to meet the requirements for an academic degree but the mentor may not. The mentor must show strong evidence of research and expertise in the proposed area. The mentor may not be a mentor on another AACN Mentorship Grant in two consecutive years.

Level of Study: Research.

Type: Grant.

Value: Up to US$10,000.

Frequency: Annual.

No. of awards offered: Varies.

Application Procedure: Applicants must submit completed application materials and a proposal. Details and forms are available directly from the organisation or from the website.

Closing Date: February 1st.

Additional Information: The novice researcher will be the principal investigator and will receive the award.

AACN Sigma Theta Tau Critical-Care Grant

Subjects: Critical care nursing practice.

Purpose: To fund research related to critical care nursing practice.

Eligibility: Applicants need not be AACN members.

Level of Study: Research.

Type: Grant.

Value: US$10,000.

Frequency: Annual.

No. of awards offered: Varies.

Application Procedure: Applicants must submit completed application materials and a proposal. Details are available directly from the organisation or from the website.

Closing Date: October 1st.

Contributor: Co-sponsored by the AACN and Sigma Theta Tau International.

Agilent Technologies - AACN Critical-Care Nursing Research Grant

Subjects: Preferred topics will address the information technology requirements of patient management in critical care.

Purpose: To fund research for study conducted by a critical care nurse.

Eligibility: Principal investigators must be nurses holding current AACN membership. Investigators who have received funding from the AACN are ineligible to receive additional funding during the lifetime of their original award. They may apply for a new award when their original award obligations have been met.

Level of Study: Research.

Type: Grant.

Value: US$35,000, providing US$33,000 for the research study and US$2,000 for travel expenses associated with presentations of the study findings.

No. of awards offered: One.

Application Procedure: Applicants must submit a completed application form and supporting materials. Details and forms are available directly from the organisation or from the website.

Closing Date: September 1st.

Contributor: Hewlett-Packard, Inc.

American Nurses Foundation Research Grant

Subjects: Clinical research.

Purpose: To encourage the research career development of nurses.

Eligibility: Principal investigators must be nurses holding current AACN membership. Investigators who have received funding from the AACN are ineligible to receive additional funding during the lifetime of their original award. They may apply for a new award when their original award obligations have been met.

Level of Study: Research.

Type: Research grant.

Value: Up to US$5,000 is awarded by the American Nurses Foundation.

No. of awards offered: Varies.

Application Procedure: Applicants must obtain information and application forms from the American Nurses Foundation, and should see the website for further details.

Closing Date: May 1st.

Contributor: The AACN.

For further information contact:

The American Nurses Foundation/NRG00
600 Maryland Avenue SW
Suite 100W, Washington, DC, 20024-2571, United States of America
Tel: (1) 202 651 7298
Email: anf@ana.org
www: http://www.nursingworld.org/anf

Medtronics Physio-Control AACN Small Projects Grants Program

Subjects: Clinical research focusing on aspects of acute myocardial infarction resuscitation, such as the use of defibrillation, synchronised cardioversion, non-invasive pacing, or interpretative 12-lead electrocardiogram.

Purpose: To provide funds to qualified individuals carrying out research.

Eligibility: Principal investigators must be nurses holding current AACN membership. Investigators who have received funding from the AACN are ineligible to receive additional funding during the lifetime of their original award. They may apply for a new award when their original award obligations have been met. Eligible projects may include patient education programmes, staff development programmes, competency based educational programmes, CQI projects, outcomes evaluation projects, or small clinical research studies. Funds may be awarded for new projects, projects in progress and projects required for an academic degree as long as all other project criteria are met. Collaborative projects are encouraged and may involve interdisciplinary teams, multiple nursing units, home health, subacute and transitional care, other institutions or community agencies.

Level of Study: Research.

Type: Grant.

Value: Up to US$1,500. Funds may be used to cover direct project expenses such as printed materials, small equipment and supplies including computer software. They may not be used to pay for salaries or institutional overheads.

No. of awards offered: Varies.

Application Procedure: Applicants must submit a completed application form and supporting materials. Details and forms are available directly from the organisation or from the website.

Closing Date: July 1st.

Additional Information: Please see the website for further information.

AMERICAN ASSOCIATION OF LAW LIBRARIES (AALL)

Scholarship Committee
Suite 940
53 West Jackson Boulevard, Chicago, IL, 60604, United States of
America
Tel: (1) 312 939 4764
Fax: (1) 312 431 1097
Email: aallhq@aall.org
www: http://www.aallnet.org
Contact: Executive Director

The American Association of Law Libraries (AALL) was founded in
1906 to promote and enhance the value of law libraries to legal and
public communities, to foster the profession of law librarianship, and
to provide leadership in the field of legal information. Today the
AALL represents law librarians and related professionals who are affiliated with a wide range of institutions including law firms, law
schools, corporate legal departments and courts, and local, state
and federal government agencies.

American Association of Law Libraries George A Strait Minority Stipend

Subjects: Law librarianship, advanced studies, law and
librarianship.
Purpose: To assist college graduates with law library experience.
Eligibility: Open to degree candidates in accredited library or law
schools. Preference is given to individuals with previous service to,
or interest in, law librarianship. Applicants must be members of a mi-
nority group as defined by the current United States of America gov-
ernment guidelines.
Level of Study: Postgraduate.
Type: Bursary.
Value: Up to US$3,500 for tuition and school-related expenses.
Frequency: Annual.
Study Establishment: Accredited library schools or accredited law
schools.
Country of Study: Any country.
No. of awards offered: Varies.
Application Procedure: Applicants must write for details or down-
load an application form from the website.
Closing Date: April 1st.

Law Librarians in Continuing Education Courses (Type V)

Subjects: Law librarianship.
Purpose: To assist law librarians.
Eligibility: Open to members of the American Association of Law Li-
braries. Preference is given to permanent residents of the United
States of America and Canada. Applicants must have a degree from
an accredited library or law school and be registrants in continuing
education courses related to law librarianship.
Level of Study: Postgraduate.
Value: Up to US$500 for tuition.
Frequency: Three times each year.
Country of Study: Any country.
No. of awards offered: Varies.
Application Procedure: Applicants must write for details or down-
load an application form from the website.
Closing Date: April 1st, October 1st or February 1st.

Library Degree for Law School Graduates (Type I)

Subjects: Law librarianship.
Purpose: To assist law school graduates working towards a degree.
Eligibility: Open to law graduates who are candidates for a library
degree.
Level of Study: Postgraduate.
Type: Scholarship.
Value: Up to US$2,000 for tuition and school-related expenses.
Frequency: Annual.

Study Establishment: Accredited library schools.
Country of Study: Any country.
No. of awards offered: Varies.
Application Procedure: Applicants must write for details.
Closing Date: April 1st.

Library Degree for Non-Law School Graduates (Type III)

Subjects: Law librarianship.
Purpose: To assist persons with meaningful law library experience.
Eligibility: Open to graduates who are degree candidates in accred-
ited library schools. Preference is given to applicants working for de-
grees with emphasis on courses in law librarianship.
Level of Study: Postgraduate.
Type: Scholarship.
Value: Up to US$2,000 for tuition and school-related expenses.
Frequency: Annual.
Study Establishment: Accredited library schools.
Country of Study: Any country.
No. of awards offered: Varies.
Application Procedure: Applicants must write for details or down-
load an application form from the website.
Closing Date: April 1st.

Library School Graduates Attending Law School (Type II)

Subjects: Law.
Purpose: To assist a library school graduate.
Eligibility: Open to library school graduates working towards a de-
gree in an accredited law school who have no more than 36 semes-
ter credit hours remaining before qualifying for the law degree and
who have law library experience. Preference is given to members of
the AALL.
Level of Study: Postgraduate.
Value: Up to US$2,000 for tuition and school related expenses.
Frequency: Annual.
Study Establishment: Accredited law schools.
Country of Study: Any country.
No. of awards offered: Varies.
Application Procedure: Applicants must write for details or down-
load an application form from the website.
Closing Date: April 1st.

AMERICAN ASSOCIATION OF NEUROLOGICAL SURGEONS (AANS)

5550 Meadowbrook Drive, Rolling Meadows, IL, 60008, United
States of America
Tel: (1) 847 378 0526
Fax: (1) 847 378 0626
Email: lms@aans.org
www: http://www.aans.org
Contact: Laurie Singer

The American Association of Neurological Surgeons (AANS) is a scientific and educational association devoted to the development of
neurological surgery, with more than 5,800 members in the United
States and Canada. The AANS is dedicated to excellence in patient
care. All active members are certified by the American Board of Neurosurgery. The Neurosurgery Research and Education Foundation
(NREF) of AANS provides research grants to residents and clinicians in neurosurgery. NREF has directed more than US$2 million to
over 62 scientific investigations since it was established in 1981.

American Association of Neurological Surgeons Research Fellowship

Subjects: Any field of neurosurgery.
Eligibility: Applicants must be MDs who have been accepted into,
or who are in, an approved residency training programmes in neurological surgery in North America.

Level of Study: Predoctorate.
Type: Fellowship.
Value: US$35,000 every year for two years.
Length of Study: Two years.
Frequency: Annual.
Country of Study: North America.
Application Procedure: Applicants must send a completed application, sponsor statement, programme director comments and letters of recommendation. The following materials must also be submitted on floppy disk using Microsoft Word format: the responses to questions 14-21, a curriculum vitae, photographic images, one hard copy of the complete application, and four copies of each video, if applicable. Faxed applications will not be accepted. Applications are available from the website.
Closing Date: December 1st.
Funding: Private.
Contributor: Corporations and membership.
No. of awards given last year: Three.
No. of applicants last year: 25.
Additional Information: Notification of awards will be made by February 28th. After notification of the award, the applicant must indicate acceptance, in writing, no later than April 1st. If unwilling to accept the award by that date, funds will be awarded to the first runner-up. A report of findings and accounting of funds will be expected at the halfway point and upon completion of the fellowship. Normally, no more than one award per year will be made to any one institution. Individuals who accept a grant from another source (NIH or private) for the same research project will become ineligible for the award. A budget must be prepared by the applicant and the sponsor indicating how the grant funds will be expended. It is the policy of the NREF to fund only direct costs involved with the research awards. This means no fringe benefits, publication costs or travel expenses. The signature representing the applicant's institution's Financial Officer on page four should be that of their chief financial officer or grants and contracts manager. The award will be made payable to the institution and disbursed by it according to its institutional policy.

Young Clinician Investigator Award

Subjects: Any field of neurosurgery.
Purpose: To fund pilot studies that could provide preliminary data that may be used to strengthen applications for permanent funding from the National Institutes of Health (NIH) or other sources.
Eligibility: Applicants must be neurosurgeons who are full-time faculty in teaching institutions in North America and in the early years of their careers.
Level of Study: Postdoctorate.
Type: Fellowship.
Value: US$40,000 for a one year period.
Length of Study: One year.
Frequency: Annual.
Country of Study: North America.
Application Procedure: Applicants must send a completed application, sponsor statement, programme director comments and letters of recommendation. The following materials must also be submitted on floppy disk using Microsoft Word format: the responses to questions 14-21, a curriculum vitae, photographic images, one hard copy of the complete application, and four copies of each video, if applicable. Faxed applications will not be accepted. Applications are available from the website.
Closing Date: December 1st.
Funding: Private.
Contributor: Corporations and membership.
No. of awards given last year: Two.
No. of applicants last year: 20.
Additional Information: Notification of awards will be made by February 28th. After notification of the award, the applicant must indicate acceptance, in writing, no later than April 1st. If unwilling to accept the award by that date, funds will be awarded to the first runner-up. A summary report and an accounting of funds will be expected upon completion of the award. Normally, no more than one award per year will be made to any one institution. Individuals who accept a grant from another source (NIH or private) for the same research project

will become ineligible for the award. The award is for those budget items necessary to pursue proper research. It may be used entirely, or in part, for stipend. A budget must be prepared by the applicant and sponsor indicating how the award funds will be expended. It is the policy of the NREF to fund only direct costs involved with the research awards. This means no fringe benefits, publication costs or travel expenses.

THE AMERICAN ASSOCIATION OF PETROLEUM GEOLOGISTS (AAPG) FOUNDATION (AAPG)

1444 South Boulder, Tulsa, OK, 74114, United States of America
Tel: (1) 918 560 2644
Fax: (1) 918 560 2642
Email: gia@aapg.org
www: http://www.aapg.org/foundation/gia/forms.html
Contact: Ms Rebecca Griffin, Grants Coordinator

Established by the American Association of Petroleum Geologists (AAPG) in 1967, the AAPG Foundation is a public foundation, qualified to receive gifts which are tax deductible to United States taxpayers, in support of worthwhile educational and scientific programmes or projects related to the geosciences.

American Association of Petroleum Geologists Foundation Grants-in-Aid

Subjects: Earth and geological sciences.
Purpose: To support graduate students whose research can be applied to the search for, and development of, petroleum and energy-minerals resources, and to related environmental geology issues.
Eligibility: Open to graduate and doctorate students of any nationality.
Level of Study: Doctorate, Graduate.
Type: Grant.
Value: A maximum of US$2,000.
Frequency: Annual.
Country of Study: Any country.
No. of awards offered: 100.
Application Procedure: Applicants must complete an application form and submit certified college academic transcripts or signed statements from professors commenting on the applicant's academic credentials and endorsements.
Closing Date: January 15th.
Funding: Private.
No. of awards given last year: 100.
No. of applicants last year: 305.
Additional Information: Grants are to be applied to expenses directly related to the student's thesis work, such as Summer field work, analytical analyses etc. Funds are not to be used to purchase capital equipment, or to pay salaries, tuition or room and board during the school year.

AMERICAN BAR FOUNDATION (ABF)

750 North Lake Shore Drive, Chicago, IL, 60611, United States of America
Tel: (1) 312 988 6580
Fax: (1) 312 988 6579
Email: fellowships@abfn.org
www: http://www.abf-sociolegal.org
Contact: Ms Jodi Polster

The American Bar Foundation (ABF) is an independent research institute and has an interdisciplinary staff of research fellows trained in law, sociology, psychology, political science, economics, anthropology and history. Current research areas include professionalism and the transformation of the legal profession in the United States of

America and abroad, the impact of civil rights on the economic progress of minorities, hate speech and its regulation, the influence of family and environmental factors on juvenile delinquency, the impact of public policy on the spread of the internet, jury decision making, historical analyses of labour and regulatory law, public interest lawyering, social reform and sentencing judgement and the effect of victim impact evidence.

ABF Fellowships in Law and Social Science

Subjects: Law and social science.

Purpose: To encourage original and significant research in law, the legal profession and legal institutions.

Eligibility: Applications are invited from outstanding students who are candidates for PhD degrees in the social sciences, or have completed their PhD within the past two years. Proposed research must be in the general area of socio-legal studies or in social scientific approaches to law, the legal profession or legal institutions. The research must address significant issues in the field and show promise of a major contribution to social scientific understanding of law and legal processes. Applicants must, at minimum, have been admitted to a candidacy for the PhD before the commencement of the fellowship. In exceptional circumstances, candidates with a JD who have substantial social science training may also be considered. Minority applicants are especially encouraged to apply.

Level of Study: Doctorate, Postdoctorate.

Type: Residential fellowship.

Value: US$30,000.

Frequency: Annual.

Study Establishment: ABF.

Country of Study: United States of America.

No. of awards offered: Varies, but usually two to three.

Application Procedure: Applications must include a letter of application, a statement describing research interests, achievements to date, plans for the fellowship period, two letters of reference, a curriculum vitae, a transcript of graduate records and a sample of written work eg. a conference paper, dissertation chapter or published article. PhD candidates should include a copy of their dissertation proposal.

Closing Date: February 1st.

Funding: Private.

No. of awards given last year: Four fellowships.

No. of applicants last year: Approx. 50.

Additional Information: Further information is available on request.

AMERICAN CHEMICAL SOCIETY (ACS)

The Petroleum Research Fund (PRF)
1155 Sixteenth Street North West, Washington, DC, 20036, United States of America
Tel: (1) 202 872 4481
Fax: (1) 202 872 6319
Email: prfinfo@acs.org
www: http://chemistry.org/prf
Contact: Dr Laurence Funke, Program Director

The Petroleum Research Fund (PRF) was established in 1944 by seven major oil companies. The American Chemical Society (ACS) must use the funds for advanced scientific education and fundamental research in the petroleum field, which may include any field of pure science which may afford a basis for subsequent research directly connected with the petroleum field. Since the first ACS/PRF grants were approved in 1954, several grant programmes have evolved to serve segments of the scientific community. PRF funding commitments in 2001 totalled US$18 million.

ACS/PRF Scientific Education Grants

Subjects: Scientific education and fundamental research in the petroleum field.

Purpose: To provide partial funding for foreign speakers at major symposia in the United States of America or Canada.

Eligibility: Open to non-profit institutions in the United States of America and other countries for speakers coming to conferences in the United States of America, Canada and Mexico on subjects within the PRF Trust.

Level of Study: Unrestricted.

Type: Grant.

Value: Up to US$1,200 per speaker or up to US$3,600 per symposium.

Frequency: Annual.

Country of Study: United States of America.

No. of awards offered: Varies.

Application Procedure: Applicants must use a PRF 'SE' form.

Closing Date: Applications are accepted at any time.

Funding: Private.

Contributor: A private trust.

ACS/PRF Type AC Grants

Subjects: Chemistry, the earth sciences, chemical engineering and related fields such as polymers and materials science.

Eligibility: Open to non-profit institutions in the United States of America and other countries. Grants are made in response to proposals. Recently, PRF support has been restricted to faculty holding tenure or a tenure track appointment. This is the largest PRF grant programme and usually funds proposals from graduate departments.

Level of Study: Professional development.

Type: Grant.

Value: Up to US$120,000 over three years. Most AC grants provide US$80,000 over two years. The budget may include stipends for graduate students, postdoctoral fellows, research supplies, travel costs and a US$500 annual departmental allocation. No overhead costs may be charged to the grant, travel may be reimbursed up to US$2,000 per year (this limit does not apply to field research), and principal investigators may receive no more than US$7,500 per year in summer salary and benefits. As PRF prefers to support people rather than purchase capital equipment, there is a limited budget for such equipment and funding will only be supplied if requested funds are matched by institutional funds.

Frequency: Annual.

Country of Study: Any country.

No. of awards offered: Varies.

Application Procedure: Applicants must use a PRF 'AC' form.

Closing Date: Applications are accepted at any time.

Funding: Private.

Contributor: A private trust.

No. of awards given last year: 201.

No. of applicants last year: 627.

Additional Information: Most grants begin on September 1st, but an earlier start can be negotiated. The PRF Advisory Board normally meets to review proposals in February, May and October. Prospective applicants should call the PRF office for current information on dates of submission and consideration.

ACS/PRF Type B Grants

Subjects: Chemistry, the earth sciences, chemical engineering and related fields such as polymers and materials science.

Eligibility: Open to non-profit institutions in the United States of America and other countries. Grants are made in response to proposals. Recently, PRF support has been restricted to faculty holding tenure or a tenure track appointment. Type B grants are restricted to departments which do not award PhDs. Graduate students may not be supported by Type B funds.

Level of Study: Professional development.

Type: Grant.

Value: Up to US$50,000 over three years. The budget may include undergraduate student stipends, summer faculty salary, supplies and equipment, travel costs and a US$500 annual departmental allocation. No overhead costs may be charged to the grant, travel may be reimbursed up to US$2,000 per year (this limit does not apply to field research), and principal investigators may receive no more than US$7,500 per year in summer salary and benefits. As PRF prefers to support people rather than purchase capital equipment, there is a

limited budget for such equipment and funding will only be supplied if requested funds are matched by institutional funds.
Frequency: Annual.
Country of Study: Any country.
No. of awards offered: Varies.
Application Procedure: Applicants must use a PRF 'B' form.
Closing Date: Applications are accepted at any time.
Funding: Private.
Contributor: A private trust.
No. of awards given last year: 50.
No. of applicants last year: 123.
Additional Information: Most grants begin on September 1st, but an earlier start can be negotiated. The PRF Advisory Board normally meets to review proposals in February, May and October. Prospective applicants should call the PRF office for current information on dates of submission and consideration.

ACS/PRF Type G 'Starter' Grants

Subjects: Chemistry, the earth sciences, chemical engineering and related fields such as polymers and materials science.
Eligibility: Open to non-profit institutions in the United States of America only. Grants are made in response to proposals. These grants are intended for new faculty within the first three years of teaching and without extensive postdoctoral research experience eg. more than five years.
Level of Study: Professional development.
Type: Grant.
Value: US$35,000 over two years, which may be used to fund student stipends, Summer faculty salary, supplies and equipment, and travel costs. Travel may be reimbursed up to US$2,000 per year, though this limit does not apply to field research, and principal investigators may receive no more than US$7,500 per year in summer salary and benefits. As PRF prefers to support people rather than purchase capital equipment, there is a limited budget for such equipment and funding will only be supplied if requested funds are matched by institutional funds. No overhead costs may be charged to the grant.
Length of Study: Two years.
Frequency: Annual.
Country of Study: United States of America.
No. of awards offered: Varies.
Application Procedure: Applicants must use a PRF 'G' form.
Closing Date: Applications are accepted at any time.
Funding: Private.
Contributor: A private trust.
No. of awards given last year: 125.
No. of applicants last year: 352.
Additional Information: Most grants begin on September 1st, but an earlier start can be negotiated. The PRF Advisory Board normally meets to review proposals in February, May and October. Prospective applicants should call the PRF office for current information on dates of submission and consideration. A detailed budget is not required.

AMERICAN COLLEGE OF OBSTETRICIANS AND GYNECOLOGISTS (ACOG)

409 12th Street South West
PO Box 96920, Washington, DC, 20090-6920, United States of America
Tel: (1) 202 863 2577
Fax: (1) 202 554 3490
Email: lcassidy@acog.org
www: http://www.acog.org
Contact: Ms Lee Cassidy, Director of Development

The American College of Obstetricians and Gynecologists (ACOG) is a membership organisation of obstetrician-gynecologists dedicated to the advancement of women's health through education, advocacy, practice and research.

ACOG/3M Pharmaceuticals Research Awards in Lower Genital Infections

Subjects: Gynaecology and obstetrics. One grant is awarded for selected research projects in the area of gynaecological infections. Examples of this would be bacterial vaginosis, trichomoniasis, candidal infections and post surgical infections. The other grant selected must focus on viral infections. Examples may include human papilomavirus (HPV), cervical intraepithelial neoplasia (CIN), genital warts and the herpes simplex virus (HSV).
Purpose: To provide seed grant funds to junior investigators for clinical research.
Eligibility: Applicants must be ACOG Junior Fellows or Fellows who are in an approved obstetrics or gynaecology residency programme, or are within three years of post residency. Applicants must be United States of America or Canadian citizens.
Level of Study: Postgraduate.
Type: Research grant.
Value: US$15,000 plus round trip coach travel to the ACOG Annual Clinical Meeting.
Length of Study: One year.
Frequency: Annual.
Country of Study: United States of America or Canada.
No. of awards offered: Two.
Application Procedure: Applicants must submit six copies of a proposal consisting of a hypothesis, objectives, specific aims, background and significance, and experimental design and methods. These must not exceed six type written pages in total. A curriculum vitae, letter of support from programme director, departmental chair or laboratory director, references and a one page budget must also be submitted.
Closing Date: October 1st.
Funding: Commercial.
Contributor: 3M Pharmaceuticals.
No. of awards given last year: Two.
No. of applicants last year: Nine.
Additional Information: Further information can be found on the website.

ACOG/Cytyc Corporation Research Award for the Prevention of Cervical Cancer

Subjects: Gynaecology and obstetrics, focusing on the prevention of cervical cancer.
Purpose: To provide seed grant funds to junior investigators for clinical research.
Eligibility: Open to ACOG Junior Fellows or Fellows who are in an approved obstetrics or gynaecology residency programme or within three years of post residency.
Level of Study: Postgraduate.
Type: Research grant.
Value: US$15,000 plus travel expenses to attend the ACOG Annual Clinical Meeting.
Length of Study: One year.
Frequency: Annual.
Country of Study: United States of America or Canada.
No. of awards offered: One.
Application Procedure: Applicants must submit six copies of a proposal consisting of a hypothesis, objectives, specific aims, background and significance, and experimental design and methods. These must not exceed six type written pages in total. A curriculum vitae, letter of support from programme director, departmental chair or laboratory director, references and a one page budget must also be submitted.
Closing Date: October 1st.
Funding: Commercial.
Contributor: The Cytyc Corporation.
No. of awards given last year: One.
No. of applicants last year: Nine.

ACOG/Organon, Inc. Research Award in Contraception

Subjects: Obstetrics and gynaecology, focusing on the area of contraception such as oestrogen supplementation during the traditional hormone free interval.

Purpose: To provide seed grant funds to junior investigators for clinical research in the area of contraception such as oestrogen supplementation during the traditional hormone free interval.

Eligibility: Applicants must be ACOG Junior Fellows or Fellows who are in an approved obstetrics or gynaecology residency programme or within three years of post residency.

Level of Study: Postgraduate.

Type: Research grant.

Value: US$25,000 plus funds for travel expenses to attend the ACOG Annual Clinical Meeting.

Length of Study: One year.

Frequency: Annual.

Country of Study: United States of America or Canada.

No. of awards offered: One.

Application Procedure: Applicants must submit six copies of a proposal consisting of a hypothesis, objectives, specific aims, background and significance, and experimental design and methods. These must not exceed six type written pages in total. A curriculum vitae, letter of support from programme director, departmental chair or laboratory director, references and a one page budget must also be submitted.

Closing Date: October 1st.

Funding: Commercial.

Contributor: Organon, Inc.

No. of awards given last year: One.

No. of applicants last year: Four.

ACOG/Ortho-McNeil Academic Training Fellowships in Obstetrics and Gynecology

Subjects: Gynaecology and obstetrics.

Purpose: To provide opportunities for especially qualified residents or Fellows to spend an extra year involved in responsibilities which will train them for academic positions in the speciality.

Eligibility: Open to ACOG Junior Fellows or Fellows who have completed at least one year of training, and are considered by the Director of their residency programme to be especially fitted for a career in medical education or academic obstetrics and gynaecology.

Level of Study: Postgraduate.

Type: Research grant.

Value: US$30,000 stipend plus travel expenses to attend the ACOG Annual Clinical Meeting.

Length of Study: One year.

Frequency: Annual.

Country of Study: United States of America or Canada.

No. of awards offered: Two.

Application Procedure: Applicants must submit six copies of a proposal consisting of a hypothesis, objectives, specific aims, background and significance, and experimental design and methods. These must not exceed six type written pages in total. A curriculum vitae, letter of support from programme director, departmental chair or laboratory director, references and a one page budget must also be submitted.

Closing Date: October 1st.

Funding: Commercial.

Contributor: Ortho-McNeil Pharmaceutical.

No. of awards given last year: Two.

No. of applicants last year: 20.

ACOG/Pharmacia Corporation Research Award on Overactive Bladder

Subjects: Gynaecology and obstetrics focusing on the area of urogynaecology of the post reproductive woman.

Purpose: To provide grant funds to junior investigators for clinical research.

Eligibility: Open to ACOG Junior Fellows or Fellows who are in an approved obstetrics or gynaecology residency programme or within three years of post residency.

Level of Study: Postgraduate.

Type: Research grant.

Value: US$15,000 plus US$1,000 travel allowance to attend the ACOG Annual Clinical Meeting.

Length of Study: One year.

Frequency: Annual.

Country of Study: United States of America or Canada.

No. of awards offered: One.

Application Procedure: Applicants must submit six copies of a proposal consisting of a hypothesis, objectives, specific aims, background and significance, and experimental design and methods. These must not exceed six type written pages in total. A curriculum vitae, letter of support from programme director, departmental chair or laboratory director, references and a one page budget must also be submitted.

Closing Date: October 1st.

Funding: Commercial.

Contributor: The Pharmacia Corporation.

No. of awards given last year: One.

No. of applicants last year: Nine.

ACOG/Solvay Pharmaceuticals Research Award in Menopause

Subjects: Gynaecology and obstetrics focusing on issues related to the menopause. Relevant subjects include the physiological changes of the post reproductive woman, hormonal receptor site distribution, or other investigation deemed appropriate to furthering the basic understanding of the menopause.

Purpose: To advance knowledge in the field through encouraging basic research.

Eligibility: Open to ACOG Fellows or Junior Fellows who are in an approved obstetrics or gynaecology residency programme or are within three years of post residency.

Level of Study: Postgraduate.

Type: Research grant.

Value: US$25,000 plus round trip coach transportation and one night's hotel stay to attend the ACOG Annual Clinical Meeting.

Length of Study: One year.

Frequency: Annual.

Country of Study: United States of America or Canada.

No. of awards offered: One.

Application Procedure: Applicants must submit six copies of a proposal consisting of a hypothesis, objectives, specific aims, background and significance, and experimental design and methods. These must not exceed six type written pages in total. A curriculum vitae, letter of support from programme director, departmental chair or laboratory director, references and a one page budget must also be submitted.

Closing Date: October 1st.

Funding: Commercial.

Contributor: Solvay Pharmaceuticals, Inc.

No. of awards given last year: One.

No. of applicants last year: 11.

Warren H Pearse/Wyeth-Ayerst Women's Health Policy Research Award

Subjects: Gynaecology and obstetrics focusing on health economics, health care patterns and health care policy as it relates to the care of women.

Purpose: To provide funds to support research.

Eligibility: The principal or co-principal investigator must be an ACOG Junior Fellow or Fellow. Proposals will be considered with regards to innovation, potential utility of the research, ability to generalise results and demonstrated capability of the investigator.

Level of Study: Postgraduate.

Type: Research grant.

Value: US$15,000 plus travel expenses to attend the ACOG Annual Clinical Meeting.

Length of Study: One year.

Frequency: Annual.

Country of Study: United States of America or Canada.

No. of awards offered: One.

Application Procedure: Applicants must submit six copies of a proposal consisting of a hypothesis, objectives, specific aims, background and significance, and experimental design and methods. These must not exceed six type written pages in total. A curriculum vitae, letter of support from programme director, departmental chair or laboratory director, references and a one page budget must also be submitted.
Closing Date: October 1st.
Funding: Commercial.
Contributor: Wyeth-Ayerst Pharmaceuticals.
No. of awards given last year: One.
No. of applicants last year: 10.

AMERICAN COUNCIL OF LEARNED SOCIETIES (ACLS)

228 East 45th Street, New York, NY, 10017, United States of America
Fax: (1) 212 949 8058
Email: grants@acls.org
www: http://www.acls.org
Contact: Grants Management Officer

ACLS American Research in the Humanities in the People's Republic of China

Subjects: The humanities.
Purpose: To enable scholars to carry out research in the People's Republic of China.
Eligibility: Open to United States citizens and permanent residents. Applicants must hold a PhD or equivalent.
Level of Study: Postdoctorate.
Type: Research grant.
Value: Monthly stipend and travel allowance.
Length of Study: 4-12 months.
Frequency: Annual.
Study Establishment: A Chinese university or research institute.
Country of Study: China.
No. of awards offered: Approx. five.
Application Procedure: Applicants must write for details.
Closing Date: November 15th.
Contributor: The National Endowment for the Humanities.

ACLS Charles A Ryskamp Research Fellowships

Subjects: Humanities or social sciences.
Purpose: To enable faculty members to conduct research under optimum conditions by providing time and resources.
Eligibility: Open to tenure track assistant professors who have successfully passed their institution's review for re-appointment or the equivalent, but have not yet been reviewed for tenure. Applicants must be employed at institutions in the United States of America and must remain so for the duration of the fellowship.
Level of Study: Postgraduate.
Type: Fellowship.
Value: US$60,000 plus US$2,500 for research and travel.
Length of Study: One academic year with the possibility of an additional Summer's support.
No. of awards offered: Up to 15.
Application Procedure: Applicants must contact the organisation.
Closing Date: October 10th.
Funding: Private.
Contributor: The Andrew W Mellon Foundation.
Additional Information: Further information is available on request.

ACLS Chinese Fellowships for Scholarly Development

Subjects: Social sciences or the humanities.
Purpose: To support scholars undertaking research.
Eligibility: Open to Chinese Scholars with the MA, PhD or equivalent from a Chinese institution who have not previously visited the United States for five months or more. Scholars involved in a degree programme are not eligible. Applicants must currently reside in China.
Level of Study: Graduate, Postdoctorate.
Type: Fellowship.
Value: Living allowance, health insurance and international airfare.
Length of Study: Up to one year.
Frequency: Annual.
Study Establishment: Approved universities or research institutions.
Country of Study: United States of America.
No. of awards offered: Approx. eight.
Application Procedure: Applicants must be nominated by the United States host. Chinese Scholars cannot apply directly.
Closing Date: November 15th.
Contributor: The Starr Foundation and the Li Foundation.
Additional Information: Further information is available on the website.

ACLS Contemplative Practice Fellowships

Subjects: Arts, humanities or social sciences.
Purpose: To restore and renew the critical contribution that contemplative practices can make to the life of the mind.
Eligibility: Open to full-time faculty members at academic institutions in the United States. There are no citizenship restrictions. First hand prior experience with contemplative practice, though encouraged, is not required.
Level of Study: Postgraduate.
Type: Fellowship.
Value: A maximum of US$20,000.
Length of Study: A summer for scholars or for a single semester's sabbatical leave.
No. of awards offered: Approx. 10.
Application Procedure: Applicants must consult the organisation.
Closing Date: November 1st.
Contributor: The Nathan Cummings Foundation and the Fetzer Institute, co-sponsored by the Center for Contemplative Mind in Society.
Additional Information: Fellows will be asked to provide reports on their research and copies of course materials to the ACLS and the Center for Contemplative Mind in Society. Contemplative practices are part of all major religious and spiritual traditions, and have long had a place in intellectual inquiry. This programme will support the study of contemplation as a historical phenomenon, as a category of religious experience, and as a method to develop concentration, deepen understanding and cultivate awareness.

ACLS Dissertation Fellowships in East European Studies

Subjects: Social sciences and humanities relating to Albania, Bulgaria, the Czech Republic, Hungary, Poland, Romania, Slovakia, and the former Yugoslavia.
Purpose: To support dissertation research and writing.
Eligibility: Open to United States citizens or permanent legal residents.
Level of Study: Doctorate.
Type: Fellowship.
Value: Up to US$15,000.
Length of Study: One academic year.
Frequency: Annual.
Study Establishment: Any approved university or research institution.
Country of Study: Outside Eastern Europe.
No. of awards offered: Approx. 10.
Application Procedure: Applicants must write for details or consult the website.
Closing Date: November 1st.
Additional Information: The product of the proposed work must be disseminated in English. Further information is available on the website.

ACLS East European Language Training Grants

Subjects: Any Eastern European language except the languages of the Commonwealth of Independent States.

Purpose: To support summer language training for students and scholars who cannot receive such training at their home institutions.

Eligibility: Open to United States citizens or permanent residents who are graduate students, or postdoctoral Scholars.

Level of Study: Doctorate, Postdoctorate, Postgraduate.

Type: Grant.

Value: Up to US$2,500.

Frequency: Annual.

Study Establishment: Any Institute of Higher Education.

Country of Study: United States of America.

No. of awards offered: Varies.

Application Procedure: Applicants must consult the website.

Closing Date: January 31st.

Additional Information: Further information is available on request.

ACLS Fellowships for Postdoctoral Research in East European Studies

Subjects: Social sciences and humanities relating to Albania, Bulgaria, the Czech Republic, Hungary, Poland, Romania, Slovakia and the former Yugoslavia.

Purpose: To allow Scholars to undertake a period of full-time research.

Eligibility: Open to United States citizens and permanent residents only.

Level of Study: Postdoctorate.

Type: Fellowship.

Value: Up to US$25,000. The funds are intended primarily as salary replacements and may be used to supplement sabbatical salaries or awards from other sources, provided they would intensify or extend the contemplated research.

Length of Study: At least six months.

Frequency: Annual.

Study Establishment: Approved universities or research institutions.

Country of Study: Outside Eastern Europe.

No. of awards offered: Approx. five-seven.

Application Procedure: Applicants must write for details.

Closing Date: November 1st.

Additional Information: The product of the proposed work must be disseminated in English. Further information is available on request.

ACLS Frederick Burkhardt Residential Fellowships for Recently Tenured Scholars

Subjects: Arts, humanities or social sciences.

Purpose: To support long-term, unusually ambitious projects.

Eligibility: Open to recently tenured humanists at institutions in the United States of America and Canada. Applicants must also be citizens of these countries.

Level of Study: Postgraduate.

Type: Fellowship.

Value: Stipend of US$65,000.

Length of Study: One academic year.

Frequency: Annual.

Study Establishment: Residential research centres.

Country of Study: United States of America or Canada.

No. of awards offered: Up to 11.

Application Procedure: Applicants must write for details or visit the website.

Closing Date: October 1st.

Funding: Private.

Contributor: The Andrew W Mellon Foundation, with additional funding from the Rockefeller Foundation.

Additional Information: Further information is available from the website.

ACLS Henry Luce Foundation/ACLS Dissertation Fellowships in American Art

Subjects: Art history, focusing on a topic in the history of the visual arts of the United States.

Purpose: To assist students at any stage of PhD dissertation research or writing.

Eligibility: Applicants must be United States citizens and have completed all requirements for a PhD except the dissertation before beginning tenure. They must also be in a department of art history, focusing on a topic in the history of the visual arts of the United States. A student whose degree will be granted by another department may be eligible if the principal dissertation advisor is in a department of the history of art. In all cases the dissertation topic should be object orientated. Students preparing theses for the Master of Fine Arts Degree are not eligible.

Level of Study: Graduate, Predoctorate.

Type: Fellowship.

Value: US$20,000.

Length of Study: One year, non renewable.

Country of Study: United States of America.

No. of awards offered: 10.

Application Procedure: Applicants must consult the organisation.

Closing Date: November 15th.

Contributor: The Henry Luce Foundation.

Additional Information: Further information is available from the website.

ACLS Library of Congress Fellowships in International Studies

Subjects: Arts, humanities or social sciences.

Purpose: To support postdoctoral research using the foreign language collections of the Library of Congress.

Eligibility: Applicants must hold a PhD and preference will be given to those at an early stage in their careers ie. within seven years of their degree. Applicants must also be United States citizens or permanent residents as of the application deadline and may be affiliated with any academic institution. Independent Scholars are also welcome to apply.

Level of Study: Postdoctorate.

Type: Fellowship.

Value: US$3,500 per month.

Length of Study: Four-nine months.

Frequency: Annual.

No. of awards offered: Up to 10.

Application Procedure: Applicants must write to the organisation or visit the website.

Closing Date: November 1st.

Contributor: The Andrew W Mellon Foundation, the Association of American Universities and the Library of Congress. The Henry Luce Foundation has enabled the Library of Congress to provide funding for research concerning East or Southeast Asia.

Additional Information: Applicants must demonstrate the need for use of the Library of Congress foreign language holdings, and must document competence in the appropriate language at a level that would suffice to conduct research, and present a record of work that promises a high quality research work of a publishable nature. Applicants will be asked to submit a general overview of the material they expect to consult, a timetable for the completion of their research and anticipated outcomes such as publications and presentations.

ACLS/Andrew W Mellon Fellowships for Junior Faculty

Subjects: Humanities or social sciences.

Eligibility: Open to citizens of America or permanent residents only. Applicants must have at least two years of teaching experience and a PhD. However, an established Scholar who can demonstrate the equivalent of a PhD in publications and professional experience may also qualify. Scholars currently enrolled for any degree are not eligible.

Level of Study: Postdoctorate, Postgraduate.

Type: Fellowship.

Value: Varies.

Length of Study: 6-12 months.
No. of awards offered: 22.
Application Procedure: Applicants must write for details.
Closing Date: October 1st.
Additional Information: Further information is available on request.

ACLS/New York Public Library Fellowships

Subjects: Arts, humanities or social sciences.
Purpose: To explore the rich and diverse collections of the NYPL Humanities and Social Sciences Library.
Eligibility: Applicants must be citizens or permanent residents of the United States of America as of the application deadline date, and hold a PhD degree. However, an established Scholar who can demonstrate the equivalent of a PhD in publications and professional experience may also qualify. Applicants will be asked to identify specific resources and benefits to be gained from affiliation with the Center. Scholars currently enrolled for any degree are not eligible.
Level of Study: Postdoctorate.
Type: Fellowship.
Value: Up to US$50,000 for full professor and equivalent, US$40,000 for associate professor and equivalent and US$30,000 for assistant professor and equivalent.
Length of Study: 6-12 months.
No. of awards offered: Up to 15.
Application Procedure: Applications must be made to the ACLS Fellowship Program. Note that application must also be made to the competition for residential fellowships administered separately by the NYPL Center for Scholars and Writers.
Closing Date: Please consult the organisation.
Additional Information: More information about the NYPL is available at http://www.nypl.org. It is possible that an application may have any one of the following outcomes: a fellowship awarded solely by the NYPL Center for Scholars and Writers, an ACLS Fellowship awarded solely by the ACLS or a joint NYPL/ACLS Residential Fellowship awarded by both organisations together.

For further information contact:

Center for Scholars and Writers
The New York Public Library Humanities and Social Sciences Library, Fifth Avenue & 42nd Street, New York, NY, 10018-2788, United States of America
Email: csw@nypl.org

ACLS/SSRC/NEH International and Area Studies Fellowships

Subjects: Research and writing on the societies and cultures of Asia, Africa, the Near and Middle East, Latin America and the Caribbean, East Europe and the Former Soviet Union.
Purpose: To encourage humanistic research in area studies.
Eligibility: Applicants must be citizens or permanent residents of the United States as of the application deadline date, and hold a PhD degree. However, an established Scholar who can demonstrate the equivalent of a PhD in publications and professional experience may also qualify. Scholars pursuing research and writing on the societies and cultures of Asia, Africa, the Near and Middle East, Latin America and the Caribbean, East Europe and the Former Soviet Union are eligible. Scholars currently enrolled for any degree are not eligible.
Level of Study: Postdoctorate.
Type: Fellowship.
Value: Up to US$50,000 for full professor and equivalent, US$40,000 for associate professor and equivalent and US$30,000 for assistant professor and equivalent.
Length of Study: 6-12 months.
No. of awards offered: Approx. 10.
Application Procedure: Applications must be made to the ACLS Fellowship Program and all requirements and provisions of that programmes must be met. The Fellow must submit a final report to both NEH and ACLS. Note that application must also be made to the competition for residential fellowships administered separately by the NYPL Center for Scholars and Writers.
Closing Date: Please consult the organisation.
Additional Information: Further information is available on request.

For further information contact:

Center for Scholars and Writers
The New York Public Library Humanities and Social Sciences Library, Fifth Avenue & 42nd Street, New York, NY, 10018-2788, United States of America
Email: csw@nypl.org

AMERICAN COUNCIL OF THE BLIND (ACB)

1155 15th Street North West
Suite 1004, Washington, DC, 20005, United States of America
Tel: (1) 202 467 5081
Fax: (1) 202 467 5085
Email: tpacheco@acb.org
www: http://www.acb.org
Contact: Mrs Terry Pacheco

The American Council of the Blind is a membership organisation that promotes the effective participation of people who are blind in all aspects of society.

ACB Scholarship Program

Subjects: All subjects.
Purpose: To provide scholarships to legally blind postsecondary students.
Eligibility: Open to United States citizens or resident aliens who are legally blind in both eyes.
Level of Study: Doctorate, Postgraduate, Postsecondary.
Type: Scholarship.
Value: US$500-4,000.
Length of Study: One year.
Frequency: Annual.
Country of Study: United States of America.
No. of awards offered: 25-30.
Application Procedure: Applicants must submit an application including an application form, a two page autobiographical sketch, transcripts, a letter of recommendation and proof of legal blindness.
Closing Date: March 1st.
Funding: Private.
Contributor: Public donations.
No. of awards given last year: 26.
No. of applicants last year: 325.

AMERICAN COUNCIL ON EDUCATION (ACE)

One Dupont Circle North West
Suite 800, Washington, DC, 20036-1193, United States of America
Tel: (1) 202 939 9420
Fax: (1) 202 785 8056
Email: fellows@ace.nche.edu
www: http://www.acenet.edu
Contact: Awards Committee

The American Council on Education (ACE), founded in 1918, is the nation's umbrella higher education association. ACE is dedicated to the belief that equal educational opportunity and a strong higher education system are essential cornerstones of a democratic society. ACE is a forum for the discussion of major issues related to higher education and its potential to contribute to the quality of American life. ACE maintains both a domestic and an international agenda and seeks to advance the interests and goals of higher and adult education in a changing environment by providing leadership and advocacy on important issues representing the views of the higher and adult education community to policy makers, and offering services to its members.

ACE Fellows Program

Subjects: Administration, leadership and governance of higher education and management of colleges and universities.

Purpose: To strengthen leadership in American higher education by identifying and preparing individuals who have shown promise for responsible positions in higher education administration.

Eligibility: Open to senior members of college faculty or mid-level staff with a minimum of five years teaching or administrative experience who show evidence of potential for senior level administration. English is the language of instruction.

Level of Study: Professional development.

Type: Fellowship.

Value: The nominating institution supports the salaries and benefits. The host institution supports the seminar and travel costs of the ACE Fellows and the Council provides support for programmatic costs. Non ACE member institutions are charged a US$4,500 tuition fee.

Length of Study: One academic year.

Frequency: Annual.

Study Establishment: A host college or university.

Country of Study: Any country.

No. of awards offered: 30-35.

Application Procedure: Applicants must be nominated by the president or vice president of a college or university. Applications must be submitted with a nomination form, along with four confidential letters of reference.

Closing Date: November 1st.

Additional Information: ACE Fellows work with a mentor, normally a president or other senior officer, at policy and practical levels. The fellowship experience is supplemented with national and regional seminars and meetings.

AMERICAN COUNCIL ON RURAL SPECIAL EDUCATION (ACRES)

Kansas State University
2323 Anderson Avenue
Suite 226, Manhattan, KS, 66502-2912, United States of America
Tel: (1) 785 532 2737
Fax: (1) 785 532 7732
Email: acres@ksu.edu
www: http://www.ksu.edu/acres
Contact: Ms Judy Weyrauch, Headquarters Co-ordinator

ACRES Scholarship

Subjects: Special education in the areas of the handicapped, those with specific learning disabilities and the socially disadvantaged.

Purpose: To give a rural teacher an opportunity to pursue education and training not otherwise affordable within his or her district.

Eligibility: Applicants must be United States citizens, currently employed by a rural school district as a certified teacher in regular or special education, working with students with disabilities or with regular education students and retraining from a career in regular education to a special education career.

Level of Study: Postgraduate.

Type: Scholarship.

Value: Varies each year. Up to US$1,000.

Length of Study: One year.

Frequency: Annual.

Country of Study: United States of America.

No. of awards offered: One.

Application Procedure: Applicants must complete and submit an application form with an essay and two letters of recommendation.

Closing Date: December 10th.

Funding: Private.

Additional Information: The award will be announced at the March ACRES Symposium.

AMERICAN DIABETES ASSOCIATION (ADA)

1701 North Beauregard Street, Alexandria, VA, 22311, United States of America
Tel: (1) 703 549 1500
Fax: (1) 703 549 1715
Email: research@diabetes.org
www: http://www.diabetes.org/research
Contact: Research Department

The American Diabetes Association is the nation's leading non-profit health organisation providing diabetes research, information and advocacy. The mission of the organisation is to prevent and cure diabetes, and to improve the lives of all people affected by diabetes. To fulfil this mission, the ADA funds research, publishes scientific findings and provides information and other services to people with diabetes, their families, health care professionals and the public.

ADA Career Development Awards

Subjects: Diabetes related research.

Purpose: To allow exceptionally promising new investigators to conduct research.

Eligibility: Open to United States citizens, permanent residents or those who have applied for permanent resident status who have MD or PhD degrees or, in the case of other health professions, an appropriate health or science related degree Applicants must hold an assistant professorship or provide documentation that he or she will receive this position upon receipt of this award. At the time of the award applicants must have at least two, but not more than five years of postdoctoral or post fellowship research experience in a diabetes related field with relevant accomplishments and publications.

Level of Study: Postdoctorate.

Type: Development award.

Value: Up to US$150,000 per year and an additional 15 per cent for indirect costs. The funds are to be divided by the recipient between the salary of the principal investigator and other grant support. Each year of funding, after the first, is contingent upon approval by the ADA of the recipient's research progress report, and the availability of funds.

Length of Study: Five years, non renewable.

Frequency: Twice a year.

Country of Study: United States of America.

No. of awards offered: Varies, depending on funds available.

Application Procedure: Applicants must write for details.

Closing Date: February 1st for July 1st funding and August 1st for January 1st funding.

No. of awards given last year: 16.

No. of applicants last year: 34.

ADA Clinical Research Grants

Subjects: Diabetes related research. For the purpose of this programme, clinical research is defined as research involving humans directly.

Purpose: To support patient orientated research.

Eligibility: Open to United States citizens, permanent residents or those who have applied for permanent resident status, who have MD or PhD degrees or, in the case of other health professions, an appropriate health or science related degree, and who hold full-time faculty positions or the equivalent at university affiliated institutions within the United States and its possessions. Support will be provided for studies that focus on intact human subjects in which the effects of a change in the individual's external or internal environment is evaluated.

Level of Study: Postdoctorate.

Type: Research grant.

Value: Up to US$100,000 per year for three years. Up to US$20,000 per year may be used for principal investigator salary support, and up to 15 per cent for indirect costs. Each year of funding after the first is contingent upon approval by the ADA of the recipient's research progress report, and the availability of funds.

Length of Study: Three years.

Frequency: Twice a year.
Country of Study: United States of America.
No. of awards offered: Varies, depending on funds available.
Closing Date: February 1st for July 1st funding and August 1st for January 1st funding.
No. of awards given last year: 15.
No. of applicants last year: 71.

ADA Junior Faculty Awards

Subjects: Diabetes related research.
Purpose: To support investigators who are establishing their independence as diabetes researchers.
Eligibility: Open to United States citizens or permanent residents, or those who have applied for permanent resident status, who have an MD or PhD degree or an appropriate health or science related degree. Applicants can hold any level of faculty appointment at university affiliated institutions within the United States and United States possessions.
Level of Study: Postdoctorate.
Type: Development award.
Value: Up to US$120,000 per year, plus up to US$10,000 per year towards repayment of the principle on loans for a doctoral degree such as the MD or PhD.
Length of Study: Three years.
Country of Study: United States of America.
No. of awards offered: Varies, depending on funds available.
Application Procedure: Applicants must write for details.
Closing Date: February 1st for July 1st funding or August 1st for January 1st funding.

ADA Medical Scholars Program

Subjects: Diabetes research.
Purpose: To produce leaders in the fields of research, teaching and patient care, by giving physicians in training the opportunity to contribute to the process of discovery in basic and clinical research laboratories. The Medical Scholars Program will supply a unique opportunity to effectively integrate medical students into the process of discovery.
Eligibility: Open to institutions within the United States and United States possessions. The application must be initiated by the student, and the student must have a qualified sponsor. The student must have completed at least one year of medical school and the sponsor must hold a faculty position within an accredited medical school in the United States and be a United States citizen or permanent resident status.
Level of Study: Postgraduate.
Type: Scholarship.
Value: The programme provides support for one year in a clinical or basic science research environment. The award will be up to US$30,000 per student, US$20,000 for the student's support, and US$10,000 for materials, supplies and travel to the Association's scientific sessions.
Frequency: Annual.
Country of Study: United States of America.
No. of awards offered: Varies.
Closing Date: February 1st for July 1st funding.
No. of awards given last year: Eight.
No. of applicants last year: Eight.

ADA Mentor-Based Postdoctoral Fellowship Program

Subjects: Diabetes research.
Purpose: To support the training of scientists in an environment most conducive to beginning a career in research. An award will also be given to an established and active investigator in diabetes research for the annual stipend support of a postdoctoral Fellow to work closely with the mentor.
Eligibility: There are no citizenship requirements for the Fellow. However, the investigator must be a United States citizen or permanent resident, and must also hold an appointment at a United States research institution and have sufficient research support to provide an appropriate training environment for the Fellow. The Fellow

selected by the investigator must hold a MD or PhD degree and must not be serving an internship or residency during the fellowship period. The Fellow must not have more than three years of postdoctoral research experience in the field of diabetes or endocrinology at the commencement of this fellowship.
Level of Study: Postdoctorate.
Type: Fellowship.
Value: Up to US$35,000 for four years.
Length of Study: Up to three years.
Frequency: Annual.
Country of Study: United States of America.
No. of awards offered: Varies, depending on funds available.
Application Procedure: Applicants must complete an application form.
Closing Date: October 1st for July 1st funding.
No. of awards given last year: 25.
No. of applicants last year: 53.

ADA Physician/Scientist Training

Subjects: Diabetes.
Purpose: To provide support for the doctoral portion of an MD or PhD degree.
Eligibility: Open to students who have a qualified sponsor and are in good academic standing. Students already enrolled in an MSTP programme are not eligible to apply for this award.
Level of Study: Postgraduate.
Type: Scholarship.
Value: Up to US$30,000 per year.
Length of Study: Three years.
Frequency: Annual.
Country of Study: United States of America.
No. of awards offered: Varies, depending on funds available.
Application Procedure: Applicants must write for details. Applications must be initiated by the student.
Closing Date: February 1st for July 1st funding.
No. of awards given last year: Five.
No. of applicants last year: 12.

ADA Research Awards

Subjects: Aetiology and pathophysiology of diabetes.
Purpose: To assist investigators, new or established, who have a particularly novel and exciting idea for which they need support.
Eligibility: Open to United States citizens or permanent residents or those who have applied for permanent resident status who have MD or PhD degrees, or, in the case of other health professions, an appropriate health or science related degree, and who hold full-time faculty positions or the equivalent at university affiliated institutions within the United States and its possessions.
Level of Study: Postdoctorate.
Type: Research grant.
Value: US$20,000-100,000 per year, for a maximum of three years, of which a maximum of US$20,000 can be used for principal investigator salary support, and up to 15 per cent for indirect costs. Each year of funding after the first is contingent upon approval by the ADA of the recipient's research progress report, and the availability of funds.
Length of Study: Up to three years.
Frequency: Twice a year.
Country of Study: United States of America.
No. of awards offered: Varies, depending on funds available.
Closing Date: February 1st for July 1st funding and August 1st for January 1st funding.
No. of awards given last year: 60.
No. of applicants last year: 226.

LCIF Clinical Research Grant Program

Subjects: New treatment regimens, epidemiology and translation research in the area of diabetic retinopathy.
Purpose: To support clinical or applied research.
Eligibility: Open to holders of an MD or PhD degree, or, in the case of other health professions, an appropriate health or science related

degree. The applicant must hold a faculty level appointment or its equivalent at a research institution. The programme is intended for any investigator with or without NIH or other significant support.
Level of Study: Postdoctorate.
Type: Research grant.
Value: Up to US$100,000 per year. The grants carry no commitment for overhead costs or tuition. The funds may be used for equipment, supplies, salary support or a combination of the three. The funds may not be used for the principal investigator's salary. Travel to diabetic retinopathy-related scientific meetings is restricted to a maximum of US$1,000 per year.
Length of Study: Three years.
Frequency: Annual.
Country of Study: Any country.
No. of awards offered: Varies, depending on funds available.
Closing Date: February 1st for July 1st funding.
No. of awards given last year: Two.
No. of applicants last year: Seven.
Additional Information: This programme is part of the Lions Sightfirst Diabetic Retinopathy Research Program, funded by the Lions Club International Foundation.

LCIF Equipment Grant Program
Subjects: Clinical research in diabetic retinopathy.
Purpose: To enable investigators to purchase equipment in order to conduct clinical research projects.
Eligibility: Open to holders of an MD or PhD degree, or, in the case of other health professions, an appropriate health or science related degree. The applicant must hold a faculty level appointment at a research institution.
Level of Study: Postdoctorate.
Type: Emergency grant.
Value: US$25,000 for the purchase of equipment. One payment is made in July.
Frequency: Annual.
Country of Study: Any country.
No. of awards offered: Varies, depending on funds available.
Application Procedure: Applicants must submit a detailed justification of the need to purchase the equipment and an explanation of its intended use.
Closing Date: February 1st for July 1st funding.
No. of applicants last year: Six.
Additional Information: This programme is part of the Lions Sightfirst Diabetic Retinopathy Research Program, funded by the Lions Club International Foundation. Applicants must submit the final disposition within six months of receipt of the award.

LCIF Training Grant Program
Subjects: Diabetic retinopathy.
Purpose: To enable foreign investigators to visit American research institutions and receive training in clinical research, the implementation of public health programmes eg. screening or epidemiology. The programme also aims to enable United States investigators to visit foreign institutions, particularly institutions in underdeveloped countries, to conduct training programmes in clinical research and implement public health programmes.
Eligibility: Open to United States citizens who have an MD or PhD degree, or, in the case of other health professions, an appropriate health or science related degree, and hold a faculty level appointment at a United States research institution. The programme is also open to non United States citizens who have an MD or PhD degree or, in the case of other health professions, an appropriate advanced degree and hold a faculty level appointment at a research institution outside the United States of America.
Level of Study: Postdoctorate.
Value: Up to US$40,000.
Length of Study: Two years.
Frequency: Annual.
Study Establishment: An approved institution.
Country of Study: Any country.
No. of awards offered: Varies, depending on funds available.
Closing Date: February 1st for July 1st funding.

Additional Information: This programme is part of the Lions Sightfirst Diabetic Retinopathy Research Program, funded by the Lions Club International Foundation.

AMERICAN DIGESTIVE HEALTH FOUNDATION (ADHF)

7910 Woodmont Avenue
Suite 610, Bethesda, MD, 20814-3015, United States of America
Tel: (1) 301 222 4005
Fax: (1) 301 222 4010
Email: desta@gastro.org
www: http://www.fdhn.org
Contact: Ms Desta Wallace, Research Awards Programme Coordinator

The American Digestive Health Foundation (ADHF) is the unified voice of the leading gastroenterology and hepatology societies, the American Gastroenterological Association (AGA) and the American Society for Gastrointestinal Endoscopy (ASGE), who are working together for better digestive health. ADHF's mission is to advance digestive health through financial support of research and education in the cause, prevention, diagnosis, treatment and cure of digestive and liver diseases.

AGA Astra Zeneca Fellowship/Faculty Transition Awards
Subjects: Medical science, specifically gastroenterology and hepathology.
Purpose: To prepare and support physicians for independent research careers in digestive diseases.
Eligibility: Applicants must be MDs currently in a gastroenterology related fellowship at an accredited North American institution, who are committed to academic careers and will have completed two years of research training at the start of this award. The additional training could be considered the equivalent of the practical training ordinarily provided in a PhD programme. Therefore, individuals who hold a PhD are ineligible. Although the host institution may supplement the award, the applicant may not concurrently hold a similar training award or grant from another organisation. However, under certain circumstances, a small pool of funds may be available to support investigators as a supplement to current funding. Women and minority investigators are strongly encouraged to apply. Applicants must be a member or be sponsored by a member of any of the ADHF partner organisations.
Level of Study: Postgraduate.
Type: Award.
Value: US$36,000 per year. Smaller amounts may be awarded as supplementary funding.
Length of Study: Two years.
Frequency: Annual.
Country of Study: United States of America, Canada or Mexico.
No. of awards offered: Four.
Application Procedure: Applicants must write for details.
Closing Date: September 10th.
Contributor: The AGA.
Additional Information: At the end of the award, the recipient will be required to indicate how the funds were used, the accomplishments made during the training project and how this training has contributed to his or her research career development. A complete financial statement and scientific progress report are required annually and upon completion of the programme. All publications arising from work funded by this programme must acknowledge support of the award.

AGA Elsevier Research Initiative Award
Subjects: Medical science, specifically gastroenterology and hepathology.
Purpose: To provide non salary funds for new investigators to help them establish their research careers and to support pilot projects that represent new research directions for established investigators.

The intent is to stimulate research in gastroenterology or hepatology related areas by permitting investigators to obtain new data that can ultimately provide the basis for subsequent grant applications of more substantial funding and duration.

Eligibility: Investigators must possess an MD or PhD degree and must hold faculty positions at accredited North American institutions. They may not hold awards on a similar topic from other agencies. In addition, applicants must be an individual member of any of the ADHF partner organisations. Women and minority investigators are strongly encouraged to apply. Applicants for this award may not apply for the AGA Miles & Shirley Fiterman Foundation Basic Research Award simultaneously.

Level of Study: Postdoctorate, Postgraduate, Predoctorate.

Type: Award.

Value: US$25,000.

Length of Study: One year.

Frequency: Annual.

Country of Study: United States of America, Canada or Mexico.

No. of awards offered: One.

Application Procedure: Applicants must write for details or visit the website.

Closing Date: January 8th.

Contributor: The AGA.

AGA June and Donald O Castell, MD Esophageal Clinical Research Award

Subjects: Clinical research in oesophageal diseases.

Purpose: To support investigators who have demonstrated a high potential to develop an independent, productive research career.

Eligibility: The recipient must be at, or below, the level of assistant professor and must have been appointed to the faculty within the past seven years. Candidates must devote at least 50 per cent of their effort to research related to oesophageal function or diseases.

Level of Study: Graduate.

Type: Research grant.

Value: US$35,000.

Country of Study: United States of America.

No. of awards offered: One.

Application Procedure: Applicants must address all documents to the Chair, AGA GI Research Committee.

Closing Date: Please contact the Foundation.

Funding: Private.

AGA Merck Clinical Research Career Development Award

Subjects: Gastroenterology or hepathology.

Purpose: To provide salary support to junior faculty members performing clinical research at the outset of their career. The award is also to ensure that at least 70 per cent of the investigator's time is protected for research in order to develop an independent and productive career as a clinical investigator in any area of gastroenterology or hepathology.

Eligibility: Applicants must hold full-time faculty positions at North American universities or professional institutes at the time of application. Applicants must also be individual members of any ADHF partner organisation.

Level of Study: Graduate.

Type: Award.

Value: One award of US$50,000 per year for two years.

Frequency: Annual.

Country of Study: United States of America.

Application Procedure: Applicants must contact the Foundation for an application form.

Closing Date: Please contact the Foundation.

Additional Information: A complete financial statement and scientific progress report are required annually and upon completion of the programme. All publications arising from work funded by this programme must acknowledge support of this award.

AGA Miles and Shirley Fiterman Foundation Basic Research Awards

Subjects: Medical science, specifically gastroenterology and hepathology.

Purpose: To provide research or salary support for junior faculty members involved in basic research in any area of gastrointestinal, liver function or related diseases.

Eligibility: Applicants must hold full-time faculty positions at a North American university or professional institute and may hold an MD and/or a PhD, or equivalent degree. Applicants must be individual members of any of the ADHF partner organisations. The recipient must be at or below the level of assistant professor, and his or her initial appointment to the faculty position must have been within seven years of the time of the application. This award is not intended for Fellows, but for junior faculty who have demonstrated unusual promise, have some record of accomplishment in research and have established an independent research programme at the award. Applicants may not simultaneously apply for the Industry Research Scholar Award or the AGA Elsevier Research Initiative Award.

Level of Study: Postgraduate.

Type: Award.

Value: US$35,000.

Length of Study: One year.

Frequency: Annual.

Country of Study: United States of America, Canada or Mexico.

No. of awards offered: Two.

Application Procedure: Applicants must write for details or visit the website.

Closing Date: January 8th.

Funding: Private.

Contributor: The Miles & Shirley Fiterman Foundation.

AGA Miles and Shirley Fiterman Foundation Clinical Research in Gastroenterology or Hepatology/Nutrition Awards

Subjects: Medical science, specifically gastroenterology and hepathology.

Purpose: To recognise excellence in clinical research and to help support the clinical research of the recipients.

Eligibility: Open to active investigators with considerable achievements to date but whose research is ongoing. In addition, the nominee must be an individual member of any of the ADHF partner organisations.

Type: Award.

Value: US$35,000.

Frequency: Annual.

Country of Study: United States of America, Canada or Mexico.

No. of awards offered: Two.

Application Procedure: Applicants must write for details or visit the website.

Closing Date: January 8th.

Funding: Private.

Contributor: The Miles & Shirley Fiterman Foundation.

Additional Information: Two awards are offered: the Joseph B Kirsner Award in Gastroenterology and the Hugh R Butt Award in Hepathology or Nutrition.

AGA R Robert and Sally D Funderburg Research Scholar Award in Gastric Biology Related to Cancer

Subjects: Gastric mucosal cell biology, regeneration and regulation of cell growth.

Purpose: To support an active established investigator working on novel approaches in the field of gastric cancer and who consequently enhances the fundamental understanding of gastric cancer pathobiology in order to ultimately develop a cure for the disease.

Eligibility: Candidates must hold faculty positions at accredited North American institutions and must have established themselves as independent investigators in the field of gastric biology. Women and minority investigators are strongly encouraged to apply. Applicants must also be individual members of any of the ADHF partner organisations.

Level of Study: Postgraduate.
Type: Award.
Value: US$25,000.
Length of Study: Two years.
Frequency: Annual.
Country of Study: United States of America, Canada or Mexico.
No. of awards offered: One.
Application Procedure: Applicants must write for details or visit the website.
Closing Date: September 10th.
Contributor: The AGA.

AGA Research Scholar Awards

Subjects: Gastroenterology and hepathology.
Purpose: To ensure that a major proportion of young investigators' time is protected for research. The overall objective is to enable young investigators to develop independent and productive research careers in gastroenterology and hepatology related fields and to support physicians or investigators who have the potential to develop independent, productive research careers in gastroenterology and hepatology.
Eligibility: The award is not intended for Fellows, but for young faculty who have demonstrated unusual promise and have some record of accomplishment in research. Candidates should be early in their careers. Those who have been at the assistant professor level or equivalent for more than five years are not eligible. However, non physician candidates with a PhD will also be considered. Candidates must devote at least 70 per cent of their effort to research related to the gastrointestinal tract or liver. Women and minority investigators are strongly encouraged to apply.
Level of Study: Graduate.
Type: Research grant.
Value: US$65,000 per year for three years.
Length of Study: Three years.
Frequency: Annual.
Country of Study: United States of America.
No. of awards offered: Six.
Application Procedure: Applicants should contact the Foundation.
Funding: Private.
Additional Information: A complete financial statement and scientific progress report are required upon completion of the programme. All publications arising from work funded by this programme must acknowledge the support of the award. Awardees must submit their work for presentation at Digestive Disease Week during the last year of the award.

AGA Sponsored Research Symposium Awards

Subjects: Medical science, specifically gastroenterology and hepathology.
Purpose: To foster interactions and enhance the exchange of information between clinical and basic science investigators and established and junior investigators working in gastrointestinal research.
Eligibility: The symposium director must be an established investigator at a North American institution and an individual member of any of the ADHF partner organisations. Women and minority organisers are encouraged to apply. Travel support may be provided for junior investigators who are less than 40 years old and are at or below the rank of assistant professor. Up to two established investigators who are invited speakers may participate. In the latter case, preference will be given to individuals whose expertise is outside mainstream gastroenterology related areas, and/or investigators who have been infrequent participants at previous AGA, ASGE, or AASLD sponsored symposia. Biosketches of these individuals and a letter addressing these issues must be submitted with the application.
Level of Study: Postgraduate.
Type: Travel grant.
Value: Varies but averages US$10,000 per symposium.
Frequency: Three times each year.
Country of Study: United States of America, Canada or Mexico.
No. of awards offered: Varies.
Application Procedure: Applicants must write for details.

Closing Date: September 4th or March 5th.
Funding: Private.
Contributor: The AGA.
Additional Information: A selection committee will review applications and rank proposals to determine the symposia to receive AGA support. Final notification of funding commitment will be made three months after the deadline.

AGA Student Research Fellowship Awards

Subjects: Medical science, specifically gastroenterology and hepathology.
Purpose: To stimulate interest in research careers in digestive diseases by providing salary support for research projects.
Eligibility: Candidates may be medical or graduate students who are not yet engaged in thesis research at accredited North American institutions. Candidates holding advanced degrees must be enrolled as medical or graduate students and they may not hold similar salary support awards from other agencies. Women and minority students are strongly encouraged to apply. The award is not intended to provide a salary for lab technicians.
Level of Study: Graduate, Postgraduate, Professional development.
Type: Award.
Value: Ranges from US$1,500-2,500.
Length of Study: A minimum of 10 weeks.
Frequency: Annual.
Country of Study: United States of America, Canada or Mexico.
No. of awards offered: 35.
Application Procedure: Applicants must write for details or visit the Foundation's website.
Closing Date: March 3rd.
Funding: Private.
Contributor: The AGA.

AMERICAN FEDERATION FOR AGING RESEARCH (AFAR)

70 West 40th Street
11th Floor, New York, NY, 10019, United States of America
Tel: (1) 212 703 9977
Fax: (1) 212 997 0330
Email: amfedaging@aol.com
www: http://www.afar.org
Contact: Grants Administrator

The American Federation for Aging Research (AFAR) is a leading non-profit organisation supporting biomedical ageing research. Since its founding in 1981, AFAR has provided some US$56 million to more than 1,600 new investigators and students conducting cutting-edge biomedical research on the ageing process and age-related diseases. The important work AFAR supports leads to a better understanding of the ageing process and to improvements in the health of all Americans as they age.

AFAR Research Grants

Subjects: Biomedical and clinical topics.
Purpose: To help students to carry out research that will serve as the basis for longer term research efforts.
Level of Study: Postdoctorate, Research.
Type: Research grant.
Value: US$50,000 to junior faculty and US$25,000 to postdoctoral fellows.
Length of Study: One-two years.
Frequency: Annual.
Country of Study: United States of America.
No. of awards offered: Up to 25 to junior faculty (MDs and PhDs) and eight for postdoctoral fellows.
Application Procedure: Applicants must complete and return the application by the annual deadline. These are available from the website.
Closing Date: December 14th.

Funding: Private.
Contributor: AFAR and the Glenn Foundation for Medical Research.
No. of awards given last year: 23 junior faculty and 25 postdoctoral fellows.

AFAR/Pfizer Research Grants in Immunology and Aging

Subjects: Immunology and ageing.
Purpose: To address specific areas of research that focus on the ageing process and age related diseases.
Eligibility: Applicants must be United States citizens or permanent residents.
Level of Study: Research.
Type: Grant.
Value: US$50,000.
Length of Study: One-two years.
Frequency: Annual.
Country of Study: United States of America.
No. of awards offered: Up to four.
Application Procedure: Applicants must complete and return the application by the annual deadline. These are available from the website.
Closing Date: December 14th.
Funding: Private.
Contributor: Pfizer Pharmaceuticals, Inc.
No. of awards given last year: Four.
No. of applicants last year: 50.
Additional Information: Projects may involve basic, clinical or epidemiological research.

Glenn/AFAR Scholarships for Research in the Biology of Aging

Subjects: Biomedical research.
Purpose: To attract potential scientists to ageing research and provide students with the opportunity to conduct a research project.
Eligibility: Candidates must be students completing MD or PhD degrees.
Level of Study: Doctorate, Research.
Type: Scholarship.
Value: US$5,000.
Length of Study: Three months.
Frequency: Annual.
No. of awards offered: 30.
Application Procedure: Applicants must complete and return the application by the annual deadline. These are available from the website.
Closing Date: February 26th.
Funding: Private.
Contributor: The Glenn Foundation for Medical Research.
No. of awards given last year: 29.
No. of applicants last year: 61.

The John A Hartford Foundation/AFAR Medical Student Geriatric Scholars Program

Subjects: Geriatrics.
Purpose: To encourage medical students, particularly budding researchers, to consider a career in academic geriatrics.
Eligibility: Applicants must be United States citizens or permanent residents.
Level of Study: Doctorate.
Type: Scholarship.
Value: US$4,000.
Length of Study: Eight weeks.
Frequency: Annual.
Country of Study: United States of America.
No. of awards offered: 100.
Application Procedure: Applicants must complete and return the application by the annual deadline. Applications are available from the website.
Closing Date: February 7th.
Funding: Private.

Contributor: The John A Hartford Foundation.
No. of awards given last year: 89.
No. of applicants last year: 135.

Merck/AFAR Junior Investigator Award in Geriatric Clinical Pharmacology

Subjects: Geriatric clinical pharmacology.
Purpose: To address the critical need of developing more physicians.
Eligibility: Open to physicians who are board certified or eligible in a primary speciality by July 1st. Applicants must be United States citizens or permanent residents.
Level of Study: Professional development, Research.
Type: Grant.
Value: US$120,000.
Length of Study: Two years.
Frequency: Annual.
Country of Study: United States of America.
No. of awards offered: Two.
Application Procedure: Applicants must complete and return the application by the annual deadline. Applications are available from the website.
Closing Date: November 1st.
Funding: Private.
Contributor: The Merck Company Foundation.
No. of awards given last year: Two.
No. of applicants last year: Five.

Merck/AFAR Research Scholarships for Medical and Pharmacy Students in Geriatric Pharmacology

Subjects: Medical sciences.
Purpose: To develop a corps of physicians and pharmacists with an understanding of medication use in the elderly.
Eligibility: Students must be United States citizens or permanent residents studying at an institution in the United States. It is open to students studying to receive their MD or PharmD degrees.
Level of Study: Doctorate, Research.
Type: Scholarship.
Value: US$4,000.
Length of Study: Two-three months.
Frequency: Annual.
Country of Study: United States of America.
No. of awards offered: Nine.
Application Procedure: Applicants must complete and submit an application form, available from the website, by the annual deadline.
Closing Date: January 22nd.
Funding: Private.
Contributor: The Merck Company Foundation.
No. of awards given last year: 11.
No. of applicants last year: 11.

Paul Beeson Physician/Faculty Scholars in Aging Research Programme

Subjects: Medical sciences.
Purpose: To bolster the current severe shortage of academic physicians who have the combination of medical, academic and scientific training relative to caring for other people.
Eligibility: Applicants must be United States citizens or permanent residents.
Level of Study: Professional development, Research.
Type: Grant.
Value: US$450,000.
Length of Study: Three years.
Frequency: Annual.
Country of Study: United States of America.
No. of awards offered: Up to 10.
Application Procedure: Applicants must complete and return the application by the annual deadline. These are available from the website.
Closing Date: November 15th.
Funding: Private.

Contributor: The John A Hartford Foundation, the Commonwealth Fund, the Alliance for Aging Research on Behalf of Donor Friends and the Starr Foundation.
No. of awards given last year: 10.
No. of applicants last year: 35.

The John A Hartford Foundation/AFAR Academic Fellowship Program in Geriatric Medicine and Geriatric Psychiatry

Subjects: Geriatric medicine.
Purpose: To foster the development of a new generation of competent and committed academic physicians.
Eligibility: Applicants must be United States citizens or permanent residents. Fellows who are eligible to sit for the Certificate of Added Qualifications in geriatrics or geriatric psychiatry may apply.
Level of Study: Postdoctorate, Research.
Type: Fellowship.
Value: US$50,000.
Length of Study: One-two years.
Frequency: Annual.
Country of Study: United States of America.
No. of awards offered: Up to 10.
Application Procedure: Applicants must complete and return the application by the annual deadline. These are available from the website.
Closing Date: February 19th.
Funding: Private.
Contributor: The John A Hartford Foundation.
No. of awards given last year: 19.
No. of applicants last year: 23.

AMERICAN FOUNDATION FOR AGING RESEARCH (AFAR)

North Carolina State University
Biochemistry Department
Polk Hall
Box 7622, Raleigh, NC, 27695, United States of America
Tel: (1) 919 515 5679
Fax: (1) 919 515 2047
Email: afar@bchserver.bch.ncsu.edu
www: http://www4.ncsu.edu/unity/users/a/agris/afar/afar.htm
Contact: Dr Paul F Agris, President

The American Foundation for Aging Research (AFAR) aims to promote and support research that will elucidate the basic processes involved in the biology of ageing and age associated disease, by awarding scholarships and fellowships to young, motivated scientists.

Wilson-Fulton and Robertson Awards in Aging Research, Cecille Gould Memorial Fund Award in Cancer Research, Richard Shepherd Fellowship

Subjects: Ageing and cancer research.
Purpose: To encourage young people to pursue research in age related health problems and the biology of ageing.
Eligibility: Open to students enrolled in graduate degree programmes eg. MS, PhD, MD or DDS at United States institutions who are working on specific projects in the fields of ageing or cancer. Applicants must have a research project which should be biological in nature. Sociological and psychological research is not accepted in these programmes.
Level of Study: Doctorate, Graduate, Postgraduate.
Type: Fellowship.
Value: US$500-1,000 per semester or summer.
Length of Study: Between four months and one year.
Frequency: Annual.
Study Establishment: Educational institutions.
Country of Study: United States of America.

No. of awards offered: 5-10.
Application Procedure: Applicants must undertake the two levels of review: a pre-application form to determine eligibility, and a full application. Applicants should submit a request for a pre-application. A cheque or money order to AFAR for US$3 to cover handling and postage should be included with the completed pre-application. There is no charge for the submission of the full application.
Closing Date: No deadline.
Funding: Private.
No. of awards given last year: Five.
No. of applicants last year: 200.
Additional Information: AFAR is a national, tax-exempt, non-profit making, educational and scientific charity not associated with North Carolina State University.

AMERICAN FOUNDATION FOR PHARMACEUTICAL EDUCATION (AFPE)

One Church Street
Suite 202, Rockville, MD, 20850-4158, United States of America
Tel: (1) 301 738 2160
Fax: (1) 301 738 2161
Email: afpe@worldnet.alt.net
www: http://www.afpend.org
Contact: Mr Bob Bachman

AAPS/AFPE Gateway Scholarships

Subjects: Pharmaceutics.
Purpose: To encourage graduates from any discipline to pursue a PhD in a pharmacy graduate programme.
Eligibility: Open to students who are enrolled in the last three years of a BS or PharmD programme at a United States school or college of pharmacy, or Baccalaureate degree programme in a related field of scientific study at any college. Candidates must have a demonstrated interest in, and potential for, a career in any of the pharmaceutical sciences and will be enrolled for at least one full academic year following the award of the scholarship. United States citizenship or permanent resident status is not required.
Level of Study: Postgraduate, Professional development.
Type: Scholarship.
Value: US$5,000 out of which US$4,500 is provided for a research project and US$500 to attend an AAPS Annual Meeting. The US$4,500 may be used for any purpose decided by the awardee and faculty sponsor that will enable the student to have a successful programme, eg. student stipend, laboratory supplies or materials related to the project, travel etc. None of the funds shall be used for indirect costs by the institution.
Length of Study: One year.
Frequency: Annual.
Country of Study: United States of America.
No. of awards offered: Six.
Application Procedure: Applicants must write for details.
Closing Date: January 28th.

AFPE Clinical Pharmacy Post-Pharm D Fellowships in the Biomedical Research Sciences Program

Subjects: Pharmacology.
Eligibility: Open to all pharmacy faculty members having a strong record of research in an area encompassing such topics as cost benefit and cost effectiveness of pharmaceuticals, the impact of current or future legislation on drug innovation and healthcare in the nation, the economics of healthcare and the quality of life in changing patterns of healthcare delivery systems, the contribution of the pharmaceutical industry, the economic impact of research and new drugs, and healthcare cost containment issues.
Level of Study: Postdoctorate.
Type: Fellowship.
Value: Up to US$27,500.
Length of Study: Up to two years.

Frequency: Annual.

Study Establishment: An Institute of Higher Education.

Country of Study: United States of America.

No. of awards offered: Three.

Application Procedure: Applicants must complete an application form and should write for details.

Closing Date: February 15th.

No. of awards given last year: Two.

AFPE Gateway Research Scholarship Program

Subjects: Pharmacology.

Purpose: To encourage graduates in a pharmacy college to pursue a PhD within a pharmacy college.

Eligibility: Open to students who are enrolled in the last three years of a BS or PharmD programme at a United States school or college of pharmacy, or Baccalaureate degree programme in a related field of scientific study at any college. Candidates must have a demonstrated interest in, and potential for, a career in any of the pharmaceutical sciences and will be enrolled for at least one full academic year following the award of the scholarship. United States citizenship or permanent resident status is not required.

Level of Study: Postgraduate, Professional development.

Type: Scholarship.

Value: US$5,000 provided for a research project. This may be used for any purpose decided by the awardee and faculty sponsor that will enable the student to have a successful programme, eg. student stipend, laboratory supplies or materials related to the project, travel etc. None of the funds shall be used for indirect costs by the institution.

Frequency: Annual.

Study Establishment: An approved college of pharmacy.

Country of Study: United States of America.

No. of awards offered: 12.

Application Procedure: Applicants must write for details.

Closing Date: January 28th.

AFPE Predoctoral Fellowships

Subjects: Any of the pharmaceutical sciences, including pharmaceutics, pharmacology, manufacturing pharmacy and medicinal chemistry.

Purpose: To offer fellowship support leading to a PhD degree.

Eligibility: Open to students who have completed at least three semesters of graduate study and who have no more than three years remaining to obtain the PhD degree in a graduate programme in the pharmaceutical sciences administered by, or affiliated with, a United States school or college of pharmacy. Also open to students enrolled in joint PharmD and PhD if the PhD degree will be awarded within three additional years. Applicants must be United States citizens or permanent residents.

Level of Study: Doctorate, Postgraduate.

Value: US$6,000. Payments are made to the university in twice yearly instalments.

Length of Study: One year, renewable for two additional years.

Frequency: Annual.

Study Establishment: An appropriate university.

Country of Study: United States of America.

No. of awards offered: Approx. 80.

Application Procedure: Applicants must write for details.

Closing Date: March 1st for fellowships beginning in September.

No. of awards given last year: 75.

AMERICAN FRIENDS OF THE UNIVERSITY OF EDINBURGH

International Office
University of Edinburgh
57 George Square, Edinburgh, EH8 9JU, Scotland
Tel: (44) 131 650 1000
Fax: (44) 131 668 4565
Email: interoff@college.ed.ac.uk
www: http://www.ed.ac.uk/internat
Contact: Administration Officer

American Friends of the University of Edinburgh Scholarship

Subjects: All subjects.

Purpose: To foster good relations with students from United States alumni contributions and to enhance graduate study opportunities for deserving students.

Eligibility: Applicants must hold a United States passport.

Level of Study: Postgraduate.

Type: Scholarship.

Value: US$5,000.

Frequency: Annual.

Country of Study: Scotland.

No. of awards offered: One.

Application Procedure: Applicants must complete an application form, available from the International Office.

Closing Date: Mid April.

Contributor: American alumni.

No. of awards given last year: One.

AMERICAN GEOPHYSICAL UNION (AGU)

2000 Florida Avenue North West, Washington, DC, 20009, United States of America
Tel: (1) 202 462 6900
Fax: (1) 202 328 0566
Email: wsinghateh@agu.org
www: http://www.agu.org
Contact: Ms Wynetta Singhateh, Education & Research Grants & Awards

The American Geophysical Union (AGU) is an international scientific society with more than 36,000 members, primarily research scientists, dedicated to advancing the understanding of the earth and solar system and making the results of the AGU's research available to the public.

Horton (Hydrology) Research Grant

Subjects: Proposals may be in hydrology including its physical, chemical or biological aspects.

Purpose: To support research in hydrology and water resources.

Eligibility: There are no restrictions.

Level of Study: Postdoctorate.

Type: Grant.

Value: US$10,000.

Frequency: Annual.

No. of awards offered: Two.

Application Procedure: Applicants must submit four copies of the application form, an executive summary, a statement of purpose, a detailed budget and two letters of recommendation. Applicants should contact the Union for further details.

Closing Date: March 1st.

No. of awards given last year: Two.

No. of applicants last year: 27.

51

AMERICAN HEALTH ASSISTANCE FOUNDATION (AHAF)

15825 Shady Grove Road, Rockville, MD, 20850, United States of America
Tel: (1) 301 948 3244
Fax: (1) 301 258 9454
Email: sgarfinkel@ahaf.org
www: http://www.ahaf.org
Contact: Dr Susan Garfinkel, Director of Research Grants

The American Health Assistance Foundation (AHAF) is a non-profit charitable organisation that funds research and public education on age related and degenerative diseases including: Alzheimer's disease, macular degeneration, glaucoma and heart and stroke diseases. The organisation also provides emergency financial assistance to Alzheimer's disease patients and their care givers.

AHAF Alzheimer's Disease Research Grant

Subjects: Neurology, biomedicine, biochemistry, biophysics, molecular biology and pharmacology.
Purpose: To enable basic research on the causes of and treatments for Alzheimer's disease.
Eligibility: The principal investigator must hold the rank of assistant professor or equivalent, or higher.
Level of Study: Doctorate.
Type: Grant.
Value: Up to US$200,000 for two years.
Length of Study: One-two years.
Frequency: Annual.
Study Establishment: Non-profit institutions and organisations.
Country of Study: Any country.
No. of awards offered: Varies.
Application Procedure: Applicants must complete an application form. The current application form should be requested for each year or can be downloaded from the website.
Closing Date: October 15th.
Funding: Private.
No. of awards given last year: 12.
No. of applicants last year: 94.
Additional Information: Further information is available on request.

AHAF Macular Degeneration Research

Subjects: Ophthalmology, biomedicine, biochemistry, biophysics, genetics, molecular biology and pharmacology.
Purpose: To enable basic research on the causes of, or the treatment for, macular degeneration.
Eligibility: The principal investigator must hold a tenure track or tenured position and the rank of assistant professor or higher.
Type: Grant.
Value: Up to US$50,000. Grants may be renewed on a competitive peer review basis.
Length of Study: One year.
Frequency: Annual.
Study Establishment: Non-profit institutions and organisations.
Country of Study: Any country.
No. of awards offered: Varies.
Application Procedure: Applicants must complete an application form. The current application form should be requested for each year or can be downloaded from the website.
Closing Date: October 23rd.
Funding: Private.
No. of awards given last year: Six.
No. of applicants last year: 10.
Additional Information: Further information is available on request.

AHAF National Glaucoma Research

Subjects: Ophthalmology, biomedicine and pharmacology.
Purpose: To enable basic research on the causes of, or treatments for, glaucoma.

Eligibility: The principal investigator must hold the rank of assistant professor or equivalent, or higher.
Level of Study: Doctorate.
Type: Grant.
Value: Up to US$35,000 per year for up to two years.
Length of Study: One-two years.
Frequency: Annual.
Study Establishment: Non-profit institutions and organisations.
Country of Study: Any country.
No. of awards offered: Varies.
Application Procedure: Applicants must complete an application form. The current application form should be requested for each year and can also be downloaded from the website.
Closing Date: November 15th.
Funding: Private.
No. of awards given last year: 10.
No. of applicants last year: 24.
Additional Information: Further information is available on request.

AHAF National Heart Foundation

Subjects: Cardiology, biomedicine, physiology, and pharmacology.
Purpose: To provide start up grants for new investigators into the causes of, or treatments for, cardiovascular disease and stroke.
Eligibility: Open to young investigators who are beginning independent research careers at the assistant professor level and are head of an independent research laboratory group.
Level of Study: Professional development.
Type: Grant.
Value: Up to US$25,000 may be requested for one year.
Length of Study: One year, renewable for a further year.
Frequency: Annual.
Study Establishment: Non-profit institutions and organisations.
Country of Study: Any country.
No. of awards offered: Varies.
Application Procedure: Applicants must complete an application form. The current application form should be requested for each year or can be downloaded from the website.
Closing Date: November 1st.
Funding: Private.
No. of awards given last year: Six.
No. of applicants last year: 19.
Additional Information: Further information is available on request.

AMERICAN HEART ASSOCIATION, INC. (AHA)

National Center
7272 Greenville Avenue, Dallas, TX, 75231-4596, United States of America
Tel: (1) 214 706 1187
Fax: (1) 214 706 1341
Email: juanita.morales@heart.org
www: http://www.americanheart.org/research
Contact: Ms Juanita Morales, Manager Promotions & Electronic Services

The American Heart Association (AHA) is a non-profit, voluntary health organisation funded by private contributions. Its mission is to reduce disability and death from cardiovascular diseases and stroke. To support this goal, the Association has given almost US$1.9 billion to heart and blood vessel research since 1949.

AHA National Established Investigator Grant

Subjects: Cardiovascular function and disease, stroke or related basic science, clinical, bioengineering or biotechnology and public health problems.
Purpose: To support the career development of highly promising clinician-scientists who have recently acquired independent status by encouraging and adequately funding high quality, innovative

research projects for which financial support has not been previously obtained from any other research granting agency.

Eligibility: At the time of application, candidates must be United States citizens or foreign nationals holding one of the following visa immigration statuses: permanent resident, exchange visitor (J-1), temporary worker in a speciality occupation (H-1, H-1B), Canadian or Mexican citizen engaging in professional activities (TC or TN), or temporary worker with extraordinary abilities in the sciences (O-1). Non citizens must submit proof of possession of a J-1, H-1, H-1B, TC, TN or O-1 visa, or permanent resident status. Applicants must have an MD, PhD, DO or equivalent doctoral degree and should be faculty or staff members initiating independent research careers, usually at the rank of Instructor or Assistant Professor or their equivalents. At the time of award activation, the investigator is usually four years but no more than nine years since their first faculty or staff appointment at the Assistant Professor level or its equivalent. Candidates must meet institutional requirements for grant submission at the time of application. Applicants cannot hold or have held any other national award.

Level of Study: Postdoctorate.

Type: Salary and project support.

Value: US$75,000 each year for salary, fringe benefits, indirect costs and project costs. At least US$40,000 must be used for the project.

Length of Study: Four years, non renewable.

Frequency: Twice a year.

Study Establishment: Non-profit institutions.

Application Procedure: Applicants must obtain an application form from the website.

Closing Date: January and July.

Funding: Private.

No. of awards given last year: 62.

No. of applicants last year: 235.

Additional Information: The most up to date information is available from the website.

AHA National Grant-in-Aid

Subjects: Cardiovascular function and disease, stroke or related basic science, clinical, bioengineering or biotechnology and public health problems.

Purpose: To encourage and adequately fund the most innovative and meritorious research projects from independent investigators.

Eligibility: At the time of application, candidates must be United States citizens or foreign nationals holding one of the following visa immigration statuses: permanent resident, exchange visitor (J-1), temporary worker in a speciality occupation (H-1, H-1B), Canadian or Mexican citizen engaging in professional activities (TC or TN), or temporary worker with extraordinary abilities in the sciences (O-1). Non citizens must submit proof of possession of a J-1, H-1, H-1B, TC, TN or O-1 visa, or permanent resident status. Applicants must have an MD, PhD, DO or equivalent doctoral degree and be faculty or staff members of any rank pursuing independent research. Candidates must meet institutional requirements for grant submission at the time of application. The principal investigator is expected to be independent.

Level of Study: Postdoctorate.

Type: Project support and salary.

Value: A maximum of US$71,500 annually for salary, fringe benefits, 10 per cent indirect costs and project costs. Up to US$32,500 per year may be requested for the principal investigator's salary and fringe benefits. All of the award may be budgeted for project support and 10 per cent indirect costs.

Length of Study: One-three years.

Frequency: Twice a year.

Study Establishment: Non-profit institutions.

Country of Study: United States of America or abroad if United States of America citizen.

No. of awards offered: Approx. 100.

Application Procedure: Applicants must obtain an application form from the website.

Closing Date: January and July.

Funding: Private.

Contributor: Public donations.

No. of awards given last year: 86.

No. of applicants last year: 685.

Additional Information: The most up to date information is available from the website.

AHA National Scientist Development Grant

Subjects: Cardiovascular function and disease, stroke or related basic science, clinical, bioengineering or biotechnology and public health problems.

Purpose: To support highly promising beginning scientists in their progress toward independence by encouraging and adequately funding research projects that can serve to bridge the gap between completion of research training and readiness for successful competition as an independent investigator.

Eligibility: At the time of application, candidates must be United States citizens or foreign nationals holding one of the following visa immigration statuses: permanent resident, exchange visitor (J-1), temporary worker in a speciality occupation (H-1, H-1B), Canadian or Mexican citizen engaging in professional activities (TC or TN), or temporary worker with extraordinary abilities in the sciences (O-1). Non citizens must submit proof of possession of a J-1, H-1, H-1B, TC, TN or O-1 visa or permanent resident status. Applicants must have an MD, PhD, DO or equivalent doctoral degree and should be faculty or staff members initiating independent research careers, usually at the rank of Instructor or Assistant Professor (or their equivalents). Applications may be submitted for review in the final year of a postdoctoral research fellowship or in the initial years of the first faculty or staff appointment. Candidates must have the faculty or staff appointment at activation and must meet institutional requirements for grant submission at the time of application. At the time of the award activation, no more than four years will have elapsed since an applicant's first faculty or staff appointment at the Assistant Professor level or its equivalent. Applicants cannot hold or have held any other national award.

Level of Study: Postdoctorate.

Type: Salary and project support.

Value: US$65,000 each year for salary, fringe benefits, indirect costs and project costs. At least US$35,000 must be used for the project.

Length of Study: Four years, non renewable.

Frequency: Twice a year.

Study Establishment: Non-profit institutions.

Application Procedure: Applicants must obtain an application form from the website.

Closing Date: January and July.

Funding: Private.

Contributor: Public donations.

No. of awards given last year: 111.

No. of applicants last year: 426.

Additional Information: The most up to date information is available from the website.

AMERICAN HISTORICAL ASSOCIATION

400 A Street South East, Washington, DC, 20003, United States of America
Tel: (1) 202 544 2422
Fax: (1) 202 544 8307
Email: ddoyle@theaha.org
www: http://www.theaha.org
Contact: Ms Debbie Ann Doyle, Convention & Administrative Assistant

The American Historical Association is a professional organisation for historians.

Albert J Beveridge Grant

Subjects: The history of the Western hemisphere.

Purpose: To support research.

Eligibility: Open to American Historical Association members only.
Level of Study: Doctorate, Postdoctorate, Postgraduate.
Type: Grant.
Value: A maximum of US$1,000.
Frequency: Annual.
Country of Study: Any country.
No. of awards offered: Varies.
Application Procedure: Applicants must contact the American Historical Association for details.
Closing Date: February 1st.
Funding: Private.
No. of awards given last year: Eight.
No. of applicants last year: 78.

Bernadotte E Schmitt Grants

Subjects: The history of Europe, Asia and Africa.
Purpose: To support research.
Eligibility: Open to American Historical Association members only.
Level of Study: Doctorate, Postdoctorate, Postgraduate.
Type: Grant.
Value: Up to US$1,000.
Frequency: Annual.
Country of Study: Any country.
No. of awards offered: Varies.
Application Procedure: Applicants must contact the American Historical Association for details.
Closing Date: September 15th.
Funding: Private.
No. of awards given last year: 16.
No. of applicants last year: 105.

J Franklin Jameson Fellowship

Subjects: The collections of the Library of Congress.
Purpose: To support significant scholarly research by new historians.
Eligibility: Open to suitably qualified applicants of any nationality.
Level of Study: Postdoctorate, Postgraduate.
Type: Fellowship.
Value: US$10,000.
Length of Study: One term.
Frequency: Annual.
Country of Study: United States of America.
No. of awards offered: One.
Application Procedure: Applicants must contact the American Historical Association for details.
Closing Date: February 15th.
Funding: Government, Private.
No. of awards given last year: One.
No. of applicants last year: Eight.

Littleton-Griswold Research Grant

Subjects: American legal history, law and society.
Purpose: To support research.
Eligibility: Open to American Historical Association members only.
Level of Study: Doctorate, Postdoctorate, Postgraduate.
Type: Research grant.
Value: Up to US$1,000.
Frequency: Annual.
Country of Study: Any country.
No. of awards offered: Varies.
Application Procedure: Applicants must contact the American Historical Association for details.
Closing Date: February 1st.
Funding: Private.
No. of awards given last year: Seven.
No. of applicants last year: 24.

AMERICAN INDIAN GRADUATE CENTER (AIGC)

4520 Montgomery Boulevard North East
Suite 1-B, Albuquerque, NM, 87109-1291, United States of America
Tel: (1) 505 881 4584
Fax: (1) 505 884 0427
www: http://www.aigc@aigc.com
Contact: Interim Executive Director

AIGC Fellowship

Subjects: All subjects.
Purpose: To support students in all professional degree programmes.
Eligibility: Open to American Indians and Alaskan Natives who are enrolled members of federally recognised tribes, attending accredited institutions and degree granting programmes. Full-time enrolment status is required.
Level of Study: Doctorate, Graduate, Postdoctorate, Postgraduate.
Type: Fellowship.
Value: US$250-3,000, dependent on funds available.
Length of Study: Depends on the degree programme.
Frequency: Annual.
Country of Study: United States of America.
No. of awards offered: Dependent on funds available.
Application Procedure: Applicants must request application forms, which are available from January each year. Applications are sent to individuals only.
Closing Date: June 1st.
Funding: Government, Private.

AMERICAN INSTITUTE FOR CANCER RESEARCH (AICR)

1759 R Street North West, Washington, DC, 20009, United States of America
Tel: (1) 202 328 7744
Fax: (1) 202 328 7226
Email: aicrweb@aicr.org
www: http://www.aicr.org
Contact: Associate Director for Research

The American Institute for Cancer Research (AICR) is the only major charitable organisation in the United States dedicated primarily to cancer prevention by promoting healthy diets and associated lifestyles.

American Institute for Cancer Research Investigator Initiator Grants

Subjects: Cancer research.
Purpose: To support research that is at the forefront of the areas of diet, nutrition and cancer.
Eligibility: The principal investigator of a grant must be an assistant professor or higher, with a PhD, MD or equivalent degree.
Level of Study: Postdoctorate, Professional development.
Type: Grant.
Value: A maximum of US$165,000.
Length of Study: Two years.
Frequency: Twice a year.
Country of Study: United States of America or Canada.
No. of awards offered: Varies.
Application Procedure: Applicants must forward applications to the AICR.
Closing Date: December 17th or July 1st.
Funding: Private.
Additional Information: The AICR also awards Postdoctoral Award Grants and Matching Grants. Interested applicants should contact the Institute for further information.

AMERICAN INSTITUTE FOR ECONOMIC RESEARCH (AIER)

PO Box 1000, Great Barrington, MA, 01230, United States of America
Tel: (1) 413 528 1216
Fax: (1) 413 528 0103
Email: info@aier.org
www: http://www.aier.org
Contact: Ms Susan J Gillette, Assistant to the President

The American Institute for Economic Research (AIER), founded in 1933, is an independent scientific educational organisation. The Institute conducts scientific enquiry into general economics with a focus on monetary issues. Attention is also given to business cycle analysis and forecasting, as well as monetary economics.

AIER Summer Fellowship

Subjects: Scientific procedures of inquiry and on monetary economics. Business cycle analysis and forecasting also receive attention.
Purpose: To further the development of economic scientists.
Eligibility: Open to graduating seniors who are entering only doctoral programmes in economics, and those enrolled in such programmes for no longer than one year. The programme is not designed for business school enrolees.
Level of Study: Postgraduate.
Type: Fellowship.
Value: US$250 weekly stipend plus room and full board.
Length of Study: Eight weeks.
Frequency: Annual.
Study Establishment: The AIER.
Country of Study: United States of America.
No. of awards offered: 10-12.
Application Procedure: Applicants must submit a completed application form, curriculum vitae, personal statement, writing sample, an outline of proposed course of study and official transcripts. Scholastic references should be sent directly to the director from the referees.
Closing Date: March 31st.
Funding: Private.
No. of awards given last year: Seven.
No. of applicants last year: 32.

AIER Summer Programme for Visiting Research Fellows

Subjects: Money, banking and credit, public and personal finance, economic and monetary history, the role of government in society, the methodology of economics and the role of individual freedom, private property and free enterprise in economic progress.
Purpose: To further the development of economic scientists.
Eligibility: Applicants who have completed all but their dissertation are preferred, but others with demonstrably strong writing skills will be considered.
Level of Study: Doctorate, Postdoctorate, Postgraduate.
Type: Fellowship.
Value: Varies.
Length of Study: Summer or longer.
Frequency: Annual.
Study Establishment: AIER.
Country of Study: United States of America.
No. of awards offered: Varies.
Application Procedure: Applicants must submit a covering letter, a 500 word outline of their proposed course of research, a curriculum vitae and a copy of a recent publication or unpublished manuscript. Applicants must also arrange for two confidential letters of reference to be sent directly to the AIER by the referees.
Closing Date: March 31st.
Funding: Private.
No. of awards given last year: Six.

AMERICAN INSTITUTE OF BAKING (AIB)

1213 Bakers Way, Manhattan, KS, 66502, United States of America
Tel: (1) 800 633 5137
Fax: (1) 913 537 1493
Email: kembers@aibonline.org
www: http://www.aibonline.org
Contact: Mr Ken Embers, Registrar

The American Institute of Baking (AIB) is a non-profit corporation, founded by the North American wholesale and retail baking industries in 1919 as a technology transfer centre for bakers and food processors. The original mission of the organisation was to put science to work for the baker and that basic theme is still central to all of the programmes, products and services provided by the AIB to baking and general food production industries worldwide.

AIB Scholarships for Study in Maintenance Engineering

Subjects: Maintenance engineering, basic mathematics and electrical concepts and practices, pulleys, levers, gears, power trains, electrical circuitry, motor starters, counters, programmable logic controllers and computers.
Purpose: To train promising individuals for positions of responsibility.
Eligibility: Open to United States candidates who meet the requirements for maintenance engineering of two years of experience and a high school diploma or CED. Applicants must also be willing to accept a position with a United States company after graduation.
Level of Study: Professional development.
Type: Scholarship.
Value: US$500-4,000.
Length of Study: 10 weeks of comprehensive instruction. The classes are held twice a year and commence around September 1st and February 1st.
Frequency: Annual.
Study Establishment: The AIB.
Country of Study: United States of America.
No. of awards offered: 10.
Application Procedure: Applicants must complete an application form available on request or from the website.
Funding: Private.
No. of awards given last year: Six.

Scholarships for Advanced Study in Baking Science and Technology and/or Maintenance Engineering

Subjects: The scientific basis of baking and the technology of modern bakery production. The maintenance engineering course emphasises electricity, electronics, motor controls, programmable controllers and computers.
Purpose: To enable scholars to advance rapidly in the baking and allied industries.
Eligibility: Open to candidates who meet entrance requirements for baking science and technology class or for maintenance engineering.
Level of Study: Professional development.
Type: Scholarship.
Value: US$500-7,000.
Length of Study: 16 weeks for the baking science and technology course, and 10 weeks for the maintenance engineering course. The classes are held twice a year and commence around September 1st and February 1st.
Frequency: Annual.
Study Establishment: The AIB.
Country of Study: United States of America.
No. of awards offered: Over 40.
Application Procedure: Applicants must complete an application form available on request or downloadable from the website.
Closing Date: May 1st or November 1st. Late applications are accepted prior to the beginning of classes in February and May.
Funding: Private.
No. of awards given last year: 40.

AMERICAN INSTITUTE OF INDIAN STUDIES (AIIS)

1130 East 59th Street, Chicago, IL, 60637, United States of America
Tel: (1) 773 702 8638
Fax: (1) 773 702 6636
Email: aiis@uchicago.edu
www: http://www.indiastudies.org
Contact: Ms Elise Auerbach, Administrator

The American Institute of Indian Studies (AIIS) is a consortium of American colleges and universities that support the understanding of India, its people and cultures. AIIS offers a range of fellowships for research in India. It also supports individuals studying the performing arts, operates language programmes in India and offers research facilities to scholars in India.

AIIS Junior Research Fellowships

Subjects: India, its people and culture.
Purpose: To support the advancement of knowledge and understanding.
Eligibility: Open to doctoral candidates at United States colleges and universities.
Level of Study: Doctorate.
Length of Study: Up to 11 months.
Frequency: Annual.
Study Establishment: An Indian university.
Country of Study: India.
Application Procedure: Applicants must write for further information.
Closing Date: July 1st.

AIIS Senior Performing and Creative Arts Fellowships

Subjects: Performing and creative arts.
Eligibility: Open to accomplished practitioners of the performing arts of India and creative artists who demonstrate that study in India would enhance their skills, develop their capabilities to teach or perform in the United States of America, enhance American involvement with India's artistic traditions and strengthen their links with peers in India.
Level of Study: Unrestricted.
Type: Fellowship.
Frequency: Annual.
Country of Study: India.
Application Procedure: Applicants must write for further information.
Closing Date: July 1st.

AIIS Senior Research Fellowships

Subjects: South Asian studies.
Purpose: To enable Scholars to pursue further research in India.
Eligibility: Open to Scholars who hold the PhD or its equivalent and are either United States citizens or resident aliens teaching full-time at United States colleges and universities.
Level of Study: Postdoctorate.
Type: Fellowship.
Length of Study: Up to nine months.
Frequency: Annual.
Country of Study: India.
Application Procedure: Applicants must write for further information.
Closing Date: July 1st.

AIIS Senior Scholarly/Professional Development Fellowships

Subjects: India, its people and culture.
Purpose: To support the advancement of knowledge and understanding.
Eligibility: Open to established Scholars who have not previously specialised in Indian studies and to established professionals who have not previously worked or studied in India.

Level of Study: Professional development.
Type: Fellowship.
Length of Study: Six-nine months.
Frequency: Annual.
Country of Study: India.
No. of awards offered: Varies.
Application Procedure: Applicants must write for further information.
Closing Date: July 1st.

AMERICAN INSTITUTE OF PAKISTAN STUDIES (AIPS)

Wake Forest University
Box 7568, Winston-Salem, NC, 27109, United States of America
Tel: (1) 336 758 5453
Fax: (1) 336 758 4809
Email: ckennedy@wfu.edu
Contact: Director

The American Institute of Pakistan Studies (AIPS), founded in 1973, is an independent scholarly organisation whose aim is to promote research in Pakistan.

American Institute of Pakistan Studies American Fellowship Program

Subjects: All fields of Pakistan studies.
Purpose: To support research.
Eligibility: All applicants must be American citizens. Predoctoral applicants must be ABD, and must be pursuing a dissertation topic relevant to Pakistan.
Level of Study: Doctorate, Postdoctorate.
Type: Research grant.
Value: US$2,500-3,000 per month.
Length of Study: Two-nine months.
Frequency: Annual.
Country of Study: Pakistan.
No. of awards offered: 10.
Application Procedure: Applicants must write for further information.
Closing Date: February 1st. Awards are announced every April.
Funding: Government.
Contributor: The United States and Pakistan governments.

AMERICAN JEWISH ARCHIVES

3101 Clifton Avenue, Cincinnati, OH, 45220, United States of America
Tel: (1) 513 221 1875
Fax: (1) 513 221 7812
Email: aja@cn.huc.edu
www: http://huc.edu/aja
Contact: Mr Kevin Proffitt, Director Fellowship Programmes

The Marcus Centre of the American Jewish Archives was founded by Dr Jacob Rader Marcus in 1947 in the aftermath of World War II and the Holocaust. It is committed to preserving a documentary heritage of the religious, organisational, economic, cultural, personal, social and family life of American Jewry.

Bernard and Audre Rapoport Fellowships

Subjects: American Jewish studies.
Eligibility: Open to postdoctoral candidates of any nationality.
Level of Study: Postdoctorate.
Type: Fellowship.
Value: US$2,000.
Length of Study: One month.
Study Establishment: The Archives.

Country of Study: Any country.
Application Procedure: Applicants must provide an up to date curriculum vitae, a research proposal, evidence of published research and two recommendations from academic colleagues.
Closing Date: April 1st.

Ethel Marcus Memorial Fellowship

Subjects: American Jewish studies.
Eligibility: Open to ABDs.
Level of Study: Postgraduate.
Type: Fellowship.
Value: US$1,000.
Length of Study: One month.
Study Establishment: The Archives.
Country of Study: Any country.
Application Procedure: Applicants must provide an up to date curriculum vitae, a research proposal and three faculty recommendations including dissertation supervisors.
Closing Date: April 1st.

Loewenstein-Wiener Fellowship Awards

Subjects: American Jewish studies.
Eligibility: Open to ABDs who have completed all but the dissertation requirement, and to postdoctoral candidates.
Level of Study: Doctorate, Postdoctorate, Postgraduate.
Type: Fellowship.
Value: US$1,000 for ABDs, US$2,000 for postdoctoral candidates.
Length of Study: One month.
Study Establishment: The Archives.
Country of Study: Any country.
Application Procedure: Applicants must provide an up to date curriculum vitae, a research proposal and evidence of published research where possible. ABDs must provide three faculty recommendations including dissertation supervisors and postdoctoral candidates must provide two recommendations from academic colleagues. These will constitute the application.
Closing Date: April 1st.

Marguerite R Jacobs Memorial Award

Subjects: American Jewish studies.
Eligibility: Open to postdoctoral candidates of any nationality.
Level of Study: Postdoctorate.
Value: US$2,000.
Length of Study: One month.
Study Establishment: The Archives.
Country of Study: Any country.
Application Procedure: Applicants must provide an up to date curriculum vitae, a research proposal, evidence of published research, where possible, and two recommendations from academic colleagues.
Closing Date: April 1st.

Rabbi Frederic A Doppelt Memorial Fellowship

Subjects: American Jewish studies.
Eligibility: Open to ABDs. Preference will be given to candidates from Eastern Europe or those working on a topic related to East European Jewry in the American context.
Level of Study: Postgraduate.
Type: Fellowship.
Value: US$1,000.
Length of Study: One month.
Study Establishment: The Archives.
Country of Study: Any country.
Application Procedure: Applicants must provide an up to date curriculum vitae, a research proposal and three faculty recommendations including dissertation supervisors.
Closing Date: April 1st.
Funding: Private.

Rabbi Levi A Olan Memorial Fellowship

Subjects: American Jewish studies.

Eligibility: Open to ABDs.
Level of Study: Postgraduate.
Type: Fellowship.
Value: US$1,000.
Length of Study: One month.
Study Establishment: The Archives.
Country of Study: Any country.
Application Procedure: Applicants must provide an up to date curriculum vitae, a research proposal and three faculty recommendations including dissertation supervisors.
Closing Date: April 1st.

Rabbi Theodore S Levy Tribute Fellowship

Subjects: American Jewish studies.
Eligibility: Open to ABDs.
Level of Study: Postgraduate.
Type: Fellowship.
Value: US$1,000.
Length of Study: One month.
Study Establishment: The Archives.
Country of Study: Any country.
Application Procedure: Applicants must provide an up to date curriculum vitae, a research proposal and three faculty recommendations including dissertation supervisors.
Closing Date: April 1st.

Starkoff Fellowship

Subjects: American Jewish studies.
Eligibility: Open to ABDs.
Level of Study: Postgraduate.
Type: Fellowship.
Value: US$1,000.
Length of Study: One month.
Study Establishment: The Archives.
Country of Study: United States of America.
Application Procedure: Applicants must provide an up to date curriculum vitae, a research proposal and three faculty recommendations including dissertation supervisors.
Closing Date: April 1st.

AMERICAN LIBRARY ASSOCIATION (ALA)

50 East Huron Street, Chicago, IL, 60611, United States of America
Tel: (1) 800 545 2433 ext. 3247
Fax: (1) 312 944 6131
Email: awards@ala.org
www: http://www.ala.org/work/awards
Contact: Ms Cheryl Malden, ALA Awards Co-ordinator

Each year the American Library Association (ALA) and its member units sponsor awards to honour distinguished service and foster professional growth.

3M/NMRT Professional Development Grant

Subjects: Library studies.
Purpose: To allow librarians to attend the annual conference of the ALA.
Eligibility: Open to members of the ALA and the New Members Round Table.
Level of Study: Professional development.
Type: Grant.
Value: Varies.
Frequency: Annual.
Country of Study: Any country.
No. of awards offered: Varies.
Application Procedure: Applicants must submit nominations to NMRT Professional Development Grant at ALA.
Closing Date: December 15th.

Funding: Commercial.
Contributor: 3M.

AASL Frances Henne Award
Subjects: Library media.
Purpose: To enable an individual to attend an AASL national conference or ALA Annual Conference for the first time.
Eligibility: Open to school library media specialists with less than five years in the profession.
Level of Study: Unrestricted.
Type: Grant.
Value: US$1,250.
Frequency: Annual.
Country of Study: Any country.
No. of awards offered: One.
Application Procedure: Applicants must write for details.
Funding: Commercial.
Contributor: R R Bowker.

AASL Highsmith Research Grant
Subjects: Library science.
Purpose: To enable an individual to conduct innovative research aimed at measuring and evaluating the impact of school library media programmes on learning and education.
Eligibility: Open to qualified researchers of any nationality.
Level of Study: Professional development.
Type: Research grant.
Value: Up to US$5,000.
Frequency: Annual.
Country of Study: Any country.
No. of awards offered: One.
Application Procedure: Applicants must write for details.
Funding: Commercial.
Contributor: The Highsmith Company.

AASL Information Technology Pathfinder Award
Subjects: Library media.
Purpose: To allow a school library media specialist, supervisor or educator to attend an ALA or AASL continuing education event.
Eligibility: Open to school library media specialists, supervisors or educators.
Level of Study: Professional development.
Type: Scholarship.
Value: US$500.
Frequency: Annual.
Country of Study: Any country.
No. of awards offered: One.
Application Procedure: Applicants must write for details.
Funding: Commercial.
Contributor: Information Plus.

ALA/Information Today Library of the Future Award
Subjects: Library science.
Purpose: To honour an individual library, library consortium, group of librarians or support organisation for innovative planning for applications of, or development of, patron training programmes about information technology in a library setting.
Type: Award.
Value: US$1,500 and a citation.
Frequency: Annual.
No. of awards offered: One.
Application Procedure: Applicants must write for details.
Contributor: Information Today, Inc.

Beta Phi Mu Award
Subjects: Education for librarianship.
Purpose: To recognise distinguished service.
Eligibility: Open to library school faculty members or others in the library profession.
Level of Study: Professional development.
Value: US$500 and a citation.

Frequency: Annual.
No. of awards offered: One.
Application Procedure: Applicants must submit six copies of nominations to the ALA Awards Programme Office.
Closing Date: December 1st.
Funding: Private.
Contributor: The Beta Phi Mu International Library Science Honorary Society.
No. of awards given last year: One.

bill boyd Literary Award
Subjects: The writing and publishing of outstanding war related fiction.
Purpose: To award an author who has written a military novel that honours the service of American veterans and military personnel during a time of war.
Type: Award.
Value: US$5,000 and a citation.
Frequency: Annual.
No. of awards offered: One.
Application Procedure: Applicants must write for details.
Closing Date: December 1st.
Contributor: William Young Boyd II.
No. of awards given last year: One.

Bogle-Pratt International Library Travel Fund
Subjects: Library science.
Purpose: To enable ALA members to attend their first international conference.
Eligibility: Open to ALA members.
Level of Study: Professional development.
Type: Travel grant.
Value: US$1,000.
Frequency: Annual.
Country of Study: Any country.
No. of awards offered: One.
Application Procedure: Applicants must write for details.
Closing Date: January 1st.
Funding: Private.
Contributor: The Bogle Memorial Fund.
No. of awards given last year: One.

Bound to Stay Bound Book Scholarships
Subjects: Library science.
Purpose: To support study in the field of library service to children toward an MLS or beyond, in an ALA accredited programme.
Eligibility: Open to qualified applicants of any nationality who have not started the programme.
Level of Study: Postgraduate.
Type: Scholarship.
Value: US$6,000 each.
Frequency: Annual.
Country of Study: United States of America or Canada.
No. of awards offered: Two.
Application Procedure: Applicants must write or email for details.
Closing Date: March 1st.
Funding: Commercial.
Contributor: Bound to Stay Bound Books, Inc.
No. of awards given last year: Two.
Additional Information: For further information please contact Ms Rebecca Singer.

Carroll Preston Baber Research Grant
Subjects: Library service.
Purpose: To encourage innovative research that could lead to an improvement in library services to any specified group or groups of people.
Level of Study: Unrestricted.
Type: Research grant.
Value: Up to US$7,500.
Frequency: Annual.

Country of Study: Any country.
No. of awards offered: One.
Application Procedure: Applicants must submit an application including a research proposal.
Funding: Private.
Contributor: Eric R Baber.
No. of applicants last year: Five.
Additional Information: The project should aim to answer a question that is of vital importance to the library community, and the researchers should plan to provide documentation of the results of their work. The jury would welcome proposals that involve innovative uses of technology and proposals that involve co-operation between libraries and other agencies, or between librarians and persons in other disciplines.

Christopher J Hoy/ERT Scholarship

Subjects: Library and information studies.
Purpose: To allow individuals to attend an ALA accredited programme of library and information studies.
Eligibility: Open to applicants who will be attending an American Library Association accredited programme of library and information studies leading to a Master's degree.
Level of Study: Postgraduate.
Type: Scholarship.
Value: US$3,000.
Frequency: Annual.
Country of Study: Any country.
No. of awards offered: One.
Application Procedure: Applicants must write for details.
Funding: Private.
Contributor: The family of Christopher J Hoy.

David H Clift Scholarship

Subjects: Library science.
Purpose: To enable a worthy Canadian or United States citizen to begin a Master's degree in an ALA accredited programme.
Eligibility: Open to qualified Canadian or United States citizens only.
Level of Study: Postgraduate.
Type: Scholarship.
Value: US$3,000.
Frequency: Annual.
Country of Study: Any country.
No. of awards offered: One.
Application Procedure: Applicants must write for details.

David Rozkuszka Scholarship

Subjects: Library science.
Purpose: To provide financial assistance to an individual who is currently working with government documents in a library.
Eligibility: Open to applicants currently completing a Master's programme in library science.
Level of Study: Postgraduate.
Type: Scholarship.
Value: US$3,000.
Frequency: Annual.
Country of Study: Any country.
No. of awards offered: One.
Application Procedure: Applicants must write for details.

Documents to the People Award

Subjects: Library science.
Purpose: To promote professional advancement in the field of librarianship and to recognise the most effective encouragement of the use of government documents in support of library services.
Eligibility: Open to individuals and libraries, organisations and other appropriate non commercial groups.
Level of Study: Unrestricted.
Value: US$2,000.
Frequency: Annual.
Country of Study: Any country.

No. of awards offered: One.
Application Procedure: Applicants must submit nominations to GODORT Staff Liaison at the ALA.
Funding: Commercial.
Contributor: The Congressional Information Service, Inc.

EBSCO ALA Conference Sponsorship

Subjects: Library science.
Purpose: To allow librarians to attend the ALA Annual Conference.
Eligibility: Open to librarians.
Level of Study: Professional development.
Type: Travel grant.
Value: Up to US$1,000 for expenses.
Frequency: Annual.
Country of Study: Any country.
No. of awards offered: 10.
Application Procedure: Applicants must write for details.
Closing Date: December 1st.
Funding: Commercial.
Contributor: EBSCO Subscription Services.

Eli M Oboler Memorial Award

Subjects: Intellectual freedom and freedom to read.
Purpose: To award the best published work in the field.
Eligibility: There are no eligibility restrictions.
Level of Study: Unrestricted.
Value: US$50,000.
Frequency: Every two years.
Country of Study: Any country.
No. of awards offered: One.
Application Procedure: Applicants must submit the nominated documents with nominating form.
Closing Date: December 1st.
Funding: Private.
No. of awards given last year: One.
No. of applicants last year: 10.

Elizabeth Futas Catalyst for Change Award

Subjects: Library science.
Purpose: To recognise and honour a librarian who invests time and talent to make positive changes in the profession of librarianship by taking risks to further the cause, helping new librarians grow and achieve, working for change within the ALA or other library organisations and inspiring colleagues to excel or make the impossible possible.
Type: Award.
Value: US$1,000 and a citation.
Frequency: Annual.
No. of awards offered: One.
Application Procedure: Applicants must write for details.
Contributor: An endowment administered by the ALA.
No. of awards given last year: One.

Equality Award

Subjects: Pay equity, affirmative action, legislative work and non sexist education.
Purpose: To recognise an outstanding contribution towards the promotion of equality in the library profession. The contribution may be either a sustained one or a single outstanding accomplishment.
Eligibility: Open to members of the library profession.
Level of Study: Professional development.
Value: US$500 plus a citation.
Frequency: Annual.
No. of awards offered: One.
Application Procedure: Applicants must submit six copies of nominations to the ALA Awards Program Office.
Funding: Commercial.
Contributor: The Scarecrow Press.
No. of awards given last year: One.

Facts on File Grant

Subjects: Library science.
Purpose: Awarded to a library for imaginative programming which would make current affairs more meaningful to an adult audience. Programmes, bibliographies, pamphlets, and innovative approaches of all types and in all media will apply.
Eligibility: Open to adult librarians.
Level of Study: Professional development.
Type: Grant.
Value: US$2,000.
Frequency: Annual.
Country of Study: Any country.
No. of awards offered: One.
Application Procedure: Applicants must submit a proposal accompanied by a statement of objective, identification of the current issues, the target audience and the extent of community involvement planned, an outline of planned activities for conducting and promoting the project, a budget summary and details of how the project will be evaluated.
Funding: Commercial.
No. of awards given last year: One.

Frances Henne/YALSA/VOYA Research Grant

Subjects: Library science.
Purpose: To provide seed money to an individual, institution or group for a project to encourage research on library service to young adults.
Eligibility: Open to applicants of any nationality.
Level of Study: Unrestricted.
Type: Research grant.
Value: US$500 minimum.
Frequency: Annual.
Country of Study: Any country.
No. of awards offered: One.
Application Procedure: Applicants must write for details.

Frederick G Melcher Scholarships

Subjects: Library service to children.
Purpose: To provide financial assistance for the professional education of men and women who intend to pursue children's librarianship.
Eligibility: Open to qualified young persons who have been accepted for admission to an appropriate school.
Level of Study: Graduate.
Type: Scholarship.
Value: US$6,000.
Frequency: Annual.
Study Establishment: An ALA accredited school.
Country of Study: United States of America or Canada.
No. of awards offered: Two.
Application Procedure: Applicants must write or email for details.
Closing Date: April 1st.
Funding: Private.

Grolier Foundation Award

Subjects: Work with children and young people to high school age.
Purpose: To recognise a librarian whose unusual contribution to the stimulation and guidance of reading by children and young people exemplifies outstanding achievement in the profession. The award is given either for outstanding for continuing service, or in recognition of one particular contribution of lasting value.
Eligibility: Open to community and school librarians.
Level of Study: Professional development.
Value: US$1,000 plus a citation.
Frequency: Annual.
No. of awards offered: One.
Application Procedure: Applicants must submit six copies of the application to the ALA Awards Program Office.
Funding: Commercial.
Contributor: Grolier Publishing Company.
No. of awards given last year: One.

The H W Wilson Library Staff Development Grant

Subjects: Library science.
Purpose: To award a library organisation whose application demonstrates greatest merit for a programme of staff development designed to further goals and objectives of the library organisation.
Type: Grant.
Value: US$3,500 and a citation.
Frequency: Annual.
No. of awards offered: One.
Application Procedure: Applicants must submit six copies of the application and documentation to the ALA Awards Program Office.
Contributor: The H W Wilson Company.
No. of awards given last year: One.

Jesse H Shera Award for Research

Subjects: Library science.
Purpose: For an outstanding and original paper reporting the results of research related to libraries.
Eligibility: Authors of nominated articles need not be Library Research Round Table (LRRT) members but the nominations must be made by LRRT members. All entries must be research articles published in English during the calendar year previous to the competition. All nominated articles must relate in at least a general way to library and information studies.
Level of Study: Unrestricted.
Type: Prize.
Value: US$500.
Frequency: Annual.
Country of Study: Any country.
No. of awards offered: One.
Application Procedure: Applicants wishing to nominate research articles for this award should send three copies of each article together with a covering letter stating that they are a current member of LRRT or that they are acting in their role as journal editor.
Closing Date: February 15th.
No. of awards given last year: One.
No. of applicants last year: 10.

John Philip Immroth Award for Intellectual Freedom

Subjects: Intellectual freedom.
Purpose: To recognise a notable contribution to intellectual freedom fuelled by personal courage.
Eligibility: Open to intellectual freedom fighters.
Level of Study: Unrestricted.
Value: US$500 plus a citation.
Frequency: Annual.
Country of Study: Any country.
No. of awards offered: One.
Application Procedure: Applicants must submit a detailed statement showing why the nominator believes that the nominee should receive the award. Nominations should be submitted to IFRT Staff Liaison at the ALA.
Closing Date: December 1st.
Funding: Private.
No. of awards given last year: One.
No. of applicants last year: Four.

Joseph W Lippincott Award

Subjects: Participation in the activities of professional library associations, notable published professional writing or other significant activity on behalf of the profession and its aims.
Purpose: To recognise distinguished service in the profession of librarianship including outstanding participation in professional library activities, notable published professional writing or other significant activities.
Eligibility: Open to librarians.
Level of Study: Professional development.
Type: Award.
Value: US$1,000 plus a citation.
Frequency: Annual.
No. of awards offered: One.

Application Procedure: Applicants must submit six copies of nominations to the ALA Awards Program Office.
Funding: Private.
Contributor: The late Joseph W Lippincott.
No. of awards given last year: One.

Loleta D Fyan Public Library Research Grant

Subjects: Library service.
Purpose: To facilitate the development and improvement of public libraries and the services they provide.
Eligibility: Applicants can include but are not limited to local, regional or state libraries, associations or organisations including units of the ALA, library schools or individuals.
Level of Study: Unrestricted.
Type: Research grant.
Value: Up to US$10,000.
Frequency: Annual.
Country of Study: Any country.
No. of awards offered: One or more.
Application Procedure: Applicants must submit an application form in addition to a proposal and budget.
Closing Date: Applications are accepted at any time.
Funding: Private.
No. of awards given last year: One.
No. of applicants last year: 10.
Additional Information: The project must result in the development and improvement of public libraries and the services they provide, have the potential for broader impact and application beyond meeting a specific local need, should be designed to effect changes in public library services that are innovative and responsive to the future, and should be capable of completion within one year.

Mary V Gaver Scholarship

Subjects: Library science.
Purpose: To assist library support staff specialising in youth services.
Eligibility: Open to library support staff who are United States or Canadian citizens.
Level of Study: Unrestricted.
Type: Scholarship.
Value: US$3,000.
Frequency: Annual.
Country of Study: Any country.
No. of awards offered: One.
Application Procedure: Applicants must write for details.

Melvil Dewey Medal

Subjects: Library science.
Purpose: To award an individual or group for recent creative professional achievement in library management, training, cataloguing, classification and the tools and techniques of librarianship.
Type: Award.
Value: Medal and citation.
Frequency: Annual.
No. of awards offered: One.
Application Procedure: Applicants must write for details.
Contributor: The OCLC Forest Press.
No. of awards given last year: One.

Miriam L Hornback Scholarship

Subjects: Library science.
Purpose: To assist an individual pursuing a Master's degree.
Eligibility: Open to ALA or library support staff who are pursuing a Master's degree in library science and who are citizens of the United States or Canada.
Level of Study: Postgraduate.
Type: Scholarship.
Value: US$3,000.
Frequency: Annual.
No. of awards offered: One.
Application Procedure: Applicants must write for details.

New Leaders Travel Grant

Subjects: Library science.
Purpose: To enhance professional development and improve the expertise of individuals new to the field by making possible their attendance at major professional development activities.
Eligibility: Open to qualified public librarians.
Level of Study: Professional development.
Type: Travel grant.
Value: Plaque and travel grant of up to US$1,500 per applicant.
Frequency: Annual.
Country of Study: Any country.
No. of awards offered: One.
Application Procedure: Applicants must write for details.

NMRT/EBSCO Scholarship

Subjects: Library science.
Purpose: To enable an individual to begin an MLS degree in an ALA accredited programme.
Eligibility: Open to United States and Canadian citizens.
Level of Study: Postgraduate.
Type: Scholarship.
Value: US$1,000.
Frequency: Annual.
Country of Study: Any country.
No. of awards offered: One.
Application Procedure: Applicants must write for details.
Closing Date: April 1st.

Penguin Putnam Books for Young Readers Award

Subjects: Library science.
Purpose: To allow children's librarians to attend the Annual Conference of the ALA.
Eligibility: Open to members of the Association for Library Service to Children with between one and ten years of experience who have never attended an American Library Association annual conference.
Level of Study: Professional development.
Type: Award.
Value: US$600.
Frequency: Annual.
Country of Study: The location of the ALA Annual Conference.
No. of awards offered: Four.
Application Procedure: Applicants must write or email for details.
Closing Date: December 1st.
Funding: Commercial.
Contributor: Penguin and Putnam Books for Young Readers.
No. of awards given last year: Four.

Primark Student Travel Award

Subjects: Library science.
Purpose: To enable a student interested in a career as a business librarian to attend an ALA Annual Conference.
Eligibility: Open to qualified Master's students in an ALA accredited programme.
Level of Study: Postgraduate.
Type: Travel grant.
Value: US$1,000.
Frequency: Annual.
Country of Study: Any country.
No. of awards offered: One.
Application Procedure: Applicants must write for details.
Funding: Commercial.
Contributor: Disclosure, Inc.

Samuel Lazerow Fellowship for Research in Acquisitions or Technical Services

Subjects: Acquisitions or technical services.
Purpose: To foster advances in acquisitions or technical services by providing a fellowship for travel or writing in those fields.
Eligibility: Open to qualified librarians.
Level of Study: Professional development.
Type: Fellowship.

Value: US$1,000 plus a citation.
Frequency: Annual.
Country of Study: Any country.
No. of awards offered: One.
Application Procedure: Applicants must write for details.

Shirley Olofson Memorial Awards

Subjects: Library science.
Purpose: To allow individuals to attend ALA conferences.
Eligibility: Open to members of the ALA who are also current or potential members of the New Members Round Table. Applicants should not have attended any more than five conferences.
Level of Study: Unrestricted.
Type: Award.
Value: Varies.
Frequency: Annual.
Country of Study: Any country.
No. of awards offered: Varies.
Application Procedure: Applicants must write for details.
Closing Date: December 15th.

Spectrum Scholarship

Subjects: Library science.
Purpose: To encourage admission to an ALA recognised Master's degree programme in library and information studies by the four largest underrepresented groups.
Eligibility: Open to United States or Canadian citizens only, from one of the largest underrepresented groups. These are African American or African Canadian, Asian or Pacific Islander, Latino or Hispanic and native people of the United States of America or Canada.
Level of Study: Postgraduate.
Type: Scholarship.
Value: US$5,000.
Frequency: Annual.
Country of Study: United States of America or Canada.
No. of awards offered: 50.
Application Procedure: Applicants must request details via fax on demand or visit the website.
Closing Date: April 1st.
No. of awards given last year: 50.
No. of applicants last year: 200.

Tom C Drewes Scholarship

Subjects: Library science.
Purpose: To assist a library support staff person.
Eligibility: Open to library support staff pursuing a Master's degree who are United States or Canadian citizens.
Level of Study: Postgraduate.
Type: Scholarship.
Value: US$3,000.
Frequency: Annual.
Country of Study: Any country.
No. of awards offered: One.
Application Procedure: Applicants must write for details.

YALSA/Baker and Taylor Conference Grants

Subjects: Library science.
Purpose: To allow young adult librarians who work directly with young adults in either a public library or a school library, to attend the Annual Conference of the ALA.
Eligibility: Open to members of the Young Adult Library Services Association with between one and ten years of library experience who have never attended an American Library Association annual conference.
Level of Study: Professional development.
Type: Grant.
Value: US$1,000.
Frequency: Annual.
Country of Study: Any country.
No. of awards offered: Two.

Application Procedure: Applicants must submit applications to the Young Adult Library Services Association, ALA.
Closing Date: December 1st.
Additional Information: The American Library Association offers a number of other awards in various fields related to library science, including the following medals and citations with no cash prizes: the Randolph Caldecott Medal, the James Bennett Childs Award, the Dartmouth Medal, the Melvil Dewey Medal, the John Newberry Medal, the Laura Ingalls Wilder Medal, the ASCLA Exceptional Service Award, the Armed Forces Librarians Achievement Citation, the Francis Joseph Campbell Citation, the Margaret Mann Citation, the Isadore Gilbert Mudge Citation, the Esther J Piercy Award, the Distinguished Library Service Award for School Administrators and the Trustees Citations. A full list of awards is available from the ALA.

AMERICAN LIVER FOUNDATION (ALF)

1425 Pompton Avenue, Cedar Grove, NJ, 07009, United States of America
Tel: (1) 973 256 2550
Fax: (1) 973 256 1560
Email: webmail@liverfoundation.org
www: http://www.liverfoundation.org
Contact: Research Department

The American Liver Foundation (ALF) is the only national, voluntary non-profit health agency dedicated to preventing, treating and curing hepatitis and all liver diseases through research, education and advocacy.

ALF Liver Scholar Award

Subjects: Liver research.
Purpose: To encourage scientific exploration into the study of liver diseases and their causes and cures.
Eligibility: Open to junior faculty only.
Level of Study: Postdoctorate, Postgraduate.
Type: Research grant.
Value: US$50,000 per year.
Length of Study: Three years.
Frequency: Annual.
Country of Study: United States of America.
No. of awards offered: Varies.
Application Procedure: Applicants must write for details.
Closing Date: January 5th.

ALF Postdoctoral Research Fellowship

Subjects: Liver research.
Purpose: To encourage scientific exploration into the study of liver diseases, their causes and cures.
Eligibility: Open to MD and PhD candidates of any nationality who are currently undertaking research in the United States of America.
Level of Study: Postgraduate.
Type: Fellowship.
Value: US$10,000.
Length of Study: One year.
Frequency: Annual.
Country of Study: United States of America.
No. of awards offered: Varies.
Application Procedure: Applicants must write for details.
Closing Date: January 5th.
Funding: Private.

ALF Student Research Fellowship

Subjects: Liver research.
Purpose: To encourage young scientists to further their studies and research in the area of hepathology.
Eligibility: Open to full-time students of United States graduate or medical school programmes.
Level of Study: Graduate.
Type: Fellowship.

Value: US$2,500.
Length of Study: Three months.
Frequency: Annual.
Country of Study: United States of America.
No. of awards offered: Varies.
Application Procedure: Applicants must write for details.
Closing Date: January 5th.

Physician Research Development Award

Subjects: Liver research.
Purpose: To support and develop clinical research training of Fellows seeking to pursue a career in hepathology.
Eligibility: Open to citizens or permanent residents of North American countries who are sponsored by non federal public or private non-profit institutions engaged in health care and health related research within the United States and its possessions. At the time of the award, the applicant must have completed at least 18 months of training in a gastroenterology or hepathology programme within the United States or its possessions. Candidates should have completed their clinical training, be eligible for junior faculty appointments or be in their first year.
Level of Study: Postdoctorate, Postgraduate.
Type: Research grant.
Value: US$225,000 for three years and up to US$270,000 for four years.
Length of Study: Three-four years.
Frequency: Annual.
Country of Study: United States of America.
Application Procedure: Applicants must write for details.
Closing Date: January 5th.
Funding: Private.

THE AMERICAN LYME DISEASE FOUNDATION, INC.

Mill Pond Offices
293 Route 100, Somers, NY, 10589, United States of America
Tel: (1) 914 277 6970
Fax: (1) 914 277 6974
Email: inquire@aldf.com
www: http://www.aldf.com
Contact: Executive Director

The American Lyme Disease Foundation is a national non-profit organisation dedicated to the diagnosis, treatment, prevention and control of Lyme disease and other tick-borne infections. The Foundation supports research and focuses on the education of the public and health care professionals.

Grants for Innovative Methods for Control of Tick-Borne Diseases

Subjects: Tick prevention and control.
Purpose: To encourage research and education into tick control.
Eligibility: Open to individuals who are within 10 years of the completion of a degree.
Level of Study: Postdoctorate.
Type: Research grant.
Value: US$10,000-25,000.
Length of Study: Two-three years.
Frequency: Annual, if funds are available.
Study Establishment: Unrestricted.
Country of Study: United States of America.
No. of awards offered: Four-seven.
Application Procedure: Applicants must contact the organisation through the website.
Closing Date: October 31st.
Funding: Commercial, Government, Private.
Additional Information: Grants are awarded in the first week of February.

AMERICAN MATHEMATICAL SOCIETY (AMS)

PO Box 6248, Providence, RI, 02940-6248, United States of America
Tel: (1) 401 455 4106
Fax: (1) 401 331 3842
Email: ams@ams.org
www: http://www.ams.org
Contact: Ms Sheila Rowland, Executive Assistant

The American Mathematical Society (AMS) was created to further mathematical research and scholarship. Founded in 1888, it now has approximately 30,000 members, including mathematicians throughout the United States and around the world. It continues to fulfil its mission with programmes that promote mathematical research, increase the awareness of its value to society and foster excellence in mathematics education.

AMS Centennial Fellowship

Subjects: Mathematics.
Purpose: To help further the research careers of outstanding mid-career mathematicians.
Eligibility: The primary selection criterion is the excellence of the candidate's research. Preference will be given to candidates who have not had extensive fellowship support in the past. Recipients may not hold the fellowship concurrently with another research fellowship such as the Sloan or NSF Postdoctoral fellowship. Under normal circumstances, the fellowship cannot be deferred. A recipient of the fellowship shall have held his or her doctoral degree for at least three years and not more than twelve years at the inception of the award. Applications will be accepted from those currently holding a tenured, tenure track, postdoctoral or comparable position, at the discretion of the selection committee, at an institution in North America.
Level of Study: Postdoctorate.
Type: Fellowship.
Value: A stipend of US$39,000 plus an expense allowance of US$1,600.
Length of Study: Full support for a year or half support over a two year period.
Frequency: Annual.
Study Establishment: At any institution selected by the Fellow or at more than one in succession.
Country of Study: Any country.
No. of awards offered: At least one, dependent on funds available.
Application Procedure: Applicants must submit an application including a cogent plan indicating how the fellowship will be used. The plan should include travel to at least one other institution and should demonstrate that the fellowship will be used for more than reduction of teaching at the candidate's home institution. The selection committee will consider the plan in addition to the quality of the candidate's research, and will try to award the fellowship to those for whom the award would make a real difference in the development of their research careers. Application forms are available from the Executive Director of the AMS or from the website. Completed applications and reference forms must not be sent to the AMS.
Closing Date: December 1st.
Funding: Private.
No. of awards given last year: Four or five.

For further information contact:

Chair, AMS Centennial Fellowship Committee
Department of Mathematics
University of California, Los Angeles, CA, 90095-1555, United States of America
Contact: Professor Thomas Liggett, Chair, AMS Centennial Fellowship Committee

AMERICAN MUSIC CENTER, INC.

30 West 26th Street
Suite 1001, New York, NY, 10010-2011, United States of America
Tel: (1) 212 366 5260
Fax: (1) 212 366 5265
Email: center@amc.net
www: http://www.amc.net
Contact: Mr Philip Rothman, Manager of Grantmaking Programs

The American Music Center is a non-profit membership and service organisation. The Center's mission is to build a national community for new American music.

Margaret Fairbank Jory Copying Assistance Program

Subjects: Musical composition.
Purpose: To assist composers with copying expenses for a première performance.
Eligibility: Open to American composers who are members of the American Music Center in good standing at the time of application. The performance must advance the professional career of the composer. Performers, presenters or ensembles are not eligible to apply. Funds are available for copying parts for the première performance of large scale works for four or more instrumental and/or vocal parts. The composer must have a written commitment for at least one public performance of the work by a professional ensemble of recognised artistic merit.
Level of Study: Professional development.
Type: Grant.
Frequency: Three times each year.
Country of Study: Any country.
No. of awards offered: Approx. 75.
Application Procedure: Applicants must complete an application form and submit this with supporting materials. These include a brief statement of the significance of this performance to the composer's career, a brief professional curriculum vitae with a list of other recent performances, written confirmation of the exact premiere performance date, background on the performing organisation, a list of estimated expenses that totals the amount requested, and the for which support is requested.
Closing Date: February 1st, June 1st or October 1st.
Funding: Private.
Contributor: The Mary Flager Cary Charitable Trust, the Helen F Whitaker Fund, JPMorgan Chase, the Arts Alive Foundation and individuals.
No. of awards given last year: Approx. 75.
No. of applicants last year: Approx. 200.

THE AMERICAN MUSIC SCHOLARSHIP ASSOCIATION, INC. (AMSA)

441 Vine Street
Suite 1030, Cincinnati, OH, 45202, United States of America
Tel: (1) 513 421 5342
Fax: (1) 513 421 2672
Email: amsa@queencity.com
www: http://www.amsa-wpc.org
Contact: Ms Gloria Ackerman, Chief Executive Officer

The American Music Scholarship Association (AMSA) produces the annual world piano competition in Cincinnati. AMSA also provides outreach programmes to Cincinnati children (eg. The Bach, Beethoven, and Brahms Club) and worldwide performances. The young artist division winners perform at Carnegie Hall and the gold medallist of the artist division performs at Lincoln Center's Alice Tully Hall.

AMSA World Piano Competition

Subjects: Musical performance on the piano.
Purpose: To encourage the careers of aspiring young pianists and expose them to the performances of great musicians.

Eligibility: Open to piano students of any nationality who are between the ages of 5 and 30.
Level of Study: Unrestricted.
Type: Scholarship.
Value: The Artist Division's first prize is US$10,000 plus a fully managed debut recital at the Lincoln Center in New York. The second prize is US$3,000, the third US$2,000, the fourth US$1,000, the fifth US$500 and the sixth US$300. The Young Artists Division grand prize at levels 9-12 is US$1,500.
Frequency: Annual, if funds are available.
Country of Study: Any country.
No. of awards offered: 58.
Application Procedure: Applicants must apply in compliance with the full competition rules and regulations, which are available on request and on the website.
Closing Date: Please refer to the website.
Funding: Private.

AMERICAN MUSICOLOGICAL SOCIETY (AMS)

Department of Music
201 South 34th Street, Philadelphia, PA, 19104-6313, United States of America
Tel: (1) 215 898 8698
Fax: (1) 215 573 3673
Email: ams@sas.upenn.edu
www: http://www.ams-net.org
Contact: Mr Robert Judd, Executive Director

The American Musicological Society (AMS) was founded in 1934 as a non-profit organisation, with the aim of advancing research in the various fields of music as a branch of learning and scholarship. In 1951 the Society became a constituent member of the American Council of Learned Societies.

Alfred Einstein Award

Subjects: Musicology.
Purpose: To honour a musicological article of exceptional merit by a Scholar in the early stages of his or her career.
Eligibility: Open to citizens or permanent residents of Canada or the United States.
Level of Study: Professional development.
Type: Prize.
Value: Varies.
Frequency: Annual.
No. of awards offered: One.
Application Procedure: Applicants must be nominated. The committee will entertain articles from any individual, including eligible authors who are encouraged to nominate their own articles. Nominations should include the name of the author, the title of the article and the name and year of the periodical or other collection in which it was published. A curriculum vitae is also required.
Closing Date: June 1st.
Funding: Private.
No. of awards given last year: One.
No. of applicants last year: 25.
Additional Information: Further information is available on request.

Alvin H Johnson 50 Dissertation One Year Fellowship

Subjects: Any field of musical research.
Purpose: To encourage research in the various fields of music as a branch of learning and scholarship.
Eligibility: Open to full-time students registered for a doctorate at a North American university, in good standing, who have completed all formal degree requirements except the dissertation at the time of full application. Open to all students without regard to nationality, race, religion or gender.
Level of Study: Doctorate, Postgraduate.
Type: Fellowship.

Value: US$12,000.
Frequency: Annual.
Country of Study: United States of America or Canada.
No. of awards offered: Five-six.
Application Procedure: Application forms will be sent via the Directors of Graduate Study at all doctorate granting institutions in North America. They will also be available directly from the Society. Applications must include a curriculum vitae, certification of enrolment and degree completed, and two supporting letters from faculty members, one of whom must be the principal adviser of the dissertation. A detailed dissertation prospectus and a completed chapter or comparable written work on the dissertation should accompany the full application. All documents should be submitted in triplicate.
Closing Date: January 15th.
Funding: Private.
Additional Information: Any submission for a doctoral degree in which the emphasis is on musical scholarship is eligible. The award is not intended for support of early stages of research and it is expected that a recipient's dissertation will be completed within the fellowship year. An equivalent major award from another source may not normally be held concurrently unless the AMS award is accepted on an honorary basis.

AMS Subventions for Publications

Subjects: Any field of musicology.
Purpose: To help individuals with expenses involved in the publication of works of musical scholarship, including books, articles and works in non-print media.
Eligibility: Open to younger Scholars and Scholars in the early stages of their careers. Proposals for projects that make use of newer technologies are welcomed.
Level of Study: Professional development.
Type: Subvention.
Value: US$500-2,000 with a maximum of US$2,500 available.
Frequency: Twice a year.
Application Procedure: Applicants must submit a short written abstract of up to 1,000 words describing the project and its contribution to musical scholarship, a copy of the article or other equivalent sample, a copy of a contract or letter of agreement from the journal editor or publisher indicating final acceptance for publication, and a detailed budget and explanation of the expenses to which the subvention would be applied. Wherever possible expenses should be itemised. If the publication is a book a representative chapter should be submitted.
Closing Date: March 15th or September 15th.
Additional Information: Further information is available on request.

The Howard Mayer Brown Fellowship

Subjects: Musicology.
Purpose: To increase the presence of minority scholars and teachers in musicology.
Eligibility: Open to candidates who have completed at least one year of academic work at an institution with a graduate programme in musicology and who intend to complete a PhD in the field. There are no restrictions on age or gender.
Level of Study: Postgraduate.
Type: Fellowship.
Value: US$12,000.
Length of Study: One year.
Frequency: Annual.
Study Establishment: An institution which offers a graduate programme in musicology.
Country of Study: United States of America or Canada.
Application Procedure: Applicants must be nominated. Nominations may come from a faculty member of the institution at which the student is enrolled, from a member of the AMS at another institution, or directly from the student. Supporting documents must include a letter summarising the candidate's academic background, letters of support from three faculty members and samples of the applicant's work such as term papers or any published material.
Closing Date: April 1st of the year in which the fellowship is awarded.

Funding: Private.
No. of awards given last year: One.
No. of applicants last year: 15.
Additional Information: The AMS encourages the institution at which the recipient is pursuing his or her degree to offer continuing financial support. Further information is available on request.

The Noah Greenberg Award

Subjects: Musicology.
Purpose: To provide a grant-in-aid to stimulate active co-operation between scholars and performers by recognising and fostering outstanding contributions to historical performing practices.
Eligibility: Both Scholars and performers may apply. Applicants need not be members of the Society.
Level of Study: Professional development.
Type: Award.
Value: US$2,000.
Frequency: Annual.
No. of awards offered: One-two.
Application Procedure: Applicants must submit three copies of a description of the project, a detailed budget and supporting materials such as articles or tapes of performances which are relevant to the project. Applications must be sent to the chair of the Noah Greenberg Award Committee.
Funding: Private.
No. of awards given last year: One.
No. of applicants last year: Eight.

The Otto Kinkeldey Award

Subjects: Musicology.
Purpose: To award the work of musicological scholarship such as a major book, edition or other piece of scholarship that best exemplifies the highest quality of originality, interpretation, logic, clarity of thought and communication.
Eligibility: The work must have been published during the previous year in any language and in any country by a Scholar who is a citizen or permanent resident of Canada or the United States.
Level of Study: Professional development.
Type: Prize.
Value: Varies.
Frequency: Annual.
Application Procedure: Applicants must write for details.
Closing Date: July 1st.
Funding: Private.
No. of awards given last year: Two.
No. of applicants last year: 45.
Additional Information: Further information is available on request.

The Paul A Pisk Prize

Subjects: Any field of musicology.
Purpose: To encourage scholarship.
Eligibility: Open to graduate students whose abstracts have been submitted to the Program Committee of the Society and papers accepted for inclusion in the Annual Meeting. Open to all students without regard to nationality, race, religion or gender.
Level of Study: Postgraduate.
Type: Prize.
Value: US$1,000.
Frequency: Annual.
Country of Study: United States of America or Canada.
No. of awards offered: One.
Application Procedure: Applicants must submit three copies of the complete text paper to the chair of the Pisk Prize Committee. The submission must be accompanied by a statement from the student's academic adviser affirming the graduate student status of the applicant.
Closing Date: September 1st.
Funding: Private.
No. of awards given last year: One.
No. of applicants last year: 25.
Additional Information: Further information is available on request.

The Philip Brett Award

Subjects: Musicology.
Purpose: To honour an exceptional musicological work such as a published article, book, edition, annotated translation, a paper read at a conference or teaching materials in the field of gay, lesbian, bisexual, transgender or transsexual studies.
Eligibility: Work must be completed during the previous two academic years (ending June 30th), in any country and in any language.
Type: Award.
Value: US$500 and a certificate.
Frequency: Annual.
Country of Study: Any country.
No. of awards offered: One.
Application Procedure: Applicants must be nominated. Nominations are accepted from any individual and should include five copies of the name of the scholar, a description of the work and a statement to the effect that the work was completed during the previous two academic years.
Closing Date: July 1st.
Funding: Private.
No. of awards given last year: One.
No. of applicants last year: 15.

AMERICAN NUCLEAR SOCIETY (ANS)

555 North Kensington Avenue, LaGrange Park, IL, 60525, United States of America
Tel: (1) 708 352 6611
Fax: (1) 708 352 0499
Email: outreach@ans.org
www: http://www.ans.org
Contact: Scholarship Programme

The American Nuclear Society (ANS) is a non-profit, international, scientific and educational organisation. It was established by a group of individuals who recognised the need to unify the professional activities within the diverse fields of nuclear science and technology.

Alan F Henry/Paul A Greebler Scholarship

Subjects: Reactor physics.
Purpose: To aid students pursuing studies in the field.
Eligibility: Applicants must be full-time graduate students at a North American university engaged in Master's or PhD research in the area of nuclear reactor physics or radiation transport. Applicants may be of any nationality.
Level of Study: Graduate, Postdoctorate.
Type: Scholarship.
Value: Varies.
Length of Study: Varies.
Frequency: Annual.
Study Establishment: An accredited institution.
Country of Study: United States of America.
No. of awards offered: Varies.
Application Procedure: Applicants must complete an application form available from the organisation. A grade transcript and three completed confidential reference forms are also required.
Closing Date: February 1st.
Additional Information: Further information is available either on request or from the website.

Arthur Holly Compton Award in Education

Subjects: Nuclear science and engineering.
Purpose: To recognise and encourage outstanding contributions to education in nuclear science and engineering.
Eligibility: Nominees do not have to be American Nuclear Society members or work primarily in the field of education.
Level of Study: Unrestricted.
Type: Prize.
Value: An engraved plaque and monetary award.

Application Procedure: Applicants must be nominated. Nomination forms are available from the website or from the American Nuclear Society headquarters.
Closing Date: March 1st.
Additional Information: This award was established in 1966 through an endowment by the wife of Edward Malinckrodt Junior, and by George E Malinckrodt in honour of the late Arthur Holly Compton. The award is presented at the American Nuclear Society Annual Meeting.

Everitt P Blizard Scholarship

Subjects: Radiation protection and shielding.
Purpose: To aid students pursuing studies in the field of radiation protection and shielding.
Eligibility: Open to full-time graduate students in a programme leading to an advanced degree in nuclear science, nuclear engineering or a nuclear related field. Applicants must be United States citizens or permanent residents and be enrolled in an accredited institution in the United States.
Level of Study: Graduate.
Type: Scholarship.
Value: Varies.
Length of Study: Varies.
Frequency: Annual.
Study Establishment: An accredited institution.
Country of Study: United States of America.
No. of awards offered: Varies.
Application Procedure: Applicants must complete an application form available from the organisation. A grade transcript and three completed confidential reference forms are also required.
Closing Date: February 1st.
Additional Information: Further information is available either on request or from the website.

James F Schumar Scholarship

Subjects: Nuclear physics and engineering, particularly materials science and technology for nuclear applications.
Purpose: To aid students pursuing graduate studies in material science and technology for nuclear applications.
Eligibility: Open to full-time graduate students in a programme leading to an advanced degree in nuclear science, nuclear engineering or a nuclear related field. Applicants must be United States citizens or permanent residents and must be enrolled in an accredited institution in the United States.
Level of Study: Graduate.
Type: Scholarship.
Value: Varies.
Length of Study: Varies.
Frequency: Annual.
Study Establishment: An accredited institution.
Country of Study: United States of America.
No. of awards offered: Varies.
Application Procedure: Applicants must complete an application form available from the organisation. A grade transcript and three completed confidential reference forms are also required.
Closing Date: February 1st.
Additional Information: Further information is available either on request or from the website.

John and Muriel Landis Scholarship Awards

Subjects: Nuclear physics and engineering.
Purpose: To aid students who have greater than average financial need.
Eligibility: Candidates should be planning to pursue a career in nuclear engineering or a nuclear related field. Candidates must have greater than average financial need, and consideration will be given to conditions or experiences that render the student disadvantaged. Applicants need not be United States citizens.
Level of Study: Graduate.
Type: Scholarship.
Value: Varies.

Frequency: Annual.
Study Establishment: An accredited institution.
Country of Study: United States of America.
No. of awards offered: Up to eight.
Application Procedure: Applicants must request an application form and include the name and a letter of commitment from the university the candidate will be attending, the year the candidate will be in in the Autumn of the award, the major course of study and a stamped addressed envelope. Completed applications must include a grade transcript and three confidential reference forms. Candidates must be sponsored by an American Nuclear Society section, division, student branch, committee, member or organisation member.
Closing Date: February 1st.

John Randall Scholarship

Subjects: Nuclear physics and engineering, particularly in the areas of science and engineering related to the nuclear fuel cycle and radioactive waste management.
Eligibility: Open to full-time graduate students in a programme leading to an advanced degree in nuclear science, nuclear engineering or a nuclear related field. Applicants must be United States citizens or permanent residents and be enrolled in an accredited institution in the United States.
Level of Study: Graduate.
Type: Scholarship.
Frequency: Annual.
Study Establishment: An accredited institution.
Country of Study: United States of America.
No. of awards offered: Varies.
Application Procedure: Applicants must complete an application form available from the organisation. A grade transcript and three completed confidential reference forms are also required.
Closing Date: February 1st.
Additional Information: Further information is available either on request or from the website.

Mark Mills Award

Subjects: Nuclear physics particularly the advancement of science and engineering related to the atomic nucleus.
Purpose: Established in 1958, to recognise the important contributions of the late Mark Mills to nuclear science and engineering. It is awarded to the author who submits the best original technical paper.
Eligibility: Applicants must have been registered in a graduate degree programme in a recognised institution of higher learning for one year prior to the award, and a certification of this fact must be made by the faculty advisor on the nomination form. Thus, this competition is open to a graduate student completing the work on which his or her paper is based from a minimum of four months prior to the award to a maximum of 16 months prior to the award. The paper should demonstrate originality and ingenuity and should be in a form suitable for publication. A thesis is not acceptable. A paper already published or submitted for publication is eligible if nominated by the faculty adviser. A paper jointly authored is eligible if the candidate has the primary responsibility.
Level of Study: Graduate.
Type: Award.
Value: An engraved plaque and US$500.
Application Procedure: Applicants must be nominated by the student faculty adviser. Multiple nominees by one nominator, nomination of past recipients of the award, and multiple year nominations of the same paper are prohibited. Forms are available from the ANS headquarters.
Closing Date: June 1st.
Additional Information: Awards are presented at the ANS Winter Meeting.

Robert A Dannels Scholarship

Subjects: Nuclear science and engineering.
Eligibility: Handicapped persons are encouraged to apply. This scholarship is open to full-time graduate students in a programme leading to an advanced degree in nuclear science, nuclear engineering, or a nuclear related field. Applicants must be United States citizens or permanent residents and must be enrolled in an accredited institution in the United States.
Level of Study: Graduate.
Type: Scholarship.
Value: Varies.
Length of Study: Varies.
Frequency: Annual.
Country of Study: United States of America.
No. of awards offered: Varies.
Application Procedure: Applicants must complete an application form available from the organisation. A grade transcript and three completed confidential reference forms are also required.
Closing Date: February 1st.
Additional Information: Further information is available either on request or from the website.

Student Design Competition

Subjects: Nuclear physics.
Purpose: To promote excellence in the design aspect of nuclear engineering education in the universities. A key feature of the programme is industry participation in the judging of the annual design problem.
Eligibility: Any university is eligible to submit solutions to nuclear engineering design problems, but participants must have a university affiliation and a faculty member as an advisor.
Level of Study: Graduate.
Type: Competition.
Value: Financial assistance is given for travel to the meeting for the competition.
Application Procedure: Each university must review solutions by its students and select the best from each category for submission.

Verne R Dapp Scholarship

Subjects: Nuclear physics and engineering.
Eligibility: Open to full-time graduate students in a programme leading to an advanced degree in nuclear science, nuclear engineering or a nuclear related field. Applicants must be United States citizens or permanent residents and be enrolled in an accredited institution in the United States.
Level of Study: Graduate.
Type: Scholarship.
Value: Varies.
Length of Study: Varies.
Frequency: Every two years.
Study Establishment: An accredited institution.
Country of Study: United States of America.
No. of awards offered: Varies.
Application Procedure: Applicants must complete an application form available from the organisation. A grade transcript and three completed confidential reference forms are also required.
Closing Date: February 1st.

Walter Meyer Scholarship

Subjects: Nuclear physics and engineering.
Eligibility: Open to full-time graduate students in a programme leading to an advanced degree in nuclear science, nuclear engineering or a nuclear related field. Applicants must be United States citizens or permanent residents and be enrolled in an accredited institution in the United States.
Type: Scholarship.
Value: Varies.
Length of Study: Varies.
Frequency: Every two years.
Study Establishment: An accredited institution.
Country of Study: United States of America.
No. of awards offered: Varies.
Application Procedure: Applicants must complete an application form available from the organisation. A grade transcript and three completed confidential reference forms are also required.

Closing Date: February 1st.
Additional Information: Further information is available either on request or from the website.

AMERICAN NUMISMATIC SOCIETY (ANS)

Broadway at 155th Street, New York, NY, 10032, United States of America
Tel: (1) 212 234 3130
Fax: (1) 212 234 3381
Email: info@amnumsoc.org
www: http://www.amnumsoc.org
Contact: Mr William E Metcalf, Chief Curator

The mission of the American Numismatic Society (ANS) is to be the pre-eminent national institution advancing the study and appreciation of coins, medals and related objects of all cultures as historical and artistic documents. It aims to do this by maintaining the foremost numismatic collection and library, supporting scholarly research and publications, and sponsoring educational and interpretative programmes for diverse audiences.

ANS Graduate Fellowship

Subjects: Numismatics.
Purpose: To further the study of numismatics as an ancillary discipline.
Eligibility: Open to persons enrolled at universities in the United States of America or Canada who have completed the general examinations (or the equivalent) for the doctoral degree and have attended one of the Society's Summer seminars.
Level of Study: Doctorate.
Type: Fellowship.
Value: US$3,500.
Length of Study: Varies.
Frequency: Dependent on funds available.
Study Establishment: An appropriate university.
Country of Study: Any country.
No. of awards offered: One.
Application Procedure: Applicants must write for details.
Closing Date: March 1st.
No. of awards given last year: One.
No. of applicants last year: Five.

Donald Groves Fund

Subjects: Early American numismatics involving material dating no later than 1800.
Purpose: To promote publications in the field.
Level of Study: Postgraduate, Research.
Value: Varies. Funding is available for travel and other expenses in association with research as well as for publication costs.
Frequency: Annual.
Country of Study: United States of America.
No. of awards offered: Varies.
Application Procedure: Applicants must address applications to the Secretary of the Society and must include an outline of the proposed research, the method of accomplishing the research, the funding requested and the specific use to which the funding will be put. Applications will be reviewed periodically by the Donald Groves Fund Committee.
Closing Date: Applications are accepted at any time.
Funding: Private.

Frances M Schwartz Fellowship

Subjects: Numismatic methodology and museum practice.
Purpose: To assist the Fellow in the study of Greek and Roman fields relevant to the subject.
Eligibility: Open to students of numismatics who possess a Bachelor of arts or equivalent degree.
Level of Study: Graduate, Postgraduate.
Type: Fellowship.

Value: Up to US$2,000.
Frequency: Annual.
Country of Study: United States of America.
No. of awards offered: Varies.
Application Procedure: Applicants must write for details.
Closing Date: March 1st.
Funding: Private.
Additional Information: Further information is available by emailing metcalf@amnumsoc.org.

Grants for ANS Summer Seminar in Numismatics

Subjects: Numismatics.
Purpose: To provide a selected number of graduate students with a deeper understanding of the contribution that this subject makes to other fields.
Eligibility: Open to persons who have had at least one year's graduate study at a university in the United States of America or Canada, and are students of classical studies, history, Near Eastern studies or other humanistic fields.
Level of Study: Postgraduate.
Type: Grant.
Value: US$2,000.
Length of Study: Nine weeks during the Summer.
Frequency: Annual.
Study Establishment: ANS.
Country of Study: United States of America.
No. of awards offered: Approx. 10.
Application Procedure: Applicants must write well in advance for details of the application process.
Closing Date: March 1st.
Funding: Private.
No. of awards given last year: 12.
No. of applicants last year: 21.
Additional Information: One or two students from overseas are usually accepted to the seminar but will not receive a grant.

Shaykh Hamad Fellowship in Islamic Numismatics

Subjects: Islamic research.
Purpose: To support training in museum practice and research on Islamic coinage.
Eligibility: Candidates are expected to have some graduate level training in medieval Near Eastern history or a related field, and some knowledge of Arabic.
Level of Study: Postgraduate.
Type: Fellowship.
Value: The stipend is US$3,000, and the student will receive training for the equivalent of one day a week for the academic year.
Frequency: Dependent on funds available.
Country of Study: Any country.
No. of awards offered: Varies.
Application Procedure: Applicants must write for details.
Closing Date: March 1st.

AMERICAN NURSES FOUNDATION (ANF)

600 Maryland Avenue South West
Suite 100W, Washington, DC, 20024-2571, United States of America
Tel: (1) 202 651 7227
Fax: (1) 202 651 7354
Email: anf@ana.org
www: http://www.nursingworld.org/anf
Contact: Grants Program Manager

ANF Nursing Research Grants

Subjects: Nursing.
Purpose: To support nursing research by new and experienced nurse researchers.

Eligibility: The principal investigator must be a registered nurse who has obtained at least one degree, either a Bachelor's or higher, in nursing.
Level of Study: Doctorate, Postdoctorate, Postgraduate.
Type: Research grant.
Value: US$3,500-10,000.
Length of Study: One year.
Frequency: Annual.
Country of Study: Any country.
No. of awards offered: Approx. 33.
Application Procedure: Applicants must submit a completed application form, available on request or from the website and a non refundable application fee of US$50.
Closing Date: May 1st.
Funding: Commercial, Private.
Additional Information: The awards vary from year to year so please contact the Foundation.

AMERICAN ORCHID SOCIETY

16700 AOS Lane
Delray Beach, West Palm Beach, FL, 33446-4351, United States of America
Tel: (1) 561 404 2000
Fax: (1) 561 404 2100
Email: theaos@aos.org
www: http://orchidweb.org
Contact: Ms Pamela Giust, Education & Research

Grants for Orchid Research
Subjects: Orchid research.
Purpose: To advance scientific study of orchids in every respect and to assist in publication of scholarly and popular scientific literature on orchids.
Eligibility: There are no eligibility restrictions.
Level of Study: Postgraduate.
Type: Grant.
Value: US$500-12,000.
Length of Study: Up to three years.
Country of Study: Any country.
No. of awards offered: Varies.
Application Procedure: Applicants must write for guidelines.
Closing Date: January 1st and July 1st.

AMERICAN ORIENTAL SOCIETY

Hatcher Graduate Library
University of Michigan, Ann Arbor, MI, 48109-1205, United States of America
Tel: (1) 734 747 4760
Email: jrodgers@umich.edu
www: http://www.umich.edu/~aos
Contact: Grants Management Officer

The American Oriental Society is primarily concerned with the encouragement of basic research in the languages and literatures of Asia.

Louise Wallace Hackney Fellowship
Subjects: Chinese art, with special relation to painting, and the translation into English of works on the subject.
Purpose: To remind scholars that Chinese art, like all art, is not a disembodied creation, but the outgrowth of the life and culture from which it has sprung. It is requested that scholars give special attention to this approach in their study.
Eligibility: Open to United States citizens who are doctoral or postdoctoral students and have successfully completed at least three years of Chinese language study at a recognised university, and

have some knowledge or training in art. In no case shall a fellowship be awarded to Scholars of well recognised standing, but shall be given to either men or women who show aptitude or promise in the said field of learning.
Level of Study: Doctorate, Postdoctorate.
Type: Fellowship.
Value: US$8,000.
Length of Study: One year.
Frequency: Annual.
Study Establishment: Any institution where paintings and adequate language guidance is available.
Country of Study: Any country.
No. of awards offered: One.
Application Procedure: Applicants must submit the following materials in duplicate: a transcript of their undergraduate and graduate coursework, a statement of personal finances, a four page summary of the proposed project to be undertaken including details of expense, and no less than three letters of recommendation.
Closing Date: March 1st.
Funding: Private.
No. of awards given last year: One.
No. of applicants last year: 10.
Additional Information: It is possible to apply for a renewal of the fellowship, but this may not be done in consecutive years.

AMERICAN ORNITHOLOGISTS' UNION (AOU)

MRC-116
National Museum of Natural History
Smithsonian Institution, Washington, DC, 20560-0116, United States of America
Tel: (1) 202 357 2051
Fax: (1) 202 633 8084
Email: aou@nmnh.si.edu
www: http://www.aou.org
Contact: Secretary

The American Ornithologists' Union (AOU) is the oldest and largest organisation in the New World devoted to the scientific study of birds. The organisation's primary function is the publication and dissemination of ornithology research results.

AOU Student Research Awards
Subjects: Avian biology or ornithology.
Purpose: To provide funding for research.
Eligibility: Open to students or other non PhDs without recourse to regular funding. Applicants must be members of the AOU.
Level of Study: Doctorate, Graduate, Postgraduate, Predoctoral.
Type: Research grant.
Value: Varies, usually US$500-2,500.
Frequency: Annual.
Country of Study: Any country.
No. of awards offered: Varies.
Application Procedure: Applicants must complete an application form available from the Union. Applicants should also submit letters of recommendation and a proposed budget.
Closing Date: February 1st.
Funding: Private.

Marcia Brady Tucker Travel Award
Subjects: Ornithology.
Purpose: To assist student AOU members planning to give a paper to attend the annual meeting.
Eligibility: Open to students in a relevant discipline. Applicants must be student members of the organisation and planning to present a paper or poster at the annual meeting.
Level of Study: Unrestricted.
Type: Travel grant.
Value: Travel expenses.

Frequency: Annual.

Country of Study: Any country.

No. of awards offered: Varies.

Application Procedure: Applicants must submit eight copies of an expanded abstract of the presentation or poster they plan to present at the meeting, a curriculum vitae and anticipated transportation costs to the Student Awards Committee.

Closing Date: Three months prior to the meeting.

Funding: Private.

AMERICAN OSTEOPATHIC ASSOCIATION (AOA)

142 East Ontario Street, Chicago, IL, 60611, United States of America

Tel: (1) 312 202 8000

Fax: (1) 312 202 8200

Email: mwhitehead@aoa-net.org

www: http://www.aoa-net.org

Contact: Ms Mary Whitehead, Administrator, Research Services

The American Osteopathic Association (AOA) is organised to advance the philosophy and practice of osteopathic medicine by promoting excellence in education and research and the delivering of quality, cost-effective healthcare in a distinct, unified profession.

AOA Research Grants

Subjects: Osteopathy.

Purpose: To support clinical and basic science projects that lead to a better understanding and a more effective application of the philosophy and concepts of osteopathic medicine.

Eligibility: Open to an osteopathic physician who holds a faculty or staff appointment at an AOA accredited, affiliated, or approved osteopathic institution, or a biomedical researcher who demonstrates evidence of professional training and experience as appropriate for his or her individual discipline and who holds a faculty or staff appointment at an AOA accredited, affiliated or approved osteopathic institution. Osteopathic physicians who hold a faculty or staff appointment at an academic or health care institution having accreditation, affiliation or approval as appropriate for that institution's activities are also eligible. Applicants must be United States citizens.

Level of Study: Doctorate.

Type: Research grant.

Value: Varies.

Length of Study: One-two years.

Frequency: Annual.

Study Establishment: A university or hospital.

Country of Study: United States of America.

No. of awards offered: Dependent on funds available.

Application Procedure: The AOA Osteopathic Research Handbook contains grant applications and describes the programmes and eligibility requirements in greater detail. The Handbook is available from the Association.

Closing Date: December 1st.

No. of awards given last year: Eight.

No. of applicants last year: 20.

AMERICAN OTOLOGICAL SOCIETY RESEARCH FUND

UCSD Otolaryngology-Head & Neck Surgery
200 West Arbor Drive
Suite 8895, San Diego, CA, 92103-8895, United States of America

Tel: (1) 619 543 7896

Fax: (1) 619 543 5521

Email: jpharris@emory.org

www: http://itsa.ucsf.edu/~ajo/AOS/AOS.html

Contact: Dr Jeffrey P Harris, Secretary & Treasurer

The purposes of the American Otological Society are to advance and promote medical and surgical otology including the rehabilitation of the hearing impaired. The Society also encourages and promotes research in otology and related disciplines, conducts an annual meeting of the members for the presentation and discussion of scientific papers and the transaction of business affairs of the Society, and publishes the papers and discussion presented during the scientific programme and the proceedings of the business meetings.

American Otological Society Research Grants

Subjects: All aspects of otosclerosis, Meniere's disease and related disorders.

Eligibility: Open to physicians and doctoral level investigators.

Level of Study: Postdoctorate, Postgraduate.

Type: Research grant.

Value: Up to US$40,000 per year. No funding is provided for the investigator's salary.

Length of Study: One year, renewable.

Frequency: Annual.

Country of Study: United States of America or Canada.

No. of awards offered: Varies.

Closing Date: January 31st.

Funding: Private.

No. of awards given last year: Three.

No. of applicants last year: 10.

American Otological Society Research Training Fellowships

Subjects: All aspects of otosclerosis, Meniere's disease and related disorders.

Purpose: To support research.

Eligibility: Open to physicians, residents and medical students in the United States of America and Canada.

Level of Study: Postgraduate.

Type: Fellowship.

Value: Up to US$40,000 depending on position and institutional norms.

Length of Study: One-two years.

Frequency: Annual.

Country of Study: United States of America or Canada.

No. of awards offered: Varies.

Closing Date: January 31st.

No. of awards given last year: One.

No. of applicants last year: One.

Additional Information: The organisation requires institutional documentation that facilities and faculty are appropriate for the requested research.

AMERICAN PHILOSOPHICAL ASSOCIATION

University of Delaware, Newark, DE, 19716, United States of
America
Tel: (1) 302 831 1112
Fax: (1) 302 831 8690
www: http://www.udel.edu/apa
Contact: Dr Elizabeth Radcliffe, Executive Director

The American Philosophical Association was founded in 1900 to promote the exchange of ideas among philosophers, to encourage creative and scholarly activity in philosophy, to facilitate the professional
work and teaching of philosophers and to represent philosophy as a
discipline.

APA Book and Article Prizes

Subjects: Philosophy.
Purpose: To award a book prize and an article prize.
Eligibility: Open to any author of a book or article on philosophy
published in the two years preceding the award year provided they
qualify as a younger Scholar ie. is 40 years of age or younger in the
year of the volume, or has received his or her PhD 10 years or less
before that year.
Type: Prize.
Value: The Book Prize is US$4,000 and the Article Prize is
US$2,000.
Frequency: Annual.
No. of awards offered: One.
Application Procedure: Applicants must write for details or visit the
website.
Funding: Private.
Additional Information: Awarded with the help of the Matchette
Foundation. The award alternates each year.

Baumgardt Memorial Lecture

Subjects: Philosophy.
Eligibility: Open to candidates of any nationality, working in any
country, whose work has some bearing on the philosophical inter-
ests of the late David Baumgardt.
Level of Study: Postgraduate.
Value: US$5,000.
Frequency: Every five years.
Country of Study: Any country.
No. of awards offered: One.
Application Procedure: Applicants must write for details or visit the
website.
Funding: Private.

Frank Chapman Sharp Memorial Prize

Subjects: The philosophy of war and peace.
Purpose: To recognise unpublished work in philosophy.
Eligibility: Open to writers of unpublished essays or monographs on
the philosophy of war and peace.
Level of Study: Postgraduate.
Value: US$1,500.
Frequency: Every two years in odd numbered years.
Country of Study: Any country.
No. of awards offered: One.
Application Procedure: Applicants must write for details or visit the
website.
Funding: Private.
No. of awards given last year: One.
No. of applicants last year: Eight.

Rockefeller Prize

Subjects: Philosophy.
Purpose: To recognise unpublished work in philosophy.
Eligibility: Open to non academically affiliated philosophers, includ-
ing those that teach part-time.
Level of Study: Postgraduate.

Value: US$1,000.
Frequency: Every two years.
Country of Study: Any country.
No. of awards offered: One.
Application Procedure: Applicants must write for details or visit the
website.
Funding: Private.
Contributor: The Rockefeller Foundation.

AMERICAN PHILOSOPHICAL SOCIETY

104 South Fifth Street, Philadelphia, PA, 19106-3387, United States
of America
www: http://www.amphilsoc.org
Contact: Ms Eleanor Roach, Research Administrator

The American Philosophical Society is an eminent scholarly organisation of international reputation, and promotes useful knowledge in
the sciences and humanities through excellence in scholarly research, professional meetings, publications, library resources, and
community outreach.

Daland Fellowships in Clinical Investigation

Subjects: Medicine, neurology, paediatrics, psychiatry or surgery.
Purpose: To award a limited number of fellowships for research in
clinical medicine including the fields of internal medicine. For the
purposes of this award, the committee emphasises patient-orien-
tated research.
Eligibility: Candidates are expected to have held the MD, or PhD
degree for less than six years. The fellowship is intended to be the
first postclinical fellowship, but each case will be decided on its merits. Preference is given to candidates who have not more than two
years of postdoctoral training. Applicants must expect to perform
their research at an institution in the United States, under the supervision of a scientific adviser.
Level of Study: Research.
Type: Fellowship.
Value: US$50,000 for the first year and US$50,000 for the second
year.
Length of Study: The term of the fellowship is one year, with renewal for a further year if satisfactory progress is demonstrated. Requests for renewal are due on the first Friday of January. Payments
are made on July 15th and January 15th.
Frequency: Annual.
Application Procedure: Applicants must complete an application
form. Information and forms are available from the website. If electronic access is denied, forms can be requested by mail and must indicate when the MD or PhD degree was awarded. A stamped
addressed envelope should also be included. Candidates must be
nominated by their department chairman in a letter providing assurance that the nominee will work with the guidance of a scientific adviser of established reputation who has guaranteed adequate space,
supplies, etc. for the Fellow. The adviser need not be a member of
the department nominating the Fellow, nor need the activities of the
Fellow be limited to the nominating department. As a general rule,
no more than one fellowship will be awarded to a given institution in
the same year of competition. Application forms must be sent to the
Daland Fellowship Committee.
Closing Date: September 1st.
Funding: Private.
No. of awards given last year: Two.
No. of applicants last year: 20.

Franklin Research Grant Program

Subjects: Scholarly research.
Purpose: To contribute towards the cost of scholarly research in all
areas of knowledge except those in which support by government or
corporate enterprise is more appropriate. Scholarly research, as the
term is used here, covers most kinds of scholarly inquiry by individuals leading to publication. It does not include journalistic or other

writing for general readership, the preparation of textbooks, case-books, anthologies, or other materials for use by students, or the work of creative and performing artists.

Eligibility: Applicants are normally expected to have a doctorate, but applications are considered from persons whose publications display equivalent scholarly achievement. Grants are rarely made to persons who have held the doctorate less than a year, and never for predoctoral study or research. It is the Society's long standing practice to encourage younger Scholars. The Committee will seldom approve more than two grants to the same person within any five year period. Applicants may be residents of the United States, American citizens on the staffs of foreign institutions, and foreign nationals whose research can only be carried out in the United States. Institutions are not eligible to apply. Applicants expecting to conduct interviews in a foreign language must possess sufficient competence in that language, and must be able to read and translate all source materials.

Level of Study: Research.

Type: Grant.

Value: The maximum grant is US$6,000 for one year or US$12,000 for two years. The budget year corresponds to the calendar year, not the academic year. If an applicant receives an award for the same project from another granting institution, the Society will consider limiting its award to costs that are not covered by the other grant.

Frequency: Annual.

Country of Study: United States of America.

Application Procedure: Applicants must complete an application form. Information and forms are available from the website. If electronic access is denied, forms can be requested by mail. These must indicate the eligibility of both applicant and project, state the nature of the research eg. laboratory, archival or fieldwork and proposed use of the grant eg. travel or purchase of microfilm. Foreign nationals must specify the objects of their research, only available in the United States eg. indigenous plants, archival materials or architectural sites. A stamped addressed envelope should also be included. If forms are downloaded from the website, applicants must ensure that the page format is maintained and must print enough copies of the form for the letters of support.

Closing Date: October 1st for a January decision.

Funding: Private.

Additional Information: If an award is made and accepted, the recipient is required to provide the Society with a 250 word report on the research accomplished during tenure of the grant, and a one page financial statement.

Library Resident Research Fellowships

Subjects: Library collections research.

Purpose: To support research in the APS library's collections.

Eligibility: Scholars who reside beyond a 75 mile radius of Philadelphia. The fellowships are open to both United States citizens and foreign nationals who are holders of the PhD or equivalent, PhD candidates who have passed their preliminary exams and independent Scholars. Applicants in any relevant field of scholarship may apply.

Level of Study: Research.

Type: Fellowship.

Value: US$2,000 per month.

Length of Study: A minimum of one month and a maximum of three months.

Frequency: Annual.

Application Procedure: Applicants must submit the following: a cover sheet stating the name, title of project, expected period of residence, institutional affiliation, mailing address, telephone numbers, and email if available, social security number, a letter (not to exceed three single spaced pages) which briefly describes the project and how it relates to existing scholarship stating the specific relevance of the American Philosophical Society's collections to the project, and indicating expected results of the research such as publications. A curriculum vitae and one letter of reference (doctoral candidates must use their dissertation advisor) must also be included. Published guides to the Society's collections are available in most research libraries, and a list of these guides is available on request. Applicants are strongly encouraged to consult the Library staff by mail or phone

regarding the collections. Further details can be found on the website.

Closing Date: March 1st for a decision by May.

Funding: Private.

No. of awards given last year: 23.

No. of applicants last year: 90.

Phillips Fund Grants for Native American Research

Subjects: Linguistics and ethnohistory.

Purpose: For research into Native American linguistics and ethnohistory, ie. the continental United States and Canada.

Eligibility: Open to graduate students who have passed their qualifying examinations for either the Master's or doctorate degrees. Postdoctoral applicants are eligible.

Level of Study: Research.

Value: The average award is approx. US$1,200 and grants rarely exceed US$1,500. This is to cover travel, tapes and informants' fees and is not for general maintenance or the purchase of permanent equipment.

Length of Study: Ordinarily for one year.

Frequency: Annual.

Application Procedure: Applicants must complete an application form. A complete application includes all information requested on the form, the correct number of copies and three confidential letters supporting the application. It is the applicant's responsibility to verify that all materials reach the Society on time. Information and forms are available from the website. If electronic access is denied, forms can be requested by mail. These must indicate eligibility of both applicant and project, and state whether the field of research is linguistics or ethnohistory. A stamped addressed envelope should also be included. Applications should be addressed to Phillips Fund for Native American Research at the main address.

Closing Date: March 1st.

Funding: Private.

Additional Information: If an award is made and accepted, the recipient is required to provide the Society Library with a brief formal report and copies of any tape recordings, transcriptions, microfilms, etc. which may be acquired in the process of the grant funded research and a release for scholarly use.

Sabbatical Fellowship for the Humanities and Social Sciences

Subjects: Humanities and social sciences.

Purpose: To support the second half of an awarded sabbatical year.

Eligibility: Open to mid career faculty of universities and four year colleges in the United States which have been granted a sabbatical or research year, but for whom financial support from the parent institution is available for only the first half of the year. Candidates must not have had a financially supported leave during the three years prior to date of application. At the discretion of the review panels, the fellowship may be used to supplement another external award of similar purpose. The total external support cannot exceed the half year salary. The Society encourages candidates to use the resources of the American Philosophical Society Library, but this is not a requirement of the fellowship. There is no restriction on where the Fellow resides during the fellowship year, but an indication of the appropriateness of the available library resources should be given. The PhD must have been awarded no fewer than five and no more than 25 years prior to date of application.

Level of Study: Research.

Type: Award.

Value: US$40,000.

Length of Study: Tenure of the fellowship is for the second half of the academic year.

Frequency: Annual.

Application Procedure: Applicants must submit an application form. Information and forms are available from the website. If electronic access is denied, applicants can request forms by mail, but must be sure to state the date that their PhD was awarded, the end date of last financially supported leave and beginning date of sabbatical. A stamped addressed envelope should also be included.

Closing Date: November 1st.

Funding: Private.

Slater Fellowship in the History of Twentieth-Century Physical Sciences

Subjects: History of physical sciences in the twentieth-century.
Purpose: To support a doctoral dissertation.
Eligibility: Open both to candidates for the doctorate in the United States and to persons in doctoral degree programmes abroad who propose to spend the fellowship year in association with an American university or other appropriate American research institution. A candidate must have passed all preliminary examinations or equivalent, and the dissertation topic must focus on the history of the physical sciences in the twentieth-century. The Society encourages candidates to use the resources of the American Philosophical Society Library, but this is not a requirement of the Fellowship. There is no restriction on where the Fellow resides during the fellowship year.
Level of Study: Research.
Type: Fellowship.
Value: US$12,000 for one year only. Payments occur in two instalments, in separate calendar years. In compliance with federal regulations, the Society issues two 1099 miscellaneous income forms.
Length of Study: Tenure of the fellowship usually coincides with the academic year, though it may begin as early as July 1st.
Frequency: Annual.
Application Procedure: Applicants must complete an application form. Information and forms are available from the website. If electronic access is denied, applicants can request forms by mail indicating the eligibility of both applicant and project. A stamped addressed envelope must also be included. Applications must be sent to the Slater Fellowship Committee.
Closing Date: December 1st for notification in March.
Funding: Private.
No. of awards given last year: One.

AMERICAN PHYSIOLOGICAL SOCIETY (APS)

9650 Rockville Pike, Bethesda, MD, 20814-3991, United States of America
Tel: (1) 301 530 7164
Fax: (1) 301 571 8305
Email: info@aps.faseb.org
www: http://www.the-aps.onawards.htm
Contact: Ms Linda Jean Comley, Executive Assistant

The American Physiological Society (APS) is a non-profit scientific society devoted to fostering education, scientific research and the dissemination of information in the physiological sciences. By providing a spectrum of physiological information, the Society strives to play a role in the progress of science and the advancement of knowledge. The Society has integrated a prestigious awards programme providing funding to outstanding APS members, young investigators and scientists in need of funding to continue their research in physiology. Through its functions and activities, the Society plays an important role in the progress of science and the advancement of knowledge. The Society maintains staff and offices on the campus of the Federation of American Societies for Experimental Biology (FASEB) in Bethesda, Maryland.

AAAS Mass Media Science and Engineering Fellowship

Subjects: Physiology or any related subject.
Purpose: To enable promising young scientists to work in the newsroom of a newspaper, magazine, radio or television, sharpening their ability to communicate complex scientific issues to non scientists and helping to improve public understanding of science.
Eligibility: Open to graduate or postgraduate students of physiology, or a related subject, preferably with a background in scientific writing.
Level of Study: Graduate, Postgraduate.
Type: Studentship.

Value: Subsistence and travel costs.
Length of Study: 10 weeks.
Frequency: Annual.
Study Establishment: The newsroom of a newspaper, magazine or radio or television station in the United States of America.
Country of Study: United States of America.
No. of awards offered: One.
Application Procedure: Applicants must complete an application form, available from Alice Ra'anan, Public Affairs Office, American Physiological Society.
Closing Date: January 15th.
No. of awards given last year: One.
Additional Information: For further details, please contact the APS or refer to the website.

APS Conference Student Award

Subjects: Biology and physiology.
Purpose: To encourage the participation of young scientists in training at the APS conferences.
Eligibility: Open to graduate students wishing to present a contributed paper at an APS conference.
Level of Study: Graduate.
Type: Award.
Value: US$500 and complimentary conference registration.
Length of Study: The duration of the conference.
Frequency: Annual.
Study Establishment: Any APS conference.
Country of Study: United States of America.
No. of awards offered: Varies.
Application Procedure: Applicants must submit an abstract to APS. Candidates must indicate on the abstract page a desire to be considered for the award and should contact the APS for further details.
Closing Date: Please write for details.

APS Minority Travel Fellowship Awards

Subjects: Biology and physiology.
Purpose: To increase the participation of predoctoral and postdoctoral minority students in the physiological sciences.
Eligibility: Open to advanced predoctoral and postdoctoral students. Students in the APS Porter Physiology Development programme are also eligible. Minority faculty members at MBRS and MARC eligible institutions may also submit applications.
Level of Study: Postdoctorate, Predoctorate.
Type: Travel grant.
Value: Funds for travel to attend either the Experimental Biology meeting or one of the APS Conferences.
Length of Study: The duration of the conference or meeting.
Frequency: Dependent upon meetings scheduled.
Country of Study: United States of America.
No. of awards offered: Varies.
Application Procedure: Applicants must contact the Education Office of the APS for further details.
Closing Date: Please write for details.
Contributor: NIDDK and NIGMS.

Caroline tum Suden/Frances Hellebrandt Professional Opportunity Awards

Subjects: Biology and physiology.
Purpose: To provide funds for junior physiologists to attend and fully participate in the Experimental Biology meeting.
Eligibility: Open to graduate students or postdoctoral fellows who are APS members or sponsored by an APS member.
Level of Study: Graduate, Postdoctorate.
Type: Award.
Value: US$500 per award, complimentary registration for the Experimental Biology meeting and a waiver of the career resources replacement fees.
Length of Study: The duration of the conference.
Frequency: Annual.
Study Establishment: An APS Experimental Biology meeting.
Country of Study: United States of America.

No. of awards offered: 36.
Application Procedure: Applicants must submit an abstract to APS and should contact the Education Office for further details.
Closing Date: Please write for details.
No. of awards given last year: 36.
Additional Information: Recipients are obliged to attend the Experimental Biology meeting and present a paper.

Procter and Gamble Professional Opportunity Awards
Subjects: Biology and physiology.
Purpose: To provide funds to predoctoral students allowing them to fully participate in the Experimental Biology meeting.
Eligibility: Open to predoctoral students who are within 12-18 months of completing a PhD degree, who wish to present a paper at the meeting. Applicants must be student members of the APS or have an adviser or supporting sponsor who is an APS member.
Level of Study: Predoctorate.
Type: Award.
Value: US$500 per award.
Length of Study: The duration of the conference.
Frequency: Annual.
Study Establishment: The APS Experimental Biology meeting.
Country of Study: United States of America.
No. of awards offered: Varies.
Application Procedure: Applicants must submit an abstract to APS and should contact the Education Office for further details.
Closing Date: Please write for details.
No. of awards given last year: 12.

William T Porter Fellowship Award
Subjects: Biology and physiology.
Purpose: To support the training of talented students entering a career in physiology and to provide predoctoral fellowships for minority students, postdoctoral fellowships and limited sabbatical leave aid for faculty members of predominantly black universities who wish to update their expertise in physiology.
Eligibility: Open to underrepresented ethnic minority applicants who are citizens or permanent residents of the United States of America or its territories (African American, Hispanics, Native Americans, Native Alaskans or Native Pacific Islanders).
Level of Study: Doctorate, Graduate, Postdoctorate, Predoctorate.
Type: Fellowship.
Value: Tuition and expenses.
Length of Study: Varies.
Frequency: Annual.
Study Establishment: Universities or research establishments in the United States of America.
Country of Study: United States of America.
No. of awards offered: Varies.
Application Procedure: Applicants must contact the Education Office of the APS for further details.
Closing Date: January 15th and June 15th.
No. of applicants last year: Varies.

AMERICAN PLANNING ASSOCIATION

Fellowships & Council Administration
122 South Michigan Avenue
Suite 1600, Chicago, IL, 60605, United States of America
Tel: (1) 312 431 9100
Fax: (1) 312 431 9985
Email: mmorrison@planning.org
www: http://www.planning.org
Contact: Ms Margo Morrison, Assistant for Divisions

The American Planning Association and its professional institute, the American Institute of Certified Planners, are organised to advance the art and science of planning and to foster the activity of planning, physical, economic, and social, at the local, regional, state, and national levels. The objective of the Association is to encourage planning that will contribute to public well being by developing communities and environments that meet the needs of people and of society more effectively.

APA Planning Fellowships
Subjects: Planning, the rational and equitable distribution of resources and opportunities.
Purpose: To encourage students of certain minority backgrounds to enter the planning profession and to help such students who would otherwise be unable to continue their studies in planning.
Eligibility: Open to United States citizens who are African American, Hispanic or Native American students enrolled in a PAB accredited graduate planning programme. The programme is open to first and second year graduate students. First year students who receive fellowships are eligible to compete for an award the following year as well. Preference will be shown to full-time students. Candidates must be able to document the need for financial assistance.
Level of Study: Postdoctorate, Postgraduate.
Type: Fellowship.
Value: US$2,000-4,000 paid to the school in two equal instalments.
Frequency: Annual.
Country of Study: Any country.
No. of awards offered: Varies.
Application Procedure: Applicants must submit an application, available from the website including a two-five page personal and background statement, describing how the student's graduate education will be applied to career goals and why planning was chosen as a career. A curriculum vitae (optional if the information is supplied in the student's personal statement) should also be supplied, as well as letter(s) of recommendation (one letter is required but two will be accepted), a completed APA financial aid application form, and official transcripts of all previous collegiate and graduate academic work (sent directly from the office of the registrar). A photocopy of the university's letter indicating that the student has been accepted for graduate study in planning, written verification from the university's financial officer or copies of a school publication indicating the average cost of one academic year of graduate school are also required.
Closing Date: May 15th.
No. of awards given last year: Eight.

Charles Abrams Scholarship
Subjects: Planning.
Purpose: To aid students who intend to pursue careers as practising planners.
Eligibility: Open to United States citizens who have been accepted into the graduate planning programme of one of the five eligible schools. Incoming students are eligible. Applicants must be in need of financial assistance as determined by a review of the applicant's financial needs and be nominated by a department chair.
Level of Study: Postgraduate.
Type: Scholarship.
Value: US$2,000.
Frequency: Annual.
Study Establishment: Columbia University, Harvard University Graduate School of Architecture and Design, Massachusetts Institute of Technology, the New School for Social Research or the University of Pennsylvania.
Country of Study: United States of America.
No. of awards offered: One.
Application Procedure: Applicants must submit an application, available from the website, including a one-two page statement containing a description of the applicant's commitment to complete the planning curriculum of the university and to pursue a career in the planning profession. An outline of the applicant's academic qualifications, extra-curricular activities and reasons for believing a scholarship award is justified should also be included, as well as a short statement by the department chair discussing the reasons why the student was chosen. This should include comments on the student's strengths, areas of interest, and other abilities as appropriate, official transcripts of all previous collegiate and graduate academic work, and an official copy of Graduate Record Examination scores. An

eligible applicant should apply through one of the five designated schools on forms supplied to the participating university by APA.
Closing Date: April 30th.
No. of awards given last year: One.

AMERICAN POLITICAL SCIENCE ASSOCIATION (APSA)

Congressional Fellowship Program
1527 New Hampshire Avenue North West, Washington, DC, 20036, United States of America
Tel: (1) 202 483 2512
Fax: (1) 202 483 2657
Email: cfp@apsanet.org
www: http://www.apsanet.org
Contact: Ms Alison Macdonald, Programme Assistant

The American Political Science Association (APSA) is the major professional society for individuals engaged in the study of politics and government. APSA brings together political scientists from all fields of enquiry, regions, and occupational endeavours. While most members teach and conduct research in universities, a quarter work outside academia in government, research organisations, consulting firms, the news media or private enterprises.

APSA Congressional Fellowship Program for Political Scientists
Subjects: Experiential programme incorporating work in unpaid positions as legislative aides for Members of Congress or congressional committees.
Purpose: To allow participants to learn more about the legislative process through direct participation.
Eligibility: Open to mid career political scientists with a PhD completed within the past 15 years or near completion who can show scholarly interest in Congress and the policy making process. Minorities are encouraged to apply.
Level of Study: Postdoctorate.
Type: Fellowship.
Value: US$38,000 stipend paid over a 10 month period.
Length of Study: 10 months.
Frequency: Annual.
Country of Study: United States of America.
No. of awards offered: Varies.
Application Procedure: Applicants must contact APSA for details, all information is available from the website.
Closing Date: December 1st for entry in the following November.
Funding: Private.
No. of awards given last year: Six.

APSA Congressional Fellowships for Journalists
Subjects: Experiential programme incorporating work in unpaid positions as legislative aides for Members of Congress or congressional committees.
Purpose: To allow participants to learn more about the legislative process through direct participation.
Eligibility: Open to mid career professionals with a Bachelor's degree and an interest in Congress. Preference is given to candidates with a background in political reporting but without extensive experience in Washington. Candidates should have an absolute minimum of two years' full-time professional level experience in newspaper, magazine, radio or TV reporting at the time of application. Candidates with more than 10 years' experience will not be considered.
Level of Study: Professional development.
Type: Fellowship.
Value: US$38,000 stipend paid over a 10 month period.
Length of Study: 10 months.
Frequency: Annual.
Country of Study: United States of America.
No. of awards offered: Varies.

Application Procedure: Applicants must visit the website for further information.
Closing Date: December 1st for entry in the following November.
Funding: Private.
No. of awards given last year: Four.

APSA/MCI Communications Congressional Fellowships
Subjects: Experiential programme incorporating work in unpaid positions for Members of Congress or congressional committees.
Purpose: To allow participants to learn more about the legislative process through direct participation.
Eligibility: Open to mid career professionals who are PhD level Scholars of any discipline or journalists with demonstrated professional interest in telecommunications and who show promise of making significant contribution to the public's understanding of the political process. Journalists must have a Bachelor's degree and two to ten years' full-time professional experience in print or broadcast reporting, which may be as writers, producers, directors or researchers.
Level of Study: Postdoctorate, Professional development.
Type: Fellowship.
Value: US$38,000.
Length of Study: 10 months.
Frequency: Annual.
Country of Study: United States of America.
No. of awards offered: Varies.
Application Procedure: Applicants must contact APSA for details, all information is available from the website.
Closing Date: December 1st for entry in the following November.
Funding: Private.
No. of awards given last year: Two.

AMERICAN PSYCHOLOGICAL ASSOCIATION MINORITY FELLOWSHIPS PROGRAM (APA/MFP)

750 First Street North East, Washington, DC, 20002-4242, United States of America
Tel: (1) 202 336 6127
Fax: (1) 202 336 6012
Email: mfp@apa.org
www: http://www.apa.org/mfp

The American Psychological Association Minority Fellowships Program's (APA/MFP) objective is to increase the knowledge of issues related to ethnic minority mental health and to improve the quality of mental health and substance abuse treatment delivered to ethnic minority populations as consistent with Healthy People 2010, the Surgeon General's report on mental health, and other federal initiatives to reduce health disparities. This is done by providing financial support and professional guidance to individuals pursuing doctoral degrees in psychology and neuroscience.

MFP Clinical Training Fellowship
Subjects: The fellowship supports students in clinical, counselling and school psychology pursuing careers as mental health practitioners and clinical research serving ethnic minority populations.
Purpose: To improve the quality of mental health treatment and research on issues of concern to ethnic minority populations by providing financial support and professional guidance to individuals pursuing doctoral degrees in psychology and by increasing the knowledge on issues related to ethnic minority health.
Eligibility: Applicants must be American citizens or permanent residents enrolled full-time in an APA accredited doctoral programme at the time the fellowship is awarded. An additional factor among many considered is one's ethnic minority group including, but not limited to, blacks or African Americans, Alaskan Natives, American Indians, Asian Americans, Hispanics or Latinos and Pacific Islanders, and/or

those who can demonstrate commitment to a career in psychology related to ethnic minority health.
Level of Study: Doctorate.
Type: Fellowship.
Frequency: Annual.
Country of Study: Any country.
Application Procedure: Applicants must submit a completed application, essay, references, transcripts, and Graduate Record Examination scores. Further information and application forms are available on request.
Closing Date: January 15th.
Funding: Government.
Contributor: The Substance Abuse and Mental Health Administration.

MFP HIV/AIDS Research Fellowship

Subjects: Students specialising in such research areas as psychoneuroimmunology, HIV prevention, AIDS treatment adherence and provider education are encouraged to apply. Students of any speciality in psychology will be considered if they plan careers in HIV or AIDS research.
Purpose: To increase the number of psychologists with expertise in HIV and AIDS prevention and research related to ethnic minority populations, to increase the number of underrepresented minorities in the area of mental health research and HIV and AIDS research and prevention, and to increase the general knowledge of issues related to ethnic minority mental health and treatment.
Eligibility: Applicants must be American citizens or permanent residents with a visa who are enrolled full-time in a doctoral programme at the time the fellowship is awarded. An important goal of the programme is to increase representation of African American, Alaskan Native, Asian American, Mexican American, Native American, Pacific Islander and Puerto Rican students within psychology.
Level of Study: Doctorate.
Type: Fellowship.
Frequency: Annual.
Country of Study: United States of America.
Application Procedure: Applicants must submit a completed application, essay, references, transcripts, and Graduate Record Examination scores. Further information and application forms are available on request.
Closing Date: January 15th.
Funding: Government.
Contributor: The National Institute of Mental Health (NIMH).

MFP HIV/AIDS Research Training Fellowship

Subjects: Psychology with a speciality in HIV or AIDS research related to ethnic minority populations. Students specialising in such areas as HIV prevention, AIDS treatment adherence, provider education or psychoneuroimmunology are encouraged to apply. Students of any other speciality in psychology will be considered if they plan careers in HIV or AIDS research.
Purpose: To improve the quality of mental health treatment and research on issues of concern to ethnic minority populations by providing financial support and professional guidance to individuals pursuing doctoral degrees in psychology and by increasing the knowledge on issues related to ethnic minority mental health.
Eligibility: Applicants must be American citizens or permanent residents enrolled full-time in a doctoral programme at the time the fellowship is awarded. An additional factor among many considered is one's member in an ethnic minority group including, but not limited to, Black or African Americans, Alaskan Natives, American Indians, Asian Americans, Hispanics or Latinos and Pacific Islanders, and/or those who can demonstrate commitment to a career in psychology with a speciality in HIV and AIDS research related to ethnic minority populations.
Level of Study: Doctorate.
Type: Fellowship.
Frequency: Annual.
Country of Study: United States of America.
Application Procedure: Applicants must submit a completed application, essay, references, transcripts, and Graduate Record

Examination scores. Further information and application forms available on request.
Closing Date: January 15th.
Funding: Government.

MFP in Neuroscience Postdoctoral Fellowship

Subjects: Behavioural neuroscience, cellular neurobiology, cognitive neuroscience, computational neuroscience, developmental neurobiology, membrane biophysics, molecular neurobiology, neuroanatomy, neurobiology of ageing, neurobiology of disease, neurochemistry, neurogenetics, neuroimmunology, neuropathology, neuropharmacology, neurophysiology, neurotoxicology or systems neuroscience.
Purpose: To increase the number of ethnic minorities in neuroscience who conduct research in areas of importance to the National Institute of Mental Health.
Eligibility: Open to those with American citizenship or permanent residency and a PhD or MD degree and prior graduate training in neuroscience or in other basic sciences.
Level of Study: Postdoctorate.
Type: Fellowship.
Application Procedure: Applicants must visit the web page.
Closing Date: January 15th.
Additional Information: Benefits include travel funds to visit universities being considered for postdoctoral training, travel funds to attend the Society for Neuroscience's annual meeting and opportunities for mentoring and networking with neuroscientists.

MFP in Neuroscience Predoctoral Fellowship

Subjects: Behavioural neuroscience, cellular neurobiology, cognitive neuroscience, computational neuroscience, developmental neurobiology, membrane biophysics, molecular neurobiology, neuroanatomy, neurobiology of ageing, neurobiology of disease, neurochemistry, neurogenetics, neuroimmunology, neuropathology, neuropharmacology, neurophysiology, neurotoxicology or systems neuroscience.
Purpose: To increase the number of ethnic minorities in neuroscience who conduct research in areas of importance to the National Institute of Mental Health.
Eligibility: Open to those with American citizenship or permanent residency and a PhD or MD degree and prior graduate training in neuroscience or other basic science.
Level of Study: Predoctorate.
Type: Fellowship.
Application Procedure: Applicants should see the web page.

MFP Mental Health and Substance Abuse Services Fellowship

Subjects: The delivery of mental health and substance abuse services to ethnic minorities. Students specialising in clinical, school, and counselling psychology are encouraged to apply.
Purpose: To improve the availability of culturally competent mental health and substance abuse services provided to ethnic minority populations, to increase the number of ethnic minority mental health and substance abuse service providers to deliver services to ethnic minority programmes and to increase the general knowledge of issues related to ethnic minority mental health and substance abuse treatment.
Eligibility: Applicants must be American citizens or permanent residents with a visa who are enrolled full-time in a doctoral programme at the time the fellowship is awarded. An important goal of the programme is to increase representation of African American, Alaskan Native, Asian American, Mexican American, Native American, Pacific Islander and Puerto Rican students within psychology.
Level of Study: Doctorate.
Type: Fellowship.
Value: Varies.
Frequency: Annual.
Country of Study: United States of America.
Application Procedure: Applicants must submit a completed application, essay, references, transcripts and Graduate Record

Examination scores. Further information and application forms are available on request.
Closing Date: January 15th.
Funding: Government.
Contributor: The Substance Abuse and Mental Health Services Administration (SAMHSA).

MFP Mental Health Research Fellowship

Subjects: Psychopathology, community, developmental, educational, health, ageing and cognitive psychology or other related areas.
Purpose: To increase the number of psychologists with expertise in psychological or mental health research or prevention related to ethnic minority populations, to increase the number of underrepresented minorities in the area of mental health research and prevention, and to increase the general knowledge of issues related to ethnic minority mental health and psychological wellbeing.
Eligibility: Applicants must be American citizens or permanent residents with a visa who are enrolled full-time in a doctoral programme at the time the fellowship is awarded. An important goal of the programme is to increase representation of African American, Alaskan Native, Asian American, Mexican American, Native American, Pacific Islander and Puerto Rican students within psychology.
Level of Study: Doctorate.
Type: Fellowship.
Frequency: Annual.
Country of Study: United States of America.
Application Procedure: Applicants must submit a completed application, essay, references, transcripts and Graduate Record Examination scores. Further information and application forms available on request.
Closing Date: January 15th.
Funding: Government.
Contributor: The National Institute of Mental Health (NIMH).

MFP Neurosciences Training Fellowship

Subjects: Behavioural neuroscience, cellular neurobiology, cognitive neuroscience, computational neuroscience, developmental neurobiology, membrane biophysics, molecular microbiology, neuroanatomy, neurobiology, neurobiology of ageing, neurobiology of disease, neurochemistry, neurogenetics, neuroimmunology, neuropathology, neurophysiology, neurotoxicology or systems neuroscience.
Purpose: To increase the representation of underrepresented ethnic minorities in neuroscience, as well as increasing the pool of researchers and teachers whose work focuses on ethnic minority persons and issues.
Eligibility: Applicants must be American citizens or permanent residents who are enrolled full-time in a doctoral programme. An important goal of the programme is to increase representation of Black or African American, Alaskan Native, American Indian, Asian American, Hispanic or Latino and Pacific Islander students within neuroscience. However, the programme welcomes applications from all students, especially those interested in increasing the representation of underrepresented ethnic minorities in neuroscience, as well as increasing the pool of researchers and teachers whose work focuses on ethnic minority persons and issues.
Level of Study: Doctorate.
Type: Fellowship.
Frequency: Annual.
Country of Study: United States of America.
Application Procedure: Applicants must submit a completed application, essay, references, transcripts, and Graduate Record Examination scores. Further information and application forms are available on request.
Closing Date: January 15th.
Funding: Government.
Contributor: The National Institute of Mental Health.

MFP Research Training Fellowship

Subjects: Students specialising in such research areas as developmental, physiological, experimental, social, industrial, organisational, quantitative and educational psychology are encouraged to apply.
Purpose: To improve the quality of mental health treatment and research on issues of concern to ethnic minority populations by providing financial support and professional guidance to individuals pursuing doctoral degrees in psychology, and by increasing the knowledge on issues related to ethnic minority health.
Eligibility: Applicants must be American citizens or permanent residents with a visa who are enrolled full-time in a doctoral programme at the time the fellowship is awarded. An important goal of the programme is to increase representation of African American, Alaskan Native, Asian American, Mexican American, Native American, Pacific Islander and Puerto Rican students within psychology.
Level of Study: Doctorate.
Type: Fellowship.
Frequency: Annual.
Country of Study: United States of America.
Application Procedure: Applicants must submit a completed application, essay, references, transcripts and Graduate Record Examination scores. Further information and application forms are available on request.
Closing Date: January 15th.
Funding: Government.
Contributor: The National Institute of Mental Health.

AMERICAN PUBLIC POWER ASSOCIATION (APPA)

2301 M Street North West, Washington, DC, 20037, United States of America
Tel: (1) 202 467 2942
Fax: (1) 202 467 2992
Email: esullivan@appanet.org
www: http://www.appanet.org
Contact: Ms Elizabeth Sullivan, DEED Assistant

The American Public Power Association (APPA) is the national trade association representing more than 2,000 municipal and other state and local government owned electric utilities. APPA provides the necessary leadership in the evolution of the electric utility industry by advancing the principles of community ownership, promoting the development of a viable and sustainable competitive wholesale power market, and protecting the public interest against the abuse of market power.

DEED Scholarship

Subjects: Engineering, mathematics or computer science.
Purpose: To promote the involvement of students studying in energy related disciplines in the public power industry and to provide host utilities with technical assistance.
Eligibility: Open to students conducting research on a project approved by the sponsoring utility who will then submit a final report on the project, describing the activities, cost, bibliography, achievements, problems, results and recommendations. In addition, the student must write a two page abstract. Only students who are studying energy related disciplines at accredited colleges or universities are eligible for scholarships. Applicants will not be discriminated against on the basis of sex, race, religion, national origin or citizenship.
Level of Study: Doctorate, Graduate, Postdoctorate, Postgraduate.
Type: Scholarship.
Value: US$4,000.
Frequency: Annual.
Country of Study: Any country.
No. of awards offered: 10.
Application Procedure: Applications must be sent from a DEED member utility and must be dated and signed on the last page by an authorised individual at that utility. Applicants must have a DEED member utility sponsor their application.

Closing Date: Please contact the foundation.
Funding: Private.
No. of awards given last year: 10.

AMERICAN RESEARCH CENTER IN EGYPT (ARCE)

Emory Briarcliff Campus
1256 Briarcliff Road North East
Building A
Suite 423W, Atlanta, GA, 30306, United States of America
Tel: (1) 404 712 9854
Fax: (1) 404 712 9849
Email: arce@emory.edu
www: http://www.arce.org
Contact: Dr Susanne Thomas, Co-ordinator of US Operations

The American Research Center in Egypt (ARCE) is the professional society in the United States for specialists on Egypt of all periods. It is also a consortium of universities and museums that support archaeological and academic research in Egypt via fellowships, and whose membership is open to the public.

ARCE Fellowships
Subjects: Arts and humanities, Far East studies and social sciences.
Purpose: For dissertation or postdoctoral research in Egypt.
Eligibility: Open to United States nationals who are predoctoral candidates. Postdoctoral candidates should be United States nationals or foreign nationals who have been teaching at an American university for three years or more.
Level of Study: Doctorate, Postdoctorate.
Type: Fellowship.
Value: Varies.
Length of Study: 3-12 months.
Frequency: Annual.
Study Establishment: ARCE.
Country of Study: Egypt.
No. of awards offered: 10.
Application Procedure: Applicants must write for materials or download them from the website.
Closing Date: November 1st.
Funding: Government.
No. of awards given last year: Nine.
No. of applicants last year: 28.

Kress Fellowship in Egyptian Art and Architecture
Subjects: Egyptian art.
Purpose: For research on any period or aspect of Egyptian art and architecture.
Eligibility: Open to PhD candidates of any nationality enrolled in a United States university at any stage but the dissertation stage.
Level of Study: Doctorate.
Type: Fellowship.
Value: US$15,000.
Length of Study: Varies.
Frequency: Annual.
Country of Study: Egypt.
No. of awards offered: One.
Application Procedure: Applicants must write for materials.
Closing Date: November 1st.
Funding: Private.
Contributor: The Samuel H Kress Foundation.
No. of awards given last year: One.

AMERICAN RESEARCH INSTITUTE IN TURKEY (ARIT)

c/o University Museum
33rd & Spruce Streets, Philadelphia, PA, 19104-6324, United States of America
Tel: (1) 215 898 3474
Fax: (1) 215 898 0657
Email: leinwand@sas.upenn.edu
www: http://mec.sas.upenn.edu/ARIT
Contact: Ms Nancy Leinwand

The American Research Institute in Turkey's (ARIT) main aim is to support scholarly research in all fields of the humanities and social sciences in Turkey through administering fellowship programmes at the doctoral and postdoctoral level and through maintaining research centres in Ankara and Istanbul.

ARIT - Bosphorus University Language Fellowships
Subjects: (Spoken) Turkish language.
Purpose: To provide students with the opportunity of studying the Turkish language at all levels.
Eligibility: Open to graduate students enrolled in a degree programme of Turkish or related language and area studies. Applicants must be United States citizens or permanent residents and have at least two years of college level Turkish language study or its equivalent.
Level of Study: Postgraduate.
Type: Fellowship.
Value: Tuition, travel and a maintenance stipend of varying amounts.
Length of Study: Eight weeks during July and August, plus additional travel time.
Frequency: Annual.
Study Establishment: Bosphorus University, Istanbul.
Country of Study: Turkey.
No. of awards offered: 10-15.
Application Procedure: Applicants must submit an application form, statement and references.
Closing Date: February 15th.
Funding: Government, Private.
Contributor: USIA.
No. of awards given last year: 15.
No. of applicants last year: 70.

ARIT - National Endowment for the Humanities for Advanced Fellowships for Research in Turkey
Subjects: All subjects of the humanities and interdisciplinary approaches of art, archaeology, language and history.
Purpose: To support research on ancient, medieval or modern times in any field of the humanities and social sciences.
Eligibility: Applicants must be citizens of the United States or three year residents.
Level of Study: Postdoctorate, Professional development.
Type: Fellowship.
Value: Stipends generally range from US$10,000-30,000.
Length of Study: Postdoctoral and dissertation research fellowships may be held for terms of two months to one year.
Frequency: Annual, if funds are available.
Study Establishment: In either of ARIT's two research establishments in Ankara and Istanbul, Turkey.
Country of Study: Turkey.
No. of awards offered: Two-four.
Application Procedure: Applicants must submit an application form, project statement and references.
Closing Date: November 15th.
Funding: Government.
Contributor: The United States Information Agency.

ARIT Humanities and Social Science Fellowships
Subjects: All fields of the humanities and social sciences.

Purpose: To encourage research on Turkey in ancient, medieval and modern times.

Eligibility: Scholars and advanced graduate students engaged in research on ancient, medieval or modern times in Turkey, in any field of the humanities and social sciences are eligible. Student applicants must have fulfilled all requirements for the doctorate except the dissertation. Applicants must be United States citizens and/or be members in good standing of educational institutions in the United States or Canada. While grants for tenures of up to one year will be considered, some preference is given to projects of shorter duration.

Level of Study: Doctorate, Postdoctorate.

Type: Fellowship.

Value: Varies, depending on the length of the study period.

Length of Study: 2-12 months, renewable only in exceptional cases.

Frequency: Annual.

Study Establishment: In either of ARIT's two research establishments in Ankara and Istanbul, Turkey.

Country of Study: Turkey.

No. of awards offered: 6-12.

Application Procedure: Applicants must submit six copies of an original application to the ARIT United States headquarters in Philadelphia. Student applicants must provide a copy of their graduate transcript. Please visit the website for further details.

Closing Date: November 15th.

Funding: Government, Private.

Contributor: The United States Information Agency.

No. of awards given last year: 16.

No. of applicants last year: 67.

Additional Information: Hostel, research and study facilities are available at ARIT's branch centres in Istanbul and Ankara.

Mellon Research Fellowship

Subjects: Humanities and social sciences.

Purpose: To bring Eastern and Central European scholars to Turkey to carry out research in the humanities and social sciences.

Eligibility: Open to Bulgarian, Czech, Slovak, Polish, Hungarian and Romanian nationals.

Level of Study: Postdoctorate.

Type: Fellowship.

Value: Up to US$11,500.

Length of Study: Two-three months.

Frequency: Annual.

Study Establishment: In either of ARIT's two research establishments in Ankara and Istanbul, Turkey.

Country of Study: Turkey.

No. of awards offered: Three-four.

Application Procedure: Applicants must submit an application form, project statement and references.

Closing Date: March 5th.

Funding: Private.

Contributor: The Mellon Foundation.

No. of awards given last year: Three-four.

No. of applicants last year: 18.

Additional Information: Further information is available on request or from the website.

Samuel H Kress Foundation Graduate Fellowships in Archaeology and the History of Art

Subjects: History of art and archaeology.

Purpose: To fund doctoral dissertation research in Turkey in the fields of art history and archaeology.

Eligibility: Applicants must be degree candidates who have completed all preliminary requirements for the PhD in art history and/or archaeology and who are enrolled at United States institutions.

Level of Study: Doctorate.

Type: Fellowship.

Value: Up to US$15,000, depending on the fellowship tenure of between 2-12 months.

Length of Study: 4-12 months.

Frequency: Annual.

Study Establishment: In either of ARIT's two research establishments in Ankara and Istanbul, Turkey.

Country of Study: Turkey.

No. of awards offered: Two-four.

Application Procedure: Applicants must submit an application form accompanied by three letters of recommendation.

Closing Date: November 15th.

Funding: Private.

Contributor: The Samuel H Kress Foundation.

No. of awards given last year: Two.

No. of applicants last year: 14.

AMERICAN SCHOOL OF CLASSICAL STUDIES AT ATHENS (ASCSA)

6-8 Charlton Street, Princeton, NJ, 08540-5232, United States of America

Tel: (1) 609 683 0800

Fax: (1) 609 924 0578

Email: ascsa@ascsa.org

www: http://www.ascsa.org

Contact: Ms Mary E Darlington, Assistant to the Executive Vice President

Established in 1881, the American School of Classical Studies at Athens (ASCSA) offers both graduate students and scholars the opportunity to study Greek civilisation, first hand in Greece. The ASCSA supports and encourages the teaching of archaeology, art, history, language and literature of Greece from early times to the present.

ASCSA Fellowships

Subjects: Classical philology and archaeology, post classical Greek studies or a related field.

Eligibility: Open to students at colleges or universities in the United States of America or Canada who have a BA but not a PhD, and who are preparing for an advanced degree in classical studies or a related field.

Level of Study: Graduate, Postgraduate.

Type: Fellowship.

Value: US$8,840 stipend plus fees, room and partial board.

Length of Study: One academic year.

Frequency: Annual.

Study Establishment: The American School of Classical Studies at Athens.

Country of Study: Greece.

No. of awards offered: Eight.

Application Procedure: Applicants must complete an official application, available on request or from the website. Applications are judged on the basis of credentials and competitive examinations in Greek language, history and archaeology. Fulbright Fellowships are also sometimes available for work at the School. Application to the School must be made simultaneously with the application for a Fulbright grant. Two fellowships may not be held concurrently.

Closing Date: January 15th.

Funding: Private.

No. of awards given last year: 13.

No. of applicants last year: 18.

Additional Information: Further information is available on request or from the website.

ASCSA Research Fellow in Faunal Studies

Subjects: Biological sciences, life sciences and archaeological sciences.

Purpose: To study faunal remains from archaeological contexts in Greece.

Eligibility: Applicants must write for details.

Level of Study: Doctorate, Postdoctorate, Postgraduate.

Type: Fellowship.

Value: Stipend of US$13,000-25,000 depending on seniority and experience.
Length of Study: One academic year.
Frequency: Annual.
Study Establishment: The Malcolm H Wiener Research Laboratory for Archaeological Science at the American School of Classical Studies at Athens.
Country of Study: Greece.
No. of awards offered: One.
Application Procedure: Applicants must contact Dr Sherry C Fox by fax on (1) 301 725 0584, or by email on sfox@ascsa.edu.gr for application guidelines and further information.
Closing Date: January 15th.
Funding: Private.
No. of awards given last year: One.
No. of applicants last year: Seven.
Additional Information: Further information can be found on the website.

ASCSA Research Fellow in Geoarchaeology

Subjects: Earth sciences, geological sciences and archaeological sciences.
Purpose: To support research on a geo-archaeological topic in Greece.
Eligibility: Applicants must write for details.
Level of Study: Doctorate, Postdoctorate, Postgraduate.
Type: Fellowship.
Value: Stipend of US$13,000-25,000 depending on seniority and experience.
Length of Study: One academic year.
Frequency: Annual.
Study Establishment: The Malcolm H Wiener Research Laboratory for Archaeological Science at the American School of Classical Studies at Athens.
Country of Study: Greece.
No. of awards offered: One.
Application Procedure: Applicants must contact Professor Nancy Wilkie by fax on (1) 507 646 4223, or by email on nwilkie@carleton.edu or Dr Sherry C Fox by fax on (1) 301 725 0584, or by email on sfox@ascsa.edu.gr for application guidelines and further information.
Closing Date: January 15th.
Funding: Private.
No. of awards given last year: One.
No. of applicants last year: Eight.

ASCSA Summer Sessions

Subjects: Archaeology, with emphasis on the topography and antiquities of Greece.
Purpose: To aid those who wish to become acquainted with Greece and its antiques in a limited time, and to improve their understanding of the relationship between the country, its monuments, landscape, climate, history, literature and culture.
Eligibility: Open to graduate students, and high school and college teachers.
Level of Study: Graduate, Postgraduate.
Type: Scholarship.
Value: To cover tuition, room and partial board up to US$2,950.
Length of Study: Six weeks.
Frequency: Annual.
Study Establishment: At one of the two Summer sessions of the School in Athens.
Country of Study: Greece.
No. of awards offered: Six.
Application Procedure: Applicants must submit a completed application form, transcripts and letters of recommendation. Applications should be made to the Committee on the Summer Sessions.
Closing Date: January 15th.
Funding: Private.
No. of awards given last year: 13.
No. of applicants last year: 60.

Additional Information: Further information can be found on the website.

J Lawrence Angel Fellowship in Human Skeletal Studies

Subjects: Biological sciences, life sciences and archaeological sciences.
Purpose: To study human skeletal remains from archaeological contexts in Greece.
Eligibility: Applicants must write for details.
Level of Study: Doctorate, Postdoctorate, Postgraduate.
Type: Fellowship.
Value: Stipend of US$13,000-25,000 depending on seniority and experience.
Length of Study: One academic year.
Frequency: Annual.
Study Establishment: The Malcolm H Wiener Research Laboratory for Archaeological Science at the American School of Classical Studies at Athens.
Country of Study: Greece.
No. of awards offered: One.
Application Procedure: Applicants must contact Professor Nancy Wilkie by fax on (1) 507 646 4223, or by email on nwilkie@carleton.edu or Dr Sherry C Fox by fax on (1) 301 725 0584, or by email on sfox@ascsa.edu.gr for application guidelines and further information.
Closing Date: January 15th.
Funding: Private.
Contributor: The Malcolm H Wiener Research Laboratory for Archaeological Sciences at the American School at Athens.
No. of awards given last year: One.
No. of applicants last year: Six.
Additional Information: Further information is available from the website.

For further information contact:

The Malcolm H Wiener Laboratory
American School of Classical Studies at Athens
54 Souidias Street, Athens, GR-10676, Greece
Tel: (30) 1 723 6313
Fax: (30) 1 729 4047
Email: sfox@asca.edu.gr
Contact: Dr Sherry Fox

Jacob Hirsch Fellowship

Subjects: Pre-classical, classical, or post-classical archaeology.
Eligibility: Open to graduate students of American or Israeli institutions writing a dissertation, or to recent PhD graduates completing a project, such as a dissertation for publication. Applications will be judged on the basis of appropriate credentials including referees.
Level of Study: Postdoctorate, Postgraduate.
Type: Fellowship.
Value: US$8,840 stipend plus room, board and waiver of fees.
Length of Study: One academic year, non renewable.
Frequency: Annual.
Study Establishment: The American School of Classical Studies at Athens.
Country of Study: Greece.
No. of awards offered: One.
Application Procedure: Applicants must submit three letters of recommendation, transcripts and a detailed description of projects to be pursued in Greece. Applicants must apply for membership at the school simultaneously with application for the Hirsch.
Closing Date: January 15th.
Funding: Private.
No. of awards given last year: One.
Additional Information: Further information can be found on the website.

M Alison Frantz Fellowship in Post-Classical Studies at The Gennadius Library (formerly known as the Gennadeion Fellowship)

Subjects: Post classical studies in late antiquity, Byzantine studies, post Byzantine studies and modern Greek studies.
Eligibility: Open to PhD candidates or recent PhDs from a United States of America or Canadian institution. Candidates must show a need to use the Gennadius Library.
Level of Study: Doctorate, Postdoctorate.
Type: Fellowship.
Value: US$8,840 stipend plus room, board and waiver of fees.
Length of Study: One academic year.
Frequency: Annual.
Study Establishment: The American School of Classical Studies at Athens, Gennadius Library.
Country of Study: Greece.
No. of awards offered: One.
Application Procedure: Applicants must submit a curriculum vitae, project description and two letters of support to the Chair of Gennadius Library Committee.
Closing Date: January 15th.
Funding: Private.
No. of awards given last year: One.
No. of applicants last year: Eight.
Additional Information: Further information can be found on the website.

NEH Research Fellowships

Subjects: Ancient, classical and post classical studies, including but not limited to, history, philosophy, language, art and archaeology of Greece and the Greek world, art history, literature, philology, architecture, archaeology, anthropology, metallurgy and environmental studies from prehistoric times to the present.
Eligibility: Open to doctoral and postdoctoral Scholars who are United States of America citizens or foreign nationals who have lived in the United States of America for the three years immediately preceding the application deadline.
Level of Study: Doctorate, Postdoctorate.
Type: Fellowship.
Value: Maximum stipend of US$16,000 for a four month project and US$40,000 for a 10 month project.
Length of Study: One academic year.
Frequency: Annual.
Study Establishment: The American School of Classical Studies at Athens.
Country of Study: Greece.
No. of awards offered: Two-five.
Application Procedure: Applicants must write for details or visit the website.
Closing Date: November 15th.
Funding: Government.
No. of awards given last year: Three.
No. of applicants last year: 16.
Additional Information: Further information can be found on the website.

Samuel H Kress Fellowship in Classical Art History

Subjects: Classical art history.
Eligibility: Open to students from the United States of America or Canadian institutions who have completed one year at the school.
Level of Study: Postgraduate.
Type: Fellowship.
Value: Varies.
Length of Study: One academic year.
Frequency: Annual.
Study Establishment: The American School of Classical Studies at Athens.
Country of Study: Greece.
No. of awards offered: One.
Application Procedure: Applicants must write to the director of the school in Athens for further information.

Closing Date: January 15th.
Funding: Private.
No. of awards given last year: One.

For further information contact:

School Director
The American School of Classical Studies at Athens
54 Soudias Street, Athens, GR-10676, Greece
Tel: (30) 1 723 6313
Fax: (30) 1 729 4047

Samuel H Kress Joint Athens-Jerusalem Fellowship

Subjects: Ancient or post classical art history, architecture and archaeology.
Purpose: To enable doctoral students to conduct research in Greece and Israel in the same academic year and to promote better understanding of interrelationships between the cultures, languages, literature and history of the Aegean and the Near East.
Eligibility: Open to any nationality but applicants must be at a college or university in the United States of America or Canada.
Level of Study: Postgraduate.
Type: Fellowship.
Value: Stipend of US$7,600 plus room and partial board at each of the two institutions.
Length of Study: One academic year.
Frequency: Annual.
Study Establishment: The American School of Classical Studies at Athens and the W F Albright Institute of Archaeological Research in Jerusalem.
Country of Study: Greece or Israel.
No. of awards offered: One.
Application Procedure: Applicants must write for details or visit the website.
Closing Date: November 15th.
Funding: Private.
No. of awards given last year: One.
No. of applicants last year: Five.
Additional Information: Further information can be found on the website.

For further information contact:

Albright Institute
c/o Department of Religious Studies
John Carroll University
20700 North Park Boulevard
University Heights, OH, 44118, United States of America
Tel: (1) 216 397 4705
Fax: (1) 216 397 4478
Email: spencer@jcu.edu
Contact: Professor John Spencer

AMERICAN SCHOOLS OF ORIENTAL RESEARCH (ASOR)

Boston University
656 Beacon Street
5th Floor, Boston, MA, 02215-2010, United States of America
Tel: (1) 617 353 6570
Fax: (1) 617 353 6575
Email: asor@bu.edu
www: http://www.asor.org
Contact: Ms Britt Hartenberger, Senior Staff Assistant

The American Schools of Oriental Research's (ASOR) mission is to initiate, encourage and support research into, and public understanding of, the peoples and cultures of the Far East from the earliest times, by fostering original research, archaeological excavations and explorations and by encouraging scholarship in the basic languages, cultural histories and traditions of the Far Eastern world.

AIAR Annual Professorship

Subjects: Near Eastern archaeology, geography, history and biblical studies.
Purpose: To support studies in Near Eastern archaeology, geography, history and biblical studies.
Eligibility: Open to qualified applicants of any nationality.
Level of Study: Postdoctorate.
Type: Professorship.
Value: US$17,200 plus US$15,800 for room and half board for appointee and spouse at the Institute (the entire award is available via USIA for an appointee who is an United States citizen).
Length of Study: 10 months.
Frequency: Annual.
Study Establishment: The W F Albright Institute of Archaeological Research in Jerusalem.
Country of Study: Israel.
No. of awards offered: One.
Application Procedure: Applicants must write for details.
Closing Date: October 12th.
No. of awards given last year: One.
No. of applicants last year: Five.
Additional Information: The professorship period should be continuous, without frequent trips outside the country.

For further information contact:

Department of Religious Studies
John Carroll University
20700 North Park Boulevard, University Heights, OH, 44118, United States of America
Email: spencer@jcu.edu
Contact: Dr John R Spencer

AIAR Islamic Studies Fellowship

Subjects: Islamic archaeology, art and architecture.
Eligibility: Candidates must have expertise in research and teaching in Islamic archaeology, art and architecture.
Level of Study: Postgraduate.
Type: Fellowship.
Value: US$20,000. The stipend is US$11,900 with the remainder for room and half board at the Institute. This amount is dependent on funding.
Length of Study: 10 months.
Frequency: Annual.
Study Establishment: The W F Albright Institute of Archaeological Research in Jerusalem.
Country of Study: Israel.
No. of awards offered: One.
Application Procedure: Applicants must write for details.
Closing Date: October 12th.
No. of awards given last year: One.
No. of applicants last year: Two.
Additional Information: During the period of the appointment the Fellow will teach regular courses in the Department of Archaeology at one of the local Palestinian universities.

For further information contact:

Department of Religious Studies
John Carrol University
20700 North Park Boulevard, University Heights, OH, 44118, United States of America
Contact: Dr John R Spencer

Andrew W Mellon Foundation Fellowships

Subjects: Humanities.
Purpose: To support Eastern European scholars.
Eligibility: Open to Bulgarian, Czech, Hungarian, Polish, Romanian and Slovak Scholars who have obtained a doctorate by the time the fellowship is awarded.
Level of Study: Postdoctorate.
Type: Fellowship.
Value: US$34,500 for the three awards.
Length of Study: Three months.

Frequency: Annual.
Study Establishment: The W F Albright Institute of Archaeological Research in Jerusalem.
Country of Study: Israel.
No. of awards offered: Three.
Application Procedure: Applicants must write for details.
Closing Date: April 1st.
No. of awards given last year: Three.
No. of applicants last year: 15.
Additional Information: Candidates should not be permanently resident outside the six countries concerned.

For further information contact:

Department of Religious Studies
John Carroll University
20700 North Park Boulevard, University Heights, OH, 44118, United States of America
Email: spencer@jcu.edu
Contact: Dr John R Spencer

ASOR Mesopotamian Fellowship

Subjects: Mesopotamian civilisation.
Purpose: To support field or museum research in ancient Mesopotamian civilisation.
Eligibility: Open to predoctoral and postdoctoral Scholars.
Level of Study: Doctorate, Postdoctorate.
Type: Fellowship.
Value: US$7,000.
Length of Study: Three-six months.
Frequency: Annual.
Study Establishment: Schools of Oriental Research in The United States of America.
Country of Study: Any country.
No. of awards offered: One.
Application Procedure: Applicants must write for details and an application form.
Closing Date: February 1st.
Funding: Private.
No. of awards given last year: One.
No. of applicants last year: Five.

CAORC Fellowships

Subjects: Humanities and social sciences.
Purpose: To support students undertaking study in the fields of humanities and social sciences in Jordan.
Eligibility: Open to predoctoral students and postdoctoral Scholars of United States nationality.
Level of Study: Doctorate, Graduate, Postdoctorate, Postgraduate, Predoctorate, Professional development.
Type: Fellowship.
Value: US$17,000 maximum for fellowships, and US$26,700 for senior fellowships.
Length of Study: Two-six months.
Frequency: Annual.
Study Establishment: The American Center of Oriental Research, Amman.
Country of Study: Jordan.
No. of awards offered: More than six.
Application Procedure: Applicants must write for details.
Closing Date: February 1st.
Funding: Government.

CAORC Senior (Postdoctoral) Fellowships

Subjects: Fields of study include anthropology, economics, history, international relations, journalism and political science.
Purpose: To support research.
Eligibility: Open to United States citizens only.
Level of Study: Postdoctorate.
Type: Fellowship.
Value: US$26,700 maximum.
Length of Study: Two-four months.

Frequency: Annual.
Study Establishment: The American Center of Oriental Research, Amman.
Country of Study: Jordan.
No. of awards offered: Three or more.
Application Procedure: Applicants must write for details.
Closing Date: February 1st.
Funding: Government.

Council of American Overseas Research Centers (CAORC) Fellowships for Advanced Multi-Country Research

Subjects: Multi-country significance in the fields of humanities, social sciences, and related natural sciences in countries in the Near and Middle East and South Asia.
Eligibility: Open to doctoral candidates and established Scholars with United States citizenship.
Level of Study: Doctorate.
Type: Fellowship.
Value: Up to US$6,000 plus an additional US$3,000 for travel.
Frequency: Annual.
Study Establishment: The W F Albright Institute of Archaeological Research in Jerusalem.
Country of Study: Near or Middle East Asia, or South Asia.
No. of awards offered: Six.
Application Procedure: Applicants must write for details.
Closing Date: December 31st.
Additional Information: Preference will be given to candidates examining comparative or cross-regional questions requiring research in two or more countries.

For further information contact:

Grants Management Officer
CAORC
Smithsonian Institution
1c 3123 MRC 705, Washington, DC, 20560, United States of America
Email: siwp01.ic.bwack@ic.si.edu
www: http://www.caorc.org

Cyprus American Archaeological Research Institute (CAARI) Anita Cecil Odonovan Fellowship

Subjects: Archaeology.
Purpose: To assist with expenses for research to be conducted in Cyprus.
Level of Study: Graduate.
Type: Fellowship.
Value: Up to US$750.
Length of Study: One-three months.
Frequency: Annual.
Study Establishment: Cyprus American Archaeological Research Institute.
Country of Study: Cyprus.
No. of awards offered: One.
Application Procedure: Applicants must submit a description of their project outlining its purpose, importance, budget and duration, and a curriculum vitae listing name, address, education, field experience and relevant publications. Two letters of recommendation should also be submitted directly from the referees.
Closing Date: February 1st.
Funding: Private.

Cyprus American Archaeological Research Institute (CAARI) Stuart Swiny & Helena Wylde Grant

Subjects: Archaeology.
Purpose: To support participation in any phase or aspect of a project in Cyprus which has been approved by ASOR's Committee on Archaeological Policy (CAP).
Eligibility: Open to Scholars of any nationality.
Level of Study: Graduate.
Type: Fellowship.

Value: Stipend of US$750 to help cover room and board.
Frequency: Annual.
Study Establishment: CAARI.
Country of Study: Cyprus.
No. of awards offered: One.
Application Procedure: Applicants must submit a description of their project outlining its purpose, importance, budget and duration, and a curriculum vitae listing name, address, education, field experience and relevant publications. Two letters of recommendation should also be submitted directly from the referees.
Closing Date: February 1st.

George A Barton Fellowship

Subjects: Near Eastern archaeology, geography, history and biblical studies.
Eligibility: Open to seminarians, predoctoral students and recent PhD recipients specialising in the appropriate subject fields. This award may not be used during the Summer.
Level of Study: Doctorate, Postdoctorate, Postgraduate.
Type: Fellowship.
Value: US$7,000. The stipend is US$2,950 and the remainder covers room and half board at the Institute.
Length of Study: Five months.
Frequency: Annual.
Study Establishment: The W F Albright Institute of Archaeological Research in Jerusalem.
Country of Study: Israel.
No. of awards offered: One.
Application Procedure: Applicants must complete an application form. Further information and forms are available on request.
Closing Date: October 12th.
No. of awards given last year: One.
No. of applicants last year: 12.
Additional Information: The research period should be continuous, without frequent trips outside the country.

For further information contact:

Department of Religious Studies
John Carroll University
North Park Boulevard, University Heights, OH, 44118, United States of America
Contact: Dr John R Spencer

Harrell Family Fellowship

Subjects: Archaeology.
Purpose: To support participation in an ACOR supported archaeological project or an ACOR funded archaeological research project.
Eligibility: Open to enrolled graduate students of any nationality.
Level of Study: Graduate.
Type: Fellowship.
Value: US$1,500.
Frequency: Annual.
Country of Study: Jordan.
No. of awards offered: One.
Application Procedure: Applicants must write for details.
Closing Date: February 1st.

Jennifer C Groot Fellowship

Subjects: Archaeology.
Purpose: To support beginners in archaeological fieldwork who have been accepted as staff members on archaeological projects with ASOR/CAP affiliation in Jordan.
Eligibility: Open to United States and Canadian citizens who are graduate students and have been accepted as staff members on archaeological projects.
Level of Study: Graduate.
Type: Fellowship.
Value: US$1,500.
Frequency: Annual.
Country of Study: Jordan.
No. of awards offered: Three.

Application Procedure: Applicants must write for details.
Closing Date: February 1st.
Funding: Private.
Additional Information: Further information is available on request.

Kress Fellowship in the Art and Archaeology of Jordan

Subjects: History of art is defined to include art history, archaeology, architectural history, and in some cases classical studies. A topic should be focused on some aspect of the artistic legacy of a specific culture, site, or period.
Purpose: To support students completing dissertation research in an art history topic.
Eligibility: Applicants must be American PhD candidates or those matriculated at United States institutions.
Level of Study: Doctorate.
Type: Fellowship.
Value: US$14,000 maximum, amount dependent on funding available.
Length of Study: Three-six months.
Frequency: Annual.
Study Establishment: The American Center of Oriental Research, Amman.
Country of Study: Jordan.
No. of awards offered: More than one.
Application Procedure: Applicants must write for details.
Closing Date: February 1st.
Funding: Private.

NEH Fellowship

Subjects: Archaeology, anthropology, geography, ancient history, philology, epigraphy, Biblical studies, Islamic studies, religion, art history, literature, philosophy or related disciplines.
Purpose: To support scholars who hold a PhD.
Eligibility: Open to Scholars in Near Eastern studies holding a PhD as of January 1st 2000, who are United States citizens or alien residents residing in the country for the last three years.
Level of Study: Postdoctorate.
Type: Fellowship.
Value: US$30,000 for one award.
Length of Study: One year.
Frequency: Annual.
Study Establishment: The W F Albright Institute of Archaeological Research in Jerusalem.
Country of Study: Israel.
No. of awards offered: One.
Application Procedure: Applicants must write for details.
Closing Date: October 12th.
Funding: Government.
No. of awards given last year: Two.
No. of applicants last year: Eight.
Additional Information: The research period should be continuous, without frequent trips outside the country.

For further information contact:

Department of Religious Studies
John Carroll University
20700 North Park Boulevard, University Heights, OH, 44118, United States of America
Email: spencer@jcu.edu
Contact: Dr John R Spencer

NEH Postdoctoral Research Award

Subjects: Fields of study include both modern and classical languages, linguistics, literature, history, jurisprudence, philosophy, archaeology, comparative religion, ethics, the history, criticism, and theory of the arts.
Purpose: To support postdoctoral scholars.
Eligibility: Open to United States citizens or foreign nationals who are living in the United States of America.
Level of Study: Postdoctorate.
Type: Fellowship.

Value: US$20,000 maximum.
Length of Study: Four-six months.
Frequency: Annual.
Study Establishment: The American Center of Oriental Research, Amman.
Country of Study: Jordan.
No. of awards offered: One.
Application Procedure: Applicants must write for details.
Closing Date: February 1st.
Funding: Government.

Pierre and Patricia Bikai Fellowship

Subjects: Archaeology.
Eligibility: Open to participants on an archaeological research project operating in Jordan.
Level of Study: Graduate.
Type: Fellowship.
Value: Room and board at ACOR and a monthly stipend of US$400.
Length of Study: One-two months.
Frequency: Annual.
Country of Study: Jordan.
No. of awards offered: One.
Application Procedure: Applicants must write for details and an application form or download it from the website.
Closing Date: February 1st.
Funding: Private.
Additional Information: This fellowship may be combined with the Groot or Harrell Fellowships.

Samuel H Kress Fellowship

Subjects: Architecture, art history and archaeology.
Purpose: To support dissertation research.
Eligibility: Open to United States citizens studying at United States universities.
Level of Study: Doctorate.
Type: Fellowship.
Value: US$16,500. The stipend is US$8,700 and the remainder is for room and half board at the Institute.
Length of Study: 10 months.
Frequency: Annual.
Study Establishment: The W F Albright Institute of Archaeological Research in Jerusalem.
Country of Study: Israel.
No. of awards offered: One.
Application Procedure: Applicants must write for details.
Closing Date: October 12th.
Funding: Private.
Contributor: The Kress Foundation.
No. of awards given last year: One.
No. of applicants last year: Seven.
Additional Information: The research period should be continuous, without frequent trips outside the country.

For further information contact:

Department of Religious Studies
John Carroll University
20700 North Park Boulevard, University Heights, OH, 44118, United States of America
Contact: Dr John R Spencer

Samuel H Kress Joint Athens-Jerusalem Fellowship

Subjects: Art history, architecture, archaeology and classical studies.
Purpose: To support predoctoral students.
Eligibility: Open to predoctoral students who are United States citizens.
Level of Study: Doctorate.
Type: Fellowship.
Value: US$15,000. The stipend is US$7,600 and the remainder covers room and board at the two institutions.

Length of Study: 10 months comprised of five months in Athens and five months in Jerusalem.
Frequency: Annual.
Study Establishment: The American School of Classical Studies in Athens and the W F Albright Institute of Archaeological Research in Jerusalem.
Country of Study: Greece or Israel.
No. of awards offered: One.
Application Procedure: Applicants must write for details and an application form.
Closing Date: October 12th.
No. of awards given last year: One.
No. of applicants last year: Four.

For further information contact:

Department of Religious Studies
John Carroll University
20700 North Park Boulevard, University Heights, OH, 44118, United States of America
Email: spencer@jcu.edu
Contact: Dr John Spencer

AMERICAN SOCIETY FOR ENGINEERING EDUCATION (ASEE)

Suite 600
1818 North Street North West, Washington, DC, 20036, United States of America
Tel: (1) 202 331 3500
Fax: (1) 202 265 8504
Email: projects@asee.org
www: http://www.asee.org
Contact: Mr Michael More, Projects Department

The American Society for Engineering (ASEE) is committed to furthering education in engineering and engineering technology. This mission is accomplished by promoting excellence in instruction, research, public service, and practice, exercising worldwide leadership, fostering the technological education of society, and providing quality products and services to members.

Army Research Laboratory Postdoctoral Fellowship Program

Subjects: Science and engineering.
Purpose: To significantly increase the involvement of creative and highly trained scientists and engineers from academia and industry in scientific and technical areas of interest and relevance to the Army.
Eligibility: Most opportunities are open to United States citizens and permanent residents, although certain opportunities for research are open only to United States citizens.
Level of Study: Postdoctorate.
Type: Fellowship.
Value: A travel and relocation allowance will be provided, as will health insurance, life assurance, disability and workers' compensation.
Frequency: Annual.
Study Establishment: Army Research Laboratory.
Country of Study: United States of America.
Application Procedure: Applicants must submit a research proposal with a completed application form.
Funding: Government.
Contributor: The United States government.
Additional Information: Participants will be permitted to carry out research pending completion of security clearance.

The Helen T Carr Fellowship Program
Subjects: Engineering.

Purpose: To increase the number of engineering professors for the historically black engineering colleges by providing financial aid for doctoral study in engineering.

Eligibility: Open to African American faculty members, graduate students and other African Americans who have completed at least the equivalent of one academic year of full-time engineering graduate study. Candidates must be sponsored by, and submit their applications through, the Dean of one of the historically black engineering colleges, at which they later intend to teach.

Level of Study: Graduate.

Value: Up to US$10,000.

Length of Study: One year, renewable as funding allows.

Frequency: Annual.

Country of Study: United States of America.

Application Procedure: Applicants must submit a letter to the Dean of a historically black engineering college asking to be sponsored, transcripts of undergraduate and graduate course credits and at least three references testifying to intellectual capacity and educational attainments which give promise of satisfactory performance in advanced study. A covering letter from the sponsoring Dean is required, transmitting a single copy of each of these documents to the committee through its secretary at ASEE headquarters.

Closing Date: Applications for Fellowships to begin in August or September should be submitted by January 15th, and by May 15th for Fellowships to begin the following January or February.

Funding: Commercial, Government, Private.

Contributor: The Allied-Signal Foundation, AMOCO Foundation, AT&T-Bell Laboratories, EI Dupont De Numours & Co, the Exxon Education Foundation, the General Electric Foundation, the IBM Corporation, the Mobil Oil Corporation, NASA, RCA and the Union Carbide.

No. of awards given last year: Three.

No. of applicants last year: Four.

ONR/ASEE Postdoctoral Fellowship Program

Subjects: Engineering.

Purpose: To significantly increase the involvement of creative and highly trained scientists and engineers from academia and industry to scientific and technical areas of interest and relevance to the navy.

Eligibility: Open to qualified United States researchers only.

Level of Study: Postdoctorate.

Type: Fellowship.

Value: US$36,000-52,000.

Length of Study: One-three years.

Frequency: Annual.

Study Establishment: Naval laboratories.

Country of Study: United States of America.

No. of awards offered: Unlimited.

Application Procedure: Applicants must submit their research proposal and transcripts. The applicant must contact the research facility at which he or she is interested in working, in order to develop a suitable research proposal.

Closing Date: January 1st, April 1st, July 1st or October 1st.

Funding: Government.

Additional Information: The applicant must be sponsored by a naval laboratory.

AMERICAN SOCIETY FOR MICROBIOLOGY (ASM)

1752 North Street North West, Washington, DC, 20036-2904, United States of America
Tel: (1) 202 942 9292
Fax: (1) 202 942 9353
Email: awards@asmusa.org
www: http://www.asmusa.org/acasrc/aca2.htm
Contact: Ms Andrea Lohse, Manager, Awards Programme

The American Society for Microbiology (ASM) is the oldest and largest single life science membership organisation in the world. Membership has grown from 59 scientists in 1899 to over 43,000 members today located throughout the world. ASM represents 24 disciplines of microbiological specialisation plus a division for microbiology educators.

Abbott Laboratories Award in Clinical and Diagnostic Immunology

Subjects: Immunology.
Purpose: To honour a distinguished scientist in the field of clinical or diagnostic immunology.
Eligibility: There are no eligibility restrictions.
Level of Study: Unrestricted.
Value: US$2,000 cash prize, a commemorative piece and domestic travel to ASM General Meeting where the Laureate serves as the Division V lecturer.
Frequency: Annual.
Country of Study: Any country.
No. of awards offered: One.
Application Procedure: Self nominations will not be accepted. Nominations must consist of a nomination cover page, a nominating letter that includes a specific description of the nominees contributions, a curriculum vitae including a list of the nominee's publications and two additional supporting letters.
Closing Date: October 1st.
Funding: Commercial.
Contributor: Abbott Laboratories, Diagnostic Division.
No. of awards given last year: One.
No. of applicants last year: Five.
Additional Information: ASM awards are granted at the discretion of award selection committees and may not be awarded every year.

Abbott-ASM Lifetime Achievement Award

Subjects: Microbiology.
Purpose: To honour a distinguished scientist for a lifetime of outstanding contributions in fundamental research in any of the microbiological sciences.
Eligibility: Open to mature scientists, both active and retired, from all relevant areas of microbiology.
Level of Study: Unrestricted.
Value: US$20,000 cash prize, a commemorative medal and travel to the ASM General Meeting where the Laureate delivers the Abbott-ASM Lifetime Achievement Award lecture.
Frequency: Annual.
Country of Study: Any country.
No. of awards offered: One.
Application Procedure: Self nominations will not be accepted. Nominations must consist of a nomination cover page, a nominating letter that includes a description of the outstanding research accomplishments, a curriculum vitae including a list of nominee's publications and two additional letters of support.
Closing Date: October 1st.
Funding: Commercial.
Contributor: Abbott Laboratories.
No. of awards given last year: One.
No. of applicants last year: 15.
Additional Information: ASM awards are granted at the discretion of the awards selection committees and may not be awarded every year.

ASM Graduate Microbiology Teaching Award

Subjects: Microbiology.
Purpose: To recognise an individual for distinguished teaching of microbiology, mentoring of students at the graduate and postgraduate level and for encouraging them to subsequent achievement.
Eligibility: Nominees must be currently teaching microbiology in a recognised college or university and have devoted a substantial portion of his or her time during the past five years to teaching graduate students in microbiology and a minimum of ten years of total teaching experience. Nominees may have engaged in research or other concerns, provided that teaching graduate students remained a substantial activity.
Level of Study: Postgraduate.
Value: A US$2,000 cash prize, a commemorative piece and travel to the ASM General Meeting, where the laureate delivers the Graduate Microbiology Teaching Award lecture.
Frequency: Annual.
Country of Study: Any country.
No. of awards offered: One.
Application Procedure: Self nominations will not be accepted. Nominations must consist of a nomination cover form, a nominating letter specifically addressing how the nominee fulfills the award eligibility, including a record of teaching responsibilities, manifests of distinguished teaching, innovations, publications, special awards, or other pertinent information, a curriculum vitae including a list of the nominee's publications and two additional supporting letters.
Closing Date: October 1st.
Funding: Private.
No. of awards given last year: One.
No. of applicants last year: Eight.
Additional Information: ASM Awards are granted at the discretion of award selection committees and may not be awarded every year.

ASM International Fellowship for Latin America

Subjects: Microbiological sciences.
Purpose: To enable a young Latin American microbiologist who has received his or her Master's, PhD or equivalent degree within the last five years, or is otherwise in the process of obtaining such a degree, to work with an ASM member in North America who is permanently employed in an accredited United States or Canadian institution for a minimum of six weeks.
Eligibility: Open to Latin American investigators who must be a member of ASM or another national microbiological society, proficient in the use of the English Language, actively involved in research in the microbiological sciences. The ASM Hosting Scientist must be actively involved in research and training and interested in sustaining international collaborations.
Level of Study: Doctorate, Postdoctorate, Predoctorate.
Type: Fellowship.
Value: Up to US$4,000.
Length of Study: Six weeks-three months.
Frequency: Annual.
Country of Study: United States of America or Canada.
No. of awards offered: Up to six.
Application Procedure: Applicants must submit a completed application form and the requested attachments. Further information is available on the website http://www.asmusa.org/international/international-fellowship-program.htm or on request from ASM at international@asmusa.org.
Closing Date: April 15th and October 15th.
Funding: Private.
Contributor: ASM.
No. of awards given last year: Six.
No. of applicants last year: 15.
Additional Information: Further information is available on request.

ASM International Professorship for Latin America

Subjects: Microbiology.
Purpose: To enable a Latin American Institute of Higher Education to invite an ASM member from North America who is an internationally recognised expert in his or her area to teach a hands on course in the microbiological sciences.

Eligibility: The host institution must be an institution with graduate students enrolled in a Master's, doctoral or equivalent programme, postdoctoral fellows or residents and teaching faculty. The institution must plan to have at least 12 students enrolled full-time in the short course. The visiting professor must be an active ASM member affiliated with an Institute of Higher Education in the United States of America or Canada, be nationally recognised for his or her microbiological expertise and actively engaged in teaching at the post secondary level.
Type: Professorship.
Value: US$4,000.
Length of Study: One-four weeks.
Frequency: Annual.
No. of awards offered: Up to five.
Application Procedure: Applicants must submit a completed application form and the requested attachments. Further information is available on the website http://www.asmusa.org/international/international-professorship.htm or on request from ASM at international@asmusa.org.
Closing Date: April 15th and October 15th.
Funding: Private.
Contributor: ASM.
No. of awards given last year: Five.
No. of applicants last year: 26.
Additional Information: Further information is available on request.

Aventis Pharmaceuticals Award
Subjects: Microbiology.
Purpose: To stimulate research in antimicrobial chemotherapy and honour outstanding sustained achievement.
Eligibility: Nominees must be actively engaged in research involving development of new agents, investigation of anti microbial action or resistance to anti microbial agents and the pharmacology, toxicology or clinical use of those agents. They must not have served on an ICAAC Program Committee within the past two years.
Level of Study: Unrestricted.
Value: US$20,000 cash prize, a commemorative medal and travel for the laureate and guest to ICAAC conference.
Frequency: Annual.
Country of Study: Any country.
No. of awards offered: One.
Application Procedure: Self nominations will not be accepted. Nominations must consist of a nomination cover page, letter of nomination which includes a specific description of the research on which the nomination is based, a curriculum vitae including a list of publications and two additional supporting letters.
Closing Date: April 1st.
Funding: Commercial.
Contributor: Aventis Pharmaceuticals.
No. of awards given last year: One.
No. of applicants last year: 15.
Additional Information: ASM awards are granted at the discretion of award selection committees and may not be awarded every year.

The BD Award for Research in Clinical Microbiology
Subjects: Clinical microbiology.
Purpose: To honour a distinguished clinical microbiologist for outstanding research accomplishments, clinical or non clinical, leading to or forming the foundation for important applications in clinical microbiology.
Eligibility: Open to distinguished clinical microbiologists.
Level of Study: Unrestricted.
Value: US$2,000 cash prize, a commemorative piece and travel expenses to the ASM General Meeting where the Laureate serves as the Division C Lecturer.
Frequency: Annual.
Country of Study: Any country.
Application Procedure: Self nominations will not be accepted. Nominations must consist of a nomination cover page, nominating letter describing the nominee's activities and accomplishments pertinent to the award, a curriculum vitae, including a list of publications and two additional supporting letters.
Closing Date: October 1st.
Funding: Commercial.
Contributor: BD Biosciences.
No. of awards given last year: One.
No. of applicants last year: Four.
Additional Information: ASM awards are granted at the discretion of award selection committees and may not be awarded every year.

BioMérieux Sonnenwirth Award for Leadership in Clinical Microbiology
Subjects: Microbiology.
Purpose: To honour a distinguished microbiologist who has exhibited exemplary leadership in clinical microbiology, recognises the promotion of innovation in clinical laboratory science, and demonstrates high dedication and commitment to ASM and to the advancement of clinical microbiology as a profession.
Eligibility: Open to distinguished microbiologists.
Level of Study: Unrestricted.
Type: Award.
Value: US$2,000 cash prize and domestic airfare to the ASM general meeting.
Frequency: Annual.
Country of Study: Any country.
No. of awards offered: One.
Application Procedure: Self nominations will not be accepted. Nominations must consist of a nomination cover page, nominating letter describing the nominee's activities and accomplishments pertinent to the award, a curriculum vitae, including a list of publications and two additional supporting letters.
Closing Date: October 1st.
Funding: Commercial.
Contributor: bioMérieux, Inc.
No. of awards given last year: One.
No. of applicants last year: Seven.
Additional Information: ASM awards are granted at the discretion of award selection committees and may not be awarded every year.

Biotechnology Research Award
Subjects: Biotechnology.
Purpose: To honour outstanding contributions to the application of biotechnology through fundamental research, developmental research or reduction to practice.
Eligibility: An outstanding contribution can be a single exceptionally significant achievement or the aggregate of a number of exemplary achievements.
Level of Study: Unrestricted.
Value: US$5,000 cash prize, a commemorative piece and travel to the ASM General Meeting where Laureate delivers the award lecture.
Frequency: Annual.
Country of Study: Any country.
No. of awards offered: One.
Application Procedure: Self nominations will not be accepted. Nominations must consist of a nomination cover page, a nominating letter that includes a description of nominees research, a curriculum vitae including a list of publications and two additional supporting letters.
Closing Date: October 1st.
Funding: Private.
No. of awards given last year: One.
No. of applicants last year: Three.
Additional Information: ASM awards are granted at the discretion of the selection committee and may not be awarded every year.

Carski Foundation Distinguished Teaching Award
Subjects: Science education.
Purpose: To recognise a mature individual for distinguished teaching of microbiology to pre-baccalaureate students and to encourage them to subsequent achievements.
Eligibility: Nominees must be currently teaching microbiology in a recognised college or university. A substantial portion of his or her

time during the past five years must have been devoted to teaching undergraduate students in microbiology and a minimum of ten years total teaching experience is required. Nominees may have engaged in research or other concerns, provided that teaching undergraduates remained a substantial activity.

Level of Study: Unrestricted.

Value: US$2,000 cash prize, commemorative piece and travel to the ASM General Meeting where the Laureate delivers the Carski Award lecture.

Frequency: Annual.

Country of Study: Any country.

No. of awards offered: One.

Application Procedure: Self nominations will not be accepted. Nominations must consist of a nomination cover page, a nominating letter detailing teaching responsibilities, manifests of distinguished teaching, innovations, publications and special awards, also a curriculum vitae and two additional supporting letters.

Closing Date: October 1st.

Funding: Private.

Contributor: Carski Foundation.

No. of awards given last year: One.

No. of applicants last year: 11.

Additional Information: ASM awards are granted at the discretion of award selection committees and may not be awarded every year.

Dade MicroScan Young Investigator Award

Subjects: Microbiology.

Purpose: To recognise research excellence and potential and to further the educational or research objectives of an outstanding young clinical scientist.

Eligibility: There are no eligibility restrictions.

Level of Study: Postdoctorate.

Value: US$2,000 cash prize, a commemorative piece and travel to the ASM General Meeting.

Frequency: Annual.

Country of Study: Any country.

Application Procedure: Self nominations will not be accepted. Nominations must consist of a nomination cover page, a curriculum vitae including a list of publications, abstracts and manuscripts in preparation, a one or two page statement from the nominee which describes how educational or research objectives will be enhanced by the award, and two additional supporting letters documenting the nominee's research excellence and anticipated impact of the award on achievement of the nominee's career objectives.

Closing Date: October 1st.

Funding: Commercial.

Contributor: Dade MicroScan.

No. of awards given last year: One.

No. of applicants last year: Eight.

Additional Information: ASM awards are granted at the discretion of award selection committees and may not be awarded every year.

Eli Lilly and Company Research Award

Subjects: Microbiology and immunology.

Purpose: To reward fundamental research of unusual merit in microbiology and immunology.

Eligibility: Nominees must be working in the United States or Canada at the time of application and must be actively involved in the line of research for which the award is to be made. They must not have reached their 40th birthday by April 30th of the year the award is given.

Level of Study: Unrestricted.

Value: US$5,000 cash prize, a commemorative medal and travel expenses to the ASM General Meeting where the laureate delivers the Eli Lilly Award lecture.

Frequency: Annual.

Country of Study: Any country.

No. of awards offered: One.

Application Procedure: Self nominations will not be accepted. Nominations must consist of a nomination cover page, a nominating letter that includes a specific description of the research on which the nomination is based, verification of the date of birth, i.e a

photocopy of driver's licence, passport or birth certificate, a curriculum vitae including a list of publications and two additional supporting letters.

Closing Date: October 1st.

Funding: Commercial.

Contributor: Lilly Research Laboratories.

No. of awards given last year: One.

No. of applicants last year: Five.

Additional Information: ASM awards are granted at the discretion of award selection committees and may not be awarded every year.

ICAAC Young Investigator Award

Subjects: Microbiology.

Purpose: To recognise and reward young investigators for excellence and research in microbiology, the discovery and application of chemotherapeutic agents and other sciences associated with infectious diseases.

Eligibility: Nominees must have completed postdoctoral research training in microbiology or infectious diseases no more than three years prior to presentation of the award, must reside in North America and have performed significant research in North America.

Level of Study: Doctorate, Postdoctorate.

Value: US$2,500 cash prize supports travel to the Interscience Conference on antimicrobial agents and chemotherapy.

Frequency: Annual.

Country of Study: Any country.

No. of awards offered: Up to two.

Application Procedure: Self nominations will not be accepted. Nominations must consist of a nomination cover page, nominating letter including a specific description of research, curriculum vitae including a list of publications and two additional supporting letters.

Closing Date: April 1st.

Funding: Commercial.

Contributor: The Human Health Division of Merck US.

No. of awards given last year: Two.

No. of applicants last year: 12.

Additional Information: ASM awards are granted at the discretion of award selection committees and may not be awarded every year.

Morrison Rogosa Award

Subjects: Microbiology.

Purpose: To recognise the outstanding research accomplishment and potential of women scientists in one of the stated countries, who would not otherwise have the opportunity to enjoy the collegiality of membership in the ASM or quick access to current scientific information in their fields.

Eligibility: The nominee must be a female scientist holding a doctorate degree and currently performing work in microbiology in one of the following countries: Armenia, Azerbaijan, Belarus, Bulgaria, Czech Republic, Georgia, Hungary, Kazakhstan, Kirghizstan, Moldova, Poland, Romania, Russia, Slovakia, Tajikistan, Turkmenistan, Ukraine, Uzbekistan and the former Yugoslavia. Outstanding research accomplishment and potential must be demonstrated. Preference will be given to those working in bacteriology, but women in other fields are also eligible.

Level of Study: Doctorate.

Type: Membership award.

Value: Two year membership of the ASM and a two year subscription to an ASM print journal of choice or all ASM online journals.

Frequency: Annual.

Country of Study: Eastern Europe.

No. of awards offered: Two.

Application Procedure: Applicants must be nominated. A letter of nomination should be accompanied by the nominee's curriculum vitae, including a list of their publications and a brief statement by the nominee of how the award will benefit her and which journal she would choose to receive. Two additional supporting letters should also be included.

Closing Date: September 1st.

Funding: Private.

Contributor: The Morrison-Rogosa Trust.

No. of awards given last year: Two.

No. of applicants last year: Three.

For further information contact:

Morrison Rogosa Awards
International & Minority Activities
American Society for Microbiology
1752 North Street North West, Washington, DC, 20036, United
States of America
Fax: (1) 202 942 9328
Email: mgranigan@asmusa.org

Procter and Gamble Award in Applied and Environmental Microbiology

Subjects: Microbiology.
Purpose: To recognise distinguished achievement in research and development in applied (excluding clinical fields) and environmental microbiology.
Eligibility: Nominees must show outstanding accomplishment in research or development in the appropriate field. They must be actively engaged in research or development at the time that the award is presented.
Level of Study: Unrestricted.
Value: US$2,000 cash prize, a commemorative piece and up to US$1,000 for travel to the ASM General Meeting where the laureate delivers the Proctor and Gamble Award lecture.
Frequency: Annual.
Country of Study: Any country.
No. of awards offered: One.
Application Procedure: Self nominations will not be accepted. Nominations must consist of a nomination cover page, a nominating letter describing the work that has stimulated the nomination, a curriculum vitae including a list of publications and awards and two additional supporting letters.
Closing Date: October 1st.
Funding: Commercial.
Contributor: Procter & Gamble.
No. of awards given last year: One.
No. of applicants last year: 10.
Additional Information: ASM awards are granted at the discretion of award selection committees and may not be awarded every year.

UNESCO-ASM Travel Award

Subjects: Microbiological sciences.
Purpose: To provide the opportunity for promising young investigators from throughout the world to travel to another country or a distant site to obtain expertise in a method, procedure, or specific topic.
Eligibility: Applicants must be students or Fellows at the predoctoral or postdoctoral level or young scientists who have completed postdoctoral training within the previous five years in any of the microbiological sciences.
Level of Study: Doctorate, Postdoctorate, Predoctorate.
Type: Travel grant.
Value: Up to US$4,000 each for travel and subsistence.
Length of Study: Usually no longer than three months.
Frequency: Annual.
Country of Study: Any country.
No. of awards offered: Up to eight.
Application Procedure: Applicants must be nominated. Nominations must be submitted in English and consist of a completed application form, a nominating letter, a letter of application from the nominee describing the nature of the training experience and the anticipated application of that training, the nominee's curriculum vitae, a letter of invitation or acceptance from the host institution describing any funds or materials to be provided, and two supporting letters addressing the nominee's achievements and potential and the impact the training will have on the nominee. Neither letter of support may be written by the nominator. Please send applications to the address below.
Closing Date: March 1st.
Funding: Private.
Contributor: UNESCO.
No. of awards given last year: Eight.

No. of applicants last year: 33.

For further information contact:

UNESCO-ASM Travel Awards
International & Minority Activities
American Society for Microbiology
1752 North Street North West, Washington, DC, 20036, United
States of America
Fax: (1) 202 942 9328
Email: mgranigan@asmusa.org

William A Hinton Research Training Award

Subjects: Microbiology.
Purpose: To honour an individual who has made outstanding significant contributions toward fostering the research training of underrepresented minorities in microbiology.
Eligibility: Nominees must have contributed to the research training of undergraduate students, graduate students, postdoctoral Fellows or health professional students. Their efforts must have led to the increased participation of underrepresented minorities in microbiology.
Level of Study: Postgraduate.
Type: Prize.
Value: US$2,000 cash prize, a commemorative piece and travel to the ASM General Meeting, where the Laureate delivers the William A Hinton Award lecture.
Frequency: Annual.
Country of Study: Any country.
No. of awards offered: One.
Application Procedure: Self nominations will not be accepted. Nominations must consist of a cover page, a nominating letter highlighting the nominee's activities and accomplishments pertinent to the award, a curriculum vitae and two additional supporting letters.
Closing Date: October 1st.
Funding: Private.
No. of awards given last year: One.
No. of applicants last year: Three.
Additional Information: ASM awards are granted at the discretion of award selection committees and may not be awarded every year.

AMERICAN SOCIETY FOR NUTRITIONAL SCIENCES

Suite L-4500
9650 Rockville Pike, Bethesda, MD, 20814-3990, United States of
America
Tel: (1) 301 530 7050
Fax: (1) 301 571 1892
Email: meyersa@asns.faseb.org
www: http://www.nutrition.org
Contact: Executive Assistant

The American Institute for Nutritional Sciences is a non-profit membership organisation.

The Bio-Serv Award in Experimental Animal Nutrition

Subjects: Nutrition research.
Purpose: To recognise meritorious research in nutrition.
Eligibility: Open to investigators who have received a doctoral degree in the 10 years preceding the award.
Level of Study: Postdoctorate.
Value: US$1,000 plus an engraved plaque.
Frequency: Annual.
Country of Study: Any country.
No. of awards offered: One.
Application Procedure: Applicants must be nominated. Nominations should include a letter stating the basis for nomination, a selected bibliography which supports the nomination, and a reprint or series of reprints on which the nomination is based.
Closing Date: September 1st.
Funding: Commercial.

Contributor: Bio-Serv, Inc.
Additional Information: This award is made available by Bio-Serv, Inc.

The Cenrium Center for Nutritional Science Award

Subjects: Nutrition science.
Purpose: To recognise investigative contributions to the understanding of human nutrition.
Eligibility: Preference is given to scientists from the Western hemisphere.
Level of Study: Professional development.
Value: US$1,500 plus an engraved plaque.
Frequency: Annual.
Country of Study: Any country.
No. of awards offered: One.
Application Procedure: Applicants must be nominated. Nominations should include a letter stating the significance of the work, a selected bibliography that supports the nomination and a reprint or series of reprints reporting such research.
Closing Date: September 1st.
Additional Information: This award is made available by American Home Products Company.

The Conrad A Elvehjem Award for Public Service in Nutrition

Subjects: Nutrition science.
Purpose: To recognise distinguished service to the public through the science of nutrition.
Eligibility: Open to qualified candidates of any nationality.
Level of Study: Unrestricted.
Value: US$1,500 plus an engraved plaque.
Frequency: Annual.
Country of Study: Any country.
No. of awards offered: One.
Application Procedure: Applicants must be nominated. Nominations must include a letter stating the basis for nomination, a selected bibliography indicating the candidate's contributions to public service and the candidate's curriculum vitae.
Closing Date: September 1st.
Additional Information: This award is made available by Nabisco, Inc.

The E L R Stokstad Award

Subjects: Nutrition science.
Purpose: To recognise outstanding fundamental research in nutrition.
Eligibility: Preference is given to scientists at relatively early stages in their careers.
Level of Study: Unrestricted.
Type: Award.
Value: US$2,500 plus an engraved plaque.
Frequency: Annual.
Country of Study: Any country.
No. of awards offered: One.
Application Procedure: Applicants must be nominated. Nominations should include a letter stating the basis for the nomination, a selected bibliography indicating the candidate's contributions to public service, and a reprint or series of reprints supporting the research.
Closing Date: September 1st.
Funding: Commercial.
Contributor: Endowment.
Additional Information: This award is made available through an endowment from the family of E L R Stokstad.

The Mead Johnson Award

Subjects: Nutrition research.
Purpose: To recognise a single outstanding piece of nutrition research.
Eligibility: Open to outstanding investigators of any nationality.
Level of Study: Postgraduate.
Value: US$2,500 plus an inscribed scroll.

Frequency: Annual.
Country of Study: Any country.
No. of awards offered: One.
Application Procedure: Applicants must be nominated. Nominations should include a letter stating the significance of the work, a selected bibliography that supports the nomination, and a reprint or series of reprints supporting this research.
Closing Date: September 1st.
Additional Information: This award is made available by the Mead Johnson Nutritionals.

The Osborne and Mendel Award

Subjects: Nutrition studies.
Purpose: To recognise outstanding basic research accomplishments in nutrition.
Eligibility: Applicants need not be members of the Institute. The awards are usually made to professionally active nutrition scientists.
Level of Study: Unrestricted.
Value: US$2,500.
Frequency: Annual.
Country of Study: Any country.
No. of awards offered: One.
Application Procedure: Applicants must be nominated. Nominations should include a letter stating the significance of the work, a selected bibliography of all papers relating to the research on which the nomination is based, and a reprint or series of reprints reporting this research. Five copies plus the original nomination material must be submitted.
Closing Date: September 1st.
Additional Information: This award is made available by ILSI North America.

AMERICAN SOCIETY OF CIVIL ENGINEERS (ASCE)

1801 Alexander Bell Drive, Reston, VA, 20191-4400, United States of America
www: http://www.civil.nwu.edu/asce
Contact: Student Services

Arthur S Tuttle Memorial National Scholarship Fund

Subjects: Civil engineering.
Purpose: To provide tuition expenses for formal civil engineering graduate study leading to a Master's degree.
Eligibility: Open to members of the Society. Financial need and educational standing will be considered.
Level of Study: Graduate.
Type: Scholarship.
Value: US$2,000 each.
Length of Study: One year.
Frequency: Annual.
Study Establishment: An approved institution.
Country of Study: Any country.
Application Procedure: Applicants must include a completed application form, a personal essay of no more than 500 words highlighting why the applicant chose to become a civil engineer, specific ASCE Student Chapter involvement, any special financial needs, and long term goals and plans along with a detailed financial statement stating the purposes for which the funds will be used and how they will assist the applicant. Applicants must also include a description of the proposed research and its objectives, as well as a statement from the institution at which the research is to be conducted indicating that the applicant and proposed research are acceptable to the institution. A minimum of two letters of recommendation must be included, one of which must be from a faculty member. Applicants must include one sealed official transcript with each application, and a one to two page curriculum vitae, including honours, activities, organisations, ASCE activities (including any offices held) and any work experience.

Closing Date: Please consult the organisation.

Freeman Fellowship

Subjects: Hydraulic science and art.
Purpose: To assist with expenses for experiments, observations and compilations to discover new and accurate data that will be useful in engineering.
Eligibility: Open to members of the Society in any grade and to applicants for membership. Preference is given to young engineers.
Level of Study: Unrestricted.
Type: Fellowship.
Value: Varies, based upon funds available from an endowment. Past awards were in the range of US$3,000-5,000.
Frequency: Annual.
Country of Study: Any country.
No. of awards offered: Varies.
Application Procedure: Applicants must include a completed application form, a personal essay of no more than 500 words highlighting why the applicant chose to become a civil engineer, specific ASCE Student Chapter involvement, any special financial needs, and long term goals and plans along with a detailed financial statement stating the purposes for which the funds will be used and how they will assist the applicant. Applicants must also include a description of the proposed research and its objectives, as well as a statement from the institution at which the research is to be conducted indicating that the applicant and proposed research are acceptable to the institution. A minimum of two letters of recommendation must be included, one of which must be from a faculty member. Applicants must include one sealed official transcript with each application, and a one to two page curriculum vitae, including honours, activities, organisations, ASCE activities (including any offices held) and any work experience.
Closing Date: Please consult the organisation.

J Waldo Smith Hydraulic Fellowship

Subjects: Experimental hydraulics.
Purpose: To encourage research.
Eligibility: Open to graduate students who are members of the Society, in any grade, though preferably an associate member.
Level of Study: Graduate.
Type: Fellowship.
Value: The award is for tuition, research and living expenses. US$4,000 is awarded, plus a maximum of US$1,000 for physical equipment.
Length of Study: One academic year.
Frequency: Every three years.
Study Establishment: Approved institutions.
Country of Study: Any country.
No. of awards offered: One.
Application Procedure: Applicants must include a completed application form, a personal essay of no more than 500 words highlighting why the applicant chose to become a civil engineer, specific ASCE Student Chapter involvement, any special financial needs, and long term goals and plans along with a detailed financial statement stating the purposes for which the funds will be used and how they will assist the applicant. Applicants must also include a description of the proposed research and its objectives, as well as a statement from the institution at which the research is to be conducted indicating that the applicant and proposed research are acceptable to the institution. A minimum of two letters of recommendation must be included, one of which must be from a faculty member. Applicants must include one sealed official transcript with each application, and a one to two page curriculum vitae, including honours, activities, organisations, ASCE activities (including any offices held) and any work experience.
Closing Date: Please consult the organisation.
Additional Information: The next award will be in 2003.

Jack E Leisch Scholarship

Subjects: Transportation and traffic engineering.

Purpose: To enable a student to enrol in a full-time transportation or traffic engineering graduate programme.
Eligibility: Open to ASCE members enrolled full-time in a transportation or traffic engineering graduate programme. Thesis topics are considered in selection.
Level of Study: Graduate.
Type: Scholarship.
Value: US$2,500.
Length of Study: One year.
Frequency: Annual.
Study Establishment: An ABET accredited university that is also a member of the Council of University Transportation Centers.
No. of awards offered: Approx. one.
Application Procedure: Applicants must write for details.
Closing Date: Please consult the organisation.

O H Ammann Research Fellowship in Structural Engineering

Subjects: Structural design and construction.
Purpose: To encourage the creation of new knowledge.
Eligibility: Open to citizens of any country who are members of the Society in any grade.
Level of Study: Unrestricted.
Type: Fellowship.
Value: US$5,000.
Length of Study: One year, renewable.
Frequency: Annual.
Study Establishment: An approved institution.
Country of Study: Any country.
No. of awards offered: One.
Application Procedure: Applicants must submit one original application and three copies.
Closing Date: Please consult the organisation.
Additional Information: Selection for the fellowship is made on the basis of transcripts of scholastic records, evidence indicating ability to conceive and explore original ideas in the field of structural engineering, description of proposed research and its objectives, including a statement from the institution at which the research is to be done that the applicant and proposed research are acceptable to the institution.

Trent R Dames and William W Moore Fellowship

Subjects: Geotechnical engineering or the earth sciences.
Purpose: For the exploration of new applications of geotechnical engineering or the earth sciences to social, economic environmental and political issues.
Eligibility: Open to practising engineers or earth scientists, professors or graduate students. Membership of the Society is not required. The fellowship may be awarded to a co-researcher in a single project or divided among multiple projects. Previous fellowship holders are eligible to reapply.
Level of Study: Graduate, Professional development.
Type: Fellowship.
Value: US$5,000-10,000.
Frequency: Every two years.
Study Establishment: An approved institution.
No. of awards offered: One.
Application Procedure: Applicants must include a completed application form, a personal essay of no more than 500 words highlighting why the applicant chose to become a civil engineer, specific ASCE Student Chapter involvement, any special financial needs, and long-term goals and plans along with a detailed financial statement stating the purposes for which the funds will be used and how they will assist the applicant. Applicants must also include a description of the proposed research and its objectives, as well as a statement from the institution at which the research is to be conducted indicating that the applicant and proposed research are acceptable to the institution. A minimum of two letters of recommendation must be included, one of which must be from a faculty member. Applicants must include one sealed official transcript with each application, and a one to two page curriculum vitae, including honours,

activities, organisations, ASCE activities (including any offices held) and any work experience.
Closing Date: Please consult the organisation.

AMERICAN SOCIETY OF HEATING, REFRIGERATING AND AIR CONDITIONING ENGINEERS, INC. (ASHRAE)

1791 Tullie Circle North East, Atlanta, GA, 30329, United States of America
Tel: (1) 404 636 8400
Fax: (1) 404 321 5478
Email: bseaton@ashrae.org
www: http://www.ashrae.org
Contact: Mr William W Seaton, Manager of Research

The American Society of Heating, Refrigerating and Air Conditioning Engineers (ASHRAE) is an international organisation of 50,000 people with chapters all over the world. The Society is organised for the sole purpose of advancing the arts and sciences of heating, ventilation, air conditioning and refrigerating for the public's benefit through research, standards writing, continuing education and publications.

ASHRAE Grants-in-Aid for Graduate Students
Subjects: Heating, refrigeration, air conditioning and ventilation.
Purpose: To stimulate interest through the encouragement of original research.
Eligibility: Open to graduate engineering students capable of undertaking appropriate and scholarly research. Grants are not restricted to United States citizens.
Level of Study: Doctorate, Postgraduate.
Type: Grant.
Value: Up to US$7,500 depending upon needs and nature of request.
Length of Study: Usually for one year or less, non renewable.
Frequency: Annual.
Study Establishment: The grantee's institution.
Country of Study: Any country.
No. of awards offered: Usually 12-18.
Application Procedure: Applicants must complete an application form which may be downloaded from the website home page under 'Student Activities'. An application form must also be obtained, completed and returned by the faculty advisor.
Closing Date: December 15th.
Funding: Private.
No. of awards given last year: 18.
No. of applicants last year: 48.

AMERICAN SOCIETY OF INTERIOR DESIGNERS EDUCATIONAL FOUNDATION, INC. (ASID)

608 Massachusetts Avenue North East, Washington, DC, 20002-6006, United States of America
Tel: (1) 202 546 3480
Fax: (1) 202 546 3240
Email: education@asid.org
www: http://www.asid.org
Contact: Education Department

The American Society of Interior Designers Educational Foundation (ASID) represents the interest of more than 30,500 members including interior design practitioners, students, and industry and retail partners. ASID's mission is to be the definitive resource for professional education and knowledge sharing, advocacy of interior designers' right to practice, and expansion of interior design markets.

ASID/Joel Polsky-Fixtures Furniture Academic Achievement Award
Subjects: Interior design.
Purpose: To recognise an outstanding undergraduate or graduate student's interior design research or thesis project.
Eligibility: Open to applicants of any nationality. Research papers or doctoral and Master's theses should address such interior design topics as educational research, behavioural science, business practice, design process, theory or other technical subjects.
Level of Study: Postgraduate.
Type: Prize.
Value: US$1,000.
Frequency: Annual.
Country of Study: Any country.
No. of awards offered: One.
Application Procedure: Applicants must write for details.
Closing Date: March 9th.
Additional Information: Entries will be judged on actual content, breadth of material, comprehensive coverage of topic, innovative subject matter and bibliography or references.

ASID/Joel Polsky-Fixtures Furniture Prize
Subjects: Interior design.
Purpose: To recognise outstanding academic contributions to the discipline of interior design through literature or visual communication.
Eligibility: Entries should address the needs of the public, designers and students on topics such as educational research, behavioural science, business practice, design process, theory or other technical subjects.
Level of Study: Unrestricted.
Type: Prize.
Value: US$1,000.
Frequency: Annual.
Country of Study: Any country.
No. of awards offered: One.
Application Procedure: Applicants must write for details.
Closing Date: March 9th.
Additional Information: Material will be judged on innovative subject matter, comprehensive coverage of topic, organisation, graphic presentation and bibliography or references.

ASID/Mabelle Wilhelmina Boldt Memorial Scholarship
Subjects: Interior design.
Purpose: To support students who are enrolled in a graduate level interior design programme at a degree granting institution.
Eligibility: Applicants must have been practising designers for a period of at least five years prior to returning to graduate level. Preference will be given to those with a focus on design research.
Level of Study: Graduate.
Type: Scholarship.
Value: US$2,000.
Frequency: Annual.
Study Establishment: A degree granting institution.
Country of Study: Any country.
No. of awards offered: One.
Application Procedure: Applicants must write for details.
Closing Date: March 9th.
Additional Information: The scholarship will be awarded on the basis of academic or creative accomplishment, as demonstrated by school transcripts and a letter of recommendation.

AMERICAN SOCIETY OF NAVAL ENGINEERS (ASNE)

1452 Duke Street, Alexandria, VA, 22314-3458, United States of America

Tel: (1) 703 836 6727

Fax: (1) 703 836 7491

Email: scholarship@navalengineers.org

www: http://www.navalengineers.org

Contact: Mr Dennis A Pignotti, Operations Manager

The American Society of Naval Engineers (ASNE) is the leading professional engineering society representing scientists, engineers and allied professionals who conceive design, develop, test, construct, outfit, operate and maintain naval and maritime surface and subsurface ships, air vehicles and their associated systems and subsystems. ASNE also serves the educators who train the professionals, researchers who renew the technology and students who bring forth new concepts. Society work helps to support the US Navy, US Coast Guard, US Army, US Marine Corps and the Merchant Marines.

American Society of Naval Engineers Scholarships

Subjects: Engineering or physical sciences. The following are some of the programmes which apply: naval architecture, marine, ocean, mechanical, civil, aeronautical, electrical and electronic engineering, the physical sciences, as well as other programmes leading to careers with both military and civilian organisations requiring these educational backgrounds.

Purpose: To encourage college students to enter the field of naval engineering and to support naval engineers seeking advanced education.

Eligibility: Open to United States citizens who are about to enter one year of graduate study leading to a designated engineering or physical science degree. A scholarship will not be awarded to a doctoral candidate or to a person who already has an advanced degree. Candidates must have demonstrated or expressed a genuine interest in a career in naval engineering.

Level of Study: Postgraduate.

Type: Scholarship.

Value: US$3,500 per year for graduate students.

Length of Study: One year.

Frequency: Annual.

Study Establishment: An accredited college or university.

Country of Study: United States of America.

No. of awards offered: Varies, usually 18-22.

Application Procedure: Applicants must submit an application form, transcripts and letters of recommendation.

Closing Date: February 15th.

Funding: Private.

Contributor: ASNE membership.

No. of awards given last year: 20.

No. of applicants last year: 90.

Additional Information: The selection criteria is based on the candidate's academic record, work history, professional promise, interest in naval engineering and extra-curricular activities as well as the recommendations of college faculty, employers and other character references. Financial need may also be considered.

AMERICAN SOCIOLOGICAL ASSOCIATION (ASA)

1307 New York Avenue North West
Suite 700, Washington, DC, 20005-4701, United States of America
Tel: (1) 202 383 9005 ext. 321
Fax: (1) 202 638 0882
Email: minority.affairs@asanet.org
www: http://www.asanet.org/student/mfp.html
Contact: Dr Alfonso R Latoni-Rodriguez, Director, ASA Minority Affairs Programme

The American Sociological Association (ASA), founded in 1905, is a non-profit membership association dedicated to advancing sociology as a scientific discipline and profession serving the public good. With over 13,200 members, ASA encompasses sociologists who are faculty members at colleges and universities, researchers, practitioners and students. About 20 per cent of the members work in government, business or non-profit organisations.

American Sociological Association Minority Fellowship Program

Subjects: Sociological research on mental health and mental illness is germane to core areas of emphasis within the National Institute of Mental Health specifically, and the national institutes of health more generally. Research on the social dimensions of mental health includes attention to prevention and to causes, consequences, adaptations and interventions.

Purpose: To support the development and training of minority sociologists in mental health, to attract talented minority students interested in mental health issues and to facilitate their placement, work and success in an appropriate graduate programme.

Eligibility: Open to citizens or non citizen nationals of the United States, or those who have been lawfully admitted to the United States for permanent residence and have in their possession an alien registration card. Applicants must have been accepted or enrolled in a full-time sociology doctoral programme in the United States. In addition, applicants must be members of a racial and ethnic group, including Black or African Americans, Latinos eg. Chicano, Cuban, Puerto Rican, American Indians or Alaskan Natives, and Asians eg. Chinese, Japanese, Korean, Southeast Asian or Pacific Islanders eg. Hawaiian, Guamanian, Samoan, Filipino. Seniors in colleges or universities, students in Master's only programmes who have been accepted by, or who are applying to, doctoral programmes and have strong interests in the sociology of mental health are encouraged to apply. If, however, a candidate is selected for an award, but not enrolled in an appropriate doctoral programme by the time the funding year begins, he or she will not be eligible to receive the award. Students already enrolled in a graduate programme can apply, provided that they fulfil the eligibility criteria and demonstrate research interests in mental health and mental illness.

Level of Study: Graduate, Predoctorate.

Type: Fellowship.

Value: Annual stipend of US$16,500.

Length of Study: One year, renewable for up to three years.

Frequency: Annual.

Study Establishment: Varies.

Country of Study: United States of America.

No. of awards offered: Varies.

Application Procedure: Applicants must submit their complete application package to the Minority Fellowship Program in one package. The complete application package consists of a fellowship application, essays, three letters of recommendation, official transcripts and other optional supporting documents such as a curriculum vitae, published research papers and Graduate Record Examination scores.

Closing Date: December 31st for announcement by April 15th.

Funding: Government, Private.

Contributor: NIMH.

No. of awards given last year: 13.

No. of applicants last year: 62.

Additional Information: Dissertation support is available through an NIMH Dissertation Research Grant to Fellows who have completed all course work and who have advanced to degree candidacy.

AMERICAN SPEECH-LANGUAGE-HEARING FOUNDATION (ASHF)

10801 Rockville Pike, Rockville, MD, 20852, United States of America
Tel: (1) 301 897 5700 ext. 4314
Fax: (1) 301 571 0457
Email: bzvirblis@asha.org
www: http://www.ashfoundation.org

The American Speech-Language-Hearing Foundation (ASHF) is a private non-profit foundation, dedicated to innovation in communication sciences and disorders. It is funded, in part, by the tax-deductible contributions of individuals, corporations and organisations. The size and quantity of funded awards are dependent on fundraising results and may vary accordingly.

ASHF Graduate Scholarship for International or Minority Student

Subjects: Communication sciences.
Purpose: To further full-time international or minority graduate studies in communications sciences and disorders in the United States.
Eligibility: This award is not open to United States citizens, but to full-time graduate students enrolled in communication sciences and disorders programmes. Master's degree candidates must be in a programme accredited by the Council on Academic Accreditation. This is not mandatory for doctoral candidates.
Level of Study: Doctorate, Graduate.
Type: Scholarship.
Value: US$4,000.
Length of Study: One year.
Frequency: Annual.
Country of Study: United States of America.
No. of awards offered: One.
Application Procedure: Applicants must obtain an official application form which is available in April.
Closing Date: Early June, please refer to the website for specific details.
Funding: Private.
Contributor: The Kala Singh Memorial Fund.
Additional Information: Visit the Foundation's website for more information.

ASHF Graduate Scholarship for Student with a Disability

Subjects: Communication sciences.
Purpose: To further full-time graduate studies in a communication sciences and disorders programme for students with a disability demonstrating outstanding academic achievement.
Eligibility: Open to full-time graduate students enrolled in communications sciences and disorders programmes. Master's degree candidates must be in a programme accredited by the Council on Academic Accreditation. This is not mandatory for doctoral students. Applicants must be United States citizens.
Level of Study: Doctorate, Graduate.
Type: Scholarship.
Value: US$2,000.
Length of Study: One year.
Frequency: Annual.
Country of Study: United States of America.
No. of awards offered: One.
Application Procedure: Applicants must obtain an official application form which is available in April.
Closing Date: Early June, please refer to the website for specific details.
Funding: Private.

Contributor: The American Business Clubs (AMBUCS) and the Leslie Isenberg Fund.
Additional Information: Visit the Foundation's website for more information.

ASHF Graduate Student Scholarship

Subjects: Communication sciences.
Purpose: For individuals demonstrating outstanding academic achievement in communication sciences and disorders programmes.
Eligibility: Open to full-time graduate students in communication sciences and disorders programmes. Master's degree candidates must be in a programme accredited by the Council on Academic Accreditation. This is not mandatory for doctoral candidates.
Level of Study: Doctorate, Graduate.
Type: Scholarship.
Value: US$4,000.
Length of Study: One year.
Frequency: Annual.
Country of Study: United States of America.
No. of awards offered: Seven.
Application Procedure: Applicants must obtain an official application form which is available in April. Application submission will include application form, transcripts, essay and recommendations. Applicants should refer to specific instructions included in the application package.
Closing Date: Early June, please refer to the website for specific details.
Funding: Private.
Contributor: The American Speech-Language-Hearing Foundation.
Additional Information: Visit the Foundation's website for more information.

ASHF New Investigator Research Grant

Subjects: Communication sciences.
Purpose: To encourage research by new scientists in communication sciences and disorders.
Eligibility: Open to new scientists earning their Master's or doctoral degree within the past five years. This is not available to students in a degree programme.
Level of Study: Doctorate, Postdoctorate, Postgraduate, Research.
Type: Grant.
Value: US$5,000.
Length of Study: One year.
Frequency: Annual.
Country of Study: United States of America.
No. of awards offered: Up to seven.
Application Procedure: Applicants must submit a proposal following the Guidelines for Preparation of Proposal which are available in April. Proposals must include, but are not limited to, the following: an abstract, research plan, management plan and budget, human subjects review approval, bibliography and letter of support.
Closing Date: Mid June. Please refer to the website for specific details.
Funding: Private.
Contributor: The Psi Iota Xi National Philanthropic Organisation and the Marni Reisberg Memorial Fund.
Additional Information: Visit the Foundation's website for more information.

ASHF Student Research Grant in Clinical or Rehabilitative Audiology

Subjects: Communication sciences.
Purpose: To further student research in audiology.
Eligibility: Open to graduate or postgraduate students in communication sciences and disorders who wish to conduct research in audiology. Applicants must be United States citizens. Master's degree candidates must be in a programme accredited by the Council on Academic Accreditation. This is not mandatory for doctoral candidates.
Level of Study: Doctorate, Graduate, Postgraduate, Research.
Type: Research grant.

Value: US$2,000.
Length of Study: One year.
Frequency: Annual.
Country of Study: United States of America.
No. of awards offered: One.
Application Procedure: Applicants must submit an official application form, abstract, research plan, management plan and budget, human subjects review approval, bibliography and a letter of support.
Closing Date: Early June, please refer to the website for specific details.
Funding: Private.
Contributor: The Ira M Ventry and Brad W Friedrich Memorial Funds.
Additional Information: Visit the Foundation's website for more information.

ASHF Student Research Grant in Early Childhood Language Development

Subjects: Communication sciences.
Purpose: To further student research in early childhood language development.
Eligibility: Open to graduate or postgraduate students in communication sciences and disorders who wish to conduct research in early childhood language development. Applicants must be United States citizens.
Level of Study: Doctorate, Graduate, Postgraduate, Research.
Type: Research grant.
Value: US$2,000.
Length of Study: One year.
Frequency: Annual.
Country of Study: United States of America.
No. of awards offered: One.
Application Procedure: Applicants must submit an official application form, abstract, research plan, management plan and budget, human subjects review approval and a letter of support. The application package is available in April.
Closing Date: Early June, please refer to the website for specific details.
Funding: Private.
Contributor: The Arlene Matkin Memorial Fund.
Additional Information: Visit the Foundation's website for more information.

AMERICAN TINNITUS ASSOCIATION (ATA)

PO Box 5, Portland, OR, 97207-0005, United States of America
Tel: (1) 503 248 9985
Fax: (1) 503 248 0024
Email: cheryl@ata.org
www: http://www.ata.org
Contact: Ms Cheryl D McGinnis

The American Tinnitus Association's (ATA) mission is to silence tinnitus through education, advocacy, research and support.

ATA Scientific and Medical Research Grants

Subjects: Tinnitus.
Purpose: To identify the mechanisms of tinnitus or to improve tinnitus treatments.
Level of Study: Postdoctorate.
Type: Research grant.
Value: Varies.
Frequency: Twice a year.
Country of Study: Any country.
No. of awards offered: Varies.
Application Procedure: Applicants must write for grant application policies and a procedures brochure. These documents can also be downloaded from the website.

Closing Date: Proposals may be sent at any time for deadlines of June 30th and December 31st.
Funding: Private.
Contributor: Sufferers of tinnitus.
No. of awards given last year: Six.
No. of applicants last year: 13.

THE AMERICAN UNIVERSITY IN CAIRO (AUC)

PO Box 2511
113 Sharia Kasr El Aini, Cairo, 11511, Egypt
Tel: (20) 2 794 2964
Fax: (20) 2 795 7565
Email: aucgrad@aucegypt.edu
www: http://www.aucegypt.edu/graduate
Contact: Mrs Sawsan Mardini, Office of Graduate Studies & Research

The American University in Cairo (AUC) provides quality higher and continuing education for students from Egypt and the surrounding region. The University is an independent, non-profit, apolitical, non-sectarian and equal opportunity institution. English is the primary language of instruction. The University is accredited in the United States of America by the Commission of Higher Education of the Middle States Association of Colleges and Schools.

AUC African Graduate Fellowship

Subjects: Arts, humanities, business administration, engineering or information science.
Purpose: To enable outstanding young men and women from Africa to study for a Master's degree at AUC.
Eligibility: Open to African nationals (not including Egyptians) with a Bachelor's degree and an academic record of not less than 'Very Good', an overall grade point average of 3.0 on a 4.0 scale or the equivalent. Candidates must also show proficiency in the English language by either submitting a Test of English as a Foreign Language with TWE score of 550 or above, or taking the AUC's ELPET exam.
Level of Study: Graduate.
Type: Tuition waiver.
Value: A waiver of tuition, incidental and graduation fees, as well as health insurance on the AUC plan. Fellows must finance their own living expenses.
Length of Study: Two academic years and the intervening Summer session.
Frequency: Annual.
Study Establishment: AUC only.
Country of Study: Egypt.
No. of awards offered: 10.
Application Procedure: Applicants must complete an application form available from the Office of Graduate Studies and Research at the address shown.
Closing Date: February 1st.
Funding: Private.
No. of awards given last year: Three.
No. of applicants last year: 45.

AUC Arabic Language Summer Fellowships

Subjects: All subjects.
Purpose: To award fully admitted international graduate students who need to satisfy their degree requirement.
Eligibility: Open to non Egyptians. Candidates must be full-time international graduate students who need to take Arabic language classes in order to satisfy their requirements at AUC and would like to enrol in the Arabic Language Institute's (ALI) full-time Summer Arabic programme.
Level of Study: Graduate, Postgraduate.
Type: Fellowship.

Value: 50 per cent waiver of tuition for the ALI intensive Arabic summer programme.
Length of Study: One Summer session.
Frequency: Annual.
Study Establishment: AUC.
Country of Study: Egypt.
No. of awards offered: Five.
Application Procedure: Applicants must submit a completed application form which can be found on the website.
Closing Date: February 1st.
No. of awards given last year: Two.
Additional Information: Fellows are assigned five hours per week of related academic or administrative work.

AUC Assistantships

Subjects: Arts, humanities, business administration, engineering or information science.
Purpose: To support graduate level teaching or research assistants who do not receive tuition waivers.
Eligibility: Fully accepted graduate students enrolled in two or more courses or actively engaged in thesis work are given preference over those not enrolled in the graduate programme. Applicants who have completed their MA or MS, are preparing for a PhD, and have or are receiving academic degree training may also receive assistantships.
Level of Study: Graduate.
Type: Award.
Value: Holders of a Master's degree receive monthly stipends of egyptian pound 33 per hour of load per week. Bachelor's degree holders receive monthly stipends of egyptian pound 27 per hour of load per week.
Length of Study: One semester, renewable.
Frequency: Three times each year.
Country of Study: Egypt.
Application Procedure: Applicants must be made to the relevant department.
Closing Date: September 7th, January 2nd or June 7th.

AUC Graduate Merit Fellowships

Subjects: Business, communication, computer science, social and behavioural sciences.
Purpose: To recognise and award outstanding new or continuing graduate students who wish to pursue full-time study in one of the graduate programmes at AUC.
Eligibility: Open to students who are fully admissible to one of the graduate programmes at AUC and who have a BA or BSc degree with a minimum overall grade point average of 3.4 on a 4.0 scale and a minimum of 3.5 in their major. Students already enrolled in one of AUC's graduate programmes and have a minimum grade point average of 3.7 in their graduate courses are also eligible to apply.
Level of Study: Graduate.
Type: Fellowship.
Value: Waiver of tuition up to approx. US$4,100 per year, student services and activities fee and a monthly stipend of egyptian pound 483 for 11 months.
Length of Study: One year, though may be renewed for a second year with the approval of the school dean.
Frequency: Annual.
Country of Study: Egypt.
No. of awards offered: 18.
Application Procedure: Applicants must write to the Office of Graduate Studies and Research or the dean's offices.
Closing Date: Mid May.

AUC International Graduate Fellowships in Arabic Studies, Middle East Studies and Sociology-Anthropology

Subjects: Arabic studies, middle east studies, sociology or anthropology.
Purpose: To recognise and award outstanding new graduate students who wish to pursue full-time study.

Eligibility: Open to candidates from any country except Egypt. Candidates must have completed an appropriate undergraduate degree with a minimum overall grade point average of 3.4 on a 4.0 scale or equivalent.
Level of Study: Graduate, Postgraduate.
Type: Fellowship.
Value: Waiver of tuition, a monthly stipend and housing allowance or accommodation in the University's dormitory. The award also includes medical insurance.
Length of Study: Two years.
Frequency: Annual.
Study Establishment: AUC.
Country of Study: Egypt.
No. of awards offered: Two.
Application Procedure: Applicants must complete an application form. Standard graduate applications are available from the website.
Closing Date: February 1st.
Additional Information: Fellows are assigned 18 hours per week of related academic or administrative work.

AUC Laboratory Instruction Graduate Fellowships in Engineering and Computer Science

Subjects: Computer science and engineering.
Purpose: To recognise and support outstanding graduate students who wish to pursue full-time study in either engineering or computer science.
Eligibility: Students must have a BSc degree with a minimum overall grade point average of 3.2 on a 4.0 scale or its equivalent. Students already enrolled in one of these graduate programmes with a minimum grade point average of 3.2 are also eligible.
Type: Fellowship.
Value: Tuition waiver of approx. US$3,200 per year, student services and activities fee and a monthly stipend of egyptian pound 460 for 10 months.
Length of Study: Reviewed every semester and may be renewed for a maximum period of two years. The fellowship may cover a Summer session.
Frequency: Annual.
Country of Study: Egypt.
No. of awards offered: 13.
Application Procedure: Application forms are available from the Departments of Engineering and Computer Science as well as the Office of Graduate Studies and Research.
Closing Date: Mid May.

AUC Nadia Niazi Mostafa Fellowship in Islamic Art and Architecture

Subjects: Islamic art and architecture.
Purpose: To recognise and award outstanding Egyptian graduate students who wish to pursue full-time study in the programme.
Eligibility: Open to Egyptians. Candidates must be a second year student enrolled in the graduate programme in Islamic Art and Architecture and have completed 12 credit hours with a minimum grade point average of 3.2.
Level of Study: Postgraduate.
Type: Fellowship.
Value: Up to US$4,100 tuition waiver and a monthly stipend over a period of 10 months.
Length of Study: One academic year.
Frequency: Annual.
Study Establishment: AUC.
Country of Study: Egypt.
No. of awards offered: One.
Application Procedure: Application forms are available from the Office of Graduate Studies and Research or the Department of Arabic Studies.
Closing Date: May 15th.
No. of awards given last year: One.
Additional Information: Fellows are assigned 12 hours per week of related academic or administrative work.

AUC Ryoichi Sasakawa Young Leaders Graduate Scholarship

Subjects: Arts, humanities or social sciences.
Purpose: To educate outstanding young men and women who have demonstrated a high potential for future leadership in international affairs, public life and private endeavour.
Eligibility: Applicants must have a Bachelor's degree with a grade point average of 3.2 or above and have actively participated in extra-curricular activities. Preference is given to those students who require four semesters to complete their degree. The award is contingent upon full admission to one of AUC's graduate programmes in the humanities and social sciences.
Level of Study: Graduate.
Type: Tuition waiver and stipend.
Value: Waiver of tuition fees, incidental and AUC medical service fees, a textbook allowance and a stipend towards living expenses of US$1,600 per year for Egyptians and US$3,600 for non-Egyptians.
Length of Study: Two years.
Frequency: Annual.
Study Establishment: AUC only.
Country of Study: Egypt.
No. of awards offered: Three.
Application Procedure: Graduate application forms are available from the Office of Graduate Studies and Research or can be downloaded from the website.
Closing Date: February 1st.
Funding: Private.

AUC Sheikh Kamal Adham Fellowship

Subjects: Television journalism.
Purpose: To assist students undertaking postgraduate study.
Eligibility: Open to non Egyptian graduate students who are MA candidates in the journalism and mass communication department, television journalism specialisation. Selection is made on the basis of financial need and academic performance. Professional experience is also considered where applicable.
Level of Study: Graduate.
Type: Fellowship.
Value: Partial tuition waiver of US$5,000 per year.
Length of Study: One year, with the possibility of one renewal.
Frequency: Annual.
Country of Study: Egypt.
No. of awards offered: One.
Application Procedure: Applicants must write to the Director of the Kamal Adham Center for Television Journalism for details, or telephone (20) 2 797 5424.
Closing Date: Mid May.
No. of awards given last year: One.
Additional Information: Applicants must serve as an assistant in the Adham Center for 40 hours per month during the academic year.

AUC Teaching Arabic as a Foreign Language Fellowships

Subjects: Arabic, education and teacher training.
Purpose: To acquire language teaching skills.
Eligibility: Open to individuals who have Teaching Arabic as a Foreign Language experience or excellent qualifications in the Arabic language.
Level of Study: Graduate.
Type: Fellowship.
Value: US$4,100 tuition waiver and a monthly stipend of egyptian pound 550 and medical insurance.
Length of Study: Two academic years and the intervening Summer session.
Frequency: Annual.
Country of Study: Egypt.
Application Procedure: Applicants must write to the Office of Graduate Admissions and the Arabic Language Institute.
Closing Date: February 1st.

AUC Teaching English as a Foreign Language Fellowships

Subjects: Education.
Purpose: To acquire language teaching experience.
Eligibility: Special consideration is given to applicants with previous Teaching Arabic as a Foreign Language experience and/or excellent qualifications in the Arabic language.
Level of Study: Graduate.
Type: Fellowship.
Value: Tuition waiver and a monthly stipend of egyptian pound 550 and medical insurance. Non-residents of Egypt are provided with accommodation in the University dormitory or with a monthly housing allowance of egyptian pound 620 and one-way home travel.
Length of Study: Two academic years and the intervening Summer session.
Frequency: Annual.
Country of Study: Egypt.
Application Procedure: Applicants must write to the English Language Institute in Cairo or the New York office on aucegypt@aucnyu.edu.
Closing Date: February 1st.

AUC University Fellowships

Subjects: Art and humanities, business administration and management, engineering, mass communication and information, mathematics and computer science, social and behavioural sciences.
Purpose: To assist new and continuing graduate students who display superior performance in their academic endeavours and who wish to pursue full time study.
Eligibility: Students must have a BSc degree with a minimum overall grade point average of 3.2 on a 4.0 scale or its equivalent. Students already enrolled in one of these graduate programmes with a minimum grade point average of 3.2 are also eligible.
Level of Study: Graduate.
Type: Fellowship.
Value: Tuition waiver of approx. US$4,100 per year, student services and activities fee and monthly stipend of egyptian pound 179 for 10 months.
Length of Study: Reviewed every semester and may be renewed for a maximum period of two years. The fellowship may cover a Summer session.
Frequency: Annual.
Country of Study: Egypt.
Application Procedure: Applicants must complete applications, available from the chosen department in May.
Closing Date: June.
Additional Information: Fellows are assigned 10 to 12 hours per week of work with faculty members in teaching and research activities.

AUC Writing Center Graduate Fellowships

Subjects: English, grammar, education and native language, literacy education, teaching and learning.
Purpose: To provide outstanding students with valuable teaching, academic experience and to involve them as tutors in AUC's Writing Center.
Eligibility: Open to students who are fully admissible to the graduate programme in English and Comparative Literature at AUC and who have a Bachelor of Arts degree with a minimum overall grade point average of 3.2 on a 4.0 scale or its equivalent. Students already enrolled in one of these graduate programmes with a minimum grade point average of 3.4 are also eligible.
Level of Study: Graduate.
Type: Fellowship.
Value: Up to US$4,100 tuition waiver, student services and activities fee and a monthly stipend of egyptian pound 230 for 10 months.
Length of Study: Reviewed every semester and may be renewed for a maximum period of two years. The fellowship may cover a Summer session.
Frequency: Annual.
Country of Study: Egypt.

Application Procedure: Applicants must write for details to the Chair of the Department of English and Comparative Literature, and the Office of Graduate Studies and Research.
Closing Date: End of April.
Additional Information: As part of their fellowship and in support of their professional training, Fellows are assigned 10 hours of work per week in the Writing Center.

AMERICAN WATER WORKS ASSOCIATION (AWWA)

6666 West Quincy Avenue, Denver, CO, 80235, United States of America
Tel: (1) 303 347 6206
Fax: (1) 303 794 6303
www: http://www.awwa.org
Contact: Scholarships Co-ordinator

The American Water Works Association (AWWA) is an international non-profit scientific and educational society dedicated to the improvement of drinking water quality and supply. The Association has more than 50,000 members who represent the full spectrum of the drinking water community eg. treatment plant operators and managers, scientists, environmentalists, manufacturers, academics, regulators and others who have a genuine interest in water supply and public health.

AWWA Abel Wolman Doctoral Fellowship
Subjects: Water supply and treatment.
Purpose: To encourage and support promising students from countries with AWWA sections to pursue advanced training and research.
Eligibility: Open to candidates who anticipate completing the requirements for their PhD degree within two years of the award. Applicants must be citizens of a country that has an AWWA section (United States of America, Canada or Mexico). Applicants will be considered without regard to colour, gender, race, creed or country of origin.
Level of Study: Doctorate.
Type: Fellowship.
Value: A stipend of US$15,000 distributed over 12 months, US$1,000 for research supplies and equipment, and an education allowance of up to US$4,000 to cover the cost of tuition and other fees.
Length of Study: Initially one year, renewable for one further year on submission of evidence of satisfactory progress and approval by a review committee.
Frequency: Annual.
Country of Study: Canada, United States of America or Mexico.
No. of awards offered: One.
Application Procedure: Applicants must submit an official application form, official transcripts of all university education, official copies of Graduate Record Examination scores, three letters of recommendation, proposed curriculum of study, and brief plans of dissertation research study.
Closing Date: January 15th, the recipient will be notified by May 1st and support will be available for the Autumn.
Funding: Private.
No. of awards given last year: One.
No. of applicants last year: 15.

AWWA Academic Achievement Award
Subjects: Water supply and treatment.
Purpose: To encourage academic excellence by recognising contributions to the field.
Eligibility: Open to all Master's theses and doctoral dissertations that are relevant to the water supply industry. The manuscript must reflect the work of a single author and be submitted during the competition year in which it was submitted for the degree. The competition is open to students majoring in any subject provided the work is directly related to the drinking water supply industry.
Level of Study: Doctorate, Postgraduate.
Type: Award.
Value: For the doctoral dissertation US$3,000 is offered for the first place and US$1,500 for second place. For the Master's thesis US$3,000 is offered for first place and US$1,500 for second place.
Frequency: Annual.
Country of Study: Any country.
No. of awards offered: Four: two for doctoral dissertations and two for Master's theses.
Application Procedure: Applicants must submit an entry form with the names of the author, school and department, major professor, the degree sought, a one page abstract of the manuscript plus a letter of endorsement from the major professor or department chair. Manuscripts submitted to the Academic Achievement Award Committee should be unbound.
Closing Date: October 1st.
Funding: Commercial.
Contributor: AWWA.
No. of awards given last year: Four.
No. of applicants last year: 15-20.
Additional Information: Further information is available on request.

AWWA Holly A Cornell Scholarship
Subjects: Water supply and treatment.
Purpose: To encourage and support outstanding female and/or minority students to pursue advanced training in the field of water supply and treatment.
Eligibility: Open to female and/or minority Master's students. Applicants must be United States citizens.
Level of Study: Postgraduate.
Type: Scholarship.
Value: US$5,000.
Frequency: Annual.
Country of Study: Any country.
No. of awards offered: One.
Application Procedure: Applicants must submit an official application form, official transcripts of all university education, official copies of Graduate Record Examination scores, three letters of recommendation, proposed curriculum of study and a brief statement describing the student's career objectives.
Closing Date: January 15th.
Funding: Commercial.
No. of awards given last year: One.
No. of applicants last year: 5-10.

AWWA Larson Aquatic Research Support Scholarships
Subjects: Including, but not limited to, corrosion control, treatment and distribution of domestic and industrial water supplies, aquatic chemistry, analytical chemistry and environmental chemistry.
Purpose: To provide support and encouragement to outstanding graduate students preparing for a career in one of the fields of science or engineering to which Dr Thurston E Larson made significant contributions and who will provide leadership in efforts to improve water quality.
Eligibility: Open to candidates pursuing an advanced degree, MS or PhD, at an Institute of Higher Education located in Canada, Guam, Puerto Rico, Mexico or the United States of America. Also the requirements for the degree must be completed in the year of the award. Selection of scholarship recipients is based upon the excellence of their academic record and their potential to provide leadership in one of the fields served by Dr Larson.
Level of Study: Doctorate, Postgraduate.
Type: Scholarship.
Value: US$5,000 for an MS student and US$7,000 for a PhD student.
Frequency: Annual.
Country of Study: Canada, Guam, Puerto Rico, Mexico or the United States of America.
No. of awards offered: Two.
Application Procedure: Applicants must submit an official application form, a curriculum vitae, official transcripts of all post secondary education, official copies of Graduate Record Examination scores,

three letters of recommendation, a proposed plan of study, and a statement of educational plans and career objectives demonstrating or declaring an interest in an appropriate field of endeavour, or, if applicable, a research plan.
Closing Date: January 15th for the MS for receipt in the following year, January 15th for the PhD for receipt in the same year.
Funding: Private.
Contributor: Private donations.
No. of awards given last year: Two.
No. of applicants last year: 30-40.
Additional Information: Scholarship recipients will be publicly recognised at the annual conference of the American Water Works Association in June.

AWWA Thomas R Camp Scholarship
Subjects: Water supply and treatment.
Purpose: To support and encourage outstanding graduate students undertaking applied research in the drinking water field.
Eligibility: Open to doctoral students in even years and to Master's students in odd years. Applicants will be considered without regard to colour, gender, race, creed or country of origin.
Level of Study: Doctorate, Postgraduate.
Type: Scholarship.
Value: US$5,000.
Frequency: Annual.
Country of Study: United States of America, Canada, Guam, Puerto Rico or Mexico.
No. of awards offered: One.
Application Procedure: Applicants must submit a completed application form, a curriculum vitae, official transcripts of all post secondary education, official copies of Graduate Record Examination scores (quantitative, verbal and analytical), three letters of recommendation, a one page statement of educational plans and career objectives demonstrating or declaring an interest in the drinking water field, and a two-page proposed plan of research.
Closing Date: January 15th.
Funding: Commercial.
Contributor: Camp Dresser and McKee, Inc.
No. of awards given last year: One.
No. of applicants last year: 10-20.
Additional Information: Further information is available on request.

THE AMERICAN-SCANDINAVIAN FOUNDATION (ASF)

58 Park Avenue, New York, NY, 10016, United States of America
Tel: (1) 212 879 9779
Fax: (1) 212 249 3444
Email: grants@amscan.org
www: http://www.amscan.org
Contact: Ms Ellen B McKey, Director of Fellowships & Grants

The American-Scandinavian Foundation (ASF) is a publicly supported, non-profit organisation that promotes international understanding through educational and cultural exchange with Denmark, Finland, Iceland, Norway and Sweden. Through its awards programmes the ASF encourages lasting academic, professional and personal ties between the United States of America and Scandinavia.

American-Scandinavian Foundation Fellowships and Grants for Advanced Study in the USA
Subjects: All subjects.
Purpose: For Scandinavians to undertake study or research programmes in the United States of America.
Eligibility: Applicants must be citizens of Denmark, Finland, Iceland, Norway or Sweden.
Level of Study: Doctorate, Graduate, Postdoctorate, Postgraduate, Predoctorate, Professional development, Research.
Type: Fellowship or grant.

Value: Varies.
Length of Study: Up to one year.
Frequency: Annual.
Country of Study: United States of America.
No. of awards offered: 50-75.
Application Procedure: Applicants must be recommended to the ASF by a co-operating organisation. Please contact one of the organisations for details.
Closing Date: Details are available on request.
Funding: Private.
No. of awards given last year: 50.

For further information contact:

The Denmark-America Foundation
Fiolstraße 24
3 sal
1171, Copenhagen, Denmark

The League of Finnish-American Societies
Mechelininkatu 10A, Helsinki, FIN-00100, Finland
www: http://www.megabaud.fi/~sayl

The Iclandic-American Society
Ravdaravstigur 25
150 Keykjavik, Iceland

The Norway-America Association
Radhusgt 23B, Oslo, N-0158, Norway
www: http://www.noram.no

The Sweden-America Foundation
Box 5280, Stockholm, S-10246, Sweden
www: http://www.sweamfo.se

American-Scandinavian Foundation Grants and Fellowships for Advanced Study or Research in Denmark, Finland, Iceland, Norway and Sweden
Subjects: All subjects.
Purpose: To encourage advanced study and research, and increase understanding between the United States of America and Scandinavia.
Eligibility: Applicants must be United States citizens or permanent residents who have a well defined research or study project that makes a stay in Scandinavia essential. Team projects are eligible but each member must apply as an individual. Some ability in the language of the host country is desirable. Priority will be given to applicants who have not previously received an ASF award.
Level of Study: Doctorate, Graduate, Postdoctorate, Postgraduate, Predoctorate, Professional development, Research.
Type: Fellowship.
Value: Grants are usually US$3,000. Fellowships up to US$18,000.
Length of Study: One year maximum.
Frequency: Annual.
Country of Study: Denmark, Finland, Iceland, Norway or Sweden.
No. of awards offered: 25-30.
Application Procedure: Applicants must complete an official application form and submit this with an application fee of US$10.
Closing Date: November 1st.
Funding: Private.
No. of awards given last year: 15 grants and 10 fellowships.
Additional Information: For further information please contact Ellen McKey via email or visit the website.

American-Scandinavian Foundation Translation Prize
Subjects: Translation.
Purpose: To award the best English translation of poetry, fiction, drama or literary prose written by a Scandinavian author since 1800.
Eligibility: Open to translators of any nationality.
Level of Study: Unrestricted.
Type: Translation prize.
Value: US$2,000, plus publication of an excerpt in an issue of Scandinavian Review and a commemorative bronze medallion.
Frequency: Annual.
No. of awards offered: One.

Application Procedure: Applicants must submit four copies of the translation, including a title page and a table of contents for the proposed book of which the manuscript submitted is a part, one copy of the work(s) in the original language, a separate sheet containing the name and contact details of the translator and the title and author of the manuscript with the original language specified. A letter or other document signed by the author, the author's agent or the author's estate granting permission for the translation to be entered in this competition and published in Scandinavian Review must also be included.

Closing Date: June 1st.

Funding: Private.

Contributor: The American-Scandinavian Foundation.

Additional Information: The Inger Sjoberg Prize of US$1,000 will be offered annually for the Honorable Mention entry.

ANGLO-AUSTRIAN MUSIC SOCIETY

Richard Tauber Memorial Scholarship Committee
c/o 158 Rosendale Road, London, SE21 8LG, England
Tel: (44) 20 8761 0444
Fax: (44) 20 8244 7355
Email: aams@averys.co.uk
Contact: J Avery, Secretary

The Anglo-Austrian Music Society promotes lectures and concerts and is closely associated with its parent organisation, the Anglo-Austrian Society, which was founded in 1944 to promote friendship and understanding between the people of Great Britain and Austria through personal contacts, educational programmes and cultural exchanges.

Richard Tauber Prize

Subjects: Vocal musical performance.

Purpose: To enable a British or Austrian singer to travel and study in order to broaden his or her musical experience prior to giving a public recital in London under the auspices of the Anglo-Austrian Music Society.

Eligibility: Open to British and Austrian residents who are singers. Men must be aged between 21 and 32 years and women between aged 21 and 30 years. Applicants must ordinarily be resident in the United Kingdom or Austria.

Level of Study: Postgraduate.

Type: Prize.

Value: A cash prize of UK £2,500 to be used in whatever way the winner prefers to further his or her career as a singer, or to study a language, or become acquainted with the Austrian or British musical scene. Advice to this end will be available from the Anglo-Austrian Music Society if required. There will also be a Wigmore Hall recital for the winner.

Length of Study: An unlimited period.

Frequency: Every two years.

Country of Study: Any country.

No. of awards offered: One.

Application Procedure: Applicants must complete an application form.

Closing Date: January 31st.

Funding: Private.

Additional Information: Preliminary auditions are held in London and Vienna in March. Applicants must attend these auditions at their own expense. A public final audition is held in London in June.

ANGLO-BRAZILIAN SOCIETY

32 Green Street, London, W1K 7AU, England
Tel: (44) 20 7493 8493
Fax: (44) 20 7493 8493
Email: anglo@braziliansociety.freeserve.co.uk
Contact: Ms Eliane Dell'Aglio, Secretary

The Anglo-Brazilian Society was formed in 1943 to promote close and friendly relations between Brazil and the United Kingdom and to further in the United Kingdom a knowledge of Brazil, its people and its culture, with the participation of Brazilians resident in the United Kingdom.

Anglo-Brazilian Society Scholarship

Subjects: Any aspect of Brazil, including the culture, history, geography, literature, economy and medicine.

Purpose: To promote close and friendly relations between Brazil and the United Kingdom. The scholarship provides a contribution to the cost of a working and/or research visit to Brazil.

Eligibility: Open to British nationals normally resident in the United Kingdom.

Level of Study: Graduate, Postgraduate.

Type: Scholarship.

Value: UK £1,000.

Frequency: Annual.

Country of Study: Brazil.

No. of awards offered: One.

Application Procedure: Applicants must contact the Scoiety and are selected by means of an essay competition and presentation of an outline of the proposed study in Brazil, of approximately 3,000 words. Recipients travel to Brazil later in the same year and are expected to deliver a lecture to the Society on their return. Final selection is by interview in London in March.

Closing Date: February 1st.

Funding: Private.

Contributor: Events run by the Anglo-Brazilian Society.

No. of awards given last year: One.

No. of applicants last year: Three.

THE ANGLO-DANISH SOCIETY

Danewood
4 Daleside, Gerrards Cross, Buckinghamshire, SL9 7JF, England
Tel: (44) 1753 884846
Contact: Mrs Anne Marie Eastwood, Secretary

The Anglo-Danish Society exists to promote closer understanding between the United Kingdom and Denmark. It provides a forum in which Britons and Danes can meet one another.

The Anglo-Danish (London) Scholarships

Subjects: Topics that are of specific value to Anglo-Danish cultural and scientific interests.

Purpose: To promote Anglo-Danish relations.

Eligibility: Open to graduates of Danish and British nationality only.

Level of Study: Doctorate, Postdoctorate, Postgraduate, Professional development.

Type: Scholarship.

Value: UK £175 per month.

Length of Study: A maximum of six months.

Frequency: Dependent on funds available.

Study Establishment: A United Kingdom university for Danish graduates and a Danish university for British graduates.

Country of Study: United Kingdom or Denmark.

No. of awards offered: Four-six.

Application Procedure: Applicants must complete an application form, available from the Secretary from October 1st to December 31st. Applicants should enclose a stamped addressed envelope or international reply coupons.

Closing Date: January 12th.
Funding: Commercial, Private.
No. of awards given last year: Six.
No. of applicants last year: 80.

The Denmark Liberation Scholarships

Subjects: Topics that are of specific value to Anglo-Danish cultural and scientific interests.
Purpose: To promote Anglo-Danish relations.
Eligibility: Open to graduates of British nationality only.
Level of Study: Doctorate, Postdoctorate, Postgraduate, Professional development.
Type: Scholarship.
Value: One major award of UK £9,000 and others at UK £6,000 each.
Length of Study: A minimum of six months.
Frequency: Annual.
Study Establishment: A Danish university or other approved institution.
Country of Study: Denmark.
No. of awards offered: Four-six.
Application Procedure: Applicants must complete an application form, available from the Secretary between October 1st and December 31st. Applicants should include a stamped addressed envelope or international reply coupons.
Closing Date: January 12th.
Funding: Private.
No. of awards given last year: Four.
No. of applicants last year: 12.

ANGLO-GERMAN FOUNDATION FOR THE STUDY OF INDUSTRIAL SOCIETY

17 Bloomsbury Square, London, WC1A 2LP, England
Tel: (44) 20 7404 3137
Fax: (44) 20 7405 2071
Email: info@agf.org.uk
www: http://www.agf.org.uk
Contact: Mr W K Dobson, Director

The Anglo-German Foundation for the Study of Industrial Society was established in 1973 by the British and German governments to support British-German research projects, seminars and conferences and disseminate the results, to cultivate and maintain understanding and closer relations between the two countries, and to establish links between industry, academics, government and the media in both countries.

Anglo-German Foundation for the Study of Industrial Society Research Grant

Subjects: Any aspect of industrial society, but especially economic and social policy. Current priority areas are employment and unemployment, the future of the welfare state, adjustment to European and global change, the environment, public spending and taxation.
Purpose: To support research projects, seminars and conferences.
Eligibility: Open to teams in the two countries who wish jointly to organise and carry out comparative research and conferences.
Level of Study: Applied research.
Type: Research grant.
Value: Up to UK £50,000.
Frequency: Major grants of over UK £4,000 are awarded three times per year. Minor grants of up to UK £3,000 are awarded throughout the year.
Country of Study: United Kingdom or Germany.
Application Procedure: Applicants must complete an application form. Teams should submit a single application.
Closing Date: The deadlines for for major projects are July, March and November.
Funding: Government, Private.

Contributor: The British Foreign Office & German Auswaertiges Amt.
No. of awards given last year: 36.
No. of applicants last year: 100.
Additional Information: No scholarships will be awarded for the completion of degrees.

ANGLO-ISRAEL ASSOCIATION

9 Bentinck Street, London, W1M 5RP, England
Tel: (44) 20 7486 2300
Fax: (44) 20 7935 4690
Email: aia@dircon.co.uk
Contact: Mr R Saunders, Administrator

Wyndham Deedes Travel Scholarships to Israel

Subjects: Intensive study of life in Israel such as the sociological, scientific, cultural and economic aspects, in the area in which the recipient is specially qualified or interested.
Eligibility: Open to United Kingdom citizens who have graduated from a British university or Institute of Higher Education, or who are experienced and qualified in their field and intend to reside permanently in the United Kingdom.
Level of Study: Graduate.
Type: Scholarship.
Value: Up to UK £2,000 to contribute towards the cost of direct travel to and from Israel and residence when there.
Length of Study: A minimum period of six weeks.
Frequency: Annual.
Country of Study: Israel.
No. of awards offered: Varies.
Application Procedure: Applicants must complete an application form. Successful applicants will be invited for interview.
Closing Date: March 1st.
Funding: Private.
No. of awards given last year: Six.
No. of applicants last year: 200.
Additional Information: Recipients must submit a report of minimum 5,000 words on their project within six months of their return. The Association has the right to publish these reports. A large stamped addressed envelope should accompany all enquiries.

ANGLO-JEWISH ASSOCIATION

Suite 5
107 Gloucester Place, London, W1U 6BY, England
Tel: (44) 20 7486 5055
Fax: (44) 20 7486 5155
Email: anglojewish@netscapeonline.co.uk
www: http://www.anglojewish.co.uk

Anglo-Jewish Association Bursary

Subjects: All subjects.
Purpose: To assist students in full-time education who are in financial need.
Eligibility: Open to Jewish students of any nationality.
Level of Study: Doctorate, Graduate, Postgraduate.
Type: Bursary.
Value: Up to UK £2,000 per year.
Frequency: Annual.
Country of Study: United Kingdom.
No. of awards offered: 100-120.
Application Procedure: Applicants must write a formal letter of application in the first instance.
Closing Date: May.
Funding: Private.
No. of awards given last year: 130.
No. of applicants last year: 950.

THE ANTI-CANCER FOUNDATION OF SOUTH AUSTRALIA

202 Grenhill Road, Eastwood, SA, 5063, Australia
Tel: (61) 8 8291 4111
Fax: (61) 8 8291 4122
Email: msmith@acf.org.au
www: http://www.acf.org.au
Contact: Ms Margaret Smith, PA to Executive Director

The Anti-Cancer Foundation of South Australia is a community-based charity independent of government control that has developed since 1928 with the support of South Australians. The Foundation's mission is to pursue the eradication of cancer through research and education on the prevention and early detection of cancer and thus, enhancing the quality of life for people living with cancer.

Anti-Cancer Foundation Research Grants

Subjects: Any scientific or medical field directly concerned with the cause, diagnosis, prevention and treatment of cancer.
Purpose: To assist postgraduate research workers undertaking research into cancer.
Eligibility: Open to postgraduate research workers who have established themselves in the field of cancer research or show promise of doing so.
Level of Study: Postdoctorate.
Type: Research grant.
Value: Varies, according to the needs of the proposed research project and available funds.
Length of Study: One-two years.
Frequency: Annual.
Study Establishment: An appropriate research organisation in South Australia.
Country of Study: Australia.
No. of awards offered: Approx. 20.
Application Procedure: Applicants must write for details.
Closing Date: June.
Funding: Private.
Contributor: SA community.
No. of awards given last year: 23.
No. of applicants last year: 67.

THE APEX FOUNDATION FOR RESEARCH INTO INTELLECTUAL DISABILITY LIMITED

PO Box 311, Mount Evelyn, VIC, 3796, Australia
Tel: (61) 3 9736 1261
Email: morrish@c031.aone.net.au
Contact: Mr Kevin E Morrish, Secretary

The Apex Foundation for Research into Intellectual Disability supports research into the prevention and treatment of intellectual disability utilising the funds raised some years ago by the Association of Apex Clubs. The Foundation manages these funds and makes annual research grants in support of selected research projects.

Apex Foundation Annual Research Grants

Subjects: Disability research.
Purpose: To support research projects which are concerned with the causes, diagnosis, prevention or treatment of intellectual disability.
Eligibility: Open to suitably qualified researchers of any nationality.
Level of Study: Research.
Type: Research grant.
Value: Varies. The total annual funds available are approx. australian $60,000.
Length of Study: Varies.
Frequency: Annual.

Country of Study: Australia.
No. of awards offered: Varies.
Application Procedure: Applicants must complete an application form, available from the Secretary of the Foundation.
Closing Date: July 31st.
Funding: Private.
No. of awards given last year: Four.
No. of applicants last year: 21.

APPRAISAL INSTITUTE

Appraisal Institute
550 West Van Buren Street
Suite 1000, Chicago, IL, 60607-3805, United States of America
Tel: (1) 312 335 4121
Fax: (1) 312 335 4200
www: http://www.appraisalinstitute.org
Contact: Ms Sheila Barnes

Educating real estate appraisers for over 60 years, the Appraisal Institute is the acknowledged leader in residential and commercial appraisal education, research, publishing and professional membership designation programmes. Appraisal Institute members are identified by their experience and knowledge of real estate valuation, and adhere to a strictly enforced code of professional ethics and standards of professional appraisal practice.

Appraisal Institute Education Trust Scholarships

Subjects: Real estate appraisal, land economics, real estate and allied fields.
Eligibility: Open to graduate students majoring in one of the designated fields.
Level of Study: Graduate, Postgraduate.
Type: Scholarship.
Value: US$3,000.
Length of Study: One year.
Frequency: Annual.
Country of Study: United States of America.
No. of awards offered: Varies.
Application Procedure: Applicants must submit a written statement from the Dean of the candidate's college. This should consist of a signed statement regarding the candidate's general activities and intellectual interests, their college training eg. college attended, number of years, and degree secured or to be secured within the next year, activities and employment outside college for the past four years or longer, if pertinent, their contemplated line of study for a degree, and the career the candidate expects to follow. This statement should not exceed 1,000 words. Official copies of all collegiate grade records, the proposed study programme, including a brief description of each course the candidate plans to pursue in working toward the degree indicated, and a certificate of approval of this programme, should also be included. Letters from two individuals regarding the candidate's qualifications and character are also required. Application forms are available in November.
Closing Date: March 15th.
Funding: Private.
Additional Information: For further information write to the attention of Olivia Carreon, Project Coordinator at the Appraisal Institute Education Trust at the address listed, email at ocarreon@appraisalinstitute.org or call on 312 335 4100.

The Minorities and Women Educational Scholarship Program

Subjects: Real estate appraisal, land economics, real estate and allied fields.
Eligibility: Applicants must be either disabled or a member of a racial, ethnic or gender group underrepresented in the appraisal profession. They must be students majoring in one of the designated fields, have proof of a cumulative grade point average of no less

than 2.5 on a 4.0 scale and the applicant must have demonstrated financial need.
Level of Study: Graduate, Postgraduate.
Type: Scholarship.
Value: Minimum of US$1,000 per person.
Frequency: Annual.
Country of Study: United States of America.
No. of awards offered: Varies.
Application Procedure: Applicants must provide an official student transcript, a 500 word written essay stating why they should be awarded the scholarship, an attestation that the scholarship will be applied towards tuition and book expenses and two letters of recommendation from previous employers and/or college professors.
Closing Date: April 15th.
Funding: Private.

ARAB-BRITISH CHAMBER CHARITABLE FOUNDATION (ABCCF)

Weathervane Cottage, Much Hadham, Hertfordshire, SG10 6BY, England
Tel: (44) 1279 842797
Fax: (44) 1279 843033
Email: 106256.2534@compuserve.com
Contact: Mr Thomas Hallawell, Secretary to the Trustees

The Arab-British Chamber Charitable Foundation (ABCCF) provides funding for Arab postgraduate students studying at British universities.

ABCCF Student Grant

Subjects: Agriculture, forestry and fishery, architecture and town planning, business administration and management, education and teacher training, engineering, mathematics and computer science, mass communication and information science, social sciences or transport.
Purpose: To assist Arab nationals in financial need whilst they are at United Kingdom universities to undertake postgraduate studies in subjects of potential value to the Arab world.
Eligibility: Restricted to nationals of an Arab League State comprised of 21 countries in the Middle East and Africa with citizenship or residency of their country. The maximum age is 40 and applicants must have United Kingdom student visa status. Applicants must show a commitment to return to the Arab world on completion of the postgraduate programme.
Level of Study: Doctorate, Postgraduate.
Type: Grant.
Value: Up to UK £2,000 per academic year.
Length of Study: Three-four years.
Frequency: Annual, if funds are available.
Study Establishment: A university in the United Kingdom.
Country of Study: United Kingdom.
No. of awards offered: Up to 30.
Application Procedure: Applicants must complete an application form which is sent only to applicants who have confirmed that their circumstances meet with our criteria. Other supportive documentation is required, eg. transcripts of degrees, academic references, citizenship and visa status, university acceptance or registration and a written undertaking to return to the Arab world after graduation.
Closing Date: April 30th for the next academic year.
Funding: Commercial.
Contributor: The Arab-British Chamber of Commerce, London.
No. of awards given last year: 30.
No. of applicants last year: 50.

THE ARC OF THE UNITED STATES

1010 Wayne Avenue
Suite 650, Silver Spring, MD, 20910, United States of America
Tel: (1) 301 565 3842
Fax: (1) 301 565 5342
Email: thearc@metronet.com
www: http://www.thearc.org
Contact: Dr Sharon Davis, Professional & Family Services Director

The Arc of the United States is the national organisation of and for people with mental retardation and related developmental disabilities and their families.

Distinguished Research Award

Subjects: Prevention or improvement of mental retardation.
Purpose: To reward an individual or individuals whose research has had a significant impact on the prevention or improvement of mental retardation.
Type: Award.
Value: The recipient of the award will receive a plaque, US$1,000 and a trip to speak at the Research and Prevention Luncheon of The Arc's National Convention.
Frequency: Annual.
No. of awards offered: One.
Application Procedure: Applicants must send a nomination, the original and five copies, to The Arc.
Closing Date: April 15th.
Funding: Private.
No. of awards given last year: One.
No. of applicants last year: Three.

THE ARCHAEOLOGICAL INSTITUTE OF AMERICA (AIA)

656 Beacon Street
4th Floor, Boston, MA, 02215-2006, United States of America
Tel: (1) 617 353 9361
Fax: (1) 617 353 6550
Email: aia@bu.edu
www: http://www.archaeological.org

The Archaeological Institute of America (AIA) is dedicated to the encouragement and support of archaeological research and publication and to the protection of the world's cultural heritage. The AIA is a non-profit cultural and educational organisation chartered by the US Congress and has more than 10,000 members around the world.

Anna C and Oliver C Colburn Fellowship

Subjects: Archaeology.
Purpose: To fund study.
Eligibility: Open to United States or Canadian citizens or permanent residents. Current officers and members of the governing board of the Institute are not eligible for this award. Applicants may not be members of the American School of Classical Studies during the year of application.
Level of Study: Doctorate, Postdoctorate.
Type: Fellowship.
Value: US$14,000.
Length of Study: One year.
Frequency: Every two years.
Country of Study: Any country.
No. of awards offered: One.
Application Procedure: Applicants must contact the AIA office for an application form.
Closing Date: January 31st.
Contributor: Anna C and Oliver C Colborn.
Additional Information: Other major fellowships may not be held during the requested tenure of the Colburn award. The fellowship is open to an applicant contingent upon his or her acceptance as an

incoming associate member or student of the American School of Classical Studies at Athens. Candidates for the fellowship must apply concurrently to the American School of Classical Studies for associate membership or student associate membership.

Harriet and Leon Pomerance Fellowship

Subjects: Archaeology.
Purpose: To enable a person to work on an individual project of a scholarly nature related to Aegean Bronze Age archaeology.
Eligibility: Applicants must be residents of the United States or Canada. Previous Harriet Pomerance Fellows are not eligible for this award. Current officers and members of the governing board of the Institute are not eligible for this award.
Level of Study: Unrestricted.
Type: Fellowship.
Value: US$4,000.
Length of Study: One academic year.
Frequency: Annual.
Country of Study: Any country, but preference is given to the Mediterranean region.
No. of awards offered: One.
Application Procedure: Applicants must contact the AIA office for an application form.
Closing Date: November 1st.
Funding: Private.
Contributor: Harriet and Leon Pomerance.

Helen M Woodruff Fellowship

Subjects: Archaeology and classical studies.
Purpose: To fund research.
Eligibility: Open to citizens or permanent residents of the United States. Current officers and members of the governing board of the Institute are not eligible for this award.
Level of Study: Doctorate, Postdoctorate.
Type: Fellowship.
Frequency: Annual.
Study Establishment: The American Academy in Rome.
Country of Study: Italy.
No. of awards offered: One.
Application Procedure: Applicants must apply for further information and application forms.
Funding: Private.
Contributor: Helen Woodruff.
Additional Information: At the conclusion of the fellowship tenure, Woodruff recipients must submit a report to the President of the Institute and the President of the American Academy in Rome.

For further information contact:

The American Academy in Rome
7 East 60th Street, New York, NY, 10022, United States of America

Kenan T Erim Award

Subjects: Archaeology.
Purpose: To fund a research or excavating Scholar working on Aphrodisias material.
Eligibility: Open to Scholars working on Aphrodisias material. Current officers and members of the governing board of the Institute are not eligible for this award.
Level of Study: Postgraduate.
Type: Award.
Value: US$4,000.
Frequency: Annual.
Country of Study: Any country.
No. of awards offered: One.
Application Procedure: Applicants must contact the AIA office for an application form.
Closing Date: November 1st.
Funding: Private.
Contributor: Kenan Erim.
Additional Information: If the project involves work at Aphrodisias, candidates must submit written approval from the Field Director with

their applications. Recipients of the Erim Award must submit a final report to the President of the AIA which will be forwarded to the President of the American Friends of Aphrodisias.

Olivia James Traveling Fellowship

Subjects: Classics, sculpture, architecture, archaeology or history.
Purpose: To enable travel and study.
Eligibility: Open to citizens or permanent residents of the United States. Current officers and members of the governing board of the Institute are not eligible for this award.
Level of Study: Doctorate, Postdoctorate.
Type: Fellowship.
Value: US$22,000.
Length of Study: At least six months.
Frequency: Annual.
Country of Study: Greece, the Aegean Islands, Sicily, Southern Italy, Asia Minor or Mesopotamia.
No. of awards offered: One.
Application Procedure: Applicants must contact the AIA office for an application form.
Closing Date: November 1st.
Funding: Private.
Contributor: Olivia James.
Additional Information: Preference will be given to individuals engaged in dissertation research, or to recent recipients of a PhD. The award is not intended to support field excavation projects. Recipients may not hold other major fellowships during the requested tenure of the Olivia James award.

ARCTIC INSTITUTE OF NORTH AMERICA (AINA)

The University of Calgary
2500 University Drive North West, Calgary, AB, T2N 1N4, Canada
Tel: (1) 403 220 7515
Fax: (1) 403 282 4609
www: http://www.ucalgary.ca/aina
Contact: Ms Karla Jesson Williamson, Executive Director

Created in 1945 the Arctic Institute of North America is a non-profit membership organisation and a multidisciplinary research institute for the University of Calgary.

AINA Grants-in-Aid

Subjects: No limitation but preference is given to natural sciences, social sciences, anthropology and economics.
Purpose: To support young investigators and provide funding to augment their research.
Eligibility: Proposed projects can include field, library or office intensive investigations.
Level of Study: Postgraduate.
Type: Grant.
Value: Up to canadian $1,000 which can be used for travel, supplies, equipment and services but not salary or wages.
Length of Study: Varies.
Frequency: Annual.
Country of Study: United States of America.
No. of awards offered: Varies.
Application Procedure: Applicants must submit proposals which must not exceed four double spaced pages. A title, introduction, objectives, methodology, anticipated results, period of performance and proposed use of the AINA award should be clearly stated. The total estimated budget for the project should be provided on a separate page and should clearly identify other anticipated and committed sources and amounts of funding.
Closing Date: February 1st.
Additional Information: A letter report to the committee will be required within one year following the award. Any report or publication

resulting from the investigation should include acknowledgement of the AINA Grant-in-Aid programme. One copy of all publications should be sent to ASTIS at the AINA Calgary office for inclusion in the ASTIS database and AINA library.

For further information contact:

Institute of Arctic Biology
University of Alaska
Fairbanks
PO Box 75700, Fairbanks, AK, 99775-7000, United States of America
Tel: (1) 907 474 7338
Fax: (1) 907 474 6967
Email: ffehf@uaf.edu
Contact: Dr Erich H Follmann

The Jim Bourque Scholarship

Subjects: Education, environmental studies or traditional knowledge of telecommunications.
Purpose: To financially support those in post secondary training.
Eligibility: Open to Canadian Aboriginal mature or matriculating students who are enrolled in post secondary training in the relevant subject areas.
Level of Study: Postgraduate.
Type: Scholarship.
Value: Canadian $1,000.
Frequency: Annual.
Country of Study: Canada.
No. of awards offered: One.
Application Procedure: There is no application form. Applicants must submit, in 500 words or less, a description of their intended programme of study and the reasons for their choice. In addition applicants must include a copy of their most recent college or university transcript, a signed letter of recommendation from a community leader eg. Town or Band Council, Chamber of Commerce, Metis Local, a statement of financial need indicating funding already received or expected and a proof of enrolment into, or application for, a post secondary institution. Applications are evaluated based on need, relevance of study, achievements, return of investment and overall presentation of the application.
Closing Date: July 15th.
Additional Information: Further information is available on request.

The Lorraine Allison Scholarship

Subjects: Canadian issues.
Purpose: To promote the study of northern issues.
Eligibility: Open to any student enrolled at a Canadian university in a programme of graduate study related to northern issues, whose application best addresses academic excellence, a demonstrated commitment to northern research and a desire for research results to be beneficial to northerners, especially Native northerners. Candidates in biological science fields will be preferred, but a social science topic will also be considered. Scholars from Yukon, the Northwest Territories and Nunavut are encouraged to apply.
Level of Study: Postgraduate.
Type: Scholarship.
Value: Canadian $2,000.
Length of Study: One year with the possibility of renewal following receipt of a satisfactory progress report and reapplication.
Frequency: Annual.
Country of Study: Canada.
Application Procedure: There is no application form. Each application must contain a two page description of the northern studies programme and relevant projects being undertaken, three letters of reference from the applicant's current or past professors, a complete curriculum vitae with academic transcripts and a separate sheet of paper listing current sources and amounts of research funding, including scholarships, grants and bursaries.
Closing Date: January 7th.
Additional Information: The selection committee will notify the winning applicant in February.

ARISTOTLE UNIVERSITY OF THESSALONIKI

School of Modern Greek Language
University Campus, Thessaloniki, GR-54006, Greece
Tel: (30) 3 199 6771
Fax: (30) 3 109 97573
www: http://www.auth.gr
Contact: Mrs E Semelidou, Studies Department

Aristotle University of Thessaloniki Scholarships

Subjects: Modern Greek language.
Purpose: To encourage foreigners to learn the modern Greek language.
Eligibility: Open to foreign citizens as well as those of Greek origin.
Level of Study: Unrestricted.
Type: Scholarship.
Value: €38,151.
Length of Study: One month.
Frequency: Annual.
Study Establishment: The School of Modern Greek.
Country of Study: Greece.
No. of awards offered: 70.
Application Procedure: Applicants must complete an application form, available on request from the Studies Department or from http://www.auth.gr/services/studies_department.en.php3.
Closing Date: February 28th.
Funding: Government.
Contributor: The Aristotle University of Thessaloniki.
No. of awards given last year: 70.
No. of applicants last year: Varies.

ARMAUER HANSEN RESEARCH INSTITUTE (AHRI)

PO Box 1005, Addis Ababa, Ethiopia
Tel: (251) 1 710 288
Fax: (251) 1 711 390
Email: ahri@telecom.net.et
www: http://www.telecom.net.et/~ahri
Contact: Dr Fisseha Haile Meskal, Acting Director

The Armauer Hansen Research Institute (AHRI) is an international biomedical research institute mainly devoted to work on bacterial infections, notably tuberculosis and leprosy. It is supported by the Ethiopian, Norwegian and Swedish Governments.

AHRI African Fellowship

Subjects: Medical sciences, parasitology or tropical medicine.
Purpose: To promote biomedical science in Africa.
Eligibility: Open to African researchers who hold an MSc, MD or PhD. Women applicants are especially encouraged to apply.
Level of Study: Doctorate.
Type: Fellowship.
Value: Accommodation and salary costs are covered.
Length of Study: One year.
Frequency: Annual.
Study Establishment: AHRI.
Country of Study: Ethiopia.
No. of awards offered: One.
Application Procedure: Applicants must contact the AHRI for details.
Closing Date: Usually October 1st.
Funding: Government.
No. of awards given last year: One.
No. of applicants last year: One.

ARTHRITIS FOUNDATION

1330 West Peachtree Street, Atlanta, GA, 30309, United States of America
Tel: (1) 404 965 7537
Fax: (1) 404 872 9559
Email: tkidd@arthritis.org
www: http://www.arthritis.org
Contact: Ms Tareyton Kidd, Grants Assistant, Research

The mission of the Arthritis Foundation is to improve lives through leadership in the prevention, control and cure of arthritis and related diseases.

Arthritis Foundation Doctoral Dissertation Award

Subjects: The research project must be related to arthritis management or comprehensive patient care in rheumatology practice, research or education. Suitable studies include, but are not limited to, functional, behavioural, nutritional, occupational and epidemiological aspects of patient care and management. Drug studies and laboratory in vitro studies are not appropriate.
Purpose: To advance the research training of men and women of promise in investigative or clinical teaching careers as they relate to the rheumatic diseases.
Eligibility: Open to doctoral candidates entering the research phase of their programmes. The doctoral chairman must approve the project. A dissertation project is preferred. A candidate must have membership or eligibility for membership in his or her professional organisation.
Level of Study: Doctorate, Postgraduate.
Value: US$10,000 per year, depending on the amount of time committed to research. Payments are made monthly.
Length of Study: One or two years.
Frequency: Annual.
Country of Study: United States of America.
No. of awards offered: Varies.
Application Procedure: Applicants must write for an application package, available from May 1st.
Closing Date: September 1st.
Funding: Private.
No. of awards given last year: Three.
No. of applicants last year: 10.
Additional Information: Individuals must pursue their research under the direction of a supervisor who possesses recognised expertise in the candidate's specific field of study. Projects are rated on the basis of proposed research environment, background and potential of the researcher, and potential significance and relevance of the project to the rheumatic diseases. All work involving human subjects must show documented compliance with NIH guidelines as provided by the sponsoring institution's committee for clinical investigation. All work involving animal experimentation should comply with NIH guidelines for care and use of laboratory animals.

Arthritis Foundation New Investigator Grant

Subjects: The research project must be related to arthritis management or comprehensive patient care in rheumatology practice, research or education. Suitable studies include, but are not limited to, functional, behavioural, nutritional, occupational and epidemiological aspects of patient care and management. Drug studies and laboratory in vitro studies are not appropriate.
Purpose: To encourage PhD level health professionals who have research expertise to design and carry out innovative research projects related to the rheumatic diseases. The grant is intended to provide support for the period between completion of doctorate work and establishment as an independent investigator.
Eligibility: Open to holders of a PhD or equivalent doctoral degree and demonstrated research experience. These awards are meant to encourage investigators who have received a doctoral degree within the last five years. MDs are not eligible. A candidate must have membership or eligibility for membership in his or her professional organisation.
Level of Study: Postdoctorate.

Type: Grant.
Value: US$35,000 per year, paid quarterly to the investigator's institution.
Length of Study: One or two years but renewable for a third.
Frequency: Annual.
Country of Study: United States of America.
No. of awards offered: Varies from year to year.
Application Procedure: Applicants must write for an application package, available from May 1st.
Closing Date: September 1st.
Funding: Private.
No. of awards given last year: Three.
No. of applicants last year: Eight.
Additional Information: Approval of each application and research project is required from an academic institution. Endorsement of an application by the institution constitutes agreement to allow the necessary time for completion of the project within the allotted term. Principal investigators do not have to be associated with an arthritis unit. Individuals with limited research experience must apply in conjunction with a supervisor or co-investigator with demonstrated research expertise in the applicant's area of study. Projects are rated on the basis of design, originality, potential significance and relevance to the rheumatic diseases, and the principal investigator's background and experience as an investigator. All work involving human subjects must show documented compliance with NIH guidelines as provided by the sponsoring institution's committee for clinical investigation. All work involving animal experimentation should comply with NIH guidelines for care and use of laboratory animals.

Arthritis Foundation Postdoctoral Fellowship

Subjects: Research in a field related to rheumatic diseases.
Purpose: To encourage qualified physicians and scientists to embark on careers in research broadly related to the understanding of arthritis and the rheumatic diseases.
Eligibility: Open to persons with an MD, PhD or equivalent doctoral degree. MDs are not eligible after six years of laboratory training, or seven years in the case of a clinical training programme which includes one year in the laboratory. PhDs are not eligible after four years of post degree laboratory experience. Individuals at or above the assistant professor level, or those who have tenured positions, are ineligible to apply for the awards. If one is promoted or establishes tenure after receiving an award, he or she may continue to receive the award for the remainder of the fellowship period under the conditions of the original award.
Level of Study: Postdoctorate.
Type: Fellowship.
Value: US$35,000 per year, plus a grant of US$500 per year to the sponsoring institution to cover health insurance, supplies, travel and publication costs.
Length of Study: Two years, with a possibility of renewal for a third year. Renewal is competitive.
Frequency: Annual.
Country of Study: United States of America.
No. of awards offered: Varies from year to year.
Application Procedure: Applicants must write for an application package, available on the website from May 1st.
Closing Date: September 1st.
Funding: Private.
No. of awards given last year: 25.
No. of applicants last year: 150.
Additional Information: A candidate must plan to pursue a programme under the supervision of a qualified supervisor. The written proposal may represent the joint effort of the applicant and the supervisor. Applications are rated on the basis of the environment in which the training programme will be conducted, specifically, the qualifications of the supervisor as an investigator, the unit, the facilities available and the potential for inter- and extra-departmental interactions, the applicant's background, training and potential as a biomedical investigator, and the proposed research project, its scientific merit and broad relevance to arthritis. Each postdoctoral Fellow is expected to devote 90 percent of his or her professional time to

activities related to the fellowship programme: laboratory research, clinical investigation, field studies, or training. The Arthritis Foundation does not award part-time fellowships. A recipient of a postdoctoral fellowship may receive salary supplementation from other sources to a total amount consistent with the ordinary institutional level for that individual's rank and position. The extent of this supplementation must be stated on the application, and the Foundation must be notified of subsequent support. All work involving human subjects must show documented compliance with NIH guidelines for human subjects, as provided by the sponsoring institution's committee for clinical investigation. All work involving animal experimentation should comply with NIH guidelines for care and use of laboratory animals.

Arthritis Investigator Award

Subjects: Research in a field related to arthritis.
Purpose: To provide support to physicians and scientists in research fields broadly related to arthritis for the period between completion of postdoctoral fellowship training and establishment as an independent investigator. The award may provide salary and/or research support.
Eligibility: Open to United States citizens and permanent residents. Applicants must have completed a minimum of three and a maximum of seven years' postdoctoral research experience as of the award date. The award is not an extended postdoctoral fellowship. Applicants must hold an MD, PhD or equivalent degree, and have demonstrated distinction and productivity in research. The applicant may not hold an NIH, RO1, NSF Grant, FIRST Award, Howard Hughes Award, Pew, Wellcome, Searle, VA Merit Award or equivalent at the time of application. If such an award is made subsequently, however, the individual may retain his or her Arthritis Foundation award. Holders of NIH Physician Scientist Awards, NIH Young Investigator Awards, VA Associate Clinical Investigatorships, and similar research training awards given by other agencies will be eligible. Individuals with tenured positions are ineligible to apply. If one establishes tenure after receiving an award, he or she may continue to receive the award for the remainder of the period under the conditions of the original award.
Level of Study: Postdoctorate.
Type: Investigator award.
Value: US$64,000 per year for stipend only, stipend plus research, or research expenses only, plus a grant of US$1,000 to the sponsoring institution to cover health insurance, supplies, travel and publication costs.
Length of Study: Three-five years.
Frequency: Annual.
Country of Study: Any country.
No. of awards offered: Varies.
Application Procedure: Applicants must write for an application package, available from May 1st.
Closing Date: September 1st.
Funding: Private.
No. of awards given last year: 17.
No. of applicants last year: 66.
Additional Information: A senior scientist familiar with the applicant's area of research should be designated as the sponsor. The sponsor and the chairman of the relevant academic department are responsible for stating the role of the applicant within the department, promising protection of time for research activities related to the award, guaranteeing space for the investigative work, and outlining future opportunities for the applicant. Applications are rated on the basis of the applicant's background, training, evidence of productivity, and potential, the proposed research project, its scientific merit and relevance to arthritis, and the environment in which the programme will be conducted, specifically, the sponsor, the academic department, the unit, available facilities, and potential for inter- and extra-departmental scientific and academic interactions. Each Arthritis Investigator is expected to devote 80 percent of his or her professional time to activities related to laboratory research. The Arthritis Foundation does not award part-time investigators. Supplementation from the sponsoring institution or other awards for salary and research expenses are permitted up to a level consistent

with institutional policies. The extent of this supplementation must be stated on the application, and the Foundation must be notified of any subsequent support. All work involving human subjects must show documented compliance with NIH guidelines for human subjects, as provided by the sponsoring institution's committee for clinical investigation. All work involving animal experimentation should comply with NIH guidelines for care and use of laboratory animals.

Physician Scientist Development Award

Subjects: Fields related to arthritis.
Purpose: To encourage qualified physicians without significant prior research experience to embark on careers in biomedical or clinical research related to the understanding of arthritis and rheumatic diseases.
Eligibility: Open to MD candidates with no research background or a limited science background.
Level of Study: Postdoctorate, Professional development.
Type: Development award.
Value: US$35,000 per year, plus a US$500 grant to the institution to cover health insurance, supplies, travel and publication costs.
Length of Study: Two years, with a possibility of renewal for two more years.
Frequency: Annual.
Country of Study: United States of America.
No. of awards offered: Varies from year to year.
Application Procedure: Applicants must write for an application package, available from May 1st.
Closing Date: September 1st.
Funding: Private.
No. of awards given last year: Six.
No. of applicants last year: Nine.
Additional Information: A candidate must plan to pursue a programme under the supervision of a qualified supervisor. The written proposal may represent the joint effort of the applicant and the supervisor. Applications are rated on the basis of the environment in which the training programme will be conducted, specifically, the qualifications of the supervisor as an investigator, the unit, the facilities available and the potential for inter- and extra-departmental interactions, the applicant's background, training and potential as a biomedical investigator, and the proposed research project, its scientific merit and broad relevance to arthritis. Each recipient is expected to devote 90 per cent of his or her professional time to activities related to the fellowship programme: laboratory research, clinical investigation, field studies, or training. The Arthritis Foundation does not award part-time fellowships. A recipient may receive salary supplementation from other sources to a total amount consistent with the ordinary institutional level for that individual's rank and position. The extent of this supplementation must be stated on the application, and the Foundation must be notified of subsequent support. All work involving human subjects must show documented compliance with NIH guidelines for human subjects, as provided by the sponsoring institution's committee for clinical investigation. All work involving animal experimentation should comply with NIH guidelines for care and use of laboratory animals.

ARTHRITIS NATIONAL RESEARCH FOUNDATION (ANRF)

200 Oceangate
Suite 400, Long Beach, CA, 90802, United States of America
Tel: (1) 800 588 2873
Fax: (1) 562 983 1410
Email: anrf@ix.netcom.com
www: http://www.curearthritis.org
Contact: Ms Helene Belisle, Executive Director

The Arthritis National Research Foundation (ANRF) provides funding for highly qualified postdoctoral researchers associated with major research institutes, universities and hospitals seeking to discover new knowledge for the prevention, treatment and cure of arthritis and related rheumatic diseases. The ANRF receives no government funding, operating solely through the generosity of individual contributions. Each year ANRF's Scientific Advisory Board determines which research studies may have the most lasting impact in the fight against the 100 forms of arthritis which afflict over 43 million Americans. The Scientific Advisory Board members, renowned scientists and physicians from the fields of rhematology and immunology, have committed their collective expertise to furthering the principles and goals of the organisation. These scientists believe that ANRF fills a much needed niche in the field of rheumatic disease research by providing support for young postdoctoral investigators, often providing the first major funding in their research careers.

ANRF Research Grants

Subjects: Research related to arthritis.
Purpose: To support research focusing on high-incidence diseases, such as osteoarthritis and rheumatoid arthritis.
Eligibility: Applicants must hold an MD and/or PhD degree. Applicants need not be United States citizens, but must conduct their research at United States institutions. Applications will be accepted from postdoctorates and faculty members, with priority going to those scientists who do not already hold awards from the NIH or from the Arthritis Foundation.
Level of Study: Research.
Type: Research grant.
Value: Grants may range from US$20,000 to US$50,000 for one year.
Length of Study: One year.
Frequency: Annual.
Study Establishment: Any non-profit institution in the United States of America.
Country of Study: United States of America.
No. of awards offered: Up to 10.
Application Procedure: Applicants must visit the website for further information.
Closing Date: January 15th.
Funding: Private.
No. of awards given last year: Eight.

ARTHRITIS RESEARCH CAMPAIGN (ARC)

Copeman House
St Mary's Court
St Mary's Gate, Chesterfield, S41 7TD, England
Tel: (44) 1246 558033
Fax: (44) 1246 558007
Email: info@arc.org.uk
www: http://www.arc.org.uk
Contact: Mr Michael Patnick, Head of Research & Education Funding

The Arthritis Research Campaign is the fifth largest medical research charity in the United Kingdom, and the only charity in the country dedicated to finding the cause of and cure for arthritis, relying entirely upon voluntary donations to sustain its wide ranging research and educational programmes.

ARC Clinical Research Fellowships

Subjects: Rheumatology, musculoskeletal diseases or a related subject.
Purpose: To encourage young physicians to enter into a career in clinical academic rheumatology. Candidates will be expected to register for a higher degree eg. MD or PhD.
Eligibility: Open to United Kingdom medical graduates at the registrar or senior registrar level.
Level of Study: Postgraduate.
Type: Fellowship.
Value: Fellow's salary plus reasonable laboratory expenses.
Length of Study: Two-three years.

Frequency: Twice a year.
Study Establishment: A university department, hospital or recognised research institution.
Country of Study: United Kingdom.
No. of awards offered: Varies.
Application Procedure: Applicants must complete an application form, available from the website.
Closing Date: Approx. February and September.
Funding: Private.
Contributor: Charitable voluntary donations.
No. of awards given last year: Seven.
No. of applicants last year: 23.

ARC Clinician Scientist Fellowship

Subjects: Rheumatology, musculoskeletal diseases or a related subject.
Purpose: To provide a period of clinical training with a period of postdoctoral research.
Eligibility: Open to medical graduates who have completed their first period of research training and, in most cases, have obtained a PhD.
Level of Study: Professional development.
Type: Fellowship.
Value: Fellow's salary plus supporting technician, running costs and essential equipment.
Frequency: Annual.
Study Establishment: A university, hospital or recognised research institute.
Country of Study: United Kingdom.
No. of awards offered: Varies.
Application Procedure: Applicants must complete an application form, available from the website.
Closing Date: March, as advertised.
Funding: Private.
Contributor: Voluntary donations.

ARC Educational Project Grants

Subjects: Rheumatology, musculoskeletal diseases or a related subject.
Purpose: To encourage education work in the field of rheumatic diseases.
Eligibility: Open to medical, scientific or educational professionals with an interest in relevant educational research.
Level of Study: Professional development.
Type: Project grant.
Value: Varies.
Length of Study: Varies.
Frequency: Three times each year.
Study Establishment: A university, hospital or recognised research institute.
Country of Study: United Kingdom.
No. of awards offered: Varies.
Application Procedure: Applicants must complete an application form, available from the website.
Closing Date: The last Monday in February, June or October.
Contributor: Voluntary contributions.
No. of awards given last year: One.

ARC Educational Research Fellowships

Subjects: Rheumatology, musculoskeletal diseases or a related subject.
Purpose: To provide an opportunity to gain training in educational research methodology and/or medical education.
Eligibility: Open to clinicians, allied health professionals and non clinicians in United Kingdom institutions.
Level of Study: Professional development.
Type: Fellowship.
Value: Fellow's salary with lecturership scale, plus supporting technician, running costs and essential equipment.
Length of Study: Two or three years full-time or part-time.
Frequency: Annual.

Study Establishment: A university, hospital or recognised research institute.
Country of Study: United Kingdom.
No. of awards offered: Varies.
Application Procedure: Applicants must complete an application form, available from the website.
Closing Date: July, as advertised.
Funding: Private.
Contributor: Voluntary contributions.
No. of awards given last year: One.
No. of applicants last year: Four.

ARC Educational Travel/Training Bursaries

Subjects: Rheumatology, musculoskeletal diseases or a related subject.
Purpose: To promote awareness and understanding of rheumatology among allied health professionals through research, practical experience, presentation of research and formal education.
Eligibility: Open to state registered allied health professionals committed to the care of patients with rheumatic diseases with at least three years' post registration work experience and one year of experience in rheumatology.
Level of Study: Postdoctorate, Professional development.
Type: Bursary.
Value: 90 percent of fares, registration, accommodation and subsistence.
Length of Study: Short courses only.
Frequency: Throughout the year.
Study Establishment: A recognised training establishment, national or international congress.
Country of Study: United Kingdom.
No. of awards offered: Varies.
Application Procedure: Applicants must complete an application form, available from the website.
Funding: Private.
Contributor: Voluntary donations.
No. of awards given last year: 22.

ARC PhD Studentships

Subjects: Rheumatology, musculoskeletal diseases or a related subject.
Purpose: To encourage the best young science graduates to embark on a research career in rheumatology.
Eligibility: Open to university departments allied to rheumatology.
Level of Study: Professional development.
Type: Studentship.
Value: Incremental stipend, United Kingdom tuition fees and limited running costs.
Length of Study: Three years.
Frequency: Annual.
Study Establishment: A university, hospital or recognised research institute.
Country of Study: United Kingdom.
No. of awards offered: Varies.
Application Procedure: Applicants must complete an application form, available from the website.
Closing Date: August, as advertised.
Funding: Private.
Contributor: Voluntary donations.
No. of awards given last year: 10.
No. of applicants last year: 20.

ARC Postdoctoral Research Fellowships

Subjects: Rheumatology, musculoskeletal diseases or a related subject.
Purpose: To attract and retain talented scientists in rheumatological research.
Eligibility: Open to United Kingdom and Commonwealth citizens. Candidates should normally be in their first or second postdoctoral appointment with between three and six years' experience.
Level of Study: Postdoctorate.

Type: Fellowship.
Value: Fellow's salary (usually within 1A or II range) plus reasonable running costs.
Length of Study: Up to five years, with a possibility of renewal subject to satisfactory review.
Frequency: Annual.
Study Establishment: A university department or similar research institute preferably within a multidisciplinary research group.
Country of Study: United Kingdom.
No. of awards offered: Varies.
Application Procedure: Applicants must complete an application form, available from the website.
Closing Date: Approx. April and November.
Funding: Private.
Contributor: Voluntary contributions.
No. of awards given last year: 10.
No. of applicants last year: 28.

ARC Postgraduate Training Bursaries

Subjects: Rheumatology, musculoskeletal diseases or a related subject.
Purpose: To promote the training of allied health professionals by financing a higher degree course.
Eligibility: Open to state registered allied health professionals committed to the care of patients with rheumatic diseases who have at least three years' relevant postgraduate experience.
Level of Study: Postgraduate, Professional development.
Type: Bursary.
Value: Fees.
Length of Study: Various, full-time or part-time.
Frequency: Twice a year.
Study Establishment: A university, hospital or recognised research institute.
Country of Study: United Kingdom.
No. of awards offered: Varies.
Application Procedure: Applicants must complete an application form, available from the website.
Closing Date: May and September as advertised.
Funding: Private.
Contributor: Voluntary donations.
No. of awards given last year: Nine.

ARC Project Grants

Subjects: Rheumatology, musculoskeletal diseases or a related subject.
Purpose: To further research into rheumatic diseases.
Eligibility: Open to candidates working within United Kingdom institutions with previous experience of investigation and research.
Level of Study: Professional development, Research.
Type: Project grant.
Value: Varies.
Length of Study: Up to three years.
Frequency: Three times each year.
Study Establishment: A university, hospital or recognised research institute.
Country of Study: United Kingdom.
No. of awards offered: Varies.
Application Procedure: Applicants must complete an application form, available from the website.
Closing Date: The last Monday of February, June or October.
Funding: Private.
Contributor: Voluntary contributions.
No. of awards given last year: 56.
No. of applicants last year: 181.
Additional Information: Grants are made in support of specific research projects.

ARC Travelling Fellowships

Subjects: Rheumatology, musculoskeletal diseases or a related subject.

Purpose: To provide training and experience for doctors committed to a career in clinical rheumatology.
Eligibility: Open to doctors up to and including senior registrar status.
Level of Study: Professional development.
Type: Fellowship.
Value: Fellow's salary and travelling costs.
Length of Study: One year.
Frequency: Annual.
Study Establishment: A centre of the Fellow's choice, subject to the campaign's approval.
Country of Study: Any country.
No. of awards offered: Two.
Application Procedure: Applicants must complete an application form, available from the website.
Closing Date: September as advertised.
Funding: Private.
Contributor: Charitable voluntary contributions.
No. of awards given last year: Two.
No. of applicants last year: Three.

Senior ARC Fellowships

Subjects: Rheumatology, musculoskeletal diseases or a related subject.
Purpose: To further research into rheumatic diseases and to attract high flying medical or scientific researchers into rheumatology.
Eligibility: Open to residents with previous experience of investigation and research. Candidates should have proven ability in establishing an independent research programme.
Level of Study: Professional development.
Type: Fellowship.
Value: Fellow's salary with lecturer B or senior lectureship scale, plus supporting technician, running costs and essential equipment.
Length of Study: Up to five years, with a possibility of renewal subject to satisfactory review.
Frequency: Annual.
Study Establishment: A university, hospital or recognised research institute.
Country of Study: United Kingdom.
No. of awards offered: Varies.
Application Procedure: Applicants must complete an application form, available from the website.
Closing Date: Approx. February to March.
Funding: Private.
Contributor: Voluntary contributions.
No. of awards given last year: Three.
No. of applicants last year: Six.

THE ARTHRITIS SOCIETY

393 University Avenue
Suite 1700, Toronto, ON, M5G 1E6, Canada
Tel: (1) 416 979 7228
Fax: (1) 416 979 1149
Email: kparker@arthritis.ca
www: http://www.arthritis.ca
Contact: Ms Kim Parker, Manager, Medical & Scientific Programs

The Arthritis Society is Canada's only non-profit agency dedicated solely to funding and promoting arthritis research and care.

Arthritis Society Industry Program

Subjects: Research relevant to arthritis.
Purpose: To foster new collaborative efforts through shared funding between The Arthritis Society and industry in research relevant to arthritis.
Eligibility: Please write for details or refer to the website.
Level of Study: Postdoctorate.
Type: Research grant.
Frequency: Annual.

Country of Study: Any country.
No. of awards offered: Varies.
Application Procedure: Applicants must write for details.
Closing Date: December 15th.
Funding: Private.

Arthritis Society Research Fellowships

Subjects: Arthritis.
Purpose: To provide financial support to allow highly qualified candidates to pursue full-time research.
Eligibility: Preference is given to candidates who intend to embark on a research career in Canada. Candidates must hold a PhD, MD, DDS, DVM, PharmD or the equivalent.
Level of Study: Postdoctorate.
Type: Fellowship.
Value: Based on the Medical Research Council scale.
Length of Study: Two years, usually beginning on July 1st, with a possibility of renewal.
Frequency: Annual.
Study Establishment: Ordinarily Canadian universities. Out of country training may be arranged in order to obtain specific expertise.
Country of Study: Canada.
No. of awards offered: Varies.
Application Procedure: Applicants must complete and submit an application form with further documentation as outlined in the regulations.
Closing Date: November 1st.
Funding: Private.
No. of awards given last year: Seven.
No. of applicants last year: 13.
Additional Information: Fellowships are awarded by the Society on the advice of the Review Panel. The Society reserves the right to approve or decline any application without stating its reasons.

Arthritis Society Research Grants

Subjects: Arthritis.
Purpose: To promote and support research operations of investigators holding staff appointments at Canadian Universities.
Eligibility: Open to investigators holding staff appointments at Canadian universities or other recognised Canadian institutions where the research is deemed relevant to arthritis. Candidates must be Canadian citizens or permanent residents.
Level of Study: Postdoctorate.
Type: Research grant.
Value: To cover research costs. Grant funds may not be used for the remuneration of grantees.
Length of Study: Usually three years. In some cases the Panel may request a progress report after one year.
Frequency: Annual.
Study Establishment: Canadian institutions.
Country of Study: Canada.
No. of awards offered: Varies.
Application Procedure: Applicants must submit an application form and other documentation as outlined in the regulations.
Closing Date: December 15th.
Funding: Private.
No. of awards given last year: 27.
No. of applicants last year: 81.

Geoff Carr Lupus Fellowship

Subjects: Lupus.
Purpose: To provide advanced training to a rheumatologist specialising in lupus at an Ontario lupus clinic.
Eligibility: Open to nationals of any country.
Level of Study: Postdoctorate.
Type: Fellowship.
Value: Canadian $55,000.
Length of Study: One year.
Frequency: Annual.
Study Establishment: An approved Ontario lupus clinic.

Country of Study: Canada.

No. of awards offered: One.

Application Procedure: Applicants must submit an application with three letters of recommendation, a letter of acceptance from a proposed supervisor to include an outline of proposed training programme and a certified transcript of their undergraduate record.

Closing Date: November 1st.

Funding: Private.

Contributor: The Ontario Lupus Association.

Additional Information: Please see the website for further information.

Metro A Ogryzlo International Fellowship

Subjects: Clinical rheumatology.

Purpose: To provide advanced training to individuals from a developing country.

Eligibility: The successful candidate will have completed his or her training in general medicine and have a substantial prospect of returning to an academic position in his or her own country. Canadian citizens or landed immigrants are not eligible.

Level of Study: Postdoctorate.

Type: Fellowship.

Value: Up to a maximum of canadian $31,000 per year.

Length of Study: One year, non renewable.

Frequency: Annual.

Study Establishment: A rheumatic disease unit or arthritis centre.

Country of Study: Canada.

No. of awards offered: One.

Application Procedure: Applicants must submit an application including letters of recommendation from three sponsors, letter of acceptance from the proposed supervisor, to include an outline of the proposed training programme, and a certified transcript of undergraduate record.

Closing Date: November 1st.

Funding: Private.

Additional Information: Fellows may not receive remuneration for any other work or hold a second major scholarship, except that, with the approval of their supervisors, they may engage in and accept remuneration for such departmental activities as are conducive to their development as clinicians, teachers or investigators. Ordinarily, a Fellow who is not a graduate of a medical school in the United States, the United Kingdom, Republic of Ireland, Australia, New Zealand or South Africa must take the Medical Council of Canada evaluating examination to obtain the Medical Council of Canada certificate before an education licence can be issued.

ARTHUR J DYER OBSERVATORY

1000 Oman Drive, Brentwood, TN, 37027, United States of America

Tel: (1) 615 373 4897

Fax: (1) 615 371 3904

Email: hall@astro.dyer.vanderbilt.edu

www: http://www.dyer.vanderbilt.edu

Contact: Director

The Arthur J Dyer Observatory is the principal astronomical facility of Vanderbilt University. The primary activities of the astronomy programme at Vanderbilt include academic training as well as scholarly research in astronomy and astrophysics. Visitors are welcome to attend demonstrations and lectures, and can view through the telescope at designated times.

Arthur J Dyer Observatory Research Assistantship

Subjects: Observational optical astronomy.

Purpose: To provide assistance in research programmes of the Dyer Observatory.

Eligibility: Open to persons holding a Bachelor's degree who are accepted to the Graduate School of Vanderbilt University.

Level of Study: Doctorate, Postgraduate.

Type: Graduate research assistantship.

Value: US$17,333 stipend, paid monthly, plus US$17,444 tuition waiver.

Length of Study: One year.

Frequency: Annual.

Study Establishment: The Dyer Observatory, Vanderbilt University.

Country of Study: United States of America.

No. of awards offered: One.

Application Procedure: Applicants must contact the Observatory Director to request application materials.

Closing Date: February 15th.

Funding: Private.

Contributor: The Vanderbilt University.

ARTHUR RUBINSTEIN INTERNATIONAL MUSIC SOCIETY

12 Huberman Street, Tel Aviv, 64075, Israel

Tel: (972) 3 685 6684

Fax: (972) 3 685 4924

Email: competition@arims.org.il

www: http://www.arims.org.il

Contact: Mr Jan Jacob Bistritzky, Director

The Arthur Rubinstein International Music Society was founded by Jan Jacob Bistritzky in 1980 in tribute to the artistry of Arthur Rubinstein (1887-1982) and to maintain his spiritual and artistic heritage in the art of the piano. The Society organises and finances the Arthur Rubinstein International Piano Master Competition, the Hommage à Rubinstein worldwide concert series and festivals, awards scholarships, runs music courses and master classes, organises lectures, seminars, exhibitions, film shows and memorial festivals, and issues publications and recordings.

Arthur Rubinstein International Piano Master Competition

Subjects: Piano.

Purpose: To reward talented pianists with the capacity for multifaceted creative interpretation of composers, ranging from the pre-classic to the contemporary era.

Eligibility: Candidates must be 18-32 years of age.

Level of Study: Professional development.

Type: Prize.

Value: First prize is a competition gold medal plus US$25,000, second prize is a competition silver medal plus US$15,000 and third prize is a competition bronze medal plus US$10,000. The fourth, fifth and sixth prizes are US$3,000 each. Additional prizes, the Audience Favorite Prize and concert engagements will be announced in future bulletins.

Frequency: Every three years.

Country of Study: Any country.

No. of awards offered: 10.

Application Procedure: Applicants must complete an application form according to the rules stipulated in the prospectus of the Arthur Rubinstein International Piano Master Competition. Details are available from the organisation.

Closing Date: September 1st.

No. of awards given last year: 16.

No. of applicants last year: 185.

ARTS AND HUMANITIES RESEARCH BOARD (AHRB)

Postgraduate Awards Division
Whitefriars
Lewins Mead, Bristol, BS1 2AE, England
Tel: (44) 117 987 6543
Fax: (44) 117 987 6544
Email: pgaenq@ahrb.ac.uk
www: http://www.ahrb.ac.uk
Contact: Vijay Chandy, Head of Postgraduate Division

The Arts and Humanities Research Board (AHRB) promotes and supports excellence in research in the arts and humanities and supports the development of highly qualified people in these fields.

AHRB Doctoral Awards in the Creative and Performing Arts (Competition C)

Subjects: Art and design, creative writing, musical performance, drama, dance or performing arts.
Purpose: To promote study for students pursuing a programme of practice board doctoral research.
Eligibility: Applicants must be resident in the United Kingdom or the European Union and be graduates of a recognised Institute of Higher Education or be expecting to graduate by the July 31st preceding the start of the course.
Level of Study: Doctorate.
Type: Studentship.
Value: A maintenance grant of UK £9,250 per year for London based students and UK £7,500 per years for students based elsewhere. Tuition fees up to UK £2,805 per year, study visit and conference costs.
Length of Study: Up to three years full-time study or up to five years part-time.
Frequency: Annual.
Study Establishment: An Institute of Higher Education.
Country of Study: United Kingdom.
Application Procedure: Applicants must complete an application form which can be downloaded from the website.
Closing Date: May 1st.
Funding: Government.
No. of awards given last year: 27.
No. of applicants last year: 77.

AHRB Professional and Vocational Awards (Competition P)

Subjects: Art and design, practice based drama and media studies, interpreting and translation, librarianship, archives and information management, museum studies and heritage management or creative writing.
Eligibility: Applicants must be resident in the United Kingdom or the European Union and be graduates of a recognised Institute of Higher Education or be expecting to graduate by the July 31st preceding the start of the course.
Level of Study: Postgraduate.
Type: Studentship.
Value: UK £5,100 in London, UK £4,300 elsewhere plus tuition fees of up to UK £2,805. These amounts are subject to change so please consult the organisation.
Length of Study: One year.
Frequency: Annual.
Study Establishment: An Institute of Higher Education.
Country of Study: United Kingdom.
Application Procedure: Applicants must download and complete an application form and guide from the website.
Closing Date: May 1st.
Funding: Government.
No. of awards given last year: 571.
No. of applicants last year: 982.

AHRB Studentships in the Humanities (Competition A)

Subjects: Archaeology, classics and ancient history, communications, cultural and media studies, English language and literature, history of art, architecture, law, linguistics, modern languages, music, drama, dance and performing arts, philosophy or religious studies.
Purpose: To promote full-time study on taught and research led Master's courses.
Eligibility: Applicants must be resident in the United Kingdom or the European Union, be graduates of a recognised Institute of Higher Education or be expecting to graduate by the July 31st preceding the start of the course.
Level of Study: Postgraduate.
Type: Studentship.
Value: A maintenance grant of UK £9,250 per year for London based students and UK £7,500 per year for students based elsewhere. Tuition fees up to UK £2,805 per year.
Length of Study: One-two years.
Frequency: Annual.
Country of Study: United Kingdom.
No. of awards offered: Varies.
Application Procedure: Applicants must download and complete an application form available on the website.
Closing Date: May 1st.
Funding: Government.
No. of awards given last year: 614.
No. of applicants last year: 1,654.
Additional Information: Further information is available on request.

AHRB Studentships in the Humanities (Competition B)

Subjects: Archaeology, classics and ancient history, communications, cultural and media studies, English language and literature, history of art, architecture, law, linguistics, modern languages, music, drama, dance and performing arts, philosophy or religious studies.
Purpose: To support full-time and part-time study by students undertaking a doctoral degree in the humanities.
Eligibility: Applicants must be resident in the United Kingdom or the European Union and be graduates of a recognised Institute of Higher Education or be expecting to graduate by the July 31st preceding the start of the course.
Level of Study: Doctorate.
Type: Scholarship.
Value: A maintenance grant of UK £9,250 per year for London based students and UK £7,500 per year for students based elsewhere. Tuition fees up to UK £2,805 per year. In addition a study visit and conference costs.
Length of Study: Up to three years full-time and five years part-time.
Frequency: Annual.
Study Establishment: Any approved Institute of Higher Education.
Country of Study: United Kingdom.
No. of awards offered: Varies.
Application Procedure: Applicants must download and complete an application form available on the website.
Closing Date: May.
Funding: Government.
Additional Information: Further information is available on request.

THE ARTS COUNCIL OF IRELAND

70 Merrion Square, Dublin, 2, Ireland
Tel: (353) 1 661 1840
Fax: (353) 1 676 1320
www: http://www.artscouncil.ie
Contact: Ms Tara Byrne, Artists' Support Executive

The Arts Council of Ireland awards grants in dance, drama, film and video, literature, music and the visual arts in order to promote artistic excellence and innovation. The Council expresses its support to the artist in a variety of ways, through grant-aid to organisations, events and production companies, and more explicitly through award schemes where the primary relationship is between the artist and the Council. Their principal strategies are improving the professional formation, practice and career development of artists, directing funding towards excellence and innovation in the promotion of the arts and supporting artists working through Irish in indigenous arts to achieve their full potential and increase audiences.

ARTFLIGHT Arts Council-Aer Lingus Travel Awards
Subjects: Creative arts, interpretative arts or arts administration.
Purpose: To offer opportunities to people working in the arts to travel outside of Ireland to benefit their artistic practice and/or career.
Eligibility: Open to creative and interpretative artists in all fields, administrators, producers and directors of Irish birth or residence. Artflights are intended to assist those individuals who have a stated reason to travel and do not have the financial resources to do so. The artist must have evidence of having produced a body of work of recognised quality and significance, or in the case of individuals with less experience, demonstrable potential. They need to be able to show evidence of artistic developmental needs, evidence of financial need, including availability of other funding and a likelihood that an award will reach the desired effect. Applicants must be practising artists or arts workers but may not necessarily earn income from their arts practice, they must identify themselves and be recognised by their peers as practising artists.
Level of Study: Professional development.
Value: A non refundable travel voucher to cover the cost of the return fare to any destination on the Aer Lingus network.
Country of Study: Any country.
No. of awards offered: Varies.
Application Procedure: Applicants must complete an application form and supply a curriculum vitae. For visual artists no more than 10 copies of slides and an accompanying slide list is required, along with supporting documentation comprising of a letter of invitation, confirmation of acceptance on course, relevant correspondence or other materials with application. Applications will be considered not eligible and returned if the eligibility criteria is not met, if all the support material specified is not included, if you have requested funding for activities that have already occurred or will be completed before the closing date and also if your application or supporting documentation is late.
Closing Date: One month before departure.
Funding: Government.
Additional Information: The Arts Council will not normally fund activities that diverge from its policies or funding criteria, projects that have already taken place, charity fund raising events, or those that are primarily competitive in nature or projects or activities that are primarily profit making. All awards are offered subject to the availability of funds and they may be withheld or divided among applicants at the discretion of The Arts Council.

The Arts Council of Ireland and Arts Council of Northern Ireland Skidmore Jazz Award
Subjects: Jazz, with the emphasis of this course being on ensemble or 'in combo' playing.
Eligibility: Open to Irish nationals and permanent residents who are of high ability in jazz. The artist must have evidence of having produced a body of work of recognised quality and significance, or in the case of individuals with less experience, demonstrable potential. They need to be able to show evidence of artistic developmental needs, evidence of financial need, including availability of other funding and a likelihood that an award will reach the desired effect. Applicants must be practising artists or arts workers but may not necessarily earn income from their arts practice, they must identify themselves and be recognised by their peers as practising artists.
Level of Study: Postgraduate.
Type: Scholarship.
Value: €2,200.
Length of Study: Summer course.
Frequency: Annual.
Study Establishment: Skidmore College, New York.

Country of Study: United States of America.
No. of awards offered: One.
Application Procedure: Applicants must submit a video recording and/or audio cassette with their application. Applications will be considered not eligible and returned if the eligibility criteria is not met, if all the support material specified is not included, if you have requested funding for activities that have already occurred or will be completed before the closing date and also if your application or supporting documentation is late.
Closing Date: March 1st.
Additional Information: The Arts Council will not normally fund activities that diverge from its policies or funding criteria, projects that have already taken place, charity fund raising events, or those that are primarily competitive in nature, or projects or activities that are primarily profit making. All awards are offered subject to the availability of funds and they may be withheld or divided among applicants at the discretion of The Arts Council.

For further information contact:

Music Department
Arts Council of Northern Ireland
77 Malone Road, Belfast, BT9 6AQ, Northern Ireland
Tel: (44) 28 9038 5200
Fax: (44) 28 9066 1715

The Arts Council of Ireland Architecture Publications Assistance Scheme
Subjects: Architecture and design.
Purpose: To support documentation of, or critical reflection on, contemporary Irish architectural design both practical and theoretical.
Eligibility: Open to publishers and publisher and writer/editor jointly. The artist must be of Irish birth or residence and have evidence of having produced a body of work of recognised quality and significance, or in the case of individuals with less experience, demonstrable potential. They need to be able to show evidence of artistic developmental needs, evidence of financial need, including availability of other funding and a likelihood that an award will reach the desired effect. Applicants must be practising artists or arts workers but may not necessarily earn income from their arts practice, they must identify themselves and be recognised by their peers as practising artists.
Level of Study: Professional development.
Type: Assistance scheme.
Value: Up to €13,000.
Frequency: Annual.
Country of Study: Ireland.
Application Procedure: Applications can be made for the publication of books, catalogues or periodicals. Some forms of digital media may also be eligible. An information sheet is available on request or see the website for further information. Applications will be considered not eligible and returned if the eligibility criteria is not met, if all the support material specified is not included, if you requested funding for activities that have already occurred or will be completed before the closing date and also if your application or supporting documentation is late.
Closing Date: April 19th.
Additional Information: The Arts Council will not normally fund activities that diverge from its policies or funding criteria, projects that have already taken place, charity fund raising events, or those that are primarily competitive in nature, or projects or activities that are primarily profit making. All awards are offered subject to the availability of funds and they may be withheld or divided among applicants at the discretion of The Arts Council.

The Arts Council of Ireland Artist-in-the-Community Scheme
Subjects: The arts.
Purpose: To enable artists and community groups to work together on projects.
Eligibility: Open to artists of Irish birth or residence and community groups. The artist must have evidence of having produced a body of work of recognised quality and significance, or in the case of

individuals with less experience, demonstrable potential. They need to be able to show evidence of artistic developmental needs, evidence of financial need, including availability of other funding and a likelihood that an award will reach the desired effect. Applicants must be practising artists or arts workers but may not necessarily earn income from their arts practice, they must identify themselves and be recognised by their peers as practising artists.

Level of Study: Professional development.

Type: Grant.

Length of Study: Varies.

Country of Study: Ireland.

No. of awards offered: Varies.

Application Procedure: Applicants must apply for the application procedure, available on request from CAFE. Applications will be considered not eligible and returned if the eligibility criteria is not met, if all the support material specified is not included, if you have requested funding for activities that have already occurred or will be completed before the closing date and also if your application or supporting documentation is late.

Closing Date: January 25th or June 21st.

Additional Information: This is a partnership scheme administered by CAFE. The Arts Council will not normally fund activities that diverge from its policies or funding criteria, projects that have already taken place, charity fund raising events, or those that are primarily competitive in nature, or projects or activities that are primarily profit making. All awards are offered subject to the availability of funds and they may be withheld or divided among applicants at the discretion of The Arts Council.

For further information contact:

CAFE
10-11 Earl Street South, Dublin 8, Ireland
Tel: (353) 1 473 6600
Fax: (353) 1 473 6577
Email: cafe@connect.ie
www: http://www.communityartsireland.com

The Arts Council of Ireland Arts Management Training Awards

Subjects: Arts management and administration.

Purpose: To raise the standard of arts professionals, enabling them to undertake in-service training or professional development to equip them with the skills necessary to manage the arts effectively, efficiently and imaginatively.

Eligibility: Open to arts managers (a person whose work within an arts organisation comprises managerial, executive or organisational duties and who is responsible for the running of the organisation or part thereof) and administrators and artists. The artist must be of Irish birth or residence and have evidence of having produced a body of work of recognised quality and significance, or in the case of individuals with less experience, demonstrable potential. They need to be able to show evidence of artistic developmental needs, evidence of financial need, including availability of other funding and a likelihood that an award will reach the desired effect. Applicants must be practising artists or arts workers but may not necessarily earn income from their arts practice, they must identify themselves and be recognised by their peers as practising artists.

Level of Study: Professional development.

Type: Award.

Value: Up to €4,000.

Length of Study: Varies.

Frequency: Annual.

Country of Study: Any country.

No. of awards offered: Varies.

Application Procedure: Applicants must complete an application form, available on request. Applications will be considered not eligible and returned if the eligibility criteria is not met, if all the support material specified is not included, if you have requested funding for activities that have already occurred or will be completed before the closing date and also if your application or supporting documentation is late.

Closing Date: May 17th or October 18th.

Additional Information: The Arts Council will not normally fund activities that diverge from its policies or funding criteria, projects that have already taken place, charity fund raising events, or those that are primarily competitive in nature, or projects or activities that are primarily profit making. All awards are offered subject to the availability of funds and they may be withheld or divided among applicants at the discretion of The Arts Council.

The Arts Council of Ireland Author's Royalty Scheme

Subjects: Contemporary literature.

Purpose: To enable publishers to pay royalties to writers in advance of publication.

Eligibility: Open to Irish nationals and permanent residents involved in publishing. The artist must have evidence of having produced a body of work of recognised quality and significance, or in the case of individuals with less experience, demonstrable potential. They need to be able to show evidence of artistic developmental needs, evidence of financial need, including availability of other funding and a likelihood that an award will reach the desired effect. Applicants must be practising artists or arts workers but may not necessarily earn income from their arts practice, they must identify themselves and be recognised by their peers as practising artists.

Level of Study: Professional development.

Type: Grants or loans.

Value: €2,000-6,500.

Frequency: Annual.

No. of awards offered: Varies.

Application Procedure: Applicants must complete an application form, available on request or visit the website for more details. Applications will be considered not eligible and returned if the eligibility criteria is not met, if all the support material specified is not included, if you have requested funding for activities that have already occurred or will be completed before the closing date and also if your application or supporting documentation is late.

Closing Date: April 26th.

Additional Information: This award ensures that important texts of contemporary literature in Irish are translated into English, making them accessible to other readers. The Arts Council will not normally fund activities that diverge from its policies or funding criteria, projects that have already taken place, charity fund raising events, or those that are primarily competitive in nature, or projects or activities that are primarily profit making. All awards are offered subject to the availability of funds and they may be withheld or divided among applicants at the discretion of The Arts Council.

The Arts Council of Ireland Bursaries

Subjects: Creative arts.

Purpose: To allow artists to pursue ideas and fulfil their artistic potential by allowing artists the time, space and freedom to concentrate on a specific body of work, particularly through releasing them from their usual commitments.

Eligibility: Open to applicants who are practising creative artists working in any context or any artform. The artist must be of Irish birth or residence and must have evidence of having produced a body of work of recognised quality and significance, or in the case of individuals with less experience, demonstrable potential. They need to be able to show evidence of artistic developmental needs, evidence of financial need, including availability of other funding and a likelihood that an award will reach the desired effect. Applicants must be practising artists or arts workers but may not necessarily earn income from their arts practice, they must identify themselves and be recognised by their peers as practising artists.

Level of Study: Unrestricted.

Type: Bursary.

Value: Up to €12,000.

No. of awards offered: Varies.

Application Procedure: Applicants must complete an application form, available on request. Applications will be considered not eligible and returned if the eligibility criteria is not met, if all the support material specified is not included, if you have requested funding for activities that have already occurred or will be completed before the closing date and also if your application or supporting documentation is late.

Closing Date: April 12th or October 25th.

Additional Information: The Arts Council will not normally fund activities that diverge from its policies or funding criteria, projects that have already taken place, charity fund raising events, or those that are primarily competitive in nature, or projects or activities that are primarily profit making. All awards are offered subject to the availability of funds and they may be withheld or divided among applicants at the discretion of The Arts Council.

The Arts Council of Ireland Cnuas

Subjects: Creative arts in visual arts, music or literature.

Purpose: To assist members in concentrating their energies on the full-time pursuit of their art.

Eligibility: Members of Aosdána resident in Ireland are eligible to apply. The artist must have evidence of having produced a body of work of recognised quality and significance, or in the case of individuals with less experience, demonstrable potential. They need to be able to show evidence of artistic developmental needs, evidence of financial need, including availability of other funding and a likelihood that an award will reach the desired effect. Applicants must be practising artists or arts workers but may not necessarily·earn income from their arts practice, they must identify themselves and be recognised by their peers as practising artists.

Level of Study: Unrestricted.

Type: Annuity.

Value: €10,000 a year.

Length of Study: Five years.

No. of awards offered: Limited to 200 members.

Application Procedure: An artist may be nominated for membership of Aosdána by two Aosdána members. Applications will be considered not eligible and returned if the eligibility criteria is not met, if all the support material specified is not included, if you have requested funding for activities that have already occurred or will be completed before the closing date and also if your application or supporting documentation is late.

Additional Information: The Arts Council will not normally fund activities that diverge from its policies or funding criteria, projects that have already taken place, charity fund raising events, or those that are primarily competitive in nature, or projects or activities that are primarily profit making. All awards are offered subject to the availability of funds and they may be withheld or divided among applicants at the discretion of The Arts Council.

The Arts Council of Ireland Critical Reflection Award

Subjects: Writing and debate on contemporary arts.

Purpose: To broaden and inform critical debate in the contemporary arts and on art in various contexts. It is also intended to develop the practise of critical writing and thinking by encouraging research into the theory and practice of contemporary arts.

Eligibility: Open to Irish nationals and permanent residents. The artist must have evidence of having produced a body of work of recognised quality and significance, or in the case of individuals with less experience, demonstrable potential. They need to be able to show evidence of artistic developmental needs, evidence of financial need, including availability of other funding and a likelihood that an award will reach the desired effect. Applicants must be practising artists or arts workers but may not necessarily earn income from their arts practice, they must identify themselves and be recognised by their peers as practising artists.

Level of Study: Graduate, Postgraduate.

Type: Award.

Value: Up to €10,000.

Frequency: Annual.

No. of awards offered: One.

Application Procedure: Applicants must complete an application form, available on request. Applications will be considered not eligible and returned if the eligibility criteria is not met, if all the support material specified is not included, if you have requested funding for activities that have already occurred or will be completed before the

closing date and also if your application or supporting documentation is late.

Closing Date: April 19th.

Additional Information: The Arts Council will not normally fund activities that diverge from its policies or funding criteria, projects that have already taken place, charity fund raising events, or those that are primarily competitive in nature, or projects or activities that are primarily profit making. All awards are offered subject to availability of funds and they may be withheld or divided among applicants at the discretion of The Arts Council.

The Arts Council of Ireland Frameworks Awards

Subjects: Animation.

Purpose: To add to the range and scope of Irish animation and encourage new and established animation, which makes use of the medium and is primarily aimed at an adult audience.

Eligibility: The artist must be of Irish birth or residence and must have evidence of having produced a body of work of recognised quality and significance, or in the case of individuals with less experience, demonstrable potential. They need to be able to show evidence of artistic developmental needs, evidence of financial need, including availability of other funding and a likelihood that an award will reach the desired effect. Applicants must be practising artists or arts workers but may not necessarily earn income from their arts practice, they must identify themselves and be recognised by their peers as practising artists.

Value: €25,000-32,000 to fund up to six animated shorts.

Country of Study: Ireland.

Application Procedure: Applicants must send completed applications to Bord Scannán na hÉireann. Applications will be considered not eligible and returned if the eligibility criteria is not met, if all the support material specified is not included, if you have requested funding for activities that have already occurred or will be completed before the closing date and also if your application or supporting documentation is late.

Closing Date: April 12th.

Contributor: The scheme is co-funded by RTÉ, Bord Scannán na hÉireann and The Arts Council.

Additional Information: Information can be obtained from both the Arts Council and the Bord Scannán na hÉireann. The Arts Council will not normally fund activities that diverge from its policies or funding criteria, projects that have already taken place, charity fund raising events, or those that are primarily competitive in nature, or projects or activities that are primarily profit making. All awards are offered subject to the availability of funds and they may be withheld or divided among applicants at the discretion of The Arts Council.

For further information contact:

Bord Scannán na hÉireann/The Irish Film Board
Rockfort House
St Augustine Street, Galway, Ireland
Tel: (353) 9 156 1398
Fax: (353) 9 156 1405
Email: info@filmboard.ie
www: http://www.filmboard.ie

The Arts Council of Ireland Margaret Arnold Scholarship

Subjects: Instrumental performance and singing.

Purpose: To facilitate high level development and training for instrumentalists and singers.

Eligibility: Open to Irish nationals and permanent residents who are musicians and are able to demonstrate that they have completed formal performance studies to an advanced level, or have attained a comparable standard in performance by other required documented means. They need to be able to show evidence of artistic developmental needs, evidence of financial need, including availability of other funding and a likelihood that an award will reach the desired effect. Applicants must be practising artists or arts workers but may not necessarily earn income from their arts practice, they must identify themselves and be recognised by their peers as practising artists.

Level of Study: Graduate, Postgraduate.

Type: Scholarship.
Value: €2,500.
Frequency: Annual.
No. of awards offered: One.
Application Procedure: Applicants must complete an application form, available on request or see the website for more details. Applications will be considered not eligible and returned if the eligibility criteria is not met, if all the support material specified is not included, if you have requested funding for activities that have already occurred or will be completed before the closing date and also if your application or supporting documentation is late.
Closing Date: August 23rd.
Additional Information: This award will be offered in rotation to instrumentalists and singers. The Arts Council will not normally fund activities that diverge from its policies or funding criteria, projects that have already taken place, charity fund raising events, or those that are primarily competitive in nature, or projects or activities that are primarily profit making. All awards are offered subject to the availability of funds and they may be withheld or divided among applicants at the discretion of The Arts Council.

The Arts Council of Ireland Music Publications and Recording Scheme

Subjects: Musical composition and performance.
Purpose: To ensure that the work of Irish composers and performers is available other than in live performance and to ensure that important or neglected materials of Irish music are preserved and disseminated to the highest professional standard.
Eligibility: The artist must be of Irish birth or residence and must have evidence of having produced a body of work of recognised quality and significance, or in the case of individuals with less experience, demonstrable potential. They need to be able to show evidence of artistic developmental needs, evidence of financial need, including availability of other funding and a likelihood that an award will reach the desired effect. Applicants must be practising artists or arts workers but may not necessarily earn income from their arts practice, they must identify themselves and be recognised by their peers as practising artists.
Type: Project grant.
Value: €3,800.
Country of Study: Ireland.
Application Procedure: Applicants must complete an application form, available on request. Applications will be considered not eligible and returned if the eligibility criteria is not met, if all the support material specified is not included, if you have requested funding for activities that have already occurred or will be completed before the closing date and also if your application or supporting documentation is late.
Closing Date: March 8th and September 27th.
Additional Information: The Scheme will assist in the making of CD recordings and in the case of traditional music, music publications. The Arts Council will not normally fund activities that diverge from its policies or funding criteria, projects that have already taken place, charity fund raising events, or those that are primarily competitive in nature, or projects or activities that are primarily profit making. All awards are offered subject to the availability of funds and they may be withheld or divided among applicants at the discretion of The Arts Council.

The Arts Council of Ireland Professional Development and Training Award

Subjects: Any area of practical arts.
Purpose: To help artists and performers to achieve the highest standards through further professional development and formation, and specifically assists any development activity that enhances creative practice and facilitates career development.
Eligibility: All practising creative and performing artists and technical personnel working in any context or any artform are eligible. The artist must have evidence of having produced a body of work of recognised quality and significance, or in the case of individuals with less experience, demonstrable potential. They need to be able to show evidence of artistic developmental needs, evidence of financial

need, including availability of other funding and a likelihood that an award will reach the desired effect.
Type: Award.
Value: Ranges from €1,000-12,000.
No. of awards offered: Varies.
Application Procedure: Applicants for courses starting in September should apply before the earlier closing date and any auditions will be held then. Please visit the website for more details and request an information sheet and application form. Applications will be considered not eligible and returned if the eligibility criteria is not met, if all the support material specified is not included, if you have requested funding for activities that have already occurred or will be completed before the closing date and also if your application or supporting documentation is late.
Closing Date: February 22nd or August 23rd.
Additional Information: Applicants may be in receipt of a maximum of two awards per year. The Arts Council will not normally fund activities that diverge from its policies or funding criteria, projects that have already taken place, charity fund raising events, or those that are primarily competitive in nature, or projects or activities that are primarily profit making. All awards are offered subject to the availability of funds and they may be withheld or divided among applicants at the discretion of The Arts Council.

The Arts Council of Ireland Projects

Subjects: All aspects of art.
Purpose: To assist the devising, exploration and implementation of creative ideas in any artform or a combination of artforms. Emphasis is on the creation of new work, experimentation and innovation. This scheme funds the development and production phases of artistic projects.
Eligibility: Open to artists, organisations and other individuals. The artist must be of Irish birth or residence and must have evidence of having produced a body of work of recognised quality and significance, or in the case of individuals with less experience, demonstrable potential. They need to be able to show evidence of artistic developmental needs, evidence of financial need, including availability of other funding and a likelihood that an award will reach the desired effect. Applicants must be practising artists or arts workers but may not necessarily earn income from their arts practice, they must identify themselves and be recognised by their peers as practising artists.
Level of Study: Professional development.
Type: Award.
Value: Up to €20,000.
Length of Study: Up to five years.
Application Procedure: Request an information sheet and application form and visit the website for more details. Applications will be considered not eligible and returned if the eligibility criteria is not met, if all the support material specified is not included, if you have requested funding for activities that have already occurred or will be completed before the closing date and also if your application or supporting documentation is late.
Closing Date: August 30th.
Additional Information: The Arts Council will not normally fund activities that diverge from its policies or funding criteria, projects that have already taken place, charity fund raising events, or those that are primarily competitive in nature, or projects or activities that are primarily profit making. All awards are offered subject to the availability of funds and they may be withheld or divided among applicants at the discretion of The Arts Council.

The Arts Council of Ireland PS1 Fellowship

Subjects: Visual arts.
Purpose: To provide a year's studio space at the Institute for Art and Urban Resources.
Eligibility: Open to Irish nationals and permanent residents. The artist must have evidence of having produced a body of work of recognised quality and significance, or in the case of individuals with less experience, demonstrable potential. They need to be able to show evidence of artistic developmental needs, evidence of financial need, including availability of other funding and a likelihood that an award

will reach the desired effect. Applicants must be practising artists or arts workers but may not necessarily earn income from their arts practice, they must identify themselves and be recognised by their peers as practising artists.

Level of Study: Professional development.

Type: Fellowship.

Value: Approx. €32,000. The award includes provision for accommodation plus a monthly stipend of $1,500.

Length of Study: One year.

Frequency: Annual.

Study Establishment: The Institute for Art and Urban Resources at PS1, New York.

Country of Study: United States of America.

No. of awards offered: One.

Application Procedure: Applicants must complete an application form, available on request. Final selection is made by a PS1 jury in New York on the basis of a shortlist provided by The Arts Council. Applications will be considered not eligible and returned if the eligibility criteria is not met, if all the support material specified is not included, if you have requested funding for activities that have already occurred or will be completed before the closing date and also if your application or supporting documentation is late.

Closing Date: Please contact the Arts Council.

Additional Information: Applicants from Northern Ireland should contact the Arts Council of Northern Ireland who provide a similar award. Further information is available on request. The Arts Council will not normally fund activities that diverge from its policies or funding criteria, projects that have already taken place, charity fund raising events, or those that are primarily competitive in nature, or projects or activities that are primarily profit making. All awards are offered subject to the availability of funds and they may be withheld or divided among applicants at the discretion of The Arts Council.

For further information contact:

Visual Arts Department
Arts Council of Northern Ireland
MacNeice House
77 Malone Road, Belfast, BT9 6AQ, Northern Ireland

The Arts Council of Ireland Publications Assistance Scheme in Visual Arts

Subjects: Visual arts.

Purpose: To contribute towards the documentation, promotion and understanding of the full range of contemporary visual arts practice through both digital and traditional publication methods.

Eligibility: Open to Irish nationals and permanent residents involved in promoting visual arts and architecture. The artist must have evidence of having produced a body of work of recognised quality and significance, or in the case of individuals with less experience, demonstrable potential. They need to be able to show evidence of artistic developmental needs, evidence of financial need, including availability of other funding and a likelihood that an award will reach the desired effect. Applicants must be practising artists or arts workers but may not necessarily earn income from their arts practice, they must identify themselves and be recognised by their peers as practising artists.

Level of Study: Professional development.

Type: Grant.

Value: €1,000-10,000.

Frequency: Annual.

Country of Study: Ireland.

No. of awards offered: Varies.

Application Procedure: Applicants must complete an application form, available on request. Applications will be considered not eligible and returned if the eligibility criteria is not met, if all the support material specified is not included, if you have requested funding for activities that have already occurred or will be completed before the closing date and also if your application or supporting documentation is late.

Closing Date: May 10th.

Additional Information: Publications may include books, catalogues, newsletters, magazines, artists' self help manuals,

directories and limited edition artists' books. Further information is available on request. The Arts Council will not normally fund activities that diverge from its policies or funding criteria, projects that have already taken place, charity fund raising events, or those that are primarily competitive in nature, or projects or activities that are primarily profit making. All awards are offered subject to the availability of funds and they may be withheld or divided among applicants at the discretion of The Arts Council.

The Arts Council of Ireland Residencies

Subjects: All aspects of art.

Purpose: To offers artists an opportunity to work on a specific project or programme and/or develop their own practice in a new environment or specific location outside their normal workplace. Other individuals working in the arts also have an opportunity to act as hosts for artists.

Eligibility: The artist must have evidence of having produced a body of work of recognised quality and significance, or in the case of individuals with less experience, demonstrable potential. They need to be able to show evidence of artistic developmental needs, evidence of financial need, including availability of other funding and a likelihood that an award will reach the desired effect. Applicants must be practising artists or arts workers but may not necessarily earn income from their arts practice, they must identify themselves and be recognised by their peers as practising artists.

Type: Residency.

Value: Up to €15,000, with most awards between €2,500-7,000.

Length of Study: From four weeks to one year.

No. of awards offered: Varies.

Application Procedure: Applicants must request an information sheet and application form and look on the website for more details. Applications will be considered not eligible and returned if the eligibility criteria is not met, if all the support material specified is not included, if you have requested funding for activities that have already occurred or will be completed before the closing date and also if your application or supporting documentation is late.

Closing Date: March 1st.

Additional Information: The Arts Council will not normally fund activities that diverge from its policies or funding criteria, projects that have already taken place, charity fund raising events, or those that are primarily competitive in nature, or projects or activities that are primarily profit making. All awards are offered subject to the availability of funds and they may be withheld or divided among applicants at the discretion of The Arts Council.

The Arts Council of Ireland Travel Grants

Subjects: Professional arts.

Purpose: To improve the professional development, formation and networking opportunities of artists and people working professionally in the arts.

Eligibility: Open to artists, performers, arts administrators and managers, arts practitioners and technical personnel in the arts. The artist must be of Irish birth or residence and must have evidence of having produced a body of work of recognised quality and significance, or in the case of individuals with less experience, demonstrable potential. They need to be able to show evidence of artistic developmental needs, evidence of financial need, including availability of other funding and a likelihood that an award will reach the desired effect. Applicants must be practising artists or arts workers but may not necessarily earn income from their arts practice, they must identify themselves and be recognised by their peers as practising artists.

Level of Study: Professional development.

Type: Travel grant.

Value: €5,000 and applicants may be in receipt of a maximum of two awards per year.

Length of Study: Up to six months.

Country of Study: Outside Ireland.

No. of awards offered: Varies.

Application Procedure: Applicants must complete an application form, available on request. Applications will be considered not eligible and returned if the eligibility criteria is not met, if all the support material specified is not included, if you have requested funding for activities that have already occurred or will be completed before the closing date and also if your application or supporting documentation is late.

Closing Date: One month before departure.

Additional Information: This grant is not intended to fund study periods or courses abroad. The Arts Council will not normally fund activities that diverge from its policies or funding criteria, projects that have already taken place, charity fund raising events, or those that are primarily competitive in nature, or projects or activities that are primarily profit making. All awards are offered subject to the availability of funds and they may be withheld or divided among applicants at the discretion of The Arts Council.

The Arts Council of Ireland Visual Artists-in-Prisons Scheme

Subjects: Visual arts.

Purpose: This scheme, which is complimentary to an existing art programme within the prison system, allows artists to work with prisoners in one of the country's prisons or detention centres.

Eligibility: Open to Irish artists (those of Irish birth or residence) who are interested in being placed on the panel of shortlisted artists to be involved in this scheme. The artist must have evidence of having produced a body of work of recognised quality and significance or in the case of individuals with less experience, demonstrable potential. They need to be able to show evidence of artistic developmental needs, evidence of financial need, including availability of other funding and a likelihood that an award will reach the desired effect. Applicants must be practising artists or arts workers but may not necessarily earn income from their arts practice, they must identify themselves and be recognised by their peers as practising artists.

Level of Study: Professional development.

Value: €1,600. €2,000 where the artist lives over 50 miles from the prison or detention centre.

Length of Study: 8-10 days.

Frequency: When the opportunity arises. Please contact the Arts Council.

Country of Study: Ireland.

No. of awards offered: Varies.

Application Procedure: Applicants must complete an application form, available on request to the Visual Arts department. Applications will be considered not eligible and returned if the eligibility criteria is not met, if all the support material specified is not included, if you have requested funding for activities that have already occurred or will be completed before the closing date and also if your application or supporting documentation is late.

Closing Date: Continuous.

Additional Information: This scheme is offered in partnership with the Department of Justice. All applications are carefully considered by both the Arts Council and the Department of Justice. As opportunities arise within the prison system an appropriate artist may be called on to undertake a project within a particular prison. The Arts Council will not normally fund activities that diverge from its policies or funding criteria, projects that have already taken place, charity fund raising events, or those that are primarily competitive in nature, or projects or activities that are primarily profit making. All awards are offered subject to the availability of funds and they may be withheld or divided among applicants at the discretion of The Arts Council.

The Arts Council of Northern Ireland Alice Berger Hammerschlag Trust Award

Subjects: The arts.

Eligibility: Open to Irish nationals and permanent residents of any age. The artist must have evidence of having produced a body of work of recognised quality and significance, or in the case of individuals with less experience, demonstrable potential. They need to be able to show evidence of artistic developmental needs, evidence of financial need, including availability of other funding and a likelihood that an award will reach the desired effect. Applicants must be practising artists or arts workers but may not necessarily earn income

from their arts practice, they must identify themselves and be recognised by their peers as practising artists.

Level of Study: Professional development.

Type: Travel grant.

Value: At least €1,000.

Frequency: Annual.

Country of Study: Any country.

No. of awards offered: One.

Application Procedure: Applicants must submit a completed application form with appropriate documentation in the form of slides or photographs. Application forms are available on request. Applications will be considered not eligible and returned if the eligibility criteria is not met, if all the support material specified is not included, if you have requested funding for activities that have already occurred or will be completed before the closing date and also if your application or supporting documentation is late.

Closing Date: May 3rd.

Additional Information: Further information is available on request. The Arts Council will not normally fund activities that diverge from its policies or funding criteria, projects that have already taken place, charity fund raising events, or those that are primarily competitive in nature, or projects or activities that are primarily profit making. All awards are offered subject to the availability of funds and they may be withheld or divided among applicants at the discretion of The Arts Council.

For further information contact:

Visual Arts Department
Arts Council of Northern Ireland
MacNeice House
77 Malone Road, Belfast, BT9 6AQ, Northern Ireland

Banff Residencies

Subjects: For creative artists, designers and technologists.

Purpose: Aims to enable artists to work on specific arts projects or programmes, observe artistic developments in their fields of interest and pursue opportunities for artistic growth and development.

Eligibility: The artist must be of Irish birth or residency and must have evidence of having produced a body of work of recognised quality and significance, or in the case of individuals with less experience, demonstrable potential. They need to be able to show evidence of artistic developmental needs, evidence of financial need, including availability of other funding and a likelihood that an award will reach the desired effect. Applicants must be practising artists or arts workers but may not necessarily earn income from their arts practice, they must identify themselves and be recognised by their peers as practising artists.

Type: Residency.

Value: The award covers the residency fee, travel, insurance and some material costs.

Frequency: Annual.

No. of awards offered: Two.

Application Procedure: Applicants must request an information sheet and application form and visit the website for more details. Applications will be considered not eligible and returned if the eligibility criteria is not met, if all the support material specified is not included, if you have requested funding for activities that have already occurred or will be completed before the closing date and also if your application or supporting documentation is late.

Closing Date: March 1st.

Additional Information: The programme is run as a partnership between An Chomhairle Ealaíon/The Arts Council, Arts Council of Northern Ireland and the Banff Centre for the Arts. The Arts Council will not normally fund activities that diverge from its policies or funding criteria, projects that have already taken place, charity fund raising events, or those that are primarily competitive in nature, or projects or activities that are primarily profit making. All awards are offered subject to the availability of funds and they may be withheld or divided among applicants at the discretion of The Arts Council.

The George Campbell Memorial Travel Award

Subjects: The arts.

Purpose: The award was established to celebrate the strong cultural contact which Irish artist George Campbell developed with Spain and is intended to allow for a period of work in Spain.

Eligibility: Open to Irish nationals and permanent residents. The artist must have evidence of having produced a body of work of recognised quality and significance, or in the case of individuals with less experience, demonstrable potential. They need to be able to show evidence of artistic developmental needs, evidence of financial need, including availability of other funding and a likelihood that an award will reach the desired effect. Applicants must be practising artists or arts workers but may not necessarily earn income from their arts practice, they must identify themselves and be recognised by their peers as practising artists.

Level of Study: Unrestricted.

Type: Travel grant.

Value: €3,800.

Frequency: Annual.

Country of Study: Spain.

No. of awards offered: One.

Application Procedure: Applicants must complete an application form, available on request. Applications will be considered not eligible and returned if the eligibility criteria is not met, if all the support material specified is not included, if you have requested funding for activities that have already occurred or will be completed before the closing date and also if your application or supporting documentation is late.

Closing Date: March 29th.

Contributor: The Arts Council/An Chomhairle Ealaion, The Arts Council of Northern Ireland and the Instituto Cervantes.

Additional Information: The award is administered on alternate years by the two Arts Councils. The Arts Council will not normally fund activities that diverge from its policies or funding criteria, projects that have already taken place, charity fund raising events, or those that are primarily competitive in nature, or projects or activities that are primarily profit making. All awards are offered subject to the availability of funds and they may be withheld or divided among applicants at the discretion of The Arts Council.

The Kevin Kieran Award

Subjects: Architecture.

Purpose: To support the artistic formation and the career development of the architect and to direct funding towards architectural excellence and innovation. It will provide an opportunity to travel, work and ultimately be contracted to design and run a building for the Office of Public Works.

Eligibility: Open to emerging and gifted graduates of architecture. The artist must be of Irish birth or residency and must have evidence of having produced a body of work of recognised quality and significance, or in the case of individuals with less experience, demonstrable potential. They need to be able to show evidence of artistic developmental needs, evidence of financial need, including availability of other funding and a likelihood that an award will reach the desired effect. Applicants must be practising artists or arts workers but may not necessarily earn income from their arts practice, they must identify themselves and be recognised by their peers as practising artists.

Level of Study: Graduate.

Value: €50,000.

Frequency: Every two years.

No. of awards offered: One.

Application Procedure: Applicants must complete an application form, available on request. Applications will be considered not eligible and returned if the eligibility criteria is not met, if all the support material specified is not included, if you have requested funding for activities that have already occurred or will be completed before the closing date and also if your application or supporting documentation is late.

Closing Date: April 19th.

Additional Information: This Award commemorates the life and work of the late Kevin Keiran, architect, tutor and former consultant to the Arts Council. The Arts Council will not normally fund activities that diverge from its policies or funding criteria, projects that have

already taken place, charity fund raising events, or those that are primarily competitive in nature, or projects or activities that are primarily profit making. All awards are offered subject to the availability of funds and they may be withheld or divided among applicants at the discretion of The Arts Council.

The Macaulay Fellowship

Subjects: Visual arts, literature and musical composition on a rotating basis.

Purpose: To further the liberal education of young creative artists. This does not refer to formal training courses.

Eligibility: Open to applicants born in Ireland and under 30 years of age on June 30th in the year of application, who have a proven track record in their discipline and have established a clearly defined career path.

Level of Study: Professional development.

Type: Fellowship.

Value: €5,000.

Frequency: Annual.

Country of Study: Any country.

No. of awards offered: One.

Application Procedure: Applicants must submit detailed plans on how they would use the award and indicate the extent to which such arrangements have been put in place. The standard application form must be completed and is available on request. Applications will be considered not eligible and returned if the eligibility criteria is not met, if all the support material specified is not included, if you have requested funding for activities that have already occurred or will be completed before the closing date and also if your application or supporting documentation is late.

Closing Date: April 19th.

Additional Information: The fellowship was established by W B Macaulay in honour of President Sean T O'Kelly. The Arts Council will not normally fund activities that diverge from its policies or funding criteria, projects that have already taken place, charity fund raising events, or those that are primarily competitive in nature, or projects or activities that are primarily profit making. All awards are offered subject to the availability of funds and they may be withheld or divided among applicants at the discretion of The Arts Council.

The Marten Toonder Award

Subjects: Music, literature and visual arts on a rotating basis.

Purpose: To honour an artist of established reputation.

Eligibility: Open to applicants of Irish birth or residence. The artist must have evidence of having produced a body of work of recognised quality and significance, or in the case of individuals with less experience, demonstrable potential. They need to be able to show evidence of artistic developmental needs, evidence of financial need, including availability of other funding and a likelihood that an award will reach the desired effect. Applicants must be practising artists or arts workers but may not necessarily earn income from their arts practice, they must identify themselves and be recognised by their peers as practising artists.

Level of Study: Unrestricted.

Value: €10,000.

Frequency: Annual.

Country of Study: Any country.

No. of awards offered: One.

Application Procedure: Applicants must complete an application form, available on request from the Council. Candidates should also enclose a detailed curriculum vitae as well as an excerpt or copy of their work and detailed plans on how the applicant proposes to use the award and the extent to which arrangements (tentative or otherwise) have been made for this purpose. Applications will be considered not eligible and returned if the eligibility criteria is not met, if all the support material specified is not included, if you requested funding for activities that have already occurred or will be completed before the closing date and also if your application or supporting documentation is late.

Closing Date: April 19th.

Additional Information: The Arts Council will not normally fund activities that diverge from its policies or funding criteria, projects that have already taken place, charity fund raising events, or those that are primarily competitive in nature, or projects or activities that are primarily profit making. All awards are offered subject to the availability of funds and they may be withheld or divided among applicants at the discretion of The Arts Council.

Splanc!

Subjects: Contemporary and traditional arts in Ireland, especially those normally overlooked by television.

Purpose: To support the making of new and innovative television programmes.

Eligibility: Open to television and film makers with specific skills in the area of video and film and others who also have a special interest in, and connection with, the arts in Ireland.

Level of Study: Professional development.

Value: Approx. €25,394.

Country of Study: Ireland.

No. of awards offered: Between six and eight.

Application Procedure: Applicants must complete an application form, available on request. Applications will be considered not eligible and returned if the eligibility criteria is not met, if all the support material specified is not included, if you have requested funding for activities that have already occurred or will be completed before the closing date and also if your application or supporting documentation is late. More information is available from the website.

Additional Information: This fund was established by TG4 (http://www.tg4.ie) and The Arts Council/An Chomhairle Ealaíon.

The Thomas Dammann Award

Subjects: Visual or applied arts, craft, design, architecture and history of art.

Purpose: To allow students to travel abroad and visit relevant sites. In honour of the late Thomas Dammann Junior.

Eligibility: Open to students studying the relevant subjects. The artist must be of Irish birth and must have evidence of having produced a body of work of recognised quality and significance, or in the case of individuals with less experience, demonstrable potential. They need to be able to show evidence of artistic developmental needs, evidence of financial need, including availability of other funding and a likelihood that an award will reach the desired effect. Applicants must be practising artists or arts workers but may not necessarily earn income from their arts practice, they must identify themselves and be recognised by their peers as practising artists.

Type: Award.

Value: Up to €2,600.

Study Establishment: Exhibitions, museums, galleries and buildings of architectural importance.

No. of awards offered: Varies.

Application Procedure: Applicants must complete an application form, available on request. Applications will be considered not eligible and returned if the eligibility criteria is not met, if all the support material specified is not included, if you have requested funding for activities that have already occurred or will be completed before the closing date and also if your application or supporting documentation is late.

Closing Date: February 22nd.

Additional Information: The Arts Council will not normally fund activities that diverge from its policies or funding criteria, projects that have already taken place, charity fund raising events, or those that are primarily competitive in nature, or projects or activities that are primarily profit making. All awards are offered subject to the availability of funds and they may be withheld or divided among applicants at the discretion of The Arts Council.

ARTS COUNCIL OF WALES

Museum Place, Cardiff, CF10 3NX, Wales
Tel: (44) 29 2037 6500
Fax: (44) 29 2022 1447
Email: information@ccc-acw.org.uk
www: http://www.ccc-acw.org.uk
Contact: Mrs Angela Blackburn, Information Officer

The Arts Council of Wales is the national organisation with specific responsibility for the funding and development of the arts in Wales. Most of its funds come from the National Assembly for Wales, but it also distributes National Lottery funds to the arts in Wales.

ACW Artform Development Scheme

Subjects: Fine art.

Purpose: To support new talent and ideas in a range of activities eg. platforms of work in process or exploratory productions in mixed artforms.

Type: Grant.

Value: UK £2,000-10,000.

Country of Study: Wales.

Application Procedure: Applicants must submit a completed application. These can be submitted at any time but early notice is needed for major projects. Applicants must contact Performing Arts at the Artform Development Division in Cardiff.

Closing Date: End of March.

ACW Arts for All

Subjects: The arts.

Purpose: To support projects that encourage people to enjoy, or participate in, the arts.

Type: Grant.

Length of Study: Up to three years.

Application Procedure: Applicants must contact the Lottery Division in Cardiff, Carmarthen or Colwyn Bay for further information.

Closing Date: January 14th, May 31st or September 29th.

Additional Information: Priority will be given to those projects which are aimed at young people and involve targeted community development or training within the arts.

ACW Awards for Advanced Study in Music

Subjects: Instrumental, vocal and conducting.

Purpose: To provide opportunities for advanced postgraduate study.

Eligibility: Open to singers and instrumentalists who will be under 28 years of age on February 1st in the year of application, who were born and educated in Wales, or who have been permanently resident in Wales for at least two years.

Level of Study: Postgraduate, Professional development.

Type: Study grant.

Value: Varies.

Frequency: Annual.

Country of Study: Any country.

No. of awards offered: Limited.

Application Procedure: Applicants must address enquiries to the Director of the Music Department at Artform Development Division in Cardiff.

Closing Date: February 1st.

Funding: Government.

Contributor: The Welsh Arts Council.

No. of awards given last year: Six.

No. of applicants last year: 45.

Additional Information: Those in full-time employment in music and students of non-Welsh origin studying at colleges in Wales are not eligible.

ACW Community Touring Night Out

Subjects: Performing arts.

Purpose: To support community-based organisations throughout Wales with access to suitable premises who wish to promote occasional professional performing arts events for their locality.

Eligibility: Schools and colleges may participate if offering a service to the wider community generally outside normal teaching time.
Type: Grant.
Country of Study: Wales.
Application Procedure: Applications may be submitted at any time to the Community Touring Manager, Access Development Division in Cardiff.
Closing Date: Please contact the Arts Council.
Additional Information: Community based organisations dedicated to the arts who wish to plan more than five events in a year may need to apply for a grant either from the Performing Arts Events Programme or the Lottery Arts For All (Fast Track) Scheme and should seek advice from their local ACW office or the Community Touring Manager.

ACW Grants to Publishers

Subjects: The publication of literary writing.
Purpose: To fund the work of publishers in producing and promoting literary books of Welsh interest or by writers living in Wales. These grants include production grants for individual books, grants for publishing programmes, grants to small presses and magazines, translation grants, commission grants, training and marketing grants.
Closing Date: Please contact the Arts Council.
Additional Information: Applicants should contact the Literature Department, Artform Development Division, Cardiff office for details.

ACW Inter-Recce

Subjects: The arts.
Purpose: To encourage contact with producers and presenters in countries outside the United Kingdom with a view to future collaborations.
Value: Financial assistance.
Country of Study: Any country except the United Kingdom.
Application Procedure: Applicants must contact the Wales Arts International Office in Cardiff for further information.
Closing Date: Applications may be submitted throughout the year.

ACW Lottery Film Grants

Subjects: Film production.
Purpose: To enable the development of scripts and production of films in Wales and to increase the level of film production and contribute to the growth of a national film industry reflecting Wales' society and culture.
No. of awards offered: Varies.
Application Procedure: Applicants must contact Performing Arts, Artform Development Division in Cardiff for more details.
Closing Date: Applications can be submitted at any time.

ACW Performing Arts Events Programme

Subjects: Performing arts.
Purpose: To help venues and presenters in Wales with the costs of an annual programme of performing arts events.
Country of Study: Wales.
Application Procedure: Applications should be sent to the Access Development Division at any ACW office.
Closing Date: November 12th.
Additional Information: These grants can assist with promoting a single event or series of events which enhance a venue's programme. They are not available to venues receiving an ACW revenue grant or to users of the Community Touring Scheme.

ACW Performing Arts Projects

Subjects: Performing arts.
Purpose: To enable production by professional artists based in Wales working with a presenting organisation.
Eligibility: Partnerships are a particular feature of this scheme and the involvement of a venue or presenter is essential. Applications may come from groups of artists, arts organisations or presenters.
Type: Grant.
Value: Grants range from UK £5,000-40,000. Quality, innovation and potential to enrich programming for the public will be priorities.

Application Procedure: Applications should be sent to Performing Arts, Artform Development Division in Cardiff.
Closing Date: February 1st.
Additional Information: Venue commissions of artists may be one form of application.

ACW Writers' Bursaries, Enabling Grants and Travel Awards

Subjects: Writing.
Purpose: To provide bursaries for several writers living in Wales or writing in Welsh, enabling them to devote more time to writing. Awards are also available for disabled writers, for travel and research and to promote international exchange.
Type: Bursaries, grants and travel awards.
Frequency: Annual.
Application Procedure: Applicants must contact Artform Development Division (Literature) in Cardiff for information.
Closing Date: November 30th.

ACW Writers' Critical Service

Subjects: Development of writing skills.
Purpose: To provide assessments of writers' work to help them develop their skills.
Eligibility: Open to any writers of Welsh and any writers of English living in Wales.
No. of awards offered: Varies.
Application Procedure: Applicants must contact Artform Development Division (Literature) in Cardiff for more details. A small fee is payable.
Closing Date: Applications may be submitted throughout the year.

ACW Writers' Mentoring

Subjects: Writing skills.
Purpose: To provide advice and assistance to promising authors to help develop their work to a publishable standard.
Eligibility: Open to any writer of Welsh and any writers of English living in Wales.
No. of awards offered: Varies.
Application Procedure: Applicants must contact Artform Development Division (Literature) in Cardiff for more details.

ARTS INTERNATIONAL

251 Park Avenue South
5th Floor, New York, NY, 10010, United States of America
Tel: (1) 212 674 9744
Fax: (1) 212 674 9092
Email: ainternational@iie.org
www: http://www.artsinternational.org
Contact: Mr Adam Bernstein, Director, Advised Funds & Regranting Programs

Arts International encourages interaction and connection in the visual and performing arts through its grant-making programmes, information services, international forums, conferences and special initiatives.

Artists Exploration Fund

Subjects: The fine arts.
Purpose: To support the development of relationships with artists and art organisations, research of significant artistic expression, the participation in international conferences and seminars, or the creation of new work.
Eligibility: Applicants must be individual performing artists who are United States citizens or permanent residents. Applications will not be accepted from students, Scholars, curators, presenters, administrators or critics. Grant decisions will be based on artistic excellence, the applicant's reasons for wanting to travel to a particular country and the scope and feasibility of the proposed activity.

Level of Study: Professional development.
Type: Award.
Value: Grants range from US$1,000-3,000. The Artists Exploration Fund will not support travel costs related to touring. Eligible expenses may include international and in-country travel, food and lodging, and other essential costs. Travel to any country outside the United States and its protectorates is eligible.
Application Procedure: Applicants must refer to the website for guidelines and application details.
Closing Date: April 23rd.
Additional Information: This fund was made possible by a generous grant from the Doris Duke Charitable Foundation, which is designed to enable individual performing artists to pursue opportunities abroad that further their artistic development.

Arts International Arts Presenters Exploration Fund

Subjects: The arts.
Purpose: To provide international travel support.
Eligibility: Open to non-profit making managers, presenters or managers with a non-profit affiliation.
Level of Study: Professional development.
Type: Award.
Value: Varies.
Application Procedure: Applicants must refer to the website for guidelines and application details.
Closing Date: Please contact the organisation.

The Fund for US Artists at International Festivals and Exhibitions

Subjects: Music, drama or dancing.
Purpose: To ensure that the excellence, diversity and vitality of the arts in the United States of America are represented at major international events. To provide grants to individual performing artists and performing arts organisations that have been invited to participate in international festivals outside the United States.
Eligibility: Open to United States citizens or permanent residents only.
Level of Study: Professional development.
Type: Grant.
Value: Up to US$25,000 to cover travel, per diem, international communication costs, shipping, and artist and agent fees.
Frequency: Three times each year.
Country of Study: Any country.
No. of awards offered: 15-20.
Application Procedure: Applicants must write to Kay Takeda the Program Manager for further details or refer to the website.
Closing Date: May 2nd, September 5th or January 16th.
Funding: Government, Private.
Contributor: The National Endowment for the Arts, the United States Department of State, the Pew Charitable Trusts and the Rockefeller Foundation, with additional support from the Doris Duke Charitable Foundation.
No. of awards given last year: 100.
No. of applicants last year: 300.
Additional Information: The Fund is particularly interested in supporting applicants invited to festivals in areas of the world where United States' work is less frequently seen, including Africa, Asia, and Latin America.

THE ASCAP FOUNDATION

One Lincoln Plaza, New York, NY, 10023, United States of America
Tel: (1) 212 621 6327
Fax: (1) 212 621 6504
Email: frichard@ascap.com
www: http://www.ascap.com
Contact: Ms Frances Richard

ASCAP, the American Society of Composers, Authors and Publishers is a membership association of over 120,000 composers, songwriters, lyricists and music publishers. ASCAP's function is to protect the rights of its members by licensing and paying royalties for the public performances of their copyrighted works.

ASCAP Foundation Morton Gould Young Composer Awards

Subjects: Music composition.
Purpose: To encourage composers, up to the age of 30, by providing recognition, appreciation and monetary awards to gifted, emerging talents.
Eligibility: Open to United States citizens or permanent residents who have not reached their 30th birthday by March 1st in the year of competition.
Level of Study: Unrestricted.
Type: Cash award.
Value: US$30,000.
Frequency: Annual.
Country of Study: Any country.
No. of awards offered: Varies from year to year.
Application Procedure: Applicants must complete an application form.
Closing Date: Postmarked March 1st.
Funding: Private.
No. of awards given last year: 30.
No. of applicants last year: 520.

ASHRIDGE MANAGEMENT COLLEGE

Berkhamsted, Hertfordshire, HP4 1NS, England
Tel: (44) 1442 841143
Fax: (44) 1442 841144
Email: doris.boyle@ashridge.org.uk
www: http://www.ashridge.org.uk
Contact: MBA Admissions Officer

Ashridge Management College's expertise, built up through many years experience as a provider of executive development, has deliberately shaped their mission to help practising and experienced managers become even more effective as leaders and in so doing fulfil their individual potential and that of the organisation.

Ashridge Essay Award

Subjects: The changing relationship between business, government and the non-profit sector, how companies balance the competing demands of different stakeholders, corporate social responsibility and corporate citizenship, transparency, accountability and corporate reporting, ethics and values in today's organisations.
Purpose: To increase managers' understanding of the changing role of business in society and how their companies can best respond to these changes.
Eligibility: Open only to full-time or part-time students studying on an MBA programme accredited by the Association of MBA's.
Level of Study: MBA.
Type: Award.
Value: A UK £3,000 prize, together with a commemorative trophy. In addition, the winning entrant's business school will be awarded a prize of UK £3,000 for developing teaching and research materials on the changing role of business and society.
Frequency: Annual.
Study Establishment: An academic institution accredited by the Association of MBAs.
Country of Study: United Kingdom.
No. of awards offered: One.
Closing Date: August 31st.
Funding: Private.
Contributor: Ashridge Management College, BT and the AMBA.
Additional Information: All papers submitted become the property of Ashridge.

ASIA CRIME PREVENTION FOUNDATION (ACPF)

7F Daiwa Bank Toranomon Building
Nishishinbashi 1-6-21, Tokyo, Minato-ku, Japan
Tel: (81) 3 3509 7732
Fax: (81) 3 3508 8870
Email: info@acpf.org
www: http://www.acpf.org
Contact: Chairman

The Asia Crime Prevention Foundation (ACPF) is a United Nations non-governmental organisation of general consultative status, working for crime prevention and improvement of criminal justice in Asia and the Pacific Region.

The Asia Crime Prevention Foundation Fellowship

Subjects: An emphasis is placed on the role of criminal justice in the alleviation of extreme poverty in the region in the coming five years.
Purpose: To encourage research on criminal justice issues in the region.
Eligibility: Open to nationals from Asia and the Pacific and the Far East.
Level of Study: Research.
Type: Fellowship.
Value: Depends on the given research.
Frequency: Dependent on funds available.
Application Procedure: Applicants must contact the Foundation for details.
Closing Date: Varies.
Contributor: Members dues.
Additional Information: The award will be a part of subsidiaries such as financial support for participation in meeting and running a project.

ASIAN CULTURAL COUNCIL (ACC)

437 Madison Avenue
37th Floor, New York, NY, 10022, United States of America
Tel: (1) 212 812 4300
Fax: (1) 212 812 4299
Email: acc@accny.org
www: http://www.asianculturalcouncil.org
Contact: Mr Ralph Samuelson, Director

The Asian Cultural Council (ACC) supports cultural exchange in the visual and performing arts between the United States and the countries of Asia. The emphasis of the ACC's programme is on providing individual fellowships to artists, scholars and specialists from Asia undertaking research, study, and creative work in the United States of America. Grants are also made to United States citizens pursuing similar work in Asia.

Asian Cultural Council Fellowship Grants Program

Subjects: Visual and performing arts.
Purpose: To provide fellowship opportunities for research, training, travel and creative work.
Eligibility: Open to individuals from East and Southeast Asia (Burma to Japan) and United States of America citizens or permanent residents. Artists seeking aid for personal exhibitions or performances cannot be considered.
Level of Study: Doctorate, Postdoctorate, Postgraduate, Professional development.
Value: Varies.
Length of Study: One month to one year.
Frequency: Annual.
Country of Study: Asians to travel to the United States of America, Americans to travel to Asia.
No. of awards offered: Approx. 130.

Application Procedure: Applicants must send a brief project description to the Council. If the proposal falls within the Council's guidelines, application forms will be forwarded to individual candidates or more detailed information will be requested from institutional applicants.
Closing Date: February 1st or August 1st.
Funding: Private.
No. of awards given last year: 120.
No. of applicants last year: 800.

ASIAN-AMERICAN JOURNALISTS ASSOCIATION (AAJA)

1182 Market Street
Street 320, San Francisco, CA, 94102, United States of America
Tel: (1) 415 346 2051
Fax: (1) 415 346 6343
Email: national@aaja.org
www: http://www.aaja.org
Contact: Professional Development Co-ordinator

The Asian-American Journalists Association (AAJA) is a national, non-profit, educational association with a network of 1,900 members and 17 chapters across the United States. The AAJA's mission is to encourage young Asian Pacific Americans to enter the ranks of journalism in order to increase the number of Asian American journalists and news managers and to work for fair and accurate coverage of Asian Americans in the industry.

Asian American Journalists Association Fellowship

Subjects: Journalism.
Purpose: To enable working journalists to further develop their professional skills by attending short-term training and skills development workshops of their choice.
Eligibility: Applicants must be full or associate members of AAJA, with at least three years of experience as a working journalist.
Level of Study: Professional development.
Type: Fellowship.
Value: Up to US$1,000 for tuition, travel, food, lodging and other related training costs.
Frequency: Twice a year.
No. of awards offered: Four.
Application Procedure: Applicants must submit two sets of fellowship application forms along with two letters of recommendation, a curriculum vitae and work samples. These should be sent to the national office at AAJA Fellowship Program.
Closing Date: Applications are accepted on a case by case basis all year round.
Additional Information: AAJA also offers scholarships for student journalists.

ASME INTERNATIONAL

Three Park Avenue, New York, NY, 10016, United States of America
Tel: (1) 212 591 8131
Fax: (1) 212 591 7143
Email: oluwanifiset@asme.org
www: http://www.asme.org/education/enged/aid
Contact: Ms Theresa Oluwanifise, Administrative Assistant

Founded in 1880 as the American Society of Mechanical Engineers, today ASME International is a non-profit educational and technical organisation serving a worldwide membership.

ASME Graduate Teaching Fellowship Program

Subjects: Mechanical engineering.
Purpose: To encourage outstanding graduate students, especially women and minorities, to pursue the doctorate in mechanical

engineering and to encourage the engineering education as a profession.

Eligibility: Open to PhD students in mechanical engineering, with a demonstrated interest in a teaching career. A Master's degree or passage of qualifying exam is required as is a lecture responsibility teaching assistantship commitment from the applicant's department. In addition, the applicant should be a United States citizen or permanent resident, with an undergraduate degree from an ABET accredited programme, and a student member of ASME.

Level of Study: Doctorate, Postgraduate.

Type: Fellowship.

Value: US$5,000 per year.

Length of Study: Two years.

Frequency: Annual.

Country of Study: United States of America.

No. of awards offered: Two.

Application Procedure: Applicants must submit an undergraduate grade point average, Graduate Record Examination scores, two letters of recommendation from faculty or their MS committee, a graduate transcript, transcripts of all academic work, a statement about faculty career, and a current curriculum vitae.

Closing Date: October 20th.

Additional Information: In the terms of the fellowship, the awardee must teach at least one lecture course. The applicant's department head must certify, prior to the award or continuation notice, the commitment of a teaching assistantship and the lecture assignment anticipated.

The Elisabeth M and Winchell M Parsons Scholarship

Subjects: Mechanical engineering.

Purpose: To assist ASME student members working towards a doctoral degree.

Eligibility: Selection is based on academic performance, character, need and ASME participation. Applicants must be United States citizens and must be enrolled in a United States school in an ABET accredited mechanical engineering department. No student may receive more than one auxiliary scholarship or loan in the same academic year.

Level of Study: Doctorate.

Type: Grant.

Value: US$2,000.

Frequency: Annual.

Country of Study: United States of America.

No. of awards offered: Approx. two.

Application Procedure: Application forms are available from the website.

Closing Date: March 15th.

Additional Information: Further information is available on request.

For further information contact:

102 Meadowridge Drive, Lynchburg, VA, 24503-3829, United States of America
Tel: (1) 434 384 1057
Email: mrsnyder@aol.com
Contact: Mrs Michael G Snyder

The Marjorie Roy Rothermel Scholarship

Subjects: Mechanical engineering.

Purpose: To assist students working toward a Master's degree.

Eligibility: Selection is based on academic performance, character, need and ASME participation. Applicants must be United States citizens and must be enrolled in a United States school in an ABET accredited mechanical engineering department. No student may receive more than one auxiliary scholarship or loan in the same academic year.

Level of Study: Graduate.

Type: Scholarship.

Value: US$2,000.

Frequency: Annual.

Country of Study: United States of America.

No. of awards offered: Six-eight.

Application Procedure: Application forms are available from the website.

Closing Date: March 15th.

Additional Information: Further information is available on request.

For further information contact:

332 Valencia Street, Gulf Breeze, FL, 32561, United States of America
Tel: (1) 850 932 3698
Email: eprocha340@aol.com
Contact: Mrs Otto Prochaska

Rice-Cullimore Scholarship

Subjects: Mechanical engineering.

Purpose: To aid a foreign student while doing graduate work for a Master's or doctoral degree in the United States.

Eligibility: Selection is based on academic performance, character, need and ASME participation. Candidates may be from any country except the United States. No student may receive more than one auxiliary scholarship or loan in the same academic year.

Level of Study: Doctorate.

Type: Scholarship.

Value: US$2,000.

Length of Study: One year.

Frequency: Annual.

Country of Study: United States of America.

Application Procedure: Applicants must apply in their home country through the local institute of International Education Embassy (IEE) or Education Offices at the United States Embassy. Only those applicants received from the IEE will be considered.

Closing Date: Please contact the organisation.

Additional Information: Further information is available on request.

ASSOCIATED BOARD OF THE ROYAL SCHOOLS OF MUSIC

24 Portland Place, London, W1B 1LU, England
Tel: (44) 20 7636 5400
Fax: (44) 20 7637 0234
Email: abrsm@abrsm.ac.uk
www: http://www.abrsm.ac.uk
Contact: Mr T P Leates, Director of Finance & Administration

The Associated Board of the Royal Schools of Music is the world's leading provider of graded music examinations with over 500,000 candidates each year in over 80 countries. It is also a major music publisher and a provider of professional development courses and seminars for music teachers.

Associated Board of the Royal Schools of Music Scholarships

Subjects: Instrumental and vocal.

Purpose: To enable exceptionally talented young musicians to study at one of the four Royal Schools of Music.

Eligibility: Open to students between the ages of 17 and 26, except in certain circumstances, eg. courses for singers and in-service teachers courses. Entries can be received from any of the countries where the Associated Board organises examinations. Candidates must have a good standard of general education and must normally have qualified by passing, with distinction, Grade 8 in a practical examination of the Board's, the Advanced Certificate or the LRSM diploma, plus one other practical examination of the Board's above Grade 5.

Level of Study: Postgraduate, Professional development.

Type: Scholarship.

Value: Full course fees, a contribution to air travel and UK £3,000 per year towards living expenses.

Length of Study: From one term to four years, according to designated course.

Frequency: Annual.

Study Establishment: The Royal Academy of Music, the Royal College of Music, the Royal Northern College of Music or the Royal Scottish Academy of Music and Drama.
Country of Study: United Kingdom.
No. of awards offered: Varies.
Application Procedure: Applicants must submit an application form, health certificate, examination marks, forms, testimonials, and an authenticated cassette tape of recent performance. Candidates should apply to the Board's representative in their own country or directly to the Board in London.
Closing Date: December 31st of the year preceding year of entry.
Funding: Private.
No. of awards given last year: Eight.
No. of applicants last year: Numerous.

ASSOCIATED WESTERN UNIVERSITIES, INC. (AWU)

4190 South Highland Drive
Suite 211, Salt Lake City, UT, 84124, United States of America
Tel: (1) 801 273 8900
Fax: (1) 801 277 5632
Email: info@awu.org
www: http://www.awu.org
Contact: Postgraduate Fellowship Programme

Associated Western Universities (AWU) is a non-profit corporation with 65 college and university members that reflect a broad diversity of roles in higher education. Established in 1959, AWU's mission is to provide a collaborative mechanism for research and educational interactions between academia, government and industry. These programmes provide scholarship, fellowship or travel support for students, graduates, postgraduates and faculty from colleges and universities throughout the United States and abroad. AWU in partnership with federal laboratories, industry and other co-operating facilities, provides fellowships for science and engineering research participation. Fellowship participants are hosted by nearly 60 federal and industrial facilities. Research participation opportunities in science, engineering and technology are available in many disciplines.

AWU Postgraduate Fellowships

Subjects: Science and engineering.
Purpose: To support recent individuals who are furthering their science or engineering careers.
Eligibility: Citizenship restrictions may apply in some facilities.
Level of Study: Doctorate, Postdoctorate, Postgraduate.
Type: Fellowship.
Value: Varies depending on the facility.
Length of Study: An initial term of one year.
Frequency: Annual.
Study Establishment: Any approved government or industry research facility.
Country of Study: United States of America.
No. of awards offered: Varies.
Application Procedure: Applicants must submit a fellowship application, two letters of reference, facility recommendation, a certificate of advanced degree and a list of publications.
Closing Date: Applications are accepted at any time.
Funding: Commercial, Government, Private.
Contributor: The Department of Energy, the Battelle Memorial Institute and Fluor Daniel.
Additional Information: AWU has been designated as an Exchange Visitor Programme Sponsor by the United States Information Agency. AWU can issue the certificate of eligibility (IAP-66 form) required for foreign nationals to receive a J-1 visa.

ASSOCIATION FOR SPINA BIFIDA AND HYDROCEPHALUS (ASBAH)

ASBAH House
42 Park Road, Peterborough, Cambridgeshire, PE1 2UQ, England
Tel: (44) 1733 555988
Fax: (44) 1733 555985
Email: lynr@asbah.org
www: http://www.asbah.org
Contact: Mrs L Rylance, Secretary to the Directorate

The Association for Spina Bifida and Hydrocephalus (ASBAH) is a voluntary organisation which works for people with spina bifida and/or hydrocephalus. The charity lobbies for improvements in legislation and provides advisory and support services to clients and their families or carers, in addition to supplying information to professionals and sponsoring medical, social and educational research.

ASBAH Bursary Fund

Subjects: Any course that will improve the chances of employment for people with spina bifida, hydrocephalus or both.
Purpose: To help with expenses of further or higher education courses approved by, but not organised by, ASBAH.
Eligibility: Open to individuals with spina bifida and hydrocephalus resident in England, Wales and Northern Ireland.
Level of Study: Unrestricted.
Type: Bursary.
Value: To cover course fees and other expenses.
Frequency: Varies, depending on funds available.
Study Establishment: Varies.
Country of Study: United Kingdom (excluding Scotland).
No. of awards offered: Varies.
Application Procedure: Applicants must complete an application form, available from M J Rollinson, the Assistant Director of Services.
Closing Date: Applications are accepted at any time.
Funding: Private.
Contributor: Charitable donations.
No. of awards given last year: Five.
No. of applicants last year: Nine.
Additional Information: Applicants are normally visited by an ASBAH Area Adviser prior to an award being considered.

ASBAH Research Grant

Subjects: Medical sciences, natural sciences, education and teacher training, recreation, welfare and protective services.
Purpose: To support research in an area directly related to spina bifida and/or hydrocephalus, and also to explore ways of improving the quality of life for people with these conditions, those being medical, scientific, educational and social research.
Eligibility: Applicants must be resident in the United Kingdom.
Level of Study: Postgraduate.
Type: Research grant.
Value: Varies.
Length of Study: Varies.
Frequency: Dependent on funds available.
Study Establishment: Varies.
Country of Study: Varies, but usually the United Kingdom.
No. of awards offered: Varies.
Application Procedure: Applicants must make an initial enquiry to the Executive Director. If the proposed research is considered to be interesting, the applicant will be asked to complete an application form. Applications should be made in good time for submission to the committees which meet in February and September to October.
Closing Date: January 1st and August 1st.
Funding: Private.
Contributor: Charitable donations.
No. of applicants last year: Three.

ASSOCIATION FOR WOMEN GEOSCIENTISTS

c/o G&H Production Company LLC
518 17th Street
Suite 930, Denver, CO, 80202, United States of America
Tel: (1) 303 534 0708
Fax: (1) 303 436 0609
Email: office@awg.org
www: http://www.awg.org
Contact: Chairwoman of Scholarship Committee

The Association for Women Geoscientists is an international organisation of geoscientists established to encourage the participation of women in the geosciences, to exchange educational, technical and professional information, and to enhance the professional growth and advancement of women in the geosciences.

Chrysalis Scholarship

Subjects: Geosciences.
Purpose: To assist women with money to use in any way that will help them complete their thesis.
Eligibility: Open to woman geoscientists who are completing their thesis, at the Master's or PhD level, in the current year who have had at least one year's interruption in their education.
Level of Study: Postgraduate.
Type: Scholarship.
Value: Two awards of US$750, plus several smaller awards of US$250-300.
Frequency: Annual.
Country of Study: Any country.
No. of awards offered: Two.
Application Procedure: Applicants must submit a letter from the candidate and two letters of reference.
Closing Date: February 28th.
Funding: Private.
Contributor: Contributions from members and businesses.

ASSOCIATION FOR WOMEN IN SCIENCE EDUCATIONAL FOUNDATION

1200 New York Avenue North West
Suite 650, Washington, DC, 20005, United States of America
Tel: (1) 202 326 8940
Fax: (1) 202 326 8960
Email: awis@awis.org
www: http://www.awis.org
Contact: Ms Krishna Shah, Corporate Liasion

Association for Women in Science Educational Foundation Predoctoral Awards

Subjects: Life, physical, behavioural or social science and engineering.
Eligibility: Open to female students enrolled in any physical, behavioural or social science or engineering programme, leading to a PhD degree.
Level of Study: Doctorate.
Value: Varies, usually US$100-1,000.
Frequency: Annual.
Study Establishment: An Institute of Higher Education.
Country of Study: United States of America citizens can study in the United States of America or abroad, non United States of America citizens can study in the United States of America.
No. of awards offered: Varies.
Application Procedure: Applicants must submit an application incuding a basic form, a two to three page summary of the candidate's dissertation research, two recommendation report forms and official transcripts of all coursework conducted at post secondary institutions.

Closing Date: Mid January.
No. of awards given last year: 10 awards, 11 citations of merit.
No. of applicants last year: 200+.
Additional Information: Winners are notified by mail in June and announced publicly in the July-August issue of the AWIS Magazine.

ASSOCIATION OF AMERICAN GEOGRAPHERS (AAG)

1710 Sixteenth Street North West, Washington, DC, 20009-3198, United States of America
Tel: (1) 202 234 1450
Fax: (1) 202 234 2744
Email: ekhater@aag.org
www: http://www.aag.org
Contact: Ms Ehsan Khater, Executive Assistant

The Association of American Geographers (AAG) is a non-profit organisation founded in 1904 to advance professional studies in geography and to encourage the application of geographic research in business, education and government. The AAG was amalgamated with the American Society of Professional Geographers (ASPG) in 1948.

AAG Dissertation Research Grants

Subjects: Geography.
Purpose: To support dissertation research.
Eligibility: Open to candidates who have been AAG members for at least one year at the time of application, who do not have a doctorate at the time of the award, and who have completed all PhD requirements except the dissertation by the end of the semester or term following the approval of the award. The candidates' dissertation supervisor must certify eligibility.
Level of Study: Postdoctorate.
Type: Research grant.
Value: Between US$100-900.
Frequency: Annual.
Country of Study: United States of America.
No. of awards offered: Three.
Application Procedure: Applicants must complete an application form, available on request. Applicants must submit six copies each of the completed application and a dissertation proposal of no more than 1,000 words.
Closing Date: December 31st.
Funding: Private.
Contributor: Members.
No. of awards given last year: Six.
No. of applicants last year: Eight.
Additional Information: By accepting an AAG dissertation grant awardees agree to submit a copy of the dissertation and a report that documents expenses charged to the grant to the AAG Executive Director. AAG support must also be acknowledged in presentations and publications. The awards include the Robert D Hodgson Memorial PhD Dissertation Fund, the Paul Vouras Fund, and the Otis Paul Starkey Fund.

AAG General Research Fund

Subjects: Geography.
Purpose: To support research and field work expenses.
Eligibility: Open to any person who has been an AAG member for at least two years at the time of application.
Level of Study: Postdoctorate, Professional development.
Type: Research fund.
Value: Between US$600-900.
Frequency: Annual, if funds are available.
Country of Study: Any country.
No. of awards offered: Varies.
Application Procedure: Applicants must complete six application forms, available on request.
Closing Date: December 31st.

Funding: Private.
Contributor: AAG members.
No. of awards given last year: Nine.
No. of applicants last year: 13.
Additional Information: No awards are made if proposals are not suitable. Guidelines are printed in the AAG Newsletter.

Anne U White Fund

Subjects: Geochemistry.
Purpose: To enable people, regardless of any formal training in geography, to engage in useful field studies and to have the joy of working alongside their partners.
Eligibility: Open to any person who has been an AAG member for at least two years at the time of application.
Level of Study: Professional development.
Type: Research fund.
Value: Between US$1,200-3,900.
Frequency: Annual.
Application Procedure: Applicants must complete an application form, available from the website.
Closing Date: December 31st.
Funding: Private.
No. of awards given last year: Two.
Additional Information: By accepting the Anne U White grant awardees agree to submit a two page report that summarises results and documents expenses underwritten by the grant to the AAG Executive Director.

Warren Nystrom Fund Awards

Subjects: Geography.
Eligibility: Open to AAG members who have received their doctorate within the last two years. The awards are made for papers presented at the annual meeting of the Association. The paper submitted should be based on the student's dissertation.
Level of Study: Doctorate, Postdoctorate.
Value: Varies.
Frequency: Annual.
Country of Study: Any country.
No. of awards offered: Varies.
Application Procedure: Applicants must apply for information.
Closing Date: Mid September for the following year.
Funding: Private.
Contributor: AAG members.
No. of awards given last year: One.
No. of applicants last year: 15.

ASSOCIATION OF COMMONWEALTH UNIVERSITIES (ACU)

John Foster House
36 Gordon Square, London, WC1H 0PF, England
Tel: (44) 20 7387 8572
Fax: (44) 20 7387 2655
www: http://www.acu.ac.uk
Contact: Ms Anna Gane, Commonwealth Awards Administrator

Founded in 1913, the Association of Commonwealth Universities (ACU) is the oldest international association of universities in the world. The ACU's aim is to promote contact and co-operation between its member institutions by encouraging and supporting the movement of academic and administrative staff between Commonwealth countries, providing information about universities, organising meetings and hosting a higher education management service.

ACU Development Fellowships

Subjects: Special preference for agriculture, forestry and food science including fisheries, nutrition and processing, biotechnology, development strategies, earth and marine sciences including mining engineering, mineral resource, oceanography, engineering, health

and related social sciences, information technology eg. computing or computer assisted learning, management for change, professional education and training eg. in accountancy, banking, business studies, insurance and law, social and cultural development, media studies and institutional management.
Purpose: To promote the development of human resources in subject areas in which the needs of developing countries are particularly great.
Eligibility: Open to Commonwealth citizens under 50 years of age. Candidates may be working in a university, in commerce, in industry or in the private sector, but must be nominated by the head of an institution which is a member of the ACU.
Level of Study: Professional development.
Type: Fellowship.
Value: Value is determined by the ACU according to the scope and location of the programme, but up to a maximum of UK £5,000 covering fares, board and lodging, local travel and medical and travel insurance. There is no allowance for spouse or dependants.
Length of Study: Up to six months, non renewable.
Frequency: Annual.
Country of Study: Commonwealth countries.
No. of awards offered: 20.
Application Procedure: Applicants must be nominated by the executive head of an institution which is a member of the ACU.
Closing Date: May 31st.
Contributor: Member institutions of the ACU.
No. of awards given last year: Nine.
No. of applicants last year: 107.
Additional Information: Countries are invited on a biennial basis.

ACU Quality of Life Awards

Subjects: Health studies, environmental management, distance education or transferable technology.
Purpose: To enhance the role that universities play both in providing higher education in the face of increasing demands for access and in addressing the wider social issues of their countries.
Eligibility: Open to staff of ACU member universities or of a Commonwealth inter-university organisation. Those working in NGOs, charities, industry, commerce or the public sector in a Commonwealth country are also eligible.
Type: Fellowship.
Value: Up to UK £5,000.
Length of Study: A maximum of six months.
Frequency: Annual.
Country of Study: Any Commonwealth country other than that in which the applicant works.
No. of awards offered: Up to 20.
Application Procedure: Applicants must be nominated by an executive head or university in ACU membership. Each executive head may make two nominations.
Contributor: ACU.
Additional Information: Special consideration will be given to projects which take place in and give benefit to the developing Commonwealth. Projects will ideally utilise personnel or expertise from at least two Commonwealth countries, and the ACU are particularly interested in receiving proposals involving south-south collaboration.

British Academy/ACU Grants for International Collaboration

Subjects: Humanities and social sciences.
Purpose: To support international joint activities, involving British Scholars in collaboration with Commonwealth partners. Priority is given to new programmes with an expectation of continued collaboration or a defined outcome such as planned joint publications.
Eligibility: Open to staff of ACU member universities for advanced research. Support will not be offered for an open ended programme involving wide spread international participation or a programme of benefit primarily to the British partner.
Level of Study: Postdoctorate.
Type: Collaboration grants.

Value: Up to UK £5,000 per year for research expenditure, travel and living costs in the partner country or countries. Awards are not intended to cover institutional overheads or permanent staff costs.
Length of Study: One year.
Frequency: Annual.
Country of Study: A Commonwealth country.
No. of awards offered: Up to 20.
Application Procedure: Applications should be submitted by the British partner. Applications received directly by overseas partners will not be considered.
Closing Date: May 31st.
Contributor: Funded jointly by the British Academy and ACU.
Additional Information: Applications must be for projects involving genuine collaborative work between a defined group of Scholars in one, or possibly two, Commonwealth countries. Priority is given to new programmes with an expectation of continued collaboration or a defined outcome such as planned joint publications.

Canada Memorial Foundation Scholarships
Subjects: All subjects.
Purpose: To allow very able British students to study at a Canadian university for a year. By this means the Canada Memorial Foundation hopes to strengthen the close association between Canada and the United Kingdom.
Eligibility: Open to United Kingdom citizens who are holders of a First Degree or equivalent ie. at least an Upper Second Class (Honours) Degree. Candidates should normally be under 30 years of age. The Foundation welcomes candidates who have left university but wish to return to academic studies with a view to enhancing their career prospects in business or industry. In all cases candidates will need to show, beside excellent academic qualifications, a record of participatory activities and to give convincing reasons as to why they wish to study in Canada, together with some knowledge of Canada and its institutions. The Foundation also wishes to actively encourage applications from students wishing to pursue an MBA in Canada.
Level of Study: Postgraduate.
Type: Scholarship.
Value: A maintenance allowance, return air fare, approved fees, a book, thesis, travel and health insurance allowance.
Length of Study: One year.
Frequency: Annual.
Study Establishment: Any university or other appropriate institution in Canada subject to the approval of the Canada Memorial Foundation.
Country of Study: Canada.
No. of awards offered: Up to two.
Application Procedure: Applications must be made through ACU, addressed to CMF Competition, Commonwealth Awards Division.
Closing Date: The third Friday in October.
Contributor: The Canada Memorial Foundation.
Additional Information: The awards are intended for persons of high academic promise and leadership potential who will play a full part in the life of the Canadian community which they visit and who will return to play a full part in their own country. The Canada Memorial Foundation also offers similar awards to Canadians so that they may study in the United Kingdom. The Scholarships are awarded in memory of the one million Canadians who served with Great Britain during World War One and World War Two.

DFID Shared Scholarship Scheme
Subjects: Subjects relating to the economic and social development of the Scholar's country of origin.
Eligibility: Open only to students from developing Commonwealth countries for study in the United Kingdom, who are not already living in and have not already studied in, a developed country. Employees of a government department or parastatal organisation are ineligible. Candidates are required to hold, or be expected to attain, a First Class or Upper Second Class Degree. Priority is given to candidates from poorer developing countries and to those aged under 30. Candidates should normally be aged under 35.
Level of Study: Postgraduate.

Type: Scholarship.
Value: Full cost of study, including a return airfare, maintenance and a thesis allowance.
Length of Study: One year.
Frequency: Annual.
Study Establishment: A list of participating institutions is available from the ACU website.
Country of Study: United Kingdom.
No. of awards offered: Up to 175 annually.
Application Procedure: Applicants must complete an application form and send it to participating institutions.
Closing Date: March-April. Candidates should check with individual institutions for precise dates.
Contributor: Funded jointly by the Department for International Development (DFID) and participating institutions in the United Kingdom.

ASSOCIATION OF CONSULTING ENGINEERS

Alliance House
12 Caxton Street, London, SW1H 0QL, England
Tel: (44) 20 7222 6557
Fax: (44) 20 7222 0750
Email: consult@acenet.co.uk
www: http://www.acenet.co.uk
Contact: Administrative Officer

The Association of Consulting Engineers (ACE) is the United Kingdom's leading trade association for engineering, technical and management consultancies. Membership is open to companies which advise on consulting engineering and related services. ACE has around 650 member firms, which range from sole practitioners to large multidisciplinary consultancy companies.

Young Consulting Engineer of the Year
Subjects: Engineering projects and the engineering profession in general.
Purpose: To encourage younger members of the profession in their work and to make them think about their role in society.
Eligibility: Candidates must be engineering consultants under the age of 30.
Level of Study: Unrestricted.
Value: UK £1,000 plus a medal. There are certificates for finalists.
Frequency: Annual.
Country of Study: Any country.
No. of awards offered: One.
Application Procedure: Applicants must complete an application form and submit this with other required documents.
Closing Date: March 30th.
Funding: Private.

ASSOCIATION OF MBAS

15 Duncan Terrace, London, N1 8BZ, England
Tel: (44) 20 7837 3375
Fax: (44) 20 7278 3634
Email: p.calladine@mba.org.uk
www: http://www.mba.org.uk
Contact: Mr Peter Calladine

Founded in 1967, the Association of MBAs is an accreditation body. It also organises MBA Fairs, produces guides to business schools and offers impartial advice. Membership is available to students and graduates of Association of MBAs' accredited courses and to those from a limited number of overseas schools.

Association of MBAs Business School Loan Scheme

Subjects: Business, administration and management.

Purpose: To encourage MBA study.

Eligibility: Open to United Kingdom residents who have been resident in the United Kingdom for three years immediately prior to study. Applicants must be graduates with more than two years' relevant work experience or, if not graduates, have more than five years' relevant work experience at an appropriate level of responsibility.

Level of Study: Postgraduate, MBA.

Type: Loan.

Value: Preferential bank loans to cover full-time study, up to two-thirds of salary plus fees for each year of study. For part-time study, fees are awarded plus study equipment and distance learning of up to UK £10,000.

Frequency: Varies.

Study Establishment: Specific courses at 36 United Kingdom and 24 continental European schools accredited by the Association of MBAs, AACSB accredited schools in the United States of America, and a limited number of schools elsewhere.

Country of Study: Any country.

No. of awards offered: Unlimited.

Application Procedure: Applicants can apply at any time provided that a place has been secured. Applications can be made via the NatWest Bank helpline on (44) 800 200 400 or via the Bank of Scotland on (44) 500 313 111.

Closing Date: Applications are accepted at any time.

Funding: Commercial.

Contributor: Natwest Bank and the Bank of Scotland.

ASSOCIATION OF RHODES SCHOLARS IN AUSTRALIA

University of Melbourne, VIC, 3010, Australia
Tel: (61) 3 8344 6937
Fax: (61) 3 9347 6739
Email: g.swafford@unimelb.edu.au
www: http://www.unimelb.edu.au/research
Contact: Dr Glenn Swafford, Director, Melbourne Research & Innovation Office

Association of Rhodes Scholars in Australia Travel Bursary

Subjects: All subjects.

Purpose: To enable an overseas Commonwealth student to undertake research for six months at one or more universities in Australia.

Eligibility: Open to graduates of a Commonwealth university approved by the committee administering the travel bursary, who are currently enrolled as a research higher degree student at their home university. Applicants must be Commonwealth citizens and may not be graduates of an Australian or New Zealand university.

Level of Study: Postgraduate, Research.

Type: Travel bursary.

Value: Currently australian $9,500 including travel expenses and a monthly stipend.

Length of Study: Six months.

Frequency: Dependent on funds available.

Study Establishment: A university.

Country of Study: Australia.

No. of awards offered: One.

Application Procedure: Applicants must apply for information and application forms, available through the website http://www.unimelb.edu.au/research/admin/rhodes/arsa.html.

Closing Date: As advertised.

Funding: Private.

Contributor: Charitable donations from former Australian Rhodes Scholars.

No. of awards given last year: One.

No. of applicants last year: 33.

ASSOCIATION OF SURGEONS OF GREAT BRITAIN AND IRELAND

c/o The Royal College of Surgeons of England
35-43 Lincoln's Inn Fields, London, WC2A 3PN, England

Tel: (44) 20 7973 0300

Fax: (44) 20 7430 9235

Contact: Mrs Nechema Lewis, Administrative Assistant

The founding objectives of the Association in 1920 were the advancement of the science and art of surgery and the promotion of friendship among surgeons. As other surgical specialists developed, the Association came to represent general surgery, encompassing breast, colorectal, endocrine, laparoscopic, transplant, upper gastro-intestinal and vascular surgery.

Moynihan Travelling Fellowship/Dinwoody Trust Travelling Scholarships

Subjects: Surgery.

Purpose: To enable specialist registrars towards the end of their higher surgical training or consultants who are within three years of appointment at the closing date for applications to broaden their education, and to present and discuss their contribution to British or Irish surgery overseas.

Eligibility: Open to specialist registrars towards the end of higher surgical training or consultants in general surgery within three years of appointment after the closing date for applications. Candidates must be nationals of and residents of the United Kingdom or the Republic of Ireland but need not be either Fellows or Affiliate Fellows of the Association. They may be engaged in general surgery or a sub-speciality thereof.

Level of Study: Postdoctorate.

Type: Fellowship.

Value: The value of the Moynihan Travelling Fellowship is up to UK £4,000, one or two Dinwoody Trust Travelling Scholarships are available up to UK £1,500.

Frequency: Annual.

Country of Study: Any country.

No. of awards offered: Three.

Application Procedure: Applicants must submit 12 copies of an application which must include a full curriculum vitae giving details of past and present appointments and publications, a detailed account of the proposed programme of travel, costs involved and the object to be achieved. Applications must be addressed to the Honorary Secretary at the Association of Surgeons.

Closing Date: October 1st.

Funding: Private.

Contributor: Charitable association funds and the Dinwoody Trust.

No. of awards given last year: Three.

No. of applicants last year: Seven.

Additional Information: Shortlisted candidates will be interviewed by the Scientific Committee of the Association who will pay particular attention to the originality, scope and feasibility of the proposed journey. The successful candidate will be expected to act as an ambassador for British and Irish surgery and should therefore be fully acquainted with the aims and objectives of the Association of Surgeons in its role in surgery. After the visit the Fellow will be asked to address the Association at its annual general meeting. A critical appraisal of the centres visited should form the basis of the report.

THE ASSOCIATION OF TEACHERS AND LECTURERS (ATL)

7 Northumberland Street, London, WC2N 5RD, England
Tel: (44) 20 7930 6441
Fax: (44) 20 7930 1359
Email: info@atl.org.uk
www: http://www.askatl.org.uk
Contact: Ms Thelma Meredith, Personal Assistant to General Secretary

The Association of Teachers and Lecturers (ATL) is the leading professional organisation and trade union for teachers and lecturers with over 150,000 members in England, Wales and Northern Ireland. The Association is committed to protecting and promoting the interests of its members and maintaining the highest quality professional support for them.

Walter Hines Page Scholarships

Subjects: Observation and study of teaching and the educational system in the United States of America.
Purpose: To promote the exchange of educational ideas between the United Kingdom and the United States.
Eligibility: Open to British teachers who are members of the Association of Teachers and Lecturers and who wish to visit the United States of America.
Level of Study: Professional development.
Type: Scholarship.
Value: UK £1,100, plus full hospitality.
Length of Study: Two weeks.
Frequency: Annual.
Country of Study: United States of America.
No. of awards offered: Two.
Application Procedure: Applicants must write to, phone or email the ATL for details.
Closing Date: November 30th.
No. of awards given last year: Two.
No. of applicants last year: 17.
Additional Information: These awards are given in conjunction with the English-Speaking Union of the Commonwealth.

ASSOCIATION OF UNIVERSITIES AND COLLEGES OF CANADA (AUCC)

International & Canadian Programs Division
350 Albert Street
Suite 600, Ottawa, ON, K1R 1B1, Canada
Tel: (1) 613 563 1236
Fax: (1) 613 563 9745
Email: awards@aucc.ca
www: http://www.aucc.ca
Contact: Ms Julie Levac, Canadian Awards Program

The Association of Universities and Colleges of Canada (AUCC) is a non-profit, non-governmental association that represents Canadian universities at home and abroad. The Association's mandate is to foster and promote the interests of higher education in the firm belief that strong universities are vital to the prosperity and wellbeing of Canada.

AUCC Cable Telecommunications Research Fellowship

Subjects: Subjects directly related to the cable television industry in a degree programme focusing on the field of engineering or computer science.
Purpose: To encourage students at the Master's or PhD level to tackle topics in the engineering of communications systems for video, voice and data signals or for computer applications to cable TV requirements.
Eligibility: Applicants must be Canadian citizens or permanent residents and enrolled or planning to enrol in a graduate degree programme at a university in Canada. Applicants must intend to use the Fellowship to assist them in completing a graduate degree which includes a thesis on a topic in the engineering of broadband communication systems or computer application to cable TV.
Level of Study: Graduate.
Type: Fellowship.
Value: Canadian $5,000.
Length of Study: One year, with the possibility of renewal for a further year.
Frequency: Annual.
Study Establishment: Any university which is a member, or affiliated to a member, of AUCC.
Country of Study: Canada.
No. of awards offered: Two.
Application Procedure: Applicants must complete an application form. Further information and application forms available on request or from the website.
Closing Date: Postmarked February 1st.
Additional Information: Further information is available on request or from the website.

AUCC Canada-Taiwan Scholarships Programme

Subjects: Mandarin language training.
Purpose: To allow 10 Canadian university students to travel to Taiwan each year for Mandarin language training.
Eligibility: Open to Canadian university students.
Level of Study: Unrestricted.
Type: Scholarship.
Value: Return airfare to Taiwan, tuition and a monthly allowance.
Length of Study: One year.
Frequency: Annual.
Study Establishment: Tenable at the Mandarin Training Centre of the National Taiwan Normal University.
Country of Study: Taiwan.
No. of awards offered: 10.
Application Procedure: Applicants must apply for information, available on request from Maria DeAlmeida.
Closing Date: March 27th.
Funding: Government.

The Canadian Wireless Telecommunications Association (CWTA) Graduate Scholarship

Subjects: All disciplines related to wireless communications including, but not limited to, engineering or business.
Purpose: To benefit students at the Master's or PhD level.
Eligibility: Candidates must be Canadian citizens or permanent residents of Canada and enrolled or planning to enrol in a graduate degree programme at a university in Canada. They must also intend to use the Scholarship to assist them in completing a graduate degree which includes a thesis on a topic related to the noted fields of study. Awards are granted on the basis of academic standing and demonstrated potential for advanced study and research.
Level of Study: Postdoctorate, Postgraduate.
Type: Scholarship.
Value: Canadian $10,000.
Length of Study: One year, with the option to renew.
Frequency: Annual.
Study Establishment: Any university or college which is a member, or affiliated to a member, of the Association of Universities and Colleges of Canada.
Country of Study: Canada.
No. of awards offered: Up to 10.
Application Procedure: Applicants must contact the organisation for details.
Closing Date: June 1st.

Department of National Defence Security and Defence Forum Internship Program

Subjects: Studies related to current and future Canadian national security and defence issues including their political, international, historical, social, military, industrial and economic dimensions.

Purpose: To help recent MA graduates with a background in security and defence studies to obtain work experience.

Eligibility: Applicants must be Canadian citizens or permanent residents at the time of application and hold a Master's degree before taking up the award.

Level of Study: Doctorate, Postgraduate.

Type: Internship.

Value: Up to canadian $24,000.

Length of Study: Up to one year, non renewable.

Frequency: Annual.

Study Establishment: In the private sector or non governmental organisations.

Country of Study: Canada.

No. of awards offered: Approx. six.

Application Procedure: Applicants must apply for information, available on request or from the website.

Closing Date: Postmarked February 1st.

Additional Information: On completion of the award a reasonable detailed account of the internship and any research undertaken must be submitted to the AUCC who will forward it to the Department of National Defence. Further information is available on request or from the website.

Department of National Defence Security and Defence Forum MA Scholarship Program

Subjects: Studies relating to current and future Canadian national security and defence issues including their political, international, historical, social, military, industrial and economic dimensions.

Eligibility: Applicants must be Canadian citizens or permanent residents at the time of application and, as a minimum requirement, hold a Bachelor's (Honours) Degree or its equivalent before taking up the award.

Level of Study: Doctorate, Postgraduate.

Type: Scholarship.

Value: Up to canadian $8,000.

Length of Study: At least one year, with possible renewal for a further year if evidence of satisfactory academic achievement is found.

Frequency: Annual.

Study Establishment: Canadian institutions.

Country of Study: Canada.

No. of awards offered: Approx. eight.

Application Procedure: Applicants must apply for information, available on request or from the website.

Closing Date: Postmarked February 1st.

Additional Information: Successful applicants may not hold more than one award from the federal government.

Frank Knox Memorial Fellowships at Harvard University

Subjects: Arts and sciences including engineering, business administration, design, divinity studies, education, law, public administration at the John F Kennedy School of Government, medicine, dental medicine and public health.

Eligibility: Applicants must be Canadian citizens or permanent residents who have recently graduated or who are about to graduate from an institution in Canada which is a member or affiliated to a member of the AUCC. Applications from students presently studying in the United States of America will not be considered, although applications will be considered from recent graduates who are working in the United States of America and will be applying to the MBA programme.

Level of Study: Postgraduate, MBA.

Type: Fellowship.

Value: US$17,000 plus tuition fees and student health insurance.

Length of Study: One academic year.

Frequency: Annual.

Study Establishment: Harvard University.

Country of Study: United States of America.

No. of awards offered: Up to three.

Application Procedure: Applicants must apply directly to the graduate school of their choice. Applicants are responsible for gaining admission to Harvard University by the deadline set by the various faculties. Further information and application forms are available on request or from the website.

Closing Date: Postmarked February 1st.

Additional Information: Holders of this award may not accept any other grant for the period of this fellowship unless approved by the Committee on General Scholarships and the Sheldon Fund of Harvard University.

Frederick T Metcalf Award Program

Subjects: Disciplines related to new media companies and delivering cable communications services in Canada such as business finance and marketing, economics, television production, mass communications and engineering.

Purpose: To support students pursuing a Master's degree in a programme related to the cable communication services.

Eligibility: Open to qualified full-time students pursuing a Master's degree in a field directly related to the development and delivery of cable in Canada.

Level of Study: Postgraduate.

Type: Scholarship.

Value: Canadian $5,000.

Length of Study: One year, non renewable.

Frequency: Annual.

Study Establishment: Any Canadian university which is a member of the AUCC, or affiliated to a member of the AUCC.

Country of Study: Canada.

No. of awards offered: One.

Application Procedure: Applicants must complete an application form, available on request or downloadable from the website.

Closing Date: Postmarked February 1st.

Office of Critical Infrastructure Protection and Emergency Preparedness (EPC) Research Fellowship in Honour of Stuart Nesbitt White

Subjects: All aspects of disaster and emergency studies as outlined in the EPC Annual Report, and especially urban and regional planning, economics, geography, risk analysis and management, systems science, social sciences, business, health administration and civil engineering.

Purpose: To encourage disaster research and emergency planning in Canada by developing a greater number of qualified professionals in this field.

Eligibility: Applicants must be Canadian citizens or permanent residents. Preference will be given to applicants who hold a Master's degree and who would normally be pursuing doctoral studies. However, applicants with a First Class (Honours) Degree will also be considered. Acceptance into a doctoral programme is normally, but not necessarily, a prerequisite.

Level of Study: Doctorate.

Type: Fellowship.

Value: Canadian $13,500 per year.

Length of Study: One year, with a possibility of renewal for a further two years.

Frequency: Annual.

Study Establishment: Normally a Canadian university, but if not the applicant must include a supplementary statement identifying the university, tuition fees and benefits deriving to the student.

Country of Study: Canada.

No. of awards offered: Varies.

Application Procedure: Applicants must write for details or refer to the website.

Closing Date: Postmarked February 1st.

Additional Information: Further information is available on request or from the website.

The Paul Sargent Memorial Linguistic Scholarship Program

Subjects: All fields at the Master's level, preferably with previous exposure to an Oriental, Middle Eastern or Eastern European language.

Purpose: To assist postgraduate level students in languages.

Eligibility: Applicants must be Canadian citizens or permanent residents at the time of application and must hold a Bachelor's degree at either the major or minor level, in the language concerned, with a high record of academic achievement. Applicants must have at least an intermediate level of competence in an Oriental, Middle Eastern or Eastern European language. The minimum proficiency required would be a consistent A in language courses.

Level of Study: Postgraduate.

Type: Scholarship.

Value: Canadian $12,000.

Length of Study: Two years.

Study Establishment: Tenable at any Canadian university which is a member, or affiliated with a member, of the AUCC.

No. of awards offered: Two.

Application Procedure: Applicants must apply for information, available on request or from the website.

Closing Date: February 7th.

Petro-Canada Graduate Research Award Program

Subjects: Sciences, engineering, social sciences and business administration.

Purpose: To recognise academic excellence and to support and encourage graduate research in specialised fields of study relating to the petroleum industry.

Eligibility: Applicants must be Canadian citizens or permanent residents and working towards a Master's or doctoral degree (on a full-time basis) on a subject related to the oil and gas industry. Awards are granted on the basis of academic standing and demonstrated potential for advanced study and research.

Level of Study: Doctorate, Postgraduate.

Type: Research grant.

Value: Canadian $10,000.

Length of Study: One year. Award holders may reapply.

Frequency: Annual.

Study Establishment: A university or college which is a member, or affiliated to a member, of the AUCC.

Country of Study: Canada.

No. of awards offered: Up to four.

Application Procedure: Applicants must apply for information, available on request or from the website.

Closing Date: Postmarked February 1st.

Additional Information: There is no restriction on the number or value of other awards that can be held concurrently by a student. However, recipients must be able to accept at least 75 per cent of the Petro-Canada award in instances where restrictions apply to other awards received.

Security and Defence Forum PhD Scholarship Program Including the Dr Ronald Baker Doctoral Scholarship

Subjects: Studies relating to current and future Canadian national security and defence issues including their political, international, historical, social, military, industrial and economic dimensions.

Eligibility: Applicants must be Canadian citizens or permanent residents at the time of application and, as a minimum requirement, hold a Master's degree or its equivalent before taking up the award.

Level of Study: Graduate.

Value: Up to canadian $16,000. The Dr Ronald Baker Doctoral Scholarship is up to canadian $17,000.

Study Establishment: Canadian institutions.

Country of Study: Canada.

No. of awards offered: Approx. four.

Application Procedure: Applicants must apply for information, available on request or from the website.

Closing Date: Postmarked February 1st.

Additional Information: On completion of the scholarship one copy of the dissertation or a reasonable detailed account of the research undertaken must be submitted to the AUCC who will forward it to the Department of National Defence.

Security and Defence Forum Postdoctoral Fellowship Program including the R B Byers Postdoctoral Fellowship

Subjects: Studies relating to current and future Canadian national security and defence issues including their political, international, historical, social, military, industrial and economic dimensions.

Eligibility: Applicants must be Canadian citizens or permanent residents at the time of application and hold a PhD or its equivalent before taking up the award. Individuals who hold a tenure or tenure track appointment at any level are not eligible.

Level of Study: Doctorate, Postgraduate.

Type: Fellowship.

Value: Up to canadian $27,000.

Length of Study: One year, non renewable.

Frequency: Annual.

Study Establishment: Educational institutions in Canada.

Country of Study: Canada.

No. of awards offered: Approx. three.

Application Procedure: Applicants must apply for information, available on request or from the website http://www.dnd.ca/eng/dp/index_e.htm.

Closing Date: Postmarked February 1st.

Additional Information: On completion of the award period a reasonably detailed account of the research undertaken, as well as copies of publications and unpublished conference presentations resulting from the award, are to be submitted to the AUCC who will forward them to the Department of National Defence. Successful applicants may not hold more than one award from the federal government.

THE ASTHMA FOUNDATION OF NEW SOUTH WALES

Unit 1/82
Pacific Highway, St Leonards, NSW, 2065, Australia
Tel: (61) 2 9906 3233
Fax: (61) 2 9906 4493
www: http://www.asthmansw.org.au
Contact: Executive Director

The vision of the Asthma Foundation of New South Wales is to eliminate asthma as a major cause of illness and disruption within the New South Wales community. Fundraising efforts assist with the promotion and funding of research activities that are aimed at helping the Foundation to achieve this vision.

Ann J Woolcock Research Fellowship

Subjects: Asthma research.

Purpose: To provide an outstanding researcher in biomedical science with an opportunity for independent research.

Eligibility: Open to Australian citizens or permanent residents who hold a PhD or equivalent doctorate in a health related field of research. Applicants must also have a demonstrated ability in research in the form of publications, and an intention to remain active in research. Candidates should have been actively engaged in research, in Australia or overseas, within the two years prior to application, and should normally have no more than eight years of postdoctoral experience from the date that the doctoral thesis was passed.

Level of Study: Postdoctorate.

Type: Fellowship.

Value: Up to australian $100,000. This sum includes salary and up to australian $15,000 for equipment, running expenses and travel. The value of a part-time fellowship will be adjusted on a pro-rata basis.

Length of Study: Applicants may elect to carry out research full or part-time with remaining time spent in clinical practice. The full-time fellowship is for a period of up to three years and the part-time fellowship is for up to four years.
Study Establishment: A recognised and approved institution, teaching hospital or university in New South Wales or the Australian Central Territories.
Country of Study: Australia.
Application Procedure: All applications must be submitted on the correct application form, which together with details of the conditions associated with the fellowship, can be found on the website.

Asthma Foundation of New South Wales Medical Research Project Grant

Subjects: Medical, scientific and clinical research into asthma, its causes, triggers and impact.
Purpose: To expand the body of knowledge towards the causes of asthma and its possible cure.
Level of Study: Postdoctorate, Postgraduate.
Type: Project grant.
Value: US$1,500-50,000.
Length of Study: One year.
Frequency: Every two years.
Country of Study: Australia.
No. of awards offered: Varies.
Application Procedure: Applicants must complete application forms. Short listed candidates wil be interviewed.
Closing Date: Mid August.
Funding: Private.
Contributor: Private donors.
No. of awards given last year: Six.
No. of applicants last year: 27.

Biomedical and Medical Postgraduate Research Scholarships

Subjects: Medical, scientific and clinical research into asthma, its causes, triggers and impact.
Purpose: To expand the body of knowledge towards the causes of asthma and its possible cure.
Level of Study: Postdoctorate, Postgraduate.
Type: Scholarship.
Value: US$1,500-50,000.
Length of Study: One year.
Frequency: Annual.
Country of Study: Australia.
No. of awards offered: Varies.
Application Procedure: Applicants must complete application forms. Short listed candidates wil be interviewed.
Closing Date: Mid August.
Funding: Private.
Contributor: Private donors.
No. of awards given last year: Three.
No. of applicants last year: Five.

ASTHMA VICTORIA

69 Flemington Road, North Melbourne, VIC, 3051, Australia
Tel: (61) 3 9326 7088
Fax: (61) 3 9326 7055
Email: afv@asthma.org.au
www: http://www.asthma.org.au
Contact: Mr Garry Irving, Manager of Services

Asthma Victoria is a community-based organisation committed to reducing the impact of asthma. Asthma Victoria provides education, training, advice, counselling and support to people with asthma, their families and community carers and educators. Asthma Victoria funds research which will have outcomes that directly benefit people living with asthma and will reduce the impact of this chronic condition.

Asthma Victoria Research Grants

Subjects: Medical or scientific research relating to increased knowledge of, and improvements in, asthma management including development and evaluation of educational programmes. Ideally projects should have direct patient application.
Purpose: To encourage and assist asthma research in Victoria, Australia.
Eligibility: Open to Australian citizens or permanent residents with appropriate qualifications and experience at various levels, from Honours graduates to postdoctoral level.
Level of Study: Doctorate, Postdoctorate, Postgraduate.
Type: Research grant and research scholarship.
Value: Varies, according to funds available.
Frequency: Annual.
Study Establishment: An approved institution in Victoria.
Country of Study: Australia.
No. of awards offered: Dependent on funds available.
Application Procedure: Applicants must complete an application form, available on request.
Closing Date: September 30th for grants awarded for the following calendar year.
Funding: Private.
Contributor: Public donations.
No. of awards given last year: Four.
Additional Information: Specific purpose grants include Helen M Schutt Trust Grants for general asthma research, Convoy for Kids Grant for research into asthma in children, Anna Jane Grant for research into adolescent asthma, and Parker Grant for research into complimentary therapies.

ATAXIA UK

10 Winchester House
Kennington Park, London, SW9 6EJ, England
Tel: (44) 20 7820 3900
Fax: (44) 20 7582 9444
Email: office@ataxia.org.uk
www: http://www.ataxia.org.uk
Contact: Ms Julia Greenfield, Research Liason Officer

Ataxia UK is the leading charity in the United Kingdom working with and for people with ataxia. It will support research projects and related activities in order to enhance scientific understanding of ataxia, develop and evaluate therapeutic and supportive strategies and encourage wider involvement with ataxia research.

Ataxia UK Research Studentships

Subjects: Any aspect of both inherited and sporadic progressive ataxias, including Friedreich's and other cerebellar ataxias.
Purpose: To enhance scientific understanding of ataxia, to develop and evaluate therapeutic and supportive strategies. To increase awareness of ataxia in the research community.
Eligibility: Proposals are accepted from academic institutions, private sector research companies and suitably qualified individuals. There are no restrictions on age, nationality or residency.
Level of Study: Doctorate.
Type: PhD studentship.
Value: Standard PhD studentship grant.
Length of Study: Three years.
Frequency: Dependent on funds available.
Study Establishment: Any academic institution.
Country of Study: Any country.
No. of awards offered: Not more than two per year.
Application Procedure: Applicants must complete an application form available from Ataxia UK's Research Liaison Officer at rlo@ataxia.org.uk.
Closing Date: April 8th, August 1st and December 2nd.
Funding: Commercial, Private.

Additional Information: There are a number of priority areas of research and these can be obtained from the Research Liaison Officer.

Ataxia UK Travel Award

Subjects: Any aspect of both inherited and sporadic progressive ataxias including Friedreich's and other cerebellar ataxias.
Purpose: To enable researchers to present their ataxia research at national and international conferences.
Eligibility: Proposals are accepted from academic institutions, private sector research companies and suitably qualified individuals. There are no restrictions on age, nationality or residency.
Level of Study: Unrestricted.
Type: Travel award.
Value: Dependent on conference.
Frequency: Dependent on funds available.
Country of Study: Any country.
No. of awards offered: Varies.
Application Procedure: Applicants must complete an application form available from Ataxia's Research Liaison Officer on rlo@ataxis.org.uk.
Closing Date: April 8th, August 1st and December 2nd.
Funding: Commercial, Private.
Additional Information: There are a number of priority areas of research and these can be obtained from the Research Liaison Officer.

Project Grant

Subjects: Any aspect of both inherited and sporadic progressive ataxias including Friedreich's and other cerebellar ataxias.
Purpose: To enhance scientific understanding of ataxia and to develop and evaluate therapeutic and supportive strategies.
Eligibility: Proposals are accepted from academic institutions, private sector research companies and suitably qualified individuals. There are no restrictions on age, nationality or residency.
Level of Study: Research.
Type: Research project grant.
Value: Varies.
Length of Study: Up to three years.
Frequency: Dependent on funds available.
Study Establishment: Any academic institution or private sector company.
Country of Study: Any country.
No. of awards offered: One.
Application Procedure: Applicants must complete an application form available from Ataxia's Research Liaison Officer on rlo@ataxis.org.uk.
Closing Date: April 8th, August 1st and December 2nd.
Funding: Commercial, Private.
Additional Information: There are a number of priority areas of research and these can be obtained from the Research Liaison Officer.

Satellite Meeting at Major Symposium on Related Disorders

Subjects: Any aspect of both inherited and sporadic progressive ataxias including Friedreich's and other cerebellar ataxias.
Purpose: To raise awareness of ataxia research and enhance collaboration with researchers within the ataxia field and in related disciplines.
Eligibility: Proposals are accepted from academic institutions, private sector research companies and suitably qualified individuals. There are no restrictions on age, nationality or residency.
Level of Study: Research.
Type: Conference award.
Value: Dependent on the meeting.
Frequency: Dependent on funds available.
Country of Study: Any country.
No. of awards offered: Varies.

Application Procedure: Applicants must complete an application form available from Ataxia's Research Liaison Officer on rlo@ataxis.org.uk.
Closing Date: April 8th, August 1st and December 2nd.
Funding: Commercial, Private.
Additional Information: There are a number of priority areas of research and these can be obtained from the Research Liaison Officer.

Short Project Grant

Subjects: Any aspect of both inherited and sporadic progressive ataxias including Friedreich's and other cerebellar ataxias.
Purpose: To enhance scientific understanding of ataxia, to develop and evaluate therapeutic and supportive strategies.
Eligibility: Proposals are accepted from academic institutions, private sector research companies and suitably qualified individuals. There are no restrictions on age, nationality or residency.
Level of Study: Research.
Type: Research project grant.
Value: A maximum of of UK £50,000.
Length of Study: Less than three years.
Frequency: Dependent on funds available.
Study Establishment: Any academic institution or private sector company.
Country of Study: Any country.
No. of awards offered: Varies.
Application Procedure: Applicants must complete an application form available from Ataxia's Research Liaison Officer on rlo@ataxis.org.uk.
Closing Date: April 8th, August 1st and December 2nd.
Funding: Commercial, Private.
No. of awards given last year: One.
No. of applicants last year: Two.
Additional Information: There are a number of priority areas of research and these can be obtained from the Research Liaison Officer.

ATHENAEUM INTERNATIONAL CULTURAL CENTRE

3 Adrianou Street, Athens, GR-10555, Greece
Tel: (30) 1 321 1987
Fax: (30) 1 321 1196
Email: athenm@attglobal.net
www: http://www.athenaeum.ids.gr
Contact: Mrs Irene Mega, Executive Secretary

The Athenaeum International Cultural Centre is a non-profit association dedicated to preserving the memory of Maria Callas. The organisation was founded in 1974 by a group of inspired artists who wanted to contribute to the development and evolution of musical education and culture in Greece.

Maria Callas Grand Prix

Subjects: Singing and the piano.
Purpose: To recognise outstanding artists.
Eligibility: Open to nationals from any country.
Level of Study: Unrestricted.
Type: Grand Prix.
Value: Please contact the organisation.
Frequency: Every two years per discipline. One year opera and the following piano.
Country of Study: Any country.
No. of awards offered: One for each category.
Application Procedure: Applicants must complete an application form and submit this with the documentation as detailed in the prospectus of the Grand Prix. There is a registration fee of US$100.
Closing Date: December 31st.
Funding: Government, Private.
No. of awards given last year: Two in opera and one in piano.

No. of applicants last year: 32 for opera and 23 for piano.
Additional Information: Concert appearances are arranged for the winners.

Maria Callas Grand Prix for Opera and Oratorio-Lied

Subjects: Three categories, which are female opera singers, male opera singers and oratorio-lied.
Purpose: To recognise outstanding singers.
Eligibility: Open to singers of any nationality. Female singers should not be older than 30 years of age and male singers not older than 32 years of age.
Level of Study: Unrestricted.
Type: Grand Prix.
Value: Please contact the organisation.
Frequency: Every two years.
Country of Study: Any country.
No. of awards offered: Three Grand Prix, one for each category.
Application Procedure: Applicants must complete an application form and pay the registration fee of US$100. Candidates must contact the Centre for further details.
Closing Date: December 31st.
Funding: Government, Private.
No. of awards given last year: Two.
No. of applicants last year: 32.
Additional Information: Concert appearances are arranged for the winners.

Maria Callas Grand Prix for Pianists

Subjects: Musical performance on the piano. Only works for the piano, orchestra or both are acceptable.
Purpose: To recognise outstanding pianists.
Eligibility: Open to pianists of any nationality, up to 32 years of age.
Level of Study: Unrestricted.
Type: Grand Prix.
Value: Please contact the organisation.
Frequency: Every two years.
Country of Study: Any country.
No. of awards offered: One.
Application Procedure: Applicants must contact the Centre for details. There is a registration fee of US$100.
Closing Date: December 31st.
Funding: Government, Private.
No. of awards given last year: One.
No. of applicants last year: 40.
Additional Information: Concert appearances are arranged for the Grand Prix winner.

Maria Callas International Music Competition

Subjects: Musical performance although disciplines vary with each competition. Singing such as opera, oratorio or lied and the piano.
Purpose: To recognise outstanding artists.
Eligibility: Open to musicians of all nationalities.
Level of Study: Unrestricted.
Type: Competition.
Value: Please contact the organisation.
Frequency: Every two years per discipline.
Country of Study: Any country.
No. of awards offered: Varies according to the discipline.
Application Procedure: Applicants must request full details and application procedures or consult the website. There is a registration fee of US$100.
Closing Date: December 31st.
Funding: Government, Private.
No. of awards given last year: Two in opera and one in piano.
No. of applicants last year: 32 for singing and 23 for the piano competition.
Additional Information: Concert appearances are arranged for the winners.

ATLANTIC SALMON FEDERATION (ASF)

PO Box 5200, St Andrews, NB, E5B 3S8, Canada
Tel: (1) 506 529 4581
Fax: (1) 506 529 4438
Email: asfres@nbnet.nb.ca
www: http://www.asf.ca/awards/awards.html
Contact: Ms Ellen Merrill, Executive Assistant

The Atlantic Salmon Federation (ASF) is an international, non-profit organisation which promotes the conservation and management of the Atlantic salmon and its environment. ASF has a network of seven regional councils, a membership of over 150 river associations and 40,000 volunteers. Regional offices cover the salmon's freshwater range in Canada and the United States of America.

Olin Fellowship

Subjects: A wide range of endeavours including salmon management, graduate study and research.
Purpose: To support individuals seeking to improve their knowledge or skills in advanced fields while looking for solutions to current problems in Atlantic salmon biology, management and conservation.
Eligibility: Open to citizens and legal residents of the United States of America or Canada. Applicants need not be enrolled in a degree programme.
Level of Study: Unrestricted.
Type: Fellowship.
Value: Canadian $1,000-3,000.
Frequency: Annual.
Study Establishment: Any accredited university, research laboratory or active management programme.
Country of Study: United States of America or Canada.
No. of awards offered: Varies.
Application Procedure: Applicants must complete an application form, available on request or from the website.
Closing Date: March 15th for notification by May 15th.
Funding: Private.
Contributor: Memberships and foundation grants.
No. of awards given last year: Three.
No. of applicants last year: Five.

For further information contact:

Executive Assistant
PO Box 807, Calais, ME, 04619-0807, United States of America
Tel: (1) 506 529 1021
Fax: (1) 506 529 4985
Email: atlsal@nbnet.nb.ca
Contact: Ms Ellen Merrill, Executive Assistant

ATLANTIC SCHOOL OF THEOLOGY

660 Fracklyn Street, Halifax, NS, B3H 3B5, Canada
Tel: (1) 902 423 6801
Fax: (1) 902 492 4048
Email: dmaclachlan@astheology.ns.ca
www: http://www.astheology.ns.ca
Contact: Mr David MacLachlan, Academic Dean

The Atlantic School of Theology is an ecumenical university committed to excellence in graduate level theological education and research. The School is also committed to the provision of information for Christian ministries, both lay and ordained, in church and society, primarily in Atlantic Canada.

The Evelyn Hilchie Betts Memorial Fellowship

Subjects: Any subject offered at the Atlantic School of Theology.
Purpose: To enable ordained clergy from the Third World to study at the School and thereby to introduce persons from other Christian communities to the church and theological education in Canada and to share their context with the School.

Eligibility: Open to ordained clergy (male or female) from developing countries, who are interested in theological education in an ecumenical atmosphere and are able to speak and write in the English language. Applicants must be interested in living and working in a Christian community and willing to share their work and experiences with the Canadian church. Since the Atlantic School of Theology is a postgraduate school they encourage applicants with university training.

Level of Study: Postgraduate.

Type: Fellowship.

Value: Approx. canadian $15,000 for transportation, tuition, room and board.

Length of Study: One academic year.

Frequency: Dependent on funds available.

Study Establishment: The Atlantic School of Theology in Halifax, Nova Scotia.

Country of Study: Canada.

No. of awards offered: One.

Application Procedure: Applicants must submit a completed application form and letters of reference to the Betts Memorial Fellowship Committee.

Closing Date: December 31st.

Funding: Private.

No. of awards given last year: One.

No. of applicants last year: 60.

Additional Information: Due to a shortage of funds for the scholarship no award will be possible until further notice.

AUSTRALIAN ACADEMY OF SCIENCE

PO Box 783, Canberra, ACT, 2601, Australia
Tel: (61) 2 6247 3966
Fax: (61) 2 6257 4620
Email: io@science.org.au
www: http://www.science.org.au/internat
Contact: International Programmes Officer

The Australian Academy of Science is an independent, non-profit organisation with a membership of 300 Fellows elected for making distinguished contributions in the area of natural sciences and their applications. The objectives of the Academy are to promote science and science education through a range of activities.

Australian Academy of Science Scientific Visits to China

Subjects: Any field of natural science, basic and applied, including mathematics and engineering science.

Purpose: To allow researchers to collaborate with researchers in China.

Eligibility: Open to Australians or residents of Australia.

Level of Study: Research.

Type: Fellowship.

Value: Air travel only up to australian $1,800. A daily allowance is provided by the Chinese counterpart.

Length of Study: Up to six weeks.

Frequency: Annual.

Country of Study: China.

No. of awards offered: Approx. five-six, depending on funding available and the length of visit.

Application Procedure: Applicants must complete an application form.

Closing Date: Between August and October. Please visit the website for details.

Funding: Government.

Contributor: The Department of Industry, Science and Resources in Australia.

Australian Academy of Science Scientific Visits to Europe

Subjects: Any field of natural science, basic and applied, including mathematics and engineering science.

Purpose: To allow Australian researchers to collaborate with researchers in Europe.

Eligibility: Open to Australians or residents of Australia.

Level of Study: Research.

Type: Fellowship.

Value: Australian $7,850.

Length of Study: Up to six weeks.

Frequency: Annual.

No. of awards offered: Approx. 20-22, depending on funds available.

Application Procedure: Applicants must complete an application form.

Closing Date: Between August and October. Please visit the website for details.

Funding: Government.

Contributor: The Department of Industry, Science and Resources in Australia.

Australian Academy of Science Scientific Visits to Japan

Subjects: Any field of natural science, basic and applied, including mathematics and engineering science.

Purpose: To allow Australian researchers to collaborate with researchers in Japan.

Eligibility: Only Australians or residents of Australia are eligible to apply.

Level of Study: Research.

Type: Fellowship.

Value: Air travel only of up to Australian $1,800. A daily allowance is provided by the Japanese counterpart.

Length of Study: Up to two months.

Frequency: Annual.

Country of Study: Japan.

No. of awards offered: Approx. 8-10.

Application Procedure: Applicants must complete an application form.

Closing Date: Between August and October. Please visit the website for details.

Funding: Government.

Contributor: The Department of Industry, Science and Resources in Australia.

Australian Academy of Science Scientific Visits to Taiwan

Subjects: Any field of natural science, basic and applied, including mathematics and engineering science.

Purpose: To allow Australian researchers to collaborate with researchers in Taiwan.

Eligibility: Open to Australians or residents of Australia.

Level of Study: Research.

Type: Fellowship.

Value: Air travel only of up to Australian $1,800. A daily allowance is provided by the Taiwanese counterpart.

Length of Study: Two-four weeks.

Frequency: Annual.

Country of Study: Taiwan.

No. of awards offered: Approx. five.

Application Procedure: Applicants must complete an application form.

Closing Date: Between August and October. Please visit the website for details.

Funding: Government.

Contributor: The Department of Industry, Science and Resources in Australia.

Australian Academy of Science Scientific Visits to the United States, Canada and Mexico

Subjects: Any field of natural science, basic and applied, including mathematics and engineering science.

Purpose: To allow Australian researchers to collaborate with researchers from the United States, Canada and Mexico.

Eligibility: Open to Australians or residents of Australia.

Level of Study: Research.
Type: Fellowship.
Value: Australian $7,850.
Length of Study: Up to six weeks.
Frequency: Annual.
Country of Study: United States, Canada or Mexico.
No. of awards offered: Approx. 20-22, depending on funds available.
Application Procedure: Applicants must complete an application form.
Closing Date: Between August and October. Please visit the website for details.
Funding: Government.
Contributor: The Department of Industry, Science and Resources in Australia.

Australian Academy of Science Scientific Visits with Korea

Subjects: Any field of natural science, basic and applied, including mathematics and engineering science.
Purpose: To allow Australian researchers to collaborate with re-searchers in Korea.
Eligibility: Open to Australians or residents of Australia.
Level of Study: Research.
Type: Fellowship.
Value: Air travel only of up to Australian $1,800. A daily allowance is provided by the Korean counterpart.
Length of Study: One-three months.
Frequency: Annual.
Country of Study: Korea.
No. of awards offered: Two-three.
Application Procedure: Applicants must complete an application form.
Closing Date: Between August and October. Please visit the website for details.
Funding: Government.
Contributor: The Department of Industry, Science and Resources in Australia.

Postdoctoral Fellowships in Science and Engineering with the Republic of Korea

Subjects: Any field of natural science, basic and applied, including mathematics and engineering science.
Purpose: To allow Australian researchers to collaborate with re-searchers in Europe.
Eligibility: Open to Australians or residents of Australia.
Level of Study: Postdoctorate.
Type: Fellowship.
Value: Won 1,300,000 per month plus the cost of the airline ticket.
Length of Study: 6-12 months.
Frequency: Annual.
Country of Study: Korea.
No. of awards offered: One-two.
Application Procedure: Applicants must complete an application form.
Closing Date: Between August and October. Please visit the website for details.
Funding: Government.
Contributor: The Korean Government, the Korea Science and Engi-neering Foundation.

Science and Technology Agency Postdoctoral Fellowships

Subjects: Any field of natural science, basic and applied, including mathematics and engineering science.
Purpose: To allow researchers to collaborate with researchers in Japan.
Eligibility: Open to Australians or residents of Australia.
Level of Study: Postdoctorate.
Type: Fellowship.
Value: Approx. australian $120,000.

Length of Study: Up to two years.
Frequency: Annual.
Country of Study: Japan.
No. of awards offered: Approx. 9-10.
Application Procedure: Applicants must complete an application form.
Closing Date: Between August and October. Please visit the website for details.
Funding: Government.
Contributor: The Japanese Government's Science and Technology Agency.

Science and Technology Agency Short-term Fellowships

Subjects: Any field of natural science, basic and applied, including mathematics and engineering science.
Purpose: To allow researchers to collaborate with researchers in Japan.
Eligibility: Open to Australians or residents of Australia.
Level of Study: Research.
Type: Fellowship.
Value: Approx. australian $15,000.
Length of Study: Up to three months.
Frequency: Annual.
Country of Study: Japan.
No. of awards offered: Approx. four-five.
Application Procedure: Applicants must complete an application form.
Closing Date: Between August and October. Please visit the website for details.
Funding: Government.
Contributor: The Japanese Government's Science and Technology Agency.

AUSTRALIAN ACADEMY OF THE HUMANITIES (AAH)

GPO Box 93, Canberra, ACT, 2601, Australia
Tel: (61) 2 6248 7744
Fax: (61) 2 6248 6287
Email: aah.office@anu.edu.au
www: http://www.asap.unimelb.edu.au/aah
Contact: Ms Tania Walker, Administration Officer

The Australian Academy of the Humanities (AAH) was established under Royal Charter in 1969 for the advancement of the scholarship, interest in and understanding of the humanities. Humanities disci-plines include, but are not limited to, history, classics, English, Euro-pean languages and cultures, Asian studies, philosophy, the arts, linguistics, prehistory and archaeology, and cultural and communica-tions studies.

Australian Academy of the Humanities Travelling Fellowships

Subjects: Humanities.
Purpose: To enable short-term study abroad.
Eligibility: Open to Scholars resident in Australia working in the field of humanities.
Level of Study: Unrestricted.
Type: Fellowship.
Value: Australian $2,500 each.
Length of Study: At least six weeks.
Frequency: Annual.
Study Establishment: An appropriate research centre.
Country of Study: Outside Australia.
No. of awards offered: Five.
Application Procedure: Applicants must write for details.
Closing Date: July 30th.
Funding: Government.
No. of awards given last year: Five.
No. of applicants last year: 19.

Additional Information: Research projects should be near completion.

AUSTRALIAN EARLY CHILDHOOD ASSOCIATION, INC. (AECA)

PO Box 105, Watson, ACT, 2602, Australia
Tel: (61) 2 6241 6900
Fax: (61) 2 6241 5547
Email: national@aeca.org.au
www: http://www.aeca.org.au
Contact: National Director

The Australian Early Childhood Association (AECA) is the national non-government organisation for the interests of children from birth to eight years of age and for older children in care. AECA promotes the provision of high quality services for young children and their families and supports the role of parents in caring for their children.

Alice Creswick and Sheila Kimpton Foundation Scholarship

Subjects: A wide range of areas of interest concerning policy, practice and research in the early childhood field.
Purpose: To provide the opportunity for travel, observation and/or major study in the early childhood field.
Eligibility: Open to Australian citizens currently employed in positions which have a direct relationship with early childhood education and care and who have qualifications in early childhood or a related field.
Level of Study: Unrestricted.
Type: Scholarship.
Value: Varies.
Frequency: Dependent on funds available.
Country of Study: Any country.
No. of awards offered: One.
Application Procedure: Applications will be called at appropriate times by AECA.
Closing Date: October 19th.
Additional Information: The successful applicant will be required to undertake certain commitments including the preparation of a written report and speaking engagements as required by AECA.

THE AUSTRALIAN FEDERATION OF UNIVERSITY WOMEN, SOUTH AUSTRALIA, INC. TRUST FUND (AFUW-SA, INC.)

GPO Box 634, Adelaide, SA, 5001, Australia
Contact: Ms Heather Latz, Fellowships Trustee

The Australian Federation of University Women's (AFUW) main activity is assisting women in tertiary education in Australia via bursaries. Funds for the bursaries are raised through volunteer work, academic dress hire, donations and bequests.

The AFUW-SA Inc Trust Fund Bursary

Subjects: All subjects.
Purpose: To assist women to complete coursework postgraduate degrees.
Eligibility: Applications are invited from women enrolled for coursework postgraduate degrees at an Australian university who are not in full-time paid employment or on fully paid study leave during the tenure of the bursary.
Level of Study: Doctorate, Postgraduate.
Type: Bursary.
Value: Australian $3,000.

Length of Study: The bursary must be used within one year of the date of the award.
Frequency: Annual.
Study Establishment: A recognised Australian tertiary institution.
Country of Study: Australia.
No. of awards offered: One.
Application Procedure: Applicants must complete an application form and submit this with evidence of enrolment at the institution at which the qualification is to be obtained, as well as copies of official transcripts, curriculum vitae and list of publications.
Closing Date: March 1st each year.
Funding: Private.
No. of awards given last year: Three.
No. of applicants last year: 30.

Barbara Crase, Doreen McCarthy, Cathy Candler and Brenda Nettle Bursaries

Subjects: All subjects.
Purpose: To assist in the completion of a Master's or PhD research degree.
Eligibility: Open to women or men of any nationality. Applicants must have completed one year of postgraduate research, excluding honours year.
Level of Study: Doctorate, Postgraduate.
Type: Bursary.
Value: Australian $2,500.
Length of Study: The bursary must be used within one year of the date of the award.
Frequency: Annual.
Study Establishment: A South Australian university.
Country of Study: Any country.
No. of awards offered: Three.
Application Procedure: Applicants must write for details. Candidates should complete an application form and submit this with evidence of enrolment at the institution at which the qualification will be obtained, as well as copies of official transcripts, curriculum vitae and list of publications.
Closing Date: March 1st each year.
Funding: Private.
No. of awards given last year: Five.
No. of applicants last year: 35.

Diamond Jubilee Bursary

Subjects: All subjects.
Purpose: To assist in the completion of a coursework postgraduate degree.
Eligibility: Open to women or men of any nationality.
Level of Study: Doctorate, Postgraduate.
Type: Bursary.
Value: Australian $2,000.
Length of Study: The bursary must be used within one year of the date of the award.
Frequency: Annual.
Study Establishment: A South Australian university.
Country of Study: Australia.
No. of awards offered: One.
Application Procedure: Applicants must write for details. Candidates should complete an application form and submit this with evidence of enrolment at the institution at which the qualification will be obtained, as well as copies of official transcripts and curriculum vitae.
Closing Date: March 1st each year.
Funding: Private.
No. of awards given last year: One.
No. of applicants last year: Seven.

Padnendadlu Bursary

Subjects: All subjects.
Purpose: To assist in the completion of a postgraduate degree.
Eligibility: Applicants must be Australian indigenous women.
Level of Study: Doctorate, Postgraduate.

Type: Bursary.
Value: Australian $2,000.
Frequency: Annual.
Study Establishment: A South Australian university.
Country of Study: Australia.
No. of awards offered: One, however, runners up may be awarded less than the bursary amount.
Application Procedure: Applicants must write for details. Candidates should complete an application form and submit this with evidence or enrolment at the institution at which the qualification will be obtained, as well as copies of official transcripts and curriculum vitae.
Closing Date: March 1st each year.
Funding: Private.
No. of awards given last year: One.
No. of applicants last year: One.
Additional Information: Eligible applicants undertaking a postgraduate degree by coursework must apply for the Diamond Jubilee Bursary and those undertaking a postgraduate degree by research must apply for the Doreen McCarthy, Barbara Crase, Cathy Candler and Brenda Nettle Bursaries. In each case, completion of a declaration of Indigenous status will ensure that applicants are considered for the Padnendadlu Bursary.

Thenie Baddams Bursary, Jean Gilmore Bursary and Daphne Elliott Bursary

Subjects: All subjects.
Purpose: To assist women to complete a Master's or PhD degree by research.
Eligibility: Open to women graduates who are enrolled in an Australian tertiary institution and have completed at least one year of postgraduate research, excluding Honours year. Applicants must hold a good Honours degree or equivalent, and not be in full-time paid employment or study leave during tenure.
Level of Study: Doctorate, Postgraduate.
Type: Bursary.
Value: Up to australian $5,000 each, however runners-up can be awarded a lesser amount.
Length of Study: The bursary must be used within one year of the date of the award.
Frequency: Annual.
Study Establishment: A recognised Australian Institute of Higher Education.
Country of Study: Any country.
No. of awards offered: Three.
Application Procedure: Applicants must complete an application form and submit this with evidence of enrolment at the institution at which the qualification is to be obtained, as well as copies of official transcripts, curriculum vitae and list of publications. There is an Australian $12 lodgement fee.
Closing Date: March 1st each year.
Funding: Private.
No. of awards given last year: Five.
No. of applicants last year: 120.

The Winifred E Preedy Postgraduate Bursary

Subjects: Dentistry or a related field.
Purpose: To assist women in the completion of a higher degree.
Eligibility: Open to women who are past or present students of the Faculty of Dentistry at the University of Adelaide and who are enrolled as graduate students in dentistry or some allied field at the University of Adelaide or such other institution of tertiary education as the trustees may approve. The applicant must have completed one year of her postgraduate degree.
Level of Study: Doctorate, Postgraduate.
Type: Bursary.
Value: Australian $5,000.
Length of Study: The bursary must be used within one year of the date of the award.
Frequency: Annual.
Study Establishment: Anywhere if the applicant is a past student at the University of Adelaide's Dental Faculty in Australia. Otherwise

the applicant must be a current student at the University of Adelaide Dental Faculty.
Country of Study: Any country if the applicant is a past or current student of the Faculty of Dentistry at the University of Adelaide, South Australia.
No. of awards offered: One.
Application Procedure: Applicants must complete an application form and submit this with evidence of enrolment at the institution at which the qualification will be obtained, as well as copies of official transcripts, curriculum vitae and list of publications.
Closing Date: March 1st each year.
Funding: Private.
No. of awards given last year: One.
No. of applicants last year: Eight.

AUSTRALIAN INSTITUTE OF ABORIGINAL AND TORRES STRAIT ISLANDER STUDIES (AIATSIS)

GPO Box 553, Canberra, ACT, 2601, Australia
Tel: (61) 2 6246 1157
Fax: (61) 2 6261 4285
Email: grants@aiatsis.gov.au
www: http://www.aiatsis.gov.au
Contact: Research Administration Team

The Australian Institute of Aboriginal and Torres Strait Islander Studies (AIATSIS) is a federally funded organisation central in Aboriginal and Torres Strait Islander research. Its principal function is to promote Australian Aboriginal and Torres Strait Islander studies. A staff of 60, directed by the Principal, engages in a range of services through the Research Programme, the Research Grants Programme, the archives and production team, and the library.

AIATSIS Research Grants

Subjects: Health, human biology, social anthropology, linguistics, ethnomusicology, material culture, rock art, prehistory, ethnobotany, psychology, education and Aboriginal history including oral history, native title and indigenous land use agreements.
Purpose: To promote research into Aboriginal and Torres Strait Islander Studies.
Eligibility: Open to nationals of any country.
Level of Study: Unrestricted.
Type: Research grant.
Value: No predetermined value.
Length of Study: Up to one year.
Frequency: Annual.
Country of Study: Australia.
No. of awards offered: Varies.
Application Procedure: Applicants must complete an application form, available from the website.
Closing Date: January 31st.
Funding: Government.
Contributor: The Australian Federal Government.
Additional Information: Permission to conduct research projects must be obtained from the appropriate Aboriginal or Torres Strait Island community or organisation.

139

AUSTRALIAN INSTITUTE OF NUCLEAR SCIENCE AND ENGINEERING (AINSE)

Private Mail Bag 1, Menai, NSW, 2234, Australia
Tel: (61) 2 9717 3376
Fax: (61) 2 9717 9268
Email: ainse@ansto.gov.au
Contact: Dr Dennis Mather, Scientific Secretary

Established in 1958, the Australian Institute of Nuclear Science and Engineering (AINSE) is a consortium of Australian universities and the University of Auckland, New Zealand, in partnership with the Australian Nuclear Science and Technology Organisation (ANSTO). Its aims are to assist research and training in nuclear science and engineering and to make the facilities of the Lucas Heights Research Laboratories available to research staff and students from member institutions.

AINSE Grants

Subjects: Fields associated with nuclear science and engineering.
Eligibility: Open to member organisations of AINSE which are undertaking projects in an appropriate field.
Level of Study: Unrestricted.
Type: Grant.
Value: Assistance is available mainly in the form of credits enabling university researchers to meet costs associated with the use of facilities, travel to and from Lucas Heights, and accommodation during periods of attachment. Direct grants for small items of equipment and materials may also be considered.
Length of Study: One year.
Frequency: Annual.
Study Establishment: Lucas Heights Science and Technology Centre, near Sydney, New South Wales.
Country of Study: Australia.
No. of awards offered: Varies.
Application Procedure: Applicants must contact the Scientific Secretary, AINSE or Research Office at member universities.
Closing Date: September 30th.
Funding: Government.
No. of awards given last year: 215.
No. of applicants last year: 240.

AINSE Postgraduate Research Awards

Subjects: Nuclear physics, neutron scattering and accelerator science including AMS, radiation biology, chemistry and physics, advanced materials, engineering and nuclear technology, environmental science, biomedicine and health and any field of research using nuclear techniques of analysis in general.
Eligibility: Open to postgraduate students whose research projects are associated with nuclear science and technology and who require access to the unique national facilities at the Lucas Heights Laboratories. Candidates must be nominated by the Australian university (and the University of Auckland) where PhD enrolment is held or proposed.
Level of Study: Postgraduate.
Type: Research grant.
Value: Australian $7,500 per year for research supplements plus australian $5,500 for research expenses.
Length of Study: One year.
Frequency: Annual.
Study Establishment: Lucas Heights Science and Technology Centre, near Sydney, New South Wales.
Country of Study: Australia.
Application Procedure: Applicants must contact the Scientific Secretary, AINSE or Research Office at member universities.
Closing Date: April 15th.
Funding: Government.
No. of awards given last year: 12.
No. of applicants last year: 22.

AUSTRALIAN KIDNEY FOUNDATION

82 Melbourne Street, Adelaide, SA, 5006, Australia
Tel: (61) 8 8334 7555
Fax: (61) 8 8334 7540
Email: teresa.taylor@adelaide.kidney.org.au
www: http://www.kidney.org.au
Contact: Ms Leanne Fardone, National Communications Manager

Founded in 1968, the Australian Kidney Foundation's mission is to be recognised as the leading non-profit national organisation providing funding for, and taking the initiative in, the prevention of kidney and urinary tract diseases.

Australian Kidney Foundation Medical Research Scholarships

Subjects: The functions and disease of the kidney, urinary tract and related organs.
Purpose: To support medical research into functions or diseases of the kidney, urinary tract and related organs.
Eligibility: Open to Australian citizens who are graduates of Australian medical schools or overseas graduates who are eligible for Australian citizenship and for registration as medical practitioners in Australia.
Level of Study: Doctorate, Postgraduate.
Type: Scholarship.
Value: Australian $26,000.
Length of Study: One year.
Frequency: Annual.
Study Establishment: Any approved medical centre, university or research institute.
Country of Study: Australia.
No. of awards offered: Up to six.
Application Procedure: Applicants must complete an application form.
Closing Date: September 30th.

Australian Kidney Foundation Seeding and Equipment Grants

Subjects: The functions or diseases of the kidney, urinary tract and related organs, or relevant problems, dialysis, transplantation, organ donation and research.
Purpose: To provide financial support for research projects related to the kidney and urinary tract.
Eligibility: Open to Australian citizens connected with Australian universities or medical centres with requisite research facilities.
Level of Study: Unrestricted.
Type: Grant.
Value: Up to australian $15,000 per year.
Frequency: Annual.
Study Establishment: Any medical centre, university or research institute.
Country of Study: Australia.
No. of awards offered: 30-35.
Application Procedure: Applicants must contact the Foundation for details.
Closing Date: June 30th.

AUSTRALIAN MUSICAL FOUNDATION

Richards Butler
Beaufort House
15 St Botolph Street, London, EC3A 7EE, England
Tel: (44) 20 7247 6555
Fax: (44) 20 7257 5091
Contact: Mr John Emmott, Secretary

AMF Award

Subjects: Any aspect of musical study, except composition, chosen by the recipient and approved by the trustees.
Purpose: To finance further studies.
Eligibility: Open to Australian singers and instrumentalists under 30 years of age who are resident in Australia or Europe.
Level of Study: Unrestricted.
Value: UK £12,000.
Length of Study: Two years, the second year being subject to assessment.
Frequency: Annual.
Country of Study: European countries.
No. of awards offered: Up to three.
Application Procedure: Applicants must complete an application form and submit this with a demo cassette.
Closing Date: End of April.
Funding: Private.
No. of awards given last year: One.
No. of applicants last year: 35.
Additional Information: Applications are considered in the first instance by the Foundation Committee, with a panel of adjudicators making the final choice. It is stressed that this award is intended for musicians of merit and ability. The Foundation will also take into account how applicants propose to use the award, should they win, to further their careers.

AUSTRALIAN NATIONAL UNIVERSITY (ANU)

Research & Scholarships Office
Building 11, Canberra, ACT, 0200, Australia
Tel: (61) 2 6249 5949
Fax: (61) 2 6125 5931
Email: ressch.enq@anu.edu.au
www: http://www.anu.edu.au
Contact: Research & Scholarships Office

The Australian National University (ANU) was founded by the Australian Government in 1946 as Australia's only completely research-orientated university. It comprises eight research schools, six teaching faculties, a graduate school and over a dozen other academic schools or centres.

Aboriginal and Torres Strait Islander Scholarship

Subjects: All subjects.
Purpose: To assist an Aboriginal or Torres Strait Islander to undertake a graduate diploma, Master's degree course, or a course leading to a PhD.
Eligibility: Open to indigenous Australians who are Aborigines or Torres Strait Islanders.
Level of Study: Postgraduate.
Type: Scholarship.
Value: Approx. australian $17,609 per year.
Length of Study: Dependent on the course to which the scholarship applies.
Frequency: Annual.
Country of Study: Australia.
No. of awards offered: Varies.
Application Procedure: Applicants must complete an application form, available on request or from the website.
Closing Date: October 31st.
Contributor: The Australian National University.
Additional Information: Initial correspondence concerning graduate courses and scholarships should be addressed to the main address or sent by email. Coursework enquiries from Australian students should be emailed to admiss.enq@anu.edu.au. All other enquiries from Australian students should be sent to the main email address. International students should send all enquiries to info.ieo@anu.edu.au or visit the website http://www.anu.edu.au/ieo.

ANU Alumni Association PhD Scholarships - HK, J, M, S +T

Subjects: All subjects.
Purpose: To assist international students with study in Australia.
Eligibility: Open to nationals from Hong Kong, Japan, Malaysia, Thailand and Singapore.
Level of Study: Doctorate.
Type: Scholarship.
Value: Approx. australian $17,609 per year, tax free.
Length of Study: Normally tenable for three years, renewable for six months.
Country of Study: Australia.
No. of awards offered: One each for nationals of eligible countries.
Application Procedure: Applicants must complete an application form, available on request or from the website.
Closing Date: Published through the Alumni Association of each country.
Contributor: The Australian National University.
Additional Information: Initial correspondence concerning graduate courses and scholarships should be addressed to the main address or sent by email. Coursework enquiries from Australian students should be emailed to admiss.enq@anu.edu.au. All other enquiries from Australian students should be sent to the main email address. International students should send all enquiries to info.ieo@anu.edu.au or visit the website http://www.anu.edu.au/ieo.

ANU Graduate School Scholarships

Subjects: All subjects.
Purpose: To fund graduate study.
Eligibility: Open to those who are on the Order of Merit list for Australian Postgraduate Awards.
Level of Study: Doctorate.
Type: Scholarship.
Value: Stipend of australian $17,609 per year tax free, travel to Canberra from within Australia and a grant for the reimbursement of some removal expenses is available.
Length of Study: Three years in the first instance, with a possible extension of six months.
Frequency: Annual.
Country of Study: Australia.
Application Procedure: Applicants must complete an application form, available on request or from the website.
Closing Date: October 31st.
Contributor: The Australian National University.
Additional Information: Initial correspondence concerning graduate courses and scholarships should be addressed to the main address or sent by email. Coursework enquiries from Australian students should be emailed to admiss.enq@anu.edu.au. All other enquiries from Australian students should be sent to the main email address. International students should send all enquiries to info.ieo@anu.edu.au or visit the website http://www.anu.edu.au/ieo.

ANU Master's Degree Scholarships (The Faculties)

Subjects: All subjects.
Purpose: To assist study in most graduate school programmes for courses leading to a Master's degree by research, by coursework or by a combination of the two.
Eligibility: Applicants must hold a Bachelor's degree with at least Upper Second Class (Honours), and, if wishing to undertake a degree by research only, must have proven capability for research.
Level of Study: Postgraduate.
Type: Scholarship.
Value: Basic stipend of australian $17,609 per year tax free, an additional allowance for dependent children of married international scholars, travel to Canberra (excluding international part of the airfare for those recruited from overseas) and a grant for the reimbursement of some removal expenses.
Length of Study: One year.
Frequency: Annual.
Study Establishment: The Faculties.
Country of Study: Australia.
No. of awards offered: Varies.

Application Procedure: Applicants must complete an application form, available on request or from the website.
Closing Date: October 31st for citizens or permanent residents of Australia and New Zealand, and August 30th for international applicants.
Contributor: The Faculties.
Additional Information: Initial correspondence concerning graduate courses and scholarships should be addressed to the main address or sent by email. Coursework enquiries from Australian students should be emailed to admiss.enq@anu.edu.au. All other enquiries from Australian students should be sent to the main email address. International students should send all enquiries to info.ieo@anu.edu.au or visit the website http://www.anu.edu.au/ieo.

ANU PhD Scholarships

Subjects: All subjects.
Purpose: To assist research.
Eligibility: Applicants should write for details.
Level of Study: Doctorate.
Type: Scholarship.
Value: Stipend of australian $17,609 per year tax free, and if applicable, an additional allowance for dependent children of unmarried international scholars plus economy travel to Canberra and a grant for the reimbursement of some removal expenses.
Length of Study: Three years, renewable for six months.
Country of Study: Australia.
No. of awards offered: Varies.
Application Procedure: Applicants must complete an application form, available on request or from the website.
Closing Date: October 31st for citizens or permanent residents of Australia and New Zealand, and August 30th for international applicants.
Additional Information: Initial correspondence concerning graduate courses and scholarships should be addressed to the main address or sent by email. Coursework enquiries from Australian students should be emailed to admiss.enq@anu.edu.au. All other enquiries from Australian students should be sent to the main email address. International students should send all enquiries to info.ieo@anu.edu.au or visit the website http://www.anu.edu.au/ieo.

ANU Re-entry Scholarships for Women

Subjects: All subjects.
Purpose: To assist women graduates who wish to resume their studies after a break of at least three years since formal enrolment in a university course, the break normally being due to fulfilment of family obligations.
Eligibility: Open to women graduates who have taken a break from their studies of at least three years since formal enrolment in a university course, the break normally being due to fulfilment of family obligations. Applicants must be Australian citizens or permanent residents. The scholarship may be awarded to undertake a graduate diploma, a Master's degree course or a PhD and applicants must hold qualifications appropriate to the level of course for which they wish to apply.
Level of Study: Doctorate, Postgraduate.
Type: Scholarship.
Value: Approx. australian $17,609 per year.
Length of Study: Tenure is dependent upon the course to which the scholarship applies.
Frequency: Annual.
Country of Study: Australia.
No. of awards offered: Varies.
Application Procedure: Applicants must submit a completed application form with a letter setting out the applicant's case for award of the scholarship and indicating their circumstances in terms of the eligibility criteria. Application forms are available on request or from the website.
Closing Date: September 30th.
Contributor: The Australian National University.
Additional Information: Initial correspondence concerning graduate courses and scholarships should be addressed to the main address or sent by email. Coursework enquiries from Australian students

should be emailed to admiss.enq@anu.edu.au. All other enquiries from Australian students should be sent to the main email address. International students should send all enquiries to info.ieo@anu.edu.au or visit the website http://www.anu.edu.au/ieo.

Australian Development Scholarships (ADS)

Subjects: All subjects.
Level of Study: Graduate.
Type: Scholarship.
Value: Return air fare to Australia, tuition fees, an establishment allowance and a living allowance are available.
Country of Study: Australia.
Application Procedure: Applicants must write to the Australian Diplomatic Mission or the Australian Education Centre in their home country.
Closing Date: Varies.

AUSTRALIAN RESEARCH COUNCIL (ARC)

GPO Box 2702, Canberra, ACT, 2601, Australia
Tel: (61) 2 6284 6600
Fax: (61) 2 6284 6601
www: http://www.arc.gov.au
Contact: Grants Management Officer

Australian Research Council Discovery Projects Australian Research Fellow/Queen Elizabeth II Fellow (ARF/QEII)

Subjects: All areas of science except clinical medicine or dentistry.
Purpose: To strengthen Australia's national research and development capability by providing opportunities for established researchers to undertake research of national and international significance.
Eligibility: Open to candidates with a PhD and an excellent academic record. Applicants should have more than three years but not more than eight years professional experience since the awarding of their PhD.
Level of Study: Postdoctorate.
Type: Fellowship.
Value: Australian Research Fellows are awarded australian $79,071 and Queen Elizabeth II Fellows are awarded australian $93,848. This includes 26 per cent on costs.
Length of Study: Five years.
Frequency: Annual.
Country of Study: Australia.
No. of awards offered: Approx. 15 of each.
Application Procedure: Applicants must submit applications through an Australian host institution. It is the responsibility of the applicant to approach potential host institutions.
Closing Date: March 8th.
Funding: Government.
No. of awards given last year: 30.
No. of applicants last year: 216.
Additional Information: Candidates must obtain Australian citizenship or temporary residency status at the time of commencing the fellowship. Further information is available from the website.

Australian Research Council Discovery Projects Postdoctoral Fellow (APD)

Subjects: All areas of science except clinical medicine or dentistry.
Purpose: To strengthen Australia's national research and development capability by providing opportunities for researchers to undertake research of national and international significance and to broaden their research experience.
Eligibility: Applicants must have submitted their PhD thesis before commencement of the fellowship. No more than three years should have elapsed since the awarding of their PhD and an excellent academic record is required.

Level of Study: Postdoctorate.
Type: Fellowship.
Value: Australian $62,523, including 26 per cent on costs.
Length of Study: Three years.
Frequency: Annual.
Country of Study: Australia.
No. of awards offered: Approx. 55.
Application Procedure: Applicants must submit applications through an Australian host institution. It is the responsibility of the applicant to approach potential host institutions.
Closing Date: March 8th.
Funding: Government.
No. of awards given last year: 110.
No. of applicants last year: 449.
Additional Information: Candidates must obtain Australian citizenship or temporary residency status at the time of commencing the fellowship. Further information is available from the website.

Australian Research Discovery Projects - Professional Fellow (APF)

Subjects: All areas of science except clinical medicine or dentistry.
Purpose: To provide opportunities for outstanding researchers with proven international reputations to undertake research which is both of major importance in its field and of significant benefit to Australia. Senior Research Fellowships are the premier fellowships offered by the Australian Research Council and, consequently, are highly sought after and extremely competitive.
Eligibility: Open to researchers who normally have more than eight years of professional experience since the awarding of their PhD and extremely high profile expatriate Australians and non Australian researchers who wish to pursue their research in Australia.
Level of Study: Postdoctorate.
Type: Fellowship.
Value: Australian $103,511-126,098 including 26 per cent on costs.
Length of Study: Five years.
Frequency: Annual.
Country of Study: Australia.
No. of awards offered: Approx. 15.
Application Procedure: Applicants must submit applications through an Australian host institution. It is the responsibility of the applicant to approach potential host institutions.
Closing Date: March 8th.
Funding: Government.
No. of awards given last year: 23.
No. of applicants last year: 165.
Additional Information: Further information is available from the website.

AUSTRALIAN-AMERICAN EDUCATIONAL FOUNDATION

GPO Box 1559, Canberra, ACT, 2601, Australia
Tel: (61) 2 6260 4460
Fax: (61) 2 6260 4461
Email: lindy@fulbright.com.au
www: http://www.fulbright.com.au
Contact: Programme Administrator

The Australian-American Educational Foundation is a bi-national commission. The major objective of the Foundation is to further mutual understanding between the peoples of Australia and the United States through educational exchanges. The Foundation also provides information for Australians wishing to study in the United States.

Coral Sea Scholarship

Subjects: Business or industry.
Purpose: To investigate a problem or opportunity relevant to Australian business or industry in the United States of America.

Eligibility: Open to Australian citizens resident in Australia who hold a degree or diploma. Candidates should have relevant business or industry experience. Applications are encouraged from those with a record of achievement who are poised for advancement in their professional field.
Level of Study: Professional development.
Type: Scholarship.
Value: Up to australian $13,000.
Length of Study: Up to three months.
Frequency: Annual.
Country of Study: United States of America.
No. of awards offered: One.
Application Procedure: Applicants must complete and submit an application form along with three reference reports, the forms are included in the application pack, and documentation of citizenship and qualifications. Further information and application packs are available from the website.
Closing Date: August 31st.
Funding: Commercial.

Fulbright Awards

Subjects: All subjects.
Eligibility: Open to Australian postgraduate and postdoctoral students, senior Scholars and professionals.
Level of Study: Doctorate, Postdoctorate, Postgraduate, Professional development.
Value: Postgraduate students receive up to australian $40,000 and postdoctoral fellows receive up to australian $40,000. Senior scholars receive up to australian $30,000 and professionals up to australian $20,000.
Length of Study: Varies.
Frequency: Annual.
Country of Study: United States of America.
No. of awards offered: Up to 16.
Application Procedure: Applicants must complete and submit an application form along with three reference reports, for which the forms are included in the application pack, documentation of citizenship and qualifications. Further information and application packs are available from the website.
Closing Date: August 31st.
Funding: Commercial, Government.

Fulbright Postdoctoral Fellowships

Subjects: All subjects.
Purpose: To enable those who have recently completed their PhD to conduct postdoctoral research, further their professional training or lecture at a university.
Eligibility: Open to Australian citizens by birth or naturalisation. Those holding dual United States of America-Australian citizenship are not eligible for this award. Applicants should have recently completed their PhD, normally less than three years prior to application, although those who have completed their PhD four or five years prior to application will be considered.
Level of Study: Postdoctorate.
Type: Fellowship.
Value: Up to australian $40,000.
Length of Study: 3-12 months.
Frequency: Annual.
Study Establishment: A university, college, research establishment or reputable private practice.
Country of Study: United States of America.
No. of awards offered: One-two.
Application Procedure: Applicants must complete and submit an application form along with three reference reports, for which the forms are included in the application pack, documentation of citizenship and qualifications. Further information and application packs are available from the website.
Closing Date: August 31st.
Funding: Government.

Fulbright Postgraduate Student Award for Aboriginal and Torres Strait Islander People

Subjects: All subjects.
Purpose: To enable candidates to undertake an approved course of study for an American higher degree, or engage in research relevant to an Australian higher degree.
Eligibility: Open to people of Aboriginal and Torres Strait Islander descent.
Level of Study: Postgraduate.
Type: Scholarship.
Value: Up to australian $40,000.
Length of Study: 8-12 months funded or up to four years unfunded.
Frequency: Annual, if funds are available.
Study Establishment: An accredited institution.
Country of Study: United States of America.
No. of awards offered: One.
Application Procedure: Applicants must complete and submit an application form along with three reference reports, for which the forms are included in the application pack, documentation of citizenship and qualifications. Further information and application packs are available from the website.
Closing Date: August 31st.
Funding: Government.
Contributor: The Aboriginal and Torres Strait Islander Commission.

Fulbright Postgraduate Student Award for Engineering

Subjects: Engineering.
Purpose: To enable candidates to undertake an approved course of study for an American higher degree, or engage in research relevant to an Australian higher degree.
Eligibility: Open to Australian citizens. Those with dual United States of America-Australian citizenship are not eligible for this award.
Level of Study: Doctorate, Postgraduate.
Value: Up to australian $40,000.
Length of Study: 8-12 months funded or up to four years unfunded.
Frequency: Annual, if funds are available.
Study Establishment: An accredited institution.
Country of Study: United States of America.
No. of awards offered: One.
Application Procedure: Applicants must complete and submit an application form along with three reference reports, for which the forms are included in the application pack, documentation of citizenship and qualifications. Further information and application packs are available from the website.
Closing Date: August 31st.
Funding: Commercial, Government.
Contributor: Clough Engineering Limited.

Fulbright Postgraduate Student Award for Science and Engineering

Subjects: Science and engineering.
Purpose: To enable candidates to undertake an approved course of study for an American higher degree, or to engage in research relevant to an Australian higher degree.
Eligibility: Open to Australian citizens. Those with dual United States of America-Australia citizenship are not eligible for this award.
Level of Study: Doctorate, Postgraduate.
Value: Up to australian $40,000.
Length of Study: 8-12 months funded or up to four years unfunded.
Frequency: Annual, if funds are available.
Study Establishment: An accredited institution.
Country of Study: United States of America.
No. of awards offered: One.
Application Procedure: Applicants must complete and submit an application form along with three reference reports, for which the forms are included in the application pack, documentation of citizenship and qualifications. Further information and application packs are available from the website.
Closing Date: August 31st.
Funding: Commercial, Government.

Contributor: BHP.

Fulbright Postgraduate Student Award for the Visual and Performing Arts

Subjects: Fine and applied arts.
Purpose: To enable candidates to undertake a higher degree, or carry out research towards an Australian higher degree.
Eligibility: Open to Australian citizens. Those with dual United States of America-Australian citizenship are not eligible for this award.
Level of Study: Doctorate, Postgraduate, Professional development.
Value: Up to australian $40,000.
Length of Study: 8-12 months funded or up to four years unfunded.
Frequency: Annual, if funds are available.
Country of Study: United States of America.
No. of awards offered: One.
Application Procedure: Applicants must complete and submit an application form along with three reference reports, for which the forms are included in the application pack, documentation of citizenship and qualifications. Further information and application packs are available from the website.
Closing Date: August 31st.
Funding: Commercial, Government.
Contributor: Anthony Joseph Pratt.

Fulbright Postgraduate Student Award to undertake an MBA

Subjects: Business administration.
Purpose: To enable applicants to undertake a higher degree or carry out research towards an Australian higher degree in the United States of America.
Eligibility: Open to Australian citizens. Those with dual United States of America-Australian citizenship are not eligible for this award.
Level of Study: MBA.
Type: Award.
Frequency: Annual, if funds are available.
Study Establishment: An approved institution in the United States of America.
Country of Study: United States of America.
No. of awards offered: One.
Application Procedure: Applicants must complete an application form and submit this with three reference reports, documentation of Australian citizenship and academic transcripts. Further information and application forms are available from the website.
Closing Date: August 31st.
Funding: Commercial, Government.
Contributor: A T Kearney.

Fulbright Postgraduate Studentships

Subjects: All subjects.
Purpose: To enable students to undertake an approved course of study for an American higher degree or its equivalent, or to engage in research relevant to an Australian higher degree.
Eligibility: Open to Australian citizens by birth or naturalisation. Those holding dual United States of America-Australian citizenship are not eligible for this award.
Level of Study: Doctorate, Postgraduate.
Type: Studentship.
Value: Up to australian $40,000.
Length of Study: 8-12 months funded, renewable for up to five years unfunded.
Frequency: Annual.
Study Establishment: An accredited institution in the United States of America.
Country of Study: United States of America.
No. of awards offered: Up to eight.
Application Procedure: Applicants must complete an application form and submit this with three reference reports, for which the forms are included in the application pack, and documentation of

citizenship and qualifications. Naturalised citizens must provide a certificate of Australian citizenship with their application, and native-born Australians must provide a copy of their birth certificate. Further information and application packs are available from the website.
Closing Date: August 31st.
Funding: Government.
Additional Information: As the award does not include any provision for maintenance payments, applicants must be able to demonstrate that they have sufficient financial resources to support themselves and any dependants during their stay in the United States of America.

Fulbright Professional Award

Subjects: All professional fields. Programmes should include an academic as well as a practical aspect.
Purpose: To support applicants undertaking a programme of professional development.
Eligibility: Open to Australian citizens resident in Australia with a record of achievement who are poised for advancement to a senior management or policy role. Those holding dual United States of America-Australian citizenship are not eligible for this award.
Level of Study: Professional development.
Type: Award.
Value: Up to australian $20,000.
Length of Study: Three-four months between July and June. Programmes of longer duration may be proposed but without additional funding.
Frequency: Annual.
Country of Study: United States of America.
No. of awards offered: One.
Application Procedure: Applicants must complete and submit an application form along with three reference reports, for which the forms are included in the application pack, documentation of citizenship and qualifications. Further information and application packs are available from the website.
Closing Date: August 31st.
Funding: Government.

Fulbright Professional Award for Vocational Education and Training

Subjects: Open to all fields but must be employed in the vocational education and training sector.
Purpose: To enable candidates to visit institutions or organisations and people in the United States of America from their own field.
Eligibility: Open to Australian citizens employed in the vocational education and training sector. Those holding dual United States of America-Australian citizenship are not eligible for this award.
Level of Study: Professional development.
Value: Up to australian $20,000.
Length of Study: Three-four months funded.
Frequency: Annual.
Country of Study: United States of America.
No. of awards offered: One.
Application Procedure: Applicants must complete and submit an application form along with three reference reports, for which the forms are included in the application pack, documentation of citizenship and qualifications. Further information and application packs are available from the website.
Closing Date: August 31st.
Funding: Government.
Contributor: The Australian National Training Authority.

Fulbright Senior Awards

Subjects: All subjects.
Purpose: To allow candidates to teach, undertake research, be an invited speaker or visit institutions within their field.
Eligibility: Open to Australian citizens by birth or naturalisation. Those holding dual United States of America-Australian citizenship are not eligible for this award. Applicants should be either Scholars of established reputation working in an academic institution who intend to teach or research in the United States of America, leaders in

the arts eg. music, drama, visual arts or senior members of the academically based professions who are currently engaged in the private practice of their profession.
Level of Study: Professional development.
Value: Up to australian $30,000.
Length of Study: Four-six months.
Frequency: Annual.
Study Establishment: A university, college, research establishment or reputable private organisation.
Country of Study: United States of America.
No. of awards offered: Two.
Application Procedure: Applicants must complete an application form and submit this with three reference reports, for which the forms are included in the application pack, documentation of citizenship and qualifications. Further information and application packs are available from the website. Naturalised citizens must provide a certificate of Australian citizenship with their application, and native-born Australians must provide a copy of their birth certificate.
Closing Date: August 31st.
Funding: Government.

Fulbright Tim Matthews Memorial Postgraduate Student Award in Statistics and Related Disciplines

Subjects: Mathematics and computer science, econometrics, statistics, finance and actuarial science.
Purpose: To enable candidates to undertake a higher degree or carry out research towards an Australian higher degree in the United States of America.
Eligibility: Open to Australian citizens. Those with dual United States of America-Australian citizenship are not eligible for this award.
Level of Study: Doctorate, Postgraduate.
Type: Award.
Value: Up to australian $50,000.
Length of Study: 8-12 months funded or up to five years unfunded.
Frequency: Annual, if funds are available.
Study Establishment: Any approved institution in the United States of America.
Country of Study: United States of America.
No. of awards offered: One.
Application Procedure: Applicants must complete an application form and submit this with three reference reports, for which the forms are included in the application pack, documentation of citizenship and qualifications. Further information and application packs are available from the website.
Closing Date: August 31st.
Funding: Commercial, Government.
Contributor: The Victorian Workcover Authority.

AUSTRIAN ACADEMY OF SCIENCES

Institute of Limnology
Mondseestraße 9
A-5310 Mondsee, Gaisberg, A-5310, Austria
Tel: (43) 623 240 79
Fax: (43) 623 235 78
Email: ipgl.mondsee@oeaw.ac.at
www: http://www.oeaw.ac.at/ipgl
Contact: Mr Gerold Winkler, IPGL Course Administrator

The Institute of Limnology of the Austrian Academy of Sciences performs ecological research on inland waters. The overall research goal is to understand the structure, function and dynamics of freshwater ecosystems. Although the Institute primarily conducts basic research, aspects of applied research are also considered. The Institute consists of two departments with a total staff of 27, including 14 scientists. The department at Mondsee located at Salzburg was established in 1981. Currently the Institute's main fields of research are trophic interactions and food web structure in lakes.

Austrian Academy of Sciences MSc Course in Limnology and Wetlands Ecosystems

Subjects: Aquatic systems.

Purpose: To give an overall insight into aquatic systems through lectures, laboratory exercises, appropriate technology, group work, role play and field studies.

Eligibility: Open to candidates from developing countries who are 25-35 years of age, have a good working knowledge of English and have an academic degree in science, agriculture or veterinary medicine from a university or other recognised Institute of Higher Education. Applicants should have practical experience within at least one special subject in their field of professional training.

Level of Study: Postgraduate.

Type: Scholarship.

Value: US$694 paid monthly to cover food, lodging and personal needs plus free tuition, health insurance, study material and equipment for laboratory work, field work and travelling expenses.

Length of Study: 18 months.

Frequency: Annual.

Study Establishment: Institute for Limnology, Mondsee, Institute IHE, Delft, The Netherlands, Makerere University, Kampala, Uganda and Egerton University, Kenya, Czech Academy of Sciences, Trebon, Czech Republic, Austrian universities and federal Institutes.

Country of Study: Austria, the Netherlands, Czech Republic, Uganda or Kenya.

No. of awards offered: Four.

Application Procedure: Applicants must obtain application forms and further information from the Austrian Diplomatic Mission, Cultural Attaché or Cultural Institute in the applicant's home country, or from the address shown. Application forms are also available from the website.

Closing Date: October 30th.

Funding: Government.

Contributor: The Austrian Development Co-operation.

No. of awards given last year: Four.

No. of applicants last year: 50.

Additional Information: No provisions are made for dependants. It is strongly advised that dependants do not accompany Fellows due to frequent moves during the course. Fellows must also provide their own transportation to and from Austria. Participants originating from certain developing countries will be further assisted by the Austrian Government so that travel expenses will be fully covered.

Austrian Academy of Sciences Postgraduate Course in Limnology

Subjects: Physical and chemical properties and processes in lakes and rivers, the role of bacteria, protozoa, phytoplankton, epilithic algae, water plants, zooplankton, macro-microbenthos and fish in aquatic ecosystems. System-ecological aspects for different aquatic systems, quantitative approaches, food web structures, trophic interactions and carbon and nitrogen budgets, the assessment of human impacts and their effect on the ecological integrity of aquatic systems. Biological indicators, methods of fish stock assessment, estimation of fish growth and fish pond management, the sustainable use of tropical and temperate wetlands, the structure and function of groundwater ecosystems eg. groundwater pollution, protection and management, biomonitoring, reconstructing the history of lakes from paleolimnological investigations, the fundamentals of water quality assessment and control, bacteriological methods for examination of water and wastewater and water as a source of disease for men and animals.

Purpose: To assist students studying the functioning of freshwater ecosystems.

Eligibility: Open to candidates from developing countries who are 25-35 years of age, have a good working knowledge of English and have an academic degree in science, agriculture or veterinary medicine from a university or other recognised Institute of Higher Education. Applicants should have practical experience within at least one special subject in their field of professional training.

Level of Study: Postgraduate.

Type: Scholarship.

Value: US$694 paid monthly to cover food, lodging and personal needs plus free tuition, health insurance, study material and equipment for laboratory work, field work and travelling expenses.

Length of Study: Six months.

Frequency: Annual.

Study Establishment: Institute for Limnology, Mondsee Austrian Academy of Sciences, Czech Academy of Sciences, Federal Institutes of the Ministry of Agriculture, University of Agricultural Sciences in Vienna, the Technical University in Vienna and the University of Vienna.

Country of Study: Austria or Czech Republic.

No. of awards offered: 10.

Application Procedure: Applicants must obtain application forms and further information from the Austrian Diplomatic Mission, Cultural Attaché or Cultural Institute in the applicant's home country, or from the address shown. Application forms are also available from the website.

Closing Date: October 30th.

Funding: Government.

Contributor: The Austrian Development Co-operation.

No. of awards given last year: Nine.

No. of applicants last year: 130.

Additional Information: No provisions are made for dependants. It is strongly advised that dependants do not accompany Fellows due to frequent moves during the course. Fellows must also provide their own transportation to and from Austria. Participants originating from certain developing countries will be further assisted by the Austrian Government so that travel expenses will be fully covered.

Institute of Limnology Postgraduate Training Fellowships

Subjects: Limnology.

Purpose: To give Fellows an overall insight into the various problems of limnology so that they may be better equipped to implement necessary research in their home countries in order to find solutions to their practical problems.

Eligibility: Open to candidates from developing countries who are 25-35 years of age, have a good working knowledge of English and have an academic degree in science, agriculture or veterinary medicine from a university or other recognised Institute of Higher Education. Applicants should have practical experience within at least one special subject in their field of professional training.

Level of Study: Postgraduate.

Type: Fellowship.

Value: Please contact the organisation.

Length of Study: Six months.

Frequency: Annual.

Country of Study: Austria.

No. of awards offered: 12.

Application Procedure: Applicants must obtain application forms and further information from the Austrian Diplomatic Mission, Cultural Attaché or Cultural Institute in the applicant's home country, or from the address shown. Application forms are also available from the website.

Closing Date: October 30th.

Additional Information: No provisions are made for dependants. It is strongly advised that dependants do not accompany Fellows due to frequent moves during the course. Fellows must also provide their own transportation to and from Austria. Participants originating from certain developing countries will be further assisted by the Austrian Government so that travel expenses will be fully covered.

AUSTRIAN SCIENCE FUND (FWF)

Weyringergasse 35, Vienna, A-1040, Austria
Tel: (43) 150 567 40
Fax: (43) 150 567 39
Email: office@fwf.ac.at
www: http://www.fwf.ac.at
Contact: Scientific Administrator

The mandate of the Austrian Science Fund (FWF) is to advance basic research in Austria. The research and funding responsibilities are as follows: the funding of research projects from all scientific areas, the funding of young scientists and scholars, and stimulations of European research co-operations.

Charlotte Bühler Habilitation Fellowships

Subjects: All subjects.
Purpose: To support and encourage young female scientists to become future university lecturers.
Eligibility: Open to female scientists up to the age of 40, who are residents of Austria.
Level of Study: Postdoctorate.
Type: A variable number of fellowships.
Value: Please contact the organisation.
Length of Study: One-two years.
Frequency: The FWF Board makes decisions on funding six times per year.
No. of awards offered: Varies.
Application Procedure: Applicants must complete an application form, available from the Austrian Science Fund, from the website or by email.
Closing Date: Applications are accepted at any time.
Funding: Government.

Erwin Schrödinger Fellowships

Subjects: All subjects.
Purpose: To offer citizens the opportunity to work in leading foreign research institutions and research programmes.
Eligibility: Open to highly qualified Austrian citizens up to the age of 35.
Level of Study: Postdoctorate.
Type: A variable number of fellowships.
Value: Please contact the organisation.
Length of Study: At least 10 months, to a maximum two years.
Frequency: The FWF Board makes decisions on funding six times per year.
Study Establishment: Universities or research institutions worldwide.
Country of Study: Any country except Austria.
No. of awards offered: Varies.
Application Procedure: Applicants must complete an application form, available from the Austrian Science Fund, from the website or by email.
Closing Date: Applications are accepted at any time.
Funding: Government.

Hertha Firnberg Research Positions for Women

Subjects: All subjects.
Purpose: To support and encourage young female scientists and expand scientific career opportunities for women.
Eligibility: Open to female scientists up to the age of 40 who are residents of Austria.
Level of Study: Postdoctorate.
Type: Research positions.
Value: Please contact the organisation.
Length of Study: Three years.
Frequency: Annual.
Study Establishment: Austrian universities.
Country of Study: Austria.
No. of awards offered: 10.

Application Procedure: Applicants must complete an application form, available from the Austrian Science Fund, from the website or by email.
Closing Date: December of every year.
Funding: Government.

Lise Meitner Fellowships

Subjects: All subjects.
Purpose: To offer foreign scientists the opportunity to carry out research in Austria and to enhance the Austrian scientific community through international contacts.
Eligibility: Open to highly qualified foreign scientists up to the age of 40.
Level of Study: Postdoctorate.
Type: Fellowship.
Value: Please contact the organisation.
Length of Study: One-two years.
Frequency: The FWF Board makes decisions on funding six times per year.
Study Establishment: Austrian universities or research institutions.
Country of Study: Austria.
No. of awards offered: Varies.
Application Procedure: Applicants must complete an application form, available from the Austrian Science Fund, from the website or by email.
Closing Date: Applications are accepted at any time.
Funding: Government.

AUSTRO-AMERICAN ASSOCIATION OF BOSTON

47 Windermere Road, Auburndale, MA, 02466-2521, United States of America
Tel: (1) 617 332 4055
Email: ghauser@hms.harvard.edu
Contact: Professor George Hauser, Chairman of Scholarship Committee

Membership of the Austro-American Association of Boston is open to any individual interested in any aspect of Austrian history, economy, culture, politics and tourism.

Austro-American Association of Boston Scholarship

Subjects: Austrian cultural studies. The project must be related to Austrian culture in the broadest sense eg. humanities, literature, music, fine and applied arts, and film.
Purpose: To promote the appreciation and dissemination of Austrian culture.
Eligibility: Students as well as faculty and staff are eligible.
Level of Study: Unrestricted.
Type: Scholarship.
Value: US$500.
Frequency: Dependent on funds available.
Country of Study: Austria or United States of America.
No. of awards offered: Two.
Application Procedure: Applicants must submit a detailed description of the project including budget, a curriculum vitae and two letters of recommendation from people familiar with the applicant's achievement and potential.
Closing Date: April 15th.
Funding: Private.
No. of awards given last year: None.
No. of applicants last year: None.
Additional Information: The award is limited to individuals living or studying in New England. Projects funded in the past have included the preparation of musical or dramatic performances, the facilitation of appropriate publications and research trips to Austria. Culture is defined to include the humanities and the arts. The recipient is expected to present the results of the project at an event of the Austro-American Association.

AVENTIS BEHRING CANADA

55 Metcalfe
Suite 1200, Ottawa, ON, K1P 6L5, Canada

Tel: (1) 613 232 3111 ext. 10

Fax: (1) 613 232 5031

Email: line.kealey@aventis.com

Contact: Research and Education Fund

Aventis Behring Canada is a world leader in plasma proteins and biotechnologies.

The Aventis Behring Canada Research and Education Fund

Subjects: Haematology.

Purpose: Aventis Behring Canada, a world leader in plasma proteins and biotechnologies, has established the Aventis Behring Canada Research and Education Fund, in collaboration with Canadian Blood Services and Hema-Quebec, to support education and research about haemophilia, von Willebrand disease and certain conditions affected by plasma protein-based therapies such as immunoglobulins, albumins, fibrinsealants, AP1, AT3 and the organisation of related services.

Eligibility: All applicants must be affiliated with a Canadian university or non-profit making health related organisation including community groups and research laboratories engaged in health research. Profit organisations with relevant proposals may contact Aventis Behring directly to discuss other sources of funding. All of the work is to be done in Canada, unless there is a specific reason to work outside Canada, such as a cross cultural study. Any exceptions should be justified. Aventis Behring Canada, in collaboration with Canadian Blood Services and Hema-Quebec, will make the final eligibility decision in these cases. Junior investigators or trainees are welcome to apply. It is the responsibility of the applicants to determine the rules of their institution about how the funds of trainees are accounted for and assigned. Requests for renewal or budget extension of a previous grant will be processed as a new application and on a par with other new applications. If a question of eligibility exists, specific justification may be required.

Value: Grants of up to canadian $30,000 will be awarded.

Country of Study: Canada.

Application Procedure: Applicants must submit a complete application form, available either in English or French by contacting Aventis Behring Canada's office.

Closing Date: January 4th.

Additional Information: Any inventions or patents that result from work in the scope of this grant shall remain the property of the investigator, subject to the rules of his or her institution. However, Aventis Behring retains the right of first refusal in respect of any such inventions or patents and the parties shall, in good faith, negotiate a licence thereto under terms and conditions that are mutually agreeable to the parties. The investigators are at liberty to publish the results of the research in a free, fair and representative manner. Publication is subject to the following provisions: that the support of Aventis Behring for the work in consideration shall be disclosed and acknowledged in each publication and/or presentation, and that 30 days prior to the submission of any manuscript, abstract, press release, or other publication in any form of work that may potentially result in a patent or otherwise commercially valuable interest, the submission will be delivered to Aventis Behring for review, for the express purpose of adequately protecting any commercial interests Aventis Behring may hold.

BACKCARE

16 Elmtree Road, Teddington, Middlesex, TW11 8ST, England
Tel: (44) 20 8977 5474
Fax: (44) 20 8943 5318
Email: info@backcare.org.uk
www: http://www.backcare.org.uk
Contact: Ms Sue Shillabeer, Communications Manager

BackCare is a national charity dedicated to educating people about how to avoid preventable back pain and to supporting those living with back pain. BackCare provides education and information through its publications, telephone helpline, local branches and self management courses. It also funds research and campaigns to raise the profile of issues surrounding back pain.

BackCare Research Grants

Subjects: Studies related to back pain such as the cause and diagnosis of back pain, identification of those most susceptible to back pain, identification of the main environmental and occupational hazards, trials of different methods of treatment to alleviate back pain, methods of preventing back pain, reduction in back pain disability by influencing health education, lifestyles, patient behaviour and clinical practice, social and psychological factors relevant to back pain, back pain and primary care.

Purpose: To encourage and support scientific research into the causes, treatment and prevention of back pain. The objective is to reduce the incidences of, and disability from, back pain and improve its treatment by gaining, through research, a better understanding of its manifestation and causes.

Eligibility: Open to appropriately qualified and experienced persons.

Level of Study: Postgraduate.

Type: Research grant.

Value: Varies, dependent on funds available. The association is not a major funding organisation.

Length of Study: Up to two years.

Study Establishment: Suitable establishments.

Country of Study: United Kingdom.

Application Procedure: Applicants must refer to the website for details of the application procedure.

Closing Date: June 1st or November 1st.

Additional Information: The organisation is unable to fund educational courses, attendance at meetings or conferences, or the purchase of computers.

THE BANFF CENTRE

Arts Programming
Box 1020
Station 28, Banff, AB, T1L 1H5, Canada
Tel: (1) 403 762 6180
Fax: (1) 403 762 6345
Email: arts_info@banffcentre.ca
www: http://www.banffcentre.ca
Contact: Ms Zarah Hofer, Information Offcier

The Banff Centre is Canada's only learning centre dedicated to the arts, leadership development and mountain culture. It serves the needs of accomplished artists, business and community leaders and members of the global mountain community through year round programmes designed to enrich professional practice beyond the realm of traditional education.

The Banff Centre Financial Assistance

Subjects: Studio art, photography, ceramics, performance art, video art, theatre production and design, stage management, opera, singing, dance, drama, music, writing, creative non fiction and cultural journalism, publishing, media arts, television and video, audio recording, computer applications, research, audio engineering work study, theatre production, design stage management work study,

Aboriginal arts programmes in dance training, programme publicity and theatre production work study and screenwriting.

Purpose: To provide financial assistance to deserving artists for a residency at The Banff Centre.

Eligibility: Open to advanced students who have been accepted for a residency at the Banff Centre.

Level of Study: Postgraduate.

Type: Financial assistance.

Value: A major contribution towards tuition.

Length of Study: Varies.

Frequency: Annual.

Study Establishment: The Banff Centre, Arts Programming.

Country of Study: Canada.

No. of awards offered: Varies.

Application Procedure: Applicants must submit a completed application form, accompanied by requested documentation.

Closing Date: Varies according to programme.

Funding: Government, Private.

Contributor: Individual donations and Banff Centre revenues.

No. of awards given last year: 1,000.

THE BANK OF SWEDEN TERCENTENARY FOUNDATION

Box 5675, Stockholm, S-11486, Sweden
Tel: (46) 85 062 6400
Fax: (46) 85 062 6430
Email: rj@rj.se
www: http://www.rj.se
Contact: Administrative Officer

Bank of Sweden Tercentenary Foundation Grants

Subjects: Scientific research.

Purpose: To support and promote research which has connections with Sweden.

Eligibility: Open to scientists of any nationality. Applicants from outside Sweden should describe a defined programme of co-operation with Swedish Scholars or research institutes.

Level of Study: Postdoctorate.

Type: Grant.

Length of Study: Two years with an option of renewal for a further two years.

Frequency: Annual.

Study Establishment: Universities or research institutions.

Country of Study: Any country.

No. of awards offered: Up to 100.

Application Procedure: Applicants must complete an application form, available from the Foundation. Applications should include a completed application form, a curriculum vitae, a detailed description of the scientific publications and competence of the applicant, a brief outline of the proposed project (no more than three pages), time required, expected results and methods the applicant will use in order to achieve them. A detailed budget is also required. Please visit the website for further details.

Closing Date: March. Please consult the awarding body for further information.

Additional Information: Priority is given to research which has fewer opportunities to receive grants. Large, long range projects and new fields of investigation requiring rapid, major supportive measures receive special attention.

BATTEN DISEASE SUPPORT & RESEARCH ASSOCIATION

120 Humphries Drive
Suite 2, Reynoldsburg, OH, 43068, United States of America
Tel: (1) 740 927 4298
Email: bdsra1@bdsra.org
www: http://www.bdsra.org
Contact: Mr Lance W Johnston, Executive Director

The Batten Disease Support & Research Association provides information, education, medical referrals and support to families that have children with NCL or Batten Disease. The Association also provides funding for research into Batten Disease.

Batten Disease Support and Research Association Research Grant Awards

Subjects: Awards are made in the field of NCL or Batten Disease in the areas of genetics, biochemistry, molecular biology and related areas with the eventual goal of developing a viable treatment.

Purpose: To support work that identifies genes, proteins, enzymes or additional NCLs and the development novel therapeutic treatments.

Eligibility: There are no eligibility restrictions.

Level of Study: Doctorate, Postdoctorate, Research.

Type: Research grant.

Value: Up to US$40,000.

Length of Study: Research is for one year and doctorate and postdoctorate are up to three years.

Frequency: Annual.

Country of Study: Any country.

Application Procedure: Applicants must complete an application form which is available online.

Closing Date: June 15th.

Funding: Private.

No. of awards given last year: 15.

No. of applicants last year: 27.

BEIT MEMORIAL FELLOWSHIPS

c/o Institute of Molecular Medicine
John Radcliffe Hospital
Headington, Oxford, Oxfordshire, OX3 9DS, England
Contact: Mrs Melanie J Goble, Administrative Secretary

Beit Memorial Fellowships for Medical Research

Subjects: Medical research.

Purpose: To promote research into medicine and allied sciences.

Eligibility: Open to graduates of postdoctoral level or medically qualified applicants from any faculty at an approved university in the United Kingdom, or in any country which is or has been since 1910 a British Dominion, Protectorate or Mandated Territory.

Level of Study: Postdoctorate.

Type: Fellowship.

Value: UK £21,290-27,273 per year plus UK £2,134 London allowance if applicable.

Length of Study: Three years.

Frequency: Every two years.

Study Establishment: An approved university, research institute or medical school.

Country of Study: United Kingdom or Ireland.

No. of awards offered: Approx. six.

Application Procedure: Applicants must write for details.

Closing Date: March 1st.

BEIT TRUST (ZIMBABWE, ZAMBIA AND MALAWI)

Beit Trust Fellowships
PO Box 76, Chisipite, Harare, Zimbabwe
Tel: (263) 4 496132
Fax: (263) 4 491046
Email: beitrust@africaonline.co.zw
Contact: B R Fieldsend, Representative

Beit Trust Postgraduate Fellowships

Subjects: All subjects.
Purpose: To support postgraduate study or research.
Eligibility: Open to persons under 30 years of age (35 in the case of medical doctors) who are university graduates domiciled in Zambia (four fellowships), Zimbabwe (four fellowships) or Malawi (two fellowships). Open to Zimbabwe, Zambia and Malawi nationals only.
Level of Study: Postgraduate.
Type: Fellowship.
Value: A variable personal allowance and fees plus book, clothing, thesis and departure allowances.
Length of Study: Two years with a possibility of renewal for a further year.
Frequency: Annual.
Study Establishment: Approved universities and other institutions.
Country of Study: United Kingdom, Ireland or South Africa.
No. of awards offered: 10.
Application Procedure: Applicants must complete an application form.
Closing Date: September 30th.
Funding: Private.
No. of awards given last year: 10.
No. of applicants last year: 400.

THE BERMUDA BIOLOGICAL STATION FOR RESEARCH, INC.

Ferry Reach, St Georges, GE 01, Bermuda
Tel: (1 441) 297 1880
Fax: (1 441) 297 8143
Email: education@bbsr.edu
www: http://www.bbsr.edu
Contact: Ms Gillian Hollis, Assistant to Director

Bermuda Biological Station for Research Grant In Aid

Subjects: Oceanography, biological and life sciences.
Purpose: To provide financial assistance to help defray the costs of in house charges for visiting scientists.
Level of Study: Doctorate, Postdoctorate, Postgraduate, Research.
Type: Grant.
Value: Varies, Bermuda $500-3,000.
Length of Study: As required.
Frequency: Annual.
Study Establishment: The Bermuda Biological Station for Research, Inc.
Country of Study: Bermuda.
No. of awards offered: Varies.
Application Procedure: Applicants must submit grant proposals with their curriculum vitae and a budget. Proposals should be concise and contain an abstract, background, objectives, methods and the significance of proposed research.
Closing Date: March 1st or October 1st for Summer or Winter projects respectively.
No. of awards given last year: 10.
No. of applicants last year: 10.

BERTHOLD LEIBINGER STIFTUNG GMBH

Johann-Maus-Straße 2, Ditzingen, D-71254, Germany
Tel: (49) 715 630 31559
Fax: (49) 715 630 3208
Email: innovationspreis@leibinger-stiftung.de
www: http://www.leibinger-stiftung.de
Contact: Mr Sven Ederer, Project Manager

Berthold Leibinger Innovationspreis

Subjects: Outstanding research work in applied laser physics in production technology and laser medicine.
Purpose: To promote the advancement of science.
Eligibility: Open to individuals and project groups who have completed a scientific paper on applied laser physics in production technology and laser medicine and have documented it with public access.
Level of Study: Unrestricted.
Type: Prize.
Value: €20,000, €10,000 and €5,000.
Frequency: Every two years.
No. of awards offered: Three.
Application Procedure: Applicants must submit a completed application form, short documentation of up to 10 pages in accordance with stipulated structure, biography and explanation describing the context of work signed by a person recognised by the scientific establishment.
Closing Date: March 31st.
Funding: Private.
Contributor: Berthold Leibinger.
No. of awards given last year: Three.
No. of applicants last year: Approx. 42.

For further information contact:

Berthold Leibinger Stiftung GmbH
Innovationspreis
Postfach, Ditzingen, D-71252, Germany

BETA PHI MU

School of Information Studies
Florida State University, Tallahassee, FL, 32306-2100, United States of America
Tel: (1) 850 644 3907
Fax: (1) 850 644 6253
Email: beta_phi_mu@lis.fsu.edu
www: http://nosferatu.cas.usf.edu/lis/bpm
Contact: Mr F William Summers, Executive Secretary

Beta Phi Mu is a library and information studies society, founded in 1948, with over 25,000 graduates of the American Library Association-accredited professional programmes initiated. Beta Phi Mu was founded at the University of Illinois in August, 1948, by a group of leading librarians and library educators. Aware of the notable achievements of honour societies in other professions, they believed that such a society would have much to offer librarianship and library education. The first initiation was held in the spring of 1949 at the University of Illinois.

Blanche E Woolls Scholarship for School Library Media Service

Subjects: Library science.
Purpose: To assist a new student who plans to become a school media specialist.
Eligibility: Open to beginning applicants who have not completed more than 12 hours by Autumn. Applicants must be accepted into an ALA-accredited programme and have three references.
Level of Study: Postgraduate.

Type: Scholarship.
Value: US$1,000.
Frequency: Annual.
Study Establishment: An ALA accredited school.
Country of Study: United States of America.
Application Procedure: Applicants must send three references and a completed application form, available by sending a stamped addressed envelope to Beta Phi Mu headquarters. Further details are available from the website.
Closing Date: March 15th.
No. of awards given last year: One.

Frank B Sessa Award

Subjects: Library science or information studies.
Purpose: To enable the continuing professional education of a Beta Phi Mu member.
Eligibility: Open to Beta Phi Mu members only.
Level of Study: Professional development.
Type: Scholarship.
Value: US$750.
Frequency: Annual.
Country of Study: Any country.
Application Procedure: Applicants must request an application form from Beta Phi Mu. Further details are available from the website.
Closing Date: March 15th.
Funding: Private.
No. of awards given last year: One.

Harold Lancour Scholarship For International Study

Subjects: Library science.
Purpose: To assist a librarian or library school student to undertake short-term research in a foreign country.
Eligibility: Open to nationals of any country.
Level of Study: Unrestricted.
Type: Scholarship.
Value: US$1,000.
Frequency: Annual.
Country of Study: Any country.
No. of awards offered: One.
Application Procedure: Applicants must write to Beta Phi Mu for further details, enclosing a stamped addressed envelope. Further details are available from the website.
Closing Date: March 15th.
Funding: Private.
No. of awards given last year: One.
No. of applicants last year: 10.

Sarah Rebecca Reed Award

Subjects: Library and information science.
Purpose: To assist a beginning student studying library and information science at an ALA-accredited school.
Eligibility: Open to beginning students who have not completed more than 12 hours by Autumn. Applicants must also be accepted on an ALA-accredited programme and have five references. Nationals of any country can apply.
Level of Study: Postgraduate.
Type: Scholarship.
Value: US$1,500.
Frequency: Annual.
Study Establishment: An ALA accredited school.
Country of Study: United States of America.
No. of awards offered: One.
Application Procedure: Applicants must request an application from the address shown, enclosing a stamped addressed envelope. Further details are also available from the website.
Closing Date: March 15th.
Funding: Private.
No. of awards given last year: One.
No. of applicants last year: 30.

BFWG CHARITABLE FOUNDATION (FORMERLY CROSBY HALL)

28 Great James Street, London, WC1N 3ES, England
Tel: (44) 20 7404 6447
Fax: (44) 20 7404 6505
Email: bfwg.charity@btinternet.com
www: http://www.bcfgrants.org.uk
Contact: Ms Jean V Collett, Grants Administrator

The BFWG Charitable Foundation offers grants to help women graduates with their living expenses (not fees) while registered for study or research at an approved Institute of Higher Education in Great Britain. The criteria for awarding grants are the proven needs of the applicants and their academic calibre.

BFWG Charitable Foundation Grants and Emergency Grants

Subjects: All subjects.
Purpose: To assist female graduates who have difficulty meeting their living expenses while studying or researching at approved Institutes of Higher Education in Great Britain. Emergency Grants are to assist graduate women facing financial crises which may prevent them completing an academic year's study.
Eligibility: Open to female graduates who have completed their first year of graduate or doctoral study or research. There is no restriction on nationality.
Level of Study: Doctorate, Postdoctorate, Postgraduate.
Type: Grant.
Value: Foundation Grants are up to UK £2,500 and Emergency Grants are up to UK £500.
Length of Study: Support for courses that exceed one year full-time in length.
Frequency: Foundation Grants are offered annually. Emergency Grants are offered three times per year.
Study Establishment: Approved institutions in the United Kingdom.
Country of Study: United Kingdom.
No. of awards offered: Approx. 50-60 foundation grants and approx. 50-60 emergency grants.
Application Procedure: Applicants must complete an application form and submit this with two references, a copy of their graduate certificate, evidence of acceptance for the year, a cheque for UK £12 or for UK £5 in the case of Emergency Grants, and a brief summary of thesis, if applicable, for Foundation Grants. Requests for application forms must be received by March 20th or downloaded from the website.
Closing Date: The deadline for Foundation Grants is April 22nd, and the deadlines for Emergency Grants are February 15th, May 15th and November 15th.
Funding: Private.
Contributor: Investment income.
No. of awards given last year: 99 Foundation Grants, 71 Emergency Grants.
No. of applicants last year: 122 for Foundation and 318 for Emergency Grants.

Theodora Bosanquet Bursary

Subjects: English literature or history.
Purpose: To support female postgraduate students who are carrying out research in English literature or history requiring the use of libraries, and archives in London.
Eligibility: Open to women only.
Level of Study: Doctorate, Postdoctorate, Postgraduate.
Type: Bursary.
Value: The Bursary provides accommodation only in a hall of residence for up to four weeks between July 1st and September 30th.
Length of Study: Up to four weeks.
Frequency: Annual.
Country of Study: United Kingdom.
No. of awards offered: One-two.

151

Application Procedure: Applicants must write to the Grants Administrator enclosing a stamped addressed envelope or international reply coupons. Envelopes should be marked 'TBB'.
Closing Date: October 31st.
Funding: Private.
Contributor: Investment income.

BIAL FOUNDATION

Avenida da Siderurgia Nacional
4745 - 457, Mamede do Coronado, Portugal
Tel: (351) 22 986 6100
Fax: (351) 22 986 6190
Email: fundacao@bial.pt
Contact: Mr Luis Portela, Chairman

The BIAL Foundation, a non-profit making institution, was set up in 1994 with the aim of encouraging and supporting research focused on humans. It manages the BIAL award, one of the most distinguished awards for Health in Europe, and the BIAL Fellowship Programme which focuses largely on psychophysiology and parapsychology.

BIAL Award in Clinical Medicine
Subjects: Medical sciences or health.
Purpose: To award intellectual written work in the subject area of health. To award work of a high quality in clinical practice.
Eligibility: At least one of the authors must be a native physician of a Portuguese speaking country.
Level of Study: Graduate.
Type: Prize.
Value: €50,000. Up to six distinctions are available of €5,000 each.
Frequency: Every two years.
No. of awards offered: Eight.
Application Procedure: Applicants must submit six copies of an original written specimen in either Portuguese or English to the Foundation. Further requirements are listed on its Regulation which will be forwarded to prospective applicants on request.
Closing Date: October 31st.
Funding: Private.
Contributor: The BIAL Foundation.
No. of awards given last year: Eight.
No. of applicants last year: 38.

BIAL Fellowship Programme
Subjects: Psychophysiology and parapsychology.
Purpose: To support research.
Level of Study: Research.
Type: Fellowship.
Value: Varies, between €5,000-50,000.
Length of Study: Between one and three years.
Frequency: Every two years.
No. of awards offered: Varies, depending on the quality of the applications and on the total amount of money available.
Application Procedure: Applicants must complete an application form.
Closing Date: August 31st.
Funding: Private.
Contributor: The BIAL Foundation.
No. of awards given last year: 41.
No. of applicants last year: 87.

BIAL Merit Award in Medical Sciences
Subjects: Medical sciences and health.
Purpose: To award intellectual written work in the subject area of health. To distinguish intellectual writing on a free medical topic.
Eligibility: Works must present research of great scientific significance and be of the highest quality. Anyone can apply to the award but at least one of the authors must be a physician.
Level of Study: Graduate.

Type: Prize.
Value: €50,000. Up to six distinctions are available of €5,000 each.
Frequency: Every two years.
No. of awards offered: Eight.
Application Procedure: Applicants must submit six copies of an original written specimen in either Portuguese or English to the Foundation. Further requirements are listed on its Regulation which will be forwarded to prospective applicants on request.
Closing Date: October 31st.
Funding: Private.
Contributor: The BIAL Foundation.
No. of awards given last year: Eight.
No. of applicants last year: 38.

BIBLIOGRAPHICAL SOCIETY OF AMERICA (BSA)

PO Box 1537
Lenox Hill Station, New York, NY, 10021, United States of America

Tel: (1) 212 452 2710

Fax: (1) 212 452 2710

Email: bsa@bibsocamer.org

www: http://www.bibsocamer.org

Contact: Ms Michele Randall, Executive Secretary

The Bibliographical Society of America (BSA) invites applications for its annual short-term fellowships, which supports bibliographical inquiry as well as research in the history of the book trades and in publishing history.

BSA Fellowship Program
Subjects: Eligible topics may concentrate on books and documents in any field, but should focus on the book or manuscript (the physical object) as historical evidence. Such topics may include establishing a text or studying the history of book production, publication, distribution, collecting or reading. Enumerative listings do not fall within the scope of this programme.
Purpose: To support bibliographical inquiry and research in the history of the book trades and publishing.
Eligibility: This programme is open to applicants of any nationality.
Level of Study: Doctorate, Postdoctorate, Postgraduate.
Type: Fellowship.
Value: US$2,000.
Length of Study: One month.
Frequency: Annual.
Country of Study: Any country.
No. of awards offered: 10.
Application Procedure: Applicants must complete an application form. The original plus six photocopies must be posted to the Executive Secretary of the Fellowship Committee at the Bibliographical Society of America.
Closing Date: December 1st.
Funding: Private.
No. of awards given last year: 10.
Additional Information: For applications contact the Executive Secretary or visit the BSA's website.

BICENTENNIAL SWEDISH-AMERICAN EXCHANGE FUND

Consulate General of Sweden in New York
1 Dag Hammarskjöld Plaza
45th Floor, New York, NY, 10017-2201, United States of America
Tel: (1) 212 583 2585
Fax: (1) 212 752 4789
Email: requests@swedeninfo.com
www: http://www.swedeninfo.com
Contact: Grants Management Officer

The Consulate General of Sweden in New York is a central resource for all persons and organisations seeking information about Sweden on subjects other than tourism and trade or business.

Bicentennial Swedish-American Exchange Fund Travel Grants

Subjects: Politics, public administration, working life, human environment, mass media, business and industry, education, research and culture.
Purpose: To provide opportunities for persons who are in a position to influence public opinion and contribute to the development of their society, to study in areas of current concern and to meet their professional counterparts.
Eligibility: Open to nationals and permanent residents of the United States of America. Applicants should have the necessary experience and education to fulfil the project. Applicants who have visited Sweden frequently will be considered only in exceptional cases.
Level of Study: Doctorate, Postdoctorate, Professional development.
Type: Travel grant.
Value: Approx. krona 25,000.
Length of Study: A research trip of two-four weeks during the year following the award.
Frequency: Annual.
Country of Study: Sweden.
No. of awards offered: Six.
Application Procedure: Applicants must submit a carefully defined research project with a detailed plan for achieving specific goals. Current year application forms must be completed and submitted with two letters of recommendation. Applicants should include a stamped addressed envelope.
Closing Date: The first Friday in February.
Funding: Government.
Additional Information: Applications are sent to Sweden where a committee of experts reviews them. Applicants are notified during May and research trips usually take place after August 20th. Acceptance of a grant carries with it the obligation to write a report within six months of return from Sweden.

BILKENT UNIVERSITY

Faculty of Business Administration
MBA Programme
Office of the Dean, Ankara, 06533, Turkey
Tel: (90) 312 266 4164
Fax: (90) 312 266 4958
Email: fba@bilkent.edu.tr
www: http://www.bilkent.edu.tr
Contact: MBA Admissions Officer

Bilkent University MBA Scholarships

Subjects: MBA.
Purpose: Bilkent University grants generous financial assistance on the basis of academic merit.
Eligibility: Open to students who have a cumulative grade point average of 3.00 over 4.00 or higher in their studies.
Level of Study: MBA.

Type: Scholarship.
Value: Varies from tuition waiver to providing a stipend.
Frequency: Annual.
Study Establishment: Bilkent University.
Country of Study: Turkey.
No. of awards offered: Varies.
Application Procedure: Applicants must apply for the MBA in the usual way and upon admission to the programme, scholarships of various degrees may be awarded.
Closing Date: Please contact the organisation.
Additional Information: For second-year students, a tuition waiver is possible based on their academic achievement during the first year.

BINATIONAL AGRICULTURAL RESEARCH AND DEVELOPMENT FUND (BARD)

PO Box 6, Bet Dagan, 50250, Israel
Tel: (972) 3 968 3230
Fax: (972) 3 966 2506
Email: bard@bard-isus.com
www: http://www.bard@bard-isus.com
Contact: Dr Edo Chalutz, Executive Director

The Binational Agricultural Research and Development Fund (BARD) promotes and supports agricultural research and development for the mutual benefits of both countries. BARD's income derives from an endowment fund contributed to in equal parts by the United States and Israel.

BARD Postdoctoral Fellowship

Subjects: Agriculture.
Purpose: To enable young scientists to acquire new skills and techniques while becoming professionally established in the agriculture community.
Eligibility: Open to United States or Israeli citizens who have completed a PhD in their home country within the last three years.
Level of Study: Postdoctorate.
Type: Fellowship.
Value: US$37,000.
Length of Study: One year, with the possibility of renewal for up to a further year.
Frequency: Annual.
Study Establishment: A non-profit research organisation, university or government.
Country of Study: United States citizens study in Israel. Israeli citizens study in the United States of America.
No. of awards offered: 8-10.
Application Procedure: Applicants must complete an application form and submit this with a written proposal. Guidelines and application forms are available from either the office or most eligible institutions.
Closing Date: January 15th.
Funding: Government.
No. of awards given last year: Eight.
No. of applicants last year: 24.

BARD Research Grant

Subjects: Agriculture.
Purpose: To support agricultural research projects of mutual interest to the United States of America and Israel. Projects cover any or all phases of research and development, including integrated research and development problems and basic and applied research.
Eligibility: Open to public or non-profit research institutions that demonstrate the necessary research and development capabilities, and whose proposals meet the objectives and criteria set down.
Level of Study: Research.
Type: Research grant.

Value: US$300,000 paid over three years.
Length of Study: Approx. three years.
Frequency: Annual.
Study Establishment: Non-profit research organisations, universities or governments.
Country of Study: Israel or United States of America.
No. of awards offered: Approx. 35.
Application Procedure: Applicants must complete an application form and submit this with a written proposal. Guidelines and application forms are available from either the office or most eligible institutions.
Closing Date: September 1st.
Funding: Government.
Contributor: The government of Israel and the government of United States of America.
No. of awards given last year: 36.
No. of applicants last year: 154.

For further information contact:

Liaison Office
USDA-ARS
5601 Sunnyside Avenue, Beltsville, MD, 20705-5134, United States of America
Tel: (1) 301 504 4584
Fax: (1) 301 504 4619

THE BIOCHEMICAL SOCIETY

59 Portland Place, London, W1N 3AJ, England
Tel: (44) 20 7580 5530
Fax: (44) 20 7637 3626
Email: alisonm@biochemsoc.org.uk
www: http://www.biochemsoc.org.uk
Contact: Assistant Director, Personnel & Administration

Serving biochemistry and biochemists since 1911, the aim of the Biochemical Society is to promote the advancement of the Science of Biochemistry. It does so in the context of cellular and molecular life sciences. Through its regular scientific meetings with special interest groups, its publishing company Portland Press Limited and its policy, professional and education contacts the Society provides a forum for current research to be shared.

Biochemical Society General Travel Fund

Subjects: Biochemistry and molecular life sciences.
Purpose: To support scientists who wish to attend scientific meetings, or make short visits to other laboratories.
Eligibility: Successful applicants must have been members of the Biochemical Society for at least one year and satisfy other requirements.
Type: Travel grant.
Value: Varies.
Frequency: Awards are made in January, March, May, July, September and November.
Country of Study: British and Irish members may apply for a grant to travel anywhere in the world, while members from elsewhere may apply for a grant to travel to the United Kingdom or Ireland.
No. of awards offered: Varies.
Application Procedure: Applicants must submit four copies of a completed form which must demonstrate that the most cost effective form of transport and accommodation are to be utilised. All parts of the form must be completed. The application needs to be supported by a copy of registration costs and an abstract of presentation. Application forms can be obtained from the Assistant Director, Personnel and Administration or via the website http://www.biochemistry.org.
Closing Date: January 1st, March 1st, May 1st, July 1st or September 1st.
Funding: Private.

Krebs Memorial Scholarship

Subjects: Biochemistry and related areas.
Purpose: To encourage students whose careers were interrupted by very special circumstances and who are unlikely to qualify for support from public agencies to work towards a PhD only.
Eligibility: Open to graduates in the top 5 per cent of PhD candidates.
Level of Study: Doctorate, Postdoctorate.
Type: Scholarship.
Value: Varies but covers all necessary fees.
Length of Study: One year, renewable possibly for a further three years. Where the scholarship has been renewed for the current holder, it will not be available to new applicants until that tenure has come to an end.
Frequency: Normally biannually, but dependent upon tenure of current scholarship.
Study Establishment: Any university in the United Kingdom.
Country of Study: United Kingdom.
No. of awards offered: One.
Application Procedure: Applicants must forward the application through the Head of Department concerned to the Assistant Director, Personnel and Administration or from the website http://www.biochemistry.org.
Closing Date: Varies, please visit the website for details.
Funding: Private.
No. of awards given last year: One.

BIOTECHNOLOGY AND BIOLOGICAL SCIENCES RESEARCH COUNCIL (BBSRC)

Polaris House
North Star Avenue, Swindon, Wiltshire, SN2 1UH, England
Tel: (44) 1793 413345
Fax: (44) 1793 413382
Email: research-grant.applications@bbsrc.ac.uk
www: http://www.bbsrc.ac.uk
Contact: Ms Margaret Henstock, Secretariat & Liaison Branch

The mission of the Biotechnology and Biological Sciences Research Council (BBSRC) is to promote and support basic, strategic applied research relating to the understanding and exploration of biological systems.

BBSRC Research Fellowships

Subjects: The Council's remit encompasses the agriculture, food, pharmaceuticals, chemical and health care industries, biotechnology, biological sciences and related areas in the physical sciences and engineering.
Purpose: To support outstanding research workers and to enable them to devote a significant period of time to full-time research.
Eligibility: Open to postdoctoral scientists.
Level of Study: Postdoctorate.
Type: Fellowship.
Frequency: Annual.
Study Establishment: Fellowships can only be held at any appropriate Institute of Higher Education or BBSRC sponsored institute in the United Kingdom which is prepared to employ the Fellow.
Country of Study: United Kingdom.
No. of awards offered: Varies.
Application Procedure: Applicants must complete an application form, available from the BBSRC website.
Closing Date: Applications are accepted once a year. Please visit the website for the deadline.
Funding: Government.
Additional Information: Full details of BBSRC's fellowship schemes and application procedures are available on the website.

BBSRC Research Grants

Subjects: Multidisciplinary with emphasis on biological sciences, biotechnology and engineering.

Purpose: To support research in United Kingdom universities, colleges and other higher education institutions. BBSRC seeks to develop and sustain high quality research within its range of interest and to encourage links between university researchers and researchers at BBSRC sponsored institutes.

Eligibility: Applicants must be resident in the United Kingdom. They must hold an appropriate appointment in a United Kingdom university, college or other similar higher education institution.

Level of Study: Postdoctorate.

Type: Research grant.

Value: Varies.

Frequency: Ongoing.

Study Establishment: A United Kingdom educational establishment, a BBSRC sponsored Institute or a BBSRC academic analogue.

Country of Study: United Kingdom.

No. of awards offered: Varies.

Application Procedure: Applicants must complete an application form. Rules, procedures and application forms are available on the BBSRC website and from the BBSRC Secretariat and Liaison Branch.

Closing Date: Applications are accepted at any time.

Funding: Government.

Additional Information: Full details are available on the website.

BBSRC Studentships

Subjects: Information on the BBSRC remit is available from the website.

Purpose: To enable graduates to study for a higher degree primarily for an MSc, MRes or PhD. There are four studentships currently available and these are BBSRC Three-Year Standard Research Studentships, Co-operative Studentships with Industry, One Year Advanced Course Studentships and Research Master's Studentships.

Eligibility: Open to candidates who have been resident in the United Kingdom for the three years immediately preceding the date of application and have graduated with a First Class (Honours) Degree or Upper Second Class (Honours) Degree. Please see the website for further eligibility details.

Level of Study: Doctorate, Postgraduate.

Type: Studentship.

Value: A maintenance grant plus a London allowance, if appropriate, dependants' and other allowances if applicable. Approved tuition fees are payable directly to the institution.

Length of Study: One or three years.

Frequency: Annual.

Study Establishment: Universities and colleges in Great Britain and BBRSC sponsored research institutes.

Country of Study: United Kingdom.

No. of awards offered: Approx. 780.

Application Procedure: Applicants must apply in the first instance to the institution where they wish to carry out their studies. The Council does not accept applications directly from students.

Closing Date: Please contact the foundation or visit the website.

Funding: Government.

No. of awards given last year: 740.

Underwood Fund

Subjects: Biotechnology and biological sciences.

Purpose: To facilitate the exchange of scientific knowledge at international level. The fund is used for the provision of grants to enable visits to be made to the United Kingdom by senior overseas scientists whose presence in the United Kingdom is likely to be of assistance to BBSRC supported research in universities or BBSRC sponsored institutes.

Eligibility: Open to senior overseas scientists. Applicants must be the holder of a BBSRC research grant at the host institution or in the case of BBSRC supported research institutes, the Institute Director.

Level of Study: Postdoctorate, Research.

Type: Grant.

Value: To cover subsistence and travel expenses as approved by the BBSRC.

Length of Study: Up to one year.

Frequency: Dependent on funds available.

Study Establishment: Universities and BBSRC sponsored institutes in the United Kingdom.

Country of Study: United Kingdom.

No. of awards offered: Varies.

Application Procedure: Applicants must complete an application form available on request from the BBRSC Secretariat and Liaison Branch. Applications should be submitted by the Director of a BBSRC supported research institute or the holder of a BBSRC research grant.

Closing Date: Applications can be submitted at any time.

Funding: Private.

Additional Information: Information on the BBSRC remit is available on the website.

Wain Fund

Subjects: Biotechnology and biological sciences.

Purpose: To provide support to United Kingdom based researchers to undertake international collaborations that are of benefit to research in the areas of agriculture including sustainable systems and fundamental research underpinning these areas within the remit of BBSRC.

Eligibility: Open to junior academic staff of United Kingdom universities and similar research institutions, but not government or government financed laboratories, and to United Kingdom based researchers who are currently approaching the end of their PhD studies.

Level of Study: Postdoctorate, Professional development, Research.

Type: Travel grant or fellowship.

Value: To cover travel and subsistence expenses as approved by the BBSRC.

Length of Study: Up to three months.

Frequency: Dependent on funds available.

Study Establishment: Approved overseas academic or industrial institutions.

Country of Study: Any country.

No. of awards offered: Up to six per year.

Application Procedure: Applicants must complete an application form, available on the BBSRC website or from the Secretariat and Liaison Branch. Applications should relate to an area of agricultural research relevant to the remit of the BBSRC.

Closing Date: Details of closing dates are on the BBSRC website.

Funding: Private.

Additional Information: Information on the BBSRC remit is available on the website.

BOARD OF ARCHITECTS OF NEW SOUTH WALES

3 Manning Street, Potts Point, NSW, 2011, Australia
Tel: (61) 2 9356 4900
Fax: (61) 2 9357 4780
Email: mail@boarch.nsw.gov.au
www: http://boarch.nsw.gov.au
Contact: Ms Mae Cruz, Deputy Registrar

Board of Architects of New South Wales Research Grant

Subjects: Any architectural topic approved by the board.

Purpose: To provide assistance to those wishing to undertake research on a topic approved by the Board to contribute to the advancement of architecture.

Eligibility: Open to candidates who are registered as architects in New South Wales.

Level of Study: Professional development.

Type: Research grant.

Value: Australian $6,000.

Length of Study: One year.

Frequency: Every two years.

Country of Study: Australia.
No. of awards offered: One.
Application Procedure: Applicants must write for details.
Closing Date: July 30th.
Funding: Government.
Additional Information: A report is to be submitted upon completion of tenure.

Byera Hadley Travelling Scholarship, Postgraduate Scholarship, Student Scholarship

Subjects: Architecture.
Purpose: To allow candidates to undertake a course of study, research or other activity approved by the Board as contributing to the advancement of architecture.
Eligibility: Open only to graduates or students of four accredited schools of architecture in New South Wales. Applicants must be Australian citizens.
Level of Study: Graduate, Research.
Type: Scholarship.
Value: The total value of the combined awards is australian $65,000.
Frequency: Annual.
Country of Study: Any country.
No. of awards offered: One postgraduate, one graduate.
Application Procedure: Applicants must write for details.
Closing Date: The deadline for Graduands and registered architects is July 30th and for students it is August 30th.
Funding: Private.
Contributor: A bequest from the estate of the late Byera Hadley an Australian architect.
No. of awards given last year: Five.
No. of applicants last year: 20.
Additional Information: A report suitable for publication must be submitted within three years of the date of the award.

BOARD OF TRUSTEES FOR THE AWARD OF THE HEINRICH WIELAND PRIZE

Boehringer Ingelheim GmbH
BIC 6th Floor, Ingelheim, D-55216, Germany
Tel: (49) 613 277 2636
Fax: (49) 613 277 6669
Email: kimmling@ing.boehringer-ingelheim.com
Contact: Ms G Kimmling, Secretary of the Kuratorium

Heinrich Wieland Prize

Subjects: Medical sciences.
Purpose: To encourage work in the areas of chemistry, biochemistry, physiology and medicine.
Eligibility: Open to nationals of any country.
Level of Study: Unrestricted.
Type: Prize.
Value: €25,000 and a medal.
Frequency: Annual.
Country of Study: Any country.
No. of awards offered: One.
Application Procedure: Application must include a curriculum vitae, reprints and copies of manuscripts.
Closing Date: March 28th.
Funding: Commercial.
Contributor: Boehringer Ingelheim.
No. of awards given last year: One.

BOISE FOUNDATION

c/o Royal Academy of Music
Marylebone Road, London, NW1 5HT, England
Contact: Ms Jean Shannon, Honorary Secretary

Boise Foundation Scholarships

Subjects: Music practical.
Purpose: To enable singers and all categories of individual instrumentalists to pursue further study in United Kingdom or abroad.
Eligibility: Open to musical students of any nationality who are under 30 years of age and ordinarily resident in the United Kingdom or Republic of Ireland, or who are Commonwealth citizens temporarily resident in the United Kingdom for their musical education. Foreign nationals who have been resident in the United Kingdom for more than three years prior to commencing musical training are eligible. Eligibility regulations must be strictly observed.
Level of Study: Postgraduate.
Type: Scholarship.
Value: Up to UK £5,000.
Frequency: Every two years.
Study Establishment: Musical centres either in the United Kingdom or abroad, subject to the approval of the Scholar's plan of study by the Trustees of the Foundation.
Country of Study: Any country.
No. of awards offered: One-two.
Application Procedure: Applicants must complete an application form which must be signed by a nominator. Awards are made on the basis of a competitive audition for which candidates must be nominated. Names of nominators are available on request from the Foundation Secretary.
Closing Date: Early March in the year of the award.
Funding: Private.
No. of awards given last year: Two.
No. of applicants last year: 46.
Additional Information: Enquiries should be made in writing only.

BOLOGNA CENTER OF THE JOHNS HOPKINS UNIVERSITY

Via Belmeloro 11, Bologna, I-40126, Italy
Tel: (39) 051 291 7811
Fax: (39) 051 228 505
Email: admission@jhubc.it
www: http://www.jhubc.it
Contact: Ms Bernadette O'Toole, Assistant Registrar

The Bologna Center, an integral part of The Johns Hopkins University, provides advanced education for students preparing for professional careers in international affairs through the study of political science, economics, history and law, and their application to international relations and foreign policy issues.

Paul H Nitze School of Advanced International Studies (SAIS) Financial Aid and Fellowships

Subjects: The Center offers an interdisciplinary programme of study in international economics, politics, history and law, with special emphasis on European studies. Language instruction is offered in several European languages.
Purpose: To allow graduates to study international relations at the Johns Hopkins Bologna Center.
Eligibility: Open to students who have completed their first university degree. Students who are in the process of completing their first degree may apply providing they are awarded the degree prior to entry to the Bologna Center in the Autumn. Ideally, candidates should have some background knowledge in economics, history, political or other social sciences. All non native English speaking students must have an excellent command of both written and spoken English as the programme is conducted entirely in English. Special fellowships

administered by the Bologna Center on behalf of other donor organisations have certain restrictions, which vary depending upon the donor.

Level of Study: Postgraduate.
Type: Fellowship and financial aid.
Value: Varies, grants may cover partial or, occasionally, full tuition. Maintenance stipends are rarely provided.
Frequency: Annual.
Study Establishment: The Bologna Center of the Johns Hopkins University, Paul H Nitze School of Advanced International Studies.
Country of Study: Italy.
No. of awards offered: Varies, depending on funds available.
Application Procedure: Applicants must submit an application form and financial aid application. Certain donor organisations require a separate application.
Closing Date: The deadline for United States students is January 15th, the deadline for non United States students is February 1st.
Funding: Commercial, Government, Private.
No. of applicants last year: 450.
Additional Information: Admission and financial aid for United States citizens and permanent residents is administered by SAIS in Washington and all enquiries from United States students should be addressed to the Admissions Office in Washington. Financial aid and admission for non United States students is administered in Bologna and all enquiries from non United States students should be addressed to the Registrar's Office in Bologna. Many of the fellowships available to non United States students are provided by government ministries and other European organisations and are reserved for citizens of the country providing the fellowship. All fellowships and financial aid awards are based on need as well as academic merit.

For further information contact:

Admissions Office
1740 Massachusetts Avenue North West, Washington, DC, 20036, United States of America
Email: admission@mail.jhuwash.jhu.edu

THE BOSTON SOCIETY OF ARCHITECTS (BSA)

52 Broad Street
4th Floor, Boston, MA, 02109-4301, United States of America
Tel: (1) 617 951 1433
Fax: (1) 617 951 0845
Contact: Awards Committee

The Boston Society of Architects (BSA) is the regional and professional association of over 3,000 architects and 1,000 affiliate members. The BSA's affiliate members include engineers, contractors, clients or owners, public officials, other allied professionals, students and lay-people. The BSA administers many programmes that enhance the public understanding of design as well as the practice of architecture.

Rotch Traveling Scholarship

Subjects: Architecture.
Purpose: To provide young architects with the opportunity to travel and study in foreign countries.
Eligibility: Open to United States of America architects who will be under 35 years of age on March 10th of the year of the competition and who have a degree from an accredited school of architecture plus one full year of professional experience in an architectural office.
Level of Study: Professional development.
Type: Fellowship.
Value: A stipend of US$30,000.
Length of Study: Nine months.
Frequency: Annual.
Country of Study: Outside the United States of America.
No. of awards offered: One-two.

Application Procedure: Applicants must complete an application form, available on written request.
Closing Date: January 1st for application requests.
Funding: Private.
Additional Information: The Scholar is selected through a two stage design competition. The one year of professional experience required should be completed prior to the beginning of the preliminary competition. Scholars are required to return to the United States of America after the duration of the scholarship and submit a report of their travels.

BRADFORD CHAMBER OF COMMERCE AND INDUSTRY

Phoenix House
Rushton Avenue, Bradford, Yorkshire, B03 7BH, England
Tel: (44) 1274 230044
Fax: (44) 1274 230042
Email: julie.astley@postwatch.co.uk
www: http://www.bradfordchamber.co.uk
Contact: Miss J Astley, Trust Administration

The Bradford Chamber of Commerce and Industry represents member companies in the Bradford and district area. It works with local partners to develop the economic health of the district and has a major voice within the British Chamber of Commerce movement in order to promote the needs of local business on a national basis.

John Speak Trust Scholarships

Subjects: Modern languages.
Purpose: To promote British trade abroad by assisting people in perfecting a basic knowledge of a foreign language.
Eligibility: Open to British born nationals intending to follow a career connected with the export trade of the United Kingdom, who are over 18 years of age. A sound, basic knowledge of a language is required.
Level of Study: Professional development.
Type: Scholarship.
Value: Approx. UK £1,800.
Length of Study: Between three and ten months abroad depending on the circumstances and each candidate's level of knowledge of the language. It is not renewable.
Frequency: Three times each year.
Country of Study: Any non English speaking country.
No. of awards offered: 10.
Application Procedure: Applicants must complete an application form and an interview.
Closing Date: February 28th, May 31st or October 31st.
Funding: Private.
No. of awards given last year: Eight.
No. of applicants last year: 14.

BRANDON UNIVERSITY

School of Music, Brandon, MB, R7A 6A9, Canada
Tel: (1) 204 727 7388
Fax: (1) 204 728 6839
Email: music@brandonu.ca
www: http://www.brandonu.ca
Contact: Professor Robert Richardson, Graduate Music Programmes

Brandon University is linked to the international community through the exchange of people and ideas. At an informal level, faculty may collaborate with researchers from around the world in pursuit of knowledge in their respective disciplines. In addition, the university has a number of joint programmes and exchange opportunities with institutions in other countries.

Brandon University Graduate Assistantships

Subjects: Music education, performance and literature (piano and strings).
Purpose: To afford graduate students the opportunity to gain professional experience while studying and to provide monetary assistance.
Eligibility: Open to candidates with a Bachelor's degree in music or music education with a minimum grade point average of 3.0 during the final year.
Level of Study: Graduate.
Value: Up to canadian $6,500.
Length of Study: Normally two years.
Frequency: Annual.
Study Establishment: The School of Music, Brandon University.
Country of Study: Canada.
No. of awards offered: Four-eight.
Application Procedure: Applicants must complete an application form.
Closing Date: May 1st.
Additional Information: Candidates for the performance and literature major are also required to show, by audition, high potential as performers. For the music education major, candidates should have adequate related professional experience, preferably teaching.

BREAD LOAF WRITER'S CONFERENCE

Middlebury College, Middlebury, VT, 05753, United States of America
Tel: (1) 802 443 5286
Fax: (1) 802 443 2087
Email: blwc@mail.middlebury.edu
www: http://www.middlebury.edu/~blwc
Contact: Mrs Carol Knauss

The Bread Loaf Writer's Conference's central purpose is to create a community in which a dialogue of converging literary voices can be sustained.

Bread Loaf Writer's Conference Fellowships and Scholarships

Subjects: Fiction, non fiction and poetry.
Purpose: To provide recognition for both established writers and writers who show unusual promise, and an atmosphere in which writing can be discussed and criticised intensively.
Eligibility: Candidates for fellowships are assumed to have published a book or to have had a book length manuscript accepted for publication. Candidates for scholarship assistance will have had articles published in periodicals. There are no restrictions regarding nationality or citizenship. All writing must be submitted in English.
Level of Study: Unrestricted.
Type: Fellowship and scholarship.
Value: Fellowships carry no cash value but cover all regular charges at the Conference. Scholarships cover full or partial tuition.
Length of Study: 11 days.
Frequency: Annual.
Study Establishment: The Bread Loaf campus, Middlebury College, Vermont.
Country of Study: United States of America.
No. of awards offered: Varies.
Application Procedure: Applicants must complete an application form.
Closing Date: March 1st.
Funding: Private.
No. of awards given last year: 35.

BREAST CANCER CAMPAIGN

Clifton Centre
110 Clifton Street, London, EC2A 4HT, England
Tel: (44) 20 7749 3700
Fax: (44) 20 7749 3701
Email: info@bcc-uk.org
www: http://www.bcc-uk.org
Contact: Grants Officer Chairman of the Trustees

Breast Cancer Campaign Project Grants

Subjects: Breast cancer research.
Purpose: To improve diagnosis and treatment of cancer, to achieve a better understanding of how it develops and ultimately to cure or prevent the disease.
Level of Study: Postdoctorate, Postgraduate.
Type: Grant.
Value: No more than UK £50,000 per year.
Length of Study: Up to three years.
Frequency: Twice a year.
Country of Study: United Kingdom.
Application Procedure: Applicants must complete an application form. These can be obtained from the campaign office and the website.
Closing Date: The beginning of June and the end of November.
No. of awards given last year: 15.
No. of applicants last year: 45.

BREAST CANCER RESEARCH TRUST (BCRT)

48 Wayneflete Tower Avenue
Esher Place, Esher, Surrey, KT10 8QG, England
Tel: (44) 1372 463235
Fax: (44) 1372 463235
Email: bcrtrust@aol.com
Contact: Ms Rosemary Sutcliffe, Secretary

The Breast Cancer Research Trust (BCRT) exists solely to raise funds for breast cancer research at a scientific laboratory level into the case of breast cancer. The project has to be within a recognised medical unit as individuals are not funded.

Breast Cancer Research Grant

Subjects: Studies into breast cancer.
Purpose: To study the causation of breast cancer.
Level of Study: Research.
Type: Research grant.
Value: UK £12,000 per year.
Length of Study: One-two years.
Frequency: Annual.
Study Establishment: A recognised medical unit.
Country of Study: United Kingdom.
Application Procedure: Applicants must request an application form.
Closing Date: End of October.
Funding: Private.
No. of awards given last year: Eight.
No. of applicants last year: 12.

For further information contact:

Royal Marsden Hospital
Downes Road, Sutton, Surrey, England
Contact: Professor Trevor Powles

THE BRITISH ACADEMY

10 Carlton House Terrace, London, SW1Y 5AH, England
Tel: (44) 20 7969 5200
Fax: (44) 20 7969 5300
Email: secretary@britac.ac.uk
www: http://www.britac.ac.uk
Contact: Ms Jane Lyddon, Assistant Secretary (International Relations)

The British Academy is the premier national learned society in the United Kingdom devoted to the promotion of advanced research and scholarships in the humanities and social sciences.

British Academy Awards

Subjects: Humanities and social sciences.
Purpose: To support individual research projects at the postdoctoral level. The Academy also offers support for conference attendance, research posts and international collaborative projects.
Eligibility: Eligibility requirements vary depending on the scheme, but they are mainly open to United Kingdom residents who specialise in humanities and social sciences.
Level of Study: Postdoctorate.
Type: Research grants, fellowships and travel grants.
Value: From UK £400-20,000 depending on the scheme.
Frequency: Annually to four times a year depending on scheme.
No. of awards offered: Varies according to scheme.
Application Procedure: Applicants must consult the website for scheme details and application forms.
Closing Date: Please contact the Academy.
Funding: Government, Private.
No. of awards given last year: 1,200.
No. of applicants last year: 2,000.
Additional Information: Please see the website.

BRITISH ASSOCIATION FOR AMERICAN STUDIES (BAAS)

American Studies Department
University of Hull, Hull, HU6 7RX, England
Tel: (44) 1482 465303
Fax: (44) 1482 465303
Email: j.virden@hull.ac.uk
www: http://www.baas.ac.uk
Contact: Dr Jenel Virden, Secretary (STA)

The British Association for American Studies (BAAS), established in 1955, promotes research and teaching in all aspects of American Studies. The Association organises annual conferences and specialist regional meetings for students, teachers and researchers. The publications produced are The Journal of American Studies with Cambridge University Press, BAAS Paperbacks with Edinburgh University Press and British Records Relating to America in Microform with Microform Publishing.

BAAS Short Term Awards

Subjects: United States of America culture and society.
Purpose: To fund travel to the United States of America for short term research projects.
Eligibility: Open to United Kingdom citizens. Preference is given to young Scholars, particularly postgraduates.
Level of Study: Doctorate, Postdoctorate, Postgraduate, Professional development.
Type: Award.
Value: UK £400.
Frequency: Annual.
Study Establishment: Anywhere in the United States of America.
Country of Study: United States of America.
No. of awards offered: 5-10.

Application Procedure: Applicants must complete an application form.
Closing Date: November 30th.
No. of awards given last year: Six.
No. of applicants last year: 35.
Additional Information: Further information is available on request.

BRITISH ASSOCIATION FOR CANADIAN STUDIES (BACS)

21 George Square, Edinburgh, EH8 9LD, Scotland
Tel: (44) 131 662 1117
Fax: (44) 131 662 1118
Email: jodie.robson@ed.ac.uk
www: http://www.canadian-studies.net
Contact: Ms Jodie Robson

In response to the growing academic interest in Canada, the British Association for Canadian Studies (BACS) was established in 1975. Its aim is to foster teaching and research on Canada and Canadian issues by locating study resources in Britain, facilitating travel and exchange schemes for professorial staff, and ensuring that the expertise of Canadian scholars who visit the United Kingdom is put to effective use. Principal activities include the publication of 'The British Journal of Canadian Studies' and the BACS Newsletter, and organisation of the Association's annual multidisciplinary conference, which attracts scholars from Canada and Europe as well as from the United Kingdom.

Molson Research Awards

Subjects: Canadian studies, humanities and social sciences.
Purpose: To encourage and fund visits to Canada directly related to the applicants' actual or proposed teaching or research. The awards are intended to increase contacts between academics and other scholars in Canada and the United Kingdom, and to assist in the preparation of teaching about Canada. The BACS administers these awards on behalf of the Foundation for Canadian Studies in the United Kingdom.
Eligibility: Open to academics from United Kingdom universities, polytechnics and colleges of higher education. Applicants must be United Kingdom citizens or long-term residents. Priority will be given to BACS members.
Level of Study: Doctorate, Postdoctorate.
Type: Travel grant.
Value: Up to UK £500.
Frequency: Annual.
Study Establishment: Universities or research institutions.
Country of Study: Canada.
No. of awards offered: Three-five.
Application Procedure: Applicants must complete an application form and submit this with a covering letter, curriculum vitae and the names of two referees.
Closing Date: October 1st, February 1st or May 1st.
No. of awards given last year: Six.
No. of applicants last year: 20.

Prix du Québec

Subjects: Humanities and social sciences.
Purpose: To assist British academics carrying out research related to Quebec in the areas of the humanities and social sciences. The award also seeks to encourage projects which incorporate Quebec in a comparative approach. The Quebec component must be more than 50 per cent.
Eligibility: Open to United Kingdom citizens or long-term residents.
Level of Study: Doctorate, Postdoctorate, Professional development.
Type: Award.
Value: UK £1,000.
Frequency: Dependent on funds available.

Study Establishment: Universities, research institutions and schools.
Country of Study: Canada.
No. of awards offered: Two, one award to doctoral and postdoctoral students and one award to full-time teaching staff.
Application Procedure: Applicants must contact Jodie Robson, Administrative Secretary of BACS, for application guidelines.
Closing Date: February 1st.
Funding: Government.
Contributor: The Office of the Government of Quebec in the United Kingdom.

BRITISH ASSOCIATION OF PLASTIC SURGEONS (BAPS)

The Royal College of Surgeons
35-43 Lincoln's Inn Fields, London, WC2A 3PN, England
Tel: (44) 20 7831 5161
Fax: (44) 20 7831 4041
Email: secretariat@baps.co.uk
www: http://www.baps.co.uk
Contact: Ms Angela Rausch, Course & Committee Administrator

The British Association of Plastic Surgeons (BAPS) is a medical education and training body for plastic surgeons.

BAPS European Travelling Scholarship
Subjects: Plastic surgery.
Purpose: To enable specialist registrars (years four to six) from Britain to visit any plastic surgery centre in Europe for training purposes.
Eligibility: Open to members of the Association who are specialist registrars in years four to six, or senior registrars enrolled in a recognised training programme. Applicants must be resident in the United Kingdom.
Level of Study: Professional development.
Type: Scholarship.
Value: Up to UK £1,000.
Length of Study: Varies.
Frequency: Annual.
Study Establishment: Any plastic surgery centre.
Country of Study: Europe, excluding the United Kingdom.
No. of awards offered: Two.
Application Procedure: Applicants must complete an application form and submit this with a proposed itinerary giving details of costs and reasons for wanting to attend a particular unit. A curriculum vitae of no more than two pages must also be submitted.
Closing Date: January 31st.
Funding: Private.
Contributor: The British Association of Plastic Surgeons.
No. of awards given last year: Two.
No. of applicants last year: Four.

BAPS Travelling Bursary
Subjects: Plastic surgery.
Purpose: To enable a plastic surgeon in the United Kingdom to study new techniques abroad.
Eligibility: Open to members of the Association who are either specialist registrars in years four to six, enrolled in a recognised training programme or consultant plastic surgeons of not more than three years standing.
Level of Study: Professional development.
Type: Bursary.
Value: Up to UK £4,000.
Length of Study: Varies.
Frequency: Annual.
Study Establishment: Any approved hospital plastic surgery units.
Country of Study: Outside the United Kingdom.
No. of awards offered: Two.
Application Procedure: Applicants must complete an application form and submit this with a proposed itinerary giving details of costs

and reasons for wanting to attend a particular unit. A curriculum vitae of no more than two pages must also be submitted.
Closing Date: January 31st.
Funding: Private.
Contributor: The British Association of Plastic Surgeons.
No. of applicants last year: Five.

Paton/Maser Memorial Fund
Subjects: Plastic surgery.
Purpose: To provide funds towards research projects.
Eligibility: Open to consultants and specialist registrars in plastic surgery working in the British Isles.
Level of Study: Research.
Type: Research grant.
Value: UK £2,500.
Length of Study: Varies.
Frequency: Annual.
Study Establishment: A hospital or research laboratory.
Country of Study: United Kingdom.
No. of awards offered: One.
Application Procedure: Applicants must submit a letter of application with a copy of research protocol.
Closing Date: January 31st.
Funding: Private.
Contributor: The British Association of Plastic Surgeons.
No. of awards given last year: One.
No. of applicants last year: One.

THE BRITISH COUNCIL

British Embassy
3100 Massachusetts Avenue North West, Washington, DC, 20008,
United States of America
Tel: (1) 202 588 7874
Fax: (1) 202 588 7918
Email: jonathan.bird@britishcouncil-usa.org
www: http://www.britishcouncil-usa.org
Contact: Mr Jonathan Bird, Scholarships & Exchanges Assistant

The British Council is Britain's international network for education, culture and development services. It co-ordinates the Marshall Scholarships Programme in the United States of America.

Atlantic Fellowships in Public Policy
Subjects: Any area of public policy.
Purpose: To provide United States mid-career professionals with an opportunity to study and gain practical experience in the United Kingdom in a wide variety of public policy areas. It was established in 1994 to commemorate the fiftieth anniversary of D-Day and the United States contribution to the liberation of Europe.
Eligibility: Open to United States mid course professionals, who are working in the area of public policy.
Level of Study: Professional development.
Type: Fellowship.
Value: Up to US$3,300 per month. The award covers a stipend, not intended to match Fellows' salary in the United States travel to and from the United Kingdom, institutional fees and family allowance.
Length of Study: 3-10 months.
Frequency: Annual.
Country of Study: United Kingdom.
No. of awards offered: Up to 10.
Application Procedure: Applicants must submit an application form and recommendation letters by the deadline announced in the Spring. Details are available from the website.
Closing Date: December of each year.
Contributor: The British Government.
No. of awards given last year: 12.
No. of applicants last year: 50.

BRITISH DENTAL ASSOCIATION

Dentsply Student Support Fund
64 Wimpole Street, London, W1G 8YS, England
Tel: (44) 20 7563 4174
Fax: (44) 20 7563 4556
Email: awards@bda-dentistry.org.uk
www: http://www.bda-dentistry.org.uk
Contact: Mr Richard Gott, Awards and Committees Officer

The British Dental Association is the national professional association for dentists. With over 20,000 members, the Association strives to enhance the science, arts and ethics of dentistry, improve the nation's oral health and promote the interests of its members.

Dentsply Scholarship Fund

Subjects: Dentistry and stomatology dentistry.
Purpose: To give financial assistance to postgraduate students of dentistry to enable them to undertake or continue studies in schools in the United Kingdom.
Eligibility: Open to British citizens studying in the United Kingdom or abroad, or citizens of any country studying in the United Kingdom.
Level of Study: Postgraduate.
Type: Mostly interest free loans.
Value: Varies.
Frequency: Annual.
Country of Study: United Kingdom.
No. of awards offered: Varies, up to ten.
Application Procedure: Applicants must complete and submit application forms, accompanied by an academic reference or supporting letter. Applications should be addressed to Mr Richard Gott.
Closing Date: May 31st.
Funding: Commercial.
No. of awards given last year: 12.
No. of applicants last year: 200.

BRITISH ECOLOGICAL SOCIETY (BES)

26 Blades Court
Putney, London, SW15 2NU, England
Tel: (44) 20 8871 9797
Fax: (44) 20 8871 9779
Email: general@ecology.demon.co.uk
www: http://www.britishecologicalsociety.org
Contact: Grants Management Officer

As a learned society and registered charity, the British Ecological Society (BES) is an independent organisation receiving no outside funds. The aims of the Society are to promote the science of ecology through research, publications and conferences and to use the findings of such research to educate the public and to influence policy decisions which involve ecological matters.

The Anne Keymer Prize

Subjects: Ecology.
Purpose: To award the best oral presentation by a postgraduate student at the Winter Meeting.
Eligibility: The candidate must present a paper at the BES Winter Meeting and should normally be a current postgraduate, or one who has recently finished and is presenting work undertaken when they were still a student.
Level of Study: Postgraduate.
Type: Prize.
Value: UK £200.
Frequency: Annual.
Application Procedure: Applicants must apply for information, available on request or from the website.
Additional Information: The prize is named in memory of Anne Keymer who was one of the first winners of the prize in 1981. Anne was a member of the Editorial Board of the Journal of Animal

Ecology, and was an exemplary scholar, teacher and citizen in her discipline.

Attendance at Conferences Run by Other Organisations

Subjects: Ecology.
Purpose: To aid attendance at the triennial European Ecological Congress and the INTECOL Congress.
Eligibility: Preference is given to those individuals who are presenting a paper or poster at the conference.
Frequency: Every four years.
Application Procedure: Applicants must refer to the 'Bulletin' where the special application procedures are advertised.
Additional Information: Further information is available from the website.

Attendance at Courses and Workshops Co-sponsored by the BES

Subjects: Ecology.
Purpose: To provide support to allow participants to attend specialist courses, workshops, or meetings organised under the auspices of the European Ecological Federation or the Tropical Biology Association.
Eligibility: Eligibility is advertised in the Bulletin.
Level of Study: Postgraduate, Research.
Value: Travel and accommodation expenses for participants, who should be prepared to play a full part in the meetings, including the possibility of giving a seminar on their work.
Application Procedure: Applicants must refer to the 'Bulletin' and in the EEF Newsletter for the application procedure.
Closing Date: Advertised in the Bulletin.
Additional Information: Courses will vary from year to year and will be advertised in the Bulletin and in the EEF Newsletter as and when details become available.

Award for the Best Paper by a Young Author

Subjects: Ecology.
Purpose: To award the best essay by a young author in each of the Society's journals.
Eligibility: The prizes are targeted at people at the start of their research career, with the normal age of eligibility being 30 or under. Papers stemming from doctoral theses are welcomed.
Type: Prize.
Value: UK £100.
Frequency: Annual.
Application Procedure: Authors wishing to be considered for an award should be the first named sole author of the paper. Details of the application procedure are included in each of the journals.
Additional Information: The Harper Prize is given for a paper in the Journal of Ecology, the Elton Prize for one in the Journal of Animal Ecology, the Southwood Prize for one in the Journal of Applied Ecology, and the Haldane Prize for one in the Journal of Functional Ecology. The journal editors decide the winner. Further information is available from the website.

BES Early Career Project Grants

Subjects: Ecological research.
Purpose: To assist promising young ecologists by supporting innovative or important research of a pure or applied nature, and to provide an opportunity for ecologists recently appointed to academic posts to establish themselves.
Eligibility: Applicants will normally be expected to have a PhD before applying. Applicants must be in their early career stage.
Type: Grant.
Value: Up to UK £15,000.
Frequency: Annual.
Application Procedure: Applicants must complete an application form, available from the BES office.
Closing Date: January 31st.
Additional Information: Successful applicants will be expected to submit a brief report within 15 months of receipt of the award. Further information is available on request or from the website.

BES Education Innovation and Research Grants

Subjects: Ecology.
Purpose: To encourage teachers and others involved in formal education to develop new approaches in communicating ecology which promote good practice and make ecology both exciting and intellectually stimulating.
Level of Study: Professional development.
Type: Grant.
Value: Up to UK £750.
Application Procedure: Applicants must complete an application form, available from the BES office. Further information is available on request and from the website.
Closing Date: September 30th.
Additional Information: Successful applicants should be prepared to attend the Winter Meeting or some other Society meeting to give a presentation, workshop or poster display to show the Society what has been achieved. Useful outcomes should be communicated to other schools, teachers and pupils through the Teaching and Communicating Ecology Group teachers' newsletter, the Internet, meetings or other appropriate ways. Any material produced should acknowledge the Society's contribution. Further information is available on request and from the website.

BES Small Ecological Project Grants

Subjects: Any aspect of ecological research and ecological survey.
Purpose: To promote all aspects of ecological research and ecological survey.
Eligibility: Open to ecological researchers.
Level of Study: Professional development.
Type: Project grant.
Value: Up to UK £1,000 for travel and up to UK £1,000 for other costs.
Frequency: Four times per year.
Country of Study: Any country.
Application Procedure: Applicants must complete an application form, available from the BES office. The original form and seven copies must be submitted.
Closing Date: January 1st, April 1st, July 1st or October 1st.
Additional Information: Support will not normally be given to projects forming part of an expedition proposal. All recipients will be required to submit a report on the work undertaken. Published papers and reports to other organisations should include an acknowledgement of the support from the BES. Other conditions may apply. The Coalbourn Trust is an independent trust which looks to the British Ecological Society to nominate suitable projects for funding. Recommendations for funding will be made from among the applicants for Small Ecological Project Grants. All applicants for Small Ecological Project Grants will automatically be eligible for funding from the Coalbourn Trust. Further information is available on request or from the website.

BES Specialist Course Grants

Subjects: Ecology.
Purpose: To help meet costs of specialist field courses.
Eligibility: The Education Training and Careers Committee decides which courses grants are available for.
Level of Study: Graduate, Postgraduate.
Type: Grant.
Value: The course fee which includes accommodation.
Length of Study: Six months between May and October.
No. of awards offered: Limited.
Application Procedure: Applicants must complete an application form, available from the BES office.
Additional Information: Successful applicants are bound by the booking conditions of the institution running the course and non attendance on a booked course will result in the applicants being personally liable for the cancellation fee. Grantees are required to produce a short report on the course. Further information is available from the website.

BES/Nordecol Student Support for Attendance at the Society's Winter Meeting

Subjects: Ecology.
Purpose: To enable students from Nordic countries to attend the BES Winter Meeting.
Eligibility: Open to students from Nordic countries.
Type: Grant.
Value: Nordecol contributes to travel costs whilst the BES provides funds for the registration fee, meals and accommodation.
No. of awards offered: Limited.
Application Procedure: Applicants must refer to the website http://www.oikos.ekol.lu.se where the details are publicised each Autumn.
Additional Information: Further information is available from the website.

The Founders' Prize

Subjects: Ecology.
Purpose: To award an outstanding ecologist in his or her early career who is making a significant contribution towards the science of ecology.
Eligibility: Nominees should be outstanding ecologists, early in their careers (normally under 30 years of age) and be making a significant contribution towards the science of ecology.
Value: UK £500 and certificate.
Frequency: Every two years.
Application Procedure: Suggestions should be made by letter from a proposer and seconder, giving a brief statement of the achievements that the individual has made to ecology plus their future potential. Suggestions should be submitted to the Executive Secretary at the BES office.
Closing Date: June 30th.

Honorary Membership of the Society

Subjects: Ecology.
Purpose: To award honorary membership of the BES, the highest honour that the Society gives.
Eligibility: Candidates must have great distinction in the science of ecology or its application.
Value: Honorary membership.
Frequency: Annual.
Application Procedure: The Society's Council is responsible for nominating and awarding honorary membership but BES members are welcome to put forward suggestions. Suggestions should include a brief statement of no more than 100 words outlining the individual's contribution to ecology and should be sent to the Executive Secretary.
Closing Date: January 31st.
Additional Information: Further information is available from the website.

The Marsh Award for Ecology

Subjects: Ecology.
Purpose: To recognise outstanding achievements and contributions to the science of ecology.
Eligibility: Open to distinguished ecologists. The Council seeks suggestions from members of the BES.
Type: Award.
Value: UK £1,000 plus a certificate.
Frequency: Annual.
Application Procedure: Applicants must send suggestions to the Executive Secretary. They should be no more than a single side of A4 and should contain the name and address of the individual and a brief statement outlining the achievements and contribution that they have made to ecology.
Closing Date: June 30th.
Additional Information: Further information is available from the website.

Prize for the Best Poster at the Winter Meeting

Subjects: Ecology.

Purpose: To award the best poster by a research student at the Winter Meeting.
Eligibility: A candidate eligible to enter must present a poster at the BES Winter Meeting and should normally be a current postgraduate, or one who has recently finished and is presenting work that was undertaken when they were still a student. The entrant must be the first author and have carried out the majority of the work presented.
Level of Study: Postgraduate.
Type: Prize.
Value: UK £200.
Frequency: Annual.
Application Procedure: Applicants must write for details.
Additional Information: Further information is available on request and from the website.

Student Support for Attendance at BES Meetings

Subjects: Ecology.
Purpose: To support students attending the Society's Winter and Annual General Meeting, Annual Symposium and Special Symposium.
Eligibility: Applicants must be students.
Level of Study: Postgraduate.
Type: Grant.
Value: 50 per cent of the cost of the registration fee plus meals and accommodation whilst at the meeting.
No. of awards offered: Varies.
Application Procedure: Applicants must complete an application form, available from the BES office. Applications must be endorsed by the student's Head of Department or research supervisor. Bulk applications on behalf of a group of students are not accepted.
Closing Date: October 31st for the Winter and Annual meeting. Other meetings are advertised in the Bulletin.
Additional Information: Further information is available from the website.

Teacher Attendance at BES Meetings

Subjects: Ecology.
Purpose: To enable teachers to attend meetings and courses organised by the British Ecological Society in cases where the applicant can show that the grant aid has been refused by the employer.
Eligibility: Open to teachers in primary and secondary education, including field centre staff and others in non school employment.
Level of Study: Professional development.
Value: Up to UK £200.
Application Procedure: Applicants must submit a letter which should specify the meeting or course to be attended, date, costs of travel and subsistence.
Closing Date: January 31st, April 30th or September 30th.
Additional Information: Further information is available from the website.

BRITISH FEDERATION OF WOMEN GRADUATES (BFWG)

4 Mandeville Courtyard
142 Battersea Park Road, London, SW11 4NB, England
Tel: (44) 20 7498 8037
Fax: (44) 20 7498 5213
Email: awards@bfwg.demon.co.uk
www: http://homepages.wyenet.co.uk/bfwg
Contact: Secretary

The British Federation of Women Graduates (BFWG) promotes women's opportunities in education and public life. BFWG works as part of an international organisation to improve the lives of women and girls, fosters local, national and international friendship, and offers scholarships for postgraduate research.

AAUW/IFUW International Fellowships

Subjects: All subjects.
Eligibility: Female applicants must be a member of BFWG or another national federation or association of the International Federation of University Women (IFUW). It is a condition that the candidate will have started her second year of research at least, to which her application refers, at the time of the application and must be studying for three or more years. Taught Master's degrees do not count as research, though research done for a MPhil may count on the assumption that it will be upgraded to a PhD.
Level of Study: Postgraduate.
Type: Fellowship.
Value: Approximately US$15,000. The fellowships do not cover travel.
Length of Study: One year.
Frequency: Annual.
Study Establishment: An American institution.
Country of Study: United States of America.
No. of awards offered: Six.
Application Procedure: Applicants must apply through their respective federation or association. Applicants studying in the United Kingdom should write for details enclosing a stamped addressed envelope. A list of IFUW national federations can be sent on request.
Closing Date: December 15th in the year preceding the competition.
Funding: Private.
Additional Information: Recipients must submit a written report within six months of completing the fellowship.

For further information contact:

The Fellowship Chair, Iowa City, IA, 52243-4030, United States of America
www: http://www.aauw.org

AFUW Georgina Sweet Fellowship

Subjects: All subjects.
Eligibility: Open to women who are members of BFWG. It is a condition that the candidate will have started her second year of research at least, to which her application refers, at the time of application and must be studying for three years or more. Taught Master's degrees do not count as research, though research done for a MPhil may count on the assumption that it will be upgraded to a PhD.
Level of Study: Postgraduate, Research.
Type: Fellowship.
Value: Approx. australian $4,500. The fellowship does not cover travel.
Length of Study: 4-12 months.
Frequency: Every two years.
Study Establishment: An Australian university.
Country of Study: Australia.
No. of awards offered: One.
Application Procedure: Applicants must write for details including a stamped addressed envelope.
Closing Date: Early April in the year preceding the competition.
Funding: Private.
Additional Information: Recipients must submit a written report within six months of concluding the research.

For further information contact:

AFUW
PO Box 14
Bullcreek, WA, 6149, Australia
www: http://www.adelaide.edu.au/afuw

Australian Capital Territory Bursary

Subjects: All subjects.
Eligibility: Female applicants must be a member of BFWG or another national federation or association of IFUW. It is a condition that the candidate will have started her second year of research, to which her application refers, at least at the time of the application, and must be studying for three or more years. Taught Master's degrees

do not count as research, though research done for a MPhil may count on the assumption that it will be upgraded to a PhD.
Level of Study: Postgraduate, Research.
Type: Bursary.
Value: Australian $1,000.
Length of Study: Three months.
Frequency: Annual.
Study Establishment: An Institute of Higher Education in Canberra.
Country of Study: Australia.
No. of awards offered: One.
Application Procedure: Applicants must write for details enclosing a stamped addressed envelope. Applicants must apply through their respective federation or association, and members of BFWG may apply for consideration by BFWG. A list of IFUW national federations can be sent upon request.
Closing Date: July 31st of the year preceding the competition.
Funding: Private.
Additional Information: Recipients must submit a written report within six months of concluding the bursary.

For further information contact:

Fellowship Convenor
AFUW (ACT), Inc.
PO Box 520, Canberra, ACT, 0201, Australia

Beryl Mavis Green Scholarship

Subjects: All subjects.
Purpose: To assist postgraduate research.
Eligibility: Open to female candidates, regardless of nationality, whose studies take place in Great Britain. It is a condition that the research student will be in her final year of formal study towards a PhD degree. Taught Master's degrees do not count as research, though MPhil research students would need to be upgraded to a PhD during the dates of the competition.
Level of Study: Postgraduate, Research.
Type: Scholarship.
Value: From UK £1,000.
Frequency: Annual.
Study Establishment: A university or institution of university status.
Country of Study: United Kingdom.
No. of awards offered: One.
Application Procedure: Applicants studying in the United Kingdom must write for details enclosing a stamped addressed envelope. Overseas applicants must include two international reply coupons.
Closing Date: Early April in the year of the competition.
Funding: Private.

BFWG Scholarships

Subjects: All subjects.
Purpose: To assist postgraduate research.
Eligibility: Open to female candidates, regardless of nationality, whose studies take place in Great Britain ie. England, Scotland or Wales. It is a condition that the research student will be in her final year of formal study towards a PhD degree. Taught Master's degrees do not count as research, though MPhil research students would need to be upgraded to a PhD during the dates of the competition.
Level of Study: Postgraduate, Research.
Type: Scholarship.
Value: From UK £750-1,000.
Frequency: Annual.
Study Establishment: A university or institution of university status.
Country of Study: United Kingdom.
No. of awards offered: More than one.
Application Procedure: Applicants studying in the United Kingdom must write for details enclosing a stamped addressed envelope. Overseas applicants must include two international reply coupons.
Closing Date: Early April in the year preceding the competition.
Funding: Private.
Additional Information: Recipients must submit a written report within six months of concluding the research.

Ellen Gleditsch Stipendiefond

Subjects: All subjects.
Eligibility: Female applicants must be a member of BFWG or another national federation or association of IFUW. It is a condition that the candidate will have started her second year of research, to which her application refers, at least at the time of the application, and must be studying for three or more years. Taught Master's degrees do not count as research, though research done for a MPhil may count on the assumption that it will be upgraded to a PhD.
Type: Bursary.
Frequency: Annual.
Study Establishment: An approved institution.
Country of Study: Norway.
No. of awards offered: One.
Application Procedure: Applicants must write for details enclosing a stamped addressed envelope. Applicants must apply through their respective federation or association, and members of BFWG may apply for consideration by BFWG. A list of IFUW national federations can be sent upon request.
Closing Date: Early April in the year preceding the competition.
Funding: Private.
Additional Information: Recipients must submit a written report within six months of concluding the research.

For further information contact:

PO Box 264, Bergen, N-5001, Norway

IFUW International Fellowships

Subjects: All subjects.
Eligibility: Female applicants must be a member of BFWG or another national federation or association of IFUW. It is a condition that the candidate will have started her second year of research at least, to which her application refers, at the time of the application and must be studying for three or more years. Taught Master's degrees do not count as research, though research undertaken may count on the assumption that it will be updated to a PhD.
Level of Study: Postgraduate.
Type: Fellowship.
Value: Varies. The awards do not cover travel.
Length of Study: Eight months.
Frequency: Every two years.
Study Establishment: An Institute of Higher Education.
Country of Study: Any country.
No. of awards offered: More than seven.
Application Procedure: Applicants must apply through their respective federation or association. Applicants studying in the United Kingdom must write for details enclosing a stamped addressed envelope to BFWG. A list of national federations can be sent on request.
Closing Date: Early November in the year preceding the competition.
Funding: Private.
Additional Information: Recipients must submit a written report within six months of concluding the research.

For further information contact:

Grants Management Officer
IFUW Headquarters
8 rue de l'Ancien-Port, Geneva, CH-1201, Switzerland
Tel: (41) 22 731 2380
Fax: (41) 22 738 0440
Email: ifuw@ifuw.org
www: http://www.ifuw.org

JAUW International Fellowships

Subjects: All subjects.
Eligibility: Open to women who are members of the International Federation of University Women or another national federation or association of IFUW. It is a condition that the candidate will have started her second year of research at least, to which her application refers, at the time of the application and must be studying for three or more years. Taught Master's degrees do not count as research,

though research done for a MPhil may count on the assumption that it will be upgraded to a PhD.
Level of Study: Postgraduate, Research.
Type: Fellowship.
Value: Yen 600,000. The fellowships do not cover travel.
Length of Study: Three months.
Frequency: Annual.
Study Establishment: An Institute of Higher Education.
Country of Study: Japan.
No. of awards offered: More than one.
Application Procedure: Applicants must write for details enclosing a stamped addressed envelope. Applicants must apply through their respective federation or association, and members of BFWG may apply for consideration by BFWG. A list of IFUW national federations can be sent upon request.
Closing Date: April 30th in the year preceding the competition.
Funding: Private.
Additional Information: Recipients must submit a written report within six months of concluding the research.

For further information contact:

The Fellowship Chair, JAUW
11-6-101 Samon-cho
Shinjuku-ku, Tokyo, 160-0017, Japan
Tel: (81) 3 3358 2882
Fax: (81) 3 3358 2889
Email: jauw@tky2.3webne.jp
www: http://www3.tky.3web.ne.jp/~jauw/jauw.htm

Johnstone and Florence Stoney Studentship

Subjects: Research in biological, geological, meteorological or radiological science undertaken preferably in Australia, New Zealand or South Africa.
Purpose: To assist postgraduate research.
Eligibility: Open to female candidates, regardless of nationality, whose studies take place in Great Britain eg. England, Scotland or Wales. It is a condition that the research student will be in her final year of formal study towards a PhD degree in biological, geological, meteorological or radiological science. Taught Master's degrees do not count as research, though MPhil research students would need to be upgraded to a PhD during the dates of the competition.
Level of Study: Postgraduate, Research.
Type: Studentship.
Value: From UK £1,000, the studentship does not cover travel.
Frequency: Annual.
Study Establishment: A university or institution of university status.
Country of Study: United Kingdom.
No. of awards offered: One.
Application Procedure: Applicants studying in the United Kingdom must write for details enclosing a stamped addressed envelope. Overseas applicants must include two international reply coupons.
Closing Date: Early April in the year of the competition.
Funding: Private.
Additional Information: The recipient must submit a written report within six months of concluding the research.

Kathleen Hall Memorial Fellowships

Subjects: All subjects.
Purpose: To assist graduates from countries of low per capita income.
Eligibility: Open to female candidates, regardless of nationality, whose studies take place in Great Britain ie. England, Scotland or Wales are eligible. Preference is given to graduates from countries of low per capita income. It is a condition that the research student will be in her final year of formal study towards a PhD degree. Taught Master's degrees do not count as research, though MPhil research students would need to be upgraded to a PhD during the dates of the competition.
Level of Study: Postgraduate, Research.
Type: Fellowship.
Value: From UK £1,000.
Frequency: Annual.

Study Establishment: A university or institution of university status.
Country of Study: United Kingdom.
No. of awards offered: More than one.
Application Procedure: Applicants studying in the United Kingdom must write for details enclosing a stamped addressed envelope, while overseas applicants must include two international reply coupons.
Closing Date: Early April in the year of the competition.
Funding: Private.
Additional Information: Recipients must submit a written report within six months of concluding the research.

M H Joseph Prize

Subjects: Architecture or engineering.
Purpose: To assist postgraduate research.
Eligibility: Open to female candidates not of United Kingdom nationality but whose studies take place in the England, Scotland or Wales. It is a condition that the research student will be in her final year of formal study towards a PhD degree. Taught Master's degrees do not count as research, though MPhil research students would need to be upgraded to a PhD during the dates of the competition.
Level of Study: Postgraduate, Research.
Type: Prize.
Value: From UK £500.
Frequency: Annual.
Study Establishment: A university or institution of university status.
Country of Study: United Kingdom.
No. of awards offered: One.
Application Procedure: Applicants studying in the United Kingdom must write for details enclosing a stamped addressed envelope. Overseas applicants must include two international mail coupons.
Closing Date: Early April in the year of the competition.
Funding: Private.
Additional Information: Recipients must submit a written report within six months of concluding the research.

Margaret K B Day Memorial Scholarship

Subjects: All subjects.
Purpose: To assist postgraduate research.
Eligibility: Open to female candidates regardless of nationality, whose studies take place in the England, Scotland or Wales. It is a condition that the research student will be in her final year of formal study towards a PhD degree. Taught Master's degrees do not count as research, though MPhil research students would need to be upgraded to a PhD during the dates of the competition.
Level of Study: Postgraduate, Research.
Type: Scholarship.
Value: From UK £1,000.
Frequency: Annual.
Study Establishment: A university or institution of university status.
Country of Study: United Kingdom.
No. of awards offered: One.
Application Procedure: Applicants studying in the United Kingdom must write for details enclosing a stamped addressed envelope. Overseas applicants must include two international reply coupons.
Closing Date: Early April in the year of the competition.
Funding: Private.

Marjorie Shaw Scholarship

Subjects: All subjects.
Purpose: To assist postgraduate research.
Eligibility: Open to female candidates, regardless of nationality, whose studies take place in Great Britain ie. England, Scotland or Wales are eligible. Preference is given to graduates from countries of low per capita income. It is a condition that the research student will be in her final year of formal study towards a PhD degree. Taught Master's degrees do not count as research, though MPhil research students would need to be upgraded to a PhD during the dates of the competition.
Level of Study: Postgraduate, Research.

Type: Fellowship.
Value: From UK £1,000.
Frequency: Annual.
Study Establishment: A university or institution of university status.
Country of Study: United Kingdom.
No. of awards offered: More than one.
Closing Date: Early April in the year of the competition.
Funding: Private.
Additional Information: Recipients must submit a written report within six months of concluding the research.

Mary Bradburn Scholarship

Subjects: All subjects.
Purpose: To assist postgraduate research.
Eligibility: Open to female candidates, regardless of nationality, whose studies take place in Great Britain ie. England, Scotland or Wales are eligible. Preference is given to graduates from countries of low per capita income. It is a condition that the research student will be in her final year of formal study towards a PhD degree. Taught Master's degrees do not count as research, though MPhil research students would need to be upgraded to a PhD during the dates of the competition.
Level of Study: Postgraduate, Research.
Type: Fellowship.
Value: From UK £1,000.
Frequency: Annual.
Study Establishment: A university or institution of university status.
Country of Study: United Kingdom.
Closing Date: Early April in the year of the competition.
Funding: Private.
Additional Information: Recipients must submit a written report within six months of concluding the research.

Rose Sidgwick Memorial Fellowship

Subjects: All subjects.
Eligibility: Open to female British candidates below 30 years of age who are members of the British Federation of Women Graduates. It is a condition that the candidate will have started her second year of research, to which her application refers, at least at the time of application and must be studying for three or more years. Taught Master's degrees do not count as research, although research undertaken for a MPhil may count on the assumption that it will be upgraded to a PhD. Preference will be given to women who show prior commitment to the advancement of women and girls through civic, community, or professional work.
Level of Study: Postgraduate, Research.
Type: Fellowship.
Value: Approximately US$15,000. The fellowship does not cover travel.
Length of Study: One year.
Frequency: Annual.
Study Establishment: An American Institute of Higher Education.
Country of Study: United States of America.
No. of awards offered: One.
Application Procedure: Applicants studying in the United Kingdom must write for details enclosing a stamped addressed envelope. Overseas applicants must include two international reply coupons.
Closing Date: Early April in the year preceding the competition.
Funding: Private.
Additional Information: Recipients must submit a written report within six months of concluding the research.

Victorian Beatrice Fincher Scholarship

Subjects: Research in any subject that will benefit mankind.
Eligibility: Open to women who are members of BFWG or another national federation or association of IFUW. A list of IFUW national federations can be sent upon request. It is a condition that the candidate will have started her second year of research at least, to which her application refers, at the time of application and must be studying for three or more years. Taught Master's degrees do not count

as research, though research done for a MPhil may count on the assumption that it will be upgraded to a PhD.
Level of Study: Postgraduate, Research.
Type: Scholarship.
Value: Approx. australian $5,000. The scholarship does not cover travel.
Frequency: Annual.
Study Establishment: An Institute of Higher Education in Victoria.
Country of Study: Australia.
No. of awards offered: One.
Application Procedure: Applicants must write for details enclosing two international reply coupons.
Closing Date: March 1st in the year preceding the competition.
Funding: Private.
Additional Information: Recipients must submit a written report within six months of concluding the research.

For further information contact:

Scholarship Secretary
AFUW (VIC), Inc.
PO Box 816, Mount Eliza, VIC, 3930, Australia
Fax: (61) 3 9787 3262
www: http://www.vicnet.net.au/~afuwvic

Western Australian Bursaries

Subjects: All subjects.
Eligibility: Woman applicants must be members of BFWG or another national federation or association of IFUW. A list of IFUW national federations is available upon request. It is a condition that the candidate will have started her second year of research at least, to which her application refers, at the time of application and must be studying for three or more years. Taught Master's degrees do not count as research, though research done for a MPhil may count on the assumption that it will be upgraded to a PhD.
Level of Study: Postgraduate, Research.
Type: Bursary.
Value: Approx. australian $1,500-2,750. The bursaries do not cover travel.
Length of Study: One year.
Frequency: Annual.
Study Establishment: An Institute of Higher Education in Western Australia.
Country of Study: Australia.
No. of awards offered: More than one.
Application Procedure: Applicants must write for details enclosing two international reply coupons.
Closing Date: July 31st of the year preceding the competition.
Funding: Private.
Additional Information: Recipients must submit a written report within six months of concluding the research.

For further information contact:

Bursary Liaison Officer
AFUW (WA), Inc.
PO Box 48, Nedlands, WA, 6909, Australia
Email: afuwwa@cygnus.uwa.edu.au

BRITISH HEART FOUNDATION (BHF)

14 Fitzharding Street, London, W1H 6DH, England
Tel: (44) 20 7935 0185
Email: research@bhf.org.uk
www: http://www.bhf.org.uk
Contact: Ms Jessica Gregory, Assistant Manager, Research Funds Department

The British Heart Foundation (BHF) exists to encourage research into the causes, diagnosis, prevention and advances of cardiovascular disease, to inform doctors throughout the country of advances in the diagnosis, cure and treatment of heart diseases, and to improve

...ties for the treatment of heart patients where the National Health ...vice is unable to help.

...F Clinical Science Fellowships

...bjects: Research relevant to the cardiovascular system.
...rpose: To enable clinicians who have demonstrated an interest ...and potential for, research to be trained.
...gibility: Open to applicants from the European Economic Area. ...plicants should be clinicians, aged approximately 25-30 years.
...vel of Study: Professional development.
...pe: Fellowship.
...lue: This award reimburses for salary commensurate with senior- ...within the health service and carries a consumables allowance of ...to UK £5,000 per year.
...ngth of Study: Up to seven years.
...equency: Three times each year.
...udy Establishment: A basic science department, preferably, but ...ot necessarily, away from the sponsoring department.
...ountry of Study: Based in the United Kingdom, but research train- ...g period can be spent overseas.
...o. of awards offered: Varies.
...pplication Procedure: Applicants must submit the appropriate ...rm with the approval of the head of department. The application ...ust include a full research protocol and/or training programme to- ...ether with the curriculum vitae of the proposed Fellow. Shortlisted ...pplicants will normally be required to attend an interview. Applica- ...ion forms and further information are available on request.
...losing Date: Available on request.

BHF Intermediate Research Fellowships

Subjects: Research projects in the field of basic or applied clinical cardiology.
Purpose: To enable highly qualified independent researchers to pur-sue their research objectives.
Eligibility: Open to applicants from the European Economic Area.
Level of Study: Professional development.
Type: Fellowship.
Value: A salary commensurate with seniority within the university and health service at registrar or first year senior registrar level, or academic equivalent, and up to UK £7,000 per year may be applied for to cover running expenses which must be fully justified.
Length of Study: Up to three years.
Frequency: Three times each year.
Country of Study: United Kingdom.
No. of awards offered: Varies.
Application Procedure: Applicants must submit the appropriate form completed by themselves or their supervisor, with the approval of the head of department. The application must include a full re-search protocol together with the curriculum vitae of the proposed Fellow.
Closing Date: Available on request.
Additional Information: These fellowships are unlikely to be awarded to those who are unable to obtain advancement within the health services.

BHF Junior Research Fellowships

Subjects: Research projects in the field of basic or applied clinical cardiology.
Purpose: To enable postgraduates to be trained in academic research.
Eligibility: Open to applicants from the European Economic Area who wish to be trained in academic research under the direct super-vision of senior and experienced research workers.
Level of Study: Postgraduate.
Type: Fellowship.
Value: A salary, not to be higher than the top of the registrar scale or equivalent, and up to UK £5,000 per year to cover running expenses.
Length of Study: A total of two years, but Junior Research Fellows may proceed to the second year only after the head of department

has submitted, and the Foundation has approved, a progress report on the first year's work.
Frequency: Three times each year.
Country of Study: United Kingdom.
No. of awards offered: Varies.
Application Procedure: Applicants must submit the appropriate form completed by the planned supervisor and with the approval of the head of department. The application must include a full research protocol together with the curriculum vitae of the proposed Fellow. The head of department must confirm that no additional financial support is necessary in order to carry out the project.
Closing Date: Available on request.

BHF Overseas Visiting Fellowships

Subjects: Basic or applied clinical cardiology.
Purpose: To enable senior overseas research workers to undertake research in the United Kingdom.
Eligibility: Open to established research workers of proven out-standing talent able to contribute to the work of the host department.
Level of Study: Professional development.
Type: Fellowship.
Value: Funds to cover the Fellow's salary and up to UK £5,000 per year as a contribution towards research expenses. The applicant must confirm that no additional financial support is necessary in or-der to carry out the project. Application may be made for funds to cover economy travel fares for the Fellow and one dependant. The latter only being eligible for travel funds if the Fellow is to be resident in the United Kingdom for one year or more.
Length of Study: Up to two years.
Frequency: Three times each year.
Study Establishment: A recognised research centre in the United Kingdom.
Country of Study: United Kingdom.
No. of awards offered: Varies.
Application Procedure: Applications must be made by the head of department in the United Kingdom institution on behalf of the Fellow and should include a full research protocol. The role of the Visiting Fellow in the research should be clearly stated. A curriculum vitae of the proposed Fellow and two letters of recommendation from the Fellow's country of origin should also be included.
Closing Date: Available on request.
Additional Information: These fellowships are not given for training.

BHF PhD Studentships

Subjects: Basic or applied clinical cardiology.
Purpose: To enable graduates to proceed to a PhD degree.
Eligibility: Open to candidates who have obtained a minimum of an Upper Second Class (Honours) Degree, who are from the European Economic Area.
Level of Study: Doctorate.
Type: Studentship.
Value: The level of stipend is set by the British Heart Foundation. Applicants may apply for funds to cover university fees. Up to UK £5,000 per year may also be applied for to cover research consumables.
Length of Study: Three years.
Frequency: Three times each year.
Study Establishment: An appropriate university.
Country of Study: United Kingdom.
No. of awards offered: Varies.
Application Procedure: Applications must be made by heads of de-partment and may be made for named or unnamed candidates, al-though priority will be given to named candidates. Applications must be made on the appropriate form and must include a full research protocol and curriculum vitae of the candidate (if known).
Closing Date: Available on request.

BHF Research Awards

Subjects: Cardiovascular research.
Purpose: To encourage and support research.

Eligibility: Open to applicants from the European Economic Area.
Level of Study: Postdoctorate.
Type: Research grant.
Value: Varies.
Length of Study: Varies.
Frequency: Varies, according to committee.
Study Establishment: Universities and medical schools.
Country of Study: United Kingdom.
No. of awards offered: Dependent on funding.
Application Procedure: Applicants must write for details.
Closing Date: Varies according to the Committee.
Additional Information: An annual report is available upon request.

BHF Senior Research Fellowships

Subjects: Research projects in the field of basic or applied clinical cardiology.
Purpose: To enable researchers with an international reputation of outstanding ability to pursue their research interests.
Eligibility: Open to applicants from the European Economic Area. The applicant should have been engaged in original research for at least two years and have published results, and should show outstanding ability both in original thought and practical application. This ability should already have been recognised outside the applicant's institution by invitations to talk to societies both at home and abroad. The applicant's career plans should be academic medicine and research. Senior Research Fellowships are awarded to those thought likely to gain high office in teaching and research institutions.
Level of Study: Professional development.
Type: Fellowship.
Value: Salary commensurate with seniority within the university and health service up to consultant level. Up to UK £10,000 per year may be applied for to cover running expenses which should be fully justified.
Length of Study: Three years initially, but it may be extended to five after submission of a progress report which has been judged to be satisfactory by the Foundation.
Frequency: Annual.
Country of Study: United Kingdom.
No. of awards offered: Varies.
Application Procedure: Applicants must complete the appropriate form and submit this, with the approval of the head of department, together with a full research protocol and curriculum vitae of the proposed Fellow. Shortlisted applicants will be required to attend an interview.
Closing Date: Available on request.
Additional Information: A Senior Research Fellow may apply to the Committee for a second five year period by the end of which it would be expected that the Fellow would have secured a permanent and more senior position. In this case an interview will be required.

BHF Travelling Fellowships

Subjects: Basic or applied clinical cardiology.
Purpose: To enable established research workers to undertake research abroad, or acquire special knowledge which would assist them in their research in the United Kingdom after their return.
Eligibility: Open to applicants from the European Economic Area who are established research workers and are of proven outstanding talent. At the time of application the proposed Fellow should hold a post in a research institution or university with tenure of more than five years.
Level of Study: Professional development.
Type: Fellowship.
Value: The proposed Fellow may apply for funds to cover the cost of economy travel and a reasonable subsistence allowance at the place of work. It is expected that the Fellow's salary would continue to be paid by the university or institution in the United Kingdom during his or her absence abroad.
Length of Study: Up to six months.
Frequency: Three times each year.
Country of Study: Outside the United Kingdom.
No. of awards offered: Varies.

Application Procedure: Applicants must submit the appropriate form together with details of the purpose of the visit and what the Fellow expects to gain as a result of the visit. The applicant's curriculum vitae and a letter of acceptance by the host institution must be included in the application.
Closing Date: Available on request.

John Fyffe Memorial Fellowship

Subjects: Research in the field of collagen disease and in particular the causes, diagnosis, treatment including surgical techniques and the eventual elimination of the disease known as Marfan's syndrome.
Purpose: To enable researchers to visit other centres working in the field in order to acquire first hand knowledge and techniques so that they may be applied to research being undertaken in the United Kingdom.
Eligibility: Open to applicants from the European Economic Area.
Level of Study: Professional development.
Type: Fellowship.
Value: Up to UK £3,000 per year.
Frequency: Three times each year.
Country of Study: Any country.
No. of awards offered: Varies.
Application Procedure: Applicants must complete an application form. Application forms and further information are available on request.
Closing Date: Available on request.

BRITISH HYPERLIPIDAEMIA ASSOCIATION

c/o Wheldon Events & Conferences
27 Honiton Way, Aldridge, West Midlands, WS9 0JS, England
Tel: (44) 1922 457984
Fax: (44) 1922 455238
www: http://www.bhaonline.org.uk
Contact: BHA Meetings Organiser

The British Hyperlipidaemia Association promotes good practice in the clinical management of hyperlipidaemia and encourages new research in the area of lipid and lipoprotein metabolism amongst the medical profession and other health care workers. It also provides advice, guidance and critical assessment.

Sue McCarthy Travelling Scholarship

Subjects: Medical sciences.
Purpose: To support the transfer of expertise and/or patient samples between international laboratories.
Eligibility: Open to medical and scientific professionals.
Level of Study: Unrestricted.
Type: Scholarship.
Value: UK £1,500.
Frequency: Annual.
Study Establishment: A university, hospital or research institution.
Country of Study: United Kingdom.
No. of awards offered: One.
Application Procedure: Applicants must request an application form from the Association.
Closing Date: Mid-March.
Funding: Private.
No. of awards given last year: One.
No. of applicants last year: 11.

BRITISH INSTITUTE IN EASTERN AFRICA

PO Box 30710, Nairobi, Kenya
Tel: (254) 2 433 30
Fax: (254) 2 433 65
Email: britinst@insightkenya.com
Contact: Dr Paul Lane, Director

The British Institute in Eastern Africa encourages research by individual scholars in African archaeology, history and cognate fields, and works closely with the universities, museums and antiquities services of the Eastern African countries. It is based in Nairobi where it maintains a centre for field research and a comprehensive reference library.

British Institute in Eastern Africa Graduate Attachments
Subjects: Pre-colonial history and archaeology in East Africa through field research.
Purpose: To provide opportunities for recent graduates in history, archaeology, anthropology and related disciplines to gain practical field experience in Eastern Africa.
Eligibility: Open to citizens of East African countries, the United Kingdom and the Commonwealth who are over 21 years of age. Candidates should have a Bachelor of Arts or equivalent degree and graduate training in African studies, archaeology, social anthropology or African history.
Level of Study: Postgraduate.
Type: Graduate attachment.
Value: Varies.
Length of Study: Three-six months.
Frequency: Annual.
Country of Study: Kenya, Tanzania, Uganda or other Eastern African countries.
No. of awards offered: Varies.
Application Procedure: Applicants must submit a letter of application to the Director with the names of two academic referees and a curriculum vitae.
Closing Date: Normally May 15th.
Funding: Government.
No. of awards given last year: Seven.
No. of applicants last year: 23.
Additional Information: Small grants and assistance may be offered on a discretionary basis to Scholars of other nationalities. Archaeological students may be required to assist in excavation carried out by the Institute's staff. Details of activities are published in the Archaeology Abroad bulletin, and in the Institute's annual report, copies of which are available on request.

BRITISH INSTITUTE IN PARIS

British Institue in Paris
11 rue de Constantine, Paris, Cedex 07, F-75340, France
Tel: (33) 1 44 11 73 91
Fax: (33) 1 45 50 31 55
Email: campos@ext.jussieu.fr
www: http://www.bip.lon.ac.uk
Contact: The Director

The British Institute in Paris is a teaching and research institute of London University specialising in English and French studies, translation and language pedagogy.

Quinn, Nathan and Edmond Scholarships
Subjects: French studies.
Purpose: To assist postgraduate research in France.
Eligibility: Open to citizens of the European Union and Commonwealth countries who are graduates and possess sufficient knowledge of French to pursue their proposed studies. Candidates in the early stages of doctoral research, or not engaged in research, are not eligible.
Level of Study: Doctorate, Postdoctorate, Postgraduate.
Type: One scholarship, one junior research fellowship.
Value: The scholarship is UK £450 per month and the junior research fellowship is UK £500 per month.
Length of Study: The Scholarship is for between one and three months, and the Junior Research Fellowship is for up to nine months.
Frequency: Annual.
Study Establishment: An approved institute in Paris.
Country of Study: France.
No. of awards offered: One or two depending on funds available.
Application Procedure: Applicants must submit applications accompanied by a written recommendation from the candidate's professor or tutor. The name of one academic referee must be given.
Closing Date: March 15th.
Funding: Private.
Contributor: Trust funds.
No. of awards given last year: One.
No. of applicants last year: Eight.
Additional Information: Scholarships cannot be held concurrently with other major awards. These Scholarships are intended for research and not for those following taught courses.

BRITISH INSTITUTE OF ARCHAEOLOGY AT ANKARA

10 Carlton House Terrace, London, SW1Y 5AH, England
Tel: (44) 20 7969 5204
Fax: (44) 20 7969 5401
Email: biaa@britac.ac.uk
www: http://www.britac.ac.uk/institutes/ankara
Contact: Research Committee

The British Institute of Archaeology at Ankara was founded in 1948 and exists to undertake, promote and encourage British research into archaeology and related subjects in Turkey and its surrounding regions.

British Institute of Archaeology at Ankara Research Grants
Subjects: Archaeology and related subjects.
Purpose: To aid research into all periods of archaeology and related subjects of Turkey and the surrounding regions.
Eligibility: Open to citizens of the United Kingdom or other Commonwealth countries who are qualified to undertake advanced research. Preference is given to research projects in areas in which the Institute is already interested. This award is also open to other nationals resident in the United Kingdom.
Level of Study: Doctorate, Postdoctorate, Postgraduate.
Type: Research grant.
Value: Determined individually in regard to the level of work involved, qualifications and seniority of the applicant, and any other relevant factors.
Length of Study: Determined individually.
Frequency: Annual.
Country of Study: Turkey or surrounding regions.
No. of awards offered: Varies.
Application Procedure: Applicants must complete an application form, available from the Assistant Secretary.
Closing Date: November 1st.
Funding: Government.

British Institute of Archaeology at Ankara Travel Grants
Subjects: Archaeology and related subjects.
Purpose: To enable students to travel to and from Turkey and the surrounding regions for the purpose of familiarising themselves with its archaeology and to visit its sites and museums.

Eligibility: Open to graduates who are nationals of the United Kingdom or a Commonwealth country and other nationals resident in the United Kingdom.
Level of Study: Doctorate, Graduate, Postdoctorate, Postgraduate.
Type: Travel grant.
Value: Up to UK £500.
Frequency: Annual.
Country of Study: Turkey or surrounding regions.
No. of awards offered: Varies.
Application Procedure: Applicants must submit a curriculum vitae, itinerary, costing and two references. There is no application form.
Closing Date: February 1st but prospective candidates should check with the organisation before applying.
Funding: Government.

BRITISH INSTITUTE OF RADIOLOGY (BIR)

36 Portland Place, London, W1N 4AT, England
Tel: (44) 20 7307 1400
Fax: (44) 20 7307 1414
Email: admin@bir.org.uk
www: http://www.bir.org.uk
Contact: Chief Executive

The British Institute of Radiology, being an independent forum, has as its aim the bringing together of all the professions in radiology, medical and scientific disciplines to share knowledge and educate the public, thereby improving the prevention and detection of disease and the management and treatment of patients.

British Institute of Radiology Travel Bursary

Subjects: Radiology.
Purpose: To enable an individual to present a paper at UKRC.
Eligibility: Open to radiographer members of the Institute who are under 35 years of age.
Level of Study: Postgraduate.
Value: Up to UK £250.
Frequency: Annual.
Country of Study: Any country.
No. of awards offered: Five.
Application Procedure: Applicants must complete a registration form.
Closing Date: November 19th.
Funding: Private.
No. of awards given last year: One.
No. of applicants last year: Two.

Health Amersham Fellowship

Subjects: Radiology and pharmaceuticals in diagnostic imaging.
Purpose: To enable a diagnostic radiologist to gain in-depth experience abroad.
Eligibility: Open to diagnostic radiologists of senior registrar or junior consultant status. Preference is given to members of the Institute.
Level of Study: Postgraduate.
Type: Fellowship.
Value: Up to UK £5,000.
Length of Study: Up to two months.
Frequency: Annual.
Study Establishment: One or more academic departments of radiology.
Country of Study: Anywhere outside the United Kingdom.
No. of awards offered: One.
Application Procedure: Applicants must submit an application letter and supporting documentation.
Closing Date: End of February.
Funding: Commercial.
No. of awards given last year: One.
No. of applicants last year: One.

Additional Information: The successful Scholar will be required to produce a report of up to 1,000 words for publication in the British Journal of Radiology.

Nic McNally Memorial Prize

Subjects: Radiology.
Eligibility: Open to young scientists who are under 35 years of age at the time of application and employed in a scientific post. Applicants need not be members of the Institute.
Level of Study: Research.
Type: Travel grant.
Value: UK £500.
Frequency: Annual.
Study Establishment: UKRC or UKRO in alternate years.
Country of Study: United Kingdom.
No. of awards offered: One.
Application Procedure: Applicants must complete a registration form and submit this with supporting material.
Closing Date: November 19th.
Funding: Private.
No. of awards given last year: None.
No. of applicants last year: Two.

Stanley Melville Memorial Award

Subjects: Radiology.
Purpose: To enable a member of the Institute to visit clinics and institutions abroad.
Eligibility: Open to members of the Institute who are under 35 years of age.
Level of Study: Unrestricted.
Value: Approx. UK £1,000.
Frequency: Annual.
Country of Study: Any country.
No. of awards offered: One.
Application Procedure: Applicants must complete an application form and submit this with supporting documentation.
Closing Date: December 31st of the year preceding the award.
Funding: Private.
No. of awards given last year: Two.
No. of applicants last year: One.
Additional Information: While the successful applicant will not be obliged to write a formal report on his or her visit, it is hoped that he or she will submit a description of the work seen during the visit in a form suitable for publication in the Journal.

BRITISH JOURNAL OF SURGERY

Blackwell Science Limited
Journals Subscriptions
PO Box 88, Oxford, Oxfordshire, OX2 0NE, England
Tel: (44) 1865 206126
Fax: (44) 1865 206219
Email: journals.cs@blacksci.co.uk
Contact: Administrative Assistant

British Journal of Surgery Research Bursaries

Subjects: Surgical research.
Purpose: To further surgical research.
Level of Study: Postgraduate.
Type: Grant.
Value: UK £10,000.
Frequency: Annual.
No. of awards offered: Up to three.
Application Procedure: Applicants must visit the website for application details.
Closing Date: July 31st.
Funding: Private.
Contributor: The British Journal of Surgery Society.
No. of awards given last year: Three.

o. of applicants last year: 91.

THE BRITISH LEPROSY RELIEF ASSOCIATION (LEPRA)

Fairfax House
Causton Road, Colchester, Essex, CO1 1PU, England
Tel: (44) 1206 562286
Fax: (44) 1206 762151
Email: lepra@lepra.org
www: http://www.lepra.org.uk
Contact: Ms Debbie Sharp

The British Leprosy Relief Association (LEPRA) is a medical development charity which works to restore health, hope and dignity to those affected by leprosy.

LEPRA Grants

Subjects: Leprosy.
Purpose: To encourage and support research which is directly relevant to the understanding, prevention and care of leprosy.
Level of Study: Postgraduate.
Type: Grant.
Value: Dependent on funds available and the nature of the research or training.
Length of Study: Up to three years.
Frequency: Dependent on funds available.
Study Establishment: As appropriate to the nature of the research or training.
Country of Study: Any country.
No. of awards offered: Varies.
Application Procedure: Applicants must complete a research application pack, available on request. Applications must be submitted using the appropriate forms and should observe the timescales involved in the approvals process.
Closing Date: Applications are accepted all year round.

THE BRITISH LIBRARY - MAP LIBRARY

96 Euston Road, London, NW1 2DB, England
Tel: (44) 20 7412 7702
Fax: (44) 20 7412 7780
Email: maps@bl.uk
www: http://ihr.sas.ac.uk/maps/wallis.html
Contact: Mr Peter Barber, Map Librarian

Helen Wallis Fellowship

Subjects: History and the history of cartography, preferably with an international dimension.
Purpose: To promote the extended and complementary use of the British Library's book and cartographic collections in historical investigation.
Eligibility: Applicants should write for details.
Level of Study: Postdoctorate.
Type: Fellowship.
Value: Up to UK £300.
Length of Study: 6-12 months.
Frequency: Annual.
Study Establishment: British Library, London.
Country of Study: United Kingdom.
No. of awards offered: One.
Application Procedure: Applicants must submit a letter indicating the proposed period and outlining the research project together with a full curriculum vitae and the names of three references.
Closing Date: May 1st.
Funding: Private.
No. of awards given last year: One.

Additional Information: The award honours the memory of Dr Helen Wallis, OBE (1924-1995), Map Librarian at the British Museum and then the British Library between the years 1967-1986. Further information can be found on the website.

BRITISH LUNG FOUNDATION

78 Hatton Garden, London, EC1N 8LD, England
Tel: (44) 20 7831 5831
Fax: (44) 20 7831 5832
Email: blf@britishlungfoundation.com
www: http://www.lunguk.org
Contact: Ms Julia Leuginger, Research Manager

The British Lung Foundation exists to fund medical research into all lung diseases in the United Kingdom. To help achieve this the Foundation provides information on lung diseases and lung health and supports people with a lung condition through the Breathe Easy Club.

British Lung Foundation Project Grants

Subjects: Respiratory diseases.
Purpose: To promote medical research into the prevention, diagnosis and treatment of all lung diseases.
Eligibility: Open to graduates working within the United Kingdom who have some experience of research. The principal applicant must be based in a research centre in the United Kingdom.
Level of Study: Doctorate, Postdoctorate, Postgraduate, Predoctorate, Professional development, Research.
Type: Project grant.
Value: Up to UK £120,000.
Length of Study: Up to three years.
Frequency: Annual.
Study Establishment: An approved research centre.
Country of Study: United Kingdom.
No. of awards offered: Approx. 10.
Application Procedure: Applicants must complete an application form, available from the British Lung Foundation.
Closing Date: Mid December for preliminary applications and mid March for full applications.
Funding: Commercial, Private.
Contributor: Voluntary donations.
No. of awards given last year: 13.
No. of applicants last year: 99.

BRITISH MEDICAL ASSOCIATION (BMA)

Board of Science & Education
Tavistock Square, London, WC1H 9JP, England
Tel: (44) 20 7383 6755
Fax: (44) 20 7383 6399
Email: info.scienceawards@bma.org.uk
www: http://www.bma.org.uk
Contact: Mrs N Jayesinghe, Head of Prizes, Awards & Fellowships

The British Medical Association (BMA) is a professional association of doctors, representing their interests and providing services for its 122,000-plus members. It is an independent trade union, a scientific and educational body, and a publishing house.

Brackenbury Award

Subjects: Research of immediate practical importance to public health, to a medico-political or medico-sociological problem, or to an educational question, whether general, medical or postgraduate.
Purpose: To assist research in the field of public health.
Eligibility: Open to members of the BMA.
Level of Study: Postdoctorate.
Type: Research grant.

Value: Approx. UK £1,250.
Length of Study: Three years.
Frequency: Every three years.
Country of Study: United Kingdom.
No. of awards offered: One.
Application Procedure: Applicants must complete an application from, available in January of the award year.
Closing Date: Mid March.
Funding: Private.
No. of awards given last year: None.

C H Milburn Research Award

Subjects: Medical jurisprudence, forensic medicine or both.
Purpose: To assist and support research.
Eligibility: Open to registered medical practitioners.
Level of Study: Research.
Type: Research grant.
Value: Approx. UK £750.
Length of Study: Three years.
Frequency: Every three years.
Country of Study: United Kingdom.
No. of awards offered: One.
Application Procedure: Applicants must complete an application form.
Closing Date: Mid March.
Funding: Private.
No. of awards given last year: None.
Additional Information: Awards are advertised in January.

Doris Hillier Award

Subjects: Rheumatism and arthritis.
Purpose: To assist and support research.
Eligibility: Open to registered medical practitioners in the United Kingdom.
Level of Study: Research.
Type: Research grant.
Value: Approx. UK £17,500.
Length of Study: Three years.
Frequency: Annual.
Country of Study: United Kingdom.
No. of awards offered: One.
Application Procedure: Applicants must complete an application form.
Closing Date: Mid March.
Funding: Private.
No. of awards given last year: One.
Additional Information: Awards are advertised in January.

Doris Odlum Award

Subjects: Mental health.
Purpose: To assist and support research.
Eligibility: Open to medical practitioners registered in the British Commonwealth or the Republic of Ireland.
Level of Study: Research.
Type: Research grant.
Value: Approx. UK £600.
Length of Study: Three years.
Frequency: Every three years.
Country of Study: United Kingdom.
No. of awards offered: One.
Application Procedure: Applicants must complete an application form.
Closing Date: Mid March.
Funding: Private.
No. of awards given last year: None.
Additional Information: Awards are advertised in January.

Elizabeth Wherry and Charlotte Eyck Research Awards

Subjects: Kidney treatment.
Purpose: To assist and support research.

Eligibility: Open to registered medical practitioners in the United Kingdom.
Level of Study: Research.
Type: Research grant.
Value: Approx. UK £7,000.
Length of Study: Three years.
Frequency: Every two years.
Country of Study: United Kingdom.
No. of awards offered: One.
Application Procedure: Applicants must complete an application form.
Closing Date: Mid March.
Funding: Private.
No. of awards given last year: One.
Additional Information: Awards are advertised in January.

Geoffrey Holt, Ivy Powell and Edith Walsh Awards

Subjects: Cardiovascular disease.
Purpose: To assist and support research.
Eligibility: Open to members of the BMA.
Level of Study: Research.
Type: Research grant.
Value: Approx. UK £4,000.
Length of Study: Three years.
Frequency: Every two years.
Country of Study: United Kingdom.
No. of awards offered: One.
Application Procedure: Applicants must complete an application form, available in January.
Closing Date: Mid March.
Funding: Private.
No. of awards given last year: None.
Additional Information: Awards are advertised in January.

H C Roscoe Fellowship

Subjects: Elimination of the common cold or other viral diseases of the human respiratory system.
Purpose: To assist and support research.
Eligibility: Open to members of the BMA and non medical scientists working in association with a BMA member.
Level of Study: Research.
Type: Fellowship.
Value: Approx. UK £62,000.
Length of Study: Three years.
Frequency: Annual.
Country of Study: United Kingdom.
No. of awards offered: One.
Application Procedure: Applicants must complete an application form.
Closing Date: Mid March.
Funding: Private.
No. of awards given last year: One.
Additional Information: Awards are advertised in January.

Helen Tomkinson and Albert McMaster Research Awards

Subjects: Cancer research including health education.
Purpose: To assist research into cancer.
Eligibility: Open to members of the BMA.
Level of Study: Research.
Type: Research grant.
Value: Approx. UK £12,000 for the Tomkinson Award and approx. UK £9,000 for the McMaster Award.
Length of Study: Three years.
Frequency: Every two years.
Country of Study: United Kingdom.
No. of awards offered: Two.
Application Procedure: Applicants must complete an application form.
Closing Date: Mid March.
Funding: Private.

No. of awards given last year: None.
Additional Information: Awards are advertised in January.

nsole Award

Subjects: The cause, prevention and treatment of disease.
Purpose: To assist and support research.
Eligibility: Open to members of the BMA.
Level of Study: Research.
Type: Research grant.
Value: Approx. UK £750.
Length of Study: Three years.
Frequency: Every three years.
Country of Study: United Kingdom.
No. of awards offered: One.
Application Procedure: Applicants must complete an application form.
Closing Date: Mid March.
Funding: Private.
No. of awards given last year: One.
Additional Information: Awards are advertised in January.

Joan Dawkins Fellowship

Subjects: Biomedicine and preference is given to particular areas which are defined on an annual basis.
Purpose: To encourage, foster and maintain the highest possible standards in medical practice, medical learning and research.
Eligibility: Open to medical practitioners. Non medical scientists mayalso apply. Projects must relate to the United Kingdom.
Level of Study: Research.
Type: Fellowship.
Value: Approx. UK £60,000.
Length of Study: Three years.
Frequency: Annual.
Country of Study: United Kingdom.
No. of awards offered: Please contact the organisation.
Application Procedure: Applicants must complete an application form.
Closing Date: Mid March.
Funding: Private.
No. of awards given last year: Two.
Additional Information: Awards are advertised in January.

John William Clark Award

Subjects: The causes of blindness.
Purpose: To assist and support research.
Eligibility: Open to members of the BMA.
Level of Study: Research.
Type: Research grant.
Value: Approx. UK £6,500.
Length of Study: Three years.
Frequency: Every two years.
Country of Study: United Kingdom.
No. of awards offered: One.
Application Procedure: Applicants must complete an application form.
Closing Date: Mid March.
Funding: Private.
No. of awards given last year: One.
Additional Information: Awards are advertised in January.

Katherine Bishop Harman Award

Subjects: The diminution and avoidance of risks to women's health and life in pregnancy and childbearing.
Purpose: To assist and support research.
Eligibility: Open to medical practitioners registered in the United Kingdom or any other country which at any time formed part of the British Empire.
Level of Study: Research.
Type: Research grant.
Value: Approx. UK £1,000.
Length of Study: Three years.

Frequency: Every three years.
Country of Study: United Kingdom.
No. of awards offered: One.
Application Procedure: Applicants must complete an application form, available in January.
Closing Date: Mid March.
Funding: Private.
No. of awards given last year: None.

Margaret Temple Fellowship

Subjects: Psychiatry and mental health.
Purpose: To assist research into schizophrenia.
Eligibility: Open to medical practitioners. Non medical scientists may also apply. Projects must relate to the United Kingdom.
Level of Study: Research.
Type: Fellowship.
Value: Approx. UK £34,000.
Length of Study: Three years.
Frequency: Annual.
Country of Study: United Kingdom.
No. of awards offered: One.
Application Procedure: Applicants must complete an application form.
Closing Date: Mid March.
Funding: Private.
No. of awards given last year: One.
Additional Information: Awards are advertised in January.

Middlemore Award

Subjects: Any branch of ophthalmic medicine or surgery.
Purpose: To assist and support research.
Eligibility: Open to registered medical practitioners in the United Kingdom.
Level of Study: Research.
Type: Research grant.
Value: Approx. UK £1,250.
Length of Study: Three years.
Frequency: Every three years.
Country of Study: United Kingdom.
No. of awards offered: One.
Application Procedure: Applicants must complete an application form.
Closing Date: Mid March.
Funding: Private.
No. of awards given last year: None.
Additional Information: Awards are advertised in January.

Nathaniel Bishop Harman Award

Subjects: Hospital practice.
Purpose: To assist research into the outcome of treatment of a specific condition in hospital practice.
Eligibility: Open to registered medical practitioners on the staff of a hospital in Great Britain or Northern Ireland who are not members of staff of a recognised undergraduate or postgraduate medical school.
Level of Study: Research.
Type: Research grant.
Value: Approx. UK £700.
Length of Study: Three years.
Frequency: Every three years.
Country of Study: United Kingdom.
No. of awards offered: One.
Application Procedure: Applicants must complete an application form.
Closing Date: Mid March.
Funding: Private.
No. of awards given last year: One.
Additional Information: Awards are advertised in January.

Sir Charles Hastings and Charles Oliver Hawthorne Awards

Subjects: General practice, observation, research and record keeping.
Purpose: To assist research in general practice.
Eligibility: Open to members of the BMA engaged in general practice.
Level of Study: Research.
Type: Research grant.
Value: Approx. UK £2,350.
Length of Study: Three years.
Frequency: Every three years.
Country of Study: United Kingdom.
No. of awards offered: One.
Application Procedure: Applicants must complete an application form.
Closing Date: Mid March.
Funding: Private.
No. of awards given last year: None.
Additional Information: Awards are advertised in January.

T P Gunton Award

Subjects: Health education with special regard to the earlier diagnosis and treatment of cancer.
Purpose: To assist research into public health education relating to cancer.
Eligibility: Open to both medical and non medical scientists.
Level of Study: Research.
Type: Research grant.
Value: Approx. UK £17,500.
Length of Study: Three years.
Frequency: Annual.
Country of Study: United Kingdom.
No. of awards offered: One.
Application Procedure: Applicants must complete an application form, available in January.
Closing Date: Mid March.
Funding: Private.
No. of awards given last year: None.
Additional Information: Awards are advertised in January.

T V James Fellowship

Subjects: The nature, cause, prevention and treatment of bronchial asthma.
Purpose: To assist research into asthma.
Eligibility: Open to members of the BMA.
Level of Study: Research.
Type: Fellowship.
Value: Approx. UK £21,000.
Length of Study: Three years.
Frequency: Annual.
Country of Study: Any country.
No. of awards offered: One.
Application Procedure: Applicants must complete an application form.
Closing Date: Mid March.
Funding: Private.
No. of awards given last year: One.
Additional Information: Awards are advertised in January.

Vera Down Award

Subjects: Neurological disorders.
Purpose: To assist research into neurological disorders.
Eligibility: Open to registered medical practitioners in the United Kingdom.
Level of Study: Research.
Type: Research grant.
Value: Approx. UK £10,500.
Length of Study: Three years.
Frequency: Every two years.
Country of Study: United Kingdom.

No. of awards offered: One.
Application Procedure: Applicants must complete an application form.
Closing Date: Mid March.
Funding: Private.
No. of awards given last year: One.
Additional Information: Awards are advertised in January.

BRITISH PHARMACOLOGICAL SOCIETY

16 Angel Gate
City Road, London, EC1V 2SG, England
Tel: (44) 20 7417 0114
Email: admin@bps.ac.uk
www: http://www.bps.ac.uk
Contact: Ms Sarah-Jane Stagg, Executive Officer

The British Pharmacological Society is a learned society concerned with research into drugs and the way they work. Its members work in academia, industry and the health services, and many are medically qualified.

A J Clark Studentship

Subjects: Pharmacology.
Purpose: To enable young scientists with degrees in pharmacology or closely related subjects to carry out research in pharmacology leading to the degree of a PhD in a recognised department in the United Kingdom.
Eligibility: Candidates should intend to follow a career in pharmacology.
Level of Study: Doctorate.
Type: PhD studentship.
Value: Annual stipend contribution of £1,500 to research costs. Fees are at European Union student rates.
Length of Study: Three years.
Frequency: Annual.
Study Establishment: A recognised department in the United Kingdom.
Country of Study: United Kingdom.
No. of awards offered: Two.
Application Procedure: Applicants must complete an application form, available from the Society.
Closing Date: February 7th.
Funding: Private.
No. of awards given last year: Two.
Additional Information: Applications must be accompanied by a covering letter from the proposed supervisor giving the agreement of the university or other organisation to accept the student if he or she receives an award. A detailed plan of the three year research project must also be submitted.

BRITISH RETINITIS PIGMENTOSA SOCIETY (BRPS)

PO Box 350, Buckingham, Buckinghamshire, MK18 1GZ, England
Tel: (44) 1280 860363
Fax: (44) 1280 815900
Email: lynda@brps.demon.co.uk
www: http://www.brps.demon.co.uk
Contact: Mrs Lynda M Cantor, Honorary Secretary

The British Retinitis Pigmentosa Society (BRPS) is a membership organisation run by volunteers with over 35 branches throughout the United Kingdom. The BRPS aims to raise funds for scientific research to provide treatments leading to a cure for Retinitis Pigmentosa. The Society provides a welfare support and guidance service to its members and their families.

BRPS Research Grants

Subjects: Retinitis Pigmentosa.

Purpose: To financially support research into treatments leading to cure for Retinitis Pigmentosa.

Eligibility: Please contact the Society.

Level of Study: Postgraduate.

Type: Research grant.

Value: Varies. Grants awarded to countries outside of the United Kingdom are made in sterling. Should sterling fall in value against the currency of the country in which the recipient of the grant works, the Society will not make good the shortfall. Unless otherwise stated the Research Grant will not provide for overheads or indirect expenses.

Length of Study: Varies.

Frequency: Annual.

Country of Study: Any country.

No. of awards offered: Varies.

Application Procedure: Applicants must submit their application to the BRPS office.

Closing Date: Grant applications should be at the BRPS office at least six weeks prior to the Board of Trustees meeting. Dates of these meetings are supplied on request from the Honorary Secretary.

Additional Information: Unless otherwise stated Research Grants are renewable annually upon recommendation of the Scientific Advisory Board, based on the recipients' annual progress reports which should be received in the 10th month of each research year. Progress reports should include a description of the work carried out for the purpose of the original project, the programme of work for the ensuring year and details of problems encountered with specific experimental methods and should cover at least two sides of an A4 sheet. At the conclusion of the project a final report must be submitted. Equipment or apparatus donated is for the purpose of RP research and should be maintained in good working order by the recipient. If a particular research project is completed, abandoned or discontinued the apparatus and equipment should be placed at the disposal of BRPS. The BRPS National Secretariat must be notified of any increase in salaries that are awarded either nationally or by the university or institution concerned at the time it is agreed. It is the responsibility of the recipient to inform the Secretariat of any relevant changes. Recipients must inform the Society of the exact date they commence work on their project.

BRITISH SCHOOL AT ATHENS

Odos Souedias 52, Athens, GR-10676, Greece
Tel: (30) 1 721 0974
Fax: (30) 1 723 6560
Email: admin@bsa.ac.uk
www: http://www.bsa.gla.ac.uk
Contact: Ms Rebecca Sweetman, Assistant Director

The British School at Athens provides facilities for research into the archaeology, architecture, art, history, language, literature, religion and topography of Greece in ancient, medieval and modern times. It consists of a hostel, library, archive, museum, the Fitch Laboratory for Archaeological Science and a second base at Knossos for excavation and research.

Hector and Elizabeth Catling Bursary

Subjects: Research in Greek studies including the archaeology, art, history, language, literature, religion, ethnography, anthropology, geography of any period and all branches of archaeological science.

Eligibility: Open to researchers of British, Irish or Commonwealth nationality.

Level of Study: Doctorate, Postdoctorate, Postgraduate.

Type: Bursary.

Value: A maximum UK £500 per bursary to assist with travel and maintenance costs incurred in fieldwork, to pay for the use of

scientific or other specialised equipment in or outside the laboratory in Greece or elsewhere and to buy necessary supplies.

Frequency: Annual, if funds are available.

Study Establishment: The British School at Athens.

Country of Study: Greece or Cyprus.

No. of awards offered: One-two.

Application Procedure: Applicants must submit a curriculum vitae and state concisely the nature of the intended work, a breakdown of budget, the amount requested from the Fund and how this will be spent. Applications should include two sealed letters of reference. Bursary holders must submit a short report to the Committee on completion of the project.

Closing Date: December 15th for notification by the end of February.

Funding: Private.

No. of awards given last year: Two.

No. of applicants last year: Five.

Additional Information: The bursary is not intended for publication costs, and can not be awarded to an excavation or field survey team.

Macmillan-Rodewald Studentship, School Studentship, Cary Studentship

Subjects: Research into the archaeology, architecture, art, history, language, literature, religion and topography of Greece in ancient, medieval and modern times.

Eligibility: Open to graduates of British, Irish or Commonwealth nationality.

Level of Study: Doctorate, Postdoctorate, Postgraduate.

Type: Studentship.

Value: Grant awards are related to British Academy postgraduate award levels.

Length of Study: One year, renewable upon reapplication.

Frequency: Annual.

Study Establishment: The British School at Athens.

Country of Study: Greece.

No. of awards offered: Three.

Application Procedure: Applicants must submit a curriculum vitae and a statement of their proposed course study with reasons for pursuing it in Greece. Applications must include the names of two referees.

Closing Date: May 1st.

No. of awards given last year: Three.

No. of applicants last year: 17.

Additional Information: The student is required to spend a minimum of eight months in Greece, normally residing in the School when in Athens, and to undertake such duties in and for the School as the Director enjoins.

For further information contact:

The British School at Athens
Senate House
Malet Street, London, WC1E 7HU, England

THE BRITISH SCHOOL AT ROME (BSR)

The British Academy
10 Carlton House Terrace, London, SW1Y 5AH, England
Tel: (44) 20 7969 5202
Fax: (44) 20 7969 5401
Email: bsr@britac.ac.uk
www: http://www.bsr.ac.uk
Contact: Dr Gillian Clark, Registrar

The British School at Rome is an interdisciplinary research centre for the humanities, visual arts and architecture. Each year the School offers a range of awards in its principal fields of interest. These interests are further promoted by public lectures, conferences, publications, archaeological research and an excellent reference library.

Abbey Fellowships in Painting

Subjects: Painting.
Purpose: To give mid-career artists the opportunity of working in Rome.
Eligibility: Open to mid-career painters with an established record of achievement. Applicants must be citizens of the United Kingdom or United States of America.
Type: Fellowship.
Value: UK £480 per month plus UK £180 travel allowance.
Length of Study: Three months.
Frequency: Annual.
Study Establishment: The British School at Rome.
Country of Study: Italy.
No. of awards offered: Three.
Application Procedure: Applicants must complete an application form and pay an application fee.
Closing Date: Early to mid January.
Funding: Private.
Contributor: The Abbey Council.
No. of awards given last year: Four.

For further information contact:

Administrator
E A Abbey Scholarship
43 Carson Road, London, SE21 8HT, England

Abbey Scholarship in Painting

Subjects: Painting.
Purpose: To give exceptionally promising emergent painters the opportunity to work in Rome.
Eligibility: Open to United Kingdom and United States citizens.
Level of Study: Unrestricted.
Type: Scholarship.
Value: UK £4,500 plus board and lodging at the British School at Rome.
Length of Study: Nine months.
Frequency: Annual.
Study Establishment: The British School at Rome.
Country of Study: Italy.
No. of awards offered: One.
Application Procedure: Applicants must complete an application form and pay an application fee.
Closing Date: Early to mid January.
Funding: Private.
Contributor: The Abbey Council.
No. of awards given last year: One.

For further information contact:

E A Abbey Scholarships
43 Carson Road, London, SE21 8HT, England

Arts Council of England Helen Chadwick Fellowship

Subjects: Visual arts.
Purpose: To allow artists to pursue a project which could be made possible or enhanced by spending periods of time in Rome and Oxford.
Eligibility: Open to visual artists who have established their practices in the years following graduation. Applicants must be United Kingdom nationals or have been continuously resident in the United Kingdom since March 1999.
Level of Study: Professional development.
Type: Fellowship.
Value: UK £600 per month plus travel and materials allowances, and board and lodging at the British School in Rome and in Oxford.
Length of Study: Six months.
Frequency: Annual.
Study Establishment: The British School at Rome and Ruskin School of Drawing and Fine Art at the University of Oxford.
Country of Study: Italy or United Kingdom.
No. of awards offered: One.

Application Procedure: Applicants must write for details of the application procedure.
Closing Date: Early January.
Funding: Private.
Contributor: The Arts Council of England.
No. of awards given last year: One.

For further information contact:

The Laboratory
Ruskin School of Drawing & Fine Art
University of Oxford
74 High Street, Oxford, Oxfordshire, OX1 4BG, England

Balsdon Fellowship

Subjects: Archaeology, art history, history and literature of Italy from prehistory to the modern period.
Purpose: To enable senior scholars engaged in research to spend a period in Rome to further their studies.
Eligibility: Open to established Scholars normally in post in a United Kingdom university. Applicants must be United Kingdom or Commonwealth nationals, or have been working professionally or studying at graduate level for more than three years within the United Kingdom or the Commonwealth. Normally applicants will be working at a university in the United Kingdom.
Level of Study: Postdoctorate.
Type: Fellowship.
Value: UK £650 plus board and lodging at the British School at Rome.
Length of Study: Three months.
Frequency: Annual.
Study Establishment: The British School at Rome.
Country of Study: Italy.
No. of awards offered: One.
Application Procedure: Applicants must complete an application form.
Closing Date: Early January.
Funding: Private.
Contributor: A bequest from the British School at Rome.
No. of awards given last year: One.

Hugh Last Fellowship

Subjects: Classical antiquity.
Purpose: To enable established scholars to collect research material concerning classical antiquity.
Eligibility: Open to established Scholars normally posted in a United Kingdom university who are United Kingdom or Commonwealth nationals, and have been working professionally or studying at graduate level for more than three years within the United Kingdom or the Commonwealth. Normally applicants should be working at a university in the United Kingdom.
Level of Study: Postdoctorate.
Type: Fellowship.
Value: Board and lodging at the British School at Rome plus a research grant.
Length of Study: One-four months.
Frequency: Annual.
Study Establishment: The British School at Rome.
Country of Study: Italy.
No. of awards offered: One-two.
Application Procedure: Applicants must complete an application form.
Closing Date: Early January.
Funding: Private.
Contributor: A bequest from the British School at Rome.
No. of awards given last year: One.

Paul Mellon Centre Rome Fellowship

Subjects: Anglo-Italian cultural and artistic relations.
Purpose: To assist research on the Grand Tour or on Anglo-Italian cultural and artistic relations.

Eligibility: Open to established Scholars in the United Kingdom, United States or elsewhere. Applicants should have fairly fluent Italian.
Level of Study: Postdoctorate.
Type: Fellowship.
Value: UK £1,000 per month plus travel allowance, board and lodging at the British School at Rome.
Length of Study: Two-six months.
Frequency: Annual.
Study Establishment: The British School at Rome.
Country of Study: Italy.
No. of awards offered: One-two.
Application Procedure: Applicants must contact the Paul Mellon Centre for Studies in British Art for details.
Funding: Private.
Contributor: The Paul Mellon Centre for Studies in British Art.

For further information contact:

The Paul Mellon Centre for Studies in British Art
16 Bedford Square, London, WC1B 3JA, England
Tel: (44) 20 7580 0311
Fax: (44) 20 7636 6730
Email: info@paul-mellon-centre.ac.uk

Rome Awards in Archaeology, History and Letters

Subjects: Archaeology, art history, history and literature of Italy from prehistory to the modern period.
Purpose: To enable persons engaged in research, either for a higher degree or at early postdoctoral level, to spend a period in Rome to further their studies.
Eligibility: Open to United Kingdom or Commonwealth citizens and to those who have been working professionally or studying at postgraduate level for more than three years in the United Kingdom or Commonwealth. Applicants should normally have begun a programme of research in the general field for which the scholarship is being sought, whether or not they are registered for a higher degree. Normally applicants should be attached to or registered at a university in the United Kingdom.
Level of Study: Doctorate, Postdoctorate, Postgraduate.
Type: Grant.
Value: UK £150 per month plus UK £180 travel, and board and lodging at the British School at Rome.
Length of Study: One-four months.
Frequency: Annual.
Study Establishment: The British School at Rome.
Country of Study: Italy.
No. of awards offered: Varies.
Application Procedure: Applicants must complete an application form.
Closing Date: Early January.
No. of awards given last year: Five.

Rome Scholarship in Architecture

Subjects: Architecture and urbanism relevant to Rome and Italy.
Purpose: To encourage the pursuit of projects in architecture and urbanism relevant to Rome and Italy.
Eligibility: Open to architects and students of architecture and associated disciplines of at least post-diploma level who are British or Commonwealth nationals, and to those who have been working professionally or studying at postgraduate level for more than three years in the United Kingdom or Commonwealth.
Level of Study: Postgraduate, Professional development.
Type: Scholarship.
Value: UK £500 per month plus board and lodging at the British School at Rome.
Length of Study: Three-nine months.
Frequency: Annual.
Study Establishment: The British School at Rome.
Country of Study: Italy.
No. of awards offered: One-two.

Application Procedure: Applicants must complete an application form and pay an application fee. Application forms are available from the British School at Rome Registrar.
Closing Date: Mid January.
No. of awards given last year: One.

Rome Scholarships in Ancient, Medieval and Later Italian Studies

Subjects: Archaeology, art history, history and literature of Italy from prehistory to the modern period.
Purpose: To enable persons engaged in research, either for a higher degree or at early postdoctoral level, to spend a period in Rome to further their studies.
Eligibility: Open to United Kingdom or Commonwealth citizens and to those who have been working professionally or studying at postgraduate level for more than three years in the United Kingdom or Commonwealth. Applicants should normally have begun a programme of research in the general field for which the scholarship is being sought, whether or not registered for a higher degree. Normally applicants should be attached to or registered at a university in the United Kingdom.
Level of Study: Doctorate, Postdoctorate, Postgraduate.
Type: Scholarship.
Value: UK £4,000 plus board and lodging at the British School in Rome.
Length of Study: Nine months.
Frequency: Annual.
Study Establishment: The British School at Rome.
Country of Study: Italy.
No. of awards offered: Four.
Application Procedure: Applicants must complete an application form.
Closing Date: Early January.
No. of awards given last year: Four.

Rome Scholarships in the Fine Arts

Subjects: Painting, printmaking, sculpture and other suitable media (including video and photography).
Purpose: To give emerging and early to mid-career artists the opportunity to work in Rome.
Eligibility: Open to United Kingdom or Commonwealth citizens who have been working professionally or studying at postgraduate level for more than three years in the United Kingdom or Commonwealth.
Level of Study: Postgraduate.
Type: Scholarship.
Value: UK £500 per month plus board and lodging at the British School at Rome.
Length of Study: Three-nine months.
Frequency: Annual.
Study Establishment: The British School at Rome.
Country of Study: Italy.
No. of awards offered: Varies.
Application Procedure: Applicants must complete an application form and pay an application fee.
Closing Date: Early December.
No. of awards given last year: Three.

Sainsbury Scholarship in Painting and Sculpture

Subjects: Painting and sculpture in which a commitment to drawing can be demonstrated clearly.
Purpose: To give emerging artists the opportunity to work in Rome.
Eligibility: Open to United Kingdom citizens and to those who have been working professionally or studying at postgraduate level for at least the last three years in the United Kingdom. Applicants must be under 28 on the first of October in the year in which they would begin to hold the scholarship.
Level of Study: Postgraduate.
Type: Scholarship.
Value: UK £750 per month plus board and lodging at the British School at Rome and a travel grant of UK £3,600.

Length of Study: Twelve months with, at the discretion of the selection committee, an opportunity for a further nine months in the following academy year.

Frequency: Annual.

Study Establishment: The British School at Rome.

Country of Study: Italy.

No. of awards offered: One.

Application Procedure: Applicants must complete an application form and pay an application fee.

Closing Date: Early December.

Funding: Private.

Contributor: The Linbury Trust.

Sargant Fellowship

Subjects: Sculpture, drawing and painting, fine art video and photography, architecture and town planning.

Purpose: To enable distinguished artists and architects to spend three to nine months in Rome developing their work.

Eligibility: Open to United Kingdom and Commonwealth nationals and to those who have been working professionally for more than three years in the United Kingdom or Commonwealth.

Level of Study: Unrestricted.

Type: Fellowship.

Value: UK £1,000 per month plus UK £500 travel and board and lodging at the British School at Rome.

Length of Study: Three-nine months.

Frequency: Annual.

Study Establishment: The British School at Rome.

Country of Study: Italy.

No. of awards offered: Varies.

Application Procedure: Applicants must write to the British School at Rome for the precise application procedure.

Closing Date: January.

Funding: Private.

Contributor: A bequest from the British School at Rome.

Wingate Rome Scholarship in the Fine Arts

Subjects: Painting, printmaking, sculpture and other suitable media including fine art video and photography.

Purpose: To give emerging and early to mid-career artists the opportunity to work in Rome.

Eligibility: Open to United Kingdom and Commonwealth nationals and to those who have been working professionally or studying at postgraduate level for more than three years in the United Kingdom or Commonwealth.

Level of Study: Postgraduate, Professional development.

Type: Scholarship.

Value: UK £500 per month plus board and lodging at the British School at Rome.

Length of Study: Three or six months.

Frequency: Annual.

Study Establishment: The British School at Rome.

Country of Study: Italy.

No. of awards offered: One-two.

Application Procedure: Applicants must complete an application form and pay an application fee.

Closing Date: Early December.

Funding: Private.

Contributor: The Harold Hyam Wingate Foundation.

No. of awards given last year: One.

BRITISH SCHOOL OF ARCHAEOLOGY IN IRAQ

10 Carlton House Terrace, London, SW1Y 5AH, England
Tel: (44) 20 7969 5274
Fax: (44) 20 7969 5401
Email: bsai@britac.ac.uk
www: http://users.ox.ac/~neareast/bsaistfo.htm
Contact: Honorary Secretary

The British School of Archaeology in Iraq's aim is to encourage and support the study of, and research relating to, the archaeology, history and languages of Iraq and its neighbouring countries including East Syria and the Gulf, from the earliest times to the end of the seventeenth-century AD.

British School of Archaeology in Iraq Grants

Subjects: Archaeology, history and the languages of Iraq and neighbouring countries from the earliest time to the eighteenth-century.

Purpose: To encourage and support research into the archaeology (and cognate subjects), history and languages of Iraq and its neighbouring countries.

Eligibility: Open to residents of the United Kingdom or Commonwealth citizens who are postgraduates with a knowledge of Western-Asiatic archaeology.

Level of Study: Postdoctorate, Postgraduate.

Type: Grant.

Value: Usually between UK £500 and UK £3,000, depending on the nature of the research.

Length of Study: One academic year.

Frequency: Annual.

Country of Study: Normally Iraq or neighbouring countries when possible, for at least some of the period of tenure. Until work in Iraq can be resumed, grants are available for studying primary material outside Iraq, whether in the field or in museums.

No. of awards offered: Varies.

Application Procedure: The School considers applications for individual research grants twice a year, in Spring and Autumn. For grants of up to UK £1,000, there is no application form. For grants of UK £1,000 or more, information and application forms are available from the Secretary. Two references are required.

Closing Date: April 15th and October 15th for grants of up to UK £1,000, and October 15th for major research grants of UK £1,000 or over.

Funding: Government.

No. of awards given last year: 14.

Additional Information: Details of the British School of Archaeology in Iraq are available on the website under Institutes Overseas and Sponsored Societies. Grantees will be required to provide a written report of their work and abstracts from these reports will be published in future issues of the BSAI Newsletter. Individual Research Grants are offered, as are Major Research Grants.

THE BRITISH SCHOOLS AND UNIVERSITIES FOUNDATION, INC. (BSUF)

12 Pilgrims Way, Guildford, Surrey, GU4 8AB, England
Tel: (44) 1483 575588
Contact: Mrs Sheila Wiltshire, Honorary Director

The British Schools and Universities Foundation (BSUF) makes grants to educational, scientific or literary institutes in the United Kingdom and in member nations of the British Commonwealth. The Foundation also fosters the education and academic work of United States scholars and students at British institutions and vice versa. It also provides a way for United States tax payers to make tax deductible gifts to the United Kingdom for colleges and schools.

British Schools and Universities Foundation May and Ward Scholarships

Subjects: All subjects.
Purpose: To promote, foster and assist the education and academic work of British scholars and students at United States educational institutions and of United States scholars and students at British educational institutions.
Eligibility: Open to Scholars from the United States of America, United Kingdom, Australia, Canada and New Zealand.
Level of Study: Doctorate, Postgraduate, Professional development.
Type: Scholarship.
Value: US$12,500 maximum.
Length of Study: A maximum of two years.
Frequency: Annual.
Study Establishment: Educational institutions in the United States for United Kingdom candidates or educational institutions in the United Kingdom for American candidates.
Country of Study: United States of America or United Kingdom.
No. of awards offered: Four-six.
Application Procedure: Applicants must obtain an application form from the representative. Please enclose a stamped addressed envelope with the request.
Closing Date: March 1st, for an award to commence the following September.
Funding: Private.
Contributor: Donors in the United States of America.
No. of awards given last year: Five.
No. of applicants last year: 150.

For further information contact:

BSUF
Suite 1006
575 Madison Avenue, New York, NY, 10022-2511, United States of America

May and Ward Scholarships British Schools and Universities

Subjects: All subjects.
Purpose: To support United States scholars at United Kingdom educational, literary and scientific institutions and British scholars in the United States.
Eligibility: Applicants must provide a strong rationale for attending an institution abroad and give evidence if possible. They must be attending or graduates (usually) of an accredited institute of learning.
Level of Study: Doctorate, Graduate, Postgraduate, Predoctorate, Professional development, Research.
Type: Scholarship.
Value: US$12,500 annually.
Length of Study: One-two years.
Frequency: Annual.
Study Establishment: A college, university or research establishment in United States of America for United Kingdom applicants and educational institutions in the United Kingdom for United States applicants.
Country of Study: United States of America or United Kingdom.
No. of awards offered: Four-six.
Application Procedure: Applicants must apply for an application form and guidelines to BSUF representative at the London address if in the United Kingdom, and at the New York address if in the United States of America.
Closing Date: March 1st.
Funding: Private.
Contributor: British Schools and Universities Foundation.
No. of awards given last year: Five.
No. of applicants last year: 150+.

For further information contact:

BSUF
Suite 1006
575 Madison Avenue, New York, NY, 10022-2511, United States of America

BRITISH SOCIOLOGICAL ASSOCIATION (BSA)

Units 3F/G
Mountjoy Research Centre
Stockton Road, Durham, DH1 3UR, England
Tel: (44) 191 383 0839
Fax: (44) 191 383 0782
Email: enquiries@britsoc.org.uk
www: http://www.britsoc.org.uk/index.htm
Contact: Henk Geertsema, Marketing/Information Officer

The British Sociological Association (BSA) is the learned society and professional association for sociology in Britain.

BSA Support Fund

Subjects: Sociology.
Purpose: To support United Kingdom BSA members who are full-time students, unwaged, or in receipt of benefits to pursue their research interests in sociology.
Eligibility: Open to current paid up and concessionary rate members of the BSA, resident in the United Kingdom.
Level of Study: Unrestricted.
Type: Support fund.
Value: Up to UK £150 per year, to cover costs associated with research, but not tuition fees, equipment or text book purchase.
Frequency: Annual.
Country of Study: United Kingdom.
No. of awards offered: Approx. 30.
Application Procedure: Applicants must obtain an application form from the BSA office.
Funding: Private.
No. of awards given last year: 28.
No. of applicants last year: 28.

THE BRITISH UNIVERSITIES NORTH AMERICA CLUB (BUNAC)

16 Bowling Green Lane, London, EC1R 0QH, England
Tel: (44) 20 7251 3472
Fax: (44) 20 7251 0215
Email: scholarships@bunac.org.uk
www: http://www.bunac.org
Contact: Ms Sarah Frampton

The British Universities North America Club (BUNAC) is a leader in the field of international work and travel exchange programmes. A non-profit, non-political organisation offering an ever-increasing range of programmes worldwide, BUNAC is dedicated to serving students and other young people everywhere by providing opportunities to live and work abroad legally overseas.

BUNAC Educational Scholarship Trust (BEST)

Subjects: All subjects. Some awards are specifically for sports and geography related courses.
Purpose: To help further Anglo-American understanding.
Eligibility: Open to United Kingdom citizens who have recently graduated from a United Kingdom university ie. within the last five years. Candidates must have a First Class Degree.
Level of Study: Postgraduate.
Type: Scholarship.
Value: From a total of US$25,000, approx. US$3,000.
Length of Study: Three months to three years.
Frequency: Annual.
Study Establishment: An American university or college.
Country of Study: United States of America or Canada.
No. of awards offered: 10.
Application Procedure: Applicants must complete an application form, available in January each year.

Closing Date: March 25th.
Funding: Commercial.
No. of awards given last year: Six.
No. of applicants last year: 90.

BRITISH VASCULAR FOUNDATION

Fides House
10 Chertsey Road, Woking, Surrey, GU21 5AB, England
Tel: (44) 1483 726511
Fax: (44) 1483 726522
Email: bvf@care4free.net
www: http://www.bvf.org.uk
Contact: K Lody, Office Manager

The British Vascular Foundation aims to provide research funding to find cures, better treatments and improve diagnosis of vascular disease. The Foundation also hopes to raise awareness of the disease's prevalence and impact and to provide information and support to sufferers, their families and friends.

Owen Shaw Award

Subjects: Applications are invited from departments of vascular surgery, interested in devising better methods of helping patients mobilise earlier.
Purpose: To improve mobility and rehabilitation of amputees.
Eligibility: Open to vascular surgical staff with an interest in amputee rehabilitation.
Level of Study: Unrestricted.
Type: Project grant for pilot study.
Value: UK £3,000.
Length of Study: One year.
Frequency: Annual.
Study Establishment: Any restricted research establishment.
Country of Study: United Kingdom.
No. of awards offered: One.
Application Procedure: Applicants must complete an outline proposal form, available from the Foundation.
Closing Date: January 31st.
Funding: Private.
Contributor: Owen Shaw.
No. of awards given last year: One.
No. of applicants last year: Five.

BRITISH VETERINARY ASSOCIATION

7 Mansfield Street, London, W1G 9NQ, England
Tel: (44) 20 7636 6541
Fax: (44) 20 7637 4769
Email: press@bva.co.uk
Contact: Mrs Helena Cotton

The British Veterinary Association's chief interests are the standards of animal health, and veterinary surgeons' working practices. The organisation's main functions are the development of policy in areas affecting the profession, protecting and promoting the profession in matters propounded by government and other external bodies, and the provision of services to members.

Harry Steele-Bodger Memorial Travelling Scholarship

Subjects: Veterinary science and agriculture.
Purpose: To further the aims and aspirations of the late Harry Steele-Bodger.
Eligibility: Open to graduates of veterinary schools in the United Kingdom or the Republic of Ireland who have been qualified for not more than three years, and to penultimate or final year students at those schools.
Level of Study: Unrestricted.

Type: Scholarship.
Value: Approx. UK £1,100.
Frequency: Annual.
Study Establishment: A veterinary or agricultural research institute or some other course of study approved by the governing committee.
Country of Study: Any country.
No. of awards offered: One.
Application Procedure: Applicants must complete an application form, available on request.
Closing Date: April 6th.
Funding: Private.
No. of awards given last year: One.
No. of applicants last year: 10.
Additional Information: Recipients must be prepared to submit a record of their study abroad.

BROAD MEDICAL RESEARCH PROGRAM (BMRP)

The Eli & Edythe L Broad Foundation
10900 Wilshire Boulevard
12th Floor, Los Angeles, CA, 90024-6532, United States of America
Tel: (1) 310 954 5091
Fax: (1) 310 954 5092
Email: info@broadmedical.org
www: http://www.broadmedical.org
Contact: Dr Daniel Hollander, Director

The Eli and Edythe L Broad Foundation was established in 1967. In 2001, the Foundation created the Broad Medical Research Program (BMRP) Inflammatory Bowel Disease (IBD) Grants. The BMRP will fund innovative and early exploratory basic and clinical projects on the aetiology, management and prevention of IBD.

Inflammatory Bowel Disease Grants

Subjects: Understanding and treating IBD.
Purpose: The BMRP seeks to stimulate innovative research that will lead to both the prevention and successful therapy of IBD. The BMRP's goal is to fund basic or clinical research projects that are in the early stages of exploration, that propose new directions or ideas that are creative, novel, cutting edge and imaginative and are not ready for funding by other more traditional granting agencies.
Eligibility: Grants will only be awarded to non-profit organisations, such as universities, hospitals and research institutes. There are no other eligibility restrictions. In addition to experienced IBD researchers, the BMRP wishes to encourage applications from well trained scientists who are not currently working in IBD to apply their knowledge, expertise and techniques to IBD research. Interdisciplinary collaboration is strongly encouraged.
Level of Study: Research.
Type: Research grant.
Value: Approx. US$100,000. Budgets should be commensurate with the scope of the work. Applicants who need less funds are encouraged to apply. Those who will need significantly more than US$100,000 should contact the BMRP before preparing their letters of interest.
Length of Study: One year, with limited renewal possible.
Country of Study: Any country.
No. of awards offered: No set number.
Application Procedure: Applicants must submit a request for funding, preceded by a brief letter of interest of between one and three pages. Please visit the website for information as to content and application process. Investigators whose letters of interest appear to fit the BMRP's aims will be invited to submit full proposals.
Closing Date: There are no deadlines for receipt of letters of interest.
Funding: Private.
Contributor: Eli and Edythe L Broad.

Additional Information: IBD refers to two chronic inflammatory disorders: Crohn's disease (ileitis) and ulcerative colitis. Both diseases result in inflammation of the intestinal wall, but differ in location and depth of inflammation. It is estimated that up to one million people in the United States are affected with IBD, which occurs predominantly in urban areas of North America and Europe. Primary symptoms include abdominal pain, bleeding, diarrhoea, weight loss and fever. There can be secondary complications, such as joint, eye, skin and liver problems. In patients with mild symptoms, medications can control the disease. However, for those with severe IBD, hospitalisations, surgery, transfusions and intravenous feeding may be needed. Although scientific advances have been made in understanding and treating IBD, the precise cause, successful treatment and prevention of IBD remain unknown.

BROADCAST EDUCATION ASSOCIATION (BEA) SCHOLARSHIP COMMITTEE

344 Moore Hall
Central Michigan University, Mount Pleasant, MI, 48859, United States of America
Tel: (1) 989 774 7279
Fax: (1) 989 774 2426
Email: peter.b.orlik@cmich.edu
www: http://www.beaweb.org
Contact: Dr Peter B Orlik, Scholarship Chair

The Broadcast Education Association (BEA) is the professional association for professors, industry professionals and graduate students interested in teaching and research relating to television, radio and the electronic media industry.

Abe Voron Scholarship
Subjects: Radio.
Purpose: To assist study towards a career in radio.
Eligibility: The applicant must be able to show substantial evidence of superior academic performance and potential to be an outstanding electronic media professional. There should be compelling evidence that the applicant possesses high integrity and a well articulated sense of personal and professional responsibility.
Level of Study: Graduate.
Type: Scholarship.
Value: US$5,000.
Frequency: Annual.
Study Establishment: Scholarships may be used only at BEA Member Institutions.
Country of Study: Any country in which a BEA Member Institution is located.
No. of awards offered: One.
Application Procedure: Applicants must obtain an official application form from the BEA or from campus faculty. Refer to the website for more details.
Closing Date: September 15th.
Funding: Private.
Contributor: The Abe Voron Committee.
No. of awards given last year: One.
No. of applicants last year: 25.

Alexander M Tanger Scholarships
Subjects: Broadcasting.
Purpose: To assist study for a career in any area of broadcasting.
Eligibility: The applicant must be able to show substantial evidence of superior academic performance and potential to be an outstanding electronic media professional. There should be compelling evidence that the applicant possesses high integrity and a well articulated sense of personal and professional responsibility.
Level of Study: Graduate.
Type: Scholarship.
Value: US$5,000.
Frequency: Annual.

Study Establishment: Scholarships may be used only at BEA Member Institutions.
Country of Study: Any country in which a BEA Member Institution is located.
No. of awards offered: One.
Application Procedure: Applicants must obtain an official application form from the BEA or from campus faculty. Refer to the website for more details.
Closing Date: September 15th.
Funding: Private.
Contributor: Alex M Tanger.
No. of awards given last year: Two.
No. of applicants last year: 60.

Andrew M Economos Scholarship
Subjects: Radio.
Purpose: To support study towards a career in radio.
Eligibility: The applicant must be able to show substantial evidence of superior academic performance and potential to be an outstanding electronic media professional. There should be compelling evidence that the applicant possesses high integrity and a well articulated sense of personal and professional responsibility.
Type: Scholarship.
Value: US$5,000.
Frequency: Annual.
Study Establishment: Scholarships may be used only at BEA Member Institutions.
Country of Study: Any country in which a BEA Member Institution is located.
No. of awards offered: One.
Application Procedure: Applicants must obtain an official application form from the BEA or campus faculty. Refer to the website for more details.
Closing Date: September 15th.
Funding: Private.
Contributor: The RCS Charitable Foundation.
No. of awards given last year: One.
No. of applicants last year: 35.

The Broadcast Education Association Neil Patterson Scholarship
Subjects: For study in the field of digital television.
Eligibility: The applicant must be able to show substantial evidence of superior academic performance and potential to be an outstanding electronic media professional. There should be compelling evidence that the applicant possesses high integrity and a well articulated sense of personal and professional responsibility.
Level of Study: Graduate.
Value: US$1,500.
Frequency: Annual.
No. of awards offered: One.
Application Procedure: Applicants must obtain an official application form from the BEA or campus faculty. Refer to the website for more details.
Closing Date: September 15th.
Funding: Private.
Contributor: Sponsored by the SilverKnight Group, New York.
No. of awards given last year: One.
No. of applicants last year: 30.

The Broadcasters' Foundation Helen J Sioussat Scholarships
Subjects: Any area of broadcasting.
Purpose: To assist study in any area of broadcasting.
Eligibility: The applicant must be able to show substantial evidence of superior academic performance and potential to be an outstanding electronic media professional. There should be compelling evidence that the applicant possesses high integrity and a well articulated sense of personal and professional responsibility.
Level of Study: Graduate.
Type: Scholarship.

Value: US$1,250 each.
Frequency: Annual.
Study Establishment: Scholarships may be used only at BEA Member Institutions.
Country of Study: Any country in which a BEA Member Institution is located.
No. of awards offered: Two.
Application Procedure: Applicants must obtain an official application form from the BEA or campus faculty. Refer to the website for moire details.
Closing Date: September 15th.
Funding: Private.
No. of awards given last year: Two.
No. of applicants last year: 80.

Country Radio Broadcasters, Inc.

Subjects: Radio broadcasting.
Purpose: To assist those who are studying towards a career in radio.
Eligibility: The applicant must be able to show substantial evidence of superior academic performance and potential to be an outstanding electronic media professional. There should be compelling evidence that the applicant possesses high integrity and a well articulated sense of personal and professional responsibility.
Level of Study: Graduate.
Value: US$3,000.
Frequency: Annual.
No. of awards offered: 10.
Application Procedure: Applicants must obtain an official application form from the BEA or campus faculty. Refer to the website for more details.
Closing Date: September 15th.
Funding: Private.
Contributor: Country Radio Broadcasters, Inc., in Nashville, Tennessee.
No. of awards given last year: 13.
No. of applicants last year: 80.

NAB Harold E Fellows Scholarships

Subjects: Broadcasting.
Purpose: To assist study in any area of broadcasting.
Eligibility: The applicant must be able to show substantial evidence of superior academic performance and potential to be an outstanding electronic media professional. There should be compelling evidence that the applicant possesses high integrity and a well articulated sense of personal and professional responsibility. Also, the applicant must have worked for pay or college credit at an NAB-member station.
Level of Study: Graduate.
Type: Scholarship.
Value: US$1,250 each.
Frequency: Annual.
Study Establishment: Scholarships may be used only at BEA Member Institutions.
Country of Study: Any country in which a BEA Member Institution is located.
No. of awards offered: Four.
Application Procedure: Applicants must obtain an official application form from the BEA or campus faculty. Refer to the website for more details.
Closing Date: September 15th.
Funding: Private.
Contributor: The National Association of Broadcasters, Washington DC.
No. of awards given last year: Four.
No. of applicants last year: 24.

NAB Walter S Patterson Scholarships

Subjects: Radio.
Purpose: To assist study towards a career in radio.

Eligibility: The applicant must be able to show substantial evidence of superior academic performance and potential to be an outstanding electronic media professional. There should be compelling evidence that the applicant possesses high integrity and a well articulated sense of personal and professional responsibility.
Level of Study: Graduate.
Type: Scholarship.
Value: US$1,250 each.
Frequency: Annual.
Study Establishment: Scholarships may be used only at BEA Member Institutions.
Country of Study: Any country in which a BEA Member Institution is located.
No. of awards offered: Two.
Application Procedure: Applicants must obtain an official application form from the BEA or campus faculty. Refer to the website for more details.
Closing Date: September 15th.
Funding: Private.
Contributor: The National Association of Broadcasters.
No. of awards given last year: Two.
No. of applicants last year: 35.

Patrick Communications Vincent T Wasilewski Scholarship

Subjects: Broadcasting.
Purpose: To assist study in any area of broadcasting.
Eligibility: The applicant must be able to show substantial evidence of superior academic performance and potential to be an outstanding electronic media professional. There should be compelling evidence that the applicant possesses high integrity and a well articulated sense of personal and professional responsibility.
Level of Study: Graduate.
Type: Scholarship.
Value: US$2,500.
Frequency: Annual.
Study Establishment: Scholarships may be used only at BEA Member Institutions.
Country of Study: Any country in which a BEA Member Institution is located.
No. of awards offered: One.
Application Procedure: Applicants must obtain an official application form from the BEA or campus faculty. Refer to the website for more details.
Closing Date: September 15th.
Funding: Private.
Contributor: The Patrick Communications Corporation, Ellicott City.
No. of awards given last year: One.
No. of applicants last year: 25.

THE BROADCASTING CORPORATIONS OF THE FEDERAL REPUBLIC OF GERMANY

International Music Competition
Bayerischer Rundfunk, Munich, D-80300, Germany
Tel: (49) 89 5900 2471
Fax: (49) 89 5900 3573
Email: ard.conc@brnet.de
www: http://www.ard-musikwettbewerb.de
Contact: Executive Secretary

International Music Competition of the ARD

Subjects: Music. Categories vary annually.
Purpose: To support and reward a selection of young musicians who are at concert standard.
Eligibility: Open to musicians of any nationality. Age restrictions apply. Further information can be found in the brochure which is available on request.

Type: Competition.
Frequency: Annual.
Study Establishment: Conservatories, university schools of music and music academies, but also advanced private studies.
Country of Study: Any country.
No. of awards offered: The competition includes either four or five categories. For each category three prizes are offered.
Application Procedure: Applicants must complete an application form and submit this with an application fee. An audio cassette is required. Further information can be found in the brochure which is available on request. There is an entry fee of €80 per soloist, €100 for duos, €130 for trios, €150 for quartets, and €175 for quintets.
Closing Date: End of April.
Contributor: Public radio stations in Germany.
No. of awards given last year: 21.
No. of applicants last year: 247.

Prize Winner of the International Music Competition of the ARD

Subjects: Music. Categories in previous years have been violin, violoncello, saxophone, percussion and wind quintet.
Purpose: To support and reward a selection of young musicians who are at concert standard.
Eligibility: Open to musicians of any nationality. Age restrictions apply. Further information can be found in the brochure which is available on request.
Type: Prize.
Value: Please contact the organisation for details.
Frequency: Annual.
Study Establishment: Conservatories, university schools of music, and music academies, but also advanced private studies.
Country of Study: Any country.
No. of awards offered: The competition includes either four or five categories. For each category three prizes are offered.
Application Procedure: Applicants must complete an application form and submit this with an application fee. An audio cassette is also required.
Closing Date: End of April.
Contributor: Public radio stations in Germany.
No. of awards given last year: 21.
No. of applicants last year: 247.

BROOKHAVEN NATIONAL LABORATORY

Brookhaven Women in Science
PO Box 183, Upton, NY, 11973-5000, United States of America
Email: pam@bnl.gov
www: http://www.bnl.gov
Contact: Ms Pamela Mansfield, Chair, Scholarship Committee

Brookhaven National Laboratory is a multi-programme national laboratory operated by Brookhaven Science Associates for the United States Department of Energy. The Laboratory's broad mission is to produce excellent science in a safe, environmentally benign manner with the co-operation, support and appropriate involvement of many communities.

Renate W Chasman Scholarship

Subjects: Natural sciences, engineering and mathematics.
Purpose: To encourage women whose education was interrupted to pursue formal studies or a career in the natural sciences, engineering or mathematics.
Eligibility: Open to re-entry women residing in Nassau County, Suffolk County, Brooklyn or Queens, who must be United States citizens or permanent residents. They must be currently enrolled in or have applied for a degree orientated programme at an accredited institution.
Level of Study: Postgraduate.
Type: Scholarship.

Value: US$2,000.
Frequency: Annual.
Country of Study: Any country.
No. of awards offered: One.
Application Procedure: Applicants must submit a completed application, academic record, letters of reference and a short essay on career goals.
Closing Date: May 1st.
Funding: Private.
No. of awards given last year: One.
Additional Information: Please write to the given address for further information.

THE BROSS FOUNDATION, LAKE FOREST COLLEGE

Religion Department
555 North Sheridan, Lake Forest, IL, 60045, United States of America
Tel: (1) 847 735 5175
Fax: (1) 847 735 6192
Contact: Mr Kyle Eichenberger, Bross Prize Assistant

The Bross Foundation at Lake Forest College was founded to present a scholarly award once every 10 years to the author who, in the opinion of a panel of judges, has written the best book or treatise on the relation between any discipline or topic of investigation and the Christian religion.

The Bross Prize

Subjects: The relationship between any discipline and the Christian religion.
Purpose: To recognise scholarly work.
Eligibility: There are no eligibility restrictions.
Level of Study: Unrestricted.
Type: Cash prize.
Value: First prize of US$15,000, second prize of US$7,000 and third prize of US$4,000.
Frequency: Every 10 years.
Country of Study: Any country.
No. of awards offered: Two.
Application Procedure: Applicants must submit three copies of their manuscript.
Closing Date: September 1st.
Funding: Private.
Contributor: The Bross Memorial.
No. of awards given last year: Two.
No. of applicants last year: 150.
Additional Information: Manuscripts must be at least 50,000 words.

BUDAPEST INTERNATIONAL MUSIC COMPETITION

Hungarofest
Nagydiofa u 10-12, Budapest, H-1072, Hungary
Tel: (36) 1 266 1459
Fax: (36) 1 342 9511
Email: hungfest@matavnet.hu
www: http://www.hungarofest.hu
Contact: Ms Maria Liszkay, Secretary

The Budapest Music Competition has been held since 1933. Competitions in different categories alternate annually.

Budapest International Music Competition

Subjects: Musical performance.

Eligibility: Open to young artists of all nationalities under 32 years of age.
Level of Study: Professional development.
Type: Competition.
Value: Total of US$13,000.
Frequency: Annual.
Country of Study: Any country.
No. of awards offered: Three.
Application Procedure: Applicants must complete an application form to be submitted with other required documentation. Please contact the office for further information.
Closing Date: May 1st.
Funding: Government.
No. of awards given last year: Three.
No. of applicants last year: 65.

THE BUSH FOUNDATION

E-900 First National Bank Building
332 Minnesota Street, St Paul, MN, 55101, United States of America
Tel: (1) 651 227 5222
Fax: (1) 651 297 6485
Email: info@bushfoundation.org
www: http://www.bushfoundation.org
Contact: Ms Kathi Polly, Program Assistant

Bush Artist Fellows Program

Subjects: Visual arts two-dimensional and three-dimensional, multimedia, performance art, music composition, film, video, scripts, literature and choreography. Categories rotate on a two-year cycle.
Purpose: To provide artists with significant financial support to enable them to advance their work and further their contribution to their communities.
Eligibility: Applicants must be at least 25 years old, be residents and have lived for at least one year of the three years preceding the application deadlines in Minnesota, North Dakota, South Dakota or counties of Northwestern Wisconsin.
Level of Study: Professional development.
Type: Fellowship.
Value: Fellows receive US$44,000 divided into monthly stipends for the selected time period.
Length of Study: 12-18 months.
Frequency: Annual.
Country of Study: United States of America.
No. of awards offered: 15.
Application Procedure: Applicants must complete an application form, available on written request from the Foundation in August of each year.
Closing Date: Deadlines are each Autumn. The fellowships will be announced in mid April.
Funding: Private.
No. of awards given last year: 15.
No. of applicants last year: 510.

BUSINESS AND PROFESSIONAL WOMEN'S FOUNDATION

Scholarships & Loans Office
2012 Massachusetts Avenue North West, Washington, DC, 20036, United States of America
Tel: (1) 202 293 1200 ext.169
Fax: (1) 202 861 0298
www: http://www.bpwusa.org
Contact: Grants Management Officer

The Business and Professional Women's Foundation was established in 1956 by members of BPW/USA to promote equity for women through education, research and training. This non-profit, non-partisan public foundation is headquartered in Washington DC.

BPW Career Advancement Scholarship Program

Subjects: Computer science, teacher education certification, paralegal studies, science, engineering or professional eg. JD, MD or DDS degrees.
Purpose: To assist women seeking the education necessary for entry or re-entry into the workforce, or career advancement in a business related field.
Eligibility: Open to women who are United States of America citizens, more than 25 years of age, can demonstrate critical financial need, are officially accepted into a programme of study at an accredited United States of America institution and are graduating within two years of the time of application for a scholarship. Candidates must be receiving a degree or certificate at the conclusion of their studies, be acquiring marketable skills that will increase their economic security and be entering the workforce after they receive their degree or certificate. Applicants should be seeking the education necessary for re-entry or advancement within the workplace.
Level of Study: Postgraduate.
Type: Scholarship.
Value: Up to US$1,000.
Length of Study: One year.
Frequency: Annual.
Study Establishment: An accredited institution.
Country of Study: United States of America.
No. of awards offered: Approx. 60.
Application Procedure: Applicants must complete an application form, available January 1st to April 1st. Please submit a business size double stamped addressed envelope.
Closing Date: Postmarked on or before April 15th.
Funding: Private.
Contributor: Business and professional Women's Foundation.
No. of awards given last year: 61.
No. of applicants last year: 498.

Wyeth Ayerst Scholarship for Women in Graduate Medical and Health Business Programs

Subjects: Emerging health fields such as biomedical engineering, biomedical research, medical technology, pharmaceutical marketing, public health and public health policy.
Purpose: To assist women in gaining entry into underrepresented and under utilised health related occupations, especially in the medical and health business professions.
Eligibility: Open to women who are United States citizens, more than 25 years of age, can demonstrate critical financial need, are officially accepted into a programme of study at an accredited United States institution and are graduating within two years of the time of application for a scholarship. Candidates must be receiving a degree or certificate at the conclusion of their studies, be acquiring marketable skills that will increase their economic security and be entering the workforce after they receive their degree or certificate. Applicants should be women seeking the education necessary for a career in a healthcare field.
Level of Study: Postgraduate.
Type: Scholarship.
Value: US$2,000.
Frequency: Annual.
Study Establishment: An accredited institution.
Country of Study: United States of America.
No. of awards offered: Varies.
Application Procedure: Applicants must complete an application form, available January 1st to April 1st. Please submit a business size double stamped addressed envelope.
Closing Date: Postmarked on or before April 15th.
Funding: Private.
Contributor: Wyeth-Ayerst Laboratories.
No. of awards given last year: 20.
No. of applicants last year: 57.
Additional Information: This award may be subject to change so please contact the institution for more details.

CAIRO UNIVERSITY

Cairo University
Faculty of Archaeology
Conservation Department
Giza, Cairo, Egypt
Tel: (20) 2 567 5640
Fax: (20) 2 758 3246
Contact: Professor Fatma Mohamed Helmi

The Conservation Department of Cairo University deals with restoration and conservation studies of different types of antiquities for postgraduate students such as stones, mural and oil paintings, metallic objects, pottery and ceramics, glass, manuscripts, icons, wood, textiles and carpets, and mastics.

Study, Restoration and Conservation of Archaeological Materials

Subjects: The preservation of cultural heritage includes the study of archaeological materials of cultural heritage and the surrounding environment to determine the causes of deterioration and to select the best materials and methods for treatment, consolidation, restoration, conservation and preservation.
Purpose: To support the study, restoration and conservation of archaeological materials.
Eligibility: Open to candidates from countries which have experience in the conservation and restoration of antiquities and monuments, and have consolidant materials and equipment such as SEM, XRD, XRF, AAS, GLC, FTIR.
Level of Study: Professional development.
Type: Grant.
Value: US$20,000.
Length of Study: Six months.
Frequency: Annual.
Country of Study: United Kingdom, Poland or United States of America.
No. of awards offered: Two.
Application Procedure: Applicants must write for further information.
Closing Date: November 11th.
Funding: Government.
Contributor: The Academy of Science.
No. of awards given last year: Two.
No. of applicants last year: Four.

THE CALEDONIAN RESEARCH FOUNDATION

The Carnegie Trust for the Universities of Scotland
Cameron House
Abbey Park Place, Dunfermline, Fife, KY12 7PZ, Scotland
Tel: (44) 1383 622148
Fax: (44) 1383 622149
Email: jgray@carnegie-trust.org
www: http://www.carnegie-trust.org
Contact: Secretary & Treasurer

The Caledonian Research Foundation is a Scottish charity which has supported independent research in Scotland since 1990.

Caledonian Scholarship

Subjects: All subjects in the university curriculum. At least one scholarship each year is made in a non scientific discipline.
Purpose: To support postgraduate research in any subject.
Eligibility: Open to persons possessing a First Class (Honours) Degree from a Scottish University.
Level of Study: Postgraduate.
Type: Scholarship.
Value: UK £7,800 plus tuition fees and allowances.
Length of Study: Up to three years subject to annual renewal.

Frequency: Annual.
Study Establishment: Any Scottish university.
Country of Study: Scotland.
No. of awards offered: Two-three.
Application Procedure: Applicants must write for details.
Closing Date: March 15th.
No. of awards given last year: Three.
No. of applicants last year: 90.
Additional Information: This award is considered along with Carnegie Scholarships.

THE CAMARGO FOUNDATION

BP 75, Cassis Cedex, F-13714, France
Tel: (33) 4 42 01 11 57
Fax: (33) 4 42 01 36 57
www: http://www.camargofoundation.org
Contact: Mr Michael Pretina Jr, Executive Director

The Camargo Foundation maintains a study centre for the benefit of scholars who wish to pursue projects in the humanities and social sciences related to French and francophone cultures. The Foundation also sponsors creative projects by visual artists, photographers, composers and writers.

Camargo Fellowships

Subjects: Humanities and social sciences.
Purpose: To assist scholars who wish to pursue projects in the humanities and social sciences related to French and Francophone cultures, and to support projects by visual artists, photographers, filmmakers, composers and writers.
Eligibility: Open to members of university and college faculties who wish to pursue special studies while on leave from their institutions, independent Scholars working on specific projects, graduate students whose academic residence and general examination requirements have been met and for whom a stay in France would be beneficial in completing the dissertation required for their degree. The awards is also open to writers, visual artists, photographers, filmmakers, video artists, multimedia artists and composers with specific projects to complete.
Level of Study: Doctorate, Postgraduate, Professional development.
Type: Residency.
Value: The use of furnished apartments, the reference library, darkroom, artist's studio and music composition studio, and a stipend of US$3,500.
Length of Study: Varies.
Frequency: Annual.
Study Establishment: Camargo Foundation study centre in Cassis.
Country of Study: France.
No. of awards offered: Varies, approx. 20-26.
Application Procedure: Applicants must submit a completed application form, a curriculum vitae, a detailed description of their project of up to 1,000 words in length and three letters of recommendation by individuals familiar with the applicant's professional work. At least two of the letters should come from persons outside the applicant's own institution, though graduate students are exempt from this requirement. Artists should submit 10 slides showing samples of their work, composers should submit a score, cassette or compact disc, and writers should send 10-20 pages of text or a copy of a published work. For further information and application forms applicants should contact the Foundation.
Closing Date: February 1st for the following academic year.
Funding: Private.
Contributor: The Jerome Hill endowment.
No. of awards given last year: 24.
Additional Information: A written report will be required at the end of the stay.

For further information contact:

Camargo Foundation
125 Park Square Court
400 Sibley Street, St Paul, MN, 55101-1928, United States of America
Tel: (1) 612 290 2237

CAMBRIDGE COMMONWEALTH TRUST, CAMBRIDGE OVERSEAS TRUST AND ASSOCIATED TRUSTS

PO Box 252, Cambridge, Cambridgeshire, CB2 1RZ, England
Tel: (44) 1223 323322
Fax: (44) 1223 351449
Email: egs10@cam.ac.uk

Aola Richards Studentships for PhD Study

Subjects: Biological sciences with preference given to those whose research is in entomology.
Purpose: To financially support study towards a PhD.
Eligibility: Applicants must be citizens of Australia or New Zealand. The Trusts cannot admit students to the University or any of its colleges. Applicants for awards from the Trusts must, therefore, also apply to the University of Cambridge and be offered a place at Cambridge in the normal way. All applicants must have a First Class or High Second Class (Honours) Degree or equivalent and normally be under 26. All applicants must be successfully nominated for an Overseas Research Student (ORS) award which covers the difference between the home and overseas rate of the University Composition Fee.
Level of Study: Doctorate, Predoctorate.
Type: Studentship.
Value: The University Composition Fee at the home rate, approved college fees, a maintenance allowance sufficient for a single student and a contribution towards a return economy airfare.
Length of Study: Up to three years.
Frequency: As available.
Study Establishment: The University of Cambridge.
Country of Study: United Kingdom.
No. of awards offered: One.
Application Procedure: Preliminary application forms should be sent to the address relevant to that particular country. The final application forms should be sent to the Secretary, the Board of Graduate Studies.
Closing Date: Please contact the organisation.
Contributor: Offered in collaboration with the Aola Richards Fund.
Additional Information: Further information is available on request.

For further information contact:

The Secretary
The Board for Graduate Studies
4 Mill Lane, Cambridge, Cambridgeshire, CB2 1RZ, England

Arab-British Chamber Charitable Foundation Scholarships

Subjects: All subjects.
Purpose: To financially support those undertaking postgraduate study.
Eligibility: Applicants must be citizens of Algeria, the Comoro Islands, Djibouti, Egypt, Jordan, Mauritania, Morocco, Palestine, Somalia, Sudan, Syria, Tunisia or the Yemen. The Trusts cannot admit students to the University or any of its colleges. Applicants for awards from the Trusts must, therefore, also apply to the University of Cambridge and be offered a place at Cambridge in the normal way. All applicants must have a First Class or High Second Class (Honours) Degree or equivalent and normally be under 26.
Type: Scholarship.

Value: The University Composition Fee at the overseas rate, approved college fees, a maintenance allowance sufficient for a single student and a contribution towards a return economy airfare.
Length of Study: One year.
Frequency: Annual.
Study Establishment: The University of Cambridge.
Country of Study: United Kingdom.
No. of awards offered: Five.
Application Procedure: Applicants must complete a preliminary application form, which can be obtained from local universities, offices of the British Council or the Trust. The preliminary application form can be downloaded from http://www.admin.cam.ac.uk/univ/gsprospectus/c7/overseas/schemes.html. Completed forms must be returned to the main address. Shortlisted candidates will be sent forms for admission to the University of Cambridge.
Closing Date: Please contact the organisation.
Contributor: Offered in collaboration with the Arab-British Chamber Charitable Foundation and the Foreign and Commonwealth Office (FCO).
Additional Information: Further information is available on request.

Argentina Cambridge Scholarships for PhD Study

Subjects: All subjects, particularly those relevant to the needs of Argentina.
Purpose: To financially support and encourage individuals to complete a PhD at the University of Cambridge.
Eligibility: Open to students from Argentina. The Trusts cannot admit students to the University or any of its colleges. Applicants for awards from the Trusts must, therefore, also apply to the University of Cambridge and be offered a place at Cambridge in the normal way. All applicants must have a First Class or High Second Class (Honours) Degree or equivalent and normally be under 26. All applicants must be successfully nominated for an Overseas Research Student (ORS) award which covers the difference between the home and overseas rate of the University Composition Fee.
Level of Study: Doctorate, Predoctorate.
Type: Scholarship.
Value: The award covers the University Composition Fee at the appropriate rate, approved college fees, a maintenance allowance sufficient for a single student and a contribution towards a return economy airfare.
Length of Study: Up to three years.
Frequency: Annual.
Study Establishment: The University of Cambridge.
Country of Study: United Kingdom.
No. of awards offered: Up to two.
Application Procedure: Applicants must complete a preliminary application form, which can be obtained from local universities, offices of the British Council or the Trust. The preliminary application form can be downloaded from http://www.admin.cam.ac.uk/univ/gsprospectus/c7/overseas/schemes.html. Completed forms must be returned to the main address. Shortlisted candidates will be sent forms for admission to the University of Cambridge.
Closing Date: Please contact the organisation.
Funding: Government.
Contributor: Offered in collaboration with the Ministry of Education in Argentina.
Additional Information: Further information is available on request.

Argentina Cambridge Scholarships for Postgraduate Study

Subjects: All subjects, particularly those relevant to the needs of Argentina.
Purpose: To financially support those undertaking postgraduate study.
Eligibility: Open to students from Argentina. The Trusts cannot admit students to the University or any of its colleges. Applicants for awards from the Trusts must, therefore, also apply to the University of Cambridge and be offered a place at Cambridge in the normal way. All applicants must have a First Class or High Second Class

(Honours) Degree or equivalent and normally be under 26. All applicants must be successfully nominated for an Overseas Research Student (ORS) award which covers the difference between the home and overseas rate of the University Composition Fee.
Level of Study: Postgraduate.
Type: Scholarship.
Value: The award covers the University Composition Fee at the overseas rate, approved college fees, a maintenance allowance sufficient for a single student and a contribution towards a return economy airfare.
Length of Study: One year.
Frequency: Annual.
Study Establishment: The University of Cambridge.
Country of Study: United Kingdom.
No. of awards offered: Up to five.
Application Procedure: Applicants must complete a preliminary application form, which can be obtained from local universities, offices of the British Council or the Trust. The preliminary application form can be downloaded from http://www.admin.cam.ac.uk/univ/gsprospectus/c7/overseas/schemes.html. Completed forms must be returned to the main address. Shortlisted candidates will be sent forms for admission to the University of Cambridge.
Closing Date: Please contact the organisation.
Funding: Government.
Contributor: Offered in collaboration with the Ministry of Education, Argentina.
Additional Information: Further information is available on request.

BAT Cambridge Scholarships for PhD Study (Russia)

Subjects: All subjects.
Purpose: To financially support study towards a PhD.
Eligibility: Open to citizens of Russia. The Trusts cannot admit students to the University or any of its colleges. Applicants for awards from the Trusts must, therefore, also apply to the University of Cambridge and be offered a place at Cambridge in the normal way. All applicants must have a First Class or High Second Class (Honours) Degree or equivalent and normally be under 26. All applicants must be successfully nominated for an Overseas Research Student (ORS) award which covers the difference between the home and overseas rate of the University Composition Fee.
Level of Study: Doctorate, Predoctorate.
Type: Scholarship.
Value: The University Composition Fee at the appropriate rate, approved college fees, a maintenance allowance sufficient for a single student and a contribution towards a return economy airfare.
Length of Study: Up to three years.
Frequency: Annual.
Study Establishment: The University of Cambridge.
Country of Study: United Kingdom.
No. of awards offered: Varies.
Application Procedure: Applicants must complete a preliminary application form, which can be obtained from local universities, offices of the British Council or the Trust. The preliminary application form can be downloaded from http://www.admin.cam.ac.uk/univ/gsprospectus/c7/overseas/schemes.html. Completed forms must be returned to the main address. Shortlisted candidates will be sent forms for admission to the University of Cambridge.
Closing Date: Please contact the organisation.
Contributor: Offered in collaboration with the British American-Tobacco (BAT) Company.
Additional Information: Further information is available on request.

BAT Cambridge Scholarships for Postgraduate Study (Russia)

Subjects: All subjects.
Purpose: To financially support those undertaking postgraduate study.
Eligibility: Open to citizens of Russia. The Trusts cannot admit students to the University or any of its colleges. Applicants for awards from the Trusts must, therefore, also apply to the University of Cambridge and be offered a place at Cambridge in the normal way. All applicants must have a First Class or High Second Class (Honours) Degree or equivalent and normally be under 26.
Level of Study: Postgraduate.
Type: Scholarship.
Value: The University Composition Fee at the appropriate rate, approved college fees, a maintenance allowance sufficient for a single student and a contribution towards a return economy airfare.
Length of Study: One year.
Frequency: Annual.
Study Establishment: The University of Cambridge.
Country of Study: United Kingdom.
No. of awards offered: Varies.
Application Procedure: Applicants must complete a preliminary application form, which can be obtained from local universities, offices of the British Council or the Trust. The preliminary application form can be downloaded from http://www.admin.cam.ac.uk/univ/gsprospectus/c7/overseas/schemes.html. Completed forms must be returned to the main address. Shortlisted candidates will be sent forms for admission to the University of Cambridge.
Closing Date: Please contact the organisation.
Contributor: Offered in collaboration with the British American-Tobacco (BAT) Company.
Additional Information: Further information is available on request.

BAT/FCO Cambridge Scholarships for PhD Study (China)

Subjects: All subjects.
Purpose: To financially support study towards a PhD.
Eligibility: Open to students from China. The Trusts cannot admit students to the University or any of its Colleges. Applicants for awards from the Trusts must therefore also apply to the University of Cambridge and be offered a place at Cambridge in the normal way. All applicants must have a First Class or High Second Class (Honours) Degree or equivalent and normally be under 26.
Level of Study: Doctorate, Postdoctorate.
Type: Scholarship.
Value: The University Composition Fee at the appropriate rate, approved college fees, a maintenance allowance sufficient for a single student and a contribution towards a return economy airfare.
Length of Study: Three years.
Frequency: Annual.
Study Establishment: The University of Cambridge.
Country of Study: United Kingdom.
No. of awards offered: Varies.
Application Procedure: Applicants must complete a preliminary application form, which can be obtained from local universities, offices of the British Council or the Trust. The preliminary application form can be downloaded from http://www.admin.cam.ac.uk/univ/gsprospectus/c7/overseas/schemes.html. Completed forms must be returned to the main address. Shortlisted candidates will be sent forms for admission to the University of Cambridge.
Closing Date: Please contact the organisation.
Contributor: Offered in collaboration with the British-American Tobacco (BAT) Company Limited.
Additional Information: Further information is available on request.

BAT/FCO Cambridge Scholarships for Postgraduate Study (China)

Subjects: All subjects.
Purpose: To financially support those undertaking postgraduate study.
Eligibility: Open to students from China. The Trusts cannot admit students to the University or any of its Colleges. Applicants for awards from the Trusts must therefore also apply to the University of Cambridge and be offered a place at Cambridge in the normal way. All applicants must have a First Class or High Second Class (Honours) Degree or equivalent and normally be under 26.
Level of Study: Postgraduate.
Type: Scholarship.

Value: The University Composition Fee at the appropriate rate, approved college fees, a maintenance allowance sufficient for a single student and a contribution towards a return economy airfare.
Length of Study: One year.
Frequency: Annual.
Study Establishment: The University of Cambridge.
Country of Study: United Kingdom.
No. of awards offered: Varies.
Application Procedure: Applicants must complete a preliminary application form, which can be obtained from local universities, offices of the British Council or the Trust. The preliminary application form can be downloaded from http://www.admin.cam.ac.uk/univ/gsprospectus/c7/overseas/schemes.html. Completed forms must be returned to the main address. Shortlisted candidates will be sent forms for admission to the University of Cambridge.
Closing Date: Please contact the organisation.
Contributor: Offered in collaboration with the British-American Tobacco (BAT) Company Limited.
Additional Information: Further information is available on request.

BP Cambridge Chevening Scholarships for Postgraduate Study (China)

Subjects: All subjects.
Purpose: To financially support those undertaking postgraduate study.
Eligibility: Open to citizens of China. The Trusts cannot admit students to the University or any of its colleges. Applicants for awards from the Trusts must, therefore, also apply to the University of Cambridge and be offered a place at Cambridge in the normal way. All applicants must have a First Class or High Second Class (Honours) Degree or equivalent and normally be under 26.
Level of Study: Postgraduate.
Type: Scholarship.
Value: The University Composition Fee at the overseas rate, approved college fees, a maintenance allowance sufficient for a single student and a contribution to a return economy airfare.
Length of Study: One year.
Frequency: Annual.
Study Establishment: The University of Cambridge.
Country of Study: United Kingdom.
No. of awards offered: Varies.
Application Procedure: Applicants must complete a preliminary application form, which can be obtained from local universities, offices of the British Council or the Trust. The preliminary application form can be downloaded from http://www.admin.cam.ac.uk/univ/gsprospectus/c7/overseas/schemes.html. Completed forms must be returned to the main address. Shortlisted candidates will be sent forms for admission to the University of Cambridge.
Closing Date: Please contact the organisation.
Additional Information: Further information is available on request.

BP Cambridge Chevening Scholarships for Postgraduate Study (Russia)

Subjects: All subjects.
Purpose: To financially support those undertaking postgraduate study.
Eligibility: Open to citizens of Russia. The Trusts cannot admit students to the University or any of its colleges. Applicants for awards from the Trusts must, therefore, also apply to the University of Cambridge and be offered a place at Cambridge in the normal way. All applicants must have a First Class or High Second Class (Honours) Degree or equivalent and normally be under 26.
Level of Study: Postgraduate.
Type: Scholarship.
Value: The University Composition Fee at the overseas rate, approved college fees, a maintenance allowance sufficient for a single student and a contribution to a return economy airfare.
Length of Study: One year.
Frequency: Annual.
Study Establishment: The University of Cambridge.

Country of Study: United Kingdom.
No. of awards offered: Varies.
Application Procedure: Applicants must complete a preliminary application form, which can be obtained from local universities, offices of the British Council or the Trust. The preliminary application form can be downloaded from http://www.admin.cam.ac.uk/univ/gsprospectus/c7/overseas/schemes.html. Completed forms must be returned to the main address. Shortlisted candidates will be sent forms for admission to the University of Cambridge.
Closing Date: Please contact the organisation.
Additional Information: Further information is available on request.

BP Cambridge Scholarships for PhD Study (China)

Subjects: All subjects.
Purpose: To financially support study towards a PhD.
Eligibility: Candidates must be citizens of China. The Trusts cannot admit students to the University or any of its colleges. Applicants for awards from the Trusts must, therefore, also apply to the University of Cambridge and be offered a place at Cambridge in the normal way. All applicants must have a First Class or High Second Class (Honours) Degree or equivalent and normally be under 26. All applicants must apply for an Overseas Research Student (ORS) award which pays the difference between the home and overseas rate of the University composition fee.
Level of Study: Doctorate, Predoctorate.
Type: Scholarship.
Value: The University Composition Fee at the overseas rate, approved college fees, a maintenance allowance sufficient for a single student and a contribution to a return economy airfare.
Length of Study: Three years.
Frequency: Annual.
Study Establishment: The University of Cambridge.
Country of Study: United Kingdom.
No. of awards offered: Varies.
Application Procedure: Applicants must complete a preliminary application form, which can be obtained from local universities, offices of the British Council or the Trust. The preliminary application form can be downloaded from http://www.admin.cam.ac.uk/univ/gsprospectus/c7/overseas/schemes.html. Completed forms must be returned to the main address. Shortlisted candidates will be sent forms for admission to the University of Cambridge.
Closing Date: Please contact the organisation.
Contributor: Offered in collaboration with BP.
Additional Information: Further information is available on request.

BP Cambridge Scholarships for PhD Study (Egypt)

Subjects: All subjects.
Purpose: To financially support study towards a PhD.
Eligibility: Candidates must be citizens of Egypt. All applicants must apply for an Overseas Research Student (ORS) award which pays the difference between the home and overseas rate of the University Composition Fee. The Trusts cannot admit students to the University or any of its colleges. Applicants for awards from the Trusts must, therefore, also apply to the University of Cambridge and be offered a place at Cambridge in the normal way. All applicants must have a First Class or High Second Class (Honours) Degree or equivalent and normally be under 26.
Level of Study: Doctorate, Predoctorate.
Type: Scholarship.
Value: The University Composition Fee at the overseas rate, approved college fees, a maintenance allowance sufficient for a single student and a contribution to a return economy airfare.
Length of Study: Up to three years.
Frequency: Annual.
Study Establishment: The University of Cambridge.
Country of Study: United Kingdom.
No. of awards offered: Two.
Application Procedure: Applicants must complete a preliminary application form, which can be obtained from local universities, offices of the British Council or the Trust. The preliminary application form

can be downloaded from
http://www.admin.cam.ac.uk/univ/gsprospectus/c7/over-seas/schemes.html. Completed forms must be returned to the main address. Shortlisted candidates will be sent forms for admission to the University of Cambridge.
Closing Date: Please contact the organisation.
Contributor: Offered in collaboration with BP Amoco.
Additional Information: Further information is available on request.

BP Cambridge Scholarships for PhD Study (Russia)
Subjects: All subjects.
Purpose: To financially support study towards a PhD.
Eligibility: Candidates must be citizens of Russia. The Trusts cannot admit students to the University or any of its colleges. Applicants for awards from the Trusts must, therefore, also apply to the University of Cambridge and be offered a place at Cambridge in the normal way. All applicants must have a First Class or High Second Class (Honours) Degree or equivalent and normally be under 26. All applicants must apply for an Overseas Research Student (ORS) award which pays the difference between the home and overseas rate of the University Composition Fee.
Level of Study: Doctorate, Predoctorate.
Type: Scholarship.
Value: The University Composition Fee at the overseas rate, approved college fees, a maintenance allowance sufficient for a single student and a contribution to a return economy airfare.
Length of Study: Three years.
Frequency: Annual.
Study Establishment: The University of Cambridge.
Country of Study: United Kingdom.
No. of awards offered: Varies.
Application Procedure: Applicants must complete a preliminary application form, which can be obtained from local universities, offices of the British Council or the Trust. The preliminary application form can be downloaded from
http://www.admin.cam.ac.uk/univ/gsprospectus/c7/over-seas/schemes.html. Completed forms must be returned to the main address. Shortlisted candidates will be sent forms for admission to the University of Cambridge.
Closing Date: Please contact the organisation.
Contributor: Offered in collaboration with BP.
Additional Information: Further information is available on request.

BP Cambridge Scholarships for Postgraduate Study (Egypt)
Subjects: All subjects.
Purpose: To financially support those undertaking postgraduate study.
Eligibility: Open to citizens of Egypt. The Trusts cannot admit students to the University or any of its colleges. Applicants for awards from the Trusts must, therefore, also apply to the University of Cambridge and be offered a place at Cambridge in the normal way. All applicants must have a First Class or High Second Class (Honours) Degree or equivalent and normally be under 26.
Level of Study: Postgraduate.
Type: Scholarship.
Value: The University Composition Fee at the appropriate rate, approved college fees, a maintenance allowance sufficient for a single student and a contribution towards a return economy airfare.
Length of Study: One year.
Frequency: Annual.
Study Establishment: The University of Cambridge.
Country of Study: United Kingdom.
No. of awards offered: Four.
Application Procedure: Applicants must complete a preliminary application form, which can be obtained from local universities, offices of the British Council or the Trust. The preliminary application form can be downloaded from
http://www.admin.cam.ac.uk/univ/gsprospectus/c7/over-seas/schemes.html. Completed forms must be returned to the main address. Shortlisted candidates will be sent forms for admission to the University of Cambridge.

Closing Date: Please contact the organisation.
Contributor: Offered in collaboration with BP Amoco.
Additional Information: Further information is available on request.

Britain-Australia Bicentennial Scholarships for Postgraduate Study
Subjects: All subjects.
Purpose: To financially support those undertaking postgraduate study.
Eligibility: Candidates must be citizens of Australia. The Trusts cannot admit students to the University or any of its colleges. Applicants for awards from the Trusts must, therefore, also apply to the University of Cambridge and be offered a place at Cambridge in the normal way. All applicants must have a First Class or High Second Class (Honours) Degree or equivalent and normally be under 26.
Level of Study: Postgraduate.
Type: Scholarship.
Value: The University Composition Fee at the overseas rate, approved college fees, a maintenance allowance sufficient for a single student and a contribution towards a return economy airfare.
Length of Study: One year.
Frequency: Annual.
Study Establishment: Jesus College, the University of Cambridge.
Country of Study: United Kingdom.
No. of awards offered: Two.
Application Procedure: Applicants must contact the Board of Graduate Studies.
Closing Date: Please contact the organisation.
Contributor: Offered in collaboration with the Foreign and Commonwealth Office (FCO) and Jesus College, Cambridge.
Additional Information: Further information is available on request.

For further information contact:

The Secretary
The Board for Graduate Studies
4 Mill Lane, Cambridge, Cambridgeshire, CB2 1RZ, England

British Chevening Brockman Cambridge Scholarships
Subjects: Engineering.
Purpose: To financially support those undertaking postgraduate study.
Eligibility: Applicants must be from Mexico. The Trusts cannot admit students to the University or any of its colleges. Applicants for awards from the Trusts must, therefore, also apply to the University of Cambridge and be offered a place at Cambridge in the normal way. All applicants must have a First Class or High Second Class (Honours) Degree or equivalent and normally be under 26.
Level of Study: Postgraduate.
Type: Scholarship.
Value: The University Composition Fee at the overseas rate, approved college fees and a maintenance allowance sufficient for a single student.
Length of Study: One year.
Frequency: Annual.
Study Establishment: The University of Cambridge.
Country of Study: United Kingdom.
No. of awards offered: Up to two.
Application Procedure: Applicants must complete a preliminary application form, which can be obtained from local universities, offices of the British Council or the Trust. The preliminary application form can be downloaded from
http://www.admin.cam.ac.uk/univ/gsprospectus/c7/over-seas/schemes.html. Completed forms must be returned to the main address. Shortlisted candidates will be sent forms for admission to the University of Cambridge.
Closing Date: Please contact the organisation.
Contributor: Offered in collaboration with the Brockman Foundation and the Foreign and Commonwealth Office (FCO).
Additional Information: Further information is available on request.

British Chevening Cambridge Australia Trust Scholarships for Postgraduate Study

Subjects: All subjects.
Purpose: To financially support those undertaking postgraduate study.
Eligibility: Applicants must be from Australia. The Trusts cannot admit students to the University or any of its Colleges. Applicants for awards from the Trusts must, therefore, also apply to the University of Cambridge and be offered a place at Cambridge in the normal way. All applicants must have a First Class or High Second Class (Honours) Degree or equivalent and normally be under 26.
Level of Study: Doctorate.
Type: Scholarship.
Value: The University Composition Fee at the overseas rate, approved College fees, a maintenance allowance sufficient for a single student and a contribution towards a return economy airfare.
Frequency: Annual.
Study Establishment: The University of Cambridge.
Country of Study: United Kingdom.
No. of awards offered: Two.
Application Procedure: Applicants must contact the Board of Graduate Studies.
Closing Date: Please contact the organisation.
Contributor: Offered in collaboration with the Foreign and Commonwealth Office (FCO) and the Cambridge Australia Trust.
Additional Information: Further information is available on request. For details of scholarships offered in collaboration with the Cambridge Australia Trust please see the website http://www.anu.edu/cabs/scholarships/cambridge/cambridge-austrust.html.

For further information contact:

The Secretary
Board of Graduate Studies
4 Mill Lane, Cambridge, Cambridgeshire, CB2 1RZ, England

British Chevening Cambridge Scholarship for PhD Study (Mexico)

Subjects: All subjects.
Purpose: To financially support study towards a PhD.
Eligibility: Open to citizens of Mexico. The Trusts cannot admit students to the University or any of its colleges. Applicants for awards from the Trusts must, therefore, also apply to the University of Cambridge and be offered a place at Cambridge in the normal way. All applicants must have a First Class or High Second Class (Honours) Degree or equivalent and normally be under 26. All applicants must be successfully nominated for an Overseas Research Student (ORS) award which covers the difference between the home and overseas rate of the University Composition Fee.
Level of Study: Doctorate.
Type: Scholarship.
Value: The University Composition Fee at the appropriate rate, approved college fees and a maintenance allowance sufficient for a single student.
Length of Study: Up to three years.
Frequency: Annual.
Study Establishment: The University of Cambridge.
Country of Study: United Kingdom.
No. of awards offered: One.
Application Procedure: Applicants for this scholarship must complete a preliminary application form which can only be obtained from the British Council in Mexico City.
Closing Date: Please contact the organisation.
Contributor: Offered in collaboration with the Foreign and Commonwealth Office (FCO).
Additional Information: Further information is available on request.

For further information contact:

The British Council
Maestro Antonio Caso 127
Col San Rafael

Delegacion Cuauhtemoc
Apartado postal 30-588, Mexico City, DF, 06470, Mexico

British Chevening Cambridge Scholarship for PhD Study (Uganda)

Subjects: All subjects.
Purpose: To financially support study towards a PhD.
Eligibility: Open to students from Uganda. The Trusts cannot admit students to the University or any of its colleges. Applicants for awards from the Trusts must, therefore, also apply to the University of Cambridge and be offered a place at Cambridge in the normal way. All applicants must have a First Class or High Second Class (Honours) Degree or equivalent and normally be under 26. All applicants must be successfully nominated for an Overseas Research Student (ORS) award which covers the difference between the home and overseas rate of the University Composition Fee.
Level of Study: Doctorate.
Type: Scholarship.
Value: The University Composition Fee at the appropriate rate, approved college fees, a maintenance allowance sufficient for a single student and a contribution towards a return economy airfare.
Length of Study: Up to three years.
Frequency: Annual.
Study Establishment: The University of Cambridge.
Country of Study: United Kingdom.
No. of awards offered: One.
Application Procedure: Applicants must complete a preliminary application form, which can be obtained from local universities, offices of the British Council or the Trust. The preliminary application form can be downloaded from http://www.admin.cam.ac.uk/univ/gsprospectus/c7/overseas/schemes.html. Completed forms must be returned to the main address. Shortlisted candidates will be sent forms for admission to the University of Cambridge.
Closing Date: Please contact the organisation.
Contributor: Offered in collaboration with the Foreign and Commonwealth Office (FCO).
Additional Information: Further information is available on request.

British Chevening Cambridge Scholarship for Postgraduate Study (Australia)

Subjects: All subjects.
Purpose: To financially support those undertaking postgraduate study.
Eligibility: Candidates must be citizens of Australia. The Trusts cannot admit students to the University or any of its colleges. Applicants for awards from the Trusts must, therefore, also apply to the University of Cambridge and be offered a place at Cambridge in the normal way. All applicants must have a First Class or High Second Class (Honours) Degree or equivalent and normally be under 26.
Level of Study: Postgraduate.
Type: Scholarship.
Value: The University Composition Fee at the overseas rate, approved college fees, a maintenance allowance sufficient for a single student and a contribution towards a return economy airfare.
Length of Study: One year.
Frequency: Annual.
Study Establishment: The University of Cambridge.
Country of Study: United Kingdom.
No. of awards offered: Two.
Application Procedure: Applicants must write for information.
Closing Date: Please contact the organisation.
Contributor: Offered in collaboration with the Foreign and Commonwealth Office (FCO).
Additional Information: Further information is available on request.

For further information contact:

The Secretary
The Board for Graduate Studies
4 Mill Lane, Cambridge, Cambridgeshire, CN2 1RZ, England

British Chevening Cambridge Scholarship for Postgraduate Study (Cyprus)

Subjects: All subjects.

Purpose: To financially support those undertaking postgraduate study.

Eligibility: Open to citizens of Cyprus. Applicants must pass a medical examination. Candidates who are currently receiving, or who have received a British Award within the past three years, are not normally eligible for this scholarship. The Trusts cannot admit students to the University or any of its colleges. Applicants for awards from the Trusts must, therefore, also apply to the University of Cambridge and be offered a place at Cambridge in the normal way. All applicants must have a First Class or High Second Class (Honours) Degree or equivalent and normally be under 26.

Level of Study: Postgraduate.

Type: Scholarship.

Value: The University Composition Fee at the overseas rate, approved college fees, a maintenance allowance sufficient for a single student and a contribution towards return economy airfare.

Length of Study: One year.

Frequency: Annual.

Study Establishment: The University of Cambridge.

Country of Study: United Kingdom.

No. of awards offered: Three.

Application Procedure: Applicants must complete a preliminary application form, which can be obtained from local universities, offices of the British Council or the Trust. The preliminary application form can be downloaded from http://www.admin.cam.ac.uk/univ/gsprospectus/c7/overseas/schemes.html. Completed forms must be returned to the main address. Shortlisted candidates will be sent forms for admission to the University of Cambridge.

Closing Date: Please contact the organisation.

Contributor: Offered in collaboration with the Foreign and Commonwealth Office (FCO) and Leventis Foundation.

Additional Information: Further information is available on request.

British Chevening Cambridge Scholarship for Postgraduate Study (East and West Africa)

Subjects: All subjects.

Purpose: To financially support those undertaking postgraduate study.

Eligibility: Applicants must be from Ghana, Sierra Leone, Tanzania or Uganda. The Trusts cannot admit students to the University or any of its colleges. Applicants for awards from the Trusts must, therefore, also apply to the University of Cambridge and be offered a place at Cambridge in the normal way. All applicants must have a First Class or High Second Class (Honours) Degree or equivalent and normally be under 26.

Level of Study: Postgraduate.

Type: Scholarship.

Value: The University Composition Fee at the overseas rate, approved college fees, a maintenance allowance sufficient for a single student and a contribution towards a return economy airfare.

Frequency: Annual.

Study Establishment: The University of Cambridge.

Country of Study: United Kingdom.

No. of awards offered: Seven. Up to three for students from Ghana, one for students from Sierra Leone, one for students from Uganda and one for students from Tanzania.

Application Procedure: Applicants must complete a preliminary application form, which can be obtained from local universities, offices of the British Council or the Trust. The preliminary application form can be downloaded from http://www.admin.cam.ac.uk/univ/gsprospectus/c7/overseas/schemes.html. Completed forms must be returned to the main address. Shortlisted candidates will be sent forms for admission to the University of Cambridge.

Closing Date: Please contact the organisation.

Contributor: Offered in collaboration with the Foreign and Commonwealth Office (FCO).

Additional Information: Further information is available on request.

British Chevening Cambridge Scholarship for Postgraduate Study (Namibia)

Subjects: All subjects.

Purpose: To financially support those undertaking postgraduate study.

Eligibility: Applicants must be from Namibia. The Trusts cannot admit students to the University or any of its colleges. Applicants for awards from the Trusts must, therefore, also apply to the University of Cambridge and be offered a place at Cambridge in the normal way. All applicants must have a First Class or High Second Class (Honours) Degree or equivalent and normally be under 26. All applicants must be successfully nominated for an Overseas Research Student (ORS) award which covers the difference between the home and overseas rate of the University Composition Fee.

Level of Study: Postgraduate.

Type: Scholarship.

Value: The University Composition Fee at the overseas rate, approved college fees and a maintenance allowance sufficient for a single student.

Length of Study: One year.

Frequency: Annual.

Study Establishment: The University of Cambridge.

Country of Study: United Kingdom.

No. of awards offered: One.

Application Procedure: Applicants must complete a preliminary application form, which can be obtained from local universities, offices of the British Council or the Trust. The preliminary application form can be downloaded from http://www.admin.cam.ac.uk/univ/gsprospectus/c7/overseas/schemes.html. Completed forms must be returned to the main address. Shortlisted candidates will be sent forms for admission to the University of Cambridge.

Closing Date: Please contact the organisation.

Contributor: Offered in collaboration with the Malaysian Commonwealth Studies Centre and the Foreign and Commonwealth Office (FCO).

Additional Information: Further information is available on request.

British Chevening Cambridge Scholarships (Hong Kong)

Subjects: All subjects.

Purpose: To financially support those undertaking postgraduate study.

Eligibility: Applicants must be from Hong Kong. The Trusts cannot admit students to the University or any of its colleges. Applicants for awards from the Trusts must, therefore, also apply to the University of Cambridge and be offered a place at Cambridge in the normal way. All applicants must have a First Class or High Second Class (Honours) Degree or equivalent and normally be under 26.

Level of Study: Postgraduate.

Type: Scholarship.

Value: The University Composition Fee at the overseas rate, approved college fees, a maintenance allowance sufficient for a single student and a contribution towards a return economy airfare.

Length of Study: One year.

Frequency: Annual.

Study Establishment: The University of Cambridge.

Country of Study: United Kingdom.

No. of awards offered: Up to eight.

Application Procedure: Applicants must complete a preliminary application form, which can be obtained from local universities, offices of the British Council or the main address. Completed forms must be returned to the main address. Shortlisted candidates will be sent forms for admission to the University of Cambridge and a scholarship application form. These forms must be returned to the Board of Graduate Studies at the address below.

Closing Date: Please contact the organisation.

Contributor: Offered in collaboration with the Foreign and Commonwealth Office (FCO).

Additional Information: Further information is available on request.

For further information contact:

The Secretary
The Board of Graduate Studies
4 Mill Lane, Cambridge, Cambridgeshire, CB2 1RZ, England

British Chevening Cambridge Scholarships (The Philippines)

Subjects: All subjects.
Purpose: To financially support those undertaking postgraduate study.
Eligibility: Applicants must be from the Philippines. The Trusts cannot admit students to the University or any of its colleges. Applicants for awards from the Trusts must, therefore, also apply to the University of Cambridge and be offered a place at Cambridge in the normal way. All applicants must have a First Class or High Second Class (Honours) Degree or equivalent and normally be under 26.
Level of Study: Postgraduate.
Type: Scholarship.
Value: The University Composition Fee at the overseas rate, approved college fees, a maintenance allowance sufficient for a single student and a contribution towards return economy airfare.
Length of Study: One year.
Frequency: Annual.
Study Establishment: The University of Cambridge.
Country of Study: United Kingdom.
No. of awards offered: Three.
Application Procedure: Applicants must complete a preliminary application form, which can be obtained from local universities, offices of the British Council or the Trust. The preliminary application form can be downloaded from http://www.admin.cam.ac.uk/univ/gsprospectus/c7/overseas/schemes.html. Completed forms must be returned to the main address. Shortlisted candidates will be sent forms for admission to the University of Cambridge.
Closing Date: Please contact the organisation.
Contributor: Offered in collaboration with the Foreign and Commonwealth Scholarships.
Additional Information: Further information is available on request.

British Chevening Cambridge Scholarships (Vietnam)

Subjects: All subjects.
Purpose: To financially support those undertaking postgraduate study.
Eligibility: Applicants must be from Vietnam. The Trusts cannot admit students to the University or any of its colleges. Applicants for awards from the Trusts must, therefore, also apply to the University of Cambridge and be offered a place at Cambridge in the normal way. All applicants must have a First Class or High Second Class (Honours) Degree or equivalent and normally be under 26. All applicants must be successfully nominated for an Overseas Research Student (ORS) award which covers the difference between the home and overseas rate of the University Composition Fee.
Level of Study: Postgraduate.
Type: Scholarship.
Value: The University Composition Fee at the overseas rate, approved college fees, a maintenance allowance sufficient for a single student and a contribution towards a return economy airfare.
Length of Study: One year.
Frequency: Annual.
Study Establishment: The University of Cambridge.
Country of Study: United Kingdom.
No. of awards offered: Two.
Application Procedure: Applicants for these scholarships should apply directly to the British Embassy in Vietnam.
Closing Date: Please contact the organisation.
Contributor: Offered in collaboration with the Foreign and Commonwealth Office (FCO).
Additional Information: Further information is available on request.

For further information contact:

The British Embassy
16 Ly Thuong Kiet, Hanoi, Vietnam

British Chevening Cambridge Scholarships for Postgraduate Study (Chile)

Subjects: All subjects.
Purpose: To financially support study towards a PhD.
Eligibility: Applicants must be from Chile. The Trusts cannot admit students to the University or any of its colleges. Applicants for awards from the Trusts must, therefore, also apply to the University of Cambridge and be offered a place at Cambridge in the normal way. All applicants must have a First Class or High Second Class (Honours) Degree or equivalent and normally be under 26. All applicants must be successfully nominated for an Overseas Research Student (ORS) award which covers the difference between the home and overseas rate of the University Composition Fee.
Level of Study: Postgraduate.
Type: Scholarship.
Value: The University Composition Fee at the overseas rate, approved college fees and a maintenance allowance sufficient for a single student.
Length of Study: One year.
Frequency: Annual.
Study Establishment: The University of Cambridge.
Country of Study: United Kingdom.
No. of awards offered: One.
Application Procedure: Applicants for this scholarship must apply directly to the British Council in Chile.
Closing Date: Please contact the organisation.
Contributor: Offered in collaboration with the Foreign and Commonwealth Office (FCO).
Additional Information: Further information is available on request.

For further information contact:

The British Council
Eliodoro Yanez 832, Santiago de Chile, Chile

British Chevening Cambridge Scholarships for Postgraduate Study (Cuba)

Subjects: All subjects.
Purpose: To financially support those undertaking postgraduate study.
Eligibility: Applicants must be from Cuba. The Trusts cannot admit students to the University or any of its colleges. Applicants for awards from the Trusts must, therefore, also apply to the University of Cambridge and be offered a place at Cambridge in the normal way. All applicants must have a First Class or High Second Class (Honours) Degree or equivalent and normally be under 26.
Level of Study: Postgraduate.
Type: Scholarship.
Value: The University Composition Fee at the overseas rate, approved college fees, a maintenance allowance sufficient for a single student and a contribution towards a return economy airfare.
Length of Study: One year.
Frequency: Annual.
Study Establishment: The University of Cambridge.
Country of Study: United Kingdom.
No. of awards offered: Two.
Application Procedure: Applicants must complete a preliminary application form, which can be obtained from local universities, offices of the British Council or the Trust. The preliminary application form can be downloaded from http://www.admin.cam.ac.uk/univ/gsprospectus/c7/overseas/schemes.html. Completed forms must be returned to the main address. Shortlisted candidates will be sent forms for admission to the University of Cambridge.
Closing Date: Please contact the organisation.
Contributor: Offered in collaboration with the Foreign and Commonwealth Office (FCO).
Additional Information: Further information is available on request.

British Chevening Cambridge Scholarships for Postgraduate Study (Eastern Europe)

Subjects: All subjects.
Purpose: To financially support those undertaking postgraduate study.
Eligibility: Open to students from Poland, Romania or Yugoslavia. The Trusts cannot admit students to the University or any of its colleges. Applicants for awards from the Trusts must, therefore, also apply to the University of Cambridge and be offered a place at Cambridge in the normal way. All applicants must have a First Class or High Second Class (Honours) Degree or equivalent and normally be under 26.
Level of Study: Postgraduate.
Type: Scholarship.
Value: The University Composition Fee at the overseas rate, approved College fees, a maintenance allowance sufficient for a single student and a contribution towards return economy airfare.
Length of Study: One year.
Frequency: Annual.
Study Establishment: The University of Cambridge.
Country of Study: United Kingdom.
No. of awards offered: Up to six.
Application Procedure: Applicants must complete a preliminary application form, which can be obtained from local universities, offices of the British Council or the Trust. The preliminary application form can be downloaded from http://www.admin.cam.ac.uk/univ/gsprospectus/c7/overseas/schemes.html. Completed forms must be returned to the main address. Shortlisted candidates will be sent forms for admission to the University of Cambridge.
Closing Date: Please contact the organisation.
Contributor: Offered in collaboration with the Foreign and Commonwealth Office (FCO).
Additional Information: Further information is available on request.

British Chevening Cambridge Scholarships for Postgraduate Study (European Union)

Subjects: All subjects.
Purpose: To financially support those undertaking postgraduate study.
Eligibility: Open to citizens of Belgium, Denmark, Finland, Germany, Greece, Ireland, Italy, Luxembourg, the Netherlands, Portugal and Sweden.
Level of Study: Postgraduate.
Type: Scholarship.
Value: Applicants must contact local offices of the British Council.
Length of Study: One year.
Frequency: Annual.
Study Establishment: The University of Cambridge.
Country of Study: United Kingdom.
No. of awards offered: Varies.
Application Procedure: Applicants must contact the local offices of the British Council for details of the application procedure. Candidates are advised to apply well in advance of their proposed date of entry to the University of Cambridge.
Closing Date: Please contact the organisation.
Contributor: Offered in collaboration with the Foreign and Commonwealth Office (FCO).
Additional Information: Further information is available on request. In Sweden these awards are known as the Prince Bertil Memorial Cambridge Scholarships.

British Chevening Cambridge Scholarships for Postgraduate Study (Hong Kong)

Subjects: All subjects.
Purpose: To financially support those undertaking postgraduate study.
Eligibility: Open to citizens of Hong Kong.
Level of Study: Postgraduate.
Type: Scholarship.

Value: The University Composition Fee at the overseas rate, approved college fees, a maintenance allowance sufficient for a single student and a contribution to a return economy airfare.
Length of Study: One year.
Frequency: Annual.
Study Establishment: The University of Cambridge.
Country of Study: United Kingdom.
No. of awards offered: Eight.
Application Procedure: Applicants must contact the organisation.
Additional Information: Further information is available on request.

British Chevening Cambridge Scholarships for Postgraduate Study (Indonesia)

Subjects: All subjects.
Purpose: To financially support those undertaking postgraduate study.
Eligibility: Applicants must be citizens of Indonesia.
Level of Study: Postgraduate.
Type: Scholarship.
Value: The University Composition Fee at the overseas rate, approved college fees, a maintenance allowance sufficient for a single student and a contribution towards a return economy airfare.
Length of Study: One year.
Frequency: Annual.
Study Establishment: The University of Cambridge.
Country of Study: United Kingdom.
No. of awards offered: Three.
Application Procedure: Applicants must apply directly to the British Embassy in Indonesia.
Closing Date: Please contact the organisation.
Contributor: Offered in collaboration with the Malaysian Commonwealth Studies Centre and the Foreign and Commonwealth Office (FCO).
Additional Information: Further information is available on request.

For further information contact:

The British Embassy
Jalan M H Thamrin 75, Jakarta, 10310, Indonesia

British Chevening Cambridge Scholarships for Postgraduate Study (Malta)

Subjects: All subjects.
Purpose: To financially support those undertaking postgraduate study.
Eligibility: Applicants must be from Malta. The Trusts cannot admit students to the University or any of its colleges. Applicants for awards from the Trusts must, therefore, also apply to the University of Cambridge and be offered a place at Cambridge in the normal way. All applicants must have a First Class or High Second Class (Honours) Degree or equivalent and normally be under 26.
Level of Study: Postgraduate.
Type: Scholarship.
Value: The University Composition Fee at the overseas rate and approved college fees.
Length of Study: One year.
Frequency: Annual.
Study Establishment: The University of Cambridge.
Country of Study: United Kingdom.
No. of awards offered: Two.
Application Procedure: Applicants must complete a preliminary application form, which can be obtained from local universities, offices of the British Council or the Trust. The preliminary application form can be downloaded from http://www.admin.cam.ac.uk/univ/gsprospectus/c7/overseas/schemes.html. Completed forms must be returned to the main address. Shortlisted candidates will be sent forms for admission to the University of Cambridge.
Closing Date: Please contact the organisation.
Contributor: Offered in collaboration with the Foreign and Commonwealth Office (FCO).
Additional Information: Further information is available on request.

193

British Chevening Cambridge Scholarships for Postgraduate Study (Mexico)

Subjects: All subjects.

Purpose: To financially support those undertaking postgraduate study.

Eligibility: Applicants must be from Mexico. The Trusts cannot admit students to the University or any of its colleges. Applicants for awards from the Trusts must, therefore, also apply to the University of Cambridge and be offered a place at Cambridge in the normal way. All applicants must have a First Class or High Second Class (Honours) Degree or equivalent and normally be under 26.

Level of Study: Postgraduate.

Type: Scholarship.

Value: The University Composition Fee at the overseas rate, approved college fees and a maintenance allowance sufficient for a single student.

Length of Study: One year.

Frequency: Annual.

Study Establishment: The University of Cambridge.

Country of Study: United Kingdom.

No. of awards offered: One.

Application Procedure: Applicants for this scholarship must complete a preliminary application form which can only be obtained from the British Council, Mexico City.

Closing Date: Please contact the organisation.

Contributor: Offered in collaboration with the Foreign and Commonwealth Office (FCO).

Additional Information: Further information is available on request.

For further information contact:

The British Council
Maestro Antonio Caso 127
Col San Rafael
Delegacion Cuauhtemoc
Apartado Postal 30-588, Mexico City, DF, 06470, Mexico

British Chevening Cambridge Scholarships for Postgraduate Study (Mozambique)

Subjects: All subjects.

Purpose: To financially support those undertaking postgraduate study.

Eligibility: Applicants must be from Mozambique. The Trusts cannot admit students to the University or any of its colleges. Applicants for awards from the Trusts must, therefore, also apply to the University of Cambridge and be offered a place at Cambridge in the normal way. All applicants must have a First Class or High Second Class (Honours) Degree or equivalent and normally be under 26. All applicants must be successfully nominated for an Overseas Research Student (ORS) award which covers the difference between the home and overseas rate of the University Composition Fee.

Level of Study: Postgraduate.

Type: Scholarship.

Value: The University Composition Fee at the overseas rate, approved college fees, a maintenance allowance sufficient for a single student and a contribution towards return economy airfare.

Length of Study: One year.

Frequency: Annual.

Study Establishment: The University of Cambridge.

Country of Study: United Kingdom.

No. of awards offered: Up to four.

Application Procedure: Applicants must complete a preliminary application form, which can be obtained from local universities, offices of the British Council or the Trust. The preliminary application form can be downloaded from http://www.admin.cam.ac.uk/univ/gsprospectus/c7/overseas/schemes.html. Completed forms must be returned to the main address. Shortlisted candidates will be sent forms for admission to the University of Cambridge.

Closing Date: Please contact the organisation.

Contributor: Offered in collaboration with the Malaysian Commonwealth Studies Centre and the Foreign and Commonwealth Office (FCO).

Additional Information: Further information is available on request.

British Chevening Cambridge Scholarships for Postgraduate Study (Peru)

Subjects: All subjects.

Purpose: To financially support those undertaking postgraduate study.

Eligibility: Open to students from Peru. The Trusts cannot admit students to the University or any of its colleges. Applicants for awards from the Trusts must, therefore, also apply to the University of Cambridge and be offered a place at Cambridge in the normal way. All applicants must have a First Class or High Second Class (Honours) Degree or equivalent and normally be under 26. All applicants must be successfully nominated for an Overseas Research Student (ORS) award which covers the difference between the home and overseas rate of the University Composition Fee.

Level of Study: Postgraduate.

Type: Scholarship.

Value: The University Composition Fee at the appropriate rate, approved college fees, a maintenance allowance sufficient for a single student and a contribution towards a return economy airfare.

Length of Study: One year.

Frequency: Annual.

Study Establishment: The University of Cambridge.

Country of Study: United Kingdom.

No. of awards offered: One.

Application Procedure: Applicants must contact the British Council in Peru.

Closing Date: Please contact the organisation.

Contributor: Offered in collaboration with the Foreign and Commonwealth Office (FCO).

Additional Information: Further information is available on request.

For further information contact:

The British Council
Calle Alberto Lynch 110
San Isidro, Lima, 27, Peru

British Chevening Cambridge Scholarships for Postgraduate Study (Thailand)

Subjects: All subjects.

Purpose: To financially support those undertaking postgraduate study.

Eligibility: Applicants must be from Thailand. The Trusts cannot admit students to the University or any of its colleges. Applicants for awards from the Trusts must, therefore, also apply to the University of Cambridge and be offered a place at Cambridge in the normal way. All applicants must have a First Class or High Second Class (Honours) Degree or equivalent and normally be under 26. All applicants must be successfully nominated for an Overseas Research Student (ORS) award which covers the difference between the home and overseas rate of the University Composition Fee.

Level of Study: Postgraduate.

Type: Scholarship.

Value: The University Composition Fee at the overseas rate, approved college fees, a maintenance allowance sufficient for a single student and a contribution to a return economy airfare.

Length of Study: One year.

Frequency: Annual.

Study Establishment: The University of Cambridge.

Country of Study: United Kingdom.

No. of awards offered: Two.

Application Procedure: Applicants must complete a preliminary application form, which can be obtained from local universities, offices of the British Council or the Trust. The preliminary application form can be downloaded from http://www.admin.cam.ac.uk/univ/gsprospectus/c7/overseas/schemes.html. Completed forms must be returned to the main address. Shortlisted candidates will be sent forms for admission to the University of Cambridge.

Closing Date: Please contact the organisation.

Contributor: Offered in collaboration with the Cambridge Thai Foundation and the Foreign and Commonwealth Office (FCO).
Additional Information: Further information is available on request.

British Chevening Malaysia Cambridge Scholarship for PhD Study

Subjects: All subjects.
Purpose: To financially support study towards a PhD.
Eligibility: Applicants must be from Malaysia. The Trusts cannot admit students to the University or any of its colleges. Applicants for awards from the Trusts must, therefore, also apply to the University of Cambridge and be offered a place at Cambridge in the normal way. All applicants must have a First Class or High Second Class (Honours) Degree or equivalent and normally be under 26. All applicants must be successfully nominated for an Overseas Research Student (ORS) award which covers the difference between the home and overseas rate of the University Composition Fee.
Level of Study: Doctorate.
Type: Scholarship.
Value: The University Composition Fee at the appropriate rate, approved college fees, a maintenance allowance sufficient for a single student and a contribution towards return economy airfare.
Length of Study: Up to three years.
Frequency: Annual.
Study Establishment: The University of Cambridge.
Country of Study: United Kingdom.
No. of awards offered: One.
Application Procedure: Applicants must complete a preliminary application form, which can be obtained from local universities, offices of the British Council or the Trust. The preliminary application form can be downloaded from http://www.admin.cam.ac.uk/univ/gsprospectus/c7/overseas/schemes.html. Completed forms must be returned to the main address. Shortlisted candidates will be sent forms for admission to the University of Cambridge.
Closing Date: Please contact the organisation.
Contributor: Offered in collaboration with the Foreign and Commonwealth Office (FCO).
Additional Information: Further information is available on request.

British Chevening Malaysia Cambridge Scholarships for Postgraduate Study

Subjects: All subjects.
Purpose: To financially support those undertaking postgraduate study.
Eligibility: Applicants must be from Malaysia. The Trusts cannot admit students to the University or any of its colleges. Applicants for awards from the Trusts must, therefore, also apply to the University of Cambridge and be offered a place at Cambridge in the normal way. All applicants must have a First Class or High Second Class (Honours) Degree or equivalent and normally be under 26.
Level of Study: Postgraduate.
Type: Scholarship.
Value: The University Composition Fee at the overseas rate, approved college fees, a maintenance allowance sufficient for a single student and a contribution towards a return economy airfare.
Length of Study: One year.
Frequency: Annual.
Study Establishment: The University of Cambridge.
Country of Study: United Kingdom.
No. of awards offered: Four.
Application Procedure: Applicants must complete a preliminary application form, which can be obtained from local universities, offices of the British Council or the Trust. The preliminary application form can be downloaded from http://www.admin.cam.ac.uk/univ/gsprospectus/c7/overseas/schemes.html. Completed forms must be returned to the main address. Shortlisted candidates will be sent forms for admission to the University of Cambridge.
Closing Date: Please contact the organisation.
Contributor: Offered in collaboration with the Foreign and Commonwealth Office (FCO).

Additional Information: Further information is available on request.

For further information contact:

The Secretary
Cambridge (Malaysia) Foundation
PO Box 10139, Kuala Lumpur, 50704, Malaysia

British Chevening Scholarships for Postgraduate Study (Pakistan)

Subjects: All subjects.
Purpose: To financially reward students of outstanding academic merit.
Eligibility: Open to citizens of Pakistan. The Trusts cannot admit students to the University or any of its colleges. Applicants for awards from the Trusts must, therefore, also apply to the University of Cambridge and be offered a place at Cambridge in the normal way. All applicants must have a First Class or High Second Class (Honours) Degree or equivalent and normally be under 26.
Level of Study: Postgraduate.
Type: Scholarship.
Value: The University Composition Fee at the overseas rate, approved college fees, a maintenance allowance sufficient for a single student and a contribution towards a return economy airfare.
Length of Study: One year.
Frequency: Annual.
Study Establishment: The University of Cambridge.
Country of Study: United Kingdom.
No. of awards offered: Five.
Application Procedure: Applicants must complete a preliminary application form, which can be obtained from local universities, offices of the British Council or the Trust. The preliminary application form can be downloaded from http://www.admin.cam.ac.uk/univ/gsprospectus/c7/overseas/schemes.html. Completed forms must be returned to the main address. Shortlisted candidates will be sent forms for admission to the University of Cambridge.
Closing Date: Please contact the organisation.
Contributor: Offered in collaboration with the Foreign and Commonwealth Office (FCO).
Additional Information: Further information is available on request.

For further information contact:

The Secretary
The Board of Graduate Studies
4 Mill Lane, Cambridge, Cambridgeshire, CB2 1RZ, England

British Prize Scholarships for Postgraduate Study

Subjects: For study in development studies, economics or international relations.
Purpose: To financially support those undertaking postgraduate study.
Eligibility: One scholarship is awarded to a student from Barbados and one from the Eastern Caribbean (Antigua and Barbuda, Dominica, Grenada, St Kitts-Nevis, St Lucia, St Vincent and the Grenadines). The Trusts cannot admit students to the University or any of its colleges. Applicants for awards from the Trusts must, therefore, also apply to the University of Cambridge and be offered a place at Cambridge in the normal way. All applicants must have a First Class or High Second Class (Honours) Degree or equivalent and normally be under 26.
Level of Study: Postgraduate.
Type: Scholarship.
Value: The University Composition Fee at the overseas rate, approved college fees, a maintenance allowance sufficient for a single student and a contribution towards return economy airfare.
Length of Study: One year.
Frequency: Annual.
Study Establishment: The University of Cambridge.
Country of Study: United Kingdom.
No. of awards offered: Two.

Application Procedure: Applicants must complete a preliminary application form, which can be obtained from local universities, offices of the British Council or the Trust. The preliminary application form can be downloaded from http://www.admin.cam.ac.uk/univ/gsprospectus/c7/overseas/schemes.html. Completed forms must be returned to the main address. Shortlisted candidates will be sent forms for admission to the University of Cambridge.
Closing Date: Please contact the organisation.
Contributor: Offered in collaboration with Her Majesty's government.
Additional Information: Further information is available on request.

C T Taylor Studentship for PhD Study

Subjects: Biotechnology, computer science, chemical engineering, engineering, earth sciences and geography, genetics, land economy, mathematics, physics and chemistry, plant sciences and zoology.
Purpose: To financially support study towards a PhD.
Eligibility: Open to citizens of Australia, New Zealand or Canada. The Trusts cannot admit students to the University or any of its colleges. Applicants for awards from the Trusts must, therefore, also apply to the University of Cambridge and be offered a place at Cambridge in the normal way. All applicants must have a First Class or High Second Class (Honours) Degree or equivalent and normally be under 26. All applicants must be successfully nominated for an Overseas Research Student (ORS) award which covers the difference between the home and overseas rate of the University Composition Fee.
Level of Study: Doctorate.
Type: Studentship.
Value: Up to UK £5,000 towards the costs of study at Cambridge, to be determined in the light of the student's own resources.
Length of Study: Up to three years.
Frequency: Annual.
Study Establishment: The University of Cambridge.
Country of Study: United Kingdom.
No. of awards offered: One.
Application Procedure: Applicants must complete a preliminary application form and send it to the address relevant to that particular country. The final application forms must be sent to The Secretary of the Board of Graduate Studies.
Closing Date: Please contact the organisation.
Contributor: The C T Taylor Fund.
Additional Information: Further information is available on request.

For further information contact:

The Secretary
The Board for Graduate Studies
4 Mill Lane, Cambridge, Cambridgeshire, CB2 1RZ, England

Cadbury's-Schweppes Cambridge Scholarship For PhD Study

Subjects: All subjects.
Purpose: To financially support study towards a PhD.
Eligibility: Open to candidates from Australia. The Trusts cannot admit students to the University or any of its colleges. Applicants for awards from the Trusts must, therefore, also apply to the University of Cambridge and be offered a place at Cambridge in the normal way. All applicants must have a First Class or High Second Class (Honours) Degree or equivalent and normally be under 26. All applicants must be successfully nominated for an Overseas Research Student (ORS) award which covers the difference between the home and overseas rate of the University Composition Fee.
Level of Study: Doctorate, Predoctorate.
Type: Scholarship.
Frequency: Varies.
Study Establishment: The University of Cambridge.
Country of Study: United Kingdom.
No. of awards offered: One.
Application Procedure: Applicants must contact the organisation.

Contributor: Offered in collaboration with the Cambridge Australia Trust.
Additional Information: Further information is available on request. For details of scholarships offered in collaboration with the Cambridge Australia Trust please see the website http://www.anu.edu/cabs/scholarships/cambridge/cambridge-austrust.html.

For further information contact:

The Secretary
The Board of Graduate Studies
4 Mill Lane, Cambridge, Cambridgeshire, CB2 1RZ, England

Cambridge Alumni Scholarship For PhD Study

Subjects: All subjects.
Purpose: To financially support study towards a PhD.
Eligibility: Open to candidates from Australia. The Trusts cannot admit students to the University or any of its colleges. Applicants for awards from the Trusts must, therefore, also apply to the University of Cambridge and be offered a place at Cambridge in the normal way. All applicants must have a First Class or High Second Class (Honours) Degree or equivalent and normally be under 26. All applicants must be successfully nominated for an Overseas Research Student (ORS) award which covers the difference between the home and overseas rate of the University Composition Fee.
Level of Study: Doctorate, Predoctorate.
Type: Scholarship.
Value: The University Composition Fee at the home rate, approved college fees, a maintenance allowance sufficient for a single student and a contribution to a return economy airfare.
Length of Study: Up to three years.
Frequency: Varies.
Study Establishment: The University of Cambridge.
Country of Study: United Kingdom.
No. of awards offered: One.
Application Procedure: Applicants must contact the Board of Graduate Studies.
Closing Date: Please contact the organisation.
Contributor: Offered in collaboration with the Cambridge Australia Trust.
Additional Information: Further information is available on request.

For further information contact:

The Secretary
The Board of Graduate Studies
4 Mill Lane, Cambridge, Cambridgeshire, CB2 1RZ, England

Cambridge DFID Scholarships for Postgraduate Study

Subjects: All subjects.
Purpose: To financially support those undertaking postgraduate study.
Eligibility: The Trusts cannot admit students to the University or any of its colleges. Applicants for awards from the Trusts must, therefore, also apply to the University of Cambridge and be offered a place at Cambridge in the normal way. All applicants must have a First Class or High Second Class (Honours) Degree or equivalent (if applying for a postgraduate course), be under the age of 35 on October 1st of the year they are applying for, return to their own country to work or study after completing the course, not be employed by a government department or by a parastatal organisation, not at present be living in a developed country, and not have taken studies lasting a year or more in a developed country. Citizens from developing countries of the Commonwealth are eligible - The Falkland Islands, St Helena, Tristan de Cunha, Brunei, Cameroon, Gambia, Ghana, Kenya, Sierra Leone, Tanzania, Uganda, India, Malta, Mauritius, the Seychelles, Fiji, Kiribati, Nauru, Papua New Guinea, Pitcairn, the Solomon Islands, Tonga, Tuvalu, Vanuatu, Western Samoa, South Africa, Botswana, Lesotho, Malawi, Mozambique, Namibia, Swaziland, Zambia, Zimbabwe and the Commonwealth countries of the Caribbean.
Level of Study: Postgraduate.
Type: Scholarship.

Value: The University Composition Fee at the overseas rate, approved college fees, a maintenance allowance sufficient for a single student and a contribution towards return economy airfare.
Length of Study: One year.
Frequency: Annual.
Study Establishment: The University of Cambridge.
Country of Study: United Kingdom.
No. of awards offered: 50.
Application Procedure: Applicants must complete a preliminary application form, which can be obtained from local universities, offices of the British Council or the Trust. The preliminary application form can be downloaded from http://www.admin.cam.ac.uk/univ/gsprospectus/c7/overseas/schemes.html. Completed forms must be returned to the main address. Shortlisted candidates will be sent forms for admission to the University of Cambridge.
Closing Date: Please contact the organisation.
Contributor: Offered in collaboration with the Department for International Development (DFID).
Additional Information: Further information is available on request.

Cambridge Foundation Scholarships for Postgraduate Study (Chile)

Subjects: All subjects, particularly those relevant to the needs of Chile.
Purpose: To financially support those undertaking postgraduate study.
Eligibility: Open to citizens of Chile. The Trusts cannot admit students to the University or any of its colleges. Applicants for awards from the Trusts must, therefore, also apply to the University of Cambridge and be offered a place at Cambridge in the normal way. All applicants must have a First Class or High Second Class (Honours) Degree or equivalent and normally be under 26. All applicants must be successfully nominated for an Overseas Research Student (ORS) award which covers the difference between the home and overseas rate of the University Composition Fee.
Level of Study: Postgraduate.
Type: Scholarship.
Value: The University Composition Fee at the appropriate rate, approved college fees, a maintenance allowance sufficient for a single student and a contribution towards a return economy airfare.
Length of Study: One year.
Frequency: Annual.
Study Establishment: The University of Cambridge.
Country of Study: United Kingdom.
No. of awards offered: Varies.
Application Procedure: Applicants must complete a preliminary application form, which can be obtained from local universities, offices of the British Council or the Trust. The preliminary application form can be downloaded from http://www.admin.cam.ac.uk/univ/gsprospectus/c7/overseas/schemes.html. Completed forms must be returned to the main address. Shortlisted candidates will be sent forms for admission to the University of Cambridge.
Closing Date: Please contact the organisation.
Contributor: Offered in collaboration with the Cambridge Foundation in Chile.
Additional Information: Further information is available on request.

Cambridge Livingstone Trust Scholarships for PhD Study

Subjects: All subjects.
Purpose: To financially support study towards a PhD.
Eligibility: Open to students from South Africa, Botswana, Lesotho, Malawi, Namibia, Swaziland, Zambia or Zimbabwe. The Trusts cannot admit students to the University or any of its colleges. Applicants for awards from the Trusts must, therefore, also apply to the University of Cambridge and be offered a place at Cambridge in the normal way. All applicants must have a First Class or High Second Class (Honours) Degree or equivalent and normally be under 26. All applicants must be successfully nominated for an Overseas Research

Student (ORS) award which covers the difference between the home and overseas rate of the University Composition Fee.
Level of Study: Doctorate, Predoctorate.
Type: Scholarship.
Value: The University Composition Fee at the appropriate rate, approved college fees, a maintenance allowance sufficient for a single student and a contribution towards a return economy airfare.
Length of Study: Up to three years.
Frequency: Annual.
Study Establishment: The University of Cambridge.
Country of Study: United Kingdom.
No. of awards offered: Varies.
Application Procedure: Applicants must complete a preliminary application form, which can be obtained from local universities, offices of the British Council or the main address. Completed forms must be returned to the main address. Shortlisted candidates will be sent forms for admission to the University of Cambridge and a scholarship application form. These forms must be returned to the Board of Graduate Studies at the address below.
Closing Date: Please contact the organisation.
Contributor: Offered by the Cambridge Livingstone Trust with the generous assistance of Anglo-American and Shell.
Additional Information: Further information is available on request.

For further information contact:

The Board of Graduate Studies
4 Mill Lane, Cambridge, Cambridgeshire, CB2 1RZ, England

Cambridge Livingstone Trust Scholarships for Postgraduate Study

Subjects: All subjects.
Purpose: To financially support those undertaking postgraduate study.
Eligibility: For students from South Africa, Botswana, Lesotho, Malawi, Namibia, Swaziland, Zambia or Zimbabwe. The Trusts cannot admit students to the University or any of its Colleges. Applicants for awards from the Trusts must, therefore, also apply to the University of Cambridge and be offered a place at Cambridge in the normal way. All applicants must have a First Class or High Second Class (Honours) Degree or equivalent and normally be under 26.
Level of Study: Postgraduate.
Type: Scholarship.
Value: The University Composition Fee at the overseas rate, approved college fees, a maintenance allowance sufficient for a single student and a contribution towards return economy airfare.
Length of Study: One year.
Frequency: Annual.
Study Establishment: The University of Cambridge.
Country of Study: United Kingdom.
No. of awards offered: Varies.
Application Procedure: Applicants must complete a preliminary application form, which can be obtained from local universities, offices of the British Council or the Trust. The preliminary application form can be downloaded from http://www.admin.cam.ac.uk/univ/gsprospectus/c7/overseas/schemes.html. Completed forms must be returned to the main address. Shortlisted candidates will be sent forms for admission to the University of Cambridge.
Closing Date: Please contact the organisation.
Contributor: Offered by the Cambridge Livingstone Trust with the generous assistance of Anglo-American and Shell.
Additional Information: Further information is available on request.

Cambridge Nehru Scholarships for PhD Study

Subjects: All subjects.
Purpose: To financially support study towards a PhD.
Eligibility: Applicants must be from India. All applicants must be successful in winning an Overseas Research Student (ORS) award, which pays the difference between the home and overseas rate of the University Composition Fee. Those who have, in addition, to a First Class (Honours) Degree, a First Class Master's Degree or its equivalent, may be given preference.

Level of Study: Doctorate, Predoctorate.
Type: Scholarship.
Value: The University Composition Fee at the home rate, approved college fees, a maintenance allowance sufficient for a single student and a contribution towards a return economy airfare.
Length of Study: Up to three years.
Frequency: Annual.
Study Establishment: The University of Cambridge.
Country of Study: United Kingdom.
No. of awards offered: Up to eight.
Application Procedure: Applicants may obtain further details and a preliminary application form by writing before August 16th of the year before entry to the Joint Secretary of the Nehru Trust for Cambridge University at the address below giving details of academic qualifications.
Closing Date: Please contact the organisation.
Contributor: Offered in collaboration with the Nehru Trust for Cambridge University.
Additional Information: Further information is available on request.

For further information contact:

The Nehru Trust for Cambridge University
Teen Murti House
Teen Murti Marg, New Delhi, 110011, India

The Nehru Trust for Cambridge University
Teen Murti House
Teen Murti Marg, New Delhi, 110011, India

Cambridge Raffles Scholarships

Subjects: All subjects.
Purpose: To financially support those undertaking postgraduate study.
Eligibility: Applicants must be from Singapore. The Trusts cannot admit students to the University or any of its colleges. Applicants for awards from the Trusts must, therefore, also apply to the University of Cambridge and be offered a place at Cambridge in the normal way. All applicants must have a First Class or High Second Class (Honours) Degree or equivalent and normally be under 26.
Level of Study: Postgraduate.
Type: Scholarship.
Value: The University Composition Fee at the overseas rate, approved college fees, a maintenance sufficient for a single student and a contribution towards return economy airfare.
Length of Study: One year.
Frequency: Annual.
Study Establishment: The University of Cambridge.
Country of Study: United Kingdom.
No. of awards offered: Two.
Application Procedure: Applicants must complete a preliminary application form, which can be obtained from local universities, offices of the British Council or the Trust. The preliminary application form can be downloaded from http://www.admin.cam.ac.uk/univ/gsprospectus/c7/overseas/schemes.html. Completed forms must be returned to the main address. Shortlisted candidates will be sent forms for admission to the University of Cambridge.
Closing Date: Please contact the organisation.
Contributor: Offered in collaboration with the Foreign and Commonwealth Office (FCO).
Additional Information: Further information is available on request.

Cambridge Thai Foundation Scholarship for PhD study

Subjects: All subjects.
Purpose: To financially support study towards a PhD.
Eligibility: Applicants must be from Thailand. The Trusts cannot admit students to the University or any of its colleges. Applicants for awards from the Trusts must, therefore, also apply to the University of Cambridge and be offered a place at Cambridge in the normal way. All applicants must have a First Class or High Second Class (Honours) Degree or equivalent and normally be under 26. For PhD study applicants must be successfully nominated for an Overseas

Research Student (ORS) award which pays the difference between the home and overseas rate of the University Composition Fee.
Level of Study: Doctorate.
Type: Scholarship.
Value: The University Composition Fee at the appropriate rate, approved college fees, a maintenance allowance sufficient for a single student and a contribution towards a return economy airfare.
Length of Study: Up to three years.
Frequency: Annual.
Study Establishment: The University of Cambridge.
Country of Study: United Kingdom.
No. of awards offered: One.
Application Procedure: Applicants must complete a preliminary application form, which can be obtained from local universities, offices of the British Council or the main address. Completed forms must be returned to the main address. Shortlisted candidates will be sent forms for admission to the University of Cambridge and a scholarship application form. These forms must be returned to The Board of Graduate Studies at the address below.
Closing Date: Please contact the organisation.
Contributor: Offered in collaboration with the Cambridge Thai Foundation.
Additional Information: Further information is available on request.

Cambridge Thai Foundation Scholarship for Postgraduate Study

Subjects: All subjects.
Purpose: To financially support those undertaking postgraduate study.
Eligibility: Applicants must be from Thailand. The Trusts cannot admit students to the University or any of its colleges. Applicants for awards from the Trusts must, therefore, also apply to the University of Cambridge and be offered a place at Cambridge in the normal way. All applicants must have a First Class or High Second Class (Honours) Degree or equivalent and normally be under 26 years of age. All applicants must be successfully nominated for an Overseas Research Student (ORS) award which covers the difference between the home and overseas rate of the University Composition Fee.
Level of Study: Postgraduate.
Type: Scholarship.
Value: The University Composition Fee at the overseas rate, approved college fees, a maintenance allowance sufficient for a single student and a contribution towards return economy airfare.
Length of Study: One year.
Frequency: Annual.
Study Establishment: The University of Cambridge.
Country of Study: United Kingdom.
No. of awards offered: Two.
Application Procedure: Applicants must complete a preliminary application form, which can be obtained from local universities, offices of the British Council or the Trust. The preliminary application form can be downloaded from http://www.admin.cam.ac.uk/univ/gsprospectus/c7/overseas/schemes.html. Completed forms must be returned to the main address. Shortlisted candidates will be sent forms for admission to the University of Cambridge.
Closing Date: Please contact the organisation.
Contributor: The Cambridge Thai Foundation.
Additional Information: Further information is available on request.

Canada Cambridge Scholarships For PhD Study

Subjects: All subjects.
Purpose: To financially support study towards a PhD.
Eligibility: For students from Canada. The Trusts cannot admit students to the University or any of its colleges. Applicants for awards from the Trusts must, therefore, also apply to the University of Cambridge and be offered a place at Cambridge in the normal way. All applicants must have a First Class or High Second Class (Honours) Degree or equivalent and normally be under 26. All applicants must be successfully nominated for an Overseas Research Student

(ORS) award which covers the difference between the home and overseas rate of the University Composition Fee.
Level of Study: Doctorate, Predoctorate.
Type: Scholarship.
Value: The University Composition Fee at the home rate and approved college fees.
Length of Study: Up to three years.
Frequency: Annual.
Study Establishment: The University of Cambridge.
Country of Study: United Kingdom.
No. of awards offered: Up to five.
Application Procedure: Application forms for the scholarship will be sent out to eligible candidates once the completed form for admission to the University of Cambridge has reached the Board of Graduate Studies.
Closing Date: Please contact the organisation.
Additional Information: Further information is available on request.

For further information contact:

The Secretary
The Board of Graduate Studies
4 Mill Lane, Cambridge, Cambridgeshire, CB2 1RZ, England

CEU Cambridge Non-Degree Research Scholarships
Subjects: All subjects.
Purpose: To financially support the pursuit of non-degree research.
Eligibility: Applicants must be current PhD students at the Central European University. They must be applying to pursue research at Cambridge in the same subject area that they are following at the Central European University.
Level of Study: Doctorate, Predoctorate.
Type: Scholarship.
Value: The University Composition Fee at the appropriate rate, approved college fees, a maintenance allowance sufficient for a single student and a return economy airfare.
Length of Study: Up to one year.
Frequency: Annual.
Study Establishment: The University of Cambridge.
Country of Study: United Kingdom.
No. of awards offered: Up to six.
Application Procedure: Applicants must apply through the Scholarships Office at the Central European University.
Closing Date: Please contact the organisation.
Contributor: Offered in collaboration with the Central European University (CEU).
Additional Information: Further information is available on request.

CIALS Cambridge Scholarships
Subjects: Law.
Purpose: To support study towards the Master of Law (LLM) degree.
Eligibility: Candidates must be Canadian citizens. Open to graduates of Canadian Law Schools who have completed a Bachelor of Law degree on or before June 1st. The Trusts cannot admit students to the University or any of its colleges. Applicants for awards from the Trusts must, therefore, also apply to the University of Cambridge and be offered a place at Cambridge in the normal way. All applicants must have a First Class or High Second Class (Honours) Degree or equivalent and normally be under 26.
Level of Study: Postgraduate.
Type: Scholarship.
Frequency: Annual.
Study Establishment: The University of Cambridge.
Country of Study: United Kingdom.
No. of awards offered: Two.
Application Procedure: Applicants must apply in writing to the Executive Director of the Canadian Institute for Advanced Legal Studies.
Closing Date: Please contact the organisation.
Contributor: Offered in collaboration with the Canadian Institute for Advanced Legal Studies (CIALS).
Additional Information: Further information is available on request.

For further information contact:

Executive Director
The Canadian Institute of Advanced Legal Studies
4 Beechwood Avenue, Ottawa, ON, K1L 8L9, Canada
Contact: Mr Frank E McArdle, Executive Director

Citibank Cambridge Scholarships
Subjects: Economics or finance.
Purpose: To financially support those undertaking postgraduate study.
Eligibility: Open to citizens of Australia, New Zealand, Sri Lanka, Brunei, Hong Kong, India, Indonesia, Malaysia, Philippines, Singapore and Thailand. The Trusts cannot admit students to the University or any of its colleges. Applicants for awards from the Trusts must, therefore, also apply to the University of Cambridge and be offered a place at Cambridge in the normal way. All applicants must have a First Class or High Second Class (Honours) Degree or equivalent and normally be under 26.
Level of Study: Postgraduate.
Type: Scholarship.
Value: The University Composition Fee at the overseas rate, approved college fees, a maintenance allowance sufficient for a single student and a contribution towards return economy airfare.
Length of Study: One year.
Frequency: As available.
Study Establishment: The University of Cambridge.
Country of Study: United Kingdom.
No. of awards offered: One.
Application Procedure: Applicants must complete a preliminary application form, which can be obtained from local universities, offices of the British Council or the Trust. The preliminary application form can be downloaded from http://www.admin.cam.ac.uk/univ/gsprospectus/c7/overseas/schemes.html. Completed forms must be returned to the main address. Shortlisted candidates will be sent forms for admission to the University of Cambridge.
Closing Date: Please contact the organisation.
Contributor: Offered in collaboration with Citibank.
Additional Information: Further information is available on request.

Citibank Cambridge Scholarships for Postgraduate Study (Czech Republic, Hungary, Poland and Slovakia)
Subjects: Economics or finance.
Purpose: To allow candidates to pursue a one year diploma at Cambridge in economics, and, subject to a satisfactory performance in the diploma, to proceed to a one year MPhil degree in finance and economics.
Eligibility: Open to students from the Czech Republic, Hungary, Poland or Slovakia. The Trusts cannot admit students to the University or any of its colleges. Applicants for awards from the Trusts must, therefore, also apply to the University of Cambridge and be offered a place at Cambridge in the normal way. All applicants must have a First Class or High Second Class (Honours) Degree or equivalent and normally be under 26.
Level of Study: Postgraduate.
Type: Scholarship.
Value: The University Composition Fee at the overseas rate, approved college fees, a maintenance allowance sufficient for a single student and a contribution towards a return economy airfare.
Length of Study: One year.
Frequency: Annual.
Study Establishment: The University of Cambridge.
Country of Study: United Kingdom.
No. of awards offered: Two.
Application Procedure: Applicants must complete a preliminary application form, which can be obtained from local universities, offices of the British Council or the Trust. The preliminary application form can be downloaded from http://www.admin.cam.ac.uk/univ/gsprospectus/c7/overseas/schemes.html. Completed forms must be returned to the main

address. Shortlisted candidates will be sent forms for admission to the University of Cambridge.
Closing Date: Please contact the organisation.
Contributor: Offered in collaboration with Citibank.
Additional Information: Further information is available on request.

Computer Laboratory ORS Equivalent Awards

Subjects: Computer science.
Purpose: To financially support study towards a PhD.
Eligibility: Open to candidates studying for a PhD in the Computer Laboratory.
Level of Study: Postgraduate.
Type: Award.
Value: Up to the difference between the home and overseas rate of the University Composition Fee.
Length of Study: Up to three years.
Frequency: As available.
Study Establishment: The University of Cambridge.
Country of Study: United Kingdom.
No. of awards offered: One.
Application Procedure: Applicants must contact the organisation.
Closing Date: Please contact the organisation.
Additional Information: Further information is available on request.

Corpus Christi ACE Scholarship for Postgraduate Study

Subjects: Conservation, development or the environment.
Purpose: To financially support those undertaking postgraduate study.
Eligibility: Open to students from the developing world with a preference for applicants from Eastern Europe. The Trusts cannot admit students to the University or any of its colleges. Applicants for awards from the Trusts must, therefore, also apply to the University of Cambridge and be offered a place at Cambridge in the normal way. All applicants must have a First Class or High Second Class (Honours) Degree or equivalent and normally be under 26.
Level of Study: Postgraduate.
Type: Scholarship.
Value: The University Composition Fee at the overseas rate, approved college fees, a maintenance allowance sufficient for a single student and a contribution towards a return economy airfare.
Length of Study: One year.
Frequency: Annual.
Study Establishment: Corpus Christi College, the University of Cambridge.
Country of Study: United Kingdom.
No. of awards offered: One.
Application Procedure: Applicants must complete a preliminary application form, which can be obtained from local universities, offices of the British Council or the Trust. The preliminary application form can be downloaded from http://www.admin.cam.ac.uk/univ/gsprospectus/c7/over-seas/schemes.html. Completed forms must be returned to the main address. Shortlisted candidates will be sent forms for admission to the University of Cambridge.
Closing Date: Please contact the organisation.
Contributor: Offered in collaboration with the Association for Cultural Exchange (ACE) and Corpus Christi College, the University of Cambridge.
Additional Information: Further information is available on request.

CSIRO Cambridge Scholarship for PhD Study

Subjects: All subjects.
Purpose: To financially support study towards a PhD.
Eligibility: Open to Australian citizens. The Trusts cannot admit students to the University or any of its colleges. Applicants for awards from the Trusts must, therefore, also apply to the University of Cambridge and be offered a place at Cambridge in the normal way. All applicants must have a First Class or High Second Class (Honours) Degree or equivalent and normally be under 26. All applicants must be successfully nominated for an Overseas Research Student

(ORS) award which covers the difference between the home and overseas rate of the University Composition Fee.
Level of Study: Doctorate.
Type: Scholarship.
Value: The University Composition Fee at the home rate, approved college fees, a maintenance allowance sufficient for a single student and a contribution towards a return economy airfare.
Length of Study: Up to three years.
Frequency: Varies.
Study Establishment: The University of Cambridge.
Country of Study: United Kingdom.
No. of awards offered: One.
Application Procedure: Applicants must contact the organisation.
Contributor: Offered in collaboration with the Cambridge Australia Trust.
Additional Information: Further information is available on request from the Board of Graduate Studies. For details of scholarships offered in collaboration with the Cambridge Australia Trust please see the website http://www.anu.edu/cabs/scholarships/cambridge/cambridge-austrust.html.

For further information contact:

The Secretary
Board of Graduate Studies
4 Mill Lane, Cambridge, Cambridgeshire, CB2 1RZ, England

Cyprus Cambridge Scholarships For PhD Study

Subjects: All subjects.
Purpose: To financially support study towards a PhD.
Eligibility: Open to citizens of Cyprus. Candidates must sign an undertaking with the Cyprus State Scholarship Authority to return to work in Cyprus for a minimum of three years. This requirement may be deferred if, eg., the Scholar obtains a subsequent award for further studies. The Trust cannot admit students to the University or any of its colleges. Applicants for awards from the Trusts must, therefore, also apply to the University of Cambridge and be offered a place at Cambridge in the normal way. All applicants must have a First Class or High Second Class (Honours) Degree or equivalent and normally be under 26. Candidates must be successfully nominated for an Overseas Research Student (ORS) award, which covers the difference between the home and overseas rate of the University Composition Fee.
Level of Study: Doctorate.
Type: Scholarship.
Value: The scholarships will take into account the financial resources of the applicant and will cover up to the University Composition Fee at the overseas rate, approved college fees, a maintenance allowance sufficient for a single student and a contribution to a return economy airfare.
Length of Study: Up to three years.
Frequency: As available.
Study Establishment: The University of Cambridge.
Country of Study: United Kingdom.
No. of awards offered: One.
Application Procedure: Applicants must complete a preliminary application form, which can be obtained from local universities, offices of the British Council or the Trust. The preliminary application form can be downloaded from http://www.admin.cam.ac.uk/univ/gsprospectus/c7/over-seas/schemes.html. Completed forms must be returned to the main address. Shortlisted candidates will be sent forms for admission to the University of Cambridge.
Closing Date: Please contact the organisation.
Contributor: Offered in collaboration with the Cyprus State Scholarship Authority.
Additional Information: Further information is available on request.

Developing World Education Fund Cambridge Scholarships for PhD Study

Subjects: All subjects.
Purpose: To financially support study towards a PhD.

Eligibility: Applicants must be citizens of Bangladesh, Pakistan, China or Sri Lanka. The Trusts cannot admit students to the University or any of its colleges. Applicants for awards from the Trusts must, therefore, also apply to the University of Cambridge and be offered a place at Cambridge in the normal way. All applicants must have a First Class or High Second Class (Honours) Degree or equivalent and normally be under 26. Applicants must be successfully nominated for an Overseas Research Student (ORS) award, which covers the difference between the home and overseas rate of the University Composition Fee.

Level of Study: Doctorate.
Type: Scholarship.
Value: The University Composition Fee at the appropriate rate, approved college fees, a maintenance allowance sufficient for a single student and a contribution towards a return economy airfare.
Length of Study: Up to three years.
Frequency: Annual.
Study Establishment: The University of Cambridge.
Country of Study: United Kingdom.
No. of awards offered: Varies.
Application Procedure: Applicants must complete a preliminary application form, which can be obtained from local universities, offices of the British Council or the Trust. The preliminary application form can be downloaded from http://www.admin.cam.ac.uk/univ/gsprospectus/c7/overseas/schemes.html. Completed forms must be returned to the main address. Shortlisted candidates will be sent forms for admission to the University of Cambridge.
Closing Date: Please contact the organisation.
Contributor: Offered in collaboration with the Developing World Education Fund.
Additional Information: Further information is available on request.

Developing World Education Fund Cambridge Scholarships for Postgraduate Study (China)

Subjects: All subjects.
Purpose: To financially support those undertaking postgraduate study.
Eligibility: Open to citizens of China. The Trusts cannot admit students to the University or any of its colleges. Applicants for awards from the Trusts must, therefore, also apply to the University of Cambridge and be offered a place at Cambridge in the normal way. All applicants must have a First Class or High Second Class (Honours) Degree or equivalent and normally be under 26.
Level of Study: Postgraduate.
Type: Scholarship.
Value: The University Composition Fee at the overseas rate, approved college fees, a maintenance allowance sufficient for a single student and a contribution towards a return economy airfare.
Length of Study: One year.
Frequency: Annual.
Study Establishment: The University of Cambridge.
Country of Study: United Kingdom.
No. of awards offered: Up to two.
Application Procedure: Applicants must complete a preliminary application form, which can be obtained from local universities, offices of the British Council or the Trust. The preliminary application form can be downloaded from http://www.admin.cam.ac.uk/univ/gsprospectus/c7/overseas/schemes.html. Completed forms must be returned to the main address. Shortlisted candidates will be sent forms for admission to the University of Cambridge.
Closing Date: Please contact the organisation.
Contributor: Offered in collaboration with the Developing World Education Fund.
Additional Information: Further information is available on request.

Dharam Hinduja Cambridge DFID Shared Scholarships

Subjects: All subjects.
Purpose: To offer financial support.
Eligibility: Applicants must be from India. All applicants must be under the age of 35 on October 1st (with priority given to those

candidates under the age of 30), undertake to return to their own country to work or study after completing the course at Cambridge, not be employed by a government department (national or local) or by a parastatal organisation, not at present be living or studying in a developed country, nor have undertaken studies lasting a year or more in a developed country. Priority will be given to candidates wishing to pursue a course of study related to the economic and social development of their country.

Level of Study: Postgraduate.
Type: Scholarship.
Value: The University Composition Fee at the appropriate rate, approved college fees, a maintenance allowance sufficient for a single student and a contribution towards a return economy airfare.
Length of Study: One year.
Frequency: Annual.
Study Establishment: The University of Cambridge.
Country of Study: United Kingdom.
No. of awards offered: Four.
Application Procedure: Applicants may obtain further details and a preliminary application form by writing before August 16th of the year before entry to the Joint Secretary of the Nehru Trust for Cambridge University at the address below giving details of academic qualifications.
Closing Date: Please contact the organisation.
Contributor: Offered in collaboration with the Hinduja Cambridge Trust and the Department for International Development.
Additional Information: Further information is available on request.

For further information contact:

The Joint Secretary
The Nehru Trust for Cambridge University
Teen Murti House
Teen Murti Marg, New Delhi, 110011, India

The Nehru Trust for Cambridge University
Teen Murti House
Teen Murti Marg, New Delhi, 110011, India

Dharam Hinduja Cambridge Scholarships

Subjects: All subjects.
Purpose: To financially support study towards a PhD.
Eligibility: Applicants must be from India. All applicants must be successful in winning an Overseas Research Student (ORS) award, which pays the difference between the home and overseas rate of the University Composition Fee. Those who have, in addition, to a First Class (Honours) Degree, a First Class Master's Degree or its equivalent, may be given preference.
Level of Study: Doctorate.
Type: Scholarship.
Value: The University Composition Fee at the home rate, approved college fees, a maintenance allowance sufficient for a single student and a contribution towards a return economy airfare.
Length of Study: Up to three years.
Frequency: Annual.
Study Establishment: The University of Cambridge.
Country of Study: United Kingdom.
No. of awards offered: Two.
Application Procedure: Applicants must obtain further details and a preliminary application form by writing before August 16th of the year before entry to The Joint Secretary of The Nehru Trust for Cambridge University at the address below giving details of academic qualifications.
Closing Date: Please contact the organisation.
Contributor: Offered in collaboration with the Hinduja Cambridge Trust.
Additional Information: Further information is available on request.

For further information contact:

The Joint Secretary
The Nehru Trust for Cambridge University
Teen Murti House
Teen Murti Marg, New Delhi, 110011, India

Downing Müller Cambridge DFID Scholarships

Subjects: All subjects.

Purpose: To offer financial support to those students from developing countries.

Eligibility: Open to students from a developing country of the Commonwealth. All applicants must be under the age of 35 on October 1st (with priority given to those candidates under the age of 30), undertake to return to their own country to work or study after completing the course at Cambridge, not be employed by a government department (national or local) or by a parastatal organisation, not at present be living or studying in a developed country, nor have undertaken studies lasting a year or more in a developed country. Priority will be given to candidates wishing to pursue a course of study related to the economic and social development of their country.

Level of Study: Postgraduate.

Type: Scholarship.

Value: The University Composition Fee at the home rate, approved college fees, a maintenance allowance sufficient for a single student and a contribution towards a return economy airfare.

Length of Study: One year.

Frequency: Annual.

Study Establishment: Downing College, the University of Cambridge.

Country of Study: United Kingdom.

No. of awards offered: Two.

Application Procedure: Applicants must complete a preliminary application form, which can be obtained from local universities, offices of the British Council or the Trust. The preliminary application form can be downloaded from http://www.admin.cam.ac.uk/univ/gsprospectus/c7/overseas/schemes.html. Completed forms must be returned to the main address. Shortlisted candidates will be sent forms for admission to the University of Cambridge.

Closing Date: Please contact the organisation.

Contributor: Offered in collaboration with Hans and Irmgard Müller Stiftung, Downing College, Cambridge and the Department for International Development.

Additional Information: From time to time, a Downing Müller Cambridge Scholarship will be offered to a candidate from Eastern Europe. Further information is available on request.

Downing Müller Cambridge Scholarships for PhD Study

Subjects: All subjects.

Purpose: To financially support study towards a PhD.

Eligibility: For students from developing countries or Eastern Europe. The Trusts cannot admit students to the University or any of its colleges. Applicants for awards from the Trusts must, therefore, also apply to the University of Cambridge and be offered a place at Cambridge in the normal way. All applicants must have a First Class or High Second Class (Honours) Degree or equivalent and normally be under 26. All applicants must be successfully nominated for an Overseas Research Student (ORS) award which covers the difference between the home and overseas rate of the University Composition Fee.

Level of Study: Doctorate, Predoctorate.

Type: Scholarship.

Value: The University Composition Fee at the home rate, approved college fees, a maintenance allowance sufficient for a single student and a contribution towards a return economy airfare.

Frequency: Annual.

Study Establishment: Downing College, the University of Cambridge.

Country of Study: United Kingdom.

No. of awards offered: One.

Application Procedure: Applicants must complete a preliminary application form, which can be obtained from local universities, offices of the British Council or the Trust. The preliminary application form can be downloaded from http://www.admin.cam.ac.uk/univ/gsprospectus/c7/overseas/schemes.html. Completed forms must be returned to the main address. Shortlisted candidates will be sent forms for admission to the University of Cambridge.

Closing Date: Please contact the organisation.

Contributor: Offered in collaboration with Hans Irmgard Müller Stiftung and Downing College of the University of Cambridge.

Additional Information: Further information is available on request.

Entente Cordiale Scholarships for Postgraduate Study

Subjects: All subjects.

Purpose: To financially support those undertaking postgraduate study.

Eligibility: Applicants must be citizens of France.

Level of Study: Postgraduate.

Type: Scholarship.

Value: Applicants must contact the British Council for details.

Length of Study: One year.

Frequency: Annual.

Study Establishment: The University of Cambridge.

Country of Study: United Kingdom.

No. of awards offered: Up to six.

Application Procedure: Applicants must obtain details of the application procedure from the British Council.

Closing Date: Please contact the organisation.

Contributor: Offered in collaboration with the United Kingdom's Foreign and Commonwealth Office (FCO).

Additional Information: Further information is available on request.

For further information contact:

British Council
9-11 rue de Constantine, Paris, F-75007, France
Tel: (33) 1 49 55 73 43
Fax: (33) 1 47 05 77 02

FCO-China Chevening Fellowships for Postgraduate Study (China)

Subjects: All subjects.

Purpose: To financially support those undertaking postgraduate study.

Eligibility: Open to citizens of China. The Trust cannot admit students to the University or any of its colleges. Applicants for awards from the Trusts must, therefore, also apply to the University of Cambridge and be offered a place at Cambridge in the normal way. All applicants must have a First Class or High Second Class (Honours) Degree or equivalent and normally be under 26.

Level of Study: Postgraduate.

Type: Scholarship.

Value: The University Composition Fee at the overseas rate, approved college fees, a maintenance allowance sufficient for a single student and a contribution towards a return economy airfare.

Length of Study: One year.

Frequency: Annual.

Study Establishment: The University of Cambridge.

Country of Study: United Kingdom.

No. of awards offered: Three.

Application Procedure: Applicants must complete a preliminary application form, which can be obtained from local universities, offices of the British Council or the Trust. The preliminary application form can be downloaded from http://www.admin.cam.ac.uk/univ/gsprospectus/c7/overseas/schemes.html. Completed forms must be returned to the main address. Shortlisted candidates will be sent forms for admission to the University of Cambridge.

Closing Date: Please contact the organisation.

Contributor: Offered in collaboration with the Foreign and Commonwealth Office (FCO).

Additional Information: Further information is available on request.

First Canadian Donner Foundation Research Cambridge Scholarships for PhD Study

Subjects: All subjects.

Purpose: To financially support study towards a PhD.

Eligibility: Applicants must be from Canada and excel at sport. Candidates must gain admission to Magdalene College, Cambridge in the normal way. All applicants must be successfully nominated for an Overseas Research Student (ORS) award which covers the difference between the home and overseas rate of the University Composition Fee.

Level of Study: Doctorate, Predoctorate.
Type: Scholarship.
Length of Study: Three years.
Frequency: Annual.
Study Establishment: Magdalene College, the University of Cambridge.
Country of Study: United Kingdom.
No. of awards offered: One.
Application Procedure: Applicants must contact the Board of Graduate Studies.
Additional Information: Further information is available on request.

For further information contact:

The Secretary
The Board of Graduate Studies
4 Mill Lane, Cambridge, Cambridgeshire, CB2 1RZ, England

French Embassy Bursaries

Subjects: Engineering.
Purpose: To financially support those undertaking postgraduate study.
Eligibility: Open to citizens of France.
Level of Study: Postgraduate.
Type: Bursary.
Value: Part-cost bursaries.
Length of Study: One year.
Frequency: Annual.
Study Establishment: The Department of Engineering at the University of Cambridge.
Country of Study: United Kingdom.
No. of awards offered: Up to four.
Application Procedure: Applicants should contact the organisation.
Contributor: Offered in collaboration with the French Embassy in London.
Additional Information: Further information is available on request.

Guy Clutton-Brock Scholarship for PhD Study

Subjects: All subjects.
Purpose: To financially support those undertaking postgraduate study.
Eligibility: For a student from Zimbabwe who has been offered a place at Magdalene College, Cambridge. The Trusts cannot admit students to the University or any of its colleges. Applicants for awards from the Trusts must, therefore, also apply to the University of Cambridge and be offered a place at Cambridge in the normal way. All applicants must have a First Class or High Second Class (Honours) Degree or equivalent and normally be under 26. All applicants must be successfully nominated for an Overseas Research Student (ORS) award which covers the difference between the home and overseas rate of the University Composition Fee.
Level of Study: Doctorate, Predoctorate.
Type: Scholarship.
Value: The University Composition Fee at the home rate, approved college fees, a maintenance allowance sufficient for a single student and a contribution towards a return economy airfare.
Length of Study: Up to three years.
Frequency: As available.
Study Establishment: Magdalene College, the University of Cambridge.
Country of Study: United Kingdom.
No. of awards offered: One.
Application Procedure: Applicants must complete a preliminary application form, which can be obtained from local universities, offices of the British Council or the Trust. The preliminary application form can be downloaded from http://www.admin.cam.ac.uk/univ/gsprospectus/c7/overseas/schemes.html. Completed forms must be returned to the main

address. Shortlisted candidates will be sent forms for admission to the University of Cambridge.
Closing Date: Please contact the organisation.
Contributor: Offered by the government of Zimbabwe in collaboration with Magdalene College, Cambridge in honour of Guy Clutton-Brock, hero of Zimbabwe.
Additional Information: Further information is available on request.

Guy Clutton-Brock Scholarship for Postgraduate Study

Subjects: All subjects.
Purpose: To financially support those undertaking postgraduate study.
Eligibility: Open to students from Zimbabwe who have been offered a place at Magdalene College, Cambridge. The Trusts cannot admit students to the University or any of its colleges. Applicants for awards from the Trusts must, therefore, also apply to the University of Cambridge and be offered a place at Cambridge in the normal way. All applicants must have a First Class or High Second Class (Honours) Degree or equivalent and normally be under 26. All applicants must be successfully nominated for an Overseas Research Student (ORS) award which covers the difference between the home and overseas rate of the University Composition Fee.
Level of Study: Postgraduate.
Type: Scholarship.
Value: The University Composition Fee at the overseas rate, approved college fees, a maintenance allowance sufficient for a single student and a contribution towards a return economy airfare.
Length of Study: One year.
Frequency: As available.
Study Establishment: The University of Cambridge.
Country of Study: United Kingdom.
No. of awards offered: One.
Application Procedure: Applicants must complete a preliminary application form, which can be obtained from local universities, offices of the British Council or the Trust. The preliminary application form can be downloaded from http://www.admin.cam.ac.uk/univ/gsprospectus/c7/overseas/schemes.html. Completed forms must be returned to the main address. Shortlisted candidates will be sent forms for admission to the University of Cambridge.
Closing Date: Please contact the organisation.
Contributor: Offered by the government of Zimbabwe in collaboration with Magdalene College at the University of Cambridge in honour of Guy Clutton-Brock, hero of Zimbabwe.
Additional Information: Further information is available on request.

Hamilton Cambridge Scholarship for PhD Study

Subjects: All subjects.
Purpose: To financially support study towards a PhD.
Eligibility: The Trusts cannot admit students to the University or any of its colleges. Applicants for awards from the Trusts must, therefore, also apply to the University of Cambridge and be offered a place at Cambridge in the normal way. All applicants must have a First Class or High Second Class (Honours) Degree or equivalent and normally be under 26. All applicants must be successfully nominated for an Overseas Research Student (ORS) award which covers the difference between the home and overseas rate of the University Composition Fee.
Level of Study: Doctorate.
Type: Scholarship.
Value: The University Composition Fee at the home rate, approved college fees, a maintenance allowance sufficient for a single student and a contribution towards a return economy airfare.
Length of Study: Up to three years.
Frequency: As available.
Study Establishment: Selwyn College, the University of Cambridge.
Country of Study: United Kingdom.
No. of awards offered: One.
Application Procedure: Applicants must complete a preliminary application form, which can be obtained from local universities, offices of the British Council or the Trust. The preliminary application form

203

can be downloaded from
http://www.admin.cam.ac.uk/univ/gsprospectus/c7/over-
seas/schemes.html. Completed forms must be returned to the main
address. Shortlisted candidates will be sent forms for admission to
the University of Cambridge.
Closing Date: Please contact the organisation.
Contributor: Offered in collaboration with Selwyn College,
Cambridge.
Additional Information: Further information is available on request.

For further information contact:

The Secretary
The Board of Graduate Studies
4 Mill Lane, Cambridge, Cambridgeshire, CB2 1RZ, England

Hong Kong Cambridge Scholarships for PhD Study
Subjects: All subjects.
Purpose: To financially support study towards a PhD.
Eligibility: Preference is given to graduates of the Chinese Univer-
sity of Hong Kong and the University of Hong Kong. The Trusts can-
not admit students to the University or any of its colleges. Applicants
for awards from the Trusts must, therefore, also apply to the Univer-
sity of Cambridge and be offered a place at Cambridge in the normal
way. All applicants must have a First Class or High Second Class
(Honours) Degree or equivalent and normally be under 26.
Level of Study: Doctorate, Predoctorate.
Type: Scholarship.
Value: The University Composition Fee at the appropriate rate, ap-
proved college fees, a maintenance allowance sufficient for a single
student and a contribution towards a return economy airfare.
Length of Study: Up to three years.
Frequency: Annual.
Study Establishment: The University of Cambridge.
Country of Study: United Kingdom.
No. of awards offered: Up to five.
Application Procedure: Applicants must complete a preliminary application form, which can be obtained from local universities, offices
of the British Council or the Trust. The preliminary application form
can be downloaded from
http://www.admin.cam.ac.uk/univ/gsprospectus/c7/over-
seas/schemes.html. Completed forms must be returned to the main
address. Shortlisted candidates will be sent forms for admission to
the University of Cambridge.
Closing Date: Please contact the organisation.
Contributor: Offered in collaboration with the Malaysian Commonwealth Studies Centre.
Additional Information: Further information is available on request.

Huntsman Tioxide Cambridge Scholarship for Postgraduate Study
Subjects: Chemical engineering.
Purpose: To financially support those undertaking postgraduate
study.
Eligibility: Applicants must be from Malaysia, South Africa or Singapore. The Trusts cannot admit students to the University or any of its
colleges. Applicants for awards from the Trusts must, therefore, also
apply to the University of Cambridge and be offered a place at Cam-
bridge in the normal way. All applicants must have a First Class or
High Second Class (Honours) Degree or equivalent and normally be
under 26.
Level of Study: Postgraduate.
Type: Scholarship.
Value: The University Composition Fee at the overseas rate, ap-
proved college fees, a maintenance allowance sufficient for a single
student and a contribution to a return economy airfare.
Length of Study: One year.
Frequency: Dependent on funds available.
Study Establishment: The University of Cambridge.
Country of Study: United Kingdom.
No. of awards offered: One.
Application Procedure: Applicants must complete a preliminary ap-
plication form, which can be obtained from local universities, offices

of the British Council or the Trust. The preliminary application form
can be downloaded from
http://www.admin.cam.ac.uk/univ/gsprospectus/c7/over-
seas/schemes.html. Completed forms must be returned to the main
address. Shortlisted candidates will be sent forms for admission to
the University of Cambridge.
Closing Date: Please contact the organisation.
Contributor: Offered in collaboration with Huntsman Tioxide.
Additional Information: Further information is available on request.

ICI Cambridge Bursaries
Subjects: Chemistry, chemical engineering, materials science and
metallurgy or physics.
Purpose: To financially support study towards a PhD.
Eligibility: Open to citizens of the Netherlands and Belgium.
Level of Study: Doctorate, Predoctorate.
Type: Bursary.
Value: Part-cost bursary.
Length of Study: Up to three years.
Frequency: Annual.
Study Establishment: The University of Cambridge.
Country of Study: United Kingdom.
No. of awards offered: One.
Application Procedure: Applicants must complete a preliminary ap-
plication form, which can be obtained from local universities, offices
of the British Council or the Trust. The preliminary application form
can be downloaded from
http://www.admin.cam.ac.uk/univ/gsprospectus/c7/over-
seas/schemes.html. Completed forms must be returned to the main
address. Shortlisted candidates will be sent forms for admission to
the University of Cambridge.
Closing Date: Please contact the organisation.
Contributor: Offered in collaboration with ICI.
Additional Information: Further information is available on request.

Isaac Newton Trust European Research Studentships for PhD Research
Subjects: All subjects.
Purpose: To financially support study towards a PhD.
Eligibility: Open to candidates from the European Union.
Level of Study: Doctorate.
Type: Studentship.
Value: UK £2,000 per year.
Length of Study: Three years.
Frequency: Annual.
Study Establishment: The University of Cambridge.
Country of Study: United Kingdom.
No. of awards offered: 33.
Application Procedure: Applicants must contact the Trust.
Closing Date: Please contact the organisation.
Contributor: Offered in collaboration with the Isaac Newton Trust
and the Cambridge European Trust.
Additional Information: Further information is available on request.

Jawaharial Nehru Memorial Fund Cambridge Scholarship for PhD Study
Subjects: The broad fields of science policy, technology, global restructuring, philosophy and history of science, comparative studies in
religion and culture, international relations and constitutional studies,
Indian history, civilisation and culture, interface of social change and
economic development, environmental ecology and sustainable
development.
Purpose: To financially support study towards a PhD.
Eligibility: Applicants must be from India. All applicants must be
successful in winning an Overseas Research Student (ORS) award,
which pays the difference between the home and overseas rate of
the University Composition Fee. Those who have, in addition, to a
First Class (Honours) Degree, a First Class Master's Degree or its
equivalent, may be given preference.
Level of Study: Doctorate, Predoctorate.
Type: Scholarship.

Value: The University Composition Fee at the home rate, approved college fees, a maintenance allowance sufficient for a single student and a contribution towards return economy airfare.

Length of Study: Up to three years.

Frequency: Annual.

Study Establishment: The University of Cambridge.

Country of Study: United Kingdom.

No. of awards offered: One.

Application Procedure: Applicants may obtain further details and a preliminary application form by writing before August 16th of the year before entry to the Joint Secretary of the Nehru Trust for Cambridge University at the address below giving details of academic qualifications.

Closing Date: Please contact the organisation.

Contributor: Offered in collaboration with the Jawaharial Nehru Memorial Fund.

Additional Information: Further information is available on request.

For further information contact:

The Joint Secretary
The Nehru Trust for Cambridge University
Teen Murti House
Teen Murti Marg, New Delhi, 110011, India

Jawaharial Nehru Memorial Trust Cambridge DFID Scholarships

Subjects: All subjects.

Purpose: To offer financial support.

Eligibility: Applicants must be from India. All applicants must be under the age of 35 on October 1st (with priority given to those candidates under the age of 30), undertake to return to their own country to work or study after completing the course at Cambridge, not be employed by a government department (national or local) or by a parastatal organisation, not at present be living or studying in a developed country, not have undertaken studies lasting a year or more in a developed country, nor have undertaken studies lasting a year or more in a developed country. Priority will be given to candidates wishing to pursue a course of study related to the economic and social development of their country.

Level of Study: Postgraduate.

Type: Scholarship.

Value: The University Composition Fee at the overseas rate, approved college fees, a maintenance allowance sufficient for a single student and a contribution towards return economy airfare.

Length of Study: One year.

Frequency: Annual.

Study Establishment: The University of Cambridge.

Country of Study: United Kingdom.

No. of awards offered: Two.

Application Procedure: Applicants may obtain further details and a preliminary application form by writing before August 16th of the year before entry to The Joint Secretary of The Nehru Trust for Cambridge University at the address below giving details of academic qualifications.

Closing Date: Please contact the organisation.

Contributor: Offered in collaboration with the Jawaharial Nehru Memorial Trust and the Department of International Development (DFID).

Additional Information: Further information is available on request.

For further information contact:

The Joint Secretary
The Nehru Trust for Cambridge University
Teen Murti House
Teen Murti Marg, New Delhi, 110011, India

The Nehru Trust for Cambridge University
Teen Murti House
Teen Murti Marg, New Delhi, 110011, India

Jawaharial Nehru Memorial Trust Cambridge Scholarships

Subjects: All subjects.

Purpose: To financially support study towards a PhD.

Eligibility: Applicants must be from India. All applicants must be successful in winning an Overseas Research Student (ORS) award, which pays the difference between the home and overseas rate of the University Composition Fee. Those who have, in addition, to a First Class (Honours) Degree, a First Class Master's Degree or its equivalent, may be given preference.

Level of Study: Doctorate.

Type: Scholarship.

Value: The University Composition Fee at the overseas rate, approved college fees, a contribution towards a maintenance allowance and a contribution to a return economy airfare.

Length of Study: Two years.

Frequency: Annual.

Study Establishment: Trinity College, the University of Cambridge.

Country of Study: United Kingdom.

No. of awards offered: One.

Application Procedure: Applicants may obtain further details and a preliminary application form by writing before August 16th of the year before entry to the Joint Secretary of the Nehru Trust for Cambridge University at the address below giving details of academic qualifications.

Closing Date: Please contact the organisation.

Contributor: Offered in collaboration with the Jawaharial Nehru Memorial Trust and Trinity College, Cambridge.

Additional Information: Further information is available on request.

For further information contact:

The Joint Secretary
The Nehru Trust for Cambridge University
Teen Murti House
Teen Murti Marg, New Delhi, 110011, India

Kalimuzo Cambridge DFID Scholarships

Subjects: All subjects.

Purpose: To offer financial support to students from Uganda.

Eligibility: Applicants must be from Uganda. All applicants must be under the age of 35 on October 1st (with priority given to those candidates under the age of 30), undertake to return to their own country to work or study after completing the course at Cambridge, not be employed by a government department (national or local) or by a parastatal organisation, not at present be living or studying in a developed country, nor have undertaken studies lasting a year or more in a developed country. Priority will be given to candidates wishing to pursue a course of study related to the economic and social development of their country.

Level of Study: Postgraduate.

Type: Scholarship.

Value: The University Composition Fee at the overseas rate, approved college fees, a maintenance allowance sufficient for a single student and a contribution towards a return economy airfare.

Length of Study: One year.

Frequency: Annual.

Study Establishment: The University of Cambridge.

Country of Study: United Kingdom.

No. of awards offered: Three.

Application Procedure: Applicants must complete a preliminary application form, which can be obtained from local universities, offices of the British Council or the Trust. The preliminary application form can be downloaded from http://www.admin.cam.ac.uk/univ/gsprospectus/c7/overseas/schemes.html. Completed forms must be returned to the main address. Shortlisted candidates will be sent forms for admission to the University of Cambridge.

Closing Date: Please contact the organisation.

Contributor: Offered in collaboration with the Department of International Development (DFID).

Additional Information: Scholarships are offered in the memory of Professor Frank Kalimuzo, former Vice Chancellor of Makerere University. Further information is available on request.

Kalimuzo Cambridge Scholarship for PhD Study

Subjects: All subjects.

Purpose: To financially support study towards a PhD.

Eligibility: Open to students from Uganda. The Trusts cannot admit students to the University or any of its colleges. Applicants for awards from the Trusts must, therefore, also apply to the University of Cambridge and be offered a place at Cambridge in the normal way. All applicants must have a First Class or High Second Class (Honours) Degree or equivalent and normally be under 26. All applicants must be successfully nominated for an Overseas Research Student (ORS) award which covers the difference between the home and overseas rate of the University Composition Fee.

Level of Study: Doctorate.

Type: Scholarship.

Value: The University Composition Fee at the appropriate rate, approved college fees, a maintenance allowance sufficient for a single student and a contribution towards return economy airfare.

Length of Study: Three years.

Frequency: Annual.

Study Establishment: The University of Cambridge.

Country of Study: United Kingdom.

No. of awards offered: One.

Application Procedure: Applicants must complete a preliminary application form, which can be obtained from local universities, offices of the British Council or the Trust. The preliminary application form can be downloaded from http://www.admin.cam.ac.uk/univ/gsprospectus/c7/overseas/schemes.html. Completed forms must be returned to the main address. Shortlisted candidates will be sent forms for admission to the University of Cambridge.

Closing Date: Please contact the organisation.

Additional Information: The scholarship is awarded in the memory of Professor Frank Kalimuzo, former Vice Chancellor of Makerere University. Further information is available on request.

Karim Rida Said Cambridge Scholarship for PhD Study

Subjects: All subjects.

Purpose: To financially support study towards a PhD.

Eligibility: Applicants must be from Jordan, Lebanon, Palestine or Syria. Scholars must undertake to return to their home country, or to another member state of the Arab League, on completion of studies at Cambridge. Candidates may be up to 40 years old. The Trusts cannot admit students to the University or any of its colleges. Applicants for awards from the Trusts must, therefore, also apply to the University of Cambridge and be offered a place at Cambridge in the normal way. All applicants must have a First Class or High Second Class (Honours) Degree, or equivalent and may be up to the age of 40. Applicants must be successfully nominated for an Overseas Research Student award which pays the difference between the home and overseas rate of the University Composition Fee.

Level of Study: Doctorate, Predoctorate.

Type: Scholarship.

Value: The University Composition Fee at the appropriate rate, approved college fees, a maintenance allowance sufficient for a single student and a contribution towards a return economy airfare.

Length of Study: Up to three years.

Frequency: Annual.

Study Establishment: The University of Cambridge.

Country of Study: United Kingdom.

No. of awards offered: Two.

Application Procedure: Applicants must complete a preliminary application form, which can be obtained from local universities, offices of the British Council or the Trust. The preliminary application form can be downloaded from http://www.admin.cam.ac.uk/univ/gsprospectus/c7/overseas/schemes.html. Completed forms must be returned to the main address. Shortlisted candidates will be sent forms for admission to the University of Cambridge.

Closing Date: Please contact the organisation.

Contributor: Offered in collaboration with the Karim Rida Said Foundation.

Additional Information: This scholarship is offered in memory of Karim Rida Said. Further information is available on request.

Karim Rida Said Cambridge Scholarship for Postgraduate Study

Subjects: All subjects.

Purpose: To financially support those undertaking postgraduate study.

Eligibility: Applicants must be from Jordan, Lebanon, Palestine or Syria. Scholars must undertake to return to their home country, or to another member state of the Arab League, on completion of studies at Cambridge. Candidates may be up to 40 years old. The Trusts cannot admit students to the University or any of its colleges. Applicants for awards from the Trusts must, therefore, also apply to the University of Cambridge and be offered a place at Cambridge in the normal way. All applicants must have a First Class or High Second Class (Honours) Degree or equivalent and may be up to the age of 40. Applicants must be successfully nominated for an Overseas Research Student (ORS) award which pays the difference between the home and overseas rate of the University Composition Fee.

Level of Study: Postgraduate.

Type: Scholarship.

Value: The University Composition Fee at the overseas rate, approved college fees, a maintenance allowance sufficient for a single student and a contribution towards a return economy airfare.

Length of Study: One year.

Frequency: Annual.

Study Establishment: The University of Cambridge.

Country of Study: United Kingdom.

No. of awards offered: Four.

Application Procedure: Applicants must complete a preliminary application form, which can be obtained from local universities, offices of the British Council or the Trust. The preliminary application form can be downloaded from http://www.admin.cam.ac.uk/univ/gsprospectus/c7/overseas/schemes.html. Completed forms must be returned to the main address. Shortlisted candidates will be sent forms for admission to the University of Cambridge.

Closing Date: Please contact the organisation.

Contributor: Offered in collaboration with the Karim Rida Said Foundation.

Additional Information: This scholarship is offered in memory of Karim Rida Said. Further information is available on request.

Kater Cambridge Scholarship for PhD Study

Subjects: All subjects.

Purpose: To financially support study towards a PhD.

Eligibility: Candidates must be citizens of Australia. The Trusts cannot admit students to the University or any of its colleges. Applicants for awards from the Trusts must, therefore, also apply to the University of Cambridge and be offered a place at Cambridge in the normal way. All applicants must have a First Class or High Second Class (Honours) Degree or equivalent and normally be under 26. All applicants must be successfully nominated for an Overseas Research Student (ORS) award which covers the difference between the home and overseas rate of the University Composition Fee.

Level of Study: Doctorate, Predoctorate.

Type: Scholarship.

Value: The University Composition Fee at the home rate, approved college fees, a maintenance allowance sufficient for a single student and a contribution towards a return economy airfare.

Length of Study: Up to three years.

Frequency: As available.

Study Establishment: The University of Cambridge.

Country of Study: United Kingdom.

No. of awards offered: One.

Application Procedure: Applicants must contact the Board of Graduate Studies.

Closing Date: Please contact the organisation.

Contributor: Offered in collaboration with the Sir Geoffrey Kater Memorial Fund and the Cambridge Australia Trust.

Additional Information: Further information is available on request. For details of scholarships offered in collaboration with the Cambridge Australia Trust please see the website http://www.anu.edu/cabs/scholarships/cambridge/cambridge-austrust.html.

For further information contact:

The Secretary
The Board of Graduate Studies
4 Mill Lane, Cambridge, Cambridgeshire, CB2 1RZ, England

Kenya Cambridge DFID Scholarship

Subjects: All subjects.

Purpose: To offer financial support to students from Kenya.

Eligibility: Applicants must be from Kenya. All applicants must be under the age of 35 on October 1st, with priority given to those candidates under the age of 30, undertake to return to their own country to work or study after completing the course at Cambridge, not be employed by a government department (national or local) or by a parastatal organisation, not at present be living or studying in a developed country, nor have undertaken studies lasting a year or more in a developed country. Priority will be given to candidates wishing to pursue a course of study related to the economic and social development of their country.

Level of Study: Postgraduate.

Type: Scholarship.

Value: The University Composition Fee at the overseas rate, approved college fees, a maintenance allowance sufficient for a single student and a contribution towards return economy airfare.

Length of Study: One year.

Frequency: Annual.

Study Establishment: The University of Cambridge.

Country of Study: United Kingdom.

No. of awards offered: One.

Application Procedure: Applicants must complete a preliminary application form, which can be obtained from local universities, offices of the British Council or the Trust. The preliminary application form can be downloaded from http://www.admin.cam.ac.uk/univ/gsprospectus/c7/overseas/schemes.html. Completed forms must be returned to the main address. Shortlisted candidates will be sent forms for admission to the University of Cambridge.

Closing Date: Please contact the organisation.

Contributor: Offered in collaboration with the Kenya Cambridge Commonwealth Trusts and the Department of International Development (DFID).

Additional Information: Further information is available on request.

Kenya Cambridge Scholarship for PhD Study

Subjects: All subjects.

Purpose: To financially support study towards a PhD.

Eligibility: Applicants must be citizens of Kenya. The Trusts cannot admit students to the University or any of its colleges. Applicants for awards from the Trusts must, therefore, also apply to the University of Cambridge and be offered a place at Cambridge in the normal way. All applicants must have a First Class or High Second Class (Honours) Degree or equivalent and normally be under 26. All applicants must be successfully nominated for an Overseas Research Student (ORS) award which covers the difference between the home and overseas rate of the University Composition Fee.

Level of Study: Doctorate.

Type: Scholarship.

Value: The University Composition Fee at the home rate, approved college fees, a maintenance allowance sufficient for a single student and a contribution towards return economy airfare.

Length of Study: Up to three years.

Frequency: Annual.

Study Establishment: The University of Cambridge.

Country of Study: United Kingdom.

No. of awards offered: One.

Application Procedure: Applicants must complete a preliminary application form, which can be obtained from local universities, offices of the British Council or the Trust. The preliminary application form can be downloaded from http://www.admin.cam.ac.uk/univ/gsprospectus/c7/overseas/schemes.html. Completed forms must be returned to the main address. Shortlisted candidates will be sent forms for admission to the University of Cambridge.

Closing Date: Please contact the organisation.

Contributor: Offered in collaboration with the Kenya Cambridge Commonwealth Trust.

Additional Information: Further information is available on request.

Kopke Cambridge Scholarship for PhD Study

Subjects: All subjects.

Purpose: To financially support study towards a PhD.

Eligibility: Candidates must be citizens of Australia. The Trusts cannot admit students to the University or any of its Colleges. Applicants for awards from the Trusts must, therefore, also apply to the University of Cambridge and be offered a place at Cambridge in the normal way. All applicants must have a First Class or High Second Class (Honours) Degree or equivalent and normally be under 26. All applicants must be successfully nominated for an Overseas Research Student (ORS) award which covers the difference between the home and overseas rate of the University Composition Fee.

Level of Study: Doctorate, Predoctorate.

Type: Scholarship.

Value: The University Composition Fee at the home rate, approved College fees, a maintenance allowance sufficient for a single student and a contribution towards return economy airfare.

Length of Study: Up to three years.

Frequency: As available.

Study Establishment: The University of Cambridge.

Country of Study: United Kingdom.

No. of awards offered: One.

Application Procedure: Applicants must contact the Board of Graduate Studies.

Closing Date: Please contact the organisation.

Contributor: Offered in collaboration with the Cambridge Australia Trust.

Additional Information: Further information is available on request. For details of scholarships offered in collaboration with the Cambridge Australia Trust please see the website http://www.anu.edu/cabs/scholarships/cambridge/cambridge-austrust.html.

For further information contact:

The Secretary
The Board of Graduate Studies
4 Mill Lane, Cambridge, Cambridgeshire, CB2 1RZ, England

Lady Noon Cambridge DFID Scholarships

Subjects: All subjects.

Purpose: To financially support those undertaking postgraduate study.

Eligibility: Open to students from Pakistan. All applicants must be under the age of 35 on October 1st, with priority given to those candidates under the age of 30, undertake to return to their own country to work or study after completing the course at Cambridge, not be employed by a government department (national or local) or by a parastatal organisation, not at present be living or studying in a developed country, nor have undertaken studies lasting a year or more in a developed country. Priority will be given to candidates wishing to pursue a course of study related to the economic and social development of their own country.

Level of Study: Postgraduate.

Type: Scholarship.

Value: The University Composition Fee at overseas rate, approved college fees, a maintenance allowance sufficient for a single student and a contribution to a return economy airfare.

Length of Study: One year.

Frequency: Annual.

Study Establishment: The University of Cambridge.
Country of Study: United Kingdom.
No. of awards offered: Varies.
Application Procedure: Applicants must complete a preliminary application form, which can be obtained from local universities, offices of the British Council or the Trust. The preliminary application form can be downloaded from http://www.admin.cam.ac.uk/univ/gsprospectus/c7/overseas/schemes.html. Completed forms must be returned to the main address. Shortlisted candidates will be sent forms for admission to the University of Cambridge.
Closing Date: Please contact the organisation.
Contributor: Offered in collaboration with the Lady Noon Trust and the Department for International Development (DFID).
Additional Information: Further information is available on request.

Link Foundation/FCO Chevening Cambridge Scholarships for Postgraduate Study

Subjects: All subjects.
Purpose: To financially support those undertaking postgraduate study.
Eligibility: Candidates must be citizens of New Zealand. The Trusts cannot admit students to the University or any of its Colleges. Applicants for awards from the Trusts must, therefore, also apply to the University of Cambridge and be offered a place at Cambridge in the normal way. All applicants must have a First Class or High Second Class (Honours) Degree or equivalent and normally be under 26.
Level of Study: Postgraduate.
Type: Scholarship.
Value: A substantial contribution of up to UK £10,000 towards the costs of study and a contribution of UK £1,000 towards the return airfare to the United Kingdom.
Length of Study: One year.
Frequency: Annual.
Study Establishment: The University of Cambridge.
Country of Study: United Kingdom.
No. of awards offered: Three.
Application Procedure: Applicants must contact the Board of Graduate Studies.
Closing Date: Please contact the organisation.
Contributor: Offered in collaboration with the Link Foundation for UK-New Zealand Relations (formerly known as the Waitangi Foundation) and the Foreign and Commonwealth Office (FCO).
Additional Information: Further information is available on request.

For further information contact:

The Secretary
The Board of Graduate Studies
4 Mill Hill, Cambridge, Cambridgeshire, CB2 1RZ, England

LMB Cambridge Scholarships for PhD Study

Subjects: Molecular biology.
Purpose: To financially support study towards a PhD.
Level of Study: Doctorate, Predoctorate.
Type: Scholarship.
Value: Full maintenance allowance at the single student rate, after taking account of other awards from public sources towards maintenance for which the students are eligible and have received.
Length of Study: Up to three years.
Frequency: Annual.
Study Establishment: The Laboratory of Molecular Biology, the University of Cambridge.
Country of Study: United Kingdom.
No. of awards offered: Up to three.
Application Procedure: Applicants must apply directly to the Laboratory of Molecular Biology. The application form and further information about the department and potential supervisors is available online at http://www.mrc-lmb.cam.ac.uk. Candidates can write to the Director of Studies at the Laboratory to request a copy of the form, details of current projects and other scholarship information.
Closing Date: Please contact the organisation.

Contributor: Offered in collaboration with the Laboratory of Molecular Biology (LMB) at the University of Cambridge.
Additional Information: Further information is available on request.

For further information contact:

Director of Studies
The MRC Laboratory of Molecular Biology
Hills Road, Cambridge, Cambridgeshire, CB2 2QH, England

LMB Newton Cambridge Scholarships

Subjects: Molecular biology.
Purpose: To support and encourage candidates to pursue a course of research leading to a PhD.
Eligibility: Open to candidates from the European Union.
Level of Study: Doctorate.
Type: Scholarship.
Value: Full maintenance allowance at the single student rate, after taking account of other awards from public sources towards maintenance for which the students are eligible and have received.
Length of Study: Three years.
Frequency: Annual.
Study Establishment: The University of Cambridge.
Country of Study: United Kingdom.
No. of awards offered: Three.
Application Procedure: Applicants must apply directly to the Laboratory of Molecular Biology. The application form and further information about the Department and potential supervisors is available online at http://www.mrc-lmb.cam.ac.uk. Candidates can also write to request an application form, details of current projects and other scholarship information.
Closing Date: Please contact the organisation.
Contributor: Offered in collaboration with the Laboratory of Molecular Biology (LMB), the Isaac Newton Trust and the Cambridge European Trust.
Additional Information: Further information is available on request.

For further information contact:

Director of Studies
The MRC Laboratory of Molecular Biology
Hills Road, Cambridge, Cambridgeshire, CB2 2QH, England

Luis López Méndez CONICIT Cambridge Scholarships for Postgraduate Study

Subjects: Social sciences or humanities.
Purpose: To financially support those undertaking postgraduate study.
Eligibility: Applicants must be citizens of Venezuela. The Trusts cannot admit students to the University or any of its colleges. Applicants for awards from the Trusts must, therefore, also apply to the University of Cambridge and be offered a place at Cambridge in the normal way. All applicants must have a First Class or High Second Class (Honours) Degree or equivalent and normally be under 26. All applicants must be successfully nominated for an Overseas Research Student (ORS) award which covers the difference between the home and overseas rate of the University Composition Fee.
Level of Study: Postgraduate.
Type: Scholarship.
Value: The University Composition Fee at the overseas rate, approved college fees, a maintenance allowance sufficient for a single student and a contribution to a return economy airfare.
Length of Study: One year.
Frequency: Annual.
Study Establishment: The University of Cambridge.
Country of Study: United Kingdom.
No. of awards offered: Four.
Application Procedure: Applicants must complete a preliminary application form, which can be obtained from local universities, offices of the British Council or the main address. Completed forms must be returned to the main address. Shortlisted candidates will be sent forms for admission to the University of Cambridge and a

scholarship application form. These forms must be returned to The Board of Graduate Studies at the address below.

Closing Date: Please contact the organisation.

Contributor: Offered in collaboration with CONICIT.

Additional Information: Successful candidates will be eligible to be considered for further funding to enable them to pursue a course of research leading to the degree of PhD at Cambridge. Two such scholarships will be awarded annually, subject to the scholars applying for an ORS award. Further information is available on request.

Malaysian Commonwealth Scholarships

Subjects: All subjects.

Purpose: To financially support students from the Commonwealth.

Eligibility: Open to students from Commonwealth countries. The Trusts cannot admit students to the University or any of its colleges. Applicants for awards from the Trusts must therefore also apply to the University of Cambridge and be offered a place at Cambridge in the normal way. All applicants must have a First Class or High Second Class (Honours) Degree or equivalent and normally be under 26. All applicants must be successfully nominated for an Overseas Research Student (ORS) award which covers the difference between the home and overseas rate of the University Composition Fee.

Level of Study: Doctorate, Predoctorate.

Type: Scholarship.

Value: Scholarships will cover the University Composition Fee at the overseas rate, approved college fees, a maintenance allowance sufficient for a single student and a contribution to a return economy airfare.

Length of Study: Three years for PhD scholarships and one year for the postgraduate scholarships.

Frequency: Annual.

Study Establishment: The University of Cambridge.

Country of Study: United Kingdom.

No. of awards offered: Varies.

Application Procedure: Applicants must complete a preliminary application form, which can be obtained from local universities, offices of the British Council or the main address. Completed forms must be returned to the main address. Shortlisted candidates will be sent forms for admission to the University of Cambridge and a scholarship application form. These forms must be returned to The Board of Graduate Studies at the address below.

Closing Date: Please contact the organisation.

Contributor: Offered in collaboration with the Malaysian Commonwealth Studies Centre and the Cambridge Commonwealth Trust.

Additional Information: These scholarships are a result of the announcement at the Commonwealth Heads of Government Meeting in Auckland, November 1995 by the Right Honourable Dato' Seri Dr Mahathir bin Mohamad, Prime Minister of Malaysia. Further information is available on request.

Mandela Cambridge Scholarships for PhD Study

Subjects: All subjects.

Purpose: To financially support study towards a PhD.

Eligibility: Applicants must be from South Africa. The Trusts cannot admit students to the University or any of its colleges. Applicants for awards from the Trusts must, therefore, also apply to the University of Cambridge and be offered a place at Cambridge in the normal way. All applicants must have a First Class or High Second Class (Honours) Degree or equivalent and normally be under 26. Applicants for study towards a PhD must be successfully nominated for an Overseas Research Student (ORS) award which pays the difference between the home and overseas rate of the University Composition Fee.

Level of Study: Doctorate, Predoctorate.

Type: Scholarship.

Value: The University Composition Fee at the appropriate rate, approved college fees, a maintenance allowance sufficient for a single student and a contribution to a return economy airfare.

Length of Study: Up to three years.

Frequency: Annual.

Study Establishment: The University of Cambridge.

Country of Study: United Kingdom.

No. of awards offered: Up to 10.

Application Procedure: Applicants must complete a preliminary application form, which can be obtained from local universities, offices of the British Council or the Trust. The preliminary application form can be downloaded from http://www.admin.cam.ac.uk/univ/gsprospectus/c7/overseas/schemes.html. Completed forms must be returned to the main address. Shortlisted candidates will be sent forms for admission to the University of Cambridge.

Closing Date: Please contact the organisation.

Contributor: Offered by the Malaysian Commonwealth Studies Centre, the Cambridge Local Examinations Syndicate, Trinity College, Cambridge, and the Cambridge University Press.

Additional Information: These scholarships are offered in honour of former South African President Nelson Mandela. Further information is available on request.

Mandela Cambridge Scholarships for Postgraduate Study

Subjects: All subjects.

Purpose: To financially support those undertaking postgraduate study.

Eligibility: Applicants must be from South Africa. The Trusts cannot admit students to the University or any of its colleges. Applicants for awards from the Trusts must, therefore, also apply to the University of Cambridge and be offered a place at Cambridge in the normal way. All applicants must have a First Class or High Second Class (Honours) Degree or equivalent and normally be under 26. Applicants for study towards a PhD must be successfully nominated for an Overseas Research Student (ORS) award which pays the difference between the home and overseas rate of the University Composition Fee.

Level of Study: Postgraduate.

Type: Scholarship.

Value: The University Composition Fee at the overseas rate, approved college fees, a maintenance allowance sufficient for a single student and a contribution to a return economy airfare.

Length of Study: One year.

Frequency: Annual.

Study Establishment: The University of Cambridge.

Country of Study: United Kingdom.

No. of awards offered: Up to 20.

Application Procedure: Applicants must complete a preliminary application form, which can be obtained from local universities, offices of the British Council or the Trust. The preliminary application form can be downloaded from http://www.admin.cam.ac.uk/univ/gsprospectus/c7/overseas/schemes.html. Completed forms must be returned to the main address. Shortlisted candidates will be sent forms for admission to the University of Cambridge.

Closing Date: Please contact the organisation.

Contributor: Offered by the Malaysian Commonwealth Studies Centre, the Cambridge Local Examinations Syndicate, Trinity College, Cambridge, and the Cambridge University Press.

Additional Information: These scholarships are offered in honour of former South African President Nelson Mandela. Further information is available on request.

Mandela Magdalene College Scholarships for Postgraduate Scholarships

Subjects: All subjects.

Purpose: To financially support those undertaking postgraduate study and research.

Eligibility: Students must have been offered a place at Magdalene College, Cambridge and be citizens of South Africa. The Trusts cannot admit students to the University or any of its colleges. Applicants for awards from the Trusts must, therefore, also apply to the University of Cambridge and be offered a place at Cambridge in the normal way. All applicants must have a First Class or High Second Class (Honours) Degree or equivalent and normally be under 26.

Level of Study: Postgraduate.

Type: Scholarship.
Value: The University Composition Fee at the overseas rate, approved college fees, a maintenance allowance sufficient for a single student and a contribution to a return economy airfare.
Length of Study: One year.
Frequency: Annual.
Study Establishment: Magdalene College, the University of Cambridge.
Country of Study: United Kingdom.
No. of awards offered: Up to three.
Application Procedure: Applicants must complete a preliminary application form, which can be obtained from local universities, offices of the British Council or the Trust. The preliminary application form can be downloaded from http://www.admin.cam.ac.uk/univ/gsprospectus/c7/overseas/schemes.html. Completed forms must be returned to the main address. Shortlisted candidates will be sent forms for admission to the University of Cambridge.
Closing Date: Please contact the organisation.
Contributor: Offered in collaboration with Magdalene College, Cambridge and Mr Chris von Christierson.
Additional Information: Further information is available on request.

Mehmed Fuad Köprülü Scholarships for Turkey

Subjects: All subjects.
Purpose: To financially support study towards a PhD.
Eligibility: Applicants must be from Turkey. All applicants must apply for an Overseas Research Student (ORS) award which pays the difference between the home and overseas rate of the University composition fee. The Trusts cannot admit students to the University or any of its colleges. Applicants for awards from the Trusts must, therefore, also apply to the University of Cambridge and be offered a place at Cambridge in the normal way. All applicants must have a First Class or High Second Class (Honours) Degree or equivalent and normally be under 26.
Level of Study: Postdoctorate.
Type: Scholarship.
Value: The University Composition Fee at the appropriate rate, approved college fees, a maintenance allowance sufficient for a single student and a contribution to a return economy airfare.
Length of Study: Up to three years.
Frequency: Annual.
Study Establishment: The University of Cambridge.
Country of Study: United Kingdom.
No. of awards offered: 10.
Application Procedure: All applicants must complete an application for admission to the University of Cambridge as a graduate student and return it to the Turkish Council for Higher Education (YÖK).
Closing Date: Please contact the organisation.
Contributor: Offered in collaboration with The Turkish Council for Higher Education (YÖK).
Additional Information: Further information is available on request.

For further information contact:

The Turkish Council for Higher Education (YÖK)
YÖK Binasi
Bilkent, Ankara, 06539, Turkey

Michael Miliffe Cambridge Scholarships

Subjects: All subjects.
Purpose: To financially support study towards a second Bachelor's degree as an affiliated student.
Eligibility: Open to citizens of India. The Trusts cannot admit students to the University or any of its colleges. Applicants for awards from the Trusts must, therefore, also apply to the University of Cambridge and be offered a place at Cambridge in the normal way. All applicants must have a First Class or High Second Class (Honours) Degree or equivalent and normally be under 26.
Level of Study: Graduate.
Type: Scholarship.

Value: A substantial contribution of up to UK £9,000 per year towards the student's costs, to be determined in the light of the student's own resources.
Length of Study: Two years.
Frequency: Annual.
Study Establishment: Gonville and Caius College, the University of Cambridge.
Country of Study: United Kingdom.
No. of awards offered: Two.
Application Procedure: Applicants must contact the organisation.
Contributor: Offered in collaboration with the Michael Miliffe Fund and Gonville and Caius College, the University of Cambridge.
Additional Information: Further information is available on request.

Ministry of Education, (Malaysia) Scholarships for Postgraduate Study

Subjects: All subjects.
Purpose: To financially support those undertaking postgraduate study.
Eligibility: Applicants must be from Malaysia. Candidates must be nominated by the Ministry of Education. The Trusts cannot admit students to the University or any of its colleges. Applicants for awards from the Trusts must, therefore, also apply to the University of Cambridge and be offered a place at Cambridge in the normal way. All applicants must have a First Class or High Second Class (Honours) Degree or equivalent and normally be under 26.
Level of Study: Postgraduate.
Type: Scholarship.
Value: The University Composition Fee at the overseas rate, approved college fees, a maintenance allowance sufficient for a single student and a contribution to a return economy airfare.
Length of Study: One year.
Frequency: Annual.
Study Establishment: The University of Cambridge.
Country of Study: United Kingdom.
No. of awards offered: Four.
Application Procedure: Applicants must complete a preliminary application form, which can be obtained from local universities, offices of the British Council or the Trust. The preliminary application form can be downloaded from http://www.admin.cam.ac.uk/univ/gsprospectus/c7/overseas/schemes.html. Completed forms must be returned to the main address. Shortlisted candidates will be sent forms for admission to the University of Cambridge.
Closing Date: Please contact the organisation.
Contributor: Offered in collaboration with the Malaysian Commonwealth Studies Centre and the Ministry of Education, Government of Malaysia.
Additional Information: Further information is available on request.

For further information contact:

The Cambridge (Malaysia) Foundation
PO Box 10139, Kuala Lumpur, 50704, Malaysia

Ministry of Science, Technology and the Environment, (Malaysia) Scholarships for Postgraduate Study

Subjects: All subjects.
Purpose: To financially support those undertaking postgraduate study.
Eligibility: Applicants must be from Malaysia. Candidates must be nominated by the Ministry of Science, Technology and the Environment. The Trusts cannot admit students to the University or any of its colleges. Applicants for awards from the Trusts must, therefore, also apply to the University of Cambridge and be offered a place at Cambridge in the normal way. All applicants must have a First Class or High Second Class (Honours) Degree or equivalent and normally be under 26.
Level of Study: Postgraduate.
Type: Scholarship.

Value: The University Composition Fee at the overseas rate, approved college fees, a maintenance allowance sufficient for a single student and a contribution to a return economy airfare.
Length of Study: One year.
Frequency: Annual.
Study Establishment: The University of Cambridge.
Country of Study: United Kingdom.
No. of awards offered: Up to 10.
Application Procedure: Applicants must complete a preliminary application form, which can be obtained from local universities, offices of the British Council or the Trust. The preliminary application form can be downloaded from http://www.admin.cam.ac.uk/univ/gsprospectus/c7/overseas/schemes.html. Completed forms must be returned to the main address. Shortlisted candidates will be sent forms for admission to the University of Cambridge.
Closing Date: Please contact the organisation.
Contributor: Offered in collaboration with the Malaysian Commonwealth Studies Centre and the Ministry of Science, Technology and the Environment, Government of Malaysia.
Additional Information: Further information is available on request.

For further information contact:

The Cambridge (Malaysia) Foundation
PO Box 10139, Kuala Lumpur, 50704, Malaysia

Nehru Centenary Chevening Cambridge Scholarships

Subjects: All subjects.
Purpose: To financially support study towards a second Bachelor's degree as an affiliated student.
Eligibility: Applicants must be from India. The Trusts cannot admit students to the University or any of its colleges. Applicants for awards from the Trusts must, therefore, also apply to the University of Cambridge and be offered a place at Cambridge in the normal way. All applicants must have a First Class or High Second Class (Honours) Degree or equivalent and normally be under 26.
Level of Study: Graduate.
Type: Scholarship.
Value: The University Composition Fee at the overseas rate, approved college fees, a contribution towards a maintenance allowance and a contribution to a return economy airfare.
Length of Study: Two years.
Frequency: Annual.
Study Establishment: The University of Cambridge.
Country of Study: United Kingdom.
No. of awards offered: Up to five.
Application Procedure: Applicants may obtain further details and a preliminary application form by writing before August 16th of the year before entry to the Joint Secretary of the Nehru Trust for Cambridge University at the address below giving details of academic qualifications.
Closing Date: Please contact the organisation.
Contributor: Offered in collaboration with the Foreign and Commonwealth Office (FCO).
Additional Information: Further information is available on request.

For further information contact:

The Joint Secretary
The Nehru Trust for Cambridge University
Teen Murti House
Teen Murti Marg, New Delhi, 110011, India

Nehru Trust for the Indian Collections V&A Cambridge DFID Scholarship

Subjects: Archaeology, focusing on archaeological heritage and museums, or social anthropology, with special reference to the work of a museum.
Purpose: To financially support those undertaking postgraduate study.
Eligibility: Applicants must be from India. All applicants must be under the age of 35 on October 1st, with priority given to those

candidates under the age of 30, undertake to return to their own country to work or study after completing the course at Cambridge, not be employed by a government department (national or local) or by a parastatal organisation, not at present be living or studying in a developed country, nor have undertaken studies lasting a year or more in a developed country. Priority will be given to candidates wishing to pursue a course of study related to the economic and social development of their country.
Level of Study: Postgraduate.
Type: Scholarship.
Value: The University Composition Fee at the overseas rate, approved college fees, a maintenance allowance sufficient for a single student and a contribution to a return economy airfare. In addition a supplementary allowance to cover a short period of practical training at the Victoria and Albert Museum, or other approved institution, will be given.
Length of Study: One year.
Frequency: Annual.
Study Establishment: The University of Cambridge.
Country of Study: United Kingdom.
No. of awards offered: One.
Application Procedure: Applicants may obtain further details and a preliminary application form by writing before August 16th of the year before entry to the Joint Secretary of the Nehru Trust for Cambridge University at the address below giving details of academic qualifications.
Closing Date: Please contact the organisation.
Contributor: Offered in collaboration with the Nehru Trust for the Indian Collections at the Victoria and Albert (V&A) Museum and the Department for International Development (DFID).
Additional Information: Further information is available on request.

For further information contact:

The Joint Secretary
The Nehru Trust for Cambridge University
Teen Murti House
Teen Murti Marg, New Delhi, 110011, India

Nepal Cambridge Scholarships

Subjects: All subjects.
Purpose: To financially support those undertaking postgraduate study.
Eligibility: Applicants must be from Nepal. The Trusts cannot admit students to the University or any of its colleges. Applicants for awards from the Trusts must, therefore, also apply to the University of Cambridge and be offered a place at Cambridge in the normal way. All applicants must have a First Class or High Second Class (Honours) Degree or equivalent and normally be under 26.
Level of Study: Postgraduate.
Type: Scholarship.
Value: The University Composition Fee at the overseas rate, approved college fees, a maintenance allowance sufficient for a single student and a contribution to a return economy airfare.
Length of Study: One year.
Frequency: Annual.
Study Establishment: The University of Cambridge.
Country of Study: United Kingdom.
No. of awards offered: One.
Application Procedure: Applicants must complete a preliminary application form, which can be obtained from local universities, offices of the British Council or the Trust. The preliminary application form can be downloaded from http://www.admin.cam.ac.uk/univ/gsprospectus/c7/overseas/schemes.html. Completed forms must be returned to the main address. Shortlisted candidates will be sent forms for admission to the University of Cambridge.
Closing Date: Please contact the organisation.
Contributor: Offered in collaboration with the British Embassy in Kathmandu.
Additional Information: Further information is available on request.

OSI Chevening Cambridge Scholarships for Postgraduate Study

Subjects: Social sciences or humanities.

Purpose: To financially support those undertaking postgraduate study.

Eligibility: Open to students from Albania, Bosnia, Croatia, Estonia, Kosovo, Latvia, Lithuania, Macedonia, Slovenia, Ukraine or the Federal Republic of Yugoslavia. The Trusts cannot admit students to the University or any of its colleges. Applicants for awards from the Trusts must, therefore, also apply to the University of Cambridge and be offered a place at Cambridge in the normal way. All applicants must have a First Class or High Second Class (Honours) Degree or equivalent and normally be under 26.

Level of Study: Postgraduate.

Type: Scholarship.

Value: The University Composition Fee at the overseas rate, approved college fees, a maintenance allowance sufficient for a single student and a contribution to a return economy airfare.

Frequency: Annual.

Study Establishment: The University of Cambridge.

Country of Study: United Kingdom.

No. of awards offered: Up to 24.

Application Procedure: Applicants must complete a preliminary application form, which can be obtained from local universities, offices of the British Council or the Trust. The preliminary application form can be downloaded from http://www.admin.cam.ac.uk/univ/gsprospectus/c7/overseas/schemes.html. Completed forms must be returned to the main address. Shortlisted candidates will be sent forms for admission to the University of Cambridge.

Closing Date: Please contact the organisation.

Contributor: Offered in collaboration with the Open Society Institute (OSI) and the Foreign and Commonwealth Office (FCO).

Additional Information: Successful applicants will be expected to return to their home country at the end of their course of study at Cambridge. Scholars should not have already spent a full academic year or more studying in a university outside Central and Eastern Europe, the former Soviet Union or Mongolia. Further information is available on request.

Oxford and Cambridge Society of Bombay Cambridge DFID Scholarship

Subjects: All subjects.

Purpose: To financially support those undertaking postgraduate study.

Eligibility: Open to a resident of Bombay City or the state of Maharashtra whose application is supported by the Oxford and Cambridge Society of Bombay. All applicants must be under the age of 35 on October 1st (with priority given to those candidates under the age of 30), undertake to return to their own country to work or study after completing the course at Cambridge, not be employed by a government department (national or local) or by a parastatal organisation, not at present be living or studying in a developed country, not have undertaken studies lasting a year or more in a developed country, nor have undertaken studies lasting a year or more in a developed country. Priority will be given to candidates wishing to pursue a course of study related to the economic and social development of their country.

Level of Study: Postgraduate.

Type: Scholarship.

Value: The University Composition Fee at the overseas rate, approved college fees, a maintenance allowance sufficient for a single student and a contribution to a return economy airfare.

Length of Study: One year.

Frequency: Annual.

Study Establishment: The University of Cambridge.

Country of Study: United Kingdom.

No. of awards offered: One.

Application Procedure: Applicants may obtain further details and a preliminary application form by writing before August 16th of the year before entry to the Joint Secretary of the Nehru Trust for Cambridge

University at the address below giving details of academic qualifications.

Closing Date: Please contact the organisation.

Contributor: Offered in collaboration with the Department for International Development (DFID).

Additional Information: Further information is available on request.

For further information contact:

The Joint Secretary
The Nehru Trust for Cambridge University
Teen Murti House
Teen Murti Marg, New Delhi, 110011, India

Pegasus Cambridge Scholarships for Postgraduate Study

Subjects: Law.

Purpose: To financially assist students who have gained an offer or a place to read for the Master of Law (LLM) degree.

Eligibility: Applicants must be from one of the following countries: Australia, New Zealand, Canada, Bermuda and the Commonwealth countries of the Caribbean, Kenya, Nigeria, Zambia, Zimbabwe, Hong Kong, Singapore or India. Applicants must have gained an offer of a place to read for the Master of Law degree (LLM). The Trusts cannot admit students to the University or any of its colleges. Applicants for awards from the Trusts must, therefore, also apply to the University of Cambridge and be offered a place at Cambridge in the normal way. All applicants must have a First Class or High Second Class (Honours) Degree or equivalent and normally be under 26. Applicants must be successful in winning an Overseas Research Student (ORS) award which pays the difference between the home and overseas rate of the University Composition Fee.

Level of Study: Postgraduate.

Type: Scholarship.

Frequency: Annual.

Study Establishment: The University of Cambridge.

Country of Study: United Kingdom.

No. of awards offered: Up to six.

Application Procedure: Applicants must complete a preliminary application form, which can be obtained from local universities, offices of the British Council or the Trust. The preliminary application form can be downloaded from http://www.admin.cam.ac.uk/univ/gsprospectus/c7/overseas/schemes.html. Completed forms must be returned to the main address. Shortlisted candidates will be sent forms for admission to the University of Cambridge.

Closing Date: Please contact the organisation.

Contributor: Offered in collaboration with the Pegasus Scholarships Trust and the Foreign and Commonwealth Office (FCO).

Additional Information: Pegasus Scholarships are held in conjunction with other awards from the Cambridge Commonwealth Trust and other sources and entitle applicants to compete for the opportunity to spend three months in London on work placements after completing the LLM at Cambridge. The London placement will be taken between July and September. By submitting one application, candidates will automatically be considered for all the awards for which they are eligible. Further information is available on request.

Pok Rafeah Cambridge Scholarship

Subjects: All subjects.

Purpose: To financially support study towards a PhD.

Eligibility: Applicants must be from Malaysia. The Trusts cannot admit students to the University or any of its colleges. Applicants for awards from the Trusts must therefore also apply to the University of Cambridge and be offered a place at Cambridge in the normal way. All applicants must have a First Class or High Second Class (Honours) Degree or equivalent and normally be under 26. Applicants for scholarships for study towards the degree of PhD must be successfully nominated for an Overseas Research Student (ORS) award, which covers the difference between the home and overseas rate of the University Composition Fee.

Level of Study: Doctorate, Postgraduate, Predoctorate.

Type: Scholarship.

Value: The University Composition Fee at the approved rate, approved college fees, a maintenance allowance sufficient for a single student and a contribution to a return economy airfare.
Length of Study: Up to three years for PhD study, and one year for postgraduate study.
Frequency: Annual.
Study Establishment: The University of Cambridge.
Country of Study: United Kingdom.
No. of awards offered: One for study towards a PhD, two for postgraduate study.
Application Procedure: Applicants must complete a preliminary application form, which can be obtained from local universities, offices of the British Council or the Trust. The preliminary application form can be downloaded from http://www.admin.cam.ac.uk/univ/gsprospectus/c7/overseas/schemes.html. Completed forms must be returned to the main address. Shortlisted candidates will be sent forms for admission to the University of Cambridge.
Closing Date: Please contact the organisation.
Contributor: Offered in collaboration with the Pok Rafeah Foundation.
Additional Information: Further information is available on request.

For further information contact:

The Secretary
The Cambridge (Malaysia) Foundation
PO Box 10139, Kuala Lumpur, 50704, Malaysia

Poynton Cambridge Scholarships for PhD Study

Subjects: All subjects.
Purpose: To financially support study towards a PhD.
Eligibility: Candidates must be citizens of Australia. The Trusts cannot admit students to the University or any of its colleges. Applicants for awards from the Trusts must, therefore, also apply to the University of Cambridge and be offered a place at Cambridge in the normal way. All applicants must have a First Class or High Second Class (Honours) Degree or equivalent and normally be under 26.
Level of Study: Doctorate.
Type: Scholarship.
Value: The University Composition Fee at the home rate, approved college fees, a maintenance allowance sufficient for a single student and a contribution towards a return economy airfare.
Length of Study: Up to three years.
Frequency: Annual.
Study Establishment: The University of Cambridge.
Country of Study: United Kingdom.
No. of awards offered: Five.
Application Procedure: Applicants must contact the Board of Graduate Studies.
Closing Date: Please contact the organisation.
Contributor: Offered in collaboration with the Cambridge Australia Trusts.
Additional Information: This award was made possible by a generous benefaction from Dr Orde Poyton. Further information is available on request. For details of scholarships offered in collaboration with the Cambridge Australia Trust please see the website http://www.anu.edu/cabs/scholarships/cambridge/cambridge-austrust.html.

For further information contact:

The Secretary
The Board of Graduate Studies
4 Mill Lane, Cambridge, Cambridgeshire, CB2 1RZ, England

President Árpád Göncz Scholarship for Postgraduate Study

Subjects: All subjects.
Purpose: To financially support those undertaking postgraduate study. The scholarship was originally set up to commemorate the visit of the President of Hungary to the University of Cambridge.
Eligibility: Applicants must be Hungarian nationals. The Trusts cannot admit students to the University or any of its colleges. Applicants for awards from the Trusts must, therefore, also apply to the University of Cambridge and be offered a place at Cambridge in the normal way. All applicants must have a First Class or High Second Class (Honours) Degree or equivalent and normally be under 26.
Level of Study: Postgraduate.
Type: Scholarship.
Value: The University Composition Fees at the overseas rate, approved college fees, a maintenance allowance sufficient for a single student and a contribution to a return economy airfare.
Length of Study: One year.
Frequency: Annual.
Study Establishment: The University of Cambridge.
Country of Study: United Kingdom.
No. of awards offered: One.
Application Procedure: Applicants must complete a preliminary application form, which can be obtained from local universities, offices of the British Council or the Trust. The preliminary application form can be downloaded from http://www.admin.cam.ac.uk/univ/gsprospectus/c7/overseas/schemes.html. Completed forms must be returned to the main address. Shortlisted candidates will be sent forms for admission to the University of Cambridge.
Additional Information: Further information is available on request.

President's Cambridge Scholarships for PhD Study

Subjects: All subjects.
Purpose: To financially support study towards a PhD.
Eligibility: Open to students from Ghana. The Trusts cannot admit students to the University or any of its Colleges. Applicants for awards from the Trusts must, therefore, also apply to the University of Cambridge and be offered a place at Cambridge in the normal way. All applicants must have a First Class or High Second Class (Honours) Degree or equivalent and normally be under 26. All applicants must be successfully nominated for an Overseas Research Student (ORS) award which covers the difference between the home and overseas rate of the University Composition Fee.
Level of Study: Doctorate.
Type: Scholarship.
Value: The University Composition Fee at the appropriate rate, approved college fees, maintenance allowance sufficient for a single student and a contribution to a return economy airfare.
Length of Study: Up to three years.
Frequency: Annual.
Study Establishment: The University of Cambridge.
Country of Study: United Kingdom.
No. of awards offered: Up to five.
Application Procedure: Applicants must complete a preliminary application form, which can be obtained from local universities, offices of the British Council or the Trust. The preliminary application form can be downloaded from http://www.admin.cam.ac.uk/univ/gsprospectus/c7/overseas/schemes.html. Completed forms must be returned to the main address. Shortlisted candidates will be sent forms for admission to the University of Cambridge.
Closing Date: Please contact the organisation.
Contributor: Offered in collaboration with the Malaysian Commonwealth Studies Centre.
Additional Information: Further information is available on request.

President's Cambridge Scholarships for Postgraduate Study

Subjects: All subjects.
Purpose: To financially support those undertaking postgraduate study.
Eligibility: Applicants must be from Ghana. The Trusts cannot admit students to the University or any of its colleges. Applicants for awards from the Trusts must, therefore, also apply to the University of Cambridge and be offered a place at Cambridge in the normal way. All applicants must have a First Class or High Second Class (Honours) Degree or equivalent and normally be under 26.

Level of Study: Postgraduate.

Type: Scholarship.

Value: The University Composition Fee at the appropriate rate, approved college fees, a maintenance allowance sufficient for a single student and a contribution towards a return economy airfare.

Length of Study: One year.

Frequency: Annual.

Study Establishment: The University of Cambridge.

Country of Study: United Kingdom.

No. of awards offered: Up to five.

Application Procedure: Applicants must complete a preliminary application form, which can be obtained from local universities, offices of the British Council or the Trust. The preliminary application form can be downloaded from http://www.admin.cam.ac.uk/univ/gsprospectus/c7/overseas/schemes.html. Completed forms must be returned to the main address. Shortlisted candidates will be sent forms for admission to the University of Cambridge.

Closing Date: Please contact the organisation.

Contributor: Offered in collaboration with the Malaysian Commonwealth Studies Centre.

Additional Information: Further information is available on request.

Prince of Wales (Cable and Wireless) Chevening Cambridge Scholarships for PhD Study

Subjects: Development studies, economics, economics and development, engineering, environment and development, finance, international relations, law or management studies.

Purpose: To financially support study in subjects related to the needs of the scholar's country.

Eligibility: Open to citizens of a number of countries including Anguilla, Antigua and Barbuda, Barbados, Bermuda, the British Virgin Islands, the Cayman Islands, Dominica, Grenada, Jamaica, Monserrat, St Kitts-Nevis, St Lucia, St Vincent, Trinidad and Tobago, and the Turks and Caicos Islands. Successful applicants will be expected to return to their home country at the end of their course of study at Cambridge. The Trusts cannot admit students to the University or any of its colleges. Applicants for awards from the Trusts must, therefore, also apply to the University of Cambridge and be offered a place at Cambridge in the normal way. All applicants must have a First Class or High Second Class (Honours) Degree or equivalent and normally be under 26. All applicants must be successfully nominated for an Overseas Research Student (ORS) award which covers the difference between the home and overseas rate of the University Composition Fee.

Level of Study: Doctorate, Predoctorate.

Type: Scholarship.

Value: The University Composition Fee at the appropriate rate, approved college fees, a maintenance allowance sufficient for a single student and a contribution towards a return economy airfare.

Length of Study: Three years.

Frequency: Annual.

Study Establishment: The University of Cambridge.

Country of Study: United Kingdom.

No. of awards offered: 10.

Application Procedure: Applicants must complete a preliminary application form, which can be obtained from local universities, offices of the British Council or the Trust. The preliminary application form can be downloaded from http://www.admin.cam.ac.uk/univ/gsprospectus/c7/overseas/schemes.html. Completed forms must be returned to the main address. Shortlisted candidates will be sent forms for admission to the University of Cambridge.

Closing Date: Please contact the organisation.

Contributor: Offered in collaboration with Cable and Wireless and the Foreign Commonwealth Office (FCO).

Additional Information: Further information is available on request.

Prince of Wales (Cable and Wireless) Chevening Cambridge Scholarships for Postgraduate Study

Subjects: Development studies, economics, economics and development, engineering, environment and development, finance, international relations, law or management studies.

Purpose: To financially support study in subjects related to the needs of the scholar's country.

Eligibility: Open to citizens of Anguilla, Antigua and Barbuda, Barbados, Bermuda, the British Virgin Islands, the Cayman Islands, Dominica, Grenada, Jamaica, Monserrat, St Kitts-Nevis, St Lucia, St Vincent, Trinidad and Tobago, and the Turks and Caicos Islands. Successful applicants will be expected to return to their home country at the end of their course of study at Cambridge. The Trusts cannot admit students to the University or any of its colleges. Applicants for awards from the Trusts must, therefore, also apply to the University of Cambridge and be offered a place at Cambridge in the normal way. All applicants must have a First Class or High Second Class (Honours) Degree or equivalent and normally be under 26.

Level of Study: Postgraduate.

Type: Scholarship.

Value: The University Composition Fee at the appropriate rate, approved college fees, a maintenance allowance sufficient for a single student and a contribution towards a return economy airfare.

Length of Study: One year.

Frequency: Annual.

Study Establishment: The University of Cambridge.

Country of Study: United Kingdom.

No. of awards offered: 10.

Application Procedure: Applicants must complete a preliminary application form, which can be obtained from local universities, offices of the British Council or the Trust. The preliminary application form can be downloaded from http://www.admin.cam.ac.uk/univ/gsprospectus/c7/overseas/schemes.html. Completed forms must be returned to the main address. Shortlisted candidates will be sent forms for admission to the University of Cambridge.

Closing Date: Please contact the organisation.

Contributor: Offered in collaboration with Cable and Wireless and the Foreign and Commonwealth Office (FCO).

Additional Information: Further information is available on request.

Prince of Wales Scholarships for PhD Study

Subjects: All subjects.

Purpose: To financially support study towards a PhD.

Eligibility: Candidates must be citizens of New Zealand. The Trusts cannot admit students to the University or any of its colleges. Applicants for awards from the Trusts must, therefore, also apply to the University of Cambridge and be offered a place at Cambridge in the normal way. All applicants must have a First Class or High Second Class (Honours) Degree or equivalent and normally be under 26. All applicants must be successfully nominated for an Overseas Research Student award, which covers the difference between the home and overseas rate of the University Composition Fee.

Level of Study: Doctorate, Predoctorate.

Type: Scholarship.

Value: The University Composition Fee at the home rate, approved college fees, a maintenance allowance sufficient for a single student and a contribution to a return economy airfare.

Length of Study: Up to three years.

Frequency: Annual.

Study Establishment: The University of Cambridge.

Country of Study: United Kingdom.

No. of awards offered: Up to five.

Application Procedure: Applicants must apply directly to the Scholarships Officer at their own university, otherwise, they should apply directly to the New Zealand Vice Chancellor's Committee.

Closing Date: Please contact the organisation.

Contributor: Offered in collaboration with the New Zealand Vice Chancellor's Committee.

Additional Information: Further information is available on request.

For further information contact:

Scholarships Officer
The New Zealand Vice Chancellor's Committee
PO Box 11-915
Manners Street, Wellington, New Zealand

Prince Philip Graduate Exhibitions For PhD Study

Subjects: All subjects.
Purpose: To financially support study towards a PhD.
Eligibility: One scholarship will go to a student who has graduated from the Chinese University of Hong Kong and one will go to a student who has graduated from the University of Hong Kong. The Trusts cannot admit students to the University or any of its colleges. Applicants for awards from the Trusts must, therefore, also apply to the University of Cambridge and be offered a place at Cambridge in the normal way. All applicants must have a First Class or High Second Class (Honours) Degree or equivalent and normally be under 26. All applicants must be successfully nominated for an Overseas Research Student (ORS) award which covers the difference between the home and overseas rate of the University Composition Fee.
Level of Study: Doctorate.
Type: Scholarship.
Value: The University Composition Fee at the appropriate rate, approved college fees, a maintenance allowance sufficient for a single student and a contribution to a return economy air fare.
Length of Study: Up to three years.
Frequency: Annual.
Study Establishment: The University of Cambridge.
Country of Study: United Kingdom.
No. of awards offered: Two.
Application Procedure: Applicants must complete a preliminary application form, which can be obtained from local universities, offices of the British Council or the Trust. The preliminary application form can be downloaded from http://www.admin.cam.ac.uk/univ/gsprospectus/c7/overseas/schemes.html. Completed forms must be returned to the main address. Shortlisted candidates will be sent forms for admission to the University of Cambridge.
Closing Date: Please contact the organisation.
Contributor: Offered in collaboration with the Friends of Cambridge University in Hong Kong.
Additional Information: Further information is available on request.

Rajiv Gandhi Cambridge Bursaries

Subjects: All subjects.
Purpose: To financially support study towards a second Bachelor's degree as an affiliated student.
Eligibility: Applicants must be from India. The Trusts cannot admit students to the University or any of its colleges. Applicants for awards from the Trusts must, therefore, also apply to the University of Cambridge and be offered a place at Cambridge in the normal way. All applicants must have a First Class or High Second Class (Honours) Degree or equivalent and normally be under 26.
Level of Study: Postgraduate.
Type: Bursary.
Value: A substantial contribution towards the student's costs, to be determined in the light of the student's own resources.
Length of Study: Two years.
Frequency: Annual.
Study Establishment: The University of Cambridge.
Country of Study: United Kingdom.
No. of awards offered: Up to four.
Application Procedure: Applicants must contact the organisation.
Contributor: Offered in collaboration with the Rajiv Gandhi Foundation.
Additional Information: Further information is available on request.

Robert S McNamara Fellowships at Cambridge

Subjects: All subjects.

Purpose: To financially support those undertaking postgraduate study.
Eligibility: Open to students from outside of the United Kingdom.
Level of Study: Postgraduate.
Type: Scholarship.
Frequency: Annual.
Study Establishment: The University of Cambridge.
Country of Study: United Kingdom.
Application Procedure: Applicants must complete a preliminary application form, which can be obtained from local universities, offices of the British Council or the Trust. The preliminary application form can be downloaded from http://www.admin.cam.ac.uk/univ/gsprospectus/c7/overseas/schemes.html. Completed forms must be returned to the main address. Shortlisted candidates will be sent forms for admission to the University of Cambridge.
Closing Date: Please contact the organisation.
Contributor: Offered in collaboration with the World Bank.
Additional Information: Further information is available on request.

Sally Mugabe Memorial Cambridge DFID Scholarship for Postgraduate Study

Subjects: Subjects relevant to the needs of Zimbabwe, in particular the broad area of social studies relating to the welfare, education and health of women and children.
Purpose: To financially support those undertaking postgraduate study.
Eligibility: Open to female graduates from Zimbabwe. All applicants must be under the age of 35 on October 1st (with priority given to those candidates under the age of 30), undertake to return to their own country to work or study after completing the course at Cambridge, not be employed by a government department (national or local) or by a parastatal organisation, not at present be living or studying in a developed country, nor have undertaken studies lasting a year or more in a developed country. Priority will be given to candidates wishing to pursue a course of study related to the economic and social development of their country.
Level of Study: Postgraduate.
Type: Scholarship.
Value: The University Composition Fee at the overseas rate, approved college fees, a maintenance allowance sufficient for a single student and a contribution to a return economy airfare.
Length of Study: One year.
Frequency: Annual.
Study Establishment: The University of Cambridge.
Country of Study: United Kingdom.
No. of awards offered: One.
Application Procedure: Applicants must complete a preliminary application form, which can be obtained from local universities, offices of the British Council or the Trust. The preliminary application form can be downloaded from http://www.admin.cam.ac.uk/univ/gsprospectus/c7/overseas/schemes.html. Completed forms must be returned to the main address. Shortlisted candidates will be sent forms for admission to the University of Cambridge.
Closing Date: Please contact the organisation.
Contributor: Offered in memory of Sally Mugabe in collaboration with the Department for International Development (DFID) and the Zimbabwe Cambridge Trust.
Additional Information: Further information is available on request.

Schlumberger Cambridge Scholarships

Subjects: All subjects.
Purpose: To offer financial assistance to a student undertaking PhD study from a developing country.
Eligibility: Open to students from a developing country. The Trusts cannot admit students to the University or any of its colleges. Applicants for awards from the Trusts must, therefore, also apply to the University of Cambridge and be offered a place at Cambridge in the normal way. All applicants must have a First Class or High Second Class (Honours) Degree or equivalent and normally be under 26. All applicants must be successfully nominated for an Overseas

Research Student (ORS) award which covers the difference between the home and overseas rate of the University Composition Fee.

Level of Study: Doctorate, Predoctorate.

Type: Scholarship.

Value: The University Composition Fee at the overseas rate, approved college fees, a maintenance allowance sufficient for a single student and a contribution to a return economy airfare.

Length of Study: Up to three years.

Frequency: Annual.

Study Establishment: The University of Cambridge.

Country of Study: United Kingdom.

No. of awards offered: One.

Application Procedure: Applicants must complete a preliminary application form, which can be obtained from local universities, offices of the British Council or the Trust. The preliminary application form can be downloaded from http://www.admin.cam.ac.uk/univ/gsprospectus/c7/overseas/schemes.html. Completed forms must be returned to the main address. Shortlisted candidates will be sent forms for admission to the University of Cambridge.

Closing Date: Please contact the organisation.

Contributor: Offered in collaboration with Schlumberger Cambridge Research Limited.

Additional Information: Further information is available on request.

Shell Centenary Chevening Scholarships for Postgraduate Study

Subjects: Applied sciences and technology, including environmental sciences, business management or economics.

Purpose: To financially support those undertaking postgraduate study.

Eligibility: Open to citizens of Pakistan, China, Russia, Nigeria, India, Malaysia, Singapore, Brazil and Thailand. The Trusts cannot admit students to the University or any of its colleges. Applicants for awards from the Trusts must, therefore, also apply to the University of Cambridge and be offered a place at Cambridge in the normal way. All applicants must have a First Class or High Second Class (Honours) Degree or equivalent and normally be under 26.

Level of Study: Postgraduate.

Type: Scholarship.

Value: The University Composition Fee at the overseas rate, approved college fees, a maintenance allowance sufficient for a single student and a contribution to a return economy airfare.

Length of Study: One year.

Frequency: Annual.

Study Establishment: The University of Cambridge.

Country of Study: United Kingdom.

No. of awards offered: Two.

Application Procedure: Applicants must complete a preliminary application form, which can be obtained from local universities, offices of the British Council or the Trust. The preliminary application form can be downloaded from http://www.admin.cam.ac.uk/univ/gsprospectus/c7/overseas/schemes.html. Completed forms must be returned to the main address. Shortlisted candidates will be sent forms for admission to the University of Cambridge.

Closing Date: Please contact the organisation.

Contributor: Offered in collaboration with Shell International Limited and the Foreign and Commonwealth Office (FCO).

Additional Information: Further information is available on request.

Shell Centenary Scholarships (Countries outside of the Commonwealth)

Subjects: Applied sciences and technology, environmental science, business management or economics.

Purpose: To financially support those undertaking postgraduate study.

Eligibility: Open to citizens from a number of non Commonwealth countries including China, Kazakhstan, Russia, Egypt, Iran, Oman, Saudi Arabia, Syria, Argentina, Brazil, Chile, Peru and Thailand. The Trusts cannot admit students to the University or any of its colleges.

Applicants for awards from the Trusts must, therefore, also apply to the University of Cambridge and be offered a place at Cambridge in the normal way. All applicants must have a First Class or High Second Class (Honours) Degree or equivalent.

Level of Study: Postgraduate.

Type: Scholarship.

Value: The University Composition Fee at the overseas rate, approved college fees, a maintenance allowance sufficient for a single student and a contribution to a return economy airfare.

Length of Study: Varies.

Frequency: Annual.

Study Establishment: The University of Cambridge.

Country of Study: United Kingdom.

No. of awards offered: Up to 12.

Application Procedure: Applicants must complete a preliminary application form, which can be obtained from local universities, offices of the British Council or the Trust. The preliminary application form can be downloaded from http://www.admin.cam.ac.uk/univ/gsprospectus/c7/overseas/schemes.html. Completed forms must be returned to the main address. Shortlisted candidates will be sent forms for admission to the University of Cambridge.

Closing Date: Please contact the organisation.

Contributor: Offered in collaboration with Shell International Limited.

Additional Information: Further information is available on request.

Shell Centenary Scholarships (Developing Countries of the Commonwealth)

Subjects: Applied sciences and technology, environmental science, business management or economics.

Purpose: To financially support those undertaking postgraduate study.

Eligibility: Open to citizens of developing countries of the Commonwealth, including Pakistan, Nigeria and India. The Trusts cannot admit students to the University or any of its colleges. Applicants for awards from the Trusts must, therefore, also apply to the University of Cambridge and be offered a place at Cambridge in the normal way. All applicants must have a First Class or High Second Class (Honours) Degree or equivalent. Applicants for all scholarships must be under 35 on October 1st in the year for which they are applying, priority will be given to those under the age of 30, return to their own country to work or study after completing the course, not be employed by a government department (local or national) or by a parastatal organisation, not at present be living or studying in a developed country, and not have taken studies lasting a year or more in a developed country. Candidates wishing to pursue a course of study related to the economic and social development of their country will be given priority.

Level of Study: Postgraduate.

Type: Scholarship.

Value: The University Composition Fee at the overseas rate, approved college fees, a maintenance allowance sufficient for a single student and a contribution to a return economy airfare.

Length of Study: Varies.

Frequency: Annual.

Study Establishment: The University of Cambridge.

Country of Study: United Kingdom.

No. of awards offered: Up to 10.

Application Procedure: Applicants must complete a preliminary application form, which can be obtained from local universities, offices of the British Council or the Trust. The preliminary application form can be downloaded from http://www.admin.cam.ac.uk/univ/gsprospectus/c7/overseas/schemes.html. Completed forms must be returned to the main address. Shortlisted candidates will be sent forms for admission to the University of Cambridge.

Closing Date: Please contact the organisation.

Contributor: Offered in collaboration with the Department for International Development (DFID) and Shell International Limited.

Additional Information: Further information is available on request.

Shell Centenary Scholarships at Cambridge (Commonwealth)

Subjects: Applied sciences and technology including environmental sciences, business management or economics.
Purpose: To financially support those undertaking postgraduate study.
Eligibility: Open to students from a number of Commonwealth countries including Malaysia, the Philippines, Singapore and South Africa. The Trusts cannot admit students to the University or any of its colleges. Applicants for awards from the Trusts must, therefore, also apply to the University of Cambridge and be offered a place at Cambridge in the normal way. All applicants must have a First Class or High Second Class (Honours) Degree or equivalent and normally be under 26.
Level of Study: Postgraduate.
Type: Scholarship.
Value: The University Composition Fee at the overseas rate, approved college fees, a maintenance sufficient for a single student and a contribution to a return economy airfare.
Length of Study: One year.
Frequency: Annual.
Study Establishment: The University of Cambridge.
Country of Study: United Kingdom.
No. of awards offered: Up to 10.
Application Procedure: Applicants must complete a preliminary application form, which can be obtained from local universities, offices of the British Council or the main address. Completed forms must be returned to the main address. Shortlisted candidates will be sent forms for admission to the University of Cambridge and a scholarship application form. These forms must be returned to the Board of Graduate Studies at the address below.
Closing Date: Please contact the organisation.
Contributor: Offered in collaboration with Shell International Limited.
Additional Information: Further information is available on request.

Shell Centenary Scholarships at Cambridge (Non-OECD Countries)

Subjects: For study in applied sciences and technology including environmental sciences, business management or economics.
Purpose: To financially support those undertaking postgraduate study.
Eligibility: Open to students from a non Organisation For Economic Co-operation and Development (OECD) countries. The Trusts cannot admit students to the University or any of its colleges. Applicants for awards from the Trusts must, therefore, also apply to the University of Cambridge and be offered a place at Cambridge in the normal way. All applicants must have a First Class or High Second Class (Honours) Degree or equivalent and normally be under 26.
Level of Study: Postgraduate.
Type: Scholarship.
Value: The University Composition Fee at the overseas rate, approved college fees, a maintenance allowance sufficient for a single student and a contribution to a return economy airfare.
Frequency: Annual.
Study Establishment: The University of Cambridge.
Country of Study: United Kingdom.
No. of awards offered: Up to 22.
Application Procedure: Applicants must complete a preliminary application form, which can be obtained from local universities, offices of the British Council or the main address. Completed forms must be returned to the main address. Shortlisted candidates will be sent forms for admission to the University of Cambridge and a scholarship application form. These forms must be returned to the Board of Graduate Studies at the address below.
Closing Date: Please contact the organisation.
Contributor: Offered in collaboration with Shell International Ltd.
Additional Information: Further information is available on request.

For further information contact:

The Board of Graduate Studies
4 Mill Lane, Cambridge, Cambridgeshire, CB2 1RZ, England

Sir Patrick Sheehy Scholarships

Subjects: International studies.
Purpose: To financially support the MPhil degree.
Eligibility: The Trusts cannot admit students to the University or any of its colleges. Applicants for awards from the Trusts must, therefore, also apply to the University of Cambridge and be offered a place at Cambridge in the normal way. All applicants must have a First Class or High Second Class (Honours) Degree or equivalent and normally be under 26. All applicants must be successfully nominated for an Overseas Research Student (ORS) award which covers the difference between the home and overseas rate of the University Composition Fee.
Level of Study: Doctorate, Predoctorate.
Type: Scholarship.
Value: The University Composition Fee at the appropriate rate, approved college fees, a maintenance allowance sufficient for a single student and a contribution to a return economy airfare.
Length of Study: Up to three years.
Frequency: Annual.
Study Establishment: The University of Cambridge.
Country of Study: United Kingdom.
No. of awards offered: Varies.
Application Procedure: Applicants must complete a preliminary application form, which can be obtained from local universities, offices of the British Council or the Trust. The preliminary application form can be downloaded from http://www.admin.cam.ac.uk/univ/gsprospectus/c7/overseas/schemes.html. Completed forms must be returned to the main address. Shortlisted candidates will be sent forms for admission to the University of Cambridge.
Closing Date: Please contact the organisation.
Additional Information: This award is offered to mark the retirement of Sir Patrick Sheehy, the Chairman of the British-American Tobacco (BAT) Company Limited. Further information is available on request.

Smuts MCSC Bursaries

Subjects: Commonwealth studies.
Purpose: To financially support study towards a PhD.
Level of Study: Doctorate, Predoctorate.
Type: Bursary.
Value: The value of the bursaries will be determined in the light of the financial circumstances of the applicant.
Frequency: Annual.
Study Establishment: The University of Cambridge.
Country of Study: United Kingdom.
No. of awards offered: Up to four.
Closing Date: Please contact the organisation.
Contributor: Offered in collaboration with the Malaysian Commonwealth Studies Centre.
Additional Information: Further information is available on request.

Smuts ORC Equivalent Awards

Subjects: Commonwealth studies.
Purpose: To financially support study towards a PhD.
Level of Study: Postdoctorate.
Type: Award.
Value: Please contact the organisation.
Frequency: Annual.
Study Establishment: The University of Cambridge.
Country of Study: United Kingdom.
No. of awards offered: Two.
Closing Date: Please contact the organisation.
Additional Information: Further information is available on request.

South African College Bursaries

Subjects: All subjects.
Purpose: To enable citizens of South and Southern Africa to take up college places at the University of Cambridge.
Eligibility: Applicants must be from South or Southern Africa. The Trusts cannot admit students to the University or any of its colleges.

Applicants for awards from the Trusts must, therefore, also apply to the University of Cambridge and be offered a place at Cambridge in the normal way. All applicants must have a First Class or High Second Class (Honours) Degree or equivalent and normally be under 26. All applicants must be successfully nominated for an Overseas Research Student (ORS) award which covers the difference between the home and overseas rate of the University Composition Fee.

Level of Study: Postgraduate.

Type: Bursary.

Value: The University Composition Fee at the overseas rate, approved college fees, a maintenance allowance sufficient for a single student and a contribution to a return economy airfare.

Length of Study: One year.

Frequency: As available.

Study Establishment: The University of Cambridge.

Country of Study: United Kingdom.

No. of awards offered: Varies.

Application Procedure: Applicants must complete a preliminary application form, which can be obtained from local universities, offices of the British Council or the Trust. The preliminary application form can be downloaded from http://www.admin.cam.ac.uk/univ/gsprospectus/c7/overseas/schemes.html. Completed forms must be returned to the main address. Shortlisted candidates will be sent forms for admission to the University of Cambridge.

Closing Date: Please contact the organisation.

Contributor: Offered in collaboration with Churchill College, Newnham College, Selwyn College, St Catherine's College and Sidney Sussex College, Cambridge.

Additional Information: The bursaries are normally held in conjunction with other awards from the Cambridge Commonwealth Trust and other sources. Further information is available on request.

Tanzania Cambridge DFID Scholarships

Subjects: All subjects.

Purpose: To offer financial support to students from Tanzania.

Eligibility: Open to candidates from Tanzania. All applicants must be under the age of 35 on October 1st, with priority given to those candidates under the age of 30, undertake to return to their own country to work or study after completing the course at Cambridge, not be employed by a government department (national or local) or by a parastatal organisation, not at present be living or studying in a developed country, nor have undertaken studies lasting a year or more in a developed country. Priority will be given to candidates wishing to pursue a course of study related to the economic and social development of their country.

Level of Study: Postgraduate.

Type: Scholarship.

Value: The University Composition Fee at the overseas rate, approved college fees, a maintenance allowance sufficient for a single student and a contribution to a return economy airfare.

Length of Study: One year.

Frequency: Annual.

Study Establishment: The University of Cambridge.

Country of Study: United Kingdom.

No. of awards offered: Up to four.

Application Procedure: Applicants must complete a preliminary application form, which can be obtained from local universities, offices of the British Council or the Trust. The preliminary application form can be downloaded from http://www.admin.cam.ac.uk/univ/gsprospectus/c7/overseas/schemes.html. Completed forms must be returned to the main address. Shortlisted candidates will be sent forms for admission to the University of Cambridge.

Closing Date: Please contact the organisation.

Contributor: Offered in collaboration with the Department of International Development (DFID).

Additional Information: Further information is available on request.

Tanzania Cambridge Scholarship for PhD Study

Subjects: All subjects.

Purpose: To financially support study towards a PhD.

Eligibility: Open to students from Tanzania. The Trusts cannot admit students to the University or any of its colleges. Applicants for awards from the Trusts must, therefore, also apply to the University of Cambridge and be offered a place at Cambridge in the normal way. All applicants must have a First Class or High Second Class (Honours) Degree or equivalent and normally be under 26. Applicants must be successfully nominated for an Overseas Research Student (ORS) award, which covers the difference between the home and overseas rate of the University Composition Fee.

Level of Study: Doctorate, Predoctorate.

Type: Scholarship.

Value: The University Composition Fee at the appropriate rate, approved college fees, a maintenance allowance sufficient for a single student, and a contribution to a return economy airfare.

Length of Study: Up to three years.

Frequency: Annual.

Study Establishment: The University of Cambridge.

Country of Study: United Kingdom.

No. of awards offered: One.

Application Procedure: Applicants must complete a preliminary application form, which can be obtained from local universities, offices of the British Council or the Trust. The preliminary Application Form can be downloaded from http://www.admin.cam.ac.uk/univ/gsprospectus/c7/overseas/schemes.html. Completed forms must be returned to the main address. Shortlisted candidates will be sent forms for admission to the University of Cambridge.

Closing Date: Please contact the organisation.

Additional Information: Further information is available on request.

Tate and Lyle/FCO Cambridge Scholarships

Subjects: All subjects.

Purpose: To financially support those undertaking postgraduate study.

Eligibility: Open to students from Barbados, Belize, the Eastern Caribbean States, Fiji, Guyana, Jamaica, Trinidad and Tobago, Hungary, Slovakia, the Ukraine, Mauritius, Mexico, Saudi Arabia, the Philippines, Swaziland, Zambia, Zimbabwe and Vietnam. The Trusts cannot admit students to the University or any of its colleges. Applicants for awards from the Trusts must, therefore, also apply to the University of Cambridge and be offered a place at Cambridge in the normal way. All applicants must have a First Class or High Second Class (Honours) Degree or equivalent and normally be under 26. Successful applicants will be expected to return to their home country at the end of the course of study at Cambridge.

Level of Study: Postgraduate.

Type: Scholarship.

Value: The University Composition Fee at the overseas rate, approved college fees, a maintenance allowance sufficient for a single student and a contribution to a return economy airfare.

Length of Study: Varies.

Frequency: Annual.

Study Establishment: The University of Cambridge.

Country of Study: United Kingdom.

No. of awards offered: Up to 10.

Application Procedure: Applicants must complete a preliminary application form, which can be obtained from local universities, offices of the British Council or the main address. Completed forms must be returned to the main address. Shortlisted candidates will be sent forms for admission to the University of Cambridge and a scholarship application form. These forms must be returned to the Board of Graduate Studies at the address below.

Closing Date: Please contact the organisation.

Contributor: Offered in collaboration with Tate and Lyle plc and the Foreign and Commonwealth Office (FCO).

Additional Information: Further information is available on request.

For further information contact:

The Board of Graduate Studies
4 Mill Lane, Cambridge, Cambridgeshire, CB2 1RZ, England

Tidmarsh Cambridge Scholarship for PhD Study

Subjects: All subjects.

Purpose: To financially support study towards a PhD.

Eligibility: Open to citizens of Canada. The Trusts cannot admit students to the University or any of its colleges. Applicants for awards from the Trusts must, therefore, also apply to the University of Cambridge and be offered a place at Cambridge in the normal way. All applicants must have a First Class or High Second Class (Honours) Degree or equivalent and normally be under 26. Applicants must have been successfully nominated for an Overseas Research Student (ORS) award, which covers the difference between the home and overseas rate of the University Composition Fee.

Level of Study: Doctorate.

Type: Scholarship.

Value: The University Composition Fee at the home rate, approved college fees and a maintenance allowance sufficient for a single student.

Frequency: As available.

Study Establishment: Trinity Hall, the University of Cambridge.

Country of Study: United Kingdom.

No. of awards offered: One.

Application Procedure: Application forms for the scholarship will be sent out to eligible candidates once the completed form for admission to the University of Cambridge has reached the Board of Graduate Studies.

Closing Date: Please contact the organisation.

Contributor: A generous benefaction from Mr Evan Schulman.

Additional Information: Further information is available on request.

For further information contact:

The Secretary
The Board of Graduate Studies
4 Mill Lane, Cambridge, Cambridgeshire, CB2 1RZ, England

UK Commonwealth (Cambridge) Scholarships for PhD Study

Subjects: All subjects.

Purpose: To offer the opportunity for individuals with proven academic merit to study towards a PhD at Cambridge.

Eligibility: Open to candidates from a number of countries including Australia, New Zealand and Canada.

Level of Study: Doctorate, Predoctorate.

Type: Scholarship.

Value: The University Composition Fee at the home rate, approved college fees, a maintenance allowance sufficient for a single student and a contribution towards a return economy airfare.

Length of Study: Three years.

Frequency: Annual.

Study Establishment: The University of Cambridge.

Country of Study: United Kingdom.

No. of awards offered: Up to 15.

Application Procedure: Candidates must apply to the local Commonwealth Scholarship agency in their home country.

Closing Date: Please contact the organisation.

Contributor: Offered in collaboration with the Association of Commonwealth Universities.

Additional Information: It is not a pre-requisite for successful United Kingdom Commonwealth Scholars to be nominated for an Overseas Research Student (ORS) award. However, candidates for the PhD will be expected to apply for an ORS award since these are competitive awards which provide evidence of proven academic merit and research potential. Further information is available on request.

UK Commonwealth (Cambridge) Scholarships for Postgraduate Study

Subjects: All subjects.

Purpose: To financially support those undertaking postgraduate study.

Eligibility: Open to candidates from a number of countries including Australia, New Zealand and Canada.

Level of Study: Postgraduate.

Type: Scholarship.

Value: The University Composition Fee at the overseas rate, approved college fees, a maintenance allowance sufficient for a single student and a contribution to a return economy airfare.

Length of Study: One year.

Frequency: Varies.

Study Establishment: The University of Cambridge.

Country of Study: United Kingdom.

No. of awards offered: Up to 10.

Application Procedure: Candidates must apply to the local Commonwealth Scholarship agency in their home country.

Closing Date: Please contact the organisation.

Contributor: Offered in collaboration with the Association of Commonwealth Universities.

Additional Information: It is not a pre-requisite for successful United Kingdom Commonwealth Scholars to be nominated for an Overseas Research Student (ORS) award. However, candidates for the PhD will be expected to apply for an ORS award since these are competitive awards which provide evidence of proven academic merit and research potential. Further information is available on request.

W A Frank Downing Studentship in Law

Subjects: Law.

Purpose: To financially support those undertaking the Master of Law (LLM) degree.

Eligibility: Open to citizens of Australia. The Trusts cannot admit students to the University or any of its colleges. Applicants for awards from the Trusts must, therefore, also apply to the University of Cambridge and be offered a place at Cambridge in the normal way. All applicants must have a First Class or High Second Class (Honours) Degree or equivalent and normally be under 26.

Level of Study: Doctorate.

Type: Studentship.

Value: The University Composition Fee at the overseas rate, approved college fees, a maintenance allowance sufficient for a single student and a contribution to a return economy airfare.

Length of Study: One academic year.

Frequency: Varies.

Study Establishment: The University of Cambridge.

Country of Study: United Kingdom.

No. of awards offered: One.

Application Procedure: Applicants must contact the Board of Graduate Studies.

Closing Date: Please contact the organisation.

Contributor: Offered in collaboration with the Cambridge Australia Trust.

Additional Information: Further information is available on request. For details of scholarships offered in collaboration with the Cambridge Australia Trust please see the website http://www.anu.edu/cabs/scholarships/cambridge/cambridge-austrust.html.

For further information contact:

The Secretary
The Board of Graduate Studies
4 Mill Lane, Cambridge, Cambridgeshire, CB2 1RZ, England

William and Margaret Brown Cambridge Scholarship for PHD Study

Subjects: Engineering, natural sciences, physical sciences or political sciences.

Purpose: To financially support study towards a PhD.

Eligibility: Open to students from Canada. The Trusts cannot admit students to the University or any of its colleges. Applicants for awards from the Trusts must, therefore, also apply to the University of Cambridge and be offered a place at Cambridge in the normal way. All applicants must have a First Class or High Second Class (Honours) Degree or equivalent and normally be under 26. All applicants must be successfully nominated for an Overseas Research

Student (ORS) award which covers the difference between the home and overseas rate of the University Composition Fee.
Level of Study: Doctorate, Predoctorate.
Type: Scholarship.
Value: The University Composition Fee at the home rate and approved college fees.
Length of Study: Up to three years.
Frequency: As available.
Study Establishment: The University of Cambridge.
Country of Study: United Kingdom.
No. of awards offered: One.
Application Procedure: Application forms for the scholarship will be sent out to eligible candidates once the completed form for admission to the University of Cambridge has reached the Board of Graduate Studies.
Closing Date: Please contact the organisation.
Contributor: A generous donation from Dr Donald Pinchin.
Additional Information: Further information is available on request.

For further information contact:

The Secretary
The Board of Graduate Studies
4 Mill Hill, Cambridge, Cambridgeshire, CB2 1RZ, England

Wolfson Bursaries

Subjects: All subjects.
Purpose: To financially support those undertaking postgraduate study.
Eligibility: The Trusts cannot admit students to the University or any of its colleges. Applicants for awards from the Trusts must, therefore, also apply to the University of Cambridge and be offered a place at Cambridge in the normal way. All applicants must have a First Class or High Second Class (Honours) Degree or equivalent and normally be under 26.
Level of Study: Unrestricted.
Type: Bursary.
Value: Part-cost bursary.
Frequency: Annual.
Study Establishment: Wolfson College, the University of Cambridge.
Country of Study: United Kingdom.
No. of awards offered: Varies.
Application Procedure: Applications should be made to the college direct.
Closing Date: Please contact the organisation.
Additional Information: Further information is available on request.

World Bank Cambridge Scholarships for Postgraduate Study

Subjects: For subjects related to development.
Purpose: To financially support those undertaking postgraduate study.
Eligibility: Candidates must be nationals of a World Bank member country, be under the age of 45, with priority given to those candidates under 35, be in good health and of good character, have or be about to obtain a First Class or high Second Class Degree from a recognised university in a development related field. Other prerequisites include two, but preferably four or five, years of recent full-time professional experience in their home country or other developing country, usually in public service. Candidates must agree to return to their home country upon completion of their studies, must not hold resident status in the United States of America or another industrialised country and must not have been given political asylum by an industrialised country. Candidates should not hold a Master's degree or diploma from an industrialised country, or at present be studying towards a Master's degree or diploma from an industrialised country.
Level of Study: Postgraduate.
Type: Scholarship.
Value: The University Composition Fee at the overseas rate, approved college fees, a maintenance allowance sufficient for a single student and a contribution to a return economy airfare.
Length of Study: One year.

Frequency: Annual.
Study Establishment: The University of Cambridge.
Country of Study: United Kingdom.
No. of awards offered: Up to 20.
Application Procedure: Applicants must contact the organisation.
Contributor: Offered in collaboration with the World Bank.
Additional Information: Further information is available on request.

Zambia Cambridge Scholarships for PhD Study

Subjects: All subjects.
Purpose: To financially support study towards a PhD.
Eligibility: Candidates must be from Zambia. The Trusts cannot admit students to the University or any of its colleges. Applicants for awards from the Trusts must, therefore, also apply to the University of Cambridge and be offered a place at Cambridge in the normal way. All applicants must have a First Class or High Second Class (Honours) Degree or equivalent and normally be under 26. All applicants must be successfully nominated for an Overseas Research Student (ORS) award which covers the difference between the home and overseas rate of the University Composition Fee.
Level of Study: Doctorate, Predoctorate.
Type: Scholarship.
Value: The University Composition Fee at the home rate, approved college fees, a maintenance allowance sufficient for a single student and a contribution to a return economy airfare.
Length of Study: Up to three years.
Frequency: As available.
Study Establishment: The University of Cambridge.
Country of Study: United Kingdom.
No. of awards offered: One.
Application Procedure: Applicants must complete a preliminary application form, which can be obtained from local universities, offices of the British Council or the Trust. The preliminary application form can be downloaded from http://www.admin.cam.ac.uk/univ/gsprospectus/c7/overseas/schemes.html. Completed forms must be returned to the main address. Shortlisted candidates will be sent forms for admission to the University of Cambridge.
Closing Date: Please contact the organisation.
Contributor: Offered in collaboration with the Zambia Cambridge Trust.
Additional Information: Further information is available on request.

Zambia Cambridge Scholarships for Postgraduate Study

Subjects: All subjects.
Purpose: To financially support those undertaking postgraduate study.
Eligibility: Candidates must be from Zambia. The Trusts cannot admit students to the University or any of its colleges. Applicants for awards from the Trusts must, therefore, also apply to the University of Cambridge and be offered a place at Cambridge in the normal way. All applicants must have a First Class or High Second Class (Honours) Degree or equivalent and normally be under 26. All applicants must be successfully nominated for an Overseas Research Student (ORS) award which covers the difference between the home and overseas rate of the University Composition Fee.
Level of Study: Postgraduate.
Type: Scholarship.
Value: The University Composition Fee at the appropriate rate, approved college fees, a maintenance allowance sufficient for a single student and a contribution to a return economy airfare.
Length of Study: One year.
Frequency: As available.
Study Establishment: The University of Cambridge.
Country of Study: United Kingdom.
No. of awards offered: One.
Application Procedure: Applicants must complete a preliminary application form, which can be obtained from local universities, offices of the British Council or the Trust. The preliminary application form can be downloaded from http://www.admin.cam.ac.uk/univ/gsprospectus/c7/overseas/schemes.html. Completed forms must be returned to the main

address. Shortlisted candidates will be sent forms for admission to the University of Cambridge.
Closing Date: Please contact the organisation.
Contributor: Offered in collaboration with the Zambia Cambridge Trust.
Additional Information: Further information is available on request.

Zimbabwe Cambridge Scholarships For PhD Study

Subjects: All subjects.
Purpose: To financially support study towards a PhD.
Eligibility: Applicants must be from Zimbabwe. The Trusts cannot admit students to the University or any of its colleges. Applicants for awards from the Trusts must, therefore, also apply to the University of Cambridge and be offered a place at Cambridge in the normal way. All applicants must have a First Class or High Second Class (Honours) Degree or equivalent and normally be under 26. All applicants for the PhD must be successfully nominated for an Overseas Research Student (ORS) award which pays the difference between home and overseas rate of the University Composition Fee.
Level of Study: Doctorate, Predoctorate.
Type: Scholarship.
Value: The University Composition Fee at the appropriate rate, approved college fees, a maintenance allowance sufficient for a single student and a contribution to a return economy airfare.
Length of Study: Up to three years.
Frequency: As available.
Study Establishment: The University of Cambridge.
Country of Study: United Kingdom.
No. of awards offered: One.
Application Procedure: Applicants must complete a preliminary application form, which can be obtained from local universities, offices of the British Council or the Trust. The preliminary application form can be downloaded from http://www.admin.cam.ac.uk/univ/gsprospectus/c7/overseas/schemes.html. Completed forms must be returned to the main address. Shortlisted candidates will be sent forms for admission to the University of Cambridge.
Closing Date: Please contact the organisation.
Contributor: Offered in collaboration with the Cambridge Local Examinations Syndicate and the Zimbabwe Cambridge Trust.
Additional Information: Further information is available on request.

Zimbabwe Cambridge Scholarships For Postgraduate Study

Subjects: All subjects.
Purpose: To financially support those undertaking postgraduate study.
Eligibility: Applicants must be from Zimbabwe. The Trusts cannot admit students to the University or any of its colleges. Applicants for awards from the Trusts must, therefore, also apply to the University of Cambridge and be offered a place at Cambridge in the normal way. All applicants must have a First Class or High Second Class (Honours) Degree or equivalent and normally be under 26. All applicants for the PhD must be successfully nominated for an Overseas Research Student (ORS) award which pays the difference between home and overseas rate of the University Composition Fee.
Level of Study: Postgraduate.
Type: Scholarship.
Value: The University Composition Fee at the overseas rate, approved college fees, a maintenance allowance sufficient for a single student and a contribution to a return economy airfare.
Length of Study: One year.
Frequency: As available.
Study Establishment: The University of Cambridge.
Country of Study: United Kingdom.
No. of awards offered: One.
Application Procedure: Applicants must complete a preliminary application form, which can be obtained from local universities, offices of the British Council or the Trust. The preliminary application form can be downloaded from http://www.admin.cam.ac.uk/univ/gsprospectus/c7/overseas/schemes.html. Completed forms must be returned to the main

address. Shortlisted candidates will be sent forms for admission to the University of Cambridge.
Closing Date: Please contact the organisation.
Contributor: Offered in collaboration with the Cambridge Local Examinations Syndicate and the Zimbabwe Cambridge Trust.
Additional Information: Further information is available on request.

CAMBRIDGE UNIVERSITY LIBRARY

West Road, Cambridge, Cambridgeshire, CB3 9DR, England
Tel: (44) 1223 333047
Fax: (44) 1223 339973
www: http://www.cam.ac.uk/libraries
Contact: D J Hall, Deputy Librarian

Cambridge University Library is a university and legal deposit library.

Munby Fellowship in Bibliography

Subjects: Historical bibliography, the history of the book trade and book collecting. There is no restriction on choice of topic within these fields, which may concern printed or manuscript material, western or oriental, in any language, although research should normally be centred on collections in Cambridge.
Purpose: To sponsor bibliographical research.
Eligibility: Open to graduates of any university. Fellows may be of any nationality.
Level of Study: Postdoctorate.
Type: Fellowship.
Value: UK £18,500 reviewed annually.
Length of Study: One year.
Frequency: Annual.
Study Establishment: The Cambridge University Library.
Country of Study: United Kingdom.
No. of awards offered: One.
Application Procedure: Applicants must submit a curriculum vitae, a statement outlining the research proposed, a list of publications, and the names and addresses of two referees. There are no interviews. Selection takes place in December for the following October.
Closing Date: September 15th for October 1st the following year.
Funding: Private.
No. of awards given last year: One.
No. of applicants last year: 14.

THE CANADA COUNCIL FOR THE ARTS

350 Albert Street
PO Box 1047, Ottawa, ON, K1P 5V8, Canada
Tel: (1) 613 566 4414 ext. 5060
Fax: (1) 613 566 4390
Email: lise.rochon@canadacouncil.ca
www: http://www.canadacouncil.ca
Contact: Ms Lise Rochon

The Canada Council for the Arts is a national agency which provides grants and services to professional Canadian artists and art organisations in dance, media arts, music, theatre, writing and publishing, interdisciplinary work, performance art and the visual arts.

Killam Research Fellowships

Subjects: Humanities, social sciences, natural sciences, health sciences, engineering and studies linking any of the disciplines within these broad fields.
Purpose: To support advanced research projects.
Eligibility: Open to Canadian citizens or permanent residents of Canada. Killam Research Fellowships are aimed at established Scholars who have demonstrated outstanding ability through substantial publications in their fields over a period of several years.
Level of Study: Postgraduate.

Type: Fellowship.
Value: Partial or full salary replacement to a maximum of canadian $53,000, based on actual salary for the year before tenure of the award. The Council does not object if the research Fellow's institution supplements the award during the year of tenure to reflect any salary increase.
Length of Study: Up to two years.
Frequency: Annual.
Country of Study: Canadians may hold the award in any country, permanent residents must use the award in Canada.
No. of awards offered: Varies.
Application Procedure: Applicants must submit requests on the appropriate application forms which are available from the Canada Council Killam Programme Section.
Closing Date: May 31st.

CANADA MEMORIAL FOUNDATION

The Association of Commonwealth Universities
John Foster House
36 Gordon Square, London, WC1H 0PF, England
Tel: (44) 20 7387 8572
Fax: (44) 20 7387 2655
Contact: Awards Division Head

Canada Memorial Foundation Scholarships

Subjects: All subjects but clinical medicine is currently excluded.
Purpose: To fund a student taking a taught postgraduate degree at a university or other appropriate institution in Canada.
Eligibility: Open to United Kingdom citizens who are permanently resident in the United Kingdom and hold, or expect to hold, an Upper Second Class (Honours) Degree or equivalent qualification. Candidates should normally be under 30 years of age and must show convincing reasons as to why they wish to study in Canada. It is not offered for study leading to PhD.
Level of Study: Postgraduate.
Type: Scholarship.
Value: Covers fees, maintenance and air fares. Other allowances for books and study travel are available.
Length of Study: One year only. Candidates wishing to take a two year course will be required to show they have funding to complete the course.
Frequency: Annual.
Study Establishment: A university or other appropriate institution.
Country of Study: Canada.
No. of awards offered: Two.
Application Procedure: Applicants must complete a preliminary application form in addition to the main application form. Curriculum vitaes are not accepted. Application forms are available June to October. Application forms are not sent out in the week prior to closing date.
Closing Date: Variable, usually October each year.
Funding: Private.
Contributor: The Canada Memorial Foundation.

CANADIAN ACADEMIC INSTITUTE IN ATHENS/CANADIAN ARCHAEOLOGICAL INSTITUTE IN ATHENS (CAIA)

59 Queens Park Crescent, Toronto, ON, M5S 2C4, Canada
Tel: (1) 416 926 7290
Fax: (1) 416 926 7292
Contact: Grants Management Officer

Thompson (Homer and Dorothy) Fellowship

Subjects: Modern Greek, classical languages and literatures, history, archaeology, history of art and music.

Purpose: To support the graduate or postdoctoral studies of a person who needs to work in Greece.
Eligibility: Open to Canadian citizens or landed immigrants.
Level of Study: Doctorate, Graduate, Postdoctorate, Postgraduate, Predoctorate.
Type: Fellowship.
Value: Canadian $4,000, plus reduced rent in the CAIA hostel for the period of the fellowship.
Length of Study: One year.
Frequency: Every two years.
Study Establishment: The Canadian Archaeological Institute at Athens.
Country of Study: Greece.
No. of awards offered: One.
Application Procedure: Applicants must write enclosing a curriculum vitae and an outline of the proposed research. Applicants must also arrange for three referees to send letters to the Canadian address.
Closing Date: March 15th.
Funding: Private.
No. of awards given last year: One.
Additional Information: In addition to studies the Fellow will assist the director of CAIA with office work (10 hours per week). Therefore some previous experience in Greece and some modern Greek is recommended.

CANADIAN ASSOCIATION OF BROADCASTERS

PO Box 627
Stn B
CP 627
Succ B, Ottawa, ON, K1P 5S2, Canada
Tel: (1) 613 233 4035
Fax: (1) 613 233 6961
Email: cab@cab-acr.ca
www: http://www.cab-acr.ca

The Canadian Association of Broadcasters is the collective voice of Canada's private radio and television stations and speciality services. The CAB develops industry wide strategic plans, works to improve the financial health of the industry, and promotes private broadcasting's role as Canada's leading programmer and local service provider.

The BBM Scholarship

Subjects: Statistical and quantitative research methodology.
Purpose: To ensure there is an investment in the development of individuals, skilled and knowledgeable in research, who may be of future benefit to the Canadian broadcasting industry.
Eligibility: Open to students enrolled in a graduate studies programme, or in the final year of an honours degree with the intention of entering a graduate programme, anywhere in Canada. Candidates will have demonstrated achievement in, and knowledge of, statistical and/or quantitative research methodology in a course of study at a Canadian university or post secondary institution.
Level of Study: Graduate.
Type: One scholarship.
Value: Canadian $2,500.
Frequency: Annual.
Country of Study: Canada.
No. of awards offered: One.
Application Procedure: Applicants must complete and application form and must submit a 250 word essay outlining their interest in audience research. Application forms are available from the Celebrating Excellence section of the website. Three references should be attached to a complete application form, including one from the course director.
Closing Date: June 30th.
Funding: Private.

Contributor: The BBM Bureau of Measurement and the Canadian Association of Broadcasters.
No. of awards given last year: One.
No. of applicants last year: Eight.

CANADIAN BAR ASSOCIATION (CBA)

50 O'Connor
Suite 902, Ottawa, ON, K1P 6LZ, Canada
Tel: (1) 613 237 2925
Fax: (1) 613 237 0185
Email: info@cba.org
www: http://www.cba.org/abc
Contact: Senior Director of Communications

The Canadian Bar Association (CBA) is the essential ally and advocate of all members of the legal profession. It is the voice of, and for, all members of the profession and its primary purpose is to serve its members. It is also the premier provider of personal and professional development and support to all members of the legal profession, promoting fair justice systems, facilitating effective law reform, and promoting equality in the legal profession. CBA is devoted to the elimination of discrimination.

Viscount Bennett Fellowship
Subjects: Law.
Purpose: To encourage a high standard of legal education, training and ethics.
Eligibility: Open to Canadian citizens only.
Level of Study: Postgraduate.
Type: Fellowship.
Value: Canadian $20,000.
Length of Study: One year.
Frequency: Annual.
Study Establishment: An approved institution.
Country of Study: Any country.
No. of awards offered: One.
Application Procedure: Applicants must write for an application form.
Closing Date: November 15th.

CANADIAN BLOOD SERVICES (CBS)

1800 Alta Vista Drive, Ottawa, ON, K1G 4J5, Canada
Tel: (1) 613 739 2408
Fax: (1) 613 739 2426
Email: cilla.perry@bloodservices.ca
www: http://www.bloodservices.ca
Contact: Ms Cilla Perry, Manager, Research & Development

Canadian Blood Services (CBS) is a non-profit, charitable organisation whose sole mission is to manage the blood system for Canadians. CBS collects approximately 740,000 units of blood annually and processes it into components and products that are administered to thousands of patients each year.

Canadian Blood Services Graduate Fellowship Program
Subjects: Blood transfusion science focuses on aspects of the collection and preparation of blood from volunteer donors, as well as on the biological materials derived from blood or their substitutes obtained through biotechnology. Such research may be basic, clinical or applied and encompass a broad variety of disciplines including, but not restricted to, epidemiology, surveillance, social sciences, blood banking, immunohaematology, haematology, infectious diseases, immunology, genetics, protein chemistry, molecular and cell biology, clinical medicine, laboratory sciences, virology, bioengineering, process engineering, or biotechnology.

Purpose: To attract and support young investigators to initiate or continue training in the field of blood or blood products research.
Eligibility: Open to graduate students who are undertaking full-time research training leading to a PhD degree. Students registering solely for a Master's degree will not be considered, only those demonstrating acceptance into a PhD programme will receive continued support. Candidates must have completed sufficient academic work to be admitted in good standing to a graduate school by the time the award is to take effect, or be already engaged in a PhD programme. Applicants possessing a medical degree but not licensed to practice medicine in Canada, are eligible to apply for this award providing they meet the above criteria.
Level of Study: Graduate.
Value: Canadian $19,030 per year plus a yearly research and a travel allowance of canadian $1,000 per year.
Length of Study: Up to four years. The initial term is for two years, with the option for a two year renewal. Renewals must be requested in the form of a complete new application.
Frequency: Twice a year.
Country of Study: Canada.
Application Procedure: Candidates are required to submit a completed application form (GFP-01) that is available either from the website or by contacting Cilla Perry at the main address or email cilla.perry@bloodservices.ca.
Closing Date: July 31st or November 15th.
Funding: Government.
No. of awards given last year: Seven.
No. of applicants last year: 11.

Canadian Blood Services Postdoctoral Fellowhip (PDF)
Subjects: Research in transfusion science.
Purpose: To support postdoctoral Fellows working with CBS affiliated research and development groups across Canada. CBS has active research programmes within transfusion science emphasising platelets, stem cells, plasma proteins, infectious disease, epidemiology and chemical transfusion practice. The CBS PDF also aims to foster careers related to transfusion science in Canada.
Eligibility: Candidates must hold a recent PhD (or equivalent research degree) or an MD/DDS/DVM, plus a recent research degree in an appropriate health field (minimum MSc) or equivalent research experience, must not be registered for a higher degree at the time of acceptance of the award, nor undertake formal studies for such a degree during the period of appointment.
Level of Study: Postdoctorate, Professional development.
Type: Fellowship.
Value: The value of each fellowship is related to the major degree(s) and experience that the applicant holds. The fellowship offers a stipend based on current Medical Research Council rates for each of the three years as well as a first year research allowance of canadian $10,000.
Length of Study: One-three years.
Frequency: Annual.
Country of Study: Canada.
No. of awards offered: Six.
Application Procedure: Applicants must complete CBS Form RD40. Applications must be made through and with the support of a CBS affiliated scientist. Application forms and guidelines are available from any of the Canadian Blood Service Centres or from the Manager, Research and Development at the main address.
Closing Date: July 1st.
Funding: Government.
No. of awards given last year: Six.
No. of applicants last year: Seven.

Canadian Blood Services Research and Development Program Individual Grants
Subjects: Research into blood.
Purpose: To carry out research into all areas of the collection, testing, processing and therapeutic use of blood and blood products in order to maximise effectiveness, to minimise risk to the health of donor and recipient, to minimise cost of products and service and to ensure that all applicable and validated scientific advances in blood

transfusion therapy and related fields are incorporated in a timely fashion for the benefit of the public.

Eligibility: Available to principal investigators who are staff members at one of the CBS centres or head office.

Type: Grant.

Value: To cover materials, supplies, equipment, travel and laboratory personnel.

Length of Study: One-three years.

Frequency: Annual.

Country of Study: Canada.

Application Procedure: Applicants must complete CBS Form RD10. Application forms and guidelines are available from any of the Canadian Blood Service Centres or from the Manager, Research and Development at the main address.

Closing Date: Deadline for the letter of intent is December 15th, and the deadline for the full application is February 15th.

Funding: Government.

No. of awards given last year: Five.

No. of applicants last year: 15.

Canadian Blood Services Research and Development Program Major Equipment Grants

Subjects: Research into blood.

Purpose: To carry out research into all areas of the collection, testing, processing and therapeutic use of blood and blood products in order to maximise effectiveness, to minimise risk to the health of donor and recipient, to minimise cost of products and service and to ensure that all applicable and validated scientific advances in blood transfusion therapy and related fields are incorporated in a timely fashion for the benefit of the public.

Eligibility: Available to principal investigators who are staff members at one of the CBS centres or head office.

Type: Grant.

Value: For the purchase of specific items of permanent and otherwise unavailable equipment costing more than canadian $10,000 necessary for research relevant to the CBS research and development programme. Less expensive items of equipment are provided for under the Individual and Group Grants and the Request for Proposal.

Frequency: Annual.

Country of Study: Canada.

Application Procedure: Applicants must complete CBS Form RD30. Application forms and guidelines are available from any of the Canadian Blood Service Centres or from the Manager of Research and Development at the main address.

Closing Date: Deadline for the letter of intent is December 15th, and the deadline for the full application is February 15th.

Funding: Government.

No. of awards given last year: One.

No. of applicants last year: Four.

Canadian Blood Services Small Projects Fund

Subjects: Any area of relevance to the Canadian Blood Services.

Purpose: The aim of this programme is to provide funding for Centre staff, including medical staff, to participate in the CBS research and development effort. Projects may address any area of obvious relevance to the mandate of CBS.

Eligibility: Projects must be based in CBS Blood Centres. Project leaders must be CBS staff members, however, co-applicants may be from other institutions. Designation as project leader implies that the individual is actively engaged in conducting the study or project and assumes the major responsibility and leadership for the project. CBS scientists (Associate Scientist, Scientist, Senior Scientists or Adjunct Scientist) are not eligible to apply to this programme as project leaders and are directed to the Intramural Grants Programme.

Value: Up to canadian $15,000.

Length of Study: One year period of research.

Frequency: Twice a year.

Study Establishment: CBS Blood Centres.

Country of Study: Canada.

Application Procedure: Requests for funding must be submitted as a completed application form (SPF-01) that is available by contacting

Cilla Perry at the main address or by email at cilla.perry@bloodservices.ca.

Closing Date: July 31st or November 15th.

Funding: Government.

No. of awards given last year: Seven.

No. of applicants last year: 10.

Canadian Blood Services Transfusion Medicine Fellowship Awards

Subjects: Transfusion medicine.

Purpose: To provide support for physicians in Canada to acquire training in transfusion medicine through exposure to the work carried out in the Canadian Blood Services Centres and Hospital Transfusion Services. It is intended that successful candidates will have some commitment to transfusion medicine in their future career plans.

Eligibility: Candidates must be in the final year of preparation for certifying examinations by the Royal College of Physicians and Surgeons of Canada, or should be newly qualified in a speciality of the Royal College. Priority will be given to those with interest and experience in areas of infectious diseases, epidemiology, public health, blood utilisation and the clinical practice of transfusion medicine.

Type: Fellowship.

Value: The fellowship offers a stipend based on the current level of house staff salaries appropriate to the level of training, provided for in the provincial scale of the province in which the fellowship is awarded, as well as a research and travel allowance of canadian $10,000.

Length of Study: Two years.

Frequency: Annual.

Country of Study: Canada.

No. of awards offered: Four.

Application Procedure: Applicants must complete an application form. Applications must be made through and with the support of the Medical Directors of the Blood Centre and the University or Hospital Training Program Director at which the applicant intends to work. Application forms are available on request from the Medical Directors at the Canadian Blood Services Centres across Canada, or from the main address.

Closing Date: November 15th.

Funding: Government.

No. of awards given last year: One.

No. of applicants last year: One.

CBS Research Fellowship In Hemostasis (RFH)

Subjects: Haemostasis management.

Purpose: Canadian Blood Services and Novo Nordisk Canada, Inc. are seeking to fund an original research proposal exploring an aspect of haemostasis management. Graduate researchers conduct the proposed research, with appropriate guidance, at a Canadian academic medical centre. The proposed research will contribute to further understanding of the processes of haemostasis and may be of a basic, pre-clinical or clinical nature. Although it is not a requirement of the award, the Fellowship may include some active participation in a clinical programme within a Canadian healthcare facility.

Eligibility: This fellowship is intended to support individuals undertaking original postgraduate research in haemostasis management. Fellowships are generally held within four years of completion of graduate or clinical fellowship training in an appropriate speciality.

Level of Study: Postdoctorate, Professional development.

Type: Fellowship.

Value: Canadian $70,000 for its one year duration.

Length of Study: One year.

Frequency: Annual.

No. of awards offered: One.

Application Procedure: Candidates for this fellowship are required to complete a NNCI/CBS RFH application form (RFH-2001). Application forms and guidelines are available from the main address, as well as in electronic format on the CBS website.

Closing Date: November 1st.

Funding: Commercial.

Contributor: Novo Nordisk Canada, Inc.

No. of awards given last year: One.
No. of applicants last year: Four.

CANADIAN BREAST CANCER RESEARCH INITIATIVE (CBCRI)

10 Alcorn Avenue
Suite 200, Toronto, ON, M4V 3BI, Canada
Tel: (1) 416 961 9406
Fax: (1) 416 961 4189
Email: cbcri@cancer.ca
www: http://www.breast.cancer.ca
Contact: Ms Pat McAulay

Established in 1993 the Canadian Breast Cancer Research Initiative (CBCRI) is Canada's primary funder of breast cancer study. As a unique partnership of groups from the public, private and non-profit sectors. CBCRI is committed to reducing the incidence of breast cancer, increasing survival, and enhancing the lives of those affected by the disease.

CBCRI Feasibility Grants

Subjects: Oncology.
Type: Grant.
Value: Varies.
Closing Date: October 15th.
Additional Information: For the most up to date information on eligibility, application procedure and grant values, applicants should refer to the website.

CBCRI Research Grants Competition

Subjects: Oncology.
Purpose: Provides research support to individuals formally affiliated with Canadian universities or institutes.
Eligibility: Applicants must write for details or refer to the website.
Type: Grant.
Value: Varies.
Application Procedure: Applicants must complete Form 801, Canadian Breast Cancer Research Institute: Application for Research Grant. Candidates must write for further details and a form or refer to the website.
Closing Date: October 15th.

CBCRI Special Programs/Idea Grants

Subjects: Oncology.
Purpose: To support initiative and new research ideas that are speculative but have the potential to advance scientific knowledge.
Frequency: Twice a year.
No. of awards offered: 6-12.
Additional Information: For the most up to date information on eligibility, application procedure and grant values, applicants should refer to the website.

CBCRI Special Programs/Streams of Excellence Grants

Subjects: Oncology.
Purpose: To move research findings forward towards translational application and ultimate impact on clinical care and the treatment of breast cancer.
Eligibility: Applicants must write for details or refer to the website.
Type: Grant.
Value: Total per year approx. canadian $1,500,000.
Length of Study: Four years with possible renewal for a further year.
Frequency: Annual.
Application Procedure: Applicants must write for details or refer to the website.

CANADIAN BUREAU FOR INTERNATIONAL EDUCATION (CBIE)

220 Laurier Avenue West
Suite 1100, Ottawa, ON, K1P 5Z9, Canada
Tel: (1) 613 237 4820
Fax: (1) 613 237 1073
Email: gbeaudoin@cbie.ca
www: http://www.cbie.ca/canstu.html
Contact: Grazyna Beaudoin, Grants Management Officer

The Canadian Bureau for International Education (CBIE) is a national non-profit association comprising educational institutions, organisations and individuals dedicated to internal education and intercultural training. CBIE's mission is to promote the free movement of learners and trainees across national borders. Activities include advocacy, research and information services, training programmes, scholarship management, professional development for international educators and a host of other services for members and learners.

CIDA Awards Program for Canadians

Subjects: Fields related to international development.
Purpose: To give individuals the opportunity to contribute to the implementation of CIDA's development priorities and to enhance the professional, technical and cross-cultural skills of those who wish to develop expertise in international development.
Eligibility: Open to Canadian citizens and permanent residents of Canada who are registered in a recognised graduate programme at the time of application. They must have relevant qualifications and substantive work experience related to the requirements of the proposed development project and must demonstrate a commitment to international development.
Level of Study: Graduate, Professional development.
Value: Canadian $10,000 maximum.
Length of Study: Up to one year.
Frequency: Annual.
Country of Study: Canada.
No. of awards offered: Approx. 60.
Application Procedure: Applicants must provide a completed application form, a personal information sheet, a curriculum vitae, proof of registration in a Master's programme, a letter of support from the host institution, a letter of support from the project advisor, a letter of reference and proof of Canadian citizenship or permanent resident status. Three sets of these documents must be provided.
Closing Date: April 15th.
Funding: Government.
Contributor: The Canadian International Development Agency.
No. of awards given last year: 64.
Additional Information: The CIDA Awards programme is for Canadian citizens who would like to participate in international development through a volunteer project of their own initiative. The project is to be carried out in collaboration with an organisation in a country eligible under Canada's Official Development Assistance (ODA) programme and must address a specific field of endeavour within CIDA's Aid Policy. The programme offers awards of up to canadian $10,000 each in three categories: Innovative Research Awards to allow Master's students to undertake field research related to their thesis or programme, Professional Leadership Awards for individuals with professional experience who wish to undertake a volunteer research or service project in international development, and International Enterprise Co-operation Awards intended for Master's students in business, commerce and management programmes to undertake an international internship or an internship combined with a semester of study in a developing country.

J Armand Bombardier Internationalist Fellowships

Subjects: All subjects.
Eligibility: Application is open to Canadians and permanent residents of Canada who hold at least one university degree, or are in the final year of a programme. College graduates (post secondary level) holding a recognised Bachelor's degree are also eligible. The

latest degree must have been awarded no longer than five years from the date of application. Applicants must have achieved a high academic standing. The fellowships are tenable anywhere in the world outside Canada.

Level of Study: Doctorate, Graduate.
Type: Fellowship.
Value: Canadian $10,000 non-renewable.
Length of Study: A minimum of eight consecutive months including at least four taught months of study courses.
Frequency: Annual.
Country of Study: Any country.
No. of awards offered: 25.
Application Procedure: Applicants must complete an application form, available at CBIE's website. To receive printed or electronic versions please write to the main address or email smelanson@cbie.ca. Applicants must submit a completed application form, a letter of intent outlining the proposed study programme abroad, a curriculum vitae, academic transcripts, and two letters of reference (one academic and one personal).
Closing Date: March 1st. This date is subject to change so please confirm before applying.
Funding: Private.
No. of awards given last year: 25.

CANADIAN CYSTIC FIBROSIS FOUNDATION (CCFF)

2221 Yonge Street
Suite 601, Toronto, ON, M4S 2B4, Canada
Tel: (1) 416 485 9149
Fax: (1) 416 485 0960
Email: kethier@cysticfibrosis.ca
www: http://www.cysticfibrosis.ca
Contact: Ms Karen Ethier, Manager, Research Programmes

Since 1960, the Canadian Cystic Fibrosis Foundation has worked to provide a brighter future for every child born with cystic fibrosis. Through its research and clinical programmes, the Foundation helps to provide outstanding care for affected individuals, while pursuing the quest for a cure or control.

Canadian Cystic Fibrosis Foundation Clinic Incentive Grants

Subjects: Medical sciences.
Purpose: To enhance the standard of clinical care available to Canadians with cystic fibrosis, by providing funds to initiate a comprehensive programme for patient care, research and teaching or to strengthen an existing programme.
Eligibility: Canadian hospitals and medical schools are eligible to apply. Applicants must demonstrate the regional need for specialised clinical care for cystic fibrosis, the need of the institution for assistance and its plans to attract complementary funding from other sources to develop a complete cystic fibrosis programme, the potential for the development of a comprehensive programme for care, clinical research, teaching and the desire to collaborate with the CCFF and with other Canadian cystic fibrosis clinics.
Level of Study: Research.
Type: Grant.
Length of Study: One year, renewable on an annual basis.
Frequency: Annual.
Country of Study: Canada.
Application Procedure: Applicants must complete an application form. Late applications will be subject to a penalty equal to 10 percent of the value of the award. This penalty will be deducted from the clinic director's honorarium.
Closing Date: October 1st.

Canadian Cystic Fibrosis Foundation Fellowships

Subjects: Biomedical or behavioural science pertinent to cystic fibrosis.

Purpose: To encourage basic or clinical research training.
Eligibility: Open to individuals who hold MD or PhD degrees. Medical graduates should have already completed their basic core years of residency training. Applications for clinical fellowships must have a strong research component in the proposed programme. Fellowships are not awarded for residency type clinical training. Canadian fellowship applicants of exceptional quality requesting funding to study abroad will be considered. Applications will be strengthened by an indication of intention to return to Canada.
Level of Study: Doctorate, Postdoctorate.
Type: Fellowship.
Value: The value is dependent upon academic qualifications and research experience. Award levels are reviewed on an annual basis and will correspond with prevailing Canadian rates.
Length of Study: Two years, with a possibility of renewal for a further year.
Frequency: Annual.
Study Establishment: Any approved university, hospital or research institute.
Country of Study: Canada.
No. of awards offered: Varies.
Application Procedure: Applicants must write for details and arrange to have three letters of recommendation submitted, one of which should be from the applicant's current or most recent supervisor. Incomplete or late applications will be returned to the applicant.
Closing Date: October 1st or April 1st.
Additional Information: One supervisor cannot submit more than two initial fellowship applications to any one competition. The supervisor should not rank the applications submitted.

Canadian Cystic Fibrosis Foundation Research Grants

Subjects: Scientific research concentrating on cystic fibrosis.
Purpose: To facilitate the scientific investigation of all aspects of cystic fibrosis.
Eligibility: A principal investigator should hold a recognised, full-time faculty appointment in a relevant discipline at a Canadian university or hospital. Under exceptional circumstances and at the discretion of the Research Subcommittee, applications from other individuals may be evaluated on a case by case basis.
Level of Study: Doctorate.
Type: Research grant.
Value: The amount of a grant will be determined by the Medical or Scientific Advisory Committee following a detailed review of the applicant's proposed budget.
Length of Study: Usually for a term of one or two years or, in a limited number of instances, three years.
Frequency: Annual.
Study Establishment: A Canadian institution.
Country of Study: Canada.
Application Procedure: Applicants must write for details. Incomplete or late applications will be returned to the applicant.
Closing Date: October 1st.
Additional Information: Investigators are eligible to hold more than one research grant. No more than one initial application may be submitted to a single competition, and it is a requirement that the focus of a second grant be clearly delineated from the first one. The specific aims of a second grant should represent new approaches to the cystic fibrosis problem and not an extension of an existing research programme.

Canadian Cystic Fibrosis Foundation Scholarships

Subjects: Cystic fibrosis.
Purpose: To provide salary support for a limited number of exceptional investigators, offering them an opportunity to develop outstanding cystic fibrosis research programmes, unhampered by heavy teaching or clinical loads. It is intended to attract gifted investigators to cystic fibrosis research.
Eligibility: Open to holders of an MD or PhD degree and must be sponsored by the chairman of the appropriate department and by the Dean of Faculty. They may recently have completed training or be established investigators wishing to devote major research effort to cystic fibrosis. The beginning investigator should have demonstrated

promise of ability to initiate and carry out independent research and the established investigator should have a published record of excellent scientific research.

Level of Study: Doctorate, Postgraduate.

Type: Scholarship.

Value: Salary support, dependent on the qualifications and experience of the successful candidate which will be determined by prevailing Canadian scholarship rates and the nominating university. The salary of the Scholar may be supplemented by the institution or by clinical income, up to 50 percent of the salary wll be paid by the foundation.

Length of Study: Three years, renewable for an additional two years on receipt of a satisfactory progress report. In no case will an award be for more than five years.

Frequency: Annual.

Study Establishment: Any approved university, hospital or research institute.

Country of Study: Canada.

No. of awards offered: Varies, subject to availability of funds.

Application Procedure: Applicants must write for details.

Closing Date: October 1st.

Canadian Cystic Fibrosis Foundation Small Conference Grants

Subjects: Medical sciences.

Purpose: To support small conferences which are focused on subjects of direct relevance to cystic fibrosis and to facilitate the exchange of special expertise between larger university based cystic fibrosis clinics and smaller, more remote clinics.

Eligibility: Applications will only be accepted from clinic directors and CCFF funded investigators.

Level of Study: Professional development.

Type: Grant.

Value: Grants to conferences focused on subjects of direct relevance to cystic fibrosis will be up to a maximum of canadian $2,500 and grants for the exchange of expertise will not normally exceed canadian $1,000.

No. of awards offered: Dependent on the availability of funds.

Application Procedure: Applicants must make applications in the form of a letter. For medical and/or scientific conferences, the application should indicate who is organising and attending the conference, and the specific topics and purpose of the conference. For inter-clinic exchanges, the application should specify the proposed arrangements for, and the specific purpose of the exchange.

Closing Date: Applications may be submitted at any time, but the Foundation should be consulted in advance with respect to the availability of funds.

Additional Information: Grants are available on a first come, first served basis. Frequency of application from any particular individual or group should be reasonable.

Canadian Cystic Fibrosis Foundation Studentships

Subjects: Biomedical and behavioural sciences relevant to the study of cystic fibrosis.

Purpose: To support highly qualified graduate students who are registered for a higher degree and who are undertaking full-time research training in areas of the biomedical or behavioural sciences relevant to cystic fibrosis.

Eligibility: Studentships are awarded for studies at the Master's or doctoral levels.

Level of Study: Doctorate, Postgraduate.

Type: Studentship.

Value: The value of a CCFF Studentship is reviewed on an annual basis, and is commensurate with prevailing Canadian rates.

Length of Study: Initial studentships are awarded for a term of two years. Routine notification will be required from the supervisor by October 1st indicating that the student has taken up the award and that he or she plans to proceed through the second year.

Frequency: Annual.

Study Establishment: Canadian universities.

Country of Study: Canada.

No. of awards offered: Varies.

Application Procedure: Applicants must write for details. Incomplete or late applications will be returned to the applicant. Applicants must arrange to have official transcripts and two letters of recommendation forwarded directly to the foundation. One of the letters of recommendations should be from the applicant's current or most recent employer.

Closing Date: October 1st or April 1st.

Additional Information: If a student receiving support for studies leading to a Master's degree elects to continue to a doctorate degree, he or she must reapply for an initial CCFF Studentship at the doctoral level. Students are expected to spend at least 75 percent of their time on the research training described in their application. Studentships may not be held in conjunction with any other award that exceeds 35 percent of the value of the Studentship.

Canadian Cystic Fibrosis Foundation Transplant Centre Incentive Grants

Subjects: Medical sciences.

Purpose: To enhance the quality of care available to cystic fibrosis transplant candidates by providing eligible centres with supplementary funding.

Eligibility: Any Canadian lung transplant centre which currently has one or more individuals with cystic fibrosis listed for transplant may apply. Please note that under no circumstances will funding be provided to more than one transplant centre in the same city. Applicants must demonstrate how funds awarded would serve to enhance the quality of care available to patients in their centre.

Level of Study: Research.

Type: Grant.

Value: Value will be determined in accordance with a formula which takes account of the number of patients assessed, accepted and followed pre-operatively, transplanted and followed post-operatively in a given centre during the calendar year ending December 31st of the year preceding the application.

Length of Study: One year.

Frequency: Annual.

Country of Study: Canada.

Application Procedure: Applicants must contact the Foundation. Applicants must provide a rationale for the funding request and a detailed report on patient care and research within the lung transplant programme. All applications will be adjudicated by the Clinic Subcommittee of the Canadian Cystic Fibrosis Foundation.

Closing Date: October 1st.

Additional Information: Late applications will be subject to a penalty equal to 10 percent of the value of the award.

Canadian Cystic Fibrosis Foundation Visiting Scientist Awards

Subjects: Biomedical and behavioural sciences relevant to the study of cystic fibrosis.

Purpose: To enable senior investigators to travel to Canada from abroad who are invited to engage in cystic fibrosis research at a Canadian institution or junior or senior investigators who wish to work in another laboratory in Canada or abroad. This experience should, in some way, benefit the Canadian cystic fibrosis research effort.

Eligibility: A senior investigator can be considered such if he or she has attained at least the position of an associate professor, or has six years of equivalent experience.

Level of Study: Doctorate, Professional development.

Type: Travel grant.

Value: Varies.

Length of Study: Varies.

Frequency: Dependent on funds available.

Study Establishment: Either a Canadian institution or another laboratory in Canada or abroad.

Country of Study: Any country.

No. of awards offered: A limited number.

Application Procedure: Applicants must send an application letter, accompanied by supporting letters from the head of the appropriate department of the host university. Supporting letters should also be provided by the head of the department and the dean of the faculty of the applicant's own university.

Closing Date: Applications are accepted at any time, but the Foundation should be consulted in advance with respect to the availability of funds.

CANADIAN EMBASSY (USA)

501 Pennsylvania Avenue North West, Washington, DC, 20001,
United States of America
Tel: (1) 202 682 1740
Fax: (1) 202 682 7791
Contact: Academic Relations Office

Canadian Embassy (USA) Faculty Enrichment Program

Subjects: Priority topics include bilateral trade and economics, Canada-United States border issues, cultural policy and values, environment, natural resources, energy issues and security co-operation. In addition, projects that examine Canadian politics, economics, culture and society as well as Canada's role in international affairs are welcome. The Embassy especially encourages the use of new Internet technology to enhance existing courses, including the creation of instructional websites, interactive technologies and distance learning links to Canadian Universities.
Purpose: To provide faculty members with the opportunity to develop or redevelop courses with substantial Canadian content that will be offered as part of their regular teaching load, or as a special offering to select audiences in continuing or distance education.
Eligibility: This programme is intended for full-time, tenured or tenure track faculty members at accredited four year United States colleges and universities. The candidates should be able to demonstrate that they are already teaching, or will be authorised to teach, courses with substantial Canadian content (33 percent or more). Team teaching applications are welcome. Applicants are ineligible to receive the same grant in two consecutive years or to receive two individual category Canadian Studies grants in the same grant period.
Value: Up to US$4,500.
Frequency: Annual.
Country of Study: United States of America.
No. of awards offered: Varies.
Application Procedure: Applicants must contact the organisation for an application form.

Canadian Embassy (USA) Graduate Student Fellowship Program

Subjects: Priority topics include business and economic issues, Canadian values and culture, communications, environment, national and international security or natural resources eg. energy, fisheries, forestry and trade.
Purpose: The Graduate Student Fellowship Program promotes research in the social sciences and humanities with a view to contributing to a better knowledge and understanding of Canada and its relationship with the United States or other countries of the world. The purpose of the fellowship is to offer graduate students the opportunity to conduct part of their doctoral research in Canada.
Eligibility: The programme is intended for full-time doctoral students at accredited four year colleges and universities in the United States or Canada whose dissertations are related in substantial part to the study of Canada, Canada/United States or Canada/North America. Candidates must be citizens or permanent residents of the United States and should have completed all doctoral requirements except the dissertation when they apply for a grant.
Level of Study: Graduate.
Type: Fellowship.
Value: A maximum amount of US$850 per month may be awarded for a designated period of up to nine months.
Frequency: Annual.
Study Establishment: An accredited four year college or university in Canada or the United States of America.
Country of Study: United States or Canada.

Application Procedure: Applicants must provide six copies of the following in the order listed: the completed application form, a concise letter (three to four pages) which will explain clearly the present status of the candidate's doctoral studies, describe the candidate's study plans in Canada, list Canadian contacts such as Scholars, research institutes, academic institutions or libraries, state clearly the exact number of months for which financial support is requested, provide a complete and detailed budget, indicate what other funding sources are available, give the names and addresses of two referees, one of which must be the dissertation advisor, contain the dissertation prospectus which must identify the key issues or the main theoretical problem, justify the methodology and indicate clearly the nature of the dissertation's contribution to the advancement of Canadian Studies. An unofficial transcript of grades, a curriculum vitae and proof of United States citizenship or permanent residency must also be included. Application forms are available on request.
Closing Date: October 31st.
Funding: Government.

Canadian Embassy (USA) Research Grant Program

Subjects: Priority subjects include business and economic issues, Canadian values and culture, communications, environment, national and international security or natural resources eg. energy, fisheries, forestry and trade.
Purpose: The Research Grant Program promotes research in the social sciences and humanities with a view to contributing to a better knowledge and understanding of Canada and its relationship with the United States or other countries of the world. The purpose of the grant is to assist individual scholars or a group of scholars in writing an article length manuscript of publishable quality and reporting their findings in scholarly publications, with a view to contributing to the development of Canadian Studies in the United States.
Eligibility: Open to full-time faculty members at accredited four year United States colleges and universities, as well as Scholars at American research and policy planning institutes who undertake significant research projects concerning Canada, Canada/United States or Canada/North America. Recent PhD recipients who are citizens or permanent residents of the United States are also eligible to apply.
Level of Study: Postgraduate.
Type: Research grant.
Value: Individual applicants may request funding for up to US$10,000. The principal investigator, on behalf of a group, may request funding for up to US$15,000.
Frequency: Annual.
Study Establishment: An accredited four year college or university in the United States of America.
Country of Study: United States of America.
Application Procedure: Applicants must provide six copies of the following in this order: the completed application form, a concise proposal (four-eight pages) which will identify all members of the research team (if a team project) and specify each member's affiliation and role in the study, identify the key issues or the main theoretical problem, describe and justify the appropriate methodology, present a general schedule of research activities, indicate clearly both the nature and scope of the projects contribution to the advancement of Canadian Studies, include a detailed budget including all other funding sources and a description of anticipated expenditures. A curriculum vitae, and the names and addresses of two Scholars from whom the applicants will solicit recommendations should also be included. Application forms are available on request.
Closing Date: September 30th.
Funding: Government.

Canadian Embassy (USA) Senior Fellowship Program

Subjects: Canadian studies, Canada or United States topics, social, political or economic issues that impact on these relationships.
Purpose: To provide senior scholars with an opportunity to complete and publish a major study which will significantly benefit the development of Canadian Studies in the United States.
Eligibility: This programme is intended for full-time tenured faculty members at accredited four year United States colleges and universities who are fully involved in Canadian Studies. These

'Canadianists' should be in the process of completing research for a book or major monograph. The study must be on a subject of widespread interest to the Canadian Studies community in the United States as well as in Canada. This fellowship is awarded only once to any one recipient and is in recognition of an academic career dedicated to the promotion of Canadian Studies.

Level of Study: Postdoctorate, Postgraduate.
Type: Fellowship.
Value: Funding not to exceed US$3,000 per month may be awarded for a period of up to six months.
Frequency: Every two years.
Study Establishment: An accredited four year college or university in the United States of America.
Country of Study: United States of America.
Application Procedure: Applicants must provide six copies of the following in the order listed: a completed application form, a concise narrative of the research project which should include a statement outlining the applicant's background, field(s) of specialisation, particular areas of interest in Canadian Studies, and courses taught in Canadian Studies, a presentation of the book's key issues, main theoretical problem, methodology, table of contents and a clear statement of both the nature and scope of the author's intended contribution to the advancement of knowledge, a detailed budget including all other funding sources, a description of anticipated expenditures, a statement of the exact number of months for which financial support is requested. Appendices to the narrative must include: a letter from the applicant's department chairperson, dean, or academic vice president attesting that the applicant will be relieved of his or her regular teaching duties throughout the designated period of time an award is sought, a curriculum vitae, and the names and addresses of two referees. Application forms are available on request.
Closing Date: June 15th.
Funding: Government.

CANADIAN FEDERATION OF UNIVERSITY WOMEN (CFUW)

251 Bank Street
Suite 600, Ottawa, ON, K2P 1X3, Canada
Tel: (1) 613 234 2732
Fax: (1) 613 234 8252
Email: cfuwfls@rogers.com
www: http://www.cfuw.org
Contact: Ms Betty Dunlop, Fellowships Programme Manager

Founded in 1919, the Canadian Federation of University Women (CFUW) is a voluntary, non-partisan, non-profit, self-funded bilingual organisation of 10,000 women university graduates. CFUW members are active in public affairs, working to raise the social, economic, and legal status of women, as well as to improve education, the environment, peace, justice, and human rights.

1989 Polytechnique Commemorative Award
Subjects: All subjects.
Purpose: To provide partial funding for graduate study.
Eligibility: Open to women who hold at least a Bachelor's degree or equivalent from a recognised university, who are Canadian citizens or have held landed immigrant status for at least one year and who are able to justify the relevance of their work to women.
Level of Study: Postgraduate.
Value: Canadian $2,800.
Frequency: Annual.
Study Establishment: A recognised university.
Country of Study: Any country.
No. of awards offered: One.
Application Procedure: Applicants must complete an application, available from the Federation website.
Closing Date: November 1st.
Funding: Private.

No. of awards given last year: One.
No. of applicants last year: 57.
Additional Information: The candidate must justify the relevance of her work to women.

Alice E Wilson Awards
Subjects: All subjects.
Purpose: To assist women's study. Special consideration is given to candidates returning to study after at least three years.
Eligibility: Open to women who are Canadian citizens or have held landed immigrant status for at least one year prior to submitting application. Candidates should have a Bachelor's degree or its equivalent from a recognised university, not necessarily in Canada. Special consideration is given to candidates returning to study after at least three years. Candidates must have been accepted into the proposed programme of study.
Level of Study: Postgraduate.
Value: Canadian $2,100.
Frequency: Annual.
Study Establishment: A recognised university.
Country of Study: Any country.
No. of awards offered: One.
Application Procedure: Applicants must complete an application, available from the Federation website.
Closing Date: November 1st.
Funding: Private.
No. of awards given last year: One.
No. of applicants last year: 50.

Beverley Jackson Fellowship
Subjects: All subjects.
Purpose: To provide partial funding for graduate study.
Eligibility: Open to women who are over the age of 35 at the time of application and who are enrolled in graduate work at an Ontario university. Candidates should hold at least a Bachelor's degree or equivalent from a recognised university and be Canadian citizens or have held landed immigrant status for at least one year prior to submission of application and must have been accepted into the proposed programme of study.
Level of Study: Postgraduate.
Type: Fellowship.
Value: Canadian $3,000.
Frequency: Annual.
Study Establishment: A recognised university in Ontario.
Country of Study: Canada.
No. of awards offered: One.
Application Procedure: Applicants must complete an application, available from the Federation website.
Closing Date: November 1st.
Funding: Private.
No. of awards given last year: One.
No. of applicants last year: 21.
Additional Information: The fellowship is funded by UWC North York.

CFUW Memorial/Professional Fellowship
Subjects: Science, mathematics or engineering.
Purpose: To provide partial funding for graduate study at the Master's degree level.
Eligibility: Open to women who are Canadian citizens or who have held landed immigrant status for at least one year prior to submitting application. Candidates should hold a Bachelor's degree or its equivalent from a recognised Canadian university and wish to pursue graduate work at Master's degree level. Candidates must have been accepted into proposed programme of study.
Level of Study: Postgraduate.
Type: Fellowship.
Value: Canadian $5,000 paid in two biannual instalments.
Frequency: Annual.
Study Establishment: A recognised university.
Country of Study: Any country.

No. of awards offered: One.
Application Procedure: Applicants must complete an application, available from the Federation website.
Closing Date: November 1st.
Funding: Private.
No. of awards given last year: One.
No. of applicants last year: 42.
Additional Information: The fellowship is not renewable.

The Dr Marion Elder Grant Fellowship

Subjects: All subjects.
Purpose: To provide partial funding for full-time graduate study.
Eligibility: Open to women who have a Bachelor's degree or equivalent from a recognised university, who are Canadian citizens or have held landed immigrant status for at least one year prior to submission of application and who have been accepted into the proposed programme of study. All things being equal, preference will be given to the holder of an Acadia University degree.
Level of Study: Postgraduate.
Type: Fellowship.
Value: Canadian $10,000.
Frequency: Annual.
Study Establishment: A recognised university.
Country of Study: Any country.
No. of awards offered: One.
Application Procedure: Applicants must complete an application, available from the Federation website.
Closing Date: November 1st.
Funding: Private.
Contributor: CFUW/Wolfville.
No. of awards given last year: One.
No. of applicants last year: 166.

Georgette Lemoyne Award

Subjects: All subjects.
Purpose: To provide partial funding for graduate study.
Eligibility: Open to women who have a Bachelor's degree or equivalent from a recognised university and who are Canadian citizens or have held landed immigrant status for at least one year prior to submission of application and who have been accepted into the proposed programme of study.
Level of Study: Postgraduate.
Value: Canadian $2,100.
Frequency: Annual.
Study Establishment: A Canadian university where one language of administration and instruction is French.
Country of Study: Canada.
No. of awards offered: One.
Application Procedure: Applicants must complete an application, available from the Federation website.
Closing Date: November 1st.
Funding: Private.
No. of awards given last year: One.
No. of applicants last year: 31.

Margaret Dale Philp Biennial Award

Subjects: The humanities or social sciences with special consideration given to candidates who wish to specialise in Canadian history.
Purpose: To provide partial funding for graduate study.
Eligibility: Open to women who are Canadian citizens or who have held landed immigrant status for at least one year prior to submission of application. Candidates should hold a Bachelor's degree or its equivalent from a recognised university, reside in Canada, and wish to embark on, or continue, a programme leading to an advanced degree and have been accepted into the proposed programme of study.
Level of Study: Postgraduate.
Value: Please contact the organisation.
Frequency: Every two years.
Study Establishment: A recognised university.
Country of Study: Canada.

No. of awards offered: One.
Application Procedure: Applicants must complete an application, available from the Federation website.
Closing Date: November 1st.
Funding: Private.
Contributor: CFUW/Kitchener-Waterloo.
No. of awards given last year: One.
No. of applicants last year: 20.

Margaret McWilliams Predoctoral Fellowship

Subjects: All subjects.
Purpose: To provide funding for doctoral study.
Eligibility: Open to women who are Canadian citizens or who have held landed immigrant status for at least one year prior to submission of application. A candidate should hold a Bachelor's degree or its equivalent from a recognised university, not necessarily in Canada, and be a full-time student at an advanced stage (at least one year) in her doctoral programme.
Level of Study: Doctorate.
Type: Fellowship.
Value: Canadian $10,000 paid in two six monthly instalments.
Frequency: Annual.
Study Establishment: A recognised university.
Country of Study: Any country.
No. of awards offered: One.
Application Procedure: Applicants must complete an application, available from the Federation website.
Closing Date: November 1st.
Funding: Private.
Contributor: Members' donations.
No. of awards given last year: One.
No. of applicants last year: 119.
Additional Information: The fellowship is not renewable.

CANADIAN FORESTRY FOUNDATION

185 Somerset Street West
Suite 203, Ottawa, ON, K2P 0J2, Canada
Tel: (1) 613 232 1815
Fax: (1) 613 232 4210
Email: lemkay@canadianforestry.com
www: http://www.canadianforestry.com
Contact: Mr Dave Lemkay

The Canadian Forestry Foundation is a registered charity whose purpose is to support the educational programmes of the Canadian Forestry Association in promoting understanding and co-operation in the wise use and environmentally sound sustainable development of Canada's forests.

Canadian Forestry Foundation Forest Capital of Canada Award

Subjects: Forestry awareness.
Purpose: To recognise, annually, one community in Canada which is distinct because of its commitment to, and dependence on, the forest (past, present and future) and the civic-minded recognition of the importance of the forest to the community.
Eligibility: Open to forest communities in Canada which fulfil the terms of the purpose of the award.
Level of Study: Unrestricted.
Type: Award.
Frequency: Annual.
Country of Study: Canada.
No. of awards offered: Three.
Application Procedure: Applicants must write for details.
Closing Date: December 31st, three years prior to the year of recognition.
No. of awards given last year: One.
Additional Information: Information on annual recipients is available on the website.

CANADIAN FOUNDATION FOR THE STUDY OF INFANT DEATHS

586 Eglinton Avenue East
Suite 308, Toronto, ON, M4P 1P2, Canada
Tel: (1) 416 488 3260
Fax: (1) 416 488 3864
Email: sidsinfo@sidscanada.org
www: http://www.sidscanada.org
Contact: Mrs Fiona Chapman, Executive Director

The Canadian Foundation for the Study of Infant Deaths is a federally incorporated charitable organisation which was set up in 1973 to respond to the needs of families experiencing a sudden and unexpected infant death. It is the only organisation in Canada solely dedicated to finding the causes of Sudden Infant Death Syndrome, its effect on families, and to the education of the public.

Dr Sydney Segal Research Grants

Subjects: Any discipline (medical, psychological, nursing, biological, sociological) which is concerned with the causes, effects or prevention of Sudden Infant Death Syndrome.
Purpose: To enable students to pursue full-time higher degree studies researching into the possible causes, effects and/or prevention of Sudden Infant Death Syndrome.
Eligibility: Open to suitably qualified graduate students who are undertaking full-time training in research in the health sciences leading to an MSc or PhD or the equivalent (studentship level) and to suitably qualified persons who are undertaking higher level training in research into Sudden Infant Death Syndrome (fellowship level).
Level of Study: Doctorate, Postdoctorate, Postgraduate.
Type: Research grant.
Value: Value is determined in accordance with current MRC stipends for studentships and fellowships.
Length of Study: Normally one year.
Frequency: Annual.
Study Establishment: A Canadian university or teaching hospital.
Country of Study: Canada.
No. of awards offered: Up to 20.
Application Procedure: Applicants must complete an application form, available from the Foundation. Completed forms should be submitted together with references from the Head of Department of the university or teaching hospital where the applicant wishes to conduct research and other documents which are listed in more detail on the application form.
Closing Date: June 1st.
Contributor: Private donations.
No. of awards given last year: Two.
No. of applicants last year: Seven.
Additional Information: Grants will be considered only for research that is directly related to Sudden Infant Death Syndrome.

CANADIAN HIGH COMMISSION

Academic Relations Unit
Canada House
Trafalgar Square, London, SW1Y 5BJ, England
Tel: (44) 20 7258 6692
Fax: (44) 20 7258 6476
www: http://www.dfait-maeci.gc.ca/london
Contact: Ms Vivien Hughes, Canadian Studies Project Officer

Canadian Department of Foreign Affairs Faculty Enrichment Program

Subjects: Social sciences and humanities, architecture and town planning, business administration and management, education and teacher training, fine art, law, mass communication and information, transport and communication, recreation, welfare and protection.

Purpose: To assist in the undertaking of studies relating to Canada or comparative Canada-United Kingdom topics in order to devise a new course on Canada or to modify or extend significantly the Canadian component (minimum 50 percent) of an existing course.
Eligibility: Open to full-time, permanent teaching members of the academic staff of a recognised Institution of Higher Education in the United Kingdom.
Level of Study: Full-time faculty.
Type: Research visit.
Value: Up to a maximum of Canadian $4,500, paid in two instalments.
Length of Study: Three-five weeks.
Frequency: Annual.
Country of Study: Canada.
No. of awards offered: Varies.
Application Procedure: Applicants must complete an application form, available from the Academic Relations Unit at the Canadian High Commission.
Closing Date: October 31st.
Funding: Government.

Canadian Department of Foreign Affairs Faculty Research Program

Subjects: Social sciences and humanities in relation to Canada and aspects of its bilateral relations with the United Kingdom. Purely scientific subjects are ineligible.
Purpose: To promote research about Canada or aspects of Canada's bilateral relations with the United Kingdom, leading to the publication of articles in the scholarly press.
Eligibility: Open to full-time academic staff members and professors emeritus of universities, colleges of higher education or equivalent degree granting institutions of the United Kingdom. Scholars at research and policy planning institutions who undertake significant Canadian projects or Canada's bilateral relations research projects may also apply.
Level of Study: Full-time faculty.
Type: Research visit.
Value: Up to a maximum of Canadian $4,500, paid in two instalments.
Length of Study: Three-five weeks.
Frequency: Annual.
Country of Study: Canada.
No. of awards offered: Varies.
Application Procedure: Applicants must complete an application form, available from the Academic Relations Unit at the Canadian High Commission.
Closing Date: October 31st.
Funding: Government.

Canadian Department of Foreign Affairs Institutional Research Program

Subjects: Canadian topics within the social sciences and humanities, comparative studies and aspects of Canada's bilateral relations with the United Kingdom.
Purpose: To assist Institutes of Higher Education to undertake, under the direction of a designated principal researcher, major team research about Canada, comparative Canada-United Kingdom topics, or on aspects of Canada's bilateral relations with the United Kingdom, leading to the publication of a substantial work.
Eligibility: Open to recognised Institutes of Higher Education, research and policy planning institutes or other established research institutions in the United Kingdom. There is a minimum of three full-time British academics.
Level of Study: Full-time faculty.
Type: Research visit.
Value: Up to Canadian $20,000.
Frequency: Annual.
Country of Study: Canada.
No. of awards offered: Varies.
Application Procedure: Applicants must complete an application form, available from the Academic Relations Unit at the Canadian High Commission.

Closing Date: October 31st.
Funding: Government.

CANADIAN HOME ECONOMICS ASSOCIATION (CHEA)

307-151 Slater Street, Ottawa, ON, K1P 5H3, Canada
Tel: (1) 613 238 8817
Fax: (1) 613 238 8972
Email: general@chea-acef.ca
www: http://www.chea-acef.ca
Contact: Ms Suzanne Boivin, Administration Assistant

The Canadian Home Economics Association (CHEA), the national organisation of home economics professionals, has worked to improve life in Canadian homes and communities since 1939. More than 60 years later, the CHEA continues to be an advocate for positive change in the home both across Canada and abroad.

Mary A Clarke Memorial Scholarship, Silver Jubilee Scholarship and Fiftieth Anniversary Scholarship

Subjects: Home economics, human ecology, textiles or consumer science.
Purpose: To promote study towards an advanced degree in home economics or an allied field such as human ecology, textiles, family and consumer science.
Eligibility: Open to Canadian citizens who are graduates in either home economics, human ecology or consumer studies. Applicants must be members of the Canadian Home Economics Association for at least two years. Proof of acceptance to a graduate programme must be available. The awards will be based on scholarship, personal qualities, past or potential contribution to the profession of home economics and financial considerations.
Level of Study: Doctorate, Postgraduate.
Type: Scholarship.
Value: Canadian $2,000-6,000 each until further notice.
Length of Study: One year.
Frequency: Annual.
Study Establishment: An appropriate institution.
Country of Study: Any country.
No. of awards offered: Three.
Application Procedure: Applicants must complete an application form, available through faculty offices or from CHEA.
Closing Date: Postmarked no later than March 31st.
Funding: Private.
Contributor: The Canadian Home Economics Association.
No. of awards given last year: Three.
No. of applicants last year: 20.

Robin Hood Multifoods Scholarship

Subjects: Home economics.
Purpose: To financially support individuals planning a career in business, consumer service, food or food service management.
Eligibility: Open to Canadian citizens who are graduates in either home economics, human ecology or consumer studies. Applicants must have been members of the Canadian Home Economics Association for at least two years. Proof of acceptance to a graduate programme must be available. The award is based on academic achievement, personal qualities and past or potential contribution to the home economics profession.
Level of Study: Doctorate, Postgraduate.
Type: Scholarship.
Value: Canadian $1,000.
Frequency: Annual.
Study Establishment: An appropriate institution.
Country of Study: Any country.
No. of awards offered: One.
Application Procedure: Applicants must complete an application form, available through faculty offices or from CHEA.
Closing Date: Postmarked no later than March 31st.

Funding: Commercial.
Contributor: Robin Hood Multifoods Inc.
No. of awards given last year: One.
No. of applicants last year: 20.

Ruth Binnie Scholarship

Subjects: Home economics or home economics education.
Purpose: The scholarship is given to graduates in home economics or home economics education who hold a professional teaching certificate and wish to obtain a Master's of Education.
Eligibility: Open to Canadian citizens who are graduates in either home economics, human ecology or consumer studies. Applicants must have been members of the Canadian Home Economics Association for at least two years. Proof of acceptance to a graduate programme must be available. First consideration will be given to applicants proceeding towards a Master's in education on a full-time basis. Second consideration will go to part-time students. The awards will be based on scholarship, personal qualities, contributions toward home economics education in junior or senior high school and potential in the education field. All candidates should have a high commitment to the teaching profession and home economics education.
Level of Study: Doctorate, Postgraduate.
Type: Scholarship.
Value: Canadian $5,000.
Frequency: Annual.
Study Establishment: An appropriate institution.
Country of Study: Any country.
No. of awards offered: Two.
Application Procedure: Applicants must complete an application form, available through faculty offices or from CHEA.
Closing Date: Postmarked no later than March 31st.
Funding: Private.
Contributor: The Ruth Binnie Bequest to the Canadian Home Economics Association.
No. of awards given last year: Three.
No. of applicants last year: 20.

CANADIAN INSTITUTE FOR ADVANCED LEGAL STUDIES

Suite 203
4 Beechwood Avenue, Ottawa, ON, K1L 8L9, Canada
Tel: (1) 613 744 6166
Fax: (1) 613 744 5766
Contact: Mr Frank McArdle, Executive Director

The Canadian Institute for Advanced Legal Studies conducts legal seminars for judges and lawyers in Cambridge, England and Strasbourg, France.

The Right Honorable Paul Martin Scholarship

Subjects: Law.
Purpose: To study for an LLM at the University of Cambridge.
Eligibility: Open to graduates of Canadian Faculty of Law at the time of application, law students in their articling year at the time of application, or to students registered in their Bar Admission course at the time of application.
Level of Study: Postgraduate.
Type: Scholarship.
Value: Canadian $14,000.
Length of Study: One year.
Frequency: Annual.
Study Establishment: The University of Cambridge.
Country of Study: England.
No. of awards offered: Two.
Application Procedure: Applicants must complete an application consisting of a letter of application, undergraduate and Faculty of Law transcripts and no more than three letters of recommendation. There is no application form.

Closing Date: December 31st.
Funding: Private.
No. of awards given last year: Two.
No. of applicants last year: 36.
Additional Information: The scholarship may be held with another small award as approved by the Institute.

CANADIAN INSTITUTE OF UKRAINIAN STUDIES (CIUS)

University of Alberta
450 Athabasca Hall, Edmonton, AB, T6G 2E8, Canada
Tel: (1) 780 492 2972
Fax: (1) 780 492 4967
Email: cius@ualberta.ca
www: http://www.ualberta.ca/~cius
Contact: Ms Khrystyna Jendyk, Administrator

The Canadian Institute of Ukrainian Studies is part of the University of Alberta under the jurisdiction of the University's Vice President of Research. It was founded in 1976 in order to provide an institutional home and to develop Ukrainian scholarship and Ukrainian language education in Canada. It also supports such studies internationally, through organising research and scholarship in Ukrainian and Ukrainian-Canadian studies, by publishing books and a scholarly journal, developing materials for Ukrainian-language education, largely for the bilingual school programme, and organising conferences, lectures and a seminar series. Policy is developed by the director in consultation with a CIUS unit, programme directors and an advisory council.

Canadian Institute of Ukrainian Studies Research Grants
Subjects: Ukrainian or Ukrainian-Canadian studies in history, literature, language, education, social sciences and library sciences.
Eligibility: Please write for details.
Level of Study: Postgraduate.
Type: Research grant.
Value: Up to canadian $8,000.
Length of Study: One year.
Frequency: Annual.
Study Establishment: None required.
Country of Study: Any country.
No. of awards offered: One.
Application Procedure: Applicants must request an application form and the guide to Research Applications from the main address.
Closing Date: March 1st.
Funding: Private.

The Helen Darcovich Memorial Doctoral Fellowship
Subjects: Ukrainian or Ukrainian-Canadian topic in education, history, law, humanities, social sciences, women's studies or library sciences.
Purpose: To aid students to complete a thesis on a Ukrainian or Ukrainian and Canadian topic in education, history, law, humanities, social sciences, women's studies or library sciences.
Eligibility: Open to qualified applicants of any nationality.
Level of Study: Doctorate.
Type: Fellowship.
Value: Up to canadian $12,000.
Length of Study: One academic year.
Frequency: Annual.
Study Establishment: Any approved Institute of Higher Education in Canada or elsewhere, although for non Canadian applicants, preference will be given to students enrolled at the University of Alberta.
Country of Study: Any country.
No. of awards offered: One.
Application Procedure: Applicants must write to the main address for details.
Closing Date: March 1st.
Funding: Private.

Contributor: The Helen Darcovich Memorial Endowment Fund.
Additional Information: Only in exceptional circumstances may an award be held concurrently with other awards.

Marusia and Michael Dorosh Master's Fellowship
Subjects: A Ukrainian or Ukrainian-Canadian topic in education, history, law, humanities, social sciences, women's studies or library sciences.
Purpose: To aid a student to complete a thesis on a Ukrainian or Ukrainian and Canadian topic in education, history, law, humanities, social sciences, women's studies or library sciences.
Eligibility: Open to qualified applicants of any nationality.
Level of Study: Postgraduate.
Type: Fellowship.
Value: Up to canadian $8,000.
Length of Study: One academic year.
Frequency: Annual.
Study Establishment: Any approved Institute of Higher Education in Canada or elsewhere, although for non Canadian applicants, preference will be given to students enrolled at the University of Alberta.
Country of Study: Any country.
No. of awards offered: One.
Application Procedure: Applicants must write to the main address for details.
Closing Date: March 1st.
Funding: Private.
Contributor: The Marusia and Michael Dorosh Endowment Fund.
Additional Information: Only in exceptional circumstances may an award be held concurrently with other awards.

Neporany Research and Teaching Fellowship
Subjects: Ukrainian studies.
Purpose: To teach one course and conduct research in Ukrainian studies.
Eligibility: Applicants must hold a doctorate, or have equivalent professional achievement, in Ukrainian studies.
Level of Study: Postdoctorate.
Type: Fellowship.
Value: Canadian $20,000.
Length of Study: One term, eg. half of the academic year.
Frequency: Annual.
Study Establishment: Tenable at any university with research facilities at which the Fellow's academic Ukrainian studies speciality may be pursued and the Fellow enabled to teach a course related to the speciality.
Country of Study: Any country.
No. of awards offered: One.
Application Procedure: Applicants must write for further details to the main address.
Closing Date: March 1st.
Funding: Private.
Contributor: The Osyp and Josaphat Neporany Educational Fund.

CANADIAN INSTITUTES OF HEALTH RESEARCH (CIHR)

9th Floor
410 Laurier Avenue West, Ottawa, ON, K1A 0W9, Canada
Tel: (1) 613 941 2672
Fax: (1) 613 954 1800
Email: info@cihr.ca
www: http://www.cihr.ca
Contact: Awards Officer

CIHR Doctoral Research Awards
Subjects: General medical sciences and health sciences.
Purpose: To provide special recognition and support to students who are pursuing a doctoral degree in the health sciences in Canada.

Eligibility: Open to students engaged in full-time research training in a Canadian graduate school, who have completed at least one year of graduate study at Master's or PhD level but have been registered for no more than two years as a full-time student in a doctoral programme. Candidates must be Canadian citizens or permanent residents of Canada.
Level of Study: Graduate.
Type: Award.
Value: A stipend of Canadian $19,030 and a travel allowance of Canadian $500 per year.
Length of Study: A maximum of three years.
Frequency: Annual.
Study Establishment: Canadian universities or research institutions.
Country of Study: Canada.
No. of awards offered: Varies.
Application Procedure: Applicants must apply for application forms and programme guidelines, available on the CIHR website.
Closing Date: October 15th.
Funding: Government.
Contributor: CIHR.
No. of awards given last year: 188.
No. of applicants last year: 518.
Additional Information: For further information please write for details. The CIHR Awards unit can be contacted via telephone on (1) 613 954 1960.

CIHR Fellowship Programme

Subjects: Applicants must be working or studying the following fields of medicine, dentistry, pharmacology, optometry, veterinary medicine, chiropractic, nursing or rehabilitative science.
Purpose: To provide support for highly qualified candidates to add to their experience by engaging in research either in Canada or abroad.
Eligibility: Open to promising postdoctoral Scholars, researchers or health professionals. Canadian citizens and permanent residents of Canada may hold an award outside of Canada.
Level of Study: Doctorate, Graduate, Postdoctorate.
Type: Fellowship.
Value: Depending on the experience, a stipend of Canadian $19,030 to Canadian $45,000 per year including a further research and travel allowance of Canadian $3,500.
Length of Study: Five years maximum.
Frequency: Twice a year.
Study Establishment: Universities or research institutions in Canada.
Country of Study: Any country.
No. of awards offered: Varies.
Application Procedure: Applicants must submit a training module, a curriculum vitae module for both the candidate and the supervisor(s), official transcripts of the candidate's graduate and/or professional training including proof of any degrees completed, proof of Canadian licensure, three assessments from persons under whom the candidate has studied and a letter of support from the proposed supervisor of foreign candidates.
Closing Date: April 1st and November 1st.
Funding: Government.
No. of awards given last year: 128 in November and 68 in April.
No. of applicants last year: 477 in November and 270 in April.
Additional Information: In addition to this fellowship programme CIHR has established the more long-term and prestigious Centennial Fellowship Programme for candidates of special academic distinction and Awards for Clinical Scientists, as well as Awards for distinguished Scientists and Senior Scientists and the Michael Smith Award for Research Personnel. Furthermore, CIHR offers the Senior Research Fellowship and Clinical Scientist programmes. For details of all of these programmes please refer to the website http://www.cihr.ca.

CIHR MD/PhD Studentships

Subjects: General medical sciences.

Purpose: To promote promising students embarking on a combined MD or PhD programme at approved Canadian Universities.
Eligibility: Candidates for this Studentship Award must be enrolled in a combined MD/PhD programme at one of the approved Canadian institutions. Research supervisors should normally be holders of operating grants or salary funding obtained through a CIHR peer review process.
Level of Study: Doctorate, Graduate, Research.
Type: Studentship.
Value: A stipend of Canadian $19,030 per year plus a yearly research allowance of US$500 is provided.
Length of Study: Six years maximum.
Study Establishment: The universities of British Columbia, Calgary, Dalhousie, Manitoba, McGill, Memorial, Montreal, Toronto and Western Ontario.
Country of Study: Canada.
No. of awards offered: Up to a maximum of 15 per year and no more than 40 studentships at any one time.
Application Procedure: Applicants must be nominated by the director of the MD/PhD programme at each institution.
Closing Date: Please write for details.
Funding: Government.
Contributor: CIHR.
No. of awards given last year: 15.
Additional Information: For further information please contact the CIHR or refer to the website.

CANADIAN LIBRARY ASSOCIATION

Scholarships & Awards Committee
CLA Membership Services
328 Frank Street, Ottawa, ON, K2P 0X8, Canada
Tel: (1) 613 232 9625
Fax: (1) 613 563 9895
www: http://www.cla.ca
Contact: B Shields, Member Services

The Canadian Library Association works to maintain a tradition of commitment to excellence in library education and to advance continuing research in the field of library and information science.

CLA Dafoe Scholarship

Subjects: Library science.
Eligibility: Open to Canadian citizens and landed immigrants.
Level of Study: Postgraduate.
Type: Scholarship.
Value: Canadian $3,000.
Length of Study: One year.
Frequency: Annual.
Study Establishment: An accredited library school.
Country of Study: Canada.
No. of awards offered: One.
Application Procedure: Applicants must complete an application form, available on request. Applicants must submit transcripts, references and proof of admission to a library school.
Closing Date: May 1st.
Funding: Commercial.
Contributor: World Book Incorporated.
No. of awards given last year: One.
Additional Information: Consideration is given to both academic standing and financial need.

CLA Research and Development Grants

Subjects: Library and information science.
Purpose: To support theoretical and applied research in library and information science.
Eligibility: Open to Canadian citizens and landed immigrants who are personal members of the CLA.
Level of Study: Unrestricted.
Type: Research grant.

Value: One or more grants totalling canadian $1,000.

Length of Study: One year.

Frequency: Annual.

Country of Study: Canada.

No. of awards offered: More than one.

Application Procedure: Applicants must apply for application guidelines, available on request.

No. of awards given last year: One.

H W Wilson Scholarship

Subjects: Library science.

Eligibility: Open to Canadian citizens or landed immigrants. Scholarship candidates must be commencing studies for their first professional library or information studies degree.

Level of Study: Postgraduate.

Type: Scholarship.

Value: Canadian $2,000.

Length of Study: One year.

Frequency: Annual.

Study Establishment: An accredited library school.

Country of Study: Canada.

No. of awards offered: One.

Application Procedure: Applicants must write, phone or visit the website for further information.

Closing Date: May 1st.

Funding: Private.

Contributor: The H W Wilson Company.

No. of awards given last year: One.

Additional Information: Consideration is given to both academic standing and financial need. The CLA acknowledges, with thanks, the generous support of the H W Wilson Company for their sponsorship of this award.

World Book Graduate Scholarship in Library Science

Subjects: Library science.

Eligibility: Open to Canadian citizens or landed immigrants with a BLS or MLS degree. In exceptional circumstances, the scholarship may be given to an outstanding candidate with a degree in another discipline who wishes to obtain a BLS or MLS degree.

Level of Study: Postgraduate.

Type: Scholarship.

Value: Canadian $2,500.

Length of Study: One year.

Frequency: Annual.

Study Establishment: An accredited library school.

Country of Study: United States of America or Canada.

No. of awards offered: One.

Closing Date: May 1st.

Funding: Private.

Contributor: World Book Incorporated.

No. of awards given last year: One.

Additional Information: Consideration is given to both academic standing and financial need. The scholarship is given for study leading to a further library degree or related to library work in which the candidate is currently engaged, or to library work which will be undertaken upon completion of the studies. The CLA gratefully acknowledges the support of World Book Incorporated for their continuing sponsorship of this award.

CANADIAN LIVER FOUNDATION

2235 Sheppard Avenue East
Suite 1500, Toronto, ON, M2J 5B5, Canada
Tel: (1) 416 491 3353
Fax: (1) 416 491 4952
Email: clf@liver.ca
www: http://www.liver.ca
Contact: Executive Director

The Canadian Liver Foundation provides support for research and education into the causes, diagnosis, prevention and treatment of diseases to the liver.

Canadian Liver Foundation Graduate Studentships

Subjects: Any discipline relevant to the objectives of the Canadian Liver Foundation.

Purpose: To enable academically superior students to undertake full-time studies in a Canadian university.

Eligibility: Candidates must be accepted into a full-time university graduate science programme in a medically related discipline related to a Master's or doctoral degree and hold a record of superior academic performance in studies relevant to the proposed training.

Level of Study: Doctorate, Postgraduate.

Type: Studentship.

Value: A stipend equivalent to that awarded by a Medical Research Council of Canada studentship award.

Length of Study: One year, renewable up to three times.

Frequency: Annual.

Country of Study: Canada.

No. of awards offered: Up to four.

Application Procedure: Applicants must write for details.

Closing Date: February 15th.

Additional Information: A student supported by the Foundation must not hold a current stipend award from another granting agency.

Canadian Liver Foundation Operating Grant

Subjects: Hepathology.

Purpose: To support research projects directed towards a defined objective.

Eligibility: Open to hepatobiliary research investigators who hold an academic appointment in a Canadian institution.

Level of Study: Professional development.

Type: Grant.

Value: Canadian $60,000 per year.

Frequency: Dependent on funds available.

Country of Study: Canada.

Application Procedure: Applicants must submit application forms along with supporting documentation.

Closing Date: December 15th.

THE CANADIAN NATIONAL INSTITUTE FOR THE BLIND (CNIB)

1929 Bayview Avenue, Toronto, ON, M4G 3E8, Canada
Tel: (1) 416 480 7707
Fax: (1) 416 480 7000
Email: hendrej@cnib.ca
www: http://www.cnib.ca
Contact: Ms Jennifer Hendren, Executive Assistant

The Canadian National Institute for the Blind (CNIB) is a voluntary, non-profit rehabilitation agency that provides services for people who are blind, visually impaired or deafblind. The CNIB provides consultation in safe and efficient travel training, braille, tape and electronic information, employment, environmental accessibility, government and community entitlements, technology, sight enhancement, eye banks and community integration. Through the EA Baker Foundation it provides fellowships and research grants into blindness prevention.

E A Baker Fellowship/Grant

Subjects: Ophthalmology and optometry.
Purpose: To further the prevention of blindness in Canada.
Eligibility: Open to Canadians for research or study in Canada, or abroad if returning to practice in Canada, with priority given to university teaching.
Level of Study: Professional development, Research.
Type: Fellowship and grant.
Value: Canadian $40,000.
Length of Study: Two years.
Frequency: Annual.
Country of Study: Any country.
No. of awards offered: Varies.
Application Procedure: Applicants must visit the website for information and an application form.
Closing Date: December 1st.
Funding: Private.

CANADIAN NURSES FOUNDATION (CNF)

50 Driveway, Ottawa, ON, K2P 1E2, Canada
Tel: (1) 613 237 2133
Fax: (1) 613 237 3520
Email: cnf@cna-nurses.ca
www: http://www.cna-nurses.ca/cnf
Contact: CNF Scholarship Co-ordinator

The Canadian Nurses Foundation (CNF) is a registered charity founded in 1962. It is committed to promoting the health of Canadians through the advancement of the nurses' profession by financially supporting Canadian nurses in pursuing further education, research, or certification in their speciality. The CNF is funded through donations from corporations, nursing associations and individuals.

CNF Scholarships and Fellowships

Subjects: All nursing specialities. Several awards are identified for neurosurgical, oncology, community health nursing, epidemiology, gerontology, child or family health care, nursing administration, occupational health, northern nursing, dialysis nursing, home care nursing and aplastic anaemia.
Purpose: To assist Canadian nurses pursuing further education and research.
Eligibility: Open to Canadian nurses who are members of the Foundation.
Level of Study: Doctorate, Postgraduate, Research, Baccalaureate.
Type: Scholarship and fellowship.
Value: Canadian $3,000-3,500 for a Master's programme, canadian $6,000 for a doctoral programme, canadian $3,000 for a baccalaureate programme and canadian $81,000 for Nightingale home care nursing.
Length of Study: One year.
Frequency: Annual.
Country of Study: Canada.
No. of awards offered: Varies.
Application Procedure: Applicants must visit the website for the application forms, criteria and requirements.
Closing Date: April 15th.
Funding: Private.
Additional Information: Recipients must submit a summary of any thesis, study or major paper undertaken as part of the course to the CNF.

CANADIAN NURSES' RESPIRATORY SOCIETY (CNRS)

The Lung Association
National Office
3 Raymond Street, Suite 300, Ottawa, ON, K1R 1A3, Canada
Tel: (1) 613 569 6411
Fax: (1) 613 569 8860
Email: info@lung.ca
www: http://www.lung.ca
Contact: President

The Canadian Nurses' Respiratory Society (CNRS) is a special nursing interest group of the Lung Association concerned with promoting a high quality of respiratory care through respiratory nursing education and research. CNRS believes in the provision of high quality respiratory nursing care which promotes respiratory health and prevents or manages respiratory illness so enhancing the quality of life for the individual, family and communities. CNRS's objectives are to promote respiratory nursing care, advance nursing education in respiratory health and disease, encourage nurses to engage in research related to respiratory health and disease, collaborate with provincial respiratory nursing societies, further the objectives of the Canadian Lung Association within the scope of the nursing profession, act as an advisory body to the Lung Association on nursing matters and maintain an affiliation with the Canadian Nurses Association and the International Council of Nurses.

Canadian Nurses' Respiratory Society Fellowships

Subjects: Respiratory nursing.
Purpose: To enable registered nurses to pursue postgraduate education with a major component of the programme involving respiratory nursing practice.
Eligibility: Applicants must be Canadian citizens or permanent Canadian residents, be a registered nurse, be enrolled or accepted for full-time studies in a graduate programme at the Master's or doctorate level and be a member of the Canadian Nurses Respiratory Society.
Level of Study: Postgraduate.
Type: Fellowship.
Value: Canadian $2,000-8,000.
Length of Study: One year.
Frequency: Annual.
Country of Study: Canada.
Application Procedure: Applicants must submit an application form available from the Canadian Lung Association or the website.
Closing Date: November 1st.

Canadian Nurses' Respiratory Society Research Grants

Subjects: Respiratory disease and symptoms.
Purpose: To enable registered nurses to undertake research investigations related to nursing management of patients with respiratory disease and symptoms.
Eligibility: The principal investigator must be a Canadian citizen or permanent resident, be a registered nurse, hold an appointment in, or have an affiliation with, a health care agency, education institution or other organisation in Canada that can administer funds in an approved manner, and be a member of the Canadian Nurses Respiratory Society.
Level of Study: Postgraduate, Research.
Type: Research grant.
Value: Canadian $3,000-30,000.
Length of Study: One year.
Frequency: Annual.
Country of Study: Canada.
Application Procedure: Applicants must submit an application form, available from the Canadian Lung Association or the website.
Closing Date: November 1st.

CANADIAN PHYSIOTHERAPY CARDIO-RESPIRATORY SOCIETY (CPCRS)

Head Office
3 Raymond Street
Suite 300, Ottawa, ON, K1R 1A3, Canada
Tel: (1) 613 569 6411
Fax: (1) 613 569 8860
Email: info@lung.ca
www: http://www.lung.ca
Contact: Ms Valoree McKay

The Canadian Physiotherapy Cardio-Respiratory Society (CPCRS) offers fellowships and Research Grants. The purpose of the CPCRS research programme is to pursue increased scientific knowledge in the area of cardiorespiratory physiotherapy practice. By supporting physiotherapists to pursue advanced degrees or by supporting the completion of research studies, the number of individuals with expertise in the cardiorespiratory area will increase, which ultimately will have a positive impact in the community, and for the cardiorespiratory client.

Canadian Physiotherapy Cardio-Respiratory Society Fellowships

Subjects: Cardiorespiratory physiotherapy.
Purpose: To pursue increased scientific knowledge in the area of cardiorespiratory physiotherapy practice.
Eligibility: Applicants must be physiotherapists pursuing postgraduate training, with respiratory research as the major component.
Level of Study: Postgraduate.
Type: Fellowship.
Value: Canadian $6,000-12,000.
Length of Study: One year.
Frequency: Annual.
Country of Study: Canada.
Application Procedure: Applicants must submit an application form, available from the Canadian Lung Association.
Closing Date: November 1st.

Canadian Physiotherapy Cardio-Respiratory Society Research Grants

Subjects: Cardiorespiratory physiotherapy practice.
Purpose: To pursue increased scientific knowledge in the area of cardiorespiratory physiotherapy practice.
Eligibility: The principal investigator must be a Canadian citizen or a permanent Canadian resident, be a registered physiotherapist, hold an appointment in or have an affiliation with a health care agency, educational institution or other organisation in Canada that can administer funds in an approved manner, and be a member of the Canadian Physiotherapy Cardio-Respiratory Society. There must be only one principal investigator responsible for the study, although there may be several co-investigators.
Level of Study: Professional development, Research.
Type: Research grant.
Value: Canadian $12,000-20,000.
Length of Study: One year.
Frequency: Annual.
Country of Study: Canada.
Application Procedure: Applicants must submit an application form, available from the Canadian Lung Association.
Closing Date: November 1st.

Canadian Physiotherapy Cardio-Respiratory Society Studentships

Subjects: Cardiorespiratory physiotherapy practice.
Purpose: To promote increased scientific knowledge and research.
Eligibility: Applicants must be Canadian citizens or permanent residents and must have completed at least the first year of study in a recognised Canadian School of Physiotherapy. Students must be working full-time on the research project during the period of the award.

Type: Studentship.
Value: Canadian $1,000 per month.
Length of Study: Two or three months.
Study Establishment: A recognised school of physiotherapy in Canada.
Country of Study: Canada.
Application Procedure: Applicants must submit an application form, available from the Canadian Lung Association.
Closing Date: November 1st.

CANADIAN SOCIETY FOR CHEMICAL ENGINEERING (CSCHE)

130 Slater Street
Suite 550, Ottawa, ON, K1P 6E2, Canada
Tel: (1) 613 232 6252 ext. 235
Fax: (1) 613 232 5862
Email: jtrohon@cheminst.ca
www: http://www.cheminst.ca
Contact: Ms Julie Trohon, Program Co-ordinator

The Canadian Society for Chemical Engineering (CSChE), one of three constituent societies of The Chemical Institute of Canada, is the national technical association of chemical engineers. As the pre-eminent technical society for chemical engineers in Canada, the CSChE provides its members with services that enhance their professional careers, contributes to the practice of chemical engineering and represents the profession to the public.

J E Zajic Postgraduate Scholarship

Subjects: Biochemical engineering.
Eligibility: Open to postgraduate students registered in chemical engineering at a Canadian university and engaged in research of a biochemical nature who will have commenced such a programme prior to application. Applicants must be members of the Canadian society for chemical engineering.
Level of Study: Postgraduate.
Type: Scholarship.
Value: Approx. canadian $1,000 per year.
Length of Study: Two years.
Frequency: Every two years (even-numbered years).
Study Establishment: A Canadian university.
Country of Study: Canada.
No. of awards offered: One.
Application Procedure: Applicants must submit an application including evidence of academic standing, a brief description of the work to be undertaken and letters of reference.
Closing Date: December 1st of even numbered years.
Additional Information: The Society is a constituent of the Chemical Institute of Canada.

CANADIAN SOCIETY FOR CHEMICAL TECHNOLOGY

130 Slater Street
Suite 550, Ottawa, ON, K1P 6E2, Canada
Tel: (1) 613 232 6252 ext. 235
Fax: (1) 613 232 5862
Email: jtrohon@cheminst.ca
www: http://www.cheminst.ca
Contact: Ms Julie Trohan, Program Co-ordinator

The Canadian Society for Chemical Technology is the national technical association of chemical and biochemical technicians and technologists with members across Canada who work in industry, government or academia. The purpose of the Society is the advancement of chemical technology, the maintenance and improvement of practitioners and educators and the continual evaluation of chemical technology in Canada. The Society hopes to maintain a dialogue with educators, government and industry, to assist in the technology content of the education process of technologists, to attract qualified people into the professions and the Society, to develop and maintain high standards and enhance the usefulness of chemical technology to both the industry and the public.

CSCT Norman and Marion Bright Memorial Award
Subjects: Chemical technology.
Purpose: To reward an individual who has made an outstanding contribution in Canada to the furtherance of Chemical Technology.
Eligibility: The person honoured must be either a chemical sciences technologist, or a person from outside the field who has made a significant or noteworthy contribution to its advancement.
Type: Award.
Value: An engraved medallion and a cash prize.
Frequency: Annual.
Country of Study: Canada.
No. of awards offered: One.
Application Procedure: Applicants must complete a nomination form.
Closing Date: October 31st.
Additional Information: Award winners are welcome to submit papers at either the CSC or CSChE conferences.

CSCT NOVA Chemicals Limited Award for Chemistry teaching in Community and Technical Colleges
Subjects: Chemistry, biochemistry, chemical engineering technology or chemical technology.
Purpose: To recognise an outstanding teacher.
Eligibility: Open to teachers who work in community or technical colleges.
Level of Study: Professional development.
Type: Award.
Value: A commemorative scroll and a cash prize.
Frequency: Annual.
Country of Study: Canada.
No. of awards offered: One.
Application Procedure: Applicants must complete a nomination form.
Closing Date: October 31st.
Funding: Private.
Contributor: NOVA Chemical Limited.
Additional Information: The CSCT Awards are not lecture awards, but award winners are welcome to submit papers at either the CSC or CSChE Conferences.

CANADIAN SOCIETY FOR CHEMISTRY (CSC)

130 Slater Street
Suite 550, Ottawa, ON, K1P 6E2, Canada
Tel: (1) 613 232 6252 ext. 235
Fax: (1) 613 232 5862
Email: jtrohon@cheminst.ca
www: http://www.cheminst.ca
Contact: Ms Julie Trohon, Program Co-ordinator

The Canadian Society for Chemistry (CSC), one of three constituent societies of The Chemical Institute of Canada, is the national scientific and educational society of chemists. The purpose of the CSC is to promote the practice and application of chemistry in Canada.

Ichikizaki Fund for Young Chemists
Subjects: Synthetic organic chemistry.
Purpose: To provide financial assistance to young chemists who are showing unique achievements in basic research by facilitating their participation in international conferences or symposia.

Eligibility: Open to members of the Canadian Society for Chemistry who have not passed their 34th birthday as of December 31st of the year in which the application is submitted, who have a research speciality in synthetic organic chemistry and are scheduled to attend within one year an international conference or symposium directly related to synthetic organic chemistry.
Level of Study: Doctorate, Postdoctorate, Postgraduate, Professional development.
Value: The maximum value of any one award is canadian $10,000. Successful applicants may re-apply in subsequent years, provided the cumulative total of all awards does not exceed canadian $15,000.
Frequency: Annual.
Country of Study: Any country.
Application Procedure: Applicants must submit an application including a curriculum vitae, copies of recent research papers, the title and brief description of the conference the applicant wishes to attend, the title and abstract, if available, of the research paper the applicant intends to present and a proposed budget. Applications from graduate students must be accompanied by a letter of reference from the research supervisor.
Closing Date: December 31st for conferences scheduled between July 1st and June 30th.
Funding: Private.
Additional Information: The number of applicants to be recommended by the Society is limited to 10 per year. Although the awards are intended primarily for established researchers, applications from postgraduate students and postdoctoral fellows will be considered. However, only one application per year from a graduate student can be recommended to the Fund.

CANADIAN SOCIETY FOR MEDICAL LABORATORY SCIENCE

PO 2830
LCD1, Hamilton, ON, L8N 3N8, Canada
Tel: (1) 905 528 8642
Fax: (1) 905 528 4968
Email: memserv@csmls.org
www: http://www.csmls.org
Contact: Mr David Dan, Administration Director

The Canadian Society for Medical Laboratory Science is the certifying body and professional association for laboratory technologists in Canada. Its purpose is to promote and maintain a nationally accepted standard of medical laboratory technology by which other health professionals and the public are assured of effective and economical laboratory services and to promote, maintain and protect the professional identity and interest of medical laboratory technologists and of the profession.

CSMLS Founders' Fund Award
Subjects: Medical laboratory technology.
Purpose: To assist members with costs of professional continuing education.
Eligibility: Open to certified members in good standing at the time of application.
Level of Study: Professional development.
Type: Study grant.
Value: Varies, at the discretion of the Founders' Fund Committee.
Frequency: Dependent on funds available.
Country of Study: Canada.
No. of awards offered: Varies.
Application Procedure: Applicants may submit applications at any time during the year and will be dealt with at the next scheduled meeting of the Founders' Fund Committee. These are held in conjunction with the meetings of the Board of Directors, usually in February, June, September, November and December. The decision to grant an award and the actual amount of the award shall be at the

discretion of the Founders' Fund Committee. Applicants may only apply for one award for any activity.

Funding: Private.

Contributor: A member supported trust fund.

Quebec CE Fund Grants

Subjects: Medical technology.

Purpose: To promote continuing education among medical laboratory technologists who are francophones.

Eligibility: Open to any person or group who is able to establish or co-ordinate the continuing education programmes for Francophone members of the CSMLS. This would include individual CSMLS members, an affiliated Society or Branch, the Ordre Professionnelle des Technologistes Médicaux du Québec (OPTMQ) and institutions which teach medical technology.

Level of Study: Postgraduate.

Type: Grant.

Value: Varies.

Country of Study: Canada.

No. of awards offered: Varies.

Application Procedure: Applicants must write for application forms. All applications must include the amount of the grant requested from the fund, an outline of the proposed programme, a comprehensive budget including a breakdown of expenses, a statement of other support to be received or being applied for, development times and the dates that progress reports will be submitted during development, evidence of the need for the programme, and a signed statement declaring that CSMLS members will be permitted to participate in the finished programme at no increased differential fee.

Funding: Private.

Additional Information: It is the policy of CSMLS that continuing education programmes should normally be financially self-supporting through the fees charged for the programme. However, there are some situations in which a programme is needed in a particular location, but the programme cannot be self-supporting without charging unacceptably high fees. There may also be a need to fund development costs for certain types of programmes. All requests for the use of the Quebec CE funds shall be reviewed and approved or rejected by the Quebec CE Fund Committee and then considered for ratification at the next CSMLS Board of Directors meeting.

CANADIAN THORACIC SOCIETY (CTS)

The Lung Association
National Office
3 Raymond Street, Suite 300, Ottawa, ON, K1R 1A3, Canada
Tel: (1) 613 569 6411
Fax: (1) 613 569 8860
Email: info@lung.ca
www: http://www.lung.ca/cts
Contact: Grants Management Officer

The Canadian Thoracic Society (CTS) is the medical section of the Canadian Lung Association. It advises the Association on scientific matters and programmes including policies regarding support for research and professional education. The CTS provides a forum whereby medical practitioners and investigators may join in the study of thoracic diseases and other medical fields which may come within the scope of the Lung Association. The CTS's objectives are to maintain the highest professional and scientific standards in all aspects of respiratory diseases, to collect, interpret and distribute scientific information, to encourage epidemiological, clinical and other scientific studies in the prevention, diagnosis and treatment of respiratory diseases, and to stimulate and support undergraduate, postgraduate and continuing medical education in respiratory diseases.

Canadian Thoracic Society Fellowships

Subjects: Pulmonary disease.

Purpose: To support research training in pulmonary disease.

Eligibility: Applicants must be Canadian citizens or permanent residents of Canada. Candidates for the award must have obtained an MD or PhD degree or the equivalent and must not hold a university level academic position. Those expected to receive a PhD degree within the following year are eligible to apply but may not begin the fellowship until the PhD requirements have been completed. CLA Fellows may not work on projects that have not been approved by the appropriate institutional ethics committees.

Level of Study: Postdoctorate, Postgraduate.

Type: Fellowship.

Length of Study: Two years, with a possibility of renewal for a further year.

Frequency: Annual.

Country of Study: Canada.

Application Procedure: Applicants must submit applications on Medical Research Council Form 18.

Closing Date: November 1st.

Funding: Commercial, Government.

Contributor: The Canadian Lung Association, the Canadian Institutes of Health Research Industry Partners eg. Glaxo Wellcome, Merck Frosst Can, Bayer Inc, Boehringer Ingelheim and Astrazeneca.

Additional Information: Recipients are selected based on priority ratings provided by the CIHR and are subject to the approval of the Canadian Thoracic Society and the Canadian Lung Association (CLA) Board of Directors. Applicants are screened to ensure proposed research areas are appropriate to the goals of the CLA. Fellowships are awarded in each case for research training in a specific institution, and may not be transferred without the explicit approval of both institutions involved.

For further information contact:

Canadian Institutes of Health Research
410 Laurier Avenue West
9th Floor
Address Locator 4209A, Ottawa, ON, KIA 0W9, Canada
www: http://www.cihr.ca

Canadian Thoracic Society Scholarships

Subjects: Respiratory disease.

Purpose: To support appropriately trained investigators to engage in full time research in the area of respiratory disease.

Eligibility: Applicants must be Canadian citizens or permanent residents of Canada who have obtained an MD or PhD degree or equivalent. Applicants must not have held a university level academic position for more than two years at the time of submission of the application.

Level of Study: Postdoctorate, Postgraduate.

Type: Scholarship.

Value: Canadian $50,000, plus an initial canadian $15,000 Establishment Award.

Length of Study: Five years.

Frequency: Annual.

Country of Study: Canada.

No. of awards offered: One.

Application Procedure: Applicants must submit applications on Medical Research Council Form 19. A letter of intent must also be submitted to the Canadian Thoracic Society.

Closing Date: Applications must be submitted by September 15th, a letter of intent must be submitted by June 15th.

Contributor: The Canadian Lung Association, and the Canadian Institutes of Health Research.

For further information contact:

CIHR
410 Laurier Avenue West
9th Floor
Address Locator 4209A, Ottawa, ON, KIA 0W9, Canada
www: http://www.cihr.ca

CANADIAN TOBACCO CONTROL RESEARCH INITIATIVE (CTCRI)

National Cancer Institute of Canada
10 Alcorn Avenue
Suite 200, Toronto, ON, M4V 3BI, Canada
Tel: (1) 416 961 7223
Fax: (1) 416 961 7327
Email: mwosnick@cancer.ca
Contact: Dr Michael A Wosnick, Research Programmes Director

The National Cancer Institute of Canada, the Canadian Cancer Society, the Social Sciences and Humanities Research Council of Canada (SSHRC) and Health Canada have joined together to create the Canadian Tobacco Control Research Initiative (CTCRI), a programme that aims to stimulate research that will have a direct impact on tobacco control policy and programming in Canada. It is hoped that the Initiative will attract other partners over time and create many new and exciting opportunities in the area of tobacco control research.

CTCRI Planning Grants

Subjects: Tobacco related cancer research.
Purpose: To aid the development of strong research teams or research networks and to support the development of multisectoral and multidisciplinary research proposals in tobacco control.
Eligibility: Applicant teams must include both researchers and those responsible for tobacco policy or programmes.
Type: Research grant.
Value: Approx. canadian $10,000-15,000, to a maximum of canadian $30,000.
Country of Study: Canada.
Application Procedure: Applicants must contact Dr Michael A Wosnick for further information.
Closing Date: September 1st.
Additional Information: Further information is available on request.

CANADIAN/SCANDINAVIAN FOUNDATION (CSF)

c/o Office of the Director of Libraries
McGill University
3459 McTavish Street, Montréal, QC, H3A 1Y1, Canada
Tel: (1) 514 398 4740
Fax: (1) 514 398 7356
Email: moller@libi.lan.mcgill.ca
www: http://www.canada-scandinavia.ca
Contact: Vice President

The Canadian/Scandinavian Foundation (CSF) was established in 1950 and offers research and study support to qualified young, talented Canadians of university age and aspiring scholars.

CSF Special Purpose Grants

Subjects: All subjects.
Purpose: To provide support for shorter study or a research visit to a Scandinavian or Nordic country destination.
Eligibility: Open to qualified Canadians and landed immigrants.
Level of Study: Postgraduate.
Type: Grant.
Value: Canadian $1,000.
Length of Study: A short period of time.
Frequency: Annual.
Country of Study: Scandinavia or Finland.
No. of awards offered: Three-four.
Application Procedure: Applicants must complete an application form.
Closing Date: January 31st.
Funding: Private.

Additional Information: Further information is available from the website.

CANCER ASSOCIATION OF SOUTH AFRICA

PO Box 2000, Johannesburg, Braamfontein, 2000, South Africa
Tel: (27) 11 616 7662
Fax: (27) 11 622 3424
Email: rbotha@cansa.org.za
www: http://www.cansa.org.za
Contact: Ms Ristie Botha, Research Administrator

It is the aim of the Cancer Association of South Africa to fight cancer and its consequences in partnership with all South African Communities and relevant stakeholders by providing direction for, and supporting the following cancer control components: health promotion through prevention and early detection, patient service facilitation, and research to enhance these components.

Cancer Association of South Africa Research Grants

Subjects: All aspects of the cancer problem, particularly those aspects which have a South African significance and can be investigated locally.
Purpose: To assist professional staff with major or specialised equipment, laboratory running expenses, skilled or unskilled laboratory or other assistants and to assist with printing and/or publishing the results of all types of research which fall within the Association's scope.
Eligibility: Open to medical graduates, biochemists, graduates in social science, etc., who are in full-time employment and can show distinct evidence of a capacity for original research or, in the case of BSc graduates, have won distinctions during their undergraduate studies. Candidates should be residents of South Africa.
Level of Study: Postgraduate.
Type: Research grant.
Value: Varies, according to merit.
Length of Study: One-three calendar years.
Frequency: Annual.
Study Establishment: A university or research institution.
Country of Study: South Africa.
No. of awards offered: Varies.
Application Procedure: Applicants must complete an application form.
Closing Date: May 31st.
Funding: Private.
Contributor: Public and corporate donors.
No. of awards given last year: 32.
No. of applicants last year: 55.
Additional Information: Of the awards given last year there were 19 research projects, nine priority research projects and consortiums and four individual projects linked to consortiums. All major equipment will remain the property of the Association. Specific details of the types of research which fall within the Association's scope as well as other additional information is available from the Association.

Cancer Association of South Africa Travel and Subsistence (Study) Grants

Subjects: Cancer projects.
Purpose: To assist workers in the cancer field to improve their academic and/or technical qualifications and experience for the furtherance of cancer research and education, and for the improvement of diagnostic and/or treatment services to cancer patients in South Africa.
Eligibility: Open to suitably qualified applicants in some aspect of the cancer field who are in full-time employment. Applicants must be South African citizens.
Level of Study: Postgraduate.
Value: Not to exceed 50 per cent of the minimum costs on condition that the applicant, through his own institution or by other means,

pays the balance of the minimum costs. Minimum costs are calculated on the basis of an economy class air fare to the furthest point of travel with such deviations as may be approved by the Association, plus a subsistence allowance appropriate to the geographical area concerned.

Frequency: Throughout the year.

Country of Study: Any country.

No. of awards offered: Varies.

Application Procedure: Applicants must complete and forward the Travel Grant application form to the executive committee for approval.

Closing Date: A minimum of two months before the departure date.

Funding: Private.

Contributor: The Cancer Association of South Africa.

No. of awards given last year: Nine.

No. of applicants last year: 16.

Additional Information: Travel Grants are awarded to suitable applicants to enable them to attend national or international conferences in the cancer field. Study Grants are awarded to suitable applicants who, by study at specialised centres, will be able to increase their knowledge in the cancer field with a view to its subsequent application in South Africa. Grantees are required to return to South Africa within a period of six months after expiration of the period for which the Grant was awarded (an extension will be considered on application) and to continue for a period of two years in the service in which they were employed at the time of the award. Grants may not be used for the purpose of studying for or obtaining degrees or diplomas. The Association also offers support to certain foreign medical scientists in the cancer field who are invited to visit South Africa to participate in scientific meetings and congresses, or for particular purposes as the need may arise.

Lady Cade Memorial Fellowship

Subjects: The cause, diagnosis or treatment of cancer.

Purpose: To encourage professional development in cancer research.

Eligibility: Open to medical graduates of senior status who are resident in South Africa, or South African nationals who are domiciled in the British Commonwealth, or in some cases, elsewhere. Preference is given to those holding senior posts at approved universities or other institutions to which the Fellows will be expected to return within six months of the termination of the Fellowship and work there for a period of not less than two years.

Level of Study: Postgraduate, Professional development.

Type: Fellowship.

Value: Rand 150,000 from the organisation and rand 150,000 from the Cancer Research Campaign in the United Kingdom.

Length of Study: Three months-one year.

Frequency: Occasionally, dependent on funds available.

Study Establishment: A university or research institution.

Country of Study: United Kingdom.

No. of awards offered: One.

Application Procedure: Applicants must complete and submit an application form with a curriculum vitae.

Closing Date: Approx. six months prior to commencement of the fellowship.

Funding: Private.

Contributor: Public and corporate donors.

Additional Information: South Africans in the United Kingdom may apply through Cancer Research Campaign.

For further information contact:

Cancer Research Campaign
2 Carlton House Terrace, London, SW1Y 5AR, England

THE CANCER RESEARCH SOCIETY, INC.

625 Avenue du President-Kennedy
Suite 402, Montréal, QC, H3A 3S5, Canada

Tel: (1) 514 861 9227

Fax: (1) 514 861 9220

Email: grants@cancer-research-society.ca

www: http://www.cancer-research-society.ca

Contact: Ms Ivy Steinberg, President

The Cancer Research Society, founded in 1945, is a national organisation which devotes its funds exclusively to research on cancer. The Society is committed to funding basic cancer research or 'seed' money for original ideas. The funds are allocated in the form of grants and fellowships to universities and hospitals across Canada.

Cancer Research Society, Inc. (Canada) Postdoctoral Fellowships

Subjects: Basic medical sciences.

Purpose: To provide financial support to recent PhD and MDs to acquire a more complete formation in research.

Eligibility: Open to holders of a PhD or MD degree, of any nationality.

Level of Study: Postdoctorate.

Type: Fellowship.

Value: Canadian $28,510.

Frequency: Annual.

Study Establishment: Canadian universities and their affiliated institutions.

Country of Study: Canada.

No. of awards offered: Varies.

Application Procedure: Applicants must visit the website for details of application procedure http://www.cancer-research-society.ca.

Closing Date: February 15th.

No. of awards given last year: Five.

No. of applicants last year: 50.

Cancer Research Society, Inc. (Canada) Research Grants

Subjects: Fundamental research on cancer.

Purpose: To provide support for new or continuing research activities by independent scientists or group of investigators in the field of cancer.

Eligibility: Candidates must hold an academic position on the staff of a Canadian university.

Level of Study: Professional development.

Type: Research grant.

Value: Canadian $30,000-60,000 to cover the cost of research. No equipment or travel is permitted.

Frequency: Annual.

Study Establishment: Canadian universities and their affiliated institutions.

Country of Study: Canada.

No. of awards offered: Varies.

Application Procedure: Applicants must visit the website for details of application procedure http://www.cancer-research-society.ca.

Closing Date: February 15th.

Funding: Commercial, Private.

No. of awards given last year: 60.

No. of applicants last year: 110.

THE CANON FOUNDATION IN EUROPE

Rijnsburgerweg 3, Leiden, NL-2334 BA, Netherlands
Tel: (31) 71 515 6555
Fax: (31) 71 515 7027
Email: foundation@canon-europa.com
www: http://www.canonfoundation.org
Contact: S H Cohen, Secretary

The Canon Foundation is a non-profit, grant making philanthropic organisation founded to promote, develop and spread science, knowledge and understanding, in particular between Europe and Japan.

Canon Foundation Award

Subjects: Academic education and cultural understanding.

Purpose: To contribute to scientific knowledge and international understanding, particularly between Japan and Europe through a teaching assignment combined with collaborative research.

Eligibility: Open to Japanese and European nationals only.

Level of Study: Postdoctorate, Professional development, Research.

Type: Award.

Value: A maximum award of €3780 per month.

Length of Study: One-three months.

Frequency: Annual.

Country of Study: Europeans study in Japan and the Japanese study in Europe.

No. of awards offered: One-three.

Application Procedure: Applicants must complete an application form which is to be submitted with two reference letters, a curriculum vitae, a list of papers, two photographs and copies of certificates of higher education.

Closing Date: October 15th.

Funding: Private.

Contributor: Canon Europa NV.

No. of awards given last year: One.

No. of applicants last year: Five.

Canon Foundation Research Fellowships

Subjects: All subjects.

Purpose: To contribute to scientific knowledge and international understanding, particularly between Japan and Europe.

Eligibility: Open to Japanese and European nationals only.

Level of Study: Doctorate, Postdoctorate, Postgraduate, Research.

Type: Fellowship.

Value: A maximum of award of €27,500.

Length of Study: One year maximum.

Frequency: Annual.

Country of Study: Europeans study in Japan and the Japanese study in Europe.

No. of awards offered: 10-12.

Application Procedure: Applicants must complete an application form which is to be submitted with two reference letters, a curriculum vitae, a list of papers, two photographs and copies of certificates of higher education.

Closing Date: October 15th.

Funding: Private.

Contributor: Canon Europa N V.

No. of awards given last year: Nine.

No. of applicants last year: 56.

CANTERBURY HISTORICAL ASSOCIATION

c/o History Department
University of Canterbury
Private Bag, Christchurch, New Zealand
Fax: (64) 3 364 2003
Contact: Dr G W Rice, Secretary

The Canterbury Historical Association (founded 1922, but in recess between 1940 and 1953) aims to foster public interest in all fields of history, by holding meetings for the discussion of historical issues and to promote historical research and writing through its administration of the J M Sherrard Award in New Zealand local and regional history.

J M Sherrard Award

Subjects: New Zealand regional and local history writing.

Purpose: To foster high standards of scholarship in New Zealand regional and local history.

Eligibility: Open to qualified applicants from New Zealand only. The major awards are normally restricted to substantial monograph length publications which meet scholarly standards. Small scale works, biographies and family histories are not eligible.

Level of Study: Unrestricted.

Type: Cash prize.

Value: New zealand $1,000.

Frequency: Dependent on funds available.

Country of Study: New Zealand.

No. of awards offered: Varies.

Application Procedure: No application is required as judges assess all potential titles appearing in the New Zealand National Biography.

Funding: Private.

No. of awards given last year: Three major awards.

No. of applicants last year: 45 works considered, but a short list of 10.

Additional Information: The prize money is often divided among two or three finalists. A commendation list is also published.

CARDIFF UNIVERSITY

Postgraduate Registry
50 Park Place
CF10 3AT, Cardiff, CF1 3XD, Wales
Tel: (44) 29 2087 4413
Fax: (44) 29 2087 4130
Email: dillonr@cf.ac.uk
Contact: Senior Assistant Registrar

Cardiff University is one of Britain's major centres of higher education, its origins date back to 1883. The University currently has some 14,500 students of whom more than 3,000 are postgraduates. Cardiff is a research led university, ranked 15th out of 102 United Kingdom universities for research activity, with 23 subject areas recognised as undertaking research of national and international excellence.

Cardiff University Postgraduate Research Studentships

Subjects: All subjects offered by the university.

Purpose: To enable selected students to pursue doctoral research to PhD level.

Eligibility: Candidates must possess at least an Upper Second Class (Honours) Degree from an approved university. For purposes of fee payment, applicants must be a home student ordinarily resident in the United Kingdom (or the European Community provided he or she is a European Community national) throughout the period of three years immediately preceding the date on which the course of study is due to begin.

Level of Study: Postgraduate, Predoctorate.

Type: Studentship.
Value: UK £2,750 fees and up to UK £6,800 maintenance allowance.
Length of Study: One year, renewable annually to a maximum of three years.
Frequency: Annual.
Study Establishment: The University.
Country of Study: United Kingdom.
No. of awards offered: Varies.
Application Procedure: Applicants must write for details.
Closing Date: June 30th.

CARNEGIE INSTITUTION OF WASHINGTON

1530 P Street North West, Washington, DC, 20005-1910, United States of America
Tel: (1) 202 939 1120
Fax: (1) 202 387 8092
Email: tmcdowell@pst.ciw.edu
www: http://www.carnegieinstitution.org
Contact: Ms Tina McDowell, Editor

The Carnegie Institution of Washington is a private, non-profit organisation engaged in basic research and advanced education in biology, astronomy, and the earth sciences. It was founded by Andrew Carnegie in 1902 and incorporated by Act of Congress in 1904. Andrew Carnegie, who provided an initial endowment of US$10 million and later gave additional millions, conceived the institution's purpose to encourage, in the broadest and most liberal manner, investigation, research, and discovery, and the application of knowledge to the improvement of mankind. Today there are five research departments: the department of terrestrial magnetism, the geophysical laboratory, the department of plant biology, the observatories and the department of embryology.

Carnegie Institution of Washington Fellowships
Subjects: Biology, astronomy and the earth sciences.
Purpose: To support advanced education.
Eligibility: Candidates are selected on an objective and non discriminatory basis through a careful process that includes assessment of the research proposal, confidential appraisal of the candidate by three or more scientists, review and comparative evaluation of each individual's qualifications and promise, review of the director's recommendations by the president of the institution, and appointment of Fellows and associates by the president. Important considerations are a candidate's apparent potential for growth and the extent that his or her development can be fostered by residence at the institution. In certain departments, a staff member agrees to act as a sponsor before a candidate is selected.
Level of Study: Doctorate, Postdoctorate, Postgraduate, Predoctorate.
Type: Fellowship.
Value: Varies.
Length of Study: Varies.
Frequency: Annual.
Study Establishment: The Carnegie Institution of Washington.
Country of Study: United States of America.
No. of awards offered: Approx. 70.
Application Procedure: Applicants must apply directly to the department of his or her interest. Procedures are explained on the website.
Closing Date: Please contact the organisation.
Additional Information: The Carnegie Institution of Washington is committed to equality of opportunity and non discrimination in all its activities, including the selection of fellows and associates. Efforts are made to recruit qualified women and minorities to help overcome the effects of past conditions that may have limited their participation in opportunities for scientific education and research.

CARNEGIE TRUST FOR THE UNIVERSITIES OF SCOTLAND

Cameron House
Abbey Park Place, Dunfermline, Fife, KY12 7PZ, Scotland
Tel: (44) 1383 622148
Fax: (44) 1383 622149
Email: jgray@carnegie-trust.org
www: http://www.carnegie-trust.org
Contact: Ms Jackie Gray, Assistant Secretary

The Carnegie Trust for the Universities of Scotland, founded in 1901, is one of the many philanthropic agencies established by Andrew Carnegie. The trust aims to offer assistance to students, to aid the expansion of the Scottish universities and to stimulate research.

Carnegie Grants
Subjects: All subjects in the university curriculum.
Purpose: To support personal research projects or aid in the publication of books likely to benefit the universities of Scotland.
Eligibility: Open to graduates of a Scottish university and to full-time members of staff of a Scottish university.
Level of Study: Postgraduate, Professional development.
Type: Grant.
Value: Varies according to requests but usually the maximum is UK £2,000.
Length of Study: Up to three months.
Frequency: Throughout the year.
Country of Study: Any country.
No. of awards offered: Varies.
Application Procedure: Applicants must complete an application form, available from the Trust office.
Closing Date: January 15th, May 15th or October 15th prior to Executive Committee meetings in February, June and November.
Funding: Private.
No. of awards given last year: 198.
No. of applicants last year: 223.

Carnegie Scholarships
Subjects: Most subjects in the university curriculum.
Purpose: To support postgraduate research.
Eligibility: Open to persons possessing a First Class (Honours) Degree from a Scottish university.
Level of Study: Postgraduate.
Type: Scholarship.
Value: UK £7,800 per year plus tuition fees and allowances.
Length of Study: Up to three years, subject to annual review.
Frequency: Annual.
Study Establishment: Any university in the United Kingdom.
Country of Study: United Kingdom.
No. of awards offered: 16.
Application Procedure: Applicants must be nominated by a senior member of staff at a Scottish university. An application form must also be completed, available from the Trust office.
Closing Date: March 15th.
Funding: Private.
No. of awards given last year: 12.
No. of applicants last year: 97.

CATCHING THE DREAM

8200 Mountain Road North East
Suite 203, Albuquerque, NM, 87110, United States of America
Tel: (1) 505 262 2351
Fax: (1) 505 262 0534
Email: nscholarsh@aol.com
Contact: Ms Zowie Banteah, Director of Recruitment

The Mathematics, Education, Science, Business, Engineering and Computer Science (MESBEC) provides scholarships to Native

Americans studying in those fields. The Native American Leadership in Education (NALE) helps Native Americans to complete their college degrees and earn teaching credentials, administrative certification and counsellor certification.

Catching The Dream

Subjects: All subjects.

Purpose: To provide scholarships to high potential Native American students in the fields that are critical for the political, economic, social and business development of American Indian tribes.

Eligibility: Restricted to United States of America citizens of Native American Indian and Alaskan Native ancestry. Students must be more than a quarter American Indian and enrolled with their tribe.

Level of Study: Unrestricted.

Type: Scholarship.

Value: US$500-5,000 per academic year.

Length of Study: Four years.

Frequency: Annual.

Study Establishment: An accredited college or university.

Country of Study: United States of America.

No. of awards offered: 230.

Application Procedure: Applicants must complete an application form, available on written request.

Closing Date: September 15th for Spring, April 15th for Autumn and March 15th for Summer.

Funding: Private.

No. of awards given last year: 210.

No. of applicants last year: 180.

CATHERINE MCCAIG'S TRUST

Clerk to the Governors
c/o McLeish Carswell
29 St Vincent Place, Glasgow, G1 2DT, Scotland
Tel: (44) 141 248 4134
Fax: (44) 141 226 3118
Contact: Ms Anne F Wilson

McCaig Postgraduate Scholarships

Subjects: Gaelic studies.

Eligibility: Bursaries are open to students enrolling in a course of Gaelic studies at any Scottish university. Postgraduate Scholarships are open to MA students of any Scottish university who have studied Gaelic among their course subjects.

Level of Study: Postgraduate.

Type: Scholarship.

Value: The bursaries are UK £250 per year for the entire course of study and the postgraduate scholarships are UK £750 per year.

Length of Study: One-three years.

Frequency: Annual.

Study Establishment: A Scottish establishment.

Country of Study: United Kingdom.

Application Procedure: Applicants must complete an application form, available from the Clerk.

Closing Date: May.

Funding: Private.

No. of awards given last year: One.

No. of applicants last year: Three.

CATHOLIC LIBRARY ASSOCIATION (CLA)

100 North Street
Suite 224, Pittsfield, MA, 01201-5109, United States of America
Tel: (1) 413 443 2252
Fax: (1) 413 442 2252
Email: cla@vgernet.net
www: http://www.cathla.org
Contact: Ms Jean R Bostley, Executive Director

The Catholic Library Association (CLA) represents all segments of the library community. Members strive to initiate, foster and encourage any activity or library programme that will promote literature and libraries, not only of a Catholic nature, but also of an ecumenical spirit.

The Rev Andrew L Bouwhuis Memorial Scholarship

Subjects: Library science.

Purpose: To encourage promising and talented individuals to enter librarianship and to foster advanced study in the library profession.

Eligibility: Open to individuals who have been accepted into a graduate school programme, show promise of success based on collegiate record and who demonstrate the need for financial aid.

Level of Study: Graduate, Postgraduate.

Type: Scholarship.

Value: US$1,500.

Frequency: Annual.

Country of Study: United States of America.

No. of awards offered: One.

Application Procedure: Applicants must complete an application form, available on request. Please send a stamped addressed envelope.

Closing Date: February 1st.

Funding: Private.

No. of awards given last year: One.

The World Book, Inc. Grant

Subjects: Continuing education in school or children's librarianship.

Eligibility: Open to national members of the CLA.

Level of Study: Postgraduate, Professional development.

Type: Grant.

Value: US$1,500 to be divided among no more than three recipients.

Frequency: Annual.

Study Establishment: Special workshops, institutes, or seminars and summer sessions at Institutes of Higher Education.

Country of Study: Any country.

No. of awards offered: One-three.

Application Procedure: Applicants must send a stamped addressed envelope for details.

Closing Date: March 15th.

Funding: Commercial.

No. of awards given last year: Three.

Additional Information: This award may not be used for study leading to a degree in library science.

THE CATHOLIC UNIVERSITY OF LOUVAIN (UCL)

Secrétariat à la Coopération Internationale
Halles Universitaires
Place de l'Université 1, Louvain-la-Neuve, B-1348, Belgium
Tel: (32) 1 047 3093
Fax: (32) 1 047 4075
Email: baeyens@sco.ucl.ac.be
www: http://www.ucl.ac.be
Contact: Mr Duque Christian

The French speaking Catholic University of Louvain (UCL) organises a yearly scholarship contest for postgraduate studies, medical specialisation and PhD.

Catholic University of Louvain Co-operation Fellowships

Subjects: Any subject relevant to Third World development.
Purpose: To promote economic, social, cultural and political progress in developing countries by training graduates from these countries.
Eligibility: Open to nationals of developing countries who hold all the requirements to be admitted at postgraduate level at UCL. Applicants should have an excellent academic background and some professional experience, they should demonstrate that their study programme is able to promote the development of their home country and they should have a good command of French ie. the Diplôme d'Études en Langue Française (DELF). Applicants must be less than 35 years of age for a PhD or 40 years of age for a specialisation. Applicants for a PhD must be members of the academic or scientific staff of a university in their own country. They should demonstrate their intent for an academic career and that they will be reintegrated into their home institution upon completion of their PhD.
Level of Study: Doctorate, Postgraduate.
Type: Fellowship.
Value: Tuition, living expenses, family allowance, medical insurance and transportation costs to the recipient's home country at the end of studies.
Length of Study: Up to four years.
Frequency: Annual.
Study Establishment: The Catholic University of Louvain.
Country of Study: Belgium.
No. of awards offered: Up to 20.
Application Procedure: Applicants must first write to the Secrétariat á la coopération internationale (SCO) at UCL. Candidiates must include a description of the programme that they wish to undertake, a short note explaining how they comply with the eligibility and selection criteria and a detailed curriculum vitae. Application forms will then be sent to those students who are eligible.
Closing Date: October 30th for letters and December 31st for application forms.
Funding: Private.
No. of awards given last year: 27.
No. of applicants last year: 300.

CDS INTERNATIONAL, INC.

871 United Nations Plaza, New York, NY, 10017-1814, United States of America
Tel: (1) 212 497 3513
Fax: (1) 212 497 3535
Email: rdelfino@cdsintl.org
www: http://www.cdsintl.org
Contact: Ms Rebecca Reagan Delfino, Programme Officer

CDS International, Inc. is a non-profit organisation which administers work exchange programmes. CDS International's goal is to further the international exchange of knowledge and technological skills, and to contribute to the development of a pool of highly trained and interculturally experienced business, academic and government leaders.

Congress Bundestag Youth Exchange for Young Professionals

Subjects: Eligible fields include business, technical, computer science, social and service fields.
Purpose: To foster the exchange of knowledge and culture between German and American youth while providing career enhancing theoretical and practical work experience.
Eligibility: Open to United States of America citizens and permanent residents aged between 18 and 24 years who are high school graduates, have well defined career goals and related part or full-time work experience, who are able to communicate and work well with others and have maturity enabling them to adapt to new situations, an intellectual curiosity and sense of diplomacy.
Level of Study: Professional development.
Type: Fellowship.
Value: International air fare and partial domestic transportation, language training and study at a German professional school, seminars, including transportation and insurance.
Length of Study: Seven months of study and a five month internship.
Frequency: Annual.
Study Establishment: A field specific postsecondary professional school.
Country of Study: Germany.
No. of awards offered: Approx. 60.
Application Procedure: Applicants must complete an application form, available on request by mail or email and downloadable from the website.
Closing Date: December 1st.
Funding: Government.
No. of awards given last year: 60.
No. of applicants last year: 300.
Additional Information: Participants must have US$300-350 pocket money per month. During their year American exchangees will have the opportunity to improve their skills through formal study and work experience. The programme also includes intensive language instruction and housing with a host family or in a dormitory.

CENTER FOR ADVANCED STUDY IN THE BEHAVIORAL SCIENCES

75 Alta Road, Stanford, CA, 94305, United States of America
Tel: (1) 650 321 2052
Fax: (1) 650 321 1192
Contact: Mr Mark Turner, Associate Director

Center for Advanced Study in the Behavioral Sciences Postdoctoral Residential Fellowships

Subjects: Behavioural sciences, biological sciences and the humanities.
Eligibility: There are no restrictions with regard to race or nationality, but applicants must hold a PhD.
Level of Study: Postdoctorate.
Type: Fellowship.
Value: Equal to up to half of a nine month university salary with an informal cap, plus travel allowance to and from the Center for recipients and their families.
Length of Study: 9-12 months.
Frequency: Annual.
Study Establishment: The Center.
Country of Study: United States of America.
No. of awards offered: Approx. 45.
Application Procedure: Applicants must contact the Center for details.
Funding: Government, Private.
No. of awards given last year: 48.

Additional Information: Fellows should be nominated by academic officers or distinguished Scholars and are expected to seek additional sources of support to share in fellowship costs. All names submitted will be kept for reviews at two year intervals. Persons authorised for fellowships are invited to indicate the year which would best suit their programme.

CENTER FOR DEFENSE INFORMATION (CDI)

1779 Massachusetts Avenue North West, Washington, DC, 20036, United States of America
Tel: (1) 202 332 0600
Fax: (1) 202 462 4559
Email: info@cdi.org
www: http://www.cdi.org
Contact: Ms Lynn Schuster, Development Director

The Center for Defense Information (CDI) provides responsible, nonpartisan analysis and criticism of the United States military and foreign policy establishment. The organisation is staffed by retired senior officers of the United States military and directed by former Senator Dale Bumpers.

CDI Internship

Subjects: Weapons proliferation, military spending, military policy, diplomacy and foreign affairs.
Purpose: To support the work of CDI's senior staff while gaining exposure to research, issues and communications related to national security and foreign policy.
Eligibility: There are no eligibility restrictions. Paid internships are for United States of America nationals or legal immigrants.
Level of Study: Unrestricted.
Type: Internship.
Value: US$700 per month. Up to US$2,100-3,500 in total.
Length of Study: Three-five months.
Frequency: Three times each year.
Study Establishment: CDI.
Country of Study: Any country.
No. of awards offered: Four per trimester, 12 per year.
Application Procedure: Applicants must submit a curriculum vitae, covering letter, brief writing sample, transcript and two letters of recommendation.
Closing Date: July 1st for the Autumn deadline, October 15th for the Spring deadline and March 15th for the Summer deadline.
Funding: Private.
No. of awards given last year: 12.
No. of applicants last year: 200.

THE CENTER FOR FIELD RESEARCH (CFR)

Earthwatch Institute
3 Clock Tower Place
Suite 100, Maynard, MA, 01754, United States of America
Tel: (1) 978 461 0081
Fax: (1) 978 461 2332
Email: cfr@earthwatch.org
www: http://www.earthwatch.org/cfr/cfr.html
Contact: Ms Johanna C Jobin, CFR

The Center for Field Research (CFR) was established in 1973 to develop a research programme for the Earthwatch Institute by encouraging and evaluating proposals from Scholars and scientists. A private non-profit organisation, CFR is served by an international advisory board of respected scientific and humanities Scholars.

Center for Field Research Grants

Subjects: Disciplines include, but are not limited to, anthropology, archaeology, biology, botany, cartography, conservation, ethnology, folklore, geography, geology, hydrology, marine sciences, meteorology, musicology, nutrition, ornithology, restoration, sociology and sustainable development.
Purpose: To provide grants for field research projects that can constructively utilise teams of non specialist field assistants in accomplishing their research goals.
Eligibility: There are no residency requirements or nomination processes. Preference is given to applicants who hold a PhD and have both field and teaching experience, however, support is also offered for outstanding projects by younger postdoctoral Scholars and, in special cases, graduate students. Women and minority applicants are encouraged. Research teams must include qualified volunteers from the Earthwatch Institute.
Level of Study: Doctorate, Postdoctorate.
Type: Grant.
Value: Varies. Grants are awarded on a per capita basis, depending upon the number of volunteer participants who are recruited by Earthwatch. The normal range of support is US$7,000-130,000.
Length of Study: Teams last for two-three weeks and projects can go on all year.
Frequency: Annual.
Study Establishment: Research sites. Approximately one quarter of the research currently funded takes place within the United States of America.
Country of Study: Any country.
No. of awards offered: Approx. 140.
Application Procedure: Applicants must complete an application form. Preliminary proposals must be submitted 13 months prior to field dates. Application forms may be obtained by contacting the Earthwatch Headquarters or visiting the website.
Closing Date: No deadline.
Funding: Private.
Contributor: Volunteers' contributions.
No. of awards given last year: 130.
No. of applicants last year: 400.
Additional Information: Further information is available on request.

CENTER FOR HELLENIC STUDIES

3100 Whitehaven Street North West, Washington, DC, 20008, United States of America
Tel: (1) 202 332 8688
Fax: (1) 202 797 3745
Email: chs@fas.harvard.edu
www: http://www.chs.harvard.edu
Contact: Ms Jennifer Reilly, Programs Officer

The Center for Hellenic Studies (Trustees for Harvard University) offers residential research fellowships for professional scholars in ancient Greek studies.

Center for Hellenic Studies Junior Fellowships

Subjects: Ancient Greek studies primarily literature, language, philosophy, history, religion, archaeology and art history, with restrictions.
Purpose: To provide selected classics scholars fairly early in their careers with an academic year free of other responsibilities to work on a publishable project.
Eligibility: Open to Scholars and teachers of Ancient Greek studies with a PhD degree or equivalent qualification and some published work, in the early stages of their career.
Level of Study: Postdoctorate.
Type: Fellowship.
Value: Up to US$24,000, plus private living quarters and a study at the Center building. Limited funds for research expenses and research related travel are available.

Length of Study: Nine months from September-June, not renewable.
Frequency: Annual.
Study Establishment: The Center for Hellenic Studies in Washington.
Country of Study: United States of America.
No. of awards offered: 12.
Application Procedure: Applicants must submit an application form, curriculum vitae, description of research project, samples of publications and three letters of recommendation. Enquiries about eligibility and early applications are encouraged. Applicants who are unable to stay for the full academic year may apply for a one semester fellowship and should include a note explaining the circumstances that make this necessary with their application.
Closing Date: October 15th.
Funding: Private.
Additional Information: Residence at the Center is required.

CENTER FOR INTERNATIONAL STUDIES, UNIVERSITY OF MISSOURI-ST LOUIS

St Louis, MO, 63121-4499, United States of America
Tel: (1) 314 516 5753
Fax: (1) 314 516 6757
Email: jglassman@umsl.edu
www: http://www.umsl.edu
Contact: Mr Robert Baumann, Assistant Director

The Center for International Studies supports a wide range of academic programmes designed to promote research and interest in international studies and to improve teaching of international affairs. The Center's Office of International Student Services co-ordinates and provides services for the University's international students, including admissions and immigration.

Theodore Lentz Postdoctoral Fellowship in Peace and Conflict Resolution

Subjects: International relations.
Purpose: To provide an opportunity for the recipient to conduct research projects in peace and conflict resolution and to teach an introductory peace studies course in the Autumn semester and one course in the Spring semester.
Eligibility: A completed PhD is required and preference is given to graduates of university programmes in peace studies and conflict resolution. Graduates of political science, international relations and other social science programmes who specialise in peace and conflict resolution are also invited to apply.
Level of Study: Postdoctorate.
Type: Fellowship.
Value: Approx. US$23,400 plus university benefits and US$1,000 travel and expense allowance.
Length of Study: Nine months.
Frequency: Annual.
Study Establishment: The University of Missouri, St Louis.
Country of Study: United States of America.
No. of awards offered: One.
Application Procedure: Applicants must submit a curriculum vitae, a letter of application, evidence of completion of PhD, three letters of recommendation and a research proposal of approximately 750 words.
Closing Date: April 15th.
Funding: Private.
Contributor: The Lentz Peace Research Association.
No. of awards given last year: One.
No. of applicants last year: 15.
Additional Information: Supported in part by the Lentz Research Association.

CENTER FOR MENTAL HEALTH SERVICES

American Psychiatric Association
1400 K Street North West, Washington, DC, 20005, United States of America
Tel: (1) 202 682 6096
Fax: (1) 202 682 6837
Email: mking@psych.org
Contact: Ms Marilyn King, Program Co-ordinator

APA/AstraZeneca Fellowship

Subjects: Psychiatry and mental health.
Purpose: To provide recipients with enriching training experiences through participation in the APA Fall Components and Annual Meetings, to provide resources to support activities that enhance culturally relevant aspects of their training programme, and to stimulate their interest in pursuing training in areas of psychiatry where minority groups are underrepresented, such as research, child psychiatry and addiction psychiatry.
Eligibility: Open to psychiatric residents in at least their PGY-2 of training. Applicants must be United States of America citizens or permanent residents.
Level of Study: Postgraduate.
Type: Fellowship.
Value: Travel expenses (transportation, hotel and incidentals) to the APA fall meeting in September, the annual meeting in May and other component related meetings as appropriate.
Length of Study: Two years.
Frequency: Annual.
Country of Study: Any country.
No. of awards offered: Up to 10.
Application Procedure: Applicants must send for an application packet, available from the APA Office of Minority and National Affairs.
Closing Date: January 1st.
Funding: Private.
Contributor: AstraZeneca Pharmaceuticals.
No. of applicants last year: 10.
Additional Information: Fellows are selected on the basis of their commitment to serve minority and underserved populations, their demonstrated leadership abilities, and their interest in the interrelationship between mental health and transcultural factors.

APA/CMHS Minority Fellowship Programme in Psychiatry

Subjects: Psychiatry and mental health.
Purpose: To provide enriching training experiences through participation in APA Fall Components and Annual Meetings, and to stimulate interest in pursuing training in areas of psychiatry where minority groups are underrepresented, such as research, child psychiatry and addiction psychiatry.
Eligibility: Open to psychiatric residents in at least their PGY-2 of training. Applicants must be United States of America citizens.
Level of Study: Postgraduate.
Type: Fellowship.
Value: Support takes the form of a partial stipend.
Length of Study: One year.
Frequency: Dependent on funds available.
Country of Study: Any country.
No. of awards offered: Varies.
Application Procedure: Applicants must complete an application form.
Closing Date: January 31st.
Funding: Government.
Contributor: The Center for Mental Health Services.
No. of applicants last year: Eight.
Additional Information: Fellows are selected on the basis of their commitment to serve minority and underserved populations, their demonstrated leadership abilities, and their interest in the interrelationship between mental health and transcultural factors.

CENTRAL QUEENSLAND UNIVERSITY (CQU)

Research Services Office, Rockhampton, QLD, 4702, Australia
Tel: (61) 7 4930 9828
Fax: (61) 7 4930 9801
Email: research-enquiries@cqu.edu.au
www: http://www.cqu.edu.au
Contact: Ms Jennifer Brett, Research Higher Degrees Officer

Central Queensland University's (CQU) higher degree programmes are characterised by open and flexible learning opportunities which provide a distinctive postgraduate research experience for students. With particular strengths in sustainable regional development and resource utilisation, industrially relevant engineering, contemporary communication and innovative teaching, learning and professional practice, the focus of higher degree programmes is the conduct of cutting edge research in areas which challenge boundaries of the traditional disciplines.

Central Queensland University Postgraduate Research Award

Subjects: Arts, health and sciences, business and law, education and creative arts, engineering and physical systems, informatics or communication.
Purpose: To enable scholars to proceed as a full-time candidate to a research Master's or doctorate.
Eligibility: Candidates must be eligible for admission to a research higher degree at CQU.
Level of Study: Doctorate, Research.
Type: Scholarship.
Value: Australian $17,267 living allowance plus australian $2,000 research support per year.
Length of Study: Two-three years.
Frequency: Annual.
Study Establishment: Central Queensland University.
Country of Study: Australia.
No. of awards offered: Six.
Application Procedure: Applicants must complete an application as prescribed. Certified academic transcripts and certified citizenship status are required. All enquiries from overseas should be directed to the CQU International Office.
Closing Date: October 31st.
Funding: Government.
No. of awards given last year: Six.
No. of applicants last year: 70.

CQU International Student Scholarship

Subjects: Arts, health and sciences, business and law, education and creative arts, engineering and physical systems, informatics or communication.
Purpose: To enable scholars to proceed as a full-time candidate to a research Master's or doctorate.
Eligibility: Candidates must be eligible for admission to a research higher degree at CQU.
Level of Study: Doctorate, Research.
Type: Award.
Value: Tuition fees plus australian $5,000 and living allowance.
Length of Study: Two-three years.
Frequency: Annual.
Study Establishment: Central Queensland University.
Country of Study: Any country.
No. of awards offered: One.
Application Procedure: Applicants must complete an application as prescribed. Certified academic transcripts and certified citizenship status are required. All enquiries from overseas should be directed to the CQU International office.
Closing Date: September 30th.
Funding: Commercial.
No. of awards given last year: One.
No. of applicants last year: 40.

CENTRE DE RECHERCHE EN SCIENCES NEUROLOGIQUES

Faculté de Médecine
Université de Montréal
CP 6128
Succ Centre-ville, Montréal, QC, H3C 3J7, Canada
Tel: (1) 514 343 6366
Fax: (1) 514 343 6113
Email: naulc@physio.umontreal.ca
www: http://www.crsn.umontreal.ca
Contact: Dr Serge Rossignol, Director

Founded in 1975, the Centre de Recherche en Sciences Neurologiques is a multidisciplinary unit based in the Department of Physiology, Faculty of Medicine, at the Université de Montreal. Educational activities at the Centre include an international symposium each spring, open to all neuroscientists, weekly research seminars in neuroanatomy, neurophysiology, and neurochemistry, and the HH Jasper and the JP Cordeau Postdoctoral Fellowships.

Herbert H Jasper Fellowship

Subjects: Neurology and neurosciences.
Purpose: To enable the use of the exceptional research facilities of the Center for Research in Neurological Sciences of the Université de Montréal. The fellowship also provides the opportunity for the recipient to work closely with the investigator of his or her choice within a large active group of neuroscientists who are members of the Center.
Eligibility: Open to Canadian citizens or permanent residents.
Level of Study: Postdoctorate.
Type: Fellowship.
Value: Canadian $25,000-30,000 per year.
Length of Study: One year.
Frequency: Annual.
Study Establishment: Centre de Recherche en Sciences Neurologiques, Université de Montréal.
Country of Study: Canada.
No. of awards offered: One.
Application Procedure: Applicants must complete an application form which can be obtained from the website, or by writing to the Fellowship Committee.
Closing Date: December 31st.
Funding: Government.
No. of awards given last year: One.
No. of applicants last year: 20.

JP Cordeau Fellowship

Subjects: Neurology and neurosciences.
Purpose: To enable the use of the exceptional research facilities of the Center for Research in Neurological Sciences of the Université de Montréal. The fellowship also provides the opportunity for the recipient to work closely with the investigator of his or her choice within a large active group of neuroscientists who are members of the Center.
Eligibility: Open to Canadian citizens or permanent residents.
Level of Study: Postdoctorate.
Type: Fellowship.
Value: Canadian $25,000-30,000.
Length of Study: One year.
Frequency: Annual.
Study Establishment: Centre de Recherche en Sciences Neurologiques, Université de Montréal.
Country of Study: Canada.
No. of awards offered: One.
Application Procedure: Applicants must complete an application form which can be obtained from the website, or by writing to the Fellowship Committee.
Closing Date: December 31st.
Funding: Commercial, Government.
No. of awards given last year: One.
No. of applicants last year: 20.

CENTRE FOR ADDICTION AND MENTAL HEALTH

250 College Street, Toronto, ON, M5T 1R8, Canada
Tel: (1) 416 535 8501 ext. 4568
Fax: (1) 416 979 4695
Email: elizabeth_cordeiro@camh.net
www: http://www.camh.net
Contact: Ms Elizabeth Cordeiro, Manager Research Grants and Awards

The Centre for Addiction and Mental Health was formed in early 1998 and involves the amalgamation of the Addiction Research Foundation, Clarke Institute, Donwood Institute and Queen Street Mental Health Centre. As a teaching hospital and research institute fully affiliated with the University of Toronto, the Centre is in a unique position to contribute to one common goal that being the better understanding, prevention and care for mental health.

Postdoctoral Training Programme in Addiction and Mental Health

Subjects: Addiction and mental health.
Purpose: To provide Fellows with a comprehensive training programme in the fields of addiction and mental health with training in research techniques.
Eligibility: Candidates must have a PhD or MD (or equivalent) at the time of taking up the appointment. Preference is given to Canadian citizens and permanent residents. Other successful applicants must obtain an appropriate visa. The successful applicant is expected to be located at the CAMH during the period of appointment. Applicants must obtain sponsorship of a supervisor at the Centre who holds an appointment as associate or full professor.
Level of Study: Postdoctorate.
Type: Fellowship.
Value: Postdoctoral salary varies depending on experience: Canadian $35,000-40,000 (based on CIHR salary scale).
Length of Study: One year, subject to renewal for a second year.
Frequency: Annual.
Study Establishment: The Centre for Addiction and Mental Health.
Country of Study: Canada.
No. of awards offered: Varies.
Application Procedure: Applicants must submit 10 copies of the application cover sheet, a description of the proposed programme of research relevant to the mission of the Centre, agreed upon by the proposed supervisor, not exceeding two pages single spaced, a curriculum vitae and two letters of reference to be sent directly to Elizabeth Cordeiro, Manager, Research Grants and Awards at the Centre for Addiction and Mental Health. Graduate School transcripts, two papers of sample writing, and a two-page biosketch of the proposed supervisor including current funding should also be sent.
Closing Date: December 3rd.
Funding: Government, Private.
Contributor: The Centre for Addiction and Mental Health Foundation and the Ontario Ministry of Health.
No. of awards given last year: Three.
No. of applicants last year: Varies.

CENTRE FOR INTERNATIONAL MOBILITY (CIMO)

PO Box 343
Hakaniemenkatu 2, Helsinki, FIN-00531, Finland
Tel: (358) 9 7747 7033
Fax: (358) 9 7747 7064
Email: cimoinfo@cimo.fi
www: http://www.cimo.fi
Contact: Grants Management Officer

The Centre for International Mobility (CIMO) is a service sector organisation whose expertise is geared to the promotion of cross-cultural communication in education, training and international mobility with the focus on education and training, work and young people. CIMO gathers, processes and distributes information and co-ordinates international education and training programmes.

CIMO Bilateral Scholarships

Subjects: Various subjects.
Eligibility: Open to applicants from Australia, Austria, Belgium, Bulgaria, Canada, China, Cuba, Czech Republic, Denmark, Egypt, France, Germany, Great Britain, Greece, Hungary, Iceland, India, Republic of Ireland, Israel, Italy, Japan, Luxembourg, Mexico, Mongolia, the Netherlands, Norway, Poland, Portugal, Republic of Korea, Romania, Slovakia, Spain, Sweden, Switzerland, Turkey and the United States of America.
Level of Study: Postgraduate.
Type: Scholarship.
Value: The bilateral scholarships usually consist of a monthly allowance. For short-term visitors there is a daily allowance, the amount of which is determined annually. Accommodation is provided for short-term visitors. There are no travel grants to or from Finland.
Length of Study: Postgraduate research of three-nine months, and study visits of one-two weeks.
Frequency: Annual.
Study Establishment: A Finnish university.
Country of Study: Finland.
Application Procedure: Applicants must make an application to the appropriate authority in the applicant's country and students can contact the CIMO in Finland for further information. Students with British nationality should apply through the Finnish Embassy in London. It is necessary that applicants establish contact with the receiving institution prior to application.
Closing Date: January 31st for United Kingdom applicants. All other candidates should consult the organisation.
Funding: Government.
Additional Information: For more information applicants can also contact Ms Liisa Matomaki at the Finnish Institute in London, 35-36 Eagle Street, London WC1R 4AJ, or by telephone on (44) 20 7404 3309, fax on (44) 20 7404 8893 or email at liisa.matomaki@finnish-institute.org.uk.

For further information contact:

Embassy of Finland
38 Chesham Place, London, SW1X 8HW, England
Tel: (44) 20 7838 6222
Contact: Pirjo Pellinen

CIMO Fellowships for Young Researchers and University Teaching Staff

Subjects: Education and research in all subjects.
Purpose: To encourage academic mobility to Finland and to promote international co-operation in teaching and research.
Eligibility: Open to nationals of any county. Applicants should be under 35.
Level of Study: Doctorate, Postdoctorate, Postgraduate, Predoctorate, Research.
Type: Scholarship.
Value: €690-1010 per month.
Length of Study: 3-12 months.
Frequency: Continuous.
Study Establishment: A university.
Country of Study: Finland.
Application Procedure: The staff of the Finnish receiving university department applies to the CIMO for the grant and they must complete an application form.
Closing Date: Applications are accepted at any time.
Funding: Government.
Additional Information: A Master's degree is a minimum requirement. Established contact with the receiving institute prior to application is required.

CIMO Scholarships for Advanced Finnish Studies and Research

Subjects: Finnish language, literature, Finno-Ugric linguistics, ethnology and folklore.

Purpose: To support postgraduate research and advanced studies of Finnish.

Eligibility: Open to nationals of any country. Applicants should be over 35.

Level of Study: Postgraduate.

Type: Scholarship.

Value: Please contact the organisation.

Length of Study: Four-nine months.

Study Establishment: A Finnish university.

Country of Study: Finland.

Application Procedure: Applicants must make an application, preferably in Finnish, on CIMO's application forms, which are available at Finnish embassies and consulates abroad. Applications should be sent to CIMO. For postgraduate studies the grant is applied for by the Finnish receiving university.

Closing Date: Applications are accepted at any time.

Funding: Government.

The Nordic Grant Scheme for Network Co-operation with the Baltic Countries and Northwest Russia

Subjects: Education and research in all fields. Priority is given to fields that promote further development in the region, as well as to fields where the special competence and experience of Nordic countries can be made use of.

Purpose: To develop long-term network collaboration projects in the fields of higher education and research and in the voluntary sector between the Nordic countries and the neighbouring states. This collaboration is designed to promote development throughout the region, the strengthening of democratic processes within the area and the reinforcement and consolidation of collaboration between the neighbouring states themselves.

Eligibility: Open to applicants from the Nordic countries and neighbouring states such as Denmark, Finland, Iceland, Norway, Sweden, Estonia, Latvia, Lithuania and the Northwest region of Russia ie. the St Petersburg and Kaliningrad areas and the Barents Region.

Level of Study: Unrestricted.

Type: Grant.

Value: Grants are awarded to cover the cost of travel and board and lodging for persons participating in a particular exchange. The scheme does not cover salary, overhead or equipment costs. The budget is approx. danish krone 13,000,000 and preliminary indications are that 85 per cent of it will be allocated to the academic sector and 15 per cent to the voluntary sector.

Length of Study: One-six months.

Frequency: Annual.

Application Procedure: Applications are to be submitted by the department serving as network co-ordinator. Documentation from each department participating in the collaboration project showing their interest in the project is to be submitted in written form in each instance. Applicants must fill in the Nordic Grant Scheme Application Form, obtainable from the website http://www.norden.org.

Closing Date: February 1st.

Funding: Government.

Contributor: The Nordic Council of Ministers.

For further information contact:

Nordic Council of Ministers
Store Strandstraede 18, Copenhagen, DK-1255, Denmark

CENTRO DE INVESTIGACIÓN Y ESTUDIOS AVANZADOS DEL IPN (CINVESTAV-IPN)

Departmento De Matemáticas Del CINVESTAV
Apartado Postal 14-740, Mexico City, 07000, Mexico
Tel: (52) 5747 3867
Fax: (52) 5747 3876
Email: matemat@math.cinvestav.mx
www: http://www.math.cinvestav.mx
Contact: Dr Enrique Ramirez de Arellano, Head

The Mathematics Department of the CINVESTAV-IPN offers the Solomon Lefschetz Instructorships to young mathematicians who show definite promise in research.

Solomon Lefschetz Instructorships

Subjects: Mathematics and statistics.

Purpose: To support young mathematicians.

Eligibility: Applicants must have a doctoral degree. Some knowledge of Spanish is also desirable.

Level of Study: Postdoctorate.

Type: Fellowship.

Value: The salary is equivalent to that of an assistant professor in the mathematics department. An allowance for moving expenses is also provided.

Length of Study: One year, with a possibility of renewal for an extra year.

Frequency: Annual, if funds are available.

Country of Study: Mexico.

No. of awards offered: Two.

Application Procedure: Applicants must submit a curriculum vitae, a short one-three page research statement and arrange for at least three letters of recommendation to be sent to the centre.

Closing Date: January 31st.

Funding: Government.

Contributor: The Mexican Office of Education.

Additional Information: Teaching duties generally include one course per semester.

CERIES (CENTRE DE RECHERCHE ED D'INVESTIGATIONS EPIDERMIQUES ET SENSORIELLES)

20 rue Victor Noir, Neuilly-sur-Seine, Cedex, F-92521, France
Tel: (33) 1 46 43 49 00
Fax: (33) 1 46 43 46 00
Email: contact@ceries.com
www: http://www.ceries.com
Contact: L Richards, Head of Communication

CERIES (Centre de Recherche ed d'Investigations Epidermiques et Sensorielles or Centre for Epidermal and Sensory Research and Investigation) is the healthy skin research centre of Chanel.

CERIES Research Award

Subjects: The biology and physiology of healthy skin and/or its reactions to environmental factors.

Purpose: To honour a scientific researcher for a fundamental or clinical research project in the field of healthy skin.

Eligibility: There are no eligibility restrictions.

Level of Study: Research.

Value: €40,000.

Length of Study: Two years.

Frequency: Annual.

Country of Study: Any country.

Application Procedure: Applicants must consult the website.

Closing Date: June 3rd.

Funding: Private.

Contributor: Chanel.
No. of awards given last year: One.
No. of applicants last year: 26.

CERN EUROPEAN LABORATORY FOR PARTICLE PHYSICS

Human Resources Division, Geneva, CH-1211, Switzerland
Tel: (41) 22 767 2735
Fax: (41) 22 767 2750
Email: recruitment.service@cern.ch
www: http://www.cern.ch/jobs

CERN European Laboratory for Particle Physics is the world's leading laboratory in its field, that being the study of the smallest constituents of matter and of the forces that hold them together. The laboratory's tools are its particle accelerators and detectors, which are among the largest and most complex scientific instruments ever built.

CERN Doctoral Student Programme

Subjects: Applied physics, electrical, electronic, mechanical or civil engineering, mathematics, computing, geotechnics, materials science, radiation protection and ultra-high vacuum.
Purpose: To assist students who are preparing a thesis at the doctoral level in a technical field.
Eligibility: Applicants must be nationals of one of the CERN member states, which are Austria, Belgium, Bulgaria, the Czech Republic, Denmark, Finland, France, Germany, Greece, Hungary, Italy, the Netherlands, Norway, Poland, Portugal, Slovakia, Spain, Sweden, Switzerland and the United Kingdom. Students must be enrolled in a doctoral programme at a university in one of these countries. Specialists in theoretical or experimental particle physics are not eligible.
Level of Study: Doctorate.
Type: Research grant.
Value: Swiss franc 3,866 per month.
Length of Study: Two years, which can be extended to three.
Frequency: Three times each year.
Study Establishment: The European Laboratory for Particle Physics.
Country of Study: Switzerland.
No. of awards offered: Varies.
Application Procedure: Applicants must submit a completed application form with two references. Forms are available on request and from the website.
Closing Date: February 22nd, July 12th or October 11th.
No. of awards given last year: Approx. 40.
No. of applicants last year: Approx. 80.
Additional Information: Selected students join a team working at CERN, and usually spend two years at the laboratory.

CERN Fellowships

Subjects: Particle physics, applied science, computing or engineering.
Purpose: To support research in particle physics and development work in applied science, computing and engineering.
Eligibility: Applicants must be aged less than 33 and be nationals from Austria, Belgium, Bulgaria, the Czech Republic, Denmark, Finland, France, Germany, Greece, Hungary, Italy, the Netherlands, Norway, Poland, Portugal, Slovakia, Spain, Sweden, Switzerland or the United Kingdom. Fellows working in research in experimental or theoretical physics should normally hold a PhD, while Fellows in applied science, computing and engineering should usually hold a Master's degree. Candidates may apply a few months before obtaining their diploma.
Level of Study: Postdoctorate, Postgraduate.
Type: Fellowship.
Length of Study: One year, normally extended for a second year.
Frequency: Twice a year.

Study Establishment: The European Laboratory for Particle Physics.
Country of Study: Switzerland.
No. of awards offered: Approx. 100.
Application Procedure: Applicants must submit a completed application form, a curriculum vitae, a list of publications and three letters of recommendation.
Closing Date: The end of October or the beginning of April.
Funding: Government.
No. of awards given last year: Approx. 100.
No. of applicants last year: Approx. 430.

CERN Technical Student Programme

Subjects: Accelerator physics, computing, mathematics, engineering, geotechnics, instrumentation for accelerators and particle physics experiments, low temperature physics and superconductivity, materials science, radiation protection, radio physics and radio chemistry, solid state, surface physics and ultra-high vacuum.
Purpose: To provide placements for students who are specialising in different technical fields.
Eligibility: Applicants must be attending an educational establishment in a CERN member state and follow a full-time course in one of the subjects listed in the subject index at university or advanced technical level. Students must have completed at least 18 months of full-time studies or studies and training periods. Students must be less than 30 years of age at the moment of the Selection Committee meeting. Candidates must be nationals of the member states of CERN, which are Austria, Belgium, Bulgaria, the Czech Republic, Denmark, Finland, France, Germany, Greece, Hungary, Italy, the Netherlands, Norway, Poland, Portugal, Slovak Republic, Spain, Sweden, Switzerland and the United Kingdom. Students specialising in theoretical or experimental particle physics are not eligible for the programme.
Value: A subsistence allowance of swiss franc 3,093 per month to cover the expenses of a single person in the Geneva area. Students will also be covered for medical costs arising from illnesses and accidents of a professional or non professional nature. Travel expenses equivalent to a second class return rail fare to Geneva for one person may be paid.
Length of Study: Appointments will last for six consecutive months, but most one year appointments can start throughout the year.
Frequency: Three times each year.
Study Establishment: The European Laboratory for Particle Physics.
Country of Study: Switzerland.
No. of awards offered: Approx. 80-90.
Application Procedure: Applicants must submit a completed application form and separate assessments by two referees. The official CERN Report on Candidate form, duly completed by the supervisor of the student at the educational establishment, must be used as one of the assessments. Any additional academic information, eg. academic records, as well as a curriculum vitae would be welcome. Candidates should write for further information.
Closing Date: February 22nd, July 12th or October 11th.
Funding: Government.
No. of awards given last year: Approx. 80-90.
No. of applicants last year: Approx. 240.
Additional Information: The official languages of CERN are English and French. A good knowledge of at least one of these languages is essential.

THE CHARLES A AND ANNE MORROW LINDBERGH FOUNDATION

2150 Third Avenue North
Suite 310, Anoka, MN, 55303-2200, United States of America
Tel: (1) 763 576 1596
Fax: (1) 763 576 1664
Email: info@lindberghfoundation.org
www: http://www.lindberghfoundation.org
Contact: Ms Shelley Nehl, Grants Co-ordinator

The Charles A and Anne Morrow Lindbergh Foundation is dedicated to furthering a balance between technological advancement and environmental preservation which was the Lindbergh's shared vision.

Lindbergh Grants

Subjects: Adaptive technology, waste minimisation and management, agriculture, aviation, aerospace, conservation of natural resources, humanities, education, arts, intercultural communication, exploration, biomedical research, health and population sciences.
Purpose: To provide grants to individuals whose initiative in a wide spectrum of disciplines seeks to actively further a better balance between technology and the natural environment.
Eligibility: Open to nationals of any country.
Level of Study: Research.
Type: Research grant.
Value: A maximum of US$10,580.
Length of Study: One year.
Frequency: Annual.
Country of Study: Any country.
No. of awards offered: Approx. 10.
Application Procedure: Applicants must complete an application form.
Closing Date: The second Tuesday in June.
Funding: Private.
Contributor: Individuals, corporations and foundations.
No. of awards given last year: 10.
No. of applicants last year: 225.

CHARLES AND JULIA HENRY FUND

University Registry
The Old Schools, Cambridge, Cambridgeshire, CB2 1TN, England
Tel: (44) 1223 332317
Fax: (44) 1223 332332
Email: mrf25@admin.cam.ac.uk
www: http://www.admin.cam.ac.uk
Contact: Ms Melanie Foster, Scholarships Clerk

Henry Fellowships (Harvard and Yale)

Subjects: Unrestricted, but subject to approval and feasibility.
Purpose: To strengthen bonds between Britain and the United States of America.
Eligibility: Candidates must be citizens of a Commonwealth country or the Republic of Ireland must be graduates of a United Kingdom university who are in their first year of postgraduate study in a United Kingdom University.
Level of Study: Postgraduate.
Type: Fellowship.
Value: US$17,500 plus a travel grant of UK £1,550 which is reviewed annually, tuition fees and health insurance.
Length of Study: One year.
Frequency: Annual.
Study Establishment: Harvard University or Yale University.
Country of Study: United States of America.
No. of awards offered: Three.
Application Procedure: Applicants must complete an application form and submit referees' reports. Applicants must also produce evidence of intellectual ability and submit a scheme of study or research not consisting of a degree course.

Closing Date: Early December.
Funding: Private.
Contributor: Trust fund.
No. of awards given last year: Two.
No. of applicants last year: 45.
Additional Information: The fellowships are awarded in conjunction with other awards to finance a continuing course of study and are not tenable for degree courses. Fellows must undertake to return to the British Isles or some other part of the Commonwealth on the expiration of their term of tenure.

CHARLES BABBAGE INSTITUTE (CBI)

University of Minnesota
211 Andersen Library
222 21st Avenue South, Minneapolis, MN, 55455, United States of America
Tel: (1) 612 624 5050
Fax: (1) 612 625 8054
Email: cbi@tc.umn.edu
www: http://www.cbi.umn.edu
Contact: Mr Jeffrey Yost, Associate Director

The Charles Babbage Institute (CBI) is a research centre dedicated to promoting the study of the history of computing, its impact on society and preserving relevant documentation. CBI fosters research and writing in the history of computing by providing fellowship support, archival resources and information to scholars, computer scientists and the general public.

Adelle and Erwin Tomash Fellowship in the History of Information Processing

Subjects: History of information processing.
Purpose: To advance the professional development of historians in the field.
Eligibility: Open to graduate students whose dissertations deal with a historical aspect of information processing.
Level of Study: Doctorate.
Type: Fellowship.
Value: US$10,000 stipend plus up to US$2,000 to be used for tuition, fees, travel and other research expenses.
Length of Study: One year.
Frequency: Annual.
Country of Study: Any country.
No. of awards offered: One.
Application Procedure: Applicants must send their curriculum vitae, a five page statement and justification of the research problem, and a discussion of methods, research materials and evidence of faculty support for the project. Applicants should also arrange for three letters of reference and certified transcripts of graduate school credits to be sent directly to the Institute.
Closing Date: January 15th.
Funding: Private.
No. of awards given last year: One.
No. of applicants last year: 15.

CHARLES H HOOD FOUNDATION

95 Berkeley Street
Suite 201, Boston, MA, 02116, United States of America
Tel: (1) 617 695 9439
Fax: (1) 617 423 4619
www: http://www.tmfnet.org/guidelines.html
Contact: Ms Gay Lockwood, Grants Administrator

Charles H Hood Foundation Child Health Research Grant

Subjects: The initiation and furtherance of medical research which will help to diminish health problems affecting large numbers of children.

Purpose: To assist junior faculty who are initiating independent research in paediatrics health and have limited federal grant experience.

Eligibility: Awards can be given to the New England states of Maine, Vermont, New Hampshire, Massachusetts, Rhode Island and Connecticut only.

Level of Study: Faculty.

Type: Research grant.

Value: US$50,000 per year for two years.

Length of Study: Two years.

Frequency: Annual.

Country of Study: United States of America.

No. of awards offered: 10 per year.

Application Procedure: Applicants must write for application forms. These must be completed and submitted along with letters of recommendation, a curriculum vitae, a non technical summary, a scientific summary and an itemised budget. Applicants should visit the website for details of guidelines.

Closing Date: April and October. Exact dates vary each year.

Funding: Private.

Contributor: The Charles H Hood Foundation.

No. of awards given last year: 10.

No. of applicants last year: 52.

CHAUTAUQUA INSTITUTION

Box 1098
Department 6
Schools Office, Chautauqua, NY, 14722, United States of America
Tel: (1) 716 357 6233
Fax: (1) 716 357 9014
www: http://www.chautauqua-inst.org/homebase.html
Contact: Mr Richard R Redington, Vice President

The Chautauqua Institution was founded in 1874. It is a is a non-profit organisation which offers nine week summer schools for the arts, education, religion and recreation.

Chautauqua Institution Awards

Subjects: Instrumental and vocal music, theatre, art and dance.

Purpose: To assist talented advanced students enrolled in the Chautauqua summer programme of fine and performing arts.

Eligibility: Open to candidates of any gender, nationality and age.

Level of Study: Postgraduate.

Type: Award.

Value: US$400-3,000.

Length of Study: Seven-eight weeks.

Frequency: Annual.

Study Establishment: The Chautauqua Institution.

Country of Study: United States of America.

No. of awards offered: Varies.

Closing Date: 10 days before the live audition, March 1st for taped auditions, and April 15th for art portfolio of slides.

Funding: Private.

Contributor: Various.

No. of awards given last year: 256.

No. of applicants last year: 1,200.

Additional Information: Walk ins are accepted for the live auditions. Most scholarships are given in music. No travel grants are provided.

CHEMICAL HERITAGE FOUNDATION (CHF)

315 Chestnut Street, Philadelphia, PA, 19106-2702, United States of America
Tel: (1) 215 925 2222
Fax: (1) 215 925 1954
Email: fellowships@chemheritage.org
www: http://www.chemheritage.org
Contact: Mr Josh McIlvain, Staff Researcher & Fellowship Coordinator

CHF Research Travel Grants

Subjects: Chemistry.

Purpose: To enable interested individuals to make use of the resources of the Beckham Centre for the History of Chemistry, the Othmer Library and its associated facilities.

Eligibility: Applicants must see the website for eligibility requirements.

Type: Travel grant.

Value: Varies.

Application Procedure: Applicants must complete an application which should include a one page statement on the proposed research and a budget.

Closing Date: For deadlines, please visit the website or contact mebowden@chemheritage.org.

Edelstein International Fellowship

Subjects: The history of chemical sciences and technology.

Purpose: To support study in the field.

Eligibility: Open to established Scholars.

Level of Study: Postgraduate.

Type: Fellowship.

Value: Varies.

Length of Study: One academic year.

Study Establishment: CHF and the Edelstein Centre for History and Philosophy of Science, Technology and Medicine in Jerusalem.

Application Procedure: Applicants must submit a letter of application which demonstrates how the CHF collection, other Philadelphia resources and the Edelstein Collection are relevant to the applicant's research. Each application must include a budget for the project. All applications must be sent to Josh McIlvain at the main address.

Closing Date: December 1st.

Edelstein International Studentship

Subjects: History of the chemical sciences and technology.

Purpose: To support dissertation research and writing.

Eligibility: Candidates must have completed all requirements for the PhD except the dissertation.

Level of Study: Predoctorate.

Type: Studentship.

Length of Study: One academic year.

Study Establishment: CHF and the Edelstein Centre for History and Philosophy of Science, Technology and Medicine in Jerusalem.

Application Procedure: Applicants must send letters of application that demonstrate how the CHF collection, other Philadelphia resources and the Edelstein Collection are relevant to the applicant's research. Each application must include a budget for the project. All applications must be addressed to Josh McIlvain at the main address.

Closing Date: December 1st.

Eugene Garfield Fellowship

Subjects: Chemical sciences, information science or the history of science, technology or medicine.

Purpose: To enable the Fellow to research the history of information science as it relates to the chemical sciences or chemical process industries.

Eligibility: Open to a student in the history of the chemical sciences and technology who has completed all requirements for the PhD except the dissertation. Time will be divided between CHF and the Edelstein Centre in Jerusalem. The studentship supports dissertation research and writing, and applicants should demonstrate how the CHF collection, other Philadelphia resources and the Edelstein Collection are relevant to their research.

Level of Study: Postdoctorate, Postgraduate.

Type: Fellowship.

Value: Varies.

Country of Study: Israel.

Application Procedure: Applications should include a proposal of no more than 1,000 words outlining the applicant's research project with specific reference to how the work advances scholarship and how the outcome might be published. Applicants must send completed application forms to Josh McIlvain at the main address.

Closing Date: December 1st.

Glenn E and Barbara Hodsdon Ullyot Scholarship

Subjects: Chemistry.

Purpose: To advance understanding of the importance of the chemical sciences to the public's welfare.

Level of Study: Postgraduate.

Type: Scholarship.

Length of Study: A minimum of two months.

Application Procedure: Applicants must submit a completed application form, a one page description of the proposed research and an outline of a specific product as an outcome of the scholarship. Application forms are available on request.

Closing Date: Please contact the organisation.

Gordon Cain Fellowship

Subjects: History of the development of the chemical industries. The outcome of the research should further understanding of the relationship between technology, policy, management and entrepreneurship and should shed light on the complex development of modern society and commerce.

Purpose: To support historical research.

Eligibility: Open to a Scholar with a PhD who will carry out historical research on the development of the chemical industries.

Level of Study: Postgraduate.

Type: Fellowship.

Value: Varies.

Length of Study: One academic year.

Application Procedure: Applications must include a proposal of no more than 1,000 words outlining the applicant's research project with specific reference to how the work advances scholarship and how the outcome might be published. All applications must be sent to Josh McIlvain at the main address.

Closing Date: December 1st.

Société de Chimie Industrielle (American Section) Fellowship

Subjects: Chemistry.

Purpose: To stimulate public understanding of the chemical industries, using both terms in their widest sense.

Eligibility: Applications are encouraged from writers, journalists, educators and historians of science, technology and business.

Type: Fellowship.

Length of Study: A minimum of two months.

Country of Study: United States of America.

Application Procedure: Applicants must submit a one page research proposal outlining the specific project to be completed while in residence at CHF, and showing how the project will further public understanding of the chemical industries.

Closing Date: February 15th.

CHEMICAL INSTITUTE OF CANADA

Suite 550
130 Slater Street, Ottawa, ON, K1P 6E2, Canada
Tel: (1) 613 232 6252 ext. 235
Fax: (1) 613 232 5862
Email: jtrohon@cheminst.ca
www: http://www.cheminst.ca
Contact: Ms Julie Trohon, Program Co-ordinator

The Chemical Institute of Canada (CIC) is an umbrella organisation for three constituent societies namely the Canadian Society for Chemistry, the Canadian Society for Chemical Engineering and the Canadian Society for Chemical Technology. The purpose of the Institute is to promote common scientific and technical interests and to provide service to all its members.

CIC Award for Environmental Improvement

Subjects: Environmental pollution, treatment and remediation.

Purpose: To award a company, individual, team or organisation in Canada for a significant achievement in pollution prevention, treatment or remediation in Canada.

Type: Award.

Value: A plaque and certificate for each nominated individual and travel assistance of up to canadian $500.

Frequency: Annual, if funds are available.

Country of Study: Canada.

No. of awards offered: One.

Application Procedure: Applicants must be nominated.

Closing Date: March 1st.

Funding: Private.

Contributor: The Environment Division.

CIC Catalysis Award

Subjects: Chemistry.

Purpose: To recognise an individual who has made a distinguished contribution to the field of catalysis while resident in Canada.

Level of Study: Professional development.

Type: Award.

Value: A rhodium plated silver medal and travel expenses to present the Award Lecture.

Frequency: Every two years.

Country of Study: Canada.

No. of awards offered: One.

Application Procedure: Applicants must be nominated.

Closing Date: October 1st.

Funding: Private.

CIC Macromolecular Science and Engineering Lecture Award

Subjects: Macromolecular science or engineering.

Purpose: To recognise an individual who has made a distinguished contribution to the field.

Level of Study: Professional development.

Type: Award.

Value: A framed scroll, a cash prize of canadian $1,500 and travel expenses.

Frequency: Annual.

Country of Study: Canada.

No. of awards offered: One.

Application Procedure: Applicants must be nominated.

Closing Date: March 1st.

Funding: Private.

Contributor: NOVA Chemicals Limited.

CIC Medal

Subjects: Chemistry and chemical engineering.

Purpose: To recognise a person who has made an outstanding contribution to the field.

Level of Study: Professional development.

Type: Award.

Value: A palladium medal and travel expenses.
Frequency: Annual.
Country of Study: Canada.
No. of awards offered: One.
Application Procedure: Applicants must be nominated.
Closing Date: March 1st.
Funding: Private.
Contributor: INCO Limited.

CIC Montreal Medal

Subjects: Chemistry and chemical engineering.
Purpose: To honour a person who has shown significant leadership in or has made an outstanding contribution to the profession of chemistry or chemical engineering in Canada.
Eligibility: Open to administrative contributions within the Chemical Institute of Canada and other professional organisations which contribute to the advancement of the professions of chemistry and chemical engineering. Contributions to the sciences of chemistry and chemical engineering are not considered.
Level of Study: Professional development.
Type: Award.
Value: A medal and travel expenses if required.
Frequency: Annual.
Country of Study: Canada.
No. of awards offered: One.
Application Procedure: Applicants must be nominated.
Closing Date: March 1st.
Contributor: Montreal CIC Local Section.

CIC Pestcon Graduate Scholarship

Subjects: Any area of pesticide research including alternative pest control strategies.
Purpose: To support postgraduate work.
Eligibility: Open to Canadian citizens, including landed immigrants, for graduate study in any area of pesticide and contaminant research. Preference will be given to students already in their second year of a PhD programme.
Level of Study: Postgraduate.
Type: Scholarship.
Value: Canadian $3,000 in two instalments.
Length of Study: One year.
Frequency: Annual.
Country of Study: Canada.
No. of awards offered: One.
Application Procedure: Applicants must submit a written application including a curriculum vitae and a brief description of no more than 500 words of the research programme undertaken and the progress to date. Applications must be accompanied by an official transcript of the candidate's academic records, the names of their supervisors and a second academic referee.
Closing Date: March 1st for notification by June 1st.
Contributor: The fifth International Congress of Pesticide Chemistry.

CIC The Bayer, Inc. Award for High School Chemistry Teachers

Subjects: Chemistry.
Purpose: To recognise excellence in the teaching of chemistry at the secondary level. This award pays tribute to outstanding contributions in high school chemistry teaching, stimulates interest in the CIC among teachers and facilitates the Institute's efforts to improve chemistry teaching at the high school level.
Level of Study: Professional development.
Type: Award.
Value: A cash prize of canadian $500 and one year's membership of the CIC.
Frequency: Annual.
Study Establishment: Any Canadian secondary school.
Country of Study: Canada.
No. of awards offered: Up to two.
Application Procedure: Applicants must be nominated.

Closing Date: December 1st.
Funding: Private.
Contributor: Bayer, Inc.

CIC Union Carbide Award for Chemical Education

Subjects: Chemistry and chemical engineering.
Purpose: To recognise a person who has made outstanding contributions in Canada to education at any level in the field of chemistry or chemical engineering.
Level of Study: Professional development.
Type: Award.
Value: A framed scroll, a cash prize of canadian $1,000 and up to canadian $400 travel expenses.
Frequency: Annual.
Country of Study: Canada.
No. of awards offered: One.
Application Procedure: Applicants must be nominated.
Closing Date: March 1st.
Funding: Private.
Contributor: Union Carbide Canada Limited.

CHIHUAHUAN DESERT RESEARCH INSTITUTE

Box 905, Fort Davis, TX, 79734, United States of America
Tel: (1) 915 364 2499
Fax: (1) 915 364 2504
Email: manager@cdri.org
www: http://www.cdri.org
Contact: Dr Cathryn A Heyt, Executive Director

The Chihuahuan Desert Research Institute is a non-profit scientific and educational organisation.

W Frank Blair Award

Subjects: The natural sciences and the Chihuahuan Desert Region.
Purpose: To support and promote excellence in written data presentation.
Eligibility: Students must be enrolled when the application is made.
Level of Study: Doctorate, Graduate, Postgraduate.
Type: Cash prize.
Value: US$500.
Frequency: Annual.
No. of awards offered: One.
Application Procedure: Applicants must contact the Institute for application instructions or see the website for more details.
Closing Date: November 1st.
Funding: Private.
No. of awards given last year: One.
No. of applicants last year: Four.

CHILDREN'S LITERATURE ASSOCIATION (CHLA)

PO Box 138, Battle Creek, MI, 49016-0138, United States of America
Tel: (1) 616 965 8180
Fax: (1) 616 965 3568
Email: kkiessling@childlitassn.org
www: http://www.childlitassn.org
Contact: Ms Kathryn Kiessling, Administrator

The Children's Literature Association (ChLA) is a non-profit organisation devoted to promoting serious scholarship and criticism in children's literature.

ChLA Beiter Scholarships for Graduate Students

Subjects: Children's literature.

Purpose: For proposals of original scholarship with the expectation that the undertaking will lead to a publication or a conference presentation and contribute to the field of children's literature criticism.

Eligibility: Winners must be, or become, members of the Children's Literature Association. Students of the ChLA Executive Board members or Scholarship Committee members are not eligible to apply. Previous recipients are not eligible to reapply until the third year from the date of the first award.

Level of Study: Doctorate, Graduate, Postdoctorate.

Type: Scholarship.

Value: Individual grants range from US$250-1,000 and may be used to purchase supplies and materials eg. books and videos, and as research support eg. photocopying, or to underwrite travel to special collections or libraries.

Frequency: Annual.

Country of Study: Any country.

No. of awards offered: One-four.

Application Procedure: Applicants should send five copies of their contact details including email address, academic institution and status, the expected date of their degree, a detailed description of the research proposal, a curriculum vitae and three letters of reference, one of which must be from the applicant's dissertation or thesis advisor.

Closing Date: February 1st.

Funding: Private.

No. of awards given last year: Two.

No. of applicants last year: 11.

Additional Information: Please see the website for further details. To receive guidelines by mail a stamped addressed envelope must be provided.

ChLA Research Fellowships and Scholarships

Subjects: Children's literature.

Purpose: To award proposals dealing with criticism or original scholarship with the expectation that the undertaking will lead to publication and make a significant contribution to the field of children's literature in the area of scholarship or criticism.

Eligibility: Applicants must be, or become, members of the Children's Literature Association.

Level of Study: Unrestricted.

Type: Fellowships and scholarships.

Value: Up to US$1,000. Individual awards may range from US$250-1,000 and may be used only for research related expenses such as travel to special collections or materials and supplies. Funds are not intended for work leading to the completion of a professional degree.

Frequency: Annual.

Country of Study: Any country.

No. of awards offered: One-four.

Application Procedure: Applicants must send five copies of the application in English including three letters of reference and a curriculum vitae. Applications must include the applicant's name, address, telephone number and email address, details of the academic institution the applicant is affiliated with and a detailed description of the research proposal, not exceeding three single spaced pages, and indicating the nature and significance of the project, where it will be carried out and the expected date of completion.

Closing Date: February 1st.

Funding: Private.

No. of awards given last year: Five.

No. of applicants last year: Seven.

Additional Information: In honour of the achievement and dedication of Dr Margaret P Esmonde, proposals that deal with critical or original work in the areas of science fantasy or science fiction for children or adolescents will be awarded the Margaret P Esmonde Memorial Scholarship. Please see the website for further details. To receive guidelines by mail applicants must provide a stamped addressed envelope.

CHILDREN'S MEDICAL RESEARCH INSTITUTE

Locked Bag 23, Wentworthville, NSW, 2145, Australia
Tel: (61) 2 9687 2800
Fax: (61) 2 9687 2120
Email: prowe@cmri.usyd.edu.au
www: http://www.cmri.com.au
Contact: Professor P B Rowe, Director

The Children's Medical Research Institute is an independent research institute affiliated with the University of Sydney and the New Children's Hospital. Supported by grants and a state government infrastructure grant, it conducts basic research in the fields of vertebrate development, cellular immortalisation and oncogenesis, cellular signalling and gene therapy.

Children's Medical Research Institute Graduate Scholarships and Postgraduate Fellowships

Subjects: Muscle genetics, the exploration of the role of genetic control systems in myogenesis and cytoarchitecture, neurosciences, the study of the physical properties and genetic control of neuronal development, oncogenesis, the role of oncogenes in leukaemogenesis and mechanisms of cellular immortalisation, embryology, cell fate designation at gastrulation, gene imprinting, gene therapy, genevector design for the treatment of inherited and acquired disease, cell signalling and membrane biology in neurotransmission.

Purpose: To allow individuals to undertake research leading to a PhD or MSc (Med) as well as to undertake postgraduate research within one of the disciplines currently under study within the Institute.

Eligibility: Open to Australian permanent residents with suitable qualifications, usually an Honours degree for postgraduate studies.

Level of Study: Postdoctorate, Postgraduate.

Type: Scholarship and fellowship.

Value: The award value is based on the National Health and Medical Research Council of Australia scale together with a Sydney loading.

Length of Study: Three-five years.

Frequency: Annual.

Study Establishment: A biomedical research institute affiliated to the University of Sydney.

Country of Study: Australia.

No. of awards offered: Up to four postgraduate scholarships and two postdoctoral fellowships.

Application Procedure: Applicants must submit a letter outlining their background, interests and referees. No application form is required.

Closing Date: Enrolment for PhD studies is in January or August.

Funding: Government, Private.

Contributor: An investment trust.

No. of awards given last year: Six.

No. of applicants last year: 32.

Additional Information: There are no course requirements.

Children's Medical Research Institute Postdoctoral Fellowship

Subjects: Biophysics and molecular biology, embryology and reproduction biology, genetics and neurosciences.

Purpose: To allow individuals to obtain further professional training in their field of interest.

Eligibility: Open to qualified applicants of any nationality, who must meet temporary visa requirements. Knowledge of English is essential.

Level of Study: Postdoctorate.

Type: Fellowship.

Value: Varies depending on experience, but is generally australian $47,000 for a first year PhD.

Length of Study: Up to three years.

Frequency: Dependent on funds available.

Study Establishment: A research centre.

Country of Study: Australia.
No. of awards offered: Two.
Application Procedure: Applicants must submit a letter of intent with a curriculum vitae, transcript, references and any other appropriate documentation.
Closing Date: Applications are accepted at any time.
Funding: Government, Private.
Contributor: Investment Trust.
No. of awards given last year: Two.
No. of applicants last year: 20.

Children's Medical Research Institute Postgraduate Scholarship

Subjects: Biophysics and molecular biology, embryology and reproduction biology, genetics and neurosciences.
Purpose: To support research based study for the award of degrees of PhD or MSc (Med) at the University of Sydney.
Eligibility: Open to Australian residents only.
Level of Study: Doctorate, Postgraduate.
Type: Scholarship.
Value: Commencing at australian $18,500 per year.
Length of Study: Three-four years.
Frequency: Dependent on funds available.
Study Establishment: A research centre.
Country of Study: Australia.
No. of awards offered: Up to four.
Application Procedure: Applicants must submit a letter of interest with a curriculum vitae, transcript, references and any other appropriate support documents. There is no application form.
Closing Date: Enrolment takes place twice a year in January and August.
Funding: Government, Private.
Contributor: Investment Trust.
No. of awards given last year: Four.
No. of applicants last year: 12.

CHINESE AMERICAN MEDICAL SOCIETY (CAMS)

281 Edgewood Avenue, Teaneck, NJ, 07666, United States of America
Tel: (1) 201 833 1506
Fax: (1) 201 833 8252
Email: hw5@columbia.edu
www: http://www.camsociety.org
Contact: Dr H H Wang, Executive Director

The Chinese American Medical Society (CAMS) is a non-profit, charitable, educational and scientific society that aims to promote the scientific association of medical professionals of Chinese descent. It also aims to advance medical knowledge and scientific research with emphasis on aspects unique to the Chinese and to promote the health status of Chinese Americans. The Society makes scholarships available to medical dental students and provides summer fellowships for students conducting research in health problems related to the Chinese.

CAMS Scholarship

Subjects: Medical or dental studies.
Purpose: To help defray the cost of study.
Eligibility: Open to Chinese Americans, or Chinese persons residing in the United States of America. Applicants must be full-time medical or dental students in approved schools in the United States of America and be able to show academic proficiency and financial hardship.
Level of Study: Doctorate.
Type: Scholarship.
Value: US$1,000-1,500.
Frequency: Annual.
Country of Study: United States of America.

No. of awards offered: Three-five.
Application Procedure: Applicants must complete an application form, and send it together with a letter for the Dean of Students verifying good standing, two to three letters of recommendation, a personal statement and curriculum vitae, plus a financial statement.
Closing Date: March 31st.
Funding: Private.
Contributor: Membership and fund raising.
No. of awards given last year: Five.
No. of applicants last year: 30.

CHOIRS ONTARIO

112 St Clair Avenue West
Suite 403, Toronto, ON, M4V 2Y3, Canada
Tel: (1) 416 923 1144
Fax: (1) 416 929 0415
Email: choirs.ontario@sympatico.ca
www: http://www.choirsontario.org
Contact: Ms Diane Phaneuf, General Manager

Choirs Ontario serves and supports those who gather together to sing. It is dedicated to the promotion of choral activities regardless of genre, language of performance or size of vocal ensemble. The organisation aims to provide services to choirs, conductors, choristers, composers, administrators and educators, and all those who have a passion for choral music.

Leslie Bell Prize

Subjects: Choral music, particularly conducting.
Purpose: To reward an emerging new conductor.
Eligibility: Candidates must be Canadian citizens or landed immigrants who are permanent residents of the province of Ontario.
Level of Study: Postgraduate.
Type: Prize.
Value: Canadian $5,000.
Frequency: Every two years (even-numbered years).
Country of Study: Any country.
No. of awards offered: One.
Closing Date: There are various deadlines.

Ruth Watson Henderson Choral Composition Competition

Subjects: Choral music, particularly composition.
Purpose: To award new choral composition.
Eligibility: Candidates must be Canadian citizens or landed immigrants who are permanent residents of the Province of Ontario.
Level of Study: Postgraduate.
Type: Prize.
Value: Canadian $1,000.
Frequency: Every two years (even-numbered years).
Country of Study: Any country.
No. of awards offered: One.
Closing Date: There are various deadlines.
Funding: Private.

CHRISTOPHER REEVE PARALYSIS FOUNDATION (CRPF)

500 Morris Avenue, Springfield, NJ, 07081, United States of America
Tel: (1) 973 379 2690
Fax: (1) 973 912 9433
Email: jnewman@crpf.org
www: http://www.paralysis.org
Contact: Ms Jennifer L Newman, Assistant Director of Research

The Christopher Reeve Paralysis Foundation (CRPF) is a national non-profit organisation whose mission is to encourage and support research in order to find a cure for paralysis caused by spinal cord injury (SCI). In addition to this the CRPF supports organisations working to improve quality of life for people with disabilities through a separate grant programme.

CRPF Research Grant

Subjects: SCI related research.
Purpose: To fund research which will lead to effective treatments and ultimately a cure, for SCI.
Eligibility: Open to American and international investigators located at institutions that have clearly established lines of accountability and fiscal responsibility. Institutional assurances regarding animal research and human subjects are required.
Level of Study: Doctorate, Postdoctorate, Research.
Type: Research grant, postdoctoral fellowship and senior investigator.
Value: US$75,000 per year for a total maximum of US$150,000.
Length of Study: A maximum of two years.
Frequency: Twice a year.
Country of Study: Any country.
No. of awards offered: Varies from year to year depending on the level of science and the amount of funds available.
Application Procedure: Applicants must complete an application form and forward 20 copies of it to the Foundation. Forms are available from the website.
Closing Date: December 15th and June 15th.
Funding: Private.
Contributor: Private sector donations.
No. of awards given last year: 20.
No. of applicants last year: 110.
Additional Information: The intent of these awards is to promote innovative and ground breaking work, not to provide ongoing long-term support. CRPF funds activities that hold promise of identifying therapies for paralysis. Areas of research that are the focus of current CRPF emphasis and funding include strategies that may promote neural growth and survival, encourage the formation of synapses, enhance production of mylein, conduction capabilities, or may otherwise lead to restoration of the compromised circuitry in the acutely and chronically injured CNS. Research that evaluates the efficiency of drugs and other interventions that protect against secondary injury or provides insight into the mechanisms causing such damage, and defines anatomical characteristics of SCI in well defined animal models and in the human spine is also encouraged as is work that specifically documents the neural systems that are most vulnerable to SCI and functional losses occurring as a result, biological mechanisms underlying approaches to improve function, eg. bladder function and sexual function, and alleviates chronic pain and spasticity.

CHRONIC DISEASE RESEARCH FOUNDATION (CDRF)

St Thomas' Hospital
1st Floor
South Wing
Lambeth Palace Road, London, SE1 7EH, England
Tel: (44) 20 7633 9990
Fax: (44) 20 7922 8154
Email: christel.barnetson@cdrf.org.uk
www: http://www.cdrf.org.uk
Contact: Ms Christel Barnetson, Chief Administrator

The Chronic Disease Research Foundation (CDRF) was set up to look at new ways of exploring the genetics of diseases associated with ageing. Its mission is to target those common diseases such as osteoporosis, arthritis, back pain, migraine, asthma and diabetes that we inherit from our parents, and prevent and alleviate them now and for future generations. Its principle focus is on comparative studies of identical and non identical twins, undertaken at the Twin Research Unit of St Thomas' Hospital.

CDRF Project Grants

Subjects: The genetic basis of diseases associates with ageing.
Purpose: To carry out comparative studies of identical and non identical twins to pinpoint the genetic cause of common diseases associated with ageing.
Level of Study: Postgraduate, Research.
Type: Project grant.
Value: UK £30,000-150,000.
Length of Study: Two-three years.
No. of awards offered: Dependent on funds.
Application Procedure: Applicants must submit a preliminary proposal of no more than one side of A4 including an outline of the proposal, a list of principle aims and objectives, and scale of funding. Provided the CDRF's panel of experts consider the project to be of relevance, applicants must then submit a full grant proposal.

CDRF Research Fellowship

Subjects: The genetic basis of disease associated with ageing.
Purpose: To promote postgraduate education and enable the charity to carry out further research projects.
Level of Study: Postgraduate.
Type: Fellowship.
Value: UK £30,000-175,000.
Length of Study: Two-five years.
Frequency: Dependent on funds available.
Country of Study: United Kingdom.
No. of awards offered: Dependent on funds.
Application Procedure: Applicants must submit a preliminary proposal of no more than one side of A4 including an outline of proposal, a list of principal aims and objectives, and scale of funding. If CDRF's panel of experts consider the project to be of relevance, applicants must then submit a full grant proposal.
Funding: Private.
No. of awards given last year: One.

CHRONIC GRANULOMATOUS DISORDER RESEARCH TRUST (CGD)

Manor Farm, Wimborne St Giles, Dorset, BH21 5NL, England
Tel: (44) 1725 517977
Fax: (44) 1725 517977
Contact: General Secretary

The Chronic Granulomatous Disorder Research Trust (CGD) exists to boost research that will lead to improved treatments and a cure for this rare, genetic, blood disorder. The Trust encourages the dissemination of knowledge and provides information for affected people and for medical professionals. The CGD also provides a point of contact to raise public awareness and moral support.

CGD Research Trust Grants

Subjects: Topics pertaining to the cause, inheritance, management and symptoms of chronic cranulomalous disorde.
Purpose: To support thorough research which aims to increase understanding of the cause, inheritance, management and symptoms of chronic cranulomalous disorder and to disseminate the useful results of such research.
Level of Study: Doctorate, Postgraduate, Predoctorate, Research.
Type: Fellowship, studentship, project, programme, travel and therapy grants.
Value: Varies according to type.
Length of Study: Usually one-three years depending on the programme, to a maximum of five years.
Frequency: Annual, if funds are available.
Application Procedure: Applicants must initially submit a one page outline. A number of these are then invited to complete full applications. These are then subject to a peer review. The medical panel then make recommendations and trustees announce grant offers the following January.
Closing Date: Grants are advertised annually every April in Nature.

Funding: Private.
Contributor: Voluntary donations.
No. of awards given last year: Three.
No. of applicants last year: Eight.

CIIT - CENTERS FOR HEALTH RESEARCH

Human Resources
PO Box 12137, Research Triangle Park, NC, 27709, United States of America
Tel: (1) 919 558 1331
Fax: (1) 919 558 1430
Email: bramlage@ciit.org
www: http://www.ciit.org
Contact: Human Resources

Founded in 1974, the CIIT - Centers for Health Research is a non-profit toxicology research institute dedicated to providing an improved scientific basis for understanding and assessing the potential adverse effects of chemicals, pharmaceuticals and consumer products on human health. Many CIIT researchers are on the faculties of the University of North Carolina at Chapel Hill, North Carolina State University in Raleigh, and Duke University in Durham, the three institutions that form North Carolina's Research Triangle. CIIT is supported by 36 major companies and the American Chemistry Council.

CIIT - Centers for Health Research Postdoctoral Fellowships
Subjects: Toxicology, including genetic toxicology, biochemical toxicology, pathology, teratology, carcinogenesis, inhalation toxicology, risk assessment and molecular biology.
Purpose: To support persons during further training in toxicology at the Institute.
Eligibility: Open to those who hold a recently awarded PhD degree in a discipline related to toxicology. Applicants holding a recently awarded DVM or MD degree are expected to have substantial research experience. Candidates on the J-1 Exchange Visitor Program are approved.
Level of Study: Postdoctorate.
Type: Fellowship.
Value: Varies, from US$34,000 depending upon the number of years of experience.
Length of Study: Two-three years.
Frequency: Varies.
Study Establishment: CIIT.
Country of Study: United States of America.
No. of awards offered: Varies.
Application Procedure: Applicants must apply for information, available on request or from the website.
Closing Date: Applications are accepted at any time.
Additional Information: Fellowships are granted only for conduct of research at the Institute's facility in Research Triangle Park, NC.

CIIT - Centers for Health Research Postdoctoral Traineeships
Subjects: Fields related to toxicology.
Purpose: To support persons holding a DVM or MD degree who are currently enrolled in a programme of study leading to the PhD degree. Trainees will pursue a PhD while conducting dissertation research at CIIT.
Eligibility: Open to persons who have recently obtained the DVM or MD degree and who have been accepted into a course of advanced study in a subject related to toxicology by a degree granting institution, and who agree to conduct their dissertation research at CIIT. The candidate must be enrolled in an accredited degree granting institution for the duration of the programme.
Level of Study: Postdoctorate.

Value: Varies, from US$34,000 depending upon the number of years of experience.
Frequency: Varies.
Study Establishment: The Institute's facility in Research Triangle Park, North Carolina.
Country of Study: United States of America.
No. of awards offered: Varies.
Application Procedure: Applicants must apply for information, available on request or from the website.
Additional Information: These traineeships are only available for conduct of research at CIIT under the guidance of a CIIT staff scientist.

CIIT - Centers for Health Research Predoctoral Traineeships
Subjects: Fields related to toxicology including biochemistry, pharmacology, chemistry, zoology and biology, etc.
Purpose: To support persons enrolled in a programme of study leading to a doctoral degree.
Eligibility: Open to persons who have been accepted into a course of graduate study in a subject related to toxicology by a degree granting institution.
Level of Study: Postgraduate.
Value: US$8,000-12,000 per year, plus tuition and fees.
Frequency: Annual.
Study Establishment: The University of North Carolina at Chapel Hill, North Carolina State University or Duke University in the Research Triangle area, for the duration of the programme.
Country of Study: United States of America.
No. of awards offered: Four-six.
Application Procedure: Applicants must apply for information, available on request or from website.
Additional Information: Preference is given to individuals who wish to conduct their dissertation research at CIIT in conjunction with local university programmes of study.

CITY UNIVERSITY BUSINESS SCHOOL (CUBS)

Frobisher Crescent
Barbican Centre, London, EC2Y 8HB, England
Tel: (44) 20 7040 8607
Fax: (44) 20 7040 8898
Email: cubs-postgrad@city.ac.uk
www: http://www.business.city.ac.uk
Contact: Ms Gina Newson

City University Business School (CUBS) has always taken pride in its academic credentials. Annually rated among the world's top business schools, it is also accredited by the Association of MBAs (AMBA and EQUIS). Located in the City of London, it is at the heart of one of the world's most dynamic business centres. The MBA programme provides extraordinary flexibility to tailor the content of programmes to suit students' goals and future plans.

CUBS MBA Studentships
Subjects: MBA.
Purpose: In collaboration with leading companies worldwide, CUBS offer an MBA studentship scheme to exceptional candidates who will add distinction to the programme. These are given to candidates who have demonstrated considerable ability in their previous studies and work experience and have gained or expect to gain high scores in the Graduate Management Admissions Test.
Level of Study: Postgraduate, MBA.
Type: Studentship.
Value: Up to full fees.
Length of Study: One year.
Frequency: Annual.
Study Establishment: CUBS.
Country of Study: England.

Application Procedure: Applicants must print out an application form from the website or contact the admissions office.

CLARA HASKIL COMPETITION

rue du Conseil 31, Vevey, CH-1800, Switzerland
Tel: (41) 21 922 6704
Fax: (41) 21 922 6734
Email: clara.haskil@smile.ch
www: http://www.regart.ch/clara-haskil
Contact: Mr Patrick Peikert, Director

The Clara Haskil Association exists to recognise and help a young pianist whose approach to piano interpretation is of the same spirit that constantly inspired Clara Haskil, and that she illustrated so perfectly.

Clara Haskil Competition

Subjects: Piano performance.
Purpose: To recognise and financially help a young pianist.
Eligibility: Open to pianists of any nationality and either sex, who are no more than 27 years of age.
Level of Study: Postgraduate.
Type: Prize.
Value: Swiss franc 20,000.
Frequency: Every two years.
Country of Study: Any country.
No. of awards offered: One.
Application Procedure: Applicants must pay an entry fee of swiss franc 250.
Closing Date: May 31st.
No. of awards given last year: One.
No. of applicants last year: 100.
Additional Information: The competition is usually held during the last weeks of August or the beginning of September.

CLAUDE HARRIS LEON FOUNDATION

PO Box 13187
Mowbray, Cape Town, Western Cape, 7705, South Africa
Tel: (27) 21 531 6910
Fax: (27) 21 531 6910
Email: tanya@conferencewise.co.za
www: http://www.leonfoundation.co.za
Contact: Mrs T Stone, Administration Officer

The Claude Harris Leon Foundation is a charitable trust resulting from a bequest by Claude Leon (1184-1972). The Foundation offers postdoctoral fellowships which are awarded for research in the faculties of science, engineering and medical sciences to be conducted at universities and technikons in South Africa.

Claude Harris Leon Foundation Postdoctoral Fellowship Award

Subjects: Science, engineering and medical sciences.
Purpose: To improve the building of research capacity at South African universities and technikons.
Eligibility: Open to South African and foreign nationals. The fellowships are awarded on a competitive basis, taking the applicant's academic achievements and potential as researchers into account.
Level of Study: Postdoctorate.
Type: Fellowship.
Value: Rand 80,000 per year.
Length of Study: Two years.
Frequency: Annual.
Study Establishment: Universities and technikons.
Country of Study: South Africa.
No. of awards offered: More than 15.

Application Procedure: Applicants must complete an application form.
Closing Date: May.
Funding: Private.
Contributor: The Claude Harris Leon Foundation.
No. of awards given last year: 15.
No. of applicants last year: 16.

CLEMSON UNIVERSITY

MBA Office
Admissions Office
124 Sirrine Hall, Clemson, SC, 29634-1315, United States of America
Tel: (1) 864 656 3975
Fax: (1) 864 656 0947
Email: mba@clemson.edu
www: http://www.clemson.edu
Contact: Ms Martha Duke, Associate Director

Clemson Graduate Assistantships

Subjects: MBA.
Eligibility: Decisions regarding the awarding of these assistantships and the duties and work period assigned are separately determined by each university department or office that employs graduate assistants.
Level of Study: MBA.
Value: The assistantships pay stipends starting at US$6.18 per hour. The pay depends upon job duties and candidate qualifications. In addition, graduate assistants are granted partial remission of academic fees and enjoy some benefits provided to University faculty and staff.
Frequency: On an annual or nine month basis.
Study Establishment: Clemson University.
Country of Study: United States of America.
No. of awards offered: Varies.
Application Procedure: Applicants must contact the various university departments or offices for information, or submit a general application with a curriculum vitae to the MBA office.
Additional Information: Due to the heavy course load required of full-time MBA students, MBAs with graduate assistantships are limited to working 10 hours per week.

Clemson University Fellowships

Subjects: MBA.
Eligibility: Candidates must be full-time first year graduate students. The fellowships will be awarded based on academic scores and departmental recommendations.
Level of Study: MBA.
Type: A variable number of fellowships.
Frequency: Annual.
Study Establishment: Clemson University.
Country of Study: United States of America.
No. of awards offered: One or two.

CLEVELAND INSTITUTE OF MUSIC

11201 East Boulevard, Cleveland, OH, 44106, United States of America
Tel: (1) 216 795 3192
Fax: (1) 216 795 3141
Email: bxd38@po.cwru.edu
www: http://www.cim.edu
Contact: Ms Beverly W Dalheim, Director of Financial Aid

The Cleveland Institute of Music's mission is to provide talented students with a professional, world class education in the art of music. The Institute ranks among the top tier music schools across the nation, granting degrees up to the doctoral level. More than 80 per cent of the Institute's alumni perform in major national and international orchestras and opera companies, while others hold prominent teaching positions.

Cleveland Institute of Music Scholarships and Accompanying Fellowships

Subjects: Music.
Eligibility: Candidates for the Teaching Fellowships should have a Bachelor of music degree or equivalent and must be proficient in English.
Level of Study: Graduate, Postgraduate.
Type: Fellowship or scholarship.
Value: US$1,000-19,000 for scholarships and U$1,000-2,500 for accompanying fellowships. No travel grants are provided.
Length of Study: One year for scholarships or from August to the following June for accompanying fellowships. Scholarships are renewable.
Frequency: Annual.
Study Establishment: The Cleveland Institute of Music.
Country of Study: United States of America.
No. of awards offered: Approx. 350 scholarships and 30 accompanying fellowships.
Application Procedure: Applicants must apply online.
Closing Date: March 1st.
Funding: Private.

COLLEGE OF OCCUPATIONAL THERAPISTS

106-114 Borough High Street
Southwark, London, SE1 1LB, England
Tel: (44) 20 7357 6480
Fax: (44) 20 7207 9612
Contact: Ms Lesley Gleaves

The College of Occupational Therapists is the professional body for occupational therapy in the United Kingdom. The College promotes the profession and standards of good practice in occupational therapy, education and research.

Agnes Storar/Constance Owens Fund

Subjects: Occupational therapy.
Purpose: To provide travel bursaries for occupational therapy teachers in recognised schools of occupational therapy to travel abroad to observe the practice and teaching of occupational therapy or to attend relevant international conferences.
Eligibility: Open to occupational therapy teachers in recognised schools of occupational therapy. Applicants must be members of the BAOT for the two years immediately prior to the date of application.
Level of Study: Unrestricted.
Value: UK £400, but may be subject to change, so please contact the organisation.
Frequency: Three times each year.
Country of Study: Outside the United Kingdom.
Application Procedure: Applicants must complete an application pack, available from the organisation or from the website.
Closing Date: Last Friday of November, March or July.
Funding: Private.

Farrer-Brown Professional Development Fund

Subjects: Occupational therapy.
Purpose: The development and improvement of professional aspects of occupational therapy.
Eligibility: Applicants must have been members of the BAOT for the two years immediately prior to the date of application.
Level of Study: Professional development.
Value: Varies.
Frequency: Annual.

Country of Study: Any country.
No. of awards offered: Varies.
Application Procedure: Applicants must complete an application pack, available from the organisation or from the website.
Closing Date: Last Friday in November.
Funding: Private.

The HAS Charitable Trust

Subjects: Occupational therapy.
Eligibility: Applicants must be state registered occupational therapists or support workers, have been members of the BAOT for at least two consecutive years immediately prior to the date of application, be working in an area which makes a significant contribution to the National Health Service, Social Services or the voluntary sector and be undertaking research or studies which will contribute to patient and client care.
Level of Study: Professional development, Research.
Type: Scholarship.
Value: Up to UK £5,000 for occupational therapists registered for a research degree (PhD or equivalent), up to UK £2,500 for occupational therapists studying for a taught Master's degree, up to UK £750 each for post-qualifying courses which contribute to professional development, and up to UK £5,000 for support workers. These amounts may be subject to change so please consult the organisation.
Frequency: Annual.
Country of Study: United Kingdom.
No. of awards offered: Varies.
Application Procedure: Applicants must complete an application pack, available from the organisation or from the website.
Closing Date: Last Friday in November.
Contributor: Charities.

Margaret Dawson Fund

Subjects: Occupational therapy.
Purpose: To provide travel bursaries for occupational therapists or final year occupational therapy students to travel abroad to observe the practice of occupational therapy or to attend relevant international conferences.
Eligibility: Open to occupational therapists in clinical practice who have been members of the BAOT for two consecutive years immediately prior to the date of application, and final year occupational therapy students.
Level of Study: Professional development.
Value: UK £200, but may be subject to change, so please consult the organisation.
Frequency: Three times each year.
Country of Study: Outside the United Kingdom.
Application Procedure: Applicants must complete an application pack, available from the organisation or from the website.
Closing Date: Last Friday in November, March or July.
Funding: Private.

Pressalit Fellowship Award

Subjects: Occupational therapy.
Purpose: To support an individual or a group of occupational therapists in their education and research.
Eligibility: Restricted to BAOT members who have held uninterrupted membership for at least two consecutive years prior to the date of application.
Level of Study: Professional development, Research.
Type: Award.
Value: UK £1,000 with an additional UK £500 available for equipment. These amounts may be subject to change, so please consult the organisation.
Frequency: Annual.
Country of Study: Any country.
No. of awards offered: One.
Application Procedure: Applicants must complete an application pack, available from the organisation or from the website.
Closing Date: Last Friday in November.

Rompa Quality of Life Award

Subjects: Occupational therapy.

Purpose: For projects, completed or planned, and a piece of research, in train or implemented, that has improved the quality of life for people with sensory impairments.

Eligibility: Restricted to BAOT members who have held uninterrupted membership for at least two years immediately prior to the date of application.

Level of Study: Graduate, Professional development.

Type: Award.

Value: UK £800 with an additional UK £500 available for equipment. These amounts may be subject to change, so please consult the organisation.

Frequency: Annual.

Country of Study: Any country.

Application Procedure: Applicants must complete an application pack, available from the organisation or from the website. Applications should be supported by a descriptive portfolio of the project or research.

Closing Date: Last Friday in November.

Speechmark Bursary

Subjects: Occupational therapy.

Purpose: To fund research visits or project work outside the applicant's country of work. The bursary favours projects that are of direct benefit to people in underprivileged circumstances.

Eligibility: Restricted to BAOT members who have held uninterrupted membership for at least two consecutive years immediately prior to the date of application.

Level of Study: Research.

Type: Bursary.

Value: UK £750 but may be subject to change, so please consult the organisation.

Frequency: Annual.

Country of Study: Any country.

No. of awards offered: One.

Application Procedure: Applicants must complete an application pack, available from the organisation or from the website.

Closing Date: Last Friday in November.

COLT FOUNDATION

New Lane, Havant, Hampshire, PO9 2LY, England
Tel: (44) 23 9249 1400
Fax: (44) 23 9249 1363
Email: jackie.douglas@uk.coltgroup.com
www: http://www.coltfoundation.org
Contact: Ms Jackie Douglas, Director

The primary interest of the Colt Foundation is the promotion of research into medical and environmental problems created by commerce and industry, particularly aimed at discovering the cause of illnesses arising from conditions at the place of work. The Foundation also makes grants to students taking higher degrees in related subjects.

Colt Foundation PhD Fellowship

Subjects: Medical and natural sciences including public health and hygiene, sports medicine, biological and life sciences, physiology or toxicology.

Purpose: To encourage the young scientists of the future.

Eligibility: Open to any student proposing to take a PhD in the correct subject area.

Level of Study: Doctorate.

Type: Fellowship.

Value: UK £46,500 over three years.

Length of Study: Normally three years.

Frequency: Annual.

Application Procedure: Applicants must visit the website.

Closing Date: Normally October 31st.

No. of awards given last year: Two.

COLUMBIA UNIVERSITY

621 Dodge Hall, New York, NY, 10027, United States of America
Tel: (1) 212 854 3331
Fax: (1) 212 678 4817
Email: webmaster@columbia.edu
www: http://www.columbia.edu
Contact: Awards Committee

Joseph H Bearns Prize in Music

Subjects: Musical composition.

Purpose: To encourage talented young people in the United States of America.

Eligibility: Open to United States citizens who are at least 18 and no more than 25 years of age on January 1st in the award year. A previous winner of the Bearns Prize may compete for a second time, but not two years in succession.

Level of Study: Unrestricted.

Type: Prize.

Value: US$3,000 and US$2,000.

Frequency: Annual.

Country of Study: United States of America.

No. of awards offered: Two.

Application Procedure: Applicants must write for details.

Closing Date: February 15th.

COMMITTEE ON SCIENCE AND TECHNOLOGY IN DEVELOPING COUNTRIES (COSTED)

24 Gandhi Mandap Road, Madras, 600025, India
Tel: (91) 44 441 9466
Fax: (91) 44 491 4543
Email: costed@vsnl.com
Contact: Scientific Secretary

The Committee on Science and Technology in Developing Countries (COSTED) of the International Council for Science is mandated to promote science and technology in developing countries, and has been striving towards its objectives by organising scientific meetings of varying levels of relevance to these countries. UNESCO is a co-sponsor of COSTED.

COSTED Travel Fellowship

Subjects: Science or agriculture.

Purpose: To provide international travel support to scientists from developing Asian countries who wish to participate in training programmes and other scientific meetings.

Eligibility: Open to scientists from developing Asian countries who have a good publication record.

Level of Study: Postdoctorate, Professional development.

Type: Travel grant.

Value: Up to US$500 per award.

Length of Study: A maximum of three months.

Frequency: Dependent on funds available.

Country of Study: Any country.

No. of awards offered: Approx. 25.

Application Procedure: Applicants must complete an application form, available on request from the scientific secretary.

Closing Date: At least three months prior to the proposed meeting or training programme.

Funding: Government.

THE COMMONWEALTH DEPARTMENT OF EDUCATION, SCIENCE AND TRAINING (DEST)

Research Grants & Training Section
Loc 731
GPO Box 9880, Canberra, ACT, 2601, Australia
Tel: (61) 2 6240 8111
Fax: (61) 2 6240 9781
Email: rbfellow@deetya.gov.au
www: http://www.deet.gov.au
Contact: Research Grants & Training Section

The Commonwealth Department of Education, Science and Training (DEST) funds the International Postgraduate Research Scholarships (IPRS) scheme to enable international students to undertake a postgraduate research qualification in Australia and gain experience with leading Australian researchers.

DEST (Department of Education, Science and Training) International Postgraduate Research Scholarships Scheme (IPRS)

Subjects: All subjects.
Purpose: To assist study leading to a PhD or to a Master's research degree at an Australian university.
Eligibility: Applicants must be citizens of an overseas country, have commenced full-time study for a higher degree by research in the year for which the award is to be allocated, be enrolled in an area of research concentration (an area of research in which the participating institute has particular strength), and satisfy all institutional academic entry requirements for a Master's by research or doctoral programme, including English proficiency levels set by the individual institutions. Applicants must not hold a PhD degree deemed equivalent of an Australian PhD degree, or hold an Australian equivalent Master's by research degree. Residents of New Zealand are not eligible.
Level of Study: Doctorate, Postgraduate, Research.
Type: Scholarship.
Value: Tuition fees at individual institutions and health insurance premiums.
Length of Study: Two years for Master's and four years for doctorate.
Frequency: Annual.
Country of Study: Australia.
No. of awards offered: 310.
Application Procedure: Applicants must apply directly to participating institutions.
Closing Date: August 30th.
Funding: Government.
No. of awards given last year: 310.
Additional Information: Further information is available from the website http://www.dest.gov.au/highered/research/aiprss.htm.

THE COMMONWEALTH FUND OF NEW YORK

Harkness House
1 East 75th Street, New York, NY, 10021-2692, United States of America
Tel: (1) 212 606 3809
Fax: (1) 212 606 3875
Email: ro@cmwf.org
www: http://www.cmwf.org
Contact: Ms Robin Osborn, International Programs in Health Policy Director

The Commonwealth Fund is a philanthropic foundation established in 1918. The Fund's national programme areas include improving health care services, bettering the health of minorities, advancing the well being of elderly people, and developing the capacities of children and youth. The Fund's international programme seeks to build a network of policy orientated health researchers to stimulate innovative policies.

Harkness Fellowships in Health Care Policy

Subjects: Health care policy and health services research.
Purpose: To encourage the professional development of promising health care policy researchers and practitioners whose multinational experience and outlook will contribute to innovation in health care policy and practice in the United States of America and their home countries.
Eligibility: Open to individuals who have completed a Master's degree or PhD in health services or health policy research. Applicants must also have shown significant promise as a policy orientated researcher or practitioner, eg. physicians or health services managers, journalists and government officials, with a strong interest in policy issues, be at the research fellow to senior lecturer level, if academically based, be in their late 20s to early 40s, and have been nominated by their department chair or the director of their institution.
Level of Study: Postgraduate, Professional development.
Type: Fellowship.
Value: Basic expenses of travel, residence and research, up to a maximum of US$75,000.
Length of Study: One year. A minimum of four months must be spent in the United States of America.
Frequency: Annual.
Study Establishment: An academic or other institution.
Country of Study: United States of America.
No. of awards offered: Two for Australia, two for New Zealand and four-five for the United Kingdom.
Application Procedure: Applicants must complete a formal application and should write to the correct country address for further information. Applicants in the United Kingdom should apply to the main address in New York.
Closing Date: October 1st.
Funding: Private.
Contributor: The Commonwealth Fund.
Additional Information: Successful candidates will have a policy orientated research project, ideally involving cross-national comparisons, on a topic relevant to the Fund's national programme areas. Projects will be supervised by senior researchers and each Fellow will be expected to produce a publishable report contributing to a better understanding of health policy issues.

For further information contact:

Associate Professor & Director
(Australia)
Center for Health Economics Research & Evaluation
University of Sydney
Mallett Street Campus
88 Mallett Street
Level 6
Building F, Camperdown, NSW, 2050, Australia
Tel: (61) 2 9351 0900
Fax: (61) 2 9351 0930
Email: sylviab@pub.health.usyd.edu.au
Contact: Dr Jane Hall, Associate Professor & Director

Policy Representative, Executive Director
(New Zealand)
New Zealand-United States Educational Foundation
PO Box 3465, Wellington, New Zealand
Tel: (64) 4 722 065
Fax: (64) 4 995 364
Email: jennifer@fulbright.org.nz
Contact: Ms Jennifer M Gill, Policy Representative, Executive Director

Ian Axford (New Zealand) Fellowships in Public Policy

Subjects: Public policy.
Purpose: To provide American professionals with the opportunity to study, travel, and gain practical experience in public policy in New

Zealand, including first hand knowledge of economic, social and political reforms, and management of the government sector.

Eligibility: Open to mid career professionals active in any part of the public, business or non-profit sectors. Applicants must be citizens of the United States of America with at least five years of experience in their professions. There are no formal age limits, but the focus of the fellowships is on mid career development and successful candidates are likely to be in their late 20s to early 40s.

Level of Study: Professional development.

Type: Fellowship.

Value: Where possible the candidates are expected to obtain paid leave. The basic award is not intended to match Fellows' United States salaries. Fellows on paid leave will receive an allowance of new zealand $1,700 per month on top of their salaries and will be entitled to family and other allowances. Fellows unable to obtain paid leave will receive a living allowance of new zealand $4,000 per month, intended to cover basic expenses of residence in New Zealand, and will be entitled to family and other allowances. Eligibility for the family allowance is based on a Fellow's family status at the time of the interview and will remain unchanged throughout the tenure.

Length of Study: Six-nine months.

Frequency: Annual.

Country of Study: New Zealand.

Application Procedure: Applicants must complete a formal application, including a project proposal. Candidates should show that their proposed project will inform policy in New Zealand and the United States and contribute something of value to the policy of their field.

Closing Date: March 15th.

Funding: Commercial, Government.

Additional Information: Applications are welcome equally from men and women, from members of any ethnic group and regardless of physical disabilities.

COMMONWEALTH OF AUSTRALIA

Participatory Programme
Australian Biological Resources Study
PO Box 787, Canberra, ACT, 2601, Australia
Tel: (61) 2 6250 9554
Fax: (61) 2 6250 9555
Email: liz.visher@ea.gov.au
www: http://www.ea.gov.au/biodiversity/abrs
Contact: Ms Liz Visher, Business Manager

The Australian Government established the Australian Biological Resources Study (ABRS) to co-ordinate research in taxonomy, the science which discovers, identifies, describes, classifies and records the distribution of flora and fauna. Since its inception, the ABRS has taken active responsibility for funding taxonomic research on Australia's diverse flora and fauna resources, and leads the world with its internationally recognised series of publications. The ABRS aims to provide fundamental and comprehensive information on all forms of Australian plants and animal life for present and future generations.

ABRS Bursaries

Subjects: Biology.

Purpose: To allow students to travel to national or international conferences.

Level of Study: Postgraduate.

Type: Travel bursary.

Country of Study: Australia.

No. of awards offered: 10.

Application Procedure: Applicants must obtain and complete an application form, available with guidelines for applicants from the contact office, or from the website.

Closing Date: Please contact the organisation.

Additional Information: Further information is available from the website.

The ABRS Postgraduate Scholarships Scheme

Subjects: Biology.

Purpose: To foster research training and provide awards for outstanding students wishing to pursue higher degrees in taxonomy.

Eligibility: Please contact the organisation for details.

Level of Study: Postgraduate.

Type: Scholarship.

Frequency: Annual.

Country of Study: Australia.

No. of awards offered: One.

Application Procedure: Applicants must obtain and complete an application form, available with guidelines for applicants from the contact office, or from the website.

Closing Date: Please contact the organisation.

Additional Information: Further information is available from the website.

The ABRS Research Grants Scheme

Subjects: Botany, zoology, taxonomy and biogeography.

Purpose: To support the documentation of Australia's biological diversity and to improve and increase the national taxonomic effort. The intent of the scheme is to support rigorous taxonomic treatment at a species level and work contributing to regional or continental generic or higher level reviews, including the development of identification tools.

Eligibility: Open to investigators of any nationality.

Level of Study: Postdoctorate, Postgraduate.

Type: Grant.

Value: Contact the organisation for details.

Frequency: Annual.

Country of Study: Australia.

No. of awards offered: Approx. 50-70 depending on funds available.

Application Procedure: Applicants must obtain and complete an application form, available with guidelines from the contact office, or from the website.

Closing Date: Please contact the organisation.

Funding: Government.

No. of awards given last year: 66.

Additional Information: Further information is available from the website.

Ebbe Nielsen Regional Scholarship

Subjects: Taxonomy.

Purpose: To foster research training in taxonomy in the Australasian region focused on Australasian flora and fauna, and thereby promoting outstanding international students pursuing higher degrees in taxonomy.

Eligibility: Eligibility requirements are available on the website.

Level of Study: Postgraduate, Predoctorate.

Type: Scholarship.

Value: A stipend, research support and relocation funding.

Length of Study: Varies.

Frequency: Annual.

Country of Study: Australia.

No. of awards offered: One.

Application Procedure: Applicants must complete an application form, available from the website.

Closing Date: Please contact the organisation.

Additional Information: This memorial training award, in the form of an international postgraduate scholarship, was established following the death in March 2001 of Dr Ebbe Nielsen, an outstanding taxonomist from CSIRO Division of Entomology.

COMMONWEALTH SCHOLARSHIP COMMISSION IN THE UNITED KINGDOM

c/o Association of Commonwealth Universities
John Foster House
36 Gordon Square, London, WC1H 0PF, England
Tel: (44) 20 7380 6700
Fax: (44) 20 7387 2655
www: http://www.acu.ac.uk
Contact: Ms Mary C Denyer, Awards Administrator

The Commonwealth Scholarship Commission in the United Kingdom was set up as the body responsible for the United Kingdom's participation in the Commonwealth Scholarship and Fellowship Plan in 1959. It is responsible for the selection and placement of recipients coming to the United Kingdom and for the selection of candidates from the United Kingdom to be put forward for awards in other Commonwealth countries.

Commonwealth Academic Staff Scholarships

Subjects: All subjects.
Purpose: To help universities in the developing countries of the Commonwealth to increase the numbers and enhance the experience of their locally born staff. The scholarships are intended to enable promising staff members from universities and similar institutions in the developing Commonwealth to obtain experience in a university or other appropriate institution in the United Kingdom.
Eligibility: Open to Commonwealth citizens or British protected persons permanently resident in a developing country of the Commonwealth, who should hold, or be about to obtain, a degree or an equivalent qualification, and should already hold a teaching appointment in a university or similar institution or have the assurance of such an appointment on his or her return. Candidates should be under 42 years of age at the time the award is taken up. All candidates must have sufficient competence in English to profit from the proposed study. These awards are not given to Indian nationals.
Level of Study: Postgraduate.
Type: Scholarship.
Value: The cost of the return air fare to the United Kingdom, approved tuition, laboratory and examination fees, a personal maintenance allowance at the rate of UK £594 per month or UK £713 a month for those studying at institutions in the London Metropolitan area, a grant for books and equipment, a grant towards the expense of preparing a thesis or dissertation, where applicable, a grant for approved travel within the United Kingdom, an initial clothing allowance in special cases, and in certain circumstances a marriage and child allowance. The emoluments are not subject to United Kingdom income tax.
Length of Study: One-three years.
Frequency: Annual.
Study Establishment: A university or comparable institution.
Country of Study: United Kingdom.
No. of awards offered: 45-50.
Application Procedure: Applicants must be nominated by the vice chancellor of a United Kingdom university, the vice chancellor of the university on whose permanent staff the applicant serves or is to serve. Heads of Bangladeshi universities should send their nominations to the University Grants Commission in Dhaka and applications from Pakistan should be channelled through the Educational Secretary, Government of Pakistan, International Co-operation Manager, Ministry of Education, Islamabad.
Closing Date: December 31st.
Additional Information: Scholars are required to sign an undertaking to return to and resume their academic post in their own country on completion of the scholarship.

Commonwealth Fellowships

Subjects: All subjects.
Purpose: To help universities in the developing countries of the Commonwealth to increase the numbers and enhance the experience of their locally born staff. The fellowships are intended to enable promising staff members from universities and similar

institutions in the developing Commonwealth to receive training and experience in a university or other appropriate institution in the United Kingdom.
Eligibility: Open to Commonwealth citizens and to British protected persons permanently resident in a developing Commonwealth country. Preference is given to candidates between 28 and 50 years of age. Candidates must have completed a Doctoral degree more than five but not more than 10 years ago, and should have had at least two years' experience as a staff member of a university or similar institution in their own country.
Level of Study: Postdoctorate.
Type: Fellowship.
Value: UK £943 per month or UK £1,132 for those studying at institutions in the London Metropolitan area, approved airfares to and from the a grant for books and equipment, a grant for approved travel within the United Kingdom, an initial clothing allowance in special cases, and in certain circumstances a marriage and child allowance. The emoluments are not subject to United Kingdom income tax.
Length of Study: 6 months.
Frequency: Annual.
Study Establishment: A university or comparable institution.
Country of Study: United Kingdom.
No. of awards offered: Approx. 50.
Closing Date: December 31st.
Funding: Government.
Additional Information: Fellows are required to sign an undertaking to return to and resume their academic post in their country on completion of the fellowships. Candidates must be nominated by the vice-chancellor of the university on whose permanent staff the applicant serves (heads of Indian universities should send their nominations to the University Grants Commission in New Delhi, heads of Pakistani universities to the Ministry of Education in Islamabad, heads of Sri Lankan universities to the Ministry of Higher Education in Colombo and heads of Bangladeshi universities to the University Grants Commission in Dhaka). The fellowship may not be held concurrently with other awards or with paid employment.

Commonwealth Scholarships

Subjects: Arts, social studies, pure science, technology, medicine, dentistry, agriculture, forestry and veterinary science.
Purpose: To enable students of high intellectual promise to pursue studies in Commonwealth countries other than their own so that on their return home they can make a distinctive contribution to life in their own countries and to mutual understanding in the Commonwealth.
Eligibility: Open to Commonwealth citizens under 35 years of age who are normally resident in some part of the Commonwealth other than the particular awarding country. Scholarships are intended for young graduates of high intellectual promise who may be expected to make a significant contribution to their own countries on their return from postgraduate study overseas. Candidates should at the time of nomination have graduated from a first or Master's degree within the last ten years.
Level of Study: Postgraduate.
Type: Scholarship.
Value: The emoluments for scholarships include fares to and from the United Kingdom, payment of tuition fees, allowances for books, special clothing and local travel, and a personal maintenance allowance.
Length of Study: One-three academic years.
Frequency: Annual.
Study Establishment: Universities, colleges and other educational institutions.
Country of Study: Designated Commonwealth countries other than candidates' own.
No. of awards offered: Approx. 300 per year.
Application Procedure: Applicants must apply to the appropriate scholarship agency in their country of normal residence. These agencies distribute prospectuses and application forms for the various awards and will, generally speaking, be the best local centres to gain information from.

Closing Date: Varies according to the country in which the candidate applies, usually some 12-18 months before the intended period of study.
Funding: Government.
Additional Information: Award holders must undertake to return to their own countries on completion of their studies overseas. Commonwealth Split-Site Doctoral Scholarships are available and intended for junior faculty or students of developing institutions who are studying for a doctoral degree at their home institution and would benefit from one year of full-time study in the United Kingdom (or, in exceptional circumstances, for two six month periods) as part of their PhD programme. Candidates must be nominated in the context of a departmental or institutional link with a United Kingdom institution already in operation or currently under negotiation. At the time of application candidates must be registered for a PhD or have been accepted to undertake PhD research at a home institution.

CONCORDIA UNIVERSITY

1455 de Maisonneuve Boulevard West, Montréal, QC, H3G 1M8, Canada
Tel: (1) 514 848 3801
Fax: (1) 514 848 2812
Email: awardsgs@vax2.concordia.ca
www: http://www.concordia.ca
Contact: Ms Patricia Verret, Graduate Awards Manager

Concordia University is the result of the 1974 merger between Sir George Williams University and Loyola College. The University incorporates superior teaching methods with an inter-disciplinary approach to learning and is dedicated to offering the best possible scholarship to the student body and to promoting research beneficial to society.

Bank of Montreal Pauline Varnier Fellowship
Subjects: Business and administration management.
Eligibility: Open to women with two years of cumulative business experience who are Canadian citizens or landed immigrants intending to pursue a full-time course of study for the MBA. This is an entrance fellowship.
Level of Study: MBA.
Type: Fellowship.
Value: Canadian $10,000 per year.
Length of Study: Two years.
Frequency: Annual.
Study Establishment: Concordia University.
Country of Study: Canada.
No. of awards offered: One.
Application Procedure: Applicants must submit a completed application form, three letters of recommendation and official transcripts of all university studies by the closing date.
Closing Date: April 30th.
Funding: Private.
No. of awards given last year: One.
Additional Information: Academic merit is the prime consideration in the granting of the awards.

Concordia University Graduate Fellowships
Subjects: All subjects.
Eligibility: Open to graduates of any nationality. Candidates must be planning to pursue full-time Master's or doctoral studies at the university.
Level of Study: Postgraduate.
Type: Fellowship.
Value: Canadian $2,900 per term for Master's level and canadian $3,600 per term for doctoral level.
Length of Study: A maximum of four terms at the Master's level and nine terms at the doctoral level, calculated from the date of entry into the programme.
Frequency: Annual.

Study Establishment: Concordia University.
Country of Study: Canada.
No. of awards offered: Varies.
Application Procedure: Applicants must submit a completed application form, three letters of recommendation and official transcripts of all university studies by the closing date.
Closing Date: February 1st.
No. of awards given last year: 19.
Additional Information: Academic merit is the prime consideration in the granting of the award.

David J Azrieli Graduate Fellowship
Subjects: All subjects.
Eligibility: Open to Master's or doctoral students of any nationality. Candidates must be planning to pursue full time Master's or doctoral study at the university.
Level of Study: Postgraduate.
Type: Fellowship.
Value: Canadian $15,000 per year.
Length of Study: One year, non renewable.
Frequency: Annual.
Study Establishment: Concordia University.
Country of Study: Canada.
No. of awards offered: One.
Application Procedure: Applicants must submit a completed application form, three letters of recommendation and official transcripts of all university studies by the closing date.
Closing Date: February 1st.
Funding: Private.
No. of awards given last year: One.
Additional Information: Academic merit is the prime consideration in the granting of the award.

J W McConnell Memorial Fellowships
Subjects: All subjects.
Eligibility: Open to Canadian citizens and permanent residents of Canada who are planning to pursue full-time Master's or doctoral study at the university. Fellowships are awarded on academic merit.
Level of Study: Postgraduate.
Type: Fellowship.
Value: Canadian $2,900 per term at the Master's level and canadian $3,600 per term at the doctoral level.
Length of Study: A maximum of four terms at the Master's level and nine terms at the doctoral level, calculated from the date of entry into the programme.
Frequency: Annual.
Study Establishment: Concordia University.
Country of Study: Canada.
No. of awards offered: Varies.
Application Procedure: Applicants must submit a completed application form, three letters of recommendation and official transcripts of all university studies by the closing date.
Closing Date: February 1st.
Funding: Private.
No. of awards given last year: 18.
Additional Information: Academic merit is the prime consideration in the granting of the awards.

John W O'Brien Graduate Fellowship
Subjects: All subjects.
Purpose: Awarded to applicants in full-time study towards a Master's or doctoral degree at Concordia University.
Eligibility: Open to full-time graduate students of any nationality. Candidates must be planning to pursue full-time Master's or doctoral study at the university.
Type: Fellowship.
Value: Canadian $3,300 per term at the Master's level and canadian $4,000 per term at the doctoral level.
Length of Study: A maximum of three terms.
Frequency: Annual.
Study Establishment: Concordia University.

Country of Study: Canada.
No. of awards offered: One.
Application Procedure: Applicants must submit a completed application form, three letters of recommendation and official transcripts of all university studies by the closing date.
Closing Date: February 1st.
Funding: Private.
No. of awards given last year: One.
Additional Information: Academic merit is the prime consideration in the granting of awards.

Stanley G French Graduate Fellowship

Subjects: All subjects.
Eligibility: Open to graduates of any nationality. Candidates must be planning to pursue full-time Master's or doctoral studies at the university.
Level of Study: Postgraduate.
Type: Fellowship.
Value: Canadian $3,300 per term for Master's level and canadian $4,000 per term for doctoral level.
Length of Study: A maximum of three terms.
Frequency: Annual.
Study Establishment: Concordia University.
Country of Study: Canada.
No. of awards offered: One.
Application Procedure: Applicants must submit a completed application form, three letters of recommendation and official transcripts of all university studies by the closing date.
Closing Date: February 1st.
Funding: Private.
No. of awards given last year: One.
Additional Information: Academic merit is the prime consideration in the granting of awards.

CONGRESSIONAL BLACK CAUCUS FOUNDATION (CBCF)

1004 Pennsylvania Avenue South East, Washington, DC, 20003, United States of America
Tel: (1) 202 675 6739
Fax: (1) 202 547 3806
Email: info@cbcfonline.org
www: http://cbcfonline.org
Contact: Office of Educational Programmes

The Congressional Black Caucus Foundation (CBCF) was established in 1976 as a non-partisan, non-profit, public policy research and educational institute. The CBCF's mission is to assist the leaders of today while helping to prepare new generations of leaders for the future. The Foundation works to broaden and elevate the influence of African-Americans in the political, legislative and public policy arenas.

CBCF Congressional Fellows Program

Subjects: Political science and government, law, public policy or international affairs.
Eligibility: Applicants must be United States of America citizens.
Level of Study: Doctorate, Graduate, Postgraduate, Professional development.
Type: Fellowship.
Value: US$20,000.
Length of Study: Nine months.
Frequency: Annual.
Country of Study: United States of America.
Application Procedure: Applicants must submit a completed application form with three letters of recommendation, all college transcripts, a writing sample of up to 10 pages, a curriculum vitae and their responses to three essay questions. Applications are available on request or from the website.
Closing Date: April 1st.

Funding: Commercial, Private.

CONSERVATION AND RESEARCH FOUNDATION

Box 5261 Connecticut College, New London, CT, 06320, United States of America
Contact: Mr Richard Goodwin, Secretary

The Conservation and Research Foundation uses its resources to support organisations, projects and activities that it hopes will have a catalytic effect in enhancing the quality of life on the planet.

Conservation and Research Foundation Grants

Subjects: Environmental studies and biological science.
Purpose: To promote the conservation and enlightened use of renewable natural resources, to encourage related research in the biological sciences, to deepen the understanding of the intricate relationships between people and the environment that supports them, and to address the problem of overpopulation by promoting methods of limiting human fertility.
Eligibility: There are no eligibility restrictions.
Level of Study: Doctorate, Postdoctorate, Postgraduate.
Type: Grant.
Value: US$100-5,000.
Length of Study: Unspecified duration.
Frequency: Dependent on funds available.
Country of Study: Any country.
No. of awards offered: Varies.
Application Procedure: The present policy of the Foundation is to invite the submission of proposals. A letter of enquiry outlining the proposal may be submitted. Unsolicited applications may not be considered.
Closing Date: Applications are accepted at any time.
Funding: Private.
Contributor: The Mary B Goodwin Trust.
No. of awards given last year: 19.
No. of applicants last year: 85.
Additional Information: The Foundation does not offer scholarships.

CONSORTIUM FOR GRADUATE STUDY IN MANAGEMENT

5585 Pershing Avenue
Suite 240, St Louis, MO, 63112, United States of America
Tel: (1) 314 877 5500
Fax: (1) 314 877 5505
Email: frontdesk@cgsm.org
www: http://www.cgsm.org
Contact: Mr Charles Harper, Executive Assistant to CEO

The aim of the Consortium for Graduate Study in Management is to provide fellowships to minorities, in order to increase the percentage of these underrepresented minority groups in corporate America.

Consortium for Graduate Study in Management Fellowships for Minorities

Subjects: Business administration.
Purpose: To hasten the entry of minority men and women into management positions in business by enabling them to obtain a Master's degree.
Eligibility: Open to United States citizens who are African American, Hispanic American or Native American and who hold a Bachelor's degree in any academic discipline.
Level of Study: Postgraduate, MBA.
Type: Fellowship.

Value: To cover full tuition and required fees over two years of full-time MBA study. Additional financial aid may also be available.
Length of Study: Two years.
Frequency: Annual.
Study Establishment: Graduate schools of management at the following universities: Indiana, Michigan, New York, North Carolina, Rochester, Southern California, Texas at Austin, Virginia, Washington, Wisconsin-Madison, California-Berkeley, Carnegie Mellon, Emory and Dartmouth.
Country of Study: United States of America.
No. of awards offered: 315.
Application Procedure: Applicants must write for details.
Closing Date: February 1st.
Funding: Private.
No. of awards given last year: 201.
No. of applicants last year: 795.

COOLEY'S ANEMIA FOUNDATION

129-09 26th Avenue
Suite 203, Flushing, NY, 11354, United States of America
Tel: (1) 718 321 2873
Fax: (1) 718 321 3340
Email: info@cooleysanemia.org
www: http://www.cooleysanemia.org
Contact: Ms Sophie Buisynski, Accounting Department

Cooley's Anemia Foundation funds research to cure this fatal blood disease, supports programmes to enhance the life and quality of patients, and educates doctors, trait carriers and the public.

Cooley's Anemia Foundation Research Fellowship Grant
Subjects: Haematology.
Purpose: To promote an increased understanding of Cooley's anaemia, develop improved treatment and achieve a final cure for this life threatening genetic blood disorder.
Eligibility: Open to researchers of any nationality.
Level of Study: Postdoctorate.
Type: Fellowship.
Value: US$40,000.
Length of Study: One year.
Frequency: Annual.
Country of Study: Any country.
No. of awards offered: 10.
Application Procedure: Applicants must submit an application to the national office.
Closing Date: March 4th.
Funding: Private.
Contributor: Donations.
No. of awards given last year: 10.
No. of applicants last year: Varies.
Additional Information: Further information is available on the website.

CORNELL UNIVERSITY

Center for the Humanities
Andrew D White House
27 East Avenue, Ithaca, NY, 14853-1101, United States of America
Tel: (1) 607 255 9274
Email: hymetr-mailbox@cornell.edu
www: http://www.arts.cornell.edu/sochum
Contact: Ms Lisa Patti, Program Administrator

Cornell University is a learning community that seeks to serve society by educating the leaders of the future and extending the frontiers of knowledge. The university aims to pursue understanding beyond the limitations of existing knowledge, ideology and disciplinary structure and to affirm the value of the cultivation and enrichment of the human mind to individuals and society.

Mellon Postdoctoral Fellowships
Subjects: Arts and humanities.
Eligibility: Open to United States of America and Canadian citizens and permanent residents who have completed requirements for the PhD within the last four to five years and before the application deadline.
Level of Study: Postdoctorate.
Type: Fellowship.
Value: US$34,000.
Length of Study: Nine months.
Frequency: Annual.
Study Establishment: Cornell University.
Country of Study: United States of America.
No. of awards offered: Three-four.
Application Procedure: Applicants must write for details.
Closing Date: Postmarked January 3rd.
No. of awards given last year: Five.
No. of applicants last year: 200.
Additional Information: While in residence at Cornell, postdoctoral Fellows have department affiliation, limited teaching duties and the opportunity for scholarly work. Areas of specialisation change each year.

Society for the Humanities Postdoctoral Fellowships
Subjects: Humanities.
Eligibility: Open to holders of a PhD degree who have at least one or two years of teaching experience at the college level. Applicants should be Scholars with interests that are not confined to a narrow humanistic speciality and whose research coincides with the focal theme for the year. Fellows of the Society devote most of their time to research writing, but they are encouraged to offer a weekly seminar related to their special projects.
Level of Study: Postdoctorate.
Type: Fellowship.
Value: US$34,000.
Length of Study: One academic year.
Frequency: Annual.
Study Establishment: Cornell University.
Country of Study: United States of America.
No. of awards offered: 8-10.
Application Procedure: Applicants must contact the office to receive information on the theme and application materials.
Closing Date: Postmarked on or before October 21st.
No. of awards given last year: 10.
No. of applicants last year: 180.
Additional Information: Information about this year's theme is available upon request.

THE CORPORATION OF YADDO

Box 395, Saratoga Springs, NY, 12866, United States of America
Tel: (1) 518 584 0746
Fax: (1) 518 584 1312
Email: yaddo@yaddo.org
www: http://www.yaddo.org
Contact: Ms Lesley M Leduc, Public Affairs Co-ordinator

The Corporation of Yaddo is an artists' community located on a 400 acre estate in Saratoga Springs, New York. Its mission is to nurture the creative process by providing an opportunity for artists to work without interruption in a supportive environment. Yaddo awards approximately 200 residences per year of between two weeks to two months in length.

Yaddo Residency

Subjects: Writing, photography, drawing, sculpture, music and drama, choreography, film, painting, performance art, printmaking or video.

Purpose: To provide uninterrupted time and space for creative artists to think, experiment and create.

Eligibility: Open to all artists who are working at the professional level in their fields. Applications are welcomed from artists from the United States of America and abroad. Open to visual artists, writers, composers and artists working in film and/or video, choreography and performance art. An abiding principle at Yaddo is that applications for residency are judged on the quality of the artists' work and professional promise.

Level of Study: Professional development.

Type: Residency.

Value: Room, board and studio space. There is no stipend.

Length of Study: From two weeks to two months.

Frequency: Annual.

Study Establishment: Yaddo.

Country of Study: United States of America.

No. of awards offered: Approx. 200.

Application Procedure: Applicants must send a large stamped addressed envelope to the Admissions Department. The requirements include a completed application form, letters from two sponsors, copies of a professional curriculum vitae, work samples and the US$20 application fee.

Closing Date: January 15th or August 1st.

Funding: Private.

Contributor: Endowment.

No. of awards given last year: 200.

No. of applicants last year: 957.

THE COSTUME SOCIETY OF AMERICA (CSA)

55 Edgewater Drive
PO Box 73, Earleville, MD, 21919, United States of America
Tel: (1) 410 275 1619
Fax: (1) 410 275 8936
Email: national.office@costumesocietyamerica.com
www: http://www.costumesocietyamerica.com

The Costume Society of America (CSA) advances the global understanding of all aspects of dress and appearance. The Society seeks as members those who are involved in the study, education, collection, preservation, presentation and interpretation of dress and appearance in past, present, and future societies.

The CSA Adele Filene Travel Award

Subjects: Cultural heritage, museum studies and related areas.

Purpose: To assis students in their travel to CSA national symposia to present either a juried paper or a poster.

Eligibility: Open to currently enrolled students with CSA membership who have been accepted for presentation of a juried paper or poster at CSA national symposium.

Level of Study: Unrestricted.

Type: Travel grant.

Value: Up to US$500.

Frequency: Annual.

Country of Study: United States of America.

No. of awards offered: One-three.

Application Procedure: Applicants must send three letters of support with a copy of the juried abstract and a one page letter of application.

Closing Date: Approx. two months before the event.

No. of awards given last year: Four.

No. of applicants last year: Three.

The CSA Stella Blum Research Grant

Subjects: North American costume.

Purpose: To help accomplish the Society's mission of advancing the global understanding of all aspects of dress and appearance.

Eligibility: Open to students who are matriculating in a degree programme at an accredited institution and who are members of the Society.

Level of Study: Unrestricted.

Type: Grant.

Value: Up to US$3,000. Allowable costs include transportation to and from the research site, living expenses at the research site, supplies such as film, photographic reproductions, books, paper, computer disks, postage and telephone, and services such as typing, computer searches and graphics. Plus up to US$500 is available for travel and related expenses to present a paper based on research at the Annual Meeting and Symposium.

Frequency: Annual.

Study Establishment: An accredited institution.

Country of Study: United States of America.

No. of awards offered: One.

Application Procedure: Applicants must complete an application form, available upon request.

Closing Date: May 1st.

No. of awards given last year: One.

No. of applicants last year: Four.

Additional Information: The award will be given based on merit rather than need. Judging criteria will include creativity and innovation, specific awareness of and attention to costume matters, impact on the broad field of costume, awareness of the interdisciplinary nature of the field, ability to successfully implement the proposed project in a timely manner, and faculty advisor recommendation.

The CSA Travel Research Grant

Subjects: Textile and fashion design, museum studies and related areas.

Purpose: To allow an individual to travel to collections for research purposes.

Eligibility: Applicants must be current non student CSA members and have held membership for two years or more. They must give proof of work in progress and indicate why the particular collection is important to the project.

Level of Study: Professional development.

Type: Research grant.

Value: US$1,000.

Frequency: Annual.

Country of Study: Any country.

No. of awards offered: One.

Application Procedure: Applicants must send a letter of application of no more than two pages and include the name of the collection and projected date of visit, a description of the project underway, evidence of work accomplished to date, reasons for visiting the designated collection, projected completion date of project, what audience the project will be directed to, as well as a current curriculum vitae.

Closing Date: September 1st.

No. of awards given last year: One.

No. of applicants last year: Three.

COUNCIL FOR BRITISH ARCHAEOLOGY (CBA)

Bowes Morrell House
111 Walmgate, York, YO1 9WA, England
Tel: (44) 1904 671417
Fax: (44) 1904 671384
Email: 100271.456@compuserve.com
www: http://www.britarch.ac.uk
Contact: Finance Officer

The Council for British Archaeology (CBA) has been campaigning for the better care of Britain's archaeology for over 50 years. It works to improve awareness and enjoyment of archaeology for the benefit of all. The Council is the leading point of contact for information about the United Kingdom's historic environment.

British Archaeological Research Trust Grants

Subjects: Archaeology.

Purpose: To support personal archaeological research, particularly that which is innovative and extends the range of techniques available to archaeologists.

Eligibility: Open to United Kingdom residents. Academic qualifications are not required.

Level of Study: Unrestricted.

Type: Research grant.

Value: Up to UK £1,000.

Frequency: Annual.

Study Establishment: An approved location.

Country of Study: United Kingdom.

No. of awards offered: Two-six.

Closing Date: June 30th.

Additional Information: Grants may be held concurrently with other income.

CBA Grant for Publication

Subjects: British archaeology.

Purpose: To finance archaeological publications which contribute significantly to research on problems of national or special regional significance.

Eligibility: Open to all institutional or individual members of the council, except those already in receipt of a direct government grant.

Level of Study: Unrestricted.

Type: Grant.

Value: Usually no more than UK £1,000 but on average UK £400.

Frequency: Three times each year.

Country of Study: United Kingdom.

No. of awards offered: 10-15.

Application Procedure: Applicants must write for an application form.

Closing Date: April 1st, July 1st or December 1st.

Additional Information: No grant will be made for the publication of records or of publications based exclusively on records, or for the publication of excavation reports where the excavation has been financed by government agencies. Grants will not normally be given to finance reports other than final excavation reports.

Council for British Archaeology Challenge Funding

Subjects: Archaeology.

Purpose: To encourage voluntary effort in making original contributions to the study and care of Britain's historic environment.

Eligibility: Open to United Kingdom residents. Academic qualifications are not required.

Level of Study: Unrestricted.

Type: Research grant.

Frequency: Varies.

Country of Study: United Kingdom.

No. of awards offered: Varies.

Application Procedure: Applicants must submit a project outline.

Closing Date: Varies.

COUNCIL FOR INTERNATIONAL EXCHANGE OF SCHOLARS (CIES)

3007 Tilden Street North West
Suite 5L, Washington, DC, 20008-3009, United States of America
Tel: (1) 202 686 8664
Fax: (1) 202 362 3442
Email: scholars@cies.iie.org
www: http://www.cies.org
Contact: Ms Judy Pehrson, Director of External Relations

The Council for International Exchange of Scholars (CIES) is a private, non-profit organisation that facilitates international exchanges in higher education. Under a co-operative agreement with the United States Department of State Bureau of Educational and Cultural Affairs, it assists in the administration of the Fulbright Scholar Program for faculty and professionals. CIES is affiliated with the Institute of International Education.

Fulbright Distinguished Chairs Program

Subjects: American studies (history, politics and literature), humanities, law, social sciences, computer science and e-commerce, business and management, fine arts, mass communications and journalism.

Purpose: To increase mutual understanding between the people of the United States and other countries and to promote international educational co-operation.

Eligibility: Open to United States citizens with a PhD or equivalent qualification. Candidates should have a prominent record of scholarly achievement.

Level of Study: Postdoctorate.

Type: Distinguished lecturing.

Value: Varies by country.

Length of Study: From three months to one academic year.

Frequency: Annual.

Country of Study: European countries, Canada or Russia.

No. of awards offered: Approx. 40.

Application Procedure: Applicants must submit a letter of interest and an eight page curriculum vitae, and should telephone CIES or visit the website for more information.

Closing Date: May 1st.

Funding: Government, Private.

No. of awards given last year: 37.

No. of applicants last year: 300.

Additional Information: Applicants must contact Dario Teutonico at dteutonico@ciess.iie.org for more information.

Fulbright Postdoctoral Research and Lecturing Awards for Non-US Citizens

Subjects: All subjects.

Eligibility: Open to nationals of countries and territories having United States diplomatic or consular posts, who have a doctoral degree or equivalent qualification. Preference is given to those persons who have not had extensive previous experience in the United States.

Level of Study: Postdoctorate.

Type: Grant.

Value: A maintenance allowance and international travel expenses.

Length of Study: From three months to one academic year.

Frequency: Annual.

Country of Study: United States of America.

No. of awards offered: Varies, approx. 700.

Application Procedure: Applicants must make applications to the Binational Educational Commission, or the United States embassy or consulate in their home country.

Closing Date: Varies by country.

Funding: Government, Private.

Contributor: The United States government and the Fulbright Commission.

No. of awards given last year: More than 700.

Fulbright Scholar Awards for Research and Lecturing Abroad for United States Citizens

Subjects: All academic disciplines and some professional fields.
Purpose: To increase mutual understanding between the people of the United States of America and the people of other nations, strengthen the ties that unite the United States of America with other nations, and promote international co-operation for educational and cultural advancement.
Eligibility: Open to United States citizens with a PhD or comparable professional qualifications. University or college teaching experience is normally expected for lecturing awards. For selected assignments, proficiency in a foreign language may be required.
Level of Study: Postdoctorate, Professional development.
Type: Lecturing or research.
Value: Varies by country.
Length of Study: From two months to one academic year.
Frequency: Annual.
Country of Study: 140 countries worldwide.
No. of awards offered: 800.
Application Procedure: Applicants must complete an application, available on request from CIES or from the website.
Closing Date: August 1st.
Funding: Government, Private.
No. of awards given last year: 800.
No. of applicants last year: 2,500.
Additional Information: Individual countries' programmes are described in the Council's publication and online. Applicants must contact apprequest@cies.iie.org for more information.

Fulbright Scholar Program for US Citizens

Subjects: The humanities, social sciences, applied, natural and physical sciences and professional fields such as architecture, business, law, museum work and creative arts, etc. Clinical medicine is excluded.
Purpose: To increase mutual understanding between the United States of America and other countries of the world.
Eligibility: Open to United States citizens only.
Level of Study: Postdoctorate.
Type: Research or lecturing.
Value: A maintenance allowance and international travel expenses.
Length of Study: From three months to one academic year.
Frequency: Annual.
No. of awards offered: Approx. 800.
Closing Date: August 1st.
No. of awards given last year: 800.
Additional Information: More information is available from the website.

Fulbright Senior Specialists Program

Subjects: Anthropology, archaeology, business administration, communications and journalism, economics, education, environmental science, information technology, law, library science, political science, public administration, sociology, social work, United States studies and urban planning.
Purpose: To offer short-term grants and encourage new types of activities in the Fulbright context. The programme also aims to advance mutual understanding, establish long-term co-operation and create opportunities for institutional linkages.
Eligibility: Open to United States citizens with a PhD or comparable professional qualifications.
Level of Study: Postdoctorate, Professional development.
Type: Grant.
Value: An honorarium and international travel expenses.
Length of Study: From two-six weeks.
Frequency: Annual.
Country of Study: 140 countries worldwide.
No. of awards offered: Varies.
Application Procedure: Applicants must complete the application, available on the CIES website.
Closing Date: Applications and grants are processed on a rolling basis.
Funding: Government.

Additional Information: Successful candidates are expected to lecture, lead seminars, work with foreign counterparts on curriculum, programme and institutional development. Applicants must contact fulspec@cies.iie.org for more information.

COUNCIL FOR THE ADVANCEMENT OF SCIENCE WRITING, INC. (CASW)

PO Box 404, Greenlawn, NY, 11740, United States of America
Tel: (1) 516 757 5664
Email: diane@casw.org
www: http://www.casw.org
Contact: Ms Diane McGurgan, Administration Secretary

Taylor/Blakeslee Fellowships for Graduate Study in Science Writing

Subjects: Journalism.
Purpose: To support graduate study in science writing.
Eligibility: Applicants must have degrees in science or journalism and must convince the CASW selection committee of their ability to pursue a career in writing science for the general public.
Level of Study: Postgraduate.
Type: Fellowship.
Value: A maximum US$2,000.
Length of Study: One year.
Frequency: Annual.
Country of Study: United States of America.
No. of awards offered: Two-four.
Application Procedure: Applicants must submit four collated sets of a completed application form, a curriculum vitae, a transcript of undergraduate studies if a student, three faculty recommendations or employer recommendations, three samples of writing on 8.5 by 11 inch sheets only, and a short statement of career goals.
Closing Date: July 1st.
Funding: Private.
No. of awards given last year: Four.
No. of applicants last year: 16.
Additional Information: Science writing is defined as writing about science, medicine, health, technology and the environment for the general public via the mass media.

COUNCIL OF LOGISTICS MANAGEMENT (CLM)

2805 Butterfield Road
Suite 200, Oak Brook, IL, 60523-1170, United States of America
Tel: (1) 630 574 0985
Fax: (1) 630 574 0989
Email: clmadmin@clm1.org
www: http://www.clm1.org
Contact: Graduate Scholarship Programme

The Council of Logistics Management (CLM) is a non-profit organisation of business personnel who are interested in improving their logistics management skills. CLM works in co-operation with private industry and various organisations to further the understanding and development of the logistics concept. This is accomplished through a continuing programme of organised activities, research and meetings designed to develop the theory and understanding of the logistics process, promote the art and science of managing logistics systems, and foster professional dialogue and development within the profession.

CLM George A Gecowets Graduate Scholarship Program

Subjects: Logistics management.

Purpose: To acknowledge the importance of logistics in a tangible way, while emphasising the Council's commitment to promote the art and science of managing logistics systems.

Eligibility: Applicants must be planning to pursue a career in logistics management, be a senior at an accredited four year college or university, and already be enrolled in the first year of a logistics or logistics related Master's degree programme.

Level of Study: Graduate.

Type: Scholarship.

Value: US$1,000.

Frequency: Annual.

No. of awards offered: 30.

Application Procedure: Applicants must submit a completed application, official college transcripts, Graduate Record Examination scores or Graduate Management Admission Test scores, and notification of any changes in address, school enrolment, or other pertinent information. The Citizens' Scholarship Foundation of America (CSFA) will then send a complete application package upon request.

Closing Date: Postmarked April 1st.

Funding: Private.

Contributor: The Council of Logistics Management.

No. of awards given last year: 32.

No. of applicants last year: 114.

Additional Information: The Council wishes to make high potential students aware of the tremendous opportunities and challenges that can await them in a career in logistics management, as the last 10 years have seen an exponential increase in the importance of the logistics manager.

For further information contact:

Council of Logistics Management
George A Gecowets Graduate Scholarship Program
Scholarship Management Services CSFA
1505 Riverview Road
PO Box 297, St Peter, MN, 56082, United States of America

COUNCIL ON FOREIGN RELATIONS (CFR)

Membership & Fellowship Affairs
58 East 68th Street, New York, NY, 10021, United States of America
Tel: (1) 212 434 9489
Fax: (1) 212 434 9801
Email: fellowships@cfr.org
www: http://www.cfr.org
Contact: Ms Elise Carlson Lewis, Vice President, Membership & Fellowship Affairs

The Council on Foreign Relations (CFR) is composed of men and women dedicated to the belief that the nation's peace and prosperity is linked to that of the rest of the world. It aims to foster America's understanding of other nations, their peoples, cultures, histories and ambitions and thus, to serve America's global interests through study and debate, both private and public.

CFR International Affairs Fellowship Programme in Japan

Subjects: International relations.

Purpose: To cultivate American understanding of Japan and to strengthen communication between emerging leaders of the two nations.

Eligibility: Open to American citizens between the ages of 27 and 45 years who have not had prior substantial experience in Japan. Fellows will be drawn form academia, government institutions, the business community and the media. The programme does not fund pre or postdoctoral scholarly research, work towards a degree, nor the completion of projects on which substantial progress has been made prior to the fellowship period. Knowledge of the Japanese language is not a requirement.

Level of Study: Professional development.

Type: Fellowship.

Value: Living expenses in Japan plus international transportation, health and travel insurance and necessary research expenses.

Length of Study: From three months to one year.

Frequency: Annual.

Country of Study: Japan.

No. of awards offered: Two-five.

Application Procedure: Application is primarily by invitation, on the recommendation of individuals in academic, government and other institutions who have occasion to know candidates particularly well suited for the experience offered by this fellowship. Others who enquire directly and who meet preliminary requirements may also be invited to apply without formal nomination. Those invited to apply will be forwarded application materials.

Closing Date: September 15th is the deadline for nominations, and October 31st is the application deadline. Nominations and applications will also be accepted out of cycle.

Funding: Private.

Contributor: Hitachi Limited.

No. of awards given last year: Two.

No. of applicants last year: Four.

Additional Information: While the Fellow is not required to produce a book, article or report, it is hoped that some written output will result.

CFR International Affairs Fellowships

Subjects: Important problems in international affairs and their implications for the interests and policies of the United States of America, foreign states or international organisations.

Purpose: To bridge the gap between analysis and action in foreign policy by supporting a variety of policy studies and active experiences in policy making.

Eligibility: Open to United States citizens between 27 and 35 years of age. While a PhD is not a requirement, successful candidates should generally hold advanced degrees and possess a solid record of work experience. The programme does not fund pre or postdoctoral research, work towards a degree, or the completion of projects for which substantial progress has been made prior to the fellowship period.

Level of Study: Postdoctorate, Professional development.

Type: Fellowship.

Value: Determined according to individual budget statements in consultation with the programme administration. The programme will attempt to meet the major portion of a Fellow's current income, up to a maximum of US$60,000. The programme does not provide support for research assistance.

Length of Study: One year.

Frequency: Annual.

Study Establishment: Usually the Fellow is not permitted to remain at his or her home institution during the fellowship period.

Country of Study: Any country.

No. of awards offered: 8-12.

Application Procedure: Application is primarily by invitation, on the recommendation of individuals in academic, government and other institutions who have occasion to know candidates particularly well suited for the experience offered by this fellowship. Others who enquire directly and who meet preliminary requirements may also be invited to apply without formal nomination. Those invited to apply will be forwarded application materials.

Closing Date: September 15th is the deadline for nominations, and October 31st is the application deadline.

Funding: Private.

No. of awards given last year: 12.

No. of applicants last year: 50.

Additional Information: While the Fellow is not required to produce a book, article or report, it is hoped that some written output will result.

Edward R Murrow Fellowship for Foreign Correspondents

Subjects: Issues in international affairs and their implications for the interests and policies of the United States, foreign states or international organisations.

Purpose: To help the Fellow increase his or her competency in reporting and interpreting events abroad and to give him or her a period of nearly a year of sustained analysis and writing, free from the daily pressures that characterise journalistic life.

Eligibility: Open to any correspondent, editor or producer for radio, television, a newspaper or a magazine widely available in the United States of America who has covered international news.

Level of Study: Professional development.

Type: Fellowship.

Value: A stipend equivalent to the salary relinquished, not to exceed US$65,000 for nine months.

Length of Study: Normally a period of nine months.

Frequency: Annual.

Study Establishment: The Fellow is expected to remain in residence at the Council headquarters in New York City for the duration of his or her tenure.

No. of awards offered: One.

Application Procedure: To receive an application, a nomination letter must be submitted to the main address. The nomination letter may be submitted by a Council member, a former or current Murrow Fellow, the candidate's employer, or the candidate him or her self. The nomination letter should confirm the candidate's eligibility as well as provide a brief description of his or her background and why the nominator believes the candidate to be an appropriate prospect for the Fellowship. For those candidates who choose to nominate themselves, their letter should address the same aforementioned issues in addition to providing a copy of his or her most recent curriculum vitae. Nominees who meet the criteria of the programme will then be forwarded an application form.

Closing Date: February.

Funding: Private.

No. of awards given last year: One.

No. of applicants last year: 12.

Additional Information: Further information is available on request.

COUNCIL ON SOCIAL WORK EDUCATION (CSWE)

1725 Duke Street
Suite 500, Alexandria, VA, 22314-3457, United States of America
Tel: (1) 703 683 8080
Fax: (1) 703 683 8099
Email: eafrancis@cswe.org
www: http://www.cswe.org
Contact: Dr E Aracelis Francis, Director, Minority Fellowship Programmes

The Council on Social Work Education (CSWE) provides national leadership and a forum for collective action designed to ensure the preparation of competent and committed social work professionals. Founded in 1952, CSWE is a non-profit, tax-exempt, national organisation representing 2,600 individual members and 119 graduate and 417 undergraduate programmes of professional social work education in major colleges and universities in the United States. CSWE's goals include improving the quality of social work education, preparing competent human service professionals and developing new programmes to meet the demands of the changing services delivery systems.

CSWE Doctoral Fellowships in Social Work for Ethnic Minority Students Preparing for Leadership Roles in Mental Health and/or Substance Abuse

Subjects: Mental health or substance abuse.

Purpose: To equip ethnic minority individuals for the provision of leadership, teaching, consultation, training, policy development and administration in mental health or substance abuse programmes and to enhance the development and dissemination of knowledge requisite for the provision of relevant clinical and social services to ethnic minority individuals and communities.

Eligibility: Applicants must be American citizens or permanent residents, including, but not limited to, persons who are American Indian or Alaskan Native, Asian or Pacific Islander (eg. Chinese, East Indian and other South Asians, Filipino, Hawaiian, Japanese, Korean or Samoan), Black or Hispanic (eg. Mexican or Chicano, Puerto Rican, Cuban, Central or South American). This programme is open to students who have a Master's degree in social work and who will begin full-time study leading to a doctoral degree in social work or who are currently enrolled as full-time students in a doctoral social work programme.

Level of Study: Doctorate.

Type: Fellowship.

Value: Monthly stipends for a one year period to help defray living expenses. Some tuition support may be provided depending upon the availability of funds.

Length of Study: One year.

Frequency: Dependent on funds available.

Study Establishment: Approved schools of social work.

Application Procedure: Applicants must write to the CSWE for an application pack and further information, or alternatively visit the website.

Closing Date: February 28th.

Funding: Government.

Contributor: The Substance Abuse and Mental Health Services Administration.

No. of awards given last year: 14.

Additional Information: Applicants should demonstrate potential for assuming leadership roles, as well as potential for success in doctoral studies and commitment to a career in providing mental health and/or substance abuse services to ethnic minority clients and communities.

CSWE Doctoral Fellowships in Social Work for Ethnic Minority Students Specialising in Mental Health

Subjects: Mental health research.

Purpose: To educate leaders of the nation's next generation of mental health researchers.

Eligibility: Applicants must be American citizens or permanent residents, including, but not limited to, persons who are American Indian or Alaskan Native, Asian or Pacific Islander (eg. Chinese, East Indian and other South Asians, Filipino, Hawaiian, Japanese, Korean or Samoan), Black or Hispanic (eg. Mexican or Chicano, Puerto Rican, Cuban, Central or South American). This programme is open to students who have a Master's degree in social work and will begin full-time study leading to a doctoral degree in social work or are currently enrolled as full-time students in a doctoral social work programme.

Level of Study: Doctorate.

Type: Fellowship.

Value: Monthly stipends for a one year period to help defray living expenses. Tuition support provided is the NIH tuition format.

Length of Study: One year, although the award is renewable upon reapplication if the Fellow maintains satisfactory progress towards degree objectives and funding is available.

Frequency: Annual, if funds are available.

No. of awards offered: 20.

Application Procedure: Applicants must write to the CSWE for an application pack and further information, or alternatively visit the website.

Closing Date: February 28th.

Funding: Government.

Contributor: The Division of Epidemology and Services Research, National Institute of Mental Health.

No. of awards given last year: 22.

No. of applicants last year: 50.

Additional Information: Applicants should demonstrate potential for, and interest in, mental health research, as well as potential for success in doctoral studies and commitment to a career in mental health.

CSWE Minority Fellowship Program

Subjects: Social work.
Purpose: To equip ethnic minority individuals for the provision of leadership, teaching, consultation, training, policy, development and administration in mental health or substance abuse programmes and to enhance the development and dissemination of knowledge necessary for the provision of relevant clinical and social services to ethnic minority individuals and communities.
Eligibility: Applicants must have Master's degree in social work and must be United States citizens.
Level of Study: Doctorate.
Type: Fellowship.
Value: US$10,008 per year, with a possible US$1,800 available towards tuition costs.
Length of Study: Renewable for up to three years.
Frequency: Dependent on funds available.
Study Establishment: Approved schools of social work.
Country of Study: United States of America.
No. of awards offered: 12.
Application Procedure: Applicants must request application materials.
Closing Date: February 28th.
Funding: Government.
No. of awards given last year: 14.
No. of applicants last year: 45.

THE COUNTESS OF MUNSTER MUSICAL TRUST

Wormley Hill, Godalming, Surrey, GU8 5SG, England
Tel: (44) 1428 685427
Fax: (44) 1428 685064
Email: munstertrust@compuserve.com
www: http://www.munstertrust.ukgateway.net
Contact: Mrs Gillian Ure, Secretary

The Trust provides financial assistance towards the cost of studies and maintenance of outstanding postgraduate students who merit further training at home or abroad. Each year the Trust is able to offer a small number of interest free loans for instrument purchase.

The Countess of Munster Musical Trust Awards

Subjects: Musical studies.
Purpose: To enable students, selected after interview and audition, to pursue a course of specialist or advanced performance studies.
Eligibility: Open to United Kingdom or British Commonwealth citizens, who are between and including the ages of 18 and 24 years for instrumentalists and composers, or under 28 for singers, who show outstanding musical ability and potential. Conductors are not considered.
Level of Study: Doctorate, Postgraduate, Professional development.
Type: Grant.
Value: By individual assessment to meet tuition fees and maintenance according to need, usually between UK £500-5,000.
Length of Study: One year, with the possibility of renewal.
Frequency: Annual.
Country of Study: Any country.
No. of awards offered: Unlimited, approx. 100 per year.
Application Procedure: Applicants must complete an application form. Candidates will have to attend an audition and interview.
Closing Date: Applications to arrive between the beginning of January and the second full week in February for awards to be applied for from the following September.
Funding: Private.

No. of awards given last year: 58.
No. of applicants last year: 315.

CRANFIELD UNIVERSITY

Silsoe, Bedfordshire, MK45 4DT, England
Tel: (44) 1525 863319
Fax: (44) 1525 863399
Email: studentenquiries.silsoe@cranfield.ac.uk
www: http://www.silsoe.cranfield.ac.uk
Contact: J L Seymour, Recruitment Manager

Cranfield University at Silsoe is an international centre for higher education, research, training and consultancy, specialising in the application of physical engineering and management sciences to agriculture, food and rural development.

Silsoe Awards

Subjects: Any MSc programme option offered by Cranfield University in the area of marketing management, information technology, natural resources, earth observation, soil and water management, environmental diagnostics, medical diagnostics and bioinformatics.
Purpose: To assist postgraduate study.
Eligibility: Open to European Union citizens who are graduates with good United Kingdom (Honours) Degree or equivalent and have been offered a place on a one year MSc programme at Cranfield University at Silsoe.
Level of Study: Postgraduate.
Type: Bursary.
Value: Tuition fees or half of tuition fees.
Length of Study: One year.
Frequency: Annual.
Study Establishment: Cranfield University at Silsoe.
Country of Study: United Kingdom.
No. of awards offered: Approx. 20.
Application Procedure: Applicants must apply direct to the university.
Closing Date: July.
Contributor: Cranfield University at Silsoe.
No. of awards given last year: 20.
No. of applicants last year: 250.

CRANFIELD UNIVERSITY, SCHOOL OF MANAGEMENT

Cranfield, Bedfordshire, MK43 0AL, England
Tel: (44) 1234 751122
Fax: (44) 1234 751806
Email: m.williams@cranfield.ac.uk
www: http://www.cranfield.ac.uk/som
Contact: Ms Maureen Williams, Senior Marketing Executive

Chevening Scholarships

Subjects: MBA.
Purpose: To enable young professionals of outstanding academic merit and leadership potential to pursue the full-time Cranfield MBA.
Eligibility: Applicants must be resident in their home country at the time of their application, and must return to that country on completion of the programme.
Level of Study: MBA.
Type: Scholarship.
Length of Study: One year.
Frequency: Annual.
Study Establishment: The Cranfield School of Management.
Country of Study: England.
Application Procedure: Applications must be made in the first instance to the appropriate British Council.

Contributor: The Foreign & Commonwealth Office and a number of leading United Kingdom companies.
No. of awards given last year: 10.
No. of applicants last year: 30.

Executive MBA (Part-time) Cranfield Scholarships

Subjects: MBA.
Purpose: To assist students who are full or partly self-funded.
Eligibility: Applicants must apply to the MBA programme in the normal way and have been offered a place before they can be considered for a scholarship.
Level of Study: MBA.
Type: Scholarship.
Value: Up to UK £8,000 towards tuition fees.
Length of Study: Two years.
Frequency: Annual.
Study Establishment: The Cranfield School of Management.
Country of Study: England.
Application Procedure: Applicants must submit an application along with an essay not exceeding 600 words on the following statement: 'The mark of a true MBA is that he is often wrong but seldom in doubt' (Robert Buzzell, Distinguished Visiting Professor, McDonough School of Business, Georgetown University, speaking in 1999).
Closing Date: November 1st.
No. of awards given last year: Eight.
No. of applicants last year: 22.

Full-Time MBA Cranfield Scholarship

Subjects: MBA.
Purpose: To assist exceptional overseas students or United Kingdom based female candidates.
Eligibility: Applicants must apply to the MBA programme in the normal way and have been offered a place before they can be considered for a scholarship.
Level of Study: MBA.
Type: Scholarship.
Value: Up to UK £8,000 towards tuition fees.
Length of Study: One year.
Frequency: Annual.
Study Establishment: The Cranfield School of Management.
Country of Study: England.
Application Procedure: Applicants must submit an application with an explanation of why they think that they should be awarded one of the scholarships in no more than 500 words.
Closing Date: April 1st.
No. of awards given last year: Four.
No. of applicants last year: 23.

The James Stuckey Scholarship

Subjects: MBA.
Purpose: To assist individuals wishing to pursue a full-time MBA course.
Eligibility: Open to anyone of New Zealand origin applying to the full-time MBA, who intends to return to work in New Zealand.
Level of Study: MBA.
Type: Scholarship.
Value: Up to UK £10,000.
Length of Study: One year.
Frequency: Annual.
Study Establishment: The Cranfield School of Management.
Country of Study: England.
Application Procedure: Applicants must include a covering letter with their MBA application, stating that they wish to be considered for the award.
Closing Date: May 1st.
No. of awards given last year: One.
No. of applicants last year: Three.

CRIMINOLOGY RESEARCH COUNCIL (CRC)

GPO Box 2944, Canberra, ACT, 2601, Australia
Tel: (61) 2 6260 9200
Fax: (61) 2 6260 9201
Email: crc@aic.gov.au
www: http://www.aic.gov.au/crc
Contact: Administrator

The Criminology Research Council (CRC) funds methodologically sound research in the areas of sociology, psychology, law, statistics, police, judiciary, corrections, mental health, social welfare, education and related fields. The research to be conducted is policy orientated, and research outcomes should have the potential for application nationally or in other jurisdictions.

Criminology Research Council (CRC) Grants

Subjects: Criminological research in the areas of sociology, psychology, law, statistics, police, judiciary and corrections, etc. From time to time the Council will call for research in specific areas.
Eligibility: Open to Australian residents or visitors (actual or intending) who are pursuing or intend to pursue studies of consequence to the furtherance of criminological research in Australia. Grants are not likely to be given for assistance with research leading to the award of postgraduate degrees.
Level of Study: Doctorate, Postdoctorate.
Type: Grant.
Value: Usually australian $25,000 paid in three instalments.
Length of Study: Usually one year, with a possibility of renewal for up to three years.
Frequency: Annual.
Country of Study: Australia.
No. of awards offered: Approx. six.
Application Procedure: Applicants must complete an application form, available from CRC.
Closing Date: Twelve weeks prior to meetings.
Funding: Government.
No. of awards given last year: Nine.
No. of applicants last year: 40.
Additional Information: The Council does not ordinarily consider applications involving travelling expenses outside of Australia. Meetings are held in March, July and November. The November meeting is for general grants, funding in any area the council deems relevant.

THE CROHN'S AND COLITIS FOUNDATION OF AMERICA, INC.

386 Park Avenue South
17th Floor, New York, NY, 10016-8804, United States of America
Tel: (1) 212 685 3440
Fax: (1) 212 779 4098
Email: info@ccfa.org
www: http://www.ccfa.org
Contact: Ms Carol M Cox, Research Co-ordinator

The Crohn's and Colitis Foundation of America, Inc. is a non-profit, voluntary health organisation dedicated to improving quality of life for persons with Crohn's disease or ulcerative colitis. It supports basic and clinical scientific research to find the causes and cure for these diseases, provides educational programmes for patients, medical and healthcare professionals, and the general public, alongside offering supportive services to patients, their families and friends.

Crohn's and Colitis Foundation Career Development Awards

Subjects: Crohn's disease and ulcerative colitis.

Purpose: To encourage the development of young outstanding scientists with research potential to help them prepare for careers of independent research into inflammatory bowel disease.

Eligibility: Open to candidates working in American laboratories who have had at least five years of postdoctoral experience, two years of which must be in research relevant to inflammatory bowel disease, prior to the beginning date of the award and not in excess of 10 years beyond the attainment of the doctoral degree. Research projects must be in the field of inflammatory bowel disease and individuals who are already well established in the field are not eligible. Proof of legal work status within the United States of America is required at the time of application.

Level of Study: Postdoctorate.

Value: Up to US$40,000 salary and US$20,000 for supplies etc. plus fringe benefits not to exceed 25 per cent of the salary award.

Length of Study: Two years.

Frequency: Every two years.

Study Establishment: Approved research institutions.

Country of Study: United States of America.

No. of awards offered: Varies.

Application Procedure: Applicants must complete an application form in accordance with the guidelines. Application material is available from the Foundation.

Closing Date: January 14th or July 1st.

Funding: Private.

No. of awards given last year: Four.

Additional Information: The awards are made to eligible institutions on behalf of qualified candidates, and each awardee is directly responsible to the institution to which the award is made.

Crohn's and Colitis Foundation First Award

Subjects: Crohn's disease and ulcerative colitis.

Purpose: To underwrite the first independent investigative efforts of an individual, to provide a reasonable opportunity to demonstrate creativity, productivity and further promise, and to help in the transition to traditional types of research project grants.

Eligibility: The applicant must be independent of a mentor yet at the same time must be at the beginning stages of his or her research career, with no more than five years of research experience since completing postdoctoral research training. The applicant must hold an MD, PhD or equivalent degree and be employed by an institution within the United States of America engaged in healthcare at the time of application.

Level of Study: Postdoctorate.

Value: A maximum of US$60,000 in direct costs per year and indirect costs of 15 per cent of direct cost.

Length of Study: A maximum of three years.

Frequency: Annual.

Study Establishment: Approved research institutions.

Country of Study: United States of America.

No. of awards offered: Varies.

Application Procedure: Applicants must complete an application form in accordance with the guidelines. Please write for details.

Closing Date: January 14th or July 1st.

Funding: Private.

No. of awards given last year: Four.

Crohn's and Colitis Foundation Research Fellowship Awards

Subjects: Crohn's disease and ulcerative colitis.

Purpose: To encourage the development of young outstanding scientists with research potential to help them prepare for careers of independent research into inflammatory bowel disease.

Eligibility: Open to candidates working in American laboratories who have had at least two years of postdoctoral experience prior to the beginning date of the award, one year of which must be in research relevant to inflammatory bowel disease, and have demonstrated an interest and capability in research. Research projects must be in the field of inflammatory bowel disease and individuals who are already well established in the field are not eligible. Proof of legal work status within the United States of America will be required at the time of application.

Level of Study: Postdoctorate.

Value: US$30,000 per year for salary plus fringe benefits not to exceed 25 per cent of the salary award.

Length of Study: One-three years.

Frequency: Every two years.

Study Establishment: Approved research institutions.

Country of Study: United States of America.

No. of awards offered: Varies.

Application Procedure: Applicants must complete an application form in accordance with the guidelines.

Closing Date: January 14th or July 1st.

Funding: Private.

No. of awards given last year: Four.

Crohn's and Colitis Foundation Research Grant Program

Subjects: Inflammatory bowel disease including the cause, pathogenesis or treatment.

Purpose: To provide financial support for innovative basic and clinical research.

Eligibility: Open to qualified investigators in the United States of America and abroad.

Level of Study: Postdoctorate.

Type: Research grant.

Value: A maximum of US$100,000 for direct costs. Requests for purchases of major equipment totalling more than US$5,000 are not generally considered. The maximum amount allowed for overhead is 15 per cent of total direct costs.

Length of Study: Two years with a possibility of renewal for a further year.

Frequency: Every two years.

Country of Study: Any country.

No. of awards offered: Varies.

Application Procedure: Applicants must complete an application form in accordance with the guidelines.

Closing Date: January 14th or July 1st.

Funding: Private.

No. of awards given last year: 13.

THE CROSS TRUST

PO Box 17
25 South Methven Street, Perth, Perthshire, PH1 5ES, Scotland
Tel: (44) 1738 620451
Fax: (44) 1738 631155
Contact: Mrs Dorothy Shaw, Assistant Secretary

The aim of the Cross Trust is to provide opportunities to young people of Scottish birth or parentage to extend the boundaries of their knowledge of human life. Proposals are to be of demonstrable merit from applicants with a record of academic distinction.

The Cross Trust Grants

Subjects: Any approved subject.

Purpose: To enable young people to extend the boundaries of their knowledge and experience or to encourage performance and participation in drama or opera. The Trust may support the pursuit of studies or research.

Eligibility: Open to graduates of Scottish universities or of central institutions in Scotland and to Scottish secondary school pupils. Applicants must be of Scottish birth or parentage.

Level of Study: Graduate, Postgraduate, Predoctorate.

Value: Varies.

Frequency: Trustees meet on average four times per year.

Study Establishment: Any approved institute.

Country of Study: Any country.

No. of awards offered: Varies.

Application Procedure: Applicants must complete an application form.

Closing Date: No deadline.

Funding: Private.

No. of awards given last year: 174.

No. of applicants last year: 528.

Additional Information: Awards will only be considered from post-graduate students who have part funding in place from another organisation.

THE CROUCHER FOUNDATION

501 Nine Queen's Road Central, Kowloon, Hong Kong

Tel: (852) 2 736 6337

Fax: (852) 2 730 0742

Email: info@croucher.org.hk

www: http://www.croucher.org.hk

Contact: Ms Elaine Sit, Administrative Officer

Founded to promote education, learning and research in the areas of natural science, technology and medicine, the Croucher Foundation operates a scholarship and fellowship scheme for individual applicants wishing to pursue doctoral or postdoctoral research. The Foundation otherwise makes grants to institutions only.

Croucher Foundation Fellowships and Scholarships

Subjects: Natural science, medicine and technology.

Purpose: To enable selected students of outstanding promise to devote themselves to full-time postgraduate study or research.

Eligibility: Open to permanent residents of Hong Kong. Fellowships are intended for PhD graduates and not for funding career vacancies in universities. Scholarships are intended for those studying for a research degree, such as a PhD programme.

Level of Study: Doctorate, Postdoctorate.

Type: Scholarship and fellowship.

Value: UK £15,300 per year for fellowships and UK £8,040 per year for scholarships. A maintenance allowance is available if the award is tenable in the United Kingdom, as well as assistance towards airfare, plus tuition fees for Scholars. Married Fellows or Scholars will be given a special spouse allowance including assistance towards air fare if he or she is dependant and accompanying the holder of the award. In addition, a child allowance will be provided if they are residing with the Fellow or Scholar. If the successful applicant is on paid study leave during the tenure of the award the maintenance allowance will not apply. A one-off grant for books or apparatus and clothing will be given during the first year of tenure. An allowance for thesis expenses will be given to final year PhD students on application, against receipts. Fellows and Scholars will be expected to devote their whole time to the objects of their award. Fellows and Scholars will not be debarred from holding another position of emolument but if, at the date of application, they hold such a position or are appointed to it at a later date, or receive concurrently any scholarship or award with monetary value, they must notify the Trustees and obtain prior approval from them. The Trustees may therefore, at their discretion, modify the value of the fellowship or scholarship.

Length of Study: One-two years for the fellowships and one-three years for the scholarships.

Frequency: Annual.

Country of Study: Hong Kong or abroad.

No. of awards offered: Approx. 20-25.

Application Procedure: Applicants must write requesting an application form stating whether they are applying for a scholarship or fellowship, and enclose a 7 by 10 inch stamped addressed envelope for 50 grammes, or download an application form from the website.

Closing Date: Mid November. Applicants should visit the website for exact date.

Funding: Private.

No. of awards given last year: 25.

No. of applicants last year: 80.

CYSTIC FIBROSIS FOUNDATION (CFF)

Office of Grants Management

6931 Arlington Road, Bethesda, MD, 20814, United States of America

Tel: (1) 301 951 4422

Fax: (1) 301 951 6378

Email: grants@cff.org

www: http://www.cff.org

Contact: Ms Monika A Last, Grants Division

The mission of the Cystic Fibrosis Foundation (CFF) is to assure the development of the means to cure and control cystic fibrosis and to improve the quality of life for those with the disease.

CFF Research Programmes in Cystic Fibrosis

Subjects: Cystic fibrosis.

Purpose: To offer competitive awards for research.

Eligibility: Some programmes have United States citizenship or permanent resident status requirements.

Level of Study: Doctorate, Professional development.

Type: Research grant.

Value: From US$36,000-100,000.

Frequency: Annual.

Country of Study: Any country.

No. of awards offered: Eight programmes.

Application Procedure: Applicants must write for an application form.

Closing Date: Varies with each award.

Additional Information: The names of the awards are as follows: Therapeutics Development Grants, Pilot Feasibility Awards, Research Grants, Leroy Matthews Physician/Scientist Award, Harry Shwachman Clinical Investigator Award, Clinical Research Grants, CFF/NIH Funding Award and Special Research Awards.

CFF Training Programmes in Cystic Fibrosis

Subjects: Cystic fibrosis.

Purpose: To support individuals interested in careers related to cystic fibrosis research and care.

Eligibility: Open to United States citizens and permanent residents only.

Level of Study: Doctorate, Professional development.

Type: Varies.

Value: From US$1,500-45,000.

Frequency: Annual.

Country of Study: Any country.

No. of awards offered: Four programmes.

Application Procedure: Applicants must write for an application form.

Closing Date: Varies with the award.

Additional Information: The names of the specific awards are: Postdoctoral Research Fellowships, Clinical Fellowships, Student Traineeships and Summer Scholarships in Epidemiology.

CYSTIC FIBROSIS RESEARCH TRUST (CFRT)

11 London Road, Bromley, Kent, BR1 1BY, England

Tel: (44) 20 8464 7211

Fax: (44) 20 8313 0472

Email: cpendry@cftrust.org.uk

www: http://www.cftrust.org.uk

Contact: Mrs Carol M Eagles, Research Manager

The Cystic Fibrosis Research Trust (CFRT) funds medical and scientific research aimed at understanding, treating and curing cystic fibrosis, and ensuring that sufferers receive the best possible care and support in all aspects of their lives.

CFRT Research Grants

Subjects: Medical and scientific research related to cystic fibrosis.
Purpose: To find a cure for cystic fibrosis and also to improve the management, care and treatment of those suffering from the disease.
Eligibility: Open to suitably qualified persons from the United Kingdom.
Level of Study: Doctorate, Postgraduate, Research.
Type: Research grants and research studentships.
Value: From a total fund of UK £1m per year, grants are made to cover such matters as salaries, expenses and equipment.
Length of Study: Up to three years, subject to annual renewal.
Frequency: Twice a year.
Country of Study: United Kingdom.
No. of awards offered: Varies.
Application Procedure: Applicants must apply by form and include justification of the support requested. Forms are available by email only.
Closing Date: Please contact the organisation.
Funding: Private.
Contributor: Charitable donations.
No. of awards given last year: 12.
No. of applicants last year: 37.

DAIWA ANGLO-JAPANESE FOUNDATION

Daiwa Foundation Japan House
13-14 Cornwall Terrace, London, NW1 4QP, England
Tel: (44) 20 7486 4348
Fax: (44) 20 7486 2914
Email: office@daiwa-foundation.org.uk
www: http://www.daiwa-foundation.org.uk
Contact: Grants & Scholarships Office

The principal aims of the Daiwa Anglo-Japanese Foundation are to enhance mutual understanding and links between the United Kingdom and Japan, to enable British and Japanese students and academics to further their education by visiting each other's countries, and to support, through grants, the work of individuals or organisations, particularly those in the fields of education and research.

Daiwa Adrian Prizes

Subjects: Medical science.
Purpose: To encourage collaborative research in the field.
Eligibility: Open to British and Japanese citizens only.
Level of Study: Doctorate.
Frequency: Every three years.
Country of Study: United Kingdom or Japan.
No. of awards offered: Up to four.
Closing Date: Usually February 1st on the appropriate year.
Funding: Private.

Daiwa Anglo-Japanese Foundation General Grants

Subjects: Cultural studies.
Purpose: To support projects that have the potential to contribute to the broader sphere of Anglo-Japanese relations.
Eligibility: Open to British and Japanese citizens only.
Value: Between UK £500-5,000.
Frequency: Annual.
Closing Date: Please contact the Foundation.
Funding: Private.

DANISH CANCER SOCIETY

Strandboulevarden 49, Copenhagen, DK-2100, Denmark
Tel: (45) 3525 7500
Fax: (45) 3525 7701
Email: info@cancer.dk
www: http://www.cancer.dk
Contact: Ms Birgit Christensen, Head Secretary

The Danish Cancer Society's mission is to fight cancer and its consequences through research, preventative measures and support for patients and their families. Patient's interests in relation to authorities are also represented.

Danish Cancer Society Psychosocial Research Award

Subjects: Psychology.
Eligibility: Only cancer related projects will be granted.
Level of Study: Research.
Type: Research grant.
Length of Study: Up to five years.
Frequency: Annual.
Country of Study: Denmark.
Application Procedure: Applicants should see the website for details.
Funding: Private.
Contributor: Legacies and Testamentary Gifts, and Investment Income Lotteries.
No. of awards given last year: 23.
No. of applicants last year: 65.

Danish Cancer Society Scientific Award

Subjects: Medical and natural sciences.
Eligibility: Only cancer related projects will be granted.
Level of Study: Research.
Type: Research grant.
Length of Study: Up to five years.
Frequency: Annual.
Country of Study: Denmark.
Application Procedure: Applicants should see the website for details.
Funding: Private.
Contributor: Legacies and Testamentary Gifts, and Investment Income Lotteries.
No. of awards given last year: 140.
No. of applicants last year: 333.

DAPHNE JACKSON TRUST

Department of Physics
University of Surrey, Guildford, Surrey, GU2 7XH, England
Tel: (44) 1483 689166
Fax: (44) 1483 689166
Email: djmft@surrey.ac.uk
www: http://www.daphnejackson.org
Contact: Mrs Jennifer Woolley, Trust Director

The Daphne Jackson Trust offers sponsored fellowships to qualified scientists, engineers and computing specialists wishing to return to their profession after having taken a career break for family reasons. Fellowships are held in universities and industrial laboratories throughout the United Kingdom.

Daphne Jackson Fellowship

Subjects: Science, engineering or computing.
Eligibility: Open to United Kingdom residents who have a minimum of a First Class Honours Degree and have taken a career break of at least three years.
Level of Study: Research.
Type: Fellowship.
Length of Study: Two years.

Country of Study: United Kingdom.
No. of awards offered: Approx. 10 per year.
Application Procedure: Applicants must send a curriculum vitae along with the names of at least two referees.
Closing Date: Applications are accepted all year round.
Funding: Commercial, Private.
No. of awards given last year: Nine.
No. of applicants last year: 31.

DATATEL SCHOLARS FOUNDATION

4375 Fair Lakes Court, Fairfax, VA, 22033, United States of America
Tel: (1) 800 486 4332
Fax: (1) 703 968 4573
Email: scholars@datatel.com
www: http://www.datatel.com
Contact: Awards Committee

The Datatel Scholars Foundation is a tax exempt foundation established by Datatel in 1990 to award scholarships to eligible students to attend an Institute of Higher Education selected from Datatel's 540 college, university and non education client sites.

Angelfire Scholarship
Subjects: All subjects.
Purpose: To support students who are Vietnam veterans or refugees.
Eligibility: Open to students attending an Institute of Higher Education selected from Datatel's list of more than 580 approved colleges, universities and non-profit client sites. United States or Canadian citizenship is not required. Candidates must be Vietnam veterans or refugees from Cambodia, Laos or Vietnam, or a spouse or child of, during the 1964-1975 time frame.
Level of Study: Doctorate, Graduate, Postgraduate.
Type: Scholarship.
Value: Applications are divided into three groups based on the undergraduate tuition at the college or university the applicant attends or is planning to attend. These amounts are US$700, US$1,300 and US$2,000.
Study Establishment: Any Datatel client site institution.
Country of Study: United States of America or Canada.
Application Procedure: Applications must be completed and forwarded by the institution's Office of Financial Aid. The Foundation does not accept applications directly from students.
Closing Date: January 31st.
Additional Information: If requesting applications from the Foundation, please visit the website and see scholar's foundation for a complete listing of eligible institutions.

Datatel Scholars Foundation Scholarship
Subjects: All subjects.
Purpose: To award scholarships to eligible students to attend an Institute of Higher Education selected from Datatel's client sites.
Eligibility: Open to students attending an Institute of Higher Education selected from Datatel's list of more than 580 approved colleges, universities and non-profit client sites. United States or Canadian citizenship is not required.
Level of Study: Doctorate, Graduate, Postgraduate.
Type: Scholarship.
Value: Applications are divided into three groups based on the undergraduate tuition at the college or university the applicant attends or is planning to attend. These amounts are US$700, US$1,300 and US$2,000.
Length of Study: One year.
Frequency: Annual.
Study Establishment: Any Datatel client site institution.
Country of Study: United States of America or Canada.
No. of awards offered: Determined annually.

Application Procedure: Applications must be completed and forwarded by the institution's Office of Financial Aid. The Foundation does not accept applications directly from students.
Closing Date: January 31st.
Funding: Private.
Contributor: Datatel, Inc.
Additional Information: If requesting applications from the Foundation, please visit the website and see scholar's foundation for a complete listing of eligible institutions.

Nancy Goodhue Lynch Scholarship
Subjects: Any technology-related subject.
Purpose: To support any student enrolled in a technology related curriculum programme.
Eligibility: Open to students attending an Institute of Higher Education selected from Datatel's list of more than 580 approved colleges, universities and non-profit client sites. United States or Canadian citizenship is not required.
Level of Study: Doctorate, Graduate, Postgraduate.
Type: Scholarship.
Value: The top rated application will be awarded US$5,000.
Study Establishment: Any Datatel client site institution.
Country of Study: United States of America or Canada.
Application Procedure: Applications must be completed and forwarded by the institution's Office of Financial Aid. The Foundation does not accept applications directly from students.
Closing Date: January 31st.
Additional Information: If requesting applications from the Foundation, please visit the website and see scholar's foundation for a complete listing of eligible institutions.

Returning Student Scholarship
Subjects: All subjects.
Purpose: To support students returning to school after an absence of five years or more.
Eligibility: Open to students attending an Institute of Higher Education selected from Datatel's list of more than 580 approved colleges, universities and non-profit client sites. United States or Canadian citizenship is not required.
Level of Study: Doctorate, Graduate, Postgraduate.
Type: Scholarship.
Value: The top rated 25 applications will be awarded US$1,000 each.
Frequency: Annual.
Study Establishment: Any Datatel client site institution.
Country of Study: United States of America or Canada.
Application Procedure: Applications must be completed and forwarded by the institution's Office of Financial Aid. The Foundation does not accept applications directly from students.
Closing Date: January 31st.

DELTA SOCIETY

289 Perimeter Road East, Renton, WA, 98055-1329, United States of America
Tel: (1) 425 226 7357
Fax: (1) 425 235 1076
Email: info@deltasociety.org
www: http://www.deltasociety.org

The Delta Society's mission is to improve human health through service and therapy animals. It does this by expanding awareness of the positive effects animals can have on family health and human development, reducing barriers to the involvement of animals in everyday life, delivering animal assisted therapy to more people and by increasing the availability of well trained service dogs.

James M Harris/Sarah W Sweatt Student Travel Grant
Subjects: Veterinary medicine, general medical sciences and general education.

Purpose: To provide an annual grant for transportation costs for a student to attend the Delta Society Training Conference.
Eligibility: Open to students who are enrolled full-time in a veterinary or human health professional training programme pursuing a Master's or doctoral degree.
Level of Study: Postgraduate.
Type: Travel grant.
Value: Transportation costs.
Frequency: Annual.
Country of Study: United States of America.
No. of awards offered: One.
Application Procedure: Applicants must contact the Society for details.
Closing Date: July.

DEMOCRATIC NURSING ORGANISATION OF SOUTH AFRICA (DENOSA)

PO Box 1280, Pretoria, 0001, South Africa
Tel: (27) 12 343 2315
Fax: (27) 12 344 0750
Email: info@denosa.org.za
www: http://www.denosa.org.za
Contact: Executive Director

The Democratic Nursing Organisation of South Africa (DENOSA) is a professional organisation and labour union for nurses in South Africa.

DENOSA Bursaries, Scholarships and Grants
Subjects: Nursing.
Purpose: To encourage post-basic studies at a South African teaching institution.
Eligibility: Open to members of the organisation in good standing who hold the required registered nursing qualifications.
Level of Study: Doctorate, Graduate, Postgraduate, Professional development.
Type: Bursary.
Value: Varies.
Frequency: Annual.
Study Establishment: A South African teaching institution.
Country of Study: South Africa.
No. of awards offered: Varies.
Application Procedure: Applicants must complete an application form.
Closing Date: January 31st.
Funding: Private.
Contributor: Donor funding.
No. of awards given last year: 125.
No. of applicants last year: 158.
Additional Information: Further information is available on request.

THE DENMARK-AMERICA FOUNDATION

Fiolstraede 24
3rd Floor, Copenhagen, DK-1171, Denmark
Tel: (45) 3312 8323
Fax: (45) 3332 5323
Email: daf-fulb@daf-fulb.dk
www: http://www.daf-fulb.dk
Contact: Ms Marie Monsted, Executive Director

The Denmark-America Foundation was founded in 1914 as a private foundation, and today its work remains based on donations from Danish firms, foundations and individuals. The Foundation offers scholarships for studies in the United States of America at the graduate and postgraduate university level and has a trainee programme.

Denmark-America Foundation Grants
Subjects: All subjects.
Purpose: To further understanding between Denmark and the United States of America.
Eligibility: Open to Danes only.
Level of Study: Postdoctorate, Postgraduate, Professional development.
Type: Bursary.
Value: Varies.
Length of Study: Between three months and one year.
Frequency: Annual.
Country of Study: United States of America.
No. of awards offered: Varies.
Application Procedure: Applicants must complete a special application form, available by contacting the secretariat.
Closing Date: To be announced.
Funding: Private.
No. of awards given last year: 40.
No. of applicants last year: 300.

DENTISTRY CANADA FUND/FONDS DENTAIRE CANADIEN (DCF)

427 Gilmour Street, Ottawa, ON, K2P 0R5, Canada
Tel: (1) 613 236 4763
Fax: (1) 613 236 3935
Email: information@dcf-fdc.ca
www: http://www.dcf-fdc.ca
Contact: Ms Donna Bierko, Co-ordinator Administration

The Dentistry Canada Fund (DCF) is the national charitable foundation dedicated to assisting in the encouragement of optimal oral health in Canada through education, research and promotion.

DCF Biennial Research Award
Subjects: Dentistry.
Purpose: To encourage research related to dentistry conducted by graduate or postgraduate students in Canada.
Eligibility: Open to graduate or postgraduate students who have conducted their research in association with a Canadian dental faculty.
Level of Study: Graduate, Postgraduate.
Type: Research grant.
Value: Canadian $2,000 plus a commemorative plaque.
Frequency: Every two years.
Country of Study: Canada.
No. of awards offered: One.
Application Procedure: One typewritten double spaced copy, not exceeding 25 pages and four copies of an original research project in the form of a paper must be submitted. The manuscript should not be a previously published paper of the candidate's graduate work currently in press or already published in a scientific journal. Each applicant must also send a current curriculum vitae.
Closing Date: October 1st biennially.
Additional Information: Each entry will be reviewed by three referees appointed by the CDA Committee on Dental Materials and Devices. The decision of the Committee is final.

DCF Fellowships for Teacher/Researcher Training
Subjects: Dentistry.
Purpose: To provide financial assistance to students who wish to pursue a career in dentistry research or teaching at graduate level.
Eligibility: Applicants must be Canadian citizens or permanent residents who have completed a course in dentistry, a dental hygiene programme or a programme in science and also be eligible for admission to a graduate or other advanced education programme.
Level of Study: Postgraduate.
Type: Fellowship.
Country of Study: Canada.

Application Procedure: Applicants must submit an application including official transcripts of previous post secondary education and letters of recommendation from a faculty member of the applicant's post secondary institution and from the administrative head of the institution and department where he or she expects to be employed. All applications must include a curriculum vitae.
Closing Date: February 1st.

DCF/Wrigley Dental Student Research Awards
Subjects: Oral biology.
Purpose: To enable applicants to undertake research projects in oral biology. Preference is given to research or community education projects concerned with the benefits of salivary stimulation and caries reduction.
Eligibility: Open to students enrolled in Canadian dental schools.
Level of Study: Graduate.
Type: Research grant.
Value: Canadian $3,000.
Frequency: Annual.
Country of Study: Canada.
No. of awards offered: Up to three.
Application Procedure: Applicants must submit an application including background on the subject matter, the research objectives, the proposed hypothesis, the research approach and the project's timetable and budget.
Closing Date: February 1st.

DEPARTMENT FOR EMPLOYMENT AND LEARNING

Adelaide House
39-49 Adelaide Street, Belfast, BT2 8FD, Northern Ireland
Tel: (44) 28 9025 7710
Fax: (44) 28 9025 7747
Contact: Mrs Siobhan Woods

The Department for Employment and Learning offers research and advanced course studentships to provide for both the payment of approved fees and the maintenance of students who are being trained in methods of research and undertaking approved postgraduate courses of instruction.

DHFETE Postgraduate Studentships and Bursaries for Study in Northern Ireland
Subjects: Science, technology, social sciences and humanities.
Purpose: To provide students ordinarily resident in the United Kingdom with bursaries similar to those given by the Arts and Humanities Research Board, the Engineering and Physical Sciences Council, the Economic and Social Research Council and the Natural Environment Research Council for attendance at courses in Northern Ireland.
Eligibility: Open to United Kingdom and European Union residents only. Applicants for studentships must have at least an Upper Second Class Degree. Bursaries are open to United Kingdom residents who must be ordinarily resident in Northern Ireland on the date of the application for an award and hold a university degree or qualification regarded by the department as equivalent to a degree.
Level of Study: Postgraduate.
Type: Studentships and bursaries.
Value: In line with the other United Kingdom awarding bodies.
Length of Study: Varies.
Frequency: Annual.
Study Establishment: Appropriate institutions.
Country of Study: Northern Ireland.
No. of awards offered: Varies but is proportional to the number available in the rest of the United Kingdom.
Application Procedure: Applicants must complete an application form, available from universities in Northern Ireland.
Closing Date: Deadlines are determined by the institution concerned.

Funding: Government.

For further information contact:

The Queen's University of Belfast
University Road, Belfast, Northern Ireland

University of Ulster
Cromore Road, Coleraine, Northern Ireland

DEPARTMENT OF EDUCATION AND SCIENCE (IRELAND)

International Section
Department of Education & Science
Training College Building
Marlborough Street, Dublin, 1, Ireland
Tel: (353) 1 889 2426
Fax: (353) 1 889 2376
Email: dolores_ronane@education.gov.ie
www: http://www.education.gov.ie
Contact: Ms Dolores Ronane, International Section

Department of Education and Science (Ireland) Exchange Scholarships and Postgraduate Scholarships Exchange Scheme
Subjects: All subjects.
Purpose: To allow students to pursue study or research in Ireland.
Eligibility: Open to Australian, Austrian, Belgian, Chinese, Finnish, German, Greek, Italian, Japanese, Dutch, Norwegian, Russian Federation, Spanish and Swiss nationals, who are university graduates and have completed at least three years of academic study. A good knowledge of English or Irish is necessary, depending on the course taken.
Level of Study: Postgraduate.
Type: Scholarship.
Value: Please contact the association for details.
Length of Study: Eight months.
Frequency: Annual.
Study Establishment: An Irish university eg. University College Dublin, University College Cork, University College Galway, Trinity College Dublin, Dublin City University, University of Limerick, St Patrick's College Maynooth or other similar Institutes of Higher Education.
Country of Study: Ireland.
No. of awards offered: 28.
Application Procedure: Applicants must apply to the appropriate institution in their home country. These are: the Federal Ministry for Science and Research in Vienna, Austria. The Ministry of Education for the Flemish Community in Brussels, Belgium. The Ministries of Foreign Affairs and Education in Beijing, China. The Finnish Centre for International Mobility (CIMO) in Helsinki, Finland. The Foreign Ministry in Paris, France. The German Academic Exchange Board (Deutscher Akademischer Austauschdienst-DAAD) in Bonn, Germany. The Ministries of Foreign Affairs and Education in Athens, Greece. The Ministry of Foreign Affairs in Rome, Italy. The Ministries of Foreign Affairs and Education in Tokyo, Japan. The Netherlands Organisation for International Co-operation in Higher Education (NUFFIC) in The Hague, The Netherlands. The Ministry of Foreign Affairs, Office of Cultural Relations in Oslo, Norway. The Ministry of Education of the Russian Federation in the Russian Federation. The Ministry of Foreign Affairs in Madrid, Spain. The Swiss University Authorities in Berne, Switzerland. Applicants in Australia should see below.
Closing Date: April 30th.
Funding: Government.

For further information contact:

Grants Management Officer
Embassy of Ireland
20 Arkana Street, Yarralumla, ACT, 2600, Australia

Tel: (61) 2 6273 3022
Fax: (61) 2 6273 3741

Department of Education and Science (Ireland) Summer School Exchange Scholarships

Subjects: All subjects.
Purpose: To allow European students to attend a summer school in Ireland.
Eligibility: Open to Belgian, French, Finnish, German, Hungarian, Italian, Dutch, Russian Federation and Spanish nationals who are university graduates. A good knowledge of English or Irish is necessary, depending on the course taken.
Level of Study: Postgraduate.
Type: Scholarship.
Value: Please contact the association for details.
Length of Study: From two weeks to one month.
Frequency: Annual.
Study Establishment: Summer schools at University College Dublin, University College Galway or University College Cork.
Country of Study: Ireland.
No. of awards offered: 32.
Application Procedure: Applicants must apply to the appropriate institution in their home country. These are: the Federal Ministry for Science and Research in Vienna, Austria. The Ministry of Education in Canberra, Australia. The Ministry of Education for the Flemish Community in Brussels, Belgium. The Ministries of Foreign Affairs and Education in Beijing, China. The Finnish Centre for International Mobility (CIMO) in Helsinki, Finland. The Foreign Ministry in Paris, France. The German Academic Exchange Board (Deutscher Akademischer Austauschdienst-DAAD) in Bonn, Germany. The Ministries of Foreign Affairs and Education in Athens, Greece. The Ministry of Foreign Affairs in Rome, Italy. The Ministries of Foreign Affairs and Education in Tokyo, Japan. The Netherlands Organisation for International Co-operation in Higher Education (NUFFIC) in The Hague, The Netherlands. The Ministry of Foreign Affairs, Office of Cultural Relations in Oslo, Norway. The Ministry of Education of the Russian Federation in the Russian Federation. The Ministry of Foreign Affairs in Madrid, Spain. The Swiss University Authorities in Berne, Switzerland.
Closing Date: April 30th.
Funding: Government.

DEUTSCHE FORSCHUNGSGEMEINSCHAFT (DFG)

Kennedyallee 40, Bonn, D-53175, Germany
Tel: (49) 228 885 1
Fax: (49) 228 885 2777
Email: postmaster@dfg.de
www: http://www.dfg.de

The Deutsche Forschungsgemeinschaft (DFG) is the central organisation for academic research in Germany. DFG supports research projects in German universities and institutions, promotes co-operation between scientists and forges support links between German academic science and industry, and with partners in foreign countries. DFG gives special attention to the education of young scientists and scholars.

Albert Maucher Prize

Subjects: Geosciences.
Purpose: To promote outstanding young scientists and scholars in the field of geosciences.
Eligibility: Open to promising young scientists and Scholars up to the age of 35 who are German nationals or permanent residents of Germany.
Level of Study: Postdoctorate.
Type: Award.
Value: Please contact the organisation.
Length of Study: Varies.

Frequency: Every two years. The next will take place in 2003.
Study Establishment: Approved universities or research institutions.
Country of Study: Germany.
No. of awards offered: Two.
Application Procedure: Applicants must write for details or visit the website. Application is by nomination.
Closing Date: Please write for details.

Deutsche Forschungsgemeinschaft (DFG) Research Training Units

Subjects: All subjects.
Purpose: To promote high quality graduate studies at doctoral level through participation of graduate students recruited through country wide calls in research programmes.
Eligibility: Open to highly qualified graduate and doctoral students of any nationality.
Level of Study: Postgraduate, Predocorate.
Type: A variable number of fellowships.
Length of Study: Up to nine years.
Study Establishment: Any approved university.
Country of Study: Germany.
No. of awards offered: Varies.
Application Procedure: Applications should be submitted in response to calls. For further information applicants must visit the website.
Closing Date: Please write for details.
Additional Information: A list of graduate colleges presently funded is available (in Germany only) from the DFG.

Deutsche Forschungsgemeinschaft Individual Grants

Subjects: All subjects.
Purpose: To foster the proposed research projects of promising academic scientists or scholars.
Eligibility: Open to promising researchers and Scholars who are German nationals or permanent residents of Germany.
Level of Study: Postdoctorate, Postgraduate, Predocorate, Research.
Type: A variable number of grants.
Value: Dependent on the requirements of the project.
Length of Study: Two-three years with the option of applying for renewal.
Frequency: Throughout the year.
Study Establishment: Universities worldwide.
Country of Study: Any country.
No. of awards offered: Varies.
Application Procedure: Applicants must submit a proposal for a research project. Applicants must write for more details or visit the website.
Closing Date: Applications are accepted at any time.

Deutsche Forschungsgemeinschaft Joint Research Projects

Subjects: All subjects.
Purpose: To foster co-operation between German scientists and scientists in Middle and Eastern European countries and countries of the former Soviet Union.
Eligibility: Open to German Scholars and Scholars from any participating Eastern European country.
Level of Study: Postdoctorate, Research.
Type: A variable number of grants.
Value: Dependent on the length of the research project and the number of participants.
Length of Study: Varies.
Frequency: Annual.
Study Establishment: Universities in any participating country.
Country of Study: Any country.
No. of awards offered: Varies.
Application Procedure: Applications must be submitted by researchers from German research institutes. Applicants must write for details or visit the website.

Closing Date: Please write for details.

Deutsche Forschungsgemeinschaft Research Groups

Subjects: All subjects.
Purpose: To promote intensive co-operation between highly qualified researchers in one or several institutions in fields of high scientific promise.
Eligibility: Open to interested groups of German nationals and permanent residents of Germany.
Level of Study: Postdoctorate, Research.
Type: Research grant.
Value: Dependent on the requirements of the project.
Length of Study: Up to six years.
Frequency: Annual.
Study Establishment: An approved university.
Country of Study: Germany.
No. of awards offered: Varies.
Application Procedure: Applicants must submit proposals to the Senate of the DFG. Applicants must write or visit the website for further information.
Closing Date: Please write for details.
Additional Information: A list of currently operating research groups is available in Germany only from the DFG.

DFG Collaborative Research Grants

Subjects: All subjects.
Purpose: To promote long term co-operative research in universities and academic research.
Eligibility: Open to promising groups of German nationals and permanent residents of Germany.
Level of Study: Postdoctorate, Research.
Type: A variable number of grants.
Value: Dependent on the requirements of the project.
Length of Study: 3-15 years.
Study Establishment: Universities and academic institutions in Germany.
Country of Study: Germany.
No. of awards offered: Varies.
Application Procedure: Applicants must write or visit the website for further information. Applications must be formally filed by the universities.
Closing Date: Please write for details.
Additional Information: A list of collaborative research centres is available in Germany only from the DFG.

Emmy Noether-Programme

Subjects: All subjects.
Purpose: To give outstanding young scholars the opportunity to obtain the scientific qualifications needed to be appointed as a lecturer within five years of receiving their PhD.
Eligibility: Open to promising young postdoctoral scientists up to the age of approximately 30, who are German nationals or permanent residents of Germany.
Level of Study: Postdoctorate.
Type: Project grant.
Value: For the two years of research spent abroad the candidate will receive a project grant in keeping with the requirements of the project including an allowance for subsistence and travel. For the three years of research spent at a German university or research institution the candidate will receive a project grant.
Length of Study: Five years.
Frequency: Annual.
Study Establishment: Universities or research institutions worldwide.
Country of Study: Any country.
No. of awards offered: 100.
Application Procedure: Applicants must complete an application form. For further information applicants must write or visit the website.
Closing Date: Please write for details.

Eugen and Ilse Seibold Award

Subjects: Arts and humanities.
Purpose: To promote outstanding young scientists and scholars who have made significant contributions to the scientific interchange between Japan and Germany.
Eligibility: Open to outstanding young German or Japanese Scholars.
Level of Study: Postdoctorate.
Type: Award.
Value: Please contact the organisation.
Length of Study: Varies.
Frequency: Every two years. The next will take place in 2003 and 2005.
Study Establishment: Universities or research institutions.
Country of Study: Germany or Japan.
No. of awards offered: Two.
Application Procedure: Applicants must write for details or visit the website. Application is by nomination.
Closing Date: Please write for details.

Gerhard Hess Programme

Subjects: All subjects.
Purpose: To promote young scientists and scholars who show exceptional promise and achievement and are seeking to establish an independent research group in a qualified research environment.
Eligibility: Open to promising young scientists and Scholars, up to the age of 35 years, who are German nationals or permanent residents of Germany.
Level of Study: Postdoctorate, Predoctorate, Research.
Type: Award.
Value: Please contact the organisation.
Length of Study: Two-five years.
Frequency: Annual.
Study Establishment: Any approved university or research institutions.
Country of Study: Germany.
No. of awards offered: 10.
Application Procedure: Applicants must write for details or visit the website. Application is by nomination.
Closing Date: Please write for details.

Gottfried Wilhelm Leibniz Prize

Subjects: All subjects.
Purpose: To promote outstanding scientists and Scholars in German universities and research institutions.
Eligibility: Open to outstanding Scholars in German universities.
Level of Study: Predoctorate, Research.
Type: Research grant.
Value: Please contact the organisation.
Length of Study: Five years.
Frequency: Annual.
Study Establishment: Any approved university or research institutions.
Country of Study: Germany.
No. of awards offered: Varies.
Application Procedure: Applicants must write for details or visit the website. Application is by nomination. Nominations are restricted to selected institutions such as DFG member organisations or individuals eg. former prize winners or chairpersons of DFG review committees.
Closing Date: Please write for details.
Additional Information: A list of prize winners is available (in Germany only) from the DFG.

Guest Professorships

Subjects: All subjects.
Purpose: To support stays of foreign scientists at German universities.
Eligibility: Open to foreign scientists whose individual research is of special interest to research and teaching in Germany.
Level of Study: Postdoctorate.

Type: A variable number of fellowships.
Value: Dependent on the duration of the stay.
Length of Study: 3-12 months.
Frequency: Annual.
Study Establishment: German universities.
Country of Study: Germany.
No. of awards offered: Varies.
Application Procedure: Applicants must submit a proposal by the university intending to host the guest professor.
Additional Information: Further information is available on the website.

Heinz Maier-Leibnitz Prize

Subjects: All subjects.
Purpose: To promote outstanding young scientists at doctorate level.
Eligibility: Open to promising young Scholars up to the age of 33, who are German nationals or permanent residents of Germany.
Level of Study: Doctorate, Postdoctorate.
Type: Award.
Value: Please contact the organisation.
Length of Study: Varies.
Frequency: Annual.
Study Establishment: Any approved university or research institution.
Country of Study: Germany.
No. of awards offered: Six.
Application Procedure: Applicants must write for details or visit the website. Application is by nomination.
Closing Date: Please write for details.

Heisenberg Programme

Subjects: All subjects.
Purpose: To promote outstanding young scientists.
Eligibility: Open to high calibre young scientists up to the age of 35 years who are German nationals or permanent residents of Germany.
Level of Study: Postdoctorate.
Type: Scholarship.
Value: Varies.
Length of Study: Five years.
Frequency: Annual.
Study Establishment: Any approved university or research institution.
Country of Study: Germany.
No. of awards offered: Varies.
Application Procedure: Applicants must submit a research proposal, a detailed curriculum vitae, copies of degree certificates, a copy of the thesis, a letter explaining the choice of host institution, a list of all previously published material and a letter outlining financial requirements in duplicate. For further information applicants must contact DFG.
Closing Date: Applications are accepted at any time.

Priority Programs

Subjects: All subjects.
Purpose: To promote proposals made by interested groups of scientists in selected fields.
Eligibility: Open to interested groups of scientists from Germany or any country participating in the scheme.
Level of Study: Postdoctorate, Research.
Type: A variable number of grants.
Value: The Senate decides on the financial ceiling for each programme.
Length of Study: Up to six years.
Study Establishment: Universities or academic establishments in the countries participating in the scheme.
Country of Study: Any country.
No. of awards offered: Varies.
Application Procedure: Applicants must write or visit the website for further information. Priority Programs are operated through calls for proposals, with all applications subject to open panel review, usually after discussion with the applicants.
Closing Date: Please write for details.

DIABETES RESEARCH & WELLNESS FOUNDATION

Office 108
Northney Marina, Hayling Island, Hampshire, PO11 0NH, England
Tel: (44) 23 9263 7808
Fax: (44) 23 9263 7308
Email: drwf@diabeteswellnessnet.org.uk
www: http://www.diabeteswellnessnet.org.uk
Contact: Ms Roslyn Elson, Executive Director

The Diabetes Research & Wellness Foundation was established in 1998 to fund research into finding a cure for diabetes. Each year this goal becomes more important as the number of people diagnosed continues to rise. Our hope is to make diabetes a thing of the past, and, until then, alleviate its awful complications.

DRWF Research Fellowship

Subjects: Endocrinology or diabetes.
Purpose: To encourage research into the causes, complications and possible cures for diabetes.
Eligibility: Open to candidates who are working at an institution within the United Kingdom in an established position.
Level of Study: Postdoctorate, Research.
Type: Fellowship, non-clinical.
Value: Up to UK £40,000 per year.
Length of Study: Up to three years.
Frequency: Every two years dependent on funds.
Study Establishment: A recognised institution or research group in the United Kingdom.
Country of Study: United Kingdom.
No. of awards offered: One.
Application Procedure: Applicants must undergo a three stage selection procedure starting with a pre-application which is a single sheet of A4 with single line spacing, using a clearly readable font in 11 or 12 point which must include the applicant's name, qualifications, contact details and present post. The pre-application must also include the name of the head of the group where the grant will be held, the post held or expected post to be held within the group and the relevant contact details. There should also be a 300 word abstract of the proposal research work including the title, research question, relevance to diabetes, expected outcome and any additional information to support the application.
Closing Date: May 25th.
Funding: Commercial, Private.
No. of awards given last year: One.
No. of applicants last year: 23.
Additional Information: Non clinical research fellowships are currently being offered in alternate years to clinical research fellowships.

DIABETES UK

10 Queen Anne Street, London, W1G 9LH, England
Tel: (44) 20 7462 2693
Fax: (44) 20 7637 5444
Email: eleanor.kennedy@diabetes.org.uk
www: http://www.diabetes.org.uk
Contact: Dr Eleanor Kennedy, Research Manager

Diabetes UK's overall aim is to help and to care for both people with diabetes and those closest to them, to represent and campaign for their interests, and to fund research into diabetes. Diabetes UK continues to encourage research into all areas of diabetes.

Diabetes UK Equipment Grant
Subjects: Endocrinology.
Purpose: To enable the purchase of equipment which is required only for a single project or programme and is solely concerned with diabetes research.
Eligibility: Open to suitably qualified members of the medical or scientific professions who are resident in the United Kingdom.
Level of Study: Postdoctorate.
Type: Emergency grant.
Value: More than UK £5,000.
Country of Study: United Kingdom.
No. of awards offered: Varies.
Application Procedure: Applicants must complete an application form which will be assessed by a peer review. Please write for details.
Closing Date: May 1st, September 1st or December 1st.
Funding: Private.
Contributor: Voluntary contributions.
No. of awards given last year: Nine.
No. of applicants last year: Three.

Diabetes UK Project Grants
Subjects: Endocrinology.
Purpose: To provide funding for a well-defined research proposal of timeliness and promise which, in terms of the application, may be expected to lead to a significant advance in our knowledge of diabetes.
Eligibility: Open to suitably qualified members of the medical or scientific professions who are resident in the United Kingdom.
Level of Study: Postdoctorate.
Type: Project grant.
Value: A maximum UK £40,000 per year.
Length of Study: One-three years.
Frequency: Annual.
Country of Study: United Kingdom.
No. of awards offered: Varies.
Application Procedure: Applicants must complete an application form which will be assessed by a peer review. Please write for details.
Closing Date: May 1st, September 1st or December 1st.
Funding: Private.
Contributor: Voluntary contributions.
No. of awards given last year: 48.
No. of applicants last year: 165.

Diabetes UK Research Fellowships
Subjects: Diabetes mellitus research.
Eligibility: Open to suitably qualified members of the medical or scientific professions who are resident in the United Kingdom.
Level of Study: Postdoctorate.
Type: Varies.
Value: Varies.
Length of Study: Two-three years.
Frequency: Annual.
Country of Study: United Kingdom.
Application Procedure: Applicants must complete an application form. Please write or telephone for details.
Closing Date: September.
Funding: Private.
Contributor: Members donations & subscriptions.
No. of awards given last year: Two.
No. of applicants last year: 25.
Additional Information: Availability is advertised annually in the scientific and medical press.

Diabetes UK Research Studentships
Subjects: Endocrinology.
Purpose: To train basic scientists in diabetes research.
Eligibility: Applications are invited from potential supervisors in single departments or in collaborative projects between departments,

pre-clinical or clinical. Applicants must be resident in the United Kingdom.
Level of Study: Postgraduate.
Type: Studentship.
Value: In London UK £11,500 maintenance and UK £5,000 laboratory expenses. Outside London UK £10,500 maintenance and UK £5,000 laboratory expenses.
Length of Study: Three years.
Frequency: Annual.
Country of Study: United Kingdom.
No. of awards offered: Varies.
Application Procedure: Applicants must complete an application form. Please write for details.
Closing Date: September.
Funding: Private.
Contributor: Voluntary contributions.
No. of awards given last year: Three.
No. of applicants last year: 14.
Additional Information: Availability is advertised annually in the scientific and medical press.

Diabetes UK Small Grant Scheme
Subjects: Endocrinology.
Purpose: To enable research workers to develop new ideas in the field of diabetes research.
Eligibility: Open to suitably qualified members of the medical or scientific professions who are resident in the United Kingdom.
Level of Study: Postdoctorate.
Type: Grant.
Value: Maximum UK £10,000.
Length of Study: One year.
Frequency: All year round.
Country of Study: United Kingdom.
No. of awards offered: Varies.
Application Procedure: Applicants must complete an application form which will be assessed by a peer review within six to eight weeks. Please write for details.
Closing Date: Applications are accepted at any time.
Funding: Private.
Contributor: Voluntary contributions.
No. of awards given last year: Seven.
No. of applicants last year: 11.

THE DIGESTIVE DISORDERS FOUNDATION

3 St Andrew's Place
Regent's Park, London, NW1 4LB, England
Tel: (44) 20 7486 0341
Fax: (44) 20 7224 2012
Email: ddf@digestivedisorders.org.uk
www: http://www.digestivedisorders.org.uk
Contact: G F Oliver

The Digestive Disorders Foundation (formerly the British Digestive Foundation) supports research into the cause, prevention and treatment of digestive disorders, including digestive cancers, ulcers, irritable bowel syndrome, inflammatory bowel disease, diverticulitis, liver disease and pancreatitis. The Foundation also provides information for the public explaining the symptoms and treatment of these and other common digestive conditions.

Digestive Disorders Foundation Fellowships and Grants
Subjects: Gastroenterology such as basic or applied clinical research into normal and abnormal aspects of the gastrointestinal tract, liver and pancreas, the prevention of and treatment for digestive disorders.
Purpose: To provide funding for gastroenterological research.

Eligibility: Applicants must have been resident in the United Kingdom for a minimum of five years. Fellowship projects must contain an element of basic science training.
Level of Study: Doctorate, Postdoctorate, Postgraduate, Research.
Type: Fellowships, research and travel grants.
Value: For fellowships, payment of a full time salary up to specialist registrar grade if medically qualified is available. Research grants are up to UK £10,000 and travel grants are up to UK £2,000.
Length of Study: One, two or three years.
Frequency: Dependent on funds available.
Study Establishment: Recognised and established research centres.
Country of Study: Primarily the United Kingdom, but training grants for overseas study by British residents can be given.
No. of awards offered: Approx. 10.
Application Procedure: Applicants must complete an application form for consideration in a research competition. Competitions are advertised in December and July each year. Details are available from the website.
Funding: Commercial, Private.
Contributor: Charitable donations.
No. of awards given last year: 10.
No. of applicants last year: Varies.
Additional Information: Conditions are advertised in the medical press. Research grants are awarded for specific projects in the same field of interest. Travel grants are awarded to assist researchers by enabling them to visit overseas institutions with the aim of learning new techniques or otherwise advancing their own research.

THE DIRKSEN CONGRESSIONAL CENTER

301 South 4th Street
Suite A, Pekin, IL, 61554-4219, United States of America
Tel: (1) 309 347 7113
Fax: (1) 309 347 6432
Email: fmackaman@pekin.net
www: http://www.pekin.net/dirksen
Contact: Mr Frank H Mackaman, Executive Director

The Dirksen Congressional Center sponsors educational and research programmes to help people better understand the United States Congress, its members and leaders, and the public policies it produces.

Dirksen Congressional Research Grants Program

Subjects: Political science and government.
Purpose: To fund the study of the United States Congress and its leaders.
Eligibility: Restricted to United States citizens or residents. Awards are to individuals only. No institutional overhead charges are permitted.
Level of Study: Doctorate, Postdoctorate, Professional development.
Type: Research grant.
Value: Up to US$3,500.
Length of Study: Not defined.
Frequency: Annual.
Study Establishment: Unrestricted.
Country of Study: United States of America.
No. of awards offered: Varies.
Application Procedure: Applicants should visit the Center's website for application information.
Closing Date: February 1st.
Funding: Private.
No. of awards given last year: 15.
No. of applicants last year: 55.

Robert H Michel Civic Education Grants

Subjects: Areas of interest include designing lesson plans, creating student activities and applying instructional technology in the classroom.
Purpose: To help teachers, curriculum developers and others improve the quality of civic instruction, with priority on the role of Congress in the United States of America Federal Government.
Eligibility: Restricted to United States citizens or residents. Awards are to individuals only. No institutional overhead charges are permitted.
Level of Study: Professional development.
Type: Grant.
Value: Varies, up to $5,000.
Length of Study: Not defined.
Frequency: Three times each year.
Study Establishment: Unrestricted.
Country of Study: United States of America.
No. of awards offered: Varies.
Application Procedure: Applicants should visit the Center's website for application information.
Closing Date: October 1st or May 1st.
Funding: Private.
No. of awards given last year: Eight.
No. of applicants last year: 65.

DOW JONES NEWSPAPER FUND, INC.

PO Box 300, Princeton, NJ, 08543-0300, United States of America
Tel: (1) 609 452 2820
Fax: (1) 609 520 5804
Email: newsfund@wsj.dowjones.com
www: http://www.dowjones.com/newsfund
Contact: Grants Management Officer

The Dow Jones Newspaper Fund is a private foundation that promotes careers in journalism.

Dow Jones Editing Intern Program

Subjects: Communication studies and journalism.
Purpose: To encourage careers in copy editing.
Eligibility: Open to United States of America citizens only.
Level of Study: Graduate, Postgraduate.
Type: Scholarship or internship.
Value: Interns returning to school at the end of the Summer receive a US$1,000 scholarship.
Length of Study: Summer programme.
Frequency: Annual.
Country of Study: United States of America.
No. of awards offered: Up to 110.
Application Procedure: Applicants must complete an application form and submit this with a curriculum vitae, list of grades or courses, essay and tests. Candidates will only be considered if an application form is submitted with the required materials. Applications are available from July 15th to November 1st.
Closing Date: All materials must be postmarked by November 15th.
No. of awards given last year: 100.
No. of applicants last year: 600.
Additional Information: This is a United States national competition.

Dow Jones Teacher Fellowship Program

Subjects: Journalism, comprising of basic courses in reporting, layout and design, newspaper publication workshops, desktop publishing and the first amendment.
Purpose: To provide education for high school journalism teachers and publication advisers.
Eligibility: Open to United States of America high school teachers who teach journalism or have advised the student newspaper.
Level of Study: Professional development.
Type: Fellowship.

Value: Varies. Up to US$500 to be used for tuition, books, fees and transportation.
Frequency: Annual.
Study Establishment: A department of journalism in a college or university approved by the Fund.
Country of Study: United States of America.
No. of awards offered: Varies.
Application Procedure: Applicants must apply directly to the school offering the workshop. A list of workshops is available on the Fund's website.
Closing Date: March 15th to June 1st.
Funding: Private.
Additional Information: Grants will be awarded to colleges, universities and journalism organisations offering Summer workshops and courses on specific topics. Directors of the workshops will select the fellowship recipients based on eligibility requirements along with additional restrictions based on the workshop. Interested teachers should request a list of workshops between March 1st-July 15th.

DR HADWEN TRUST FOR HUMANE RESEARCH

84A Tilehouse Street, Hitchin, Hertfordshire, SG5 2DY, England
Tel: (44) 1462 436819
Fax: (44) 1462 436844
Email: info@drhadwentrust.org.uk
www: http://www.drhadwentrust.org.uk
Contact: Dr G Langley

The Dr Hadwen Trust for Humane Research is a registered charity, established in 1970, to promote research into techniques and procedures to replace the use of living animals in biomedical research, teaching and testing.

Dr Hadwen Trust for Humane Research Plus PhD Studentship

Subjects: Developing alternatives to animal experiments in biomedical fields.
Purpose: To encourage young graduates with good honours degrees to train in non animal methods.
Eligibility: Applicants must be resident in the United Kingdom.
Level of Study: Postgraduate.
Type: Studentship.
Value: Value outside London is UK £7,250 per year and in London is UK £9,580 plus an allowance for consumables.
Length of Study: Three years.
Frequency: Dependent on funds available.
Country of Study: United Kingdom.
No. of awards offered: Varies.
Application Procedure: Applicants must make initial enquiries in writing to the Scientific Adviser, Dr G Langley. Applications must be submitted by the project supervisor.
Funding: Private.
Contributor: Donations from the general public.

Dr Hadwen Trust Research Assistant or Technician

Subjects: The development, validation or implementation of a technique or procedure which would replace one currently using living animals.
Purpose: To provide additional scientific or technical support for a research project.
Eligibility: Applicants must be resident in the United Kingdom.
Value: Salary for research assistant or technician plus an allowance for consumables.
Length of Study: Three years.
Frequency: Dependent on funds available.
Study Establishment: Varies.
Country of Study: United Kingdom.
No. of awards offered: Varies.

Application Procedure: Applicants must make initial enquiries in writing to the Scientific Adviser, Dr G Langley. Applications must be made by the Senior Researcher who will oversee the work.
Funding: Private.

Dr Hadwen Trust Research Fellowship

Subjects: The development, validation or implementation of a technique or procedure which would replace one currently using living animals.
Purpose: To attract and retain talented young scientists in non-animal research fields. The funds provide personal support and a contribution to direct research costs.
Eligibility: Applicants must be resident in the United Kingdom.
Level of Study: Postdoctorate.
Type: Fellowship.
Value: Salary on research analogous salary scale grade 1A, up to spinal point 9 plus a London allowance where appropriate and an allowance for consumables.
Length of Study: Three years.
Frequency: Dependent on funds available.
Study Establishment: Varies.
Country of Study: United Kingdom.
No. of awards offered: Varies.
Application Procedure: Applicants must make initial enquiries in writing to the Scientific Adviser, Dr G Langley. Application forms must be submitted by a Senior Researcher who will oversee the work.
Funding: Private.
Contributor: Public donations.

DR M AYLWIN COTTON FOUNDATION

c/o Albany Trustee Company Ltd
PO Box 232
Pollet House, St Peter Port, GY1 4LA, Guernsey
Tel: (44) 1481 724136
Fax: (44) 1481 710478
Contact: Ms Anne McMillan, Administrator

Cotton Research Fellowships

Subjects: Archaeology, architecture, history, language and the arts of the Mediterranean.
Eligibility: Open to senior Scholars.
Level of Study: Professional development.
Type: Fellowship.
Value: Up to UK £10,000.
Frequency: Annual.
Country of Study: Any country.
No. of awards offered: Varies.
Application Procedure: Applicants must complete an application form, available on request.
Closing Date: February 28th.
Funding: Private.
Contributor: Dr M Aylwin Cotton.
No. of awards given last year: Eight.
No. of applicants last year: 42.
Additional Information: The Foundation also provides grants annually to finance the publication costs of a completed work or a work due for publication in the immediate future.

DUBLIN INSTITUTE FOR ADVANCED STUDIES

10 Burlington Road, Dublin, 4, Ireland
Tel: (353) 1 668 0748
Fax: (353) 1 668 0561
Email: registrar@admin.dias.ie
www: http://www.dias.ie
Contact: Ms Kathy Carr, Administrative Assistant

The Dublin Institute for Advanced Studies is a statutory corporation established in 1940 under the Institute for Advanced Studies Act of that year. It is a publicly funded independent centre for research in basic disciplines. Research is currently carried out in the fields of celtic studies and cosmic physics including astronomy, astrophysics, geophysics and theoretical physics.

Dublin Institute for Advanced Studies Scholarship in Astronomy, Astrophysics and Geophysics

Subjects: Astronomy, astrophysics or geophysics.
Purpose: To enable training in advanced research methods in the fields of astronomy, astrophysics and geophysics.
Eligibility: Open to candidates from any country.
Level of Study: Doctorate, Postdoctorate, Postgraduate.
Type: Scholarship.
Value: Please contact the Institute for details.
Length of Study: One year.
Frequency: Annual.
Study Establishment: The Dublin Institute for Advanced Studies.
Country of Study: Ireland.
No. of awards offered: Three.
Application Procedure: Applicants must complete an application form, available upon request.
Closing Date: Please write for details.
Funding: Government.
Contributor: State funded.
No. of awards given last year: Two.
No. of applicants last year: 12.

Dublin Institute for Advanced Studies Scholarship in Celtic Studies

Subjects: Celtic studies, futurology or anthropology.
Purpose: To enable training in advanced research methods in the field of Celtic studies.
Eligibility: Open to nationals of any country.
Level of Study: Doctorate, Postdoctorate, Postgraduate.
Type: Scholarship.
Value: Please contact the Institute for details.
Length of Study: One year.
Frequency: Annual.
Study Establishment: The Dublin Institute for Advanced Studies.
Country of Study: Ireland.
No. of awards offered: One.
Application Procedure: Applicants must complete an application form, available upon request.
Closing Date: Applications are accepted at any time.
Funding: Government.
No. of awards given last year: Three.
No. of applicants last year: 10.

Dublin Institute for Advanced Studies Scholarship in Theoretical Physics

Subjects: Physics.
Purpose: To enable training in advanced research methods in the field of theoretical physics.
Eligibility: Open to candidates of any country.
Level of Study: Postdoctorate.
Type: Scholarship.
Value: Please contact the Institute for details.
Length of Study: One year.
Frequency: Annual.

Study Establishment: The Dublin Institute for Advanced Studies.
Country of Study: Ireland.
No. of awards offered: Five.
Application Procedure: Applicants must complete an application form, available upon request.
Closing Date: Please write for details.
Funding: Government.
Contributor: State funded.
No. of awards given last year: Three.
No. of applicants last year: 30.

DUKE UNIVERSITY CENTER

Box 2908, Durham, NC, 27710, United States of America
Tel: (1) 919 681 8777
Fax: (1) 919 681 8744
Email: grm@duke.edu
www: http://www.geri.duke.edu/educate/rtp.html
Contact: Co-ordinator

Duke University Center Postdoctoral Training in Aging Research

Subjects: Social and behavioural sciences, natural sciences and medical sciences.
Purpose: To train research scientists in the methods used in research on ageing in any scientific field.
Eligibility: Open to United States of America citizens and permanent residents.
Level of Study: Postdoctorate.
Type: Training award.
Value: US$28,260-44,412 depending on experience. This amount is reviewed annually.
Length of Study: Two years.
Frequency: Annual.
Study Establishment: Duke University.
Country of Study: United States of America.
No. of awards offered: Approx. four.
Application Procedure: Applicants must submit a curriculum vitae and letter requesting further application materials. Applicants must also submit a project description, three letters of reference, a training plan, a career plan and graduate transcripts. Further information and application forms are available from the website.
Closing Date: April 1st.
Funding: Government.
Contributor: The National Institute on Aging.

DUMBARTON OAKS: TRUSTEES FOR HARVARD UNIVERSITY

1703 32nd Street North West, Washington, DC, 20007, United States of America
Tel: (1) 202 339 6410
www: http://www.doaks.org
Contact: Ms Carol A Sellery, Fellowship Program Manager

Dumbarton Oaks houses important research and study collections in the areas of Byzantine and Medieval studies, landscape architecture studies and pre-Columbian studies. While the gallery holds exhibitions and the gardens are open to the public, the research facilities exist primarily to serve scholars who hold appointments at Dumbarton Oaks.

Dumbarton Oaks Fellowships and Junior Fellowships

Subjects: Byzantine civilisation in all its aspects, including the late Roman and Early Christian period and the Middle Ages generally, studies of Byzantine cultural exchanges with the Latin West, Slavic and Near Eastern Countries, pre-Columbian studies and studies in landscape architecture.

Purpose: To promote study and research or to support writing of doctoral dissertations.

Eligibility: Junior Fellowships are open to persons of any nationality who have passed all preliminary examinations for a higher degree and are writing a dissertation. Candidates must have a working knowledge of any languages required for research. Fellowships are open to Scholars of any nationality holding a PhD or relevant advanced degree and wishing to pursue research on a project of their own at Dumbarton Oaks.

Level of Study: Doctorate, Postdoctorate.

Type: Fellowship.

Value: US$13,900 per year for junior fellowships and US$25,325 per year for fellowships. Both junior and regular Fellows receive furnished accommodation or a housing allowance and US$1,900, if needed, to assist with the cost of bringing and maintaining dependants in Washington and an expense account of US$900 for approved research expenditure during the academic year. Fellows are also provided with travel assistance.

Length of Study: Up to one academic year of full-time study, non renewable.

Frequency: Annual.

Study Establishment: Dumbarton Oaks.

Country of Study: United States of America.

No. of awards offered: 10-11 fellowships in Byzantine studies, three-four in each of the other fields.

Application Procedure: Applicants must contact Dumbarton Oaks for the current application brochure.

Closing Date: November 1st of the academic year preceding that for which the fellowship is required.

No. of awards given last year: 35 between Summer, Junior and Regular Fellowships.

No. of applicants last year: 200.

Additional Information: Dumbarton Oaks also awards a limited number of Summer Fellowships.

DUQUESNE UNIVERSITY, DEPARTMENT OF PHILOSOPHY

Pittsburgh, PA, 15282, United States of America
Tel: (1) 412 396 6500
Fax: (1) 412 396 5353
Email: thompson@duq.edu
www: http://www.duq.edu
Contact: Ms Joan Thompson, Administrative Assistant

The PhD programme in the Department of Philosophy at Duquesne University emphasises continental philosophy, ie. phenomenology and twentieth-century French and German philosophy, as well as the history of philosophy.

Duquesne University Graduate Assistantship

Subjects: Philosophy.

Purpose: To provide a stipend to enable students to obtain a PhD in philosophy.

Eligibility: Open to holders of a Bachelor's degree in philosophy, or its equivalent, who have a grade point average of at least 3.7 and an excellent Graduate Record Examination score. Candidates should have knowledge of a second language.

Level of Study: Doctorate.

Type: Graduate assistantship.

Value: A stipend of approximately US$9,000 plus all tuition for coursework.

Length of Study: Five-six years.

Frequency: Annual.

Study Establishment: McAnulty College and Graduate School of Liberal Arts.

Country of Study: United States of America.

No. of awards offered: 13 each year, two for first year students.

Application Procedure: Applicants must complete an application including a statement of intent and three letters of recommendation, Graduate Record Examination scores and application form and fee, plus Test Of English as a Foreign Language scores.

Closing Date: February 15th before the Autumn term.

Funding: Private.

Contributor: Duquesne University.

No. of awards given last year: 13.

No. of applicants last year: 75.

DYSTROPHIC EPIDERMOLYSIS BULLOSA RESEARCH ASSOCIATION (DEBRA)

DEBRA House
13 Wellington Business Park
Dukes Ride, Crowthorne, Berkshire, RG45 6LS, England
Tel: (44) 1344 771961
Fax: (44) 1344 762661
Email: debra.uk@btinternet.com
www: http://www.debra.org.uk
Contact: Mr John Dart, Director

The Dystrophic Epidermolysis Bullosa Research Association (DEBRA) is a voluntary organisation working on behalf of people with epidermolysis bullosa. The main activities of the organisation are funding research into epidermolysis bullosa, and providing services to people whose lives are affected by epidermolysis bullosa.

DEBRA Medical Research Grant Scheme

Subjects: Dermatology, treatment techniques or genetics.

Purpose: To fund research into all aspects of Epidermolysis Bullosa.

Eligibility: Open to qualified researchers who are able to demonstrate the ability to undertake a specific project in Epidermolysis Bullosa.

Level of Study: Postdoctorate.

Type: Project grant.

Value: Approx. UK £30,000 per year.

Length of Study: Up to three years.

Frequency: Twice a year.

Country of Study: Any country.

No. of awards offered: Varies.

Application Procedure: Applicants must complete an application form, available from the DEBRA office and the website.

Closing Date: April 1st or October 1st.

Funding: Private.

Contributor: Private donations.

No. of awards given last year: 10.

No. of applicants last year: 16.

EARLY AMERICAN INDUSTRIES ASSOCIATION

1324 Shallcross Avenue, Wilmington, DE, 19806, United States of America
Tel: (1) 302 652 7297
Contact: Ms Justine J Mataleno, Co-ordinator

The Early American Industries Association seeks to encourage the study and better understanding of early American industries in the home, in the shop, on the farm and on the sea. It also wishes to discover, identify, classify, and exhibit obsolete tools, implements, and mechanical devices which were used in early America.

Early American Industries Association Research Grants Program

Subjects: Early American industrial development, including craft practices, industrial technology and identification and use of obsolete tools, implements and mechanical devices used in early America.
Purpose: To encourage graduate or postgraduate research on the preservation and classification of obsolete tools and mechanical devices prior to 1900, leading to a publication, exhibition or audio-visual material for educational purposes.
Eligibility: Open to United States citizens or permanent residents. Individuals may be sponsored by an institution or be engaged in self directed projects. Research is restricted to American tools and industrial technology prior to 1900.
Level of Study: Postgraduate.
Type: Grant.
Value: Up to US$2,000.
Length of Study: One year, non renewable.
Frequency: Annual.
Country of Study: United States of America.
No. of awards offered: Three-five.
Application Procedure: Applicants must submit a completed application form plus three letters of recommendation.
Closing Date: March 15th.
Funding: Private.
Contributor: Membership dues and donations.
Additional Information: Awards may be used to supplement existing financial awards. Successful applicants are required to file a project report on forms supplied by the Association. These are not scholarship funds.

EARTHWATCH INSTITUTE

3 Clocktower Place Suite 100
Box 75, Maynard, MA, 01754-0075, United States of America
Tel: (1) 978 461 0081 ext. 116
Fax: (1) 978 461 2332
Email: mmarino@earthwatch.org
www: http://www.earthwatch.org
Contact: Mr Matt Marino, Fellowships Assistant

Earthwatch Institute is a non-profit organisation formed in 1972 which supports scientific field research by placing paying volunteers in two-week expeditions worldwide. Earthwatch's mission is to promote sustainable conservation of the world's natural resources and cultural heritage by creating partnerships between scientists, educators, and the general public.

Earthwatch Education Awards

Subjects: Science education, historical and cultural education.
Purpose: To give teachers and students the opportunity to experience field research first hand and share this experience with their students and local communities.
Eligibility: Open to full time, elementary, middle or high school students aged 16 or over.
Level of Study: Professional development.
Type: Participation fellowship.
Value: Partial to full funding for over 300 teachers and students to participate in Earthwatch expeditions.
Length of Study: Two-three weeks.
Frequency: Annual.
Country of Study: Any country.
No. of awards offered: 265.
Application Procedure: Applicants must complete an application form and submit it with the other requested documents. Incomplete applications will not be considered. Letters of recommendation are required and should explain how long and in what respect they know the applicant. There is an application fee of US$20.
Closing Date: Applications are accepted on an ongoing basis.
Funding: Private.

Contributor: Over 40 donors including foundations and corporations.
No. of awards given last year: 250.
No. of applicants last year: 700.
Additional Information: Recipients are limited to two Education Awards and cannot receive an award in two consecutive years. Applicants will not be considered if they have already reserved a space on an expedition.

EAST LOTHIAN EDUCATIONAL TRUST

Finance Department
John Muir House, Haddington, East Lothian, EH41 3HA, Scotland
Tel: (44) 1620 892314
Fax: (44) 1620 827446
Contact: Kim Stirrat, Clerk

The East Lothian Educational Trust provides grants to individuals who are undertaking studies, courses or projects of an educational nature, including scholarships abroad and educational travel. Applicants must be residents of East Lothian.

East Lothian Educational Trust General Grant

Subjects: All subjects, but must be of an educational nature.
Purpose: To provide supplementary support to individuals who undertake studies.
Eligibility: Open to residents of East Lothian, excluding Musselburgh, Wallyford and Whitecraig.
Level of Study: Unrestricted.
Type: Supplementary bursary.
Value: Variable.
Length of Study: Unrestricted.
Frequency: Annual.
No. of awards offered: Variable.
Application Procedure: Applicants must complete an application form.
Closing Date: August 20th and November 20th each year.
Funding: Private.

EASTMAN DENTAL CENTER

University of Rochester
625 Elmwood Avenue, Rochester, NY, 14620, United States of America
Tel: (1) 716 275 8315
Fax: (1) 716 256 3153
Email: mfoy@edc.rochester.edu
Contact: Ms Marilyn Foy, Residency Co-ordinator

Eastman Dental Center Clinical Fellowships

Subjects: General dentistry.
Purpose: To enable suitably qualified dental graduates to undertake training and/or research at the Center.
Eligibility: Open to recent dental graduates who have a DDS degree or equivalent qualification. Candidates from overseas must show evidence of high academic achievement and of their intention to follow an academic or research career.
Level of Study: Postdoctorate.
Type: Fellowship.
Value: International students pay tuition for peridontics prosthodontics and orthodontics. Scholarships are sometimes available for General Dentistry.
Length of Study: One-two year programmes from June to June.
Frequency: Annual.
Study Establishment: The University of Rochester, Eastman Dental Center.
Country of Study: United States of America.
No. of awards offered: Approx. 25.

Application Procedure: Applicants must submit a completed application form, curriculum vitae, dental transcripts, undergraduate transcripts and three letters of recommendation from dental professors and Dean of Dental School.

Closing Date: October 15th for Advanced Education in General Dentistry, General Practice Residency, Prosthodontics and Paediatric Dentistry, and September 1st for Orthodontics and Periodontics.

No. of awards given last year: 10.

No. of applicants last year: 200.

EASTMAN SCHOOL OF MUSIC OF THE UNIVERSITY OF ROCHESTER

26 Gibbs Street, Rochester, NY, 14604, United States of America
Tel: (1) 716 274 1060
Fax: (1) 716 232 8601
Email: esmadmit@uhura.cc.rochester.edu
www: http://www.rochester.edu/eastman
Contact: Ms Theresa K Gieseke, Acting Director of Financial Aid

In its 16-year history the Eastman School of Music has remained faithful to its founding mission to develop articulate and literate musicians. The breadth and depth of the accomplishments of its graduates is testimony to the strength and value of an Eastman education.

Eastman School of Music Graduate Awards

Subjects: Music.

Purpose: To support the School's academic programmes.

Eligibility: Open to nationals of all countries. Candidates should have the qualifications necessary for admission to the Eastman School of Music. Non United States citizens are usually offered service scholarships in ensemble work at graduate level.

Level of Study: Doctorate, Postgraduate.

Type: Tuition scholarships and stipends.

Value: Up to US$25,685.

Length of Study: One academic year, renewable.

Frequency: Annual.

Study Establishment: At the School.

Country of Study: United States of America.

No. of awards offered: Approx. 200.

Application Procedure: Applicants must complete an application form. In addition, most awards require an interview in Rochester.

Closing Date: January 1st.

Funding: Private.

Contributor: The Institution.

No. of awards given last year: 214.

No. of applicants last year: 735.

Additional Information: Further information is available on request.

ECONOMIC AND SOCIAL COMMISSION FOR ASIA AND THE PACIFIC (ESCAP)

United Nations Building
Rajadamnern Avenue, Bangkok, 10200, Thailand
Tel: (66) 2 288 1502
Fax: (66) 2 288 3036
www: http://www.unescap.org
Contact: Ms Evelyn Domingo-Barker, Chief Librarian

The Economic and Social Commission for Asia and the Pacific (ESCAP), located in Bangkok, is the largest of the five United Nation's Regional Commissions, comprising 51 members and nine associate members and representing some 60 per cent of the world's population, or 3.5 billion people.

ESCAP HRD Award

Subjects: Each year the award carries a different theme. Previous themes include HRD for empowering the urban poor, HRD for women in extreme poverty and HRD aspects of the environment. Please consult the organisation for specific details.

Purpose: To recognise exemplary work in the field of human resources development and to encourage exemplary training, research or other innovative achievement.

Eligibility: Open to individuals, resident nationals, organisations and institutions in both the government and non governmental sectors of developing and transitional countries and areas of the ESCAP region who/which have undertaken practical research, training or other innovative HRD work.

Type: Award.

Value: US$30,000.

Frequency: Annual.

Application Procedure: Applications should include an overview of activities related to the theme of the award with a maximum of 3,000 words, a summary of 600 words of the most significant features of the applicant's HRD work for each of the five criteria. These criteria are the degree of HRD commitment, responsiveness, innovativeness, impact and sustainability. They should also contain letters from two independent referees and a project proposal with a maximum of five pages on A4 size paper. No applications sent by email will be accepted. Applications should be addressed to Human Resources Development Section, Social Development Division.

Closing Date: November 30th, but please check with the organisation.

Funding: Government.

No. of awards given last year: One.

No. of applicants last year: 129.

ECONOMIC AND SOCIAL RESEARCH COUNCIL (ESRC)

Polaris House
North Star Avenue, Swindon, Wiltshire, SN2 1UJ, England
Tel: (44) 1793 413000
Fax: (44) 1793 413056
Email: ptd@esrc.ac.uk
www: http://www.esrc.ac.uk/postgrad.html
Contact: Ms Zoë Grimwood, Divisional Administrator

The Economic and Social Research Council (ESRC) is an independent, government funded body set up by royal charter. The mission of ESRC is to promote and support, by any means, high-quality basic, strategic and applied research and related postgraduate training in the social sciences. It also aims to advance knowledge and provide trained social scientists which meet the needs of users and beneficiaries, thereby contributing to the economic competitiveness of the United Kingdom, the effectiveness of public services and policy, and quality of life. ESRC also provides advice, disseminates knowledge and promotes public understanding of the social sciences.

The ESRC 1+3 Awards

Subjects: Social sciences.

Purpose: To promote social science research and postgraduate training. The ESRC aims to provide continuous support for high quality postgraduate training and research on issues of importance to business, the public sector and government.

Eligibility: Open to United Kingdom or European Community nationals with a First or Upper Second Class (Honours) Degree in any subject, a United Kingdom professional qualification acceptable to the ESRC as of degree standard plus three years' subsequent full-time relevant professional work experience. Candidates must have ordinarily been resident in Great Britain throughout the three year period preceding the date of application and not have been so resident during any part of that period wholly or mainly for the purpose of receiving full-time education.

Level of Study: Postgraduate.

Type: Standard research studentship which includes 1+3 scholarships, Case research studentship, ESRC/NERC studentship.

Value: ESRC 1+3 awards cover fees and maintenance, depending on the student's situation, circumstances and the type of award.

Length of Study: Up to three years.

Frequency: Annual.

Study Establishment: Institutional outlets and courses which have been given recognition by ESRC.

Country of Study: United Kingdom.

No. of awards offered: Varies.

Application Procedure: Applicants must complete an application form. Information sheets and application forms are available from February each year and must be collected from the social science department of any university or Institute of Higher Education or career guidance outlet.

Closing Date: May 1st.

Funding: Government.

ESRC Research Studentships

Subjects: Social sciences.

Purpose: To promote social science research and postgraduate training. The ESRC aims to provide funding for high quality postgraduate training and research on issues of importance to business, the public sector and government.

Eligibility: Open to United Kingdom or European Community nationals with a First or Upper Second Class (Honours) Degree in any subject, a Master's degree or a degree from a United Kingdom university or the CNAA, a United Kingdom professional qualification acceptable to the ESRC as of degree standard plus three years' subsequent full-time relevant professional work experience. Candidates must have ordinarily been resident in Great Britain throughout the three year period preceding the date of application and not have been so resident during any part of that period wholly or mainly for the purpose of receiving full-time education.

Level of Study: Postgraduate.

Type: Standard research studentship, CASE research studentship, ESRC/NERC studentship.

Value: ESRC studentship awards can cover fees and maintenance, depending on the student's situation, circumstances and the type of award.

Length of Study: Up to three years.

Frequency: Annual.

Study Establishment: Institutional outlets and courses which have been given recognition by ESRC.

Country of Study: United Kingdom.

No. of awards offered: Varies.

Application Procedure: Applicants must complete an application form. Information sheets and application forms are available from February each year and must be collected from the social science department of any university or Institute of Higher Education or career guidance outlet.

Closing Date: May 1st for competition applications and June 1st for quota nominations.

Funding: Government.

No. of awards given last year: 900.

No. of applicants last year: 1,500.

Additional Information: Guidance notes are available from social science departments, Registrars and university careers services from the middle of February each year.

ECONOMIC HISTORY ASSOCIATION (EHA)

University of Kansas
Department of Economics
226A Summerfield Hall, Lawrence, KS, 66049, United States of America
Tel: (1) 785 864 2847
Fax: (1) 785 864 5270
Email: eha@falcon.cc.ukans.edu
www: http://www.eh.net/eha
Contact: Mr Thomas Weiss, Executive Director

The Economic History Association (EHA) was founded in 1940. Its mission is to stimulate interest in the study of economic history, to encourage research in economic history and ideas, to co-operate with societies devoted to the study of agricultural, industrial, technological, or business history and to collaborate with economists, historians, statisticians, geographers and all other students of economic change.

Arthur H Cole Grants-in-Aid

Subjects: Economic history.

Purpose: To support research in economic history.

Eligibility: Applicants must have completed a PhD and be a member of the EHA.

Level of Study: Postdoctorate.

Type: Grant in aid.

Value: Typically US$1,500 award.

Frequency: Annual.

Country of Study: Any country.

Application Procedure: Applicants must supply seven copies of the following: a description of the project of no more than five pages, a curriculum vitae and a brief budget for the project. Applications must be marked for the attention of Professor Kerry Odell.

Closing Date: April 1st.

Funding: Private.

Contributor: EHA Members.

No. of awards given last year: Three.

Additional Information: Membership enquiries should be addressed to the Department of Economics.

For further information contact:

Caltech (California Institute of Technology)
Department of Economics
MC 228-77, Pasadena, CA, 91125, United States of America
Contact: Professor Caroline Fohlin

EDMUND NILES HUYCK PRESERVE, INC.

PO Box 189, Rensselaerville, NY, 12147, United States of America
Tel: (1) 518 797 3440
Fax: (1) 518 797 3440
Email: rlwyman@capital.net
www: http://www.huyckpreserve.org/ggl.htm
Contact: Grants Management Officer

The Edmund Niles Huyck Preserve is a 2,000 acre nature preserve and biological research station with a newly expanded laboratory and housing for 20. The habitat is the north eastern hardwood-hemlock forest with lakes, streams, bogs and plantations.

Edmund Niles Huyck Preserve, Inc. Graduate and Postgraduate Grants

Subjects: Ecology, behaviour, evolution and natural resources of the area, and conservation biology.

Purpose: To promote scientific research on the flora and fauna of the Huyck Preserve and vicinity.

Eligibility: Awards are made without regard to sex, colour, religion, ethnic origin or academic affiliation of the applicant. Support is based

solely on the quality of the proposed research and its appropriateness to the natural resources and facilities of the Preserve.
Level of Study: Doctorate, Graduate, Postdoctorate, Postgraduate.
Type: Grant.
Value: A maximum of US$2,500 plus laboratory space and lodging. The grants are renewable.
Length of Study: Varies.
Frequency: Annual.
Study Establishment: At the Preserve.
Country of Study: United States of America.
No. of awards offered: 10.
Application Procedure: Applicants must complete an application form, available on written request. Proposals must contain an abstract of not more than 200 words describing the background and significance of the proposal. A literature cited section should be included and an up to date curriculum vitae should be provided. The researcher should submit three references that deal specifically with the work proposed to be done at the Preserve.
Closing Date: February 1st.
Funding: Private.
No. of awards given last year: Six.
No. of applicants last year: 12.
Additional Information: Further information is available from the website.

EDUCATIONAL COMMISSION FOR FOREIGN MEDICAL GRADUATES (ECFMG)

3624 Market Street, Philadelphia, PA, 19104-2685, United States of America
Tel: (1) 215 823 2105
Fax: (1) 215 387 9963
www: http://www.ecfmg.org
Contact: Director, Programme Planning & Development

The Educational Commission for Foreign Medical Graduates (ECFMG) serves the public interest through a programme of evaluation of foreign trained physicians. ECFMG also sponsors foreign national physicians as exchange visitors in accredited graduate medical education programmes. The organisation's aims and missions include promoting excellence in international medical education and contributing to the exchange of medical knowledge among nations.

International Fellowships in Medical Education
Subjects: Eligible areas of study include educational methodology, curriculum design, evaluation systems, medical school governance and the development of basic and clinical science departments.
Purpose: To facilitate the placement of faculty from foreign medical schools in United States academic institutions able to provide educational opportunities of high quality. This is in order to match educational opportunities in the United States of America with the determined needs of nations abroad, and to provide opportunities for faculty from schools of medicine outside the United States to study aspects of medical education in the United States that have the potential to improve medical education in their home country institutions and departments.
Eligibility: Applicants must reside and work in their home countries both at the time of application and at the time of acceptance of the Fellowship. They must also hold an academic appointment as a faculty member in a school of medicine or postgraduate medical education institute and have a graduate or professional degree in clinical medicine, a basic science or education. More than three years of experience as a faculty member, the ability to communicate effectively in the English language and the endorsement of a home country medical school or postgraduate medical education institute are also required. Candidates must have a position to return to in the home country on completion of the Fellowship.
Level of Study: Professional development.

Type: Fellowship.
Value: US$2,400 monthly stipend, round trip air fare for the Fellow only, and health insurance for the Fellow and any accompanying family members.
Length of Study: 6-12 months.
Frequency: Annual.
Study Establishment: Medical institutions in the United States.
Country of Study: United States of America.
No. of awards offered: 15-20.
Application Procedure: Applicants must request and complete an application form. Two reference reports must also be submitted. EFCMG screens applications, matches approved candidates with appropriate United States faculty mentors and provides formal recognition for the educational programme upon its completion.
Closing Date: August 15th.
Funding: Private.
Additional Information: Fellowships are not provided for programmes in basic or clinical research, degree granting educational programmes, programmes that require tuition payments, grants for short-term courses or conference attendance, speciality training in residency programmes, clinical fellowships, or training solely in clinical procedures or educational programmes in schools of public health.

EDUCATIONAL FOUNDATION OF THE NATIONAL RESTAURANT ASSOCIATION

175 West Jackson Boulevard
Suite 1500, Chicago, IL, 60604-2702, United States of America
Tel: (1) 312 715 5385
Email: dramos@foodtrain.org
www: http://www.nraef.org
Contact: Mrs Dalilah Torres-Ramos, Scholarship Programme Specialist

The Educational Foundation of the National Restaurant Association is the educational branch of the National Restaurant Association, the largest provider of food service and hospitality scholarships, grants and fellowships.

National Restaurant Association Teacher Work-Study Grants
Subjects: Hotel, restaurant and institutional management, food service, culinary arts and commercial foods.
Purpose: To provide the opportunity for educators in the food service and hospitality industry to gain hands on work experience during the summer.
Eligibility: Open to United States citizens who are full-time teachers or administrators at an educational institution at the high school or college level who will continue to be full-time teachers or administrators in a food service or hospitality orientated programme, or who will be full-time students pursuing an advanced degree during the next academic year.
Level of Study: Postgraduate.
Type: Grant.
Value: US$2,000.
Frequency: Annual.
Study Establishment: An appropriate institution.
Country of Study: United States of America.
No. of awards offered: 28.
Application Procedure: Applicants must complete applications, available from November 1st.
Closing Date: February 18th.
Funding: Private.
Contributor: The National Restaurant Association.
No. of awards given last year: 17.
No. of applicants last year: 20.
Additional Information: Applicants must arrange for 300 hours of full-time or part-time employment in the food service or hospitality

industry in a line or staff position and at a pay commensurate with the position.

EDUCATIONAL TESTING SERVICE (ETS)

Mail Stop 0 9 R, Princeton, NJ, 08541-0001, United States of America
Tel: (1) 609 734 1806
Fax: (1) 609 734 1755
Email: ldelauro@ets.org
www: http://www.ets.org
Contact: Ms Linda J DeLauro

The Educational Testing Service (ETS) is a non-profit organisation whose goal is to help advance quality and equity in education by providing valid assessments, research, projects and services.

ETS National Assessment of Educational Progress (NAEP) Visiting Scholar Program

Subjects: Educational policy using NAEP data for large scale assessment.
Purpose: To provide research opportunities for scholars, encourage secondary analyses of NAEP data and increase the number of minority professionals in educational measurement and related fields.
Eligibility: Applicants must hold a doctorate degree in a related discipline and provide evidence of scholarship. The main criteria for selection will be scholarship, importance or research questions and relevance to the National Assessment of Educational Progress (NAEP).
Level of Study: Postdoctorate.
Type: Research programme.
Value: Comparable to that of an ETS researcher who possesses similar training and experience. Scholars will be reimbursed for relocation expenses, concurrent with ETS guidelines, upon presentation of receipts.
Length of Study: 10 months. Timing is flexible but usually coincides with an academic year.
Frequency: Annual.
Country of Study: United States of America.
No. of awards offered: One.
Application Procedure: Applicants must submit a letter of application, a curriculum vitae, detailed proposal of research the applicant will conduct while at ETS, which should be about five pages, and references of three individuals who are familiar with the applicant's work. There is no formal application form.
Closing Date: Postmarked on or before January 5th.
Funding: Private.
Contributor: Educational Testing Service.
No. of awards given last year: None.
No. of applicants last year: Six.
Additional Information: Studies focused on issues concerning the education of minority students are especially encouraged. Scientific enquiries should be directed to Dr John Mazzeo (email: jmazzeo@ets.org).

ETS Postdoctoral Fellowships

Subjects: Psychology, education, sociology of education, psychometrics, statistics, computer science, policy research or special education.
Purpose: To provide research opportunities to individuals who hold a doctorate in education and related fields, and to increase the number of women and minority professionals conducting research in educational measurement.
Eligibility: The applicant should hold a doctorate in second language testing or a related field, such as applied linguistics. A background in second language education and assessment is highly desirable. The applicant should show evidence of a commitment to research, especially language testing research and to achieving excellence in this field. Recommendations from established Scholars in second language education and assessment would be highly valued.

Level of Study: Postdoctorate.
Type: Fellowship.
Value: US$38,000. In addition, limited relocation expenses, consistent with ETS guidelines, will be reimbursed upon presentation of receipts.
Length of Study: One year.
Frequency: Annual.
Country of Study: United States of America.
No. of awards offered: Up to three.
Application Procedure: Applicants must submit a curriculum vitae, a five page typed research proposal, a description of relevant work, interests and experience, publications and other relevant documents and materials, official transcripts of undergraduate and graduate studies and letters of recommendation from three people who are familiar with the applicant's work. There is no formal application form.
Closing Date: Materials must be postmarked to ETS by February 1st.
Funding: Private.
Contributor: The Educational Testing Service.
No. of awards given last year: One.
No. of applicants last year: 86.
Additional Information: Proposed research must be relevant to that which is conducted at ETS.

ETS Summer Program in Research for Graduate Students

Subjects: Psychology, education, teaching, learning, psychometrics, statistics, computer science, linguistics, psycholinguistics, educational technology, minority issues, testing issues, including alternate forms of assessment for special populations, testing issues associated with new forms of assessment or policy research.
Purpose: To increase the number of women and minority professionals in educational measurement and related fields and to provide graduate students with the opportunity to conduct independent research under the mentorship of an ETS researcher.
Eligibility: Open to graduate students who are pursuing a doctorate in a relevant discipline. The main criteria for selection will be scholarship and the match of applicant interests with participating ETS staff. Affirmative action goals will also be considered.
Level of Study: Doctorate, Predoctorate.
Type: Research programme.
Value: US$4,000 for the eight week period. Participants will be reimbursed for limited travel to and from Princeton, consistent with the ETS travel policy.
Length of Study: June-July.
Frequency: Annual.
Country of Study: United States of America.
No. of awards offered: Up to 16.
Application Procedure: Applicants must submit an application including a statement of interest, a curriculum vitae, letters of reference from two individuals who are familiar with the applicant's academic work and official transcripts of undergraduate and graduate studies.
Closing Date: February 15th.
Funding: Private.
Contributor: The Educational Testing Service.
No. of awards given last year: 27.
No. of applicants last year: 109.

THE EDWARD F ALBEE FOUNDATION, INC.

14 Harrison Street, New York, NY, 10013, United States of America
Tel: (1) 212 226 2020
Email: albeefdtn@aol.com
www: http://www.pipeline.com/~jtnyc/albeefdtn.html
Contact: Mr Jacob Holder, Foundation Secretary

The Edward F Albee Foundation provides residence and working space to writers and visual artists at its facilities in Montauk, New

York. The residency is offered at no charge to the participants and imposes no obligations, except diligent application to their work and respect for the privacy of others.

William Flanagan Memorial Creative Persons Center

Subjects: Writing, painting, sculpting and musical composition.
Purpose: To provide accommodation.
Eligibility: Available to artists and writers in need who have displayed talent.
Level of Study: Unrestricted.
Value: Accommodation only.
Length of Study: Four months between June 1st and October 1st.
Frequency: Annual.
Study Establishment: The Center in Montauk, Long Island.
Country of Study: United States of America.
No. of awards offered: 20 places.
Application Procedure: Applicants must complete an application form. Forms are available upon request and should be accompanied by a pre-paid return envelope. Other materials are also required, please write for further details.
Closing Date: January 1st to April 1st.
Funding: Private.
No. of awards given last year: 20.
No. of applicants last year: 300.
Additional Information: The environment is communal and residents are expected to do their share in maintaining the conditions of the Center.

THE ELECTROCHEMICAL SOCIETY, INC.

65 South Main Street, Pennington, NJ, 08534, United States of America
Tel: (1) 609 737 1902
Fax: (1) 609 737 2743
Email: ecs@electrochem.org
www: http://www.electrochem.org
Contact: Ms Erin Grow

The Electrochemical Society is an international non-profit educational organisation concerned with a broad range of phenomena relating to electrochemical and solid state science and technology. The Society has more than 7,000 individual members worldwide as well as roughly 100 corporations and laboratories which hold contributing membership.

Electrochemical Society Summer Fellowships

Subjects: Electrochemical and solid state science.
Purpose: To fund a student's research through the Summer months.
Eligibility: Open to nationals of any country who are enrolled in either an American or Canadian university or college.
Level of Study: Unrestricted.
Type: Fellowship.
Value: US$4,000.
Length of Study: Three months over one Summer.
Frequency: Annual.
Study Establishment: An approved university.
Country of Study: United States of America or Canada.
No. of awards offered: Four.
Application Procedure: Applicants must submit an application and supporting materials.
Closing Date: January 1st.
Funding: Private.
No. of awards given last year: Three.
No. of applicants last year: 30.

ELIZABETH GLASER PEDIATRIC AIDS FOUNDATION

2950 31st Street
Suite 125, Santa Monica, CA, 90405, United States of America
Tel: (1) 310 314 1459
Fax: (1) 310 314 1469
Email: research@pedaids.org
www: http://www.pedaids.org
Contact: Resource Co-ordinator

The Elizabeth Glaser Pediatric AIDS Foundation funds basic medical research in paediatric HIV and AIDS.

EGSA Scholar Awards

Subjects: Paediatric HIV or AIDS research.
Purpose: To encourage young investigators to select paediatric HIV and AIDS as a research focus for their career.
Eligibility: Applicants must have two-three years of postdoctoral experience. Tenured investigators are not eligible. Applicants must work with a qualified sponsor.
Type: Research grant.
Value: US$66,000 indirect costs, for two years of salary support. Renewable for a third year at US$36,000.
Length of Study: Two years, with a possibility of renewal for a further year.
Frequency: Annual.
Country of Study: Any country.
Application Procedure: Applicants must send requests for applications in March. Only one application for any Scholar, sponsor, laboratory or department.
Closing Date: Please contact the organisation.
Additional Information: Further information is available on the website.

Elizabeth Glaser Pediatric AIDS Foundation Basic Research Grants One-Year and Two-Year

Subjects: Paediatrics.
Purpose: To provide initial funding to investigators to enable them to gather preliminary data to answer questions quickly or obtain sufficient results to apply to other granting agencies.
Type: Research grant.
Value: Up to US$80,000 per year in direct costs for a period of performance not to exceed two years. Research using animal models may apply for supplemental funds directly related to the purchase and care of animals, total direct cost is US$100,000 per year with supplement. Indirect cost allowed is 20 per cent of total direct.
Length of Study: Determination as to the duration of the support will be made by the Scientific Advisory Committee during peer review. Renewals for one year are completely reviewed based on progress. Two year grants are not renewable.
Frequency: Annual.
Country of Study: Any country.
Application Procedure: Applicants must write for details.
Closing Date: Requests for applications should arrive no later than March.
Funding: Private.
Additional Information: Further information is available on the website.

Elizabeth Glaser Scientist Award

Subjects: Paediatric HIV or AIDS research and investigation.
Purpose: To build a network of scientists focusing on issues of paediatric HIV and AIDS, and to create a generation born free of this infection.
Eligibility: Applicants must have an MD, PhD, DDS or DVM degree and must be at assistant professor level or above.
Level of Study: Doctorate.
Type: Award.
Value: Up to US$650,000 in direct costs over a period of five years.
Frequency: Annual.

Country of Study: Any country.
No. of awards offered: Up to five.
Application Procedure: Applicants must write for details.
Closing Date: Please contact the organisation.
Funding: Private.
Additional Information: Further information is available on the website.

Pediatric AIDS Foundation Student Intern Awards

Subjects: Medical research particularly paediatrics.
Purpose: To encourage students to enter clinical and research programmes related to paediatric AIDS.
Eligibility: Open to highly motivated high school, college, graduate and medical students who have a sponsor recognised for his or her contributions to paediatric AIDS. The programme may be orientated to either fundamental research or clinical research and care.
Level of Study: Doctorate, Postgraduate.
Type: Award.
Value: US$2,000 for 320 hours work.
Length of Study: One year.
Frequency: Annual.
Country of Study: Any country.
No. of awards offered: 50.
Application Procedure: Applicants must contact the Grant Department for information as the application procedure differs for each specific programme.
Closing Date: March 28th.
Funding: Private.
Additional Information: Further information is available on the website.

Short-Term Scientific Awards

Subjects: Research.
Purpose: To provide funding for travel or short-term study in the United States of America, to initiate a critical research project, obtain preliminary data, learn new techniques in an established laboratory, or sponsor an important workshop.
Eligibility: Foreign investigators may apply.
Level of Study: Research.
Type: Award.
Value: Up to US$5,000. Indirect costs are not applicable. Funds are intended for travel, yearly stipend, housing, research supplies or other costs as needed for short-term projects. Renewals are not granted.
Frequency: Annual.
Study Establishment: Institutions in the United States, unless being used for travel.
Country of Study: United States of America, unless being used for travel.
Application Procedure: Applicants must send requests for applications in March.
Closing Date: Please contact the organisation.
Funding: Private.
Additional Information: Renewals are not granted. Further information is available on the website.

ELIZABETH GREENSHIELDS FOUNDATION

1814 Sherbrooke Street West
Suite 1, Montréal, QC, H3H 1E4, Canada
Tel: (1) 514 937 9225
Fax: (1) 514 937 0141
Email: egreen@total.net
Contact: Ms Micheline Leduc, Administrator

The purpose of the Elizabeth Greenshields Foundation is to aid artists in the early stages of their careers. Awards are limited to candidates working in the areas of painting, drawing, printmaking, and sculpture. Work must be figurative or representational, as abstract art is precluded by the terms of the Foundation's charter.

The Elizabeth Greenshields Grant

Subjects: Painting, drawing, printmaking and sculpture.
Purpose: To assist talented artists in the early stages of their careers.
Eligibility: Open to nationals of any country and there is no age limit. Candidates must have already started or completed training at an established school of art or demonstrate, through past work and future plans, a commitment to making art a lifetime career. The Foundation will not accept applications from commercial artists, photographers, video artists, filmmakers, craftmakers or any artist whose work falls primarily into these categories. Applicants may reapply to the Foundation, whether or not they have previously received a grant, but candidates who have previously been declined must wait for a period of two years before reapplying. Grantees may reapply for a second grant one year after the first grant was awarded.
Level of Study: Unrestricted.
Type: Grant.
Value: Canadian $10,000.
Frequency: Throughout the year.
Country of Study: Any country.
No. of awards offered: 45-55 per year.
Application Procedure: Applicants must complete an application form and submit this with six slides (12 for sculptors), completed no longer than three years ago. Requests for application forms can be made in writing with return postage paid, or by phone, fax or email.
Closing Date: Grants are awarded throughout the year.
Funding: Private.
No. of awards given last year: 49.
No. of applicants last year: 1,588.
Additional Information: Application forms are sent to individuals only. The Foundation is not a school or a gallery.

EMBLEM CLUB SCHOLARSHIP FOUNDATION

PO Box 712, San Luis Rey, CA, 92068, United States of America
Tel: (1) 619 757 0619
Fax: (1) 619 757 0619
Email: perky2@home.com
Contact: Ms Shirley Perkins, Administrative Secretary

Emblem Club Scholarship Foundation Grant

Subjects: Education and teacher training.
Purpose: To assist teachers who are working towards their Master's degree and accreditation in order to teach the deaf and hearing impaired. This does not include audiology or speech therapy.
Eligibility: Applicants must be United States citizens of no more than 50 years of age, and must agree to teach within the United States of America. There are no other restrictions as to minority, religion, or language.
Level of Study: Postgraduate.
Type: Grant.
Value: Varies, US$1,000-5,000.
Frequency: Four times per year.
Country of Study: United States of America.
No. of awards offered: 40.
Application Procedure: Applicants must apply to the schools concerned.
Closing Date: March 1st, June 1st, September 1st or January 1st.
Funding: Private.
No. of awards given last year: 32.
No. of applicants last year: 35.

EMIGRÉ MEMORIAL GERMAN INTERNSHIP PROGRAMS

PO Box 345, Durham, NH, 03824, United States of America
Email: gkr@hopper.unh.edu
Contact: Professor George K Romoser, Director

The Emigré Memorial German Internship Programs rest on the co-operation of North American and German affairs specialists with German government offices. Interns are placed in German offices to encourage training or future specialists on Germany and German-United States of America contacts in particular. It is independent of governments and universities.

Emigré Memorial German Internship Programs

Subjects: Government service and social sciences.
Purpose: To promote professional study and work on German government and society.
Eligibility: Open to advanced graduate students who are not natural German speakers. High fluency in German is required.
Level of Study: Graduate, Postgraduate, Predoctorate, Professional development.
Type: Grants and stipends.
Value: Please contact the organisation.
Length of Study: Up to three months.
Frequency: Dependent on funds available.
Study Establishment: Parliamentary offices in German government institutions.
Country of Study: Germany.
No. of awards offered: 10-12.
Application Procedure: Applicants must complete an application form available by email. Interviews will be held in English and German.
Closing Date: Varies but usually February.
Funding: Government.
Contributor: German offices and the German Academic Exchange Service.
No. of awards given last year: 11.
No. of applicants last year: 35.

EMILY ENGLISH SCHOLARSHIP

16 Ogle Street, London, W1W 6JA, England
Tel: (44) 20 7636 4481
Fax: (44) 20 7637 4307
Email: education@mbf.org.uk
www: http://www.mbf.org.uk
Contact: Mrs Susan Dolton

Emily English Scholarship

Subjects: Musical performance on the violin.
Purpose: To assist the studies of outstanding postgraduate violinists.
Eligibility: Open to violinists under the age of 24 years of any nationality, who have been resident in the United Kingdom for three years.
Level of Study: Postgraduate.
Value: UK £5,000.
Frequency: Annual.
Country of Study: Any country.
No. of awards offered: One.
Application Procedure: Applicants must complete an application form and provide two references.
Closing Date: February 21st.
Funding: Private.
Additional Information: Selected students will be asked to audition in April.

ENGINEERING AND PHYSICAL SCIENCES RESEARCH COUNCIL (EPSRC)

Polaris House
North Star Avenue, Swindon, Wiltshire, SN2 1ET, England
Tel: (44) 1793 444040
Fax: (44) 1793 444007
www: http://www.epsrc.ac.uk
Contact: Mr Alan Harrison

The Engineering and Physical Sciences Research Council (EPSRC) promotes and supports high quality, basic, strategic and applied research and related postgraduate training in engineering and physical sciences. It aims to advance knowledge and technology by providing trained scientists and engineers, in order to meet the needs of users and beneficiaries, and thereby contribute to economic competitiveness and quality of life.

EPSRC Advanced Fellowships

Subjects: Engineering, mathematics, physics, chemistry, materials and information technology.
Purpose: To support outstanding young academic research workers in order that they may devote themselves to full-time research projects.
Eligibility: Open to research workers normally under 35 years of age. Candidates must hold a PhD or be of equivalent standing in their profession and have at least three years of experience at post-doctoral level at the expected start date of the award.
Level of Study: Postdoctorate.
Type: Fellowship.
Value: Funding for the basic salary costs. The successful candidates receive National Insurance and superannuation plus a Fellowship Support Fund (FSF). This is at a level of UK £8,000 and UK £10,000 per year respectively. The use of the FSF, which is at the discretion of the Fellow, will vary according to the nature of the research programme, but may include small items of equipment including computers, software, travel and subsistence expenses, such as visits to collaborators and conferences, and small amounts of research and technical effort. Up to UK £2,000 may be used in the first year to cover relocation and removal costs associated with taking up the fellowship. The FSF must not be used to meet any university overheads or indirect or unspecified costs. A full account of the use of the FSF will be required at the end of the fellowship. Please note that payment of salary and relevant FSF for all fellowships are administered via the university hosting the award. The salary is paid on an 'age for wage' basis.
Length of Study: A maximum of five years.
Frequency: Annual.
Study Establishment: Any academic institution acceptable to the Council.
Country of Study: United Kingdom.
No. of awards offered: 40.
Application Procedure: Applicants must complete an application form, available on the website. The subject area panel shortlists those candidates to be invited for interview. The interviewees are usually the top ranked 25-33 per cent of candidates and interviews are usually held in December or January. The remaining candidates not selected for interview are informed of this decision as soon as possible. Applications are limited to one per year and applications for more than one type of fellowship will not be accepted.
Closing Date: September 8th to take up the award on October 1st of the following year.
Funding: Government.
No. of awards given last year: 40.
No. of applicants last year: 200.
Additional Information: A degree of mobility during the course of a Research Fellowship may be beneficial. Any proposal to transfer the fellowship to a different organisation would need to be discussed with the existing and proposed organisations. If the new organisation agrees to host the fellowship, the EPSRC will normally be agreeable to a transfer. In such cases the original award would be closed down and a new award issued for the balance of the funding period.

Fellows are expected to devote their whole working time to research. Up to one day a week may, however, be spent on teaching and demonstrating. The period of the fellowship may also be extended to compensate for an agreed abeyance, sick leave in excess of three months and maternity leave. At the end of the fellowship, a complete account of the research undertaken is required. The format of the fellowship final report is likely to change in the near future. In due course these will be known as the Individual Fellowship Report (IFR). The IFR format will allow a report of the outcomes of the research undertaken by the Fellow and will also include an element for reporting how the Fellowship Support Funding was spent. Submission of the form is required within three months of the termination date of the fellowship. Any request to extend the submission date must be made in writing and agreed by the EPSRC. EPSRC will not consider further applications from Fellows who are in default of submitting an IFR.

EPSRC Doctoral Training Grants

Subjects: Engineering, mathematics, information technology, materials, chemistry or physics.
Purpose: To provide funds directly to universities to support doctoral training in subjects which lie broadly within the remit of the EPSRC.
Eligibility: Candidates must be at a university whose standards of training, supervision and career advice meet those set by the EPSRC.
Level of Study: Postgraduate, Predoctorate.
Type: Research grant.
Value: Payments will be profiled over the first three years, save an element held back to the final quarter pending reconciliation of actual expenditure against payments made. A separate grant will be awarded for each subsequent annual output from the research algorithm. Funds can be used for the following types of expenditure: fees, consumables, part-time study and industrial placements, extended support and broadening skills training and career advice. Funds must not be used for academic salaries, premises costs, administration charges, indirect costs or overheads.
Length of Study: Three years to provide flexibility over the duration of research studentships and to allow for late and deferred starts and breaks through illness.
Frequency: Annual.
Country of Study: United Kingdom.
Application Procedure: Students are selected in accordance with the university's postgraduate admission requirements and must meet the eligibility requirements of the Education (Fees and Awards) Regulations 1997.
Funding: Government.
Additional Information: Students are selected and paid by the university. Further information is available from the website.

EPSRC Masters Training Packages (MTP)

Subjects: Engineering, mathematics, physics, chemistry, materials and information technology.
Purpose: To enable universities to meet better the changing needs of students, employees and employers and to draw together and extend the support available through the current mechanisms, providing opportunities for greater flexibility in course design and delivery. Training packages can include full or part-time training and continuing professional development courses leading to appropriate postgraduate qualifications.
Eligibility: Candidates must be shown to be in critical need of EPSRC support.
Level of Study: Postgraduate, Professional development.
Type: Training grant.
Length of Study: A maximum of five years for the requesting university and one year for the awardee. There is no minimum funding period. Subsequent periods of funding may be requested in the form of new bids against later calls for proposals.
Frequency: Dependent on funds available.
Country of Study: United Kingdom.
No. of awards offered: Varies.
Application Procedure: Calls for proposals are normally made annually, in the Autumn, and are placed on the website. Full details of

how to apply are provided in the call documentation. ESPRC does not accept applications outside the published calls. Complete details are provided on the website.
Closing Date: Please consult the website for dates.
Funding: Government.
Additional Information: For further information please see the website or contact Janet Edwards, Programme Operations on (44) 1793 444 098 or janet.edwards@epsrc.ac.uk.

EPSRC Postdoctoral Fellowships in Mathematics

Subjects: Mathematics.
Purpose: To provide support for outstanding individuals at various stages of their careers to give them the freedom to pursue their research interests full-time, free from the burden of academic duties.
Eligibility: Candidates are usually within three years of completing their PhD and should not hold permanent academic posts nor have more than four years' postdoctoral experience. This Fellowship is open to European Union citizens.
Level of Study: Postdoctorate.
Type: Fellowship.
Value: Funding for the basic salary costs. The successful candidates receive National Insurance and superannuation plus a Fellowship Support Fund (FSF). This is at a level of UK £8,000 and UK £10,000 per year respectively. The use of the FSF, which is at the discretion of the Fellow, will vary according to the nature of the research programme, but may include small items of equipment including computers, software, travel and subsistence expenses, such as visits to collaborators and conferences, and small amounts of research and technical effort. Up to UK £2,000 may be used in the first year to cover relocation and removal costs associated with taking up the fellowship. The FSF must not be used to meet any university overheads or indirect or unspecified costs. A full account of the use of the FSF will be required at the end of the fellowship. Please note that payment of salary and relevant FSF for all fellowships are administered via the university hosting the award. The salary is paid on an 'age for wage' basis.
Length of Study: Two-three years.
Frequency: Annual.
Study Establishment: Normally universities or research institutions in the United Kingdom.
Country of Study: United Kingdom, but up to one year may be spent abroad.
No. of awards offered: 10.
Application Procedure: Applicants must complete an application form, available on the website. The subject area panel shortlists those candidates to be invited for interview. The interviewees are usually the top ranked 25-33 per cent of candidates and interviews are usually held in December or January. The remaining candidates not selected for interview are informed of this decision as soon as possible. Applications are limited to one per year and applications for more than one type of fellowship will not be accepted.
Closing Date: January 8th.
Funding: Government.
No. of applicants last year: 50.
Additional Information: A degree of mobility during the course of a Research Fellowship may be beneficial. Any proposal to transfer the Fellowship to a different organisation would need to be discussed with the existing and proposed organisations. If the new organisation agrees to host the Fellowship, the EPSRC will normally be agreeable to a transfer. In such cases the original award would be closed down and a new award issued for the balance of the funding period. Fellows are expected to devote their whole working time to research. Up to one day a week may, however, be spent on teaching and demonstrating. The period of the Fellowship may also be extended to compensate for an agreed abeyance, sick leave in excess of three months and maternity leave. At the end of the Fellowship, a complete account of the research undertaken is required. The format of the Fellowship final report is likely to change in the near future. In due course these will be known as the Individual Fellowship Report (IFR). The IFR format will allow a report of the outcomes of the research undertaken by the Fellow and will also include an element for reporting how the Fellowship Support Funding was spent.

Submission of the form is required within three months of the termination date of the Fellowship. Any request to extend the submission date must be made in writing and agreed by the EPSRC. EPSRC will not consider further applications from Fellows who are in default of submitting an IFR.

EPSRC Postdoctoral Theory Fellowship in Physics

Subjects: Physics.

Purpose: To provide support for outstanding individuals at various stages of their careers to give them the freedom to pursue their research interests full-time, free from the burden of academic duties, normally shortly or immediately after completing a PhD.

Eligibility: Candidates are usually within three years of completing their PhD and should not hold permanent academic posts nor have more than four years' postdoctoral experience. This Fellowship is open to European Union citizens.

Level of Study: Postdoctorate.

Type: Fellowship.

Value: Funding for the basic salary costs: the successful candidates receive National Insurance and superannuation plus a Fellowship Support Fund (FSF). This is at a level of UK £8,000 and UK £10,000 per year respectively. The use of the FSF, which is at the discretion of the Fellow, will vary according to the nature of the Funding for the basic salary costs. The successful candidates receive National Insurance and superannuation plus a Fellowship Support Fund (FSF). This is at a level of UK £8,000 and UK £10,000 per year respectively. The use of the FSF, which is at the discretion of the Fellow, will vary according to the nature of the research programme, but may include small items of equipment including computers, software, travel and subsistence expenses, such as visits to collaborators and conferences, and small amounts of research and technical effort. Up to UK £2,000 may be used in the first year to cover relocation and removal costs associated with taking up the fellowship. The FSF must not be used to meet any university overheads or indirect or unspecified costs. A full account of the use of the FSF will be required at the end of the fellowship. Please note that payment of salary and relevant FSF for all fellowships are administered via the university hosting the award. The salary is paid on an 'age for wage' basis.

Length of Study: Two-three years.

Frequency: Annual.

Study Establishment: Normally universities or research institutions in the United Kingdom.

Country of Study: United Kingdom, but up to one year may be spent abroad.

No. of awards offered: 10.

Application Procedure: Applicants must complete an application form, available on the website. The subject area panel shortlists those candidates to be invited for interview. The interviewees are usually the top ranked 25-33 per cent of candidates and interviews are usually held in December or January. The remaining candidates not selected for interview are informed of this decision as soon as possible. Applications are limited to one per year and applications for more than one type of fellowship will not be accepted.

Closing Date: January 8th.

Funding: Government.

No. of awards given last year: Four.

No. of applicants last year: 20.

Additional Information: A degree of mobility during the course of a Research Fellowship may be beneficial. Any proposal to transfer the fellowship to a different organisation would need to be discussed with the existing and proposed organisations. If the new organisation agrees to host the fellowship, the EPSRC will normally be agreeable to a transfer. In such cases the original award would be closed down and a new award issued for the balance of the funding period. Fellows are expected to devote their whole working time to research. Up to one day a week may, however, be spent on teaching and demonstrating. The period of the fellowship may also be extended to compensate for an agreed abeyance, sick leave in excess of three months and maternity leave. At the end of the fellowship, a complete account of the research undertaken is required. The format of the fellowship final report is likely to change in the near future. In due course these will be known as the Individual Fellowship Report

(IFR). The IFR format will allow a report of the outcomes of the research undertaken by the Fellow and will also include an element for reporting how the Fellowship Support Funding was spent. Submission of the form is required within three months of the termination date of the fellowship. Any request to extend the submission date must be made in writing and agreed by the EPSRC. EPSRC will not consider further applications from Fellows who are in default of submitting an IFR.

EPSRC Senior Research Fellowships

Subjects: Engineering, mathematics, physics, chemistry, materials and information technology.

Purpose: To enable outstanding established scientists and engineers at the peak of their capabilities to devote themselves to full-time research free of the restrictions imposed by their normal academic duties.

Eligibility: Open to scientists and engineers who are already established in their careers, having proved their exceptional research and interpretative ability. Applicants must be members of permanent staff of United Kingdom universities, technical colleges or similar United Kingdom academic institutions. Fellows are expected to return to their normal employment at the termination of the Fellowship.

Level of Study: Professional development.

Type: Fellowship.

Value: A Senior Research Fellowship provides a replacement of the Fellow's basic academic salary, but not the superannuation or National Insurance contributions as these will need to be covered by the academic host institution. Please note that payment of salary is administered via the university hosting the award.

Length of Study: A maximum of five years.

Frequency: Annual.

Study Establishment: Any institution which has a firm working link with a university or similar academic establishment.

Country of Study: United Kingdom.

No. of awards offered: Three.

Application Procedure: Applicants must complete an application form, available on the EPSRC website. The application forms can be downloaded via the links within section three of the guidance notes. An applicant is limited to one application for a Research Fellowship each year. Applications for more than one type of fellowship will not be accepted.

Closing Date: September 8th to take up the award on October 1st of the following year.

Funding: Government.

No. of awards given last year: Three.

No. of applicants last year: 35.

Additional Information: A degree of mobility during the course of a Research Fellowship may be beneficial. Any proposal to transfer the fellowship to a different organisation would need to be discussed with the existing and proposed organisations. If the new organisation agrees to host the fellowship, the EPSRC will normally be agreeable to a transfer. In such cases the original award would be closed down and a new award issued for the balance of the funding period. Fellows are expected to devote their whole working time to research. Up to one day a week may, however, be spent on teaching and demonstrating. The period of the fellowship may also be extended to compensate for an agreed abeyance, sick leave in excess of three months and maternity leave. At the end of the fellowship, a complete account of the research undertaken is required. The format of the fellowship final report is likely to change in the near future. In due course these will be known as the Individual Fellowship Report (IFR). The IFR format will allow a report of the outcomes of the research undertaken by the Fellow and will also include an element for reporting how the Fellowship Support Funding was spent. Submission of the form is required within three months of the termination date of the fellowship. Any request to extend the submission date must be made in writing and agreed by the EPSRC. EPSRC will not consider further applications from Fellows who are in default of submitting an IFR.

MOD Joint Grants Scheme

Subjects: All subjects.

Purpose: To support high quality research that has relevance to defence.
Eligibility: Permanent employees of an eligible organisation.
Type: Research grant.
Value: Varies.
Length of Study: Varies.
Frequency: Dependent on funds available.
Study Establishment: Universities and similar institutions.
Country of Study: United Kingdom.
No. of awards offered: Varies.
Application Procedure: Applicants must visit the website for information.
Closing Date: No closing date.
Additional Information: Further information available on the website.

Royal Society EPSRC BBSRC PPARC and Rolls Royce PLC Industry Fellowships

Subjects: Science and technology outside the fields of agriculture including horticulture, agricultural economics, agricultural engineering, and the more applied aspects of agricultural science, natural environment sciences which may be defined broadly as geology and geophysics including seismology and geomagnetism, meteorology, hydrology, oceanography, marine and freshwater biology, terrestrial ecology, medicine, food science, social science, and those aspects of psychology which are closely related to fundamental biology and to the engineering and biological aspects of ergonomics and cybernetics.
Purpose: To provide opportunities for academic scientists, mathematicians and engineers to hold a job in an industrial environment and undertake a project at any stage in the chain from fundamental science to industrial innovation, and, conversely, for industrial scientists, mathematicians and engineers to undertake research or course development work in a university.
Eligibility: Open to individuals ordinarily resident in the United Kingdom, the Channel Islands or the Isle of Man. Candidates should be of PhD status or equivalent, normally holding a tenured post in a university, or employed as a scientist, mathematician or engineer in industry, an industrial research organisation or an organisation in the public service. Candidates should preferably be at the mid career stage. Additional consideration may be shown to applicants who have already had previous contact with or interest in the opposite sector of employment.
Level of Study: Postdoctorate.
Type: Fellowship.
Value: Payment of salary but not employers' national insurance and pension contributions.
Length of Study: For periods of between six months and two years full-time. A part-time equivalent is available.
Frequency: Every six months.
Country of Study: United Kingdom, although proposals to hold fellowships overseas will be considered.
No. of awards offered: Varies.
Application Procedure: Applicants must complete an application form available from the website http://www.sst.ph.ic.ac.uk/trust. Details are available from the Royal Society Research Appointments Department.
Closing Date: June or December.
Funding: Commercial, Government, Private.
No. of awards given last year: Nine.
No. of applicants last year: 28.

For further information contact:

The Royal Society
Research Appointments Department
6 Carlton House Terrace, London, SW1Y 5AG, England
Tel: (44) 20 7451 2547
Fax: (44) 20 7930 2170
Email: ukresearch.appointments@royalsoc.ac.uk
www: http://www.royalsoc.ac.uk

ENGLISH-SPEAKING UNION (ESU)

Dartmouth House
37 Charles Street, London, W1J SED, England
Tel: (44) 20 7529 1550
Fax: (44) 20 7495 6108
Email: esu@esu.org
www: http://www.esu.org
Contact: Mr Tim Rolph, Cultural Affairs Officer

The English Speaking Union (ESU) is an independent, non-political educational charity with members throughout the world, promoting international and human achievement through the worldwide use of the English language.

English Speaking Union Chautauqua Scholarships

Subjects: Art (painting, ceramics and sculpture), music education, literature and international relations and drama.
Purpose: To enable British teachers to study at the Chautauqua Summer School.
Eligibility: Open to British teachers with a particular interest in the arts, who are between 25 and 35 years of age.
Level of Study: Professional development.
Type: Scholarship.
Value: UK £850 plus board, room, tuition and lecture sessions at the Summer School.
Length of Study: Six weeks.
Frequency: Annual.
Study Establishment: Chautauqua Institution's Summer School in Chautauqua, New York.
Country of Study: United States of America.
No. of awards offered: Two.
Application Procedure: Applicants must write for details.
Closing Date: November 30th.
Funding: Private.
No. of awards given last year: Two.
No. of applicants last year: 15.

ESU Music Scholarships

Subjects: Music.
Purpose: To enable musicians of outstanding ability to study at summer schools in the United States, Canada, France, United Kingdom, Czech Republic and Hungary.
Eligibility: Candidates must be aged 30 or under, and be students or graduates from a recognised United Kingdom conservatory or university music department.
Level of Study: Professional development.
Type: Scholarship.
Value: Tuition, board and lodging and relevant flight costs.
Length of Study: Three-nine weeks, depending on the particular scholarship.
Frequency: Annual.
Study Establishment: Summer school.
Country of Study: United States of America, Canada, France, Czech Republic, Hungary or the United Kingdom.
No. of awards offered: 10.
Application Procedure: Applications must be supported by a teacher's reference.
Closing Date: November 1st.
Funding: Commercial, Private.
Contributor: Private trust funds.
No. of awards given last year: Six.
No. of applicants last year: 52.

ESU Travelling Librarian Award

Subjects: Library science.
Purpose: To encourage United States and United Kingdom contacts in the library world and establish links between pairs of libraries.
Eligibility: Open to professionally qualified United Kingdom and American librarians.
Level of Study: Professional development.
Type: Travel grant.

Value: This Award covers board and lodging and relevant flight costs.
Length of Study: A minimum of three weeks.
Frequency: Annual.
Country of Study: United States of America or the United Kingdom.
No. of awards offered: One.
Application Procedure: Applicants must submit a curriculum vitae and covering letter explaining why they are the ideal candidate for the award.
Closing Date: Please write for details.
Funding: Commercial, Private.
No. of awards given last year: One.
No. of applicants last year: 30.

Lindemann Trust Fellowships

Subjects: Astronomy, chemistry, engineering, geology, geophysics, mathematics, physics and biophysics.
Purpose: To enable graduates in the field of pure and applied physical sciences, to carry out research.
Eligibility: Open to United Kingdom and Commonwealth citizens who are graduates of a United Kingdom university and to United Kingdom and Commonwealth citizens who are pursuing postgraduate research at a United Kingdom university although not graduates of that institution. Preference is given to those who have demonstrated their capacity for original research and who will be under 30 years of age on September 1st of the fellowship year, but candidates up to 35 years of age are not debarred.
Level of Study: Postdoctorate, Postgraduate.
Type: Fellowship.
Value: A stipend of US$30,000, round trip travel expenses, and, where appropriate, a spouse's allowance.
Length of Study: One year.
Frequency: Annual.
Study Establishment: A university.
Country of Study: United States of America.
No. of awards offered: Two.
Application Procedure: Applicants must write for details.
Closing Date: October 15th.
Funding: Private.
No. of awards given last year: Three.
No. of applicants last year: 20.
Additional Information: Fellows are not required to work for an American degree but are expected to be attached to a university, college or seat of advanced learning and technical repute in the United States of America. The place of study and research programme must be approved by the Committee. A limited amount of teaching as an adjunct to research activities is not excluded.

ENTENTE CORDIALE SCHOLARSHIPS

French Cultural Department
23 Cromwell Road, London, SW7 2EL, England
Tel: (44) 20 7073 1300
Fax: (44) 20 7073 1326
Email: entente.cordiale@ambafrance.org.uk
www: http://www.francealacarte.org.uk/entente
Contact: Administrative Officer

Launched by an agreement between the United Kingdom and French governments in 1995, the Entente Cordiale Scholarships enable outstanding British postgraduates to study or carry out research on the other side of the Channel, with a view to dispel preconceived ideas and promote good relations between the two countries.

Bourses Scholarships

Subjects: All subjects.
Purpose: To study or carry out research in France.
Eligibility: Open to British postgraduates who wish to study in France.
Level of Study: Postgraduate.

Type: Scholarship.
Value: UK £8,000 for students living in Paris and UK £7,500 for those studying outside Paris.
Length of Study: One academic year.
Frequency: Annual.
Study Establishment: Approved universities or grande écoles.
Country of Study: France.
No. of awards offered: 20.
Application Procedure: Applicants must complete an application form, available from the website.
Closing Date: March.
Funding: Private.
Contributor: AXA UK, Blue Circle (Lafarge), BP Amoco, CGNU plc, Kingfisher plc, London Electricity, L'Oreal, Reuters Foundation, UBS Warburg and Xerox.
No. of awards given last year: 18.
No. of applicants last year: 60.
Additional Information: The scheme is run by the French Embassy and the British Council, but is privately funded. Scholarships are also awarded to French postgraduates to study in the United Kingdom. Interested parties should contact the British Council in Paris.

EPILEPSY FOUNDATION

4351 Garden City Drive, Landover, MD, 20785, United States of America
Tel: (1) 301 459 3700
Fax: (1) 301 577 2684
www: http://www.efa.org
Contact: Ms Liz Bryson

The Epilepsy Foundation is a national, charitable organisation, founded in 1968 as the Epilepsy Foundation of America. It is the only organisation wholly dedicated to the welfare of people with epilepsy and to working on their behalf through research, education, advocacy and service.

Dreifuss International Travel Programme

Subjects: Epilepsy research.
Purpose: To provide an opportunity for a visiting professor to spend time at a host institution to promote the exchange of medical and scientific information and expertise on epilepsy between the United States of America and other countries.
Eligibility: Either the visitor or the host institution must be from the United States of America.
Level of Study: Professional development.
Type: Tuition waiver and stipend.
Value: To cover travel expenses and minor incidental expenses.
Length of Study: Three-six weeks.
Frequency: Throughout the year.
Study Establishment: An approved facility.
Country of Study: Any country.
No. of awards offered: Up to 10 depending on funds available.
Application Procedure: Applicants must write for details.
Closing Date: Applications are accepted at any time.
Funding: Private.

EF Behavioral Sciences Research Training Fellowship

Subjects: Epilepsy research relative to the behavioural sciences. Appropriate fields of study include sociology, social work, psychology, anthropology, nursing, political science and others relevant to epilepsy research and practice.
Purpose: To offer qualified individuals the opportunity to develop expertise in epilepsy research through a training experience or involvement in an epilepsy research project.
Eligibility: Open to individuals who have received their doctoral degree in a field of the behavioural sciences by the time the Fellowship commences and desire additional postdoctoral research experience in epilepsy. Applications from women and minorities are encouraged.

Level of Study: Postdoctorate.

Type: Fellowship.

Value: A stipend of up to US$30,000, depending on the experience and qualifications of the applicant and the scope and duration of the proposed project.

Length of Study: One year.

Frequency: Annual.

Study Establishment: An approved facility.

Country of Study: United States of America.

No. of awards offered: One.

Application Procedure: Applicants must complete an application form, available from the Foundation on request.

Closing Date: February 1st.

Funding: Private.

No. of awards given last year: One.

Additional Information: The closing date for applications may vary from year to year. Applicants should email cmorris@efa.org for details.

EF Junior Investigator Research Grants

Subjects: Basic biomedical, behavioural and social sciences. Particular encouragement is given to applications in the behavioural sciences.

Purpose: To support basic and clinical research which will advance the understanding, treatment and prevention of epilepsy.

Eligibility: Open to United States researchers. Priority is given to beginning investigators just entering the field of epilepsy, to new or innovative projects, and to investigators whose research is relevant to developmental or paediatric aspects of epilepsy. Applications from women and minorities are encouraged, whilst applications from established investigators with other sources of support are discouraged. Research grants are not intended to provide support for postdoctoral Fellows.

Level of Study: Postdoctorate, Postgraduate.

Type: Research grant.

Value: Varies. Support is limited to US$40,000.

Length of Study: One year.

Frequency: Annual.

Country of Study: United States of America.

No. of awards offered: Varies.

Application Procedure: Applicants must complete an application form, available from the Foundation on request.

Closing Date: September 1st.

Funding: Private.

Additional Information: The closing date for applications may vary from year to year. Applicants should email cmorris@efa.org for details.

EF Research Training Fellowships

Subjects: Basic or clinical epilepsy research, which must address a question of fundamental importance. A clinical training component is not required.

Purpose: To offer qualified individuals the opportunity to develop expertise in epilepsy research through involvement in an epilepsy research project.

Eligibility: Open to physicians and PhD neuroscientists who desire postdoctoral research experience. Preference is given to applicants whose proposals have a paediatric or developmental emphasis. Applications from women and minorities are encouraged.

Level of Study: Postdoctorate.

Type: Fellowship.

Value: A stipend of US$40,000.

Length of Study: One year.

Frequency: Annual.

Study Establishment: A facility where there is an ongoing epilepsy research programme.

Country of Study: United States of America or Canada.

No. of awards offered: Varies.

Application Procedure: Applicants must complete an application form, available from the Foundation upon request. Applicants may also look at the website under research for details.

Closing Date: September 1st.

Funding: Private.

EF Research/Clinical Training Fellowships

Subjects: Basic or clinical epilepsy research, with an equal emphasis on clinical training and clinical epileptology.

Purpose: To offer qualified individuals the opportunity to develop expertise in epilepsy research through a training experience and involvement in an epilepsy research project.

Eligibility: Open to individuals who have received their MD degree and completed residency training. Applications from women and minorities are encouraged.

Level of Study: Postdoctorate, Postgraduate.

Type: Fellowship.

Value: A stipend of US$40,000.

Length of Study: One year.

Frequency: Annual.

Study Establishment: A facility where there is an ongoing epilepsy research programme.

Country of Study: United States of America.

No. of awards offered: Varies.

Application Procedure: Applicants must write for details.

Closing Date: September 1st.

Funding: Private.

Additional Information: These fellowships include the Merritt-Putnam Fellowship.

EPILEPSY RESEARCH FOUNDATION

Research & Information Executive
PO Box 3004, London, W4 1XT, England

Tel: (44) 20 8400 6108

Fax: (44) 20 8995 4781

Email: info@erf.org.uk

www: http://www.erf.org.uk

Contact: L Slocombe, Executive Director

The Epilepsy Research Foundation promotes and supports basic and clinical scientific research into epilepsy. It seeks to identify medical research needs in epilepsy and raise money for independent research to be carried out by the best available research teams.

Epilepsy Research Foundation Research Grant

Subjects: Epilepsy.

Purpose: To promote and support basic and clinical research into epilepsy.

Eligibility: Open to researchers resident in the United Kingdom.

Level of Study: Research.

Type: Research grant.

Value: A maximum of UK £60,000.

Length of Study: One-three years.

Frequency: Annual.

Country of Study: United Kingdom.

Application Procedure: Applications are invited by advertisements in scientific journals. A one page summary is requested initially.

Closing Date: End of November.

Funding: Private.

No. of awards given last year: 11.

No. of applicants last year: 40.

EPISCOPAL CHURCH FOUNDATION

815 Second Avenue, New York, NY, 10017, United States of
America
Tel: (1) 212 697 2858
Fax: (1) 212 297 0142
Email: all@episcopalfoundation.org
www: http://www.episcopalfoundation.org
Contact: Fellows Program Manager

The Episcopal Church Foundation is an independent, lay-led organisation which offers innovative programmes in leadership development, education and philanthropy for the clergy and laity of the Episcopal Church.

Episcopal Church Foundation Graduate Fellowship Program

Subjects: Religious studies.
Purpose: To support doctoral study for Episcopalians planning teaching careers in theological education in the Episcopal church in the United States.
Eligibility: Open to recent graduates of an accredited seminary who have been nominated by one of the 11 Episcopal seminaries, by Harvard Divinity School or the Union Theological Seminary of New York. Scholars who are not graduates of these institutions must also have a letter of nomination from the Dean of their degree granting seminary as well as a nomination by one of the seminaries named above. Neither ordination nor a Master of Divinity degree is required. Priority consideration is given to applicants who are in the early stages of their doctoral studies.
Level of Study: Doctorate.
Type: Fellowship.
Value: US$10,000 regardless of financial need.
Length of Study: One year, renewable for a further two years.
Frequency: Annual.
Study Establishment: At accredited institutions in the United States of America and abroad.
Country of Study: Any country.
No. of awards offered: Four.
Application Procedure: Applicants must contact the Dean's office at any of the 11 accredited Episcopal seminaries or the Harvard Divinity School or the Union Theological Seminary for application materials.
Closing Date: December 1st.
Funding: Private.

THE ERIC THOMPSON TRUST

c/o The Royal Philharmonic Society
10 Stratford Place, London, W1C 1BA, England
Tel: (44) 20 7491 8110
Fax: (44) 20 7493 7463
www: http://www.royalphilharmonicsociety.org.uk/ericthompson.htm
Contact: Mr Richard Fisher, Clerk to The Trustees

The Eric Thompson Trust aims to provide modest grants to help aspiring professional organists. Preference will be given to students seeking assistance towards specific projects, rather than continuing academic tuition eg. summer schools or special lessons in addition to normal studies and opportunities to play on historical instruments in the context of further study.

Eric Thompson Trust Grants-in-Aid

Subjects: The organ.
Purpose: To provide aspiring professional organists with financial assistance for special studies such as summer schools, travel and subsistence for auditions or performance, or other incidental costs incurred in their work.
Eligibility: Some professional training as an organist is required.
Level of Study: Professional development.

Type: Grant in aid.
Value: Determined by Trustees but normally limited to a contribution towards costs.
Frequency: Twice a year.
Country of Study: Any country.
No. of awards offered: Varies.
Application Procedure: Applicants must send full details of their needs together with information on their training and career, two written references from organists of good standing in the profession and other relevant material to the Clerk to the Trustees.
Closing Date: December 31st or June 30th for consideration in January and July respectively.
Funding: Private.
Contributor: Personal and corporate donors.

ESADE

MBA Office
Avenue d'espluges 92-96, Barcelona, E-08034, Spain
Tel: (34) 93 495 2088
Fax: (34) 93 495 3828
Email: mba@esade.edu
www: http://www.esade.edu
Contact: Ms Nuria Guilera, MBA Admissions Director

Established in 1958, ESADE is a private non-profit Institution of Higher Education with a distinctly international outlook. It consists of three schools: the Business School, the Law School and the Language School. Located in one of Barcelona's most attractive residential areas, ESADE's three buildings provide a total of 26,850 square metres of space for teaching and study.

ESADE MBA Scholarships

Subjects: MBA.
Purpose: To assist full-time MBA students with tuition fees.
Eligibility: Scholarships are awarded on the basis of applicants' academic records, professional experience, personal merits and how well they fit the required profile of the programme.
Level of Study: MBA.
Type: Scholarship.
Value: The scholarship covers up to 50 per cent of the programme tuition fees.
Length of Study: 18 months.
Frequency: Annual.
Study Establishment: ESADE.
Country of Study: Spain.
Application Procedure: Applicants must apply for a scholarship along with their course application. Scholarship applications are reviewed once candidates have been admitted to the MBA programme by the admissions committee.
Closing Date: May.

ESTHER A AND JOSEPH KLINGENSTEIN CENTER FOR INDEPENDENT EDUCATION

Box 125
Teachers College
Columbia University, New York, NY, 10027, United States of
America
Tel: (1) 212 678 3156
Fax: (1) 212 678 3254
Email: crf17@columbia.edu
www: http://www.klingenstein.org
Contact: Grants Management Officer

The mission of the Esther A and Joseph Klingenstein Center for Independent Education is to improve the quality of independent school education by strengthening leadership among teachers and administrators who work in, and with, independent schools. The Center aims to attract educators who have demonstrated outstanding accomplishment or potential for excellence. The goal is to equip these educators with the knowledge, skills and values necessary for informed practice using the resources of Colombia University and drawing upon a wide range of experts in education.

Esther A and Joseph Klingenstein Fellowship Awards

Subjects: Education, administrative or academic disciplines.
Purpose: To foster educational leadership skills for teachers and administrators in independent elementary, middle and secondary schools.
Eligibility: Open to qualified applicants who have at least five years of teaching experience in grades 5 to 12 in an independent school and who plan to return to their home school following the fellowship year.
Level of Study: Professional development.
Type: Fellowship.
Value: US$18,330 tuition allowance, a US$25,000 stipend and other benefits.
Length of Study: One academic year.
Frequency: Annual.
Study Establishment: The Klingenstein Center, Teachers College, Columbia University.
Country of Study: United States of America.
No. of awards offered: 12.
Application Procedure: Applicants must complete an application form.
Closing Date: January 15th.
Funding: Private.

Klingenstein Summer Institute

Subjects: Educational science.
Purpose: To provide professional development for teachers in independent elementary, middle and secondary schools.
Eligibility: Restricted to teachers currently employed in independent secondary schools with two to five years of experience in grades 9 to 12.
Level of Study: Graduate, Professional development.
Type: Fellowship.
Value: Room and board plus four graduate credits from Teachers College, approx. US$2,820.
Length of Study: Two weeks.
Frequency: Annual.
Study Establishment: A residential boarding school.
Country of Study: United States of America.
No. of awards offered: 70.
Application Procedure: Applicants must telephone for application materials.
Closing Date: January 15th.
Funding: Private.

EUROPEAN GARDENS SCHOLARSHIP SCHEME

1 Townsend Yard
Highgate, London, N6 5JF, England
Tel: (44) 20 8348 5054
Fax: (44) 20 8342 8578
Contact: Administrator

The aim of the European Gardens Scholarship scheme is to enable individuals to develop their knowledge and understanding of the care, conservation and history of gardens and parks by visiting and learning in a different European country from their own.

European Gardens Horticulture Scholarships
Subjects: Horticulture.

Purpose: To enable individuals to develop their knowledge by visiting other European countries, to exchange ideas and form links with the aim of making practical improvements.
Eligibility: Open to persons from continental Europe or the United Kingdom, who are professionals or equivalent, have two years of experience, are over 25 years of age and are actively involved in the care, conservation or history of gardens and parks.
Level of Study: Postgraduate.
Type: Scholarship.
Value: UK £1,000.
Length of Study: Two-three weeks.
Frequency: Annual.
Country of Study: European countries.
No. of awards offered: Two.
Application Procedure: Applicants must complete an application form available from the organisation.
Closing Date: January 31st.
Funding: Private.
Additional Information: The European Gardens Scholarship scheme is for exchanges between the United Kingdom and continental Europe on the basis of short study visits or tours.

EUROPEAN MOLECULAR BIOLOGY ORGANISATION (EMBO)

Postfach 1022.40, Heidelberg, D-69012, Germany
Tel: (49) 6221 383 031
Fax: (49) 6221 384 879
Email: embo@embl-heidelberg.de
www: http://www.embo.org
Contact: Mr Andrew Moore, Project Manager

The European Molecular Biology Organisation (EMBO) was established in 1962 and is an international academy focusing on molecular biology in its broadest sense, responding to developing areas that use molecular biology to describe biological events at the molecular level.

EMBO Long-Term Fellowships in Molecular Biology

Subjects: Molecular biology and disciplines relying on molecular biology.
Purpose: To promote the development of molecular biology and allied research in Europe and Israel.
Eligibility: Open to holders of a doctorate degree. EMBO Fellowships are not awarded for exchanges between laboratories within any one country. Applicants must be a national from a European Molecular Biology Conference (EMBC) member state or wishing to travel from one EMBC member state to another.
Level of Study: Postdoctorate.
Type: Fellowship.
Value: Return travel allowance for the Fellow and any dependants plus a stipend and dependants allowance.
Length of Study: One year, renewable for a further year.
Frequency: Twice a year.
Study Establishment: A suitable laboratory.
Country of Study: Any country.
No. of awards offered: Varies.
Application Procedure: Applicants must include a self addressed adhesive label when making enquiries. Further information is available on the website.
Closing Date: February 15th and August 15th.
Funding: Government.
Contributor: The 24 member states.
No. of awards given last year: 147.
No. of applicants last year: 645.
Additional Information: The following countries form the European Molecular Biology Conference (EMBC): Austria, Belgium, Croatia, Czech Republic, Denmark, Finland, France, Germany, Greece, Hungary, Iceland, Ireland, Israel, Italy, Netherlands, Norway, Poland, Portugal, Slovenia, Spain, Sweden, Switzerland, Turkey and the

United Kingdom. Special provision is also made for applications involving Cyprus.

EMBO Restart Fellowship

Subjects: Molecular biology and disciplines relying on molecular biology.
Purpose: To promote the development of molecular biology and allied research in Europe and Israel.
Eligibility: Candidates must hold a PhD degree and should have some postdoctoral training with a proven track record, with at least one first author paper. They should have the support of a host laboratory which will provide space and facilities for the duration of the fellowship. The candidate must also have taken a break from research for childcare for at least one year and the post previously held must have been terminated during pregnancy or maternity leave. The applicant must have a research plan for the duration of the award.
Level of Study: Postdoctorate.
Type: Fellowship.
Value: Return travel allowance for the fellow and any dependants plus a stipend and dependants' allowance.
Length of Study: Two years.
Frequency: Annual.
Study Establishment: A suitable laboratory.
Country of Study: Any European Molecular Biology Conference (EMBC) member country.
No. of awards offered: Eight.
Application Procedure: Applicants must visit the website for further information.
Closing Date: August 15th.
Funding: Government.
Contributor: 24 member states.
Additional Information: The following countries form the European Molecular Biology Conference (EMBC): Austria, Belgium, Croatia, Czech Republic, Denmark, Finland, France, Germany, Greece, Hungary, Iceland, Ireland, Israel, Italy, Netherlands, Norway, Poland, Portugal, Slovenia, Spain, Sweden, Switzerland, Turkey and the United Kingdom. Special provision is also made for applications involving Cyprus.

EMBO Short-Term Fellowships in Molecular Biology

Subjects: Molecular biology and disciplines relying on molecular biology.
Purpose: To promote the development of molecular biology and allied research in Europe and Israel.
Eligibility: EMBO Fellowships are not awarded for exchanges between laboratories within any one country. Applicants must be nationals from a European Molecular Biology Conference (EMBC) member state or wishing to travel from one EMBC member state to another.
Level of Study: Doctorate, Postdoctorate, Postgraduate, Research.
Type: Fellowship.
Value: Return travel allowance for the Fellow only for duration of fellowship.
Length of Study: One week to three months.
Frequency: Throughout the year.
Study Establishment: A suitable laboratory.
Country of Study: Any European Molecular Biology Conference (EMBC) member state.
Application Procedure: Applicants must visit the website for information on applications.
Funding: Government.
Contributor: 24 member states.
No. of awards given last year: 176.
No. of applicants last year: 274.
Additional Information: The following countries form the European Molecular Biology Conference (EMBC): Austria, Belgium, Croatia, Czech Republic, Denmark, Finland, France, Germany, Greece, Hungary, Iceland, Ireland, Israel, Italy, Netherlands, Norway, Poland, Portugal, Slovenia, Spain, Sweden, Switzerland, Turkey and the United Kingdom. Special provision is also made for applications involving Cyprus.

EMBO Young Investigator

Subjects: Molecular biology and disciplines relying on molecular biology.
Purpose: To promote the development of molecular biology and allied research in Europe and Israel.
Eligibility: Applicants should be a leading member of an independent laboratory for at least one and not more than three years in a European Molecular Biology Conference (EMBC) member country. They must have two to eight years of post PhD scientific experience and an excellent track record. The applicants must have demonstrated physical mobility and have enough funds to run their laboratories.
Level of Study: Postdoctorate.
Value: €15,000.
Length of Study: Three years.
Frequency: Annual.
Study Establishment: The applicant's own independent laboratory.
Country of Study: A European Molecular Biology Conference (EMBC) member state.
Application Procedure: Applicants must visit the website.
Closing Date: April 1st.
Funding: Government.
Contributor: 24 member states.
No. of awards given last year: 23.
No. of applicants last year: 150.
Additional Information: The following countries form the European Molecular Biology Conference (EMBC): Austria, Belgium, Croatia, Czech Republic, Denmark, Finland, France, Germany, Greece, Hungary, Iceland, Ireland, Israel, Italy, Netherlands, Norway, Poland, Portugal, Slovenia, Spain, Sweden, Switzerland, Turkey and the United Kingdom. Special provision is also made for applications involving Cyprus.

EUROPEAN SOUTHERN OBSERVATORY (ESO)

Karl-Schwarzschild-Straße 2, Garching bei Muenchen, D-85748, Germany
Tel: (49) 893 200 60
Fax: (49) 893 202 362
Email: abeller@eso.org
www: http://www.eso.org
Contact: Ms Angelika Beller

The European Southern Observatory (ESO) is an intergovernmental organisation for research in astronomy. At present ESO is constructing the Very Large Telescope (VLT) at Cerro Paranal in Chile, the world's most powerful facility for optical astronomy.

ESO Fellowship

Subjects: Astronomy and astrophysics.
Purpose: To provide a unique opportunity to learn and participate in the process of observational astronomy while pursuing a research programme.
Level of Study: Postdoctorate.
Type: Fellowship.
Value: Basic monthly salary of not less than €2,755, to which is added an expatriation allowance as well as some family allowances, if applicable. The Fellow will also have an annual travel budget for scientific meetings, collaborations and observing trips.
Length of Study: One year, with a possible extension to three years.
Frequency: Annual.
Study Establishment: The European Southern Observatory.
Country of Study: Germany or Chile.
No. of awards offered: Six-nine.
Application Procedure: Applicants must visit the ESO website for an application form and further information.
Closing Date: October 15th.
Funding: Government.

Contributor: France, Germany, Sweden, Denmark, Netherlands, Belgium, Switzerland, Portugal and Italy.
Additional Information: Fellowships begin between April and October of the year in which they are awarded. Selected Fellows can join ESO only after having completed their doctorate.

EUROPEAN SYNCHROTRON RADIATION FACILITY (ESRF)

BP 220, Grenoble, F-38043, France
Tel: (33) 4 76 88 20 00
Fax: (33) 4 76 88 20 20
Email: stuck@esrf.fr
www: http://www.esrf.fr
Contact: Ms Elizabeth Moulin

The European Synchrotron Radiation Facility (ESRF) supports scientists in the implementation of fundamental and applied research on the structure of condensed matter in fields such as physics, chemistry, crystallography, earth science, biology, medicine, surface science and materials science.

ESRF Postdoctoral Fellowships

Subjects: Physics, biology, chemistry, mineralogy and crystallography, computer engineering, and accelerators science.
Purpose: To enable postdoctoral fellows to develop their own research programme. In addition, they should be motivated to collaborate with external users.
Eligibility: Preference is given to member country nationals but other nationals may be accepted for the postdoctoral positions. Member countries are Belgium, Denmark, Finland, France, Germany, Italy, the Netherlands, Norway, Spain, Sweden, Switzerland and the United Kingdom. New associated members are the Czech Republic, Israel, Portugal and the Republic of Hungary.
Level of Study: Postdoctorate.
Value: €2,975 each month, plus a possible relocation allowance of up to €371 each month. These amounts correspond to a gross remuneration and are subject to social charges and income tax in France.
Length of Study: Two-three years.
Frequency: Dependent on funds available.
Study Establishment: Postdoctoral scientists are not linked to a university as research is carried out at the ESRF.
No. of awards offered: Up to 20.
Application Procedure: Applicants must complete an application form, available on request from the personnel department of the ESRF.
Closing Date: Individual deadlines exist for each position. Please contact the organisation.
Funding: Private.
Contributor: Public funds from 16 countries, mostly European.
No. of awards given last year: 25.
No. of applicants last year: 304.
Additional Information: Further information can be found on the website.

For further information contact:

Personnel Department, France
Fax: (33) 4 76 88 24 60
Email: recruitm@esrf.fr

ESRF Thesis Studentships

Subjects: Physics, biology, chemistry, mineralogy and crystallography, computer engineering, and accelerators science. The ESRF proposes subjects related to the use of synchrotron radiation or to synchrotron or storage ring technology.
Purpose: To enable grant holders to prepare a PhD at the ESRF, and to enable young scientists to acquire knowledge of the use of Synchrotron Radiation or its generation.

Eligibility: Preference is given to member country nationals but other nationals may be accepted for the postdoctoral positions. Member countries are Belgium, Denmark, Finland, France, Germany, Italy, the Netherlands, Norway, Spain, Sweden, Switzerland and the United Kingdom. New associated members are the Czech Republic, Israel, Portugal and the Republic of Hungary.
Level of Study: Doctorate.
Value: €1,959 per month. These amounts correspond to a gross remuneration and are subject to social charges and income tax in France.
Length of Study: Two-three years.
Frequency: Dependent on funds available.
Study Establishment: PhD students are free to choose a university in or outside France.
Country of Study: The research is carried out at the ESRF but the academic programme of studies depends on the university which is chosen.
No. of awards offered: Up to 10.
Application Procedure: Applicants must complete an application form, available on request from the personnel department of the ESRF.
Closing Date: There is an individual deadline for each position.
Funding: Private.
Contributor: Public funds from 16 countries, mainly European.
No. of awards given last year: 12.
No. of applicants last year: 202.
Additional Information: Further information can be found on the website.

For further information contact:

Personnel Department, France
Fax: (33) 4 76 88 24 60
Email: recruitm@esrf.fr

EUROPEAN UNIVERSITY INSTITUTE (EUI)

Via dei Roccettini 9
50016 San Domenico di Fiesole, Florence, Italy
Tel: (39) 055 468 51
Fax: (39) 055 468 5444
Email: applyres@iue.it
www: http://www.iue.it
Contact: Mr Kenneth Hulley, Assistant Administrator (Academic Service)

The European University Institute's (EUI) main aim is to make a contribution to the intellectual life of Europe. Created by the European Union member states, it is a postgraduate research institution, pursuing interdisciplinary research programmes on the main issues confronting European society and the construction of Europe.

European University Institute Postgraduate Scholarships

Subjects: History and civilisation, economics, law or political and social sciences.
Purpose: To provide the opportunity for study leading to the doctorate degree or Master's in law from the Institute.
Eligibility: Open to nationals of the 15 European Union member states. Candidates must possess a good Honours Degree or its equivalent, and have full written and spoken command of at least two of the Institute's official languages. Under certain conditions, nationals of countries other than the European Union may also be admitted to the Institute and be eligible for a scholarship.
Level of Study: Doctorate, Postgraduate.
Type: Scholarship.
Value: Varies but approx. €1,060 per month.
Length of Study: One year, renewable for up to an additional two years.
Frequency: Annual.

Study Establishment: The Institute.
Country of Study: Italy.
No. of awards offered: Approx. 115-125.
Application Procedure: Applicants must complete an application form, available from the Institute and from the Institute's website.
Closing Date: January 31st.
Funding: Government.
Contributor: Member states of the European Union.
No. of awards given last year: 110.
No. of applicants last year: 1,200.
Additional Information: The Scholarships are granted over two academic years, by the governments of the 15 European Union member states to nationals of their own countries. The awards are currently distributed as follows: Federal Republic of Germany 29, France 25, Italy 29, United Kingdom 26, Spain 25, the Netherlands 15, Denmark 10, Belgium 10, Republic of Ireland 10, Greece 10, Luxembourg 5, Portugal 13, Austria 12, Finland 5 and Sweden 10.

Jean Monnet Fellowships

Subjects: Humanities and social sciences, with special attention to problems related to the European Community and to the development of Europe's cultural and academic heritage.
Purpose: To encourage postdoctoral research.
Eligibility: Open mainly to candidates with a doctoral degree at an early stage of their academic career. Established academics on leave are also eligible.
Level of Study: Postdoctorate.
Type: Fellowship.
Value: €12,000-21,500 per year, depending on age, plus allowances for dependants, travel and medical insurance. Flat-rate basis of approx. €1,000 per month for academics with paid sabbatical is available.
Length of Study: One year, possibly renewable for a further year.
Frequency: Annual.
Study Establishment: European University Institute.
Country of Study: Italy.
No. of awards offered: 40-50.
Application Procedure: Applicants must complete an application form available by contacting the office at the EUI via the Internet or by contacting the Jean Monnet Fellowships Officer at the general EUI address.
Closing Date: October 25th.
Funding: Government.
Contributor: Member states of the European Union.
No. of awards given last year: 50.
No. of applicants last year: 230.
Additional Information: Further information is available from the website.

EUROTOX

Turku University Hospital
Department of Clinical Physiology, Turku, FIN-20520, Finland
Tel: (358) 2 2612 664
Fax: (358) 2 2611 666
Email: eino.hietanen@utu.fi
www: http://www.eurotox.com
Contact: Professor Eino Hietanen, Secretary General

Eurotox is a non-profit organisation promoting research teaching and expertise in toxicology.

Eurotox Merit Award

Subjects: Toxicology.
Purpose: To recognise a distinguished career in European toxicology.
Eligibility: Open to a European toxicologist.
Level of Study: Unrestricted.
Frequency: Annual.
Country of Study: Any country.

No. of awards offered: One.
Application Procedure: Nominations must be submitted in writing by National Society Eurotox members, by Eurotox speciality sections or by at least 10 individual Eurotox members. Nominations have to be motivated, including a short curriculum vitae and a list of 5-10 key publications.
Closing Date: November 30th preceding the year for consideration.
Funding: Private.
Contributor: Eurotox.
No. of awards given last year: One.
No. of applicants last year: Four-five.
Additional Information: The awardee is invited to the congress where he or she will be presented with a diploma. The registration fee for the awardee will be waived.

Eurotox Young Scientist's Award

Subjects: Toxicology, clinical or experimental.
Purpose: To encourage young scientists to conduct research and to present high quality posters at Eurotox Congresses.
Eligibility: Open to scientists who live in Europe and who are of no more than 35 years of age on December 31st of the year of the Congress.
Level of Study: Unrestricted.
Type: Award.
Value: Please contact the organisation.
Frequency: Annual.
Country of Study: Any country.
No. of awards offered: One.
Application Procedure: Applicants must contact Eurotox for details.
Closing Date: To be determined at the Eurotox Congress.
Funding: Private.
Contributor: Eurotox.
No. of awards given last year: One.
No. of applicants last year: Approx. 90.

Gerhard Zbinden Memorial Lecture

Subjects: Toxicology.
Purpose: To recognise scientific excellence in the area of drug and chemical safety.
Eligibility: Open to scientists who have made recent outstanding research contributions to this field.
Level of Study: Unrestricted.
Type: Diploma.
Frequency: Annual.
Country of Study: Any country.
No. of awards offered: One.
Application Procedure: Nominations must be submitted in writing by National Society Eurotox members, by Eurotox speciality sections or by at least 10 individual members. Nominations have to be motivated including a short curriculum vitae and a list of 5-10 key publications.
Closing Date: November 30th preceding the year for consideration.
Funding: Private.
Contributor: Eurotox.
No. of awards given last year: One.
No. of applicants last year: Six.

EVANGELICAL LUTHERAN CHURCH IN AMERICA (ELCA)

Division for Ministry
8765 West Higgins Road, Chicago, IL, 60631-4195, United States of America
Tel: (1) 773 380 2873
Fax: (1) 773 380 2829
Email: pwilder@elca.org
www: http://www.elca.org
Contact: Pat Wilder, Executive Secretary

ELCA Educational Grant Program

Subjects: Theological studies.
Purpose: To provide financial assistance to graduate students in advanced degree PhD or ThD programmes in theological education.
Eligibility: Open to members of the Evangelical Lutheran Church in America who are enrolled in an accredited graduate institution for study in a PhD or ThD programme in a theological area appropriate to seminary teaching.
Level of Study: Doctorate.
Type: Grant.
Value: US$500-5,000.
Length of Study: Four years and an additional year for a dissertation.
Frequency: Annual.
Country of Study: United States of America.
No. of awards offered: 40-50.
Application Procedure: Applications are sent out to applicants in January.
Closing Date: March 15th.
Funding: Private.
No. of awards given last year: 61.
No. of applicants last year: 70.
Additional Information: Priority is given to women and minority students. Funds are distributed according to need and the contribution the applicant will make towards the future of the church. Grants are awarded for a maximum of four years with a fifth year award for the dissertation. Two recommendations are required for each applicant.

EVRIKA FOUNDATION

PO Box 615
1 Patriarch Evtimii Boulevard, Sofia, BG-1000, Bulgaria
Tel: (359) 2 981 5181
Fax: (359) 2 981 5483
Email: evrika@einet.bg
www: http://www.evrika.org
Contact: Mr Vassil Velev, Executive Director

The Evrika Foundation was established in 1990 by state and public organisations to promote the development of youth technical and scientific creativity, and to encourage youth economic enterprise and to assist youth education, specialisation and training. The Evrika Foundation is a non-governmental, non-religious and apolitical organisation.

Evrika Foundation Awards

Subjects: Agriculture and farm management, management systems and techniques, engineering or natural sciences.
Purpose: To support young people with proven abilities and skills.
Eligibility: Open to Bulgarian nationals only, up to the age of 35. Scholarships are available to postgraduate students and grants and awards are reserved for Scholars who hold a Master's degree or PhD.
Level of Study: Doctorate, Graduate.
Type: Scholarships, grants and awards.
Value: Dependent on the type of award.
Frequency: Annual.
Country of Study: Bulgaria, except for travel grants.
No. of awards offered: Three-four.
Application Procedure: Applicants must complete and submit an application form with references.
Closing Date: December 15th.
Funding: Private.
No. of awards given last year: Three.
No. of applicants last year: 285.

EXETER COLLEGE

Oxford, Oxfordshire, OX1 3DP, England
Tel: (44) 1865 279660
Fax: (44) 1865 279630
Email: joan.himpson@exeter.ox.ac.uk
www: http://www.exeter.ox.ac.uk
Contact: Ms Joan Himpson, Academic Administrator

Exeter College is one of the University of Oxford's oldest Colleges. Founded in 1314, the College currently has 429 students, of which 310 are undergraduates and 119 are postgraduate students.

Exeter College Senior Scholarship in Theology

Subjects: Theology or theology and philosophy.
Purpose: To support a graduate who wishes to read for the Final Honour School of theology or philosophy and theology.
Eligibility: Applicants must hold by the time of admission at least a Second Class (Honours) Degree in a subject other than theology.
Level of Study: Postgraduate.
Type: Scholarship.
Value: Minimum value UK £200 may be supplemented up to a maximum of all college fees, university fees to the amount charged to home and European Union students, and maintenance to the current maximum Local Education Authority maintenance grant.
Length of Study: Two years.
Frequency: Every two years.
Study Establishment: Exeter College, the University of Oxford.
Country of Study: United Kingdom.
No. of awards offered: One.
Application Procedure: Applicants must apply in writing to the chaplain, with a curriculum vitae and the names of two academic references.
Funding: Private.
Contributor: Endowment.
No. of awards given last year: One.
No. of applicants last year: Seven.

Monsanto Senior Research Fellowship

Subjects: Molecular biology, cellular biology, or biochemistry.
Purpose: To support research into molecular or cellular biology, or biochemistry.
Eligibility: Open to qualified applicants of any nationality.
Level of Study: Postdoctorate.
Type: Fellowship.
Value: Stipend between UK £13,895 and UK £22,726 per year. Fellows are entitled to free lunch and dinner, free rooms in college if unmarried, and housing allowance if not resident in college.
Length of Study: Three-five years.
Frequency: Every three to five years.
Study Establishment: Exeter College, the University of Oxford.
Country of Study: United Kingdom.
No. of awards offered: One.
Application Procedure: Applicants must address enquiries to the Academic Administrator.
Funding: Private.
No. of awards given last year: One.
No. of applicants last year: 22.
Additional Information: The next award is not expected to be given until 2004.

Queen Sofia Research Fellowship

Subjects: Spanish literature.
Purpose: To support research into peninsular Spanish literature.
Eligibility: Applicants should be close to completing doctoral or postdoctoral work and must be under 31 at the time of taking up the fellowship. They must also be fluent in Spanish.
Level of Study: Doctorate, Postdoctorate.
Type: Fellowship.
Value: Stipend of UK £10,240 per year. Fellows are entitled to free lunch and dinner, free rooms in college if unmarried, and housing allowance if not resident in the college.

Length of Study: Two-three years.
Frequency: Every two to three years.
Study Establishment: Exeter College, the University of Oxford.
Country of Study: United Kingdom.
No. of awards offered: One.
Application Procedure: Applicants must address enquiries to the Academic Administrator.
Funding: Private.
Contributor: Endowment.
No. of awards given last year: One.
No. of applicants last year: 23.

Staines Medical Research Fellowship

Subjects: Medical science widely construed.
Purpose: To support research into medical science.
Eligibility: Applicants should be close to completing doctoral or postdoctoral work and must be under 31 at the time of taking up the fellowship.
Level of Study: Doctorate, Postdoctorate.
Type: Fellowship.
Value: Stipend of between UK £300 and UK £10,240 per year. Fellows are entitled to free lunch and dinner, free rooms in college if unmarried and housing allowance if not resident in college.
Length of Study: Two-three years.
Frequency: Every two to three years.
Study Establishment: Exeter College, the University of Oxford.
Country of Study: United Kingdom.
No. of awards offered: One.
Application Procedure: Applicants must address enquiries to the Academic Administrator.
Funding: Private.
Contributor: Endowment.
No. of awards given last year: One.
No. of applicants last year: 19.

F BUSONI FOUNDATION

Conservatorio Statale di Musica 'C Monteverdi'
Piazza Domenicani 25, Bolzano, I-39100, Italy
Tel: (39) 047 197 6568
Fax: (39) 047 197 3579
Email: info@concorsobusoni.it
www: http://www.concorsobusoni.it
Contact: Ms Maria Pia Venturi, Secretary

The Busoni International Piano Competition was first held in 1949 to commemorate the 25th anniversary of the death of composer Ferruccio Busoni. The aim of the competition is to create a forum for Busoni's music as well as for promising young pianists.

F Busoni International Piano Competition

Subjects: Piano performance.
Purpose: To award excellence in piano performance.
Eligibility: Open to pianists of any nationality under 28 years of age.
Level of Study: Unrestricted.
Type: Prize.
Value: First prize is €22,000 plus 60 important concert contracts, second prize is €10,000, third prize is €5,000, fourth prize is €4,000, fifth prize is €3,000 and sixth prize is €2,500, plus other special prizes.
Frequency: Every two years.
Country of Study: Italy.
No. of awards offered: 10.
Application Procedure: Applicants must complete an application form and submit this with a birth certificate, reports or certificates of study, a brief curriculum vitae and documentation of any artistic activity. Three recent photographs, entrance fee and written evidence of any prizes and international competitions should also be included.
Closing Date: May 31st.
Funding: Commercial, Government, Private.

Contributor: The municipality of Bolzano.
No. of awards given last year: 10.
No. of applicants last year: 120.
Additional Information: The competition lasts for two years, with the preselection phase taking place in the first year.

FANCONI ANEMIA RESEARCH FUND, INC.

1801 Willamette Street
Suite 200, Eugene, OR, 97401, United States of America
Tel: (1) 541 687 4658
Fax: (1) 541 687 0548
Email: info@fanconi.org
www: http://www.fanconi.org
Contact: Ms Mary Ellen Eiler, Executive Director

Fanconi Anemia Research Award

Subjects: Fanconi anaemia.
Purpose: To support research into effective treatments and a cure for Fanconi anaemia.
Eligibility: There are no restrictions on eligibility in terms of nationality, residency, age, gender, sexual orientation, race, religion or politics.
Level of Study: Doctorate, Postdoctorate.
Type: Research grant.
Value: US$5,000-1000,000.
Length of Study: Two years.
Frequency: As required.
Country of Study: Any country.
No. of awards offered: Unlimited.
Application Procedure: Applicants must contact info@fanconi.org to obtain information about the application process and to complete an application form.
Closing Date: There is no closing date.
Funding: Commercial, Government, Private.
No. of awards given last year: Four.
No. of applicants last year: Six.
Additional Information: The Internal Revenue Service has confirmed that the fund are not a private foundation for the purposes of tax exempt donations but a public charitable organisation under 501(c) 3 of the Internal Revenue Code.

FANNIE AND JOHN HERTZ FOUNDATION

2456 Research Drive, Livermore, CA, 94550, United States of America
Tel: (1) 925 373 1642
Email: askhertz@aol.com
www: http://www.hertzfoundation.org
Contact: Ms Linda Kubiak, Fellowship Administrator

The Fannie and John Hertz Foundation runs a national competition for graduate fellowships in the applied physical sciences.

Fannie and John Hertz Foundation Fellowships

Subjects: Applied physical and biophysical sciences.
Purpose: To promote the education and enhancement of the technological stature of the United States, by aiding in the education of the most capable students, working for PhDs in the applied physical and biophysical sciences.
Eligibility: Open to United States citizens or permanent residents who have received a Bachelor's degree by the start of tenure and propose to complete a programme of graduate study leading to a PhD. Students who have commenced graduate study are also eligible. The Foundation does not support candidates pursuing joint PhD and professional degree programmes.
Level of Study: Doctorate.

Type: Fellowship.

Value: US$25,000 per nine month academic year plus up to US$15,000 towards the cost of tuition.

Length of Study: One academic year and may be renewed annually for up to five years.

Frequency: Annual.

Study Establishment: Specified universities listed on the website.

Country of Study: United States of America.

No. of awards offered: 20.

Application Procedure: Applicants must complete a Hertz application form, four reference reports on the supplied specific forms and official transcripts of all college work must be submitted. The application form is available from the Foundation's website.

Closing Date: The first Friday in November.

Funding: Private.

No. of awards given last year: 21.

No. of applicants last year: Approx. 570.

THE FEDERATION OF AMERICAN SOCIETIES FOR EXPERIMENTAL BIOLOGY (FASEB)

9650 Rockville Pike, Bethesda, MD, 20814-3998, United States of America

Tel: (1) 301 530 7020

Fax: (1) 301 571 0699

www: http://www.faseb.org

Contact: Ms Cheryl Wright, Programme Co-ordinator

The Federation of American Societies for Experimental Biology (FASEB), founded in 1912, provides educational meetings and disseminates biological research results. The FASEB runs the Minority Access to Research Careers (MARC) programme, which aims to encourage minority students in the pursuit of graduate training leading to a PhD degree in the biomedical sciences.

Minority Scientist Scholarships to FASEB Summer Research Conferences

Subjects: Biological and life sciences.

Purpose: To provide an opportunity for full time minority faculty members to attend FASEB Summer Research Conferences.

Eligibility: Open to full-time minority faculty members at academic or research institutions in the United States of America.

Level of Study: Doctorate, Postdoctorate.

Type: Travel grant.

Value: Conference registration, travel costs and a subsistence allowance.

Length of Study: Varies.

Frequency: Annual.

Study Establishment: FASEB Summer Research Conferences.

Country of Study: United States of America.

No. of awards offered: 30.

Application Procedure: Applicants must complete an application form available from the organisation.

Closing Date: Please write for details.

Funding: Government.

Additional Information: Further information is available on the website.

FEDERATION OF EUROPEAN MICROBIOLOGICAL SOCIETIES (FEMS)

Poortlandplein 6, Delft, NL-2628 BM, Netherlands

Tel: (31) 15 278 5604

Fax: (31) 15 278 5696

Email: fems@fems-microbiology.org

www: http://www.fems-microbiology.org

Contact: Dr D Van Rossum, Executive Officer

The Federation of European Microbiological Societies (FEMS) is devoted to the promotion of microbiology in Europe. FEMS advances research and education in the science of microbiology within Europe, for example, by encouraging joint activities and facilitating communication among microbiologists, supporting meetings and laboratory courses and publishing books and journals.

FEMS Fellowship

Subjects: Microbiology.

Purpose: To foster transnational research in microbiology and to support young scientists to pursue a short term research project in another European country.

Eligibility: The award is restricted to members of FEMS member societies.

Level of Study: Doctorate, Graduate, Postdoctorate, Postgraduate, Predoctorate, Professional development, Research.

Type: Fellowship.

Value: A maximum of €3,500.

Length of Study: A maximum of three months.

Frequency: Twice a year.

Study Establishment: None.

No. of awards offered: Approx. 50.

Application Procedure: Applicants must complete and submit an application form to a society which is a member of FEMS. The delegate of the member society will handle the application and submit it to the Federation for funding. FEMS will then make a decision on the application. Addresses of the Federation's delegates are published on the website.

Closing Date: December 1st and June 15th.

Funding: Private.

No. of awards given last year: 44.

THE FIELD PSYCH TRUST

301 Dixie Street, Carrollton, GA, 30117, United States of America

Tel: (1) 770 834 8143

Email: arichards@westga.edu

www: http://www.fieldpsychtrust.org

Contact: Ms Anne C Richards, Trustee

The Field Psych Trust is a charitable trust honouring the professional life and contributions of psychologist/educator Dr Arthur W Combs. It provides grant funding to encourage graduate student research grounded in perceptual (field) psychology perspectives. It also supports publication of manuscripts related to Dr Combs' professional life and work.

Field Psych Trust Grant

Subjects: As a psychological theory, perceptual (field) psychology is applicable to any subject area in which links between human experience, meaning and/or perception and human behaviour can be explored. Hence applicants representing a wide range of subject areas may qualify for grant funding. Those which explore the history, contributions and further development of perceptual (field) psychology as related to the research and writings of Arthur W Combs, PhD will be favoured.

Purpose: To encourage graduate research exploring the history, contributions and further development of perceptual (field) psychology as related to the research and writings of Arthur W Combs, PhD.

Eligibility: Open to graduate students in good standing through a competitive review process.

Level of Study: Doctorate, Graduate, Postdoctorate, Predoctorate.

Type: Research grant.

Value: Varies according to the itemised budget request of successful applicants and their projects. Awards range from US$500-1,500.

Length of Study: Varies, although one year is preferable.

Frequency: Twice a year.

Study Establishment: An accredited Institute of Higher Education, preferably in the United States of America or the United Kingdom.

Country of Study: Any country.

No. of awards offered: Two.

Application Procedure: Applicants must complete an application form and submit references. Application forms can be found on the website. Applications are judged with respect to the relevance of the proposed project to the mission of the Field Psych Trust, substance, conceptual quality and clarity of the proposal, significance of the project in addressing matters of consequence to the human condition, and the degree of confidence that the prospective grant recipient has the ability to produce the proposed project.

Closing Date: January 31st and October 5th of each year.

Funding: Private.

Contributor: The estate of Arthur W Combs, PhD.

Additional Information: Awards are subject to conditions which are described and include an obligation to submit a final report upon conclusion of the project (which can take the form of a completed Master's thesis, research project report, doctoral dissertation or published manuscript). More information is available from the website, or by contacting Anne Rochards at the main address.

FIGHT FOR SIGHT, INC.

Research Division of Prevent Blindness America
500 East Remington Road, Schaumburg, IL, 06173, United States of America

Tel: (1) 847 843 2020
Fax: (1) 847 843 8458
Email: info@preventblindness.org
www: http://www.preventblindness.org
Contact: Program Co-ordinator

The goal of the Fight For Sight programme is to restore and preserve sight through research in detection, prevention, treatment and curing of visual disorders, as well as diseases leading to impaired sight and partial or total blindness.

Fight for Sight Grants-in-Aid

Subjects: Ophthalmology, vision and related sciences.

Purpose: To award investigators who are interested in conducting research in vision and vision related sciences.

Eligibility: Applicants must be residents of the United States of America or Canada.

Level of Study: Research.

Type: Research grant.

Value: By individual assessment. A maximum of US$1,000-12,000 to help defray the cost of personnel, equipment and supplies needed for a specific research investigation.

Length of Study: One year. Support may be renewed.

Frequency: Annual.

Study Establishment: Any institution which offers research facilities suitable for the research project in question.

Country of Study: United States of America or Canada.

No. of awards offered: Approx. 20-25.

Application Procedure: Applicants must write for an application form and programme details.

Closing Date: March 1st.

Funding: Private.

Contributor: Private donations from individuals.

Additional Information: It is the responsibility of candidates to make arrangements with the institutions of their choice. Applications for support of pilot projects are welcome.

Fight for Sight Postdoctoral Research Fellowships

Subjects: Ophthalmology, vision and related sciences.

Purpose: To support investigators who are interested in conducting research into vision or vision related sciences.

Eligibility: Applicants must be residents of the United States of America or Canada.

Level of Study: Postdoctorate, Research.

Type: Fellowship.

Value: US$5,000-14,000 per year. Recipients may supplement this stipend with institutional funds from another source, not to exceed US$28,000 per year.

Length of Study: One year, possibly renewable.

Frequency: Annual.

Study Establishment: At any approved institution.

Country of Study: United States of America or Canada.

No. of awards offered: Approx. 15-20.

Application Procedure: Applicants must write for an application form and programme details.

Closing Date: March 1st.

Funding: Private.

Contributor: Donations from private individuals.

Additional Information: It is the responsibility of candidates to make arrangements with the institutions of their choice.

Fight for Sight Student Research Fellowships

Subjects: Ophthalmology, vision and related sciences.

Purpose: To support new investigators who are interested in conducting research in vision and vision related sciences.

Eligibility: Open to graduate students who are interested in eye related clinical or basic research. Student fellowships are not offered to Americans who wish to study abroad.

Level of Study: Doctorate, Graduate, Predoctorate, Research.

Type: Fellowship.

Value: US$700 per month.

Length of Study: Two-three months, usually during the Summer.

Frequency: Annual.

Study Establishment: Approved institutions.

Country of Study: United States of America or Canada.

No. of awards offered: Approx. 20.

Application Procedure: Applicants must write for an application form and programme details.

Closing Date: March 1st.

Funding: Private.

Contributor: Donations from private individuals.

Additional Information: It is the responsibility of candidates to make arrangements with the institutions of their choice.

FINE ARTS WORK CENTER IN PROVINCETOWN, INC.

24 Pearl Street, Provincetown, MA, 02657, United States of America
Tel: (1) 508 487 9960
Fax: (1) 508 487 8873
Email: info@fawc.org
www: http://www.fawc.org
Contact: Mr Hunter O'Hanian, Executive Director

Established in 1968, the Fine Arts Work Center offers seven month fellowships to emerging visual artists and creative writers. Housing, studios and monthly stipends are provided to create a community of peers as a catalyst for artistic growth.

Fine Arts Work Center in Provincetown Fellowships

Subjects: Visual arts and creative writing both fiction and poetry.

Purpose: To give artists and writers the opportunity to work at the Center in a congenial and stimulating environment and to devote most of their time to their art and writing.

Eligibility: Open to all, but preference is given to emerging artists of outstanding promise. Applicants are accepted on the basis of work submitted.

Level of Study: Unrestricted.

Type: Fellowship.

Value: US$375-650 per month, plus housing and studio space.

Length of Study: Seven months.

Frequency: Annual.

Study Establishment: Provincetown, Massachusetts.

Country of Study: United States of America.

No. of awards offered: 10 for the visual arts, 10 for writing.

Application Procedure: Applicants must send a stamped addressed envelope for applications, the fee for which is US$35. Alternatively, applications can be downloaded from the website.

Closing Date: February 1st for visual artists and December 1st for writers.

Funding: Government, Private.

No. of awards given last year: 20.

No. of applicants last year: 1,000.

Additional Information: The Center is a working community, not a school.

FIRST (FLORICULTURE INDUSTRY RESEARCH AND SCHOLARSHIP TRUST)

PO Box 280, East Lansing, MI, 48826-0280, United States of America
Tel: (1) 517 333 4617
Fax: (1) 517 333 4494
Email: willbrandt@firstinfloriculture.org
www: http://www.firstinfloriculture.org
Contact: Mr William Willbrandt, Executive Director

FIRST (Floriculture Industry Research and Scholarship Trust) is a leading organisation for funding research and education in floriculture to improve the production and marketability of plants.

FIRST Scholarship Program

Subjects: Horticulture and the horticultural industry.

Eligibility: Open to students who are studying horticulture or have a career interest in any aspect of the horticultural industry. Further information is available on request.

Type: Scholarship.

Value: Varies.

Frequency: Annual.

Study Establishment: An accredited college or university.

Country of Study: United States of America.

No. of awards offered: Varies.

Application Procedure: Applicants must contact FIRST directly to obtain the latest scholarship application form which lists all of the current scholarships and requirements. Application forms are available from January 1st to May 1st from the website or by sending a stamped addressed envelope or printed self addressed mailing label to the main address.

Closing Date: May 1st.

Additional Information: Applicants are requested to contact the Foundation directly for information on individual scholarships. Information regarding the Foundation's research grant programme is also available from the website.

FLEMISH COMMUNITY

c/o Embassy of Belgium
3330 Garfied Street North West, Washington, DC, 20008, United States of America
Tel: (1) 202 625 5850
Fax: (1) 202 342 8346
www: http://www.diplobel.org
Contact: Flemish Community Fellowships Office

Fellowship of the Flemish Community

Subjects: Art, music, humanities, social and political sciences, law, economics, science and medicine.

Purpose: To assist American college students who wish to continue their postgraduate education in Flanders, Belgium.

Eligibility: Open to United States citizens of no more than 35 years of age, who hold a Bachelor's or Master's degree, and who have no other Belgian sources of income.

Level of Study: Postgraduate.

Type: Fellowship.

Value: A monthly stipend, tuition fees at a Flemish institution, health insurance and public liability insurance in accordance with Belgian law. There is no reimbursement of travel expenses.

Length of Study: 10 months.

Frequency: Annual.

Study Establishment: Universities, conservatories of music or art academies affiliated with the Flemish Community.

Country of Study: Belgium.

No. of awards offered: Five.

Application Procedure: Applicants must complete and submit a typed application form in triplicate with a certified true copy of the applicant's birth certificate, copies of diplomas, a summary of the thesis, official transcripts, two recommendations from current teachers or employers and latest grade point average where applicable.

Closing Date: January 31st.

Additional Information: Applicants will be notified of the result of applications no later than the end of July. The academic year for most Institutes of Higher Education in Flanders starts at the end of September.

FONDATION FYSSEN

194 Rue de Rivoli, Paris, F-75001, France
Tel: (33) 1 42 97 53 16
Fax: (33) 1 42 60 17 95
Email: secretariat@fondation-fyssen.org
www: http://www.fondation-fyssen.org
Contact: Ms Anne Kergraisse, Secretary

The aim of the Fyssen Foundation is to encourage all forms of scientific enquiry into cognitive mechanisms, including thought and reasoning, that underly animal and human behaviour; their biological and cultural bases, and phylogenetic and ontogenetic development.

Fondation Fyssen Postdoctoral Study Grants

Subjects: Disciplines relevant to the aims of the Foundation such as ethology, paleontology, archaeology, anthropology, psychology, epistemology, logic or the neurosciences.

Purpose: To fund scientific research.

Eligibility: Open to French research scientists who wish to work in laboratories abroad and foreign research scientists who wish to work in French laboratories.

Type: Grant.

Value: €20,124.

Length of Study: Two years for researchers of neurobiology who are coming from the United States of America to France and one year for all others.

Frequency: Annual.

Application Procedure: Applicants must complete an application form, available from the secretariat of the Foundation or from the website.
Closing Date: March 30th.
Funding: Private.

FONDATION PHILIPPE WIENER-MAURICE ANSPACH

39 avenue Franklin D Roosevelt
CP 172, Brussels, B-1050, Belgium
Tel: (32) 2 650 4996
Fax: (32) 2 650 4546
Email: fwa@ulb.ac.be

Fondation Philippe Wiener-Maurice Anspach Postdoctorate Grants

Subjects: All subjects.
Purpose: For doctors of all disciplines who have completed their thesis at the Universite Libre de Bruxelles and want to continue at the University of Oxford or the University of Cambridge.
Eligibility: Eligible candidates must have completed the doctorate at the Universite Libre de Bruxelles, having passed with a minimum of grand distinction.
Level of Study: Postdoctorate.
Type: Grant.
Value: Belgian franc 100,000 per month. Fees and laboratory costs are paid by the Foundation.
Length of Study: A maximum of one year.
Frequency: Annual.
Study Establishment: The University of Oxford or Cambridge.
Country of Study: United Kingdom.
Application Procedure: Applicants must complete an application form which can be obtained from the secretariat, to be submitted with a full curriculum vitae and photocopies of certificates. Information should be given on the research planned including a timetable and the name of someone who will supervise the research in the United Kingdom. A letter of recommendation also needs to be provided from an English sponsor and two letters of recommendation from members of university staff.
Closing Date: March 25th.
Funding: Private.
No. of awards given last year: Six.
No. of applicants last year: 15.

Fondation Philippe Wiener-Maurice Anspach Predoctorate Grants for Students at Oxford or Cambridge Universities

Subjects: All subjects.
Purpose: To allow students at the University of Oxford or the University of Cambridge to continue their studies at the Université Libre de Bruxelles.
Eligibility: Open to students who have finished the second stage of their predoctoral course and who want to develop their studies or research during an academic year at the Université Libre de Bruxelles. Access to the grants is dependent on their having completed the first stages of study at the University of Oxford or the University of Cambridge.
Level of Study: Predoctorate.
Type: Grant.
Value: Please contact the organisation. University fees are paid by the Foundation.
Frequency: Annual.
Study Establishment: The Université Libre de Bruxelles.
Country of Study: Belgium.
Application Procedure: Applicants must complete an application form, available from the secretariat, to be submitted with a curriculum vitae and photocopies of certificates, university grades and details of specific projects completed so far. Also, information on the

type of study or research the applicant wishes to undertake and two letters of academic reference should be included.
Closing Date: January 7th.
Funding: Private.
No. of awards given last year: Four.
No. of applicants last year: Six.

Fondation Philippe Wiener-Maurice Anspach Predoctorate Grants for Students at the Université Libre de Bruxelles

Subjects: All subjects.
Purpose: To allow students at the Université Libre de Bruxelles to continue their studies at the University of Oxford or the University of Cambridge.
Eligibility: Open to students who have finished the second stage of their predoctoral course at the Université Libre de Bruxelles and who want to develop their studies or research. Access to the grants is dependent on their having completed the first stages of study at the Université Libre de Bruxelles, having passed with a minimum of grand distinction.
Level of Study: Predoctorate.
Type: Grant.
Value: UK £9,250 per academic year. College fees are paid by the Foundation.
Frequency: Annual.
Study Establishment: The University of Oxford or Cambridge.
Country of Study: United Kingdom.
Application Procedure: Applicants must complete an application form, available from the secretariat, to be submitted with a curriculum vitae and photocopies of certificates, university grades and details of specific projects completed so far. Information on the type of study or research the applicant wishes to undertake and two letters of academic reference should be included.
Closing Date: December 1st.
Funding: Private.
No. of awards given last year: 15.

FOOD AND DRUG LAW INSTITUTE (FDLI)

1000 Vermont Avenue North West
Suite 200, Washington, DC, 20005-4903, United States of America
Tel: (1) 202 371 1420
Fax: (1) 202 371 0649
Email: cat@fdli.org
www: http://www.fdli.org
Contact: Ms M Cathryn Butler, Academic Programs

The Food and Drug Law Institute (FDLI) is a non-profit educational association dedicated to advancing the public health by providing a neutral forum for critical examination of the laws, regulations and policies related to drugs, medical devices, other healthcare technologies and food.

H Thomas Austern Memorial Writing Competition - Food and Drug Law

Subjects: An in-depth analysis of a current issue relevant to the food and drug field including a relevant case law, legislative history and other authorities, particularly where the United States Food and Drug Administration is involved. Additional topic possibilities are available from the website.
Purpose: To encourage law students interested in the areas of law affecting foods, drugs, devices, cosmetics and biologics.
Eligibility: Entrants must currently be enrolled in a JD programme at any of the United States law schools.
Level of Study: Postgraduate.
Value: First prize of US$1,500, second prize of US$1,000 and third prize of US$500.
Frequency: Annual.
Country of Study: United States of America.
No. of awards offered: Three.

Application Procedure: Applicants must submit a typewritten, double-spaced paper on 8½ x 11 inch paper. The cover sheet must list the applicant's full name, address and telephone number, law school and year, and the date of submission of the paper. Papers must not exceed 40 pages in length, including footnotes.
Closing Date: May 17th.
Funding: Private.
Contributor: Association funds and Association member dues.
No. of awards given last year: Three.
No. of applicants last year: Approx. 40.
Additional Information: Winning papers will be considered for publication in the Food and Drug Law Journal.

FOREST ROBERTS THEATRE

Panowski Playwriting Competition
Northern Michigan University
1401 Presque Isle, Marquette, MI, 49855-5364, United States of America
Tel: (1) 906 227 2559
Fax: (1) 906 227 2567
Contact: Ms Lindsey Harman, Award Co-ordinator

Mildred and Albert Panowski Playwriting Award

Subjects: Playwriting.
Purpose: To encourage and stimulate artistic growth among educational and professional playwrights.
Eligibility: Open to amateur, pre-professional and professional playwrights. There is no restriction as to theme or genre, but plays must be written in English. Entries must be original, full length plays. One act plays and previously submitted works are unacceptable. Submissions must not have been previously produced or published. Story adaptations and translations are eligible.
Level of Study: Unrestricted.
Value: US$2,000 cash award and production of the winning script plus travel costs and a one week summer workshop.
Frequency: Annual.
Country of Study: United States of America.
No. of awards offered: One.
Application Procedure: Applicants must send a stamped addressed envelope for rules and application form.
Closing Date: Plays must be received by the Friday before Thanksgiving.
Funding: Private.
Contributor: Dr James Panowski.
No. of awards given last year: One.
No. of applicants last year: 350.
Additional Information: Please write for a complete copy of the rules.

FORT COLLINS SYMPHONY ASSOCIATION

PO Box 1963, Fort Collins, CO, 80522, United States of America
Tel: (1) 970 482 4823
Fax: (1) 970 482 4858
Email: note@fcsymphony.org
www: http://www.fcsymphony.org
Contact: Executive Director

The Fort Collins Symphony Orchestra is conducted by Fusao Kajima and performs throughout the year, presenting a full concert season in the performance hall at the Lincoln Center. There are also special performances and concerts for all fourth and sixth graders and high school students in the Poudre R-1 School District to help introduce children to the delights of the symphony.

Adeline Rosenberg Memorial Prize Competition

Subjects: Music performance.
Purpose: To foster excellence in young performers of classical music.
Eligibility: Open to musicians of 25 years of age or under.
Level of Study: Unrestricted.
Value: First prize of US$3,000, second prize of US$2,000 and a third prize of US$1,000.
Frequency: Annual.
Country of Study: Any country.
No. of awards offered: Three.
Application Procedure: Applicants must submit an application form and include an application fee of US$35. Applications are available after October 1st and applicants should send a stamped addressed envelope.
Closing Date: January 20th.
Funding: Commercial, Private.
Additional Information: The Competition alternates between orchestral instruments (odd years) and piano (even years) and winning contestants are invited to perform with the Fort Collins Symphony Orchestra.

FOULKES FOUNDATION

37 Ringwood Avenue, London, N2 9NT, England
Tel: (44) 20 8444 2526
Fax: (44) 20 8444 2526
www: http://www.cbcu.cam.ac.uk/foulkes/ff.html
Contact: M Foulkes, The Registrar

The aim of the Foulkes Foundation Fellowship is to promote medical research by providing financial support for postdoctoral science graduates who need a medical degree before they can undertake medical research, and similarly for medical graduates who need a science degree.

Foulkes Foundation Fellowship

Subjects: All aspects of medical research, especially in the areas of molecular biology and biological sciences.
Purpose: To promote medical research by providing financial support for postdoctoral science graduates needing a medical degree before they can undertake medical research or for medical graduates in need of a science PhD degree.
Eligibility: Open to recently qualified scientists and medical graduates who have a PhD or equivalent degree or proven research ability and who intend to contribute to medical research. The applicant must study in the United Kingdom.
Level of Study: Postdoctorate.
Type: Fellowship.
Value: Varies. The amount of the fellowship depends on individual need, but the scale for the basic SRC Studentship is used as a guideline. Fellowships do not cover fees.
Length of Study: Up to three years.
Frequency: Annual.
Country of Study: United Kingdom.
No. of awards offered: Varies.
Application Procedure: Applicants must send a stamped addressed envelope to the Registrar for additional information and an application form.
Closing Date: March 15th.
Funding: Private.
No. of awards given last year: Seven.
No. of applicants last year: 75.

FOUNDATION FOR ANESTHESIA EDUCATION AND RESEARCH (FAER)

Charlton Building 1-128
Mayo Clinic
200 First Street South West, Rochester, MN, 55905, United States
of America
Tel: (1) 507 266 6866
Fax: (1) 507 284 0120
Email: todd.kerry@mayo.edu
www: http://www.faer.org
Contact: Ms Kerry Todd, Assistant Director

The Foundation for Anesthesia Education and Research (FAER) strives to foster progress in anaesthesiology, critical care, pain and all areas of perioperative medicine. We aim to generate new knowledge that advances health and patient care by facilitating the career development of anaesthesiologists dedicated to research and education. FAER offers four types of grants to anaesthesiologists. They range from US$25,000 to US$175,000. A 20 member committee consisting of both clinical and basic science anaesthesiologists reviews proposals. Clinical and outcomes projects are encouraged.

FAER Research Education Grant
Subjects: Anaesthesiology.
Purpose: To improve the quality and productivity of education and research in anaesthesiology.
Eligibility: Open to anaesthesiology residents or faculty.
Level of Study: Postgraduate.
Type: Grant.
Value: US$25,000.
Length of Study: Two years.
Frequency: Annual.
Application Procedure: Applicants must visit the website.
Closing Date: February 15th and August 15th.
Additional Information: Further information is available on request.

FAER Research Fellowship Grant
Subjects: Anaesthesia.
Purpose: To provide significant training in research techniques and scientific methods.
Eligibility: Open to anaesthesiology residents after CA-1 training and six months of Clinical Scientist Track.
Level of Study: Postdoctorate.
Type: Fellowship.
Value: US$50,000.
Length of Study: One year.
Frequency: Annual.
Application Procedure: Applicants must visit the website.
Closing Date: February 15th or August 15th.
Additional Information: Further information is available on request.

FAER Research Starter Grants
Subjects: Anaesthesiology.
Purpose: To support and initiate a project for which investigator will seek further support.
Eligibility: Applicants must be instructors or assistant professors who are within five years of their initial appointment.
Level of Study: Postdoctorate.
Type: Grant.
Value: US$35,000 in the first year and US$50,000 in the second.
Length of Study: Two years.
Frequency: Annual.
Application Procedure: Applicants must visit the website.
Closing Date: February 15th or August 15th.
Additional Information: Further information is available on request.

FAER Research Training Grant (RTG)
Subjects: Anaesthesiology.
Purpose: To allow the applicant to become an independent investigator.

Eligibility: Applicants must be instructors or assistant professors who are within five years of their initial appointment.
Level of Study: Postdoctorate.
Type: Training grant.
Value: US$75,000 in the first year and US$100,000 in the second.
Length of Study: Two years.
Frequency: Annual.
Application Procedure: Applicants must visit the website.
Closing Date: February 15th or August 15th.
Additional Information: Further information is available on request.

FOUNDATION FOR HIGH BLOOD PRESSURE RESEARCH

PO Box 13F
Monash University, VIC, 3800, Australia
Tel: (61) 3 9905 2555
Fax: (61) 3 9905 2566
Email: fhbpr@med.monash.edu.au
Contact: Ms Jan Morrison, Administrative Officer

The Foundation for High Blood Pressure Research was established to support research into any aspects of blood pressure, hypertension and associated cardiovascular diseases.

Foundation for High Blood Pressure Research Postdoctoral Fellowship
Subjects: Hypertension research or areas relevant to the understanding of the causes, prevention, treatment or effects of hypertension.
Purpose: To fund an Australian or New Zealand scientist to perform research into the causes or treatment of hypertension.
Eligibility: Open to applicants from Australia or New Zealand, who have a degree in medicine or science, with an appropriate PhD. The research must be performed in Australia.
Level of Study: Postdoctorate.
Type: Fellowship.
Value: Salary and associated costs, plus project maintenance.
Length of Study: Two years.
Frequency: Annual.
Study Establishment: An approved institute, university or hospital.
Country of Study: Australia.
No. of awards offered: One.
Application Procedure: Applicants must complete and submit an application with a curriculum vitae and relevant publications.
Closing Date: Usually July 31st.
Funding: Private.
Contributor: The Foundation for High Blood Pressure Research.
No. of awards given last year: One.
No. of applicants last year: 15.
Additional Information: The award is advertised in Australia and overseas. Interested applicants should contact the Honorary Secretary for further information.

ISH Postdoctoral Fellowship
Subjects: Hypertension research or areas relevant to the understanding of the causes, prevention, treatment or effects of hypertension.
Purpose: To fund an international scientist to perform research.
Eligibility: Open to applicants who have a degree in medicine or science, or appropriate PhD. The research must be performed in Australia.
Level of Study: Postdoctorate.
Type: Fellowship.
Value: Some assistance is provided to the employing institution comprising of part salary only.
Length of Study: Two years.
Frequency: Every two years.
Study Establishment: An approved institute, university or hospital.
Country of Study: Australia.

No. of awards offered: One.
Application Procedure: Applicants must complete and submit an application with a curriculum vitae and relevant publications.
Closing Date: Usually July 31st.
Funding: Private.
Contributor: The Foundation for High Blood Pressure Research.
No. of awards given last year: One.
No. of applicants last year: Three.
Additional Information: Details are advertised in Australia and overseas. Interested applicants should contact the Honorary Secretary for further information.

FOUNDATION FOR PHYSICAL THERAPY

1111 North Fairax Street, Alexandria, VA, 22314, United States of America
Tel: (1) 800 999 2782 ext. 8505
Fax: (1) 703 706 8519
Email: foundation@apta.org
www: http://www.apta.org/foundation
Contact: Ms Lucy Dickson, Scientific Review Administrator

The Foundation for Physical Therapy is a national, independent, non-profit corporation to support the physical therapy profession's research needs in the following three areas of scientific research, clinical research and health services research.

New Investigator Fellowships Training Initiative (NIFTI)

Subjects: Physical therapy, rehabilitation medicine, neuroscience, sports medicine, paediatrics, medical sciences and social or preventative medicine.
Purpose: To fund doctorally prepared physical therapists as developing researchers and improve their competitiveness in securing external funding for future research.
Eligibility: Open to candidates who possess a licence to practice physical therapy in the United States of America, have received the required post professional doctoral degree no earlier than five years prior to the year of application and have completed a research experience as part of their post professional doctoral education.
Level of Study: Postdoctorate.
Type: Fellowship.
Value: US$30,000.
Length of Study: One year.
Frequency: Annual.
Country of Study: United States of America.
No. of awards offered: Varies.
Application Procedure: Applicants must complete an application form.
Closing Date: January 15th.
Funding: Private.
No. of awards given last year: One.

Promotion of Doctoral Studies (PODS)

Subjects: Physical therapy, rehabilitation medicine, neuroscience, sports medicine, paediatrics, medical sciences and social or preventative medicine.
Purpose: To fund doctoral students who, having completed one full year of coursework, wish to continue their coursework or enter the dissertation phase.
Eligibility: Open to candidates who possess a licence to practice physical therapy in the United States of America and are enrolled as students in a regionally accredited post professional doctoral programme. The content of this programme should have a demonstrated relationship to physical therapy. Applicants must also demonstrate continuous progress towards the completion of his or her post professional doctoral programme in a timely fashion and a commitment to further the physical therapy profession through research and teaching in the United States and its territories.
Level of Study: Doctorate.
Type: Scholarship.

Value: Two levels at US$7,500 or US$15,000.
Length of Study: One year.
Frequency: Annual.
Country of Study: United States of America.
No. of awards offered: Varies.
Application Procedure: Applicants must complete an application form.
Closing Date: January 15th.
Funding: Private.
No. of awards given last year: 22.

FOUNDATION FOR SCIENCE AND DISABILITY, INC.

503 North West 89 Street, Gainesville, FL, 32607, United States of America
Tel: (1) 352 374 5774
Fax: (1) 352 374 5781
Email: rmankin@gainesville.usda.ufl.edu
www: http://www.as.wvu.edu~scidis/organizations
Contact: Dr Richard Mankin, Grants Committee Chair

The Foundation for Science and Disability aims to promote the integration of scientists with disabilities into all activities of the scientific community and of society as a whole, and to promote the removal of barriers in order to enable students with disabilities to choose careers in science.

Foundation for Science and Disability Student Grant Fund

Subjects: Engineering, mathematics, medicine, computer science and natural sciences or computer science.
Purpose: To increase opportunities in science for physically disabled students at the graduate or professional level.
Eligibility: Open to candidates from all countries.
Level of Study: Doctorate, Postdoctorate, Postgraduate.
Type: Grant.
Value: US$1,000.
Length of Study: One year.
Frequency: Annual.
Country of Study: Any country.
No. of awards offered: One-three.
Application Procedure: Applicants must submit a completed application form, copies of official college transcripts, a letter from the research or academic supervisor in support of the request and a second letter from another faculty member.
Closing Date: December 1st.
Funding: Private.
No. of awards given last year: Two.
No. of applicants last year: Eight.
Additional Information: The award may be used for an assistive device or instrument, or as financial support to work with a professor, or on an individual research project, or for some other special need.

FOUNDATION FOR THE ADVANCEMENT OF MESOAMERICAN STUDIES, INC. (FAMSI)

268 South Suncoast Boulevard, Crystal River, FL, 34429-5498,
United States of America
Tel: (1) 352 795 5990
Fax: (1) 352 795 1970
Email: famsi@famsi.org
www: http://www.famsi.org
Contact: Dr Sandra Noble, Executive Director

The Foundation for the Advancement of Mesoamerican Studies (FAMSI) was created in 1993 to foster increased understanding of ancient Mesoamerican cultures. The Foundation aims to assist and promote qualified scholars who might otherwise be unable to undertake or complete their programmes of research and synthesis. FAMSI provides research funds and research materials.

FAMSI Research Grant

Subjects: Mesoamerican Studies, investigations concerning the ancient pre-Columbian cultures of Mexico, Guatemala, Belize, Honduras and El Salvador.
Purpose: To support scholarly works with the potential for significant contributions to the understanding of ancient Mesoamerican cultures and to provide monies for projects that might otherwise not continue.
Eligibility: Preference is for recent graduates, degree candidates or active professionals who are involved in fully developed programmes of Mesoamerican study. FAMSI does not provide funds for equipment, salary or stipends. FAMSI does not fund other institutions.
Level of Study: Unrestricted.
Type: Research grant.
Value: General Research Grants: maximum US$10,000. Contingency Grants: maximum US$2,000.
Length of Study: One year.
Frequency: Annual.
Study Establishment: Unrestricted.
Country of Study: Pre-Columbian Mesoamerica: Mexico, Guatemala, Belize, Honduras or El Salvador.
No. of awards offered: 25-35.
Application Procedure: Applicants must complete a current application form and submit this with three letters of reference, a curriculum vitae, a budget, a statement of purpose and an abstract in English. Application forms are available on written request or from the website.
Closing Date: September 30th.
Funding: Private.
Contributor: Anonymous individuals.
No. of awards given last year: 36.
No. of applicants last year: 110.

FOUNDATION FOR THE STUDY OF INFANT DEATHS (FSID)

14 Halkin Street, London, SW1X 7DP, England
Tel: (44) 20 7235 0965
Fax: (44) 20 7823 1986
Email: fsid@sids.org.uk
www: http://www.sids.org.uk/fsid
Contact: Dr S Levene, Secretary, Scientific Advisory Committee

The Foundation for the Study of Infant Deaths (FSID), a United Kingdom cot death charity, raises funds for research, supports families whose babies have died and disseminates information about cot death and infant care to health professionals and the public.

FSID Research Grant Award

Subjects: Paediatrics, including developmental physiology, pathology, infection, metabolism, statistics, epidemiology, immunology, infant care practices and genetics.
Purpose: To support research into postneonatal infant health, morbidity and mortality, taking account of recent epidemiological studies in the field and giving consideration to the relevance of psychosocial factors.
Eligibility: Open to any graduate research worker employed by an academic or medical institution within the United Kingdom.
Level of Study: Unrestricted.
Type: Research grant.
Value: There is no fixed upper limit but applications are unlikely to succeed if recurrent expenditure exceeds UK £30,000 and total annual expenditure in any one year exceeds UK £50,000.
Length of Study: For the duration of the project, normally up to three years.
Frequency: Twice a year, dependent on funds available.
Study Establishment: An academic or medical institute.
Country of Study: United Kingdom.
No. of awards offered: Varies.
Application Procedure: Applicants must complete an application form and submit 10 copies.
Closing Date: Late February. Please telephone for confirmation.
Funding: Commercial, Government, Private.
Contributor: Donations and covenants from the public.
No. of awards given last year: Two.
No. of applicants last year: Six.

FSID Short Term Training Fellowship

Subjects: Paediatrics.
Purpose: To allow research workers to visit and work in other specialist laboratories for a short period to acquire new technical skills which can be applied to their own work, to apply new methods of data analysis, to establish collaborative research not possible by other means, or to undertake pilot studies in support of a more detailed application. The work must have relevance to sudden infant death.
Eligibility: Open to graduate research workers employed by an academic or medical institution within the United Kingdom.
Level of Study: Unrestricted.
Type: Fellowship.
Value: Approx. UK £2,500, up to a maximum of UK £5,000.
Length of Study: 6-26 weeks.
Frequency: Dependent on funds available.
Study Establishment: An academic or medical institute.
Country of Study: United Kingdom.
No. of awards offered: Varies.
Application Procedure: Applicants must complete an application form.
Closing Date: Applications are accepted at any time.
Funding: Commercial, Government, Private.
Contributor: Donations and covenants from the public.
No. of awards given last year: Two.
No. of applicants last year: Five.
Additional Information: Meeting attendance does not fall within the scope of the fellowships.

FOUNDATION OF THE AMERICAN COLLEGE OF HEALTHCARE EXECUTIVES

Suite 1700
One North Franklin Street, Chicago, IL, 60606-3491, United States of America
Tel: (1) 312 424 2800
Fax: (1) 312 424 0023
Email: srauchenecker@ache.org
www: http://www.ache.org
Contact: Mr Steven M Rauchenecker, Membership Associate Director

It is the mission of the Foundation of the American College of Healthcare Executives to be the professional membership society for healthcare executives, to meet its members' professional, educational and leadership needs, to promote high ethical standards and conduct, and to advance healthcare leadership and management excellence.

Albert W Dent Student Scholarships

Subjects: Healthcare management.
Purpose: To provide financial aid and increase the enrolment of minority students in healthcare management graduate programmes, and to encourage students through structured, formalised study to obtain positions in middle and upper levels of healthcare management.
Eligibility: Open to United States and Canadian citizens who are student associates of the American College of Healthcare Executives and are in good standing. Applicants must also be minority students enrolled for full-time study for the upcoming Autumn term (which is the final year of a healthcare management graduate programme), be able to demonstrate financial need and must not be previous recipients.
Level of Study: Graduate.
Type: Scholarship.
Value: US$3,500.
Frequency: Annual.
Country of Study: United States of America or Canada.
No. of awards offered: Varies.
Application Procedure: Applicants must complete an application form, available from their programme director or the main address.
Closing Date: Applications are accepted between January 1st and March 31st.
No. of awards given last year: Six.
No. of applicants last year: 25.

Foster G McGaw Student Scholarships

Subjects: Healthcare management.
Purpose: To help students to better prepare themselves for healthcare management, thereby contributing to improvements in the field.
Eligibility: Open to United States and Canadian citizens who are student associates of the American College of Healthcare Executives and are in good standing. Applicants must also be minority students enrolled for full-time study for the upcoming Autumn term (which is the final year of a healthcare management graduate programme), be able to demonstrate financial need and must not be previous recipients.
Level of Study: Graduate.
Type: Scholarship.
Value: US$3,500.
Frequency: Annual.
Country of Study: United States of America or Canada.
No. of awards offered: Varies.
Application Procedure: Applicants must complete an application form, available from their programme director or the main address.
Closing Date: Applications are accepted between January 1st and March 31st.
No. of awards given last year: Eight.

No. of applicants last year: 37.

FOUNDATION PRAEMIUM ERASMIANUM

Jan van Goyenkade 5, Amsterdam, NL-1075 HN, Netherlands
Tel: (31) 20 676 0222
Fax: (31) 20 675 2231
Email: spe@erasmusprijs.org
www: http://www.erasmusprijs.org
Contact: Y C Goester, Secretary

The Foundation Praemium Erasmianum operates internationally in the fields of social studies and the arts and humanities, as well as through the awarding of the Erasmus Prize and other activities.

ERASMUS Prize

Subjects: Arts, humanities or social studies.
Purpose: To honour persons who have made an exceptional contribution to European culture.
Eligibility: There are no eligibility restrictions.
Level of Study: Unrestricted.
Value: €150,000.
Frequency: Annual.
Country of Study: Any country.
No. of awards offered: One.
Application Procedure: Applications by third parties only are considered.
Funding: Private.

Foundation Praemium Erasmianum Study Prize

Subjects: Humanities or social sciences.
Purpose: To honour young academics who have written an excellent thesis in the field of humanities or social sciences.
Eligibility: Open to students of Dutch universities.
Level of Study: Postdoctorate.
Value: €3,000.
Frequency: Annual.
Country of Study: Any country.
No. of awards offered: Five.
Application Procedure: Relevant faculties or universities nominate candidates, from which the Foundation selects five winners.
Closing Date: July 15th.
Funding: Private.
No. of awards given last year: Four.
No. of applicants last year: 21.

FRANCIS CHAGRIN FUND

c/o Society for the Promotion of New Music (SPNM)
9th Floor
18-20 Southwark Street, London, SE1 1TJ, England
Tel: (44) 20 7407 1640
Fax: (44) 20 7403 7652
Email: spnm@spnm.org.uk
www: http://www.spnm.org.uk
Contact: Ms Jo-Anne Naish, Administrator

From contemporary jazz, classical and popular music to that written for film, dance and other creative media, the Francis Chagrin Fund is one of the main advocates of new music in the United Kingdom today.

Francis Chagrin Award

Subjects: Composition.
Purpose: To help cover the costs of photocopying incurred by composers in reproducing performance materials for unpublished works awaiting their first performance.

Eligibility: Applicants must be British composers, or composers resident in the United Kingdom. Their works must be unpublished.
Level of Study: Unrestricted.
Type: Grant.
Value: UK £250 maximum.
Frequency: Dependent on funds available.
No. of awards offered: Unlimited.
Application Procedure: Applicants must complete and submit an application form to the SPNM, with receipts. Application forms are available from the SPNM.
Funding: Private.

Francis Chagrin Fund Awards

Subjects: Subjects relevant to musical compositions or electronic tapes awaiting their first performance.
Purpose: To cover the costs of reproducing performance materials for works awaiting their first performance.
Eligibility: Open to United Kingdom nationals and those living in the United Kingdom.
Level of Study: Unrestricted.
Type: Grant.
Value: UK £250 maximum.
Frequency: Awards are considered once a month by committee.
Country of Study: United Kingdom.
No. of awards offered: Varies.
Application Procedure: Applicants must submit an application form as well as a curriculum vitae, two references and relevant invoices. Application forms are available from the SPNM.
Closing Date: Applications are accepted at any time. The committee meets once a month.
Funding: Government, Private.
Contributor: The Arts Council of England.
No. of awards given last year: 21.
No. of applicants last year: 24.

FRANK KNOX MEMORIAL FELLOWSHIPS

48 Westminster Palace Gardens
Artillery Row, London, SW1P 1RR, England
Tel: (44) 20 7222 1151
Fax: (44) 20 7222 5355
www: http://www.franknox.demon.co.uk
Contact: Ms Anna Mason, Secretary

The Frank Knox Memorial Fellowships were established at Harvard University in 1945 by a gift from Mrs Annie Reid Knox, widow of the late Colonel Frank Knox, to allow students from the United Kingdom to participate in an educational exchange programme.

Frank Knox Fellowships at Harvard University

Subjects: Arts, sciences including engineering and medical sciences, business administration and management, design, divinity, education, law, public administration and public health.
Eligibility: Open to United Kingdom citizens who, at the time of application, have spent at least two of the last four years at a United Kingdom university or university college and will have graduated by the start of tenure.
Level of Study: Postgraduate.
Type: Fellowship.
Value: US$17,500 plus tuition fees. Unmarried Fellows may be accommodated in one of the university dormitories or halls.
Length of Study: One academic year. Depending on the availability of sufficient funds fellowships may be renewed for those Fellows registered for a degree programme of more than one year.
Frequency: Annual.
Study Establishment: Harvard University.
Country of Study: United States of America.
No. of awards offered: Four.

Application Procedure: Applicants must file an admissions application directly with the graduate school of their choice at an early date. Harvard University will try to arrange a suitable course for each individual. Fellowships are not awarded for postdoctoral study and no application will be considered from persons already in the United States. A period of full-time work since graduation is necessary prior to embarking on the MBA programme. Travel grants are not awarded, although in cases of extreme hardship applications can be made to Harvard University for travel cost assistance.
Closing Date: October 27th.
Funding: Private.
Contributor: Estate of the late Frank Knox.
No. of awards given last year: Six.
No. of applicants last year: 130.

FRANKLIN AND ELEANOR ROOSEVELT INSTITUTE

Franklin D Roosevelt Library
4079 Albany Post Road, Hyde Park, NY, 12538, United States of America
Tel: (1) 845 229 5321
Fax: (1) 845 229 9046
Email: emurphy@idsi.net
www: http://www.feri.org
Contact: Chairman, Grants Committee

The Franklin and Eleanor Roosevelt Institute is a private non-profit corporation dedicated to preserving the legacy and promoting the ideals of Franklin and Eleanor Roosevelt.

Roosevelt Institute Grant-in-Aid

Subjects: The Roosevelt years and clearly related subjects.
Purpose: To encourage younger scholars to expand their knowledge and understanding of the Roosevelt period and to give continued support to more experienced researchers who have already made a mark in the field.
Eligibility: Open to qualified researchers of any nationality with a viable plan of work. Proposals are recommended for funding by an independent panel of Scholars which reports to the Institute Board.
Level of Study: Doctorate, Graduate, Postdoctorate.
Type: Grant.
Value: Up to US$2,500.
Frequency: Twice a year.
Study Establishment: The Franklin D Roosevelt Library, Hyde Park in New York.
Country of Study: United States of America.
No. of awards offered: 15-20.
Application Procedure: Applicants must submit two copies of each of the following: an application face sheet, research proposal, relevance of holdings, travel plans, time estimate, curriculum vitae, three letters of reference and budget. Application forms and guidelines are available from the website or by emailing, faxing, or writing to the Roosevelt Institute.
Closing Date: February 15th and September 15th.
Funding: Private.
No. of awards given last year: 23.
No. of applicants last year: 41.

FRAXA RESEARCH FOUNDATION

45 Pleasant Street, Newburyport, MA, 01950, United States of America
Tel: (1) 978 462 1866
Fax: (1) 978 463 9985
Email: info@fraxa.org
www: http://www.fraxa.org
Contact: Ms Katherine Clapp, President

The FRAXA Research Foundation funds postdoctoral fellowships and investigator initiated grants to support medical research aimed at the treatment of Fragile X Syndrome. FRAXA is particularly interested in preclinical studies of potential pharmacological and genetic treatments and studies aimed at understanding the function of the FMRI gene.

FRAXA Grants and Fellowships

Subjects: Medical research aimed at the treatment of Fragile X Syndrome. Preclinical studies of potential pharmacological and genetic treatments and studies aimed at understanding the function of the FMRI gene.
Purpose: To promote research aimed at finding a specific treatment for Fragile X syndrome.
Eligibility: There are no eligibility restrictions.
Level of Study: Postdoctorate, Research.
Type: Fellowship and investigator initiated grant.
Value: Up to US$35,000 for postdoctoral fellowships. No limit for investigator initiated grants.
Length of Study: One year, renewable.
Frequency: Twice a year.
Country of Study: Any country.
No. of awards offered: 8-15.
Application Procedure: Applicants must complete an application form, available from the FRAXA Research Foundation or from the website. Potential applicants are welcome to submit a one page initial inquiry letter describing the proposed research before submitting a full application.
Closing Date: May 1st or December 1st every year.
Funding: Private.
No. of awards given last year: 25.
No. of applicants last year: 50.
Additional Information: Further information is available on request.

FREDERICK DOUGLASS INSTITUTE FOR AFRICAN AND AFRICAN-AMERICAN STUDIES

University of Rochester
302 Morey Hall, Rochester, NY, 14627-0440, United States of America
Tel: (1) 585 275 7235
Fax: (1) 585 256 2594
Email: fdi@troi.cc.rochester.edu
www: http://www.cc.rochester.edu/college/aas
Contact: G R Radegonde-Eison, Administrative Assistant

The Frederick Douglass Institute for African and African-American Studies was established in 1986 to promote the development of African and African-American studies and graduate education through advanced research at the University of Rochester. It has served as an interdisciplinary centre, with its focus on the social sciences, though not excluding the humanities and the natural sciences.

FDIRFP Postdoctoral Fellowship

Subjects: Historical and contemporary topics on the economy, society, politics and culture of Africa and its diaspora. Broadly conceived projects on human and technological aspects of energy development and agriculture in Africa are welcomed.
Purpose: To support the completion of a project.
Eligibility: Open to Scholars who hold a PhD degree in a field related to the African and African-American experience.
Level of Study: Postdoctorate.
Type: Fellowship.
Value: A stipend of US$35,000 as well as full access to the university's facilities and office space in the Institute. It also supports the completion of a research project for one academic year.
Frequency: Annual.
Country of Study: Any country.
No. of awards offered: One.
Application Procedure: Applicants must submit a completed application, a curriculum vitae, a three-five page description of the project plus a short bibliography and a sample of published or unpublished writing on a topic related to the proposal. Three letters of recommendation that comment upon the value and feasibility of the work proposed are to be sent by referees.
Closing Date: January 31st.
Additional Information: All Fellows receive office space in the Institute and opportunities to interact and collaborate with Scholars of their respective disciplines within the University. Fellows must be in full-time residence during the tenure of their awards and are expected to be engaged in scholarly activity on a full-time basis. They must be available for consultation with students and professional colleagues, make at least two formal presentations based upon their research and contribute generally to the intellectual discourse on African and African-American Studies.

FDIRFP Predoctoral Dissertation Fellowship

Subjects: Historical and contemporary topics on the economy, society, politics and culture of Africa and its diaspora. Broadly conceived projects on human and technological aspects of energy development and agriculture in Africa are additionally welcomed.
Purpose: To support the completion of a dissertation.
Eligibility: Open to graduate students of any university who study aspects of the African and African-American experience.
Level of Study: Predoctorate.
Type: Fellowship.
Value: A stipend of US$15,000.
Frequency: Annual.
Country of Study: Any country.
Application Procedure: Please visit the website for more details.
Closing Date: January 31st.
Additional Information: All Fellows receive office space in the Institute and opportunities to interact and collaborate with Scholars of their respective disciplines within the University. Fellows must be in full-time residence during the tenure of their awards and are expected to be engaged in scholarly activity on a full-time basis. They must be available for consultation with students and professional colleagues, make at least two formal presentations based upon their research and contribute generally to the intellectual discourse on African and African-American Studies.

Frederick Douglass Institute for African and African-American Studies Fellowships for Graduate Study

Subjects: Historical and contemporary topics on the economy, society, politics, and culture of Africa and its diaspora. Broadly conceived projects on human and technological aspects of energy development and agriculture in Africa are additionally welcomed.
Eligibility: Open to students who want to begin their graduate work in African and African-American studies. The award is only available to those who hold a Bachelor's degree and who have been admitted into a University of Rochester graduate degree programme.
Level of Study: Postgraduate.
Type: Fellowship.
Value: Tuition plus academic year stipends ranging from US$10,000-12,000.
Length of Study: Four years.
Frequency: Annual.
Study Establishment: The University of Rochester.
Country of Study: Any country.
No. of awards offered: Varies.

Application Procedure: Applicants must write directly to the department and PhD programme of their choice in the first instance and then the second set of application materials comes to the Frederick Douglass Institute. A typical package would consist of the completed FDI fellowship application form, a copy of the application to the University of Rochester graduate programme, a curriculum vitae, a transcript and a statement of up to two typed pages describing the research interest.

Closing Date: January 31st.

Additional Information: All Fellows receive office space in the Institute and opportunities to interact and collaborate with Scholars of their respective disciplines within the University. Fellows must be in full-time residence during the tenure of their awards and are expected to be engaged in scholarly activity on a full-time basis. They must be available for consultation with students and professional colleagues, make at least two formal presentations based upon their research and contribute generally to the intellectual discourse on African and African-American Studies.

FREDERICK SODDY TRUST

25 Henry Burt Way, Burgess Hill, West Sussex, RH15 9UX, England
Contact: Mr Peter J Bunker, Chairman

Frederick Soddy Trust Grants

Subjects: Sociological sciences are preferred.

Purpose: To encourage group study of the whole life of a specified area.

Eligibility: Open to groups, not individuals, studying the whole life of a particular area in Great Britain, or elsewhere, with major emphasis on the human community therein. Preference is given to students of the sociological sciences and particularly to younger men and women, both teachers and students.

Level of Study: Unrestricted.

Type: Grant.

Value: UK £200-350.

Frequency: Dependent on funds available.

Country of Study: Any country.

No. of awards offered: Up to eight.

Application Procedure: Applicants must apply by letter to the Chairman.

Closing Date: Applications are accepted at any time.

Funding: Private.

No. of awards given last year: 10.

FRENCH EMBASSY LINGUISTIC SECTION

6 Perth Avenue
Yarralumla, Canberra, ACT, 2600, Australia
Tel: (61) 2 6216 0100
Fax: (61) 2 6216 0156
Email: language@france.net.au
www: http://www.france.net.au/language/program
Contact: Mr Christian Depierre, Attaché de Co-opération pour le Français

French Government Postgraduate Scholarships

Subjects: French language, literature and civilisation.

Eligibility: Open to Australian citizens, who hold a Bachelor of arts degree and have completed three years of French university.

Level of Study: Postgraduate.

Type: Scholarship.

Value: A monthly maintenance allowance of €730 plus medical cover.

Length of Study: One year.

Frequency: Annual.

Study Establishment: An approved French university.

Country of Study: France.

No. of awards offered: Two.

Application Procedure: Applicants must submit an application after their admission to the postgraduate programme of a French university. Application forms are available from the French departments of universities.

Closing Date: December 31st.

Funding: Government.

No. of awards given last year: Two.

Language Assistantships in Australia

Subjects: French language studies.

Purpose: To enable French assistants to take up positions supporting the teaching of French in Australian schools.

Eligibility: Open to French citizens only.

Level of Study: Postgraduate.

Type: Assistantship.

Value: Please contact the organisation.

Length of Study: One year, non renewable.

Frequency: Annual.

Study Establishment: Australian schools.

Country of Study: Australia.

No. of awards offered: 25.

Application Procedure: Applicants must apply to the French Ministry of Education in Paris through the French Embassy in Canberra.

Closing Date: Applications are accepted at any time.

Funding: Government.

No. of awards given last year: 25.

Additional Information: These awards are organised by the Bureau de Co-opération pour le Francais of the Embassy of France in Australia (BCLE).

Language Assistantships in France and New Caledonia

Subjects: French language studies.

Purpose: To enable young Australian graduates who intend to teach French in the future or beginning teachers of French to improve their language skills.

Eligibility: Open to young Australian graduates only.

Level of Study: Graduate.

Type: Assistantship.

Value: A living allowance of €891.83 and medical cover.

Length of Study: Seven months.

Frequency: Annual.

Study Establishment: Any approved high school in France or New Caledonia.

Country of Study: France or New Caledonia.

No. of awards offered: 50 in France and three in New Caledonia.

Application Procedure: Applicants must write for details.

Closing Date: October 15th.

Funding: Government.

No. of awards given last year: 28.

Additional Information: These awards are organised by the Bureau de Co-opération pour le Francais (BCF) of the Embassy of France in Australia. Successful applicants will conduct English conversation classes with small groups of students for 12 hours per week.

Ministry of Foreign Affairs (France) International Teaching Fellowships

Subjects: French language education.

Purpose: To enable experienced teachers of French to spend one year at a French college.

Eligibility: Open to Australian teachers of French employed by state education authorities.

Level of Study: Professional development.

Type: Fellowship.

Length of Study: One year.

Frequency: Annual.

Study Establishment: A lycée, collège, primary school or Institut Universitarie de Formation de Maîtres (IUFM).

Country of Study: France.

No. of awards offered: Two.

Application Procedure: Applicants must complete an application form, available from state Departments of Education.
Closing Date: April 30th.
Funding: Government.
No. of awards given last year: Two.
Additional Information: These awards are organised by the Bureau de Co-opération pour le Francais of the Embassy of France in Australia (BCF).

Ministry of Foreign Affairs (France) Stage de la Réunion (One Month Scholarships)

Subjects: French language teaching.
Purpose: To enable school teachers of French to attend a course on the methodology specific to the teaching of French at primary or secondary level.
Eligibility: Open to Australian teachers of French only.
Level of Study: Professional development.
Type: Scholarship.
Value: All costs except travel costs between Australia and Réunion Island.
Length of Study: One month.
Frequency: Annual.
Study Establishment: Cifept in Le Tampon.
Country of Study: Reunion Island.
No. of awards offered: Four-five.
Application Procedure: Applicants must write for details.
Closing Date: March 15th.
Funding: Government.
No. of awards given last year: Five.
Additional Information: These awards are organised by the Bureau de Co-opération pour le Francais of the Embassy of France in Australia (BCF).

Ministry of Foreign Affairs (France) Stage de Nouméa (Three Week Course)

Subjects: French language, and French and Melanesian culture.
Purpose: To enable primary and secondary teachers of French to refresh and consolidate their knowledge of French, to improve their teaching skills and to increase their knowledge of French and Melanesian cultures.
Eligibility: Open to primary and secondary teachers of French and final year Diploma of Education or Bachelor of Education students.
Level of Study: Professional development.
Value: Australian $4,000.
Length of Study: Three weeks.
Frequency: Annual.
Study Establishment: CREIPAC, Nouméa.
Country of Study: New Caledonia.
No. of awards offered: Up to 30.
Application Procedure: Applicants from state schools must apply through their local Department of Education, please check the deadline with the Department. Teachers from Catholic or Independent schools must refer to their State authorities.
Closing Date: August 1st.
No. of awards given last year: 25.

Ministry of Foreign Affairs (France) Stage de Paris/Toulon

Subjects: French.
Eligibility: Open to experienced primary and secondary teachers of French, especially those holding positions of responsibility in language departments.
Level of Study: Professional development.
Type: Course.
Value: Australian $4,000.
Length of Study: Four weeks.
Frequency: Annual.
Study Establishment: The Centre International d'Etudes Pédagogiques (CIEP) de Sévres and the Campus International de Toulon.
Country of Study: France.

No. of awards offered: Up to 20.
Application Procedure: Applicants must write for details.
Closing Date: August 1st.
No. of awards given last year: 14.

Ministry of Foreign Affairs (France) Support for Associations of Independent Schools

Subjects: French.
Purpose: To financially assist independent schools which have a particular project related to the teaching of French.
Eligibility: Applicants must be French teachers from independent schools.
Level of Study: Professional development.
Type: Grant.
Value: Varies.
Frequency: Annual.
No. of awards offered: Seven.
Application Procedure: Applicants must submit their projects to their State Association before May 15th. Each State Association of Independent Schools will then sort the projects according to its own priorities and forward them along with the statement of priorities to the BCLE of the French Embassy before May 31st.
Closing Date: May 15th for project submissions from teachers. May 31st for forwarded projects and priorities list from Associations.
Funding: Government.
No. of awards given last year: Seven.

Ministry of Foreign Affairs (France) Support for French Teachers' Associations

Subjects: French.
Purpose: To support initiatives in the teaching of French.
Eligibility: Open to Australian associations of French teachers.
Level of Study: Professional development.
Type: Grant.
Value: Varies.
Frequency: Annual.
No. of awards offered: Six.
Application Procedure: Applicants must write for details.
Closing Date: May 15th.
Funding: Government.
No. of awards given last year: Four.

Ministry of Foreign Affairs (France) Tertiary Studies in French Universities (Bandin Travel Grants)

Subjects: French language.
Purpose: To encourage graduate and postgraduate students to study for at least one semester at a French university.
Eligibility: Applicants must be graduate or postgraduate students with a double major in French and in another subject.
Level of Study: Graduate, Postgraduate.
Type: Grant.
Value: Australian $2,000.
Length of Study: A minimum of one semester.
Frequency: Annual.
Study Establishment: A university in France.
Country of Study: France.
No. of awards offered: 16.
Application Procedure: Applicants must complete an application form, available on request from every Australian university's department or section of French studies.
Closing Date: May 15th.
Funding: Government.
No. of awards given last year: 16.
Additional Information: Students must apply for a course of study approved for credit by their home institution.

Ministry of Foreign Affairs (France) University Study Tours (Nouméa)

Subjects: French language.

Purpose: To assist French language students to attend a French course in Nouméa.
Eligibility: Open to French language students.
Level of Study: Graduate.
Value: Australian $500-1,000.
Length of Study: Two-three weeks.
Frequency: Annual.
Study Establishment: CREIPAC, Nouméa.
Country of Study: New Caledonia.
No. of awards offered: 25.
Application Procedure: Applicants must write for details.
Closing Date: April 30th.
Funding: Government.
No. of awards given last year: 25.
Additional Information: The tours are currently organised at different times of the year by the French departments of the James Cook University of North Queensland, Australian National University, Flinders University, Macquerie University, Melbourne and Monash Universities. Students from other universities are entitled to join one of these groups. Please contact the relevant French department for further information.

FRIEDRICH EBERT FOUNDATION

Godesberger Allee 149, Bonn, D-53175, Germany
Tel: (49) 228 883 648
Fax: (49) 228 883 697
www: http://www.fes..de
Telex: 885479 fest d
Contact: Dr Friedrich Wilhem

The Friedrich Ebert Foundation is a non-profit, cultural institution aiming to promote art and culture as elements of a vigorous democracy, to conduct and sponsor research both within the Foundation and outside, to support gifted and motivated young scholars, to cultivate international understanding and partnership with developing countries and to educate people from all walks of life in the spirit of democracy.

Friedrich Ebert Foundation Fellowship Program
Subjects: Any subject in the social sciences and related disciplines.
Purpose: To offer study and research fellowships.
Eligibility: Open to highly qualified applicants with a good knowledge of German.
Level of Study: Doctorate, Postgraduate.
Type: Fellowship.
Value: €588-920 per month.
Length of Study: 5-12 months.
Frequency: Annual.
Study Establishment: German universities.
Country of Study: Germany.
Application Procedure: Applicants must complete and submit an application form with a curriculum vitae and short description of research programme.
Closing Date: April 30th.
Funding: Government.
Additional Information: The Friedrich Ebert Foundation is the first and earliest German foundation with a socio-economic and political background. Its constitution of March 3rd 1925 was based upon the political legacy of Friedrich Ebert, the first President of the Weimar Republic.

FRIENDS OF FRENCH ART

100 Vanderlip Drive
Villa Narcissa, Rancho Palos Verdes, CA, 90275, United States of America
Tel: (1) 310 377 4444
Fax: (1) 310 377 4584
Email: villacisssa@aol.com
Contact: Ms Elin Vanderlip, President

Friends of French Art restore art in peril, both in France and the United States of America.

Summer Art Restoration Program
Subjects: Art restoration and conservation.
Purpose: To give graduate students in the field of art conservation the opportunity to spend the summer in France.
Eligibility: Open to graduate students in the field of art restoration.
Level of Study: Postgraduate.
Value: Approx. US$5,000 air fare to France and accommodation while working on a specific project.
Length of Study: Summer programme.
Frequency: Annual.
Country of Study: France.
No. of awards offered: Varies.
Application Procedure: Applicants should contact the organisation for details.
Funding: Private.
Contributor: Private donations through the Friends of French Art.

For further information contact:

University of Delaware
Winterthur Art Conservation Department, Winterthur, DE, 19735, United States of America

FRIENDS OF ISRAEL EDUCATIONAL TRUST

Academic Study Group
PO Box 7545, London, NW2 2QZ, England
Tel: (44) 20 7435 6803
Fax: (44) 20 7794 0291
Email: info@foi-asg.org
Contact: Mr John D A Levy

The Friends of Israel Educational Trust and its sister operation, the Academic Study Group, aim to encourage a critical understanding of the achievements, hopes and problems of modern Israel, and to forge new collaborative working links between the United Kingdom and Israel.

Friends of Israel Educational Trust Academic Study Bursary
Subjects: All subjects.
Purpose: To provide funding for British academics planning to pay a first research or study visit to Israel.
Eligibility: Open to research or teaching postgraduates. The Academic Study Group will only consider proposals from British academics who have already linked up with professional counterparts in Israel and agreed terms of reference for an initial visit.
Level of Study: Postdoctorate.
Type: Bursary.
Value: UK £300 per person.
Frequency: Annual.
Country of Study: Israel.
No. of awards offered: 30.
Application Procedure: Applicants must contact the organisation, there is no application form.
Closing Date: November 15th or March 15th.
Funding: Private.

Contributor: Trusts and individual donations.
No. of awards given last year: Five.
No. of applicants last year: 50+.

Friends of Israel Educational Trust Young Artist Award

Subjects: Fine arts.
Purpose: To enable a promising British painter to pay a working visit to Israel and prepare work for an exhibition on Israeli themes in the United Kingdom.
Eligibility: Open to promising young British painters and illustrators.
Level of Study: Postgraduate, Professional development.
Value: To cover airfare, accommodation and basic living costs.
Length of Study: A minimum of two months.
Frequency: Annual.
Study Establishment: A kibbutz.
Country of Study: Israel.
No. of awards offered: One-two.
Closing Date: Mid April.
Funding: Private.
Contributor: Individual donations.
No. of awards given last year: Two.
No. of applicants last year: 25.

Jerusalem Botanical Gardens Scholarship

Subjects: Botany and horticulture.
Purpose: To provide opportunities for botanists and horticulturists to work at the Jerusalem Botanical Gardens.
Eligibility: Open to United Kingdom graduates of recognised colleges and universities who hold a degree in a relevant subject.
Level of Study: Postgraduate, Professional development.
Type: Scholarship.
Value: To cover round trip air fare, accommodation and basic living costs.
Length of Study: 3-12 months.
Frequency: Annual.
Study Establishment: The Jerusalem Botanical Gardens.
Country of Study: Israel.
No. of awards offered: Several.
Application Procedure: Applicants must contact the organisation, there is no application form.
Closing Date: March 31st.
Funding: Private.
Contributor: Trusts and individual donations.
No. of awards given last year: Four.
No. of applicants last year: 30.

FRIENDS OF JOSE CARRERAS INTERNATIONAL LEUKEMIA FOUNDATION

1100 Fairview Avenue North
D5-100, Seattle, WA, 98109-1024, United States of America
Tel: (1) 206 667 7108
Fax: (1) 206 667 6124
Email: friendsjc@fhcrc.org
www: http://www.carrerasfoundation.org
Contact: Ms Karen Carbonneau, Administrator

E D Thomas Fellowship

Subjects: Medical sciences or leukaemia.
Purpose: To support research in the field of leukaemia or related haematological disorders.
Eligibility: Candidates must hold an MD or PhD degree and have completed at least three years of postdoctoral training but must be less than 10 years past their first doctoral degree when the award begins.
Type: Fellowship.
Value: US$50,000.

Length of Study: One year, renewable for an additional two years.
Frequency: Annual.
Study Establishment: A suitable institution with the academic environment to provide adequate support for the proposal project.
Country of Study: Any country.
No. of awards offered: One.
Application Procedure: Applicants must complete an application form, available from the website. All applications must be typed, single spaced, in English and must follow the format specified in the application packet. Award announcements will be made by letter in January. Do not contact the Foundation for results. Reapplication by unsuccessful candidates will be necessary for the following year.
Closing Date: November.
No. of awards given last year: One.
No. of applicants last year: 15.

FROMM MUSIC FOUNDATION

c/o Department of Music
Harvard University, Cambridge, MA, 02138, United States of America
Tel: (1) 617 495 2791
Fax: (1) 617 496 8081
Email: moncrieff@fas.harvard.edu
www: http://www.fas.harvard.edu
Contact: Ms Jean Moncrieff

Fromm Foundation Commission

Subjects: Music, composition only.
Purpose: To support compositions by young and lesser known composers. The award includes a stipend for premiere performance of commissioned work.
Eligibility: There are no eligibility restrictions.
Level of Study: Unrestricted.
Frequency: Annual.
Country of Study: Any country.
No. of awards offered: Up to 10.
Application Procedure: Applicants must obtain guidelines from the Fromm Music Foundation.
Closing Date: June 1st.
Funding: Private.
No. of awards given last year: 10.
No. of applicants last year: 150.

FULBRIGHT COMMISSION (ARGENTINA)

Viamonte 1653
2 Piso, Buenos Aires, Capital Federal, 1055, Argentina
Tel: (54) 11 4814 3561
Fax: (54) 11 4814 1377
Email: gabarca@fulbright.com.ar
www: http://www.fulbright.edu.ar
Contact: Ms M Graciela Abarca, Programme Officer, Educational Advisor

The Fulbright Programme is an educational exchange programme which sponsors awards for individuals approved by the J William Fulbright Board. The programme's major aim is to promote international co-operation and contribute to the development of friendly, sympathetic and peaceful relations between the United States and other countries in the world.

Fulbright Commission (Argentina) Awards for US Lecturers and Researchers

Subjects: All subjects except medical science.
Purpose: To enable United States lecturers to teach at an Argentine university for one semester, and to enable United States researchers to conduct research at an Argentine institution for three months.

Eligibility: Open to United States researchers and lecturers. Applicants must be proficient in spoken Spanish.
Level of Study: Professional development.
Value: Varies according to professional experience.
Length of Study: Three months.
Frequency: Annual.
Country of Study: Argentina.
No. of awards offered: 10-12.
Application Procedure: Applicants must contact Ralph Blessing at CIES, Washington DC at la3@ciesnet.cies.org for information.
Closing Date: August 1st.
Funding: Government.
Contributor: The United States of America and the Argentine government.
No. of awards given last year: 14.
No. of applicants last year: 30.

For further information contact:

Council for International Exchange of Scholars (CIES)
3007 Tilden Street North West
Suite 5L, Washington, DC, 20008, United States of America
Email: crobles@iie.org
www: http://www.cies.org
Contact: Ms Carol Robles

Fulbright Commission (Argentina) Master's Program
Subjects: All subjects except medical sciences.
Purpose: To support Argentines pursuing a Master's degree in the United States of America.
Eligibility: Open to Argentines only.
Level of Study: Postgraduate.
Value: US$12,000-15,000 per year.
Length of Study: Two years.
Frequency: Annual.
Country of Study: United States of America.
No. of awards offered: 40.
Application Procedure: Applicants must contact the Fulbright Commission in Argentina between February 1st and April 30th.
Closing Date: April 30th.
Funding: Government, Private.
Contributor: The Binational Commission ie. between the United States of America and Argentina, and private sources.
No. of awards given last year: 42.
No. of applicants last year: 300.

Fulbright Commission (Argentina) US Students Research Grant
Subjects: All subjects except medical science.
Purpose: To enable American students to study in Argentina.
Eligibility: Open to United States of America citizens who hold a Bachelor's degree, are writing a Master's thesis or PhD dissertation and are proficient in Spanish.
Level of Study: Doctorate, Graduate, Postgraduate.
Type: Research grant.
Value: Approx. US$17,350.
Length of Study: Eight months.
Frequency: Annual.
Country of Study: Argentina.
No. of awards offered: 10-12.
Application Procedure: Applicants must complete an application form. For further information contact Rachel Goldberg at IIE, New York at rgoldberg@iie.org.
Funding: Government.
Contributor: The United States of America and Argentine government.
No. of awards given last year: Eight.
No. of applicants last year: 150.

For further information contact:

Institute of International Education
809 United Nations Plaza, New York, NY, 10017-3580, United States of America

Email: adegroot@iie.org
www: http://www.iie.org/fulbright
Contact: Mr Andrew de Groot

FULBRIGHT TEACHER AND ADMINISTRATOR EXCHANGE

600 Maryland Avenue SW
Room 320, Washington, DC, 20024, United States of America
Tel: (1) 202 314 3527
Fax: (1) 202 479 6806
Email: fulbright@grad.usda.gov
www: http://www.fulbrightexchanges.org
Contact: Administrative Officer

Sponsored by the United States Department of State, the Fulbright Teacher and Administrator Exchange arranges direct one to one classroom exchanges to over 30 countries for teachers at the elementary, secondary, two-year and four-year college levels. Administrators may participate in six-week seminars in eleven countries.

Fulbright Teacher and Administrator Exchange
Subjects: Education or cultural exchange.
Purpose: To promote cultural understanding between peoples of other countries and the people of the United States of America through educational exchange.
Eligibility: Open to administrators and teachers of all subjects and levels from elementary through to community college. Applicants must be United States citizens.
Level of Study: Professional development.
Type: Grant.
Value: Varies by country.
Length of Study: Six weeks to one year.
Frequency: Annual.
Study Establishment: K-12 Schools, two year colleges and four year colleges.
Country of Study: Any country.
No. of awards offered: Varies.
Application Procedure: Applicants must submit a basic application which includes a two page essay, three letters of recommendation, administrative approval and a peer interview.
Closing Date: October 15th.
Funding: Government.
No. of awards given last year: 250.
No. of applicants last year: 800.
Additional Information: Applicants must be fluent in English, have a current full-time academic position, be in at least their third year of teaching and hold a Bachelor's degree.

FUND FOR EDUCATION AND TRAINING (FEAT)

1830 Connecticut Avenue North West, Washington, DC, 20009-5732, United States of America
Tel: (1) 202 483 1242
Fax: (1) 202 483 1246
Email: nisbco@nisbco.org
www: http://www.nisbco.org/feat.htm
Contact: Ms Rachel S Zuses, Administrator

The Fund for Education and Training (FEAT) assists young men who, for reasons of conscience, do not comply with United States laws requiring registration for the draft. FEAT Loans allow these men to receive education and training that they would otherwise not be able to afford without federal or state aid.

FEAT Loan
Subjects: Education and training.

Purpose: To assist young people who believe it is wrong to comply with registration with the Selective Service System.
Eligibility: FEAT loans are a last resort for those who are denied government aid because they have refused to register for the draft. This presently pertains only to male United States citizens over 18 years of age.
Level of Study: Unrestricted.
Type: Loan.
Value: US$2,500.
Frequency: Annual.
Country of Study: United States of America.
No. of awards offered: Varies.
Application Procedure: Applicants must write for details.
Funding: Private.
No. of awards given last year: Seven.

FUND FOR THEOLOGICAL EDUCATION, INC.

825 Houston Mill Road
Suite 250, Atlanta, GA, 30329, United States of America
Tel: (1) 404 727 1450
Fax: (1) 404 727 1490
Email: fte@thefund.org
www: http://www.thefund.org
Contact: Ms Sharon Watson Fluker, Director

The Fund for Theological Education (FTE) exists to promote excellence in the profession of ministry and scholarship by inspiring, recruiting and supporting gifted women and men from diverse backgrounds in their theological formation. The mission of FTE is to respond to the continuing need for outstanding persons for Christian leadership as pastors, educators and citizens.

Expanding Horizons - Dissertation Fellowship for African Americans

Subjects: Religion and theology.
Purpose: To support African American students in PhD and ThD programmes in the final writing stage of their dissertation.
Eligibility: Students must be an African-American in the writing stages of their dissertation and the dissertation proposal must have been approved prior to application.
Level of Study: Doctorate.
Type: Fellowship.
Value: Up to US$15,000 per academic year.
Length of Study: One year, non renewable.
Frequency: Annual.
Study Establishment: Graduate schools or theological schools.
Country of Study: United States of America.
No. of awards offered: Up to 10 per year.
Application Procedure: Applicants must complete an application form, available from the programme office or the website.
Closing Date: February 1st.
Funding: Private.
Contributor: Lilly Endowment, Inc.
No. of awards given last year: Seven.
No. of applicants last year: Varies.

Expanding Horizons - Doctoral Fellowship for African Americans

Subjects: Religion and theology.
Purpose: To support African American students in PhD and ThD programmes in religion and theology.
Eligibility: Students must be entering the first year of a PhD or ThD programme and studying at an ATS (Association of Theological Schools) or in another accredited graduate programme. Applicants must be African-American.
Level of Study: Doctorate.
Type: Fellowship.

Value: Up to US$15,000.
Length of Study: One year, with a possibility of renewal for a second year.
Frequency: Annual.
Study Establishment: Graduate schools or theological schools.
Country of Study: United States of America.
No. of awards offered: Up to 10.
Application Procedure: Applicants must complete an application form, available from the programme office or the website.
Closing Date: March 1st.
Funding: Private.
Contributor: Lilly Endowment, Inc.
No. of awards given last year: Seven.
No. of applicants last year: Varies.

Ministry Fellowship

Subjects: Religion, theology and divinity.
Purpose: To enrich theological education in a Master of Divinity degree programme.
Eligibility: The award is to be used for the design and implementation of creative projects during the Summer. Applicants must be aged 35 or younger and entering a Master of Divinity degree programme in the Autumn semester.
Level of Study: Postgraduate.
Type: Fellowship.
Value: US$5,000 plus conference attendance.
Frequency: Annual.
Study Establishment: An American or Canadian school accredited by the Association of Theological Schools of North America.
Country of Study: United States of America or Canada.
No. of awards offered: 40.
Application Procedure: Applicants must complete and submit an application form together with supporting documentation. Forms are available online or by request.
Closing Date: April 1st.
Funding: Private.
No. of awards given last year: 39.
No. of applicants last year: 125.

North American Doctoral Fellowship

Subjects: Religion and theology.
Purpose: To support students from African American, Asian American, Hispanic American and Native American populations already in doctoral programmes leading towards completion of a PhD or ThD.
Eligibility: Open to students from targeted racial or ethnic groups at any point in their graduate programme, though preference is given to students further along in their programmes. Students must be currently enrolled in programmes of religion or theology.
Level of Study: Doctorate.
Type: Fellowship.
Value: US$5,000.
Length of Study: One year.
Frequency: Annual.
No. of awards offered: 10-12 per year.
Application Procedure: Applicants must complete an application form, available from the programme office or the website.
Closing Date: March 1st.
Funding: Private.
No. of awards given last year: 12.
No. of applicants last year: Varies.

FUND FOR UFO RESEARCH, INC.

PO Box 277, Mount Rainier, MD, 20712, United States of America
Tel: (1) 703 684 6032
Fax: (1) 703 684 6032
Email: swiman@pop.dn.net
www: http://www.fufor.com
Contact: Mr Donald L Berliner, Chairman

The Fund for UFO Research is a non-profit corporation established in 1979 to raise funds to support scientific research and public education related to the mystery of unidentified flying objects. The Fund takes no stand on any proposed explanation, but is convinced that unexplained, high performance craft have long been in the skies.

Fund for UFO Research Grants
Subjects: Possible topics for research include analysis of sighting reports, physical trace and photographic cases, government involvement in UFOs and abduction cases.
Purpose: To provide financial assistance for scientific research and public education projects relating to the phenomenon of unidentified flying objects.
Eligibility: Open to anyone wishing to undertake scientific research or public education projects related to UFOs. There are no restrictions, except that reports must be written in English.
Level of Study: Unrestricted.
Type: Research grant.
Value: Awards can cover not only out of pocket expenses, but also supplies, equipment, publication costs and fees for services in the case of professional consultants.
Length of Study: Varies.
Frequency: Dependent on funds available.
Country of Study: Any country.
No. of awards offered: Unlimited.
Application Procedure: Applicants must complete an application form, available upon request.
Closing Date: Applications are accepted at any time.
Funding: Private.
Contributor: Individuals.
No. of awards given last year: Four.
No. of applicants last year: 10.

FUNGAL RESEARCH TRUST

27 Regina Terrace, London, W13 9HY, England
www: http://www.fungalresearchtrust.org
Contact: Secretary

The Fungal Research Trust is a small charity that funds small research and travel grants and the aspergillus website (www.aspergillus.man.ac.uk). The website is the most comprehensive source of data on the fungus aspergillus and the diseases it causes.

Fungal Research Trust Travel Grants
Subjects: Fungal diseases and fungi.
Purpose: To enable researchers to attend the national and international fungal meetings.
Eligibility: There are no restrictions.
Level of Study: Doctorate, Postdoctorate, Postgraduate, Professional development, Research.
Value: UK £750.
Frequency: Dependent on funds available.
No. of awards offered: Up to three.
Application Procedure: Applicants must submit a letter of application.
Closing Date: Applications are considered at any time, but three months notice before travel is required.
Funding: Commercial, Private.
No. of awards given last year: Two.

No. of applicants last year: Two.
Additional Information: Advertisements for other awards are placed in the Lancet.

GATES CAMBRIDGE TRUST

PO Box 252, Cambridge, Cambridgeshire, CB2 1TZ, England
Tel: (44) 1223 338467
Fax: (44) 1223 351449
Email: info@gates.scholarships.cam.ac.uk
www: http://www.gates.scholarships.cam.ac.uk
Contact: Board of Graduate Studies

Cambridge Gates Scholarships
Subjects: All subjects including MBA.
Purpose: The programme will offer a substantial number of scholarships for study as an affiliated student or to pursue taught or research courses of postgraduate study at the University of Cambridge.
Eligibility: Candidates must hold, or expect to be able to obtain, a First Class or exceptionally a High Second Class (Honours) Degree or its equivalent from a recognised university. Applicants must also gain admission to the University of Cambridge and to a constituent college in due course, be able to meet the conditions set by the university for admission, ie. academic qualifications and evidence of proficiency in the English language, and must normally be under the age of 30. These scholarships are not available to citizens of the United Kingdom.
Level of Study: Graduate, Postgraduate, MBA.
Type: Scholarship.
Value: University and College fees at applicable rates, a maintenance allowance sufficient for a single student, a contribution towards return airfare, other discretionary allowances and a contribution to Colleges for a mentoring programme.
Frequency: Annual.
Study Establishment: The University of Cambridge.
Country of Study: United Kingdom.
Application Procedure: Applicants from the United States of America, Canada, Australia, New Zealand or the European Union must fill in the CIGAS Form A, available from the Board of Graduate Studies at the address below. Applicants from all other countries must fill in and submit the Gates Cambridge Trust Preliminary Application Form.
Closing Date: Please contact the organisation.
Funding: Private.

For further information contact:

Board of Graduate Studies
4 Mill Lane, Cambridge, Cambridgeshire, CB2 1RZ, England

GENERAL BOARD OF HIGHER EDUCATION AND MINISTRY

PO Box 340007, Nashville, TN, 37203-0007, United States of America
Tel: (1) 615 340 7388
Fax: (1) 615 340 7395
Email: rkohler@gbhem.org
Contact: Reverend Robert F Kohler

The General Board of Higher Education and Ministry of the United Methodist Church prepares and assists those whose ministry in Christ is exercised through ordination, the diaconate, licensing or certification. It also provides general oversight and care for united methodist institutions of higher education and campus ministries as well as financial resources for students to attend institutions of higher education through church offerings and investments.

Dempster Fellowship

Subjects: Theology.

Purpose: To increase the effectiveness of teaching in United Methodist schools of theology by assisting worthy PhD candidates who are committed to serving the church through theological education.

Eligibility: Open to members of the United Methodist Church who plan to teach in seminaries, or to teach religion and related subjects in universities or colleges. The applicant must have received the Master of Divinity degree or its equivalent from one of the United Methodist Seminaries, or be in a PhD programme or its equivalent at one of these schools at the time of application. Verification of study towards the PhD or an equivalent degree is required prior to the distribution of the stipend. A person already holding a PhD degree is not excluded from candidacy.

Level of Study: Doctorate.

Type: Fellowship.

Value: Up to US$10,000.

Length of Study: One year, with a possibility of renewal at the discretion of the Committee on Awards.

Frequency: Annual.

Country of Study: Any country.

No. of awards offered: Five.

Application Procedure: Applicants must submit a completed application form, transcripts of all previous academic work, secure letters of reference, term or other paper of essay length, results of the Graduate Record Examination scores, summary statement of academic plans and a curriculum vitae. Further information is available on request.

Closing Date: February 1st.

Funding: Private.

Contributor: The United Methodist Church.

No. of awards given last year: Five.

No. of applicants last year: 20.

GENERAL SOCIAL CARE COUNCIL

General Social Care Council
Goldings House
2 Hay's Lane, London, SE1 2HB, England
Tel: (44) 20 7397 5100
Fax: (44) 20 7397 5101
Email: info@bursaries.gscc.org.uk
Contact: Administrative Officer

The General Social Care Council is the first ever regulatory body for the social care profession in England. It was set up to establish codes of conduct and practice for social care workers, a register of practising professionals and to regulate and support social work, education and training. It takes forward some of the work of the Central Council for Education and Training in Social Work, which closed on September 28th 2001. Similar councils exist for Northern Ireland, Scotland and Wales.

General Social Care Council Postgraduate Bursary

Subjects: Social work.

Purpose: To support those seeking the qualifications required for social work.

Eligibility: Open to graduates who are aged 22 on completion of the course, who have ordinarily been a resident in the United Kingdom for three years and comply with the LEA regulations for Mandatory Awards.

Level of Study: Postgraduate.

Type: Bursary.

Length of Study: Two years.

Frequency: Annual.

Study Establishment: Universities.

Country of Study: United Kingdom.

No. of awards offered: Approx. 1,000.

Closing Date: June 29th.

Funding: Government.

Contributor: The Department of Health.

No. of awards given last year: 1,000.

GEOLOGICAL SOCIETY OF AMERICA (GSA)

3300 Penrose Place
PO Box 9140, Boulder, CO, 80301-9140, United States of America
Tel: (1) 303 337 1037
Fax: (1) 303 447 1133
Email: lcarter@geosociety.org
www: http://www.geosociety.org
Contact: Ms Leah J Carter, Program Officer Grants, Awards and Medals

Established in 1888, the Geological Society of America (GSA) is a non-profit organisation dedicated to the advancement of the science of geology. GSA membership is for the generalist and the specialist in the field of geology, and offers something for everyone.

Gladys W Cole Memorial Research Award

Subjects: Investigation of the geomorphology of semi-arid and arid terrains in the United States of America and Mexico.

Purpose: To provide financial support for research.

Eligibility: Open to GSA members or Fellows between 30 and 65 years of age who have published one or more significant papers in geomorphology.

Level of Study: Postdoctorate.

Type: Research grant.

Value: US$9,500.

Frequency: Annual.

Country of Study: United States of America or Mexico.

No. of awards offered: One.

Application Procedure: Applicants must complete an application form, available from the website.

Closing Date: February 1st.

Funding: Private.

Contributor: Dr W Storrs Cole.

No. of awards given last year: One.

No. of applicants last year: Three.

Additional Information: Funds cannot be used to pay for work already accomplished, but previous recipients may reapply if additional support is needed to complete their work. All qualified applicants are urged to apply.

GSA Research Grants

Subjects: Earth science.

Purpose: To provide partial support for Master's and doctoral thesis research.

Eligibility: Open to students attending colleges and universities within the United States of America, Canada, Mexico and Central America. Applicants must be members of the Geological Society of America in order to apply.

Level of Study: Graduate.

Type: Research grant.

Value: No set limits.

Length of Study: One year, renewable.

Frequency: Annual.

Country of Study: United States, Canada, Mexico or Central America.

No. of awards offered: Varies from year to year.

Application Procedure: Applicants must complete current application forms.

Closing Date: February 1st.

Funding: Government, Private.

Contributor: GSA's Penrose and Pardee endowments, the National Science Foundation, industry, individual GSA members through the GEOSTAR and Research Grants funds, and numerous dedicated research funds that have been endowed at the GSA Foundation by members.

No. of awards given last year: 224.
No. of applicants last year: 583.
Additional Information: Grants are awarded on the basis of the scientific merits of the problem, the capability of the investigator and how reasonable the budget is. Grants are awarded as an aid to a research project and not to sustain the entire cost.

W Storrs Cole Memorial Research Award

Subjects: Invertebrate micropalaeontology.
Purpose: To support research into invertebrate micropalaeontology.
Eligibility: Open to GSA members or Fellows between 30 and 65 years of age who have published one or more significant papers on micropalaeontology. Funds cannot be used for work already accomplished, but recipients of previous awards may reapply if additional support is needed to complete their work.
Level of Study: Postdoctorate.
Type: Research grant.
Value: US$8,700.
Frequency: Annual.
Application Procedure: Applicants must write for further details and an application form, or access the website.
Closing Date: Applications must be postmarked before February 1st.
Funding: Private.
Contributor: Dr W Storrs Cole.
No. of applicants last year: One.
Additional Information: All qualified applicants are urged to apply.

GEORGE A AND ELIZA GARDNER HOWARD FOUNDATION

Brown University
Box 1867
42 Charlesfield Street, Providence, RI, 02912, United States of America
Tel: (1) 401 863 2640
Fax: (1) 401 863 7341
Email: howard_foundation@brown.edu
www: http://www.brown.edu/divisions/graduate_school/howard
Contact: Ms Susan M Clifford, Co-ordinator

The George A and Eliza Gardner Howard Foundation was established in 1952 by Nicea Howard in memory of her grandparents. Although Miss Howard had a special interest in the arts, her stated purpose was to aid the personal development of promising individuals at the crucial middle stages of their careers.

Howard Foundation Fellowships

Subjects: The Foundation awards a limited number of fellowships each year for independent projects in fields selected on a rotational basis.
Purpose: To assist individuals in the middle stages of their careers.
Eligibility: Nominees should normally have the rank of assistant or associate professor or their non academic equivalents. Support is intended to augment paid sabbatical leaves, making it financially possible for grantees to have an entire year in which to pursue their projects, free of any other professional responsibilities. Accepted nominees should therefore be eligible for sabbaticals or other leave with guaranteed additional support. Candidates must be professionally based in the United States of America either by affiliation with an institution or by residence, regardless of their country of citizenship.
Level of Study: Postdoctorate.
Type: Fellowship.
Value: US$20,000.
Length of Study: One year.
Frequency: Annual.
Country of Study: United States of America.
No. of awards offered: 10.

Application Procedure: Applicants must be nominated. Details of the nomination procedure are available from the Foundation. Fellowships are not available for work leading to any academic degree.
Closing Date: October 15th for nominations and November 30th for completed applications. Fellowships will be announced May 1st, for commencement of tenure July 1st.
Funding: Private.
No. of awards given last year: 13.
No. of applicants last year: 160.

GEORGE WALFORD INTERNATIONAL ESSAY PRIZE (GWIEP)

Rue de la Longue Haie 35-39, Bruxelles, B-1000, Belgium
Tel: (32) 2 642 9733
Email: richenda@hartleywalford.com
www: http://www.geocities.com/sysiedo
Contact: Ms Richenda Walford, Trustee

The George Walford International Essay Prize (GWIEP) is a registered charity which awards a cash prize each year to the winner of an essay on the subject of systematic ideology.

The George Walford International Essay Prize

Subjects: Systematic ideology, which seeks to understand the origin and development of ideologies, how ideologies and ideological groups work together, and the possibilities of guiding the development of ideologies on a global scale.
Purpose: To award the best essay on systematic ideology.
Eligibility: Everyone is eligible, with the exception of the trustees and judges themselves. Applicants do not need to be current students. There are no bars regarding age, race, nationality or gender.
Level of Study: Unrestricted.
Type: Prize.
Value: UK £3,000.
Length of Study: Varies.
Frequency: Annual.
Country of Study: Any country.
No. of awards offered: One.
Application Procedure: Applicants must contact GWIEP for details. Information can be requested by mail though communication via email and the website is greatly preferred.
Closing Date: May 31st.
Funding: Private.
Contributor: The family of the late George Walford.
No. of awards given last year: One.
Additional Information: For more information about the prize and systematic ideology please visit the website.

GEORGIA LIBRARY ASSOCIATION (GLA)

c/o GLA Administrative Services
1438 W Peachtree Street North West
Suite 200, Atlanta, GA, 30309-2955, United States of America
Tel: (1) 800 999 8558
Fax: (1) 404 892 7879
Email: gla@solinet.net
www: http://www.lib.gsu.edu/gla
Contact: The Scholarship Committee

The Georgia Library Association's (GLA) mission is to provide an understanding of the place that libraries should take in advancing the educational, cultural and economic life of the state, to promote the expansion and improvement of library service and to stimulate activities toward these ends.

Hubbard Scholarship

Subjects: Library science.

Purpose: To provide financial aid to a qualified candidate completing a Master's degree.

Eligibility: Open to United States citizens accepted for admission to a Master's programme at an American Library Association (ALA) accredited library school, who intend to complete the course of study within two years.

Level of Study: Postgraduate.

Type: Scholarship.

Value: US$3,000, paid in equal instalments at the beginning of each term, semester or quarter.

Length of Study: Two years.

Frequency: Annual.

Study Establishment: An ALA accredited school.

Country of Study: United States of America.

No. of awards offered: One.

Application Procedure: Applicants must write for details.

Closing Date: May 1st.

No. of awards given last year: One.

No. of applicants last year: Five.

Additional Information: The Scholar is required to work in a library or library related capacity in Georgia for one year following completion of the programme, or agree to pay back a pro-rated amount of the scholarship plus interest within a two year period.

For further information contact:

Dunwoody Campus Library
Georgia Perimeter College
2101 Womack Road, Dunwoody, GA, 30338, United States of America
Contact: Ms Sylvia George-Williams

GERMAN ACADEMIC EXCHANGE SERVICE (DAAD)

950 Third Avenue
19th Floor, New York, NY, 10022, United States of America
Tel: (1) 212 758 3223
Fax: (1) 212 755 5780
Email: daadny@daad.org
www: http://www.daad.org
Contact: Grants Management Officer

The German Academic Exchange Service is the New York office of the Deutscher Akademischer Austauschdienst (DAAD), a private, publicly funded self-governing organisation of the Institutes of Higher Education in Germany. The DAAD promotes international academic relations especially through the exchange of students and faculty. The New York office assists residents of the United States of America or Canada who are enrolled or employed full time at an Institute of Higher Education and would like to study or conduct research in Germany.

Contemporary German Literature Grant

Subjects: Research in contemporary German literature.

Purpose: To aid faculty planning to work in the field.

Eligibility: Open to suitably qualified Scholars of any nationality.

Level of Study: Postgraduate.

Type: Grant.

Value: US$3,000.

Length of Study: Three months.

Frequency: Annual.

Study Establishment: The Max Cade Center for Contemporary German Literature at Washington University in St Louis.

Country of Study: United States of America.

No. of awards offered: One.

Application Procedure: Applicants must write for details.

Closing Date: March 1st.

Additional Information: The Center is administered by the German Department in conjunction with the Olin Library at Washington University. Further information is available from the website.

For further information contact:

Director
The Max Kade Center for Contemporary German Literature
Campus Box 1104
Washington University, St Louis, MO, 63130, United States of America
Tel: (1) 314 935 4784
Fax: (1) 314 935 7255
Email: jahrbuch@artsci.wustl.edu
Contact: Professor Paul Michael Lutzeler, Director

DAAD German Studies Research Grant

Subjects: The cultural, political, historical, economic and social aspects of modern and contemporary German affairs.

Purpose: To promote study in the field from an interdisciplinary and multidisciplinary perspective.

Eligibility: Open to Master's and PhD candidates working on a Certificate in German Studies and PhD candidates doing preliminary dissertation research. Nominees must have completed two years of college level German and a minimum of three German studies courses by the deadline. Support cannot be provided for stays in Germany in the context of study abroad programmes.

Type: Grant.

Value: To offset possible additional research costs or summer earnings requirements.

Country of Study: North America or Germany.

Application Procedure: Department and/or programme chairs should nominate candidates to the DAAD. Applicants must visit the website for further information.

Closing Date: November 1st or May 1st.

DAAD Guest Lectureships

Subjects: All subjects.

Purpose: For universities and colleges to invite German academics in all fields, notably university faculty, to teach at the host institution. The programme is designed to help fill a curricular gap or to act as a stimulus for teaching and research in the department concerned.

Eligibility: United States and Canadian universities and colleges. Funds cannot be made available to replace faculty on sabbatical.

Level of Study: Postdoctorate, Postgraduate.

Length of Study: One-six months.

Application Procedure: Applicants must contact the DAAD New York office or visit the website.

Closing Date: Applications are accepted at any time.

DAAD Information Visits

Subjects: All subjects.

Purpose: To increase knowledge of specific German topics and institutions within the framework of an academic study tour.

Eligibility: Preference will be given to groups with a homogeneous academic background. Visits within the context of study abroad programmes cannot be funded and tours cannot be funded during July and August and between December 22nd and January 8th.

Level of Study: Graduate.

Length of Study: 7-21 days.

Frequency: Annual.

Country of Study: Germany.

Application Procedure: Applicants must obtain forms from the DAAD New York office or download them from the website.

Closing Date: Applications may be filed at any time but should reach the DAAD New York office at least six months before the beginning date of the planned visit.

Additional Information: Further information is available from the website.

DAAD Research Grants for Recent PhD Recipients and PhD Candidates

Subjects: All subjects.

Purpose: To enable PhD candidates and recent PhDs to carry out dissertation or postdoctoral research at libraries, archives, institutes or laboratories in Germany.

Eligibility: Open to recent PhDs (up to two years after the degree) of no more than 35 years of age and PhD candidates of no more than 32 years of age. Applicants should possess knowledge of the German language commensurate with the demands of their research project.
Level of Study: Doctorate, Postdoctorate.
Type: Grant.
Value: A monthly maintenance allowance, an international travel subsidy and health insurance.
Length of Study: Two-six months.
Frequency: Annual.
Country of Study: Germany.
No. of awards offered: Varies.
Application Procedure: Applicants must request forms from the DAAD New York office or download them from the website.
Closing Date: August 1st.
Additional Information: Further information is available from the website.

DAAD Temporary Teaching Assignments for Highly Qualified Academics at German Universities

Subjects: All subjects.
Purpose: To strengthen the international dimensions of teaching.
Eligibility: Open to foreign academics of any discipline, except language teaching.
Level of Study: Postdoctorate, Postgraduate.
Value: DAAD provides funding based on the terms of the cost sharing plans of the home and host institutions. In addition supplemental funding may be provided for health insurance, living, travel, a German course at a language institute and conference participation.
Length of Study: One semester to two years.
Study Establishment: Various types of German Institutes of Higher Education including universities, Fachhochschulen, colleges of fine arts etc.
Country of Study: Germany.
Application Procedure: Applicants must consult the organisation.
Closing Date: June 15th or December 15th.
Additional Information: This grant is part of a German federal and Länder initiative.

DAAD-AICGS Grant

Subjects: Topics dealing with post war Germany.
Eligibility: Open to PhD candidates, recent PhDs and junior faculty members.
Level of Study: Doctorate, Postdoctorate.
Type: Fellowship.
Value: Funds for summer residency.
Frequency: Annual.
Study Establishment: The American Institute for Contemporary German Studies (AICGS).
Country of Study: United States of America.
No. of awards offered: One.
Application Procedure: Applicants must write for details.
Closing Date: April 15th.
Additional Information: Further information is available from the website.

For further information contact:

AICGS
1400 16th Street North West
Suite 420, Washington, DC, 20036-2217, United States of America
Tel: (1) 202 332 9312
Fax: (1) 202 265 9531
Email: info@aicgs.org
www: http://www.aicgs.org

Hochschulsommerkurse at German Universities

Subjects: German studies and language courses.
Purpose: To provide a broad range of language courses with an integrated thematic focus on literary, cultural, political and economic aspects of modern and contemporary Germany.

Eligibility: In general, graduate students in all disciplines, enrolled full-time and between 18 and 32 years of age are eligible to apply. Two years of college level German or equivalent at the time of application are a prerequisite.
Level of Study: Graduate, Postgraduate.
Type: Scholarship.
Value: Tuition, room and board in whole or in part and a small international travel subsidy.
Length of Study: Three-four weeks.
Frequency: Annual.
Study Establishment: German universities.
Country of Study: Germany.
Application Procedure: Applicants must obtain a course catalogue, available from the DAAD New York office or from the website. Applicants must specify the national category.
Closing Date: January 31st.

International Lawyers: Study and Training Program

Subjects: German law.
Purpose: To give young lawyers the opportunity to gain a unique insight into the structure and function of German law. Through this programme the DAAD aims to support and encourage closer international links in the area of law and to improve mutual knowledge of the legal systems in other countries.
Eligibility: Open to applicants from the United Kingdom, France, Belgium, the Netherlands, Luxembourg, Poland, the Commonwealth of Independent States, Japan, South Korea, the United States and Canada. The DAAD encourages applications from North American lawyers who hold JD or LLB degrees and who have or will have passed the bar examination by the beginning of the scholarship period, proof of which is required prior to departure to Germany. The importance of gaining a knowledge of German law should be evident from the applicant's stated professional or research goals. Applicants must have a very good command of German, which would enable them to take an active part in all lectures and discussions. In general, applicants should be younger than 30 years of age. Students currently in their last year of law school who will obtain a JD or LLB and will have passed the bar examination by the beginning of the scholarship period may apply. Applicants should preferably have some relevant professional experience.
Level of Study: Postgraduate.
Type: Scholarship.
Value: A monthly stipend to cover board and a single room in university housing.
Length of Study: Eight months.
Country of Study: Germany.
Application Procedure: Applicants must complete an application form, available from the website.

Learn German in Germany for Faculty

Subjects: All fields.
Purpose: To enable recipients to attend intensive language courses.
Eligibility: Applicants must have a basic knowledge of German and should be able to demonstrate a need for acquiring a better proficiency in the German language for their future research. Students in the fields of English and German or any other modern languages or literatures are not eligible.
Level of Study: Faculty.
Type: Scholarship.
Value: Course fees, room and partial board.
Length of Study: Four and eight weeks.
Frequency: Annual.
Study Establishment: Goethe Institutes.
Country of Study: Germany.
Application Procedure: Applicants must obtain forms from the DAAD office in New York or download them from the website.
Closing Date: January 31st.
Additional Information: Further information is available from the website.

Leo Baeck Institute-DAAD Grants

Subjects: The social, communal and intellectual history of German speaking Jewry.
Purpose: To assist students in their research.
Eligibility: Open to American doctoral students and recent PhDs.
Level of Study: Doctorate, Postdoctorate.
Type: Fellowship.
Value: Varies.
Frequency: Annual.
Study Establishment: The Leo Baeck Institute in New York or in Germany.
Country of Study: United States of America or Germany.
No. of awards offered: Six.
Application Procedure: Applicants must write for details.
Closing Date: November 1st.
Additional Information: Further information is available form the website.

For further information contact:

The Leo Baeck Institute
129 East 73rd Street, New York, NY, 10021, United States of America
Tel: (1) 212 744 6400
Fax: (1) 212 988 1305
Email: lbi1@lbi.com

Munich University Summer Training in European and German Law (MUST)

Subjects: German and continental European law.
Purpose: To allow students to receive intensive training in general subjects like private and constitutional law and the law of the European Union, as well as providing an introduction to corporate, securities and antitrust law.
Eligibility: Open to graduate students enrolled full-time in a law programme at an accredited university in the United States of America or Canada. Applicants should have completed at least one year of law school at the time of application. Applicants must be American or Canadian citizens or hold permanent resident status in one of these countries.
Level of Study: Postgraduate.
Type: Scholarship.
Value: Tuition and part of living and housing expenses. A small international travel subsidy will also be paid.
Length of Study: Four weeks.
Study Establishment: Munich University Law School.
Country of Study: Germany.
No. of awards offered: A limited number.
Application Procedure: Applicants must complete an application form, available from the website.
Closing Date: March 15th.

NSF(National Science Foundation)-DAAD Grants for the Natural, Engineering and Social Sciences

Subjects: Natural, engineering and social sciences.
Purpose: To provide support for scholars and scientists who wish to carry out joint research projects with colleagues at German universities and Fachhochschulen.
Eligibility: For Scholars and scientists at United States universities as well as university affiliated research institutes.
Type: Grant.
Value: Support for travel and living expenses.
Study Establishment: German universities and Fachhochschulen.
Country of Study: Germany.
Application Procedure: Applicants must visit the NSF website for further information.
Closing Date: June 15th.

For further information contact:

NSF
4201 Wilson Boulevard, Arlington, VA, 22230, United States of America

Tel: (1) 703 292 8705
Fax: (1) 703 292 9177
Email: msuskin@nsf.gov
www: http://www.nsf.gov/sbe/int
Contact: Dr Mark A Suskin

Study Visit Research Grants for Faculty

Subjects: All subjects.
Purpose: To allow scholars to pursue research at universities and other institutions in Germany.
Eligibility: Open to individuals with at least two years of teaching or research experience after the PhD or equivalent and a research record in the proposed field.
Level of Study: Faculty.
Type: Grant.
Value: A monthly maintenance allowance.
Length of Study: One-three months.
Frequency: Annual.
Country of Study: Germany.
No. of awards offered: Varies.
Application Procedure: Applicants must obtain forms from the DAAD New York office or download them from the website.
Closing Date: August 1st for visits during the first half of the year, February 1st for visits during the second half of the year.
Additional Information: Grants are awarded for specific research projects and cannot be used for travel only, attendance at conferences or conventions, editorial meetings, lecture tours or extended guest professorships. Further information is available from the website.

Summer Language Courses at Goethe-Instituts

Subjects: All fields, but students in the fields of English and German or any other modern languages or literatures are not eligible.
Purpose: To allow students to attend intensive eight week language courses.
Eligibility: Open to students pursuing full time study at any accredited graduate or professional school in the United States or Canada, with the exception of those in the fields of English, German or any other modern languages or literatures. As a rule, applicants must be citizens of the United States of America or Canada. Foreign nationals may be eligible if they have been full-time graduate students at an American or Canadian university for at least one academic year at the time of application. Preference will be given to students who are under 33 years of age. Applicants must have completed three semesters of college level German or have an equivalent level of language proficiency. Applicants should not have previously studied in a German speaking country for more than two months or been granted a German language course scholarship by the DAAD or any other organisation within the last three years. Recipients of the scholarships are selected on the basis of an outstanding academic record and potential, as well as a demonstrated need for acquiring a better proficiency in the German language for their future studies and research.
Level of Study: Postgraduate.
Type: Scholarship.
Value: Tuition and fees, room and partial board.
Length of Study: Eight weeks.
Frequency: Annual.
Study Establishment: Goethe Institutes.
Country of Study: Germany.
Application Procedure: Applicants must obtain forms from the DAAD New York office or download them from the website.
Closing Date: January 31st.
Additional Information: Further information is available from the website.

GERMAN HISTORICAL INSTITUTE

1607 New Hampshire Avenue North West, Washington, DC, 20009,
United States of America
Tel: (1) 202 387 3355
Fax: (1) 202 483 3430
Email: info@ghi-dc.org
www: http://www.ghi-dc.org
Contact: Mr Christof Mauch, Director

The German Historical Institute is an independent research institute dedicated to the promotion of historical research in the Federal Republic of Germany and the United States. The Institute supports and advises German and American historians and political scientists and encourages co-operation between them.

German Historical Institute Collaborative Research Programme for Postdoctoral Scholars

Subjects: German and United States post World War II history, transatlantic studies and comparative studies in social, cultural and political history.
Purpose: To support a research programme for postdoctoral Scholars on the topic of continuity, change and globalisation in post-war Germany and the United States.
Eligibility: Open to German and United States postdoctoral students. Applications from women and minorities are especially encouraged.
Level of Study: Postdoctorate.
Type: Scholarship.
Value: Depends on length of study.
Length of Study: 6-12 months.
Frequency: Dependent on funds available.
Country of Study: United States of America.
Application Procedure: Applicants must refer to the website for details.
Funding: Government.
Contributor: The National Endowment for Humanities.
No. of awards given last year: Four.

German Historical Institute Courses in German Handwriting and Archives

Subjects: German handwriting, German archives, German history and transatlantic studies.
Purpose: To introduce students to German handwriting of previous centuries by exposing them to a variety of German archives, familiarising them with major research topics in German culture, history, and encouraging the exchange of ideas among the next generation of United States Scholars.
Eligibility: Open to United States doctoral students. Applications from women and minorities are especially encouraged.
Level of Study: Doctorate.
Type: Scholarship.
Value: US$2,500.
Length of Study: Two weeks.
Frequency: Annual.
Country of Study: Germany.
Application Procedure: Applicants must refer to the website for details.
Closing Date: December 31st.
Funding: Government.
No. of awards given last year: 10.
No. of applicants last year: 25.

German Historical Institute Dissertation Scholarships

Subjects: Humanities and social sciences, comparative studies in social, cultural and political history, studies of German-American relations and transatlantic studies.
Purpose: To give support to German and United States doctoral students working on topics related to the Institute's general scope of interest.

Eligibility: Open to German and United States doctoral students. Applications from women and minorities are especially encouraged.
Level of Study: Doctorate.
Type: Scholarship.
Value: US$1,100 per month.
Length of Study: Up to six months.
Frequency: Annual.
Country of Study: United States of America.
No. of awards offered: 12.
Application Procedure: Applicants must refer to the website for details.
Closing Date: May 31st.
Funding: Government.
No. of awards given last year: 14.
No. of applicants last year: 50.
Additional Information: United States candidates are expected to evaluate source material in the United States of America that is important for their research on German history. At the end of the scholarship they are required to report on their findings.

German Historical Institute Transatlantic Doctoral Seminar in German History

Subjects: German history and transatlantic studies.
Purpose: To bring together young Scholars from Germany and the United States who are nearing completion of their doctoral degrees. It provides an opportunity to debate doctoral projects in a transatlantic setting.
Eligibility: Open to German and United States doctoral students. Applications from women and minorities are especially encouraged.
Level of Study: Doctorate.
Type: Scholarship.
Value: US$2,000.
Length of Study: Four days.
Frequency: Annual.
Country of Study: United States of America or Germany.
Application Procedure: Applicants must refer to the website for details.
Closing Date: December 1st.
Funding: Government.
No. of awards given last year: 16.
No. of applicants last year: 35.

GERMAN MARSHALL FUND OF THE UNITED STATES (GMF)

11 Dupont Circle North West
Suite 750, Washington, DC, 20036, United States of America
Tel: (1) 202 745 3950
Fax: (1) 202 265 1662
Email: info@gmfus.org
www: http://www.gmfus.org

The German Marshall Fund of the United States (GMF) is an American institution that stimulates the exchange of ideas and promotes co-operation between the United States and Europe in the spirit of the post war Marshall Plan. GMF was created in 1972 by a gift from Germany as a permanent memorial to Marshall Plan Aid.

GMF Research Fellowships Program

Subjects: Either comparative analysis of a specific issue in more than one country or the exploration of an issue in a single country in ways that can be expected to have relevance to other countries. The geographical scope of the programme includes Western, Central and Eastern Europe, including Russia and Turkey as they relate to Europe, but not the Central Asian countries that were formerly part of the Soviet Union.
Purpose: To support research projects that seek to improve the understanding of significant contemporary economic, political and social developments involving the United States of America and Europe.

Eligibility: Only citizens of the United States and permanent residents are eligible. Special consideration will be given to applicants seeking support for dissertation fieldwork in one or more European countries and to projects involving parallel or collaborative research by both established and younger Scholars, including projects designed on a transatlantic basis.

Level of Study: Doctorate, Postdoctorate, Postgraduate.

Type: Fellowship.

Value: For dissertation fieldwork in Europe the grants are worth US$20,000. The support for advanced research grants will not exceed US$40,000.

Length of Study: For dissertation fieldwork in Europe up to one year, and for advanced research support not less than one semester and not greater than one year.

Frequency: Annual.

Study Establishment: There is no restriction on the place of tenure.

Country of Study: United States of America or Europe.

No. of awards offered: Approx. 20.

Application Procedure: Applicants must visit the website for information and downloadable application forms.

Closing Date: November 15th for dissertation or advanced research.

No. of awards given last year: 22.

No. of applicants last year: 120.

Additional Information: All award recipients are responsible for arranging their own housing, insurance, benefits and travel, including a visa if applicable. Submissions will be reviewed by a committee of established Scholars from various disciplines. An independent selection committee of Scholars will make recommendations to the Fund.

GERMANISTIC SOCIETY OF AMERICA

Institute of International Education
809 United Nations Plaza, New York, NY, 10017, United States of America

Tel: (1) 212 984 5330

www: http://www.iie.org

Contact: W Jackson, Manager

Germanistic Society of America Fellowships

Subjects: German language, literature, philosophy, history, art history, political science, economics and banking, international law and public affairs.

Eligibility: Open to United States citizens who have a good academic record and capacity for independent study. Preference is given to candidates with a Master's degree.

Level of Study: Postgraduate.

Type: Fellowship.

Value: US$11,000 per academic year.

Length of Study: One academic year of nine months.

Frequency: Annual.

Country of Study: Germany.

No. of awards offered: Four.

Application Procedure: Applicants must apply for information, available on request.

Closing Date: October 25th.

Funding: Private.

Additional Information: Candidates selected will be considered for Fulbright Travel Grants.

THE GETTY GRANT PROGRAM, J PAUL GETTY TRUST

1200 Getty Center Drive
Suite 800, Los Angeles, CA, 90049-1685, United States of America
Tel: (1) 310 440 7320
Fax: (1) 310 440 7703
Email: researchgrants@getty.edu
www: http://www.getty.edu/grants
Contact: Dr Joan Weinstein, Senior Programme Officer

The Getty Grant Program is part of the J Paul Getty Trust, a private operating foundation dedicated to the visual arts and the humanities. The Grant Program supports a wide range of projects that promote research in the history of art related fields, advancement of the understanding of art and the conservation of cultural heritage.

The Getty Grant Program Collaborative Research Grants

Subjects: History of art or related fields.

Purpose: To provide opportunities for teams of Scholars to collaborate on interpretative research projects that offer new explanations of art and its history.

Eligibility: Collaborative Research Grant teams must consist of two or more art historians, or of an art historian and one or more Scholars from other disciplines. Funding is also available for the research and planning of scholarly exhibitions. Teams for these projects must include Scholars from both museums and universities.

Level of Study: Postdoctorate.

Type: Research grant.

Value: Varies according to the needs of the project.

Length of Study: One-two years.

Frequency: Annual.

Country of Study: Any country.

No. of awards offered: Varies.

Application Procedure: Applicants must complete an application form. Additional information, detailed guidelines and application forms are available from the website or by contacting the Getty Grant Program office.

Closing Date: November 1st.

Funding: Private.

No. of awards given last year: Four.

No. of applicants last year: 50.

Additional Information: Further information is available on request.

The Getty Grant Program Curatorial Research Fellowships

Subjects: History of art or related fields.

Purpose: To support the professional scholarly development of curators by providing them with time off from regular museum duties to undertake short-term research or study projects.

Eligibility: Open to full-time curators who have a minimum of three years of professional experience and are employed at museums with art collections.

Level of Study: Professional development.

Type: Fellowship.

Value: US$3,500 per month plus up to US$3,000 for travel and research materials.

Length of Study: One-three months.

Frequency: Annual.

Country of Study: Any country.

No. of awards offered: Varies.

Application Procedure: Applicants must complete an application form. Additional information, detailed guidelines and application forms are available from the website or by contacting the Getty Grant Program office.

Closing Date: November 1st.

Funding: Private.

No. of awards given last year: Varies.

Additional Information: Further information is available on request.

The J Paul Getty Postdoctoral Fellowships in the History of Art and Humanities

Subjects: History of art or related fields.
Purpose: To provide support for outstanding Scholars in the early stages of their careers to pursue interpretative research projects that make a substantial and original contribution to the understanding of art and its history.
Eligibility: Open to Scholars of all nationalities who have earned a doctoral degree within the past six years.
Level of Study: Postdoctorate.
Type: Fellowship.
Value: US$40,000.
Length of Study: One year.
Frequency: Annual.
Country of Study: Any country.
No. of awards offered: 15.
Application Procedure: Applicants must complete an application form. Additional information, detailed guidelines and application forms are available from the website or by contacting the Getty Grant Program office.
Closing Date: November 1st.
Funding: Private.
No. of awards given last year: 15.
No. of applicants last year: 150.
Additional Information: Further information is available on request.

Residential Grants at the Getty Centre

Subjects: Arts and humanities.
Purpose: To provide support for established scholars to undertake research related to a specific theme while in residence at the Getty Center in Los Angeles.
Eligibility: Open to established Scholars who are working on projects which address the given scholarly theme.
Level of Study: Postdoctorate, Research.
Type: Grant.
Frequency: Annual.
Country of Study: Any country.
No. of awards offered: Varies.
Application Procedure: Applicants must complete an application form. Additional information, detailed guidelines and application forms are available from the website or by contacting the Getty Grant Program office.
Closing Date: November 1st.
Funding: Private.

GÉZA ANDA FOUNDATION

Bleicherweg 18, Zurich, CH-8002, Switzerland
Tel: (41) 1 205 1423
Fax: (41) 1 205 1205
Email: info@gezaanda.org
www: http://www.gezaanda.org
Contact: Ms Ruth Bossart

The Géza Anda Foundation was established in 1977 in memory of the pianist, Géza Anda. It holds an international piano competition, every three years, awarding three prize winners, special prizes and provides the opportunity for the laureates to appear as soloists in concerts and recitals.

International Géza Anda Piano Competition

Subjects: The piano.
Purpose: To sponsor young pianists in the musical spirit of Géza Anda.
Eligibility: Open to pianists who were born after June 11th, 1971.
Level of Study: Unrestricted.
Type: Prize.
Value: Cash prizes of swiss franc 60,000 and other benefits such as free concert management services for three years.
Frequency: Every three years.

Country of Study: Switzerland.
No. of awards offered: Three.
Application Procedure: Applicants must complete four rounds in the competition: audition, recital, Mozart and a final concert with orchestra.
Closing Date: March 1st.
Funding: Private.
No. of awards given last year: Three official and four special.

GILBERT MURRAY TRUST

International Studies Committee
5 Warnborough Road, Oxford, Oxfordshire, OX2 6HZ, England
Tel: (44) 1865 556633
Contact: Mrs Mary Bull, Secretary, International Studies Committee

Gilbert Murray Trust Junior Awards

Subjects: International affairs or international law.
Purpose: To study the purposes and work of the United Nations.
Eligibility: Open to persons of any nationality who are, or have been, postgraduate students at a university or similar institution in the United Kingdom. Candidates should be taking or should have taken part in a course of international affairs or international law and must not be over 25 years of age, although consideration will be given to those over that age in special cases.
Level of Study: Postgraduate.
Type: Award.
Value: UK £300.
Frequency: Annual.
Country of Study: Any country.
No. of awards offered: 10.
Application Procedure: Applicants must submit five copies (in typed form and on one side only) of a letter of application, a curriculum vitae, an outline of their intention with regards to a future career, full particulars of the purpose for which the award would be used and a supporting testimonial from a person capable of judging the candidate's ability to use the award profitably.
Closing Date: April 1st in the year of award.
Funding: Private.
Contributor: Small individual contributions.
No. of awards given last year: 10.
No. of applicants last year: 30.
Additional Information: Awards are only given to support a specific project, such as a visit to the headquarters of an international organisation, a research visit to a particular country or a short course at an institution abroad, which will assist the applicant in his or her study of international affairs in relation to the purpose and work of the United Nations. The Junior Awards are not intended as general financial support for the study of international affairs.

GILCHRIST EDUCATIONAL TRUST

Mary Trevelyan Hall
10 York Terrace East, London, NW1 4PT, England
Tel: (44) 20 7631 8300 ext. 773
Contact: Mrs Everidge, Secretary

GET Grants

Subjects: All subjects.
Purpose: To promote the advancement of education and learning in every part of the world.
Eligibility: Open to students in the United Kingdom who are within sight of the end of a course and are facing unexpected financial difficulties which may prevent completion of their studies, students who are required to spend a short period studying abroad as part of their course, recognised British university expeditions and pioneer educational establishments. Individuals entitled to student loans are not

eligible. Students studying at a United Kingdom university are required to spend a short period abroad.
Level of Study: Doctorate, Postgraduate.
Type: Grant.
Value: Modest.
Frequency: Dependent on funds available.
Study Establishment: Any university in the United Kingdom.
Country of Study: United Kingdom.
No. of awards offered: Varies.
Application Procedure: University expeditions are required to complete an application form. Eligible individuals are sent a list of information required.
Closing Date: For university expeditions the deadline is February 28th, and for all other categories applications can be made at any time.
Funding: Private.

Gilchrist Fieldwork Award
Subjects: All scientific subjects.
Purpose: To fund a period of fieldwork by established scientists or academics.
Eligibility: Open to teams of not more than 10 members, most of whom should be British, with the majority holding established positions in research departments at universities or similar establishments, wishing to undertake a field season of over six weeks in relation to one or more scientific objectives. The proposed research must be original and challenging, achievable within the timetable and preferably of benefit to the host country or region.
Type: Grant.
Value: UK £10,000.
Frequency: Every two years.
Country of Study: Any country.
No. of awards offered: One.
Application Procedure: Applicants must write for details.
Closing Date: March 15th.
Funding: Private.
Additional Information: The award is competitive.

GLADYS KRIEBLE DELMAS FOUNDATION

521 Fifth Avenue
Suite 1612, New York, NY, 10175-1699, United States of America
Tel: (1) 212 687 0011
Fax: (1) 212 687 8877
Email: info@delmas.org
www: http://www.delmas.org
Contact: Ms Shirley Lockwood

The Gladys Krieble Delmas Foundation promotes the advancement and perpetuation of humanistic enquiry and artistic creativity by encouraging excellence in scholarship and in the performing arts, and by supporting research libraries and other institutions that preserve the resources which transmit this cultural heritage.

Gladys Krieble Delmas Foundation Grants
Subjects: The history of Venice, the former Venetian empire and contemporary Venetian society and culture. Disciplines of the humanities and social sciences are eligible areas of study including, but not limited to, art, architecture, archaeology, theatre, music, literature, political science, economics and law.
Purpose: To promote research into Venice and the Veneto.
Eligibility: Open to United States of America citizens and permanent residents who have some experience in advanced research. Graduate students must have fulfilled all doctoral requirements except for completion of the dissertation, but including acceptance of the dissertation proposal, at the time of application. There is also a programme for Scholars from Commonwealth countries.
Level of Study: Postdoctorate, Predoctorate.
Type: Grant.

Value: US$500-16,500 depending on length of study. At the discretion of the trustees and advisory board of the Foundation, funds may be made available for aid on the publication of results.
Length of Study: Up to one academic year.
Frequency: Annual.
Country of Study: Italy.
No. of awards offered: Usually 15-25.
Application Procedure: Applicants must complete an application form. Instruction sheets and forms are available from the Foundation.
Closing Date: December 15th.
Funding: Private.

GLASGOW EDUCATIONAL AND MARSHALL TRUST

21 Beaton Road, Glasgow, G41 4NW, Scotland
Tel: (44) 141 423 2169
Fax: (44) 141 424 1731
Contact: R R McLean, Administrator

The Glasgow Educational and Marshall Trust is a charitable trust which meets quarterly and awards bursaries to, amongst others, mature students and postgraduate students and to aid travel and school trips within the Glasgow area.

Glasgow Educational and Marshall Trust Bursary
Subjects: All subjects.
Purpose: To offer financial support to those living within the Glasgow Municipal Boundary.
Eligibility: Applicants must have a minimum of five years of residence within the Glasgow Municipal Boundary (as it was prior to 1975). Years spent within the Boundary purely for the purpose of study do not count.
Level of Study: Unrestricted.
Type: Bursary.
Value: UK £100-1,000.
Frequency: Annual.
Country of Study: United Kingdom.
Application Procedure: Applicants must complete and submit an application form together with two written references prior to the start of the course. No retrospective awards are available.
Closing Date: July 31st.
Funding: Private.
No. of awards given last year: 68.
No. of applicants last year: 240.
Additional Information: Further information is available on request.

GLAUCOMA RESEARCH FOUNDATION

200 Pine Street
Suite 200, San Francisco, CA, 94104, United States of America
Tel: (1) 415 986 3162
Fax: (1) 415 986 3763
Email: research@glaucoma.org
www: http://www.glaucoma.org
Contact: Ms Jennifer Rulon, Research Manager

The Glaucoma Research Foundation is a national non-profit organisation working to protect the sight and independence of people with glaucoma, through research and education.

Pilot Project Grants Program
Subjects: Glaucoma.
Purpose: To provide funds for research.
Eligibility: Applicants must hold a graduate degree.
Level of Study: Postgraduate.
Type: Research grant.

Value: US$15,000-50,000.
Length of Study: One year.
Frequency: Annual.
Country of Study: United States of America.
No. of awards offered: Varies.
Application Procedure: Applicants must write, phone, or visit the website for details.
Closing Date: December 1st.

GLAXOSMITHKLINE

Medicines Research Centre
Gunnels Wood Road, Stevenage, SG1 2NY, England
Tel: (44) 1438 763280
Fax: (44) 1438 763276
Email: ms3845@gsk.com
www: http://www.glaxosmithkline.co.uk
Contact: Dr Malcolm Skingle, Director, European Academic Liaison

GlaxoSmithKline is a pharmaceutical and health care company, committed to improving the quality of human life by enabling people to do more, feel better and live longer. The focus of the company is health care, the treatment, prevention and diagnosis including the concept of proactive health living. GlaxoSmithKline is comprised of three integrated businesses: pharmaceuticals, consumer health care and clinical diagnostics.

GlaxoSmithKline Collaborative Research Projects

Subjects: Pharmaceuticals, consumer health care and clinical diagnostic services.
Purpose: To target people whose research activities fit into the company's own research programme.
Eligibility: Open to groups who are carrying out relevant research activities. Speculative approaches are also welcome from the academic sector.
Level of Study: Doctorate, Graduate.
Type: Studentship.
Value: Approx. UK £3,000-6,000 per year, but can be higher depending on the type of research carried out.
Length of Study: One-three years.
Frequency: Annual.
Study Establishment: Any university.
Country of Study: Any country.
No. of awards offered: 160.
Application Procedure: Applicants must write for details.
Closing Date: Applications are accepted at any time.
Funding: Commercial, Government.
Contributor: The majority of studentships are jointly funded with the Research Councils and a small number are totally funded by them.
No. of awards given last year: 105.
Additional Information: The company also operates a scheme whereby postdoctoral workers are employed by GlaxoSmithKline on a contract basis for two years.

Services to Academia

Subjects: Pharmacology, chemistry, biotechnology and toxicology.
Eligibility: Open to students excelling in the listed subject areas during their studies.
Level of Study: Professional development.
Type: Prizes, sponsored lectures and scholarship.
Value: Varies.
Length of Study: Varies.
Frequency: Annual.
Country of Study: Any country.
No. of awards offered: Varies.
Application Procedure: Organisations must approach the company in writing.
Closing Date: Applications are accepted at any time.
Funding: Commercial.

THE GOLDA MEIR MOUNT CARMEL INTERNATIONAL TRAINING CENTRE (MCTC)

PO Box 6111, Haifa, 31060, Israel
Tel: (972) 4 837 5904
Fax: (972) 4 837 5913
Email: mctc@mctc.co.il
Contact: Mrs Mazal Renford, Director

The Golda Meir Mount Carmel International Training Centre (MCTC) devotes its resources to training women and men from developing countries and societies in transition. Its underlying philosophy stresses the importance of grassroots development and recognition of women's contribution. It conducts courses and workshops at MCTC and abroad in three key areas: community development, early childhood education and management of microenterprises.

Golda Meir Mount Carmel International Training Centre Assistance for Courses

Subjects: Courses in community organisation and management of human services, pre school education, organisation and management of income generating projects and small scale industries, and management of non-governmental organisations (NGOs).
Purpose: To assist developing countries and transitional societies in training personnel engaged in socio-economic development.
Eligibility: Open mainly to women aged 25-45 years of age from developing countries. Male students are also accepted. Participants must have completed at least 12 years of schooling, have undergone relevant professional training, and have work experience. A good knowledge of the language in which the course will be given is essential.
Level of Study: Postgraduate, Professional development.
Value: Tuition, lodging and board, plus a monthly pocket money allowance.
Length of Study: Four and eight weeks, accordingly.
Frequency: Annual.
Study Establishment: MCTC.
Country of Study: Israel.
No. of awards offered: 28.
Application Procedure: Applicants must apply to the Israeli diplomatic representative in their country for admission to the course.
Closing Date: Three months prior to the commencement of the course.
Funding: Government.
No. of awards given last year: 400.
No. of applicants last year: 1,400.
Additional Information: Courses are given in English, French or Spanish and include lectures, discussion groups, study tours and fieldwork.

Golda Meir Mount Carmel International Training Centre Tuition and Maintenance Scholarships

Subjects: Community organisation and management of human services, pre-school education, organisation and management of income generating projects and small-scale industries or management of non-governmental organisations (NGOs).
Eligibility: Open to nationals of developing countries and transitional societies.
Level of Study: Postgraduate, Professional development.
Type: Tuition and maintenance scholarship.
Value: US$3,000 per month.
Length of Study: Four or eight weeks.
Frequency: Annual.
Study Establishment: MCTC.
Country of Study: Israel.
No. of awards offered: 28.
Application Procedure: Applicants must complete an application form, and include a health form and copies of their diplomas. Forms can be obtained from the nearest Israeli diplomatic representative.
Closing Date: Three months prior to the course opening.

Funding: Government.

No. of awards given last year: 400.

No. of applicants last year: 1,400.

Additional Information: Courses are given in English, French or Spanish and include lectures, discussion groups, study tours and fieldwork.

GOLDEN KEY NATIONAL HONOR SOCIETY

International Headquarters
1189 Ponce de Leon Avenue North East, Atlanta, GA, 30306-4624, United States of America
Tel: (1) 404 377 2400
Fax: (1) 404 373 4033
Email: scholarships@goldenkey.gsu.edu
www: http://goldenkey.gsu.edu/gk
Contact: Mr Luke Anderson, Co-ordinator of Scholarships and Awards

Golden Key National Honor Society is a non-profit academic honours organisation that recognises the top 15 per cent of juniors and seniors in all undergraduate fields. Membership of the Society is by invitation only and there are various benefits available to members. The Society has a five part mission to recognise scholastic achievement and excellence in all undergraduate fields of study, unite collegiate faculty and administrators with students to foster a network of scholars, to award scholarships for the pursuit of knowledge, to serve the campus and community for personal growth and leadership development and to connect members with career opportunities.

Golden Key National Honor Society Art International

Subjects: Painting, drawing, photography, sculpture, computer generated art, graphic design and illustration, applied art such as jewellery, textiles, ceramics and set design, printmaking and mixed media.

Purpose: To recognise and reward the creative talents of members and to reward their superlative works of art through their visual arts scholarship programme.

Eligibility: Open to Golden Key members.

Level of Study: Unrestricted.

Type: Scholarship.

Value: Ten finalists in each category will receive US$100 and one winner in each of eight categories will receive a scholarship of US$1,000.

Frequency: Annual.

No. of awards offered: Eight.

Application Procedure: Applicants must submit an original work on a slide. Participants in the photography category may submit a slide or a matted print of the photograph. The top ten finalists in each category will submit their original work to Golden Key for final judging. Entries must arrive matted or framed in order to be considered and shipping costs must be paid by entrants. Finalists will receive US$100 to offset shipping costs. Due to the high number of entries, the slides are not returned so applicants should not send their only copies. Applicants in North America should submit applications to the main address and applicants in the Asia-Pacific region should submit applications to the Australian address.

Closing Date: April 1st.

Funding: Private.

Contributor: Society members.

No. of awards given last year: Eight.

No. of applicants last year: 100.

Additional Information: Wining entries may be displayed at the Golden Key International Convention and will be published in Concepts, the society's award-winning annual magazine.

For further information contact:

Art International
Golden Key International Honour Society
PO Box 302, Glebe, NSW, 2037, Australia

Golden Key National Honor Society Business Achievement Awards

Subjects: Business administration and management.

Purpose: To honour students for their excellence in the field of business study.

Eligibility: Open to Golden Key members.

Level of Study: Unrestricted.

Type: Scholarship.

Value: The winner will receive a US$1,000 award, the second place applicant will receive US$750 and the third place applicant will receive US$500.

Length of Study: Varies.

Frequency: Annual.

No. of awards offered: Three.

Application Procedure: Applicants will be asked to respond to a problem posed by an honorary member within the discipline. The response will be in the form of a new business plan. Applications will be judged by honorary members in the field of business based on the creativity and viability of the business plan. Applicants must develop a business plan for an new venture that would meet a current need in society but one that is not currently being met by an existing company, product or service. Applicants must submit a creative, viable business plan based on their fundamental knowledge of business and marketing. The business plan must not exceed three typewritten pages in length and must be accompanied by an application form, an academic transcript and a letter of recommendation from a professor in the relevant discipline. Applicants in North America should submit applications to the main address and applicants in the Asia-Pacific region should submit applications to the Australian address.

Closing Date: March 1st.

Funding: Private.

Contributor: Society members.

No. of awards given last year: Three.

No. of applicants last year: 50.

Additional Information: Further information is available from the website.

For further information contact:

Art International
Golden Key International Honour Society
PO Box 302, Glebe, NSW, 2037, Australia

Golden Key National Honor Society Claes Nobel Earth Ethics Award

Subjects: All subjects.

Purpose: To recognise a member who exhibits exemplary dedication to environmental awareness and responsibility.

Eligibility: Open to Golden Key members.

Level of Study: Unrestricted.

Type: Scholarship.

Value: US$1,000.

Frequency: Annual.

No. of awards offered: One.

Application Procedure: Applicants must complete a specific assignment, details of which are available from the organisation. Applicants must send the essay along with their contact details to the society. Applicants in North America should submit applications to the main address and applicants in the Asia-Pacific region should submit applications to the Australian address.

Closing Date: February 15th.

Funding: Private.

Contributor: Society members.

No. of awards given last year: One.

No. of applicants last year: 50.

Additional Information: The winning earth ethics essay will be published in Concepts magazine.

For further information contact:

Art International
Golden Key International Honour Society
PO Box 302, Glebe, NSW, 2037, Australia

Golden Key National Honor Society Education Achievement Awards

Subjects: Education study.
Purpose: To honour students for excellence in the field.
Eligibility: Open to Golden Key members.
Level of Study: Unrestricted.
Type: Scholarship.
Value: The winner will receive a US$1,000 award, the second place applicant will receive US$750 and the third place applicant will receive US$500.
Frequency: Annual.
No. of awards offered: Three.
Application Procedure: Applicants are asked to complete a specific assignment, details of which are available by contacting the organisation. The thematic unit must be accompanied by an application form, an academic transcript and a letter of recommendation from a professor in the discipline. Applicants in North America should submit applications to the main address and applicants in the Asia-Pacific region should submit applications to the Australian address.
Closing Date: March 1st.
Contributor: Society members.
No. of awards given last year: Three.
No. of applicants last year: 30.

For further information contact:

Art International
Golden Key International Honour Society
PO Box 302, Glebe, NSW, 2037, Australia

Golden Key National Honor Society Engineering Achievement Award

Subjects: Engineering.
Purpose: To honour students for excellence in the field.
Eligibility: Open to Golden Key members.
Level of Study: Unrestricted.
Type: Scholarship.
Value: The winner will receive a US$1,000 award, the second place applicant will receive US$750 and the third place applicant will receive US$500.
Frequency: Annual.
No. of awards offered: Three.
Application Procedure: Applicants must provide a solution to one of three design problems. Topics are available by contacting the Society. Applicants in North America should submit applications to the main address and applicants in the Asia-Pacific region should submit applications to the Australian address.
Closing Date: March 1st.
Funding: Private.
Contributor: Society members.
No. of awards given last year: Three.
No. of applicants last year: 30.

For further information contact:

Art International
Golden Key International Honour Society
PO Box 302, Glebe, NSW, 2037, Australia

Golden Key National Honor Society Excellence in Speech and Debate Awards

Subjects: All subjects. Applicants are assessed on the viability of their argument, as well as on their verbal and non verbal communication skills.
Purpose: To recognise talented members for their oratory skills.

Eligibility: Open to Golden Key members.
Level of Study: Unrestricted.
Type: Scholarship.
Value: Varies.
Frequency: Annual.
No. of awards offered: Two.
Application Procedure: Applicants must submit a videotaped monologue of no more than five minutes in length responding to the following topic: universities have a moral responsibility to prohibit hate speech on their campuses. Applicants in North America should submit applications to the main address and applicants in the Asia-Pacific region should submit applications to the Australian address.
Closing Date: April 1st.
Funding: Private.
Contributor: Society members.
No. of awards given last year: Two.
No. of applicants last year: 30.

For further information contact:

Art International
Golden Key International Honour Society
PO Box 302, Glebe, NSW, 2037, Australia

Golden Key National Honor Society GEICO Adult Scholar Awards

Subjects: All subjects.
Purpose: To recognise academic achievement in students from all backgrounds and from all disciplines. The Society recognises that returning students are an important component of their member population and this award hopes to reward motivated students for their commitment to maintaining academic excellence while balancing additional responsibilities.
Eligibility: Candidates must be more than 25 years of age and must have completed at least 12 credit hours since their return to the university and be enrolled at the time of application. Candidates must be working towards a Baccalaureate degree.
Level of Study: Unrestricted.
Type: Scholarship.
Value: US$1,000.
Frequency: Annual.
No. of awards offered: 10.
Application Procedure: Applicants must submit an official application form, an academic transcript and a personal essay of no more than 500 words describing their educational goals, their other commitments and the obstacles they have overcome to achieve academic excellence. Candidates must submit a letter of recommendation either from an employer or from a professor in their major field of study. Applicants in North America should submit applications to the main address and applicants in the Asia-Pacific region should submit applications to the Australian address.
Closing Date: April 1st.
Funding: Commercial.
Contributor: GEICO Insurance.
No. of awards given last year: 10.
No. of applicants last year: 35.

For further information contact:

Art International
Golden Key International Honour Society
PO Box 302, Glebe, NSW, 2037, Australia

Golden Key National Honor Society Information Systems Achievement Awards

Subjects: Information systems study.
Purpose: To honour students for excellence in their field.
Eligibility: Open to Golden Key members.
Level of Study: Unrestricted.
Type: Scholarship.
Value: Varies from US$500-1,000.
Frequency: Annual.
No. of awards offered: Three.

Application Procedure: Applicants are asked to respond a specific assignment, the details of which can be obtained from the organsiation. This solution must be accompanied by an application form, an academic transcript and a letter of recommendation from a professor in the discipline. Applications will be judged by honorary members in the field of information systems based on the creativity and viability of the response. Applicants in North America should submit applications to the main address and applicants in the Asia-Pacific region should submit applications to the Australian address.
Closing Date: March 1st.
Funding: Private.
Contributor: Society members.
No. of awards given last year: Three.
No. of applicants last year: 35.

For further information contact:

Art International
Golden Key International Honour Society
PO Box 302, Glebe, NSW, 2037, Australia

Golden Key National Honor Society International Student Leader

Subjects: All subjects.
Purpose: To recognise a talented member for outstanding commitment to Golden Key, as well as for campus and community leadership and academic achievement.
Eligibility: Open to Golden Key members who are in good standing and are currently enrolled in an accredited graduate programme.
Level of Study: Unrestricted.
Type: Scholarship.
Value: US$1,000.
Frequency: Annual.
No. of awards offered: One.
Application Procedure: Applicants must submit an official application form, a personal statement of no more than 1,000 words explaining why the student feels that he or she should receive the award, a detailed list of Golden Key involvement, a list of extracurricular activities listing involvement in other organisations, honours and awards received, community service activities and work experience, and a letter of recommendation from the Golden Key chapter advisor. Applicants in North America should submit applications to the main address and applicants in the Asia-Pacific region should submit applications to the Australian address.
Closing Date: May 1st.
Funding: Private.
Contributor: Society members.
No. of awards given last year: One.
No. of applicants last year: 30.
Additional Information: The award will be presented at the international convention.

For further information contact:

Art International
Golden Key International Honour Society
PO Box 302, Glebe, NSW, 2037, Australia

Golden Key National Honor Society Literary Achievement Awards

Subjects: Fiction, non-fiction, poetry and feature writing.
Purpose: To recognise and encourage members' literary talents.
Eligibility: Open to Golden Key members. Each entry must be an original composition and previously published works will not be accepted. Only one composition per member, per category will be accepted.
Level of Study: Unrestricted.
Type: Scholarship.
Value: US$1,000.
Frequency: Annual.
No. of awards offered: Four.
Application Procedure: Entries must be accompanied by a separate Literary Achievement Awards application form. The applicant's

name or other identification must not appear on any page other than the application as a numbering system will be used to track entries and applications.
Closing Date: April 1st.
Funding: Private.
Contributor: Society members.
No. of awards given last year: Four.
No. of applicants last year: 250.
Additional Information: Winning entries will be published in Concepts, the Society's award winning annual magazine.

Golden Key National Honor Society Performing Arts Showcase

Subjects: Dance, drama, film making, instrumental performance, original musical composition and vocal performance.
Purpose: To recognise and encourage creative talents.
Eligibility: Open to Golden Key members. Only one entry per member, per category will be accepted.
Level of Study: Unrestricted.
Type: Scholarship.
Value: US$1,000 and the opportunity to perform at the Golden Key international convention.
Frequency: Annual.
No. of awards offered: Eight.
Application Procedure: Each entry must be accompanied by a separate Performing Arts Showcase application form, available from the Society. Entries must be submitted on VHS videotape and may not exceed ten minutes in length. Applicants in North America should submit applications to the main address and applicants in the Asia-Pacific region should submit applications to the Australian address.
Closing Date: March 1st.
Funding: Private.
Contributor: Society members.
No. of awards given last year: Eight.
No. of applicants last year: 250.

For further information contact:

Art International
Golden Key International Honour Society
PO Box 302, Glebe, NSW, 2037, Australia

Golden Key National Honor Society Research Travel Grants

Subjects: All subjects.
Purpose: To assist students who need funding to pursue field research related to an honours thesis.
Eligibility: Open to Golden Key members. The student must be able to show that they have been invited to present their research as a specific conference.
Level of Study: Unrestricted.
Type: Grant.
Value: US$500.
Frequency: Every two years.
Country of Study: Any country.
No. of awards offered: 10.
Application Procedure: The student must submit documentation supported by the thesis advisor that the trip is highly relevant to the research to be conducted, as well as a documented budget that summarises the overall cost of attending the conference or of travelling to undertake necessary research. Applications must include a statement of personal particulars, details of Golden Key activities, a description of the proposed research presentation and documented evidence that the applicant has been invited to present at a specified professional association conference or research symposia, or a documented research proposal related to progress in the applicant's honours thesis, a brief statement of the relevance of this request signed by the applicant's academic departmental chairperson or thesis advisor, and a recent academic transcript. Applicants in North America should submit applications to the main address and

applicants in the Asia-Pacific region should submit applications to the Australian address.
Closing Date: October 15th and April 15th.
Funding: Private.
Contributor: Society members.
No. of awards given last year: 10.
No. of applicants last year: 50.

For further information contact:

Art International
Golden Key International Honour Society
PO Box 302, Glebe, NSW, 2037, Australia

Golden Key National Honor Society Scholar Award

Subjects: All subjects.
Purpose: To support members' graduate study at accredited universities.
Eligibility: Open to lifetime members of the Golden Key National Honor Society who are in good standing at the time of the application, have graduated no earlier than five years prior to the application deadline from an institution with an active chapter of the Golden Key International Honor Society, hold Baccalaureate degrees or the equivalent by the time they receive their scholarships or enrol in a post-baccalaureate program of study at an accredited Institute of Higher Education during the academic year of application as a full-time student.
Level of Study: Graduate.
Type: Scholarship.
Value: US$10,000.
Frequency: Annual.
Study Establishment: Any accredited university.
Country of Study: Any country.
No. of awards offered: 12.
Application Procedure: Applicants must submit an application form and four sets of the required documents to the Society's headquarters. Applicants in North America should submit applications to the main address and applicants in the Asia-Pacific region should submit applications to the Australian address.
Closing Date: January 15th.
Funding: Private.
Contributor: Society members.
No. of awards given last year: 12.
No. of applicants last year: 100.
Additional Information: Previous Golden Key Scholar Award recipients are not eligible to reapply. The Society does not discriminate on the basis of race, religion, national origin, disability, gender, age or sexual orientation. The Golden Key Scholar Award is an equal opportunity scholarship.

For further information contact:

Art International
Golden Key International Honour Society
PO Box 302, Glebe, NSW, 2037, Australia

Golden Key National Honor Society Service Award

Subjects: All subjects.
Purpose: To recognise an individual for outstanding commitment to community service.
Eligibility: Open to Golden Key members who has been enrolled as a student during the previous academic year.
Level of Study: Unrestricted.
Type: Scholarship.
Value: US$500.
Frequency: Annual.
No. of awards offered: One.
Application Procedure: The application packet must include an official application form, a 250-500 word statement describing the service project and the applicant's philosophy of community service, two letters of recommendation from the applicant's chapter advisor and one from a representative of the beneficiary of the service. Applicants in North America should submit applications to the main

address and applicants in the Asia-Pacific region should submit applications to the Australian address.
Closing Date: February 15th.
Funding: Private.
Contributor: Society members.
No. of awards given last year: One.
No. of applicants last year: 20.

For further information contact:

Art International
Golden Key International Honour Society
PO Box 302, Glebe, NSW, 2037, Australia

Golden Key National Honor Society Student Scholastic Showcase

Subjects: All subjects.
Purpose: To highlight the research of Society members across the broad spectrum of academic disciplines.
Eligibility: Open to Golden Key members. Alumni are eligible. Only one entry per member is permitted. Each entry must be accompanied by an official Student Scholastic Showcase application. Winners of the Golden Key Scholar Award are not eligible.
Level of Study: Unrestricted.
Type: Scholarship.
Value: US$1,000.
Frequency: Annual.
No. of awards offered: Four.
Application Procedure: Applicants must submit an abstract, not to exceed 250 words, which describes the nature of the study. The abstract should be written in language that is suitable for a reader who is unfamiliar with the discipline. Each entry must contain a complete copy of the paper or research and a letter of support from a faculty member related to, or familiar with, the research project. Recipients must be able to present their research at the Golden Key International Convention. Convention registration including lodging and most meals will be provided. Applicants in North America should submit applications to the main address and applicants in the Asia-Pacific region should submit applications to the Australian address.
Closing Date: March 1st.
Funding: Private.
Contributor: Society members.
No. of awards given last year: Four.
No. of applicants last year: 50.

For further information contact:

Art International
Golden Key International Honour Society
PO Box 302, Glebe, NSW, 2037, Australia

Golden Key National Honor Society Study Abroad Scholarships

Subjects: All subjects.
Purpose: To assist members to study abroad during their undergraduate programme.
Eligibility: Open to Golden Key members. The programme must be approved by the home university as credit towards the home degree. The candidate must meet tuition and living costs at the host university and must secure entry to the programme at the host university.
Level of Study: Unrestricted.
Type: Scholarship.
Value: US$2,000.
Length of Study: One semester of study, a full academic year or an industry placement.
Frequency: Twice a year.
No. of awards offered: 10.
Application Procedure: The selection of scholarship recipients will be assessed on active participation in Golden Key activities, academic record and contribution of the planned study programme to the candidate's home degree. Applications must include an application form, details of Golden Key activities, a description of the planned academic programme at the host university, a brief

statement of the relevance of this programme to the applicants' degree and a recent academic transcript. Candidates will be expected to participate in the activities of the Golden Key chapter at their host university or, if there is no chapter, to pursue interests in the establishment of a chapter. Candidates will be expected to contribute an article to Concepts magazine based on their study abroad experience. Applicants in North America should submit applications to the main address and applicants in the Asia-Pacific region should submit applications to the Australian address.

Closing Date: October 15th and April 15th.
Funding: Private.
Contributor: Society members.
No. of awards given last year: 10.
No. of applicants last year: 75.

For further information contact:

Art International
Golden Key International Honour Society
PO Box 302, Glebe, NSW, 2037, Australia

GRADUATE INSTITUTE OF INTERNATIONAL STUDIES, GENEVA

Institut Universitaire de Hautes Études Internationales
Case Postale 36
132 rue de Lausanne, Geneva, CH-1211, Switzerland
Tel: (41) 22 908 5700
Fax: (41) 22 908 5710
Email: info@hei.unige.ch
www: http://heiwww.unige.ch
Telex: 412 151 Pax Ch
Contact: Ms Isabelle Gerardi, Secretary General

The Graduate Institute of International Studies is a teaching and research establishment devoted to the scientific study of contemporary international relations. The international character of the Institute is emphasised by the use of both English and French as working languages. Its plural approach, which draws upon the method of history and political science, of law and of economics, reflects its aim to promote a broad approach and in depth understanding of international relations.

Graduate Institute of International Studies (Geneva) Scholarships

Subjects: History and international politics, international economics, international law and political science.
Eligibility: Open to any person who can give evidence of a sound knowledge of the French language and of sufficient prior study in political science, economics, law or modern history by the presentation of a college or university degree.
Level of Study: Doctorate, Postgraduate.
Type: Scholarship.
Value: Swiss franc 1,000 per month.
Length of Study: One year, possibly renewable.
Frequency: Annual.
Study Establishment: The Graduate Institute of International Studies, Geneva.
Country of Study: Switzerland.
No. of awards offered: 12.
Application Procedure: Applicants must contact the Institute for details.
Closing Date: March 1st.
Funding: Government.
Contributor: The Canton of Geneva and the Swiss Confederation.
No. of awards given last year: 24.
No. of applicants last year: 49.
Additional Information: Scholarships are normally awarded to more advanced students of the Institute. As a general rule, they are not granted during the first year of studies. Scholars are exempt from Institute fees, but not from the obligatory fees of the University of

Geneva which confers the doctorate (doctorat en relations internationales).

GRAINS RESEARCH AND DEVELOPMENT CORPORATION (GRDC)

PO Box E6, Kingston, ACT, 2604, Australia
Tel: (61) 2 6272 5525
Fax: (61) 2 6271 6430
Email: grdc@grdc.com.au
www: http://www.grdc.com.au
Contact: Mrs Katie Poidomani, Program Co-ordinator

The Grains Research and Development Corporation's (GRDC) mission is to invest in research and development for the greatest benefit to its stakeholders, grain growers and the Commonwealth. The GRDC links innovative research with industry needs. The Corporation's vision is for a profitable, internationally competitive and ecologically sustainable grains industry.

Grains Industry Research Scholarships

Subjects: Fields of high priority to the grains industry.
Eligibility: Open to permanent Australian residents who hold academic qualifications equivalent to a First Class (Honours) Degree or have otherwise demonstrated a high level of postgraduate achievement in research, teaching or extension activities.
Level of Study: Doctorate, Postgraduate.
Type: Fellowship.
Value: A tax free stipend of australian $25,000 with no allowances for dependants. An additional grant of up to australian $5,000 per year may be provided to the host organisation to support the work.
Length of Study: Up to three years.
Frequency: Annual.
Study Establishment: Any university with a record of achievement for full-time research in the subject area leading to a Dphil.
Country of Study: Australia.
No. of awards offered: Up to six.
Application Procedure: Applicants must complete an application form, available on request. Applications (10 copies) should include the curriculum vitae of the applicant and the report of at least two referees. Evidence that the university and collaborating organisations will provide facilities and supervision of the project must also be supplied.
Closing Date: October for the following year.
Funding: Government.
Contributor: The government and Australian grain growers.
No. of awards given last year: 10.
No. of applicants last year: Approx. 50.
Additional Information: The Corporation's five year research and development plan outlines the objectives and programmes to be covered. Copies of this may be obtained from the Secretariat.

GRDC In-Service Training

Subjects: Grains research and development.
Purpose: To support training on an industry wide basis by funding younger scientists, technical staff or other persons engaged in work relevant to the Corporation's objectives who may not be eligible for other forms of support. Funds may be provided for travel, secondment or interchange between institutions.
Eligibility: Open to permanent Australian residents only.
Level of Study: Unrestricted.
Type: Training.
Value: To cover personal travel costs, including economy class air fares and contribution to living expenses for a maximum of six months.
Length of Study: Up to six months.
Frequency: Annual.
Country of Study: Any country.
Application Procedure: Applicants must submit an application including 10 copies of a curriculum vitae, details of the proposed in-

service training, the names, positions and locations of the proposed collaborators and training venue, and approximate dates for the programme, which must fall within the appropriate funding year. Details of any travel directly related to the proposed programme, a proposed budget, including the cost of travel and expected accommodation and living expenses, an indication of other forms of support available to the applicant, evidence that the proposed collaborators are agreeable to the training programme, supporting comments from two referees, and a covering letter should also be included.
Closing Date: October for the following year.
Contributor: The government and Australian grain growers.
Additional Information: On completion of their award, trainees must provide the Board with a report.

GRDC Industry Development Awards
Subjects: Grains research and development.
Purpose: To fund study tours or for other purposes approved by the Corporation.
Eligibility: Open to permanent Australian residents who are experienced growers, processors or other contributors to the work of the Corporation who are not engaged in research and development activity.
Level of Study: Unrestricted.
Type: Development award.
Value: Up to a total of australian $15,000 towards personal travel costs, including economy class air fares and contribution to living expenses.
Frequency: Annual.
Country of Study: Any country.
Application Procedure: Applicants must submit an application including five copies of the nominee's curriculum vitae, details of the proposed programme, the names, positions and locations of the proposed collaborators, approximate dates for the programme, and details of any internal travel directly related to the proposed programme. A proposed budget, including the cost of international and internal travel, and expected accommodation and living expenses, an indication of other forms of support available to the nominee, evidence that the proposed collaborators are agreeable to the programme, supporting comments from two referees, and a covering letter should also be included.
Closing Date: End of October for the following year.
Contributor: The government and Australian grain growers.
Additional Information: On completion of the award, a report must be given to the Board. Preference may be given to applicants who have access to matching funds.

GRDC Postdoctoral Fellowships
Subjects: Grains research and development.
Purpose: To allow individuals of exceptional calibre to enhance their experience and to contribute to the work of the Corporation.
Eligibility: Open to postdoctoral fellows from any country.
Level of Study: Doctorate, Postdoctorate.
Type: Fellowship.
Value: A stipend in the vicinity of australian $45,000 a year with costs and a provision for fare and removal costs to the Australian institution as required.
Length of Study: Up to three years.
Frequency: Annual.
Study Establishment: Approved institutions.
Country of Study: Australia.
No. of awards offered: Up to five.
Application Procedure: Applicants must complete an application form, available upon request. Applications (10 copies) should include the curriculum vitae of the applicant and a report from at least two referees. Evidence that the university and collaborative organisations will provide facilities and supervision of the project must be supplied.
Closing Date: October for the following year.
Funding: Government.
Contributor: The government and Australian grain growers.
No. of awards given last year: Five.

No. of applicants last year: Approx. 50.

GRDC Senior Fellowships
Subjects: Grains research and development.
Purpose: To allow experienced research and development personnel to enhance their experience and their potential to contribute to the work of the Corporation by working at an institution in Australia or overseas.
Eligibility: Open to permanent Australian residents only.
Level of Study: Unrestricted.
Type: Fellowship.
Value: Up to a total of australian $50,000 towards personal travel costs, including economy class air fares and a contribution to living expenses.
Length of Study: Up to one year.
Frequency: Annual.
Country of Study: Any country.
Application Procedure: Applicants must submit an application including 10 copies of the following documentation: the nominee's curriculum vitae, including a list of publications, details of the nominee's research project and its relationship to the host institution's programme of research (this should include evidence that the host institution already has an interest and competence in the area of research proposed by the applicant and that it is relevant to the Corporation's objectives), the names, positions and major publications of the proposed collaborators, together with a letter of invitation from the Head of the host institution. They should also include approximate dates for the programme, which must fall within the appropriate funding year, details of any internal travel directly related to the proposed programme, a proposed budget, including the cost of international and internal travel, and expected accommodation and living expenses, an indication of other forms of support available to the applicant, evidence that the host institution has available the necessary facilities and is willing to accept the Fellow, supporting comments from two referees, and a covering letter. On completion of their award Fellows must furnish the Board with a report. Preference may be given to applicants who have access to matching funds.
Closing Date: October for the following year.
Funding: Government.
Contributor: The government and Australian grain growers.

GRDC Visiting Fellowships and Industry Awards
Subjects: Grains research and development.
Purpose: To give support and stimulus to research programmes supported by the Corporation by funding visits by overseas personnel who could enhance those programmes.
Eligibility: Open to candidates of any nationality.
Level of Study: Postgraduate.
Type: Fellowship.
Value: The Corporation will consider paying the nominee's personal travel costs, contributing to living expenses and providing some support to the host institution or company. The maximum total level of support will normally be australian $17,500.
Length of Study: Up to one year.
Frequency: Annual.
Country of Study: Australia.
Application Procedure: Applicants must submit an application including 10 copies of the following documentation: the nominee's curriculum vitae, details of the nominee's research project or itinerary for study and its relationship to the host institution's or company's programme of research, development or other industry contribution, the name, position and industry contributions of the person proposing the nominee, together with a letter of support from the head of the host institution or company, where appropriate, the names, positions and institutions of collaborators of the proposed project or study tour. They should also include approximate dates for the programme, which must fall within the appropriate funding year, details of any travel directly related to the proposed programme, a proposed budget, including the cost of international and internal travel, and expected accommodation and living expenses, an indication of other forms of support available to the nominee, including those from the home institution or company, evidence that the host institution or

company has accepted the nomination, supporting comments from two referees, and a covering letter.
Closing Date: October for the following year.
Contributor: The government and Australian grain growers.
Additional Information: On completion of the award, a report must be given to the Board. Preference may be given to nominees who have access to matching funds.

GRIFFITH UNIVERSITY

Postgraduate Centre
Office for Research & International Projects
Griffith University, Nathan Campus, QLD, 4111, Australia
Tel: (61) 7 3875 6596
Fax: (61) 7 3875 3885
Email: m.mitchell@mailbox.gu.edu.au
www: http://www.gu.edu.au/postgrad
Contact: Ms Marianne Mitchell, Postgraduate Scholarships Officer

In the pursuit of excellence in teaching, research and community service, Griffith University is committed to innovation, bringing disciplines together, internationalisation, equity and social justice and life-long learning, for the enrichment of Queensland, Australia and the international community.

Griffith University Postgraduate Research Scholarships
Subjects: All subjects.
Purpose: To provide financial support for candidates undertaking full-time research leading to the award of the degree of Doctor of Philosophy or Master of Philosophy.
Eligibility: Open to any person, irrespective of nationality, holding or expecting to hold a First Class (Honours) Degree or equivalent, from a recognised institution. Applicants must demonstrate proficiency in the English language by scoring an overall score of 6.5 in the IELTS test, or have a score of at least 580 on the Teaching English As a Foreign Language or hold a test score of 237 (new Teaching English As a Foreign Language) with an essay rating of 5.0 (Teaching English As a Foreign Language).
Level of Study: Postgraduate.
Type: Scholarship.
Value: Australian $17,609 per year tax exempt, plus a dependent child allowance of australian $1,500 per year for some overseas students, a relocation allowance, travel allowance and a thesis production allowance.
Length of Study: Up to two years for Research Master's and up to three years for PhD candidates, with a possible extension of up to six months for the PhD, subject to satisfactory progress.
Frequency: Annual.
Study Establishment: Griffith University.
Country of Study: Australia.
No. of awards offered: Varies.
Application Procedure: Applicants must complete an application form.
Closing Date: October 30th for commencement by March 30th of the following year.
No. of awards given last year: 48.
Additional Information: The scholarship does not cover the cost of tuition fees which range between australian $12,000 and australian $16,000 per year. Applicants must demonstrate proficiency in the English language by scoring an overall score of 6.5 in the IELTS test, or have a score of at least 580 on the Teaching English As a Foreign Language or hold a test score of 237 (new Teaching English As a Foreign Language) with an essay rating of 5.0 (Teaching English As a Foreign Language).

Jackson Memorial Fellowship
Subjects: Preference will be given to those with an interest in the application of the social, political, economic, environmental or technological sciences to the analysis and resolution of substantial policy issues at the national or regional levels.

Purpose: To consolidate links with a variety of institutions in South East Asia and to provide funding to facilitate visits to Griffith University by faculty staff of the Association of South East Asian Institution of Higher Learning (ASAIHL) member institutions.
Eligibility: Open to senior members of faculty staff of the ASAIHL member institutions.
Level of Study: Professional development.
Type: Fellowship.
Value: Australian $2,500 to assist with travel to and from Australia. A stipend of australian $350 per week during period of residence, accommodation expenses, travel assistance to other tertiary institutions in Australia up to a total of australian $1,200 is also available.
Length of Study: One-three months during a teaching semester February-June or July-October.
Frequency: Annual.
Study Establishment: A faculty of Griffith University.
Country of Study: Australia.
No. of awards offered: One.
Application Procedure: Applicants must apply through the heads of their employing institutions.
Closing Date: October 28th of the year preceding that award.
Funding: Private.
No. of awards given last year: One.

Sir Allan Sewell Visiting Fellowship
Subjects: Available for all faculties of Griffith University.
Purpose: To commemorate the distinguished service of Sir Allan Sewell to Griffith University by offering awards to enable visits by distinguished scholars engaged in academic work who can contribute to the research and teaching in one or more areas of interest to a faculty or college of the university.
Eligibility: Open to researchers of any nationality.
Level of Study: Professional development.
Type: Fellowship.
Value: Up to australian $6,000.
Length of Study: A minimum of eight weeks.
Frequency: Annual.
Study Establishment: Griffith University.
Country of Study: Australia.
No. of awards offered: Four.
Application Procedure: Applicants must be invited by faculties or colleges of the University to apply.
Closing Date: October 28th of the year preceding the award.
Funding: Private.
No. of awards given last year: Four.

THE GRUNDY EDUCATIONAL TRUST

Springhill Cottage
Shirley Holms, Lymington, Hampshire, SO41 8NG, England
Contact: Mr P G Grundy, Secretary to the Trustees

Grundy Educational Trust
Subjects: Courses leading to degrees in technologically or scientifically based disciplines in industry, commerce or the professions.
Purpose: To assist in covering maintenance costs whilst obtaining postgraduate or second degrees.
Eligibility: Open to United Kingdom citizens under 30 years of age.
Level of Study: Doctorate, Postgraduate.
Type: Award.
Value: Up to UK £3,000.
Length of Study: One-three years.
Frequency: Annual.
Study Establishment: Birmingham, Loughborough, Imperial College, Southampton, Surrey, UMIST or Nottingham.
Country of Study: United Kingdom.
No. of awards offered: 12-15.
Application Procedure: Applicants must apply only through the seven selected universities.
Closing Date: May 31st.

Funding: Private.
No. of awards given last year: 15.
No. of applicants last year: 32.

GUIDE DOGS FOR THE BLIND ASSOCIATION

Hillfields
Burghfield Common, Reading, Berkshire, RG7 3YG, England
Tel: (44) 118 983 5555
Fax: (44) 118 983 5433
www: http://www.guidedogs.org.uk
Contact: Ms Fiona Reilly, Opthalmic Research Officer

Founded in 1931, the Guide Dogs for the Blind Association's mission is to provide guide dogs, mobility and other rehabilitation services that meet the needs of blind and partially sighted people. The Association also supports other activities which enhance the quality of life of visually impaired people including funding research into eye conditions.

Guide Dogs Opthalmic Research Fellowship Grant
Subjects: The causes, treatment, prevention and cure of sight threatening diseases and conditions, more especially those that involve large numbers of people, require improved therapeutic regimens or that are likely to lead to a clinical application.
Purpose: To promote high quality research into the causes, treatment, prevention and cure of sight threatening diseases and conditions.
Eligibility: Applicants must be resident in the United Kingdom.
Level of Study: Research.
Type: Fellowship.
Value: Salary and other running costs.
Length of Study: Two years.
Frequency: Annual.
Study Establishment: Specialist ophthalmic departments or organisations.
Country of Study: United Kingdom.
No. of awards offered: Dependent on funds.
Application Procedure: Applicants must submit an application in accordance with Guide Dogs Opthalmic Research Fellowship Grant application guidelines.
Closing Date: The last Friday in February.
Funding: Private.
Contributor: Donations to the Guide Dogs for the Blind Association.
Additional Information: The Guide Dogs for the Blind Association is committed to avoiding the use of experimental animals or tissues from laboratory animals in funded research and will not accept any application which involves these procedures.

Guide Dogs Opthalmic Research Grant
Subjects: The causes, treatment, prevention and cure of sight threatening diseases and conditions, more especially those that involve large numbers of people, require improved therapeutic regimens or that are likely to lead to a clinical application.
Purpose: To promote high quality research into the causes, treatment, prevention and cure of sight threatening diseases and conditions.
Eligibility: Applicants and any research workers must be resident in the United Kingdom. The principal applicant must be in a tenured post for the duration of the requested grant.
Level of Study: Research.
Type: Research grant.
Value: Up to UK £50,000 per year for up to three years.
Length of Study: Three years.
Frequency: Annual.
Study Establishment: Specialist ophthalmic departments or organisations.
Country of Study: United Kingdom.
No. of awards offered: 6-10 annually, depending of funds.

Application Procedure: Applicants must submit an application in accordance with Guide Dogs Opthalmic Research Fellowship Grant application guidelines.
Closing Date: The last Friday in February.
Funding: Private.
Contributor: Donations to the Guide Dogs for the Blind Association.
No. of awards given last year: Six.
No. of applicants last year: 50.
Additional Information: The Guide Dogs for the Blind Association is committed to avoiding the use of experimental animals or tissues from laboratory animals in funded research and will not accept any application which involves these procedures.

GUILLAIN-BARRÉ SYNDROME SUPPORT GROUP

Lincolnshire County Council
Council Offices
Eastgate, Sleaford, Lincolnshire, NG34 8NR, England
Tel: (44) 1529 300328
Fax: (44) 1529 300328
Email: admin@gbs.org
Contact: Ms Glennys Sanders, Honorary President

The Guillain-Barré Syndrome Support Group provides emotional support, personal visits and comprehensive literature to patients, relatives and friends. The Group also educates the public and the medical community about the Support Group and maintains their awareness of the illness. The Group fosters research into the cause, treatment and other aspects of the illness and encourages fund raising and support for its activities.

Guillain-Barré Syndrome Support Group Research Fellowship
Subjects: Any aspect of Guillain-Barré syndrome (GBS) or related diseases including chronic inflammatory demyelinating polyradiculoneuropathy (CIDP).
Purpose: To advance research into the prevention and cure of GBS and CIDP.
Eligibility: Interested candidates should propose a research project to be carried out in an appropriate United Kingdom and Ireland laboratory or department.
Level of Study: Doctorate, Postgraduate, Professional development, Research.
Type: Fellowship.
Value: Up to UK £65,000.
Length of Study: Up to three years.
Frequency: Dependent on funds available.
Study Establishment: Any suitable hospital or university laboratory or department.
Country of Study: United Kingdom or Ireland.
No. of awards offered: One.
Application Procedure: Applicants must write for an application form.
Closing Date: Please contact the organisation.
Contributor: Members' donations, fundraising and trust funds.
Additional Information: Further information is available on request.

HAGLEY MUSEUM AND LIBRARY

PO Box 3630, Wilmington, DE, 19807, United States of America
Tel: (1) 302 658 2400 ext. 243
Fax: (1) 302 655 3188
Email: crl@udel.edu
www: http://www.hagley.org
Contact: Ms Carol Ressler Lockman, Center Coordinator

Located along the Brandywine River on the site of the first du Pont black powder works, Hagley Museum and Library provides a unique glimpse into American life at home and at work in the nineteenth-century. Set among more than 230 acres of trees and flowering shrubs, Hagley offers a diversity of restorations, exhibits and live demonstrations for visitors of all ages.

Hagley Museum and Library Grants-in-Aid of Research

Subjects: American economic and technological history and French eighteenth-century history.
Purpose: To support travel to the Hagley Library for scholarly research in the collections.
Eligibility: Open to degree candidates and advanced Scholars of any nationality. Research must be relevant to Hagley's collections.
Level of Study: Doctorate, Postdoctorate.
Type: Research grant.
Value: Up to US$1,400 per month.
Length of Study: Two-eight weeks.
Frequency: Four times per year.
Study Establishment: The Hagley Library.
Country of Study: United States of America.
No. of awards offered: 25 grants in aid each year.
Application Procedure: Applicants must submit a completed application form with a five page proposal.
Closing Date: March 30th, June 29th or October 30th.
Funding: Private.
Contributor: Foundation funds.
No. of awards given last year: 19.
No. of applicants last year: 40.
Additional Information: Candidates may apply for research in the imprint, manuscript, pictorial and artefact collections of the Hagley Museum and Library. In addition the resources of the 125 libraries in the greater Philadelphia area will be at the disposal of the visiting scholar. The Research Fellowship is to be used only in the Hagley Library.

Hagley/Winterthur Arts and Industries Fellowship

Subjects: Business and economics, design, architecture, crafts, fine arts, technology and industrial history, focusing onon historical and cultural relationships between economic life and the arts.
Purpose: To support scholarly research at Hagley and Winterthur Libraries.
Eligibility: Open to advanced Scholars, graduate students and independent researchers.
Level of Study: Doctorate, Postdoctorate, Professional development.
Type: Residential travel grant.
Value: US$1,400 per month.
Length of Study: Up to three months.
Frequency: Annual.
Country of Study: United States of America.
No. of awards offered: Six.
Application Procedure: Applicants must submit a completed application form with a five page proposal and two recommendations.
Closing Date: December 1st.
Funding: Private.
Contributor: Foundation funds.
No. of awards given last year: Four.
No. of applicants last year: 15.
Additional Information: The Scholar must travel to Delaware to use the collections at both the Hagley and Winterthur libraries.

The Henry Belin du Pont Dissertation Fellowship in Business, Technology and Society

Subjects: Business and technology.
Purpose: To aid graduate students and PhD candidates whose research on important historical questions would benefit from use of Hagley's research collections.
Eligibility: Recipients are expected to have no other obligations during the term of the fellowship, to maintain continuous residence at Hagley for its duration and to participate in events organised by Hagley's Center for the History of Business, Technology and Society. Towards the end of the residency the recipient will make a presentation at Hagley based on research conducted during the Fellowship. Hagley should also receive a copy of the dissertation, as well as any publications aided by the Fellowship.
Type: Fellowship.
Value: US$6,000, free housing, use of computer, email and Internet access and an office.
Length of Study: Four months.
Frequency: Annual.
Study Establishment: The Center for the History of Business, Technology and Society at Hagley.
Country of Study: United States of America.
Application Procedure: Applicants must submit an application dossier including a dissertation prospectus, a statement concerning the relevance of Hagley's research collections to the project and at least two letters of recommendation. Writing samples are also welcome. Potential applicants are strongly encouraged to consult with Hagley staff prior to submitting their dossier.
Closing Date: November 15th.

The Henry Belin du Pont Fellowship

Subjects: Areas of study relevant to the Library's archival and artefact collections.
Purpose: To support access to and use of Hagley's research collections, and to enable individual out of state scholars to pursue their own research and to participate in the interchange of ideas among the Center's scholars.
Eligibility: Open to persons who have already completed their formal professional training. Consequently, degree candidates and persons seeking support for degree work are not eligible to apply. Applicants must not be residents of Delaware and preference will be given to those whose travel costs to Hagley will be higher. Research must be relevant to Hagley's collections.
Level of Study: Doctorate, Postdoctorate.
Type: Fellowship.
Value: A stipend of US$1,500 per month.
Length of Study: Two-six months.
Frequency: Annual.
Study Establishment: The Library.
Country of Study: United States of America.
No. of awards offered: Varies.
Application Procedure: Applicants must submit a completed application form with a five page proposal.
Closing Date: March 31st, June 30th or October 30th.
Funding: Private.
Contributor: Foundation funds.
No. of awards given last year: Three.
No. of applicants last year: 10.
Additional Information: Fellows must devote all their time to their studies and may not accept teaching assignments or undertake any other major activities during the tenure of their fellowships. At the end of their tenure, Fellows must submit a final report on their activities and accomplishments. As a centre for advanced study in the humanities, Hagley is a focal point of a community of Scholars. Fellows are expected to participate in seminars which meet periodically, as well as attend colloquia, lectures, concerts, exhibits, and other public programmes offered during their tenure. Research fellowships are to be used in the Hagley Library only, not as scholarships for college.

THE HAGUE ACADEMY OF INTERNATIONAL LAW

Peace Palace
Carnegieplein 2, The Hague, NL-2517 KJ, Netherlands
Tel: (31) 70 302 4154
Fax: (31) 70 302 4153
Email: hagueacademy@registration
www: http://www.hagueacademy.nl
Contact: The Secretariat

The Hague Academy of International Law's purpose is to gather to-gether young international lawyers of a high standard from all parts of the world who will undertake original research work within the framework of the subject matter of the concerned year. The results of this research work may, if appropriate, be published collectively.

Hague Academy of International Law Doctoral Scholarships

Subjects: International law.
Purpose: To aid individuals with the completion of their theses through the assistance of the Academy.
Eligibility: Open to doctoral candidates up to the age of 40 years from developing countries who reside in their home country and who do not have access to scientific sources.
Level of Study: Doctorate.
Type: Scholarship.
Value: Please contact the Academy for details.
Length of Study: Two months from July 1st.
Frequency: Annual.
Study Establishment: The Hague Academy of International Law.
Country of Study: Netherlands.
No. of awards offered: Four.
Application Procedure: Applicants must submit applications with a letter of recommendation from the professor under whose direction the thesis is being written. The thesis may be concerned with either private or public international law and the title of should be mentioned.
Closing Date: March 1st.
Funding: Private.
Contributor: The Levi Lassen Foundation.
No. of awards given last year: Four.
No. of applicants last year: 30.

Hague Academy of International Law Scholarships for Sessions or Courses

Subjects: International private or public law.
Purpose: To assist students with living expenses during summer courses including the registration fee.
Eligibility: Open to persons up to the age of 40 years who have not received an Academy Scholarship before. Applicants must have suf-ficient knowledge of English or French.
Level of Study: Doctorate.
Type: Scholarship.
Value: Please contact the Academy for details. Scholars are exempt from registration and examination fees. Travelling expenses will not be refunded.
Length of Study: Three weeks.
Frequency: Annual.
Study Establishment: The Hague Academy of International Law.
Country of Study: Netherlands.
No. of awards offered: Varies.
Application Procedure: Applicants must apply personally and sub-mit a curriculum vitae, one photograph and statement of the evi-dence which he or she considers to be of value in support of candidature. Every application must be typed and accompanied by a recommendation from a professor of international law. Applicants should, if possible, attach copies of any scientific publications. As documents forwarded by applicants are not returned, university cer-tificates or other documents must be submitted in the form of copies,

duly verified by a competent authority. The teaching period for which the candidate wants to be registered should be stated clearly.
Closing Date: March 1st.
Funding: Private.
Contributor: Foundations, institutions and personalities.
No. of awards given last year: 121.
No. of applicants last year: 326.

THE HAMBIDGE CENTER

PO Box 339, Rabun Gap, GA, 30568, United States of America
Tel: (1) 706 746 5718
Fax: (1) 706 746 9933
Email: hambidge@rabun.net
www: http://www.hambidge.org
Contact: Mr Bob Thomas, Residency Director

The Hambidge Center's primary function is an artist residency programme with the following aims: to provide artists with time and space to pursue their work, to enhance their communities' art envi-ronment, provide public accessibility and to protect and sustain natu-ral environment, land and endangered species. The Center is set in 600 acres of mountain and valley terrain with waterfalls and nature trails.

Hambidge Center Residency Program Scholarships

Subjects: Any field or discipline of creative work.
Purpose: To provide applicants with an environment for creative work in the arts and sciences. Scholarships offered are the Nellie Mae Rowe Fellowship, the Fulton County Arts Council Fellowship and the CGR Advisors Fellowship.
Eligibility: Open to qualified applicants in all disciplines who can demonstrate seriousness, dedication and professionalism. Interna-tional residents are welcome. Applicants for the CGR Advisors Fel-lowship must be visual artists from the state of Georgia.
Level of Study: Unrestricted.
Type: Fellowship.
Length of Study: Two weeks to two months.
Frequency: Dependent on space available.
Study Establishment: The Hambidge Center.
Country of Study: United States of America.
Application Procedure: Applicants must complete an application form and should send a stamped addressed envelope to the centre marked for the attention of the Residency Program. The application form can be downloaded from the website. Applicants for the Fulton County Arts Council Fellowship should contact the Council at the ad-dress below.
Closing Date: November 1st for residencies from March to August and May 1st for residencies from September to February.
Funding: Government, Private.

For further information contact:

The Fulton County Arts Council
121 Pryor Street South West, Atlanta, GA, 30303, United States of America
Tel: (1) 404 730 5780

HARRY FRANK GUGGENHEIM FOUNDATION (HFG)

527 Madison Avenue, New York, NY, 10022-4301, United States of America
Tel: (1) 212 644 4907
Fax: (1) 212 644 5110
www: http://www.hfg.org

The Harry Frank Guggenheim Foundation (HGF) sponsors scholarly research on problems of violence, aggression and dominance. The

Foundation provides both research grants to established scholars and dissertation fellowships to graduate students during the dissertation writing year. The HFG review of research is published twice a year.

Harry Frank Guggenheim Dissertation Fellowship

Subjects: Any discipline which includes the study of dominance, aggression and violence.

Purpose: To support a PhD candidate in the writing stage of a dissertation. Work must be relevant to HFG programme interests in the study of violence and aggression.

Eligibility: Open to PhD candidates of any nationality.

Level of Study: Doctorate.

Type: Fellowship.

Value: US$15,000.

Length of Study: One year.

Frequency: Annual.

Study Establishment: Any university.

Country of Study: Any country.

No. of awards offered: 10.

Application Procedure: Applicants must submit an application form, research proposal and letter from advisor. Candidates should contact the Foundation for application materials.

Closing Date: February 1st.

No. of awards given last year: 10.

No. of applicants last year: 150.

Additional Information: A final report to the Foundation is mandatory. Recipients of Dissertation Fellowships must submit a copy of the dissertation, approved and accepted by the home university or college, within six months of the end of the award year. The award is only available in circumstances where all necessary research has been done and the dissertation will be complete within one year.

Harry Frank Guggenheim Research Program

Subjects: Support is provided mainly for basic research in the social, behavioural and biological sciences. However, research which is related to the Foundation's programme will be considered regardless of the disciplines involved.

Purpose: To promote understanding of the human social condition through the study of the causes and consequences of dominance, aggression and violence.

Eligibility: Open to individuals or institutions in any country.

Level of Study: Postdoctorate, Postgraduate.

Type: Research grant.

Value: Up to US$35,000 per year. Contact the organisation for more details.

Length of Study: One year. Two or three year projects may be considered.

Frequency: Annual.

Country of Study: Any country.

No. of awards offered: Between 15 and 35 grants per year. Awards are based predominately on merit.

Application Procedure: Applicants must submit an application form and research proposal along with a curriculum vitae and budget request. Application materials are available by contacting the Foundation.

Closing Date: August 1st.

No. of awards given last year: 46.

No. of applicants last year: 324.

Additional Information: The Foundation operates a programme of specific and innovative study and research. Proposals should be for a specific project and should describe well defined aims and methods, not general institutional support. Grants will be considered for salaries, employee benefits, research assistantships, computer time, supplies and equipment, field work, reasonable secretarial and technical help and other items necessary to the successful completion of a project. The Foundation cannot supply funds for overhead costs of institutions, travel to professional meetings, publication subsidies, self education or elaborate fixed equipment.

THE HARRY S TRUMAN LIBRARY INSTITUTE

500 West US Highway 24, Independence, MO, 64050, United States of America
Tel: (1) 816 833 0425
Fax: (1) 816 833 2715
Email: library@truman.nara.gov
www: http://www.trumanlibrary.org/grants
Contact: Ms Lisa Sullivan, Grants Administrator

The Harry S Truman Library Institute is a non-profit partner of the Harry S Truman Library.

Harry S Truman Library Institute Dissertation Year Fellowships

Subjects: The public career of Harry S Truman and the history of the Truman administration.

Purpose: To encourage historical scholarship in the Truman era.

Eligibility: Open to individuals who have completed their dissertation research and are ready to begin writing. Dissertations must be on some aspect of the life and career of Harry S Truman or of the public and policy issues which were prominent during the Truman years.

Level of Study: Postgraduate.

Type: Fellowship.

Value: US$16,000, payable in two instalments.

Frequency: Annual.

Country of Study: United States of America.

No. of awards offered: One-two.

Application Procedure: Application forms are available from the website.

Closing Date: February 1st for notification in April.

Funding: Private.

No. of awards given last year: One.

No. of applicants last year: Eight.

Additional Information: Recipients will not be required to come to the Truman Library but will be expected to furnish the Library with a copy of their dissertation.

Harry S Truman Library Institute Research Grants

Subjects: The public career of Harry S Truman and the history of the Truman administration.

Purpose: To enable graduate students and postdoctoral scholars to come to the library to use its archival facilities.

Eligibility: Open to graduate students and postdoctoral Scholars who are working on a project pertaining to Truman's public career or to some facet of his administration.

Level of Study: Doctorate, Graduate, Postdoctorate, Postgraduate, Research.

Type: Research grant.

Value: Up to US$2,500, to cover round trip air fare between the applicant's home and Independence, and a modest sum to cover living expenses while working at the Library.

Length of Study: One-three weeks.

Study Establishment: The Library.

Country of Study: United States of America.

No. of awards offered: Varies.

Application Procedure: Application forms are available from the website.

Closing Date: April 1st or October 1st.

Funding: Private.

No. of awards given last year: 21.

No. of applicants last year: 42.

Harry S Truman Library Institute Scholar's Award

Subjects: Some aspect of the life and career of Harry S Truman or of the public and foreign policy issues which were prominent during the Truman years.

Purpose: To free a Scholar from teaching or other employment for a substantial period of time for the purpose of writing a book length manuscript on some aspect of Harry S Truman or his era.
Eligibility: Open to established Scholars and Scholars about to embark on their careers.
Level of Study: Postgraduate.
Value: Up to US$30,000.
Frequency: Every two years if funds are available.
Study Establishment: An applicant's work should be based in part on extensive research at the Truman Library.
Country of Study: United States of America.
No. of awards offered: One.
Application Procedure: Applicants must write for details.
Closing Date: December 15th.
Funding: Private.
No. of awards given last year: One.
Additional Information: The research should result in a book length manuscript intended for publication. One copy of the publication resulting from work done under the award is to be provided by the author to the Library.

HARRY S TRUMAN SCHOLARSHIP FOUNDATION

712 Jackson Place North West, Washington, DC, 20006, United States of America
Tel: (1) 202 395 4831
Fax: (1) 202 395 6995
Email: staff@truman.gov
www: http://www.truman.gov

The Harry S Truman Scholarship Foundation was established by Congress in 1975 as the official federal memorial to honour the 33rd President of the United States of America. The Foundation recognises President Truman's contributions to the nation, his commitment to public service and his interest in education.

Harry S Truman Scholarship Foundation Scholarships
Subjects: Public service. The Foundation defines this as employment in the following: government at any level, uniformed services, public interest organisations, non-governmental research or educational organisations, and public service oriented non-profit organisations such as those whose primary purposes are to help needy or disadvantaged persons or to protect the environment. A wide variety of fields of study can lead to public service careers, for example, agriculture, biology, engineering, environmental management, physical and social sciences, as well as traditional fields such as economics, education, government, history, international relations, law, political science, public administration, public health and public policy.
Purpose: To reward outstanding students who intend to pursue careers in public service.
Eligibility: Open to United States citizens or, in the case of nominees from American Samoa or the Commonwealth of the Northern Mariana Islands, United States nationals. Candidates should be at college or university pursuing a Bachelor's degree as full-time students. Applicants must have a college grade point average of at least B (or equivalent) and be in the upper fourth of their class.
Level of Study: Graduate.
Type: Scholarship.
Value: Up to US$30,000.
Frequency: Annual.
Country of Study: United States of America, some programmes abroad are upon approval of the Executive Secretary.
No. of awards offered: 75-85.
Application Procedure: Applicants must be nominated by a faculty representative at their Institute of Higher Education. The Foundation neither solicits nor accepts direct candidate applications. Junior means a student who has one more year of full-time study to complete the requirements for a Baccalaureate degree.
Closing Date: January 29th.

Funding: Government.

HARVARD BUSINESS SCHOOL

Morgan 295
Soldiers Field, Boston, MA, 02163, United States of America
Tel: (1) 617 495 9102
Fax: (1) 617 496 5985
Email: kabdelmeguid@hbs.edu
www: http://www.hbs.edu
Contact: Grants Management Officer

Alfred D Chandler Jr Travelling Fellowships in Business History and Institutional Economic History
Subjects: Business history and institutional economic history. Topics such as labour relations and government regulation will also be considered if the approach is primarily institutional.
Purpose: To facilitate library and archival research.
Eligibility: Open to Harvard University graduate students in history, economics, business administration or a related discipline such as sociology, government or law, whose research requires travel to distant archives or repositories. Graduate students or non tenured faculty in those fields from other North American universities, whose research requires travel to the Boston and Cambridge area. Study of the collections at the Baker, Widener, McKay, Law, Kress or Houghton libraries is also eligible.
Level of Study: Postgraduate.
Type: Fellowship.
Value: US$1,000-3,000 from a total of approx. US$15,000.
Frequency: Annual.
Country of Study: Any country.
No. of awards offered: Varies.
Application Procedure: Applicants must complete an application form, available on request.
Closing Date: December 1st.
Funding: Private.

Harvard-Newcomen Fellowship in Business History
Subjects: Any research project connected with economic and business history.
Purpose: To assist young scholars in improving their professional acquaintance with business and economic history and to allow them to engage in research that will benefit from the resources of the Harvard Business School and the Boston-Cambridge scholarly community.
Eligibility: Open to applicants who have received a PhD within the 10 years preceding the start of the fellowship. Harvard University is an equal opportunity, affirmative action employer.
Level of Study: Postdoctorate.
Type: Fellowship.
Value: US$46,000.
Length of Study: One year.
Frequency: Annual.
Study Establishment: Harvard Business School for one year, including participation in the business history course and seminar, one semester each, plus other courses the applicant wishes to audit.
Country of Study: United States of America.
No. of awards offered: One.
Application Procedure: Applicants must complete an application form, available on request.
Closing Date: November 1st.
Funding: Private.

HARVARD LAW SCHOOL

ILS 331
1557 Massachusetts Avenue, Cambridge, MA, 02138, United States of America
Tel: (1) 617 495 3356
Fax: (1) 617 495 1110
Email: mcpherso@law.harvard.edu
www: http://www.law.harvard.edu
Contact: Grants Management Officer

Established in 1817, Harvard Law School is the oldest existing law school in the United States of America. The School provides comprehensive and enlightened training to prepare its graduates for law practice, public service at the local, state, federal and international levels, law teaching and legal scholarship.

Harvard Law School Liberal Arts Fellowship

Subjects: Law.
Purpose: To enable teachers in the social sciences or humanities to study fundamental techniques, concepts and aims of law so that in their teaching and research they will be better able to use legal materials and legal insights which are relevant to their own disciplines.
Eligibility: Open to college and university teachers in the arts and sciences. There are no further eligibility restrictions.
Level of Study: Professional development.
Type: Fellowship.
Value: Tuition and a health clinic fee only, as well as provision of office space.
Length of Study: One year.
Frequency: Annual.
Country of Study: United States of America.
No. of awards offered: Four-five.
Application Procedure: Applicants must submit a curriculum vitae including an academic record and a list of biological publications, a statement explaining what the applicant hopes to achieve through the year of study and two letters of recommendation. These letters must be mailed directly to the Chair from the referees.
Closing Date: January 15th.

HARVARD UNIVERSITY

Weatherhead Center for International Affairs
1737 Cambridge Street, Cambridge, MA, 02138, United States of America
Tel: (1) 617 495 3671
Fax: (1) 617 495 8292
www: http://www.harvard.edu
Contact: CFIA Fellowship Office

Harvard University, which celebrated its 350th anniversary in 1986, is the oldest Institute of Higher Education in the United States. Founded 16 years after the arrival of the pilgrims at Plymouth, the university has grown from nine students with a single master to an enrolment of more than 18,000 degree candidates, including undergraduates and students in 10 graduate and professional schools.

The Harvard Academy Program for International and Area Studies Predoctoral and Postdoctoral Fellowships

Subjects: The programme focuses on training social scientists in area studies, especially those areas of the world that require the use of difficult languages, or conversely, assisting area specialists in developing expertise in an established discipline.
Purpose: To identify young scholars at the start of their careers whose work combines disciplinary excellence in the social sciences with an in-depth grounding in particular countries or regions outside the United States or Canada.
Eligibility: Open to predoctoral applicants who have completed all course work and general examinations by the beginning of the first year for which they seek support, and also to postdoctoral Scholars.

Level of Study: Doctorate, Postdoctorate, Predoctorate.
Type: Fellowship.
Value: Predoctoral awards are US$24,000, plus university facilities. Postdoctoral awards are US$34,000, plus health insurance.
Length of Study: Two years.
Frequency: Annual.
Study Establishment: The Weatherhead Center for International Affairs (WCFIA), Harvard University.
Country of Study: United States of America.
No. of awards offered: Varies, four to six for two year appointments.
Application Procedure: Applicants must contact Jeana Flahive at the Weatherhead Center for more information on (1) 617 495 2137 or email jflahive@cfia.harvard.edu.
Closing Date: October 15th, but contact the organisation for confirmation.
Funding: Private.

The Harvard University Graduate Student Associate Program

Subjects: Fields of study include anthropology, economics, government, history, East Asian history and languages, law, Middle Eastern studies, public policy, sociology, population and international health, inner Asian and Altaic studies.
Purpose: To provide a supportive and stimulating environment in which promising graduate students can interact with one another as well as with faculty and fellows of the Center, as they complete their dissertations and begin the transition to a career.
Eligibility: Students in a PhD programme or similarly advanced degree programme at any of Harvard's academic departments or professional schools may apply. Students who are accepted will have finished their coursework, completed general exams and have a focus relating to the core interests of the Weatherhead Center. Preference is then given to those applicants whose work is related to current research projects at the Center.
Level of Study: Doctorate, Predoctorate.
Type: Associateship.
Value: Graduate student associates receive research grants of US$500-2,000 and are provided with office space equipped with computers and printers.
Study Establishment: The Weatherhead Center for International Affairs (WCFIA), Harvard University.
Country of Study: United States of America.
Application Procedure: Applicants should contact Clare Putnam at the Weatherhead Center for more information on (1) 617 495 9899, or email cputnam@cfia.harvard.edu.
Closing Date: March 1st, but please contact the university for confirmation.
Funding: Private.
Additional Information: Selected GSAs are expected to participate in the programme's seminars and activities, including support of undergraduate associates of the Center. GSAs may renew their affiliation for up to three years. The interests of the Weatherhead Center are broadly defined to encompass research on international, transnational and comparative topics, both contemporary and historical, including rigorous policy analysis as well as the study of countries and regions other than the United States.

John M Olin Institute for Strategic Studies Predoctoral and Postdoctoral Fellowships in National Security

Subjects: The causes and conduct of war, military strategy and history, defence policy and institutions, economic security, defence economics and the defence industrial base.
Purpose: To support young scholars conducting basic research in the broad area of security and strategic affairs, including the economics of these issues.
Eligibility: Open to predoctoral candidates who have completed all course work and general examinations by the beginning of the year for which they seek support. Also open to postdoctoral Scholars.
Level of Study: Doctorate, Postdoctorate.
Type: Fellowship.

Value: Predoctoral awards are up to US$20,000 plus university facilities, fees and health insurance. Postdoctoral awards are up to US$35,000 plus health insurance.
Frequency: Annual.
Study Establishment: The Weatherhead Center for International Affairs (WCFIA), Harvard University.
Country of Study: United States of America.
No. of awards offered: Up to 10 but may vary.
Application Procedure: Applicants must contact Ann Townes at the Weatherhead Center for more information on (1) 617 496 5495, or email atownes@cfia.harvard.edu.
Closing Date: January 15th, but please contact the organisation for confirmation.

Program on US-Japan Relations Advanced Research Fellowships

Subjects: Issues or problems in contemporary United States-Japanese relations, Japan's international relations and other studies of Japan that contribute to an understanding of Japan's international behaviour.
Purpose: To support the work of scholars engaged in the study of contemporary Japan and/or the relations between the United States of America and Japan.
Eligibility: Preference is given to non Japanese citizens, but others, especially from Pacific Rim countries, may apply. Applicants must hold a doctoral or other terminal degree in a discipline bearing on the study of contemporary United States of America and Japanese relations, other aspects of Japan's foreign relations, or domestic Japanese politics and policy. Applicants must demonstrate significant scholarly achievement or potential.
Level of Study: Postdoctorate.
Type: Fellowship.
Value: Up to US$35,000 plus health insurance and shared office space.
Frequency: Annual.
Study Establishment: The Weatherhead Center for International Affairs (WCFIA), Harvard University.
Country of Study: United States of America.
No. of awards offered: Two or three.
Application Procedure: Applicants must contact Frank Schwartz at the Weatherhead Center for more information on (1) 617 495 1890, or email fschwart@cfia.harvard.edu. Applications can also be downloaded from http://data.fas.harvard.edu/cfia/us-japan/pdapplication.htm.
Closing Date: March 1st, but please contact the organisation for confirmation.
Funding: Private.

Sidney R Knafel Dissertation Completion Grant

Subjects: The core interests of the Weatherhead Center. These interests are broadly defined as research on international, transnational and comparative topics (both contemporary and historical) including rigorous policy analysis as well as the study of countries and regions other than the United States.
Purpose: To aid a Harvard doctoral candidate who is completing a dissertation related to the core research interests of the Centre.
Eligibility: Applicants must be currently enrolled at Harvard University, PhD candidates (or doctoral degree candidates from other Harvard faculties) and likely to complete their degree by the end of the academic year for which the Fellowship is awarded. The recipient may not accept any other grants or teaching fellowships during the tenure of this Fellowship.
Level of Study: Doctorate, Predoctorate.
Type: Fellowship.
Value: A stipend of US$18,200 plus facilities fees and individual health insurance. Office space and access to computer facilities at the Weatherhead Center will also provided.
Length of Study: One year.
Frequency: Annual.
Study Establishment: The Weatherhead Center for International Affairs (WCFIA), Harvard University.
Country of Study: United States of America.

Application Procedure: Applicants must contact Clare Putnam at the Weatherhead Center for more information on (1) 617 495 9899, or email cputnam@cfia.harvard.edu.
Closing Date: March 1st, but please contact the organisation for confirmation.
Funding: Private.
Additional Information: Named after Sidney R Knafel who served as chairman of the Centre's Visiting Committee from 1991-2000.

Thyssen Postdoctoral Fellowship

Subjects: Transnational security issues.
Purpose: To assist young German scholars and to form an interdisciplinary group studying transnational security issues.
Eligibility: Applicants must be German nationals. Fellowships are offered for research conducted while in residence at the Weatherhead Center for International Affairs, Harvard University.
Level of Study: Postdoctorate.
Type: Fellowship.
Value: US$40,000 plus health insurance plus shared office space.
Frequency: Annual.
Country of Study: United States of America.
No. of awards offered: One.
Application Procedure: Applicants must contact Clare Putnam at the Weatherhead Center for more information on (1) 617 495 9899, or email cputnam@cfia.harvard.edu.
Closing Date: February 15th, but please contact the organisation for confirmation.
Funding: Private.

Weatherhead Center Predissertation Grants

Subjects: The core interests of the Weatherhead Center. These interests are broadly defined as research on international, transnational and comparative topics (both contemporary and historical) including rigorous policy analysis as well as the study of countries and regions other than the United States.
Purpose: To aid graduate students who have passed preliminary exams and who are exploring or beginning research on a project related to the core research interests of the Center.
Eligibility: Applicants must be currently enrolled at Harvard University and of predoctoral, or similarly advanced, degree status who will have finished their preliminary exams.
Level of Study: Predoctorate.
Type: Grant.
Value: Approx. US$3,000.
Frequency: Annual.
Study Establishment: The Weatherhead Center for International Affairs (WCFIA), Harvard University.
Country of Study: United States of America.
No. of awards offered: Up to seven.
Application Procedure: Applicants must contact Clare Putnam at the Weatherhead Center for more information on (1) 617 495 9899, or email cputnam@cfia.harvard.edu.
Closing Date: March. Please contact the organisation for confirmation.

Weatherhead Grants for Graduate Student Conferences

Subjects: International politics.
Purpose: To offer financial resources for graduate student conferences at Harvard that address topics relating to international affairs.
Eligibility: Open to graduates who need funds to support conferences related to international affairs that directly benefit graduate students. Preference will be given to conferences that have not been previously funded.
Level of Study: Graduate.
Type: Grant.
Value: Up to US$1,000.
Frequency: Twice a year.
Study Establishment: Harvard University.
Country of Study: United States of America.

Application Procedure: Applicants must contact Clare Putnam at the Weatherhead Center for more information on (1) 617 495 9899, or email cputnam@cfia.harvard.edu.
Closing Date: Mid October and mid-February.

HARVARD UNIVERSITY, CENTER FOR THE STUDY OF WORLD RELIGIONS

42 Francis Avenue, Cambridge, MA, 02138, United States of America
Tel: (1) 617 496 5834
Fax: (1) 617 496 5411
Email: brooke_palmer@harvard.edu
www: http://www.hds.harvard.edu/cswr
Contact: Ms Brooke Palmer, Co-ordinator of Educative Planning

Harvard University, Center for the Study of World Religions fosters excellence in the study of religions of the world. Two characteristics mark the Center, the first being the international scope of its subject matter and constituency, and the second the encouragement of multiple disciplinary approaches towards the study of religion. The Center offers no scheduled courses of instruction but rather is distinguished by the quality of scholars in residence, senior Fellows and others, affiliated faculty, and visiting lecturers.

Harvard University, Center for the Study of World Religions, Senior Fellowship

Subjects: Religious studies including the historical and comparative study of religions.
Purpose: To provide individual scholars from many nations with time for investigation and access to the resources of Harvard University. It also facilitates the exchange of ideas growing out of such research.
Eligibility: Open to postdoctoral Scholars who, in their research projects, utilise multiple disciplinary approaches toward the study of religion, whether from the point of view of arts, medicine, law, music, economics or cosmological sciences.
Level of Study: Postdoctorate.
Type: Fellowship.
Value: Senior Fellowships include admission to the Director's Seminar, University library access, a US$4,000 stipend per academic year and the option of residence at the Center. In recognition of the Center's 40th Anniversary, up to four awards will be designated as 40th Anniversary Fellowships. Stipend awards for the 40th Anniversary Fellowships will range from US$25,000-50,000 per academic year, and also include a research assistant allowance of US$1,000, a relocation allowance of US$1,500, use of a shared office at the Center, and the option of residence at the Center.
Length of Study: One academic year.
Frequency: Annual.
Study Establishment: Harvard University Center for the Study of World Religions, in Cambridge Massachusetts.
Country of Study: United States of America.
No. of awards offered: Varies.
Application Procedure: Applicants must complete an application form, arrange for two letters of recommendation, the form for which are available on the website, and provide a research proposal and curriculum vitae.
Closing Date: January 15th.
Funding: Private.
No. of awards given last year: 12.
Additional Information: Funds are limited and the fellowship stipend awarded covers only a small fraction of the expenses facing visiting Center Fellows. Therefore, Scholars admitted as Fellows need to seek the bulk of their financial support from sources other than the Center.

THE HASTINGS CENTER

21 Malcolm Gordon Road, Garrison, NY, 10524, United States of America
Tel: (1) 914 424 4040
Fax: (1) 845 424 4545
Email: visitors@thehastingscenter.org
www: http://www.thehastingscenter.org
Contact: Mr Lori P Knowles, Executive Vice President

The Hastings Center is an independent, non-profit research and educational institute that studies ethical, social and legal issues in medicine, the life sciences, health policy and environment policy.

The Hastings Center International Visiting Scholars Program

Subjects: Ethical, legal and policy issues in medicine, the life sciences and the professions.
Purpose: To enable international visiting scholars to spend time at the Center for advanced study and research.
Eligibility: Open to international Scholars.
Level of Study: Doctorate, Postdoctorate, Predoctorate.
Type: Stipend.
Value: Some financial aid is available based on need.
Length of Study: Usually four-six weeks.
Frequency: Annual.
Study Establishment: The Hastings Center.
Country of Study: United States of America.
No. of awards offered: Varies.
Application Procedure: Applicants must visit the website for applications. A detailed description of a research topic and work plan is also required as well as a copy of a recent writing sample, a curriculum vitae and the names and addresses of two referees.
Closing Date: Applications are accepted at any time, but should be submitted at least three months prior to the proposed stay.
No. of awards given last year: 13.
No. of applicants last year: 15.
Additional Information: Participation in the ongoing activities of the Center such as conferences, seminars and workshops is encouraged.

HATTORI FOUNDATION

72E Leopold Road, London, SW19 7JQ, England
Tel: (44) 20 8944 5319
Fax: (44) 20 8946 6970
Contact: Ms Sarah C Hallan, Administrator

The chief aim of the Hattori Foundation is to encourage and assist exceptionally talented young instrumental soloists or chamber ensembles who are British nationals or resident in the United Kingdom, and whose talent and achievement give promise of an international career.

Hattori Foundation Awards

Subjects: Solo performance, instrumental and ensembles.
Purpose: To assist young instrumentalists of exceptional talent in establishing a solo or chamber music career at international level.
Eligibility: Open to British or foreign nationals, aged 21-27 years, studying full-time in the United Kingdom. Foreign applicants must have won a major prize in an international competition or won a national competition. Candidates should be of postgraduate performance status.
Level of Study: Postgraduate, Professional development.
Type: Individual project assistance.
Value: No pre-determined amounts. The grant is based on the requirements of the approved project.
Length of Study: Varies, one year maximum.
Frequency: Annual.

Country of Study: British nationals can study in any country. Foreign nationals must be resident in the United Kingdom only.
No. of awards offered: Up to 20.
Application Procedure: Applicants must submit a completed application form with reference forms, plus 30 minutes of performance (recital) on cassette tape or compact disc.
Closing Date: April 30th.
Funding: Private.
Contributor: Hattori family.
No. of awards given last year: 16.
No. of applicants last year: 59.
Additional Information: Grants may be made for study, concert experience, and international competitions. Projects must be submitted for approval and discussion with the Director of Music and the trustees. Auditions take place in June and are in two stages.

HAYSTACK MOUNTAIN SCHOOL OF CRAFTS

PO Box 518, Deer Isle, ME, 04627, United States of America
Tel: (1) 207 348 2306
Fax: (1) 207 348 2307
Email: haystack@haystack-mtn.org
www: http://www.haystack-mtn.org
Contact: Ms Jacqueline Michaud, Development Director

The Haystack Mountain School of Crafts studio programme in the arts offers two and three week workshops in a variety of craft and visual mediums including clay, wood, glass, metals, fibres and graphics.

Haystack Scholarship
Subjects: Instruction in fine crafts.
Purpose: To allow craftspeople of all skill levels to study at Haystack sessions for two or three week periods. Technical Assistant and work study positions as well as minority scholarships and fellowships are awarded.
Eligibility: Open to nationals of any country, who are 18 or older.
Level of Study: Unrestricted.
Type: Scholarship and fellowship.
Value: US$500-1,000.
Length of Study: Two week and three week sessions.
Frequency: Annual.
Country of Study: Any country.
No. of awards offered: 100.
Application Procedure: Applicants must include references and supporting materials in their application.
Closing Date: March 25th.
Funding: Private.
No. of awards given last year: 100.
No. of applicants last year: 300.

HEALTH RESEARCH BOARD (HRB)

73 Lower Baggot Street, Dublin, 2, Ireland
Tel: (353) 1 676 1176
Fax: (353) 1 661 1856
Email: hrb@hrb.ie
www: http://www.hrb.ie
Contact: Medical & Health Service Research Manager

The Health Research Board (HRB) is comprised of 16 members appointed by the Minister of Health, with eight of the members being nominated on the co-joint nomination of the universities and colleges. The main functions of the HRB are to promote or commission health research, to promote and conduct epidemiological research as may be appropriate at national level, to promote or commission health services research, to liase and co-operate with other research bodies in Ireland and overseas in the promotion of relevant research, and to undertake such other cognate functions as the Minister may from time to time determine.

Health Research Board and British Council Research Visits Scheme
Subjects: Medicine and health biomedical sciences, epidemiology, dentistry, psychology, social sciences and economics.
Purpose: To facilitate Irish and British researchers in developing collaborative research projects in the biomedical and health research fields, by supporting travel and subsistence associated with short-term research visits. There is particular interest in supporting new research links.
Eligibility: Open to full-time research staff, although part of the funding may be used to support travel and subsistence of research students. Collaboration must be based on a joint research proposal and achievable objectives. At least one of the collaborating partners must be a member of staff of an Institute of Higher Education. The focus of the subvention requested should be on the travel and subsistence necessary for bringing the partners together. Priority will be given to projects which demonstrate clear additional benefits which will arise from support.
Value: UK £500-1,000 to cover travel, subsistence and, in exceptional circumstances, consumables.
Length of Study: Six weeks.
Frequency: Annual.
No. of awards offered: 20-30.
Application Procedure: Applicants must complete an application form, available from the website.
Funding: Government.
Contributor: Irish participants are supported by the Health Research Board and United Kingdom participants by the British Council.

Health Services Research Fellowships
Subjects: Clinical, epidemiological, public health, statistics, health economics, social science, operational and management disciplines.
Purpose: To enable graduates with some appropriate relevant experience to pursue a career in health devices and research in Ireland.
Eligibility: Candidates must normally hold a primary degree in a discipline relevant to health services research, have acquired appropriate postgraduate experience in the field of health services and research, have support from an approved academic department or centre, have obtained the prior approval of a head of department for the research study being proposed, be Irish citizens or graduates from overseas with a permanent Irish resident status.
Level of Study: Graduate.
Type: Fellowship.
Value: Please consult the organisation.
Length of Study: Normally the maximum period of the award will be three years, with renewal being subject to appropriate annual review.
Frequency: Annual.
Study Establishment: Institutions approved by the Board, such as teaching hospitals, universities, research institutes and health boards in Ireland.
Country of Study: Ireland.
No. of awards offered: Varies.
Application Procedure: Applicants must complete an application form, available from the website.
Funding: Government.
Additional Information: It is envisaged that Fellows will spend up to 30 per cent of their time in an advisory or resource centre role.

HRB Clinical Research Training Fellowships
Subjects: Biomedicine.
Purpose: To enable medical and dental graduates at any stage in their career to gain specialised research training in the biomedical field in Ireland.

Eligibility: Candidates should be graduates in medicine or dentistry from post registration up to and including senior registrar or equivalent academic level.
Level of Study: Graduate, Postdoctorate, Postgraduate.
Value: Please consult the organisation.
Length of Study: Normally two years.
Frequency: Annual.
Study Establishment: At an appropriate academic department in the Republic of Ireland.
Country of Study: Ireland.
No. of awards offered: Varies.
Application Procedure: Applicants must apply with the support of the head of an appropriate sponsoring laboratory in the Republic of Ireland. Candidates may apply to remain in their current laboratory, to return to one where they have worked before, or move to a new laboratory. Applicants must write to the Research Grants Section at the Health Research Board for more information.
Funding: Government.
Additional Information: Proposals may be submitted for specialised research training or for training in a basic subject relevant to a particular clinical interest.

HRB Equipment Grants

Subjects: Health and health related biological sciences.
Purpose: To facilitate the purchase of medium sized items of equipment aimed at improving the quality or broadening the scope of a scientific research investigation being undertaken.
Eligibility: Applicants should hold a full-time academic post in an Irish university or college and be actively engaged in biomedical research in Ireland.
Level of Study: Postdoctorate, Research.
Type: Grant.
Value: Varies.
Study Establishment: An Irish academic institution.
No. of awards offered: Varies, depending on the quality of the applications received.
Application Procedure: Applicants must write for details. Applications for equipment that is essential for the conduct of biomedical research may be made and applications will be assessed on the basis of the research case presented.
Funding: Government.
Additional Information: Applications reflecting interdepartmental collaboration are particularly welcome. A matching funds contribution from the receiving institution is encouraged.

HRB Postdoctoral Research Fellowships

Subjects: Biomedicine.
Eligibility: Applicants must be postdoctorates with less than five years of postdoctoral experience.
Level of Study: Postdoctorate.
Type: Fellowship.
Value: Please consult the organisation.
Length of Study: Up to three years.
Frequency: Annual.
Study Establishment: A university, research hospital or institute.
Country of Study: Ireland.
No. of awards offered: Varies.
Application Procedure: Applicants must complete an application form, available from the website.

HRB Project Grants Co-Funded in Health Services Research

Subjects: Any discipline relevant to health services research.
Purpose: To facilitate the development of health services research by providing support for research projects and pilot studies which might lead to larger research proposals.
Eligibility: Open to applicants from any of the health professions, academic disciplines or other relevant backgrounds.
Value: Please contact the organisation.
Length of Study: Varies, but it is expected that most projects will be completed within one year.

Frequency: Annual.
Country of Study: Ireland.
Application Procedure: Applicants must obtain an application form, available by on written request or from the website.
Funding: Government.

HRB Project Grants-General

Subjects: Biomedical sciences, public health and epidemiology, health services research or health research.
Purpose: To facilitate research in biomedical sciences, public health, epidemiology and health service research.
Eligibility: The principal must hold a full-time academic post in an Irish academic institution and his or her speciality should be within the range of disciplines stated in the subject index. Applicants must reside in the Republic of Ireland and grants are tenable in this country.
Value: Please consult the organisation.
Frequency: Annual.
Study Establishment: An Irish academic institution.
Country of Study: Ireland.
No. of awards offered: Varies.
Application Procedure: Applicants must complete an application form, available on request or downloadable from the website.
Funding: Government.

HRB Research Project Grants Inter-Disciplinary

Subjects: Engineering, information technology, humanities, medicine, science and the social sciences.
Purpose: To promote interdisciplinary research in addressing research topics directly related to improving human health.
Eligibility: At least one applicant should hold a full-time academic post in an Irish university or college and be actively engaged in research on a relevant health research topic.
Value: Please consult the organisation.
Length of Study: Two years.
Frequency: Annual.
Study Establishment: Recognised academic and health services centres.
Country of Study: Ireland.
No. of awards offered: Varies.
Application Procedure: Applicants must obtain an application form, available by writing or from the website.
Funding: Government.

HRB Research Project Grants North-South Co-operation

Subjects: Biomedical sciences, public health and epidemiology, health services research or health research.
Purpose: To stimulate co-operation between research investigators in the Republic of Ireland and in Northern Ireland by making grant support available for joint health research projects of a high quality.
Eligibility: Applicants should hold a full-time academic post in an Irish university or college and be actively engaged in medical, epidemiological, health service or health research in Ireland.
Value: Please consult the organisation.
Length of Study: One-three years.
Frequency: Annual.
Study Establishment: Recognised academic institutions and health service centres.
Country of Study: Ireland.
No. of awards offered: Varies.
Application Procedure: Applicants must complete an application form, available from the website.
Funding: Government.

HRB Summer Student Grants

Subjects: Medical, dental science, health service and science.
Purpose: To develop interest in research and give the student the opportunity to become familiar with research techniques.
Eligibility: Open to students from medical, dental science or health service related disciplines.
Type: Grant.

Value: Please consult the organisation.
Length of Study: Eight weeks.
Frequency: Annual.
Study Establishment: A university, research hospital or institution.
Country of Study: Ireland.
No. of awards offered: One per director.
Application Procedure: Applicants must obtain an application form, available by writing or from the website.
Funding: Government.

HEBREW IMMIGRANT AID SOCIETY (HIAS)

333 Seventh Avenue, New York, NY, 10001, United States of America
Tel: (1) 212 613 1358
Fax: (1) 212 629 0921
Email: info@hias.org
www: http://www.hias.org
Contact: Ms Phoebe Lewis, Scholarship Co-ordinator

The Hebrew Immigrant Aid Society (HIAS) is the international migration agency of the organised Jewish community.

HIAS Scholarship Awards Competition
Subjects: All subjects.
Purpose: To help HIAS-assisted refugees and their children in pursuing higher education.
Eligibility: Open to refugees and their children who were assisted by HIAS to come to the United States. Applicants must have completed one year ie. two semesters at a United States of America high school, college or graduate school.
Level of Study: Doctorate, Graduate, Postdoctorate, Postgraduate, Predoctorate, Professional development, Research.
Type: One time grant.
Value: Average US$1,500.
Length of Study: One year must be completed.
Frequency: Annual.
Country of Study: United States of America.
No. of awards offered: Varies.
Application Procedure: Applicants must complete an official application. Application requests must be in writing and include a stamped addressed envelope. Application forms are available from mid December each year.
Closing Date: March 15th.
Funding: Private.
No. of awards given last year: 143.
No. of applicants last year: 775.
Additional Information: Applications are judged on financial need, academic scholarship and community service.

HEBREW UNIVERSITY OF JERUSALEM

Institute of Jewish Studies
Mount Scopus Campus, Jerusalem, Israel
Tel: (972) 2 588 008
Fax: (972) 2 588 3004
www: http://www.huji.ac.il/unew/main.html
Contact: Mr Joel Alpert, Academic Secretary

Moritz and Charlotte Warburg Prizes
Subjects: Jewish studies.
Eligibility: Open to nationals of all countries. Candidates for PhD degrees should be 35 years of age or younger, postdoctoral candidates may be up to 40 years of age.
Level of Study: Doctorate, Postgraduate.
Type: Prize.
Value: US$5,000-7,000 per year.

Length of Study: One year, renewable.
Frequency: Annual.
Study Establishment: The Institute of Jewish Studies.
Country of Study: Israel.
No. of awards offered: Eight.
Application Procedure: Applicants must write for details.
Closing Date: End of December.

HEED OPHTHALMIC FOUNDATION

Cleveland Clinic Foundation
Desk I-32
9500 Euclid Avenue, Cleveland, OH, 44195, United States of America
Tel: (1) 216 445 8145
Fax: (1) 216 444 8968
Contact: Executive Secretary

Heed Award
Subjects: Diseases and surgery of the eye or research in ophthalmology.
Purpose: To provide assistance to men and women who desire to further their education or to conduct research in ophthalmology.
Eligibility: Open to United States citizens who are graduates of an institution approved by the AMA.
Level of Study: Postgraduate.
Type: Fellowship.
Value: US$1,250 per month for up to one year.
Length of Study: One year, non renewable.
Frequency: Annual.
Study Establishment: Universities or research institutions in the United States.
Country of Study: United States of America.
No. of awards offered: Approx. 25.
Application Procedure: Applicants must write for details.
Closing Date: January 15th.
Funding: Private.

HENRY A MURRAY RESEARCH CENTER

Radcliffe Institute for Advanced Study
Harvard University
10 Garden Street, Cambridge, MA, 02138, United States of America
Tel: (1) 617 495 8140
Fax: (1) 617 496 3993
Email: mrc@radcliffe.edu
www: http://www.radcliffe.edu/murray
Contact: Programme Co-ordinator

The Henry A Murray Research Center is a centre for research on the changing lives of American women. The Center's purpose is to promote the use of existing social science data to explore human development and social change. The archive holds over 230 studies available for new research.

Adolescent and Youth Research Award
Subjects: Social and behavioural sciences.
Purpose: To support predoctoral and postdoctoral researchers who focus on adolescent development projects drawing on the Center's data.
Eligibility: Predoctoral applicants must be enrolled in a doctoral programme in a relevant field, and must have their dissertation proposal approved by an advisor or committee before the grant application is made.
Level of Study: Doctorate, Postdoctorate, Predoctorate.
Type: Research grant.
Value: Predoctoral US$5,000 and postdoctoral US$10,000.
Frequency: Predoctoral is annual and postdoctoral is twice a year.

Country of Study: Any country.
No. of awards offered: Six.
Application Procedure: Applicants must submit six copies of a curriculum vitae including social security number, permanent home address and the name and address of a referee who has been asked to send a letter of recommendation directly to the programme. Also, an application for the Use of Data form and a Computer Data Request form should be submitted if applicable, as well as six copies of a proposal that describes the intended research and a covering letter.
Closing Date: The deadline for predoctoral applications is April 1st, and for postdoctoral applications is October 15th or March 15th.
Contributor: The W T Grant Foundation.
No. of applicants last year: Varies.

Henry A Murray Dissertation Award Program

Subjects: Social and behavioural studies.
Purpose: To enable doctoral students to undertake projects which focus on some aspect of the study of lives, concentrating on issues in human development or personality. Priority will be given to projects drawing on Center data.
Eligibility: Applicants must be enrolled in a doctoral programme in a relevant field and must have had their dissertation proposal approved by an advisor or committee before the grant application is made.
Level of Study: Doctorate, Predoctorate.
Type: Research grant.
Value: US$5,000.
Length of Study: One year.
Frequency: Annual.
Country of Study: Any country.
No. of awards offered: Three-four.
Application Procedure: Applicants must submit six copies of a curriculum vitae including their social security number, permanent home address and the name and address of a referee who has been asked to send a letter of recommendation directly to the programme. Also, an application for the Use of Data form and a Computer Data Request form should be submitted if applicable, as well as six copies of a proposal that describes the intended research and a covering letter.
Closing Date: April 1st.
Funding: Private.
Contributor: The Radcliffe Institute.
No. of awards given last year: Four.
No. of applicants last year: Varies.

Jeanne Humphrey Block Dissertation Award

Subjects: Social and behavioural studies.
Purpose: To enable a female doctoral student to undertake research on gender differences or some developmental issue of particular concern to girls or women. Projects drawing on Center data will be given priority, although this is not a requirement.
Eligibility: Applicants must be enrolled in a doctoral programme in a relevant field and must have had their dissertation proposal approved by an advisor or committee before the grant application is made.
Level of Study: Doctorate, Predoctorate.
Type: Award.
Value: US$5,000.
Length of Study: One year.
Frequency: Annual.
Country of Study: Any country.
No. of awards offered: One.
Application Procedure: Applicants must submit six copies of a curriculum vitae including their social security number, permanent home address and the name and address of a referee who has been asked to send a letter of recommendation directly to the programme. Also, an application for the Use of Data form and a Computer Data Request form should be submitted if applicable, as well as six copies of a proposal that describes the intended research and a covering letter.
Closing Date: April 1st.

Contributor: Murray Center Endowment.
No. of awards given last year: One.
No. of applicants last year: Varies.

The Mother/Child Interaction in Low Income Families Research Award

Subjects: Social and behavioural sciences.
Purpose: To support predoctoral and postdoctoral researchers using data from the Manpower Demonstration Research Corporation's Observational Studies for secondary analysis and comparative research which focuses on parenting and child development.
Eligibility: Predoctoral applicants must be enrolled in a doctoral programme in a relevant field, and must have their dissertation proposal approved by an advisor or committee before the grant application is made.
Level of Study: Doctorate, Postdoctorate, Predoctorate.
Type: Research grant.
Value: Predoctoral US$5000 and postdoctoral US$10,000.
Frequency: Annual.
Country of Study: Any country.
No. of awards offered: Two.
Application Procedure: Applicants must submit six copies of a curriculum vitae including their social security number, permanent home address and the name and address of a referee who has been asked to send a letter of recommendation directly to the programme should be attached to the proposal. Also, an application for the Use of Data form and a Computer Data Request form should be submitted if applicable, as well as six copies of a proposal that describes the intended research and a covering letter.
Closing Date: April 1st for predoctoral, October 15th and March 15th for postdoctoral.
Funding: Private.
Contributor: The Manpower Demonstration Research Group.

Studying Diverse Lives

Subjects: Social sciences.
Purpose: To allow social science researchers to use the Henry A Murray Research Center's Diversity Archive.
Eligibility: Open to postdoctoral researchers looking for data with racially and ethnically diverse samples to use in their work who have received their doctorate within the last ten years.
Level of Study: Postdoctorate.
Type: Research grant.
Value: US$10,000.
Frequency: Annual.
Country of Study: Any country.
No. of awards offered: Three.
Application Procedure: Applicants must submit six copies of a curriculum vitae including their social security number, permanent home address and the name and address of a referee who has been asked to send a letter of recommendation directly to the programme should be attached to the proposal. Also, an application for the Use of Data form and a Computer Data Request form should be submitted if applicable, as well as six copies of a proposal that describes the intended research and a covering letter.
Closing Date: February 1st and October 15th.
Contributor: The National Institute of Mental Health.
Additional Information: Grant recipients will be required to attend one of two research meetings at Harvard to discuss their work.

THE HENRY MOORE INSTITUTE

74 The Headrow, Leeds, West Yorkshire, LS1 3AA, England
Tel: (44) 113 246 7467
Fax: (44) 113 246 1481
Email: hmi@henry-moore.ac.uk
www: http://www.henry-moore-fdn.co.uk
Contact: Grants Management Officer

The Henry Moore Institute aims to enlarge the understanding of how sculpture makes meaning at different times and in different places through a programme of exhibitions, talks, conferences, publications and its collections.

Henry Moore Institute Research Fellowship

Subjects: Sculpture, both historical and contemporary.
Purpose: To enable scholars to use the Institute's facilities which include the sculpture collection, library, archive and slide library to assist them in researching their particular field.
Level of Study: Doctorate, Postdoctorate, Postgraduate, Research.
Type: Fellowship.
Value: Accommodation, travel and daily living expenses.
Length of Study: Usually one month.
Frequency: Annual.
Study Establishment: The Henry Moore Institute.
Country of Study: United Kingdom.
No. of awards offered: Usually four.
Application Procedure: Applicants must write to the research coordinator at the Henry Moore Institute, including a proposal and a curriculum vitae.
Closing Date: December 3rd.
Contributor: The Henry Moore Foundation.
No. of awards given last year: Four.
No. of applicants last year: 70.

THE HERB SOCIETY OF AMERICA, INC.

9019 Kirtland Chardon Road, Kirtland, OH, 44094, United States of America
Tel: (1) 440 256 0514
Fax: (1) 440 256 0541
Email: herbs@herbsociety.com
www: http://www.herbsociety.org
Contact: Ms Michelle Milks, Office Administrator

The aim of the Herb Society of America is to promote the knowledge, use and delight of herbs through educational programmes, research and sharing the experience of its members with the community.

Herb Society of America Research Grant

Subjects: Research on herbal projects.
Purpose: To further the knowledge and use of herbs and to contribute the results of the study and research to the records of horticulture, science, literature, history, art or economics.
Eligibility: Open to persons with a proposed programme of scientific, academic or artistic investigation of herbal plants.
Level of Study: Unrestricted.
Type: Research grant.
Value: Up to US$5,000.
Length of Study: Up to one year.
Frequency: Annual.
Country of Study: Any country.
Application Procedure: Applicants must submit an application in which all research must be defined clearly in 500 words or less and a proposed budget must be included with specific budget items listed. No requests for funds will be considered unless accompanied by five copies of the application form and proposal.
Closing Date: January 31st.
Contributor: Members.

No. of awards given last year: Two.
No. of applicants last year: 45.
Additional Information: Finalists will be interviewed.

HERBERT HOOVER PRESIDENTIAL LIBRARY ASSOCIATION

302 Parkside Drive
PO Box 696, West Branch, IA, 52358, United States of America
Tel: (1) 319 643 5327
Fax: (1) 319 643 2391
Email: info@hooverassociation.org
www: http://www.hooverassociation.org
Contact: Ms Patricia A Hand, Manager of Promotions & Academic Programs

The Herbert Hoover Presidential Library Association is a private non-profit support group for the Herbert Hoover Presidential Library Museum and National Historic Site in West Branch, Iowa.

Herbert Hoover Presidential Library Association Travel Grants

Subjects: American history, journalism, political science or economic history.
Purpose: To encourage scholarly use of the holdings, to promote the study of subjects of interest and concern to Herbert Hoover, Lou Henry Hoover and other public figures.
Eligibility: Open to current graduate students, postdoctoral students and qualified independent Scholars. Priority is given to well developed proposals that utilise the resources of the Hoover Presidential Library and which have the greatest likelihood of publication and subsequent use by educators, students and policy makers.
Level of Study: Doctorate, Graduate, Postdoctorate, Postgraduate, Professional development.
Type: Travel grant.
Value: Usually US$500-1,200 to cover the cost of a trip to the Library, but requests will be considered for longer research stays.
Frequency: Annual.
Study Establishment: The Herbert Hoover Presidential Library-Museum in West Branch, Iowa.
Country of Study: United States of America.
No. of awards offered: Varies.
Application Procedure: Applicants must submit a completed application form, a project proposal of up to 1,200 words, and three letters of reference mailed separately.
Closing Date: March 1st.
Funding: Private.
No. of awards given last year: Six.
No. of applicants last year: Eight.
Additional Information: For archival holdings information please contact the Association on (1) 319 643 5301.

HILDA MARTINDALE EDUCATIONAL TRUST

c/o Registry
Royal Holloway University of London, Egham, Surrey, TW20 0EX, England
Tel: (44) 1784 434455
Fax: (44) 1784 437520
Contact: Miss J L Hurn, Secretary to the Trustees

The Hilda Martindale Educational Trust was set up by Miss Hilda Martindale in order to help women of the British Isles with the costs of vocational training for any profession or career likely to be of use or value to the community. Applications are considered annually by six women trustees.

Hilda Martindale Exhibitions

Subjects: Any vocational training for a profession or career likely to be of value to the community.

Purpose: To assist with the costs of vocational training.

Eligibility: Open to women of the British Isles aged over 21 years.

Level of Study: Postgraduate, Professional development.

Type: Grant.

Value: Varies, normally UK £200-1,000.

Length of Study: One year.

Frequency: Annual.

Study Establishment: Any establishment in the United Kingdom approved by the trustees.

Country of Study: United Kingdom.

No. of awards offered: 25-35.

Application Procedure: Applicants must complete an application form (two copies), to be obtained from and returned to the Secretary to the Trustees.

Closing Date: March 1st for the following academic year. Late or retrospective applications will not be considered.

Funding: Private.

Contributor: Private trust.

No. of awards given last year: 26.

No. of applicants last year: 114.

Additional Information: Assistance is not given for short courses, courses abroad, elective studies, intercalated BSc years, access courses, or academic research. Awards are not given to those who are eligible for grants from LEAs, research councils, British Academy or other public sources.

HILGENFELD FOUNDATION FOR MORTUARY EDUCATION

PO Box 4311, Fullerton, CA, 92834, United States of America
Contact: Mr Chester Gromaki, President

Hilgenfeld Foundation Grant

Subjects: Mortuary science education.

Purpose: To support scholarships and research.

Eligibility: Open only to nationals of the United States.

Level of Study: Graduate, Postgraduate, Professional development.

Type: Research grant and research scholarship.

Length of Study: Varies.

Frequency: Annual.

Country of Study: United States of America.

No. of awards offered: Approx. 20.

Application Procedure: Applicants must submit an application on forms provided by the Hilgenfeld Foundation.

Closing Date: Applications are accepted at any time.

Funding: Private.

Contributor: The Hilgenfeld Family.

No. of awards given last year: 26.

No. of applicants last year: 100.

Additional Information: Scholarship grants are awarded through a co-operative effort between the Hilgenfeld Foundation and the American Board of Funeral Service.

For further information contact:

American Board of Funeral Service Education
38 Florida Avenue, Portland, ME, 04103, United States of America

THE HINRICHSEN FOUNDATION

10-12 Baches Street, London, N1 6DN, England
Contact: L E Adamson, Administrator

Hinrichsen Foundation Awards

Subjects: Contemporary music composition, performance and research.

Purpose: To promote the written areas of music by assisting contemporary composition, its performance and musical research.

Eligibility: Preference will be given to United Kingdom applicants and projects taking place in the United Kingdom. Grants are not given for recordings, for the funding of commissions, for degree or other study courses or for the purchase of instruments or equipment.

Value: Varies.

Frequency: Dependent on funds available.

No. of awards offered: Varies.

Application Procedure: Applicants must submit a completed application form with two references.

Closing Date: Applications are accepted at any time.

No. of awards given last year: 53.

No. of applicants last year: 117.

HISTORIC NEW ORLEANS COLLECTION

533 Royal Street, New Orleans, LA, 70130, United States of America
Tel: (1) 504 523 4662
Fax: (1) 504 598 7108
Email: info@hnoc.org
www: http://www.hnoc.org
Contact: Mr John Lawrence, Director of Museum Programmes

The Historic New Orleans Collection was established in 1966 by General and Mrs L Kemper Williams, private collectors of Louisiana material, to maintain and expand their collection and make it available to the public through research facilities and exhibitions.

The Kemper and Leila Williams Prize in Louisiana History

Subjects: History.

Purpose: To honour the best contribution to historical work about Louisiana.

Eligibility: There are no eligibility restrictions.

Level of Study: Unrestricted.

Type: Cash and plaque.

Value: US$1,500.

Frequency: Annual.

Country of Study: Any country.

No. of awards offered: One.

Application Procedure: Applicants must submit four copies of work and four copies of the application form.

Closing Date: January 15th for works published from the previous calendar year.

Funding: Private.

No. of awards given last year: One.

No. of applicants last year: 40.

Additional Information: The administration of these prizes is determined by a committee of Scholars chosen by the Louisiana Historical Association. Funding is provided by the Historic New Orleans Collection.

HISTORY OF SCIENCE SOCIETY (HSS)

HSS Executive Office
Box 351330
University of Washington, Seattle, WA, 98195, United States of America
Tel: (1) 206 543 9366
Fax: (1) 206 685 9544
Email: hssexec@u.washington.edu
www: http://www.hssonline.org
Contact: Mr Robert J Malone, Executive Director

The History of Science Society (HSS) is the world's largest society dedicated to understanding science, technology, medicine, and their interactions with society within their historical context.

HSS Travel Grant

Subjects: History, the history of science from ancient to modern times.
Purpose: For travel to the annual HSS meeting.
Eligibility: Eligibility is restricted to those who participate in the annual meeting. Preference is given to HSS members and those who have not been awarded a travel grant in the past two years.
Level of Study: Doctorate, Postdoctorate, Postgraduate.
Type: Travel grant.
Value: US$10-1,000.
Frequency: Annual.
Country of Study: United States of America.
No. of awards offered: Approx. 50.
Application Procedure: Applicants must apply to the HSS Executive Office.
Closing Date: June 1st.
Funding: Government.
Contributor: The National Science Foundation.
No. of awards given last year: 43.
No. of applicants last year: 48.
Additional Information: Applicants must book their ticket through the HSS affiliated travel agency, or show proof that a less expensive fare has been obtained. Other awards include the History of Women in Science Prize, Watson Davis and Helen Miles Davis Prize, Derek Price Award, Ida and Henry Schuman Prize, Pfizer Prize, Joseph H Hazen Education Prize.

HONDA FOUNDATION

6-20 Yaesu 2-chome
Chuo-ku, Tokyo, 104, Japan
Tel: (81) 3 3274 5125
Fax: (81) 3 3274 5103
Email: lej07727@nifty.ne.jp
www: http://www.soc.nii.ac.jp/hf/eng
Contact: Yutaka Ishihara, Secretary General

The Honda Foundation was established in December 1977 to contribute to the creation of true human civilisation on the basis of the philosophy of the late Mr Soichiro Honda, the founder of Honda Motor Company Limited.

Honda Prize

Subjects: To propose eco-technology, the new concept which harmonises the progress of technology and civilisation, rather than pursuing technology only designed for efficiency and profit.
Purpose: To be awarded annually to an individual or organisation, irrespective of nationality, for a distinguished achievement in the field of eco-technology.
Type: Prize.
Value: The prize includes a donation of yen 10,000,000 and an original medal.
Frequency: Annual.
Closing Date: March 31st every year.

Funding: Private.
Contributor: The late Mr Soichiro Honda, the founder of Honda Motor Company Limited.
No. of awards given last year: One.
No. of applicants last year: One.

HORTICULTURAL RESEARCH INSTITUTE

1000 Vermont Street North West
Suite 500, Washington, DC, 20005, United States of America
Tel: (1) 202 789 2900 ext. 3014
Fax: (1) 202 789 1893
Email: tjodon@anla.org
www: http://www.anla.org/research
Contact: Ms Teresa A Jodon, Research Communications & Grants Manager

The aim of the Horticultural Research Institute is to direct, fund, promote and communicate research which increases the quality and value of plants, improves the productivity and profitability of the nursery and landscape industry, and protects and enhances the environment.

Horticultural Research Institute Grants

Subjects: Nursery and landscape industry, especially concerning woody and perennial landscape plants, their production, marketing, landscape, water management or the environment.
Purpose: To support necessary research for the advancement of the nursery, greenhouse and landscape industry.
Eligibility: Open to nationals and permanent residents of the United States and Canada, who submit an appropriate project which the Institute feels is deserving of support.
Level of Study: Unrestricted.
Type: Grant.
Value: Varies US$5,000-125,000.
Length of Study: One year, occasionally renewable by reapplication.
Frequency: Annual.
Study Establishment: At state or federal research laboratories, land grant universities, forest research stations, botanical gardens and arboreta.
Country of Study: United States of America.
No. of awards offered: Over 35.
Application Procedure: Applicants must submit the application electronically.
Closing Date: May 15th.
Funding: Private.
Contributor: Nursery and landscape firms, as well as state and regional nursery and landscape associations.
No. of awards given last year: 37.
No. of applicants last year: 184.
Additional Information: Contact the Institute for a grant application packet, now available via the website.

THE HOSPITAL FOR SICK CHILDREN FOUNDATION

555 University Avenue
Suite 1725, Toronto, ON, M5G 1X8, Canada
Tel: (1) 416 813 6101
Fax: (1) 416 813 8142
Email: gwen.burrows@sickkids.on.ca
www: http://www.sickkids.on.ca/foundation
Contact: Ms Gwen Burrows, Grants Officer

The Hospital for Sick Children Foundation is a fundraising and granting organisation, dedicated to the betterment of the health of children. The Foundation is committed to supporting the broader aims of child health in Canada through an annual allocation to the National Grants Programme for paediatric research, health promotion, public education, postgraduate training and innovative community projects.

Duncan L Gordon Fellowships

Subjects: Paediatric health care, both clinical training and research training.
Purpose: To provide postdoctoral training.
Eligibility: Open to physicians and scientists wishing to obtain postdoctoral training, who are Canadian citizens or landed immigrants, are of outstanding academic achievement and can provide evidence of special aptitude for teaching and research.
Level of Study: Postdoctorate.
Type: Fellowship.
Value: Up to canadian $47,000 per year, dependent on the number of years of postdoctoral experience.
Length of Study: One-three years.
Frequency: Annual.
Study Establishment: Any agreed institution.
Country of Study: Any country.
No. of awards offered: Up to three.
Application Procedure: Applicants must be nominated by the head of the department in which they are involved. A project proposal and three letters of reference are required. Applicants should contact the office for current guidelines and application forms. Applicants must supply an outline of the course of study and detailed study plans indicating the location and facilities which will be available and the individual who would supervise his or her study. Application forms, guidelines and additional information can be found on the website.
Closing Date: October 1st.
Funding: Commercial, Private.
Contributor: A broad base of individual and corporate donors.
No. of awards given last year: One.
No. of applicants last year: Seven.
Additional Information: The candidate must indicate his or her objectives in paediatrics upon completion of the fellowship period.

Hospital for Sick Children Foundation External Research Grants

Subjects: All areas of paediatric health, including research into paediatric home care, native health, psychosocial health, clinical research or biomedical research.
Purpose: To support innovative research and research by new investigators.
Eligibility: Open to researchers in Canada who are working on projects which have significant potential to impact positively on child health in Canada.
Level of Study: Research.
Type: Grant.
Value: From canadian $1,000 per project, not to exceed canadian $65,000 per year for two years.
Length of Study: One-two years.
Frequency: Twice a year.
Study Establishment: Any agreed Canadian institution.
Country of Study: Canada.
No. of awards offered: Approx. 20.
Application Procedure: Applicants must make applications through the institution or organisation under whose auspices the project will be carried out. For further information, guidelines and application forms applicants should refer to the website.
Closing Date: There are two cycles, one in the Spring and one in the Autumn. Please contact the office or visit the website for exact dates.
Funding: Commercial, Private.
Contributor: A broad base of individual and corporate donors.
No. of awards given last year: 22.
No. of applicants last year: 95.
Additional Information: Grants will not be made to support annual campaigns, operating expenses, operating deficits, general

endowment or sustaining funds, projects which might result in gain or profit to the organisation, or building construction or improvement. The grant cycle takes about six months from letter of intent to the final decision.

For further information contact:

180 Dundas Street West
20th floor, Toronto, ON, M5G 1Z8, Canada

HOUBLON-NORMAN FUND

Secretary's Department HO-3
c/o Bank of England
Threadneedle Street, London, EC2R 8AH, England
Tel: (44) 20 7601 4751
Fax: (44) 20 7601 3210
Email: margot.wilson@bankofengland.co.uk
www: http://www.bankofengland.co.uk/houblonnorman
Contact: Miss Margot F Wilson, Secretary to the Fund

Houblon-Norman Fellowships

Subjects: Economics and finance.
Purpose: To promote research into and disseminate knowledge and understanding of the working, interaction and function of financial and business institutions in Great Britain and elsewhere and the economic conditions affecting them.
Eligibility: Open to distinguished research workers as well as younger postdoctoral or equivalent applicants of any nationality. Preference will be shown to British and EU nationals for fellowships.
Level of Study: Postdoctorate.
Type: Fellowship.
Value: The value of a fellowship is dependent on the candidate's circumstances and will be of such amount as seems necessary for undertaking the work. It might take the form of payment to the individual's employer.
Length of Study: From one month to one year.
Frequency: Annual.
Study Establishment: The Bank of England.
Country of Study: United Kingdom.
No. of awards offered: Varies.
Application Procedure: Applicants must complete an application form.
Closing Date: As advertised in the press.
No. of awards given last year: Three.
No. of applicants last year: 14.
Additional Information: Please see the website.

HOWARD HUGHES MEDICAL INSTITUTE (HHMI)

National Research Council
2101 Constitution Avenue, Washington, DC, 20418, United States of America
Tel: (1) 202 334 2872
Fax: (1) 202 334 3419
Email: infofell@nas.edu
www: http://national-academies.org/fellowships
Contact: Ms Judith O Willis, HHMI Programme Co-ordinator

Founded in 1953, the Howard Hughes Medical Institute (HHMI) is a medical research organisation whose scientists include many of the world's leaders in the fields of cell biology, genetics, immunology, neuroscience and structural biology. HHMI investigators carry out research at universities and academic medical centres across the United States.

Howard Hughes Medical Institute Predoctoral Fellowships

Subjects: Biological sciences.
Purpose: To promote excellence in biomedical research by helping prospective researchers with exceptional promise to obtain high quality graduate education.
Eligibility: Open to students at or near the beginning of their graduate study towards a PhD or ScD in any field of biological science.
Level of Study: Doctorate.
Type: Fellowship.
Value: US$31,000 includes US$21,000 stipend and US$16,000 cost of education allowance.
Length of Study: Up to five years.
Frequency: Annual.
Study Establishment: An Institute of Higher Education.
Country of Study: United States of America.
No. of awards offered: 80.
Application Procedure: Applicants must obtain application forms and instructions from the address shown or alternatively, may download them from the National Academy's website.
Closing Date: Early November. Awards are announced in April.
Funding: Private.
No. of awards given last year: 80.
No. of applicants last year: 1,110.

HUDSON RIVER FOUNDATION (HRF)

40 West 20th Street
9th Floor, New York, NY, 10011, United States of America
Tel: (1) 212 924 8290
Fax: (1) 212 924 8325
Email: info@hudsonriver.org
www: http://www.hudsonriver.org
Contact: Grants Management Officer

The Hudson River Foundation (HRF) supports scientific and public policy research, education, and projects to enhance public access to the Hudson River. The Foundation was established in 1981 under the terms of an agreement among environmental groups, government regulatory agencies and utility companies seeking the constructive resolution of a long series of legal controversies concerning the environmental impacts of power plants on the Hudson River.

The Hudson River Foundation Graduate Fellowships

Subjects: Research on the Hudson River system.
Eligibility: Applicants must be enrolled in an accredited programme, have a thesis advisor and advisory committee (if appropriate to the institution), and have a thesis research plan approved by the student's institution or department.
Level of Study: Doctorate, Graduate.
Type: Fellowship.
Value: Fellowships awarded to doctoral students will consist of a stipend of up to US$15,000 for one year and an incidentals research budget up to US$1,000. Fellowships awarded to Master's level students will consist of a stipend of up to US$11,000 for one year and an incidentals research budget of up to US$1,000.
Frequency: Annual.
No. of awards offered: Up to six.
Application Procedure: Applicants must obtain an HRF Call for Proposals booklet, available on request or from the website. Applications must include an HRF Proposal Cover Page, letter of interest, description of the project of up to 10 pages, timetable, statement of the significance and relevance of the project to the HRF's objectives, an estimate of the cost of supplies and travel using the HRF's Proposal Budget Summary Page, and a letter from the university stating that the student will receive a tuition waiver or reimbursement for the period of the fellowship. Two letters of recommendation, sent under separate cover are also required, one of which must be from the student's advisor and should certify the student's current status, evaluate the student's capabilities, and rate the student's project on

technical merit. The original and 10 copies of the proposal must be submitted to the Science Director.
Closing Date: March 5th.
Additional Information: The award is conditional upon a full tuition waiver or reimbursement by the University.

Tibor T Polgar Fellowship

Subjects: All aspects of the environment of Hudson River, from Troy, New York, to New York Harbor and Bight. Previous projects have studied hydrodynamics, larval fish, zooplankton, terrapins, landscape ecology, nutrients and public policy.
Purpose: To fund Summer research on the Hudson River.
Eligibility: There are no eligibility restrictions.
Level of Study: Graduate.
Type: Fellowship.
Value: US$3,500 stipend, plus small materials and travel budget. US$500 to sponsoring professors.
Length of Study: From May-June to August-September.
Frequency: Annual.
Country of Study: United States of America.
No. of awards offered: Eight every Summer.
Application Procedure: Applicants must submit the original and five copies of their application which must include letters of interest from the student and of support from the sponsor, a short description of the research project including its significance of between four and six pages, a detailed timetable for the completion of the project, a detailed budget with estimated cost of supplies, travel and other expenses, and the student's curriculum vitae.
Closing Date: March 4th.
Funding: Private.
No. of awards given last year: Three.
No. of applicants last year: Five.
Additional Information: To acquire copies of previous fellowship programme annual reports, or for general queries, applicants should contact Dr John Waldman at the main address or Chuck Nieder, on (1) 845 758 7010.

HUMANE RESEARCH TRUST

Brook House
29 Bramhall Lane South
Bramhall, Stockport, Cheshire, SK7 2DN, England
Tel: (44) 161 439 8041
Fax: (44) 161 439 3713
Contact: Mr David Greenfield, Trust Secretary

The Humane Research Trust is a national charity which funds a range of unique medical research programmes into human illness at hospitals and universities around the country. In keeping with the philosophy of the Trust, none of the research involves animals, and much of it seeks to establish and develop pioneering techniques which will replace animal intensive experiments currently undertaken elsewhere.

Humane Research Trust Grant

Subjects: Humane research.
Purpose: To encourage scientific programmes where the use of animals is replaced by other methods.
Eligibility: Open to established scientific workers engaged in productive research. Nationals of any country are considered but for the sake of overseeing, projects should be undertaken in a United Kingdom establishment.
Level of Study: Unrestricted.
Type: Grant.
Value: Varies.
Frequency: Dependent on funds available.
Study Establishment: Various.
Country of Study: United Kingdom.
No. of awards offered: Varies.

Application Procedure: Applicants must complete an application form, available on request.
Closing Date: Varies, the trustees meet every three to four months.
Funding: Private.
Contributor: Supporters and legacies.
No. of awards given last year: Five.
No. of applicants last year: 18.
Additional Information: The Trust is a registered charity and donations are encouraged.

HUMANITARIAN TRUST

27 St James Place, London, SW1A 1NR, England
Contact: Mrs M Myers, Secretary of Trustees

Humanitarian Trust Awards

Subjects: Unrestricted, subject to the discretion of the trustees. Awards are not made for journalism, theatre, music or any arts subjects. All aspects of medical sciences are eligible apart from nursing, medical auxiliaries, midwifery, radiology, treatment techniques or medical technology. Candidates are only considered when studying academic subjects. The award cannot be used for travel, overseas courses and fieldwork excluded.
Purpose: For general charitable purposes beneficial to the community.
Eligibility: Open to persons already holding an original grant.
Level of Study: Graduate, Postgraduate.
Type: Award.
Value: Approx. UK £200.
Length of Study: One year, non renewable.
Study Establishment: Any approved institution.
Country of Study: United Kingdom.
No. of awards offered: Approx. 15.
Application Procedure: Applicants must write in, submit two references preferably from tutors or heads of department, a breakdown of anticipated income and expenditure, and a curriculum vitae.
Funding: Private.
No. of awards given last year: 18.
No. of applicants last year: 100.
Additional Information: Awards are not made for travel or overseas courses. They are intended only as supplementary assistance and are to be held concurrently with other awards. Candidates are only considered when studying academic subjects.

HUMANITIES RESEARCH CENTRE (HRC)

Australian National University (ANU), Canberra, ACT, 0200, Australia
Tel: (61) 2 6125 2700
Fax: (61) 2 6248 0054
Email: administration.hrc@anu.edu.au
www: http://www.anu.edu.au/hrc
Contact: Ms Judy Buchanan, Assistant Office Administrator & Programme Manager

The Humanities Research Centre (HRC) was established in 1972 specifically to stimulate humanities research and debate at the Australian National University (ANU), within Australia and beyond.

HRC Visiting Fellowships

Subjects: The HRC interprets the humanities generously, recognising that new methods of theoretical enquiry have done much to break down the traditional distinction between the humanities and the social sciences, recognising too, the importance of establishing dialogue between the humanities and the natural and technological sciences and the creative arts.
Purpose: To provide scholars with time to pursue their own work in congenial and stimulating surroundings.

Eligibility: Open to candidates of any nationality who are at the postdoctoral level.
Level of Study: Postdoctorate.
Type: Fellowship with grant, partial grant or no grant.
Value: Return economy airfare up to australian $2,500, plus accommodation for 13 weeks.
Length of Study: Three-six months, not renewable.
Frequency: Annual.
Study Establishment: The Humanities Research Centre at the Australian National University.
Country of Study: Australia.
No. of awards offered: Up to 20.
Application Procedure: Applicants must complete a formal application, available from the website.
Closing Date: January 25th.
Funding: Government.
Additional Information: Fellows are required to spend all of their time in residence at the Centre, but are encouraged to visit other institutions.

THE HUNTINGTON

Committee on Awards
1151 Oxford Road, San Marino, CA, 91108, United States of America
Tel: (1) 626 405 2194
Fax: (1) 626 449 5703
Email: cpowell@huntington.org
www: http://www.huntington.org
Contact: Ms Carolyn Powell, Assistant to Director of Research

Barbara Thom Postdoctoral Fellowship

Subjects: British and American history, literature, art history or history of science.
Purpose: To support a non tenured faculty member while they are revising a manuscript for publication.
Eligibility: Preference will be given to Scholars who are four or five years beyond the award of PhD.
Level of Study: Postdoctorate.
Type: Fellowship.
Value: US$30,000.
Length of Study: One year.
Frequency: Annual.
Study Establishment: The Huntington.
Country of Study: United States of America.
No. of awards offered: Two.
Application Procedure: Applicants must contact the Chair of the Committee on Awards at the main address.
Closing Date: Applications are accepted between October 1st and December 15th.
Funding: Private.

Huntington Short-Term Fellowships

Subjects: British and American history, literature, art history or history of science.
Purpose: To enable outstanding scholars to carry out significant research in the collections of the Library and Art Gallery by assisting in balancing budgets of such persons on leave at reduced pay and living away from home.
Eligibility: Open to nationals of any country who have demonstrated, to a degree commensurate with their age and experience, unusual abilities as Scholars through publications of a high order of merit. Attention is paid to the value of the candidate's project and the degree to which the special strengths of the Library and Art Gallery will be used.
Level of Study: Postdoctorate, Postgraduate.
Type: Fellowship.
Value: US$2,000 per month.
Length of Study: One-five months.
Frequency: Annual.

Study Establishment: The Huntington.
Country of Study: United States of America.
No. of awards offered: Approx. 100, depending on funds available.
Application Procedure: Applicants must contact the Chair of the Committee on Awards at the main address.
Closing Date: Applications are accepted between October 1st and December 15th.
Funding: Private.
Additional Information: Fellowships are available for work towards doctoral dissertations.

Mellon Postdoctoral Research Fellowships

Subjects: British and American history, literature, art history or history of science.
Purpose: To support scholarship study in a field appropriate to the Huntington's collections.
Eligibility: Preference will be given to Scholars who have not held a major award in the three years preceding the year of this award.
Level of Study: Postdoctorate.
Type: Fellowship.
Value: US$30,000.
Length of Study: One year.
Frequency: Annual.
Study Establishment: The Huntington.
Country of Study: United States of America.
No. of awards offered: Two.
Application Procedure: Applicants must contact the Committee on Fellowships at the main address.
Closing Date: Applications are accepted between October 1st and December 15th.
Funding: Private.

National Endowment for the Humanities Fellowships

Subjects: British and American history, literature, art history or history of science.
Purpose: To support scholarship in a field appropriate to the Huntington's collections.
Eligibility: Preference will be given to Scholars who have not held a major award in the three years preceding the year of this award.
Level of Study: Postdoctorate.
Type: Fellowship.
Value: Up to US$30,000.
Length of Study: 4-12 months.
Frequency: Annual.
Study Establishment: The Huntington.
Country of Study: United States of America.
No. of awards offered: Three.
Application Procedure: Applicants must contact the Chair of the Committee on Awards at the main address.
Closing Date: Applications are accepted between October 1st and December 15th.
Funding: Government.

The W M Keck Foundation Fellowship for Young Scholars

Subjects: British and American history, literature, art history or history of science.
Purpose: To encourage outstanding young scholars to pursue their own lines of enquiry, completing dissertation research or beginning a new project in the fields of British and American history, literature, art history and the history of science.
Eligibility: There are no restrictions on age, nationality or citizenship.
Level of Study: Postdoctorate, Postgraduate.
Type: Fellowship.
Value: US$2,300 per month.
Length of Study: One-three months.
Frequency: Annual.
Study Establishment: The Huntington.
Country of Study: United States of America.
No. of awards offered: Varies.

Application Procedure: Applicants must contact the Chair of the Committee on Awards.
Closing Date: Applications are accepted between October 1st and December 15th.
Funding: Private.

HUNTINGTON'S DISEASE ASSOCIATION

108 Battersea High Street, London, SW11 3HP, England
Tel: (44) 20 7223 7000
Fax: (44) 20 7223 9489
Email: sue_watkin@hda.org.uk
www: http://www.hda.org.uk
Contact: Ms Sue Watkin, Chair

Huntington's Disease Association Research Grant

Subjects: Subjects aimed at furthering the understanding of Huntington's disease, improving its treatment, or otherwise improving the quality of life of patients and carers.
Purpose: To support medical or social research.
Eligibility: Open to suitably qualified researchers of any nationality.
Level of Study: Postgraduate.
Type: Project grant and studentship.
Value: Studentship is up to UK £12,000 per year, and project grants are up to UK £25,000 for one-three years.
Frequency: Annual.
Country of Study: United Kingdom.
No. of awards offered: Varies, depending on the annual budget.
Application Procedure: Applicants must complete an application form, please write for details.
Closing Date: March 1st.

HUNTINGTON'S DISEASE SOCIETY OF AMERICA (HDSA)

158 West 29th Street
7th Floor, New York, NY, 10001-5300, United States of America
Tel: (1) 212 242 1968 ext. 13
Fax: (1) 212 239 3430
Email: dlowen@hdsa.org
www: http://www.hdsa.org
Contact: Co-ordinator of Medical & Scientific Programmes

The Huntington's Disease Society of America (HDSA) is dedicated to the care and cure of families afflicted with Huntington's disease. HDSA is a non-profit volunteer health agency whose mission statement is three-fold: to eradicate Huntington's disease by promoting and supporting research, to help families cope with the problems presented by the disease and to educate the public and professionals about it.

HDSA Fellowships

Subjects: The cure and treatment of Huntington's disease at the basic and clinical level.
Purpose: To help promising young investigators in the early stages of their careers.
Eligibility: Open to MDs or PhDs from accredited medical schools and universities.
Level of Study: Postdoctorate.
Type: Fellowship.
Value: Up to US$80,000 over two years.
Length of Study: Up to two years.
Frequency: Annual.
Country of Study: Any country.
No. of awards offered: Varies.
Application Procedure: Applicants must email with a request for application.
Closing Date: December 15th.

Funding: Private.
Contributor: Private donations from individuals.

HDSA Research Grants

Subjects: Cure and treatment of Huntington's disease at the basic and clinical level.
Purpose: To provide seed money for new or innovative research projects in the hope that they will develop sufficiently to attract funding from other sources.
Eligibility: Open to MDs or PhDs from accredited medical schools and universities.
Level of Study: Postdoctorate.
Type: Research grant.
Value: Up to US$100,000 over two years.
Length of Study: Up to two years.
Frequency: Annual.
Country of Study: Any country.
No. of awards offered: Varies.
Application Procedure: Applicants must email with a request for application.
Closing Date: December 15th.
Funding: Private.
Contributor: Private individuals.

HDSA Research Initiative Grants

Subjects: Cure and treatment of Huntington's disease at the basic and clinical level.
Purpose: To swiftly investigate a novel idea with very little preliminary data.
Eligibility: Open to MDs or PhDs from accredited medical schools and universities.
Level of Study: Postdoctorate.
Type: Grant.
Value: Up to US$20,000.
Length of Study: One year.
Frequency: Annual.
Country of Study: Any country.
No. of awards offered: Varies.
Application Procedure: Applicants must email with a request for application.
Closing Date: December 15th, March 15th, June 15th or September 15th.
Funding: Private.

HYPERTENSION TRUST

127 High Street, Teddington, Middlesex, TW11 8HH, England
Tel: (44) 20 8977 0011
Fax: (44) 20 8977 0055
Email: gmccarthy@hamptonmedical.com
www: http://www.hypertensiontrust.org
Contact: Mrs G McCarthy, Administrator

The Hypertension Trust is a registered charity established to support research in hypertension and related cardiovascular conditions. Funds are available to support annual awards for Research Fellowships and Research Studentships.

Hypertension Trust Fellowship

Subjects: Hypertension and related cardiovascular conditions.
Purpose: To support research into hypertension and related cardiovascular conditions.
Eligibility: Applicants must hold a medical degree or higher degree in science (eg. doctorate) and have evidence of research aptitude or clinical experience in hypertension. The Fellowship is open to United Kingdom citizens or European Union nationals working in the United Kingdom.
Level of Study: Graduate, Postgraduate.
Type: Fellowship.

Value: A salary of approx. UK £20,000-30,000 per year. Up to UK £5,000 per year in expenses is available.
Length of Study: Two years.
Frequency: Annual.
Country of Study: United Kingdom.
No. of awards offered: One.
Application Procedure: Applicants must complete an application form.
Closing Date: March 1st.
Contributor: Surplus funds following the 16th Scientific Meeting of the International Society of Hypertension in June 1996.
No. of awards given last year: One.
No. of applicants last year: Seven.
Additional Information: Please see the website for additional information.

Hypertension Trust Studentship

Subjects: Hypertension and related cardiovascular conditions.
Purpose: To support research into hypertension and related cardiovascular conditions.
Eligibility: Open to graduates of a European Union university or those currently working in a United Kingdom or Republic of Ireland hospital or institution.
Level of Study: Graduate, Postgraduate.
Type: Studentship.
Value: A salary based on MRC rates and PhD fees. Up to UK £5,000 in expenses.
Length of Study: Three years.
Frequency: Annual.
Country of Study: United Kingdom or Republic of Ireland.
No. of awards offered: One.
Application Procedure: Applicants must complete an application form.
Closing Date: March 1st.
Contributor: Surplus funds following the 16th Scientific Meeting of the International Society of Hypertension in June 1996.
Additional Information: Please see the website for additional information.

IAN FLEMING CHARITABLE TRUST MUSIC EDUCATION AWARDS

1-16 Ogle Street, London, W1W 6JA, England
Tel: (44) 20 7636 4481
Fax: (44) 20 7637 4307
Email: education@mbf.org.uk
www: http://www.mbf.org.uk
Contact: Mrs Susan Dolton

Ian Fleming Charitable Trust Music Education Awards

Subjects: Musical performance.
Purpose: To help exceptionally talented young musicians.
Eligibility: Open to singers and instrumentalists possessing the potential to become first class performers, who have been resident in the United Kingdom for three years. Instrumentalists must be under 25, female singers under 27 and male singers under 28.
Level of Study: Postgraduate, Professional development.
Value: Varies, to cover tuition, maintenance and the purchase of instruments. Award range from UK £2,000-5,000.
Frequency: Annual.
Country of Study: Any country.
No. of awards offered: Approx. 10.
Application Procedure: Applicants must complete application forms and provide two references.
Closing Date: February 21st.
Funding: Private.
No. of awards given last year: 14.
No. of applicants last year: 310.

Additional Information: Selected applicants will be asked to audition in April.

IEEE (INSTITUTE OF ELECTRICAL AND ELECTRONICS ENGINEERS, INC.) HISTORY CENTER

39 Union Street, New Brunswick, NJ, 08901, United States of America
Tel: (1) 732 932 1066
Fax: (1) 732 932 1193
Email: history@ieee.org
www: http://www.ieee.org/history_center
Contact: Director

IEEE Fellowship in Electrical History

Subjects: The history of electrical engineering and technology.
Purpose: To support graduate work in the history of electrical engineering.
Eligibility: Open to suitably qualified graduate students.
Level of Study: Doctorate, Postdoctorate, Postgraduate.
Type: Fellowship.
Value: US$17,000 plus US$3,000 research budget.
Length of Study: One year.
Frequency: Annual.
Study Establishment: A college or university of recognised standing.
Country of Study: Any country.
No. of awards offered: One.
Application Procedure: Applicants must submit a completed application, transcripts, three letters of recommendation and a research proposal.
Closing Date: February 1st.
Funding: Commercial.
Additional Information: The fellowship is made possible by a grant from the IEEE Life Member Fund and is awarded by the IEEE History Committee. Application materials become available in October. Materials may be requested from the Center directly. Applicants should contact the IEEE Center for the History of Electrical Engineering for further information.

IMC GRADUATE SCHOOL OF MANAGEMENT

Zrinyi utca 14, Budapest, H-1051, Hungary
Tel: (36) 1 235 6117
Fax: (36) 1 327 3282
Email: tokat@imc.hu
www: http://www.imc.hu
Contact: Tibor Toka, Admissions Co-ordinator

IMC Graduate School of Management is a non-profit educational institution, which offers a postgraduate academic programme leading to the MBA degree conducted entirely in English with a curriculum based on those of leading edge western graduate business schools, and a broad range of management development programmes leading to specialised training certificates. These certificates are given in English and Hungarian, usually custom tailored to the needs of corporations.

Soros Scholarship

Subjects: MBA.
Purpose: To provide a modest living stipend to an MBA student.
Eligibility: Open to candidates from the following countries: Albania, Armenia, Azerbaijan, Bulgaria, Croatia, Czech Republic, Estonia, Georgia, Kazakhstan, Kyrgyzstan, Latvia, Lithuania, Moldova, Mongolia, Poland, Romania, Russian Federation, Slovak Republic,

Slovenia, Tajikistan, Turkmenistan, Ukraine, Uzbekistan or Yugoslavia.
Level of Study: MBA.
Type: Scholarship.
Value: Up to 100 per cent of tuition fees and may provide a modest living stipend.
Length of Study: Up to four semesters.
Study Establishment: The IMC Graduate School of Management.
Country of Study: Hungary.
Application Procedure: Applicants must complete an application form, available from the website.
Closing Date: Please contact the organisation.
Additional Information: Applicants should visit the website for further information.

IMPERIAL CANCER RESEARCH FUND

PO Box 123
Lincoln's Inn Fields, London, WC2A 3PX, England
Tel: (44) 20 7269 3328
Fax: (44) 20 7269 3585
www: http://www.icnet.uk
Contact: Ms Johanna Higgins, Administration Manager

The Imperial Cancer Research Fund is a registered United Kingdom charity dedicated to saving lives through research into the causes, prevention, treatment and cure of cancer.

Imperial Cancer Research Fund Clinical Research Fellowships

Subjects: All areas of cancer research.
Purpose: To enable research training.
Eligibility: Open to medical graduates of registrar or senior registrar status who have obtained MRCP, FRCS or other higher medical qualifications.
Level of Study: Doctorate, Postdoctorate.
Type: Fellowship.
Value: Remuneration is based on current NHS salary scales.
Length of Study: Up to four years.
Frequency: Annual.
Study Establishment: Imperial Cancer Research Fund laboratories and clinical units.
Country of Study: United Kingdom.
No. of awards offered: Approx. three.
Application Procedure: Applicants must refer to the advertisements which list procedure information or make direct applications to laboratory heads.
Additional Information: Fellowships are advertised in scientific and medical journals.

Imperial Cancer Research Fund Graduate Studentships

Subjects: All areas of cancer research.
Purpose: To enable research training.
Eligibility: Candidates should normally have been resident in the United Kingdom for more than three years, and have, or be about to obtain, a First or Upper Second Class (Honours) Degree in science, and not be over 25 years of age. Non residents are not excluded from consideration.
Level of Study: Doctorate.
Type: Studentship.
Value: Approx. UK £12,882-13,908 per year, depending on location.
Length of Study: Three years.
Frequency: Annual.
Study Establishment: Imperial Cancer Research Fund laboratories and clinical units.
Country of Study: United Kingdom.
No. of awards offered: Approx. 20.
Application Procedure: Applicants must refer to the advertisements which list procedure information.

Imperial Cancer Research Fund Research Fellowships

Subjects: All areas of cancer research.

Purpose: To assist postdoctoral research.

Eligibility: Applicants must have been awarded a PhD or equivalent, or show written proof of submission of their thesis.

Level of Study: Postdoctorate.

Type: Fellowship.

Value: Starting salary approx. UK £19,945-26,839 plus location allowances per year depending on experience.

Length of Study: Up to three years.

Frequency: Every two months.

Study Establishment: Imperial Cancer Research Fund laboratories and clinical units.

Country of Study: United Kingdom.

No. of awards offered: Approx. 30.

Application Procedure: Applicants must refer to the advertisements which list procedure information or make direct applications to laboratory heads.

IMPERIAL COLLEGE OF SCIENCE, TECHNOLOGY AND MEDICINE

London, SW7 2AZ, England
Tel: (44) 20 7594 8015
Fax: (44) 20 7594 8004
Email: d.atkins@ic.ac.uk
Contact: Mr D N Atkins, Senior Assistant Registrar, Admissions

The Imperial College of Science, Technology and Medicine is a college of the University of London and provides university education at first degree and postgraduate level.

Beit Fellowship For Scientific Research

Subjects: Science, engineering or technology.

Purpose: To enable a student of outstanding research ability to undertake research in a scientific, technological or biomedical field at Imperial College.

Eligibility: Candidates must hold a First Class (Honours) Degree awarded by a recognised university in a territory which is currently part of the British Commonwealth (or formed part of the British Empire on 20th September 1913) and must have been accepted for admission to Imperial College.

Level of Study: Doctorate.

Type: Fellowship.

Value: UK £9,300 per year plus college fees. These fees are reviewed annually.

Length of Study: One year, renewable for up to two additional years.

Frequency: Annual.

Study Establishment: Imperial College, for research leading to the PhD degree of the University of London.

Country of Study: United Kingdom.

No. of awards offered: One.

Application Procedure: Applicants must complete an application form and submit this with two references. A transcript and academic record are required from non United Kingdom students.

Closing Date: April 30th.

No. of awards given last year: One.

Additional Information: Applicants should state desired subject of study. Further information is available on request.

John Stanley Scholarship

Subjects: Environmental technology.

Purpose: To facilitate postgraduate study or research.

Eligibility: Applicants must be undertaking a programme of postgraduate study in environmental technology in the Department of Environmental Science and Technology at Imperial College, London.

Level of Study: Postgraduate.

Type: Scholarship.

Value: To cover fees at the home student rate only and maintenance at the research council studentship basic rates.

Length of Study: One, year, renewable for up to two additional years.

Frequency: Dependent on funds available.

Study Establishment: The Department of Environmental Science and Technology at Imperial College, London.

Country of Study: United Kingdom.

No. of awards offered: Two.

Application Procedure: Applicants must state that they wish to apply on Section 9 of their admissions application form (PG1) and attach an additional letter asking to be considered for the award.

Closing Date: June 30th.

Contributor: Offered in collaboration with the Holly Hill Charitable Trust.

No. of awards given last year: Two.

Additional Information: Further information is available on request.

Rees Jeffreys Road Fund Bursaries

Subjects: Transport.

Purpose: To facilitate postgraduate study or research by supporting attendance on the one year Intercollegiate MSc in Transport run in conjunction with University College London.

Eligibility: Open to United Kingdom citizens who hold at least an Upper Second Class (Honours) Degree.

Level of Study: Postgraduate.

Type: Bursary.

Value: To cover fees and maintenance at the research council studentship basic rates.

Frequency: Annual.

Study Establishment: The Department of Civil Engineering at Imperial College.

Country of Study: United Kingdom.

No. of awards offered: Two at the discretion of the Trustees.

Application Procedure: Applicants must complete an application form and submit this with two references. This must be accompanied by a short written statement.

Closing Date: June 15th.

Additional Information: Research into transport leading to the PhD of the University of London is also a programme eligible for support under this scheme.

Stephen and Anna Hui Fellowship

Subjects: The fields of earth sciences, defined as geology, extractive metallurgy, minerals, mining engineering or petroleum engineering.

Purpose: To facilitate postgraduate study or research.

Eligibility: Candidates must be graduates with a First or Upper Second Class (Honours) Degree from universities of China including Hong Kong and Taiwan.

Level of Study: Doctorate, Postgraduate.

Type: Fellowship.

Value: Fees, plus a maintenance allowance based on the United Kingdom's research council studentship rates.

Length of Study: One year, renewable for up to two additional years.

Frequency: Every two to three years.

Study Establishment: Imperial College.

Country of Study: United Kingdom.

No. of awards offered: One.

Application Procedure: Applicants must complete an application form and submit this with two references and a transcript or academic record.

Closing Date: January 31st.

Funding: Private.

Additional Information: Further information is available on request.

INDIAN COUNCIL OF SOCIAL SCIENCE RESEARCH (ICSSR)

Aruna Asaf Ali Marg, New Delhi, 110067, India
Tel: (91) 11 617 9838
Fax: (91) 11 617 9850
www: http://www.icssr.org
Contact: Deputy Director

The Indian Council of Social Science Research is an autonomous organisation, funded by the Indian Government to promote research in the social sciences. It provides grants in aid for research projects, fellowships and study grants for young people, and gives publication grants. It established the National Social Science Documentation Centre and Archives for providing information to social scientists.

Indian Council of Social Science Research Centrally Administered Doctoral Fellowships

Subjects: Social sciences.
Eligibility: Applicants should consult the organisation as eligibility varies according to the category that the award falls into. These categories are Open Doctoral Fellowship, Physically Handicapped Scholars, Priority Areas Fellowships and Fellowships for North-Eastern Region.
Level of Study: Doctorate.
Type: Fellowship.
Value: Indian rupee 2,500 per month for the first two years and indian rupee 2,800 for the third and fourth year. Indian rupee 5,000 is paid to each Scholar per year as contingency.
Length of Study: Two years.
Frequency: Annual.
No. of awards offered: Varies.
Application Procedure: Applications are invited each year through advertisements in national newspapers and employment news.
Closing Date: Please consult the organisation.

Indian Council of Social Science Research Contingency Grant

Subjects: Social sciences.
Eligibility: Open to students working towards a PhD who are not already in receipt of a fellowship from the ICSSR.
Level of Study: Doctorate, Postdoctorate.
Value: A maximum of indian rupee 5,000.
No. of awards offered: Varies.
Application Procedure: Applicants must complete an application form, available from the website.

Indian Council of Social Science Research Doctoral Fellowships for Foreign Nationals

Subjects: Social sciences.
Purpose: To enable foreign students to undertake research in India.
Eligibility: Open to Scholars from any country other than India, though preference is given to countries neighbouring India.
Level of Study: Doctorate.
Type: Fellowship.
Value: Indian rupee 2,500 per month for the first two years and indian rupee 2,800 for the third and fourth year. Salary protected doctoral fellowships for foreign Scholars are for two years, and indian rupee 5,000 is paid to each Scholar per year as contingency. Employed foreign doctoral fellows are paid indian rupee 3,500 per month.
Frequency: Annual.
Country of Study: India.
No. of awards offered: Varies.
Application Procedure: Applicants must consult the organisation.

Indian Council of Social Science Research General Fellowships

Subjects: All social sciences and social science aspects of other sciences eg. economics, commerce, education, management,

business administration, psychology, political science, international relations, public administration, sociology, social work, criminology, social science aspects of anthropology, demography, geography, history, law or linguistics.
Purpose: To enable scholars to devote all their time to research in their area of interest.
Eligibility: Open to young Scholars who have shown significant promise and potential for research and have completed their doctoral degree or have done equivalent research work of merit and intend to work on approved research projects at the institution of excellence under the guidance of senior social scientists. Superannuated and retired Scholars are not eligible.
Level of Study: Postdoctorate.
Type: Fellowship.
Value: Indian rupee 2,500 under revision in the case of unemployed scholars and to the extent of protection of salary in the case of employed scholars. Allowances as per roles of the affiliating institution. In addition a contingency grant of indian rupee 7,500 per year is admissible for the fellowship period.
Length of Study: Two years.
Frequency: Annual.
Study Establishment: Any registered research body or university in India.
Country of Study: India.
No. of awards offered: Varies.
Application Procedure: Applicants must submit four copies of a detailed self-contained research proposal and bio-data.
Closing Date: April and October.
Funding: Government.
Additional Information: Funds are released every six months. Further instalments of the grant are released after assessing progress reports. More information is available on request.

Indian Council of Social Science Research Institutional Fellowship

Subjects: Social sciences.
Purpose: To enable a Scholar to undertake research for a doctoral degree.
Level of Study: Doctorate.
Type: Fellowship.
Value: Indian rupee 2,500 per month for the first two years and indian rupee 2,800 for the third and fourth year. Salary protected doctoral fellowship is for two years, and indian rupee 5,000 is paid to each Scholar per year as contingency.
Frequency: Annual.
Study Establishment: Any research institution approved by the ICSSR.
Application Procedure: Applicants must consult the organisation.

Indian Council of Social Science Research National Fellowships

Subjects: Social sciences.
Purpose: To provide opportunities for social scientists to engage themselves in full time research, and to assist young scholars who have the potential and competence for research to work on a full time basis on their approved research degrees.
Eligibility: Open to social scientists of eminence who have made outstanding contributions to research in their respective fields and would like to continue with their academic pursuits. Awards are made purely on the basis of merit, irrespective of age and status of the Scholar.
Level of Study: Postgraduate.
Type: Fellowship.
Value: Employed scholars salary will be protected, retired and unemployed scholars will be paid indian rupee 7,300 per month minus the pension equivalent. In addition a contingency grant of indian rupee 15,000 per year is admissible.
Length of Study: Two years.
Country of Study: India.
No. of awards offered: 15.

Application Procedure: The ICSSR does not entertain any direct applications for the award of national fellowships. The awards are made on its own initiative.
Closing Date: August 16th.
Funding: Government.
Additional Information: National fellowships fall under the categories of Mahatma Gandhi National Fellowship for Peace Studies and Conflict Resolution, Jawaharial Nehru National Fellowship for Diplomatic Studies, B R Ambedkar National Fellowship for Constitutional Studies, J P Naik National Fellowship for Educational Studies and Community Health, Irawati Karve National Fellowship for Women Studies, Patrick Geddes National Fellowship for Urban Studies, Khan Abdul Gaffar Khan National Fellowship for South Asian Studies, Sarojini Naidu National Fellowship for Political Studies, Bhikaji Kama National Fellowship for Studies on Minorities, Sister Nivedita National Fellowship for Studies in Social Culture and Religious Tolerance, Dadabhai Naoroji National Fellowship for Economic Studies, Patanjali National Fellowship in Psychology, C V Raman National Fellowship on Interface Between Science and Social Sciences or Science and Society, J C Bose National Fellowship for Environmental Studies, and Ananda K Coomaraswamy National Fellowship on Society and Culture. Further information is available on request.

Indian Council of Social Science Research Partial Assistance to PhD Scholars for Doctoral Studies

Subjects: Social sciences.
Eligibility: Open to Scholars who have completed at least two years of their doctoral work.
Level of Study: Doctorate.
Type: Fellowship.
Value: Indian rupee 2,800 per month plus a contingency grant of indian rupee 2,500. College teachers and research staff are provided with full salary protection for six months.
Length of Study: Six months.
No. of awards offered: Varies.
Application Procedure: Applicants must consult the organisation.

Indian Council of Social Science Research Senior Fellowships

Subjects: All social sciences and social science aspects of other sciences eg. economics, commerce, education, management, business administration, psychology, political science, international relations, public administration, sociology, social work, criminology, social science aspects of anthropology, demography, geography, history, law or linguistics.
Purpose: To enable scholars to devote all their time to research in their area of interest.
Eligibility: Open to professional social scientists who have significant publications to their credit, including books or papers in professional journals. Social workers and civil servants known for their academic interests with record of publications may also be considered. Employed, unemployed and superannuated Scholars under the age of 65 years who are Indian social scientists and who would like to undertake full-time research in India, are also eligible, as are Indian Scholars who would like to undertake a research project outside India and Scholars from outside India who would like to undertake research in India.
Level of Study: Postgraduate.
Type: Fellowship.
Value: Indian rupee 3,000-4,000 per month, under revision, in the case of scholars who are unemployed and under the age of superannuation and indian rupee 3,000 per month in the case of scholars who are retired on superannuation, to the extent of protection of salary in the case of employed scholars. In addition a contingency grant of indian rupee 7,500 per year is admissible for the fellowship period.
Length of Study: Two years.
Frequency: Annual.
Study Establishment: Any registered research body or university in India.
Country of Study: India.
No. of awards offered: Varies.

Application Procedure: Applicants must submit four copies of a detailed self-contained research proposal and bio-data.
Closing Date: April and October.
Funding: Government.
Additional Information: Funds are released every six months. Further instalments of the grant are released after assessing progress reports. More information is available on request.

INDIANA UNIVERSITY CENTER ON PHILANTHROPY

550 West North Street
Suite 301, Indianapolis, IN, 46202-3162, United States of America
Tel: (1) 317 278 2700
Fax: (1) 317 278 2701
Email: jafellow@iupui.edu
www: http://www.philanthropy.iupui.edu
Contact: Mr Robert Payton

The Center on Philanthropy at Indiana University is dedicated to education, research and public service in philanthropy. An academic unit of Indiana University, the Center is located on the Indiana University Purdue University at Indianapolis (IUPUI) campus.

Jane Addams/Andrew Carnegie Fellowships in Philanthropy

Subjects: The theory and practice of the philanthropic tradition, its history and societal role, its ethics and values, its opportunities and limitations, and its responsibilities. Fellows spend a portion of their time working under appropriate supervision at a local non-profit organisation in their field of interest.
Purpose: To advance and renew interest in public service by engaging recent college graduates in intensive study and voluntary action.
Eligibility: Open to recent graduates with a Bachelor's degree or equivalent from another country. The programme is not intended for students who already have committed to a graduate programme, or who have received a graduate degree.
Level of Study: Postgraduate.
Type: Fellowship.
Value: US$15,000 plus all tuition and mandatory fees will be waived.
Length of Study: 10 months.
Frequency: Annual.
Study Establishment: Indiana University Center on Philanthropy.
Country of Study: United States of America.
No. of awards offered: Six.
Application Procedure: Applicants must write for details.
Closing Date: January 31st.
Funding: Private.
No. of awards given last year: Six.
No. of applicants last year: 100.
Additional Information: Candidates should have a special interest in some aspect of the non-profit community. Fellows must be able to spend the full programme period in Indianapolis.

INSEAD

Boulevard de Constance, Fontainebleau, Cedex, F-77305, France
Tel: (33) 1 60 72 43 92
Fax: (33) 1 60 74 55 35
Email: mba.info@insead.fr
www: http://www.insead.edu/mba
Contact: Ms Helen Henderson, Director, Financial Aid

INSEAD is widely recognised as one of the most influential business schools in the world. With a brand new campus in Asia to complement its established presence in Europe, INSEAD is setting the pace in globalising the MBA. The one year intensive MBA programme is focused on international general management.

Giovanni Agnelli Scholarship

Subjects: MBA.
Purpose: To support MBA participants.
Eligibility: Open to Italian candidates of high merit, admitted to the INSEAD MBA programme.
Level of Study: MBA.
Type: Scholarship.
Value: €1,500.
Frequency: Annual.
Study Establishment: INSEAD.
Country of Study: France or Singapore.
No. of awards offered: One-two.
Application Procedure: Applicants must complete an application form, available from the website.
Closing Date: May 15th for the September class of the same year and September 15th for the January class of the following year.
Contributor: Fiat.
Additional Information: This scholarship is offered by Giovanni Agnelli, President of the Fiat Group.

INSEAD A T Kearney Scholarship

Subjects: MBA.
Eligibility: Open to candidates admitted to the MBA programme who are beginning their studies at INSEAD's Asian campus.
Level of Study: MBA.
Type: Scholarship.
Value: €10,000.
Frequency: Annual.
Study Establishment: INSEAD.
Country of Study: Singapore.
No. of awards offered: One.
Application Procedure: Applicants must complete a specific assignment, details of which are available from the organisation or from the website.
Closing Date: September 15th for the January class of the following year.
Contributor: A T Kearney.
Additional Information: This merit based scholarship has been created by A T Kearney for MBA participants studying at INSEAD's Asian campus, in recognition of the group's commitment to developing top management talent for the Asia Pacific region. Founded in Chicago, in 1928, A T Kearney (http://www.atkearney.com) is one of the world's largest and fastest growing management consulting firms. With a global presence that includes nearly 60 offices, spanning major and emerging markets, A T Kearney provides strategic, operational, organisational and information technology consulting and executive search services to the world's leading companies. A T Kearney has operated in Europe since 1969 and in Asia since 1972.

INSEAD Alumni Fund (IAF) Scholarship for the Asian campus

Subjects: MBA.
Eligibility: Open to candidates admitted and starting their course on INSEAD's Asian campus.
Level of Study: MBA.
Type: Scholarship.
Value: Varies.
Frequency: Annual.
Study Establishment: INSEAD.
Country of Study: Singapore.
No. of awards offered: Three.
Application Procedure: Applicants must complete a specific assignment, details of which are available from the organisation or from the website.
Closing Date: May 15th for the September intake of the same year and September 15th for the January intake of the following year.
Contributor: Alumni and a gift from a private individual.

INSEAD Alumni Fund (IAF) Scholarships

Subjects: MBA.

Purpose: To assist candidates from emerging or developing countries admitted to the MBA programme.
Eligibility: Open to applicants from emerging or developing countries.
Level of Study: MBA.
Type: Scholarship.
Value: From €3,000-10,000.
Frequency: Annual.
Study Establishment: INSEAD.
Country of Study: France or Singapore.
No. of awards offered: Varies.
Application Procedure: Applicants must complete a specific assignment, details of which are available from the organisation or from the website.
Closing Date: May 15th for the September intake of the same year and September 15th for the January intake of the following year.
Contributor: Alumni.

INSEAD Antoine Rachid Irani/Bissada Scholarship

Subjects: MBA.
Purpose: To financially support MBA candidates.
Eligibility: Open to candidates of Lebanese or Egyptian nationality who are fluent in Arabic, preferably have a minimum of three years in a Lebanese University, who have obtained excellent academic and professional results and have been admitted to the INSEAD MBA programme.
Level of Study: MBA.
Type: Scholarship.
Value: Full tuition fees, but in order to lengthen the period of the scholarship, winners must pledge to repay 10 per cent of the value of the scholarship two years after graduating from INSEAD and an additional 10 per cent three years after graduating.
Frequency: Annual.
Study Establishment: INSEAD.
Country of Study: France or Singapore.
No. of awards offered: One.
Application Procedure: Applicants must complete a specific assignment, details of which are available from the organisation or from the website.
Closing Date: May 15th for the September class of the same year and September 15th for the January class of the following year.
Contributor: Bissada Management.

INSEAD Belgian Alumni and Council Scholarship Fund

Subjects: MBA.
Purpose: To assist MBA participants.
Eligibility: Open to candidates of merit of Belgian nationality and those who have lived in Belgium for at least five years. Priority will be given to admitted applicants who intend to return to Belgium after their MBA.
Level of Study: MBA.
Type: Scholarship.
Value: €6,400.
Frequency: Annual.
Study Establishment: INSEAD.
Country of Study: France or Singapore.
No. of awards offered: Two.
Application Procedure: Applicants must complete a specific assignment, details of which are available from the organisation or from the website.
Closing Date: May 15th for the September class of the same year and September 15th for the January class of the following year.
Contributor: Alumni and the Belgian Council.

INSEAD Børsen/Danish Council Scholarship

Subjects: MBA.
Purpose: To assist MBA participants.
Eligibility: Open to candidates of Danish nationality, admitted to the INSEAD MBA programme.
Level of Study: MBA.
Type: Scholarship.

Value: Please contact the organisation.
Frequency: Annual.
Study Establishment: INSEAD.
Country of Study: France or Singapore.
No. of awards offered: Two.
Application Procedure: Applicants must complete an application form, available from the website.
Closing Date: May 15th for the September class of the same year and September 15th for the January class of the following year.
Contributor: The Danish Council/Børsen.

INSEAD Broadview Scholarship

Subjects: MBA.
Purpose: To further personal development in the fields of finance and technology management.
Eligibility: Open to candidates admitted to the MBA programme in the September class. Candidates of any nationality who have professional backgrounds in corporate finance or technology or media and communications and who demonstrate high academic achievement, together with strong personal qualities may apply.
Level of Study: MBA.
Type: Scholarship.
Value: €9,600.
Frequency: Annual.
Study Establishment: INSEAD.
Country of Study: France or Singapore.
No. of awards offered: One.
Application Procedure: Applicants must complete a specific assignment, details of which are available from the organisation or from the website.
Closing Date: May 15th for candidates admitted to the September class of the same year.
Contributor: Broadview.
Additional Information: The scholarship is offered to commemorate the leading global M&A investment organisation Broadview's 25 years of serving the IT, communications and media industries.

INSEAD Canadian Foundation Scholarship

Subjects: MBA.
Purpose: To provide financial assistance and scholarships to deserving Canadians admitted to the INSEAD MBA programme.
Eligibility: Open to candidates of Canadian nationality, preferably resident in Canada, who have been admitted to the INSEAD MBA programme and are intending to return to Canada.
Level of Study: MBA.
Type: Scholarship.
Value: Up to canadian $10,000.
Frequency: Annual.
Study Establishment: INSEAD.
Country of Study: France or Singapore.
No. of awards offered: Varies.
Application Procedure: Applicants must submit the following in support of their application, a covering letter requesting scholarship specifying which campus, a budget detailing the need for financial assistance including current and expected sources of funding, a copy of a completed INSEAD admission form with essay and supporting documents, a copy of reference letters submitted in support of application to INSEAD, a copy of Graduate Management Admissions Test results, a copy of university transcripts, and a copy of confirmation of admittance to INSEAD.
Closing Date: June 30th for candidates admitted to the September intake of the same year, and October 31st for candidates admitted to the January class of the following year.
Contributor: Alumni.
Additional Information: The Canadian INSEAD Foundation is a non-profit corporation whose purpose is to encourage Canadian students to develop an international business understanding and perspective. The Foundation's board members include many prominent Canadian business leaders and INSEAD alumni. Foundation members also act as the de facto representatives of Canada on INSEAD's International Council. The Foundation's financial assistance has to date already benefited over 50 Canadian alumni. It is hoped that this financial assistance and scholarship programme, while benefiting its Canadian recipients, will also impact favourably on the Canadian economy.

For further information contact:

The Board of Trustees
Canadian INSEAD Foundation
c/o Richard Tarte
Société générale de financement du Québec
600 de La Gauchetière Street West Suite 1700, Montréal, QC, H3B 4L8, Canada
Tel: (1) 514 876 9290 ext. 2171

INSEAD Christian Thams Scholarship

Subjects: MBA.
Purpose: To aid MBA participants.
Eligibility: Open to candidates of Norwegian nationality who have been admitted to the INSEAD MBA programme.
Level of Study: MBA.
Type: Scholarship.
Value: €9,600. US$10,000 towards tuition, providing approx. one third of fees.
Frequency: Annual.
Study Establishment: INSEAD.
Country of Study: France or Singapore.
No. of awards offered: One.
Application Procedure: Applicants must complete an application form, available from the website.
Closing Date: May 15th for the September class of the same year and September 15th for the January class of the following year.
Contributor: Orkla.

INSEAD Danuta Scholarship

Subjects: MBA.
Purpose: To assist MBA participants.
Eligibility: Open to Polish nationals resident in Poland who fulfil the INSEAD MBA admission requirements.
Level of Study: MBA.
Type: Scholarship.
Value: €3,000.
Frequency: Annual.
Study Establishment: INSEAD.
Country of Study: France or Singapore.
No. of awards offered: One-two.
Application Procedure: Applicants must complete an application form, available from the website.
Closing Date: May 15th for the September class of the same year and September 15th for the January class of the following year.
Contributor: Danuta.
Additional Information: The winning Scholar may also be requested to submit a short essay on a given topic prior to entry in the INSEAD MBA programme. Michel Marbot, an INSEAD alumnus (MBA 1983), President and Chief Executive Officer, Danuta South Africa, created this Scholarship.

INSEAD Edmond Israel Foundation Scholarships

Subjects: MBA.
Purpose: To assist MBA participants.
Eligibility: Open to candidates of merit admitted to the INSEAD MBA programme who are nationals of a Central and Eastern European country or of the Commonwealth of Independent States. The candidates must have resided in the region for at least five years and intend to return after the MBA.
Level of Study: MBA.
Type: Scholarship.
Value: €6,800.
Frequency: Annual.
Study Establishment: INSEAD.
Country of Study: France or Singapore.
No. of awards offered: Four.

Application Procedure: Applicants must complete a specific assignment, details of which are available from the organisation or from the website.
Closing Date: May 15th for the September class of the same year and September 15th for the January class of the following year.
Contributor: The Edmond Israel Foundation.

INSEAD Eli Lilly and Company Innovation Scholarship
Subjects: MBA.
Eligibility: Scholarships will be awarded to students of merit and who demonstrate the capacity for innovative thinking and actions. Nationals from Africa, Asia, Central and Eastern Europe, Middle East, Central and South America, Turkey and Canada may apply.
Level of Study: MBA.
Type: Scholarship.
Value: Full tuition.
Frequency: Annual.
Study Establishment: INSEAD.
Country of Study: France or Singapore.
No. of awards offered: Four, two to candidates in Fontainebleau (one per class ie. September and January) and two for candidates in Singapore in January.
Application Procedure: Applicants must complete a specific assignment, details of which are available from the organisation or from the website.
Closing Date: May 15th for the September intake of the same year and September 15th for the January intake of the following year.
Contributor: Eli Lilly.
Additional Information: Eli Lilly creates and delivers innovative pharmaceutical based health care solutions that enable people worldwide to live longer, healthier, more active lives. The key driver of our success is the ability to innovate, both in the discovery and acquisition of new compounds, and deliver these to our customers around the world.

INSEAD Elmar Schulte Diversity Scholarship
Subjects: MBA.
Purpose: To encourage diversity in the INSEAD MBA programme.
Eligibility: Open to candidates from non traditional MBA backgrounds admitted to the programme.
Level of Study: MBA.
Type: Scholarship.
Value: Varies.
Frequency: Annual.
Study Establishment: INSEAD.
Country of Study: France or Singapore.
No. of awards offered: Varies.
Application Procedure: Applicants must complete an application form, available from the website.
Closing Date: May 15th for the September intake of the same year and September 15th for the January intake of the following year.
Contributor: Alumni.

INSEAD Elof Hansson Scholarship Fund
Subjects: MBA.
Purpose: To assist MBA participants.
Eligibility: Open to candidates of Swedish nationality who have been admitted to the INSEAD MBA programme.
Level of Study: MBA.
Type: Scholarship.
Value: €6,000.
Frequency: Annual.
Study Establishment: INSEAD.
Country of Study: France or Singapore.
No. of awards offered: Two.
Application Procedure: Applicants must complete an application form, available from the website.
Closing Date: May 15th for the September class of the same year and September 15th for the January class of the following year.
Contributor: The Elof Hansson Foundation.

INSEAD Freshfields Scholarship
Subjects: MBA.
Eligibility: Open to candidates of Asian nationality admitted to the INSEAD MBA programme and who will spend some time studying at INSEAD's Asian campus.
Level of Study: MBA.
Type: Scholarship.
Value: €17,500.
Frequency: Annual.
Study Establishment: INSEAD.
Country of Study: Singapore.
No. of awards offered: Two.
Application Procedure: Applicants must complete an application form, available from the website.
Closing Date: May 15th for the September class of the same year and September 15th for the January class of the following year.
Contributor: Freshfields.
Additional Information: Freshfields is a major international law firm and market leader in international transactions that has an appreciation of the importance of the Asia-Pacific region.

INSEAD Gesellschaft Deutschland Scholarship
Subjects: MBA.
Eligibility: At least one scholarship per year will be awarded to candidates of German nationality admitted to the INSEAD MBA programme. Awards will be made on the basis of both financial need and managerial potential. Eligible candidates admitted to the MBA programme will be interviewed by a scholarship committee.
Level of Study: MBA.
Type: Scholarship.
Value: Please contact the organisation.
Frequency: Annual.
Study Establishment: INSEAD.
Country of Study: France or Singapore.
No. of awards offered: At least one.
Application Procedure: Applicants must complete an application form, available from the website.
Closing Date: May 15th for the September intake of the same year and September 15th for the January intake of the following year.
Additional Information: The INSEAD Gesellschaft Deutschland is composed of leading German alumni and companies associated with INSEAD. It grants several scholarships and interest free loans to German participants in the MBA programme. At least one scholarship per year will be awarded, the Dr Paul Wagner Scholarship, additional awards being based on availability of funds.

For further information contact:

INSEAD Gesellschaft Deutschland e V
c/o Gerling-Konzern
Gereonshof, Köln, D-50597, Germany

INSEAD Henry Grunfeld Foundation Scholarship
Subjects: MBA.
Purpose: To aid MBA students who can demonstrate a commitment to a career in investment banking.
Eligibility: Open to participants from a United Kingdom background with an interest in pursuing a career in investment banking.
Level of Study: MBA.
Type: Scholarship.
Value: €38,000.
Frequency: Annual.
Study Establishment: INSEAD.
Country of Study: France or Singapore.
No. of awards offered: One.
Application Procedure: Applicants must complete a specific assignment, details of which are available from the organisation or from the website.
Closing Date: May 15th for the September class of the same year and September 15th for the January class of the following year.
Contributor: The Henry Grunfeld Foundation.
Additional Information: Henry Grunfeld was a co-founder of S G Warburg, the United Kingdom investment bank that became one of

the largest securities firms in the world, combining merchant banking, securities broking and market making.

INSEAD Jean François Clin MBA Scholarship

Subjects: MBA.
Purpose: To assist MBA participants from Francophone Africa.
Eligibility: Scholarships will be awarded to candidates for either the September or January classes, on the basis of both merit and need. Applicants from Burkino Faso, Guinea, Côte D'Ivoire, Mali, Niger, Senegal or Togo, who have already gained admission to the INSEAD MBA programme and have close ties with his or her country of origin are eligible. Candidates must have had at least secondary education in his or her country of origin although university level education may have been spent abroad.
Level of Study: MBA.
Type: Scholarship.
Value: Partial tuition.
Frequency: Annual.
Study Establishment: INSEAD.
Country of Study: France or Singapore.
No. of awards offered: Three.
Application Procedure: Applicants must complete a specific assignment, details of which are available from the organisation or from the website.
Closing Date: May 15th for the September intake of the same year and September 15th for the January intake of the following year.
Contributor: Jean François Clin.
Additional Information: Jean-François Clin, an alumnus of INSEAD who has a general interest in the economic development of francophone West Africa, believes that managers in the region will need to be better equipped to face increasing competition, globalisation of businesses and demands on productivity.

INSEAD Judith Connelly Delouvrier Scholarship

Subjects: MBA.
Purpose: To support females undertaking the MBA.
Eligibility: Open to deserving American women admitted to the September MBA programme.
Level of Study: MBA.
Type: Scholarship.
Value: US $15,000.
Frequency: Annual.
Study Establishment: INSEAD.
Country of Study: France or Singapore.
No. of awards offered: One.
Application Procedure: Applicants must complete a specific assignment, details of which are available from the organisation or from the website.
Closing Date: May 15th for the September class of the same year.
Contributor: Alumni.
Additional Information: This Scholarship is offered to remember Judith Connelly Delouvrier, wife of Phillippe Delouvrier, an INSEAD MBA of 1977, who was a victim of the TWA Flight 800 tragedy in 1996.

INSEAD L'Oréal Scholarship

Subjects: MBA.
Purpose: To foster creativity, diversity and entrepreneurial spirit within the MBA population.
Eligibility: Open to candidates of any nationality who demonstrate a capacity for creativity, innovation and entrepreneurial activity.
Level of Study: MBA.
Type: Scholarship.
Value: Full tuition fees.
Length of Study: One year.
Frequency: Annual.
Study Establishment: INSEAD.
Country of Study: France or Singapore.
No. of awards offered: Two per year, one per intake.
Application Procedure: Applicants must submit an essay giving any relevant examples of a particularly creative personal

achievement, an example of a very ambitious and even risky objective, and summaries of educational and professional experiences and achievements, reasons for applying (financial and other) and professional ambitions. Application forms are available from the website.
Closing Date: May 15th for the September class of the same year and September 15th for the January class of the following year.
Contributor: L'Oréal.

INSEAD Lister Vickery Memorial Award

Subjects: MBA.
Purpose: To assist MBA participants from emerging countries.
Eligibility: Open to Russian nationals who demonstrate the potential for pursuing a career in industry.
Level of Study: MBA.
Type: Scholarship.
Value: €5,300.
Frequency: Annual.
Study Establishment: INSEAD.
Country of Study: France or Singapore.
No. of awards offered: One.
Application Procedure: Applicants must complete a specific assignment, details of which are available from the organisation or from the website.
Closing Date: May 15th for the September intake of the same year and September 15th for the January intake of the following year.
Contributor: Alumni.
Additional Information: This scholarship was created in memory of Lister Vickery (MBA of 1966) by two of his INSEAD class-mates and close friends. After a career in Venture Capital and some years with the IFC in Washington and Asia, Lister Vickery returned to INSEAD in 1980 as an Affiliate Professor, introducing the first entrepreneurship courses into the MBA curriculum. He left INSEAD again in 1987 to become president of a start-up company he developed with some of his students. He later sold the business and returned to Fontainebleau in 1994. He again gave generously of his time and effort in support of entrepreneurship and alumni activities at INSEAD. He died in 1995 after fighting cancer for two years.

INSEAD Lord Kitchener National Memorial Scholarship

Subjects: MBA.
Purpose: To assist MBA participants from the United Kingdom.
Eligibility: To be eligible, a candidate must be a British subject and have served, or be the son or daughter of a parent who has at any time served or is serving on a full-time engagement in HM Armed Forces. This includes members and former members of the Territorial Army and other Reserve Forces of the Crown, and their sons and daughters, providing that the former have served an element of full-time or permanent service for a minimum consecutive period of three months.
Level of Study: MBA.
Type: Scholarship.
Value: UK £2,000 each.
Frequency: Annual.
Study Establishment: INSEAD.
Country of Study: France or Singapore.
No. of awards offered: Two per year, one per intake.
Application Procedure: Applicants must complete an application form, available from the website and send it to the main address, with documentary evidence of the candidates' parent's service in the British Armed Forces.
Closing Date: May 15th for the September class of the same year, and September 15th for the January class of the following year.
Additional Information: The Lord Kitchener National Memorial Fund was created in memory of the first Earl Kitchener of Khartoum who died in action in June 1916 when he went down with his ship. Earl Kitchener had a national reputation as Secretary of State for War and as the organiser of 'Kitchener's Army'. The Council of the Fund regards that the acquisition of an MBA would benefit not only the individual but also the United Kingdom as a whole as it is relevant to overseas trade and is a worthy memorial to the first Earl Kitchener, a great patriot and also a far-seeing internationalist.

INSEAD Louis Franck Scholarship

Subjects: MBA.

Eligibility: Open to candidates of United Kingdom nationality admitted to INSEAD. Financial need is neither a necessary nor a sufficient condition for being granted an award. Nevertheless, the candidate's financial position will be taken into account, and awards will not necessarily be granted to the best candidates if there is a sound candidate who is in financial need. Selected Scholars are required to write a thesis or report (the subject of which to be agreed with the trustees) to be presented to the trustees within three months of graduation.

Type: Scholarship.

Value: Varies.

Frequency: Annual.

Study Establishment: INSEAD.

Country of Study: France or Singapore.

No. of awards offered: Up to eight.

Application Procedure: Applicants must complete a specific assignment, details of which are available from the organisation or from the website. These should be emailed to mba.finance@insead.fr, accompanied by a digital photograph.

Closing Date: May 15th for the September class of the same year and September 15th for the January class of the following year.

Contributor: The Louis Franck Trust.

Additional Information: This scholarship was established in 1983 by Louis Franck, who served for many years on the Board of INSEAD, to mark his gratitude for the opportunities in life which the United Kingdom gave him. Louis Franck was born in Belgium in 1907 and came to work in England as a young man. He became a prominent banker in the City of London and was responsible for transforming Samuel Montagu (now part of HSBC Investment Bank) from a quiet firm of bullion and foreign exchange dealers into a leading merchant bank. During World War II, Louis Franck had a distinguished record in the British Army, including involvement in the clandestine Special Operations Executive, and was awarded the CBE in recognition of his services. Louis Franck died in Switzerland in September 1988.

INSEAD Mette Røed Heyerdahl Memorial Scholarship

Subjects: MBA.

Eligibility: Open to female candidates of Palestinian, Nepalese or Ugandan nationality admitted to the MBA programme.

Level of Study: MBA.

Type: Scholarship.

Value: €9,600. If need is demonstrated there is a possibility of further funding towards tuition fees and a contribution to a living allowance.

Frequency: Annual.

Study Establishment: INSEAD.

Country of Study: France or Singapore.

No. of awards offered: One.

Application Procedure: Applicants must complete an application form, available from the website.

Closing Date: May 15th for the September intake of the same year and September 15th for the January intake of the following year.

Contributor: Alumni.

Additional Information: This scholarship is awarded in memory of Mette Røed Heyerdahl, who was a lawyer in Norway working, amongst other things, with women's legal rights in co-operation with local law organisations in Palestine, Nepal and Uganda.

INSEAD Misys Foundation Scholarship

Subjects: MBA.

Eligibility: Open to candidates from developing countries admitted to the MBA programme.

Level of Study: MBA.

Type: Scholarship.

Value: €12,000.

Frequency: Annual.

Study Establishment: INSEAD.

Country of Study: France or Singapore.

No. of awards offered: Two.

Application Procedure: Applicants must complete a specific assignment, details of which are available from the organisation or from the website.

Closing Date: May 15th for the September class of the same year and September 15th for the January class of the following year.

Contributor: Misys plc.

Additional Information: The Misys Charitable Foundation was set up in 1997, with the object of furthering education in information technology both domestically and internationally. The Foundation is funded by Misys plc, one of the 10 largest applications software companies in the world.

INSEAD SAPEC MBA Scholarship

Subjects: MBA.

Purpose: To assist MBA participants.

Eligibility: Open to candidates of Spanish, Portuguese or Brazilian nationality admitted to the MBA programme.

Level of Study: MBA.

Type: Scholarship.

Value: €6,000.

Frequency: Annual.

Study Establishment: INSEAD.

Country of Study: France or Singapore.

No. of awards offered: Two.

Application Procedure: Applicants must complete a specific assignment, details of which are available from the organisation or from the website.

Closing Date: May 15th for the September intake of the same year and September 15th for the January intake of the following year.

Contributor: SAPEC.

INSEAD Sasakawa (SYLLF) Scholarships

Subjects: MBA.

Purpose: To encourage candidates to broaden their knowledge and enhance their career leadership through the INSEAD MBA programme.

Eligibility: Candidates of any nationality are eligible. The awards will be made on a competitive basis.

Level of Study: MBA.

Type: Scholarship.

Value: €3,000-11,000 depending on the number and quality of applications.

Frequency: Annual.

Study Establishment: INSEAD.

Country of Study: France or Singapore.

No. of awards offered: One or more per intake.

Application Procedure: Applicants must complete a specific assignment, details of which are available from the organisation or from the website.

Closing Date: May 15th for the September class of the same year and September 15th for the January class of the following year.

Contributor: The Sasakawa Young Leaders Fellowship Fund (SYLFF).

INSEAD Sisley-Marc d'Ornano Scholarship

Subjects: MBA.

Purpose: To support young graduates seeking further education in order to contribute to the economic development of Poland.

Eligibility: Open to Polish nationals admitted to the INSEAD MBA programme who demonstrate a commitment to work in Poland for three years after the INSEAD MBA programme. The winner of the scholarship will agree to take up a professional activity in Poland for at least three years, as if not, the candidate is obliged to reimburse the scholarship.

Level of Study: MBA.

Type: Scholarship.

Value: Tuition fees and a living allowance. Partial scholarships, ie. tuition fees only, may be awarded in the case of residence outside Poland.

Frequency: Annual.

Study Establishment: INSEAD.

Country of Study: France or Singapore.
No. of awards offered: One.
Application Procedure: Applicants must submit an essay addressing the following question: 'Give the main reason for your applying for the scholarship and describe your aspirations for your future career development'. Scholarship applications may be submitted with the admissions application form. Application forms are available from the website.
Closing Date: May 15th for the September intake of the same year and September 15th for the January intake of the following year.
Contributor: Sisley.
Additional Information: This scholarship is offered in memory of the late Marc d'Ornano, who lost his life in a car accident while at the start of an excellent career.

INSEAD Spanish Council Scholarship

Subjects: MBA.
Purpose: To assist MBA participants.
Eligibility: Open to candidates from Spain, admitted to the INSEAD MBA programme.
Level of Study: MBA.
Type: Scholarship.
Value: €12,000.
Frequency: Annual.
Study Establishment: INSEAD.
Country of Study: France or Singapore.
No. of awards offered: Two.
Application Procedure: Applicants must complete a specific assignment, details of which are available from the organisation or from the website.
Closing Date: May 15th for the September class of the same year and September 15th for the January class of the following year.
Contributor: The Spanish Council.

INSTITUT FRANÇAIS DE WASHINGTON

234 Dey Hall
CB 3170
UNC-CH, Chapel Hill, NC, 27599-3170, United States of America
Tel: (1) 919 962 0154
Fax: (1) 919 962 5457
Email: cmaley@email.unc.edu
www: http://www.unc.edu/depts/institut
Contact: Dr Catherine A Maley, President

The purpose of the Institut Français de Washington is to promote the study of French civilisation, history, literature and art in the United States of America.

Edouard Morot-Sir Fellowship in Literature

Subjects: French studies in the areas of art, economics, history, history of science, linguistics, literature or social sciences.
Eligibility: Open to those in the final stage of the PhD dissertation, or who have held a PhD for no longer than six years before the application deadline.
Level of Study: Doctorate, Postdoctorate.
Type: Fellowship.
Value: US$1,500.
Length of Study: At least two months.
Frequency: Annual.
Country of Study: France.
Application Procedure: Applicants must write a maximum of two pages describing the research project and planned trip and enclose a curriculum vitae. A letter of recommendation from the dissertation director is also required.
Closing Date: January 15th.
No. of awards given last year: One.
No. of applicants last year: 45.
Additional Information: Awards are for maintenance during research in France and should not be used for travel.

Gilbert Chinard Fellowships

Subjects: French studies in the areas of art, economics, history, history of science, linguistics, literature or social sciences.
Eligibility: Open to those in the final stage of the PhD dissertation, or who have held a PhD for no longer than six years beforethe application deadline.
Level of Study: Doctorate, Postdoctorate.
Type: Fellowship.
Value: US$1,500.
Length of Study: At least two months.
Frequency: Annual.
Country of Study: France.
No. of awards offered: Three.
Application Procedure: Applicants must write a maximum of two pages describing the research project and planned trip and enclose a curriculum vitae. A letter of recommendation from the dissertation director is also required for PhD candidates.
Closing Date: January 15th.
No. of awards given last year: Two.
No. of applicants last year: 45.
Additional Information: Awards are for maintenance during research in France and should not be used for travel.

Harmon Chadbourn Rorison Fellowship

Subjects: French studies in the areas of art, economics, history, history of science, linguistics, literature or social sciences.
Eligibility: Open to those in the final stage of the PhD dissertation, or who have held a PhD for no longer than six years before the application deadline.
Level of Study: Doctorate, Postdoctorate.
Type: Fellowship.
Value: US$1,500.
Length of Study: At least two months.
Frequency: Every two years.
Country of Study: France.
No. of awards offered: One.
Application Procedure: Applicants must write a maximum of two pages describing the research project and planned trip and enclose a curriculum vitae. A letter of recommendation from the dissertation director is also required for PhD candidates.
Closing Date: January 15th.
No. of awards given last year: One.
No. of applicants last year: 45.
Additional Information: Awards are for maintenance during research in France and should not be used for travel.

INSTITUTE FOR ADVANCED STUDIES IN THE HUMANITIES

University of Edinburgh
Hope Park Square, Edinburgh, EH8 9NW, Scotland
Tel: (44) 131 650 4671
Fax: (44) 131 668 2252
Email: iash@ed.ac.uk
www: http://www.ed.ac.uk/iash
Contact: Ms Anthea Taylor, Assistant to Director

The Institute aims to promote scholarship in the humanities, and wherever possible to foster interdisciplinary enquiries. This is achieved by means of fellowships awarded for the pursuit of relevant research and by the public dissemination of findings in seminars, lectures, conferences, exhibitions, cultural events and publications.

Andrew W Mellon Foundation Fellowships in the Humanities

Subjects: The humanities. No limitation will be placed on the area of research within the humanities, but preference will be given to scholars, from any discipline, whose work concerns one of the Institute's themes eg. The New Information Order; Scotland in Europe and Europe in Scotland.

Purpose: To promote advanced research within the field of humanities, broadly understood, and to sponsor interdisciplinary research.

Eligibility: Restricted to Bulgarian, Czech, Hungarian, Polish Romanian and Slovak Scholars. Fellows must be able to speak English and must be under 45.

Level of Study: Postdoctorate.

Type: Grant.

Length of Study: Three months.

Frequency: Annual.

Study Establishment: The Institute for Advanced Studies in the Humanities at the University of Edinburgh.

Country of Study: Scotland.

No. of awards offered: Three.

Application Procedure: Applicants must complete an application form, available from the Institute.

Closing Date: March 28th.

Funding: Private.

No. of awards given last year: Four.

No. of applicants last year: 65.

Institute for Advanced Studies in the Humanities Visiting Research Fellowships

Subjects: Archaeology, history of art, classics, English literature, history, European and oriental languages and literature, linguistics, philosophy, Scottish studies, history of science, law, divinity, music and the social sciences. Preference will be given to scholars, from any discipline, whose work concerns one of the Institute's themes eg. The New Information Order; Scotland in Europe and Europe in Scotland.

Purpose: To promote advanced research within the field of the humanities, broadly understood, and also to sponsor interdisciplinary research.

Eligibility: Open to Scholars of any nationality holding a doctorate or offering equivalent evidence of aptitude for advanced studies. Degree candidates are not eligible.

Level of Study: Postdoctorate.

Type: Fellowship.

Value: Most fellowships are honorary, but limited support towards expenses is available to a small number of candidates.

Length of Study: Two-six months.

Frequency: Annual.

Study Establishment: The Institute for Advanced Studies in the Humanities at the University of Edinburgh.

Country of Study: United Kingdom.

No. of awards offered: 15.

Application Procedure: Applicants must complete an application form, available from the Institute.

Closing Date: December 1st.

Funding: Private.

No. of awards given last year: 11.

No. of applicants last year: 20.

Additional Information: Fellows have the use of study rooms at the Institute, near the library and within easy reach of the National Library of Scotland, the Central City Library, the National Galleries and Museums, the Library of the Society of Antiquaries in Scotland, and the Scottish Record Office. Candidates should advise their referees to write on their behalf direct to the Institute and to ensure that references are received in Edinburgh before January 7th.

INSTITUTE FOR ADVANCED STUDY

Einstein Drive, Princeton, NJ, 08540, United States of America
Tel: (1) 609 734 8000
Fax: (1) 609 924 8399
Email: gwhidden@ias.edu
www: http://www.ias.edu
Contact: Ms Georgia Whidden, Public Affairs Officer

The Institute for Advanced Study is an independent, private institution whose mission is to support advanced scholarship and fundamental research in historical studies, mathematics, natural sciences, social science and theoretical biology. It is a community of scholars where theoretical research and intellectual enquiry are carried out under the most favourable conditions.

Institute for Advanced Study Postdoctoral Residential Fellowships

Subjects: Social science, history, astronomy, theoretical physics, mathematics or theoretical biology.
Purpose: To support advanced study and scholarly exploration.
Eligibility: There are no restrictions on eligibility.
Level of Study: Postdoctorate.
Type: Stipend.
Value: US$30,000-50,000.
Length of Study: Generally one year.
Frequency: Annual.
Country of Study: United States of America.
No. of awards offered: 180.
Application Procedure: Applicants must complete an application. Materials are available from the school administrative officers.
Closing Date: Varies, between November 15th and December 15th.
No. of awards given last year: 180.
No. of applicants last year: 2,400.

INSTITUTE FOR ECUMENICAL AND CULTURAL RESEARCH

PO Box 6188, Collegeville, MN, 53621-6188, United States of America
Tel: (1) 320 363 3366
Fax: (1) 320 363 3313
Email: iecr@iecr.org
www: http://www.iecr.org
Contact: Executive Director

The Institute for Ecumenical and Cultural Research seeks to discern the meaning of Christian identity and unity in a religiously and culturally diverse nation and world and to communicate that meaning for the mission of the church and the renewal of human community. The Institute is committed to research, study, prayer, reflection and dialogue, in a place shaped by the Benedictine tradition of worship and work.

Institute for Ecumenical and Cultural Research Resident Scholars Program

Subjects: Religious studies.
Purpose: To encourage constructive and creative thought in a community setting, not only in theology and religious studies, but also more generally in scholarly research as it relates to the Christian tradition, including the interplay of Christianity and culture.
Eligibility: The normal prerequisite is possession of the academic doctorate, but the Admission Committee will, on occasion, consider candidates with some other preparation, or those writing a dissertation.
Level of Study: Postdoctorate.
Length of Study: One academic year or semester.
Frequency: Annual.
Study Establishment: The Institute.
Country of Study: United States of America.

No. of awards offered: 9-18.
Application Procedure: Applicants must complete the form provided.
Closing Date: January 15th prior to the intended period of stay.

INSTITUTE FOR HOUSING AND URBAN DEVELOPMENT STUDIES (IHS)

PO Box 1935, Rotterdam, NL-3000 BX, Netherlands
Tel: (31) 10 402 1544
Fax: (31) 10 404 5671
Email: ihs@ihs.nl
www: http://www.ihs.nl
Contact: Head PC&M Bureau

The Institute for Housing and Urban Development Studies (IHS), is an international educational institute offering postgraduate education in the field of urban management, housing and urban environmental management. Established in 1958, IHS has long worked in the training of urban professionals from developing countries and Central and Eastern Europe.

Institute for Housing and Urban Development Studies Fellowships for Courses

Subjects: Housing planning and building.
Eligibility: Open to participants from any country who have relevant professional experience and are engaged in work related to urban management, housing or urban environment and are proficient in English, the language of the course.
Level of Study: Postgraduate.
Type: Fellowship.
Value: Varies.
Length of Study: Three months for the postgraduate courses, and 17 months for the Master's degree.
Frequency: Dependent on funds available.
Study Establishment: The Institute for Housing and Urban Development Studies.
Country of Study: Netherlands.
No. of awards offered: Varies.
Application Procedure: Applicants must apply for IHS application forms, available from the Institute.
Closing Date: Varies depending on the course.
Funding: Commercial, Government.

INSTITUTE FOR HUMANE STUDIES (IHS)

3301 North Faifax Drive
Suite 440, Arlington, VA, 22201-4432, United States of America
Tel: (1) 703 993 4880
Fax: (1) 703 993 4890
Email: ihs@gmu.edu
www: http://theihs.org
Contact: Mr Steve Sinicula, Student Co-ordinator

The Institute for Humane Studies (IHS) is a unique organisation that assists graduate students worldwide with a special interest in individual liberty. IHS awards over US$400,000 a year in scholarships to students from universities around the world. They also sponsor the attendance of hundreds of students at free summer seminars, and provide various forms of career assistance. Through these and other programmes, IHS and a network of faculty associates promote the study of liberty across a broad range of disciplines, encouraging understanding, open enquiry, rigorous scholarship and creative problem solving.

Charles G Koch Summer Fellowship

Subjects: Current public policy issues, career development workshops, writing projects with a professional editor, and the experience of spending an exciting summer in the Washington DC policy community.
Purpose: To offer intensive eight week internship experiences with Washington DC free market public policy think tanks alongside two week seminars in public policy.
Eligibility: Recent graduates may apply.
Value: US$1,500 plus furnished housing, stipend and travel expenses.
Length of Study: Ten weeks consisting of a full-time eight week internship with a Washington DC free market public policy organisation and a two week intensive seminar on the Summer Fellow Programme.
Application Procedure: Applicants must contact the Charles G Koch Summer Fellow Program at the IHS or visit the website.
Closing Date: February 15th.

Felix Morley Journalism Competition

Subjects: The principles include inalienable individual rights eg. their protection through the institutions of private property, contract, the rule of law, voluntarism in all human relations, the self-ordering market, free trade, free migration, and peace.
Purpose: To award journalists for demonstrated ability, potential for development as a writer and appreciation of classical liberal principles evidenced in submitted publications.
Eligibility: Applicants must be full-time students and 25 years of age or younger.
Type: Competition.
Value: First prize is US$2,500, second prize is US$1,000, third prize is US$750 and the runners up prize is US$250.
Application Procedure: Applicants must contact the Morley Journalism Competition Secretary at the IHS.
Closing Date: December 1st.

Humane Studies Fellowships

Subjects: Arts and humanities, fine and applied art, law, mass communication and information, religion and theology or social and behavioural science.
Purpose: To support outstanding students with a demonstrated interest in the classical liberal tradition intent on pursuing an intellectual and scholarly career.
Eligibility: Open to graduate students with junior or senior standing in the next academic year at accredited colleges and universities.
Level of Study: Graduate, Postgraduate.
Type: Fellowship.
Value: Up to US$12,000.
Frequency: Annual.
Country of Study: Any country.
Application Procedure: Applicants must complete and submit an application form with three completed evaluations, three essays, official test scores, official transcripts and a term paper or writing sample.
Closing Date: December 30th.
No. of awards given last year: 90.
No. of applicants last year: 400.

IHS Film & Fiction Scholarships

Subjects: Film making, fiction writing or playwriting.
Eligibility: Open to graduate students pursuing a Master of Fine Arts degree. Applicants should have a demonstrated interest in classical liberal ideas and their application in contemporary society and demonstrate the desire, motivation and creative ability to succeed in their chosen profession.
Level of Study: Graduate.
Type: Scholarship.
Value: Up to US$10,000.
Application Procedure: Applicants must contact the Film and Fiction Scholarship Secretary at the IHS.

IHS Summer Graduate Research Fellowship

Subjects: Research within the humane sciences eg. history, political and moral philosophy, political economy, economic history, legal and social theory.

Purpose: To give students who share an interest in scholarly research in the classical liberal tradition the opportunity to work on a thesis chapter or a paper of publishable quality and to participate in interdisciplinary seminars under the guidance of a faculty supervisor.

Eligibility: Open to graduate students in the humanities, social sciences and law, who intend academic careers and are pursuing research in the classical liberal tradition.

Level of Study: Doctorate, Graduate, Postgraduate.

Type: Fellowship.

Value: US$5,000.

Frequency: Annual.

Study Establishment: George Mason University.

Country of Study: United States of America.

No. of awards offered: 8-10.

Application Procedure: Applicants must submit a proposal, current curriculum vitae, a copy of Graduate Record Examination scores or Law School Admission Test scores and transcripts, a writing sample and reference details.

Closing Date: January 15th.

Funding: Private.

Liberty & Society Summer Seminars

Subjects: Seminars include: Foundations of Liberty, Exploring Libertarian Perspectives, Liberty and Culture, The First Amendment and Beyond, Liberty and Current Issues, and Scholarship and the Free Society.

Purpose: To allow individuals who share an interest in the scope of individual rights, free markets, the rule of law, peace and tolerance to learn and exchange ideas.

Eligibility: Recent graduates may apply.

Level of Study: Graduate.

Value: All free summer seminars include room and board, lectures and seminars materials and books. Each seminar spot is worth approximately US$1,000.

Study Establishment: The IHS.

Country of Study: United States of America.

Application Procedure: Applicants must visit the website or email for specific seminar information or to request an application.

Closing Date: The no fee deadline is March 1st and the final deadline is March 30th.

THE INSTITUTE FOR SUPPLY MANAGEMENT (ISM)

2055 East Centennial Circle
PO Box 22160, Tempe, AZ, 85285-2160, United States of America
Tel: (1) 480 752 6276
Fax: (1) 480 752 7890
Email: jcavinato@napm.org
www: http://www.napm.org
Contact: Dr Joseph L Cavinato, Senior Vice President

The Institute for Supply Management (ISM) is a non-profit association that provides national and international leadership in purchasing and supply management research and education. ISM provides more than 46,000 members with opportunities to expand their professional skills and knowledge.

ISM Doctoral Grants

Subjects: Purchasing materials and supply management.

Purpose: To provide individuals with financial assistance in preparation for a career in the field or for university teaching, and to encourage research.

Eligibility: Applicants must be doctoral candidates who are pursuing a PhD or DBA in purchasing, business, logistics, management, economics, industrial engineering or a related field, and be at the dissertation stage. Applicants must be enrolled in accredited United States universities to be eligible for the grant.

Level of Study: Doctorate.

Type: Grant.

Value: Up to US$10,000.

Frequency: Annual.

Country of Study: United States of America.

No. of awards offered: Four.

Application Procedure: Applicants must submit an application form and documents, including letters of recommendation and transcripts, and a research proposal.

Closing Date: January 31st.

Funding: Private.

Contributor: ISM.

No. of awards given last year: Four.

No. of applicants last year: 20.

Additional Information: Upon successful completion of the research, the ISM will be interested in the publication of material from the study. Nominations are invited from departments of economics, management, marketing and business administration at United States universities offering a doctoral degree in appropriate fields.

ISM Senior Research Fellowship Program

Subjects: Research topics include but are not limited to the following: the integration of purchasing with other functions, the impact of globalisation on purchasing, the role of purchasing in supply chain management, measuring purchasing effectiveness, historical analysis of trends in purchasing, objective measures of supplier performance, the application of electronic commerce in purchasing and supply, the use of purchasing as a strategic tool, the identification of educational or training tools and skills for purchasing and supply management, forecasting methods, ERP and purchasing, alliances and supplier development.

Purpose: To help support emerging, high potential scholars who teach and conduct research in purchasing and supply management, and to help produce useful research that can be applied to the advancement of purchasing and supply management.

Eligibility: Open to those who are assistant or associate professors, or of equivalent status, at their institutions and have demonstrated exceptional academic productivity in research and teaching. An assistant professor should have three or more years of post degree experience. Candidates must be full-time faculty members within or outside the United States and current or past members of NAPM committees, groups, forums or affiliated organisations. Previous awardees are ineligible.

Level of Study: Predoctorate.

Type: Fellowship.

Value: US$5,000.

Frequency: Annual.

Country of Study: United States of America.

No. of awards offered: Two.

Application Procedure: Applicants must submit four copies of each of the following items in one complete package: a letter of application explaining qualifications for the Fellowship, a research proposal of no more than five pages including a problem statement or hypothesis, research methodology with data sources, collection and analysis, value to the field of purchasing and supply and a curriculum vitae including works in progress.

Closing Date: April 1st.

Funding: Private.

Contributor: ISM.

No. of applicants last year: 5-10.

Additional Information: It is expected that the ISM Fellows will present the results of this research at an ISM forum eg. research symposium, ISM Annual International Purchasing Conference, and/or an NAPM publication such as 'The Journal of Supply Chain Management'.

THE INSTITUTE FOR THE STUDY OF AGING

767 Fifth Avenue
Suite 4600, New York, NY, 10153, United States of America
Tel: (1) 212 572 4116
Fax: (1) 212 572 4094
Email: tlee@rslmgmt.com
www: http://www.aging-institute.org
Contact: Ms Tanya Lee, Grants Manager

The Institute for the Study of Aging is a non-profit foundation based in New York City. The Institute supports research on Alzheimer's disease and cognitive decline.

The Institute for the Study of Aging Grants Program

Subjects: The Institute has three priority areas for grant support, these being early identification, prevention and treatment of Alzheimer's disease and cognitive decline. The Institute focuses its efforts in supporting drug discovery and development in this field.
Purpose: To promote the research and development of technology and therapies to identify, treat and prevent cognitive decline in ageing, Alzheimer's disease and related dementias.
Eligibility: There are no eligibility restrictions.
Level of Study: Unrestricted.
Type: Grant.
Value: Negotiable.
Length of Study: One-three years.
Frequency: No funding cycle.
Study Establishment: A non-profit foundation.
Country of Study: Any country.
No. of awards offered: Not limited by number.
Application Procedure: Applicants must submit a brief lay summary, a research proposal of up to five pages including background, aims, supporting data and experimental design and methods, a biosketch, a summary of resources and a budget with justification.
Closing Date: Applications are accepted any time as grants are received continuously.
Funding: Private.
No. of awards given last year: 28.
No. of applicants last year: 68.
Additional Information: In addition to funding reassert activities the Institute sponsors and/or co-sponsors conferences and scientific or medical workshops to advance knowledge on issues related to the cognitive health and vitality of the elderly. For further information please contact Alan O'Connell, Scientific Officer, email: rslmgmt.com, or Howard Fillit, Executive Director, email: hfillit@rslmgmt.com.

INSTITUTE FOR THE STUDY OF MAN IN AFRICA

Room 2B17
Medical School
University of the Witwatersrand
York Road
Parktown, Johannesburg, Braamfontein, 2193, South Africa
Tel: (27) 11 647 2203
Fax: (27) 11 643 4318
Contact: Secretary

P V Tobias International Essay Competition

Subjects: Anthropology.
Purpose: To recognise the work of Professor P V Tobias, University of Witwatersrand, in the study of human evolution.
Eligibility: There are no eligibility restrictions.
Level of Study: Postgraduate, Professional development.
Value: US$1,000.
Frequency: Annual.

Country of Study: Any country.
No. of awards offered: One.
Application Procedure: Applicants must submit a letter of application.
Closing Date: By registration.
Funding: Private.
Contributor: The Anglo-American and De Beers Chairman's Fund.

THE INSTITUTE MITTAG-LEFFLER

Auravägen 17, Djursholm, S-18260, Sweden
Tel: (46) 87 551 809
Fax: (46) 86 220 589
Email: koskull@ml.kva.se
www: http://www.ml.kva.se
Contact: Assistant to the Director

The Institute Mittag-Leffler is a Nordic research institute for mathematics, under the auspices of the Royal Swedish Academy of Sciences, created by Gösta and Signe Mittag-Leffler who donated their house, library and fortune to the Academy.

Institute Mittag-Leffler Grants

Subjects: Mathematics. The specific topics vary each year.
Eligibility: Open to recent PhDs and advanced graduate students. Preference will be given to applications for long stays.
Level of Study: Doctorate.
Type: Grant.
Value: Krona 12,000 per month or krona 108,000 for those who stay for the full duration of the programme plus family allowance.
Length of Study: One academic year, from September through to June 15th.
Frequency: Annual.
Country of Study: Sweden.
No. of awards offered: Varies.
Application Procedure: Applicants must complete an application form.
Closing Date: January 31st.
Additional Information: Further information is available on request.

INSTITUTE OF ADVANCED LEGAL STUDIES (IALS)

17 Russell Square, London, WC1B 5DR, England
Tel: (44) 20 7862 5883
Fax: (44) 20 7862 5850
Email: dphillip@sas.ac.uk
www: http://www.ials.sas.ac.uk
Contact: Mr D E Phillips, Administrative Secretary

The Institute of Advanced Legal Studies (IALS) has a national and international role in the promotion and facilitation of legal research. It possesses one of the leading research libraries in Europe and organises a regular programme of conferences, seminars and lectures. It also offers postgraduate taught and research programmes and specialised training courses.

Howard Drake Memorial Fund

Subjects: Law and library science.
Purpose: To encourage collaboration and exchanges between legal scholars and law librarians, especially between those of different countries and to promote the study of law librarianship and the training of law librarians.
Eligibility: There are no restrictions on eligibility.
Level of Study: Professional development.
Type: Grant.
Value: Up to approx. UK £800 per grant.
Frequency: Dependent on funds available.

Study Establishment: The IALS.
Country of Study: United Kingdom.
No. of awards offered: One-two.
Application Procedure: Applicants must make applications to the Administrative Secretary. There is no official application form.
No. of awards given last year: None.

IALS Visiting Fellowship in Law Librarianship
Subjects: Law and library science.
Purpose: To enable experienced law librarians, who are undertaking research in appropriate fields, to relate their work to activities in which the Institute's own library is involved.
Eligibility: Open to experienced law librarians from any country.
Level of Study: Unrestricted.
Type: Fellowship.
Value: Non-stipendary.
Length of Study: A minimum of three months and a maximum of one year.
Frequency: Annual.
Study Establishment: The IALS.
Country of Study: United Kingdom.
No. of awards offered: One.
Application Procedure: Applicants must submit a full curriculum vitae, the names, addresses and telephone numbers of two referees and a brief statement of the research programme to be undertaken to the Administrative Secretary.
Closing Date: January 31st in respect of the following academic year.
No. of awards given last year: One.
No. of applicants last year: One.

IALS Visiting Fellowship in Legislative Studies
Subjects: Law.
Purpose: To enable experienced academics or practitioners in the field to undertake research.
Eligibility: Open to established academics and practitioners from any country.
Level of Study: Unrestricted.
Type: Fellowship.
Value: Non-stipendary.
Length of Study: A minimum of three months and a maximum of one year.
Frequency: Annual.
Study Establishment: The IALS.
Country of Study: United Kingdom.
No. of awards offered: One.
Application Procedure: Applicants must submit a full curriculum vitae, the names, addresses and telephone numbers of two referees and a brief statement of the research programme to be undertaken.
Closing Date: January 31st in respect of the following academic year.
No. of awards given last year: None.
No. of applicants last year: One.
Additional Information: This award is not available for postgraduate research.

IALS Visiting Fellowships
Subjects: Law.
Purpose: To enable established legal scholars, who are undertaking research in appropriate fields, to relate their work with the Institute's own research programmes.
Eligibility: Open to nationals of any country.
Level of Study: Unrestricted.
Type: Fellowship.
Value: Non-stipendary.
Length of Study: A minimum of three months and a maximum of one year.
Frequency: Annual.
Study Establishment: The IALS.
Country of Study: United Kingdom.
No. of awards offered: Up to six.

Application Procedure: Applicants must submit a full curriculum vitae, the names, addresses and telephone numbers of two referees and a brief statement of the research programme to be undertaken.
Closing Date: January 31st in respect of the following academic year.
No. of awards given last year: Six.
No. of applicants last year: Eight.
Additional Information: This award is not available for postgraduate research.

Inns of Court Fellowship
Subjects: Law.
Purpose: To enable established legal scholars, who are undertaking research in appropriate fields, to relate their work with the Institute's own research programmes.
Eligibility: Open to nationals of any country.
Level of Study: Unrestricted.
Type: Fellowship.
Value: Non-stipendary, but free accommodation is provided by the Inns of Court.
Length of Study: A minimum of three months and a maximum of one year.
Frequency: Annual.
Study Establishment: The IALS.
Country of Study: United Kingdom.
No. of awards offered: Up to three.
Application Procedure: Applicants must submit a full curriculum vitae, the names, addresses and telephone numbers of two referees and a brief statement of the research programme to be undertaken.
Closing Date: January 31st in respect of the following academic year.
No. of awards given last year: Three.
No. of applicants last year: 12.
Additional Information: This award is not available for postgraduate research.

INSTITUTE OF BIOLOGY

20 Queensberry Place, London, SW7 2DZ, England
Tel: (44) 20 7581 8333
Fax: (44) 20 7823 9409
Email: info@iob.org
www: http://www.iob.org
Contact: Ms Georgina Day, Education Officer

The Institute of Biology's mission is to promote biology and the biological sciences, to foster the public understanding of science, to enhance the status of the biology profession and to represent its members as a whole to government and other bodies worldwide. The Institute is the 'voice' of British biology.

Dax Copp Travelling Fellowship
Subjects: Biological sciences.
Purpose: To support overseas travel in connection with biological study, teaching or research and to aid those who would otherwise not have this opportunity.
Eligibility: Open to students in the biological sciences studying in the United Kingdom.
Level of Study: Unrestricted.
Type: Sponsorship.
Value: UK £500.
Frequency: Annual.
No. of awards offered: Varies.
Application Procedure: Applicants must complete an application form, available from the Expeditions Grants Manager. Applicants are also required to produce a reasoned statement of the purpose to which the Fellowship will be put, supported by three referees.
Closing Date: Mid January.
Funding: Private.
Contributor: Membership.

No. of awards given last year: One.
No. of applicants last year: 20.
Additional Information: Applicants receiving a fellowship will be expected to provide the Institute with a report within six months of its end.

For further information contact:

Expedition Grants Manager
Royal Geographical Society
1 Kensington Gore, London, SW7 2AR, England
Tel: (44) 20 7591 3073
Email: grants@rsg.org

THE INSTITUTE OF CANCER RESEARCH (ICR)

E Block
15 Cotswold Road, Sutton, Surrey, SM2 5NG, England
Tel: (44) 20 8643 8901 ext. 4656
Fax: (44) 20 8643 6940
Email: lindy@icr.ac.uk
www: http://www.icr.ac.uk/icrhome.htm
Contact: Ms Renate Divers, Assistant Registrar

Over the past 90 years, the Institute of Cancer Research has become one of the largest, most successful and innovative cancer research centres in the world. The Institute and the Royal Marsden NHS Trust exist side by side in Chelsea and on a joint site at Sutton, and this close association allows for maximum interaction between fundamental laboratory work and clinical environment.

ICR Research Studentships

Subjects: Cancer research.
Purpose: To encourage research into the causes, prevention and treatment of cancer.
Eligibility: There is a minimum entry requirement of a First or Upper Second Class (Honours) Degree or equivalent in a relevant subject.
Level of Study: Postgraduate.
Type: Studentship.
Value: Equivalent to CRC Studentship rates.
Length of Study: Up to three years.
Frequency: Annual.
Study Establishment: The Institute.
Country of Study: United Kingdom.
No. of awards offered: 15-20.
Application Procedure: Applicants must complete an application form and attend an interview.
Closing Date: January.
Funding: Government.
Contributor: The CRC.
No. of awards given last year: 17.
No. of applicants last year: 202.
Additional Information: A limited number of Institute Postdoctoral Fellowships are offered from time to time as vacancies occur.

INSTITUTE OF CLASSICAL STUDIES

3rd Floor
Senate House
Malet Street, London, WCIE 7HU, England
Tel: (44) 20 7636 8700
Fax: (44) 20 7862 8722
Contact: Ms Margaret Packer, Institute Secretary

Michael Ventris Memorial Award

Subjects: Mycenaean studies.
Purpose: To promote the study of Mycenaean civilisation.

Eligibility: Open to applicants from all countries who are postgraduate students or young Scholars who have obtained a doctorate in the last eight years.
Level of Study: Postdoctorate, Postgraduate.
Value: UK £1,500.
Frequency: Annual.
Country of Study: Any country.
No. of awards offered: One.
Application Procedure: Applicants must send a typewritten letter with two references.
Closing Date: February 28th.
Additional Information: A second Michael Ventris Award is made annually for Architecture and is administered by the Architectural Association.

INSTITUTE OF CURRENT WORLD AFFAIRS

4 West Wheelock Street, Hanover, NH, 03755, United States of America
Tel: (1) 603 643 5548
Fax: (1) 603 643 9599
Email: icwa@valley.net
www: http://www.icwa.org

Institute of Current World Affairs Fellowships

Subjects: International affairs.
Purpose: To enable young adults of outstanding promise and character to study and write about areas or issues of the world outside the United States.
Eligibility: Open to individuals under 36 who have finished their formal education. Applicants must have a good command of spoken and written English.
Level of Study: Unrestricted.
Type: Fellowship.
Value: Full support for Fellows and their immediate families.
Length of Study: A minimum of two years.
Frequency: Annual.
Country of Study: Outside United States of America.
No. of awards offered: Four.
Application Procedure: Applicants must write to the Executive Director and explain briefly the personal background and professional experience that would qualify them in the Institute's current areas of concern, details of which are available upon request. They should also describe the activities they would like to carry out during the two years overseas. This initial letter is followed by a more detailed written application process and must be completed prior to the deadline.
Closing Date: Deadlines for completed applications are April 1st for a June decision and September 1st for a December decision.
Funding: Private.
No. of awards given last year: Three.
No. of applicants last year: 68.
Additional Information: Fellowships are not awarded to support work toward academic degrees nor to underwrite specific studies or research projects. The institute is also known as the Crane-Rogers Foundation.

INSTITUTE OF EUROPEAN HISTORY

Institut für Europäische Geschichte
Alte Universitätsstraße 19, Mainz, D-55116, Germany
Tel: (49) 6131 393 9360
Fax: (49) 6131 393 0154
Email: ieg2@inst-euro-history.uni-mainz.de
www: http://www.inst-euro-history.uni-mainz.de
Contact: Dr Andreas Kunz, Deputy Director

The Institute of European History in Mainz, founded in 1950, is dedicated to the promotion of historical research. Its Abteilung für Religionsgeschichte specialises in the history of occidental religion and has developed into a centre for ecumenical research on the Reformation. The Abteilung für Universalgeschichte concentrates its research on the history of Europe between the sixteenth and twentieth-centuries.

Institute of European History Fellowships
Subjects: Scientific research on Western religious history and on modern and contemporary European history generally.
Purpose: To support young scientists in the completion of their doctoral work or in the execution of shorter postdoctoral projects.
Eligibility: Open to holders of a Master's degree and to Fellows in the advanced stages of graduate work, at least two years after admission to doctoral candidacy, and who have successfully completed their comprehensive oral examinations.
Level of Study: Doctorate, Postdoctorate.
Type: Fellowship.
Value: In line with the guidelines of the German Academic Exchange Service (DAAD), a monthly stipend, a family allowance, health insurance and a travel allowance.
Frequency: Three times each year.
Study Establishment: The Institute of European History.
Country of Study: Germany.
Application Procedure: Applicants must contact the Director of the Section of World History or of the History of Occidental Religion.
Closing Date: February, June or October.
Funding: Government.
No. of awards given last year: 20.
No. of applicants last year: 100.

INSTITUTE OF FOOD TECHNOLOGISTS (IFT)

221 North LaSalle Street, Chicago, IL, 60601, United States of America
Tel: (1) 312 782 8424
Fax: (1) 312 782 8348
Email: info@ift.org
www: http://www.ift.org
Contact: Scholarship Department

The Institute of Food Technologists (IFT), founded in 1939, is a non-profit scientific society with 29,000 members working in food science, technology and related professions in industry, academia and government. IFT's mission is to advance the science and technology of food through the exchange of knowledge. As the society for food science and technology, IFT brings the scientific perspective to the public discussion of food issues.

IFT Freshman/Sophomore Scholarships
Subjects: Food technology and food science.
Purpose: To support study in food science.
Eligibility: Open to previous graduates entering college for the first time, who are enrolled in an approved programme in food science or technology.
Level of Study: Postgraduate.
Type: Scholarship.
Value: US$1,000-1,500.

Frequency: Annual.
Study Establishment: An approved educational institution.
Country of Study: United States of America or Canada.
No. of awards offered: 15 freshman scholarships and 14 sophomore scholarships.
Application Procedure: Applicants must submit applications to their own department head.
Closing Date: The deadline for Freshman Scholarships is February 15th. The deadline for the Sophomore Scholarships is March 1st.

IFT Graduate Fellowships
Subjects: Food technology and food science.
Purpose: To encourage and support outstanding research in food science and technology.
Eligibility: Open to current graduates pursuing a course of study leading to an MS or PhD degree. Candidates must possess an above average interest in research together with demonstrated scientific aptitude.
Level of Study: Doctorate, Graduate, Postgraduate.
Type: Fellowship.
Value: Varies, from US$1,250-5,000.
Frequency: Annual.
Study Establishment: Any educational institution that is conducting fundamental investigations in the advancement of food science and technology.
Country of Study: United States of America or Canada.
No. of awards offered: 27.
Application Procedure: Applicants must contact IFT for details.
Closing Date: February 1st.
Funding: Commercial, Private.
Contributor: Contributors include General Mills, Inc., the Coca-Cola Foundation and Proctor & Gamble Company.

INSTITUTE OF HISTORICAL RESEARCH (IHR)

Senate House
Malet Street, London, WC1E 7HU, England
Tel: (44) 20 7862 8740
Fax: (44) 20 7862 8811
Email: ihrsec@sas.ac.uk
www: http://www.ihr.sas.ac.uk
Contact: Director

The Institute of Historical Research (IHR) is the University of London's centre for advanced study in history. It is an important meeting place for scholars from all over the world and has an open-access library, common room and computer training room, publishes works of reference, administers several research projects and runs courses, conferences and seminars.

Isobel Thornley Research Fellowship
Subjects: Arts and humanities, medieval history, modern history or contemporary history.
Purpose: To help candidates at an advanced stage of a PhD to complete their doctorates.
Eligibility: Open to candidates without regard to nationality, but only to those registered for a PhD at the University of London.
Level of Study: Doctorate, Postgraduate.
Type: Fellowship.
Value: UK £6,200.
Length of Study: One year.
Frequency: Dependent on funds available.
Study Establishment: IHR.
Country of Study: United Kingdom.
No. of awards offered: One.
Application Procedure: Applicants must complete an application form, available from the Assistant Secretary in early January.
Closing Date: Approx. mid February.
Funding: Private.

Contributor: Isobel Thornley bequest.
No. of awards given last year: One.

Past and Present Postdoctoral Fellowships in History
Subjects: History.
Purpose: To provide one year of postdoctoral study in history.
Eligibility: Applicants may be of any nationality and their PhD may have been awarded in any country. Those who have previously held another postdoctoral fellowship will not normally be eligible. The fellowship may not be held in conjunction with any other award. Fellowships will begin on October 1st each year and it is a strict condition of these awards that the PhD thesis should have been submitted by that date.
Level of Study: Postdoctorate.
Type: Fellowship.
Value: UK £13,000.
Length of Study: One year.
Frequency: Dependent on funds available.
Study Establishment: IHR.
Country of Study: England.
No. of awards offered: One.
Application Procedure: Applicants must complete an application form, available from the Assistant Secretary in early January.
Closing Date: Approx. end of February.
Funding: Private.
Contributor: The Past and Present Society.
No. of awards given last year: One.

Royal History Society Fellowship
Subjects: Arts and humanities, medieval history, modern history or contemporary history.
Purpose: To help candidates at an advanced stage of a PhD to complete their doctorates.
Eligibility: Open to nationals of any country.
Level of Study: Doctorate, Postgraduate.
Type: Fellowship.
Value: Approx. UK £6,200.
Length of Study: One year.
Frequency: Annual.
Study Establishment: IHR.
Country of Study: United Kingdom.
No. of awards offered: One.
Application Procedure: Applicants must complete an application form, available from the Assistant Secretary in early January.
Closing Date: Approx. mid February.
Funding: Private.
Contributor: The Royal Historical Society.
No. of awards given last year: One.

Scouloudi Fellowships
Subjects: Arts and humanities, medieval history, modern history or contemporary history.
Purpose: To help candidates at an advanced stage of a PhD to complete their doctorates.
Eligibility: Only open to United Kingdom citizens or to candidates with a first degree from a United Kingdom university.
Level of Study: Doctorate, Postgraduate.
Type: Fellowship.
Value: Approx. UK £6,200.
Length of Study: One year.
Frequency: Annual.
Study Establishment: IHR.
Country of Study: United Kingdom.
No. of awards offered: Seven.
Application Procedure: Applicants must complete an application form, available from the Assistant Secretary in early January.
Closing Date: Approx. mid February.
Funding: Private.
Contributor: The Scouloudi Foundation.
No. of awards given last year: Seven.

Yorkist History Trust Fellowship
Subjects: Arts and humanities or medieval history.
Purpose: To help candidates at an advanced stage of a PhD to complete their doctorates.
Eligibility: Open to candidates without regard to nationality, but only to those researching British history or topics relevant to British history from the late fourteenth-century to the early sixteenth-century.
Level of Study: Doctorate, Postgraduate.
Type: Fellowship.
Value: Approx. UK £6,200.
Length of Study: One year.
Frequency: Dependent on funds available.
Study Establishment: IHR.
Country of Study: United Kingdom.
No. of awards offered: One.
Application Procedure: Applicants must complete an application form, available from the Assistant Secretary in early January.
Closing Date: Approx. mid February.
Funding: Private.
Contributor: The Richard III and Yorkist History Trust.
No. of awards given last year: One.

INSTITUTE OF HORTICULTURE (IOH)

14/15 Belgrave Square, London, SW1X 8PS, England
Tel: (44) 20 7245 6943
Fax: (44) 20 7245 6943
Email: ioh@horticulture.org.uk
www: http://www.horticulture.org.uk
Contact: A Clarke, General Secretary

The Institute of Horticulture (IOH) is the professional institute for horticulturists of all disciplines in the industry.

Martin McLaren Horticultural Scholarship
Subjects: Horticulture, botany or landscape architecture.
Purpose: To fund one year of an MSc course at an American university.
Eligibility: Applicants must have gained a botany, horticulture or landscape architecture degree, and be in the early stages of their career. The age limit is 27 years of age.
Level of Study: Postgraduate.
Type: Scholarship.
Length of Study: One year.
Frequency: Annual.
Study Establishment: A university.
Country of Study: United States of America.
No. of awards offered: One.
Application Procedure: Applicants must complete an application form, available from the IOH.
Closing Date: November 10th.
Funding: Private.
Contributor: The Martin McLaren Trust.
No. of awards given last year: One.
Additional Information: The Martin McLaren Horticultural Scholarship/Garden Club of America Interchange Fellowship is one year spent in an United Kingdom or United States of America university.

INSTITUTE OF IRISH STUDIES

Queen's University
8 Fitzwilliam Street, Belfast, BT9 6AW, Northern Ireland
Tel: (44) 28 9027 3386
Fax: (44) 28 9043 9238
Email: irish.studies@qub.ac.uk
www: http://www.qub.ac.uk/iis
Contact: Dr B M Walker, Director

The Institute of Irish Studies at Queen's University was established in 1965 and was one of the first of its kind. It is one of the leading centres for research based teaching in Irish studies and is an internationally renowned centre of interdisciplinary Irish scholarship attracting academics from all over the world.

Institute of Irish Studies Research Fellowships
Subjects: Any field of Irish studies.
Purpose: To promote research.
Eligibility: Candidates must hold at least a Second Class (Honours) Degree, have research experience and a viable research proposal.
Level of Study: Postdoctorate.
Type: Fellowship.
Value: UK £16,500.
Length of Study: One year.
Frequency: Annual.
Study Establishment: The Institute of Irish Studies.
Country of Study: Northern Ireland.
No. of awards offered: Up to three.
Application Procedure: Awards are usually advertised in February to March.
Closing Date: Varies.
No. of awards given last year: Three.
No. of applicants last year: 50.

Institute of Irish Studies Senior Visiting Research Fellowship
Subjects: Any field of Irish studies.
Purpose: To promote research.
Eligibility: Open to established Scholars of senior standing with a strong publication record.
Level of Study: Postdoctorate.
Type: Fellowship.
Value: UK £16,500.
Length of Study: One year.
Frequency: Annual.
Study Establishment: The Institute of Irish Studies.
Country of Study: Northern Ireland.
No. of awards offered: Up to two.
Application Procedure: Awards are usually advertised in February to March.
Closing Date: Varies.
No. of awards given last year: Two.
No. of applicants last year: 12.

Mary McNeill Scholarship in Irish Studies
Subjects: Irish studies.
Eligibility: Open to well qualified students enrolled in the one year MA course in Irish Studies at Queen's University. Applicants must be citizens of the United States or Canada and be enrolled as overseas students on this course.
Level of Study: Postgraduate.
Type: Scholarship.
Value: UK £3,000.
Length of Study: One year.
Study Establishment: Queen's University of Belfast.
Country of Study: Ireland.
Closing Date: May 31st.

THE INSTITUTE OF LOGISTICS AND TRANSPORT

11-12 Buckingham Gate, London, SW1E 6LB, England
Tel: (44) 20 7467 9400
Fax: (44) 20 7467 9440
Email: enquiry@iolt.org.uk
www: http://www.iolt.org.uk
Contact: Mr Richard Smith

The Institute of Logistics and Transport is the leading professional body for transport and integrated supply chain management with over 23,000 members. The Institute aims to meet the professional needs and promote the interests of all who work in these areas and encourage the adoption of policies which are both efficient and sustainable. The Institute is the United Kingdom territorial organisation of the International Chartered Institute of Logistics and Transport.

CMUA Road Transport Research Fellowship
Subjects: Road transport.
Purpose: To enable the candidate to examine and report upon road transport arrangements abroad.
Eligibility: Open to members of the Institute of Logistics and Transport (ILT).
Level of Study: Postgraduate, Professional development.
Type: Fellowship.
Value: Up to UK £1,300.
Frequency: Annual.
Country of Study: Outside the United Kingdom.
No. of awards offered: One.
Application Procedure: Applicants must submit an application form, available from the Institute in January. An outline research proposal must also be submitted.
Closing Date: May 31st.
Funding: Private.
Additional Information: The fellowship is sponsored by the Commercial Motor Users' Association.

Henry Spurrier Travelling Scholarship
Subjects: Fields connected with road transport, including traffic engineering.
Purpose: To encourage study and research in the sphere of road transport.
Eligibility: Open to members of the CILT or Institute of Logistics and Transport (ILT) who are employed in, or in connection with road transport (administration, operation, engineering, staff, and traffic).
Level of Study: Postgraduate, Professional development.
Type: Scholarship.
Value: Up to UK £2,000.
Frequency: Annual.
Country of Study: Any country.
No. of awards offered: Varies.
Application Procedure: Applicants must complete an application form, available from the Institute in January. An outline research proposal must also be submitted.
Closing Date: May 31st.
Funding: Private.
Additional Information: The money available can be awarded to one person or divided between more than one, according to the merit of the applications. Funds may be used for full-time study to assist with books and subsistence, part-time study for books and non local travelling expenses, or research, to cover subsistence, clerical assistance and other expenses. The award is not available for the payment of tuition fee.

John F Hooper Bursary Scheme
Subjects: Transport.
Purpose: To assist people wishing to undertake distance learning study for the ILT Diploma in Transport.
Eligibility: Open mainly to overseas students who encounter financial problems in their country. United Kingdom candidates may be

eligible where justified as special need. Applicants must be members of the Institute.
Level of Study: Professional development.
Type: Bursary.
Value: Up to UK £300 a year to cover study material, tuition and examination fees for qualifying examinations.
Length of Study: Up to three years.
Frequency: Annual.
Country of Study: Any country.
No. of awards offered: Varies.
Application Procedure: Applicants must apply by application form with references. At the second stage of selection an assignment must be completed.
Closing Date: May 31st.
Funding: Private.

John Gilbraith Award

Subjects: Road freight transport, logistics or distribution.
Purpose: To enable candidates to undertake research or travel to investigate transport practice and operation.
Eligibility: Open to members of any grade in the Northern Area, who are directly engaged in road freight transport, logistics or distribution.
Level of Study: Postgraduate, Professional development.
Value: Up to UK £500.
Frequency: Annual.
Country of Study: Any country.
No. of awards offered: Varies.
Application Procedure: Applicants must submit an application form, available from the Institute in January. An outline research proposal must also be submitted.
Closing Date: May 31st.
Funding: Commercial.

National Port Employers' Fund

Subjects: Any aspect of transport and communications relating to ports and port operations, including airports.
Purpose: To encourage the study of ports and port operations.
Eligibility: Applicants must be members of the Institute.
Level of Study: Postgraduate, Professional development.
Value: Up to UK £2,000 per year.
Frequency: Annual.
Country of Study: Any country.
Application Procedure: Applicants must submit an application form, available from the Institute from January.
Closing Date: May 31st.
Funding: Private.
Additional Information: The money available can be awarded to one person or divided between more than one, according to the merit of the applications. Funds may be used for full-time study to assist with books and subsistence, part-time study for books and non-local travelling expenses, or research, to cover subsistence, clerical assistance and other expenses. The award is not available for the payment of tuition fees.

Robert Bell Travelling Scholarship

Subjects: Overseas railway practice.
Purpose: To allow a candidate to travel abroad.
Eligibility: Open to members of the Institute engaged in railway transport in the United Kingdom.
Level of Study: Postgraduate, Professional development.
Type: Scholarship.
Value: Up to UK £500.
Frequency: Annual.
Country of Study: Outside the United Kingdom.
No. of awards offered: One.
Application Procedure: Applicants must complete an application form, available from the Institute in January. An outline research proposal must also be submitted.
Closing Date: May 31st.
Funding: Private.

Sir William Chamberlain Awards

Subjects: Fields connected with road transport.
Purpose: To encourage study and research in road transport.
Eligibility: Open to persons engaged, or intending to be engaged, in road transport in the North West traffic area, which is defined as Cheshire, Clwyd, Cumbria, Derbyshire, Greater Manchester, Gwynedd, Merseyside or Lancashire. Applicants must be members of the Institute.
Level of Study: Postgraduate, Professional development.
Value: Up to UK £1,350.
Frequency: Annual.
Study Establishment: A university, recognised college or a correspondence college.
Country of Study: Any country.
No. of awards offered: Varies.
Application Procedure: Applicants must complete an application form, available from the Institute in January. An outline research proposal must also be submitted.
Closing Date: May 31st.
Funding: Private.
Additional Information: The money available can be awarded to one person or divided between more than one, according to the merit of the applications. Funds may be used for full-time study to assist with books and subsistence, part-time study for books and non local travelling expenses, or research, to cover subsistence, clerical assistance and other expenses. The award is not available for the payment of tuition fees.

THE INSTITUTE OF SPORTS MEDICINE

Royal Free & University College Medical School
Charles Bell House
67-73 Riding House Street, London, W1W 7EJ, England
Tel: (44) 20 7813 2832
Fax: (44) 20 7813 2832
Email: m.hobsley@ucl.ac.uk
Contact: Miss D Meynell, Secretary

The Institute of Sports Medicine is a postgraduate medical institute which was established to develop research, teaching and treatment in sports medicine. It offers national awards to medical practitioners and runs courses on different aspects of this specialist subject. Now that it is based at University College London the Institute hopes to work closely with the College in the fulfilment of its objectives.

Duke of Edinburgh Prize for Sports Medicine

Subjects: Clinical or research work in the field of sports medicine in the community.
Purpose: To promote postgraduate work and to signify standards of excellence.
Eligibility: Open to medical practitioners in the United Kingdom.
Level of Study: Postgraduate.
Value: Varies, but is usually a substantial cash prize.
Frequency: Annual.
Country of Study: United Kingdom.
No. of awards offered: One.
Application Procedure: Applicants must write for an entry or nomination form in the first instance.
Closing Date: Varies annually. The exact date is specified in the conditions of entry.
Funding: Private.
No. of applicants last year: Two.

The Robert Atkins Award

Subjects: Sports medicine.
Purpose: To increase medical support for, and active involvement in, sports medicine and to recognise a doctor who has provided, for not less than five years, the most consistently valuable medical, clinical or preventive service to a national sporting organisation or sport in general.

Eligibility: Open to medical practitioners in the United Kingdom.
Level of Study: Postgraduate.
Value: Varies, but is usually a substantial cash prize.
Frequency: Annual.
Country of Study: United Kingdom.
No. of awards offered: One.
Application Procedure: Applicants must write for an entry or nomination form in the first instance.
Closing Date: Varies annually.
Funding: Private.
No. of awards given last year: One.
No. of applicants last year: Two.

THE INSTITUTION OF CIVIL ENGINEERS

1-7 Great George Street
Westminster, London, SW1P 3AA, England
Tel: (44) 20 7665 2110
Fax: (44) 20 7233 0515
Email: helen.moger@ice.org.uk
www: http://www.ice.org.uk
Contact: Ms Ellen Ryan, Education Officer

QUEST C H Roberts Bequest

Subjects: Civil engineering.
Purpose: To promote the exchange of engineering graduates between the United Kingdom and Spain for the purpose of furthering their academic studies and engineering training.
Eligibility: Open to British or Spanish nationals who are members or associate members of the Institution.
Level of Study: Postgraduate.
Type: Bursary.
Value: Approx. UK £2,000.
Length of Study: Six-nine months.
Frequency: Annually, alternately to each country.
Country of Study: Spain for United Kingdom candidates or the United Kingdom for Spanish candidates.
No. of awards offered: Two.
Application Procedure: Applicants must complete an application form, available from Ms Coverdale.
Closing Date: March 31st.
Funding: Private.
Contributor: The British Council.
Additional Information: Successful applicants are encouraged under the terms of the bequest to learn the language of the other country (some prior knowledge is essential) and to acquire a knowledge of its people by residence, study and engineering experience. They will be required to further their knowledge of the language by spending one to two hours weekly on additional language study with an approved institute or teacher, whose fees will be covered by the award. Practical experience gained in Spain under the award will be accepted towards the experience required for permission to take the professional examination.

QUEST Institution of Civil Engineers Continuing Education Award

Subjects: Civil engineering.
Purpose: To enable approved persons to undertake MSc courses after some years industrial experience.
Eligibility: Open to graduates of any nationality who hold an accredited First Class Degree in civil engineering and have been members of the Institution (any grade) for not less than two years.
Level of Study: Postgraduate.
Type: Award.
Value: Up to UK £2,000.
Frequency: Annual.
Country of Study: United Kingdom.
No. of awards offered: 10-15.
Application Procedure: Applicants must complete an application form, available from Ms Coverdale.

Closing Date: March 31st.
No. of awards given last year: 13.
No. of applicants last year: 20.

QUEST Institution of Civil Engineers Overseas Travel Awards

Subjects: Civil engineering, environmental engineering, transportation and agricultural engineering.
Purpose: To support overseas travel by institution members to overseas universities, specific overseas projects and mid-career support and development.
Eligibility: Open to institution members, preference being given to postgraduate applicants proposing individual overseas projects or requiring mid career support.
Level of Study: Postgraduate.
Value: Up to UK £2,000.
Length of Study: 3-12 months.
Frequency: Annual.
Study Establishment: Exchange visits with overseas universities, specific overseas projects proposed by individual applicants, or mid career support and development.
Country of Study: Any country.
No. of awards offered: Approx. 15.
Application Procedure: Applicants must complete an application form, available from Mrs Coverdale.
Closing Date: March 31st.
Additional Information: Applications are not necessarily restricted to technical developments, but may be concerned with organisational, managerial or financial aspects of civil engineering. Awards will be judged on merit.

THE INSTITUTION OF ELECTRICAL ENGINEERS (IEE)

Grants Management Office
Qualifications Department
Savoy Place, London, WC2R 0BL, England
Tel: (44) 20 7240 1871
Fax: (44) 20 7497 3633
Email: twalter@iee.org.uk
www: http://www.iee.org.uk
Contact: Grants Management Officer

The Institution of Electrical Engineers (IEE) seeks to promote the advancement of electrical, manufacturing and information engineering and facilitate the exchange of knowledge and ideas. IEE wishes to provide a broad range of services to members, to assist them in developing their careers by improving their capabilities as engineers, and to play their full part in contributing to society.

The D H Thomas Travel Bursary

Subjects: Electrical, electronic, information and manufacturing engineering and related disciplines.
Purpose: To support IEE members undertaking research in Europe related to either their postgraduate education or their professional interests eg. historical or biographical work leading to a publication.
Eligibility: Open to IEE members underrating personal and professional research. Preference is given to research taking place in Germany.
Level of Study: Doctorate, Postdoctorate, Postgraduate, Professional development, Research.
Type: Scholarship.
Value: UK £500.
Length of Study: Up to three years.
Frequency: Every two years.
Country of Study: Germany or another European country.
No. of awards offered: One.
Application Procedure: Applicants must complete an application form.

Closing Date: Applications may be received from January 1st to December 15th. Given that there are a limited number of awards, applicants are advised to apply as early in the year as possible.

Additional Information: Further information can be found on the website.

Hudswell Bequest Travelling Fellowships

Subjects: Electrical, electronic, manufacturing engineering and related disciplines.

Purpose: To allow IEE members to pursue study overseas.

Eligibility: Open to IEE members undertaking postgraduate research in the United Kingdom.

Level of Study: Postgraduate.

Type: Fellowship.

Value: Up to UK £1,000.

Frequency: Annual.

Country of Study: United Kingdom.

No. of awards offered: Four.

Application Procedure: Applicants must make enquiries with the IEE.

Closing Date: Applications may be received from January 1st to December 15th. Given that there are a limited number of awards, applicants are advised to apply as early in the year as possible.

No. of awards given last year: Two.

Additional Information: Further information can be found on the website.

Hudswell International Research Scholarships

Subjects: Electrical, electronic, information technology and manufacturing engineering and related disciplines.

Purpose: To assist members of the Institution with advanced research work, leading to the award of a doctorate, to be undertaken outside the applicant's home country.

Eligibility: Applicants must have been a member of the IEE for a minimum period of two years before an application is submitted. It is expected that applicants should have attained Corporate Membership of the IEE, but applications may be accepted from applicants whose research studies may lead to Corporate Membership on completion of the approved doctorate.

Level of Study: Doctorate, Postgraduate.

Type: Scholarship.

Value: UK £5,000.

Length of Study: One year.

Frequency: Every two years.

Study Establishment: Internationally recognised universities or research establishments with a high reputation for research.

Application Procedure: Applicants must complete an application form.

Closing Date: For consideration in May applications must be received by April 30th, for consideration in September applications must be received by August 2nd and for consideration in November applications must be received by October 30th.

Additional Information: Given that there are a limited number of awards available, applicants are advised to apply as early as possible.

IEE Management Scholarship

Subjects: MBA in management studies or equivalent degree.

Purpose: To encourage IEE corporate members to undertake formal management training leading to the award of an MBA or equivalent degree.

Eligibility: Open to corporate members of the IEE.

Level of Study: Postgraduate, MBA.

Type: Scholarship.

Value: UK £1,000 per year.

Length of Study: A maximum of two years.

Frequency: Annual.

Study Establishment: A suitable university.

Country of Study: United Kingdom.

No. of awards offered: One.

Application Procedure: Applicants must complete an application form.

Closing Date: For consideration in May applications must be received by April 30th, for consideration in September applications must be received by August 2nd and for consideration in November applications must be received by October 30th.

No. of awards given last year: One.

Additional Information: Given that there is a single award available, applicants are advised to apply as early as possible.

IEE Master's Degree Research Scholarship

Subjects: Electrical, electronic, manufacturing or information engineering.

Purpose: To assist IEE members undertaking advance postgraduate research studies for MRes or MPhil degrees.

Eligibility: Applicants must be IEE members who have satisfied the IEE educational requirements for Corporate Membership, or whose course of studies will lead to Corporate Membership of the IEE. Applicants must have been an IEE member, in any class, for not less than two years.

Level of Study: Postgraduate.

Type: Scholarship.

Value: UK £2,500 for one year of full time study or UK £1,250 per year for part time study.

Frequency: Annual.

Country of Study: United Kingdom.

No. of awards offered: Two.

Application Procedure: Applicants must make enquiries with the IEE.

Closing Date: For consideration in May applications must be received by April 30th, for consideration in September applications must be received by August 2nd and for consideration in November applications must be received by October 30th.

Additional Information: Given that there are a limited number of awards available, applicants are advised to apply as early as possible. This award is subject to complete revision and substantial changes in terms and conditions.

IEE Postgraduate Scholarships

Subjects: Electrical, electronic, communications, manufacturing or power engineering.

Purpose: To assist IEE members with research studies.

Eligibility: Open to research students holding qualifications which have been accepted by the Institution as fulfilling the IEE educational requirements for Corporate Membership, or to assist members to complete a research programme that will lead to Corporate Membership.

Level of Study: Doctorate, Postgraduate, Research.

Type: Scholarship.

Value: UK£1,250.

Length of Study: One year.

Frequency: Annual.

Country of Study: United Kingdom.

No. of awards offered: Three.

Application Procedure: Applicants must complete an application form.

Closing Date: Applications may be received from January 1st to October 30th. Applicants are advised to apply as early in the year as possible.

No. of awards given last year: Three.

Additional Information: Further details are available from the website.

IEE Younger Members Conference Bursary

Subjects: Electrical engineering and related disciplines.

Purpose: To assist IEE members with presenting papers at IEE conferences.

Eligibility: Open to members of the IEE who are full-time students and/or aged under 30, who have had papers accepted for presentation at an IEE conference and have no other sources of funding towards the registration fee and accommodation whilst attending the event.

Level of Study: Postgraduate, Professional development.
Type: Travel grant.
Frequency: Annual.
No. of awards offered: Two per conference.
Application Procedure: Applicants must make enquiries with the IEE.
Closing Date: Two months prior to the date of the conference.
No. of awards given last year: Three.
Additional Information: This award is subject to complete revision and substantial changes in terms and conditions.

J R Beard Travelling Fund Awards

Subjects: Electrical, electronic, manufacturing and related engineering.
Purpose: To enable members of the Institution to travel overseas to broaden their professional experience.
Eligibility: Open to IEE members intending to expand their experience in the field of manufacturing techniques conducted overseas. Grants are available to assist, in particular, younger IEE members to broaden their professional experience through overseas travel. Applicants must be studying in the United Kingdom.
Level of Study: Unrestricted.
Type: Travel grant.
Value: Up to UK £500.
Frequency: Annual.
Country of Study: Any country.
No. of awards offered: Six.
Application Procedure: Applicants must complete an application form.
Closing Date: Applications for these scholarships may be received from January 1st to December 15th. Given that there are a limited number of awards applicants are advised to apply as early in the year as possible.
Additional Information: Further information can be found on the website.

The Leonard Research Grant

Subjects: Electrical, electronic, manufacturing or related engineering.
Purpose: To assist engineering graduates who might not otherwise be able to undertake or complete work leading to a higher degree.
Eligibility: Applicants should currently be resident in the United Kingdom and must have satisfied the Institution's educational requirement for corporate membership.
Level of Study: Doctorate, Postgraduate.
Type: Research grant.
Value: Please contact the organisation.
Frequency: Dependent on funds available.
Study Establishment: A suitable university.
Country of Study: United Kingdom.
No. of awards offered: One.
Application Procedure: Applicants must complete an application form.
Closing Date: Please contact the organisation.

Leslie H Paddle Fellowship

Subjects: Electrical or radio engineering.
Purpose: To assist IEE members with research studies.
Eligibility: Applicants must currently be resident in the United Kingdom and must possess qualifications which have been accepted by the IEE as fulfilling the educational requirements for Corporate Management. Applicants must be first year research students.
Level of Study: Doctorate, Postgraduate.
Type: Scholarship.
Value: UK £10,000.
Length of Study: Two years.
Frequency: Annual.
Study Establishment: A suitable university.
Country of Study: United Kingdom.

No. of awards offered: One.
Application Procedure: Applicants must make enquiries with the IEE.
Closing Date: Applications may be received from January 1st to October 30th. Applicants are advised to apply as early in the year as possible.
No. of awards given last year: One.
Additional Information: It is hoped that the fellowship will encourage co-operation between industry and the higher education sector and that an industrial organisation will be associated with the fellowship. Leslie H Paddle Fellowship holders who satisfactorily complete their research studies may use the appendage 'IEE Scholar'. Further details can be found on the website.

The Lord Lloyd of Kilgerran Memorial Prize (Postgraduate Award)

Subjects: Mobile radio or RF engineering.
Purpose: To aid a candidate who intends to undertake a MSc, MPhil or PhD in mobile radio and RF engineering.
Eligibility: Applicants should currently be resident in the United Kingdom and should have been practising professional engineers for a minimum of three years.
Level of Study: Postgraduate.
Type: Scholarship.
Value: UK £2,000.
Length of Study: One year for full time study or two years for part time study.
Frequency: Every two years.
Study Establishment: A suitable university.
Country of Study: United Kingdom.
No. of awards offered: One.
Application Procedure: Applicants must complete an application form.
Closing Date: Applications may be received from January 1st to October 30th.

The Princess Royal Scholarship

Subjects: Engineering work commensurate with the activities of the Institution.
Purpose: To enable an IEE member to use his or her professional knowledge and experience in a way that is beneficial to an underprivileged community in a developing country.
Eligibility: Open to applicants undertaking a specific programme of work with a charitable organisation. The nature of the work must be commensurate with the activities of the IEE. The programme must be undertaken for a period of not less than three months and conducted in co-operation with an organisation in the receiving country.
Level of Study: Postgraduate.
Type: Scholarship.
Value: UK £1,000.
Frequency: Annual.
Country of Study: Developing nations.
No. of awards offered: One.
Application Procedure: Applicants must complete an application form.
Closing Date: Applications may be received from January 1st to October 30th. Given that there are a limited number of awards, applicants are advised to apply as early in the year as possible.
No. of awards given last year: One.
Additional Information: Further information can be found on the website.

Robinson Research Scholarship

Subjects: Electrical, electronic, communications, information or manufacturing engineering and related disciplines.
Purpose: To assist IEE members with research leading to the award of a PhD or postdoctoral qualification.
Eligibility: Applicants must currently be resident in the United Kingdom and must possess qualifications which have been accepted by the IEE as fulfilling the educational requirements for Corporate Management. If not already a member, the candidate must apply for

admission to the class of Associate Member (AMIEE) of the IEE. Applicants must be first year research students.
Level of Study: Doctorate, Postdoctorate, Postgraduate.
Type: Scholarship.
Value: UK £1,250 per year.
Length of Study: Two years.
Frequency: Annual.
Study Establishment: A suitable university or research establishment.
Country of Study: United Kingdom.
No. of awards offered: Two.
Application Procedure: Applicants must make enquiries with the IEE.
Closing Date: For consideration in May applications must be received by April 30th, for consideration in September applications must be received by August 2nd and for consideration in November applications must be received by October 30th.
Additional Information: Given that there are a limited number of awards available, applicants are advised to apply as early as possible.

INSTITUTION OF MECHANICAL ENGINEERS (IMECHE)

1-3 Birdcage Walk, London, SW1H 9JJ, England
Tel: (44) 20 7222 7899
Fax: (44) 20 7222 4557
Email: enquiries@imeche.org.uk
www: http://www.imeche.org.uk/prizes
Contact: Council Officer

The Institution of Mechanical Engineers (IMechE) was founded in 1847 by engineers. They formed an institution to promote the exchange of ideas and encourage individuals or groups in creating inventions that would be crucial to the development of the world as a whole. Now, over 150 years later, IMechE is one of the largest engineering institutions in the world with over 88,000 members in 120 countries.

Bramah Scholarship

Subjects: Hydraulic mechanisms, particularly hydrostatic transmissions and servomechanisms.
Purpose: To encourage engineers to study hydraulic engineering, obtain special experience or to carry out studies at approved centres or laboratories.
Eligibility: Candidates must be members of the Institution and must satisfy, or be making adequate progress towards satisfying, the academic requirements for graduate membership and preferably have had two years or more of acceptable professional training.
Level of Study: Postgraduate.
Type: Research grant.
Value: Up to UK £1,500.
Length of Study: One year, with a possibility of renewal for a maximum of two years. Shorter periods of study will also be considered.
Frequency: Annual.
Study Establishment: An approved centre or laboratory.
Country of Study: United Kingdom.
No. of awards offered: Up to two.
Application Procedure: Applicants must complete and submit an application form with three references.
Closing Date: Three months before a decision is required.
Additional Information: At the completion of a scholarship, or at the end of each 12 month period, a report of work must be submitted. It is one of the major objectives of the Institution to publish new or original work. The Institution has the copyright and the right to publish any report made by a scholar.

For further information contact:

Educational Services
The Institution for Mechanical Engineers (IMechE)

Northgate Avenue, Bury St Edmunds, Suffolk, IP32 6BN, England
Tel: (44) 1284 716617

Bryan Donkin Award

Subjects: The science or practice of mechanical engineering.
Purpose: To assist members of the Institution to carry out original research in the science or practice of mechanical engineering.
Eligibility: Open to British born members of the Institution. Applicants should not have less than two years acceptable practical training in mechanical engineering.
Level of Study: Doctorate, Postdoctorate, Postgraduate.
Value: Up to UK £7,000.
Frequency: Annual.
Country of Study: Any country.
No. of awards offered: Varies.
Application Procedure: Applicants must submit a completed application form with three references.
Closing Date: Three months before a decision is required.
Additional Information: The award may be made to supplement grants from other sources. A report of the work must be submitted.

For further information contact:

Educational Services
The Institution of Mechanical Engineers (IMechE)
Northgate Avenue, Bury St Edmunds, Suffolk, IP32 6BN, England
Tel: (44) 1284 718617

Donald Julius Groen Prizes

Subjects: Engineering.
Purpose: To award the author of outstanding papers or for outstanding achievements in the group's sphere of activity.
Eligibility: Open to authors of papers or achievements of a sufficiently high standard to warrant the award of a IMechE prize. As a general rule, but with certain exceptions, grants are normally awarded only to members of the Institution.
Type: Prize.
Value: UK £250.
Frequency: Annual.
No. of awards offered: Eight.
Application Procedure: Applicants must contact the Institution of Mechanical Engineers for details.

Flatman Grants

Subjects: Mechanical engineering.
Purpose: To help students, graduates and members to further their education or obtain special experience overseas.
Eligibility: Open to members under 30 years of age.
Level of Study: Postgraduate, Professional development.
Type: Grant.
Value: Up to UK £750.
Frequency: Annual.
Country of Study: Any country.
No. of awards offered: Approx. 10.
Application Procedure: Applicants must submit a completed application form with three references.
Closing Date: Three months before a decision is required.
Funding: Private.
Additional Information: A report is required within three months of completion of project.

For further information contact:

Educational Services
The Institution of Mechanical Engineers (IMechE)
Northgate Avenue, Bury St Edmunds, Suffolk, IP32 6BN, England
Tel: (44) 1284 718617

James Bates Grants

Subjects: Engineering.
Purpose: To promote mechanical engineering and the professional development of young members of the Institution.
Eligibility: Open to young members of the Institution.

Type: Grant.
Value: 50 per cent of the cost of travel, accommodation, meals and appropriate fees will be made to the young members of the Institution who attend the railway division technical meetings and industrial visits arranged by young members' panels.
Frequency: Annual.
No. of awards offered: Varies.
Application Procedure: Applicants must contact the Institution of Mechanical Engineers for details.

The James Bates Prize

Subjects: Engineering.
Purpose: For technical contributions submitted by young members under the age of 31.
Eligibility: Awarded for technical contributions submitted by graduates or students and read before a local meeting of the Institution providing that the paper or contribution is of sufficient merit. As a general rule, but with certain exceptions, grants are normally awarded only to members of the Institution.
Type: Prize.
Value: First Prize is UK £100 and the second prize is UK £50.
Frequency: Annual.
No. of awards offered: Two per branch.
Application Procedure: Applicants must contact the IMechE for details.
Funding: Private.
Contributor: James Bates.

For further information contact:

Educational Services
The Institution of Mechanical Engineers (IMechE)
Northgate Avenue, Bury St Edmunds, Suffolk, IP32 6BN, England
Tel: (44) 1284 718617

James Clayton Awards

Subjects: Mechanical engineering.
Purpose: To enable the recipient to pursue advanced postgraduate studies or programmes of research.
Eligibility: Open to Institution members who hold an accredited engineering degree, or have satisfied the academic requirements for IMechE membership by other means, and have had not less than two years of acceptable professional training in mechanical engineering.
Level of Study: Postgraduate.
Type: Grant.
Value: Up to UK £1,000 per year.
Length of Study: Up to three years.
Frequency: Annual.
Study Establishment: An approved centre.
Country of Study: United Kingdom.
No. of awards offered: Approx. 10.
Application Procedure: Applicants must complete and submit an application form with three references.
Closing Date: Three months before a decision is required.
Additional Information: A report is required within three months of completion of the project.

For further information contact:

Educational Services
The Institution of Mechanical Engineers (IMechE)
Northgate Avenue, Bury St Edmunds, Suffolk, IP32 6BN, England
Tel: (44) 1284 718617

James Clayton Lectures

Subjects: Mechanical engineering.
Purpose: To provide for the expenses of the person presenting the lecture which is to take place at an ordinary meeting of the Institution on a subject relating to mechanical engineering science, research, invention or experimental work.
Level of Study: Postgraduate.
Type: Grant.

Value: UK £500.
Frequency: Annual.
Country of Study: United Kingdom.
No. of awards offered: One.
Application Procedure: Applicants must write for details.
Funding: Private.

James Clayton Overseas Conference Travel for Senior Engineers

Subjects: Mechanical engineering.
Purpose: To assist members of the Institution who have been invited to contribute in some way to a conference or who could be expected to make a significant contribution to the aims of a conference by their attendance.
Eligibility: Open to members over the age of 40 years.
Level of Study: Professional development.
Type: Travel grant.
Value: Up to UK £1,000.
Country of Study: Any country.
No. of awards offered: Varies.
Application Procedure: Applicants must submit a completed application form with three references.
Funding: Private.
Additional Information: A report is required three months after the conference.

For further information contact:

Educational Services
The Institution of Mechanical Engineers (IMechE)
Northgate Avenue, Bury St Edmunds, Suffolk, IP32 6BN, England
Tel: (44) 1284 718617

James Clayton Postgraduate Hardship Award

Subjects: Mechanical engineering.
Purpose: To assist outstanding postgraduates who experience hardship while undertaking courses of advanced study, training or research work on a course approved by the Institution.
Eligibility: Open to candidates who have completed a degree course in mechanical engineering accredited by IMechE and have gained graduate membership of IMechE.
Level of Study: Postgraduate.
Type: Grant.
Value: Up to UK £1,000.
Length of Study: One year.
Frequency: Annual.
Country of Study: United Kingdom.
No. of awards offered: Up to three.
Application Procedure: Applicants must complete and submit an application form with three references.
Closing Date: Three months before a decision is required.
Additional Information: A report is required three months after the activity has been completed.

For further information contact:

Educational Services
The Institution of Mechanical Engineers (IMechE)
Northgate Avenue, Bury St Edmunds, Suffolk, IP32 6BN, England
Tel: (44) 1284 718617

James Watt International Medal

Subjects: Mechanical engineering.
Purpose: To award an eminent engineer who has attained worldwide recognition in mechanical engineering.
Eligibility: Nominations are invited from overseas. Eminent United Kingdom engineers are also eligible.
Type: Medal.
Frequency: Awarded in odd numbered years.
No. of awards offered: One.
Application Procedure: Applicants must write for details.
Additional Information: This award is the premier international award of the Institution.

Labrow Grants

Subjects: Mechanical engineering.
Purpose: To assist research in the science or practice of mechanical engineering.
Eligibility: Open to members of the IMechE. Applicants should have no less than two years of acceptable practical training in mechanical engineering.
Level of Study: Unrestricted.
Type: Grant.
Value: Up to UK £7,000.
Frequency: Varies.
Country of Study: Any country.
No. of awards offered: Varies.
Application Procedure: Applicants must submit a completed application form with three references.
Additional Information: A report is required three months after the activity has been completed.

For further information contact:

Educational Services
The Institution of Mechanical Engineers (IMechE)
Northgate Avenue, Bury St Edmunds, Suffolk, IP32 6BN, England
Tel: (44) 1284 718617

Neil Watson Grants

Subjects: Mechanical engineering, power generation or internal combustion engines.
Purpose: To enable young engineers to attend conferences and seminars, travel abroad to study engineering practices overseas, or to attend suitable training courses in the field of power generation in general and internal combustion engines in particular.
Eligibility: Normally only open to non corporate members of the IMechE under the age of 31.
Level of Study: Postgraduate.
Type: Grant.
Value: UK £500.
Frequency: Annual.
Country of Study: Any country.
No. of awards offered: Varies.
Application Procedure: Applicants must submit a completed application form with three references.
Additional Information: A report is required three months after the activity has been completed.

For further information contact:

Educational Services
The Institution of Mechanical Engineers (IMechE)
Northgate Avenue, Bury St Edmunds, Suffolk, IP32 6BN, England
Tel: (44) 1284 718617

Solids Handling Award

Subjects: Bulk solids technology.
Purpose: To recognise an individual's professional excellence in the field.
Eligibility: Open to people from any nationality, who do not have to be members of IMechE. The award is for either a paper published by the Institution, or for research, design or development work in the field, or in recognition of an individual's professional excellence.
Type: Award.
Value: UK £250 and a plaque.
Frequency: Annual.
No. of awards offered: One.
Application Procedure: Nominations for the award are made by the Bulk Materials Handling Committee and are approved by the Process Industries Division Board.
Funding: Commercial.
Contributor: Trinity Publishing Limited.

Spencer Wilks Scholarship/Fellowship

Subjects: Mechanical engineering.

Purpose: To promote or encourage the study of automobile engineering.
Level of Study: Postgraduate.
Type: Scholarship.
Value: Up to UK £10,000.
Frequency: Annual.
Country of Study: Any country.
No. of awards offered: One.
Application Procedure: Applicants must write for details.
Funding: Private.

Thomas Andrew Common Grants

Subjects: Areas related to mechanical engineering.
Purpose: To provide assistance to members of the Institution to attend conferences.
Eligibility: Open to members under the age of 40 who have been invited to contribute in some way to a conference or who could be expected to make a significant contribution to the aims of a conference by attending.
Level of Study: Postgraduate, Professional development.
Type: Grant.
Value: Up to UK £1,000.
Frequency: Varies.
Study Establishment: Approved conferences.
Country of Study: Any country.
No. of awards offered: Approx. 35.
Application Procedure: Applicants must complete and submit an application form with three references.
Closing Date: Three months before a decision is required.
Additional Information: A report is required within three months of return from the conference.

For further information contact:

Educational Services
The Institution of Mechanical Engineers (IMechE)
Northgate Avenue, Bury St Edmunds, Suffolk, IP32 6BN, England
Tel: (44) 1284 718617

THE INSTITUTION OF MINING AND METALLURGY

Danum House
South Parade, Doncaster, South Yorkshire, DN1 2DY, England
Tel: (44) 1302 380912
Fax: (44) 1302 380900
Email: hq@imm.org.uk
www: http://www.imm.org.uk
Contact: Ms Carol MacKenzie, Professional Affairs Assistant

The Institution of Mining and Metallurgy is a qualifying body and learned society for individuals seeking to be recognised, or already practising as, professionals in the international minerals industry.

Bosworth Smith Trust Fund

Subjects: Metal mining and non ferrous extraction metallurgy or mineral dressing.
Purpose: To assist postgraduate research.
Eligibility: Open to persons who possess a degree in a relevant subject.
Level of Study: Postgraduate.
Value: Approx. UK £5,500 is available for grants toward working expenses, the costs of visits to mines and plants in connection with such research, and the purchase of apparatus.
Length of Study: One year.
Frequency: Annual.
Study Establishment: An approved university.
Country of Study: United Kingdom.
No. of awards offered: Varies.
Application Procedure: Applicants must complete an application form, available on request.

Closing Date: March 15th.

For further information contact:

The Institution of Mining and Metallurgy
Hallam Court
77 Hallam Street, London, W1W 5BS, England

Edgar Pam Fellowship

Subjects: All subjects within the Institution's fields of interest, which range from explorative geology to extractive metallurgy.
Purpose: To enable postgraduate study.
Eligibility: Open to young graduates domiciled in Australia, Canada, New Zealand, South Africa or the United Kingdom who wish to undertake advanced study or research in the United Kingdom.
Level of Study: Postgraduate.
Type: Fellowship.
Value: UK £2,000.
Length of Study: One year.
Frequency: Annual.
Study Establishment: Approved universities in the United Kingdom.
Country of Study: United Kingdom.
No. of awards offered: One.
Application Procedure: Applicants must complete an application form, available on request.
Closing Date: March 15th.

For further information contact:

The Institution of Mining and Metallurgy
Hallam Court
77 Hallam Street, London, W1W 5BS, England

G Vernon Hobson Bequest

Subjects: Mining geology.
Purpose: To advance the teaching and practice of geology as applied to mining.
Eligibility: Open to members of university staffs in the United Kingdom.
Level of Study: Professional development.
Value: From a total of approx. UK £1,300 for travel, research or other objects in accordance with the terms of the bequest.
Frequency: Annual.
Country of Study: United Kingdom.
No. of awards offered: More than one.
Application Procedure: Applicants must complete an application form, available on request.
Closing Date: March 15th.

For further information contact:

The Institution of Mining and Metallurgy
Hallam Court
77 Hallam Street, London, W1W 5BS, England

Mining Club Award

Subjects: Mineral industry operations.
Purpose: To enable candidates to study mineral industry operations in the United Kingdom or overseas, to present a paper at an international minerals industry conference or to assist the candidate in attending a full-time course of study related to the minerals industry outside the United Kingdom.
Eligibility: Open to British citizens aged 21 to 35 years who are actively engaged (in full or part-time postgraduate study or employment) in the minerals industry.
Level of Study: Postgraduate, Professional development.
Type: Award.
Value: Approx. UK £1,500.
Frequency: Annual.
Country of Study: Any country.
No. of awards offered: Varies.
Application Procedure: Applicants must complete an application form, available on request.
Closing Date: March 15th.

For further information contact:

The Institution of Mining and Metallurgy
Hallam Court
77 Hallam Street, London, W1W 5BS, England

Stanley Elmore Fellowships

Subjects: Research into all branches of extractive metallurgy and mineral processing.
Eligibility: Open to persons who are fully qualified to undertake postdoctoral research. In general, preference will be given to applicants who are members of the Institution.
Level of Study: Postdoctorate.
Type: Fellowship.
Value: UK £12,000-16,000. Lesser amounts are available for approved short-term assignments.
Length of Study: One year, with a possibility of renewal to a maximum of three years.
Frequency: Annual.
Study Establishment: An approved university in the United Kingdom.
Country of Study: United Kingdom.
No. of awards offered: One-two.
Application Procedure: Applicants must complete an application form, available on request.
Closing Date: March 15th.

For further information contact:

The Institution of Mining and Metallurgy
Hallam Court
77 Hallam Street, London, W1W 5BS, England

INSTITUTO NACIONAL DE METEOROLOGIA (INM)

Camino de las Morenas
S/N Ciudad Universitaria, Madrid, E-28040, Spain
Tel: (34) 91 581 9860
Fax: (34) 91 581 9892
Email: carlos.legaz@inm.es
www: http://www.inm.es
Telex: 2247 LEMMC
Contact: Dr Carlos Garcia-Legaz Martinez

INM Fellowship for Curso Internacional de Meteorologia Clase II OMM

Subjects: Atmospheric sciences and meteorology.
Eligibility: Candidates should have a background of training and professional experience in sciences, engineering or meteorology. A good knowledge of the Spanish language is required.
Level of Study: Professional development.
Type: Fellowship.
Value: Please contact the association for details.
Length of Study: 21 months.
Frequency: Every two years.
Study Establishment: INM training centre.
Country of Study: Spain.
No. of awards offered: 15-20.
Application Procedure: Applicants must complete an application form, distributed by the INM. Candidates should be supported by a meteorological or academic authority. Applications can be submitted through the WMO in Geneva.
Funding: Government.
No. of awards given last year: 15.
No. of applicants last year: 60.

INM Short-term Fellowship

Subjects: Atmospheric sciences and meteorology.

Purpose: To support on the job training in different departments of the INM.

Eligibility: Candidates must be staff of the meteorological service in their country. A good knowledge of English or the Spanish language is required.

Level of Study: Professional development.

Type: Fellowship.

Value: Please contact the association for details.

Length of Study: Two months.

Frequency: Annual.

Study Establishment: INM technical departments.

Country of Study: Spain.

No. of awards offered: 10-15.

Application Procedure: Applicants must complete an application, but no form is required, through the permanent representatives of their countries with WMO expressing their support of the candidate.

Closing Date: Beginning of February for fellowships to be initiated in the first semester, beginning of June for fellowships to be initiated in the second semester.

Funding: Government.

No. of awards given last year: 15.

No. of applicants last year: 100.

INTENSIVE CARE SOCIETY

9 Bedford Square, London, WC1B 3RE, England

Tel: (44) 20 7631 8890

Fax: (44) 20 7631 8897

Email: admin@ics.ac.uk

Contact: N R Webster, Chair of Research Committee

The Intensive Care Society is a charitable organisation promoting advances in the care of the critically ill. This is largely accomplished through educational means and promoting research activity.

Intensive Care Society Project Grant

Subjects: Any aspect of intensive care medicine and care of the critically ill.

Purpose: To promote research into pump priming.

Eligibility: Applicants must be ICS members.

Level of Study: Unrestricted.

Type: Project grant.

Value: Up to UK £5,000.

Length of Study: Up to one year.

Frequency: Dependent on funds available.

Country of Study: Any country.

No. of awards offered: Varies.

Application Procedure: Applicants must complete an application form, available from the website.

Closing Date: Please contact the foundation.

Funding: Private.

No. of awards given last year: Four.

No. of applicants last year: 12.

Additional Information: Further information is available on the Foundation's website.

INTER AMERICAN PRESS ASSOCIATION (IAPA)

IAPA Scholarship Fund, Inc.
2911 North West 39th Street, Miami, FL, 33142, United States of America
Tel: (1) 305 376 3522
Fax: (1) 305 376 8950
Email: zulaydominguez@aol.com
www: http://www.sipiapa.org
Contact: Ms Zulay Dominguez Chirinos, Scholarships Director

The Inter-American Press Association was established in 1942 to defend and promote the right of the peoples of the Americas to be fully and freely informed through an independent press.

IAPA Scholarship Fund, Inc.

Subjects: Journalism in the print media.

Purpose: To help develop more rounded journalists through cultural exposure and study in a foreign country.

Eligibility: Open to natives of North America, Latin America and the West Indies who are between 21 and 35 years of age and are either professional journalists with at least three years' experience in the print media, or graduates of a school of journalism.

Level of Study: Postgraduate, Professional development.

Type: Scholarship.

Value: US$13,000.

Length of Study: Nine months.

Frequency: Annual.

Study Establishment: An American or Canadian university school of journalism approved by the Fund for Latin American and West Indian candidates, or an approved university or field work in a Latin American country for United States and Canadian candidates.

Country of Study: United States of America, Canada or Latin American countries.

No. of awards offered: Four-six.

Application Procedure: Applicants must complete an application form, available from the Scholarships Director.

Closing Date: December 31st.

Additional Information: Candidates should have good command of the language of the country they intend to visit. United States and Canadian Scholars must take a minimum of three university courses, participate in the Fund's Reporting Program, and undertake a major research project. The Association also gives IAPA awards of US$500-1,000 and a scroll or plaque to Latin American and American journalists.

INTERART FESTIVAL CENTER

PO Box 80
1051 Vörösmarty Tér 1, Budapest, H-1366, Hungary
Tel: (36) 1 317 9838
Fax: (36) 1 317 9910
Contact: Grants Management Officer

The Hungarian Television and Interart Festival Center has organised the International Conductors' Competition every third year since 1974. The goal of the competition is to discover gifted young conductors from Hungary and abroad, to introduce them to the possible audience and to stimulate public interest in musical performance, musical values and modes and possibilities of interpretation.

Hungarian Television, Interart Festival Center International Conductors' Competition

Subjects: Conducting.

Purpose: To hold a competition in memory of Jànos Ferencsik.

Eligibility: Open to conductors of all nationalities.

Level of Study: Professional development.

Type: Competition.

Value: First prize is US$5,000, the second prize is US$3,000 and the third prize is US$2,000.
Frequency: Every three years.
Country of Study: Any country.
No. of awards offered: Three.
Application Procedure: Applicants must complete an application form and submit this with study documents, two photographs and a video recording.
Closing Date: January 1st.
Funding: Commercial, Government.
Contributor: Hungarian television.
No. of awards given last year: Three.
No. of applicants last year: 50.

INTERNATIONAL AGENCY FOR RESEARCH ON CANCER (IARC)

150 cours Albert Thomas, Lyon, Cedex 08, F-69372, France
Tel: (33) 4 72 73 84 48
Fax: (33) 4 72 73 80 80
Email: fel@iarc.fr
www: http://www.iarc.fr
Telex: 380 023
Contact: Ms Eve Elakroud, Administrative Assistant IARC Fellowship Programme

The International Agency for Research on Cancer (IARC) is part of the World Health Organisation. IARC's mission is to co-ordinate and conduct research into the causes of human cancer and the mechanisms of carcinogenesis, and to develop scientific strategies for cancer control. The Agency is involved in both epidemiological and laboratory research and disseminates scientific information through publications, meetings, courses and fellowships.

IARC Postdoctoral Fellowships for Research Training in Cancer

Subjects: Environmental carcinogenesis such as biostatistics, epidemiology of cancer, all aspects of chemical and viral carcinogenesis, cancer prevention, molecular cell biology, molecular genetics, molecular biology, biochemistry, immunology and mechanisms of carcinogenesis. Applications are encouraged from epidemiologists and laboratory scientists for interdisciplinary training that will facilitate the conduct of genetic and molecular epidemiological research. Applicants requiring basic training in cancer epidemiology or in laboratory research will also be considered.
Purpose: To provide training in cancer research to junior scientists who are actively engaged in research in medical or allied sciences, and who wish to pursue a career in cancer research.
Eligibility: Fellows will, in general, be selected from applicants with a recent doctoral degree PhD or MD in medicine or the natural sciences or who are in the final phase of completing their doctoral degree. Applications cannot be accepted and will not be considered if the applicant has previously received postdoctoral training abroad, or has already started postdoctoral work at the host institute. Fellowships must be taken up by December 31st of the year of award and cannot be started before the doctoral degree is formally obtained. Applicants should have an adequate knowledge of the working language of the host laboratory as well as the ability to read and write English as a level sufficient for scientific communication.
Level of Study: Postdoctorate.
Type: Fellowship.
Value: Travel for the Fellow and for one dependant if accompanying the Fellow for at least eight months. Stipends vary according to country of tenure. Annual family allowance of US$400 for spouse and US$450 for each child.
Length of Study: One year.
Frequency: Annual.
Study Establishment: An institution in any country abroad where suitable research facilities and material exist.
Country of Study: Any country.

No. of awards offered: Approx. 15.
Application Procedure: Applicants must complete an application form. Applications must be supported by the Director of the applicant's own institution. A letter of acceptance from the host laboratory should be included.
Closing Date: December 31st.
No. of awards given last year: 10.
No. of applicants last year: 80.
Additional Information: Applicants should provide reasonable assurance that they will return to a post in their own country at the end of the fellowship.

INTERNATIONAL AGRICULTURAL CENTRE (IAC)

PO Box 88, Wageningen, NL-6700 AB, Netherlands
Tel: (31) 31 749 5495
Fax: (31) 31 749 5395
Email: iac@iac.agro.nl
www: http://www.iac.wageningen-ur.nl
Contact: Marketing Co-ordinator

The Netherlands Ministry of Agriculture, Nature Management and Fisheries Fellowship Programme

Subjects: Agricultural sciences.
Purpose: To promote exchange of knowledge in agricultural sciences and those fields that are related to the work carried out at the governmental research and training institutions in the Netherlands.
Eligibility: Open to candidates who hold the nationality of one of the European countries, the United States of America, Argentina, Australia, Brazil, Canada, China, Indonesia, Iran, Israel, Japan, New Zealand or South Africa. Applicants should be educated to at least MSc level, be employed by a government institution and have several years of professional experience in the research subject concerned. Candidates from member states of the European Union and the former Yugoslavian Republics are not eligible.
Level of Study: Doctorate, Postgraduate.
Type: Fellowship.
Value: When staying at the Wageningen International Residence hotel, free lodging and a daily allowance of €15 is available and when staying in accommodation elsewhere, a daily allowance of €24.50 per day, insurance, a book allowance and an allowance for study tours in the Netherlands. International travel costs from, and to, the home country are not paid.
Length of Study: Between three and six months, renewable for a further six months in some cases.
Frequency: Annual.
Country of Study: Netherlands.
No. of awards offered: Approx. 40.
Application Procedure: Applicants must submit an application form, available from the IAC, two letters of recommendation regarding the candidate's professional experience and, where applicable, a certificate of proficiency in the English language. The application should be accompanied by a letter of invitation from a host institution in the Netherlands.
Closing Date: August 31st of the year preceding the award.
Funding: Government.
No. of awards given last year: 34.
No. of applicants last year: 79.

INTERNATIONAL AIRLINE TRAINING FUND

IATA Centre
Route de l'Aeroport 33
PO Box 416, Geneva, CH-1215, Switzerland
Tel: (41) 22 799 2605
Fax: (41) 22 799 2682
Email: iatf@iata.org
Contact: Mr Jacquard Caladec, IATF Co-ordinator

The International Airline Training Fund's mission is to provide vocational training opportunities for staff of IATA member airlines based in countries with developing economies. It does so by providing scholarships and other training opportunities to enable worthy candidates to follow vocational training courses conducted by the IATA Aviation Training & Development Institute, the Aviation MBA at Concordia University, as well as several other courses.

IATF Aviation MBA Scholarship

Subjects: Aviation law, business administration and management.
Purpose: To allow candidates to study for their global aviation MBA course.
Eligibility: Open to staff from IATA member airlines from countries with developing economies. Applications for IATF Scholarships will be considered only after the applicant has gained acceptance onto the course by Concordia University.
Level of Study: Postgraduate, MBA.
Type: Scholarship.
Value: US$25,000.
Length of Study: One academic year.
Frequency: Annual.
Study Establishment: Concordia University.
Country of Study: Canada.
No. of awards offered: Five.
Application Procedure: Applicants must first complete a course application form, available from Concordia University, followed by a scholarship application form, available from the human resources director of the applicant's airline or from the IATF secretariat.
Closing Date: May 31st.
Funding: Commercial.
Contributor: IATA member airlines and aviation industry suppliers.
Additional Information: All applicants have to take the Graduate Management Admissions Test and should accordingly make timely arrangements to do so at the nearest testing point to their place of residence.

For further information contact:

Concordia University
Annex FB 801
1455 de Maisonneuve Boulevard West, Montréal, H3G 1M8,
Canada

IATF Global Aviation MBA Scholarship (GAMBA)

Subjects: Business administration and management.
Purpose: To allow candidates to study for their global aviation MBA course.
Eligibility: Open to staff from IATA member airlines from countries with developing economies. Applications must first complete a course application form, available from Concordia University. Applicants must complete a scholarship application form, available from the Human Resources Director of the applicant's airline or from the IAFT Secretariat.
Level of Study: Postgraduate, MBA.
Type: Scholarship.
Value: US$12,500 and a guarantee on a loan for the balance of the tuition fee.
Length of Study: Two academic years.
Frequency: Annual.
No. of awards offered: Six.
Application Procedure: Applicants must first complete a course application form, available from Concordia University. They must then complete a scholarship application form, available from the human resources director of the applicant's airline or from the IAFT secretariat.
Closing Date: May 31st.
Funding: Commercial.
Additional Information: All applicants have to take the Graduate Management Admissions Test and should accordingly make timely arrangements to do so at the nearest testing point to their place of residence. This programme is the same as the Aviation MBA but has a distance learning format and runs over two academic year.

IATF IATA Aviation Training and Development Institute (ATDI) Scholarships

Subjects: Business administration and management in the field of aviation training and development.
Purpose: To enable staff of IATA member airlines based in countries with developing economies to follow short courses of specialist vocational training provided under the auspices of the IATA Aviation Training & Development Institute (ATDI).
Eligibility: Open to staff from IATA member airlines from countries with developing economies.
Level of Study: Postgraduate.
Type: Scholarship.
Value: Full tuition and accommodation costs for the duration of the course. Subsistence costs are for the account of the trainee's employer airline.
Length of Study: 3-30 days per course.
Frequency: Throughout the year.
Country of Study: Switzerland, United States of America or Singapore.
No. of awards offered: Varies.
Application Procedure: Applicants must channel applications through the human resources director of the IATA member airline which employs the applicant for an IATF-IATDI scholarship.
Funding: Commercial, Private.
Contributor: IATA member airlines and aviation industry suppliers.
Additional Information: The scholarship committee meets quarterly to assess accumulated applications as of that date and to make awards. The ATDI seeks to offer skills training for managers, supervisors and other airline industry specialist staff who wish to add to their professional knowledge and ability. The range of courses taught is wide, with courses in heavy demand being repeated during the course of the year.

INTERNATIONAL ASSOCIATION FOR THE STUDY OF INSURANCE ECONOMICS

53 Route de Malagnou, Geneva, CH-1208, Switzerland
Tel: (41) 22 707 6600
Fax: (41) 22 736 7536
Email: secretariat@genevaassociation.org
www: http://www.genevaassociation.org
Contact: Professor Patrick Liedtke, Secretary General

The International Association for the Study of Insurance Economics was established in 1973 for the purpose of promoting economic research in the sector of risk and insurance.

Ernst Meyer Prize

Subjects: Risk and insurance economics.
Purpose: To recognise research work which makes a significant and original contribution to the study of risk and insurance economics.
Eligibility: Open to professors, researchers or students of economics.
Level of Study: Unrestricted.
Type: Prize.
Value: Swiss franc 5,000.

Frequency: Annual.
Country of Study: Any country.
No. of awards offered: One.
Application Procedure: Applicants must write for details.
Closing Date: September 30th.
Funding: Private.

Geneva Association

Subjects: Topics of interest in risk management or insurance.
Purpose: To defray printing costs of university theses.
Eligibility: Open to authors of university theses already submitted.
Level of Study: Doctorate, Postdoctorate.
Type: Subsidy.
Value: Swiss franc 3,000 to help defray printing costs.
Frequency: Annual.
Application Procedure: Applicants must write for further information.
Closing Date: September 30th.
Funding: Private.

International Association for the Study of Insurance Economics Research Grants

Subjects: Risk management and insurance economics.
Purpose: To promote economic research.
Eligibility: Open to graduates involved in research for a thesis leading to a doctoral degree in economics.
Level of Study: Postgraduate.
Type: Research grant.
Value: Swiss franc 10,000.
Length of Study: 10 months.
Frequency: Annual.
Country of Study: Any country.
No. of awards offered: Two.
Application Procedure: Applicants must submit an application accompanied by a personal history, a description of the research undertaken and a letter of recommendation from two professors of economics.
Closing Date: September 30th.
Funding: Private.
Additional Information: The Association reserves the right to support research on other subjects which may be submitted. The Association also grants authors of university theses already submitted, dealing in depth with a subject in the field of risk and insurance economics, a subsidy of up to swiss franc 3,000 towards printing costs.

INTERNATIONAL ASTRONOMICAL UNION (IAU)

98 bis boulevard Arago, Paris, F-75014, France
Tel: (33) 1 43 25 83 58
Fax: (33) 1 43 25 26 16
Email: iau@iap.fr
www: http://www.iau.org
Contact: Administrative Assistant

The mission of the International Astronomical Union (IAU), founded in 1919, is to promote and safeguard the science of astronomy in all its aspects through international co-operation. The IAU, through its 11 scientific divisions and 40 commissions covering the full spectrum of astronomy, continues to play a key role in promoting and co-ordinating worldwide co-operation in astronomy.

International Astronomical Union Travel Grant

Subjects: Astronomy and astrophysics.
Purpose: To provide funds to qualified individuals to enable them to visit institutions abroad. It is intended that the visitors have ample time and opportunity to interact with intellectual life of the host institution. It is a specific objective of the programme that astronomy in the home country is enriched after the applicant returns.

Eligibility: Candidates must be faculty or staff members, postdoctoral Fellows or graduate students at any recognised educational or research institution.
Level of Study: Graduate, Postdoctorate, Postgraduate, Research.
Value: One return economy fare between home and host institutions.
Length of Study: Normally more than three months at a single host institution.
Application Procedure: Applicants must submit an application including a curriculum vitae, a plan of scientific activity, letters of support from the home and host institutions, information on responsibility for subsistence at the host institution, and information on the lowest available fare. Applications should be submitted in time for the Officers of the Commission to consult by post.
Closing Date: No deadline.

For further information contact:

Vice President
ESO
Karl-Schwarzschild-Straße 2, Garching bei Muenchen, D-85748, Germany
Fax: (49) 893 202 362
Email: rwest@eso.org

President
NRAO
Edgemont Road, Charlottesville, VA, 22903, United States of America
Fax: (1) 804 296 0278
Email: mroberts@nrao.edu
Contact: Dr Morton S Roberts, President

INTERNATIONAL BANK FOR RECONSTRUCTION AND DEVELOPMENT

1818 H Street North West, Washington, DC, 20433, United States of America
Tel: (1) 202 473 1817
Fax: (1) 202 522 4036
Email: jjwbgsp@worldbank.org
www: http://www.worldbank.org/wbi/scholarships
Contact: Mr Abdul-Monen Al-Mashat, Scholarships Administrator

The Joint Japan/World Bank Graduate Scholarship Program (JJ/WBGSP)

Subjects: Development related fields.
Purpose: To promote economic and social development by awarding scholarships.
Eligibility: Eligibility criteria can be found on the programme's website.
Level of Study: Postgraduate.
Type: Scholarship.
Value: No limitation.
Length of Study: One-two years.
Frequency: Annual.
Study Establishment: All universities in the member countries of World Bank.
Country of Study: All member countries of the World Bank.
No. of awards offered: 400.
Application Procedure: Applicants must complete an application form and submit it along with admission letters and supporting documents.
Closing Date: April 1st.
Funding: Government.
Contributor: Japan.
No. of awards given last year: 128.
No. of applicants last year: 4,500.

INTERNATIONAL BEETHOVEN PIANO COMPETITION

Anton-Von-Webernplatz 1, Vienna, A-1030, Austria
Tel: (43) 171 155 6050
Fax: (43) 171 155 6059
Email: beethoven-comp@mdw.ac.at
www: http://www.mdw.ac.at/beethoven-competition
Contact: Ms Elga Ponzer, Secretary General

International Beethoven Piano Competition Vienna

Subjects: Piano.
Purpose: To encourage the artistic development of young pianists.
Eligibility: Open to pianists of all nationalities born between January 1st 1973 and December 31st 1988.
Level of Study: Unrestricted.
Type: Competition.
Value: The first prize is €7,122 a Bosendorfer Model 200 piano and engagements. The second prize is €5,087, the third prize is €4,069, plus three further prizes of €1,500.
Frequency: Every four years.
Country of Study: Austria.
No. of awards offered: Six.
Application Procedure: Applicants must write for details.
Closing Date: September 30th.
Funding: Government, Private.
No. of awards given last year: Six.
No. of applicants last year: 248.
Additional Information: For more information please visit the website at http://www.mdw.ac.at/beethoven-competition.

For further information contact:

Universität für Musik und darstellende Kunst Wien
Anton-von-Webern-Platz 1, Vienna, A-1030, Austria
Tel: (43) 711 556 050
Fax: (43) 711 556 059
Email: beethoven-comp@mdw.ac.at
www: http://www.mdw.ac.at/beethoven-competition

INTERNATIONAL CENTRE FOR GENETIC ENGINEERING AND BIOTECHNOLOGY (ICGEB)

Padriciano 99, Trieste, I-34012, Italy
Tel: (39) 040 375 71
Fax: (39) 040 226 555
Email: vincent@icgeb.trieste.it
www: http://www.icgeb.trieste.it
Contact: Ms Susan Vincent, Office of the Director General

The International Centre for Genetic Engineering and Biotechnology (ICGEB) is an organisation devoted to advanced research and training in molecular biology, with special regard to the needs of the developing world. The component host countries are Italy and India. The full member states of ICGEB are the following: Afghanistan, Algeria, Argentina, Bangladesh, Bhutan, Brazil, Bulgarian States, Chile, China, Colombia, Costa Rica, Côte d'IvoireCroatia, Cuba, Ecuador, Egypt, Hungary, Iraq, Kuwait, Macedonia, Mauritius, Mexico, Morocco, Nigeria, Pakistan, Panama, Peru, Poland, Romania, Russia, Senegal, Slovakia, Slovenia, Sri Lanka, Sudan, Syria, Tanzania, Tunisia, Turkey, Uruguay, Venezuela, Vietnam and Yugoslavia.

ICGEB Long-Term Postdoctoral Fellowship Programme

Subjects: The following subjects in the New Delhi laboratory: mammalian biology, virology, immunology, Malaria, recombinant gene products, plant biology, plant molecular biology, insect resistance, and plant resistance. In Trieste: molecular biology, molecular medicine, virology, microbiology, bacteriology, protein structure and function, molecular pathology, molecular immunology. At the Italian Institutes: enzymology, human genetics, immunology, molecular biology, plant molecular biology and virology.

Purpose: To provide long-term training in genetic engineering and biotechnology for scientists from the member states and to promote state of the art academic and industrial research training in an international context. The fellowship aims to effectively contribute to the scientific development of the Fellow's home country. Training is proposed within the scope of biotechnological and genetic engineering research and offers an opportunity for individuals to broaden their scientific background or to extend their research in health, nutrition, industrial development, environmental protection and energy production.

Eligibility: Open to promising postdoctoral or established research students under the age of 35, who are nationals of one of the member states.
Level of Study: Postdoctorate.
Type: Fellowship.
Value: US$13,000-21,000 per Fellow per year, depending on the place of study, as well as travel costs and medical insurance.
Length of Study: One year, with the possibility of an extension for a further year.
Frequency: Annual.
Study Establishment: ICGEB laboratories in Trieste, Italy, New Delhi, India and in selected Italian research institutes.
Country of Study: Italy or India.
No. of awards offered: Varies.
Application Procedure: Applicants must submit a completed application form through, and endorsed by, the respective National Liasion Officer in his or her country of origin.
Closing Date: June 30th for the first review and December 31st for the second review.
Additional Information: For further information please write to the main address or refer to the website.

ICGEB Short-Term Postdoctoral Fellowship Programme

Subjects: Molecular biology, molecular medicine, virology, microbiology, bacteriology, protein structure and function or bioinformatics, molecular pathology, molecular immunology, mammalian biology, malaria, biotechnology, plant biology, plant molecular biology, plant transformation, insect resistance and plant resistance.
Purpose: To provide short-term training in genetic engineering and biotechnology for scientists from the member states of ICGEB, and to promote academic and industrial research in an international context.
Eligibility: Open to promising postdoctoral students, who are nationals of one of the member states of ICGEB and have already made contact with an ICGEB research group or affiliated centres involved in an ongoing collaborative research project.
Level of Study: Postdoctorate.
Type: Fellowship.
Value: An allowance to cover travel costs as well as board and lodging.
Length of Study: A maximum of three months.
Frequency: Annual.
Study Establishment: ICGEB laboratories in Trieste, Italy, New Delhi, India and at ICGEB affiliated centres involved in an ongoing collaborative research project funded by the ICGEB.
Country of Study: Italy or India.
No. of awards offered: Varies.
Application Procedure: Applicants must submit a completed application form through the ICGEB Liasion officer of the applicant's country of origin. Application forms can be found on the website.
Closing Date: Applications are accepted at any time.

Predoctoral Fellowship Programme ICGEB JNU PhD Course in Molecular Biology

Subjects: Mammalian biology, virology, immunology, malaria and biotechnology, plant biology, molecular biology, transformation, or insect and plant resistance.
Purpose: To offer postgraduate training with the aim of obtaining a PhD degree in the field of molecular biology at the Jawaharlal Nehru University in New Delhi, in collaboration with the ICGEB.

Eligibility: Open to promising young students in possession of an MSc from a recognised university, who are nationals of one of the member states.
Level of Study: Postgraduate, Predoctorate.
Type: Fellowship.
Value: US$10,200.
Length of Study: Four-five years, depending on the academic qualification the individual student has achieved prior to embarking on the course.
Frequency: Annual.
Study Establishment: Jawaharlal Nehru University in New Delhi.
Country of Study: India.
No. of awards offered: Three-four.
Application Procedure: For details of the application process, applicants must contact Ms Susan Vincent, Office of the Director General (Programme and Training Unit), ICGEB, on (39) 40 37 57 30 5, or one of the ICGEB Group Leaders in New Delhi, India, by faxing (91) 11 616 23 16.
Closing Date: Please write for details.
Additional Information: For more information on this course please refer to the website.

Predoctoral Fellowship Programme ICGEB SISSA PhD Course in Molecular Genetics

Subjects: Molecular biology, molecular medicine, virology, microbiology, bacteriology, protein structure and function or bioinformatics, molecular pathology or molecular immunology.
Purpose: To enable promising young students to attend and complete the PhD course in molecular genetics at ICGEB Trieste in Italy. The course is validated by the Open University's life sciences programme in the United Kingdom, or by a suitable national university.
Eligibility: Open to promising predoctoral students under the age of 30 from any member state of the ICGEB.
Level of Study: Predoctorate.
Type: Fellowship.
Value: US$13,200 per year.
Length of Study: Three-four years.
Frequency: Annual.
Study Establishment: ICGEB component laboratories in Trieste.
Country of Study: Italy.
No. of awards offered: Five.
Application Procedure: Applicants must submit a complete application to ICGEB Trieste.
Closing Date: March 31st for preselection or September 30th for the entrance exams in October.
Additional Information: For further information please refer to the website.

INTERNATIONAL CENTRE FOR PHYSICAL LAND RESOURCES

Geological Institute
University Ghent
Krijgslaan 281/S8, Ghent, B-9000, Belgium
Tel: (32) 9 264 4626
Fax: (32) 9 264 4991
Email: plrprog.adm@rug.ac.be
www: http://allserv.rug.ac.be/~amtanghe/main.html
Contact: Professor E Van Ranst

The International Centre for Physical Land Resources has a long standing tradition in the academic formation and training in physical land resources, including soil science, soil survey, land evaluation, agricultural applications and eremology eg. dryland and desertification. Since 1997 the scope of courses has been recently widened with courses on the non-agricultural use and application of physical land resources.

Postgraduate Studies in Physical Land Resources Scholarship

Subjects: Analysis of physical land resources, fundamental soil science, micropedology, archaeopedology. Use of physical land resources, non-agricultural use and applications of land and soils, soil mechanics and hydrogeology. Management of physical and land resources, agricultural applications, soil fertility, soil erosion, conservation or land evaluation.
Purpose: To provide postgraduate training opportunities to nationals from developing countries.
Eligibility: Candidates are eligible if they are nationals of the developing world or non European Union members.
Level of Study: Postgraduate.
Type: Scholarship.
Value: €500.
Length of Study: One year, with maximum extension to two years.
Frequency: Annual.
Study Establishment: The University of Gent.
Country of Study: Belgium.
No. of awards offered: Approx. two.
Application Procedure: Applicants must complete an application form and submit this with certified diplomas and transcripts to the Programme Secretariat to obtain academic admission.
Closing Date: March 31st.
Funding: Government.
No. of awards given last year: Two.

INTERNATIONAL CHAMBER MUSIC COMPETITION

UFAM
8 rue du Dôme, Paris, F-75116, France
Tel: (33) 1 47 04 76 38
Fax: (33) 1 47 27 35 03
Email: ufam@wanadoo.fr
www: http://www.infoservice.fr/ufam
Contact: Mrs Dominique Bertrand, President

International Chamber Music Competition

Subjects: Groups of wind and string instruments, with or without piano, harp, guitar or percussion instruments. String instruments accompanying wind instruments are also permitted.
Purpose: To enable musicians to play engagements across the world.
Eligibility: Open to groups of musicians of any nationality, who are no more than 36 years of age. The average age of the group should not exceed 34 years.
Level of Study: Postgraduate.
Type: Prize.
Value: Please contact the organisation. Winners are also offered important performance engagements.
Frequency: Every two years.
Country of Study: Any country.
No. of awards offered: Varies.
Application Procedure: Applicants must request a brochure.
Closing Date: September 20th in the year of the competition.
Funding: Private.
Additional Information: The competition includes various sections for groups of various sizes, who may perform with or without piano accompaniment.

Paris International Singing Competition

Subjects: Singing, opera or melody.
Purpose: To help young singers to start their career.
Eligibility: Open to female singers of no more than 32 years of age and to male singers of no more than 34 years of age. The competition is open to singers of all nationalities.
Level of Study: Unrestricted.
Type: Prize.

Value: Please contact the organisation. There is free accommodation for competitors and winners are offered important singing engagements.
Frequency: Every two years.
Country of Study: Any country.
No. of awards offered: Eight.
Application Procedure: Applicants must request a brochure.
Closing Date: May.

INTERNATIONAL COLLEGE OF SURGEONS

1516 North Lake Shore Drive, Chicago, IL, 60610-1694, United States of America
Tel: (1) 312 642 3555
Fax: (1) 312 787 1624
Email: max@icsglobal.org
www: http://www.icsglobal.org
Contact: Mr Max Downham, International Executive Director

ICS Scholarship

Subjects: Medical research and surgery.
Purpose: To support education and research.
Eligibility: Open to surgeons from third world countries travelling to developed nations to further their education.
Level of Study: Doctorate, Postdoctorate, Postgraduate, Professional development.
Type: Scholarship.
Value: US$500-1,500.
Length of Study: Varies.
Frequency: Dependent on funds available.
Country of Study: Any country.
No. of awards offered: Varies.
Application Procedure: Applicants must send requests to ICS headquarters.
No. of awards given last year: Five.
No. of applicants last year: 15.
Additional Information: Further information is available on request.

INTERNATIONAL COUNCIL FOR CANADIAN STUDIES (ICCS)

75 Albert S-908, Ottawa, ON, K1P 5E7, Canada
Tel: (1) 613 789 7828
Fax: (1) 613 789 7830
Email: general@iccs-ciec.ca
www: http://www.scholarships-bourses-ca.org
Contact: Ms Stephanie Poitras, Programme Assistant

The International Council for Canadian Studies (ICCS) administers programmes for Canadian students (CSFP, FGA, OAS AND PRA) on behalf of the Department of Foreign Affairs and International Trade (DFAIT). The ICCS is also responsible for the administration aspects of scholarships and study programmes offered to students of foreign countries, funded by DFAIT.

Canadian Commonwealth Scholarship Program

Subjects: All subjects, except medicine or introduction to languages.
Purpose: To provide opportunities for students of other Commonwealth countries to pursue advanced studies in Canada. The scholarships are intended for men and women of high intellectual promise who may be expected to make a significant contribution to their own countries on their return from study in Canada.
Eligibility: Open to members of the British Commonwealth.
Level of Study: Doctorate, Graduate, Postgraduate, Research.
Type: Scholarship.

Value: Each scholarship is intended to cover the expenses of travel, living and study for the Scholar only. No dependent allowance is payable.
Length of Study: Varies, depending on where the applicant is applying from, however scholarships are offered for one degree only. An award will not be granted for less than one semester.
Frequency: Annual.
Study Establishment: AUCC member institution.
Country of Study: Canada.
No. of awards offered: Varies.
Application Procedure: Applicants must contact the designated Commonwealth agency in their home country for application guidelines. In most countries the agency is part of the national government's Department of Ministry of Education. Citizens of New Zealand and the United Kingdom must contact different organisations. Addresses are listed on the website. Please note, the Canadian Commonwealth agency, the ICCS, does not accept applications and supporting documents sent directly by applicants.
Closing Date: Varies in each country.
Funding: Government.
Contributor: The Department of Foreign Affairs and International Trade.

Foreign Government Awards

Subjects: Most subjects, except introduction to languages.
Purpose: To assist Canadians to study or conduct research abroad at the Master's, doctoral or postdoctoral level.
Eligibility: Open to Canadian citizens with a working knowledge of the host country's language and a Bachelor's degree (or PhD for postdoctoral fellowships), completed before the beginning of the award term.
Level of Study: Doctorate, Graduate, Postdoctorate, Postgraduate, Research.
Type: Scholarship.
Value: Generally to cover tuition fees, living allowance, transportation and medical insurance.
Frequency: Annual.
Country of Study: Chile, Colombia, Finland, France, Mexico, Korea, Germany, Italy, Japan, the Netherlands, the Philippines, Russia or Spain.
No. of awards offered: Varies.
Application Procedure: Applications are initially evaluated by a 'preselection committee' of Canadian academics. The committee submits a list of recommended candidates and alternates to each host country where award recipients are chosen. A list of participating countries is available on request.
Closing Date: Varies, October to January.
Funding: Government.

ICCS Commonwealth Scholarship Plan

Subjects: As specified by each country.
Purpose: To assist the pursuit of graduate studies or research abroad in a Commonwealth country other than Canada.
Eligibility: Open to Canadian citizens, or permanent residents who are graduates of a Canadian university, who have completed a university degree or expect to graduate prior to the tenure of the award. There are no age restrictions, but preference will be given to applicants who have obtained a university degree within the last five years.
Level of Study: Doctorate, Graduate, Postgraduate, Research.
Type: Scholarship.
Value: Most awards include the scholar's return travel from Canada to the awarding country, a monthly living allowance, tuition and compulsory academic fees and medical insurance. Various other allowances may be available, depending on the host country.
Length of Study: As specified by each country.
Frequency: Annual.
Country of Study: India, Malaysia, New Zealand, Sri Lanka, Trinidad and Tobago, Uganda, United Kingdom or Fiji.
No. of awards offered: Varies.
Application Procedure: Applicants can download an application form from the website, apply online or pick up an application from

the graduate studies or student awards office at any Canadian university.
Closing Date: New Zealand and Fiji at the end of December, other countries at the end of October. Exact dates will be posted on the website.
Funding: Government.
Additional Information: The Canadian Scholarship and Fellowship Selection Committee will select nominations to be forwarded to the awarding country. The number of nominations varies, but will be approximately double the number of awards expected to be made. The decision of the Canadian Committee is final and not open to appeal. The actual offer of a scholarship will be made by the Commonwealth Scholarship Agency in the awarding country. In general, the Agency tries to place selected candidates in the institutions of their choice, however, where this is not possible, an alternative institution offering opportunities for the proposed course of study will be chosen.

INTERNATIONAL CROPS RESEARCH INSTITUTE FOR THE SEMI-ARID TROPICS (ICRISAT)

Learning Systems Unit
Patancheru
PO 502 324, Andhra Pradesh, India
Tel: (91) 40 329 6161
Fax: (91) 40 324 1239
Email: icrisat@cgiar.org
www: http://www.icrisat.org
Contact: Learning Systems Unit

The International Crops Research Institute for the Semi-Arid Tropics (ICRISAT) is a non-profit, apolitical, international organisation that helps developing countries apply science to increase crop productivity and food security, reduce poverty and protect the environment. ICRISAT carries out its mission by forming research partnerships with government, non-governmental and private sector organisations in developing countries and linking these partners to advanced research institutions worldwide.

International Crops Research Institute Apprenticeship
Subjects: Research, administration, computer services, information and library services, farm services and engineering.
Purpose: To provide an opportunity for students to carry out their student project work.
Eligibility: Open to students pursuing their degree or diploma courses. There are no nationality restrictions.
Level of Study: Graduate, Postdoctorate.
Type: Apprenticeship.
Value: Generally self-supporting. Nominal financial assistance is provided subject to availability of funds.
Length of Study: One-six months.
Frequency: Depends on project work.
Study Establishment: The Institute.
Country of Study: India, Nigeria, Mali, Zimbabwe, Kenya, Malawi or Niger.
No. of awards offered: Dependent on project work.
Application Procedure: Applicants must obtain an application form from the Institute.

International Crops Research Institute Research Fellowships
Subjects: Genetic resources management, genetics, plant breeding, cytogenetics, biotechnology, physiology, agronomy, land and water management, soil science, modelling, agroclimatology, entomology, pathology, virology, socio-economics, and statistics, related to sorghum, pearl millet, groundnut, pigeonpea and chickpea, and rain-fed semi-arid tropical resource management.

Purpose: To provide opportunities for scientists, PhD or Master's degree, to work with senior research scientists on research problems of the semi-arid tropics with ICRISAT's mandate.
Eligibility: There are no nationality restrictions. This programme is for NARS scientists with a MSC, PhD or equivalent science degree. It presents an opportunity to work with scientists in an international research and development environment.
Level of Study: Doctorate, Postdoctorate.
Type: Fellowship.
Value: Award will be provided subject to availability of funds.
Length of Study: Generally for a short-term period.
Frequency: Dependent on funds available.
Study Establishment: The Institute.
Country of Study: India, Nigeria, Mali, Zimbabwe, Niger, Kenya or Malawi.
No. of awards offered: Dependent on research project needs.
Application Procedure: Applicants must obtain an application form from the Institute.
Closing Date: Applications are accepted at any time.
Funding: Government, Private.

International Crops Research Institute Research Scholarships
Subjects: Genetic resources management, genetics, plant breeding, cytogenetics, biotechnology, physiology, agronomy, land and water management, soil science, modelling, agroclimatology, entomology, pathology, virology, socio-economics, and statistics, related to sorghum, pearl millet, groundnut, pigeonpea and chickpea, and rain-fed semi-arid tropical resource management.
Purpose: To provide an opportunity for students to conduct research for an MSc or PhD thesis.
Eligibility: There are no nationality restrictions. Applicants must have completed all coursework and preliminary examinations for an MSc or PhD in agricultural or related sciences. The Scholar's university must accept the Institute's research guide.
Level of Study: Doctorate, Postgraduate.
Type: Fellowship.
Value: Varies, stipends are intended to meet the scholar's expenses.
Length of Study: 18-36 months.
Frequency: Annual.
Study Establishment: The Institute.
Country of Study: India, Nigeria, Mali, Zimbabwe, Kenya, Malawi or Niger.
No. of awards offered: Varies.
Application Procedure: Applicants must obtain an application form from the Institute.
Funding: Government, Private.

INTERNATIONAL DEVELOPMENT RESEARCH CENTRE (IDRC)

Centre Training & Awards Unit
250 Albert Street
PO Box 8500, Ottawa, ON, K1G 3H9, Canada
Tel: (1) 613 236 6163
Fax: (1) 613 563 0815
Email: cta@idrc.ca
www: http://www.idrc.ca/awards
Contact: Ms Danielle Reinhardt, Programme Assistant

The International Development Research Centre (IDRC) is a public corporation created by the Canadian government to help communities in the developing world find solutions to social, economic and environmental problems through research.

Canadian Window on International Development
Subjects: Proposals must indicate comparative research in Canada and a developing region of the world to better understand the common, interrelated problem or issue identified for in-depth study.

Purpose: In recognition of the challenges posed in defining international development in a world which continues to change drastically, IDRC offers one award for doctoral research that explores the relationship between Canadian aid, trade, immigration and diplomatic policy, and international development and the alleviation of global poverty. A second award will be granted for doctoral or Master's research into a problem that is common to First Nations or Inuit communities in Canada and a developing region of the world.
Eligibility: Successful candidates will propose comparative research requiring data from both Canada and a developing region of the world to better understand the common, interrelated problem or issue identified for in depth study. Selection will favour those proposals which demonstrate the relevance of the research topic for Canada and for the less developed country or countries being studied, and the close linkage between the international.
Level of Study: Doctorate, Postgraduate.
Value: Up to canadian $20,000.
Length of Study: Four-eight months.
Frequency: Annual.
Study Establishment: Canadian universities.
Country of Study: Canada.
No. of awards offered: One or two.
Application Procedure: Applicants must complete an application form.
Closing Date: April 1st.
Funding: Government.
Contributor: The Canadian Government.
No. of applicants last year: Varies.
Additional Information: Further information is available on the website.

Community Forestry: Trees and People - John G Bene Fellowship

Subjects: Forestry management.
Purpose: To assist Canadian graduate students in undertaking research on the relationship of forest resources to the social, economic and environmental welfare of people in developing countries.
Eligibility: Open to Canadian citizens and permanent residents who are registered at a Canadian university at the Master's or doctoral level. Applicants must have an academic background that combines forestry or agroforestry with social sciences.
Level of Study: Doctorate, Postgraduate.
Type: Fellowship.
Value: Canadian $15,000.
Frequency: Annual.
Study Establishment: Canadian universities.
Country of Study: Canada.
No. of awards offered: One.
Application Procedure: Applicants must submit a summary of their research proposal, budget of proposed research, application form, curriculum vitae, two references, a letter from the institution confirming affiliation, transcripts, confirmation from their academic advisor that coursework is complete and proof of Canadian citizenship or permanent residency.
Closing Date: March 1st.
Funding: Private.
Contributor: Endowment.
No. of awards given last year: One.
Additional Information: Further information is available on the website.

IDRC Doctoral Research Awards

Subjects: Food security, uses of natural resources, biodiversity conservation, sustainable employment, strategies and policies for healthy societies, information and communication.
Purpose: To promote the growth of Canadian capacity in research on sustainable and equitable development from an international perspective.
Eligibility: Open to Canadian citizens and permanent residents. Applicants must be registered at a Canadian university, have a research proposal for a doctoral thesis and provide evidence of affiliation and complete coursework prior to taking on research.

Level of Study: Doctorate.
Type: Award.
Value: Up to canadian $20,000.
Length of Study: Four-twelve months.
Frequency: Twice a year.
Study Establishment: Canadian universities. Normally such research is conducted in Latin America, Africa, the Middle East or Asia.
Country of Study: Canada.
No. of awards offered: Varies.
Application Procedure: Applicants must complete and submit an application form with a research proposal, budget, curriculum vitae, two references, a letter from the institution of affiliation, approval of thesis by committee, transcripts, confirmation from advisor that coursework will be complete before the start of research, and proof of Canadian citizenship or permanent residency.
Closing Date: May and November.
Funding: Government.
Contributor: The Canadian government.
No. of applicants last year: Varies.
Additional Information: Further information is available on the website.

Use of Fertility Enhancing Food, Forage and Cover Crops in Sustainably Managed Agroecosystems: The Bentley Fellowship

Subjects: Use of forage crops, agricultural production and soil fertility.
Purpose: To provide assistance to Canadian or developing country students or researchers with a university degree in agriculture, forestry or biology, who wish to undertake postgraduate study into farm research in a developing country with co-operating farmers.
Level of Study: Doctorate, Graduate, Postdoctorate, Postgraduate.
Type: Fellowship.
Value: Up to canadian $20,000.
Length of Study: Four-twelve months.
Frequency: Annual.
Study Establishment: Canadian universities.
Country of Study: Canada or developing countries.
No. of awards offered: One-two.
Application Procedure: Applicants must complete an application form, available on request.
Closing Date: October.
Funding: Government.
Additional Information: Further information is available on the website.

INTERNATIONAL EYE FOUNDATION

Tv 21 No 100-20 Piso 7, Bogota, Colombia
Tel: (57) 1 611 1711
Fax: (57) 1 256 8274
Email: earenas@cable.net.co
www: http://www.interaction.org/members/ief.html
Contact: Dr Eduardo Arenas

International Eye Foundation (Colombia) Fellowship

Subjects: Anterior segment surgery.
Purpose: To bring ophthalmologists up to date with advances in procedures of cornea, glaucoma and cataract.
Eligibility: Open to ophthalmologists from any country.
Level of Study: Postdoctorate.
Type: Fellowship.
Value: US$200.
Length of Study: Six months.
Frequency: Twice a year.
Study Establishment: Santa Fe de Bogota Foundation.
Country of Study: Colombia.
No. of awards offered: Two.

Application Procedure: Applicants must write for details.

Closing Date: June or September.

INTERNATIONAL FEDERATION OF LIBRARY ASSOCIATIONS AND INSTITUTIONS (IFLA)

PO Box 95312, The Hague, NL-2509 CH, Netherlands

Tel: (31) 70 314 0884

Fax: (31) 70 383 4827

Email: ifla@ifla.org

www: http://www.ifla.org

Contact: Ms Josche Neven, Co-ordinator of Professional Activities

Established in 1927, the primary function of the International Federation of Library Associations (IFLA) and Institutions is to encourage, sponsor and promote research and development in all aspects of library activity, and to share its findings with the library community as a whole for the greater good of librarianship.

The Guust van Wesemael Literacy Prize

Subjects: Library science.

Purpose: To recognise an achievement in the field of literacy promotion in a developing country.

Eligibility: Open to candidates from developing countries.

Level of Study: Unrestricted.

Value: €2,725.

Frequency: Every two years.

Country of Study: Any country.

No. of awards offered: One.

Application Procedure: Applicants must complete an application form, available from IFLA headquarters.

Closing Date: March 1st every odd numbered year.

Funding: Private.

No. of awards given last year: Two.

Additional Information: The prize should be used for follow up activities such as purchasing targeted collections of appropriate books.

Hans-Peter Geh Grant for Conference Participation

Subjects: Library and information science.

Purpose: To sponsor a librarian from the former Soviet region, including the Baltic States, to attend an IFLA seminar or conference in Germany in order to become acquainted with new developments in the field of information.

Eligibility: Applicants must be IFLA affiliates, or employees of IFLA members. Open only to librarians from the former Soviet region or the Baltic States.

Level of Study: Professional development.

Value: €1,135.

Frequency: Annual.

Country of Study: Any country.

Application Procedure: Applicants must complete an application form, available from IFLA headquarters.

Closing Date: February 1st.

Funding: Private.

No. of awards given last year: One.

INTERNATIONAL FEDERATION OF UNIVERSITY WOMEN (IFUW)

8 rue de l'Ancien-Port, Geneva, CH-1201, Switzerland

Tel: (41) 22 731 2380

Fax: (41) 22 738 0440

Email: ifuw@ifuw.org

www: http://www.ifuw.org

Contact: Grants Management Officer

The International Federation of University Women (IFUW) is a non-profit, non-governmental organisation comprising of graduate women working locally, nationally and internationally to advocate the improvement of the status of women and girls at the international level, to promote lifelong education and to enable graduate women to use their expertise to effect change.

The British Federation Crosby Hall Fellowship

Subjects: All subjects.

Purpose: To encourage advanced scholarship and original research.

Eligibility: Women applicants for all awards must be either a member of one of IFUW's national federations or associations or, in the case of women graduates living in countries where there is not yet a national affiliate, an independent member of IFUW.

Level of Study: Doctorate, Postdoctorate, Research.

Type: Fellowship.

Value: UK £2,500.

Frequency: Every two years.

Study Establishment: An approved Institute of Higher Education.

Country of Study: United Kingdom.

No. of awards offered: One.

Application Procedure: Applicants must apply through their respective federation or association. A list of IFUW national federations can be sent upon request or obtained from the Internet. IFUW independent members and international individual members must apply directly to IFUW headquarters in Geneva.

Closing Date: Early September in the year preceding the competition.

Funding: Private.

No. of awards given last year: One.

Additional Information: Applicants in the United States and the United Kingdom should write to the addresses shown for those countries, all others should write to the main address. Further information is available from the website.

For further information contact:

BFWG
4 Mandeville Courtyard
142 Battersea Park Road, London, SW11 4NB, England
Tel: (44) 20 7498 8037
Fax: (44) 20 7498 8037

AAUW/IFUW Liason
1111 Sixteenth Street NW, Washington, DC, 28036, United States of America
Fax: (1) 202 872 1425

Ida Smedley Maclean, CFUW/A Vibert Douglas, IFUW and Action Fellowship

Subjects: All subjects.

Purpose: To encourage advanced scholarship and original research.

Eligibility: Women applicants for all awards must be either a member of one of IFUW's national federations or associations or, in the case of women graduates living in countries where there is not yet a national affiliate, an independent member of IFUW. Applicants should be well started on a research programme and should have completed at least one year of graduate work.

Level of Study: Doctorate, Postdoctorate, Postgraduate.

Type: Fellowship.

Value: The Maclean Fellowship is swiss franc 8,000-10,000, the Douglas Fellowship is canadian $6,000 and the SAAP Fellowship is swiss franc 8,000-10,000.
Length of Study: More than eight months.
Frequency: Every two years.
Study Establishment: An approved Institute of Higher Education other than that in which the applicant received her education or habitually resides.
Country of Study: Any country.
No. of awards offered: One of each fellowship.
Application Procedure: Applicants must write for details enclosing a stamped addressed envelope. Applicants should apply through their respective federation or association. A list of IFUW national federations can be sent upon request or obtained from the Internet.
Closing Date: Early September in the year preceding the competition.
Funding: Private.
No. of awards given last year: One of each.
Additional Information: Applicants in the United States and the United Kingdom should write to the addresses shown for those countries, all others should write to the main address. Further information is available from the website.

For further information contact:

BFWG
4 Mandeville Courtyard
142 Battersea Park Road, London, SW11 4NB, England
Tel: (44) 20 7498 8037
Fax: (44) 20 7498 8037

AAUW/IFUW Liaision
1111 Sixteenth Street NW, Washington, DC, 28036, United States of America
Fax: (1) 202 872 1425

Winifred Cullis and Dorothy Leet Grants, NZFUW Grants
Subjects: All subjects.
Purpose: To enable recipients to carry out research, obtain specialised training essential to research or training in new techniques.
Eligibility: Women applicants for all awards must be either a member of one of IFUW's national federations or associations or, in the case of women graduates living in countries where there is not yet a national affiliate, an independent member of IFUW.
Level of Study: Doctorate, Graduate, Postdoctorate, Postgraduate.
Type: Grant.
Value: Varies, swiss franc 3,000-6,000.
Length of Study: A minimum of two months.
Frequency: Every two years.
Country of Study: Any country.
No. of awards offered: Varies.
Application Procedure: Applicants must write for details enclosing a stamped addressed envelope. Applicants should apply through their respective federation or association. A list of IFUW national federations can be sent upon request or obtained from the Internet.
Closing Date: Early September in the year preceding the competition.
Funding: Private.
No. of awards given last year: 15-20.
Additional Information: Applicants in the United States and the United Kingdom should write to the addresses shown for those countries, all others should write to the main address. Further information is available from the website.

For further information contact:

BFWG
4 Mandeville Courtyard
142 Battersea Park Road, London, SW11 4NB, England
Tel: (44) 20 7498 8037
Fax: (44) 20 7498 8037

AAUW/IFUW Liason
1111 Sixteenth Street NW, Washington, DC, 28036, United States of America
Fax: (1) 202 872 1425

INTERNATIONAL FOUNDATION FOR ETHICAL RESEARCH (IFER)

53 West Jackson Boulevard
Suite 1552, Chicago, IL, 60604, United States of America
Tel: (1) 312 427 6025
Fax: (1) 312 427 6524
www: http://www.ifer.org
Contact: Mr Peter O'Donovan, Deputy Director

The International Foundation for Ethical Research (IFER) supports the development and implementation of viable, scientifically valid alternatives to the use of animals in research, product testing, and classroom education. IFER is dedicated to the belief that through new technologies and diligent research, solutions can be found that will create a better world for all, without using animals.

International Foundation for Ethical Research Fellowship for Alternatives in Scientific Research
Subjects: Tissue cultures, cell cultures, organ cultures, gas chromatography, mathematical and computer models, clinical and epidemiological surveys are examples of some of the research areas previously awarded grants.
Purpose: To develop, validate and disseminate alternatives to the use of live animals in research, education and product testing. Alternatives are defined as methods which replace, refine or reduce the number of animals traditionally used.
Eligibility: Open to students enrolled in Master's and PhD programmes in the sciences, humanities, psychology and journalism.
Level of Study: Graduate.
Type: Fellowship.
Value: US$12,500 and US$2,500 for supplies.
Length of Study: One year, renewable for up to three years based on eligibility and funding.
Frequency: Annual.
Country of Study: Any country.
No. of awards offered: Varies.
Application Procedure: Applicants must write for details or refer to the website.
Additional Information: Further information can be found on the website.

INTERNATIONAL FOUNDATION FOR SCIENCE (IFS)

Grev Turegatan 19, Stockholm, S-11438, Sweden
Tel: (46) 85 458 1800
Fax: (46) 85 458 1801
Email: info@ifs.se
www: http://www.ifs.se
Contact: Ms Eva Gerson, Head of Finance & Administration

The International Foundation for Science (IFS) shall contribute to the strengthening of capacity in developing countries to conduct relevant and high quality research on the management, use and conservation of biological resources and the environment in which these resources occur and upon which they depend.

IFS Grant
Subjects: Research relating to the renewable utilisation of biological resources such as projects in agriculture, forestry, natural products and aquatic resources, as well as research on the sustainable utilisation and conservation of natural ecosystems.
Purpose: To build scientific capacity in developing countries.
Eligibility: Open to scientists who are citizens of a developing country, in possession of an academic degree (not less than an MSc or the equivalent), currently working at a university or research institution in a developing country, young (normally under 40 at the time of

first application for a grant) and at the beginning of their research careers. Candidates from Argentina and Uruguay are not eligible.

Level of Study: Research.

Type: Research grant.

Value: Awards are limited to US$12,000 per research period and may be renewed twice. IFS also gives other support to help grantees further their research. IFS funding is not intended for travel or study, but should be used for purchasing the basic tools of research such as equipment, expendable supplies and literature.

Frequency: Twice a year.

Country of Study: Developing countries.

No. of awards offered: One-three.

Application Procedure: Applicants must complete an application form. This is available on request in English or French.

Closing Date: Applications are accepted at any time.

Funding: Government.

No. of awards given last year: 180.

No. of applicants last year: 665.

Additional Information: Research proposed by applicants shall be conducted in a developing country and relevant to the needs of a developing country. Application forms (in English or French) are available on request. Regular financing comes from: Australia, Denmark, France, Germany, the Netherlands, Norway, Sweden, and Switzerland. A number of national and international development agencies contribute to the IFS granting and supporting programmes.

INTERNATIONAL FREDERIC CHOPIN COMPETITION

Frederic Chopin Society in Warsaw
Ostrogski Castle
ul Okólnik 1, Warsaw, PL-00 368, Poland

Tel: (48) 82 754 71

Fax: (48) 82 795 99

www: http://www.chopin/pl

The Frederic Chopin Society organises The International Chopin Piano Competition, Scholarly Piano Competition for Polish Pianists, Grand Prix du Disque Frederic Chopin, courses in Chopin's music interpretation and Chopin music recitals, as well running as a museum and collection.

International Frederic Chopin Piano Competition

Subjects: Piano performance of Chopin music.

Purpose: To recognise the best artistic interpretation of Chopin's music and to encourage professional development.

Eligibility: Open to pianists of any nationality, born between 1977 and 1988.

Level of Study: Unrestricted.

Type: Prize.

Frequency: Every five years (the next will be in 2005).

Country of Study: Any country.

No. of awards offered: Six.

Closing Date: March 1st.

No. of awards given last year: 18.

No. of applicants last year: 250.

INTERNATIONAL HARP CONTEST IN ISRAEL

4 Aharonowitz Street, Tel Aviv, 63566, Israel
Tel: (972) 3 528 233
Fax: (972) 3 629 9524
Email: harzimco@netvision.net.il
www: http://bigfoot.com/~harzimco
Contact: Ms Esther Herlitz, Director

The International Harp Contest takes place in Israel every three years and is judged by a jury of internationally known musicians.

International Harp Contest in Israel

Subjects: Harp playing.

Purpose: To encourage excellence in harp playing.

Eligibility: Open to harpists of any nationality who are no more than 35 years of age.

Level of Study: Professional development.

Type: Harp and a monetary award.

Value: The first prize is a grand concert harp from the House of Lyon and Healy, Chicago. The second prize is US$5,000 and the third prize is US$3,000. The Propes Prize is US$1,500 and the Herlitz Prize is US$1,000. Board and lodging is provided by the Contest Committee.

Frequency: Every three years.

Country of Study: Any country.

No. of awards offered: Five.

Application Procedure: Applicants must complete an application form and submit this with recommendations, a record of concert experience, curriculum vitae and birth certificate. There is a registration fee of US$200.

Closing Date: May 1st.

Funding: Government, Private.

Contributor: Culture authority, the government of Israel, the Ministry of Culture, foundations and donors.

No. of awards given last year: Five.

No. of applicants last year: 36.

Additional Information: The next contest will be held between October 24th and November 6th 2003.

INTERNATIONAL HUMAN FRONTIER SCIENCE PROGRAM ORGANIZATION (HFSP)

Bureaux Europe
20 Place des Halles, Strasbourg, F-67080, France
Tel: (33) 3 88 21 51 12
Fax: (33) 3 88 32 88 97
Email: info@hfsp.org
www: http://www.hfsp.org
Contact: Mr Patrick Vincent, Director of Administration & Finance

The International Human Frontier Science Program (HFSP) promotes basic research into the complex mechanisms underlying the function of living organisms, including humans, by supporting interdisciplinary and international collaboration. The programme only supports research that transcends national boundaries.

International Human Frontier Science Programme Organization Long-Term Fellowships

Subjects: Interdisciplinary research in the life sciences to elucidate the complex mechanisms of living organisms, emphasising brain functions and molecular approaches.

Purpose: To provide a period of postdoctoral training for researchers who are expected to play an important role in originating and pursuing creative research. The third year of support can be used for postdoctoral research in the home country.

Eligibility: Applicants must be within five years of receiving their PhD at the start of the fellowship. Applicants cannot go to a country of which they are a national or in which he or she received the PhD degree.

Level of Study: Postdoctorate, Research.

Type: A variable number of fellowships.

Value: Approx. US$45,000 per year per Fellow.

Length of Study: Three years.

Frequency: Annual.

Study Establishment: Outstanding academic or non-profit research institutions in any member country.

Country of Study: Any country.

No. of awards offered: 110.

Application Procedure: Applicants must refer to the website.

Closing Date: Please refer to the website.

Funding: Government.

International Human Frontier Science Programme Organization Research Grants

Subjects: Interdisciplinary research in the life sciences to elucidate the complex mechanisms of living organisms, emphasising brain functions and molecular approaches.

Purpose: To foster international co-operation between the best scientists from different disciplines to reach new frontiers in biology and life sciences.

Eligibility: Open to teams of scientists from different countries who wish to combine their expertise to approach questions that could not be answered by individual laboratories. The principal investigator must be from one of the G7 countries, European Union countries or Switzerland. Co-investigators may be from any country.

Level of Study: Research.

Type: Programme grants and young investigator's grants.

Value: Up to US$500,000 per year for the whole team.

Length of Study: Up to three years.

Frequency: Annual.

Study Establishment: Laboratories worldwide.

Country of Study: Any country.

No. of awards offered: Varies.

Application Procedure: Applicants must refer to the website.

Closing Date: Please refer to the website.

Funding: Government.

International Human Frontier Science Programme Organization Short Term Fellowships

Subjects: Interdisciplinary research in the life sciences to elucidate the complex mechanisms of living organisms, emphasising brain functions and molecular approaches.

Purpose: To enable researchers to learn state of the art techniques already in use abroad or to establish new research collaborations.

Eligibility: Open to promising researchers.

Level of Study: Postdoctorate, Research.

Type: A variable number of fellowships.

Value: Dependent on the length of time spent abroad.

Length of Study: Two weeks to three months.

Frequency: Annual.

Study Establishment: Laboratories in any member country.

Country of Study: Any country.

Application Procedure: Applicants must refer to the website.

Closing Date: Please refer to the website.

Funding: Government.

INTERNATIONAL INSTITUTE FOR MANAGEMENT DEVELOPMENT (IMD)

Chemin de Bellerive 23
PO Box 915, Lausanne, CH-1001, Switzerland
Tel: (41) 21 618 0298
Fax: (41) 21 618 0615
Email: mbainfo@imd.ch
www: http://www.imd.ch/mba

Contact: Ms Suzanne Laurent, MBA Marketing Officer

The International Institute for Management Development (IMD), created by industry to serve industry develops cutting-edge research and programmes that meet real world needs. Their clients include dozens of leading, international companies and their experienced faculty incorporate new management practices into the small and exclusive MBA programme. With no nationality dominating IMD is truly global, practical and relevant.

IMD MBA Alumni Scholarship

Subjects: MBA.

Eligibility: Candidates must have gained acceptance into the MBA programme, provide evidence of financial need, demonstrate that all other financing options have been exhausted and show high potential for successful careers in private, public or governmental sectors of business.

Level of Study: MBA.

Type: Scholarship.

Value: Swiss franc 40,000 towards tuition fees and book expenses.

Study Establishment: The International Institute for Management Development.

Country of Study: Switzerland.

Application Procedure: Applicants must complete and submit the IMD MBA application form for financial assistance and the MBA application form.

Closing Date: September 30th.

No. of awards given last year: One.

Nestlé Scholarship for Women

Subjects: MBA.

Purpose: To financially support women undertaking a MBA.

Eligibility: Candidates must be female, have gained acceptance onto the MBA course and show financial need.

Level of Study: MBA.

Type: Scholarship.

Value: Swiss franc 20,000 towards tuition and living expenses.

Frequency: Annual.

Study Establishment: The International Institute for Management Development.

Country of Study: Switzerland.

Application Procedure: Applicants must submit an additional essay of a maximum 750 words, on the topic Diversity in Management along with their completed application.

Closing Date: September 30th.

Funding: Commercial.

No. of awards given last year: One.

INTERNATIONAL INSTITUTE FOR POPULATION SCIENCES (IIPS)

Govandi Station Road
Deonar, Bombay, Maharashtra, 400088, India
Tel: (91) 22 556 3254
Fax: (91) 22 556 3257
Email: diriips@bom8.vsnl.net.in
www: http://www.iipsindia.org
Contact: Professor T K Roy, Director

The International Institute for Population Sciences (IIPS) is one of the few institutes set up solely for the purpose of studying demography. The only institute of its kind in the world, it was declared a deemed university on August 15, 1985. The IIPS offers academic courses in population sciences and takes major initiatives to strengthen reproductive health, research and training programmes.

IIPS Master of Population Studies

Subjects: Population studies.
Eligibility: Open to all those with a Master's degree from a recognised university in any of the following disciplines: statistics, mathematics, economics, sociology, anthropology, psychology or geography.
Level of Study: Postgraduate.
Type: Fellowship.
Value: US$6,000.
Length of Study: One year.
Frequency: Annual, if funds are available.
Study Establishment: The International Institute for Population Sciences.
Country of Study: India.
Application Procedure: Applicants must complete an application form, available from the website.
Closing Date: Please contact the organisation.
Funding: Government, Private.

IIPS PhD Programme in Population Studies

Subjects: Population studies.
Purpose: To promote the knowledge of population studies.
Eligibility: Applicants must have a Master's degree in population studies or a Master's degree of any recognised university in a social science subject.
Level of Study: Postgraduate.
Type: Fellowship.
Frequency: Annual.
Study Establishment: The International Institute for Population Sciences.
Country of Study: India.
No. of awards offered: Varies.
Application Procedure: Applicants must complete an application form which is available from the website.
Closing Date: Please contact the organisation.
Funding: Government, Private.

UNPFA Diploma Course in Population Studies

Subjects: Population studies.
Purpose: To provide a higher level of understanding of the population sciences and to provide in depth understanding of the links between population and various socioeconomic phenomena.
Eligibility: Open to those who have a Bachelor's degree and some experience of handling population data. Generally, two types of students are admitted to this course: United Nations sponsored Fellows, usually from countries of the Asia and Pacific region, and sponsored candidates from various departments of the government of India, the United States of America and other research organisations.
Level of Study: Professional development, Research.
Type: Fellowship.
Value: US$6,000 as a course fee and some amount of fellowship for students, depending upon the sponsoring agency, plus return travel.

Length of Study: Two semesters beginning on the second Monday of July until mid-May of the following year.
Frequency: Annual.
Country of Study: India.
No. of awards offered: Flexible, depending upon the availability of fellowships to the students from the United Nations and other international agencies.
Application Procedure: Applicants must make an application through UNFPA country directors or representatives in their own country.
Closing Date: April.
Funding: Government, Private.
Contributor: UNFPA and other international funding agencies.
No. of awards given last year: One.
Additional Information: Further information on this programme is also available from Dr Tim Dyson at the London School of Economics, on (44) 20 7405 7686.

INTERNATIONAL M LONG-J THIBAUD COMPETITION

32 Avenue Matignon, Paris, F-75008, France
Tel: (33) 1 42 66 66 80
Fax: (33) 1 42 66 06 43
Email: longthi@club-internet.fr
www: http://www.concours.long.thibaud.org
Contact: Mrs Claude Perin, General Secretary

Premier Grand Prix Marguerite Long, Premier Grand Prix Jacques Thibaud

Subjects: Piano (Prix Marguerite Long) and violin (Prix Jacques Thibaud).
Eligibility: Open to musicians under 30 years of age, of all nationalities.
Level of Study: Professional development.
Value: Please contact the organisation. The prize also includes 30 concert engagements and a tour of Asia, North and South America.
Frequency: Every three years.
Country of Study: France.
No. of awards offered: Six.
Application Procedure: Applicants must complete and submit a registration form and copies of Diplomas. Full particulars are given on the application form which is available on request. There is a registration fee of french franc 500.
Closing Date: September 1st.
Funding: Commercial, Government.
Contributor: BNP Fujisankei Network Incorporated.
No. of awards given last year: Five.
No. of applicants last year: 50.

INTERNATIONAL MATHEMATICAL UNION (IMU)

Institute for Advanced Study
Einstein Drive, Princeton, NJ, 08540, United States of America
Tel: (1) 609 734 8200
Fax: (1) 609 683 7605
Email: imu@ias.edu
www: http://www.mathunion.org
Contact: Ms Linda Geraci

The International Mathematical Union (IMU) is an international non-governmental and non-profit making scientific organisation, with the purpose of promoting international co-operation in mathematics. It belongs to the International Council of Scientific Unions (ICSU).

IMU Fields Medals

Subjects: Mathematics.
Purpose: To reward outstanding achievements.
Eligibility: Open to young mathematicians (up to 40 years old) of any nationality.
Level of Study: Unrestricted.
Type: Medal.
Frequency: Every four years.
Country of Study: Any country.
No. of awards offered: Two-four.
Application Procedure: Applicants must be nominated by other mathematicians.
Contributor: The Fields Foundation.

Rolf Nevanlinna Prize

Subjects: Mathematical aspects of information science.
Eligibility: Open to young mathematicians (up to 40 years old) of any nationality.
Level of Study: Unrestricted.
Type: Prize.
Frequency: Every four years.
Country of Study: Any country.
No. of awards offered: One.
Application Procedure: Applicants must be nominated by other mathematicians.
Contributor: The University of Helsinki/IMU.

INTERNATIONAL NAVIGATION ASSOCIATION (PIANC)

Graaf de Ferraris
11th Floor
Box 3
20 Avenue Roi Albert II, Brussels, B-1000, Belgium
Tel: (32) 2 553 7160
Fax: (32) 2 553 7145
Email: info@pianc-aipcn.org
www: http://www.pianc-aipcn.org
Contact: Secretary General

The International Navigation Association (PIANC) is a worldwide non-political and non-profit making technical and scientific organisation of private individuals, corporations and national governments. PIANC's objective is to promote the maintenance and operation of both inland and maritime navigation by fostering progress in the planning, design, construction, improvement, maintenance and operations of inland and maritime waterways, ports and coastal areas for general use in industrialised and industrialising countries. Facilities for fisheries, sport and recreational navigation are included in PIANC's activities.

Gustave Willems Award

Subjects: The design, construction, improvement, maintenance or operation of inland and maritime waterways such as rivers, estuaries, canals, port approaches, inland and maritime ports and coastal areas, and related fields.
Purpose: To encourage young engineers, research workers and others to pursue studies in fields of interest of the Association and to submit articles on these subjects suitable for publication in the PIANC Bulletin.
Eligibility: Open to members of PIANC or candidates sponsored by a member, who are under the age of 35.
Level of Study: Unrestricted.
Type: Award.
Value: A monetary award (€5,000) and free membership of PIANC for a five year period. Free hotel accommodation will be provided, together with a coverage of travel expenses to the venue of the General Assembly.
Frequency: Annual.
Country of Study: Any country.

No. of awards offered: One.
Application Procedure: Applicants must complete an application form, available on request from the PIANC General Secretariat or on the PIANC website, and submit this together with the article. Articles must be written by a single author, not have been previously published elsewhere, not exceed 12,000 words, be in type script, and in English or French with a summary in the same language. Articles may be accompanied by illustrations or diagrams.
Closing Date: October 31st.
Funding: Government, Private.
No. of awards given last year: One.
Additional Information: The prize will be awarded to the individual candidate who submits the most outstanding article in the calendar year preceding the Annual General Assembly at which the prize is awarded, provided the article is judged to be of sufficiently high standard. The prize winner will be invited to present a commentary on his or her article during the General Assembly of the PIANC or during the Congress. In judging the articles the jury shall take into account their technical level, originality and practical value and the quality of presentation. Candidates are advised that the Bulletin is designed for readers with a wide range of engineering interests and highly specialised articles should be written with this in mind.

INTERNATIONAL ORGAN COMPETITION 'GRAND PRIX DE CHARTRES'

Concours international d'orgue
75 rue de Grenelle, Paris, F-75007, France
Tel: (33) 1 45 48 31 74
Fax: (33) 1 45 49 14 34
Email: orgues.chartres@free.fr
www: http://orgues.chartres.free.fr/
Contact: Ms Colette Morillon, Director

Under the patronage of the President of the Republic, the Association of the Great Organ of Chartres has been active for the past 30 years. After saving the great organ of the cathedral, the Association has since taken charge of the artistic life around it. The Association's aims are: to help in the regular maintenance of the instrument, to organise the international organ competition called the Grand Prix of Chartres, to organise each Summer the International Organ Festival of Chartres, to encourage and promote creation of new organ music through commissions for the Grand Prix de Chartres and to favour the diffusion of organ music in general.

International Organ Competition 'Grand Prix de Chartres'

Subjects: Organ performance, in two categories of interpretation and improvisation.
Purpose: To recognise and promote young, talented organists.
Eligibility: Open to organists of any nationality who are 35 years of age or under in the year of the competition. Any contestant who has previously been awarded a second prize may compete but they must succeed in all rounds of the competition.
Level of Study: Unrestricted.
Type: Prize plus concerts in France and other countries.
Value: The first prize is €5,000, the second prize is €3,100 and the public prize is €1,525. The winners are offered approx. 70 concerts in the most famous places in France and abroad.
Frequency: Every two years.
Country of Study: France.
No. of awards offered: Two.
Application Procedure: Applicants must send the following documents to the Secretariat: a completed registration form, curriculum vitae, certificate from the institution (national or private conservatory, academy or other institution) where the applicant studied music indicating the honours obtained, if studies have taken place partially or wholly under private tuition, the applicant must produce a certificate signed by their teacher, any documents such as programmes, reviews or press articles giving evidence of the applicants' musical

ability, an official document establishing the applicants age, nationality and place of residence, two passport sized photographs and the non refundable registration fee of €65. In a separate envelope applicants should also submit: an anonymous sound recording of the highest possible quality on audiocassette, DAT, CD or minidisk. It must contain only the performance of the requested works and not contain any other sounds (words or acoustical references), and must not be edited in any fashion, a detailed description of the specialisations of the instrument(s) used for the recording, without indicating where the organ(s) are located, and a statement on the applicants' honour stipulating that they are indeed the performer on the recorded works.

Closing Date: April 15th.
Funding: Government, Private.
No. of awards given last year: Three.
No. of applicants last year: 62.
Additional Information: The contestants selected for the final round who are not prize winners will receive a finalist's certificate and a medal, but are not allowed to claim the title prize winner. Contestants may not claim any other award than the one they actually received. Unjustified claims for titles will be denied and the Board of Directors of the Association will prosecute such claimants according to the common law.

INTERNATIONAL PEACE SCHOLARSHIP FUND

c/o PEO
3700 Grand Avenue, Des Moines, IA, 50312, United States of America
Tel: (1) 515 255 3153
Fax: (1) 515 255 3820
www: http://peointernational.org
Contact: Ms Carolyn J Larson, Project Supervisor

PEO International Peace Scholarship

Subjects: All subjects.
Purpose: To support international women studying for graduate degrees eg. the Master's or PhD in the United States of America or Canada.
Eligibility: Any nationality may apply apart from candidates from United States of America or Canada. Eligibility is based on financial need, nationality, degree, full-time status and residence the entire term of study.
Level of Study: Doctorate, Graduate, Postgraduate.
Type: Grant in aid.
Value: US$6,000 maximum per year.
Length of Study: A maximum of two years.
Frequency: Annual.
Country of Study: United States of America or Canada.
No. of awards offered: Approx. 170.
Application Procedure: Eligibility must be established before application material is sent. Candidates should write to IPS Office and request an eligibility form. If the applicant is deemed eligible an application form is sent.
Closing Date: December 15th for receipt of eligibility form, January 31st for receipt of application form.
Funding: Private.
Contributor: PEO Members.
No. of awards given last year: 167.
No. of applicants last year: 340.
Additional Information: Scholarships cannot be used for travel, research dissertations, internships or practical training. An applicant must have a contact person who is a citizen of the United States or Canada and who will act as a non academic advisor. Applicants must also have round trip return travel expense guaranteed at the time of the application and must return to their own country on completion of their studies.

INTERNATIONAL READING ASSOCIATION

800 Barksdale Road
PO Box 8139, Newark, DE, 19714-8139, United States of America
Tel: (1) 302 731 1600 ext. 423
Fax: (1) 302 731 1057
Email: research@reading.org
www: http://www.reading.org
Contact: Ms Marcella Moore, Projects Manager, Division of Research & Policy

The International Reading Association seeks to promote high levels of literacy for all by improving the quality of reading instruction through studying the reading processes and teaching techniques, serving as a clearinghouse for the dissemination of reading research through conferences, journals and other publications and actively encouraging the lifetime reading habit.

Albert J Harris Award

Subjects: Reading and literacy.
Purpose: To recognise outstanding published works on the topics of reading disabilities and the prevention, assessment or instruction of learners experiencing difficulty learning to read.
Eligibility: Articles must be single or joint authored research based articles. Nominees for this award do not need to be members of the International Reading Association. Publications that have appeared in a refereed professional journal or monograph within the last 18 months are eligible and may be submitted by the author or anyone else.
Level of Study: Postgraduate.
Type: Literacy prize.
Value: US$1,000.
Frequency: Annual.
Country of Study: Any country.
No. of awards offered: One.
Application Procedure: Applicants must obtain guidelines with specific information from the main address, by contacting Marcella Moore via email or on extension 423 or by visiting the website.
Closing Date: September 15th.
Funding: Private.
No. of awards given last year: One annually since 1975.

Dina Feitelson Research Award

Subjects: Literacy.
Purpose: To recognise an outstanding empirical study, or a literacy or reading related topic published in a refereed journal.
Eligibility: Articles must have been published in a refereed journal within the past 18 months and may be submitted by the author or anyone else. Nominees for this award do not need to be members of the International Reading Association.
Level of Study: Unrestricted.
Type: Literacy prize.
Value: US$500.
Frequency: Dependent on funds available.
Country of Study: Any country.
No. of awards offered: One.
Application Procedure: Applicants must obtain guidelines with specific information from the main address, by contacting Marcella Moore via email or on extension 423 or by visiting the website.
Closing Date: September 15th.
Funding: Private.
Additional Information: This award began in 1997.

Elva Knight Research Grant

Subjects: Literacy education and education research.
Purpose: To assist a researcher in a reading and literacy project. Research is defined as an enquiry which addresses significant questions about literacy instruction and practice.
Eligibility: Applicants must be members of the International Reading Association and projects should be completed within two years.

Level of Study: Postgraduate.
Type: Research grant.
Value: A maximum of US$10,000 for each award.
Length of Study: Two years.
Frequency: Annual.
Country of Study: Any country.
No. of awards offered: Up to seven awards.
Application Procedure: Applicants must obtain guidelines with specific information from the main address, by contacting Marcella Moore via email or on extension 423 or by visiting the website.
Closing Date: January 15th.
Funding: Private.
Additional Information: This award began in 1982. One annual award will go to a researcher outside the United states and/or Canada and one to a teacher-initiated research project. There are also up to five additional grants.

Helen M Robinson Award

Subjects: Literacy education.
Purpose: To support International Reading Association members at the early stages of their dissertation research in the field of reading and literacy.
Eligibility: Open to all doctoral students worldwide who are members of the International Reading Association.
Level of Study: Doctorate.
Type: Reading or literacy research grant.
Value: US$1,000.
Frequency: Annual.
Country of Study: Any country.
No. of awards offered: One.
Application Procedure: Applicants must obtain guidelines with specific information from the main address, by contacting Marcella Moore via email or on extension 423 or by visiting the website.
Closing Date: January 15th.
Funding: Private.
Additional Information: This award began in 1991.

International Reading Association Outstanding Dissertation of the Year Award

Subjects: Reading and literacy.
Purpose: To recognise dissertations in the field of reading and literacy.
Eligibility: Open to all doctoral students worldwide who are members of the International Reading Association.
Level of Study: Doctorate.
Type: Reading and/or literacy prize.
Value: US$1,000.
Frequency: Annual.
Country of Study: Any country.
No. of awards offered: One.
Application Procedure: Applicants must obtain guidelines with specific information from the main address, by contacting Marcella Moore via email or on extension 423 or by visiting the website.
Closing Date: October 1st.
Funding: Private.
Additional Information: This award began in 1964. Should there be more than one winner the US$1,000 prize will be split.

International Reading Association Teacher as Researcher Grant

Subjects: Literacy.
Purpose: To support teachers in their enquiries about literacy learning and instruction.
Eligibility: All applicants must be members of the International Reading Association and practising pre K-12 teachers with full-time teaching responsibilities (includes librarians, classroom teachers and resource teachers). Applicants are limited to one proposal per year. There must be a span of three years before past grant recipients can apply for another Teacher as Researcher Grant.
Level of Study: Professional development.
Type: Research grant.

Value: Up to US$5,000 maximum, but priority is given to smaller grants (US$1,000-2,000).
Frequency: Several awarded annually.
Country of Study: Any country.
No. of awards offered: Several.
Application Procedure: Applicants must obtain guidelines with specific information from the main address, by contacting Marcella Moore via email or on extension 423 or by visiting the website.
Closing Date: October 15th.
Funding: Private.
Additional Information: This award began in 1997.

Jeanne S Chall Research Fellowship

Subjects: Reading and literacy research.
Purpose: To encourage and support doctoral research investigating issues in beginning research, readability, reading difficulty and stages of reading development.
Eligibility: Open to doctoral students who are members of the International Reading Association and are planning or beginning dissertations.
Level of Study: Doctorate, Research.
Type: Fellowship.
Value: US$6,000 maximum.
Frequency: Annual.
Country of Study: Any country.
No. of awards offered: One.
Application Procedure: Applicants must obtain guidelines with specific information from the main address, by contacting Marcella Moore via email or on extension 423 or by visiting the website.
Closing Date: January 15th.
Funding: Private.
Additional Information: This award began in 1997.

Nila Banton Smith Research Dissemination Support Grant

Subjects: Reading and literacy research.
Purpose: To facilitate the dissemination of literacy research to the educational community.
Eligibility: Open to all members of the International Reading Association worldwide.
Level of Study: Professional development.
Type: Reading and/or literacy research dissemination grant and professional development.
Value: US$5,000.
Frequency: Annual.
No. of awards offered: One.
Application Procedure: Applicants must obtain guidelines with specific information from the main address, by contacting Marcella Moore via email or on extension 423 or by visiting the website.
Closing Date: January 15th.
Additional Information: This award began in 1991.

Reading/Literacy Research Fellowship

Subjects: Literacy education and education research.
Purpose: To provide support to a researcher who has shown exceptional promise in reading or literacy research.
Eligibility: Open to any International Reading Association member outside the United States or Canada.
Level of Study: Postdoctorate.
Type: Fellowship.
Value: US$1,000.
Frequency: Annual.
Country of Study: Outside United States of America or Canada.
No. of awards offered: One.
Application Procedure: Applicants must obtain guidelines with specific information from the main address, by contacting Marcella Moore via email or on extension 423 or by visiting the website.
Closing Date: January 15th.
Funding: Private.
Additional Information: This award began in 1974.

INTERNATIONAL RESEARCH AND EXCHANGE BOARD (IREX)

2121 K Street North West
Suite 700, Washington, DC, 20037, United States of America
Tel: (1) 202 628 8188
Fax: (1) 202 628 8189
Email: irex@info.irex.org
www: http://www.irex.org
Contact: Ms Michelle Duplissis, Senior Program Officer

Since 1958, the International Research and Exchange Board (IREX) and its predecessor organisation, the Inter-University Committee on Travel Grants, have administered advanced field research and professional training exchanges between the United States and countries in Europe, Asia and the Near East. Committed to international education in its broadest sense, IREX's efforts encompass academic research, professional training, institution building, technical assistance and policy programmes with universities and other organisational partners in the region.

ECA/IREX Contemporary Issues Fellowship Program

Subjects: Sustainable growth and economic development in the NIS, democratisation, human rights and the rule of law, political, military, security and public policy issues, strengthening civil society in the NIS, and the communications revolution and access to information.
Purpose: To provide opportunities to qualified individuals of all 12 New Independent States to conduct research, write studies and deliver lectures in the United States.
Eligibility: Applicants must be citizens of, and residing in the New Independent States of Armenia, Azerbaijan, Belarus, Georgia, Kazakhstan, Kyrgyzstan, Moldova, the Russian Federation, Tajikistan, Turkmenistan, Ukraine or Uzbekistan. Candidates must also be aged 25 to 55 years, have an academic degree at least equivalent to a United States Master's degree, have at least three years experience in the listed topic of research, and possess a high level of proficiency in written and spoken English. Applicants must not have participated in a United States government sponsored grant of more than six weeks in the past two years.
Level of Study: Professional development.
Type: Travel grant.
Value: Housing, a stipend, medical insurance, a research allowance and return trip transportation from home city to placement city in United States.
Length of Study: Four months.
Frequency: Annual, if funds are available.
Study Establishment: An American university, research centre, government institution or NGO.
Country of Study: United States of America.
No. of awards offered: 100.
Application Procedure: Applicants must submit a completed application form, research proposal, two letters of recommendation, curriculum vitae, and short personal biography. For further information please contact Courteney Dunn, Senior Program Officer or Jessica Bagdonis, Program Officer, email irex@irex.org.
Closing Date: November.
Funding: Government.
Contributor: The Bureau of Cultural and Educational Affairs, at the United States Department of State.
No. of awards given last year: 75.
No. of applicants last year: 750.
Additional Information: Prospective applicants are encouraged to contact IREX's NIS field offices and educational advising centres before submitting an application. Further information and field offices contact information is available from the website.

IREX Grant Opportunities for US Scholars

Subjects: Arts, humanities or social sciences.
Purpose: To provide long-term and short-term field access for United States specialists to scholars, policymakers and research resources of Central and Eastern Europe, the New Independent States, Turkey, Iran, Afghanistan, Pakistan, China, Mongolia and North Korea.
Eligibility: Open to United States citizens and permanent residents. Applicants must have a good command of the host country language.
Level of Study: Doctorate, Graduate, Postgraduate, Professional development.
Type: Grant.
Value: Up to US$50,000.
Length of Study: Varies, depending on the programme.
Frequency: Annual.
Country of Study: Countries of Central or Eastern Europe, Eurasia or Mongolia.
No. of awards offered: Varies.
Application Procedure: Applicants must contact IREX for application forms and information on current programmes.
Closing Date: Dates vary depending on the programme.
Funding: Government, Private.
Contributor: The American Department of State's Bureau of Educational and Cultural Affairs, the American Department of State's Title VIII Program, John J and Nancy Lee Roberts, IREX Scholar Support Fund and the National Endowment for the Humanities.
Additional Information: Further information is available on request.

IREX Individual Advanced Research Opportunities

Subjects: Humanities or social sciences.
Purpose: To provide opportunities for American scholars wishing to pursue research in humanities and social sciences, policy research and development and cross-disciplinary studies with a strong focus on Central and Eastern Europe and Eurasia.
Eligibility: Open to United States citizens or residents who should normally have a full-time affiliation with a North American college or university and be faculty members or advanced doctoral candidates who will have completed all requirements for the PhD (or equivalent professional degree) except the thesis by the time of application. However, many Scholars not academically employed and candidates for the MA degree may also be qualified if they are proposing professional level, independent research projects. Normally, command of the host country language sufficient for advanced research is required of all applicants.
Level of Study: Doctorate, Professional development.
Type: Grant.
Value: Travel and visa fees, plus dollar stipend and a housing allowance. Up to a maximum of US$30,000.
Length of Study: Two-nine months.
Frequency: Annual.
Study Establishment: Appropriate institutions in the NIS and Central and Eastern Europe.
Country of Study: Albania, Armenia, Azerbaijan, Belarus, Bosnia, Bulgaria, Croatia, Czech Republic, Estonia, Kazakhstan, Kyryzstan, Latvia, Lithuania, Macedonia, Moldova, Poland, Romania, Russian Federation, Slovakia, Slovenia, Tajikistan, Turkmenistan, Ukraine, Uzbekistan.
No. of awards offered: Varies.
Application Procedure: Applicants must visit the website for application forms and further information or email irex@irex.org.
Closing Date: November 1st.
Funding: Government, Private.
Contributor: The Department of State (Title 8), NEH and the IREX Scholar Support Fund.
No. of awards given last year: 36.
Additional Information: Please contact IREX for programme information well in advance of the deadline.

IREX Russian/US Young Leadership Fellows for Public Service Program

Subjects: Russian area studies for United States participants. Corporate affairs, community affairs, or governmental affairs for Russian participants. Includes course work in conflict resolution, economics, government studies, history, international relations or political sciences.

Purpose: To promote leadership and public service in both the United States and Russia.

Eligibility: Applicants must be a citizen and current resident of the United States or of the Russian Federation. United States applicants must have received equivalent of Bachelor's degree, have a working knowledge of the Russian language, and be aged no more than 30 years. Russian applicants must lack a source of funding for study in the United States, be aged no more than 30 years, hold an undergraduate degree from a four to five year programme, and have achieved a minimum Test Of English as a Foreign Language score of 550. In addition Russian applicants must not have participated in another United States government sponsored academic exchange programme since October 1st 1997 for a period of more than six weeks, be married to a United States citizen or citizens of countries other than the countries of NIS, be enrolled in academic training or research programmes outside of Russia, earn a living or salary outside of Russia, or have applied for an immigrant visa or political asylum to any country.

Level of Study: Graduate, Postgraduate, Professional development.
Type: Fellowship.
Length of Study: One year.
Frequency: Annual, if funds are available.
Study Establishment: Universities throughout the Russian Federation and the United States.
Country of Study: Russian Federation or United States of America.
No. of awards offered: Varies.
Application Procedure: Applicants must submit a completed application form, two letters of recommendation, transcripts, a curriculum vitae, and a proposal.
Closing Date: November 30th.
Funding: Government.
Contributor: The United States Department of State (Bureau of Educational and Cultural Affairs).
Additional Information: This programme also includes a public service component and a professional internship. Further information is available on the website.

IREX Short-Term Travel Grants

Subjects: Humanities or social sciences.
Purpose: All projects should seek to advance the public cultural and historical knowledge of Central and Eastern Europe, the New Independent States, Turkey and Iran.
Eligibility: Open to United States citizens who have a PhD or equivalent professional degree and need project support. Funding from the National Endowment for the Humanities is available for applicants who are not United States citizens or permanent residents, but who have been resident in the United States for at least three years.
Level of Study: Doctorate, Postdoctorate, Postgraduate.
Type: Travel grant.
Value: Travel expenses up to a maximum of US$3,000. Airfare on a United States flag carrier is provided through IREX Travel, as well as per diems for up to 14 days, not to exceed US$100 per day for food, lodging and local transport. The grant may also cover incidental expenses such as conference registration fees, visa fees and research expenses.
Length of Study: A maximum of 60 days.
Frequency: Annual.
Country of Study: Albania, Armenia, Azerbaijan, Belarus, Bosnia, Bulgaria, Croatia, Czech Republic, Estonia, Kazakhstan, Kyrgyzstan, Latvia, Lithuania, Macedonia, Molodova, Mongolia, Poland, Romania, Russian Federation, Slovakia, Slovenia, Tajikistan, Turkmenistan, Ukraine.
No. of awards offered: Varies.
Application Procedure: Applicants must contact Jessica Bagdonis, Program Officer, by email irex@irex.org for details of the application guidelines. Application forms are also available on the IREX website.
Closing Date: February 1st.
Funding: Government.
Contributor: The United States government and the United States Department of State's Title VIII Program.
No. of awards given last year: Approx. 95.
No. of applicants last year: Varies.

Additional Information: In order to encourage wider participation in East-West scholarly contacts, grants may be awarded to United States Scholars outside the field of Soviet, Eurasian, and Central and East European studies. The programmes are designed to facilitate collaborative projects with East European colleagues, lectures or seminars in Eurasia, and Central and Eastern Europe, or individual research in Eurasia, and Central and Eastern Europe. Grant recipients are responsible for their own visa, travel and academic arrangements.

INTERNATIONAL ROAD EDUCATIONAL FOUNDATION

1010 Massachusetts Avenue North West
Suite 410, Washington, DC, 20001, United States of America
Tel: (1) 202 371 5544
Fax: (1) 202 371 5565
Email: aschuurman@mindspring.com
www: http://www.irfnet.org
Contact: Director General

The International Road Educational Foundation is a non-profit, non-political service organisation. Its purpose and continuing objective is to encourage better road and transportation systems worldwide and to help apply technology and management practices which will give maximum economic and social returns from national road investments.

IREF Fellowship

Subjects: Engineering and management.
Purpose: To support technology transfer in selected countries.
Eligibility: Each year a specific list of countries is identified and the fellowship is offered to organisations within those countries.
Level of Study: Graduate.
Type: Fellowship.
Value: US$16,000.
Length of Study: A minimum of one year.
Frequency: Annual.
Study Establishment: Unrestricted.
Country of Study: Any country.
No. of awards offered: 15.
Application Procedure: Applicants must secure a form from an organisation, being either a road association or government agency, within their country.
Closing Date: January 30th.
Funding: Private.

THE INTERNATIONAL SCHOOL FOR ADVANCED STUDIES (SISSA)

Via Beirut 2-4, Trieste, I-34014, Italy
www: http://www.sissa.it
Contact: Ms Alex Poretti, Scientific Secretariat

The International School for Advanced Studies (SISSA) is a centre for research and postgraduate studies leading to the PhD degree (equivalent to the Italian Dottore di Ricerca) in the fields of astrophysics, mathematics, neuroscience, elementary particles and condensed matter physics and functional and structural genomics.

SISSA Fellowship

Subjects: Applied mathematics, astrophysics, functional and structural genomics, mathematical analysis, mathematical physics, statistical and biological physics, neurosciences, theory of elementary particles or the theory of computational physics of condensed matter.
Purpose: To financially support PhD studies.

Eligibility: Open to candidates over the age of 30 at the beginning of the academic year.
Level of Study: Doctorate.
Type: Fellowship.
Value: Please contact the School for details.
Length of Study: Three-four years.
Frequency: Annual.
Study Establishment: The International School for Advanced Studies (SISSA).
Country of Study: Italy.
No. of awards offered: 58.
Application Procedure: Applicants must complete the application form which can be found on SISSA's website http://www.sissa.it.
Closing Date: March 20th for pre-selection of non European Union citizens, April 5th for the first session, July 8th for the theory of elementary particles and September 30th for the second session.
Funding: Government.
Contributor: The Italian Government.
No. of awards given last year: 54.
No. of applicants last year: 181.

INTERNATIONAL SCHOOL OF CRYSTALLOGRAPHY, E MAJORANA CENTRE

c/o Dip to Scienze Della Terra Geo Ambientoli
Pza Porta San Donato 1, Bologna, I-40126, Italy
Tel: (39) 051 243 556
Fax: (39) 051 243 336
Email: riva@geomin.unibo.it
www: http://www.geomin.unibo.it/orgv/erice/erice.htm
Contact: Professor L Riva Di Sanseverino

The International School of Crystallography is an international organising committee which offers, once a year, short advanced courses (10-13 days) on frontier topics in crystallography, solid state chemistry, materials science, structure activity relationship, molecular biology and biophysics.

International School of Crystallography Grants

Subjects: Frontier topics in crystallography eg. high pressure crystallography, polymorphism and drug design via crystallography.
Purpose: To enable postgraduates to attend short courses held at Erice once a year.
Eligibility: Open to all who have scientific interests related to the topic chosen each year at a PhD or postdoctoral level. English language is mandatory.
Level of Study: Doctorate, Postdoctorate, Postgraduate.
Type: Grant.
Value: Fees, board and lodging during the course.
Length of Study: 8-12 days.
Frequency: Annual.
Study Establishment: E Majorana Centre, Erice, Sicily.
Country of Study: Italy.
No. of awards offered: Approx. 30-40.
Application Procedure: Applicants must submit a letter of recommendation stating financial needs, personal data and details of scientific interests.
Closing Date: End of November.
Funding: Government.
Contributor: NATO, the British Council, the European Commission and the Italian National Research Council.
No. of awards given last year: 130.
No. of applicants last year: 170.

For further information contact:

Department of Organic Chemistry
Via Marzolo 1, Padova, I-35131, Italy
Tel: (39) 049 827 5275
Fax: (39) 049 827 5239

Email: paola@chor00.unipd.it
Contact: Dr Paola Spadon

INTERNATIONAL SOCIETY OF ARBORICULTURE RESEARCH TRUST (ISA)

PO Box 3129
1400 W Anthony, Campaign, IL, 61826-3129, United States of America
Tel: (1) 217 355 9411
Fax: (1) 217 355 9516
Email: isa@isa-arbor.com
www: http://isa-arbor.com
Contact: Mr John A Geissal

The mission of the International Society of Arboriculture Research Trust (ISA) is to identify significant environmental, biological, social and economic needs of arboriculture and urban forestry, including the management, maintenance and care of urban trees, and provide funding for innovative basic and applied research, and education projects.

The Hyland R Johns Grant Program

Subjects: Forestry and arboriculture.
Purpose: To provide funding for arboricultural and urban forestry research.
Eligibility: Open to qualified researchers of any nationality.
Level of Study: Postgraduate.
Type: Research grant, no scholarships.
Value: In excess of US$5,000.
Length of Study: Two-three years.
Frequency: Annual.
Country of Study: Any country.
Application Procedure: Applicants must complete an application form.
Closing Date: May 1st.
Funding: Private.
Contributor: ISA members.
No. of awards given last year: Seven.
No. of applicants last year: 39.

The John Z Duling Grant Program

Subjects: Forestry and arboriculture.
Purpose: To provide seed money to support research projects in arboriculture and urbane forestry.
Eligibility: Open to qualified researchers of any nationality.
Level of Study: Postgraduate.
Type: Research grant, no scholarships.
Value: A maximum of US$5,000. Funds cannot be used for expenses associated with attendance at colleges and universities eg. tuition, books or laboratory fees.
Length of Study: One-three years.
Frequency: Annual.
Country of Study: Any country.
No. of awards offered: 5-10.
Application Procedure: Applicants must complete a two page application form, available from the ISA Research Trust.
Closing Date: November 1st.
Funding: Private.
Contributor: International Society of Arboriculture Research Trust (ISA).
No. of awards given last year: 10.
No. of applicants last year: Approx. 60.

INTERNATIONAL SOCIETY OF NEPHROLOGY (ISN)

Academic Medical Centre
Department of Pathology
Meibergdreef 9, Amsterdam, NL-1105 AZ, Netherlands
Tel: (31) 20 566 4939
Fax: (31) 20 696 0389
Email: isn@amc.uva.nl
www: http://www.isn-online.org
Contact: Sanchita Mukherjee, Administrative Assistant

The International Society of Nephrology (ISN) pursues the goal of worldwide advancement of education, science and patient care in nephrology. ISN achieves this through its journal Kidney International, organising international congresses, symposia, specific programmes and fellowships. As a result ISN helps to improve renal science and renal patient care worldwide especially in emerging countries.

ISN Fellowship Awards

Subjects: Nephrology.
Purpose: To offer training opportunities to young nephrologists in emerging countries with the ultimate goal of improving the standards of their home institutions upon their return.
Eligibility: Open to young nephrologists from emerging countries (as defined by World Bank criteria). Applicants must have received sufficient training in internal medicine or other fields to pass all host country exams that are necessary for the care of patients. Fellowships are primarily offered for clinical training in nephrology, but in some circumstances research training may be allowed.
Level of Study: Postdoctorate, Predoctorate.
Type: Fellowship.
Value: US$22,500 for one year and less for shorter periods. If the host country is contributing funds then this is subtracted from the standard fund.
Length of Study: Short-term fellowships are for three months and long-term fellowships are for one-two years.
Frequency: Annual.
Study Establishment: Any suitable university, scientific institution or hospital.
No. of awards offered: Up to 55 each year.
Application Procedure: Applicants must complete an application form for both full-time fellowship and the short-term fellowship award. Applicants must provide evidence of a guaranteed position in a medical institution upon return to their home country. The applicant must agree to return to their home country upon completion of the training, if not then the recipient will have to refund the ISN fellowship in full.
Closing Date: Deadlines are the end of January and the end of July each year. The selection is made in May and November each year.
Funding: Commercial, Private.
Contributor: Offered in collaboration with sister societies and industry, the American Society of Nephrology, the Japanese Society of Nephrology, the National Kidney Research Fund in the United Kingdom and Fresenius in Germany.
No. of awards given last year: 44.
No. of applicants last year: 62.
Additional Information: The selection procedure has three parts: data verification, where information provided by applicants is verified and evaluated through correspondence, then evaluation, where five members of the Committee (one from each Continent) score each application according to standard format, and finally selection, which is largely based on the aforementioned scores but also considers the geographical balance, urgent needs in certain regions and the preference of certain sponsors.

For further information contact:

Secretary General
Cairo Kidney Centre
3 Hussein El-Memar Street
Antikhana

PO Box 91
Bab El-Louk, Cairo, 11513, Egypt
Tel: (20) 2 579 0267
Email: isn@rwsys.eg.net
Contact: Dr Rashad Barsoum, Secretary General

ISN Travel Grants

Subjects: Nephrology.
Purpose: To encourage young physicians and scientists to attend conferences especially those from emerging countries. Travel grants are offered to facilitate attendance at the ISN International Congress and the ISN Forefronts Commission Conference.
Eligibility: Applicants must have training and experience in an area of research relevant to the conference and an infrastructure at their home institutions to allow the pursuit of techniques and approaches discussed at the conference. Young physicians and scientists are preferred as are ISN fellows. A portion of the grants are reserved for applicants from emerging countries.
Level of Study: Doctorate, Postdoctorate, Postgraduate, Research.
Type: Travel grant.
Value: The size of the grant is decided according to each conference and congress.
Length of Study: Varies.
Frequency: To coincide with the conference and congress.
No. of awards offered: 120 travel grants for each International Congress of Nephrology and six travel grants for young scientists from emerging countries to attend each ISN Forefront Conference.
Application Procedure: Applicants must complete an application form which can be downloaded from the ISN website or requested from the ISN Secretary General a year prior to the Congress. Applications can also be obtained from the Directors of the ISN Forefront Programmes.
Closing Date: Please contact the organisation.
Funding: Commercial, Private.
Contributor: Offered in collaboration with sponsors of ISN.
No. of awards given last year: 120.
No. of applicants last year: 395.
Additional Information: Further information is available on request.

For further information contact:

ISN Secretary General
Cairo Kidney Centre
3 Hussein El-Memar Street
Antikhana
PO Box 91
Bab El-Louk, Cairo, 11513, Egypt
Tel: (20) 2 579 0267
Email: Isn@rusys.eg.net
Contact: Dr Rashad Barsoum, ISN Secretary General

ISN Visiting Scholars Program

Subjects: Nephrology.
Purpose: To improve the long-term quality of patient care, education and research in fields relevant to the kidney at the host institution. To enable senior physicians or scientists who are experts in nephrology and related disciplines to spend between six weeks and three months at an institution in the developing world.
Eligibility: Applicants must focus primarily on 'hands-on' activities which are the focus of this award eg. the establishment of a new clinical programme, research programme or laboratory technique. ISN visiting Scholars should spend the duration of their study time at an institution in the developing world. Applicants must be experts in nephrology and related disciplines.
Level of Study: Postdoctorate, Research.
Type: Scholarship.
Value: US$25,000 (inclusive of travel and expenses) for three months or a pro rata amount for a shorter period of time.
Length of Study: Six weeks to three months.
Frequency: At the discretion of the ISN.
No. of awards offered: At the discretion of the ISN but usually up to two scholarships per year.

Application Procedure: Applicants must send a description of the programme, its objectives, personal references and a letter of acceptance from the host institution to the ISN Secretary General.
Closing Date: Please contact the organisation.
Funding: Commercial, Private.
No. of awards given last year: Two.
No. of applicants last year: Two.
Additional Information: Further information is available on request.

For further information contact:

Cairo Kidney Centre
3 Hussein El-Memar Street
Antikhana
PO Box 91
Bab El-Louk, Cairo, 11513, Egypt
Tel: (20) 2 579 0267
Email: isn@rusys.eg.net

THE INTERNATIONAL SPINAL RESEARCH TRUST (ISRT)

Unit 8a
Bramley Business Centre
Station Road
Bramley, Guildford, Surrey, GU5 0AZ, England
Tel: (44) 1483 898786
Fax: (44) 1483 898763
Email: research@spinal-research.org
www: http://www.spinal-research.org
Contact: Mr John Cavanagh, Head of Research

The International Spinal Research Trust (ISRT) organises fundraising to support research projects that have the aim of repairing or restoring the loss of function that occurs as a result of injury to the spinal cord. A structured research strategy has been developed to target funds towards relevant research topics.

ISRT Project Grant

Subjects: Topics relevant to furthering the understanding of mammalian spinal cord injury and approaches towards the repair and restoration of function.
Purpose: To provide support for laboratory or clinically based projects.
Eligibility: Open to suitably qualified and experienced principal investigators.
Level of Study: Postdoctorate, Research.
Type: Grant.
Value: Up to UK £250,000 over three years.
Length of Study: Up to three years.
Frequency: Dependent on funds but at least once a year.
Study Establishment: An appropriate university or research institution.
Country of Study: Any country.
No. of awards offered: Approx. six-eight or more per year according to funds.
Application Procedure: Calls for proposals on a specific theme will be advertised periodically. Short listed applicants will be required to complete a full application form.
Closing Date: Variable, as advertised.
Funding: Private.
No. of awards given last year: Four.
No. of applicants last year: 44.
Additional Information: Each call for proposals is on a specific theme. Proposals must be within the charity's remit.

Nathalie Rose Barr PhD Studentship

Subjects: Topics relevant to ISRT's research strategy. Projects will be between collaborative laboratories involved in spinal cord injury research based in the United Kingdom. Both clinical and basic research projects are considered.

Purpose: To support basic and clinical students while working towards a research based PhD degree.
Eligibility: Applicants must hold relevant positions at a United Kingdom university or research establishment.
Level of Study: Postgraduate.
Type: Studentship.
Value: Starts in line with the Wellcome Trust.
Length of Study: Four years for the basic research studentship, and three years for the clinical research fellowship.
Frequency: Annual, if funds are available.
Study Establishment: Universities in the United Kingdom.
Country of Study: United Kingdom.
No. of awards offered: Approx. two-four each year.
Application Procedure: Following advertisement, supervisors will submit project proposals on an ISRT application form. Supervisors of successful projects will then advertise for students.
Closing Date: To be advertised, usually December.
Funding: Private.
No. of awards given last year: Four.
No. of applicants last year: 44.
Additional Information: The advertisement is for supervisors to submit project proposals, not for PhD students themselves.

INTERNATIONAL UNION AGAINST CANCER (UICC)

Fellowships Department
3 rue de Conseil-Général, Geneva, CH-1205, Switzerland
Fax: (41) 22 809 1810
Email: bbaker@uicc.org
www: http://fellows.uicc.org
Contact: Mr Brita M Baker, Head

The International Union Against Cancer (UICC) Fellowships Programme provides long, medium and short-term fellowships abroad to qualified investigators, clinicians, and nurses, who are actively involved in cancer research, clinical oncology or oncology nursing.

UICC Asia-Pacific Cancer Society Training Grants (APCASOT)

Subjects: Non-medical aspects of cancer society work, such as fundraising, media relations, organisation and managerial skills, surveillance of cancer statistics, behavioural research, advocacy, non-medical patient services, preventions and early detection education programmes.
Purpose: To support the training of qualified individuals in non-practical aspects of cancer society work.
Eligibility: Open to staff and accredited volunteers from cancer societies in the Asia-Pacific region.
Level of Study: Unrestricted.
Type: Grant.
Value: US$1,800 to the least expensive round trip fare or other appropriate form of transport and to the living costs. Extra costs for visa, passports, airport taxes and insurance are the responsibility of the grant recipient. No financial support is provided for dependants.
Length of Study: One-two weeks.
Frequency: Annual.
Study Establishment: Cancer Society.
Country of Study: Any country in the Asia Pacific region.
No. of awards offered: Five.
Application Procedure: Applicants must complete an application form, available from the Fellowships Department or from the website.
Closing Date: September 1st for December selection.
Funding: Private.
Contributor: The William Rudder Memorial Fund (Australia).
No. of awards given last year: Three.
No. of applicants last year: Seven.

UICC International Cancer Research Technology Transfer Project (ICRETT)

Subjects: Cancer control and prevention, epidemiology and cancer registration, public education, and behavioural sciences.

Purpose: To enable recipients to learn or teach up to date research techniques, transfer appropriate technology, or acquire advanced clinical management, diagnostic and therapeutic skills.

Eligibility: Open to qualified investigators and experienced clinicians.

Level of Study: Professional development.

Type: Fellowship.

Value: The average stipend is US$3,000.

Length of Study: One-three months with stipend support for one month.

Frequency: Annual.

Country of Study: Any country.

No. of awards offered: 120.

Application Procedure: Applicants may submit an application at any time. Awardees are normally notified within 60 days of registration of a complete application. Application forms can be obtained from the Fellowships Department or downloaded from the website.

Closing Date: Applications are accepted at any time.

Funding: Commercial, Government, Private.

No. of awards given last year: 143.

No. of applicants last year: 300.

Additional Information: The fellowships are funded by the National Cancer Institute, USA, Norwegian Agency for Development (NORAD), Norwegian Cancer Society, Cancer Research Campaign, UK, Imperial Cancer Research Fund, UK, Swedish Cancer Society, Nordic Cancer Union, National Cancer Institute of Canada/Cancer Society of Canada, Italian Cancer Research Foundation, Dutch Cancer Society, French National League Against Cancer, Dr Mildred Scheel Foundation Deutsche Krebshilfe, Germany, Finnish International Development Agency (FINNIDA), Cancer Society of Finland, Australian Cancer Society Inc., Israel Cancer Association, Cancer Association of South Africa, Association of UICC Fellows, UICC Roll of Honour.

UICC International Cancer Technology Transfer Fellowships (ICRETT) for Bilateral Exchanges Between Indonesia and the Netherlands

Subjects: Cancer control and prevention, epidemiology and cancer registration, public education or behavioural sciences.

Purpose: To foster the acquisition of up to date clinical management, diagnostic and therapeutic expertise, exchange knowledge and enhance skills in cancer control and prevention, and facilitate rapid transfer of cancer research and technology.

Eligibility: Eligible to nationals of Indonesia. Qualified cancer investigators should be in the early stages of their careers whilst clinicians should be well established in their oncology practice. Experts from any country who have been invited to teach these specialised skills at institutes abroad are also eligible to apply.

Level of Study: Postdoctorate, Postgraduate, Professional development, Research.

Type: Fellowship.

Value: One month stipend and travel of US$3,000. Home and or host institutions are expected to cover living costs for any additional periods. UICC also contributes to the least expensive international return air fares or other appropriate form of transport. Travel estimates should not include costs for internal travel within the home and/or host countries. These and extra costs for visa, passports, airport taxes and insurance, are the responsibility of the Fellow. No allowances are made for accompanying dependants.

Length of Study: A maximum of three months.

Frequency: Annual.

Study Establishment: A suitable host institution abroad.

Country of Study: Netherlands.

No. of awards offered: 10.

Application Procedure: Applicants must complete an application form, available from the Fellowships Department or from the website.

Closing Date: Applications are accepted at any time.

Funding: Private.

No. of awards given last year: Three.

No. of applicants last year: Six.

UICC International Fellowships for Beginning Investigators (ACSBI)

Subjects: Epidemiology, prevention, cause, detection, diagnosis, treatment and psycho-oncology.

Purpose: To enable investigators and clinicians who are in the early stages of their careers to carry out basic, translational, or clinical projects and to develop, acquire and apply advance research procedures and techniques that foster a bi-directional flow of knowledge, experience, expertise and innovation to and from the United States of America.

Eligibility: Candidates should be in the early stages of their careers and applications that are geared to the development of specific cancer control measures in developing and central and east European countries are particularly encouraged. Candidates should hold assistant professorships or similar positions at their home institutes and ordinarily have a minimum of two and a maximum of 10 years' postdoctoral experience after obtaining their MD or PhD degrees or equivalents. Awards are conditional on the return of the Fellow to the home institute at the end of the fellowship and on the availability of appropriate facilities and resources to apply newly acquired skills. Candidates who are physically present at the proposed host institute whilst their applications are under consideration are not eligible for UICC Fellowships.

Level of Study: Postdoctorate, Professional development, Research.

Type: Fellowship.

Value: Average value of US$35,000 for travel and stipend support. Calculation of travel and stipend awards are based on the candidate's estimates which are adjusted, if need be, to published fares and UICC scales. Travel awards contribute to least expensive international return air fares or other appropriate form of transport. Travel estimates should not include costs for internal travel within the home and/or host countries. These and extra costs for visa, passports, airport taxes, and insurance, are the responsibility of the Fellow. No allowances are made for accompanying dependants.

Length of Study: One year, extendable by a further year at no additional cost to UICC.

Frequency: Annual.

Country of Study: United States of America.

No. of awards offered: 8-10.

Application Procedure: Applicants must submit completed applications with all supporting documentation to reach the UICC by the application closing date. Application forms may be obtained from the Fellowships Department or from the website.

Closing Date: December 1st, selection results are notified in mid April of the following year.

Funding: Private.

Contributor: The American Cancer Society.

No. of awards given last year: 10.

No. of applicants last year: 21.

UICC Latin America COPES Training and Education Fellowships (LACTEF)

Subjects: Non-medical aspects of cancer society work.

Purpose: To support the training of qualified individuals in non-medical aspects of cancer society work.

Eligibility: Open to staff and accredited volunteers from cancer societies in the Latin American region.

Level of Study: Unrestricted.

Type: Fellowship.

Value: US$1,800.

Length of Study: One-two weeks.

Frequency: Annual.

Country of Study: Any country within the Latin American region.

No. of awards offered: Five.

Application Procedure: Applicants must complete an application form, available from the Fellowships Department or from the website.

Closing Date: May 1st, with selection in mid August.
Funding: Private.
No. of awards given last year: Six.
No. of applicants last year: Eight.

UICC Translational Cancer Research Fellowships (TCRF)

Subjects: The bridging of areas that effectively connect the cell and molecular biologists to the patients in the clinic.
Purpose: To accelerate the translation of basic, experimental, and applied research insights into their clinical or population applications in the form of new ideas, drugs and treatments for solid tumours.
Eligibility: The Fellowships are subject to the UICC general conditions for fellowships.
Level of Study: Postdoctorate, Research.
Type: Fellowships.
Value: The average award value is US$55,000.
Length of Study: One year.
Frequency: Annual.
Country of Study: Any country.
No. of awards offered: Two.
Application Procedure: Applicants must complete an application form, available from the Fellowships Department or from the website.
Closing Date: December 1st.
Funding: Commercial.
Contributor: Novartis (Switzerland) and AstraZeneca (UK).
No. of awards given last year: One.
No. of applicants last year: 20.
Additional Information: Further information is available on request.

UICC Trish Greene International Oncology Nursing Fellowships

Subjects: Cancer nursing training.
Purpose: To support English speaking nurses who are actively engaged in the care of cancer patients and who come from developing and Eastern European countries.
Eligibility: Open to English speaking nurses who are actively engaged in the care of cancer patients in their home institutes and who come from developing or Eastern European countries where specialist cancer nursing training is not yet widely available.
Level of Study: Professional development.
Type: Fellowship.
Value: The average stipend is US$2,800.
Length of Study: One-three months with stipend support for one month.
Frequency: Annual.
Country of Study: Any country.
No. of awards offered: 11.
Application Procedure: Applicants must submit applications complete with supporting documentation to the UICC Geneva Office by the application closing date. Application forms can be obtained from the Fellowships Department or from the website.
Closing Date: November 1st for notification in mid February.
Funding: Private.
Contributor: The Oncology Nursing Society (USA) and the Norwegian Cancer Society.
No. of awards given last year: 11.
No. of applicants last year: 24.

UICC Yamagiwa-Yoshida Memorial International Cancer Study Grants

Subjects: Cancer research.
Purpose: To enable cancer investigators from any country to carry out bilateral research projects which exploit complementary materials or skills, including advanced training in experimental methods or special techniques.
Eligibility: Open to appropriately qualified investigators from any country who are actively engaged in cancer research. Candidates who are already physically present at the proposed host institute are not eligible.
Level of Study: Professional development.

Type: Grant.
Value: The average stipend is US$9,000 (if a Fellow's return to home is delayed beyond the extra approved period, 50 per cent of the travel award, the return portion has to be reimbursed to the UICC). Calculation of travel and stipend awards are based on the candidate's estimates which are adjusted, if need be, to published fares and UICC scales. Travel awards contribute to the least expensive international return air fares or other appropriate form of transport. Travel estimates should not include costs for internal travel within the home or host countries. These and extra costs for visa, passports, airport taxes and insurance are the responsibility of the Fellow. No financial support is provided for dependants.
Length of Study: One-three months, and may be extended by their original duration, subject to written approval of the home and host supervisors. Funding for these additional periods may be secured from other funding agencies.
Frequency: Annual.
Country of Study: Any country.
No. of awards offered: 15.
Application Procedure: Applicants must complete an application form, available from the Fellowships Department or from the website.
Closing Date: January 1st for notification by mid April, July 1st for notification by mid October.
Funding: Commercial, Private.
Contributor: Kyowa Hakko Kyoga Company, Limited, Toray Industries, Inc. and the Japan National Committee for UICC.
No. of awards given last year: 14.
No. of applicants last year: 34.
Additional Information: These grants are funded by the Kyowa Hakko Kogyo Company Ltd, Toray Industries Incorporated, Tokyo, and the Japan National Committee for UICC.

Yamagiwa-Yoshida Memorial (YY) UICC International Cancer Study Grants

Subjects: Cancer study.
Purpose: To enable cancer investigators to carry out bilateral research projects abroad which exploit complementary materials or skills.
Eligibility: Open to candidates who are actively involved in cancer research, with appropriate scientific or medical qualifications and recent publications in international peer reviewed periodicals.
Level of Study: Postgraduate.
Type: Grant.
Value: Up to US$9,000. Calculation of travel and stipend awards is based on the candidates' estimates which are adjusted, if need be, to published fares and UICC scales. Travel awards contribute to the least expensive international two-way return air fare or other appropriate form of transport. Travel estimates should not include costs for internal travel within the home or host countries. These and extra costs for visa, passports, airport taxes, insurances etc. are the responsibility of the Fellow. Stipend estimates should indicate living expenses per month. No financial support is provided for dependants.
Length of Study: One-three months, with the possibility of extension subject to the written approval of the home and host supervisors. Funding for such extension periods may be secured from other funding agencies.
Frequency: Annual.
Country of Study: Any country.
No. of awards offered: Approx. 15.
Application Procedure: Applicants must complete an application form which can be obtained from the Fellowships Department or from the website.
Closing Date: January 1st and July 1st.
Contributor: The Kyowa Hakko Kogyo Company Limited, Toray Industries Incorporated, Tokyo and the Japan National Committee for UICC.
Additional Information: Selection results are available in mid April and mid October. Further information is available upon request.

INTERNATIONAL UNION FOR THE SCIENTIFIC STUDY OF POPULATION (IUSSP)

3-5 rue Nicolas, Paris, Cedex 20, F-75080, France
Tel: (33) 5 60 62 17 3
Fax: (33) 5 60 62 20 4
Email: iussp@iussp.org
www: http://www.iussp.org
Contact: Grants Management Officer

The International Union for the Scientific Study of Population (IUSSP) promotes scientific studies in population problems through encouraging research into demographic issues worldwide, stimulating interest in population questions among governments, international and national organisations, the scientific community and the general public. The IUSSP fosters exchanges between population specialists and those in related disciplines and disseminates scientific knowledge on population as widely as possible.

International Union for the Study of Population Travel Grants for Junior Demographers

Subjects: Demography.
Purpose: To promote the participation of junior demographers in the activities of the Union by enabling the successful candidate to attend a seminar organised or co-sponsored by the Union.
Eligibility: Open to members who are junior in demography and hold an MA or PhD degree in demography. Preference is normally given to applicants from a developing country.
Level of Study: Doctorate, Postgraduate.
Type: Travel grant.
Value: Full travel and daily allowance.
Frequency: Dependent on funds available.
Country of Study: Dependent on the venue of the seminar.
No. of awards offered: Four.
Application Procedure: Applicants must write for details.
Closing Date: Please write for details.
Additional Information: Applicants must be sponsored by two Union members. Details are available on the website.

INTERNATIONAL UNION FOR VACUUM SCIENCE AND TECHNOLOGY (IUVSTA)

7 Mohawk, Nepean, ON, K2H 7G7, Canada
Tel: (1) 613 829 5790
Fax: (1) 613 829 3061
Email: westwood@istar.ca
www: http://www.vacuum.org/iuvsta.html
Contact: Dr William D Westwood, Secretary General

The International Union for Vacuum Science and Technology (IUVSTA) is a non-government organisation whose member societies represent all vacuum scientists, engineers and technologists in their country.

Welch Foundation Scholarship

Subjects: Vacuum science.
Purpose: To encourage promising scholars who wish to study vacuum science, techniques or their application in any field.
Eligibility: Open to applicants of any nationality who hold at least a Bachelor's degree, although a doctoral degree is preferred.
Level of Study: Doctorate, Postdoctorate, Postgraduate.
Type: Scholarship.
Value: US$15,500.
Length of Study: One year.
Frequency: Annual.
Study Establishment: An appropriate laboratory overseas.
Country of Study: Any country.
No. of awards offered: One.

Application Procedure: Applicants must complete and submit an application form with a research proposal, a curriculum vitae and two letters of reference. More information and application forms can be obtained from the website under Welch headings.
Closing Date: April 15th.
Funding: Private.
Contributor: IUVSTA.
No. of awards given last year: One.
No. of applicants last year: Four.

For further information contact:

Administrator
Nortel Networks
Box 3511
Station C, Ottawa, ON, K1Y 4H7, Canada
Email: frsims@nortelnetworks.com
Contact: Dr FR Shepherd, Administrator

INTERNATIONALER ROBERT-SCHUMANN-WETTBEWERB ZWICKAU

Organisationsbüro
Münzstraße 12, Zwickau, D-08056, Germany
Tel: (49) 375 212 636
Fax: (49) 375 834 130
Email: kulturbuero@zwickau.de
www: http://www.zwickau.de/robert-schumann.htm
Contact: Ms Hannelore Heil

International Robert Schumann Competition

Subjects: Piano performance or individual singing.
Purpose: To support the interpretation of the work of Robert Schumann.
Eligibility: Open to pianists up to the age of 30 and to individual singers up to the age of 32.
Level of Study: Professional development.
Type: Competition.
Value: Please contact the organisation.
Frequency: Every four years.
Country of Study: Any country.
No. of awards offered: 10.
Application Procedure: Applicants must write for further details.
Funding: Commercial, Government.

IRIS FUND FOR PREVENTION OF BLINDNESS

York House
199 Westminster Bridge Road, London, SE1 7UT, England
Tel: (44) 20 7928 7743
Fax: (44) 20 7928 7919
Email: info@irisfund.org.uk
www: http://www.irisfund.org.uk
Contact: Mr Michael Roberts, Executive Director

The Iris Fund for Prevention of Blindness supports nationwide research into the prevention, treatment and cure of all forms of blindness and serious eye disorders, whether inherited, congenital or acquired. The Fund also focuses on current needs by sponsoring screening programmes and helping ophthalmology departments purchase vital innovative equipment when funds are unavailable from other sources.

Iris Fund Award

Subjects: Ophthalmology.
Purpose: In recognition of distinction either in training or in the chosen area of ophthalmic research.

Eligibility: Open to United Kingdom citizens only who are under the age of 40.
Level of Study: Professional development.
Value: UK £10,000.
Frequency: Every three years.
Country of Study: United Kingdom.
No. of awards offered: One.
Application Procedure: Applicants must submit six copies of the application form as well as supporting paperwork.
Closing Date: Please contact the Iris Fund for confirmation.
Funding: Commercial, Private.
No. of awards given last year: One.
No. of applicants last year: Six.

Iris Fund Grants for Research and Equipment (Ophthalmology)

Subjects: Ophthalmology.
Purpose: To prevent and cure blindness and serious eye disorders.
Eligibility: Open to suitably qualified individuals. Applications must be submitted by qualified consultant ophthalmologists or equivalent for research under his or her supervision. Research projects can only take place in the United Kingdom.
Level of Study: Unrestricted.
Type: Grant.
Value: As funds become available.
Length of Study: Usually for a maximum of three years.
Frequency: Annual.
Country of Study: United Kingdom.
No. of awards offered: Varies.
Application Procedure: Applicants must submit eight copies of the application form as well as supporting paperwork.
Closing Date: March 31st.
Funding: Commercial, Private.
No. of awards given last year: Seven.
No. of applicants last year: 19.

IRISH-AMERICAN CULTURAL INSTITUTE (IACI)

1 Lackawanna Place, Morristown, NJ, 07960, United States of America
Tel: (1) 973 605 1991
Fax: (1) 973 605 8875
Email: irishwaynj@aol.com
www: http://www.irishaci.org
Contact: Ms Anne-Marie Crowell

The Irish American Cultural Institute (IACI), a non-profit educational institute, is dedicated to preserving and promoting the highest standards of artistic development, education, research and entertainment in fostering the cultural understanding of Irish heritage in America. With international headquarters in Morristown, New Jersey, the Institute has a long history of supporting the arts and humanities through grants and awards as well as through programming. The Institute is strictly non-political and non-sectarian. Founded in 1962, the IACI is the sole United States of America organisation with the distinction of having the President of Ireland as patron.

Irish Research Funds

Subjects: All subjects. Historical research has predominated, but other areas of research will be considered equally.
Purpose: To promote scholarly enquiry and publication regarding the Irish-American experience.
Eligibility: Open to individuals of any nationality. Media production costs and journal subventions will not be considered for funding.
Level of Study: Postgraduate.
Type: Grant.
Value: US$1,000-5,000.
Frequency: Annual.
Country of Study: Any country.

No. of awards offered: Varies.
Application Procedure: Applicants must complete an application form. Information is available on request.
Closing Date: October 1st.
Funding: Private.
No. of awards given last year: Up to 10.
No. of applicants last year: 40.

Irish-American Cultural Institute Visiting Fellowship in Irish Studies at National University of Ireland, Galway

Subjects: Irish studies.
Purpose: To allow scholars to spend a semester at UI-Galway and whose work relates to any aspect of Irish studies.
Eligibility: Open to Scholars who normally reside in the United States of America, whose work relates to any aspect of Irish studies.
Level of Study: Postgraduate.
Type: Fellowship.
Value: Stipend of US$13,000 plus transatlantic transportation.
Length of Study: A period of not less than four months.
Frequency: Annual.
Country of Study: Ireland.
No. of awards offered: One.
Application Procedure: Applicants must complete an application form and submit this with a current curriculum vitae and list of publications. Application forms are available on request.
Closing Date: December 31st for the forthcoming academic year.
Contributor: Jointly funded with University College Galway (UCG).
Additional Information: The holder of the fellowship will be provided with services appropriate to a visiting faculty member during his or her time at UCG. There are certain relatively minor departmental responsibilities expected of the holder during his or her time at UCG, and certain other expectations regarding publication, upon completion of the fellowship.

ISMA CENTRE

The University of Reading
Whiteknights Park
PO Box 242, Reading, Berkshire, RG6 6BA, England
Tel: (44) 118 931 8239
Fax: (44) 118 931 4741
Email: admin@ismacentre.rdg.ac.uk
www: http://www.ismacentre.rdg.ac.uk
Contact: Ms Julie Stewart, Marketing & Recruitment Manager

The ISMA Centre at the University of Reading is a leader in the research and education of applied securities and investment banking education. Its graduate study opportunities include Master's degrees and doctoral research programmes. The Centre is part of the School of Business at the University, but is housed in its own facilities with two financial dealing rooms.

ISMA Centre Doctoral Scholarship

Subjects: A topic related to the following research areas: financial econometrics, market microstructure, interest rates or credit risk.
Purpose: To support research in the field.
Eligibility: Candidates should have an excellent academic background and have, or be in the process of completing, a Master's degree, with grade averages at distinction level, in a course containing a significant proportion of finance.
Level of Study: Doctorate.
Type: Scholarship.
Value: UK £10,000 (paid quarterly) plus PhD fee waiver.
Length of Study: Three years.
Frequency: Annual.
Study Establishment: ISMA Centre, the University of Reading.
Country of Study: United Kingdom.
No. of awards offered: Three.
Application Procedure: Applicants must complete an application form, available from the Centre.

Funding: Commercial.
Contributor: ISMA Centre and the University of Reading.
No. of awards given last year: Three.
No. of applicants last year: 120.

ITALIAN INSTITUTE FOR HISTORICAL STUDIES

Via Benedetto Croce 12, Naples, I-80134, Italy
Tel: (39) 081 551 7159
Fax: (39) 081 551 2390
Email: direzione.iiss@iol.it
www: http://www.iiss.it
Contact: Ms Marta Herling, Secretary

The Italian Institute for Historical Studies is a postgraduate institute for the study of history and philosophy. The study of history is seen in connection with the disciplines of philosophy, the arts, economics and literature. The Institute offers two annual scholarships for non-Italian postgraduates specialising in humanities and social sciences.

Adolfo Omodeo Scholarship

Subjects: History and philosophy. The study of history is seen in connection with the disciplines of philosophy, the arts, economics and literature.
Purpose: To allow students to participate in life at the Institute while completing a personal research project with the assistance of its staff.
Eligibility: Open to nationals of all countries. Applicants must possess a Bachelor's degree.
Level of Study: Postgraduate.
Type: Scholarship.
Value: Please contact the Institute for details.
Length of Study: Eight months.
Frequency: Annual.
Study Establishment: The Italian Institute for Historical Studies.
Country of Study: Italy.
No. of awards offered: One.
Application Procedure: Applicants must submit an application including birth certificate, proof of citizenship, university diploma, scholarly work, curriculum vitae, programme of research, letters of reference, and copies of publications.
Closing Date: September 30th.
Funding: Government, Private.
No. of awards given last year: Two.
No. of applicants last year: Two.

Frederico Chabod Scholarship

Subjects: History and philosophy. The study of history is seen in connection with the disciplines of philosophy, the arts, economics and literature.
Purpose: To allow students to participate in life at the Institute, while completing a personal research project with the assistance of its staff.
Eligibility: Open to nationals of all countries. Applicants must possess a Bachelor's degree.
Level of Study: Postgraduate.
Type: Scholarship.
Value: Please contact the Institute for details.
Length of Study: Eight months.
Frequency: Annual.
Study Establishment: The Italian Institute for Historical Studies.
Country of Study: Italy.
No. of awards offered: One.
Application Procedure: Applicants must submit an application including birth certificate, proof of citizenship, university diploma, scholarly work, curriculum vitae, programme of research, letters of reference, and copies of publications.
Closing Date: September 30th.
Funding: Government, Private.

No. of awards given last year: Two.
No. of applicants last year: Two.

THE J B HARLEY RESEARCH FELLOWSHIPS TRUST

c/o British Library Map Library
96 Euston Road, London, NW1 2DB, England
Fax: (44) 20 7412 7780
Email: t.campbell@ockendon.clara.co.uk
www: http://ihr.sas.ac.uk/maps/harley.html
Contact: Mr Tony Campbell

The J B Harley Research Fellowships in the History of Cartography

Subjects: The history of cartography.
Purpose: To promote the use of the great wealth of historical and cartographical material available in London.
Eligibility: Open to anyone pursuing advanced research in the history of cartography, irrespective of nationality, discipline or profession. Advanced research is taken to mean work towards a doctorate, postdoctoral research or work of an equivalent level regardless of the applicant's formal qualifications. Preference will be given to interpretative studies in map history, irrespective of area, theme or period.
Level of Study: Doctorate, Postdoctorate.
Type: Grant.
Value: Normally UK £250 per week.
Length of Study: Up to four weeks.
Frequency: Annual.
Study Establishment: London libraries.
Country of Study: United Kingdom.
No. of awards offered: Three.
Application Procedure: Details are available from the website.
Funding: Private.

J N TATA ENDOWMENT

Bombay House
24 Homi Mody Street, Bombay, 400001, India
Tel: (91) 20 491 31
Fax: (91) 20 454 32
Email: gjkerawalla@tata.com
Contact: Professor Gulistan J Kerawalla Kerawalla, Chief Executive Officer

The J N Tata Endowment awards one time loan scholarships to scholars of conspicuous distinction for postgraduate, PhD or post-doctoral studies abroad in all fields. Mid-career professionals with an outstanding academic background and experience in the field going abroad for further specialisation are also considered for the scholarship.

J N Tata Endowment Loan Scholarship

Subjects: All subjects.
Purpose: To provide an opportunity to the gifted to pursue higher studies abroad in all disciplines.
Eligibility: Open only to Indian nationals. Applicants must be graduates with a sound academic and extra curricular record. Deserving mid-career professionals are also eligible.
Level of Study: Doctorate, Postdoctorate, Postgraduate.
Type: Loan scholarship.
Value: Up to indian rupee 100,000.
Frequency: Annual.
Country of Study: Any country except India.
No. of awards offered: 100+.

Application Procedure: Applicants must complete an application form. Forms are issued against an application fee of indian rupee 50.
Closing Date: February 15th for the Autumn and Spring semesters.
Funding: Private.
Contributor: Tata Trusts.
No. of awards given last year: 168.
No. of applicants last year: 979.
Additional Information: The award is primarily for the Autumn semester. Selection of Scholars is made on the basis of a personal interview which assesses the student's competence in the field of graduation, general knowledge, maturity and suitability for the proposed field of study. Interviews are conducted between March and June for the Autumn and Spring semesters.

For further information contact:

Administrative Office
J N Tata Endowment
Mulla House
4th Floor
51 M G Road, Bombay, 400001, India

J W DAFOE FOUNDATION

Faculty of Graduate Studies
500 University Centre
University of Manitoba, Winnipeg, MB, R3T 2N2, Canada
Tel: (1) 204 474 9836
Fax: (1) 204 474 7553
Email: ilse_krentz@umanitoba.ca
www: http://www.umanitoba.ca
Contact: Awards Officer

The J W Dafoe Foundation was established by admirers of John Wesley Dafoe, who was editor of the Winnipeg Free Press from 1901 until his death in 1944. He was Canada's most distinguished journalist and editor with a special interest in Canada's place in the world.

J W Dafoe Graduate Fellowship
Subjects: International relations.
Purpose: To encourage graduate study in international relations.
Eligibility: Open to graduates with a First Class (Honours) Degree from a recognised university or equivalent who intend to work for a higher degree in the field of international studies at the University of Manitoba in the departments of economics, political studies or history.
Level of Study: Doctorate, Graduate, Postgraduate.
Type: Fellowship.
Value: Canadian $15,000 renewable for one year.
Frequency: Annual.
Study Establishment: Departments of political studies, economics or history at the University of Manitoba.
Country of Study: Canada.
No. of awards offered: One.
Application Procedure: Applicants must apply for and obtain a University of Manitoba Graduate Fellowship (UMGF) form. The UMGF application form must be completed and should include an additional page outlining a detailed research proposal in the field of international relations to be carried out in the departments stated. The completed application form must be submitted to the department requested for study by the applicant by their specified deadline which is usually two to four weeks prior to February 15th. Application forms can be obtained directly from the departments or from the website.
Closing Date: February 15th.

JACOB'S PILLOW DANCE FESTIVAL, INC.

Box 287, Lee, MA, 01238, United States of America
Tel: (1) 413 637 1322
Fax: (1) 413 243 4744
Email: info@jacobspillow.org
www: http://www.jacobspillow.org
Contact: Ms J R Glover, Education Director

The Jacob's Pillow Dance Festival seeks to nurture and sustain artistic creation, presentation, education and preservation. To engage and deepen public appreciation and support for dance. Founded in 1932 by modern dance pioneer Ted Shawn, the School provides rigorous dance training and education for some 100 pre-professionals, artists and teachers seeking professional development in a residential artist community.

Jacob's Pillow Education Fund Scholarship
Subjects: Dance traditions, techniques, repertory and theory. Classes are offered in all forms of dance and vary from year to year. Ballet, modern, jazz and cultural traditions are four core school programmes offered annually. In addition, one or two programmes with an emphasis on choreographic development are part of each summer's offerings.
Purpose: To allow advanced dancers an opportunity to participate in summer dance workshops with world renowned faculty and artists.
Eligibility: Open to United States of America and foreign nationals who are over 16 years of age, have advanced dance training and complete application requirements for the programme the applicant wishes to attend.
Level of Study: Unrestricted.
Type: Scholarship.
Value: Room, board, tuition and performance tickets. There is no travel allowance.
Length of Study: Varies, usually one-three weeks.
Frequency: Annual.
Study Establishment: The School at Jacob's Pillow Dance Festival.
Country of Study: United States of America.
No. of awards offered: 50-60 percent of students are provided with partial scholarships.
Application Procedure: Applicants must contact the School after December 1st for audition requirements for the upcoming Summer programme. Applicants can write, phone or visit the website.
Closing Date: The deadline for videotape auditions is March 22nd.
Funding: Private.
Contributor: Private contributions.
No. of awards given last year: Approx. 100.
No. of applicants last year: Varies.
Additional Information: Scholarships are only offered to enable dancers to attend the School at Jacob's Pillow Dance Festival and are non transferable. Scholarship awards apply towards the total programme fee which includes tuition, room and board and access to performances.

For further information contact:

(For UPS/Express Mail)
The School at Jacob's Pillow
358 George Carter Road, Becket, MA, 01233, United States of America

JAMES COOK UNIVERSITY

Research Higher Degrees, Townsville, QLD, 4811, Australia
Tel: (61) 7 4781 4575
Fax: (61) 7 4781 6204
www: http://www.jcu.edu.au
Contact: Ms Susan Meehan, Manager

James Cook University prides itself on its international reputation for research and discovery and the teaching is enhanced and enlivened by that research activity. Students will experience at first hand the process of producing new knowledge, which will provide them with the confidence and the ability to become the entrepreneurs and innovators of tomorrow.

James Cook University Postgraduate Research Scholarship

Subjects: Marine sciences, earth sciences, tropical biology and conservation, biotechnology and molecular sciences, computational experimental mechanics, health and medicine in the tropics, gender studies and social change in the tropics tourism.
Purpose: To encourage full-time postgraduate research leading to a Master's or PhD degree.
Eligibility: Open to any student who has attained at least a Second Class (Honours) Bachelor's Degree.
Level of Study: Postgraduate.
Type: Scholarship.
Value: Australian $17,071 per year. The award does not cover annual tuition fees for overseas students.
Length of Study: Three years with a possible additional six months in exceptional circumstances for the PhD, or two years for the Master's programme.
Frequency: Annual.
Study Establishment: James Cook University.
Country of Study: Australia.
No. of awards offered: Up to seven.
Closing Date: October 31st.

Noel and Kate Monkman Postgraduate Award

Subjects: Marine biology.
Purpose: To encourage full-time study towards a MSc or PhD degree in marine biology.
Eligibility: Open to persons holding or expecting to hold a Second Class (Honours) Degree, or its equivalent, in marine biology or a related science. Applicants must be Australian citizens or have permanent resident status in Australia.
Level of Study: Postgraduate.
Type: Scholarship.
Value: To be determined.
Length of Study: Three years for the PhD or two years for the Master's programme.
Frequency: Dependent on funds available.
Study Establishment: James Cook University.
Country of Study: Australia.
No. of awards offered: One.

JAMES MADISON MEMORIAL FELLOWSHIP FOUNDATION

2000 K Street North West
Suite 303, Washington, DC, 20006, United States of America
Tel: (1) 202 653 8700
Fax: (1) 202 653 6111
Email: madison@act.org
www: http://www.jamesmadison.com
Contact: Mr Lewis F Larsen, Director of Programs

The mission of the James Madison Memorial Fellowship Foundation is to strengthen secondary school teaching of the principles, framing and development of the United States of America Constitution.

James Madison Fellowship Program

Subjects: History, political science or the arts.
Purpose: For graduate study leading to a Master's degree.
Eligibility: Applicants must be United States of America citizens.
Level of Study: Graduate.
Type: Fellowship.
Value: Up to US$24,000.
Length of Study: Up to five years.
Frequency: Annual.

Country of Study: United States of America.
No. of awards offered: Up to 60.
Application Procedure: Applicants must obtain an application form by calling (1) 800 525 6928. Applications may also be downloaded from the Foundation's website.
Closing Date: March 1st.
Funding: Government, Private.
No. of awards given last year: 70.

JAMES PANTYFEDWEN FOUNDATION GRANTS AND LOANS

Pantyfedwen
9 Market Street, Aberystwyth, Ceredigion, SY23 1DL, Wales
Tel: (44) 1970 612806
Fax: (44) 1970 612806
Email: pantyfedwen@btinternet.com
Contact: Mr Richard H Morgan, Executive Secretary

The James Pantyfedwen Foundation Grants and Loans

Subjects: All subjects.
Purpose: To promote mainly postgraduate research.
Eligibility: Open to Welsh nationals, especially those who wish to train to become ministers of religion of any denomination (qualifying criteria is defined by benefactor).
Level of Study: Postgraduate.
Type: Grants and loans.
Value: Varies, usually up to a maximum of UK £6,000.
Length of Study: Up to a maximum of three years.
Frequency: Annual.
Country of Study: United Kingdom.
No. of awards offered: Varies.
Application Procedure: Applicants must submit applications on the appropriate forms, accepted on an ongoing basis.
Closing Date: July 31st.
Funding: Private.
Contributor: Exclusive to private investment portfolio.
No. of awards given last year: 60.
No. of applicants last year: 250.

JANE COFFIN CHILDS MEMORIAL FUND FOR MEDICAL RESEARCH

333 Cedar Street, New Haven, CT, 06510, United States of America
Tel: (1) 203 785 4612
Fax: (1) 203 785 3301
Email: info@jccfund.org
www: http://www.jccfund.org
Contact: Director's Office

Jane Coffin Childs Memorial Fund for Medical Research Fellowships

Subjects: Medical and related sciences relevant to the causes, origins and treatment of cancer.
Eligibility: Open to persons who possess an MD or PhD degree in the field in which they propose to work.
Level of Study: Postdoctorate.
Type: Fellowship.
Value: US$33,500 in the first year, US$35,000 in the second year, US$37,000 in the third year plus dependant child allowance of US$750 each and usually US$1,500 per year departmental grant.
Length of Study: Two-three years.
Frequency: Annual.
Study Establishment: Laboratories and other institutions where the candidate's proposed research is acceptable and where adequate facilities for work exist.

Country of Study: Any country for United States of America citizens. The United States of America for the citizens of other countries.
No. of awards offered: 20-25.
Application Procedure: Applicants must contact the Fund for information.
Closing Date: February 1st.
Funding: Private.

JANSON JOHAN HELMICH OG MARCIA JANSONS LEGAT

Blommeseter
Norderhov, Hönefoss, N-3512, Norway
Tel: (47) 3 213 5465
Fax: (47) 3 213 5626
Email: janlegat@online.no
www: http://www.jansonslegat.no
Contact: Mr Reidun Haugen, Manager

Janson Johan Helmich Scholarships and Travel Grants
Subjects: All subjects.
Purpose: To support practical or academic training.
Eligibility: Open to qualified Norwegian postgraduate students with practical experience for advanced study abroad.
Level of Study: Doctorate, Postgraduate, Professional development.
Type: Scholarship.
Value: A maximum of norwegian krone 75,000.
Frequency: Annual.
Country of Study: Any country.
No. of awards offered: 30.
Application Procedure: Applicants must complete an application form.
Closing Date: March 15th.
No. of awards given last year: 34.
No. of applicants last year: 176.

JAPAN SOCIETY FOR THE PROMOTION OF SCIENCE (JSPS)

Jochi Kioizaka Building
6-26-3 Kioi-cho
Chiyoda-ku, Tokyo, 102-0094, Japan
Tel: (81) 3 3263 9094
Fax: (81) 3 3263 1854
www: http://www.jsps.go.jp/e-home.htm

The Japan Society for the Promotion of Science (JSPS) is a quasi-governmental organisation established by a national law for the purpose of contributing to the advancement of science. JSPS plays a key role in the administration of various scientific and academic programmes.

JSPS Invitation Fellowship Programme for Research in Japan
Subjects: All fields of the humanities, social sciences, natural sciences, engineering or medicine.
Purpose: To promote international co-operation and mutual understanding in scientific research.
Eligibility: Open to university professors and associate and assistant professors, senior scientists, and other persons with substantial professional experience.
Level of Study: Professional development.
Type: Fellowship.
Value: The short-term programme consists of a round trip air ticket, a daily maintenance allowance of yen 18,000 and a domestic research travel allowance of yen 150,000. The long-term programme consists of a round trip air ticket, a monthly maintenance allowance of yen 369,000, a domestic research travel allowance of yen 100,000, and a research expenses of yen 40,000. Overseas travel accident and sickness insurance coverage will be provided for both programmes.
Length of Study: The short-term programme is for between 14 and 60 days and the long-term programme is 2-10 months.
Frequency: Annual.
Study Establishment: Japanese universities and research institutions.
Country of Study: Japan.
No. of awards offered: Varies.
Application Procedure: Applications must be submitted to JSPS by the inviting scientist in Japan.
Closing Date: The deadlines for the short-term programme are May and September, and the deadline for the long-term programme is September.
Funding: Government.
No. of awards given last year: 380 for the short-term and 79 for the long term.
No. of applicants last year: 811 short-term and 228 long-term.
Additional Information: A short-term programme is also available with a fellowship period of 14-60 days, and a reduced award amount.

JSPS Postdoctoral Fellowships for Foreign Researchers
Subjects: Humanities, social sciences, natural sciences, engineering or medicine.
Purpose: To assist promising and highly qualified young foreign researchers wishing to conduct research in Japan.
Eligibility: Open to citizens of countries which have diplomatic relations with Japan. Applicants must have a doctoral degree.
Level of Study: Postdoctorate.
Type: Fellowship.
Value: A round trip ticket is provided with a monthly maintenance allowance of yen 392,000, a settling in allowance of yen 200,000, an annual domestic research travel allowance of yen 58,500 and accident and sickness insurance coverage for the Fellow only.
Length of Study: Two years but a minimum of one year.
Frequency: Annual.
Study Establishment: Japanese universities and research institutions.
Country of Study: Japan.
No. of awards offered: Varies.
Application Procedure: Applicants must write for details. Application must be submitted to JSPS by the host researcher in Japan.
Funding: Government.
No. of awards given last year: 520.
No. of applicants last year: 2032.

JAPANESE AMERICAN CITIZENS LEAGUE (JACL)

1765 Sutter Street, San Francisco, CA, 94115, United States of America
Tel: (1) 415 921 5225
Fax: (1) 415 931 4671
Email: jacl@jacl.org
www: http://www.jacl.org
Contact: Akiko Schelske, Scholarships Officer

The Japanese American Citizens League (JACL) was founded in 1929 to fight discrimination against people of Japanese ancestry. It is the largest and one of the oldest Asian American organisations in the United States. The JACL has over 24,500 members in 112 chapters located in 25 states, Washington DC, and Japan. The organisation operates within a structure of eight district councils, with headquarters in San Francisco, California.

Japanese American Citizens League Scholarship and Award Program

Subjects: Six categories are offered, they are entering freshman, undergraduate, graduate, law, financial aid and creative or performing arts.

Purpose: To recognise education as a key to greater opportunities for JACL members.

Eligibility: Open to members of the Japanese American Citizens League (JACL). Applicants must be enrolled or planning to enrol full-time in an accredited school for the following semester. Membership of the JACL is not race restrictive. Only applicants that exhibit severe financial need will be considered for the student aid award (Hagiwara).

Level of Study: Doctorate, Graduate, Postdoctorate.

Type: Scholarship and award programme.

Value: Awards vary between US$1,000-5,000.

Frequency: Annual.

Study Establishment: Any accredited college, university, trade school, business school, law school, art school or other Institute of Higher Education.

Country of Study: Any country.

No. of awards offered: Eight for the graduate programme, two for the law programme, one for the student aid award and two for the performing arts programme.

Application Procedure: Applicants must request an application form from JACL, enclosing a stamped addressed envelope, and stating the category which they would like to apply for, or download an application form and eligibility information from the website.

Closing Date: April 1st.

Funding: Private.

No. of awards given last year: 38.

No. of applicants last year: 500.

Additional Information: Selection is based upon scholastic achievement, community involvement, extracurricular activities, personal statement and letters of recommendation. For the Student Aid award a Financial Aid Statement is required, for the creative and performing arts award sample works are required.

JAPANESE GOVERNMENT

Embassy of Japan
112 Empire Circuit, Yarralumla, ACT, 2600, Australia
Tel: (61) 2 6273 3244
Fax: (61) 2 6273 1848
Email: cultural@japan.org.au
www: http://www.japan.org.au
Contact: Ms Eriko Prior, Monbukagakusho Scholarship Co-ordinator

Japanese Government (Monbukagakusho) Scholarships In-Service Training for Teachers Category

Subjects: Teacher training.

Eligibility: Open to Australians under 35 years of age who are university or teacher training college graduates and are teachers in active service of primary or secondary schools, or on the staff at teacher training institutions or educational administrative institutions. Applicants must also have at least five years of experience in their terms of service. In principle, a university academic staff member should not be selected as a grantee.

Level of Study: Postgraduate.

Type: Scholarship.

Value: Return air fare plus yen 184,000 per month.

Length of Study: 18 months.

Frequency: Annual.

Study Establishment: A Japanese university.

Country of Study: Japan.

No. of awards offered: One-two.

Application Procedure: Applicants must complete an application form available from the Embassy of Japan in their own country. Applications are not available from the main organisation itself.

Closing Date: April.

Funding: Government.

No. of awards given last year: Two.

No. of applicants last year: Six.

Additional Information: Applicants must be willing to study the Japanese language.

Japanese Government (Monbukagakusho) Scholarships Research Category

Subjects: Humanities, social sciences, literature, history, aesthetics, law, politics, economics, commerce, pedagogy, psychology, sociology, music and fine arts, natural sciences, pure science, engineering, agriculture, fisheries, pharmacology, medicine, dentistry or home economics.

Eligibility: Open to Australian graduates under 35 years of age.

Level of Study: Doctorate, Postgraduate.

Type: Scholarship.

Value: Return air fare plus yen 184,000 per month.

Length of Study: 18-24 months.

Frequency: Annual.

Study Establishment: A Japanese university.

Country of Study: Japan.

No. of awards offered: Approx. 20.

Application Procedure: Applicants must complete an application form available from the Embassy of Japan in their own country. Applications are not available from the main organisation itself.

Closing Date: June.

Funding: Government.

No. of awards given last year: 15.

No. of applicants last year: 80.

Additional Information: Applicants must be willing to study the Japanese language.

JEAN SIBELIUS INTERNATIONAL VIOLIN COMPETITION

PB 31, Helsinki, FIN-00101, Finland
Tel: (358) 9 4114 3443
Fax: (358) 9 2200 2680
Email: violin.competition@kolumbus.fi
www: http://www.siba.fi/sibeliuscompetition
Contact: Mr Harri Pohjolainen, Competition Secretary

The International Jean Sibelius Violin Competition is organised by the Sibelius Society. The first competition was held in 1965 to mark the 100th anniversary of the maestro's birth.

Jean Sibelius International Violin Competition

Subjects: Musical performance on the violin.

Purpose: To recognise and reward exceptional young violinists.

Eligibility: Open to violinists of any nationality born in 1970 or later.

Level of Study: Unrestricted.

Type: Prize.

Value: The first prize is €16,000, the second prize is €12,500, the third prize is €9,000 plus five prizes of €1,800. A further prize of €1,800 is given by the Finnish Broadcasting Company for the best performance of Sibelius' Violin Concerto.

Frequency: Every five years. The next will be in 2005.

Country of Study: Any country.

No. of awards offered: Nine.

Application Procedure: Applicants must refer to the competition brochure for the rules, application forms and programme which is published in March of the preceding year. The brochure will be sent to schools around the world, but can also be sent directly on request. Applicants should contact the competition Secretary.

Closing Date: August 18th.

Funding: Government.

Contributor: The Ministry of Education.

No. of awards given last year: 12.

No. of applicants last year: 121.

Additional Information: For further information please contact the Competition Secretary.

JENNY MOORE FUND FOR WRITERS

George Washington University
English Department, Washington, DC, 20052, United States of America
Tel: (1) 202 994 6180
Fax: (1) 202 994 7915
Email: ckibler@gwis2.circ.gwu.edu
www: http://www.gwu.edu/~english
Contact: Professor & Director of Creative Writing

The George Washington English Department sponsors the Jenny Moore Writer-in-Washington programme and a reading series.

Jenny Moore Writer-in-Washington

Subjects: Authorship. Genre alternates between fiction and poetry with the occasional year for creative non-fiction or playwriting.
Purpose: To offer a free writing workshop and teach one writing course to GW students.
Eligibility: There are no eligibility restrictions, although significant publications are necessary.
Level of Study: Professional development.
Type: Residency.
Frequency: Annual.
Country of Study: Any country.
No. of awards offered: One.
Application Procedure: Applicants must submit a 25 page writing sample, curriculum vitae and letters of recommendation.
Closing Date: November 15th.
Funding: Private.
Contributor: Jenny McKean Moore.

JEUNESSES MUSICALES OF SERBIA

Terazije 26/11, Belgrade, 11000, Yugoslavia
Tel: (381) 11 686 380
Fax: (381) 11 235 1517
Email: ijmcbyu@music-competition.co.yu
www: http://www.music-competition.co.yu
Contact: Mrs Mirjana Tomic, Assistant Director

The International Jeunesses Musicales Competition was created in Belgrade in 1969. It is dedicated to the most promising young musicians at the beginning of their international careers. The categories which are solo instruments, chamber ensembles and composers are repeated each five or six years so that each generation will have an equal chance.

International Jeunesses Musicales Competition

Subjects: Musical performance, oboe and woodwind quintet.
Purpose: To award the most promising young musicians at the beginning of their international careers.
Eligibility: Open to young musicians ready for international appearances.
Level of Study: Professional development.
Type: Competition.
Value: Cash prizes in new dinar, special prizes and concert engagements.
Frequency: Annual.
Country of Study: Any country.
No. of awards offered: Three in each category.
Application Procedure: Applicants must submit a completed application form, recommendations, a ten inch by eight inch glossy photograph and a curriculum vitae.
Closing Date: December 31st.

Funding: Commercial, Government, Private.
Contributor: Ministry for Culture of Serbia, Secretariat for culture of Belgrade, The City Hall of Belgrady.
No. of awards given last year: Three.
No. of applicants last year: 24.
Additional Information: There are three winners in each category with several prizes. This competition has been organised for 31 years.

JEWISH COMMUNITY CENTERS ASSOCIATION (JCC)

15 East 26th Street, New York, NY, 10010-1579, United States of America
Tel: (1) 212 532 4949 ext. 246
Fax: (1) 212 481 4174
www: http://www.jcca.org
Contact: Ms Joy Brand, Scholarships Co-ordinator

The Jewish Community Centers Association (JJCC) of North America is the leadership network of, and central agency for, over 275 Jewish Community Centers, YM-YWHAs and camps in the United States and Canada, which annually serve more than one million members. The Association offers a wide range of services and resources to enable its affiliates to provide educational, cultural and recreational programmes to enhance the lives of North American Jewry. The JCC Association is also the United States government accredited agency for serving the religious and social needs of Jewish military personnel, their families and patients, in Virginia hospitals through JWB Chaplains Council.

JCC Association Scholarships

Subjects: Social work, Jewish education, health, physical education, recreation, education and non-profit business administration.
Purpose: To provide scholarships for graduate study at the Master's level in areas leading to full-time professional employment at a Jewish Community Center.
Eligibility: Open to applicants who have a BA with at least a 3.0 grade point average and a strong commitment to the Jewish Community Center movement. It is preferred that applicants have knowledge of Jewish community practices, customs, rituals and organisation. The recipients must make the commitment of working at a JCC following completion of graduate work.
Level of Study: Postgraduate.
Type: Scholarship.
Value: Up to US$7,500 for tuition costs.
Length of Study: One year, renewable for one more year based on satisfactory academic performance.
Frequency: Annual.
Country of Study: United States of America or Canada.
No. of awards offered: 8-10.
Application Procedure: Applicants must submit an application, reference letters, personal statement and transcripts.
Closing Date: February 1st.
Funding: Private.
No. of awards given last year: 14.
No. of applicants last year: 100.

JEWISH FOUNDATION FOR EDUCATION OF WOMEN

135 East 64th Street, New York, NY, 10021, United States of America
Tel: (1) 212 288 3931
Fax: (1) 212 288 5798
Email: fdnscholar@aol.com
www: http://www.jfew.org
Contact: Ms Marge Goldwater, Executive Director

The Jewish Foundation for Education of Women is a private, non-sectarian organisation. It provides scholarship assistance for higher education to women with financial need within a 50 mile radius of New York City through several specific programmes.

Fellowship Programme for Émigrés Pursuing Careers in Jewish Education

Subjects: Religious education and Jewish studies.
Purpose: To provide fellowships for graduate work to women from the former Soviet Union who are interested in pursuing careers in Jewish education.
Eligibility: Women must be residents of New York City or a 50 mile radius thereof. Students entering or enrolled in full-time rabbinical and cantorial programmes, or Master's and doctoral programmes in Jewish education or Jewish studies are eligible.
Level of Study: Doctorate, Graduate, Professional development.
Type: Fellowship.
Value: US$10,000-20,000 per year.
Length of Study: Two years for the Master's degree and four years for the rabbinical, cantorial programmes and PhD.
Frequency: Annual.
Study Establishment: Study must take place in New York City.
Country of Study: United States of America.
No. of awards offered: 5-10.
Application Procedure: Applicants must request an application in writing or by email. In the application request the candidate must indicate current educational status and the programme for which financial aid is required.
Closing Date: March 15th.
Funding: Private.
Additional Information: The Foundation also provides recipients with the opportunity to meet with the programme supervisor for enriched learning on a monthly basis and to productively share experiences as a means of learning how to teach more effectively.

Scholarships for Émigrés in the Health Professions

Subjects: Medicine, dentistry, nursing, pharmacy, occupational therapy, physical therapy, physician assistant and dental hygiene.
Eligibility: Applicants must be female, émigrés from the former Soviet Union, who live within a 50 mile radius of New York City and demonstrate financial need.
Level of Study: Graduate.
Type: Scholarship.
Value: US$5,000 per year.
Frequency: Annual.
Study Establishment: Schools within a 50 mile radius of New York City.
Country of Study: United States of America.
No. of awards offered: Approx. 80.
Application Procedure: Applicants must request an application in writing or email the Federation Scholar. Application forms are available in late October.
Closing Date: May 15th.
Funding: Private.

JILA (FORMERLY JOINT INSTITUTE FOR LABORATORY ASTROPHYSICS)

440 UCB
University of Colorado, Boulder, CO, 80309-0440, United States of America
Tel: (1) 303 492 7789
Fax: (1) 303 492 5235
Email: jilavf@jila.colorado.edu
www: http://jilawww.colorado.edu
Contact: Ms Cheryl Glenn, Programme Assistant

JILA's interests at present are research and applications in the fields of laser technology, opto-electronics, precision measurement, surface science and semiconductors, information and image processing, and materials and process science, as well as basic research in atomic, molecular and optical physics, precision measurement, gravitational physics, chemical physics, astrophysics, and geophysical measurements. To provide an opportunity for persons actively contributing to these fields, JILA operates the Visiting Fellowship Programme as well as the Postdoctoral Research Associate Programme.

JILA Postdoctoral Research Associateship and Visiting Fellowships

Subjects: Natural sciences.
Purpose: To support additional training beyond the PhD and sabbatical research.
Eligibility: There are no restrictions other than those which might be required by the grant which supports the research.
Level of Study: Postdoctorate, Professional development.
Type: Fellowship.
Value: Varies.
Length of Study: Visiting Fellowships are for between 4 and 12 months. Postdoctoral Research Associateships are for one year.
Frequency: Annual.
Country of Study: United States of America.
No. of awards offered: Varies.
Application Procedure: Applicants must complete an application form available from the website.
Closing Date: November 1st for visiting fellowships. There is no closing date for postdoctoral applications.
Funding: Government.
Contributor: Varies.

JOHN AND MARY R MARKLE FOUNDATION

10 Rockefeller Plaza
Floor 16, New York, NY, 10020, United States of America
Tel: (1) 212 489 6655
Fax: (1) 212 765 9690
Email: info@markle.org
www: http://www.markle.org
Contact: Grants Manager

The John and Mary R Markle Foundation is a private non-profit grant making foundation that was incorporated in 1927 in the state of New York by John Markle and his wife Mary R Markle. The Foundation has assets of US$200 million, and makes charitable contributions of approximately US$10 million per year which seek to realise the potential of communications media and information technology to improve people's lives.

John and Mary R Markle Foundation Grants

Subjects: The current programme of the Markle Foundation is focused on the following areas policy for a networked society, interactive media for children and information technology for better health.

Purpose: To realise the potential of emerging communications media and information technology to improve people's lives and to promote the development of communications industries that address public needs.
Eligibility: Open to non governmental organisations or other institutions operating in the field. Grants are not made to individuals.
Type: Grant.
Value: Varies.
Country of Study: There are no geographical restrictions, but most of the Foundation's work is in the United States of America.
No. of awards offered: Varies.
Application Procedure: Applicants must submit grant proposals in a informal letter and must include the purpose for which aid is sought, resources needed, personnel involved and a description of methods to be used in completing the project.
Closing Date: Proposals are evaluated at any time during the year and are awarded in March, June and November.
Funding: Private.

JOHN CARTER BROWN LIBRARY AT BROWN UNIVERSITY

Box 1894, Providence, RI, 02912, United States of America
Tel: (1) 401 863 2725
Fax: (1) 401 863 3477
Email: jcbl_fellowships@brown.edu
www: http://www.jcbl.org
Contact: Ms Nan Sumner-Mack, Programme Administration

The John Carter Brown Library, an independently funded and administered institution for advanced research in history and the humanities, is located on the campus of Brown University. The Library supports research focused on the colonial history of the Americas, including all aspects of the European, African and Native American involvement.

Alexander O Vietor Memorial Fellowship

Subjects: European and American maritime history between 1450 and 1800.
Purpose: To assist students conducting research into early maritime history.
Eligibility: Open to Americans and foreign nationals who are engaged in predoctoral, postdoctoral, or independent research. Graduate students must have passed their preliminary or general examinations at the time of application.
Level of Study: Doctorate, Postdoctorate, Predoctorate.
Type: Fellowship.
Value: US$1,300 per month.
Length of Study: Two-four months.
Frequency: Annual.
Country of Study: United States of America.
No. of awards offered: One.
Application Procedure: Applicants must complete an application form. Please write to or email the Director at the main address.
Closing Date: January 15th.
Funding: Private.
No. of awards given last year: One.
Additional Information: Further information is available on request.

Barbara S Mosbacher Fellowship

Subjects: All aspects of the discovery, exploration, settlement and development of the new world and the related history of Europe and Africa prior to 1825.
Purpose: To assist scholars in any area of research related to the Library's holdings.
Eligibility: Open to Americans and foreign nationals who are engaged in predoctoral, postdoctoral, or independent research. Graduate students must have passed their preliminary or general examinations at the time of application.
Level of Study: Postdoctorate, Predoctorate, Research.

Type: Fellowship.
Value: US$1,300 per month.
Length of Study: Two-four months.
Frequency: Annual.
Country of Study: United States of America.
No. of awards offered: Varies.
Application Procedure: Applicants must complete an application form. Candidates should write or email to the Director at the main address.
Closing Date: January 15th.
Funding: Private.
No. of awards given last year: One.
Additional Information: Further information is available on request.

Center for New World Comparative Studies Fellowship

Subjects: The early history of the Americas from the late fifteenth-century to 1830 and research relating to materials at the Library regarding all aspects of the discovery, exploration, settlements and development of the new world.
Purpose: To enable research with a definite comparative dimension relating to the history of the Americas before 1825.
Eligibility: Open to Americans and foreign nationals who are engaged in predoctoral, postdoctoral or independent research. Graduate students must have passed their preliminary or general examinations at the time of application.
Level of Study: Doctorate, Postdoctorate, Predoctorate.
Type: Fellowship.
Value: US$1,300 per month.
Length of Study: Two-four months.
Frequency: Annual.
Country of Study: United States of America.
No. of awards offered: Two.
Application Procedure: Applicants must complete an application form. Please write to or email the Director at the main address.
Closing Date: January 15th.
Funding: Private.
No. of awards given last year: One.

Charles H Watts Memorial Fellowship

Subjects: All aspects of the discovery, exploration, settlement and development of the new world and the related history of Europe and Africa prior to 1825.
Purpose: To assist scholars in any area of research related to the Library's holdings.
Eligibility: Open to Americans and foreign nationals who are engaged in predoctoral, postdoctoral, or independent research. Graduate students must have passed their preliminary or general examinations at the time of application.
Level of Study: Postdoctorate, Predoctorate, Research.
Type: Fellowship.
Value: US$1,300 per month.
Length of Study: Two-four months.
Frequency: Annual.
Country of Study: United States of America.
No. of awards offered: Varies.
Application Procedure: Applicants must complete an application form. Please write to or email the Director at the main address.
Closing Date: January 15th.
Funding: Private.
No. of awards given last year: One.

Helen Watson Buckner Memorial Fellowship

Subjects: All aspects of the discovery, exploration, settlement, and development of the new world and the related history of Europe and Africa prior to 1825.
Purpose: To assist scholars in any area of research related to the Library's holdings.
Eligibility: Open to Americans and foreign nationals who are engaged in predoctoral, postdoctoral, or independent research. Graduate students must have passed their preliminary or general examinations at the time of application.

Level of Study: Postdoctorate, Predoctorate, Research.
Type: Fellowship.
Value: US$1,300 per month.
Length of Study: Two-four months.
Country of Study: United States of America.
No. of awards offered: Varies.
Application Procedure: Applicants must complete an application form. Candidates should write or email the Director at the main address.
Closing Date: January 15th.
Funding: Private.
No. of awards given last year: One.
Additional Information: Further information is available on request.

JCB William Reese Company Fellowship

Subjects: Bibliography of books that deal with the discovery, exploration, settlement and development of the new world and the related history of Europe and Africa prior to 1825.
Purpose: To enable the study of American bibliography and the history of the book in the Americas.
Eligibility: Open to Americans and foreign nationals who are engaged in predoctoral, postdoctoral or independent research. Graduate students must have passed their preliminary or general examinations at the time of application.
Level of Study: Postdoctorate, Predoctorate.
Type: Fellowship.
Value: US$1,300 per month.
Length of Study: Two-four months.
Frequency: Annual.
No. of awards offered: One.
Application Procedure: Applicants must contact the organisation for details.
Closing Date: January 15th.
Funding: Commercial.
Additional Information: Further information is available on request.

Jeannette D Black Memorial Fellowship

Subjects: The early history of the Americas from the late fifteenth-century to 1830 and research relating to materials at the Library regarding all aspects of the discovery, exploration, settlements and development of the new world.
Purpose: To enable research into the history of cartography or a closely related area.
Eligibility: Open to Americans and foreign nationals who are engaged in predoctoral, postdoctoral, or independent research. Graduate students must have passed their preliminary or general examinations at the time of application.
Level of Study: Doctorate, Postdoctorate, Predoctorate.
Type: Fellowship.
Value: US$1,300 per month.
Length of Study: Two-four months.
Frequency: Annual.
Country of Study: United States of America.
No. of awards offered: One.
Application Procedure: Applicants must write to or email the Director at the main address to request an application form.
Closing Date: January 15th.
Funding: Private.
No. of awards given last year: One.

John Carter Brown Library at Brown University Long Term Fellowships

Subjects: All aspects of the discovery, exploration, settlement and development of the new world, including the related history of Europe and Africa prior to 1825.
Purpose: To assist scholars in any area of research related to the Library's holdings.
Eligibility: Applicants must be American citizens or have been resident in the United States for three years immediately preceding the term of the fellowship. Those living within commuting distance of the

library which is classed as a distance of approx. 50 miles are ordinarily not eligible for JCB fellowships.
Level of Study: Postdoctorate.
Type: Fellowship.
Value: US$3,000 per month.
Length of Study: 5-10 months.
Frequency: Annual.
Study Establishment: The John Carter Brown Library.
Country of Study: United States of America.
No. of awards offered: Approx. four.
Application Procedure: Applicants must complete an application form. Please write to or email the Director at the main address.
Closing Date: January 15th.
Funding: Government, Private.
Contributor: The Andrew W Mellon Foundation and the National Endowment for the Humanities.
No. of awards given last year: Four.
No. of applicants last year: 15.
Additional Information: Recipients are expected to relocate to Providence and be in continuous residence at the John Carter Brown Library for the entire term of the award.

The Lampadia/Adams Fellowship

Subjects: Colonial history prior to 1825.
Purpose: To support research into the colonial history of Argentina, Brazil and Chile.
Eligibility: Restricted to senior Scholars from Argentina, Brazil or Chile.
Level of Study: Postdoctorate, Research.
Type: Fellowship.
Value: US$20,000.
Length of Study: Five months.
Frequency: Annual.
Study Establishment: The John Carter Brown Library.
Country of Study: United States of America.
No. of awards offered: One.
Application Procedure: Applicants must complete an application form. Please write to or email the Director at the main address.
Closing Date: January 15th.
Funding: Private.
No. of applicants last year: Four.
Additional Information: Further information is available on request.

Library Associates Fellowship

Subjects: All aspects of the discovery, exploration, settlement and development of the new world and the related history of Europe and Africa prior to 1825.
Purpose: To assist scholars in any area of research related to the Library's holdings.
Eligibility: Open to Americans and foreign nationals who are engaged in predoctoral, postdoctoral, or independent research. Graduate students must have passed their preliminary or general examinations at the time of application.
Level of Study: Postdoctorate, Predoctorate, Research.
Type: Fellowship.
Value: US$1,300 per month.
Length of Study: Two-four months.
Frequency: Annual.
Country of Study: United States of America.
No. of awards offered: One.
Application Procedure: Applicants must complete an application form. Please write to or email the Director at the main address.
Closing Date: January 15th.
Funding: Private.
Contributor: Associates of the John Carter Brown Library.
Additional Information: Further information is available on request.

Maria Elena Cassiet Fellowships

Subjects: The history of the colonial period of the Americas.
Purpose: To sponsor historical research relating to Spanish America.

Eligibility: Restricted to Scholars who are permanent residents of countries in Spanish America who are engaged in predoctoral, post-doctoral or independent research. Graduate students must have passed their preliminary or general examinations at the time of application.
Level of Study: Postdoctorate, Predoctorate, Research.
Type: Fellowship.
Value: US$1,300 per month.
Length of Study: Two-four months.
Frequency: Annual.
Study Establishment: The John Carter Brown Library.
Country of Study: United States of America.
No. of awards offered: One-two.
Application Procedure: Applicants must complete an application form. Please write to or email the Director at the main address.
Closing Date: January 15th.
Funding: Private.
No. of awards given last year: One.

Paul W McQuillen Memorial Fellowship

Subjects: All aspects of the discovery, exploration, settlement and development of the new world and the related history of Europe and Africa prior to 1825.
Purpose: To assist scholars in any area of research related to the Library's holdings.
Eligibility: Open to Americans and foreign nationals who are engaged in predoctoral, postdoctoral, or independent research. Graduate students must have passed their preliminary or general examinations at the time of application.
Level of Study: Postdoctorate, Predoctorate, Research.
Type: Fellowship.
Value: US$1,300 per month.
Length of Study: Two-four months.
Frequency: Annual.
Country of Study: United States of America.
No. of awards offered: Varies.
Application Procedure: Applicants must complete an application form. Please write to or email the Director at the main address.
Closing Date: January 15th.
Funding: Private.
No. of awards given last year: One.
Additional Information: Further information is available on request.

Ruth and Lincoln Ekstrom Fellowship

Subjects: The history of women and the family in the Americas prior to 1825, including the question of cultural influences on gender formation.
Purpose: To sponsor historical research.
Eligibility: Open to Americans and foreign nationals who are engaged in predoctoral, postdoctoral, or independent research. Graduate students must have passed their preliminary or general examinations at the time of application.
Level of Study: Postdoctorate, Predoctorate, Research.
Type: Fellowship.
Value: US$1,300 a month.
Length of Study: Two-four months.
Frequency: Annual.
Country of Study: United States of America.
No. of awards offered: One-two.
Application Procedure: Applicants must complete an application form. Please write to or email the Director at the main address.
Closing Date: January 15th.
Funding: Private.
No. of awards given last year: One.
Additional Information: Further information is available on request.

Touro National Heritage Trust Fellowship

Subjects: Research on some aspect of the Jewish experience in the western hemisphere prior to 1830.
Purpose: To sponsor historical research.

Eligibility: Open to Americans and foreign nationals who are engaged in predoctoral, postdoctoral or independent research. Graduate students must have passed their preliminary or general examinations at the time of application.
Level of Study: Doctorate, Postdoctorate, Predoctorate.
Type: Fellowship.
Value: US$1,300 per month.
Length of Study: Two-four months.
Frequency: Annual.
Country of Study: United States of America.
No. of awards offered: One.
Application Procedure: Applicants must complete an application form. Please write to or email the Director at the main address.
Closing Date: January 15th.
Funding: Private.
No. of awards given last year: One.
Additional Information: The Touro Fellow will be selected by an academic committee consisting of representatives from Brown University, the American Jewish Historical Society, Brandeis University, the Newport Historical Society, and the John Carter Brown Library, as well as a representative of the Executive Committee of the Touro National Heritage Trust. The Touro Fellow must be prepared to participate in symposia or other academic activities organised by these institutions and may be called upon to deliver one or two public lectures.

JOHN DOUGLAS FRENCH ALZHEIMER'S FOUNDATION (JDFAF)

11620 Wiltshire Boulavard
Suite 270, Los Angeles, CA, 90025, United States of America

Tel: (1) 310 445 4654

Fax: (1) 310 479 0516

www: http://www.jdfaf.org

Contact: Fellowship Administrator

French Foundation Fellowships

Subjects: Alzheimer's disease.

Purpose: To aid the development of young scientists with demonstrated promise for a research career in Alzheimer's disease.

Eligibility: Candidates who are more than six research years out from a PhD or residency are not ordinarily eligible.

Level of Study: Doctorate.

Type: Fellowship.

Value: US$35,000 for a maximum of two years.

Frequency: Annual.

Country of Study: Any country.

No. of awards offered: One.

Application Procedure: Applicants must complete an application form, available from the website.

Closing Date: November 1st.

JOHN E FOGARTY INTERNATIONAL CENTER (FIC) FOR ADVANCED STUDY IN THE HEALTH SCIENCES

Division of International Training & Research
Building 31
Room B2C39
Fogarty International Center
31 Center Drive
MSC 2220, Bethesda, MD, 20892, United States of America
Tel: (1) 301 496 1653
Fax: (1) 301 402 0779
www: http://www.nih.gov/fic/programs.html
Contact: Programme Specialist

The John E Fogarty International Center (FIC) for Advanced Study in the Health Sciences, a component of the National Institutes of Health (NIH), promotes international co-operation in the biomedical and behavioural sciences. This is accomplished primarily through long and short-term fellowships, small grants and training grants. This compendium of international opportunities is prepared by the FIC with the hope that it will stimulate scientists to seek research enhancing experiences abroad.

AIDS International Training and Research Programme (AITRP)

Subjects: Biomedical and behavioural research related to AIDS.
Purpose: To enable scientists from developing countries to increase their proficiency to undertake biomedical and behavioural research related to AIDS and HIV, related TB infections and to develop these acquired skills in clinical trials, prevention and related research.
Eligibility: Decisions about whom to accept for training are made by the programme directors. All current programme directors have developed collaborative activities with specific countries. The relevant United States programme director should be contacted for country specific information, necessary qualifications, eligibility and application procedures. Scientists from the participating countries are eligible to apply for these training programmes.
Level of Study: Research.
Type: Research grant.
Frequency: Annual.
No. of awards offered: Varies.
Application Procedure: Applications are accepted from United States institutions in response to a specific request for applications. Individuals who wish to become trainees must apply to the project director of an awarded grant. Application forms are available from the website.
Funding: Government.

Fogarty International Research Collaboration Award (FIRCA)

Subjects: Biomedical and behavioural sciences.
Purpose: To foster international research partnerships between NIH supported United States scientists and their collaborators in regions of the developing world.
Eligibility: Open to principal investigators of a United States based NIH sponsored research project grant that will be active for at least one year beyond the submission date of the FIRCA application. It is also open to scientists affiliated with public and private research institutions in Africa, Asia (except Japan, Singapore, South Korea and Taiwan), Central and Eastern Europe, Russia and the Newly Independent States of the Former Soviet Union, Latin America and the non United States Caribbean, the Middle East and the Pacific Islands except Australia and New Zealand. The United States scientist will apply as principal investigator with a colleague from a single laboratory or research site in an eligible country.
Level of Study: Unrestricted.
Type: Research grant.
Value: Up to US$32,000 in direct costs per year are available for up to three years. Additional funds are available for the purchase of supplies and equipment necessary to the collaborative research

project, for the foreign collaborator's laboratory only, funds for travel for the United States principal investigator, the foreign collaborator and/or their research associates. In addition up to US$2,000 is allowed for conference travel for the foreign collaborator. No salaries are offered under these awards, but a stipend of up to US$5,000 may be allocated for the foreign collaborator, if justified.
Length of Study: One-three years.
Frequency: Three times each year.
Study Establishment: Awards are made to the American applicant's institution to support a collaborative research project that will be carried out mainly at the foreign collaborator's research site.
Country of Study: Developing countries.
No. of awards offered: Approx. 35 depending on funds available.
Application Procedure: Applicants must submit applications on the grant application form PHS 398. Special instructions and conditions apply. Please refer to the website for further information.
Closing Date: March 25th, July 25th or November 25th.
Funding: Government.
No. of awards given last year: 40.
No. of applicants last year: 102.

HIV-AIDS and Related Illnesses Collaboration Award (AIDS-FIRCA)

Subjects: HIV and AIDS research.
Purpose: To support co-operative research between NIH grant recipients and foreign institutions throughout the world.
Eligibility: Open to principal investigators of a United States based NIH sponsored research project grant that will be active during the proposed grant award period. The award is also open to scientists affiliated with public and private research institutions in other countries, who serve as co-investigators.
Type: Institution training grant.
Value: Up to US$32,000 in direct costs per year, for a maximum of three years to support direct costs. Funds are also available for supplies and equipment necessary to support the collaborative studies at the foreign and United States sites and for travel for the principal investigator, the foreign collaborator and/or their research associates. In addition, up to US$2,000 is allowed for conference travel for a foreign collaborator from a developing country. No salaries are offered under these awards, but a stipend of up to US$50,000 may be allocated for a foreign collaborator from a developing country, if required.
Length of Study: Up to three years.
Application Procedure: Applicants must refer to the website for further information and application details.
Closing Date: September 1st, January 2nd or May 1st.

John E Fogarty International Research Scientist Development Award

Subjects: Medical research.
Purpose: To forge working relationships between future heads of health research programmes in the United States of America and established researchers in developing countries that will lead to ongoing collaborations in the study of health problems of mutual interest.
Eligibility: Applicants must be American citizens or permanent residents, have a doctoral or medical degree, or the equivalent, in a health science field earned within the last seven years. Applicants must have a demonstrated commitment and competence in health research, and have an invitation from a sponsor affiliated with an internationally recognised research facility in Africa, Asia (except Japan, Singapore, South Korea and Taiwan), Central and Eastern Europe, Russia and the Newly Independent States of the Former Soviet Union, Latin America and the non United States Caribbean, the Middle East and the Pacific Islands except Australia and New Zealand. Applications to work in institutions in Sub-Saharan Africa are especially encouraged. Applicants must have a United States sponsor or mentor at a research institution with ongoing collaborative research funding in one of the eligible countries listed above.
Value: Up to US$50,000 for three years based on level of experience, an allowance of up to US$20,000 for materials and an administrative supplement of up to US$20,000 during the third year if

candidate is promoted to junior faculty status upon return. An economy class round trip airfare.

Application Procedure: Applicants must refer to the website for further information and application forms.

JOHN F AND ANNA LEE STACEY SCHOLARSHIP FUND

c/o National Cowboy Hall of Fame
1700 North East 63rd Street, Oklahoma City, OK, 73111, United States of America
Tel: (1) 405 478 2250
Contact: Mr Ed Muno

In accordance with the will of the late Anna Lee Stacey, a trust fund has been created for the education of young men and women who aim to make art their profession.

John F and Anna Lee Stacey Scholarships

Subjects: Painting and drawing in the classical tradition of western culture.

Purpose: To foster a high standard in the study of form, colour, drawing, painting, design, and technique, as these are expressed in modes showing patent affinity with the classical tradition of western culture.

Eligibility: Open to United States citizens of 18-35 years of age who are skilled in, and devoted to, the classical or conservative tradition of western culture.

Level of Study: Postgraduate.

Type: Scholarship.

Value: A total of approx. US$5,000.

Length of Study: One year.

Frequency: Annual.

Country of Study: Any country.

No. of awards offered: One-three.

Application Procedure: Applicants must complete and submit an application form with up to 10 35mm slides of their work. Slides and completed application forms should be sent by United States mail, not rail or air express. Applicants should also enclose a recent photograph, a letter outlining plans and objectives and at least four letters of reference.

Closing Date: February 1st.

Funding: Private.

Contributor: A bequest from the John F and Anna Lee Stacey Foundation.

No. of awards given last year: Three.

No. of applicants last year: 63-75.

Additional Information: The Committee does not maintain storage facilities, so applicants must not send slides or any materials before October 1st. Each successful competitor will be required to submit a brief quarterly report together with 35mm slides of their work and a more complete report at the termination of the scholarship.

JOHN SIMON GUGGENHEIM MEMORIAL FOUNDATION

90 Park Avenue, New York, NY, 10016, United States of America
Tel: (1) 212 687 4470
Fax: (1) 212 697 3248
Email: fellowships@gf.org
www: http://www.gf.org
Contact: Ms Patricia E O'Sullivan, Assistant Secretary

The John Simon Guggenheim Memorial Foundation is concerned with encouraging and supporting scholars and artists to engage in research in any field of knowledge and creation within the arts. The Foundation was established by United States Senator Simon

Guggenheim and his wife as a memorial to their son who died April 26th, 1922.

Guggenheim Fellowships to Assist Research and Artistic Creation (Latin America and the Carribbean)

Subjects: Sciences, humanities, social sciences and creative arts.

Purpose: To further the development of scholars and artists by assisting them to engage in research in any field of knowledge and creation in any of the arts, under the freest possible conditions irrespective of race, colour or creed.

Eligibility: Open to citizens and permanent residents of countries of Latin America and the Caribbean who have demonstrated an exceptional capacity for productive scholarship or exceptional creative ability in the arts.

Level of Study: Postdoctorate, Professional development.

Type: Fellowship.

Value: Grants will be adjusted to the needs of Fellows, taking into consideration their other resources and the purpose and scope of their plans. The average grant in 2000 was US$35,000.

Length of Study: Ordinarily for one year, but in no instance for a period shorter than six consecutive months.

Frequency: Annual.

Country of Study: Any country.

No. of awards offered: 48.

Application Procedure: Applicants must complete an application form. Further information is available on the Foundation's website.

Closing Date: December 1st.

Funding: Private.

Contributor: The Foundation.

No. of awards given last year: 48.

No. of applicants last year: 516.

Additional Information: Members of the teaching profession receiving sabbatical leave on full or part salary are eligible for appointment, as are holders of other fellowships and of appointments at research centres. Fellowships are awarded by the Trustees upon nominations made by a committee of selection.

Guggenheim Fellowships to Assist Research and Artistic Creation (USA and Canada)

Subjects: Sciences, humanities, social sciences and creative arts.

Purpose: To further the development of scholars and artists by assisting them to engage in research in any field of knowledge and creation in any of the arts, under the freest possible conditions irrespective of race, colour or creed.

Eligibility: Open to citizens and permanent residents of the United States of America and Canada who have demonstrated an exceptional capacity for productive scholarship or exceptional creative ability in the arts.

Level of Study: Postdoctorate, Professional development.

Type: Fellowship.

Value: Grants will be adjusted to the needs of Fellows taking into consideration their other resources and the purpose and scope of their plans. The average grant in 2001 was US$36,000.

Length of Study: Ordinarily for one year, but in no instance for a period shorter than six consecutive months.

Frequency: Annual.

Country of Study: Any country.

No. of awards offered: 183.

Application Procedure: Applicants must complete an application form. Further information is available on the Foundation's website.

Closing Date: October 1st.

Funding: Private.

Contributor: The Foundation.

No. of awards given last year: 183.

No. of applicants last year: 2,728.

Additional Information: Members of the teaching profession receiving sabbatical leave on full or part salary are eligible for appointment, as are holders of other fellowships and of appointments at research centres. Fellowships are awarded by the Trustees upon nominations made by a committee of selection.

JOHNS HOPKINS UNIVERSITY

Bloomberg School of Public Health
Center for Alternatives to Animal Testing
111 Market Place
Suite 840, Baltimore, MD, 21202, United States of America
Tel: (1) 410 223 1618
Fax: (1) 410 223 1603
Email: caat@jhsph.edu
www: http://caat.jhsph.edu
Contact: Ms Nakita Lewis, Grants Co-ordinator

The vision of the Johns Hopkins Center for Alternatives to Animal Testing is to be a leading force in the development and use of reduction, refinement and replacement alternatives in research, testing and education to protect and enhance the health of the public.

CAAT Research Grants

Subjects: Alternatives to current testing methods to replace, reduce and refine the use of animals.
Purpose: To serve as starter grants.
Eligibility: There are no eligibility restrictions.
Level of Study: Unrestricted.
Type: Research grant.
Value: A maximum of US$20,000.
Length of Study: One year.
Frequency: Annual.
Country of Study: United States of America.
No. of awards offered: Approx. 12.
Application Procedure: Applicants must complete a preproposal. After review, those which are applicable are invited to submit a full application.
Closing Date: Preproposal deadline is March 15th.
Funding: Private.
No. of awards given last year: 12.
No. of applicants last year: 30.

JOSEPH COLLINS FOUNDATION

787 7th Avenue
Room 3950, New York, NY, 10019-6099, United States of America
Fax: (1) 212 728 8111
Contact: Ms Augusta L Packer, Secretary & Treasurer

The Joseph Collins Foundation was established in 1951 as the result of a bequest by the late Dr Joseph Collins, physician and pioneer neurologist, for the purpose of allowing needy medical students to complete their medical education with an MD degree without sacrificing all other interests in the broad field of learning.

Joseph Collins Foundation Grants

Subjects: Medicine.
Purpose: To aid needy medical students with broad cultural interests who wish to receive an adequate medical education and obtain an MD degree without sacrificing other interests.
Eligibility: Open to anyone attending an accredited medical school in the United States of America, located east of the Mississippi River, who intends to specialise in neurology, psychiatry or general practice. Applicants must have successfully completed their first year at an accredited medical school. No grants are available to students attending medical schools west of the Mississippi River. Awards are not made to pre-medical or postgraduate medical students or to chiropracter, osteopathic, or podiatry students.
Level of Study: Postgraduate.
Type: Grant.
Value: Varies, up to a maximum of US$10,000 annually, to be used towards tuition.
Length of Study: One year, renewable at the discretion of the Foundation.

Study Establishment: Any accredited medical school, located east of the Mississippi River.
Country of Study: United States of America.
No. of awards offered: Varies.
Application Procedure: Applicants must complete an application form, available to accredited medical schools upon request by the medical school authorities. Applicants must obtain and return application forms from the medical school authorities for forwarding to the Foundation. Application forms must be accompanied by a separate letter from the Dean or other officer of the medical school, approving the application on the basis of qualification, merit and need. This letter must contain a specific recommendation as to the amount of financial assistance required by the student to enter or continue in medical school.
Closing Date: March 1st.
Funding: Private.
Additional Information: Consideration of all applicants will be based on financial need, scholastic record and demonstrated interest in arts and letters or other cultural pursuits or to outside the field of medicine. Preference is given to students who reside within 200 miles of the medical school they attend.

JOURNALISTS IN EUROPE

The Journalists in Europe Fund
4 rue du Faubourg Monmartre, Paris, F-75009, France
Tel: (33) 1 55 77 20 00
Fax: (33) 1 48 24 40 02
Email: europmag@europmag.com
www: http://www.europmag.com
Contact: Grants Management Officer

Journalists in Europe Study Programme on European Affairs

Subjects: Journalism.
Purpose: The programmes combine lectures, seminars, workshops and reporting assignments in the field of journalism.
Eligibility: Open to working journalists between the ages of 25 and 35. Applicants must have a minimum of four years of full-time experience as a journalist, and must speak both English and French.
Level of Study: Professional development.
Length of Study: Eight months, or three-eight modules according to needs.
Frequency: Dependent on funds available.
Country of Study: France.
Application Procedure: Applicants must submit a completed application form with a curriculum vitae, samples of work, copies of diplomas and three letters of reference.
Closing Date: January 31st.
Additional Information: Three self-contained programmes are offered in October-December, January-March and April-May.

JUNE BAKER TRUST

5 Forest Road, Kintore, Aberdeenshire, AB51 0US, Scotland
Tel: (44) 1467 632337
Email: ramseyph@goosecroft.u-net.com
Contact: Mrs Priscilla Ramsey, Chairman

June Baker collected, refurbished and arranged a collection of artefacts in her domestic environment. In 1990 her friends established the Trust, in memory of her life and death, to help individuals in the conservation of historic and artistic artefacts in Scotland, or those training with the intention to do so.

June Baker Trust Awards

Subjects: Conservation of historic and artistic artifacts.
Purpose: To assist with travel, training and equipment.

Eligibility: Open to individuals from Scotland working in conservation in Scotland, or training with the intention of doing so.
Type: Grant.
Value: Up to UK £500 towards travel, training and purchase of equipment.
Frequency: Annual.
Country of Study: Scotland.
No. of awards offered: One-three.
Application Procedure: Applicants must complete an application form, available from the Chairman.
Closing Date: June 1st.
Funding: Private.
Contributor: Trust investments.
No. of awards given last year: Three.
No. of applicants last year: Eight.

KAY KENDALL LEUKAEMIA FUND

9 Red Lion Court, London, EC4A 3EF, England
Tel: (44) 20 7410 7045
Fax: (44) 20 7410 0332
Email: liz.storer@sfct.org
Contact: Ms Elizabeth Storer, Trust Secretary

Kay Kendall Leukaemia Fund Research Fellowship

Subjects: Aspects of leukaemia or relevant studies on related haematological malignancies.
Purpose: To encourage younger researchers in the field of leukaemia research to submit applications on their own account.
Eligibility: Open to applicants who will be under 35 years old on the date the fellowship commences. Applicants can be of any nationality but intending to work mainly in the United Kingdom. Applicants must hold a recognised higher degree but need not be medically qualified.
Level of Study: Postgraduate.
Type: Fellowship.
Value: Salary and laboratory expenses.
Frequency: Annual.
Country of Study: United Kingdom.
No. of awards offered: Two-three.
Application Procedure: Applicants must submit a research proposal form and support from the intended institution.
Closing Date: January.
Funding: Private.
Additional Information: Further information is available on request.

KENNAN INSTITUTE FOR ADVANCED RUSSIAN STUDIES

Woodrow Wilson International Center for Scholars
One Woodrow Wilson Plaza
1300 Pennsylvania Avenue North West, Washington, DC, 20004-3027, United States of America
Tel: (1) 202 691 4100
Fax: (1) 202 691 4247
Email: kiars@wwic.si.edu
www: http://www.wilsoncenter.org
Contact: Ms Jennifer Giguo, Program Associate

The Kennan Institute for Advanced Russian Studies sponsors advanced research on the successor states to the USSR, and encourages Eurasian studies with its public lecture and publication programmes, maintaining contact with scholars and research centres abroad. The Institute seeks to function as a forum where the scholarly community can interact with public policymakers.

Kennan Institute Research Scholarship

Subjects: Social sciences and humanities. Research proposals examining topics in Eurasian studies are eligible, with those topics relating to regional Russia, the NIS and contemporary issues especially welcome.
Purpose: To offer support to junior scholars studying the former Soviet Union, allowing them time and resources in the Washington DC area to work on their first published work, or to continue their research.
Eligibility: Open to academic participants in the early stages of their career before tenure, or Scholars whose careers have been interrupted or delayed. For non academics, an equivalent degree or professional achievement is expected. Grants must have a doctoral degree prior to taking up residency at the Institute.
Level of Study: Postdoctorate.
Type: Scholarship.
Value: US$3,000 per month plus research facilities, word processing support and some research assistance.
Length of Study: Three-nine months.
Frequency: Dependent on funds available.
Study Establishment: The Kennan Institute.
Country of Study: The former Soviet Union: Russia, Ukraine, Belarus, Moldova, Georgia, Armenia, Azerbaijan, Kazakhstan, Kirgizia, Uzbekistan, Turkmenistan or Tajikistan.
No. of awards offered: Four.
Application Procedure: Applicants must complete an application form. The application must include project proposals, biographical data and three letters of recommendation specifically in support of the research to be conducted at the Institute. Applications received by fax or email will not be accepted.
Closing Date: All materials must be received by October 1st.
Funding: Government.
No. of awards given last year: Three.
No. of applicants last year: 25.

Kennan Institute Short Term Grants

Subjects: Eurasian studies in the social sciences and humanities.
Purpose: To support scholars in need of the academic and archival resources of the Washington DC area in order to complete their research.
Eligibility: Open to academic participants with a doctoral degree or those who have nearly completed their dissertations. For non academic participants, an equivalent level of professional development is required. Applicants can be citizens of any country, but must note their citizenship when applying.
Level of Study: Doctorate, Postdoctorate.
Type: Scholarship.
Value: US$100 per day.
Length of Study: Up to 31 days.
Frequency: Dependent on funds available.
Study Establishment: The Kennan Institute.
Country of Study: The former Soviet Union: Russia, Ukraine, Belarus, Moldova, Georgia, Armenia, Azerbaijan, Kazakhstan, Kirgizia, Uzbekistan, Turkmenistan or Tajikistan.
No. of awards offered: In each competition round, four are available to non United States citizens and four to United States citizens.
Application Procedure: There is no application form required for short-term grants. Each applicant should submit a concise description of his or her research project of 700-800 words, a curriculum vitae, a statement on preferred dates of residence in Washington DC and two letters of recommendation specifically in support of the research to be conducted at the institute.
Closing Date: March 1st, June 1st, September 1st or December 1st.
Funding: Government, Private.
No. of awards given last year: 40.
No. of applicants last year: 230.

KENNEDY MEMORIAL TRUST

48 Westminster Palace Gardens
Artillery Row, London, SW1P 1RR, England

Tel: (44) 20 7222 1151

Fax: (44) 20 7222 5355

www: http://www.kentrust.demon.co.uk

Contact: Ms Anna Mason, Secretary

As part of the British national memorial to President Kennedy, the Kennedy Memorial Trust awards scholarships to British postgraduate students for study at Harvard University or the Massachusetts Institute of Technology. The awards are offered annually following a national competition and cover tuition costs and a stipend to meet living expenses.

Kennedy Scholarships

Subjects: All fields of arts, science, social science or political studies.

Purpose: As part of the British National Memorial to President Kennedy, to enable students to undertake a course of postgraduate study in the United States.

Eligibility: Open to United Kingdom citizens who are resident in the United Kingdom and who have been wholly or mainly educated in the United Kingdom. At the time of application, candidates must have spent at least two of the last five years at a United Kingdom university or university college and must have graduated by the start of tenure in the following year, or have graduated not more than three years prior to the commencement of studies.

Level of Study: Postgraduate.

Type: Scholarship.

Value: US$17,500 to cover support costs, special equipment and some travel in the United States of America, plus tuition fees and travelling expenses to and from the United States.

Length of Study: One year. In certain circumstances, students who are applying for PhD or two year Master's programmes may be considered for extra funding to help support a second year of study.

Frequency: Annual.

Study Establishment: Harvard University and the Massachusetts Institute of Technology in Cambridge, Massachusetts.

Country of Study: United States of America.

No. of awards offered: 12.

Application Procedure: Applicants must submit a form, statement of purpose, references and letter of endorsement from the applicant's British university. Applications should come via the applicant's British university.

Closing Date: November 3rd.

Funding: Private.

Contributor: Public donation.

No. of awards given last year: 14.

No. of applicants last year: 160.

Additional Information: No application will be considered from persons already in the United States. Scholarships for the study of an MBA will only be granted in exceptional circumstances and candidates must have completed two years of employment in business or public service since graduation. An independent application to Harvard or MIT is necessary. Scholars are not required to study for a degree in the United States but are encouraged to do so if they are eligible and able to complete the requirements for it.

THE KIDNEY FOUNDATION OF CANADA

300-5165 Sherbrooke Street West
Suite 300, Montréal, QC, H4A 1T6, Canada

Tel: (1) 514 369 4806

Fax: (1) 514 369 2472

Email: research@kidney.ca

www: http://www.kidney.ca

Contact: Co-ordinator, Research Grants & Awards

The Kidney Foundation of Canada is a national volunteer organisation dedicated to improving the health and quality of life of people living with kidney disease. Supported by the public and responsive to its beneficiaries, the Foundation funds research and related clinical education, provides services for the special needs of individuals living with kidney disease, advocates access to high quality health care, and actively promotes awareness of and commitment to organ donation.

The Kidney Foundation of Canada Allied Health Doctoral Fellowship

Subjects: Nephrology, urology nursing, social work or dietetics.

Purpose: To provide for full-time academic and research preparation at the doctoral level and to promote and enhance the development of nephrology and urology allied health investigators in Canada.

Eligibility: Open to Canadian citizens who are nephrology or urology nurses or technicians, social workers, dieticians, transplant coordinators and other allied health professionals. Applicants must intend to return to Canada.

Level of Study: Doctorate.

Type: Fellowship.

Value: Up to canadian $31,000.

Length of Study: Up to four years.

Frequency: Annual.

Country of Study: Any country.

Application Procedure: Applicants must apply for application forms and guidelines, available on request.

Closing Date: April 1st.

The Kidney Foundation of Canada Allied Health Research Grant

Subjects: Social or preventive medicine, dietetics, nephrology, urology, nursing and organ donation.

Purpose: To encourage research relevant to clinical practice in the area of nephrology and urology by allied health professionals.

Eligibility: Open to Canadian citizens.

Level of Study: Research.

Type: Grant.

Value: Up to canadian $50,000.

Length of Study: Up to two years.

Frequency: Annual.

Country of Study: Canada.

Application Procedure: Application forms and guidelines are available on request.

Closing Date: October 15th.

The Kidney Foundation of Canada Allied Health Scholarship

Subjects: Social or preventive medicine, dietetics, nephrology, urology and nursing.

Purpose: To assist students in pursuing education at the Master's, doctoral or nurse practitioner level.

Eligibility: Open to Canadian citizens who are nurses and technicians, social workers, dieticians, transplant co-ordinators, or other allied professionals who demonstrate commitment to the area of nephrology, urology or organ donation. Applicants must intend to return to Canada after the scholarship ends.

Level of Study: Graduate, Postgraduate, Professional development.

Type: Scholarship.

Value: Canadian $5,000 for the full-time scholarship and canadian $2,500 for the part-time. A maximum of canadian $10,000 is offered.
Length of Study: One year, renewable.
Frequency: Annual.
Country of Study: Any country.
Application Procedure: Applicants must apply for application forms and guidelines, available on request.
Closing Date: April 1st.

The Kidney Foundation of Canada Biomedical Fellowship

Subjects: Nephrology or urology.
Purpose: To provide for full-time postdoctoral research training in the renal and urinary tract field.
Eligibility: Open to Canadian citizens and those with landed immigrant status.
Level of Study: Postdoctorate, Research.
Type: Fellowship.
Value: Up to canadian $45,000.
Length of Study: Up to three years, plus the possibility of renewal for a further year.
Frequency: Annual.
Country of Study: Any country.
Application Procedure: Application forms and guidelines are available on request.
Closing Date: October 15th.

The Kidney Foundation of Canada Biomedical Research (Operating) Grant

Subjects: Nephrology or urology.
Purpose: To assist in defraying the cost of research.
Eligibility: Open to Canadian citizens and those holding landed immigrant status.
Level of Study: Postdoctorate, Research.
Type: Grant.
Value: Up to canadian $50,000.
Length of Study: Up to two years.
Frequency: Annual.
Country of Study: Canada.
Application Procedure: Application forms and guidelines are available on request.
Closing Date: October 15th.

The Kidney Foundation of Canada Biomedical Scholarship

Subjects: Nephrology or urology.
Purpose: To provide salary support for two years of an initial faculty appointment at the rank of Assistant Professor, or its equivalent, at an approved medical school.
Eligibility: Open to Canadian citizens.
Level of Study: Postdoctorate.
Type: Scholarship.
Value: Canadian $45,000 per year.
Length of Study: Two years.
Frequency: Annual.
Study Establishment: An approved medical school.
Country of Study: Canada.
Application Procedure: Application forms and guidelines are available on request.
Closing Date: October 15th.

KING EDWARD VII BRITISH-GERMAN FOUNDATION

10 Langton Street, London, SW10 0JH, England
Email: helle.browne@virgin.net
Contact: Ms Helle Browne, Secretary

The King Edward VII British-German Foundation provides scholarships to postgraduate students of British nationality under the age of 30 to study in Germany and promote Anglo-German relations and understanding.

King Edward VII Scholarships

Subjects: All subjects.
Purpose: To promote Anglo-German relations.
Eligibility: Open to British nationals who are graduates of British universities, are under 30 years of age and who wish to study further in Germany.
Level of Study: Postgraduate.
Type: Scholarship.
Value: Please contact the organisation.
Length of Study: 10 months.
Frequency: Annual.
Study Establishment: A university or other Institute of Higher Education.
Country of Study: Germany.
No. of awards offered: Up to three.
Application Procedure: Applicants must write for application form, enclosing an A5 stamped addressed envelope.
Closing Date: December 31st.
Funding: Private.
No. of awards given last year: Three.
No. of applicants last year: 50.

KOREA FOUNDATION

Fellowship Programme Team
The Korean Foundation
Seocho PO Box 227
Diplomatic Center Building
1376-1
Seocho-2-Dong, Seocho-gu, Seoul, 137-072, Korea, Republic (South)
Tel: (82) 2 346 35614
Fax: (82) 2 346 36075
Email: fellow@kf.or.kr
www: http://www.kf.or.kr
Contact: Ms Jung-Min Lee, Programme Officer

The Korea Foundation seeks to improve awareness and understanding of Korea worldwide as well as to foster co-operative relationships between Korea and foreign countries through a variety of exchange programmes.

Korea Foundation Advanced Research Grant

Subjects: Korean related research in the humanities and social sciences, culture and arts, and comparative research related to Korea.
Purpose: To support scholarly research and writing activities of Korean studies students during their sabbatical leave to advance scholarship in Korean studies.
Eligibility: Open to overseas Korean studies Scholars with a PhD degree in a subject related to Korea, who are currently engaged in Korea related teaching and research activities. In the case of Korean nationals, only those with foreign residency status and regular faculty positions at foreign universities are eligible to apply. Candidates who are receiving support from other programmes administered by the Korea Foundation are not eligible to receive this grant at the same time.
Level of Study: Postdoctorate, Professional development, Research.

Type: Research grant.
Value: The grant amount is designed to be flexible to satisfy the various circumstances of Korean studies scholars at different stages in their careers to supplement a scholar's sabbatical compensation.
Length of Study: 6-12 months.
Frequency: Annual.
Country of Study: Outside of Korea.
Application Procedure: Applicants must complete an application form. Application forms are available from the Foundation or the website.
Closing Date: February 28th.
Additional Information: Further information is available from the website.

Korea Foundation Fellowship for Field Research

Subjects: Korea related research in the humanities and social sciences, culture and arts, and comparative research related to Korea.
Purpose: To promote Korean studies and support professional researchers in Korean studies by facilitating their research activities in Korea.
Eligibility: Open to university professors and instructors, doctoral candidates, researchers and other professionals. Candidates must be proficient in Korean or English. In the case of Korean nationals, only those with foreign residency status and regular faculty positions at foreign universities are eligible to apply. Fellows in this programme must concentrate on their research and may not enrol in any language courses or other university courses during the fellowship period. Candidates who are receiving support from other organisations or programmes administered by the Korea Foundation are not eligible to receive this fellowship at the same time.
Level of Study: Doctorate, Postdoctorate, Professional development, Research.
Type: Fellowship.
Value: The grant amount will be determined by the Foundation according to the Fellow's research experience and current position. Awards range between US$1,000 and US$1,200. The Foundation will also provide an international economy class airline ticket for round trip transportation between the airport nearest to the Fellow's residence and Korea. Travellers' insurance is also provided.
Length of Study: Three months to one year.
Frequency: Annual.
Country of Study: Korea.
No. of awards offered: Varies.
Application Procedure: Applicants must complete an application form. Application forms are available from the Foundation and the website.
Closing Date: May 31st.
No. of awards given last year: 42.
No. of applicants last year: 80.
Additional Information: Further information is available from the website.

Korea Foundation Fellowship for Graduate Studies

Subjects: Korean related research in the humanities and social sciences, culture and arts, and comparative research related to Korea.
Purpose: To promote Korean studies and foster young scholars in this field by providing graduate students majoring in Korean studies with scholarships for their coursework and/or research while enrolled at their home institutions.
Eligibility: Open to MA or PhD level students majoring in Korean studies at any university in the United States of America, Canada, Europe, Australia, New Zealand, China and Japan. Korean nationals are eligible to apply only if they have permanent residency status overseas. Candidates who are receiving support from other programmes administered by the Korea Foundation are not eligible to receive this fellowship at the same time.
Level of Study: Doctorate, Graduate, Postgraduate, Predoctorate.
Type: Scholarship.
Value: A stipend intended to cover living expenses and/or tuition costs, of an amount to be determined based on the country, region, institution and academic level of applicants.
Length of Study: One academic year.

Frequency: Annual.
Country of Study: United States of America, Canada, Europe, Australia, New Zealand, China or Japan.
No. of awards offered: Up to 110.
Application Procedure: Applicants must complete an application form available from the Foundation or from the website.
Closing Date: Varies according to the region. Please contact the Foundation for details.
No. of awards given last year: 89.
No. of applicants last year: 200.
Additional Information: Further information is available from the website.

Korea Foundation Fellowship for Korean Language Training

Subjects: Korean studies related to the humanities, culture and arts, social sciences or comparative research.
Purpose: To provide foreign scholars and graduate students who need systematic Korean language education with the opportunity to enrol in a Korean language programme at a language institute affiliated to a Korean university.
Eligibility: Candidates must have a basic knowledge of, and an ability to communicate in, the Korean language. In the case of Korean nationals, only those with foreign residency status are eligible to apply. Candidates who are receiving support from other organisations or programmes administered by the Korea Foundation are not eligible to receive this fellowship at the same time.
Level of Study: Graduate, Postgraduate.
Type: Fellowship.
Value: The grant amount will be determined by the Foundation according to the Fellow's academic experience and current position. Awards range between US$900 and US$1,000. The tuition for language training will be paid by the Foundation directly to the Korean language institute that the Foundation designates. Travellers' insurance is also provided. Please note that the cost of an international round trip airline ticket is not covered under this fellowship.
Length of Study: Six months, nine months or one year.
Frequency: Annual.
Study Establishment: A language institute affiliated to a Korean university. Currently the Korean language Institute at Yonsei University.
Country of Study: Korea.
No. of awards offered: Varies.
Application Procedure: Applicants must complete an application form. Application forms are available from the Korean Foundation. Applicants must request an application form by supplying their curriculum vitae including Korean language ability and previous study of Korean.
Closing Date: May 31st.
No. of awards given last year: 54.
No. of applicants last year: 91.
Additional Information: Further information is available from the website.

Korea Foundation Postdoctoral Fellowship

Subjects: Korea related research in the humanities and social sciences, culture and arts, and comparative research related to Korea.
Purpose: To provide promising and highly qualified PhD recipients with the opportunity to conduct research at leading universities in the field of Korean studies so that they can further develop their scholarship as well as have their dissertations published as manuscripts.
Eligibility: Open to non Korean Scholars who have received the PhD degree in a subject related to Korea within five years of their application but do not currently hold a regular faculty position. Korean nationals with permanent resident status in foreign countries may apply. Candidates who are receiving support form other programmes administered by the Korea Foundation are not eligible to receive this fellowship at the same time.
Level of Study: Postdoctorate.
Type: Fellowship.

Value: A stipend support for a 12 month period, of an amount to be determined based on the country, region and institution where the fellow will conduct his or her research.
Length of Study: One year.
Frequency: Annual.
Country of Study: Any country.
No. of awards offered: Four.
Application Procedure: Applicants must complete an application form. Application forms are available from the website.
Closing Date: February 28.
Additional Information: Further information is available from the website.

KOSCIUSZKO FOUNDATION

New York Office
15 East 65th Street, New York, NY, 10021-6595, United States of America
Tel: (1) 212 734 2130
Fax: (1) 212 628 4552
Email: thekf@aol.com
www: http://www.kosciuszkofoundation.org
Contact: Mr Thomas J Pniewski, Director Cultural Affairs

The Kosciuszko Foundation, founded in 1925, is dedicated to promoting educational and cultural relations between the United States and Poland, and to increasing American awareness of Polish culture and history. In addition to its grants and scholarships, which total more than US$1 million annually, the Foundation presents cultural programmes including lectures, concerts and exhibitions, promoting Polish culture in the United States, and nurturing the spirit of multicultural co-operation.

Chopin Piano Competition

Subjects: Piano performance of Chopin or other composers.
Purpose: To encourage highly talented students of piano to study and play works of Chopin and other Polish composers.
Eligibility: Open to students between the ages of 16 and 22 who are United States citizens or full-time international students in the United States with a valid visa who wish to pursue a career in piano performance.
Level of Study: Unrestricted.
Type: Prize.
Value: First prize of US$2,500, a second prize of US$1,500 and a third prize of US$1,000. Scholarships may be awarded in the form of shared prizes.
Frequency: Annual.
Country of Study: United States of America.
No. of awards offered: Three.
Application Procedure: Applicants must complete an application form, available in December via the Kosciuszko Foundation's Cultural Department. Applications should be marked Chopin Piano Competition.
Closing Date: The first week of March.
No. of awards given last year: Three.
No. of applicants last year: 25.
Additional Information: The required repertoire is as follows: Chopin: one mazurka of the contestant's choice, two major works chosen from the following Ballades, scherzi, sonatas, f-sharp minor polonaise, a-flat major polonaise-fantasy, andante spianato and grande polonaise, barcarolle, f-minor fantasy, introduction and rondo op 16, allegro de concert, op 46, a group of 3 consecutive etudes, Szymanowski: one mazurka of the contestant's choice, a major work by Bach (excluding The Well-Tempered Clavier), a complete sonata by Beethoven, Hadyn, Mozart or Schubert, a major nineteenth-century work (including Debussy, Ravel, Prokofiev, Rachmaninoff but excluding those already mentioned) and a substantial work by an American, Polish or Polish-American composer written within the last 75 years. All works are to be complete and played from memory. The competition is held on three consecutive days in mid April.

Kosciuszko Foundation Graduate and Postgraduate Studies and Research in Poland Program

Subjects: All subjects.
Purpose: To enable American students to pursue a course of graduate or postgraduate study and research in Poland for an academic year or semester.
Eligibility: Open to United States graduate and postgraduate students who wish to pursue a course of graduate or postgraduate study and research at institutes of higher education in Poland. University faculty members who wish to spend a sabbatical pursuing research in Poland are also eligible. All entrants must have the requisite Polish language ability commensurate with the proposed research project.
Level of Study: Graduate, Postgraduate.
Type: Grant.
Value: Housing, plus a monthly stipend from the Polish Ministry in Polish currency for living expenses, and additional funding of US$250 per month from the Foundation for expenses.
Length of Study: One academic year or semester.
Frequency: Annual.
Country of Study: Poland.
No. of awards offered: Varies.
Application Procedure: Applicants must complete application forms, available in the Autumn by mail or from the website.
Closing Date: January 15th.
Contributor: The Foundation and the Polish Ministry of National Education.
No. of awards given last year: 13.
Additional Information: Applicants must have a working knowledge of the Polish language and are reviewed based on academic background, motivation for pursuing graduate studies and/or research in Poland, and the proposal of studies and research in Poland. Applicants must have the agreement of a university and must be under the advice of a Polish university academic advisor. If the applicant is required to pay tuition for a study programme it is their responsibility to secure a tuition waiver as this grant does not cover tuition. Students must also pass a medical.

Kosciuszko Foundation Tuition Scholarships

Subjects: Polish-American related issues and activities.
Purpose: To provide financial aid to students in the United States of America and Poland.
Eligibility: Candidates must be United States citizens of Polish descent for graduate studies in any field of study at an institution in the United States or Polish citizens who are legal permanent residents for graduate studies in any field at a United States Institute of Higher Education, or United States citizens who are pursuing a major in polish studies on graduate level. All entrants must have a grade point average of 3.0.
Level of Study: Graduate.
Type: Scholarship.
Value: US$1,000-5,000.
Length of Study: One academic year, renewable for a further academic year.
Frequency: Annual.
Country of Study: United States of America.
No. of awards offered: Varies.
Application Procedure: Applicants must write for details or see the website.
Closing Date: January 15th.
No. of awards given last year: 156.
Additional Information: Information and guidelines are available all year round.

The Kosciuszko Foundation Year Abroad Programme at the Jagiellonian University in Krakow

Subjects: Polish language, history, literature, and culture.
Purpose: To offer American Junior and Senior undergraduates the opportunity to study Polish language, history, literature, and culture for credit at undergraduate level.

Eligibility: Open to United States citizens. Students may participate in this programme during their junior or senior year of college. Although it is an undergraduate programme, students in a MA or PhD programme (but not at the dissertation level) can also apply.
Level of Study: Doctorate, Graduate, Postgraduate.
Type: Grant.
Value: Tuition and housing, plus a monthly stipend in Polish currency for living expenses from the Polish Ministry of National Education plus a monthly stipend of US$150 from the Foundation.
Length of Study: One year.
Frequency: Annual.
Study Establishment: Polonia Institute at Jagiellonian University in Krakow.
Country of Study: Poland.
No. of awards offered: Varies.
Application Procedure: Applicants must complete application forms, available in the Autumn by mail, or from the website.
Closing Date: January 16th.
No. of awards given last year: 12.
Additional Information: Candidate should mention 'Year Abroad Program' in their request letter. Applicants must complete a physician's certificate as part of the application procedure.

The Polish American Club of North Jersey Scholarships

Subjects: All subjects.
Purpose: To financially aid full-time graduate students in the United States.
Eligibility: Applicants must be a United States Citizen or a permanent resident of Polish descent, an active member of the Polish American Club of North Jersey, have a minimum grade point average of 3.0 and be children or grandchildren of Polish American Club of North Jersey members.
Level of Study: Postgraduate, Predoctoral.
Type: Scholarship.
Value: US$1,000.
Length of Study: One year only.
Frequency: Annual.
Country of Study: United States of America.
Application Procedure: Applicants must complete an application form, available from October to the end of December on the website with the full application procedure.
Closing Date: January 15th.

KPMG FOUNDATION

3 Chestnut Ridge Road, Montvale, NJ, 07645, United States of America
Tel: (1) 201 307 7932
Fax: (1) 201 307 7093
Email: tperino@kpmg.com
www: http://www.kpmgfoundation.com
Contact: Grant Support Programme

Minority Accounting and Information Systems Doctoral Scholarship Program

Subjects: Accounting and information systems.
Purpose: To support African Americans, Hispanic Americans and Native Americans studying for a PhD.
Eligibility: Candidates must be African American, Hispanic American, or Native American and studying full-time for a doctorate degree in either accountancy or information systems.
Level of Study: Doctorate.
Type: Scholarship.
Value: US$10,000 per year, renewable for a total of five years.
Length of Study: Up to five years.
Frequency: Annual.
Study Establishment: A full-time AACSB accredited university.
Country of Study: United States of America.
No. of awards offered: Up to 20.

Application Procedure: Applicants must submit a curriculum vitae together with a covering letter.
Closing Date: May 1st.
Funding: Private.
Additional Information: The awards are to be announced in early May.

THE KURT WEILL FOUNDATION FOR MUSIC

7 East 20 Street
3rd Floor, New York, NY, 10003, United States of America
Tel: (1) 212 505 5240
Fax: (1) 212 353 9663
Email: kwfinfo@kwf.org
www: http://www.kwf.org
Contact: Mr Brian Butcher, Office Manager

The Kurt Weill Foundation for Music is a non-profit, private foundation chartered to preserve and perpetuate the legacies of the composer Kurt Weill (1900-1950) and his wife, singer and actress Lotte Lenya (1898-1981). The Foundation awards grants and prizes, sponsors print and on-line publications, maintains the Weill-Lenya Research Center and administers Weill's copyrights.

Kurt Weill Foundation for Music Grants Program

Subjects: Any subject related to the perpetuation of Kurt Weill's artistic legacy. This includes performances or recordings of his compositions in their original form, scholarly projects focusing on Kurt Weill and other related activities as outlined in the printed guidelines.
Purpose: To fund projects that aim to perpetuate Kurt Weill's artistic legacy.
Eligibility: There are no eligibility restrictions.
Level of Study: Doctorate, Postdoctorate, Postgraduate, Professional development.
Value: College and university production performances maximum US$5,000 otherwise no restrictions on requested amounts.
Frequency: Annual.
Country of Study: Any country.
No. of awards offered: Varies.
Application Procedure: Applicants must complete an application form for all but performances over US$5,000. Guidelines and forms are available from the website or from the Foundation directly.
Closing Date: November 1st. There is no deadline for professional proposals over US$5,000.
Funding: Private.

Kurt Weill Prize

Subjects: Music theatre of the twentieth-century.
Purpose: To encourage scholarship focusing on musical theatre in the twentieth-century.
Eligibility: Open to nationals of any country.
Level of Study: Unrestricted.
Type: Cash prize.
Value: US$2,500 for books, US$500 for articles.
Frequency: Every two years.
Country of Study: Any country.
No. of awards offered: Two.
Application Procedure: Applicants must submit five copies of their published work. Works must have been published within the two years preceding the award year.
Closing Date: April 30th.
Funding: Private.
Additional Information: Award years are 2003, 2005 etc.

KUWAIT FOUNDATION FOR THE ADVANCEMENT OF SCIENCE (KFAS)

PO Box 25263, Safat, Kuwait City, 13113, Kuwait

Tel: (965) 242 5912

Fax: (965) 240 3912

Email: prize@kfas.org.kw

www: http://www.kfas.org

Contact: Dr Ali A Al-Shamlan, Director General

The Kuwait Foundation for the Advancement of Science (KFAS) aims to support efforts for modernisation and for scientific development within Kuwait by sponsoring basic and applied research, awarding grants to support and encourage research, and awarding grants, prizes and recognition to enhance intellectual development. KFAS also grants scholarships and fellowships for academic or training purposes, holds symposiums and scientific conferences, and encourages, supports and develops research projects and scientific programmes.

Islamic Organisation for Medical Sciences Prize

Subjects: Medical practice addressing professional and well-documented clinical and laboratory experiments, appropriate documentation of Islamic medical heritage including Islamic jurisprudence.

Purpose: To support and promote scientific research in the field of Islamic medical sciences.

Level of Study: Unrestricted.

Type: Prize.

Frequency: Every two years.

No. of awards offered: Two.

Application Procedure: Nominations must be proposed by universities, scientific institutes, international organisations, individuals, past recipients of the prize and academic bodies.

Closing Date: December 31st.

Funding: Private.

Contributor: KFAS.

No. of awards given last year: Three.

No. of applicants last year: 31.

KFAS Kuwait Prize

Subjects: Basic sciences, applied sciences, economics and social sciences, arts and letters, and Arabic and Islamic scientific heritage.

Purpose: To recognise the scientific achievements of outstanding Arab and Kuwaiti researchers and scientists worldwide.

Level of Study: Unrestricted.

Type: Prize.

Value: Kuwaiti dinar 30,000 which is approx. US$100,000 for each prize. The combined value of the prizes is more than US$1 million.

Frequency: Annual.

No. of awards offered: 10.

Application Procedure: Applicants must apply themselves or through non political organisations and may also be recommended by Search Committees.

Closing Date: October 31st.

Funding: Private.

Contributor: KFAS.

No. of awards given last year: One.

No. of applicants last year: 190.

Additional Information: Further information is available on request.

L S B LEAKEY FOUNDATION

PO Box 29346, San Francisco, CA, 94129-9911, United States of America

Tel: (1) 415 561 4646

Fax: (1) 415 561 4647

Email: info@leakeyfoundation.org

www: http://www.leakeyfoundation.org

Contact: Mr Shawn Kallio, Membership & Marketing Officer

The Leakey Foundation was formed to further research into human origins. Recent priorities include research into the environments, archaeology and human palaeontology of the Miocene, Pliocene, and Pleistocene. Other concerns are the behaviour, morphology and ecology of the great apes and other primate species when it contributes to the development or testing of models of human evolution, and the behavioural ecology of contemporary hunter gatherers.

L S B Leakey Foundation Fellowship for Great Ape Research

Subjects: Ecology, primatology of great apes which contributes to understanding human evolution.

Purpose: To promote long-term research on the behaviour and ecology of wild populations of great apes.

Eligibility: Open to postdoctoral and senior scientists for exceptional research projects.

Level of Study: Postdoctorate, Research.

Type: Research grant.

Length of Study: Initially one year. Funding for subsequent years is not guaranteed.

Country of Study: Any country.

No. of awards offered: One.

Application Procedure: Applicants must submit a completed application form with required materials. Application guidelines and forms are available on request from the Foundation or from the website.

Closing Date: Please contact the foundation.

Funding: Private.

Contributor: Charitable donations.

Additional Information: Strong preference is given to candidates prepared to make a long-term commitment. Applicants should contact the organisation for availability.

L S B Leakey Foundation Fellowship for the Study of Foraging Peoples

Subjects: Behavioural observation and socioecology.

Purpose: To initiate research among a particular group or to continue a study already underway. Priority is given to research directed towards long-term, systematic behavioural observations and research which attempts to elucidate evolutionary theory or specific socioecological adaptations.

Eligibility: Applicants must be postdoctoral or senior scientists.

Level of Study: Postdoctorate, Research.

Type: Fellowship.

Length of Study: One-two years.

Country of Study: Any country.

No. of awards offered: One.

Application Procedure: Applicants must submit a completed application form with required materials. Application guidelines and forms are available on request from the Foundation or from the website.

Closing Date: Please contact the foundation.

Funding: Private.

Contributor: Charitable donations.

Additional Information: The Foundation especially seeks proposals for urgent research that ordinarily might not be funded by other granting agencies. The fellowship was last awarded in 1994. Applicants should contact the organisation for availability.

L S B Leakey Foundation General Research Grant

Subjects: Research related to human evolution.

Purpose: Human evolution.

Eligibility: There are no age, nationality, or residency restrictions. Research must be at least at the graduate level of studies.
Level of Study: Doctorate, Postdoctorate, Postgraduate, Research.
Type: Grant.
Value: US$3,000-12,000, although most awards are in the US$3,000-7,000 range.
Length of Study: Varies with field season.
Frequency: Twice a year.
Country of Study: Any country.
No. of awards offered: Approx. 70.
Application Procedure: Applicants must complete an application form. Application guidelines and forms are available on request from the Foundation or from the website.
Closing Date: January 5th or August 15th.
Funding: Private.
Contributor: Charitable donations.
No. of awards given last year: Approx. 60.
No. of applicants last year: Approx. 160.

L S B Leakey Foundation Paleoanthropology Award

Subjects: Paleoanthropology.
Purpose: To support long-term, multidisciplinary research projects which seek to recover the physical or cultural remains of early humans and their hominid ancestors.
Eligibility: Candidates must be senior scientists or postdoctorates.
Level of Study: Postdoctorate, Research.
Country of Study: Any country.
Application Procedure: Applicants must submit a completed application form with required materials. Application guidelines and forms are available on request from the Foundation or from the website.
Funding: Private.
Contributor: Charitable donations.
Additional Information: Applicants should contact the organisation for availability.

LA TROBE UNIVERSITY

Bundoora Campus, Melbourne, VIC, 3083, Australia
Tel: (61) 3 9479 2971
Fax: (61) 3 9479 1464
Email: c.cocks@latrobe.edu.au
www: http://www.latrobe.edu.au/www/rgso
Contact: Scholarships & Candidature Co-ordinator

La Trobe University is one of the leading research universities in Australia. The University has internationally regarded strengths across a diverse range of disciplines. It offers a detailed and broad research training programme and provides unique access to technology transfer and collaboration with end users of its research and training via its Research and Development Park.

Australian Postgraduate Awards

Subjects: Health sciences, humanities, social sciences, science, technology, engineering, law or management.
Purpose: To support research leading to Master's or doctoral degrees.
Eligibility: Applicants must have completed at least four years of tertiary education studies at a high level of achievement eg. First Class (Honours) Degree or equivalent at an Australian university. Applicants must be Australian citizens or have permanent resident status and have lived in Australia continuously for the year prior to the closing date for application. Applicants who have previously held an Australian Government Award (APA, APRA or CPRA) for more than three months are not eligible for an APA. Applicants who have previously held an Australian Postgraduate Course Award (APCA) may apply only for an APA to support PhD research.
Level of Study: Doctorate, Postgraduate, Research.
Type: Award.

Value: Australian $17,267 per year full-time which is tax exempt plus allowances. Australian $9,173 per year part-time taxable plus allowances.
Length of Study: The Master's is for two years and the PhD is three years in length. Periods of study already undertaken towards the degree will be deducted from the tenure of the award.
Frequency: Annual.
Study Establishment: Bundoora Campus, La Trobe University.
Country of Study: Australia.
No. of awards offered: Varies.
Application Procedure: Applicants must apply for application kits, available from the school in which the candidate wishes to study. Applications must be submitted in duplicate to the Research and Graduate Studies Office.
Closing Date: October 31st.
Funding: Government.
No. of awards given last year: 44.
Additional Information: APA holders are required to pay the annual General Service Fee of australian $341 (Bundoora Campus), or australian $296 (Bendigo Campus). The awards may be held concurrently with other non Australian government awards. Paid work may be permitted for up to a maximum of eight hours per week for the full-time award or up to four hours per week for the part-time award.

International Postgraduate Research Scholarships (IPRS)

Subjects: Health sciences, humanities, social sciences, science, technology, engineering, law or management.
Purpose: To attract top quality overseas postgraduate students to areas of research strength in Institutes of Higher Education and to support Australia's research effort.
Eligibility: IPRS are awarded on the basis of academic merit and research capacity to suitably qualified overseas graduates eligible to commence a doctoral or Master's degree by research. The IPRS may be held concurrently with a university research scholarship and applicants for an IPRS are advised to apply for La Trobe University Postgraduate Research Scholarship (LTUPRS). The scheme is open to citizens of all overseas countries (excluding New Zealand). Successful applicants will research specialisation and, in most instances, will become members of a research team working under the direction of senior researchers. Applicants who have already commenced a Master's or PhD candidature are not eligible to apply for an IPRS to support the degree course for which they have already enrolled. Applicants for Master's candidature by coursework and minor thesis are not eligible to apply for the IPRS.
Level of Study: Doctorate, Postgraduate.
Type: Scholarship.
Value: Tuition fees, basic health care cover.
Length of Study: Two years for the Master's and three years for the PhD.
Study Establishment: Bundoora Campus, La Trobe University.
Country of Study: Australia.
No. of awards offered: Varies.
Application Procedure: Applicants must submit the application form for international candidates available from the International Programmes Office. Email international@latrobe.edu.au for further information.
Contributor: The Australian government.
Additional Information: APA holders are required to pay the annual General Service Fee of australian $341 for the Bundoora Campus, or australian $296 the Bendigo Campus.

La Trobe University Postdoctoral Research Fellowship

Subjects: All subjects.
Purpose: To advance research activities on the various campuses of the university by bringing to or retaining promising scholars in Australia.
Eligibility: Open to students who have been awarded their doctorates within the last five years. Applicants must hold a doctoral degree or equivalent at the date of appointment. The university may also take into account the proposed area of research having regard

to the university's research promotion and management strategy policies.

Level of Study: Postdoctorate.

Type: Fellowship.

Value: Australian $34,030-46,181 per year, plus air fares and a re-settlement allowance.

Length of Study: Two years.

Frequency: Annual.

Country of Study: Australia.

No. of awards offered: One.

Application Procedure: Applicants must complete an application form, available either upon request in writing or via email, or they can be downloaded from the University's website. The administrative contact is Ms Jennie Somerville, Grants Administrator, Research and Graduate Studies Office, tel (61) 3 9479 2049, fax (61) 3 9479 1464, or email j.somerville@latrobe.edu.au.

Closing Date: August.

Funding: Government.

No. of awards given last year: Two.

No. of applicants last year: 55.

Additional Information: A project must be proposed by the applicant in collaboration with a La Trobe University research worker or team. The approved project will be designated in the letter of offer and the major objectives of a Fellow's project shall not be altered without the written approval of the university.

La Trobe University Postgraduate Scholarship

Subjects: Aboriginal studies, accountancy, agriculture, archaeology, art history, Asian studies, Australian studies, behavioural health sciences, biochemistry, botany, chemistry, cinema studies, communication disorders, computer science, drama, economic history, economics, econometrics, education, electronic and communication sciences, English, genetics and human variation, geology, gerontology, health administration, health education, history, history and philosophy of science, Italian, legal studies, linguistics, Latin American studies, mathematics, microbiology, nursing, occupational therapy, orthoptics, pacific studies, peace studies, philosophy, philosophy of science, physics, physiotherapy, podiatry, politics, prosthetics and orthotics, psychology, religious studies, revolutionary studies, romance languages, social work, sociology, statistics, Spanish, women's studies or zoology.

Purpose: To provide financial assistance.

Eligibility: Open to applicants of any nationality having qualifications deemed to be equivalent to a First Class Australian (Honours) Degree.

Level of Study: Doctorate, Postgraduate.

Type: Scholarship.

Value: Approx. australian $16,432 per year, no spouse allowance, australian $919 per year per dependant child, a thesis allowance and partial removal and travel allowances, all dependent on funds available.

Length of Study: Up to two years for Master's candidates and up to three years for PhD candidates.

Frequency: Annual.

Country of Study: Australia.

No. of awards offered: Approx. 50.

Application Procedure: Applicants must complete an application form, available directly from the department offering the relevant course of study.

Closing Date: September 30th for overseas applicants, and October 31st for Australian citizens and permanent residents.

THE LADY DAVIS FELLOWSHIP TRUST

Hebrew University
Givat Ram, Jerusalem, 91904, Israel
Tel: (972) 2 658 4723
Fax: (972) 2 566 3848
Email: LDFT@vms.huji.ac.il
www: http://sites.huji.ac.il/LDFT
Contact: Mr M Mark Sopher, Executive Secretary

The Lady Davis Trust Doctoral Student Fellowships

Subjects: All subjects.

Purpose: To advance the interests of international scholarship and Israeli higher education.

Eligibility: Applicants must be enrolled in a recognised doctoral programme at a university outside of Israel.

Level of Study: Doctorate.

Type: Fellowship.

Value: A stipend of shekel 3,450.

Length of Study: 9-12 months, with possible renewal for a further year.

Frequency: Annual.

No. of awards offered: Varies.

Application Procedure: Applicants must write for details or visit the website.

Closing Date: January 31st.

Additional Information: Further information is available from the website.

The Lady Davis Trust Postdoctoral Research Fellowship

Subjects: All subjects.

Purpose: To advance the interests of international scholarship and Israeli higher education.

Eligibility: Applicants must have received their doctorate not earlier than October 1st 1996.

Level of Study: Postdoctorate.

Type: Fellowship.

Value: Stipend of shekel 5,000 plus US$250 rent allowance or US$150 for single Fellows.

Length of Study: 9-12 months, with possible renewal for a further year.

Frequency: Annual.

No. of awards offered: Varies.

Application Procedure: Applicants must write for details or visit the website.

Closing Date: December 31st.

Additional Information: Further information is available from the website.

The Lady Davis Trust Visiting Professorships

Subjects: All subjects.

Purpose: To advance the interests of international scholarship and Israeli higher education.

Eligibility: Open to full or associate professors.

Level of Study: Doctorate, Postdoctorate, Postgraduate.

Type: Fellowship.

Value: Associate professors receive a stipend of US$2,000, full professors receive a stipend of US$2,400 and a rent allowance of US$250.

Length of Study: Two-four months.

Frequency: Annual.

Study Establishment: The Hebrew University in Jerusalem, or the Israel Institute of Technology in Haifa.

Country of Study: Israel.

Application Procedure: Applicants must write for details or visit the website.

Closing Date: November 30th.

Additional Information: Similar awards are available to promising students of the Hebrew University or the Technikon to study or undertake research in outstanding institutions abroad. Further information is available from the website.

LALOR FOUNDATION

c/o Grants Management Associates
77 Summer Street
8th Floor, Boston, MA, 02110, United States of America
Tel: (1) 617 426 7122
Fax: (1) 617 426 5441
Email: lalorfoundation@grantsmanagement.com
www: http://www.lalorfound.org

The Lalor Foundation was incorporated in Delaware in 1935 under bequests from members of the Lalor family. A major objective of the Foundation has been to give assistance and encouragement to capable, young investigators who have embarked on teaching and research careers in universities and colleges.

Lalor Foundation Postdoctoral Fellowships

Subjects: Basic postdoctoral research in reproductive biology as related to the regulation of fertility.
Purpose: To promote intensive research and to assist and encourage able young investigators in academic positions to follow research careers in reproductive physiology.
Eligibility: Open to tax exempt institutions within or outside the United States of America. Candidates should apply for details. The individual nominated by the applying institution for the postdoctoral fellowship may be a citizen of any country and should have training and experience at least equal to PhD or MD level. People who have held a doctoral degree for less than five years are preferred. The institution applying may make its nomination of a Fellow from among its own personnel or elsewhere, but, qualifications being equal, candidates from other than the proposing institution itself may carry modest preference. The application must name the institution's nominee for the fellowship and include his or her performance record.
Level of Study: Postdoctorate.
Type: Fellowship.
Value: Up to US$30,000 per year to cover a fellowship stipend, institutional overheads and miscellaneous expenses.
Frequency: Annual.
Study Establishment: An institution which is tax exempt.
Country of Study: Any country.
No. of awards offered: Approx. 30.
Application Procedure: Applicants must submit an application form, available on request or from the website.
Closing Date: January 15th.
Funding: Private.
No. of awards given last year: Approx. 30.
No. of applicants last year: Approx. 75.

LANCASTER UNIVERSITY

Student Support Office
University House
Bailrigg, Lancaster, LA1 4YW, England
Tel: (44) 1524 65201
Fax: (44) 1524 594294
www: http://www.lancs.ac.uk
Contact: Ms Kathleen Bird, Student Finance Manager

Cartmel College Scholarship Fund

Subjects: All subjects offered by the university.
Purpose: To assist students unable to obtain adequate grants from other bodies.
Eligibility: Open to candidates of any nationality who have a place at Lancaster University. Priority is given to members of Cartmel College and to new students.
Level of Study: Graduate, Postgraduate.
Type: Scholarship.
Value: UK £300-500 not including fees.
Frequency: Annual.
Study Establishment: Lancaster University.

Country of Study: United Kingdom.
No. of awards offered: Varies.
Application Procedure: Applicants must write to Kathleen Bird at the Student Support Office for details.
Closing Date: June 1st.
Funding: Government.
No. of awards given last year: Four.

Lancaster University County College Awards

Subjects: All subjects offered by the university.
Purpose: To assist students whose course of study will lead to financial hardship.
Eligibility: Open to candidates of any nationality who have a place at Lancaster University. Candidates must be former members of the County College and must be prepared to reside in the College.
Level of Study: Postgraduate.
Value: The amount is offset against residence charges.
Frequency: Annual.
Study Establishment: Lancaster University.
Country of Study: United Kingdom.
No. of awards offered: Varies.
Application Procedure: Applicants must write to Kathleen Bird at the Student Support Office for details.
Closing Date: June 1st.
Funding: Government.
No. of awards given last year: Three.

Lancaster University International Bursaries

Subjects: All subjects.
Purpose: To offer financial support.
Eligibility: Open to nationals of India and the People's Republic of China who have not previously studied at Lancaster University.
Level of Study: Postgraduate.
Type: Bursary.
Value: UK £2,000, offset against fees.
Length of Study: One year minimum.
Frequency: Annual.
Study Establishment: Lancaster University.
Country of Study: United Kingdom.
No. of awards offered: Three.
Application Procedure: Applicants must complete an application, available on request from the International Office.
Closing Date: June 1st.
Funding: Government.

Peel Awards

Subjects: All subjects offered by the university.
Purpose: To enable students who are unable to secure finance from other sources to study at Lancaster University.
Eligibility: Open to candidates of any nationality who have a place at Lancaster University and will be over 21 years of age at the commencement of the course.
Level of Study: Postgraduate.
Value: Varies. Awards do not cover fees.
Frequency: Annual.
Study Establishment: Lancaster University.
Country of Study: United Kingdom.
No. of awards offered: Varies.
Application Procedure: Applicants must complete an application form, available on request from Kathleen Bird at the Student Support Office.
Closing Date: June 1st.
Funding: Private.
No. of awards given last year: 21.

LANCASTER UNIVERSITY, THE MANAGEMENT SCHOOL

MBA Office
Lancaster University Management School, Lancaster, LA1 4YX,
England
Tel: (44) 1524 594068
Fax: (44) 1524 592417
Email: mba@lancaster.ac.uk
www: http://www.lums.lancs.ac.uk
Contact: M C Witt

The Management School at Lancaster University is one of three United Kingdom business schools to be rated five star (international excellence in most areas) for research quality. It is also rated 'excellent' for teaching quality and was included in the Financial Times top 75 business schools in North America and Europe.

Lancaster MBA Scholarships

Subjects: MBA.
Purpose: To assist exceptional candidates to pursue the full-time MBA.
Level of Study: MBA.
Type: Scholarship.
Value: Varies, UK £1,000-7,500.
Length of Study: One year.
Frequency: Annual.
Study Establishment: The Management School at Lancaster University.
Country of Study: England.
Application Procedure: Applicants must contact the organisation.
Closing Date: July.
No. of awards given last year: Eight.

LANDSCAPE ARCHITECTURE FOUNDATION

818 18th Street
Suite 810, Washington, DC, 20006, United States of America
Tel: (1) 202 331 7070
Email: rfigura@lafoundation.org
www: http://www.laprofession.org
Contact: Mr Ron Figura, Development Co-ordinator

The mission of the Landscape Architecture Foundation is to support the preservation, improvement and enhancement of the quality of the environment.

AILA/Yamagani/Hope Fellowship

Subjects: Landscape architecture.
Purpose: To support credit or non credit courses, seminars or workshops, for travel or related expenses in support of an independent research project, or for the development of post secondary educational materials or curriculum plans.
Eligibility: Open to students with a Bachelor's or Master's degree in landscape architecture.
Level of Study: Postgraduate, Professional development.
Type: Fellowship.
Value: US$1,000.
Frequency: Annual.
Country of Study: Any country.
No. of awards offered: One.
Application Procedure: Applicants must submit a 500 word essay, a 100 word statement of intent, two letters of recommendation and a completed application form. A statement of intent, which should be a maximum of 100 words, detailing how the funds would be used and a line item budget should also be included if applicable. Two letters of recommendation from licensed landscape architects are also required.

Closing Date: August 1st.

The Douglas Dockery Thomas Fellowship In Garden History and Design

Subjects: New techniques of garden restoration eg. studying how small gardens created by community groups have impacted public gardens, exploring and documenting physical, emotional and spiritual healing properties of the garden and instigating the development of gardens that use ecological and regenerative concepts.
Purpose: To stimulate the knowledge and love of gardening, to share the advantages of association by means of educational meetings, conferences, correspondences and publications, and to restore, improve and protect the quality of the environment through educational programmes and action in the fields of conservation and civic improvement.
Eligibility: Open to graduate students studying at United States institutions. Selection criteria will include the degree to which the proposed fellowship work addresses GAC objectives, as well as the excellence of the student's academic qualifications and person.
Type: Fellowship.
Value: US$4,000.
No. of awards offered: One.
Application Procedure: Please visit the website for more information.
Closing Date: January 15th.

Edith H Henderson Scholarship

Subjects: Landscape architecture.
Purpose: To assist students with skills in public presentation.
Eligibility: Applicants must be participating in a class in public speaking or creative writing.
Type: Scholarship.
Value: US$1,000.
Frequency: Annual.
Country of Study: United States of America.
No. of awards offered: One.
Application Procedure: Applicants must submit three copies each of a completed application form and a typewritten essay, of a maximum 400 words, plus a review of Mrs Henderson's book entitled Edith Henderson's Home Landscape Companion.
Closing Date: Applications should be postmarked no later than April 1st.
Funding: Private.
Additional Information: Please visit the website for more information.

Hawaii Chapter/David T Woolsey Scholarship

Subjects: Landscape architecture.
Purpose: To provide funds and support study.
Eligibility: Open to students from Hawaii.
Level of Study: Postgraduate.
Type: Scholarship.
Value: US$1,000.
Frequency: Annual.
Country of Study: Any country.
No. of awards offered: One.
Application Procedure: Applicants must provide a typed, double spaced autobiography and statement of personal and professional goals, which must be a maximum of 500 words, a sample of design work, three 8x10 colour or black and white photographs, two letters of recommendation including one from a design instructor and proof of Hawaii residency.
Closing Date: April 1st.
Additional Information: LAF/CLASS Fund scholarships and Internships are also available for architecture students from UCLA and CaL Poly. These include the University Program, which consists of six scholarships at US$1,500, the Landscape Architecture Program, of five scholarships at US$500, the Internship Program, of two scholarships for US$2,000 and the Ornamental Horticulture Program, of three scholarships at US$1,000. Enquiries should be directed to the LAF/CLASS Fund Program Administrator at the given address.

William J Locklin Scholarship

Subjects: Landscape architecture.

Purpose: To emphasise the importance of 24 hour lighting in landscape designs.

Eligibility: Open to students pursuing a programme in lighting design, or landscape architecture students focusing on lighting design in studio projects.

Level of Study: Postgraduate.

Type: Scholarship.

Value: US$1,000.

Frequency: Annual.

Country of Study: United States of America.

No. of awards offered: One.

Application Procedure: Applicants must submit a typed, double spaced essay of a maximum of 300 words, highlighting the design project, visual samples including schematics, renderings, sketches or other plans and one letter of recommendation relevant to the proposed project and applicant, preferably from a current professor.

Closing Date: Postmarked no later than April 1st.

Funding: Private.

Additional Information: Visit the website for more details.

LAW AND JUSTICE FOUNDATION OF NEW SOUTH WALES

GPO Box 4264, Sydney, NSW, 2001, Australia

Tel: (61) 2 9221 3900

Fax: (61) 2 9221 6280

Email: if@lawfoundation.net.au

www: http://www.lawfoundation.net.au

Contact: Mr Simon Rice, Director

The Law and Justice Foundation's objectives are to contribute to the development of a fair and equitable justice system which addresses the legal needs of the community, and to improve access to justice by the community, in particular by economically and socially disadvantaged people.

Law and Justice Foundation of New South Wales Grants Program

Subjects: Law.

Purpose: To promote community understanding of, and access to, the legal system in New South Wales. The Law Foundation invests in community based projects that promote research into, and the understanding of, the legal system.

Type: Grant.

Value: Varies.

Frequency: Varies.

No. of awards offered: Varies.

Application Procedure: Applicants must seek grant guidelines, which are available from the website.

Closing Date: Please contact the Foundation for details.

Contributor: Users of legal services in New South Wales.

LEAGUE FOR THE EXCHANGE OF COMMONWEALTH TEACHERS (LECT)

Commonwealth House
7 Lion Yard
Tremadoc Road
Clapham, London, SW4 7NF, England
Tel: (44) 20 7498 1101
Fax: (44) 20 7720 5403
Email: tedwards.lect@virgin.net
www: http://www.lect.org.uk
Contact: Publicity

The aim of the League for the Exchange of Commonwealth Teachers (LECT) is to develop and support a wide range of exchanges for teachers and others in all sectors of the educational profession in the United Kingdom with similarly qualified colleagues in other parts of the Commonwealth for a fixed period, so that shared experiences may be of benefit to students, teachers and their employing institutions.

UK Government Grants

Subjects: All subjects.

Purpose: To facilitate the exchange of British teachers to other Commonwealth countries.

Eligibility: Open to teachers in all types of schools (primary, secondary, special, technical colleges, colleges of education) from the United Kingdom who are accepted for exchange with teachers in selected Commonwealth countries. Teachers should be aged 25-45 years and have not less than five years of teaching experience in the United Kingdom, with at least two years under the current employing authority.

Level of Study: Professional development.

Type: Grant.

Value: Return air fare.

Length of Study: One academic year.

Frequency: Annual.

Study Establishment: Schools or colleges in selected Commonwealth countries.

Country of Study: Australia, Bahamas, Bermuda, Canada, India, Jamaica, Kenya (Nairobi), New Zealand, Sierra Leone or Trinidad.

No. of awards offered: Approx. 300.

Application Procedure: Applicants must complete an application form.

Funding: Government.

Additional Information: There is also a separate programme to support teacher exchanges between different parts of the United Kingdom.

LEARNING, EMPLOYMENT AND HUMAN DEVELOPMENT DIRECTORATE

15 Eddy Street
Room 1402, Ottawa, ON, K1A 0H4, Canada
Tel: (1) 819 994 7436
Fax: (1) 819 994 0443
Email: reference@inac.gc.ca
www: http://www.inac.gc.ca
Contact: Indian Programming & Funding Allocations Director

Inuit Cultural Grants Program

Subjects: Inuit literature, music and art, cross cultural crafts and cultural exchange.

Purpose: To enable Inuit people to share their cultural heritage with other Canadians to promote awareness of Canada's cultural diversity.

Eligibility: Open to Canadian Inuits whose applications meet the purpose of the programme. Grants are made to Inuit individuals and organisations only. Applicants, wherever possible, should have the support of a community organisation. Applicants are encouraged to seek financing for their projects from other appropriate sources in addition to the Cultural Grants Program. Grants are made available on a one time basis only and are not intended to provide direct on going support to projects or activities of a regular nature such as annually occurring festivities, workshops or conferences.

Level of Study: Unrestricted.

Type: Grant.

Value: Averaging canadian $2,000 and not to exceed canadian $5,000 per award.

Frequency: Annual, if funds are available.

Country of Study: Canada.

No. of awards offered: Approx. 15.

Application Procedure: Applicants must describe their projects in full, mentioning how they intend to carry out the project and the contribution the completed project will make to the promotion of Inuit culture. A detailed budget, listing the costs of carrying out the project is also required. Finally, the approaches made to other possible funding sources should also be mentioned. No application forms are required.

Closing Date: Applications are accepted at any time.

Funding: Government.

LEEDS INTERNATIONAL PIANOFORTE COMPETITION

Piano Competition Office
The University of Leeds, Leeds, West Yorkshire, LS2 9JT, England
Tel: (44) 113 244 6586
Fax: (44) 113 244 6586
Email: info@leedspiano.bdx.co.uk
www: http://www.leedspiano.com
Contact: Mr David T Lewis, Honorary Treasurer

The aim of the Leeds International Pianoforte Competition is to offer talented young professional pianists of all nationalities the chance to be recognised by the musical world and the media and to help them build their professional careers.

Leeds International Pianoforte Competition

Subjects: Piano performance.

Purpose: To promote the careers of talented professional pianists.

Eligibility: Open to professional pianists who were born on or after September 1st 1971.

Level of Study: Professional development.

Type: Prize.

Value: Total prizes of up to UK £58,000 and a number of national and international engagements for all six finalists.

Frequency: Every three years.

Country of Study: Any country.

No. of awards offered: 36.

Application Procedure: Applicants must complete an application form.

Closing Date: March 15th.

Funding: Commercial, Private.

Contributor: Halifax plc.

No. of awards given last year: 27.

No. of applicants last year: 298.

Additional Information: The competition is to be held during September 2003.

LENTZ PEACE RESEARCH ASSOCIATION (LPRA)

c/o University of Missouri-St Louis
8001 Natural Bridge Road, St Louis, MO, 63121-4499, United States of America
Tel: (1) 314 516 6040
Fax: (1) 314 516 5268
Email: miranda@umsl.edu
Contact: Mr Robert Baumann, Board Member

The Lentz Peace Research Association (LPRA) was established in 1930 in St Louis as the Character Research Association by Dr Theodore F Lentz with an aim towards conducting scientific research on the causes of war and conditions for peace. In 1993 LPRA initiated the Lentz Post-Doctoral Fellowship in Peace and Conflict Resolution in residence at the University of Missouri-St Louis.

Theodore Lentz Postdoctoral Fellowship in Peace and Conflict Studies

Subjects: International relations.

Purpose: To support research projects in peace and conflict resolution and to enable the recipient to teach an introductory peace studies course in the fall semester and one course in the Spring semester at the University of Missouri-St Louis.

Eligibility: A completed PhD is required and preference is given to graduates of university programmes in peace studies and conflict resolution. Graduates of political science, international relations and other social science programmes who specialise in peace and conflict resolution are also invited to apply.

Level of Study: Postdoctorate.

Type: Fellowship.

Value: Approx. US$23,400 plus university benefits and US$1,000 travel and expense allowance.

Length of Study: Nine months.

Frequency: Annual.

Study Establishment: The University of Missouri, St Louis.

Country of Study: United States of America.

No. of awards offered: One.

Application Procedure: Applicants must send a curriculum vitae, a letter of application, evidence of completion of the PhD, three letters of recommendation and a research proposal of approximately 750 words to the Center for International Studies.

Closing Date: April 15th.

Funding: Private.

Contributor: The Lentz Peace Research Association.

No. of awards given last year: One.

No. of applicants last year: 18.

Additional Information: The fellowship is supported in part by the University of Missouri-St Louis.

LEO BAECK INSTITUTE (LBI)

15 West 16th Street, New York, NY, 10011-6301, United States of America
Tel: (1) 212 744 6400
Fax: (1) 212 988 1305
Email: lbi1@interport.net
Contact: Secretary

The Leo Baeck Institute (LBI) is a research, study and lecture centre, and a library and repository for archival and art materials. It is devoted to the preservation of original materials pertaining to history and culture of German speaking Jewry.

David Baumgardt Memorial Fellowship

Subjects: Modern intellectual history of German speaking Jewry.

Purpose: The fellowship provides financial support to scholars whose research projects are connected with the writings of Professor David Baumgardt or his scholarly interests.

Level of Study: Doctorate, Postdoctorate, Postgraduate.
Type: Fellowship.
Value: US$3,000.
Length of Study: One year.
Frequency: Annual.
Study Establishment: The Leo Baeck Institute.
Country of Study: United States of America.
No. of awards offered: One.
Application Procedure: Applicants must submit an application consisting of the application form, a curriculum vitae and a full description of the research project. Doctoral students must submit official transcripts of graduate and undergraduate work, written evidence that they are enrolled in a PhD programme and two letters of recommendation, one by their doctoral advisor and one by another Scholar familiar with the work. Postdoctoral candidates must submit evidence of their degree of which transcripts are not required, and two letters of recommendation from two colleagues familiar with their research.
Closing Date: November 1st.
Funding: Private.
Contributor: The Leo Baeck Institute.

Fritz Halbers Fellowship

Subjects: Culture and history of German speaking Jewry.
Purpose: To provide financial assistance to scholars whose projects are connected with the culture and history of the German speaking Jewry.
Level of Study: Doctorate, Graduate, Postdoctorate, Postgraduate, Predoctorate.
Type: Fellowship.
Value: US$3,000.
Length of Study: One year.
Frequency: Annual.
Country of Study: United States of America.
No. of awards offered: More than one.
Application Procedure: Applicants must submit an application consisting of the application form, a curriculum vitae and a full description of the research project. Doctoral students must submit official transcripts of graduate and undergraduate work, written evidence that they are enrolled in a PhD programme and two letters of recommendation, one by their doctoral advisor and one by another Scholar familiar with the work. Postdoctoral candidates must submit evidence of their degree of which transcripts are not required, and two letters of recommendation from two colleagues familiar with their research.
Closing Date: November 1st.
Funding: Private.
Contributor: The Leo Baeck Institute.

LBI, DAAD Fellowship for Research at the Leo Baeck Institute, New York

Subjects: Social, communal and intellectual history of German speaking Jewry.
Purpose: To provide assistance to students for dissertation research and to academics for writing a scholarly essay or book.
Level of Study: Doctorate, Graduate, Postdoctorate.
Type: Fellowship.
Value: US$2,000.
Length of Study: One year.
Frequency: Annual.
Study Establishment: The Leo Baeck Institute.
Country of Study: United States of America.
No. of awards offered: Two.
Application Procedure: Applicants must submit an application consisting of the application form, a curriculum vitae and a full description of the research project. Doctoral students must submit official transcripts of graduate and undergraduate work, written evidence that they are enrolled in a PhD programme and two letters of recommendation, one by their doctoral advisor and one by another Scholar familiar with the work. Postdoctoral candidates must submit evidence of their degree of which transcripts are not required, and two

letters of recommendation from two colleagues familiar with their research.
Closing Date: November 1st.
Funding: Private.
Contributor: The Leo Baeck Institute.
Additional Information: The fellowship holders agree to submit a brief report on their research activities after the period for which the fellowship was granted.

LBI/DAAD Fellowships for Research in the Federal Republic of Germany

Subjects: Social, communal and intellectual history of German speaking Jewry.
Purpose: To provide financial assistance to doctoral students doing research for their dissertation and to academics in the preparation of a scholarly essay or book.
Eligibility: Applicants must be United States citizens and PhD candidates or recent PhDs who have received their degrees within the preceding two years.
Level of Study: Doctorate, Postdoctorate.
Type: Fellowship.
Value: Please contact the organisation.
Length of Study: One year.
Frequency: Annual.
Country of Study: Germany.
No. of awards offered: One-two.
Application Procedure: Applicants must submit an application consisting of the application form, a curriculum vitae and a full description of the research project. Doctoral students must submit official transcripts of graduate and undergraduate work, written evidence that they are enrolled in a PhD programme and two letters of recommendation, one by their doctoral advisor and one by another Scholar familiar with the work. Postdoctoral candidates must submit evidence of their degree of which transcripts are not required, and two letters of recommendation from two colleagues familiar with their research.
Closing Date: November 1st.
Funding: Private.
Contributor: The Leo Baeck Institute.
Additional Information: The fellowship holders agree to submit a brief report on their research activities upon conclusion of their fellowship. These awards are in conjunction with awards offered by the German Academic Exchange Service (DAAD) in New York, United States of America.

LEUKAEMIA RESEARCH FUND

43 Great Ormond Street, London, WC1N 3JJ, England
Tel: (44) 20 7405 0101
Fax: (44) 20 7242 1488
Email: info@lrf.org.uk
www: http://www.lrf.org.uk
Contact: Dr David Grant

The Leukaemia Research Fund is devoted exclusively to leukaemia, Hodgkin's disease and other lymphomas, myeloma, myelodysplastic syndromes, aplastic anaemia and the myeloproliferative disorders. The Fund is committed to finding causes, improving and developing new treatments and diagnostic methods, as well as supplying free information booklets and answering written and telephone enquiries.

Gordon Piller Studentships

Subjects: All life science disciplines. The research topic must be applicable to leukaemia.
Purpose: To train graduates in life sciences in research and allow them to submit for a PhD degree.
Eligibility: Open to graduates of any nationality who work and reside in the United Kingdom.
Level of Study: Postgraduate.
Type: Studentship.

Value: Varies.
Length of Study: Three years.
Frequency: Annual.
Study Establishment: Universities, medical schools and research institutes.
Country of Study: United Kingdom.
No. of awards offered: Four.
Application Procedure: Applicants must be invited to apply and must complete the appropriate form.
Closing Date: August.
No. of awards given last year: Four.
No. of applicants last year: 14.

Leukaemia Research Fund Clinical Research Fellowship

Subjects: All life science disciplines. The research topic must be applicable to leukaemia.
Purpose: To train registrar grade clinicians in research and allow them to submit for a higher degree (MD or PhD).
Eligibility: Open to researchers of any nationality who work and reside in the United Kingdom.
Level of Study: Clinical.
Type: Fellowship.
Value: Varies.
Length of Study: Three years.
Frequency: Annual.
Study Establishment: Universities, medical schools, research institutes and teaching hospitals.
Country of Study: United Kingdom.
No. of awards offered: Four.
Application Procedure: Applicants must complete an application form.
Closing Date: March.
No. of awards given last year: Four.
No. of applicants last year: 10.

Leukaemia Research Fund Clinical Training Fellowship

Subjects: Haematology, oncology.
Purpose: To train registrar grade clinicians in the care and treatment of patients with a haematological malignancy.
Eligibility: Open to researchers of any nationality who work and reside in the United Kingdom.
Level of Study: Clinical.
Type: Fellowship.
Value: Varies.
Length of Study: Two years.
Frequency: Three times each year.
Study Establishment: Any United Kingdom centre of excellence for leukaemia medicine.
Country of Study: United Kingdom.
No. of awards offered: 11.
Application Procedure: Applicants must complete an application form.
Closing Date: Available on request.
No. of awards given last year: Five.
No. of applicants last year: 15.

Leukaemia Research Fund Grant Programme

Subjects: All life science disciplines.
Purpose: To give long-term support to research groups studying the causes and treatment of haematological malignancies.
Eligibility: Open to researchers who work and reside in the United Kingdom.
Level of Study: Unrestricted.
Type: Research grant.
Value: Varies.
Length of Study: Varies.
Frequency: Three times each year.
Study Establishment: Universities, medical schools, research institutes and teaching hospitals.
Country of Study: United Kingdom.
No. of awards offered: Varies.

Application Procedure: Applicants must complete an application form only after discussion with Scientific Director.
Closing Date: Available on request.

Leukaemia Research Fund Grant Project

Subjects: All life science disciplines.
Purpose: To support laboratory and clinical based research into the causes and treatment of the haematological malignancies.
Eligibility: Open to researchers of any nationality who work and reside in the United Kingdom.
Level of Study: Postdoctorate, Postgraduate.
Type: Grant.
Value: Varies.
Length of Study: Varies.
Frequency: Three times each year.
Study Establishment: Universities, medical schools, research institutes and teaching hospitals.
Country of Study: United Kingdom.
No. of awards offered: Varies.
Application Procedure: Applicants must complete an application form.
Closing Date: Available on request.
No. of awards given last year: 56.
No. of applicants last year: 160.

LEUKEMIA AND LYMPHOMA SOCIETY

1311 Mamoroneck Avenue, White Plains, NY, 10605, United States of America
Tel: (1) 914 821 8843
Fax: (1) 914 949 6691
Email: doyle-wandellg@leukemia-lymphoma.org
www: http://www.leukemia-lymphoma.org
Contact: Director of Research Administration

The Leukemia and Lymphoma Society is a national voluntary health agency dedicated to the conquest of leukaemia, lymphoma and myeloma through research. Through its research programme, the Society hopes to encourage and promote research activity of the highest quality. In addition, the Society also supports patient aid, public and professional education and community service programmes.

Leukemia and Lymphoma Society Scholarships, Special Fellowships and Fellowships

Subjects: Leukaemia, lymphoma, Hodgkin's disease and myeloma research.
Purpose: To provide support for individuals pursuing careers in basic, clinical or translational research.
Eligibility: Applications may be submitted by individuals working in domestic or non-profit organisations such as universities, hospitals or units of state and local governments.
Level of Study: Postdoctorate.
Type: Career development.
Value: US$40,000-100,000 per year for up to five years plus 8 per cent institutional overhead.
Length of Study: Three-five years, based on experience and training.
Frequency: Annual.
Study Establishment: International and domestic non-profit organisations.
Country of Study: International or domestic.
No. of awards offered: Varies.
Application Procedure: Applicants may visit the website for details of the Career Development Award Application Packet.
Closing Date: September 15th is the deadline for the preliminary application, and October 1st is the deadline for the complete application.

Leukemia and Lymphoma Society Translational Research Award

Subjects: Leukaemia, lymphoma, Hodgkin's disease and myeloma research.

Purpose: To encourage and provide early stage support for clinical research.

Eligibility: Open to individuals working in domestic or foreign non-profit organisations such as universities, hospitals or units of state and local governments.

Level of Study: Postdoctorate.

Type: Research grant.

Value: Annual maximum of US$100,000 in direct costs plus 8 per cent overhead.

Length of Study: Three years, with the possibility of two additional years.

Frequency: Annual.

Study Establishment: International and domestic non-profit organisations.

Country of Study: International or domestic.

No. of awards offered: Varies.

Application Procedure: Applicants must contact the Director of Research Administration at the Leukemia Society of America or visit the website for details of the Translational Research Grant Application Packet.

Closing Date: March 1st for the preliminary application and March 15th for the complete application.

LEUKEMIA RESEARCH FUND OF CANADA (LRFC)

1110 Finch Avenue West
Suite 220, Toronto, ON, M3J 2T2, Canada
Tel: (1) 416 661 9541
Fax: (1) 416 661 7799
Email: leukemia@istar.ca
www: http://www.leukemia.ca
Contact: Executive Director

The Leukemia Research Fund of Canada (LRFC) is a volunteer driven organisation with branches across Canada whose goal is to raise money to support Canadian research for the cure of leukaemia and related blood diseases.

Leukemia Research Fund Awards

Subjects: Research on leukaemia and related blood diseases.

Purpose: To provide funds for researchers and to provide a limited number of research operating grants, postdoctoral fellowships and Summer studentships in the same field.

Eligibility: Open to researchers and postdoctoral students engaged in work in Canada in the relevant fields.

Level of Study: Postdoctorate, Research.

Type: Operating grants, fellowships and studentships.

Value: Varies.

Length of Study: One year. Fellowships are renewable for a further year.

Frequency: Annual.

Country of Study: Canada.

No. of awards offered: Varies.

Application Procedure: Applicants must complete an official application. Applications are available from Deans of Medicine, the LRFC Office, the website, on (1) 800 268 2144 or by email.

Closing Date: February 1st.

Funding: Private.

Additional Information: A special grant is available for the study of CLL, gene therapy at a maximum of canadian $50,000 for up to two years. The deadline is March 1st.

THE LEVERHULME TRUST

Research Awards Advisory Committee
1 Pemberton Row, London, EC4A 3BG, England
Tel: (44) 20 7822 6964
Fax: (44) 20 7822 5084
Email: jcater@leverhulme.org.uk
www: http://www.leverhulme.org.uk
Contact: Mrs Bridget Kerr, Grants Administrative Officer

The Leverhulme Trust awards grants mainly for research but also, to a limited extent, for the support of students and areas of educational activity.

Leverhulme Trust Emeritus Fellowships

Subjects: All subjects.

Purpose: To assist experienced researchers in the completion of research already begun.

Eligibility: Open to persons who have retired during the last three years or are about to retire, who hold or have recently held teaching and/or research posts in universities or institutions of similar status in the United Kingdom and who have an established record of research. Applicants must be aged 59 or over at the age of retirement.

Level of Study: Postdoctorate.

Type: Fellowship.

Value: By individual assessment but not exceeding UK £17,350.

Length of Study: Between three months and two years.

Frequency: Annual.

Study Establishment: In the United Kingdom or abroad.

Country of Study: Any country.

No. of awards offered: Approx. 30.

Application Procedure: Applicants must complete an application form. Requests for application forms must be accompanied by an A4 size stamped addressed envelope.

Closing Date: Mid November.

Funding: Private.

No. of awards given last year: 36.

No. of applicants last year: 84.

Additional Information: The awards are to meet incidental costs and do not provide a personal allowance or pension supplementation.

Leverhulme Trust Research Fellowships and Grants

Subjects: All subjects.

Purpose: To assist experienced researchers pursuing investigations who are prevented by routine duties or other cause, from undertaking or completing a research programme.

Eligibility: Open to persons educated in the United Kingdom or in any other part of the Commonwealth or who are permanent members of the United Kingdom scholarly community and who are normally resident in the United Kingdom. Awards are not normally made to those under 30 and are never made to those registered for first or higher degrees, professional or vocational qualifications.

Type: Fellowship and grant.

Value: By individual assessment but not exceeding UK £20,000.

Length of Study: Between three months and two years.

Frequency: Annual.

Country of Study: Any country.

No. of awards offered: Approx. 150.

Application Procedure: Applicants must complete an application form. Requests for application forms must be accompanied by an A4 size stamped addressed envelope.

Closing Date: Mid November.

Funding: Private.

No. of awards given last year: 149.

No. of applicants last year: 480.

Leverhulme Trust Study Abroad Studentships

Subjects: All subjects, but students wishing only to improve knowledge of modern languages are not eligible.

Purpose: To fund advanced study or research at a centre of learning.

Eligibility: At the time of application candidates must hold a first degree from a United Kingdom university, or be able to show evidence of equivalent education in the United Kingdom. They must also have been educated at a school or schools in the United Kingdom or other part of the Commonwealth. They must be normally resident in the United Kingdom and under 30 years of age on June 1st, or if older, must make a strong and appropriate case for special consideration.

Level of Study: Doctorate, Postdoctorate, Postgraduate, Professional development.

Type: Studentship.

Value: UK £13,100 per year plus return air passage and other allowances at the discretion of the Committee.

Length of Study: One or two years.

Frequency: Annual.

Study Establishment: Any centre of learning.

Country of Study: Any country, except the United Kingdom or United States of America.

No. of awards offered: Approx. 20.

Application Procedure: Applicants must complete an application form. Requests for application forms must be accompanied by an A4 size stamped self addressed envelope.

Closing Date: Early January.

Funding: Private.

No. of awards given last year: 29.

No. of applicants last year: 129.

LEWIS WALPOLE LIBRARY

154 Main Street, Farmington, CT, 06032-2958, United States of America
Tel: (1) 860 677 2140
Fax: (1) 860 677 6369
Email: walpole@yale.edu
www: http://www.library.yale.edu/Walpole
Contact: Ms Margaret K Powell, The Librarian

The Lewis Walpole Library is a research centre for the study of all aspects of English eighteenth-century studies and is a prime centre for the study of Horace Walpole and Strawberry Hill.

Lewis Walpole Library Fellowship

Subjects: Eighteenth-century British studies including history, literature, theatre, drama, art, architecture, politics, philosophy or social history.

Purpose: To fund study into any aspect of British eighteenth-century studies in the Library's collection of eighteenth-century British prints, paintings, books and manuscripts.

Eligibility: Applicants should normally be pursuing an advanced degree or must be engaged in postdoctoral research or equivalent research.

Level of Study: Doctorate, Postdoctorate, Postgraduate, Research.

Type: Fellowship.

Value: US$1,800 plus a modest travel allowance.

Length of Study: One month.

Frequency: Annual.

Study Establishment: Lewis Walpole Library, Yale University.

Country of Study: United States of America.

No. of awards offered: More than two.

Application Procedure: Applicants must submit a curriculum vitae, a brief outline of research proposal of up to three pages and two confidential letters of recommendation.

Closing Date: January 15th.

Funding: Private.

No. of awards given last year: 13.

No. of applicants last year: 35.

LIBRARY COMPANY OF PHILADELPHIA

1314 Locust Street, Philadelphia, PA, 19107, United States of America
Tel: (1) 215 546 3181
Fax: (1) 215 546 5167
Email: jgreen@librarycompany.org
www: http://www.librarycompany.org
Contact: Fellowship Office

Founded in 1731, the Library Company of Philadelphia was the largest public library in America until the 1850s and contains printed materials on aspects of American culture and society in that period. It is a research library of 450,000 books, pamphlets, newspapers and periodicals, 75,000 prints, maps, photographs and 150,000 manuscripts.

Library Company of Philadelphia Program in Early American Economy and Society

Subjects: Pre-1860 American economic and business history.

Purpose: Designed to promote scholarship by offering long term dissertation and advanced research fellowships.

Eligibility: The fellowship supports both postdoctoral and dissertation research. The project proposal should demonstrate that the Library Company has a primary source central to the research topic.

Level of Study: Postdoctorate, Research.

Type: Fellowship.

Value: US$15,000-30,000.

Length of Study: Three months.

Frequency: Annual.

Study Establishment: An independent research library.

Country of Study: United States of America.

No. of awards offered: Two.

Application Procedure: Applicants must send four copies each of a curriculum vitae, a description of the proposed project of two-four pages in length, two letters of recommendation and a relevant writing sample of up to 24 pages in length. Candidates are encouraged to enquire about the appropriateness of a proposed topic before applying by email to economics@librarycompany.org.

Closing Date: March 1st. Fellows may take up residence at any time from the following September through to May of the next year.

Funding: Private.

Additional Information: Further information can be found on the website.

Library Company of Philadelphia Research Fellowships in American History and Culture

Subjects: Eighteenth-century and nineteenth-century American social and cultural history, African American history, literary history or the history of the book in America.

Purpose: To offer short-term fellowships for research in residence in its collections.

Eligibility: The fellowship supports both postdoctoral and dissertation research. The project proposal should demonstrate that the Library Company has primary source central to the research topic. Candidates are encouraged to enquire about the appropriateness of a proposed topic before applying.

Level of Study: Doctorate, Postdoctorate.

Type: Fellowship.

Value: US$1,500.

Length of Study: One month.

Frequency: Annual.

Study Establishment: An independent research library.

Country of Study: United States of America.

No. of awards offered: Usually 12-15.

Application Procedure: Applicants must send four copies each of a curriculum vitae, a description of the proposed project of two-four pages in length) and a letter of reference.

Closing Date: March 1st. Fellows may take up residence at any time from the following June through to May of the next year.

Funding: Private.

Contributor: The Andrew W Mellon Foundation, the Barra Foundation and McLean Contributionship.
No. of awards given last year: 15.
No. of applicants last year: 85.
Additional Information: Fellows will be assisted in finding reasonably priced accommodation. International applications are especially encouraged since one fellowship, jointly sponsored with the Historical Society of Pennsylvania, is reserved for Scholars whose residence is outside the United States of America. A partial catalogue of the Library's holdings is available through the website.

LIFE SCIENCES RESEARCH FOUNDATION (LSRF)

Lewis Thomas Labs
Princeton University
Washington Road, Princeton, NJ, 08544, United States of America
Tel: (1) 609 258 3551
Email: sdirenzo@molbio.princeton.edu
www: http://www.lsrf.org
Contact: Ms Susan DiRenzo, Assistant Director

The Life Sciences Research Foundation (LSRF) solicits monies from industry, foundations and individuals to support postdoctoral fellowships in the life sciences. The LSRF recognises that discoveries and the application of innovations in biology for the public's good will depend upon the training and support of the highest quality young scientists in the very best research environments. LSRF awards fellowships across the spectrum of life sciences: biochemistry, cell, developmental, molecular, plant, structural, organismic population and evolutionary biology, endocrinology, immunology, microbiology, neurobiology, physiology and virology.

LSRF Three Year Postdoctoral Fellowships

Subjects: Biological and life sciences.
Purpose: To offer research support for aspiring scientists.
Eligibility: Open to researchers of any nationality, who are graduates of medical or graduate schools in the biological sciences and who hold an MD or PhD. Awards will be based solely on the quality of the individual applicant's previous accomplishments and on the merit of the proposal for postdoctoral research.
Level of Study: Postdoctorate.
Type: Fellowship.
Value: US$50,000 per year. The salary scale begins at US$30,000 for a first year postdoctoral and 5 per cent raise thereafter. The Fellow will control expenditure of the remainder. It can be used for fringe benefits, travel to the host institution, travel to visit the sponsor and to the LSRF annual meeting. However, its main purpose is to support the Fellow's research expenses.
Length of Study: Three years.
Frequency: Annual.
Study Establishment: Appropriate research institutions.
Country of Study: United States of America citizens can conduct research anywhere in the world, non United States of America citizens can conduct research in a United States of America laboratory.
No. of awards offered: 16-18.
Application Procedure: Applicants must submit a form, a curriculum vitae, not exceeding three pages, a five page research proposal, letter from sponsoring lab supervisor, three sealed letters of reference and a stamped addressed envelope. One application plus three copies are to be submitted. The entire proposal must be printed in standard size type ie. 10-12 point. No condensed print is allowed. Application information and forms are available from the website.
Closing Date: October 1st.
Funding: Private.
No. of awards given last year: 20.
No. of applicants last year: 430.
Additional Information: LSRF Fellows must carry out their research at non-profit institutions. The fellowship cannot be used to support research that has any patent commitment or other kind of agreement with a commercial profit making company.

LIGHT WORK

316 Waverly Avenue, Syracuse, NY, 13244, United States of America
Tel: (1) 315 443 1300
Fax: (1) 315 443 9516
Email: jjhoone@syr.edu
www: http://www.lightwork.org
Contact: Ms Marianne Stavenhagen, Administrative Assistant

Light Work is an artist run space which focuses on providing direct support for artists working in photography through its Artist-in-Residence Program, exhibitions and publications.

Light Work Artist-in-Residence Program

Subjects: Photography.
Purpose: To support and encourage the production of new work by emerging and mid-career artists.
Eligibility: Open to artists of any nationality working in photography with a demonstrated, serious intent and experience in the field. Students are not eligible.
Level of Study: Professional development.
Type: Residency.
Value: US$2,000 stipend plus darkroom and apartment for one month.
Length of Study: One month, not renewable.
Frequency: Annual.
Country of Study: United States of America.
No. of awards offered: 15.
Application Procedure: Applicants must write for guidelines as there are no application forms. A covering letter, curriculum vitae, 20 slides, other support materials and an stamped addressed envelope should be submitted for the return of support materials.
Closing Date: Applications are accepted at any time.
Funding: Government, Private.
No. of awards given last year: 15.
No. of applicants last year: 300.
Additional Information: The residencies are non academic. Artists will be asked to give one informal lecture about their work and to contribute work produced in Syracuse to the Light Work collection. Work by participating artists is published in the Contact Sheet. Light Work also curates two photography galleries at Syracuse University.

THE LINNEAN SOCIETY OF NEW SOUTH WALES

PO Box 137, Matraville, NSW, 2036, Australia
Tel: (61) 2 9662 6196
Fax: (61) 2 9662 6196
Email: linnsoc@acay.com.au
www: http://www.acay.com.au/~linnsoc/welcome.html
Contact: Grants Management Award

The Linnean Society of New South Wales is concerned with the publication of original scientific research papers and the encouragement of scientific research through grants and public lectures.

Betty Mayne Scientific Research Fund

Subjects: Earth sciences.
Purpose: To support worthy research.
Level of Study: Unrestricted.
Value: Not exceeding australian $700.
Length of Study: Up to one year.
Frequency: Annual.
Country of Study: Australia.

No. of awards offered: Dependent on funds available.
Application Procedure: Applicants must submit an application form, plus references and a list of publications over the previous five years.
Closing Date: March 31st.
Funding: Private.
Contributor: Bequests and donations.
Additional Information: Research must be in English.

Joyce W Vickery Scientific Research Fund

Subjects: Natural history.
Purpose: To support worthy research.
Level of Study: Unrestricted.
Value: Not exceeding australian $700.
Length of Study: Up to one year.
Frequency: Annual.
Country of Study: Australia.
No. of awards offered: Dependent on funds available.
Application Procedure: Applicants must submit an application form, plus references and a list of publications over the previous five years.
Closing Date: March 31st.
Funding: Private.
Contributor: Bequests and donations.
Additional Information: Research must be in English.

Linnean Macleay Fellowship

Subjects: Animal and plant physiology and pathology, anthropology, biochemistry, botany, comparative anatomy and embryology, general biology, geography, geology, palaeontology, zoology and research.
Purpose: To encourage the study of natural history in New South Wales.
Eligibility: Candidates must be residents of New South Wales, Australia, have taken a degree in science or agricultural science at the University of Sydney and be members of the Society.
Level of Study: Postgraduate.
Type: Fellowship.
Value: Australian $3,200.
Length of Study: One year.
Frequency: Annual.
Study Establishment: The University of Sydney or elsewhere, subject to the approval of the Council of the Linnean Society.
Country of Study: Australia.
No. of awards offered: One.
Closing Date: November 15th.
Funding: Private.
Contributor: Bequests and donations.

THE LISTER INSTITUTE OF PREVENTIVE MEDICINE

The White House
70 High Road, Bushey Heath, Hertfordshire, WD23 1GG, England
Tel: (44) 20 8421 8808
Fax: (44) 20 8421 8818
Email: secretary@lister-institute.org.uk
www: http://www.lister-institute.org.uk
Contact: Mr Keith Cowey, Secretary

Originally founded in 1891, the Lister Institute now operates as a medical research charity whose sole function is to sponsor research fellowships in the area of biomedicine. A rolling portfolio of 25 to 30 research fellowships, supported by investment income, is maintained within United Kingdom universities and research institutions.

Lister Institute Senior Research Fellowships

Subjects: Biomedical and biological science. There are no priority diseases or scientific disciplines, provided that the proposed research has implications for preventive medicine. The research is primarily laboratory based and is targeted at generating understanding and underpinning knowledge through fundamental research.
Purpose: To promote biomedical excellence in the United Kingdom through the support of postdoctoral scientific research into the causes and prevention of disease in man thereby enhancing the state of public health.
Eligibility: Open to United Kingdom residents with a PhD, DPhil, MD, or MB BCh with membership of the Royal College of Physicians, who must be aged 33 or under for non clinicians, and 35 or under for clinicians (subject to appeal, up to 40 years of age for both classes). Applicants must have at least two years postdoctoral experience. Research must be performed in the United Kingdom. Applicants must not be permanent employees of research councils or charities. Applications for part-time ie. 80 per cent fellowships will also be considered.
Level of Study: Postdoctorate.
Type: Senior postdoctoral fellowship.
Value: Full salary plus employer's superannuation and national insurance costs reimbursed, together with up to UK £8,500 per year consumables allowance.
Length of Study: Five years.
Frequency: Annual.
Study Establishment: An employing university, research institute or unit, or research hospital.
Country of Study: United Kingdom.
No. of awards offered: Five.
Application Procedure: Applicants must complete an application form which is to be submitted with a curriculum vitae and two letters of reference.
Closing Date: End of the third week in January.
Funding: Private.
Contributor: Investment income.
No. of awards given last year: Five.
No. of applicants last year: 46.
Additional Information: Research topics are of the applicant's own choosing. Projects are assessed on scientific merit and potential. The awards are personal fellowships and are transferable within the United Kingdom.

LLOYD'S OF LONDON TERCENTENARY FOUNDATION

Lloyd's of London
One Lime Street, London, EC3M 7HA, England
Tel: (44) 20 7327 5925
Fax: (44) 20 7327 6368
Contact: Ms Linda Harper, Assistant Secretary

Lloyds Fellowship

Subjects: Science, medicine, environmental safety or engineering.
Purpose: To facilitate postdoctoral research.
Eligibility: Open to individuals who gained their PhD within the last four years and are under the age of 30.
Level of Study: Postdoctorate.
Type: Fellowship.
Value: Calculated salary according to age and experience.
Frequency: Annual.
Country of Study: United Kingdom.
No. of awards offered: Two-three.
Application Procedure: Applicants must complete an application form.
Closing Date: March 29th.
Funding: Private.
No. of awards given last year: Two.
No. of applicants last year: 46.

LONDON ARTS

2 Pear Tree Court, London, EC1R 0DS, England
Tel: (44) 20 7608 6100
Fax: (44) 20 7608 4100
Email: info@lonab.co.uk
www: http://www.arts.org.uk/londonarts
Contact: Ms Hazel Speed, Public Affairs Administrator

The London Arts Board (LAB) is the Arts Funding and Regional Development Agency for the capital city. It is one of 10 English Arts Boards.

London Arts Awards and Schemes for Artists

Subjects: The arts.
Purpose: To help artists in the London area to reach a new and wider audience.
Eligibility: Open to individual writers, artists, composers and photographers who wish to undertake an arts project in London. London Arts is unable to offer fees or grants for any individual undertaking education in the statutory further or higher education sectors.
Level of Study: Professional development.
Type: Award.
Value: Varies.
Length of Study: Varies.
Country of Study: United Kingdom.
No. of awards offered: Varies.
Application Procedure: Applicants must submit an application form.
Closing Date: Please write for details.
Funding: Government.
Additional Information: For information on the awards and schemes administered by the other Regional Arts Boards, please contact the listed address.

For further information contact:

Grants Management Officer
West Midlands Arts
82 Granville Street, Birmingham, West Midlands, B1 2LH, England
Tel: (44) 121 631 3121
Fax: (44) 121 643 7239

Grants Management Officer
Eastern Arts
Cherry Hinton Hall
Cherry Hinton Road, Cambridge, Cambridgeshire, CB1 4DW, England
Tel: (44) 1223 215355
Fax: (44) 1223 248075
Email: info@eastern-arts.co.uk
www: http://www.metro-net.co.uk

Grants Management Officer
Yorkshire Arts
21 Bond Street, Dewsbury, West Yorkshire, WF13 1AX, England
Tel: (44) 1924 455555
Fax: (44) 1924 466522

Grants Management Officer
South West Arts
Bradninch Place
Gandy Street, Exeter, Devon, EX4 3LS, England
Tel: (44) 1392 218188
Fax: (44) 1392 413554

Grants Management Officer
East Midlands Arts
Mountfields House
Forest Road, Loughborough, Leicestershire, LE11 3HU, England
Tel: (44) 1509 218292
Fax: (44) 1509 262214

Grants Management Officer
Arts Board: North West
12 Harter Street, Manchester, M1 6HY, England

Tel: (44) 161 228 3062
Fax: (44) 161 236 1257

Grants Management Officer
Northern Arts
(Arts North Limited)
10 Osborne Terrace, Newcastle upon Tyne, NE2 1NZ, England
Tel: (44) 191 281 6334
Fax: (44) 191 281 3276

Grants Management Officer
South East Arts
10 Mount Ephraim, Tunbridge Wells, Kent, TN4 8AS, England
Tel: (44) 1892 515210
Fax: (44) 1892 549383

Grants Management Officer
Southern Arts
13 St Clement Street, Winchester, Hampshire, SO23 9DQ, England
Tel: (44) 1962 855099
Fax: (44) 1962 861186

THE LONDON BUSINESS SCHOOL

Regents Park, London, NW1 4SA, England
Tel: (44) 20 7262 5050
Fax: (44) 20 7724 7875
Email: mferreira@lbs.lon.ac.uk
www: http://www.lbs.ac.uk
Contact: MBA Admissions Officer

British Chevening and London Business School Scholarship

Subjects: MBA.
Purpose: In conjunction with the British Council India, one scholarship will be awarded to an outstanding Indian National.
Eligibility: Applicants who are shortlisted by the London Business School will be interviewed by the British Council in India and may be required to travel.
Level of Study: MBA.
Type: Scholarship.
Value: The scholarship covers all tuition and living expenses for the duration of the MBA programme.
Study Establishment: The London Business School.
Country of Study: England.
No. of awards offered: One.
Application Procedure: Applicants must apply for the MBA course in the usual way. Candidates who are offered a place on the MBA will be contacted after an offer is made to invite them to apply for the specific Class and Company scholarships. These scholarships require specific characteristics from candidates who fit certain criteria. The Class and Company scholarships will be considered and awarded in the Summer.
Additional Information: Please note that applicants will have to meet any travel expenses they incur.

Elof Hansson Foundation Scholarship

Subjects: MBA.
Purpose: To provide funds to enable Swedish students to pursue the full-time MBA programme at London Business School.
Eligibility: Candidates must be of Swedish nationality and should demonstrate a financial need for this award. This award will be made at the discretion of the Scholarships Committee to a candidate who fits the eligibility criteria, and who in the opinion of the committee, is a deserving scholar.
Level of Study: MBA.
Type: Scholarship.
Value: 50 per cent of first year tuition fees.
Study Establishment: The London Business School.
Country of Study: England.
Application Procedure: Applicants must apply for the MBA course in the usual way. Candidates who are offered a place on the MBA

will be contacted after an offer is made to invite them to apply for the specific Class and Company scholarships. These scholarships require specific characteristics from candidates who fit certain criteria. The Class and Company scholarships will be considered and awarded in the Summer.
Closing Date: Please contact the organisation.

Elton Family Scholarship
Subjects: MBA.
Purpose: This scholarship was funded by friends and colleagues of the late David Elton (MSc1) as a token of sympathy, and in remembrance of his achievements and friendships.
Eligibility: Applications are welcome from all applicants, with priority given to those with proven financial need.
Level of Study: MBA.
Type: Scholarship.
Value: UK £1,000.
Study Establishment: The London Business School.
Country of Study: England.
No. of awards offered: One.
Application Procedure: Applicants must apply for the MBA course in the usual way. Candidates who are offered a place on the MBA will be contacted after an offer is made to invite them to apply for the specific Class and Company scholarships. These scholarships require specific characteristics from candidates who fit certain criteria. The Class and Company scholarships will be considered and awarded in the Summer.
Closing Date: Please contact the organisation.

Eugene Klouza Scholarship
Subjects: MBA.
Purpose: Eugene Klouza was a Czechoslovakian entrepreneur who set up this scholarship to enable Central European applicants to study at the London Business School.
Eligibility: Preference will be given to Czech applicants, with other Central European applicants also welcome to apply.
Level of Study: MBA.
Type: Scholarship.
Value: The scholarship covers all tuition and living expenses for the duration of the MBA programme.
Study Establishment: The London Business School.
Country of Study: England.
Application Procedure: Applicants must apply for the MBA course in the usual way. Candidates who are offered a place on the MBA will be contacted after an offer is made to invite them to apply for the specific Class and Company scholarships. These scholarships require specific characteristics from candidates who fit certain criteria. The Class and Company scholarships will be considered and awarded in the Summer.
Closing Date: Please contact the organisation.

Ford Finance Scholarships
Subjects: MBA.
Purpose: To support people who can demonstrate the enthusiasm and ability to work in industry.
Eligibility: Applicants must have a background in finance and the personal and intellectual qualities to fulfil the aim of working in an international industrial environment.
Level of Study: MBA.
Type: Scholarship.
Value: UK £5,000.
Study Establishment: The London Business School.
Country of Study: England.
No. of awards offered: Two.
Application Procedure: Applicants must apply for the MBA course in the usual way. Candidates who are offered a place on the MBA will be contacted after an offer is made to invite them to apply for the specific Class and Company scholarships. These scholarships require specific characteristics from candidates who fit certain criteria. The Class and Company scholarships will be considered and awarded in the Summer.

Closing Date: Please contact the organisation.
Contributor: The Ford Motor Company.
Additional Information: The aim is to establish an ongoing relationship with Ford throughout the year, and if appropriate, the longer term. Scholarship recipients are under no obligation to undertake employment with Ford.

Friends of London Business School Scholarships
Subjects: MBA.
Purpose: To assist outstanding candidates to pursue an MBA.
Eligibility: The scholarships are awarded on the basis of merit to applicants who possess a strong academic and professional background, and can demonstrate the capability to contribute to all aspects of the MBA programme.
Level of Study: MBA.
Type: Scholarship.
Value: UK £1,000-6,500.
Study Establishment: The London Business School.
Country of Study: England.
Application Procedure: Applicants must apply for the MBA course in the usual way. All applicants are automatically considered for the Friends of London Business School scholarships when they apply. These scholarships will be considered at the end of each of the four stages. Candidates will be notified if they are successful.
Closing Date: Please contact the organisation.
Contributor: Alumni.

Henry Grunfield Foundation Scholarships
Subjects: MBA.
Purpose: To enable students to pursue a career in international banking.
Eligibility: Applications are particularly welcome from candidates who have the profile and desire to enter, or further a career in investment banking. Applicants should also have experience of working in more than one culture. Candidates must have worked in the City of London.
Level of Study: MBA.
Type: Scholarship.
Value: UK £20,000 split over two years.
Length of Study: Two years.
Study Establishment: The London Business School.
Country of Study: England.
No. of awards offered: Two.
Application Procedure: Applicants must apply for the MBA course in the usual way. Candidates who are offered a place on the MBA will be contacted after an offer is made to invite them to apply for the specific Class and Company scholarships. These scholarships require specific characteristics from candidates who fit certain criteria. The Class and Company scholarships will be considered and awarded in the Summer.
Closing Date: Please contact the organisation.
Additional Information: The Foundation was set up by Henry Grunfeld who, together with Siegmund Warburg, founded SG Warburg & Company.

London Business School Scholarships
Subjects: MBA.
Purpose: To assist outstanding students in financial need.
Level of Study: MBA.
Type: Scholarship.
Value: Varies, UK £1,000-12,500.
Frequency: Annual.
Study Establishment: The London Business School.
Country of Study: England.
No. of awards offered: More than eight.
Application Procedure: Applicants must apply for the MBA course in the usual way. Candidates who are offered a place on the MBA will be contacted after an offer is made to invite them to apply for the specific Class and Company scholarships. These scholarships require specific characteristics from candidates who fit certain criteria.

The Class and Company scholarships will be considered and awarded in the Summer.
Closing Date: Please contact the organisation.

Maurice Forshaw Scholarships
Subjects: MBA.
Eligibility: Candidates must be citizens of the United Kingdom.
Level of Study: MBA.
Type: Scholarship.
Value: Two scholarships of UK £6,500 each.
Study Establishment: The London Business School.
Country of Study: England.
No. of awards offered: Two.
Application Procedure: Applicants must apply for the MBA course in the usual way. Candidates who are offered a place on the MBA will be contacted after an offer is made to invite them to apply for the specific Class and Company scholarships. These scholarships require specific characteristics from candidates who fit certain criteria. The Class and Company scholarships will be considered and awarded in the Summer.
Closing Date: Please contact the organisation.

Peter Curtis Memorial Scholarship
Subjects: MBA.
Purpose: To enable a student to undertake the London Business School MBA.
Eligibility: Candidates must have a strong academic background, a proven financial need and be citizens of the United Kingdom.
Level of Study: MBA.
Type: Scholarship.
Value: UK £4,000.
Frequency: Annual.
Study Establishment: The London Business School.
Country of Study: England.
No. of awards offered: One.
Application Procedure: Applicants must apply for the MBA course in the usual way. Candidates who are offered a place on the MBA will be contacted after an offer is made to invite them to apply for the specific Class and Company scholarships. These scholarships require specific characteristics from candidates who fit certain criteria. The Class and Company scholarships will be considered and awarded in the Summer.
Closing Date: Please contact the organisation.
Additional Information: Established at the 25 year reunion of the year in which they graduated, this particular MBA class founded this scholarship in memory of their classmate and friend Peter Curtis.

Robert Fleming Scholarships
Subjects: MBA.
Purpose: To assist students with a background in finance or a career interest in working in that area to pursue the London Business School MBA.
Eligibility: Candidates must have a background in finance or a have a career interest in working in that area. Candidates should also have experience or an interest in working in the Asia Pacific Rim (including Australasia) and intend to be active participants on the programme, both in academic and extracurricular activities.
Level of Study: MBA.
Type: Scholarship.
Value: The scholarships comprise of UK £2,500 in the first year, the opportunity to carry out a summer internship with Flemings, and UK £2,500 in the second year (subject to certain conditions).
Frequency: Annual.
Study Establishment: The London Business School.
Country of Study: England.
No. of awards offered: Two.
Application Procedure: Applicants must apply for the MBA course in the usual way. Candidates who are offered a place on the MBA will be contacted after an offer is made to invite them to apply for the specific Class and Company scholarships. These scholarships require specific characteristics from candidates who fit certain criteria.

The Class and Company scholarships will be considered and awarded in the Summer.
Closing Date: Please contact the organisation.

THE LONDON CHAMBER OF COMMERCE AND INDUSTRY EXAMINATIONS BOARD (LCCIEB)

Athena House
112 Station Road, Sidcup, Kent, DA15 7BJ, England
Tel: (44) 20 8302 0261
Fax: (44) 20 8309 1473
Email: custerv@lccieb.org.uk
www: http://www.lccieb.com
Contact: Ms Valerie Brasier, Secretary to Director of Commercial Development

London Chamber of Commerce and Industry Examinations Board (LCCIEB) is a leading international awarding body for business, information technology, secretarial, financial and marketing qualifications. Established over a century ago by the London Chamber of Commerce and Industry, the Board is active today in more than 86 countries worldwide.

LCCIEB Examinations Board Scholarships
Subjects: Business studies, marketing or finance.
Purpose: To award scholarships to qualified candidates wishing to take higher level qualifications or desiring to pursue LCCIEB qualifications.
Eligibility: Open to suitable candidates of any nationality.
Level of Study: Unrestricted.
Type: Scholarship.
Value: Varies according to student requirements.
Frequency: Annual.
Country of Study: Any country.
Application Procedure: Applicants must complete an application form subject to recommendation from a registered LCCIEB centre, who must process the application on the applicant's behalf.
Closing Date: December.
Funding: Private.

LONDON STRING QUARTET FOUNDATION

Royal College of Music
Prince Consort Road, London, SW7 2BS, England
Tel: (44) 20 7591 4847
Fax: (44) 20 7591 4848
Email: lsqf@compuserve.com
www: http://www.lsqf.com
Contact: Ms Madeleine Milne, Administrator

The London String Quartet Foundation is a registered charity whose purpose is to promote the discovery and development of talent and audiences for the string quartet. The main activity of the Foundation is organising the triennial London International String Quartet Competition.

London International String Quartet Competition
Subjects: Musical performance.
Purpose: To encourage young string quartets to develop further on the world stage and take part in this prestigious competition.
Eligibility: There are no restrictions except each musician in the quartet must be under 35 years on 9th April.
Level of Study: Unrestricted.

Value: Prizes total UK £28,000, split into five different awards of differing amounts and a menu of development prizes for three prize winners.
Frequency: Every three years.
Country of Study: Any country.
No. of awards offered: Six major monetary prizes with concerts organised for the first three prize winners.
Application Procedure: Applicants must complete an application form, available on the website.
Closing Date: October 1st in the year preceding the award.
Funding: Commercial, Private.
No. of awards given last year: Eight.
No. of applicants last year: 30.

THE LONDON SYMPHONY ORCHESTRA (LSO)

Barbican Centre
Barbican, London, EC2Y 8DS, England
Tel: (44) 20 7588 1116
Fax: (44) 20 7374 0127
Email: hthompson@lso.co.uk
www: http://www.lso.co.uk
Contact: Ms Helen Thompson, Administrator, LSO Music Scholarship

The London Symphony Orchestra (LSO) continues to build a formidable reputation, attracting the world's top performers, touring the world, initiating ground breaking and original education and access projects, and playing to large audiences in Britain and abroad.

LSO Music Scholarship
Subjects: Musical training.
Purpose: To be used in the best interests of the winner's development, and to facilitate his or her entry into the musical profession.
Eligibility: Open to British nationals, or persons normally resident in the United Kingdom for at least the past three years, who are aged between 14 and 23 years.
Level of Study: Unrestricted.
Type: Scholarship.
Value: The scholarship is UK £6,000 and a gold medal. There is a second prize of UK £3,000 and a silver medal and two third prizes of UK £1,500 each and a bronze medal. The Gerald McDonald Prize is UK £750.
Frequency: Annually, in a four year cycle covering each section of the orchestra.
Country of Study: United Kingdom.
No. of awards offered: One scholarship and four cash prizes.
Application Procedure: Applicants must submit application forms plus two references.
Closing Date: December.
Funding: Private.
Contributor: The Candide Charitable Trust, the Esmee Fairbairn Foundation, the Musicians Benevolent Fund, the Musicians Union and Shell UK Limited.
No. of awards given last year: Five.
No. of applicants last year: 200.
Additional Information: Candidates take part in auditions, master classes and workshops with principals of the LSO. Four finalists perform with the LSO and the scholarship is awarded to the winner.

For further information contact:

Scholarship Administrator
15 Ashley Way, Sawston, Cambridgeshire, CB2 4DY, England
Tel: (44) 1223 501709
Fax: (44) 1223 501709
Contact: Ms Helen Thompson, Scholarship Administrator

LORD DOWDING FUND FOR HUMANE RESEARCH

261 Goldhawk Road, London, W12 9PE, England
Tel: (44) 20 8846 9777
Fax: (44) 20 8846 9712
Email: info@ldf.org.uk
www: http://www.ldf.org.uk
Contact: Head of Research

Lord Dowding Fund for Humane Research is a department of the National Anti-Vivisection Society. It aims to support, sponsor and fund better methods of research for testing products and curing disease, which work towards replacing the use of laboratory animals.

Lord Dowding Fund for Humane Research
Subjects: Medical research, veterinary science, toxicology and teaching. A wide range of techniques are supported, including cell, tissue or organ culture, computer simulation mathematical modelling, quantum pharmacology chemical analysis, epidemiology, genetic or tissue engineering, virology and pain research.
Purpose: To support research aimed at replacing the use of laboratory animals.
Eligibility: Applications on behalf of junior scientists must be made by a senior scientist eg. a PhD supervisor or Head of Research. Projects must not involve the use of animals and applicants must not hold a Home Office licence.
Level of Study: Research.
Type: Award.
Value: Up to UK £75,000.
Length of Study: Up to three years.
Frequency: Four times per year.
Study Establishment: Academic departments or hospitals.
Country of Study: United Kingdom.
No. of awards offered: Varies.
Application Procedure: Applicants must complete an application form and a project proposal is required. An information pack can be requested from the organisation, or is available by visiting the website.
Closing Date: February 1st, May 1st, August 1st and November 1st each year.
Funding: Private.
Contributor: Private subscribers, legacies and fundraising events.
No. of awards given last year: Seven.

LOREN L ZACHARY SOCIETY FOR THE PERFORMING ARTS

2250 Gloaming Way, Beverly Hills, CA, 90210, United States of America
Tel: (1) 310 276 2731
Fax: (1) 310 275 8245
Contact: Mrs Nedra Zachary, National Vocal Competition Director

The Loren L Zachary Society for the Performing Arts was founded in 1972 by the late Dr Loren L Zachary and Nedra Zachary. The purpose of the organisation is to help further the careers of young opera singers by providing financial assistance. The National Vocal Competition, now in its 30th year, has assisted over 70 singers to embark on international careers.

Loren L Zachary Society National Vocal Competition for Young Opera Singers
Subjects: Operatic singing.
Purpose: To assist in the careers of young opera singers through competitive auditions and monetary awards.
Eligibility: Open to female singers between 21 and 33 years of age and male singers between 21 and 35 years of age who have

completed operatic training and are fully prepared to pursue professional stage careers.

Level of Study: Professional development.

Type: Competition.

Value: US$10,000 for the top winner. A round trip flight to Europe for opera auditioning purposes may be awarded to a finalist.

Frequency: Annual.

Country of Study: Any country.

No. of awards offered: 10.

Application Procedure: Applicants must complete an application form accompanied by proof of age and an application fee of US$35. For application forms and exact dates, singers should send a stamped addressed business sized envelope to the Society in November. Faxed requests will not be accepted.

Closing Date: Deadline for the New York auditions is in January and the Los Angeles deadline is in March.

Funding: Private.

No. of awards given last year: 10.

No. of applicants last year: 200.

Additional Information: Applicants must be present at all phases of the auditions. Tapes are not acceptable. Auditions take place in New York in Feburary, and in Los Angeles in April. The concert for the grand final occurs on May 19th.

LOWE SYNDROME ASSOCIATION (LSA)

222 Lincoln Street, West Lafayette, IA, 47906-2732, United States of America

Tel: (1) 765 743 3634

Email: info@lowesyndrome.org

www: http://www.lowesyndrome.org

Contact: Ms Kaye McSpadden, Director of Public & Scientific Affairs

The Lowe Syndrome Association (LSA) is an international non-profit organisation made up of families, friends and professionals dedicated to helping children with Lowe Syndrome and their families. Its main purposes are to foster communication among families, provide information and support research.

LSA Medical Research Grant

Subjects: Understanding and treatment of Lowe Syndrome.

Purpose: To support research projects that will lead to a better understanding of the metabolic basis of Lowe Syndrome, to better treatments of the major complications of the disease and to the prevention of and/or a cure for it.

Eligibility: Open to researchers who are affiliated with a non-profit institution.

Level of Study: Unrestricted.

Type: Grant.

Value: Varies. The most recent was US$30,000.

Length of Study: One year.

Frequency: Dependent on funds available.

No. of awards offered: Varies.

Application Procedure: Applicants must submit their application in writing. Specific instructions are available in the grant proposal guidelines document.

Closing Date: Varies.

Funding: Private.

Contributor: Members of the LSA and fundraising events.

No. of awards given last year: One.

No. of applicants last year: One.

THE LYNDON BAINES JOHNSON FOUNDATION

2313 Red River, Austin, TX, 78705, United States of America

Tel: (1) 512 478 7829

Fax: (1) 512 478 9104

Contact: Mr Lawrence Reed, Assistant Director

Lyndon Baines Johnson Foundation Grants-in-Aid of Research

Subjects: Any subject relevant to the Library's collections.

Purpose: To defray living and travel expenses incurred through conducting research while at the Johnson Library.

Eligibility: There are no restrictions in regard to age, sex, academic background, citizenship or residency.

Level of Study: Unrestricted.

Type: Research grant.

Value: Calculated on the basis of US$110 per day, plus actual travel costs. Air travel should be by the least expensive route.

Length of Study: One year, non renewable.

Frequency: Twice a year.

Study Establishment: The Johnson Library.

Country of Study: United States of America.

No. of awards offered: Varies.

Application Procedure: Applicants must complete an application form.

Closing Date: March 31st or October 1st.

Funding: Private.

Contributor: The Lyndon Baines Johnson Foundation.

No. of awards given last year: 35.

No. of applicants last year: 60.

Additional Information: It should be agreed that the product of the research, made possible through the grant, will not be used for any political purposes. A copy of any publication, article or book resulting from this grant-in-aid will be presented to the chief archivist of the Library. Funds are not awarded for reproduction expenses, secretarial or research assistance. Prior to submitting a grant proposal, applicants are recommended to write to the Chief Archivist at the Foundation to obtain information on the materials available.

THE MACDOWELL COLONY

100 High Street, Peterborough, NH, 03458, United States of America

Tel: (1) 603 924 3886

Fax: (1) 603 924 9142

Email: info@macdowellcolony.org

www: http://www.macdowellcolony.org

Contact: Ms Courtney Bethel, Admissions Coordinator

The MacDowall Colony was founded in 1907 to provide creative artists with uninterrupted time and seclusion to work and enjoy the experience of living in a community with gifted artists. Residences are up to eight weeks for writers, composers, film and video makers, visual artists, architects and interdisciplinary artists. Artists in residence receive room, board and the exclusive use of a studio.

MacDowell Colony Residencies

Subjects: Creative writing, visual arts, musical composition, film or video making, architecture and interdisciplinary arts.

Purpose: To provide a place where creative artists can take advantage of uninterrupted work time and seclusion in which to work and enjoy the experience of living in a community of gifted artists.

Eligibility: Open to established and emerging artists in the fields specified.

Level of Study: Unrestricted.

Type: Residency.

Value: Up to US$1,000 for writers in need of financial assistance during a residency at MacDowell. Limited travel grants are also available.
Length of Study: Usually six weeks.
Frequency: Three application reviews each year.
Study Establishment: The Colony.
Country of Study: United States of America.
No. of awards offered: A total of 32 studios are available each application period for individual residencies.
Application Procedure: Applicants must write or telephone for details or refer to the website for an application.
Closing Date: January 15th, April 15th and September 15th for residencies to become tenable in Summer, Autumn-Winter, and Winter-Spring respectively.
Funding: Private.
Additional Information: The studios are offered for the independent pursuit of the applicant's art. No workshops or courses are given. There are no stipends. Requests for information should be accompanied by a stamped addressed envelope.

MACKENZIE KING SCHOLARSHIP TRUST

MacKenzie King Scholarship Selection Committee
Faculty of Law
University of British Columbia
1822 East Mall, Vancouver, BC, V6T 1Z1, Canada
Tel: (1) 604 822 4564
Fax: (1) 604 822 8108
Email: blom@law.ubc.ca
Contact: Professor Joost Blom, Chair

The Mackenzie King Scholarship Trust consists of two funds established under the will of the Right Honourable William Lyon Mackenzie King (1874-1950). Both scholarships are to support postgraduate study by graduates of Canadian universities.

Mackenzie King Open Scholarship
Subjects: All subjects.
Eligibility: Open to graduates of any Canadian university. Applicants should be persons of unusual worth or promise. Awards are determined on the basis of academic achievement, personal qualities and demonstrated aptitudes. Consideration is also given to the applicant's proposed programme of postgraduate study.
Level of Study: Postgraduate.
Type: Scholarship.
Value: Canadian $7,500.
Length of Study: One year, non renewable.
Frequency: Annual.
Country of Study: Any country.
No. of awards offered: One.
Application Procedure: Applicants must complete an application form, available from the Faculty of Graduate Studies at each Canadian university and from the Trust. Applications must be submitted to the Dean of Graduate Studies at the Canadian university from which the candidate most recently graduated.
Closing Date: February 1st.
Funding: Private.
No. of awards given last year: One.

Mackenzie King Travelling Scholarships
Subjects: International or industrial relations, including the international or industrial relations, aspects of law, history, politics and economics.
Purpose: To give Canadian students the opportunity to broaden their outlook and sympathies and contribute in some measure to the understanding of the problems and policies of other countries.
Eligibility: Open to graduates of any Canadian university who propose to engage in postgraduate studies in the given fields.
Level of Study: Postgraduate.
Type: Scholarship.

Value: Canadian $10,000.
Length of Study: One year, non renewable.
Frequency: Annual.
Study Establishment: Suitable institutions.
Country of Study: United States of America or the United Kingdom.
No. of awards offered: Four.
Application Procedure: Applicants must complete an application form, available from the Faculty of Graduate Studies in each Canadian university or from the Trust. Applications must be submitted to the Dean of Graduate Studies at the Canadian university from which the candidate most recently graduated.
Closing Date: February 1st.
Funding: Private.
No. of awards given last year: Four.

THE MACQUARIE BANK RECRUITMENT AND CAREERS

GPO Box 4294, Sydney, NSW, 1164, Australia
Tel: (61) 2 8232 3333
Fax: (61) 2 8232 4544
Email: mbaschol@macquarie.com
www: http://www.macquarie.com.au
Contact: Ms Gina A Sennitt, Associate Director Recruitment & Careers

Formed in 1985 from one of the leading Australian Merchant Banks, Macquarie Bank Limited has been an innovator in the Australasian banking industry, offering outstanding products and services and regularly leading the field in market development initiatives. It is now Australia's leading investment bank and one of the top 25 companies listed on the Australian Stock Exchange. The bank employs approx. 5,000 people and has around 43 offices worldwide.

The Macquarie Bank Graduate Management Scholarship
Subjects: MBA.
Purpose: To encourage and contribute to a higher standard of management education and to the effectiveness of Australasia's future managers.
Eligibility: Open to citizens or permanent residents of Australia or New Zealand who have work experience which reflects management expertise or potential, who indicate a firm intention to reside in Australia or New Zealand within a reasonable period after completion of the course and who are bona fide candidates for full-time study on an MBA course at an institution approved by the Trustees. The applicants must not have yet commenced the relevant course on either a full or part-time basis.
Level of Study: Postgraduate, MBA.
Type: Scholarship.
Value: US$35,000, payable over the study period.
Length of Study: A maximum of two years, the normal term of an MBA course.
Frequency: Annual.
Study Establishment: Any well known business school approved by the trustees.
Country of Study: Australia, the United Kingdom, Europe or United States of America.
No. of awards offered: One.
Application Procedure: Applicants must complete application forms with references. These are available from August.
Closing Date: The last Friday in October.
Funding: Commercial.
Contributor: The Macquarie Bank Foundation.
No. of awards given last year: One.
No. of applicants last year: 50-60.
Additional Information: Successful applicants will be required to attend initial and final interviews in Australia in November or December.

MAKING MUSIC, THE NATIONAL FEDERATION OF MUSIC SOCIETIES (NFMS)

7-15 Rosebery Avenue, London, EC1R 4SP, England
Tel: (44) 870 872 3300
Fax: (44) 870 872 3400
Email: info@makingmusic.org.uk
www: http://www.nfms.org.uk
Contact: Ms Kate Fearnley, Award Administrator

The National Federation of Music Societies (NFMS) represents and supports amateur choirs, orchestras and music promoters of all kinds throughout the United Kingdom. The 1,750 member societies represent over 135,000 musicians and music lovers, present 7,500 concerts each year to an audience of 1.7 million, and spend in excess of UK £16.5 million each year.

Making Music Award for Young Concert Artists

Subjects: The award alternates, on an annual basis, between singers and instrumentalists.
Purpose: To support young musicians at the start of their professional careers.
Eligibility: Open to singers under 30 years of age and instrumentalists under 28 years of age. All applicants must be European Community citizens normally resident in the United Kingdom.
Level of Study: Professional development.
Type: Award.
Value: Up to 60 engagements with affiliated societies.
Frequency: Annual.
No. of awards offered: Three-four.
Application Procedure: Applicants must submit a completed application form with their curriculum vitae.
Closing Date: As advertised in the national press and on the website.
Funding: Private.
Contributor: The Worshipful Company of Musicians.
No. of awards given last year: Five.
No. of applicants last year: 60+.

MANHATTAN SCHOOL OF MUSIC

120 Claremont Avenue, New York, NY, 10027, United States of America
Tel: (1) 212 749 2802 ext. 449
Fax: (1) 212 749 3025
Contact: Ms Amy A Anderson, Director of Financial Aid

The Manhattan School of Music is a major national and international force in the education of professional musicians. It is the largest private conservatory in the nation offering both classical and jazz training.

Manhattan School of Music Scholarships

Subjects: Music.
Purpose: To recognise outstanding talent, achievements and performance.
Eligibility: Open to all students who demonstrate through performance that they have attained excellence in the field of music and have the capacity for further development.
Level of Study: Doctorate, Graduate, Postgraduate.
Type: Scholarship.
Value: Tuition expenses only, awards range from US$1,000 to full tuition costs, payable in equal instalments by semester.
Length of Study: One academic year, renewable for a total of two years.
Frequency: Annual.
Study Establishment: The Manhattan School of Music.
Country of Study: United States of America.

No. of awards offered: 400.
Application Procedure: Applicants must submit a completed PROFILE and FAFSA form (United States citizens and permanent residents). For international students an International Application for MSM Scholarship in house form must be submitted.
Closing Date: March 15th for March auditions and April 15th for May auditions.
Funding: Private.
No. of awards given last year: 335.
No. of applicants last year: 1000.
Additional Information: Students must demonstrate financial need and provide the necessary income documents in order to qualify.

MANOUG PARIKIAN AWARD

16 Ogle Street, London, W1W 6JA, England
Tel: (44) 20 7636 4481
Fax: (44) 20 7637 4307
Email: education@.mbf.org.uk
www: http://www.mbf.org.uk
Contact: Mrs Susan Dolton

Manoug Parikian Award

Subjects: Musical performance on the violin.
Purpose: To assist the studies of an outstanding young violinist.
Eligibility: Open to violinists under the age of 21 years, of any nationality, who have been resident in the United Kingdom for three years.
Level of Study: Professional development.
Value: UK £3,000.
Frequency: Annual.
Country of Study: Any country.
No. of awards offered: One.
Application Procedure: Applicants must complete an application form and provide two references.
Closing Date: October.
Funding: Private.
No. of awards given last year: Five.
No. of applicants last year: 21.
Additional Information: Selected students will be asked to audition.

MARCH OF DIMES BIRTH DEFECTS FOUNDATION

1275 Mamaroneck Avenue, White Plains, NY, 10605, United States of America
Tel: (1) 914 997 4555
Fax: (1) 914 997 4560
Email: research-grants@modimes.org
www: http://www.modimes.org
Contact: Grants Administration

Four major problems threaten the health of America's babies: birth defects, infant mortality, low birth weight and lack of prenatal care. The goal of the March of Dimes Birth Defects Foundation is to eliminate these problems so that all babies can be born healthy.

Basil O'Connor Starter Scholar Research Award Program

Subjects: The broader aspects of pregnancy outcome eg. factors underlying the birth and survival of a healthy infant, the cognitive development of low birth weight infants, as well as the function of chromosomes, their subunits, genes or supporting structures.
Purpose: To support young scientists who are just embarking on their independent research careers.
Eligibility: Open to young investigators (MDs or PhDs) who are interested in undertaking independent research after the completion of

their doctoral and postdoctoral training. Applicants may not be recipients of a major grant exceeding US$100,000 at the time of their application.
Level of Study: Faculty.
Type: Research grant.
Value: Up to US$75,000. This award is not intended to cover the applicant's salary but to provide support for technical help and supplies.
Length of Study: Two years.
Frequency: Annual.
Study Establishment: An appropriate institution.
Country of Study: Any country.
No. of awards offered: Varies.
Application Procedure: Applicants must be nominated. Nominations must be accompanied by the candidate's full name, appointment, full mailing address, telephone and fax numbers, email designation, curriculum vitae and an abstract of the proposed research. A hard copy should not be submitted if the application is transmitted by fax.
Closing Date: An abstract is due by February 15th, with the full application due on May 31st.
Additional Information: Further information is available on request.

March of Dimes Research Grants
Subjects: Basic biological processes governing development, genetics, clinical studies, studies of reproductive health, environmental toxicology, and social or behavioural studies.
Purpose: To encourage research directed at the prevention of birth defects.
Eligibility: Open to qualified scientists from universities, hospitals and research institutions.
Level of Study: Faculty.
Type: Research grant.
Value: Approx. US$65,000 per year.
Frequency: Annual.
Study Establishment: An appropriate institution.
Country of Study: Any country.
No. of awards offered: Varies.
Application Procedure: Applicants must submit four copies of a letter of intent, of no more than two pages, summarising their proposed studies addressed to the Vice President for Research, as well as a curriculum vitae.
Closing Date: Letter of intent is due on April 30th, and the full application is due on September 30th.
Additional Information: Further information is available on request.

MARGARET MCNAMARA MEMORIAL FUND

1818 H Street North West
Room Q5 - 080, Washington, DC, 20433, United States of America
Tel: (1) 202 473 8751
Fax: (1) 202 522 3142
Email: wservices1@worldbank.org
Contact: Chairman of the MMMF Selection Committee

The Margaret McNamara Memorial Fund was established in 1981 to honour the late Margaret McNamara and her commitment to the well being of women and children in developing countries.

Margaret McNamara Memorial Fund
Subjects: Agriculture, architecture and urban planning, civil engineering, education, forestry, journalism, nursing, nutrition, paediatrics, public administration, public health, social sciences, social work and others.
Purpose: To support the education of women from developing countries who are committed to improving the lives of women and children in their home countries.
Eligibility: Open to women who are nationals of a developing country residing in the United States, but not as permanent residents.

Candidates must also be enrolled in an accredited educational institution in the United States where the grant will be used. They must be at least 25 years old and must not be related to any World Bank Group staff member or their spouse.
Level of Study: Postgraduate.
Type: Grant.
Value: US$11,000. This amount is revised annually.
Length of Study: One-two years.
Frequency: Annual.
Study Establishment: Universities or research institutions.
Country of Study: United States of America.
No. of awards offered: Up to six.
Application Procedure: Applicants must write for application forms. This must be submitted along with two recommendations and an academic transcript.
Closing Date: February 1st.
Funding: Private.
Contributor: Private donations.
No. of awards given last year: Six.
No. of applicants last year: 250.

MARINE CORPS HISTORICAL CENTER

History & Museums Division
Building 58
901 M Street South East
Washington Navy Yard, Washington, DC, 20374-5040, United States of America
Tel: (1) 202 433 4244
Fax: (1) 202 433 7265
Contact: Grants & Fellowships Co-ordinator

The Marine Corps Historical Center houses the History and Museums Divisions. The Historical Branch provides reference services to the public and government agencies, maintains the Marine Corps' archives and oral history collection, and produces official histories of Marine activities, units and bases. The Museums Branch maintains the artefact and personal papers collection, and operates the Marine Corps Museum and the Air-Ground Museum.

Beeler-Raider Fellowship
Subjects: Topics in United States military and naval history, as well as history and history based studies in the social and behavioural sciences with a direct relationship to the United States Marine Corps.
Purpose: To encourage graduate level and advanced study of the combat contributions of enlisted Marines.
Eligibility: The competition is limited to citizens or nationals of the United States of America. While the programme concentrates on graduate students, fellowships are available to other qualified persons.
Level of Study: Postgraduate.
Type: Fellowship.
Value: US$2,500.
Frequency: Annual.
Study Establishment: Fellowship recipients are expected to conduct a portion of their research in Washington, DC. Fellows will also receive access to the Historical Center's facilities and collections.
No. of awards offered: One.
Application Procedure: Applicants must submit a preliminary application to the Director of Marine Corps History and Museums outlining their qualifications, and either proposing a specific topic or requesting a suggested topic based on the applicant's interests and qualifications. If the evaluation of the preliminary application is favourable, the applicant will be asked to make a formal application on a form provided by the Historical Center. The applicant is responsible for insuring that all required documentation is mailed before the closing date.
Closing Date: May 1st.

Funding: Private.

Contributor: The Marine Corps Heritage Foundation.

Additional Information: The Director of Marine Corps History and Museums will notify all applicants individually of their decision not later than mid July.

Marine Corps Historical Center College Internships

Subjects: History.

Purpose: To offer opportunities for college students to participate on a professional level in the Marine Corps Historical Center many historical and museum activities. The intent of the programme is to give promising and talented student interns a chance to earn college credit while gaining meaningful experience in fields in which they might choose to seek employment after school or pursue a vocational interest.

Eligibility: Applicants must be registered students at a college or university which will grant academic credit for work experience as interns in subject areas related to the students' course of study. While there are no restrictions on individuals applying for intern positions, it has been found that mature and academically superior students are most successful. The agreement of the academic institution to the internship for credit is essential.

Level of Study: Professional development.

Type: Internship.

Value: A small grant of daily expense money is provided. Any other costs of the internship must be made by the student.

Study Establishment: Internships are served either at the Marine Corps Historical Center, in Washington or the Marine Corps Air Ground Museum, Marine Corps Development and Education Command, Quantico, Virginia.

Country of Study: United States of America.

No. of awards offered: Varies.

Application Procedure: Applicants must contact the Chief Historian at the Center for further details.

Closing Date: Please contact the organisation.

Marine Corps Historical Center Dissertation Fellowships

Subjects: Topics in United States military and naval history, as well as history and history based studies in the social and behavioural sciences with a direct relationship to the United States Marine Corps.

Purpose: To award a qualified graduate student working on a doctoral dissertation relevant to Marine Corps history.

Eligibility: Applicants must be citizens of the United States, enrolled in a recognised graduate school, have completed by September all requirements for the doctoral degree except the dissertation and have an approved, pertinent dissertation topic. A fellowship will not be awarded to an applicant who has held or accepted an equivalent fellowship from any other Department of Defence agency, however, recipients of the Marine Corps' Master's Thesis Fellowships may apply.

Level of Study: Doctorate.

Type: Fellowship.

Value: A stipend of US$10,000.

Frequency: Annual.

Study Establishment: Fellowship recipients are expected to conduct a portion of their research in Washington, DC. Fellows will also receive access to the Historical Center's facilities and collections.

No. of awards offered: One.

Application Procedure: Applicants must complete an application form, available from the Chairman of the History Department of the applicant's university, or by writing to the Director of the Marine Corps History and Museums at the Center. The applicant is responsible for insuring that all required documentation is mailed before the closing date.

Closing Date: May 1st.

Funding: Private.

Contributor: The Marine Corps Historical Foundation.

Additional Information: Evaluation of applicants is on the basis of academic achievements, faculty recommendations, and demonstrated research and writing ability. The nature of the topic must be

of benefit to the study and understanding of Marine Corps history. All awards will be based on merit, without regard to race, creed, colour, or sex. The Director of Marine Corps History and Museums will notify all applicants individually of their decision not later than mid July.

Marine Corps Historical Center Master's Thesis Fellowships

Subjects: Topics in United States military and naval history, as well as history and history based studies in the social and behavioural sciences, with a direct relationship to the United States Marine Corps. This programme gives preference to projects covering the pre-1975 period where records are declassified or can be most readily declassified and made available to scholars.

Purpose: To award a number of fellowships to qualified graduate students working on topics pertinent to Marine Corps history.

Eligibility: Applicants must be actively enrolled in an accredited Master's degree programme which requires a Master's thesis. The competition is limited to citizens or nationals of the United States of America. A fellowship will not be awarded to anyone who has held or accepted an equivalent fellowship from any other Department of Defence agency.

Level of Study: Postgraduate.

Type: Fellowship.

Value: A stipend of US$3,500.

Frequency: Annual.

Study Establishment: Fellowship recipients are expected to conduct a portion of their research in Washington, DC. Fellows will also receive access to the Historical Center's facilities and collections.

No. of awards offered: Varies.

Application Procedure: Applicants must complete an application form, available from the chairman of the history department of the applicant's university, or by writing to the Director of the Marine Corps History and Museums, at the Center. The applicant is responsible for insuring that all required documentation is mailed before the closing date.

Closing Date: May 1st.

Funding: Private.

Contributor: The Marine Corps Historical Foundation.

Additional Information: The Director of Marine Corps History and Museums will notify all applicants individually of their decision not later than mid July.

Marine Corps Historical Center Research Grants

Subjects: Topics in United States military and naval history, as well as history and history based studies in the social and behavioural sciences, with a direct relationship to the United States Marine Corps. This programme gives preference to projects covering the pre-1975 period where records are declassified or can be most readily declassified and made available to scholars.

Purpose: To encourage graduate level and advanced study in Marine Corps history and related fields.

Eligibility: While the programme concentrates on graduate students, grants are available to other qualified persons. Applicants for grants should have the ability to conduct advanced study in those aspects of American military history and museum activities related to the United States Marine Corps.

Level of Study: Research.

Type: Grant.

Value: Varies, US$400-3,000.

Frequency: Annual.

Application Procedure: Applicants must submit a preliminary application to the Director of Marine Corps History and Museums outlining their qualifications, and either proposing a specific topic or requesting a suggested topic based on the applicant's interests and qualifications. If the evaluation of the preliminary application is favourable, the applicant will be asked to make a formal application on a form provided by the Center.

Closing Date: Please contact the organisation.

Funding: Private.

Contributor: The Marine Corps Historical Foundation.

MARQUETTE UNIVERSITY, GRADUATE SCHOOL

PO Box 1881, Milwaukee, WI, 53201-1881, United States of America
Tel: (1) 414 288 7137
Fax: (1) 414 288 1902
Email: mugs@marquette.edu
www: http://www.grad.marquette.edu
Contact: Mr Thomas Marek, Student Services Coordinator

Marquette University is a private, Jesuit university situated about 100 miles north of Chicago. It is a graduate research institution with 18 doctoral and over 40 Masters and certificate programmes.

Alpha Sigma Nu Graduate Scholarship
Subjects: All subjects.
Purpose: To offer tuition scholarships for members of Alpha Sigma Nu.
Eligibility: Applicants must be first year graduate students and members of Alpha Sigma Nu.
Level of Study: Graduate.
Type: Scholarship.
Value: US$10,000.
Length of Study: Two years.
Frequency: Annual.
Country of Study: United States of America.
No. of awards offered: Two.
Application Procedure: Applicants must send a letter of application to the Graduate School.
Closing Date: February 15th.
Funding: Private.
No. of awards given last year: Two.

Johnson's Wax Research Fellowship
Subjects: Engineering, chemistry or biology.
Eligibility: Applicants must be admitted to a doctoral programme in engineering, biology or chemistry.
Level of Study: Doctorate.
Type: Fellowship.
Value: US$5,500 stipend plus 18 credits of scholarship (approx. value US$10,000).
Length of Study: One year.
Frequency: Annual.
No. of awards offered: One.
Application Procedure: Qualified applicants will be contacted by their department.
Closing Date: February 15th.
Funding: Private.
No. of awards given last year: One.
Additional Information: The award is offered to a different programme each year.

Marquette University Women's Club Fellowship
Subjects: All subjects.
Purpose: To support students who received their baccalaureate degrees from Marquette University.
Eligibility: Applicants must be admitted to a degree programme and must have received a Bachelor's degree from Marquette University.
Level of Study: Graduate.
Type: Fellowship.
Value: US$2,000 stipend plus 18 credits of scholarship (approx. value US$10,000).
Length of Study: One year.
Frequency: Annual.
No. of awards offered: One.
Application Procedure: Qualified students will be contacted by their department.
Closing Date: February 15th.
Funding: Private.
No. of awards given last year: One.

Additional Information: The award is offered to a different graduate programme each year.

Marquette University's Graduate Assistantship
Subjects: All subjects.
Purpose: To support teaching and research.
Eligibility: Open to full-time Master's and doctoral students.
Level of Study: Graduate.
Type: Assistantship and scholarship.
Value: Stipends range from US$10,520-15,650 plus an 18 credit tuition scholarship (approx. value $10,000).
Length of Study: One year.
Frequency: Annual.
No. of awards offered: 289.
Application Procedure: Applicants must submit an application to graduate school by the deadline. Please see the graduate bulletin for details or visit the website.
Closing Date: February 15th for the Autumn deadline and November 15th for the Spring deadline.
Funding: Private.
Contributor: Marquette University.
No. of awards given last year: 289.

Milwaukee Foundation's Frank Rogers Bacon Research Assistantship
Subjects: Electrical engineering.
Purpose: To provide research support for students.
Eligibility: Open to full-time Master's and doctoral students.
Level of Study: Graduate.
Type: Fellowship.
Value: US$10,520 Stipend.
Length of Study: Varies.
Frequency: Varies.
Country of Study: United States of America.
No. of awards offered: Varies depending on funds.
Application Procedure: Applicants must contact the Department of Electrical and Computer Engineering at the University.
Closing Date: February 15th.
Funding: Private.
No. of awards given last year: Seven.

R A Bournique Memorial Fellowship
Subjects: Chemistry.
Eligibility: Applicants must be graduate students in chemistry.
Level of Study: Graduate.
Type: Fellowship.
Value: US$1,250 stipend.
Length of Study: For the Summer.
Frequency: Annual.
No. of awards offered: Two.
Application Procedure: Applicants must contact the Department of Chemistry.
Funding: Private.
No. of awards given last year: Two.

MARSHALL AID COMMEMORATION COMMISSION

c/o ACU
John Foster House
36 Gordon Square, London, WC1H 0PF, England
Tel: (44) 20 7380 6700
Fax: (44) 20 7387 2655
Email: info@marshallscholarship.org
www: http://www.marshallscholarship.org

Marshall Scholarships
Subjects: All subjects.

Purpose: To provide intellectually distinguished young Americans with the opportunity to study in the United Kingdom and thus, to understand and appreciate the British way of life.
Eligibility: Open to United States citizens, who have graduated with a minimum grade point average of 3.7 or A- from an accredited United States college not more than two years previously. Recipients are required to take a degree at their United Kingdom university. Preference is given to candidates who combine high academic ability with the capacity to play an active part in the United Kingdom university.
Level of Study: Postgraduate.
Type: Scholarship.
Value: Approximately UK £19,000 per year, which comprises tuition fees, residence, travel and related costs.
Length of Study: Two academic years, with a possible extension for a third year.
Frequency: Annual.
Study Establishment: Any suitable institution.
Country of Study: United Kingdom.
No. of awards offered: 40.
Application Procedure: Applicants must submit an application form, university or college endorsement, and four references. Information and application forms can be obtained from the various consulate addresses.
Closing Date: October annually.
Funding: Government.
No. of awards given last year: 40.
No. of applicants last year: 800.

For further information contact:

British Consulate-General
Federal Reserve Plaza
600 Atlantic Avenue, Boston, MA, 02210, United States of America

British Consulate-General
33 North Dearborn Street, Chicago, IL, 60602, United States of America

British Consulate-General
Wells Fayo Plaza
1000 Louisiana No 1900, Houston, TX, 77002, United States of America

British Consulate-General
11766 Wiltshire Boulevard
Suite 400, Los Angeles, CA, 90025, United States of America

British Consulate-General
845 Third Avenue, New York, NY, 10022, United States of America

British Consulate-General
1 Sansome Street, San Francisco, CA, 94104, United States of America

Cultural Department
British Embassy
3100 Massachusetts Avenue North West, Washington, DC, 20008, United States of America

MARY ROBERTS RINEHART FUND

MSN 3E4
English Department
George Mason University
4400 University Drive, Fairfax, VA, 22030-4444, United States of America
Tel: (1) 703 993 1180
Email: bgompert@gmu.edu
www: http://www.gmu.edu/departments/writing/rinehart.htm
Contact: Mr William Miller, Director of Graduate Writing Program

The Mary Roberts Rinehart Fund is housed within a public university and was established to support and encourage unpublished writers.

Mary Roberts Rinehart Awards
Subjects: Writing eg. works of fiction, poetry, biography, autobiography or history with a strong narrative quality.
Purpose: To encourage developing writers who need financial assistance, not otherwise available, to complete works in progress.
Eligibility: Open to new and relatively unknown writers, without regard to citizenship, sex, colour or creed. Published writers are ineligible. Applicants from any country are eligible, although only works in English will be read and awards will only be made in United States dollars.
Level of Study: Unrestricted.
Type: Contest.
Value: US$2,000.
Frequency: Annual.
Country of Study: Any country.
No. of awards offered: Three.
Application Procedure: There are no formal application forms. The only way to have a work considered is to have it submitted, in manuscript form, by a sponsoring writer, agent, writing teacher or editor who is familiar with the author. Candidates are requested to provide their address and telephone number with their submission and should also include brief biographical information.
Closing Date: November 30th for announcement in the following March.
Funding: Private.
Contributor: The Mary Roberts Rinehart Foundation.
No. of awards given last year: Three.
No. of applicants last year: 500+.

MARYLAND INSTITUTE COLLEGE OF ART (MICA)

1300 West Mount Royal Avenue, Baltimore, MD, 21217, United States of America
Tel: (1) 410 225 2255
Fax: (1) 410 225 2408
Email: graduate@mica.edu
www: http://www.mica.edu
Contact: Mr Scott G Kelly, Director of Graduate Studies

The Maryland Institute College of Art (MICA) offers a Master of Fine Arts (MFA) degree in painting, sculpture, mixed media, photography and digital imaging. It also offers excellent art education degrees such as MAT, MA, and an MFA for art educators. The college has private studios, a strong visiting artists programme, housing and excellent exhibition opportunities. A new MA degree in digital arts is also available.

MICA Fellowship
Subjects: Arts.
Purpose: To serve as a tuition scholarship.
Level of Study: Graduate.
Type: Fellowship.
Value: US$5,000-12,000 per year.
Length of Study: One-two years.
Frequency: Annual.
Study Establishment: MICA.
Country of Study: United States of America.
No. of awards offered: 10.
Application Procedure: Applicants must contact the Institute.
Closing Date: March 1st.
Funding: Private.
Contributor: MICA.
No. of awards given last year: 10.
No. of applicants last year: 250.

MICA International Fellowship Award
Subjects: Fine and applied arts.
Purpose: To serve as a tuition scholarship.
Eligibility: Open to qualified applicants of any nationality.

Level of Study: Postgraduate.
Type: Fellowship.
Value: US$12,000 per year.
Length of Study: One-two years.
Frequency: Annual.
Study Establishment: MICA.
Country of Study: Any country.
No. of awards offered: One.
Application Procedure: All accepted applicants are automatically considered.
Closing Date: March 1st.
Funding: Private.
Contributor: MICA.
No. of awards given last year: One.
No. of applicants last year: 57.

MASSEY UNIVERSITY

National Student Administration & Teaching Support
Private Bag 11-222, Palmerston North, New Zealand
Tel: (64) 6 350 5799 ext. 2909
Fax: (64) 6 350 2263
Email: m.e.gilbert@massey.ac.nz
www: http://www.massey.ac.nz
Contact: Ms Margeret E Gilbert, Scholarships Officer

Massey University has over 30,000 students, 12,000 of which study on campus with the remaining 18,000 studying by correspondence. The five colleges of business, education, science, design, fine arts and music, and humanities and social sciences, provide a comprehensive range of undergraduate and graduate degrees and diplomas all tailored to meeting national and international needs.

Massey Doctoral Scholarship

Subjects: Agriculture, forestry, town planning, arts and humanities, business administration and management, education and teacher training, engineering, commercial law, media studies, mathematics and computer science, nursing, midwifery, natural sciences, social welfare and social work, environmental studies, religious studies, tourism, social and behavioural studies and air transport, design, fine arts or music.
Purpose: To fund research towards a PhD degree.
Eligibility: Open to those with a minimum qualification of a First Class (Honours) Degree.
Level of Study: Doctorate.
Type: Scholarship.
Value: New zealand $18,000 per year.
Length of Study: Three years.
Frequency: Annual.
Study Establishment: The University.
Country of Study: New Zealand.
No. of awards offered: 20-30.
Application Procedure: Applicants must complete an application form.
Closing Date: October 1st or July 1st.
No. of awards given last year: 33.
No. of applicants last year: 70.
Additional Information: Applicants who are not New Zealand citizens or permanent residents must have additional funding to meet the cost of tuition fees (approximately new zealand $16,000-30,000, depending on the programme undertaken) as the value of the scholarship is sufficient only for living expenses.

THE MATSUMAE INTERNATIONAL FOUNDATION

Room 6-002
New Marunouchi Building
1-5-1 Marunouchi
Chiyoda-ku, Tokyo, 100-0005, Japan
Tel: (81) 3 3214 7611
Fax: (81) 3 3214 7613
Email: contact@matsumae-if.org
www: http://www.matsumae-if.org
Contact: Mr S Nakajima

Matsumae International Foundation Research Fellowship

Subjects: Engineering, mathematics, medicine, natural sciences or agriculture.
Purpose: To provide the opportunity for foreign scientists to conduct research at Japanese institutions.
Eligibility: Open to applicants under 40 years of age, of non Japanese nationality, who hold a doctorate or have two years of research experience after receipt of a Master's degree, and who have not been to Japan previously.
Level of Study: Postdoctorate, Professional development.
Type: Fellowship.
Value: An air ticket, personal accident or sickness insurance and a research stipend plus yen 300,00 on arrival in addition to yen 200,000 monthly.
Length of Study: Three-six months.
Frequency: Annual.
Study Establishment: Unrestricted.
Country of Study: Japan.
No. of awards offered: 20.
Application Procedure: Applicants must obtain the current issue of the Fellowship announcement from the Foundation.
Closing Date: July 31st.
Funding: Private.
Contributor: Charitable donations from individuals.
No. of awards given last year: 21.
No. of applicants last year: 132.
Additional Information: Priority will be given to the fields of science, engineering and medicine.

MCGILL UNIVERSITY

3644 Peel Street, Montréal, QC, H3A 1W9, Canada
Tel: (1) 514 398 6604
Fax: (1) 514 398 4659
www: http://www.mcgill.ca
Contact: Ms Linda Coughlin, Secretary

Maxwell Boulton QC Fellowship

Subjects: Any legal subject, especially those having significance to the Canadian legal system and legal community.
Purpose: To provide younger scholars with an opportunity to pursue a major research project or to complete the research requirement for a higher degree.
Eligibility: Open to candidates who have completed residency requirements for a doctoral degree in law.
Level of Study: Doctorate, Postdoctorate.
Type: Fellowship.
Value: Canadian $30,000-35,000 per year.
Length of Study: One year.
Frequency: Annual.
Country of Study: Canada.
No. of awards offered: Two.
Application Procedure: Applicants must write for details.
Closing Date: February 1st.
No. of awards given last year: Two.

No. of applicants last year: 20.

MEDICAL LIBRARY ASSOCIATION (MLA)

65 East Wacker Place
Suite 1900, Chicago, IL, 60601, United States of America
Tel: (1) 312 419 9094
Fax: (1) 312 419 8950
Email: mlapd2@mlahq.org
www: http://www.mlanet.org
Contact: Professional Development Department

The Medical Library Association (MLA) is organised exclusively for scientific and educational purposes, and is dedicated to the support of health sciences research, education and patient care. MLA fosters excellence in the professional achievement and leadership of health sciences library and information professionals to enhance the quality of health care, education and research.

Cunningham Memorial International Fellowship

Subjects: Medical librarianship.
Purpose: To provide a foreign medical librarian with the opportunity to observe and perform specialised work in the United States of America or Canada.
Eligibility: Open to those with a Baccalaureate degree and a library degree who are working in a medical library. The applicant must submit a signed statement from a home country official stating that he or she is guaranteed a position in a medical library upon returning home. A satisfactory score must be achieved on the Test Of English as a Foreign Language competency examination. Nationals of the United States of America or Canada are not eligible.
Level of Study: Professional development.
Type: Fellowship.
Value: US$8,000 to cover living expenses and travel within the United States of America and Canada.
Length of Study: Four months.
Frequency: Annual.
Study Establishment: Medical libraries.
Country of Study: United States of America or Canada.
No. of awards offered: One.
Application Procedure: Applicants must submit a completed application form with three letters of reference in English, a project overview, certificate of health, Test of English as a Foreign Language examination result, and audio or video tape.
Closing Date: December 1st.
No. of awards given last year: One.

MLA Continuing Education Grants

Subjects: The theoretical, administrative and technical aspects of library and information science.
Purpose: To provide professional health science librarians with the opportunity to continue their education.
Eligibility: Candidates must be United States or Canadian citizens, or permanent residents who are medical librarians with a graduate degree in library science and at least two years of work experience at the professional level.
Level of Study: Professional development.
Type: Fellowship.
Value: US$100-500.
Length of Study: One year.
Frequency: Annual.
Country of Study: United States of America.
No. of awards offered: Usually one.
Application Procedure: Applicants must complete and submit an application form along with three references. Candidiates should also identify a continuing education programme.
Closing Date: December 1st.
No. of awards given last year: One.
Additional Information: The award is not to support work towards a degree or certificate.

MLA Doctoral Fellowship

Subjects: Medical librarianship or information science.
Purpose: To encourage superior students to conduct doctoral work in an area of health sciences librarianship or information services.
Eligibility: Open to citizens or permanent residents of the United States of America or Canada who are graduates of an ALA accredited library school and are in a PhD programme with an emphasis on biomedical and health related information science.
Level of Study: Doctorate.
Type: Fellowship.
Value: US$2,000.
Length of Study: One year, non renewable.
Frequency: Every two years.
Country of Study: United States of America or Canada.
No. of awards offered: One.
Application Procedure: Applicants must submit a completed application form with two letters of reference, transcripts of graduate work completed, summary of project and detailed budget plus signed statement of terms and conditions.
Closing Date: December 1st.
Contributor: The Institute for Scientific Information.
No. of awards given last year: One.
Additional Information: The award supports research or travel applicable to the candidate's study and may not be used for tuition.

MLA Research, Development and Demonstration Project Award

Subjects: Health science librarianship or the information sciences.
Purpose: To provide support for research, development or demonstration projects that will help to promote excellence in the field of health sciences, librarianship and information services.
Eligibility: Open to members of the Association who have a graduate degree in library science, are practising medical librarians with at least two years' experience at the professional level and are citizens or permanent residents of the United States of America or Canada.
Level of Study: Postgraduate.
Type: Award.
Value: US$100-1,000.
Length of Study: One year.
Frequency: Annual.
Country of Study: United States of America or Canada.
No. of awards offered: Usually one.
Application Procedure: Applicants must submit a completed application form with three references, detailed description of project design and budget.
Closing Date: December 1st.
No. of awards given last year: One.
Additional Information: Grants will not be given to support an activity which is operational in nature or has only local usefulness.

MLA Scholarship

Subjects: Library science.
Purpose: To provide an opportunity to study at an ALA accredited library school.
Eligibility: Open to citizens and permanent residents of the United States of America or Canada who are entering an ALA accredited library school or have at least one half of the academic requirements of the programme to finish in the scholarship year.
Level of Study: Graduate.
Type: Scholarship.
Value: US$5,000.
Length of Study: One full academic year.
Frequency: Annual.
Country of Study: United States of America or Canada.
No. of awards offered: One.
Application Procedure: Applicants must contact submit a completed application form with two letters of reference, official transcripts and a statement of career objectives.
Closing Date: December 1st.
Funding: Private.
No. of awards given last year: One.

MLA Scholarship for Minority Students

Subjects: Medical librarianship.

Purpose: To provide a minority student with the opportunity to begin or continue graduate study in the field of library and information science.

Eligibility: Open to Black, Hispanic, Asian, Pacific Island or Native American students who are entering an ALA accredited library school and have at least one half of the academic requirements of the programme to finish in the scholarship year.

Level of Study: Graduate.

Type: Scholarship.

Value: US$5,000.

Length of Study: One academic year.

Frequency: Annual.

Study Establishment: An ALA accredited library school.

Country of Study: United States of America or Canada.

No. of awards offered: One.

Application Procedure: Applicants must submit a completed application form with two letters of reference, official transcripts and a statement of career objectives.

Closing Date: December 1st.

No. of awards given last year: One.

MEDICAL RESEARCH COUNCIL (MRC)

20 Park Crescent, London, W1B 1AL, England
Tel: (44) 20 7636 5422
Fax: (44) 20 7670 5002
Email: robert.hay@headoffice.mrc.ac.uk
www: http://www.mrc.ac.uk
Contact: Mr Robert Hay, Research Career Awards

The Medical Research Council (MRC) offers support for talented individuals who want to pursue a career in the biomedical sciences, public health and health services research. It provides its support through a variety of personal award schemes that are aimed at each stage in a clinical or non clinical research career.

MRC Career Development Award

Subjects: Biomedical sciences.

Purpose: To award outstanding researchers who wish to consolidate and develop their research skills and make the transition from postdoctoral research and training to becoming independent investigators, but who do not hold established positions.

Eligibility: It is normally expected that all applicants will hold a PhD or MPhil in a basic science and will have at least three years' postdoctoral research experience. Residence requirements apply.

Level of Study: Postdoctorate, Research.

Type: Fellowship.

Value: Competitive personal salary support plus research support staff at technical level, research expenses, capital equipment and a travel allowance for attendance at scientific conferences.

Length of Study: Up to four years.

Frequency: Annual.

Study Establishment: A suitable university department or similar institution.

Country of Study: United Kingdom including one year in a recognised research establishment overseas, a second United Kingdom centre or in United Kingdom industry.

No. of awards offered: Up to 10.

Application Procedure: Applicants must submit a personal application. Forms and further details are available from the MRC.

Closing Date: October to December, but applicants are advised to check the website for details.

Funding: Government.

No. of awards given last year: 10.

No. of applicants last year: 68.

MRC Clinical Research Training Fellowships

Subjects: Biomedical sciences.

Purpose: To provide an opportunity for specialised or further research training in the biomedical sciences within the United Kingdom leading to the submission of a PhD, DPhil or MD.

Eligibility: Open to hospital doctors, dentists, general practitioners, nurses, midwives and members of the Professions Allied to Medicine (PAMS). Residence requirements apply.

Level of Study: Postgraduate.

Type: Fellowship.

Value: An appropriate clinical academic salary will be provided along with a fixed sum for research expenses and a travel allowance for attendance at scientific conferences.

Length of Study: Up to three years.

Frequency: Annual.

Study Establishment: A suitable university department or similar institution.

Country of Study: United Kingdom.

No. of awards offered: Up to 58.

Application Procedure: Applicants must submit a personal application. Forms and further details are available from the MRC.

Closing Date: Round one is August-September, and round two is January-March, but applicants are advised to check the MRC website for details.

Funding: Government.

No. of awards given last year: 58.

No. of applicants last year: 215.

Additional Information: In addition to this scheme, the MRC also offers Joint Training Fellowships with the Royal Colleges of Surgeons of England and Edinburgh, the Royal College of Obstetricians and Gynaecologists and the Royal Colleges of Physicians and Pathologists. These awards are aimed at individuals whose long-term career aspirations involve undertaking academic clinical research.

MRC Clinician Scientist Fellowship

Subjects: Biomedical sciences.

Purpose: To provide an opportunity for outstanding clinical researchers who have already secured a PhD in a basic science subject who wish to consolidate their research skills and make the transition from postdoctoral research and training to becoming independent investigators, but who do not hold established positions.

Eligibility: The scheme is open to hospital doctors, dentists, general practitioners, nurses, midwives and members of the Professions Allied to Medicine (PAMS). All applicants must have obtained their PhD or MD in a basic science or clinical project, or expect to have received their doctorate by the time they intend to take up an award.

Level of Study: Postdoctorate, Research.

Type: Fellowship.

Value: Competitive personal salary support plus research support staff at technical level, research expenses, capital equipment and a travel allowance for attendance at scientific conferences.

Length of Study: Up to four years.

Frequency: Annual.

Study Establishment: A suitable university department or similar institution.

Country of Study: United Kingdom, including one year in a recognised research establishment overseas, a second United Kingdom centre or in United Kingdom industry.

No. of awards offered: Up to 12.

Application Procedure: Applicants must submit a personal application. Forms and further details are available from the MRC.

Closing Date: August to December, but applicants are advised to check the website for details.

Funding: Government.

No. of awards given last year: 12.

No. of applicants last year: 57.

MRC Collaborative/Industrial Collaborative Studentships

Subjects: Any biomedical science.

Purpose: To enhance links between academia and industry in the provision of high quality research training.

Eligibility: Candidates should have graduated with a good honours degree from a United Kingdom academic institution in a subject relevant to MRC's scientific remit. This should be Upper Second Class

Degree or higher. MRC will however consider qualifications or a combination of qualifications and experience which demonstrates equivalent ability and attainment eg. a Lower Second Class Degree can be enhanced by a Master's degree. A copy of the regulations governing residence eligibility may be obtained from the Council.
Level of Study: Postgraduate.
Value: Tax free maintenance stipend depending on United Kingdom location, university tuition fees up to the current DFEE recommended limit plus college fees where applicable. Awards also include a fixed sum for conference travel expenses and a support grant to the university department to help cover incidental costs of students' training. As a measure of interest and involvement the industrial company is expected to make a financial contribution to the cost of the studentship.
Length of Study: Up to three years.
Frequency: Annual.
Study Establishment: Universities, medical schools, industry and other academic institutions in the UK.
Country of Study: United Kingdom.
No. of awards offered: Approx. 50.
Application Procedure: The MRC does not make awards directly to students. Awards are made to departments who apply for studentships by application. Departments will then advertise for students to apply for their awards. Students who wish to apply for a studentship are advised to contact the department where they wish to study to see if it has an allocation of awards.
Closing Date: Departments should submit student nomination forms to the MRC no later than July 31st each year.
Funding: Commercial.
No. of awards given last year: Approx. 50.
Additional Information: The industrial company is expected to make a contribution.

MRC Masters Studentships

Subjects: Any biomedical science.
Purpose: To enable students to undertake early research training relevant to strategic research or strategic employment in a research related capacity in academia or industry.
Eligibility: Candidates should have graduated with a good honours degree. A copy of the regulations governing residence eligibility may be obtained from the Council.
Level of Study: Postgraduate.
Type: Studentship.
Value: Tax free maintenance stipend, depending on United Kingdom location, and university tuition fees up to the current DFEE recommended limit. Awards also include a fixed sum for conference travel expenses.
Length of Study: One year.
Frequency: Annual.
Study Establishment: Universities, medical schools and other academic organisations in the United Kingdom.
Country of Study: United Kingdom.
No. of awards offered: Approx. 120.
Application Procedure: The MRC does not make awards directly to students. Awards are made to departments who apply for studentships by application. Departments will then advertise for students to apply for their awards. Students who wish to apply for a studentship are advised to contact the department where they wish to study to see if it has an allocation of awards.
Closing Date: Departments must submit student nomination forms to the MRC no later than July 31st each year.
Funding: Government.
No. of awards given last year: Approx. 120.
Additional Information: The MRC also has awards in strategic scientific priority areas from time to time. Further details are available from the MRC website.

MRC Patient Oriented Clinician Scientist Fellowship

Subjects: Biomedical sciences.
Purpose: To allow outstanding clinical researchers who have already secured a PhD in a basic science subject to consolidate their research skills and make the transition from postdoctoral research

and training to becoming independent investigators. These awards allow for a greater proportion of time (up to 40 per cent) to be spent in clinical work, at least some of which should be of direct relevance to the project.
Eligibility: Open to hospital doctors, dentists, general practitioners, nurses, midwives and members of the Professions Allied to Medicine (PAMS).
Level of Study: Postdoctorate.
Type: Fellowship.
Value: Competitive personal salary support plus research support staff at technical level, research expenses, capital equipment and a travel allowance for attendance at scientific conferences.
Length of Study: Up to five years.
Frequency: Annual.
Study Establishment: A suitable university department or similar institution.
Country of Study: United Kingdom, including one year in a recognised research establishment overseas, a second United Kingdom centre or in a United Kingdom industry.
No. of awards offered: Up to four.
Application Procedure: Applicants must submit a personal application. Forms and further details are available from the MRC.
Closing Date: August to December, but applicants are advised to check the website for details.
Funding: Government.
No. of awards given last year: Two.
No. of applicants last year: 14.

MRC Research Fellowship in Clinical Psychology

Subjects: Clinical psychology.
Eligibility: Information about eligibility is available on request.
Level of Study: Postdoctorate.
Type: Fellowship.
Value: An appropriate academic salary will be provided along with a fixed sum for research expenses and a travel allowance for attendance at scientific conferences. Additional support is provided for overseas training periods.
Length of Study: Up to four years.
Frequency: Annual.
Study Establishment: A suitable university or similar institute.
Country of Study: United Kingdom.
No. of awards offered: Please contact the organisation.
Application Procedure: Applicants must complete a personal application. Forms and further details are available from MRC.
Closing Date: Applicants should contact the Council for details.
Funding: Government.
Additional Information: Further information is available on request or from the website.

MRC Research Studentships

Subjects: Any biomedical science.
Purpose: To enable individuals to undertake a training programme under the guidance of named supervisors that includes a research project plus training in research methods and personal key skills.
Eligibility: Candidates should have graduated with a good honours degree from a United Kingdom academic institution in a subject relevant to MRC's scientific remit. This should be an Upper Second Class Degree or higher. MRC will however consider qualifications or a combination of qualifications and experience which demonstrates equivalent ability and attainment eg. a Lower Second Class Degree can be enhanced by a Master's degree. A copy of the regulations governing residence eligibility may be obtained from the Council.
Level of Study: Postgraduate.
Type: Research studentship.
Value: Tax free maintenance stipend depending on United Kingdom location, university tuition fees up to the current DFEE recommended limit plus college fees where applicable. Awards also include a fixed sum for conference travel expenses and a support grant to the university department to help cover incidental costs of students' training.
Length of Study: Most studentships are three years, but they can be linked to a Master's course, making it a four year programme.

Frequency: Annual.
Study Establishment: Universities, medical schools, MRC research establishments and other academic organisations in the United Kingdom.
Country of Study: United Kingdom.
No. of awards offered: 357 including studentships in strategic priority areas.
Application Procedure: The MRC does not make awards directly to students. Awards are made to departments who apply for studentships by application. Departments will then advertise for students to apply for their awards. Students who wish to apply for a studentship are advised to contact the department where they wish to study to see if it has an allocation of awards.
Closing Date: Departments must submit student nomination forms to the MRC no later than July 31st each year.
Funding: Government.

MRC Research Training Fellowship
Subjects: Biomedical sciences.
Purpose: To provide an opportunity for high calibre non-clinical postdoctoral scientists, who wish to develop their careers in biomedical and public health research, to gain specialised or further research training.
Eligibility: Residence requirements apply. Applicants would normally be expected to hold a PhD or DPhil in basic science, or expect to receive their doctorate by the time they intend to take up an award. Applicants who hold a research orientated Master's degree and who have at least three years of appropriate postgraduate research experience may, exceptionally, be considered eg. medical statisticians.
Level of Study: Postdoctorate.
Type: Fellowship.
Value: Competitive personal salary support plus research support staff at technical level, research expenses, capital equipment and a travel allowance for attendance at scientific conferences.
Length of Study: Up to three years.
Frequency: Annual.
Study Establishment: A suitable university department or similar institution.
Country of Study: United Kingdom, but one year may be spent in a recognised second United Kingdom centre, industry or research establishment overseas.
Application Procedure: Applicants must complete a personal application. Forms and further details are available from the MRC.
Closing Date: Please contact the Council for details.
Funding: Government.
No. of awards given last year: 15.
No. of applicants last year: 41.
Additional Information: The fellowship also allows the opportunity to spend a fourth year on a period of focused training in clinical psychology. It is expected that this training will be undertaken in the first or second year of the award and will be incorporated into a research project.

MRC Royal College of Obstetricians and Gynaecologists Training Fellowship
Subjects: Biomedical sciences.
Purpose: To provide members of the Royal College with an opportunity for specialist or further research training in a basic science relevant to obstetrics and gynaecology leading to the submission of a PhD, a DPhil or an MD.
Eligibility: Open to members of the Royal College of Obstetrics and Gynaecology wishing to pursue research at PhD or MD level. Applicants must have a minimum of one year's experience in clinical obstetrics and gynaecology and hold part one membership of the college. Resident requirements apply.
Level of Study: Postgraduate.
Type: Fellowship.
Value: An appropriate clinical academic salary will be provided along with a fixed sum for research expenses and a travel allowance for attendance at scientific conferences.
Length of Study: Up to three years.

Frequency: Annual.
Study Establishment: A suitable university or similar institution.
Country of Study: United Kingdom.
No. of awards offered: One-two per year.
Application Procedure: Applicants must contact the Fellowships Section, Research Career Awards of the MRC for details.
Closing Date: Applicants are advised to check the MRC website for details.
Funding: Government.
No. of awards given last year: Two.
No. of applicants last year: Two.

MRC Royal College of Physicians and Pathologists Training Fellowships
Subjects: Medicine and surgery. This scheme is intended to encourage promising young clinicians who are pursuing clinical training under RCP or RCPath schemes to undertake a period of research training in clinical infection and medical microbiology which involves work in the clinic as well as in the laboratory.
Purpose: To encourage and promote research of direct relevance to surgery and to provide members of these Royal Colleges with an opportunity for specialised or further research training leading to the submission of a PhD, and MPhil or an MD.
Eligibility: Applicants must fulfil the eligibility criteria for the Clinical Research Training Fellowship scheme, preferably having obtained their MRCP or be participating in an approved training programme. The project must also involve research training which crosses the boundary between the clinic and the laboratory. Residence requirements apply.
Level of Study: Postgraduate.
Type: Fellowship.
Value: An appropriate clinical academic salary along with a fixed sum for research expenses and a travel allowance for attendance at scientific conferences.
Length of Study: Up to four years.
Frequency: Annual.
Study Establishment: A suitable university or similar institution.
Country of Study: United Kingdom.
No. of awards offered: Up to two.
Application Procedure: Applicants must contact the Fellowships Section, Research Career Awards of the MRC for details.
Closing Date: Round one is August-September, and round two is January-March, but applicants are advised to check the website for details.
Funding: Government.

MRC Royal College of Surgeons of Edinburgh Training Fellowship
Subjects: Biomedical sciences.
Purpose: To provide an opportunity for specialised or further research training within the United Kingdom leading to the submission of a PhD, DPhil or MD.
Eligibility: Open to members of the Royal College of Surgeons of Edinburgh wishing to pursue research at PhD or MD level. Residence requirements apply.
Level of Study: Postgraduate.
Type: Fellowship.
Value: An appropriate clinical academic salary will be provided along with a fixed sum for research expenses and a travel allowance for attendance at scientific conferences.
Length of Study: Up to three years.
Frequency: Annual.
Study Establishment: A suitable university department or similar institution.
Country of Study: United Kingdom.
No. of awards offered: One-two per year.
Application Procedure: Applicants must submit a personal application. Forms and further details are available from the MRC.
Closing Date: Applicants are advised to check the MRC website for details.
Funding: Government.
No. of awards given last year: Two.

No. of applicants last year: 15.

MRC Royal College of Surgeons of England Training Fellowship

Subjects: Biomedical sciences.

Purpose: To provide an opportunity for specialised or further research training within the United Kingdom leading to the submission of a PhD, DPhil or MD.

Eligibility: Open to members of the Royal College of Surgeons of England wishing to pursue research at PhD or MD level. Residence requirements apply.

Level of Study: Postgraduate.

Type: Fellowship.

Value: An appropriate clinical academic salary will be provided along with a fixed sum for research expenses and a travel allowance for attendance at scientific conferences.

Length of Study: Up to three years.

Frequency: Annual.

Study Establishment: A suitable university department or similar institution.

Country of Study: United Kingdom.

No. of awards offered: Up to two a year.

Application Procedure: Applicants must submit a personal application. Forms and further details are available from the MRC.

Closing Date: Round One is August to September, and round Two is in January to March, but applicants are advised to check the website for details.

Funding: Government.

No. of awards given last year: Two.

No. of applicants last year: 34.

MRC Senior Clinical Fellowship

Subjects: Biomedical sciences.

Purpose: To provide an opportunity for clinical researchers of exceptional ability to concentrate on a period of research.

Eligibility: Open to nationals of any country. Applicants are expected to have proven themselves to be independent researchers, be well qualified for an academic research career and demonstrate the promise of becoming future research leaders. The scheme is open to hospital doctors, dentists, general practitioners, nurses, midwives and members of the Professions Allied to Medicine (PAMS). Applicants must hold a PhD or MD in a basic science or clinical project and have at least three years of postdoctoral research experience.

Level of Study: Postdoctorate, Research.

Type: Fellowship.

Value: Competitive personal salary support is provided plus research support staff at technical level and postdoctoral level, research expenses, capital equipment and a travel allowance for attendance at scientific conferences.

Length of Study: Up to five years, with a possibility of renewal through open competition for a further five years.

Frequency: Annual.

Study Establishment: A suitable university department or similar institution.

Country of Study: United Kingdom.

No. of awards offered: Up to four.

Application Procedure: Applicants must complete a personal application. Forms and further details are available from MRC.

Closing Date: August, but applicants are advised to check the website for details.

Funding: Government.

No. of awards given last year: Four.

No. of applicants last year: 13.

MRC Senior Non-Clinical Fellowship

Subjects: Biomedical sciences.

Purpose: To provide support for non-clinical scientists of exceptional ability to concentrate on a period of research.

Eligibility: Open to nationals of any country. Applicants are expected to have proven themselves to be independent researchers, be well qualified for an academic research career and demonstrate the promise of becoming future research leaders. It is usually expected that all applicants will hold a PhD or DPhil in a basic science project, have at least six years of relevant postdoctoral research experience and not hold a tenured position.

Level of Study: Postdoctorate, Research.

Type: Fellowship.

Value: Competitive personal salary support is provided plus research support staff at technical and postdoctoral level, research expenses, capital equipment and a travel allowance for attendance at scientific conferences.

Length of Study: Up to five years, with a possibility of renewal through open competition for a further five years.

Frequency: Annual.

Study Establishment: A suitable university department or similar institution.

Country of Study: United Kingdom.

No. of awards offered: Up to eight.

Application Procedure: Applicants must complete a personal application. Forms and further details are available from MRC.

Closing Date: October to December, but applicants are advised to check the MRC website for details.

Funding: Government.

No. of awards given last year: Eight.

No. of applicants last year: 51.

MRC Special Training Fellowship in Bioinformatics and Neuroinformatics

Subjects: Biomedical sciences.

Purpose: To provide specialist, multidisciplinary research training at the doctoral or postdoctoral level. Fellows may undertake a Master's degree during the first part of their fellowship, followed by a period of specialist research training.

Eligibility: The scheme is aimed at individuals from a variety of backgrounds such as non biological as well as biological, non clinical as well as clinical, and individuals with PhDs or MDs or with informatics research experience at a predoctoral level.

Level of Study: Postgraduate.

Type: Fellowship.

Value: An appropriate academic salary will be provided along with a fixed sum for research expenses and a travel allowance for attendance at scientific conferences.

Length of Study: Up to four years.

Frequency: Annual.

Study Establishment: A suitable university department or similar institution.

Country of Study: United Kingdom but up to one year may be spent in United Kingdom industry or a second United Kingdom centre.

No. of awards offered: Up to six.

Application Procedure: Applicants must complete a personal application. Forms and further details are available from the MRC.

Closing Date: Applicants are advised to check the website for details.

Funding: Government.

No. of awards given last year: Six.

No. of applicants last year: 13.

Additional Information: Award holders are encouraged to apply for a PhD or MD if they do not already have one.

MRC Special Training Fellowships in Health Services and Health of the Public Research

Subjects: Biomedical sciences in health services research and health of the public. Applications must be within the health services and health of the public remit as defined by the MRC.

Purpose: To provide support for researchers wishing to gain further training in multidisciplinary research to address problems of direct relevance to the health services within the United Kingdom.

Eligibility: The scheme is open to non medical graduates, hospital doctors, dentists, general practitioners, nurses, midwives and members of the Professions Allied to Medicine (PAMS) who are seeking a research career in health services and research.

Level of Study: Postdoctorate.

Type: Fellowship.
Value: An appropriate academic salary will be provided along with a fixed sum for research expenses and a travel allowance for attendance at scientific conferences.
Length of Study: Up to four years.
Frequency: Annual.
Study Establishment: A suitable university department or similar institution.
Country of Study: United Kingdom, but one year may be spent at a recognised research establishment overseas.
No. of awards offered: Up to 15.
Application Procedure: Applicants must complete a personal application. Forms and further details are available from the MRC.
Closing Date: October to November, but applicants are advised to check the MRC website for details.
Funding: Government.
No. of awards given last year: 19.
No. of applicants last year: 59.
Additional Information: Some awards are jointly funded with the Department of Health and NHS regions.

MRC/Academy of Medical Sciences Tenure Track Clinician Scientist Fellowship

Subjects: Biomedical sciences.
Purpose: To allow outstanding clinical researchers to consolidate their research skills and make the transition from postdoctoral research and training to becoming independent investigators, and to support career development and promote recruitment into clinical academic medicine.
Eligibility: Open to hospital doctors, dentists and general practitioners.
Level of Study: Postdoctorate, Research.
Type: Fellowship.
Value: Competitive personal salary support plus research support staff at technical level, research expenses, capital equipment and a travel allowance for attendance at scientific conferences.
Length of Study: Up to five years.
Frequency: Annual.
Study Establishment: A suitable university department or similar institution.
Country of Study: United Kingdom, including one year in a recognised research establishment overseas and a second United Kingdom centre or a year in a United Kingdom industry.
No. of awards offered: One.
Application Procedure: Applicants must submit a personal application. Forms and further details are available from the MRC.
Closing Date: August-December, but applicants are advised to check the website for details.
Funding: Government.
No. of awards given last year: Two.
No. of applicants last year: 14.

MRC/PPARC Research Training Fellowship

Subjects: Biomedical sciences.
Purpose: To provide an opportunity for high calibre non clinical scientists at the early postdoctoral stage to further develop their research skills and experience in the biomedical and public health research within the United Kingdom. The scheme provides the opportunity to spend time in a research establishment overseas or in the United Kingdom.
Eligibility: Residence requirements apply. Applicants would normally be expected to hold a PhD or MPhil in basic science, or expect to receive their doctorate by the time they intend to take up an award. Applicants who hold a research orientated Master's degree and who have more than three years of appropriate postgraduate research experience may exceptionally be considered.
Level of Study: Postdoctorate.
Type: Fellowship.
Value: Competitive personal salary support plus research support staff at technical level, research expenses, capital equipment and a travel allowance for attendance at scientific conferences.
Length of Study: Up to three years.

Frequency: Annual.
Study Establishment: A suitable university department or similar institution.
Country of Study: United Kingdom, but one year may be spent in a recognised second United Kingdom centre, industry or research establishment overseas.
Application Procedure: Applicants must complete a personal application. Forms and further details are available from the MRC.
Closing Date: Please contact the Council for details.
Funding: Government.
No. of applicants last year: None.
Additional Information: The scheme has been specifically designed to allow individuals to make the transition from physical to biomedical science and is aimed at researchers with skills such as imaging, data analysis, optical analysis, informatics and modelling.

MEET THE COMPOSER, INC.

2112 Broadway
Suite 505, New York, NY, 10023, United States of America
Tel: (1) 212 787 3601
Fax: (1) 212 787 3745
Email: mtrevino@meetthecomposer.org
www: http://www.meetthecomposer.org
Contact: Mr Mark D Trevino, Senior Programme Manager

Meet The Composer's mission is to increase artistic and financial opportunities for American composers by fostering the creation, performance, dissemination and appreciation of their music.

Commissioning Music/USA

Subjects: Music commissioning.
Purpose: To support the commissioning of new works by American composers in orchestral, chamber, opera, music theatre, choral, jazz, experimental and avant garde music.
Eligibility: Open to United States citizens only. Organisations that have been producing or presenting for at least three years are eligible and may be opera, theatre and music-theatre companies, festivals, arts presenters, public radio and television stations, Internet providers, soloists and small performing ensembles of all kinds (jazz, chamber, new music etc.).
Level of Study: Unrestricted.
Value: A single organisation may apply for up to US$10,000 and a consortium up to US$30,000.
Frequency: Annual.
Country of Study: United States of America.
Application Procedure: Individuals cannot apply themselves. Host organisations must submit completed application forms and accompanying materials.
Closing Date: January 15th.
Contributor: Offered in partnership with the National Endowment for the Arts.

JP Morgan Chase Fund for Small Ensembles

Subjects: Musical performance.
Purpose: To support small New York based ensembles and music organisations with a commitment to performing work of living composers and contemporary music.
Eligibility: Applicants must write for details.
Level of Study: Predoctorate.
Type: Award.
Value: Varies.
Frequency: Annual.
Country of Study: United States of America.
Application Procedure: Applicants must contact the organisation.
Closing Date: April 30th.
Additional Information: Further information is available on request.

Meet The Composer American Symphony Orchestra League

Subjects: Musical performance.

Purpose: To financially support orchestras.

Eligibility: Open to all league professional and youth member orchestras. The residencies must be scheduled in conjunction with performance(s) of the composer's work. The work(s) may be a world premiere or an existing work by a living American composer. The performance of a world premiere or commissioned work is not a requirement of the programme. Residency weeks may be scheduled contiguously or divided into multiple visits but must be of a one week minimum duration.

Level of Study: Professional development.

Type: Grant.

Value: Grant for composer's fee of up to US$2,500 per residency per week, composer's expenses of up to one round trip for every two week residency and up to US$175 per day for food and lodging, and orchestra expenses of up to US$1,000 per residency week.

Length of Study: Two-eight weeks.

Frequency: Annual.

Country of Study: United States of America.

Application Procedure: Individuals cannot apply themselves. Performing organisations must apply on behalf of the composer.

Closing Date: August 16th.

Additional Information: Further information is available on request.

Meet The Composer Fund

Subjects: Music.

Purpose: To enable composers to participate actively in performances of their work and consequently build audiences for new music. Participation may include performing, conducting, speaking with the audience, presenting workshops, giving interviews and coaching performances.

Eligibility: Open to United States citizens only. Organisations may be choruses, dance, opera, theatre and music theatre companies, symphonies, arts presenters, musical organisations, festivals, television production companies, radio stations and performing ensembles of all kinds (jazz, chamber, new music etc.). Awards are based solely on the overall quality of the application which includes: merit of composer participation, level of audience or community involvement and general strength of the compositions.

Level of Study: Professional development.

Value: Up to US$250 per composer.

Frequency: Four times per year.

Country of Study: United States of America.

Application Procedure: Varies from region to region but individuals cannot apply themselves, as performing organisations apply on behalf of the composer. Interested parties should contact the organisation for further details.

Closing Date: Application deadlines are quarterly: January 2nd, April 1st, June 1st and October 1st.

Additional Information: Further information is available on request.

Music Alive

Subjects: For professional composers to work with teachers, students and their families, nurturing creativity in the classroom while writing works for students to play and sing.

Purpose: To support composer residencies.

Eligibility: Open to all American Symphony Orchestra League and youth member orchestras.

Level of Study: Professional development.

Type: Residency.

Value: A composer's fee of US$2,500 per residency week, composer's expenses of up to one round trip for every two week residency and up to US$175 per day for food and lodging, and orchestra expenses of up to US$1,000 per residency week.

Length of Study: Two-eight week residencies.

Frequency: Annual.

Country of Study: United States of America.

Application Procedure: Individuals cannot apply themselves, as performing organisations apply on behalf of the composer.

Closing Date: August 16th.

Contributor: Offered in partnership with the American Symphony Orchestra League.

Additional Information: Further information is available on request.

MEMORIAL FOUNDATION FOR JEWISH CULTURE

Room 1703
15 East 26th Street, New York, NY, 10010, United States of America
Tel: (1) 212 679 4074
Fax: (1) 212 889 9080
www: http://www.mfjc.org
Contact: Dr Jerry Hochbaum, Executive Vice President

The Memorial Foundation for Jewish Culture was established in 1965 to help assure a creative future for Jewish life throughout the world. The Foundation encourages Jewish scholarship, Jewish cultural creativity, and makes possible the training of professionals to serve in communities deprived of a large Jewish presence.

International Fellowships in Jewish Studies

Subjects: A field of Jewish specialisation which will make a significant contribution to the understanding, preservation, enhancement or transmission of Jewish culture.

Purpose: To allow well qualified individuals to carry out independent scholarly, literary or artistic projects.

Eligibility: Open to recognised or qualified Scholars, researchers or artists of any nationality who possess the knowledge and experience to formulate and implement a project in a field of Jewish specialisation.

Level of Study: Unrestricted.

Type: Fellowship.

Value: Varies, depending on the country in which the project is undertaken, usually US$1,000-4,000.

Length of Study: One academic year, in exceptional cases renewable for a further year.

Frequency: Annual.

Country of Study: Any country.

No. of awards offered: Varies.

Application Procedure: Applicants must write requesting an application.

Closing Date: October 31st.

International Scholarship Programme for Community Service

Subjects: The rabbinate, Jewish education, communal service or religious functionaries, eg. shohatim, mohalim.

Purpose: To assist well qualified individuals for career training.

Eligibility: Open to any individual, regardless of country of origin, who is presently receiving, or plans to undertake training in his or her chosen field in a recognised Yeshiva, teacher training seminary, school of social work, university or other educational institution.

Level of Study: Unrestricted.

Type: Scholarship.

Value: Varies, depending on the country in which the recipient is trained and other considerations, usually US$1,000-4,000.

Length of Study: One year, renewable.

Frequency: Annual.

Study Establishment: Diaspora Jewish communities in need of such personnel.

Country of Study: Any country except the United States of America, Canada or Israel.

No. of awards offered: Varies.

Application Procedure: Applicants must write for details.

Closing Date: November 30th.

Additional Information: Recipients must commit themselves to serve a community of need. They should also be knowledgeable in the language and culture of that country or be prepared to learn it.

Memorial Foundation for Jewish Culture International Doctoral Scholarships

Subjects: Jewish studies.

Purpose: To assist in the training of future Jewish scholars for careers in Jewish scholarship and research, and to enable religious, educational and other Jewish communal workers, to obtain advanced training for leadership positions.

Eligibility: Open to graduate students of any nationality who are specialising in a Jewish field and are officially enrolled or registered in a doctoral programme at a recognised university.

Level of Study: Doctorate.

Type: Scholarship.

Value: Varies, depending on the country where study is undertaken, usually US$2,000-5,000 per year.

Length of Study: One academic year, renewable for a maximum of four years.

Frequency: Annual.

Study Establishment: A recognised university.

Country of Study: Any country.

No. of awards offered: Varies.

Application Procedure: Applicants must write requesting an application.

Closing Date: October 31st.

Scholarships for Post-Rabbinical Students

Subjects: Jewish studies.

Purpose: To assist in the training of future Jewish religious scholars and leaders, and to help newly ordained rabbis obtain advanced training for careers as head of Yeshivot, as Dayanim, and in other leadership positions.

Eligibility: Open to a recently ordained rabbi engaged in full-time studies at a Yeshiva, Kollel or rabbinical seminary.

Level of Study: Unrestricted.

Type: Scholarship.

Value: US$1,000-4,000.

Length of Study: One year.

Frequency: Annual.

Country of Study: Any country.

No. of awards offered: Varies.

Application Procedure: Applicants must write for details.

Closing Date: November 30th.

Additional Information: The following institutional support programme is also available: Grants for Jewish Research and Publication. Grants are awarded to universities and recognised scholarly bodies for research and publication in Jewish fields, and to universities and Jewish educational organisations for the preparation of textbooks and educational literature for children and youth. The Foundation also provides grants to bolster Jewish educational programmes in areas of need. Grants are awarded on the understanding that the recipient institution will assume responsibility for the programme following the initial limited period of Foundation support. Grants are made only for team or collaborative projects.

MENDELSSOHN SCHOLARSHIP FOUNDATION

c/o Royal Academy of Music
Marylebone Road, London, NW1 5HT, England
Contact: Ms Jean Shannon, Honorary Secretary

Mendelssohn Scholarship

Subjects: Musical composition.

Purpose: To enable postgraduate composition students to pursue their study.

Eligibility: Open to music students of any nationality under 30 years of age on the closing date who are resident in the United Kingdom or Republic of Ireland. Eligibility regulations must be strictly observed.

Level of Study: Postgraduate.

Type: Scholarship.

Value: UK £3,000-5,000.

Frequency: Every two years.

Country of Study: Any country.

No. of awards offered: One.

Application Procedure: Applicants must complete an application form and submit this with a photocopy of their birth certificate, registration fee and two compositions.

Closing Date: Usually the first half of March in the scholarship year.

Funding: Private.

No. of awards given last year: One.

No. of applicants last year: 50.

Additional Information: Candidates compete for the scholarship by submitting two compositions plus one tape which are assessed by independent judges. There is a small entrance fee for the competition. All enquiries should be in writing only.

MENINGITIS RESEARCH FOUNDATION

Midland Way, Thornbury, Bristol, BS35 2BS, England
Tel: (44) 1454 281811
Fax: (44) 1454 281094
Email: lindaglennie@meningitis.org
www: http://www.meningitis.org
Contact: Mrs Joy Pepper, Research Administrator

Meningitis Research Foundation is a registered charity that supports an international programme of independently peer reviewed research into prevention, detection and treatment of meningitis and septicaemia. The Foundation also provides information for the public and health professionals, runs medical and scientific meetings and provides support to people affected by the disease.

Meningitis Research Foundation Project Grant

Subjects: Research into meningitis and associated infections that focus on prevention, including vaccine directed research, improving the speed and accuracy of diagnosis, improving treatment and outlook for patients, in particular, development of more effective therapies, epidemiology and disease surveillance, and basic scientific research.

Purpose: To fight death and disability from meningitis and septicaemia by supporting research with the potential to produce results in immediate problem areas. This may include basic research that contributes to understanding their pathophysiology or epidemiology but priority is given to work that is likely to bring clinical or public health benefit.

Eligibility: There are no eligibility restrictions.

Level of Study: Research.

Type: Project grant.

Value: Up to UK £150,000 per year.

Length of Study: Up to five years.

Frequency: Twice a year.

Study Establishment: Universities, research institutes and teaching hospitals.

No. of awards offered: Two.

Application Procedure: Applicants must submit a two or three page outline proposal by email summarising the work planned, the approximate cost and the duration of the project. The Scientific Advisory Panel will then decide whether to request a full application according to whether it conforms to the Foundation's aims and policies, is feasible and original. Researchers who are invited to submit a full application are sent grant application forms which must be completed with reference to the guidance for applicants. Full applications are considered twice a year at Scientific Advisory Panel meetings, scheduled for May and October. All applications are reviewed by external referees whose comments are considered along with the applications when the Panel meets.

Closing Date: February 28th or 31st August.

Funding: Private.

Contributor: Public donations.

No. of awards given last year: 13.

No. of applicants last year: 46.

Meningitis Research Foundation Small Project Grant

Subjects: Research into meningitis and associated infections that focus on prevention, including vaccine directed research, improving the speed and accuracy of diagnosis, improving treatment and outlook for patients, in particular, development of more effective therapies, epidemiology and disease surveillance, and basic scientific research.

Purpose: To fight death and disability from meningitis and septicaemia by supporting research with the potential to produce results in immediate problem areas. This may include basic research that contributes to understanding their pathophysiology or epidemiology but priority is given to work that is likely to bring clinical or public health benefit.

Eligibility: There are no eligibility restrictions.

Level of Study: Research.

Type: Project grant.

Value: Up to UK £30,000 per year.

Length of Study: Up to three years.

Frequency: Twice a year.

Study Establishment: Universities, research institutes and teaching hospitals.

No. of awards offered: Two.

Application Procedure: Applicants should submit a two or three page outline proposal by email summarising the work planned, the approximate cost and the duration of the project. The Scientific Advisory Panel will then decide whether to request a full application according to whether it conforms to the Foundation's aims and policies, is feasible and original. Researchers who are invited to submit a full application are sent grant application forms which must be completed with reference to the guidance for applicants. Full applications are considered twice a year at Scientific Advisory Panel meetings, scheduled for May and October. All applications are reviewed by external referees whose comments are considered along with the applications when the Panel meets.

Closing Date: February 28th or August 31st.

Funding: Private.

Contributor: Public donations.

No. of awards given last year: Six.

No. of applicants last year: Twelve.

MENINGITIS TRUST

Fern House
Bath Road, Stroud, Gloucestershire, GL5 3TJ, England
Tel: (44) 1453 768000
Fax: (44) 1453 768001
Email: support@meningitis-trust.org.uk
Contact: Ms Sarah Booker, Education & Research Co-ordinator

The Meningitis Trust is an internationally respected charity with a strong community focus. It has three main aims which are to provide care and support for people affected by meningitis, to educate both public and professionals and to fund life saving medical research.

Meningitis Trust Research Award

Subjects: Current priorities for research are the development of meningococcal vaccines, surveillance and diagnosis of meningococcal disease, the effectiveness of early treatment, management of after effects, pathogenesis and hospital therapy.

Purpose: To contribute to the funding of research into all strains of meningitis whether bacterial or viral.

Eligibility: Please contact the Trust for eligibility requirements.

Level of Study: Unrestricted.

Type: Research grant.

Value: Up to UK £400,000 per year.

Frequency: Annual.

Application Procedure: Applicants must submit a précis and if accepted they will be required to submit a completed full application.

Closing Date: Please contact the organisation.

Additional Information: As a funding body the Trust contribute monies to research projects. Generally funding is given to postgraduate study but applications from those studying for a doctorate will be considered.

THE MENTAL HEALTH FOUNDATION

20-21 Cornwall Terrace, London, NW1 4QL, England
Tel: (44) 20 7535 7400
Fax: (44) 20 7535 7474
Email: mhf@mhf.org.uk
www: http://www.mentalhealth.org.uk
Contact: Grants Management Officer

The Mental Health Foundation is the leading charity in the United Kingdom working for the needs of people with mental health problems and those with learning disabilities. The Foundation's work includes funding research and community projects, promoting the development of good services and providing easily accessible information to the general public.

Mental Health Foundation Project Grant

Subjects: Mental health and learning disabilities.

Purpose: To allow individuals to undertake community or social projects in the areas of mental health and learning disabilities.

Eligibility: Awards are made under specific advertised programmes.

Level of Study: Unrestricted.

Type: Project grant.

Value: Varies.

Length of Study: Special programmes run for three-five years.

Frequency: Dependent on funds available.

Country of Study: United Kingdom.

No. of awards offered: Varies.

Application Procedure: Applicants must submit an application form and any other documentation deemed a requirement for a specific grant giving round. New grant rounds are advertised in the national press.

Closing Date: Variable, throughout the financial year.

Funding: Commercial.

Additional Information: Current programmes include community projects and clinical research in the field of dementia, older people with learning disabilities and children and young people's mental health. Further information can be found on the website.

Mental Health Foundation Research Grant

Subjects: Mental health and learning disabilities.

Purpose: To further research.

Eligibility: There are no restrictions within the United Kingdom. Awards are made under specific programmes.

Level of Study: Research.

Type: Research grant.

Value: Normally to a maximum of UK £70,000.

Length of Study: Special projects run for three-five years.

Frequency: Dependent on funds available.

Country of Study: United Kingdom.

No. of awards offered: Varies.

Application Procedure: Applicants must submit an application form and any other documentation deemed a requirement for a specific grant giving round. New grant rounds are advertised in the national press.

Closing Date: Variable, throughout the financial year.

Funding: Commercial, Government, Private.

Additional Information: Information on current programmes of work can be obtained from the Foundation's website. Current programmes include community projects and clinical research in the field of dementia, older people with learning disabilities and children and young people's mental health. The majority of funding is allocated in research within themed programmes.

MENZIES CENTRE FOR AUSTRALIAN STUDIES

28 Russell Square, London, WC1B 5DS, England
Tel: (44) 20 7862 8854
Fax: (44) 20 7580 9627
Email: menzies.centre@kcl.ac.uk
www: http://www.kcl.ac.uk/menzies
Contact: Ms Kirsten McIntyre

The Menzies Centre for Australian Studies is located at King's College, University of London. There are six broad areas of activity which form the core of the Centre's operations. These are teaching, postgraduate seminars, public lectures, conferences, research and external lecturing. The Centre also offers scholarship and fellowship programmes.

Australian Bicentennial Scholarships and Fellowships
Subjects: All subjects.
Purpose: To promote scholarship, intellectual links and mutual awareness and understanding between the United Kingdom and Australia. The awards also aim to enable United Kingdom graduates to study in approved courses or undertake approved research in Australia and to enable Australian graduates to study in approved courses or undertake approved research in the United Kingdom.
Eligibility: Open to candidates registered as postgraduate students at a British tertiary institution or eligible for registration at an Australian tertiary institution and usually resident in the United Kingdom. The fellowship is open to holders of a good postgraduate degree or similar who are seeking to further their education or professional experience but not through taking a further degree.
Level of Study: Postdoctorate, Postgraduate, Professional development.
Type: Scholarship and fellowship.
Value: Up to UK £4,000.
Frequency: Annual.
Study Establishment: Any approved Australian Institute of Higher Education for United Kingdom applicants or any approved United Kingdom Institute of Higher Education for Australian applicants.
Country of Study: Australia or the United Kingdom.
No. of awards offered: One-four.
Application Procedure: Applicants must submit a completed application form, three references and a letter of acceptance from the proposed host institution.
Closing Date: June 7th for United Kingdom and October 29th for Australian applicants.
Funding: Private.
Contributor: The Australian Bicentennial Trust.

Northcote Graduate Scholarship
Subjects: All subjects.
Purpose: To enable students to undertake a higher degree at an Australian University.
Eligibility: Open to applicants resident in the United Kingdom who are under 30 years old.
Level of Study: Postgraduate.
Type: Scholarship.
Value: Allowance of australian $17,427 per year plus return economy air fare and payment of compulsory fees.
Length of Study: Up to three years.
Frequency: Annual.
Study Establishment: Any approved Australian tertiary institution.
Country of Study: Australia.
No. of awards offered: Up to two.
Application Procedure: Applicants must submit a completed application form, two references and a letter of acceptance from their chosen Australian university.
Closing Date: August 31st.
Funding: Private.
Contributor: The Northcote Trust.
No. of awards given last year: Two.
No. of applicants last year: 30.

THE METROPOLITAN MUSEUM OF ART

1000 Fifth Avenue, New York, NY, 10028-0198, United States of America
Tel: (1) 212 650 2763
Fax: (1) 212 570 3782
Email: communications@metmuseum.org
www: http://www.metmuseum.org
Contact: Internship Programmes & Education

The Metropolitan Museum of Art is one of the world's largest and finest art museums. Its collections include more than two million works of art spanning 5,000 years of world culture, from prehistory to the present, and from every part of the world. As one of the greatest research institutions in the world, the Metropolitan Museum welcomes the responsibility to train future scholars and museum professionals. The Museum offers opportunities for students at several stages in their academic careers, from high school to the postgraduate level. Internships and apprenticeships can be either paid or unpaid, full or part-time and can last from nine weeks to an academic year.

The Metropolitan Museum of Art Andrew W Mellon Fellowships in Art History
Subjects: History of art.
Purpose: To reward promising young scholars with commendable research projects related to the Museum's collections, as well as distinguished visiting scholars from the United States of America and abroad who can serve as teachers and advisors and make their expertise available to refine and catalogue the collections.
Eligibility: Applicants should have received the doctorate or have completed substantial work towards it. Fellowships for senior Scholars are also available for as short a term as one month.
Level of Study: Postdoctorate.
Type: Fellowship.
Length of Study: Usually one year.
Frequency: Annual.
Study Establishment: The Metropolitan Museum of Art, New York.
Country of Study: United States of America.
No. of awards offered: Varies.
Application Procedure: A typed application in triplicate should include the following: name, home and present address, telephone number, curriculum vitae, details of professional experience, a statement (not to exceed 1,000 words) describing what the applicant expects to accomplish in the Fellowship period and how the Museum's facilities can be utilised to achieve these objectives, a tentative schedule of work to be accomplished, proposed starting and ending dates, and three letters of recommendation (at least one professional and one academic). Master's degree and predoctoral applicants should only send official undergraduate and graduate transcripts (original transcripts plus two copies).
Closing Date: November.
Funding: Private.
Additional Information: Predoctoral Fellows, with the exception of the Theodore Rousseau, will generally be expected to assist the hosting curatorial departments with projects that complement and are incidental to their approved scholarly subject. They will be asked to give a gallery talk during their Fellowship term and be expected to participate in a Fellows' colloquium in the second half of their term, in which they will give a 20 minute presentation on their work-in-progress. Senior Fellows will also be invited to participate in these activities.

The Metropolitan Museum of Art Andrew W Mellon Foundation Fellowships in Conservation
Subjects: Paintings conservation, objects conservation including sculpture, metalwork, glass, ceramics, furniture and archaeological objects, musical instruments, arms and armour, paper conservation including photographs, textile conservation, costume and Asian art.
Eligibility: Applicants to this programme should have reached an advanced level of experience or training.
Level of Study: Postgraduate.
Type: Fellowship.

471

Length of Study: One year.
Frequency: Annual.
Study Establishment: The Metropolitan Museum of Art, New York.
Country of Study: United States of America.
No. of awards offered: A limited number.
Application Procedure: A typed application in triplicate should include the following: name, home and present address, telephone number, curriculum vitae, details of professional experience, a statement (not to exceed 1,000 words) describing what the applicant expects to accomplish in the Fellowship period and how the Museum's facilities can be utilised to achieve these objectives, a tentative schedule of work to be accomplished, proposed starting and ending dates, and three letters of recommendation (at least one professional and one academic). Master's degree and predoctoral applicants should only send official undergraduate and graduate transcripts (original transcripts plus two copies).
Closing Date: January.
Funding: Private.
Contributor: The Andrew W Mellon Foundation.
Additional Information: Shorter-term Fellowships for senior Scholars are also available. All Fellowship recipients will be expected to spend the Fellowship in residence in the department with which they are affiliated. Most applicants for Fellowships need not contact the Conservation department to which they are applying before submission of the application unless it is the Department of Textile or Paper Conservation.

The Metropolitan Museum of Art Annette Kade Art History Fellowship

Subjects: Fine art.
Purpose: To allow foreign students to study in the United States, who would not otherwise be able to do so.
Eligibility: Open to predoctoral art history students.
Level of Study: Predoctorate.
Type: Fellowship.
Length of Study: One year.
Frequency: Annual.
Study Establishment: The Metropolitan Museum of Art, New York.
Country of Study: United States of America.
No. of awards offered: One.
Application Procedure: A typed application in triplicate should include the following: name, home and present address, telephone number, curriculum vitae, details of professional experience, a statement (not to exceed 1,000 words) describing what the applicant expects to accomplish in the Fellowship period and how the Museum's facilities can be utilised to achieve these objectives, a tentative schedule of work to be accomplished, proposed starting and ending dates, and three letters of recommendation (at least one professional and one academic). Master's degree and predoctoral applicants should only send official undergraduate and graduate transcripts (original transcripts plus two copies).
Closing Date: November.
Funding: Private.
Contributor: Annette Kade.
Additional Information: Predoctoral Fellows, with the exception of the Theodore Rousseau, will generally be expected to assist the hosting curatorial departments with projects that complement and are incidental to their approved scholarly subject. They will be asked to give a gallery talk during their Fellowship term and be expected to participate in a Fellows' colloquium in the second half of their term, in which they will give a 20 minute presentation on their work-in-progress. Senior Fellows will also be invited to participate in these activities.

The Metropolitan Museum of Art Bothmer Fellowship

Subjects: Greek or Roman art.
Purpose: To reward an outstanding student.
Eligibility: Applicants must have been admitted to a doctoral programme of a university in the United States of America and have submitted an outline of their thesis. Preference will be given to the applicant who, in the opinion of the Grants Committee, will profit most from utilising the resources of the Department of Greek and Roman Art, its collections, library, photographic and other archives and the guidance of its curatorial staff. Fellowships generally cannot be given for projects involving exhibitions to be organised and installed during the fellowship period.
Level of Study: Postdoctorate, Postgraduate.
Type: Fellowship.
Length of Study: One year.
Frequency: Annual.
Study Establishment: The Metropolitan Museum of Art, New York.
Country of Study: United States of America.
No. of awards offered: One.
Application Procedure: A typed application in triplicate should include the following: name, home and present address, telephone number, curriculum vitae, details of professional experience, a statement (not to exceed 1,000 words) describing what the applicant expects to accomplish in the Fellowship period and how the Museum's facilities can be utilised to achieve these objectives, a tentative schedule of work to be accomplished, proposed starting and ending dates, and three letters of recommendation (at least one professional and one academic). Master's degree and predoctoral applicants should only send official undergraduate and graduate transcripts (original transcripts plus two copies).
Closing Date: November.
Additional Information: Predoctoral Fellows, with the exception of the Theodore Rousseau, will generally be expected to assist the hosting curatorial departments with projects that complement and are incidental to their approved scholarly subject. They will be asked to give a gallery talk during their Fellowship term and be expected to participate in a Fellows' colloquium in the second half of their term, in which they will give a 20 minute presentation on their work-in-progress. Senior Fellows will also be invited to participate in these activities.

The Metropolitan Museum of Art Chester Dale Fellowships

Subjects: Fine Arts of the Western World.
Purpose: To recognise those whose fields of study are related to the fine arts of the Western world.
Eligibility: Open to United States of America citizens who are under the age of 40 years.
Level of Study: Postgraduate.
Type: Fellowship.
Length of Study: Three months to one year.
Frequency: Annual.
Study Establishment: The Metropolitan Museum of Art, New York.
Country of Study: United States of America.
No. of awards offered: Varies.
Application Procedure: A typed application in triplicate should include the following: name, home and present address, telephone number, curriculum vitae, details of professional experience, a statement (not to exceed 1,000 words) describing what the applicant expects to accomplish in the Fellowship period and how the Museum's facilities can be utilised to achieve these objectives, a tentative schedule of work to be accomplished, proposed starting and ending dates, and three letters of recommendation (at least one professional and one academic). Master's degree and predoctoral applicants should only send official undergraduate and graduate transcripts (original transcripts plus two copies).
Closing Date: November.
Funding: Private.
Additional Information: Predoctoral Fellows, with the exception of the Theodore Rousseau, will generally be expected to assist the hosting curatorial departments with projects that complement and are incidental to their approved scholarly subject. They will be asked to give a gallery talk during their Fellowship term and be expected to participate in a Fellows' colloquium in the second half of their term, in which they will give a 20 minute presentation on their work-in-progress. Senior Fellows will also be invited to participate in these activities.

The Metropolitan Museum of Art Douglass Foundation Fellowship in American Art

Subjects: American art.
Eligibility: Open to graduate students who have been enrolled in an advanced degree programme in the field of American art or culture for at least one year.
Level of Study: Postgraduate.
Type: Fellowship.
Length of Study: One year.
Frequency: Annual.
Application Procedure: A typed application in triplicate should include the following: name, home and present address, telephone number, curriculum vitae, details of professional experience, a statement (not to exceed 1,000 words) describing what the applicant expects to accomplish in the Fellowship period and how the Museum's facilities can be utilised to achieve these objectives, a tentative schedule of work to be accomplished, proposed starting and ending dates, and three letters of recommendation (at least one professional and one academic). Master's degree and predoctoral applicants should only send official undergraduate and graduate transcripts (original transcripts plus two copies).

The Metropolitan Museum of Art J Clawson Mills Scholarships

Subjects: Fine arts.
Purpose: To enable one year's study or research at the Museum in any branch of the fine arts.
Eligibility: Open to mature Scholars of demonstrated ability.
Level of Study: Postdoctorate.
Type: Scholarship.
Length of Study: One year, with the possibility of renewal for a further year.
Frequency: Annual.
Study Establishment: The Metropolitan Museum of Art, New York.
Country of Study: United States of America.
No. of awards offered: Varies.
Application Procedure: A typed application in triplicate should include the following: name, home and present address, telephone number, curriculum vitae, details of professional experience, a statement (not to exceed 1,000 words) describing what the applicant expects to accomplish in the Fellowship period and how the Museum's facilities can be utilised to achieve these objectives, a tentative schedule of work to be accomplished, proposed starting and ending dates, and three letters of recommendation (at least one professional and one academic). Master's degree and predoctoral applicants should only send official undergraduate and graduate transcripts (original transcripts plus two copies).
Closing Date: November.
Funding: Private.
Contributor: J Clawson Mills.
Additional Information: Predoctoral Fellows, with the exception of the Theodore Rousseau, will generally be expected to assist the hosting curatorial departments with projects that complement and are incidental to their approved scholarly subject. They will be asked to give a gallery talk during their Fellowship term and be expected to participate in a Fellows' colloquium in the second half of their term, in which they will give a 20 minute presentation on their work-in-progress. Senior Fellows will also be invited to participate in these activities.

The Metropolitan Museum of Art Jane and Morgan Whitney Art History Fellowships

Subjects: Fine art.
Purpose: To recognise study, work or research to students of the fine arts whose fields are related to the Museum's collections.
Eligibility: Preference is given to students in the decorative arts who are under 40 years of age.
Level of Study: Postdoctorate.
Type: Fellowship.
Length of Study: One year. The fellowship carries the possibility of renewal for one additional year.
Frequency: Annual.
Study Establishment: The Metropolitan Museum of Art, New York.
Country of Study: United States of America.
No. of awards offered: Varies.
Application Procedure: A typed application in triplicate should include the following: name, home and present address, telephone number, curriculum vitae, details of professional experience, a statement (not to exceed 1,000 words) describing what the applicant expects to accomplish in the Fellowship period and how the Museum's facilities can be utilised to achieve these objectives, a tentative schedule of work to be accomplished, proposed starting and ending dates, and three letters of recommendation (at least one professional and one academic). Master's degree and predoctoral applicants should only send official undergraduate and graduate transcripts (original transcripts plus two copies).
Closing Date: November.
Funding: Private.
Contributor: Jane and Morgan Whitney.
Additional Information: Predoctoral Fellows, with the exception of the Theodore Rousseau, will generally be expected to assist the hosting curatorial departments with projects that complement and are incidental to their approved scholarly subject. They will be asked to give a gallery talk during their Fellowship term and be expected to participate in a Fellows' colloquium in the second half of their term, in which they will give a 20 minute presentation on their work-in-progress. Senior Fellows will also be invited to participate in these activities.

The Metropolitan Museum of Art L W Frohlich Charitable Trust

Subjects: Objects conservation.
Purpose: To encourage conservators, art historians or scientists who are at an advanced level in their training.
Eligibility: Applicants to this programme should be employed as conservators, art historians or scientists, and have reached an advanced level of training or experience.
Level of Study: Postgraduate.
Type: Fellowship.
Length of Study: Two years.
Frequency: Annual.
Study Establishment: The Metropolitan Museum of Art, New York.
Country of Study: United Kingdom.
No. of awards offered: One.
Application Procedure: A typed application in triplicate should include the following: name, home and present address, telephone number, curriculum vitae, details of professional experience, a statement (not to exceed 1,000 words) describing what the applicant expects to accomplish in the fellowship period and how the Museum's facilities can be utilised to achieve these objectives, a tentative schedule of work to be accomplished during the fellowship period and proposed starting and ending dates, and three letters of recommendation (at least one professional and one academic). Master's degree and Predoctoral applicants should only send official undergraduate and graduate transcripts (original transcripts plus two copies).
Funding: Private.
Contributor: The L W Frohlich Charitable Trust.

The Metropolitan Museum of Art Leo and Julia Forchheimer Fellowship

Subjects: Textiles.
Purpose: To enable study and research at the Antonio Ratti Textile Center on any aspect of the Museum's textile collections.
Eligibility: Open to graduate students or mature Scholars of demonstrated ability.
Level of Study: Postdoctorate.
Type: Fellowship.
Length of Study: Three-six months.
Frequency: Annual.
Study Establishment: The Antonio Ratti Textile Center.
Country of Study: United States of America.
No. of awards offered: Varies.

Application Procedure: A typed application in triplicate should include the following: name, home and present address, telephone number, curriculum vitae, details of professional experience, a statement (not to exceed 1,000 words) describing what the applicant expects to accomplish in the Fellowship period and how the Museum's facilities can be utilised to achieve these objectives, a tentative schedule of work to be accomplished, proposed starting and ending dates, and three letters of recommendation (at least one professional and one academic). Master's degree and predoctoral applicants should only send official undergraduate and graduate transcripts (original transcripts plus two copies).

Closing Date: November.

Funding: Private.

Contributor: Leo and Julia Forchheimer.

Additional Information: Predoctoral Fellows, with the exception of the Theodore Rousseau, will generally be expected to assist the hosting curatorial departments with projects that complement and are incidental to their approved scholarly subject. They will be asked to give a gallery talk during their Fellowship term and be expected to participate in a Fellows' colloquium in the second half of their term, in which they will give a 20 minute presentation on their work-in-progress. Senior Fellows will also be invited to participate in these activities.

The Metropolitan Museum of Art Polaire Weissman Fund

Subjects: Fine arts, costume history and conservation.

Purpose: To recognise students who are interested in pursuing costume history in a museum or teaching career related to the field of costume.

Eligibility: Open to qualified graduate students.

Level of Study: Postdoctorate.

Type: Fellowship.

Length of Study: Generally nine months.

Frequency: Annual.

Study Establishment: The Metropolitan Museum of Art, New York.

Country of Study: United States of America.

No. of awards offered: Varies.

Application Procedure: A typed application in triplicate should include the following: name, home and present address, telephone number, curriculum vitae, details of professional experience, a statement (not to exceed 1,000 words) describing what the applicant expects to accomplish in the Fellowship period and how the Museum's facilities can be utilised to achieve these objectives, a tentative schedule of work to be accomplished, proposed starting and ending dates, and three letters of recommendation (at least one professional and one academic). Master's degree and predoctoral applicants should only send official undergraduate and graduate transcripts (original transcripts plus two copies).

Closing Date: November.

Funding: Private.

Contributor: The Polaire Weissman Fund.

Additional Information: Predoctoral Fellows, with the exception of the Theodore Rousseau, will generally be expected to assist the hosting curatorial departments with projects that complement and are incidental to their approved scholarly subject. They will be asked to give a gallery talk during their Fellowship term and be expected to participate in a Fellows' colloquium in the second half of their term, in which they will give a 20 minute presentation on their work-in-progress. Senior Fellows will also be invited to participate in these activities.

The Metropolitan Museum of Art Sherman Fairchild Foundation

Subjects: Paintings conservation, objects conservation including sculpture, metalwork, glass, ceramics, furniture, and archaeological objects, musical instruments, arms and armour, paper conservation including photographs, textile conservation, costume and Asian art conservation.

Purpose: To support qualified candidates from the United States of America and abroad who have already reached an advanced level of training or experience.

Eligibility: Applicants to this programme should have reached an advanced level of experience or training.

Level of Study: Postgraduate.

Type: Fellowship.

Length of Study: One year.

Frequency: Annual.

Study Establishment: The Metropolitan Museum of Art, New York.

Country of Study: United States of America.

No. of awards offered: Varies.

Application Procedure: A typed application in triplicate should include the following: name, home and present address, telephone number, curriculum vitae, details of professional experience, a statement (not to exceed 1,000 words) describing what the applicant expects to accomplish in the Fellowship period and how the Museum's facilities can be utilised to achieve these objectives, a tentative schedule of work to be accomplished, proposed starting and ending dates, and three letters of recommendation (at least one professional and one academic). Master's degree and predoctoral applicants should only send official undergraduate and graduate transcripts (original transcripts plus two copies).

Funding: Private.

Contributor: The Sherman Fairchild Foundation.

The Metropolitan Museum of Art Theodore Rousseau Art History Fellowships

Subjects: Fine art.

Purpose: To develop the skills of connoisseurship by supporting first hand examination of paintings in major European collections, rather than by supporting library research. The fellowship is awarded to those whose goal it is to enter museums as curators of painting.

Eligibility: Applicants should have been enrolled for at least one year in an advanced degree programme in the field of art history.

Level of Study: Postgraduate, Predoctorate.

Type: Fellowship.

Length of Study: One year.

Frequency: Annual.

Country of Study: Any country.

No. of awards offered: Varies.

Application Procedure: A typed application in triplicate should include the following: name, home and present address, telephone number, curriculum vitae, details of professional experience, a statement (not to exceed 1,000 words) describing what the applicant expects to accomplish in the Fellowship period and how the Museum's facilities can be utilised to achieve these objectives, a tentative schedule of work to be accomplished, proposed starting and ending dates, and three letters of recommendation (at least one professional and one academic). Master's degree and predoctoral applicants should only send official undergraduate and graduate transcripts (original transcripts plus two copies).

Closing Date: November.

Funding: Private.

Contributor: Theodore Rousseau.

MMA Polaire Weissman Fund Fellowship in Conservation

Subjects: Costume history.

Purpose: To encourage those who are interested in pursuing costume history in a museum or teaching career, or other career related to the field of costume.

Eligibility: Applicants to this programme should have reached an advanced level of experience or training.

Level of Study: Postgraduate.

Type: Fellowship.

Length of Study: Varies.

Frequency: Annual.

Study Establishment: The Costume Institute at the Metropolitan Museum of Art.

Country of Study: United States of America.

No. of awards offered: Varies.

Application Procedure: A typed application in triplicate should include the following: name, home and present address, telephone number, curriculum vitae, details of professional experience, a statement (not to exceed 1,000 words) describing what the applicant expects to accomplish in the Fellowship period and how the Museum's facilities can be utilised to achieve these objectives, a tentative schedule of work to be accomplished, proposed starting and ending dates, and three letters of recommendation (at least one professional and one academic). Master's degree and predoctoral applicants should only send official undergraduate and graduate transcripts (original transcripts plus two copies).

Closing Date: January.
Funding: Private.
Contributor: The Polaire Weissman Fund.

MICHIGAN SOCIETY OF FELLOWS

University of Michigan
3030 Rackham Building
915 E Washington Street, Ann Arbor, MI, 48109-1070, United States of America
Tel: (1) 734 763 1259
Email: society.of.fellows@umich.edu
www: http://www.rackham.umich.edu/Faculty/society.html

The Michigan Society of Fellows, founded in 1970, promotes academic and creative excellence in the humanities and the arts, the social, physical and life sciences and the professions. The objective of the Society is to provide financial and intellectual support for individuals selected for outstanding achievement, professional promise and interdisciplinary interests.

Michigan Society of Fellows Postdoctoral Fellowships

Subjects: All subjects offered by the University of Michigan.
Purpose: To provide financial and intellectual support for individuals selected for outstanding achievement, professional promise and interdisciplinary interests.
Eligibility: Applicants must be near the beginning of their professional careers and have completed the PhD or comparable professional or artistic degree three years prior to application.
Level of Study: Postdoctorate.
Type: Fellowship.
Value: Stipend of US$42,000 per year.
Length of Study: Three years.
Frequency: Annual.
Study Establishment: The University of Michigan.
Country of Study: United States of America.
No. of awards offered: Four.
Application Procedure: Applicants must complete an application form available from the website.
Closing Date: Postmarked the first Friday in October.
Funding: Private.
Contributor: The University of Michigan.
No. of awards given last year: Four.
No. of applicants last year: 322.

MIGRAINE TRUST

45 Great Ormond Street, London, WC1N 3HZ, England
Tel: (44) 20 7831 4818
Fax: (44) 20 7831 5174
Email: research@migrainetrust.org
www: http://www.migrainetrust.org
Contact: Ms Tamars Khan, Research Officer

Established in 1965, the Migraine Trust is a research charity. The Trust aims to fund and promote research into migraine, improve the diagnosis and treatment of migraine, and provide information and advice on managing migraine.

Migraine Trust Grants

Subjects: All aspects of migraine and associated headaches.
Purpose: To fund research into migraine and other headaches.
Eligibility: Grants are awarded on merit and not according to predetermined criteria.
Level of Study: Doctorate, Postdoctorate, Postgraduate.
Type: Research grant, fellowship and studentship.
Value: Varies.
Length of Study: Up to three years.
Frequency: Annual.
Study Establishment: Approved universities or research institutions.
Country of Study: Unrestricted except for the Studentships which must be United Kingdom only.
No. of awards offered: Varies.
Application Procedure: Applicants must write for a project, fellowship, studentship or grant application form and research grant conditions in the first instance. Studentship applications must be made by the host institution and not directly by the student.
Closing Date: March 31st.
Funding: Private.
Contributor: Migraine sufferers.
No. of awards given last year: One.
No. of applicants last year: Three.

THE MILLAY COLONY FOR THE ARTS, INC. (MCA)

East Hill Road
PO Box 3, Austerlitz, NY, 12017-0003, United States of America
Tel: (1) 518 392 3103
Email: application@millaycolony.org
www: http://www.millaycolony.org
Contact: Ms Martha Hodewell, Executive Director

The Millay Colony for the Arts, Inc. (MCA) provides fully funded one month residencies to writers, visual artists and composers at Steepletop, the national historic landmark home of poet Edna St Vincent Millay.

MCA Residencies

Subjects: Visual arts, musical composition and creative writing.
Eligibility: Open to visual artists, composers and writers.
Level of Study: Unrestricted.
Type: Residency.
Value: Room, board and studio space for one month. The Millay Colony does not provide financial assistance of any kind.
Length of Study: One month.
Frequency: Monthly from April to November.
Study Establishment: Steepletop, the former home of Edna St Vincent Millay.
Country of Study: United States of America.
No. of awards offered: 48 residencies per year.
Application Procedure: Applicants must complete an application form, available on request when a stamped addressed envelope is provided or via email.
Closing Date: November 1st.
Funding: Government, Private.
No. of awards given last year: 48-50.
No. of applicants last year: 600.
Additional Information: Applications are reviewed by selection committees comprised of professional artists. Applicants are invited to the Colony strictly on the basis of artistic merit.

MINISTRY OF EDUCATION, SCIENCE AND CULTURE (ICELAND)

Sölvhólsgata 4, Reykjavik, IS-150, Iceland
Tel: (354) 560 9500
Fax: (354) 562 3068
Email: postur@mrn.stjr.is
www: http://www.menntamalaraduneyti.is
Contact: Mrs Pórunn Bragadóttir, Division for Higher Education, Science & Research

Scholarships in Icelandic Studies

Subjects: Icelandic language, literature and history.
Level of Study: Unrestricted.
Type: Scholarship.
Value: Krona 490,000 plus tuition.
Length of Study: Eight months.
Frequency: Annual.
Study Establishment: The University of Iceland, Reykjavik.
Country of Study: Iceland.
No. of awards offered: 25.
Application Procedure: The Ministry decides each year in which countries these scholarships are to be made available and requests that the Ministry of Education in each of the recipient countries select a candidate for the award. Applicants must therefore apply to the relevant government department in their own country. United States candidates should apply to the Institute of International Education. United Kingdom candidates should apply to the Icelandic Embassy. Candidates of Icelandic origin from Canada or the United States should apply to the Icelandic National League.
Closing Date: Nomination of candidates must reach the Ministry of Culture and Education, Iceland, before May 15th.
Funding: Government.
No. of awards given last year: 25.

For further information contact:

Icelandic National League
103-94 1st Avenue
Gimli, Manitoba, MB, R0C 1B1, Canada
Email: inl@ecn.mb.ca

Icelandic Embassy
2A Hans Street, London, SW1X 0JE, England
Email: icemb.london@utn.stjr.is
www: http://www.iceland.org/uk

Institute of International Education
809 United States Plaza, New York, NY, 10017-3580, United States of America

MINISTRY OF FOREIGN AFFAIRS (ITALY)

Italian Cultural Institute
39 Belgrave Square, London, SW1X 8NX, England
Tel: (44) 20 7235 1461
Fax: (44) 20 7235 4618
Email: ici@italcultura.org.uk
www: http://www.italcultur.org.uk
Contact: Ms Lina Panetta, Cultural & Education Officer

The Italian Cultural Institute is the official Italian government agency for the promotion of cultural exchanges between Great Britain and Italy. The Institute promotes collaboration between universities, academies and learned societies in the two countries and assists in the organisation of major Italian cultural events in Britain.

Italian Government Scholarships

Subjects: Any subject connected with Italian culture.
Purpose: To further cultural exchanges, in the frame of the cultural agreement between Italy and the United Kingdom.

Eligibility: Open to British nationals who are university students with good academic records, researchers, or musicians. Applicants must be artists under 38 years of age.
Level of Study: Doctorate, Postgraduate, Professional development, Research.
Type: Scholarship.
Value: €619,75 per month.
Length of Study: Two-three months between June and October for short-term, or four-eight months starting in November for long-term.
Frequency: Annual.
Study Establishment: Italian universities, institutions or research centres.
Country of Study: Italy.
No. of awards offered: Dependent on funds available.
Application Procedure: Applicants must complete an application form.
Closing Date: End of February.
Funding: Government.
No. of awards given last year: Five.
No. of applicants last year: Eight.
Additional Information: Further information is available on request.

MINNESOTA HISTORICAL SOCIETY (MHS)

345 Kellogg Boulevard West, St Paul, MN, 55102, United States of America
Tel: (1) 651 297 4464
Fax: (1) 651 297 1345
Email: debbie.miller@mnhs.org
www: http://www.mnhs.org
Contact: Ms Deborah L Miller, Research Supervisor

The Minnesota Historical Society (MHS) is a private, non-profit educational and cultural institution established in 1849 to preserve and share Minnesota history. The Society collects, preserves and tells the story of Minnesota's past through interactive and engaging museum exhibits, extensive libraries and collections, 23 historic sites, and educational programmes and book publishing.

Minnesota Historical Society Research Grant

Subjects: The history of Minnesota and its region, which includes the bordering Canadian provinces as well as the American Midwest.
Purpose: To support original research and interpretative writing on the history of Minnesota by academics, independent Scholars and professional or non professional writers.
Eligibility: Open to applicants of any nationality with English reading and writing ability.
Level of Study: Unrestricted.
Type: Research support.
Value: Varies. Up to US$1,500 for research that will result in an article, up to US$5,000 for research that will result in a book, up to US$500 for mini grants, or up to US$1,000 for visiting Scholar grants.
Length of Study: Varies.
Frequency: Annual.
Country of Study: Any country.
No. of awards offered: Varies.
Application Procedure: Applicants must complete an application form. Other documentation is also required. Guidelines and applications are available by writing to the given address, by sending an email message to Ms Miller or from the website.
Closing Date: April 1st and October 1st.
Funding: Government.
Contributor: The state of Minnesota.
No. of awards given last year: 22.
No. of applicants last year: 45.

MINTEK

Human Resources Division
Private Bag X3015, Randburg, 2125, South Africa
Tel: (27) 11 709 4648
Fax: (27) 11 709 4465
Email: bobt@mintek.co.za
www: http://www.mintek.co.za
Contact: Mr Bob Tait, Head of Academic Support

Mintek is the partially state funded South African metallurgical research organisation. Its mission is to serve the national interest through high calibre research, development and technology transfer that promotes mineral technology, and fosters the establishment of small, medium and large industries in the field of minerals and products derived from them.

Mintek Bursaries
Subjects: Chemical engineering, electrical engineering, light current and electronics, metallurgical engineering, chemistry, with the emphasis on inorganic, physical or analytical chemistry, metallurgy, extraction and physical, mineralogy, geology or physics.
Purpose: To promote the training of research workers for the minerals industry in general and to meet its own needs for technically trained people.
Eligibility: Open to graduates of any nationality who possess an appropriate four year degree or higher qualification. A knowledge of English is essential. Preference is given to South African citizens. Merit and excellence are the criteria for selection. The project should be a promising development that will contribute to Mintek's activities and is in line with its strategic purpose, the student must have a strong academic background and show the potential to develop expertise that would benefit Mintek and the institution where the project is carried out should be a centre of excellence in the subject.
Level of Study: Postgraduate.
Type: Bursary.
Value: Rand 32,400 per year for a MSc degree and rand 40,200 per year for a PhD degree.
Length of Study: Up to two years. Extension of this period can be granted by the President of Mintek.
Frequency: Annual.
Study Establishment: Any South African university or technikons in fields that complement its own activities.
Country of Study: South Africa.
No. of awards offered: 10-15.
Application Procedure: Applicants must write for details.
Closing Date: No deadline.
Funding: Government.
No. of awards given last year: 17.
Additional Information: Candidates are requested to sign a contract before starting their project. Usually Mintek insists on a service commitment from the bursar on completion of his or her studies on a year-for-year basis. Bursars are paid a monthly bursary-salary and Mintek pays the institution an amount to cover the project's running costs.

MIRIAM LICETTE SCHOLARSHIP

16 Ogle Street, London, W1W 6JA, England
Tel: (44) 20 7636 4481
Fax: (44) 20 7637 4307
Email: education@mbf.org.uk
www: http://www.mbf.org.uk
Contact: Mrs Susan Dolton

Miriam Licette Scholarship
Subjects: Musical performance and song.
Purpose: To assist a female student of French song.
Eligibility: Open to soprano, mezzo soprano or contralto singers for advanced study in France. Applicants should be under 30 years of age and British or have been resident in the United Kingdom for three years. Applicants' mother tongue must not be French.
Level of Study: Postgraduate, Professional development.
Type: Scholarship.
Value: UK £5,000.
Frequency: Annual.
Country of Study: France.
No. of awards offered: One.
Application Procedure: Selected students will be asked to audition. An application form must be completed and two references provided.
Closing Date: December 1st.
Funding: Private.
No. of awards given last year: One.
No. of applicants last year: 20.

MIZUTANI FOUNDATION FOR GLYCOSCIENCE

Sen-I Kaikan Suite 5F
3-1-11 Nihonbashi-honcho
Chuo-ku, Tokyo, 103-0023, Japan
Tel: (81) 3 3246 0224
Fax: (81) 3 3246 1265
Email: info@mizutanifdn.or.jp
www: http://www.mizutanifdn.or.jp
Contact: Keiichi Yoshida, Executive Secretary

The Mizutani Foundation for Glycoscience undertakes major programmes such as the worldwide distribution of research grants to qualified glycoscientists for their outstanding basic research, assistance of international exchanges between Japanese and foreign glycosciences, contributions to glycoscience related meetings in Japan and practice of other activities that are necessary to achieve the aim of the Foundation.

Mizutani Foundation for Glycoscience Research Grants
Subjects: Glycoscience.
Purpose: To contribute to human welfare through the enhancement of glycoscience by awarding grants for creative research into glycoscience conducted by domestic and overseas researchers, and awarding grants for international exchanges and for convening conferences in the field of glycoscience.
Eligibility: Open to those with a doctorate (corresponding to PhD or MD in the United States of America) in a field relevant to the proposed project who have documented capability of performing independent studies and are a member of a scientific institution where he or she can carry out the proposed study. An applicant who has been awarded the grant previously may re-apply after five years.
Level of Study: Postgraduate.
Type: Research grant.
Value: Yen 3,000,000-10,000,000.
Length of Study: One year.
Frequency: Annual.
Country of Study: Any country.
No. of awards offered: 10-15.
Application Procedure: Applicants must download an application form from the website and the complete application package should be sent to the Foundation.
Closing Date: July 1st-September 1st.
Contributor: The Seikagaku Corporation.
No. of awards given last year: 14.
No. of applicants last year: 100.
Additional Information: Further information is available on request.

MMA HEALTHSERVE

First Floor
106-110 Watney Street, London, E1W 2QE, England
Tel: (44) 20 7790 1336
Fax: (44) 20 7790 1384
Email: grants@healthserve.org.uk
www: http://www.healthserve.org.uk
Contact: Dr Peter Arton, Medical Director

The MMA HealthServe is developing a health resource centre to promote Christian medical mission. Other support includes elective days, a refresher course, overseas update publications and grants.

Medical Missionary Association Grants

Subjects: Medical mission, church related or Christian healthcare.
Purpose: To assist doctors and nurses and other paramedicals who have served at least one tour in a mission or church related medical post in the developing world, to gain a postgraduate qualification.
Eligibility: Open to committed Christians (United Kingdom based) who have spent at least one tour working in a mission or church related medical post and who will be going back to continue this work for at least one further tour of three years.
Level of Study: Postgraduate.
Type: Grant.
Value: Up to UK £750.
Frequency: Varies.
Country of Study: United Kingdom or developing world countries.
Application Procedure: Applicants must complete an application form available on written request.
Closing Date: At least six months before the course is due to start.
Funding: Private.
No. of awards given last year: Three.
No. of applicants last year: Three.
Additional Information: Each request is discussed on its own merit.

MODERN LANGUAGE ASSOCIATION OF AMERICA (MLA)

26 Broadway 3rd Floor, New York, NY, 10004-1789, United States of America
Tel: (1) 646 576 5141
Fax: (1) 646 458 0030
Email: awards@mla.org
www: http://www.mla.org
Contact: Ms Alicia Walker, Co-ordinator, MLA Book Prizes

The Modern Language Association of America (MLA) is a non-profit membership organisation that promotes the study and teaching of language and literature in English and foreign languages.

Aldo and Jean Scaglione Prize for a Translation of a Literary Work

Subjects: Translation.
Purpose: For an outstanding translation into English of a book length literary work.
Eligibility: Open to translations published in the year preceding the year in which the award is given.
Type: Prize.
Value: US$2,000.
Frequency: Every two years (even-numbered years).
No. of awards offered: One.
Application Procedure: Applicants must send four copies. For detailed information about specific prizes, applicants should contact the MLA.
Closing Date: April 1st.

Aldo and Jeanne Scaglione Prize for Comparative Literary Studies

Subjects: Comparative literary and cultural studies involving at least two literatures.
Purpose: To recognise outstanding scholarly work.
Eligibility: Open to books published in the year before the award is given. Authors must be members of the MLA.
Level of Study: Postdoctorate.
Type: Prize.
Value: US$2,000.
Frequency: Annual.
No. of awards offered: One.
Application Procedure: Applicants must send four copies of the work. For detailed information about specific prizes, applicants should contact the MLA.
Closing Date: May 1st.

Aldo and Jeanne Scaglione Prize for French and Francophone Literary Studies

Subjects: French and Francophone linguistic or literary studies.
Purpose: To recognise outstanding scholarly work.
Eligibility: Open to books published in the year before the prize is given. Authors must be members of the MLA.
Level of Study: Postdoctorate.
Type: Prize.
Value: US$2,000.
Frequency: Annual.
No. of awards offered: One.
Application Procedure: Applicants must send four copies of the work. For detailed information about specific prizes, applicants should contact the MLA.
Closing Date: May 1st.
Funding: Private.

Aldo and Jeanne Scaglione Prize for Italian Studies

Subjects: Italian literature and culture.
Eligibility: Open to books published in the year before the award is to be given. Authors must be members of the MLA.
Level of Study: Postdoctorate.
Type: Prize.
Value: US$2,000.
Frequency: Odd numbered years.
No. of awards offered: One.
Application Procedure: Applicants must send four copies of the work. For detailed information about specific prizes, applicants should contact the MLA.
Closing Date: May 1st.
Funding: Private.

Aldo and Jeanne Scaglione Prize for Studies in Germanic Languages and Literatures

Subjects: The linguistics or literatures of any of the Germanic languages including Danish, Dutch, German, Norwegian, Swedish or Yiddish.
Purpose: To recognise an outstanding scholarly work.
Eligibility: Authors must be members of the MLA.
Level of Study: Postdoctorate.
Type: Prize.
Value: US$2,000.
Frequency: Every two years (even-numbered years).
No. of awards offered: One.
Application Procedure: Applicants must send four copies of the work. For detailed information about specific prizes, applicants should contact the MLA.
Closing Date: May 1st.

Aldo and Jeanne Scaglione Prize for Studies in Slavic Languages and Literatures

Subjects: Linguistic or literary study of a work in a Slavic language.
Purpose: To recognise an outstanding scholarly work.

Eligibility: Open to books published in the year or two before the prize is given. Authors need not be members of the MLA.
Level of Study: Postdoctorate.
Type: Prize.
Value: US$2,000.
Frequency: Odd numbered years.
No. of awards offered: One.
Application Procedure: Applicants must send four copies of the work. For detailed information about specific prizes, applicants should contact the MLA.
Closing Date: May 1st.

Aldo and Jeanne Scaglione Prize for Translation of a Scholarly Study of Literature

Subjects: Translation.
Purpose: To recognise an outstanding translation into English of a book length work of literary history, literary criticism, philology or literary theory.
Eligibility: Open to books published in the year or two before the prize is given. Authors need not be members of the MLA.
Level of Study: Postdoctorate.
Type: Prize.
Value: US$2,000.
Frequency: Odd numbered years.
No. of awards offered: One.
Application Procedure: Applicants must send four copies of the work. For detailed information about specific prizes, applicants should contact the MLA.
Closing Date: May 1st.

Fenia and Yaakov Leviant Memorial Prize

Subjects: English translation of a Yiddish literary work and/or Yiddish literature and culture.
Purpose: To recognise an outstanding translation into English or an outstanding scholarly work in the field of Yiddish.
Eligibility: The prize is awarded alternatively to a translational or scholarly work in the field of Yiddish. In 2004 the prize will be awarded to a scholarly work in English translation between 1999 and 2003. Cultural studies, critical biographies, edited works in the field of Yiddish folklore or linguistic studies are eligible.
Level of Study: Postdoctorate.
Type: Prize.
Value: US$500.
Frequency: Every two years (even-numbered years).
No. of awards offered: One.
Application Procedure: Applicants must send four copies of the work. For detailed information about specific prizes, applicants should contact the MLA.
Closing Date: May 1st.
Funding: Private.

Howard R Marraro Prize

Subjects: Italian literature.
Purpose: For an outstanding scholarly work on any phase of Italian literature or comparative literature involving Italian.
Eligibility: Authors must be members of the MLA.
Level of Study: Postdoctorate.
Type: Prize.
Value: US$1,000.
Frequency: Every two years.
No. of awards offered: One.
Application Procedure: Applicants must send four copies of the work. For detailed information about specific prizes, applicants should contact the MLA.
Closing Date: May 1st.
Additional Information: The two prizes have the same criteria. Members compete for both simultaneously.

James Russell Lowell Prize

Subjects: Open to studies dealing with literary theory, media, cultural history or interdisciplinary topics.

Purpose: To recognise an outstanding literary or linguistic study, a critical edition of an important work or a critical biography.
Eligibility: Open to books published the year before the award is due to be given. Authors must be current members of the MLA.
Level of Study: Postdoctorate.
Type: Prize.
Frequency: Annual.
No. of awards offered: One.
Application Procedure: Applicants must send six copies of the work. For detailed information about specific prizes, applicants should contact the MLA.
Closing Date: March 1st.

Katherine Singer Kovacs Prize

Subjects: Latin American or Spanish literatures and cultures.
Purpose: To recognise an outstanding book published in English.
Eligibility: Open to books published in the year before the prize is given. Competing books should be broadly interpretative works that enhance understanding of the interrelations among literature, the arts and society.
Level of Study: Postdoctorate.
Type: Prize.
Value: US$1,000.
Frequency: Annual.
No. of awards offered: One.
Application Procedure: Applicants must send six copies of the work. For detailed information about specific prizes, applicants should contact the MLA.
Closing Date: May 1st.
Funding: Private.

Kenneth W Mildenberger Prize

Subjects: Teaching foreign languages and literatures.
Purpose: To support a research publication.
Eligibility: Open to articles published in refereed journals or books published in the two years prior to the prize being given. Authors need not be members of the MLA.
Level of Study: Postdoctorate.
Type: Prize.
Value: For articles US$500 and for books US$1,000.
Frequency: Annual.
No. of awards offered: One.
Application Procedure: Applicants must send four copies of the work. For detailed information about specific prizes, applicants should contact the MLA.
Closing Date: May 1st.
Additional Information: The prize is give for a research article in odd numbered years and a book in even numbered years.

Lois Roth Award for a Translation of Literary Work

Subjects: Translation.
Purpose: To recognise an outstanding translation into English of a book length literary work.
Eligibility: Open to translations published in the year before the prize is given. Translators need not be members of the MLA.
Level of Study: Postdoctorate.
Type: Prize.
Value: US$1,000.
Frequency: Odd numbered years.
No. of awards offered: One.
Application Procedure: Applicants must send six copies of the work. For detailed information about specific prizes, applicants should contact the MLA.
Closing Date: April 1st.
Funding: Private.

Mina P Shaughnessy Prize

Subjects: Writing.
Purpose: To recognise a research publication in the field of teaching English language, literature, rhetoric and composition.

Eligibility: Open to books published in the year prior to the prize being given. Authors need not be members of the MLA.
Level of Study: Postdoctorate.
Type: Prize.
Value: US$1,000.
Frequency: Annual.
No. of awards offered: One.
Application Procedure: Applicants must send four copies of the work. For detailed information about specific prizes, applicants should contact the MLA.
Closing Date: May 1st.

MLA Prize for a Distinguished Bibliography

Subjects: Bibliography.
Purpose: To award an outstanding enumerative or descriptive bibliography.
Eligibility: Editors need not be members of the MLA.
Level of Study: Postdoctorate.
Type: Prize.
Value: US$1,000.
Frequency: Every two years (even-numbered years).
No. of awards offered: One.
Application Procedure: Applicants must send four copies of the work. For detailed information applicants should contact the MLA.
Closing Date: May 1st.
Funding: Private.

MLA Prize for a Distinguished Scholarly Edition

Subjects: Scholarly edition of a work in any of the modern languages.
Purpose: To recognise an outstanding scholarly edition.
Eligibility: At least one volume must have been published in the year or two prior to the award being given. Editors need not be members of the MLA. Editions may be single or multiple volumes.
Level of Study: Postdoctorate.
Type: Prize.
Value: US$1,000.
Frequency: Odd numbered years.
No. of awards offered: One.
Application Procedure: Applicants must send four copies of the work. For detailed information about specific prizes, applicants should contact the MLA.
Closing Date: May 1st.

MLA Prize for a First Book

Subjects: Literary theory, media, cultural history or interdisciplinary topics.
Purpose: To recognise an outstanding literary or linguistic study, a critical edition of an important work, or a critical biography.
Eligibility: Open to books published in the year before the prize is given as the first book length publication of a current MLA member.
Level of Study: Postdoctorate.
Type: Prize.
Value: US$1,000.
Frequency: Annual.
No. of awards offered: One.
Application Procedure: Applicants must send six copies of the work. For detailed information about specific prizes, applicants should contact the MLA.
Closing Date: April 1st.

MLA Prize for Independent Scholars

Subjects: English or other modern languages and literatures.
Purpose: To award a scholarly book in the field of English or other modern languages and literatures.
Eligibility: Open to books published the year before the prize is given. At the time of publication of the book the author must not be enrolled in a programme leading to an academic degree or hold a tenured, tenure accruing or tenure track position in post secondary education. Authors or publishers must request an application form from the MLA. Authors need not be members of the MLA.

Level of Study: Postdoctorate.
Type: Prize.
Value: US$1,000.
Frequency: Annual.
No. of awards offered: One.
Application Procedure: Applicants must send six copies of the work. For detailed information about specific prizes, applicants should contact the MLA.
Closing Date: May 1st.

Morton N Cohen Award for Distinguished Edition of Letter

Subjects: Edition of letters in any of the modern languages.
Purpose: To recognise an outstanding edition of letters.
Eligibility: At least one volume must have been published in the year or two prior to the award being given. Editors need not be members of the MLA. Editions may be single or multiple volumes.
Level of Study: Postdoctorate.
Type: Award.
Value: US$1,000.
Frequency: Odd numbered years.
No. of awards offered: One.
Application Procedure: Applicants must send four copies of the work. For detailed information about specific prizes, applicants should contact the MLA.
Closing Date: May 1st.

William Sanders Scarborough Prize

Subjects: Black American literature and culture.
Purpose: To recognise an outstanding book in the field.
Eligibility: Books that are primarily translation will not be considered.
Level of Study: Postdoctorate.
Type: Prize.
Value: US$1,000.
Frequency: Annual.
No. of awards offered: One.
Application Procedure: Applicants must send four copies of the work. For detailed information about specific prizes, applicants should contact the MLA.
Closing Date: May 1st.

MONASH UNIVERSITY

Wellington Road, Clayton, VIC, 3168, Australia
Tel: (61) 3 9905 3012
Fax: (61) 3 9905 3831
Email: offres@adm.monash.edu.au
www: http://www.monash.edu.au
Contact: Ms Rosalba Drummond, Grants Officer, Research Grants & Ethics Branch

Monash University is one of Australia's largest universities with 10 faculties covering every major area of intellectual activity, six campuses in Australia and an increasing global presence. Research at Monash covers the full spectrum from fundamental to applied and ranges across the arts and humanities, social, natural, health and medical sciences and the technological sciences. The University is determined to preserve its strength in fundamental research, which underpins its successes in applied research and to continue to make a distinguished contribution to intellectual and cultural life.

Monash University International Postgraduate Research Scholarship (MIPRS)

Subjects: All subjects.
Purpose: To provide support for supervised full-time research at Master's and doctoral level.

Eligibility: Open to graduates of any Australian or overseas university, who should hold a First Class (Honours) Bachelor's Degree or equivalent.
Level of Study: Doctorate, Postgraduate, Research.
Type: Scholarship.
Value: The award meets the full cost of international tuition fees.
Length of Study: Up to two years for the Master's degree, and up to three years with the possibility of an additional six month extension for the doctoral degree.
Frequency: Annual.
Study Establishment: Monash University.
Country of Study: Australia.
No. of awards offered: Nine.
Application Procedure: Applicants must complete an application kit, which is available four months before closing date.
Closing Date: October 31st.

Monash University Silver Jubilee Postgraduate Scholarship

Subjects: Engineering or information technology in 2003.
Purpose: To provide supervised full-time research at Master's and doctoral level.
Eligibility: Open to graduates of any Australian or overseas university, who should hold a First Class (Honours) Bachelor's Degree or equivalent.
Level of Study: Doctorate, Research.
Type: Scholarship.
Value: Australian $22,030 per year plus establishment, relocation, incidentals and thesis allowance.
Length of Study: Up to two years for the Master's degree, and up to three years with the possibility of an additional six month extension for the doctoral degree.
Frequency: Annual.
Study Establishment: Monash University.
Country of Study: Australia.
No. of awards offered: One.
Application Procedure: Applicants must complete an application kit, which is available four months before the closing date.
Closing Date: October 31st.
No. of awards given last year: One.
No. of applicants last year: 225.
Additional Information: International students must meet English language proficiency requirements.

Sir James McNeill Foundation Postgraduate Scholarship

Subjects: Engineering, medicine, music or science.
Purpose: To enable a PhD Scholar to pursue a full-time programme of research which is both environmentally responsible and socially beneficial to the community.
Eligibility: Open to graduates of any Australian or overseas university, who should hold a First Class (Honours) Bachelor's Degree or equivalent.
Level of Study: Doctorate.
Type: Scholarship.
Value: Australian $22,530 per year, plus allowances.
Length of Study: Up to four years.
Frequency: Annual.
Study Establishment: Monash University.
Country of Study: Australia.
No. of awards offered: One.
Application Procedure: Applicants must complete an application kit, which is available four months before the closing date.
Closing Date: October 31st.
Funding: Private.
No. of awards given last year: One.
No. of applicants last year: 400.
Additional Information: International students must meet English language proficiency requirements.

Vera Moore International Postgraduate Research Scholarships

Subjects: All subjects.
Purpose: To provide support for supervised full-time research at Master's and doctoral level.
Eligibility: Open to graduates of any Australian or overseas university, who should hold a First Class (Honours) Bachelor's Degree or equivalent.
Level of Study: Doctorate, Research.
Type: Scholarship.
Value: The full cost of tuition fees plus a research allowance of Australian $550 per year.
Length of Study: Up to two years for the Master's degree, and up to three years with the possibility of an additional six month extension for the doctoral degree.
Frequency: Annual.
Study Establishment: Monash University.
Country of Study: Australia.
No. of awards offered: 110.
Application Procedure: Applicants must complete an application kit, which is available four months before closing date.
Closing Date: October 31st.
Additional Information: International students must meet English language proficiency requirements.

THE MONGOLIA SOCIETY, INC.

Hangin Scholarship Committee
322 Goodbody Hall
Indiana University, Bloomington, IN, 47405-7005, United States of America
Tel: (1) 812 855 4078
Fax: (1) 812 855 7500
Email: monsoc@indiana.edu
www: http://www.indiana.edu/~mongsoc
Contact: Ms Susie Drost

The Mongolia Society was founded in late 1961 as a private, non-profit, non-political organisation interested in promoting and furthering the study of Mongolia, its history, language and culture. The aims of the Society are exclusively scholarly, educational and charitable.

Dr Gombojab Hangin Memorial Scholarship

Subjects: All subjects.
Purpose: To give a student of Mongolian nationality a chance to pursue studies in the United States of America.
Eligibility: Open to students of Mongolian heritage, defined as an individual of Mongolian ethnic origin who has permanent residency in the Mongolian People's Republic, the People's Republic of China, or the former Soviet Union.
Level of Study: Unrestricted.
Type: Scholarship.
Value: Up to US$2,400. The award does not include transportation from the recipient's country to the United States, nor does it include board and lodging at the university where the recipient will study.
Length of Study: One year.
Frequency: Annual.
Country of Study: United States of America.
No. of awards offered: One.
Application Procedure: Applicants must request the scholarship application form in English and return it written in English, accompanied by a photocopy of the applicant's identification card and passport, complete with photograph, and a curriculum vitae. If letters of recommendation are available, these should also be enclosed.
Closing Date: January 1st.
Funding: Private.
Additional Information: Upon conclusion of the award year, the recipient must write a report of his or her activities which resulted from receipt of the scholarship.

MONTREAL NEUROLOGICAL INSTITUTE

McGill University
3801 University Street, Montréal, QC, H3A 2B4, Canada
Tel: (1) 514 398 8998
Fax: (1) 514 398 8248
Email: fil@mni.lan.mcgill.ca
www: http://www.mcgill.ca/mni
Contact: Ms Filomena Lumia, Personnel Liaison Officer

The Montreal Neurological Institute is dedicated to the study of the nervous system and neurological disorders. Its 70 principal researchers hold teaching positions at McGill University. The Institute is characterised by close interaction between basic science researchers and the clinicians at its affiliated hospital.

Jeanne Timmins Costello Fellowships

Subjects: Neurology, neurosurgery, neuroscience research and study.
Purpose: To support research.
Eligibility: Open to candidates of any nationality who have an MD or PhD degree. Those with MD degrees will ordinarily have completed clinical studies in neurology or neurosurgery.
Level of Study: Doctorate, Postgraduate.
Type: Fellowship.
Value: Canadian $25,000 per year.
Length of Study: One year, with the possibility of renewal for further year.
Frequency: Annual.
Study Establishment: The Montreal Neurological Institute.
Country of Study: Canada.
No. of awards offered: Four.
Application Procedure: Applicants must write for details.
Closing Date: October 15th.
Funding: Private.
Contributor: Jean Timmins Costello.
No. of awards given last year: Four.

Preston Robb Fellowship

Subjects: Neurology, neurosurgery or neuroscience.
Purpose: To support research.
Eligibility: Open to researchers of any nationality.
Level of Study: Doctorate, Postdoctorate, Postgraduate.
Type: Fellowship.
Value: Canadian $25,000.
Length of Study: One year.
Frequency: Annual.
Country of Study: Canada.
No. of awards offered: One.
Application Procedure: Applicants must write for details.
Closing Date: October 15th.
Funding: Private.
Contributor: Preston Robb.
No. of awards given last year: One.

MOTOR NEURONE DISEASE ASSOCIATION

PO Box 246, Northampton, Northamptonshire, NN1 2PR, England
Tel: (44) 1604 250505
Fax: (44) 1604 638289
Email: research@mndassociation.org
Contact: Mrs M D Reicale, Research Administrator

The Motor Neurone Disease Association supports research on fundamental aspects of motor neurone disease (MND) and on its management and alleviation. It provides information and advice to patients and carers and runs a nationwide care service. MND paralyses selectively or generally and is fatal, irreversible and at present, incurable.

MND PhD Studentship Award

Subjects: Research on all aspects of MND in all relevant disciplines.
Purpose: To stimulate interest in MND research by encouraging young scientists into the field.
Eligibility: Restricted to United Kingdom laboratories.
Level of Study: Postdoctorate.
Type: Studentship.
Value: Approx. UK £65,000 for three years.
Length of Study: Three years.
Frequency: Annual.
Country of Study: United Kingdom.
No. of awards offered: One-two.
Application Procedure: Applicants must submit a summary of their proposal that is first considered by three members of the Research Advisory Panel (RAP). Full applications are invited thereafter and application forms provided. Full applications are submitted to two or more independent referees and then to the RAP for consideration.
Closing Date: Summary applications must be received by May 17th.
No. of awards given last year: Two.
No. of applicants last year: Four.
Additional Information: The studentships are awarded on the basis of scientific merit and the value of research training offered.

MND Research Project Grant

Subjects: Research into all aspects of MND in all disciplines.
Purpose: To understand and research the cause and effective treatments of MND.
Eligibility: Overseas applicants must have a project that is unique in concept or design, that involves some aspect of collaboration with a United Kingdom institute.
Type: Grant.
Value: Approx. UK £60,000 per year.
Length of Study: Three years.
Frequency: Twice a year.
Study Establishment: A research institution.
No. of awards offered: Varies.
Application Procedure: Applicants must submit a summary of their proposal that is first considered by three members of the Research Advisory Panel (RAP). Full applications are invited thereafter and application forms provided. Full applications are submitted to two or more independent referees and then to the RAP for consideration.
Closing Date: Summary applications must be received by May 17th.
No. of awards given last year: Five.
No. of applicants last year: 13.

MOUNT VERNON HOTEL MUSEUM AND GARDEN

421 East 61st Street, New York, NY, 10021, United States of America
Tel: (1) 212 838 6878
Fax: (1) 212 838 7390
Email: mvhmdev@aol.com
www: http://www.mvhmuseum.freeyellow.com/newyork.html
Contact: Development Officer

The Mount Vernon Hotel Museum and Garden is located on Manhattan's Upper East Side, and was originally constructed in 1799 as the Carriage House for an elegant country estate planned by Abigail Adams Smith, daughter of President John Adams. Accredited by the American Association of Museums since 1983, the Museum's period rooms represent its existence as the Mount Vernon Hotel, which is dated approximately 1830.

William Randolph Hearst Foundation Fellowship

Subjects: American social history, material culture, historic preservation and museum education.
Purpose: To provide fellowships to college or university students who are interested in American social history, material culture, historic preservation and museum education.

Eligibility: Applicants must currently be enrolled in a college, university or graduate programme.
Level of Study: Postgraduate.
Type: Fellowship.
Value: US$2,750.
Length of Study: Nine weeks.
Frequency: Annual.
Study Establishment: A museum.
Country of Study: United States of America.
No. of awards offered: Two.
Application Procedure: Applicants must complete an application form and submit this with an essay explaining their interest in the fellowship and three letters of recommendation.
Closing Date: The first Friday in March.
Funding: Private.
Contributor: The William Randolph Hearst Foundation.

MRS GILES WHITING FOUNDATION

Writers' Program
1133 Avenue of the Americas, New York, NY, 10036-6710, United States of America
Tel: (1) 212 336 2138
Contact: Ms Kellye Rosenheim, Associate Director

Whiting Fellowships in the Humanities

Subjects: Humanities.
Purpose: To recognise and award outstanding doctoral candidates in the humanities during the final year of dissertation writing.
Eligibility: Open to students selected by their participating institutions which consist of Bryan Mar, the University of Chicago, Columbia, Harvard, Princeton, Stanford and Yale.
Level of Study: Doctorate.
Type: Fellowship.
Value: Varies. The amount of the stipend is set by each school (usually US$17,500).
Frequency: Annual.
Country of Study: Any country.
No. of awards offered: Varies.
Application Procedure: Direct applications are not accepted by the Foundation.
Funding: Private.

Whiting Writers' Awards

Subjects: Writing.
Purpose: To identify and support emerging writers of exceptional promise.
Eligibility: Nominated candidates may be writers of fiction, poetry or non fiction, essayists, literary Scholars, playwrights, novelists, poets or critics. Selections are based on the quality of the nominee writing accomplishment and the likelihood of outstanding future work. The programme places special emphasis on promising emerging talent. To qualify, writers need not be young, given that new talent may emerge at any age.
Level of Study: Unrestricted.
Value: US$35,000.
Frequency: Annual.
Country of Study: Any country.
No. of awards offered: 10.
Application Procedure: Direct applications and informal nominations are not accepted by the Foundation. Recipients are nominated by writers, educators and editors from communities across the United States of America whose experience and vocations bring them into contact with individuals of unusual talent. The nominators and selectors are appointed by the Foundation and serve anonymously. Nominees are not informed of their candidacies.
Funding: Private.

MULTIPLE SCLEROSIS SOCIETY OF CANADA (MSSC)

250 Bloor Street East
Suite 1000, Toronto, ON, M4W 3PG, Canada
Tel: (1) 416 967 3001
Fax: (1) 416 967 3040
Email: jackie.munroe@mssociety.ca
www: http://www.mssociety.ca
Contact: Ms Jackie Munroe, Research Grants Programme Manager

The mission of the Multiple Sclerosis Society of Canada (MSSC) is to be a leader in finding a cure for multiple sclerosis and enabling people affected by the disease to enhance their quality of life.

MSSC Career Development Award

Subjects: Multiple sclerosis.
Purpose: To encourage full-time research.
Eligibility: Open to individuals holding a doctoral degree who have recently completed their training in research and are capable of carrying out independent research relevant to multiple sclerosis on a full-time basis.
Level of Study: Postdoctorate.
Value: The salary scale, conditions of remuneration and allowable involvement in non-research activities will be similar to Medical Research Council (MRC) scholarships.
Length of Study: Three years initially, with the opportunity for renewal twice.
Frequency: Annual.
Study Establishment: A Canadian school of medicine.
Country of Study: Canada.
No. of awards offered: Limited.
Closing Date: October 1st.
Funding: Private.
No. of awards given last year: One.
No. of applicants last year: One.

MSSC Postdoctoral Fellowship

Subjects: Multiple sclerosis and allied diseases.
Purpose: To encourage research.
Eligibility: Open to qualified persons holding an MD or PhD degree and intending to pursue research work relevant to multiple sclerosis and allied diseases. The applicant must be responsible to an appropriate authority in the field he or she wishes to study.
Level of Study: Postdoctorate.
Type: Fellowship.
Value: Salary scales will be similar to those suggested by the Canadian Institutes for Health Research.
Length of Study: Three years, but may be extended for one additional year under exceptional circumstances.
Frequency: Annual.
Study Establishment: A recognised institution which deals with problems relevant to multiple sclerosis.
Country of Study: Canadian citizen applicants proposing to go abroad are encouraged to seek the advice of the panel members regarding suitable laboratories for advanced training. Non Canadian citizens' studies are limited to Canada.
No. of awards offered: Varies.
Closing Date: October 1st.
Funding: Private.
No. of awards given last year: 11.
No. of applicants last year: 16.

MSSC Research Grant

Subjects: Multiple sclerosis.
Purpose: To fund research projects.
Eligibility: Open to researchers working in Canada or intending to return to Canada.
Level of Study: Postgraduate.
Type: Research grant.
Value: Varies.

Length of Study: One, two or three years. If further funding is requested reapplication must be made in full.
Frequency: Annual.
Study Establishment: An approved institution.
Country of Study: Any country.
No. of awards offered: Limited.
Closing Date: October 1st.
Funding: Private.
No. of awards given last year: 23.
No. of applicants last year: 32.

MSSC Research Studentship

Subjects: Multiple sclerosis research.
Purpose: To provide further training in a specialised area related to research in multiple sclerosis and allied diseases.
Eligibility: Open to qualified persons holding an MD or PhD degree. Applicants directed towards understanding the pathogenesis and potential treatment of multiple sclerosis will receive priority.
Level of Study: Postgraduate.
Type: Studentship.
Value: Salary scales will be similar those suggested by the Canadian Institutes for Health Research.
Length of Study: Four years, but may be extended under exceptional circumstances. Renewal must be obtained each year.
Frequency: Annual.
Study Establishment: A recognised institution.
Country of Study: Any country for Canadian citizens. Canada for non Canadian citizens.
No. of awards offered: Varies.
Closing Date: October 1st.
No. of awards given last year: 23.
No. of applicants last year: 32.

MULTIPLE SCLEROSIS SOCIETY OF GREAT BRITAIN AND NORTHERN IRELAND

372 Edgware Road, London, NW2 6ND, England
Tel: (44) 20 8438 0700
Email: researchadmin@mssociety.org.uk
www: http://www.mssociety.org.uk
Contact: Mr D Bartram, Assistant Information Officer

The Multiple Sclerosis Society of Great Britain and Northern Ireland is the United Kingdom's largest charity for people affected by multiple sclerosis (MS). The study funds research, runs holiday homes and respite care, provides grants, education and training, publishes various publications and runs a freephone specialist helpline.

Multiple Sclerosis Society Research Grants

Subjects: Multiple sclerosis.
Purpose: To promote medical research into the cause and treatment of multiple sclerosis.
Eligibility: Open to nationals of all countries.
Level of Study: Doctorate, Postdoctorate.
Type: Research grant.
Value: Research Grants may be awarded in the form of fellowships and PhD studentships, to provide remuneration for research workers. They may also be awarded for the provision of scientific assistance in connection with some particular aspect of research by a qualified medical or graduate scientist, to meet the entire or part cost of technical laboratory assistance, equipment and materials.
Length of Study: Innovative Awards are for one year, PhD and Junior Fellowships are for four years, Project Grants are for two years and Senior Fellowships are for five years.
Frequency: Twice a year.
Study Establishment: Suitable institutions.
Country of Study: Any country.
No. of awards offered: Varies.

Application Procedure: Applicants must complete an application form.
Closing Date: Please contact the Society.
Funding: Commercial, Private.
Contributor: Charitable donations.
No. of awards given last year: 12.
No. of applicants last year: 50.
Additional Information: Applications should, where applicable, be sponsored by the Head of the hospital department or laboratory in which the work is to be carried out.

MURIEL TAYLOR SCHOLARSHIP FUND FOR CELLISTS

The Warehouse
13 Theed Street, London, SE1 8ST, England
Tel: (44) 1892 782220
Contact: Ms Kate Beresford, Honorary Secretary

Muriel Taylor Cello Scholarship

Subjects: The cello.
Purpose: To help talented young cellists continue their studies, usually following study at a recognised tertiary college of music, the Royal Academy of Music or the Royal College of Music.
Eligibility: Open to candidates of any nationality, with any qualifications who are between 17 and 23 years of age on March 31st in the year of competition.
Level of Study: Unrestricted.
Type: Scholarship.
Value: UK £3,500 for tuition fees.
Frequency: Annual.
Study Establishment: A recognised tertiary college of music.
Country of Study: Any country.
No. of awards offered: One.
Application Procedure: Applicants must write to the Competition Secretary for details.
Closing Date: January 7th.
Funding: Private.
Contributor: The Ralph Vaughan Williams Trust, the London Festival Orchestra and Warehouse Records.
No. of awards given last year: One.
No. of applicants last year: Eight.
Additional Information: The competition is usually held in mid-April. The trustees committee organises adjudication of usually four finalists chosen from cassette presentation for preliminary adjudication by two first time adjudicators. The four finalists are invited to play to the competition adjudicator in London. The prize is awarded on the day of the competition, the adjudicator speaking individually to each entrant.

MUSCULAR DYSTROPHY ASSOCIATION (MDA)

Research Department
3300 East Sunrise Drive, Tucson, AZ, 85718, United States of America
Tel: (1) 520 529 2000
Fax: (1) 520 529 5300
Email: grants@mdausa.org
www: http://www.mdausa.org
Contact: Ms Karen Mashburn, Grants Manager

The Muscular Dystrophy Association (MDA) supports research into over 40 diseases of the neuromuscular system to identify the causes of, and effective treatments for, the muscular dystrophies and related diseases which include spinal muscular atrophies and motor neurone diseases, peripheral neuropathies, inflammatory myopathies, metabolic myopathies and diseases of the neuromuscular junction.

Muscular Dystrophy Association Grant Programs

Subjects: The muscular dystrophies and related diseases which include spinal muscular atrophies and motor neurone diseases, peripheral neuropathies, inflammatory myopathies, metabolic myopathies and diseases of the neuromuscular junction.
Purpose: To support research into over 40 diseases of the neuromuscular system, and to identify the causes of, and effective treatments for, the muscular dystrophies and related diseases.
Eligibility: Open to persons who are professional or faculty members at appropriate educational, medical or research institutions and qualified to conduct and supervise programmes of original research, who have access to institutional resources necessary to conduct the proposed research project and who hold a MD, PhD, MSc or equivalent degree.
Level of Study: Postdoctorate.
Type: Grant.
Value: Please contact the Association.
Length of Study: One year, renewable for a further two and three years.
Frequency: Annual.
Country of Study: Any country.
No. of awards offered: Varies.
Application Procedure: Applicants must complete the Request for Research Grant Application.
Closing Date: Pre-applications are due no later than December 15th or June 15th.
Funding: Private.
Contributor: Voluntary contributions.
Additional Information: Proposals from applicants outside the United States of America will only be considered for projects of highest priority to the MDA. Other conditions apply. Research is sponsored under the following grant programmes: Neuromuscular Disease Research and Neuromuscular Disease Research Development. Further information is available from the website.

MUSCULAR DYSTROPHY CAMPAIGN OF GREAT BRITAIN AND NORTHERN IRELAND

Room 400F
Mezzanine Floor
Cambridge Regional College
Newmarket Road, Cambridge, Cambridgeshire, CB5 8FG, England
Tel: (44) 1223 351161
Fax: (44) 1223 306566
Email: joycelyna@muscular-dystrophy.org
www: http://www.muscular-dystrophy.org
Contact: Ms Joycelyn Amponsah

The Muscular Dystrophy Campaign is a United Kingdom based charity funding medical research and support services for people with neuromuscular conditions.

Muscular Dystrophy Programme Grant

Subjects: Biomedicine.
Purpose: To provide continuity of funding for high quality research of central importance to the muscular dystrophy group's research objectives.
Eligibility: This grant is only awarded in exceptional circumstances. A site visit would be made prior to approval.
Level of Study: Postdoctorate, Professional development, Research.
Type: Programme grant.
Value: Salary of research staff, equipment and consumables. Salary of grant holder is not funded.
Length of Study: One-three years.

Frequency: Annual.
Study Establishment: A university or hospital.
Country of Study: United Kingdom.
No. of awards offered: Varies.
Application Procedure: Applicants must contact the Director of Scientific Affairs with a summary of proposed research.
Closing Date: To be announced.
Funding: Commercial.

Muscular Dystrophy Project Grant

Subjects: Biomedicine, muscular dystrophy and allied neuromuscular diseases.
Purpose: To support medical research.
Eligibility: Open to United Kingdom nationals who are research workers with appropriate qualifications and experience. Grant holders must have a tenured position.
Level of Study: Postdoctorate, Research.
Type: Project grant.
Value: Salary of research staff, equipment and consumables.
Length of Study: Three years.
Frequency: Annual.
Study Establishment: A university or hospital.
Country of Study: Any country.
No. of awards offered: Varies.
Application Procedure: Applicants must contact the Director of Scientific Affairs with a summary of proposed research.
Closing Date: To be announced.
No. of awards given last year: 29.
No. of applicants last year: 15.

Muscular Dystrophy Research Grants

Subjects: Muscular dystrophy and allied neuromuscular diseases.
Purpose: To support research into neuromuscular function in health and in disease.
Eligibility: Open to United Kingdom nationals who have the appropriate qualifications and experience. Grant holders must have a tenured position.
Level of Study: Postdoctorate.
Type: Research grant.
Value: Varies, according to the nature of the research and the qualifications and experience of the applicant.
Length of Study: Three years.
Frequency: Annual.
Study Establishment: Universities, hospitals or research institutions.
Country of Study: United Kingdom.
No. of awards offered: Varies.
Application Procedure: Applicants must contact the Director of Scientific Affairs with a summary of proposed research.
Closing Date: To be announced.
No. of awards given last year: 15.
No. of applicants last year: 25.

MUSEUM OF COMPARATIVE ZOOLOGY

26 Oxford Street, Cambridge, MA, 02138, United States of America
Tel: (1) 617 495 2460
Fax: (1) 617 496 8308
Email: ernstmayrgrant@oeb.harvard.edu
www: http://www.mcz.harvard.edu
Contact: Ms Andrea Prill, Assistant to the Director

The Museum of Comparative Zoology was founded in 1859, through the efforts of Louis Agassiz (1807-1873). Agassiz, a zoologist from Neuchatel, Switzerland, served as the Director of the Museum from 1859 until his death in 1873. A brilliant lecturer and scholar, he established the Museum and its collections as a centre for research and education.

Ernst Mayr Grants

Subjects: Zoology.
Purpose: To enable systematists to make short visits to museums in order to undertake research needed for the completion of taxonomic revisions and monographs.
Eligibility: There are no restrictions on eligibility.
Level of Study: Unrestricted.
Type: Travel grant.
Value: Typical expenses that may be covered by this award include travel, lodging and meals for up to a few months while conducting research, services purchased from the host institution and research supplies.
Length of Study: Varies, short visits.
Frequency: Twice a year.
Study Establishment: Museums.
Country of Study: Any country.
No. of awards offered: Varies.
Application Procedure: Applicants must submit a short project description, itinerary, budget, curriculum vitae and three letters of support. No proposal forms are required or provided. Proposals may be submitted through standard mail or electronically. Submissions through standard mail must include four copies of all materials and be postmarked by the closing date. Proposals submitted electronically must be created in Microsoft Word or plain ASCII text format.
Closing Date: April 15th and September 15th.
Funding: Private.
Additional Information: Announcements of awards will be made within two months of the closing date.

THE MYASTHENIA GRAVIS FOUNDATION OF AMERICA

5841 Cedar Lake Road
Suite 204, Minneapolis, MN, 55416, United States of America
Tel: (1) 800 541 5454
Fax: (1) 952 646 2028
Email: myastheniagravis@msn.com
www: http://www.myasthenia.org
Contact: Ms Debora K Boelz, Chief Executive

The Myasthenia Gravis Foundation of America was established in order to find a cure for myasthenia gravis and related disorders of the neuromuscular junction, and to improve the lives of all people affected, through programmes of medical research, patient care, professional education and public information.

Henry R Viets Medical/Graduate Student Research Fellowship

Subjects: The scientific basis of myasthenia gravis or related neuromuscular conditions.
Purpose: To promote research into the cause and cure of myasthenia gravis.
Eligibility: There are no eligibility restrictions.
Level of Study: Doctorate, Postgraduate.
Type: Stipend.
Value: US$3,000.
Length of Study: Short-term.
Frequency: Annual.
Country of Study: Any country.
No. of awards offered: Four-eight.
Application Procedure: Applicants must briefly describe, in abstract form, the question proposed for study, its association to myasthenia gravis or related neuromuscular conditions and research methodology. Further information may then be requested by the Foundation.
Closing Date: March 15th.
Funding: Private.
No. of awards given last year: Four.
No. of applicants last year: Eight.

Myasthenia Gravis Nursing Fellowship

Subjects: Myasthenia gravis.
Purpose: To strengthen the linkages between myasthenia gravis treatment and the nursing profession.
Eligibility: There are no eligibility restrictions.
Level of Study: Postgraduate.
Type: Stipend.
Value: US$3,000.
Length of Study: Short-term.
Frequency: Annual.
Country of Study: Any country.
No. of awards offered: Two-three.
Application Procedure: Applicants must contact the Foundation for further details.
Closing Date: Applications are accepted at any time.
Funding: Private.
No. of awards given last year: One.
No. of applicants last year: Three.

Osserman/Sosin/McClare Research Fellowship

Subjects: Research pertinent to myasthenia gravis, concerned with neuromuscular transmission, immunology, molecular cell biology of the neuromuscular synapse, the aetiology or pathogenesis, diagnosis or treatment of the disease.
Purpose: To investigate the fundamental nature of myasthenia gravis.
Eligibility: There are no eligibility restrictions.
Level of Study: Postdoctorate.
Type: Fellowship.
Value: US$50,000.
Length of Study: One year.
Frequency: Annual.
Country of Study: Any country.
No. of awards offered: Two-four.
Application Procedure: Applicants must complete an application form.
Closing Date: November 15th.
Funding: Private.
No. of awards given last year: Two.
No. of applicants last year: Five.

MYRA HESS TRUST

16 Ogle Street, London, W1W 6JA, England
Tel: (44) 20 7636 4481
Fax: (44) 20 7637 4307
Email: education@mbf.org.uk
www: http://www.mbf.org.uk
Contact: Mrs Susan Dolton, Administrator

Myra Hess Trust

Subjects: Musical performance on strings and piano.
Purpose: To give assistance for the purchase of instruments, for tuition, maintenance and towards the cost of first recitals.
Eligibility: Open to outstanding young instrumentalists between 20 and 27 years of age inclusive. Preference is given to those entering a professional career as a soloist. Open to piano, violin, viola, cello and double bass students.
Level of Study: Postgraduate, Professional development.
Value: Up to UK £3,000 each.
Frequency: Annual.
Country of Study: Any country.
No. of awards offered: 5-10.
Application Procedure: Applicants must complete an application form with two references. Selected applicants are asked to audition in June.
Closing Date: May 14th.
Funding: Private.
No. of awards given last year: 10.
No. of applicants last year: 71.

NANTUCKET HISTORICAL ASSOCIATION (NHA)

PO Box 1016, Nantucket, MA, 02554, United States of America
Tel: (1) 508 228 1655
Fax: (1) 508 325 7968
Email: library@nha.org
www: http://www.nha.org
Contact: Library Director

The Nantucket Historical Association (NHA) is the principal repository of Nantucket history, with extensive archives, collections of historic properties and art and artifacts that broadly illustrate
Nantucket's past. The Research Library at the NHA contains a rich
collection of primary and secondary sources that document all facets
of Nantucket's cultural, social, economic and spiritual history for
more than three centuries. More than 400 manuscript collections relate to Nantucket individuals and families, ships, businesses and
trades, churches, schools and organisations. Searchable inventories
of the library's manuscript, map and book holdings can be accessed
via the NHA website. The NHA art and artifacts collections include
paintings, drawings, prints, baskets, silver, whaling tools, scrimshaw,
furniture and textiles. Particular strengths of the collection lie in artifacts that document Nantucket's whaling industry.

E Geoffrey and Elizabeth Thayer Verney Research Fellowship

Subjects: History.
Purpose: To enhance the public's knowledge and understanding of
the heritage of Nantucket, Massachusetts.
Eligibility: Open to graduate students and independent Scholars in
any field to conduct research in the collections of the NHA.
Level of Study: Graduate.
Type: Residency.
Value: The NHA will provide housing in the historic property,
Thomas Macy House. Housing is available January-May or October-
December. The NHA will also provide a weekly stipend of US$250
and will reimburse for reasonable travel expenses.
Length of Study: Three-four weeks.
Frequency: Annual.
Study Establishment: The NHA.
Country of Study: United States of America.
No. of awards offered: One.
Application Procedure: Applicants must send a full description of
the proposed project, a preliminary bibliography and a complete cur-
riculum vitae. An account of travel expenses must also be included
with the anticipated time and duration of stay. Applications must be
addressed to the Library Director.
Closing Date: November 21st.
No. of awards given last year: One.
Additional Information: Applicants will be notified by December
22nd.

NANYANG TECHNOLOGICAL UNIVERSITY (NTU)

Nanyang Business School
MBA Office
Nanyang Avenue, 639798, Singapore
Tel: (65) 799 4722
Fax: (65) 791 3561
Email: nbsmba@ntu.edu.sg
www: http://www.ntu.edu.sg
Contact: Ms Pearl Yap, Administrative Officer

NTU AEH Exchange Studentships

Subjects: MBA and information technology.
Purpose: To promote student exchanges between Asia and Europe
and to enable students from the ASEM (Asia-Europe Meeting)
member countries to participate in an exchange programme with
NTU. Applicants will join NTU as non-graduating exchange students
for a period of one to two semesters.
Eligibility: Open to candidates from member countries of the ASEM
which are Austria, Belgium, Denmark, Finland, France, Germany,
Greece, Ireland, Italy, Luxembourg, The Netherlands, Portugal,
Spain, Sweden and the United Kingdom. This exchange is to facili-
tate Asia-Europe student mobility. NTU will not consider applicants
from the Asia region.
Level of Study: Graduate, MBA.
Type: Studentship.
Value: NTU will waive the tuition fees and provide on-campus ac-
commodation and a monthly living allowance of singaporean $500.
Length of Study: One or two semesters or trimesters.
Frequency: Annual.
Study Establishment: NTU.
Country of Study: Singapore.
No. of awards offered: Two for MBA and two for information
technology.
Application Procedure: Applicants must submit applications for the
studentships on the prescribed form which can be found at
http://www.ntu.edu.sg/aeh-earn. For enquiries please contact Agnes
Yap at aeh-aern@ntu.edu.sg.
Closing Date: March 15th.
Funding: Government.
Contributor: The Nanyang Technological University.
No. of awards given last year: One.
No. of applicants last year: One.

NTU APEC Scholarship

Subjects: MBA.
Purpose: To allow outstanding candidates from the APEC member
economies to pursue the Master of Business Administration
Programme at NTU on a full-time basis.
Eligibility: Only candidates from the following APEC (Asia Pacific
Economic Co-operation) member economies are eligible to apply:
Australia, Brunei Darussalam, Canada, Chile, People's Republic of
China, Hong Kong, Indonesia, Japan, Republic of Korea, Malaysia,
Mexico, New Zealand, Papua New Guinea, Peru, Philippines, Rus-
sia, Chinese Taipei, Thailand, United States of America and Viet-
nam. Singaporeans and Singapore permanent residents and
recipients of other scholarships or bursaries are not eligible to apply.
Level of Study: MBA.
Type: Scholarship.
Value: A monthly stipend of singaporean $1,400, a book allowance
of singaporean $500, tuition fees, health insurance, examination
fees and other approved fees, allowances and expenses, the cost of
one overseas Business Study Mission, cost of travel from home
country to Singapore on award of the scholarship and cost of travel
from Singapore to home country on successful completion of the
MBA programme.
Length of Study: Full-time for 16 months.
Frequency: Annual.
Study Establishment: NTU.
Country of Study: Singapore.
No. of awards offered: Two.
Application Procedure: Applicants must submit their applications
from September onwards. Invitations for applications will be placed
in the newspapers in the capital cities of APEC countries and on the
university's website.
Closing Date: December 31st.
Funding: Government.
No. of awards given last year: Two.
No. of applicants last year: 30.
Additional Information: International students have to apply for a
Student's Pass to pursue a course of full-time study in Singapore un-
less they are holders of a valid immigration pass eg. Employment
Pass, Dependent Pass and Work Permit issued by the Singapore
Immigration and Registration Department. The Student's Pass is
only issued to full-time students and not to part-time students. Inter-
national students may, therefore, only apply for admission as full-
time students. International students who wish to pursue

programmes on a part-time basis should obtain employment in Singapore first before applying for admission to the University and should ensure that they are permitted to work and reside in Singapore throughout the course of their study by the Singapore Immigration and Registration. Passport holders of specific countries including China and India must have a valid visa before entering Singapore.

NTU ASEAN Postgraduate Scholarahip

Subjects: MBA.

Purpose: To allow outstanding candidates from the ASEAN (Association of South-East Asian Nations) member economies (except Singapore) to pursue the Master of Business Administration programme at NTU on a full-time basis.

Eligibility: Only candidates from the following ASEAN member economies are eligible to apply: Brunei Darussalam, Cambodia, Indonesia, Laos, Malaysia, Myanmar, Philippines, Thailand and Vietnam. Singaporeans, Singapore permanent residents and recipients of other scholarships or bursaries are not eligible to apply.

Level of Study: MBA.

Type: Scholarship.

Value: A monthly stipend of singaporean $1,350, a book allowance of singaporean $500, tuition fees, health insurance, examination fees and other approved fees, allowances and expenses, cost of travel from the home country to Singapore on award of the scholarship and cost of travel from Singapore to the home country on successful completion of the MBA programme.

Length of Study: Full-time for 16 months.

Frequency: Annual.

No. of awards offered: One or two.

Application Procedure: Applicants must submit their applications from September onwards. Invitations for applications will be placed in the newspapers in the capital cities of ASEAN countries and on the university's website.

Closing Date: December 31st.

Funding: Government.

No. of awards given last year: One.

No. of applicants last year: 31.

Additional Information: International students have to apply for a Student's Pass to pursue a course of full-time study in Singapore unless they are holders of a valid immigration pass eg. Employment Pass, Dependent Pass and Work Permit issued by the Singapore Immigration and Registration Department. The Student's Pass is only issued to full-time students and not to part-time students. International students may, therefore, only apply for admission as full-time students. International students who wish to pursue programmes on a part-time basis should obtain employment in Singapore first before applying for admission to the University and should ensure that they are permitted to work and reside in Singapore throughout the course of their study by the Singapore Immigration and Registration. Passport holders of specific countries including China and India must have a valid visa before entering Singapore.

NTU MBA Scholarship

Subjects: MBA.

Purpose: To enable outstanding overseas candidates to pursue the MBA programme on a full-time basis.

Eligibility: Open to outstanding candidates who are admitted to the NTU MBA programme. Singaporeans and Singapore permanent residents and recipients of other scholarships or bursaries are not eligible to apply. Selection is based on the applicant's scholastic achievements as well as financial circumstances and other factors.

Level of Study: MBA.

Type: Scholarship.

Value: Up to singaporean $16,000 payable over four trimesters to cover the tuition fees only.

Length of Study: Full-time for 16 months.

Frequency: Annual.

Study Establishment: NTU.

Country of Study: Singapore.

No. of awards offered: Three.

Application Procedure: Applicants must submit the application for the scholarship to the MBA Office together with the application for admission to the MBA programme. Application forms may be obtained from the website or from the MBA Office when applications for the MBA programme open in October each year. The award of the scholarship will be made together with the offer of admission.

Closing Date: February.

Funding: Private.

No. of awards given last year: Three.

No. of applicants last year: 45.

Additional Information: International students have to apply for a Student's Pass to pursue a course of full-time study in Singapore unless they are holders of a valid immigration pass eg. Employment Pass, Dependent Pass and Work Permit issued by the Singapore Immigration and Registration Department. The Student's Pass is only issued to full-time students and not to part-time students. International students may, therefore, only apply for admission as full-time students. International students who wish to pursue programmes on a part-time basis should obtain employment in Singapore first before applying for admission to the University and should ensure that they are permitted to work and reside in Singapore throughout the course of their study by the Singapore Immigration and Registration. Passport holders of specific countries including China and India must have a valid visa before entering Singapore.

NTU SCCCF Business Scholarship

Subjects: MBA.

Purpose: To provide financial support to Singaporeans and permanent residents of Singapore who are admitted onto the MBA programme on either a full-time or part-time basis.

Eligibility: Open to Singaporeans and Singapore permanent residents admitted to the MBA programme on either a full-time or part-time basis. Selection is on the basis of merit. Applicants with a keen interest and knowledge in the local Chinese business community will have an added advantage. Recipients of other scholarships or bursaries are not eligible to apply.

Level of Study: MBA.

Type: Scholarship.

Value: Singaporean $5,000.

Length of Study: Full-time is 16 months and part-time is 24-32 months.

Frequency: Annual.

Study Establishment: NTU.

Country of Study: Singapore.

No. of awards offered: Three.

Application Procedure: Applicants must apply in September and October each year. Invitations for applications will be put up at the notice boards at the MBA Office and Registrar's Office.

Closing Date: Please contact the organisation.

Funding: Commercial.

Contributor: The Singapore Chinese Chamber of Commerce Foundation Business Scholarship.

No. of awards given last year: Three.

No. of applicants last year: Fifteen.

THE NATIONAL ACADEMY OF EDUCATION

New York University
School of Education
726 Broadway
5th Floor, New York, NY, 10003-9580, United States of America
Tel: (1) 212 998 9035
Fax: (1) 212 995 4435
Email: nae.info@nyu.edu
www: http://www.nae.nyu.edu
Contact: Ms Jessica Claire, Programme Assistant

The National Academy of Education consists of up to 125 members who are elected on the basis of outstanding scholarship or contributions to education. From its establishment in 1965, the Academy has sponsored a variety of commissions and study panels that have published proceedings and reports. Since 1986, the National Academy of Education has administered a Postdoctoral Fellowship Programme designed to support young scholars.

National Academy of Education Spencer Postdoctoral Fellowships

Subjects: Education and educational research.
Purpose: To ensure the future of research in education by supporting young scholars working in critical areas of educational scholarship. The Academy seeks to fund proposals which promise to make significant scholarly contributions to the field of education as well as to advance the careers of its recipients.
Eligibility: Open to candidates who have obtained doctoral degrees in the past five years and are conducting research relevant to the improvement of education in all its forms. United States citizenship is not required.
Level of Study: Postdoctorate.
Type: Fellowship.
Value: US$50,000.
Length of Study: One academic year full-time or two academic years part-time.
Frequency: Annual.
Study Establishment: Any establishment.
Country of Study: Any country.
No. of awards offered: Up to 30.
Application Procedure: Applicants must complete an application form. Please see the website for a more detailed description and updated application forms for downloading.
Funding: Private.
Contributor: The Spencer Foundation.
No. of awards given last year: 30.
No. of applicants last year: 200.
Additional Information: The fellowship is non residential.

NATIONAL ACADEMY OF SCIENCES INSTITUTE OF MEDICINE

2101 Constitution Avenue North West, Washington, DC, 20418, United States of America
Tel: (1) 202 334 2872
Fax: (1) 202 334 3419
Email: infofell@nas.edu
www: http://national-academies.org/osep/fo
Contact: Programme Assistant

Ford Foundation Dissertation Fellowships for Minorities

Subjects: All subjects.
Purpose: To increase the presence of underrepresented minorities in the nation's college and university faculties, to enhance diversity on campuses and to address the persisting effects of past discrimination, whilst providing individuals of demonstrated ability with the opportunity to complete a dissertation.

Eligibility: Applicants must have finished all requirements for their degree except for writing and defending their dissertation. Eligibility is limited to citizens or nationals of the United States (must have become a citizen by the application deadline) who are members of the following groups: Alaskan natives, black/African Americans, Mexican Americans/Chicanas/Chicanos, native American Indians, native Pacific Islanders and Puerto Ricans. Only those individuals who are PhD or ScD degree candidates at United States institutions studying one of the eligible fields, aspire to a teaching and research career and have not earned a doctoral degree may apply.
Level of Study: Postdoctorate.
Type: Fellowship.
Value: Stipend of US$24,000 and expenses paid to attend three conferences of Ford Fellows.
Length of Study: No less than nine months and no more than twelve.
Study Establishment: Any fully accredited, non-profit Institute of Higher Education in the United States of America offering PhDs or ScDs.
Country of Study: United States of America.
No. of awards offered: Approx. 40.
Application Procedure: Applicants must submit a confidential information form, a fellowship application form, a personal statement, an abstract of the dissertation, a proposed plan for completion of the doctoral degree, a statement of previous research experience, a working bibliography, an annotated bibliography, a list of publications, a list of presentations and posters, an official copy of all undergraduate and graduate transcripts, four letters of reference and verification of doctoral degree candidacy form. Applicants are strongly advised to use the online application form if possible.
Closing Date: Please consult the website.

Ford Foundation Postdoctoral Fellowships for Minorities

Subjects: A comprehensive list of eligible fields is included with the application.
Purpose: To foster diversity on the nation's college and university faculties and campuses and identify outstanding researchers and scholars who are members of minority groups, who can then engage in a year of research and scholarship in an environment free from the interference of their normal professional responsibilities.
Eligibility: Eligibility is limited to citizens or nationals of the United States (must have become a citizen by the application deadline) who are members of the following groups: Alaskan natives, black/African Americans, Mexican Americans/Chicanas/Chicanos, native American Indians, native Pacific Islanders and Puerto Ricans. Only those individuals already engaged in a teaching career or those planning such a career may apply. Previous Fellows are not eligible.
Level of Study: Postdoctorate.
Type: Fellowship.
Value: US$35,000 stipend, US$3,000 travel and relocation allowance, US$2,000 cost-of-research allowance and US$2,000 employing institution allowance which will be forwarded to the employing institution after tenure is completed.
Length of Study: These one year fellowships may be held for either nine or twelve months.
Study Establishment: Appropriate non-profit Institutes of Higher Education or research, normally in the United States of America.
Country of Study: United States of America.
No. of awards offered: Approx. 30.
Application Procedure: Applicants must submit a confidential application form, a fellowship application form, a one page abstract of the dissertation, a one page abstract of the proposed plan of study or research, a working bibliography, an annotated bibliography, a list of publications, a list of presentations and posters, a list of grants, a teaching load and a writing sample. The supporting materials required are a host letter endorsing the applicant's prospective affiliation with the fellowship institution, four letters of reference and a transcript from the PhD or ScD institution. Applicants are strongly advised to use the online application form if possible.
Closing Date: Please consult the website.

Ford Foundation Predoctoral Fellowships for Minorities

Subjects: Research based programmes in the behavioural and social sciences, humanities, engineering, mathematics, physical sciences or life sciences.

Purpose: To increase the presence of underrepresented minorities on the nation's college and university faculties, to enhance diversity on campuses and to address the persisting effects of past discrimination. The Ford Foundation offers fellowships to members of six minority groups whose underrepresentation in the professiorate has been severe and longstanding.

Eligibility: Eligibility is limited to citizens or nationals of the United States (must have become a citizen by the application deadline) who are members of the following groups: Alaskan natives, black/African Americans, Mexican Americans/Chicanas/Chicanos, native American Indians, native Pacific Islanders and Puerto Ricans, who have not earned a doctoral degree at any time, in any field.

Level of Study: Predoctorate.

Type: Fellowship.

Value: Annual stipend of US$15,500 and an allowance of US$8,500 to the fellowship institution in lieu of tuition and fees, and expenses paid to attend three conferences of Ford Fellows.

Length of Study: Three years of support to be used within five years.

Frequency: Varies.

Study Establishment: Fellowships are tenable at any fully accredited, non-profit Institute of Higher Education in the United States of America offering PhDs or ScDs in the fields eligible for support in this programme.

Country of Study: United States of America.

No. of awards offered: Approx. 60.

Application Procedure: Applicants must submit a confidential information form, a fellowship application form, a proposed plan of graduate study, a personal statement, a statement of previous research experience, a list of publications, if any, a list of presentations and posters, if any, an undergraduate grade point average form, a verification of predoctoral status form (required for applicants already enrolled in a PhD or ScD programme), official undergraduate and graduate transcripts, four letters of reference, Graduate Record Examination general test scores and an official copy of the transcript showing previous grades. The applicant is responsible for ensuring that their application is complete, but all applicants will receive a data sheet listing information to be verified and any materials missing before the deadline. Applicants are strongly advised to use the online application form if possible.

Closing Date: Please consult the website.

Howard Hughes Medical Institute Predoctoral Fellowships in Biological Sciences

Subjects: Biomedical sciences.

Purpose: To promote excellence in biomedical research by helping prospective researchers with exceptional promise to obtain high quality graduate education.

Eligibility: Open to applicants who are citizens or nationals of the United States or who are foreign citizens or nationals. Eligibility will be determined by the Howard Hughes Medical Institute on an individual basis.

Level of Study: Predoctorate.

Type: Fellowship.

Value: Annual stipend of US$18,000 and an allowance of US$16,000 to the fellowship institution in lieu of tuition and fees.

Length of Study: Five years.

Study Establishment: Any Institute of Higher Education offering advanced degrees in biomedical sciences.

Country of Study: Any country.

No. of awards offered: Over 80.

Application Procedure: Applicants must submit eligibility, medical student support if applicable, education, honours, awards and employment, educational objectives, previous research experience, proposed plan of research and study, contact information, personal and confidential information, participation in science education programmes, reference reports, undergraduate grade point average report, academic transcripts, Graduate Record Examination test

scores attained, Graduate Record Examination test-fee payment/reimbursement request, if applicable and Test of English As a Foreign Language scores attained, if applicable. Applicants are strongly advised to use the online application form if possible.

Closing Date: Please consult the website.

Additional Information: Note that Fellows who are United States citizens or nationals may study in the United States or abroad while those who are not United States citizens or nationals must enrol in a doctoral degree programme at a United States institution.

The NASA Administrator's Fellowship Program

Subjects: Science, mathematics and engineering.

Purpose: To enhance the professional development of NASA employees and the science, mathematics and engineering faculty of minority serving institutions. Minority serving institutions include Historically Black Colleges and Universities, Hispanic-Serving Institutions and Tribal Colleges and Universities.

Eligibility: NASA employees must be full-time career employees at the GS13 level or above, and must sign a service agreement to work at NASA for at least two years following the fellowship tenure. For the minority serving institutions faculty, applicants must be United States citizens, tenure track faculty at minority serving institutions, hold a PhD or ScD for less than 15 years in science, engineering or mathematics, with expertise in NASA related fields and must agree to return to home institution for at least two years following the fellowship tenure.

Type: Fellowship.

Value: NASA employees retain their current salaries and minority serving institutions' faculty receive a stipend equal to their current salary.

Length of Study: One year followed by 15-18 months of developmental assignments for NASA employees and 12-18 months for minority serving institutions faculty.

Study Establishment: NASA headquarters, field centres or other appropriate organisations, or another government agency, a research university or private sector organisation.

No. of awards offered: Six for NASA employees and six for minority serving institutions' faculty research.

Application Procedure: Applicants must use the online application form.

Closing Date: Please consult the website.

NATIONAL AIR AND SPACE MUSEUM, SMITHSONIAN (NASM)

Room 3306, Washington, DC, 20560, United States of America
Tel: (1) 202 633 8002
www: http://www.nasm.edu
Contact: Ms Anita Mason

The Smithsonian Institution's National Air and Space Museum (NASM) maintains the largest collection of historic air and spacecraft in the world. It is also a vital centre for research into the history, science and technology of aviation and space flight.

CEPS Fellowship

Subjects: Geology.

Purpose: To assist postdoctoral candidates interested in scientific research in planetary and terrestrial geological and geophysical studies.

Eligibility: There are no eligibility restrictions.

Level of Study: Postdoctorate.

Type: Fellowship.

Value: Competitive with the National Research Council Awards.

Length of Study: One-two years.

Frequency: Dependent on funds available.

Study Establishment: In residence at the NASM.

Country of Study: United States of America.

Application Procedure: Applicants must complete an application form.

Closing Date: Please contact the organisation.
No. of awards given last year: One.
No. of applicants last year: 21.

NATIONAL ALLIANCE FOR RESEARCH ON SCHIZOPHRENIA AND DEPRESSION (NARSAD)

60 Cutter Mill Road
Suite 404, Great Neck, NY, 11021, United States of America
Tel: (1) 516 829 5576
Fax: (1) 516 487 6930
Email: amoran@narsad.org
www: http://www.narsad.org
Contact: Ms Audra Moran, Director, Research Grants Programme

The National Alliance for Research on Schizophrenia and Depression (NARSAD) raises and distributes funds for scientific research into the causes, cures, treatments and prevention of neurobiological disorders, primarily the schizophrenias, depressions and bipolar disorders. NARSAD is the largest donor supported organisation devoted exclusively to supporting scientific research on brain disorders in the world.

NARSAD Distinguished Investigator Awards

Subjects: Schizophrenia, major affective disorders or other serious mental illnesses including bipolar disease, borderline disorders with depression or suicide plus research with children.
Purpose: To encourage experienced scientists to pursue innovative projects in diverse areas of neurobiological research.
Eligibility: Open to senior researchers of any nationality who are of professor status or equivalent and maintain their own laboratory.
Level of Study: Postdoctorate, Research.
Type: Grant.
Value: Up to US$100,000.
Length of Study: One year.
Frequency: Annual.
Country of Study: Any country.
No. of awards offered: Varies.
Application Procedure: Applicants must refer to the website for guidelines and a face sheet.
Closing Date: May 15th.
Funding: Private.
Contributor: Donors.
No. of awards given last year: Nine.
No. of applicants last year: 82.
Additional Information: Further information is available from the website.

NARSAD Independent Investigator Awards

Subjects: Schizophrenia, major affective disorders or other serious mental illnesses including bipolar disease, borderline disorders with depression or suicide plus research with children.
Purpose: To facilitate innovative research opportunities in diverse areas of neurobiological research.
Eligibility: This award is intended for scientists at the academic level of associate professor or equivalent, who have won national competitive support as a principal investigator.
Level of Study: Postdoctorate, Research.
Type: Grant.
Value: Up to US$50,000 maximum per year.
Length of Study: Two years.
Frequency: Annual.
Country of Study: Any country.
No. of awards offered: Varies.
Application Procedure: Applicants must refer to the website for guidelines and a face sheet.
Closing Date: March 5th.
Funding: Private.

Contributor: Donors.
No. of awards given last year: 40.
No. of applicants last year: 88.
Additional Information: Further information is available from the website.

NARSAD Young Investigator Awards

Subjects: Schizophrenia, major affective disorders or other serious mental illnesses including bipolar disease, borderline disorders with depression or suicide plus research with children.
Purpose: To enable promising investigators to either extend their research fellowship training or to begin careers as independent research faculty.
Eligibility: Open to investigators who have attained a doctorate or equivalent degree, are affiliated with a specific research institution and who have a mentor or senior collaborator who is performing significant research in an area relevant to schizophrenia, depression or other serious mental illnesses. Candidates should be at the postdoctoral through to assistant professor level.
Level of Study: Postdoctorate, Research.
Type: Grant.
Value: Up to US$30,000 maximum per year.
Length of Study: Up to two years.
Frequency: Annual.
Country of Study: Any country.
No. of awards offered: Varies.
Application Procedure: Applicants must refer to the website for guidelines and a face sheet.
Closing Date: July 25th.
Funding: Private.
Contributor: Donors.
No. of awards given last year: 131.
No. of applicants last year: 324.
Additional Information: This award is intended to support only advanced Fellows and assistant professors or their equivalent. Further information is available from the website.

NATIONAL ASSOCIATION OF BROADCASTERS (NAB)

1771 N Street North West, Washington, DC, 20036-2891, United States of America
Tel: (1) 202 429 5389
www: http://www.nab.org/research/grants/grants.asp
Contact: Ms Molly Fink, Office Manager

The National Association of Broadcasters (NAB) aims to make high quality academic research available to industry practitioners as well as other researchers.

NAB Grants for Research in Broadcasting

Subjects: Broadcast research, especially research on economic, business, social or policy issues of importance to the United States of America's commercial broadcast industry.
Purpose: To stimulate interest in broadcast research.
Eligibility: Open to all academic personnel working in the several disciplines that relate to the social, cultural, political and economic aspects of broadcasting. Graduate students are invited to submit proposals.
Level of Study: Doctorate, Graduate, Postdoctorate, Postgraduate.
Type: Grant.
Value: US$5,000 average.
Length of Study: One year.
Frequency: Annual.
Country of Study: United States of America.
No. of awards offered: Varies.
Application Procedure: Applicants must complete an application form, available on written request, or from the website.
Closing Date: Please write for details.
No. of awards given last year: Six.

No. of applicants last year: 41.

NATIONAL ASSOCIATION OF COMPOSERS

PO Box 49256
Barrington Station, Los Angeles, CA, 90049, United States of
America
Tel: (1) 310 541 8213
Fax: (1) 310 544 1413
Email: bia@flash.net
www: http://www.music-usa.org/nacusa
Contact: Mr Marshall Bialosky, President

The National Association of Composers presents concerts of the members' music throughout the United States, mainly the West Coast (Los Angeles and San Francisco) and the East Coast (New York, Philadelphia and Boston).

National Association of Composers Young Composers Competition

Subjects: Music composition.
Purpose: To foster the creation of new American concert hall music.
Eligibility: Open to nationals of any country between the ages of 18 and 30.
Level of Study: Postdoctorate, Postgraduate.
Type: Cash and musical performance.
Value: US$200 first place, US$50 second place.
Frequency: Annual.
Country of Study: Any country.
No. of awards offered: Two.
Application Procedure: Applicants must send in their music as there are no application forms.
Closing Date: October 30th.
Funding: Private.
No. of awards given last year: Two.
No. of applicants last year: 35.

NATIONAL ASSOCIATION OF DENTAL ASSISTANTS

900 South Washington Street
G-13, Falls Church, VA, 22046, United States of America
Tel: (1) 703 237 8616
Fax: (1) 703 533 1153
Contact: Scholarship Department

National Association of Dental Assistants Annual Scholarship Award

Subjects: Dental assistant certification, recertification, dental training, continuing dental education seminars or any course that is related to, or required in, the dental degree programme.
Purpose: To enable dental assistants to further their education.
Eligibility: Open to dental assistants who have a minimum of two years' membership in good standing. Applicants may also be a member's dependant, spouse or grandchild. All courses must be approved by the board.
Level of Study: Unrestricted.
Type: Scholarship.
Value: US$250.
Frequency: Annual.
Study Establishment: Appropriate institutions.
Country of Study: Any country.
No. of awards offered: One-two.
Application Procedure: Applicants must submit one recommendation from their current or previous employer, one recommendation from someone other than a member (if a member's dependant) such as a school counsellor or another dental assistant, a completed application form and an up to date student transcript.
Closing Date: May 31st.
No. of awards given last year: Two.
No. of applicants last year: Approx. 10.

NATIONAL ASSOCIATION OF SCHOLARS (NAS)

221 Witherspoon Street
2nd Floor, Princeton, NJ, 08542-3215, United States of America
Tel: (1) 609 683 7878
Fax: (1) 609 683 0316
Email: nas@nas.org
www: http://www.nas.org
Contact: G C Brasor, Associate Director

The National Association of Scholars (NAS) is an organisation of professors, graduate students, college administrators and independent scholars committed to rational discourse as the foundation of academic life in a free democratic society. The NAS works to enrich the substance and strengthen the integrity of scholarship and teaching, convinced that only through an informed understanding of the western intellectual heritage and the realities of the contemporary world, can citizen and scholar be equipped to sustain civilisation's achievements.

The Barry R Gross Memorial Award

Subjects: Academic reform.
Purpose: To reward an NAS member for outstanding service, through the medium of the organisation or responsible citizenship, to the cause of academic reform.
Eligibility: Candidates must be NAS nominated.
Type: Award.
Value: US$1,000, a plaque and travel expenses to attend the national conference and present a speech.
Frequency: Every 18 months.
Funding: Private.
Additional Information: Established to honour the memory of Barry R Gross.

The Peter Shaw Memorial Award

Subjects: Writing on issues pertaining to higher education and American intellectual culture.
Purpose: To recognise exemplary writing on issues pertaining to higher education and American intellectual culture.
Eligibility: Candidates must be NAS nominated.
Type: Award.
Value: US$1,000, a plaque and travel expenses to attend the national conference and present a speech.
Frequency: Every 18 months.
Funding: Private.
Additional Information: Established to honour the memory of Peter Shaw.

The Sidney Hook Memorial Award

Subjects: Defence of academic freedom and integrity of academic life.
Purpose: To award an individual for distinguished contributions to the defence of academic freedom and the integrity of academic life.
Eligibility: Candidates must be NAS nominated.
Type: Award.
Value: US$2,500, a plaque and travel expenses to attend the national conference and present a speech.
Frequency: Every 18 months.
Funding: Private.

NATIONAL ASTHMA CAMPAIGN

Providence House
Providence Place, London, N1 0NT, England
Tel: (44) 20 7226 2260
Fax: (44) 20 7704 0740
Email: pmajor@asthma.org.uk
www: http://www.asthma.org.uk
Contact: Office for Funding

The National Asthma Campaign is an independent United Kingdom charity, working to conquer asthma in partnership with people with asthma and all who share their concern. Their work is achieved by a combination of research, education and support.

National Asthma Campaign Project Grants

Subjects: Research into delivery or care, interaction of asthma and the environment, evaluation of complementary therapies, genetics, mechanisms of severe asthma and primary prevention.
Purpose: To fund research in applied, basic or clinical research relevant to asthma or a related allergy.
Eligibility: Open to tenured individuals working in the United Kingdom.
Level of Study: Research.
Type: Project grant.
Value: Varies.
Length of Study: A maximum of three years.
Frequency: Annual.
Country of Study: Normally the United Kingdom.
No. of awards offered: 18-20 per year.
Application Procedure: Applicants must complete an application form, available directly from the website.
Closing Date: Late November.
Funding: Private.
No. of awards given last year: 18.
No. of applicants last year: 65.

NATIONAL ATAXIA FOUNDATION

2600 Fernbrook Lane
Suite 119, Minneapolis, MN, 55447, United States of America
Tel: (1) 763 553 0020
Fax: (1) 763 553 0167
Email: naf@mail.ataxia.org
www: http://www.ataxia.org
Contact: Ms Donna Gruetzmacher, Executive Director

The National Ataxia Foundation is dedicated to improving the lives of persons affected by ataxia through support, education and research.

Ataxia Research Grant

Subjects: Neurology and genetics in relation to the study of ataxia.
Purpose: To support research projects.
Eligibility: There are no eligibility restrictions.
Level of Study: Unrestricted.
Type: Research grant.
Value: US$5,000-35,000.
Length of Study: One year.
Frequency: Annual.
Country of Study: Any country.
No. of awards offered: Approx. nine.
Application Procedure: Applicants must apply for application forms and guidelines, available on request or from the website.
Closing Date: August 15th.
Funding: Private.
Contributor: Members of the Foundation.
No. of awards given last year: 10.
No. of applicants last year: 18.

NATIONAL BLACK MBA ASSOCIATION (NBMBAA)

180 North Michigan
Suite 1400, Chicago, IL, 60601, United States of America
Tel: (1) 312 236 2622
Fax: (1) 312 236 4131
Email: lori@nbmbaa.org
www: http://www.nbmbaa.org
Contact: Director of Education

The National Black MBA Association (NBMBAA) is a business organisation which leads in the creation of economic and intellectual wealth for the black community. Started in 1970, it has 39 chapters and one international affiliate.

NBMBAA MBA Scholarships

Subjects: An essay topic is selected annually by the scholarship committee.
Eligibility: Open to minority full-time students enrolled in an accredited United States business programme pursuing an MBA degree.
Level of Study: MBA.
Type: Scholarship.
Value: From US$2,500-4,000, plus travel, accommodation and registration to the annual conference and a three year membership in the NBMBAA.
Frequency: Annual.
Country of Study: United States of America.
No. of awards offered: 25.
Application Procedure: Applicants must submit a completed application form with official transcripts, a curriculum vitae, a two page essay on a topic determined by their office and a black and white photograph. Application forms are available from the website.
Closing Date: March 31st.
Funding: Commercial.
Additional Information: Further information is available on the website.

NATIONAL BRAIN TUMOR FOUNDATION (NBTF)

414 Thirteenth Street
Suite 700, Oakland, CA, 94612-2603, United States of America
Tel: (1) 510 839 9777
Fax: (1) 510 839 9779
Email: nbtf@braintumor.org
www: http://www.braintumor.org
Contact: Mr Robert Tufel, Director of Patient Services

Charles B Wilson Brain Tumor Research Excellence Grant

Subjects: Neuro-oncology and neuro-science.
Purpose: To provide funding for general research.
Eligibility: Preference is given to translational research but all type of applications are accepted.
Level of Study: Research.
Type: Research grant.
Value: A total value of US$100,000.
Country of Study: United States of America or Canada.

NABTC/NABTT Research Grant

Subjects: Brain tumour research.
Purpose: To fund research.
Eligibility: Applicants must be researchers at a member institution of the North American Brain Tumor Consortium (NABTC) or New Approaches to Brain Tumor Therapy (NABTT).
Level of Study: Research.
Type: Grant.
Value: US$100,000.

Study Establishment: A member institution of the North American Brain Tumor Consortium (NABTC) or New Approaches to Brain Tumor Therapy (NABTT).
Country of Study: United States of America or Canada.
No. of awards offered: One.
Application Procedure: Applicants must visit the website for further information.

NBTF Quality of Life Research Grant

Subjects: Brain tumour research.
Purpose: To provide support for research into quality of life issues affecting both brain tumour patients and their caregivers.
Level of Study: Research.
Type: Research grant.
Value: US$15,000.
Country of Study: United States of America or Canada.
No. of awards offered: One.
Application Procedure: Applicants must visit the website for further information.

The Oligo Brain Tumor Fund

Subjects: Neurology.
Purpose: To support research into oligodendroglioma tumours.
Level of Study: Research.
Type: Research grant.
Value: US$50,000.
Country of Study: United States of America or Canada.
No. of awards offered: Varies.
Application Procedure: Applicants must visit the website for further information.
Closing Date: February.
Funding: Private.
Contributor: The Jeffrey Bein Family.

Richard Anthony Hollow, Jr Memorial Grant for NABTC Institutions

Subjects: Brain tumour research.
Purpose: To support the work of a researcher at one of the North American Brain Tumor Consortium (NABTC) member institutions.
Eligibility: Applicants must be a researcher at a NABTC member institution.
Level of Study: Research.
Type: Grant.
Value: US$25,000.
Study Establishment: A North American Brain Tumor Consortium (NABTC) member institution.
Country of Study: United States of America or Canada.
No. of awards offered: One.
Application Procedure: Applicants must visit the website for further information.
Contributor: The family of Richard Anthony Hollow, Junior.

The Steven J Bryant Research Grant

Subjects: Medical research.
Purpose: This grant, funded by the Steven J. Bryant Foundation, will be awarded to the best result-orientated research project.
Eligibility: Applicants must be practising healthcare professionals conducting research in the Northern Ohio and/or Western Pennsylvania area. Specific preferences given for academic medical institutions and translational research but all applicants are considered.
Level of Study: Research.
Type: Research grant.
Value: US$25,000.
Country of Study: United States of America or Canada.
No. of awards offered: One.
Application Procedure: Applicants must visit the website for further information.
Funding: Private.
Contributor: The Steven J Bryant Foundation.

NATIONAL CANCER INSTITUTE OF CANADA (NCIC)

Suite 200
10 Alcorn Avenue, Toronto, ON, M4V 3B1, Canada
Tel: (1) 416 961 7223
Fax: (1) 416 732 7327
Email: ncic@cancer.ca
www: http://www.ncic.cancer.ca
Contact: Dr Michael A Wosnick, Research Programmes Director

The National Cancer Institute of Canada (NCIC) and the Canadian Cancer Society (CCS) are organisations that have evolved from the need for a co-ordinated attack on the problem of cancer in Canada and have formed a 50 year partnership. The Terry Fox Foundation has also entered into partnership with the NCIC, which is the sole recipient of funds raised by the Foundation for Cancer Research.

CCS Feasibility Grants

Subjects: Cancer research.
Purpose: To provide a modest level of funding as the NCIC recognises that it is difficult to submit a full application for a research grant without having first conducted preliminary studies.
Eligibility: This programme is open to all applicants but priority will be given where it is apparent that no other resources are available. These grants will not be awarded to support travel to conduct planning meetings. These funds will also not be awarded for conference travel or for the purchase of permanent equipment.
Level of Study: Postgraduate.
Type: Grant.
Value: Up to canadian $35,000.
Length of Study: One year, but funds may be spent over a two year period.
Frequency: Annual.
Country of Study: Canada.
No. of awards offered: Varies.
Application Procedure: Applicants must write for details or refer to the website.
Closing Date: Please contact the organisation.
Funding: Private.
Contributor: The Canadian Cancer Society.
Additional Information: Further information is available from the website.

Equipment Grants for New Investigators

Subjects: Cancer research.
Purpose: To make it possible for new investigators to set up cancer research facilities in Canada. The award is designed to assist young investigators beginning their career.
Eligibility: Applicants should be new investigators who have no more than two years' experience as an independent investigator and have not received an operational research grant from the National Cancer Institute or another comparable agency.
Level of Study: Postgraduate.
Type: Grant.
Value: Up to canadian $75,000, plus an additional canadian $75,000.
Frequency: Dependent on funds available.
Country of Study: Canada.
No. of awards offered: Varies.
Application Procedure: Applicants must write for details or refer to the website.
Closing Date: Please contact the organisation.
Funding: Private.
Contributor: The Terry Fox Foundation.
Additional Information: The award is not intended to facilitate the relocation of individuals from one laboratory to another. Further information is available from the website.

NCIC Clinical Research Fellowships

Subjects: Clinical cancer research.

Purpose: To assist outstanding individuals who hold a doctoral degree in medicine and who seek specialised training.
Eligibility: Applicants must be Canadian citizens or residents at the time of application, possess a doctoral degree in medicine from a recognised institution and be licensed to practice in Canada. Preference will be given to those who can demonstrate research commitment by having completed, or being enrolled in, a relevant graduate course.
Level of Study: Postdoctorate, Professional development.
Type: Research fellowship.
Value: Minimum US$25,000 rising for each year of postdoctoral experience to a maximum of US$47,500 per year.
Length of Study: Up to three years.
Frequency: Annual.
Study Establishment: A teaching hospital.
Country of Study: Canada, or abroad as approved.
No. of awards offered: Varies.
Application Procedure: Applicants must write for details or refer to the website.
Closing Date: February 1st.
Funding: Private.
Contributor: The Terry Fox Foundation and the Canadian Cancer Society.
No. of awards given last year: One.
No. of applicants last year: Three.
Additional Information: Further information is available from the website. Stipends are subject to annual review. Recipients of these fellowships are eligible to apply for a contribution of canadian $1,200 towards the cost of conference travel per award year.

NCIC Research Grants for New Investigators

Subjects: Cancer research.
Purpose: To facilitate the greatest possibility for new investigators to obtain grant support for cancer research. The award is designed to assist new investigators who are beginning a career in cancer research.
Eligibility: Applicants should be new investigators who have no more than two years' experience as an independent investigator and have not previously received a research grant from the National Cancer Institute of Canada or another comparable agency.
Level of Study: Postgraduate.
Type: Research grant.
Value: Varies.
Frequency: Annual.
Study Establishment: An approved institution.
Country of Study: Canada.
No. of awards offered: Varies.
Application Procedure: Applicants must write for details or refer to the website.
Closing Date: October 15th.
Funding: Private.
Contributor: The Terry Fox Foundation.
No. of awards given last year: Seven.
No. of applicants last year: 26.
Additional Information: Grantees are asked to play a direct role in the Institute's efforts to provide more funds for research in the future. Recipients of the award are expected to acknowledge the support of the Institute and its financial partners in all scientific communications and press releases related to the award.

NCIC Research Grants to Individuals

Subjects: Cancer research.
Purpose: To stimulate Canadian investigators in a very broad spectrum of research.
Eligibility: A researcher who is designated as the principal investigator must be based in, or formally affiliated with, but not necessarily receive salary support from, an eligible Canadian host institution such as a university, research institute or health care agency. Graduate students, postdoctoral Fellows, research associates, technical support staff, or investigators based outside of Canada are not eligible to be a principal investigator.
Level of Study: Postgraduate.

Type: Research grant.
Value: Awards will be granted for the purchase and maintenance of animals, for expendable supplies, minor items of equipment, for payment of graduate students, postdoctoral Fellows and technical and professional assistants, and for research travel and permanent equipment. An allocation for conference travel will be added automatically by the NCIC. These grants do not provide for personal salary support of the principal investigator and/or co-applicants nor for institutional overhead costs.
Length of Study: Three years in the first instance, with possible renewals for periods of one-five years.
Frequency: Annual.
Study Establishment: Universities or other institutions.
Country of Study: Canada.
No. of awards offered: Varies.
Application Procedure: Applicants must complete an application form. Further details are available on request or from the website.
Closing Date: Please contact the organisation.
Funding: Private.
Contributor: The Terry Fox Foundation and the Canadian Cancer Society.
Additional Information: Further information is available from the website. Grants will be awarded to projects deemed worthy of support, provided that the basic equipment and research facilities are available in the institution concerned and that it will provide the necessary administrative services. Grants are made only with the consent and knowledge of the administrative head of the institution at which they are to be held and applications must be countersigned accordingly.

NCIC Research Scientist Awards

Subjects: Cancer research.
Purpose: To provide a career development opportunity for individuals committed to a high standard of cancer research.
Eligibility: Applicants must hold a PhD, MD or comparable degree and be conducting research in a field relevant to cancer or cancer control. An intention to remain in Canada is required. Candidates must have a minimum of three years' postdoctoral training in research and may not have more than five years' research experience calculated from the beginning of their independent research career. Applicants must also hold a nationally peer reviewed research grant relevant to cancer at the time of application.
Level of Study: Postdoctorate.
Type: Research grant.
Value: The initial salary will depend on the experience and competence of the individual. The University must be willing to provide space and two years' salary at the end of the award.
Length of Study: A maximum of six years.
Frequency: Annual.
Study Establishment: An approved university or research establishment.
Country of Study: Canada.
No. of awards offered: Varies.
Application Procedure: Applicants must refer to the website for details. Applications are made by the university in which the candidate will hold an academic appointment, and not directly from the applicants themselves.
Closing Date: Please contact the organisation.
Funding: Private.
Contributor: The Canadian Cancer Society.
No. of awards given last year: Three.
No. of applicants last year: 10.
Additional Information: Further information is available from the website.

NCIC Research Studentships

Subjects: Cancer research.
Purpose: To award outstanding PhD students who plan a career in cancer research in Canada.
Eligibility: Applicants must be Canadian residents enrolled in a PhD programme at a Canadian institute. Applicants must have completed

at least two years of research training at graduate level or have equivalent research experience.

Level of Study: Postgraduate.

Type: Research grant.

Value: Canadian $21,500 per year.

Length of Study: A maximum of four years.

Frequency: Annual.

Study Establishment: An approved institution.

Country of Study: Canada.

No. of awards offered: Varies.

Application Procedure: Applicants must refer to the website for details and application forms.

Closing Date: Please contact the organisation.

Funding: Private.

Contributor: The Terry Fox Foundation and the Canadian Cancer Society.

Additional Information: Further information is available from the website. The NCIC invite all members of the research community to identify and approach qualified individuals, and encourage them to apply.

NCIC Travel Award for Senior Level PhD Students

Subjects: Cancer research.

Purpose: To provide financial assistance by helping to defray the travel costs associated with making a scientific presentation at a conference, symposium or other appropriate professional gathering.

Eligibility: Applicants must be students enrolled in a PhD or MD programme at a Canadian institution and be in the final phase of their studies. Candidates must be attending a conference for the purpose of presenting data from a cancer related project on a first author basis.

Level of Study: Postgraduate.

Type: Travel grant.

Value: Up to canadian $1,500.

Frequency: Three times each year.

Country of Study: Canada.

No. of awards offered: Up to 20 per calendar year.

Application Procedure: Applicants must refer to the website.

Closing Date: April 1st, September 1st or December 1st.

Funding: Private.

Contributor: The Canadian Cancer Society.

No. of awards given last year: 10.

No. of applicants last year: 14.

Additional Information: Further information is available from the website.

Post-PhD and Post-MD Research Fellowships

Subjects: Cancer research.

Purpose: To provide training in cancer research for outstanding candidates who plan a career in Canada in this field of investigation.

Eligibility: Candidates must be graduates of a university recognised by the NCIC and must be accepted for postdoctoral training in the field of cancer research in an academic environment also recognised. If the Fellowship is to be taken outside Canada the applicant must be either a Canadian citizen or Canadian landed immigrant. Post MD candidates must be licensed to practice in Canada. For applicants with both PhD and MD degrees, the degree obtained most recently will determine the Fellowship category for which they should apply.

Level of Study: Postgraduate.

Type: Fellowship.

Value: Minimum canadian $25,000 rising for each year of postdoctoral experience to a maximum of canadian $47,500 per year.

Length of Study: Up to a maximum of three years.

Frequency: Annual.

Study Establishment: A Canadian institute or abroad if the applicant is Canadian or a Canadian landed immigrant.

Country of Study: Canada or abroad.

No. of awards offered: Varies.

Application Procedure: Applicants must refer to the website.

Closing Date: February 1st.

Funding: Private.

Contributor: The Terry Fox Foundation and the Canadian Cancer Society.

No. of awards given last year: 19.

No. of applicants last year: 70.

Additional Information: Further information is available from the website.

NATIONAL CENTER FOR ATMOSPHERIC RESEARCH (NCAR)

PO Box 3000, Boulder, CO, 80307-3000, United States of America

Tel: (1) 303 497 1601

Fax: (1) 303 497 1646

Email: barbm@ucar.edu

www: http://www.asp.ucar.edu/asp

Contact: Ms Barbara Hansford, Co-ordinator

The National Center for Atmospheric Research (NCAR) is a national research centre focused on atmospheric science.

NCAR Postdoctoral Appointments in the Advanced Study Program

Subjects: Atmosphere sciences.

Purpose: To assist and support research.

Eligibility: Open to those who have recently received their PhD and scientists with no more than four years' applicable experience since receiving their PhD. Foreign nationals may apply. NCAR is an equal opportunity employer with an affirmative action programme.

Level of Study: Postdoctorate.

Type: Fellowship.

Value: Minimum of US$40,000 per year (for recent PhDs) and US$42,200 for appointees in the second year at NCAR/ASP. All appointees are eligible for life and health insurance. Travel expenses to the Center are reimbursed for the appointee and family. Fellows living abroad will have round trip travel expenses for themselves and their families paid up to a maximum of US$2,500. A small allowance for moving and storing personal belongings is provided. Scientific travel and registration fees that cost up to US$1,500 per year are normally available.

Length of Study: Up to one year, with a possibility of renewal for a further year.

Frequency: Annual.

Study Establishment: The Center.

Country of Study: United States of America.

No. of awards offered: 8-10.

Application Procedure: Applicants must send transcripts of graduate university courses, a curriculum vitae including any scientific work experience, an abstract of doctoral thesis, four references, a short statement describing the applicant's interest in the atmospheric sciences and the work he or she would like to do during their visit to the National Center for Atmospheric Research. Applications should be addressed to Barbara Hanford, Advanced Study Programme at the main address or sent express mail to the address below.

Closing Date: January 5th.

Funding: Government.

No. of awards given last year: 10.

No. of applicants last year: 100.

For further information contact:

1850 Table Mesa Drive, Boulder, CO, 80305, United States of America

THE NATIONAL COLLEGIATE ATHLETIC ASSOCIATION

700 West Washington Avenue
PO Box 6222, Indianapolis, IN, 46206-6222, United States of America
Tel: (1) 317 917 6222
Fax: (1) 317 917 6888
www: http://www.ncaa.org

The National Collegiate Athletic Association is the organisation through which the nation's colleges and universities speak and act on athletics matters at the national level. It is a voluntary association of more than 1,200 institutions, conferences, organisations and individuals devoted to the sound administration of intercollegiate athletics.

NCAA Postgraduate Scholarship

Subjects: All subjects.
Purpose: To honour outstanding student athletes who are also outstanding scholars.
Eligibility: Open to student athletes enrolled at an NCAA member institution, in the last year of intercollegiate competition and with a minimum grade point average of 3,200 on a 4,000 scale or its equivalent.
Level of Study: Postgraduate.
Type: Grant.
Value: One time grant of US$5,000. This is not earmarked for a specific area of postgraduate study but the awardee must use it as a full-time graduate student in a graduate or professional school of an academically accredited institution, part-time or full-time within three years of winning the award.
Frequency: This grant is not renewable.
Country of Study: Any country.
No. of awards offered: 174.
Application Procedure: Applicants must be nominated by their faculty athletics representative or director of athletics.
Closing Date: Three deadlines, may vary slightly each year.
Funding: Private.
No. of awards given last year: 174.

NATIONAL ENDOWMENT FOR THE HUMANITIES (NEH)

Room 318
1100 Pennsylvania Avenue North West, Washington, DC, 20506, United States of America
Tel: (1) 202 606 8400
Fax: (1) 202 606 8204
Email: research@neh.gov
www: http://www.neh.gov
Contact: Programme Officer

Through grants to educational institutions, fellowships to scholars and teachers, and through the support of significant research, this division is designed to strengthen sustained, thoughtful study of the humanities at all levels of education and promote original research into the humanities.

NEH Centers for Advanced Study Grants

Subjects: The humanities.
Purpose: To support co-ordinated research in well defined subject areas through block fellowship grants.
Eligibility: Open to independent research libraries and museums, American research centres overseas and centres for advanced study.
Level of Study: Postgraduate.
Type: Grant.
Value: Varies.

Frequency: Annual.
Study Establishment: Any approved centres for advanced study.
Country of Study: Any country.
No. of awards offered: Varies.
Application Procedure: Applicants must contact the organisation for details.
Closing Date: September 1st.
Funding: Government.
Additional Information: Individuals should apply directly to the centres, a list of which is available from the Division of Research or on the NEH website.

NEH Collaborative Research

Subjects: Arts and humanities.
Purpose: To support original research undertaken by two or more scholars, which because of its scope, complexity or duration, cannot be sponsored through one year fellowships.
Eligibility: Applicants must visit the website for eligibility requirements.
Level of Study: Postdoctorate.
Type: Research grant.
Value: Varies depending on the project.
Length of Study: Up to three years.
Frequency: Annual.
Country of Study: Any country.
No. of awards offered: Varies.
Application Procedure: Applicants must complete a NEH application form in addition to project material.
Closing Date: September 1st.
Funding: Government.
Additional Information: People seeking further information on the full range of programmes in the Division of Research should contact NEH.

NEH Extending the Reach: Faculty Research Awards

Subjects: The humanities.
Purpose: To strengthen and improve teaching.
Eligibility: Open to faculty members of historically black United States colleges and universities, Hispanic serving colleges and universities and tribally controlled colleges.
Level of Study: Doctorate, Postdoctorate.
Type: Fellowship.
Value: Up to US$30,000.
Length of Study: 9-12 months.
Frequency: Annual.
Study Establishment: The target institutions noted above.
Country of Study: United States of America.
No. of awards offered: Varies.
Application Procedure: Applicants must obtain application materials, available directly from the NEH or from the website.
Closing Date: April 10th.
Funding: Government.
Additional Information: Further information is available on request and questions should be directed to the Division of Research.

NEH Fellowships for College Teachers and Independent Scholars

Subjects: Projects which may contribute to scholarly knowledge, to the conception and substance of individual courses in the humanities, or to the general public's understanding of the humanities. Projects may address broad topics or consist of study and research in a specialised field.
Purpose: To encourage and support full-time independent advanced study and research by people of diverse interests, backgrounds and circumstances.
Eligibility: Open to teachers in two year, four year and five year colleges and universities, faculty members of university departments and programmes that do not grant the PhD, individuals affiliated with institutions other than colleges and universities, and Scholars and writers working independently. Applicants need not have advanced degrees, but candidates for degrees and persons seeking support

for work leading towards degrees are not eligible. Applicants should be United States citizens or foreign nationals who have resided in the United States of America for at least three years.
Level of Study: Postdoctorate.
Type: Fellowship.
Value: The maximum stipend is US$35,000.
Length of Study: 6-12 consecutive months.
Frequency: Annual.
Country of Study: Any country.
No. of awards offered: Approx. 86.
Application Procedure: Applicants must complete an application form. Application guidelines are available from the Division of Research at the main address, or by visiting the NEH website.
Closing Date: May 1st.
Funding: Government.

NEH Fellowships for University Teachers
Subjects: Projects which may contribute to scholarly knowledge, to the conception and substance of individual courses in the humanities, or to the general public's understanding of the humanities. Projects may address broad topics or consist of study and research in a specialised field.
Purpose: To encourage and support full-time independent advanced study and research by people of diverse interests, backgrounds and circumstances.
Eligibility: Open to faculty members of departments and programmes in universities that grant the PhD and faculty members of postgraduate professional United States schools. Applicants need not have advanced degrees, but candidates for degrees and persons seeking support for work leading towards degrees are not eligible. Applicants should be United States citizens or foreign nationals who have resided in the United States for at least three years.
Level of Study: Postdoctorate.
Type: Fellowship.
Value: The maximum stipend is US$35,000.
Length of Study: 6-12 consecutive months.
Frequency: Annual.
Country of Study: Any country.
No. of awards offered: Approx. 86.
Application Procedure: Applicants must complete an application form. Application guidelines are available from the Public Affairs Office on (1) 202 606 8446 at the main address or by visiting the NEH website. Enquiries should be directed to the Division of Research.
Closing Date: May 1st.
Funding: Government.

NEH Humanities Focus Grants
Subjects: Arts and humanities.
Purpose: To support curriculum and materials development efforts, faculty study programmes within and among educational institutions, and the dissemination of significant development in humanities and education.
Eligibility: Open to institutions from the United States of America.
Level of Study: Unrestricted.
Type: Grant.
Value: Varies depending upon the project.
Length of Study: Varies.
Frequency: Annual.
Country of Study: Any country.
No. of awards offered: Approx. 30.
Application Procedure: Applicants must complete a NEH application form in addition to project material. Forms are available from NEH or from the website.
Funding: Government.
Additional Information: Enquiries should be directed to the Administrative Officer at the main address.

NEH National Education Projects
Subjects: Art and humanities.
Purpose: To support curriculum and materials development efforts, faculty study programmes within and among educational institutions,

and the dissemination of significant developments in humanities education.
Eligibility: Open to institutions from the United States of America. Projects should be national in scope and utilise, when appropriate, new technologies.
Level of Study: Unrestricted.
Type: Grant.
Value: Varies depending upon the project.
Length of Study: Varies.
Frequency: Annual.
Country of Study: Any country.
No. of awards offered: Approx. 20.
Application Procedure: Applicants must complete an NEH application form in addition to project materials. Forms are available from NEH or from the Endowment's website.
Closing Date: October 15th.
Funding: Government.
Additional Information: Enquiries should be directed to the Administrative Officer at the main address.

NEH Preservation and Access Grants
Subjects: Arts and humanities.
Purpose: To support projects that will describe, organise, preserve and increase the availability of resources supporting research, education and public programming in the humanities.
Eligibility: Open to individuals, non-profit institutions, cultural organisations, state agencies and institutional consortia.
Level of Study: Postgraduate.
Type: Grant.
Value: Varies.
Frequency: Annual.
Country of Study: Any country.
Application Procedure: Applicants must complete an application. Guidelines and instructions are available upon request from the Division of Preservation and Access, Room 411 on (1) 202 606 8570, by fax on (1) 202 606 8639, or by email preservation@neh.gov.
Closing Date: July 1st.
Funding: Government.
Additional Information: Further information is available on request.

NEH Seminars and Institutes for College Teachers
Subjects: All disciplines of the humanities and the humanistic social sciences.
Purpose: To provide American college and university teachers with the opportunity for intense collaborative study.
Eligibility: Open to individuals who primarily teach undergraduates and have not recently had the opportunity to use the resources of a major library. Independent Scholars are also eligible. Applicants must have completed their professional training by March 1st. Candidates for degrees and persons seeking support for work leading towards a degree are ineligible. Applicants should be United States citizens or foreign nationals who have resided in the United States for at least three years.
Level of Study: Postgraduate, Professional development.
Type: Summer seminar and institute.
Value: Varies, to cover travel expenses to and from the seminar centre, books and other research expenses and living expenses.
Length of Study: Four-six weeks.
Frequency: Annual.
Study Establishment: Various institutions under the direction of distinguished scholars and teachers.
Country of Study: Any country.
No. of awards offered: Approx. 12 seminars each with 15 members, and 12 institutes each with 25 members.
Application Procedure: Applicants must obtain an application form, available from individual seminar directors. A list of directors and a programme description are available from NEH.
Closing Date: March 1st.
Funding: Government.
Additional Information: Enquiries should be directed to the Administrative Officer.

NEH Seminars and Institutes for School Teachers

Subjects: The humanities.

Purpose: To provide opportunities for United States teachers to work with master teachers and distinguished scholars, studying important works in a systematic and thorough way.

Eligibility: Open to United States citizens who are full-time teachers at United States public, private or parochial schools, of grades K through to 12. Other school personnel may also apply.

Level of Study: Professional development.

Value: Varies depending on the length of the seminar or institute, to cover travel expenses to and from the host institution, books, other research expenses and living expenses.

Length of Study: Four-six weeks.

Frequency: Annual.

Country of Study: Any country.

No. of awards offered: Approx. 20 seminars each with 15 members, and 10 institutes each with 25 members.

Application Procedure: Applicants must submit application forms and essays. Interested school teachers should write directly to the Division of Education. Applications are then submitted to the seminar or institute director, and not to the NEH.

Closing Date: March 1st.

Funding: Government.

Additional Information: A list of the seminars and institutes is distributed widely in late Autumn and is also available from the Education division. Seminars range from Mozart to Beowulf, American history to Shakespeare. Institutes range from the American Civil Rights Movement to Mexican American Literature.

NEH Summer Stipends

Subjects: The humanities, the work proposed may be within the applicant's special areas of interest, or in some field that will enable them to understand their own fields better and enlarge their competence.

Purpose: To allow college and university staff to pursue two consecutive months of full-time study and research.

Eligibility: Each college and university in the United States of America and its territorial possessions may nominate two members of its faculty and staff. One nominee should be in the early stages of his or her career ie. a junior Scholar. For the purposes of the programme, instructors and assistant professors will be considered junior nominees and associate professors and professors will be considered senior nominees. Writers and independent Scholars may apply without nomination. All applicants should be United States citizens or foreign nationals who have resided in the United States for at least three years.

Level of Study: Unrestricted.

Type: Stipend.

Value: US$4,500.

Length of Study: Full-time study or research, for two consecutive months.

Frequency: Annual.

Country of Study: United States of America.

No. of awards offered: Approx. 130.

Application Procedure: Applicants must complete an application. Guidelines are available from the Division of Research and Education at the main address or from the website.

Closing Date: October 1st.

Funding: Government.

Additional Information: Further information is available on request.

NEH Tools Program

Subjects: The creation of dictionaries, historical and linguistic atlases, encyclopaedias, concordances, catalogues and raisonnés, linguistic grammars, descriptive catalogues, databases, and other materials that serve to codify information essential to research in the humanities. Grants are also given to projects that provide access to materials that are national or international in scope.

Purpose: To provide support for projects that promise to facilitate research in the humanities by organising essential resources for scholarship and by preparing reference works that can improve scholarly access to information and collections.

Eligibility: Open to Institutes of Higher Education, non-profit professional associations and scholarly societies and also individuals.

Level of Study: Postgraduate.

Type: Grant.

Value: Dependent upon proposal.

Frequency: As required.

Country of Study: United States of America.

No. of awards offered: Varies.

Application Procedure: Applicants must contact the organisation.

Closing Date: July 1st.

Funding: Government.

Additional Information: For information, applicants should write to the Division of Preservation and Access, Room 411, telephone on (1) 202 606 8570, fax on (1) 202 606 8639, or email preservation@neh.gov.

Schools for a New Millennium Grants

Subjects: Arts and humanities.

Purpose: To support whole schools, in partnership with colleges and communities, to implement professional development activities that integrate digital technology into the humanities classroom.

Eligibility: Open to institutions from the United States of America.

Level of Study: Unrestricted.

Type: Grant.

Value: Varies depending upon the project.

Length of Study: Varies.

Frequency: Annual.

Country of Study: Any country.

No. of awards offered: Approx. 20.

Application Procedure: Applicants must complete an NEH application form in addition to project materials. Forms are available from NEH or from the Endowment's website.

Funding: Government.

Additional Information: Enquiries should be directed to the Administrative Officer at the main address.

NATIONAL FEDERATION OF STATE POETRY SOCIETIES, INC.

310 South Adams Street, Beverly Hills, FL, 34465, United States of America
Tel: (1) 352 746 2919
Fax: (1) 352 746 7817
Email: verdure@digitalusa.net
Contact: Scholarship Chair

The National Federation of State Poetry Societies is a national coalition of state poetry societies which promotes the creation and appreciation of poetry.

The Edna Meudt Memorial Award

Subjects: Poetry.

Purpose: To encourage the study and writing of poetry.

Level of Study: Unrestricted.

Type: Scholarship.

Value: US$500, plus publication and travel stipend for awards ceremony.

Frequency: Annual.

Country of Study: Any country.

No. of awards offered: One.

Application Procedure: Applicants must complete and submit a 10 poem manuscript (titled) plus an application form.

Closing Date: February 1st.

Funding: Private.

Contributor: Individual donations.

Additional Information: Three anonymous, highly qualified judges will evaluate, judge and select scholarship winners on or before March 1st.

The Florence Kahn Memorial Award

Subjects: Poetry.
Purpose: To encourage the study and writing of poetry.
Type: Award.
Value: US$500, plus publication and travel stipend for awards ceremony.
Frequency: Annual.
Country of Study: Any country.
No. of awards offered: One.
Application Procedure: Applicants must complete and submit a 10 poem manuscript (titled) plus an application form.
Closing Date: February 1st.
Funding: Private.
Contributor: Individual donations.
Additional Information: Three anonymous, highly qualified judges will evaluate, judge and select scholarship winners on or before March 1st.

NATIONAL FEDERATION OF THE BLIND (NFB)

Scholarship Committee
805 Fifth Avenue, Grinnell, IA, 50112, United States of America
Tel: (1) 641 236 3366
Email: epc@roudley.com
www: http://www.nfb.org
Contact: Mrs Peggy Elliott, Chairman

Founded in 1940, the National Federation of the Blind (NFB) is the nation's largest and most influential membership organisation of blind people. With 50,000 members, the NFB has affiliates in all 50 states plus Washington DC and Puerto Rico, and over 700 local chapters. As a consumer and advocacy organisation, the NFB is considered the leading force in the blindness field today.

E U Parker Scholarship

Subjects: All subjects.
Purpose: To honour a long time leader of the National Federation of the Blind whose participation in the organisation stood for strong principles and strong support of the Federation's work.
Eligibility: Open to legally blind persons pursuing, or planning to pursue, a full-time post secondary course of training. The Scholarship is awarded on the basis of academic excellence, service to the community and financial need. Candidates need not be members of the Federation.
Level of Study: Postgraduate.
Type: Scholarship.
Frequency: Annual.
Country of Study: United States of America.
No. of awards offered: One.
Application Procedure: Applicants must complete an application form, available on request.
Closing Date: March 31st.
Funding: Private.

Hermione Grant Calhoun Scholarship

Subjects: All subjects.
Eligibility: Open to legally blind women pursuing, or planning to pursue, a full-time post secondary course of training. The Scholarship is awarded on the basis of academic excellence, service to the community and financial need. Candidates need not be members of the Federation.
Level of Study: Graduate.
Type: Scholarship.
Value: US$3,000.
Frequency: Annual.
Country of Study: United States of America.
No. of awards offered: One.
Application Procedure: Applicants must complete an application form, available on request.

Closing Date: March 31st.
Additional Information: Dr Isabelle Grant endowed this scholarship in memory of her daughter.

Howard Brown Rickard Scholarship

Subjects: Law, medicine, engineering, architecture or the natural sciences.
Eligibility: Open to legally blind persons pursuing, or planning to pursue, a full-time post secondary course of training. The Scholarship is awarded on the basis of academic excellence, service to the community and financial need. Candidates need not be members of the Federation.
Level of Study: Graduate.
Type: Scholarship.
Frequency: Annual.
Country of Study: United States of America.
No. of awards offered: One.
Application Procedure: Applicants must complete an application form, available on request.
Closing Date: March 31st.
Funding: Private.

Jennica Ferguson Memorial Scholarship

Subjects: All subjects.
Purpose: To keep the memory of Jennica Ferguson alive, a young woman who dealt with her blindness and terminal illness with a grace and strength she frequently assured others she drew from the Federation and from her faith in God.
Country of Study: United States of America.
Application Procedure: Applicants must complete an application form, available on request.

Kenneth Jernigan Scholarship

Subjects: All subjects.
Purpose: To keep fresh and current in the twenty first-century the understandings that Kenneth Jernigan brought to the field. To do this, the NFB has endowed this scholarship dedicated to his memory and to the continuation of the work he began.
Eligibility: Open to legally blind persons pursuing, or planning to pursue, a full-time post secondary course of training. The Scholarship is awarded on the basis of academic excellence, service to the community and financial need. Candidates need not be members of the Federation.
Type: Scholarship.
No. of awards offered: One.
Application Procedure: Applicants must complete an application form, available on request.
Closing Date: March 31st.
Additional Information: Given by the American Action Fund for Blind Children and Adults, a non-profit making organisation which works to assist blind persons, in memory of the man who changed perceptions regarding the capabilities of the blind in this country and throughout the world. Kenneth Jernigan is viewed as the most important figure in the twentieth-century in the lives of blind persons.

Kuchler-Killian Memorial Scholarship

Subjects: All subjects.
Eligibility: Open to legally blind persons pursuing, or planning to pursue, a full-time post secondary course of training. The Scholarship is awarded on the basis of academic excellence, service to the community and financial need. Candidates need not be members of the Federation. There are no additional restrictions.
Level of Study: Graduate.
Type: Scholarship.
Value: US$3,000.
Frequency: Annual.
Country of Study: United States of America.
No. of awards offered: One.
Application Procedure: Applicants must complete an application form, available on request.
Closing Date: March 31st.

Funding: Private.
Additional Information: Given in loving memory of her parents, Charles Albert Kuchler and Alice Helen Kuchler, by Junerose Killian, a dedicated member of the National Federation of the Blind in Connecticut.

Lora E Dunetz Scholarship

Subjects: All subjects.
Purpose: To assist the winner in achieving a lifetime of employment through higher education.
Eligibility: There are no restrictions but preference will be given to those studying to enter the medical field.
Country of Study: United States of America.
Application Procedure: Applicants must complete an application form, available on request.

Michael and Marie Marucci Scholarship

Subjects: All subjects that involve study abroad.
Eligibility: Open to candidates studying a foreign language or comparative literature pursuing a degree in history, geography or political science with a concentration in international studies, or majoring in any other discipline that involves study abroad. The winner's file must also show evidence of competence in a foreign language.
Type: Scholarship.
Country of Study: United States of America.
Additional Information: Given by two dedicated and valued members of the National Federation of the Blind of Maryland.

National Federation of the Blind Computer Science Scholarship

Subjects: Computer science.
Eligibility: Open to legally blind persons pursuing, or planning to pursue, a full-time post secondary course of training. The Scholarship is awarded on the basis of academic excellence, service to the community and financial need. Candidates need not be members of the Federation.
Level of Study: Postgraduate.
Type: Scholarship.
Frequency: Annual.
Country of Study: United States of America.
No. of awards offered: One.
Application Procedure: Applicants must complete an application form, available on request.
Closing Date: March 31st.
Funding: Private.

National Federation of the Blind Educator of Tomorrow Award

Subjects: Teaching.
Eligibility: Open to legally blind persons pursuing, or planning to pursue, a full-time post secondary course of training. The winner must be planning a career in elementary, secondary or post secondary teaching. The Scholarship is awarded on the basis of academic excellence, service to the community and financial need. Candidates need not be members of the Federation.
Level of Study: Graduate.
Type: Scholarship.
Frequency: Annual.
Country of Study: United States of America.
No. of awards offered: One.
Application Procedure: Applicants must complete an application form, available on request.
Closing Date: March 31st.
Funding: Private.

National Federation of the Blind Humanities Scholarship

Subjects: The traditional humanities such as art, English, foreign languages, history, philosophy or religion.
Eligibility: Open to legally blind persons pursuing, or planning to pursue, a full-time post secondary course of training. The

Scholarship is awarded on the basis of academic excellence, service to the community and financial need. Candidates need not be members of the Federation.
Level of Study: Graduate.
Type: Scholarship.
Frequency: Annual.
Country of Study: United States of America.
No. of awards offered: One.
Application Procedure: Applicants must complete an application form, available on request.
Closing Date: March 31st.
Funding: Private.

National Federation of the Blind Scholarships

Subjects: All subjects.
Eligibility: Open to legally blind persons pursuing, or planning to pursue, a full-time post secondary course of training. The Scholarship is awarded on the basis of academic excellence, service to the community and financial need. Candidates need not be members of the Federation. There are no additional restrictions, except that one scholarship may be given to a person working full-time who is attending or planning to attend a part-time course of study which will result in a new degree and broader opportunities in present or future work if a suitable candidate applies.
Level of Study: Unrestricted.
Type: Scholarship.
Value: US$3,000.
Frequency: Annual.
Country of Study: United States of America.
No. of awards offered: 13.
Application Procedure: Applicants must complete an application form, available on request.
Closing Date: March 31st.

NATIONAL FOUNDATION FOR INFECTIOUS DISEASES (NFID)

4733 Bethesda Avenue
Suite 750, Bethesda, MD, 20814, United States of America
Tel: (1) 301 656 0003
Fax: (1) 301 907 0878
Email: info@nfid.org
www: http://www.nfid.org
Contact: Mr John Han, Grants Manager

The National Foundation for Infectious Diseases (NFID) is a non-profit, non-governmental organisation whose mission is public and professional education and promotion of research on the causes, treatment and prevention of infectious diseases.

Colin L Powell Minority Postdoctoral Fellowship in Tropical Disease Research

Subjects: Tropical diseases.
Purpose: To encourage and assist a qualified minority researcher to become a specialist and investigator in the field of tropical diseases.
Eligibility: The applicant must hold a doctorate from a recognised university and be a permanent resident or citizen of the United States, or a spouse of a citizen or permanent resident of the United States. Each applicant is required to have arranged for an American or foreign laboratory in which to conduct his or her research. The laboratory should be supervised by a recognised leader in tropical disease research qualified to oversee the work of the selected Fellow. The Fellowship may not be awarded if the applicant has received or will receive a major fellowship, research grant, or traineeship from the federal government or another foundation in excess of the total amount of this award.
Level of Study: Postdoctorate.
Type: Fellowship.
Value: A stipend of US$30,000 for the year, of which US$3,000 may be used for travel and supplies, at the investigator's discretion.

Although it is anticipated that the award will be tax exempt, no guarantee of inland revenue service rulings can be made. No overhead to the sponsoring institution will be paid. The stipend may be supplemented by other monies up to US$30,000 to achieve salary levels consistent with other Fellows within the supporting institution.
Length of Study: One year.
Frequency: Annual.
No. of awards offered: One.
Application Procedure: Applicants must submit the original application and four copies no later than the deadline and addressed to the Grants Manager.
Closing Date: January.
Contributor: NFID, the Foundation for Microbiology, and Glaxo Wellcome, Inc.
Additional Information: Minority in the context of this fellowship refers to underrepresented minorities in the biomedical sciences eg. black, Hispanic, American Indian, or Alaskan Native, and Asian or Pacific Islander from the United States Bureau of the Census.

John P Utz Postdoctoral Fellowship in Medical Mycology

Subjects: Medical mycology.
Purpose: To encourage and assist a qualified physician to become a specialist and investigator in medical mycology.
Eligibility: Open to physicians who are citizens of the United States. Applicants must demonstrate aptitude and training in research, and must confirm arrangements for conduct of the proposed research in a recognised host laboratory. The applicant must be sponsored by a university affiliated medical centre. The Fellowship may not be awarded if the applicant has received or will receive a major fellowship, research grant or traineeship from the Federal government or another foundation in excess of the amount of this award.
Level of Study: Postdoctorate.
Type: Fellowship.
Value: A stipend of US$30,000 for the year and an additional US$1,000 for travel and supplies. Although it is anticipated that the award will be tax exempt, no guarantee of inland revenue service rulings can be made. No overhead will be paid to the sponsoring institution.
Length of Study: One year.
Frequency: Annual.
Study Establishment: Approved research institutions.
Country of Study: United States of America.
No. of awards offered: One.
Application Procedure: Applicants must submit four copies of an original application including a letter from laboratory director, curriculum vitae, description of applicant's proposed research project and a signed statement indicating that the applicant will acknowledge support received from the grant.
Closing Date: January.
Contributor: NFID and Pfizer, Inc.
No. of awards given last year: One.

NFID Fellowship in Infectious Diseases

Subjects: Infectious diseases.
Purpose: To encourage and assist qualified physicians to become specialists and investigators in the field of infectious diseases.
Eligibility: Open to physicians who are citizens of the United States and have satisfactorily completed three or more years of postgraduate medical training (internal medicine, surgery, paediatrics, epidemiology). The applicant must be sponsored by a university affiliated medical centre. This fellowship may not be awarded if the applicant has received or will receive a major fellowship, research grant or traineeship in excess of the amount of this award from the Federal government or another foundation.
Level of Study: Postdoctorate.
Type: Fellowship.
Value: A stipend of US$24,000 for the year and an additional US$1,000 for travel and supplies. Although it is anticipated that the award will be tax exempt, no guarantee of inland revenue service rulings can be made. No overhead will be paid to the sponsoring institution.
Length of Study: One year.

Frequency: Annual.
Country of Study: United States of America.
No. of awards offered: One.
Application Procedure: Applicants must submit four copies of an original application including a letter from laboratory director, curriculum vitae, description of applicant's proposed research project and a signed statement indicating that the applicant will acknowledge support received from the grant.
Closing Date: January.
Contributor: NFID and Glaxo Wellcome Inc.
No. of awards given last year: One.

NFID New Investigator Matching Grants

Subjects: The proposal must be based on research relevant to infectious diseases, microbiology, clinical medicine, epidemiology, and nursing. Those topics included in the top ten infectious diseases problems as recognised by the NFID will receive highest priority for funding, as follows, HIV and AIDS, antimicrobial resistance and emerging infections, vaccine preventable diseases, hospital acquired and opportunistic infections, viral hepatitis, gastrointestinal, diarrheal and foodborne diseases, sexually transmitted diseases, tuberculosis, zoonotic diseases and tropical infectious diseases.
Purpose: To assist new investigators who are beginning their research.
Eligibility: Open to young investigators, defined as individuals with full-time junior faculty (Instructor or Assistant Professor) status at a recognised and accredited institution of higher learning. Priority will be given to those who do not have research grants and whose studies represent pilot work with intent to further develop their research.
Level of Study: Postgraduate.
Type: Grant.
Value: US$2,000. Each application must be accompanied by an agreement from the applicant's sponsoring institution to match the award with equal funds. No indirect costs may be included.
Frequency: Annual.
Country of Study: United States of America or Canada.
No. of awards offered: Varies.
Application Procedure: Applicants must complete a four page application proposal, available from the NFID or downloadable from the website.
Closing Date: February 16th and awarded in May.
Contributor: NFID and Schering Plough.
No. of awards given last year: Eight.

NFID Postdoctoral Fellowship in Emerging Infectious Diseases

Subjects: Epidemiology research.
Purpose: To encourage and assist a qualified physician to become a recognised authority on emerging infectious diseases and epidemiology.
Eligibility: Open to physicians who are United States citizens and have completed an infectious diseases fellowship.
Level of Study: Postdoctorate.
Type: Fellowship.
Value: US$50,000.
Length of Study: One year.
Frequency: Annual.
Study Establishment: The National Center for Infectious Diseases, CDC Atlanta, Georgia.
Country of Study: United States of America.
No. of awards offered: One.
Application Procedure: Applicants must submit four copies of an original application including a letter from the laboratory director, curriculum vitae, description of applicant's proposed research project and a signed statement indicating that the applicant will acknowledge support received from the grant.
Closing Date: January.
Contributor: NFID, Centers for Disease Control and Prevention-Merck & Co, Inc.
No. of awards given last year: One.

NFID Postdoctoral Fellowship in Nosocomial Infection Research and Training

Subjects: Medical research into nosocomial infections.
Purpose: To encourage and assist a qualified physician researcher to become a specialist and investigator in the field of nosocomial infections.
Eligibility: Open to physicians in training who are citizens of the United States. Applicants must demonstrate aptitude or accomplishments in laboratory or epidemiologic research, and must confirm arrangements for the site of the proposed research in a recognised host laboratory. Applicants receiving or to be awarded grants in the same academic year in excess of the amount of this award are not eligible for funding under this proposal.
Level of Study: Postdoctorate.
Type: Fellowship.
Value: A stipend of US$25,000 for the year, of which US$1,000 may be used for travel and supplies (at investigator's discretion). Although it is anticipated that the award will be tax exempt, no guarantee of inland revenue service rulings can be made. No overhead to the sponsoring institution will be paid. The stipend may be supplemented by other monies to achieve salary levels consistent with other Fellows within the supporting institutions.
Length of Study: One year.
Frequency: Annual.
Country of Study: United States of America.
No. of awards offered: One.
Application Procedure: Applicants must submit four copies of an original application including a letter from laboratory director, curriculum vitae, description of applicant's proposed research project and a signed statement indicating that the applicant will acknowledge support received from the grant.
Closing Date: January.
Contributor: NFID and Aventis Pharmaceuticals, Inc.
No. of awards given last year: One.

NATIONAL HEADACHE FOUNDATION

428 West Saint James Place
2nd Floor, Chicago, IL, 60614, United States of America
Tel: (1) 773 388 6399
Fax: (1) 773 525 7357
www: http://www.headaches.org
Contact: Ms Suzanne E Simons, Executive Director

The National Headache Foundation disseminates information, funds research, sponsors public and professional education programmes and has a nationwide network of support groups, with 20,000 members. The Foundation is the recognised authority in headache and head pain, and offers the award winning newsletter 'NHF Head Lines', patient education brochures, and audio and video tapes.

National Headache Foundation Research Grant

Subjects: Causes of, and treatments for, headache.
Purpose: To encourage better understanding and treatment of headache and head pain.
Eligibility: Open to researchers in neurology and pharmacology departments in United States medical schools. Submissions from other departments and individual investigators are also welcome.
Level of Study: Doctorate, Postdoctorate, Postgraduate.
Type: Research grant.
Value: Amount is dependent on funds available. Grant covers only direct costs of carrying out research, no overhead or salaries.
Frequency: Annual.
Country of Study: United States of America.
No. of awards offered: Varies, depending on funds available and worthy projects submitted.
Application Procedure: Applicants must complete an application form.
Closing Date: December 1st for notification by the following March.
Funding: Private.

Contributor: Dues and donations.
No. of awards given last year: Seven.
No. of applicants last year: 11.

NATIONAL HEALTH AND MEDICAL RESEARCH COUNCIL (NHMRC)

Research Management Unit (MDP 33)
GPO Box 9848, Canberra, ACT, 2601, Australia
Tel: (61) 2 6289 1070
Fax: (61) 2 6289 1329
Email: research@health.gov.au
www: http://www.health.gov.au/nhmrc

The National Health and Medical Research Council (NHMRC) consolidates within a single national organisation the often independent functions of research funding and development of advice. One of its strengths is that it brings together and draws upon the resources of all components of the health system, including governments, medical practitioners, nurses and allied health professionals, researchers, teaching and research institutions, public and private programme managers, service administrators, community health organisations, social health researchers and consumers.

Australian Clinical Research Postdoctoral Fellowship

Subjects: Scientific research, including the social and behavioural sciences, which can be applied to any area of clinical or community medicine.
Purpose: To provide training in scientific research methods.
Eligibility: Open to Australian citizens or graduates from overseas with permanent Australian resident status, who are not under bond to any foreign government. Candidates should hold a doctorate in a health related field of research or have submitted a thesis for such by December of the year of application and be actively engaged in such research in Australia or overseas and have no more than two years' postdoctoral experience at the time of application.
Level of Study: Postdoctorate.
Type: Fellowship.
Value: Varies.
Length of Study: Four years.
Frequency: Annual.
Study Establishment: Institutions approved by the NHMRC, such as teaching hospitals, universities and research institutes.
Country of Study: Australia.
No. of awards offered: Varies.
Application Procedure: Applicants must write for details.
Closing Date: July 27th.
Funding: Government.
Additional Information: Enquiries should be directed to the Training Awards Office at the main address or by telephone on (61) 2 6289 9115 or by fax on (61) 2 6289 913.

Burnet Fellowships

Subjects: Any field of health and medical sciences.
Purpose: To attract back to Australia health and medical researchers of a high calibre who have spent considerable time overseas and who have not returned because of the lack of suitable opportunities.
Eligibility: Open to Australian citizens or permanent residents who are not under bond to any foreign government. Candidates should have a current academic or hospital appointment overseas (for at least seven years) equivalent to an Australian Professor or Associate Professor, be actively engaged in research and apply in conjunction with a host institution which must undertake to provide infrastructural support and administer the award. Normal access procedures for receipt of NHMRC funds will apply.
Level of Study: Professional development.
Type: Fellowship.
Value: A setting up grant of up to australian $250,000 per year to cover the senior investigator's salary at the appropriate level on the NHMRC Research Fellowship scales, maintenance or equipment

and/or salaries for a limited number of associate investigators who wish to return with the senior investigator, plus appropriate travel and removal allowances.
Length of Study: Five years.
Frequency: Dependent on funds available.
Study Establishment: Australian research institutions.
Country of Study: Australia.
No. of awards offered: Varies.
Application Procedure: Applicants must submit applications in writing with a curriculum vitae attached. There is no application form.
Closing Date: Applications are accepted at any time.
Funding: Government.
Additional Information: Enquiries should be directed to the Fellowships Office at the main address or by telephone on (61) 2 6289 5034 or by fax on (61) 2 6289 9131.

C J Martin Fellowships

Subjects: Biomedical sciences.
Purpose: To enable Fellows to develop their research skills and work overseas on specific research projects within the biomedical sciences under nominated advisers.
Eligibility: Open to Australian citizens or graduates from overseas with permanent Australian resident status who are not under bond to any foreign government. Candidates should hold a doctorate in a medical, dental or related field of research, be actively engaged in such research in Australia and have no more than two years' postdoctoral experience at the time of application.
Level of Study: Postdoctorate.
Type: Fellowship.
Value: Varies.
Length of Study: Four years, the first two of which are to be spent overseas and the final two in Australia.
Frequency: Annual.
Study Establishment: Institutions approved by the NHMRC, such as teaching hospitals, universities and research institutes.
Country of Study: Any country.
No. of awards offered: Varies.
Application Procedure: Applicants must complete an application form.
Closing Date: July 27th.
Funding: Government.
Additional Information: Enquiries should be directed to the Training Awards Office at the main address, by telephone on (61) 2 6289 9115, or fax on (61) 2 6289 9131.

Dora Lush (Biomedical) and Public Health Postgraduate Scholarships

Subjects: Biomedical sciences.
Purpose: To encourage science honours or equivalent graduates of outstanding ability to gain full-time medical research experience.
Eligibility: Open to Australian citizens who have already completed a science degree (or equivalent) at the time of submission of the application, science honours graduates and unregistered medical or dental graduates from overseas, who have permanent resident status and are currently residing in Australia. The scholarship shall be held within Australia.
Level of Study: Postgraduate.
Type: Scholarship.
Value: The stipend varies annually and includes an allowance of australian $1,500 per year, payable to the department where the Scholar is working.
Length of Study: One year, renewable for up to two further years.
Frequency: Annual.
Study Establishment: An Institute of Higher Education.
Country of Study: Australia.
No. of awards offered: Varies.
Application Procedure: Applicants must write for details.
Closing Date: August 17th.
Funding: Government.
Additional Information: Enquiries should be directed to the Training Awards Office at the main address, by telephone on (61) 2 6289 9115, or fax on (61) 2 6289 9131.

Eccles Awards

Subjects: Any field of the health and medical research. Preference will be given to fields recognised as high priority to the health of the nation.
Purpose: To assist in the appointment of distinguished and productive expatriate medical and dental researchers to an academic position in Australia.
Eligibility: Open to investigators with an outstanding record in research, who have potential for an appointment at a level equivalent to Australian Professor or Associate Professor, and who are Australian citizens currently working overseas or have permanent Australian resident status and are not under bond to any foreign government. Applicants must have been working overseas for at least seven years.
Level of Study: Professional development.
Type: Award.
Value: No more than australian $150,000 per year to be used for equipment, maintenance and/or salaries for associate investigators, excluding the salary of the potential appointee. This grant must be matched by the appointing institution in an appropriate and adequate way.
Length of Study: Three years.
Frequency: Dependent on funds available.
Study Establishment: Australian research institutions.
Country of Study: Australia.
No. of awards offered: Varies.
Application Procedure: Applicants must submit applications in writing with a curriculum vitae attached. There is no application form.
Closing Date: Applications are accepted at any time.
Funding: Government.
Additional Information: Enquiries should be directed to the Fellowships Office at the main address or by telephone on (61) 2 6289 5034 or by fax on (61) 2 6289 9131.

Neil Hamilton Fairley Fellowships

Subjects: Scientific research, including the social and behavioural sciences, which can be applied to any area of clinical or community medicine.
Purpose: To provide training in scientific research methods.
Eligibility: Open to Australian citizens or graduates from overseas with permanent Australian resident status who are not under bond to any foreign government. Candidates should hold a doctorate in a health related field of research or have submitted a thesis for such by December of the year of application and be actively engaged in such research in Australia and have no more than two years' postdoctoral experience at the time of application.
Level of Study: Postdoctorate.
Type: Fellowship.
Value: Varies.
Length of Study: Four years, the first two of which are to be spent overseas and the final two in Australia.
Frequency: Annual.
Study Establishment: Institutions approved by the NHMRC, such as teaching hospitals, universities and research institutes.
Country of Study: Any country.
No. of awards offered: Varies.
Application Procedure: Applicants must complete an application form.
Closing Date: July 27th.
Funding: Government.
Additional Information: Enquiries should be directed to the Training Awards Office at the main address, by telephone on (61) 2 6289 9115, or fax on (61) 2 6289 9131.

NHMRC Equipment Grants

Subjects: All fields of medicine and dentistry.
Purpose: To provide funding support for the purchase of items of equipment required for biomedical research.
Eligibility: Open to individuals, groups or institutions which are normally eligible for NHMRC support. Grants will be made on the basis of scientific merit, taking into consideration factors including whether the applicants hold NHMRC grants, the institutional ranking of the

application, and institutional or regional availability of major equipment.
Level of Study: Unrestricted.
Type: Grant.
Value: To cover the cost of equipment in excess of australian $10,000.
Frequency: Annual.
Country of Study: Australia.
No. of awards offered: Varies.
Application Procedure: Applicants must complete an application form.
Closing Date: Please contact the organisation.
Funding: Government.

For further information contact:

Equipment Grants Officer
MDP 33
Project Grants Office
GPO Box 9848, Canberra, ACT, 2601, Australia
Tel: (61) 2 6289 8278
Fax: (61) 2 6289 8617
Email: jean.sewell@hhlgcs.ausgovhhcs.telememo.au

NHMRC Medical and Dental and Public Health Postgraduate Research Scholarships

Subjects: Medical or dental research.
Purpose: To encourage medical and dental graduates to gain full-time research experience.
Eligibility: Open to Australian citizens who are medical or dental graduates registered to practice in Australia, with the proviso that medical graduates can also apply during their intern year and that dental postgraduate research scholarships may be awarded prior to graduation provided that the evidence of high quality work is shown. Also open to medical and dental graduates from overseas who hold a qualification that is registered for practice in Australia and who have permanent resident status and are currently residing in Australia. Evidence of residence status must be provided. The scholarship shall be held within Australia.
Level of Study: Postgraduate.
Type: Scholarship.
Value: The stipend varies annually and includes an allowance of australian $1,500 per year, payable to the department where the Scholar is working.
Length of Study: One year, renewable for up to two further years.
Frequency: Annual.
Study Establishment: An Institute of Higher Education.
Country of Study: Australia.
No. of awards offered: Varies.
Application Procedure: Applicants must complete an application form.
Closing Date: August 17th.
Funding: Government.
Additional Information: Enquiries should be directed to the Training Awards Office at the main address, by telephone on (61) 2 6289 9115, or fax on (61) 2 6289 9131.

NHMRC Type II Research Grants

Subjects: All fields of health and medical research.
Purpose: To provide guaranteed support for a collaborative research team.
Eligibility: Open to research teams that would normally comprise several outstanding established investigators. Essential criteria include evidence of significant and innovating research on a broad central theme over a lengthy period and evidence of collaboration.
Level of Study: Unrestricted.
Type: Grant.
Value: Varies.
Length of Study: Five years.
Frequency: Annual.
Study Establishment: Australian research institutions.
Country of Study: Australia.
No. of awards offered: Varies.

Application Procedure: Application forms and information kits are available from the Programme Management Section on (61) 2 6289 9120 or by fax on (61) 2 6289 9131.
Closing Date: February 9th.
Funding: Government.

NHMRC/INSERM Exchange Fellowships

Subjects: Biomedical sciences.
Purpose: To enable Fellows to work overseas on specific research projects.
Eligibility: Open to Australian citizens and permanent residents, who are not under bond to any foreign government, who hold a doctorate in a medical, dental or related field of research or have submitted a thesis for such by December in the year of application, are actively engaged in such research in Australia and have no more than two years' postdoctoral experience at the time of application.
Level of Study: Postdoctorate.
Type: Fellowship.
Value: Varies.
Length of Study: Four years, the first two of which are to be spent in France and the final two in Australia.
Frequency: Annual.
Study Establishment: Institutions approved by the NHMRC, such as teaching hospitals, universities and research institutes, and INSERM laboratories in France.
Country of Study: France or Australia.
No. of awards offered: One.
Application Procedure: Applicants must complete an application form.
Closing Date: July 27th.
Additional Information: Enquiries should be directed to the Training Awards Office at the main address, or by telephone on (61) 2 6289 9115 or fax on (61) 2 6289 9131. This fellowship is awarded in association with l'Institut National de la Santé et de la Recherche Médicale (INSERM), France.

Peter Doherty Fellowships

Subjects: Biomedical sciences.
Purpose: To provide a vehicle for training in clinical and basic research in Australia, and to encourage persons of outstanding ability to make medical research a full-time career.
Eligibility: Open to Australian citizens or graduates from overseas with permanent Australian resident status who are not under bond to any foreign government. Candidates should hold a doctorate in a medical, dental or related field of research or have submitted a thesis for such by December in the year of application, be actively engaged in such research in Australia or overseas and have no more than two years' postdoctoral experience at the time of application.
Level of Study: Postdoctorate.
Type: Fellowship.
Value: Varies.
Length of Study: Four years.
Frequency: Annual.
Study Establishment: Institutions approved by the NHMRC, such as teaching hospitals, universities and research institutes.
Country of Study: Australia.
No. of awards offered: Varies.
Application Procedure: Applicants must complete an application form.
Closing Date: July 27th.
Funding: Government.
Additional Information: Enquiries should be directed to the Training Awards Office at the main address, or by telephone on (61) 2 6289 9115, by fax on (61) 2 6289 9131 or by email on marian.blake@health.gov.au.

NATIONAL HEART FOUNDATION (USA), (NHF)

15825 Shady Grove Road
Suite 140, Rockville, MD, 20850, United States of America
Tel: (1) 301 948 3244
Fax: (1) 301 258 9454
Email: sgarfinkel@ahaf.org
www: http://www.ahaf.org
Contact: Dr Susan Garfinkel, Director of Research Grants

AHAF's National Heart Foundation (NHF) programme was established in 1976 to fund research on and educate the public about coronary heart disease. As the programme has grown and changed over the years, its name has changed accordingly, from Atherosclerosis Research Fund to Coronary Heart Disease Research Project to Coronary Heart Disease Research to its current name, National Heart Foundation. The programme became the National Heart Foundation in 1992 to reflect its expanded mission to fund research on stroke and all cardiovascular diseases.

National Heart Foundation Grant

Subjects: Cardiology, biomedicine, physiology, or pharmacology.
Purpose: To provide start up grants for new investigators in cardiovascular disease and stroke.
Eligibility: The principal investigator must hold the academic rank of assistant professor or the equivalent.
Level of Study: Professional development.
Type: Grant.
Value: Up to US$25,000 may be requested for one year.
Length of Study: One year, renewable for a further year.
Frequency: Annual.
Country of Study: Any country.
No. of awards offered: Varies.
Application Procedure: Applicants must complete an application form, available on request or from the website.
Closing Date: November 1st or the following Tuesday if it falls on a weekend or Monday.
Funding: Private.
Contributor: Many small contributions.
No. of awards given last year: Six.
No. of applicants last year: 20.

NATIONAL HEART FOUNDATION OF AUSTRALIA

411 King Street, West Melbourne, VIC, 3003, Australia
Tel: (61) 3 9329 8511
Fax: (61) 3 9326 3190
Email: research@heartfoundation.com.au
www: http://www.heartfoundation.com.au
Contact: Research Manager

The National Heart Foundation of Australia is a non-government, non-profit health organisation funded mostly by public donation. The Foundation's mission is to prevent early death and disability from heart disease and stroke. The Foundation funds biomedical research, provides clinical leadership and develops health promotion strategies and initiatives.

National Heart Foundation of Australia Career Development Fellowship

Subjects: Basic, clinical or public health research on cardiovascular disease and related disorders.
Purpose: To enable a senior Australian researcher of exceptional merit and proven record in the cardiovascular field to undertake independent research.
Eligibility: Open to Australian citizens and permanent residents only.

Level of Study: Research.
Type: Fellowship.
Value: Australian $65,831 plus a travel allowance of australian $5,000 per year for the duration of the fellowship.
Length of Study: Five years, non renewable.
Frequency: Annual.
Study Establishment: Universities, hospitals or research institutions.
Country of Study: Australia.
No. of awards offered: One.
Application Procedure: Applicants must be nominated by the head of the host department or institution.
Closing Date: May 31st.
Funding: Private.

National Heart Foundation of Australia Clinical Research Fellowship

Subjects: Clinical research on cardiovascular disease and related disorders.
Purpose: To award graduates who have demonstrated expertise and significant achievement in cardiovascular research.
Eligibility: Open to Australian citizens and permanent residents only.
Level of Study: Postdoctorate.
Type: Fellowship.
Value: SR06, RF3 Level: australian $55,345 per year if full-time. Clinical loading will be paid as appropriate.
Frequency: Annual.
Study Establishment: Universities, hospitals or research institutions.
Country of Study: Australia.
No. of awards offered: One.
Closing Date: May 31st.
Funding: Private.

National Heart Foundation of Australia Overseas Research Fellowships

Subjects: Clinical or basic medical sciences related to cardiovascular disease and related disorders.
Purpose: To allow Fellows to obtain skills in cardiovascular research.
Eligibility: Open to Australian citizens or permanent residents who are actively engaged in research in Australia on December 31st of the year prior to application.
Level of Study: Postdoctorate.
Type: Fellowship.
Value: Australian $39,886-48,449 plus cost of living allowance, rent allowance and travel costs.
Length of Study: Three years.
Frequency: Annual.
Study Establishment: Approved institutions.
Country of Study: Overseas for the first two years and Australia for the third year.
No. of awards offered: One-two.
Application Procedure: Applicants must be nominated by the head of the host department or institution.
Closing Date: May 31st.
Funding: Private.
Additional Information: Fellowships are awarded on the understanding that the Fellow will return to Australia to continue his or her career upon completion of the fellowship.

National Heart Foundation of Australia Postgraduate Biomedical Research Scholarship

Subjects: Basic research on cardiovascular research and related disorders.
Purpose: To allow graduates to undertake a period of training in research under the full-time supervision and tuition of a responsible investigator.
Eligibility: Open to Australian citizens and permanent residents only.

Level of Study: Postgraduate.
Type: Scholarship.
Value: Australian $19,755, australian $1,070 departmental allowance and australian $535 conference travel allowance (conditions apply) per year, plus up to australian $860 thesis allowance (final year).
Length of Study: Up to three years.
Frequency: Annual.
Study Establishment: Universities, hospitals or research institutions.
Country of Study: Australia.
Application Procedure: Applicants must submit an application outlining a research proposal accompanied by the supervisor's reference and backing.
Closing Date: October 31st.
Funding: Private.

National Heart Foundation of Australia Postgraduate Clinical Research Scholarship

Subjects: Cardiovascular research.
Purpose: To enable medical graduates to undertake a period of training in research under the full-time supervision and tuition of a responsible investigator.
Eligibility: Open to Australian citizens and permanent residents only.
Level of Study: Postgraduate.
Type: Scholarship.
Value: Australian $26,118, australian $1,070 departmental allowance and australian $535 conference travel allowance (conditions apply) per year plus up to australian $860 thesis allowance (final year).
Length of Study: Three years.
Frequency: Annual.
Study Establishment: Universities, hospitals and research institutions.
Country of Study: Australia.
No. of awards offered: Varies.
Application Procedure: Applicants must submit an application outlining a research proposal accompanied by the supervisor's reference and backing.
Closing Date: May 31st.
Funding: Private.

National Heart Foundation of Australia Postgraduate Public Health Research Scholarship

Subjects: Basic research on cardiovascular research and related disorders.
Purpose: To allow graduates to undertake a period of training in research under the full-time supervision and tuition of a responsible investigator.
Eligibility: Open to Australian citizens and permanent residents only.
Level of Study: Postgraduate.
Type: Scholarship.
Value: Australian $19,755, australian $1,070 departmental allowance and australian $535 conference travel allowance (conditions apply) per year, plus up to australian $860 thesis allowance (final year).
Length of Study: Up to three years.
Frequency: Annual.
Study Establishment: Universities, hospitals or research institutions.
Country of Study: Australia.
Application Procedure: Applicants must submit an application outlining a research proposal accompanied by the supervisor's reference and backing.
Closing Date: August 2nd.
Funding: Private.

National Heart Foundation of Australia Research Grants-in-Aid

Subjects: Basic, clinical or public health research.
Purpose: To support research in the cardiovascular field.
Eligibility: Open to Australian citizens and permanent residents only.
Level of Study: Research.
Type: Grant.
Value: Maximum australian $50,000 per year.
Length of Study: Up to two years.
Frequency: Annual.
Study Establishment: An approved Australian institution.
Country of Study: Australia.
No. of awards offered: 50.
Application Procedure: Applicants must submit an application outlining research proposal. References are also required.
Closing Date: April 2nd.
Funding: Private.

NATIONAL HEART FOUNDATION OF NEW ZEALAND

PO Box 17-160
Greenlane
Newmarket, Auckland, New Zealand
Tel: (64) 9 571 9191
Fax: (64) 9 571 9190
Email: helens@nhf.org.nz
www: http://www.nhf.org.nz
Contact: Ms Helen Stewart, Research Grants Administrator

The National Heart Foundation of New Zealand aims to promote good health and to reduce suffering and premature death from diseases of the heart and circulation.

National Heart Foundation of New Zealand Fellowships

Subjects: Any aspect of cardiovascular disease including research, rehabilitation and education.
Purpose: To promote the aims of the National Heart Foundation of New Zealand.
Eligibility: Normally open to New Zealand graduates only.
Level of Study: Postgraduate.
Type: Fellowship.
Value: Varies, according to the determination of the Scientific Committee and within an annual budget.
Frequency: Annual.
Study Establishment: New Zealand institutions.
Country of Study: New Zealand.
No. of awards offered: Varies.
Application Procedure: Applicants must apply to the Foundation for the publication 'A Guide to Applicants for Research and Other Grants'.
Closing Date: June 1st.
Funding: Private.
No. of awards given last year: Four.

National Heart Foundation of New Zealand Limited Budget Grants

Subjects: Any aspect of cardiovascular disease including research, rehabilitation and education. Priority areas include modification of lifestyle with regards to cardiovascular disease, the socio-economic determinants of heart disease, Maori health and Pacific Island health.
Purpose: To further the aims of the National Heart Foundation of New Zealand.
Eligibility: Normally open to New Zealand graduates only.
Level of Study: Postgraduate.
Type: Grant.

Value: Varies, according to the determination of the Scientific Committee and within an annual budget.
Frequency: Three times each year.
Study Establishment: New Zealand institutions.
Country of Study: New Zealand.
No. of awards offered: Varies.
Application Procedure: Applicants must write for details.
Closing Date: February 1st, June 1st or October 1st.
Funding: Private.
No. of awards given last year: 13.
Additional Information: These grants cover small projects eg. less than new zealand $15,000 and grants-in-aid.

National Heart Foundation of New Zealand Maori Cardiovascular Research Fellowship

Subjects: Cardiovascular health.
Purpose: To financially support graduates who propose to engage in research to improve Maori cardiovascular health.
Eligibility: Open to medical graduates or non medical graduates enrolled for a higher degree. Preference will be given to those with a working knowledge of 'Te Reo Maori' and who are committed to Maori health.
Level of Study: Doctorate, Postgraduate, Predoctorate.
Type: Fellowship.
Value: New Zealand $30,000.
Length of Study: Two years.
Frequency: Annual.
Country of Study: New Zealand.
No. of awards offered: One.
Application Procedure: Applications will be considered at the annual meeting of the Scientific Committee.
Closing Date: February 1st.

National Heart Foundation of New Zealand Project Grants

Subjects: Any aspect of cardiovascular disease including research, rehabilitation and education. Priority areas include modification of lifestyle with regards to cardiovascular disease, the socio-economic determinants of heart health, Maori health and Pacific Island health.
Purpose: To provide short-term support for a single individual or small group working on a clearly defined research project which will promote the aims of the National Heart Foundation of New Zealand.
Eligibility: Normally open to New Zealand graduates only.
Level of Study: Postgraduate.
Type: Grant.
Value: Varies, according to the determination of the scientific committee and within an annual budget.
Frequency: Annual.
Study Establishment: New Zealand institutions.
Country of Study: New Zealand.
No. of awards offered: Varies.
Application Procedure: Applicants must write for details.
Closing Date: March 1st.
Funding: Private.
No. of awards given last year: Eight.

National Heart Foundation of New Zealand Travel Grants

Subjects: Any aspect of cardiovascular disease including research and education.
Purpose: To enable medical or non-medical workers to travel in New Zealand or overseas for short-term study or to attend conferences.
Eligibility: Normally open to New Zealand graduates only.
Level of Study: Postgraduate.
Type: Grant.
Value: Varies, according to the determination of the scientific committee and within an annual budget.
Frequency: Three times each year.
Country of Study: Any country.
No. of awards offered: Varies.
Application Procedure: Applicants must write for details.

Closing Date: February 1st, June 1st or October 1st.
Funding: Private.
No. of awards given last year: 12.

NATIONAL HISTORICAL PUBLICATIONS AND RECORDS COMMISSION (NHPRC)

Room 111
National Archives & Records Administration
700 Pennsylvania Avenue North West, Washington, DC, 20408-0001, United States of America
Tel: (1) 202 501 5605 ext. 253
Fax: (1) 202 501 5601
Email: nhprc@nara.gov
www: http://www.nara.gov
Contact: Dr Mary A Giunta, Director for Communications & Outreach

The National Historical Publications and Records Commission (NHPRC) is the grant making affiliate of the National Archives and Records Administration (NARA). The Commission has defined its purpose to carry out its statutory mission to ensure understanding of the nation's past by promoting, nationwide, the identification, preservation and dissemination of essential historical documentation.

NHPRC Fellowship in Archival Administration

Subjects: Library and archive studies.
Purpose: To provide experience in management and administration for archivists.
Eligibility: Individuals must have spent two-five years working as an archivist and be United States of America citizens. While not required, it is desirable that applicants have the equivalent of two semesters of full-time graduate training in a programme containing an archival education component.
Level of Study: Professional development.
Type: Fellowship.
Value: A stipend of US$35,000 plus an additional US$7,000 for fringe benefits.
Length of Study: 9-12 months.
Frequency: Annual.
Country of Study: United States of America.
No. of awards offered: One.
Application Procedure: Applicants must contact the Commission for guidelines and host institution information. This information is available before December of the preceding year.
Closing Date: Postmarked March 15th.
Funding: Government.

NHPRC Fellowship in Documentary Editing

Subjects: Documentary editing.
Purpose: To provide individuals with training in the field of historical documentary editing.
Eligibility: Applicants should hold a PhD or have completed all requirements for the doctorate except the dissertation. Applicants may be working on their dissertation and must be United States of America citizens.
Level of Study: Doctorate, Postdoctorate.
Type: Fellowship.
Value: US$41,250 including funds for fringe benefits.
Length of Study: 11 months.
Frequency: Annual.
Country of Study: United States of America.
No. of awards offered: One.
Application Procedure: Applicants must contact the Commission for guidelines and host institution information. This information is available before December of the preceding year.
Closing Date: Postmarked March 15th.
Funding: Government.
Additional Information: Further information is available from the website.

NATIONAL HUMANITIES CENTER (NHC)

PO Box 12256, Research Triangle Park, NC, 27709-2256, United States of America
Tel: (1) 919 549 0661
Fax: (1) 919 990 8535
Email: nhc@ga.unc.edu
www: http://www.nhc.rtp.nc.us:8080
Contact: Mr Kent Mullikin, Deputy Director

The National Humanities Center (NHC) is a residential institute for advanced study in history, languages and literature, philosophy and other fields of the humanities. Each year it awards approximately 35 to 40 fellowships to Scholars of demonstrated achievement and to promising younger Scholars.

NHC Fellowships

Subjects: History, philosophy, languages and literature, classics, religion, history of the arts and other fields in the liberal arts.
Purpose: To support advanced postdoctoral scholarship in the humanities.
Eligibility: Open to Scholars of any nationality. Social scientists, natural scientists, or professionals whose work has a humanistic dimension may also apply. Applicants must hold a doctorate or have equivalent professional accomplishments. Fellowships are awarded to senior Scholars of recognised accomplishment and to promising young Scholars engaged in research beyond the revision of their dissertations.
Level of Study: Postdoctorate.
Type: Fellowship.
Value: Ranges from US$30,000 to US$50,000. Fellowships are individually determined in accordance with the needs of each Fellow and the Center's ability to meet them. As the Center cannot in most instances replace full salaries, applicants are urged to seek partial funding in the form of sabbatical salaries or grants from other sources. In addition to stipends, the Center provides round trip travel expenses for Fellows and their immediate families to and from North Carolina.
Length of Study: One academic year, although a few fellowships may be awarded for a single semester.
Frequency: Annual.
Study Establishment: The Center.
Country of Study: United States of America.
No. of awards offered: 40.
Application Procedure: Applicants must submit the Center's form supported by their curriculum vitae, a 1,000 word project proposal and three letters of recommendation.
Closing Date: October 15th.
Funding: Private.
Contributor: Private foundation grants, income from the Center's endowment and the National Endowment for the Humanities.
No. of awards given last year: 34.
No. of applicants last year: 534.

NATIONAL INSTITUTE OF GENERAL MEDICAL SCIENCES (NIGMS)

45 Center Drive
MSC 6200, Bethesda, MD, 20892-6200, United States of America
Tel: (1) 301 496 7301
Fax: (1) 301 402 0224
Email: pub_info@nigms.nih.gov
www: http://www.nigms.nih.gov
Contact: Ms Susan J Athey, Public Affairs

The National Institute of General Medical Sciences (NIGMS) is a component of the National Institutes of Health, the principal biomedical research agency of the United States government. NIGMS supports basic biomedical research that is not targeted to specific diseases, but that increases the understanding of life processes and lays the foundation for advances in disease diagnosis, treatment and prevention.

MARC Faculty Predoctoral Fellowships

Subjects: Biomedical or behavioural sciences.
Purpose: To provide an opportunity for faculty who lack the PhD degree or equivalent to obtain the research doctorate.
Eligibility: Applicants must be full-time, permanent faculty members in a biomedically related science or mathematics programme and have been at the minority or minority serving institution for at least three years at the time of application. Candidates must be enrolled in, or have been accepted into, a PhD or combined MD-PhD training programme in the biomedical or behavioural sciences. Candidates must intend to return to the minority institution at the end of the training period.
Level of Study: Postgraduate.
Type: Fellowship.
Value: An applicant may request a stipend equal to his or her annual salary, but not to exceed the stipend of a level one postdoctoral Fellow (currently at US$29,832). The applicant may also request tuition and fees as determined by the training institution as well as an allowance of US$2,500 per year for training related costs.
Frequency: Annual.
Study Establishment: An institution in the United States of America.
Country of Study: United States of America.
No. of awards offered: Varies.
Application Procedure: Applicants must write to the main address for details or telephone Dr Adolphus Toliver, on (1) 301 594 3900. Further details are also available from the website.
Funding: Government.

NIGMS Fellowship Awards for Minority Students

Subjects: Biomedical or behavioural sciences.
Purpose: Awards support research training leading to a PhD or equivalent research degree, a combined MD-PhD degree or another combined professional doctorate-research PhD.
Eligibility: Open to highly qualified students who are members of minority groups that are under represented in the biomedical or behavioural sciences in the United States. These groups include African Americans, Hispanic Americans, Native Americans (including Alaska Natives) and natives of the United States Pacific Islands.
Level of Study: Postgraduate, Predoctorate.
Type: Fellowship.
Value: An annual stipend of US$16,500, a tuition and fee allowance, and an annual institution fee of US$2,500, which may be used for travel to scientific meetings and for laboratory and other training expenses.
Length of Study: Up to five years.
Frequency: Annual.
Country of Study: United States of America.
No. of awards offered: Varies.
Application Procedure: Applicants must write to the main address for details or telephone Dr Adolphus Toliver, on (1) 301 594 3900. Further details are also available from the website.
Funding: Government.

NIGMS Fellowship Awards for Students With Disabilities

Subjects: Biomedical or behavioural sciences.
Purpose: To address the problem of the low participation rate of Americans with disabilities in biomedical research. The programme provides funding at several different stages in a research career. This includes post Baccalaureate, post Master's, graduate students, individuals in postdoctoral research training, investigators developing independent research careers and established investigators who become disabled.
Eligibility: Open to principal investigators at domestic institutions holding an active NIGMS research grant, programme project grant, centre grant or co-operative agreement research programme with a reasonable period of research support remaining.

Level of Study: Doctorate, Graduate, Postdoctorate, Postgraduate, Predoctorate.
Type: Research supplements.
Value: Varies.
Length of Study: Two years or more.
Frequency: Annual.
Study Establishment: An institution in the United States of America.
Country of Study: United States of America.
No. of awards offered: Varies.
Application Procedure: Applicants must write to the main address for details or telephone Dr Anthony René, on (1) 301 594 3833. Further details are also available from the website.
Funding: Government.

NIGMS Postdoctoral Awards

Subjects: Biomedical or behavioural sciences.
Purpose: NIGMS welcomes NRSA applications from eligible individuals who seek postdoctoral biomedical research training in areas related to the scientific programmes of the Institute.
Eligibility: Applicants must have received the doctoral degree (domestic or foreign), by the beginning date of the proposed award.
Level of Study: Postdoctorate.
Type: Research grant.
Value: Up to US$44,412 per year, based on the salary of the applicant at the time of the award.
Frequency: Annual.
Study Establishment: The institutional setting may be domestic or foreign, public or private.
Country of Study: Any country.
No. of awards offered: Varies.
Application Procedure: Applicants must write to the main address for details or telephone Dr John Norvell, on (1) 301 594 0533. Further details are also available from the website.
Funding: Government.

NIGMS Research Project Grants

Subjects: Biomedical or behavioural sciences.
Purpose: To support a discrete project related to the investigator's area of interest and competence.
Eligibility: Research grants may be awarded to non-profit organisations and institutions, governments and their agencies, and occasionally to individuals who have access to adequate facilities and resources for conducting the research, as well as profit making organisations. Foreign institutions and international organisations are also eligible to apply for these grants.
Level of Study: Postgraduate.
Type: Research grant.
Value: These grants may provide funds for reasonable costs of the research activity, as well as for salaries, equipment, supplies, travel and other related expenses.
Frequency: Annual.
Country of Study: United States of America.
No. of awards offered: Varies.
Application Procedure: Applicants must contact the Office of Extramural Outreach and Information Resources for details.
Funding: Government.

For further information contact:

Office of Extramural Outreach & Information Resources, NIH, 6701 Rockledge Drive, MSC 7910, Room 6207, Bethesda, MD, 20892-7910, United States of America
Tel: (1) 301 435 0714
Email: grantsinfo@nih.gov

NIGMS Research Supplements for Underrepresented Minorities

Subjects: Biomedical or behavioural sciences.
Purpose: To help minority scientists and students develop their capabilities for independent research careers. Supplements are available to post Baccalaureate and post Master's degree and predoctoral students as well as minority individuals in postdoctoral training and minority staff and faculty.
Eligibility: Open to principal investigators at domestic institutions holding an active NIGMS research grant, programme project grant, centre grant or co-operative agreement research programme with a reasonable period of research support remaining.
Level of Study: Unrestricted.
Type: Research supplements.
Value: Varies.
Length of Study: Two years or more.
Frequency: Annual.
Study Establishment: An institution in the United States of America.
Country of Study: United States of America.
No. of awards offered: Varies.
Application Procedure: Applicants must write to the main address for details or telephone Dr Anthony René, on (1) 301 594 3833. Further details are also available from the website.
Funding: Government.

NATIONAL INSTITUTE OF JUSTICE (NIJ)

810 Seventh Street, Washington, DC, 20531, United States of America
Tel: (1) 202 307 0648
Fax: (1) 202 307 6394
www: http://www.ojp.usdoj.gov/nij

The National Institute of Justice (NIJ), a component of the Office of Justice Programs, is the research arm of the United States Department of Justice. Created by the Omnibus Crime Control and Safe Streets Act of 1968, the NIJ is authorised to support research, evaluation, and demonstration programmes, development of technology, and both national and international information dissemination.

NIJ Graduate Research Fellowship Program

Subjects: The subject of the proposed doctoral dissertation should constitute the research for this fellowship. This research must focus on a topic relevant to criminal justice policy that fills in key gaps in scientific knowledge.
Purpose: To provide dissertation research support to outstanding doctoral students undertaking independent research on issues of crime and justice.
Eligibility: Individuals may not receive awards directly, as grant awards will be made only to educational institutions. To be eligible to administer a fellowship on behalf of a doctoral candidate, an institution must be fully accredited by one of the regional institutional accreditation commissions recognised by the United States commissioner of education.
Level of Study: Doctorate.
Value: US$15,000 stipend for costs associated with the dissertation.
Frequency: Dependent on funds available.
Study Establishment: NIJ.
Application Procedure: The application procedure is set forth in detail on the website under 'funding opportunities'.
Closing Date: Applications may be submitted at any time.
Funding: Government.

NIJ Visiting Fellowship Program

Subjects: Criminal justice issues relevant to the NIJ and public policy.
Purpose: To support research and development on high priority topics that enhance the capabilities of criminal justice systems to combat crime, violence and substance abuse.
Eligibility: The NIJ awards grants and co-operative agreements to educational institutions, non-profit making organisations, public agencies, individuals, and profit making organisations that are willing to waive their fees. For this programme, no indirect costs are allowable.
Level of Study: Postgraduate.

Type: Fellowship.

Value: Varies, dependent on funds available.

Length of Study: Six-eight months.

Frequency: Dependent on funds available.

Country of Study: United States of America.

No. of awards offered: Varies, dependent on funds available.

Application Procedure: Applicants must write to the NIJ director expressing their interest in fellowship opportunities. They should enclose a curriculum vitae and a brief concept paper of four-five double spaced pages, that describes research objectives and how the work would contribute to the work of the Institute. The Institute will review each concept paper and selectively invite the development of a full proposal reflecting a scope and work plan of mutual interest.

Closing Date: Applications are accepted at any time.

Contributor: The Government of the United States of America.

Additional Information: Through the programme, Fellows may investigate new approaches for resolving operational problems and become involved in NIJ's criminal justice research national programme.

NATIONAL INSTITUTE ON AGING

GW 218, Bethesda, MD, 20892, United States of America

Tel: (1) 301 496 9322

Fax: (1) 301 402 2945

Email: mk46u@nih.gov

www: http://www.nih.gov

Contact: Dr Miriam Kelty, Associate Director

The National Institute on Aging conducts and supports research and research training in all facts of biological ageing, the neuroscience and neuropsychology of ageing, geriatrics and the social and behavioural sciences of ageing.

NIH Research Grants

Subjects: The biology of aging neuroscience and neuropsychology of aging, geriatrics, and the social and behavioural sciences of aging.

Purpose: To support research and training in biological, clinical, behavioural and social aspects of ageing mechanisms and processes.

Eligibility: Varies, depending on mechanism, but generally open to United States citizens only.

Level of Study: Postdoctorate, Professional development.

Type: Research grants, fellowships, career development awards and institutional training awards.

Value: Varies.

Length of Study: One-five years.

Frequency: Annual.

Country of Study: United States of America or others depending on mechanism.

No. of awards offered: Varies.

Application Procedure: Applicants must write for application form PHS 398 or access it on the website.

Closing Date: Deadlines are staggered. Please see form PHS 398.

Funding: Government.

Contributor: The United States government.

Additional Information: Some award mechanisms are limited to citizens and permanent residents of the United States of America. Others are open to applicants from any country. Further information is available on the website.

NATIONAL KIDNEY RESEARCH FUND (NKRF)

King's Chambers
Priestgate, Peterborough, Cambridgeshire, PE1 1FG, England
Tel: (44) 1733 704658
Fax: (44) 1733 704685
Email: grants@nkrf.org.uk
www: http://www.nkrf.org.uk
Contact: Mrs Elaine Davies, Grants Administration Manager

The National Kidney Research Fund aims to advance and promote research into kidney and renal disease generally, the acute failure of kidneys and chronic renal failure, and congenital malformations of the kidney and bladder. The Fund's research also incorporates the development of artificial kidney and dialysis machines.

NKRF Research Project Grants

Subjects: Renal research projects.

Purpose: To support both basic and scientific and clinical research projects, improving the understanding of renal disease, its causes, treatment and management.

Eligibility: Open to suitably qualified researchers of any nationality. Work must be carried out in the United Kingdom.

Level of Study: Unrestricted.

Type: Project grant.

Value: Up to UK £100,000 over one-three years for a full research project and up to UK £30,000 for a start up research project.

Length of Study: One-three years.

Frequency: Twice a year.

Study Establishment: Any institution in the United Kingdom.

Country of Study: United Kingdom.

No. of awards offered: Varies.

Application Procedure: Applicants must complete application forms, available from the Grants Department and also via the website or email.

Closing Date: The round one deadline is March 1st and the round two deadline is August 30th.

Funding: Private.

Contributor: Public donations.

No. of awards given last year: 21.

No. of applicants last year: 110.

NKRF Senior Fellowships

Subjects: Renal medicine and related scientific studies.

Eligibility: Open to postdoctoral researchers in the biomedical field with evidence of independent research, including two years' postdoctoral research. Applicants may be of any nationality, but project work must be carried out in the United Kingdom.

Level of Study: Postdoctorate, Research.

Type: Fellowship.

Value: Up to UK £250,000 over a maximum of five years. Salary will be at the Registrar or Senior Registrar level or at the appropriate university scale includes a UK £12,000 per year bench allowance for consumables, minor equipment and technical support.

Length of Study: Three-five years, subject to review in the third year.

Frequency: Annual.

Study Establishment: Any institution in the United Kingdom.

Country of Study: United Kingdom.

No. of awards offered: Varies.

Application Procedure: Applicants must complete an application form, available from the Grants Department or the website.

Closing Date: November 29th.

Funding: Private.

Contributor: Public donations.

No. of awards given last year: One.

No. of applicants last year: Three.

NKRF Studentships

Subjects: Renal medicine.

Purpose: To enable postgraduates to commence a career in renal medicine by completing a course of training including submitting a PhD thesis.

Eligibility: Open to applicants of any nationality. Project work must take place in the United Kingdom.

Level of Study: Postgraduate.

Type: Studentship.

Value: Up to UK £50,000. University fees are met by the NKRF, and a bench fee is available to the host institution.

Length of Study: Three years, subject to a satisfactory annual report.

Frequency: Annual.

Study Establishment: Any institution in the United Kingdom.

Country of Study: United Kingdom.

No. of awards offered: Varies.

Application Procedure: Applicants must complete an application form, available from the Grants Department or the website.

Closing Date: November 29th.

Funding: Private.

Contributor: Public donations.

No. of awards given last year: Three.

No. of applicants last year: Eight.

NKRF Training Fellowships

Subjects: Renal medicine and related scientific studies.

Purpose: To enable medical or scientific graduates to undertake specialised training in renal research.

Eligibility: Open to medical candidates of immediate post registration to registrar level and to science candidates with a PhD or DPhil and at least two years' postdoctoral experience. Project work must be carried out in the United Kingdom.

Level of Study: Graduate, Predoctorate.

Type: Fellowship, clinical and non-clinical.

Value: Up to UK £150,000. The level of financial support will be based on an appropriate point on current NHS or university pay scales and includes a UK £5,000 per year bench allowance and fees where applicable.

Length of Study: One-three years, subject to annual review.

Frequency: Annual.

Study Establishment: Any institution in the United Kingdom.

Country of Study: United Kingdom.

No. of awards offered: Varies.

Application Procedure: Applicants must complete application forms, available from the Grants Department or via the website or email.

Closing Date: November 29th.

Funding: Private.

Contributor: Public donations.

No. of awards given last year: Four.

No. of applicants last year: 15.

NATIONAL LEAGUE OF AMERICAN PEN WOMEN, INC. (NLAPW)

1300 17th Street NW, Washington, DC, 20036-1973, United States of America
Tel: (1) 202 785 1997
Fax: (1) 202 452 6868
Email: nlapw1@juno.com
Contact: Ms Mary Jane Hillery, National Scholarship Chairperson

The National League of American Pen Women exists to promote women in the creative arts including art, writing and music.

National League of American Pen Women Grants for Mature Women

Subjects: Art, writing and music.

Purpose: To further creative purpose in art, writing and music.

Eligibility: Current and past recipients are not eligible for this award. Open to women over 35 years of age who wish to pursue special work in their field of art, letters and music. Applicants must be United States citizens.

Level of Study: Unrestricted.

Type: Grant.

Value: US$1,000. The award may be used for college, framing, research or any creative purpose that furthers a career in the creative arts.

Frequency: Every two years.

Country of Study: United States of America.

No. of awards offered: One in each category.

Application Procedure: Applicants must send a letter stating their age, background and creative purpose and include proof of their citizenship. There are no application forms. No applications will be accepted by telephone or email.

Closing Date: Even numbered years.

Funding: Private.

Contributor: NLAPW.

No. of awards given last year: Three.

No. of applicants last year: 1000+.

Additional Information: Interested parties must send a stamped addressed envelope to receive current information.

For further information contact:

66 Willow Road, Sudbury, MA, 01776-2663, United States of America

NATIONAL LIBRARY OF AUSTRALIA

Canberra, ACT, 2600, Australia
Tel: (61) 2 6262 1258
Fax: (61) 2 6262 1516
Email: g.powell@nla.gov.au
Contact: Mr Graeme Powell, Manuscript Librarian

The National Library of Australia is responsible for developing and maintaining a comprehensive collection of Australian library materials, a strong collection of non-Australian publications, and for administering and co-ordinating a range of national bibliographical activities.

Harold White Fellowships

Subjects: Few subject limitations, but most fellowships fall within the categories of arts and humanities, fine and applied arts or social sciences.

Purpose: To promote the Library as a centre of scholarly activity and research, to encourage scholarly and literary use of the collection and the production of publications based on them, to publicise the Library's collections.

Eligibility: Open to established Scholars, writers and librarians from any country. Fellowships are not normally offered to candidates working for a higher degree.

Level of Study: Unrestricted.

Type: Fellowship.

Value: Australian $700 per week.

Frequency: Annual.

Study Establishment: The National Library of Australia.

Country of Study: Australia.

No. of awards offered: Three-five.

Application Procedure: Applicants must complete an application form, available from the National Library.

Closing Date: April 30th.

Funding: Government.

No. of awards given last year: Five.

Additional Information: Normally Fellows will be expected to give a public lecture and at least one seminar during their tenure on the subject of their research. At least three quarters of the fellowship time should be spent in Canberra.

NATIONAL MARFAN FOUNDATION

382 Main Street, Port Washington, NY, 11050, United States of
America
Tel: (1) 516 883 8712 ext. 17
Fax: (1) 516 883 8040
Email: research@marfan.org
www: http://www.marfan.org
Contact: Ms Josephine Grima, Director of Research

The National Marfan Foundation was founded in 1981 by people
who have Marfan syndrome and their families. It is a voluntary organisation that has three objectives: to disseminate accurate and
timely information about Marfan syndrome to patients, family members and physicians; to provide a network of communications for patients and relatives to share experiences, support one another and
improve their medical care; and to support and foster research. In
1995, the Foundation's mission was expanded to include Marfan
syndrome and related connective tissue disorders. These genetic
disorders of connective tissue affect approximately 200,000 people
in the United States and strike men and women of any race or ethnic
group without discrimination.

National Marfan Foundation Clinical Fellowship Grant

Subjects: Special areas of interest are basic research, translational
studies and clinical studies in cardiovascular, orthopaedic and
ophthalmologic issues of Marfan syndrome.
Purpose: To provide the opportunity for Fellows to gain formal education and experience in research methodologies so that the recipient will be able to conduct independent research and compete for
extramural funding.
Eligibility: The Fellow should possess an MD and be licensed to
practice medicine. Fellows should be eligible at their institution for
speciality training in the field of Marfan syndrome including but not
limited to genetics, cardiology, orthopaedics and ophthalmology.
Level of Study: Professional development.
Type: Fellowship.
Value: US$100,000 over two years.
Length of Study: One or two years.
Frequency: Annual.
Country of Study: United States of America.
No. of awards offered: One.
Application Procedure: Application guidelines and forms are avail-
able from the website.
Closing Date: January 1st.
Funding: Private.
Additional Information: The Fellow should work in an active, pro-
gressive research environment that intimately involves them in the
conception, planning, execution and reporting of MFS research. It is
expected that the Fellow receive formal education in such topics as
biomedical statistics, research design, grant writing and safety, regulatory and ethical concerns.

National Marfan Foundation Research Grant

Subjects: Basic and clinical research related to the Marfan syndrome and related connective tissue disorders. Areas include basic,
translational and clinical research in genetics, cardiology, ophthalmology and orthopaedic issues of the Marfan syndrome.
Purpose: To provide financial support for investigators, scientists
and physicians studying any or all disciplines involved in Marfan syn-
drome research.
Eligibility: The principal investigator must hold an MD, DO, PhD,
ScD, DDS, DVM or equivalent degree. The investigator must have
proven ability to pursue independent research publications in peer-
reviewed journals.
Level of Study: Doctorate, Postdoctorate, Research.
Type: Research grant.
Value: US$50,000-100,000.
Length of Study: One or two years.
Frequency: Annual.
Country of Study: Any country.
No. of awards offered: Three-four.

Application Procedure: Applicants must complete an application
form, available from the website.
Closing Date: July 1st.
Funding: Private.
No. of awards given last year: Four.
No. of applicants last year: 10.

THE NATIONAL MULTIPLE SCLEROSIS SOCIETY

733 Third Avenue, New York, NY, 10017, United States of America
Tel: (1) 212 986 3240
Fax: (1) 212 986 7981
Email: nat@nmss.org
www: http://www.nationalmssociety.org
Contact: Grants Management Officer

The National Multiple Sclerosis Society is dedicated to ending the
devastating effects of multiple sclerosis.

National Multiple Sclerosis Society Junior Faculty Awards

Subjects: Neurosciences related to multiple sclerosis.
Purpose: To enable highly qualified persons who have concluded
their research training and have begun academic careers as inde-
pendent investigators to undertake independent research.
Eligibility: Open to United States citizens holding a doctoral degree
who have had sufficient research training at the pre or postdoctoral
levels to be capable of independent research. Individuals who have
already carried out independent research for more than five years
are not eligible.
Level of Study: Professional development.
Value: Approx. US$75,000 per year.
Length of Study: Five years.
Frequency: Annual.
Study Establishment: An approved university, professional or re-
search institute in the United States of America.
Country of Study: United States of America.
No. of awards offered: Varies.
Application Procedure: Applicants must complete an application
form.
Closing Date: February 1st for awards to become effective on Au-
gust 1st.
Funding: Private.
No. of awards given last year: One.
No. of applicants last year: Four.
Additional Information: The candidate will not be an employee of
the Society, but rather of the institution. It is expected that the institution will develop plans for continuing the candidate's appointment
and for continued salary support beyond the five year period of the
award. Fellows may not supplement their salary through private
practice or consultation, nor accept another concurrent award. The
grantee institution holds title to all equipment purchased with award
funds.

National Multiple Sclerosis Society Pilot Research Grants

Subjects: Multiple sclerosis.
Purpose: To provide limited short-term support of novel high risk
research.
Eligibility: Open to suitably qualified investigators.
Level of Study: Established investigator.
Type: Research grant.
Value: Up to US$30,000 in direct costs may be requested for the
one year period.
Length of Study: One year.
Frequency: Dependent on funds available.
Country of Study: Any country.
No. of awards offered: Varies.

Application Procedure: Applicants must complete an application form.
Closing Date: Applications are accepted at any time.
Funding: Private.
No. of awards given last year: 40.
No. of applicants last year: 74.
Additional Information: Grants are awarded to an institution to support the research of the principal investigator. Progress reports are required.

National Multiple Sclerosis Society Postdoctoral Fellowships

Subjects: Training in research applicable to multiple sclerosis.
Purpose: To provide postdoctoral training which will enhance the likelihood of performing meaningful and independent research relevant to multiple sclerosis.
Eligibility: Open to unusually promising recipients of MD or PhD degrees. The programme of training to be supported by the grant must materially enhance the likelihood of the trainee performing meaningful and independent research on multiple sclerosis and obtaining a suitable position which will enable him to do so. Foreign nationals are welcome to apply for fellowships in the United States of America only. Besides its attention to younger researchers, the Society will also consider applications from established investigators who seek support to obtain specialised training in some field in which they are not expert, when such training will materially enhance their capacity to conduct more meaningful research on multiple sclerosis. United States citizenship is not required for training in United States institutions, but applicants who plan to train in other countries must be United States citizens. These fellowships are awarded to support training in research and are not awarded to support clinical training directed towards the completion of internship or speciality board certification. Similarly, they cannot be used to provide support for individuals whose primary responsibility is teaching or service, although Fellows are encouraged to spend a reasonable amount of their time (up to 10 percent) in teaching.
Level of Study: Postdoctorate.
Type: Fellowship.
Value: Varies according to professional status, previous training, accomplishments in research and the pay scale of the institution in which the training is provided. Fellowships may be supplemented by other forms of support, with prior approval.
Length of Study: One-three years.
Frequency: Annual.
Study Establishment: An institution of the candidate's choice.
Country of Study: United States of America for foreign postdoctoral applicants.
No. of awards offered: Varies.
Application Procedure: Applicants must complete an application form.
Closing Date: February 1st for grants to become effective on August 1st or thereafter.
Funding: Private.
No. of awards given last year: 28.
No. of applicants last year: 50.
Additional Information: Fellows are not considered as employees of the Society, but rather of the institution where the training is provided. The fellowship is to be administered in accordance with the prevailing policies of the sponsoring institution. It is the responsibility of the applicant to make all the necessary arrangements for his training with the mentor and institution of his choice.

National Multiple Sclerosis Society Research Grants

Subjects: Multiple sclerosis, the cause, prevention, alleviation and cure.
Purpose: To stimulate, co-ordinate and support fundamental or applied, clinical or non-clinical research.
Eligibility: Open to suitably qualified investigators.
Level of Study: Professional development.
Type: Research grant.
Value: Funds may be used to pay the salaries of associated professional personnel, technical assistants and other non-professional personnel in proportion to their time spent directly on the project, in whole or in part. Salaries are made in accordance with the prevailing policies of the grantee institution. If requested, other expenses, such as travel costs and fringe benefits, may also be paid.
Length of Study: Three years.
Frequency: Twice a year.
Country of Study: Any country.
No. of awards offered: Varies.
Application Procedure: Applicants must complete an application form.
Closing Date: February 1st or August 1st for grants to become effective on October 1st and April 1st respectively.
Funding: Private.
No. of awards given last year: 59.
No. of applicants last year: 162.
Additional Information: Grants are awarded to an institution to support the research of the principal investigator. Scientific equipment and supplies bought with grant funds become the property of the grantee institution. Progress reports are required, and appropriate publication is expected.

NATIONAL ORCHESTRAL INSTITUTE

Clarice Smith Performing Arts Center
University of Maryland, College Park, MD, 20742-1620, United States of America
Tel: (1) 301 405 2317
Fax: (1) 301 314 9504
Email: noi@accmail.umd.edu
www: http://www.nationalorchestralinstitute.com

National Orchestral Institute Scholarships

Subjects: Orchestral performance and chamber music.
Purpose: To provide an intensive three week orchestral training programme to enable musicians to rehearse and perform under internationally acclaimed conductors and study with principal musicians of the United States' foremost orchestras in preparation for careers as orchestral musicians.
Eligibility: Open to advanced musicians between 18-28 years of age, primarily students and postgraduates of United States universities, conservatories and colleges. Others, however, are welcome to apply but must appear at an audition centre. String players, including harpists, who live more than 100 miles away from an audition centre may audition by tape.
Level of Study: Professional development.
Type: Scholarship.
Value: Full tuition, room and board.
Length of Study: Three weeks.
Frequency: Annual.
Study Establishment: The University of Maryland.
Country of Study: United States of America.
No. of awards offered: Approx. 90.
Application Procedure: Applicants must submit an application, a fee of US$35, curriculum vitae and letter of recommendation.
Closing Date: Before regional auditions.
Funding: Government.
Contributor: The University of Maryland.
No. of awards given last year: 90.
No. of applicants last year: 800.
Additional Information: Personal auditions are required at one of the audition centres throughout the country.

THE NATIONAL ORGANIZATION FOR RARE DISORDERS (NORD)

PO Box 8923, New Fairfield, CT, 06812-8923, United States of America
Tel: (1) 203 746 6518
Fax: (1) 203 746 5418
Email: lcataldo@rarediseases.org
www: http://www.rarediseases.org
Contact: Ms Linda M Cataldo, Research Grant Co-ordinator

The National Organization for Rare Disorders (NORD) is a federation of voluntary health organisations dedicated to helping people with rare (orphan) diseases and assisting the organisations that serve them. NORD is committed to the identification, treatment and cure of rare disorders through programmes of advocacy, education, research and service. For more information on current research funding opportunities please visit the website.

NORD Clinical Research Grants
Subjects: New treatments for rare diseases or medical research.
Purpose: To support small clinical trials on rare diseases.
Eligibility: Open to academic scientists in the United States of America, Canada and Europe, or any country that adheres to the most recent guidelines for human subject protection as set forth by the NIH.
Level of Study: Doctorate, Postdoctorate, Professional development, Research.
Type: Research grant.
Value: US$30,000-50,000 per year.
Length of Study: Up to two years.
Frequency: Annual.
Country of Study: United States of America, Canada, Europe Middle East, Australia or South America.
No. of awards offered: Three-four.
Application Procedure: Applicants must submit an application form, letter of intent and proposals. Forms are available from the website.
Closing Date: Enquiries are accepted at any time for future announcements and should be sent by email.
Funding: Private.
Contributor: Public donations.
No. of awards given last year: 10.
No. of applicants last year: 100.
Additional Information: Funding opportunities are announced January-March.

NORD/ROSCOE BRADY Lysosomal Storage Diseases Fellowship
Subjects: Genetics, new treatments and diagnostics, and/or epidemiology of lysosomal storage diseases in general, or for a specific lysosomal storage disease.
Purpose: To assist physicians who desire to establish careers in lysosomal storage diseases and clinical medicine.
Eligibility: Open to all countries that adhere to the most recent guidelines for human subject protection as set forth by the NIH. Applicants will have an MD or MD/PhD earned in or after 1992.
Level of Study: Doctorate, Postdoctorate, Professional development, Research.
Type: Fellowship.
Value: US$50,000-70,000 per year.
Length of Study: One year but renewable for a second year.
Frequency: Dependent on funds available.
Country of Study: United States of America, Canada, Europe, Middle East, Australia, or South America.
No. of awards offered: Three-four.
Application Procedure: Application forms and required attachments may be obtained directly from the website.
Closing Date: February 28th.
Funding: Commercial.
Contributor: Public donations.

No. of awards given last year: Five.
No. of applicants last year: Eight.

NATIONAL RADIO ASTRONOMY OBSERVATORY (NRAO)

520 Edgemont Road, Charlottesville, VA, 22903-2475, United States of America

Tel: (1) 434 296 0221

Fax: (1) 434 296 0278

Email: info@nrao.edu

www: http://www.nrao.edu

Contact: Ms Sheila Marks, Secretary

Jansky Postdoctorals

Subjects: Areas of present interest include theoretical and observational studies of discrete radio sources, galaxies, the interstellar medium, planets, millimetre wave instrumentation and research, interferometry, aperture, synthesis, large antenna arrays, radio astronomy instrumentation (HFET and SIS amplifiers, radiometer systems, cryogenics), data processing, information theory, computer system applications or digital and online techniques.

Purpose: To provide outstanding opportunities to qualified young PhDs who wish to devote themselves to full-time research.

Eligibility: Open to astronomers, physicists, electrical engineers and computer specialists. Preference will be given to recent PhD recipients.

Level of Study: Postdoctorate.

Value: US$35,000 per year, plus a liberal vacation allowance, authorised travel expenses and a moving allowance.

Length of Study: Two years, with a possibility of renewal for one further year.

Frequency: Annual.

Study Establishment: The Observatory's centres in Charlottesville, Virginia; Green Bank, West Virginia; Tucson, Arizona; and Socorro, New Mexico.

Country of Study: Any country.

No. of awards offered: Four.

Application Procedure: Applications normally commence in September or October. There is no application form. The initial letter should include a statement of the individual's research interests together with his or her own appraisal of his or her qualifications for carrying out research. Applications should be single sided with no staples. The applicant should have three letters of recommendation sent directly to the NRAO.

Closing Date: December 15th.

Funding: Government.

Contributor: The National Science Foundation.

No. of awards given last year: Four.

No. of applicants last year: 54.

Additional Information: Research Associates may formulate and carry out investigations either independently or in collaboration with others.

NATIONAL RESEARCH COUNCIL (NRC) OFFICE FOR CENTRAL EUROPE AND EURASIA

2101 Constitution Avenue North West, Washington, DC, 20418, United States of America
Tel: (1) 202 334 2644
Fax: (1) 202 334 2614
Email: ocee@nas.edu
www: http://www.nas.edu/oia
Contact: Ms Kelly Robbins, Senior Programme Officer

The National Research Council (NRC) was organised by the National Academy of Sciences in 1916 to associate the broad community of science and technology with the Academy's purposes of further knowledge and advising the federal government.

COBASE Collaboration in Basic Science and Engineering

Subjects: History, philosophy of science, social science or science and technology policy.
Purpose: Primarily to prepare new partnerships of American specialists with their colleagues from Central or Eastern Europe.
Eligibility: Open to United States citizens or permanent residents, but not to United States government employees. American and foreign colleagues must possess a PhD or equivalent.
Level of Study: Postdoctorate.
Type: Travel grant.
Value: US$3,000-10,000.
Length of Study: Two-eight weeks.
Frequency: Annual.
Country of Study: Eastern Europe.
No. of awards offered: 30-40.
Application Procedure: Applicants must submit the original and five copies of the completed application form, a three to four page statement of objectives, a curriculum vitae, a publication list, a statement from a collaborator and a budget.
Closing Date: There are three deadlines each year in January, April and August.
Funding: Government.
Contributor: NSF.
No. of awards given last year: 59.
No. of applicants last year: 166.
Additional Information: Further information is available on the website.

NRC Twinning Program

Subjects: Fields supported by NSF. No disease related topics.
Purpose: To yield significant publications and long-term sustained linkages between researchers in the United States of America and underrepresented countries in Eastern Europe.
Eligibility: Open to American citizens or permanent residents but not to employees of the United States' government. Principal investigators must hold a PhD or equivalent.
Level of Study: Postdoctorate.
Type: Travel grant.
Value: US$12,000-15,000.
Length of Study: Two years.
Frequency: Annual, if funds are available.
Country of Study: Eastern Europe. A specific country is selected annually, please refer to the website.
No. of awards offered: Generally 8-12 per year.
Application Procedure: Applicants must submit five copies of a description of their proposed research, a budget, a curriculum vitae, a list of publications, a curriculum vitae of foreign counterparts, letters of support from United States applicants' institutions, correspondence with prospective twinning partner and a list of potential peer reviewers.
Closing Date: Varies.
Funding: Government.
Contributor: NSF.

No. of awards given last year: Eight.
No. of applicants last year: 26.
Additional Information: Further information is available on the website.

NATIONAL RESEARCH COUNCIL OF CANADA (NRC)

Recruitment Unit, Montreal Road, M58, Ottawa, ON, K1A 0R6, Canada
Tel: (1) 613 993 9150
Fax: (1) 613 990 7669
Email: ra.coordinator@nrc.ca
www: http://www.nrc.ca/careers
Contact: Research Associates Co-ordinator

The National Research Council of Canada (NRC) is a dynamic, nationwide research and development organisation committed to helping Canada realise its potential as an innovative and competitive nation.

National Research Council Laboratories Research Associateships

Subjects: Biological sciences, biotechnology, chemistry, molecular science, chemical engineering and process technologies, electrical engineering, astrophysics, industrial materials research, marine dynamics, construction, mechanical engineering, aeronautics, physics, photonics, microstructural sciences, plant biotechnology, biochemistry, microbiology or advanced structural ceramics.

Purpose: To give promising scientists and engineers an opportunity to work on challenging research problems in fields of interest to NRC as a stage in the development of their research careers.

Eligibility: Open to nationals of all countries, although preference will be given to Canadians and permanent residents of Canada. Applicants should have acquired a PhD in natural science or a Master's degree in an engineering field within the last five years or should expect to obtain the degree before taking up the associateship. Selections will be made on a competitive basis. Demonstrated ability to perform original research of high quality in the chosen field will be the main criterion used in selecting candidates and in considering extensions of their term.

Level of Study: Postgraduate.

Type: Research associateship.

Value: Canadian $43,890 for a new PhD. Salaries are revised annually.

Frequency: Annual.

Study Establishment: The laboratories in the National Research Council of Canada.

Country of Study: Any country.

No. of awards offered: Approx. 50.

Application Procedure: Applicants must fill out an electronic application on the Internet or write for details.

Closing Date: Applications are accepted at any time.

Funding: Government.

Additional Information: Further information is available from the website.

NATIONAL RESEARCH FOUNDATION (NRF)

PO Box 2600, Pretoria, 0001, South Africa
Tel: (27) 12 481 4097
Fax: (27) 12 349 1179
Email: anke@nrf.ac.za
www: http://www.nrf.ac.za
Contact: Ms A Rädel, Manager, Bursary & Fellowship Programme

The National Research Foundation (NRF) is responsible for funding South African research and other expertise in the fields of the social, natural and applied sciences, humanities, engineering and technology. The NRF is funded by the government, but also pursues joint ventures and collaboration with industry and the international community to increase the impact of its activities.

NRF Bursaries for Study towards an Honours Degree

Subjects: Natural and applied sciences, engineering and the social sciences and humanities.
Purpose: To foster studies in the fields of applied and natural sciences, engineering, the social sciences and the humanities.
Eligibility: Restricted to South African citizens studying towards an Honours or BTech degree at a South African university or technikon.
Level of Study: Postgraduate.
Type: Bursary.
Value: A maximum of rand 8,000.
Length of Study: One year, non renewable.
Frequency: Annual.
Study Establishment: Any South African university or technikon for full-time study.
Country of Study: South Africa.
No. of awards offered: 200.
Application Procedure: Applicants must complete and submit an application form and full academic record. Forms are available from the bursary offices of universities and technikons.
Closing Date: October 31st of the year preceding the award.
Funding: Government.
No. of awards given last year: 200.
No. of applicants last year: 600.
Additional Information: The award of a bursary does not bind the candidate to enter the Foundation's service. However, candidates are expected to obtain the degree for which the award was made.

NRF Doctoral Scholarships and Postdoctoral Fellowships for Study Abroad

Subjects: Natural and applied sciences, engineering and the social sciences and humanities.
Purpose: To foster postgraduate studies and research in the fields of applied and natural sciences, engineering, the social sciences and the humanities.
Eligibility: Open to South African citizens who are in the process of obtaining or who have obtained their doctoral degree. Applicants for postdoctoral fellowships should have obtained their doctorate in the last five years.
Level of Study: Doctorate, Postdoctorate, Postgraduate.
Type: Scholarships and fellowships.
Value: Scholarships are US$12,000, and postdoctoral awards are up to US$16,500.
Length of Study: Up to three years of doctoral study, or up to two years of postdoctoral research.
Frequency: Scholarships are offered annually and fellowships are offered twice a year.
Study Establishment: Approved institutions abroad for full-time study or research.
Country of Study: Outside South Africa.
No. of awards offered: 20.
Application Procedure: Applicants must complete and submit an application form, full academic record, and referee's reports. Forms are available from the bursary offices of the universities and technikons or can be downloaded from the website.
Closing Date: The deadline for scholarships is July 31st of the year preceding the award, and for fellowships the deadlines are March 31st and September 30th.
Funding: Government.
No. of awards given last year: 20.
No. of applicants last year: 50.
Additional Information: Candidates should motivate their choice of overseas institution.

NRF Fellowships for Postdoctoral Research

Subjects: Natural and applied sciences, engineering, technology, social sciences and humanities.
Purpose: To foster postdoctoral research in the natural and applied sciences, engineering, social sciences and the humanities.
Eligibility: Open to South African citizens or holders of permanent residence permits who have recently received their PhD degrees (in the last five years).
Level of Study: Postdoctorate.
Type: Fellowship.
Value: Up to rand 60,000 plus a contribution of rand 10,000 towards the running cost of the project.
Length of Study: Up to two years.
Frequency: Twice a year.
Study Establishment: Any South African university, technikon or research institution for full-time research.
Country of Study: South Africa.
No. of awards offered: 50.
Application Procedure: Applicants must complete and submit an application form, full academic record, and the names of referees. Forms are available from the bursary offices of universities and technikons or can be downloaded from the website.
Closing Date: March 31st or September 30th.
Funding: Government.
No. of awards given last year: 30.
No. of applicants last year: 90.
Additional Information: A limited number of postdoctoral fellowships are also available for outstanding foreign candidates for full-time research in South Africa.

NRF Scholarships for Doctoral Study

Subjects: Natural and applied sciences, engineering and the social sciences and humanities.
Purpose: To foster postgraduate studies in the fields of natural and applied sciences, engineering, the social sciences and the humanities.
Eligibility: Open to South African citizens for full-time doctoral studies at South African universities or technikons.
Level of Study: Doctorate, Postgraduate.
Type: Scholarship.
Value: Rand 50,000 per year.
Length of Study: Up to three years.
Frequency: Annual.
Study Establishment: Any South African university or technikon for full-time study.
Country of Study: South Africa.
No. of awards offered: Approx. 30.
Application Procedure: Applicants must complete and submit an application form, full academic record, and referee's reports. Forms are available from the bursary offices of universities and technikons.
Closing Date: July 31st of the year preceding the award.
Funding: Government.
No. of awards given last year: 35.
No. of applicants last year: 110.
Additional Information: The award of a scholarship does not bind the candidate to enter the Foundation's service. However, candidates are expected to obtain the degree for which the award was made. In addition, one contribution will be made towards travel costs during the entire duration of the study to either attend a conference (locally or abroad) with the proviso that the student will be making a contribution to the conference, and/or visit a laboratory for two to three months, provided it is linked to the student's research.

NRF Scholarships for Master's Study

Subjects: Natural and applied sciences, engineering and the social sciences and humanities.

Purpose: To foster studies in the fields of applied and natural sciences, engineering, the social sciences and the humanities.

Eligibility: Open to South African citizens for full-time Master's study at South African universities or technikons.

Level of Study: Postgraduate.

Type: Scholarship.

Value: Rand 33,000 per year.

Length of Study: Two years. Where Master's registration is upgraded to PhD, the maximum period of support for Master's and doctoral study will be four years in total.

Frequency: Annual.

Study Establishment: Any South African university or technikon for full-time study.

Country of Study: South Africa.

No. of awards offered: 50.

Application Procedure: Applicants must complete and submit an application form, full academic record, and referee's reports. Forms are available from the bursary offices of universities and technikons.

Closing Date: July 31st of the year preceding the award.

Funding: Government.

No. of awards given last year: 50.

No. of applicants last year: 200.

Additional Information: The award of a scholarship does not bind the candidate to enter the Foundation's service. However, candidates are expected to obtain the degree for which the award was made. In addition, one contribution will be made towards travel costs during the entire duration of the study to either attend a conference (locally or abroad) with the proviso that the student will be making a contribution at the conference, or visit a laboratory for two to three months, provided it is linked to the student's research.

NATIONAL RIGHT TO WORK COMMITTEE

National Institute for Labour Relations Research
5211 Port Royal Road
Suite 510, Springfield, VA, 22151, United States of America
Tel: (1) 703 321 9606
Fax: (1) 703 321 7342
Email: kml@nilrr.org
www: http://www.nilrr.org
Contact: Public Relations Department

William B Ruggles Right to Work Award

Subjects: Journalism.

Purpose: To support promising young journalists.

Eligibility: Open to students majoring in journalism or mass communication who exemplify the dedication to the principle and high journalistic standards of William B Ruggles.

Level of Study: Doctorate, Postgraduate.

Type: Award.

Value: US$2,000.

Frequency: Annual.

Study Establishment: An Institute of Higher Education.

Country of Study: United States of America.

No. of awards offered: One.

Application Procedure: Applicants must send a recent transcript of grades, a completed application form, a 500 word essay on the right to work as well as a student financial aid form, and a projection of the expected education expenses. Application forms are available from the website.

Closing Date: January 1st to March 31st.

Additional Information: Applications must be received, not postmarked, by March 31st, or they will not be considered. Only the first 150 applicants will be considered. For further information please contact the National Institute for Labour Relations Research.

NATIONAL SCIENCE FOUNDATION (NSF)

Division of Earth Sciences
4201 Wilson Boulevard, Arlington, VA, 22230, United States of America
Tel: (1) 703 292 8550
Fax: (1) 703 292 9025
Email: hzimmer@nsf.gov
www: http://www.geo.nsf.gov/ear
Contact: Dr Herman Zimmerman, Division Director

The National Science Foundation (NSF) supports research in the areas of geology, geophysics, geochemistry, paleobiology and hydrology, including interdisciplinary or multidisciplinary proposals that may involve one or more of these disciplines. Proposals for research in newly emerging areas of science that may not fit easily into one of these categories are especially welcome.

NSF Division of Earth Sciences

Subjects: Emphasis is on research aimed at an improved understanding of the earth's structure, properties, processes and evolution, including basic research in areas of practical importance. Support is provided in most fields of the solid-earth sciences including geology, geophysics, geochemistry and hydrology in response to unsolicited, investigator initiated proposals.

Purpose: To advance the state of knowledge in the earth sciences and enhance the ability of United States colleges and universities to conduct research and education in these fields.

Eligibility: Open to qualified research scientists at United States universities, colleges and other research institutions.

Level of Study: Unrestricted.

Value: Award sizes vary greatly depending on the project proposed, but most awards are US$50,000-100,000.

Frequency: Annual.

Study Establishment: Appropriate sites and institutions.

Country of Study: Any country.

No. of awards offered: Approx. 500.

Application Procedure: Applicants must consult the following publications: 'NSF Guide to Programs' and 'Earth Sciences Research at NSF'. Latest editions of these publications may be requested by mail from the Forms and Publications Unit.

Closing Date: June 1st or December 1st.

Funding: Government.

No. of awards given last year: 462.

No. of applicants last year: 1,592.

Additional Information: For detailed information on general application procedure, preparation of proposals and budgeting, please refer to the website http://www.nsf.gov. The Division is a participant in the National Earthquake Hazard Prevention Programme and the United States of America Global Change Research Program.

NATIONAL STRENGTH AND CONDITIONING ASSOCIATION (NSCA)

1955 N Union, Colorado Springs, CO, 80909-2229, United States of America
Tel: (1) 719 632 6722
Fax: (1) 719 632 6367
www: http://www.nsca-lift.org
Contact: Ms Karri Todd Baker, Membership Director

As the worldwide authority on strength and conditioning, the National Strength and Conditioning Association (NSCA) supports and disseminates research based knowledge and its practice to improve athletic performance and fitness.

NSCA Challenge Scholarship

Subjects: A strength and conditioning related field.

Purpose: To financially assist members in their pursuit of a career in strength and conditioning.

Eligibility: Applicants must have been NSCA members for at least one year from the application deadline and seeking a graduate degree in a strength and conditioning related field.
Level of Study: Graduate, Postgraduate.
Type: Scholarship.
Value: US$1,000.
Frequency: Annual.
Study Establishment: Unrestricted.
Country of Study: Any country.
No. of awards offered: 12.
Application Procedure: Applicants must submit a current curriculum vitae, a cover letter of application and three current letters of recommendation, an original copy of an authorised transcript from all post secondary schools attended, and an essay of no more than 500 words describing course of study, career goals and need. All material must be mailed together and postmarked by March 1st. Applicants may also apply via the website.
Closing Date: March 1st.
Funding: Private.
Contributor: Funding is made possible by the Bob Hoffman Foundation, NSCA Certification Commission and the NSCA National Office.
No. of awards given last year: 11.
No. of applicants last year: 15.

NSCA Student Grant Research Grant
Subjects: Strength and conditioning.
Purpose: To fund graduate student research in strength and conditioning that is directed by a graduate faculty member.
Eligibility: Open to NSCA members who have been members for at least one year from the application deadline. Graduate student members who are studying in the field of strength and conditioning are invited to apply. A graduate faculty member is required to serve as co-investigator in the study.
Level of Study: Graduate, Postgraduate, Research.
Type: Grant.
Value: Up to US$2,500.
Length of Study: One year.
Frequency: Annual.
Study Establishment: Unrestricted.
Country of Study: Any country.
No. of awards offered: Varies, dependent on the number of applications.
Application Procedure: Applicants must submit a grant application to the NSCA Student Grant Programme containing the following sections not to exceed 10 single spaced pages containing the following information: project title, name of student investigator with NSCA membership number, proof of enrolment, institution, address, phone, fax and email, abstract, brief review of literature, importance of project to the field, limited bibliography, methods, statistical analysis, itemised budget, Human Subjects Consent Form and proof of institutional review board approval, proposed time schedule and a curriculum vitae of faculty co-investigator. Candidates may also apply via the website.
Closing Date: The letter of intent is due on February 3rd, and the application is due on March 17th.
Funding: Private.
Contributor: The NSCA Certification Commission and NSCA National Office.
No. of awards given last year: Six.
No. of applicants last year: Nine.
Additional Information: Application forms can be accessed via the website or by telephoning the organisation.

Power Systems Professional Scholarship
Subjects: Strength and conditioning.
Purpose: To financially assist members in their pursuit of a career as a strength and conditioning coach.
Eligibility: Open to any NSCA member who has been a member for at least one year from the application deadline and is pursuing a career as a strength and conditioning coach.
Level of Study: Graduate, Postgraduate.

Type: Scholarship.
Value: US$1,000.
Frequency: Annual.
Study Establishment: Unrestricted.
Country of Study: Any country.
No. of awards offered: One-two depending on the amount of applications.
Application Procedure: The head strength coach from the applicant's school must submit a letter of application. The applicant must submit an original, official transcript from all secondary schools attended, current curriculum vitae and an essay of no more than 500 words describing career goals and objectives. The transcript must be mailed directly to the NSCA office by the school. To obtain an application form applicants should telephone or visit the website. Only one candidate per school is permitted.
Closing Date: All materials must be postmarked by the application deadline of May 1st.
Funding: Private.
Contributor: Power Systems, Inc.
No. of awards given last year: One.
No. of applicants last year: Five.

NATIONAL UNION OF TEACHERS (NUT)

Central Co-ordinating Unit
Hamilton House
Mabledon Place, London, WC1H 9BD, England
Tel: (44) 20 7380 4704
Fax: (44) 20 7387 8458
www: http://www.teachers.org.uk
Contact: Ms Angela Bush

NUT Page Scholarship
Subjects: A specific aspect of American education relevant to the recipient's own professional responsibilities.
Purpose: To promote the exchange of educational ideas between Britain and America.
Eligibility: Open to teachers who are members of the National Union of Teachers and between 25 and 60 years of age (25 to 55 is preferred).
Level of Study: Professional development.
Type: Scholarship.
Value: Up to UK £1,700 (pro-rata daily rate), with complete hospitality in the United States of America provided by the English speaking Union of the United States.
Length of Study: Two weeks. The scholarship must be taken during the American academic year, September-April, whilst the American educational institutions are in session.
Frequency: Annual.
Country of Study: United States of America.
No. of awards offered: One.
Application Procedure: Applicants must complete an application form. An outline and synopsis of the project must accompany the form (1,000-1,500 words), along with a curriculum vitae and scholastic and personal testimonials.
Closing Date: December 22nd.
Funding: Private.
Contributor: NUT.
No. of awards given last year: One.
No. of applicants last year: 120.
Additional Information: The scholarship is limited to the individual teacher and neither the spouse nor partner can be included in the travelling, accommodation or study arrangements. Recipients are required to report on their visit to teacher groups and educational meetings in the United States of America and on their return home.

NATIONAL UNIVERSITY OF SINGAPORE (NUS)

National University of Singapore
Registrar's Office
10 Kent Ridge Crescent, 119260, Singapore
Tel: (65) 874 2301
Fax: (65) 778 6371
Email: gradenquiry@nus.edu.sg
www: http://www.nus.edu.sg
Contact: Associate Professor Khoo Hoon Eng, Grants Management Officer

NUS Graduate Scholarships for ASEAN Nationals

Subjects: Public policy, architecture, arts in Chinese studies, arts in English studies, arts in Southeast Asian studies, arts in urban design, business administration (English or Chinese), clinical embryology, computing, dental surgery in endodontics, dental surgery in oral and maxillofacial surgery, dental surgery in orthodontics, dental surgery in periodontology, dental surgery in prosthodontics, laws, medicine in internal medicine, medicine in anaesthesia, medicine in diagnostic radiology, medicine in obstetrics and gynaecology, medicine in occupational medicine, medicine in ophthalmology, medicine in paediatric medicine, medicine in psychiatry, medicine in public health, medicine in surgery. Other subject areas include science in building science, science in chemical engineering, science in civil engineering, science in electrical engineering, science in environmental engineering, science in industrial and systems engineering, science in management of technology, science in materials science and engineering, science in mathematics, science in mechanical engineering, science in mechatronics, science in project management, science in real estate, science in safety, health and environmental technology, science in transportation systems and management, social sciences in applied psychology, social sciences in economics, social sciences in international studies, and social sciences in social work.
Purpose: To provide outstanding candidates with an opportunity to pursue postgraduate studies at the National University of Singapore.
Eligibility: Open to citizens of ASEAN member countries (except Singapore).
Level of Study: Postgraduate.
Type: Scholarship.
Value: Stipend of singaporean $1,350 each month, a once only book allowance of singaporean $500, approved fees and expenses.
Frequency: Annual.
Study Establishment: National University of Singapore.
Country of Study: Singapore.
No. of awards offered: 40.
Application Procedure: Applicants must complete and submit application forms for the designated degrees with supporting documents to the respective faculties and graduate schools.
Closing Date: Concurrent with the closing date of graduate courses of the respective faculties or graduate schools.
No. of awards given last year: 40.
No. of applicants last year: 600.
Additional Information: ASEAN is the abbreviation for the Association of South East Asian Nations and comprises the following nations in South East Asia - Brunei, Cambodia, Indonesia, Laos, Malaysia, Myanmar, Philippines, Singapore, Thailand and Vietnam.

NUS Postgraduate Research Scholarship

Subjects: Engineering, science, medicine, humanities, business or law.
Purpose: To encourage qualified candidates to pursue postgraduate research in their fields of interest in the National University of Singapore.
Eligibility: Open to graduates with at least an Upper Second Class (Honours) Bachelor's Degree, or equivalent.
Level of Study: Doctorate, Postgraduate.
Type: Scholarship.

Value: Singaporean $1,200-1,400 plus a full fee subsidy over two-three years.
Length of Study: Two or three years.
Frequency: Annual.
Study Establishment: National University of Singapore.
Country of Study: Singapore.
No. of awards offered: Varies.
Application Procedure: Applicants must complete an application form, available on request.
Closing Date: Usually mid May and mid December.
Funding: Government.

NATURAL ENVIRONMENT RESEARCH COUNCIL (NERC)

Polaris House
North Star Avenue, Swindon, Wiltshire, SN2 1EU, England
Tel: (44) 1793 411500
Fax: (44) 1793 411501
www: http://www.nerc.ac.uk/funding
Contact: Dr A M McFarlane, Schemes Policy Officer

The Natural Environment Research Council (NERC) is one of the seven United Kingdom Research Councils which fund and manage research in the United Kingdom. NERC is the leading body in the United Kingdom for research, survey, monitoring and training in the environmental sciences. NERC supports research and training in universities and in its own centres, surveys and units.

NERC Advanced Course Studentships

Subjects: Environmental sciences.
Purpose: To allow postgraduate students to take courses recognised by NERC, which usually lead to an MSc. These courses are essentially vocational and are designed to prepare students for employment in industry or the public sector, or to further study.
Eligibility: Open to persons who, at the closing date of application for an award, have been ordinarily resident in Great Britain or Northern Ireland throughout the three year period preceding that date. Ordinarily resident means that no period of the candidate's residence during those three years has been wholly, or mainly, for the purpose of receiving full-time education. Candidates must hold a First or Second Class (Honours) Degree in an appropriate branch of science or technology. An alternative qualification or combination of qualifications and experience which clearly demonstrate equivalent knowledge and ability may exceptionally be accepted at the Council's discretion. There is no age limit for studentships but the Council reserves the right to decline an application from an older candidate if it considers that an award would not represent a good investment of public funds.
Level of Study: Postgraduate, Predoctorate.
Type: Studentship.
Value: A maintenance grant of UK £6,970 per year for students outside London and UK £8,720 per year for students in London, the payment of approved fees, and assistance with travel and subsistence expenses under specified conditions (fieldwork).
Length of Study: One year.
Frequency: Annual.
Study Establishment: Any approved Institute of Higher Education in the United Kingdom.
Country of Study: United Kingdom.
No. of awards offered: Varies, approx. 290.
Application Procedure: All applications for studentships must be submitted by the head of the department in which the student proposes to work. Applications will not be accepted directly from individual candidates. Awards are tenable only for those courses which are currently recognised by NERC for the purposes of its studentship scheme. The number of NERC awards given to each of these courses is detailed in the display notice. A review of the portfolio of NERC supported advanced courses is undertaken every five years.
Closing Date: July 31st for student nominations.

Funding: Government.
No. of awards given last year: 349.

NERC Advanced Research Fellowships

Subjects: Novel research within the sciences of the natural environment.
Purpose: To support outstanding research workers who are well qualified for academic careers, but who do not hold tenured posts at the time of application.
Eligibility: Candidates must hold a PhD and have had at least two years' research experience at postdoctoral level at the time of application, though not necessarily in the United Kingdom. They must also have proved their ability as individual research workers.
Level of Study: Postdoctorate.
Type: Fellowship.
Value: Awards are based on the United Kingdom universities non-clinical academic and related research staff scale and are related to age when taking up appointment. Increments are awarded on the anniversary of the day the award is taken up. Up to UK £8,000 per year is also available for small items of equipment, consumables and United Kingdom fieldwork.
Length of Study: Depends on the individual scheme. Generally up to five years with a possible extension of a further five years.
Frequency: Annual.
Country of Study: United Kingdom.
No. of awards offered: Varies.
Application Procedure: Applicants must refer to the fellowship booklet and application forms, available on request or via the NERC website.
Closing Date: September 15th.
Funding: Government.
No. of awards given last year: Eight.
Additional Information: All applications must carry the full support of the host institution, which will be expected to act as the Fellow's employer. As part of NERC's commitment to promoting equal opportunities, all fellowships may be held by suitably qualified candidates on a full or part-time basis, subject to the agreement of the host institution. The NERC is particularly keen to attract applications from scientists in the areas of applied mathematics, physics, or strongly quantitative disciplines wishing to develop a career in environmental science.

NERC Postdoctoral Research Fellowships

Subjects: Novel research within the sciences of the natural environment.
Purpose: To enable a small number of outstanding research workers to devote the majority of their time to research so that they may further develop their research potential.
Eligibility: Candidates should normally be under 35 years of age. Applications may be accepted from candidates over 35 where the candidate intends to return to study after a considerable absence from a research environment or where the candidate has come late to higher education. However, such consideration would be subject to the requirement that there should be a substantial career ahead of the Fellow. Candidates must hold a PhD. Applications will be accepted from PhD students but, if successful, awards may not start until NERC has received written confirmation of the outcome of the applicant's PhD viva. However, applicants are advised that some post PhD experience can be an advantage when seeking a postdoctoral fellowship.
Level of Study: Postdoctorate, Postgraduate.
Type: Fellowship.
Value: Awards are based on the United Kingdom universities non-clinical academic and related research staff scale. Starting stipend is related to age when taking up appointment, up to a maximum of the age 30 point on the scale. Increments are awarded on the anniversary of the day the award is taken up. Up to UK £7,000 per year is also available for the purchase of small items of equipment and consumables.
Length of Study: Three years, with the possibility of extension for up to two further years.
Frequency: Annual.

Study Establishment: At universities, government funded research institutes or other approved research institutes in the United Kingdom.
Country of Study: United Kingdom.
Application Procedure: Applicants must refer to the fellowship booklet and application forms, available on request or via the NERC website.
Closing Date: September 15th.
Funding: Government.
No. of awards given last year: Eight.
Additional Information: All applications must carry the full support of the host institution, which will be expected to act as the Fellow's employer. As part of the NERC's commitment to promoting equal opportunities, all fellowships may be held by suitably qualified candidates on a full or part-time basis, subject to the agreement of the host institution. The NERC is particularly keen to attract applications from scientists in the areas of mathematics, physics or other strongly quantitative disciplines wishing to develop a career in environmental science.

NERC Research Grants

Subjects: Research projects concerned with the natural environment.
Purpose: To support a specific investigation in which the applicant will be engaged personally, to enter promising new or modified fields of research, or to take advantage of developments in apparatus offering improved techniques in promising lines of research already established.
Eligibility: Open to research workers ordinarily resident in the United Kingdom who are also members of the academic staff of universities, colleges and similar institutions within the United Kingdom recognised by the NERC. Research assistants and technicians are not eligible to apply. Holders of Research Council Fellowships at an Institute of Higher Education are eligible to apply for research grants.
Level of Study: Postdoctorate, Professional development.
Type: Grant.
Value: The Standard Research Grant offers amounts over UK £30,000, for periods not usually in excess of three years. The Small Research Grant offers a more rapid response for applications costing UK £2,000-30,000. Applications for less than UK £2,000 will not be accepted. The new investigator scheme offers up to the UK £50,000.
Frequency: Throughout the year.
Study Establishment: Any approved Institute of Higher Education in the United Kingdom.
Country of Study: United Kingdom.
No. of awards offered: Varies.
Application Procedure: Applicants must complete an application form, available on request. Application forms and further information can be found on the NERC website.
Closing Date: The deadlines for the Standard Research Grant are July 1st and December 1st. The deadlines for the Small Research Grant are February 1st, June 1st or October 1st.
Funding: Government.
No. of awards given last year: 307.

NERC Research Studentships

Subjects: Environmental sciences.
Purpose: To enable postgraduate students to receive training in methods of research and to undertake research in particular scientific areas under the guidance of named supervisors. It is expected that the awards will lead to the submission of a PhD thesis.
Eligibility: Open to persons who, at the closing date of application for an award, have been ordinarily resident in Great Britain or Northern Ireland throughout the three year period preceding that date. Ordinarily resident means that no period of the candidate's residence during those three years has been wholly, or mainly, for the purpose of receiving full-time education. Candidates must hold a First or Upper Second Class (Honours) Degree in an appropriate branch of science or technology. An alternative qualification or combination of qualifications and experience which clearly demonstrate equivalent knowledge and ability may exceptionally be accepted at the

Council's discretion. Possession of an MSc degree will not be accepted by itself as an adequate qualification for candidates who do not have at least an Upper Second Class (Honours) Degree. Strong and specific reasons will still be needed for an exception to be made. There is no age limit for studentships but the Council reserves the right to decline an application from an older candidate if it considers that an award would not represent a good investment of public funds.

Level of Study: Postgraduate.

Type: Studentship.

Value: A maintenance grant of UK £7,500 per year for students outside London and UK £9,250 per year for students in London, the payment of approved fees, and assistance with travel and subsistence expenses under specified conditions (fieldwork).

Length of Study: Up to three years, part of which may be spent at an institution in Europe.

Frequency: Annual.

Study Establishment: Any approved Institute of Higher Education in the United Kingdom.

Country of Study: United Kingdom or Europe.

No. of awards offered: Varies, approx. 310.

Application Procedure: All applications for studentships must be submitted by the head of the department in which the student proposes to work. Applications will not be accepted directly from individual candidates. To encourage research students to gain additional experience outside the academic sphere some of these awards are made as Co-operative Awards in Sciences of the Environment (CASE Studentships). CASE awards involve the joint supervision of the student by a member of staff of an academic institution and a scientist from industry, a public authority or government research institute.

Closing Date: November 1st for departments to apply for quotas and July 31st for student nominations.

Funding: Government.

No. of awards given last year: 366.

NERC Senior Research Fellowships

Subjects: Environmental sciences.

Purpose: To support environmental scientists of exceptional ability who have an established reputation and who have won, and are likely to continue to win, NERC or other research grants on a regular basis.

Eligibility: Researchers who have already been awarded research grants.

Level of Study: Postdoctorate, Research.

Type: A variable number of fellowships.

Value: Awards are based on the United Kingdom universities non-clinical academic and related research staff scale and are related to the age when taking up the appointment. Up to UK £10,000 per year is also available for small items of equipment, United Kingdom fieldwork and consumables.

Length of Study: Five-ten years.

Frequency: Annual.

Study Establishment: Universities or research institutions in the United Kingdom.

Country of Study: United Kingdom.

No. of awards offered: Varies.

Application Procedure: Applicants must refer to the fellowship booklet and application forms, available on request or via the NERC website.

Closing Date: September 15th.

Funding: Government.

No. of awards given last year: Two.

Additional Information: All applications must carry the full support of the host institution, which is expected to act as the Fellow's employer. As part of NERC's commitment to promoting equal opportunities, all fellowships may be held by suitably qualified candidates on a full or part-time basis, subject to the agreement of the host institution.

NATURAL HISTORY MUSEUM

Cromwell Road, London, SW7 5BD, England

Tel: (44) 20 7942 5530

Fax: (44) 20 7942 5841

Email: l.houseage@nhm.ac.uk

www: http://www.nhm.ac.uk/science

Contact: L Houseage, Liaison Officer

The Museum's mission is to maintain and develop its collections and use them to promote the discovery, understanding, responsible use and enjoyment of the natural world.

Natural History Museum Sys-Resource

Subjects: Biomedical sciences to explain the taxonomy, molecular diversity, distribution and ecology of various organisms detrimental to human and animal health, the impact of mineralogical, geochemical and human disturbances on environmental quality, earth materials, history and processes to study the properties and relationships of minerals, meteorites, rocks and fossils so as to further the understanding of the origin and history of the Earth. Other areas of interest are ecological patterns and processes to investigate the distribution of organisms in space and through time, and the processes by which these patterns are generated, thereby providing a sound scientific basis for the conservation and management of biological diversity, fauna and flora to make known the diversity of the natural world through description and naming of animals and plants with particular emphasis on those from threatened habitats, and systematics and evolution to discover and investigate the broad patterns of biodiversity and evolution as a foundation for comparative biology and its uses.

Purpose: To provide access for researchers to undertake short visits to utilise the facilities of the Natural History Museum and its associates the Royal Botanical Gardens, Kew and the Linnean Society.

Eligibility: Applicants must be from European Union Member states, associated and accession states.

Level of Study: Doctorate, Postdoctorate, Research.

Value: International travel, accommodation, local travel and subsistence along with all access and facility costs.

Length of Study: Up to 60 working days.

Frequency: Twice a year.

Study Establishment: The Natural History Museum, London.

Country of Study: United Kingdom.

No. of awards offered: 25 per call.

Application Procedure: Applicants must contact the Natural History Museum by telephone or email, or visit the website.

Closing Date: Please refer to the website.

Funding: Government.

Contributor: The European Union IHP Programme.

No. of awards given last year: 51.

No. of applicants last year: 250.

Additional Information: During the visit the User is assigned, according to their speciality, a Mentor. The role of the Mentor is to familiarise the User with the department, collections and facilities, and to give training where necessary. The visits are often collaborative in which case the Mentor will work directly with the User. Please note that projects which include one of the associated institutions must be collaborative with the Natural History Museum.

NATURAL SCIENCES AND ENGINEERING RESEARCH COUNCIL OF CANADA (NSERC)

350 Albert Street, Ottawa, ON, K1A 1H5, Canada
Tel: (1) 613 995 5521
Fax: (1) 613 996 2589
Email: schol@nserc.ca
www: http://www.nserc.ca
Contact: Scholarships & Fellowships Division

The Natural Sciences and Engineering Research Council of Canada (NSERC) is the national instrument for making strategic investments in Canada's capability in science and technology. NSERC supports both basic university research through research grants and project research through partnerships of universities with industry, as well as advanced training of highly qualified people in both areas.

NSERC Chairs in the Management of Technological Change

Subjects: Technology creation, technology application for a defined purpose and management of the impacts of technological change on the individual, on the workplace and on society as a whole.
Purpose: To encourage and manage the process of change as well as to increase technological entrepreneurship and facilitate the integration of new knowledge and technology in the workplace and other realms of society.
Eligibility: Open to Canadian post secondary institutions that meet the general eligibility requirements for NSERC or SSHRC.
Type: Fellowship.
Value: Varies.
Length of Study: Each Chair is funded for an initial period of five years.
Study Establishment: Any Canadian university.
Country of Study: Canada.
No. of awards offered: Varies.
Application Procedure: Application is by submission of a proposal by the university and should include Forms 10, 100 and 183A. For advice on how to prepare a proposal please contact the NSERC or SSHRC. Proposals must include confirmed private and public sector support sufficient to make the chair viable in combination with the Council's funding. An application must include firm commitments from the private sector sponsor or sponsors to make a cash contribution equalling at least one third of all direct costs associated with the chair.
Closing Date: December 15th.

NSERC Doctoral Prizes

Subjects: Engineering or natural sciences.
Purpose: To recognise high quality research conducted by students completing their doctoral degree in the relevant field.
Eligibility: Doctoral students who have successfully defended their doctoral thesis between September 6th of the previous year and September 5th of the current year and are either Canadian citizens or permanent residents in Canada at the time of nomination, are eligible to apply.
Level of Study: Doctorate.
Type: Prize.
Value: Canadian $5,000 per student.
Length of Study: Varies.
Frequency: Annual.
Study Establishment: Any Canadian university.
Country of Study: Canada.
No. of awards offered: Up to four.
Application Procedure: Deans of Graduate Studies at Canadian Universities can nominate one eligible candidate from each of the two categories.
Closing Date: October 2nd.
Additional Information: For further information telephone (1) 613 995 5521 or fax (1) 613 996 2589.

NSERC Equipment Grants

Subjects: Engineering or natural sciences.
Purpose: To foster and enhance the research and research training capability of university researchers by supporting the purchase of research equipment and installations.
Eligibility: Open to Research Fellows.
Level of Study: Postdoctorate, Research.
Type: Bursary.
Value: Equipment grants are canadian $7,001-150,000, major equipment grants are canadian $150,000-325,000 and major installation grants are more than canadian $325,500.
Frequency: Annual, if funds are available.
No. of awards offered: Varies.
Application Procedure: Applicants must submit an application form for a grant and a personal data form for the applicant and each co-applicant. Applications for major installation grants must be accompanied by a letter from the university president indicating the importance and priority placed on the proposed equipment or facilities.
Closing Date: October 1st for Major Equipment and Major Installation Grants, and November 1st for Equipment Grants.

NSERC EWR Steacie Memorial Fellowships

Subjects: Engineering or natural sciences.
Purpose: To enhance the career development of outstanding and highly promising scientists and engineers who are faculty members of Canadian universities and who, at an early stage of their career, are enjoying a reputation for original research in their field.
Eligibility: Outstanding faculty members of Canadian universities, who have obtained their doctorate in engineering or natural sciences within the last 12 years and hold a grant from NSERC, are eligible to apply.
Level of Study: Postdoctorate.
Type: A variable number of fellowships.
Value: Canadian $90,000 per year.
Length of Study: Varies.
Frequency: Annual.
Study Establishment: Any approved university.
Country of Study: Canada.
No. of awards offered: Up to six.
Application Procedure: Applicants must be nominated by senior members of the department or university and the nomination must be endorsed by the executive head of the candidate's university.
Closing Date: July 1st.
Additional Information: For further information telephone (1) 613 995 5992 or fax (1) 613 992 5337.

NSERC Industrial Research Chairs

Subjects: Engineering or natural sciences.
Purpose: To assist universities in building on existing strengths to achieve the critical mass required for a major research endeavour in science and engineering of interest to industry, and/or to assist in the development of research efforts in fields that have not yet been developed in Canadian universities but for which there is an important industrial need.
Eligibility: Open to persons who hold a senior administrative position in a Canadian university such as Head of Department, Dean, Vice President, or President. The applicant cannot be the candidate for the Chair.
Level of Study: Research.
Type: A variable number of fellowships.
Value: Varies.
Length of Study: Chairholders are initially appointed for five years, with the option of renewing the position for another five years if progress is satisfactory and industrial support continues.
Frequency: Varies.
Study Establishment: Any Canadian university.
Country of Study: Canada.
No. of awards offered: Varies.
Application Procedure: Applicants must submit a proposal which includes a personal data form for each candidate, a detailed research proposal and budget for each candidate, a completed Appendix F for each collaborating company, a letter from each

collaborating company in support of the application, a copy of the latest Annual Report for each company, three letters of reference for each candidate and a list of suggested reviewers Appendix E. As there is no application form for an IRC Grant, applicants are strongly advised to contact university industry project staff before submitting a proposal.
Closing Date: Applications are accepted at any time.

NSERC Industrial Research Fellowships (IRF)
Subjects: Industrial research and development within the natural sciences and engineering disciplines.
Purpose: To encourage highly qualified scientists and engineers to seek careers in Canadian industry.
Eligibility: Open to Canadian citizens or permanent residents who have recently completed a doctorate degree and who are seeking employment in industry in Canada for the first time.
Level of Study: Postdoctorate.
Type: Fellowship.
Value: NSERC's contribution to the Fellow's salary is canadian $30,000 per year for two years, plus a company contribution of a minimum of canadian $10,000 per year.
Length of Study: Two years maximum.
Frequency: Approx. every three months.
Study Establishment: Approved industrial organisations.
Country of Study: Canada.
Application Procedure: Applicants must negotiate the terms of employment and proposed research with the sponsoring industrial organisation. Form 200 is to be completed by the candidate and their referees, and Form 183C must be completed by the nominating organisation. Both forms should be submitted together by the nominating organisation. Please refer to the NSERC website for further details.
Closing Date: Varies, please visit the website.
Contributor: NSERC.
Additional Information: There are four competitions each year.

NSERC International Opportunity Fund
Subjects: Engineering or natural sciences.
Purpose: To promote new Canadian participation in international research collaborations. A guiding principle is that such Canadian participation must have the potential to be of significant benefit to Canada.
Application Procedure: Applicants must contact the NSERC for details.
Additional Information: Programme details are available from the website.

NSERC NATO Science Fellowships
Subjects: Engineering or natural sciences.
Purpose: To offer opportunities for emerging scientists and engineers to pursue research.
Eligibility: Open to recent doctoral graduates who are citizens of one of the following Nato Partner countries including Albania, Armenia, Azerabijan, Belarus, Bulgaria, Croatia, Czech Republic, Estonia, Georgia, Hungary, Kazakhstan, Kyrgyz Republic, Latvia, Lithuania, Moldova, Poland, Romania, Russian Federation, Slovak Republic, Slovenia, Tajikstan, the former Yugoslav Republic of Macedonia, Turkmenistan, Ukraine and Uzbekistan. Candidates must not be Canadian citizens or permanent residents of Canada. Candidates must engage in full-time postdoctoral research in one of the fields of research supported by NSERC and be supervised by an NSERC award holder. Candidates must hold, or expect to receive prior to the award, a doctorate from a recognised university outside Canada, in one of the fields supported by NSERC. Applicants must have obtained their first PhD equivalent degree no more than two years before the deadline date of the year in which they apply.
Level of Study: Postdoctorate.
Type: A variable number of fellowships.
Value: Canadian $33,000 per year.
Length of Study: Six months, one year or two years.
Frequency: Annual.

Study Establishment: Any Canadian university that can provide the research facilities and environment appropriate for the proposed research activity.
Country of Study: Canada.
Application Procedure: Applicants must be nominated by the proposal supervisor and the host university.
Closing Date: October 1st, though applicants do have to meet an earlier University deadline.

NSERC Postdoctoral Fellowships
Subjects: Engineering or natural sciences.
Purpose: To provide support to a core of the most promising researchers at a pivotal time in their careers. The fellowships are also intended to secure a supply of highly qualified Canadians with leading edge scientific and research skills for Canadian industry, government and universities.
Eligibility: Open to Canadian citizens or permanent residents residing in Canada, who have recently received, or will shortly receive, a PhD.
Level of Study: Postdoctorate.
Type: Fellowship.
Value: Canadian $35,000 per year.
Length of Study: One year, renewable for one additional year.
Frequency: Annual.
Study Establishment: A university or research institution of the Fellow's choice.
Country of Study: Any country.
Application Procedure: Applicants must complete Form 200. Information is available on request.
Closing Date: November 15th.
Funding: Government.

NSERC Postgraduate Scholarships
Subjects: Engineering or natural sciences.
Purpose: To provide financial support to high calibre scholars who are or will be engaged in Master's or doctoral level studies in the natural sciences or engineering.
Eligibility: Open to Canadian citizens or permanent residents who will undertake a programme of postgraduate studies and research leading to an advanced degree. Specific eligibility conditions apply for PGSA and PGSB awards. Applicants must have obtained a first class average in the last two completed years of study.
Level of Study: Doctorate, Graduate, Postgraduate, Predoctorate.
Type: Scholarship.
Value: The PGSA Master's is canadian $17,300 per year for two years, and the PGSB, PhD is canadian $19,100 per year for two years.
Length of Study: Two years for the MSc or PhD, with a possibility of renewal for a further two years for PhDs only.
Frequency: Annual.
Study Establishment: Universities.
Application Procedure: Applicants must complete Application Form 200. Applicants who are, or have recently been, registered at a Canadian university must submit their application through the graduate studies office of the university. There may be an earlier deadline at the university for these applications.
Closing Date: November 15th.
Funding: Government.

NSERC Project Research Grants
Subjects: Engineering or natural sciences.
Purpose: To promote and maintain a diversified base of high quality research capability in the natural sciences and engineering in Canadian universities, to foster research excellence and to provide a stimulating environment for research training.
Eligibility: Individual researchers or groups of researchers at Canadian universities.
Level of Study: Research.
Type: A variable number of grants.
Value: According to the budget requirements described in the application.

Length of Study: One-five years.
Frequency: Annual.
Study Establishment: Any approved university.
Country of Study: Canada.
No. of awards offered: Varies.
Application Procedure: Applicants must submit a Notification of Intent to Apply for a Research Grant form and a list of contributions for the last six years as early in the year as possible. By May, most potential applicants should receive a memo providing instructions for the preparation of the documents to be submitted. Applicants should submit an application for a grant and a Personal Data Form for the applicant and each co-applicant, samples of contributions such as reprints and/or manuscripts, excerpts from the applicant's thesis, and technical reports which will be used by the reviewers to assess the quality of the work. These documents should be chosen to represent the applicant's most significant recent contributions or those most relevant to the proposed work in the last six years, and a list of samples of contributions submitted within the application.
Closing Date: November 1st.
Additional Information: Additional programme information is available by emailing resgrant@nserc.ca.

NSERC Strategic Project Grants (SPG)

Subjects: Engineering, mathematics, computer science, natural sciences, biotechologies, energy efficiency, information technologies, environmental technologies, manufacturing and processing or materials.
Purpose: To support early stage research projects that have the potential to lead to breakthrough discoveries.
Eligibility: Individuals or groups undertaking research in natural sciences or engineering at Canadian universities in conjunction with a partner organisation from the commercial sector, are eligible to apply.
Level of Study: Research.
Type: A variable number of grants.
Value: Varies.
Length of Study: Up to five years.
Frequency: Annual.
Study Establishment: Any Canadian university.
Country of Study: Canada.
No. of awards offered: Varies.
Application Procedure: Applicants must submit the relevant forms as well as letters of support.
Closing Date: April 15th.

THE NEA FOUNDATION FOR THE IMPROVEMENT OF EDUCATION

1201 16th Street North West
Suite 234, Washington, DC, 20036-7840, United States of America
Tel: (1) 202 822 7840
Fax: (1) 202 822 7779
Email: kwillis@nea.org
www: http://www.nea.org
Contact: Ms Kathryn Willis, Communications Officer

National Education Association Fine Arts Grants

Subjects: Art, music, theatre, dance, design, media or folk arts.
Purpose: To enable teachers to create and implement fine arts programmes that promote learning by students at risk of school failure.
Eligibility: Open to NEA member teachers of art, music, theatre, dance, design, media or folk arts is designated to implement the grant work.
Type: Grant.
Value: US$2,000.
No. of awards offered: 10.

Application Procedure: Applications must be submitted by local affiliates of the National Education Association. The local affiliate accepts the grant and administers the project.
Closing Date: Please contact the organisation.

NEA Foundation Innovation Grants

Subjects: Education.
Purpose: To promote collaborative, innovative ideas that lead to student achievement of high standards.
Eligibility: Open to teams of two or more practising United States public school teachers in grades K-12, public school education support personnel, public higher education faculty and staff.
Type: Grant.
Value: US$2,000.
Length of Study: 18 months.
Frequency: Annual.
Country of Study: United States of America.
No. of awards offered: Up to 200.
Application Procedure: Applicants must consult the organisation for details.
Closing Date: March 15th.
Additional Information: Preference will be given to National Education Association members, and to educators who serve economically disadvantaged and/or underserved students.

The NEA Foundation Learning and Leadership Grants

Subjects: All subjects.
Purpose: To support high quality professional development that addresses specific student learning needs. Recipients must also exercise professional leadership by sharing their new learning with their colleagues.
Eligibility: Open to practising public school classroom teachers, public school education support personnel and faculty and staff of public higher education institutions. Two or more collaborating educators may also apply for a group grant.
Level of Study: Professional development.
Type: Grant.
Value: Up to 45 individual grants of US$1,000 each and up to 10 group grants of US$3,000 each.
Length of Study: One year.
Frequency: Annual.
Country of Study: United States of America.
No. of awards offered: Up to 55.
Application Procedure: Applicants should consult the organisation for details.
Closing Date: March 1st and October 15th.
Additional Information: Preference will be given to members of the National Education Association.

NETHERLANDS GOVERNMENT

Royal Netherlands Embassy
120 Empire Circuit, Yarralumla, ACT, 2600, Australia
Tel: (61) 2 6273 3111
Fax: (61) 2 6273 3206
Email: can@minbuza.nl
www: http://www.netherlandsconsulate.org.au
Contact: Press & Cultural Affairs

Huygens Scholarships Programme

Subjects: All subjects.
Purpose: To foster an influx of outstanding foreign students from countries with which the Netherlands has concluded a cultural agreement and from countries with which the Dutch Ministry of Education, Culture and Science has concluded agreements regarding the award of scholarships.
Eligibility: To be eligible, students must intend to pursue a specialisation at a higher education institution recognised by the Dutch government or at a research institute carrying out work related to the

academic work the person is doing in their own country. They must also have been provisionally admitted to a Dutch higher education institution or research institute, be in the final stages of their studies and have graduated no longer than two years previously or be working on a PhD in their own country. Candidates should also show promise and have an outstanding academic record, and must be able to demonstrate that they are sufficiently skilled in speaking or writing the language in which the course is taught (generally English or Dutch). Applicants should also be no older than 35 years at the start of the period in the Netherlands and be a national of one of the following eligible countries: Albania, Australia, Austria, Belarus, Bosnia-Herzegovina, Brazil, Bulgaria, Canada, Czech Republic, China, Colombia, Croatia, Denmark, Egypt, Estonia, Finland, Former Yugoslav Republic of Macedonian, France, Georgia, Germany, Greece, Hungary, Iceland, India, Indonesia, Ireland, Israel, Italy, Japan, Jordan, Latvia, Lithuania, Luxembourg, Mexico, Moldova Republic, Morocco, New Zealand, Norway, Poland, Portugal, Romania, Russian Federation, Slovakia, Slovenia, South Africa, Spain, Sweden, Switzerland, Turkey, Ukraine, United Kingdom or Yugoslavia.

Level of Study: Postdoctorate, Postgraduate.

Type: Scholarship.

Value: A monthly allowance for board, lodging and books sufficient for one person only, a single payment to cover travel costs from and to the student's country, exemption from the statutory tuition fee at Dutch institute of higher education and medical insurance premiums. As a rule this will not include dental treatment or the treatments of conditions that existed before the person came to the Netherlands.

Length of Study: 3-10 months.

Frequency: Annual.

Study Establishment: A university, art academy, school of music or other Institute of Higher Education.

Country of Study: Netherlands.

No. of awards offered: Varies.

Application Procedure: Applicants must submit applications together with the required documents to the Dutch embassy in the country where the student is a permanent resident. Students from China are an exception as they must first apply to the China Scholarship Council. Application forms can be obtained from the Dutch Embassy in the applicant's country of nationality or they can be downloaded from the website.

Closing Date: February 1st.

Funding: Government.

Contributor: The Netherlands government.

Additional Information: NUFFIC the Netherlands organisation for international co-operation in higher education is responsible for managing and implementing the Huygens Programme.

NETHERLANDS ORGANISATION FOR INTERNATIONAL CO-OPERATION IN HIGHER EDUCATION (NUFFIC)

NUFFIC
PO Box 29777, The Hague, NL-2502 LT, Netherlands
Tel: (31) 70 426 0260
Fax: (31) 70 426 0399
Email: nuffic@nuffic.nl
www: http://www.nuffic.nl
Contact: Ms Rosalien van Santen, Information Officer

Since its founding in 1952, the Netherlands Organisation for International Co-operation in Higher Education (NUFFIC) has been an independent non-profit organisation. Its mission is to foster international co-operation in higher education. Special attention is given to development co-operation.

European Development Fund Awards for Citizens of ACP Countries

Subjects: All subjects.

Eligibility: Open to citizens of the African, Caribbean and Pacific countries associated with the European Union.

Level of Study: Unrestricted.

Value: Course fees, books and field trips, international travel expenses, insurance, a monthly allowance and stipend to cover the initial expense of becoming established.

Length of Study: For the duration of the course.

Country of Study: Countries associated with the European Union, ACP countries.

No. of awards offered: Varies.

Application Procedure: Applicants must obtain information and application forms from the Netherlands Embassy in the candidate's country and the European Union Delegations and offices of the Commission. The application is submitted through the candidate's employer and government. Delegations of the Commission can be found usually in the capital cities in the following countries: Angola, Barbados and the Eastern Caribbean, Benin, Botswana, Burkina Faso, Burundi, Cameroon, Cape Verde, Central African Republic, Chad, Congo (Democratic Republic), Congo (Republic), Côte d'Ivoire, Djibouti, Dominican Republic, Eritrea, Ethiopia, Gabon, Gambia, Ghana, Guinea, Guinea Bissau, Guyana, Haiti, Jamaica, Kenya, Lesotho, Liberia, Madagascar, Malawi, Mali, Mauritania, Mauritius, Mozambique, Namibia, Niger, Nigeria, Papua New Guinea, Rwanda, Senegal, Sierra Leone, Solomon Islands, Somalia, Sudan, Surinam, Swaziland, Tanzania, Togo, Trinidad and Tobago, Uganda, Zambia and Zimbabwe. Offices of the Commission can be found in the following countries: Antigua and Barbuda, Bahamas, Belize, Comoros, Equatorial Guinea, Netherlands Antilles and Aruba, New Caledonia, Samoa, Sao Tome and Principe, Seychelles, Tonga and Vanuatu.

Closing Date: Please contact the Commission for details.

Additional Information: NUFFIC (the Netherlands organisation for international co-operation in higher education) does not administer these awards and will not accept applications.

NFP Netherlands Fellowships Programme of Development Co-operation

Subjects: Most of the courses offered by the Institutes for International Education in the Netherlands.

Purpose: To develop human potential through education and training mainly in the Netherlands with a view to diminish qualitative and quantitative deficiencies in the availability of trained manpower in developing countries.

Eligibility: Open to candidates who have the education and work experience required for the course, as well as an adequate command of the language in which it is conducted (usually English, sometimes French). The age limit is 40 for men and 45 for women. It is intended that candidates, upon completion of training, return to their home countries and resume their jobs. When several candidates with comparable qualifications apply, priority will be given to women. Candidates for a fellowship must be nominated by their employer, and formal employment should be continued during the fellowship period. As a rule the candidate's government is required to state its formal support, except in the case of certain development orientated non government organisations.

Level of Study: Postgraduate.

Type: Fellowship.

Value: Normal living expenses, fees and health insurances. International travel expenses are provided only when the course lasts three months or longer.

Length of Study: For the duration of the course.

Country of Study: Mainly in the Netherlands.

No. of awards offered: Varies.

Application Procedure: Applicants must contact the Netherlands Embassy in their own country for information on the nationality eligibility for these fellowships and on the application procedure. Information on the courses for which the fellowships are available can be obtained from the website.

Funding: Government.

Additional Information: More information is available from the website http://www.studyin.nl.

THE NETHERLANDS ORGANISATION FOR SCIENTIFIC RESEARCH (NWO)

Lann van Nieuw Oost Indie 131
PO Box 93138, The Hague, NL-2509 AC, Netherlands
Tel: (31) 70 344 0852
Fax: (31) 70 385 0971
Email: nwo@nwo.nl
www: http://www.nwo.nl
Contact: Mr Weyma, Head Of Central Programmes

The Netherlands Organisation for Scientific Research (NWO) is the central Dutch organisation in the field of fundamental and strategic scientific research. NWO encompasses all fields of scholarship and consequently plays a key role in the development of science, technology and culture in the Netherlands. NWO is an independent organisation which acts as the national research council in the Netherlands. NWO is the largest national sponsor of fundamental scientific research undertaken in the 13 Dutch universities and provides many types of funding for research driven by intellectual curiosity.

TALENT Programme

Subjects: All subjects.
Purpose: To promote highly qualified young postdoctoral students who wish to conduct research at a reputable research institute outside the Netherlands. The programme is designed to make a major contribution to the market value of the recipients of TALENT scholarships.
Eligibility: Open to highly qualified, young postdoctoral students who are Dutch nationals or permanent residents of the Netherlands.
Level of Study: Postdoctorate.
Type: Scholarship.
Length of Study: Up to one year.
Frequency: Three times each year.
Study Establishment: A university or research institute outside the Netherlands.
Country of Study: Any country outside of the Netherlands.
No. of awards offered: Varies.
Application Procedure: Applicants must contact Ms Consolini at the Grants Division for details, on (31) 70 344 06 30.
Closing Date: January 15th, May 15th or October 15th.
Funding: Government.
No. of awards given last year: 42.
No. of applicants last year: 79.

NETHERLANDS-SOUTH AFRICA ASSOCIATION

Studiefonds voor Zuidafrikanse Studenten NZAV
Keizersgradet 141, Amsterdam, NL-1015 CK, Netherlands
Tel: (31) 20 624 9318
Fax: (31) 20 638 2596
Email: studiefonds@zuidafrikahuis.nl
www: http://www.zuidafrikahuis.nl
Contact: Dr S B I Veltkamp-Visser, Secretary

Netherlands-South Africa Study Fund

Subjects: All subjects.
Purpose: To support postgraduate study in Holland.
Eligibility: Open to nationals of South Africa.
Level of Study: Postgraduate.
Value: Please contact the association for details.
Length of Study: Up to one year.
Frequency: Twice a year.
Country of Study: Netherlands.
No. of awards offered: 5-10.
Application Procedure: Applicants must write for details.
Closing Date: May 15th or December 15th.

Funding: Private.
No. of awards given last year: 13.
No. of applicants last year: 28.

NEW ENGLAND THEATRE CONFERENCE (NETC)

Northeastern University
360 Huntington Avenue, Boston, MA, 02115, United States of America
Tel: (1) 617 424 9275
Fax: (1) 617 424 1057
Email: info@netconline.org
www: http://www.netconline.org

The New England Theatre Conference (NETC) works to develop, expand and assist theatre activity at the community, educational and professional levels. Script competitions have a national and international reach.

Aurand Harris Memorial Playwriting Award

Subjects: Playwriting for young audiences.
Purpose: To support new full length plays for young audiences.
Eligibility: Open to all playwrights in New England who wish to submit a full length play for young audiences which is both commercially unpublished and unproduced. Playwrights living outside New England may participate by joining NETC.
Level of Study: Unrestricted.
Type: Prize.
Value: First prize of US$1,000 and second prize of US$500.
Frequency: Annual.
Country of Study: Any country.
No. of awards offered: Two.
Application Procedure: Applicants must send a stamped addressed envelope for current guidelines. There is a processing fee of US$20.
Closing Date: May 1st.
Funding: Private.
Additional Information: This is a competition and not a financial aid programme.

John Gassner Memorial Playwriting Award

Subjects: Playwriting, particularly new full length plays.
Eligibility: Open to all playwrights in New England, or NETC members, who wish to submit a full length play which is both commercially unpublished and unproduced. Playwrights living outside New England may participate by joining NETC.
Level of Study: Unrestricted.
Type: Prize.
Value: First prize of US$1,000 and second prize of US$500.
Frequency: Annual.
Country of Study: Any country.
No. of awards offered: Two.
Application Procedure: Applicants must send a stamped addressed envelope for current guidelines. There is a processing fee of US$10.
Closing Date: April 15th.
Funding: Private.
Contributor: Donations from members.
Additional Information: Portions of winning plays are given staged readings. This is a competition and not a financial aid programme.

NEW SOUTH WALES CANCER COUNCIL

PO Box 572, Kings Cross, NSW, 2011, Australia
Tel: (61) 2 9334 1735
Fax: (61) 2 9326 9328
Email: gillianm@nswcc.org.au
www: http://www.cancercouncil.com.au
Contact: Ms Gillian Mackay, Programme Co-ordinator, Cancer Control Network

The New South Wales Cancer Council is one of the leading cancer charity organisation in New South Wales. Their mission is to defeat cancer and to do that they are working to build a cancer smart community. In building a cancer smart community, the Council undertakes high quality research and is an advocate on cancer issues, providing information and services to the public and raising funds for cancer programmes.

New South Wales Cancer Council Research Programme Grant

Subjects: Cancer research.
Purpose: To provide relatively long-term, flexible support for cancer researchers.
Eligibility: Open to investigators with a sufficient record of research achievement in any field of cancer research.
Level of Study: Unrestricted.
Type: Research grant.
Value: Varies, depending on requirements.
Length of Study: Three-five years, potentially renewable based on results.
Frequency: Varies, depending on other priorities.
Study Establishment: An approved institution in New South Wales.
Country of Study: Australia.
No. of awards offered: Varies.
Application Procedure: Applicants must complete an application form, available on request or from the website.
Closing Date: To be advised.
Funding: Private.
Contributor: Community fundraising.
No. of awards given last year: Three.
No. of applicants last year: 32.

New South Wales Cancer Council Research Project Grants

Subjects: Research projects in all aspects of cancer which elucidate its origin, cause and control at a fundamental and applied level. Grants are open to researchers from all research disciplines relevant to cancer including behavioural, biomedical, clinical, epidemiological, psychosocial and health services.
Purpose: To support research into all aspects of cancer, including its cause, mechanism, prevention, treatment and care, and the organisation and performance of cancer control services.
Eligibility: Open to Australian residents from New South Wales. Recipients of tobacco sponsorship are ineligible.
Level of Study: Unrestricted.
Type: Research grant.
Value: Varies, depending on requirements.
Length of Study: One-three years.
Frequency: Annual.
Study Establishment: An approved institution in New South Wales.
Country of Study: Australia.
No. of awards offered: Varies.
Application Procedure: Applicants must complete an application form, available on request or from the website.
Closing Date: Early May, please visit the website for confirmation.
Funding: Private.
Contributor: Community fundraising.
No. of awards given last year: Six.
No. of applicants last year: 68.

NEW YORK STATE HISTORICAL ASSOCIATION

PO Box 800
Lake Road, Cooperstown, NY, 13326-0800, United States of America
Tel: (1) 607 547 1491
Fax: (1) 607 547 1405
Email: goodwind@nysha.org
www: http://www.nysha.org
Contact: Mr Daniel Goodwin, Editor

The mission of the New York State Historical Association is to instil and cultivate, in a broad public audience, an informed appreciation of the diversity of the American past, especially as represented and exemplified by the history of New York State, in order to better understand the present.

Dixon Ryan Fox Manuscript Prize of the New York State Historical Association

Subjects: History.
Purpose: To honour the best unpublished book length monograph dealing with the history of New York State.
Eligibility: Open to nationals of any country.
Level of Study: Doctorate, Postdoctorate, Postgraduate, Professional development.
Type: Financial support.
Value: US$3,000 plus assistance in publishing.
Length of Study: Dependent on the book length.
Frequency: Annual.
Country of Study: United States of America (New York State).
No. of awards offered: One.
Application Procedure: Applicants must submit two copies of the manuscript, typed and double spaced with at least one inch margins.
Closing Date: January 20th.
Funding: Private.
No. of awards given last year: One.
No. of applicants last year: Eighteen.

NEW ZEALAND COMMONWEALTH SCHOLARSHIPS AND FELLOWSHIPS COMMITTEE

PO Box 11-915, Wellington, New Zealand
Tel: (64) 4 381 8510
Fax: (64) 4 381 8501
Email: schols@nzvcc.ac.nz
www: http://www.nzvcc.ac.nz
Contact: Scholarships Officer

The New Zealand Commonwealth Scholarships and Fellowships Committee is a secretariat which provides administrative and policy services to the eight vice chancellors of the New Zealand Universities.

New Zealand Commonwealth Scholarships

Subjects: Study undertaken should be of developmental relevance to the candidate's home country.
Purpose: To enable persons of high intellectual promise to study in New Zealand in the expectation that they will make a significant contribution to life in their own countries on their return.
Eligibility: Open to graduates who are citizens of a Commonwealth country and who have graduated within the last five years.
Level of Study: Postgraduate.
Type: Scholarship.
Value: New zealand $1,000 per month plus travel and allowances.
Length of Study: Up to three years.
Frequency: Annual.
Country of Study: New Zealand.

No. of awards offered: Approx. 10.

Application Procedure: Applicants must send nominations to the appropriate agency in their home country.

Closing Date: Differs from country to country. Applications close in New Zealand on August 1st.

Funding: Government.

Additional Information: Scholarships are provided by the New Zealand government and fall within the framework of the Commonwealth Scholarship and Fellowship Plan.

NEW ZEALAND VICE-CHANCELLORS COMMITTEE (NZVCC)

PO Box 11-915, Wellington, New Zealand
Tel: (64) 4 381 8510
Fax: (64) 4 381 8501
Contact: Scholarships Officer

Claude McCarthy Fellowships

Subjects: Literature, science or medicine.

Purpose: To enable graduates to undertake original work or research.

Eligibility: Open to any graduate of a New Zealand university.

Level of Study: Postgraduate.

Type: Fellowship.

Value: Varies, according to country of residence during tenure, and the project itself. Assistance for expenses incurred in travel, employment of technical staff, special equipment, etc. may be provided.

Length of Study: Usually no more than one year.

Frequency: Annual.

Country of Study: Any country.

No. of awards offered: Varies, depending upon funds available, but there is usually 12-15.

Application Procedure: Applicants must write for details.

Closing Date: August 1st.

Funding: Private.

Contributor: The Claude McCarthy Trust.

Additional Information: Further information is available on request.

Gordon Watson Scholarship

Subjects: International relationships or social and economic conditions.

Purpose: To facilitate study abroad.

Eligibility: Candidates must be New Zealand citizens or permanent residents. Open to holders of an honours degree, or a degree in theology from a university in New Zealand. Candidates must undertake to return to New Zealand after the scholarship period for not less than two years.

Level of Study: Postgraduate.

Type: Scholarship.

Value: New zealand $10,200 per year.

Length of Study: Three years.

Frequency: Annual.

Study Establishment: Any approved university.

Country of Study: United Kingdom, Europe, Asia or United States of America.

No. of awards offered: One.

Application Procedure: Applicants must write for details.

Closing Date: October 1st.

Funding: Private.

Contributor: The Gordon Watson Trust.

Additional Information: Further information is available on request.

L B Wood Travelling Scholarship

Subjects: All subjects.

Purpose: To allow graduates to undertake doctoral studies in the United Kingdom.

Eligibility: Open to all holders of postgraduate scholarships from any faculty of any university in New Zealand, provided that application is made within three years of the date of graduation.

Level of Study: Doctorate.

Type: Scholarship.

Value: New zealand $3,000 per year, as a supplement to another postgraduate scholarship.

Length of Study: Up to three years.

Frequency: Annual.

Study Establishment: A university or institution of university rank.

Country of Study: United Kingdom.

No. of awards offered: One.

Application Procedure: Applicants must write for details.

Closing Date: October 1st.

Funding: Private.

Contributor: The L B Wood Trust.

Additional Information: Further information is available on request.

Shirtcliffe Fellowship

Subjects: Arts, science, law, commerce or agriculture.

Purpose: To provide further aid for New Zealand doctoral students.

Eligibility: Open to graduates of New Zealand universities.

Level of Study: Doctorate.

Type: Fellowship.

Value: New zealand $2,000 as a supplement to the postgraduate scholarship emolument.

Length of Study: Up to three years.

Frequency: Annual.

Study Establishment: A suitable Institute of Higher Education.

Country of Study: New Zealand or a Commonwealth country overseas.

No. of awards offered: Three.

Application Procedure: Applicants must write for details.

Closing Date: October 1st.

Additional Information: Further information is available on request.

William Georgetti Scholarships

Subjects: All subjects.

Purpose: To encourage postgraduate study and research in a field which is important to the social, cultural or economic development of New Zealand.

Eligibility: Candidates must be New Zealand citizens or permanent residents. Open to graduates who have been resident in New Zealand for five years immediately before application and who are preferably aged between 21 and 28.

Level of Study: Postgraduate.

Type: Scholarship.

Value: Up to new zealand $6,000 for study in New Zealand and up to new zealand $12,000 for study overseas.

Frequency: Annual.

Study Establishment: Suitable universities.

Country of Study: Any country.

No. of awards offered: Varies.

Application Procedure: Applicants must write for details.

Closing Date: October 1st.

Funding: Private.

Contributor: The Georgetti Trust.

Additional Information: Further information is available on request.

529

THE NEWBERRY LIBRARY

60 West Walton Street, Chicago, IL, 60610, United States of
America
Tel: (1) 312 255 3666
Fax: (1) 312 255 3680
Email: research@newberry.org
www: http://www.newberry.org
Contact: Ms Nadia E Joseph, Administrative Assistant

The Newberry Library, open to the public without charge, is an independent research library and educational institution dedicated to the expansion and dissemination of knowledge in the humanities. With a broad range of books and manuscripts relating to the civilisations of Western Europe and the Americas, the Library's mission is to acquire and preserve research collections of such material, and to provide for and promote their effective use by a diverse community of users.

American Society for Eighteenth-Century Studies (ASECS) Fellowship

Subjects: Arts and humanities.
Purpose: To support scholars wanting to use the Newberry's collections to study the period 1660-1815.
Eligibility: Applicants must be a member of the Society.
Level of Study: Doctorate, Postdoctorate.
Type: Fellowship.
Value: US$1,200 per month, pro-rata.
Length of Study: From one week to two months.
Frequency: Annual.
Study Establishment: The Newberry Library.
Country of Study: United States of America.
No. of awards offered: Varies.
Application Procedure: Applicants must submit a completed application form, a description of the project and three letters of reference.
Closing Date: February 20th.
Funding: Private.
Contributor: ASECS.
No. of awards given last year: One.
No. of applicants last year: Eight.

Arthur Weinberg Fellowship for Independent Scholars

Subjects: Humanities.
Purpose: To award scholars working outside the academy who have demonstrated excellence through publishing and are working in a field appropriate to the Newbury's collections.
Eligibility: Preference is given to Scholars working on historical issues related to social justice or reform. Applicants for this Fellowship need not be from outside the Chicago area.
Level of Study: Graduate, Postgraduate.
Type: Fellowship.
Value: US$1,200.
Length of Study: One month.
Frequency: Annual.
Study Establishment: The Newberry Library.
Country of Study: United States of America.
No. of awards offered: Varies.
Application Procedure: Applicants must write for details. Application forms may also be downloaded from the website.
Closing Date: January 20th.
Funding: Private.

Audrey Lumsden-Kouvel Fellowship

Subjects: Late medieval or renaissance studies.
Purpose: To enable scholars to use the Newberry's extensive holdings in late medieval and renaissance history and literature. The fellowship is intended to encourage scholars to pursue research at the Newberry during sabbaticals.
Eligibility: Open to postdoctoral Scholars wishing to carry out extended research in late medieval or renaissance studies. Applicants must plan to be in continuous residence for at least three months. Preference will be given to projects focusing on romance cultures.
Level of Study: Postdoctorate.
Type: Fellowship.
Value: A stipend of up to US$4,000.
Length of Study: At least three months.
Frequency: Annual.
Study Establishment: The Newberry Library.
Country of Study: United States of America.
No. of awards offered: One.
Application Procedure: Applicants must write for details. Application forms may also be downloaded from the website.
Closing Date: February 20th.
Funding: Private.
No. of awards given last year: One.
No. of applicants last year: Six.

Center for Great Lakes Culture/Michigan State University Fellowship

Subjects: The cultural history and expressions of the diverse peoples of the Great Lakes or Ohio Valley region eg. Michigan, Illinois, Wisconsin, Minnesota, Ohio, Indiana, West Virginia, Kentucky, and Ontario.
Purpose: To support projects using the Newberry Library collections to understand and interpret the cultural history and expressions of the diverse people of the Great Lakes and Ohio Valley region.
Eligibility: Open to Scholars with a PhD or the equivalent or an established record of scholarly research. Candidates for degrees are not eligible.
Level of Study: Postdoctorate.
Type: Fellowship.
Value: US$1,250.
Length of Study: One month.
Frequency: Annual.
Study Establishment: The Newberry Library.
Country of Study: United States of America.
No. of awards offered: Two.
Application Procedure: Applicants must write for details. Application forms may also be downloaded from the website.
Closing Date: February 20th.
Funding: Government, Private.
Contributor: The Center for Great Lakes Culture and Michigan State University.

Frances C Allen Fellowships

Subjects: Humanities or social sciences.
Purpose: To encourage women of Native American heritage in their studies through financial support.
Eligibility: Open to women of American Indian heritage who are pursuing an academic programme in any graduate or pre-professional field.
Level of Study: Postgraduate.
Type: Fellowship.
Value: Varies according to need and may include travel expenses. Up to US$8,000 in approved expenses is available.
Length of Study: One month to one year.
Frequency: Annual.
Study Establishment: The Newberry Library.
Country of Study: United States of America.
No. of awards offered: Varies.
Application Procedure: Applicants must write for details. Application forms may also be downloaded from the website.
Closing Date: February 20th.
Funding: Private.
Contributor: The Frances C Allen Fund.
No. of awards given last year: Four.
No. of applicants last year: Six.
Additional Information: Allen Fellows are expected to spend a significant part of their tenure in residence at the Newberry's D'Arcy McNickle Center for American Indian History.

Herzog August Bibliothek Wolfenbüttel Fellowship
Subjects: Humanities.
Purpose: To enable a period of residence in Wolfenbüttel, Germany for study of the collections housed in the Herzog August Bibliothek.
Eligibility: Applicants for long and short term fellowships at the Newberry may ask to also be considered for this joint fellowship which provides a period of residence in Wolfenbüttel, Germany. The proposed project should link the collections of both libraries. Applicants should plan to hold both fellowships sequentially to ensure continuity of research.
Level of Study: Postdoctorate.
Type: Fellowship.
Value: Please contact the organisation.
Length of Study: Three months.
Frequency: Annual.
Study Establishment: Herzog August Bibliothek Wolfenbüttel.
Country of Study: Germany.
No. of awards offered: One.
Application Procedure: Applicants must write for details. Application forms may also be downloaded from the website.
Closing Date: January 21st.
Funding: Private.

Lester J Cappon Fellowship in Documentary Editing
Subjects: Editing and archiving.
Purpose: To support historical editing projects based on Newberry materials and carried out while in residence at the library.
Eligibility: Open to Scholars who live outside the Chicago area.
Level of Study: Postdoctorate.
Type: Fellowship.
Value: US$1,200 per month.
Length of Study: One week to two months.
Frequency: Annual.
Study Establishment: The Newberry Library.
Country of Study: United States of America.
No. of awards offered: One.
Application Procedure: Applicants must write for details. Application forms may also be downloaded from the website.
Closing Date: February 20th.
Funding: Private.
Contributor: Lester J Cappon.
No. of awards given last year: One.
No. of applicants last year: Five.

Lloyd Lewis Fellowships in American History
Subjects: Any field of American history appropriate to the collections of the Newberry Library.
Eligibility: Open to established Scholars, holding the PhD, who have demonstrated, through publications, excellence in the field. Foreign nationals may apply if they have resided in the United States for three or more years.
Level of Study: Postdoctorate.
Type: Fellowship.
Value: Up to US$30,000.
Length of Study: 6-11 months.
Frequency: Annual.
Study Establishment: In residence at the Library with participation in the Library's scholarly community.
Country of Study: United States of America.
No. of awards offered: Varies.
Application Procedure: Applicants must write for details. Application forms may also be downloaded from the website.
Closing Date: January 21st.
Funding: Private.
Contributor: The Lloyd Lewis Memorial Fund.
No. of awards given last year: One.
No. of applicants last year: 19.
Additional Information: Lewis Fellows participate in the Library's scholarly community through regular participation in seminars, colloquia, and other events. Lewis Fellowships may be combined with sabbaticals or other stipendiary support. Applicants may ask to be considered for NEH and Mellon Fellowships at the time of their application.

Mellon Postdoctoral Research Fellowships
Subjects: Humanities.
Purpose: To support residential postdoctoral research and writing.
Eligibility: Applications are invited from postdoctoral Scholars in any field of relevant to the Library's collection for awards to support their research and writing.
Level of Study: Postdoctorate.
Type: Fellowship.
Value: Up to US$30,000.
Length of Study: 6-11 months.
Frequency: Annual.
Study Establishment: The Newberry Library.
Country of Study: United States of America.
No. of awards offered: Varies.
Application Procedure: Applicants must write for details. Application forms may also be downloaded from the website. Completed applications must include three letters of recommendation.
Closing Date: January 21st.
Funding: Private.
Contributor: The Mellon Foundation.
No. of awards given last year: Four.
No. of applicants last year: 74.
Additional Information: Fellows will become part of Newberry's community of Scholars, participating in bi-weekly fellows seminars, colloquia and other events. Applicants may combine this award with sabbatical or other stipendiary support. Individuals applying for National Endowment for the Humanities and Lloyd Lewis Fellowships at the Newberry Library will also be considered for the Mellon Research Fellowships.

Monticello College Foundation Fellowship for Women
Subjects: Any field appropriate to the Library's collections.
Purpose: To offer young women the opportunity to undertake work in residence at the Library and to significantly enhance their careers through research and writing.
Eligibility: Open to women who hold the PhD who are in the early stages of their academic careers. This academic award is designed for a woman whose work gives clear promise of scholarly productivity and who would benefit significantly from six months of research, writing and participation in the intellectual life of the library.
Level of Study: Postdoctorate.
Type: Fellowship.
Value: US$15,000.
Length of Study: Six months.
Frequency: Annual.
Study Establishment: The Newberry Library.
Country of Study: United States of America.
No. of awards offered: One.
Application Procedure: Applicants must write for details. Application forms may also be downloaded from the website.
Closing Date: January 21st.
Funding: Private.
Contributor: The Monticello College Foundation.
No. of awards given last year: One.
No. of applicants last year: 24.
Additional Information: Other things being equal, preference is given to the applicant whose proposed study is concerned with the study of women.

National Endowment for the Humanities (NEH) Fellowships
Subjects: Any field appropriate to the Library's collections.
Purpose: To encourage scholarly research, and to deepen and enrich the opportunities for serious intellectual exchange through the active participation of Fellows in the Library community.
Eligibility: Open to United States citizens or foreign nationals who have been resident in the United States for three years, who are established Scholars at the postdoctoral level or its equivalent.

Preference is given to applicants who have not held major Fellowships for three years preceding the proposed period of residency.
Level of Study: Postdoctorate.
Type: Fellowship.
Value: Up to US$30,000 for 11 months' residency.
Length of Study: 6-11 months.
Frequency: Annual.
Study Establishment: The Newberry Library.
Country of Study: United States of America.
No. of awards offered: Varies.
Application Procedure: Applicants must write for an application form. Completed application forms must include all letters of reference. Application forms may also be downloaded from the website.
Closing Date: January 21st.
Funding: Government.
Contributor: The NEH.
No. of awards given last year: Four.
No. of applicants last year: 53.
Additional Information: Applicants may combine this award with sabbatical or other stipendiary support. Scholars conducting research in American history may also ask to be considered for the Lloyd Lewis Fellowship at the time of their application.

Newberry Library British Academy Fellowship for Study in Great Britain

Subjects: Humanities.
Purpose: To allow an individual to study in Great Britain in any field in which the Newberry's collections are strong.
Eligibility: Open to established Scholars at the postdoctoral level or equivalent. Preference is given to readers and staff of the Newberry Library and to established Scholars who have previously used the Newberry Library.
Level of Study: Postdoctorate.
Type: Fellowship.
Value: A stipend of UK £40 per day while in the United Kingdom.
Length of Study: Three months.
Frequency: Annual.
Country of Study: United Kingdom.
No. of awards offered: Varies.
Application Procedure: Applicants must write for details. Application forms may also be downloaded from the website.
Closing Date: February 20th.
Funding: Private.
Contributor: The British Academy.
No. of awards given last year: Two.
No. of applicants last year: Five.
Additional Information: The home institution is expected to continue to pay the Fellow's salary.

Newberry Library Ecole des Chartes Exchange Fellowship

Subjects: Renaissance studies.
Purpose: To enable a graduate student to study at the Ecole des Chartes in Paris.
Eligibility: Preference is given to graduate students at institutions in the Renaissance Center Consortium.
Level of Study: Doctorate.
Type: Fellowship.
Value: Varies, but provides a monthly stipend and free tuition.
Length of Study: Three months.
Frequency: Annual.
Study Establishment: Ecole des Chartes.
Country of Study: France.
No. of awards offered: Varies.
Application Procedure: Applicants must write for details. Application forms may also be downloaded from the website.
Closing Date: January 21st.
Funding: Private.
Contributor: The Ecole des Chartes.
No. of awards given last year: One.
No. of applicants last year: Five.

Additional Information: The Ecole des Chartes is the oldest institution in Europe specialising in the archival sciences, including palaeography, bibliography, textual editing and the history of the book.

Newberry Library Short-Term Resident Fellowships for Individual Research

Subjects: Any field appropriate to the Library's collections.
Purpose: To provide access to Newberry's collections for those who live beyond commuting distance from Chicago.
Eligibility: Open to nationals of any country who hold a PhD degree or have completed all requirements for the degree except the dissertation.
Level of Study: Doctorate, Postdoctorate.
Type: Fellowship.
Value: US$1,200 per month.
Length of Study: One week-two months.
Frequency: Annual.
Study Establishment: The Newberry Library.
Country of Study: United States of America.
No. of awards offered: Varies.
Application Procedure: Applicants must write for details. Application forms may also be downloaded from the website.
Closing Date: February 20th.
Funding: Private.
No. of awards given last year: 18.
No. of applicants last year: 98.
Additional Information: Preference is given to those who particularly need the facilities of the Library and live outside Chicago.

Short-Term Fellowship in the History of Cartography

Subjects: The history of cartography.
Purpose: To financially support work in residence at the Newberry on projects related to the history of cartography.
Eligibility: Open to established Scholars of any nationality, but limited to Scholars who live outside the Chicago area.
Level of Study: Doctorate, Postdoctorate.
Type: Fellowship.
Value: US$1,200.
Length of Study: One week to two months.
Frequency: Annual.
Study Establishment: The Newberry Library.
Country of Study: United States of America.
No. of awards offered: One-two.
Closing Date: January 20th.
Funding: Private.
Contributor: Arthur Holzheimer.
No. of awards given last year: One.
No. of applicants last year: 11.

South Central Modern Language Association Fellowship

Subjects: Humanities.
Purpose: To support residential research at the Library by members of the South Central Modern Language Association.
Eligibility: Limited to Scholars who live outside the Chicago area.
Level of Study: Doctorate, Postdoctorate.
Type: Fellowship.
Value: US$2,000.
Length of Study: One month.
Frequency: Annual.
Study Establishment: The Newberry Library.
Country of Study: United States of America.
No. of awards offered: One.
Application Procedure: Applicants must write for details. Application forms may also be downloaded from the website.
Closing Date: February 20th.
Funding: Private.
Contributor: The South Central Modern Language Association.
No. of awards given last year: One.
No. of applicants last year: Three.

Weiss/Brown Publication Subvention Award

Subjects: Humanities, particularly European civilisation before 1700 in the areas of music, theatre, French or Italian literature or cultural studies.

Purpose: To subsidise the publication of a scholarly book or books on European civilisation before 1700.

Eligibility: Open to authors of scholarly books already accepted for publication.

Type: Award.

Value: Variable, up to US$15,000.

Frequency: Annual.

No. of awards offered: Varies.

Application Procedure: Applicants must write for details. Application guidelines may also be downloaded from the website. Applicants will be asked to provide detailed information regarding the publication and the subvention request.

Closing Date: January 21st.

Funding: Private.

No. of awards given last year: Two.

No. of applicants last year: Three.

NEWBY TRUST LIMITED

Hill Farm
Froxfield, Petersfield, Hampshire, GU32 1BQ, England
Tel: (44) 1730 827557
Fax: (44) 1730 827557
Contact: Miss W Gillam, Company Secretary

The Newby Trust Limited is a grant giving charity working nationally, whose principal aims are to promote medical welfare, education and training and the relief of poverty.

Newby Trust Awards

Subjects: All subjects.

Eligibility: Open to students of any nationality. Overseas students must have commenced their course in the United Kingdom before applying.

Level of Study: Doctorate, Postgraduate, Professional development.

Type: Grant.

Value: A maximum of UK £1,000 for fees or maintenance.

Frequency: Annual.

Study Establishment: A suitable university.

Country of Study: United Kingdom.

No. of awards offered: Varies.

Application Procedure: Applicants must submit a personal letter with a curriculum vitae, two letters of reference, a statement of income and expenditure (including fees) and a stamped self addressed envelope. Application forms are not supplied. Applications intended for the start of an academic year should be submitted at least four months in advance.

Closing Date: Applications need to arrive at least two weeks prior to a Director's meeting which are on either April 24th, July 17th or a date in October.

Funding: Private.

Contributor: Funds from the Trust.

No. of awards given last year: 144.

No. of applicants last year: 1,100.

Additional Information: Funding is not available for the CPS law exam, BSc intercalculated with a medical degree, or postgraduate medical or veterinary degrees in the first or second years.

northumbria
UNIVERSITY

NEWCASTLE BUSINESS SCHOOL (NBS), UNIVERSITY OF NORTHUMBRIA AT NEWCASTLE

International Office
Ellison Place, Newcastle upon Tyne, NE1 8ST, England
Tel: (44) 191 227 4274
Fax: (44) 191 261 1264
Email: er.scholarships@northumbria.ac.uk
www: http://www.northumbria.ac.uk/nbs
Contact: Mr Walter Fraser, School of Strategy, Marketing & Tourism

Newcastle Business School (NBS) is part of the University of Northumbria which is widely recognised as one of the United Kingdom's leading modern universities. Quality assessors of the Higher Education Funding Council for England have rated the standard of education provided by NBS as 'excellent'. The School offers programmes at levels from University Certificate, through first degree to Master's, MBA, DBA and PhD.

Northumbria University International Scholarships

Subjects: All subjects.

Eligibility: Open to non European Union students beginning a full-time course of at least one year's duration. This does not include English language (ELAN) courses, distance learning programmes, exchange programmes, short courses or any courses delivered outside the United Kingdom.

Level of Study: Postgraduate, Research, MBA.

Type: Scholarship.

Length of Study: At least one year.

Study Establishment: The University of Northumbria.

Country of Study: England.

No. of awards offered: Varies.

Application Procedure: Applicants must obtain application forms from the main address.

Closing Date: June, July or August.

Additional Information: Please visit the website for further information.

NEWCOMEN SOCIETY IN THE UNITED STATES

412 Newcomen Road, Exton, PA, 19341, United States of America
Tel: (1) 610 363 6600
Fax: (1) 610 363 0612
Email: newcomen@libertynet.org
Contact: Ms Maureen Hayes, Controller

Harvard/Newcomen Postdoctoral Award

Subjects: Business history.

Purpose: To improve the scholar's professional acquaintance with business and economic history, to increase his or her skills as they relate to this field, and to enable him or her to engage in research that will benefit from the resources of the Harvard Business School and the Boston scholarly community.

Eligibility: Open to Scholars who have received the PhD in history, economics or a related discipline within the past 10 years, and who would not otherwise be able to attend Harvard Business School.

Level of Study: Postdoctorate.

Type: Fellowship.

Value: US$46,000.

Length of Study: One year.

Frequency: Annual.
Study Establishment: Harvard Business School in Cambridge, Massachusetts.
Country of Study: United States of America.
No. of awards offered: One.
Application Procedure: Applicants must contact Mr Thomas K McCraw at Harvard University for further details.
Closing Date: March 15th.

For further information contact:

Straus Professor of Business History
Harvard University
Graduate School of Business Administration
Soldiers Field Road, Boston, MA, 02163, United States of America
Tel: (1) 617 495 6354
Email: tmccraw@hbs.edu
Contact: Mr Thomas K McCraw, Straus Professor of Business History

Newcomen Society Dissertation Fellowship in Business and American Culture

Subjects: American business history.
Purpose: To encourage doctoral students to pursue careers in studying and teaching the history of American business.
Eligibility: Open to United States doctoral students only.
Level of Study: Doctorate.
Type: Fellowship.
Value: US$10,000.
Length of Study: Nine months full-time.
Frequency: Annual.
Country of Study: United States of America.
No. of awards offered: One.
Application Procedure: Applicants must submit five copies of their curriculum vitae and a research programme which must not exceed 10 double spaced pages, including references. Faxed proposals cannot be accepted. University transcripts and two letters of recommendation must be sent in support of applications.
Closing Date: February 1st.

NICOLO PAGANINI INTERNATIONAL VIOLIN COMPETITION

Comune di Genova
Settore Promozione della Citta, Turismo e Spettacolo
Ufficio Conservazione, Promozione Violini Storici e Premio Paganini
Via Sottoripa 5, Genova, I-16124, Italy
Tel: (39) 010 557 4215
Fax: (39) 010 246 9272
Email: violinopaganini@comune.genova.it
www: http://www.comune.genova.it/turismo/paganini/welcome.htm
Contact: Miss Anna Rita Cero, Secretary

Premio Paganini is an international violin competition for young violinists between 16 and 33 years old. It offers a first prize of the amount of €12,000 and the possibility for the winner to play Paganini's violin on October 12th, on the occasion of the closing ceremony of the 'Columbian Celebrations'.

Nicolo Paganini International Violin Competition

Subjects: Violin.
Purpose: To discover new talented young violinists and to encourage them to spread the music values which Paganini himself, and his music, stands for.
Eligibility: Open to violinists of any nationality born after May 31th 1969 and before May 31th 1986.
Level of Study: Unrestricted.
Type: Prize.
Value: First prize €12,000, second prize €7,000, third prize €4,500, fourth prize €2,700, fifth prize €2,200 and sixth prize €1,600.
Frequency: Annual.

Country of Study: Any country.
No. of awards offered: Six.
Application Procedure: Applicants must write for an application and registration form. A registration fee must be paid. Forms can be downloaded from the website, but must be mailed to the competition.
Closing Date: May 31st.
Funding: Government.
Contributor: Comune di Genova.
No. of awards given last year: Six.
No. of applicants last year: 91.
Additional Information: The competition is held from late September to early October.

For further information contact:

Comune di Genova
Premio Paganini
c/o Archivio Generale
S ta S Francesco, Genova, Italy

NIEMAN FOUNDATION

1 Francis Avenue, Cambridge, MA, 02138, United States of America
Tel: (1) 617 495 2237
Fax: (1) 617 495 8976
Email: nieman@harvard.edu
www: http://www.nieman.harvard.edu
Contact: Program Assistant

The Nieman Foundation's fellowships provide a mid-career opportunity for journalists to spend a year of learning and reflection at Harvard University. Fellows design an individual course of study and participate in Nieman seminars.

Nieman Fellowships for Journalists

Subjects: Each Fellow is free to design an individual course of study. Some pursue courses in a reporting speciality, whereas others explore the breadth of Harvard's schools and departments.
Purpose: To provide an opportunity for journalists to spend a year at Harvard University, where Fellows experience discovery and enrichment, learning and reflection in Harvard classrooms, in Nieman seminars and from the close friendships that emerge during the Nieman year.
Eligibility: Applicants must be full-time staff or freelance journalists working for the news or editorial departments of newspapers, news services, radio, television, magazines of general public interest or Internet news sites. They must also have at least three years of professional experience in the news media and their employer's consent for a leave of absence for that academic year. There are no age, nationality or residency restrictions.
Level of Study: Postgraduate.
Type: Fellowship.
Value: Tuition, a stipend of US$50,000, housing allowance and childcare support. Please note that special funding arrangements apply to international Fellows.
Length of Study: One academic year.
Frequency: Annual.
Study Establishment: Harvard University.
Country of Study: United States of America.
No. of awards offered: 12 to journalists from the United States, and 12 to journalists from other countries.
Application Procedure: Applicants must obtain information and an application form by contacting the Program Officer at the Nieman Foundation. The completed application form must include supporting materials, letters of recommendation, essays on journalism experience and proposed course of study, and work samples.
Closing Date: January 31st for United States journalists and March 1st for international journalists.
Funding: Private.
Additional Information: No course credits are given or degrees granted. Further information is available on request.

NORTH ATLANTIC TREATY ORGANIZATION (NATO)

NATO Information Service
NB 110, Brussels, B-1110, Belgium
Tel: (32) 2 728 5014
Fax: (32) 2 728 5457
www: http://www.nato.int
Contact: Academic Affairs Officer

The North Atlantic Treaty was signed in Washington on April 4th 1949, creating an alliance of 12 independent nations committed to each other's defence. Four more European nations later acceded to the Treaty between 1952 and 1982. On March 12th 1999, the Czech Republic, Hungary and Poland were welcomed into the Alliance, which now numbers 19 members.

Manfred Wörner Fellowship
Subjects: International relations.
Purpose: To honour the memory of the late Secretary General by focusing attention on his leadership in the transformation of the alliance, including efforts at extending NATO's relations with CEE countries and promoting the principles and image of the Transatlantic partnership.
Eligibility: Please contact the organisation.
Level of Study: Professional development.
Type: Fellowship.
Frequency: Annual.
Country of Study: Any country.
Funding: Government.

NORTH DAKOTA UNIVERSITY SYSTEM

600 East Boulevard, Bismarck, ND, 58505, United States of America
Tel: (1) 701 328 2960
www: http://www.ndus.nodak.edu
Contact: Ms Rhonda Shaver, Coordinator

The North Dakota University System, governed by the State Board of Higher Education, is comprised of 11 public campuses.

North Dakota Indian Scholarship
Subjects: All subjects.
Purpose: To assist Native American students in obtaining a basic college education.
Eligibility: Open to residents of North Dakota with a quarter degree of Indian blood, who are accepted for admission at an Institute of Higher Education or state vocational programme. Recipients must be enrolled full-time and have a grade point average above 2.00.
Level of Study: Doctorate, Postgraduate.
Type: Scholarship.
Value: US$700.
Frequency: Annual.
Country of Study: United States of America.
No. of awards offered: 140.
Application Procedure: Applicants must complete an application form.
Closing Date: July 15th.
Funding: Government.
Contributor: The state.
No. of awards given last year: 140.

NORTHERN TERRITORY UNIVERSITY (NTU)

Research Branch, Darwin, NT, 0909, Australia
Tel: (61) 8 8946 6405
Fax: (61) 8 8946 7075
Email: charles.webb@ntu.edu.au
www: http://www.ntu.edu.au
Contact: Professor Charles Webb

The Northern Territory University (NTU) offers programmes from PhD to certificate level, incorporating the full range of vocational education courses. NTU has a distinctive research profile, reflecting the priorities appropriate to its location. It is a participating member of several CRCs and hosts the Centre for Indigenous and Natural Cultural Resource Management and the Arc Key Centre for Tropical Wildlife Management.

Deputy Chancellors Postdoctoral Research
Subjects: Indigenous resource management, alternative energy, Aboriginal education, geographic information systems or remote sensing, tropical environmental science including ecophysiolgy and environmental chemistry, tropical plant science, Southeast Asian studies, Aboriginal legal issues, Southeast Asian law, education in diverse contexts, tourism and hospitality, tropical aquaculture, tropical built environment, visual and performing arts of the Asia Pacific region and indigenous health and culture.
Purpose: To foster research in designated areas of research strength and developing priority.
Eligibility: All applicants must have completed their PhD within three years of the date of application.
Level of Study: Postdoctorate.
Type: Fellowship.
Value: Australian $43,731-49,414 per year plus allowances, and australian $3,500 per year research support.
Length of Study: Three years.
Frequency: Dependent on funds available.
Study Establishment: NTU.
Country of Study: Australia.
Application Procedure: Applicants must contact the Research Branch at the University for application forms, which are also available from the website.
Closing Date: October 31st.
Funding: Private.

NTU One Year Postdoctoral Fellowship
Subjects: Indigenous resource management, alternative energy, Aboriginal education, geographic information systems or remote sensing, tropical environmental science including ecophysiology and environmental chemistry, tropical plant science, Southeast Asian studies, Aboriginal legal issues, Southeast Asian law, education in diverse contexts, tourism and hospitality, tropical aquaculture, tropical built environment, visual and performing arts of the Asia Pacific region and indigenous health and culture.
Purpose: To foster research in designated areas of research strength and developing priority.
Eligibility: All applicants must have completed their PhD within five years of the date of application.
Level of Study: Postdoctorate.
Type: Fellowship.
Value: Australian $43,731-49,414 per year plus allowances, and australian $3,500 per year research support.
Length of Study: One year.
Frequency: Dependent on funds available.
Study Establishment: NTU.
Country of Study: Australia.
Application Procedure: Applicants must contact the Research Branch at the University for application forms, which are also available from the website.
Closing Date: October 31st.
Funding: Private.
Contributor: The University.

NTU Senior Research Fellowship

Subjects: Indigenous resource management, alternative energy, Aboriginal education, geographic information systems or remote sensing, tropical environmental science including ecophysiolgy and environmental chemistry, tropical plant science, Southeast Asian studies, Aboriginal legal issues, Southeast Asian law, education in diverse contexts, tourism and hospitality, tropical aquaculture, tropical built environment, visual and performing arts of the Asia Pacific region and indigenous health and culture.

Purpose: To provide opportunities for outstanding researchers with proven international reputations to undertake research which is of both major importance in its field and of benefit to Australia.

Eligibility: All applicants must have an outstanding track record in a relevant field of research.

Level of Study: Postdoctorate.

Type: Fellowship.

Value: Australian $60,532-69,799 per year plus allowances, and australian $20,000 establishment grant.

Length of Study: Three years.

Frequency: Dependent on funds available.

Study Establishment: NTU.

Country of Study: Australia.

Application Procedure: Applicants must contact the Research Branch at the University for application forms, which are also available from the website.

Closing Date: October 31st.

Funding: Private.

NTU Three Year Postdoctoral Fellowship

Subjects: Indigenous resource management, alternative energy, Aboriginal education, geographic information systems or remote sensing, tropical environmental science including ecophysiology and environmental chemistry, tropical plant science, Southeast Asian studies, Aboriginal legal issues, Southeast Asian law, education in diverse contexts, tourism and hospitality, tropical aquaculture, tropical built environment, visual and performing arts of the Asia Pacific region and indigenous health and culture.

Purpose: To foster research in designated areas of research strength and developing priority.

Eligibility: All applicants must have completed their PhD within five years of the date of application.

Level of Study: Postdoctorate.

Type: Fellowship.

Value: Australian $43,731-49,414 per year plus allowances, and australian $3,500 per year research support.

Length of Study: Three years.

Frequency: Dependent on funds available.

Study Establishment: NTU.

Country of Study: Australia.

No. of awards offered: One.

Application Procedure: Applicants must contact the Research Branch at the University for application forms, which are also available from the website.

Closing Date: October 31st.

Funding: Private.

Contributor: The University.

NORWEGIAN INFORMATION SERVICE IN THE UNITED STATES

825 Third Avenue
38th Floor, New York, NY, 10022-7584, United States of America
Tel: (1) 212 421 7333
Fax: (1) 212 754 0583
Email: norcons@interport.net
www: http://www.norway.org
Contact: Grants & Scholarships Department

The America-Norway Heritage Fund Grant

Subjects: All subjects.

Purpose: To award special grants to Americans of Norwegian descent who have made significant contributions to American culture, enabling them to visit Norway to share the results of their work through lectures, exhibitions or performances. In this way, it is hoped that Norwegians will become better acquainted with the cultural, economic, political and religious contributions made by Norwegian-Americans in the building of America.

Eligibility: Open to Americans of Norwegian descent who have made significant contributions to American culture.

Level of Study: Unrestricted.

Type: Travel grant.

Value: To cover travel expenses as well as a honorarium.

Length of Study: One-two weeks. Activities should be scheduled between October-April.

Frequency: Annual.

Country of Study: Norway.

Application Procedure: Applications are not accepted. Candidates will be selected by the Board of Directors of the Fund in co-operation with its connections in the United States of America. However, proposals for possible candidates will be appreciated.

Contributor: The Lutheran Brotherhood Insurance Company.

For further information contact:

Nordmanns-Forbundet
Rådhusgt 23 B, Oslo, N-0158, Norway

Norge-Amerika Foreningen
Rådhusgt 23 B, Oslo, N-0158, Norway

The American-Scandinavian Foundation (ASF)

Subjects: All subjects.

Purpose: To encourage advanced study and research in the Scandinavian countries.

Eligibility: Applicants must be United States citizens or permanent residents. Team projects are eligible, but each member must apply as an individual, submitting a separate, fully-documented application. First priority will be given to applicants who have not previously received an ASF award. Only in exceptional cases will a third award be considered. The ASF considers it desirable that all candidates have at least some ability in the language of the host country, even if it is not essential for the execution of the research plan. For projects that require a command of one or more Scandinavian (or other) languages, candidates should defer application until they have the necessary proficiency.

Level of Study: Postgraduate.

Type: Grants and fellowships.

Value: Grants are normally US$3,000, and fellowships can be up to US$18,000.

Frequency: Annual.

Country of Study: Scandinavian countries.

No. of awards offered: Varies.

Application Procedure: Applicants must complete an application on ASF application forms, available on request from the Foundation.

Closing Date: November 1st.

For further information contact:

Grants Management Officer
American Scandinavian Foundation
56 Park Avenue, New York, NY, 10016, United States of America
Tel: (1) 212 879 9779
Fax: (1) 212 249 3444
www: http://www.amscan.org

The Fulbright Stipend

Subjects: All subjects.

Level of Study: Graduate, Postdoctorate, Postgraduate.

Length of Study: Three months to one year.

Application Procedure: Applicants must contact the organisation.

Funding: Government.

For further information contact:

US Student Program
Institute of International Education
809 United Nation Plaza, New York, NY, 10017, United States of America
www: http://www.iie.org

For applicants with a PhD or more
Fulbright Senior Scholars Programme
Council of International Exchange of Scholars
3007 Tilden Street North West
Suite 5M, Washington, DC, 20008-3009, United States of America
Email: scholars@cies.iie.org

The John Dana Archbold Fellowship Program

Subjects: All subjects.
Purpose: To support educational exchange between the United States and Norway.
Eligibility: Open to United States citizens aged 20-35, in good health and of good character. Qualified applicants must show evidence of a high level of competence in their chosen field, indicate a seriousness of purpose, and have a record of social adaptability. There is ordinarily no language requirement.
Level of Study: Postdoctorate, Postgraduate, Professional development, Research.
Type: Fellowship.
Value: Up to US$5,000. Individual grants vary, depending on the projected costs. Note that there will be no tuition at the University of Oslo. The maintenance stipend is sufficient to meet expenses for a single person. The travel allowance covers round trip airfare to Oslo.
Length of Study: One year.
Frequency: Annual.
Study Establishment: The University of Oslo.
Country of Study: Norway or United States of America.
No. of awards offered: Two.
Application Procedure: Applicants must write to the Nansen Fund, Inc. for an application form.
Closing Date: January 15th.
Funding: Private.
Additional Information: The University of Oslo International Summer School offers orientation and Norwegian languages courses six weeks before the start of the regular academic year. For Americans, tuition is paid. Attendance is required. Americans visit Norway in even numbered years and Norwegians visit the United States of America in odd numbered years. For further information please contact the Nansen Fund, Inc.

For further information contact:

The Nansen Fund, Inc.
77 Saddlebrook Lane, Houston, TX, 77024, United States of America
Tel: (1) 713 680 8255

The Memorial Fund of May 8th 1970

Subjects: All subjects.
Purpose: To promote cultural exchange between foreign countries and Norwegian folk high schools by providing scholarships for residence. The folk high schools have no set curricula or examinations, and serve as Life Laboratories whose objective is to help prepare young people for everyday life in the community.
Eligibility: Open to candidates aged between 18 and 22 years old who do not have a permanent residence in Norway, and who do not hold a Norwegian passport. Candidates must be planning to return to their home country after a year in Norway. Candidates must be aware of the kind of education the Memorial Fund bursaries cover, that being a year in a Norwegian folk high school, not admission to education on a higher level, such as a university, or specialised training.
Level of Study: Unrestricted.
Type: Scholarship.
Value: The scholarship will cover board and lodging. In addition it is possible to apply for extra funds. Applicants from some countries

may apply for required books and excursions arranged by the school. Also, extra support may be provided for short study trips and short courses before or after the school year. A fixed amount towards spending money may also be given. Normally the students must pay their own travelling expenses. The folk high s   do not charge tuition fees.
Length of Study: One year.
Frequency: Annual.
Study Establishment: Norwegian folk high schools.
Country of Study: Norway.
No. of awards offered: Approx. 25.
Application Procedure: Applicants must request more information and application forms from the Memorial Fund of 8th of May 1970 or to the nearest Norwegian Embassy. Applicants who require a Memorial Fund scholarship to attend a folk high school, should not apply to a folk high school themselves. In this case, the Board will place successful applicants at a folk high school based on their hobbies and interest. Residence permits must be applied by each individual student when scholarship has been granted.
Closing Date: March 15th.
Funding: Government.
No. of awards given last year: 25.
No. of applicants last year: 700.
Additional Information: A folk high school is a one year independent residential school, primarily for young adults, offering many non traditional subjects of study. Each school has its own profile, but as a group, the Norwegian folk high schools teach classes covering almost all interest areas, including history, arts, crafts, music, sports, philosophy, theatre, photography etc.

For further information contact:

c/o IKF
Grensen 9a
N-0159 Oslo
Norway, Oslo, N-0159, Norway
Email: ikf@ikf.no

The Norwegian Emigration Fund of 1975

Subjects: Emigration history and relations between the United States of America and Norway.
Purpose: To award grants for advanced or specialised study in Norway.
Eligibility: Open to citizens and residents of the United States of America. The fund may also give grants to institutions in the United States whose activities are primarily centred on the subjects mentioned.
Level of Study: Graduate, Postgraduate.
Type: Grant.
Value: Norwegian krone 5,000-20,000.
Frequency: Annual.
Country of Study: Norway.
No. of awards offered: Varies.
Application Procedure: Applicants must complete an application form and return it clearly marked Emigration Fund to Nordmanns-Forbundet. Applications as well as enclosures will not be returned.
Closing Date: February 1st.
Funding: Government.
Additional Information: Please see the website http://www.folkehogskole.no/undersider/engminnefond.html.

For further information contact:

Nordmanns-Forbundet
Rådhusgt 23B, Oslo, N-0158, Norway
Tel: (47) 2 335 7170
Fax: (47) 2 242 5163
Email: norseman@online.no
www: http://www.norseman.no

The Norwegian Marshall Fund

Subjects: Science and humanities.
Purpose: To provide financial support for Americans to come to Norway to conduct postgraduate study or research in areas of

mutual importance to Norway and the United States, thereby increasing knowledge, understanding and strengthening the ties of friendship between the two countries.
Eligibility: Open to citizens of the United States, who have arranged with a Norwegian sponsor or research institution to pursue a research project or programme in Norway. Under special circumstances, the awards can be extended to Norwegians for study or research in the United States.
Level of Study: Postgraduate, Research.
Type: Research grant.
Value: The size of the individual grants depends on the research subject, purpose and the intended length of stay in Norway. In previous years, the grants have varied from norwegian krone 10,000 to 30,000.
Length of Study: Varies.
Frequency: Annual.
Study Establishment: Norwegian universities.
Country of Study: Norway.
No. of awards offered: 5-15.
Application Procedure: Applicants must contact the Norway-America Association to receive an application. Application forms must be typewritten in either English or Norwegian and submitted in duplicate, including all supplementary materials. Each application must also be accompanied by a letter of support from the project sponsor or affiliated research institution in Norway. There is an application fee of norwegian krone 350.
Closing Date: March 23rd.
Funding: Government.

For further information contact:

The Norway-America Association
Rådhusgt 23 B, Oslo, N-0158, Norway
Fax: (47) 2 335 7160
Email: namerika@online.no
www: http://www.noram.no/index_am.html

Norwegian Ministry of Foreign Affairs Travel Grants
Subjects: Norwegian culture and society.
Purpose: To give financial assistance to teachers and graduate students visiting Norway for study and research purposes.
Eligibility: Open to citizens and residents of the United States who are members of NORTANA. They must be university or college teachers of Norwegian or other courses in Norwegian culture or society, or graduate students who have passed their preliminary examinations in these fields.
Level of Study: Graduate, Professional development.
Type: Travel grant.
Value: US$750-1,500.
Frequency: Annual.
Country of Study: Norway.
No. of awards offered: Varies.
Application Procedure: Applicants must send a letter of application including the following information: their contact details, their date and place of birth, the length of time that they have been a member of NORTANA, the suggested amount of funds, the outline of the subject to be studied in Norway, what kind of grants, if any, have been previously received from the Norwegian government, a brief description of the applicant's professional position and education, and any other factors that they consider relevant. This should be addressed to the Royal Norwegian Consulate General at the main address. There is no application form.
Closing Date: February 15th.
Funding: Government.
Contributor: The Norwegian Ministry of Foreign Affairs.

The Norwegian Thanksgiving Fund Scholarship
Subjects: Fisheries, geology, glaciology, astronomy, social medicine or Norwegian culture.
Eligibility: Open to American graduate students.
Level of Study: Graduate.
Type: Scholarship.
Value: Up to US$3,000.

Country of Study: Norway.
No. of awards offered: One.
Application Procedure: Applicants must contact the American Scandinavian Foundation.

For further information contact:

The American Scandinavian Foundation
58 Park Avenue, New York, NY, 10016, United States of America
Tel: (1) 212 879 9779
Fax: (1) 212 249 3444
Email: grants@amscan.org
www: http://www.amscan.org

NORWICH JUBILEE ESPERANTO FOUNDATION

37 Granville Court
Cheney Lane, Oxford, Oxfordshire, OX3 0HS, England
Tel: (44) 1865 245509
Contact: Dr Kathleen M Hall, Secretary to the Foundation

A registered charitable trust established in 1967 (registration number 313190) the Norwich Jubilee Esperanto Foundation was founded for the advancement of education in the study and practice of Esperanto. It can pay travelling expenses to enable young persons who have shown efficiency in the study of Esperanto to visit foreign countries. It also awards prizes and encourages research.

Norwich Jubilee Esperanto Foundation Grants-in-Aid
Subjects: Esperanto.
Purpose: To encourage thorough study of Esperanto by enabling young students to travel abroad and to promote research into the teaching of Esperanto.
Eligibility: Open to citizens of any country under 26 years of age who require financial assistance and have a high standard of competence in Esperanto. An efficiency test may be required. There are no set academic or age requirements for research grants.
Level of Study: Unrestricted.
Type: Travel grant.
Value: Approx. UK £50-200, to a maximum of UK £1,000.
Length of Study: From one week to several months.
Frequency: Dependent on funds available.
Study Establishment: Any venue approved by the Foundation.
Country of Study: Outside the United Kingdom for United Kingdom applicants. The United Kingdom for other applicants.
No. of awards offered: Varies.
Application Procedure: Applicants must submit a letter of application in Esperanto. An application may be completed later.
Closing Date: Applications are accepted at any time provided an adequate margin is left for processing.
Funding: Private.
Contributor: Legacies from past supporters.
No. of awards given last year: 10.
No. of applicants last year: 11.
Additional Information: Visitors to the United Kingdom will be expected to speak in Esperanto to schools or clubs.

NOVARTIS FOUNDATION

41 Portland Place, London, W1B 4BN, England
Tel: (44) 20 7636 9456
Fax: (44) 20 7436 2840
Email: dchadwick@novartisfound.org.uk
www: http://www.novartisfound.org.uk
Contact: Dr D J Chadwick, Director

A scientific and educational charity, the Novartis Foundation was established in 1997 as the direct successor to the Ciba Foundation which was created in 1947 by Ciba of Basle. There are three main functions, those being the organisation of scientific meetings, the publishing of books and the provision of accommodation and hospitality for visiting scientists and their societies.

Novartis Foundation Symposium Bursaries
Subjects: Biomedicine, chemistry and related topics.
Purpose: To enable young scientists to attend Novartis Foundation symposia and, immediately following the meeting, spend time in the laboratory of one of the symposium participants.
Eligibility: Open to applicants of any nationality, aged between 23 and 35 on the closing date for application, and who are actively engaged in research on the topic covered by the symposium of their choice.
Level of Study: Doctorate, Postdoctorate.
Type: Symposium bursary.
Value: Travel expenses, by the most economical means, bed and breakfast during the symposium, and board and lodging while in the host's laboratory.
Length of Study: One-three months, including travel, attendance at a Novartis Foundation symposium and up to four-twelve weeks in the participant's laboratory or institution.
Frequency: Twice a year.
Country of Study: Any country.
No. of awards offered: Approx. eight.
Application Procedure: Applicants must send a full curriculum vitae and statement of current research, stating their symposium of choice from current advertisements.
Closing Date: Please refer to advertisements.
Funding: Commercial.
Contributor: Novartis AG, Basle.
No. of awards given last year: Six.
No. of applicants last year: 75.
Additional Information: The availability of the awards is advertised by circular to overseas members of the Novartis Foundation's Scientific Advisory Panel and invited symposiasts, and by an advertisement in 'Nature', or other journals if more appropriate. Awards are advertised every three to six months, and at least six months before the date of the relevant meetings. The awardee is selected by the senior staff of the Foundation, usually four months before the symposium. Offers to host an awardee are sought from symposiasts at the time of the invitation to the symposium. The successful awardee is asked to select three names from the membership list of the symposium and every effort is made by the Novartis Foundation to accommodate the awardee's choice. Successful candidates are expected to submit a short report following their return home.

NURSES' EDUCATIONAL FUNDS, INC.

555 West 57th Street
Suite 1327, New York, NY, 10019, United States of America
Tel: (1) 212 399 1428
Fax: (1) 212 581 2368
Email: bbnef@aol.com
www: http://www.n-e-f.org
Contact: Ms Barbara Butler, Scholarship Co-ordinator

Nurses' Educational Funds, Inc. is an independent, non-profit organisation which grants scholarships to registered nurses for graduate study. It is governed by a board of trustees of nursing and business leaders, and is supported by contributions from corporations, foundations, nurses and individuals interested in the advancement of nursing.

Nurses' Educational Funds Fellowships and Scholarships
Subjects: Administration, supervision, education, clinical specialisation and research.
Purpose: To provide the opportunity to registered nurses who seek to qualify through advanced study in a degree programme.

Eligibility: Open to full-time Master's degree students or full or part-time doctoral students who are United States citizens or have officially declared the intention of becoming United States citizens. Applicants must be members of a professional nursing association.
Level of Study: Doctorate, Graduate, Postgraduate.
Type: Fellowship.
Value: US$2,500-10,000.
Length of Study: One year.
Frequency: Annual.
Study Establishment: Any college or university offering Master's programmes in nursing accredited by the NLNAC or CCNE, or at the doctoral level in nursing or a nursing related programme.
Country of Study: United States of America.
No. of awards offered: Varies.
Application Procedure: Applicants must send a US$10 cheque to cover postage and handling to receive an application kit. Completed applications must be accompanied by official transcripts of academic records, Graduate Record Examination scores or management admissions test scores, references, proof of membership in a professional nursing association, and proof of admission to an academic programme. Application forms are available from the Fund from August 1st-February 1st.
Closing Date: March 1st preceding the academic year for which funds are sought.
Funding: Private.

OFFICE OF NAVAL RESEARCH (ONR)

American Society of Engineering Education (ASEE)
1818 N Street North West
Suite 600, Washington, DC, 20036, United States of America
Tel: (1) 202 331 3509
Fax: (1) 202 265 8504
Email: projects@asee.org
www: http://www.asee.org/postdoc
Contact: Associate Programme Director

As manager of the Navy's exploratory development programme, the Office of Naval Research (ONR) is charged with developing technologies that will support naval forces in meeting future operational needs. Scientists and engineers at ONR help shape and execute the Navy's programme for meeting future operational need by pursuing scientific research and technologies development to address problems in many diverse fields, eg. acoustics, hydrodynamics, chemistry, aerodynamics, astrophysics, electron devices, biotechnology, oceanography, communications and command control and intelligence.

ONR Postdoctoral Fellowship
Subjects: Engineering.
Purpose: To encourage the involvement of creative, capable and highly trained scientists and engineers from academia and industry in areas of interest and relevance to the navy.
Eligibility: Open to citizens of the United States, or permanent residents with a 'green card' at the time of application. Security clearance participants must be eligible for a Department of Defense security clearance. Before appointment participants must provide evidence of having received a PhD or equivalent within seven years of the date of application.
Level of Study: Postdoctorate.
Type: Fellowship.
Value: US$36,000-53,000.
Length of Study: One year, renewable for up to three years.
Frequency: Annual.
Study Establishment: Naval laboratories.
Country of Study: United States of America.
No. of awards offered: Up to 40.
Application Procedure: Applicants must submit an application form, which can be obtained from ASEE, a current curriculum vitae, three letters of reference, transcripts from all schools attended, and

a 5-10 page research proposal which has been developed with the help of the proposed host facility.
Closing Date: January 1st, April 1st, July 1st or October 1st.
Funding: Government.
Contributor: The ONR.

OKLAHOMA STATE UNIVERSITY (OSU)

Department of Financial Aid
119 Student Union, Stillwater, OK, 74078-0212, United States of America
Tel: (1) 405 744 6604
Fax: (1) 405 744 6438
Email: finaid@okstate.edu

OSU Graduate Assistantships

Subjects: MBA.
Purpose: To enable qualified domestic and international applicants to undertake the MBA programme.
Level of Study: MBA.
Type: Assistantship.
Value: A monthly stipend and a waiver of the out of state portion of tuition and fees.
Length of Study: Varies.
Frequency: Annual.
Study Establishment: OSU.
Country of Study: United States of America.
No. of awards offered: Varies.
Application Procedure: Applicants must contact the Department for Financial Aid for more details.
Closing Date: Please contact the organisation.
Funding: Government.
Additional Information: Graduate assistants normally work 10 hours per week.

OSU Tuition Aid Grants

Subjects: MBA.
Purpose: To enable Oklahoma residents to undertake graduate study.
Eligibility: Open to Oklahoma residents enrolled in a minimum of six graduate hours per semester. Grants are based on demonstrated financial need.
Level of Study: MBA.
Type: Assistantship.
Value: Varies.
Length of Study: Varies.
Frequency: Annual.
Study Establishment: OSU.
Country of Study: United States of America.
No. of awards offered: Varies.
Application Procedure: Applicants must contact the Department of Financial Aid for more details.
Closing Date: Please contact the organisation.
Funding: Government.

OMAHA SYMPHONY GUILD

1605 Howard Street, Omaha, NE, 68102, United States of America
Tel: (1) 402 342 3836
Fax: (1) 402 342 3819
Email: bravo@omahasymphony.org
www: http://www.omahasymphony.org
Contact: Ms Kimberly Mettenbrink, Volunteer Co-ordinator

The purpose of the Omaha Symphony Guild is to promote the growth and development of the Omaha Symphony Orchestra.

Omaha Symphony Guild International New Music Competition

Subjects: Music theory and composition.
Purpose: To award composers of unpublished compositions which have never been performed by a professional orchestra.
Eligibility: Open to composers aged 25 and over.
Level of Study: Postgraduate.
Type: Competition.
Value: US$3,000 award and premiere performance.
Frequency: Annual.
Country of Study: United States of America.
No. of awards offered: One.
Application Procedure: Applicants must write for an application form. Two copies of the composition score must be submitted. Photocopies are acceptable but no tapes are accepted. The entry fee is US$30 and cheques should be made payable to the Omaha Symphony Guild. Application forms can also be downloaded from the website.
Closing Date: April 15th.
Funding: Private.
Contributor: The Omaha Symphony Guild.
No. of awards given last year: One.
No. of applicants last year: 35.
Additional Information: Compositions must be no longer than 20 minutes. If applicants require the score to be returned they must include US$10 postage.

OMOHUNDRO INSTITUTE OF EARLY AMERICAN HISTORY AND CULTURE

PO Box 8781, Williamsburg, VA, 23187-8781, United States of America
Tel: (1) 757 221 1110
Fax: (1) 757 221 1047
Email: ieahc1@wm.edu
www: http://www.wm.edu/oieahc
Contact: Ms Sally D Mason, Assistant to the Director

The Omohundro Institute of Early American History and Culture publishes books in its field of interest, the William and Mary Quarterly, and a biannual newsletter, Uncommon Sense. It also sponsors conferences and colloquia, and annually awards a two year NEH Postdoctoral Fellowship and a one year Andrew W Mellon Postdoctoral Research Fellowship.

Andrew W Mellon Postdoctoral Research Fellowship

Subjects: The history and culture of North America's indigenous and immigrant peoples during the colonial, revolutionary and early national periods of the United States of America and the related histories of Canada, the Caribbean, Latin America, the British Isles, Europe and Africa from 1500 to approx. 1815.
Purpose: To revise the applicant's book manuscript into a first book that will make a distinguished contribution to scholarship, with publication by the Institute intended.
Eligibility: Applicants must not have previously published a book or have a book under contract, and must also have received their PhD at least one year prior to the application deadline.
Level of Study: Postdoctorate.
Type: Fellowship.
Value: US$45,000.
Length of Study: One year, residential recommended.
Frequency: Annual.
Study Establishment: Omohundro Institute of Early American History and Culture.
Country of Study: United States of America.
No. of awards offered: One.
Application Procedure: Applicants must complete an application form and submit this with a completed manuscript. Application forms are available on request and from the web pages.
Closing Date: November 1st.

Funding: Private.
Contributor: The Andrew W Mellon Foundation and the College of William and Mary.
No. of awards given last year: One.
No. of applicants last year: 14.

NEH Institute Postdoctoral Fellowship

Subjects: The history and culture of North America's indigenous and immigrant peoples during the colonial, revolutionary, and early national periods of the United States and the related histories of Canada, the Caribbean, Latin America, the British Isles, Europe and Africa from 1500 to approx. 1815.
Purpose: To revise a dissertation into a first book that will make a major contribution to the field of early American history and culture, for publication by the Institute.
Eligibility: Applicants must have been United States of America citizens for three years prior to applying.
Level of Study: Postdoctorate.
Type: Fellowship.
Value: US$40,000.
Length of Study: Two years.
Frequency: Annual.
Study Establishment: The Omohundro Institute of Early American History and Culture.
Country of Study: United States of America.
No. of awards offered: One.
Application Procedure: Applicants must complete an application form, available on written request or from the web pages.
Closing Date: November 1st.
Funding: Government.
Contributor: The National Endowment for Humanities (NEH) and the College of William and Mary.
No. of awards given last year: One.
No. of applicants last year: 21.

ONCOLOGY NURSING FOUNDATION (ONS)

501 Holiday Drive, Pittsburgh, PA, 15220-2749, United States of America
Tel: (1) 412 921 7373
Fax: (1) 412 921 6565
Email: found@ons.org
www: http://www.ons.org
Contact: Dr Gail A Mallory, Director of Research

The mission of the Oncology Nursing Society (ONS) is to promote excellence in oncology nursing and quality cancer care. The Foundation works to fulfil this mission by providing nurses and healthcare professionals with access to the highest quality educational programmes, cancer care resources, research opportunities, and networks for peer support.

ONS Foundation Research Awards

Subjects: Oncology nursing research, including research proposals related to AIDS, neuro-oncology, community health, cancer related genetics, nursing outcomes, oncology nursing education, symptom assessment and management, pain, palliative care, nausea and vomiting, neutropenia or biotherapy.
Eligibility: Open to health professionals working in the field of oncology.
Level of Study: Unrestricted.
Type: Research grant.
Value: Generally US$3,000-10,000, though some awards are up to US$100,000.
Length of Study: Two years.
Frequency: Dependent on funds available.
Country of Study: Any country.
No. of awards offered: 28.

Application Procedure: Applicants must complete an application form, available on request. They must also include a research proposal.
Closing Date: November 1st.
No. of awards given last year: 35.
No. of applicants last year: 50+.

THE ONTARIO INSTITUTE FOR STUDIES IN EDUCATION (OISE)

University of Toronto (UT)
252 Bloor Street West, Toronto, ON, M5S 1V6, Canada
Tel: (1) 416 923 6641 ext. 8157
Fax: (1) 416 926 4765
Email: mbrennan@oise.utoronto.ca
www: http://www.oise.utoronto.ca
Contact: Ms Margaret Brennan

The Ontario Institute for Studies in Education/University of Toronto (OISE/UT) is an educational institution dedicated to the establishment of a learning society, through immersing itself in the world of applied problem solving and expanding the knowledge and capacities of individuals to lead productive lives.

OISE/UT Graduate Assistantships

Subjects: Adult education, applied psychology, curriculum, educational administration, higher education, history and philosophy of education, sociology in education or human development.
Purpose: To provide remuneration and financial assistance for graduate students who are engaged in research and/or field development oriented projects contributing to their academic and professional development.
Eligibility: Open to persons of any nationality who are suitably qualified for admission to a Master's or doctoral degree programme in graduate studies at the OISE/UT. Applicants must be registered full-time students at OISE/UT.
Level of Study: Doctorate, Postgraduate.
Type: Assistantship.
Value: Canadian $9,180 per year, plus 4 per cent vacation pay.
Length of Study: Eight months, renewable for one additional year in certain programmes.
Frequency: Annual.
Study Establishment: OISE/UT.
Country of Study: Canada.
No. of awards offered: 182.
Application Procedure: Applicants must submit a completed application form and an application for admission.
Closing Date: December 3rd.
No. of awards given last year: 182.
Additional Information: The award is for employment, at an average of 10 hours per week.

OISE/UT Local Support

Subjects: Adult education, applied psychology, curriculum, educational administration, higher education, history and philosophy of education, sociology in education or human development.
Purpose: To support students studying at OISE/UT.
Eligibility: Open to persons of any nationality who are suitably qualified for admission to a MA or a PhD programme in graduate studies at the OISE/UT.
Level of Study: Doctorate, Postgraduate.
Type: Scholarship.
Value: Canadian $1,500-12,000.
Length of Study: Eight months, renewable for one additional year in certain programmes.
Frequency: Annual.
Study Establishment: OISE/UT.
Country of Study: Canada.
No. of awards offered: Variable, depending on funds available.

Application Procedure: Applicants must not apply, as they are nominated by each OISE/UT department at the time of admission.
Closing Date: December 3rd.

ONTARIO MINISTRY OF EDUCATION AND TRAINING

PO Box 4500
189 Red River Road
4th Floor, Thunder Bay, ON, P7B 6G9, Canada
Tel: (1) 807 343 7257
Fax: (1) 807 343 7278
www: http://osap.gov.on.ca
Contact: G Vibert, OGS Officer

Ontario Graduate Scholarship Programme

Subjects: All subjects.
Purpose: To encourage excellence in graduate studies.
Eligibility: Open to Canadian residents with an overall A average or equivalent during the previous two years of study. 60 awards may be allocated to students holding a student authorisation.
Level of Study: Doctorate, Graduate, MBA.
Type: Scholarship.
Value: Approx. canadian $5,000 per term.
Length of Study: Two or three consecutive terms of full-time graduate study.
Frequency: Annual.
Study Establishment: An university in Ontario.
Country of Study: Canada.
No. of awards offered: 2,000.
Application Procedure: Applicants currently registered at a university in Ontario must submit their applications and supporting documentation through that institution.
Closing Date: November 15th.
Funding: Government.
Contributor: The Ministry of Training, and colleges and universities.
No. of awards given last year: 2,000.
No. of applicants last year: 6,500.
Additional Information: Students may hold another award up to canadian $10,000 and may accept research assistantships or part-time teaching or demonstrating appointments, providing that the total amount paid to the Scholars within the period of the award shall not interfere with their status as full-time graduate students. The total amount of time spent by the student in connection with such an appointment, including preparation, marking examinations, etc. must not exceed an average of 10 hours per week. Students must reapply each year and may receive a maximum of four awards.

OPEN SOCIETY FOUNDATION - SOFIA

56 Solunska Street, Sofia, BG-1000, Bulgaria
Tel: (359) 2 930 6619
Fax: (359) 2 951 6348
Email: info@osf.bg
www: http://www.osf.bg
Contact: Ms Iliana Bobova, Education Consultant

The goal of the Open Society Foundation network is to promote an open society. The concept of open society is based on the recognition that people act on the basis of imperfect knowledge and nobody is in possession of the ultimate truth. This leads to a respect for the rule of law, to a society which is not dominated by the state, to the existence of democratic government, to a market economy and, above all, to respect for minorities and minority opinions.

Curriculum Resource Centre of the Central European University Scholarship

Subjects: Political science, medical studies, gender and culture, philosophy, history, international relations and European studies, economics, legal studies, management, environmental science and policy.
Purpose: To support curriculum development.
Eligibility: Open to university teachers and/or professionals who teach part-time in the social sciences and humanities with sufficient knowledge of English.
Level of Study: Professional development.
Type: Scholarship.
Value: Full scholarship, travel and book allowance.
Length of Study: One week.
Study Establishment: The Curriculum Resource Centre of the Central European University.
Country of Study: Hungary.
No. of awards offered: 20.
Application Procedure: Applicants must submit an application form and accompanying documents are needed.
Closing Date: Varies.
Funding: Private.
Contributor: The Central European University and the Open Society Institute.
No. of awards given last year: 20.
Additional Information: For more information see the Centre's website at http://www.ceu.hu/crc.

Open Society Sofia Central European University Scholarship

Subjects: Economics, environmental sciences and policy, gender and culture, history, international relations and European studies, legal studies, mathematics and its applications, medieval studies, nationalism, philosophy, political science or sociology.
Purpose: To contribute to the development of open societies by promoting a system of education in which ideas are creatively, critically and comparatively exhausted.
Eligibility: Open to nationals from countries of Central and Eastern Europe and the former Soviet Union.
Level of Study: Doctorate, Graduate, Postgraduate, Research.
Type: Scholarship.
Value: Approx. US$11,000 to cover tuition fees, living expenses and travel to and from the teaching site.
Length of Study: One-three years.
Frequency: Annual.
Study Establishment: The Central European University.
Country of Study: Hungary or Poland.
No. of awards offered: Varies.
Application Procedure: Applicants must submit a completed application form, a curriculum vitae, two recommendations and their language proficiency test results.
Closing Date: January.
Funding: Private.
Contributor: George Soros.
No. of awards given last year: 33.
No. of applicants last year: 311.
Additional Information: Programme availability and format are reviewed on an annual basis. Changes may occur from year to year. For the most up to date information please contact the Central European University.

For further information contact:

Central European University
Nador u 9-1051, Budapest, Hungary
Tel: (36) 1 327 3000
Fax: (36) 1 327 3007
www: http://www.ceu.hu

OSI Global Supplementary Grant Program (Grant SGP)

Subjects: Humanities or social sciences.

Purpose: To enable qualified students to pursue doctoral studies in the humanities and social sciences.

Eligibility: Open to candidates from selected countries from Eastern and Central Europe and the former Soviet Union. Bulgarian nationals under the age of 40 who have been accepted into a full-time doctoral programme at an accredited university in Western Europe, Asia, Australia or North America and have already been awarded partial or full tuition, room and board stipends or other types of financial aid are also eligible.

Level of Study: Doctorate.

Type: Grant.

Value: 50 per cent of tuition and fees or living expenses or additional expenses.

Length of Study: Up to one year of study with the option to apply for a second year.

Frequency: Annual.

Study Establishment: Accredited universities.

Country of Study: Western Europe, Asia, Australia or North America.

No. of awards offered: Varies.

Application Procedure: Applicants must complete an application form and provide the required supporting documents.

Closing Date: April 1st.

Funding: Private.

Contributor: The Open Society Institute in New York.

No. of awards given last year: 22.

Additional Information: Programme availability and format are reviewed on an annual basis. Changes may occur from year to year. For the most up to date information please contact the Open Society Institute in New York.

For further information contact:

Open Society Institute
Network Scholarship Programs
400 West 59th Street, New York, NY, 10019, United States of America
Tel: (1) 212 548 0175
Fax: (1) 212 548 4652
Email: vjohnson@sorosny.org
www: http://www.soros.org

Oxford Colleges Hospitality Scheme for East European Scholars

Subjects: All subjects offered by the University of Oxford and the University of Cambridge.

Purpose: To enable overseas scholars to work in Oxford or Cambridge libraries or to consult Oxbridge specialists in their subjects.

Eligibility: Open to Scholars from Eastern and Central Europe, who have a good knowledge of English and who are in the process of completing work for an advanced degree, or who are working on a book, or a new course of lectures.

Level of Study: Professional development.

Type: Scholarship.

Value: Full scholarship.

Length of Study: One-three months.

Frequency: Annual.

Study Establishment: The University of Oxford and the University of Cambridge.

Country of Study: United Kingdom.

No. of awards offered: Up to six.

Application Procedure: Applicants must submit a completed application form, a curriculum vitae, a list of publications and two recommendation letters.

Closing Date: November.

Funding: Government, Private.

Contributor: FCO, OSI-Budapest, University of Oxford.

No. of awards given last year: Seven.

No. of applicants last year: 45.

Additional Information: Programme availability and format are reviewed on an annual basis. Changes may occur from year to year. For the most up to date information please contact the Open Society Institute in Budapest.

For further information contact:

Open Society Institute
Network Scholarship Programmes
Nador Utca 11, Budapest, H-1051, Hungary
www: http://www.osi.hu

Salzburg Medical Seminars

Subjects: Medicine and surgery.

Purpose: To promote the exchange of ideas between physicians from Eastern Europe and the United States of America.

Eligibility: Open to English speaking Bulgarian advanced level medical doctors under the age of 40.

Level of Study: Professional development.

Length of Study: One week, plus three one month internships in the following years.

Frequency: Annual.

Study Establishment: Salzburg Seminars, Leopoldskron Salzburg, Austria.

Country of Study: Austria.

No. of awards offered: Varies.

Application Procedure: Applicants must submit a curriculum vitae, higher education diploma and diploma for acknowledged medical speciality, letters of reference, a statement of purpose and a photograph.

Closing Date: Varies.

Funding: Commercial, Government, Private.

Contributor: The Open Society Institute, New York, the Hurrican Austrian Foundation and the Austrian government.

No. of awards given last year: 20.

No. of applicants last year: 40+.

Additional Information: Programme availability and format are reviewed on an annual basis. Changes may occur from year to year. For the most up to date information please contact the Open Society Institute in New York or visit the website.

Scholarships at the University of Manchester

Subjects: Political science, European politics and policy, third world political development, political theory, international political economy or international relations.

Purpose: To support students of postgraduate courses.

Eligibility: Open to Bulgarian nationals who have a university degree in political science, history, philosophy, sociology, economics or law. Candidates should be not more than 35 years of age, with the highest level of competence in English.

Level of Study: Graduate, Postgraduate.

Type: Scholarship.

Value: Full scholarship.

Length of Study: One year.

Frequency: Annual.

Study Establishment: The University of Manchester.

Country of Study: United Kingdom.

No. of awards offered: Two-four.

Application Procedure: Applicants must submit a completed application form, two letters of recommendation, evidence of English proficiency and a statement of intent.

Closing Date: February.

Funding: Government, Private.

Contributor: FCO, Open Society Institute - Budapest, University of Manchester.

No. of awards given last year: Three.

No. of applicants last year: 92.

Additional Information: Programme availability and format are reviewed on an annual basis. Changes may occur from year to year. For the most up to date information please contact the Open Society Institute in Budapest.

For further information contact:

Open Society Institute
Network Scholarship Programs
Nador Utca 11, Budapest, H-1051, Hungary
www: http://www.osi.hu

543

Soros Supplementary Grants Programme (SSGP)

Subjects: Social sciences, humanities, fine and performing arts.

Purpose: To provide assistance to citizens of the countries of central and eastern Europe who are pursuing advanced study within the region but outside of their home countries.

Level of Study: Graduate.

Type: Grant.

Value: US$1,000-5,000.

Frequency: Annual.

Country of Study: Eastern European countries, the former Soviet Union or Mongolia.

No. of awards offered: Varies.

Application Procedure: Applicants must complete an application form, available on request.

Closing Date: April.

Funding: Private.

Contributor: The Open Society Institute - Budapest.

No. of awards given last year: 18.

No. of applicants last year: 34.

Additional Information: Programme availability and format are reviewed on an annual basis. Changes may occur from year to year. For the most up to date information please contact the Open Society Institute in Budapest.

For further information contact:

Open Society Institute
Soros Supplementary Grants Program
99-2000
Nador Utca 11, Budapest, H-1051, Hungary

Soros/FCO Chevening Scholarships

Subjects: All subjects offered by the University of Oxford and political philosophy at York University.

Purpose: To support young scholars who wish to use the experience gained from studying in Britain to benefit higher education, research, or public life in their home country.

Eligibility: Open to Bulgarian nationals, who have completed five years of university study, are not older than 28 and who have an excellent knowledge of English.

Level of Study: Graduate, Postgraduate, Professional development.

Type: Scholarship.

Value: Full scholarship.

Length of Study: One academic year.

Frequency: Annual.

Study Establishment: The University of Oxford or the University of York.

Country of Study: United Kingdom.

No. of awards offered: Varies.

Application Procedure: Applicants must submit a completed application form, a copy of their official diploma, a summary of their dissertation, two confidential evaluation forms, proof of English proficiency, and a list of any publications.

Closing Date: Mid December.

Funding: Government, Private.

Contributor: FCO, Open Society Institute - Budapest and the University of Oxford.

No. of awards given last year: Five.

No. of applicants last year: 57.

Additional Information: Programme availability and format are reviewed on an annual basis. Changes may occur from year to year. For the most up to date information please contact the Open Society Institute in Budapest.

For further information contact:

Open Society Institute
Network Scholarship Programs
Nador Utca 11, Budapest, H-1051, Hungary
www: http://www.osi.hu

Summer University of The Central European University Scholarship

Subjects: Arts and humanities, mathematics and computer science, environmental studies, social sciences, lax, educational science or business administration.

Purpose: To encourage and promote regional academic co-operation and curriculum development by drawing together young faculty.

Eligibility: Open to university teachers, administrators, professionals and students in Master's degree programmes with teaching experience. Knowledge of English is required.

Level of Study: Professional development.

Type: Scholarship.

Value: Tuition fees, accommodation, travel, health insurance and a book allowance.

Length of Study: Two, three or four weeks.

Frequency: Annual.

Study Establishment: Central European University.

Country of Study: Hungary.

No. of awards offered: Approx. 30 for Bulgaria.

Application Procedure: Applicants must submit an application form including statement of purpose and letters of recommendation.

Closing Date: January 15th.

Funding: Private.

Contributor: The Central European University and the Open Society Institute in Hungary.

No. of awards given last year: 28.

No. of applicants last year: 53.

Additional Information: For further information see the University's website at http://www.ceu.hu/sun/sunindx.html.

University of Warwick Scholarships for East Europe

Subjects: All subjects offered by the University of Warwick.

Purpose: To support postgraduate study.

Eligibility: Open to Bulgarian nationals. Applicants must have a good command of English and must be under 35 years of age.

Level of Study: Graduate, Postgraduate.

Type: Scholarship.

Value: Full scholarship.

Length of Study: One year.

Frequency: Annual.

Study Establishment: The University of Warwick.

Country of Study: United Kingdom.

No. of awards offered: Up to four.

Application Procedure: Applicants must complete and submit an application form with two letters of recommendation and evidence of English proficiency.

Closing Date: January.

Funding: Government, Private.

Contributor: FCO, Open Society Institute - Budapest, University of Warwick.

No. of awards given last year: Three.

No. of applicants last year: 160.

Additional Information: Programme availability and format are reviewed on an annual basis. Changes may occur from year to year. For the most up to date information please contact the Open Society Institute in Budapest.

For further information contact:

Open Society Institute
Network Scholarship Programs
Nador Utca 11, Budapest, H-1051, Hungary
www: http://www.osi.hu

ORCHESTRE SYMPHONIQUE DE MONTRÉAL

260 de Maisoneurve Boulevard West, Montréal, QC, H2X 1Y9, Canada
Tel: (1) 514 842 3402
Fax: (1) 514 842 0728
Email: concoursosm@osm.ca
www: http://www.osm.ca
Contact: Ms Marianne Perron, Associate Music Administrator

Founded in 1934, the Orchestre Symphonique de Montréal is one of the greatest orchestras in the world. Under the guidance of its Artistic Director, Maestro Charles Dutoit, it gives about 100 concerts each year and has produced more than 85 recordings.

Orchestre Symphonique de Montréal Competitions

Subjects: Piano, singing, string or wind instrument performance.
Purpose: To award the best performances in strings, wind instruments and percussion, and piano.
Eligibility: Open to Canadian citizens and landed immigrants only.
Level of Study: Unrestricted.
Type: Scholarship.
Value: Canadian $30,000.
Frequency: Annual.
Country of Study: Any country.
No. of awards offered: Nine.
Application Procedure: Applicants must complete a registration form showing proof of eligibility and submit a curriculum vitae and registration fee.
Closing Date: October 4th.
Funding: Private.
Contributor: Standard Life.
No. of awards given last year: 14.
No. of applicants last year: 26.

ORENTREICH FOUNDATION FOR THE ADVANCEMENT OF SCIENCE, INC. (OFAS)

855 Route 301
Box 375, Cold Spring, NY, 10516-9802, United States of America
Tel: (1) 845 265 4200
Fax: (1) 845 265 4210
Email: ofas1@juno.com
Contact: Dr Rozlyn A Krajcik, Assistant Director Scientific Affairs

The Orentreich Foundation for the Advancement of Science (OFAS) is an operating private foundation that performs its own research and collaborates on projects of mutual interest.

OFAS Grants

Subjects: Areas of interest to the Foundation including ageing, dermatology, endocrinology and serum markers for human diseases.
Purpose: To conduct collaborative biomedical research, or research at the Foundation.
Eligibility: Applicants must be at or above the postgraduate level in science or medicine at accredited research institutions in the United States of America. There are, however, no citizenship restrictions.
Level of Study: Postgraduate.
Type: Grant.
Value: Amounts vary depending on the needs, nature and level of OFAS interest in the project.
Country of Study: United States of America.
Application Procedure: Applicants must submit an outline of proposed joint or collaborative research, including, as a minimum, a brief overview of the current research in the field of interest, a statement of scientific objectives, a protocol summary, the curriculum vitae of principal investigator, funding needed and total estimated

project funding. Confirming applications are reviewed at least quarterly. OFAS is usually the initiator of joint projects.
Closing Date: Applications for collaborative research projects may be submitted at any time.
Funding: Private.
Additional Information: If you have a research question relating to a human disease or disease prevention factor for which there is adequate scientific basis for a serum marker to justify use of the Serum Treasury, please submit a brief overview of your proposal. Researchers will be asked for additional information after the initial screening process. Proposals will be evaluated on an ongoing basis. In certain cases where the research applies directly to the primary interests of OFAS in ageing, dermatology or endocrinology, limited grants to fund collaborative studies are available.

ORGANIZATION OF AMERICAN HISTORIANS (OAH)

112 North Bryan Avenue, Bloomington, IN, 47408-4199, United States of America
Tel: (1) 812 855 9852
Fax: (1) 812 855 0696
Email: awards@oah.org
www: http://www.oah.org

The Organization of American Historians (OAH) was founded in 1907 as the Mississippi Valley Historical Association and originally focused on the history of the Mississippi Valley. Now national in scope and, with approximately 11,000 members, it is a large professional organisation created and sustained for the investigation, study and teaching of American history.

ABC-Clio America History and Life Award

Subjects: American history.
Purpose: To recognise and encourage scholarship in American history as documented in journal literature, and to advance new perspectives on accepted interpretations or previously unconsidered topics.
Eligibility: Open to entrants who have published an article in an American historical journal. Nominations and applications are welcome from both individuals and editors. Each entry must have been published during the period November 16th 2000 to November 15th 2002.
Type: Award.
Value: US$750 and a certificate.
Frequency: Every two years.
No. of awards offered: One.
Application Procedure: Applicants must send a copy of each entry to each member of the award committee by the deadline. Individuals as well as editors are encouraged to submit nominations.
Closing Date: December 1st.
Contributor: OAH.
No. of awards given last year: One.
No. of applicants last year: Approx. 26.

For further information contact:

Johns Hopkins University
3400 North Charles Street, Baltimore, MD, 21218, United States of America
Contact: Ms Jane Dailey

Graduate History Programme
School of Liberal Studies
Roosevelt University, Chicago, IL, 60605-1394, United States of

America
Contact: Mr Christopher R Reed

Committee Chair
308 Glenwood Court, Martinez, CA, 94553, United States of America
Contact: Mr Christopher Waldrep, Committee Chair

Department of History
Rutgers University
16 Seminary Place, New Brunswick, NJ, 08901, United States of America
Contact: Ms Mia Bay

Avery O Craven Award

Subjects: The Civil War.
Purpose: Awarded for the most original book on the coming of the Civil War, the Civil War years or the Era of Reconstruction, with the exception of works of purely military history. The exception recognises and reflects the Quaker convictions of Craven, President of the Organisation of American Historians 1963-64.
Type: Award.
Value: US$500 and a certificate.
Frequency: Annual.
No. of awards offered: One.
Application Procedure: Applicants must send a copy of each entry to each member of the prize committee by October 1st of the year the entry must be published. Publishers are urged to enter one or more books in the competition.
Closing Date: October 1st.
Contributor: OAH.
No. of awards given last year: One.
No. of applicants last year: 34.

David Thelen Prize

Subjects: Concerned with past issues of continuity and change, also with events or processes that began, developed or ended in what is now the United States of America.
Purpose: To award a prize for the best article on American history published in a foreign language.
Eligibility: Comparative and international studies that fall within these guidelines are welcomed. This prize is not open to articles whose manuscripts were originally submitted for publication in English or by other people for whom English is their first language.
Type: Prize.
Value: The winning article will be printed in the Journal of American History and its author awarded US$500 subvention for refining the article's English translation.
Frequency: Annual.
No. of awards offered: One.
Application Procedure: Applicants must write a one-two page essay in English explaining why their article is a significant and original contribution to our understanding of American history. This and five copies of the article should be sent to Professor David Thelen. The application must include the following information: name, mailing address, institutional affiliation, fax number and email address if available, and the language of submitted article. Authors of eligible articles are invited to nominate their work. Scholars who know of eligible publications written by others are urged to inform others of the prize.
Closing Date: May 1st.
Contributor: OAH.
No. of awards given last year: One.

For further information contact:

Chair
Journal of American History
1215 East Atwater, Bloomington, IN, 47401, United States of America
Contact: Ms Joanne Meyerowitz, Chair

Ellis W Hawley Prize

Subjects: Political economy, politics or institutions of the United States of America in its domestic or international affairs, from the Civil War to the present.
Purpose: To award the best book length historical study in the field.
Eligibility: Eligible works shall include book length historical studies, written in English and published during a given calendar year.
Type: Prize.
Value: US$500 and a certificate.
Frequency: Annual.
No. of awards offered: One.
Application Procedure: Applicants must send one copy of each entry to each member of the award committee.
Closing Date: October 1st.
No. of awards given last year: One.
No. of applicants last year: 62.

The Erik Barnouw Award

Subjects: American history.
Purpose: To recognise outstanding reporting or programming on network television, cable television or in documentary film, concerned with American history, the study of American history or the promotion of history.
Level of Study: Professional development.
Type: Award.
Value: A certificate.
Frequency: Annual.
No. of awards offered: One-two.
Application Procedure: Applicants must submit each entry on half inch video cassette and a copy must be sent to each committee member. Instructions regarding the preferred medium in which you would like the film shown, should it win, must be included with the copy of the film sent to the chair of the committee. Otherwise, the half inch video cassette sent to the chair will be used for the screening at the annual meeting.
Closing Date: December 1st.
No. of awards given last year: One.
No. of applicants last year: 16.

For further information contact:

Robinson Hall
Department of History
Harvard University, Cambridge, MA, 02138, United States of America
Contact: Ms Laurel Thatcher Ulrich

Committee Chair
Associate Dean for Policy & Development
Columbia Journalism School
Room 701-A
2950 Broadway, New York, NY, 10027, United States of America
Contact: Mr Evan W Cornog, Committee Chair

American Social History Project
Graduate Center
City University of New York
365 Fifth Avenue
Room 7301.09, New York, NY, 10027, United States of America
Contact: Mr Joshua Brown

Frederick Jackson Turner Award

Subjects: History.
Purpose: To award an author's first book on some significant phase of American history and also to the press that publishes it.
Eligibility: The work must be the first book length study of history published by the author. If the author has a PhD, he or she must have received it no more than seven years prior to submission of the manuscript for publication. The work must be published in the calendar year before the award is given and must deal with some significant phase of American history.
Type: Award.
Value: A medal, a certificate and US$1,000.
Frequency: Annual.

No. of awards offered: One.
Application Procedure: Applicants must send one copy of each entry to each member of the award committee by September 1st of the same year the book is published. Final page proofs may be used for books to be published after September 1st and before January 1st. If the final page proof is submitted, a bound copy of the entry must be submitted no later than January 7th. Publishers are urged to enter one or more books to the competition.
Closing Date: September 1st.
No. of awards given last year: One.
No. of applicants last year: 66.

Horace Samuel and Marion Galbraith Merrill Travel Grants in Twentieth Century American Political History

Subjects: History, American political history.
Purpose: To promote access of younger scholars to the Washington DC region's rich primary source collections in late nineteenth and twentieth-century American political history.
Level of Study: Graduate.
Type: Travel grant.
Value: US$500-3,000.
Frequency: Annual.
Application Procedure: Applicants must visit the website for complete application requirements. There is no standard application form.
Closing Date: December 1st.
No. of awards given last year: Five.
No. of applicants last year: 23.

For further information contact:

Women Studies Programme
University of California, Santa Barbara, CA, 93106, United States of America
Contact: Ms Eileen Boris

Committee Chair
United States Senate Historical Office, Washington, DC, 20510-7108, United States of America
Contact: Mr Richard A Baker, Committee Chair

Huggins-Quarles Awards

Subjects: History, ethnic studies, whiteness studies, Afro-Caribbean studies, cultural studies (post-colonialism), feminist studies, popular culture and media studies, immigration history, environmental studies or diplomatic history.
Eligibility: Open to minority graduate students at the dissertation research stage of their PhD.
Level of Study: Postgraduate.
Type: Award.
Value: Up to US$1,000.
Frequency: Annual.
Application Procedure: Applicants must submit a brief two page abstract of the dissertation project, along with a one page budget explaining the travel and research plans for the funds requested. Each application must be accompanied by a letter from the dissertation adviser attesting to the student's status and the ways in which the award will facilitate the completion of the dissertation project.
Closing Date: December 1st.
No. of awards given last year: Two.

For further information contact:

Women's Studies Program
203 Flinn Hall
University of South Carolina, Columbia, SC, 29208, United States of America
Contact: Ms Wanda A Hendricks

Department of History
Colgate University
13 Oak Drive, Hamilton, NY, 13346-1398, United States of America
Contact: Ms Charles Pete Banner-Haley

Department of History
University of Rhode Island

80 Upper College Road, Kingston, RI, 02881, United States of America
Contact: Peniel E Joseph

Curator, Special Collections
Department of History
Williams College, Williamstown, MA, 01267, United States of America
Contact: Ms Emma J Lapansky, Curator, Special Collections

Committee Chair
Department of History
Williams College, Williamstown, MA, 01267, United States of America
Contact: Mr Craig Steven Wilder, Committee Chair

James A Rawley Prize

Subjects: History.
Purpose: To reward a book dealing with the history of race relations in the United States.
Type: Prize.
Value: US$1,000 and a certificate.
Frequency: Annual.
No. of awards offered: One.
Application Procedure: One copy of each entry must be received by each member of the prize committee. Final page proofs may be used for books to be published after October 1st and before January 1st. If a final page proof is submitted, a bound copy of the entry must be submitted no later than January 7th.
Closing Date: October 1st.
No. of awards given last year: One.
No. of applicants last year: 42.

Jamestown Scholars: New Dissertation Fellowships from the National Park Service and OAH

Subjects: Local American history.
Purpose: To support PhD research that contributes to understanding the development and legacy of seventeenth-century Jamestown.
Eligibility: Entrants must be United States graduate students pursing PhDs in history, American studies and related fields. Proposals will be judged on their relevance and scholarly contribution to the understanding of seventeenth-century Jamestown.
Level of Study: Doctorate.
Type: Fellowship.
Value: US$5,000.
Frequency: Annual.
Country of Study: United States of America.
Application Procedure: Applicants must provide a curriculum vitae, a letter of recommendation and a two page abstract of the dissertation project. Applications may be emailed to jamestown@oah.org.
Closing Date: December 15th.

La Pietra Dissertation Travel Fellowship in Transnational History

Subjects: American history.
Purpose: To provide financial assistance to graduate students whose dissertation topics deal with aspects of American history that extend beyond the United States' borders.
Eligibility: Applicants must be currently enrolled in a United States or foreign graduate programme.
Level of Study: Graduate.
Type: Travel fellowship.
Value: US$1,250.
Frequency: Annual.
No. of awards offered: One.
Application Procedure: Applicants must submit a two or three page project description indicating the dissertation's significance, including a statement of the major collections to be examined abroad and their relevance to the dissertation as well as two letters of recommendation including one from the dissertation advisor and a current curriculum vitae indicating language proficiency.
Closing Date: December 1st.

Lerner-Scott Prize

Subjects: United States women's history.
Purpose: To award the best doctoral dissertation.
Level of Study: Postdoctorate.
Type: Prize.
Value: US$1,000 and a certificate.
Frequency: Annual.
No. of awards offered: One.
Application Procedure: Each application must contain a letter of support from a faculty member at the degree granting institution, along with an abstract, table of contents and sample chapter from the dissertation. Email addresses for the applicants and the adviser should also be included if available.
Closing Date: December 1st.
No. of awards given last year: One.
No. of applicants last year: 31.

For further information contact:

2325 South Seventh Street, Ann Arbor, MI, 48103, United States of America
Contact: Mr Kevin Gaines

301 Morrill Hall
Department of History
Michigan State University, East Lansing, MI, 48824, United States of America
Contact: Ms Lisa M Fine

Committee Chair
236 Munroe Hall
Department of History
University of Delaware, Newark, DE, 19716, United States of America
Contact: Ms Anne M Boylan, Committee Chair

Louis Pelzer Memorial Award

Subjects: Any period or topic in the history of the United States.
Purpose: To promote and encourage strong essay writing with special emphasis on literary craftsmanship, subject significance and competent handling of evidence.
Type: Award.
Value: The winning essay will be published in the Journal of American History. The organisation offers a prize of US$500, a certificate and a medal to the winner.
Frequency: Annual.
Application Procedure: Applicants must submit five copies of essays which should not exceed 7,000 words in length. The footnotes at the end of the text should be triple spaced. Manuscripts are judged anonymously therefore the author's name and graduate programme should appear only on a separate cover page.
Closing Date: December 1st.
No. of awards given last year: One.
No. of applicants last year: 20.

For further information contact:

Committee Chair
Louis Pelzer Award Committee
Journal of American History
1215 East Atwater Avenue, Bloomington, IN, 47401, United States of America
Contact: Ms Joanne Meyerowitz, Committee Chair

Mary K Bonsteel Tachau Pre-Collegiate Teaching Award

Subjects: History.
Purpose: To recognise the contributions made by pre-collegiate and classroom teachers to improve history education.
Eligibility: Open to pre-collegiate teachers engaged at least half time in history teaching, whether in history or social studies. Successful candidates shall demonstrate exceptional ability in initiating or participating in projects which involve students in historical research, writing, or other means of representing their knowledge of history, or in school, district, regional, state or national projects which enhance the professional development of teachers. They should also show ability in initiating or participating in projects which aim to build bridges between pre-collegiate and collegiate teachers, in working with museums, historical preservation societies or other public history associations to enhance the place of public history in pre-collegiate schools, in developing innovative history criteria which foster a spirit of enquiry and emphasise critical skills, and in publishing or otherwise publicly presenting scholarship that advances education or knowledge.
Level of Study: Professional development.
Type: Award.
Value: A certificate, US$750, one year OAH membership and a one year subscription to the OAH Magazine of History. If the winner is an OAH member, the award will include a one year renewal of membership in the awardee's usual membership category. Finally, the winner's school will receive a plaque suitable for permanent public display.
Frequency: Annual.
No. of awards offered: One.
Application Procedure: Applicants must submit one application packet to each of the three committee members that includes copies of the following in the order given: a covering letter of no more than two pages written by a colleague indicating why the teacher merits the award, two letters written by former or present students of no more than two pages each, a curriculum vitae of no more than three pages, samples of the nominee's written work, a narrative prepared by the nominee describing the goals and effects of the candidate's work in the classroom and elsewhere for history education (no more than three pages) and the names, addresses and telephone numbers of at least three professional referees, including the writer of the covering letter, at least one of whom must be a colleague or supervisor.
Closing Date: December 1st.
No. of awards given last year: One.
No. of applicants last year: Six.

For further information contact:

HUMB 344
Department of History
University of South Alabama, Mobile, AL, 36688, United States of America
Contact: Ms Betty Brandon

Committee Chair
Martha's Vineyard Regional High School
Box 1385, Oak Bluffs, MA, 02557, United States of America
Contact: Ms Margaret Harris, Committee Chair

162 Plains Road, Salisbury, VT, 05769, United States of America
Contact: Ms Michele Forman

Merle Curti Award in American Intellectual History

Subjects: History.
Purpose: To recognise books in the field of American intellectual history.
Type: Award.
Value: US$1,000, a certificate and a medal.
Frequency: Every two years.
No. of awards offered: One.
Application Procedure: Applicants must send a copy of each entry to the committee members. Publishers are urged to enter one or more books in the competition.
Closing Date: October 1st.
Contributor: OAH.
No. of awards given last year: One.
No. of applicants last year: 95.

For further information contact:

California Institute of Technology
Mail Code 228-77, Pasadena, CA, 91125, United States of America
Contact: Mr Daniel J Kevles

Committee Chair
Department of History
129 Dickinson Hall

Princeton University, Princeton, NJ, 08544, United States of America
Contact: Mr Daniel T Rodgers, Committee Chair

Merle Curti Award in American Social History
Subjects: History.
Purpose: To recognise books in the field of American social history.
Type: Award.
Value: US$1,000, a certificate and a medal.
Frequency: Every two years (even-numbered years).
No. of awards offered: One.
Application Procedure: Applicants must send a copy of each entry to the committee members Professor Leon Fink and Professor Judith Sealander. Publishers are urged to enter one or more books in the competition.
Closing Date: October 1st in the year the book was published.
Contributor: OAH.
No. of awards given last year: One.
No. of applicants last year: 218.

OAH Awards and Prizes
Subjects: American history.
Purpose: To recognise scholarly and professional achievement in the field of American history.
Eligibility: Open to applicants of any nationality.
Level of Study: Unrestricted.
Value: Varies, depending on award.
Frequency: Varies, depending on award.
Application Procedure: Applicants must obtain flyers for each award from the OAH office. The names and addresses of committee members are listed and submissions are sent directly to these members. There are no application forms to fill out and no application fees.
Closing Date: Deadlines vary.

OAH Foreign-Language Book Prize
Subjects: American history, namely the past and issues of continuity and change, as well as events or processes that began, developed or ended in what is now the United States of America.
Purpose: To award a prize to the best book on American history published in a foreign language.
Eligibility: This prize is not open to books whose manuscripts were originally submitted for publication in English or by people for whom English is their first language.
Type: Prize.
Value: Includes a subsidy of at least US$1,000 to support the costs of translation into an English language edition, to be matched by the publisher if translation can be arranged.
Frequency: Every two years.
No. of awards offered: One.
Application Procedure: Applicants must write a two page essay in English explaining why the book is a significant and original contribution to understanding American history. This and four copies of the book should be sent to the Foreign-Language Book Prize Committee at the main address. Authors of eligible books are invited to nominate their work. Scholars who know of eligible publications written by others are urged to inform those authors of the prize.
Closing Date: May 1st of even numbered years.
Contributor: OAH.
No. of awards given last year: One.
No. of applicants last year: Eight.

Ray Allen Billington Prize
Subjects: American frontier history.
Purpose: To award the best book in American frontier history, defined broadly so as to include the pioneer periods of all geographical areas and comparisons between American frontiers and others.
Type: Award.
Value: US$1,000, a certificate and a medal.
Frequency: Every two years (even-numbered years).
No. of awards offered: One.

Application Procedure: Applicants must send a copy of each entry to each member of the award committee by October 1st of the second year of the two year period. Final page proofs may be used for books to be published after October 1st and before January 1st. If a final page proof is submitted, a bound copy of the entry must be submitted no later than January 7th.
Closing Date: October 1st.
Contributor: OAH.
No. of awards given last year: Two.
No. of applicants last year: 67.

Richard W Leopold Prize
Subjects: Foreign policy, military affairs broadly construed, the historical activities of the federal government or biography in one of the foregoing areas.
Purpose: To improve contacts and interrelationships within the historical profession, where an increasing number of historically trained scholars hold distinguished positions in governmental agencies. It is awarded to the best book written by a historian connected with federal, state or municipal government.
Eligibility: The winner must have been employed in a government position for the last five years. If the author has accepted an academic position the book must have been published within two years from the time of the change.
Type: Prize.
Value: US$1,500 and a certificate.
Frequency: Every two years.
No. of awards offered: One.
Application Procedure: Applicants must send one copy of each entry to each member of the award committee.
Closing Date: September 1st.
No. of awards given last year: One.
No. of applicants last year: 21.

ORGANIZATION OF AMERICAN STATES (OAS)

1889 F Street North West, Washington, DC, 20006-3897, United States of America
Tel: (1) 202 458 3000
Fax: (1) 202 458 3897
Email: portal@iacd.oas.org
www: http://www.oas.org
Contact: Mr Santos Mahung

PRA Fellowships
Subjects: All fields except medicine and related fields and languages.
Purpose: To promote the economic, social, scientific and cultural development of the member states in order to achieve a stronger bond and better understanding among the peoples of the Americas.
Eligibility: Candidates must be citizens or permanent residents of an OAS member state and hold a university degree or have demonstrated the ability to pursue advanced studies in the chosen field.
Level of Study: Postgraduate.
Type: Fellowship.
Value: A round trip ticket, tuition fees, study materials, health insurance and subsistence allowance (which varies from country to country), depending on the circumstances of each fellow.
Length of Study: From three months to two years.
Frequency: Annual.
Study Establishment: The candidate must choose the university or study centre in their chosen country of study and make the necessary contacts to secure acceptance.
Country of Study: Any member country of the OAS.
No. of awards offered: Varies.
Application Procedure: Applicants must present the fellowship form to the general secretariat of the OAS through the official channels established by each government. United States citizens can

send applications directly to the OAS headquarters in Washington, DC.

Closing Date: March 1st.
No. of awards given last year: 360.
No. of applicants last year: 1,500.

ORIENTAL CERAMIC SOCIETY

30B Torrington Square, London, WC1E 7JL, England
Tel: (44) 20 7636 7985
Fax: (44) 20 7580 6749
Contact: Ms Jean Martin

The Oriental Ceramic Society was established in 1921 and aims to increase knowledge and appreciation of Asian ceramics and other arts. The Society is open to anyone interested in the arts of Asia. Membership is worldwide, and meetings, lectures and exhibitions are held regularly.

George De Menasce Memorial Trust Bursary

Subjects: Any aspect of oriental art.
Purpose: To promote research into oriental art.
Eligibility: Awards are only given to applicants of the highest calibre. The last recipient of the bursary wrote on his extensive research into Mamluk Ceramics. Please contact the Society for more details.
Level of Study: Postgraduate.
Type: Bursary.
Value: Up to UK £2,000.
Frequency: The award is dependent on funds available and is only offered once every four to five years.
Country of Study: Any country.
No. of awards offered: One.
Application Procedure: Applicants must write for details.
Funding: Private.
Additional Information: The recipient is required to read a paper on the research they have undertaken which is then published so their research should be of an unusual and highly interesting nature. Applicants are required to complete a form giving complete academic qualifications. Research connected with a PhD degree is not normally considered adequate for the bursary.

ORTHOPAEDIC RESEARCH AND EDUCATION FOUNDATION (OREF)

6300 N River Road
Suite 700, Rosemont, IL, 60018-4261, United States of America
Tel: (1) 847 698 9980
Fax: (1) 847 698 7806
Email: mcguire@oref.org
www: http://www.oref.org
Contact: Mrs Jean McGuire, Vice President Grants

In 1955, leaders of the major professional organisations in the speciality, the American Orthopaedic Association, the American Academy of Orthopaedic Surgeons and the Orthopaedic Research Society, established the Orthopaedic Research and Education Foundation as a means of supporting research and building the scientific base of clinical practice. Today, the Foundation raises over US$5 million per year and holds a unique place in United States medicine.

AAOS/OREF Fellowship in Health Services Research

Subjects: Orthopaedics.
Purpose: To enable orthopaedic surgeons with research skills to manage health services and outcomes research.
Eligibility: Applicants must be orthopaedic surgeons in either Canada or United States of America.
Level of Study: Postdoctorate.
Type: Fellowship.

Value: US$70,000 per year for up to two years.
Length of Study: Two years.
Frequency: Annual.
Study Establishment: At participating institutions.
Country of Study: United States of America.
No. of awards offered: One.
Application Procedure: Applicants must make a formal application.
Closing Date: August 1st.
Funding: Private.
Contributor: Orthopaedic surgeons.
No. of awards given last year: One.
No. of applicants last year: Five.

OREF Career Development Award

Subjects: Orthopaedic surgery.
Purpose: To encourage a commitment to scientific research in orthopaedic surgery.
Eligibility: Applicants must be orthopaedic surgeons, and are not eligible if they are holders of NIH ROI award.
Level of Study: Professional development.
Type: Basic or clinical research.
Value: Up to US$75,000 per year.
Length of Study: Three years.
Frequency: Annual.
Country of Study: United States of America or Canada.
No. of awards offered: One-three.
Application Procedure: Applicants must make a formal application with letters of recommendation.
Closing Date: August 1st.
Funding: Private.
Contributor: Orthopaedic surgeons.
No. of awards given last year: Two.
No. of applicants last year: 13.

OREF Clinical Research Award

Subjects: Orthopaedics.
Purpose: To recognise outstanding clinical research related to musculoskeletal disease or injury.
Eligibility: Restricted to members of American Academy of Orthopaedic Surgeons, Orthopaedic Research Society (ORS), Canadian Orthopaedic Association, or Canadian ORS. Alternatively, candidates may be sponsored by a member.
Level of Study: Professional development.
Type: Award.
Value: US$20,000.
Length of Study: One year.
Frequency: Annual.
Country of Study: United States of America or Canada.
No. of awards offered: One.
Application Procedure: Applicants must submit an original manuscript.
Closing Date: July 1st.
Funding: Private.
Contributor: Orthopaedic surgeons.
No. of awards given last year: One.
No. of applicants last year: Nine.

OREF Prospective Clinical Research

Subjects: Orthopaedics.
Purpose: To provide funding for promising prospective clinical proposals in orthopaedics.
Eligibility: Applicants must be orthopaedic surgeons.
Level of Study: Professional development.
Type: Award.
Value: Up to US$50,000 per year.
Length of Study: Three years.
Frequency: Annual.
Study Establishment: Medical centre.
Country of Study: United States of America.
No. of awards offered: One-three.
Application Procedure: Applicants must make a formal application.

Closing Date: August 1st.
Funding: Private.
Contributor: Orthopaedic surgeons.
No. of awards given last year: One.
No. of applicants last year: Nine.

OREF Research Grants

Subjects: Sports medicine, surgery, rheumatology and treatment techniques.
Purpose: To encourage new investigators by providing seed money and start up funding.
Eligibility: Open to orthopaedic surgeons who are PI or co PI. PI cannot have NIH ROI awards.
Level of Study: Postdoctorate.
Type: Research grant.
Value: Up to US$50,000 per year.
Length of Study: Two years.
Frequency: Annual.
Study Establishment: A medical centre.
Country of Study: United States of America.
No. of awards offered: 8-12.
Application Procedure: Applicants must make a formal application.
Closing Date: August 1st.
Funding: Private.
Contributor: Orthopaedic surgeons and orthopaedic corporations.
No. of awards given last year: 12.
No. of applicants last year: 64.

OREF Resident Research Award

Subjects: Orthopaedics.
Purpose: To encourage the development of research interests for residents and Fellows.
Eligibility: Applicants must be orthopaedic surgeon residents or Fellows in an approved residency programme in the United States.
Level of Study: Professional development.
Type: Basic research training.
Value: US$15,000.
Length of Study: One year.
Frequency: Annual.
Study Establishment: Medical centre.
Country of Study: United States of America.
No. of awards offered: Up to 10.
Application Procedure: Applicants must make a formal application.
Closing Date: August 1st.
Funding: Private.
Contributor: Orthopaedic surgeons.
No. of awards given last year: 12.
No. of applicants last year: 34.

OSTEOGENESIS IMPERFECTA FOUNDATION, INC.

804 W Diamond Avenue
Suite 210, Gaithersburg, MD, 20878, United States of America
Tel: (1) 301 947 0083
Fax: (1) 301 947 0456
Email: bonelink@oif.org
www: http://www.oif.org
Contact: Mr Heller An Shapiro, Executive Director

The Osteogenesis Imperfecta Foundation works to improve the quality of life for individuals affected by osteogenesis imperfecta, through research to find treatments and a cure, and awareness, education and mutual support.

Michael Geisman Memorial Fellowship Fund

Subjects: Osteogenesis imperfecta.
Purpose: To encourage research scientists to develop expertise in osteogenesis imperfecta.

Eligibility: Open to suitably qualified investigators with less than five years of postdoctoral research training.
Level of Study: Postdoctorate.
Type: Fellowship.
Value: US$50,000 per year salary comprised of US$35,000 per year for salary and US$15,000 per year for supplies.
Length of Study: Two years.
Frequency: Annual.
Country of Study: Any country.
No. of awards offered: Two-three.
Application Procedure: Applicants must complete an application form, available on request or from the website.
Closing Date: November 1st.
Funding: Private.
No. of awards given last year: One.
No. of applicants last year: Three.

Osteogenesis Imperfecta Foundation Seed Research Grant

Subjects: Basic research or clinical studies on osteogenesis imperfecta to investigate causes, treatment or cure.
Purpose: To fund seed projects which can then be submitted to larger funding bodies.
Eligibility: Open to qualified researchers in the field of osteogenesis imperfecta.
Level of Study: Postdoctorate.
Type: Research grant.
Value: Up to US$60,000 (indirect costs and salaries will not be covered).
Length of Study: One year.
Frequency: Annual.
Country of Study: Any country.
No. of awards offered: Two-three.
Application Procedure: Applicants must complete an application form, available on request or from the website.
Closing Date: November 1st.
Funding: Private.
No. of awards given last year: Two.
No. of applicants last year: Six.

PALOMA O'SHEA SANTANDER INTERNATIONAL PIANO COMPETITION

Calle Hernán Cortés 3, Santander, E-39003, Spain
Tel: (34) 94 231 1451
Fax: (34) 94 231 4816
Email: concurso@albeniz.com
www: http://www.albeniz.com
Contact: A Kaufmann, Secretariat General

The Paloma O'Shea Santander International Piano Competition is one of the best rated competitions in the world. It provides an opportunity for exceptionally talented pianists to enhance their careers. The jury is composed of renowned musicians in order to ensure that grants are made in a fair and unbiased manner.

Paloma O'Shea Santander International Piano Competition

Subjects: Piano performance.
Purpose: To give support to young pianists of exceptional talent.
Eligibility: Open to pianists of any nationality under the age of 29 years.
Level of Study: Unrestricted.
Type: Competition.
Value: Please contact the association for details.
Length of Study: July 27th-August 7th.
Frequency: Every three years.

Study Establishment: The pre-selection will be held in London, Madrid, Moscow, New York and Paris. The competition will be held in Santander.

No. of awards offered: Seven.

Application Procedure: Applicants in the United States should contact Mrs Brookes McIntyre at the address given. Applicants from all other countries must contact the Secretariat General for details at the main address.

Closing Date: December 15th.

Funding: Commercial, Government, Private.

No. of awards given last year: Seven.

Additional Information: In general 20 pianists will participate in Santander. Each one will be chosen from the pre-selection phase which is recorded and filmed on video. Six participants will be selected for the semi-finals and later three participants go through to the final. The competition consists of three stages: first stage, recital and chamber music (a quintet for piano and strings), second phase, semi-finals, concerto with chamber orchestra and recital and third phase, final, concerto with symphony orchestra.

For further information contact:

PO Box 82743, Alberquerque, NM, 87198, United States of America
Tel: (1) 505 250 2341
Fax: (1) 505 265 8932
Contact: Mrs Brookes McIntyre

PAN AMERICAN HEALTH ORGANIZATION (PAHO) REGIONAL OFFICE OF THE WORLD HEALTH ORGANIZATION (WHO)

Regional Office for the Americas/Pan-American Sanitary Bureau
525 23rd Street North West, Washington, DC, 20037-2895, United States of America
Tel: (1) 202 974 3117
Fax: (1) 202 974 3680
Email: rgp@paho.org
www: http://www.paho.org
Contact: M González, Grants Administrator

The Pan American Health Organization (PAHO) is an international public health agency working to improve health and living standards of the countries of the Americas. It serves as the specialised organisation for health of the Inter-American System and as the regional office for the Americas of the World Health Organization.

PAHO Grants

Subjects: Public health studies.

Purpose: To contribute to the public health of the region of the Americas (individual programme objectives vary). Programmes include graduate thesis grants, research training grants, regional research competitions (announced yearly) and special initiatives announced via the PAHO website.

Eligibility: Open to citizens and residents of Latin America and the Caribbean.

Level of Study: Doctorate, Graduate, Postgraduate, Research.

Type: Research grant.

Value: Graduate thesis grants of up to US$5,000 for Master's and up to US$10,000 for the doctoral level, research training grants (mid-level researchers) of US$40,000 or less, and regional research competitions usually of US$30,000.

Length of Study: Usually six months-two years. For research training programmes training lasts for three-six months.

Frequency: Varies.

Study Establishment: Varies.

Country of Study: Latin America or Caribbean countries only.

No. of awards offered: Varies according to programme.

Application Procedure: Applicants must complete an application form. Guidelines and application forms are available from the website.

Closing Date: Varies according to programme.

Funding: Government.

Contributor: Member states and their agencies.

No. of awards given last year: 51.

No. of applicants last year: Varies.

Additional Information: Special initiatives arise every year and are announced on the PAHO website. Conditions for these vary according to each individual initiative. Information on other regional offices of the World Health Organization can be found on the WHO website. Each office will have their own grant offers generally limited to that geographical region.

For further information contact:

WHO Regional Office for Africa
PO Box No 6, Brazzaville, Congo
www: http://www.whoafr.org

WHO Regional Office for Europe
8 Scherfigsvej, Copenhagen, DK-2100, Denmark
www: http://www.who.dk

WHO Regional Office for the Eastern Mediterranean
PO Box No 1517, Alexandria, 21511, Egypt
www: http://www.who.sci.eg

Regional Office for South East Asia
Indraprstha Estate
Mahatma Gandhi Road, New Delhi, 110002, India
Tel: (91) 11 331 7804
Fax: (91) 11 331 8607
www: http://www.w3.whosea.org

Regional Office for the Western Pacific
PO Box 2932, Manila, Laguna, 1099, Philippines
www: http://www.who.org.ph

WHO Headquarters
Avenue Appia 20, Geneva, CH-1211, Switzerland
www: http://www.who.int

PARALYZED VETERANS OF AMERICA, SPINAL CORD RESEARCH FOUNDATION

801 18th Street North West, Washington, DC, 20006, United States of America
Tel: (1) 202 416 7651
Fax: (1) 202 416 7641
Email: scrf@pva.org
www: http://www.pva.org/scrf
Contact: Administrative Officer

The Spinal Cord Research Foundation was established in 1976 by the Paralyzed Veterans of America for the purpose of supporting research directed to spinal cord injury and disease.

Paralyzed Veterans of America Research Grants

Subjects: Laboratory research in the basic sciences related to spinal cord injury or disease, clinical and functional studies of the medical, psychological and economic effects of spinal cord injury or disease, as well as interventions proposed to alleviate these effects, design and development of new and improved rehabilitative and assistive devices for individuals with spinal dysfunction. Fellowships for postdoctoral scientists, clinicians, or engineers designed to encourage the training and specialisation of these individuals in the field of spinal dysfunctional research.

Purpose: To improve the quality of life of individuals with spinal cord injuries, and to hasten the discovery of a cure of spinal cord injury.

Eligibility: Open to qualified individuals who are seeking funds to develop a project in the field of spinal cord injury. Please visit the website for further eligibility requirements.

Level of Study: Postdoctorate.

Type: Research grant and fellowship.
Value: Up to US$75,000 per year.
Length of Study: Two years, with a chance to resubmit after the second year is completed.
Frequency: Annual.
No. of awards offered: Approx. 30.
Application Procedure: Applicants must obtain a brochure, guidelines and applications for a grant request, which can be downloaded from the website or are available from the Foundation.
Closing Date: June 1st.
Funding: Private.
Additional Information: All grant recipients must submit biannual and annual progress reports, a photo and an article in layman's language for publications in PVA's monthly publication, Paraplegia News and other publications.

PARAPSYCHOLOGY FOUNDATION, INC.

228 East 71st Street, New York, NY, 10021, United States of America
Tel: (1) 212 628 1550
Fax: (1) 212 628 1559
Email: info@parapsychology.org
www: http://www.parapsychology.org
Contact: Ms Lisette Coly, Vice President

Established in 1951, the Parapsychology Foundation acts as a clearinghouse for information about parapsychology. Essentially an administrative organisation, it maintains one of the largest libraries to do with parapsychology, the Eileen J Garret Library, as well as supporting various programmes which include the library, a grant and scholarship programme, a conference and lecture programme, and a speaker's bureau and publishing programme.

D Scott Rogo Award for Parapsychological Literature

Subjects: Parapsychology.
Purpose: To provide support to authors working on a manuscript pertaining to the science of parapsychology.
Eligibility: Open to nationals of any country.
Level of Study: Unrestricted.
Type: Award.
Value: US$3,000.
Length of Study: One year.
Frequency: Annual.
Country of Study: Any country.
No. of awards offered: One.
Application Procedure: Applicants must submit a brief synopsis of the proposed contents of manuscript, a list of previous writings and a sample writing of assistance.
Closing Date: April 15th for notification on May 1st.
No. of awards given last year: One.
No. of applicants last year: 12.

Eileen J Garrett Scholarship

Subjects: Parapsychology.
Purpose: To assist students attending an accredited college or university in pursuing the academic study of the science of parapsychology.
Eligibility: Open to nationals of any country.
Level of Study: Unrestricted.
Type: Scholarship.
Value: US$3,000.
Length of Study: One year.
Frequency: Annual.
Study Establishment: An accredited college or university.
Country of Study: Any country.
No. of awards offered: One.
Application Procedure: Applicants must submit samples of writings on the subject with an application form from the Foundation. Letters

of reference are required from three individuals, familiar with the applicant's work and/or studies in parapsychology.
Closing Date: July 15th for notification on August 1st.
No. of awards given last year: One.
No. of applicants last year: 25.

Parapsychology Foundation Grant

Subjects: Parapsychology.
Purpose: To support original study, research and experiments in parapsychology.
Eligibility: Open to nationals of any country.
Level of Study: Unrestricted.
Type: Grant.
Value: Up to US$3,000.
Length of Study: One year.
Frequency: Annual.
Country of Study: Any country.
No. of awards offered: 10.
Application Procedure: Applicants must submit a proposal outlining the aims of the project, the time required to complete it, likely expenditure, educational background, references, past work and publications.
Closing Date: Applications are accepted at any time.
No. of awards given last year: 10.

PARENTERAL DRUG ASSOCIATION FOUNDATION FOR PHARMACEUTICAL SCIENCES, INC. (PDA)

6 Sunset Lane, Garden City, NY, 11530, United States of America
Tel: (1) 516 248 6713
Fax: (1) 516 483 1011
Email: hndemuth@aol.com
www: http://www.pdafoundation.org
Contact: Awards & Grants Programme

Charles P Schaufus Grant

Subjects: Pharmaceutics, quality assurance, biotechnology processing, pharmaceutical process engineering or other appropriate disciplines.
Purpose: To stimulate research in the area of parenteral processing technology and to provide a stipend for a student.
Eligibility: Open to suitably qualified researchers of any nationality.
Level of Study: Postgraduate.
Type: Grant.
Value: US$10,000 in cash per year, plus an equipment grant of US$10,000 per year.
Length of Study: Up to three years.
Country of Study: United States of America.
No. of awards offered: One.
Application Procedure: Applicants must refer to the website for full eligibility and application requirements.
Closing Date: June 15th.
Contributor: The Millipore Corporation, Bedford, Massachusetts.
Additional Information: First publication rights are reserved by the foundation for possible publication in the Journal of Parenteral Science and Technology.

PDA Foundation Grant in Biotechnology

Subjects: Biotechnology, and the research into developing analytical methodology for peptides, polypeptides and proteins. It is expected that the methodology will be used in formulation and stability studies on bioengineered products.
Purpose: To provide a stipend for a student.
Eligibility: There are no eligibility restrictions.
Level of Study: Postgraduate.
Type: Grant.
Value: US$15,000 per year.

Length of Study: Two years.
Frequency: Annual.
Country of Study: Any country.
No. of awards offered: One.
Application Procedure: Applicants must submit a completed application form with eight copies of the proposal. Full eligibility and application requirements are available on request.
Closing Date: Early June.
Contributor: The PDA Foundation and the Kapoor Charitable Foundation.
Additional Information: First publication rights are reserved by the Foundation for possible publication in the Journal of Parenteral Science and Technology.

PDA Foundation Research Grants

Subjects: Parenteral technology and related disciplines including pharmaceutics, microbiology, biology, chemistry, pharmacy, quality assurance, pharmacology, manufacturing, engineering, formulation or stability studies.
Purpose: To provide a stipend for a student.
Eligibility: Open to suitably qualified researchers of any nationality.
Level of Study: Postgraduate.
Type: Grant.
Value: US$15,000.
Length of Study: One year.
Country of Study: United States of America.
No. of awards offered: One.
Application Procedure: Applicants must refer to the website for full eligibility and application requirements.
Closing Date: June 15th.
Contributor: The PDA Foundation, the Pall Corporation and the Warner Lambert Company.
Additional Information: The grants are funded by the PDA Foundation, Glaxo Wellcome, The Pall Corporation and the Parke Davis Division of Warner-Lambert.

PARKER B FRANCIS FELLOWSHIP PROGRAM

Physiology Program
Harvard School of Public Health
Room 1411 Building 1
665 Huntington Avenue, Boston, MA, 02115, United States of America
Tel: (1) 617 432 4099
Fax: (1) 617 277 2382
Email: brain@hsph.harvard.edu
www: http://www.hsph.harvard.edu/pbf
Contact: Ms Gail Weidner, Administrator

Parker B Francis Fellowship Program

Subjects: Pulmonary research.
Purpose: To support rising stars in the field of pulmonary research as they make the transition from postdoctoral trainee to independent researcher.
Eligibility: The ideal applicant has between two and seven years of postdoctoral research experience, has published articles in leading journals and has a clear trajectory in pulmonary research.
Level of Study: Postdoctorate.
Type: Fellowship.
Value: The total budget is limited to US$38,000 for the first, US$40,000 for the second, and US$42,000 for the third years. These totals include stipend plus fringe benefits and may include travel to a maximum of US$1,500. Direct research project costs and indirect costs are not allowed. These expenses ought to be supported by research project grants which are an essential part of the application in documenting the availability of sufficient research project support to make possible fulfilment of the Fellow's research aims.

Length of Study: Three years.
Frequency: Annual.
Country of Study: United States of America or Canada.
No. of awards offered: 18.
Application Procedure: Applicants must submit a completed application form, biographical sketch and brief statement of their career goals. They must also include a letter from the mentor evaluating the applicant's qualifications and indicating career goals in the field of pulmonary research, three letters of recommendation, a summary of the past training record of the primary mentor (including names of former trainees and their current positions, sources and level of support (including grants pending) and the extent of equipment and space for research training available to the primary mentor and trainee, and (on the face page) signatures of the primary mentor, department or division head, and fiscal officer responsible for administering the grant.
Closing Date: Mid October.
Funding: Private.
Contributor: The Francis Families Foundation.
No. of awards given last year: 18.
No. of applicants last year: 50.
Additional Information: Further information is available from the website.

PARKINSON'S DISEASE FOUNDATION, INC. (PDF)

650 West 168th Street, New York, NY, 10032, United States of America
Tel: (1) 212 923 4700
Fax: (1) 212 923 4778
Email: info@pdf.org
www: http://www.pdf.org
Contact: Ms Patricia Arroyo, Business Administrator

The Parkinson's Disease Foundation (PDF) was founded in 1957 to encourage and promote research into Parkinson's disease, a chronic, degenerative neurological disorder that exhibits itself in such symptoms as tremor, stiffness and slowness of movement.

H Houston Merritt Fellowship

Subjects: Parkinson's disease research.
Eligibility: Open to established scientists at the level of associate professor or above.
Level of Study: Postgraduate.
Type: Fellowship.
Value: US$15,000.
Length of Study: 6-12 months.
Frequency: Annual.
Study Establishment: The College of Physicians and Surgeons, Columbia University, New York.
Country of Study: United States of America.
No. of awards offered: One.
Application Procedure: Applicants must send applications, including a curriculum vitae, directly to Dr Stanley Fahn at the Foundation. There is no application form.
Closing Date: April 1st.

Parkinson's Disease Foundation Extramural Research Grants

Subjects: Parkinson's disease research.
Eligibility: Open to PhDs and MDs.
Level of Study: Postgraduate.
Type: Grant.
Value: US$25,000.
Frequency: Annual.
Study Establishment: Any institution.
Country of Study: Any country.
No. of awards offered: 12-14.
Application Procedure: Applicants must write for details.

Closing Date: April 1st.

Parkinson's Disease Foundation Postdoctoral Fellowships
Subjects: Parkinson's disease research.
Eligibility: Open to physicians who have completed their residency in neurology.
Level of Study: Postdoctorate.
Type: Fellowship.
Value: US$35,000.
Length of Study: One year.
Frequency: Annual.
Study Establishment: The College of Physicians and Surgeons, Columbia University, New York.
Country of Study: United States of America.
No. of awards offered: Three.
Application Procedure: Applicants must send applications, including a curriculum vitae, directly to Dr Stanley Fahn at the Foundation. There is no application form.
Closing Date: April 1st.

Parkinson's Disease Foundation Summer Fellowships
Subjects: Parkinson's disease research.
Purpose: To allow students to study under the supervision of an established investigator.
Eligibility: Open to premedical and medical students and to doctoral candidates.
Level of Study: Doctorate, Postgraduate.
Type: Fellowship.
Value: US$1,800-2,200.
Length of Study: 10 weeks.
Frequency: Annual.
Study Establishment: Any college or university.
Country of Study: United States of America.
No. of awards offered: 10-15.
Application Procedure: Applicants must complete an application form, available from the Foundation.
Closing Date: April 1st.

THE PARKINSON'S DISEASE SOCIETY OF THE UNITED KINGDOM (PDS)

215 Vauxhall Bridge Road, London, SW1V 1EJ, England
Tel: (44) 20 7931 8080
Fax: (44) 20 7233 9908
Email: research@parkinsons.org.uk
www: http://www.parkinsons.org.uk
Contact: Ms Catherine Fleming, Research Officer

The Parkinson's Disease Society of the United Kingdom (PDS) works with people who have Parkinson's, their families, and health and social care professionals. The mission of the PDS is the conquest of Parkinson's and the alleviation of the suffering and distress it causes through research. The work of the PDS includes research into the cause, cure and prevention of Parkinson's, and improvements in treatments, a helpline staffed by nurses offering advice on all aspects of Parkinson's including drug treatments, surgery, therapies, social and health care rights, benefits, driving, insurance and employment. The PDS also provides a wide range of publications, audio tapes and videos, a comprehensive education and training programme and a national network of field staff, branches and welfare visitors, offering local information, support, advice and social activities.

Parkinson's Disease Society Research Project Grant
Subjects: Medical sciences, neurology, neurosciences, biochemistry, toxicology, pathology, genetics, geriatrics or pharmacy.
Purpose: To support research into the causes, cure and prevention of Parkinson's disease, and care and effective treatments.
Eligibility: Restricted to United Kingdom residency. The principal applicant must hold a tenured position for the duration of the award and hold suitable qualifications.
Level of Study: Postdoctorate, Professional development.
Type: Project grant.
Value: To include at least one salary plus consumables and equipment.
Length of Study: Up to three years.
Frequency: As available.
Study Establishment: A recognised research institution, university or hospital in the United Kingdom.
Country of Study: United Kingdom.
No. of awards offered: Varies.
Application Procedure: Applicants must complete an application form which is available from the Society's website.
Closing Date: Please refer to the website.
Funding: Private.
Contributor: Donations.
No. of awards given last year: 14.
No. of applicants last year: 38.
Additional Information: Please note that the Society is implementing a new research strategy, for further details of this please visit the Society's website.

Parkinson's Disease Society Studentships and Junior/Senior Fellows
Subjects: Medical sciences, neurology, neurosciences, biochemistry, toxicology, pathology, genetics, geriatrics or pharmacy.
Purpose: To support research into the causes, cure and prevention of Parkinson's disease, and care and effective treatments.
Eligibility: Restricted to United Kingdom residents with suitable qualifications and a salaried position for the duration of the award.
Level of Study: Doctorate.
Type: Studentship and fellowship.
Value: Funding ranges from UK £55,000 (non-clinical) to UK £105,000 (clinical).
Length of Study: Up to three years.
Frequency: As available.
Study Establishment: A recognised teaching, research or clinical institution in the United Kingdom.
Country of Study: United Kingdom.
No. of awards offered: Varies.
Application Procedure: Applicants must complete an application form which is available from the Society's website.
Closing Date: November 30th.
Funding: Private.
Contributor: Donations.
No. of awards given last year: Three.
No. of applicants last year: 21.
Additional Information: Please note that the Society is implementing a new research strategy, for further details of this please visit the Society's website.

PARTICLE PHYSICS AND ASTRONOMY RESEARCH COUNCIL (PPARC)

Polaris House
North Star Avenue, Swindon, Wiltshire, SN2 1SZ, England
Tel: (44) 1793 442026
Fax: (44) 1793 442036
Email: steve.cann@pparc.ac.uk
www: http://www.pparc.ac.uk
Contact: Mr Steve Cann, E & T Section

The mission of the Particle Physics and Astronomy Research Council (PPARC) is to pursue a programme of high quality basic research in astronomy, planetary science and particle physics which furthers the understanding of fundamental questions, trains high quality scientists and engineers, increases the United Kingdom industry's competitiveness, attracts future generations of scientists and engineers and stimulates public interest.

PPARC Advanced Fellowships

Subjects: Particle physics, astronomy or astrophysics.
Purpose: To give outstanding researchers the opportunity to pursue full-time research. The intention is to further the careers of individuals of outstanding potential.
Eligibility: Candidates must hold a PhD or be of equivalent standing in their profession and have at least two years of research experience at postdoctoral level when the application is made and have proved their ability as an individual and independent researcher.
Level of Study: Postdoctorate.
Type: Fellowship.
Value: Awards are made on the first 18 points on the UFC scale for non-clinical academic and related staff in United Kingdom universities.
Length of Study: Up to five years.
Frequency: Annual.
Study Establishment: Any academic institution in the United Kingdom which is acceptable to PPARC.
Country of Study: United Kingdom.
No. of awards offered: Up to 13.
Application Procedure: Applicants must refer to the PPARC website for application information.
Closing Date: November 1st.
Funding: Government.
Additional Information: Further information is available on request by emailing fellowships@pparc.ac.uk.

PPARC Daphne Jackson Memorial Fellowships

Subjects: Particle physics or astronomy.
Purpose: To enable high level engineers and scientists to return to their professions after a career break for family or other reasons.
Eligibility: Open to promising engineers and scientists who have taken a career break.
Level of Study: Postdoctorate, Research.
Type: Fellowship.
Value: Dependent on age and experience.
Length of Study: Two years.
Frequency: Annual.
Study Establishment: Universities and research institutions in the United Kingdom that are convenient for the candidate.
Country of Study: United Kingdom.
No. of awards offered: Varies.
Application Procedure: Applicants must contact Dr E A Johnson, Trust Co-ordinator, or Jennifer Woolley, Administrator, for application forms and further information.
Closing Date: Please write for details.
Additional Information: The Daphne Jackson Memorial Fellowship is also administered by the BBSRC and the EPSRC.

For further information contact:

The Daphne Jackson Memorial Fellowships Trust
Department of Physics
University of Surrey, Guildford, Surrey, GU2 5XH, England
Tel: (44) 1483 259166

PPARC Postdoctoral Fellowships

Subjects: Particle physics or astronomy.
Purpose: To enable less experienced researchers to devote themselves to independent and original research.
Eligibility: Applicants must have, or expect to have, a PhD.
Level of Study: Postdoctorate.
Type: Fellowship.
Length of Study: Up to three years.
Frequency: Annual.
Study Establishment: Any academic institution in the United Kingdom which is acceptable to PPARC.
Country of Study: United Kingdom.
No. of awards offered: Approx. 10.

Application Procedure: Applicants must refer to the PPARC website for application information.
Closing Date: November 1st.
Funding: Government.
Additional Information: Further information is available on request by emailing fellowships@pparc.ac.uk.

PPARC Postgraduate Studentships

Subjects: Particle physics or astronomy.
Eligibility: Open to postgraduates from the United Kingdom and European Union countries.
Level of Study: Postgraduate.
Type: Studentship.
Length of Study: Up to three years.
Frequency: Annual.
Study Establishment: Any academic institution in the United Kingdom which is acceptable to PPARC.
Country of Study: United Kingdom.
No. of awards offered: Approx. 170.
Application Procedure: Applicants must refer to the PPARC website for application information.
Closing Date: July 31st.
Funding: Government.
Additional Information: Further information is available on request by emailing studentships@pparc.ac.uk.

PPARC Research Grants in Astronomy and Particle Physics

Subjects: Particle physics or astronomy.
Eligibility: For requirements please refer to the website.
Level of Study: Postdoctorate, Research.
Type: Research grant.
Value: Varies.
Frequency: Twice a year.
Study Establishment: Any academic institution in the United Kingdom which is acceptable to PPARC.
Country of Study: United Kingdom.
No. of awards offered: Varies.
Application Procedure: Applicants must refer to the PPARC website for application information.
Funding: Government.

PPARC Royal Society Industry Fellowships

Subjects: Particle physics or astronomy.
Purpose: To enhance interaction between those in industry and the research base, to the benefit of United Kingdom industry.
Eligibility: Senior academic scientists and industrial employees with a project proposal central to their own research programme for which a collaborative effort would bring benefits.
Level of Study: Postdoctorate, Professional development.
Type: Fellowship.
Value: Varies.
Length of Study: Six months-two years full-time, or part-time over a period of up to four years.
Frequency: Annual.
Study Establishment: An appropriate academic institution or position in the industry.
Country of Study: United Kingdom.
No. of awards offered: Up to 15.
Application Procedure: Applicants must find a suitable industrial or academic partner to host their project before submitting an application. Applications and further information are available from the Research Appointments Department of The Royal Society.
Closing Date: June or December.
Funding: Commercial, Private.
Contributor: The Royal Society, EPSRC, BBSRC, Rolls-Royce and PPARC.
Additional Information: Apart from the Royal Society Fellowships Programme the following fellowship programmes are administered by the PPARC in collaboration with other partners: The European Organisation for Nuclear Research (CERN) Fellowships, The

European Space Agency (ESA) Fellowships, The Anglo-Australian Postdoctoral Research Fellowships, and the Daphne Jackson Fellowships. Further information on these programmes is available on the PPARC website.

For further information contact:

Research Appointments Department
The Royal Society, 6 Carlton House Terrace, London, SW1Y 5AG, England
Tel: (44) 20 7451 2542
Email: ukresearch.appointments@royalsoc.ac.uk
www: http://www.royalsoc.ac.uk/gr_ifs.html

PPARC Senior Research Fellowships

Subjects: Particle physics or astronomy.
Purpose: To enable a small number of outstanding scientists at the peak of their capabilities to devote themselves full-time to research and scholarship, free of the restrictions imposed by their normal employment.
Eligibility: Open to scientists who are already established in their careers, having proved their exceptional research and interpretative ability. Applicants must be members of permanent staff of United Kingdom universities, technical colleges or similar institutions. Fellows are expected to return to their normal employment at the termination of the fellowship.
Level of Study: Postdoctorate.
Type: Fellowship.
Value: The Council will pay the salary, but not superannuation or National Insurance contributions, as if the Fellow is continuing in his or her normal employment at his or her home institution.
Length of Study: Up to three years.
Frequency: Annual.
Study Establishment: Any academic institution in the United Kingdom which is acceptable to PPARC.
Country of Study: United Kingdom.
No. of awards offered: Up to 10.
Application Procedure: Applicants must refer to the PPARC website for application information.
Closing Date: November 1st.
Funding: Government.
Additional Information: Fellowships are not intended to replace sabbatical leave. Further information is available on request or by emailing fellowships@pparc.ac.uk.

PATERSON INSTITUTE FOR CANCER RESEARCH

Christie Hospital NHS Trust, Manchester, M20 4BX, England
Tel: (44) 161 446 3136
Fax: (44) 161 446 3109
Email: gcowling@picr.man.ac.uk
www: http://www.paterson.man.ac.uk
Contact: Dr G J Cowling, Scientific Administrator

The Paterson Institute is a Cancer Research campaign funded centre for cancer research and forms the research arm of a specialist cancer hospital, the Christie Hospital NHS Trust. It carries out cancer research in a large number of areas and has 12 research groups and around 200 scientists.

CRC Studentship

Subjects: Several different projects offered each year which are advertised in December or January to start in the following September.
Purpose: To support the study towards a PhD.
Eligibility: Candidates must have a First or Upper Second Class Bachelor of Science Degree.
Level of Study: Doctorate, Postgraduate.
Type: Studentship.
Value: UK £10,000 per year stipend, university fees and bench fees.
Length of Study: Three years.

Frequency: Annual.
Study Establishment: The University of Manchester.
Country of Study: United Kingdom.
No. of awards offered: Two-six per year.
Application Procedure: Applicants must apply to advertisements in Nature and the New Scientist, or visit the website.
Closing Date: Usually before January 31st.
Contributor: Cancer Research Campaign (UK).
No. of awards given last year: Six.
No. of applicants last year: 100.
Additional Information: All positions are advertised on the website. Self-funded students are accepted subject to qualifications and three year funding.

PAUL LOWIN PRIZES

Perpetual Trustees Australia Limited
39 Hunter Street, Sydney, NSW, 2000, Australia
Tel: (61) 2 9229 3951
Fax: (61) 2 9229 3957
Email: lowinprizes@perpetual.com.au
www: http://www.paullowin.perpetual.com.au
Contact: Charitable Planning Services Administration

The Paul Lowin Prizes are administered by the Perpetual Trustees Australia Limited, which is a public trustee company operating in all mainland states of Australia. It is the sole or co-trustee of 360 charitable trusts and foundations with a value of approximately australian $580 million. Income generated from investment of this capital is distributed annually to charitable organisations to fulfil the intent of the trusts under management.

Paul Lowin Prizes - Orchestral Prize

Subjects: Music composition and orchestral work.
Purpose: To recognise original composition.
Eligibility: The composer must be at least 18 years of age and an Australian citizen or a resident of Australia for not less than three years prior to the closing date.
Level of Study: Unrestricted.
Type: Prize.
Value: Australian $25,000.
Frequency: Every two years.
Country of Study: Any country.
No. of awards offered: One.
Application Procedure: Applicants must refer to the website for details.
Funding: Private.
No. of awards given last year: One.
No. of applicants last year: 10.
Additional Information: Works must be scored for modern chamber or symphony orchestras of at least 30 players and at least 15 independent lines, with a duration of not less than 12 to 15 minutes. The work may include instrumental or vocal soloists and/or choral, electronically produced or pre-recorded elements, but works for string ensemble alone will not be considered.

For further information contact:

c/o Australian Music Centre
Level 4, The Arts Exchange
18 Hickson Road
The Rocks, Sydney, NSW, 2001, Australia

Paul Lowin Prizes - Song Cycle Prize

Subjects: Music composition vocal.
Purpose: To recognise original composition. For the purposes of the competition, a song cycle is music suitable for chamber performance.
Eligibility: The composer must be at least 18 years of age and an Australian citizen or a resident of Australia for not less than three years prior to the closing date.

Level of Study: Unrestricted.
Type: Prize.
Value: Australian $15,000.
Frequency: Every two years.
Country of Study: Any country.
No. of awards offered: One.
Application Procedure: Applicants must refer to the website for details.
Closing Date: June 30th.
Funding: Private.
No. of awards given last year: One.
No. of applicants last year: 10.
Additional Information: Works should use no more than one-eight independent vocal lines, which may be accompanied by up to 10 instrumental players. The text of the work may have a unifying theme, and the composer and the author of the text may or may not be different people, but the author of the text is not eligible for the prize. The work may be no less than 15 minutes and no more than 60 in duration.

For further information contact:

c/o Australian Music Centre
Level 4, The Arts Exchange
18 Hickson Road
The Rocks, Sydney, NSW, 2001, Australia

PAUL MELLON CENTRE FOR STUDIES IN BRITISH ART, LONDON

16 Bedford Square, London, WC1B 3JA, England
Tel: (44) 20 7580 0311
Fax: (44) 20 7636 6730
Email: info@paul-mellon-centre.ac.uk
www: http://www.paul-mellon-centre.ac.uk
Contact: Mr Brian Allen, Director of Studies

The Paul Mellon Centre for Studies in British Art is an art and architectural research institution, based in London but part of Yale University.

Paul Mellon Centre Grants

Subjects: Any aspect of British art or architecture before 1960.
Purpose: To support scholarship in British art or architecture and to disseminate knowledge through publications, exhibitions and educational programmes.
Eligibility: Open to candidates of any nationality.
Level of Study: Graduate, Postdoctorate, Postgraduate, Predoctorate, Professional development, Research.
Type: Grant.
Value: UK £500-20,000 curatorial research, publication, educational and research support grants.
Length of Study: A maximum of one academic year.
Frequency: Annual.
Country of Study: United States of America or United Kingdom.
No. of awards offered: Varies, usually 15-20.
Application Procedure: Applicants must submit their name, address and telephone number, an outline proposal of not more than three pages, a detailed breakdown of estimated costs, the proposed completion and/or publication date where appropriate, a curriculum vitae and three letters of recommendation. These should be sent directly to the Paul Mellon Centre in London.
Closing Date: September 15th.
Funding: Private.
No. of awards given last year: 25.
No. of applicants last year: 80.

THE PAULO FOUNDATION

PL 1105, Helsinki, FIN-00101, Finland
Tel: (358) 4 0528 4876
Fax: (358) 9 2243 2879
Email: cello@paulo.fi
www: http://www.cellocompetitionpaulo.org

The Paulo Foundation organises an international competition for cellists of all nations.

International Paulo Cello Competition

Subjects: Cello performance.
Eligibility: Open to cellists born between 1969 and 1986 inclusive.
Level of Study: Unrestricted.
Type: Competition and prize.
Value: The first prize is €15,000, the second prize is €12,000, the third prize is €9,000 and the fourth, fifth and sixth prizes are €2,000.
Frequency: Approx. every five years.
Country of Study: Finland.
No. of awards offered: Six.
Application Procedure: Applicants must send for a brochure containing details of the application and audition pieces.
Closing Date: May 15th.
Funding: Private.
Contributor: The Paulo Foundation.
Additional Information: Further information is available on request.

PEN AMERICAN CENTER

568 Broadway, New York, NY, 10012, United States of America
Tel: (1) 212 334 1660
Fax: (1) 212 334 2181
Email: victoria@pen.org
www: http://www.pen.org
Contact: Ms Victoria Kupchinetsky

PEN American Center is a fellowship of writers dedicated to defending free expression and advancing the cause of literature and literacy. The American Center is the largest of 130 international PEN Centers worldwide.

PEN Writers Fund

Subjects: Writing and translation.
Purpose: To assist professional published writers facing emergency situations.
Eligibility: Open to published professional writers and produced playwrights who have a traceable record of writing and publication.
Level of Study: Unrestricted.
Type: Emergency grants.
Value: Up to US$1,000.
Frequency: Every three months.
Country of Study: Any country.
Application Procedure: Applicants must submit an application which consists of a two-page form, published writing samples, documentation of financial emergency (bills etc.), and professional curriculum vitae.
Closing Date: Applications are accepted all year round.
Funding: Private.
Additional Information: A separate fund exists for writers and editors with AIDS in need of emergency assistance. The funds are not for research purposes, to enable writers to complete unfinished projects, or to fund writing publications or organisations. Grants and loans are for unexpected emergencies only, and not for the support of working writers. PEN also offers numerous annual awards to recognise distinguished writing, editing and translation.

PENN HUMANITIES FORUM

University of Pennsylvania
3619 Locust Walk, Philadelphia, PA, 19104-6213, United States of America
Tel: (1) 215 898 8220
Fax: (1) 215 746 5946
Email: humanities@sas.upenn.edu
www: http://humanities.sas.upenn.edu
Contact: Ms Wendy Steiner, Director

The Penn Humanities Forum promotes interdisciplinary collaboration across University of Pennsylvania departments and schools and between the University and the Philadelphia region. Each year, a broad topic sets the theme for a research seminar for resident and visiting scholars, courses and public events involving Philadelphia cultural institutions.

Mellon Postdoctoral Fellowships in the Humanities

Subjects: Humanities.
Purpose: To support research for untenured junior scholars.
Eligibility: Open to younger Scholars who, at the time of application, have received the PhD, but have not yet held it for more than eight years nor been granted tenure. Research proposals are invited in all areas of humanistic studies except educational curriculum building and performing arts. Preference is given to proposals that are interdisciplinary and directly related to the annual topic, and to candidates who have not previously utilised the resources of this university and whose work would allow them to take advantage of the research strengths of the institution and to make contribution to its intellectual life. The requirements are residency at the University of Pennsylvania and the teaching of one course per semester.
Level of Study: Postdoctorate.
Type: Fellowship.
Value: US$34,000 plus health insurance.
Length of Study: One academic year and possibly the Summer term before or after, not renewable.
Frequency: Annual.
Study Establishment: The University of Pennsylvania.
Country of Study: United States of America.
No. of awards offered: Five.
Application Procedure: Applicants must complete an application, available for downloading at the Forum's website.
Closing Date: Applications must be postmarked no later than October 15th.
Funding: Private.
No. of awards given last year: Five.
No. of applicants last year: 120.
Additional Information: Fellows may not normally hold other concurrent awards.

PERCY SLADEN MEMORIAL FUND

c/o The Linnean Society
Burlington House
Piccadilly, London, W1V 0LQ, England
Tel: (44) 20 7434 4479
Fax: (44) 20 7287 9364
Email: gina@linnean.demon.co.uk
Contact: Secretary to the Trustees

The Percy Sladen Memorial Fund supports field work in the life and earth sciences.

Percy Sladen Memorial Fund Grants

Subjects: Natural and earth sciences, including botany, zoology, geology, anthropology, archaeology, experimental physiology, pathology and therapeutics.
Purpose: To assist field research or investigations overseas.
Eligibility: There are no eligibility restrictions.

Level of Study: Postdoctorate.
Type: Grant.
Value: UK £100-650.
Length of Study: Varies.
Frequency: Twice a year.
Country of Study: Any country, provided it is not the applicant's native country.
No. of awards offered: 30-40.
Application Procedure: Applicants must complete an application form, available from the Secretary to the Trustees by post or email. This must be submitted with two references.
Closing Date: January 30th or September 30th.
Funding: Private.
Additional Information: Preference is given to individual research projects either as part of an expedition or independently. This must not be essential fieldwork for a higher degree. No coursework of any kind is supported. Trustees usually meet mid-March and mid-November.

PERMANENT

35 Clarence Street, Sydney, NSW, 2001, Australia
Tel: (61) 2 8295 8191
Fax: (61) 2 8295 8659
Email: linda.ingaldo@permanentgroup.com.au
www: http://www.permanentgroup.com.au
Contact: Ms Linda Ingaldo

Permanent is a publicly listed financial services group offering outsourcing solutions to companies and the full suite of financial products to create and manage wealth for individuals. With the mission to be the respected and trusted financial services partner to corporate Australia and wealthy individuals and their families, Permanent has embraced a culture of providing smart advice by people that can be trusted with a commitment to proven delivery along with the benefits of over 110 years of experience. The group has two businesses; a multi faceted private clients unit and a corporate clients unit, tailoring solutions to meet the needs of individuals and companies.

The Kathleen Mitchell Award

Subjects: Literature.
Purpose: To encourage the advancement and betterment of Australian literature.
Eligibility: Entries must be published during the two years previous to the Award, the entrant must be resident in Australia during the year preceding the entry date, and must be under 30 years in the year such entry is published.
Type: Award.
Value: Australian $5,000.
Frequency: Every two years.
No. of awards offered: One.
Application Procedure: Applicants must complete an application form and enter their book or books.
Funding: Private.
Contributor: The estate of the late Kathleen Adele Mitchell.
No. of awards given last year: One.
No. of applicants last year: 14.

Lady Mollie Askin Ballet Travelling Scholarship

Subjects: Dancing or classical ballet.
Purpose: To support the advancement of culture and education in Australia and elsewhere. To reward Australian citizens of outstanding ability and promise in ballet.
Eligibility: Open to Australian citizens who are between the ages of 17 and 30 at the closing date for entries for the award.
Level of Study: Unrestricted.
Type: Scholarship.
Value: Australian $15,000.
Length of Study: More than two years.

Frequency: Every two years.
Country of Study: Any country.
No. of awards offered: One.
Application Procedure: Applicants must complete an application form to be submitted with specified documents and enclosures.
Closing Date: The last Friday in April.
Funding: Private.
Contributor: The estate of Lady Mollie Askin.
No. of awards given last year: One.
No. of applicants last year: 30.

The Marten Bequest Travelling Scholarships

Subjects: Instrumental music, painting, singing, sculpture, architecture, ballet, prose, poetry or acting.
Purpose: To augment a Scholar's own resources towards affording them a cultural education by means of a travelling scholarship.
Eligibility: Applicants must have been born in Australia, and be between the ages of 21 and 35 , or 17 and 35 for ballet.
Level of Study: Unrestricted.
Type: Scholarship.
Value: Australian $18,000 over two years.
Length of Study: Two years.
Frequency: Annual.
Country of Study: Any country.
No. of awards offered: Six.
Application Procedure: Applicants must complete an application form and submit this with a study outline and supporting material as required.
Closing Date: The last Friday in October of the year preceding the award.
Funding: Private.
Contributor: The Estate of the late John Chisholm Marten.
No. of awards given last year: Six.
No. of applicants last year: 200.

Miles Franklin Literary Award

Subjects: Authorship. The prize is directed to be awarded for the novel of the year which is of the highest literary merit and which presents Australian life in any of its phases.
Purpose: To award a novel or play first published in the year preceding the award.
Eligibility: Genres not eligible for the award are farce, musical comedy, biographies, collections of short stories, poetry and children's books.
Level of Study: Unrestricted.
Type: Award.
Value: Australian $28,000.
Frequency: Annual.
Country of Study: Any country.
No. of awards offered: One.
Application Procedure: Applicants must complete an application form and enter their novel.
Closing Date: December 15th in the year preceding the awards.
Funding: Private.
Contributor: The estate of the late Miss S M S Miles Franklin.
No. of awards given last year: One.
No. of applicants last year: 55.
Additional Information: If there is no novel worthy of the prize the award may be given to the author of a play.

Portia Geach Memorial Award

Subjects: Fine and applied arts.
Purpose: To award the best portraits painted from life of some man or woman distinguished in art, letters or the sciences by any female artists.
Eligibility: Entrants must be female Australian residents who are either Australian born or naturalised or British born. Works must be executed entirely in the previous year.
Type: Award.

Value: Australian $18,000. The winning portrait and selected works are exhibited for one month at the S H Ervin Gallery in Sydney, Australia.
Frequency: Annual.
No. of awards offered: One.
Application Procedure: Applicants must complete an application form and submit this with an entry fee and the works.
Closing Date: The last Friday in August for applications.
Funding: Private.
Contributor: The estate of the late Miss Florence Kate Geach.
No. of awards given last year: One.
No. of applicants last year: 315.

Sir Robert Askin Operatic Travelling Scholarship

Subjects: Operatic singing.
Purpose: To support the advancement of culture and education in Australia and elsewhere. To reward male Australian citizens of outstanding ability and promise as an operatic singer.
Eligibility: Applicants must be male Australian citizens and be between the ages of 18 and 30 at the time of application.
Level of Study: Unrestricted.
Type: Scholarship.
Value: Australian $15,000.
Length of Study: Two years.
Frequency: Every two years.
Country of Study: Any country.
No. of awards offered: One.
Application Procedure: Applicants must complete an application form to be submitted with specified documents and enclosures.
Closing Date: The last Friday in September.
Funding: Private.
Contributor: The estate of Sir Robert Askin.
No. of awards given last year: One.
No. of applicants last year: 30.

THE PERRY FOUNDATION

31 Rossendale, Chelmsford, Essex, CM1 2UA, England
Tel: (44) 1245 260805
Fax: (44) 1245 260805
www: http://www.perryfoundation.co.uk
Contact: Mr D J Naylor, Secretary & Chief Executive

The Perry Foundation offers research awards and postgraduate scholarships in agriculture and related disciplines. Research awards are offered to universities and institutes in the United Kingdom and are normally for a three year period. Postgraduate scholarships are offered to holders of First or Second Class Degrees and are for a three year period leading to a PhD. Both research awards and postgraduate scholarships must be undertaken at a university, college or research establishment in the United Kingdom.

Perry Postgraduate Scholarships and Research Awards

Subjects: The production and utilisation of crops for food and non food uses, ecologically acceptable and sustainable farming systems, including in particular, water and nutrient balances, integrated disease and pest control systems for both crops and livestock, socio-economic studies in the occupation and use of land, the rural economy and infrastructure and developments in marketing.
Purpose: To enable postgraduates to undertake research projects and investigative work into agriculture and related fields, and to build and develop a pool of highly competent researchers in the United Kingdom.
Eligibility: Open to holders of First and Upper Second Class Degrees in appropriate subjects, gained in the United Kingdom.
Level of Study: Postgraduate, Research.
Type: Scholarship and research awards.
Value: Currently UK £7,380 stipend, UK £2,740 tuition fees, plus bench fees to a maximum of UK £2,500 per year for postgraduate

scholarships. Research awards are normally UK £15,000 per year maximum.

Length of Study: Normally three years leading to a doctorate or completion of a research award.

Frequency: Annual.

Study Establishment: Universities, colleges, institutes and research establishments in the United Kingdom.

Country of Study: United Kingdom.

No. of awards offered: Three-four depending on the availability of funds.

Application Procedure: Applicants must apply for a brochure and application forms, containing details of procedure, available from the Foundation Secretary. Applications submitted by individuals must be supported by their university, college, institute or other establishment.

Closing Date: November 30th for the postgraduate scholarships and October 31st for the research awards.

Funding: Private.

No. of awards given last year: Four.

No. of applicants last year: 20.

Additional Information: Both the postgraduate scholarships and the research awards must be of definable benefit to United Kingdom agriculture.

PETER WHITTINGHAM AWARD

16 Ogle Street, London, W1W 6JA, England
Tel: (44) 20 7636 4481
Fax: (44) 20 7637 4307
Email: education@mbf.org.uk
www: http://www.mbf.org.uk
Contact: Administrator

Peter Whittingham Award

Subjects: Popular music or jazz. Applications should bear in mind the chosen idiom of such artists as Gershwin, Cole Porter, Jerome Kern, Bernstein, Hamlisch, Sondheim, George Shearing, Art Tatum and Oscar Peterson.

Purpose: To promote both composition and performance in the field of popular music or jazz.

Eligibility: Open to individuals, ordinarily resident in the United Kingdom, of any age group, to work independently or with a project group of any size. The project should be in creation, performance, teaching or research in the field of quality popular music or jazz. Money is not given for course fees.

Level of Study: Postgraduate.

Value: UK £4,000.

Frequency: Annual.

No. of awards offered: One.

Application Procedure: Selected applicants are asked to attend an interview. A written description of the project must be provided together with a budget and a reference.

Closing Date: October.

Funding: Private.

No. of awards given last year: Two.

No. of applicants last year: 44.

PETERHOUSE

Cambridge, Cambridgeshire, CB2 1RD, England
Tel: (44) 1223 338200
Fax: (44) 1223 766147
www: http://www.pet.cam.ac.uk
Contact: Ms Julie Petrucci, College Secretary

Friends of Peterhouse Bursary

Subjects: All subjects except clinical medicine.

Purpose: To fund study for a postgraduate one or two year taught course as a registered graduate student at Peterhouse.

Eligibility: Open to those who are required to pay university fees at the overseas rate. Applicants should be under 25 years of age on December 1st in the year in which they hope to come into residence.

Level of Study: Postgraduate.

Type: Bursary.

Value: University fees only.

Length of Study: One year.

Frequency: Annual.

Study Establishment: Peterhouse only.

Country of Study: United Kingdom.

No. of awards offered: One.

Application Procedure: Applicants must complete an application form and submit this with a curriculum vitae and two references.

Closing Date: April 1st.

Funding: Private.

Contributor: The Friends of Peterhouse.

No. of awards given last year: One.

No. of applicants last year: 21.

Peterhouse Research Fellowship

Subjects: All subjects.

Purpose: To support a young Scholar in postdoctoral research at Peterhouse.

Eligibility: Applicants must hold, or be studying for, a degree from Cambridge or Oxford universities.

Level of Study: Postdoctorate.

Type: Fellowship.

Value: Maintenance and allowances.

Length of Study: Three years.

Frequency: Annual.

Study Establishment: Peterhouse only.

Country of Study: United Kingdom.

No. of awards offered: Two-three.

Application Procedure: Applicants must complete an application form, available on request.

Closing Date: Early February.

Funding: Private.

Contributor: Peterhouse.

No. of awards given last year: Two.

No. of applicants last year: 132.

Peterhouse Research Studentship

Subjects: All subjects.

Purpose: To assist study for a PhD at Peterhouse.

Eligibility: Applicants should be under 25 years of age on December 1st in the year in which they hope to come into residence.

Level of Study: Postgraduate.

Type: Studentship.

Value: Full fees and maintenance subject to deduction of any other emoluments that may be awarded.

Length of Study: Three years.

Frequency: Annual.

Study Establishment: Peterhouse only.

Country of Study: United Kingdom.

No. of awards offered: Two-three.

Application Procedure: Applicants must complete an application form and submit this with a curriculum vitae and two references.

Closing Date: April 1st.

Funding: Private.

Contributor: Peterhouse.

No. of awards given last year: Three.

No. of applicants last year: 23.

Additional Information: Details are also available from the website.

PETSAVERS

Woodrow House, 1 Telford Way
Waterwells Business Park, Quedgeley, Gloucester, Gloucestershire,
GL2 4AB, England
Tel: (44) 1452 726700
Fax: (44) 1452 726701
Email: adminoff@bsava.com
www: http://www.bsava.com
Contact: M J Berriman, Administrator

Petsavers was established in 1970 to promote clinical investigations into the many unsolved diseases of dogs, cats, rabbits and other small animals. In the past 20 years Petsavers has given over UK £1 million towards numerous clinical studies, clinical research studentships and residencies. The running costs are paid for by the British Small Animal Veterinary Association, which allows all monies donated to flow directly into the fund.

Petsavers Award

Subjects: Small animal veterinary medicine and surgery.
Purpose: To advance the science of small animal medicine and surgery.
Eligibility: Open to veterinary surgeons currently working in United Kingdom universities, centres of learning or veterinary practices.
Level of Study: Postgraduate, Professional development.
Type: Award.
Value: Varies.
Length of Study: One-three years.
Frequency: Annual.
Study Establishment: Universities, veterinary schools and veterinary practices.
Country of Study: United Kingdom.
No. of awards offered: Varies.
Application Procedure: Applicants must write for details.
Funding: Private.
Contributor: Donations by practice clients.
No. of awards given last year: Six.
No. of applicants last year: 14.
Additional Information: Projects must involve clinical cases only and no experimental animals.

PHARMACEUTICAL RESEARCH AND MANUFACTURERS OF AMERICA FOUNDATION (PHRMA)

1100 Fifteenth Street North West, Washington, DC, 20005, United
States of America
Tel: (1) 202 835 3470
Fax: (1) 202 467 4823
Email: foundation@phrma.org
www: http://www.phrmafoundation.org
Contact: Ms Eileen M McCarron, Director of Development

The Pharmaceutical Research and Manufacturers of America Foundation (PhRMA) is a non-profit making organisation established in 1965 to promote public health through scientific and medical research. It provides funding for research and for the education and training of scientists and physicians who have selected pharmacology, pharmaceutics, toxicology, informatics or health outcomes as a career choice.

PhRMA Center of Excellence in Clinical Pharmacology

Subjects: Clinical pharmacology.
Purpose: To encourage the further development of, and provide unrestricted financial support for, relatively new clinical pharmacology programmes with potential for significant expansion in faculty and training.

Eligibility: A Center of Excellence may be administratively based in a department of internal medicine or pharmacology, although the former will be given preference. For a programme to be eligible for this award, it must meet either or both of the following criteria. It must be a new programme, with a new director or a division head named within the past two years at the time of the application or it must be a small division, having no more than two full-time faculty members. Preference will be given to programmes meeting the first criteria. Programmes meeting only the second criteria will also be eligible but will need to provide additional justification for entering into a building phase.
Level of Study: Professional development.
Type: Grant.
Value: A total of US$250,000 payable over a one year period in accordance with the submitted budget and in a fashion mutually agreed to by the recipient and the Foundation.
Length of Study: One-two years.
Frequency: Varies.
Country of Study: United States of America.
Application Procedure: Applicants must visit the organisation's website where detailed application requirements are stated and application forms can be downloaded. Applications for this grant are to be submitted by the appropriate representative of the school or university to the Director of Development at PhRMA. Applications should be submitted by the chair of the department in which the division is, or will be, located.
Closing Date: October 1st.
Additional Information: This award is designed to provide substantial flexible support over a relatively brief time frame to permit the programme to become an essential and viable entity within the institution.

PhRMA Fellowships for Careers in Pharmacology or Clinical Pharmacology

Subjects: Clinical pharmacology.
Purpose: To generate interest in, and assist those who are vitally interested in, careers in pharmacology or clinical pharmacology.
Eligibility: Candidates must be enrolled in a United States medical or dental school and have finished at least one year of the school curriculum. Priority consideration will be given to those candidates who project strong commitments to careers in the field of clinical pharmacology. The applicant must be sponsored by the pharmacology or clinical pharmacology programme in which the investigative project is to be undertaken. The sponsoring unit must have a demonstrated commitment to training in the fields of pharmacology or clinical pharmacology. All applicants must be United States citizens or permanent residents.
Level of Study: Postdoctorate.
Type: Fellowship.
Value: Up to US$1,500 per month with a maximum US$18,000 available.
Length of Study: Three months-two years.
Frequency: Annual.
Study Establishment: An appropriate institution.
Country of Study: United States of America.
Application Procedure: Applicants must write for details or visit the website. Before an individual is eligible to apply for a PhRMA Foundation award, the applicant must first have a firm commitment from a university in the United States.
Closing Date: September 15th.
Funding: Private.
No. of awards given last year: Two.
No. of applicants last year: 20.

PhRMA Fellowships in Pharmacology-Morphology

Subjects: Pharmacology-morphology, including cell biology.
Purpose: To advance understanding of drug action through discovery of specifically related cellular and tissue changes and to uncover associations between normal and abnormal function in particular tissue and cellular structures.
Eligibility: Candidates must be sponsored by the school or university at which the research is to be conducted.

Level of Study: Postdoctorate.
Type: Fellowship.
Value: Varies.
Length of Study: Two years.
Frequency: Annual.
Study Establishment: An American school of medicine.
Country of Study: United States of America.
No. of awards offered: Three.
Application Procedure: Applicants must write for details or visit the website.
Closing Date: January 15th.
Funding: Private.
No. of awards given last year: Three.
No. of applicants last year: 35.

PhRMA Medical Student Fellowships in Pharmacology/Toxicology

Subjects: Pharmacology or toxicology.
Purpose: To support medical, dental or veterinary students who have substantial interests in research and teaching careers in pharmacology or clinical pharmacology and who are willing to work full-time in a specific research effort.
Eligibility: Before an individual is eligible to apply for a PhRMA Foundation award, the applicants must first have a firm commitment from a university in the United States. All applicants must be citizens of the United States of America or permanent residents.
Level of Study: Graduate, Postgraduate.
Type: Fellowship.
Value: Varies.
Length of Study: Varies.
Frequency: Annual.
Country of Study: United States of America.
Application Procedure: Applications are to be submitted by the appropriate representative of the school or university to the Director of Development at PhRMA. Detailed application requirements are stated on the Foundation's website where the applicant can download an application form and read the specific requirements for each award.
Additional Information: Research projects involving animal subjects require a statement that the project will follow the guidelines set forth by the NIH Guide for the Care and Use of Laboratory Animals and that the project will be performed, reviewed and approved by a faculty committee of the university. The recipient school is expected to submit an annual report on the disposition of the funds awarded by PhRMA. A progress report is to be submitted by the recipient within 30 days after the conclusion of each year of the fellowship. A final report is due within 60 days after the conclusion of the grant. These reports must be signed by the recipient's sponsor. Any publications, speeches, presentations, and all other materials that stem directly from the research supported by this grant must acknowledge the support of the PhRMA Foundation. Three reprints of each publication should be forwarded to the PhRMA Foundation.

PhRMA Medical Student Research Fellowships

Subjects: Clinical pharmacology.
Purpose: To generate interest in research careers among medical students.
Eligibility: Candidates must be sponsored by the school or university at which the research is to be conducted.
Type: Fellowship.
Value: US$18,000.
Length of Study: 3-24 months.
Frequency: Annual.
Study Establishment: A school of medicine or dentistry in the United States of America.
Country of Study: United States of America.
No. of awards offered: Four.
Application Procedure: Applicants must write for details or visit the Foundation's website.
Closing Date: September 15th.

PhRMA Postdoctoral Fellowships in Health Outcomes Research

Subjects: Health outcomes research, patient reported outcomes or pharmacoeconomics.
Purpose: To support well trained graduates from PharmD, MD and PhD programmes who seek to further develop and refine their research skills through formal postdoctoral training.
Eligibility: Before an individual is eligible to apply for a PhRMA Foundation award, the applicants must first have a firm commitment from a university in the United States. Applicants must be full-time students and the department's chair is expected to verify the applicant's doctoral candidacy. All applicants must be citizens of the United States of America or permanent residents.
Level of Study: Graduate, Postgraduate.
Type: Fellowship.
Value: Stipend funding.
Frequency: Annual.
Country of Study: United States of America.
Application Procedure: Applications must include a research plan written by the applicant, the mentor's research record and a description of how the mentored experience will enhance the applicant's career development in health outcomes research. Applications are to be submitted by the appropriate representative of the school or university to the Director of Development at PhRMA. Detailed application requirements are stated on the Foundation's website where applicant can download an application form and read the specific requirements for each award.
Closing Date: October 1st.
Additional Information: Research projects involving animal subjects require a statement that the project will follow the guidelines set forth by the NIH Guide for the Care and Use of Laboratory Animals and that the project will be performed, reviewed and approved by a faculty committee of the university. The recipient school is expected to submit an annual report on the disposition of the funds awarded by PhRMA. A progress report is to be submitted by the recipient within 30 days after the conclusion of each year of the fellowship. A final report is due within 60 days after the conclusion of the grant. These reports must be signed by the recipient's sponsor. Any publications, speeches, presentations, and all other materials that stem directly from the research supported by this grant must acknowledge the support of the PhRMA Foundation. Three reprints of each publication should be forwarded to the PhRMA Foundation.

PhRMA Postdoctoral Fellowships in Informatics

Subjects: Informatics.
Purpose: To support well-trained graduates from PhD programmes who seek to further develop and refine their informatics research skills through formal postdoctoral training.
Eligibility: Before an individual is eligible to apply for a PhRMA Foundation award, the applicants must first have a firm commitment from a university in the United States. Applicants must be full-time students and the department's chair is expected to verify the applicant's doctoral candidacy. All applicants must be citizens of the United States of America or permanent residents.
Level of Study: Predoctorate.
Type: Fellowship.
Value: Varies.
Length of Study: Varies.
Frequency: Annual.
Country of Study: United States of America.
Application Procedure: Applicants must submit an application including a research plan written by the applicant, the mentor's research record and a description of how the mentored experience will enhance the applicant's career development in informatics. Applications are to be submitted by the appropriate representative of the school or university to the Director of Development at PhRMA. Detailed application requirements are stated on the Foundation's website where the applicant can download an application form and read the specific requirements for each award.
Closing Date: October 1st.
Additional Information: Research projects involving animal subjects require a statement that the project will follow the guidelines set

forth by the NIH Guide for the Care and Use of Laboratory Animals and that the project will be performed, reviewed and approved by a faculty committee of the university. The recipient school is expected to submit an annual report on the disposition of the funds awarded by PhRMA. A progress report is to be submitted by the recipient within 30 days after the conclusion of each year of the fellowship. A final report is due within 60 days after the conclusion of the grant. These reports must be signed by the recipient's sponsor. Any publications, speeches, presentations, and all other materials that stem directly from the research supported by this grant must acknowledge the support of the PhRMA Foundation. Three reprints of each publication should be forwarded to the PhRMA Foundation.

PhRMA Postdoctoral Fellowships in Pharmaceutics

Subjects: Pharmaceutics.
Purpose: To encourage graduates to continue to develop and refine their pharmaceutics research skills through formal postdoctoral training.
Eligibility: Open to graduates from PhD programmes in pharmaceutics. Before an individual is eligible to apply for a PhRMA Foundation award, the applicants must first have a firm commitment from a university in the United States. Applicants must be full-time students and the department's chair is expected to verify the applicant's doctoral candidacy. All applicants must be citizens of the United States of America or permanent residents.
Level of Study: Postdoctorate.
Type: Fellowship.
Value: Stipend funding.
Length of Study: One year.
Frequency: Annual.
Study Establishment: Schools of pharmacy and public health in the United States.
Country of Study: United States of America.
No. of awards offered: Varies.
Application Procedure: Applicants must visit the organisation's website where detailed application requirements are stated and application forms can be downloaded. Applications must include a research plan written by the applicant, the mentor's research record and a description of how the mentored experience will enhance the applicant's career development in pharmaceutics.
Closing Date: October 1st.
Funding: Private.
Additional Information: Research projects involving animal subjects require a statement that the project will follow the guidelines set forth by the NIH Guide for the Care and Use of Laboratory Animals and that the project will be performed, reviewed and approved by a faculty committee of the university. The recipient school is expected to submit an annual report on the disposition of the funds awarded by PhRMA. A progress report is to be submitted by the recipient within 30 days after the conclusion of each year of the fellowship. A final report is due within 60 days after the conclusion of the grant. These reports must be signed by the recipient's sponsor. Any publications, speeches, presentations, and all other materials that stem directly from the research supported by this grant must acknowledge the support of the PhRMA Foundation. Three reprints of each publication should be forwarded to the PhRMA Foundation.

PhRMA Postdoctoral Fellowships in Pharmacology/Toxicology

Subjects: Pharmacology or toxicology.
Purpose: To facilitate career entry into pharmacology or toxicology at the level of postdoctoral training and to provide funding for recent graduates from PhD programmes who seek to develop research skills through formal postdoctoral training.
Eligibility: Before an individual is eligible to apply for a PhRMA Foundation award, the applicants must first have a firm commitment from a university in the United States. Applications must be submitted by an accredited United States school. All applicants must be citizens of the United States of America or permanent residents.
Level of Study: Postdoctorate.
Type: Fellowship.
Value: Stipend funding.

Frequency: Annual.
Study Establishment: An accredited school in the United States of America.
Country of Study: United States of America.
Application Procedure: Applicants must visit the organisation's website where detailed application requirements are stated and application forms can be downloaded. Applications must be submitted by the appropriate representative of the school or university to the Director of Development at PhRMA. An application must include a research plan written by the applicant, a mentor's research record, and a description of how the mentored experience will enhance the applicant's career development on pharmacology or toxicology.
Closing Date: September 15th.
Additional Information: Research projects involving animal subjects require a statement that the project will follow the guidelines set forth by the NIH Guide for the Care and Use of Laboratory Animals and that the project will be performed, reviewed and approved by a faculty committee of the university. The recipient school is expected to submit an annual report on the disposition of the funds awarded by PhRMA. A final report is due within 60 days after the conclusion of the grant. These reports must be signed by the recipient's sponsor. Any publications, speeches, presentations, and all other materials that stem directly from the research supported by this grant must acknowledge the support of the PhRMA Foundation. Three reprints of each publication should be forwarded to the PhRMA Foundation.

PhRMA Predoctoral Fellowships in Health Outcomes Research

Subjects: Health outcomes research, patient reported outcomes or pharmacoeconomics.
Purpose: To support a student's PhD doctoral programme after coursework has been completed and the remaining training activity is the student's research project.
Eligibility: Before an individual is eligible to apply for a PhRMA Foundation award, the applicants must first have a firm commitment from a university in the United States. Applicants must be full-time students and the department's chair is expected to verify the applicant's doctoral candidacy. All applicants must be citizens of the United States of America or permanent residents.
Level of Study: Postgraduate.
Type: Fellowship.
Value: Stipend funding.
Length of Study: Two years.
Frequency: Annual.
Country of Study: United States of America.
Application Procedure: Applications are to be submitted by the appropriate representative of the school or university to the Director of Development at PhRMA. Detailed application requirements are stated on the Foundation's website where the applicant can download an application form and read the specific requirements for each award.
Closing Date: October 1st.
Additional Information: Research projects involving animal subjects require a statement that the project will follow the guidelines set forth by the NIH Guide for the Care and Use of Laboratory Animals and that the project will be performed, reviewed and approved by a faculty committee of the university. The recipient school is expected to submit an annual report on the disposition of the funds awarded by PhRMA. A progress report is to be submitted by the recipient within 30 days after the conclusion of each year of the fellowship. A final report is due within 60 days after the conclusion of the grant. These reports must be signed by the recipient's sponsor. Any publications, speeches, presentations, and all other materials that stem directly from the research supported by this grant must acknowledge the support of the PhRMA Foundation. Three reprints of each publication should be forwarded to the PhRMA Foundation.

PhRMA Predoctoral Fellowships in Pharmaceutics

Subjects: Pharmaceutics.
Purpose: To support promising students during their thesis research.
Eligibility: Before an individual is eligible to apply for a PhRMA Foundation award, the applicants must first have a firm commitment

from a university in the United States. Applicants must be full-time students and the department's chair is expected to verify the applicant's doctoral candidacy. All applicants must be citizens of the United States of America or permanent residents.

Level of Study: Postgraduate.

Type: Fellowship.

Value: Stipend funding.

Length of Study: Two years.

Frequency: Annual.

Study Establishment: An American school of pharmacy.

Country of Study: United States of America.

Application Procedure: Applicants must visit the organisation's website where detailed application requirements are stated and application forms can be downloaded. Applications must be submitted by the appropriate representative of the school or university to the Director of Development at PhRMA.

Closing Date: October 1st.

Funding: Private.

Additional Information: Research projects involving animal subjects require a statement that the project will follow the guidelines set forth by the NIH Guide for the Care and Use of Laboratory Animals and that the project will be performed, reviewed and approved by a faculty committee of the university. The recipient school is expected to submit an annual report on the disposition of the funds awarded by PhRMA. A progress report is to be submitted by the recipient within 30 days after the conclusion of each year of the fellowship. A final report is due within 60 days after the conclusion of the grant. These reports must be signed by the recipient's sponsor. Any publications, speeches, presentations, and all other materials that stem directly from the research supported by this grant must acknowledge the support of the PhRMA Foundation. Three reprints of each publication should be forwarded to the PhRMA Foundation.

PhRMA Predoctoral Fellowships in Pharmacology/Toxicology

Subjects: Pharmacology or toxicology.

Purpose: To support promising students during their thesis research.

Eligibility: This fellowship seeks to support advanced students who will have completed the bulk of their pre-thesis requirements and are starting their thesis research by the time the award is activated. Students just starting in graduate school should not apply. Before an individual is eligible to apply for a PhRMA Foundation award, the applicant must have a firm commitment form a university in the United States of America. The applicant must be a United States citizen.

Level of Study: Predoctorate.

Type: Fellowship.

Value: A stipend of US$20,000 per year plus US$500 for expenses associated with thesis research.

Length of Study: One or two years.

Frequency: Annual.

Country of Study: United States of America.

Application Procedure: Applicants must visit the organisation's website where detailed application requirements are stated and application forms can be downloaded.

Closing Date: September 15th.

Additional Information: Research projects involving animal subjects require a statement that the project will follow the guidelines set forth by the NIH Guide for the Care and Use of Laboratory Animals and that the project will be performed, reviewed and approved by a faculty committee of the university. The recipient school is expected to submit an annual report on the disposition of the funds awarded by PhRMA. A progress report is to be submitted by the recipient within 30 days after the conclusion of each year of the fellowship. A final report is due within 60 days after the conclusion of the grant. These reports must be signed by the recipient's sponsor. Any publications, speeches, presentations, and all other materials that stem directly from the research supported by this grant must acknowledge the support of the PhRMA Foundation. Three reprints of each publication should be forwarded to the PhRMA Foundation.

PhRMA Research Starter Grants in Health Outcomes Research

Subjects: Health outcomes research, patient reported outcomes or pharmacoeconomics.

Purpose: To support individuals beginning independent research careers in academia.

Eligibility: Applicants must be sponsored by the school or university at which the research is to be conducted. Applicants must be appointed to an entry level tenure track or equivalent permanent position in a department or unit responsible for pharmaceutical activities as part of its core mission.

Level of Study: Graduate, Postgraduate.

Type: Grant.

Value: Varies.

Length of Study: Varies.

Frequency: Annual.

Country of Study: United States of America.

Application Procedure: Applicants must visit the organisation's website where detailed application requirements are stated and application forms can be downloaded. Applications must be submitted by the appropriate representative of the school or university to the Director of Development at PhRMA. The description of an applicant's career goals and the departmental chair's description of institutional support for the applicant's salary are all important when evaluating an application.

Closing Date: October 1st.

Additional Information: Research projects involving animal subjects require a statement that the project will follow the guidelines set forth by the NIH Guide for the Care and Use of Laboratory Animals and that the project will be performed, reviewed and approved by a faculty committee of the university. The recipient school is expected to submit an annual report on the disposition of the funds awarded by PhRMA. A final report is due within 60 days after the conclusion of the grant. These reports must be signed by the recipient's sponsor. Any publications, speeches, presentations, and all other materials that stem directly from the research supported by this grant must acknowledge the support of the PhRMA Foundation. Three reprints of each publication should be forwarded to the PhRMA Foundation.

PhRMA Research Starter Grants in Informatics

Subjects: Informatics.

Purpose: To offer support to new investigators beginning their independent research careers in academia.

Eligibility: Applicants must be sponsored by the school or university at which the research is to be conducted. Applicants must be appointed to an entry level tenure track or equivalent permanent position in a department or unit responsible for informatics activities as part of its core mission.

Level of Study: Graduate, Postgraduate.

Type: Grant.

Value: Varies.

Length of Study: Varies.

Frequency: Annual.

Country of Study: United States of America.

Application Procedure: Applicants must visit the organisation's website where detailed application requirements are stated and application forms can be downloaded. Applications must be submitted by the appropriate representative of the school or university to the Director of Development at PhRMA. The description of an applicant's career goals and the departmental chair's description of institutional support for the applicant's salary are all important when evaluating an application.

Closing Date: October 1st.

Additional Information: Research projects involving animal subjects require a statement that the project will follow the guidelines set forth by the NIH Guide for the Care and Use of Laboratory Animals and that the project will be performed, reviewed and approved by a faculty committee of the university. The recipient school is expected to submit an annual report on the disposition of the funds awarded by PhRMA. A final report is due within 60 days after the conclusion of the grant. These reports must be signed by the recipient's sponsor. Any publications, speeches, presentations, and all other materials that stem directly from the research supported by this grant must acknowledge the support of the PhRMA Foundation. Three reprints of each publication should be forwarded to the PhRMA Foundation.

PhRMA Research Starter Grants in Pharmaceutics

Subjects: Pharmaceutics.
Purpose: To offer support to new investigators beginning their independent research careers in academia.
Eligibility: Applicants must be sponsored by the school or university at which the research is to be conducted. Applicants must be appointed to an entry level tenure track or equivalent permanent position in a department or unit responsible for pharmaceutics activities as part of its core mission.
Level of Study: Professional development.
Type: Grant.
Length of Study: One year.
Frequency: Annual.
Study Establishment: United States schools of medicine, pharmacy and public health in the United States.
Country of Study: United States of America.
Application Procedure: Applicants must visit the organisation's website where detailed application requirements are stated and application forms can be downloaded. Applications must be submitted by the appropriate representative of the school or university to the Director of Development at PhRMA. The description of an applicant's career goals and the departmental chair's description of institutional support for the applicant's salary are all important when evaluating an application.
Closing Date: September 1st.
Funding: Private.
Additional Information: Research projects involving animal subjects require a statement that the project will follow the guidelines set forth by the NIH Guide for the Care and Use of Laboratory Animals and that the project will be performed, reviewed and approved by a faculty committee of the university. The recipient school is expected to submit an annual report on the disposition of the funds awarded by PhRMA. A final report is due within 60 days after the conclusion of the grant. These reports must be signed by the recipient's sponsor. Any publications, speeches, presentations, and all other materials that stem directly from the research supported by this grant must acknowledge the support of the PhRMA Foundation. Three reprints of each publication should be forwarded to the PhRMA Foundation.

PhRMA Research Starter Grants in Pharmacology/Toxicology

Subjects: Pharmacology or toxicology.
Purpose: To support individuals beginning independent research careers in academia.
Eligibility: Applicants must be sponsored by the school or university at which the research is to be conducted. Applicants must be appointed to an entry level tenure track or equivalent permanent position in a department or unit responsible for pharmacology or toxicology activities as part of its core mission.
Level of Study: Graduate, Postgraduate.
Type: Grant.
Value: Varies.
Length of Study: Varies.
Frequency: Annual.
Country of Study: United States of America.
Application Procedure: Applicants must visit the organisation's website where detailed application requirements are stated and application forms can be downloaded. Applications must be submitted by the appropriate representative of the school or university to the Director of Development at PhRMA. The description of an applicant's career goals and the departmental chair's description of institutional support for the applicant's salary are all important when evaluating an application.
Closing Date: September 15th.
Additional Information: Research projects involving animal subjects require a statement that the project will follow the guidelines set forth by the NIH Guide for the Care and Use of Laboratory Animals

and that the project will be performed, reviewed and approved by a faculty committee of the university. The recipient school is expected to submit an annual report on the disposition of the funds awarded by PhRMA. A final report is due within 60 days after the conclusion of the grant. These reports must be signed by the recipient's sponsor. Any publications, speeches, presentations, and all other materials that stem directly from the research supported by this grant must acknowledge the support of the PhRMA Foundation. Three reprints of each publication should be forwarded to the PhRMA Foundation.

PhRMA Sabbatical Fellowships in Health Outcomes Research

Subjects: Health outcomes research, patient reported outcomes or pharmacoeconomics.
Purpose: To support faculty members at all levels with active research programmes and the opportunity to work at other institutions to learn new skills or develop new collaborations that will enhance their research and research training activities in health outcomes.
Eligibility: Applicants are expected to have approval for a sabbatical leave from their home institution and provide an endorsement from the mentor who will sponsor their visiting scientific activity. Matching funds must be provided through the university. All applicants must be citizens of the United States of America or permanent residents.
Level of Study: Graduate, Postdoctorate, Postgraduate, Predoctorate.
Type: Fellowship.
Value: Stipend funding.
Length of Study: Six months-one year.
Frequency: Annual.
Country of Study: United States of America.
Application Procedure: Applications are to submitted by the appropriate representative of the school or university to the Director of Development at PhRMA. Detailed application requirements are stated on the Foundation's website where applicant can download an application form and read the specific requirements for each award.
Closing Date: October 1st.
Additional Information: Research projects involving animal subjects require a statement that the project will follow the guidelines set forth by the NIH Guide for the Care and Use of Laboratory Animals and that the project will be performed, reviewed and approved by a faculty committee of the university. The recipient school is expected to submit an annual report on the disposition of the funds awarded by PhRMA. A progress report is to be submitted by the recipient within 30 days after the conclusion of each year of the fellowship. A final report is due within 60 days after the conclusion of the grant. These reports must be signed by the recipient's sponsor. Any publications, speeches, presentations, and all other materials that stem directly from the research supported by this grant must acknowledge the support of the PhRMA Foundation. Three reprints of each publication should be forwarded to the PhRMA Foundation.

PhRMA Sabbatical Fellowships in Informatics

Subjects: Informatics.
Purpose: To give pharmaceutics faculty members at all levels with active research programmes an opportunity to work at other institutions and to develop new collaborations that will enhance their research and research training activities in informatics.
Eligibility: Applicants are expected to have approval for a sabbatical leave from their home institution and provide an endorsement from the mentor who will sponsor their visiting scientific activity. Matching funds must be provided through the university. All applicants must be citizens of the United States of America or permanent residents.
Level of Study: Professional development.
Type: Fellowship.
Value: Varies.
Length of Study: Six months-one year.
Frequency: Annual.
Country of Study: United States of America.
Application Procedure: Applications are to submitted by the appropriate representative of the school or university to the Director of Development at PhRMA. Detailed application requirements are stated

on the Foundation's website where the applicant can download an application form and read the specific requirements for each award.

Closing Date: October 1st.

Additional Information: Research projects involving animal subjects require a statement that the project will follow the guidelines set forth by the NIH Guide for the Care and Use of Laboratory Animals and that the project will be performed, reviewed and approved by a faculty committee of the university. The recipient school is expected to submit an annual report on the disposition of the funds awarded by PhRMA. A progress report is to be submitted by the recipient within 30 days after the conclusion of each year of the fellowship. A final report is due within 60 days after the conclusion of the grant. These reports must be signed by the recipient's sponsor. Any publications, speeches, presentations, and all other materials that stem directly from the research supported by this grant must acknowledge the support of the PhRMA Foundation. Three reprints of each publication should be forwarded to the PhRMA Foundation.

PhRMA Sabbatical Fellowships in Pharmaceutics

Subjects: Pharmaceutics.

Purpose: To enable pharmaceutics faculty members at all levels with active research programmes an opportunity to work at other institutions and to develop new collaborations that will enhance their research and research training activities in pharmaceutics.

Eligibility: Applicants are expected to have approval for a sabbatical leave from their home institution and provide an endorsement from the mentor who will sponsor their sabbatical activity. Matching funds must be provided through the university. All applicants must be citizens of the United States of America or permanent residents.

Type: Fellowship.

Value: Stipend funding.

Length of Study: Six months to one year.

Frequency: Annual.

Study Establishment: An approved institute.

Country of Study: United States of America.

No. of awards offered: Varies.

Application Procedure: Applicants must visit the organisation's website where detailed application requirements are stated and application forms can be downloaded.

Additional Information: Research projects involving animal subjects require a statement that the project will follow the guidelines set forth by the NIH Guide for the Care and Use of Laboratory Animals and that the project will be performed, reviewed and approved by a faculty committee of the university. The recipient school is expected to submit an annual report on the disposition of the funds awarded by PhRMA. A progress report is to be submitted by the recipient within 30 days after the conclusion of each year of the fellowship. A final report is due within 60 days after the conclusion of the grant. These reports must be signed by the recipient's sponsor. Any publications, speeches, presentations, and all other materials that stem directly from the research supported by this grant must acknowledge the support of the PhRMA Foundation. Three reprints of each publication should be forwarded to the PhRMA Foundation.

PhRMA Sabbatical Fellowships in Pharmacology/Toxicology

Subjects: Pharmacology or toxicology.

Purpose: To give faculty members at all levels with active research programmes an opportunity to work at other institutions to learn new skills or develop new collaborations that will enhance their research and research training activities in pharmacology or toxicology.

Eligibility: Applicants are expected to have approval for a sabbatical leave from their home institution and provide an endorsement from the mentor who will sponsor their visiting scientific activity. Matching funds must be provided through the university. All applicants must be citizens of the United States of America or permanent residents.

Level of Study: Professional development.

Type: Fellowship.

Value: Stipend funding.

Length of Study: Six months-one year.

Frequency: Annual.

Country of Study: United States of America.

Application Procedure: Applicants must visit the organisation's website where detailed application requirements are stated and application forms can be downloaded. Applications must be submitted by the appropriate representative of the school or university to the Director of Development at PhRMA.

Additional Information: Research projects involving animal subjects require a statement that the project will follow the guidelines set forth by the NIH Guide for the Care and Use of Laboratory Animals and that the project will be performed, reviewed and approved by a faculty committee of the university. The recipient school is expected to submit an annual report on the disposition of the funds awarded by PhRMA. A final report is due within 60 days after the conclusion of the grant. These reports must be signed by the recipient's sponsor. Any publications, speeches, presentations, and all other materials that stem directly from the research supported by this grant must acknowledge the support of the PhRMA Foundation. Three reprints of each publication should be forwarded to the PhRMA Foundation.

THE PHI BETA KAPPA SOCIETY

1785 Massachusetts Avenue NW
Fourth Floor, Washington, DC, 20036, United States of America
Tel: (1) 202 265 3808
Fax: (1) 202 986 1601
Email: ccurtis@pbk.org
www: http://www.pbk.org
Contact: Ms Cameron Curtis, Program Officer

The Phi Beta Kappa Society has pursued its mission of fostering and recognising excellence in the liberal arts and sciences since 1776.

Mary Isabel Sibley Fellowship

Subjects: French language or literature in even years. Greek language, literature, history or archaeology in odd years.

Purpose: To recognise female scholars who have demonstrated their ability to carry out original research.

Eligibility: Open to unmarried women aged 25 to 35 (inclusive) who have demonstrated their ability to carry out original research. Candidates must hold the doctorate or have fulfilled all the requirements for the doctorate except the dissertation. There are no restrictions as to nationality and the award is not restricted to members of Phi Beta Kappa.

Level of Study: Doctorate, Postdoctorate, Postgraduate.

Type: Fellowship.

Value: US$20,000.

Length of Study: One year, non renewable.

Frequency: Annual.

Country of Study: Any country.

No. of awards offered: One.

Application Procedure: Applicants must complete an application form, available from Phi Beta Kappa, and submit this with transcripts and references.

Closing Date: January 15th.

Funding: Private.

No. of awards given last year: One.

No. of applicants last year: 50.

PHILHARMONIA ORCHESTRA / MARTIN MUSICAL SCHOLARSHIP FUND

'Beeches'
Well Hill, Chelsfield, Kent, BR6 7PR, England
Tel: (44) 20 8658 9432
Fax: (44) 20 8658 9432
www: http://www.philharmonia.co.uk
Contact: Mr Martyn Jones, Administrator

The Emanual Hurwitz Award for Violinists of British Nationality

Subjects: Musical performance on violin only.
Purpose: To reward exceptional musical talent.
Eligibility: Open to British nationals only.
Level of Study: Postgraduate.
Type: Award.
Value: Varies.
Frequency: Annual.
Country of Study: Any country.
No. of awards offered: Varies.
Application Procedure: Applicants must write for details.
Closing Date: Please contact the organisation.
Additional Information: Further information is available on request.

Gillian Sinclair Music Trust

Subjects: Musical performance, all instruments.
Purpose: To reward exceptional musical talent.
Eligibility: Applicants must write for details.
Level of Study: Postgraduate.
Type: Award.
Value: Two recitals and two UK £500 awards.
Frequency: Twice a year.
Country of Study: Any country.
No. of awards offered: Varies.
Application Procedure: Applicants must complete an application form and submit this with a stamped addressed envelope and a non refundable registration fee of UK £10.
Closing Date: December 1st.
Additional Information: Further information is available on request.

John E Mortimer Foundation Awards

Subjects: Musical performance, all instruments.
Purpose: To reward exceptional musical talent.
Eligibility: Applicants must write for details.
Level of Study: Postgraduate.
Type: Award.
Value: Prizes are of varying value.
Frequency: Annual.
Country of Study: Any country.
No. of awards offered: Varies.
Application Procedure: Applicants must complete an application form and submit this with a stamped addressed envelope and a non returnable registration fee of UK £10.
Closing Date: December 1st.
Additional Information: Further details are available on request.

The June Allison Award

Subjects: Musical performance on woodwind only.
Purpose: To assist exceptional musical talent with specialist and advanced study, and to help bridge the gap between study and fully professional status.
Eligibility: Applicants must write for details.
Level of Study: Postgraduate.
Type: Award.
Value: UK £500 plus recital.
Frequency: Annual.
Country of Study: Any country.
Application Procedure: Applicants must complete an application form and submit this with a stamped addressed envelope and a non returnable registration fee of UK £10.
Closing Date: December 1st.
Additional Information: Further details are available on request.

KPMG Scholarship

Subjects: Musical performance.
Purpose: To assist with tuition fees and maintenance whilst studying.
Eligibility: Open to nationals of any country.
Level of Study: Unrestricted.
Type: Scholarship.

Value: UK £2,000.
Frequency: Annual.
Country of Study: Any country.
No. of awards offered: One.
Application Procedure: Applicants must complete an application form.
Closing Date: October 1st.
No. of awards given last year: One.
No. of applicants last year: 71.
Additional Information: Further details are available on request.

The LDF Casbolt Memorial Award

Subjects: Musical performance on violin only.
Purpose: To reward exceptional musical ability.
Eligibility: Applicants must write for details.
Level of Study: Postgraduate.
Type: Award.
Value: UK £500.
Frequency: Annual.
Country of Study: Any country.
Application Procedure: Applicants must complete an application form and submit this with a stamped addressed envelope and a non returnable registration fee of UK £10.
Closing Date: Please contact the organisation.
Additional Information: Further information is available on request.

Martin Musical Scholarships

Subjects: Musical performance.
Purpose: To assist exceptional musical talent with specialist and advanced study and to help in bridging the gap between study and fully professional status.
Eligibility: Open to practising musicians as well as students who are instrumental performers (including pianists) preparing for a career on the concert platform either as a soloist or orchestral player, and of no more than 25 years of age. Preference is given to United Kingdom citizens.
Level of Study: Postgraduate.
Type: Scholarship.
Value: Varies.
Length of Study: Two years, with a possibility of renewal.
Frequency: Annual.
Country of Study: United Kingdom, Europe or United States of America.
No. of awards offered: Varies.
Application Procedure: Applicants must complete an application form.
Closing Date: October 1st.
Funding: Private.
No. of awards given last year: 50.
No. of applicants last year: 71.
Additional Information: It is not the present policy of the Fund to support organists, singers, conductors, composers, academic students or piano accompanists. Further information is available on request.

The Reginald Conway Memorial Award for String Performers

Subjects: Musical performance on strings only.
Purpose: To reward exceptional musical talent.
Eligibility: Applicants must write for details.
Level of Study: Postgraduate.
Type: Award.
Value: Varies.
Frequency: Annual.
Country of Study: Any country.
Application Procedure: Applicants must write for details.
Closing Date: Please contact the organisation.
Additional Information: Further information is available on request.

Sidney Perry Scholarship

Subjects: Musical performance.

Purpose: To support postgraduate study.
Eligibility: Open to nationals of any country.
Level of Study: Postgraduate.
Type: Scholarship.
Value: Varies.
Length of Study: Up to two years.
Frequency: Annual.
Country of Study: Any country.
No. of awards offered: Varies.
Application Procedure: Applicants must complete an application form.
Closing Date: October 1st.
No. of awards given last year: Three.
Additional Information: Further information is available on request.

TotalFinaElf Ensemble Award

Subjects: Musical performance.
Purpose: To reward exceptional musical talent.
Eligibility: Open to any ensemble of three to eight performers. Applicants must be 25 years old or younger. Applicants must write for details.
Level of Study: Postgraduate.
Type: Award.
Value: Varies.
Length of Study: Varies.
Frequency: Annual.
Country of Study: United Kingdom.
Application Procedure: Applicants must write for details.
Closing Date: Please contact the organisation.
Additional Information: Further information is available on request.

TotalFinaElf in Association with Arts & Business New Partners, Outreach and Access Ensemble Award

Subjects: Musical performance.
Purpose: To reward exceptional musical talent.
Eligibility: Open to ensembles of three to eight people who are specialising in educational work. Applicants must be 25 years old or younger.
Level of Study: Postgraduate.
Type: Award.
Value: Varies.
Frequency: Annual.
Country of Study: United Kingdom.
Application Procedure: Applicants must write for details.
Closing Date: Please contact the organisation.
Additional Information: Further information is available on request.

TotalFinaElf Recital Series

Subjects: Musical performance.
Purpose: To reward exceptional musical talent.
Eligibility: Applicants must be 25 years old or younger.
Level of Study: Postgraduate.
Value: A recital series at the Royal Festival Hall.
Frequency: Annual.
Country of Study: United Kingdom.
Application Procedure: Applicants must write for details.
Closing Date: Please contact the organisation.
Additional Information: Further information is available on request.

Trevor Snoad Memorial Trust

Subjects: Music performance on the viola.
Purpose: To reward exceptional musical talent.
Eligibility: Open to outstanding viola players. There is no limit to the number of times an unsuccessful candidate may apply. Each candidate is eligible to apply for two awards.
Level of Study: Postgraduate.
Type: Award.
Value: UK £500.
Frequency: Annual.
Country of Study: Any country.
No. of awards offered: One.

Application Procedure: Applicants must complete an application form.
Closing Date: October 1st.
No. of awards given last year: One.
No. of applicants last year: Three.
Additional Information: An award is valid for two years and must be taken up within that time. Selection of candidates is by audition. Preliminary auditions are held in the Autumn with final auditions in the Spring. Further information is available on request.

PHILLIPS EXETER ACADEMY

20 Main Street, Exeter, NH, 03833-2460, United States of America
Tel: (1) 603 777 3405
Fax: (1) 603 777 4393
Email: beggers@exeter.edu
www: http://www.exeter.edu
Contact: Ms Barbara Eggers, Dean of Faculty

Philips Exeter Academy is a private secondary school with over 1,000 students.

George Bennett Fellowship

Subjects: Creative writing.
Purpose: To allow a person commencing a career as a writer the time and freedom from material considerations to complete a manuscript in progress.
Eligibility: Preference is given to writers who have not published a book with a major commercial publisher. Works must be in English.
Level of Study: Unrestricted.
Type: Fellowship.
Value: US$6,000 per year.
Frequency: Annual.
Study Establishment: Phillips Exeter Academy in Exeter, New Hampshire.
Country of Study: United States of America.
No. of awards offered: One.
Application Procedure: Applicants must send a manuscript, together with an application form, personal statement and US$5.
Closing Date: December 1st for the following academic year.
Funding: Private.
No. of awards given last year: One.
No. of applicants last year: 150.
Additional Information: Duties include being in residence for one academic year while working on the manuscript and informal availability to student writers. Requests for further information should be accompanied by a stamped addressed envelope. Information can also be obtained from the Academy website.

PITT RIVERS MUSEUM

University of Oxford
South Parks Road, Oxford, Oxfordshire, OX1 3PP, England
Tel: (44) 1865 284651
Fax: (44) 1865 270943
Email: peter.mitchell@prm.ox.ac.uk
www: http://www.prm.ox.ac.uk
Contact: Dr Peter Mitchell, Secretary of the Swan Fund

The Pitt Rivers Museum was founded in 1884 when General Pitt Rivers, an influential figure in the development of archaeology and evolutionary anthropology, gave his collection to the University of Oxford. The conditions of his gift were that a museum was built to house it and that a lecturer be appointed in anthropology.

James A Swan Fund

Subjects: The later stone age prehistory of southern Africa and the study of the contemporary Bushman and Pygmy peoples of Africa.

Purpose: To provide support for research sponsored by the Pitt Rivers Museum on the later stone age prehistory of southern Africa and the study of the contemporary Bushman and Pygmy peoples of Africa.

Eligibility: Awards are not restricted by nationality.

Level of Study: Doctorate, Graduate, Research.

Type: Research grant.

Value: Varies, usually UK £500-2,000.

Length of Study: Varies.

Frequency: Annual.

Country of Study: Any country.

No. of awards offered: Varies.

Application Procedure: Applicants must submit three copies of the following: a statement of the proposed research (up to 2,000 words), an itemised budget indicating which items are for funding from the Swan Fund and details of all other grant applications, a full curriculum vitae including publications and the names and addresses (including email where possible) of two academic referees. Applications should be addressed to the Secretary of the Swan Fund. References must be sent independently to the Secretary by the closing date.

Closing Date: March 1st.

Funding: Private.

Contributor: The James A Swan benefaction.

No. of awards given last year: 10-12.

No. of applicants last year: 20.

Additional Information: Successful applicants must acknowledge the Swan Fund in all publications arising from their grant, submit a report of their work to the Secretary of the Fund and provide the Balfour Library of the Pitt Rivers Museum with one copy of all publications, including theses and dissertations.

PITTSBURGH NEW MUSIC ENSEMBLE

PO Box 99476, Pittsburgh, PA, 15233, United States of America

Tel: (1) 412 682 2955

Fax: (1) 412 682 2955

www: http://www.pnme.org

Contact: Mr Kevin Noe, Artistic Director

Harvey Garl Composition Contest

Subjects: Music composition.

Purpose: To award a commission for the Pittsburgh New Music Ensemble.

Eligibility: Open to United States citizens only.

Level of Study: Unrestricted.

Type: Commission.

Value: US$3,000.

Frequency: Every two years.

Country of Study: United States of America.

No. of awards offered: One.

Application Procedure: Applicants must complete an application form, available on request.

Closing Date: April 1st.

Funding: Private.

No. of awards given last year: One.

No. of applicants last year: 130.

Additional Information: There is a US$50 application fee.

PLASTIC SURGERY EDUCATIONAL FOUNDATION (PSEF)

444 East Algonquin Road, Arlington Heights, IL, 60005, United States of America

Tel: (1) 847 228 9900

Fax: (1) 847 228 9131

Email: ml@plasticsurgery.org

www: http://www.plasticsurgery.org

Contact: Ms Mary Lewis

The mission of the Plastic Surgery Educational Foundation is to develop and support domestic and international education, as well as research and public service activities of plastic surgeons.

Plastic Surgery Basic Research Grant

Subjects: Clinical and basic research in plastic surgery.

Purpose: To encourage young investigators to perform clinical research.

Eligibility: Open to plastic surgeons and holders of an MD or PhD working in plastic surgery. Residents, Fellows and non members of ASPRS or PSEF require sponsorship of a member or candidate for membership of ASPRS or PSEF or the American Society for Aesthetic Plastic Surgery.

Level of Study: Postgraduate, Professional development.

Type: Research grant.

Value: Research seed money US$5,000.

Length of Study: One year.

Frequency: Annual.

Country of Study: Any country.

No. of awards offered: Approx. 40.

Application Procedure: Applicants must complete an application, available on the website under medical professionals, PSEF funded programmes.

Closing Date: Mid January.

Funding: Private.

Contributor: The Plastic Surgery Educational Foundation.

Plastic Surgery Educational Foundation Scientific Essay Contest

Subjects: Plastic surgery. One award category is to focus on theory, history, ethics, socio-economic issues relating to the art and science of plastic surgery, and three prizes in the non-plastic surgeon category.

Eligibility: Open to persons involved in research in the field of plastic surgery.

Level of Study: Postgraduate, Professional development.

Type: Prize.

Value: US$500-3,000.

Length of Study: One year.

Frequency: Annual.

Country of Study: Any country.

No. of awards offered: Eight.

Application Procedure: Applicants must submit manuscripts which should contain the result of original clinical or basic science research in an area of importance to plastic and reconstructive surgery. Information on essay content and format are available on the website under medical professionals, PSEF funded programmes.

Closing Date: February 15th.

Funding: Private.

Contributor: Bernard G Sarnat MD, D Ralph Millard from the Plastic Surgery Society and the Plastic Surgery Educational Foundation.

Plastic Surgery Research Fellowship Award

Subjects: Unrestricted, any area related to plastic surgery.

Purpose: To encourage research and academic career development in plastic and reconstructive surgery.

Eligibility: Open to surgical residents or Fellows preparing for a plastic surgery residency, or plastic surgery residents planning to interrupt their training for a research experience, or recent residency graduates wishing to supplement their clinical training with a research experience. Residents, Fellows and non members of ASPRS or PSEF require sponsorship of a member or candidate for membership of ASPRS or PSEF.

Level of Study: Postgraduate, Professional development.
Type: Fellowship.
Value: Each award underwrites the salary of the investigator for a one year period (US$30,000).
Length of Study: One year.
Frequency: Annual.
Country of Study: Any country.
No. of awards offered: Two, one in each category.
Application Procedure: Applicants must complete an application, available on the website under medical professionals, PSEF funded programmes.
Closing Date: December 14th.
Funding: Private.
Contributor: Lyndon Peer, Pharmacia, Fresh Start Surgical Gifts, PSEF, Mercedes-Benz and LLC.
No. of awards given last year: One in each category.

PLAYMARKET

Independent Newspapers Limited
PO Box 9767, Wellington, New Zealand
Tel: (64) 4 382 8462
Fax: (64) 4 382 8461
Email: info@playmarket.org.nz
www: http://www.playmarket.org.nz
Contact: Ms Dilys Grant, Director

Playmarket was founded in 1973 to assist New Zealand playwrights with a professional production of their scripts. For 25 years Playmarket have offered script assessment, development and agency services. Playmarket are at the heart of New Zealand theatre and its focus is playwrights.

The Sunday Star Times/Bruce Mason Playwriting Award
Subjects: Playwriting.
Purpose: To recognise achievement at the beginning of a career.
Eligibility: Open to New Zealand playwrights.
Level of Study: Unrestricted.
Type: Award.
Value: New Zealand $7,000.
Length of Study: One year.
Frequency: Annual.
Country of Study: New Zealand.
No. of awards offered: One.
Application Procedure: Applicants must submit their name and address, plus two references. No scripts need to be submitted.
Closing Date: Varies annually.
Funding: Commercial.
Contributor: Independent Newspapers Limited.
No. of awards given last year: One.
No. of applicants last year: 13.
Additional Information: It is expected that the award will be used to write or complete a work for the theatre.

POLISH EMBASSY

47 Portland Place, London, W1B 1JH, England
Tel: (44) 20 7636 6032
Fax: (44) 20 7637 2190
Email: polishembassy@polishembassy.org.uk
www: http://www.polishembassy.org.uk
Contact: Ms Monika Lawacz, First Secretary for Science & Education

The Polish Embassy helps establish links between scientific and educational institutions in Poland and the United Kingdom. It awards Polish government scholarships (postgraduate bursaries, short-term visits and language programmes) and also offers grants within the framework of the British-Polish Research Partnership Programme which is designed to support joint scientific research.

Polish Embassy Scholarship for Polonicum
Subjects: Polish language course.
Eligibility: Priority in the scholarship allocation will be given to applicants studying Central European or Polish history, language and literature.
Level of Study: Doctorate, Graduate, Postgraduate, Professional development.
Type: Scholarship.
Value: Students are provided with accommodation, but will have to pay for return travel to Poland.
Length of Study: Four weeks during the Summer.
Frequency: Annual.
Study Establishment: The University of Warsaw, Jagiellonian University in Cracow, the Maria Curie-Skodowska University in Lublin and the University of Silesia in Katowice.
Country of Study: Poland.
No. of awards offered: Eight.
Application Procedure: Applicants must complete an application form and submit this with a covering letter and one letter of reference to the Polish Embassy. Application forms and further information are available from the Polish Embassy.
Closing Date: April 15th.
Funding: Government.
Contributor: The Polish Ministry of Education.
No. of awards given last year: Eight.

Polish Embassy Short Visits Grants
Subjects: Research.
Purpose: To allow academics and professionals to establish contacts, develop programmes of joint research and exchange scientific information.
Eligibility: The age limit is 50. Candidates should be experienced academics in their professional field in a way which could contribute to research in the candidate's subject area.
Level of Study: Doctorate, Postdoctorate, Postgraduate, Professional development, Research.
Type: Grant.
Value: Internal travel cost related to the visitors' itinerary plus accommodation and daily rate for subsistence, or a lump sum grant in aid will be paid by the Polish side. Recipients are expected to pay their return travel to Poland.
Length of Study: One week to one month.
Frequency: Annual.
Study Establishment: Universities and other Institutes of Higher Education and research.
Country of Study: Poland.
No. of awards offered: Unspecified.
Application Procedure: Applicants must submit with their application their curriculum vitae, an explanation of the purpose of their visit and a letter of invitation from an academic institution in Poland expressing willingness to receive the visiting applicant. Applications must be sent to the Polish Embassy no later than 12 weeks prior to the proposed date of arrival in Poland.
Funding: Government.
Contributor: The Polish Ministry of Education.

Polish Embassy Short-Term Bursaries
Subjects: All subjects.
Purpose: To provide financial support for British students wishing to study in Poland.
Eligibility: Candidates must be British citizens with a university degree or equivalent qualification who have some postgraduate research or lecturing experience. Preference is given to those undertaking doctoral or postdoctoral work. Married candidates must indicate whether they are prepared to go unaccompanied. Candidates wishing to study Polish philology, Slavonic languages and the

history and the geography of Poland must be conversant with Polish or any other appropriate Slavonic language.

Level of Study: Doctorate, Postdoctorate, Postgraduate, Professional development.

Type: Bursary.

Value: A monthly allowance, free accommodation in student hostels (or possibly in hotels) or a monthly allowance towards accommodation found privately, free meals in a student canteen or a monthly allowance in lieu, a modest book grant, exemption from tuition fees and free medical care. The Polish authorities will pay for necessary travel expenses within Poland from one academic centre to another, but recipients will be required to pay their own fares to and from Poland.

Length of Study: Three-nine months.

Frequency: Annual.

Study Establishment: A University or another Institute of Higher Education.

Country of Study: Poland.

No. of awards offered: 40.

Application Procedure: Applicants must complete an application form and submit this with a curriculum vitae, a copy of their diploma, research proposal, medical statement and two letters of recommendation.

Closing Date: April 15th.

Funding: Government.

No. of awards given last year: 20.

No. of applicants last year: 35.

Additional Information: This scheme is new under agreement between Poland and the United Kingdom on exchanges in the fields of science, humanities and arts. Bursaries cannot normally be taken up during the university Summer, except for the Summer vacation courses 'Polonicum' and 'Polish Language'.

Polish Government Postgraduate Scholarships Scheme

Subjects: Unrestricted. The following subjects in particular are taught to a high standard in Polish universities: sociology, mathematics, geography and geology, history of Polish architecture, music both performance and composition, the arts and scientific topics.

Purpose: To provide financial support for British students wishing to study in Poland.

Eligibility: Candidates must be British citizens with a university degree or equivalent qualification. Priority is given to candidates who hold an honours degree and have had some experience of research, laboratory techniques or teaching since graduation. Married candidates must indicate whether they are prepared to go unaccompanied. Candidates wishing to study Polish philology, Slavonic languages and the history and geography of Poland must be conversant with Polish or the appropriate Slavonic language. Applicants should be under 35 years of age.

Level of Study: Doctorate, Postgraduate, Professional development.

Type: Scholarship.

Value: A monthly allowance, free accommodation in student hostels or a monthly allowance towards accommodation found privately, free meals in a student canteen or a monthly allowance in lieu, a modest book grant, exemption from tuition fees and free medical care.

Length of Study: Three-nine months.

Frequency: Annual.

Study Establishment: A University or another Institute of Higher Education.

Country of Study: Poland.

No. of awards offered: Varies.

Application Procedure: Applicants must complete an application form and submit this with a curriculum vitae, a copy of their diploma, research proposal, medical statement and two letters of recommendation. Application forms are available from the Education Officer.

Closing Date: April 15th.

Funding: Government.

Contributor: The Polish Ministry of Education.

No. of awards given last year: 17.

Additional Information: This scheme is run under agreement between Poland and the United Kingdom on exchange in the fields of science, humanities and arts.

POLLOCK-KRASNER FOUNDATION, INC.

863 Park Avenue, New York, NY, 10021, United States of America
Tel: (1) 212 517 5400
Fax: (1) 212 288 2836
Email: grants@pkf.org
www: http://www.pkf.org
Contact: Ms Caroline Black, Program Officer

The Pollock-Krasner Foundation's mission is to aid, internationally, those individuals who have worked as professional artists over a significant period of time.

Pollock-Krasner Foundation Grant

Subjects: Painting, sculpting, print-making, mixed media or installation art.

Purpose: To aid, internationally, individual artists of artistic merit with financial need.

Eligibility: Applicants may be painters, sculptors, print-makers, mixed media or installation artists. The Foundation has no age or geographic limits. Commercial artists, photographers, filmmakers, craft-makers and students are not eligible.

Level of Study: Professional development.

Type: Grant.

Frequency: Annual.

Application Procedure: Applicants must write, fax or email the Foundation for an application and guidelines.

Closing Date: No deadline as grants are awarded throughout the year.

Funding: Private.

Additional Information: The Foundation does not fund academic study.

PONTIFICAL INSTITUTE OF MEDIEVAL STUDIES

59 Queen's Park Crescent East, Toronto, ON, M5S 2C4, Canada
Tel: (1) 416 926 7290
Fax: (1) 416 926 7276
Email: sheila.campbell@utoronto.ca

Council of the Institute Awards

Subjects: Medieval studies.

Eligibility: Open to Scholars engaged in medieval studies.

Level of Study: Postdoctorate.

Type: Bursary, scholarship.

Value: Varies depending on funds available.

Length of Study: One year.

Frequency: Annual.

Study Establishment: The Institute.

Country of Study: Canada.

No. of awards offered: Varies.

Application Procedure: Applicants must complete an application form, available on request.

Closing Date: January 15th.

Additional Information: The Institute also offers a small number of Research Associateships (without stipend) annually to postdoctoral students and senior Scholars who wish to use the Institute library for their research.

THE POPULATION COUNCIL

Policy Research Division, One Dag Hammarskjold Plaza, New York, NY, 10017, United States of America
Tel: (1) 212 339 0671
Fax: (1) 212 755 6052
Email: ssfellowship@popcouncil.org
www: http://www.popcouncil.org
Telex: 9102900660 POPCO
Contact: Jude Lam-Garrison, Fellowship Co-ordinator

The Population Council is an international non-profit, non-governmental institution that seeks to improve the wellbeing and reproductive health of current and future generations around the world and to help achieve a humane, equitable and sustainable balance between people and resources. The Council conducts biomedical, social science and public health research and helps build research capacities in developing countries.

Population Council Fellowships in Population and Social Sciences

Subjects: Fellowships will be awarded for advanced training in population studies (including demography and public health) in combination with a social science discipline, such as economics, sociology, anthropology, or geography. Awards will be made only to applicants whose proposals deal with the developing world.
Purpose: To make a significant contribution to the advanced training of professionals in the broad field of population studies through the awarding of fellowships on a competitive basis, with particular emphasis on the training of nationals from developing countries.
Eligibility: Predoctoral fellowships are open to applicants who have completed all coursework requirements toward the PhD or an equivalent degree in one of the social sciences in combination with population studies. Applications requesting support for either the dissertation fieldwork or the dissertation writing period will be considered. Postdoctoral fellowships are open to persons having a PhD or equivalent degree who wish to undertake postdoctoral training and research at an institution other than the one at which they received their PhD degree. Awards are open to all qualified persons, but strong preference will be given to applicants from developing countries who have a firm commitment to return home upon completion of their training programmes. Applications by women are particularly encouraged.
Level of Study: Doctorate, Postdoctorate, Professional development.
Type: Fellowship.
Value: For predoctoral the value is US$24,000, for postdoctoral US$32,000, and for midcareer the value varies. A monthly stipend (based on the type of fellowship and place of study), tuition payments and related fees, transportation expenses (for Fellow only) and health insurance are also included. Some research related costs may also be part of the award. Tuition at the postdoctoral and midcareer academic levels is not included in the award.
Length of Study: Up to one year.
Frequency: Annual.
Study Establishment: A training or research institution with a strong programme in population studies, regardless of geographic location.
Country of Study: Any country.
No. of awards offered: 15-20.
Application Procedure: Applicants must submit an application and supporting documents in English. Application forms can be obtained from the website. Requests for application forms should include a brief description of candidates' academic and professional qualifications and a short statement about their research or study plans for the proposed fellowship period.
Closing Date: December 15th of each year for notification in March. If the 15th falls on a weekend or holiday then the due date is the next business day.
No. of awards given last year: 14.
No. of applicants last year: 98.

Additional Information: Selection will be based on the recommendation of the Fellowship Committee which consists of three distinguished Scholars in the field of population. Selection criteria will stress academic excellence and prospective contribution to the population field. Application for independent research funds, or for fieldwork not related to a dissertation, will not be considered. The Bernard Berelson Fellowships are for training at The Population Council's New York office. Prior to submitting a formal application to the Fellowship Office for consideration, the Berelson applicants are required to seek sponsorship from at least one council staff member from the New York office. There are two types of Bernard Berelson Fellowships, Postdoctoral and Midcareer.

PRAGUE SPRING INTERNATIONAL MUSIC COMPETITION

Hellichova 18, Prague, CS-118 00, Czech Republic
Tel: (42) 2 5732 0468
Fax: (42) 2 5731 3725
Email: info@festival.cz
www: http://www.festival.cz
Contact: Mrs J Nedvedová

Prague Spring International Music Competition

Subjects: Music. Competition categories for 2003 are the violin and the trumpet, and in 2004 the competition will be for the piano and trombone.
Purpose: To encourage and assist outstanding young musicians.
Eligibility: Open to musicians of any nationality who do not exceed the main age limit of 30 (string quartet 120 years combined, conducting 35 years).
Level of Study: Unrestricted.
Value: Prizes range from koruna 10,000-120,000. Accommodation is paid for those who qualify for the second round and final.
Frequency: Annual.
Country of Study: Czech Republic.
No. of awards offered: Three main prizes.
Application Procedure: Applicants must complete an application form, available from the website, and enclose an audio tape with a recording of the setting compositions, a copy of their birth certificate and a photograph. There is an application fee of US$100.
Closing Date: December 15th of the year preceding the award.

PREHISTORIC SOCIETY

University College London
Institute of Archaeology
31-34 Gordon Square, London, WC1H 0PY, England
Fax: (44) 20 7383 2572
Contact: Administrative Assistant

The Prehistoric Society is open to professionals and amateurs alike and has over 2,000 members worldwide. Its main activities are lectures, study tours and conferences and it publishes an annual journal (PPS) and a newsletter (PAST) which is published three times a year.

Prehistoric Society Conference Fund

Subjects: Archaeology, especially prehistoric.
Purpose: To finance attendance at international conferences.
Eligibility: Preference is given first to Scholars from developing countries, whether they are members of the Society or not, then to members of the Society not qualified to apply for conference funds available to university staff. Other members of the Society are also eligible.
Level of Study: Postgraduate.
Type: Travel grant.
Value: A maximum of UK £250.

Length of Study: One year. Renewals are considered.
Frequency: Annual.
Country of Study: Any country.
No. of awards offered: Two.
Application Procedure: Applicants must contact the Honorary Secretary for an application form.
Closing Date: December 31st.
Funding: Private.
Additional Information: Recipients are required to submit a short report on the conference to PAST, the Society's newsletter and their papers for the Society's proceedings if these are not to be included in a conference volume.

Prehistoric Society Research Fund Grant

Subjects: Prehistoric archaeology.
Purpose: To further research in prehistory by excavation or other means.
Eligibility: Open to all members of the Society. The Society may make specific conditions relating to individual applications.
Level of Study: Unrestricted.
Type: Grant.
Value: At the discretion of the Society.
Length of Study: One year. Renewals are considered.
Frequency: Annual.
Country of Study: Any country.
No. of awards offered: Varies.
Application Procedure: Applicants must include the names of two referees in their application.
Closing Date: December 31st.
Funding: Private.
Additional Information: Awards are made on the understanding that a detailed report will be made to the Society as to how the grant was spent.

Prehistoric Society Research Grant Conference Award

Subjects: Prehistoric archaeology.
Purpose: To fund initial projects and visits to conferences.
Eligibility: There are no eligibility restrictions.
Level of Study: Unrestricted.
Value: Variable (usually under UK £500).
Frequency: Annual.
Application Procedure: Applicants must complete an application form.
Closing Date: January 1st.
Funding: Private.

PRINCETON UNIVERSITY PROCTER FELLOWSHIPS

University Registry
The Old Schools, Cambridge, Cambridgeshire, CB2 1TN, England
Tel: (44) 1223 332317
Fax: (44) 1223 332332
Email: mrf25@admin.cam.ac.uk
www: http://www.admin.cam.ac.uk
Contact: Ms Melanie Foster, Scholarships Clerk

Procter Visiting Fellowships

Subjects: Fellows will be required to devote themselves to advanced study and investigation in a branch of subjects of one of the liberal arts and sciences, exclusive of professional, technical or commercial subjects.
Purpose: To support study in the liberal arts and sciences.
Eligibility: Open to Commonwealth citizens who hold a First Class (Honours) BA or equivalent from a United Kingdom university and are able to prove exceptional scholarly power. Preference is normally given to candidates who would be in their second or third year of postgraduate research when, if elected, they take up tenure of the award.

Level of Study: Postgraduate.
Type: Fellowship.
Value: US$15,000 (for 10 months) plus full tuition fees and medical insurance.
Length of Study: One year.
Frequency: Annual.
Study Establishment: Princeton University, New Jersey.
Country of Study: United States of America.
No. of awards offered: Two.
Application Procedure: Applicants must complete an application form, available on request.
Closing Date: Early December.
No. of awards given last year: One.
No. of applicants last year: 16.
Additional Information: The fellowship is normally tenable for one year as a visiting award, but provision also exists exceptionally for a Fellow to be nominated for admission to a PhD programme at Princeton. Candidates who wish to be considered for nomination for the PhD programme should state so on the application form.

PROFESSOR CHARLES LEGGETT TRUST

16 Ogle Street, London, W1W 6JA, England
Tel: (44) 20 7636 4481
Fax: (44) 20 7637 4307
Email: sdolton@mbf.org.uk
www: http://www.mbf.org.uk
Contact: Mrs Susan Dolton

Professor Charles Leggett Trust

Subjects: Musical performance of brass and woodwind instruments.
Purpose: To provide annual awards for talented young brass and wind players.
Eligibility: Open to players of any nationality who have been resident in the United Kingdom for three years and are aged under 25 on the closing date. The award is open to individual woodwind and brass players.
Level of Study: Postgraduate, Professional development.
Value: Up to UK £5,000 each.
Frequency: Annual.
Country of Study: Any country.
No. of awards offered: Two.
Application Procedure: Applicants must complete an application form and provide two references. Leggett awards are made as a result of the MBF Music Education Awards auditions.
Closing Date: February 21st.
Funding: Private.
No. of awards given last year: Three.
Additional Information: Selected applicants are asked to audition in April.

PYMATUNING LABORATORY OF ECOLOGY (PLE)

The University of Pittsburgh
13142 Hartstown Road, Linesville, PA, 16424, United States of America
Tel: (1) 814 683 5813
Fax: (1) 814 683 2302
Email: ple@toolcity.net
www: http://www.pitt.edu/~biology/pymatuning
Contact: Dr Gail F Johnston, Associate Director

The Pymatuning Laboratory of Ecology (PLE) is a University of Pittsburgh field station dedicated to environmental education and ecological research. Situated on the shores of the Pymatuning Reservoir in North Western Pennsylvania, PLE's land includes woods, wetlands, successional fields and experimental agricultural lands. Researchers from nine institutions conduct projects ranging from community and ecosystem ecology to evolutionary genetics and behaviour.

Darbaker Botany Prize

Subjects: Botany.
Purpose: To award funds for the pursuit of excellent graduate and recent postdoctoral research in botany at Pymatuning Laboratory of Ecology.
Eligibility: Applicants must conduct research and reside at Pymatuning Laboratory.
Level of Study: Doctorate, Postdoctorate, Postgraduate.
Type: Research grant.
Value: US$500-1,500.
Length of Study: One year.
Frequency: Annual.
Study Establishment: Pymatuning Laboratory of Ecology.
Country of Study: United States of America.
No. of awards offered: One-three.
Application Procedure: Applicants must request guidelines from the Pymatuning Laboratory of Ecology or refer to the website.
Closing Date: February 1st.
Funding: Private.
No. of awards given last year: One.
No. of applicants last year: Two.

G M McKinley Research Fund

Subjects: Ecology.
Purpose: To fund research at the graduate and recent postdoctoral level in ecological science at the Pymatuning Laboratory of Ecology.
Eligibility: Applicants must conduct research and reside at the Pymatuning Laboratory of Ecology.
Level of Study: Doctorate, Postdoctorate, Postgraduate.
Type: Research grant.
Value: US$500-3,000.
Length of Study: One year.
Frequency: Annual.
Study Establishment: Pymatuning Laboratory of Ecology.
Country of Study: United States of America.
No. of awards offered: One-five.
Application Procedure: Applicants must request guidelines from the Pymatuning Laboratory of Ecology or refer to the website.
Closing Date: February 1st.
Funding: Private.
Contributor: Dr G M McKinley.
No. of awards given last year: Eight.
No. of applicants last year: 10.

QUEEN ELISABETH INTERNATIONAL MUSIC COMPETITION OF BELGIUM

20 rue aux Laines, Brussels, B-1000, Belgium
Tel: (32) 2 513 0099
Fax: (32) 2 514 3297
Email: info@concours-reine-elisabeth.be
www: http://www.concours-reine-elisabeth.be
Contact: Secretariat

The Queen Elisabeth International Music Competition of Belgium is a non-profit association, located in Brussels, whose principal aim is to organise major international competitions for music virtuosos. In this way, the competition participates in the Belgian and international music world, and gives its support to young musicians.

Queen Elisabeth International Music Competition of Belgium

Subjects: Piano and composition.
Purpose: To provide career support for young pianists, singers, violinists and composers.

Eligibility: Open to musicians of any nationality who are at least 17 years of age and not older than 27 (violin and piano) or 30 years of age for singing.
Level of Study: Unrestricted.
Type: Prize.
Value: From a total amounting to more than €800,000.
Frequency: A competition for each category is held at four yearly intervals.
Country of Study: Any country.
No. of awards offered: Six.
Application Procedure: Applicants must obtain an application form from the Secretariat of the Competition.
Closing Date: January 15th.
Funding: Private.
No. of awards given last year: Six.
Additional Information: There are also master classes with jury members.

QUEEN MARIE JOSÉ INTERNATIONAL PRIZE FOR MUSICAL COMPOSITION

Prix de Composition Musicale Reine Marie-José
Case Postale 19
Meinier, Geneva, CH-1525, Switzerland
www: http://musnov1.unige.ch/prixrmj
Contact: Mr Jean Rémy Berthoud, General Secretary

In order to encourage gifted musicians, Her Majesty Queen Marie José decided to create an international prize for musical composition.

Queen Marie José Prize International Prize for Musical Composition

Subjects: Musical composition.
Purpose: To reward a new musical composition never performed before.
Eligibility: Open to composers of all nationalities and of any age.
Level of Study: Unrestricted.
Type: Prize.
Value: Swiss franc 15,000.
Frequency: Every two years.
Country of Study: Any country.
No. of awards offered: One.
Application Procedure: Applicants must apply for information, available on request or from the website.
Closing Date: May 31st.
Funding: Private.
Contributor: Her Majesty the Queen Marie José.
No. of awards given last year: One.
No. of applicants last year: 60.
Additional Information: The award winning work remains its author's exclusive property but, if possible, is performed as part of the Merlinge concerts.

QUEEN MARY UNIVERSITY OF LONDON

Admissions & Research Student Office, London, E1 4NS, England
Tel: (44) 20 7882 3657
Fax: (44) 20 7882 5588
Email: admissions@qmul.ac.uk
www: http://www.qmul.ac.uk
Contact: Mr Peter Smith, Admissions Assistant

Queen Mary is the fourth largest college in the University of London. Located on an attractive campus they have more than 8,000 students studying in four facilities plus St Bartholomew's and the Royal London School of Medicine and Dentistry. Of these, more than 1,600 are following postgraduate courses and undertaking research.

Queen Mary Research Studentships

Subjects: Arts, sciences, engineering, social sciences, law, medicine or dentistry.
Purpose: To provide the opportunity for full-time research leading towards an MPhil or PhD.
Eligibility: Open to suitably qualified candidates who hold at least an Upper Second Class (Honours) or equivalent at First Degree level.
Level of Study: Research.
Type: Studentship.
Value: Maintenance at the current research council rate plus tuition fees.
Length of Study: Three years full-time, subject to a satisfactory academic report.
Frequency: Dependent on funds available.
Study Establishment: Queen Mary, the University of London.
Country of Study: United Kingdom.
No. of awards offered: 10+.
Application Procedure: Applicants must write to the Admission and Recruitment Office for details.
Closing Date: Mid Summer.
No. of awards given last year: 25.
No. of applicants last year: 200.
Additional Information: These studentships are not available to existing Queen Mary research students.

THE QUEEN'S UNIVERSITY OF BELFAST

Academic Council Office, Level 6
Administration Building, Belfast, BT7 1NN, Northern Ireland
Tel: (44) 28 9024 5133
Fax: (44) 28 9031 3537
Email: academic.council@qub.ac.uk
www: http://www.qub.ac.uk
Contact: Academic Registrar

Queen's University is over 150 years old and offers degree programmes in all major subject areas, organised for teaching and research purposes into five faculties. The University is located just south of Belfast city centre, although it has opened an outreach campus in Armagh. Queen's employs over 1,000 academic staff and 20,000 students attend full and part-time courses.

Musgrave Research Studentships

Subjects: Biology, chemistry, pathology, physics or physiology.
Purpose: To fund personal research.
Eligibility: Open only to British applicants who are graduates, with preference being given to graduates of universities in the United Kingdom, a United Kingdom colony, protectorate, trust or mandated territory or any territory within or associated with the Commonwealth or Republic of Ireland. Candidates must be engaged in, or show marked capacity for, research in biology, chemistry, pathology, physics or physiology.
Level of Study: Doctorate, Postgraduate.
Type: Studentship.
Value: Dependent upon trust income.
Length of Study: One year, with a possibility of renewal for a further one-two years.
Frequency: Annual.
Study Establishment: Queen's University of Belfast.
Country of Study: United Kingdom.
No. of awards offered: Three-four.
Application Procedure: Applicants must complete an application form.
Closing Date: June 1st.
Funding: Private.
Contributor: Endowment.
No. of awards given last year: Four.
No. of applicants last year: Five.

Additional Information: The selection panel will take into account other sources of funding for the research.

Queen's University of Belfast Research and Senior Visiting Research Fellowships

Subjects: Irish studies.
Purpose: To fund personal research at the Institute of Irish Studies.
Eligibility: Research fellowships normally go to postdoctoral applicants, but strictly speaking applicants need an Upper Second Class (Honours) Degree and research experience for senior posts. Senior academics must have held a university post for at least 10 years.
Level of Study: Postdoctorate.
Type: Fellowship.
Value: Research is UK £12,500 and Senior Visiting Research is UK £16,500.
Length of Study: One year.
Frequency: Annual.
Study Establishment: Queen's University of Belfast.
Country of Study: United Kingdom.
No. of awards offered: Three research fellowships and one-two senior visiting research fellowships.
Application Procedure: Applicants must complete an application form.
Closing Date: February 7th but this varies.
Funding: Government.
No. of awards given last year: Five.
No. of applicants last year: 70.

QUEENSLAND UNIVERSITY OF TECHNOLOGY (QUT)

Grants & Fellowships Office
GPO Box 2434, Brisbane, QLD, 4001, Australia
Tel: (61) 7 3864 1844
Fax: (61) 7 3864 1304
Email: c.depinna@qut.edu.au
www: http://www.qut.edu.au
Contact: Ms Cherie de Pinna

Queensland University of Technology Postdoctoral Research Fellowship

Subjects: All disciplines supported by research centres at QUT.
Purpose: To foster effective and productive interdisciplinary group research and to encourage excellence in individual research.
Eligibility: Open to holders of the PhD who have less than five years full-time postdoctoral experience and have submitted their thesis for examination prior to closing date.
Level of Study: Postdoctorate.
Type: Fellowship.
Value: Australian $46,021-49,397.
Length of Study: Two years, with a possible extension for a further year.
Frequency: Annual.
Study Establishment: Queensland University of Technology in a specified centre or area of research concentration.
Country of Study: Australia.
No. of awards offered: Usually six-eight.
Application Procedure: Applicants must complete an application form. Further information and application forms are available from the website.
Closing Date: Mid August.
No. of awards given last year: Eight.
No. of applicants last year: 50.

THE RADCLIFFE INSTITUTE FOR ADVANCED STUDY

34 Concord Avenue, Cambridge, MA, 02138, United States of America
Tel: (1) 617 495 8212
Fax: (1) 617 495 8136
Email: bunting_fellowships@radcliffe.harvard.edu
www: http://www.radcliffe.edu
Contact: Ms Paula Sores, Administrator of Fellowships

The Radcliffe Institute for Advanced Study is a scholarly community where individuals pursue advanced work across a wide range of academic disciplines, professions and creative arts. Within this broad purpose, the Radcliffe Institute sustains a continuing commitment to the study of women, gender and society.

Radcliffe Institute for Advanced Study Fellowship Programme

Subjects: Any discipline, including creative writing, visual and performing arts.
Purpose: To support women of exceptional promise and demonstrated accomplishment who wish to pursue independent work in professional and academic fields and in the creative arts.
Eligibility: Open to female Scholars in any field who gained a doctorate or appropriate terminal degree at least two years prior to appointment, female creative writers and visual or performing artists with a record of significant accomplishment and equivalent professional experience (special eligibility requirements apply to creative artists).
Level of Study: Postdoctorate.
Type: Fellowship.
Value: Around US$45,000 for a year appointment starting on September 15th. Fellows may not simultaneously hold another major fellowship which provides more than US$20,000.
Length of Study: Nine months from September to June.
Frequency: Annual.
Study Establishment: Harvard University.
Country of Study: United States of America.
No. of awards offered: 15-30.
Application Procedure: Applicants must visit the website.
Closing Date: Please consult the organisation.
Additional Information: Applications are judged on the quality and significance of the proposed project, the applicant's record of accomplishment, and the difference the fellowship might make in advancing the applicant's career. Residence in the Boston area is required during the fellowship appointment. Fellows are expected to present their work in progress.

RADIO AND TELEVISION NEWS DIRECTORS FOUNDATION (RTNDF)

1000 Connecticut Avenue North West
Suite 615, Washington, DC, 20036, United States of America
Tel: (1) 202 659 6510
Fax: (1) 202 223 4007
Email: walts@rtndf.org
www: http://www.rtndf.org
Contact: Ms Walt Swanston, Senior Project Director

The mission of the Radio and Television News Directors Foundation (RTNDF) is to promote excellence in electronic journalism through research, education and professional training in four principal programme areas: journalistic ethics and practices, the impact of technological change on electronic journalism, the role of electronic news in politics and public policy, and cultural diversity in the electronic journalism profession.

Capitol Hill News Internships

Subjects: Electronic journalism.
Purpose: To provide an opportunity for students to make future contacts and learn the ropes of political coverage.
Eligibility: Open to recent college graduates whose career objective is electronic journalism. Preference is given to minority students.
Level of Study: Postgraduate.
Type: Internship.
Value: US$1,000 per month. Travel, housing and other living expenses are the responsibility of the intern.
Length of Study: Three months.
Frequency: Annual.
Country of Study: United States of America.
No. of awards offered: Four.
Application Procedure: Applicants must write or email for an application form, including a curriculum vitae and a one page essay on why they are interested in this programme. Late, incomplete, or faxed applications will not be accepted.
Closing Date: The deadline for the Spring internships is January 19th and April 1st for the Summer internships.
Funding: Private.
Contributor: The Radio-Television Correspondent's Association.
Additional Information: Interns will be responsible for following newsworthy congressional activities and helping to co-ordinate these activities. Excellent writing skills are essential. Interns will get hands on experience in the House and Senate Radio or TV galleries, working with the Washington press and congressional staff to cover the political process.

RTNDF Fellowships

Subjects: Electronic journalism.
Eligibility: For young journalists in radio or television with up to 10 years' experience.
Level of Study: Postgraduate, Professional development.
Type: Fellowship.
Value: Up to US$2,500.
Frequency: Annual.
Country of Study: United States of America.
No. of awards offered: Eight.
Application Procedure: Applicants must write for application form.
Closing Date: May 4th.
Funding: Private.
Additional Information: The awards include: the Sandra Freeman Geller and Alfred Geller Fellowship, the Shirlee Barish Fellowship, the Michele Clark Fellowship for Minority News Professionals, the Jacque I Minotte Health Reporting Fellowship, the Vada and Barney Oldfield National Security Fellowship, RTNDF Environment and Science Reporting Fellowship, the Michael Burke News Management Fellowship and the NS Bienstock Fellowship for Minority Journalists.

RADIOLOGICAL SOCIETY OF NORTH AMERICA, INC. (RSNA)

820 Jorie Boulevard, Oak Brook, IL, 60523-2251, United States of America
Tel: (1) 630 571 2670
Fax: (1) 630 571 7837
www: http://www.rsna.org
Contact: Mr Scott A Walter, Grant Review Process Manager

RSNA Educational Scholar Program

Subjects: Radiology or related disciplines.
Purpose: To fund board certified individuals who are seeking an opportunity to develop their expertise in the discipline of education in the radiological sciences.
Eligibility: Open to board certified individuals in radiology or related disciplines who hold an MD, have a demonstrated interest in teaching and show that the pursuit of advanced training in education will impact the future education of radiologists. Applicants must be

citizens of a North American country or have permanent resident status.
Level of Study: Postgraduate, Predoctorate.
Type: Grant.
Value: Up to US$75,000 per year.
Length of Study: Two years.
Frequency: Annual.
No. of awards offered: One.
Application Procedure: Applicants must complete an application form, available from the website.
Closing Date: June 1st.

RSNA Institutional Clinical Fellowship in Cardiovascular Imaging

Subjects: Cardiovascular imaging.
Purpose: To provide opportunities for radiologists early in their careers to gain experience and expertise in cardiovascular imaging.
Eligibility: Fellows must be citizens or permanent residents of a North American country and must have completed their residency training in the radiological sciences. Fellows must also hold an MD or the equivalent as recognised by the American Medical Association and must be ACGME certified in radiology or be eligible to sit for such certification.
Type: Fellowship.
Value: US$50,000 per year paid to a department. The Foundation does not pay overhead or indirect costs.
Length of Study: Three years.
Frequency: Annual.
No. of awards offered: One.
Application Procedure: Applications must be submitted by a department in preparation for the recruitment of a Fellow into an existing cardiovascular imaging training programme. Application forms are available from the website.
Closing Date: June 1st.

RSNA International Radiology Program Educational Grant To "Teach the Teachers" from Emerging Nations

Subjects: Radiology or related disciplines.
Purpose: To provide an opportunity for scientists and physicians working within the radiological sciences in developed countries to use or develop educational materials specifically to educate the teachers in emerging countries who will return to their respective countries to improve clinical practice and education.
Eligibility: Open to individuals in the radiological sciences in developed countries throughout the world with the facilities and institutional support to establish the programme required to successfully compete for this grant.
Level of Study: Postgraduate.
Type: Grant.
Value: Up to US$100,000 per year. Each year's funding is based on successful progress toward the stated goals of the proposal. The Foundation does not pay institutional overhead costs or indirect costs.
Length of Study: Three years.
Frequency: Annual.
No. of awards offered: One.
Application Procedure: Applicants must complete an application form, available from the website.
Closing Date: June 1st.

RSNA Medical Student Departmental Grant Program

Subjects: Diagnostic radiology, radiation oncology or nuclear medicine.
Purpose: To provide matching grants to enable departments of diagnostic radiology, radiation oncology or nuclear medicine allied with North American medical schools to offer research opportunities to medical students.
Eligibility: Open to departments of diagnostic radiology, radiation oncology or nuclear medicine who have been allied with fully accredited North American medical schools for five consecutive years.
Type: Grant.

Value: US$1,000 per month for three or more months to be matched by the department.
Frequency: Annual.
Application Procedure: Applicants must complete an application form, available from the website. Departments must describe their commitment to research, provide details of the medical student's proposed activity and participation, and identify the method by which the student will be selected. They must also designate a scientific advisor to oversee the medical student's participation in the research programme.
Closing Date: January 8th.

RSNA Medical Student/Scholar Assistant Program

Subjects: Radiology or related disciplines.
Purpose: To make radiology research opportunities available for medical students early in their training and encourage them to consider academic radiology as a career option.
Eligibility: Open to full time medical students at an accredited North American medical school. Nominees must be citizens of a North American country or hold permanent resident status.
Type: Grant.
Value: US$5,000.
Length of Study: One year.
Application Procedure: Applicants must be nominated by a current RSNA Scholar grant recipient and work with the Scholar on his/her designated research project.
Closing Date: There is no specific deadline. The Scholar is notified of the option to nominate a medical student. The application must be prepared with the assistance of the nominating Scholar.

RSNA Research Fellow Program

Subjects: Medical sciences.
Purpose: To provide opportunities for physicians early in their careers to gain insight into scientific investigation and to develop competence in research, educational techniques and methods.
Eligibility: Open to citizens or permanent residents of a North American country who have an MD, DO, DVM, DDS, DMD degree or the equivalent as recognised by the American Medical Association. Individuals with a PhD or ScD, in addition to the appropriate medical degree, are not eligible for this award, though MD or PhDs who have their PhDs in areas other than medical research are eligible. Applicants should be near the end of their prescribed training and/or have completed the prerequisite training to sit for qualifying exams. Preference will be given to candidates who have a commitment from a North American educational institution for a faculty appointment after the fellowship is completed.
Level of Study: Doctorate, Postdoctorate, Postgraduate, Predoctorate.
Type: Fellowship.
Value: US$45,000 for one year with US$5,000 to the institution, on request, to be applied to direct expenses. Applications for renewal for a second year at US$50,000, plus US$5,000 to the institution, on request, will be considered. The Foundation does not pay overhead or indirect costs.
Frequency: Annual.
No. of awards offered: One.
Application Procedure: Applicants must complete an application form, available from the website.
Closing Date: January 9th.

RSNA Research Resident Program

Subjects: Radiology, radiation oncology and nuclear medicine.
Purpose: To provide opportunities for radiology, radiation oncology and nuclear medicine residents to gain further insight into scientific investigation, and to develop competence in research and educational techniques and methods.
Eligibility: Open to citizens or permanent residents of a North American country. Applicants should be in residency training so that the award can occur during any year after the first year of training and should have an academic degree acceptable for a radiology residency.

Level of Study: Postgraduate.
Type: Grant.
Value: US$30,000, designed to replace a portion of the resident's salary.
Length of Study: One year, non renewable.
Frequency: Annual.
No. of awards offered: One.
Application Procedure: Applicants must complete an application form, available from the website.
Closing Date: January 9th.

RSNA Scholars Program

Subjects: Medical sciences.
Purpose: To support junior clinical faculty members and allow them to gain experience in research early in their academic careers.
Eligibility: Open to citizens or permanent residents of a North American country who have completed advanced training and are within five years of an initial faculty appointment at a North American educational institution. Applicants must also be board certified or eligible to sit for certifying exams and have not served or not currently be serving as principal investigator or co-principal investigator on grants or contracts totalling US$50,000 or more in a single calendar year.
Level of Study: Doctorate, Postdoctorate.
Value: US$75,000 annually for two years, payable to the institution, to be used exclusively as a stipend for the Scholar. In unusual circumstances, a third year may be granted to provide bridge funding between the Scholar award and additional funding obtained from other sources. A separate application is required to be considered for a third year of funding.
Frequency: Annual.
No. of awards offered: One.
Application Procedure: Scholar applicants must be nominated by their host institution. If awarded, Scholars will be required to take the Advanced Grant Writing Course offered through the RSNA Office of Research Development (ORD). Personal interviews will be conducted for selected finalists. Three letters of recommendation are needed as is a budget with details of the project and all sources of support.
Closing Date: January 9th.

RSNA World Wide Web Based Educational Program

Subjects: Radiology and related disciplines.
Purpose: To provide an opportunity for scientists and physicians in the radiological sciences to develop educational materials specifically for wide spread distribution through the Internet.
Eligibility: Open to anyone in the radiological sciences from any country. Individuals who are not in the radiological sciences such as computer or web specialists may be involved as co-investigators.
Level of Study: Postgraduate, Professional development.
Type: Grant.
Value: Up to US$75,000 for one year with the possibility of a second year of support at the level of up to US$75,000.
Length of Study: One-two years.
Application Procedure: Applicants must complete an application form, available from the website.
Closing Date: June 1st.

Seed Grant Research Program

Subjects: Diagnostic radiology, radiation oncology or nuclear medicine.
Purpose: To assist investigators in defining objectives and testing hypotheses before they apply for major grants from corporations, foundations, or government agencies.
Eligibility: Applications are accepted from any country. Applicants must hold a full-time faculty position in an educational institution at the time the award commences and be in a department of diagnostic radiology, radiation oncology or nuclear medicine having completed all advanced training. Applicants must not have served as a principal investigator, co-principal investigator, or co-investigator on grants totalling US$50,000 or more in a single calendar year. Any area of

radiology related research is eligible including basic, clinical, developmental and health care planning, delivery and evaluation.
Type: Research grant.
Value: US$30,000 or less, payable to the recipient's department in two equal instalments.
Length of Study: One year.
Frequency: Twice a year.
Application Procedure: Applicants must complete an application form, available from the website.
Closing Date: January 15th and September 15th.

RAGDALE FOUNDATION

1260 North Green Bay Road, Lake Forest, IL, 60045, United States of America
Tel: (1) 847 234 1063
Fax: (1) 847 234 1075
Email: ragdale1@aol.com
www: http://www.ragdale.org
Contact: Ms Sylvia Brown, Marketing & Programming Director

The Ragdale Foundation is an independent, non-profit organisation whose mission is to provide a peaceful place for artists of all disciplines to work. Residences offered range from two weeks to two months.

Frances Shaw Fellowship

Subjects: Writing, particularly authorship.
Purpose: To support women over the age of 55 who are beginning to write seriously.
Eligibility: Open to women over the age of 55 only. Applicants must be United States citizens.
Level of Study: Unrestricted.
Type: Residency.
Value: US$1,500.
Length of Study: Two months.
Frequency: Annual.
Country of Study: United States of America.
No. of awards offered: One.
Application Procedure: Applicants must write for guidelines enclosing a stamped addressed envelope.
Closing Date: February 1st.
Funding: Private.
No. of awards given last year: One.
No. of applicants last year: 75.

Ragdale Foundation Residencies

Subjects: Creative writing, musical composition, film-making or the visual arts.
Purpose: To provide a peaceful place and uninterrupted time for writers, artists, and composers to do their work.
Eligibility: Open to all creative writers, Scholars, composers, film makers and visual artists. Professional recognition is helpful for admission, but it is not essential. Selections are based on the peer panel's rankings of work samples.
Level of Study: Unrestricted.
Type: Residency.
Length of Study: Periods of between two weeks and two months.
Frequency: Throughout the year, except May and December 15th to January 1st.
Study Establishment: Ragdale House and Barnhouse, Friend's Studio.
Country of Study: United States of America.
No. of awards offered: Up to 12 places at any one time, approx. 160 per year.
Application Procedure: Applicants must submit slides, tapes or samples of writing and two references.
Closing Date: January 15th for June to December and June 1st for January to April.
Contributor: Private donors, the NEA, and the Illinois Arts Council.

Additional Information: Couples are not accepted unless each qualifies independently. Ragdale is in Lake Forest, 30 miles north of Chicago on Lake Michigan. The Ragdale House and Barnhouse were designed by Howard Van Doren Shaw. Much of his landscaping also remains intact such as a garden, lanes through a meadow and prairie, a wide lawn and large trees. Ragdale is on the National Register of Historic Places and the property overlooks a large nature preserve. A new studio building was constructed in 1991.

RAMSAY MEMORIAL FELLOWSHIPS TRUST

University College London
Gower Street, London, WC1E 6BT, England
Tel: (44) 20 7380 7815
Fax: (44) 20 7380 7327
Email: g.hawes@ucl.ac.uk
Contact: Mr Gary Hawes, Executive Secretary

The Ramsay Memorial Fellowships Trust was constituted in 1920 to administer the Ramsay Fellowships which were founded in memory of the late Sir William Ramsay.

British (General) Fellowship

Subjects: Chemistry.
Purpose: To assist postdoctoral research.
Eligibility: Usually open to United Kingdom or Commonwealth citizens who have had training in research methods as evidenced by the possession of a PhD or its equivalent, preferably from a university in the United Kingdom or Commonwealth and who can demonstrate their capacity for original research in chemical science. The maximum age for candidates is 35 years.
Level of Study: Postdoctorate.
Type: Fellowship.
Value: Normally equivalent to the lower part of the Lecturer scale for United Kingdom universities, plus superannuation benefits and a maximum of UK £500 for research expenses.
Length of Study: Two years.
Frequency: Annual.
Study Establishment: A university, university college or other Institute of Higher Education.
Country of Study: Mainly the United Kingdom.
No. of awards offered: Approx. one-two.
Application Procedure: Applicants must complete an application form, available from August.
Closing Date: November 15th.
Funding: Private.
No. of awards given last year: Two.
No. of applicants last year: 46.
Additional Information: Recipients are encouraged to undertake a small amount of teaching work, not exceeding three hours per week.

REES JEFFREYS ROAD FUND

13 The Avenue, Chichester, West Sussex, PO19 4PX, England
Tel: (44) 1243 787013
Fax: (44) 1243 790622
Contact: Mr B Fieldhouse, Secretary

The Rees Jeffreys Road Fund makes grants for courses or research connected with roads and transportation. Within those subjects, it endows university teaching posts, pays bursaries for postgraduate students, sponsors research and contributes to research projects put forward. It has a small budget for the provision of roadside rests and improving roadside environment.

Rees Jeffreys Road Fund Bursaries

Subjects: Transport.
Purpose: To facilitate postgraduate study or research into transport.
Eligibility: Open to candidates of any nationality who hold at least an Upper Second Class (Honours) Degree.
Level of Study: Doctorate, Postgraduate.
Type: Bursary.
Value: To cover fees and equivalent of SERC maintenance for MSc courses in transportation.
Frequency: Annual.
Study Establishment: Universities in the United Kingdom.
Country of Study: United Kingdom.
No. of awards offered: Approx. 10.
Application Procedure: Applicants must be recommended by the intended institution of study.
Closing Date: July 1st for study courses.
Funding: Private.
No. of awards given last year: Nine.
No. of applicants last year: 15.

Rees Jeffreys Road Fund Research Grants

Subjects: Transport.
Purpose: To facilitate research projects into roads and transportation.
Level of Study: Research.
Type: Contribution to research project costs.
Value: UK £1,000 to UK £20,000, depending on the project.
Frequency: Annual.
No. of awards offered: Approx. 12 per year.
Application Procedure: Applicants must write a letter to the secretary.
Closing Date: Any date. Applications will be considered by the trustees at one of five meetings each year.
Funding: Private.
No. of awards given last year: 29.
No. of applicants last year: 40.

THE REID TRUST FOR THE HIGHER EDUCATION OF WOMEN

53 Thornton Hill, Exeter, Devon, EX4 4NR, England
Contact: Mrs H M Harvey, Honorary Treasurer

The Reid Trust for the Higher Education of Women was founded in 1868 in connection with Bedford College for Women for the promotion and improvement of women's education. It is administered by a small committee of voluntary trustees.

The Reid Trust For the Higher Education of Women

Subjects: All subjects.
Purpose: To promote the education of women.
Eligibility: Open to female United Kingdom nationals who have the appropriate academic qualifications and who wish to undertake further study or research.
Level of Study: Unrestricted.
Type: Grant.
Value: UK £50-750 each.
Length of Study: Unrestricted.
Frequency: Annual.
Country of Study: United Kingdom.
No. of awards offered: Usually 10-12.
Application Procedure: Applicants must complete an application form, obtained by sending a stamped addressed envelope with a request.
Closing Date: May 31st.
Funding: Private.
No. of awards given last year: 16.
No. of applicants last year: 200.

REMEDI

The Old Rectory
Stanton Prior, Bath, BA2 9HT, England
Tel: (44) 1761 472662
Fax: (44) 1761 470662
Email: g.coles_remedi@btinternet.com
www: http://www.remedi.org.uk
Contact: Lt Colonel P D Mesquita OBE, Director

REMEDI, founded in 1973, supports pioneering research into all aspects of disability in the widest sense of the word, with special emphasis on handicaps and the way in which they limit the activities and lifestyle of all ages.

REMEDI Research Grants

Subjects: Arthritis, osteoporosis, prostatic disease, rehabilitation of the elderly, speech therapy, stroke, autism or head injury.
Purpose: To support pioneering research into all aspects of disability, in the widest sense of the word, with special emphasis on handicap and the way in which it limits the activities and lifestyle of people of all ages. The Trustees are particularly interested in funding or part funding initial grants where applicants find it difficult to obtain funding through larger organisations.
Eligibility: Open to English speaking applicants living and working in the United Kingdom.
Level of Study: Unrestricted.
Type: Research grant.
Value: Varies.
Length of Study: One-three years.
Frequency: Annual, if funds are available.
Study Establishment: A hospital or university.
Country of Study: United Kingdom.
No. of awards offered: Varies.
Application Procedure: Applicants must email the Director with a summary including costs and start date on one side of A4 paper. If the Chairman considers the research project to be of interest the Director will email an application form to be completed. Completed applications are sent to independent referees for peer review. The Trustees normally make awards twice a year in June and December.
Closing Date: Applications are accepted at any time.
Funding: Private.
Contributor: Trusts, companies and individuals.
No. of awards given last year: 12.
No. of applicants last year: 174.
Additional Information: Grants will not be awarded for course fees, administration and university overheads. Cancer and cancer related diseases are not normally supported. Trustees have decided to reduce the number of awards, but substantially increase the size of the grants.

REPORTERS COMMITTEE FOR FREEDOM OF THE PRESS

1815 North Forte Myer Drive
Suite 900, Arlington, VA, 22209-1817, United States of America
Tel: (1) 703 807 2100
Fax: (1) 703 807 2109
Email: rcfp@rcfp.org
www: http://www.rcfp.org
Contact: Ms Maria Gowen, Office Manager

The Reporters Committee for Freedom of the Press is a voluntary, unincorporated association of reporters and editors, dedicated to protecting the First Amendment interests of the news media. From its Arlington, Virginia office the Reporters Committee staff provide cost free legal defence and research services to journalists and their attorneys throughout the United States and also operate the FOI service centre to assist the news media with federal and state open records and open meetings issues.

Jack Nelson Legal Fellowship

Subjects: Media law.
Eligibility: To be eligible for the programme, candidates must have been granted a law degree no later than August 1999. Significant experience in print or electronic news reporting and strong legal research and writing skills are required.
Type: Fellowship.
Value: US$30,000 plus fully paid health benefits.
Length of Study: One year, September-August.
Frequency: Annual.
Country of Study: United States of America.
No. of awards offered: One.
Application Procedure: Applicants must submit a covering letter, curriculum vitae, contact details of three referees, news clips and a short legal writing sample to the attention of Gregg P Leslie, Acting Executive Director. There is no application form.
Closing Date: February 1st.
Funding: Private.
No. of awards given last year: One.
No. of applicants last year: 40.
Additional Information: The Fellow will monitor significant developments in First Amendment media law, assist with legal defence requirements from reporters, prepare legal memoranda, amicus briefs and other special projects. He or she will also write for The Reporter's Committee's publications, the quarterly magazine The News Media and The Law and the bi-weekly newsletter News Media Update.

The Reporters Committee Legal Fellowship

Subjects: Media law.
Eligibility: Candidates must have received a law degree no later than August 2000. Strong legal research and writing skills are required and a background in news reporting is very strongly preferred.
Type: Fellowship.
Value: US$30,000 plus fully paid health benefits.
Length of Study: One year, September-August.
Frequency: Annual.
Country of Study: United States of America.
No. of awards offered: One.
Closing Date: February 1st.
Funding: Private.
No. of awards given last year: One.
No. of applicants last year: 40.
Additional Information: Legal fellows monitor significant developments in First Amendment media law, assist with legal defence requests from reporters, prepare legal memoranda, amicus briefs and other special projects. They write for the Committee's publications, the quarterly magazine The News Media and The Law and the bi-weekly newsletter, News Media Update.

Robert R McCormick Tribune Foundation Journalism Fellowship

Subjects: Media law.
Purpose: The McCormick Tribune Journalism Fellow will be responsible for ensuring that their publications are appealing to, and understandable by, the core readers, those being journalists who do not have any special legal knowledge. The Fellow will serve as the primary editor of the single topic guides and the daily news product, making sure the website is updated regularly. The Fellow will be responsible for helping identify media law topics that should be addressed in analytical pieces or in enterprise reporting projects, drawing from his or her experience concerning what newsrooms need to know about developments in free press law. In addition, the journalism Fellow will write, edit and design for the Committee's flagship publications, the quarterly magazine, The News Media and The Law, and the bi-weekly newsletter, News Media Update. The Fellow will also be able to audit a course on First Amendment or media law at one of the Washington area universities.
Eligibility: Candidates must possess a law degree and be admitted to the bar of any state. They must have a minimum of two or three years' postgraduate legal experience in a law firm, public interest

group, government agency, or judicial clerkship. Substantial experience in appellate brief writing is mandatory and strong legal research and writing skills is required. A background in news reporting is strongly preferred.

Type: Fellowship.

Value: US$40,000.

Length of Study: One year.

Frequency: Annual.

Country of Study: United States of America.

No. of awards offered: One.

Application Procedure: Applicants must submit a covering letter, curriculum vitae and contact details of three referees, a sample appellate brief and news clips or another short non legal writing sample to Gregg P Leslie, Acting Executive Director. There is no application form.

Closing Date: February 1st.

Funding: Private.

No. of awards given last year: One.

No. of applicants last year: 10.

Additional Information: The Fellow will be expected to draft approx. six appellate amicus briefs in significant cases involving First Amendment media law issues during the fellowship. The legal Fellow will also monitor significant developments in media law, assist with responding to legal defence requests from reporters, prepare legal memoranda and other special projects.

Robert R McCormick Tribune Foundation Legal Fellowship

Subjects: Media law.

Eligibility: Candidates must possess a law degree and be admitted to the bar of any state. They must have a minimum of two or three years of postgraduate legal experience in a law firm, public interest group, government agency or judicial clerkship. Substantial experience in appellate brief writing is mandatory and strong legal research and writing skills is required. A background in news reporting is strongly preferred.

Type: Fellowship.

Value: US$40,000.

Length of Study: One year.

Frequency: Annual.

Country of Study: United States of America.

No. of awards offered: One.

Application Procedure: Applicants must submit a coveing letter, curriculum vitae and contact details of three referees, a sample appelate brief and news clips or another short non legal writing sample to Gregg P Leslie, Acting Executive Director. There is no application form.

Closing Date: February 1st.

Funding: Private.

No. of awards given last year: One.

No. of applicants last year: 10.

Additional Information: The Fellow will be expected to draft approx. six appellate amicus briefs in significant cases involving First Amendment media law issues during the fellowship. The legal Fellow will also monitor significant developments in media law, assist with responding to legal defence requests from reporters, prepare legal memoranda and other special projects. In addition, the legal Fellow will write for the Committee's publications, the quarterly magazine The News Media and The Law and the bi-weekly newsletter News Media Update.

RESEARCH CORPORATION (USA)

101 North Wilmot Road
Suite 250, Tucson, AZ, 85711, United States of America
Tel: (1) 520 571 1111
Fax: (1) 520 571 1119
Email: awards@rescorp.org
www: http://www.rescorp.org
Contact: Ms Carmen Vitello, Editor, Science Advancement Programme

The Research Corporation was one of the first United States of America foundations, and is the only one wholly devoted to the advancement of academic science. An endowed organisation, it makes grants totalling US$5-7 million annually for independently proposed research in chemistry, physics and astronomy at United States of America and Canadian colleges and universities.

Cottrell College Science Awards

Subjects: Physics, chemistry or astronomy.

Purpose: To support significant research.

Eligibility: Open to faculty members at public and private institutes of higher education in the United States of America or Canada. The principal investigator must have an appointment in a department of astronomy, chemistry or physics and the department must offer at least Baccalaureate, but not doctoral degrees. The institution must demonstrate its commitment by providing facilities and opportunities for faculty and student research.

Level of Study: Professional development.

Type: Research grant.

Value: Equipment and supplies, student Summer stipends of up to US$3,500 and a faculty Summer stipend of up to US$7,500.

Length of Study: One-two years, possibly renewable for a further one-two years.

Frequency: Twice a year.

Study Establishment: Public and private universities and non-PhD granting departments of astronomy, chemistry or physics.

Country of Study: United States of America or Canada.

No. of awards offered: 100+.

Application Procedure: Applicants must complete an application form and should visit the website for guidelines and application request forms.

Closing Date: November 15th or May 15th.

Funding: Private.

Contributor: Foundation endowment.

No. of awards given last year: 79.

No. of applicants last year: 239.

Cottrell Scholars Awards

Subjects: Physics, chemistry or astronomy in graduate university departments.

Purpose: To encourage excellence in both research and teaching.

Eligibility: Open to faculty in the third year of a first tenure track position.

Level of Study: Professional development.

Type: Award.

Value: US$75,000, which may be flexibly applied in keeping with the applicants' approved programme.

Frequency: Annual.

Study Establishment: Universities with PhD granting departments of physics, chemistry and astronomy.

Country of Study: United States of America or Canada.

No. of awards offered: Varies.

Application Procedure: Applicants must complete an application form and should visit the website for guidelines and application request forms.

Closing Date: September 1st.

Funding: Private.

Contributor: Foundation endowment.

No. of awards given last year: 18.

No. of applicants last year: 91.

Additional Information: Candidates must provide both a research and teaching plan for peer review.

Research Corporation (USA) Research Innovation Awards

Subjects: Physics, chemistry or astronomy.

Purpose: To assist innovative research programmes in physics, chemistry and astronomy, for faculty of PhD granting departments of United States and Canadian research universities.

Eligibility: Open to faculty members whose first tenure track position began in either the preceding or the current calendar year are eligible to apply.

Level of Study: Professional development.

Type: Research grant.

Value: Up to US$35,000 for equipment and supplies, graduate stipends and some other expenses (no overheads).

Frequency: Annual.

Study Establishment: Research universities with PhD granting departments of physics, chemistry and astronomy.

Country of Study: United States of America or Canada.

No. of awards offered: Varies.

Application Procedure: Applicants must complete an application form. Guidelines and an application request are available from the website http://www.rescorp.org.

Closing Date: May 1st.

Funding: Private.

Contributor: Foundation endowment.

No. of awards given last year: 46.

No. of applicants last year: 143.

Additional Information: Research proposals are sought after that transcend the ordinary and promise significant discoveries.

Research Corporation (USA) Research Opportunity Awards

Subjects: Physics, chemistry or astronomy.

Purpose: To assist mid-career faculty scientists in launching new research programmes.

Eligibility: Open to established faculty members in PhD departments in the United States of America or Canada.

Level of Study: Professional development.

Type: Research grant.

Value: Up to US$75,000.

Frequency: Annual.

Study Establishment: Universities with PhD granting departments of physics, chemistry and astronomy.

Country of Study: United States of America or Canada.

No. of awards offered: Varies, there is no fixed number.

Application Procedure: Applicants must be nominated by the department chair and selected nominees are invited to submit applications on the forms provided. Interested parties should visit the website or write for printed guidelines.

Closing Date: May 1st or October 1st are the target dates for nominations.

Funding: Private.

Contributor: Foundation endowment.

No. of awards given last year: Eight.

No. of applicants last year: 16.

Additional Information: The chair of each PhD granting physics and chemistry department in the United States of America or Canada may make two nominations annually from tenured faculty without major research funding. Applications are invited from a selected group of these nominees.

RESEARCH INTO AGEING

PO Box 32833, London, N1 9ZQ, England
Tel: (44) 20 7404 6878
Fax: (44) 20 7404 6816
Email: ria@ageing.co.uk
www: http://www.ageing.org
Contact: Dr S Sorensen, Research Manager

Research into Ageing's purpose is to advance the prevention, or improvement in treatment, of diseases and disabilities which become more common in later life. This is done by funding high quality research, supporting the education of scientists, raising awareness of the potential of research and lobbying for implementation of results.

Queen Elizabeth the Queen Mother Fellowship Award

Subjects: Geriatric medicine, gerontology, cell and molecular biology of ageing processes.

Purpose: To provide an opportunity for postdoctoral scientists or those who are medically qualified to become independent researchers and to undertake research of high quality.

Eligibility: Applicants should normally have no more than 10 years of postdoctoral experience and intend to maintain a long-term interest in ageing research. Applicants must be able to speak English. The award is only tenable at United Kingdom institutions.

Level of Study: Postdoctorate.

Type: Fellowship.

Value: Up to UK £50,000 per year for the duration of the award.

Length of Study: Three years.

Frequency: Annual.

Study Establishment: An institution in the United Kingdom.

Country of Study: United Kingdom.

No. of awards offered: Four-six.

Application Procedure: Applicants must initially submit a two page outline proposal on a form available on request. Shortlisted applicants will be sent a full application form. Fellowships are considered annually in May and November.

Closing Date: Outline proposal forms are due in Winter and Summer. Please check the exact date with the Research Department. This can be found on the website where forms are also available to download.

No. of awards given last year: Four-six.

Research into Ageing Prize Studentships

Subjects: Geriatric medicine, gerontology, cell and molecular biology of ageing processes or related disciplines.

Purpose: To ensure a flow of first class students into the field of ageing research.

Eligibility: Open to potential supervisors wishing to enable a postgraduate to obtain a further degree, usually to PhD standard, through work on a topic connected with age related illness or the ageing process. Applicants must be able to speak English and must be employed by a United Kingdom institution.

Level of Study: Postgraduate.

Type: Studentship.

Value: Stipend, university fees up to UK £3,000 per year, expenses for consumables and travel up to UK £3,000 per year.

Length of Study: Three years.

Frequency: Annual.

Study Establishment: Suitable United Kingdom establishments.

Country of Study: United Kingdom.

No. of awards offered: Three.

Application Procedure: Applicants must initially submit a two page outline proposal on a form available on request. Shortlisted applicants will be sent a full application form. Studentships are considered annually in November for start the following year.

Closing Date: Outline proposal forms must be returned between July and August. Check the exact date with the Research Department.

No. of awards given last year: Three.

No. of applicants last year: 15-20.

Additional Information: Awards should be applied for by supervisors.

Research into Ageing Programme Grants

Subjects: Geriatric medicine, gerontology or related disciplines.
Purpose: To provide support for research that cannot be carried out in the short-term. The programme is designed to enable researchers to establish longer term programmes of work and retain teams of research workers without having to repeatedly seek funds.
Eligibility: Individuals, groups of researchers or interdisciplinary teams. Applicants should normally hold an established post at a university or institution within the United Kingdom and have a good track record of research in the proposed field of work.
Level of Study: Postdoctorate.
Type: Programme grant.
Value: Up to UK £500,000 over five years.
Length of Study: Up to five years.
Frequency: Annual.
Study Establishment: Universities, medical colleges, hospitals and general practices in the United Kingdom.
Country of Study: United Kingdom.
No. of awards offered: Dependent on funds available.
Application Procedure: Applicants must initially submit a two page outline proposal on a form available on request. Shortlisted applicants will be sent a full application form. Research project grants are considered annually in May.
Closing Date: Once a year. Outline applications are due in November.
No. of awards given last year: Two.
No. of applicants last year: 29.

RESOURCES FOR THE FUTURE (RFF)

1616 P Street North West, Washington, DC, 20036, United States of America
Tel: (1) 202 328 5043
Fax: (1) 202 939 3460
Email: macauley@rff.org
www: http://www.rff.org
Contact: Ms Molly Macauley, Co-ordinator for Academic Programmes

Resources for the Future (RFF) is a non-profit and non-partisan think tank located in Washington, DC that conducts independent research rooted primarily in economics and other social sciences on environmental and natural resource issues.

Gilbert F White Postdoctoral Fellowship

Subjects: Social and policy sciences, environmental studies, energy and natural resources.
Purpose: To enable postdoctoral researchers to spend a year in residence conducting research in the social or policy sciences in areas related to the environment, energy or natural resources.
Eligibility: A strong economics (or closely related discipline in the social or policy sciences) background is required. Applicants must be of postdoctorate level.
Level of Study: Postdoctorate.
Type: Fellowship.
Value: US$35,000 plus living expenses.
Length of Study: One year.
Frequency: Annual.
Country of Study: United States of America.
No. of awards offered: Two.
Application Procedure: Applicants must submit a covering letter and curriculum vitae with a proposal relating to budget and three letters of recommendation. No application form is required.
Closing Date: February 28th.
No. of awards given last year: Two.
No. of applicants last year: 25.

Joseph L Fisher Dissertation Award

Subjects: Economics, policy sciences, environment and natural resources.
Purpose: To support PhD students in their last year of dissertation research in economics or other policy sciences on issues related to the environment, energy or natural resources.
Eligibility: Open to all nationalities. Students must be in the final year of dissertation research or writing.
Level of Study: Doctorate.
Type: Dissertation award.
Value: US$12,000.
Length of Study: One year.
Frequency: Annual.
Country of Study: Any country.
No. of awards offered: Five.
Application Procedure: Applicants must submit a letter of application, a curriculum vitae, graduate transcripts, a one page abstract of the dissertation, a technical summary of the dissertation, a letter from the department chair and two letters of recommendation.
Closing Date: February 28th.
No. of awards given last year: Five.
No. of applicants last year: 150.

RFF Fellowships in Environmental Regulatory Implementation

Subjects: Environment, natural resources or a descriptive study.
Purpose: To support research that documents the implementation and outcomes of environmental regulations.
Eligibility: Open to Scholars from universities and research establishments who have a doctorate or equivalent degree or professional research experience.
Level of Study: Postdoctorate.
Type: Fellowship.
Value: Negotiable stipend.
Length of Study: One-two years.
Frequency: Annual.
Country of Study: United States of America.
No. of awards offered: Two.
Application Procedure: Applicants must submit a pre-proposal containing their full name, title and address including telephone number and email address, a descriptive name or title of the project, a concise description of the research to be addressed, the importance of the problem, the product eg. book or monograph expected to result from the project, a list of the major tasks involved in conducting the project, a schedule for start and completion of the project, a brief statement of prior experience of the applicant and an estimated budget. The pre-proposal should be limited to two pages, single spaced with no smaller than 11 point font and one inch margins. Applicants whose pre-proposals are selected for further review will then be invited to submit final proposals. These are limited to ten pages and are to follow a similar format. They must include all of the information contained in the pre-proposal but should offer further detailed description of the proposed research, anticipated contribution of the project and the importance of the results. They should also include a curriculum vitae with the applicant's educational background, professional experience, a list of most relevant publications and honours and awards received. In addition, final proposals must include three letters of recommendation from fellow faculty members or colleagues and these are not included in the 10 page limit.
Closing Date: January 4th for pre-proposals and February 28th for final proposals.
Funding: Private.

RHODES UNIVERSITY

PO Box 94, Grahamstown, 6140, South Africa
Tel: (27) 46 603 8055
Fax: (27) 46 622 8444
Email: research-admin@ru.ac.za
www: http://www.ru.ac.za/research
Contact: Miss Moira Pogrund, Dean of Research

Rhodes University is a small university of two campuses in Grahamstown and East London. The University plans to continue to offer excellent undergraduate and postgraduate education, provide opportunities for research and to foster personal development and leadership as well as team, social and communication skills among its diverse student body.

Allan Gray Senior Scholarship

Subjects: Any discipline at Rhodes University.
Purpose: To encourage and enable previously disadvantaged South Africans to pursue their studies at Honours and Master's level.
Eligibility: Open to previously disadvantaged South African students with the appropriate qualifications.
Level of Study: Postgraduate.
Type: Scholarship.
Value: Rand 25,000.
Length of Study: One year, renewable upon reapplication.
Frequency: Annual.
Study Establishment: Rhodes University, Grahamstown.
Country of Study: South Africa.
No. of awards offered: Four.
Application Procedure: Applicants must submit a curriculum vitae and a full academic record by August 1st in the year preceding registration at Rhodes University. Shortlisted applicants will be required to complete an application form providing additional information and referee reports.
Closing Date: August 1st in the year preceding registration.
Funding: Private.
Contributor: Donor and investments.
No. of awards given last year: Four.
No. of applicants last year: 103.
Additional Information: Postgraduate Scholars must assist with teaching and/or research duties up to a maximum of six hours a week in their department of study, without additional remuneration. Awards are for full-time study in attendance at Rhodes University only.

Andrew Mellon Foundation Scholarship

Subjects: Applicants may pursue studies in any of the six faculties at Rhodes University which are humanities, commerce, education, law, pharmacy and science.
Purpose: To encourage and enable previously disadvantaged people to pursue their studies at Master's or doctoral level at Rhodes University, as well as to enhance the recipients' ability to contribute to higher education in South Africa.
Eligibility: Open to those previously disadvantaged with the appropriate qualifications.
Level of Study: Postgraduate.
Type: Scholarship.
Value: Rand 25,000 for Master's and rand 40,000 for doctoral.
Length of Study: One year, renewable upon reapplication.
Frequency: Annual.
Study Establishment: Rhodes University, Grahamstown.
Country of Study: South Africa.
No. of awards offered: 10.
Application Procedure: Applicants must submit a curriculum vitae and a full academic record by August 1st in the year preceding registration at Rhodes University. Shortlisted applicants will be required to complete an application form providing additional information and referee reports.
Closing Date: August 1st in the year preceding registration.
Funding: Private.
Contributor: Donor and investments.

No. of awards given last year: 10.
No. of applicants last year: 103.
Additional Information: Scholars must assist with teaching and/or research duties up to a maximum of six hours a week in their department of study, without additional remuneration. Awards are for full-time study in attendance at Rhodes University only.

The Guy Butler Research Award

Subjects: Applicants may pursue research in English language, English literature, South African English drama, South African journalism in English, and cultural studies focusing on English related topics in South Africa.
Purpose: To attract outstanding graduate students to the University, thereby extending the tradition of originality and innovation which has characterised the discipline of the University, for the benefit of South Africa.
Level of Study: Postgraduate.
Type: Scholarship.
Value: Rand 25,000 at Master's level and rand 40,000 at doctoral level.
Length of Study: One year, renewable upon reapplication.
Frequency: Annual.
Study Establishment: Rhodes University, Grahamstown.
Country of Study: South Africa.
No. of awards offered: One.
Application Procedure: Applicants must submit a curriculum vitae and a full academic record by August 1st in the year preceding registration at Rhodes University. Shortlisted applicants will be required to complete an application form providing additional information and referee reports.
Closing Date: August 1st.
Funding: Private.
Contributor: Donor and investments.
No. of awards given last year: One.
No. of applicants last year: 40.
Additional Information: Applicants must register full-time attendance at Rhodes University. The Guy Butler Research Award must be acknowledged in the thesis and any publication derived from it.

Henderson Postgraduate Scholarships

Subjects: Applicants may pursue the following fields of mathematical, physical, earth, life and pharmaceutical sciences, accountancy or information systems.
Purpose: To encourage and enable students to pursue their studies at the Master's and doctoral levels. Also to enhance recipients' research abilities and produce internationally competitive graduates with an innovative, analytical, articulate and well rounded desire to learn.
Eligibility: Open to South African citizens with appropriate qualifications.
Level of Study: Postgraduate.
Type: Scholarship.
Value: Rand 25,000 for Master's and rand 40,000 for doctoral.
Length of Study: One year, renewable upon reapplication.
Frequency: Annual.
Study Establishment: Rhodes University, Grahamstown.
Country of Study: South Africa.
No. of awards offered: One.
Application Procedure: Applicants must submit a curriculum vitae and a full academic record by August 1st in the year preceding registration at Rhodes University. Shortlisted applicants will be required to complete an application form, providing additional information and referee reports.
Closing Date: August 1st in the year preceding registration.
Funding: Private.
Contributor: Donor and investments.
No. of awards given last year: One.
No. of applicants last year: 29.
Additional Information: Scholars must assist with teaching and/or research duties up to a maximum of six hours a week in their department of study, without additional remuneration. Awards are for full-time study in attendance at Rhodes University only.

Hobart Houghton Research Fellowship

Subjects: Social and behavioural sciences or economics.
Purpose: To promote work of scientific value relevant to the economic problems of the Eastern Cape Province, Republic of South Africa, which could contribute to the betterment of the people of the region.
Eligibility: Open to English speakers who hold at least a Master's degree in economics and who exhibit successful research experience.
Level of Study: Doctorate, Postdoctorate.
Type: Fellowship.
Value: Rand 25,000.
Length of Study: 2-12 months.
Frequency: Annual.
Study Establishment: Rhodes University, Grahamstown.
Country of Study: South Africa.
No. of awards offered: One.
Application Procedure: Applicants must complete an application form, available from Dean of Research. Enquiries may also be addressed to Professor H Nel, Department of Economics and Economic History, email h.nel@ru.ac.za or from the website.
Closing Date: September 30th.
Funding: Commercial.
No. of awards given last year: One.
No. of applicants last year: One.

Hugh Kelly Fellowship

Subjects: Biochemistry and microbiology, botany, chemistry, computer science, statistics, mathematics both pure and applied, pharmaceutical sciences, physics and electronics, zoology and entomology, ichthyology, fisheries science, geography or geology.
Purpose: To enable senior scientists to devote themselves to advanced work.
Eligibility: Open to suitable postdoctoral scientists. Preference is given to candidates willing to accept appointments for at least six months. Applicants must be English speakers.
Level of Study: Postdoctorate.
Type: Fellowship.
Value: Currently under review, but a package of approx. US$11,000 per year depending on exchange rate at the time of the award is available. If the Fellow accepts an appointment for at least six months and is accompanied by a spouse, the spouse's air or rail fares will also be paid. University accommodation will be provided free of charge, but the provision of a telephone (if available) at the place of residence will be for the Fellow's personal account.
Length of Study: Up to one year.
Frequency: Every two years.
Study Establishment: Rhodes University, Grahamstown.
Country of Study: South Africa.
No. of awards offered: One.
Application Procedure: Applicants must complete an application form, available from the Dean of Research or from the website.
Closing Date: July 31st of the year preceding the award.
Funding: Private.
Contributor: Donor and investments.
No. of awards given last year: One.
No. of applicants last year: Six.
Additional Information: The Fellow will be required to present a concise report on the work completed at the conclusion of the term of the fellowship.

Hugh Le May Fellowship

Subjects: Philosophy, theology, classics, ancient, modern or medieval history, classical, biblical, medieval or modern languages, political theory or law.
Purpose: To enable scholars to devote themselves to advanced work.
Eligibility: Open to any postdoctoral Scholars of standing, with research publications to their credit. Applicants must be English speakers.
Level of Study: Postdoctorate.
Type: Fellowship.

Value: Return economy air ticket, furnished accommodation and small monthly cash stipend.
Length of Study: Three-four months. This may be extended by mutual agreement, subject to availability of funds.
Frequency: Every two years (even-numbered years).
Study Establishment: Rhodes University, Grahamstown.
Country of Study: South Africa.
No. of awards offered: One.
Application Procedure: Applicants must complete an application form, available from the Dean of Research or from the website.
Closing Date: July 31st of the year preceding the award.
Funding: Private.
Contributor: Donor and investments.
No. of awards given last year: One.
No. of applicants last year: 15.
Additional Information: Fellows are not expected to undertake teaching duties.

Patrick and Margaret Flanagan Scholarship

Subjects: All subjects.
Purpose: To enable South African women graduates to attend a university in the United Kingdom in order to obtain a higher postgraduate qualification.
Eligibility: Women graduates are eligible, preferably who are English speaking applicants of South African descent. Selection is based initially on academic merit, as well as broader qualities of intellect and character.
Type: Scholarship.
Value: Rand 140,000 per year.
Length of Study: Two years.
Frequency: Annual.
Study Establishment: Rhodes University, Grahamstown.
Country of Study: United Kingdom.
No. of awards offered: One.
Application Procedure: Applicants must submit a curriculum vitae and full academic record by August 1st. Candidates shortlisted will be sent an application form or additional information and referee reports.
Closing Date: August 1st of the year prior to registration abroad.
Funding: Private.
Contributor: Donor and investments.
No. of awards given last year: One.
No. of applicants last year: 113.

Rhodes University Postdoctoral Fellowship

Subjects: All subjects.
Purpose: To enable scholars to devote themselves to advanced work which will closely complement existing programmes in the host department.
Eligibility: Open to any postdoctoral Scholars of standing, with research publications to their credit and of exceptional merit. Applicants must be English speakers.
Level of Study: Postdoctorate.
Type: Fellowship.
Value: Rand 55,000 per year with an additional allocation of a maximum of rand 5,000 to be used at the discretion of the head of department for running costs for the postdoctoral project or the transport of the candidate to Grahamstown.
Length of Study: One year, but may be extended by mutual agreement, subject to the availability of funds.
Frequency: Annual.
Study Establishment: Rhodes University, Grahamstown.
Country of Study: South Africa.
No. of awards offered: One.
Application Procedure: Applicants must be nominated. Nominations should be made through heads of departments and directors of research institutes at Rhodes University. Nominations must include a full curriculum vitae and the name of three referees who may be consulted. Further information may be obtained from the Dean of Research.
Closing Date: July 31st of the year preceding the award.
Funding: Private.

Contributor: Donor and investments.
No. of awards given last year: Four.
No. of applicants last year: 12.
Additional Information: Fellows are not expected to undertake teaching duties.

Rhodes University Postgraduate Scholarship

Subjects: Applicants may pursue studies in any of the six faculties at Rhodes University: humanities, commerce, education, law, pharmacy or science.
Purpose: To encourage and enable students to pursue their studies at Master's and doctoral levels, enhancing recipients' research abilities and producing internationally competitive graduates with an innovative, analytical, articulate, adaptable and well rounded desire to learn.
Eligibility: Students with the appropriate qualifications are eligible. Academic merit will override criterion.
Level of Study: Postgraduate.
Type: Scholarship.
Value: Rand 25,000 for Master's and rand 40,000 for doctoral.
Length of Study: One year, renewable upon reapplication.
Frequency: Annual.
Study Establishment: Rhodes University, Grahamstown.
Country of Study: South Africa.
No. of awards offered: Four.
Application Procedure: Applicants must submit a curriculum vitae and a full academic record by August 1st in the year preceding registration at Rhodes University. Shortlisted applicants will be required to complete an application form providing additional information and referee reports.
Closing Date: August 1st in the year preceding registration.
Funding: Private.
Contributor: Donor and investments.
No. of awards given last year: Four.
No. of applicants last year: 31.
Additional Information: Scholars must assist with teaching and/or research duties up to a maximum of six hours per week in their department of study, without additional remuneration. Awards are for full-time study in attendance at Rhodes University only.

RICHARD III SOCIETY, AMERICAN BRANCH

2041 Christian Street, Philadelphia, PA, 19146, United States of America
Email: feedback@r3.org
www: http://www.r3.org
Contact: Ms Laura Blanchard, Schallek Fellowships

The Richard III Society was founded in 1924 in England as The Fellowship of the White Boar and was renamed the Richard III Society in 1959. The American Branch was founded in 1961. Today the Society has more than 4,000 members worldwide and American Branch membership is more than 800.

William B Schallek Memorial Graduate Fellowship Award

Subjects: Medieval history.
Purpose: To support graduate study of fifteenth-century English history and culture.
Eligibility: Applicants must be United States citizens or have made application for first citizenship papers, or be permanent resident aliens, enrolled at a recognised educational institution.
Level of Study: Doctorate.
Type: Fellowship.
Value: US$500-2,000 depending on the need and/or quality of applicant.
Length of Study: One year, although renewals will be considered.
Frequency: Annual.
Study Establishment: Recognised and accredited degree granting institutions.

Country of Study: Any country.
No. of awards offered: Varies.
Application Procedure: Applicants must visit the website for guidelines, lists of past awards, their topics and application forms.
Closing Date: February 28th for the following academic year.
No. of awards given last year: Three.
No. of applicants last year: Seven.

RICHARD TUCKER MUSIC FOUNDATION

1790 Broadway
Suite 715, New York, NY, 10019, United States of America
Tel: (1) 212 757 2218
Fax: (1) 212 757 2347
www: http://www.rtucker.com
Contact: Executive Director

The Richard Tucker Music Foundation is a non-profit cultural organisation designed to perpetuate the memory of the great American tenor principally through the support and advancement of the careers of promising and talented American opera singers. In addition, the Foundation seeks to heighten public awareness of the art of opera.

Richard Tucker Award

Subjects: Operatic singing.
Purpose: To further the career development of an artist on the brink of international acclaim.
Eligibility: Open to American born opera singers who are recommended to the Foundation by a person other than the artist or the artist's manager. Awarded by a conferral not a competition. The operative guideline for the Richard Tucker Award is that it be awarded to an American singer poised on the edge of a major national and international career.
Level of Study: Professional development.
Type: Award.
Value: US$30,000.
Length of Study: One year, non renewable.
Frequency: Annual.
Country of Study: Any country.
No. of awards offered: One.
Application Procedure: Applicants must be recommended.
Closing Date: November 30th of the year preceding the award.
Funding: Private.

Richard Tucker Career Grant

Subjects: Operatic singing.
Purpose: To further the career of young American artists.
Eligibility: Open to American born opera singers. Candidates must be recommended by a professional in the operatic field with whom they have worked. A Career Grant candidate must be 36 years old or younger and should have a fair amount of performing experience in professional companies.
Level of Study: Professional development.
Type: Grant.
Value: At least US$7,500.
Length of Study: One year, renewable.
Frequency: Annual.
Country of Study: Any country.
No. of awards offered: Four.
Application Procedure: Applicants must be recommended.
Closing Date: November 30th of the year preceding the award.
Funding: Private.

Sara Tucker Study Grant

Subjects: Operatic singing.
Purpose: To help an artist at the earliest stage of his or her career.
Eligibility: Open to American born opera singers who are at an early level of their career. Candidates must be recommended for the grant and should be completing an apprentice programme, or have

recently graduated from a conservatory. A Study Grant candidate must be 27 years old or younger and should be making the transition from student to professional singer. A candidate should have recently completed a graduate degree programme, or recently completed or soon to complete work in a young artist or apprentice programme at a regional company.

Level of Study: Postgraduate.
Type: Grant.
Value: US$5,000.
Length of Study: One year, non renewable.
Frequency: Annual.
Country of Study: Any country.
No. of awards offered: Four.
Application Procedure: Applicants must be recommended.
Closing Date: November 30th of the year preceding the award.
Funding: Private.

RICS FOUNDATION

12 Great George Street, London, SW1P 3AD, England
Tel: (44) 20 7334 3725
Fax: (44) 20 7334 3894
Email: stephen@rics-foundation.org
www: http://www.rics-foundation.org
Contact: Mr Stephen Brown

The Royal Institution of Chartered Surveyors (RICS) is the professional institution for the surveying profession.

RICS Education Trust Award

Subjects: The theory and practice of surveying in any of its disciplines including general practice, quantity surveying, building surveying, rural practice, planning and development, land surveying or minerals surveying.
Eligibility: Open to chartered surveyors and others carrying out research studies in relevant subjects.
Level of Study: Unrestricted.
Type: Research grant.
Value: Usually up to UK £5,000.
Frequency: Twice a year.
Country of Study: Any country.
Application Procedure: Applicants must complete an application form.
Closing Date: September 30th or February 28th.
Funding: Commercial.
Contributor: RICS.
No. of awards given last year: 20.
No. of applicants last year: 40.

ROB AND BESSIE WELDER WILDLIFE FOUNDATION

PO Drawer 1400, Sinton, TX, 78387, United States of America
Tel: (1) 361 364 2643
Fax: (1) 361 364 2650
Email: welderwf@aol.com
www: http://hometown.aol.com/welderwf/welderweb.html
Contact: Dr Lynn Drawe, Director

The Rob and Bessie Welder Wildlife Foundation is a private nonprofit operating foundation whose mission is to conduct research and education in wildlife management and closely related fields. The Welder Foundation operates a wildlife refuge on a commercial ranch in the midst of an active oil field.

Welder Wildlife Foundation Fellowship

Subjects: Wildlife ecology and management.

Purpose: To provide support to individual graduate student research.
Eligibility: Open to United States of America citizens or aliens registered in a United States of America university for a graduate degree. Priority is given to students who wish to work at the Welder Foundation Refuge or in the Coastal Bend Region of Texas.
Level of Study: Graduate.
Type: Fellowship.
Value: Up to US$15,000 per year, according to individual needs.
Length of Study: The duration of a graduate degree programme.
Frequency: Annual.
Study Establishment: Any legitimate wildlife management or wildlife ecological department at any accredited university in the United States of America.
Country of Study: United States of America.
No. of awards offered: 20 at any given time, approx. five each year.
Application Procedure: Applicants must write for details.
Closing Date: October 1st for fellowships to begin in January.
Funding: Private.
Contributor: Private endowment.
No. of awards given last year: Five.
No. of applicants last year: 25.

THE ROBERT A TOIGO FOUNDATION

1211 Preservation Park Way, Oakland, CA, 94612, United States of America
Tel: (1) 510 763 5771
Fax: (1) 510 763 5778
Email: nsimsrtf@aol.com
www: http://www.rtf.org
Contact: Fellowship Administrator

Robert A Toigo Foundation Fellowships

Subjects: MBA.
Purpose: To increase minority representation in the investment community.
Eligibility: Open to minority students of outstanding academic record who show a dedication to furthering the goals of the finance industry.
Level of Study: MBA.
Type: Fellowship.
Study Establishment: The Wharton School.
Country of Study: United States of America.
Application Procedure: Applicants must contact the organisation.
Closing Date: Please contact the organisation.
Additional Information: Further information is available on request.

ROBERT BOSCH FOUNDATION

c/o CDS International, Inc.
871 United Nations Plaza, 15th Floor
First Avenue 49th Street, New York, NY, 10017-1814, United States of America
Tel: (1) 212 497 3500
Fax: (1) 212 497 3535
Email: info@cdsintl.org
www: http://www.cdsintl.org
Contact: Program Officer

The Robert Bosch Stiftung is one of the largest German industry foundations. Many of the Foundation's international exchange programmes are aimed at providing young people with opportunities to improve their knowledge of other countries and cultures and to build up networks among the future elite in Europe and the United States.

Robert Bosch Foundation Fellowship Program

Subjects: Business and administration management, law, journalism, mass communication and media studies.
Eligibility: Open to United States of America nationals.
Level of Study: Postgraduate, Professional development.
Type: Fellowship.
Length of Study: Nine months from September-May.
Frequency: Annual.
Country of Study: Germany.
No. of awards offered: 20.
Application Procedure: Applicants must visit the website for details.
Closing Date: October 15th.
Funding: Private.
Contributor: Private foundation.

Robert Bosch Foundation Fellowships

Subjects: Business administration, economics, public affairs, public policy, political science, law, journalism and mass communication.
Purpose: To promote the advancement of American and German-European relations, and to broaden the participants' professional competence and cultural horizons.
Eligibility: Open to United States citizens with a graduate or professional degree or equivalent work experience in the above subject areas. Candidates must provide evidence of outstanding professional or academic achievement and a strong knowledge of the German language. For those candidates who are outstanding in other areas but lack sufficient knowledge of German, the Foundation will provide language training prior to programme participation.
Level of Study: Postgraduate, Professional development.
Type: Internship.
Value: Deutsche mark 3,500 per month stipend, extra funding for family, language training and business travel.
Length of Study: Nine months from September-May.
Frequency: Annual.
Country of Study: Germany.
No. of awards offered: 20.
Application Procedure: Applicants must complete an application form and attend a personal interview.
Closing Date: October 15th.
Funding: Private.
Additional Information: Programme participants receive internships in German institutions such as the Federal Parliament, private corporation headquarters, mass media and other elements within the framework of government or commerce. Internships will be at a high level, closely related to senior officials. The programme will follow the following schedule: an intensive course on German language, political, economic and cultural affairs, work experience, a visit to Berlin and the former East Germany, a visit to the European Economic Community and NATO headquarters in Brussels, a group visit to France for an overview of the political, economic and cultural perspective of another European country, and a final programme evaluation in Stuttgart. All activities are conducted in German.

ROBERTO LONGHI FOUNDATION

Via Benedetto Fortini 30, Florence, I-50125, Italy
Tel: (39) 055 658 0794
Fax: (39) 055 658 0794
www: http://www.firenze.it/frl
Contact: Ms Mina Gregori, President

The aim of the Robert Longhi Foundation is to advance art historical studies. Applications are accepted annually from prospective fellows who hold an advanced degree in art history. Fellows pursue individual and group research projects using the library and photo archive, participate in seminars and lectures by distinguished scholars at the Foundation and visit galleries, restorations and exhibitions.

Roberto Longhi Foundation Fellowships

Subjects: History of art.
Purpose: To aid those who want to seriously dedicate themselves to research in the history of art.
Eligibility: Open to Italian citizens who possess a degree from an Italian university with a thesis in the history of art, and to non Italian citizens who have fulfilled the preliminary requirements for a doctoral degree in the history of art at an accredited university or an institution of equal standing. Students who have reached their 30th birthday before the application deadline are not eligible.
Level of Study: Doctorate, Postgraduate.
Type: Fellowship.
Value: The monthly rate is €565.
Length of Study: Nine months.
Frequency: Annual.
Study Establishment: The Institute.
Country of Study: Italy.
No. of awards offered: Up to 10.
Application Procedure: Applicants must submit an application containing their biographical data (place and date of birth, domicile, citizenship), transcript of undergraduate and graduate records, a copy of the degree thesis (if available) and of other original works, a curriculum vitae including knowledge of foreign languages both spoken and written, letters of reference from at least two persons of academic standing who are acquainted with the applicant's work, the subject of the research proposed, and two passport photographs.
Closing Date: May 15th.
Funding: Private.
Contributor: Private funds and capital endowment.
No. of awards given last year: Six.
Additional Information: Successful candidates must give the assurance that they can dedicate their full-time to the research for which the fellowship is assigned. They may not enter into any connection with other institutions, they must live in Florence for the duration of the fellowship, excepting travels required for their research. They may not exceed the periods of vacations fixed by the Institute. They are required to attend seminars, lectures and other activities arranged by the Institute. The Fellows must in addition submit a written report at the end of their stay in Florence, relating the findings of their individual research undertaken at the Longhi Foundation. Once approved by the scientific committee the Fellow's research must be published only in the Foundation's annual journal Proporzioni. The non compliance of the above conditions will be considered sufficient grounds for the cancellation of a fellowship. Further information is available on request.

ROCHE RESEARCH FOUNDATION

Building 92/8.08
F Hoffmann-La Roche Limited, Basel, CH-4070, Switzerland
Tel: (41) 61 688 5227
Fax: (41) 61 688 1460
Email: research.foundation@roche.com
www: http://www.research-foundation.org
Contact: Ms Margrit Freiburghaus

The Roche Research Foundation is a charity sponsored by F Hoffmann-La Roche Limited, subsidising experimental scientific research in the life sciences.

Roche Research Foundation

Subjects: Biology, medicine or chemistry.
Purpose: To promote scientific research at Swiss universities and hospitals in the biomedical field, and to sponsor experimental research of Swiss Fellows in biology, chemistry and medicine at universities and laboratories abroad.
Eligibility: Open to all qualified researchers (for fellowships at Swiss universities or hospitals) and to qualified Swiss students (for fellowships abroad).
Level of Study: Doctorate, Postdoctorate, Postgraduate.

589

Type: Fellowship.
Value: Living costs.
Frequency: Quarterly.
Country of Study: Any country.
No. of awards offered: 100.
Application Procedure: Applicants must complete an application form in English.
Closing Date: January 15th, April 15th, July 15th or October 15th.
Funding: Private.

ROCK ISLAND ARSENAL MUSEUM

Attn: SIORI-CFS-M
Rock Island Arsenal Historical Society
R Maguire Scholarship Committee
Rock Island Arsenal, Rock Island, IL, 61299-5000, United States of America
Tel: (1) 309 782 5021
Fax: (1) 309 782 3598

Richard C Maguire Scholarship

Subjects: History (United States, world, military, religion) or related fields such as archaeology and museum study.
Purpose: To financially support a student working for a Master's or doctorate degree.
Eligibility: Applicants must be United States citizens. Grants will be awarded on an objective and non discriminatory basis without regard to age, sex, race, religion or affiliation.
Level of Study: Postdoctorate, Postgraduate.
Type: Scholarship.
Value: US$1,000.
Length of Study: One year.
Frequency: Annual.
Study Establishment: A United States college of the candidate's choice.
Country of Study: United States of America.
No. of awards offered: One.
Application Procedure: For an application form applicants must write to the Rock Island Arsenal Museum, enclosing a stamped addressed envelope. Completed applications must include proof of citizenship, a letter of acceptance into a postgraduate programme in an accredited college or university and complete transcript of college grades.
Closing Date: March 31st.
Funding: Private.
No. of awards given last year: One.
No. of applicants last year: 53.

ROCKEFELLER ARCHIVE CENTER

15 Dayton Avenue, Sleepy Hollow, NY, 10591-1598, United States of America
Tel: (1) 914 631 4505
Fax: (1) 914 631 6017
Email: archive@rockvax.rockefeller.edu
www: http://www.rockefeller.edu/archive.ctr
Contact: Mr Darwin H Stapleton, Director

The Rockefeller Archive Center holds the archives of the Rockefeller family and its philanthropies, and assists scholarly researchers who visit the Center to examine documents in the archives.

Rockefeller Archive Center Research Grant Program

Subjects: Developments and issues of the twentieth-century in the United States of America and throughout the world.
Purpose: To foster research in the records of the Rockefeller Foundation, Rockefeller University, the Rockefeller Brothers Fund and the Rockefeller family, as well as in the collections of other institutions and individuals deposited at the Rockefeller Archive Center.
Eligibility: Open to applicants of any discipline, usually graduate students or postdoctoral Scholars, who are engaged in projects which require substantial use of the collections.
Level of Study: Unrestricted.
Type: Grant.
Value: Up to US$2,500 for applicants within the United States of America and US$3,000 for applicants from outside the United States of America, depending upon travel, lodging and research expenses of the applicant.
Length of Study: One year, renewable through application.
Frequency: Annual.
Study Establishment: The Rockefeller Archive Center.
Country of Study: United States of America.
No. of awards offered: Varies.
Application Procedure: Applicants must complete an application form.
Closing Date: November 30th for notification in March.
Funding: Private.
No. of awards given last year: 41.
No. of applicants last year: 80.

ROSL (ROYAL OVER-SEAS LEAGUE) ARTS

Royal Over-Seas League
Over-Seas House
Park Place
St James's Street, London, SW1A 1LR, England
Tel: (44) 20 7408 0214 ext. 219
Fax: (44) 20 7499 6738
Email: culture@rosl.org.uk
www: http://www.rosl.org.uk
Contact: Ms Elaine Mitchener, Promotions Officer

The principal aim of the ROSL (Royal Over-Seas League) ARTS is to provide performance and exhibition opportunities for prize winning artists and musicians early in their careers, bringing their work to the attention of the professional arts community, the media and the general public.

Royal Over-Seas League Annual Music Competition

Subjects: Musical performance, in four solo classes such as strings including the harp and guitar, woodwind and brass, keyboard, singers and an ensemble class.
Purpose: To support and promote young Commonwealth musicians.
Eligibility: Open to citizens of the Commonwealth, including the United Kingdom, and former Commonwealth countries, who are no more than 28 years of age for instrumentalists or 30 years of age for singers.
Level of Study: Professional development.
Type: Competition.
Value: Over UK £30,000 in prizes, including a UK £5,000 first prize.
Frequency: Annual.
Country of Study: Any country.
No. of awards offered: Varies.
Application Procedure: Applicants must write or email for an application form.
Closing Date: December 20th.
Funding: Commercial, Private.
No. of awards given last year: 19.
No. of applicants last year: 500.

ROSWELL ARTIST-IN-RESIDENCE PROGRAM

PO Box 1, Roswell, NM, 88202, United States of America
Tel: (1) 505 622 6037
Fax: (1) 505 623 5603
Email: rswelair@dfn.com
www: http://www.rair.org
Contact: Mr Stephen Fleming, Programme Director

The Roswell Artist-in-Residence Program was established in 1967 to provide professional studio artists with the unique opportunity to concentrate on their work in a supportive, collegial environment for a period of one year. This 'gift of time' allows artists to work without distraction in an effort to break new ground and focus on individual goals. The Artist-in-Residence Program serves as a contemporary counterpoint to the traditional arts of the south west, reinforces the programme's interest in strengthening the vitality of art in New Mexico and has been a catalyst in broadening community understanding of modern art.

Roswell Artist-in-Residence Program

Subjects: Drawing, painting, sculpture, photography, printmaking, and other fine art media.
Purpose: To provide time for artists to focus on their work, without distractions or interruptions.
Eligibility: Not open to all students, except those whose degrees will be completed before the beginning of the grant period.
Level of Study: Unrestricted.
Type: Residency.
Value: US$500 per month, plus housing, studio and utilities and US$100 per dependant.
Length of Study: One year.
Frequency: Annual.
Country of Study: United States of America.
No. of awards offered: Approx. five.
Application Procedure: Applicants must complete the current application form. Please send a stamped addressed envelope for application materials or visit the website.
Closing Date: December 15th.
Funding: Private.
Contributor: The Roswell Museum and the Art Center Foundation.
Additional Information: For further information please contact the organisation through the website.

ROTARY FOUNDATION

One Rotary Center, 1560 Sherman Avenue, Evanston, IL, 60201-3698, United States of America
Tel: (1) 847 866 3000
Fax: (1) 847 328 8554
www: http://www.rotary.org
Contact: Ms Liliana Ware

Through the Rotary Foundation, Rotarians worldwide strive to promote international understanding and relations between peoples of different nations.

Rotary Foundation Academic Year Ambassadorial Scholarships

Subjects: All subjects.
Purpose: To further international understanding and friendly relations among people of different countries.
Eligibility: All applicants must be citizens of a country in which there are rotary clubs and have completed more than two years of college level coursework or equivalent professional experience before commencing their scholarship studies. Applicants must be proficient in the language of the proposed host country.
Level of Study: Unrestricted.
Type: Scholarship.

Value: Round trip transportation, tuition, room and board expenses, some educational supplies and one month of language training if necessary, totalling up to US$25,000 or its equivalent.
Length of Study: One academic year.
Frequency: Annual, if funds are available.
Study Establishment: A study institution assigned by the Trustees of the Rotary Foundation.
Country of Study: Any country other than that in which the Scholar resides, providing there are Rotary clubs there.
No. of awards offered: Varies.
Application Procedure: Applicants must make the initial application through a local Rotary club in the applicant's legal or permanent residence or place of full-time study or employment. Applicants must submit a completed application form, two recommendations, college transcripts, an autobiographical essay, statement of purpose, and a language ability form verifying applicant's background in the language of the proposed host country.
Closing Date: Varies according to the local Rotary club, but between March and July 15th. Applicants must apply over a year in advance.
Funding: Private.
Additional Information: Scholars will not be assigned to study in areas of a country where they have previously lived or studied for more than six months. During the study year, Scholars are expected to be outstanding ambassadors of goodwill through appearances before Rotary clubs, schools, civic organisations and other forums. Upon completion of the scholarship, Scholars are expected to share the experiences of understanding acquired during the study year with the people of their home countries. Candidates should contact local Rotary clubs for information on the availability of particular scholarships. Not all Rotary districts are able to offer scholarships. Further details are available from the website.

Rotary Foundation Cultural Ambassadorial Scholarships

Subjects: For cultural immersion and intensive language study.
Purpose: To further international understanding and friendly relations among people of different countries, and to make possible intensive language study and cultural immersion in another country.
Eligibility: All applicants must be citizens of a country in which there are rotary clubs and have completed more than two years of college level coursework or equivalent professional experience before commencing their scholarship studies. Applicants must have completed more than one year of college level coursework or equivalent in the proposed language of study.
Level of Study: Unrestricted.
Type: Scholarship.
Value: Round trip transportation, language training expenses, and homestay living arrangements, totalling up to US$12,000 and US$19,000 respectively.
Length of Study: Three-six months.
Frequency: Annual, if funds are available.
Study Establishment: A language school assigned by the Trustees of the Rotary Foundation.
Country of Study: Determined by the Rotary Foundation, according to the language of study.
No. of awards offered: Varies.
Application Procedure: Applicants must submit a completed application form, two recommendations, college transcripts, an autobiographical essay and statement of purpose. Applications are considered for candidates interested in studying Arabic, English, French, German, Hebrew, Italian, Japanese, Korean, Mandarin Chinese, Polish, Portuguese, Russian, Spanish, Swahili and Swedish. Initial applications must be made through a local Rotary club in the applicant's legal or permanent residence, or place of full time study or employment.
Closing Date: Varies according to the local Rotary club, but between March and July 15th. Applicants must apply over a year in advance.
Funding: Private.
Additional Information: Wherever possible, Scholars will reside with host families. During the study year, Scholars are expected to be outstanding ambassadors of goodwill through appearances

before Rotary clubs, schools, civic organisations and other forums. Candidates should contact local Rotary clubs for information on the availability of particular scholarships. Not all Rotary districts are able to offer scholarships. Further details are available from the website.

Rotary Foundation Multi-Year Ambassadorial Scholarships

Subjects: All subjects.

Purpose: To further international understanding and friendly relations among people of different countries and help defray the cost of pursuing a degree.

Eligibility: All applicants must be citizens of a country in which there are rotary clubs and have completed more than two years of college level coursework or equivalent professional experience before commencing their scholarship studies. Applicants must be proficient in the language of the proposed host country.

Level of Study: Unrestricted.

Type: Scholarship.

Value: The award provides a flat grant of US$12,000, or its equivalent, per year to be applied towards the cost of a degree programme.

Length of Study: Two-three years.

Frequency: Annual, if funds are available.

Study Establishment: A foreign study institution approved by the trustees of the Rotary Foundation.

Country of Study: Any country other than that in which the Scholar resides, providing there are Rotary clubs there.

No. of awards offered: Varies.

Application Procedure: Applicants must make the initial applications through a local Rotary club in the applicant's legal or permanent residence, or place of full-time study or employment. Applicants must submit a completed application form, two recommendations, college transcripts, an autobiographical essay and a statement of purpose.

Closing Date: Varies according to the local Rotary club, but between March and July 15th. Applicants must apply over a year in advance.

Funding: Private.

Additional Information: Scholars will not be assigned to study in areas of a country where they have previously lived or studied for more than six months. During the study year, Scholars are expected to be outstanding ambassadors of goodwill through appearances before Rotary clubs, schools, civic organisations and other forums. Upon completion of the scholarship, Scholars are expected to share the experiences of understanding acquired during the study year with the people of their home countries. Candidates should contact local Rotary clubs for information on the availability of particular scholarships. Not all Rotary districts are able to offer scholarships. Further details are available from the website.

Rotary Grants for University Teachers

Subjects: Fields taught must have practical use to the host country.

Purpose: To build international understanding while strengthening higher education in low income countries.

Eligibility: Applicants must hold a college or university appointment for three or more years and must be proficient in the language of their prospective host country. Rotarians and relatives of rotarians are eligible.

Level of Study: Professional development.

Type: Grant.

Value: Up to US$12,500 for three-five months or up to US$22,500 for six-ten months.

Length of Study: Three-five months or six-ten months.

Frequency: Dependent on funds available.

Country of Study: Developing countries in which there are Rotary clubs.

No. of awards offered: A set number.

Application Procedure: Applicants must apply through a local Rotary club. Applications should include a completed application form, current curriculum vitae, statement of intent and two letters of recommendation. Prospective candidates must contact a local Rotary club to confirm the availability of awards, to obtain application materials, and to enquire about the local deadline.

Closing Date: Varies according to the local Rotary club, but between March and July 15th. Applicants must apply over a year in advance.

Funding: Private.

Additional Information: Grant recipients are expected to be outstanding ambassadors of goodwill to the people of their host and home countries through appearances to Rotary clubs. Not all Rotary districts are able to offer scholarships. Further details are available from the website.

ROTARY YONEYAMA MEMORIAL FOUNDATION, INC.

8F abc Building
2-6-3 Shiba Koen
Minato-ku, Tokyo, 105-0011, Japan
Tel: (81) 3 3434 8681
Fax: (81) 3 3578 8281

The Rotary Yoneyama Memorial Foundation, Inc. has been growing in service and organisation annually through the endorsement and co-operation of Japanese Rotaries. It awards scholarships to students not only from Asian countries but also from the rest of the world who are residents of Japan and studying or conducting research at Japanese Institutes of Higher Education.

Rotary Yoneyama Scholarship

Subjects: All subjects.

Eligibility: Applicants must be non Japanese with a 'college student' visa for the purpose of studies and research, and be under 40 years old.

Level of Study: Doctorate, Postgraduate.

Type: Scholarship.

Value: Yen 150,000 per month.

Length of Study: A maximum of two years.

Frequency: Annual.

Study Establishment: Colleges and universities.

Country of Study: Japan.

No. of awards offered: 1000.

Application Procedure: Applicants must carry out selection procedures in Japanese.

Closing Date: October 7th.

Funding: Private.

Contributor: Rotarians in Japan.

No. of awards given last year: 1,000.

No. of applicants last year: 1,600.

Additional Information: It is recommended that applicants contact the Foundation directly, since requirements for certain applicants can be conditional. Selection is extremely competitive, as the number of awards is limited.

THE ROYAL ACADEMY OF ENGINEERING

29 Great Peter Street, London, SW1P 3LW, England
Tel: (44) 20 7222 2688
Fax: (44) 20 7233 0054
www: http://www.raeng.org.uk
Contact: Mr Keith Davies, MacRobert Award Scheme

The Royal Academy of Engineering's objectives may be summarised as the pursuit, encouragement and maintenance of excellence in the whole field of engineering in order to promote the advancement of the science, art and the practice of engineering for the benefit of the public.

Exxon Mobil Engineering Teaching Fellowships

Subjects: Chemical, petroleum or mechanical engineering.

Purpose: To encourage able young engineering lecturers to remain in the education sector in their early years.

Eligibility: Applicants must be well qualified graduates, preferably with industrial experience and must hold full-time lecturing posts at Institutes of Higher Education in the United Kingdom. They should have been in their current posts for at least one year. The post must include the teaching of chemical, petroleum, or mechanical engineering to undergraduates on courses which are accredited for registration as chartered engineers. These courses must include substantial elements of chemical, petroleum, or mechanical engineering, but need not be entirely devoted to these subjects. For applicants whose career path has been graduation at the age of 22, followed by academic or industrial posts, the age limit is generally 32 years (at the closing date). Older candidates who have taken time out, eg., for industrial experience, parenthood or voluntary service, will also be considered. Applicants should preferably be chartered engineers, or of equivalent professional status, or should be making progress towards this.

Level of Study: Postdoctorate.

Type: Fellowship.

Value: UK £9,000 over four years: UK £3,000 in the first calendar year, UK £2,500 in the second year, UK £2,000 in the third, and UK £1,500 in the fourth year.

Length of Study: Four years.

Frequency: Annual.

Study Establishment: The applicant's current university in the United Kingdom. Two weeks will be spent at an Esso site.

Country of Study: United Kingdom.

No. of awards offered: Up to six.

Application Procedure: Applicants must complete an application form.

Closing Date: October 1st.

Funding: Commercial.

Contributor: Esso UK Plc.

No. of awards given last year: 622.

Additional Information: A brochure is available on request. Enquiries about Esso University contacts should be made to the Esso Recruitment Centre on (44) 1372 222000. Email bowbricki@raeng.co.uk for more information.

Panasonic Trust Awards

Subjects: Engineering, particularly new engineering developments and new technologies.

Purpose: To encourage the technical updating and continuous professional development of qualified engineers through courses provided by United Kingdom Institutes of Higher Education at Master's level.

Eligibility: Applicants must be United Kingdom citizens, be qualified to degree level in engineering or a related discipline. HND,HNC, OND, ONC or City and Guilds Full Technological Certificate qualifications are acceptable as a minimum. Applicants must be members, at any grade, of an engineering institution, working at the professional level in engineering in the United Kingdom and have several years' experience working at this level. Preference is given to those undertaking part-time modular Master's courses. The intended course of study must be relevant to the applicant's current or future career plans.

Level of Study: Professional development.

Type: Award.

Value: Usually to cover 50 percent of course fees up to a maximum of UK £1,000.

Length of Study: The duration of the course.

Frequency: Dependent on funds available.

Country of Study: United Kingdom.

No. of awards offered: Varies.

Application Procedure: Applicants must apply for application instructions, the application form and guidelines for employers and course co-ordinators, available from the main address.

Closing Date: Offered all year round.

Additional Information: Employers are expected to support an application in writing. The Trustees hope that the employer, once approached, might pay the full fees for the course. However, if this is not possible, a contribution from the employer is desirable. Applications must be supported by the course director or co-ordinator to confirm that the applicant is suitable for the course. Applications for grants of less than UK £1,000 should be submitted at least four weeks before the start of the course. Applications for larger grants should be submitted at least six weeks before the start of the course.

The Royal Academy of Engineering Industrial Secondment Scheme

Subjects: All fields of engineering.

Purpose: To provide financial support for the secondment of academic engineering staff to industrial companies within the United Kingdom.

Eligibility: Open to permanent members of United Kingdom Institutes of Higher Education with an approved engineering qualification, teaching some aspects of engineering. Preference may be given to junior staff without previous industrial experience, or to more senior members whose industrial experience may have been some time ago.

Level of Study: Unrestricted.

Type: Grant.

Value: Varies.

Length of Study: Usually three-six months.

Frequency: Dependent on funds available.

Study Establishment: An industrial or commercial company within the United Kingdom.

Country of Study: United Kingdom.

No. of awards offered: Varies.

Application Procedure: Applicants must submit a completed application form with a curriculum vitae, personal statement outlining the nature and objectives of the proposed secondment, letter of support from the applicant's head of department, statement from the applicant's employer detailing the financial aspects of the application, statement from the host company confirming the agreed work programme and defining the benefits of the secondment to the company and detailing any contribution costs which the company may wish to make. Application forms are available from the Royal Academy of Engineering.

Funding: Government.

No. of awards given last year: 18.

No. of applicants last year: 26.

Additional Information: The main objective is to obtain up to date industrial experience, to improve teaching capabilities and generally to foster academic industrial links. Contact Mr A Eades for further information.

The Royal Academy of Engineering International Travel Grants

Subjects: Engineering, materials technology or computing.

Purpose: To facilitate study visits overseas, generally for attendance at conferences, research institutions and/or industrial sites.

Eligibility: The scheme is open to postgraduate students, postdoctoral researchers, lecturers involved in research and chartered engineers in United Kingdom Institutes of Higher Education and in United Kingdom industry. Grants are not given to Fellows of The Royal Academy of Engineering, civil servants, employees of the British Museum or other government bodies. To be eligible for funding applicants must be United Kingdom or European Union nationals or United Kingdom permanent residents. There are no age restrictions.

Level of Study: Postdoctorate, Postgraduate.

Type: Travel grant.

Value: 30-50 percent of approved costs.

Frequency: Dependent on funds available.

Country of Study: Outside the United Kingdom.

No. of awards offered: Varies.

Application Procedure: Applicants must submit a completed application form (nominating two referees of their choice), an abstract if an essay is being presented at a conference, publication list, photocopy of the personal details page form their passport, short paragraph of no more than 200 words (on a separate sheet of A4) justifying the relevance of the activity to their current work.

Closing Date: Applications are accepted at any time.

No. of awards given last year: 550.
No. of applicants last year: 750.
Additional Information: Applicants are urged to submit their forms at least two months prior to the departure date to enable APEX fares to be used.

The Royal Academy of Engineering MacRobert Award

Subjects: The successful development of innovation in engineering or the other physical sciences.
Purpose: To recognise and reward outstanding contributions relating to innovation in engineering.
Eligibility: Open to individuals, independent teams and teams working for a firm, organisation or laboratory (no more than five members in a team).
Level of Study: Unrestricted.
Type: Award.
Value: UK £50,000 and a gold medal.
Frequency: Annual.
Country of Study: United Kingdom.
No. of awards offered: One.
Application Procedure: Applicants must submit a 200-500 word summary of the engineering achievement, supported by relevant technical documentation (15 copies of each). Further details and rules and conditions are available from the Royal Academy of Engineering.
Closing Date: February 28th.
Funding: Private.
No. of awards given last year: One.

The Royal Academy of Engineering Senior Research Fellowships

Subjects: Engineering research projects of direct relevance to the sponsoring industrial company. Research must be precompetitive.
Purpose: To provide additional funds for a senior research Fellow working in an Institute of Higher Education in the United Kingdom on a research project of direct relevance to the sponsoring company, and the industry as a whole.
Eligibility: Open to individuals holding qualifications commensurate with those required for a senior research post. Applicants must be employed in the United Kingdom.
Level of Study: Postdoctorate, Research.
Type: Fellowship.
Value: One-third of gross salary from The Royal Academy of Engineering and two-thirds from the industrial sponsor.
Length of Study: Three-five years.
Frequency: Annual.
Study Establishment: Any university in the United Kingdom.
Country of Study: United Kingdom.
No. of awards offered: Varies.
Application Procedure: Applicants must contact the Manager, Research Support for further details.
Closing Date: Applications are accepted at any time.
Funding: Government.
Contributor: An industrial sponsor and the Academy.
Additional Information: The award of a fellowship is dependent upon a suitable industrial sponsor being identified.

Sainsbury Management Fellowship Scheme

Subjects: Engineering.
Purpose: To enable young chartered engineers of the highest career potential to undertake MBA courses at European business schools.
Eligibility: Applicants must be United Kingdom citizens, hold a First or Upper Second Class (Honours) Degree in engineering or a closely allied subject, have Chartered Engineer Status or be making substantial progress towards it, have the potential and ambition to achieve senior management responsibility at an early age and be aged 26-34 years at the commencement of the proposed MBA course.
Level of Study: Postgraduate, MBA.
Type: Fellowship.

Value: To cover course fees.
Length of Study: One year.
Frequency: Annual.
Study Establishment: Awards are normally tenable at the following business schools: North America - Harvard, MIT, Stanford, Wharton, Columbia, Kellogg, University of Chicago. In Europe: INSEAD France, IMD Switzerland, Erasmus The Netherlands, IESE Spain, SDA Bocconi Italy.
Country of Study: Any country.
No. of awards offered: 12.
Application Procedure: Applicants must complete an application form, please contact the office for details.
Closing Date: Applications are accepted at any time.
Contributor: The Gatsby Charitable Foundation.
No. of awards given last year: 12.
No. of applicants last year: 60.

ROYAL ACADEMY OF MUSIC

Marylebone Road, London, NW1 5HT, England
Tel: (44) 20 7873 7393
Fax: (44) 20 7873 7394
www: http://www.ram.ac.uk
Contact: Ms Marie Hopps, Examinations Officer

The Royal Academy of Music is a music college offering courses in music at postgraduate level. The Academy is part of the University of London.

Royal Academy of Music General Bursary Awards

Subjects: All relevant branches of music education and training.
Purpose: To help defray tuition fees and general living expenses for study at the Royal Academy of Music.
Eligibility: Open to any student offered a place at the Academy, irrespective of race, creed and gender.
Level of Study: Postgraduate.
Type: Bursary.
Value: According to need and availability of funds.
Length of Study: Normally for a complete academic year. Individual requirements may be imposed.
Frequency: Annually, funds are often available on a continuing basis.
Study Establishment: The Royal Academy of Music.
Country of Study: United Kingdom.
No. of awards offered: Varies.
Application Procedure: Applicants must complete an application form which is sent automatically to all postgraduate students who are offered places.
Closing Date: January 31st for the following academic year.
No. of awards given last year: 237.
No. of applicants last year: 351.

ROYAL AERONAUTICAL SOCIETY

4 Hamilton Place, London, W1J 7BQ, England
Tel: (44) 20 7670 4300
Fax: (44) 20 7670 4309
Email: careers@raes.org.uk
www: http://www.aerosociety.com
Contact: Miss Vanissa Amliwala, Careers Centre Manager

The Royal Aeronautical Society was founded in 1866 and is the only professional institution which covers all aspects of the aerospace industry including research, manufacture, operations and maintenance. Society membership unlocks a host of benefits for both the individual and organisations. Membership is open to anyone with an association or interest in aerospace.

Handley Page Award

Subjects: Aeronautics. The award is for original work leading to advancement and progress in the art and science of aeronautics, with special reference to the practical application of a device, or the long-term implications of a new concept, directed towards the safety of those who work with or travel in aircraft. The award can also be given to encourage interest in aerospace technology in schools and colleges and by young people generally.

Purpose: To encourage the advancement of safety and reliability in air transport.

Eligibility: Open to citizens of the United Kingdom and the British Commonwealth who are suitably qualified to undertake the proposed work.

Level of Study: Professional development.

Type: Financial support.

Value: Approx. UK £5,000 to be awarded in whole or in part to an individual or group.

Frequency: Annual.

Country of Study: United Kingdom or Commonwealth countries.

No. of awards offered: One.

Application Procedure: Applicants must complete an application form, available on request.

Closing Date: May 31st.

Funding: Private.

Contributor: The Society Trust Fund.

No. of applicants last year: 12.

ROYAL AGRICULTURAL COLLEGE, SCHOOL OF BUSINESS

Cirencester, Gloucestershire, GL7 6JS, England
Tel: (44) 1285 652531
Fax: (44) 1285 650219
www: http://www.royagcol.ac.uk
Contact: Dr Johnathon Turner, Dean of Business

The Royal Agricultural College, School of Business, is a privately owned Higher Education Institution, established in 1845, and now publicly funded. It has strong food chain links and an excellent national and international network of companies and university partners.

Alltech Biotechnology, Inc. MSc/MBA Studentships

Subjects: Agricultural biotechnology, animal science and agrifood, agribusiness management, equine business management or wine business management.

Eligibility: Applicants should have obtained or expect to obtain, a First or Upper Second Class Honours Degree (or equivalent) in an appropriate biological science, agri-food business or business degree. Furthermore, they should be highly motivated, possess good interpersonal skills and be willing to travel. Candidates must be competent in the English language. A good command of a continental European language would also be an advantage.

Level of Study: Postgraduate, MBA.

Type: Studentship.

Value: Tuition, accommodation and subsistence.

Length of Study: Nine months.

Frequency: Annual.

Study Establishment: The Royal Agricultural College.

Country of Study: United Kingdom, Netherlands, United States of America or Uruguay.

No. of awards offered: Five.

Application Procedure: Applicants can apply on the website or alternatively, contact the college.

No. of awards given last year: Two.

No. of applicants last year: 200.

ROYAL ANTHROPOLOGICAL INSTITUTE

50 Fitzroy Street, London, WTP 5BT, England
Tel: (44) 20 7387 0455
Fax: (44) 20 7383 4235
Email: admin@therai.org.uk
www: http://www.therai.org.uk
Contact: Director of Grants

The Royal Anthropological Institute is a non-profit making registered charity. It is entirely independent, with a Director and a small staff accountable to the Council, elected annually from the Fellowship. Council and Committee members and the editorial team of the Institute's principal journal 'The Journal of the Royal Anthropological Institute' (Incorporating MAN), give their services without remuneration.

Emslie Horniman Anthropological Scholarship Fund

Subjects: Anthropology.

Purpose: To provide predoctoral grants for fieldwork in anthropology with a preference for research outside the United Kingdom.

Eligibility: Open to citizens of the United Kingdom, Commonwealth or Irish Republic who are university graduates or who can satisfy the trustees of their suitability for the study proposed. Preference is given to applicants whose proposals include field work outside the United Kingdom. Graduates who already hold a doctorate in anthropology are not eligible. Open to individuals only, as no grants are given to expeditions or teams.

Level of Study: Postgraduate, Predoctorate.

Type: Scholarship.

Value: UK £1,000-9,500.

Frequency: Annual.

Country of Study: Any country.

No. of awards offered: Approx. 10.

Application Procedure: Applicants must request an application form.

Closing Date: March 31st.

Funding: Private.

Additional Information: No grants are available for library research, university fees or subsistence in the United Kingdom.

ROYAL COLLEGE OF MUSIC

Prince Consort Road, London, SW7 2BS, England
Tel: (44) 20 7591 4377
Fax: (44) 20 7591 4856
Email: cpartridge@rcm.ac.uk
www: http://www.rcm.ac.uk
Contact: Ms Celia Partridge, International & Awards Officer

The Royal College of Music provides specialised musical education and professional training at the highest international level for performers and composers. This enables talented students to develop the musical skills, knowledge, understanding and resourcefulness which will equip them to contribute significantly to musical life in the United Kingdom and internationally.

Royal College of Music Scholarships

Subjects: Music performance, composition or conducting.

Purpose: To recognise merit in music performance, composition or conducting.

Eligibility: Unrestricted, but only for study at the College.

Level of Study: Unrestricted.

Type: Scholarship.

Value: Up to UK £11,400 (up to full fees).

Length of Study: One-four years.

Frequency: Annual.

Study Establishment: Music conservatoire.

Country of Study: United Kingdom.

No. of awards offered: Approx. 50.

Application Procedure: Applicants must apply only by application for a place of study.
Closing Date: October 1st.
Funding: Private.
No. of awards given last year: 150.
No. of applicants last year: 1,500.

ROYAL COLLEGE OF OBSTETRICIANS AND GYNAECOLOGISTS (RCOG)

27 Sussex Place
Regent's Park, London, NW1 4RG, England
Tel: (44) 20 7772 6263
Fax: (44) 20 7772 6359
Email: rdeshmukh@rcog.org.uk
www: http://www.rcog.org.uk
Contact: Ms Erin Jones, Awards Secretary

The Royal College of Obstetricians and Gynaecologists' principal objects stated in the Charter are the encouragement of the study and the advancement of the science and practice of obstetrics and gynaecology.

Endometriosis Millennium Fund Award

Subjects: Research into endometriosis.
Purpose: To stimulate and encourage research, clinical or laboratory based, in the field of endometriosis, or to encourage clinicians to acquire extra clinical skills to manage patients with the disease.
Eligibility: Open to members of the College or members of the RCOG Trainees Register, who are resident and working within the British Isles.
Level of Study: Postgraduate.
Type: Research grant.
Value: Up to UK £5,000.
Frequency: Annual.
Country of Study: United Kingdom.
No. of awards offered: More than one.
Application Procedure: Applicants must submit an application on the requisite form, which can be downloaded from the website or can be obtained from the Awards Secretary at the RCOG. Applications must be accompanied by two references from supervisors or senior colleagues and written confirmation of availability of laboratory space or access for surgical training in the host institution must be provided with the application. An undertaking will be given that a structured typewritten report will be provided at the end of the grant period and that the source of grant will be acknowledged in any related publications.
Closing Date: February 18th.
Contributor: The Endometriosis Millennium Fund.
Additional Information: The award may only be used for the purpose approved by the Assessment Committee.

RCOG Bernhard Baron Travelling Scholarships

Subjects: Obstetrics or gynaecology.
Purpose: To expand the recipient's knowledge in areas in which he or she already has some experience.
Eligibility: Open to Fellows and members of the College.
Level of Study: Postgraduate.
Type: Scholarship.
Value: Up to UK £6,000.
Frequency: Annual.
Country of Study: Any country.
No. of awards offered: One.
Application Procedure: Applicants must contact the Awards Secretary for details.
Closing Date: July 31st.
No. of awards given last year: One.
No. of applicants last year: 16.

RCOG Eden Travelling Fellowship

Subjects: Obstetrics or gynaecology.
Purpose: To enable the recipient to gain additional knowledge and experience in the pursuit of a specific research project in which he or she is currently engaged.
Eligibility: Open to medical graduates of not less than two years' standing from any approved university in the United Kingdom or Commonwealth.
Level of Study: Postgraduate.
Type: Fellowship.
Value: Up to UK £5,000, according to the project undertaken.
Length of Study: For a specified period of time.
Frequency: Annual.
Study Establishment: At another department of obstetrics and gynaecology or of closely related disciplines.
Country of Study: Any country.
No. of awards offered: One.
Application Procedure: Applicants must include information on qualifications, areas of interest and/or publications in a specified area, centre(s) to be visited with confirmation of arrangements from the head of that centre, estimated costs, and the names of two referees.
Closing Date: July 31st.
Additional Information: Further information is available on request.

RCOG Edgar Gentilli Prize

Subjects: Obstetrics or gynaecology.
Purpose: To recognise original work done on the cause, nature, recognition and treatment of any form of cancer of the female genital tract.
Eligibility: Eligibility is unrestricted.
Type: Prize.
Value: UK £750 plus book tokens to the value of UK £250.
Frequency: Annual.
No. of awards offered: One.
Application Procedure: Applicants must submit results of their research in the form of an original manuscript, adequately referenced and written in a format comparable to those used for submission to a learned journal, or by means of reprint of a published article.
Closing Date: July 31st.
Additional Information: Further information is available on request.

RCOG Ethicon Foundation Fund Travel

Subjects: Obstetrics or gynaecology.
Purpose: To aid attendance of postgraduate training courses and visits to research centres, and to promote international goodwill in the speciality of obstetrics and gynaecology.
Eligibility: Open to RCOG members who have passed both Part I and II of the membership exams. Members from the British Isles must be trainees and overseas members must not be in independent practice.
Level of Study: Postgraduate.
Type: Travel grant.
Value: Up to UK £750.
Frequency: Twice a year.
No. of awards offered: Up to 15.
Application Procedure: Applicants must complete an application form, available from the Awards Secretary or from the website.
Closing Date: January 31st or July 31st.
No. of awards given last year: 13.
No. of applicants last year: 42.

RCOG Green-Armytage and Spackman Travelling Scholarship

Subjects: Obstetrics or gynaecology.
Purpose: To allow applicants to visit centres where similar work is carried out to their own.
Eligibility: Open to Fellows and members of the College. Applicants should have shown a special interest in some particular aspect of obstetrical or gynaecological practice.
Level of Study: Postgraduate.

Type: Scholarship.
Value: Up to UK £4,000.
Frequency: Every two years.
Study Establishment: At centres where similar work is being carried out.
Country of Study: Any country.
No. of awards offered: One.
Application Procedure: Applicants must include information on qualifications, area of interest and/or publications in a specified area, centre(s) to be visited with confirmation from the head of that centre, estimated costs, and the names of two referees.
Closing Date: July 31st.
Additional Information: Further information is available on request.

RCOG Harold Malkin Prize

Subjects: Obstetrics or gynaecology.
Purpose: To award those undertaking best original work whilst holding a Specialist Registrar post in a hospital.
Eligibility: Open to RCOG members or membership candidates.
Level of Study: Professional development.
Type: Prize.
Value: First prize UK £250 and second prize UK £150.
Frequency: Annual.
No. of awards offered: One first prize and one second prize.
Application Procedure: Applicants must contact the Awards Secretary for details.
Closing Date: July 31st.
Additional Information: Further information is available on request.

RCOG Medical Student Prizes

Subjects: Obstetrics or gynaecology.
Purpose: Awarded to medical students in the United Kingdom showing the greatest understanding of a clinical problem in obstetrics and gynaecology.
Eligibility: Open to medical students in the United Kingdom.
Type: Prize.
Value: First prize is UK £500, second prize is UK £250 and the third prize is UK £100.
Frequency: Annual.
Country of Study: United Kingdom.
No. of awards offered: One first prize, one second prize and four third prizes.
Application Procedure: Applicants must contact the Awards Secretary for details.
Closing Date: January 31st.

RCOG Menopause Travel Award

Subjects: Menopause.
Purpose: To study advances in clinical practice in the area of the menopause.
Eligibility: Open to either Fellows or members of the College, or those training for the MRCOG, or clinical assistants with a special interest in the menopause.
Level of Study: Postgraduate.
Type: Travel award.
Value: Up to UK £1,000.
Frequency: Annual.
Country of Study: Any country.
No. of awards offered: Up to six.
Application Procedure: Applicants must complete an application form, available from the website or from Mrs Roopa Deshmukh at the main address.
Closing Date: August.
Additional Information: It is a condition of the award that a typewritten report (approx. 300 words) is submitted to the College within eight weeks of travel. The award is available to attend United Kingdom, Irish or international symposia or to visit institutions to advance clinical practice. The awards are sponsored by Solvay Healthcare.

RCOG Overseas Fund (Founded by the Aileen Dickens Bequest)

Subjects: Obstetrics or gynaecology.
Purpose: To allow individuals to travel to the United Kingdom for further training.
Eligibility: Open to RCOG members or the equivalent, working in obstetrics and gynaecology overseas.
Level of Study: Professional development.
Type: Travel grant.
Value: Up to UK £2,000.
Frequency: Annual.
No. of awards offered: Up to six.
Application Procedure: Applicants must contact Mrs Roopa Deshmukh on (44) 20 7772 6263 or by email rjeffs@rcog.org.uk for further information.
Closing Date: December 1st.
No. of awards given last year: Seven.
No. of applicants last year: 13.

RCOG USA/British Isles Visiting Fellowship

Subjects: Obstetrics or gynaecology.
Purpose: To enable the recipient to visit, make contact with and gain knowledge from a specific centre offering new techniques or methods of clinical management within the speciality of obstetrics and gynaecology.
Eligibility: Open to specialist Registrars in the British Isles or junior Fellows or those in residency programmes in obstetrics and gynaecology in the United States of America.
Level of Study: Professional development.
Type: Fellowship.
Value: Up to UK £1,000.
Frequency: Annual.
Country of Study: United States of America or United Kingdom.
No. of awards offered: One.
Application Procedure: Applicants must contact the Awards Secretary for details.
Closing Date: July 31st.

RCOG William Blair-Bell Memorial Lectureships in Obstetrics and Gynaecology

Subjects: Gynaecology or obstetrics.
Purpose: To allow an individual to give a lecture on either obstetrics or gynaecology with preference given to original work.
Eligibility: Open to Fellows or members of not more than two years standing.
Type: Lectureship.
Value: Honorarium of UK £500.
Frequency: Annual.
No. of awards offered: One.
Application Procedure: Applicants must contact the Awards Secretary.
Closing Date: July 31st.

RCOG/Wyeth Historical Lecture

Subjects: Gynaecology or obstetrics with a strong historical content.
Purpose: To give a lecture on a current development in obstetrics and gynaecology with a strong historical content.
Eligibility: Open to RCOG Fellows and members.
Type: Lecture.
Value: Honorarium of UK £200. This amount may be subject to change and applicants should contact the organisation.
Frequency: Annual.
No. of awards offered: One.
Application Procedure: Applicants must contact the Awards Secretary for details.
Closing Date: July 31st.
Funding: Private.
Contributor: Wyeth Laboratories.
No. of awards given last year: One.
No. of applicants last year: Eight.

ROYAL COLLEGE OF ORGANISTS (RCO)

7 St Andrew Street
Holborn, London, EC4A 3LQ, England
Tel: (44) 20 7936 3606
Fax: (44) 20 7353 8244
Contact: Mr Alan Dear, Senior Executive

The Royal College of Organists (RCO) is membership based. It promotes the art of organ playing as choral directing, and provides an organisation with a library, events and examinations to further that object.

RCO Grants and Travel Scholarships

Subjects: Organ playing.
Eligibility: Open to promising pupils of any nationality who are training to be organists. Some of the grants are restricted to applicants under 20 years of age.
Level of Study: Unrestricted.
Type: Grant and travel scholarship.
Value: Not less than UK £50.
Length of Study: One year, renewable.
Frequency: Annual.
Country of Study: Any country.
No. of awards offered: Varies.
Application Procedure: Applicants must write for an application form.
Closing Date: May 1st.
Funding: Commercial, Private.

RCO Scholarships and Awards

Subjects: Organ playing.
Purpose: To assist organists with professional playing.
Eligibility: Open to members of the College (only in exceptional circumstances will awards be made to non members). Membership is open to all upon payment of an annual subscription.
Level of Study: Unrestricted.
Type: Grant.
Value: Not less than UK £50.
Length of Study: One year, renewable.
Frequency: Annual.
Study Establishment: Varies.
Country of Study: Any country.
No. of awards offered: Varies.
Application Procedure: Applicants must write for an application form.
Closing Date: April.
Funding: Private.
Contributor: College Trusts.
No. of awards given last year: 28.
No. of applicants last year: 40.

ROYAL COLLEGE OF PAEDIATRICS AND CHILD HEALTH

50 Hallam Street, London, W1W 6DE, England
Tel: (44) 20 7307 5650
Fax: (44) 20 7307 5652
Email: amanda.leighton@rcpch.ac.uk
www: http://www.rcpch.ac.uk
Contact: Miss Amanda Leighton, Conference Organiser

The Royal College of Paediatrics and Child Health works to advance the art and science of paediatrics, to raise the standard of medical care provided to children, to educate and examine those concerned with health of children, and to advance the education of the public and, in particular, medical practitioners in child health.

Heinz Visiting and Travelling Fellowships

Subjects: Paediatrics.

Purpose: To enable paediatricians from any part of the Commonwealth to spend up to 12 weeks in the United Kingdom and to attend the Spring meeting of the College (visiting), or to enable British paediatricians in the early years of professional life to spend up to three months in a developing country (travelling).
Eligibility: Visiting Fellowships are open to paediatricians from any part of the Commonwealth who will benefit from meeting United Kingdom paediatricians and seeing something of their work. Preference is given, in general, to applicants from developing countries who are not otherwise likely to visit the United Kingdom. Travelling Fellowships are open to United Kingdom paediatricians in the early years of professional life.
Level of Study: Professional development.
Type: Fellowship.
Value: To cover the cost of air fares and living expenses.
Length of Study: Up to 12 weeks, or a short working visit to a centre for up to three months teaching or conducting research that will benefit the Fellow and hosts.
Frequency: Annual.
Country of Study: United Kingdom for the Visiting Fellowship and developing countries for the Travelling Fellowship.
No. of awards offered: Varies.
Application Procedure: Applicants must complete an application form, available from Amanda Leighton. The application form is to be submitted with a letter of support from the applicant's head of department.
Closing Date: Please write for details.
Funding: Private.
No. of awards given last year: Three.

ROYAL COLLEGE OF SURGEONS OF ENGLAND

35-43 Lincoln's Inn Fields, London, WC2A 3PE, England
Tel: (44) 20 7869 6611
Fax: (44) 20 7869 6644
Email: research@rcseng.ac.uk
www: http://www.rcseng.ac.uk
Contact: Miss Bumbi Singh, Research Board

The Royal College of Surgeons of England is an independent professional body committed to promoting and advancing the highest standards of surgical care for patients.

Ethicon Foundation Fund

Subjects: Surgery.
Purpose: To promote international goodwill in surgery and to assist Fellows travelling abroad for research or training purposes.
Eligibility: Open to Fellows of the Royal College of Surgeons of England, preferably specialist registrars in training or within one year from their appointment as a consultant.
Level of Study: Professional development.
Type: Grant.
Value: Varies according to the number of awards and travel costs.
Length of Study: Varies.
Frequency: Twice a year.
Country of Study: Any country.
No. of awards offered: Varies.
Application Procedure: Applicants must send 10 copies of the application form to the Research Board of the College and should include a letter of support from the head of department or consultant under whom the applicant is currently working and a letter of support from another independent referee.
Closing Date: Please contact the organisation.

Lionel Colledge Memorial Fellowship in Otolaryngology

Subjects: Head and neck surgery, with an emphasis on laryngology, rhinology or otology.
Purpose: To encourage research in the area of head and neck surgery with an emphasis on laryngology, rhinology or otology.

Eligibility: Open to candidates who are Fellows of the Royal College of Surgeons and between 25 and 35 years of age. Candidates must be senior trainees or recently appointed consultants, or of similar status in otolaryngology, rhinology or otology.

Level of Study: Professional development.

Type: Fellowship.

Value: Up to UK £3,000.

Length of Study: Varies.

Frequency: Annual.

Study Establishment: Appropriate research institutions outside the United Kingdom.

Country of Study: Any country.

No. of awards offered: One.

Application Procedure: Applicants must address applications (eight copies) to the Research Board of the College and should include an application form and letters of support from the applicant's present consultant (or if already a consultant, the name of an independent referee in the United Kingdom) and from the head(s) of the department(s) to be visited.

Closing Date: April 1st.

Norman Capener Travelling Fellowships

Subjects: Surgery.

Purpose: To provide travel expenses to and from the United Kingdom for the study of orthopaedic surgery and surgery of the hand.

Eligibility: Open to medical practitioners. Preference is given to candidates enrolled for higher surgical training or those who have recently completed a course in orthopaedic or hand surgery.

Level of Study: Professional development.

Type: Fellowship.

Value: Varies according to travel costs. The award is paid in one lump sum.

Frequency: Annual.

Country of Study: Any country.

No. of awards offered: Varies.

Application Procedure: Applicants must submit applications to the Research Board of the College and should include six copies of the application form, available from the main address, and a letter of support from the consultant under whom the applicant is currently working, or in the case of the applicant being a consultant, a letter of support from an independent referee.

Closing Date: September 30th.

Royal College of Surgeons, New York Travelling Fellowships

Subjects: Surgery or dentistry.

Purpose: To enable young surgeons and dental surgeons to visit the United States of America to observe medical procedures first hand.

Eligibility: Open to United Kingdom surgeons, usually between 30 and 36 years of age, who are qualified practitioners in their speciality and Fellows of the Royal College of Surgeons of England.

Level of Study: Professional development.

Type: Fellowship.

Value: Up to US$7,000.

Length of Study: Four-six weeks.

Frequency: Annual.

Country of Study: United States of America.

No. of awards offered: Three.

Application Procedure: Applicants must complete an application form, available from the main address, and include letters of support from the applicant's present consultant and a statement of expenses to be incurred.

Closing Date: April 1st.

ROYAL COMMISSION FOR THE EXHIBITION OF 1851

Sherfield Building
Imperial College, London, SW7 2AZ, England
Tel: (44) 20 7594 8790
Fax: (44) 20 7594 8794
Email: royalcom1851@ic.ac.uk
www: http://www.royalcommission1851.org.uk
Contact: Mr J P W Middleton, Secretary

The Royal Commission for the Exhibition of 1851 is an educational trust supporting innovation and creativity in science, technology and occasionally the arts, almost always at graduate level. Apart from the competitive schemes listed, assistance is sometimes given to suitable charities or individuals.

1851 Research Fellowships

Subjects: Natural sciences.

Purpose: To give young scientists or engineers of exceptional promise the opportunity to conduct research for a further period of two years.

Eligibility: Open to citizens of the British Commonwealth, Republic of Ireland or Pakistan.

Level of Study: Postdoctorate.

Type: Fellowship.

Value: Approx. UK £18,000 per year.

Length of Study: Two years.

Frequency: Annual.

Study Establishment: Any approved university.

Country of Study: Any country.

No. of awards offered: Approx. six.

Application Procedure: Applicants must complete an application form, available from all United Kingdom universities or from the website. Applications must be made by professors of United Kingdom universities on behalf of the applicants.

Closing Date: March 2nd.

Funding: Private.

Contributor: The profits from the Great Exhibition.

No. of awards given last year: Six.

No. of applicants last year: 50.

Royal Commission Industrial Design Studentship

Subjects: Industrial design.

Purpose: To fund engineering and science graduates for a postgraduate industrial design course.

Eligibility: Open to United Kingdom nationals only with a first degree in engineering.

Level of Study: Postgraduate.

Type: Studentship.

Value: Approx. UK £8,000 per year and tuition.

Length of Study: One-two years.

Frequency: Annual.

Study Establishment: Universities in the United Kingdom or universities abroad.

Country of Study: Any country.

No. of awards offered: Approx. six.

Application Procedure: Applicants must complete an application form and submit this with the required enclosures.

Closing Date: April 20th.

Funding: Private.

Contributor: The profits from the Great Exhibition.

No. of awards given last year: Six.

No. of applicants last year: 24.

Royal Commission Industrial Fellowships

Subjects: Industrial and management engineering.

Purpose: To allow able science or engineering graduates working in industry to carry out research and development leading to a higher degree or other career milestone.

Eligibility: Open to United Kingdom nationals only with a degree in science or engineering who are working in for a British company.
Level of Study: Doctorate, Postgraduate.
Type: Fellowship.
Value: Approx. UK £18,000.
Length of Study: Three years.
Frequency: Annual.
Study Establishment: A United Kingdom company.
Country of Study: United Kingdom.
No. of awards offered: Approx. six.
Application Procedure: Applicants must complete an application form.
Closing Date: January 26th.
Funding: Private.
Contributor: The profits from the Great Exhibition.
No. of awards given last year: Six.
No. of applicants last year: 30.

ROYAL GEOGRAPHICAL SOCIETY (WITH THE INSTITUTE OF BRITISH GEOGRAPHERS)

1 Kensington Gore, London, SW7 2AR, England
Tel: (44) 20 7591 3073
Fax: (44) 20 7591 3031
Email: grants@rgs.org
www: http://www.rgs.org
Contact: Grants Co-ordinator

The Royal Geographical Society (with the Institute of British Geographers) is the United Kingdom's learned society for geography and geographers and a professional body. It supports and promotes many aspects of geography including geographical research, education and teaching, field training and small expeditions, the public understanding and popularisation of geography, and the provision of geographical information.

Gilchrist Fieldwork Award

Subjects: Natural sciences or geography.
Purpose: To finance an overseas research proposal which will enable original and challenging research to take place, preferably of potential applied benefit to the host country.
Eligibility: Open to teams of up to 10 members, the majority of which must be British and hold established posts in university departments.
Level of Study: Doctorate, Postdoctorate.
Type: Grant.
Value: UK £10,000.
Length of Study: More than six weeks.
Frequency: Every two years.
Country of Study: Outside United Kingdom.
No. of awards offered: One.
Application Procedure: Applicants must submit a proposal, following the guidelines, to the Grants Co-ordinator by the closing date. There is no application form. Details can be found on the website http://www.rgs.org/grants.
Closing Date: March 15th.
Funding: Commercial.

For further information contact:

The Secretary
Gilchrist Educational Trust
Mary Trevewyan Hall
10 York Terrace East, London, NW1 4PT, England

Monica Cole Research Grant

Subjects: Earth and geological sciences.
Purpose: To enable the winner to undertake original fieldwork overseas.

Eligibility: Open to female physical geographers only. Applicants must be registered at a United Kingdom university.
Level of Study: Doctorate, Postdoctorate, Postgraduate.
Type: Grant.
Value: UK £1,000.
Frequency: Every three years (next in 2004).
Country of Study: Outside the United Kingdom.
No. of awards offered: One.
Application Procedure: Applicants must download guidelines from the website http://www.rgs.org/grants or contact the Grants Co-ordinator. There is no application form.
Closing Date: January 25th.
Funding: Private.

Neville Shulman Challenge Award

Subjects: The geographical sciences and exploration.
Purpose: To further the understanding and exploration of the planet, while promoting personal development through the intellectual or physical challenges involved.
Eligibility: Open to any United Kingdom national over the age of 25.
Level of Study: Unrestricted.
Type: Grant.
Value: Normally up to UK £5,000.
Length of Study: Unrestricted.
Frequency: Annual.
Country of Study: Any country.
No. of awards offered: Normally one.
Application Procedure: Applicants must submit a proposal, following the guidelines, to the Grants Co-ordinator by the closing date. There is no application form. Details are available on the website http://www.rgs.org/grants.
Closing Date: October 31st.
Funding: Private.
No. of awards given last year: One.
No. of applicants last year: 24.

Ralph Brown Expedition Award

Subjects: Natural sciences.
Purpose: To support and encourage objectives that involve the study of rivers, inland or coastal wetlands or shallow marine environments.
Eligibility: Open to applicants over 25 from any country who must be a Fellow or associate Fellow of the society.
Level of Study: Postgraduate, Research.
Type: Grant.
Value: UK £15,000.
Frequency: Annual.
Country of Study: Any country.
No. of awards offered: One.
Application Procedure: Applicants must contact the Grants Co-ordinator or refer to the website http://www.rgs.org/grants for detailed guidelines.
Closing Date: November 30th.
Funding: Private.
No. of awards given last year: One.
No. of applicants last year: 15.

Royal Geographical Society Expedition Research Grants

Subjects: Geographical, earth, life and human sciences.
Purpose: To support British expeditions carrying out geographical field research and exploration overseas.
Eligibility: Open to multidisciplinary teams, rather than individuals, the majority of which must be British and over 19 years of age.
Level of Study: Unrestricted.
Type: Grant.
Value: UK £750-3,000.
Length of Study: Must be over five weeks.
Frequency: Twice a year.
Country of Study: Unrestricted, but preference is given to remote and challenging environments.
No. of awards offered: 60-70.

Application Procedure: Applicants must complete an application form. These can be obtained from the Society's website or by writing to the Grants Co-ordinator.
Closing Date: January 25th or August 25th.
Funding: Commercial, Private.
No. of awards given last year: 52.
No. of applicants last year: 61.

Swawson Awards

Subjects: Social and behavioural sciences or development studies.
Purpose: For PhD students intending to carry out geographical field research outside the United Kingdom to increase knowledge, awareness and understanding of the world in which we live.
Eligibility: Applicants must normally be United Kingdom citizens, currently be registered for a PhD at a United Kingdom Institute of Higher Education and be Fellows of the Society.
Level of Study: Postgraduate.
Type: Grant.
Value: Normally up to UK £3,000.
Frequency: Annual.
Country of Study: Outside the United Kingdom, preferably in developing countries.
Application Procedure: Applicants must submit a proposal, following the guidelines, to the Grants Co-ordinator by the closing date. There is no application form and more details are available from the website.
Closing Date: February 22nd.
Funding: Private.
No. of awards given last year: Three.
No. of applicants last year: 40.

Violet Cressey-Marcks Fisher Travel Scholarship

Subjects: Natural sciences or geography.
Purpose: To finance geographical research in the field.
Eligibility: Applicants must be registered at a United Kingdom university. There is no age limit.
Level of Study: Postgraduate, Research.
Value: UK £500.
Length of Study: More than six months.
Frequency: Annual.
Country of Study: Outside the United Kingdom.
No. of awards offered: One.
Application Procedure: Applicants must submit a formal proposal following guidelines to the Grants Co-ordinator. Guidelines can be downloaded from the website. There is no application form.
Closing Date: January 25th.
Funding: Private.
No. of awards given last year: One.
No. of applicants last year: 16.

ROYAL HOLLOWAY, UNIVERSITY OF LONDON

Egham, Surrey, TW20 0EX, England
Tel: (44) 1784 434455
Fax: (44) 1784 473662
Email: graduateoffice@rhbnc.ac
www: http://www.rhbnc.ac.uk
Contact: Ms Claire Collingwood, Schools & International Liasion Officer

All departments of Royal Holloway, University of London seek to provide taught programmes which reflect the latest developments and are responsive to the needs of students and society, together with research and scholarship which contribute to the advancement of knowledge and the enhancement of public policy, wealth creation and the quality of life.

Royal Holloway, University of London College Overseas Entrance Scholarships

Subjects: All subjects.
Purpose: To award outstanding academic achievement.
Eligibility: For overseas students only, full time Master's or research.
Level of Study: Postgraduate, Research.
Type: Scholarship.
Value: Up to a maximum of UK £10,000 depending on the number of awards available and the strength of the applicant. This award pays fees and/or some maintenance depending on level of award.
Frequency: Annual.
Application Procedure: Students who accept the offer of a place will automatically receive an application form.
Closing Date: February 1st.
Additional Information: Further details of the awards can be found on the University's website or in the booklet 'Funding Postgraduate Studies', available from the college.

Royal Holloway, University of London College Research Studentship

Subjects: All subjects.
Level of Study: Postgraduate.
Type: Studentship.
Value: Tuition fees at the home rate.
Length of Study: Tenable for three years full-time or six years part-time.
Frequency: Annual.
Application Procedure: Applicants must indicate if they wish to be considered, but departments nominate their candidates.
Closing Date: Applicants should contact the relevant academic department.
Additional Information: These studentships cannot be held with a research council, AHRB or similar major award. Further details of the awards can be found on the University's website or in the booklet 'Funding Postgraduate Studies', available from the college.

Royal Holloway, University of London Departmental Assistantships

Subjects: All subjects.
Level of Study: Postgraduate.
Type: Assistantship.
Value: Up to UK £3,000 per year for a maximum of six hours work per week, 48 weeks per year.
Length of Study: Tenable for one year full-time or two years part-time.
Frequency: Annual.
Application Procedure: Applicants must indicate on their application form that they wish to be considered.
Closing Date: Applicants should contact the relevant academic department.
Additional Information: These Assistantships cannot be held with a research council, AHRB or similar major award. Departmental Assistantships require research students to support teaching and research in the department for up to six hours each week. Further details of the awards can be found on the University's website or in the booklet 'Funding Postgraduate Studies', available from the college.

Royal Holloway, University of London Endowed Postgraduate Scholarships

Subjects: All subjects.
Eligibility: This cannot be held with a research council, AHRB or similar major award.
Level of Study: Postgraduate.
Type: Scholarship.
Value: Varies.
Length of Study: Tenable for three years full-time. For part-time maintenance elements are reduced pro-rata.
Frequency: Annual.
No. of awards offered: Varies.

Application Procedure: Applicants must indicate if they wish to be considered, but departments nominate their candidates.
Closing Date: Applicants should contact the relevant academic department.
Additional Information: Availability varies from year to year and is restricted to certain departments. Contact the academic department for availability. More details of the awards can be found on the University's website or in the booklet 'Funding Postgraduate Studies', available from the college.

Royal Holloway, University of London Master's Studentship
Subjects: All subjects.
Level of Study: Postgraduate.
Type: Studentship.
Value: Up to UK £3,000 each year in return for a maximum of six hours per week, 48 weeks per year supporting teaching, research or administrative duties as required within the department.
Application Procedure: Applicants must indicate if they wish to be considered, but opportunity and availability varies between departments.
Closing Date: Applicants should contact the relevant academic department.
Additional Information: This may be incorporated within the Thomas Holloway Research Studentship, held in conjunction with College Research Studentships or with Departmental Awards. Further details of the awards can be found on the University's website or in the booklet 'Funding Postgraduate Studies', available from the college.

Thomas Holloway Research Studentship
Subjects: Arts and humanities, business administration and management, music, drama, cinema and television, mathematics and computer science, natural sciences and social science or behavioural science.
Eligibility: This studentship cannot be held with a research council, AHRB or similar major award.
Type: Studentship.
Value: Tuition fees at the home rate plus maintenance of up to UK £9,000 per year (rates vary between departments).
Length of Study: Tenable for three years full-time. For part-time maintenance elements are reduced pro-rata.
Frequency: Annual.
Application Procedure: Applicants must indicate if they wish to be considered, but departments nominate their candidates.
Closing Date: Applicants should contact the relevant academic department.

ROYAL HORTICULTURAL SOCIETY (RHS)

Wisley, Woking, Surrey, GU23 6QB, England
Tel: (44) 1483 212380
Fax: (44) 1483 212382
Contact: Mr M R Pollock, Head of Education

The Royal Horticultural Society (RHS) is a membership charity holding a Royal Charter for horticulture. The Society promotes the science, art and practice of horticulture in all its branches through a wide range of educational, research and advisory activities. It also maintains some major gardens, shows and the internationally renowned Lindley Library.

Blaxall Valentine Trust Award
Subjects: To help finance worldwide plant collecting expeditions which will provide real benefits to horticulture.
Purpose: To support plant collection.
Eligibility: Submissions are welcomed from applicants worldwide, but preference is given to United Kingdom and Commonwealth

citizens. Applicants should preferably be within the age bracket of 20-35 years and satisfy the Society that their health enables them to undertake the project proposed. Financial sponsorship will be available to both professional and amateur horticulturists and consideration for an award is not restricted to RHS members.
Level of Study: Unrestricted.
Value: Funds are limited. High cost projects are expected to receive supplementary finance from other sources, including personal contributions.
Frequency: Four times per year.
Country of Study: Any country.
Application Procedure: Applicants must complete an application form available on request. Candidates may be called for interview.
Closing Date: December 24th, March 31st, June 30th or September 30th.
Funding: Private.

Coke Trust Award
Subjects: Broadening of professional gardeners' and student gardeners' horticultural knowledge, skills and experience, and horticultural projects which demonstrate a distinct educational or historic value, as submitted by horticultural institutions, charities or gardens.
Purpose: To help finance horticulture related projects.
Eligibility: Submissions are welcomed from applicants worldwide, but preference is given to United Kingdom and Commonwealth citizens. Applicants should preferably be within the age bracket of 20-35 years and satisfy the Society that their health enables them to undertake the project proposed. Financial sponsorship will be available to both professional and amateur horticulturists and consideration for an award is not restricted to RHS members.
Value: Funds are limited. High cost projects are expected to receive supplementary finance from other sources, including personal contributions.
Frequency: Four times per year.
Country of Study: United Kingdom.
No. of awards offered: Unlimited.
Application Procedure: Applicants must complete an application form, available on request.
Closing Date: December 24th, March 31st, June 30th or September 30th.
Funding: Private.

The Osaka Travel Award
Subjects: Horticultural related study or work experience will be considered.
Purpose: To allow young people from the United Kingdom and Japan to study in each other's country and benefit from a cross-cultural exchange of ideas.
Eligibility: Open to British and Japanese citizens with a horticultural background. Applicants should preferably be within the age bracket of 20-35 years. Financial sponsorship will be available to both professional and amateur horticulturists and consideration for an award is not restricted to RHS Members. The awards are made to individuals, not to groups or expeditions.
Level of Study: Unrestricted.
Type: Bursary.
Value: Funds are limited. High cost projects are expected to receive supplementary finance from other sources, including personal contributions.
Frequency: Four times per year.
Country of Study: Japan or the United Kingdom.
No. of awards offered: One.
Application Procedure: Applicants must complete an application form, available on request. Candidates may be called for interview.
Closing Date: December 24th, March 31st, June 30th or September 30th.
Funding: Private.
Additional Information: Recipients must submit a brief factual report within six weeks of completion, along with an outline of achievements or difficulties and an account of expenses.

The Queen Elizabeth the Queen Mother Bursary

Subjects: Horticulture eg. study tours, horticulturally related expeditions, minor research projects, possibly working with an acknowledged expert on short-term research, taxonomic studies, specialised courses and programmes of study such as specific subject symposia.

Purpose: To help finance horticulture related projects.

Eligibility: Submissions are welcomed from applicants worldwide but preference is given to United Kingdom and Commonwealth citizens. Applicants should preferably be within the age bracket of 20-35 years and satisfy the Society that their health enables them to undertake the project proposed. Financial sponsorship will be available to both professional and amateur horticulturists and consideration for an award is not restricted to RHS members. The awards are made to individuals, not to groups or expeditions.

Level of Study: Unrestricted.

Type: Bursary.

Value: Funds are limited. High cost projects are expected to receive supplementary finance from other sources, including personal contributions.

Frequency: Considered four times a year.

Country of Study: Any country.

No. of awards offered: One-three.

Application Procedure: Applicants must complete an application form, available on request. Candidates may be called for interview.

Closing Date: December 24th, March 31st, June 30th or September 30th.

Funding: Private.

Additional Information: Recipients must submit a brief factual report within six weeks of completion, along with an outline of achievements or difficulties, including any unusual problems eg. medical or political, and an account of expenses. Recipients must also be prepared to give a lecture on their project at the Society's Headquarters, Vincent Square, London, within 18 months of completing the project.

RHS Financial Award

Subjects: All aspects of horticultural related study or work experience.

Purpose: To help finance horticulture related projects.

Eligibility: Submissions are welcomed from applicants worldwide, but preference is given to United Kingdom and Commonwealth citizens. Applicants should preferably be within the age bracket of 20-35 years and satisfy the Society that their health enables them to undertake the project proposed. Financial sponsorship will be available to both professional and amateur horticulturists and consideration for an award is not restricted to RHS members. The awards are made to individuals, not to groups or expeditions.

Level of Study: Unrestricted.

Type: Bursary.

Value: Funds are limited. High cost projects are expected to receive supplementary finance from other sources, including personal contributions.

Frequency: Four times per year.

Country of Study: Any country.

No. of awards offered: Unlimited.

Application Procedure: Applicants must complete an application form, available on request. Candidates may be called for interview.

Closing Date: December 24th, March 31st, June 30th or September 30th.

Funding: Private.

Additional Information: Recipients must submit a brief factual report within six weeks of completion, along with an outline of achievements or difficulties, including any unusual problems eg. medical or political, and an account of expenses.

ROYAL INCORPORATION OF ARCHITECTS IN SCOTLAND (RIAS)

15 Rutland Square, Edinburgh, EH1 2BE, Scotland
Tel: (44) 131 229 7545
Fax: (44) 131 228 2188
Contact: Ms Linda Connolly, Awards Administrator

The Martin Jones Memorial Scholarship and Award

Subjects: Architecture.

Purpose: To support an outstanding student in pursuing a personal line of creative investigation and research.

Eligibility: Open to students and graduates of the School of Architecture in Duncan of Jordanstone College of Art, Dundee University.

Level of Study: Postgraduate.

Type: Scholarship.

Value: UK £7,500.

Frequency: Annual.

Country of Study: Any country.

No. of awards offered: One.

Application Procedure: Invitations are issued in the Autumn each year.

Closing Date: End of January.

Funding: Private.

For further information contact:

The Martin Jones Award
c/o School of Architecture
Duncan of Jordanstone
Perth Road, Dundee, DD1 4HT, Scotland

RIAS Award for Measured Drawing

Subjects: Architecture and measured drawing.

Purpose: To encourage and recognise original hand measured drawing as essential to an architect's training.

Eligibility: Open to student members and members of the RIAS.

Level of Study: Postgraduate.

Value: The Premier Award for student members is UK £200 and the prize for full members is UK £100.

Frequency: Annual.

Country of Study: Any country.

No. of awards offered: One.

Closing Date: End of January.

Additional Information: The Committee will judge competitors on the following points: the choice of architectural fabric for the measured study, such as buildings under threat (the building need not be old), the clarity of understanding and accuracy revealed by the drawing and the elegance with which the analysis is presented. Adjudication will normally take place in March. If confirmed by the RIAS council the result of the competition will be notified to the competitors. The presentation of the award will be made at the RIAS Annual Convention. The winning drawing will form part of a travelling exhibition of RIAS Awards and Prizes and may, at the Incorporation's discretion, subsequently form part of the RIAS Archive.

RIAS John Maclaren Travelling Fellowship

Subjects: Architecture.

Purpose: To assist study at a school of architecture or engineering, or to assist an individual in taking up a paid position in practice in the country chosen for study, or to reward work which has involved study overseas.

Eligibility: Applicants must be on the Register of Registered Architects and be corporate members of the RIAS.

Level of Study: Postgraduate.

Type: Fellowship.

Value: UK £600 and a certificate.

Frequency: Every two years.

Country of Study: Outside the United Kingdom.

No. of awards offered: One.

Closing Date: End of January.

Additional Information: It is the preference of the RIAS that the outcome of the fellowship should be a presentation at the RIAS Convention of the results of the study with a lodgement in the RIAS Library of such manuscript and slides or photographs as may be appropriate. The fellowship requires both scholarship and analysis, and submission to the RIAS of evidence of lasting value. Applicants, both in their proposal and in the subsequent presentation, are expected to have adopted an investigative and critical attitude towards their proposed subject of study in the manner of a learned society dissertation. The option of presenting the results orally at the Convention (with the deposit of the material in the Library), or the simple deposit of written material in the Library, will be a matter for determination between the Fellow and the RIAS Awards Committee.

RIAS/Whitehouse Studios Award for Architectural Photography

Subjects: Architectural photography inspired by the topic a building and its people.
Purpose: To recognise that architectural photography is a distinct art, and to encourage its appreciation and development.
Eligibility: Open to student members and members of the RIAS.
Level of Study: Postgraduate.
Value: A certificate and UK £250.
Frequency: Annual.
Country of Study: Any country.
No. of awards offered: One.
Closing Date: January 31st.
Additional Information: At the Incorporation's discretion the winning photograph may also form part of the RIAS Archives.

The Sir John Burnet Memorial Award

Subjects: Architecture.
Purpose: To test a student's skill in architectural design and communicating by drawing, prepared within a predetermined time limit, their proposals in response to a client's brief.
Eligibility: Competitors must be student members of the RIAS and should be first year full-time post Part I.
Level of Study: Postgraduate.
Value: UK £150 and a certificate.
Frequency: Annual.
Country of Study: Any country.
No. of awards offered: One.
Additional Information: Submissions will be judged by the RIAS Awards Committee. The Committee may be assisted by distinguished critics, co-opted by the Committee. The judges will consider skills in interpreting a brief within a time deadline, flair in architectural design and skill in methods of communication and presentation. The drawings will remain the property of the RIAS.

The Sir Robert Lorimer Memorial Award

Subjects: Architecture.
Purpose: To encourage students to keep sketch books or notebooks, as in Lorimer's time.
Eligibility: Open to student members and members of the RIAS under the age of 29.
Level of Study: Postgraduate.
Value: A book voucher to the value of UK £125 and a certificate.
Frequency: Annual.
Country of Study: Any country.
No. of awards offered: One.
Closing Date: End of January.
Additional Information: The assessors prefer working sketch book(s), which are a record of study and travel, and will look for careful observation and sensitive draughtsmanship. Adjudication will normally take place in March. If confirmed by the RIAS Council the result of the competition will be notified to the competitors. The presentation of the award will be made at the RIAS Annual Convention.

The Sir Rowand Anderson Silver Medal

Subjects: Architecture.
Purpose: To recognise the best student member in Scotland.

Eligibility: Open to student members of the RIAS within a year of passing Part II.
Level of Study: Postgraduate.
Value: A silver medal and a certificate.
Frequency: Annual.
Country of Study: Scotland.
No. of awards offered: One.
Closing Date: October 31st.
Additional Information: The RIAS Awards Committee may require to interview candidates before making their selection. The award and presentation will be made at the RIAS Annual Convention, for which the winner may be asked to make available a selection of his or her portfolio for exhibition.

The Thomas Ross Award

Subjects: Architecture pertaining particularly to Scotland, Scottish architecture and environment or the study of ancient Scottish buildings or monuments.
Purpose: To recognise post qualification research.
Eligibility: Candidates must be members of the RIAS, be of graduate status or possess and produce evidence of such other qualifications as may satisfy the requirements of the RIAS.
Level of Study: Postgraduate.
Value: UK £600, a certificate and the possibility of additional help towards publication.
Frequency: Every two years.
Country of Study: Any country.
No. of awards offered: One, though the Committee, at its discretion, may make more than one award, provided that the total number of awards in a six year period does not exceed three.
Closing Date: End of January.
Additional Information: The Committee will judge applicants upon the clarity of the proposal or completed work, upon the candidates' ability to write and to present material and upon the extent to which the study covers ground not covered by existing material. The Committee may require applicants to attend an interview.

THE ROYAL INSTITUTION OF NAVAL ARCHITECTS (RINA)

10 Upper Belgrave Street, London, SW1X 8BQ, England
Tel: (44) 20 7235 4622
Fax: (44) 20 7245 6959
Email: hq@rina.org.uk
www: http://www.rina.org.uk
Contact: Mr D Bragger, Professional Affairs Manager

The Royal Institution of Naval Architects (RINA) exists to promote and serve the interests and needs of its members, who are those involved in the design, construction, repair and operation of ships, boats and marine structures.

Froude Research Scholarship in Naval Architecture

Subjects: Research into hydrodynamic or other problems connected with marine technology.
Purpose: To support marine engineering research.
Eligibility: Open to applicants from any country, normally under 30 years of age, who have shown unusual promise in the study of naval architecture and are members of RINA.
Level of Study: Postgraduate.
Type: Scholarship.
Value: UK £700.
Length of Study: Two years with a possibility of renewal for a further year.
Frequency: Annual, if funds are available.
Study Establishment: An approved institution.
Country of Study: Any country.
No. of awards offered: Usually one.
Application Procedure: Applicants must complete an application form and submit this with a letter of support from the Head of

Department of the applicant's university or college and evidence of the offer of a postgraduate placement. Applications should be returned to RINA. Candidates may be required to attend an interview in London. Application forms are available from the Director of Professional Affairs.

Closing Date: July 31st prior to commencement.
Funding: Private.
Contributor: Trust fund.
No. of awards given last year: Two.
No. of applicants last year: Five.
Additional Information: The holder is required to submit a report on the work done during the first year accompanied by a letter stating satisfactory progress from the Head of Department. The holder is also required to submit a report on satisfactory completion of the research and is not permitted to accept payment from a company in respect of work done in connection with the research for which the scholarship was awarded.

Sir William White Postgraduate Scholarship in Naval Architecture

Subjects: Marine engineering and naval architecture.
Purpose: To enable students to follow a postgraduate course or carry out research work into problems connected with the design and construction of ships.
Eligibility: Open to applicants from any country who have passed a course of study recognised by the Institute and who have at some time been employed in the marine industry.
Level of Study: Postgraduate.
Type: Scholarship.
Value: UK £700 payable at commencement of first year of study.
Length of Study: One-two years.
Frequency: Annual, if funds are available.
Study Establishment: An approved university, college or research establishment.
Country of Study: United Kingdom.
No. of awards offered: One-two.
Application Procedure: Applicants must complete an application form and submit this with qualification certificates, a letter of support from the applicant's university and evidence of the offer of a postgraduate placement. Applications should be returned to RINA. Candidates may be required to attend an interview in London. Application forms are available from the Director of Professional Affairs.
Closing Date: July 31st prior to commencement.
Funding: Private.
Contributor: Trust fund.
No. of awards given last year: One.
Additional Information: The holder is required to submit a report on satisfactory completion of the research and is not permitted to accept payment from a company in respect of work done in connection with the research for which the scholarship was awarded.

ROYAL IRISH ACADEMY

19 Dawson Street, Dublin, 2, Ireland
Tel: (353) 1 676 2570
Fax: (353) 1 676 2346
Email: admin@ria.ie
www: http://www.ria.ie
Contact: Ms Laura Mahoney, Assistant Executive Secretary

The Royal Irish Academy is the senior institution in Ireland for both the sciences and humanities. It publishes a number of journals and monographs. It is Ireland's national representative in a large number of international unions, and through its national committees runs conferences, lectures and workshops. It also manages a number of long-term research projects.

Eoin O'Mahony Bursary
Subjects: History.

Purpose: To assist Irish scholars undertaking overseas research on historical subjects of Irish interest.
Level of Study: Unrestricted.
Type: Bursary.
Value: Varies.
Length of Study: Varies.
Frequency: Annual.
Country of Study: Any country.
No. of awards offered: One.
Application Procedure: Applicants must complete an application form available from the Academy.
Closing Date: End of January.
Funding: Private.
Contributor: Trust fund.
No. of awards given last year: Eight.
Additional Information: Preference will be given to projects concerning family history, in particular those which are associated with the 'Wild Geese' (genealogy). Special consideration will be given to those who have been active in local learned societies.

Royal Irish Academy Award in Biochemistry
Subjects: Biochemistry.
Eligibility: Open to anyone who is actively engaged in biochemical research in Ireland.
Level of Study: Postdoctorate, Professional development.
Value: Silver medal.
Frequency: Annual.
Country of Study: Ireland.
No. of awards offered: One.
Application Procedure: Applicants must be nominated. Nomination must be made by two scientists who also supply the names of two independent referees, one of whom must reside outside Ireland.
Closing Date: Please contact the Academy.
Funding: Private.
Contributor: Schering Plough (Brinny) Company.
No. of awards given last year: One.
Additional Information: The award may be made to scientists at any stage of their scientific career and will primarily recognise scientific work carried out in the past decade. A silver medal is awarded and the recipient delivers a review lecture at the Royal Irish Academy and also at a meeting of the Irish Area Section of the Biochemical Society.

Royal Irish Academy Award in Microbiology
Subjects: Microbiology.
Purpose: To recognise research contributions in microbiology in referred international journals.
Eligibility: Open to people who are resident in either Northern Ireland or the Republic of Ireland. Only applicants less than 40 years of age on January 1st of the year of the award are eligible.
Level of Study: Unrestricted.
Value: Silver medal.
Frequency: Every two years.
Country of Study: Ireland.
No. of awards offered: One.
Application Procedure: Applicants must be nominated independently by two scientists who are familiar with the work of the nominee.
Closing Date: February 23rd.
Funding: Private.
No. of awards given last year: One.
Additional Information: The recipient will deliver a review lecture at the Royal Irish Academy. A copy of the lecture must be deposited in the Academy's library.

Royal Irish Academy Award in Nutritional Sciences
Subjects: Dietetics or microbiology.
Purpose: To recognise research contributions in nutritional sciences in referred international journals.
Eligibility: Open to people who are resident in either Northern Ireland or the Republic of Ireland. Only applicants who are less than 45 years of age on January 1st of the year of the award are eligible.

605

Level of Study: Postdoctorate, Professional development.
Value: Silver medal.
Frequency: Every two to four years.
Country of Study: Ireland.
No. of awards offered: One.
Application Procedure: Applicants must be nominated independently by two scientists who are familiar with the work of the nominee.
Closing Date: Applications are accepted at any time.
Funding: Private.
Additional Information: The recipient will deliver a review lecture at the Royal Irish Academy. A copy of the lecture must be deposited in the Academy's library.

Royal Irish Academy Award in Pharmacology and Toxicology

Subjects: Pharmacology and toxicology.
Purpose: To recognise achievement.
Eligibility: Open to all those who work in or close to the areas of pharmacology and toxicology and who are resident in either Northern Ireland or the Republic of Ireland.
Level of Study: Postdoctorate, Professional development.
Value: Silver medal.
Frequency: Every two years.
Country of Study: Ireland.
Application Procedure: Applicants must be nominated by not less than two persons who will have obtained the prior agreement of the nominee.
Closing Date: Applications are accepted at any time.
Funding: Private.
Contributor: The Élan Corporation.
No. of awards given last year: One.
Additional Information: The medal will be presented at a function to be held at the Royal Irish Academy. The recipient will be required to speak on this occasion and a copy of the address must be deposited in the Academy's library.

Royal Irish Academy European Exchange Fellowship

Subjects: Humanities, social sciences or natural sciences.
Purpose: To promote academic exchange between Ireland and Austria, Great Britain, Hungary, France and Poland.
Eligibility: Irish applications must come from applicants who are resident in the Republic of Ireland. Researchers from other countries must apply to their own academy or learned society.
Level of Study: Postdoctorate, Professional development.
Type: Fellowship.
Value: Varies.
Length of Study: Varies.
Frequency: Annual.
Country of Study: United Kingdom, France, Hungary, Poland or Austria.
Application Procedure: Applicants must complete an application form, available form the Academy.
Closing Date: October 30th.
Funding: Government.
No. of awards given last year: 17.

Royal Irish Academy Science Writing Competition

Subjects: Biochemistry.
Eligibility: Open to graduate students in third level institutions in either Northern Ireland or the Republic of Ireland.
Level of Study: Postgraduate, Predoctorate, Research.
Value: €1,000 for the winner and €400 for the runner-up.
Frequency: Annual.
Country of Study: Ireland.
No. of awards offered: Two.
Application Procedure: Applicants must submit five copies of the article.
Closing Date: March 26th.
Funding: Private.
Contributor: Yamanouchi Ireland and the Irish Times newspaper.
No. of awards given last year: Two.

Additional Information: The newspaper article must be suitable for a non scientific reader explaining the development of any new topic in biochemistry and its significance to medical, agricultural or industrial practices. The winner's article will appear in the Irish Times newspaper.

Royal Irish Academy Senior Visiting Fellowships

Subjects: Scientific research other than in social sciences, dentistry and theoretical and clinical medicine.
Purpose: To enable a new scientific research technique or development to be introduced into the Republic of Ireland.
Eligibility: Open to senior researchers from member countries of the Organization for Economic Co-operation and Development (OECD) only.
Level of Study: Postdoctorate, Professional development.
Type: Fellowship.
Value: Varies.
Frequency: Annual.
Country of Study: Ireland or other (OECD) member countries.
No. of awards offered: Varies.
Application Procedure: Applicants must complete an application form.
Closing Date: October 15th.
Funding: Government.
No. of awards given last year: 10.
Additional Information: The Academy participates in the Royal Society European Science Exchange Programmes in pure and applied science, in the British Academy European Exchange Programmes in the humanities, and in the Austrian, Hungarian, or Polish academy exchange schemes in science and the humanities. Small grants for work in all disciplines are available annually from the Academy's own funds. The Senior Visiting Fellowship Awards are made on behalf of the Irish government.

ROYAL PHILHARMONIC SOCIETY (RPS)

10 Stratford Place, London, W1C 1BA, England
Tel: (44) 20 7491 8110
Fax: (44) 20 7493 7463
Email: admin@rps-uk.demon.co.uk
www: http://www.royalphilharmonicsociety.org.uk
Contact: Ms Rosemary Johnson, General Administrator

The Royal Philharmonic Society (RPS) offers support for young musicians and composers, sponsorship of new music events, debate and discussion about the future of music and has an active commissioning policy. It recognises achievement through the prestigious annual RPS Music Awards and with the Society's Gold Medal. Full information is available on the RPS website.

Julius Isserlis Scholarship

Subjects: Musical performance in varying instrumental categories.
Purpose: To facilitate musical study abroad, starting within 16 months of the award being made.
Eligibility: Open to students of any nationality, permanently resident in the United Kingdom, who are 15-25 years of age.
Level of Study: Unrestricted.
Type: Scholarship.
Value: UK £25,000.
Length of Study: Two years.
Frequency: Every two years.
Country of Study: Outside the United Kingdom.
No. of awards offered: One main award with the additional possibility of smaller discretionary awards.
Application Procedure: Applicants must complete an application form. There is a UK £20 entry fee.
Closing Date: March.
Funding: Private.
Additional Information: The winner must take up residence for a period of study in the country designated on the application.

Royal Philharmonic Society Composition Prize

Subjects: Musical composition.

Purpose: To encourage young composers.

Eligibility: Open to past and present registered students of any conservatoire or university within the United Kingdom, of any nationality, under the age of 29. Former winners are not eligible.

Level of Study: Postgraduate.

Type: Prize.

Value: UK £5,000 commission plus a guaranteed performance of commissioned work.

Frequency: Annual.

No. of awards offered: One.

Application Procedure: Applicants must complete an application form. There is a UK £20 entry fee but this is free to RPS members.

Closing Date: March 31st annually.

Funding: Private.

No. of awards given last year: One.

No. of applicants last year: 70.

THE ROYAL SCOTTISH ACADEMY (RSA)

17 Waterloo Place, Edinburgh, EH1 3BG, Scotland
Tel: (44) 131 558 7097
Fax: (44) 131 557 6417
Email: info@royalscottishacademy.org
www: http://www.royalscottishacademy.org
Contact: Secretary

Founded in 1826, the Royal Scottish Academy (RSA), Scotland's foremost body of artists, has promoted the works of leading contemporary painters, sculptors, printmakers and architects. It also gives practical and financial help to young artists through scholarships as well as the annual Student's Exhibition.

The Alastair Salvesen Art Scholarship

Subjects: Painting, sculpture, architecture or printmaking.

Purpose: To encourage young painters who have already made the transition from college to a working environment.

Eligibility: Applicants must be painters who have been trained at one of four Scottish Colleges of Art (Aberdeen, Dundee, Edinburgh or Glasgow) and are currently living and working in Scotland.

Level of Study: Postgraduate.

Type: Travel scholarship.

Value: Up to UK £10,000 depending on the plan submitted, and an exhibition that lasts about three weeks to take place in November or December in a gallery.

Length of Study: Three-six months.

Frequency: Annual.

Country of Study: Any country.

No. of awards offered: One.

Application Procedure: Applicants must contact the RSA.

Closing Date: End of December.

Funding: Private.

Contributor: The Alastair Salvesen Trust.

The John Kinross Memorial Fund Student Scholarships

Subjects: Painting, sculpture, architecture or printmaking.

Purpose: To allow young artists from the established training centres in Scotland to spend time in Italy.

Eligibility: The painting, printmaking and sculpture scholarship is open to students in final or postgraduate years of study at one of the Scottish Colleges of Art. The architecture scholarship is open to senior students at one of the six Scottish Schools of Architecture presenting work which would normally be related to the requirements of RIBA Part 1 or Part 2 Syllabus. Group work is not acceptable. Students at Scottish Colleges studying painting, sculpture, printmaking and architecture are eligible to apply for a three month scholarship to Florence in memory of the late John Kinross.

Level of Study: Postgraduate.

Type: Scholarship.

Value: Varies.

Length of Study: Three months.

Frequency: Annual.

Study Establishment: In Florence or the surrounding area.

Country of Study: Italy.

No. of awards offered: Varies, usually 10-15.

Closing Date: Late April.

Funding: Private.

Contributor: The Kinross Scholarship Fund which is administered by the RSA.

No. of awards given last year: 15.

No. of applicants last year: 80.

RSA Annual Student Competition

Subjects: Painting, sculpture, architecture or printmaking.

Eligibility: Candidates should be residents of Scotland. Painting, printmaking and sculpture students should be in their final or postgraduate years of study at a college of art in Scotland. Applicants should submit one work. Architecture students should be in their final year and present work normally related to the requirements of the RIBA Part II syllabus.

Level of Study: Postgraduate.

Type: Competition.

Value: Varies. UK £400 for printmaking, painting, sculpture, architecture and the Carnegie Travelling Scholarship of UK £200.

Frequency: Annual.

Study Establishment: All Scottish colleges of Art and Architecture.

Country of Study: Scotland.

No. of awards offered: Varies.

Application Procedure: Applicants must submit applications via their college, which must be countersigned by the tutor.

Closing Date: February.

Funding: Commercial.

Contributor: The RSA.

No. of awards given last year: 15.

No. of applicants last year: 400.

Additional Information: The Academy also sponsors an Annual Exhibition of painting including oils, water colours, pastels, and black and white, sculpture, architectural drawings and prints. Various monetary awards are also made from May 2nd-July 5th.

Sir William Gillies Bequest-Hospitalfield Residencies

Subjects: Painting, sculpture, architecture or printmaking.

Purpose: To provide young professional artists who are Scottish or have studied in Scotland, with a period for personal development and the exploration of new directions.

Eligibility: Applicants should have completed a period of formal study in an area of the visual arts by at least one year, have continued to practice and exhibit and wish to continue to develop ideas and concepts which they regard as important.

Level of Study: Postgraduate.

Type: Residency.

Value: Accommodation, studio space and access to the private collection of Patrick Allan-Fraser.

Length of Study: One or three months.

Frequency: Annual.

Study Establishment: Hospitalfield House, Arbroath.

Country of Study: Scotland.

No. of awards offered: Usually three.

Application Procedure: Applicants must contact the RSA.

Closing Date: End of November.

Funding: Private.

Contributor: The Bequest Fund administered by Royal Scottish Academy.

THE ROYAL SOCIETY

6 Carlton House Terrace, London, SW1Y 5AG, England
Tel: (44) 20 7451 2547
Fax: (44) 20 7930 2170
Email: ukresearch.appointments@royalsoc.ac.uk
www: http://www.royalsoc.ac.uk
Contact: Mr Keith Wylde, Research Appointments Officer

The Royal Society is an independent academy promoting the natural and applied sciences. The Society has a dual role, as the United Kingdom Academy of Science acting nationally or internationally and as the provider of a broad range of services for the scientific community in the national interest, responsive to individual demand with selection by merit, not by field. The Royal Society supports over 300 research appointments, covering all disciplines and at all levels: research professorships, senior research fellowships, research fellowships, university research fellowships, Leverhulme Trust and Amersham fellowships for one year research 'sabbaticals' and Industry fellowships to enhance industry-academia links.

Copus Public Understanding of Science Development Fund

Subjects: All areas of science.
Purpose: Grants are awarded to encourage and support major new initiatives which aim to improve the public understanding of science and technology.
Eligibility: Applicants must be resident in the United Kingdom.
Level of Study: Unrestricted.
Type: Grant.
Value: Up to UK £20,000.
Frequency: Annual.
Study Establishment: Varies.
Country of Study: Varies.
No. of awards offered: Varies.
Application Procedure: Applicants must complete an application form. Further information is available on request. Requests must quote the name of the scheme or programme. If requests are made by email applicants must include their full name and postal address.
Closing Date: To be determined.
Funding: Government.
Contributor: OST.
No. of awards given last year: Seven.
No. of applicants last year: 34.
Additional Information: Further information is available on the website or by contacting Scott Kier on (44) 20 7451 2513.

Copus Public Understanding of Science Seed Fund

Subjects: All areas of science.
Purpose: To assist pump priming activities or initiatives directly concerned with the promotion of the public understanding of science at a local level.
Eligibility: Open to residents of the United Kingdom.
Level of Study: Unrestricted.
Type: Grant.
Value: Up to UK £3,000.
Frequency: Annual.
Study Establishment: Varies.
Country of Study: United Kingdom.
No. of awards offered: Varies.
Application Procedure: Applicants must complete an application form. Further information is available from the website or by contacting Natasha Martineau on (44) 20 7451 2579. Requests must quote the name of the scheme or programme. If requests are made by email applicants must include their full name and postal address.
Closing Date: To be determined.
Funding: Government.
Contributor: OST.
No. of awards given last year: 25.
No. of applicants last year: 68.
Additional Information: Further information is available on the website or by contacting Scott Kier on (44) 20 7451 2513.

Dorothy Hodgkin Fellowships

Subjects: Natural sciences including mathematics or engineering.
Purpose: To provide the first step into a research career for excellent young scientists and engineers.
Eligibility: Open to applicants under the age of 35 years with postdoctoral status and no more than four years of postdoctoral research experience. Applicants must either be currently employed in the United Kingdom or have been resident in the United Kingdom for a continuous period of at least three years, not including time spent in full-time education. Those already holding a substantive post in an European Union university are not eligible.
Level of Study: Postdoctorate.
Type: Fellowship.
Value: Salaries at research staff IIA/II scales.
Length of Study: Four years.
Frequency: Annual.
Study Establishment: Universities and Institutes of Higher Education.
Country of Study: United Kingdom.
No. of awards offered: Varies.
Application Procedure: Applicants must complete an official application. Further information and application forms are available from the website. If any problems occur applicants should contact the Research Appointments Department on (44) 20 7451 2542 or by email. Requests must quote the name of the scheme or programme. If requests are made by email applicants must include their full name and postal address.
Closing Date: February 8th.
Funding: Commercial, Government, Private.
No. of awards given last year: 10.
No. of applicants last year: 200.
Additional Information: Further information is available on request and on the website.

James Ellis Research Fellowship

Subjects: Quantum information processing.
Purpose: To assist research focused on the practical implementation of quantum computation rather than other possible applications in the field of quantum information processing.
Eligibility: Applicants must have a PhD or equivalent research experience. Applicants for both fellowship schemes must have between two and seven years of full-time postdoctoral experience. Career breaks such as maternity leave, European Union national service and voluntary service overseas can be discounted, but teaching experience or time spent in industry since the award of a PhD should be included in the total amount of postdoctoral experience. Part-time work will be counted pro-rata.
Level of Study: Postdoctorate.
Type: Fellowship.
Value: Salaries on the university lecturers' A or B scale for non-clinical academic and related staff.
Length of Study: Five years in the first instance.
Frequency: Annual.
Study Establishment: Appropriate university departments.
Country of Study: United Kingdom.
No. of awards offered: Varies.
Application Procedure: Applicants must complete an official form. Further information and application forms are available from the website.
Closing Date: Early January.
Funding: Government.

Leverhulme Trust Senior Research Fellowships

Subjects: Natural sciences including mathematics or science.
Purpose: To enable senior scientists in academia to be relieved of all teaching and administration duties to undertake full-time research.
Eligibility: Open to senior scientists at the mid career stage who hold a permanent post in Institutes of Higher Education or universities in the United Kingdom.
Level of Study: Postdoctorate.
Type: Fellowship.

Value: The Fellow's employing institution will be reimbursed for full salary costs of a younger academic employed to take over the Fellow's teaching and administration duties for the fellowship period.
Length of Study: One academic term to one academic year.
Frequency: Annual.
Study Establishment: Usually the applicant's own institution but it may be held at any Institute of Higher Education or industrial research organisation in the United Kingdom which is approved by the Council of the Royal Society.
Country of Study: United Kingdom.
No. of awards offered: Seven.
Application Procedure: Applicants must complete an official application. Further information is available on the website. Application forms are downloadable from the website. If any problems occur contact the Research Appointments Department on (44) 20 7451 2542 or by email. Requests must quote name of scheme or programme. If requests are made by email applicants must include their full name and postal address.
Closing Date: December 7th.
Funding: Private.
No. of awards given last year: Seven.
No. of applicants last year: 55.
Additional Information: Further information is available on request and on the website.

Olga Kennard Research Fellowship Scheme

Subjects: Crystallography or structural molecular biology.
Eligibility: Open to citizens of the European Union, Norway, Israel and Switzerland. Applicants must have at least three years of post-doctoral experience and be aged between 26-40 years.
Level of Study: Postdoctorate.
Type: Fellowship.
Value: Salary with London allowance where appropriate, together with annual research expenses, travel expenses and a contribution to baggage costs for overseas applicants.
Length of Study: Five years.
Frequency: As vacancies occur.
Study Establishment: Appropriate university departments.
Country of Study: United Kingdom.
No. of awards offered: One.
Application Procedure: Applicants must complete an official application. Further information and application forms are available from the website. If any problems occur applicants should contact the Research Appointments Department on (44) 20 7451 2542 or by email. Requests must quote the name of the scheme or programme. If requests are made by email applicants must include their full name and postal address.
Closing Date: No fixed deadline.
Additional Information: Further information is available on the website.

Paul Instrument Fund

Subjects: Instrument development for pure or applied physical science.
Purpose: To assist the design, construction and maintenance of novel, unusual or much improved types of physical instruments and apparatus needed for an investigation in pure or applied physical science.
Eligibility: Open to British subjects or persons domiciled or ordinarily resident in the United Kingdom. Applicants must be employed and working in the United Kingdom.
Level of Study: Postdoctorate, Research.
Type: Grant.
Value: Varies.
Frequency: Three times each year.
Country of Study: United Kingdom.
No. of awards offered: Varies.
Application Procedure: Applicants must contact Jane Lewis on (44) 20 7451 2538. Requests must quote name of the scheme or programme. If requests are made by email applicants must include their full name and postal address.
Closing Date: January 15th, May 15th or September 15th.

Funding: Private.
No. of awards given last year: 10.
No. of applicants last year: 27.

Rink Research Fellowship Scheme

Subjects: Clinical science, particularly degenerative disorders or diseases of later life.
Eligibility: Open to citizens of the European Union who are either employed in the United Kingdom or have been resident in the United Kingdom for at least three consecutive years, not including time spent in full-time education. Applicants must be medically qualified and must have a PhD or MD, be aged between 26-40 years and have no more than seven years of research experience. Those who hold a substantive post in such a department or in a European Union university are not eligible.
Level of Study: Postdoctorate.
Type: Fellowship.
Length of Study: Five years.
Frequency: As vacancies occur.
Study Establishment: A department in a British university or a recognised clinical research establishment.
No. of awards offered: One.
Application Procedure: Applicants must apply for information, available on request. Requests must quote the name of the scheme or programme. If requests are made by email applicants must include their full name and postal address.
Funding: Private.
Additional Information: Further information is available on request or on the website.

Royal Society Conference Grants

Subjects: Natural and applied sciences or technology.
Purpose: To assist with expenses in participating at a conference overseas.
Eligibility: Open to non government scientists of PhD status who are normally resident in the United Kingdom. Applicants must be presenting their own paper or poster at a meeting or chairing a session.
Level of Study: Postdoctorate.
Type: Grant.
Value: Varies.
Length of Study: Varies.
Frequency: Four times per year.
Country of Study: Outside the United Kingdom.
No. of awards offered: Varies.
Application Procedure: Applicants must complete an official application. Further information and forms are available from the website and on request from Sandra Goodall by telephoning (44) 20 7451 2540 or emailing sandra.goodall@royalsoc.ac.uk. Requests must quote the name of the scheme or programme.
Closing Date: March 1st, June 1st, October 1st and December 1st.
Funding: Government.
No. of awards given last year: 1,138.
No. of applicants last year: 1,752.

Royal Society History of Science Meetings

Subjects: The history of science.
Purpose: To support the funding of meetings on the history of science.
Eligibility: Open to scientific bodies or learned societies concerned with the history of science.
Level of Study: Graduate, Postdoctorate, Postgraduate.
Type: Grant.
Value: Up to UK £5,000.
Frequency: Annual.
Country of Study: United Kingdom.
No. of awards offered: Varies.
Application Procedure: Applicants must contact Karen Peters on (44) 20 7451 2595 or by email on karen.peters@royalsoc.ac.uk. Information is also available on the website. Requests must quote the

name of the scheme or programme. If requests are made by email applicants must include their full name and postal address.

Closing Date: August 15th.

Funding: Government.

No. of awards given last year: One.

Royal Society Industry Fellowships Scheme

Subjects: All areas of natural science.

Purpose: To provide opportunities for industrial scientists and engineers to carry out research or course development in a university or polytechnic. The scheme also provides similar opportunities for corresponding academic employees to undertake a project in industry.

Eligibility: Open to applicants of any nationality at the mid career stage who hold a PhD or equivalent. Applicants must hold either a substantive academic post in an Institute of Higher Education in the United Kingdom or be employed as a scientist, mathematician or engineer in an industry in the United Kingdom.

Level of Study: Postgraduate.

Type: Fellowship.

Value: The Fellow's employer will be reimbursed for the salary only.

Length of Study: Six months to two years. Part-time appointments are permitted.

Frequency: Twice a year.

Country of Study: United Kingdom.

No. of awards offered: Varies, approx. eight.

Application Procedure: Applicants must complete an official application. Further information and application forms are available from the website. If any problems occur applicants should contact the Research Appointments Department on (44) 20 7451 2542 or by email. Requests must quote the name of the scheme or programme. If requests are made by email applicants must include their full name and postal address.

Closing Date: December or June.

Funding: Commercial, Government, Private.

Additional Information: Further information is available on request and from the website.

Royal Society Research Grants Scheme

Subjects: Any scientific or technological discipline within the remit of the Royal Society. Natural sciences including mathematics, engineering, agricultural and medical research, scientific aspects of archaeology, geography, experimental psychology and the history of science.

Purpose: To allow the purchase of specialised equipment or essential consumable materials for use in research projects of 'timeliness and promise'. The scheme aims to support those new into research, or researchers moving into a new field of research. The scheme also aims to meet the requests for support to enable a new facet of research or new directions in an existing research programme and to provide support for research in the history of science.

Eligibility: Open to academic workers in United Kingdom universities, Institutes of Higher Education and research institutions. Further information is available on request or on the website.

Level of Study: Postdoctorate, Research.

Type: Grant.

Value: Up to UK £10,000.

Frequency: Twice a year.

Country of Study: United Kingdom.

No. of awards offered: Varies.

Application Procedure: Applicants must complete an official application. Further information and application forms are available on the website or by contacting Miss Susan Moss on (44) 20 7451 2539, or by email on susan.moss@royalsoc.ac.uk. Applications cannot be accepted if sent by fax or email.

Closing Date: April 1st and November 1st.

Funding: Private.

Contributor: The public.

No. of awards given last year: 341.

No. of applicants last year: 899.

Royal Society University Research Fellowships

Subjects: Science including agriculture, medicine, mathematics, engineering or technology.

Purpose: To provide support for young, high quality research workers to work in university departments, possibly leading to a permanent post.

Level of Study: Postdoctorate.

Type: Fellowship.

Value: Salaries on the university lecturers' A or B scale for non clinical academic and related staff.

Length of Study: Five years in the first instance, with two possible further renewals for three and then two years.

Frequency: Annual.

Study Establishment: Appropriate university departments.

Country of Study: United Kingdom.

No. of awards offered: Varies.

Application Procedure: Applicants must complete an official application form. Further information and application forms are available from the website.

Closing Date: Early January.

Funding: Government.

No. of awards given last year: 40.

No. of applicants last year: 300.

The Royal Society-Wolfson Foundation Laboratory Refurbishment Scheme

Subjects: The subject area is chosen each year and is always within the natural sciences.

Purpose: To support the physical infrastructure in universities for basic research in a specific field which is chosen each year.

Eligibility: Open to scientists who hold a substantive post in a United Kingdom university.

Level of Study: Postdoctorate, Research.

Type: Grant.

Value: Varies.

Frequency: Annual.

Country of Study: United Kingdom.

No. of awards offered: Approx. 20.

Application Procedure: Applicants must submit 15 copies of the complete application. Further information is available on request or from the website. Applications cannot be accepted if sent by fax. Requests must quote the name of the scheme or programme.

Closing Date: Please contact the organisation.

Funding: Private.

Contributor: The Wolfson Foundation.

No. of awards given last year: 21.

No. of applicants last year: 48.

Additional Information: Applications and all enquiries should be addressed to Elaine Potter on (44) 20 7451 2541 or by email to elaine.potter@royalsoc.ac.uk. Enquiries are preferred to be made by email. Further information is available on request or on the website.

ROYAL SOCIETY FOR THE ENCOURAGEMENT OF ARTS, MANUFACTURES AND COMMERCE (RSA)

8 John Adam Street, London, WC2N 6EZ, England
Tel: (44) 20 7930 5115
Fax: (44) 20 7839 5805
Email: lizzie.tulip@rsa.org.uk
www: http://rsa.org.uk/afa
Contact: Ms Lizzie Tulip, Project Co-ordinator

The Royal Society for the Encouragement of Arts, Manufactures and Commerce (RSA), is an instrument of change, working to create a civilised society based on a sustainable economy. It is a charity which uses its independence and the resources of its international fellowship to stimulate discussion, develop ideas and encourage action. Its main fields of interest today are business and industry, design and technology, education, the arts and the environment.

RSA Art for Architecture

Subjects: Art and architecture.
Purpose: To encourage collaboration between artists and architects or other design professionals, by giving grants to support the artist's place in a design team at the early stage of the design process.
Eligibility: Open to visual artists who are to be employed at the earliest stage of a building project as part of the design team. Restricted to projects within the British Isles, but open to individuals of any nationality if attached to a project.
Type: Varies.
Value: UK £2,000-15,000. Awards are in the form of payment towards the design fees of artists appointed.
Frequency: Three times each year.
Country of Study: United Kingdom.
No. of awards offered: Two.
Application Procedure: Applicants must complete an application form. Other documentation such as slides, plans, and letters of support should be submitted with all applications to Lizzie Tulip.
Closing Date: Three times per year on January 18th, April 19th and September 13th.
Funding: Commercial, Government.
Contributor: The Commission for Architecture and the Built Environment (CABE).
No. of awards given last year: 12.
No. of applicants last year: 50.
Additional Information: There is also a Publication Award, intended to help fund publications that focus on issues and practice relating to collaboration.

RSA Student Design Awards

Subjects: Design.
Purpose: To give the winning students the opportunity to undertake research or study abroad, or to undertake periods of attachment in industry.
Eligibility: Open to students who have studied for at least one term at a recognised college of design within the United Kingdom and some in other European Community countries.
Level of Study: Postgraduate.
Type: Travel bursaries and work placements.
Value: UK £250-5,000.
Frequency: Annual.
Study Establishment: An appropriate institution or in industry.
Country of Study: Travel awards may be used to fund study tours abroad.
No. of awards offered: Varies.
Application Procedure: Applicants must visit the website for project briefs and details for application.
Closing Date: November 30th.
Funding: Commercial, Government, Private.
No. of awards given last year: 152.
No. of applicants last year: 2,444.
Additional Information: The Student Design Awards scheme is not a grant, but an annual competition open to design students. The majority of periods of attachment are with companies in the United Kingdom, while some are with companies abroad.

ROYAL SOCIETY OF CANADA

283 Sparks Street, Ottawa, ON, K1R 7XG, Canada
Tel: (1) 613 991 6990
Fax: (1) 613 991 6996
Email: adminrsc@rsc.ca
www: http://www.rsc.ca
Contact: Dr Andrew D Miall, FRSC Programme Chair

The primary objective of the Royal Society of Canada is to promote learning and research in the arts and sciences. It draws on the breadth of knowledge and expertise of its members from all disciplines to recognise and honour distinguished accomplishments, to advise on the state of scholarship and culture across the country, and to inform the public of newsworthy social, scientific and ethical questions of the day.

CCMS (Committee on the Challenges of Modern Society) Fellowships

Subjects: Subjects related to the natural or social environment.
Purpose: To allow Fellows to contribute to the work of the CCMS pilot studies. The purpose of these studies is to suggest, on the basis of existing knowledge, solutions to problems relating to the natural and social environment. To achieve this objective, the programme provides support to Fellows who wish to conduct research under the guidance of pilot study directors or to work as members of the CCMS pilot study teams or both.
Eligibility: Open to citizens of NATO countries who have demonstrated research interest or have experience in a subject area related to one of the ongoing CCMS pilot studies, and willingness to work under the guidance of the respective pilot study director. Candidates must have a suitable background which is acceptable to the pilot study director, a connection with a research unit or government agency having an active interest in the subject with a view to ensuring the useful application of the experience gained to the needs of the home country, and a good working knowledge of the language of the CCMS pilot study Director with whom the Fellow will be working, or English or French, if either of them is sufficient and mutually convenient.
Level of Study: Postdoctorate, Professional development.
Type: Research fellowship.
Frequency: Annual.
Country of Study: Any country.
No. of awards offered: Varies.
Application Procedure: Applicants must complete an application form. Application forms and a list of pilot studies are available on request. Consultation with the pilot study director prior to the preparation of the application is recommended.
Closing Date: December 31st.
Contributor: NATO.

THE ROYAL SOCIETY OF CHEMISTRY

Burlington House
Piccadilly, London, W1J 0BA, England
Tel: (44) 20 7437 8656
Fax: (44) 20 7734 1227
Email: langers@rsc.org
www: http://www.rsc.org
Contact: Mr S S Langer

The Royal Society of Chemistry is the learned society for chemistry and the professional body for chemists in the United Kingdom with 46,000 members worldwide. The Society is a major publisher of chemical information, supports the teaching of chemistry at all levels, organises hundreds of chemical meetings a year and is a leader in communicating science to the public. It is now the United Kingdom National Adhering Organisation (NAO) to the International Union of Pure and Applied Chemistry (IUPAC).

Corday-Morgan Memorial Fund

Subjects: Chemistry.
Purpose: To assist members of any established chemical society or institute in the Commonwealth to visit chemical establishments in another Commonwealth country.
Eligibility: Open to citizens of, and those domiciled in, any Commonwealth country.
Level of Study: Professional development.
Type: Grant.
Value: Up to UK £500. The grants will complement, where appropriate, those for visits to developing countries available from the

International Committee's fund, and funding would cover the additional travel costs involved, together with appropriate subsistence. Applicants should also see the Visits to Developing Countries awards.
Frequency: Dependent on funds available.
Country of Study: Any country.
No. of awards offered: Approx. 10.
Application Procedure: Applicants must submit applications on the official form and will normally be considered within one month of receipt.
Closing Date: Applications are accepted at any time.
No. of awards given last year: Six.
No. of applicants last year: Eight.
Additional Information: Applicants must be travelling to another country (not necessarily in the Commonwealth) and would normally stop en route to visit a third country which must be in the Commonwealth.

Hickinbottom/Briggs Fellowship

Subjects: Chemistry.
Purpose: To assist research into organic chemistry.
Eligibility: Open to applicants domiciled in the United Kingdom or Republic of Ireland. Candidates must already hold a PhD or equivalent in chemistry and be not more than 36 years of age on October 31st.
Level of Study: Postdoctorate.
Type: Fellowship.
Value: Approx. UK £17,000.
Length of Study: Three years.
Frequency: Dependent on funds available.
Study Establishment: A British or Irish university or college.
Country of Study: United Kingdom or Ireland.
No. of awards offered: One.
Application Procedure: Applicants must apply by application forms or be nominated.
Closing Date: June 1st.
No. of awards given last year: One.

J W T Jones Travelling Fellowship

Subjects: Chemistry.
Purpose: To promote international co-operation in chemistry, to enable chemists to carry out short-term studies in well established scientific centres abroad and to learn and use techniques not accessible to them in their own country.
Eligibility: Open to members of the Royal Society of Chemistry who hold at least a Master's or PhD degree in chemistry or a related subject and are already actively engaged in research. Candidates must produce evidence that the theoretical and practical knowledge or training to be acquired in the foreign laboratory will be beneficial to their scientific development and must also return to their country of origin upon termination of the Fellowship.
Level of Study: Professional development.
Type: Fellowship.
Value: A lump sum of up to UK £5,000, designed to cover part or all of an economy class air or rail ticket and a subsistence allowance. It is expected that the institution of origin and/or the host institution will contribute to defray any remaining expenses incurred by the fellowship holder.
Length of Study: Normally one-three months.
Frequency: Four times per year.
Country of Study: Any country.
No. of awards offered: Approx. six.
Application Procedure: Applicants must apply for application forms, together with full details, from the International Affairs Officer.
Closing Date: January 1st, April 1st, July 1st or October 1st.
No. of awards given last year: Four.
No. of applicants last year: Five.
Additional Information: Fellowships will not be awarded to attend scientific meetings. Applications will be considered by a Fellowship Committee and the holder will be required to submit a formal report on the work accomplished.

Royal Society of Chemistry Journals Grants for International Authors

Subjects: Chemistry.
Purpose: To allow international authors to visit other countries in order to collaborate in research, exchange research ideas and results, and to give or receive special expertise and training.
Eligibility: Open to anyone with a recent publication in any of the the Society's journals. Those from the United Kingdom or Republic of Ireland are excluded.
Level of Study: Professional development.
Type: Grant.
Value: A lump sum of up to UK £2,000, designed to cover part or all of an economy class air or rail ticket and a subsistence allowance. It is expected that the institution of origin and/or the host institution will contribute to defray any remaining expenses incurred by the grant holder.
Length of Study: Normally one-three months.
Frequency: Four times per year.
Country of Study: Any country.
No. of awards offered: 100.
Application Procedure: Applicants must apply for application forms, together with full details, from the International Affairs Officer.
Closing Date: January 1st, April 1st, July 1st or October 1st.
No. of awards given last year: 83.
No. of applicants last year: 107.

Royal Society of Chemistry Research Fund

Subjects: Chemistry research and chemical education.
Purpose: To provide financial support to those working in less affluent institutions.
Eligibility: Open to members of the Society.
Level of Study: Professional development.
Type: Grant.
Value: Up to UK £1,200 for the purchase of chemicals, equipment or for running expenses of research.
Length of Study: One year.
Frequency: Annual.
Country of Study: Any country.
No. of awards offered: 20-30.
Closing Date: October 31st.
No. of awards given last year: 30.
No. of applicants last year: 50.
Additional Information: Funds are limited, so preference will be given to those working in less well-endowed institutions. The Selection Committee is especially anxious to see inventive applications of a 'pump priming' nature. Members in developing countries should note particularly that additional funds have been made available by the Society's International Committee to provide grants for successful applicants from such countries. Preference will be given to those able to cite collaborative research projects with United Kingdom institutions.

Royal Society of Chemistry Visits to Developing Countries

Subjects: Chemistry.
Purpose: To promote international co-operation in chemistry, specifically, to enable chemists to carry out short-term studies in well established scientific centres abroad and to learn and use techniques not accessible to them in their own country.
Eligibility: Open to members of the Society.
Level of Study: Professional development.
Type: Grant.
Value: Up to UK £500. The grants will complement, where appropriate, those for visits to Commonwealth countries, and funding would cover the additional travel costs involved, together with appropriate subsistence. Applicants should also see the 'Corday-Morgan' Memorial Fund.
Frequency: Dependent on funds available.
Country of Study: Any country.
No. of awards offered: Approx. 10.

Application Procedure: Applicants must submit applications on the official form and will normally be considered within one month of receipt.

Closing Date: Applications are accepted at any time.

Additional Information: Applicants must be travelling to another country and would normally stop en route to visit a third country which must be a developing country.

THE ROYAL SOCIETY OF EDINBURGH (RSE)

22-26 George Street, Edinburgh, EH2 2PQ, Scotland
Tel: (44) 131 240 5000
Fax: (44) 131 240 5024
Email: resfells@royalsoced.org.uk
www: http://www.ma.hw.ac.uk/RSE
Contact: Ms Anne D G Ferguson, Research Fellowships Secretary

The Royal Society of Edinburgh (RSE) is Scotland's National Academy. It is an independent body, founded in 1783 by Royal Charter for the Advancement of Learning and Useful Knowledge and governed by an elected council of Fellows.

Auber Bequest

Subjects: All subjects.

Purpose: To provide assistance for the furtherance of academic research but not industrial research.

Eligibility: Open to naturalised British citizens or individuals wishing to acquire British nationality who are over 60 years of age, resident in Scotland or England and are bona fide Scholars engaged in academic (but not industrial) research. Applicants should not have been British nationals at birth, nor held dual British nationality. Applicants must have since acquired British nationality.

Level of Study: Unrestricted.

Value: Varies, not normally exceeding UK £3,000.

Length of Study: Up to two years.

Frequency: Every two years.

Country of Study: Scotland or England.

No. of awards offered: Varies.

Application Procedure: Applicants must complete an application form, available from the Research Fellowships Secretary.

Closing Date: October 31st.

Funding: Private.

Contributor: The Auber Bequest.

No. of awards given last year: None.

No. of applicants last year: None.

BP/RSE Research Fellowships

Subjects: Mechanical engineering, chemical engineering, control engineering, solid state sciences, information technology, non-biological chemistry and geological sciences.

Purpose: To support independent research in specific fields.

Eligibility: Open to persons of all nationalities who have a PhD or equivalent qualification. Applicants should be aged under 35 on the date of appointment (October 1st) and must show they have a capacity for innovative research and have a substantial volume of published work relevant to their proposed field of study.

Level of Study: Postdoctorate.

Type: Fellowship.

Value: Salaries within the scales RGIA-2 for research and analogous staff in Institutes of Higher Education with annual increments and superannuation benefits. Financial support towards expenses involved in carrying out the research is available, including a start up grant of UK £1,000 in the first year only and a further allowance of up to UK £1,500 for travel and subsistence each year. Up to £2,500 is also available by competitive bid from the support fund pool each year.

Length of Study: Up to three years.

Frequency: Annual.

Study Establishment: Any Institute of Higher Education in Scotland approved for the purpose by the Council of the Society.

Country of Study: Scotland.

No. of awards offered: One.

Application Procedure: Applicants must complete an application form, available from the Research Fellowships Secretary. Candidates must negotiate directly with the relevant Head of Department of the proposed host institution.

Closing Date: Mid March.

Funding: Private.

Contributor: British Petroleum.

No. of awards given last year: One.

No. of applicants last year: 26.

Additional Information: The Fellowships are offered with the support of British Petroleum (BP). Fellows will be expected to devote their full time to research and will not be allowed to hold other paid appointments without the express permission of the Council of the RSE.

CRF (Caledonian Research Foundation)/RSE European Visiting Research Fellowships

Subjects: Within one of the following arts and letters subjects of archaeology, art and architecture, economics and economic history, geography, history, jurisprudence, linguistics, literature and philology, philosophy or religious studies.

Purpose: To create a two way flow of visiting scholars in arts and letters between Scotland and continental Europe.

Eligibility: Open to members of the academic staff of a Scottish Institute of Higher Education or equivalent continental European institution. Applicants must be aged 60 or under on the date of the appointment, which is variable, but must be within 16 months of date of award. Applicants from continental Europe must be nominated by members of staff from a Scottish Institute of Higher Education.

Level of Study: Professional development.

Type: Fellowship.

Value: Up to UK £6,000 for visits of six months which is reduced pro-rata for shorter visits, to cover actual costs of travel, subsistence and relevant study costs.

Length of Study: Up to six months.

Frequency: Annual.

Study Establishment: A Scottish Institute of Higher Education or a recognised Institute of Higher Education in a continental European country.

Country of Study: European countries.

No. of awards offered: Eight.

Application Procedure: Applicants must complete an application form, available from the Research Fellowships Secretary in August and September each year.

Closing Date: Early November.

Funding: Private.

Contributor: The Caledonian Research Foundation.

No. of awards given last year: Six.

No. of applicants last year: 10.

Additional Information: Successful applicants will be required to submit a report within two months of the end of the visit.

CRF (Caledonian Research Foundation)/RSE Personal Research Fellowships

Subjects: Biological, biochemical, physical or clinical sciences.

Purpose: To aid independent research in the biomedical sciences.

Eligibility: Open to students of all nationalities who have a PhD and are aged 32 or under on the date of appointment, or who have two to six years' postdoctoral experience.

Level of Study: Postdoctorate.

Type: Fellowship.

Value: Salary according to age, qualifications and experience. Salaries are within the scales RGIA-2 for research staff in Institutes of Higher Education. Financial support towards expenses involved in carrying out the research is available, including a start-up grant of UK £1,000 in the first year only. Fellows receive UK £1,000 for travel and subsistence each year.

Length of Study: Up to three years.

Frequency: Annual.
Study Establishment: Any Institute of Higher Education in Scotland.
Country of Study: Scotland.
No. of awards offered: Varies.
Application Procedure: Applicants must complete an application form, available from the CRF. Candidates must negotiate with the relevant Head of Department of the proposed host institution.
Closing Date: Mid March.
Funding: Private.
Contributor: The CRF.
No. of awards given last year: Two.
No. of applicants last year: 20.
Additional Information: The Fellowships are administered by the Caledonian Research Foundation (CRF). Fellows will be expected to devote their full time to research and will not be allowed to hold other paid appointments without the express permission of the Council of the RSE.

For further information contact:

Grants Management Officer
The Caledonian Research Foundation (CRF)
39 Castle Street, Edinburgh, EH2 3BH, Scotland

CRF (Caledonian Research Foundation)/RSE Support Research Fellowship

Subjects: Biology, biochemical, physical and clinical sciences related to medicine.
Purpose: To enable Fellows to take study leave, either in their own institution or elsewhere, whilst remaining in continuous employment with their present employer.
Eligibility: Open to existing members of academic staff aged 40 or under on date of appointment and employed on the lecturer scale, who have held a permanent appointment for at least five years in any Scottish Institute of Higher Education.
Level of Study: Professional development.
Type: Fellowship.
Value: The actual cost for non-clinical staff will be reimbursed according to the lecturer 'A' scale (maximum RGI-3) with the placement determined by the employer. If clinically qualified, the salary will be within clinical senior lecturer grade. A provision of UK £1,000 is made for a start up grant. There is also a grant of UK £1,000 for travel and subsistence.
Length of Study: One year.
Frequency: Annual.
Study Establishment: Any Institute of Higher Education in Scotland.
Country of Study: Scotland.
No. of awards offered: One.
Application Procedure: Applicants must complete an application form, available from the CRF.
Closing Date: Mid March.
Funding: Private.
Contributor: The CRF.
No. of awards given last year: One.
No. of applicants last year: Four.

For further information contact:

Grants Management Officer
The Caledonian Research Foundation (CRF)
39 Castle Street, Edinburgh, EH2 3BH, Scotland

Henry Dryerre Scholarship

Subjects: Medical or veterinary physiology.
Purpose: To support postgraduate research.
Eligibility: Open to European Community citizens holding a First Class (Honours) Degree from a Scottish university.
Level of Study: Postgraduate.
Type: Scholarship.

Value: Fees, research costs and travel expenses up to UK £850 per year and a maintenance grant of UK £5,956 if living away from home.
Length of Study: Three years full-time research.
Frequency: Every four years.
Study Establishment: A Scottish institution.
Country of Study: Scotland.
No. of awards offered: One.
Application Procedure: Applicants must be nominated by a professor, reader or lecturer in a Scottish university.
Funding: Private.
No. of awards given last year: One.
No. of applicants last year: One.
Additional Information: The scholarships are administered by the Carnegie Trust for the Universities of Scotland.

For further information contact:

Carnegie Trust for the Universities of Scotland
Cameron House
Abbey Park Place, Dunfermline, Fife, KY12 7PZ, Scotland
Tel: (44) 1383 622148
Fax: (44) 1383 622149
Email: carnegie.trust@ed.ac.uk
Contact: Miss J Gray

John Moyes Lessells Scholarships

Subjects: All forms of engineering.
Purpose: To enable well qualified engineering graduates of Scottish Institutes of Higher Education to study some aspect of their profession overseas.
Eligibility: Applicants must be graduates of a Scottish Institute of Higher Education.
Level of Study: Postgraduate, Professional development.
Type: Scholarship.
Value: Normally up to UK £15,000 per year. Additional research or travel expenditure may be sanctioned.
Length of Study: Initially for one year but shorter periods or extension for a second year may be considered. Acceptance of a scholarship implies a willingness to spend at least two years in the United Kingdom following the period of tenure.
Frequency: Annual.
Country of Study: Outside United Kingdom, but awardees must return to Scotland at the end of the scholarship.
No. of awards offered: Varies.
Application Procedure: Applicants must complete an application form, available from the Research Fellowships Secretary or the RSE website.
Closing Date: February 28th.
Funding: Private.
No. of awards given last year: Three.
No. of applicants last year: Three.

SEELLD Personal Research Fellowships

Subjects: All subjects. The Fellowships are awarded in fields likely to enhance the development of industry and encourage better uses of resources in Scotland.
Purpose: To encourage independent research in any discipline.
Eligibility: Open to persons of all nationalities who have a PhD or equivalent qualification. Applicants must be aged 32 or under on the date of appointment (October 1st) or have between two and six years of postdoctoral experience. They must also show they have a capacity for innovative research and have a substantial volume of published work relevant to their proposed field of study.
Level of Study: Postdoctorate.
Type: Fellowship.
Value: Annual stipends are within the scales RGIA-2 for research and analogous staff in Institutes of Higher Education with annual increments and superannuation benefits. Expenses of up to UK £2,500 in year one, UK £1,000 in years two and three for travel and attendance at meetings or incidentals may be reimbursed. No support payments are available to the institution but Fellows may seek support for their research from other sources.

Length of Study: Up to three years full-time research.

Frequency: Annual.

Study Establishment: Any Institute of Higher Education, research institution or industrial laboratory approved for the purpose by the Council of the Society.

Country of Study: Scotland.

No. of awards offered: Four.

Application Procedure: Applicants must complete an application form, available from the Research Fellowships Secretary. Applicants should negotiate directly with the proposed host institution.

Closing Date: Mid March.

Funding: Government.

Contributor: The Scottish Executive.

No. of awards given last year: Five.

No. of applicants last year: Approx. 80.

Additional Information: Fellows may not hold other paid appointments without the express permission of the Council, but teaching or seminar work appropriate to their special knowledge may be acceptable. The Fellowships are offered with the support of the Scottish Executive Enterprise and Lifelong Learning Department.

SEELLD/RSE Support Research Fellowships

Subjects: All subjects. The fellowships are awarded in fields likely to enhance the development of industry and encourage better uses of resources in Scotland.

Purpose: To enable support Fellows to take study leave, either in their own institution or elsewhere, whilst remaining in continuous employment with their present employer.

Eligibility: Candidates must be existing members of staff who have held a permanent appointment for not less than five years in any Institution of Higher Education in Scotland. Applicants should be aged under 40 on the date of appointment (January 1st) and employed on the lecturer (or equivalent) grade.

Level of Study: Professional development.

Type: Fellowship.

Value: The actual cost of replacement staff will be reimbursed according to the Lecturer A scale (maximum RGI-3) with the placement determined by the employer. Superannuation costs and employer's national insurance contributions will also be reimbursed.

Length of Study: Up to one year of full-time research.

Frequency: Annual.

Study Establishment: Any Institute of Higher Education, research institution or industrial laboratory in Scotland approved for the purpose by the Council of the Society.

Country of Study: Scotland.

No. of awards offered: Four.

Application Procedure: Applicants must complete an application form, available from the Research Fellowships Secretary. Applicants must negotiate directly with the proposed host institution.

Closing Date: Mid March.

Funding: Government.

Contributor: The Scottish Executive.

No. of awards given last year: Two.

No. of applicants last year: Approx. 15.

Additional Information: The Fellowships are offered with the support of the Scottish Executive Enterprise and Lifelong Learning Department (SEELLD). Further information is available on request or on the website.

THE ROYAL SOCIETY OF MEDICINE (RSM)

1 Wimpole Street, London, W1M 8AE, England
Tel: (44) 20 7290 2900
Fax: (44) 20 7290 2909
Email: anne-marie.fisker@roysocmed.ac.uk
www: http://www.roysocmed.ac.uk
Contact: Ms Anne-Marie Fisker, Manager

The Royal Society of Medicine (RSM) provides academic services and club facilities for its members as well as publishing a monthly journal and a quarterly bulletin, and providing over 300 educational conferences and meetings per year.

Colyer Prize

Subjects: Odontology.

Purpose: To reward the best original work in dental science completed during the previous five years.

Eligibility: Open to dental surgeons educated at a United Kingdom dental school who have not been qualified for more than 10 years.

Level of Study: Postdoctorate.

Type: Research prize.

Value: Varies, at least UK £100.

Frequency: Every three years.

Country of Study: United Kingdom.

No. of awards offered: One.

Application Procedure: Applicants must submit a general brief account of their research of not more than 800 words.

Closing Date: March 31st.

No. of applicants last year: One.

John of Arderne Medal

Subjects: Coloproctology.

Purpose: To award the presenter of the best paper presented at the short papers meeting of the section of coloproctology. Applicants have to submit an abstract for presentation at the meeting.

Eligibility: Open to applicants of any nationality.

Level of Study: Professional development.

Type: Medal and travelling fellowship.

Value: Approx. UK £500.

Frequency: Annual.

Study Establishment: Varies.

Country of Study: Any country.

No. of awards offered: One.

Application Procedure: Applicants must write for details.

Closing Date: September and December.

No. of awards given last year: One.

No. of applicants last year: 80.

Karl Storz Travelling Scholarship

Subjects: Laryngology and rhinology.

Purpose: To assist with the cost of travel to overseas centres.

Eligibility: Open to senior registrars or consultants of not more than two years standing, who must be members of the section of laryngology and rhinology of the RSM.

Level of Study: Postdoctorate.

Type: Scholarship.

Value: UK £1,000.

Frequency: Annual.

Country of Study: Any country.

No. of awards offered: One.

Application Procedure: Applicants must submit a paper to the RSM Section of Laryngology and Rhinology.

Closing Date: January 31st.

Funding: Commercial.

Contributor: Karl Storz Endoscopy Limited.

No. of awards given last year: One.

Additional Information: The recipient will be required to submit a brief report on the visit within three months of his or her return.

Medical Insurance Agency Prize

Subjects: Surgery.
Purpose: To enable the recipient to travel to a recognised institution to further his or her knowledge of surgery, or to attend an overseas conference in the speciality.
Eligibility: Open to surgeons in training, holding the post up to the grade of registrar or senior registrar.
Level of Study: Professional development.
Type: Prize.
Value: UK £500.
Frequency: Annual.
Study Establishment: A recognised institution in the United Kingdom or overseas.
Country of Study: Any country.
No. of awards offered: One.
Application Procedure: Applicants must write for details.
Additional Information: The recipient will be required to submit a brief report on the visit within three months of his or her return.

Mental Health Foundation Essay Prize

Subjects: Psychiatry.
Eligibility: Open to candidates practising medicine in the United Kingdom or the Republic of Ireland who are in training at any grade from senior house officer to senior registrar or equivalent.
Level of Study: Unrestricted.
Type: Essay prize.
Value: Varies, approx. UK £500 depending on available finance. It also includes a subscription to RSM if funds are available.
Frequency: Annual.
Country of Study: United Kingdom.
No. of awards offered: One.
Application Procedure: Applicants need not be members of RSM. The prize is awarded for an essay on psychiatry, submitted to the RSM section of psychiatry, in triplicate.
Closing Date: March 31st.
No. of applicants last year: One.
Additional Information: The subject is left to the candidate. Essays should be approx. 5,000 words in length.

Nichols Fellowship

Subjects: Obstetrics and gynaecology.
Purpose: To encourage research to advance knowledge in obstetrics and gynaecology.
Eligibility: Open to suitably qualified United Kingdom citizens.
Level of Study: Postdoctorate.
Type: Fellowship.
Value: UK £500 per year for two years, the second year being at the discretion of the Section Council.
Length of Study: Two years.
Frequency: Every three years.
Country of Study: Any country.
No. of awards offered: One.
Application Procedure: Applicants must write for details.

Norman Gamble Fund and Research Prize

Subjects: Otology.
Purpose: To support specific research projects in otology.
Eligibility: Open to British nationals.
Level of Study: Unrestricted.
Type: Prize.
Value: UK £300 for research prize and UK £1,000 for grant-in-aid.
Frequency: Every four years (the next will be in 2004).
Country of Study: Any country.
No. of awards offered: One.
Application Procedure: Applicants must write for details.
Closing Date: May 31st.
Funding: Private.

Norman Tanner Medal and Prize

Subjects: Surgery.

Purpose: To enable the recipient to travel to a recognised institution to further his or her knowledge of surgery, or to attend an overseas conference in the speciality.
Eligibility: Open to applicants of any nationality.
Level of Study: Professional development.
Type: Medal and travel grant.
Value: UK £500.
Frequency: Annual.
Country of Study: Any country.
No. of awards offered: One.
Application Procedure: Applicants must present papers at a meeting.

Ophthalmology Travelling Fellowship

Subjects: Ophthalmology.
Purpose: To enable British ophthalmologists to travel abroad with the intention of furthering the study or advancement of ophthalmology, or to enable foreign ophthalmologists to visit the United Kingdom for the same purpose.
Eligibility: Open to ophthalmologists in the British Isles of any nationality who have not attained an official consultant appointment, nor undertaken professional clinical work or equivalent responsibility for any substantial period before or during the execution of original work.
Level of Study: Professional development.
Type: Fellowship.
Value: UK £500-2,000.
Frequency: Twice a year.
Study Establishment: Varies.
Country of Study: Any country.
No. of awards offered: Varies.
Application Procedure: Applicants must apply to the Academic Administrator at RSM.
Closing Date: Entries are evaluated in December and May.
No. of awards given last year: Four.
No. of applicants last year: Six.

Royal Society of Medicine President's Prize

Subjects: Clinical neurosciences.
Purpose: To reward summaries of cases for clinical presentation.
Eligibility: Open to applicants of any nationality.
Level of Study: Professional development.
Type: Prize.
Value: UK £100.
Frequency: Annual.
Country of Study: Any country.
No. of awards offered: One.
Application Procedure: Applicants must write for details.
Closing Date: January.
Funding: Private.
No. of awards given last year: One.
No. of applicants last year: 12.
Additional Information: Presentations take place in April.

Royal Society of Medicine Travelling Fellowship

Subjects: Urology.
Purpose: To enable the holder to enhance his or her knowledge and experience by visiting an overseas unit.
Eligibility: Open to members of the section of urology of RSM, who should be in urological training or within three years of a consultant appointment.
Level of Study: Professional development.
Type: Travelling fellowship.
Value: UK £1,000.
Frequency: Annual.
Country of Study: Any country.
No. of awards offered: Varies.
Application Procedure: Applicants must write for details.
Closing Date: October 9th.

Sylvia Lawler Prize

Subjects: Oncology.

Purpose: To provide prizes in the field of oncology intended to go to medically qualified or scientifically qualified trainees.

Eligibility: Open to medically or scientifically qualified trainees.

Level of Study: Postgraduate.

Type: Prize.

Value: Details on application.

Frequency: Annual.

Country of Study: United Kingdom.

No. of awards offered: Two.

Application Procedure: Applicants must submit an abstract of one side of A4 to the annually held Sylvia Lawler prize meeting. Abstract forms are available from Louisa Bendela.

Closing Date: Please contact the foundation.

ROYAL TOWN PLANNING INSTITUTE

41 Botolph Lane, London, EC3R 8DL, England

Tel: (44) 20 7929 9473

Fax: (44) 20 7929 8197

Email: judy.woollett@rtpi.org.uk

Contact: Ms Judy Woollett

The Royal Town Planning Institute was founded in 1914 and is a registered charity. Its aim is to advance the science and art of town planning in all its aspects, including local, regional and national planning for the benefit of the public. The Institute is primarily concerned with maintaining high standards of competence and conduct within the profession, promoting the role of planning within the country's social, economic and political structures, and presenting the profession's views on current planning issues.

George Pepler International Award

Subjects: Town and country planning or some particular aspect of planning theory and practice.

Purpose: To enable young people of any nationality to visit another country for a short period to study the theory and practice of town and country planning.

Eligibility: Open to persons under 30 years of age of any nationality.

Level of Study: Professional development.

Value: Up to UK £1,500.

Length of Study: Short-term travel outside the United Kingdom for United Kingdom residents or for visits to the United Kingdom for applicants from abroad.

Frequency: Every two years.

Country of Study: Any country.

No. of awards offered: One.

Application Procedure: Applicants must submit a statement showing the nature of the study visit proposed, together with an itinerary. Application forms are available on request from the RTPI.

Closing Date: March 31st.

Funding: Private.

Contributor: Trust fund.

No. of awards given last year: One.

No. of applicants last year: 20.

Additional Information: At the conclusion of the visit the recipient must submit a report.

RUSSELL SAGE FOUNDATION

112 East 64th Street, New York, NY, 10021, United States of America

Tel: (1) 212 750 6012

Fax: (1) 212 371 4761

Email: info@rsage.org

www: http://www.russellsage.org

Contact: Ms Madeline G Spitaleri, Vice President of Administration

The Russell Sage Foundation is the principal American foundation devoted exclusively to research in the social sciences. Located in New York City, the Foundation is a research centre, a funding source for studies by scholars at other academic and research institutions, and an active member of the nation's social science community.

Russell Sage Foundation Visiting Fellowships

Subjects: Social sciences.

Eligibility: Open to Scholars in the social sciences. The Foundation particularly welcomes groups of visiting Scholars who wish to collaborate on a specific project during their residence at the Foundation. In order to develop these projects fully, support is sometimes provided for working groups prior to their arrival at the Foundation. Awards are not made for the support of graduate degree work, nor for institutional support.

Level of Study: Doctorate, Postdoctorate.

Type: Fellowship.

Value: Varies.

Length of Study: One academic year.

Frequency: Annual.

Study Establishment: The Foundation.

Country of Study: Any country.

No. of awards offered: 18 visiting Scholar appointments.

Application Procedure: Applicants must submit a four-five page description plus their curriculum vitae.

Closing Date: November 15th prior to the year of residence.

No. of awards given last year: 18.

No. of applicants last year: 120.

Additional Information: Awardees are expected to offer the Foundation the right to publish any book length manuscripts resulting from Foundation support.

RUTH ESTRIN GOLDBERG MEMORIAL FOR CANCER RESEARCH

885 Gloucester Road, Union, NJ, 07083, United States of America

Tel: (1) 908 688 1725

Contact: Mrs Myrna Abramson, Past President

Ruth Estrin Goldberg Memorial for Cancer Research

Subjects: Cancer research.

Eligibility: Open to candidates from the eastern United States of America, preferably New York, New Jersey, Pennsylvania, Connecticut, Massachusetts, Delaware or Maryland.

Level of Study: Unrestricted.

Value: US$10,000-15,000.

Frequency: Annual.

Country of Study: United States of America.

No. of awards offered: Two.

Application Procedure: Applicants must write for application and guidelines.

Closing Date: February 28th.

Funding: Private.

Contributor: Members and friends.

No. of awards given last year: Two.

No. of applicants last year: 10-15.

Additional Information: The Ruth Estrin Goldberg Memorial for Cancer Research is a volunteer organisation.

RYAN DAVIES MEMORIAL FUND

1 Squire Court
The Marina, Swansea, SA1 3XB, Wales
Tel: (44) 1792 301500
Fax: (44) 1792 301500
Contact: Mr Michael D Evans, Secretary

The Ryan Davies Memorial Fund honours the memory of the great Welsh performer, Ryan Davies, and gives awards in the performing arts to postgraduate students of Welsh extraction.

Ryan Davies Memorial Fund Scholarship Grants

Subjects: Music, drama and all performing arts.
Purpose: To enable Welsh artists to continue studies following their formal training.
Eligibility: Open to Welsh artists or artists of Welsh extraction only.
Level of Study: Up to postgraduate.
Type: Grant.
Value: Up to UK £2,500 each.
Length of Study: Up to one year.
Frequency: Annual.
Study Establishment: Unrestricted.
Country of Study: Any country.
No. of awards offered: Up to eight.
Application Procedure: Applicants must apply by forwarding all relevant information including their reason for application, qualifications, referees and any further background information to the Secretary.
Closing Date: May 30th for notification by July 31st.
Funding: Private.
Contributor: The general public.
No. of awards given last year: Eight.
No. of applicants last year: 50.
Additional Information: The Fund was set up in memory of Ryan Davies, Wales' most versatile entertainer.

S S HUEBNER FOUNDATION FOR INSURANCE EDUCATION

430 Vance Hall, Philadelphia, PA, 19104-6301, United States of America
Tel: (1) 215 898 9631
Fax: (1) 215 573 2218
Email: harowitl@wharton.upenn.edu
www: http://rider.wharton.upenn.edu/~sshuebne
Contact: Ms Linda Harowitz, Assistant Director

The S S Huebner Foundation is an educational foundation with the objective of promoting education and research in risk management and insurance. It provides PhD fellowships for the study of risk management and insurance economics at the Wharton School of the University of Pennsylvania, and publishes books and working papers.

S S Huebner Foundation for Insurance Education Predoctoral Fellowships

Subjects: Managerial science and applied economics, with specialisation in risk management and insurance economics.
Purpose: To increase the supply of college professors specialising in risk management and insurance economics.
Eligibility: Open to citizens of the United States of America and Canada who hold a Bachelor's degree from an accredited United States or Canadian university or college and intend to pursue an insurance teaching career.
Level of Study: Doctorate.
Type: Fellowship.
Value: Full tuition and fees of the Wharton School of the University of Pennsylvania plus an annual living stipend of US$15,000.
Length of Study: Four years.

Frequency: Annual.
Study Establishment: The Wharton School of the University of Pennsylvania.
Country of Study: United States of America.
No. of awards offered: Varies.
Application Procedure: Applicants must contact the Foundation for further details.
Closing Date: February 1st.
Funding: Private.
Contributor: Leading insurance companies in the United States of America and Canada.
No. of awards given last year: One.
Additional Information: Candidates are required to certify that it is their intention to follow an insurance teaching career and that they will major in insurance and risk management for a graduate degree. Applicants must take the admission test for graduate study in business. For information concerning these examinations candidates should write directly to the Educational Testing Service. Applicants should apply separately and directly to the Wharton School Doctoral Program Office for admission into the Insurance and Risk Management Doctoral Program.

For further information contact:

The Educational Testing Service
20 Nassau Street, Princeton, NJ, 08540, United States of America

SAINT MARY'S UNIVERSITY

MBA Program
923 Robie Street, Halifax, NS, B3H 3C3, Canada
Tel: (1) 902 420 5415
Fax: (1) 902 496 8184
Email: admit.international@stmarys.ca
www: http://www.stmarys.ca
Contact: Office of Financial Aid

The Ronald Wong Scholarship

Subjects: MBA.
Eligibility: Open to students whose university performance gives promise of successful graduate studies. Candidates must be enrolled in the MBA programme on a full-time basis and have completed five credits at Saint Mary's University. They must also be Canadian citizens who have lived in Nova Scotia for at least 10 years and be able to show evidence of financial need, academic ability and possess those qualities of character and initiative which indicate potential leadership in the business world.
Level of Study: MBA.
Type: Scholarship.
Value: One of canadian $1,500 or two of canadian $750 each.
Study Establishment: Saint Mary's University.
Country of Study: Canada.
Application Procedure: Applicants must seek advice on the availability of scholarships by contacting the Secretary of the Senate, Room MM216A, McNally Building and the relevant academic department at the University.
Additional Information: Scholarships are awarded by the University's Graduate Awards Committee based on the recommendation of the MBA Director and Dean of Commerce. Please see the website for further information.

Saint Mary's University Entrance Scholarships

Subjects: MBA.
Eligibility: Open to students from any country. The awards are based on previous academic achievements and Graduate Management Admissions Test scores. In some cases financial need is considered.
Level of Study: MBA.
Type: Scholarship.
Value: Ranges from canadian $500-4,000.
Study Establishment: Saint Mary's University.

Country of Study: Canada.
Closing Date: Please contact the organisation.
Additional Information: Please see the website for further details.

Saint Marys University MBA Scholarships
Subjects: MBA.
Eligibility: Open to successful and promising second year students.
Level of Study: MBA.
Type: Scholarship.
Value: Varies, please consult the organisation for specific details.
Study Establishment: Saint Mary's University.
Country of Study: Canada.
Application Procedure: Applicants must seek advice on the availability of scholarships by contacting the Secretary of the Senate, Room MM216A, McNally Building and the specific academic department at the University.
Closing Date: Please contact the organisation.
Additional Information: There are a number of named scholarships sponsored by leading organisations and very generous donors available. Applicants should consult the website or the organisation for details.

SAMRO (SOUTHERN AFRICAN MUSIC RIGHTS ORGANISATION) ENDOWMENT FOR THE NATIONAL ARTS

PO Box 31609, Braamfontein, 2017, South Africa
Tel: (27) 11 489 5000
Fax: (27) 11 403 1934
Telex: 4 24653 SAMROSA
Contact: J C Otto, Liaison & Research Officer

SAMRO (Southern African Music Rights Organisation) is Southern Africa's Society of Composers and Lyricists, with special reference to the performing and broadcasting rights in their music. Through the SAMRO Endowment for the National Arts, it currently supports music study at home and abroad for citizens of South Africa, Botswana, Lesotho and Swaziland.

SAMRO Intermediate Bursaries for Composition Study In Southern Africa
Subjects: Music.
Purpose: To support music composition study in either the serious or jazz popular music genres.
Eligibility: Open to citizens of South Africa, Botswana, Lesotho and Swaziland, who have met the requirements for proceeding to the third, fourth or honours of a senior undergraduate degree or equivalent diploma course. Applicants must have been born after February 15th 1970. For entering any year of a Master's or doctorate degree, the age limit is 30. Older students are considered in special circumstances.
Level of Study: Postgraduate.
Type: Bursary.
Value: Rand 8,250 for third, fourth and honours year and rand 5,250 for Master's or doctorate degrees.
Length of Study: One year.
Frequency: Annual.
Study Establishment: A university, technikon or other recognised statutory institute of tertiary education approved by the trustees.
Country of Study: South Africa, Botswana, Lesotho or Swaziland.
No. of awards offered: 10.
Application Procedure: Applicants must complete an application form.
Closing Date: February 15th.
Funding: Private.
Contributor: SAMRO.
No. of awards given last year: Seven.
No. of applicants last year: 10.

Additional Information: Applicants must produce an official letter of acceptance for entering any year of Master's or doctoral degrees.

SAMRO Overseas Scholarship
Subjects: Music.
Purpose: To encourage music study at postgraduate level in the serious or jazz popular music genres.
Eligibility: Open to postgraduate students who are citizens of South Africa, Botswana, Lesotho or Swaziland. The age limit is 30 years.
Level of Study: Postgraduate.
Type: Scholarship.
Value: Rand 100,000 plus travel expenses of up to rand 10,000.
Length of Study: Two years.
Frequency: Annual.
Study Establishment: An institute or educational entity approved by the SAMRO Endowment for the National Arts.
Country of Study: Europe or North America.
No. of awards offered: Two.
Application Procedure: Applicants must complete an application form.
Closing Date: April 30th.
Funding: Private.
Contributor: SAMRO.
No. of awards given last year: Two.
No. of applicants last year: 11.
Additional Information: These awards rotate on a quadrennial basis as follows: 2003 is singers, 2004 is instrumentalists and 2005 is pianists and other keyboard players.

SAMRO Postgraduate Bursaries for Indigenous African Music Study
Subjects: Music.
Purpose: To encourage the study of indigenous African music at the postgraduate level in either the traditional serious or jazz popular music genres.
Eligibility: Open to postgraduate students who are citizens of South Africa, Botswana, Lesotho or Swaziland. The age limit is 40 years.
Level of Study: Postgraduate.
Type: Bursary.
Value: Rand 4,750.
Length of Study: Five years.
Frequency: Annual.
Study Establishment: A university or other recognised statutory institute of tertiary education approved by the trustees and situated in SAMRO's current territory of operation.
Country of Study: South Africa, Botswana, Lesotho or Swaziland.
No. of awards offered: Six.
Application Procedure: Applicants must complete an application form.
Closing Date: February 15th.
Contributor: SAMRO.
No. of awards given last year: Five.
No. of applicants last year: Six.
Additional Information: Applicants must produce an official letter of acceptance from a recognised tertiary institute of learning. They must have acceptance into the first year, or of entry into any subsequent year, of a postgraduate degree in indigenous African music at such an institute.

SAMUEL H KRESS FOUNDATION

174 East 80th Street, New York, NY, 10021, United States of America
Tel: (1) 212 861 4993
www: http://www.kressfoundation.org
Contact: Ms Lisa Ackerman, Vice President

Over the past 72 years, the Samuel H Kress Foundation has established a record of philanthropy in three related areas: the collection and distribution of works of art from the great European traditions, the preservation of significant European monuments of art and architecture, and the nurturing of professional expertise in art history and art conservation.

Kress Fellowships for Advanced Training in Fine Arts Conservation

Subjects: Specific areas of fine arts conservation.
Purpose: To enable young American conservators to undertake post MA advanced internships.
Eligibility: Open to those who have completed their academic training in conservation.
Level of Study: Postgraduate.
Type: Fellowship.
Value: US$25,000.
Frequency: Annual.
Study Establishment: Appropriate institutions.
Country of Study: United States of America.
No. of awards offered: 10.
Application Procedure: Applicants must write for details. The Foundation does not accept grant materials by fax.
Closing Date: February 28th.
No. of applicants last year: Approx. 25.
Additional Information: Emphasis is on hands on training. These grants are not for completion of degree programmes. Enquiries should be directed to Ms Ackerman or Wymen Meers.

Samuel H Kress Foundation Travel Fellowships

Subjects: Art history.
Purpose: To facilitate travel for PhD candidates in the history of art to view materials essential for the completion of dissertation research.
Eligibility: Open to predoctoral candidates at American universities.
Level of Study: Doctorate.
Type: Fellowship.
Value: Varies between US$1,000-10,000.
Frequency: Annual.
Country of Study: Any country.
No. of awards offered: 10-15.
Application Procedure: Applicants must be nominated by their art history department. There is a limit of two applicants per department and the Foundation does not accept grant materials by fax.
Closing Date: November 30th.
Funding: Private.
No. of awards given last year: 10.
No. of applicants last year: Approx. 50.

Samuel H Kress Foundation Two-Year Research Fellowships at Foreign Institutions

Subjects: Art history.
Purpose: To facilitate advanced dissertation research in association with a selected art historical institute in Florence, Jerusalem, Leiden, London, Munich, Nicosia, Paris, Rome or Zurich.
Eligibility: Restricted to PhD candidates in the history of art for completion of dissertation research. Candidates must be United States citizens or matriculated at a United States institution.
Level of Study: Predoctorate.
Type: Fellowship.
Value: US$18,000 per year.
Length of Study: Two years.
Frequency: Annual.
Study Establishment: One of a number of art historical institutes in Florence, Jerusalem, Leiden, London, Munich, Nicosia, Paris, Rome or Zurich.
Country of Study: Outside United States of America.
No. of awards offered: Four.
Application Procedure: Applicants must be nominated by their art history department. There is a limit of one applicant per department and the Foundation does not accept grant materials by fax.
Closing Date: November 30th.
Funding: Private.
No. of awards given last year: Four.

No. of applicants last year: Approx. 25.

SAN ANGELO SYMPHONY SOCIETY

PO Box 5922, San Angelo, TX, 76902, United States of America
Tel: (1) 915 658 5877
Fax: (1) 915 653 1045
Email: mercyla@sanangelosymphony.org
www: http://www.sanangelosymphony.org
Contact: Ms Mercyla Shelburne, Manager

The San Angelo Symphony provides the only source of classical music in a 90 mile radius. Eight concerts, a Summer pop concert, two children's concerts and the International Sorantin Competition comprise the annual season. The Symphony also supports a 100 voice chorale and a 300 member guild.

Sorantin Young Artist Award

Subjects: Piano performance, vocal performance or instrumental performance.
Purpose: To recognise and reward talent.
Eligibility: Open to instrumentalists and pianists under 28 years of age and vocalists under 31 years of age by November in the year of the competition.
Level of Study: Postgraduate.
Type: Competition.
Value: The overall winner receives US$3,000 plus his or her division prize and a guest appearance with the San Angelo Symphony Orchestra. The division winner receives US$1,000 and the division runner up, US$400.
Frequency: Annual.
Country of Study: Any country.
No. of awards offered: Varies.
Application Procedure: Applicants must complete an application form by the entry deadline. At the time of application, all entry fees must be paid.
Closing Date: October 6th.
Funding: Private.
Contributor: Mr and Mrs Norman Roussuliet.
No. of awards given last year: Six.
No. of applicants last year: 74.

SAN FRANCISCO CONSERVATORY OF MUSIC

1201 Ortega Street, San Francisco, CA, 94122, United States of America
Tel: (1) 415 759 3422
Fax: (1) 415 759 3499
Email: cmk@sfcm.edu
www: http://www.sfcm.edu
Contact: Ms Colleen Katzowitz, Director of Studies

The San Francisco Conservatory of Music is a college of music which trains students for careers as professional symphony musicians, concert artists, opera singers, composers, conductors and teachers.

San Francisco Conservatory Performance Scholarships in Music

Subjects: Musical performance.
Purpose: To permit talented students to attend the Conservatory.
Eligibility: Open to United States and foreign nationals who will be attending the Conservatory on a full-time basis. Candidates must have had considerable experience in musical performance.
Level of Study: Graduate, Postgraduate.
Type: Scholarship.
Value: US$300-19,600.

Length of Study: One year, renewable.
Frequency: Annual.
Study Establishment: San Francisco Conservatory of Music.
Country of Study: United States of America.
No. of awards offered: Varies.
Application Procedure: Applicants must audition and complete both admission and scholarship applications.
Closing Date: February 15th.
Funding: Private.
No. of awards given last year: 150.
No. of applicants last year: 500.
Additional Information: Further information is available on request.

SAVOY FOUNDATION

PO Box 69
230 Foch, St Jean Sur Richelieu, QC, J3B 2B2, Canada
Tel: (1) 450 358 9779
Fax: (1) 450 346 1045
Email: epilepsy@savoy-foundation.ca
www: http://www.savoy-foundation.ca
Contact: Ms Caroline Savoy, Secretary

The Savoy Foundation's main activity is to support and encourage research into epilepsy.

Savoy Foundation Post Doctoral and Clinical Research Fellowships

Subjects: Medical and behavioural science, as they relate to epilepsy.
Purpose: To support a full-time research project in the field of epilepsy.
Eligibility: Candidates must be scientists or medical specialists with a PhD or MD.
Level of Study: Postdoctorate, Postgraduate, Research.
Type: Research grant.
Value: Canadian $25,000.
Length of Study: One year, in the first instance, but will be renewable once and, exceptionally, twice upon request.
Frequency: Annual.
Country of Study: Canada.
No. of awards offered: Varies.
Application Procedure: Applicants must contact the Foundation or visit the website for application forms and further information.
Closing Date: January 15th.
Funding: Private.
Contributor: The Savoy Foundation endowments.
No. of awards given last year: Four.
No. of applicants last year: 13.
Additional Information: The period of support may begin at any time between May and October.

Savoy Foundation Research Grants

Subjects: Medical and behavioural science, as they relate to epilepsy.
Purpose: To support further research into epilepsy.
Eligibility: Only available to clinicians and established scientists.
Level of Study: Postdoctorate, Postgraduate, Research.
Type: Research grant.
Value: Up to canadian $25,000.
Frequency: Annual.
Country of Study: Any country for Canadian citizens, otherwise Canada only.
No. of awards offered: Varies.
Application Procedure: Applicants must contact the Foundation or visit the website for application forms and further information.
Closing Date: January 15th.
Funding: Private.
Contributor: The Savoy Foundation endowments.

No. of awards given last year: Five.
No. of applicants last year: 10.
Additional Information: The grant is only available to Canadian citizens or for projects conducted in Canada.

Savoy Foundation Studentships

Subjects: Biomedicine, neurology and epileptology.
Purpose: To support training and research in a biomedical discipline, the health sciences or social sciences related to epilepsy.
Eligibility: Candidates must have a good university record eg. a BSc, MD or equivalent diploma and have ensured that a qualified researcher affiliated to a university or hospital will supervise his or her work. Concomitant registration in a graduate programme is encouraged. The awards are available to Canadian citizens or for projects conducted in Canada.
Level of Study: Doctorate, Postgraduate, Predoctorate.
Type: Studentship.
Value: The stipend will be canadian $12,000 for the first year, with a canadian $1,000 increase for each year of renewal. An annual sum of canadian $1,000 will be allocated to the laboratory or institution as additional support for the research project.
Length of Study: One-four years.
Frequency: Annual.
Country of Study: Any country for Canadian citizens, otherwise Canada only.
No. of awards offered: Varies.
Application Procedure: Applicants must contact the Foundation or visit the website for application forms and further information.
Closing Date: January 15th.
Funding: Private.
Contributor: The Savoy Foundation endowments.
No. of awards given last year: 10.
No. of applicants last year: 22.

SCHOLARSHIP FOUNDATION OF THE LEAGUE OF FINNISH-AMERICAN SOCIETIES

Mechelininkatu 10, Helsinki, FIN-00100, Finland
Tel: (358) 9 4133 3700
Fax: (358) 9 4089 74
Email: sayl@sayl.fi
Contact: Ms Tuula Nuckols, Project Manager

Scholarship Foundation of the League for Finnish-American Societies

Subjects: All subjects.
Purpose: To enable Finns to study in the United States.
Eligibility: Open to citizens of Finland only.
Level of Study: Doctorate, Postdoctorate, Postgraduate.
Type: Scholarship.
Value: US$3,000-15,000.
Length of Study: One academic year.
Frequency: Annual.
Study Establishment: A university.
Country of Study: United States of America.
No. of awards offered: Approx. 12.
Application Procedure: Applicants must submit a completed application with references.
Closing Date: The first week in January.
Funding: Private.
No. of awards given last year: 12 including TTS and ASF scholarships.
No. of applicants last year: Varies.
Additional Information: The Scholarship Foundation also handles awards given to Finns by the American-Scandinavian Foundation and Thanks to Scandinavia Inc. both based in New York.

SCHOOL OF ORIENTAL AND AFRICAN STUDIES (SOAS)

University of London
Thornhaugh Street
Russell Square, London, WC1H 0XG, England
Tel: (44) 20 7637 2388
Fax: (44) 20 7436 4211
Email: dg1@soas.ac.uk
www: http://www.soas.ac.uk
Telex: 262433 W6876
Contact: Mrs Deirdre Goodman, Assistant Registrar

The School of Oriental and African Studies (SOAS) regards its role as advancing the knowledge and understanding of the cultures and societies of Asia and Africa and of the School's academic disciplines, through high quality teaching and research.

Bernard Buckman Scholarship

Subjects: Chinese studies with the emphasis on modern and contemporary China, although it is possible to study aspects of pre-modern China.
Purpose: To provide fee remission for a student taking an MA in Chinese studies.
Eligibility: Open to those candidates who qualify to pay for home or European Union tuition fees.
Level of Study: Postgraduate.
Type: Scholarship.
Value: Home or European Union postgraduate fee.
Length of Study: One year.
Frequency: Annual.
Study Establishment: SOAS.
Country of Study: United Kingdom.
No. of awards offered: One.
Application Procedure: Applicants must complete an application form, which can be obtained from the registry.
Closing Date: March 31st.
Funding: Private.
No. of awards given last year: One.
No. of applicants last year: 12.

SOAS Bursary

Subjects: Oriental and African studies in archaeology area studies, economics, ethnomusicology, geography, history, law, languages, linguistics, phonetics, politics, religious studies, social anthropology or development studies.
Purpose: To provide financial assistance to study for a Master's or postgraduate diploma.
Eligibility: There are no eligibility restrictions.
Level of Study: Postgraduate.
Type: Bursary.
Value: UK £7,060.
Length of Study: One year, non renewable.
Frequency: Annual.
Study Establishment: SOAS.
Country of Study: United Kingdom.
No. of awards offered: Six.
Application Procedure: Applicants must complete and submit an application form obtainable from the registrar, with two references plus a 500 word submission.
Closing Date: March 31st.
Funding: Government.
No. of awards given last year: Eight.
No. of applicants last year: 250.

SOAS Research Student Fellowships

Subjects: Languages and cultures of East Asia, Southeast Asia, South Asia, Near and Middle East and Africa, anthropology and sociology, art and archaeology, economics, geography, history, law, linguistics, political studies, study of religions, development studies and ethnomusicology.

Purpose: To support research study at SOAS.
Eligibility: There are no eligibility restrictions.
Level of Study: Doctorate.
Type: Fellowship.
Value: UK £7,020 plus remission of home or European Union fees.
Length of Study: Three years.
Frequency: Annual.
Study Establishment: SOAS.
Country of Study: United Kingdom.
No. of awards offered: Five.
Application Procedure: Applicants must complete and submit an application form which is obtainable from the registrar, with two references, a 500 word submission and five photocopies.
Closing Date: March 31st.
Funding: Government.
No. of awards given last year: Five.
No. of applicants last year: 160.

SCHOOL OF VETERINARY MEDICINE, HANNOVER

Postfach 71 11 80, Hannover, D-30545, Germany
Tel: (49) 511 953 6
Fax: (49) 511 953 8050
Email: bhuesch@vw.tiho-hannover.de
www: http://www.tiho-hannover.de
Contact: Mr Hans Linneman, Executive Member of the Board

The School of Veterinary Medicine, Hannover is a centre of teaching and research in veterinary medicine and zoology with approximately 300 scientists and 2,000 students. Among the 26 institutes and clinics is the Institute for Parasitology where the Karl-Enigk-Stiftung was founded.

Karl-Enigk-Stipendium

Subjects: Parasitology, mainly veterinary parasitology.
Purpose: To support research in experimental parasitology, mainly veterinary parasitology.
Eligibility: Applicants must not be older than 32 years and must be from European countries where German is spoken.
Level of Study: Doctorate, Postdoctorate.
Type: Scholarship.
Value: Postdoctoral is €1,720 per month, and up to €2,850 per month according to country of study. Doctoral is €920 per month.
Length of Study: One-two years.
Frequency: Annual.
Country of Study: Any country.
No. of awards offered: Two.
Application Procedure: Applicants must submit a curriculum vitae, publication list, short research proposal and references from the head of the research institute. Applications must be addressed to Karl Enigk-Stiftung c/o School of Veterinary Medicine Hannover.
Closing Date: Applications are accepted at any time.
Funding: Private.
No. of awards given last year: Four.
No. of applicants last year: Five.

THE SCOTTISH AGRICULTURAL COLLEGE

Auchincruive, Ayr, KA6 5HW, Scotland
Tel: (44) 1292 525350
Fax: (44) 1292 525357
Email: etsu@au.sac.ac.uk
www: http://www.sac.ac.uk
Contact: Mr Gary Wallace, Education Information Manager

The Scottish Agricultural College is engaged in education and training, research and development and advisory and consultant work related to food, the land and the environment.

William John Thomson Scholarship

Subjects: Agriculture, horticulture and related areas in which the college can provide appropriate resources.
Purpose: To fund students who would benefit from training in methods of research.
Eligibility: Open to any graduate in agricultural science from a United Kingdom university who is qualified to carry out research for a higher degree from either Glasgow or Strathclyde University.
Level of Study: Postgraduate.
Type: Scholarship.
Value: Varies.
Length of Study: Three years.
Frequency: Every three years.
Study Establishment: The Scottish Agricultural College, Auchincruive.
Country of Study: United Kingdom.
No. of awards offered: One.
Application Procedure: Applicants must write for details.

SCOTTISH RITE CHARITABLE FOUNDATION OF CANADA

4 Queen Street South, Hamilton, ON, L8P 3R3, Canada
Tel: (1) 905 522 0033
Fax: (1) 905 522 3716
Email: srfoundation@scottishritemasons-can.org
www: http://scottishritemasons-can.org/foundation
Contact: Manager, Information Services

College Diploma/Certificate Bursaries for Students Enrolled in a Programme of Study Relating to Intellectual Impairment

Subjects: Intellectual disability and related fields.
Purpose: To support the work of The Canadian Association for Community Living by funding study into the causes, treatment and palliative care of the various forms of intellectual impairment.
Eligibility: Applications are invited from full-time students at a recognised community college who are enrolled in the second or third year of a programme of studies leading to certification to work in the field of intellectual disability. Applicants must be a Canadian citizen and permanent resident of Canada from one of the provinces or territories.
Level of Study: Doctorate.
Type: Research grant.
Value: Up to canadian $10,000.
Length of Study: One academic year.
Country of Study: Canada.
No. of awards offered: One bursary is made available to a student from each province and territory.
Application Procedure: Application forms should be sent to the local office of the provincial or territorial association of the Canadian Association for Community Living, including personal information data, a letter of reference from a senior official of the college, a letter of recommendation from the regional office of the Canadian

Association for Community Living, transcripts of academic records and a summary of past involvement in the field of intellectual impairment.
Closing Date: June 30th.
Additional Information: For additional information on other categories of award please contact the Bursaries and Grants Awards Committee at the listed address.

For further information contact:

Bursaries & Grants Awards Committee
c/o The Roeher Institute
Kinsmen Building
York University
4700 Keele Street, North York, ON, M3J 1P3, Canada
Tel: (1) 416 661 9611
Fax: (1) 416 661 5701

Major Research Grant for Biomedical Research into Intellectual Impairment

Subjects: Focuses on the causes and eventual cure of intellectual impairment, such as autism and Down syndrome, especially as it affects children. Also, the causes and eventual care of Alzheimer's disease.
Purpose: To support postdoctoral biomedical research.
Eligibility: Applicants must be Canadian citizens and permanent residents. Candidates are required to hold a firm offer of an academic appointment or a postdoctoral appointment at a Canadian university or similar. Research projects must be endorsed by the Research Services Department or equivalent of the university, hospital or research institute and must be carried out in Canada.
Level of Study: Postgraduate.
Type: Research grant.
Value: Up to canadian $35,000.
Length of Study: One year, and may be renewed for a total of three years.
Country of Study: Canada.
No. of awards offered: Approx. 10.
Application Procedure: Application forms are available from the Foundation. Applicants must submit two copies of a personal data form, a research proposal, documents of approval, a budget and three letters of reference.
Closing Date: April 30th.
Additional Information: Grant recipients may be asked to assist in a peer review of future applications.

Scottish Rite Charitable Foundation of Canada Graduate Student Grants for Master's and Doctoral Programes

Subjects: Focuses on the causes and eventual cure of intellectual impairment, such as autism and Down syndrome, especially as it affects children. Also, the causes and eventual care of Alzheimer's disease, early identification and intervention in potentially disabling conditions, minimising long-term disability and lessening the effect of the disability.
Purpose: To enable principal researchers to examine issues affecting people with intellectual disabilities.
Eligibility: Applicants must be Canadian citizens and permanent residents. Applicants are required to hold a firm offer of an academic appointment or a postdoctoral appointment at a Canadian university or similar. Research projects must be endorsed by the Research Services Department or equivalent of the university, hospital or research institute and must be carried out in Canada.
Level of Study: Professional development.
Type: Research grant.
Value: Up to canadian $10,000.
Length of Study: One year, and may be renewed for a total of three years.
Country of Study: Canada.
No. of awards offered: Approx. 16.
Application Procedure: Application forms are available from the Foundation. Applicants must submit two copies of a personal data form, a research proposal, documents of approval, a budget and three letters of reference.

Closing Date: April 30th.

Scottish Rite Charitable Foundation Research Grants in Intellectual Disability

Subjects: A broad range of fields relating to human services and intellectual disability.

Purpose: To enable principal researchers to examine issues affecting people with intellectual disabilities.

Eligibility: Applicants must be Canadian citizens and permanent residents.

Level of Study: Professional development.

Type: Research grant.

Value: Up to canadian $10,000.

Length of Study: One academic year.

Study Establishment: Research projects must be under the responsibility of the Roeher Institute academic associates or other university faculty or researchers approved by the Roeher Institute.

Country of Study: Canada.

No. of awards offered: Varies.

Application Procedure: Applicants must submit a research plan, their budget and their financial requirements.

Closing Date: April 30th.

Additional Information: Funding for research assistants and equipment is not provided through this programme.

THE SCOULOUDI FOUNDATION

c/o The Institute of Historical Research
University of London
Senate House, London, WC1E 7HU, England
Tel: (44) 20 7636 0272
Fax: (44) 20 7436 2183
Email: g-younan@sas.ac.uk
Contact: Secretary

Economic History Society Research Fellowships

Subjects: Economic and social history.

Purpose: To help candidates at an advanced stage of a PhD to complete their doctorates or to provide one year's postdoctoral study in history.

Eligibility: Fellowships will be awarded to postdoctoral candidates who must have recently completed a doctoral degree in economic or social history or to graduates who are engaged in the completion of a doctoral degree in economic or social history and who must have completed two years, but not more than four years' full-time or eight years part-time, research on their chosen topics. Fellowships are open to citizens of the United Kingdom or to candidates with a degree from a university in the United Kingdom.

Level of Study: Doctorate, Postdoctorate, Postgraduate.

Type: Fellowship.

Value: UK £7,000.

Length of Study: One year.

Frequency: Dependent on funds available.

Study Establishment: An institute of historical research.

Country of Study: England.

Application Procedure: Applicants must complete an application form, available from the Assistant Secretary in early January.

Closing Date: Approx. end of March.

Contributor: The Economic History Society.

No. of awards given last year: Three.

Scouloudi Foundation Historical Awards

Subjects: History or a related subject.

Purpose: To provide subsidies towards the cost of publishing a book or article in the field of history, incorporating an academic thesis or other scholarly work already accepted by a reputable publisher or learned journal, or to pay for special expenses incurred in the completion of advanced historical work such as the cost of fares and subsistence during visits to libraries or record repositories.

Eligibility: Open to graduates of United Kingdom universities who possess a relevant Honours degree or United Kingdom citizens with a similar qualification from a university outside the United Kingdom. These awards are not made for study or research towards a post-graduate qualification eg work on theses for higher degrees are not eligible.

Level of Study: Doctorate, Postdoctorate.

Type: Varies.

Value: UK £100-1,000. Applicants should not ask for more than their minimum requirements for the year concerned.

Frequency: Annual.

Country of Study: Any country.

No. of awards offered: Varies.

Application Procedure: Applicants must complete an application form.

Closing Date: March 1st.

Funding: Private.

Contributor: The Scouloudi Foundation.

SEMICONDUCTOR RESEARCH CORPORATION (SRC)

PO Box 12053, Research Triangle Park, NC, 27709, United States of America
Tel: (1) 919 941 9453
Fax: (1) 919 941 9450
Email: poe@src.org
www: http://www.src.org
Contact: Fellowships Office

The Semiconductor Research Corporation (SRC) is a consortium of about 60 semiconductor manufacturers and equipment makers. The SRC manages a research portfolio in major research universities throughout the United States. At any given time it supports about 700 advanced degree students on contract research, 45 graduate Fellows and 15 Master's scholars. The SRC supports a pragmatic approach to developing student programmes and provides industry interactions, presentation and other opportunities for its students.

SRC Graduate Fellowship Program

Subjects: Electrical engineering, computer engineering, chemical engineering, mechanical engineering, materials science, physics and some related areas.

Purpose: To attract academically outstanding students with United States citizenship or permanent resident status to doctoral programmes in areas of interest to the semiconductor industry.

Eligibility: Open to students who have United States citizenship or permanent resident status. Students are also required to be performing their doctoral research under the guidance of an SRC funded faculty member.

Level of Study: Doctorate.

Type: Fellowship.

Value: Tuition and fees, US$1,550 per month stipend, US$2,000 unrestricted gift to the department in which the student is enrolled.

Length of Study: Three years or until completion of the PhD degree, whichever comes first.

Frequency: Annual.

Study Establishment: Universities having SRC funded contracts. A list is available on the website.

Country of Study: United States of America.

No. of awards offered: Varies.

Application Procedure: Applicants must complete an application form. Applications are distributed through SRC funded faculty in November. Applications are also distributed through other venues outside the SRC community and applications are encouraged from non SRC funded colleges.

Closing Date: February 3rd.

Funding: Commercial.

Contributor: The semiconductor industry.

Additional Information: Recipients are required to be associated with an SRC funded contract. Resources are available to assist qualified students in identifying suitable faculty within SRC funded universities. SRC contract support precompetitive research areas of interest to the semiconductor industry.

SRC Master's Scholarship Program

Subjects: Electrical engineering, computer engineering, chemical engineering, mechanical engineering, materials science, physics and some related areas.
Purpose: To attract underrepresented minorities and women to disciplines of interest to the semiconductor industry.
Eligibility: Open to students having United States citizenship or permanent resident status. Students are also required to be from underrepresented minorities eg. African American, Native American, Hispanic or female.
Level of Study: Postgraduate.
Type: Scholarship.
Value: Tuition and fees, US$1,550 per month stipend and US$2,000 unrestricted gift to the department in which the student is enrolled.
Length of Study: Two years or until completion of the Master's degree, whichever comes first.
Frequency: Annual.
Study Establishment: Universities having SRC funded contracts. A list is available on the website.
Country of Study: United States of America.
No. of awards offered: Five.
Application Procedure: Applicants must complete an application form. Applications are distributed through SRC funded faculty in November with a due date early in February. Applications are also distributed through other avenues outside the SRC community and applications are encouraged from non SRC funded colleges.
Closing Date: February 3rd.
Funding: Commercial.
Contributor: The semiconductor industry.
Additional Information: Recipients are required to be associated with an SRC funded contract. Resources are available to assist qualified students in identifying suitable faculty within SRC funded universities. SRC contracts support precompetitive research in areas of interest to the semiconductor industry.

SHASTRI INDO-CANADIAN INSTITUTE (SICI)

Room 1402 Education Tower
2500 University Drive North West, Calgary, AB, T2N 1N4, Canada
Tel: (1) 403 220 7467
Fax: (1) 403 289 0100
Email: sici@ucalgary.ca
www: http://www.ucalgary.ca/~sici
Contact: Ms Lori Mudrick-Donnon, Programme Officer

The Shastri Indo-Canadian Institute (SICI) is a unique educational enterprise that promotes understanding between Canada and India, mainly through facilitating academic activities. The Institute funds research, links institutions in the two countries and organises seminars and conferences.

India Studies Fellowship Competition

Subjects: Subjects relating to India in the social sciences and humanities including education, law, management and the arts.
Purpose: To support candidates wishing to undertake research or training in India.
Eligibility: Applicants must be Canadian citizens or landed immigrants.
Level of Study: Doctorate, Postdoctorate, Postgraduate, Professional development, Research.
Type: Fellowship.
Value: Varies.
Length of Study: Three months to one year.

Frequency: Annual.
Study Establishment: Varies.
Country of Study: India.
No. of awards offered: Varies from year to year.
Application Procedure: Applicants must contact the Canada head office for the application procedure.
Closing Date: July 3rd.
Funding: Government.

SHEFFIELD HALLAM UNIVERSITY

Graduate Studies Team
City Campus
Howard Street, Sheffield, S1 1WB, England
Tel: (44) 114 225 4054
Fax: (44) 114 225 4055
Email: resenq@shu.ac.uk
www: http://registry.shu.ac.uk/gst
Contact: Ms Irene Benevicius, Senior Administrative Officer

Sheffield Hallam University received the highest rating of all the new universities in the 1996 Research Assessment Exercise. The university has a postgraduate population of 4,500 students and is one of the United Kingdom's major providers of postgraduate and research opportunities.

Sheffield Hallam University Research Studentships

Subjects: All subject areas covered by the university, eg. business, computing, construction, cultural studies, education, finance, health studies, materials sport and leisure management, science, mathematics, engineering, urban and regional studies, and social studies courses.
Purpose: To support study towards an MPhil or PhD degree.
Eligibility: Open to European Union nationals only.
Level of Study: Doctorate, Postgraduate.
Type: Bursaries and studentships.
Value: UK £7,500 maintenance award and fees.
Length of Study: Up to three years full-time.
Frequency: Dependent on funds available.
Study Establishment: Sheffield Hallam University.
Country of Study: United Kingdom.
Application Procedure: Applicants must direct initial enquiries to the Graduate Studies Team. If there are studentships for the chosen area of study then an application form must be completed.
Closing Date: Applications are accepted at any time.
Funding: Commercial, Government.

SHELBY CULLOM DAVIS CENTER FOR HISTORICAL STUDIES

Department of History
G-13 Dickinson Hall
Princeton University, Princeton, NJ, 08544-1017, United States of America
Tel: (1) 609 258 4997
Fax: (1) 609 258 5326
www: http://www.princeton.edu/~davisctr
Contact: Ms Kari Hoover

Since 2001 the Shelby Cullom Davis Center for Historical Studies has focused on the study of migration in history.

Shelby Cullom Davis Center Research Projects, Research Fellowships

Subjects: Migration.
Eligibility: Applicants must have completed a PhD.
Level of Study: Postdoctorate.
Type: Fellowship.

Length of Study: One-two semesters.
Frequency: Annual.
Study Establishment: Shelby Cullom Davis Center.
Country of Study: United States of America.
No. of awards offered: Varies.
Application Procedure: Applicants must complete an application form.
Closing Date: December 1st.
Funding: Private.
No. of awards given last year: Seven-eight.

SIDNEY SUSSEX COLLEGE, CAMBRIDGE

Cambridge, Cambridgeshire, CB2 3HU, England
Tel: (44) 1223 338800
Fax: (44) 1223 338884
Email: aga22@cam.ac.uk
www: http://www.sid.com.ac.uk
Contact: Tutor for Graduate Students

Founded in 1596, Sidney Sussex College admits men and women as undergraduates and graduates. The college presently has 150 graduate students, including 75 working for the PhD degree. The college has excellent sporting, dramatic, and musical facilities and can house the majority of its graduate students in college rooms.

Evan Lewis Thomas Law Studentships
Subjects: Law.
Purpose: To support students carrying out research or taking advanced courses in law or cognate subjects.
Eligibility: There are no eligibility restrictions.
Level of Study: Doctorate, Postgraduate.
Type: Studentship.
Value: UK £1,000-4,000 per year.
Length of Study: One-three years.
Frequency: Annual.
Study Establishment: The University of Cambridge.
Country of Study: United Kingdom.
No. of awards offered: Three-four.
Application Procedure: Applicants must obtain application forms from the tutor for graduate studies. Applicants must also apply for a postgraduate place at the University of Cambridge.
Closing Date: February 1st.
Funding: Private.
Contributor: Trust fund.

Sidney Sussex College Research Studentship
Subjects: All subjects.
Purpose: To provide full support for research leading a PhD degree.
Eligibility: Applicants must also apply for a postgraduate place at the University of Cambridge. Preference is given to candidates under 26 years of age. Candidates must be members of Sidney Sussex College.
Level of Study: Doctorate.
Type: Studentship.
Value: UK £6,620 maintenance per year plus fees.
Length of Study: Three years.
Frequency: Annual.
Study Establishment: The University of Cambridge.
Country of Study: United Kingdom.
No. of awards offered: One.
Application Procedure: Applicants must complete an application form, available from the tutor for graduate studies.
Closing Date: March 1st.
Funding: Private.
Contributor: Sidney Sussex College.

SIGMA ALPHA IOTA

5133 Latrobe Drive, Windermere, FL, 34786, United States of America
Tel: (1) 407 876 8986
Fax: (1) 407 876 8985
Email: barbarastaton@earthlink.net
www: http://www.sai-national.org/phil/philiama.html
Contact: Ms Barbara Staton, Director

Sigma Alpha Iota, International Music Fraternity, was organised in 1903 to form chapters of music students and musicians who shall by their influence and their musical interest uphold the highest ideals of a music education. To raise the standard of productive musical work among the women students of colleges, conservatories and universities.

Sigma Alpha Iota Inter-American Music Awards
Subjects: Musical composition but the specifications vary. Entries must be original works for a solo string instrument, violin, viola or cello with or without piano accompaniment.
Purpose: To promote contemporary composers of the Americas and their music.
Eligibility: Open to any composer residing in North, Central or South America. Prior winners are not eligible. Applicants' previous compositions shall not have been published by nationally or internationally known music publishers.
Level of Study: Unrestricted.
Type: Award.
Value: US$1,000. Transportation to the convention and lodging for two nights will also be provided to the winning composer.
Frequency: Every three years.
Country of Study: Any country.
No. of awards offered: One.
Application Procedure: Applicants must submit a manuscript. Applicants may enter more than one work for the competition and an entry fee of US$35 must accompany each manuscript submitted.
Closing Date: Applications must be postmarked by May 1st.
Funding: Private.
Contributor: Organisation members.
No. of awards given last year: One.
No. of applicants last year: 84.
Additional Information: Compositions shall be for solo string instruments eg. the violin, viola and cello, and piano accompaniment is optional. They must be no longer than 10 minutes in duration and represent an advanced difficulty level for college performers. Once submitted, works shall not be announced, performed or recorded until the IAMA winner is presented at the National Convention.

SIGMA THETA TAU INTERNATIONAL

550 West North Street, Indianapolis, IN, 46202, United States of America
Tel: (1) 317 634 8171
Fax: (1) 317 634 8188
Email: research@stti.iupui.edu
www: http://www.nursingsociety.org
Contact: Research Grant Programme

Sigma Theta Tau International exists to promote the development, dissemination and utilisation of nursing knowledge. It is committed to improving the health of people worldwide through increasing the scientific base of nursing practice. In support of this mission, the society advances nursing leadership and scholarship and furthers utilisation of nursing research in health care delivery as well as in public policy.

Rosemary Berkel Crisp Research Award
Subjects: Women's health, oncology and infant or child care.
Purpose: To support nursing research in the critical areas of women's health, oncology and infant and child care.

Eligibility: Applicants must be registered nurses with a current license, have a Master's or higher degree (those with Baccalaureate degrees may be co-investigators), have submitted a complete research application package, be ready to initiate the research project and be a member of the Sigma Theta Tau International. Some preference is given to applicants residing in Illinois Missouri, Arkansas, Kentucky and Tennessee. Applicants must be a member of Sigma Theta Tau International.

Level of Study: Doctorate, Predoctorate.

Type: Award.

Value: US$5,000.

Frequency: Annual.

Country of Study: Any country.

No. of awards offered: One.

Application Procedure: Applicants must submit a completed Sigma Theta Tau research application and agreement.

Closing Date: December 1st.

Funding: Private.

Contributor: The Harry L Crisp, II and Rosemary Berkel Crisp Foundation to Sigma Theta Tau International's Research Endowment.

No. of awards given last year: One.

No. of applicants last year: 52.

Additional Information: The allocation of funds is based upon a research project in the area of women's health, oncology or paediatrics that is ready for implementation, the quality of the proposed research, future potential of the application, appropriateness of the research budget and feasibility of the time frame.

Sigma Theta Tau International Association of Perioperative Registered Nurses Foundation Grant

Subjects: Perioperative nursing practice. All relevant topics will be considered although priority will be given to research studies that relate to the AORN research priorities, the relationship of nursing interventions to quality and cost effective outcomes, prevention of wound infections, protection from injury, thermal, electric, laser, chemical or physical, maintenance of skin integrity, patient satisfaction with care, nursing care, pain management and anxiety management. Patient and family satisfaction with communication and teaching, the relationship of staff mix, cost and length of stay to quality outcomes, the impact of technology on patient outcomes, the conduct and utilisation of research related to AORN's standards, recommendation and practice guidelines and ethical issues related to patient outcomes are also relevant subjects.

Purpose: To encourage qualified nurses to conduct research related to perioperative nursing practice and contribute to the development of perioperative nursing science.

Eligibility: The principal investigator is required to be a registered nurse with a current license in the perioperative setting, or a registered nurse who demonstrates interest in or significant contributions to nursing practice. The principal investigator must have, as a minimum, a Master's degree in nursing. Applicants must submit a completed AORN research application. Membership of either organisation is acceptable, but not required.

Level of Study: Postgraduate.

Type: Research grant.

Value: US$10,000. Allocation of funds is based on the quality of the research, the future promise of the applicant, and the applicant's research budget.

Frequency: Annual.

Country of Study: Any country.

No. of awards offered: One.

Application Procedure: Applicants must write to the AORN for an application form and general instructions.

Closing Date: April 1st.

Funding: Private.

Contributor: The Association of Perioperative Registered Nurses and Sigma Theta Tau International.

Additional Information: July is the funding date.

For further information contact:

Association of Perioperative Registered Nurses
2170 South Parker Road
Suite 300, Denver, CO, 80231-5711, United States of America
Tel: (1) 800 755 2676 ext. 277
Fax: (1) 303 750 2927
Email: sbeya@aorn.org
www: http://www.aorn.org

Sigma Theta Tau International Small Research Grants

Subjects: Nursing.

Purpose: To encourage qualified nurses to contribute to the advancement of nursing through research.

Eligibility: Applicants must be a registered nurse with a current license, have submitted a complete research application package, have the project ready for implementation, hold a Master's degree and/or be enrolled in a Doctoral programme and have signed a Sigma Theta Tau International.

Level of Study: Predoctorate.

Type: Research grant.

Value: Up to US$5,000.

Frequency: Annual.

Country of Study: Any country.

No. of awards offered: 10-15.

Closing Date: December 1st.

Sigma Theta Tau International/American Association of Critical Care Nurses

Subjects: Critical care nursing practice.

Purpose: To encourage qualified nurses to contribute to the advancement of nursing.

Eligibility: Applicants must be registered nurses with a current licence, have received a Master's degree and submit grant proposals relevant to critical care nursing practice. Research must be related to critical care nursing practice.

Level of Study: Postgraduate.

Type: Research grant.

Value: Up to US$10,000.

Frequency: Annual.

Study Establishment: Unrestricted.

Country of Study: Any country.

No. of awards offered: One.

Application Procedure: Applicants must write for an information booklet and application form.

Closing Date: October 1st.

Funding: Private.

Contributor: The American Association of Critical Care Nurses and Sigma Theta Tau International.

Additional Information: January 1st is the funding date.

For further information contact:

American Association of Critical Care Nurses
Department of Research
101 Columbia, Aliso Viejo, CA, 92656-1491, United States of America
Tel: (1) 949 362 2000
Fax: (1) 949 362 2020

Sigma Theta Tau International/American Association of Diabetes Educators Grant

Subjects: Research relating to diabetes education and care.

Purpose: To encourage qualified nurses to contribute to the enhancement of quality and increase the availability of diabetes education and care.

Eligibility: The principal investigator must be a registered nurse but team members may be from other disciplines. The principal investigator must also have received a Master's degree, have the ability to complete the project in one year from funding date. Preference will be given to Sigma Theta Tau members, other qualifications being equal. The grant must be dedicated to diabetes education and care research.

Level of Study: Postgraduate.
Type: Research grant.
Value: Up to US$6,000.
Frequency: Annual.
Country of Study: Any country.
No. of awards offered: One.
Application Procedure: Applicants must write for an information booklet and an application form.
Closing Date: October 1st.
Funding: Private.
Contributor: The American Association of Diabetes Educators and Sigma Theta Tau International.
Additional Information: January 1st is the funding date.

For further information contact:

AADE Foundation Awards
100 West Monroe Street
Suite 400, Chicago, IL, 60603, United States of America
Tel: (1) 312 424 2426
Fax: (1) 312 424 2427

Sigma Theta Tau International/American Nephrology Nurses Association Grant

Subjects: Nephrology nursing.
Purpose: To encourage research.
Eligibility: Applicants must be registered nurses with a current licence and have received a Master's degree. Preference will be given to Sigma Theta Tau members, other qualifications being equal.
Level of Study: Postgraduate.
Type: Research grant.
Value: Up to US$6,000.
Frequency: Annual.
Study Establishment: Unrestricted.
Country of Study: Any country.
No. of awards offered: One.
Application Procedure: Applicants must send application forms to the American Nephrology Nurses Association and must write for an information booklet and application form.
Closing Date: October 31st.
Funding: Private.
Contributor: The American Nephrology Nurses Association and Sigma Theta Tau International.
Additional Information: April 1st is the funding date.

For further information contact:

American Nephrology Nurses' Association
East Holly Avenue
PO Box 56, Pitman, NJ, 08071-0056, United States of America
Tel: (1) 856 256 2320
Fax: (1) 888 600 2662

Sigma Theta Tau International/American Nurses Foundation Grant

Subjects: Any clinical topic.
Purpose: To encourage the research career development of nurses through the support of research conducted by beginning nurse researchers, or experienced nurse researchers who are entering a new field of study.
Eligibility: Applicants must be registered nurses with a current licence and a Master's degree, have submitted a complete research application package, be ready to start the research project and have signed a Sigma Theta Tau research agreement.
Level of Study: Postgraduate.
Type: Research grant.
Value: Up to US$7,500.
Frequency: Annual.
Study Establishment: Unrestricted.
Country of Study: Any country.
No. of awards offered: One.
Application Procedure: Applicants must write for an information booklet and application form. Proposals should be sent to the Sigma

Theta Tau International headquarters in even numbered years, for which applicants should use the STTI application and to the American Nurses Foundation in odd numbered years, for which applicants should use the ANF application.
Closing Date: May 1st.
Funding: Private.
Contributor: The American Nurses Foundation and Sigma Theta Tau International.
Additional Information: Preference will be given to Sigma Theta Tau members, other qualifications being equal. Allocation of funds is based on the quality of the proposed research, the future promise of the applicant and the applicant's research budget. October is the funding date.

For further information contact:

(Odd-numbered years)
American Nurses Foundation
600 Maryland Avenue South West
Suite 100 West, Washington, DC, 20024-2571, United States of America
Tel: (1) 202 651 7071
Fax: (1) 202 651 7354

Sigma Theta Tau International/Association of Operating room Nurses Foundation Grant

Subjects: Perioperative Nursing.
Purpose: To encourage nurses to conduct research related to perioperative nursing practice and contribute to the development of perioperative nursing science.
Eligibility: The principal investigator should be a registered nurse with a current license in the perioperative setting and have received a Master's degree in nursing. Membership of either funding organisation is acceptable but not required.
Level of Study: Predoctorate.
Type: Research grant.
Value: US$10,000.
Frequency: Annual.
Country of Study: Any country.
No. of awards offered: One.
Application Procedure: Applicants should submit a completed application package for the relavent institution for that year.
Closing Date: April 1st.
No. of awards given last year: One.

For further information contact:

Association of Operating Room Nurses
2170 South Parker Road
Suite 300, Denver, CO, 80231-5711, United States of America
Tel: (1) 800 755 2676 ext. 277
Fax: (1) 303 750 2927
Email: sbeyea@aorn.org
www: http://www.aorn.org
Contact: Ms Suzanne Beyea

Sigma Theta Tau International/Emergency Nurses Association Foundation Grant

Subjects: Topics relating to specialised practice of emergency nursing. All relevant subjects will be considered, although priority will be given to studies which relate to ENA Research Initiatives which include, but are not limited to, mechanisms to assure effective, efficient and quality emergency nursing care delivery systems, factors affecting health care cost, productivity, and market forces to emergency services, ways to enhance health promotion and injury prevention and mechanisms to assure quality and cost effective educational programmes for emergency nursing.
Purpose: To support research.
Eligibility: The principal investigator is required to be a registered nurse, but team members may be from other disciplines. Applicants must have a Master's degree, submit a complete application with signed research agreement and be ready to or have already started the research project.
Level of Study: Postgraduate.

Type: Research grant.
Value: Up to US$6,000.
Frequency: Annual.
Study Establishment: Unrestricted.
Country of Study: Any country.
No. of awards offered: One.
Application Procedure: Applicants must write for an information booklet and application form.
Closing Date: February 1st.
Funding: Private.
Contributor: The Emergency Nursing Foundation and Sigma Theta Tau International.
Additional Information: July 1st is the funding date.

For further information contact:

ENA Foundation
915 Lee Street, Des Plaines, IL, 60016-6569, United States of America
Tel: (1) 847 460 4100
Fax: (1) 847 460 4005

Sigma Theta Tau International/Oncology Nursing Society Grant

Subjects: Clinical oncology.
Purpose: To encourage the research career development of nurses through the support of clinically orientated oncology research.
Eligibility: Applicants must be registered nurses actively involved in some aspect of cancer patient care, education or research who hold a Master's degree. Preference will be given to Sigma Theta Tau members, other qualifications being equal.
Level of Study: Postgraduate.
Type: Research grant.
Value: Up to US$10,000.
Frequency: Annual.
Study Establishment: Unrestricted.
Country of Study: Any country.
No. of awards offered: One.
Application Procedure: Applicants must send proposals for this grant to the Oncology Nursing Society and must write for an information booklet and application form.
Closing Date: November 1st.
Funding: Private.
Contributor: The Oncology Nursing Society and Sigma Theta Tau International.
Additional Information: The funding date is in May.

For further information contact:

Oncology Nursing Foundation
501 Holiday Drive, Pittsburgh, PA, 15220-2749, United States of America
Tel: (1) 412 921 7373
Fax: (1) 412 921 6565

Sigma Theta Tau International/Rehabilitation Nursing Foundation Grant

Subjects: Rehabilitation nursing.
Purpose: To encourage research related to rehabilitation nursing.
Eligibility: The principal investigator is required to be a registered nurse in rehabilitation or a registered nurse who demonstrates interest in and significant contributions to rehabilitation nursing. Proposals that address the clinical practice, educational or administrative dimensions of rehabilitation nursing are requested. Quantitative and qualitative research projects will be accepted for review. The principal investigator must have Master's degree in nursing and an ability to complete the project within two years of initial funding.
Level of Study: Postgraduate.
Type: Research grant.
Value: Up to US$6,000.
Frequency: Annual.
Country of Study: Any country.
No. of awards offered: One.

Application Procedure: Applicants must write for details.
Closing Date: April 1st.
Funding: Private.
Contributor: The Rehabilitation Nursing Foundation and Sigma Theta Tau International.
Additional Information: The funding date is the following January.

For further information contact:

Rehabilitation Nursing Foundation
4700 West Lake Avenue, Glenview, IL, 60025, United States of America
Tel: (1) 847 375 4710
Fax: (1) 847 375 4710
Email: info@rehabnurse.org

Virginia Henderson/Sigma Theta Tau International Clinical Research Grant

Subjects: Clinical research.
Purpose: To encourage the research career development of clinically based nurses through support of clinically orientated research.
Eligibility: Applicants must be registered nurses actively involved in some aspect of health care delivery, education or research in a clinical setting, be a member of Sigma Theta Tau International, hold a Master's degree in nursing or be enrolled in a doctoral programme. Allocation of funds is based on a research project ready for implementation, the quality of the proposed research, the future potential of the applicant, appropriateness of the research budget and feasibility of the time frame.
Level of Study: Doctorate, Postgraduate, Predoctorate.
Type: Research grant.
Value: US$5,000.
Frequency: Every two years.
Country of Study: Any country.
No. of awards offered: One.
Application Procedure: Applicants must complete a Sigma Theta Tau International research grant application.
Closing Date: December 1st in odd numbered years.
Funding: Private.
Contributor: The Virginia Henderson Clinical Research Endowment Fund.
Additional Information: June is the funding date.

SIGMA XI, THE SCIENTIFIC RESEARCH SOCIETY

Sigma Xi Headquarters
Box 13975
99 Alexander Drive, Research Triangle Park, NC, 27709, United States of America
Tel: (1) 919 549 4691
Fax: (1) 919 549 0090
Email: giar@sigmaxi.org
www: http://www.sigmaxi.org
Contact: Grant Programme Co-ordinator

Sigma Xi, The Scientific Research Society is the international honour society for scientists and engineers. Founded in 1886, its goals are to foster worldwide interactions among science, technology, and society, to encourage appreciation and support of original work in science and technology, and to honour scientific accomplishments.

Sigma Xi Grants-in-Aid of Research

Subjects: Scientific investigation in any field eg. physical sciences and engineering, behavioural and life sciences, astronomy, cell biology, chemistry, computer science, mathematics, ecology, engineering, geology, physics, psychology, anthropology, ophthalmology and blood plasma research.
Eligibility: Open to graduate students in degree programmes.
Level of Study: Doctorate, Graduate, Postgraduate, Predoctorate, Research.

Type: Grant.
Value: Awards are made in amounts up to a maximum of US$1,000 except in the fields of astronomy and eye or vision research where special funds allow for awards up to a maximum of US$2,500. No part of an award may be used for the payment of indirect costs to the recipient's institution. All funds must be expended directly in support of the proposed investigation. Any equipment purchased shall be the property of the institution.
Frequency: Twice a year.
Country of Study: Any country.
No. of awards offered: Approx.1,000 awards annually.
Application Procedure: Applicants must visit the website for up to date guidelines and to fill out an interactive form.
Closing Date: March 15th or October 15th.
Funding: Private.
Additional Information: The following are not granted support: educational programmes and curriculum development, stipends for applicants or assistants, manuscript preparation and publication costs, purchase of standard equipment and supplies that should normally be available in an institutional research laboratory, travel to scientific meetings or symposia, and requests for a third year of support. The Committee attaches low priority to support for use of institutional and departmental equipment and facilities.

SIMON FRASER UNIVERSITY

MBA Program
8888 University Drive, Burnaby, BC, V5A 1S6, Canada
Tel: (1) 604 291 3047
Fax: (1) 604 291 3404
Email: mba@sfu.ca
www: http://www.bus.sfu.ca/mba
Contact: MBA Admissions Officer

SFU Graduate Fellowships

Subjects: MBA.
Purpose: To offer financial support to SFU MBA students.
Eligibility: Open to current or entering MBA students with a grade point average of 3.5 or above. Successful students typically receive one graduate fellowship per year.
Level of Study: MBA.
Type: Fellowship.
Value: US$4,400.
Length of Study: One semester.
Frequency: Annual.
Study Establishment: Simon Fraser University.
Country of Study: United States of America.
No. of awards offered: 30.
Application Procedure: Applicants must contact the organisation for application details.
Closing Date: April 15th.
Additional Information: Please note that most graduate fellowships are available to visa students as well as Canadian citizens and residents. However, when applying to SFU's Professional MBA Program, foreign applicants must provide evidence that they have sufficient financial resources to complete their graduate education at SFU without additional financial support.

SFU Teaching Assistantships

Subjects: MBA.
Purpose: To offer financial support to SFU MBA students.
Eligibility: Applicants must have already been accepted onto the MBA course.
Level of Study: MBA.
Type: Teaching assistantships.
Value: From US$2,500-4,500.
Length of Study: One-two semesters.
Frequency: Annual.
Study Establishment: Simon Fraser University.
Country of Study: United States of America.

Application Procedure: Applicants must contact the organisation for application details.
Closing Date: Please contact the organisation.
Additional Information: Please note that most teaching assistantships are available to visa students as well as Canadian citizens and residents. However, when applying to SFU's Professional MBA Program, foreign applicants must provide evidence that they have sufficient financial resources to complete their graduate education at SFU without additional financial support. Those who receive teaching assistantships are responsible for preparation and instruction in course tutorial sessions, marking, consultation with students, attendance at course orientation and lectures, consultation with the faulty member responsible for the course and other related duties. Recipients gain valuable teaching experience, usually in their area of specialisation, while earning income.

SIR ERNEST CASSEL EDUCATIONAL TRUST

199 West Malvern Road, Malvern, Worcestershire, WR14 4BB, England
Tel: (44) 1684 572437
Email: casseltrust@sherborn.demon.co.uk
Contact: D N Constable, Secretary

The Sir Ernest Cassel Educational Trust awards oversees research grants, through the British Academy, in the language, literature or civilisation of any country. The Trust also awards the Mountbatten Memorial Grants to Commonwealth university students in their final year of study in the United Kingdom.

Mountbatten Memorial Grants to Commonwealth Students

Subjects: All subjects.
Purpose: To assist overseas students from the Commonwealth who encounter unforeseen financial difficulties in their final year of study.
Eligibility: Open to Commonwealth students who are pursuing a course of study at postgraduate level at universities or other recognised Institutes of Higher Education in the United Kingdom.
Level of Study: Postgraduate.
Type: Grant.
Value: Up to UK £500.
Frequency: Annual.
Country of Study: United Kingdom.
No. of awards offered: Varies.
Application Procedure: Applicants must apply in writing and include a brief curriculum vitae.
Funding: Private.
Contributor: Cassel Trust investments.
No. of awards given last year: 80.
No. of applicants last year: 580.
Additional Information: Grants are administered and awarded, on the Trust's behalf, by a number of universities and other Institutes of Higher Education. Applicants should consult their university or college student welfare officer for further information. The Trust does not sponsor or award scholarships, or pay fees. There are no grants for one year courses.

Sir Ernest Cassel Educational Trust Overseas Research Grants

Subjects: Language, literature or civilisation of any country.
Purpose: To help towards the expenses of approved research abroad.
Eligibility: Open to the more junior teaching members of faculties of universities and other recognised Institutes of Higher Education in the United Kingdom, regardless of country of birth.
Level of Study: Unrestricted.
Type: Research grant.
Value: UK £100-500.

Frequency: Annual.
Country of Study: Outside the United Kingdom.
No. of awards offered: Varies.
Application Procedure: Applicants must write to the British Academy for information.
Closing Date: September 30th, December 31st, February 28th or April 30th.
Funding: Private.
Contributor: Cassel Trust investments.
No. of awards given last year: 10.
No. of applicants last year: Unknown.
Additional Information: Grants are administered by the British Academy.

For further information contact:

10 Carlton House Terrace, London, SW1Y 5AH, England

SIR HALLEY STEWART TRUST

22 Earith Road
Willingham, Cambridge, Cambridgeshire, CB4 5LS, England
Tel: (44) 1954 260707
www: http://www.sirhalleystewart.org
Contact: Mrs Sue West, Administrator

The Sir Halley Stewart Trust has a Christian basis and is concerned with the development of body, mind and spirit, a just environment and international goodwill. The Trust aims to promote innovative research activities or developments. It emphasises prevention rather than alleviation of human suffering.

Sir Halley Stewart Trust Grants

Subjects: Medical, social or religious research within certain priority areas.
Purpose: To assist pioneering research.
Eligibility: Not open to general appeals, building, capital, running costs or personal education including educational and travel costs.
Level of Study: Doctorate, Postgraduate, Predoctorate, Research.
Type: Research grant.
Value: Salaries and relevant costs for innovative and imaginative young researchers in the region of UK £15,000-20,000.
Length of Study: Limited to two or three years.
Frequency: Dependent on funds available.
Study Establishment: Under the auspices of a charitable institution eg. a hospital, laboratory, university department or charitable organisation.
Country of Study: Certain priorities operate. These are reviewed annually. Studies are based mainly in institutions in the United Kingdom.
Application Procedure: Applicants must contact the Trust for further details. There is no application form and applications will not be accepted if sent by fax or email.
Closing Date: Applications are accepted at any time.
Funding: Private.
No. of awards given last year: 51.
No. of applicants last year: 818.
Additional Information: Further information is available from the Trust office by obtaining a copy of 'Notes for those Seeking Grants'. The website contains the most up to date details.

SIR HENRY RICHARDSON AWARDS

16 Ogle Street, London, W1W 6JA, England
Tel: (44) 20 7636 4481
Fax: (44) 20 7647 4307
Email: education@mbf.org.uk
www: http://www.mbf.org.uk
Contact: Mrs Susan Dolton

Sir Henry Richardson Awards

Subjects: Musical performance.
Purpose: To assist accompanists and repetiteurs.
Eligibility: Open to postgraduates of up to 30 years. Applicants should be British, Indian, Pakistani or Bangladeshi nationals or have been resident in the United Kingdom for three years.
Level of Study: Postgraduate, Professional development.
Value: UK £8,000-12,000 in total.
Frequency: Annual.
Country of Study: Any country.
No. of awards offered: 5-10.
Application Procedure: Selected students will be asked to audition.
Closing Date: March 27th.
Funding: Private.
No. of awards given last year: Nine.
No. of applicants last year: 34.

SIR JOHN SOANE'S MUSEUM FOUNDATION

636 Broadway
Suite 720, New York, NY, 10012, United States of America
Tel: (1) 646 654 0085
Fax: (1) 646 654 0089
Email: soane@mindspring.com
Contact: Mrs Dale S Cunningham, Executive Director

The Sir John Soane's Museum Foundation assists the Museum in London to further Soane's commitment to educate and inspire the general and professional public in architecture and the fine and decorative arts. Programmes have attracted students, collectors, architects, decorators and arts enthusiasts since 1991 to its events, lectures, tours and dinners.

Sir John Soane's Museum Foundation Travelling Fellowship

Subjects: Art, architecture and the decorative arts.
Purpose: To enable scholars to pursue research projects related to the work of Sir John Soane's Museum and its collections.
Eligibility: Applicants must be enrolled in a graduate degree programme in a field appropriate to the Foundation's purpose.
Level of Study: Postgraduate.
Type: Fellowship.
Value: US$4,000.
Frequency: Annual.
Study Establishment: The choice of the fellowship recipient.
Country of Study: Usually the United States of America or the United Kingdom. The Scholar usually spends some time at Sir John Soane's Museum at 13 Lincoln's Inn Fields, London, studying architectural drawings, models, and paintings.
No. of awards offered: One.
Application Procedure: Applicants must submit a formal proposal of not more than five pages describing the goal, scope and purpose of the research project, in addition to three letters of recommendation. An interview may be required.
Closing Date: February 1st.
Funding: Private.
Contributor: The Board of Directors and the Advisory Board.
No. of awards given last year: One.
No. of applicants last year: Six.
Additional Information: At the end of each research project the award recipient must submit written documentation or a sketch book on the progress of the research as outlined in the original proposal with respect to goal, scope and allocation of funds, and give a lecture on the research, arranged by the Foundation.

SIR RICHARD STAPLEY EDUCATIONAL TRUST

North Street Farmhouse, Sheldwich, Near Faversham, Kent, ME13 0LN, England
Email: admin@stapleytrust.org
www: http://www.stapleytrust.org
Contact: Mrs Christine Ford, Administrator

The Sir Richard Stapley Educational Trust awards grants to students studying for higher degrees, or an equivalent academic qualification, degrees in medicine, veterinary science or dentistry at a university in the United Kingdom.

Sir Richard Stapley Educational Trust Grants

Subjects: Medical, dental or veterinary science and higher degrees in other subjects.
Purpose: To support postgraduate study.
Eligibility: Open to graduates holding a First Class (Honours) Degree or an Upper Second Class (Honours) Degree and are more than 24 years of age on October 1st of the proposed academic year. Students in receipt of a substantial award from local authorities, Research Councils, the British Academy or other, similar public bodies will not normally receive a grant from the Trust. Courses not eligible include electives, diplomas, professional training and intercalated degrees. The Trust does not normally support students for full-time PhD studies beyond a third year.
Level of Study: Postgraduate.
Type: Grant.
Value: From UK £300 to UK £1,300.
Length of Study: Not defined, but PhD studies are not more than three years. Grants are awarded for one full academic year in the first instance.
Frequency: Annual.
Study Establishment: Any appropriate university.
Country of Study: United Kingdom.
No. of awards offered: Dependent on funds available.
Application Procedure: Applicants making enquiries should include a large stamped addressed envelope or international reply coupons. Application forms will be sent and must be returned complete with two academic references in sealed envelopes. Applicants will be notified in May.
Closing Date: March 31st.
Funding: Commercial, Private.
No. of awards given last year: 177.
No. of applicants last year: 231.
Additional Information: Grants are paid upon receipt of official confirmation of participation in the course. All matters concerning application are by correspondence only.

SIR ROBERT MENZIES MEMORIAL FOUNDATION

210 Clarendon Street, East Melbourne, VIC, Australia
Tel: (61) 3 9419 5699
Fax: (61) 3 9417 7049
Email: menzies@vicnet.net.au
www: http://www.vicnet.net.au/~menzies
Contact: Ms S K Mackenzie, General Manager

The Sir Robert Menzies Memorial Foundation was formed as a memorial to Sir Robert Menzies in 1979. It is a non-profit and non-political organisation with two principal activities. One is directed to the health and fitness of the Australian community and the other to the promotion of academic excellence.

The Sir Robert Menzies Memorial Research Scholarships in the Allied Health Sciences

Subjects: Occupational therapy, speech pathology, physiotherapy, psychology, nursing, optometry or physical education.
Purpose: To allow an outstanding applicant to carry out doctoral research work that is likely to improve the health of Australians.
Eligibility: Open to Australian citizens of at least five years' standing. Applicants will generally have completed the first year of their PhD project.
Level of Study: Doctorate, Postgraduate.
Type: Scholarship.
Value: Australian $24,000 free of income tax.
Length of Study: Two years.
Frequency: Annual.
Study Establishment: A tertiary institute with appropriate facilities.
Country of Study: Australia.
No. of awards offered: One.
Application Procedure: Applicants must complete an application form and submit this with academic transcripts and other documents. Further information is available on request.
Closing Date: June 30th.
Funding: Private.
Contributor: The Sir Robert Menzies Memorial Foundation.
No. of awards given last year: One.
No. of applicants last year: 30.

The Sir Robert Menzies Scholarships in Law

Subjects: Law.
Purpose: To enable Australian citizens to pursue postgraduate studies in the United Kingdom, generally leading to a higher degree.
Eligibility: Open to Australian citizens of five years' standing, with at least an Upper Second Class (Honours) Degree in Law at the time of application.
Level of Study: Postgraduate.
Type: Scholarship.
Value: Payment of tuition fees, or a research grant equivalent, examination and other compulsory fees, a grant of UK £300 for books and equipment in the first year and UK £150 in the second year, a grant of up to UK £120 towards the typing and binding of a thesis, a quarterly living allowance of UK £2,000 plus additional allowance of UK £150 per month for spouse and UK £30 per month each for dependant children under 16. Return airfares will also be paid for.
Length of Study: One-two years.
Frequency: Annual.
Study Establishment: The universities of St Andrews, Edinburgh, Cambridge or Oxford, or occasionally elsewhere.
Country of Study: United Kingdom.
No. of awards offered: One or two.
Application Procedure: Applicants must complete and submit an application form along with academic transcripts and other documents.
Closing Date: August 31st.
Funding: Private.
Contributor: The Trust, the Foreign and Commonwealth Office and the Foundation in Australia.
No. of awards given last year: Two.
No. of applicants last year: 40.

THE SKIDMORE, OWINGS AND MERRILL FOUNDATION

224 South Michigan Avenue
Suite 1000, Chicago, IL, 60604, United States of America
Tel: (1) 312 427 4202
Fax: (1) 312 360 4551
Contact: Ms Lisa Westerfield, Administrative Director

The mission of the Skidmore, Owings and Merrill Foundation is to help young architects and engineers broaden their professional education, instil a heightened sense of responsibility as future practitioners to improve the quality of the built and natural environments, and to encourage them to appreciate the influence of place-making, culture and technology on the design of buildings and their settings.

Architecture Travelling Fellowship

Subjects: Recognises progressive achievement.
Purpose: To help young architects to broaden their education and take an enlightened view of society's need to improve the built and natural environments.
Eligibility: Applicants must be graduating from a United States of America school but may be of any citizenship. For the Bachelor of Architecture Travelling Fellowship applicants must receive, prior to application, a Bachelor of Architecture degree. For the Master of Architecture First Professional Degree Fellowship applicants must receive, prior to application, a Master of Architecture degree. For the Master of Architecture Second Professional Degree Fellowship applicants must receive, prior to application, a Master of Architecture degree.
Level of Study: Graduate.
Type: Fellowship.
Value: US$10,000 per fellowship.
Frequency: Annual.
Study Establishment: Accredited schools, colleges or universities.
Country of Study: United States of America.
No. of awards offered: Three, one for Bachelor of Architecture graduating student and two for Master of Architecture.
Application Procedure: Applicants must submit a portfolio with a proposed travel itinerary and a signed copyright release statement provided by the Foundation. Full guidelines are available on request. Students must be nominated by a United States of America school of attendance.
Funding: Private.
No. of awards given last year: Four.
Additional Information: Information is sent to schools between February and March.

Chicago Institute for Architecture and Urbanism Award

Subjects: Reversal of decentralisation, gridlocked traffic, urban sprawl, diminishing open spaces for agriculture and recreation. Recognition of the value of irreplaceable resources. Setting strategies for growth, focusing new development in existing centres and subcentres, and using transportation investments to improve the quality of existing districts and neighbourhoods.
Purpose: To encourage writing and research on the question of how architecture, infrastructure, urban design and planning can contribute to improving the quality of life of the American city.
Level of Study: Graduate.
Type: Prize.
Value: US$5,000.
Study Establishment: Accredited schools in the United States of America.
Country of Study: United States of America.
No. of awards offered: One.
Application Procedure: Applicants must submit a curriculum vitae, copyright release statement, and one original and five copies of the paper and its synopsis. Full guidelines are available on request.
Funding: Private.
No. of awards given last year: One.
No. of applicants last year: 10.
Additional Information: Information is sent to schools between February and March of each year and the award is announced in September. Finalist and winning papers become the property of the Foundation, which will hold the copyright for their publication in any media. The Foundation may also publish an anthology of winning and finalist papers in the future.

Interior Architecture Travelling Fellowship

Subjects: Recognises awareness and skilful handling of the full range of elements that support a designed interior space, including furniture and finishes, lighting and artwork.

Purpose: To encourage young designers to explore the relationship between architecture and interiors, with particular emphasis on the three dimensional modelling of space and the integration of interior spaces and elements with building architecture and systems.
Eligibility: Applicants must be graduating with a Bachelor's or Master's degree from an accredited United States of America architectural school or Foundation for Interior Design Education Research (FIDER). Applicants must be nominated by the faculty and endorsed by the Chair of the department from which they will receive the degree.
Level of Study: Graduate.
Type: Fellowship.
Value: US$7,500.
Frequency: Annual.
Study Establishment: Accredited schools in the United States of America.
Country of Study: United States of America.
No. of awards offered: One.
Application Procedure: Applicants must submit a portfolio with two copies each of a letter of recommendation, proposed travel itinerary and a signed copyright release statement provided by the SOM Foundation. Full guidelines are available on request. Students must be nominated by the United States school of attendance.
Funding: Private.
No. of awards given last year: One.
Additional Information: Information is sent to schools between February and March.

Mechanical/Electrical Building Systems Travelling Fellowship

Subjects: Recognises research on such topics as energy efficient design, the application of new technologies, the appropriate use or re-use of natural resources and the integration of building systems as components of a work of architecture.
Purpose: To expand the vision and imagination of young engineers.
Eligibility: Candidates must receive, prior to application, a Bachelor or Master of Science engineering degree specialising in architectural, mechanical or electrical engineering from a United States of America school but can be of any citizenship. Candidates must be nominated by the faculty and endorsed by the Chair of the department from which they will receive the degree. Candidates must intend to enter the professional practice of mechanical or electrical engineering of buildings.
Level of Study: Graduate.
Type: Fellowship.
Value: US$7,500.
Frequency: Annual.
Study Establishment: Accredited schools in the United States of America.
Country of Study: United States of America.
No. of awards offered: One.
Application Procedure: Applicants must submit four copies of a letter of recommendation, a curriculum vitae, recent transcript, brief original paper no more than 10 pages in length, proposed travel itinerary, a computer disk containing the paper, abstract and travel itinerary and a signed copyright release statement provided by the Foundation. Full guidelines are available on request.
Funding: Private.
No. of awards given last year: One.
No. of applicants last year: Six.
Additional Information: Information is sent to schools in October.

Structural Engineering Travelling Fellowship

Subjects: An essay concerning the applicant's interest in the role of aesthetics, innovation, efficiency and economy in the structural design of buildings, bridges and other structures.
Purpose: To foster an appreciation of the aesthetic potential inherent in the structural design of buildings, bridges and other major works of architecture and engineering.
Eligibility: Applicants must be graduating with a Master's or PhD degree in civil or architectural engineering with a specialisation in structural engineering from a United States of America school but

can be of any citizenship. Applicants must be nominated by the faculty and endorsed by the Chair of the department from which they will receive the degree. Applicants must intend to enter the professional practice of structural engineering in the field of buildings or bridges.

Level of Study: Doctorate, Graduate.
Type: Competition.
Value: US$7,500.
Frequency: Annual.
Study Establishment: Accredited schools in the United States of America.
Country of Study: United States of America.
No. of awards offered: One.
Application Procedure: Applicants must submit four copies of a letter of recommendation, curriculum vitae, recent graduate and undergraduate transcripts, a brief essay between two and four pages in length plus figures, a proposed travel itinerary, a computer disk containing the essay and itinerary and a signed copyright release provided by the Foundation. Full guidelines are available on request.
Funding: Private.
No. of awards given last year: One.
Additional Information: The fellowship hopes to encourage an awareness of their visual impact among engineering students and their schools. It also helps to strengthen the connection between aesthetics and efficiency, economy and innovation in structural design.

Urban Design Travelling Fellowship

Subjects: Pertinent urban design issues such as appropriate development character, sense of place, preservation and adaptive reuse, way finding and ease of access and movement, and sustainable patterns of densification and growth.
Purpose: To encourage young architects with an interest in urban design to broaden their knowledge of the design of modern, high density cities.
Eligibility: Applicants must be graduating with a Bachelor's degree in architecture, landscape architecture or urban design and a Master's degree in urban design from a United States of America school but can be of any citizenship. Applicants must be nominated by the faculty and endorsed by the Chair of the department from which they will receive the degree.
Level of Study: Graduate.
Type: Fellowship.
Value: US$7,500.
Frequency: Annual.
Study Establishment: Accredited schools in the United States of America.
Country of Study: United States of America.
No. of awards offered: One.
Application Procedure: Applicants must submit a portfolio with two copies each of a letter of recommendation, curriculum vitae, recent transcript, proposed travel itinerary and a signed copyright release statement provided by the Foundation. Full guidelines are available on request.
Funding: Private.
No. of awards given last year: One.
Additional Information: Information is sent to schools between February and March.

SME EDUCATION FOUNDATION

PO Box 930, Dearborn, MI, 48121-0930, United States of America
Tel: (1) 313 271 1500 ext. 1702
Fax: (1) 313 240 6095
Email: quinste@sme.org
www: http://www.sme.org/foundation
Contact: Mr Steve Quinlan, Grants Program Officer

SME Education Foundation Grants Program

Subjects: Manufacturing engineering.

Purpose: To establish a process that will stimulate the academic community to help improve the competency of the manufacturing workforce. It focuses on identifying and then closing competency gaps between industry's manufacturing workforce needs and what is currently provided by educational programmes.
Eligibility: Open to full-time university faculty representing manufacturing engineering or manufacturing engineering technology programmes which offer manufacturing courses.
Level of Study: Postgraduate.
Type: Grant.
Value: Funds are reimbursed upon receipt of an invoice and narrative report.
Frequency: Annual.
Country of Study: United States of America or Canada.
No. of awards offered: Varies.
Application Procedure: Applicants must submit a signed original application with seven copies to coincide with the request. Further information is available from the website.
Closing Date: December 7th.
Funding: Private.
Contributor: SME members, chapters, regions and corporations.
No. of awards given last year: 58.
No. of applicants last year: 120.
Additional Information: Capital equipment and research initiation grants must be matched dollar for dollar by the educational institution.

THE SMITH AND NEPHEW FOUNDATION

Heron House
15 Adam Street, London, WC2N 6LA, England
Tel: (44) 20 7960 2276
Fax: (44) 20 7960 2298
Email: barbara.foster1@smith-nephew.com
www: http://www.snfoundation.org.uk
Contact: Ms Barbara Foster, Foundation Administrator

The Smith and Nephew Foundation aims to improve health care in the United Kingdom by offering awards to individuals in the medical and nursing professions undertaking educational or research projects.

Smith and Nephew Foundation Nursing Research Fellowships

Subjects: Projects which have been designed to enhance the evidence base for nursing and midwifery practice and which clearly evaluate the effectiveness and outcomes of nursing and midwifery interventions.
Purpose: To aid nursing research as part of a PhD programme.
Eligibility: For eligibility requirements please telephone, write or email for details.
Level of Study: Postgraduate.
Type: Fellowship.
Value: Up to UK £30,000 each for one year.
Length of Study: One year, usually during the final year of their PhD study.
Frequency: Annual.
Country of Study: United Kingdom.
No. of awards offered: Varies.
Application Procedure: Applicants must apply for details by telephone, email or post. The fellowships are advertised in the relevant nursing journals.
Closing Date: Advertised at the beginning of March with closing date at the beginning of May.
Funding: Commercial.
Contributor: Smith & Nephew plc.
No. of awards given last year: Four.
No. of applicants last year: 26.
Additional Information: Further information is available on request.

Smith and Nephew Foundation Postdoctoral Nursing Research Fellowship

Subjects: The awards will focus on projects which have been designed to enhance the evidence base for nursing and midwifery practice and which clearly evaluate the effectiveness and outcomes of nursing and midwifery interventions.

Purpose: To aid nursing postdoctoral research and support outstanding career nurse researchers.

Eligibility: Applicants must be based in a university, school, faculty or department of nursing within a multidisciplinary environment which also has an established reputation and proven track record for research and development in one or both of the specified areas eg. nursing care of patients receiving minimally invasive or orthopaedic surgery, patients with skin or tissue damage.

Level of Study: Postdoctorate.

Type: Fellowship.

Value: UK £120,000 for three years.

Length of Study: Up to three years.

Frequency: Dependent on funds available.

Country of Study: United Kingdom.

No. of awards offered: One.

Application Procedure: Applicants must apply for details by telephone, email or post. The fellowships are advertised in the relevant nursing journals.

Closing Date: The beginning of June.

Funding: Commercial.

Contributor: Smith and Nephew plc.

No. of awards given last year: One.

No. of applicants last year: Seven.

SMITHSONIAN ASTROPHYSICS OBSERVATORY (SAO)

60 Garden Street
Mail Stop 47, Cambridge, MA, 02138, United States of America
Email: predoc@cfa.harvard.edu
www: http://cfa-www.harvard.edu/newtop/saohome.html

SAO Predoctoral Fellowships

Subjects: Astronomy, astrophysics, atomic and molecular physics, planetary science, radio and geoastronomy, solar and stellar physics or theoretical astrophysics.

Purpose: To allow students from other institutions throughout the world to undertake their thesis research at SAO.

Eligibility: Applicants must have completed their preliminary course work and examinations and be ready to begin dissertation research at the time of the award.

Level of Study: Predoctorate.

Type: Fellowship.

Value: Stipend of US$21,500. Some funds may also be available for relocation, travel and other expenses.

Length of Study: One year, with a possibility of renewal for up to a further three years.

Frequency: Annual.

Study Establishment: The Smithsonian Astrophysical Observatory.

Country of Study: United States of America.

No. of awards offered: Varies.

Application Procedure: Applicants must contact directly Smithsonian scientists in their area of interest to discuss possible research topics. Applicants must complete an application form, available on request from email predoc@cfa.harvard.edu and downloadable from the website.

Closing Date: April 15th.

No. of awards given last year: Five.

No. of applicants last year: 15.

Additional Information: Further information can be found on the website.

SMITHSONIAN INSTITUTION

750 9th Street North West
Suite 9300
MRC 902, Washington, DC, 20560-0902, United States of America
Tel: (1) 202 275 0655
Fax: (1) 202 275 0489
Email: siofg@ofg.si.edu
www: http://www.si.edu/ofg
Contact: Mr Bryan T Fair, Office of Fellowships

The Smithsonian Institution was established in 1846 with funds bequeathed to the United States by James Smithson. The Institution is as an independent trust instrumentality of the United States holding some 140 million artifacts and specimens in its trust for the increase and diffusion of knowledge.

Postdoctoral Fellowships at the Smithsonian Astrophysical Observatory

Subjects: Various fields of astrophysics and astronomy, including atomic and molecular physics, the solar system, stars, galaxies or cosmology.

Purpose: To financially support those undertaking postdoctoral scholarships.

Eligibility: Open to recent PhD recipients of any nationality in a relevant field with interests in theory, observation, instrumentation or laboratory research. Only applicants who receive their degrees in the academic year preceding application will be considered unless there are special circumstances such as illness or national service. A short postdoctoral period, especially at the PhD institution, is not a disqualification.

Level of Study: Postdoctorate.

Type: Fellowship.

Value: US$35,000 per year plus US$8,000 research allowance.

Length of Study: Two years, with a possibility of renewal for a further year.

Frequency: Annual.

Study Establishment: The Smithsonian Astrophysical Observatory.

Country of Study: United States of America.

No. of awards offered: Varies.

Application Procedure: Applicants must complete an application form.

Closing Date: December 15th for notification by February 15th.

Additional Information: Techniques used range from computer simulations through observations in the radio, infrared, optical, ultraviolet, X- and gamma-ray bands to instrument development and laboratory experiments. Facilities include the Multiple Mirror Telescope, many local computers, an image processing laboratory, the Einstein Observatory data archive, the EUV/Skylab solar data archive, a number of specialised laboratories and an outstanding astronomical library, but above all, a large and vigorous staff involved in almost every branch of astrophysical and solar system research.

Smithsonian Institution Graduate Student Fellowships

Subjects: Animal behaviour, ecology, environmental science, anthropology, archaeology, astrophysics, astronomy, earth sciences, paleobiology, evolutionary and systematic biology, history of science and technology, history of art and folklife.

Purpose: To enable graduate students to conduct individual research under the guidance of Smithsonian staff members. Projects must be related to the research and interests of the Institution's professional staff.

Eligibility: Open to graduate students of any nationality who are formally enrolled and engaged in a graduate programme of study at a degree granting institution and have completed at least one semester before the appointment period, and have not yet been advanced to candidacy. Projects proposed will be approved in advance by a Smithsonian staff member who will serve as the appointee's advisor. Fluency in English is required.

Level of Study: Graduate.

Type: Fellowship.

Value: US$3,700.

Length of Study: 10 weeks.
Frequency: Annual.
Study Establishment: Smithsonian Institution facilities.
Country of Study: United States of America.
No. of awards offered: Varies.
Application Procedure: Applicants must complete an application pack, available from the office or the website.
Closing Date: January 15th.

Smithsonian Institution Postdoctoral Fellowships

Subjects: American social and cultural history, history of science and technology, history of art, anthropology, biological sciences, earth sciences, history of African art and culture.
Purpose: To offer appointments to those who wish to pursue postdoctoral research training at the Smithsonian Institution in collaboration with a member of the professional staff of the Institution.
Eligibility: Open to candidates of any nationality who have received the PhD or equivalent within seven years of the application date. Recipients must have completed the degree or certificate at the time the Fellowship commences. Fluency in English is required.
Level of Study: Postdoctorate.
Type: Fellowship.
Value: US$30,000 per year plus research and travel allowances.
Length of Study: 3-12 months, usually one year.
Frequency: Annual.
Study Establishment: Smithsonian Institution facilities.
Country of Study: United States of America.
No. of awards offered: Varies.
Application Procedure: Applicants must complete an application form. Further information and application forms are available from the Institution.
Closing Date: January 15th.
No. of awards given last year: Varies.
No. of applicants last year: Varies.

Smithsonian Institution Predoctoral Fellowships

Subjects: Anthropology, biological sciences, earth sciences, history of art, history of science and technology, American social and cultural history, and the history of African art and culture.
Purpose: To financially support those undertaking predoctoral fellowships.
Eligibility: Open to students of any nationality who are enrolled in a university as candidates for the PhD or equivalent. At the time of appointment the university must approve the undertaking of dissertation research at the Smithsonian Institution and indicate that requirements for the doctorate, other than dissertation, have been met. Fluency in English is required.
Level of Study: Postgraduate, Predoctorate.
Type: Fellowship.
Value: US$17,000 per year plus research and travel allowances.
Length of Study: 3-12 months.
Frequency: Annual.
Study Establishment: Smithsonian Institution facilities.
Country of Study: United States of America.
No. of awards offered: Varies.
Application Procedure: Applicants must complete an application form.
Closing Date: January 15th.
Additional Information: Projects proposed will be approved in advance by a Smithsonian staff member who will serve as the appointee's advisor. Projects must be related to the research and interest of the Institution's professional staff.

Smithsonian Institution Senior Fellowships

Subjects: Anthropology, biological sciences, American social and cultural history, history of science and technology, history of art, and the history of African art and culture.
Purpose: To offer appointments to senior scholars who wish to pursue research at the Smithsonian Institution. Projects must be related to the research and interests of the Institution's professional staff.

Eligibility: Open to applicants of any nationality who are seven or more years beyond the degree of PhD or equivalent. Projects proposed will be approved in advance by a Smithsonian staff member who will serve as the appointee's advisor. Fluency in English is required.
Level of Study: Postdoctorate.
Type: Fellowship.
Value: US$30,000 per year plus allowances.
Length of Study: 3-12 months.
Frequency: Annual.
Study Establishment: Smithsonian Institution facilities.
Country of Study: United States of America.
No. of awards offered: Varies.
Application Procedure: Applicants must complete an application pack, available from the office or the website.
Closing Date: January 15th.

SMITHSONIAN INSTITUTION - NATIONAL AIR AND SPACE MUSEUM

Room 3313, Washington, DC, 20560-0312, United States of America
Tel: (1) 202 357 2515
Fax: (1) 202 786 2447
Email: collette.williams@nasm.si.edu
www: http://www.nasm.edu/nasm/joinnasm/fellow/fellow.htm
Contact: Ms Collette Williams, Fellowships Coordinator

A Verville Fellowship

Subjects: The history of aviation and space flights.
Purpose: To fund the analysis of major trends, developments and accomplishments in the history of aviation or space studies.
Eligibility: Open to all interested candidates who can demonstrate skills in research and writing. An advanced degree is not a requirement.
Level of Study: Postgraduate.
Type: Fellowship.
Value: Stipend US$45,000 for a one year period with limited additional funds available for travel and miscellaneous expenses.
Length of Study: 9-12 months, normally beginning June 1st-October 1st.
Country of Study: United States of America.
No. of awards offered: One.
Application Procedure: Applicants must submit a summary description, research proposal, bibliography, estimated schedule, research budget, curriculum vitae and letters from three referees. Six copies of the complete application must be submitted. Further information and an application pack are available on request or downloadable from the website.
Closing Date: January 15th.
Additional Information: Residence in the Washington DC, Metropolitan area during the fellowship term is a requirement of this fellowship. Further information is available on the website.

The Guggenheim Fellowships

Subjects: Historical research related to aviation and space.
Purpose: To promote research into, and writing about, the history of aviation and space flight.
Eligibility: Postdoctoral Fellowships are open to applicants who have received the PhD degree or equivalent within seven years of the beginning of the fellowship period. Predoctoral Fellowships are open to applicants who have completed preliminary course and examinations and are engaged in dissertation research. All applicants must be able to speak and write fluently in English.
Level of Study: Postdoctorate, Predoctorate.
Type: Fellowship.
Value: Postdoctoral stipend US$30,000 for one year term and predoctoral stipend US$20,000 for one year term, with limited additional funds available for travel and miscellaneous expenses.

Length of Study: 3-12 months.

Frequency: Annual.

Study Establishment: A major portion of research must be conducted at Smithsonian.

Country of Study: United States of America.

No. of awards offered: Varies.

Application Procedure: Applicants must submit a summary description, research proposal, bibliography, estimated schedule, research budget, transcripts from all graduate institutions, English training with test scores and level of proficiency in reading, conversing and writing, if English is not native language, curriculum vitae and letters from three referees. Six copies of the complete application must be submitted.

Closing Date: January 15th.

Additional Information: Further information is available on the website.

National Air and Space Museum Aviation/Space Writers Award

Subjects: Aerospace topics.

Purpose: To support research leading towards publication.

Eligibility: Applicants for NASM or Smithsonian Fellowships are encouraged to apply for the Aviation/Space Writers Award but recipients of the award need not be in residence at the National Air and Space Museum.

Type: Grant.

Value: US$5,000 to support research travel and expenses, or the publication of research.

Frequency: Every two years.

Country of Study: United States of America.

Application Procedure: Applicants must submit a letter of proposal stating the subject of their research and publication goals not exceeding five pages.

Closing Date: January 15th.

Ramsay Fellowship in Naval Aviation History

Subjects: Aviation history.

Purpose: Focusing on the history of aviation at sea and in naval service, particularly the United States Navy.

Eligibility: Open to all interested candidates who can demonstrate skills in research and writing. An advanced degree is not a requirement.

Level of Study: Postgraduate.

Type: Fellowship.

Value: Stipend US$45,000 will be awarded for a one year fellowship, with additional limited funds available for travel and miscellaneous expenses.

Length of Study: 9-12 months.

Country of Study: United States of America.

No. of awards offered: One.

Application Procedure: Applicants must submit a summary description, research proposal, bibliography, estimated schedule, research budget, curriculum vitae and letters from three referees. Six copies of the complete application must be submitted. Further information and an application pack are available on request or downloadable from the website.

Closing Date: January 15th.

Additional Information: Residence in the Washington DC, Metropolitan area during the fellowship term is a requirement of this fellowship. Further information is available on the website.

SOCIAL SCIENCE RESEARCH COUNCIL (SSRC)

810 Seventh Avenue, New York, NY, 10019, United States of America
Tel: (1) 212 377 2700
Fax: (1) 212 377 2727
Email: info@ssrc.org
www: http://www.ssrc.org
Contact: Ms Elsa Dixler, Publications Director

Founded in 1923, the Social Science Research Council (SSRC) is an independent, non-governmental, non-profit, international association devoted to the advancement of interdisciplinary research in the social sciences. The aim of the organisation is to improve the quality of publicly available knowledge around the world.

ACLS/SSRC/NEH International and Area Studies Fellowships

Subjects: Humanities.

Purpose: To encourage humanistic research in area studies.

Eligibility: Applicants must be United States citizens who must have completed their PhD more than two years prior to application.

Level of Study: Postdoctorate.

Type: Fellowship.

Length of Study: 6-12 months.

Frequency: Annual.

Country of Study: Africa, Asia, the Near and Middle East, Latin America, Eastern Europe, or the former Soviet Union.

No. of awards offered: Eight.

Application Procedure: Applicants must apply for information, available on request from ACLS.

Closing Date: October.

Contributor: The National Endowment for the Humanities.

For further information contact:

ACLS
228 East 45th Street, New York, NY, 10017-3398, United States of America
Fax: (1) 212 949 8058
Email: grants@acls.org

SSRC Abe Fellowship Program

Subjects: Research in the social sciences and humanities relevant to any one or combination of the following themes: global issues, problems common to advanced industrial societies and issues that relate to improving United States-Japanese relations.

Purpose: To develop a new generation of researchers who study policy relevant topics of long range importance and who will become members of bilateral and global research networks. The programme promotes a new level of intellectual co-operation between the Japanese and American academic and professional research communities concerned with, and trained for, advancing global understanding and problem solving.

Eligibility: Open to Japanese and American citizens,and other nationals, who can demonstrate serious and long-term affiliations in Japanese or American research communities. Applicants must hold a PhD or have attained an equivalent level of professional experience as evaluated in their country of residence. Applications from researchers in non academic professions are welcome.

Level of Study: Postdoctorate.

Type: Fellowship.

Value: To include a base award and supplementary research and travel expenses as necessary for completion of the research project.

Length of Study: Up to one year.

Frequency: Annual.

Study Establishment: An appropriate institution.

Country of Study: United States of America or Japan.

Application Procedure: Applicants must submit a reference and a optional language evaluation form.

Closing Date: September 1st.

Funding: Private.
Contributor: The Japan Foundation Center for Global Partnership.
No. of awards given last year: 16.
No. of applicants last year: 84.
Additional Information: In addition to receiving fellowship awards, Fellows will attend annual conferences and other events sponsored by the programme, which will promote the development of an international network of Scholars concerned with research on contemporary policy issues. Funds are provided by the Japan Foundation's Center for Global Partnership.

SSRC Berlin Programme for Advanced German and European Studies

Subjects: The economic, political and social aspects of modern and contemporary German and European affairs.
Purpose: To encourage the comparative and interdisciplinary study by supporting anthropologists, economists, political scientists, sociologists and all scholars in German social science and cultural studies fields, including historians working on the period since the mid nineteenth-century.
Eligibility: Open to citizens and permanent residents of the United States of America and Canada who, at the dissertation level, have completed all requirements, except the dissertation, for the PhD at the time the Fellowship begins, or at the postdoctoral level, have received the PhD or its equivalent in the last two years.
Level of Study: Doctorate, Postdoctorate.
Value: Please contact the organisation.
Length of Study: Nine months to one year.
Frequency: Annual.
Study Establishment: The Free University of Berlin.
Country of Study: Germany.
No. of awards offered: 12.
Application Procedure: Applicants must apply for information, available on request by emailing berlin@ssrc.org.
Closing Date: February 1st.
Funding: Government, Private.
Contributor: The Berlin Government and the German Marshall Fund of the United States of America.
Additional Information: Fellows are expected to produce a research monograph dealing with one or more aspects of German or European affairs, including United States-European relations. The programme is funded by the Berlin government, and the German Marshall Fund of the United States. Applicants must contact the programme for further information.

The SSRC Eurasia Program Dissertation and Postdoctoral Fellowships

Subjects: The humanities and social sciences relating to Eastern Europe, the Soviet Union and its successor states.
Purpose: To provide support to students who have completed research for their doctoral dissertations and expect to complete the writing during the next academic year, and to improve the academic employment and tenure opportunities of new PhDs.
Eligibility: Open to United States citizens who have received their PhDs after 1993 and are untenured. Applicants must have the PhD in hand at the time of application.
Level of Study: Doctorate, Postdoctorate.
Type: Fellowship.
Value: US$15,000 for dissertation fellowships. A stipend of US$24,000 to provide two years of Summer support plus one semester free of teaching for scholars.
Length of Study: Two years.
Frequency: Annual.
Country of Study: Any country in Eastern Europe or the former Soviet Union.
No. of awards offered: Varies.
Application Procedure: Applicants must apply for information, available on request by emailing oneurasia@ssrc.org.
Closing Date: November.
Funding: Government.

The SSRC Eurasia Program Dissertation Fellowships

Subjects: The humanities and social sciences relating to the former Soviet Union and its successor states.
Purpose: To provide support to students who have completed research for their doctoral dissertations and expect to complete the writing of their dissertations during the next academic year.
Eligibility: Open to United States citizens.
Level of Study: Doctorate.
Type: Fellowship.
Value: Up to US$15,000.
Length of Study: Up to one year.
Frequency: Annual.
Country of Study: Any country in Eastern Europe or former Soviet Union.
Application Procedure: Applicants must submit a completed application form, three letters of recommendation, one official copy of all relevant post secondary study, language self evaluation, and a narrative statement.
Closing Date: February 3rd.
Funding: Government.
Additional Information: Applicants must contact the programme for further information by emailing eurasia@ssed.org.

SSRC International Dissertation Field Research Fellowship Program

Subjects: Social sciences or humanities.
Purpose: To provide support for dissertation field research in all areas and regions of the world.
Eligibility: Applicants must have completed all PhD requirements except fieldwork and must provide evidence of language fluency adequate to complete the project.
Level of Study: Doctorate, Postdoctorate.
Type: Fellowship.
Value: Support in the field, plus travel expenses. Awards rarely exceed US$17,000.
Length of Study: 9-12 months.
Frequency: Annual.
Country of Study: Any country except the United States of America.
No. of awards offered: Approx. 50.
Application Procedure: Applicants must complete an application form, available from the SSRC website.
Closing Date: November.
Funding: Private.
Contributor: The Andrew W Mellon Foundation.
Additional Information: Applicants must contact the programme for further information by emailing idfr@ssrc.org.

SSRC International Migration Program Dissertation Fellowships

Subjects: Study of migration to the United States.
Purpose: To foster innovative research that will advance theoretical understandings of voluntary and forced migration to the United States, the process of settlement and outcomes for immigrants, refugees and native born Americans.
Eligibility: Open to United States citizens, permanent residents or international students in PhD programmes in the social sciences, at United States universities.
Level of Study: Doctorate.
Type: Fellowship.
Value: US$12,000 with up to US$3,000 in research expenses.
Length of Study: One year.
Country of Study: United States of America.
No. of awards offered: Seven.
Application Procedure: Applicants must apply for information, available from the website or the International Migration Program.
Closing Date: January.
Additional Information: Applicants must contact the programme for further information by emailing migration@ssrc.org.

SSRC International Migration Program Postdoctoral Fellowships

Subjects: Study of migration to the United States.
Purpose: To foster innovative research that will advance theoretical understandings of voluntary and forced migration to the United States, the process of settlement and outcomes for immigrants, refugees and native born Americans.
Eligibility: Open to United States citizens, permanent residents or international Scholars affiliated with a United States academic or research institution during the time of the award. Applicants must hold a PhD or equivalent in one of the social sciences including history or an allied professional field.
Level of Study: Postdoctorate.
Type: Fellowship.
Value: US$20,000.
Length of Study: Funds may be spent over the period of one year, but the expectation is that awardees will engage in full-time research for at least six months.
Country of Study: United States of America.
No. of awards offered: Five.
Application Procedure: Applicants must apply for information, available on request from the programme.
Closing Date: January.
Funding: Private.
Additional Information: Research should result in publication. Applicants must contact the programme for further information by emailing migration@ssrc.org.

SSRC International Migration Program Summer Dissertation Workshop

Subjects: Arts, humanities, social and behavioural sciences.
Purpose: To offer intensive training to students of minority backgrounds in developing dissertation and funding proposals.
Eligibility: Applicants must be United States citizens or permanent residents who are of African, Latino, Asian, Pacific Island, or native American ancestry. Applicants have to be graduate students who are matriculated in doctoral programmes in the social sciences including history, have taken coursework related to international migration and have developed a preliminary research focus for their dissertation.
Level of Study: Postgraduate.
Length of Study: Three weeks, two in June and one in August.
Frequency: Annual.
No. of awards offered: 10-15.
Application Procedure: Applicants must apply for information, available on request by emailing migration@ssrc.org.
Closing Date: January 10th.
Funding: Private.
Contributor: The Andrew W Mellon Foundation.

The SSRC Japan Program Advanced Research Grants

Subjects: Social sciences or humanities.
Purpose: To encourage innovative research which is comparative and contemporary in nature, and has long-term applied policy implications, or which engages Japan in wider regional and global debates.
Eligibility: Open to holders of a PhD or an equivalent degree who are United States citizens or have been resident in the United States of America for at least three consecutive years at the time of application.
Level of Study: Postdoctorate.
Type: Research grant.
Value: Grants are disbursed in United States dollars and/or yen depending on the location of the research.
Length of Study: 2-12 months.
Frequency: Annual.
Country of Study: Any country.
No. of awards offered: Varies.
Application Procedure: Applicants must email brooks@ssrc.org for further information.

Closing Date: January. Please contact the Research Council for confirmation.
Funding: Private.
Contributor: The Japan-US Friendship Commission.
Additional Information: Special attention will be given to Japanists who are interested in broadening their skills and expertise through additional training or comparative work in an additional geographic area, and to non Japanists who use Japan as a case study or those who draw Japan into wider global debates.

The SSRC Japan Program Dissertation Workshop

Subjects: Dissertation work.
Purpose: To create a network of advanced graduate students and faculty.
Eligibility: Open to full-time advanced graduate students, regardless of citizenship, who are enrolled at United States institutions. Applicants must have an approved dissertation prospectus, but cannot have completed writing for final submission. A narrative description of the dissertation topic and a letter of reference from the student's advisor are required as part of the application.
Level of Study: Doctorate.
Value: In most cases, the SSRC will fully cover participants' travel, lodging and meals for the duration of the workshop.
Frequency: Annual.
Country of Study: Japan.
No. of awards offered: 10-12.
Application Procedure: Applicants must apply for information, available on request by emailing japan@ssrc.org.
Closing Date: October 1st.
Funding: Private.
Contributor: The Japan Foundation.

The SSRC Japan Program JSPS Postdoctoral Fellowship Program

Subjects: Social sciences and humanities.
Purpose: To provide qualified researchers with the opportunity to conduct research with leading universities and other research institutions in Japan.
Eligibility: Open to United States citizens or permanent residents. Applicants will need proof of an affiliation with an eligible host research institution. For one to two years of study, Scholars must have received the PhD no more than six years prior to April 1st of the year for which they are applying. For 3-11 months of study, Scholars must have received the PhD no more than 10 years prior to April 1st of the year for which they are applying.
Level of Study: Postdoctorate.
Type: Fellowship.
Value: Round trip airfare, insurance coverage for accidents and illness, a monthly stipend of yen 270,000, a settling in allowance of yen 200,000, a monthly housing allowance of yen 100,000 and a monthly family allowance of yen 50,000. Applicants will also be eligible for up to an additional yen 1,500,000 annually for research expenses.
Length of Study: One-two years.
Frequency: Annual.
Study Establishment: An approved institution.
Country of Study: Japan.
No. of awards offered: One.
Application Procedure: Applicants must apply for information, available on request by emailing japan@ssrc.org.
Closing Date: December. Please contact the SSRC for the exact date.
Contributor: The Japan Society for the Promotion of Science.

SSRC Latin American Program Research and Training Fellowship on Collective Memory of Repression: Comparative Perspectives on Democratization Processes in Latin America's Southern Core

Subjects: Latin American history and politics.
Purpose: To enable junior researchers based in the Southern Cone of Latin America and PhD candidates at United States universities to

participate in a series of training workshops and to conduct field research on issues related to the collective memory of repression.
Eligibility: Applicants from the Southern Cone eg. Argentina, Brazil, Chile, Paraguay, and Uruguay must have completed the Master's degree or its equivalent and have research experience. Applicants from United States universities must be candidates for the PhD in any discipline of the social sciences or humanities, have completed all requirements for the degree except the dissertation fieldwork in the Southern Cone on a memory related topic.
Level of Study: Doctorate, Postgraduate.
Type: Fellowship.
Value: A minimum of half time support.
Length of Study: One year, including two intensive training workshops.
Country of Study: The Southern Cone of Latin America eg. Argentina, Brazil, Chile, Paraguay, or Uruguay.
No. of awards offered: 15 for applicants from the Southern Cone, and four for United States applicants.
Application Procedure: Applicants must apply for information, available from the relevant page of the SSRC website.
Closing Date: October.
Funding: Private.
Additional Information: Applicants must contact the programme for further information.

SSRC Latin American Program Working Group on Cuba Grant Competition

Subjects: Cuba.
Purpose: To promote academic collaboration between scholars in Cuba and North America. To promote the acquisition and transfer of information among libraries, museums and archives, the dissemination of work by Cuban researchers through the provision of funds to defray costs of publication or translation of scholarly volumes, research projects conducted jointly by scholars at institutions in the United States and Cuba, international travel by Cuban researchers to conferences and travel by North American academics invited by Cuban institutions to present lectures in Cuba.
Eligibility: Open to Scholars in Cuba and the United States.
Level of Study: Postgraduate, Professional development.
Value: Varies. Usually travel grants will not exceed US$2,500 per researcher, grants in support of museums, libraries and archives will not exceed US$5,000, and awards for institutional partnerships will range from US$10,000-15,000.
Length of Study: Varies.
Frequency: Twice a year.
No. of awards offered: Varies.
Application Procedure: Applicants must apply for information, available from the Latin America page on SSRC website.
Closing Date: Varies.
Funding: Private.
No. of awards given last year: 16.
Additional Information: Applicants must contact the programme for further information via email on cuba@ssrc.org.

SSRC Program in Applied Economics Fellowship in Applied Economics

Subjects: Economics.
Purpose: To prepare students to write accomplished and innovative dissertations that address vital and complex economic and social issues.
Eligibility: Open to students of any citizenship or nationality entering the third year of a PhD programme in economics at a United States university. Applicants must have completed coursework and qualifying examinations.
Level of Study: Doctorate, Postgraduate.
Value: US$15,000 and a modest contribution to tuition and health insurance.
Length of Study: One year.
Frequency: Annual.
No. of awards offered: 20-25.
Application Procedure: Applicants must complete an application form, available from the SSRC website.

Closing Date: February.
Funding: Private.
Contributor: The John D and Catherine T MacArthur Foundation.
Additional Information: Applicants must contact the programme for further information via email on pae@ssrc.org.

SSRC Program in Applied Economics Summer Workshop in Applied Economics

Subjects: Economics.
Purpose: To help students develop research skills that build on and extend their training in economic theory and to apply these skills to deepen their theoretical understanding of real world problems.
Eligibility: Open to full-time graduate students enrolled in economics PhD programmes in a United States university. There are no citizenship, residency or nationality requirements. Intended for students after the first year of graduate study, although second year students may also apply.
Level of Study: Postgraduate.
Type: Workshop.
Value: Transportation, room, board and tuition.
Length of Study: One week.
Frequency: Annual.
Country of Study: United States of America.
No. of awards offered: 50.
Application Procedure: Applicants must apply for information, available on request by email on pae@ssrc.org.
Closing Date: March.
Funding: Private.
Additional Information: Modest research grants for students to pursue independent or collaborative research projects based on issues discussed in the workshop are also available.

SSRC Program on Philanthropy and the Nonprofit Sector Fellowships

Subjects: Philanthropy and the non-profit sector. This can include psychology, public policy, political economy, organisational demography and history.
Purpose: To provide greater visibility, coherence and direction to the study of philanthropy and the non-profit sector in the United States through annual fellowship competitions.
Eligibility: There are no citizenship requirements, but applicants must be enrolled in doctoral programmes at United States universities and must have completed all requirements for the PhD including an approved dissertation prospectus except the research component.
Level of Study: Doctorate.
Type: Fellowship.
Value: US$18,000. An additional US$5,000 for dissertation write up may be requested.
Length of Study: Nine months to one year.
Country of Study: United States of America.
No. of awards offered: Seven.
Application Procedure: Applicants must apply for information, available on request from Contact Program on Philanthropy and the Non profit Sector at the main address or from the website.
Closing Date: December.
Additional Information: Fellowship winners will attend a multidisciplinary dissertation workshop. Applicants must contact the programme for further information via email on phil-np@ssrc.org.

SSRC Program on the Arts Dissertation Fellowship

Subjects: Arts.
Purpose: To foster research on the social dimension of art in relation to a number of key issues including globalisation, multiculturalism and new technologies.
Eligibility: Full-time students in the social sciences and other relevant fields enrolled in doctoral programmes in the United States are eligible to apply.
Level of Study: Doctorate.
Type: Fellowship.
Value: US$16,500.

Length of Study: Nine-12 months.
Frequency: Annual.
Country of Study: Any country.
No. of awards offered: 14.
Application Procedure: Applicants must apply to the Program on Arts, all information is on the website.
Closing Date: March.
Funding: Private.
Contributor: The Rockefeller Foundation.
No. of awards given last year: 14.
Additional Information: The programme sponsors workshops for fellowship holders.

SSRC Program on the Corporation as a Social Institution Fellowships

Subjects: Economic sociology, political economy, business history and corporate law.
Purpose: To develop a stronger, conceptually richer and potentially more interdisciplinary approach to the study of firms and other business institutions.
Eligibility: Open to graduate students from all fields conducting research in economic sociology, political economy, business history, corporate law or related fields who must be advanced by PhD candidacy before taking up the Fellowship.
Level of Study: Doctorate.
Type: Fellowship.
Value: US$10,000.
Length of Study: Two years.
Frequency: Annual.
Application Procedure: Applicants must submit an approved dissertation proposal, a two page summary of the project, a budget, and two letters of recommendation to the Program on the Corporation as a Social Institution, Social Science Research Council at the main address.
Closing Date: January.
Contributor: The Alfred P Sloan Foundation.
Additional Information: Students will participate in four workshops over the course of two years with senior Scholars working in sociology, economics, law and business.

SSRC Religion and Immigration Predoctoral Fellowships

Subjects: Religion and immigration to United States.
Purpose: To foster innovative research that will advance theoretical understandings of the relationship between religion and the incorporation of immigrants into American society.
Eligibility: Open to United States citizens, permanent residents or international students who are matriculated in a United States university. Applicants must have approval for their proposed research from their dissertation committees and must have completed all course and examination requirements for the PhD before taking up the Fellowship.
Level of Study: Doctorate, Postgraduate.
Type: Fellowship.
Value: US$20,000.
Length of Study: Six months of full-time research.
Frequency: Annual.
Application Procedure: Applicants must apply for information, available on request by email on religion@ssrc.org.
Closing Date: January.
Funding: Private.
Contributor: Pew Charitable Trusts.
Additional Information: Fellowship winners will meet prior to undertaking the SSRC funded research and to report their findings at a conference once the research is completed. Applicants must contact the programme for further information.

SSRC Sexuality Research Fellowship Program

Subjects: Human sexuality research.
Purpose: To fund social and behavioural research.
Eligibility: There are no citizenship, residency, or nationality requirements. Dissertation students must have completed all

requirements for the PhD, except the dissertation, in a full-time graduate programme leading to the PhD in a social, health or behavioural science department of a nationally accredited United States college or university. Postdoctoral candidates must hold the PhD or its equivalent in a social or behavioural science from a state or nationally accredited university in the United States, or an equivalent PhD degree from an accredited non United States university.
Level of Study: Doctorate, Postdoctorate.
Type: Fellowship.
Value: US$28,000 at doctoral level and US$38,000 at postdoctoral level.
Length of Study: One-two years.
Frequency: Annual.
Country of Study: United States of America.
No. of awards offered: 10 dissertation fellowships and four post-doctoral fellowships.
Application Procedure: Applicants must apply for information, available on request by email on srfp@ssrc.org.
Closing Date: December.
Funding: Private.
Contributor: The Ford Foundation.
No. of awards given last year: 14.
No. of applicants last year: 70.
Additional Information: Women and members of minority groups are especially encouraged to apply. Applicants must contact the programme for further information.

The SSRC South Asia Program Bangladesh Dissertation Fellowships

Subjects: Bangladesh or Bengal related studies.
Purpose: To support PhD candidates' doctoral dissertation field research.
Eligibility: Open to Bangladeshi citizens enrolled in full-time accredited doctoral programmes anywhere outside Bangladesh. Applicants must complete all requirements for the PhD except the dissertation by the Spring after they submit their application.
Level of Study: Doctorate.
Type: Fellowship.
Length of Study: 9-15 months.
Frequency: Annual.
Country of Study: Bangladesh.
Application Procedure: Applicants must write to the Bangladesh Studies Program at the main address for information.
Closing Date: November 1st.
Funding: Private.
Contributor: The Ford Foundation.
Additional Information: Scholars pursuing pan-Bengal research of a comparative nature can divide their research time between Bangladesh and India, but would be expected to spend at least two thirds of their research period in Bangladesh. This programme is funded by the Ford Foundation. Applicants must contact the programme for further information via email on s-asia@ssrc.org.

The SSRC South Asia Program Bangladesh Predissertation Fellowships

Subjects: Bangladesh or Bengal related studies.
Purpose: To support short-term field trips to Bangladesh designed for preliminary dissertation field activities, such as investigating potential research sites, archival and other research materials, development of language skills and establishing local research contacts.
Eligibility: Open to students of any nationality who, at the time of application, have completed at least one year of graduate study in a programme leading to a PhD in the social sciences or humanities at a North American university.
Level of Study: Doctorate.
Type: Fellowship.
Value: US$5,200.
Length of Study: Three-four months.
Frequency: Annual.
Country of Study: Bangladesh.
Application Procedure: Applicants must apply for information, available on request by email on s-asia@ssrc.org.

Closing Date: December 1st.
Funding: Private.
Contributor: The Ford Foundation.
Additional Information: Applicants must contact the programme for further information (email: s-asia@ssrc.org).

The SSRC Southeast Asia Program Vietnam Dissertation Field Research Fellowships

Subjects: Doctoral dissertation research in the social sciences and humanities in Vietnam.
Purpose: To help fund doctoral dissertation research.
Eligibility: Graduate students enrolled full-time in PhD programmes in any of the social sciences or humanities at accredited universities in the United States or Canada are eligible. Awards are subject to proof of completion of all departmental requirements other than the dissertation. There are no citizenship restrictions.
Level of Study: Doctorate.
Type: Fellowship.
Value: Up to US$15,000.
Length of Study: One-two years.
Frequency: Annual.
Country of Study: Vietnam.
Application Procedure: Applicants must email lam@ssrc.org for further information.
Closing Date: Please write for details.
Funding: Private.
Contributor: The Ford Foundation.

The SSRC/ACLS Eastern European Program Dissertation Fellowships

Subjects: The social sciences and humanities relating to Albania, Bulgaria, the Baltic States, the Czech Republic, Hungary, Poland, Romania, Slovakia or the former Yugoslavia.
Purpose: To fund dissertation research.
Eligibility: Open to United States citizens or permanent legal residents.
Level of Study: Postgraduate.
Type: Varies.
Value: Up to US$15,000 plus expenses.
Length of Study: One academic year.
Frequency: Annual, if funds are available.
Study Establishment: Any university or institution.
Country of Study: Outside Eastern Europe.
Application Procedure: Applicants must contact the American Council of Learned Societies (ACLS) for further information.
Closing Date: November.
Additional Information: The product of the proposed work must be disseminated in English.

For further information contact:

ACLS
Office of Fellowships & Grants
228 East 45th Street, New York, NY, 10017, United States of America
Email: grants@acls.org

The SSRC/ACLS Eastern European Program Fellowships for Postdoctoral Research

Subjects: The social sciences and humanities relating to Albania, Bulgaria, the Baltic States, the Czech Republic, Hungary, Poland, Romania, Slovakia or the former Yugoslavia.
Purpose: To provide free time for research.
Eligibility: Applicants must be United States citizens or permanent legal residents and hold a PhD or its equivalent as of the application deadline.
Level of Study: Doctorate, Postdoctorate.
Type: Fellowship.
Value: Up to US$25,000. The funds may be used to supplement sabbatical salaries or awards from other sources, provided they would intensify or extend the contemplated research.
Length of Study: Six months-one year.

Frequency: Annual.
Country of Study: Albania, Bulgaria, the Baltic States, Czech Republic, Hungary, Poland, Romania, Slovakia or the former Yugoslavia. For research undertaken outside Eastern Europe.
Application Procedure: Applicants must contact the American Council of Learned Societies (ACLS) for information.
Closing Date: November.
Additional Information: The product of the proposed work must be disseminated in English.

For further information contact:

ACLS
Office of Fellowships & Grants 228 East 45th Street, New York, NY, 10017, United States of America
Email: grants@acls.org

SOCIAL SCIENCES AND HUMANITIES RESEARCH COUNCIL OF CANADA (SSHRC)

350 Albert Street
PO Box 1610, Ottawa, ON, K1P 6G4, Canada
Tel: (1) 613 992 0691
Fax: (1) 613 992 1787
Email: info@sshrc.ca
www: http://www.sshrc.ca
Contact: Mr Joel Tatelman, English Editor

The Social Sciences and Humanities Research Council of Canada (SSHRC) is a federal agency responsible for promoting and supporting research and research training in the social sciences and humanities in Canada. SSHRC support research on the economic, political, social and cultural dimensions of human activity.

The Bora Laskin National Fellowship in Human Rights Research

Subjects: Human rights, as relevant to Canada.
Purpose: To support research, preferably of a multidisciplinary or interdisciplinary nature, and to develop Canadian expertise in the field of human rights, with an emphasis on themes and issues relevant to the Canadian human rights scene.
Eligibility: Open to Canadian citizens or permanent residents of Canada. Preference will be given to applicants with at least five years of proven research experience in their field, as this Fellowship is not intended for Scholars just beginning their research careers.
Level of Study: Postdoctorate, Research.
Type: Fellowship.
Value: Canadian $45,000, plus a research and travel allowance of canadian $10,000.
Length of Study: One year, non renewable.
Frequency: Annual.
Country of Study: Canada but travel abroad will be permitted for research purposes.
No. of awards offered: One.
Application Procedure: Applicants must complete an application form, available from the website.
Closing Date: October 1st.
Funding: Government.

Canada Tobacco Research Initiative Fellowship Doctoral Fellowship Supplements

Subjects: Controlling the health threats caused by tobacco.
Purpose: To supplement the awards of SSHRC doctoral fellowship holders.
Eligibility: Open to SSHRC doctoral Fellows entering their third or fourth year of studies who are conducting research on tobacco control.
Level of Study: Doctorate.
Type: Supplement.

Value: Canadian $5,000 per year.
Length of Study: Up to two years.
Frequency: Annual.
Country of Study: Canada.
Application Procedure: Applicants must visit the website. Candidates should contact Jacques Critchley on jacques.critchley@sshrc.ca to indicate their interest and desire to be considered.
Closing Date: Please consult the organisation.

Canada Tobacco Research Initiative Postdoctoral Fellowship Supplements

Subjects: Controlling the health threats caused by tobacco.
Purpose: To supplement the awards of SSHRC postdoctoral fellowship holders who are conducting research relevant to the Canadian Tobacco Control Research Initiative programme.
Eligibility: Applicants must be SSHRC postdoctoral Fellows conducting research on tobacco control.
Level of Study: Postdoctorate.
Type: Supplement.
Value: Canadian $10,000 per year.
Length of Study: Up to two years.
Frequency: Annual.
Country of Study: Canada.
Application Procedure: Applicants must visit the website or contact Jacques Critchley on jacques.critchley@sshrc.ca.
Closing Date: Please consult the organisation.
Funding: Government.

Canadian Forest Service Graduate Supplements

Subjects: Forestry and related fields.
Purpose: To promote Canadian doctoral research into forestry, to encourage the use of Canadian Forest Service (CFS) centres and to increase contacts between CFS researchers and Canadian universities.
Eligibility: Open to SSHRC doctoral Fellows who are conducting research in an area related to forestry in Canada and who are in the third or fourth year of their programme. Candidates must have at least one CFS scientist on their supervisory committee and must carry out all or part of their research at a CFS forestry centre.
Level of Study: Doctorate, Research.
Type: Graduate supplements.
Value: Canadian $5,000 supplement to the canadian $17,700 doctoral fellowship.
Length of Study: Up to two years.
Frequency: Annual.
No. of awards offered: Five.
Application Procedure: Applicants must visit the website.
Closing Date: Interested doctoral students should contact their department for the SSHRC Doctoral Fellowship application deadline.
Contributor: The Canadian Forest Service.

For further information contact:

Program Co-ordinator
Canadian Forest Service Graduate Supplements
Science Branch
Natural Resources Canada
580 Booth Street, Ottawa, ON, K1A 0E4, Canada
Tel: (1) 613 947 8992
Fax: (1) 613 947 9090
Email: mlamarch@nrcan.gc.ca

Canadian Tobacco Control Research Initiative Planning Grants

Subjects: Tobacco control policies and practices from the perspectives of the social sciences, humanities, education and health.
Purpose: To support investigators in developing strong proposals for grants in tobacco control research.
Eligibility: Experts in programme and policy development as well as researchers may apply. Teams must include both researchers and policy or programme specialists.

Level of Study: Research.
Type: Grant.
Value: Up to canadian $30,000.
Length of Study: Up to one year.
Frequency: Dependent on funds available.
Country of Study: Canada.
Application Procedure: Applicants must complete an application form available with instructions on the National Cancer Institute of Canada website http://www.ncic.cancer.ca.
Closing Date: March 1st.
Funding: Government, Private.
No. of awards given last year: Six.

For further information contact:

Research Programs Department
National Cancer Institute of Canada (NCIC)
10 Alcorn Avenue, Suite 200, Toronto, ON, M4V 3B1, Canada
Tel: (1) 416 961 7223
Email: mwosnick@cancer.ca

Canadian Tobacco Control Research Initiative: Best Practices in Tobacco Control Grants

Subjects: Public health, policy and intervention.
Purpose: To allow researchers and research teams to identify interventions that are likely to reduce tobacco use in China.
Eligibility: One investigator must be named as the principal applicant. This applicant need not be affiliated with a university, but must identify an organisation as the administrative agent for the grant. This organisation must be able to demonstrate an ability to administer funds awarded. This is normally determined by a review of the financial statements provided by the organisation.
Level of Study: Research.
Type: Grant.
Value: Up to canadian $65,000.
Length of Study: One year.
Frequency: Annual.
Application Procedure: Applicants must contact the Canadian Tobacco Control Research Initiative in the Strategic Programmes and Joint Initiatives Division at the main address. All applications will be adjudicated by a peer review committee comprising academics, policy analysts and policy makers who have demonstrated expertise in the field of tobacco-related public policy and programmes. Further information is available on the website or by emailing Jacques Critchley, Senior Program Officer on jacques.critchley@sshrc.ca.
Closing Date: Please contact the organisation.
Funding: Government, Private.
Contributor: The SSHRC and the National Cancer Institute of Canada.
Additional Information: At the end of the grant researchers are expected to provide CTCRI with a set of concrete recommendations ready for dissemination to target audiences. Recommendations must be based on currently available evidence and experience, and should be compelling, timely and relevant to the tobacco control community at large. These recommendations are the primary focus of this initiative. Researchers must prepare a short report for the CTCRI, which will oversee the dissemination. Recommendations for research to address gaps in current knowledge are also required. This may include general and specific topics or questions, as well as suggestions for appropriate investigative methods or funding mechanisms. Researchers should prepare these recommendations for dissemination and present them to the CTCRI, which will share them with the tobacco research community. Researchers must provide feedback on uses of the best practices process itself. Finally, researchers must submit to the CTCRI a short report describing their experience of using the model, including any suggestions for its improvement.

Canadian Tobacco Control Research Initiative: Policy Research Grants

Subjects: Tobacco reduction policy research that aims to understand, stimulate, inform, support, direct and/or evaluate policy making that will contribute to the reduction of tobacco use in Canada.

Purpose: To allow researchers to analyse public policy issues relevant to tobacco control.

Eligibility: Applicants should see the website for eligibility requirements.

Level of Study: Research.

Type: Grant.

Value: A maximum of canadian $50,000 for up to three years or a maximum of canadian $25,000 for one year.

Length of Study: Up to three years for annual competitive cycle grants and one year for fast track grants.

Frequency: Annual.

Application Procedure: Applicants must visit the website.

Closing Date: April 30th for annual competitive cycle grants and all year round for fast track grants.

Additional Information: Candidates should contact Jacques Critchley on jacques.critchley@sshrc.ca for further details.

Federalism and Federations Program Research Grants

Subjects: Federalism in Canada and public policy Canadian federalism including intergovernmental processes, globalisation and multi-level governance processes.

Purpose: To support research that will enhance understanding of Canadian federalism by drawing on a scholarship that documents and analyses developments in both domestic and comparative contexts.

Eligibility: Applicants must meet the eligibility criteria of SSHRC's standard Research Grants Program and propose research on federalism and federations that meets the overall objectives of the Program.

Level of Study: Research.

Type: Grant.

Value: Up to canadian $20,000 annually.

Length of Study: Up to two years.

Frequency: Annual.

Country of Study: Canada.

Application Procedure: Applicants must obtain application forms and instructions from the website. For further information contact Luc Lebrun, Program Officer at the Strategic Programs and Joint Initiatives Division, Federalism and Federations Program at the normal address, or telephone (1) 613 947 9652, fax (1) 613 947 0223 or via email on federations@sshrc.ca.

Closing Date: Varies. Please visit the website for dates.

Funding: Government.

Federalism and Federations Program: New Patterns of Interactions, Interests and Community Component Research Grants

Subjects: Humanities and social sciences.

Purpose: To support research that will enrich the understanding of internal and external linkages, interactions and contacts among individuals and groups in and between Canada and other federations.

Eligibility: Applicants must meet the eligibility criteria for SSHRC's Standard Research Grants Program and propose research that meets the overall objectives of the Federations Program. See the website for more details.

Level of Study: Research.

Type: Grant.

Value: Up to canadian $20,000 annually.

Length of Study: Two years.

Frequency: Annual.

Country of Study: Canada.

Application Procedure: Applicants must obtain an application form and instructions from the SSHRC website. For further information contact Luc Lebrun, Program Officer at the Strategic Programs and Joint Initiatives Division, Federalism and Federations Program at the normal address, or on telephone (1) 613 947 9652, fax (1) 613 947 0223 or via email on federations@sshrc.ca.

Closing Date: January-February. Please visit the website for exact dates.

Funding: Government.

INE Collaborative Research Initiatives

Subjects: Research and research training in general issues, management and entrepreneurship, education and lifelong learning as they apply to the knowledge based economy.

Purpose: To support collaborative research initiatives that bring together critical masses of research talent on complex new economy issues that require both breadth and depth of perspective.

Eligibility: Applications must be submitted by a team of at least two researchers led by a project director who meets all eligibility requirements for a principal investigator, as set out in the SSHRC Grants Guide and also elsewhere. Researchers may be from Canadian post secondary institutions, eligible non academic sectors or both. The teams may include co-applicants and collaborators who may be of any nationality.

Level of Study: Research.

Type: Grant.

Value: Up to canadian $3 million over the four years.

Length of Study: Up to four years.

Frequency: Annual.

Country of Study: Canada.

Application Procedure: Applicants must appreciate that this is a two stage process where a letter of intent must be sent and then, by invitation only, a formal application. Please visit the website for details.

Closing Date: The letter of intent is due by November 8th and formal application by July 14th.

Funding: Government.

Additional Information: For further information contact Jo Ann Levesque, Program Officer on (1) 613 996 6972 or at joann.levesque@sshrc.ca.

Initiative on the New Economy: INE Research Alliances

Subjects: General new economy issues, management and entrepreneurship, education or lifelong learning.

Purpose: To encourage research partnerships between academic institutions and Canadian community organisations, that will undertake diverse programmes of research, focusing on new economy themes of mutual importance.

Eligibility: Applications must be submitted by one or more universities and one or more community organisations such as NGOs, community groups, labour unions, businesses, voluntary organisations, industry organisations, think tanks and local or provincial governments. Principal applicants must be Canadian but co-applicants and collaborators may be of any nationality.

Level of Study: Research.

Type: Grant.

Value: Maximum of canadian $300,000 per year.

Length of Study: Up to three years.

Frequency: Annual.

Country of Study: Canada.

Application Procedure: Applicants must appreciate that this is a two stage application which consists of a letter of intent, and by invitation only, a formal application. Visit the website for more details.

Closing Date: The letter of intent is due by 6th December and a formal application by 4th August.

Funding: Government.

Additional Information: For further details contact Allen Middleborough, Programme Officer on (1) 613 992 5353 or at allen.middlebro@sshrc.ca.

Initiative on the New Economy: INE Research Grants

Subjects: The four research theme areas are general issues, management and entrepreneurship, education and lifelong learning as they apply to the new or knowledge based economy.

Purpose: To support research projects relevant to the Initiative on the new economy.

Eligibility: Open to researchers affiliated with post secondary institutions and those from the non-profit sector provided that they meet all academic requirements and that their institutions meet certain criteria. Applicants must be citizens or permanent residents of Canada and be affiliated with a suitable Canadian institution. Co-applicants and collaborators may be of any nationality.

Level of Study: Research.
Type: Grant.
Value: Maximum canadian $100,000 per year.
Length of Study: Up to three years.
Frequency: Annual.
Country of Study: Canada.
Application Procedure: Applicants must complete a web based application form. Applicants must refer to the website for forms and further instructions.
Closing Date: October 15th.
Funding: Government.
Additional Information: For further information applicants can contact Yves Mougeot, Director of Research and Dissemination Grants Programs on (1) 613 992 3145 or via email on yves.mougeot@sshrc.ca.

The Jules and Gabrielle Léger Fellowship

Subjects: The Crown and Governor General in a parliamentary democracy.
Purpose: To encourage research and writing on the historical and contemporary contribution of the Crown and its representatives, federal and provincial, to the political, constitutional, cultural, intellectual and social life of the country, including comparisons between Canadian and Commonwealth systems.
Eligibility: Applicants must be Canadian citizens or permanent residents of Canada, have proven experience in the proposed field of research and not be under SSHRC sanction for financial or research misconduct.
Level of Study: Postdoctorate, Research.
Type: Fellowship.
Value: Canadian $40,000, plus canadian $10,000 for research and travel costs.
Length of Study: One year, non renewable.
Frequency: Every two years.
Study Establishment: A recognised university or research institute.
Country of Study: Any country.
No. of awards offered: One.
Application Procedure: Applicants must write for details.
Closing Date: October 1st.
Funding: Government.

Queen's Fellowships

Subjects: Canadian studies.
Purpose: To assist a candidate who intends to enter a doctoral programme in the relevant field.
Eligibility: Open to Canadian citizens and permanent residents who, by the time of taking up the Fellowship, will have completed one year of graduate study or all the requirements for the Master's degree beyond the honours BA or its equivalent, and will be registered in a programme of studies leading to the PhD or its equivalent. This award is offered to one or two outstanding successful doctoral fellowship candidates.
Level of Study: Doctorate.
Type: Fellowship.
Value: Tuition fees and travel to the main place of tenure and travel for research purposes.
Length of Study: One year, non renewable.
Frequency: Annual.
Study Establishment: A recognised university.
Country of Study: Canada.
No. of awards offered: One-two.
Application Procedure: Applicants cannot apply for this award but are automatically eligible if they intend to study Canadian studies at a Canadian university.The Queen's Fellowship is not a programme but a special award given to a doctoral Fellow.
Funding: Government.
Additional Information: Further information is available on the website.

SSHRC Aid to Occasional Research Conferences and International Congresses in Canada

Subjects: Arts and humanities and social sciences.
Purpose: To encourage and facilitate the communication of research, within and between disciplines, among Canadian researchers, international experts and foreign researchers through occasional regional and national conferences and workshops, as well as through congresses of major international scholarly associations held in Canada.
Eligibility: For applicants to be eligible they must be either Canadian citizens or permanent residents of Canada at the time of application, be researchers in the social sciences or humanities, be members of the conference's or congress' organising committee. Applicants for congress grants must also be members in good standing of the international scholarly association in question, be affiliated with a Canadian university that agrees to administer the grant and not be under SSHRC sanction for financial or research misconduct. For a conference to be eligible, it must take place after the date specified for SSHRC's announcement of competition results, have a defined theme and be devoted to scholarly research issues in the social sciences or humanities, be held in Canada or at a Canadian academic institution abroad, not be receiving support for the same activity under another SSHRC programme, and not be an association's annual general meeting. Please note that a conference that is held by an association and that coincides with that association's annual general meeting is eligible only if the organisers can demonstrate that the conference is a distinct, independent and self-contained event, and that it will address an audience different from, or broader than, that of the annual general meeting. For a congress to be eligible, it must be sponsored by an international scholarly association that has as its main objective the furthering of advanced scholarly research in a discipline of the social sciences or the humanities, and that shows evidence of a membership with broad international representation eg. a minimum of three countries, take place in Canada after the date specified for SSHRC's announcement of competition results, include a fully constituted business meeting of its members, and have a defined research theme in areas within the association's purview.
Type: Grant.
Value: The maximum value and period of tenure of a grant is canadian $10,000 for a conference held within the 12 months following the announcement of results and canadian $50,000 for a congress held within three years following the announcement of results. The actual amount of the grant depends on the merit of the application, the financial need and the appropriateness of the proposed budget.
Length of Study: One year.
Frequency: Twice a year.
Country of Study: Canada.
Application Procedure: Applicants must consult the organisation or visit the website.
Closing Date: May 1st or November 1st.
Funding: Government.

SSHRC Aid to Research and Transfer Journals

Subjects: Social sciences and humanities.
Purpose: To assist in the effective dissemination of original research findings and in the transfer of knowledge to practitioners. The programme offers two types of grants: General Grants, to help defray part of the costs related to the production of a journal, and Special Initiative Grants, to assist with the establishment of electronic publishing or other initiatives or improvements, and to defray the costs of initiatives of exceptional quality and interest.
Eligibility: Applicants must be either Canadian citizens or permanent residents of Canada at the time of application and be established researchers in the social sciences or in the humanities. They must also be a member of the sponsoring institution or organisation and not be under SSHRC sanction for financial or research misconduct. A research or transfer journal must have as its main objective the publishing of the results of advanced research and scholarly work by specialists for a readership of specialists or practitioners, normally appear at least twice a year and have published a minimum of four issues in the last two years prior to the application deadline,

and have as its primary focus a discipline or disciplines within SSHRC's mandate. The journal must also have a subscription level over 200, be in either English or French and be sponsored, edited and published in Canada, by a Canadian institution or a Canadian association.

Type: Grant.

Value: The maximum value of a General Grant is canadian $30,000 per year or canadian $90,000 over three years, and the maximum value of a Special Initiative Grant is canadian $10,000.

Frequency: Every three years.

Country of Study: Canada.

Application Procedure: Applicants must make the case for the funding requested.

Closing Date: June 30th.

Funding: Government.

Additional Information: Further information is available on the website.

SSHRC Aid to Scholarly Publications

Subjects: Social sciences or humanities.

Purpose: To promote the sharing of research results by assisting the publication of individual works that make an important contribution to the advancement of knowledge.

Eligibility: Candidates must see the website for eligibility requirements.

Type: Grant.

Application Procedure: Applicants must refer to the website or email the Federation on secaspp@hssfc.ca. Applicants may apply at any time.

Additional Information: The programme is administered on behalf of the SSHRC by the Humanities and Social Sciences Federation of Canada (HSSFC). Detailed information concerning application requirements, eligibility, value etc. can be obtained by contacting them.

For further information contact:

The Humanities & Social Sciences Federation of Canada (HSSFC)
151 Slater Street
Ottawa, ON, K1P 5H3, Canada
Tel: (1) 613 238 6112 ext. 350
Email: secaspp@aspp.hssfc.ca
www: http://www.hssfc.ca/aspp/homee.htm

SSHRC Aid to Small Universities

Subjects: Arts, humanities or social sciences.

Purpose: To promote the focused development of social sciences and humanities research capacity in small universities by encouraging them to critically assess their most promising potential areas for research concentration, develop effective strategies for strengthening their research capabilities in these areas and to develop ongoing focal points or research centres where appropriate.

Eligibility: Institutions must have active degree granting status for social sciences and humanities disciplines at the graduate level or beyond, be an institutional member of the Association of Universities and Colleges of Canada (AUCC), or member of the AUCC and be affiliated with an institution itself too large to be eligible for the ASU Program. They must also operate in an official language other than that of the larger parent institution, have fewer than 250 full-time faculty in SSHRC fields and be independent of the federal government for the purpose of faculty employment status.

Type: Grant.

Value: Determined using a formula based on the number of full-time social sciences and humanities faculty at the institution. Usually up to canadian $30,000 for three years.

Length of Study: Three years.

Frequency: Every three years.

Country of Study: Canada.

Application Procedure: Applicants must consult the organisation or see the website.

Closing Date: December.

Funding: Government.

SSHRC Doctoral Fellowships

Subjects: Social sciences or humanities.

Purpose: To develop research skills and to assist in the training of highly qualified academic personnel by supporting students who demonstrate a high standard of scholarly achievement.

Eligibility: Applicants must be Canadian citizens or permanent residents living in Canada at the time of application, and must not be under SSHRC sanction resulting from financial or research misconduct, or have already received SSHRC, NSERC, or MRC (now CIHR) funding to undertake or complete a previous doctoral degree. At the time of taking up the award applicants must have completed either a Master's degree or at least one year of doctoral study, and be pursuing either full-time studies leading to a PhD, or equivalent, with the intention of pursuing an academic career. Candidates wishing to study at a foreign university may only do so if one of their previous degrees was earned in Canada.

Level of Study: Doctorate.

Type: Fellowship.

Value: Canadian $17,700 per year, up to and including the fourth year of doctoral study.

Length of Study: 6-48 months.

Frequency: Annual.

Study Establishment: Recognised universities.

Country of Study: Canada, or abroad under certain conditions.

No. of awards offered: Varies.

Application Procedure: Applicants must complete an application form.

Closing Date: Completed application forms must be mailed to the Council by November 15th for applicants not registered at a Canadian university and by January 15th for applicants registered at Canadian universities.

Funding: Government.

No. of awards given last year: 572.

No. of applicants last year: 1,521.

SSHRC Institutional Grants

Subjects: Social sciences or humanities.

Purpose: To help universities develop and maintain a solid base of research and research-related activities.

Eligibility: Open to Canadian post secondary institutions.

Level of Study: Postgraduate.

Type: Research grant.

Value: Varies, calculated on the number of faculty in each university. Universities may award not more than canadian $5,000 to individual researchers to help cover small research expenses, cost of travel to conferences and other similar costs. SSHRC guarantees a minimum annual grant of canadian $2,000.

Length of Study: Three years.

Frequency: Every three years.

Country of Study: Canada.

No. of awards offered: Varies.

Application Procedure: Applicants must complete an application form, available from the website.

Closing Date: December 1st.

Funding: Government.

Additional Information: Further information is available on the website.

SSHRC Major Collaborative Research Initiatives (MCRI)

Subjects: Arts, humanities or social sciences.

Purpose: To strengthen Canadian research capacity by promoting high quality, innovative, collaborative research and unique student training opportunities in a collaborative research environment.

Eligibility: The programme is intended for leading scholars with a solid track record and past experience in collaborative research, student training and grant management. Please consult the organisation for criteria.

Level of Study: Research.

Type: Grant.

Value: Up to canadian $500,000 per year with a minimum budget of canadian $100,000 per year. A canadian $5,000 development fund will also be offered to assist the research team's planning and preparation for its formal application.

Length of Study: Five years.

Frequency: Annual.

Application Procedure: Applications must be submitted by the Project Director on behalf of the research team. There is a two stage application process, the first being a letter of intent, followed by a formal application. For further information contact Pierrette Tremblay, Research Grants Co-ordinator on (1) 613 996 2994, at the organisation address or at pierrette.tremblay@sshrc.ca.

Closing Date: January 31st for the first stage and September 1st for the second.

Funding: Government.

Additional Information: Further information is available on the website.

SSHRC Postdoctoral Fellowships

Subjects: Social sciences or humanities.

Purpose: To support the most promising new scholars and to assist them in establishing a research base at an important time in their research career.

Eligibility: Applicants must be Canadian citizens or permanent residents living in Canada at the time of application. They must also be able to demonstrate skill in research, not be under SSHRC sanction resulting from financial or research misconduct and have earned their doctorate from a recognised university no more than 36 months prior to the competition deadline or have completed their degree within six years prior to the competition deadline but have had their career interrupted or delayed for the purpose of childrearing. Candidates must also have finalised arrangements for affiliation with a university or a research institution and have applied only once before for a postdoctoral fellowship. At the time of taking up the award, applicants must have completed all requirements for the doctoral degree, must intend to engage in full-time postdoctoral research and not hold a tenure or tenure track position.

Level of Study: Postdoctorate.

Type: Fellowship.

Value: Up to canadian $35,028, plus a research allowance of up to canadian $5,000.

Length of Study: A minimum of 12 months and a maximum of 24 months.

Frequency: Annual.

Study Establishment: There is no restriction on the location of tenure, but fellowships will normally be awarded to candidates affiliated with a university other than that which awarded the PhD.

Country of Study: Any country, under certain conditions.

No. of awards offered: Approx. 100.

Application Procedure: Applicants must complete an application form.

Closing Date: October 1st.

Funding: Government.

No. of awards given last year: 100.

No. of applicants last year: 380.

Additional Information: Applicants wishing to hold their award at a foreign university may do so only if their PhD was earned at a Canadian university.

SSHRC Relationships in Transition

Subjects: Public policy issues relating to law reform.

Purpose: To support the writing of research papers.

Eligibility: Participants must meet SSHRC's general eligibility criteria as detailed in the SSHRC Grants Guide, available from the organisation.

Level of Study: Research.

Type: Grant.

Value: Average canadian $25,000, but up to canadian $40,000 per paper.

Length of Study: One year.

Frequency: Annual.

No. of awards offered: Varies.

Application Procedure: Applications must consist of a research proposal and a budget proposal. Applicants must visit the website for further details.

Closing Date: Please contact the organisation.

Additional Information: Each year the focus is on one of the following four themes of economic relationships, personal relationships, social relationships and governance relationships. Successful candidates will be invited to present their papers at a conference held in the Spring. Further information is available on the website.

SSHRC Research Development Initiatives

Subjects: Humanities, the social and cognitive sciences or the educational sciences.

Purpose: To support research that defines new conceptual and methodological perspectives and challenges. Research should define new priorities to be taken into account when conducting research, disseminating research results or training new researchers. The programme supports research that both addresses and elicits the changing directions of research and the evolution of the relevant disciplines.

Eligibility: Candidates should see the website for eligibility requirements.

Level of Study: Research.

Value: Maximum of canadian $50,000 per year.

Length of Study: Three years.

Frequency: Annual.

Application Procedure: Applicants must visit the website for further details as there are two parts to the application process, a form and a project description. Applications must be addressed to the Strategic Programmes and Joint Initiatives Division at the main address or emailed to collaborative@sshrc.ca.

Closing Date: February 28th, July 15th or October 31st.

Funding: Government.

Additional Information: Further information is available on the website.

SSHRC Standard Research Grants

Subjects: Social sciences or humanities.

Purpose: To support research and develop excellence in research activities.

Eligibility: Open to career Scholars who are Canadian citizens or permanent residents of Canada affiliated with a Canadian university or a recognised post secondary institution.

Level of Study: Research.

Type: Research grant.

Value: Up to a maximum of canadian $100,000 per year but not totalling more than canadian $250,000 over a three year period. A minimum of canadian $5,000 in at least one of the years is required unless the applicant is at an institution not receiving a General Research Grant.

Length of Study: Grants in support of research programmes will ordinarily be expected to cover three year periods.

Frequency: Annual.

Study Establishment: An approved institution.

Country of Study: Any country.

No. of awards offered: Varies.

Application Procedure: Applicants must complete an application form which are available on request.

Closing Date: October 15th.

Funding: Government.

SSHRC Strategic Research Grants

Subjects: Social sciences and humanities.

Purpose: To support research and research related activities in areas of national importance.

Eligibility: Applicants should visit the website for requirements.

Level of Study: Research.

Type: Grant.

Country of Study: Canada.

SSHRC Valuing Literacy in Canada Doctoral and Postdoctoral Fellowship Supplements

Subjects: Literacy education.
Purpose: To aid SSHRC postdoctoral fellows conducting research on adult literacy, workplace literacy or family literacy.
Eligibility: Applicants must be SSHRC doctoral or postdoctoral Fellows and therefore have satisfied their eligibility criteria.
Level of Study: Postdoctorate.
Type: Supplement.
Value: Canadian $5,000, supplementary to the regular fellowship award.
Length of Study: Up to two years.
Frequency: Annual.
No. of awards offered: Five.
Application Procedure: Applicants must indicate their interest in this supplement on their initial application form for SSHRC's Postdoctoral Fellowships.
Closing Date: Please contact the organisation.

SSHRC Valuing Literacy in Canada Strategic Partnership Development Grants

Subjects: Literacy education.
Purpose: To allow researchers to seek and develop potential partnerships for research activities relating to adult literacy.
Eligibility: Please see the website of the SSHRC Grants Guide.
Level of Study: Research.
Type: Grant.
Value: Up to canadian $5,000.
Length of Study: One year.
Country of Study: Canada.
Application Procedure: Applicants must submit a letter of intent.
Closing Date: Applications may be submitted at any time.
Additional Information: Results are announced within four months of the submission date.

SSHRC Valuing Literacy in Canada Strategic Research Grants

Subjects: Applicants may submit proposals on a wide range of research topics, including research on existing literacy programmes.
Purpose: To stimulate research into key areas in the field of adult literacy, develop research capacity in Canada in the field of adult literacy, to encourage and assist co-operation between researchers and adult literacy practitioners, to improve the dissemination and application of research results, to encourage the training of future researchers in the field of adult literacy, to stimulate collaboration among researchers from different disciplines and to stimulate research that will influence and guide policy decisions in literacy or that will have a direct impact on policy decisions.
Eligibility: All proposals must involve significant collaboration between at least one researcher affiliated with a Canadian post secondary institution and at least one literacy organisation or practitioner. Proposals for programme development and programme start up are not eligible. Participants must meet the specific eligibility criteria provided in the definitions section of the SSHRC Grants Guide, which is available from the website. In addition, proposals must focus on adult literacy only.
Level of Study: Research.
Type: Grant.
Value: Maximum of canadian $50,000 each year.
Length of Study: Three years.
Frequency: Annual.
Country of Study: Canada.
Application Procedure: Applicants must use the web based application or the form-fillable PDF. A partnership agreement form must be appended to the application. This form should outline the objectives of the partnership and the roles and responsibilities of each partner.
Closing Date: November 21st.
Additional Information: Further information is available on the website or in the SSHRC Grants Guide.

SSHRC Virtual Scholar in Residence Program

Subjects: The area of study varies from year to year.
Purpose: To allow an individual to work with the Law Commission of Canada (LCC) to advance research in a particular area.
Eligibility: The LCC invites applications from researchers affiliated to a Canadian post secondary educational institution.
Level of Study: Research.
Type: Research grant.
Value: A maximum of canadian $50,000 to cover a period of intensive research with the LCC. Financial details regarding this grant will be negotiated between the LCC, SSHRC and the successful applicant's institution following the second stage of the competition. In addition the Commission will also provide up to canadian $10,000 for research expenses.
Length of Study: Six months.
Frequency: Annual.
No. of awards offered: One.
Application Procedure: Applicants must visit the website for application details.
Closing Date: January 2nd.

Thérèse F Casgrain Fellowship

Subjects: Research into Canadian women and social change.
Purpose: To carry out research in the field of social justice, particularly in defence of individual rights and the promotion of the economic and social interests of Canadian women.
Eligibility: Applicants must be Canadian citizens or permanent residents. At the time of taking up the Fellowship, the successful candidate must have obtained a doctorate or an equivalent advanced professional degree, as well as have proven research experience and not be under SSHRC sanction for financial or research misconduct.
Level of Study: Postdoctorate.
Type: Fellowship.
Value: Canadian $40,000, paid in three instalments, of which up to canadian $10,000 may be used for travel and research expenses.
Length of Study: One year, non renewable.
Frequency: Every two years.
Country of Study: Canada.
No. of awards offered: One.
Application Procedure: Applicants must complete an application form, available from the website.
Closing Date: June 15th.
Funding: Private.
Contributor: The Thérèse F Casgrain Foundation.
No. of awards given last year: One.
No. of applicants last year: 21.
Additional Information: The fellowship was created by the Thérèse F Casgrain Foundation and is administered by the Social Sciences and Humanities Research Council. Affiliation with a university or an appropriate research institute or similar organisation is desirable, but is not a condition of the award. Recipients must submit a final report to the Foundation outlining conclusions of the research, accompanied by a complete financial statement for all expenses. Further information is available on the website.

SOCIAL WORKERS EDUCATIONAL TRUST

British Association of Social Workers
16 Kent Street, Birmingham, West Midlands, B5 6RD, England
Tel: (44) 121 622 3911
Fax: (44) 121 622 4860
www: http://www.basw.co.uk/swet
Contact: Ms Gill Aslett, Honorary Secretary

The Social Workers Educational Trust offers grants to experienced social workers for post-qualifying training or research, with the overall aim of improving social work practice in the United Kingdom.

Anne Cummins Scholarship

Subjects: Competitive submission of proposals for research and practice development in health related social work.
Purpose: To support study or research on health related social work practice.
Eligibility: Open to qualified social workers who have completed two years' work practice post qualification.
Level of Study: Postgraduate, Professional development.
Type: Award.
Value: UK £1,500.
Frequency: Annual.
Country of Study: United Kingdom.
No. of awards offered: One.
Application Procedure: Applicants must complete an application form. Details and forms are available on written request from the Social Workers' Educational Trust or from the website. Applicants should state whether their application is for a grant or scholarship.
Funding: Private.
No. of awards given last year: One.

SOCIETY FOR THE PROMOTION OF HELLENIC STUDIES

Senate House
Malet Street, London, WC1E 7HU, England
Tel: (44) 20 7862 8730
Fax: (44) 20 7862 8731
Email: hellenic@sas.ac.uk
www: http://www.sas.ac.uk/icls/hellenic
Contact: Secretary

The Society for the Promotion of Hellenic Studies, generally known as the Hellenic Society, was founded in 1879 to advance the study of Greek language, literature, history, art and archaeology in the Ancient, Byzantine and Modern periods.

Dover Fund

Subjects: Greek language and papyri.
Purpose: To further the study of the history of the Greek language in any period from the Bronze Age to the fifteenth-century AD, and to further the edition and exegesis of Greek texts from any period within those same limits.
Eligibility: Open to currently registered research students and within the first five years of their appointment, to lecturers, teaching Fellows, research Fellows, postdoctoral Fellows and research assistants.
Level of Study: Doctorate, Postdoctorate, Postgraduate.
Type: Grant.
Value: Grants will be made for such purposes as books, photography, including microfilm and photocopying, and towards the costs of visits to libraries, museums and sites. The sums awarded will vary according to the needs of the applicant, but most grants will be in the range of UK £50-250. Larger grants may be made from time to time at the discretion of the awards committee.
Frequency: Annual.
Study Establishment: The Society for the Promotion of Hellenic Studies.
Country of Study: United Kingdom.
No. of awards offered: Varies.
Application Procedure: Applicants must complete an application form, available from the Society. Applications should be marked for the attention of the Dover Fund and sent to the main address.
Closing Date: February 14th of the year in which the award is sought.
Funding: Private.
Contributor: Membership subscriptions.
No. of awards given last year: Four.
No. of applicants last year: 10.

SOCIETY FOR THE PROMOTION OF ROMAN STUDIES

Senate House
Malet Street, London, WC1E 7HU, England
Tel: (44) 20 7862 8727
Fax: (44) 20 7862 8728
Email: romansoc@sas.ac.uk
www: http://www.sas.ac.uk/icls/roman
Contact: Dr Helen M Cockle, Secretary of Society

The Society for the Promotion of Roman Studies aims to promote the study of history, architecture, archaeology, language, literature and the art of Italy and the Roman Empire, including Roman Britain, from the earliest times to about 700 AD.

Hugh Last and Donald Atkinson Funds Committee Grants

Subjects: The history, archaeology, language, literature or art of Italy and the Roman Empire.
Purpose: To assist in the undertaking, completion or publication of work that relates to any of the general scholarly purposes of the Roman Society, which promotes the study of the history, archaeology, language, literature and art of Italy and the Roman Empire, from the earliest times down to about AD 700. In addition, postgraduate students may apply for small grants for visits to conferences and for other research purposes.
Eligibility: Open to applicants of graduate, postgraduate or postdoctoral status or the equivalent, usually of United Kingdom nationality.
Level of Study: Graduate, Postdoctorate, Postgraduate.
Type: Grant.
Value: Varies, but usually UK £200-1,500.
Frequency: Annual.
Country of Study: Not specified, but usually a country formerly in the Roman Empire.
No. of awards offered: 20.
Application Procedure: Applicants must ensure that two references are sent directly to the Society. Completion of an application form is not essential.
Closing Date: January 15th.
Funding: Private.
No. of awards given last year: 20.
No. of applicants last year: 26.
Additional Information: Grants for the organisation of conferences of colloquia and symposia will only be considered in exceptional circumstances.

SOCIETY FOR THE PSYCHOLOGICAL STUDY OF SOCIAL ISSUES (SPSSI)

SPSSI Central Office
1901 Pennsylvania Avenue North West
Suite 901, Washington, DC, 20006-3405, United States of America
Tel: (1) 202 223 5100
Fax: (1) 202 223 5555
Email: spssi@spssi.org
www: http://www.spssi.org
Contact: Ms Brenda Stanard, Administrative Associate

The Society for the Psychological Study of Social Issues (SPSSI) is an interdisciplinary, international organisation of over 3,000 social scientists who share an interest in research on the psychological aspects of important social issues. The Society's goals are to increase understanding of social issues through research and its dissemination and to support policy efforts consistent with such research.

Clara Mayo Grants

Subjects: Aspects of sexism, racism or prejudice.

Purpose: To support the writing of a Master's thesis or predissertation research.
Eligibility: Open to individuals who have matriculated in graduate programmes in psychology, applied social science and related disciplines.
Level of Study: Graduate, Postgraduate.
Type: Research grant.
Value: Up to US$1,000.
Frequency: Annual.
Country of Study: United States of America.
No. of awards offered: Four.
Application Procedure: Applicants must send five copies of a cover sheet with the title of the thesis and address details, an abstract of no more than 100 words, a budget request and other relevant details.
Closing Date: March 31st.
Funding: Private.

Gordon Allport Intergroup Relations Prize

Subjects: Intergroup relations. Originality of the contribution, whether theoretical or empirical, will be given special weight. The research area of intergroup relations includes such dimensions as age, sex, and socio-economic status, as well as race.
Purpose: To recognise the best paper or article of the year on intergroup relations.
Eligibility: Open to non members, as well as members of SPSSI. Graduate students are especially urged to submit papers.
Level of Study: Doctorate, Graduate, Postdoctorate, Postgraduate.
Type: Prize.
Value: US$1,000.
Frequency: Annual.
Country of Study: Any country.
No. of awards offered: One.
Application Procedure: Entries can be either papers published during the current year or unpublished manuscripts. Entries cannot be returned and four copies must be sent. Applicants must include contact information for all authors.
Closing Date: December 31st.
No. of awards given last year: One.

Louise Kidder Early Career Award

Subjects: Social and community psychology.
Purpose: To recognise social issues researchers who have made substantial contributions to the field early in their careers.
Eligibility: Nominees should be social issues investigators who have made substantial contributions to social issues research within five years of receiving a graduate degree and who have demonstrated the potential to continue such contributions.
Level of Study: Postdoctorate, Professional development.
Value: US$500 plus plaque.
Frequency: Annual.
Country of Study: Any country.
No. of awards offered: One.
Application Procedure: Applicants must send three copies of a covering letter stating the nominee's accomplishments to date and future contributions, a curriculum vitae, and three letters of support.
Closing Date: May 1st.
No. of awards given last year: One.

Otto Klineberg Intercultural and International Relations Award

Subjects: Intercultural or international relations. The originality of the contribution, whether theoretical or empirical, will be given special weight.
Purpose: To recognise the best paper or article of the year.
Eligibility: Open to non members, as well as members of SPSSI. Graduate students are especially urged to submit papers.
Level of Study: Doctorate, Graduate, Postdoctorate, Postgraduate.
Type: Prize.
Value: US$1,000.
Frequency: Annual.

Country of Study: Any country.
No. of awards offered: One.
Application Procedure: Entries can be either papers published during the current year or unpublished manuscripts. Entries cannot be returned and five copies must be sent. Applicants must include contact information for all authors.
Closing Date: February 1st.

SPSSI Applied Social Issues Internship Program

Subjects: Proposals are invited for applying social science principles to social issues in co-operation with a community, city or state government organisation, public interest group or other non-profit entity.
Purpose: To encourage intervention projects, non-partisan advocacy projects, applied research and writing and implementing policy.
Eligibility: Open to graduate students and first year postdoctorates in psychology, applied social science and related disciplines.
Level of Study: Graduate, Postdoctorate, Postgraduate.
Type: Grant.
Value: US$300-2,500 to cover research costs, community organising, Summer stipends etc.
Frequency: Annual.
Country of Study: Any country.
No. of awards offered: Varies.
Application Procedure: Applicants must submit an application including three copies of a two-five page proposal including a budget, a short curriculum vitae, a letter from a faculty sponsor or supervisor of the project including a statement concerning protection for participants if relevant, and a letter from an organisational sponsor, though this is waived if the applicant is proposing to organise a group.
Closing Date: Postmarked November 10th for awards announced in January and postmarked April 1st for awards announced in June.

SPSSI Grants-in-Aid Program

Subjects: Scientific research in social problem areas related to the basic interests and goals of SPSSI and particularly those that are not likely to receive support from traditional sources.
Eligibility: Open to students at the dissertation stage of a graduate career or beyond.
Level of Study: Doctorate, Graduate, Postdoctorate, Postgraduate.
Type: Grant.
Value: Up to US$2,000. Up to US$1,000 for graduate students, which must be matched by the student's university. Funds are not normally provided for travel to conventions, travel or living expenses while conducting research, stipends of principal investigators, or costs associated with manuscript preparation.
Frequency: Twice a year.
Country of Study: Any country.
No. of awards offered: Varies.
Application Procedure: Applicants must submit four copies of a statement that includes a cover sheet stating the title of the proposal, the contact details of the investigator, an abstract of 100 words or less summarising the proposed research, project purposes, theoretical rationale and specific procedures to be employed, the relevance of research to SPSSI goals and grants-in-aid criteria, the curriculum vitae of the investigator and the specific amount requested including a budget. A faculty sponsor's recommendation must be provided if the investigator is a graduate student as support is seldom awarded to students who have not yet reached the dissertation stage. A recommended length for the entire proposal is five-seven double spaced, typed pages. The entire submission should be sent to the SPSSI Central Office. The programme is sponsored in part by the Sophie and Shirley Cohen Memorial Fund and through membership contributions.
Closing Date: April 1st and November 13th.

SPSSI Social Issues Dissertation Award

Subjects: Doctoral dissertations on social issues in psychology or in a social science with psychological subject matter.

Eligibility: Open to doctoral dissertations on a relevant topic accepted between March 1st of the year preceding that of application and March 1st of the year of application.
Level of Study: Postgraduate.
Type: Prize.
Value: First prize of US$750 and a second prize of US$550.
Frequency: Annual.
Country of Study: Any country.
No. of awards offered: Two.
Application Procedure: Applications should include four copies of a 500 word dissertation summary with all identification deleted, one copy of the summary with identification including the candidate's name, address, phone and school, the dissertation title and certification by the dissertation advisor of the acceptance date of the dissertation. Dissertations will be judged according to scientific excellence and potential application to social problems.
Closing Date: April 1st.
No. of awards given last year: Two.

SPSSI Sponsored Research Workshop

Subjects: Social policy.
Purpose: To foster awareness of the state of social research in important areas of social policy.
Type: Award.
Value: Up to US$4,000.
Frequency: Annual.
Application Procedure: Applicants must write for details.
Closing Date: October 5th.

THE SOCIETY FOR THE SCIENTIFIC STUDY OF SEXUALITY (SSSS)

PO Box 416, Allentown, PA, 18105, United States of America
Tel: (1) 319 895 8407
Fax: (1) 319 895 6203
Email: thesociety@inetmail.att.net
www: http://www.sexscience.org
Contact: Mr David L Fleming, Executive Director

The Society for the Scientific Study of Sexuality (SSSS) is an international organisation dedicated to the advancement of knowledge about sexuality. The Society brings together an interdisciplinary group of professionals who believe in the importance of both production of quality research and the clinical, educational and social applications of research related to all aspects of sexuality.

SSSS Student Research Grant Award

Subjects: Related to the field of human sexuality from any discipline: psychology, anthropology, social work, biology, theology and medical research.
Purpose: To support research in the field of human sexuality.
Eligibility: Open to students of any nationality who are enrolled in a degree granting programme.
Level of Study: Unrestricted.
Type: Grant.
Value: US$1,000.
Frequency: Twice a year.
Study Establishment: An appropriate institution.
Country of Study: Any country.
No. of awards offered: Three.
Application Procedure: Applicants must send a stamped addressed envelope for further details and application forms.
Closing Date: February 1st or September 1st.
Funding: Private.
Contributor: The Foundation for the Scientific Study of Sexuality.
No. of awards given last year: Three.
Additional Information: The purpose of the research can be a Master's thesis or doctoral dissertation, but this is not a requirement.

SOCIETY FOR THE STUDY OF FRENCH HISTORY

Department of History
University of Stirling, Stirling, FK9 4LA, Scotland
Tel: (44) 1786 467580
Fax: (44) 1786 467581
Email: mgr1@stir.ac.uk
Contact: Dr Michael Rapport, Secretary

The Society for the Study of French History was established to encourage research into French history. It offers a forum where scholars, teachers and students can meet and exchange ideas. It also offers bursaries for research and conferences to postgraduates registered in the United Kingdom undertaking research into French history.

Society for the Study of French History Bursaries

Subjects: Any aspect of French history.
Purpose: To enable postgraduates to complete research in French history.
Eligibility: Open to postgraduate students registered at a United Kingdom university. Preference will be given to those applicants who are in the later stages of research.
Level of Study: Postgraduate.
Type: Bursary.
Value: UK £500.
Length of Study: Dependent on the project for which the award is given.
Frequency: Annual.
Country of Study: France.
No. of awards offered: Two-three.
Application Procedure: Applicants must give details of the research being pursued and the use to which the money would be put, along with names of two referees. There is no application form and applications by email are acceptable. Applicants are responsible for writing to their referees. Successful applicants will be required to submit, in the first instance, a brief outline of their research proposal and then, after the research trip, a synopsis of their findings, both for publication in the society's bulletin, The French Historian.
Closing Date: June 30th.
Funding: Private.
Contributor: The Society for the Study of French History.
No. of awards given last year: Three.
No. of applicants last year: 10.

Society for the Study of French History Conference Bursaries

Subjects: Any aspect of French history.
Purpose: To enable postgraduates to attend conferences related to research.
Eligibility: Open to postgraduate students registered at a United Kingdom university.
Level of Study: Postgraduate.
Type: Bursary.
Value: Up to UK £100 each.
Frequency: Annual.
Country of Study: France.
No. of awards offered: Five.
Application Procedure: Applicants must give details of the conference being attended and the use to which the money will be put, along with names of two referees. There is no application form and applications by email are acceptable.
Closing Date: September 30th.
Funding: Private.
Contributor: The Society for the Study of French History.
No. of awards given last year: Five.
No. of applicants last year: Five.

THE SOCIETY FOR THEATRE RESEARCH

c/o The Theatre Museum
1E Tavistock Street, London, WC2E 7PA, England
Email: e.cottis@btinternet.com
www: http://www.str.org.uk
Contact: Research Awards Sub-Committee Chairman

The Society for Theatre Research was founded in 1948 for all interested in the history and technique of British theatre. It publishes annually one or more books, newsletters, and three issues of the journal Theatre Notebook, holds lecture meetings and other events, and gives an annual book prize as well as grants for theatre research.

Society for Theatre Research Awards

Subjects: The history and practice of the British theatre, including music hall, opera, dance and other associated performing arts. Exclusively literary topics are not eligible.
Purpose: To aid research into the history and practice of British theatre.
Eligibility: Applicants should normally be aged 18 or over but there is no other restriction on their status, nationality or the location of the research.
Level of Study: Unrestricted.
Value: From a total of approx. UK £4,000: major awards are normally UK £1,000-1,500 and other awards are normally UK £200-500.
Frequency: Annual.
Country of Study: Any country.
No. of awards offered: Two major awards and a number of lesser awards.
Application Procedure: Applicants must write to the Chairman of the Research Awards Sub-Committee after October 1st of the preceding year for an application form and guidance notes. All applications and enquiries must be made by post to the Society's accommodation address.
Closing Date: February 1st.
Funding: Private.
Contributor: Members' subscriptions, donations, and bequests.
No. of awards given last year: Nine.
No. of applicants last year: 25.
Additional Information: While applications will need to show evidence of the value of the research and a scholarly approach, they are by no means restricted to professional academics. Many awards, including major ones, have previously been made to theatre practitioners and 'amateur' researchers, who are encouraged to apply. The Society also welcomes proposals which in their execution extend methods and techniques of historiography. In coming to its decisions, the Society will consider the progress already made by the applicants and the possible availability of other grants.

SOCIETY OF APOTHECARIES OF LONDON

Black Friars Lane, London, EC4V 6EJ, England
Tel: (44) 20 7236 1180
Fax: (44) 20 7329 3177
Email: clerk@apothecaries.org
www: http://www.apothecaries.org
Contact: R J Stringer, The Clerk

Gillson Scholarship in Pathology

Subjects: Pathology.
Purpose: To encourage original research in any branch of pathology.
Eligibility: Open to candidates under 35 years of age who are either licenciates or freemen of the Society, or who obtain the licence or the freedom within six months of election to the scholarship.
Level of Study: Postgraduate.
Type: Scholarship.

Value: UK £1,800 in total. Payments are made twice annually for the duration of the scholarship.
Length of Study: Three years, renewable for a second term of three years.
Frequency: Every three years.
Country of Study: Any country.
No. of awards offered: One.
Application Procedure: Applicants must submit two testimonials and present evidence of their attainments and capabilities as shown by any papers already published, and/or a detailed record of any pathological work already done. Candidates should also state where the research will be undertaken.
Closing Date: December 1st.
Funding: Private.
No. of awards given last year: One.
No. of applicants last year: Two.
Additional Information: Preference is given to the candidate who is engaged in the teaching of medical science or in its research. Scholars are required to submit an interim report at the end of the first six months of tenure, and a complete report one month prior to the end of the third year. Any published results should also be submitted to the Society.

SOCIETY OF ARCHITECTURAL HISTORIANS (SAH)

1365 North Astor Street, Chicago, IL, 60610-2144, United States of America
Tel: (1) 312 573 1365
Fax: (1) 312 573 1141
Email: info@sah.org
www: http://www.sah.org
Contact: Ms Angela Fitzsimmons, Director of Programs

A national, non-profit, membership organisation established in 1940, the Society of Architectural Historians (SAH) promotes discussion among those interested in architecture and its related disciplines, encourages scholarly research in the history of architecture and the built environment, and supports the preservation of architectural monuments worldwide.

Carroll LV Meeks Fellowship

Subjects: Architectural history.
Purpose: To enable an outstanding student to participate in the annual SAH domestic tour.
Eligibility: Open to SAH members who are students engaged in graduate work in architecture, or architectural history, city planning or urban history, landscape or the history of landscape design.
Level of Study: Postgraduate.
Type: Scholarship.
Value: A surcharge on non-student participants' registrations is applied toward such tour scholarships to defray the cost of the tour itself.
Frequency: Annual.
Country of Study: Any country.
No. of awards offered: One.
Application Procedure: Applicants must complete an application form, available on request by writing to SAH for guidelines or visiting the SAH website.
Closing Date: The date changes each year, please contact the organisation.
Funding: Commercial.
No. of awards given last year: One.
No. of applicants last year: Four.

Edilia and François-Auguste de Montequin Fellowship in Iberian and Latin American Architecture

Subjects: Spanish, Portuguese or Ibero-American architecture, including colonial architecture produced by the Spaniards in the Philippines and what is today the United States of America.

Purpose: To fund travel for research into Spanish, Portuguese or Ibero-American architecture.

Eligibility: Open to SAH members who are junior Scholars, including graduate students, and senior Scholars.

Level of Study: Doctorate, Postdoctorate, Postgraduate.

Type: Fellowship.

Value: US$2,000 for junior scholars and US$6,000 for senior scholars which is offered every two years.

Frequency: Annual.

Country of Study: Any country.

No. of awards offered: Two.

Application Procedure: Applicants must complete an application form, available on request by writing to SAH for guidelines or visiting the SAH website.

Closing Date: November 15th.

Funding: Private.

No. of awards given last year: One.

No. of applicants last year: Five.

Keepers Preservation Education Fund Fellowship

Subjects: Historic preservation.

Purpose: To enable a graduate student to attend the annual meeting of the Society, held each April.

Eligibility: Open to members of any nationality who are currently engaged in the study of historic preservation.

Level of Study: Postgraduate.

Type: Fellowship.

Value: Registration fee for the meeting itself is waived, plus reimbursement for travel, lodging and meals directly related to the meeting, up to a combined total of US$500.

Frequency: Annual.

Country of Study: Any country.

No. of awards offered: One.

Application Procedure: Applicants must write to SAH for application guidelines or download an application from the society's website.

Closing Date: November 15th.

Funding: Private.

No. of awards given last year: One.

No. of applicants last year: Seven.

Rosann Berry Fellowship

Subjects: Architectural history or an allied field eg. city planning, landscape architecture, decorative arts or historic preservation.

Purpose: To enable a student engaged in advanced graduate study to attend the annual meeting of the Society.

Eligibility: Open to persons of any nationality who have been members of SAH for at least one year prior to the meeting, and who are currently engaged in advanced graduate study, normally beyond the Master's level, that involves some aspect of the history of architecture or of one of the fields closely allied to it.

Level of Study: Postgraduate.

Type: Fellowship.

Value: Registration fee connected with the meeting is waived, plus reimbursement for travel, lodging and meals directly related to the meeting, up to a combined total of US$500.

Frequency: Annual.

Country of Study: Any country.

No. of awards offered: One.

Application Procedure: Applicants must complete an application form, available on request by writing to SAH for guidelines or visiting the SAH website.

Closing Date: November 15th.

Funding: Private.

No. of awards given last year: One.

No. of applicants last year: 15.

Sally Kress Tompkins Fellowship

Subjects: Architectural history and historic preservation.

Purpose: To enable an architectural history student to work as an intern on an Historic American Buildings Survey project, during the summer.

Eligibility: Open to architectural history and historic preservation students.

Level of Study: Doctorate, Postgraduate.

Type: Fellowship.

Value: US$8,800.

Frequency: Annual.

Country of Study: United States of America.

No. of awards offered: One.

Application Procedure: Applicants must submit an application including a sample of work, a letter of recommendation from a faculty member, and a United States Government Standard Form 171, available from HABS or most United States government personnel offices. Applications should be sent to the Sally Kress Tompkins Fellowship, care of HABS/HAER. Applicants not selected for the Tomkins Fellowship will be considered for other HABS Summer employment opportunities. For more information, please contact E Blaine Cliver, Chief at HABS/HAER.

Closing Date: January 13th.

Funding: Government.

No. of awards given last year: One.

No. of applicants last year: Seven.

For further information contact:

The Sally Kress Tompkins Fellowship
c/o HABS/HAER
National Park Service
PO Box 37127, Washington, DC, 20013-7127, United States of America

Spiro Kostof Annual Meeting Fellowship

Subjects: Architectural history.

Purpose: To enable an advanced graduate student in architectural history to attend the annual meeting of the Society of Architectural Historians.

Eligibility: Open to doctoral candidates only who have been members of the SAH for at least one year.

Level of Study: Doctorate, Predoctorate.

Type: Fellowship.

Value: US$500.

Frequency: Annual.

No. of awards offered: One.

Application Procedure: Applicants must write for an application form, available after June 1st by mail or by visiting the website.

Closing Date: November 15th.

Funding: Commercial.

Contributor: The Society of Architectural Historians.

No. of awards given last year: One.

No. of applicants last year: 15.

SOCIETY OF ARCHITECTURAL HISTORIANS OF GREAT BRITAIN

6 Fitzroy Square, London, W1T 5DX, England
Tel: (44) 20 7387 1720
Fax: (44) 20 7387 1721
Contact: Mr Andrew Martindale, Honorary Secretary

The Society of Architectural Historians of Great Britain encourages the study and enjoyment of architectural history. It was founded in 1956. Through its membership, the Society provides a forum for the interchange of ideas and information, acting as a valuable link between architectural historians both in Great Britain and abroad. Membership is open to all who are interested in architecture and its history.

Ramsden Bursaries

Subjects: Any aspect of the history of architecture.

Purpose: To support postgraduate research in the field of architectural history.

Eligibility: Candidates may apply for a second award, but in cases of equal merit, priority will be given to the first time applicant. No one may receive more than two awards.

Level of Study: Postgraduate.

Type: Bursary.

Value: To support research expenses including travel, building survey, photography and conference attendance. Bursaries are not awarded for maintenance at home, purchase of books or equipment, secretarial help or tuition fees. Value does not normally exceed UK £500, and the maximum is UK £1,000.

Length of Study: Projects are normally to be completed within one year.

Frequency: Twice a year.

Country of Study: Applicants must either be resident in the United Kingdom, or working on the history of British architecture.

No. of awards offered: Up to five.

Application Procedure: Applicants must submit an application including the title and description of the project, a curriculum vitae, detailed estimated costs, the date of the start of the project and estimated completion date, as well as two letters of recommendation to be sent directly by referees to the Secretary. Applicants are responsible for asking their referees to write. Five copies of the application should be submitted to the Honorary Secretary of the Society with a stamped addressed envelope if acknowledgement is required.

Closing Date: April 30th or October 31st each year.

Funding: Private.

Contributor: Endowment.

Additional Information: The award decisions will be made annually in May and November, and announced in the Society's Newsletter. Payments to successful applicants will only be made after documentary evidence of each major item of expenditure has been supplied. This may be in receipt or invoice, or confirmation of travel booking or conference enrolment. The Society must be acknowledged in any published work arising out of the application. Copies of books, or in the case of shorter publications, an offprint or photocopy should be sent to the Honorary Secretary of the Society. A brief report of the use made of the grant must be submitted to the Honorary Secretary within a year of its receipt and, if the work extends beyond a year, a second report should be submitted on its completion. For further details please contact the Honorary Secretary.

Stroud Bursaries

Subjects: The topic in the application may relate to any aspect of the history of architecture.

Purpose: To support publication in the field of architectural history.

Eligibility: Candidates may apply for a second award, but in cases of equal merit, priority will be given to the first time applicant. No one may receive more than two awards.

Level of Study: Unrestricted.

Type: Bursary.

Value: Subsidy to defray publication costs, cost of purchase of illustrations, payment of copyright fees, contribution to the costs of mounting an exhibition. The amount does not normally exceed UK £500, and the maximum is UK £1,000.

Length of Study: Projects are normally to be completed within one year.

Frequency: Twice a year.

Country of Study: Applicants must either be resident in the United Kingdom, or working on the history of British architecture.

No. of awards offered: Up to five.

Application Procedure: Applicants must submit an application including the title and description of the project, a curriculum vitae, detailed estimated costs, the date of the start of the project and estimated completion date, as well as two letters of recommendation to be sent directly by referees to the Secretary. Applicants are responsible for asking their referees to write. Five copies of the application should be submitted to the Honorary Secretary of the Society with a stamped addressed envelope if acknowledgement is required.

Closing Date: April 30th or October 31st each year.

Funding: Private.

Contributor: Endowment.

Additional Information: The award decisions will be made annually in May and November, and announced in the Society's Newsletter. Payments to successful applicants will only be made after documentary evidence of each major item of expenditure has been supplied. The Society must be acknowledged in any published work arising out of the application. Copies of books, or in the case of shorter publications, an offprint or photocopy should be sent to the Honorary Secretary within a year of receipt and, if the work extends beyond a year, a second report should be submitted on its completion. For further details please contact the Honorary Secretary.

SOCIETY OF CHILDREN'S BOOK WRITERS AND ILLUSTRATORS (SCBWI)

8271 Beverly Boulevard, Los Angeles, CA, 90048, United States of America
Tel: (1) 323 782 1010
Fax: (1) 323 782 1892
Email: scbwi@scbwi.org
www: http://www.scbwi.org
Contact: Mr Stephen Mooser, President

The Society of Children's Book Writers and Illustrators (SCBWI) is an organisation of 17,000 writers, illustrators, editors, agents, and publishers of children's books, television, film and multimedia.

Barbara Karlin Grant

Subjects: Children's picture-books.

Purpose: To assist picture book writers in the completion of a specific project.

Eligibility: Open to both full and associate members of the Society who have never had a picture book published. The grant is not available for a project on which there is already a contract.

Level of Study: Unrestricted.

Type: Grant.

Value: The full grant is US$1,500 and the runner up grant is US$500.

Frequency: Annual.

Country of Study: Any country.

No. of awards offered: One.

Application Procedure: Applicants must write for details.

Closing Date: May 15th.

Funding: Private.

No. of awards given last year: Two.

No. of applicants last year: 75.

Don Freeman Memorial Grant-in-Aid

Subjects: Children's picture-books.

Purpose: To enable picture book artists to further their understanding, training and work in the picture book genre.

Eligibility: Open to both full and associate members of the Society who, as artists, seriously intend to make picture books their chief contribution to the field of children's literature.

Level of Study: Unrestricted.

Type: Grant.

Value: The full grant is US$1,500 and the runner up grant is US$500.

Frequency: Annual.

Country of Study: Any country.

No. of awards offered: Two.

Application Procedure: Applicants must submit an application to the Society. Receipt of application will be acknowledged.

Closing Date: Application requests should be submitted by June 15th and completed application should be submitted by February 10th.

Funding: Private.

No. of awards given last year: Two.

No. of applicants last year: 48.

SCBWI General Work-in-Progress Grant

Subjects: Children's literature.
Purpose: To assist children's book writers in the completion of a specific project.
Eligibility: Open to both full and associate members of the Society. The grant is not available for projects on which there is already a contract. Recipients of previous grants are not eligible to apply for any further SCBWI Grants.
Level of Study: Unrestricted.
Type: Grant.
Value: The full grant is US$1,500 and the runner up grant is US$500.
Frequency: Annual.
Country of Study: Any country.
No. of awards offered: One full grant and one runner up grant.
Application Procedure: Applicants must write for details.
Closing Date: May 1st.
Funding: Private.
No. of awards given last year: Two.
No. of applicants last year: 123.

SCBWI Grant for a Contemporary Novel for Young People

Subjects: Children's literature.
Purpose: To assist children's book writers in the completion of a specific project.
Eligibility: Open to both full and associate members of the Society. The grant is not available for projects on which there is already a contract. Recipients of previous grants are not eligible to apply for any further SCBWI Grants.
Level of Study: Unrestricted.
Type: Grant.
Value: The full grant is US$1,500 and the runner up grant is US$500.
Frequency: Annual.
Country of Study: Any country.
No. of awards offered: One full grant and one runner up grant.
Application Procedure: Applicants must write for details.
Closing Date: May 1st.
Funding: Private.
No. of awards given last year: Two.
No. of applicants last year: 110.

SCBWI Grant for Unpublished Authors

Subjects: Children's literature.
Purpose: To assist children's book writers in the completion of a specific project.
Eligibility: Open to both full and associate members of the Society who have never had a book published. The grant is not available for a project on which there is already a contract. Recipients of previous grants are not eligible to apply for any further SCBWI Grants.
Level of Study: Unrestricted.
Type: Grant.
Value: The full grant is US$1,500 and the runner up grant is US$500.
Frequency: Annual.
Country of Study: Any country.
No. of awards offered: One full grant and one runner up grant.
Closing Date: May 1st.
Funding: Private.
No. of awards given last year: Two.
No. of applicants last year: 45.

SCBWI Non-Fiction Research Grant

Subjects: Children's literature.
Purpose: To assist children's book writers in the completion of a specific project.
Eligibility: Open to both full and associate members of the Society. The grant is not available for projects on which there is already a contract. Recipients of previous grants are not eligible to apply for any further SCBWI Grants.

Level of Study: Unrestricted.
Type: Grant.
Value: The full grant is US$1,500 and the runner up grant is US$500.
Frequency: Annual.
Country of Study: Any country.
No. of awards offered: One full grant and one runner up grant.
Application Procedure: Applicants must write for details.
Closing Date: May 1st.
Funding: Private.
No. of awards given last year: One.
No. of applicants last year: 75.

SOCIETY OF EXPLORATION GEOPHYSICISTS FOUNDATION (SEG)

Box 702740, Tulsa, OK, 74170, United States of America
Tel: (1) 918 497 5530
Fax: (1) 918 497 5557
Email: slobianco@seg.org
Contact: Ms Sue LoBianco

The Society of Exploration Geophysicists (SEG) began a programme of encouraging the establishment of scholarship funds by companies and individuals in the field of geophysics. In 1963, the Foundation's activities were expanded to include grants-in-aid.

SEG Scholarships

Subjects: Geophysics and related earth sciences.
Purpose: To encourage careers in the exploration of geophysics and related earth sciences.
Eligibility: Open to citizens of any country who are entering graduate level and have above average grades and an aptitude for physics, mathematics and geology.
Level of Study: Doctorate.
Type: Scholarship.
Value: Usually US$500-3,000 per academic year. Average awards are approx. US$2,000.
Length of Study: One academic year, renewable.
Frequency: Annual.
Study Establishment: Any college offering a course of study in geophysics.
Country of Study: Any country.
No. of awards offered: Varies.
Application Procedure: Applicants must submit a completed application form accompanied by three years worth of transcripts and two letters of recommendation from the mathematics and science faculty.
Closing Date: March 1st of the year in which the award is made.
Funding: Commercial, Private.
No. of awards given last year: 115.
No. of applicants last year: 201 and 51 renewals.

SOCIETY OF NAVAL ARCHITECTS AND MARINE ENGINEERS

601 Pavonia Avenue
Suite 400, Jersey City, NJ, 07306, United States of America
Tel: (1) 201 798 4800 ext. 3033
Fax: (1) 201 798 4975
Contact: Mr Philip B Kimball, Executive Director

The objectives of the Society of Naval Architects and Marine Engineers are to advance the state of the art, to afford facilities for the exchange of information and ideas, to disseminate the results of the research, experience and information among the members, to encourage and sponsor such research, to co-operate with educational institutions and to promote the professional integrity and status of members.

Society of Naval Architects and Marine Engineers Graduate Scholarships

Subjects: Awards are primarily for advanced study in naval architecture, marine engineering and ocean engineering, but are not necessarily limited to these subjects.
Purpose: To encourage young men and women to enter marine industry related fields.
Eligibility: Open to citizens of any country who are college graduates of a recognised technical institution. Applicants must be members of the Society in good standing for one year.
Level of Study: Graduate.
Type: Scholarship.
Value: Varies, usually to cover tuition costs at the selected school.
Length of Study: One year.
Frequency: Annual.
Country of Study: Any country.
No. of awards offered: Varies.
Application Procedure: For details applicants must write to Erlinda Faustino, the Scholarship Co-ordinator, or email efaustino@sname.org.
Closing Date: February 1st.
Funding: Private.
No. of awards given last year: Varies.
No. of applicants last year: 20.

SOCIETY OF WOMEN ENGINEERS (SWE)

230 East Ohio Street
Suite 400, Chicago, IL, 60611, United States of America
Tel: (1) 312 596 5223
Fax: (1) 312 644 8557
Email: hq@swe.org
www: http://www.swe.org
Contact: Ms Gina Ryan, Executive Director

The Society of Women Engineers (SWE) was founded in 1950 and is a non-profit educational service organisation of graduate engineers and women and men with equivalent engineering experience. SWE has an international membership of more than 16,000 in 95 local sections and 300 student sections. SWE corporate membership is available to organisations which employ engineers and are interested in supporting the goals of the Society.

BK Krenzer Memorial Re-entry Scholarship

Subjects: Engineering.
Purpose: To assist women in obtaining the credentials necessary to re-enter the job market as engineers.
Eligibility: Open to women who have been out of the job market as well as out of school for a minimum of two years. Recipients may be entering any year of an engineering programme, as full or part-time students. Preference is given to graduate engineers desiring to return to the workforce following a period of temporary retirement.
Level of Study: Graduate, Postgraduate.
Type: Scholarship.
Value: US$2,000.
Frequency: Annual.
Country of Study: United States of America.
No. of awards offered: One.
Application Procedure: Application forms are available from the website.
Closing Date: May 15th.
Funding: Private.
Additional Information: Recipients will be notified in September. Further information is available on request.

Lydia I Pickup Memorial Scholarship

Subjects: Engineering and computer science.

Purpose: To advance the applicant's career in engineering or computer science.
Eligibility: Open only to women majoring in engineering or computer science in a college or university with an ABET accredited programme.
Level of Study: Graduate.
Type: Scholarship.
Value: US$2,000.
Frequency: Annual.
No. of awards offered: One.
Application Procedure: Application forms are available from the website.

Microsoft Corporation Scholarships

Subjects: Computer science or computer engineering.
Purpose: To encourage women engineers to attain a high level of education and professional achievement.
Eligibility: Open only to women majoring in engineering or computer science in a college or university with an ABET accredited programme. Applicants must be United States citizens.
Level of Study: Graduate, Postgraduate.
Type: Scholarship.
Value: US$2,500.
Frequency: Annual.
Study Establishment: A four year college or university.
Country of Study: United States of America.
No. of awards offered: Two.
Application Procedure: Application forms are available from the website.
Closing Date: February 1st.
Funding: Commercial.
Contributor: Microsoft Corporation.
Additional Information: Further information is available on the website.

Olive Lynn Salembier Scholarship

Subjects: Engineering and computer science.
Purpose: To aid women who have been out of the engineering market and out of school to obtain the credentials necessary to re-enter the job market as an engineer.
Eligibility: Open to women who have not practiced engineering or been enrolled in an engineering or other university or college programme in the past two years. Applicants must be United States citizens. Recipients may be entering any graduate year, including doctoral programmes, as full or part-time students.
Level of Study: Doctorate, Graduate.
Type: Scholarship.
Value: US$2,000.
Frequency: Annual.
Country of Study: United States of America.
No. of awards offered: One.
Application Procedure: Application forms are available from the website.
Closing Date: May 15th.
Funding: Private.
Additional Information: Further information is available on request.

Past Presidents Scholarships

Subjects: Engineering.
Eligibility: Open only to women majoring in engineering or computer science in a college or university with an ABET accredited programme. United States citizenship is required.
Level of Study: Graduate, Postgraduate.
Type: Scholarship.
Value: US$1,500.
Frequency: Annual.
Country of Study: United States of America.
No. of awards offered: Two.
Application Procedure: Application forms are available from the website.
Closing Date: Please contact the organisation.

Additional Information: Further information is available on request.

SWE General Motors Foundation Graduate Scholarship

Subjects: Mechanical engineering, electrical engineering, chemical engineering, industrial engineering, materials science and engineering or manufacturing engineering.

Purpose: To encourage women engineers to attain high levels of education and professional achievement.

Eligibility: Open only to women students entering the first year of a Master's degree programme. Applicants must have a career interest in the automotive industry or manufacturing, and have demonstrated leadership potential.

Level of Study: Graduate, Postgraduate.

Type: Scholarship.

Value: US$1,000, plus a travel grant of US$5,00 for each recipient to attend the SWE National Convention and Student Conference.

Frequency: Annual.

Country of Study: United States of America.

No. of awards offered: One.

Application Procedure: Application forms are available from the website.

Closing Date: February 1st.

Funding: Commercial.

Contributor: General Motors.

Additional Information: Further information is available on request.

SOIL AND WATER CONSERVATION SOCIETY

7515 Northeast Ankeny Road, Ankeny, IA, 50021-9764, United States of America

Tel: (1) 515 289 2331

Fax: (1) 515 289 1227

Email: judyh@swcs.org

www: http://www.swcs.org

The Soil and Water Conservation Society fosters the science and the art of soil, water and related natural resource management to achieve sustainability. The Society promotes and practices an ethic recognising the interdependence of people and the environment.

Kenneth E Grant Research Scholarship

Subjects: Soil conservation.

Purpose: To provide financial aid to members of SWCS for graduate level research on a specific topic that will help SWCS carry out its mission of advocating the protection, enhancement and wise use, of soil, water and related natural resources.

Eligibility: Open to members of the SWCS who have demonstrated integrity, ability and competence to complete the specified study topic.

Level of Study: Postgraduate.

Type: Research grant.

Value: Up to US$1,300.

Length of Study: One year.

Frequency: Annual.

Country of Study: Any country.

No. of awards offered: One.

Application Procedure: Applicants must submit a proposal and evidence of their ability to meet eligibility requirements. There are no specific application forms.

Closing Date: February 12th.

Funding: Private.

SONS OF THE REPUBLIC OF TEXAS

1717 8th Street, Bay City, TX, 77414, United States of America

Tel: (1) 979 245 6644

Fax: (1) 979 244 3819

Email: srttexas@srttexas.org

www: http://www.srttexas.org

Contact: Ms Janet Hickl, Administrative Assistant

Presidio La Bahia Award

Subjects: History.

Purpose: To promote suitable preservation of relics, appropriate dissemination of data, and research into Texas heritage, with particular emphasis on the Spanish colonial period.

Eligibility: Open to all persons interested in the Spanish colonial influence on Texas culture.

Level of Study: Unrestricted.

Type: Cash award.

Value: First place is a minimum of US$1,200, and second and third place prizes are the divided balance from the total amount available of US$2,000 at the discretion of the judges.

Frequency: Annual.

Country of Study: Any country.

No. of awards offered: Three.

Application Procedure: Applicants must submit four copies of published writings to the office. Galley proofs are not acceptable.

Closing Date: Entries are accepted from June 1st until September 30th.

Funding: Private.

No. of awards given last year: Three.

Additional Information: Research writings have, in the past, proved to be the most successful type of entry. However, consideration will be given to other literary forms, art, architecture and archaeological discovery. For projects other than writing, contestants should furnish a description of the proposed entry, so that the Chairman may issue specific instructions.

Summerfield G Roberts Award

Subjects: History.

Purpose: To encourage literary effort and research about historical events and personalities during the days of the Republic of Texas (1836-1846), and to stimulate interest in the period.

Eligibility: Open to all writers.

Level of Study: Unrestricted.

Type: Cash award.

Value: US$2,500.

Frequency: Annual.

Country of Study: Any country.

No. of awards offered: One.

Application Procedure: Manuscripts must be written or published during the calendar year for which the award is given. There is no word limit.

Closing Date: January 15th.

Funding: Private.

No. of awards given last year: One.

SOROPTIMIST INTERNATIONAL OF GREAT BRITAIN AND IRELAND

127 Wellington Road South, Stockport, Cheshire, SK1 3TS, England

Tel: (44) 161 480 7686

Fax: (44) 161 477 6152

Contact: Ms Georgina Coad, Administrative Officer

Soroptomist International of Great Britain and Ireland Golden Jubilee Fellowship

Subjects: All subjects, but preference is given to women seeking to train or retrain for a business or profession as mature students. However all applications will be considered by the committee.

Eligibility: Open to women residing within the boundaries of Soroptimist International of Great Britain and Ireland, who need not be Soroptimists. The countries are Anguilla, Antigua and Barbuda, Bangladesh, Barbados, British Virgin Islands, Cameroon, Gambia, Grenada, Guernsey, India, Isle of Man, Jamaica, Jersey, Republic of Ireland, Malawi, Malta, Mauritius, Nigeria, Pakistan, Seychelles, Sierra Leone, South Africa, Sri Lanka, St Vincent and the Grenadines, Thailand, Trinidad and Tobago, Turks and Caicos Islands, Uganda, United Kingdom and Zimbabwe.
Level of Study: Unrestricted.
Type: Fellowship.
Value: Normally within range UK £100-500 per year, from a fund of UK £6,000.
Frequency: Annual.
Study Establishment: Any agreed institution, providing the residential stipulation is met.
Country of Study: Any country.
No. of awards offered: Approx. 40.
Application Procedure: Applicants must enclose a stamped addressed envelope or international reply coupon for details. Applications in writing must be made on a personal basis to the Secretary.
Closing Date: April 30th for the academic year beginning the following Autumn.
Funding: Private.
No. of awards given last year: Approx. 20.
No. of applicants last year: 750.
Additional Information: Preference is given to women improving their skills or acquiring new ones to either seek employment after years in the home or to enter a field in which prospects for employment or advancement are greater.

SOUTH AFRICAN ASSOCIATION OF WOMEN GRADUATES (SAAWG)

Suite 329
Post Bag X18, Rondebosch, 7701, South Africa
Tel: (27) 21 447 8989
Fax: (27) 21 447 8989
Email: hbowen@sn.apc.org
www: http://www.ifuw.org/southafrica
Contact: Mrs Hazel Bowen, National President

The South African Association of Women Graduates (SAAWG) promotes the tertiary education of women and their self development over their life span. It seeks and facilitates equity for women graduates, cross cultural insights and co-operation, and societal advancement. Its great underlying purpose is world peace, brought about through education and international friendship.

Bertha Stoneman Memorial Award for Botanical Research
Subjects: Botany or any related subject including environmental studies.
Purpose: To provide assistance for women undertaking research in the biological sciences.
Eligibility: Open to members of the South African Association of Women Graduates.
Level of Study: Postgraduate.
Type: Research grant.
Value: Rand 1,000.
Frequency: Annual.
Country of Study: Any country.
No. of awards offered: One.
Application Procedure: Applicants must write for application forms.
Closing Date: October 31st.
Funding: Private.
No. of awards given last year: One.
Additional Information: The award is made when a suitable applicant applies.

For further information contact:

21 Templeton Drive, Grahamstown, 6140, South Africa
Contact: Miss V Henley

Edna Machanick Award
Subjects: All subjects.
Purpose: To provide assistance to women at tertiary institutions, other than a university.
Eligibility: Open to South African women of all races who have successfully completed one year of a course of study and are in need of financial assistance to complete their studies towards a non degree qualification eg. diploma or certificate at the tertiary education level.
Level of Study: Graduate.
Type: Award.
Value: Rand 500 per year.
Frequency: Annual.
Study Establishment: Any Institute of Higher Education.
Country of Study: Any country.
No. of awards offered: Three-four.
Application Procedure: Applicants must complete an application form, available on written request.
Closing Date: October 31st.
Funding: Private.
Additional Information: The awards are generally made by the institutions concerned. SAAUW provides the funding.

Hansi Pollak Scholarship
Subjects: Any branch of the social sciences.
Purpose: To assist postgraduate study or research devoted to the practical purpose of ameliorating social conditions in South Africa.
Eligibility: Open to South African women graduates of all races who are, or have become, members of the Association.
Level of Study: Doctorate, Postgraduate.
Type: One scholarship.
Value: Rand 6,000 paid in six month instalments.
Length of Study: Two years, non renewable.
Frequency: Every two years.
Study Establishment: Any recognised university.
Country of Study: Any country.
No. of awards offered: One.
Application Procedure: Applicants must write for application forms.
Funding: Private.
No. of awards given last year: One.
No. of applicants last year: 50.
Additional Information: Fellows must spend at least two years in South Africa after completing a Master's or doctoral degree, in order to put into practice the results of the research.

For further information contact:

PO Box 6638, Johannesburg, Braamfontein, 2000, South Africa
Email: jocelynbell@iafrica.com
Contact: Ms Jocelyn Bell

Isie Smuts Research Award
Subjects: All subjects.
Purpose: To assist postgraduate women in research.
Eligibility: Open to members of the South African Association of Women Graduates.
Level of Study: Postgraduate.
Type: Award.
Value: Rand 1,000.
Frequency: Annual.
Study Establishment: Any university.
Country of Study: South Africa.
No. of awards offered: One.
Application Procedure: Applicants must write to Miss V Henley.
Closing Date: October 31st.
Funding: Private.
No. of awards given last year: One.

For further information contact:

21 Templeton Drive, Grahamstown, 6140, South Africa
Contact: Miss V Henley

Joan Whitmore Scholarship
Subjects: Engineering.
Purpose: To assist postgraduate study or research in the broad field of engineering.
Level of Study: Postgraduate.
Type: One scholarship.
Frequency: Annual, if funds are available.
Study Establishment: An approved university or technikon.
Country of Study: South Africa.
Application Procedure: Applicants must contact Joan Whitmore showing evidence of the relevance of their study or research to the development of South Africa and of their community service.
Funding: Private.

For further information contact:

201 Sheraton
605 Pretorius Street, Arcadia, Pretoria, 0083, South Africa
Contact: Ms Joan Whitmore

SAAWG International Fellowship
Subjects: All subjects for postgraduate research.
Purpose: To assist women, who wish to study in South Africa.
Eligibility: Open to members of the International Federation of University Women, foreign students enrolled at a South African university for at least one year for postgraduate research.
Level of Study: Postgraduate.
Type: Fellowship.
Value: At least rand 1,000.
Length of Study: Not less than six months.
Frequency: Every three years.
Study Establishment: A university in South Africa.
Country of Study: South Africa.
No. of awards offered: One.
Application Procedure: Applicants must write for application forms.
Closing Date: August 31st.
Funding: Private.
Additional Information: The award is made when a suitable applicant applies.

For further information contact:

21 Templeton Drive, Grahamstown, 6140, South Africa
Contact: Miss V Henley

SOUTH AFRICAN COUNCIL FOR ENGLISH EDUCATION (SACEE)

PO Box 660, Pretoria, 0001, South Africa
Tel: (27) 12 429 8616
Fax: (27) 12 429 8616
Email: ueng6@unisa.ac.za
www: http://www.sacee.org.za
Contact: Ms Patricia Bootland, Administrative Secretary

The South African Council for English Education's mission statement is to support the teaching, learning and appreciation of English. They have branches throughout South Africa, and major national projects are the English Alive publication, English olympiad, language challenge, oracy programme and plays festival.

Norah Taylor Bursary
Subjects: Speech training, oral communication, and the teaching of English as a second language.
Purpose: To assist teachers to further their training.

Eligibility: Open to qualified teachers teaching English or other subjects in English, with three years' post matriculation study, at least four years' teaching experience and leadership potential.
Level of Study: Graduate, Postgraduate, Professional development, Unrestricted.
Type: Bursary.
Value: Varies, depending upon type of course taken.
Frequency: Annual.
Study Establishment: Any educational institution for correspondence.
Country of Study: South Africa.
No. of awards offered: Varies.
Application Procedure: Applicants must write for details.
Closing Date: July 31st of the year preceding that for which the bursary is required.
Funding: Private.
No. of awards given last year: Two.
No. of applicants last year: 10.
Additional Information: Applicants not conforming to the requirements cannot be considered and will not be replied to.

South African Council for English Education (EX-PCE Bursary)
Subjects: English and subjects in English, including literature, drama or radio.
Purpose: To assist teachers in service who wish to improve their qualifications. To assist those who wish to take up postgraduate study specialising in the English language.
Eligibility: Open to nationals and residents of South Africa. Applicants' normal place of residence should be Gauteng RSA.
Level of Study: Postgraduate.
Type: Bursary.
Value: Varies, depending upon type of course taken.
Length of Study: Varies.
Frequency: Annual.
Study Establishment: Any academic institution.
Country of Study: South Africa.
No. of awards offered: Varies.
Application Procedure: Applicants must write for details.
Closing Date: Applications are accepted at any time.
Funding: Private.
No. of awards given last year: None.
No. of applicants last year: None.

SOUTH AFRICAN DENTAL ASSOCIATION

Private Bag 1
Houghton, Johannesburg, Braamfontein, 2041, South Africa
Tel: (27) 11 484 5288
Fax: (27) 11 642 5718
Email: rswanepoel@sada.co.za
www: http://www.sadanet.co.za
Contact: Ms Rita Swanepoel, Secretary

The South African Dental Association's main objective is to promote the interests of its members in order to promote optimal oral health for all.

The DDF Scholarship for the Development of a Research Technique for Dentistry/Dental Research
Subjects: Dentistry.
Purpose: To enable a qualified person to spend time in a laboratory to study a research technique.
Eligibility: Open to individuals with a proven record of research or who are sponsored by such an individual. The applicant must undertake to live and work in South Africa for at least two years after the tenure of the Scholarship, or to refund the money.
Level of Study: Postgraduate.
Type: Scholarship.
Value: Rand 8,000.

Length of Study: At least one month. The scholarship must be held during the year it is awarded.
Frequency: Annual.
Country of Study: Any country.
No. of awards offered: One.
Application Procedure: Applicants must write for details.
Closing Date: January 31st.
Funding: Private.
No. of applicants last year: One.
Additional Information: This award does not render itself solely to the specific support of research nor to the study of research techniques.

Lever Pond's Postgraduate Fellowship

Subjects: Any biological field related to dentistry.
Purpose: To promote dental research and ensure its continuation in South Africa.
Eligibility: Open to residents of South Africa, who are either dentists registered with the South African Medical and Dental Council wishing to qualify themselves further or to equip themselves for research by taking an additional degree, or who are suitably qualified persons wishing to concentrate on dental research.
Level of Study: Postgraduate.
Type: Fellowship.
Value: Up to rand 25,000.
Length of Study: One year, renewable in special circumstances.
Frequency: Annual.
Country of Study: South Africa unless facilities are not available.
No. of awards offered: One.
Application Procedure: Applicants must complete an application form which must be supported by and submitted through a university or other such institution. An award may be made for research overseas, provided that the application is accompanied by a statement from the sponsoring institution that the proposed project can best be carried out in another country.
Closing Date: January 31st.
Funding: Private.
Contributor: Dentists.
No. of applicants last year: Three.
Additional Information: A Fellow working overseas must undertake to return to South Africa for a minimum period of two years after completing the project under the award, or refund the Fellowship Fund any money he or she has received.

THE SOUTH AFRICAN INSTITUTE OF INTERNATIONAL AFFAIRS (SAIIA)

Jan Smuts House
PO Box 31596, Johannesburg, Braamfontein, 2017, South Africa
Tel: (27) 11 339 2021
Fax: (27) 11 339 2154
Email: saiiagen@global.co.za
www: http://www.wits.ac.za/saiia.html
Contact: Ms Gillian Large, Programme Manager & Assistant to National Director

The South African Institute of International Affairs (SAIIA) is an independent, self-governing institute, whose purpose is to encourage wider and more informed interest in international affairs.

SAIIA Bradlow Fellowship

Subjects: Social and behavioural sciences.
Purpose: To provide limited travel costs and a stipend to enable a senior Scholar to reside at the Institute in order to research a subject of importance to South Africa's international relations.
Eligibility: Open to senior Scholars.
Level of Study: Research.
Type: Fellowship.
Value: The stipend covers a return economy class airfare from place of residence as well as living expenses.

Length of Study: Four-six months.
Frequency: Annual.
Study Establishment: South African Institute of International Affairs.
Country of Study: South Africa.
No. of awards offered: One.
Application Procedure: Applicants must send a curriculum vitae including a short research proposal of not more than 1,000 words to the Director of Studies.
Funding: Private.
Contributor: The Bradlow Foundation.
No. of awards given last year: One.

SOUTHERN CROSS UNIVERSITY

Graduate Research College
PO Box 157, Lismore, NSW, 2480, Australia
Tel: (61) 2 6620 3705
Fax: (61) 2 6626 9145
Email: jrussell@scu.edu.au
www: http://www.scu.edu.au
Contact: Mr John Russell, Administrative Officer

Southern Cross University is one of Australia's most modern, creative and innovative universities founded on traditions of academic excellence, with national and international industry links. The University's courses emphasise real world skills and vocational training and are designed to give graduates a competitive edge in today's demanding employment market.

Southern Cross University Postgraduate Research Scholarships

Subjects: All subjects.
Purpose: To support a student while undertaking postgraduate research study.
Eligibility: There are no eligibility restrictions.
Level of Study: Postgraduate.
Type: Scholarship.
Value: Up to australian $12,000.
Length of Study: Up to three years.
Frequency: Twice a year.
Study Establishment: Southern Cross University.
Country of Study: Australia.
No. of awards offered: 15-20.
Application Procedure: Applicants must complete an application form.
Closing Date: October 31st or May 31st.
Funding: Government.
No. of awards given last year: 12.
No. of applicants last year: 92.

SOUTHWEST MISSOURI STATE UNIVERSITY

College of Business Administration
400 David D Glass Hall, Springfield, MO, 65801, United States of America
Tel: (1) 417 836 5646
Fax: (1) 417 836 4407
Email: dmf603f@smsu.edu
www: http://www.coba.smsu.edu
Contact: MBA Admissions Officer

The Master of Business Administration (MBA) degree at SMSU is a College of Business Administration degree with courses taken in various departments. The programme will provide the background knowledge necessary for professional practice in the field of business. In the eyes of MBA students at SMSU, educational value is defined by a high quality programme, low tuition rates and low living costs in an attractive locale.

SMSU Carr Foundation Scholarship

Subjects: MBA.
Purpose: To assist students with expenses and enhance learning.
Eligibility: Students must be enrolled on the MBA programme and display financial need.
Level of Study: Graduate.
Type: Scholarship.
Value: US$600.
Length of Study: Varies.
Frequency: Annual, if funds are available.
Study Establishment: Southwest Missouri State University.
Country of Study: United States of America.
No. of awards offered: One.
Application Procedure: Applicants must contact the organisation for application details.
Closing Date: Please contact the organisation.

SMSU Graduate Assistantships

Subjects: All subjects.
Purpose: To assist students with expenses and to enhance learning while studying for advanced degrees at SMSU.
Eligibility: Applicants must be admitted to a graduate programme at SMSU to be eligible. A minimum grade point average of 3.00 on the last 60 hours of undergraduate course work or a minimum grade point average of 3.00 on nine or more hours of graduate course work is required. Graduate students who did not receive both their primary and secondary education where English was the primary language must meet the following requirements to qualify for graduate assistantships: successful completion of one semester of graduate studies at SMSU, during which they complete cultural orientation to prepare them for a teaching appointment and pass an SMSU juried examination in which the candidate must demonstrate his or her ability to interpret written English passages and to communicate orally in English in a classroom setting.
Level of Study: Graduate, MBA.
Type: Graduate assistantships.
Value: A minimum stipend of US$6,150 for the academic year. In a few situations a stipend of US$8,200 may be awarded.
Length of Study: A maximum of two years.
Frequency: Annual.
Study Establishment: Southwest Missouri State University.
Country of Study: United States of America.
No. of awards offered: Varies.
Application Procedure: Applicants must submit an application directly to the department in which the assistantship is sought. It is wise to check with the department before applying. Applications are available from the Graduate College and on the website http://www.smsu.edu/grad. Information from an applicant must include employment history, academic history and the addresses of referees.
Additional Information: Graduate assistantships are offered in both administrative and academic areas and involve administrative, research or teaching responsibilities. Whenever feasible, the assistantship assignment is closely related to the student's programme of study. A graduate assistant is required to complete a minimum of six hours of graduate course work during each semester of appointment. Some departments or units may require assistants to take more than six hours of course work. Graduate assistants are not eligible to work at any other paid position at SMSU during the time of their assistantship. A limited number of graduate assistantships are available during the Summer session. A graduate assistant appointed for the Summer session will receive a stipend of either US$1,537 or US$2,050. Summer graduate assistants are required to complete a minimum of three hours of graduate course work during the Summer session.

SMSU Graduate of Business Professional Honor Society Scholarship

Subjects: MBA.
Purpose: To assist students with expenses and enhance learning.
Eligibility: Applicants must be enrolled in either the MBA program or the Macc Program, have a grade point average of not less than 3.33, have active membership in Graduate of Business Professional Honor Society and have been a member of the society for at least two semesters.
Level of Study: MBA.
Type: Scholarship.
Frequency: Annual.
Study Establishment: Southwest Missouri State University.
Country of Study: United States of America.
No. of awards offered: One.
Application Procedure: Applicants must contact the organisation for application details.
Closing Date: Please contact the organisation for details.

SMSU Robert and Charlotte Bitter Graduate Scholarship

Subjects: MBA.
Purpose: To assist students with expenses and enhance learning.
Eligibility: Applicants must have been admitted to the MBA or Macc programme and have a Graduate Management Admissions Test score of 1,100 or higher, be enrolled in 12 hours each semester and have a grade point average of 3.33.
Level of Study: Graduate, MBA.
Type: Scholarship.
Value: US$1,200.
Length of Study: Varies.
Frequency: Annual, if funds are available.
Study Establishment: Southwest Missouri State University.
Country of Study: United States of America.
No. of awards offered: One.
Application Procedure: Applicants must contact the organisation for application details.
Closing Date: Please contact the organisation.

SPALDING TRUSTS

PO Box 85, Stowmarket, Suffolk, IP14 3NY, England
Fax: (44) 1359 240739
Contact: Mrs T Rodgers, General Secretary

The Spalding Trust supports academic research on comparative inter-faith projects. Consideration is also given to applications which are not academically orientated, provided that they will have a practical and beneficial effect on inter-religious understanding.

Spalding Trusts Grants-in-Aid of Research

Subjects: World religions other than that of the holder. Such study should be the principal, not a subsidiary, object.
Purpose: To promote a better understanding between the great cultures of the world by encouraging the study of the religious principles on which they are based.
Eligibility: Open to those engaged in academic studies or in study which will have practical benefit in promoting inter-religious understanding. No grant may be offered for a study or project within the context of the applicant's own religion unless there is likely to be a significant result in the improvement of inter-religious understanding. The trustees are reluctant to approve requests for assistance with the expenses of undertaking or completing first degree courses. The Trust's resources do not permit assistance to applicants to whom other adequate sources of finance are available. Consideration is also given to applications which are not academically orientated, provided that they will have a practical and beneficial effect on inter-religious understanding.
Level of Study: Doctorate, Postdoctorate, Postgraduate, Research.
Type: Varies.

Value: Limited amounts in the form of grants for subsistence to-wards tuition fees, purchase of books or for travel.
Length of Study: Short periods of up to three years.
Frequency: According to research project.
Country of Study: Any country.
Application Procedure: Applicants must submit a research pro-posal, a budget including other possible sources of funding, an aca-demic reference and curriculum vitae. Applications take two-three months to be considered.
Closing Date: Applications are considered throughout the year but major applications are considered in April.
Funding: Private.
Contributor: Mr and Mrs H N Spalding.
No. of awards given last year: 50.
No. of applicants last year: 92.
Additional Information: Trustees are particularly interested in re-search projects which are backed by professional ability to raise the standard of knowledge of religious principles and practices, and to interpret their relation to contemporary society. On completion of the project, the Trustees expect to receive a report on what has been achieved.

SPINAL CORD INJURY EDUCATION AND TRAINING FOUNDATION (ETF)

Paralyzed Veterans of America Education & Training Foundation
801 18th Street North West, Washington, DC, 20006, United States of America
Tel: (1) 202 416 7651
Fax: (1) 202 416 7641
Email: etf@pva.org
www: http://www.pva.org
Contact: Administrative Officer

Spinal Cord Injury Grants

Subjects: Spinal cord injury: continuing education and training, post professional traineeships, patient or client education, conferences.
Purpose: To provide funds for grants to institutions, agencies and organisations that will improve the knowledge and abilities of health professionals, people with SCI or disease and those significant to them.
Eligibility: Open to suitably qualified persons working in the field of spinal cord injury.
Level of Study: Doctorate, Graduate, Postgraduate, Predoctorate.
Type: Grant.
Value: Varies.
Frequency: Annual.
Country of Study: Any country.
No. of awards offered: Varies.
Application Procedure: Applicants must write for details.
Closing Date: December 1st or June 1st.

ST ANDREW'S SOCIETY OF THE STATE OF NEW YORK

3 West 51st Street, New York, NY, 10019, United States of America
Tel: (1) 212 223 4248
Fax: (1) 212 223 0748
Email: standrewsny@msn.com
Contact: Mr Stephen James White

St Andrew's Society of the State of New York's constitution states, 'For the relief of natives of Scotland and their descendants who might be in want or distress and to promote social intercourse among its members'.

St Andrew's Society of the State of New York Scholarship

Subjects: General, no field of endeavour requirement.
Purpose: To promote cultural and intellectual interchange and good-will between Scotland and the United States of America.
Eligibility: Open to students of Scottish-American descent who have graduated from an American university and have New York state address (within a 250 mile radius).
Level of Study: Postgraduate.
Type: Scholarship.
Value: US$10,000.
Length of Study: One year.
Frequency: Annual.
Study Establishment: Any university in Scotland.
Country of Study: Scotland.
No. of awards offered: Two.
Application Procedure: Applicants must submit an application form, documentation of transcripts and letters of recommendation. The president of each college or university must recommend one student only from that institution.
Closing Date: December 15th.
Funding: Private.
No. of awards given last year: Two.
No. of applicants last year: 25.

ST ANDREW'S SOCIETY OF THE STATE OF NEW YORK

36 St Andrew Square, Edinburgh, EH2 2YE, Scotland
Fax: (44) 131 557 9178
Contact: Chairman of the Scottish Selection Committee

St Andrew's Society of the State of New York Scholarship Fund

Subjects: All subjects.
Purpose: To support advanced study exchanges between the United States of America and Scotland by individuals with Scottish backgrounds.
Eligibility: Open to newly qualified graduates of a Scottish university or of Oxford or Cambridge. Candidates are required to have a Scot-tish background. The possession of an Honours degree is not es-sential. Personality and other qualities will influence the selection.
Level of Study: Postgraduate.
Type: Scholarship.
Value: US$20,000 to cover university tuition fees, room and board, and transportation expenses.
Length of Study: One academic year.
Frequency: Annual.
Study Establishment: An American university within 250 miles of New York City. Only in unusual circumstances will the Society con-sider other locations. Thereafter, the Scholar is expected to spend a little time travelling in America before returning to Scotland.
Country of Study: United States of America, restricted to a radius of 250 miles from New York City.
No. of awards offered: Two.
Application Procedure: Applicants must write for details.
Closing Date: Early January.
Funding: Private.
No. of awards given last year: Two.
No. of applicants last year: 10.
Additional Information: Each Scottish university will vet its own ap-plicants and nominate one candidate to go forward to the Final Se-lection Committee to be held in Edinburgh in early March. Oxford and Cambridge applicants should apply directly to the Society.

ST JOHNS UNIVERSITY

Rome Campus
MBA Programme
Via Santa Maria Mediatrice 24, Rome, I-00165, Italy
Tel: (39) 066 369 37
Fax: (39) 066 369 01
Email: info@stjohns.edu
www: http://www.stjohns.edu
Contact: MBA Admissions Officer

St John's University was founded by the Vincentian community in 1870. Today it is the largest Catholic university in the United States of America. Through its outstanding faculty, exciting programmes and state of the art facilities, the University remains on the cutting edge of contemporary theory and technology. Its graduate students are afforded every opportunity to achieve their goals as initial thinkers and career minded individuals.

SJG Graduate Assistantships

Subjects: Arts and humanities, medical studies, natural sciences, or MBAs.
Purpose: To offer financial support to students undertaking graduate programmes.
Eligibility: Candidates are selected on academic ability.
Level of Study: Graduate, MBA.
Type: Assistantships.
Value: A stipend plus full tuition remission for up to 12 credits a semester is awarded.
Length of Study: One year.
Frequency: Annual.
Study Establishment: St John's University.
Country of Study: United States of America.
No. of awards offered: Varies.
Application Procedure: Applicants must write to the Office of Admissions for an application form.
Closing Date: April 1st.
Additional Information: Successful applicants are not permitted to accept employment or other appointments either inside or outside the University during the period of their contract.

STANFORD HUMANITIES CENTER

Mariposa House
546 Salvatierra Walk
Stanford University, Stanford, CA, 94305-8630, United States of America
Tel: (1) 650 723 3052
Fax: (1) 650 723 1895
Email: sebbard@stanford.edu
www: http://shc.stanford.edu
Contact: Ms Susan Sebbard

The Stanford Humanities Center was founded in 1980 to promote humanistic research and education, both at Stanford University and nationally. To this aim it provides fellowships, public presentations and research workshops.

External Faculty Fellowships

Subjects: Humanities.
Purpose: To offer research opportunities both to members of humanities departments as traditionally defined and to other scholars seriously interested in humanistic issues.
Eligibility: Candidates should be at least three years beyond receipt of their PhD. These Fellowships are intended primarily for persons currently teaching or affiliated with an academic institution, but others may apply.
Level of Study: Postdoctorate.
Type: Fellowship.

Value: Up to US$25,000 for junior scholars and up to US$40,000 for senior scholars. In addition, up to US$12,500 will be offered as a housing or travel subsidy. Applicants are expected to seek supplementary financial support and are required to contribute this support, together with any sabbatical earnings, to their stipend.
Length of Study: One year residency, not renewable.
Frequency: Annual.
Study Establishment: Stanford Humanities Center.
Country of Study: United States of America.
No. of awards offered: Six-eight.
Application Procedure: Applicants must complete an application form available from the Center.
Closing Date: November 15th.
Funding: Government, Private.
No. of awards given last year: Nine.
No. of applicants last year: 187.

Rockefeller Fellowships in Black Performing Arts

Subjects: Arts, humanities or the performing arts.
Purpose: To support scholars with an interest in the arts whose research examines the character and global influences of black arts and culture with a specific focus on performance. In addition these fellowships will support research which furthers the understanding of links between humanities, performance and arts generally within the specific area of black studies, or by placing black performance in a comparative context.
Eligibility: Junior Scholars should be at least three years but no more than 10 years beyond receipt of their PhD or MFA.
Level of Study: Postdoctorate, Research.
Type: Fellowship.
Value: Up to US$25,000 for junior scholars and up to US$40,000 for senior scholars. In addition, up to US$12,500 will be offered as a housing and moving allowance. Applicants are expected to seek supplementary financial support and are required to contribute this support, together with any sabbatical earnings, to their stipend.
Frequency: Annual.
Study Establishment: Stanford Humanities Center.
Country of Study: United States of America.
No. of awards offered: Two, one to a senior and one to a junior.
Application Procedure: Applicants must complete an application form available from the Center.
Closing Date: November 1st.
Funding: Private.
Contributor: The Rockefeller Foundation, the Stanford Humanities Center and in conjunction with the Stanford Committee on Black Performing Arts.
No. of awards given last year: Two.
No. of applicants last year: 11.

STANLEY SMITH (UK) HORTICULTURAL TRUST

Cory Lodge
PO Box 365, Cambridge, Cambridgeshire, CB2 1HR, England
Tel: (44) 1223 336299
Fax: (44) 1223 336278
Contact: Mr James Cullen, Director

Stanley Smith (UK) Horticultural Trust Awards

Subjects: Horticulture. The Trust supports individual projects in all aspects of amenity horticulture and some aspects of commercial horticulture.
Purpose: To support amenity horticulture and horticultural education.
Eligibility: Open to institutions and individuals. All projects are judged entirely on merit and there are no eligibility requirements, but grants are not awarded for students to take academic or diploma courses of any kind.
Level of Study: Unrestricted.

Type: Varies.
Value: Varies.
Length of Study: Dependent on the nature of the project.
Frequency: Twice a year.
Country of Study: Any country.
No. of awards offered: Varies.
Application Procedure: Applicants must apply to the Trust. Trustees allocate awards in Spring and Autumn.
Closing Date: February 15th and September 15th.
Funding: Private.
Contributor: Donations.
No. of awards given last year: 46.
No. of applicants last year: 218.

STATE FARM COMPANIES FOUNDATION

One State Farm Plaza
B-4, Bloomington, IL, 61710-0001, United States of America
Tel: (1) 309 766 2161
Fax: (1) 309 766 2314
Email: home.sf-foundation.494b00@statefarm.com
www: http://www.statefarm.com/foundati/doctoral.htm
Contact: Graduate Office

The State Farm Companies Foundation provides support for higher education through grants to college and universities, the Matching Gift Program and established scholarship programmes.

Doctoral Dissertation Award

Subjects: Insurance, business and risk management. Eligible dissertation topics include insurance and risk management topics that directly relate to, or affect, the insurance industry, and business topics that relate to general business principles and issues.
Purpose: To stimulate research and develop knowledge in business and insurance related fields.
Eligibility: Open to candidates who have completed a major portion of their doctoral programme and are at the dissertation stage. Applicants must be nominated by their supervising professor or faculty advisor and must be United States citizens.
Level of Study: Doctorate.
Type: Award.
Value: US$10,000 for the individual and the winner's school receives a US$3,000 grant.
Frequency: Annual.
Country of Study: United States of America.
No. of awards offered: Up to three awards in each category.
Application Procedure: Applicants must request an application form from the dean or director of doctoral programmes at their university. Alternatively they can contact State Farm Companies Foundation at the main address. A completed application form, nomination forms and required attachments must be submitted. The Foundation will not accept faxed materials.
Closing Date: March 31st.
Contributor: The State Farm Companies Foundation.
No. of awards given last year: Six.
No. of applicants last year: 34.
Additional Information: The State Farm Companies Foundation is not involved in the evaluation or selection of the award winners. An independent committee of educators selects the winners using the following criteria: academic achievement, quality of dissertation proposal, and recommendations from dissertation advisor and faculty.

STATE LIBRARY OF NEW SOUTH WALES

Macquarie Street, Sydney, NSW, 2000, Australia
Tel: (61) 2 9273 1766
Fax: (61) 2 9273 1248
Email: library@slnsw.gov.au
www: http://www.slnsw.gov.au
Contact: State Librarian

The State Library of New South Wales is the premier reference and research library in the state. The Library consists of the State Reference Library and the Mitchell Library which contains the famous Australian Research Collections pertaining to the history of Australia and the South West Pacific region.

C H Currey Memorial Fellowship

Subjects: Australian history.
Purpose: To promote the writing of Australian history from original sources.
Eligibility: Open to individuals of any nationality.
Level of Study: Unrestricted.
Type: Fellowship.
Value: Approx. australian $20,000.
Frequency: Annual.
Country of Study: Australia.
No. of awards offered: One.
Application Procedure: Applicants must complete an application form, available from the State Librarian.
Closing Date: Varies.
Funding: Private.
No. of awards given last year: One.
No. of applicants last year: Nine.
Additional Information: Proposed work must conform to the purpose of the award.

Nancy Keesing Fellowship

Subjects: Australian history, literature, life and culture.
Purpose: To encourage the use of the State Library's collections for original research.
Eligibility: Open to researchers of any nationality.
Level of Study: Unrestricted.
Type: Fellowship.
Value: Australian $10,000.
Frequency: Annual.
Study Establishment: The State Library of New South Wales.
Country of Study: Australia.
No. of awards offered: One.
Application Procedure: Applicants must complete an application form, available on request.
Closing Date: Varies.
Funding: Private.
No. of awards given last year: One.
No. of applicants last year: Nine.

STATISTICAL SOCIETY OF CANADA

1485 Laperriere Avenue, Ottawa, ON, K1Z 7S8, Canada
Tel: (1) 613 725 2253
Fax: (1) 613 729 6206
Email: ssc@thewillowgroup.com
www: http://www.ssc.ca
Contact: Secretary

The Statistical Society of Canada provides a forum for discussion and interaction among individuals involved in all aspects of the statistical sciences. It publishes a newsletter, Liaison, as well as a scientific journal, The Canadian Journal of Statistics. The Society also organises annual scientific meetings and short courses on professional development.

Pierre Robillard Award

Subjects: Statistics.
Purpose: To recognise the best PhD thesis defended at a Canadian university and written in a field covered by the Canadian Journal of Statistics.
Level of Study: Doctorate.
Type: Award.
Value: A certificate, monetary prize of canadian $400 and one year membership in the Society.
Frequency: Annual.
Country of Study: Canada.
No. of awards offered: Varies.
Application Procedure: Applicants must submit four copies of the thesis together with a covering letter from the thesis supervisor.
Closing Date: February 15th.
No. of awards given last year: One.
No. of applicants last year: 10.
Additional Information: The committee may decide that none of the submitted theses merits the award.

STIFTELSEN LARS HIERTAS MINNE

Eriksbergsg 3 2tr, Stockholm, S-11430, Sweden
Tel: (46) 86 116 401
Fax: (46) 86 110 527
Email: hierta@brevet.nu
www: http://go.to/hierta
Contact: Ms Elisabeth Norlander, Secretary

Stiftelsen Lars Hiertas Minne Scientific Research Award

Subjects: Any scientific field.
Purpose: To support scientific research.
Eligibility: Open to all nationalities.
Level of Study: Doctorate, Postdoctorate, Postgraduate.
Value: Krona 10,000-50,000.
Frequency: Annual.
Study Establishment: Any institution.
Country of Study: Sweden.
No. of awards offered: Varies.
Application Procedure: Applicants must complete an application form.
Closing Date: October 1st.
Funding: Private.
No. of awards given last year: 240.
No. of applicants last year: 717.
Additional Information: Foreigners must conduct their research in Sweden.

STOUT RESEARCH CENTRE, VICTORIA UNIVERSITY OF WELLINGTON

PO Box 600, Wellington, New Zealand
Tel: (64) 4 465 5305
Fax: (64) 4 463 5439
Email: stout-centre@vuw.ac.nz
www: http://www.vuw.ac.nz/stout-centre
Contact: Ms Margarita Ivanova, Administrator

J D Stout Fellowship

Subjects: New Zealand society, history or culture.
Purpose: To encourage research.
Eligibility: Open to distinguished Scholars from New Zealand and abroad.
Level of Study: Postdoctorate.
Type: Fellowship.
Value: Up to new zealand $56,000.
Length of Study: One year.

Frequency: Annual, if funds are available.
Study Establishment: The Stout Research Centre.
Country of Study: New Zealand.
No. of awards offered: One.
Application Procedure: Applicants must write for details.
Closing Date: August 1st of the year preceding the fellowship.

THE STROKE ASSOCIATION

Stroke House
Whitecross Street, London, EC1Y 8JJ, England
Tel: (44) 20 7566 0300
Fax: (44) 20 7490 4768
Email: research@stroke.org.uk
www: http://www.stroke.org.uk
Contact: Dr Sharon Crossen, Research Office

The Stroke Association raises funds for research, prevention, welfare, information and community services.

Stroke Association Clinical Fellowships

Subjects: Stroke research.
Purpose: To equip a trainee for a career in the prevention, treatment or rehabilitation of strokes.
Eligibility: Open to departments that can demonstrate a track record in providing an educational training programme which may include a research project.
Level of Study: Professional development.
Type: Fellowship.
Value: UK £35,000 for one year.
Frequency: Annual.
Study Establishment: Suitable universities and medical schools.
Country of Study: United Kingdom.
No. of awards offered: Two.
Application Procedure: Applicants must respond to advertisements in the British Medical Journal in January of each year. Application forms are available from the Research Secretary.
Closing Date: Please contact the organisation.
Funding: Private.
Additional Information: Fellowships are assessed by peer review. Awards are made in June.

Stroke Association Stroke Therapy Research Bursaries

Subjects: Stroke research.
Purpose: To provide a research training programme and appropriate supervision to equip a trainee for a career in stroke research.
Eligibility: These bursaries are primarily intended for nurses and therapists, but consideration will be given to other health professionals. They will be awarded to departments that can demonstrate a track record and current participation in stroke research.
Level of Study: Postgraduate, Professional development.
Type: Bursary.
Value: UK £20,000 per year.
Length of Study: Up to three years.
Frequency: Annual.
Study Establishment: Suitable universities and hospitals.
Country of Study: United Kingdom.
No. of awards offered: Three.
Application Procedure: Applicants must respond to advertisements in Therapy Weekly in January of each year. Application forms are available from the Research Secretary.
Closing Date: Please contact the organisation.
Funding: Private.
Additional Information: Further information is available on request.

Stroke Research Awards

Subjects: Stroke research. Applied research in epidemiology, prevention, acute treatment, assessment and rehabilitation, psychology of stroke and stroke in ethnic minorities.
Purpose: To advance research into stroke.

Eligibility: Open to medically qualified and other clinically active researchers in the United Kingdom, in the relevant fields. Applications are judged by peer review on their merit without limitations of age. Applicants can be from any country but must be based in the United Kingdom.
Level of Study: Postdoctorate, Research.
Type: Project grant.
Value: Awards cover salaries for researchers and support staff, some equipment costs, consumables and essential travel. No other overheads, advertising etc. are covered. The maximum award is normally UK £60,000 per year to a total of UK £180,000 over three years.
Length of Study: One-three years.
Frequency: Annual.
Study Establishment: A suitable university or hospital in the United Kingdom.
Country of Study: United Kingdom.
No. of awards offered: Usually 20-30.
Application Procedure: Application forms are available on request from the Research Secretary.
Closing Date: As advertised, usually in July and November.
Funding: Private.
Contributor: Donations.
No. of awards given last year: 11.
No. of applicants last year: 80.

SUDAN CIVIC FOUNDATION (SCF)

SCF House
37 Monkswell Road, Cambridge, Cambridgeshire, CB2 2JU, England
Tel: (44) 1223 504393
Fax: (44) 1223 501125
Email: equiano@sudan21.net
www: http://www.sudan21.net/equiano.html
Contact: Dr Salah Al Bander, Director

The Sudan Civic Foundation (SCF) is an independent non-profit making group whose purpose is to contribute to public understanding of socio-economic and political issues through research, discussion and publications. It was established in 1996 to provide, among other things, a network for those who share a common concern for better race relations.

Equiano Memorial Award

Subjects: The promotion of race relations.
Purpose: To support a person engaged in the study or promotion of tolerance and peaceful co-existence between communities, and to support research or practical field investigations, leading to a report, essay or dissertation.
Eligibility: There are no eligibility restrictions.
Level of Study: Unrestricted.
Type: Research grant.
Value: UK £2,000.
Length of Study: One year.
Frequency: Annual.
Study Establishment: An academic or professional establishment.
Country of Study: Any country.
No. of awards offered: Two.
Application Procedure: Applicants must complete an application form and should write for details.
Closing Date: March 31st.
Funding: Private.
Contributor: Dr Salah Al Bander.
No. of awards given last year: One.
No. of applicants last year: 152.
Additional Information: Applicants must be registered at a recognised educational institution. The award is based on need as well as academic merit. The area of study must fit in with research priorities of the Foundation. Applicants who are awarded the grant may reapply for a second year of funding.

THE SUSAN G KOMEN BREAST CANCER FOUNDATION

5005 LBJ Freeway
Suite 250, Dallas, TX, 75244, United States of America
Tel: (1) 972 855 1656
Fax: (1) 972 855 1640
Email: grants@komen.org
www: http://www.komen.org
Contact: Ms Elizabeth Lopez Lyon, Grants Co-ordinator

It is the mission of the Susan G Komen Breast Cancer Foundation to eradicate breast cancer as a life threatening disease by advancing research, education, screening and treatment.

Basic Clinical and Translational Breast Cancer Research

Subjects: Studies may be clinical, basic or translational design. The Foundation does not target funding to any specific area of breast cancer study, geographic area or institution.
Purpose: This programme is intended to foster investigations into the cause, treatment, prevention and cure of breast cancers.
Level of Study: Research.
Type: Research grant.
Value: US$250,000 (combined direct and indirect costs) over a two year period.
Length of Study: Two years.
Frequency: Annual.
Country of Study: Any country.
No. of awards offered: Dependent on funding per project.
Application Procedure: Applicants must register before submitting an application. Registration is available on the website. Candidates should contact the National Grants and Sponsored Programs Office for more information at the main address. All applications must be submitted electronically.
Closing Date: Electronic abstracts are due by 11.59pm Central Standard Time on October 18th and applications must be posted to the Komen website by 11.59pm Central Standard Time on November 1st.
Funding: Private.
No. of awards given last year: 50.
No. of applicants last year: 364.

Imaging Technology

Subjects: Advanced imaging technology.
Purpose: To fund research and develop new methods for early detection and diagnosis of breast cancer.
Eligibility: Applicants from any country may apply.
Type: Research grant.
Value: US$250,000 combined direct and indirect costs over a two year period.
Length of Study: Two years.
Frequency: Annual.
Country of Study: Any country.
No. of awards offered: Varies.
Application Procedure: Applicants must register before submitting an application. Registration is available on the website. Candidates should contact the National Grants and Sponsored Programs Office for more information at the main address. All applications must be submitted electronically.
Closing Date: Electronic abstracts are due by 11.59pm Central Standard Time on October 18th and applications must be posted to the Komen website by 11.59pm Central Standard Time on November 1st.
Funding: Private.
No. of awards given last year: 10.
No. of applicants last year: 52.

Population Specific Research Project

Subjects: Unique needs, trends and barriers to breast health care among populations such as African American, Asian Pacific Islander,

Hispanic Latino, Native American, lesbian, low literacy, breast cancer survivors and other defined communities.

Purpose: For innovative research projects addressing breast cancer and epidemiology within specific populations at risk from disease.
Eligibility: Applicants from any country may apply.
Level of Study: Research.
Type: Research grant.
Value: US$250,000 per year for combined direct and indirect costs.
Length of Study: Two years.
Frequency: Annual.
Country of Study: Any country.
No. of awards offered: Varies.
Application Procedure: Applicants must register before submitting an application. Registration is available on the website. Candidates should contact the National Grants and Sponsored Programs Office for more information at the main address. All applications must be submitted electronically.
Closing Date: Electronic abstracts are due by 11.59pm Central Standard Time on October 18th and applications must be posted to the Komen website by 11.59pm Central Standard Time on November 1st.
Funding: Private.
No. of awards given last year: 11.
No. of applicants last year: 76.

Postdoctoral Fellowship in Breast Cancer Research, Public Health or Epidemiology

Subjects: Particular emphasis will be given to projects that are innovative, non duplicative of other efforts and have the potential to lay the ground work for continuing study.
Purpose: To encourage young scientists to begin a career in breast cancer research or to support continued research and continued independent investigations in breast health and breast cancer.
Eligibility: Applicants from any country may apply.
Level of Study: Postdoctorate.
Type: Fellowship.
Value: US$35,000.
Length of Study: Three years.
Frequency: Annual.
Country of Study: Any country.
No. of awards offered: Varies.
Application Procedure: Applicants must register before submitting an application. Registration is available on the website. Candidates should contact the National Grants and Sponsored Programs Office at the main address for more information. All applications must be submitted electronically.
Closing Date: Electronic abstracts are due by 11.59pm Central Standard Time on October 18th and applications must be posted to the Komen website by 11.59pm Central Standard Time on November 1st.
Funding: Private.
No. of awards given last year: 17.
No. of applicants last year: 96.

The Susan G Komen Breast Cancer Foundation Dissertation Research Award

Subjects: Particular emphasis will be given to projects offering an indication of the potential to help the Foundation meet its mission to eradicate breast cancer as a life threatening disease.
Purpose: Funding is available for doctoral candidates in the fields of health and social sciences to conduct dissertation research on breast health and breast cancer. Applications will be considered in health sciences and basic research.
Level of Study: Doctorate.
Type: Award.
Value: US$20,000-30,000 over a two year period.
Length of Study: Two years.
Frequency: Annual.
Country of Study: Any country.
No. of awards offered: Varies.
Application Procedure: Applicants must register before submitting an application. Registration is available on the website. Candidates

should contact the National Grants and Sponsored Programs Office for more information at the main address. All applications must be submitted electronically.
Closing Date: Electronic abstracts are due by 11.59pm Central Standard Time on October 18th and applications must be posted to the Komen website by 11.59pm Central Standard Time on November 1st.
Funding: Private.
No. of awards given last year: 19.
No. of applicants last year: 49.

SWEDISH INFORMATION SERVICE

1 Dag Hammarskjold Plaza
45th Floor, New York, NY, 10017-2201, United States of America
Tel: (1) 212 583 2550
Fax: (1) 212 752 4789
Email: requests@swedeninfo.com
www: http://www.swedeninfo.com/sis
Contact: Academic Liaison Officer

The Swedish Information Service, part of the Culture and Public Affairs Office of the Consulate General of Sweden in New York, works to promote awareness in the United States of Swedish cultural achievement and advancement in scientific research and development, and contributes to the formation of public opinion and policy in an international context.

Bicentennial Swedish-American Exchange Fund

Subjects: Priority is given to politics, public administration, working life, human environment, mass media, business and industry, education or culture.
Purpose: To provide an opportunity for those in a position to influence public opinion and contribute to the development of their society to make an intensive research trip to Sweden.
Eligibility: Applicants should be citizens or permanent residents of the United States. People who have made recurrent visits to, or resided in Sweden, will only be considered in exceptional circumstances. The grant may not be used to finance participation in conferences or regular ongoing vocational or academic courses. If co-applicants on the same project are selected, the grant will be divided between them. The grant may be used in conjunction with scholarships from other sources.
Level of Study: Research.
Type: Travel grant.
Value: Krona 25,000 (or the equivalent in United States dollars) to partially cover transportation and living expenses.
Length of Study: Two-four weeks.
Frequency: Annual.
Country of Study: Sweden.
No. of awards offered: Two.
Application Procedure: Application forms are available from the website or can be requested directly from the Swedish Information Service. Two letters of recommendation are also required.
Closing Date: The first Friday in February.
Funding: Government.
Contributor: The Swedish Institute in Stockholm, Sweden.
No. of awards given last year: Five.
No. of applicants last year: 40.
Additional Information: The project must be completed within one year of receipt of the grant. Six months after the completed research trip a report must be submitted to the Swedish Information Service.

The Swedish Government 'SASS' Travel Grants

Subjects: Study of, or research into, Swedish language, literature or linguistics.
Purpose: To encourage the in depth study of topics relating to Sweden.
Eligibility: Open to members in good standing of the Society for the Advancement of Scandinavian Studies (SASS). Priority will be given

to graduate students and untenured faculty. Applicants must be nationals or permanent residents of the United States of America.
Level of Study: Doctorate, Postdoctorate, Postgraduate, Professional development.
Type: Travel grant.
Value: A sum of US$5,000 will be divided among the grantees. Awards vary depending upon individual need.
Frequency: Annual.
Country of Study: Sweden or United States of America.
No. of awards offered: Varies.
Application Procedure: Applicants must submit a self written application following a specific pattern, a project description and two letters of recommendation.
Closing Date: March 15th to be taken up during the calendar year.
Funding: Government.
No. of awards given last year: Two.
No. of applicants last year: 10.
Additional Information: Graduate students in the social sciences may use the grants for intensive Swedish language study in Sweden. Otherwise grants may be used for projects either in North America or Sweden.

SWEDISH NATURAL SCIENCE RESEARCH COUNCIL (NFR)

Box 7142, Stockholm, S-10387, Sweden
Tel: (46) 85 464 400
Fax: (46) 85 464 4180
www: http://www.nfr.se
Contact: Grants Management Officer

NFR FRN Grants for Scientific Equipment
Subjects: Natural sciences.
Purpose: To assist researchers.
Eligibility: Open to individuals holding a research grant from any Swedish research council.
Level of Study: Research.
Type: A variable number of grants.
Value: Up to krona 10,000,000.
Length of Study: Dependent on the requirements of the projects.
Frequency: Annual.
Study Establishment: Universities.
Country of Study: Sweden.
No. of awards offered: Varies.
Application Procedure: Applicants must contact the organisation for details.
Closing Date: Please contact the organisation.
Funding: Government.

For further information contact:

Grant Office, Sweden
Tel: (46) 84 544 254
Email: lars@nfr.se

Grant Office, Sweden
Tel: (46) 84 544 132
Email: kerstin.hagwall@nfr.se
Contact: Ms Kerstin Hagwell

NFR Junior Research Fellowships
Subjects: Natural sciences and mathematics.
Eligibility: Open to promising young scientists.
Level of Study: Postdoctorate.
Type: A variable number of fellowships.
Value: A grant of up to krona 200,000 and a salary of krona 500,000 per year.
Length of Study: Two years, with a possibility of renewal for a further two years.
Frequency: Annual.

Study Establishment: A university or research institution of the candidate's choice.
Country of Study: Sweden.
No. of awards offered: Approx. 10.
Application Procedure: Applicants must complete an application form, available from the end of March from the NFR or from the website.
Closing Date: May 15th.
Funding: Government.
Additional Information: Further information is available on request.

NFR Open Postdoctoral Fellowships
Subjects: Natural sciences and mathematics.
Purpose: To provide research group leaders in Sweden with the opportunity to co-operate with postdoctoral Fellows.
Eligibility: Open to postdoctoral researchers who have held their doctoral degree for no more than three years.
Level of Study: Postdoctorate, Research.
Type: Fellowship.
Value: Krona 150,000-200,000.
Length of Study: One year, with a possibility of renewal for a further year.
Frequency: Annual.
Study Establishment: Appropriate institutions.
Country of Study: Any country.
No. of awards offered: Varies.
Application Procedure: Applicants must be nominated by a senior scientist at the Swedish host institution.
Closing Date: May 15th.
Funding: Government.
Additional Information: Further information is available on request.

NFR Research Grants
Subjects: Mathematics, natural sciences.
Purpose: To promote outstanding young scientists.
Eligibility: Open to promising postdoctoral students who live and work in a Swedish university or research institution.
Level of Study: Postdoctorate.
Type: Research grant.
Value: Depends on the project requirements. Approx. krona 200,000-500,000 per year to a maximum of krona 1,000,000.
Length of Study: Three years.
Frequency: Annual.
Study Establishment: Suitable universities or research institutions.
Country of Study: Sweden.
No. of awards offered: Varies.
Application Procedure: Applicants must complete an application form, available from February from the NFR or from the website.
Closing Date: May 15th.
Funding: Government.

NFR Senior Research Positions
Subjects: Applications are especially invited from researchers in the following fields: aquatic ecology, advanced simulations in condensed matter physics from electronic structure to material properties, bioanalytical chemistry relevant to proteomics, ecological consequences of energy based production with special reference to biodiversity, experimental astroparticle physics related to the AMANDA experiment, combinatorics, co-ordination chemistry and reactivity of solid surfaces, quantum chaos, organism biology-higher plants, sediments as environmental archives, statistical inference, theoretical biochemistry and zoological tissue biology.
Purpose: To contribute to the recruitment of researchers and to the renewal of research in Sweden.
Eligibility: Open to promising scientists with a doctorate and several years of postgraduate research.
Level of Study: Postdoctorate.
Type: Residency.
Value: Krona 300,000-390,000 per year.
Length of Study: Three years, with the option for renewal for a further three years.

Frequency: Annual.
Study Establishment: Universities or research institutions of the candidate's choice.
Country of Study: Sweden.
No. of awards offered: Varies.
Application Procedure: Positions are announced in leading relevant journals.
Closing Date: December 15th.
Funding: Government.
Additional Information: For further information please contact the secretariat of NFR, by telephoning (46) 84 544 232 or faxing (46) 84 544 250.

NFR Travel Grants

Subjects: Natural sciences.
Purpose: To give financial support to researchers attending conferences or wishing to undertake short-term research abroad.
Eligibility: Open to Swedish researchers and foreign national researchers who have completed their PhD at a Swedish university and have embarked on postdoctoral studies.
Level of Study: Postdoctorate, Research.
Type: Travel grant.
Value: Travelling expenses and subsistence.
Length of Study: Up to two months.
Frequency: Throughout the year.
Study Establishment: Universities or academic institutions abroad.
Country of Study: Any country.
No. of awards offered: Varies.
Application Procedure: Applicants must complete an application form.
Closing Date: Any time excluding June 15th to August 15th.
Funding: Government.

For further information contact:

Grant Office, Sweden
Tel: (46) 84 544 229
Email: elisa@nfr.se

SWISS FEDERAL INSTITUTE OF TECHNOLOGY ZÜRICH

Eidgenössische Technische Hochschule Zürich
Austauschdienst
ETH Zentrum, Zurich, CH-8092, Switzerland
Tel: (41) 1 632 2141
Fax: (41) 1 632 1264
Email: doc.exchange@rektorat.ethz.ch
www: http://www.mobilitaet.ethz.ch
Contact: Silke Jonda, Student Exchange Office

Swiss Federal Institute of Technology Scholarships

Subjects: Architecture, engineering (civil, mechanical, electrical, production, rural and surveying), computer science, materials science, chemistry, physics, mathematics, biology, environmental sciences, earth sciences, pharmacy, agriculture and forestry.
Eligibility: Open primarily, but not exclusively, to nationals of Canada, Italy, Japan, Poland, Spain, the United Kingdom and the United States of America. Candidates should be 20-30 years of age, have had at least two years of university study and have a good working knowledge of German.
Level of Study: Unrestricted.
Type: Scholarship.
Value: Swiss franc 1,300-1,500 per month, plus tuition.
Length of Study: One academic year between October and July.
Frequency: Annual.
Study Establishment: The Institute.
Country of Study: Switzerland.
No. of awards offered: 15.

Application Procedure: Applications must be made to the appropriate address.
Closing Date: February 15th.
Funding: Government.

For further information contact:

Université Laval
Faculté des études supérieures
Pavillon Jean-Charles Bonenfant, QC, G1K 7P4, Canada

Imperial College of Sciences, Technology & Medicine
Scholarships Co-ordinator (Admissions)
Exhibition Road, London, SW7 2AZ, England

Ministero degli Affari Esteri
Direzione Generale delle Relazioni Culturali
Piazzale della Farnesia 1, Rome, I-00194, Italy

Foreign Student Office
Tokyo Institute of Technology
2-12-1 O-okoyama
Meguro-ku, Tokyo, 152-8550, Japan

Warsaw University of Technology
Akademisches Auslandamt Noakowskiego
18/20, Warsaw, PL-00 668, Poland

Consejo Superior de Investigaciones Cientificas
Dpto de Relaciones Internacionales
Calle Serrano 117
28006, Madrid, Spain

World Student Fund
Georgia Institute of Technology
756 West Peachtree Street North West, Atlanta, GA, 30308, United States of America

Center for International Education
Michigan Technological University, Houghton, MI, 49931, United States of America

University of Kansas
International Programs, Lawrence, KS, 66045, United States of America

Kansas State University
International Programs, Manhattan, KS, 66506, United States of America

Exchange Co-ordinator
Department of Decision Sciences & Engineering Systems
Rensselaer Polytechnic Institute
Troy, New York, NY, 12180, United States of America

International Programs
Union College, Schenectady, NY, 12308, United States of America

Humanities and Arts Department
Worcester Polytechnic Institute, Worcester, MA, 01609, United States of America
Contact: Professor D Dollenmayer, Humanities and Arts Department

SYBIL TUTTON AWARDS

16 Ogle Street, London, W1W 6JA, England
Tel: (44) 20 7636 4481
Fax: (44) 20 7637 4307
Email: education@mbf.org.uk
www: http://www.mbf.org.uk
Contact: Mrs Susan Dolton

Sybil Tutton Awards

Subjects: Musical performance in opera.
Purpose: To assist exceptionally talented students on a recognised course of operatic study.
Eligibility: Open to opera students under 30 years who have been resident in the United Kingdom for three years.
Level of Study: Postgraduate, Professional development.

Value: From a total of UK £15,000.
Frequency: Annual.
Country of Study: Any country.
Application Procedure: Applicants must complete an application form and provide two references.
Closing Date: May 7th.
Funding: Private.
No. of awards given last year: Seven.
No. of applicants last year: 54.
Additional Information: Selected students will be asked to audition in June.

SYMPHONY ORCHESTRA ASSOCIATION OF KINGSPORT

Kingsport Symphony Orchestra
Renaissance Center
Box 13
1200 East Center Street, Kingsport, TN, 37660, United States of America
Tel: (1) 423 392 8423
Fax: (1) 423 392 8428
Email: ksorch@aol.com
www: http://www.kso.bigstep.com
Contact: Ms Ann Myers, General Manager

Elizabeth Harper Vaughn Concerto Competition

Subjects: Three categories alternating annually in the following sequence: percussion, wind instruments and brass, strings or piano.
Eligibility: Open to musicians who are 26 years of age or under.
Level of Study: Postgraduate.
Type: Competition.
Value: US$1,500 plus a concert performance with the orchestra and accommodation.
Frequency: Annual.
Country of Study: Any country.
No. of awards offered: One.
Application Procedure: Applications must be accompanied by a letter of recommendation from a qualified teacher, the entrance fee of US$20, payable to Kingsport Symphony Orchestra, and a cassette tape. The tape recording must be a concerto, or work of similar importance, written with orchestral accompaniment.
Closing Date: December 31st.
Funding: Private.
Contributor: Women's Symphony Committee.
No. of awards given last year: One.
No. of applicants last year: 30.
Additional Information: The competition is held in March.

SYRACUSE UNIVERSITY

SU Graduate School
303 Bowne Hall, Syracuse, NY, 13244-1200, United States of America
Tel: (1) 315 443 4492
Fax: (1) 315 443 3423
Email: grad@gwmail.syr.edu
www: http://cwis.syr.edu
Contact: Ms Lynn Carno, Graduate Awards Specialist

Syracuse University is a non-profit, private student research university.

Syracuse University African American Fellowship

Subjects: African American studies.
Purpose: To provide support to students who will tie African American studies in with their programmes of study.
Eligibility: Open to United States citizens who are African American.
Level of Study: Unrestricted.
Type: Fellowship.
Value: US$31,723.
Length of Study: One-six years.
Frequency: Annual.
Study Establishment: Syracuse University.
Country of Study: United States of America.
No. of awards offered: Six.
Application Procedure: Applicants must apply through admission application.
Closing Date: January 10th.
Funding: Private.
Contributor: The Syracuse University Graduate School.
No. of awards given last year: Six.
No. of applicants last year: 20.

Syracuse University Fellowship

Subjects: All subjects.
Purpose: To provide a full support package during a student's term of study.
Eligibility: Open to nationals of any country.
Level of Study: Unrestricted.
Type: Fellowship.
Value: US$31,723.
Length of Study: One-six years.
Frequency: Annual.
Study Establishment: Syracuse University.
Country of Study: United States of America.
No. of awards offered: 101.
Application Procedure: Applicants must apply through admission application.
Closing Date: January 10th.
Funding: Private.
Contributor: The Syracuse University Graduate School.
No. of awards given last year: 101.
No. of applicants last year: 250.

Whitney Young Fellowships

Subjects: Social welfare and social work.
Purpose: To provide support to students studying social work.
Eligibility: Open to African American students.
Level of Study: Postgraduate.
Type: Fellowship.
Value: US$28,168.
Length of Study: Two-three years.
Frequency: Annual.
Study Establishment: Syracuse University.
Country of Study: United States of America.
No. of awards offered: Two.
Application Procedure: Applicants must apply through admission application.
Closing Date: August 5th.
Funding: Private.
Contributor: The Syracuse University Graduate School.
No. of awards given last year: Two.
No. of applicants last year: Six.

TEAGASC (IRISH AGRICULTURE AND FOOD DEVELOPMENT AUTHORITY)

19 Sandymount Avenue, Dublin, 4, Ireland
Tel: (353) 1 637 6000
Fax: (353) 1 668 8023
Email: corourke@hq.teagasc.ie
www: http://www.teagasc.ie
Contact: Dr C O'Rourke, Manager

Teagasc (Irish Agriculture and Food Development Authority) is the parastatal body responsible for agricultural and food research, farm advisory services and farmer education in the Republic of Ireland. Its research programme includes foods, dairy cows, beef cattle, pigs, sheep, crops, horticulture, environment and rural economics and sociology at eight research centres.

The Walsh Fellowships
Subjects: Any subject relevant to food and agriculture: animal sciences, plant sciences, physical or earth sciences, environment, economics and rural development.
Purpose: To support MSc and PhD projects in universities on topics relevant to the overall Teagasc research programme on agriculture and food.
Eligibility: Applicants must be college faculty members who, in co-operation with Teagasc researchers, submit proposals relevant to the Teagasc programme on agriculture and food in Ireland. If successful, they then select postgraduate students for MSc or PhD programmes as Walsh Fellows. Applications are not accepted from individual students, or for taught (non research) postgraduate courses.
Level of Study: Doctorate, Postgraduate, Research.
Type: Fellowship.
Value: €15,000 per year to cover a postgraduate stipend and all fees. A limited provision for materials and travel is also available.
Length of Study: One and a half to three years.
Frequency: Annual.
Study Establishment: Any third level college, in association with a Teagasc Research Centre.
Country of Study: Mainly Ireland (Northern and Republic), or some other countries.
No. of awards offered: Approx. 40.
Application Procedure: Applicants must apply for an information brochure which includes an application form, available on request.
Closing Date: Mid December.
Funding: Government.
Contributor: Teagasc's own resources, via the Irish government and the European Union.
No. of awards given last year: 40.
No. of applicants last year: 100.

TELLURIDE ASSOCIATION

217 West Avenue, Ithaca, NY, 14850, United States of America
Tel: (1) 607 273 5011
Fax: (1) 607 272 2667
Email: telluride@cornell.edu
www: http://www.telluride.cornell.edu
Contact: Administrative Director

The Telluride Association is a private, non-profit organisation whose trustees are young men and women committed to providing educational opportunities for others through a variety of programmes for gifted high school, undergraduate and postgraduate students. The Association seeks out young people with the desire and the ability to contribute to society and helps them develop intellectually and as community members.

Telluride Scholarship
Subjects: All subjects.

Purpose: To provide room and board scholarships to gifted students who attend Cornell University or the University of Michigan.
Eligibility: Open to students of Cornell University or the University of Michigan.
Level of Study: Postgraduate.
Type: Scholarship.
Value: Room and board.
Frequency: Annual.
Country of Study: United States of America.
No. of awards offered: Up to 10 at each institution.
Application Procedure: Applicants must submit essays and attend an interview.
Closing Date: December.
Funding: Private.
Contributor: The Telluride Association.

THE TEXTILE INSTITUTE

1st Floor
St James's Buildings
Oxford Street, Manchester, M1 6FQ, England
Tel: (44) 870 876 0100
Fax: (44) 870 876 0700
Email: hyeowart@textileinst.org.uk
www: http://www.texi.org
Contact: Miss E H Yeowart, Professional Affairs Manager

The Textile Institute has an international membership covering almost 100 countries and spanning every sector and occupation relating to fibres and their uses. The mission of the Textile Institute is to promote professionalism in all areas associated with the textile industries, including clothing and footwear, worldwide.

Cotton Industry War Memorial Trust Scholarships
Subjects: Textile technology or design.
Purpose: To assist students to study on a full-time or sandwich course basis for the Associateship of The Textile Institute, or for a textile degree in technology or design, or to assist professionally qualified people and degree holders in textile technology or design, related sciences or other disciplines to undertake a full-time course for a Master's degree or PhD.
Eligibility: All applicants must reside in the United Kingdom and undertake to be employed in, and to benefit, the United Kingdom textile industry.
Level of Study: Doctorate, Graduate, Postgraduate.
Type: Scholarship.
Value: Up to UK £1,000.
Frequency: Annual.
Country of Study: Any country.
No. of awards offered: Varies.
Application Procedure: Applicants must complete an application form.
Closing Date: Mid July.
No. of awards given last year: 13.
No. of applicants last year: 90 in total for all scholarships.

Lord Barnby Foundation Bursaries
Subjects: Textiles.
Purpose: To assist those who are or who have been employed in the textile industry and who are studying on a full-time or part-time course of study leading to a qualification in a textile related field.
Eligibility: Open to United Kingdom nationals previously employed for at least two years in the United Kingdom textile industry.
Level of Study: Unrestricted.
Type: Bursary.
Value: Varies, up to UK £500.
Frequency: Annual.
Country of Study: United Kingdom.
No. of awards offered: Two.

Application Procedure: Applicants must complete an application form.
Closing Date: Mid July.
No. of awards given last year: Two.
No. of applicants last year: 90 in total for all scholarships.

Textile Institute Scholarship

Subjects: Any textile related subject.
Purpose: To assist students who are studying or undertaking research in a related field.
Eligibility: Open to students or professionally qualified individuals wishing to undertake further study in the fields of textile technology or design.
Level of Study: Doctorate, Graduate, Postgraduate.
Type: Scholarship.
Value: Generally UK £100-400.
Frequency: Annual.
Country of Study: Any country.
No. of awards offered: Varies.
Application Procedure: Applicants must complete an application form.
Closing Date: Mid July.
No. of awards given last year: 12.
No. of applicants last year: 90 in total for all scholarships.

The Worshipful Company of Weavers' Scholarships

Subjects: All subjects relevant to weaving, including design.
Purpose: To assist students who are studying or undertaking research in a related field.
Eligibility: All applicants must undertake to be employed in, and to benefit, the United Kingdom textile industry. Open to United Kingdom nationals only.
Level of Study: Doctorate, Postgraduate.
Type: Scholarship.
Value: Varies, up to UK £1,200.
Frequency: Annual.
Country of Study: United Kingdom.
No. of awards offered: Varies.
Application Procedure: Applicants must complete an application form.
Closing Date: Mid July.
No. of awards given last year: 23.
No. of applicants last year: 90 in total for all scholarships.

THIRD WORLD ACADEMY OF SCIENCES (TWAS)

c/o The Abdus Salam International Centre for Theoretical Physics
Strada Costiera, Trieste, I-34014, Italy
Tel: (39) 040 224 0327
Fax: (39) 040 224 559
Email: info@twas.org
www: http://www.twas.org
Contact: Mr Mohamed H A Hassan, Executive Director

The Third World Academy of Sciences (TWAS) is an autonomous international organisation promoting excellence in scientific research in the South.

CSIR (The Council of Scientific & Industrial Research)/TWAS Fellowship for Postdoctoral Research

Subjects: Newly emerging areas of science and technology.
Purpose: To enable scholars who wish to pursue postdoctoral research to undertake research in laboratories or institutes of the CSIR.
Eligibility: The minimum qualification requirement is a PhD degree in science or technology. Applicants must be regular employees in a developing country and should hold a research assignment.
Level of Study: Postdoctorate.

Type: Fellowship.
Value: A monthly stipend of indian rupees 5,000 for the first two years, extendable for a third year with rupees 5,600 per month.
Frequency: Annual.
Study Establishment: CSIR research laboratories or institutes.
Country of Study: India.
No. of awards offered: Varies.
Application Procedure: Applicants must complete an application form, available on request or from the website http://www.ictp.trieste.it/~twas/CSIR.html.
Closing Date: June 1st.
Funding: Government.
Contributor: CSIR, India, the Italian Ministry of Foreign Affairs and the Directorate General for Development Co-operation.
Additional Information: CSIR is the premier civil scientific organisation of India, which has a network of research laboratories covering wide areas of industrial research. Further information is available on the website.

For further information contact:

Senior Deputy Advisor
The Council of Scientific & Industrial Research (CSIR)
Anusandhan Bhavan - 2 Rafi Marg, New Delhi, 110001, India
Tel: (91) 11 331 6751
Fax: (91) 11 371 0618
Email: rprasad@csirhq.ren.nic.in
Contact: Dr B K Ramaprasad, Senior Deputy Advisor

TWAS Awards in Basic Sciences

Subjects: Basic medical sciences, biology, chemistry, mathematics and physics.
Purpose: To recognise and support outstanding achievements made by scientists from developing countries. They are awarded to those individual scientists in developing countries whose research work has significantly contributed to the advancement of sciences.
Eligibility: Open to nationals of developing countries who are, as a rule, working and living in these countries. Consideration is given to proven achievements judged particularly by their national and international impact. Fellows of the Academy of Sciences are not eligible for such awards.
Level of Study: Doctorate, Postdoctorate, Postgraduate, Professional development.
Type: Prize.
Value: US$10,000 plus a plaque on which major contributions of the award winner are mentioned.
Frequency: Annual.
Country of Study: Developing countries.
No. of awards offered: Five.
Application Procedure: Applicants must be designated on the nomination form. The nomination must be accompanied by a one-two page biographical sketch of the nominee including their major scientific accomplishments, a list of 12 of the candidate's most significant publications as well as a complete list of publications and a curriculum vitae. Nominations for the awards are invited from all members of the TWAS as well as from academies, national research councils, universities and scientific institutions in developing countries and advanced countries.
Closing Date: March 1st. Nominations received after the deadline will be considered in the next year.
Funding: Government.
Contributor: The Italian Ministry of Foreign Affairs and the Directorate General for Development Co-operation.
Additional Information: The awards are usually presented on a special occasion, normally coinciding with the general meeting of the Academy and/or a general conference organised by the Academy. Recipients of awards are expected to give lectures about the work for which the awards have been made. Further information is available on the website.

TWAS Grants for Scientific Meetings in Developing Countries

Subjects: Agricultural, biological, chemical, engineering or geological and medical sciences.

Purpose: To encourage the organisation of international scientific meetings in Third World countries.

Eligibility: Open to organisers of international scientific meetings in developing countries. Special consideration is given to those meetings which are likely to benefit the scientific community in the Third World and to promote regional and international co-operation in developing science and its applications to the problems of the Third World.

Level of Study: Postgraduate, Professional development.

Type: Travel grant.

Value: Travel expenses of principal speakers from abroad and/or participants from the region, up to US$4,000.

Frequency: Annual.

Country of Study: Developing countries.

No. of awards offered: Varies.

Application Procedure: Applicants must complete an application form, available on request or from the website.

Closing Date: June 1st for meetings held between January and June of the following year, and December 1st for meetings held between July and December of the following year.

Funding: Government.

Contributor: The Italian Ministry of Foreign Affairs and the Directorate General for Development Co-operation.

Additional Information: Further information is available on the website.

TWAS Prizes to Young Scientists in Developing Countries

Subjects: Biology, chemistry, mathematics or physics, rotated annually.

Purpose: To enable academies and research councils in over 20 Third World countries to institute prizes and medals for young scientists in their countries.

Eligibility: Open to academies and research councils in developing countries. The age limit for prize winners is 40 years.

Level of Study: Postgraduate.

Type: Prize.

Value: Usually US$2,000.

Frequency: Annual.

Country of Study: Developing countries.

No. of awards offered: Over 20.

Application Procedure: Applicants must write for details.

Funding: Government.

Contributor: The Italian Ministry of Foreign Affairs and the Directorate General for Development Co-operation.

Additional Information: Further information is available on the website.

TWAS Research Grants

Subjects: Biology, chemistry, mathematics or physics.

Purpose: To reinforce and promote scientific research in basic sciences in the Third World, to strengthen the endogenous capacity in science and to reduce the exodus of scientific talents from the South.

Eligibility: Applicants must be nationals of developing countries with an advanced academic degree, some research experience, and must hold positions at universities or research institutions in developing countries.

Level of Study: Doctorate, Postdoctorate, Postgraduate, Professional development.

Type: Research grant.

Value: Up to US$10,000. Grants are to be used to purchase scientific equipment, consumable laboratory supplies and scientific literature (textbooks and proceedings only).

Length of Study: One year.

Frequency: Annual.

Country of Study: Developing countries.

No. of awards offered: Varies.

Application Procedure: Applicants must complete an application form available on request or from the website. Applications must be submitted in English.

Closing Date: July 1st or December 1st.

Funding: Government.

Contributor: The Italian Ministry of Foreign Affairs, the Directorate General for Development Co-operation and the Swedish Agency for Research Co-operation with Developing Countries.

Additional Information: Further information is available on the website or on request.

TWAS South-South Fellowship Scheme

Subjects: All fields of basic sciences.

Purpose: To facilitate and promote mutual contacts of research scientists in the Third World and to further relations between their scientific institutions.

Eligibility: Open to nationals of developing countries, normally with some research experience, and with permanent positions in universities or research institutes in developing countries.

Level of Study: Postgraduate.

Type: Fellowship.

Value: Travel support. Living expenses are usually obtained from local sources.

Length of Study: One-three months.

Frequency: Continuous.

Country of Study: Developing countries.

No. of awards offered: Varies.

Application Procedure: Applicants must complete an application form, available on request or from the website.

Closing Date: Applications are accepted at any time.

Funding: Government.

Contributor: The Italian Ministry of Foreign Affairs and the Directorate General for Development Co-operation.

Additional Information: Special consideration will be given to visits which can be expected to promote co-operation among scientists of the same region and yield substantial benefits to the visitors, their host and their respective scientific communities. Further information is available on the website.

TWAS Spare Parts for Scientific Equipment

Subjects: Spare parts for scientific equipment regarding biology, chemistry and physics.

Purpose: The programme has been established in response to the current difficulty faced by several laboratories in the Third World to obtain badly needed spares and replacement parts for scientific equipment which often interrupts their experimental research for long periods.

Eligibility: Applicants must be research group leaders at universities or research institutes in developing countries.

Level of Study: Professional development.

Type: Grant.

Value: Up to US$1,000 including insurance and freight charges.

Country of Study: Developing countries.

No. of awards offered: Varies.

Application Procedure: Applicants must first contact the suppliers and obtain a proforma invoice, valid for three to six months, including cost, insurance and freight charges for the items they require. Applicants must submit a completed application form with the proforma invoice from the supplier. Application forms are available on request or from the website.

Closing Date: Applications are accepted at any time.

Funding: Government.

Contributor: The Italian Ministry of Foreign Affairs and the Directorate General for Development Co-operation.

Additional Information: Applications for computer parts will not be accepted. Further information is available on the website.

TWAS UNESCO Associate Membership Scheme

Subjects: Biology, chemistry, physics, mathematics, engineering, agricultural sciences and medical sciences.

Purpose: To alleviate the problem of isolated talented scientists in developing countries, and strengthen the research programmes of Centres of Excellence in the South.

Eligibility: Open to associates among the most eminent and promising researchers in developing countries. Special consideration is given to scientists from isolated institutions in developing countries.

Level of Study: Postdoctorate, Professional development.

Value: Varies.

Length of Study: Three years, plus the entitlement to visit the Centre twice for a period of two-three months each time. There is a possibility of renewal for a further three years depending on funds available.

Frequency: Annual.

Study Establishment: There are over 80 centres.

Country of Study: Developing countries.

No. of awards offered: Varies.

Application Procedure: Applicants must complete an application form, available on request or from the website.

Closing Date: December 1st.

Funding: Government.

Contributor: UNESCO, the Italian Ministry for Foreign Affairs and the Directorate General for Development Co-operation.

Additional Information: Further information is available on the website.

THIRD WORLD NETWORK OF SCIENTIFIC ORGANIZATIONS (TWNSO)

c/o TWAS & The Abdus Salam ICTP, Trieste, I-34014, Italy
Tel: (39) 040 224 0683
Fax: (39) 040 224 0689
Email: info@twnso.org
www: http://www.twnso.org
Contact: Secretariat

The Third World Network of Scientific Organizations (TWNSO) is a non-governmental organisation founded in 1988 to promote science based sustainable economic development in the South. It was founded on the initiative of the Third World Academy of Sciences (TWAS), and by ministers of science, technology and higher education and heads of science academies and research councils in developing countries. In 1990 TWNSO acquired consultative status with UNESCO.

The Celso Furtado Award

Subjects: The understanding and promotion of the socio-economic development of countries in the South.

Purpose: To give recognition, encouragement and support to outstanding work in the field of the political economy of developing countries.

Eligibility: Applicants must have worked in the field of political economy resulting in a fundamental contribution to the advancement of socioeconomic development and the developing world in the global context.

Type: Prize.

Value: US$10,000 and a medallion.

Frequency: Every two years.

Country of Study: Any country.

Application Procedure: Applicants must be designated on the nomination form. The nomination should be accompanied by one-two page profile of the nominated individual, a list of significant publications relevant to the award, a complete list of publications and a curriculum vitae of candidate.

Closing Date: January 31st.

Funding: Government.

Contributor: The Federal Republic of Brazil.

Additional Information: Further information is available on the website. The award is named after Celso Furtado, one of the leading Latin American economists from Brazil.

TWNSO Grants to Institutions in the South for Joint Research Projects

Subjects: Biotechnology, new materials, microelectronics, information technology, space technology, new and renewable energies, soil erosion and desertification, floods and earthquakes, biodiversity, atmosphere pollution, toxic and chemical waste or fresh water resources.

Purpose: To award grants to joint research projects with well defined objectives.

Eligibility: Open to institutions in developing countries in the South. Applications must be joint proposals from two to three institutions.

Level of Study: Professional development.

Type: Grant.

Value: Up to US$30,000.

Length of Study: Up to two years.

Frequency: Annual.

Country of Study: Developing countries.

No. of awards offered: Varies.

Application Procedure: Applicants must complete and submit an application form, available on request or from the website. Applications must be submitted from two or three institutions in the South.

Closing Date: December 1st.

Funding: Government.

Contributor: The OPEC Fund for international Development.

Additional Information: Further information is available on the website.

TWNSO Prizes in Applied Sciences

Subjects: Major Third World problems related to agriculture and technology.

Purpose: To honour and support distinguished individuals or institutions whose scientific and technical innovations have provided significant and sustainable solutions to some important economic and social problems in the Third World and have brought, or will bring, substantial benefits to the wellbeing of the people.

Eligibility: Open to individuals or institutions whose scientific and technological innovations have had, or will have, a beneficial effect on the nations of the Third World in the fields of agriculture or technology. Nominees may be from either developing or developed countries. Fellows and Associate Fellows of the Third World Academy of Sciences (TWAS) are not eligible.

Level of Study: Unrestricted.

Type: Prize.

Value: US$10,000 per prize, plus a TWNSO Medal on which major contributions of the prize winner will be mentioned.

Frequency: Every two years.

Country of Study: Any country.

No. of awards offered: Two.

Application Procedure: Nominations for the TWNSO prizes are invited from all members of TWNSO and TWAS as well as from science academies, national research councils, universities and research institutions in developing and developed countries. They should be made on special TWNSO forms, available from the TWNSO Secretariat, and should clearly state the contributions made in one of the fields of applied science for which the prize would be given. The nomination should be accompanied by a one or two page profile of the nominated individual or institution, and a list of significant publications relevant to the award. For nominated individuals a complete list of publications and the biodata of the candidate are required. Nominations must be submitted in the English language. Nominations for each of these prizes are judged by an international committee of distinguished scientists and technologists appointed by the President of the Network.

Closing Date: March 1st.

Funding: Government.

Contributor: The Foreign Ministry and the Directorate General for Development Cooperation.

Additional Information: Further information is available on the website.

THE THIRD WORLD ORGANISATION FOR WOMEN IN SCIENCE (TWOWS)

Enrico Fermi Building
Room 109
Via Beirut 6, Trieste, I-34014, Italy
Tel: (39) 040 224 0321
Fax: (39) 040 224 559
Email: info@twows.org
www: http://www.twows.org
Contact: Ms Leena Mungapen, Secretariat

TWOWS Postgraduate Fellowships for Women from Sub-Saharan Africa and Least Developed Countries (LDC) at Centres of Excellence in the South

Subjects: All subjects.
Purpose: To strengthen the research efforts of qualified women scientists working and living in Third World countries and to recognise, support and encourage the scientific and technological achievements of women in the Third World. The fellowships also aim to facilitate access to educational and training opportunities for young and promising women scientists in Third World countries, and to promote the involvement of women in science and technology professions, in scientific leadership and in the decision making processes, both at the national and international level.
Eligibility: Open to female students in Sub-Saharan Africa and Least Developed Countries (LDC).
Level of Study: Postgraduate.
Type: Fellowship.
Length of Study: Up to four years.
Frequency: Annual.
Country of Study: Any developing country.
No. of awards offered: Up to 50.
Application Procedure: Applicants must complete an application form, available from the website.
Closing Date: May 31st.
Funding: Government.
Contributor: The Department for Research Co-operation of the Swedish International Development Co-operation Agency (Sida-SAREC).
No. of awards given last year: 50.
No. of applicants last year: 322.

THE THOMSON FOUNDATION

37 Park Place, Cardiff, CF10 3BB, Wales
Tel: (44) 29 2035 3060
Fax: (44) 29 2035 3061
Email: enquiries@thomfound.co.uk
www: http://www.thomsonfoundation.co.uk
Contact: Mr Gareth Price

The Thomson Foundation provides practical, intensive training both in the United Kingdom and abroad, along with a wide range of consultancies to journalists, managers, technicians and production staff in television, radio and the press.

Thomson Foundation Scholarship

Subjects: Journalism, radio or television broadcasting, internet publishing and photojournalism.
Purpose: To enable recipients to attend Thomson Foundation training courses in Britain.
Eligibility: Open to professional journalists and broadcasters with at least three years of full-time experience.
Level of Study: Professional development.
Type: Scholarship.
Value: Varies.
Length of Study: Varies, usually a 12 week Summer course or a shorter four week course.

Study Establishment: The Thomson Foundation.
Country of Study: United Kingdom.
No. of awards offered: Varies.
Application Procedure: Applicants must complete an application form, available from the Foundation, for the courses they wish to apply for.
Closing Date: Varies.
No. of awards given last year: Four.
No. of applicants last year: 20.

THOURON-UNIVERSITY OF PENNSYLVANIA FUND FOR BRITISH-AMERICAN STUDENT EXCHANGE

Thouron Awards
University of Glasgow
Court Office, Glasgow, G12 8QQ, Scotland
Tel: (44) 141 330 5853
Fax: (44) 141 307 4920
Email: dmaddern@mis.gla.ac.uk
www: http://www.upenn.edu
Contact: Ms D H Maddern, Administrator

The University of Glasgow is host to the United Kingdom operation of the Thouron Awards and organises the annual competition for the selection of United Kingdom graduates applying for awards tenable at the University of Pennsylvania, Philadelphia, in the United States of America.

Thouron Awards

Subjects: All subjects.
Purpose: To promote better understanding between the people of the United Kingdom and the United States of America.
Eligibility: Open to United Kingdom citizens who are graduates, normally resident in the United Kingdom and who have followed a regular school education in the United Kingdom. Postdoctoral candidates are not eligible unless their proposed study is in a field different from that in which they undertook their previous postgraduate study. No application will be considered from a student already in the United States of America or who has previously spent an academic year at the University of Pennsylvania.
Level of Study: Postgraduate.
Type: Scholarship.
Value: US$1,300 per month plus tuition fees.
Length of Study: One-two years.
Frequency: Annual.
Study Establishment: The University of Pennsylvania, Philadelphia.
Country of Study: United States of America.
No. of awards offered: Up to 10.
Application Procedure: Applicants for the award must submit three application forms, three passport sized photographs and three referee forms. Applications for admission to individual postgraduate courses are dealt with separately and should be sent directly to the University of Pennsylvania.
Closing Date: Varies, but is around mid November each year.
Funding: Private.
Contributor: Sir John R H Thouron and the late Lady Thouron (Esther Dupont).
No. of awards given last year: Eight.
No. of applicants last year: 170.
Additional Information: United States citizens interested in studying in the United Kingdom should write to the University of Pennsylvania for further details.

THRASHER RESEARCH FUND

15 East South Temple Street, Salt Lake City, UT, 84150-6910,
United States of America
Tel: (1) 801 240 4753
Fax: (1) 801 240 1625
Email: brownrj@thrasherresearch.org
www: http://www.thrasherresearch.org
Contact: Mr Justin Brown, Research Manager

The Thrasher Research Fund provides grants for paediatric medical research that addresses problems in children's health that are significant in terms of either magnitude or severity. Priority is given to clinical and/or translational research that has a relatively shorter distance to application. The Fund assumes that significant solutions to children's health problems remain undiscovered and invites a broad array of applications designed to remedy these deficiencies.

Thrasher Research and Field Demonstration Project Grants

Subjects: Paediatrics.
Purpose: To promote international and national child health research and child health related projects. Emphasis is on practical and applied interventions with the potential to improve the health of children worldwide.
Eligibility: Open to research scientists and private voluntary organisations. Pre and postdoctoral students may be employed on Thrasher funded projects, but the principal investigator is expected to take an active role in the project and assume full responsibility for it. The principal investigator must have a connection with a university, research institution or appropriate private voluntary organisation.
Level of Study: Postdoctorate.
Type: Grant.
Value: Up to US$500,000.
Length of Study: Up to three years.
Frequency: Four times per year.
Country of Study: Any country.
No. of awards offered: Varies.
Application Procedure: Application guidelines are available on the Fund's website. Potential applicants are encouraged to contact Fund staff prior to a formal submission to determine how a potential project will fit with current Fund interests.
Closing Date: Proposals that have completed the external review process will be considered at the subsequent quarterly meeting.
Funding: Private.
Contributor: The Thrasher Research Fund.
Additional Information: Historically the Fund has primarily supported international research. In an effort to achieve greater balance, the Fund is currently emphasising research conducted in the United States.

TIBOR VARGA INTERNATIONAL COMPETITION FOR VIOLIN

Case postale 1429, Sion, CH-1951, Switzerland
Tel: (41) 27 323 4317
Fax: (41) 27 323 4662
Email: festivargasion@vtx.ch
www: http://www.festival-varga.ch
Contact: Ms Veronique Moreillon, Secretary

The Tibor Varga International Competition for Violin is an annual music festival held from the middle of July to the beginning of September with more than 20 concerts.

Tibor Varga International Competition for Violin

Subjects: Violin, an interpretative performance.

Purpose: To help discover a new talent, to enrich the musical experience and practice of the participants, and to encourage and support prize winners in their future careers.
Eligibility: Open to violinists of any nationality aged between 15-32 years.
Level of Study: Unrestricted.
Type: Prize.
Value: The first prize is swiss franc 10,000, the second is swiss franc 7,500, the third is swiss franc 5,000 and the fourth is swiss franc 2,500. There are also other special prizes totalling approx. swiss franc 35,000.
Length of Study: 10 days.
Frequency: Annual.
Country of Study: Switzerland.
No. of awards offered: Four prizes and several special prizes.
Application Procedure: Applicants must complete an application form and submit this with three passport sized photographs, a curriculum vitae and a receipt showing payment of the entrance fee of swiss franc 100.
Closing Date: May 1st.
Funding: Government, Private.
No. of awards given last year: 10.
No. of applicants last year: 84.
Additional Information: Participants will compete in Sion during August. Prize winners are obliged to remain in Sion for the awards presentation at the end of the competition. They will also be expected to perform in the presentation concert. The first prize winner will be presented as soloist with a symphony orchestra at the Festival. Other winners will be presented at chamber music concerts in Geneva and Vienna.

TOKYU FOUNDATION FOR INBOUND STUDENTS

1-21-6 Dogenzaka
Shibuya Ku, Tokyo, 150, Japan
Tel: (81) 3 3461 0844
Fax: (81) 3 5458 1696
Email: tqzaiden@246.ne.jp
Contact: Mr Yasushi Teranaka, Secretary General

Tokyu Scholarship

Subjects: All subjects in a Japanese university postgraduate course.
Purpose: To promote international exchange by fostering the development of international goodwill between Japan and her neighbours in the Pacific and Asia, and contributing to international co-operation and cultural exchange in the broadest possible sense.
Level of Study: Postgraduate.
Type: Scholarship.
Value: Yen 160,000 per month per student.
Length of Study: Up to two years.
Frequency: Annual.
Country of Study: Japan.
No. of awards offered: 24-25.
Application Procedure: Applicants must complete an application form.
Closing Date: Please consult the organisation.
Funding: Commercial.
Contributor: The Tokyu Corporation.
No. of awards given last year: 25.
No. of applicants last year: 924.
Additional Information: Applicants must travel to Japan at their own cost and be admitted to enter university postgraduate school. With over 900 applicants competition for these places is very high.

TOURETTE SYNDROME ASSOCIATION, INC. (TSA)

42-40 Bell Boulevard
Suite 205, Bayside, NY, 11361-2874, United States of America
Tel: (1) 718 224 2999
Fax: (1) 718 279 9596
Email: ts@tsa-usa.org
www: http://tsa-usa.org
Contact: Ms Sue Levi-Pearl, Liaison for Medical & Scientific Programmes

The Tourette Syndrome Association, Inc. (TSA), founded in 1972, is the only national voluntary non-profit membership organisation dedicated to identifying the cause, finding the cure and controlling the effects of Tourette Syndrome. Members include individuals with the disorder, their relatives and other interested, concerned people. The Association develops and disseminates educational material to individuals, professionals and to agencies in the fields of health care, education and government, co-ordinates support services to help people and their families cope with the problems that occur with Tourette Syndrome, and funds research that will ultimately find the cause of and cure for it and, at the same time, lead to improved medications and treatments.

Tourette Syndrome Association Research Grants

Subjects: Basic neuroscience specifically relevant to Tourette Syndrome, clinical studies and training of postdoctoral Fellows.
Purpose: To foster basic and clinical research related to the causes or treatment of Tourette Syndrome.
Eligibility: Open to candidates who have an MD, PhD or equivalent qualifications. Previous experience in the field of movement disorders is desirable, but not essential. Fellowships are intended for young postdoctoral investigators in the early stages of their careers.
Level of Study: Doctorate, Postdoctorate.
Type: Research grant.
Value: Varies depending upon the category and applicants' experience within that category, and is usually US$5,000-75,000. Postdoctoral is up to US$40,000.
Length of Study: One-two years.
Frequency: Annual.
Study Establishment: Any institution with adequate facilities.
Country of Study: Any country.
No. of awards offered: Varies.
Application Procedure: Applicants must submit a letter of intent briefly describing the scientific basis of the proposed project.
Closing Date: Please contact the Association.
Funding: Private.
Additional Information: The Association provides up to 10 per cent of overhead or indirect costs within the total amount budgeted.

TRANSPORTATION ASSOCIATION OF CANADA (TAC)

Secretariat
2323 St Laurent Boulevard, Ottawa, ON, K1G 4J8, Canada
Tel: (1) 613 736 1350
Fax: (1) 613 736 1395
Email: gmorier@tac-atc.ca
www: http://www.tac-atc.ca
Contact: Mr Gilbert Morier

The Transportation Association of Canada (TAC) is a non-profit association of government and industry members which acts as a neutral forum for the gathering and exchanging of information on technical guidelines and best practices. Its areas of interest are roads, their links with other modes of transportation and urban transformation.

TAC Scholarships

Subjects: Road and transportation related disciplines.
Purpose: To promote transportation related disciplines at the postgraduate level.
Eligibility: Open to Canadian citizens and landed immigrants who hold university degrees and who are acceptable to the university at which they plan to carry out their postgraduate studies in the transportation field.
Level of Study: Postgraduate.
Type: Scholarship.
Value: Canadian $3,000-6,000.
Length of Study: One year.
Frequency: Annual.
Study Establishment: Universities.
Country of Study: Varies, depending on the scholarship.
No. of awards offered: Six.
Application Procedure: Applicants must submit all applications electronically via TAC's website.
Closing Date: The first working day in March. Applicants should telephone for the exact date, which varies each year.
Funding: Commercial, Government, Private.
No. of awards given last year: Six.
Additional Information: Scholarships currently offered are from the DELCAN Corporation, Stantec Consulting Limited, federal, provincial or territorial governments of Canada, the Emery Family (Caledon East, Ontario), ND LEA Consultants, ND LEA Engineers and Planners, and EBA Engineering Consultants Limited.

TROPICAL AGRICULTURAL RESEARCH AND HIGHER EDUCATION CENTER (CATIE)

CATIE Graduate School
PO Box 7170, Turrialba, Costa Rica
Tel: (506) 556 1016
Fax: (506) 556 0914
Email: posgrado@catie.ac.cr
www: http://www.catie.ac.cr
Contact: Dean of the Graduate School

The Tropical Agricultural Research and Higher Education Center (CATIE) is an international, non-profit, regional, scientific and educational institution. Its main purpose is research and education in agricultural sciences, natural resources and related subjects in the American tropics, with emphasis on Central America and the Caribbean.

CATIE Scholarships

Subjects: Ecological agriculture, biotechnology and genetic resources, management and conservation of tropical forestry and biodiversity, tropical woodlands, tropical agroforestry, tropical crop protection and improvement, integrated watershed management and protected areas, and environmental socioeconomics.
Purpose: To develop specialised intellectual capital the field.
Eligibility: Priority is given to citizens of Belize, Guatemala, El Salvador, Honduras, Nicaragua, Panama, Costa Rica, Mexico, Venezuela, Colombia and the Dominican Republic.
Level of Study: Doctorate, Postdoctorate, Postgraduate.
Type: Scholarship.
Value: Tuition and fees.
Length of Study: One year of coursework, one year for a Master's thesis and three-four years for a PhD.
Frequency: Annual.
Country of Study: Costa Rica.
No. of awards offered: 40.
Application Procedure: Applicants must undertake an admission process which constitutes 75 per cent for curricular evaluation and 25 per cent for a domiciliary examination.

Closing Date: Applications are accepted at any time, but the evaluation deadline is October.
Funding: Government.
Contributor: ASDI, DANIDA, OAS, CATIE, AID and others.
No. of awards given last year: 40.
No. of applicants last year: 350.

TRUSTEES OF THEODORA BOSANQUET BURSARY

c/o 28 Great James Street, London, WC1N 3ES, England
Tel: (44) 20 7404 6447
Fax: (44) 20 7404 6505
Email: bfwg.charity@btinternet.com
www: http://www.bcfgrants.org.uk
Contact: Mrs Considine, Company Secretary

The Trustees of Theodora Bosanquet Bursary was set up to support female postgraduate students carrying out research in English literature or history requiring the use of libraries and archives in London.

Theodora Bosanquet Bursary

Subjects: English or history.
Purpose: To support female postgraduate students who are carrying out research in English literature or history requiring the use of libraries and archives in London.
Eligibility: Open to women only.
Level of Study: Doctorate, Postdoctorate, Postgraduate.
Type: Accommodation.
Value: Up to UK £600. The award provides accommodation only in a hall of residence for up to four weeks in mid June and mid September.
Length of Study: Up to four weeks.
Frequency: Annual.
Study Establishment: London Hall of Residence.
Country of Study: United Kingdom.
No. of awards offered: One-two.
Application Procedure: Applicants must send requests for applications to the grants administrator accompanied by a large stamped addressed envelope or international reply coupons. The envelope should be marked with TBB.
Closing Date: October 31st.
Funding: Private.
Contributor: Investment income.
No. of awards given last year: One.
No. of applicants last year: Two.

TURKU CENTRE FOR COMPUTER SCIENCE (TUCS)

TUCS Office
DataCity
Lemminkäisenkatu 14 A
4th Floor, Turku, FIN-20520, Finland
Tel: (358) 2 2154 049
Fax: (358) 2 2410 154
Email: tucs@abo.fi
www: http://www.tucs.fi
Contact: Mr Thomas Sund, Administrative Officer

The Turku Centre for Computer Science (TUCS) and its Graduate School are situated in the Turku Technology Centre. The computer science departments of three universities are all located in this centre, together with a number of other university departments and companies in computer and communication technology, electronics, biotechnology and material sciences. It is an independent research organisation.

TUCS Postgraduate Grant

Subjects: Computer science, information systems or computer engineering.
Purpose: To support students studying for a doctoral degree.
Eligibility: Applicants should have a Test of English as a Foreign Language score of at least 550 points or a corresponding level of English proficiency and an MSc or BSc in computer science or a related field. The Graduate Record Examination test is not required but can be sent voluntarily.
Level of Study: Postgraduate.
Type: Grant.
Value: €1,180 per month for postgraduate and €1,430 per month for postdoctoral. Both grants are tax free.
Length of Study: Four-six years.
Frequency: Annual.
Study Establishment: An approved graduate school.
Country of Study: Finland.
No. of awards offered: 4-10 each year.
Application Procedure: Applicants must submit a free form application, curriculum vitae, financing plan for studies, application for financial support, letters of recommendation with full contact details, official copies of examinations gained with official English translations, a certificate of English proficiency and a statement of research interests.
Closing Date: Applications are accepted at any time. The deadline for studies starting in September is May 15th and for studies starting in January the deadline is October 31st.
Funding: Government.
No. of awards given last year: Four.
No. of applicants last year: 56.

UCLA CENTER FOR 17TH AND 18TH CENTURY STUDIES AND THE WILLIAM ANDREWS CLARK MEMORIAL LIBRARY

310 Royce Hall
UCLA, Los Angeles, CA, 90095-1404, United States of America
Tel: (1) 310 206 8552
Fax: (1) 310 206 8577
Email: c1718cs@humnet.ucla.edu
www: http://www.humnet.ucla.edu/humnet/c1718cs
Contact: Fellowship Co-ordinator

The UCLA Center for 17th and 18th Century Studies provides a forum for discussion of central issues in the field of early modern studies, facilitates research and publication, supports scholarship and encourages the creation of interdisciplinary, cross cultural programmes that advance the understanding of this important period. The William Andrews Clark Memorial Library, administered by the Center, is known for its collections of rare books and manuscripts concerning seventeenth and eighteenth-century Britain and Europe, Oscar Wilde and the 1890s, the history of printing, and certain aspects of the American West.

Ahmanson and Getty Postdoctoral Fellowships

Subjects: Arts and humanities, religious studies and social sciences.
Purpose: To encourage participation eg. the research for and reading of a paper in the Center's annual interdisciplinary, cross cultural programmes.
Eligibility: Open to postdoctoral Scholars who have received their PhD in the last six years.
Level of Study: Postdoctorate.
Type: Fellowship.
Value: US$18,400.
Length of Study: Two consecutive academic quarters.
Frequency: Annual.
Study Establishment: UCLA and the William Andrews Clark Memorial Library.

Country of Study: United States of America.
No. of awards offered: Up to four.
Application Procedure: Applicants must submit an application form, curriculum vitae, proposal statement, a bibliography and three letters of reference.
Closing Date: February 1st.
Funding: Private.
Contributor: The Ahmanson Foundation of Los Angeles and the Getty Trust.
No. of awards given last year: Four.
No. of applicants last year: 30.
Additional Information: The award is theme based and is announced each year.

ASECS (American Society for Eighteenth-Century Studies)/Clark Library Fellowships

Subjects: The Restoration or the eighteenth-century.
Eligibility: Open to members of ASECS who are postdoctoral Scholars and hold a PhD or equivalent degree at the time of application.
Level of Study: Postdoctorate.
Type: Fellowship.
Value: US$2,000.
Length of Study: One month.
Frequency: Annual.
Study Establishment: UCLA and the William Andrews Clark Memorial Library.
Country of Study: United States of America.
No. of awards offered: Varies.
Application Procedure: Applicants must submit an application form, curriculum vitae, proposal statement, a bibliography and three letters of reference.
Closing Date: February 1st.
Funding: Government.
Contributor: ASECS and the Clark Library Endowment.
No. of awards given last year: One.
No. of applicants last year: 40.

Clark Library Short-Term Resident Fellowships

Subjects: Research relevant to the Library's holdings.
Eligibility: Open to Scholars holding a PhD or equivalent degree who are involved in advanced research.
Level of Study: Postdoctorate.
Type: Fellowship.
Value: US$2,000 per month.
Length of Study: One-three months.
Frequency: Annual.
Study Establishment: UCLA and the William Andrews Clark Memorial Library.
Country of Study: United States of America.
No. of awards offered: Varies.
Application Procedure: Applicants must submit an application form, curriculum vitae, proposal statement, a bibliography and three letters of reference.
Closing Date: February 1st.
Funding: Government, Private.
Contributor: The Ahmanson Foundation and the Clark Library Endowment.
No. of awards given last year: 16.
No. of applicants last year: 60.

Clark Predoctoral Fellowships

Subjects: Any area represented in the Clark's collections.
Purpose: To support dissertation research.
Eligibility: Restricted to advanced doctoral students at the University of California, whose dissertation concerns an area appropriate to the collections of the Clark Library.
Level of Study: Predoctorate.
Type: Fellowship.
Value: US$6,000.
Length of Study: Three months.

Frequency: Annual.
Study Establishment: UCLA and the William Andrews Clark Memorial Library.
Country of Study: United States of America.
No. of awards offered: Varies.
Application Procedure: Applicants must submit an application form, curriculum vitae, proposal statement, a bibliography and three letters of reference.
Closing Date: February 1st.
Funding: Private.
Contributor: The Ahmanson Foundation.
No. of awards given last year: Three.
No. of applicants last year: Nine.

Clark-Huntington Joint Bibliographical Fellowship

Subjects: Early modern literature and history and in other areas where the sponsoring libraries have common strengths.
Purpose: To support bibliographical research.
Level of Study: Postdoctorate, Professional development.
Type: Fellowship.
Value: US$4,000.
Length of Study: Two months.
Frequency: Annual.
Study Establishment: The Clark Library and the Huntington Library.
Country of Study: United States of America.
No. of awards offered: One.
Application Procedure: Applicants must submit an application form, curriculum vitae, proposal statement, a bibliography and three letters of reference.
Closing Date: February 1st.
No. of awards given last year: One.
No. of applicants last year: 15.

For further information contact:

Fellowship Co-ordinator
William Andrews Clark Memorial Library
2520 Cimarron Street, Los Angeles, CA, 90018-2098, United States of America

Kanner Fellowship In British Studies

Subjects: Research relevant to the Library's holdings in an area pertaining to British history and culture.
Eligibility: Open to both postdoctoral and predoctoral Scholars.
Level of Study: Postdoctorate, Predoctorate.
Type: Fellowship.
Value: US$6,000.
Length of Study: Three months.
Frequency: Annual.
Application Procedure: Applicants must submit an application form, curriculum vitae, proposal statement, a bibliography and three letters of reference.
Closing Date: February 1st.
Funding: Private.
Contributor: Penny Kanner.
No. of awards given last year: One.
No. of applicants last year: Five.

UCLA CENTER FOR MEDIEVAL AND RENAISSANCE STUDIES (CMRS)

Box 951485, Los Angeles, CA, 90095-1485, United States of America
Tel: (1) 310 825 1880
Fax: (1) 310 825 0655
Email: cmrs@humnet.ucla.edu
www: http://www.humnet.ucla.edu/cmrs
Contact: Ms Susanne Kahle, Assistant Director

Through its activities and programmes, the UCLA Center for Medieval and Renaissance Studies promotes interdisciplinary and cross cultural studies of modern civilisation in its formative period from late antiquity to the middle of the seventeenth-century.

CMRS Summer Fellowship

Subjects: Medieval and early modern history, culture, literature, philosophy or religion.
Purpose: To defray expenses for a Scholar conducting research at UCLA.
Eligibility: There are no restrictions, except that applicants must have a PhD or similar degree from a recognised and accredited university.
Level of Study: Postdoctorate.
Type: Stipend.
Value: US$500.
Length of Study: Not to exceed three months.
Frequency: Annual.
Study Establishment: CMRS.
Country of Study: United States of America.
No. of awards offered: One.
Application Procedure: Applicants must submit a curriculum vitae, a two page project description and one letter of recommendation.
Closing Date: Early February for Summer notification.
No. of awards given last year: One.

UCLA INSTITUTE OF AMERICAN CULTURES (IAC)

Institute of American Cultures
1237 Murphy Hall
Box 951419, Los Angeles, CA, 90095-1419, United States of America
Tel: (1) 310 206 2557
Fax: (1) 310 825 8099
Email: pjohnson@gdnet.ucla.edu
www: http://www.gdnet.ucla.edu/iacweb/iachome.htm
Contact: Mr Parker Johnson, Co-ordinator

The UCLA Institute of American Cultures (IAC) is committed to advancing knowledge, strengthening and integrating interdisciplinary research and enriching instruction on African Americans, American Indians, Asian Americans and Chicanos. Since 1971 the IAC has been responsible for developing and expanding graduate studies, research and training in ethnic studies, and is a major contributor to the academic and intellectual life of the university.

UCLA IAC Postdoctoral/Visiting Scholar Fellowships

Subjects: Arts and humanities, education and teacher training, fine arts, applied arts, law, social sciences and sciences.
Purpose: To enable PhD scholars wishing to work in association with the American Indian Studies Center, the Center for African American Studies, the Asian American Studies Center and the Cicano Studies Research Center, in order to conduct research and publish books or manuscripts relating to American Indian Studies.
Eligibility: Open to United States citizens and permanent residents.
Level of Study: Doctorate, Postdoctorate.
Type: Fellowship.
Value: US$27,000-32,000 stipend plus health benefits and up to US$4,000 in research support.
Length of Study: Up to one year.
Frequency: Annual.
Country of Study: United States of America.
No. of awards offered: Four.
Application Procedure: Applicants must complete an application form, available from one of the ethnic studies centres or the IAC.
Closing Date: December 31st.
No. of awards given last year: Four.
Additional Information: Further information is available on request or from the website.

For further information contact:

Fellowship Director
Center for African American Studies
160 Haines Hall
Box 951545, Los Angeles, CA, 90095-1545, United States of America
Tel: (1) 310 206 8267
Fax: (1) 310 206 3421
www: http://www.sscnet.ucla.edu/caas

Fellowship Director
American Indian Studies Center
3220 Campbell Hall
Box 951548, Los Angeles, CA, 90095-1548, United States of America
Tel: (1) 310 825 7315
Fax: (1) 310 206 7060
Email: aisc@ucla.edu
www: http://www.sscnet.ucla.edu/indian

Fellowship Director
Asian American Studies Center
3230 Campbell Hall
Box 951546, Los Angeles, CA, 90095-1546, United States of America
Tel: (1) 310 825 2974
Fax: (1) 310 206 9844
www: http://www.sscnet.ucla.edu/aasc

Fellowship Director
Chicano Studies Research Center
180 Haines Hall
Box 951544, Los Angeles, CA, 90095-1544, United States of America
Tel: (1) 310 825 2363
Fax: (1) 310 206 1784
www: http://www.sscnet.ucla.edu/csrc

UNITED DAUGHTERS OF THE CONFEDERACY

328 North Boulevard, Richmond, VA, 23220-4057, United States of America
Tel: (1) 804 355 1636
Fax: (1) 804 353 1396
Email: hqudc@rcn.com
www: http://www.hqudc.org
Contact: Executive Secretary

The objectives of the United Daughters of the Confederacy are historical, educational, benevolent, memorial and patriotic, to honour the memory of those who served and those who fell in the service of the Confederate States of America.

Mrs Simon Baruch University Award

Subjects: Southern United States history in or near the period of the Confederacy or bearing upon the causes that led to secession and the War Between the States. The life of an individual, a policy or a phase of life may be eligible.

Purpose: To encourage research and to assist scholars in the publication of their theses, dissertations and other writings.

Eligibility: Open to individuals who have graduated with an advanced degree from a United States university or college within the previous 15 years, or whose thesis or dissertation has been accepted by such institutions as part of graduation requirements. Book length manuscripts should contain at least 75,000 words and monographs 25,000-50,000 words.

Level of Study: Postgraduate.

Value: US$2,000 to aid in defraying the costs of publication and US$500 to the author.

Frequency: Every two years (even-numbered years).

Country of Study: Any country.

No. of awards offered: One.

Application Procedure: Applicants must write for details.

Closing Date: May 1st of the award year.

Funding: Private.

UNITED STATES BUSINESS SCHOOL

José Martí 2, Prague, Veleslavín, CS-162 00, Czech Republic
Tel: (42) 2 3535 8307
Fax: (42) 2 3536 0484
Email: usbsp@usbsp.cz
www: http://www.usbsp.cz
Contact: Ms Monika Supilhova, Business Development Director

The United States Business School in Prague offers one of the preeminent Western MBA programmes under professors from leading business colleges throughout the United States. The MBA degree is awarded by the Rochester Institute of Technology and accredited by the Association to Advance Collegiate Schools of Business (AACSB).

United States Business School (Prague) MBA Scholarships

Subjects: MBA.

Purpose: To provide financial support to exceptional students.

Eligibility: Open only to students enrolled in the full-time MBA programme.

Level of Study: Postgraduate, MBA.

Type: Scholarship.

Value: Scholarships are awarded on the basis of results of the Graduate Management Admissions Test scores. For scores of 650-699 US$1,000 is awarded and for scores of 700 or above, US$2,000 is awarded. The funds are provided as a discount from the tuition fee.

Length of Study: 10 months.

Frequency: Annual.

Study Establishment: The United States Business School (Prague).

Country of Study: Czech Republic.

Application Procedure: Applicants must contact the organisation or visit the website for details.

Closing Date: July 31st.

Funding: Private.

Contributor: Czech Relecom, the Czech Insurance Company and McKinsey & Company.

Additional Information: As the United States Business School in Prague was established to help Central and Eastern Europe in the transformation of their economies, financial support is available mainly to the citizens of these countries. For Czech and Slovak citizens up to US$8,000 is available, and for citizens of other Central and Eastern European countries up to US$7,000 is allocated. Please contact the organisation for further information.

UNITED STATES DEPARTMENT OF STATE

2201C Street North West
Room 5643, Washington, DC, 20520, United States of America
Tel: (1) 202 736 7022
Fax: (1) 202 647 8743
www: http://www.state.gov

Fulbright Study and Research Grants for US Citizens

Subjects: All subjects.

Purpose: To increase mutual understanding between the people of the United States of America and people of other countries by means of educational and cultural exchange.

Eligibility: Open to United States citizens who have a Bachelor's degree or equivalent qualification. Candidates must have a high scholastic record, have an acceptable plan of study, demonstrate proficiency in the language of the host country and be in good health. In some cases special language training is provided as part of a grant. Preference is given to persons who have not had prior experience of, or opportunity for, extended foreign study, residence or travel.

Level of Study: Postgraduate.

Value: Full grants cover international transportation, a language or orientation course where appropriate, tuition, book and maintenance allowances, and health and accident insurance. Travel grants will consist of travel expenses supplementing students' personal funds or maintenance allowances and tuition scholarships which are granted to students by universities and other organisations.

Length of Study: One academic year.

Frequency: Annual.

Study Establishment: Institutes of Higher Education.

Country of Study: Outside the United States of America. A list of participating countries in a given year may be obtained from the Institute of International Education.

No. of awards offered: Varies.

Application Procedure: Applicants enrolled in a college or university must apply to the Fulbright Programme Adviser on their campus. Applicants not enrolled in a college or university should apply to the Institute of International Education. Applications should be requested at least 15 days prior to the closing date.

Closing Date: October 25th.

Funding: Government.

Hubert H Humphrey Doctoral Fellowships in Arms Control, Non-proliferation and Disarmament

Subjects: Academic disciplines including, but not limited to, political science, economics, law, sociology, psychology, physics, chemistry, biology, public policy, philosophy, international relations, engineering and operations control may apply, providing the research proposal is designed to contribute to a better understanding of current and future arms control issues.

Purpose: To encourage specialised training and research in the arms control field.

Eligibility: Open only to applicants who are citizens or nationals of the United States at the time of application and who, by the date the fellowship begins, will have completed academic requirements for the doctorate, except the dissertation, at a United States college or university, and whose dissertation proposals have been approved in accordance with university procedures. JD candidates preparing to enter their third or final year of law school are eligible if the proposed research project would represent a substantial amount of credit towards third year requirements and would result in a paper that would, eg., be appropriate for publication in a law journal.

Level of Study: Doctorate.

Type: Fellowship.

Value: A stipend of US$8,000 and the payment of tuition fees to a maximum of US$6,000 maximum.

Length of Study: One year.

Frequency: Annual.

Study Establishment: An approved institution.

Country of Study: Any country.
No. of awards offered: One-two.
Application Procedure: Applicants must submit a signed and completed application, dissertation or JD research proposal not exceeding five pages, describing the topic, the research design, the methodology to be employed in the research and the relevance of the research to arms control, non proliferation and disarmament issues and policies, a concise bibliography of works related to the research topic, official transcripts of all graduate school course work, a signed statement by the applicant's research or dissertation adviser or dissertation committee, as appropriate, stating that the proposal has been approved in accordance with university or departmental procedures, and evaluation forms from three academic references who must be familiar with both the applicant's abilities and the research proposal, one of whom should be the dissertation or research adviser. These forms must be sent directly to the Hubert H Humphrey Fellowship Program office.
Closing Date: March 31st.
Funding: Government.
Additional Information: Each Fellow will be required to submit quarterly progress reports to the Department of State, as well as a copy of the final dissertation or research paper, when completed and approved by the academic institution, together with a 5-10 page summary of the principal findings. The thesis and summary may be circulated to interested readers inside and outside the government. Potential applicants should note that supported research dealing with foreign relations or with foreign areas and peoples must be approved in advance by the Department if the project involves foreign travel or contact with foreign nationals.

UNITED STATES EDUCATIONAL FOUNDATION IN INDIA (USEFI)

Fulbright House
12 Hailey Road, New Delhi, 110001, India
Tel: (91) 11 332 8944
Fax: (91) 11 332 9718
Email: info@fulbright-india.org
www: http://www.fulbright-india.org
Contact: Programme Officer

The activities of the United States Educational Foundation in India (USEFI) may be broadly categorised as the administration of the Fulbright Exchange Fellowships for Indian and United States scholars and professionals, and the provision of educational advising services to help Indian students wishing to pursue higher education in the United States.

Fulbright-CII Fellowships for Leadership in Management
Subjects: Leadership in management.
Purpose: To enable business managers to attend a management course in the United States of America.
Eligibility: Open to Indian business managers.
Level of Study: Professional development.
Type: Fellowship.
Length of Study: 10 weeks.
Study Establishment: Usually the Graduate School of Administration, Carnegie Mellon University, Pittsburgh.
Country of Study: United States of America.
No. of awards offered: Three-four.
Application Procedure: Applicants must complete an application form, available from the CII.
Funding: Private.
Contributor: The Confederation of Indian Industry (CII) and USEFI.
Additional Information: For further information contact the CII.

For further information contact:

Deputy Director
Confederation of Indian Industry (CII)
23 Institutional Area

Lodi Road, New Delhi, 110003, India
Tel: (91) 46 299 9497
Fax: (91) 46 012 98
Email: kavita.kohli@ciionline.org
Contact: Ms Kavita Kohli, Deputy Director

Fulbright-TATA Travel Fellowships
Subjects: Humanities, social sciences including administration, economics, education, environmental science, language and literature, population studies and women's studies are especially welcome. Applications in subjects that would help in the development of India and its national resources are encouraged.
Purpose: To assist academics and professionals who have invitations to visit the United States of America for either a research or teaching assignment.
Eligibility: Open to Indian citizens resident in India at the time of application who have not been to the United States of America in the previous three years. Applicants must have a high level of academic and professional achievement, proficiency in English and be in good health. Applicants must be permanent full-time faculty members at an Indian college, university or research institute, hold a PhD degree or have equivalent published work and be no more than 50 years of age. In addition, applicants must be accepted by a recognised United States university or research institution for postdoctoral research and/or as a visiting lecturer and have assurance of dollar support to cover the expenses in the United States for the duration of the assignment. The letter of acceptance must show the nature and duration of the assignment, and must be accompanied by evidence of dollar support of not less than US$2,000 per month and not more than US$25,000 per academic year. American universities, Indian universities or research institutions could offer the evidence of dollar support in the form of a grant or fellowship. The letters of invitation or sponsorship from United States host institutions must indicate that all expenses towards room and board, local transportation, and related personal expenses will be met. No personal funding or financial support from family or friends is permitted.
Level of Study: Postdoctorate, Professional development.
Type: Travel grant.
Value: Round trip economy class airfare and health insurance.
Length of Study: Research or teaching assignments are 4-12 months and professional visits are two-six months.
Frequency: Annual.
Country of Study: United States of America.
No. of awards offered: Four.
Application Procedure: Applicants must complete an application form. Requests for application materials must state the applicant's academic and professional qualifications, date of birth, current position and grant category and be accompanied by a 7 by 10 inch stamped addressed envelope. Requests for application materials must be sent to the USEFI offices in the applicant's region or to the J N Tata Endowment (JNTE) by October 15th.
Closing Date: November 1st.
Additional Information: Further information is available on request.

For further information contact:

Director
J N Tata Endowment (JNTE)
Bombay House
24 Homi Modi Street, Mumbai, 400001, India
Tel: (91) 20 491 31

Hubert H Humphrey Fellowships
Subjects: Agriculture, planning, resource management, public health and public administration. Subject to availability of funds, fellowships may also be offered to working journalists and to medical practitioners in the area of drug abuse.
Eligibility: Open to Indian citizens resident in India at time of application who have not been to the United States of America in the previous three years. Applicants must have a high level of academic and professional achievement, proficiency in English and be in good health. Preferably applicants will have a First Class Master's or a professional degree of at least four years duration. Applicants must

have at least five years of substantial professional experience in the respective field and not be more than 40 years of age. Applicants applying for the fellowships in drug abuse must hold a PhD or equivalent degree in the health, behavioural or social sciences or an MD.
Level of Study: Doctorate, Postgraduate, Professional development.
Type: Fellowship.
Value: Tuition and fees, a monthly maintenance allowance, modest allowance for books and supplies, round trip international travel to the host institution and domestic travel to Washington DC and/or Minnesota workshops.
Length of Study: 10 months.
Frequency: Annual.
Country of Study: United States of America.
No. of awards offered: Varies.
Application Procedure: Applicants must complete an application form. Requests for application materials must state the applicant's academic and professional qualifications, date of birth, current position and grant category and be accompanied by a 7 by 10 inch stamped addressed envelope. Requests for application materials must be sent to the USEFI offices in the applicant's region.
Closing Date: June 30th.
Funding: Government.
No. of awards given last year: Three.
No. of applicants last year: 90.
Additional Information: Further information is available on request.

USEFI Postdoctoral Research Scholar Grants

Subjects: American studies, special education, development studies or business administration.
Purpose: To provide scholars with the opportunity to undertake research on contemporary issues and concerns.
Eligibility: Open to Indian citizens resident in India at time of application who have not been to the United States of America in the preceding three years. Applicants must have a high level of academic and professional achievement, proficiency in English and be in good health. Applicants must be employed as full-time faculty members in an Indian college, university or research institution, hold a PhD degree or have equivalent published work and be under 50 years of age.
Level of Study: Postdoctorate.
Type: Grant.
Value: Round trip travel, monthly stipend, university affiliation fees, health insurance and a modest settling in allowance, dependent allowance and round trip travel for one dependent.
Length of Study: Up to eight months.
Frequency: Annual.
Study Establishment: A university or research institution in the United States of America.
Country of Study: United States of America.
No. of awards offered: Limited.
Application Procedure: Applicants must complete an application form. Requests for application materials must state the applicant's academic and professional qualifications, date of birth, current position and grant category and be accompanied by a 7 by 10 inch stamped addressed envelope. Requests for application materials must be sent to the USEFI offices in the applicant's region.
Closing Date: July 1st.
Additional Information: Applicants must demonstrate the relevance of the proposed research to India and/or the United States, its applicability in India, its benefit to the applicant's institution and the need to carry it out in the United States. Further information is available on request.

USEFI Postdoctoral Travel-Only Grants

Subjects: Social sciences, humanities, fine arts or the performing arts.
Eligibility: Open to Indian citizens resident in India at the time of application who have not been to the United States of America in the preceding three years. Applicants must have a high level of academic and professional achievement, proficiency in English and be in good health. Applicants must be full-time faculty members of an

Indian college, university or research institution, hold a PhD degree or have equivalent published work and be no more than 50 years of age. Applicants must be accepted by a recognised United States university or research institution for postdoctoral research and/or as a visiting lecturer and have assurance of dollar support to cover the expenses in the United States for the duration of the assignment. The letter of acceptance must show the nature and duration of the assignment, and must be accompanied by evidence of dollar support and of not less that US$2,000 per month and not more than US$25,000 per academic year. United States universities, Indian universities or research institutions could offer the evidence of dollar support in the form of a grant or fellowship. The letter(s) of invitation or sponsorship from United States host institutions must indicate that all expenses (towards room and board, local transportation, and related personal expenses) will be met.
Level of Study: Postdoctorate, Professional development.
Type: Travel grant.
Value: Round trip economy class airfare and health insurance.
Length of Study: Research or teaching assignments are 4-12 months. Inter-institutional collaboration is for two-three months and social science, humanities, fine arts or performing arts candidates are for two-three months.
Frequency: Annual.
Study Establishment: Travel only, for varying periods.
Country of Study: United States of America.
No. of awards offered: Two.
Application Procedure: Applicants must complete an application form. Requests for application materials must state the applicant's academic and professional qualifications, date of birth, current position and grant category and be accompanied by a 7 by 10 inch stamped addressed envelope. Requests for application materials must be sent to the USEFI offices in the applicant's region.
Closing Date: November 1st.
Funding: Government.
Additional Information: Further information is available on request.

USEFI Postdoctoral Visiting Lecturer Grants

Subjects: Contemporary issues significant to India and the United States of America in the fields of humanities or the social sciences.
Purpose: To allow scholars to share their expertise on contemporary issues significant to India and the United States of America.
Eligibility: Open to Indian citizens resident in India at the time of application who have not been to the United States of America in the preceding three years. Applicants must have a high level of academic and professional achievement, proficiency in English and be in good health. Applicants must be permanent full-time faculty members at an Indian college, university or research institute, hold a PhD degree or have equivalent published work, have at least 10 years of college or university level teaching experience and be no more than 50 years of age.
Level of Study: Postdoctorate.
Type: Grant.
Value: Round trip travel, monthly stipend, university fees, health insurance and a modest settling in allowance.
Length of Study: Three months.
Frequency: Annual.
Country of Study: United States of America.
No. of awards offered: Two-three.
Application Procedure: Applicants must complete an application form. Requests for application materials must state the applicant's academic and professional qualifications, date of birth, current position and grant category and be accompanied by a 7 by 10 inch stamped addressed envelope. Requests for application materials must be sent to the USEFI offices in the applicant's region.
Closing Date: July 15th.
Additional Information: Further information is available on request.

USEFI Predoctoral Fellowships

Subjects: American studies, intellectual property rights or special education.
Eligibility: Open to Indian citizens resident in India at the time of application who have not been to the United States of America in the

previous three years. Applicants must have a high level of academic and professional achievement, proficiency in English and be in good health. Applicants must be registered for a PhD at an Indian institution at least one year prior to application. The fellowship is also open to professionals with postgraduate degrees who are working in areas where study of IPR or special education would be helpful to their institutions.

Level of Study: Predoctorate, Professional development.
Type: Fellowship.
Value: Maintenance in the United States of America, affiliation fees, health insurance and round trip economy class airfare.
Length of Study: Up to six months.
Frequency: Annual.
Country of Study: United States of America.
No. of awards offered: Four-five.
Application Procedure: Applicants must complete an application form. Requests for application materials must state the applicant's academic and professional qualifications, date of birth, current position and grant category and be accompanied by a 7 by 10 inch stamped addressed envelope. Requests for application materials must be sent to the USEFI offices in the applicant's region.
Closing Date: June 30th.
Funding: Government.
No. of awards given last year: Five.
No. of applicants last year: 50.
Additional Information: Further information is available on request.

USEFI Professional Fellowships in Information Science and Technology

Subjects: Information science and technology.
Eligibility: Open to Indian citizens resident in India at the time of application who have not been to the United States of America in the preceding three years. Applicants must have a high level of academic and professional achievement, proficiency in English and be in good health. Applicants must be permanently employed as a librarian, assistant librarian, documentation officer, manager of information systems or equivalent position, hold a Master's degree in library and information science, management of information systems or other equivalent qualifications and be no more than 45 years of age.
Level of Study: Professional development.
Type: Fellowship.
Value: Maintenance in the United States of America, affiliation fees, health insurance and round trip economy or excursion air fare.
Length of Study: Up to six months.
Frequency: Annual.
Country of Study: United States of America.
No. of awards offered: Three-four.
Application Procedure: Applicants must complete an application form. Requests for application materials must state the applicant's academic and professional qualifications, date of birth, current position and grant category and be accompanied by a 7 by 10 inch stamped addressed envelope. Requests for application materials must be sent to the USEFI offices in the applicant's region.
Closing Date: June 30th.
Funding: Government.
No. of awards given last year: Three.
No. of applicants last year: 50.
Additional Information: Further information is available on request.

USEFI Professional Fellowships in Plastics and Performing Arts, Museum Studies and Arts/Culture Management

Subjects: Museum studies, arts or culture management, plastics or performing arts.
Purpose: To enable museum professionals or those employed in Arts and Culture organisations to attend non degree courses at United States of America universities or institutions in the relevant areas, and to gain practical work experience in suitable settings in the United States of America.

Eligibility: Open to Indian citizens resident in India at the time of application who have not been to the United States of America in the preceding three years. Applicants must have a high level of academic and professional achievement, proficiency in English and be in good health. Applicants must have completed their formal education, preferably having a postgraduate degree in the relevant area. Museum Studies applicants must be employed in museums in India. Arts and Culture Management applicants must be employed in Indian art and culture institutions or organisations. Applicants must be aged between 25 and 40 years. Plastics and performing arts applicants should have completed their formal education, or have substantial training under the auspices of the traditional Guru-Shishya Parampara.
Level of Study: Postgraduate, Professional development.
Type: Fellowship.
Value: Round trip travel, moderate monthly stipend, university fees, health insurance and a modest settling in allowance.
Length of Study: Two-six months.
Frequency: Dependent on funds available.
Country of Study: United States of America.
No. of awards offered: Four.
Application Procedure: Applicants must complete an application form. Requests for application materials must state the applicant's academic and professional qualifications, date of birth, current position and grant category and be accompanied by a 7 by 10 inch stamped addressed envelope. Requests for application materials must be sent to the USEFI offices in the applicant's region.
Closing Date: July 15th.
Funding: Government.
Additional Information: Further information is available on request.

UNITED STATES FOUNDATION

Fondation des États-Unis
15 boulevard Jourdan, Paris, Cedex 14, F-75690, France
Tel: (33) 1 53 80 68 80
Fax: (33) 1 53 80 68 99
Email: fondusa@iway.fr
Contact: Mr Terence Murphy, Director

Harriet Hale Woolley Scholarships

Subjects: Art and music.
Purpose: To support the study of visual fine arts in Paris.
Eligibility: Open to United States citizens, who are 21-29 years of age and have graduated with high academic standing from a United States college, university or professional school of recognised standing. Preference is given to mature students who have already completed graduate study. Applicants should provide evidence of artistic or musical accomplishment. Applicants should have a good working knowledge of French, sufficient to enable the student to benefit at once from study in France, good moral character, personality and adaptability and good physical health and emotional stability. Grants are for those doing painting, printmaking or sculpture and for instrumentalists, not for research in art history, musicology or composition, nor for students of dance or of theatre.
Level of Study: Graduate, Postgraduate.
Type: Scholarship.
Value: A stipend of US$8,500.
Length of Study: One academic year.
Frequency: Annual.
Country of Study: France.
No. of awards offered: Four-five.
Application Procedure: Applicants must write for details.
Closing Date: January 31st.
Funding: Private.
No. of awards given last year: Four.
No. of applicants last year: 25.

UNITED STATES INSTITUTE OF PEACE (USIP)

1200 17th Street North West
Suite 200, Washington, DC, 20036-3011, United States of America
Tel: (1) 202 429 3842
Fax: (1) 202 429 6063
Email: grant_program@usip.org
www: http://www.usip.org
Contact: Ms Elizabeth Drakulich, Administration Assistant

The United States Institute of Peace (USIP) is mandated by Congress to promote education and training, research and public information programmes on means to promote international peace, and resolve international conflicts without violence. The Institute meets this mandate through an array of programmes, including grants, fellowships, conferences and workshops, library services, publications and other educational activities.

Jennings Randolph Program for International Peace Dissertation Fellowship

Subjects: A broad range of disciplines and interdisciplinary fields are eligible.
Purpose: To support dissertations that explore the sources and nature of international conflict, and strategies to prevent or end conflict and to sustain peace.
Eligibility: Open to applicants of all nationalities who are enrolled in an accredited college or university in the United States of America. Applicants must have completed all requirements for the degree except the dissertation by the commencement of the award.
Level of Study: Doctorate.
Type: Fellowship.
Value: US$17,000 which may be used to support writing or field research.
Length of Study: One year.
Frequency: Annual.
Study Establishment: The student's home university or site of fieldwork.
Country of Study: United States of America.
No. of awards offered: 10-12.
Application Procedure: Applicants must complete an application form, available on request from the Institute or from the website.
Closing Date: November 1st.
Funding: Government.
Additional Information: The programme does not support work involving partisan political and policy advocacy or policy making for any government or private organisation. Further information is available on the website.

Jennings Randolph Program for International Peace Senior Fellowships

Subjects: Preventive diplomacy, ethnic and regional conflicts, peacekeeping and peace operations, peace settlements, post conflict reconstruction and reconciliation, democratisation and the rule of law, cross cultural negotiations, United States policy in the twenty first-century and related subjects.
Purpose: To use the recipient's existing knowledge and skills towards a fruitful endeavour in the international peace and conflict management field, and to help bring the perspectives of this field into the Fellow's own career.
Eligibility: Open to outstanding practitioners and Scholars from a broad range of backgrounds. The competition is open to citizens of any country who have specific interest and experience in international peace and conflict management. Candidates would typically be senior academics, however applicants who hold at least a Bachelor's degree from a recognised university will also be considered.
Level of Study: Doctorate, Postdoctorate, Postgraduate.
Type: Fellowship.
Value: A stipend, an office with computer and voicemail and a part-time research assistant.
Length of Study: Up to 10 months.

Frequency: Annual.
Study Establishment: USIP.
Country of Study: United States of America.
No. of awards offered: 10-12.
Application Procedure: Applicants must complete an application form, available on request from the Institute or from the website.
Closing Date: September 15th.
Funding: Government.

USIP Solicited Grants

Subjects: Special priority topics identified in advance by the Institute. Current grant topics can be found on the website.
Purpose: To provide financial support for research, education and training, and the dissemination of information on international peace and conflict resolution.
Eligibility: The Institute may provide grant support to non-profit organisations and individuals, both American and foreign. These include institutions of post secondary, community and secondary education, public and private education, training or research institutions and libraries. Although the Institute can provide grant support to individuals, it prefers that an institutional affiliation be established. The Institute will not accept applications that list as participants, consultants, or project personnel members of the Institute's Board of Directors or staff. In addition, any application that lists the Institute as a collaborator in the project will not be accepted.
Level of Study: Postdoctorate, Research.
Type: Grant.
Value: Most awards fall in the range of US$25,000 to US$45,000, although somewhat larger grants are also awarded. The amount of any grant is based on the proposed budget and on negotiations with successful applicants.
Length of Study: One-two years.
Frequency: Annual.
Application Procedure: Applicants must complete an application form, available on request from the Institute or from the website.
Closing Date: March 1st for the Spring competition and October 1st for the Autumn competition.
Funding: Government.
No. of awards given last year: 38.
No. of applicants last year: 212.

USIP Unsolicited Grants

Subjects: Topic areas of interest to the Institute include, but are not restricted to, international conflict resolution, diplomacy, negotiation theory, functionalism and track two diplomacy, methods of third party dispute settlement, international law, international organisations and collective security, deterrence and balance of power, arms control, psychological theories about international conflict, the role of non violence and non violent sanctions, moral and ethical thought about conflict and conflict resolution, and theories about relationships among political institutions, human rights and conflict.
Purpose: To provide financial support for research, education and training, and the dissemination of information on international peace and conflict resolution.
Eligibility: The Institute may provide grant support to non-profit organisations and individuals, both American and foreign. These include institutions of post secondary, community and secondary education, public and private education, training or research institutions and libraries. Although the Institute can provide grant support to individuals, it prefers that an institutional affiliation be established. The Institute will not accept applications that list members of the Institute's Board of Directors or staff as participants, consultants or project personnel. In addition, any application that lists the Institute as a collaborator in the project will not be accepted.
Level of Study: Postdoctorate, Research.
Type: Grant.
Value: Most awards fall in the range of US$25,000-45,000, although somewhat larger grants are also awarded. The amount of any grant is based on the proposed budget and on negotiations with successful applicants.
Length of Study: One-two years.
Frequency: Annual.

Application Procedure: Applicants must complete an application form, available on request from the Institute or from the website.
Closing Date: October 1st or March 1st.
Funding: Government.
No. of awards given last year: 63.
No. of applicants last year: 419.

UNITED STATES TROTTING ASSOCIATION

750 Michigan Avenue, Columbus, OH, 43215, United States of America
Tel: (1) 614 224 2291
Fax: (1) 614 228 1385
Email: jpawlak@ustrotting.com
www: http://www.ustrotting.com
Contact: Mr John Pawlak, Publicity/PR Director

The United States Trotting Association promotes the sport of harness racing and the Standardbred breed. It also maintains and disseminates racing information and records and serves as the registry for the breed.

John Hervey, Broadcasters and Smallsreed Awards

Subjects: Journalism, television broadcasting and photography.
Purpose: To honour the best media stories on harness racing in the categories of newspaper, magazines, television and photo journalism.
Eligibility: Stories must have been published or aired in North America.
Level of Study: Unrestricted.
Type: Cash prize.
Value: First prize is US$500, second prize is US$100 and third prize is US$100 in each division.
Frequency: Annual.
Country of Study: Any country.
No. of awards offered: 15.
Application Procedure: Applicants must submit entries to the address shown. There is no application form.
Closing Date: February 1st.
Funding: Private.
Contributor: The United States Trotting Association.
No. of awards given last year: 12.
No. of applicants last year: 75.
Additional Information: Articles, television programmes and photographs must be published or broadcast in North America.

UNIVERSAL ESPERANTO ASSOCIATION

Nieuwe Binneweg 176, Rotterdam, NL-3015 BJ, Netherlands
Tel: (31) 10 436 1044
Fax: (31) 10 436 1751
Email: uea@inter.nl.net
www: http://www.uea.org
Contact: Mr P Zapelli

Universal Esperanto Association Awards

Subjects: Esperanto.
Purpose: To train young volunteer workers for the advancement of the language and literature of Esperanto.
Eligibility: Open to individuals of all nationalities who are between 18-29 years of age. A fluent knowledge of Esperanto, both written and spoken, is essential prior to qualification.
Level of Study: Unrestricted.
Type: Award.
Value: A monthly stipend of €280 plus accommodation.
Length of Study: Up to one year, non renewable.
Frequency: Annual.

Study Establishment: The Head Office of the Association.
Country of Study: Netherlands.
No. of awards offered: One-two.
Closing Date: Applications are accepted at any time.

UNIVERSITA' PER STRANIERI DI PERUGIA

Palazzo Gallenga
Piazza Fortebraccio 4, Perugia, I-06122, Italy
Tel: (39) 075 574 61
Fax: (39) 075 573 0901
Email: borse@unistrapg.it
www: http://www.unistrapg.it
Contact: Anpiolo Boncompagni, Press Office

Of all the Italian institutions which conduct research into the teaching and acquisition of the Italian language and which foster the knowledge of Italian culture, the Universita' Per Stranieri Di Perugia is the oldest and the most prestigious. The University is the only Italian member of ALTE (Association of Language Testers in Europe).

University for Foreigners Scholarships

Subjects: Italian language and culture.
Eligibility: Open to foreign citizens and Italians resident abroad. Preference is given to students of Italian at schools and universities abroad, and to teachers of the Italian language.
Level of Study: Postgraduate.
Type: Scholarship.
Value: To cover one month's study and living expenses.
Length of Study: One-six months.
Frequency: Monthly.
Study Establishment: The University.
Country of Study: Italy.
No. of awards offered: 350.
Application Procedure: Applications for scholarships must be made through the Italian Institutes of Culture in the country of residence. Direct application to the University for Foreigners may be made only by applicants residing in countries where there are no Italian Institutes of Culture. Further information is available on request or from the website.
Closing Date: At least four months before the start of the course.
No. of awards given last year: 350.
No. of applicants last year: 6,000.

UNIVERSITA' PER STRANIERI DI SIENA

Via Pantaneto N 45, Siena, I-53100, Italy
Tel: (39) 057 724 0111
Fax: (39) 057 728 3163
Email: info@unistrasi.it
www: http://www.unistrasi.it
Contact: Ms Giuseppina Grassiccia, Head of Promotions & International Division

The Universita' Per Stranieri Di Siena is a state university which undertakes research and instruction in the fields of Italian language and culture. It is located in the heart of Tuscany, Italy, and offers Italian language courses for foreigners, graduate courses related to Italian culture and language, and training courses for teachers of Italian as a foreign language.

Regional Agency for the Right to University Study (DSU) Grants

Subjects: Linguistics, philology, history, literature, education and teacher training.
Purpose: To give university students the financial means necessary to fulfil their study programme.

Eligibility: This award is restricted by merit and family or personal income.
Level of Study: Graduate.
Type: Scholarship.
Value: University fees and lodging in the students' halls of residence.
Length of Study: One year.
Frequency: Annual.
Study Establishment: The University of Siena for Foreigners.
Country of Study: Italy.
No. of awards offered: Varies.
Application Procedure: Applicants must apply to the DSU after the enrolment to the second year of the course at the university in Italy.
Closing Date: September.
Funding: Government.
No. of awards given last year: 16.

For further information contact:

Azienda Regionale per il Diritto Allo Studio
Via dei Termini 6, Siena, I-53100, Italy

Universita' Per Stranieri Di Siena CILS Grants

Subjects: Italian language and culture.
Purpose: To exempt students from the payment for the CILS Exam.
Eligibility: Applicants must hold a certificate of merit.
Level of Study: Unrestricted.
Type: Grant.
Value: The examination fee.
Frequency: Dependent on funds available.
Study Establishment: Conventional institutions throughout the world.
No. of awards offered: Varies.
Application Procedure: Applicants must apply for information, available on request.
Closing Date: Please write for details.
Funding: Private.
Contributor: The University of Siena for Foreigners and Bank Monte dei Paschi of Siena.
No. of awards given last year: 46.
Additional Information: The CILS (Certification of Italian as a Foreign Language) is an examination established by the University and aimed to assess student's proficiency in Italian. It is recognised by the Italian Ministry of Foreign Affairs.

For further information contact:

CILS Certification Centre
Via S Bandini 35, Siena, I-53100, Italy

Universita' Per Stranieri Di Siena Doctorate in Italian Language and Culture (with an intertextual approach)

Subjects: Language, literature and education.
Purpose: To further research into the Italian language with an intertextual approach.
Eligibility: Applicants must be citizens of the European Union and hold a university degree equivalent to the Italian 'Laurea' degree.
Level of Study: Doctorate.
Type: Scholarship.
Value: Established by law.
Length of Study: Three years.
Frequency: Annual.
Study Establishment: The University of Siena for Foreigners and the consorted university 'La Sapienza' of Rome.
Country of Study: Italy.
No. of awards offered: Two.
Application Procedure: This is a public competition and regulations are published in the Gazzetta Ufficiale of the Italian Republic every year.
Closing Date: Usually late Spring or early Summer. Deadlines are published each year in the official document Gazzetta Ufficiale.
Funding: Government.
Contributor: The University of Siena for foreigners.

No. of awards given last year: Two.

Universita' Per Stranieri Di Siena Doctorate in the Teaching of Italian to Foreigners

Subjects: Italian language.
Purpose: To further research into the teaching of Italian to foreigners.
Eligibility: Applicants must be citizens of the European Union and hold a university degree considered equivalent to the Italian 'Laurea' degree.
Level of Study: Doctorate.
Type: Scholarship.
Value: Established by law.
Length of Study: Three years.
Frequency: Annual.
Study Establishment: The University of Siena for Foreigners.
Country of Study: Italy.
No. of awards offered: Two.
Application Procedure: This is a public competition and regulations are published in the Gazzetta Ufficiale of the Italian Republic every year.
Closing Date: Usually late Spring or early Summer. Deadlines are published each year in the official document Gazzetta Ufficiale.
Funding: Government.
Contributor: The University of Siena for Foreigners.
No. of awards given last year: Two.
Additional Information: Further information is available on request.

Universita' Per Stranieri Di Siena PVS Grants

Subjects: Italian language and culture.
Purpose: To support study at regular and special Italian language courses for students coming from developing countries.
Eligibility: Applicants must hold a study qualification valid for admission to university level studies in their home country and be a citizen of a developing country.
Level of Study: Graduate.
Type: Scholarship.
Value: Fees and lodging.
Length of Study: One-two months.
Frequency: Annual.
Study Establishment: The University of Siena for Foreigners.
Country of Study: Italy.
No. of awards offered: Up to 50.
Application Procedure: Applicants must apply directly to the Italian Cultural Institutes in their home country.
Closing Date: End of February.
Funding: Private.
Contributor: The University of Siena for Foreigners and the Bank Monte dei Paschi di Siena.
No. of awards given last year: 50.
Additional Information: Further information is available on request.

Universita' Per Stranieri Di Siena Socrates Erasmus Students Mobility

Subjects: Arts and humanities.
Purpose: To provide an opportunity for someone to study abroad.
Eligibility: Applicants must be enrolled in the University for Foreigners of Siena and be European Union citizens.
Level of Study: Graduate.
Type: Grant.
Value: €120 per month.
Length of Study: From 3-12 months.
Frequency: Annual.
Study Establishment: The University of Birmingham in the United Kingdom, Heidelberg Universität in Germany, the University of Poitiers and University of Rennes in France.
Country of Study: United Kingdom, Germany or France.
No. of awards offered: Varies according to the partnerships established with European universities. There are eight for students and two for teachers.

687

Application Procedure: Applicants must complete an application form which will be submitted to the examination of the relevant commission. Applications should be addressed to the Divisione Promozione E Relazioni Internazionali.

Closing Date: End of May.

Contributor: The European Union and the University of Siena for Foreigners.

No. of awards given last year: One.

No. of applicants last year: Two.

Additional Information: The grants support students abroad while they attend one or more terms at the host university, choosing courses offered there and taking the appropriate examinations.

Universita' Per Stranieri Di Siena Unstra Grants

Subjects: Italian language and culture.

Purpose: To support study at regular courses.

Eligibility: Applicants must hold a study qualification valid for admission to university level studies in their home country.

Level of Study: Graduate.

Type: Scholarship.

Value: Course fees.

Length of Study: One-three months.

Frequency: Annual.

Study Establishment: The University of Siena for Foreigners.

Country of Study: Italy.

No. of awards offered: Approx. 50.

Application Procedure: Applicants must apply directly to the Italian Cultural Institutes in their home country.

Closing Date: End of February.

Funding: Private.

Contributor: The University of Siena for Foreigners and the Bank Monte dei Paschi di Siena.

No. of awards given last year: 133.

Additional Information: Further information is available on request.

UNIVERSITY INSTITUTE OF EUROPEAN STUDIES

Via Maria Vittoria 26, Turin, I-10123, Italy
Tel: (39) 011 839 4660
Fax: (39) 011 839 4664
Email: iuseinfo@inrete.it
www: http://www.iuse.it
Contact: Ms Maria Grazia Goiettina, Course Secretariat

The University Institute of European Studies promotes international relations and European integration by organising academic activities. The Institute has a comprehensive library in international law and economics. Since 1952 the Institute has been a European Documentation Centre (EDC), thus receiving all official publications of European institutions.

University Institute of European Studies Postgraduate Scholarships

Subjects: International trade law. The programme deals with the origin and evolution of international trade, instruments and rules of the main economic international organisations, sources of law in international trade, legal aspects of international contracts in international trade, conflict of laws, modes of payment taxation, arbitration and dispute resolution.

Purpose: To allow students to attend the postgraduate course on International Trade Law.

Eligibility: Open to Italian and foreign graduates in law, business and economics. Candidates from Turin are not eligible.

Level of Study: Postgraduate.

Type: Scholarship.

Value: To cover part of the accommodation expenses.

Length of Study: Three months (one term).

Frequency: Annual.

Study Establishment: The ILO Turin Centre.

Country of Study: Italy.

No. of awards offered: Varies.

Application Procedure: Candidates should fill in the application form obtainable from the Secretariat or the website. A copy of the degree, including a transcript of academic records and a certificate of English knowledge should be attached.

Closing Date: Mid January.

Funding: Private.

No. of awards given last year: Seven.

No. of applicants last year: 300.

Additional Information: The course aims to provide candidates with a common legal approach to the main legal issues in international trade law and contract drafting. Lecturers are prominent Italian and international experts, university professors or practitioners and senior officials of international institutions. The course, usually held in Spring, is in English. The number of participants is limited and full-time participation is required throughout the programme.

UNIVERSITY OF ADELAIDE

Graduate School of Management
3rd Floor Security House
233 North Terrace, Adelaide, SA, 5005, Australia
Tel: (61) 8 3035 525
Fax: (61) 8 8223 4782
Email: cmchugh@gsm.adelaide.edu.au
www: http://www.gsm.adelaide.edu.au
Contact: MBA Admissions Officer

Adelaide Postgraduate Coursework Scholarships International (APCS)

Subjects: All subjects.

Purpose: To financially support outstanding international students from any country undertaking a postgraduate coursework programme in any academic discipline.

Eligibility: Citizens and permanent residents of Australia, and citizens of New Zealand are ineligible. Candidates are required to enrol in Adelaide University as international students and must maintain this status for the duration of their enrolment in the University.

Level of Study: Postgraduate, MBA.

Type: Scholarship.

Value: Payment of full tuition fees plus an annual living allowance of Australian $17,267.

Length of Study: The duration of the postgraduate course.

Frequency: Annual.

Study Establishment: Adelaide University.

Country of Study: Australia.

No. of awards offered: Four.

Application Procedure: There is no separate application process for the scholarships. An application for admission to the University will constitute an application for a scholarship. All applications for admission consistent with the eligibility and selection criteria will be considered automatically for a scholarship. An application fee of Australian $50 must accompany the application for admission.

Closing Date: Please contact the organisation.

Additional Information: All successful recipients will be required to pay their own Overseas Student Health Cover each year.

UNIVERSITY OF ALBERTA

Faculty of Graduate Studies & Research
105 Administration Building, Edmonton, AB, T6G 2M7, Canada
Tel: (1) 780 492 3499
Fax: (1) 780 492 0692
Email: grad.awards@ualberta.ca
www: http://gradfile.fgsro.ualberta.ca
Contact: A Andrews, Awards Assistant

Opened in 1908, the University of Alberta has a long tradition of scholarly achievements and commitment to excellence in teaching, research and service to the community. It is one of Canada's five largest research intensive universities, with an annual research income from external sources of more than canadian $112 million. It participates in all 14 of the Federal Networks of Centres of Excellence which link industry, universities and government in applied research and development.

Grant Notley Memorial Postdoctoral Fellowship

Subjects: Research in the politics, history, economy or society of Western Canada, or related fields.
Purpose: To encourage scholars of superior research ability who graduated within the last three years.
Eligibility: Open to persons who have recently completed a PhD programme or will do so in the immediate future. Applicants should be active and promising young Scholars who will perform significantly in fields associated with Grant Notley's broad interests in the politics, history, economy or society of Western Canada or related fields. Applicants who have received their PhD degree from the University of Alberta, will be on sabbatical leave, or have held or will have held postdoctoral fellowships at other institutions for two years are not eligible.
Level of Study: Postdoctorate.
Type: Fellowship.
Value: Canadian $38,000 per year, a non renewable research grant of canadian $4,000, and return travel from the point of residence at the time of application.
Length of Study: Two years.
Frequency: Annual.
Study Establishment: The University of Alberta.
Country of Study: Canada.
No. of awards offered: One.
Application Procedure: Applicants must visit the website for application information.
Closing Date: January 2nd.
Funding: Private.
No. of awards given last year: One.
No. of applicants last year: Four.

Izaak Walton Killam Memorial Postdoctoral Fellowships

Subjects: All subjects.
Purpose: To attract scholars of superior research ability who graduated within the last three years.
Eligibility: Open to candidates of any nationality who have recently completed a PhD programme or will do so in the immediate future. Applicants who have received their PhD degree from the University of Alberta, will be on sabbatical leave, or have held or will have held postdoctoral fellowships at other institutions for two years are not eligible.
Level of Study: Postdoctorate.
Type: Fellowship.
Value: Canadian $38,000 per year, a non renewable research grant of canadian $4,000 and a return airfare.
Length of Study: Two years.
Frequency: Annual.
Study Establishment: The University of Alberta.
Country of Study: Canada.
No. of awards offered: Six.
Application Procedure: Applicants must visit the website for application information.
Closing Date: January 2nd.

Funding: Private.
No. of awards given last year: Six.
No. of applicants last year: 33.

Izaak Walton Killam Memorial Scholarships

Subjects: All subjects.
Eligibility: Open to candidates of any nationality who are registered in, or are admissible to, a doctoral programme at the University. Scholars must have completed at least one year of graduate work prior to beginning the scholarship. Applicants must be nominated by the department in which they plan to pursue their doctoral studies.
Level of Study: Doctorate, Postgraduate.
Type: Scholarship.
Value: Canadian $19,100 per year, a non renewable research grant of canadian $2,000, tuition and fees.
Length of Study: Two years from May 1st or September 1st, subject to review after the first year.
Frequency: Annual.
Study Establishment: The University of Alberta.
Country of Study: Canada.
No. of awards offered: Approx. 20.
Application Procedure: Applicants must contact the university departments for application information.
Closing Date: February 1st for submission of nominations from departments. Please check with the department for their internal deadline.
Funding: Private.
No. of awards given last year: 20.
No. of applicants last year: 137.

Province of Alberta Graduate Fellowships

Subjects: All subjects.
Eligibility: Open to Canadian citizens or permanent residents at the date of application who have completed at least one year of graduate study and are registered in a full-time doctoral programme at the University of Alberta.
Level of Study: Doctorate, Postgraduate.
Type: Fellowship.
Value: Canadian $10,500 for commencement in May and canadian $7,000 for commencement in September.
Length of Study: One year from May 1st or September 1st.
Frequency: Annual.
Study Establishment: The University of Alberta.
Country of Study: Canada.
No. of awards offered: Approx. 35.
Application Procedure: Applicants must be nominated by the department in which they plan to pursue their doctoral studies.
Closing Date: February 1st for submission of nominations from departments. Please check with the department for their internal deadline.
Funding: Government.
No. of awards given last year: 34.
No. of applicants last year: 252.
Additional Information: Recipients must carry out a full-time research programme during the Summer months.

Province of Alberta Graduate Scholarships

Subjects: All subjects.
Eligibility: Open to Canadian citizens or permanent residents who are entering or continuing in a full-time Master's programme at the University of Alberta at the date of application. Applicants must be nominated by the department in which they plan to pursue their studies. Students registered as qualifying graduate or probationary students are not eligible.
Level of Study: Postgraduate.
Type: Scholarship.
Value: Canadian $9,300 for commencement in May, canadian $6,200 for commencement in September.
Length of Study: One year from May 1st or eight months from September 1st. Partial awards may be recommended at a reduced value

and the award may be terminated earlier by either the student or the university and the amount reduced proportionately.

Frequency: Annual.

Study Establishment: The University of Alberta.

Country of Study: Canada.

No. of awards offered: Approx. 35.

Application Procedure: Applicants must complete an application form available from the relevant university department.

Closing Date: February 1st for submission of nominations from departments. Please check with the department for their internal deadline.

Funding: Government.

No. of awards given last year: 44.

No. of applicants last year: 162.

UNIVERSITY OF BATH

Graduate Office
Claverton Down, Bath, BA2 7AY, England
Tel: (44) 1225 323234
Fax: (44) 1225 826366
Email: grad-office@bath.ac.uk
www: http://www.bath.ac.uk
Contact: Dr Lisa Isted, Assistant Registrar

The School of Management at the University of Bath is one of only seven out of 100 business schools to achieve top ratings for both teaching and research in HEFCE assessments. In 2000 it came fifth out of 90 business schools in the 'Times Good University Guide'. It has 100 academic staff and 1,400 students.

University of Bath Research Studentships

Subjects: All subjects offered by the University.

Purpose: To provide funds for well qualified candidates to pursue full-time research leading to a research degree.

Eligibility: Open to candidates of any nationality with a First Class (Honours) Degree or good Second Class (Honours) Degree or equivalent. Candidates must have applied or been accepted for study for a research degree.

Level of Study: Doctorate, Research.

Type: Scholarship.

Value: Home fees plus a minimum annual stipend of UK £7,004.

Length of Study: Up to three years.

Frequency: Annual.

Study Establishment: The University of Bath.

Country of Study: United Kingdom.

No. of awards offered: Approx. 20.

Application Procedure: Applicants must state that they wish to apply for the Studentship when applying for a higher degree and must contact the appropriate academic department or the graduate office.

Closing Date: August 1st.

Funding: Government.

Contributor: The University of Bath.

No. of awards given last year: 15.

Additional Information: Other studentships are available from the University of Bath including Overseas Research Students awards. Please contact the Graduate Office for further details.

UNIVERSITY OF BIRMINGHAM

Student Services & Admissions
Edgbaston, Birmingham, West Midlands, B15 2TT, England
Tel: (44) 121 414 3344
Fax: (44) 121 414 3907
www: http://www.bham.ac.uk
Telex: 333762 UOBHAM G
Contact: Ms Gillian M York, Financial Support Assistant

The University of Birmingham is a leading research institution, offering a wide range of programmes, high teaching and research standards, and excellent facilities for academic work.

Kenward Memorial Fellowship

Subjects: Engineering production.

Purpose: To provide financial assistance to those wishing to undertake research in manufacturing and mechanical engineering at the University of Birmingham.

Eligibility: Open to graduates in suitable disciplines.

Level of Study: Doctorate.

Type: Fellowship.

Value: Varies but dependent on funds available.

Length of Study: One year, possibly renewable for a further one or two years.

Frequency: Dependent on funds available.

Study Establishment: The University of Birmingham.

Country of Study: United Kingdom.

No. of awards offered: Dependent on funds available.

Application Procedure: Applicants must apply through recommendation by school and evidence of academic achievement.

Closing Date: Advertised with vacancies.

Funding: Private.

Contributor: Friends of the late Sir Harold Leslie Kenward.

No. of awards given last year: One.

Additional Information: The holder of the fellowship, as well as undertaking research, will undertake a limited amount of teaching in the school, not exceeding two hours each week.

Neville Chamberlain Scholarship

Subjects: Humanities subjects. Preference will be given to studies focusing on modern political, social and economic history, especially concerning Great Britain and its nineteenth-century sphere of influence.

Purpose: To provide financial assistance to students wishing to study for a higher degree in a humanities subject.

Eligibility: Preferably open to non United Kingdom students with a good honours degree who have been offered and have accepted admission to study for a higher degree in a humanities subject. Proficiency in English is essential.

Level of Study: Postgraduate.

Type: Scholarship.

Value: A supplement to student's resources should these be inadequate for taking the degree. An award may be given towards both tuition fees and maintenance but normally should not exceed UK £7,000 per year.

Length of Study: One year, renewable as funding allows.

Study Establishment: The University of Birmingham.

Country of Study: United Kingdom.

No. of awards offered: One, depending on funds available.

Application Procedure: Applicants must be nominated by the school that they intend to study at.

Closing Date: Mid June.

Funding: Private.

Contributor: The family of Neville Chamberlain.

No. of awards given last year: Two.

No. of applicants last year: Eight.

UNIVERSITY OF BRISTOL

Student Finance Office
Students Union
Queen's Road, Bristol, BS8 1LN, England
Tel: (44) 117 954 5886
Fax: (44) 117 954 5709
Email: stdfin@bris.ac.uk
www: http://www.bristol.ac.uk/depts/stdfin
Contact: Ms J Tyler, Student Finance Officer

The University of Bristol is committed to providing high quality teaching and research in all its designated fields.

University of Bristol Postgraduate Scholarships

Subjects: Any research topic which is covered in the work of the department within the University.
Purpose: To recruit high quality research students.
Eligibility: Open to new research students with normally at least an Upper Second Class (Honours) Degree or equivalent and full-time or part-time students who are not in full-time employment. All University Scholars must be registered and in attendance for a research degree at the University.
Level of Study: Postgraduate.
Type: Scholarship.
Value: UK £7,000-10,000 plus home tuition fees of UK £2,805.
Length of Study: Three years.
Frequency: Annual.
Study Establishment: The University of Bristol.
Country of Study: United Kingdom.
No. of awards offered: 30.
Application Procedure: Applicants must complete the appropriate form and submit this to the department of their field of interest.
Closing Date: Normally May 1st.
Funding: Private.
Contributor: The University of Bristol.
No. of awards given last year: 30.
Additional Information: Overseas students need to find the difference between home and overseas fees. To do this they can apply for an overseas research scholarship (ORS).

For further information contact:

Postgraduate Admissions
University of Bristol
Senate House
Tyndall Avenue
Clifton, Bristol, BS8 1TH, England

UNIVERSITY OF BRITISH COLUMBIA (UBC)

Faculty of Graduate Studies
180-6371 Crescent Road, Vancouver, BC, V6T 1Z2, Canada
Tel: (1) 604 822 4556
Fax: (1) 604 822 5802
Email: gradawards@mercury.ubc.ca
www: http://www.grad.ubc.ca
Contact: Ms Jiffin Arboleda, Killam Secretary

The University of British Columbia (UBC) is one of North America's major research universities. The faculty of Graduate Studies has 6,500 students and is a national leader in interdisciplinary study and research, with 98 departments, 18 interdisciplinary research units, nine interdisciplinary graduate programmes, two graduate residential colleges and one scholarly journal.

Izaak Walton Killam Postdoctoral Fellowships

Subjects: All subjects.
Purpose: To support all areas of academic research.

Eligibility: Open to candidates who show superior ability in research and have obtained, within two academic years of the anticipated commencement date of the fellowship, a doctorate at a university other than the University of British Columbia. Graduates of the University of British Columbia are not normally eligible.
Level of Study: Postdoctorate.
Type: Fellowship.
Value: Canadian $41,000 per year and canadian $3,000 travel allowance for duration of the award.
Length of Study: Two years, subject to satisfactory progress at the end of the first year.
Frequency: Annual.
Study Establishment: UBC.
Country of Study: Canada.
No. of awards offered: Eight.
Application Procedure: Applicants must submit an application form, academic transcripts and three reference letters to the appropriate department. For information and application forms, please visit the website.
Closing Date: November 15th.
Funding: Private.
No. of awards given last year: Four.
No. of applicants last year: 200.
Additional Information: Candidates are responsible for contacting the appropriate department at the University to ensure their proposed research project is acceptable and may be undertaken under the supervision of a member of the department. Candidates can email killam@mercury.ubc.ca for further details.

Izaak Walton Killam Predoctoral Fellowship

Subjects: All subjects.
Purpose: To assist doctoral students with full-time studies and research.
Eligibility: Open to students of any nationality, discipline, age or sex. This award is given at the PhD level only and is strictly based on academic merit. Students must have a first class standing in their last two years of study.
Level of Study: Doctorate.
Type: Fellowship.
Value: Canadian $22,000 per year and a canadian $1,500 travel allowance for the duration of the award.
Frequency: Annual.
Study Establishment: UBC.
Country of Study: Canada.
No. of awards offered: Approx. 15.
Application Procedure: Top ranked students are selected from the University Graduate Fellowship competition. Application forms can be obtained from departments or the Faculty of Graduate Studies or the website http://www.grad.ubc.ca. Students must submit their applications to the departments, not to Graduate Studies.
Closing Date: Each department has its own internal deadline, usually in early Autumn.
Funding: Private.
No. of awards given last year: 12.
No. of applicants last year: 200.

University of British Columbia Graduate Fellowship (UGF)

Subjects: All subjects.
Purpose: To assist graduate students with their studies and research.
Eligibility: Open to students of any nationality, discipline, age or sex. This award is strictly based on academic merit. Students must have a first class standing in their last two years of study.
Level of Study: Graduate.
Type: Fellowship.
Value: Canadian $16,000 per year for two years full renewable fellowships, canadian $16,000 for one year fellowships, or canadian $8,000 for one year partial fellowships.
Frequency: Annual.
Study Establishment: UBC.
Country of Study: Canada.

691

No. of awards offered: Approx. 450.
Application Procedure: Applicants must be nominated by their departments based on academic merit. Students must submit their applications to the UBC department by the department deadline date, not to the Faculty of Graduate Studies. UGF applications are available from the website.
Closing Date: Early Autumn.
Funding: Government.
No. of awards given last year: 460.
No. of applicants last year: Approx. 2,500.
Additional Information: Please check for internal departmental deadlines.

THE UNIVERSITY OF CALGARY

Faculty of Graduate Studies
Earth Sciences Building
Room 720
2500 University Drive North West, Calgary, AB, T2N 1N4, Canada
Tel: (1) 403 220 5690
Fax: (1) 403 289 7635
Email: cbusch@ucalgary.ca
www: http://www.ucalgary.ca
Contact: Ms Connie Busch, Graduate Scholarship Assistant

The University of Calgary is a place of education and scholarly inquiry. Its mission is to seek truth and disseminate knowledge and it aims to pursue this mission with integrity for the benefit of the people of Alberta, Canada and the world.

Alberta Art Foundation Graduate Scholarships in The Department of Art

Subjects: Major fields of study in the department of art.
Purpose: To support study.
Eligibility: Open to students entering the second year of the MFA programme in the categories of painting, printmaking, sculpture, drawing or photography.
Level of Study: Postgraduate.
Type: Scholarship.
Value: Canadian $6,000.
Frequency: Annual.
Study Establishment: The University of Calgary.
Country of Study: Canada.
No. of awards offered: Three.
Application Procedure: Applicants must be nominated by the Department of Art.
Closing Date: February 1st.

The Alberta Law Foundation Graduate Scholarship

Subjects: Natural resources, energy and environmental law.
Eligibility: Open to full-time graduates who are registered in or admissible to a programme of studies leading to a Master's degree in the Faculty of Law at the University of Calgary.
Level of Study: Postgraduate.
Type: Scholarship.
Value: Canadian $13,000 each.
Length of Study: One year, non renewable.
Frequency: Annual.
Study Establishment: The University of Calgary.
Country of Study: Canada.
No. of awards offered: Two.
Application Procedure: Applicants must complete an application form, available from the director of the graduate programme at the Faculty of Law.
Additional Information: In cases where no suitable application is received no awards will be made.

The Alberta Research Council Scholarship

Subjects: Agriculture, forestry, fishery, transport, communications, energy engineering, natural sciences or home economics.

Eligibility: Open to graduate students engaged in thesis research at Master's or PhD level in the relevant fields.
Level of Study: Doctorate, Postgraduate.
Type: Scholarship.
Value: Approx. canadian $17,300 which is equal to PGSA level NSERC Scholarship.
Length of Study: One year. Students may apply in open competition for a subsequent year's award.
Frequency: Annual.
Study Establishment: The University of Calgary.
Country of Study: Canada.
No. of awards offered: One.
Application Procedure: Applicants must complete an application form, available from the graduate programme directors of the departments concerned, which include engineering, natural sciences and economics.
Closing Date: February 1st.

Canadian Natural Resources Limited Graduate Scholarship

Subjects: Engineering, earth and geological sciences, home economics or MBA.
Eligibility: Open to full-time graduate students, registered or eligible to register full-time in economics, geology and geophysics, engineering or management.
Level of Study: Postgraduate.
Type: Scholarship.
Value: Up to canadian $10,000.
Length of Study: One year.
Frequency: Annual.
Study Establishment: The University of Calgary.
Country of Study: Canada.
No. of awards offered: One.
Application Procedure: Applicants must complete an application form, available from the graduate co-ordinators of the departments concerned of the University of Calgary.
Closing Date: February 1st.

Craigie (Peter C) Memorial Scholarship

Subjects: The humanities.
Eligibility: Open to full-time registrants from any country who are registered in and have completed one term of study in a programme of studies leading to an MA degree in a department of the Faculty of Humanities. The recipient must have an outstanding scholastic record and will have been or be involved in activities contributing to the general welfare of the university committee.
Level of Study: Postgraduate.
Type: Scholarship.
Value: Canadian $5,000.
Frequency: Every two years.
Study Establishment: The University of Calgary.
Country of Study: Canada.
No. of awards offered: One.
Application Procedure: Applicants must apply to the Faculty of Humanities in the first instance. Recommendations from the Faculty will be submitted for consideration and approval by the University Graduate Scholarship Committee.
Closing Date: February 1st.

Davies (William H) Medical Research Scholarship

Subjects: Medicine.
Eligibility: Open to qualified graduates of any recognised university who will be registered in the Faculty of Graduate Studies at the University of Calgary. Successful candidates must conduct their research programme within the Faculty of Medicine. Others cannot be considered.
Level of Study: Postgraduate.
Type: Scholarship.
Value: Canadian $3,000-11,000 depending on qualifications, experience and graduate programme.
Length of Study: 4-12 months, renewable in open competition.

Study Establishment: The University of Calgary.
Country of Study: Canada.
No. of awards offered: More than one.
Application Procedure: Applicants must apply to the Assistant Dean of Medical Science in the first instance. The Graduate Scholarship Committee will make the final decision based on departmental recommendations. Awards are made on the basis of academic excellence.
Closing Date: April 1st.

The Honourable N D McDermid Graduate Scholarship in Law

Subjects: Law.
Eligibility: Open to graduate students enrolled on a full-time basis in the LLM programme in the Faculty of Law at the University of Calgary.
Level of Study: Postgraduate.
Type: Scholarship.
Value: Canadian $10,000.
Frequency: Annual.
Study Establishment: The University of Calgary.
Country of Study: Canada.
No. of awards offered: Two.
Application Procedure: Applicants must complete an application form, available from the Dean's Office, Faculty of Law.
Closing Date: February 1st.
Additional Information: The scholarship is not renewable. In cases where no suitable applications are received the award will not be made.

Izaak Walton Killam Memorial Scholarships

Subjects: All subjects.
Eligibility: Open to qualified graduates of any university who are admissible to a doctoral programme at the University of Calgary. Applicants must have completed at least one year of graduate study prior to taking up the award.
Level of Study: Doctorate, Postgraduate.
Type: Scholarship.
Value: Canadian $20,100. If approved, award holders may also receive up to canadian $3,000 over the full term of appointment for special equipment and/or travel in direct connection with the PhD research.
Length of Study: One year, renewable for a further year upon presentation of evidence of satisfactory progress. Further renewal in open competition.
Frequency: Annual.
Study Establishment: The University of Calgary.
Country of Study: Canada.
No. of awards offered: Four-five.
Application Procedure: Applicants must complete an application form, available from the graduate scholarship secretary at the university.
Closing Date: February 1st annually.
No. of awards given last year: Four-five.

Province of Alberta Graduate Scholarships and Fellowships

Subjects: All subjects.
Eligibility: Candidates must be registered in, or admissible to, a programme leading to a Master's or doctoral degree. It is restricted to Canadian citizens and landed immigrants.
Level of Study: Doctorate, Postgraduate.
Type: Fellowship and scholarship.
Value: The scholarship consists of canadian $9,300 per year and the fellowship of canadian $10,500 per year.
Length of Study: One year, renewable in open competition.
Frequency: Annual.
Study Establishment: The University of Calgary.
Country of Study: Canada.
No. of awards offered: 60-70.

Application Procedure: Applicants must complete an application form, available from the directors of graduate studies of the departments concerned.
Closing Date: February 1st.
Additional Information: Students whose awards begin in May are expected to carry out a full-time research programme during the Summer months.

The Robert A Willson Doctoral Management Scholarship

Subjects: MBA.
Eligibility: Open to candidates who are registered in or admissible to a full-time programme leading to a doctoral degree in management at the University of Calgary. While academic excellence is essential, candidates should also present evidence of leadership in their academic or professional background.
Level of Study: Doctorate.
Type: Scholarship.
Value: Up to canadian $10,000.
Length of Study: One year.
Frequency: Annual.
Study Establishment: The University of Calgary.
Country of Study: Canada.
No. of awards offered: One.
Application Procedure: Applicants must apply to the Faculty of Management.
Closing Date: May 30th.

Sheriff Willoughby King Memorial Scholarship

Subjects: Prevention of family violence and the treatment of the victims of family violence.
Eligibility: Open to candidates registered in the Faculty of Graduate Studies at the University of Calgary who are pursuing a Master of social work degree. Candidates must be Canadian citizens.
Level of Study: Postgraduate.
Type: Scholarship.
Value: Canadian $5,000.
Length of Study: One year.
Frequency: Annual.
Study Establishment: The University of Calgary.
Country of Study: Canada.
No. of awards offered: One to a candidate studying in the area of treatment, and one to a candidate studying in the area of prevention.
Application Procedure: Applicants must apply to the Faculty of Social Work. Recommendations from the Faculty will be considered by the University Graduate Scholarship Committee at its annual meeting. Awards are made on the basis of academic excellence.
Closing Date: February 1st.

University of Calgary Cogeco Inc Graduate Scholarship

Subjects: Mass communication or information sciences.
Eligibility: Open to students admissible to or registered in an MA programme, either thesis or course based, in communication studies programmes at the University of Calgary.
Level of Study: Postgraduate.
Type: Scholarship.
Value: Canadian $5,000.
Length of Study: One year.
Frequency: Annual.
Study Establishment: The University of Calgary.
Country of Study: Canada.
No. of awards offered: One.
Application Procedure: Applicants must apply to the MA of communications studies programme.
Closing Date: February 1st.
Additional Information: The Graduate Scholarship Committee makes the final decision based on departmental recommendations. Awards will be made on the basis of academic excellence.

University of Calgary Dean's Special Entrance Scholarship

Subjects: All subjects.

Eligibility: Open to women admissible to the Faculty of Graduate Studies in a programme of study leading to either the Master's or doctoral degree. Applicants must be entering a first year of graduate work after an absence from full-time study at a university for more than three years for the purpose of raising children, caring for elderly parents or other demanding family responsibilities.
Level of Study: Doctorate, Postgraduate.
Type: Scholarship.
Value: Canadian $8,000.
Length of Study: One year, non renewable.
Frequency: Annual.
Study Establishment: The University of Calgary.
Country of Study: Canada.
No. of awards offered: Four.
Application Procedure: Applicants must complete the graduate scholarship application form and submit this with a description, of up to one page in length, of the family responsibilities, to the chairperson of the Graduate Scholarship Committee.
Closing Date: February 1st.

University of Calgary Dean's Special Master's Scholarship

Subjects: Disciplines where the Master's degree is the terminal degree at the University of Calgary.
Eligibility: Open to candidates who are or will be registered in a full-time thesis based MA programme in a relevant discipline.
Level of Study: Postgraduate.
Type: Scholarship.
Value: Canadian $5,000.
Length of Study: One year, renewable in open competition.
Frequency: Annual.
Study Establishment: The University of Calgary.
Country of Study: Canada.
No. of awards offered: Up to five.
Application Procedure: Applicants must apply to the appropriate departments at the University of Calgary.
Closing Date: February 1st.

University of Calgary Faculty of Law Graduate Scholarship

Subjects: Natural resources, energy and environmental law.
Eligibility: Open to full-time graduate students who are registered in or admissible to a programme of studies leading to a Master's degree in the Faculty of Law.
Level of Study: Postgraduate.
Type: Scholarship.
Value: Up to canadian $10,000.
Length of Study: One year, non renewable.
Frequency: Annual.
Study Establishment: The University of Calgary.
Country of Study: Canada.
No. of awards offered: One.
Application Procedure: Applicants must complete an application form, available from the graduate programme director at the Faculty of Law. Awards will be recommended by a committee of the Faculty of Law based upon academic excellence.
Closing Date: February 1st.
Additional Information: In cases where no suitable applications are received no awards will be made.

University of Calgary Silver Anniversary Graduate Fellowships

Subjects: All subjects.
Eligibility: Open to qualified graduates of any recognised university who are registered in or admissible to a doctoral programme at the University of Calgary. The award is restricted to Canadian residents only.
Level of Study: Doctorate.
Type: Fellowship.
Value: Up to canadian $20,000 but in no case less than canadian $16,000.

Length of Study: One year, renewable for a further year upon presentation of evidence of satisfactory progress.
Frequency: Annual.
Study Establishment: The University of Calgary.
Country of Study: Canada.
No. of awards offered: More than two.
Application Procedure: Applicants must apply to their department.
Closing Date: February 1st.
Additional Information: Awards are granted on the basis of academic standing and demonstrated potential for advanced study and research.

UNIVERSITY OF CALIFORNIA DAVIS

Graduate School of Management
One Shields Avenue, Davis, CA, 95616-8609, United States of America
Tel: (1) 530 752 7399
Fax: (1) 530 752 2924
Email: gsm@ucdavis.edu
www: http://www.gsm.ucdavis.edu
Contact: Recruitment & Outreach Co-ordinator

UCD GSM Scholar's Grants

Subjects: MBA.
Purpose: To reward excellent academic performance and potential for success in MBA study.
Eligibility: Applicants must have already been accepted onto the MBA programme with an excellent academic record and must display potential for success in MBA study.
Level of Study: MBA.
Type: Grant.
Value: Please contact the organisation for details.
Length of Study: Varies.
Frequency: Annual.
Study Establishment: The University of California Davis, Graduate School of Management.
Country of Study: United States of America.
No. of awards offered: 15.
Application Procedure: Applicants must file a Free Application for Federal Student Aid (FAFSA) available from either the Graduate Financial Aid office or the Graduate School of Management Admissions and Student Services office.
Closing Date: Please contact the organisation.

UNIVERSITY OF CAMBRIDGE

University Registry
The Old Schools, Cambridge, Cambridgeshire, CB2 1TN, England
Tel: (44) 1223 332317
Fax: (44) 1223 332332
Email: mrf25@admin.cam.ac.uk
www: http://www.admin.cam.ac.uk
Contact: Ms Melanie Foster, Scholarships Clerk

The University of Cambridge is a loose confederation of faculties, colleges and other bodies. The Colleges are mainly concerned with the teaching of their undergraduate students through tutorials and supervisions and the academic support of both graduate and undergraduate students, while the University employs professors, readers, lecturers and other teaching and administrative staff who provide the formal teaching in lectures, seminars and practical classes. The University also administers the University Library.

Broodbank Fellowship

Subjects: Biochemistry or biophysics, with special reference to the principles and practice of food preservation. These terms will be interpreted broadly to include fundamental research including molecular processes.

Purpose: To further research in biochemistry and biophysics.
Eligibility: Open to graduates of any university, but strong preference will be given to postdoctoral applicants.
Level of Study: Postdoctorate.
Type: Fellowship.
Value: Determined according to a Fellow's experience and qualifications, from UK £17,626-26,491 (under review) plus possible grants to cover expenses incurred by the Fellow in his or her work.
Length of Study: Not to exceed three years as determined by the managers.
Frequency: Every three years.
Study Establishment: The University of Cambridge.
Country of Study: United Kingdom.
No. of awards offered: Two-three.
Closing Date: End of April.
Funding: Private.
Contributor: The Broodbank Fund.
No. of awards given last year: Two.
No. of applicants last year: Nine.

For further information contact:

Manager's Secretary
The Broodbank Fund
Department of Plant Sciences
Downing Street, Cambridge, Cambridgeshire, CB2 3EA, England

Cambridge Overseas Studentship in Social Anthropology (ORS Equivalent)

Subjects: Social anthropology.
Purpose: To support study in social anthropology for the degree of PhD at the University of Cambridge.
Eligibility: Open to all overseas students.
Level of Study: Doctorate.
Type: Studentship.
Value: Fees only, to cover fees at rate equivalent to ORS.
Length of Study: Three years.
Frequency: Annual.
Study Establishment: The University of Cambridge.
Country of Study: United Kingdom.
No. of awards offered: One.
Application Procedure: Applicants must submit an application form with a declaration form signed by a supervisor, together with an academic paper of up to 5,000 words, including a bibliography, footnotes, and an abstract of 100 words. A two-page curriculum vitae and a 1,000 word statement of research interests including a 100 word abstract should also be included.
Closing Date: April 15th.
Funding: Private.
Contributor: Trinity College, Cambridge.
Additional Information: Applicants should have a first degree in social (or cultural) anthropology, or a Master's degree in the same subject. Applicants must also apply for an Overseas Research Student award to cover the difference between overseas and home fees.

For further information contact:

Admissions Secretary
Department of Social Anthropology
Free School Lane, Cambridge, Cambridgeshire, CB2 3RF, England
Tel: (44) 1223 334599
Fax: (44) 1223 335993
Contact: Ms Margaret Story, Admissions Secretary

Churchill College Research Studentships

Subjects: All subjects for which research supervision can be provided at the University.
Purpose: To assist research for candidates who intend to register for the degree of PhD at the University of Cambridge.
Eligibility: Open to any person who has graduated from a university or, if not a graduate, can show evidence of exceptional qualifications for research.

Level of Study: Doctorate.
Type: Studentship.
Value: University and college fees, plus maintenance based on recommended rates.
Length of Study: Three years.
Frequency: Annual.
Study Establishment: Churchill College, the University of Cambridge.
Country of Study: United Kingdom.
No. of awards offered: Varies, depending on funds available.
Application Procedure: Applicants must complete an application form, available from the given address.
Closing Date: February 15th.
Funding: Private.
No. of awards given last year: Four.
No. of applicants last year: 85.

For further information contact:

Tutor for Advanced Students
Churchill College, Cambridge, Cambridgeshire, CB3 0DS, England
Tel: (44) 1223 336157
Fax: (44) 1223 336177
Email: hrh21@hermes.cam.ac.uk
www: http://www.chu.cam.ac.uk

Clare Hall Foundation Fellowship

Subjects: All subjects.
Purpose: To help a promising Scholar from either a developing country, a centrally planned economy or a country in transition to a market economy.
Eligibility: Open to persons who already hold academic posts in their own country, have not previously studied in the United Kingdom or North America and are able to demonstrate that a period of study in Cambridge would be of special benefit. There is no restriction as to gender or age, although preference may be given to applicants under the age of 40.
Level of Study: Postdoctorate.
Type: Fellowship.
Value: Normally sufficient for three months' residence in Cambridge.
Length of Study: Three months, although by supplementing other funds the fellowship would possibly permit a longer stay of up to six months.
Frequency: Annual.
Study Establishment: Normally Clare Hall, but probably attached to one of the university departments.
Country of Study: United Kingdom.
No. of awards offered: One.
Application Procedure: Applicants must address applications, accompanied by a curriculum vitae, to the Chairman of the Fellowship Committee at the College, to whom three referees should write direct. One reference should be from a referee whose work is recognised in the United Kingdom.
Closing Date: Applications are accepted at any time.
No. of awards given last year: One.
No. of applicants last year: Unknown.
Additional Information: The fellowship is awarded on the grounds of academic suitability.

For further information contact:

College Secretary
Clare Hall
Herschel Road, Cambridge, Cambridgeshire, CB3 9AL, England
Tel: (44) 1223 332360
Fax: (44) 1223 332333
Contact: Ms Elizabeth Ramsden, College Secretary

Corpus Christi College Research Scholarships

Subjects: All subjects.
Purpose: To enable the successful candidate to pursue, as a member of the College, a course of study in any subject leading to a research based higher degree, normally the PhD, at the University of Cambridge.

Eligibility: Open to all those who have been offered a place at the college by June 15th.
Level of Study: Postgraduate.
Type: Scholarship.
Value: Awards are made usually in collaboration with the Cambridge Commonwealth and Overseas Trusts. The amount of the awards varies but substantial contributions up to UK £7,000 towards fees or maintenance costs are made.
Length of Study: Usually three years.
Frequency: Annual.
Study Establishment: Corpus Christi College, the University of Cambridge.
Country of Study: United Kingdom.
No. of awards offered: More than one.
Application Procedure: All those eligible are considered. There is no application form.
Closing Date: June 15th.
Funding: Private.
Contributor: Dr John Taylor.
No. of awards given last year: 13.
No. of applicants last year: 200.

For further information contact:

Tutor for Advanced Students
Corpus Christi College, Cambridge, Cambridgeshire, CB2 1RH, England
Tel: (44) 1223 338038
Fax: (44) 1223 765589
Contact: Dr C J B Brookes, Tutor for Advanced Students

The Cropwood Fellowship Programme

Subjects: Criminology and related fields.
Purpose: To enable practitioners in the British criminal justice system to undertake research or study under the guidance of experienced academic researchers.
Eligibility: There are no formal qualifications other than that candidates should be experienced practitioners in their field and should currently be working within the British Criminal Justice system.
Level of Study: Unrestricted.
Type: Fellowship.
Value: An allowance towards living expenses. The reimbursement of travelling expenses if any in connection with the research is considered.
Length of Study: One year, with up to a maximum of 12 weeks in Cambridge, not renewable.
Frequency: Annual.
Study Establishment: The Institute of Criminology at the University of Cambridge.
Country of Study: United Kingdom.
No. of awards offered: Three-four.
Application Procedure: Applicants must contact the Cropwood Secretary for further information.
Closing Date: September 30th.
Funding: Private.
Contributor: The Barrow Cadbury Trust.
No. of awards given last year: Four.
No. of applicants last year: 13.

For further information contact:

Cropwood Secretary
Institute of Criminology
University of Cambridge
7 West Road, Cambridge, Cambridgeshire, CB3 9DT, England
Tel: (44) 1223 335364
Fax: (44) 1223 335356
Email: hmr21@cam.ac.uk

Downing College Research Fellowships

Subjects: As advertised, but generally arts and science subjects in alternate years.
Purpose: To enable promising young scholars to undertake research, undistracted by other duties, to consolidate their reputations.

Eligibility: Open to graduates who have completed or are on the point of completing a PhD. Applicants must normally be under 30 on taking up the award, or if over 30, must normally not have completed more than 12 terms of research as a registered research student.
Level of Study: Postdoctorate.
Type: Fellowship.
Value: For resident pre PhD UK £14,473 is available and for resident post PhD UK £15,449 is available. A living out allowance of UK £2,000 is also offered.
Length of Study: Three years.
Frequency: Annually at present.
Study Establishment: Normally based in Cambridge.
Country of Study: United Kingdom.
No. of awards offered: One.
Application Procedure: Applicants must complete an application form, available from the Senior Tutor, following advertisements.
Closing Date: December 1st for the following October.
Funding: Private.
Contributor: Downing College.
No. of awards given last year: One.
No. of applicants last year: 83.
Additional Information: The application form indicates that candidates must ask referees to write to the college.

For further information contact:

Tutorial Office Manager
Downing College, Cambridge, Cambridgeshire, CB2 1DQ, England
Tel: (44) 1223 334811
Fax: (44) 1223 362279
Email: magzz@cam.ac.uk
www: http://www.dow.cam.ac.uk
Contact: Ms Jane Perks, Tutorial Office Manager

E D Davies Scholarship

Subjects: All subjects.
Purpose: To enable graduates to undertake a course of research in any subject area.
Eligibility: Open to graduates of any university who have been admitted to a course of research.
Level of Study: Postgraduate.
Type: Scholarship.
Value: UK £1,250 per year. The award is designed to supplement funding from other sources.
Length of Study: A maximum of three years. Candidates must reapply annually.
Frequency: Annual.
Study Establishment: Fitzwilliam College, the University of Cambridge.
Country of Study: England.
No. of awards offered: One.
Application Procedure: Applicants must complete an application form, available on request.
Closing Date: October 1st.
Funding: Private.
No. of awards given last year: One.
No. of applicants last year: 10.

For further information contact:

Tutor for Graduate Students
Fitzwilliam College, Cambridge, Cambridgeshire, CB3 0DG, England
Tel: (44) 1223 332035
Fax: (44) 1223 332082
Contact: Dr W Alison, Tutor for Graduate Students

Evans Fund

Subjects: All aspects of anthropology and archaeology of South East Asia, especially in relation to Borneo, the Malay Peninsula, Singapore and Thailand.
Purpose: To support research.
Eligibility: Open to graduates of any university who intend to engage in research in any aspect of anthropology and the archaeology

of Southeast Asia, especially in relation to Borneo, the Malay Peninsula, Singapore and Thailand.
Level of Study: Doctorate, Postdoctorate, Postgraduate.
Type: Fellowship.
Value: Up to UK £6,000 per year.
Length of Study: One or two years in the first instance, up to a maximum of three years.
Frequency: Annual.
Study Establishment: The University of Cambridge.
Country of Study: Any country.
No. of awards offered: More than one.
Application Procedure: Applicants must obtain an application form from the Secretary which must be returned together with an outline of the applicant's proposed scheme of travel and research, a curriculum vitae and the names and addresses of two referees.
Closing Date: March 7th.
Funding: Private.
Contributor: Legacy.
No. of awards given last year: One.
No. of applicants last year: Two.
Additional Information: It is expected that the successful candidate will either be based in Cambridge, or will spend a substantial period of time in Cambridge during or after their period of research.

For further information contact:

Secretary of the Evans Fund Advisory Committee
Department of Social Anthropology
University of Cambridge
Free School Lane, Cambridge, Cambridgeshire, CB2 3RF, England
Tel: (44) 1223 334599
Fax: (44) 1223 335993
Email: ms127@hermes.cam.ac.uk

Fitzwilliam College Graduate Scholarship
Subjects: All subjects.
Eligibility: Open to candidates who are carrying out research for a PhD at any British or Irish university, or who have recently completed their course of study for this degree. Candidates should not have completed four years of full-time research by the April preceding the commencement of the Scholarship.
Level of Study: Postgraduate.
Type: Fellowship.
Length of Study: A maximum of three years. Candidates must re-apply annually.
Frequency: Annual.
Study Establishment: Fitzwilliam College, the University of Cambridge.
Country of Study: United Kingdom.
No. of awards offered: Varies.
Application Procedure: Applicants must write for details.
Closing Date: Early September.
No. of awards given last year: One.
No. of applicants last year: 10.
Additional Information: Fellowships are awarded for new research only and not to enable candidates to complete their PhD dissertation. Preference is given to candidates conducting research in an arts subject.

For further information contact:

Tutor for Graduate Students
Fitzwilliam College, Cambridge, Cambridgeshire, CB3 0DG, England
Contact: Dr W Alison, Tutor for Graduate Students

Fitzwilliam College Hirst-Player Studentship
Subjects: Research in the Faculty of Divinity or, exceptionally, on a theological topic in another faculty. Preference is given to those intending to take holy orders in a Christian church.
Purpose: To support students who need assistance with payment of fees and who would otherwise be unable to read for a degree in Cambridge.
Eligibility: Open to graduates of any university. The awards are only available to candidates who have applied for admission to the

University through the Board of Graduate Studies and subsequently satisfied the conditions of admission made by the Board. Candidates should also place Fitzwilliam College as their first preference in their application.
Level of Study: Postgraduate.
Type: Studentship.
Value: UK £1,250 per year. The award is designed to supplement other funds.
Length of Study: One year.
Frequency: Annual.
Study Establishment: Fitzwilliam College, the University of Cambridge.
Country of Study: United Kingdom.
No. of awards offered: One.
Application Procedure: Applicants must complete the application form, available on request.
Closing Date: October 1st.
Funding: Private.
No. of awards given last year: One.

For further information contact:

Tutor for Graduate Students
Fitzwilliam College, Cambridge, Cambridgeshire, CB3 0DG, England
Tel: (44) 1223 332035
Fax: (44) 1223 332082
Contact: Dr W Alison, Tutor for Graduate Students

Fitzwilliam College J R W Alexander Studentship in Law
Subjects: Law (LLM degree).
Eligibility: Open to graduates from a British university who will have graduated by the time they come into residence.
Level of Study: Postgraduate.
Type: Studentship.
Value: UK £1,000. The award is designed to supplement funding from other sources.
Length of Study: One year.
Frequency: Dependent on funds available.
Study Establishment: Fitzwilliam College, the University of Cambridge.
Country of Study: United Kingdom.
No. of awards offered: One.
Application Procedure: Applicants must have applied for admission to the University through the Board of Graduate Studies and subsequently satisfied the conditions of admission made by the Board. Candidates should also place Fitzwilliam College as their first preference in their application.
Closing Date: October 1st.
Funding: Private.
No. of awards given last year: One.

For further information contact:

Tutor for Graduate Students
Fitzwilliam College, Cambridge, Cambridgeshire, CB3 0DG, England
Tel: (44) 1223 332035
Fax: (44) 1223 322082
Contact: Dr W Alison, Tutor for Graduate Students

Fitzwilliam College Leathersellers' Graduate Scholarship
Subjects: Physical or biological sciences, mathematics or engineering.
Purpose: To support students who wish to undertake research.
Eligibility: Open to home graduates from any British university who have been admitted to a course of research in one of the appropriate faculties.
Level of Study: Postgraduate.
Type: Scholarship.
Value: UK £2,000 per year. The award is designed to supplement funding from other sources.
Length of Study: Three years, subject to an annual review.
Frequency: Annual.
Study Establishment: Fitzwilliam College, the University of Cambridge.

Country of Study: United Kingdom.
No. of awards offered: One.
Application Procedure: Applicants must complete an application form, available on request.
Closing Date: June 13th.
No. of awards given last year: One.
No. of applicants last year: Three.

For further information contact:

Tutor for Graduate Students
Fitzwilliam College, Cambridge, Cambridgeshire, CB3 0DG, England
Tel: (44) 1223 332035
Fax: (44) 1223 332082
Contact: Dr W Alison, Tutor for Graduate Students

Fitzwilliam College Research Fellowship

Subjects: To be advised in further particulars as this is arranged on a triennial subject rota.
Purpose: To enable scholars to carry out a programme of new research.
Eligibility: Open to candidates who are carrying out research for a PhD at any British or Irish university, or who have recently completed their course of study for this degree. Candidates should not have completed four years of full-time research by the April preceding the commencement of the fellowship.
Level of Study: Doctorate.
Type: Fellowship.
Value: Varies. Non stipendiary funding is also offered.
Frequency: Annual.
Study Establishment: Fitzwilliam College, the University of Cambridge.
Country of Study: United Kingdom.
No. of awards offered: Varies.
Application Procedure: Applicants must write for details.
Closing Date: January.
Additional Information: Fellowships are awarded for new research only and not to enable candidates to complete their PhD dissertation.

For further information contact:

The Master's Secretary
Fitzwilliam College, Cambridge, Cambridgeshire, CB3 0DG, England
Tel: (44) 1223 332029
Fax: (44) 1223 332074
Email: jmw65@cam.ac.uk

Fitzwilliam College Shipley Studentship

Subjects: Research in the Faculty of Divinity or exceptionally, on a theological topic in another faculty, for graduates who wish to undertake research.
Purpose: To enable graduates to undertake research.
Eligibility: Open to graduates of any university. The awards are only available to candidates who have applied for admission to the University through the Board of Graduate Studies and subsequently satisfied the conditions of admission made by the Board. Candidates should also place Fitzwilliam College as their first preference in their application.
Level of Study: Postgraduate.
Type: Studentship.
Value: UK £1,250 per year. The award is designed to supplement other funds.
Length of Study: One year.
Frequency: Annual.
Study Establishment: Fitzwilliam College, the University of Cambridge.
Country of Study: United Kingdom.
No. of awards offered: One.
Application Procedure: Applicants must complete an application form, available on request.
Closing Date: October 1st.
Funding: Private.
No. of awards given last year: One.

No. of applicants last year: Three.

For further information contact:

Tutor for Graduate Students
Fitzwilliam College, Cambridge, Cambridgeshire, CB3 0DG, England
Tel: (44) 1223 332035
Fax: (44) 1223 332082
Contact: Dr W Alison, Tutor for Graduate Students

Girton College Research Fellowships

Subjects: Arts and humanities and natural sciences.
Purpose: To provide the opportunity for graduate students to conduct research in their chosen field of study.
Eligibility: Open to qualified graduates of any university who are able to provide evidence of outstanding research abilities. There is no age limit, but Fellowships will normally be awarded to candidates at an early stage of their academic careers who have recently completed their PhD or are close to completion.
Level of Study: Doctorate.
Type: Fellowship.
Value: UK £9,475 per year for predoctoral Fellows and UK £11,895-12,525 per year for postdoctoral Fellows for over three years. The stipend is reviewed annually.
Length of Study: Up to three years.
Frequency: Annual.
Study Establishment: Girton College, the University of Cambridge.
Country of Study: United Kingdom.
No. of awards offered: Two-four.
Application Procedure: Applicants must submit a completed application form, which is available from the Mistress' secretary from around July or August each year.
Closing Date: Usually the end of September to the beginning of the first week of October.
Funding: Private.
Contributor: College endowment.
No. of awards given last year: Four.
No. of applicants last year: 300.
Additional Information: The arts and science competitions will be run in different terms.

For further information contact:

Mistress' Secretary
Girton College, Cambridge, Cambridgeshire, CB3 0JG, England
Tel: (44) 1223 338951
Fax: (44) 1223 338896
Email: ic208@cam.ac.uk
www: http://www.cl.cam.ac.uk

Gonville and Caius College Gonville Bursary

Subjects: All subjects offered by the University.
Purpose: To help outstanding students from outside the EU to meet the costs of degree courses at the University of Cambridge.
Eligibility: Open to candidates who have been accepted by the College through its normal admissions procedures, and who are classified as overseas students for fees purposes. A statement of financial circumstances is required.
Level of Study: Doctorate, Postgraduate.
Type: Bursary.
Value: Reimbursement of college fees.
Length of Study: Up to three years, with a possibility of renewal, dependent on satisfactory progress.
Frequency: Annual.
Study Establishment: Gonville and Caius College, the University of Cambridge.
Country of Study: United Kingdom.
No. of awards offered: Up to six.
Application Procedure: Applicants must contact the Admissions Tutor for further information. There are no application forms.
Closing Date: Deadlines are the same as for the University's courses.

For further information contact:

Admissions Tutor
Gonville & Caius College, Cambridge, Cambridgeshire, CB2 1TA, England
Tel: (44) 1223 332447
Fax: (44) 1223 332456
Email: admissions@cai.cam.ac.uk
www: http://www.cai.cam.ac.uk

Gonville and Caius College W M Tapp Studentship in Law

Subjects: Law.
Purpose: To encourage the study of law.
Eligibility: Open to candidates who are not already members of the College, but who propose to register as graduate students at the University of Cambridge. Candidates must be under 30 years of age as of October 1st of the studentship year and be graduates, or expect to be, no later than August of the same year. Preference is given to applicants nominating Gonville and Caius College as their first choice when applying under the Cambridge Intercollegiate Graduate Application Scheme.
Level of Study: Doctorate, Postgraduate.
Type: Studentship.
Value: A stipend similar to that of a state studentship for research, plus fees and certain allowances, dependant allowance, allowance for a period of approved postgraduate experience, travelling contribution for foreign students and a research allowance for research students.
Length of Study: One year, renewable for up to a maximum of three years.
Frequency: Annual.
Study Establishment: Gonville and Caius College, the University of Cambridge.
Country of Study: United Kingdom.
No. of awards offered: Approx. six.
Application Procedure: Applicants must complete an application form, available from the Admissions Tutor.
Closing Date: January 15th.
No. of awards given last year: Seven.
No. of applicants last year: 61.

For further information contact:

Admissions Tutor
Gonville & Caius College, Cambridge, Cambridgeshire, CB2 1TA, England
Tel: (44) 1223 332447
Fax: (44) 1223 332456
Email: admissions@cai.cam.ac.uk
www: http://www.cai.cam.ac.uk

Isaac Newton Studentship

Subjects: Astronomy (especially gravitational astronomy, but also including other branches of astronomy and astronomical physics) and those branches of physical optics which, in the opinion of the electors, have a direct bearing on astronomy or astronomical techniques.
Purpose: To further advanced study and research in astronomy and astrological physics.
Eligibility: Open to graduates of any university who should normally be under 26 years of age on January 1st prior to the beginning of tenure.
Level of Study: Postgraduate.
Type: Studentship.
Value: Approx. UK £8,200. Married students will receive an allowance under PPARC conditions. The electors may also award grants for fees, books or other expenses incurred by the student in the course of study or research.
Length of Study: Up to three years.
Frequency: Annual.
Study Establishment: The University of Cambridge.
Country of Study: United Kingdom.
No. of awards offered: More than one.

Application Procedure: Applicants must send applications to the university registry together with evidence of age and other evidence of qualifications as thought fit. Applicants should request that three referees send letters of recommendation by the deadline. It is recommended that an account of any work bearing on astronomy or astrophysics, and copies of the papers published on these subjects should be included, plus a clear statement of the course of study and/or research proposed for the tenure of the studentship.
Closing Date: February 13th.
No. of awards given last year: Four.
No. of applicants last year: 15.

Magdalene College Leslie Wilson Research Scholarships

Subjects: All subjects offered by the University.
Purpose: To assist study for a doctorate degree.
Eligibility: Open to graduates from the United Kingdom and overseas who will be studying at Cambridge for a PhD degree. Consideration is normally restricted to those who have obtained, or who have a strong prospect of obtaining, a First Class (Honours) Bachelor's Degree. Preference is given to those nominating Magdalene College as their first choice.
Level of Study: Doctorate.
Type: Scholarship.
Value: A maximum of UK £12,144 (at October 2001 values) for a Scholar who has no other sources of finance including a maintenance grant of UK £7,500, university fees of UK £2,805 and college fees of UK £1,839. Rented accommodation in or near Magdalene College will be made available during the first year of residence for unmarried Scholars. Married Scholars will be offered rented accommodation near to the college.
Length of Study: Up to three years.
Frequency: Annual.
Study Establishment: Magdalene College, the University of Cambridge.
Country of Study: United Kingdom.
No. of awards offered: One.
Application Procedure: Applicants must obtain a CIGAS form from the Board of Graduate Studies. United Kingdom candidates are expected to apply, if eligible, for State or Research Council Studentships. Overseas candidates are expected to apply for United Kingdom government support as well as Overseas Student Bursaries awarded by the University of Cambridge and administered by the Board of Graduate Studies. In addition, all candidates should obtain a Leslie Wilson Research Scholarship form from the address below.
Closing Date: May 1st.
No. of awards given last year: One major award, eight minor awards.
No. of applicants last year: 84.

For further information contact:

Admissions Tutor for Graduates
Magdalene College
University of Cambridge, Cambridge, Cambridgeshire, CB3 0AG, England
Tel: (44) 1223 332135
Fax: (44) 1223 462589

The Board of Graduate Studies, Cambridge, Cambridgeshire, CB2 1RZ, England

Oliver Gatty Studentship

Subjects: Biophysical and colloid science.
Purpose: To assist full-time study and training for research.
Eligibility: Open to graduates of all universities, preference being given to graduates of universities outside the United Kingdom. Both graduate and postdoctoral students may apply.
Level of Study: Postgraduate.
Type: Studentship.
Value: To be determined by the electors after taking into account the student's circumstances and the funds available.
Length of Study: One year, renewable for up to two additional years.

Frequency: Advertised when available, usually every three years.
Study Establishment: The University of Cambridge.
Country of Study: United Kingdom.
No. of awards offered: One.
Application Procedure: Applicants must contact Melanie Foster for details.
Closing Date: Usually April 30th.
No. of awards given last year: One.
No. of applicants last year: Eight.

Pembroke College Graduate Awards

Subjects: All subjects offered by the University.
Eligibility: Open to candidates of any nationality who are accepted by Pembroke College and who intend to register for a PhD degree at the University of Cambridge. Candidates must make Pembroke their first choice college.
Level of Study: Doctorate, Postgraduate.
Type: Studentship.
Value: Full support.
Length of Study: Three years.
Frequency: Annual.
Study Establishment: Pembroke College, the University of Cambridge.
Country of Study: United Kingdom.
No. of awards offered: One.
Application Procedure: Applicants must complete an application form for financial assistance, available from the graduate admissions office at Pembroke College. There is no specific form for the research studentship.
Closing Date: May 1st.
Funding: Private.
Contributor: Pembroke College.
No. of awards given last year: One.
Additional Information: There are also a number of fees only scholarships and bursaries available.

For further information contact:

Graduate Admissions Secretary
Pembroke College, Cambridge, Cambridgeshire, CB2 1RZ, England
Tel: (44) 1223 338115
Fax: (44) 1223 338163
Email: graduates@pem.cam.ac.uk
www: http://www.pem.cam.ac.uk
Contact: Mrs Frances Kentish, Graduate Admissions Secretary

Queen's College Research Fellowships

Subjects: The competition is open to all Queen's College graduates in any discipline and to graduates of other institutions. However, for candidates who are not members of the college the subject areas are restricted and are specified in the advertising for the competition each year.
Purpose: To provide the opportunity for postdoctoral research in various fields of study.
Eligibility: Open to graduates of any university who should normally not have completed more than four years of research including time on research degrees.
Level of Study: Postdoctorate.
Type: Fellowship.
Value: The current stipend is UK £11,650 for the first year.
Length of Study: Three years.
Frequency: Annual.
Study Establishment: Queen's College.
Country of Study: United Kingdom.
No. of awards offered: Two.
Application Procedure: Applicants must complete and submit an application form and research proposal. Written work will be requested from short listed candidates.
Closing Date: Usually October 8th.
Funding: Private.
Contributor: Endowed funds.
No. of awards given last year: Two.
No. of applicants last year: 40.

Additional Information: Interviews take place in November of the academic year prior to that in which the fellowship will commence.

For further information contact:

Clerk to the Tutors
Queens' College, Cambridge, Cambridgeshire, CB3 9ET, England
Tel: (44) 1223 335601
Fax: (44) 1223 335522
www: http://www.quns.cam.ac.uk

St John's College Benefactors' Scholarships for Research

Subjects: All subjects offered by the University.
Purpose: To fund candidates for PhD and MPhil degrees.
Eligibility: Open to candidates of any nationality with a First Class (Honours) Degree or equivalent.
Level of Study: Postgraduate.
Type: Scholarship.
Value: UK £7,500, plus approved college and university fees, a book allowance of UK £315 and other expenses.
Length of Study: Up to three years.
Frequency: Annual.
Study Establishment: St John's College, the University of Cambridge.
Country of Study: United Kingdom.
No. of awards offered: Six.
Application Procedure: Applicants must see the Cambridge University Graduate Studies Prospectus for particulars.
Closing Date: May 1st.
No. of awards given last year: Six.

For further information contact:

Secretary to Tutor for Graduate Affairs
St John's College, Cambridge, Cambridgeshire, CB2 1TP, England
Tel: (44) 1223 338612
Fax: (44) 1223 766419
Email: graduate_admissions@joh.cam.ac.uk
Contact: A M Mansfield, Secretary to Tutor for Graduate Affairs

Westminster College Lewis and Gibson Scholarship

Subjects: Theology.
Purpose: To enable Scholars to study for a theology degree at the University of Cambridge as an integral part of his or her training for the ministry of a church in the reformed tradition which has a Presbyterian order.
Eligibility: Open to graduates of a recognised university who are members of the United Reformed Church in the United Kingdom or of any church not established by the state which is a member of the World Alliance of Reformed Churches and has a Presbyterian form of government. Applicants must have been recognised by their churches as candidates for the Ministry of Word and Sacrament, but should not yet have been ordained.
Level of Study: Postgraduate.
Type: Scholarship.
Value: One scholarship of UK £6,000 or two scholarships of UK £3,000 approx.
Length of Study: One year, renewable for up to two further years.
Frequency: Annually, except when the current holders are likely to have the award renewed for the following year.
Study Establishment: The University of Cambridge.
Country of Study: United Kingdom.
No. of awards offered: One-two.
Application Procedure: If it is the intention to study at the postgraduate level, an application should be made at the same time to the Board of Graduate Studies of the university. The Scholar will normally study for one of the following degrees: BA or MPhil in theology, or PhD. He or she will be a member of both Westminster College and one of the University's constituent colleges.
Closing Date: December 24th.
Funding: Private.
Contributor: A legacy controlled by the United Reformed Church.
No. of awards given last year: Two.

Additional Information: Scholars from outside the United Reformed Church have usually been theology graduates and have used the scholarship for postgraduate work.

For further information contact:

Director of Studies
Westminster College, Cambridge, Cambridgeshire, CB3 0AA, England
Tel: (44) 1223 741084
Fax: (44) 1223 300765
Email: jp225@cam.ac.uk
Contact: Reverend John Proctor, Director of Studies

William Wyse Master of Philosophy Bursary in Social Anthropology

Subjects: Social anthropology.
Purpose: To support study in social anthropology for the degree of MPhil (SAA) at the University of Cambridge.
Eligibility: Open to United Kingdom and European Union students.
Level of Study: Graduate.
Type: Bursary.
Value: UK £2,500 per year as a part cost maintenance grant and fees for three years.
Length of Study: One year.
Frequency: Annual.
Study Establishment: The University of Cambridge.
Country of Study: United Kingdom.
No. of awards offered: One.
Application Procedure: Applicants must submit an application form and a 1,000 word statement of background information about their reasons for wishing to study the course at this level. This must include any special interests and past experience and any future plans.
Closing Date: Please write for details.
Funding: Private.
Contributor: Trinity College Wyse Fund.
No. of awards given last year: One.
No. of applicants last year: Nine.
Additional Information: The bursary is a nomination award by the Department of Social Anthropology. Applicants must show that they are actively seeking funding from other sources for the course of study.

For further information contact:

Admissions Secretary
Department of Social Anthropology
Free School Lane, Cambridge, Cambridgeshire, CB2 3RF, England
Tel: (44) 1223 334599
Fax: (44) 1223 335993
Contact: Ms Margaret Story, Admissions Secretary

William Wyse Studentship in Social Anthropology

Subjects: Social anthropology.
Purpose: To support study.
Eligibility: Open to United Kingdom and European Union students.
Level of Study: Doctorate.
Type: Studentship.
Value: Equivalent to a United Kingdom state award.
Length of Study: Three years.
Frequency: Annual.
Study Establishment: The University of Cambridge.
Country of Study: United Kingdom.
No. of awards offered: One.
Application Procedure: Applicants must complete and submit an application form with a declaration form signed by a supervisor, together with an academic paper of up to 5,000 words, including a bibliography, footnotes and a 100 word abstract. A 1,000 word statement of research interests accompanied by a 100 word abstract and a two-page curriculum vitae must also be included.
Closing Date: April 15th.
Funding: Private.
Contributor: Trinity College, the University of Cambridge.

No. of awards given last year: One.
No. of applicants last year: Nine.
Additional Information: Applicants should show evidence that they are seeking funding for PhD support from the ESRC.

For further information contact:

Admissions Secretary
Department of Social Anthropology
Free School Lane, Cambridge, Cambridgeshire, CB2 3RF, England
Tel: (44) 1223 334599
Fax: (44) 1223 335993
Contact: Ms Margaret Story, Admissions Secretary

UNIVERSITY OF CAMBRIDGE, JUDGE INSTITUTE OF MANAGEMENT

Trumpington Street, Cambridge, Cambridgeshire, CB2 1AG, England
Tel: (44) 1223 339700
Fax: (44) 1223 339701
Email: enquiries@jims.cam.ac.uk
www: http://www.jims.cam.ac.uk
Contact: Ms Louise Freckleton

The Judge Institute of Management is the University of Cambridge's business school. Founded in 1990 it offers a portfolio of management programmes, including the Cambridge MBA. Accredited by AMBA and EQUIS, the business school now hosts one of the largest concentrations of interdisciplinary business and management research activity in Europe.

Browns Restaurant Scholarships

Subjects: MBA.
Purpose: The Browns Restaurant Scholarships provide funds for United Kingdom citizens with a strong interest in the hospitality and tourism industries to study for an MBA at the Judge Institute of Management.
Eligibility: Open to candidates with at least three years of experience in the hospitality or tourism industries. Candidates must show evidence of a career plan showing how they would use skills and knowledge gained on the MBA course to develop their career within the hospitality or tourism industries. Where an applicant opts for the two year integrated version of the MBA course, arrangements should be in place for the placement year to be in an organisation in the hospitality or tourism industries. Applicants must be United Kingdom citizens.
Level of Study: MBA.
Type: Scholarship.
Value: One scholarship of UK £20,000 to cover the University fees for the Cambridge MBA course and two scholarships of UK £10,000 to cover roughly half the University fees for the Cambridge MBA course.
Length of Study: One year.
Frequency: Annual.
Study Establishment: The Judge Institute of Management, the University of Cambridge.
Country of Study: England.
No. of awards offered: Two.
Application Procedure: Applicants must complete and submit an application form, together with a covering letter indicating that they would like to apply for a Browns Restaurant Scholarship, to the Judge Institute of Management.
Closing Date: End of March.
Funding: Commercial.
Contributor: Browns Restaurants Limited.

Margaret Thatcher Scholarships

Subjects: MBA.
Purpose: The Margaret Thatcher Scholarship Scheme supports Cambridge MBA students who are resident in Russia and citizens of

a country of the former Soviet Union, with particular encouragement to Russian nationals. It provides an opportunity for the business leaders of tomorrow to gain a thorough business education in an international environment at a world class University. The aim of the Scheme is to ensure that lessons learned in Cambridge and more broadly in Western Europe can be widely disseminated to future business leaders in Russia.

Eligibility: Open to Russian candidates with at least three years of work experience in Russia or elsewhere in the former Soviet Union. Applicants must have strong support from their current employer and have evidence of a career plan showing how they would use the skills and knowledge gained on the MBA course to develop their career within Russia. Applicants for the two year integrated programme must have a work placement set up within a work organisation.

Level of Study: MBA.
Type: Scholarship.
Value: Varies from UK £3,000-30,000.
Length of Study: One year.
Frequency: Annual.
Study Establishment: The Judge Institute of Management, the University of Cambridge.
Country of Study: England.
No. of awards offered: Up to five.
Application Procedure: Applicants must complete and submit an application form, together with a covering letter indicating that they would like to apply for a Margaret Thatcher Scholarship, to the Judge Institute of Management.
Closing Date: End of March.
Funding: Private.
No. of awards given last year: Five.
No. of applicants last year: 10.

Sainsbury Bursaries

Subjects: MBA.
Purpose: The Sainsbury Bursary Scheme provides bursaries for candidates from the non-profit or public sector to study for a Cambridge MBA. To support students engaged in charitable, voluntary or public sector work in areas such as housing, health and education, local economic development and social services, as it is difficult for such candidates to secure sponsorship from their employers.
Eligibility: Preference will be given to applicants from the United Kingdom but exceptional candidates working for international aid agencies based outside the United Kingdom will be given consideration. It is expected that applicants will contribute to the sectors in the United Kingdom after completion of the MBA. Candidates must have completed three years of work experience within the charitable, voluntary or public sector prior to submitting their application. The applicants for the two year integrated course must have a placement set up within an organisation in the charitable, voluntary or public sector. Candidates must also show evidence of a career plan showing how they would use skills and knowledge gained on the MBA course to develop their career within the charitable, voluntary or public sector.
Level of Study: MBA.
Type: Bursary.
Value: Ranges from UK £10,000-20,000 at the discretion of The Sainsbury Bursary Scheme Committee. The Committee is also willing to consider higher awards of up to UK £25,000 for candidates who show exceptional ability and potential.
Length of Study: One year.
Frequency: Annual.
Study Establishment: The Judge Institute of Management, the University of Cambridge.
Country of Study: England.
No. of awards offered: Four-seven.
Application Procedure: Applicants must complete and submit an application form for the MBA along with a covering letter indicating that they would also like to apply for a Sainsbury Bursary, to the Judge Institute.
Closing Date: The end of March.
Funding: Private.
Contributor: The Monument Trust.

No. of awards given last year: Four.
No. of applicants last year: Five.
Additional Information: The Monument Trust is one of the Sainsbury Family Charitable Trusts.

UNIVERSITY OF CANTERBURY

Private Bag 4800, Christchurch, New Zealand
Tel: (64) 3 364 2808
Fax: (64) 3 364 2325
Email: hr@regy.canterbury.ac.nz
www: http://www.canterbury.ac.nz
Contact: Ms Hazel Reeves, Human Resources Administrator

The University of Canterbury offers a variety of subjects in a few flexible degree structures; first and postgraduate degrees in arts, commerce, education, engineering, fine arts, forestry, law, music and science. At Canterbury, research and teaching are closely related and while this feature shapes all courses it is very marked at postgraduate level.

University of Canterbury and Creative New Zealand Ursula Bett Residency in Creative Writing

Subjects: Creative writing, fiction, drama or poetry.
Purpose: To foster New Zealand writing by providing a full-time opportunity for a writer to work in an academic environment.
Eligibility: Open to authors of proven merit who are normally resident in New Zealand and to New Zealand nationals temporarily resident overseas.
Level of Study: Unrestricted.
Type: Fellowship.
Value: Emolument at the rate of new zealand $46,500.
Length of Study: Up to one year.
Frequency: Dependent on funds available.
Study Establishment: The University of Canterbury.
Country of Study: New Zealand.
No. of awards offered: One.
Application Procedure: Applicants must submit details of published writings and work in progress, and include a proposal of work to be undertaken during the appointment only.
Closing Date: Usually October 31st.
Funding: Government.
No. of awards given last year: 27 since 1979.
Additional Information: The appointment will be made on the basis of published or performed writing of high quality. Conditions of appointment should be obtained from the Human Resources Department before applying, available in August.

UNIVERSITY OF CAPE TOWN

MBA Program
International Academic Programs Office
Private Bag, Rondebosch, 7701, South Africa
Tel: (27) 21 650 9111
Fax: (27) 21 650 2138
Email: fadomi@bremner.uct.ac.za
www: http://www.gsb.uct.ac.za
Contact: MBA Admissions Officer

Allan and Jill Gray Charitable Trust

Subjects: MBA.
Eligibility: Open to South Africans from disadvantaged backgrounds. Selection is based on financial need and academic ability.
Level of Study: MBA.
Type: Scholarship.
Value: Partial funding.
Frequency: Annual, if funds are available.
Study Establishment: The University of Cape Town.

Country of Study: South Africa.
No. of awards offered: Limited.
Application Procedure: Applicants must apply in writing to the main address. Applications must include a motivation for the particular assistance required, details of any financial assistance already obtained or applied for, even if declined, and full details of the applicant's personal financial circumstances and anticipated expenses.
Closing Date: Please contact the organisation.
Additional Information: There are limited funds available and in almost all cases, students will need to have made their own funding arrangements.

CAM (Centre for African Management) Fund
Subjects: MBA.
Eligibility: Open to South Africans from disadvantaged backgrounds. Selection is based on both financial need and academic ability.
Level of Study: MBA.
Value: Please consult the organisation for details.
Frequency: As available.
Study Establishment: The University of Cape Town.
Country of Study: South Africa.
Application Procedure: Applicants must apply in writing to the main address. Applications must include a motivation for the particular assistance required, details of any financial assistance already obtained or applied for, even if declined, and full details of the applicant's personal financial circumstances and anticipated expenses.
Closing Date: Please contact the organisation.

Executive Women's Club
Subjects: MBA.
Eligibility: Open to South African women with the desire to succeed as corporate managers and the ability to equip themselves appropriately.
Level of Study: MBA.
Value: Please consult the organisation.
Frequency: As available.
Study Establishment: The University of Cape Town.
Country of Study: South Africa.
Application Procedure: Applicants must apply in writing to the main address. Applications should include a motivation for the particular assistance required, details of any financial assistance already obtained or applied for (even if declined), and full details of the applicant's personal financial circumstances and anticipated expenses.
Closing Date: Please contact the organisation.
Additional Information: There are limited funds available and in almost all cases, students will need to have made their own funding arrangements.

Molteno Brothers' Trust Scholarship
Subjects: MBA.
Eligibility: Open to South Africans with an agricultural or economics background who have the stated intention of working in the agriculture sector.
Level of Study: MBA.
Type: Scholarship.
Value: Please consult the organisation for details.
Frequency: As available.
Study Establishment: The University of Cape Town.
Country of Study: South Africa.
No. of awards offered: Limited.
Application Procedure: Applicants must apply in writing to the main address. Applications must include a motivation for the particular assistance required, details of any financial assistance already obtained or applied for even if declined, and full details of the applicant's personal financial circumstances and anticipated expenses.
Closing Date: Please contact the organisation.

Additional Information: There are limited funds available and in almost all cases, students will need to have made their own funding arrangements.

Old Mutual Scholarship
Subjects: MBA.
Eligibility: Open to academically excellent South Africans who come from disadvantaged backgrounds.
Level of Study: MBA.
Type: Scholarship.
Value: Please consult the organisation for details.
Frequency: As available.
Study Establishment: The University of Cape Town.
Country of Study: South Africa.
No. of awards offered: One-two.
Application Procedure: Applicants must apply in writing to the main address. Applications must include a motivation for the particular assistance required, details of any financial assistance already obtained or applied for, even if declined, and full details of the applicant's personal financial circumstances and anticipated expenses.
Closing Date: Please contact the organisation.
Additional Information: Recipients are required to work for Old Mutual for a period after graduation. There are limited funds available and in almost all cases, students will need to have made their own funding arrangements.

Reuters
Subjects: MBA.
Eligibility: Open to South Africans from disadvantaged backgrounds.
Level of Study: MBA.
Value: Please consult the organisation for details.
Frequency: As available.
Study Establishment: The University of Cape Town.
Country of Study: South Africa.
No. of awards offered: Limited.
Application Procedure: Applicants must apply in writing to the main address. Applications should include a motivation for the particular assistance required, details of any financial assistance already obtained or applied for even if declined, and full details of the applicant's personal financial circumstances and anticipated expenses.
Closing Date: Please contact the organisation.

The Sainsbury Trust Fellowship
Subjects: MBA.
Eligibility: Open to South Africans who come from disadvantaged backgrounds and have previous education in an engineering discipline.
Level of Study: MBA.
Type: Fellowship.
Value: Please consult the organisation for details.
Frequency: As available.
Study Establishment: The University of Cape Town.
Country of Study: South Africa.
No. of awards offered: Limited.
Application Procedure: Applicants must write to the Scientific and Industrial Leadership Initiative, enclosing a full curriculum vitae.
Closing Date: Please contact the organisation.
Additional Information: There are a limited number of scholarships available and in almost all cases, students will need to have made their own funding arrangements.

For further information contact:

Scientific & Industrial Leadership Initiative
c/o Leaf College
46 Rouwkoop Road, Rondebosch, 7700, South Africa

The University of Cape Town Graduate School of Business Association (GSBA)
Subjects: MBA.

Eligibility: Open to South African residents or exceptional candidates from neighbouring countries.
Level of Study: MBA.
Type: Grant.
Value: Please consult the organisation for details.
Frequency: As available.
Study Establishment: The University of Cape Town.
Country of Study: South Africa.
No. of awards offered: Limited.
Application Procedure: Applicants must apply in writing to the main address. Applications must include a motivation for the particular assistance required, details of any financial assistance already obtained or applied for, even if declined, and full details of the applicant's personal financial circumstances and anticipated expenses.
Closing Date: Please contact the organisation.
Additional Information: There are limited funds available and in almost all cases, students will need to have made their own funding arrangements.

UNIVERSITY OF DELAWARE

Department of History
University of Delaware, Newark, DE, 19716, United States of America
Tel: (1) 302 831 8226
Fax: (1) 302 831 1538
Email: pato@udel.edu
www: http://www.udel.edu
Contact: Ms Patricia H Orendorf, Administrative Assistant

The University of Delaware maintains more than 30 research centres which provide students with the opportunity to use state of the art equipment and computing facilities while conducting research at the University. A high proportion of full-time graduates receive financial assistance through fellowships, tuition scholarships and assistantships.

E Lyman Stewart Fellowship
Subjects: History.
Purpose: To provide a programme of graduate study leading to a MA or PhD degree for students who plan careers as museum professionals, historical agency administrators, or seek careers in college teaching and public history.
Eligibility: Open to nationals of any country.
Level of Study: Doctorate, Graduate, Postgraduate, Predoctorate.
Type: Fellowship.
Value: US$10,000 plus tuition.
Frequency: Annual.
Study Establishment: The University of Delaware.
Country of Study: United States of America.
No. of awards offered: Four-six.
Application Procedure: Applicants must apply by University of Delaware application, transcripts, Graduate Record Examination scores, Test Of English as a Foreign Language scores where applicable, plus three letters of recommendation and a writing sample.
Closing Date: January 31st.
Funding: Private.
No. of awards given last year: Seven.
No. of applicants last year: 16.
Additional Information: This is a residential programme.

Fellowships in the University of Delaware Hagley Program
Subjects: The history of industrialisation, broadly defined to include business, economic, labour and social history and the history of science and technology.
Purpose: To provide a programme of graduate study leading to an MA or PhD degree for students who seek careers in college teaching and public history.

Eligibility: Open to graduate students of any nationality seeking degrees in American or European history or the history of science and technology.
Level of Study: Doctorate, Graduate, Postgraduate, Predoctorate.
Type: Fellowship.
Value: US$10,000 for Master's candidates and doctoral candidates. All tuition fees for university courses are paid.
Length of Study: One year, renewable once for those seeking a terminal MA, and up to three times for those seeking the doctorate.
Frequency: Annual.
Study Establishment: The University of Delaware.
Country of Study: United States of America.
No. of awards offered: Approx. two-three.
Application Procedure: Fellows are selected upon Graduate Record Examination scores, recommendations, undergraduate grade index, work experience and personal interviews.
Closing Date: January 31st.
Funding: Government, Private.
No. of awards given last year: Two.
No. of applicants last year: 22.
Additional Information: This is a residential programme.

UNIVERSITY OF DUNDEE

Nethergate, Dundee, DD1 4HN, Scotland
Tel: (44) 1382 345028
Fax: (44) 1382 345343
Email: j.e.nicholson@dundee.ac.uk
www: http://www.dundee.ac.uk
Contact: Postgraduate Office

The University of Dundee believes emphatically in the 'traditional' mission of universities, that being the pursuit of excellence in the twin activities of learning and discovery. The University is well placed to fulfil these objectives as it has an established record in teaching and research.

University of Dundee Research Awards
Subjects: Medicine, dentistry, science, engineering, law, arts, social sciences, environmental studies, town planning, architecture, management and consumer studies, nursing, fine art, television and imaging.
Purpose: To assist full-time research leading to a PhD.
Eligibility: Open to holders of a First Class or Upper Second Class (Honours) Degree or equivalent.
Level of Study: Doctorate, Postgraduate.
Type: Studentship.
Value: UK £7,050 plus tuition fees at the home rate.
Length of Study: One year, renewable annually for up to a maximum of two additional years.
Frequency: Dependent on funds available.
Study Establishment: The University of Dundee, Tayside.
Country of Study: United Kingdom.
No. of awards offered: Dependent on funds available.
Application Procedure: Applicants must contact the relevant faculty office for information on the availability of awards.
Closing Date: March 2nd.
No. of awards given last year: Seven.
No. of applicants last year: 70.

UNIVERSITY OF EAST ANGLIA (UEA)

Norwich, Norfolk, NR4 7TJ, England
Tel: (44) 1603 592810
Fax: (44) 1603 507728
Email: v.striker@uea.ac.uk
www: http://www.uea.ac.uk
Contact: Ms Val Striker, Dean's Secretary

The University of East Anglia (UEA) is organised into 17 Schools of Study encompassing the sciences, humanities and social sciences, and professional studies. These are supported by central service and administration departments.

David T K Wong Fellowship

Subjects: Writing.
Purpose: To support promising writers in producing a work of fiction set in the Far East.
Eligibility: Open to any writer who wishes to produce a work of fiction in English which deals seriously with some aspect of life in the Far East.
Level of Study: Unrestricted.
Type: Fellowship.
Value: UK £25,000.
Length of Study: One year.
Frequency: Annual.
Study Establishment: The University of East Anglia.
Country of Study: United Kingdom.
No. of awards offered: One.
Application Procedure: Applicants must obtain further information and application forms by writing to the School of English and American Studies at UEA.
Closing Date: October 31st.
Funding: Private.
Contributor: David T K Wong.
No. of awards given last year: One.
No. of applicants last year: 75.
Additional Information: The Far East is defined as China, Hong Kong, Macau, Taiwan, Japan, Korea, Mongolia, Laos, Cambodia, Vietnam, Thailand, Burma, Philippines, Singapore, Malaysia, Indonesia and Brunei.

UEA Writing Fellowship

Subjects: Creative writing.
Purpose: To enable a creative writer to work in a university atmosphere and with a regional arts board on a reciprocal basis.
Eligibility: Open to practising, published writers in fiction and poetry. Applicants must be English speaking.
Level of Study: Professional development.
Type: Fellowship.
Value: UK £7,500 plus free accommodation.
Length of Study: The Spring semester of each academic year.
Frequency: Annual.
Study Establishment: The University of East Anglia.
Country of Study: United Kingdom.
No. of awards offered: One.
Application Procedure: Applicants must submit a completed application form, curriculum vitae and two examples of recent work.
Closing Date: October. For exact dates each year, see advertisements in the press, or telephone. Interviews take place in November.
Funding: Government.
Contributor: Eastern England Arts and the University of East Anglia.
No. of awards given last year: One.
No. of applicants last year: 16.
Additional Information: A driving licence and access to a car would be an advantage.

For further information contact:

Personnel Office
University Plain, Norwich, Norfolk, NR4 7TJ, England

Tel: (44) 1603 593809
Fax: (44) 1603 507728

UNIVERSITY OF EDINBURGH FACULTY OF SCIENCE AND ENGINEERING

Weir Building
The King's Buildings, Edinburgh, EH9 3JY, Scotland
Tel: (44) 131 650 5765
Fax: (44) 131 650 5738
www: http://www.scieng.ed.ac.uk
Contact: Mr Chris Jowett, Administrator

University of Edinburgh Faculty of Science and Engineering Scholarship

Subjects: Science or engineering.
Purpose: To provide funds for well qualified candidates to pursue full-time research leading to a PhD.
Eligibility: Open to individuals of any nationality with a First or Upper Second Class (Honours) Degree or its equivalent. Candidates must have applied or have been accepted to study for a research degree.
Level of Study: Doctorate.
Type: Scholarship.
Value: Stipend of UK £7,500 tuition fees at home rate and research costs to the department of UK £1,000.
Length of Study: Three years.
Frequency: Dependent on funds available.
Study Establishment: The University of Edinburgh.
Country of Study: United Kingdom.
No. of awards offered: 4-10.
Application Procedure: Applicants must make an application for admission as a postgraduate student and indicate a wish to be considered for a scholarship.
Closing Date: Varies according to the department.
No. of awards given last year: 10.
Additional Information: Further information is available from the department in which the candidate intends to study.

UNIVERSITY OF EXETER

The Graduate School
Northcote House
The Queen's Drive, Exeter, Devon, EX4 4QJ, England
Tel: (44) 1392 263044
Fax: (44) 1392 263313
Email: gradschool@exeter.ac.uk
www: http://www.exeter.ac.uk/gradschool
Contact: Mr Dan Cook, Administrative Officer

The University of Exeter is representative of the best of British university education. It combines research of international standing across all departments with excellence in teaching, and is one of the most popular in the country among applicants.

Andrew Stratton Scholarship

Subjects: Engineering and science.
Eligibility: Open to postgraduate students in engineering or science.
Level of Study: Postgraduate.
Type: Scholarship.
Value: UK £1,000.
Length of Study: One year.
Study Establishment: The University of Exeter.
Country of Study: United Kingdom.
Application Procedure: Applicants must consult the University.
Closing Date: Please contact the organisation.
Additional Information: Further information is available on request.

Anning-Morgan Bursary

Subjects: All subjects.
Purpose: To financially support postgraduate study.
Eligibility: Students must have been resident in the Duchy of Cornwall prior to entry or must be resident there during their postgraduate studies.
Level of Study: Postgraduate.
Type: Bursary.
Value: Fees only.
Length of Study: A maximum of two years.
Study Establishment: The University of Exeter.
Country of Study: United Kingdom.
Application Procedure: Applicants must consult the University.
Closing Date: Please contact the organisation.
Additional Information: Further information is available on request.

Anthony Parsons Memorial Scholarship

Subjects: Arabic, Islamic or Middle East studies.
Purpose: To financially support those undertaking postgraduate study.
Eligibility: Open to students doing research into Arabic, Islamic or Middle East studies.
Level of Study: Postgraduate.
Type: Scholarship.
Value: Up to UK £3,000.
Study Establishment: The University of Exeter.
Country of Study: United Kingdom.
Application Procedure: Applicants must consult the University.

British Council Awards and Scholarships for International Students

Subjects: Any subject offered by the university if the School has scholarship funding available.
Purpose: To allow international students to pursue certain postgraduate study at the university.
Eligibility: Open to candidates for research degrees who have obtained at least an Upper Second Class (Honours) Degree or its equivalent.
Level of Study: Postgraduate.
Type: Scholarship.
Value: Varies.
Study Establishment: The University of Exeter.
Country of Study: United Kingdom.
No. of awards offered: Varies.
Application Procedure: Applicants must obtain details from the British Council representative in the applicant's own country.
Closing Date: Please contact the organisation.
Additional Information: Further information is available on request.

Commonwealth Scholarship Plan

Subjects: All subjects.
Purpose: To allow Commonwealth students to pursue postgraduate study at the university.
Eligibility: Available to students from Commonwealth countries who do not already hold scholarships from their own country.
Level of Study: Postgraduate.
Type: Scholarship.
Value: Includes payment of tuition fees.
Study Establishment: The University of Exeter.
Country of Study: United Kingdom.
Application Procedure: Applicants must apply well in advance in their country of permanent residence, through the Commonwealth Scholarship Agency.
Closing Date: Please contact the organisation.
Additional Information: Further information is available on request.

Cornwall Heritage Trust Scholarship

Subjects: Any aspect of Cornwall's heritage.
Purpose: To assist a Master's degree student with their dissertation.
Eligibility: Open to students working towards a Master's degree and producing a dissertation.

Level of Study: Postgraduate.
Type: Scholarship.
Value: UK £1,000.
Length of Study: One year.
Frequency: Annual.
Study Establishment: The University of Exeter.
Country of Study: United Kingdom.
No. of awards offered: One.
Application Procedure: Applicants must inform the Graduate School when applying for a place on a programme.
Closing Date: Please contact the organisation.
Additional Information: Further information is available on request.

University of Exeter Graduate Research Assistantships

Subjects: All subjects.
Purpose: To assist students by offering them a top quality scheme that offers excellent career development opportunities.
Eligibility: Available for MPhil and PhD students.
Level of Study: Postgraduate.
Type: Assistantship.
Value: Fees and maintenance at research council rates currently UK £7,500 per year.
Length of Study: Four years.
Study Establishment: The University of Exeter.
Country of Study: United Kingdom.
Application Procedure: Applicants must visit the website.
Additional Information: Further details of this scheme are available from the Graduate School website. GRAs are required to undertake two days a week of research for a research team in addition to their own research.

University of Exeter Graduate Teaching Assistantships

Subjects: All subjects.
Purpose: To assist students by offering them a top quality scheme that offers excellent career development opportunities.
Eligibility: Available for MPhil and PhD students.
Level of Study: Postdoctorate, Postgraduate.
Type: Assistantship.
Value: Fees and maintenance at research council rates currently UK £7,500 per year.
Length of Study: Up to four years.
Study Establishment: The University of Exeter.
Country of Study: United Kingdom.
Application Procedure: Applicants must visit the website.
Closing Date: Please contact the organisation.
Additional Information: Further details of this scheme are available from the Graduate School website. GTAs are given full training with SEDA accreditation and are expected to teach for up to 150 hours per year.

University of Exeter Overseas Research Students Award Scheme

Subjects: All subjects.
Purpose: To assist international students of outstanding merit and research potential undertaking research degrees.
Eligibility: For overseas students only undertaking research degrees.
Level of Study: Postdoctorate, Postgraduate, Research.
Type: Award.
Value: The difference between the tuition fees for a home or European Union postgraduate student and that for an international postgraduate student.
Length of Study: Three years.
Frequency: Annual.
Study Establishment: The University of Exeter.
Country of Study: United Kingdom.
No. of awards offered: Varies.
Application Procedure: Applications forms and details are sent to all applicants offered a place before mid April for MPhil or PhD study.

University of Exeter Research Scholarships

Subjects: All subjects.
Purpose: For MPhil and PhD study.
Eligibility: Open to students of the university who are studying for a PhD or MPhil and who have already completed one year's study.
Level of Study: Postgraduate.
Type: Scholarship.
Value: Varies.
Study Establishment: The University of Exeter.
Country of Study: United Kingdom.
Application Procedure: Nominations are made by academic schools. If you wish to be considered you should inform the postgraduate admissions tutor or the head of the appropriate school.
Closing Date: Please contact the organisation.
Additional Information: Further information is available on request.

University of Exeter Sports Scholarships

Subjects: Sports.
Purpose: To assist students of outstanding sporting ability who show evidence of achievement or potential at national level.
Level of Study: Graduate, Postgraduate.
Type: Scholarship.
Value: Free university residential accommodation and UK £1,000 per year for sporting expenses.
Length of Study: One year initially, but may be renewed for a further two years.
Frequency: Annual.
Study Establishment: The University of Exeter.
Country of Study: United Kingdom.
No. of awards offered: Varies.
Application Procedure: Applicants must contact the Secretary of the Sports Scholarship Board at the University.
Closing Date: February 15th.
Additional Information: Students will be provided with a mentor with whom an annual programme of training and competition will be agreed.

UNIVERSITY OF GLASGOW

Glasgow, G12 8QQ, Scotland
Tel: (44) 141 330 4515
Fax: (44) 141 330 4413
Email: sras@gla.ac.uk
www: http://www.gla.ac.uk/sras/pg.html
Contact: Ms Hazel Sydeserff, Graduate Assistant Director

The University of Glasgow is a major research led university operating in an international context which aims to provide education through the development of learning in a research environment, to undertake fundamental, strategic and applied research and to sustain and add value to Scottish culture, to the natural environment and to the national economy.

James Houston Scholarship

Subjects: Veterinary medicine.
Purpose: To assist the advanced study or research into bovine animals, with particular reference to bloodstock breeding and its improvement.
Eligibility: Open to university graduates of veterinary medicine and qualified veterinary surgeons.
Level of Study: Postgraduate.
Type: Scholarship.
Value: Approx. UK £9,130.
Length of Study: One year, with the possibility of renewal for up to two additional years.
Frequency: Every two years.
Study Establishment: The University of Glasgow.
Country of Study: United Kingdom.
No. of awards offered: One.
Application Procedure: Applicants must write for details.

Closing Date: February.
Additional Information: Preference is given to graduates in veterinary medicine of the University of Glasgow.

For further information contact:

Faculty of Veterinary Medicine
University of Glasgow Veterinary School
Bearsden, Glasgow, G61 1QH, Scotland
Email: gvmx04@udcf.gla.ac.uk
Contact: Mr T W Mathieson

John Crawford Scholarship

Subjects: Veterinary medicine.
Purpose: To assist the advanced study or research into equine animals, with particular reference to bloodstock breeding and its improvement.
Eligibility: Open to university graduates of veterinary medicine and qualified veterinary surgeons.
Level of Study: Postgraduate.
Type: Scholarship.
Value: Approx. UK £9,130 including a home fee plus stipend of £6,456.
Length of Study: One year, with the possibility of renewal for up to two additional years.
Frequency: Every two years.
Study Establishment: The University of Glasgow.
Country of Study: United Kingdom.
No. of awards offered: One.
Application Procedure: Applicants must write for details.
Closing Date: February 28th.
Additional Information: Preference is given to graduates in veterinary medicine of the University of Glasgow.

For further information contact:

Faculty of Veterinary Medicine
University of Glasgow Veterinary School
Bearsden, Glasgow, G61 1QH, Scotland
Email: gvmx04@udcf.gla.ac.uk
Contact: Mr T W Mathieson

University of Glasgow Postgraduate Research Scholarships

Subjects: All subjects.
Purpose: To assist with research toward a PhD degree.
Eligibility: Open to candidates of any nationality who are proficient in English and who have obtained a First or an Upper Second Class (Honours) Degree or equivalent.
Level of Study: Postgraduate.
Type: Scholarship.
Value: A maintenance allowance of UK £6,804, plus home fees of UK £2,740.
Length of Study: Three years, subject to satisfactory progress.
Frequency: Annual.
Study Establishment: The University of Glasgow.
Country of Study: Scotland.
No. of awards offered: 27.
Application Procedure: Applicants must refer to the University's application for graduate studies form which covers application for admission and scholarship. Please refer to the notes for applicants booklet issued with the application form for address details.
Closing Date: The deadline for the faculties of medicine and science is January 31st, for the arts, divinity, and veterinary medicine the deadline is February 28th. The education, engineering, law and financial studies, and social sciences deadline is March 31st.
Funding: Private.
Contributor: Endowments.
No. of awards given last year: 27.
No. of applicants last year: 500+.
Additional Information: Scholars from outside the European Union will be expected to make up the difference between the home fee and the overseas fee.

William Barclay Memorial Scholarship

Subjects: Biblical studies, theology and church history or any subject falling within the faculty of the divinity.
Purpose: To provide an opportunity for a Scholar to undertake research or graduate study.
Eligibility: Open to any suitably qualified graduate of theology from a university outside the United Kingdom.
Level of Study: Postgraduate.
Type: Scholarship.
Value: Up to approx. UK £5,000.
Length of Study: Study length depends on degree. A one year award is not normally renewable.
Frequency: Annual.
Study Establishment: In the Faculty of Divinity, University of Glasgow.
Country of Study: Scotland.
No. of awards offered: Two.
Application Procedure: Applicants must request postgraduate study application material. The PG form is used for the Barclay application.
Closing Date: March 31st.
Funding: Private.
No. of awards given last year: Two.
No. of applicants last year: 15-20.

For further information contact:

Faculty of Divinity, Glasgow, G12 8QQ, Scotland
Tel: (44) 141 330 6525
Fax: (44) 141 330 4943
Email: gvmx04@udcf.gla.ac.uk
Contact: Ms A O'Neil

THE UNIVERSITY OF KENT AT CANTERBURY

The Graduate Office
The Registry, Canterbury, Kent, CT2 7NZ, England
Tel: (44) 1227 824040
Fax: (44) 1227 827077
Email: recruitment@ukc.ac.uk
www: http://www.ukc.ac.uk
Contact: Ms Hayley Mills, Secretary, Student Office

The University of Kent at Canterbury aims to provide higher education of excellent quality characterised by flexibility and interdisciplinarity, informed by research and scholarship, and meeting the lifelong needs of a diversity of students.

EB Spratt Bursary

Subjects: Computer science with particular reference to programming languages. Formal methods, software and systems engineering, object technology, data analysis and exploration, database technology, intelligent systems, networks and distributed systems, concurrency and computers and education.
Purpose: To support postgraduate studies towards PhD.
Eligibility: Open to candidates of all countries, but the fees component is sufficient for home fees only. Non European Community citizens require further monies for overseas fees.
Level of Study: Postgraduate.
Type: Bursary.
Value: Up to four awards of fees plus UK £10,000 maintenance for United Kingdom and European Union applicants, and up to seven awards of fees only for home or overseas applicants, as well as the possibility of a contribution to maintenance for outstanding overseas applicants, particularly those who may be in receipt of funding from other sources.
Length of Study: Three years.
Frequency: Annual.
Study Establishment: The University of Kent.
Country of Study: United Kingdom.

No. of awards offered: Up to eight.
Application Procedure: Applicants must enclose a covering letter and indicate their area of interest.
Closing Date: June.
Funding: Government.
No. of awards given last year: Two.

EPSRC Grant

Subjects: Physical sciences.
Purpose: To support research.
Eligibility: Candidates should hold or expect to obtain a First Class (Honours) Degree. They should also be citizens of one of the European Union countries.
Level of Study: Postgraduate.
Type: Grant.
Value: Tuition fees plus the maintenance bursary at the same rate as provided by the EPSRC.
Length of Study: Three years.
Frequency: Annual.
Study Establishment: The University of Kent.
Country of Study: United Kingdom.
No. of awards offered: Six.
Application Procedure: Applicants must complete an application form.
Closing Date: There is no fixed closing date.
Contributor: EPSRC.
No. of awards given last year: Six.
No. of applicants last year: 20.
Additional Information: Holders of the studentships are required to undertake a small amount of teaching assistance.

EPSRC Quota

Subjects: Computer science with particular reference to programming languages. Formal methods, software and systems engineering, object technology, data analysis and exploration, database technology, intelligent systems, networks and distributed systems, concurrency, computers and education.
Purpose: To support postgraduate studies towards a PhD.
Eligibility: Primarily open to United Kingdom nationals although European Community citizens may qualify in special circumstances.
Level of Study: Postgraduate.
Type: Research grant.
Value: Home fees plus maintenance grant of approx. UK £10,000 per year.
Length of Study: Three years.
Frequency: Annual.
Study Establishment: The University of Kent.
Country of Study: United Kingdom.
No. of awards offered: Two.
Application Procedure: Applicants must indicate their interest on postgraduate application forms.
Closing Date: June.
Funding: Government.
Contributor: EPSRC.
No. of awards given last year: Two.

Ian Gregor Scholarship

Subjects: English.
Purpose: To support a candidate registered for the taught or research MA programmes in English.
Eligibility: Candidates are expected to hold at least an Upper Second Class (Honours) Degree or equivalent. Candidates should also have applied for an external scholarship, such as AHRB.
Level of Study: Graduate.
Type: Scholarship.
Value: Home fees plus UK £500. An equivalent contribution towards fees will be made in the case of overseas students.
Length of Study: One year.
Frequency: Annual.
Study Establishment: The University of Kent.
Country of Study: United Kingdom.

No. of awards offered: One.
Application Procedure: Candidates must complete the UKC Postgraduate Application Form, indicating in the appropriate section that they are interested in being considered for departmental scholarships. A covering letter supporting the scholarship application should be attached.
Closing Date: May 30th.
No. of awards given last year: One.

Kent Law School MPhil Studentships

Subjects: Law, particularly socio-legal studies, legal theory, feminist legal studies, comparative law, corporate governance, environmental law, criminal justice, military justice, international law and international commercial law.
Eligibility: Candidates should hold an Upper Second Class (Honours) Degree and be a citizen of one of the European Union countries.
Level of Study: Postgraduate.
Type: Studentship.
Value: Home fees plus the Research Council equivalent of a maintenance grant.
Length of Study: One-three years.
Frequency: Annual.
Study Establishment: The University of Kent.
Country of Study: United Kingdom.
No. of awards offered: Two.
Application Procedure: Applicants must submit, to the Graduate Office, a research proposal, a curriculum vitae, a covering letter and two references.
Closing Date: June.
Funding: Private.
No. of awards given last year: Seven.
Additional Information: Holders of the studentships will be expected to teach for a maximum of six hours per week in term time on an undergraduate law module.

Maurice Crosland History of Science Studentship

Subjects: The history of science, technology or medicine.
Purpose: To fund research to PhD level.
Eligibility: Open to qualified applicants of any nationality.
Level of Study: Postgraduate.
Type: Studentship.
Value: Home fees plus a maintenance bursary.
Length of Study: Three years.
Frequency: Dependent on funds available.
Study Establishment: The University of Kent.
Country of Study: United Kingdom.
No. of awards offered: One.
Application Procedure: Applicants must apply to Professor Crosbie Smith.
Closing Date: June 1st.
Funding: Private.
No. of awards given last year: Two.
No. of applicants last year: Five.

For further information contact:

Centre for History & Cultural Studies of Science
Rutherford College
University of Kent at Canterbury, Canterbury, Kent, CT2 7NX, England
Tel: (44) 1227 764000
Fax: (44) 1227 827258
Contact: Professor Crosbie Smith

Tizard Centre Departmental Scholarships

Subjects: Mental health and learning disabilities.
Purpose: To support research studies in mental health or learning disabilities.
Eligibility: Candidate should hold or expect to obtain a First or Second Class (Honours) Degree. They must also be citizens of one of the European Union countries.
Level of Study: Postgraduate.

Type: Studentship.
Value: Home tuition fees plus a maintenance bursary at the same rate as the EPSRC.
Length of Study: Three years.
Frequency: Dependent on funds available.
Study Establishment: The University of Kent.
Country of Study: United Kingdom.
No. of awards offered: Two.
Application Procedure: Applicants must complete an application form.
Closing Date: Usually late Spring or early Summer for entry at the beginning of the academic year.
No. of awards given last year: Two.
No. of applicants last year: Seven.

The University of Kent at Canterbury Anthropology Bursaries

Subjects: Social anthropology, environmental anthropology, ethnobotany, conservation biology, tourism, conservation, visual anthropology and biodiversity management.
Purpose: To support both research and taught programmes.
Eligibility: Candidates are expected to hold an Upper Second Class (Honours) Degree.
Level of Study: Research.
Type: Bursary.
Value: Home fees only.
Length of Study: Three years.
Frequency: Annual.
Study Establishment: The University of Kent.
Country of Study: United Kingdom.
No. of awards offered: Three.
Closing Date: Please write for details.
No. of awards given last year: Two.

For further information contact:

Department of Anthropology
Eliot College, Canterbury, Kent, England
Email: n.a.kerry-yoxall@ukc.ac.uk
Contact: Ms Nicola Kerry-Yoxall

The University of Kent at Canterbury Department of Biosciences

Subjects: Biosciences.
Purpose: To support research.
Eligibility: Primarily open to United Kingdom nationals although European Union citizens may qualify in special circumstances. Candidates should hold an Upper Second Class (Honours) Degree and be a national of one of the European Union countries.
Level of Study: Postgraduate.
Type: Research grant.
Value: Home tuition fees and a maintenance bursary at the same rate as that provided by the Research Councils for a three year period.
Length of Study: Three years.
Frequency: Annual.
Study Establishment: The University of Kent.
Country of Study: United Kingdom.
No. of awards offered: 10.
Application Procedure: Applicants should contact Dr Andrew MacGregor, Department of Biosciences for further information via email on a.n.macgregor@ukc.ac.uk.
Closing Date: July 31st.
Contributor: BBSRC.
No. of awards given last year: Seven.

The University of Kent at Canterbury Department of Economics Bursaries

Subjects: Economics.
Purpose: To support research.
Eligibility: Candidates should hold an Upper Second Class (Honours) Degree and a Master's degree in economics.

Level of Study: Postgraduate.
Type: Research grant.
Value: Up to the equivalent of home fees plus a maintenance grant equivalent to that of the ESRC.
Length of Study: Three years.
Frequency: Annual.
Study Establishment: The University of Kent.
Country of Study: United Kingdom.
No. of awards offered: Up to six.
Closing Date: June.
Funding: Government.
Additional Information: A maximum of four hours of teaching per week will be required.

For further information contact:

Department of Economics
Keynes College, Canterbury, Kent, England
Email: r.w.vickerman@ukc.ac.uk
Contact: Mr Roger Vickerman

The University of Kent at Canterbury Department of Electronics Studentships

Subjects: Any aspect of electronic engineering relating to the current research interests of the Department. These include antennas, optical communication, microwave networks, radio astronomy, CAD tools, image processing and computer vision, ASIC design, document processing, neural network engineering, multi-media applications, medical image processing, medical electronics and multimedia tools and systems.
Purpose: To enable well qualified students to undertake research programmes within the department.
Eligibility: Candidates are expected to hold an Upper Second Class (Honours) Degree or equivalent in an appropriate subject, and be nationals of one of the European Union countries.
Level of Study: Doctorate, Postgraduate.
Type: Studentship.
Value: Research Council studentships are at a fixed rate determined annually by EPSRC. Departmental bursaries depend on individual circumstances.
Length of Study: Three years.
Frequency: Annual.
Study Establishment: The University of Kent.
Country of Study: United Kingdom.
No. of awards offered: Varies.
Application Procedure: Applicants should contact the Department of Electronics.
Closing Date: June.
Funding: Government.
Contributor: EPSRC.

For further information contact:

Electronic Engineering Laboratory
University of Kent, Canterbury, Kent, CT2 7NT, England
Email: m.c.fairhurst@ukc.ac.uk
Contact: Professor M C Fairhurst

The University of Kent at Canterbury Department of Politics and International Relations Bursary

Subjects: Politics and international relations.
Purpose: To support research.
Eligibility: Candidates must be citizens of one of the European Union countries. Please write for further details with regards to academic eligibility.
Level of Study: Postgraduate.
Type: Bursary.
Value: Home fees.
Length of Study: Three years.
Frequency: Annual.
Study Establishment: The University of Kent.
Country of Study: United Kingdom.
No. of awards offered: Approx. three.

Application Procedure: Applicants must apply by letter to the head of department after being accepted for research study.
Closing Date: Applications may be submitted at any time.
No. of awards given last year: One.
No. of applicants last year: Four.
Additional Information: A maximum of six hours of teaching per week will be required.

The University of Kent at Canterbury Department of Psychology Studentships

Subjects: Research areas considered include cognitive neuroscience, developmental, forensic, group or intergroup processes and health.
Purpose: To support research studies in psychology.
Eligibility: Candidates should hold or expect to obtain at least an Upper Second Class (Honours) Degree in psychology.
Level of Study: Postgraduate.
Type: Studentship.
Value: Tuition fees plus the maintenance bursary at the same rate as provided by the ESRC.
Length of Study: Three years.
Frequency: Annual.
Study Establishment: The University of Kent.
Country of Study: United Kingdom.
No. of awards offered: Three.
Application Procedure: Applicants must complete an application form.
Closing Date: The deadline changes according to when studentships are advertised. This is usually the end of July.
No. of awards given last year: Three.
No. of applicants last year: 20-30.
Additional Information: A maximum of six hours of teaching per week will be required.

The University of Kent at Canterbury English Scholarship

Subjects: English.
Purpose: To support research.
Eligibility: Candidates are expected to hold at least an Upper Second Class (Honours) Degree or equivalent. Candidates should also have applied for an external scholarship, such as AHRB.
Level of Study: Postgraduate.
Type: Research grant.
Value: Home tuition fees and UK £2,500 stipend. An equivalent contribution towards fees will be made will be made in the case of overseas students.
Length of Study: Three years.
Frequency: Annual.
Study Establishment: The University of Kent.
Country of Study: United Kingdom.
No. of awards offered: One.
Application Procedure: Candidates must complete the UKC Postgraduate Application Form, indicating in the appropriate section that they are interested in being considered for departmental scholarships. A covering letter supporting the scholarship application should be attached.
Closing Date: May 30th.
No. of awards given last year: One.
Additional Information: Holders of the scholarship are expected to undertake a small amount of teaching or research assistance each week.

The University of Kent at Canterbury School of European Culture and Language Scholarships

Subjects: Various subjects from the School of European Culture and Languages.
Purpose: To support research.
Eligibility: Candidates are expected to hold an Upper Second Class (Honours) Degree and be a citizen of one of the European Union countries.
Level of Study: Postgraduate.

Type: Research grant.
Value: UK £1,500.
Length of Study: Three years.
Frequency: Annual.
Study Establishment: The University of Kent.
Country of Study: United Kingdom.
No. of awards offered: Varies, up to four.
Application Procedure: Applicants must contact Professor Robin Gill at the School of European Culture and Languages, Cornwallis West Building or by email at r.gill@ukc.ac.uk.
Closing Date: June.
No. of awards given last year: Three.
No. of applicants last year: Seven.
Additional Information: Some part-time teaching will be required.

The University of Kent at Canterbury Second English Scholarship

Subjects: English.
Purpose: To support research.
Eligibility: Candidates are expected to hold at least an Upper Second Class (Honours) Degree or equivalent. Candidates should also have applied for an external scholarship, such as AHRB.
Level of Study: Postgraduate.
Type: Research grant.
Value: Home tuition fees and UK £1,500 stipend. An equivalent contribution towards fees will be made will be made in the case of overseas students.
Frequency: Annual.
Study Establishment: The University of Kent.
Country of Study: United Kingdom.
Application Procedure: Candidates must complete the UKC Postgraduate Application Form, indicating in the appropriate section that they are interested in being considered for departmental scholarships. A covering letter supporting the scholarship application should be attached.
Closing Date: May 30th.
Additional Information: One.

The University of Kent at Canterbury Social and Public Policy Studentships

Subjects: Social and public policy.
Purpose: To support research.
Eligibility: Candidates should hold an Upper Second Class (Honours) Degree and be a citizen of one of the European Union countries.
Level of Study: Postgraduate.
Type: Studentship.
Value: Home fees and UK £6,250 per year for maintenance.
Length of Study: Three years.
Frequency: Annual.
Study Establishment: The University of Kent.
Country of Study: United Kingdom.
No. of awards offered: Two.
Application Procedure: Applicants must contact Professor John Butler in the Department of Social and Public Policy, Darwin College or email him at j.r.butler@ukc.ac.uk.
Closing Date: June.
Funding: Government.
No. of awards given last year: Two.
Additional Information: A maximum of two hours of teaching per week will be required.

For further information contact:

The School of Social Policy, Sociology & Social Research
Darwin College, Canterbury, Kent, England
Email: c.g.pickvance@ukc.ac.uk
Contact: Professor C Pickvance

The University of Kent at Canterbury Sociology Studentship

Subjects: Sociology.

Purpose: To support research.
Eligibility: Candidates should hold an Upper Second Class (Honours) Degree and be a citizen of one of the European Union countries.
Level of Study: Postgraduate.
Type: Research grant.
Value: Tuition fees.
Length of Study: Three years.
Frequency: Annual.
Study Establishment: The University of Kent.
Country of Study: United Kingdom.
No. of awards offered: One.
Application Procedure: Applicants must contact Anne Phillips at the Department of Sociology, Darwin College for further information or email her at a.e.phillips@ukc.ac.uk.
Closing Date: June.
Funding: Government.
No. of awards given last year: Two.

For further information contact:

Director of Graduate Studies
School of Social Policy, Sociology & Social Research
Darwin College, Canterbury, Kent, England
Email: m.s.evans@ukc.ac.uk
Contact: Professor Mary Evans, Director of Graduate Studies

The University of Kent IMS Studentships

Subjects: Mathematics or statistics.
Purpose: To support PhD studies at the Institute of Mathematics and Statistics.
Eligibility: Candidates for scholarships should hold (or be expected to obtain) a First Class (Honours) Degree in mathematics or a related subject.
Level of Study: Doctorate.
Type: Studentship.
Value: Tuition fees plus the maintenance bursary at the same rate as provided by the EPSRC.
Length of Study: Three years.
Frequency: Dependent on funds available.
Study Establishment: The University of Kent.
Country of Study: United Kingdom.
No. of awards offered: Three.
Application Procedure: Candidates should complete an application form for postgraduate study and indicate that they wish to be considered for this award.
Closing Date: April 19th.
No. of awards given last year: Two.
No. of applicants last year: 11.
Additional Information: Holders of the studentships are required to undertake a small amount of teaching assistance. For more information please email imspg-admiss@ukc.ac.uk.

THE UNIVERSITY OF LEEDS

Research Degrees & Scholarships Office, Leeds, West Yorkshire, LS2 9JT, England
Tel: (44) 113 233 4007
Fax: (44) 113 233 3941
Email: ajmorrison@adm.leeds.co.uk
www: http://www.leeds.ac.uk
Contact: Ms J Y Findlay, Senior Assistant Registrar

The University of Leeds aims to promote excellence and to achieve and sustain international standing in higher education teaching, learning and research and to serve a wide range of student constituencies, social and professional communities and industrial, commercial and government agencies, locally, nationally and internationally.

BEIT Trust FCO Chevening Leeds University Scholarship

Subjects: All subjects.
Purpose: To provide awards to students of high academic calibre from Malawi, Zambia and Zimbabwe.
Eligibility: Open to candidates who have obtained, or are about to obtain, the equivalent of a United Kingdom First Class or Good Second Class (Honours) Degree. Candidates must be nationals of Malawi, Zambia and Zimbabwe and aged between 20 and 35.
Level of Study: Postgraduate.
Type: Scholarship.
Value: Academic fees, living expenses, books, equipment, arrival and departure allowance, economy return airfares and the production of a dissertation.
Length of Study: One year.
Frequency: Annual.
Study Establishment: The University of Leeds.
Country of Study: United Kingdom.
No. of awards offered: Three.
Application Procedure: Applications must be made to the BEIT Trust.
Closing Date: August to October.
Funding: Private.
No. of awards given last year: None.
No. of applicants last year: Not known.

For further information contact:

The BIET Trust
BEIT House
Grove Road, Woking, Surrey, GU21 5JB, England

BPAmoco-Leeds University-FCO Chevening Scholarship

Subjects: Exploration geophysics, geochemistry, environmental engineering and project management, economics, finance and accounting, business administration and management, international studies, politics of international resources and development and waste management.
Purpose: To provide postgraduate scholarships to Vietnamese students of high academic calibre.
Eligibility: Open to candidates who have obtained, or be about to obtain, a United Kingdom First Class or good Second Class Degree or equivalent. Candidates must be nationals of Vietnam and be aged between 20 and 35.
Level of Study: Postgraduate.
Type: Scholarship.
Value: To cover academic fees and living expenses, books equipment, arrival and departure allowance, economy return airfares and the production of a dissertation.
Length of Study: One year.
Frequency: Annual.
Study Establishment: The University of Leeds.
Country of Study: United Kingdom.
No. of awards offered: Four.
Application Procedure: Applicants must apply by application form after acceptance on to a taught course. Application forms are available from the University.
Closing Date: January 10th.
Funding: Commercial, Government, Private.
No. of awards given last year: Four.
No. of applicants last year: 41.

Canon Collins Educational Trust FCO Chevening-Leeds University Scholarships

Subjects: Any one year full-time taught Master's programme.
Purpose: To provide awards to students of high academic calibre from the following countries of Botswana, Lesotho, Mozambique, Namibia, South Africa and Swaziland.
Eligibility: Open to candidates who have obtained or are about to obtain the equivalent of a United Kingdom First Class or good Second Class Honours Degree. Candidates must be nationals of

Botswana, Lesotho, Mozambique, Namibia, South Africa or Swaziland and must be aged between 20 and 35.
Level of Study: Postgraduate.
Type: Scholarship.
Value: Academic fees, living expenses, books, equipment, arrival and departure allowance, economy return airfares and the production of a dissertation.
Length of Study: One year.
Frequency: Annual.
Study Establishment: The University of Leeds.
Country of Study: United Kingdom.
No. of awards offered: 10.
Application Procedure: Applicants must complete an application form available on request from the Canon Collins Education Trust for Southern Africa.
Closing Date: March 1st.
Funding: Private.
No. of awards given last year: Two.

For further information contact:

Canon Collins Educational Trust for Southern Africa (CCETSA)
22 The Ivories
6 Northampton Street, London, N1 2HY, England

Derek Fatchett Memorial Scholarships (Palestine)

Subjects: Politics or international studies.
Purpose: To provide awards to students of high academic calibre from Palestine.
Eligibility: Open to candidates who have obtained or are about to obtain the equivalent of a United Kingdom First Class or Second Class (Honours) Degree. Candidates must be nationals of Palestine.
Level of Study: Postgraduate.
Type: Scholarship.
Value: Academic fees, living expenses, books, equipment, arrival and departure allowance, economy return airfares and the production of a dissertation.
Length of Study: One year.
Frequency: Annual.
Study Establishment: The University of Leeds.
Country of Study: United Kingdom.
No. of awards offered: Three.
Application Procedure: Applicants must contact the Institute for Politics and International Studies at the University of Leeds.
Closing Date: May 31st.
Funding: Private.
No. of awards given last year: None.
No. of applicants last year: Not known.

For further information contact:

The Director
Institute for Politics & International Studies
ESS Building
University of Leeds, Leeds, West Yorkshire, LS2 9JT, England

Hong Kong Arts Development Council FCO Chevening-Leeds University Scholarships

Subjects: Courses relating to the performing and studio arts, art gallery and museum studies, social history and theory of art, art history, sculpture studies, feminist theory and practice in the visual arts, theatre studies, music, film music studies, music and liturgy, arts education or performance studies.
Purpose: To provide awards to students of high academic calibre from Hong Kong.
Eligibility: Open to candidates who have obtained or are about to obtain the equivalent of a United Kingdom First Class or Second Class (Honours) Degree in a relevant subject. Candidates must be permanent residents of Hong Kong.
Level of Study: Postgraduate.
Type: Scholarship.
Value: Academic fees, living expenses, books, equipment, arrival and departure allowance, economy return airfares and the production of a dissertation.

Length of Study: One year.
Frequency: Annual.
Study Establishment: The University of Leeds.
Country of Study: United Kingdom.
No. of awards offered: Four.
Application Procedure: Applicants must complete an application form, available from the Hong Kong Arts Development Council.
Closing Date: Please contact the organisation.
Funding: Government, Private.
No. of awards given last year: Two.
No. of applicants last year: Not known.

For further information contact:

HKADC Arts Scholarship
Hong Kong Arts Development Council
11F Soundwill Plaza
38 Russell Street
Causeway, Hong Kong

International Fee Bursaries (India)

Subjects: Information systems, distributed multimedia systems, international communications or communications studies.
Purpose: To provide postgraduate scholarships to Indian students of high academic calibre.
Eligibility: Open to candidates who have obtained, or be about to obtain, a United Kingdom First Class Degree, good Second Class Degree or equivalent. Candidates must be nationals of India.
Level of Study: Postgraduate.
Type: Scholarship.
Value: UK £4,000 towards the cost of the overseas fee.
Length of Study: One year.
Frequency: Annual.
Study Establishment: The University of Leeds.
Country of Study: United Kingdom.
No. of awards offered: Two, one in computing and one in communication studies or international communications.
Application Procedure: Applicants must address a letter of application to the relevant department clearly stating that the applicant wishes to be considered for the scholarship. Applications should include a postgraduate taught study application form, references, full academic transcripts and details of English language qualifications.
Closing Date: May 31st.

Jordan-Leeds University-Chevening Scholarship

Subjects: Courses within the science or engineering areas.
Purpose: For study on a one year taught Master's programme.
Eligibility: Candidates must have obtained, or be about to obtain, a United Kingdom First Class or Upper Second Class (Honours) Degree or similar standard. Candidates must also be nationals of Jordan.
Level of Study: Postgraduate.
Type: Scholarship.
Value: Academic fees and some maintenance.
Length of Study: One year.
Frequency: Annual.
Study Establishment: The University of Leeds.
Country of Study: United Kingdom.
No. of awards offered: One.
Application Procedure: Applicants must complete an application form from the British Council in Jordan and have been accepted on to a taught course.
Closing Date: To be announced.
Funding: Government, Private.
No. of awards given last year: One.

For further information contact:

British Council
First Circle
Jebel Amman
Post Office Box 634, Amman, 11118, Jordan
Contact: Ms Hind Samman

Kulika-Leeds University FCO Chevening Scholarships

Subjects: All subjects.
Purpose: To provide postgraduate scholarships to students of a high academic calibre.
Eligibility: Open to candidates who have obtained a United Kingdom First or Second Class Degree or equivalent. Candidates must be nationals of Uganda.
Level of Study: Postgraduate.
Type: Scholarship.
Value: To cover academic fees and living expenses, books equipment, arrival and departure allowance, economy return airfares and the production of a dissertation.
Length of Study: One year.
Frequency: Annual.
Study Establishment: The University of Leeds.
Country of Study: United Kingdom.
No. of awards offered: Three.
Application Procedure: Applicants must apply via application form after acceptance on to a taught course. Application forms for the scholarship are available from the British Council in Kampala.
Closing Date: Approx. mid January.
Funding: Government, Private.
No. of awards given last year: Three.

For further information contact:

British Council in Uganda
IPS Building
Parliament Avenue
PO Box 7070, Kampala, Uganda

Tetley and Lupton Scholarships for Overseas Students

Subjects: All subjects.
Purpose: To provide awards to overseas students of high academic calibre.
Eligibility: Open to candidates liable to pay tuition fees for Master's degrees and research degrees at the full cost rate for overseas students. Applicants must be of a high academic standard.
Level of Study: Doctorate, Postgraduate.
Type: Scholarship.
Value: UK £3,000 per year to be credited towards academic fees.
Length of Study: One year, may be renewed for second or third year according to duration of course. It may also be held concurrently with other awards except those providing full payment of fees.
Frequency: Annual.
Study Establishment: The University of Leeds.
Country of Study: United Kingdom.
No. of awards offered: Up to 64.
Application Procedure: Applicants must apply for a course and then apply for a Scholarship. Research candidates need to apply concurrently with the national Overseas Research Student competition.
Closing Date: Postgraduates are required to submit applications by March 1st and research postgraduates by March 30th.
Funding: Private.
No. of awards given last year: 57.
No. of applicants last year: Unknown.

University of Leeds International Fee Bursaries (Vietnam)

Subjects: Development studies, international political economy, international studies or international resources.
Purpose: To provide scholarships to Vietnamese students of high academic calibre.
Eligibility: Applicants must already hold a degree of equivalent standard to a good Second Class (Honours) Degree. An adequate standard of English is also required. Applicants must be nationals of Vietnam.
Level of Study: Postgraduate.
Type: Scholarship.

Value: Academic fees, living expenses, books, equipment, arrival and departure allowance, economy return airfares and the production of a dissertation.
Length of Study: One year.
Frequency: Annual.
Study Establishment: The University of Leeds.
Country of Study: United Kingdom.
No. of awards offered: One.
Application Procedure: Applicants must address a letter of application to the Institute for Politics and International Studies.
Closing Date: June 14th.
Funding: Private.
No. of awards given last year: One.

For further information contact:

Institute for Politics & International Studies
University of Leeds, Leeds, West Yorkshire, LS2 9JT, England
Contact: Mr C Wise

University of Leeds International Fee Bursary (Vietnam)

Subjects: Information systems or multimedia systems.
Purpose: To provide scholarships to students of high academic calibre from Vietnam.
Eligibility: Applicants must already hold a degree of equivalent standard to a good Second Class (Honours) Degree. An adequate standard of English is also required. Applicants must be nationals of Vietnam.
Level of Study: Postgraduate.
Type: Scholarship.
Value: Academic fees, living expenses, books, equipment, arrival and departure allowance, economy return airfares and the production of a dissertation.
Length of Study: One year.
Frequency: Annual.
Study Establishment: The University of Leeds.
Country of Study: United Kingdom.
No. of awards offered: One.
Application Procedure: Applicants must make an application in letter form to the Taught Postgraduate Secretary in the School of Computing.
Closing Date: June 14th.
Funding: Private.
No. of awards given last year: One.

For further information contact:

Taught Postgraduate Secretary
The School of Computing
University of Leeds, Leeds, West Yorkshire, LS2 9JT, England

University of Leeds International Fee Bursary (Vietnam)

Subjects: Accounting, finance, economics or human resource management.
Purpose: To provide scholarships to students of high academic calibre from Vietnam who wish to study in the Business School.
Eligibility: Applicants must already hold a degree of equivalent standard to a good Second Class (Honours) Degree. An adequate standard of English is also required. Applicants must be nationals of Vietnam.
Level of Study: Postgraduate.
Type: Scholarship.
Value: Academic fees, living expenses, books, equipment, arrival and departure allowance, economy return airfares and the production of a dissertation.
Length of Study: One year.
Frequency: Annual.
Study Establishment: The University of Leeds.
Country of Study: United Kingdom.
No. of awards offered: Two.
Application Procedure: Applicants must make an application in letter form to the Taught Postgraduate Secretary at Leeds University Business School.
Closing Date: June 14th.

Funding: Private.
No. of awards given last year: One.

For further information contact:

Taught Postgraduate Secretary
Leeds University Business School
University of Leeds, Leeds, West Yorkshire, LS2 9JT, England

University of Leeds Overseas Research Students Awards Scheme - National Competition

Subjects: All subjects.
Purpose: To provide postgraduate scholarships for international students of high calibre.
Eligibility: Applicants must already hold a degree of equivalent standard to a good United Kingdom Second Class (Honours) Degree. An adequate standard of English is required.
Level of Study: Doctorate, Postgraduate.
Type: Scholarship.
Value: Academic fees, living expenses, books, equipment, arrival and departure allowance, economy return airfares and the production of a dissertation.
Length of Study: One year.
Frequency: Annual.
Study Establishment: The University of Leeds.
Country of Study: United Kingdom.
Application Procedure: Applicants must complete an application form, available from the Research Degrees and Scholarships Office at the University of Leeds.
Closing Date: March 30th.
Funding: Government.
No. of awards given last year: 40.
No. of applicants last year: 201.

For further information contact:

The Research Degrees & Scholarships Office
The University of Leeds, Leeds, West Yorkshire, LS2 9JT, England

University of Leeds Shared Scholarship Scheme

Subjects: All subjects.
Purpose: To provide postgraduate scholarships to students of high academic calibre from developing commonwealth countries.
Eligibility: Applicants must already hold a degree of equivalent standard to a good United Kingdom Second Class (Honours) Degree. An adequate standard of English is also required. Candidates must be nationals of a developing commonwealth country.
Level of Study: Postgraduate.
Type: Scholarship.
Value: Academic fees, living expenses, books, equipment, arrival and departure allowance, economy return airfares and the production of a dissertation.
Length of Study: One year.
Frequency: Annual.
Study Establishment: The University of Leeds.
Country of Study: United Kingdom.
Application Procedure: Applicants must complete an application form, available from the Research Degrees and Scholarships Office at the University of Leeds.
Closing Date: Please contact the organisation.
No. of awards given last year: Seven.
No. of applicants last year: 241.

For further information contact:

Research Degrees & Scholarships Office
The University of Leeds, Leeds, West Yorkshire, LS2 9JT, England

UNIVERSITY OF LOUISIANA AT MONROE

The College of Business Administration
ULM CBA
700 University Avenue, Monroe, LA, 71209-1110, United States of America
Tel: (1) 318 342 1100
Fax: (1) 318 342 1101
Email: dbasexton@ulm.edu
Contact: Mrs Jackie W O'Neal, MBA Director

University of Louisiana at Monroe Graduate Assistantships
Subjects: MBA.
Eligibility: Open to full-time applicants who have been accepted for admission to the MBA programme.
Level of Study: Graduate.
Type: Assistantship.
Value: Full tuition waiver and a stipend of up to US$2,500 per semester.
Study Establishment: The University of Louisiana at Monroe.
Country of Study: United States of America.
Application Procedure: Applicants must submit an application form and three letters of recommendation. Forms are available by phone, fax and email from the organisation.
Funding: Government.
Additional Information: Graduate assistants must work 20 hours per week in a variety of research, educational and administrative activities.

UNIVERSITY OF MANCHESTER

Oxford Road, Manchester, M13 9PL, England
Tel: (44) 161 275 2736
Fax: (44) 161 275 2445
Email: sara.duncalf@man.ac.uk
www: http://www.man.ac.uk
Contact: Mr Nick Church, Senior Administrative Assistant

The University of Manchester is an international provider of quality research and graduate education across a variety of disciplines and has a wide range of good support facilities.

Frederick Craven Moore Awards
Subjects: Biological sciences and medicine.
Purpose: To support postgraduate research.
Eligibility: Open to graduates of any approved university, or other suitably qualified persons, who can furnish satisfactory evidence of their qualifications to pursue research in clinical medicine.
Level of Study: Doctorate, Postgraduate.
Type: Scholarships and fellowships.
Value: The value of the Scholarship varies, but it is normally not less than the annual value of a state or research council postgraduate award in medicine. The value of the fellowship is determined on an individual basis in accordance with the qualifications and experience of the Fellow.
Length of Study: One year. The scholarships are renewable for up to a maximum of two additional years.
Frequency: Annual, if funds are available.
Study Establishment: Manchester University.
Country of Study: United Kingdom.
No. of awards offered: Varies.
Application Procedure: Applicants must contact the Graduate School of Science, Engineering and Medicine.
Closing Date: May 1st.

University of Manchester Research Studentships and Scholarships
Subjects: Any area of study within the purview of the Graduate Schools of Arts including social sciences, education, science, engineering, biological sciences, medicine, dentistry, nursing and pharmacy.
Purpose: To support postgraduate research and provide funding for high quality United Kingdom, European and overseas graduates wishing to study for a PhD.
Eligibility: Open to graduates of any approved university, or other suitably qualified persons, who can furnish satisfactory evidence of their qualifications to pursue research. Applicants must hold at least an Upper Second Class Degree to be eligible. Applicants must have applied and been accepted onto a programme of study before they can be considered.
Level of Study: Doctorate, Postgraduate.
Type: Studentship and scholarship.
Value: Varies. Some full studentships including maintenance and United Kingdom fees. Part scholarships are also available.
Length of Study: Normally three years.
Frequency: Annual.
Study Establishment: Manchester University.
Country of Study: United Kingdom.
No. of awards offered: Up to 30.
Application Procedure: Applicants must complete an application form. Further information is available on request from the Research and Graduate Support Unit.
Closing Date: April 19th.
No. of awards given last year: Approx. 50.
No. of applicants last year: Approx. 900.

UNIVERSITY OF MANITOBA

Faculty of Graduate Studies
500 University Centre, Winnipeg, MB, R3T 2N2, Canada
Tel: (1) 204 474 9836
Fax: (1) 204 474 7553
Email: ilse_krentz@umanitoba.ca
www: http://www.umanitoba.ca/faculties/graduate_studies/awards
Contact: Awards Officer

The Faculty of Graduate Studies at the University of Manitoba offers 120 graduate programmes leading to diplomas, Master's and PhD degrees. Their graduate programmes have a long and distinguished tradition in teaching and cutting edge research. The 120 programmes are delivered in 20 faculties. These faculties provide for over 2,800 Canadian and international students, a rich and varied choice of graduate programmes, including the Interdisciplinary Program (IDP) administered by the Faculty of Graduate Studies. IDP students are provided with an opportunity to tailor their own programme under the guidance of an advisory committee.

University of Manitoba Graduate Fellowships
Subjects: Any discipline taught at graduate level at the university.
Purpose: To reward academic excellence.
Eligibility: At the time of application, students do not need to have been accepted by the department or faculty, but at the time of taking up the award must be regular full-time graduate students who have been admitted to and registered in advanced degree programmes eg. Master's or PhD, but not pre-Master's in any field of study or faculty of the University of Manitoba. Students beyond the second year in the Master's programme or beyond the fourth year in the PhD programme are not eligible to apply for or hold a University of Manitoba Graduate Fellowship. Part-time PhD students enrolled for a four year course will be eligible for two years of funding.
Level of Study: Doctorate, Postgraduate.
Type: Fellowship.
Value: Canadian $16,000 for the PhD and canadian $10,000 for the Master's.
Frequency: Annual.

Study Establishment: The University of Manitoba.

Country of Study: Canada.

No. of awards offered: 80-90.

Application Procedure: Applicants must request application forms from the department to which they are applying at the University of Manitoba and must be returned to that department. Forms are available from the beginning of December and can be requested either by phoning or writing or from the website.

Closing Date: February 15th, with earlier departmental deadlines.

Contributor: The University of Manitoba and the government of Manitoba.

UNIVERSITY OF MELBOURNE

Melbourne Scholarships Office, VIC, 3010, Australia

Tel: (61) 3 8344 8747

Fax: (61) 3 9349 1740

Email: pg-schools@unimelb.edu.au

www: http://www.services.unimelb.edu.au

Contact: Ms Kris Day, Manager, Postgraduate Scholarships

The University of Melbourne has a long and distinguished tradition of excellence in teaching and research. It is the leading research institution in Australia and enjoys a reputation for the high quality of its research programmes, consistently winning the largest share of national competitive research funding.

Melbourne Research Scholarships

Subjects: All subjects offered by the university.

Purpose: To enable graduates to undertake research in any discipline.

Eligibility: Open to candidates from Australia and foreign countries.

Level of Study: Doctorate, Postgraduate, Research.

Type: Scholarship.

Value: Australian $17,067 per year, payable fortnightly.

Length of Study: Up to two years at the Master's level and up to three years at the PhD level. A six month extension is possible at the PhD level.

Frequency: Annual.

Study Establishment: The University of Melbourne.

Country of Study: Australia.

No. of awards offered: 210 of which up to 83 may be awarded to international students.

Application Procedure: Applicants must complete an application form. Please contact the Melbourne Scholarships Office.

Closing Date: October 31st for Australian citizens and residents in the main selection round, and September 15th for international students. A small number of scholarships may be available throughout the year subject to availability.

Funding: Government.

Contributor: Scholarship fund.

No. of awards given last year: 232.

No. of applicants last year: 1,321.

Additional Information: Further information is available from the website.

For further information contact:

Melbourne Scholarships Office
John Smyth Building
University of Melbourne, Parkville, VIC, 3010, Australia

UNIVERSITY OF MICHIGAN

Mike & Mary Wallace House
620 Oxford Road, Ann Arbor, MI, 48104, United States of America

Tel: (1) 734 998 7666

Fax: (1) 734 998 7979

Email: drath@umich.edu

www: http://www.umich.edu/~mjfellow

Contact: Director

Michigan Journalism Fellows

Subjects: Journalism.

Purpose: To provide mid-career professionals with the opportunity to indulge in a sabbatical of study and reflection. The fellowship is designed to broaden perspectives, nurture intellectual growth and inspire personal transformation. To this end, Fellows must devise a plan of study and select classes from the full range of courses offered at the University of Michigan.

Eligibility: Open to full-time print or broadcast journalists, including freelancers, who have a minimum of five years' experience. Applicants must be United States citizens.

Level of Study: Professional development.

Type: Fellowship.

Value: US$45,000 plus tuition, paid directly to the University.

Length of Study: September-April.

Frequency: Annual.

Study Establishment: The University of Michigan.

Country of Study: United States of America.

No. of awards offered: 12.

Application Procedure: Applicants must write for details.

Closing Date: February 1st.

Additional Information: Further information is available on request.

UNIVERSITY OF MICHIGAN BUSINESS SCHOOL

701 Tappan Street
Room 2260, Ann Arbor, MI, 48109-1234, United States of America

Tel: (1) 734 763 5796

Fax: (1) 734 763 7804

Email: umbusmba@umich.edu

www: http://www.bus.umich.edu

Contact: MBA Admissions Officer

University of Michigan Business School International Student Scholarships

Subjects: MBA.

Eligibility: All admitted international applicants are eligible for these scholarships, which are merit-based.

Level of Study: MBA.

Type: Scholarship.

Value: Varies, from partial to full tuition.

Study Establishment: The University of Michigan Business School.

Country of Study: United States of America.

Application Procedure: Applicants must apply to the MBA in the usual way, no separate application is required.

Closing Date: Please contact the organisation.

Additional Information: Students are usually informed of their financial award in May.

UNIVERSITY OF MINNESOTA, TWIN CITIES

Department of Sociology
1014A Social Sciences Building
Life Course Centre
267-19 Avenue S, Minneapolis, MN, 55455, United States of America

Tel: (1) 612 624 4064

Fax: (1) 612 624 7020

Email: morti002@atlas.socsci.umn.edu

www: http://www.soc.umn.edu

Contact: Dr Jeylan R Mortimer

The Life Course Centre, Department of Sociology, University of Minnesota, supports scholarly enquiry related to the life course. Through research, seminars and courses offered by Centre faculty and visiting scholars, the Centre provides an intellectual forum that enriches the research and educational activities of a broad range of faculty and students, as research assistants, in the department of sociology, as well as in other units of the University.

National Research Service Award Mental Health and Adjustment in the Life Course

Subjects: Topics include early work experience, mental health and the transition to adulthood, the joint development of autonomy and intimacy, the sources of competence and resilience in the face of adversity, physical and relational aggression, the life course consequences of victimisation, cognitive and emotional factors in decision making in criminal, delinquent and work behaviour, perceptions of criminal sanctions and their efficacy in inhibiting offending, female inmates' adaptations to prison life as a function of prior life experience or trajectories of deviance and reintegration.

Purpose: To provide opportunities for students to carry out longitudinal research into the psycho-social determinants of mental health and adjustment, with emphasis on childhood, adolescence, and the transition to adulthood.

Eligibility: Open to United States citizens or residents. Postdoctoral candidates must have received a PhD in a social science discipline or an equivalent degree such as an MD, public health or nursing degree.

Level of Study: Postdoctorate, Predoctorate.

Type: Fellowship.

Value: Stipend in accordance with NRSA guidelines, providing tuition, fees and medical insurance.

Length of Study: A maximum of two years. This award is subject to review at the end of the first year.

Frequency: Every two years.

Study Establishment: The University of Minnesota.

Country of Study: United States of America.

No. of awards offered: Four: three predoctoral and one postdoctoral.

Application Procedure: Applicants must provide a letter describing current research interests, a complete curriculum vitae, university transcript, three letters of recommendation and samples of written work.

Closing Date: November 1st, applications will be accepted until the position is filled.

Funding: Government.

Contributor: The National Institute of Mental Health.

Additional Information: The University of Minnesota is committed to the policy that all persons shall have equal access to its programmes, facilities and employment without regard to race, colour, creed, religion, national origin, sex, age, marital status, disability, public assistance status or sexual orientation.

UNIVERSITY OF NEBRASKA AT OMAHA (UNO)

Business Adminstration
Office of Graduate Studies
Eppley Administration Building
Room 204, Omaha, NE, 68182, United States of America

Tel: (1) 402 554 2341

Email: mba@unomaha.edu

www: http://mba.unomaha.edu

Contact: MBA Admissions Officer

The University of Nebraska at Omaha's College of Business Administration offers a dynamic, challenging Master's programme designed to help students acquire the knowledge, perspective and skills necessary for success in the marketplace of today and tomorrow. The goal of the programme is to develop leaders who have the ability to incorporate change, use information technology to resolve problems and make sound business decisions. The curriculum focuses on results with an emphasis on how to excel in a rapidly changing world.

UNO Graduate Assistantships

Subjects: All subjects.

Eligibility: The graduate assistantships are available for qualified students who are enrolled in a graduate degree programme.

Level of Study: Graduate, MBA.

Type: Assistantship.

Value: A Graduate Assistantship entitles the holder to a waiver of tuition costs up to 12 hours of graduate credit per semester.

Study Establishment: The University of Nebraska at Omaha.

Country of Study: United States of America.

Application Procedure: Applicants must make enquiries in their department about the availability of assistantships, the procedures for applying, the details of when the application and supporting credentials should be on file in the department or school for consideration.

Closing Date: June 1st.

No. of awards given last year: Four.

No. of applicants last year: 25.

UNIVERSITY OF NEVADA, LAS VEGAS

School of Business
MBA Programme
4505 Maryland Parkway
Box 456031, Las Vegas, NV, 89154-6031, United States of America

Tel: (1) 702 895 3655

Email: cobmba@ccmail.nevada.edu

www: http://www.unlv.edu

Contact: Ms Lisa R Davis, Recruitment Director

UNLV Alumni Association Graduate Scholarships

Subjects: All subjects.

Purpose: To reward outstanding graduate students.

Eligibility: Applicants must have completed at least 12 credits of graduate study at UNLV, have minimum undergraduate and graduate grade point average of 3.5 and enrol for six or more graduate credits in each semester of the scholarship year.

Level of Study: Graduate, MBA.

Type: Scholarship.

Value: US$1,000.

Length of Study: One year.

Frequency: Annual.

Study Establishment: The University of Nevada, Las Vegas.

Country of Study: United States of America.

No. of awards offered: Three.

Application Procedure: Applicants must telephone (1) 702 895 3320 or write to the Graduate College for application forms or further information.

Closing Date: March 1st.

UNLV Graduate Assistantships

Subjects: All subjects.
Purpose: To offer financial assistance and support to students admitted to any graduate degree programme.
Eligibility: The graduate assistantship positions are available on a competitive basis to students who have already been admitted to any graduate degree programme.
Level of Study: Graduate, MBA.
Type: Assistantship.
Value: A nine month stipend of US$8,500 for Master's level assistantships plus tuition and fee waivers.
Length of Study: One year.
Frequency: Annual.
Study Establishment: The University of Nevada, Las Vegas.
Country of Study: United States of America.
No. of awards offered: Varies.
Application Procedure: Applicants must send applications and all supporting materials to the dean of the graduate college no later than March 1st preceding the Autumn semester in which an assistantship is sought. Applications may be accepted after this date in the event of an unexpected opening for the Autumn semester. On some rare occasions an assistantship is available for the Spring semester.
Closing Date: March 1st or November 1st for the Spring assistantship.
Additional Information: Graduate assistants must carry a minimum of six semester hours of credit and are expected to spend 20 hours per week on departmental duties such as instruction or research.

UNLV James F Adams/GSA Scholarship

Subjects: All subjects.
Purpose: To recognise academic achievement of graduate students.
Eligibility: Applicants must have completed at least 12 credits of graduate study at UNLV, have a minimum undergraduate and graduate grade point average of 3.5 and enrol for six or more credits in each semester of the scholarship year.
Level of Study: Graduate, MBA.
Type: Scholarship.
Value: US$1,000.
Length of Study: Varies.
Frequency: Annual.
Study Establishment: The University of Nevada, Las Vegas.
Country of Study: United States of America.
No. of awards offered: Six.
Application Procedure: Applicants must telephone (1) 702 895 3320 or write to the Graduate College for application forms or further information.
Closing Date: March 1st.

UNIVERSITY OF NEW BRUNSWICK FREDERICTON

School of Graduate Studies
PO Box 4400
Station A, Fredericton, NB, E3B 5A3, Canada
Tel: (1) 506 453 4766
Fax: (1) 506 453 3561
Email: kivey@unb.ca
www: http://www.unb.ca
Contact: Ms Liz Lemon-Mitchell, Information/Office Manager

The MBA Programme in the Faculty of Administration at the University of New Brunswick Fredericton provides a balanced approach to the study of management problems. It is designed to educate people for positions as middle or senior level managers. The emphasis is on both problem solving and decision making skills.

UNBF Atkinson Prize in Accounting

Subjects: MBA.

Eligibility: Applicants must have excellent academic performance and an aptitude for accounting.
Level of Study: MBA.
Type: Prize.
Value: Canadian $500.
Frequency: Annual.
Study Establishment: The University of New Brunswick, Fredericton.
Country of Study: Canada.
No. of awards offered: One.
Application Procedure: Applicants must contact the University.
Funding: Private.

UNBF Brydone Deblois Millidge Memorial Scholarship

Subjects: MBA.
Purpose: To recognise and reward an excellent MBA student.
Eligibility: Applicants must have excellent academic records, be a second year full-time student and display financial need.
Level of Study: MBA.
Type: One scholarship.
Value: Approx. canadian $1,500.
Length of Study: Please contact the University.
Frequency: Annual.
Study Establishment: The University of New Brunswick, Fredericton.
Country of Study: Canada.
No. of awards offered: One.
Application Procedure: Applicants must contact the University.
Closing Date: Please contact the University.
Funding: Private.

UNBF E D Maher Graduate Student Prize

Subjects: MBA.
Purpose: To recognise and reward an excellent MBA student.
Eligibility: Applicants must have the highest CGPA on graduate work completed during the programme and be a full-time student during their final year.
Level of Study: MBA.
Type: Prize.
Value: A wall plaque.
Frequency: Annual.
Study Establishment: The University of New Brunswick, Fredericton.
Country of Study: Canada.
No. of awards offered: One.
Application Procedure: Applicants must contact the University.
Funding: Private.

UNBF Frank H Sobey Fund for Excellence Scholarship

Subjects: MBA.
Purpose: To recognise an excellent MBA student.
Eligibility: Applicants must have an outstanding academic performance, full-time status and the first year courses of the MBA programme completed. Extra-curricular and community activities, entrepreneurial interest, employment history and career aspirations are positively considered.
Level of Study: MBA.
Type: Scholarship.
Value: Canadian $6,000.
Frequency: Annual.
Study Establishment: The University of New Brunswick, Fredericton.
Country of Study: Canada.
No. of awards offered: Five.
Application Procedure: Applicants must contact the University.
Funding: Private.

UNBF Graduate Research Assistantships

Subjects: MBA.

Eligibility: Candidates must have excellent academic performances in the first year of their MBA programme and be registered as a full-time student in MBA6996 (Project) or MBA6779 (Thesis).
Level of Study: MBA.
Type: Research grant.
Value: Up to canadian $4,500.
Frequency: Annual.
Study Establishment: The University of New Brunswick, Fredericton.
Country of Study: Canada.
No. of awards offered: Six.
Application Procedure: Applicants must contact the University.
Funding: Government.

UNBF Graduate Teaching Assistantships
Subjects: MBA.
Eligibility: Applicants must have an excellent academic performance in the first year of the MBA programme and be registered as full-time students.
Level of Study: MBA.
Type: Teaching assistantship.
Value: Up to canadian $1,500.
Frequency: Annual.
Study Establishment: The University of New Brunswick, Fredericton.
Country of Study: Canada.
No. of awards offered: Varies.
Application Procedure: Applicants must send a written request to the MBA Office (T332) stating their areas of interest.
Closing Date: Please contact the University.
Funding: Government.

UNBF Merrithew-De Grandpré Prize in Entrepreneurial
Subjects: MBA.
Purpose: To recognise an MBA student with an excellent academic record.
Eligibility: Applicants must be graduates of a New Brunswick High School and have prepared an outstanding business plan in the MBA course 6312 Entrepreneurship and Small Business II.
Level of Study: MBA.
Type: Prize.
Value: Canadian $1,000.
Frequency: Annual.
Study Establishment: The University of New Brunswick, Fredericton.
Country of Study: Canada.
No. of awards offered: One.
Application Procedure: Applicants must contact the University.
Closing Date: Please contact the University.
Funding: Private.
Contributor: Michael Merrithew and Louise de Gradpré.

UNBF Research Assistantships from Research Grant-Holders
Subjects: MBA.
Eligibility: Please contact the organisation for eligibility requirements.
Level of Study: MBA.
Type: Research assistantships.
Value: Varies, but canadian $500 per month is quite common.
Frequency: Annual, if funds are available.
Study Establishment: The University of New Brunswick, Fredericton.
Country of Study: Canada.
No. of awards offered: Varies.
Application Procedure: Applicants must contact the University.

UNBF Singer Graduate Bursary
Subjects: MBA.
Purpose: To recognise an excellent MBA student.

Eligibility: Applicants must have an acceptable academic performance, be a second year full-time student and display financial need.
Level of Study: MBA.
Type: Bursary.
Value: Up to canadian $500.
Length of Study: Please contact the University.
Frequency: Annual.
Study Establishment: The University of New Brunswick, Fredericton.
Country of Study: Canada.
No. of awards offered: One.
Application Procedure: Applicants must contact the University.
Closing Date: Please contact the University.
Funding: Private.

UNBF Summer Internships
Subjects: MBA.
Eligibility: Applicants must be a full-time student between their first and second year of the MBA Programme.
Level of Study: MBA.
Type: Internship.
Value: Up to canadian $4,000.
Length of Study: Please contact the University.
Frequency: Annual.
Study Establishment: The University of New Brunswick, Fredericton.
Country of Study: Canada.
No. of awards offered: Varies.
Application Procedure: Applicants must contact the University.

UNBF Teaching Assistantships (Markers)
Subjects: MBA.
Eligibility: All relevant courses must be completed.
Level of Study: MBA.
Type: Teaching assistantships.
Value: Varies.
Length of Study: Please contact the University.
Frequency: Annual.
Study Establishment: The University of New Brunswick, Fredericton.
Country of Study: Canada.
No. of awards offered: Varies.
Application Procedure: Applications must be made to the individual instructor.
Closing Date: Please contact the University.
Funding: Government.

UNIVERSITY OF NEW ENGLAND (UNE)

Research Grants Office
Research Services, Armidale, NSW, 2351, Australia
Tel: (61) 2 6773 2239
Fax: (61) 2 6773 3543
Email: aharris@metz.une.edu.au
www: http://www.une.edu.au
Contact: Mr Paul McFarland, Manager, Research Office

The University of New England (UNE) is Australia's oldest regional university. UNE has a reputation for quality research with students undertaking research in the arts, education, environmental engineering, health studies, rural science and science. The UNE PhD is over 40 years old and has 550 PhD students currently enrolled.

University of New England Research Scholarships
Subjects: Arts, education, economics, sciences, social science, resource sciences, archaeology, environmental engineering, humanities, geography, animal science, psychology, agricultural or resource economics.

Purpose: To provide assistance toward the completion of a research Master's degree, PhD or EdD.

Eligibility: Open to candidates of any nationality who have at least a First Class (Honours) Bachelor's Degree or equivalent. Candidates from non English speaking countries must successfully pass an English test.

Level of Study: Doctorate, Postgraduate.

Type: Scholarship.

Value: Approx. australian $15,000 per year.

Length of Study: Two years for the Master's degree or for an initial period of three years which may be renewed for six months for the PhD.

Frequency: Annual.

Study Establishment: The University of New England.

Country of Study: Australia.

No. of awards offered: 10.

Application Procedure: Applicants must submit an application form with certified copies of academic transcripts and academic referees. Candidates who are not permanent residents or citizens of Australia must provide evidence of additional financial support of at least australian $10,000.

Closing Date: October 31st.

Funding: Government.

No. of awards given last year: 15.

No. of applicants last year: 150.

Additional Information: The research proposal must be approved by the head of the relevant department. Initial enquiries from overseas students should be directed to the International Students Officer at the University. Further information can be found on the website.

UNIVERSITY OF NEW HAMPSHIRE

The Family Research Laboratory
Department of Sociology
Horton Social Science Center, Durham, NC, 03824, United States of America
Tel: (1) 603 862 2594
Fax: (1) 603 862 1122
Email: murray.straus@unh.edu
www: http://www.unh.edu
Contact: Mr Murray Strauss, Co-Director

The Family Research Laboratory conducts research studies of interest to state and national policy makers and citizens. Studies include a national survey of families and youth, and a recent dating violence awareness survey conducted in two New Hampshire high schools. Staff and faculty members associated with the laboratory give lectures and workshops to professionals and provide information to the public about family violence and related family issues. The Family Violence Research Program, which is part of the laboratory, is the first and only research programme concerned with all aspects of family violence and related phenomena. The laboratory maintains a library of about 2,500 books and sponsors a number of regional and national conferences.

University of New Hampshire Postdoctoral Fellowships For Research on Family Violence

Subjects: Family violence including physical, sexual and psychological maltreatment of children, partners in marital, cohabiting and dating relationships, and maltreatment of the elderly by members of their family.

Purpose: To provide training and experience in research into all aspects of family violence.

Eligibility: Applicants must be citizens or permanent residents of the United States of America.

Level of Study: Postdoctorate.

Type: Fellowship.

Length of Study: One or two years.

Frequency: Annual.

Study Establishment: The Family Research Laboratory at the University of New Hampshire.

Country of Study: United States of America.

No. of awards offered: Four.

Application Procedure: Applicants must send a brief letter, publications and arrange for three letters of recommendation.

Closing Date: Continuous.

Funding: Government.

Contributor: The National Institute of Mental Health.

No. of awards given last year: Four.

No. of applicants last year: 35.

For further information contact:

Family Research Laboratory
University of New Hampshire, Durham, NH, 03824, United States of America
Contact: Ms Victoria Benn

THE UNIVERSITY OF NEWCASTLE

Graduate School of Business, Callaghan, NSW, 2308, Australia
Tel: (61) 2 4921 6537
Fax: (61) 2 4921 6908
Contact: Research Branch Director

The University of Newcastle is one of Australia's top ten research universities. There are 12 special research centres, over 50 research programmes of international standing and 900 research candidates spread over 10 faculties which include architecture, building and design, arts and social science, economics and commerce, education, engineering, law, medicine and health sciences, music, nursing, science and mathematics.

Australian Government Postgraduate Awards

Subjects: All academic disciplines.

Purpose: To support students undertaking full-time higher research degree programmes.

Eligibility: Open to Australian citizens and permanent residents who have lived in Australia for one year prior to application. Applicants must have completed four years of full-time undergraduate study and gained a First Class Honours Degree or equivalent award.

Level of Study: Doctorate, Postgraduate.

Type: Research grant and research scholarship.

Value: A living allowance of approximately australian $16,000 per year. The allowance is tax exempt and index linked. Allowances for relocation and thesis production are available as are exemption of HECS payments.

Length of Study: Two years full-time study for research Master's candidates, or three years full-time for PhD candidates.

Frequency: Annual.

Study Establishment: Australian universities.

Country of Study: Australia.

No. of awards offered: Approx. 40.

Application Procedure: Applicants must complete an application form.

Closing Date: October 31st.

Funding: Government.

THE UNIVERSITY OF NOTTINGHAM

Graduate School
University Park, Nottingham, Nottinghamshire, NG7 2RD, England
Tel: (44) 115 951 4664
Fax: (44) 115 951 4668
Email: postgraduate-enquiries@nottingham.ac.uk
www: http://www.nottingham.ac.uk/gradschool
Contact: Ms Jane Watson, Senior Assistant Registrar

The University of Nottingham is a community of students and staff dedicated to bringing out the best in all of its members. It aims to provide the finest possible environment for teaching, learning and research and has a well known record of success.

University of Nottingham Research Scholarships

Subjects: All subjects offered by the University.
Purpose: To promote research.
Eligibility: Open to graduates of all nationalities. The Scholarships are allocated to schools or institutes, to whom students should apply for further information.
Level of Study: Postgraduate, Predoctorate.
Type: Scholarship.
Value: UK £8,000 per year maintenance and payment of fees at home or European Union rate.
Length of Study: Three years leading to PhD submission given adequate academic progress.
Frequency: Annual.
Study Establishment: The University of Nottingham.
Country of Study: United Kingdom.
No. of awards offered: More than 75.
Application Procedure: Applicants must contact the individual schools for information.
Closing Date: Please contact the individual schools for information.
Contributor: The University of Nottingham.
No. of awards given last year: 117.
Additional Information: The scholarships are awarded internally to the schools and/or institutes that bid for them. It is then up to those schools receiving awards to advertise the scholarship and set an application deadline.

University of Nottingham Weston Scholarships

Subjects: Any subject from a prescribed list.
Purpose: To provide promising students with home and European Union fees.
Eligibility: There are no eligibility restrictions.
Level of Study: Postgraduate.
Type: Studentship.
Value: Home or European Union fees only.
Length of Study: Usually one year full-time or the part-time equivalent.
Frequency: Annual.
Study Establishment: The University of Nottingham.
Country of Study: United Kingdom.
No. of awards offered: Approx. four.
Application Procedure: Applicants must submit applications to the individual schools and should contact them for details.
Closing Date: Applications are accepted at any time.
No. of awards given last year: 14.
Additional Information: The scholarships are awarded internally to the schools and/or institutes that bid for them. It is then up to those schools receiving awards to advertise the scholarship and set an application deadline.

UNIVERSITY OF OTAGO

Scholarships Office
PO Box 56, Dunedin, New Zealand
Tel: (64) 3 479 1100 ext. 5291
Fax: (64) 3 479 8367
Email: pgschols@nimrodel.otago.ac.nz
www: http://www.otago.ac.nz
Contact: Mrs Margaret Sykes, Postgraduate Administrator

The University of Otago has over 17,000 students, most of whom are based at the Dunedin campus, which is the oldest campus in New Zealand. The University has four divisions: the Division of Commerce (School of Business), the Division of Health Sciences, the Division of Humanities and the Division of Science. The University has a School of Medicine in Christchurch and Wellington, and a campus in Auckland.

University of Otago Dr Sulaiman Daud 125th Jubilee International Postgraduate

Subjects: All subjects.
Purpose: To fund research towards a PhD or Master's degree.
Eligibility: Open to citizens of Malaysia with a minimum qualification of a First Class Honours Degree.
Level of Study: Doctorate, Postgraduate.
Type: Scholarship.
Value: New zealand $20,000 per year for doctoral study and new zealand $13,000 per year for Master's study.
Length of Study: Three years for doctoral study and two years for Master's study.
Frequency: Annual.
Study Establishment: The University of Otago.
Country of Study: New Zealand.
No. of awards offered: One.
Application Procedure: Applicants must complete an application form, available from the website.
Closing Date: June 30th.

University of Otago International Scholarships

Subjects: All subjects.
Purpose: To assist with funding for study at Otago.
Eligibility: Open to all international applicants intending to study at the University of Otago.
Level of Study: Doctorate, Graduate.
Type: Scholarship.
Value: Master's scholarships US$7,500 per year for up to two years and PhD scholarships US$12,500 per year for three years.
Length of Study: Two years for Master's study and three for doctoral study.
Frequency: Annual.
Study Establishment: The University of Otago.
Country of Study: New Zealand.
No. of awards offered: Four Master's scholarships and four PhD scholarships.
Application Procedure: Applicants must complete the application for International study at the University of Otago, available from the website.
Closing Date: October 15th.

University of Otago Masters Awards

Subjects: All subjects.
Purpose: To fund research towards a Master's degree.
Eligibility: Open to permanent residents or citizens of New Zealand or Australia, and to citizens of France and Germany with a minimum qualification of a First Class Honours Degree who are entering the thesis year of a Master's degree.
Level of Study: Postgraduate.
Type: Scholarship.
Value: New zealand $13,000 per year.
Length of Study: One year.
Frequency: Annual.
Study Establishment: The University of Otago.

Country of Study: New Zealand.
No. of awards offered: Between 40-50.
Application Procedure: Applicants must complete an application form, available from the website.
Closing Date: October 1st.

University of Otago PhD Scholarships

Subjects: All subjects.
Purpose: To fund research towards a PhD degree.
Eligibility: Open to permanent residents or citizens of New Zealand or Australia and to citizens of France and Germany with a minimum qualification of a First Class Honours Degree.
Level of Study: Doctorate.
Type: Scholarship.
Value: New zealand $20,000.
Length of Study: Three years.
Frequency: Annual.
Study Establishment: The University of Otago.
Country of Study: New Zealand.
No. of awards offered: Between 40-50.
Application Procedure: Applicants must complete an application form, available from the website.
Closing Date: October 1st.

University of Otago Prestigious PhD Scholarships

Subjects: All subjects.
Purpose: To fund research towards a PhD degree.
Eligibility: Open to permanent residents or citizens of New Zealand or Australia, and to citizens of France and Germany with a minimum qualification of a First Class Honours Degree.
Level of Study: Doctorate.
Type: Scholarship.
Value: New zealand $25,000.
Length of Study: Three years.
Frequency: Annual.
Study Establishment: The University of Otago.
Country of Study: New Zealand.
No. of awards offered: 10.
Application Procedure: Applicants must complete an application form, available from the website.
Closing Date: October 1st.

UNIVERSITY OF OXFORD

University Offices
Wellington Square, Oxford, Oxfordshire, OX1 2JD, England
Tel: (44) 1865 270000
Fax: (44) 1865 270708
www: http://www.ox.ac.uk
Contact: Ms Clare Woodcock, Information Officer

Artal Scholarships

Subjects: Law and political science.
Purpose: To provide assistance for those studying a MPhil degree or for the MJuris degree.
Eligibility: Open to citizens of Belgium.
Level of Study: Postgraduate.
Type: Scholarship.
Value: UK £6,000.
Study Establishment: The University of Oxford.
Country of Study: United Kingdom.
No. of awards offered: Up to four.
Application Procedure: Applicants must complete an application form.
Closing Date: April 1st.
Additional Information: Please contact the International Office for further information.

Balliol College Dervorguilla Scholarship

Subjects: Arts or sciences.
Eligibility: Eligible to overseas students only.
Level of Study: Postgraduate.
Type: Scholarship.
Value: College and university fees and a full maintenance grant.
Length of Study: Two years, with a possibility of renewal for a third year.
Frequency: Annual.
Study Establishment: Balliol College, the University of Oxford.
Country of Study: United Kingdom.
No. of awards offered: Two, one in arts and one in science.
Application Procedure: Applicants must write for details.
Closing Date: January 31st.
Funding: Private.

For further information contact:

Tutor for Graduate Admissions
Balliol College, Oxford, Oxfordshire, OX1 3BJ, England

Balliol College Domus Graduate Scholarships

Subjects: All subjects.
Eligibility: Overseas students only.
Type: Scholarship.
Value: UK £2,000.
Length of Study: Two years, with a possibility of renewal for a third year.
Frequency: Annual.
Study Establishment: The University of Oxford.
Country of Study: United Kingdom.
No. of awards offered: Varies.

For further information contact:

Tutor for Graduate Admissions
Balliol College, Oxford, Oxfordshire, OX1 3BJ, England

Balliol College Marvin Bower Scholarship

Subjects: International relations, politics or economics.
Eligibility: Open to home and European students only.
Type: Scholarship.
Value: UK £2,000.
Length of Study: Two years, with a possibility of renewal for a third year.
Country of Study: United Kingdom.
No. of awards offered: One.
Closing Date: Please contact the College.

For further information contact:

Tutor for Graduate Admissions
Balliol College, Oxford, Oxfordshire, OX1 3BJ, England

Balliol College Snell Exhibition

Subjects: All subjects.
Eligibility: Open to graduates from Glasgow University only.
Level of Study: Graduate, Postgraduate.
Type: Exhibition.
Value: UK £1,000 per year.
Length of Study: Three years.
Study Establishment: Balliol College, the University of Oxford.
Country of Study: United Kingdom.
Application Procedure: Applicants must contact the Tutor for Graduate Admissions at Balliol College.
Closing Date: Please contact the College.

For further information contact:

Tutor for Graduate Admissions
Balliol College, Oxford, Oxfordshire, OX1 3BJ, England

Brasenose College Michael Woods Senior Scholarship

Subjects: Philosophy.

Eligibility: Open to applicants reading for the BPhil or DPhil in Philosophy.
Level of Study: Postgraduate.
Type: Scholarship.
Value: UK £1,600 per year plus some dining rights and guaranteed accommodation in the College for the first year of the course.
Length of Study: Two years.
Frequency: Varies.
Study Establishment: Brasenose College, the University of Oxford.
Country of Study: United Kingdom.
Application Procedure: Applicants must write for details.
Closing Date: Please write for details.
Additional Information: This scholarship is not available again before October 2004.

For further information contact:

Tutor for Graduates
Brasenose College, Oxford, Oxfordshire, OX1 4AJ, England

Brasenose College Senior Germaine Scholarship

Subjects: All subjects.
Eligibility: Open to home and European Union students only.
Level of Study: Postgraduate.
Type: Scholarship.
Value: College and university fees plus maintenance equal to a state maintenance grant and a college room for the first year.
Length of Study: One year, annually renewable for a further two years.
Study Establishment: Brasenose College, the University of Oxford.
Country of Study: United Kingdom.
No. of awards offered: Two, offered in conjunction with the Oxford University Graduate Scholarship Scheme.
Application Procedure: Applicants must contact the Tutor for Graduates at Brasenose College.

For further information contact:

Tutor for Graduates
Brasenose College, Oxford, Oxfordshire, OX1 4AJ, England

Brasenose Hector Pilling Scholarship

Subjects: All subjects.
Eligibility: Open to graduates of any Commonwealth university, excluding the United Kingdom. Preference will be given to applicants who are serving or who have served in the Royal Air Force or the Air Force of a Commonwealth country, or to the children or dependants of such persons.
Level of Study: Postgraduate.
Type: Scholarship.
Value: College and university fees plus maintenance equal to a state maintenance grant, plus a college room for the first year.
Length of Study: One year, renewable for a further two years.
Frequency: Varies, not available every year.
Study Establishment: Brasenose College, the University of Oxford.
Country of Study: United Kingdom.
No. of awards offered: One.
Application Procedure: Applicants must write for details.
Closing Date: Please write for details.
Funding: Private.
Additional Information: This scholarship is offered in conjunction with the Clarendon Fund in Studentship Scheme.

For further information contact:

Tutor for Graduates
International Office
University Offices
Wellington Square, Oxford, Oxfordshire, OX1 2JD, England
Email: international.office@admin.ox.ac.uk

British Chevening Scholarships (formerly known as Foreign and Commonwealth Office Scholarships and Awards)

Subjects: All subjects.
Purpose: To enable future leaders, decision makers and opinion formers to study in the United Kingdom.
Eligibility: Preference is given to postgraduates or those already established in a career.
Level of Study: Postgraduate.
Type: Scholarship.
Value: All or part of the student's costs.
Length of Study: Usually one year.
Study Establishment: The University of Oxford.
Country of Study: United Kingdom.
Application Procedure: Applicants must apply for information, which is available on request from the British Council in the applicant's home country. Candidates are selected by British diplomatic missions overseas. Applicants must apply independently for admission to the University through the Graduate Admissions Office.
Closing Date: Please write for details.
Funding: Government.
Contributor: The Foreign and Commonwealth Office.
Additional Information: The scholarships are administered by the British Council on behalf of the Foreign Office. Further information is available on request or from the website http://www.britishcouncil.org.

Chevening Oxford-Australia Scholarships

Subjects: Economics, environmental studies, human rights or law.
Purpose: To assist individuals with overseas study.
Eligibility: Open to Australian nationals.
Level of Study: Postgraduate.
Type: Scholarship.
Value: Up to australian $24,000. Australian $12,000 is for fees and australian $12,000 is for living expenses.
Length of Study: One year.
Frequency: Annual.
Study Establishment: The University of Oxford.
Country of Study: United Kingdom.
No. of awards offered: Two.
Application Procedure: Applicants must write for details.

For further information contact:

Chairman, Oxford-Australia Scholarships Committee
Research School for Chemistry
Australian National University, Canberra, ACT, 0200, Australia
Tel: (61) 2 6125 3578
Fax: (61) 2 6125 4903
Email: jww@rsc.anu.edu.au
Contact: Professor J W White

Christ Church American Friends Scholarship

Subjects: All subjects.
Eligibility: Open to graduate students from the United States of America only.
Level of Study: Postgraduate.
Type: Scholarship.
Value: US$7,000 per year.
Length of Study: One year.
Frequency: Annual.
Study Establishment: Christ Church, the University of Oxford.
Country of Study: United Kingdom.
No. of awards offered: Varies.
Application Procedure: Applicants must apply for the scholarship when applying for admission.
Closing Date: Please write for details.
Funding: Private.

For further information contact:

The Tutor for Graduates' Secretary
Christ Church, Oxford, Oxfordshire, OX1 1DP, England

723

Christ Church DFID Shared Scholarship

Subjects: All subjects.
Eligibility: Open to citizens of developing Commonwealth countries only.
Level of Study: Postgraduate.
Type: Scholarship.
Value: Fees and maintenance.
Length of Study: Up to three years.
Frequency: Annual.
Study Establishment: Christ Church, the University of Oxford.
Country of Study: United Kingdom.
No. of awards offered: One.
Application Procedure: Applicants must write for details.
Funding: Private.

For further information contact:

International Office
University Offices
Wellington Square, Oxford, Oxfordshire, OX1 2JD, England
www: http://www.admin.ox.ac.uk/io

Christ Church Hugh Pilkington Scholarship

Subjects: All subjects.
Eligibility: Open to graduate students from outside the United States.
Level of Study: Postgraduate.
Type: Scholarship.
Value: UK £3,000 per year.
Length of Study: One year.
Frequency: Annual.
Study Establishment: Christ Church, the University of Oxford.
Country of Study: United Kingdom.
Application Procedure: Applicants must write to the Tutor for Graduates' Secretary at Christ Church for further information. Applications should be made when applying for admission.

For further information contact:

Dean's Secretary
Christ Church, Oxford, Oxfordshire, OX1 1DP, England

Christ Church Senior Scholarship

Subjects: All subjects.
Purpose: To enable graduate scholars to undertake some definite course of literary, educational, scientific or professional study or training.
Eligibility: Open to candidates who will have been reading for a higher degree in the University of Oxford for at least one year, but not more than two years, by October 1st of the year in which the award is sought.
Level of Study: Postgraduate.
Type: Scholarship.
Value: Rooms and maintenance at Research Council level, subject to deduction of grants from other sources.
Length of Study: Two years, with a possibility of renewal for a further year.
Frequency: Annual.
Study Establishment: Christ Church, the University of Oxford.
Country of Study: United Kingdom.
No. of awards offered: Varies.
Application Procedure: Applicants must write for details. Applications should be made in February.
Additional Information: Normally, the scholarship is held in conjunction with an award from a government agency which pays the university fees.

For further information contact:

Tutor of Graduates' Secretary
Christ Church, Oxford, Oxfordshire, OX1 1DP, England

Citibank/Chevening Scholarships

Subjects: Economics, European politics and society or international relations.
Eligibility: Open to students from Argentina, Brazil, Colombia, India, Indonesia, Malaysia, Vietnam, China, Czech Republic, Hungary, Poland and South Africa.
Level of Study: Postgraduate.
Type: Scholarship.
Value: University and college fees and maintenance costs.
Length of Study: Two years.
Frequency: Annual.
Country of Study: United Kingdom.
No. of awards offered: Up to three partial awards.
Application Procedure: Applicants must write for details.
Closing Date: April 1st.
Contributor: Citibank, the Foreign and Commonwealth Office and the University of Oxford.

For further information contact:

International Office
University Offices
Wellington Square, Oxford, Oxfordshire, OX1 2JD, England

Clarendon Fund Bursaries

Subjects: All subjects.
Purpose: To enable outstanding candidates who have been accepted for admission to the University to take up their places.
Eligibility: Open to students who are liable for fees at the overseas rate, and therefore, not home or European Union students.
Level of Study: Doctorate, Postgraduate.
Type: Bursary.
Value: The financial circumstances of applicants will be taken into account in determining the level of awards. It is expected that most awards will be partial although full scholarships will occasionally be provided.
Frequency: Annual.
Study Establishment: The University of Oxford.
Country of Study: United Kingdom.
No. of awards offered: Varies.
Application Procedure: Applicants should complete the application form available from the International Office.
Closing Date: End of January.
Contributor: Oxford University Press.
Additional Information: Candidates must apply for an Overseas Research Students (ORS) award if the course they intend to follow makes them eligible.

Corpus Christi College EK Chambers Studentship

Subjects: English literature.
Eligibility: Candidates should have graduated in the United Kingdom, have read and been examined in some Latin or Greek at university, and have an Honours Degree in a subject other than Single Honours English.
Level of Study: Postgraduate.
Type: Studentship.
Value: Full fees and graduate maintenance grant plus some dining rights.
Length of Study: Two-three years.
Frequency: Varies.
Study Establishment: Corpus Christi College or Somerville College, the University of Oxford.
Country of Study: United Kingdom.
No. of awards offered: One.
Application Procedure: Applicants must write for details.
Closing Date: Please write for details.

For further information contact:

Tutor for Graduates
Corpus Christi College, Oxford, Oxfordshire, OX1 4JF, England

DFID Shared Scholarship Scheme

Subjects: Related to the economic and social development of the student's home country.

Eligibility: Open to students from developing Commonwealth countries. Candidates must not be living or studying in a developed country, or be employed by a government department (national or local) or a parastatal organisation. Candidates must certify that they would be otherwise unable to afford the cost of study in Britain, and that they will return to work or study in their home country as soon as their award ends. Candidates should normally be under the age of 35 years at the time the award begins.

Level of Study: Postgraduate.

Type: Scholarship.

Value: University and college fees, maintenance and return air travel to Britain.

Study Establishment: The University of Oxford.

Country of Study: United Kingdom.

No. of awards offered: Varies.

Application Procedure: Applicants must complete application forms available on request from the International Office, Wellington Square, or from the website.

Closing Date: May.

Dolabani Fund for Syriac Studies

Subjects: Syriac studies or area studies.

Purpose: To assist students in meeting the cost of engaging in courses involving Syriac studies at the University, and for the provision of grants for the purchase of Syriac manuscripts for the Bodleian Library and the Oriental Institute Library. The award also wishes to further Syriac studies within the University, and support students from Syriac churches studying their own tradition in working for formal qualifications of the University.

Eligibility: Open to graduate students of the University who are nationals of the Middle East or the region of the Indian state of Kerala.

Level of Study: Postgraduate.

Type: Grant.

Value: Varies.

Study Establishment: The University of Oxford.

Country of Study: United Kingdom.

No. of awards offered: Varies.

Application Procedure: Applicants must submit a statement of purpose for which the grant is requested and, in the case of graduate students, the name of the applicant's supervisor.

Closing Date: March 9th.

Funding: Private.

For further information contact:

Secretary
Board of the Faculty of Oriental Studies
Oriental Institute
Pusey Lane, Oxford, Oxfordshire, OX1 2LE, England

Dulverton Scholarships

Subjects: All subjects.

Purpose: To provide assistance for students of outstanding academic merit and financial need.

Eligibility: Open to students from Eastern European Countries, namely Albania, Armenia, Azerbaijan, Belarus, Bosnia, Bulgaria, Croatia, Czech Republic, Estonia, Georgia, Hungary, Latvia, Lithuania, Macedonia, Moldova, Poland, Romania, the Russian Federation, Slovakia, Ukraine and Yugoslavia.

Level of Study: Postgraduate.

Value: Full scholarships will cover university and college fees and maintenance for the length of the proposed course of study. Partial scholarships will be awarded on the basis of financial need.

Study Establishment: The University of Oxford.

Country of Study: United Kingdom.

No. of awards offered: Varies.

Application Procedure: Applicants must apply separately for admission to Oxford through the Graduate Admissions Office, and should write for further particulars and an application form.

Closing Date: March 1st.

Funding: Private.

Contributor: The Dulverton Trust.

For further information contact:

International Office
University Offices
Wellington Square, Oxford, Oxfordshire, OX1 2JD, England

Exeter College Usher-Cunningham Senior Studentship

Subjects: Alternately awarded for medical science and medieval or modern history.

Purpose: To support graduate study.

Eligibility: The Modern History Studentship is only open to graduates of Irish universities.

Level of Study: Postgraduate.

Type: Studentship.

Value: Home level fees plus maintenance up to the equivalent of a Research Council Award.

Length of Study: Usually awarded for three years.

Frequency: Every three years.

Study Establishment: Exeter College, the University of Oxford.

Country of Study: United Kingdom.

No. of awards offered: One.

Application Procedure: Applicants must address enquiries to the Academic Administrator.

Closing Date: Please write for details.

Funding: Private.

Contributor: An endowment.

Additional Information: The medical sciences scholarship is held jointly with a University studentship in a particular preclinical or clinical department and will probably be next awarded in 2003. Modern history includes any period from the fourth-century AD and will probably be next awarded in 2006.

For further information contact:

Academic Administrator
Exeter College, Oxford, Oxfordshire, OX1 3DP, England

Felix Scholarships

Subjects: All subjects.

Purpose: To enable graduates accepted for entry to Oxford to read for taught graduate courses or for a Master's or DPhil degree by research, who would be unable, without financial assistance, to take up their place.

Eligibility: Open to Indian nationals under 30 years of age who must have at least a First Class Bachelor's Degree from an Indian university or comparable institution. Those who already hold degrees from universities outside India are not eligible to apply.

Level of Study: Doctorate, Postgraduate.

Value: University and college fees and maintenance costs.

Length of Study: For two years in the first instance, with a possible extension for three years for those initially registered for a DPhil degree.

Study Establishment: The University of Oxford.

Country of Study: United Kingdom.

No. of awards offered: Up to six.

Application Procedure: Applicants must apply separately for admission to Oxford through the Graduate Admissions Office and should write for further details. Applicants for Felix Scholarships are expected to apply for an Overseas Research Student (ORS) award if the course they intend to take makes them eligible.

Closing Date: March 1st.

For further information contact:

International Office
University Offices
Wellington Square, Oxford, Oxfordshire, OX1 2JD, England

Fulbright Oxford University Scholarships

Subjects: All subjects.

Level of Study: Postgraduate.

Value: Full funding covering round trip travel, a maintenance allowance and approved tuition fees. A candidate gaining three awards ie. the Fulbright, Overseas Research Award (ORS) and Oxford bursary) will have adequate funding for two years.
Length of Study: Two-three years.
Study Establishment: The University of Oxford.
Country of Study: United Kingdom.
Application Procedure: Applicants must complete an application form.
Closing Date: October 25th. Those enrolled in United States institutions must file applications with their Fulbright Programme Advisor by the deadline set by the campus advisor.
Additional Information: The course must lead to a higher degree and qualify for funding under the Overseas Research Student (ORS) award scheme. Candidates must apply for this award.

For further information contact:

US Student Programs
Institute of International Education (IIE)
809 United Nations Plaza, New York, NY, 10017-3580, United States of America

Hertford College Senior Scholarships

Subjects: All subjects.
Eligibility: Restricted to students about to commence a new research degree course or those about to upgrade their current course.
Level of Study: Postgraduate.
Type: Scholarship.
Value: UK £500 per year, plus priority for housing.
Length of Study: Two years in the first instance, with a possibility of renewal for a further year.
Study Establishment: Hertford College, the University of Oxford.
Country of Study: United Kingdom.
Application Procedure: Applicants must write to the College for further details.
Closing Date: February.

For further information contact:

College Secretary
Hertford College, Oxford, Oxfordshire, OX1 3BW, England

Hill Foundation Scholarships

Subjects: All subjects.
Eligibility: Open to students from the Russian Federation studying for a postgraduate or a second Bachelor of Arts degree. Candidates should not normally be more than 25 years of age and should be intending to return to Russia at the end of their period of study.
Level of Study: Postgraduate.
Type: Scholarship.
Value: University and college fees, travel to and from the United Kingdom and a grant for maintenance.
Study Establishment: The University of Oxford.
Country of Study: United Kingdom.
No. of awards offered: Up to four.
Application Procedure: Applicants must complete the form for scholarships and bursaries for international students available from the International Office.
Closing Date: November 30th.

Hong Kong Oxford Scholarship Fund Bursaries (China)

Subjects: All subjects.
Eligibility: Open to nationals of the People's Republic of China. It is a condition of the award that students should be planning to return to and to benefit their home country on completion of their studies.
Level of Study: Postgraduate.
Value: Up to UK £4,000.
Study Establishment: The University of Oxford.
Country of Study: United Kingdom.
No. of awards offered: Varies.

Application Procedure: Applicants must apply for admission to Oxford through the Graduate Admissions Office and should write for further details.
Closing Date: July 1st.

For further information contact:

International Office
University Offices
Wellington Square, Oxford, Oxfordshire, OX1 2JD, England

James Fairfax and Oxford-Australia Fund

Subjects: Oxford-Australia Fund scholarships are open to any discipline whereas James Fairfax Scholarships are intended for those wishing to study in the arts or social sciences.
Level of Study: Postgraduate.
Value: University fees at the home and European Union rate, college fees and a living allowance of the order of australian $12,000 per year.
Length of Study: Oxford-Australia Fund scholarships are for two years, or in the case of DPhil for three years, and James Fairfax Scholarships will generally be of two years duration.
Study Establishment: The University of Oxford.
Country of Study: United Kingdom.
No. of awards offered: One-two.
Application Procedure: Applicants must write for details.
Closing Date: February.
Funding: Private.
Contributor: Australian scholars who have studied at Oxford, and in particular, Mr James Fairfax.
Additional Information: Candidates are also expected to apply for an Overseas Research Student (ORS) award if the course they intend to follow makes them eligible.

For further information contact:

International Office
University Offices
Wellington Square, Oxford, Oxfordshire, OX1 2JD, England

James Ingham Halstead Scholarship in Music

Subjects: Music.
Eligibility: Open to graduates of any university who intend to proceed to one of the university's advanced degrees in music eg. MLitt, MPhil or DPhil, or are intending to supplicate for the BMus or DMus.
Level of Study: Doctorate, Postdoctorate, Postgraduate.
Type: Scholarship.
Value: Usually UK £300 per year.
Length of Study: One year, with a possibility of renewal for a further two years subject to reports of satisfactory progress.
Frequency: Annual.
Study Establishment: The University of Oxford.
Country of Study: United Kingdom.
No. of awards offered: Varies.
Application Procedure: Applicants must submit an application which includes their date of birth, a brief statement of their academic career, an example of original work eg. compositions, theses, essays, articles etc., whether published or not, a brief statement of proposed research, and the names of two referees. If applicants submit pieces of research whose purpose and relationship to their main plan of research is not immediately clear, a short introduction should be included to set the work in the context of larger aims.
Closing Date: March 1st.
Funding: Private.
Contributor: The James Ingham Halstead Bequest.
Additional Information: Halstead Scholars may qualify for awards supplementary to their financial circumstances and the state of the fund.

For further information contact:

Secretary
Board of the Faculty of Music
Humanities Divisional Office
34 St Giles, Oxford, Oxfordshire, OX1 3LH, England

Jesus College Graduate Scholarship

Subjects: All subjects.
Level of Study: Postgraduate.
Type: Scholarship.
Value: Up to UK £500 per year.
Length of Study: Up to three years.
Frequency: Varies.
Study Establishment: Jesus College, the University of Oxford.
Country of Study: United Kingdom.
Application Procedure: Applicants must contact the Tutor for Graduates.

For further information contact:

Tutor for Graduates
Jesus College, Oxford, Oxfordshire, OX1 3DW, England

Jesus College Meyricke Graduate Scholarships

Subjects: All subjects.
Eligibility: Open to graduates of the University of Wales who have been accepted by the College.
Level of Study: Graduate.
Type: Scholarship.
Value: UK £500 per year.
Length of Study: Up to three years.
Study Establishment: Jesus College, the University of Oxford.
Country of Study: United Kingdom.
Application Procedure: Applicants must write for details.

For further information contact:

Tutor for Graduates
Jesus College, Oxford, Oxfordshire, OX1 3DW, England

Jesus College The Alun Hughes' Graduate Scholarship

Subjects: Polynesia or Micronesia.
Eligibility: Applicants must have been accepted by the University of Oxford to undertake research towards a DPhil in the correct subject area.
Level of Study: Doctorate.
Type: Scholarship.
Value: Home and European Union fees.
Length of Study: Up to three years.
Study Establishment: Jesus College, the University of Oxford.
Country of Study: United Kingdom.
No. of awards offered: Normally only one holder at a time.
Application Procedure: Applicants must write for details.
Closing Date: Please write for details.

For further information contact:

Tutor for Graduates
Jesus College, Oxford, Oxfordshire, OX1 3DW, England

K C Wong Scholarships

Subjects: All subjects.
Purpose: To assist students studying at doctorate level.
Eligibility: Open to residents of the People's Republic of China only.
Level of Study: Doctorate.
Value: University and college fees and maintenance for a maximum of three years.
Study Establishment: The University of Oxford.
Country of Study: United Kingdom.
No. of awards offered: Three.
Application Procedure: Applicants must write for further details and an application form or visit the website.
Closing Date: April 1st.
Funding: Private.
Contributor: The K C Wong Foundation.
Additional Information: Applicants for the K C Wong Scholarships are also expected to apply for an Overseas Research Students (ORS) award.

For further information contact:

International Office
University Offices
Wellington Square, Oxford, Oxfordshire, OX1 2JD, England

Karim Rida Said Foundation Scholarships

Subjects: All subjects.
Purpose: To assist students with either a taught Master's degree, a Master's degree by research or for the DPhil degree.
Eligibility: Open to students from Iraq, Jordan, Lebanon, Palestine or Syria.
Level of Study: Postgraduate.
Value: University and college fees plus a maintenance grant for the duration of the student's course.
Study Establishment: The University of Oxford.
Country of Study: United Kingdom.
No. of awards offered: Varies.
Application Procedure: Applicants must apply separately for admission to Oxford through the Graduate Admissions Office and should write for further details.
Closing Date: April 1st.
Funding: Private.
Contributor: The Karim Rida Said Foundation.
Additional Information: Applicants are expected to apply for an Overseas Research Student (ORS) award if the course they intend to follow makes them eligible.

For further information contact:

International Office
University Offices
Wellington square, Oxford, Oxfordshire, OX1 2JD, England

Keble College Gwynne-Jones Scholarship

Subjects: All subjects.
Eligibility: Eligible to nationals of Sierra Leone, or among the Yoruba speaking people of Nigeria.
Level of Study: Postgraduate.
Type: Scholarship.
Value: Up to UK £4,000 per year.
Length of Study: Up to three years.
Frequency: Varies.
Study Establishment: Keble College, the University of Oxford.
Country of Study: United Kingdom.
No. of awards offered: Varies.
Application Procedure: Applicants must write for details.
Closing Date: June.
Funding: Private.

For further information contact:

Tutor for Graduates
Keble College, Oxford, Oxfordshire, OX1 3PG, England

Keble College Ian Palmer Graduate Scholarship in Information Technology

Subjects: Computer science and related fields concerning the practical uses of computer systems.
Eligibility: Please write for details.
Level of Study: Postgraduate.
Type: Scholarship.
Value: To the value of college fees.
Length of Study: Up to three years.
Frequency: Varies, may not be available every year.
Study Establishment: Keble College, the University of Oxford.
Country of Study: United Kingdom.
No. of awards offered: Varies.
Application Procedure: Applicants must write for details.
Closing Date: Late March.
Funding: Private.

For further information contact:

Tutor for Graduates
Keble College, Oxford, Oxfordshire, OX1 3PG, England

Keble College Ian Tucker Memorial Bursary

Subjects: All subjects.
Eligibility: Candidates must demonstrate sporting prowess in principally the field of rugby football, together with qualities that will make a contribution to both the College and University.
Type: Bursary.
Value: UK £3,000.
Length of Study: One year.
Frequency: Varies, not available every year.
Study Establishment: Keble College, the University of Oxford.
Country of Study: United Kingdom.
No. of awards offered: One.
Application Procedure: Applicants must contact the Tutor for Graduates at Keble College.

For further information contact:

Tutor for Graduates
Keble College, Oxford, Oxfordshire, OX1 3PG, England

Keble College Keble Association Graduate Scholarship

Subjects: All subjects.
Level of Study: Postgraduate.
Type: Scholarship.
Value: To the value of college fees.
Length of Study: Up to two years.
Frequency: Annual.
Study Establishment: Keble College, the University of Oxford.
Country of Study: United Kingdom.
No. of awards offered: More than one.
Application Procedure: Applicants must write for details.
Closing Date: Late March.
Funding: Private.

For further information contact:

Tutor for Graduates
Keble College, Oxford, Oxfordshire, OX1 3PG, England

Keble College Paul Hayes Graduate Scholarship

Subjects: All subjects.
Eligibility: Candidates must demonstrate sporting excellence.
Level of Study: Doctorate, Graduate.
Type: Scholarship.
Value: Up to the value of college fees.
Length of Study: Up to three years.
Frequency: Varies, not available every year.
Study Establishment: Keble College, the University of Oxford.
Country of Study: United Kingdom.
No. of awards offered: One.
Application Procedure: Applicants must contact the Tutor for Graduates at Keble College.
Closing Date: Please contact the College.

For further information contact:

Tutor for Graduates
Keble College, Oxford, Oxfordshire, OX1 3PG, England

Keble College Water Newton and Gosden Graduate Scholarship

Subjects: All subjects.
Eligibility: Open to students intending to seek ordination in a church in communion with the Church of England.
Level of Study: Postgraduate.
Type: Scholarship.
Value: Up to UK £5,000 per year.
Length of Study: Two years.
Study Establishment: Keble College, the University of Oxford.

Country of Study: United Kingdom.
Application Procedure: Applicants must contact the Tutor for Graduates, in the first instance at Keble College.

For further information contact:

Tutor for Graduates
Keble College, Oxford, Oxfordshire, OX1 3PG, England

Kellogg College Graduate Studentships

Subjects: All subjects.
Eligibility: Open to part-time DPhil students at Kellogg College.
Level of Study: Doctorate.
Type: Studentship.
Value: Approx. UK £600 per year.
Frequency: Annual.
Study Establishment: Kellogg College, the University of Oxford.
Country of Study: United Kingdom.
Application Procedure: Applicants must contact the Tutor for Admissions at Kellogg College.

For further information contact:

Tutor for Admissions
Kellogg College, Oxford, Oxfordshire, OX1 2JA, England

Kellogg College Kellogg Scholarships

Subjects: All subjects.
Eligibility: Restricted to those offered a place at Kellogg College, Oxford.
Level of Study: Postgraduate.
Type: Scholarship.
Value: Approx. UK £300 per year.
Length of Study: Two years or more.
Study Establishment: Kellogg College, the University of Oxford.
Country of Study: United Kingdom.
Application Procedure: Applicants must contact the Tutor for Admissions, in the first instance at Kellogg College.

For further information contact:

Tutor for Admissions
Kellogg College, Oxford, Oxfordshire, OX1 2JA, England

Lady Noon/Oxford University Press (Pakistan) Scholarship

Subjects: All subjects.
Eligibility: Open to nationals of Pakistan, with preference being given to those who have not previously studied outside Pakistan.
Level of Study: Postgraduate.
Study Establishment: The University of Oxford.
Country of Study: United Kingdom.
No. of awards offered: Varies. There are a small number of full or partial awards.
Application Procedure: Applicants must apply separately for admission to Oxford through the Graduate Admissions Office and should write for further details.
Closing Date: April 1st.
Contributor: The Lady Noon Educational Trust, the Foreign and Commonwealth Office and the University of Oxford.

For further information contact:

International Office
University Offices
Wellington Square, Oxford, Oxfordshire, OX1 2JD, England

Linacre College A J Hosier Studentship

Subjects: Husbandry, agricultural economics or statistics and applied agricultural science.
Purpose: To fund graduate study.
Eligibility: Candidates must be honours graduates of a university in the United Kingdom and be citizens of the United Kingdom.
Level of Study: Postgraduate.

Type: Studentship.
Value: UK £3,500 per year which may be divided between more than one person.
Length of Study: One year.
Study Establishment: Linacre College, the University of Oxford.
Country of Study: United Kingdom.
No. of awards offered: Varies.
Application Procedure: Applicants must contact the Tutor for Admissions for further details.

For further information contact:

Tutor for Admissions
Linacre College, Oxford, Oxfordshire, OX1 3JA, England

Linacre College Applied Materials Scholarships

Subjects: Materials science, environmental studies.
Eligibility: Open to candidates reading for the BCL or the MJuris, with an emphasis or special interest in European or public law.
Level of Study: Postgraduate.
Type: Scholarship.
Value: Up to UK £2,000 per year.
Length of Study: Up to three years.
Frequency: Varies, not available every year.
Study Establishment: Linacre College, the University of Oxford.
Country of Study: United Kingdom.
No. of awards offered: Up to five.
Application Procedure: Applicants must contact the Tutor for Admissions at Linacre College.

For further information contact:

Tutor for Admissions
Linacre College, Oxford, Oxfordshire, OX1 3JA, England

Linacre College Canadian National Scholarship

Subjects: All subjects.
Eligibility: Open to suitably qualified students of Canadian nationality reading or intending to read for a postgraduate degree.
Level of Study: Graduate, Postgraduate.
Type: Scholarship.
Value: Approx. UK £3,600 per year.
Length of Study: Up to three years.
Frequency: May not be available every year.
Study Establishment: Linacre College, the University of Oxford.
Country of Study: United Kingdom.
Application Procedure: Applicants must write for details.
Closing Date: Please write for details.

For further information contact:

Tutor for Admissions
Linacre College, Oxford, Oxfordshire, OX1 3DR, England

Linacre College Domus Studentships

Subjects: All subjects.
Purpose: To assist postgraduate study.
Eligibility: Open to students with a good first degree, who intend to begin reading for a higher degree, or to current members of Linacre College.
Level of Study: Postgraduate.
Type: Studentship.
Value: UK £250 per year plus priority for accommodation.
Length of Study: Up to three years.
Frequency: Annual.
Study Establishment: Linacre College, the University of Oxford.
Country of Study: United Kingdom.
No. of awards offered: Varies.
Application Procedure: Applicants must write for details.
Closing Date: Please write for details.
Funding: Private.
Contributor: College funds.

For further information contact:

Tutor for Admissions
Linacre College
St Cross Road, Oxford, Oxfordshire, OX1 3JA, England
Email: jane.edwards@linacre.ox.ac.uk
www: http://www.linacre.ox.ac.uk

Linacre College European Blaschko Visiting Research Scholarship

Subjects: Pharmacology or anatomical neuropharmacology.
Purpose: To allow a student to study in Oxford as a visiting student at the department of pharmacology or the MRC anatomical neuropharmacology unit.
Eligibility: Open to European students intending to study at Linacre College.
Level of Study: Postgraduate.
Type: Scholarship.
Value: College and university fees for visiting student status, a stipend and the cost of return travel.
Length of Study: One year.
Frequency: Annual.
Study Establishment: Linacre College, the University of Oxford.
Country of Study: United Kingdom.
No. of awards offered: One.
Application Procedure: Applicants must write for details.
Funding: Private.
Contributor: Mrs Mary Blaschko.

For further information contact:

Department of Pharmacology
Mansfield Road, Oxford, Oxfordshire, OX1 3QT, England
Contact: Professor A D Smith

Linacre College Heselton Legal Research Scholarship

Subjects: English or European Union law research degrees.
Purpose: To fund graduate research.
Level of Study: Postgraduate.
Type: Scholarship.
Value: UK £1,000 per year.
Length of Study: Up to three years.
Frequency: Varies.
Study Establishment: Linacre College, the University of Oxford.
Country of Study: United Kingdom.
Application Procedure: Applicants must contact the Tutor for Admissions, in the first instance at Linacre College.
Additional Information: This scholarship may not be available every year.

For further information contact:

Tutor for Admissions
Linacre College, Oxford, Oxfordshire, OX1 3JA, England

Linacre College Lloyd African Scholarship DFID Shared Scholarships

Subjects: A subject which will be beneficial in aiding the economic or social development of the student's country.
Purpose: To enable a qualified graduate student from an African university to pursue a one or two year taught Master's course.
Eligibility: Open to qualified graduate students from African universities.
Level of Study: Postgraduate.
Type: Scholarship.
Value: University and college fees, maintenance and return air travel.
Length of Study: One-two years.
Frequency: Annually or biannually.
Study Establishment: Linacre College, the University of Oxford.
Country of Study: United Kingdom.
No. of awards offered: Two.
Application Procedure: Applicants must write for details.

Funding: Private.

For further information contact:

Tutor for Admissions
Linacre College, Oxford, Oxfordshire, OX1 3JA, England

Linacre College Mary Blaschko Graduate Scholarship

Subjects: Arts and humanities.
Eligibility: Open to suitably qualified students reading or intending to read for a research degree in the arts and humanities.
Level of Study: Postgraduate, Research.
Type: Scholarship.
Value: UK £2,000 per year.
Length of Study: One-two years.
Frequency: May not be available every year.
Study Establishment: Linacre College, the University of Oxford.
Country of Study: United Kingdom.
No. of awards offered: Three.
Application Procedure: Applicants must write for details.
Closing Date: Please write for details.

For further information contact:

Tutor for Admissions
Linacre College, Oxford, Oxfordshire, OX1 3UA, England

Linacre College Norman and Ivy Lloyd Scholarship/DFID Shared Scholarship

Subjects: Forestry and its relation to land use.
Purpose: To enable a student from to undertake the MSc.
Eligibility: Open to nationals of developing Commonwealth countries.
Level of Study: Postgraduate.
Type: Scholarship.
Value: University and college fees, maintenance and return air travel from the scholar's home country.
Length of Study: One year.
Frequency: Annual.
Study Establishment: The Oxford Forestry Institute, Linacre College, the University of Oxford.
Country of Study: United Kingdom.
No. of awards offered: Varies.
Application Procedure: Applicants must write for details.
Closing Date: Please write for details.
Funding: Private.

For further information contact:

Oxford Forestry Institute
South Parks Road, Oxford, Oxfordshire, OX1 3RB, England
Contact: Dr P S Savill

Linacre College Rausing Scholarships

Subjects: Subjects vary from year to year, the Scholarship is offered in conjunction with the faculties and departments of the University.
Level of Study: Postgraduate.
Type: Scholarship.
Value: Up to UK £2,000 per year.
Length of Study: Up to three years.
Frequency: Varies, not available every year.
Study Establishment: Linacre College, the University of Oxford.
Country of Study: United Kingdom.
No. of awards offered: Two.
Application Procedure: Applicants must contact the Tutor for Admissions at Linacre College.
Closing Date: Please contact the College.

For further information contact:

Tutor for Admissions
Linacre College, Oxford, Oxfordshire, OX1 3JA, England

Linares Rivas Scholarship

Subjects: All subjects.
Eligibility: Open to students from Spain, studying at or recently graduated from a Spanish university.
Value: University and college fees and a grant towards living costs.
Length of Study: One year.
Study Establishment: The University of Oxford.
Country of Study: United Kingdom.
No. of awards offered: One.
Application Procedure: Applicants must complete the application form, available from the International Office.
Closing Date: April.
Funding: Private.
Contributor: The trustees of the late Lady Consuelo Maria Allen.

For further information contact:

International Office
University Offices
Wellington Square, Oxford, Oxfordshire, OX1 2JD, England

Lincoln College Berrow Scholarships

Subjects: All subjects.
Purpose: To permit graduates of certain Swiss universities to undertake postgraduate study at Oxford.
Eligibility: Open to graduates of the Swiss universities Berne, Geneva, Lausanne, Fribourg, Neuchätel, or the Ecole Polytechnique Fédérale de Lausanne.
Level of Study: Doctorate, Postgraduate.
Type: Scholarship.
Value: All university and college fees are covered, plus a generous maintenance allowance.
Length of Study: Two years, with a possibility of renewal for a further year.
Frequency: Annual.
Study Establishment: Lincoln College, the University of Oxford.
Country of Study: United Kingdom.
No. of awards offered: Three.
Application Procedure: Applicants must write for details.
Closing Date: Please write for details.
Funding: Private.

For further information contact:

Tutor for Graduates
Lincoln College, Oxford, Oxfordshire, OX1 3DR, England

Lincoln College Erich and Rochelle Endowed Prize in Music

Subjects: Open to graduates in any discipline other than music.
Eligibility: Open to graduate students of exceptional and proven musical ability. The successful candidate will be expected to play a prominent part in the musical life of the college and in particular to act, if requested, as organising secretary of the college's active Music Society.
Level of Study: Postgraduate.
Value: UK £1,000.
Length of Study: One year only.
Frequency: Annual.
Study Establishment: Lincoln College, the University of Oxford.
Country of Study: United Kingdom.
No. of awards offered: One.
Closing Date: Please write for details.
Funding: Private.

For further information contact:

Tutor for Graduates
Lincoln College, Oxford, Oxfordshire, OX1 3DR, England

Lincoln College Keith Murray Senior Scholarship

Subjects: Varies from year to year.
Purpose: To permit students from outside the European Union to undertake postgraduate study at Oxford University.

Eligibility: Open to holders of a very good first degree, who are citizens of any country outside the European Community.
Level of Study: Doctorate, Postgraduate.
Type: Scholarship.
Value: All university and college fees are covered, plus a generous maintenance allowance.
Length of Study: Two years with the possibility of renewal for a third year.
Frequency: Dependent on funds available.
Study Establishment: Lincoln College, the University of Oxford.
Country of Study: United Kingdom.
No. of awards offered: More than one depending on funds available.
Application Procedure: Applicants must write for details.
Closing Date: December of the year preceding commencement of study.
Funding: Private.

For further information contact:

Tutor for Graduates
Lincoln College, Oxford, Oxfordshire, OX1 3DR, England

Lincoln College Overseas Graduate Entrance Scholarship

Subjects: All subjects.
Eligibility: Restricted to those offered a place for graduate study at Lincoln College.
Level of Study: Graduate.
Type: Scholarship.
Value: UK £1,500.
Length of Study: One year only.
Frequency: Annual.
Study Establishment: Lincoln College, the University of Oxford.
Country of Study: United Kingdom.
Application Procedure: Applicants must write for details.
Closing Date: Please write for details.

For further information contact:

Tutor for Graduates
Lincoln College, Oxford, Oxfordshire, OX1 3DR, England

Lincoln College Supperstone Law Scholarship

Subjects: Law.
Eligibility: Open to candidates reading for the BCL or the Mjuris, with an emphasis or special interest in European or Public Law.
Type: Scholarship.
Value: UK £600 per year.
Length of Study: One year only.
Study Establishment: Lincoln College, the University of Oxford.
Country of Study: United Kingdom.
No. of awards offered: One.
Application Procedure: Applicants must contact the Tutor for Graduates at Lincoln College.
Closing Date: Please contact the College.

For further information contact:

Tutor for Graduates
Lincoln College, Oxford, Oxfordshire, OX1 3DR, England

Magdalen College Hichens Scholarship

Subjects: MBA.
Level of Study: Postgraduate, MBA.
Type: Scholarship.
Value: The cost of college accommodation.
Length of Study: One year.
Frequency: Annual.
Study Establishment: Magdalen College, the University of Oxford.
Country of Study: United Kingdom.
No. of awards offered: Up to three.
Application Procedure: Applicants must contact the Tutor for Graduates, in the first instance at Magdalen College.

For further information contact:

Tutor for Graduates
Magdalen College, Oxford, Oxfordshire, OX1 4AU, England

Mansfield College Elfan Rees Scholarship

Subjects: Alternates between politics and theology.
Level of Study: Postgraduate.
Type: Scholarship.
Value: UK £2,300 per year.
Length of Study: Two years.
Frequency: Every four years.
Study Establishment: Mansfield College, the University of Oxford.
Country of Study: United Kingdom.
No. of awards offered: Varies.
Application Procedure: Applicants must write for details.
Funding: Private.
Additional Information: The next award will be made in 2005 for politics.

For further information contact:

Tutor for Admissions
Mansfield College, Oxford, Oxfordshire, OX1 3TF, England

Merton College Domus Graduate Scholarships A

Subjects: All subjects accepted by the college.
Eligibility: Open to non United Kingdom students.
Level of Study: Graduate.
Type: Scholarship.
Value: Fees, housing and maintenance.
Length of Study: Three years.
Frequency: Annual.
Study Establishment: Merton College, the University of Oxford.
Country of Study: United Kingdom.
No. of awards offered: Two.
Application Procedure: Applicants must write for details.
Closing Date: Please write for details, the deadline is usually in late February.

For further information contact:

Assistant Tutorial Secretary
Merton College, Oxford, Oxfordshire, OX1 4JD, England

Merton College Domus Graduate Scholarships B

Subjects: All subjects accepted by the College.
Eligibility: Open to United Kingdom students who hold a First Class Degree and are still unfunded in September.
Level of Study: Graduate.
Type: Scholarship.
Value: Fees, housing and maintenance.
Length of Study: Three years.
Frequency: Annual.
Study Establishment: Merton College, the University of Oxford.
Country of Study: United Kingdom.
No. of awards offered: One-two.
Application Procedure: Applicants must write for details.
Closing Date: Early September.

For further information contact:

Assistant Tutorial Secretary
Merton College, Oxford, Oxfordshire, OX1 4JD, England

Merton College Greendale Scholarship

Subjects: All subjects.
Eligibility: Open to nationals and permanent residents of Switzerland who have a degree from a Swiss university.
Level of Study: Postgraduate.
Type: Scholarship.
Value: Fees, housing and maintenance.
Length of Study: For a course length of up to three years.
Frequency: Annual.

Study Establishment: Merton College, the University of Oxford.
Country of Study: United Kingdom.
No. of awards offered: One.
Closing Date: Early January. Applicants should confirm this with the college.
Funding: Private.

For further information contact:

Assistant Tutorial Secretary
Merton College, Oxford, Oxfordshire, OX1 4JD, England

Merton College Leventis Scholarship

Subjects: Greek studies from the Bronze Age to AD 1453.
Eligibility: Open to citizens of Greece or the Republic of Cyprus.
Level of Study: Postgraduate.
Type: Scholarship.
Value: Fees, housing and maintenance.
Length of Study: Three years.
Frequency: Every two years.
Study Establishment: Merton College, the University of Oxford.
Country of Study: United Kingdom.
No. of awards offered: One.
Closing Date: Please contact the College.
Funding: Private.

For further information contact:

Warden's Secretary
Merton College, Oxford, Oxfordshire, OX1 4JD, England

Merton College Reed Foundation Scholarship

Subjects: All subjects except medicine.
Eligibility: Open to nationals of underdeveloped countries, which are decided on a rotational basis.
Type: Scholarship.
Value: Fees, housing and maintenance.
Length of Study: Two years.
Frequency: Every two years.
Study Establishment: Merton College, the University of Oxford.
Country of Study: United Kingdom.
No. of awards offered: One.
Application Procedure: Applicants must write for details.
Closing Date: Early January.
Funding: Private.

For further information contact:

Assistant Tutorial Secretary
Merton College, Oxford, Oxfordshire, OX1 4JD, England

Michael Foster Scholarships

Subjects: All subjects.
Eligibility: Open to citizens of Germany who are aged 21-25 years. Candidates should not have already been studying at a university in the United Kingdom for more than one year at the time of application.
Level of Study: Postgraduate.
Value: University and college fees and a maintenance grant.
Length of Study: Up to two years.
Study Establishment: The University of Oxford.
Country of Study: United Kingdom.
No. of awards offered: One.
Closing Date: End of October.

For further information contact:

Dept 313
DAAD
Kennedyallee 50, Bonn, D-53175, Germany
Tel: (49) 228 882 239
Contact: Mrs H Kowalczich

Nuffield College Funded Studentships

Subjects: Social sciences.

Purpose: To assist students on a postgraduate degree course.
Eligibility: Open to persons with at least an Upper Second Class (Honours) Degree, or equivalent.
Level of Study: Postgraduate.
Type: Studentship.
Value: University and college fees plus maintenance.
Length of Study: For the length of the course.
Frequency: Annual.
Study Establishment: Nuffield College, the University of Oxford.
Country of Study: United Kingdom.
No. of awards offered: Varies.
Application Procedure: Applicants must submit a completed Nuffield application form with two pieces of recent academic written work. Applications must be made to the relevant faculty board of the university via the Graduate Admissions Office of the University.
Additional Information: Requests for information should be addressed to the Student Administrator. The studentships are offered in August for commencement in October. Candidates are advised to apply as early as possible.

For further information contact:

College Secretary
Nuffield College, Oxford, Oxfordshire, OX1 1NF, England
Email: glynis.baleham@nuf.ox.ac.uk
www: http://www.hicks.nuf.ox.ac.uk

Nuffield College ODA Shared Scholarship

Subjects: Social sciences in taught postgraduate courses.
Eligibility: Graduates from developing countries of the Commonwealth are eligible to apply.
Level of Study: Postdoctorate.
Type: Studentship.
Value: Fees and maintenance.
Length of Study: Up to three years.
Frequency: Annual.
Study Establishment: Nuffield College, the University of Oxford.
Country of Study: United Kingdom.
Application Procedure: Applicants must submit a list of publications, a curriculum vitae, a synopsis of the proposed research and the names and addresses of three referees when the post is advertised.

For further information contact:

College Secretary
Nuffield College, Oxford, Oxfordshire, OX1 1NF, England
Email: marion.rogers@nuf.ox.ac.uk

Oriel College Graduate Scholarships

Subjects: Arts or sciences.
Eligibility: Open to all graduates in residence in the College reading for a higher degree.
Level of Study: Postgraduate.
Type: Scholarship.
Value: UK £1,250.
Length of Study: Two years.
Study Establishment: Oriel College, the University of Oxford.
Country of Study: United Kingdom.
Application Procedure: Applicants must contact the Tutor for Graduates, in the first instance at Oriel College.

For further information contact:

Tutor for Graduates
Oriel College, Oxford, Oxfordshire, OX1 4EW, England

ORISHA (Oxford Research in the Scholarship and Humanities of Africa) Studentships

Subjects: Humanities.
Purpose: To support postgraduate study of Africa.
Eligibility: Applicants may be candidates for admission, or already registered as graduate students. The successful applicant, if not

already a member of an Oxford college, may be offered a place at St Antony's College or St Cross College.

Level of Study: Postgraduate.

Type: Studentship.

Value: College and university fees plus maintenance allowance. University fees will normally be covered at the home rate, although in exceptional circumstances supplemental grants may be made in order to meet, or to go some way towards meeting, the difference between home and overseas fee.

Length of Study: Two years with the possibility of extension for three and, very occasionally, four years.

Frequency: Annual.

Study Establishment: The University of Oxford.

Country of Study: United Kingdom.

No. of awards offered: One.

Application Procedure: Applicants must write to the Secretary of the Interfaculty Committee for African Studies at the the University Offices for further details.

Closing Date: February 25th.

OSI (Open Society Institute) Chevening Scholarships

Subjects: Humanities, social sciences, environmental sciences, public health or policy related areas of medical sciences.

Purpose: To assist candidates studying for a one year Master's degree in certain subjects or conducting research.

Eligibility: Open to citizens of central and eastern Europe namely Albania, Belarus, Bosnia, Bulgaria, Croatia, Estonia, Kazakhstan, Latvia, Lithuania, Macedonia, Moldova, Poland, Romania, Russia, Slovakia and the Ukraine.

Level of Study: Postgraduate.

Type: Scholarship.

Value: University and college fees, basic maintenance costs and travel to and from Oxford.

Length of Study: One year.

Frequency: Annual.

Study Establishment: The University of Oxford.

Country of Study: United Kingdom.

No. of awards offered: Up to 40.

Application Procedure: Applicants must submit a single application which will serve for both the Scholarship and for entry to the University. Application forms and further details are available from the OSI/SOROS Foundation office in the applicants country of residence. Addresses are listed on the website http://www.soros.org.

Closing Date: November 30th.

Funding: Government, Private.

Contributor: The OSI and the Foreign and Commonwealth Institute.

For further information contact:

International Office
University Offices
Wellington Square, Oxford, Oxfordshire, OX1 2JD, England

Overseas Research Student (ORS) Awards Scheme

Subjects: All subjects.

Level of Study: Postgraduate.

Value: Equivalent to the difference between home and overseas fees.

Length of Study: Renewable for as long as a student is liable for university fees.

Study Establishment: The University of Oxford.

Country of Study: United Kingdom.

No. of awards offered: Varies.

Application Procedure: Applicants must write for further details.

Closing Date: April 20th.

Funding: Government.

Contributor: The British Government.

Additional Information: Overseas Research Students awards can be held in conjunction with many other scholarships, and can be seen as an element of a package of financial support assembled by a prospective student. The degrees at Oxford which qualify as research courses for Overseas Research Students support are DPhil, MLitt, MSc by research, BPhil, MPhil (where an applicant intends to submit a dissertation), and those MSts in Research or Research Methods which are an integral part of a research programme in a particular subject. Therefore, students who are applying for admission as a Probationer Research Student (leading to a degree of DPhil, MLitt or MSc by research) or as a BPhil or MPhil are eligible to apply. Students applying for an MSt (other than the Research MSts defined above), MBA, MSc by coursework, MJur, BCL, Diploma or Certificate, or who will not submit a dissertation as part of an MPhil, are not eligible for an Overseas Research Student award. Competition for these awards is fierce and candidates should be aware that acceptance for study at Oxford does not necessarily mean the University will nominate them for an award. Nomination by the University does not guarantee success in the national Overseas Research Students competition. Candidates who gain an Overseas Research Students award may take it up at any time in the academic year for which it is initially awarded, but cannot defer the award for a full academic year. For further information please see the website.

For further information contact:

International Office
University Offices
Wellington Square, Oxford, Oxfordshire, OX1 2JD, England

Oxford Kobe Scholarships (Japan)

Subjects: All subjects.

Eligibility: Open to citizens of Japan taking up places to study for a graduate degree.

Level of Study: Graduate.

Type: Scholarship.

Value: University and college fees plus a maintenance allowance of UK £625 per month, as well as the cost of travel to and from Japan at the start and end of the course.

Length of Study: One year, with a possibility of renewal for a further two years.

Frequency: Annual.

Study Establishment: The University of Oxford. One of the scholarships will normally be tenable at St Catherine's College.

Country of Study: United Kingdom.

No. of awards offered: Two.

Application Procedure: Applicants must write for details or refer to the website.

Closing Date: December.

Additional Information: Further information and application details are available from the International Office.

For further information contact:

International Office
University Offices
Wellington Square, Oxford, Oxfordshire, OX1 2JD, England

Oxford University Graduate Studentships

Subjects: Dependent on the faculty or department offering the studentship.

Eligibility: Open to United Kingdom and European Union students only.

Type: Studentship.

Study Establishment: The University of Oxford in association with particular colleges.

Country of Study: United Kingdom.

No. of awards offered: Varies.

Application Procedure: Applicants must apply as directed on the standard application form for graduate study.

Additional Information: Studentships are awarded by a number of faculties and departments, in association with particular colleges. Potential applicants are asked to note that these studentships cannot be held in conjunction with other full cost awards and must be taken at the college which is associated with the studentship. Applicants should not rely on receiving a university graduate studentship in order to fund their study.

Oxford University Theological Scholarships in Eastern and Central Europe

Subjects: Theology.
Purpose: To enable students to pursue further studies in the University's Faculty of Theology.
Eligibility: Open to candidates, normally between the ages of 22 and 40, who will already have, or expect to obtain, a theological degree from a recognised university or theological college. Applications are invited from citizens of Russia, the Ukraine and any other countries of the former Soviet Union, apart from the Baltic States, Slovakia, Slovenia, Croatia, Bosnia, Macedonia, Bulgaria, Albania and Yugoslavia.
Level of Study: Graduate.
Type: Scholarship.
Value: Fees, a maintenance allowance and, where necessary, a return air fare.
Length of Study: Up to one year.
Study Establishment: The Faculty of Theology, the University of Oxford.
Country of Study: United Kingdom.
No. of awards offered: Up to four.
Application Procedure: Applicants must contact Mrs Elizabeth Macallister for further information.
Closing Date: December 31st.
Funding: Government, Private.
Contributor: Member churches of the Council of Churches for Britain and Ireland, the Foreign and Commonwealth Office and Oxford University.

For further information contact:

Humanities & Social Sciences Division
University of Oxford
34 St Giles, Oxford, Oxfordshire, OX1 3LH, England
Tel: (44) 1865 270117
Fax: (44) 1865 270553
Contact: Mrs Elizabeth Macallister

Pembroke College Australian Graduate Scholarship

Subjects: Classics, law, medicine, philosophy or theology.
Eligibility: Open to male graduates of Melbourne University.
Level of Study: Postgraduate.
Type: Scholarship.
Value: UK £4,000 per year.
Length of Study: Two years.
Frequency: Annual.
Study Establishment: Pembroke College, the University of Oxford.
Country of Study: United Kingdom.
No. of awards offered: Varies.
Application Procedure: Applicants must write for details.
Funding: Private.

For further information contact:

Dean of Graduate Students
Pembroke College, Oxford, Oxfordshire, OX1 1DW, England

Pembroke College Jose Gregorio Hernandez Award of the Venezuelan National Academy of Medicine

Subjects: Medicine or the biological sciences.
Eligibility: Open to nationals of Venezuela.
Level of Study: Postgraduate.
Type: Scholarship.
Value: Full fees and maintenance.
Length of Study: One year, renewable.
Frequency: Annual.
Study Establishment: Pembroke College, the University of Oxford.
Country of Study: United Kingdom.
No. of awards offered: Varies.
Application Procedure: Applicants must write for details.
Funding: Private.

For further information contact:

Dean of Graduate Students
Pembroke College, Oxford, Oxfordshire, OX1 1DW, England

Pembroke College TEPCO Senior Studentship

Subjects: Japanese studies.
Eligibility: Open to nationals from any country.
Level of Study: Postgraduate.
Type: Studentship.
Value: Fees and maintenance, where the holder has no other means of support.
Length of Study: One year, renewable for a further year.
Frequency: Annual.
Study Establishment: Pembroke College, the University of Oxford.
Country of Study: United Kingdom.
No. of awards offered: Varies.
Application Procedure: Applicants must write for details.
Funding: Private.

For further information contact:

Dean of Graduate Studies
Pembroke College, Oxford, Oxfordshire, OX1 1DW, England

Pirie-Reid Scholarships

Subjects: All subjects.
Purpose: To enable persons who would otherwise be prevented by lack of funds to begin a course of study at Oxford.
Level of Study: Postgraduate.
Type: Scholarship.
Value: University and college fees normally at the home rate plus maintenance grant, subject to assessment of income from other sources.
Length of Study: Renewable from year to year, subject to satisfactory progress and continuance of approved full-time study.
Frequency: Annual.
Study Establishment: The University of Oxford.
Country of Study: United Kingdom.
No. of awards offered: Up to two.
Application Procedure: Applicants must write for application forms. Candidates must apply for admission to the University through the Graduate Admissions Office.
Closing Date: May 1st.
Funding: Private.
Additional Information: Preference will be given to candidates applying from other universities ie. not matriculated at Oxford, and to those domiciled or educated in Scotland. Candidates not fulfilling these criteria are unlikely to be successful.

For further information contact:

Life & Environmental Sciences Divisional Office
2 South Parks Road, Oxford, Oxfordshire, OX1 3UB, England
Contact: Mrs J Brown

Prendergast Bequest

Subjects: All subjects.
Eligibility: Open to persons born in the Republic of Ireland whose parents are also citizens of the Republic of Ireland. Applicants must already be at Oxford, or have received a firm offer of both faculty and college place for a one year taught Master's course.
Level of Study: Postgraduate.
Type: Grant.
Value: Varies, approx. UK £500-2,000. The grant is means tested.
Length of Study: One year.
Frequency: Varies.
Study Establishment: The University of Oxford.
Country of Study: United Kingdom.
No. of awards offered: Varies.
Application Procedure: Applicants must complete an application form. Further information and application forms are available on written request.
Funding: Private.

For further information contact:

Secretary to the Board of Management
Prendergast Bequest
University Offices
Wellington Square, Oxford, Oxfordshire, OX1 2JD, England

The Queen's College Cyril and Phillis Long Studentship

Subjects: Varies.
Eligibility: Open to graduates of any country.
Level of Study: Postgraduate.
Type: Studentship.
Value: College and university fees plus the equivalent of a Research Council maintenance grant.
Length of Study: Three years, with a possibility of renewal for a fourth.
Frequency: Annual.
Study Establishment: The Queen's College, the University of Oxford.
Country of Study: United Kingdom.
No. of awards offered: Varies.
Closing Date: Please write for details.
Funding: Private.

For further information contact:

Tutor for Admissions
The Queen's College, Oxford, Oxfordshire, OX1 4AW, England

The Queen's College Florey EPA Scholarship

Subjects: Medical, biological or chemical sciences.
Eligibility: Open to nationals of European Union countries excluding United Kingdom and Ireland, Finland, Norway or Sweden.
Level of Study: Postgraduate.
Type: Scholarship.
Value: UK £2,000 per year. Assistance may also be given with fees to a maximum of half the cost.
Length of Study: One year, renewable for a second and third year.
Frequency: Annual.
Study Establishment: The Queen's College, the University of Oxford.
Country of Study: United Kingdom.
No. of awards offered: Varies.
Closing Date: Please contact the organisation.
Funding: Private.

For further information contact:

Tutor for Graduates
The Queen's College, Oxford, Oxfordshire, OX1 4AW, England

The Queen's College George Oakes Senior Scholarship

Subjects: Aspects of the culture of the United States of America.
Eligibility: Open to United Kingdom citizens.
Level of Study: Postgraduate.
Type: Scholarship.
Value: UK£5,000 per year.
Length of Study: One year, renewable for a second and third year.
Frequency: Varies, not available every year.
Study Establishment: The Queen's College, the University of Oxford.
Country of Study: United Kingdom.
No. of awards offered: One.

For further information contact:

Tutor for Graduates
The Queen's College, Oxford, Oxfordshire, OX1 4AW, England

The Queen's College Hastings Senior Scholarship

Subjects: All subjects.
Eligibility: Open to graduates with First Class (Honours) Degrees from the Universities of Bradford, Hull, Leeds, Sheffield or York.
Level of Study: Postgraduate.

Type: Scholarship.
Value: UK £2,000 per year (under review). Assistance may be given with fees if the holder is not eligible for Research Council or British Academy Studentships.
Length of Study: One year, renewable for a second and third year.
Study Establishment: The Queen's College, the University of Oxford.
Country of Study: United Kingdom.
Application Procedure: Applicants must contact the Tutor for Graduates, in the first instance at Queen's College.

For further information contact:

Tutor for Graduates
The Queen's College, Oxford, Oxfordshire, OX1 4AW, England

The Queen's College Holwell Studentship

Subjects: Religion and theology.
Eligibility: Open to home and overseas students.
Level of Study: Postgraduate.
Type: Studentship.
Value: UK £2,000 per year.
Length of Study: One year, renewable for a second and third year.
Study Establishment: The Queen's College, the University of Oxford.
Country of Study: United Kingdom.
No. of awards offered: One.

For further information contact:

Tutor for Graduates
The Queen's College, Oxford, Oxfordshire, OX1 4AW, England

The Queen's College ODA Shared Scholarship

Subjects: Forestry.
Eligibility: Open to graduates of developing countries of the Commonwealth.
Level of Study: Postgraduate.
Type: Scholarship.
Value: Fees and maintenance.
Length of Study: One year.
Frequency: Annual.
Study Establishment: The Queen's College, the University of Oxford.
Country of Study: United Kingdom.
No. of awards offered: One.
Closing Date: Please write for details.
Funding: Private.

For further information contact:

Tutor for Graduates
The Queen's College, Oxford, Oxfordshire, OX1 4AW, England

The Queen's College Wendell Herbruck Studentship

Subjects: All subjects.
Eligibility: Preference will be given to residents of Ohio, although the award is open to other United States residents, no older than 26 when appointed.
Level of Study: Postgraduate.
Type: Studentship.
Value: UK £2,000 per year.
Length of Study: One year, renewable for a second or third year.
Frequency: Varies.
Study Establishment: The Queen's College, the University of Oxford.
Country of Study: United Kingdom.
No. of awards offered: Varies.
Application Procedure: Applicants must write for details.
Funding: Private.
Additional Information: The next election is expected for entry in 2003.

For further information contact:

Tutor for Graduates
The Queen's College, Oxford, Oxfordshire, OX1 4AW, England

Radhakrishnan/British Chevening Scholarships

Subjects: All subjects.
Eligibility: Open to nationals of India.
Level of Study: Postgraduate.
Value: University and colleges fees and maintenance for the duration of the student's course.
Frequency: Annual.
Study Establishment: The University of Oxford.
Country of Study: United Kingdom.
No. of awards offered: Two.
Application Procedure: Applicants must write for further information and an application form or refer to the website.
Closing Date: April 1st.
Additional Information: For further details please contact the University Offices.

For further information contact:

International Office
University Offices
Wellington Square, Oxford, Oxfordshire, OX1 2JD, England

Regent's Park College (Permanent Private Hall) Asheville Scholarship

Subjects: Theology.
Eligibility: Open to men and women from Baptist seminaries in the United States of America.
Level of Study: Postgraduate.
Type: Scholarship.
Value: Up to UK £1,000 per year.
Length of Study: The second and third year of the course.
Frequency: Annual.
Study Establishment: Regents Park College (Permanent Private Hall), the University of Oxford.
Country of Study: United Kingdom.
No. of awards offered: Varies.
Application Procedure: Applicants must contact the College for further information.
Funding: Private.

For further information contact:

Regent's Park College
Pusey Street, Oxford, Oxfordshire, OX1 2LB, England

Regent's Park College (Permanent Private Hall) Eastern European Scholarship

Subjects: Theology.
Eligibility: Open to students from Central and Eastern Europe, with a preference given (but not restricted to), members of the Baptist denomination.
Level of Study: Postgraduate.
Type: Scholarship.
Value: Up to UK £1,800 per year.
Length of Study: Up to three years.
Frequency: Annual.
Study Establishment: Regent's Park College (Permanent Private Hall), the University of Oxford.
Country of Study: United Kingdom.
No. of awards offered: One.
Application Procedure: Applicants must contact the College for further information.
Funding: Private.

For further information contact:

Regent's Park College
Pusey Street, Oxford, Oxfordshire, OX1 2LB, England

Regent's Park College (Permanent Private Hall) Ernest Payne Scholarship

Subjects: Theology.
Eligibility: Open to men and women resident in the United Kingdom preparing for Baptist ministry.
Level of Study: Postgraduate.
Type: Scholarship.
Value: Up to UK £1,500 per year towards fees.
Length of Study: Two years, extendable to three.
Frequency: Annual.
Study Establishment: Regent's Park College (Permanent Private Hall), the University of Oxford.
Country of Study: United Kingdom.
No. of awards offered: One.
Application Procedure: Applicants must contact the College for further information.
Funding: Private.

For further information contact:

Regent's Park College
Pusey Street, Oxford, Oxfordshire, OX1 2LB, England

Regent's Park College (Permanent Private Hall) Henman Scholarship

Subjects: Theology.
Eligibility: Open to overseas students.
Level of Study: Postgraduate.
Type: Scholarship.
Value: Up to UK £1,800 per year.
Length of Study: Up to three years.
Frequency: Annual.
Study Establishment: Regents Park College (Permanent Private Hall), the University of Oxford.
Country of Study: United Kingdom.
No. of awards offered: Varies.
Application Procedure: Applicants must contact the College for further information.
Funding: Private.

For further information contact:

Regent's Park College
Pusey Street, Oxford, Oxfordshire, OX1 2LB, England

Regent's Park College (Permanent Private Hall) J W Lord Scholarship

Subjects: Medicine or theology.
Eligibility: Open to men and women preparing to serve Christian churches in India, Hong Kong and China, or otherwise in Asia, Africa, Central and South America and the Caribbean, also available for in-service training or sabbatical study for similar candidates.
Level of Study: Postgraduate.
Type: Scholarship.
Value: Up to UK £1,500 per year.
Length of Study: Up to three years.
Frequency: Annual.
Study Establishment: Regent's Park College (Permanent Private Hall), the University of Oxford.
Country of Study: United Kingdom.
No. of awards offered: Varies.
Application Procedure: Applicants must contact the College at the address below for further information.
Funding: Private.

For further information contact:

Regent's Park College
Pusey Street, Oxford, Oxfordshire, OX1 2LB, England

Regent's Park College (Permanent Private Hall) Organ Scholarship

Subjects: All subjects but with a preference for music.

Eligibility: Open to suitably qualified candidates in any subject, but preference will be given to graduate students in music.
Level of Study: Postgraduate.
Type: Scholarship.
Value: UK £2,000 per year.
Length of Study: Up to three years, with a possibility of renewal annually.
Frequency: Annual.
Study Establishment: Regent's Park College (Permanent Private Hall), the University of Oxford.
Country of Study: United Kingdom.
No. of awards offered: Varies.
Application Procedure: Applicants must contact the College for further information.
Funding: Private.
Additional Information: The scholarship includes duties as musical director and organist at New Road Baptist Church.

For further information contact:

Regent's Park College
Pusey Street, Oxford, Oxfordshire, OX1 2LB, England

Regent's Park College Studentships of the Centre for the Study of Christianity and Culture

Subjects: Any area concerning the relation of the Christian faith to culture.
Level of Study: Postgraduate.
Type: Studentship.
Value: College fees.
Length of Study: Up to three years.
Study Establishment: Regent's Park College, (Permanent Private Hall), the University of Oxford.
Country of Study: United Kingdom.

For further information contact:

The Tutor for Graduates
Regent's Park College
Pusey Street, Oxford, Oxfordshire, OX1 2LB, England

Rhodes Scholarships

Subjects: All subjects.
Eligibility: Candidates must be aged 19-25 years, though in Kenya the upper age limit is 27. Rhodes Scholars must have graduated from a university and have resided for a number of years in their country of origin. The annual distribution of awards is as follows: Australia - nine, Bermuda - one, Commonwealth Caribbean - two, Canada - 11, Germany - four, Hong Kong - one, India - six, Jamaica - one, Kenya - two, Malaysia - one, New Zealand - three, Pakistan - two, Singapore - one, South Africa - 10, Uganda - one, United States of America - 32, Zambia - one, Zimbabwe - two, Bangladesh - one.
Level of Study: Doctorate, Graduate, Postgraduate.
Type: Scholarship.
Value: University and college fees and maintenance stipend.
Length of Study: Two-three years.
Frequency: Annual.
Study Establishment: The University of Oxford.
Country of Study: United Kingdom.
No. of awards offered: 90.
Application Procedure: Rhodes Scholars are chosen by local Selection Committees in each constituency. There is no formal written examination as Scholars are chosen for their academic all round qualities on the evidence of testimonials from responsible persons and after personal interviews by the Selection Committee concerned. Elections usually take place in November and December and the Scholars come into residence the following October. After election, application is made on behalf of Scholars for admission to individual colleges and faculties in Oxford and the election is not confirmed by the Rhodes Trustees until the Scholar-elect has been accepted for admission by the college.
Funding: Private.
Contributor: The Rhodes Trust.

Additional Information: All applications should be made to the Secretary of the local Selection Committee. A separate memorandum explaining the regulations in details is published for each country and may be obtained from the local secretaries. See http://www.rhodesscholar.org for further information.

For further information contact:

Civil & Environmental Engineering Department
University of Melbourne
Parkville, VIC, 3052, Australia
Contact: Professor G L Hutchinson

Secretary
The Rhodes Scholarship Selection Committee
Department of Political Science
University of Dhaka, Dhaka, 1000, Bangladesh
Contact: Professor T Maniruzzaman

c/o Conyers, Dill & Pearman
PO Box HM 319
Clarendon House
Church Street, Hamilton, HM BX, Bermuda
Contact: Mr J C Collis

General Secretary
Rhodes Scholarship Trust
PO Box 48
Toronto - Dominion Centre, Toronto, ON, M5K 1E6, Canada
Contact: Mr A R A Scace QC

Scherneck
Alteschlostraße 9, Untersiemau, D-96253, Germany
Contact: Mr T F M Böcking

Rhodes Scholarship Selection Committee
Office of Student Affairs
The Chinese University of Hong Kong, Shatin, NT, Hong Kong
Contact: Mrs C Lee

International Centre for Genetic Engineering & Biotechnology
Aruna Asaf Ali Marg, New Delhi, 110067, India
Contact: Professor V S Chauhan

Secretary
Rhodes Scholarship Selection Committee
PO Box 417, Kingston, 6, Jamaica
Contact: Mr Peter S Goldson

Secretary
Rhodes Scholarship Selection Committee
PO Box 2588
Kenyatta National Hospital, Nairobi, Kenya

Scholarships & Training Officer
The British Council
Jalan Bukit Aman
PO Box10539, Kuala Lumpur, 50916, Malaysia
Contact: Miss M Chow

Scholarships Officer
New Zealand Vice Chancellors' Committee
PO Box 11-915, Wellington, New Zealand

Secretary
Rhodes Scholarship Selection Committee
PO Box 2939, Islamabad, Pakistan

Secretary
Rhodes Scholarship Selection Committee
c/o 119 Dover Road, 139656, Singapore
Contact: Dr Ong Teck Chin

General Secretary
Rhodes Scholarships in Southern Africa
PO Box 41468
Craighill, Gauteng, 2024, South Africa

The British Council
PO Box 7070, Kampala, Uganda

Rhodes Scholarship Trust
8229 Boone Boulevard

Suite 240, Vienna, VA, 22182-2623, United States of America
Contact: Mr E F Gerson

Director
Institute for African Studies
University of Zambia
PO Box 30900, Lusaka, Zambia
Contact: Professor A S Saasa

Secretary
Rhodes Scholarships Selection Committee
PO Box 53, Harare, Zimbabwe
Contact: Mr D L L Morgan

Sasakawa Fund Scholarships

Subjects: All subjects which require some period of study in Japan.
Eligibility: Candidates must be Japanese nationals or students from countries other than Japan whose course at Oxford University requires some period of study in Japan.
Level of Study: Doctorate, Graduate.
Type: Scholarship.
Value: Up to UK £5,000.
Length of Study: One year in the first instance, with the possibility of renewal for a maximum of three years, subject to satisfactory progress.
Frequency: Varies.
Study Establishment: The University of Oxford.
Country of Study: United Kingdom.
No. of awards offered: Up to two.
Application Procedure: Applicants from outside the United Kingdom must complete the Scholarships and Bursaries for International Student form available from the International Office or the university website. Applicants from the United Kingdom should contact the Secretary of the Sasakawa Fund.
Closing Date: May 1st.

For further information contact:

Secretary
The Sasakawa Fund
The Oriental Institute
Pusey Lane, Oxford, Oxfordshire, OX1 2LE, England
Tel: (44) 1865 278225
Fax: (44) 1865 278190
Email: alix.slater@orinst.ox.ac.uk

Scatcherd European Scholarships

Subjects: All subjects.
Eligibility: Open to nationals of any European country, excluding the United Kingdom and Turkey, but including the Russian Federation and other countries to the west of the Urals. Applicants must be taking up places to read either for a postgraduate degree or a second BA or to spend a period of study as a Graduate Visiting Student at the University of Oxford.
Level of Study: Postgraduate.
Type: Scholarship.
Value: University and college fees, plus maintenance grant.
Study Establishment: The University of Oxford.
Country of Study: United Kingdom.
No. of awards offered: Varies.
Application Procedure: Applicants must complete the application form obtainable from the International Office.
Closing Date: March.

For further information contact:

International Office
University Offices
Wellington Square, Oxford, Oxfordshire, OX1 2JD, England

Shell Centenary Scholarships and Shell Centenary Chevening Scholarships

Subjects: Applied statistics, computer science, mathematics and foundations of computer science, environmental change and management, economics for development, industrial relations and human resources management, public policy in Latin America, forced migration, or forestry and its relation to land use.
Purpose: To assist with Master's degrees.
Eligibility: Open to students from countries which are not present or applicant members of the Organisation for Economic Co-operation and Development (OECD). Candidates should normally be aged 20-35 years and be intending to return to the home country at the end of the period of study. They should normally already hold a degree of an equivalent standard to a United Kingdom First Class (Honours) Degree or be expecting to obtain such a degree before the start of their proposed course.
Level of Study: Postgraduate.
Value: University and college fees, maintenance and return air travel to the United Kingdom.
Study Establishment: The University of Oxford.
Country of Study: United Kingdom.
No. of awards offered: At least eight.
Application Procedure: Applicants must apply separately for admission to Oxford through the Graduate Admissions Office. Please write for further particulars and an application form or visit the website.
Closing Date: January 31st.

For further information contact:

International Office
University Offices
Wellington Square, Oxford, Oxfordshire, OX1 2JD, England

Sir John Rhys Studentship in Celtic Studies

Subjects: Celtic studies.
Purpose: To enable the successful candidate to complete a research programme on which he or she is already engaged.
Eligibility: Open to persons engaged in graduate research in Celtic studies who need financial support in respect of living expenses or fees. The award is not intended for those who hold full-time university posts.
Level of Study: Postgraduate.
Type: Studentship.
Value: Dependent on circumstances. The value is normally similar to that of a graduate studentship from a United Kingdom research council.
Length of Study: One year, renewable only in exceptional circumstances.
Frequency: Annual.
Study Establishment: The University of Oxford, normally Jesus College.
Country of Study: United Kingdom.
No. of awards offered: One.
Application Procedure: Applicants must send applications to the Secretary of the Taylor Institution and should include: a curriculum vitae, a brief outline of the research proposed, an indication of the size of grant required ie. any necessary expenses in addition to the normal living costs of a graduate student and of other sources of financial support, brief details of any other awards or appointments for which the candidate is applying, the names of two academic referees, and the candidate's address for the Easter period if different from the term time address. Applicants who are not already members of the University should apply for admission through the Graduate Admissions Office.
Closing Date: March 1st.
Funding: Private.
Contributor: The Sir John Rhys Fund.
Additional Information: The successful applicant, if not already a member of the University of Oxford, would normally become a member of Jesus College and would be expected to reside in Oxford for the greater part of the academic year.

For further information contact:

Secretary of the Taylor Institution
37 Wellington Square, Oxford, Oxfordshire, OX1 2JF, England
Email: enquiries@modern-languages.ox.ac.uk

Somerville College Graduate Scholarships

Subjects: All subjects offered by the College.
Eligibility: Open to students of any nationality who are reading for a higher degree at Somerville College, University of Oxford.
Level of Study: Postgraduate.
Type: Scholarship.
Value: UK £1,500 per year minimum.
Length of Study: Two years, with the possibility of renewal for a third year.
Frequency: Annual.
Study Establishment: Somerville College, the University of Oxford.
Country of Study: United Kingdom.
No. of awards offered: Two.
Application Procedure: Applicants must contact the College Secretary.

For further information contact:

College Secretary
Somerville College, Oxford, Oxfordshire, OX2 6HD, England

Somerville College Margaret Pelly Scholarship

Subjects: Biochemistry, experimental psychology, human anatomy and genetics, pathology, pharmacology, physiology, plant sciences or zoology.
Level of Study: Postgraduate.
Type: Scholarship.
Value: At least UK £2,000 per year.
Length of Study: Two years in the first instance.
Study Establishment: Somerville College, the University of Oxford.
Country of Study: United Kingdom.

For further information contact:

College Secretary
Somerville College, Oxford, Oxfordshire, OX2 6HD, England

Somerville College Oxford Bursary for American Graduates (Janet Watson Bursary)

Subjects: All subjects.
Eligibility: For those reading for a higher degree or diploma.
Level of Study: Postgraduate.
Type: Bursary.
Value: Approximately one quarter of total fees to a maximum of UK £3,500 per year.
Length of Study: Two years.
Study Establishment: Somerville College, the University of Oxford.
Country of Study: United Kingdom.
Application Procedure: Applicants must contact the College Secretary.
Funding: Private.

For further information contact:

College Secretary
Somerville College, Oxford, Oxfordshire, OX2 6HD, England

St Anne's College Ethics Scholarship

Subjects: Philosophy.
Level of Study: Postgraduate.
Type: Scholarship.
Value: UK £1,500.
Length of Study: One year.
Frequency: Annual.
Study Establishment: St Anne's College, the University of Oxford.
Country of Study: United Kingdom.
No. of awards offered: One.
Application Procedure: All graduate students with an interest in ethics who have accepted a place at St Anne's by June 20th to read for a higher degree in philosophy of more than one year's duration will automatically be considered without any further application being necessary.
Closing Date: June 20th.

For further information contact:

St Anne's College, Oxford, Oxfordshire, OX2 6HS, England
Contact: Dr R Crisp

St Anne's College Irene Jamieson Research Scholarship

Subjects: Any arts or social science subject offered by the College.
Purpose: To fund graduate research.
Eligibility: Open to United Kingdom or European Community citizens who are graduates of any university, or individuals who can show some other proof of their ability to undertake advanced work. Candidates who are graduates of a British university must have obtained a First or Upper Second Class (Honours) Degree. All candidates must be accepted by the University of Oxford to read for a higher degree of at least two years duration, and by the college by June 1st. Candidates for one year courses or for second BA degrees are not eligible.
Level of Study: Postgraduate.
Type: Scholarship.
Value: Equal to the college fee.
Length of Study: One year, renewable for a further year.
Frequency: Annual.
Study Establishment: St Anne's College, the University of Oxford.
Country of Study: United Kingdom.
No. of awards offered: One.
Application Procedure: All graduates who have accepted a place at St Anne's by June 20th will automatically be considered without any further application being necessary. For more information contact the College Secretary.
Closing Date: June 20th.

For further information contact:

College Secretary
St Anne's College, Oxford, Oxfordshire, OX2 6HS, England

St Anne's College Olwen Rhys Research Scholarship

Subjects: Medieval romance language, literature or medieval history.
Purpose: To fund graduate research.
Eligibility: Open to United Kingdom or European Community citizens who are graduates of any university, or individuals who can show other proof of their ability to undertake advanced work. Candidates who are graduates of a British university must have obtained a First or Upper Second Class (Honours) Degree. All candidates must be accepted by the University of Oxford to read for a higher degree of at least two years duration, and by the college by June 1st. Candidates for one year courses and for a second BA degrees are not eligible.
Level of Study: Postgraduate.
Type: Scholarship.
Value: Equal to the college fee.
Length of Study: One year, renewable for a further year.
Frequency: Annual.
Study Establishment: St Anne's College, the University of Oxford.
Country of Study: United Kingdom.
No. of awards offered: One.
Application Procedure: All graduates who have accepted a place at St Anne's by June 20th will automatically be considered without any further application being necessary. For more information contact the College Secretary.
Closing Date: June 20th.

For further information contact:

College Secretary
St Anne's College, Oxford, Oxfordshire, OX2 6HS, England

St Anne's College Overseas Scholarship

Subjects: All subjects offered by the university.
Purpose: To fund graduate research.
Eligibility: Open to graduates of any university who are not United Kingdom or European Community citizens. All candidates must be accepted by the college by June 1st, by the University of Oxford to

read for a higher degree of at least two years duration. Candidates for one year courses or second BA degrees are not eligible.
Level of Study: Postgraduate.
Type: Scholarship.
Value: Equal to the college fee.
Length of Study: One year, renewable for a further year.
Frequency: Annual.
Study Establishment: St Anne's College, the University of Oxford.
Country of Study: United Kingdom.
No. of awards offered: Three.
Application Procedure: All graduates who have accepted a place at St Anne's by June 20th will automatically be considered without any further application being necessary. For more information contact the College Secretary.
Closing Date: June 20th.

For further information contact:

College Secretary
College Secretary
St Anne's College, Oxford, Oxfordshire, OX2 6HS, England

St Anne's College Research Scholarship

Subjects: Arts or social science subjects.
Eligibility: Candidates for one year courses or second BAs will not be eligible.
Level of Study: Postgraduate.
Type: Scholarship.
Value: Equal to the college fee.
Length of Study: One year, renewable for a further year.
Frequency: Annual.
Study Establishment: St Anne's College, the University of Oxford.
Country of Study: United Kingdom.
No. of awards offered: One.
Application Procedure: All graduate students who have accepted a place at St Anne's will automatically be considered without any further application being necessary. For further information contact the College Secretary.
Closing Date: June 30th.
Funding: Private.

For further information contact:

College Secretary
St Anne's College, Oxford, Oxfordshire, OX2 6HS, England

St Anne's College Una Goodwin Research Scholarship

Subjects: Any science subject offered by the College.
Purpose: To fund graduate research.
Eligibility: Open to United Kingdom or European Community citizens who are graduates of any university, or individuals who can show other proof of their ability to undertake advanced work. Candidates who are graduates of a British university must have obtained a First or Upper Second Class (Honours) Degree. All candidates must be accepted by the University of Oxford to read for a higher degree of at least two years duration, and by the college by June 1st. Candidates for one year courses or second BA degrees are not eligible.
Level of Study: Postgraduate.
Type: Scholarship.
Value: Equal to the college fee.
Length of Study: One year, renewable for a further year.
Frequency: Annual.
Study Establishment: St Anne's College, the University of Oxford.
Country of Study: United Kingdom.
No. of awards offered: One.
Application Procedure: All graduates who have accepted a place at St Anne's by June 20th will automatically be considered without any further application being necessary. For more information contact the College Secretary.
Closing Date: June 20th.

For further information contact:

College Secretary
St Anne's College, Oxford, Oxfordshire, OX2 6HS, England

St Antony's College EFG Bank Group Scholarship

Subjects: Any of the subjects in which the college specialises.
Eligibility: Open to graduate students of Greek nationality reading for a higher degree in any of the subjects in which the college specialises.
Level of Study: Graduate.
Type: Scholarship.
Value: Fees, maintenance and travel costs.
Length of Study: Two years.
Study Establishment: St Antony's College, the University of Oxford.
Country of Study: United Kingdom.
Application Procedure: Applicants must contact the College Secretary.
Funding: Private.

For further information contact:

College Secretary
St Anthony's College, Oxford, Oxfordshire, OX2 6JF, England

St Antony's College Fay and Geoffrey Elliott Graduate Studentship in Russian and East European Studies

Subjects: Russian and East European studies, especially in the social sciences or modern history with particular reference to the former Soviet Union and its successor states.
Eligibility: Open to United Kingdom students studying for a doctorate.
Level of Study: Postgraduate.
Type: Studentship.
Value: Fees and maintenance.
Length of Study: Varies.
Study Establishment: St Antony's College, the University of Oxford.
Country of Study: United Kingdom.

For further information contact:

Director
The Russian & East European Studies Centre
St Anthony's College, Oxford, Oxfordshire, OX2 6JF, England

St Antony's College Ismene Fitch Scholarship

Subjects: Humanities.
Eligibility: Open to graduate students of Greek nationality reading for a doctorate in the humanities.
Level of Study: Doctorate.
Type: Scholarship.
Value: Fees and maintenance.
Length of Study: Three years.
Frequency: Every six years.
Study Establishment: St Antony's College, the University of Oxford.
Country of Study: United Kingdom.

For further information contact:

College Secretary
St Anthony's College, Oxford, Oxfordshire, OX2 6JF, England

St Antony's College Ronaldo Falconer Scholarship

Subjects: All subjects in which the College specialises.
Eligibility: Open to graduate students from Costa Rica studying for a higher degree.
Level of Study: Graduate.
Type: Scholarship.
Value: Fees, maintenance and some travel costs.
Length of Study: One-three years depending on course.

Study Establishment: St Antony's College, the University of Oxford.
Country of Study: United Kingdom.
Application Procedure: Applicants must write for details.
Closing Date: Please write for details.

For further information contact:

CIAPA
PO Box 4224, San Jose, Costa Rica
Fax: (506) 224 9280
Email: enquiries@lac.ox.ac.uk

Director
Latin American Centre
St Antony's College, Oxford, Oxfordshire, England

St Antony's College Sassoon Scholarship

Subjects: All subjects in which the College specialises.
Eligibility: Open to graduate students reading for a doctorate.
Level of Study: Doctorate.
Type: Scholarship.
Value: University and college fees.
Length of Study: Three years.
Frequency: Annual.
Study Establishment: St Antony's College, the University of Oxford.
Country of Study: United Kingdom.

For further information contact:

College Secretary
St Anthony's College, Oxford, Oxfordshire, OX2 6JF, England

St Antony's College Sir John Swire Scholarship

Subjects: All subjects in which the College specialises.
Eligibility: Open to graduate students from north east and south east Asia studying for a higher degree.
Level of Study: Graduate.
Type: Scholarship.
Value: Fees, maintenance and some travel costs.
Length of Study: Two years, with a possibility of renewal for a further year.
Frequency: Every three years.
Study Establishment: St Antony's College, the University of Oxford.
Country of Study: United Kingdom.
Application Procedure: Applicants must write for details.
Funding: Commercial.

For further information contact:

College Secretary
St Antony's College, Oxford, Oxfordshire, OX2 6JF, England

St Antony's College Swire Centenary and Cathay Pacific Scholarship (Japan)

Subjects: All subjects in which the College specialises.
Eligibility: Open to students from Japan studying for a higher degree.
Level of Study: Graduate.
Type: Scholarship.
Value: Fees, maintenance and some travel costs.
Length of Study: Two years, with a possibility of renewal for a further year.
Frequency: Annual.
Study Establishment: St Antony's College, the University of Oxford.
Country of Study: United Kingdom.
Application Procedure: Applicants must write for details.
Closing Date: Please write for details.
Funding: Commercial.

For further information contact:

John Swire & Sons Japan Limited
Level 16
Shiroyama JT Mori Building
4-3-1 Toranomon
Minato-ku, Tokyo, 105-6016, Japan

St Antony's College Swire/Cathay Pacific Scholarship (Hong Kong)

Subjects: All subjects in which the College specialises.
Eligibility: Open to permanent residents of Hong Kong who have completed the majority of their education there.
Level of Study: Graduate.
Type: Scholarship.
Value: Fees, maintenance and some travel costs.
Length of Study: Two years, with a possibility of renewal for a further year.
Frequency: Annual.
Study Establishment: St Antony's College, the University of Oxford.
Country of Study: United Kingdom.
Application Procedure: Applicants must write for details.
Closing Date: Please write for details.
Funding: Commercial.

For further information contact:

Staff Co-ordinator
John Swire & Sons (HK) Limited
35/F Two Pacific Place
88 Queensway, Hong Kong

St Antony's College Swire/Cathay Pacific Scholarship (Republic of Korea)

Subjects: All subjects in which the College specialises.
Eligibility: Open to graduate students from the Republic of Korea studying for a higher degree.
Level of Study: Graduate.
Type: Scholarship.
Value: Fees, maintenance and some travel costs.
Length of Study: Two years, with a possibility of renewal for a further year.
Frequency: Annual.
Study Establishment: St Antony's College, the University of Oxford.
Country of Study: United Kingdom.
Application Procedure: Applicants must write for details.
Closing Date: Please write for details.
Funding: Commercial.

For further information contact:

Personnel & Administration Department
Cathay Pacific Airways Limited
5th Floor Chase Plaza Building
34-35 Jung-dong, Choong-ku, Seoul, 100-120, Korea, Republic (South)

St Antony's College Swire/Chevening Scholarship (Hong Kong)

Subjects: All subjects in which the College specialises.
Eligibility: Open to graduate students who are permanent residents of Hong Kong and who have completed the majority of their education there.
Level of Study: Graduate.
Type: Scholarship.
Value: Fees, maintenance and some travel costs.
Length of Study: Two years, with a possibility of renewal for a further year.
Frequency: Annual.
Study Establishment: St Antony's College, the University of Oxford.
Country of Study: United Kingdom.

Application Procedure: Applicants must write for details.
Closing Date: Please write for details.
Funding: Commercial.

For further information contact:

Staff Co-ordinator
John Swire & Sons (HK) Limited
35/F Two Pacific Place
88 Queensway, Hong Kong

St Catherine's College Glaxo Scholarship in Medicine (2nd BM)

Subjects: Medicine.
Eligibility: Open to any student who has a confirmed place on the clinical medicine course (2nd BM) in the Oxford Medical School. Preference will be given to students who are not eligible for full funding eg. graduates who have already completed an honours degree before embarking on the pre-clinical course (1st BM) or the fast track graduate medical course.
Value: UK £1,500 per year.
Length of Study: Up to three years.
Study Establishment: St Catherine's College, the University of Oxford.
Country of Study: United Kingdom.
Closing Date: February.

For further information contact:

Tutor for Graduates
St Catherine's College, Oxford, Oxfordshire, OX2 6JF, England

St Catherine's College Great Eastern Scholarship

Subjects: All subjects.
Eligibility: Open to Indian nationals.
Level of Study: Graduate.
Type: Scholarship.
Value: UK £2,000 per year.
Length of Study: Up to three years.
Frequency: Varies, not available every year.
Study Establishment: St Catherine's College, the University of Oxford.
Country of Study: United Kingdom.
Closing Date: July.

For further information contact:

Tutor for Graduates
St Catherine's College, Oxford, Oxfordshire, OX2 6HD, England

St Catherine's College Leathersellers' Company Graduate Scholarship

Subjects: Research in the physical or biological sciences, mathematics or engineering.
Eligibility: Open to graduates of any British university who wish to undertake research in the physical or biological sciences, mathematics and engineering. This may be held in conjunction with another award.
Level of Study: Graduate.
Type: Scholarship.
Value: UK £2,000 per year.
Length of Study: Up to three years.
Frequency: Annual.
Study Establishment: St Catherine's College, the University of Oxford.
Country of Study: United Kingdom.
Application Procedure: Applicants must contact the Tutor for Graduates or see the website.
Closing Date: April.
Funding: Private.

For further information contact:

Tutor for Graduates
St Catherine's College

Manor Road, Oxford, Oxfordshire, OX1 3UJ, England
www: http://www.stcatz.ox.ac.uk

St Catherine's College Overseas Graduate Scholarship

Subjects: All subjects.
Purpose: To assist graduates studying for a research degree, usually in their first year at the University of Oxford.
Eligibility: Open to qualified individuals who are citizens of non European Union countries.
Level of Study: Postgraduate.
Type: Scholarship.
Value: UK £1,500.
Length of Study: Two years. Current holders may reapply for a third year.
Frequency: Varies.
Country of Study: United Kingdom.
No. of awards offered: One.
Application Procedure: Applicants must write for details.
Closing Date: July 31st.

For further information contact:

Tutor for Graduates
St Catherine's College, Oxford, Oxfordshire, OX1 3UJ, England

St Cross College Major College Scholarships

Subjects: All subjects.
Purpose: To support postgraduate study.
Level of Study: Postgraduate.
Type: Scholarship.
Value: UK £1,819 per year.
Length of Study: One-three years.
Frequency: Annual.
Study Establishment: St Cross College, the University of Oxford.
Country of Study: United Kingdom.
Closing Date: February and March.

For further information contact:

Tutor for Admissions
St Cross College, Oxford, Oxfordshire, OX1 3LZ, England

St Cross College Paula Soans O'Brian Scholarships

Subjects: All subjects.
Purpose: To support postgraduate study.
Level of Study: Postgraduate.
Type: Scholarship.
Value: UK £1,819 per year.
Length of Study: One-three years.
Frequency: Varies.
Study Establishment: St Cross College, the University of Oxford.
Country of Study: United Kingdom.
Closing Date: Please write for details.

For further information contact:

Tutor for Admissions
St Cross College, Oxford, Oxfordshire, OX1 3LZ, England

St Cross College Unilever Scholarship

Subjects: Science, particularly biochemistry or engineering.
Purpose: To support postgraduate study.
Eligibility: Open to any student from Oxford or from other Institutes of Higher Education who intends to study, or is studying, for a postgraduate degree in science.
Level of Study: Postgraduate.
Type: Scholarship.
Value: UK £1,819 per year.
Length of Study: One-three years.
Frequency: Annual.
Study Establishment: St Cross College, the University of Oxford.
Country of Study: United Kingdom.
No. of awards offered: One.
Application Procedure: Applicants must write for details.

Funding: Commercial.
Contributor: Unilever.

For further information contact:

Tutor for Admissions
St Cross College, Oxford, Oxfordshire, OX1 3LZ, England

St Edmund Hall William R Miller Graduate Awards

Subjects: All subjects.
Level of Study: Postgraduate.
Value: Accommodation.
Length of Study: Two years.
Frequency: Annual.
Study Establishment: St Edmund Hall, the University of Oxford.
Country of Study: United Kingdom.
No. of awards offered: Three per year.
Application Procedure: Applicants must contact the Senior Tutor at St Edmund Hall for further information.
Closing Date: May 1st.

For further information contact:

Senior Tutor
St Edmund Hall, Oxford, Oxfordshire, OX1 4AR, England

St Hilda's College Dame Helen Gardner Scholarship

Subjects: Humanities.
Purpose: To support study in the humanities.
Eligibility: Open to women who have been accepted to read for a higher research degree at Oxford in the humanities.
Level of Study: Postgraduate.
Type: Scholarship.
Value: Up to UK £5,000 per year.
Length of Study: One-three years.
Frequency: Usually every three years.
Study Establishment: St Hilda's College, the University of Oxford.
Country of Study: United Kingdom.
No. of awards offered: One.
Application Procedure: Applicants must write for details.
Funding: Private.
Contributor: Dame Helen Gardner Bequest.
Additional Information: The next scholarship will be available in 2004.

For further information contact:

Admissions Secretary
St Hilda's College, Oxford, Oxfordshire, OX4 1DY, England

St Hilda's College Graduate Scholarships

Subjects: All subjects offered by the University.
Eligibility: Open to female graduates from any country working for a higher research degree.
Level of Study: Postgraduate.
Type: Scholarship.
Value: Up to UK £1,000 per year.
Length of Study: One-three years.
Frequency: Annual.
Study Establishment: St Hilda's College, the University of Oxford.
Country of Study: United Kingdom.
Funding: Private.
Contributor: St Hilda's College.

For further information contact:

Admissions Secretary
St Hilda's College, Oxford, Oxfordshire, OX4 1DY, England

St Hilda's College New Zealand Bursaries

Subjects: All subjects offered by the University.
Eligibility: Open to female students who are New Zealand citizens and who have been accepted for a graduate research degree.
Level of Study: Postgraduate.

Type: Bursary.
Value: Up to UK £2,000 per year.
Length of Study: One-three years.
Frequency: Annual.
Study Establishment: St Hilda's College, the University of Oxford.
Country of Study: United Kingdom.
No. of awards offered: Varies.
Funding: Private.
Contributor: The Raymond and Sisam Funds.
Additional Information: Though the main criteria for the award is academic merit, financial circumstances are also considered. Applicants must show evidence of sufficient funding to complete their course.

For further information contact:

Admissions Secretary
St Hilda's College, Oxford, Oxfordshire, OX4 1DY, England

St Hugh's College Bursaries for Students from PRC

Subjects: All subjects offered at the College.
Eligibility: Open to nationals of the People's Republic of China.
Level of Study: Postgraduate.
Type: Scholarship.
Value: UK £2,000 per year.
Length of Study: Two years, with the possibility of renewal for the fee paying duration of the course.
Study Establishment: St Hugh's College, the University of Oxford.
Country of Study: United Kingdom.
Application Procedure: Applicants must contact the Academic Administrator in the first instance.

For further information contact:

Academic Administrator
St Hugh's College, Oxford, Oxfordshire, OX2 6LE, England

St Hugh's College Dorothea Gray Scholarship

Subjects: Classics.
Eligibility: Open to candidates of any nationality.
Level of Study: Postgraduate.
Type: Scholarship.
Value: UK £2,000 per year.
Length of Study: For the fee paying duration of the course.
Study Establishment: St Hugh's College, the University of Oxford.
Country of Study: United Kingdom.
Application Procedure: Applicants must contact the Academic Administrator in the first instance.

For further information contact:

Academic Administrator
St Hugh's College, Oxford, Oxfordshire, OX2 6LE, England

St Hugh's College Graduate Scholarships

Subjects: All subjects by research.
Purpose: To provide financial support to graduates reading for a degree by research.
Eligibility: Open to British nationals and candidates from overseas.
Level of Study: Postgraduate.
Type: Scholarship.
Value: UK £2,000 per year plus accommodation and some dining rights.
Length of Study: For the fee paying duration of the course.
Frequency: Annual.
Study Establishment: St Hugh's College, the University of Oxford.
Country of Study: United Kingdom.
No. of awards offered: Up to 12.
Application Procedure: Applicants must contact the College Secretary in the first instance.

For further information contact:

Academic Administrator
St Hugh's College, Oxford, Oxfordshire, OX2 6LE, England
Fax: (44) 1865 274912

St Hugh's College William Thomas and Gladys Willing Scholarship

Subjects: Modern languages.
Eligibility: Open to candidates of any nationality.
Level of Study: Postgraduate.
Type: Scholarship.
Value: UK £2,000 per year.
Length of Study: For the fee paying duration of the course.
Study Establishment: St Hugh's College, the University of Oxford.
Country of Study: United Kingdom.
Application Procedure: Applicants must contact the Academic Administrator in the first instance.

For further information contact:

Academic Administrator
St Hugh's College, Oxford, Oxfordshire, OX2 6LE, England

St Hugh's College Yates Senior Scholarship

Subjects: Theology research degrees.
Eligibility: Open to candidates of any nationality.
Level of Study: Postgraduate.
Type: Scholarship.
Value: UK £2,000 per year.
Length of Study: For the fee paying duration of the course.
Study Establishment: St Hugh's College, the University of Oxford.
Country of Study: United Kingdom.
Application Procedure: Applicants must contact the Academic Administrator in the first instance.

For further information contact:

Academic Administrator
St Hugh's College, Oxford, Oxfordshire, OX2 6LE, England

St John's College Beeston Scholarships

Subjects: All subjects.
Eligibility: Normally restricted to graduates with United Kingdom degrees, who have already begun research.
Level of Study: Postgraduate.
Type: Scholarship.
Value: Fees and accommodation and the equivalent of a Research Council grant when the candidate's grant expires. The award is not intended as a sole source of funding.
Length of Study: Normally two years.
Study Establishment: St John's College, the University of Oxford.
Country of Study: United Kingdom.
Application Procedure: Applicants must contact the Tutor for Graduates at St John's College in the first instance.
Closing Date: Advertised in November and December and tenable from the following October.

For further information contact:

Secretary to the Tutor for Graduates
St John's College, Oxford, Oxfordshire, OX1 3JP, England

St John's College North Senior Scholarships

Subjects: All subjects.
Eligibility: Normally restricted to graduates with United Kingdom degrees, who have already begun research, advertised in November and December and tenable from the following October.
Level of Study: Postgraduate.
Type: Scholarship.
Value: Fees and accommodation and the equivalent of a Research Council grant. Not intended as a sole source of income.
Length of Study: Usually two years.
Study Establishment: St John's College, the University of Oxford.

Country of Study: United Kingdom.
No. of awards offered: Two.
Application Procedure: Applicants must contact the Secretary to the Tutor for Graduates in the first instance.

For further information contact:

Secretary to the Tutor for Graduates
St John's College, Oxford, Oxfordshire, OX1 3JP, England

St Peter's College Bodossaki Foundation Graduate Scholarship in Science

Subjects: Natural sciences.
Eligibility: Open to nationals of Greece.
Level of Study: Postgraduate.
Type: Scholarship.
Value: Fees and maintenance.
Length of Study: Up to three years.
Study Establishment: St Peter's College, the University of Oxford.
Country of Study: United Kingdom.
Application Procedure: Applicants must contact the Tutor for Graduates at St Peter's College in the first instance.
Funding: Private.
Contributor: The Bodossaki Foundation.

For further information contact:

Tutor for Graduates
St Peter's College, Oxford, Oxfordshire, OX1 2DL, England

St Peter's College Leonard J Theberge Memorial Scholarship

Subjects: All subjects offered at the College.
Eligibility: Open to United States citizens. Preference will be given to mature students over 30, or those who have been employed for five years. Only students who have been admitted to the College will be considered.
Level of Study: Postgraduate.
Type: Scholarship.
Value: A modest contribution to maintenance and personal expenses.
Length of Study: One-two years.
Study Establishment: St Peter's College, the University of Oxford.
Country of Study: United Kingdom.
Application Procedure: Applicants must contact the Tutor for Graduates in the first instance.

For further information contact:

Tutor for Graduates
St Peter's College, Oxford, Oxfordshire, OX1 2DL, England

Templeton College Barclay MBA Scholarship

Subjects: MBA.
Eligibility: Open to students from the United Kingdom.
Level of Study: MBA.
Type: Scholarship.
Value: UK £5,000.
Length of Study: One year.
Frequency: Annual.
Study Establishment: Templeton College, the University of Oxford.
Country of Study: United Kingdom.
No. of awards offered: One.
Application Procedure: Applicants must contact the Senior Tutor.

For further information contact:

Senior Tutor
Templeton College, Oxford, Oxfordshire, OX1 5NY, England

Templeton College Leyland Scholarships

Subjects: Management studies.
Eligibility: Preference is given to United Kingdom students and those registered for, or intending to go on to, the DPhil.

Level of Study: Postgraduate.
Type: Scholarship.
Value: UK £1,500.
Length of Study: One year.
Frequency: Annual.
Study Establishment: Templeton College, the University of Oxford.
Country of Study: United Kingdom.
No. of awards offered: Up to three.
Application Procedure: Applicants must contact the Senior Tutor for further information.

For further information contact:

Senior Tutor
Templeton College, Oxford, Oxfordshire, OX1 5NY, England

Templeton College MBA Scholarship

Subjects: MBA.
Level of Study: MBA.
Type: Scholarship.
Value: UK £5,000.
Length of Study: One year.
Frequency: Annual.
Study Establishment: Templeton College, the University of Oxford.
Country of Study: United Kingdom.
No. of awards offered: Up to three.
Application Procedure: Applicants must contact the Senior Tutor.

For further information contact:

Senior Tutor
Templeton College, Oxford, Oxfordshire, OX1 5NY, England

Trinity College Birkett Scholarship in Environmental Studies

Subjects: Environmental change and management.
Eligibility: Open to any graduate accepted for the MSc.
Level of Study: Postgraduate.
Type: Scholarship.
Value: UK £2,400.
Length of Study: One year.
Frequency: Annual.
Study Establishment: Trinity College, the University of Oxford.
Country of Study: United Kingdom.
No. of awards offered: One.
Application Procedure: Applicants must contact the Academic Administrator in the first instance.

For further information contact:

Academic Administrator
Trinity College, Oxford, Oxfordshire, OX1 3BH, England

Trinity College Cecil Lubbock Memorial Scholarship

Subjects: Humanities or social sciences.
Type: Scholarship.
Value: UK £5,000.
Length of Study: One-three years, depending on the course.
Frequency: Varies, not available every year.
Study Establishment: Trinity College, the University of Oxford.
Country of Study: United Kingdom.

For further information contact:

Dean of Graduates
Trinity College, Oxford, Oxfordshire, OX1 3BN, England

Trinity College Kandiah Thirunavukkarasu Graduate Scholarship

Subjects: Engineering or materials science.
Level of Study: Doctorate.
Type: Scholarship.
Value: UK £500.
Length of Study: One year.

Study Establishment: Trinity College, the University of Oxford.
Country of Study: United Kingdom.

For further information contact:

Academic Administrator
Trinity College, Oxford, Oxfordshire, OX1 3BN, England

Trinity College Max Beloff Scholarship in History

Subjects: History.
Eligibility: Open to candidates intending to read for a research degree in history.
Level of Study: Graduate, Research.
Type: Scholarship.
Value: University and college fees at the home or European Union rate plus a contribution towards living expenses.
Length of Study: Up to three years.
Frequency: When the Scholarship becomes vacant.
Study Establishment: Trinity College, the University of Oxford.
Country of Study: United Kingdom.
No. of awards offered: One.
Application Procedure: Applicants must write for details.
Closing Date: Please write for details.
Funding: Private.

For further information contact:

Tutor for Graduates
Graduate Studies Office
Modern History Faculty
Broad Street, Oxford, Oxfordshire, OX1 3BD, England

University College Applied Materials Research Studentship

Subjects: Science or engineering.
Level of Study: Doctorate.
Type: Studentship.
Value: UK £2,500 per year.
Length of Study: Two years in the first instance.
Study Establishment: The University College, the University of Oxford.
Country of Study: United Kingdom.

For further information contact:

Dean of Graduates
University College, Oxford, Oxfordshire, OX1 4BH, England

University College Chellgren Scholarship

Subjects: All subjects, but with a preference for those studying economics.
Level of Study: Graduate.
Type: Scholarship.
Value: UK £1,500 per year.
Length of Study: Up to three years.
Study Establishment: The University College, the University of Oxford.
Country of Study: United Kingdom.

For further information contact:

Dean of Graduates
University College, Oxford, Oxfordshire, OX1 4BH, England

University College Loughman Scholarship

Subjects: All subjects.
Eligibility: Preference is given to those who can demonstrate excellence in, and who will make a significant contribution to college life through non academic pursuits (arts, community service, sport etc.).
Level of Study: Graduate.
Type: Scholarship.
Value: UK £2,500 per year.
Length of Study: Up to three years.

Study Establishment: The University College, the University of London.
Country of Study: United Kingdom.

For further information contact:

Dean of Graduates
University College, Oxford, Oxfordshire, OX1 4BH, England

Varley-Gradwell Travelling Fellowship in Insect Ecology

Subjects: Insect ecology.
Purpose: To support field work, travel and other activity of direct benefit to the field of insect ecology.
Level of Study: Doctorate, Postdoctorate, Postgraduate.
Type: Travel fellowship.
Value: Up to UK £2,000.
Length of Study: One year.
Frequency: Annual.
Study Establishment: The University of Oxford.
Country of Study: United Kingdom.
No. of awards offered: One.
Application Procedure: Applicants must send applications, including a curriculum vitae and a research proposal. The research should include a budget and should not exceed two sides of A4 in length. Applicants should arrange for two referees to write in confidence to the Board of Management for the Varley-Gradwell Travelling Fellowship by the closing date. In the case of graduate students one of the referees should be the supervisor.
Closing Date: February 28th.
Funding: Private.

For further information contact:

Assistant to the Secretary
The Board of Management
Vasley-Gradwell Travelling Fellowship in Insect Ecology
2 South Parks Road, Oxford, Oxfordshire, OX1 3UB, England

Wadham College Norwegian Scholarship

Subjects: All subjects.
Eligibility: Open to registered students or graduates of Oslo University, who are Norwegian citizens.
Level of Study: Postgraduate.
Type: Scholarship.
Value: Fees and maintenance.
Length of Study: One year.
Frequency: Annual.
Study Establishment: Wadham College, the University of Oxford.
Country of Study: United Kingdom.
Application Procedure: Applicants must submit applications in August of each year to the committee for the Norsk Oxford-Stipendium ved Wadham College at the University of Oslo.

Wolfson College Department for International Development Shared Scholarship Scheme (formerly ODASSS)

Subjects: All subjects.
Eligibility: Open to nationals of developing Commonwealth countries only.
Level of Study: Graduate.
Type: Scholarship.
Value: Full fees and maintenance.
Length of Study: Normally one year.
Frequency: Annual.
Study Establishment: Wolfson College, the University of Oxford.
Country of Study: United Kingdom.
Application Procedure: Applicants must write for details.

For further information contact:

International Office
University Offices
Wellington Square, Oxford, Oxfordshire, OX1 2JD, England

Wolfson College Graduate Studentships

Subjects: Specific subjects set by the College.
Level of Study: Doctorate.
Type: Studentship.
Value: Varies depending on faculty affiliation.
Length of Study: Up to three years.
Study Establishment: Wolfson College, the University of Oxford.
Country of Study: United Kingdom.
Application Procedure: Applicants must write for details. Applications should be sent to the faculty or department admissions officer.
Closing Date: Please write for details.
Additional Information: A small number of studentships are offered to DPhil students in specific subjects.

THE UNIVERSITY OF QUEENSLAND

Office of Research & Postgraduate Studies
Cumbrae-Stewart Building
Research Road, Brisbane, QLD, 4072, Australia
Tel: (61) 7 3365 2033
Fax: (61) 7 3365 4455
www: http://www.uq.edu.au
Contact: Director

The University of Queensland is recognised internationally as a premier research institution. The University attracts world class students and staff, and has numerous notable alumni. Its teaching, learning and research activities are underpinned by state of the art computing and it has received numerous awards.

University of Queensland Postdoctoral Research Fellowship

Subjects: All subjects offered by the University.
Purpose: To assist persons wishing to conduct full-time research at the University in any of its disciplines.
Eligibility: Open to candidates of any nationality. Applicants must not have had more than five years of full-time professional experience since the award of a doctoral degree as at June 30th of the year before the fellowship commences. Fellowships may be offered to applicants who do not hold a doctoral degree provided that evidence is given that a doctoral thesis has been submitted by June 30th (for candidates from Australia, New Zealand or Papua New Guinea) or September 1st (for all other candidates) and that the selection committee is satisfied that the degree will be awarded by June 30th of the Fellowship year.
Level of Study: Postdoctorate, Professional development.
Type: Fellowship.
Value: Australian $43,284-48,234 per year plus excursion return airfare for the recipient only.
Length of Study: Three years, with a possibility of renewal for a further year.
Frequency: Annual.
Study Establishment: The University of Queensland.
Country of Study: Australia.
No. of awards offered: Approx. nine.
Application Procedure: Applicants must complete an application form available from the heads of the relevant department or from the Director of Research Services. Application forms are also available from the website.
Closing Date: May 31st of the year preceding the award.
Funding: Government.
Additional Information: Further information is available on request.

University of Queensland Postgraduate Research Scholarships

Subjects: Philosophy.
Purpose: To support full-time study towards a Master of Philosophy degree or a Doctor of Philosophy degree.
Eligibility: Open to candidates of any nationality who are acceptable as full-time internal students for a research degree at the University.

Applicants should hold an Australian First Class Degree, a Master's degree, or the equivalent. Candidates must have a sound knowledge of both written and spoken English.
Level of Study: Research.
Type: Scholarship.
Value: Australian $17,267.
Length of Study: The Master of Philosophy degree is two years, and the Doctor of Philosophy degree is up to three years.
Frequency: Annual.
Study Establishment: The University of Queensland.
Country of Study: Australia.
No. of awards offered: Approx. 100.
Application Procedure: International applicants must apply through the University's International Education Directorate. Australian applicants must apply through the Scholarships Officer.
Closing Date: The deadline for international applicants is August 31st and Australian applicants is October 31st.
Funding: Government.
Additional Information: To assist with tuition fee expenses international students may apply for the International Postgraduate Research Scholarships (IPRS) which are administered through the International Education Directorate.

University of Queensland Travel Scheme for International Collaborative Research

Subjects: All subjects offered by the University.
Purpose: To facilitate visits by scholars from institutions in other countries.
Eligibility: Open to any suitably qualified Scholar actively engaged in academic work at a university or internationally recognised research institution who will be able to contribute substantially to research activity in the department to which he or she is attached at the University of Queensland.
Level of Study: Postdoctorate.
Type: Grant.
Value: Return economy airfare.
Length of Study: Applicants must spend at least four weeks during the semester at the University of Queensland in the year of the award.
Frequency: Annual.
Study Establishment: The University of Queensland.
Country of Study: Australia.
No. of awards offered: Approx. 15.
Application Procedure: Applicants must complete an application form, available from the heads of the relevant department or from the Director of Research Services. Application forms are also available from the website.
Closing Date: August 1st of the year preceding the award year.
Funding: Government.
Additional Information: Further information is available on request.

THE UNIVERSITY OF READING

Whiteknights
PO Box 217, Reading, Berkshire, RG6 6AH, England
Tel: (44) 118 931 8115
Fax: (44) 118 987 4722
Email: k.h.dickinson@reading.ac.uk
www: http://www.rdg.ac.uk
Contact: Scholarship Administrator

The University of Reading offers postgraduate taught and research degree courses in all the traditional subject areas except medical sciences. Other, more vocational courses are also offered. Research work in many areas is of international renown.

BPF Lord Samuel of Wych Cross Memorial Award

Subjects: Land management.
Purpose: To assist students who would otherwise be unable financially to follow the MSc course.

Eligibility: Open to candidates who hold a first degree and are, at the time of the award, ordinarily resident in the United Kingdom.
Level of Study: Postgraduate.
Type: Scholarship.
Value: UK £1,000.
Length of Study: One year.
Frequency: Annual.
Study Establishment: The University of Reading.
Country of Study: United Kingdom.
No. of awards offered: One-three.
Application Procedure: Applicants must submit curriculum vitaes by invitation to Mr N French, Senior Acacia Lecturer, or Mr Jonathon Edwards, Consulting Fellow in Corporate Real Estate at the University of Reading, on (44) 118 931 6336, by fax on (44) 118 931 8172 or by email n.s.french@reading.ac.uk.
Funding: Private.
Additional Information: Scholars must intend to remain resident in the United Kingdom after the term of the scholarship has ended.

The University of Reading China Scholarship

Subjects: All subjects, subject to the availability of appropriate supervision at the university.
Purpose: To enable students to obtain a doctoral degree.
Eligibility: Open to Chinese students who hold an offer of a place on a research degree by April 30th in the year of entry.
Level of Study: Doctorate, Postgraduate.
Type: Studentship.
Value: Tuition fees at the full overseas rate.
Length of Study: Up to three years.
Frequency: Annual.
Study Establishment: The University of Reading.
Country of Study: United Kingdom.
No. of awards offered: One.
Application Procedure: Applicants must fulfil the eligibility criteria and express an interest in the scholarships to be considered.
Closing Date: Please contact the University.
Funding: Private.
Contributor: The University of Reading.
No. of awards given last year: One.

The University of Reading General Overseas Scholarships

Subjects: All subjects, subject to the availability of appropriate supervision at the university.
Purpose: To enable students to obtain a postdoctoral degree.
Eligibility: Open to applicants paying tuition fees at the full overseas rate, who hold an offer of a place on a research degree by April 30th in the year of entry.
Level of Study: Doctorate, Postgraduate.
Type: Studentship.
Value: UK £5,000 per year.
Length of Study: Up to three years.
Frequency: Annual.
Study Establishment: The University of Reading.
Country of Study: United Kingdom.
No. of awards offered: Three.
Application Procedure: Applicants must fulfil the eligibility criteria and express an interest in the scholarships to be considered.
Closing Date: Please contact the University.
Funding: Private.
Contributor: The University of Reading.
No. of awards given last year: Three.
No. of applicants last year: 135.

The University of Reading Postgraduate Studentship

Subjects: There are no restrictions on subject area, subject to the availability of appropriate supervision at the university.
Purpose: To enable students to obtain a doctoral degree.
Eligibility: Candidates must hold a first degree qualification.
Level of Study: Doctorate, Postgraduate.
Type: Studentship.

Value: Composition fee (at home standard rate) plus maintenance award as for Research Council Postgraduate Studentships.
Length of Study: Up to three years.
Frequency: Annual.
Study Establishment: The University of Reading.
Country of Study: United Kingdom.
No. of awards offered: Four.
Application Procedure: Applicants must complete an application form, available from Mr D A Stannard and submit this with a confidential academic reference.
Closing Date: February of the year of entry.
Funding: Private.
Contributor: The University of Reading.
No. of awards given last year: Four.
No. of applicants last year: 90.
Additional Information: At present the studentships are awarded on the nomination of the Head of School or Department.

The University of Reading Research Studentships in Arts and Humanities

Subjects: Research areas within the arts and humanities.
Purpose: To enable students to obtain a doctoral degree.
Level of Study: Doctorate, Postgraduate.
Type: Studentship.
Value: Composition fee at the home standard rate plus a maintenance award as for Research Council Postgraduate Studentships.
Frequency: Annual.
Study Establishment: The University of Reading.
Country of Study: United Kingdom.
No. of awards offered: Up to 12.
Application Procedure: Applicants must complete an application form, available from the University.
Closing Date: February of the year of entry.
Funding: Private.

The University of Reading Research Studentships within the Social Sciences

Subjects: Research areas within the social sciences.
Purpose: To enable students to obtain a doctoral degree.
Level of Study: Doctorate, Postgraduate.
Type: Scholarship.
Value: Composition fee at the home standard rate plus a maintenance award as for Research Council Postgraduate Studentships.
Length of Study: Up to three years.
Frequency: Annual.
Study Establishment: The University of Reading.
Country of Study: United Kingdom.
No. of awards offered: Up to 10.
Application Procedure: Applicants must complete an application form available from Joanna Nyirenda, Senior Assistant Registrar, at the University, by email on J.M.Nyirenda@reading.ac.uk.
Closing Date: February of the year of entry.
Funding: Private.
Contributor: The University of Reading.
No. of awards given last year: Four.
No. of applicants last year: 17.

The University of Reading Taiwan Scholarship

Subjects: All subjects, subject to the availability of appropriate supervision at the university.
Purpose: To enable students to obtain a doctoral degree.
Eligibility: Open to students from Taiwan who hold the offer of a place on a research degree by April 30th in the year of entry.
Level of Study: Doctorate, Postgraduate.
Type: Studentship.
Value: Tuition fees at the full overseas rate.
Length of Study: Up to three years.
Frequency: Annual.
Study Establishment: The University of Reading.
Country of Study: United Kingdom.

No. of awards offered: One.
Application Procedure: Applicants must fulfil the eligibility criteria and express an interest in the scholarships to be considered.
Closing Date: Please contact the University.
Funding: Private.
Contributor: The University of Reading.
No. of awards given last year: One.

UNIVERSITY OF RHODE ISLAND

College of Business Administration
210 Flagg Road, Kingston, RI, 02881-0802, United States of America
Tel: (1) 401 874 4241
Fax: (1) 401 874 7047
Email: mba@etal.uri.edu
www: http://www.cba.uri.edu/graduate/mba.htm
Contact: Ms Lisa Lancellotta, MBA Co-ordinator

The University of Rhode Island, College of Business Administration offers three AACSB accredited MBA programmes to fit students' needs: the one year full-time MBA, the providence evening part-time MBA and the 18 month executive weekend MBA. The College also offers an MS in Accounting and a PhD in business.

URI Assistantships

Subjects: All subjects.
Purpose: To award degree candidates for services rendered to a department or a particular research project.
Eligibility: Applicants must hold Bachelor's degrees and must have been admitted as degree candidates by the Graduate School.
Level of Study: Graduate, MBA.
Type: Assistantships.
Value: Stipends vary.
Length of Study: Varies.
Frequency: Annual.
Study Establishment: The University of Rhode Island.
Country of Study: United States of America.
No. of awards offered: Varies.
Application Procedure: Applicants must contact the Graduate School.
Closing Date: Please contact the organisation.
Funding: Government.
Additional Information: The duties of those holding assistantships consist of assisting, under supervision, with the instructional or research activity of a department. Assistants will be required to devote a maximum of 20 hours a week to departmental work, not more than 10 hours of which may be in classroom contact.

URI Fellowships

Subjects: All subjects.
Purpose: To recognise Scholars' achievement and promise. To enable Scholars to pursue graduate study and research full-time without rendering services to the University.
Eligibility: Applicants must be full-time students.
Level of Study: Graduate, MBA.
Type: Competition.
Value: Stipends vary with the nature and tenure of each fellowship. In most instances, Fellows have tuition and registration fees paid by the University.
Length of Study: Varies.
Frequency: Annual.
Study Establishment: The University of Rhode Island.
Country of Study: United States of America.
No. of awards offered: Varies.
Application Procedure: Fellows are selected from lists of nominees submitted by department chairpersons.
Closing Date: Please contact the organisation.

UNIVERSITY OF SOUTHAMPTON

Highfield, Southampton, Hampshire, SO17 1BJ, England
Tel: (44) 23 8059 4741
Fax: (44) 23 8059 3037
Contact: Academic Registrar

The University of Southampton was founded as the Hartley Institute in the mid nineteenth-century and was granted its Royal Charter in 1952. Today, the University offers a range of postgraduate and research courses in the following faculties: arts, engineering and applied science, law, mathematics, medicine, health and biological science, science and social sciences.

University of Southampton Studentships

Subjects: All subjects offered by the university.
Purpose: To support postgraduate research study.
Eligibility: Open to candidates who hold a good Honours Degree and are eligible for admission to the department in which they intend to study.
Level of Study: Postgraduate, Research.
Type: Studentship.
Value: Based on Research Council Studentship rates.
Length of Study: The duration of the course of study and research.
Frequency: Annual.
Study Establishment: The University of Southampton.
Country of Study: United Kingdom.
No. of awards offered: Varies.
Application Procedure: Applicants must make initial enquiries to the head of the academic department in which research is to be undertaken.
Closing Date: Varies, enquiries should be made by January for the following October.

World Universities Network (WUN) Scholarship Scheme

Subjects: Selected areas within chemistry, engineering sciences, geography, law, ocean and earth science, physics, politics and biological sciences.
Purpose: To support postgraduate research visits to partner American universities.
Eligibility: Open to candidates currently registered for an MPhil or PhD degree in one of the University of Southampton's departments participating in the WUN scheme.
Level of Study: Postgraduate, Research.
Type: Travel scholarship.
Value: Up to UK £10,000.
Length of Study: The duration of the research visit, which is normally three months.
Frequency: Annual.
Study Establishment: Partner American universities.
Country of Study: United States of America.
No. of awards offered: Varies.
Application Procedure: Applicants must make initial enquiries to the head of the academic department in which they are registered for their research degree.
Closing Date: Varies.
Contributor: The University of Southampton.
No. of awards given last year: Five.
No. of applicants last year: Seven.

UNIVERSITY OF SOUTHERN CALIFORNIA (USC)

University Park
Mail Code 4012, Los Angeles, CA, 90089, United States of America
Tel: (1) 213 740 5294
Fax: (1) 213 740 8607
www: http://www.usc.edu/dept/LAS/Faculty/mellon.htm
Contact: Mr Richard Tithecott, Assistant Administrative Director

Located near the heart of Los Angeles, the University of Southern California (USC) is a private research university. It maintains a tradition of academic strength at all levels, from the earliest explorations of the undergraduate to the advanced scholarly research of the postdoctoral Fellow.

Andrew W Mellon Postdoctoral Fellowships in the Humanities

Subjects: The humanities.
Purpose: To encourage junior scholars to develop their research.
Eligibility: Open to Scholars who received their PhD within the past seven years and who do not hold tenure at an academic institution.
Level of Study: Postdoctorate.
Type: Fellowship.
Value: Approx. US$30,000, plus full faculty fringe benefits and modest research expense support.
Frequency: Annual.
Study Establishment: The University of Southern California.
Country of Study: United States of America.
No. of awards offered: One-two.
Application Procedure: This information varies each year so applicants should consult the website.
Funding: Private.
Contributor: The Mellon Foundation.
No. of awards given last year: Two.
No. of applicants last year: 100.

USC College Dissertation Fellowship

Subjects: Arts and humanities, natural sciences, social and behavioural sciences.
Purpose: To provide financial assistance to students who are about to begin, or are in the process of, writing their doctoral dissertation in the College of Letters, Arts and Sciences at USC.
Eligibility: Open to outstanding students of any nationality, who present evidence of achievement and promise as Scholars and have completed all but the dissertation stage of their degree.
Level of Study: Postgraduate, Predoctorate.
Type: Fellowship.
Value: US$15,000 plus four units of tuition.
Length of Study: One year.
Frequency: Annual.
Study Establishment: The University of Southern California.
Country of Study: United States of America.
No. of awards offered: 29.
Application Procedure: Application dossiers are collated by department.
Closing Date: March 10th.
No. of awards given last year: 19.

USC College of Letters, Arts and Sciences Merit Award

Subjects: Arts and humanities, natural sciences and social or behavioural sciences.
Purpose: To provide an opportunity for students working towards a PhD degree who intend to pursue a career in university teaching and research.
Eligibility: Open to outstanding seniors and graduates of any nationality who present evidence of achievement and promise as Scholars.
Level of Study: Postdoctorate.
Type: Fellowship.
Value: US$15,000 per year, plus full tuition.

Length of Study: Up to five years. This consists of two years of fellowship and three years of teaching.
Frequency: Annual.
Study Establishment: The University of Southern California.
Country of Study: United States of America.
No. of awards offered: 100.
Application Procedure: Application forms are available from the USC academic department to which the student is applying for admission.
Closing Date: February 1st.
No. of awards given last year: 75.

UNIVERSITY OF STIRLING

Research Office, Stirling, FK9 4LA, Scotland
Tel: (44) 1786 407041
Fax: (44) 1786 466688
Email: research@stir.ac.uk
www: http://www.stir.ac.uk
Contact: Research Services Officer

The University of Stirling offers the following postgraduate awards: Doctor of Philosophy, Master of Letters and Master of Science. The University is organised into four faculties: Arts, Human Science, Management and Natural Sciences. Most research degrees are available on a full-time or part-time basis. Further information is given in the relevant departmental entries.

University of Stirling Research Studentships
Subjects: The arts, human sciences eg. applied social science, psychology, education, and nursing and midwifery, and management and natural sciences, including aquaculture.
Purpose: To support postgraduate study.
Eligibility: Applicants must also apply to external funding bodies.
Level of Study: Doctorate, Postgraduate.
Type: Studentship.
Value: UK £6,800 per year.
Length of Study: A maximum of three years.
Frequency: Annual.
Study Establishment: The University of Stirling.
Country of Study: Scotland.
No. of awards offered: 12 new studentships per academic year.
Application Procedure: Applicants must complete an application form for the individual faculty. Further information and application forms are available from the relevant faculty office, to which the completed application forms must be returned.
Closing Date: Please consult the relevant Faculty Office for details.
Funding: Private.
Contributor: The University of Stirling.
Additional Information: Further information is available on request.

UNIVERSITY OF SUSSEX/ASSOCIATION OF COMMONWEALTH UNIVERSITIES

Postgraduate Office
Sussex House
Falmer, Brighton, East Sussex, BN1 9RH, England
Tel: (44) 1273 606755
Fax: (44) 1273 678335
Email: t.o-donnell@sussex.ac.uk
www: http://www.sussex.ac.uk
Contact: Mr Terry O'Donnell

The University of Sussex is one of the top 12 United Kingdom universities for research. The University boasts a distinguished faculty that includes 17 Fellows of the Royal Society and four Fellows of the British Academy. The University has around 10,000 students, 25 per cent of whom are postgraduates.

Geoff Lockwood Scholarship
Subjects: All subjects.
Eligibility: Open to United Kingdom students.
Level of Study: Postgraduate.
Type: Scholarship.
Value: UK £1,000.
Frequency: Annual.
No. of awards offered: One.
Additional Information: Applicants should see the website.

Sasakawa Scholarship
Subjects: Science, economic and environmental policy, internationalism or gender roles in modern society.
Purpose: To educate graduate students with high potential for future leadership in international life as well as in private endeavour.
Eligibility: Applications are usually accepted from students from United Kingdom, China, Eastern Europe or former Soviet Republics.
Level of Study: Postgraduate.
Type: Scholarship.
Value: Fees, maintenance award and return airfare.
Length of Study: One year.
Frequency: Annual.
Study Establishment: Sussex University.
Country of Study: United Kingdom.
No. of awards offered: Three.
Application Procedure: Applicants must complete and submit an application form with transcripts and academic references.
No. of awards given last year: Three.
No. of applicants last year: 90.

University of Sussex Overseas Development Administration Shared Scholarship Scheme
Subjects: Subjects related to the economic and social development of overseas countries.
Purpose: To help students of high academic calibre in developing Commonwealth countries who would not be eligible for awards to study in the United Kingdom under existing British Government schemes, and would not be able to afford to pay for the cost themselves.
Eligibility: Candidates must be below the age of 35, have sufficient fluency in English, not have studied in the United Kingdom before, be a national of a developing Commonwealth country, not be living in a developed country and not be employed by a government department.
Level of Study: Postgraduate.
Type: Scholarship.
Value: Fees and maintenance grant.
Length of Study: One year.
Frequency: Annual.
Study Establishment: Sussex University.
Country of Study: United Kingdom.
No. of awards offered: Two.
Application Procedure: Applicants must complete and submit an application form with academic transcripts and references.
Closing Date: Usually mid March.
No. of awards given last year: Two.
No. of applicants last year: 10.
Additional Information: Only applicants from targeted countries are eligible to apply and this information is usually known in the January preceding the start of the academic year. Targeted countries are decided annually. Successful applicants must agree to return to their home country on completion of studies.

University of Sussex Overseas Research Studentships
Subjects: Arts and humanities, education science, English, law, mathematics and computer science, communication and information science, natural sciences or social sciences.
Purpose: To assist overseas students of outstanding merit and research potential.
Eligibility: Open to students applying for research degrees eg. the MPhil or the DPhil who are assessed as liable to the overseas rate

of fee. Applicants are allowed to submit an award through only one institution.
Level of Study: Postgraduate.
Type: Scholarship.
Value: Part of tuition fee.
Length of Study: Up to three years.
Frequency: Annual.
Study Establishment: The University of Sussex.
Country of Study: United Kingdom.
No. of awards offered: 15.
Application Procedure: Applicants must complete and submit an application form with academic transcripts and references.
Closing Date: Early April.
No. of awards given last year: 14.
No. of applicants last year: 60.

University of Sussex/Association of Commonwealth Universities Access Fund Bursaries
Subjects: All subjects.
Eligibility: Open to United Kingdom students.
Level of Study: Postgraduate.
Type: Bursary.
Value: UK £2,000.
Frequency: Annual.
No. of awards offered: 20.
Additional Information: Applicants should visit the website for further details.

University of Sussex/Association of Commonwealth Universities Graduate Teaching Assistantships
Subjects: All subjects.
Eligibility: Applicants must visit the website for full eligibility requirements.
Level of Study: Postgraduate.
Type: Assistantship.
Value: Includes at least a fee waiver but possibly more, depending on whether the student undertakes teaching.
Length of Study: Varies.
Frequency: Annual.
No. of awards offered: 20.
Application Procedure: Applicants must visit the website for details of the application procedure.
Closing Date: Please contact the organisation.

THE UNIVERSITY OF SYDNEY

Research Office
Main Quadrangle A14, Sydney, NSW, 2006, Australia
Tel: (61) 2 9351 3250
Fax: (61) 2 9351 3256
Email: scholars@reschols.usyd.edu.au
www: http://www.usyd.edu.au/su/reschols/welcome.html
Contact: Ms Carmen Ng, Research Training

The role of the University of Sydney is to preserve, transmit, extend and apply knowledge through teaching, research, creative works and other forms of scholarship. In carrying out its role, the University affirms its commitment to the values and goals of institutional autonomy, recognises the importance of ideas and intellectual freedom to pursue critical and open enquiry, as well as social responsibility, tolerance, honesty and respect, as the hallmarks of relationships throughout the University community. It also understands the needs and expectations of those whom it serves and constantly improves the quality and delivery of its services.

Australian Postgraduate Award (APA)
Subjects: All subjects.
Purpose: To enable candidates with exceptional research potential to undertake a higher degree by research.

Eligibility: Open to Australian citizens and permanent residents who are resident in Australia continuously for one year prior to the closing date of each year.
Level of Study: Doctorate, Postgraduate, Research.
Type: Scholarship.
Value: Australian $17,606 per year (in 2001).
Length of Study: Two years for Master's by research candidates, and three years with a possible six month extension for PhD candidates.
Frequency: Annual.
Study Establishment: The University of Sydney.
Country of Study: Australia.
No. of awards offered: Varies from year to year.
Application Procedure: Applicants must complete a form, available from the Research Office between August and October. Forms can also be downloaded from the website or emailed on request.
Closing Date: October 31st.
Funding: Government.
No. of awards given last year: 150.

International Postgraduate Research Scholarships (IPRS) and University of Sydney International Postgraduate Awards (IPA)
Subjects: All subjects.
Purpose: To support candidates with exceptional research potential.
Eligibility: Open to suitably qualified graduates eligible to commence a higher degree by research. Australia and New Zealand citizens and Australian permanent residents are not eligible to apply.
Level of Study: Doctorate, Postgraduate, Research.
Type: Scholarship.
Value: IPRS tuition fees and for IPA australian $17,609 (in 2002).
Length of Study: Two years for the Master's by research candidates, and three years with a possible six month extension for the PhD candidates.
Frequency: Annual.
Study Establishment: The University of Sydney.
Country of Study: Australia.
No. of awards offered: Varies from year to year.
Application Procedure: Applicants must complete an application form, available between May and August from the International Office.
Closing Date: August 31st.
Funding: Government.
No. of awards given last year: 24.

For further information contact:

International Scholarships Officer
International Office
Services Building G12, Sydney, NSW, 2006, Australia
Tel: (61) 2 9351 4161
Fax: (61) 2 9351 4013
Email: infoschol@io.usyd.edu.au
www: http://www.usyd.edu.au/homepage/exterel/intgeninfo.html

University of Sydney Postgraduate Award (UPA)
Subjects: All subjects.
Purpose: To enable candidates with exceptional research potential to undertake a higher degree by research.
Eligibility: Open to Australian citizens and permanent residents and New Zealand citizens.
Level of Study: Doctorate, Postgraduate, Research.
Type: Scholarship.
Value: Australian $17,609 per year (in 2002).
Length of Study: Two years for the Master's by research candidates, and three years with a possible six month extension for the PhD candidates.
Frequency: Annual.
Study Establishment: The University of Sydney.
Country of Study: Australia.
No. of awards offered: Varies from year to year.

Application Procedure: Applicants must complete a form, available from the Research Office between August and October. Forms can also be downloaded from the website or emailed on request.
Closing Date: October 31st.
Funding: Government.
No. of awards given last year: 40.

UNIVERSITY OF TASMANIA

GPO Box 252-01, Hobart, TAS, 7001, Australia
Tel: (61) 3 6226 2768
Fax: (61) 3 6226 2765
Email: info@research.utas.edu.au
www: http://www.research.utas.edu.au
Contact: Research & Development Office

The Research and Development Office (RDO) of the University of Tasmania is an administrative section of the Research College and assists staff in grants, fellowships, tenders, consultancies, ethics and research infrastructure matters. The office co-ordinates the annual research data collections for DETYA and the Australian Bureau of Statistics and produces the annual research report.

Merle Weaver Postgraduate Scholarship

Subjects: All subjects.
Purpose: To fund research leading to a higher degree.
Eligibility: Open to women graduates from SouthEast Asia and the Pacific region.
Level of Study: Postgraduate.
Type: Scholarship.
Value: Australian $16,135 per year.
Length of Study: Up to three years.
Frequency: Dependent on funds available.
Study Establishment: The University of Tasmania.
Country of Study: Australia.
No. of awards offered: One.
Application Procedure: Applicants must write for details.
Closing Date: October 31st.
Funding: Private.

UNIVERSITY OF TORONTO

Admissions & Awards
315 Bloor Street West, Toronto, ON, M5S 1A3, Canada
Tel: (1) 416 978 7960
Fax: (1) 416 978 7022
Email: ask@adm.utoronto.ca
www: http://www.utoronto.ca
Contact: Grants Management Officer

The University of Toronto, an institution with an impressive history and a future of remarkable promise, was ranked Canada's top research intensive University for the fourth consecutive year by Maclean's magazine and is one of the leading universities of its kind in the world. The University provides its students with access to extraordinary professors and a diverse array of rigorous programmes. Moreover, the University offers students the best of both worlds, as nine colleges offer the experience of a rich liberal arts education within the larger setting of a great research university.

Taylor Statten Memorial Fund

Subjects: Any professional field or career related to youth services such as, but not restricted to, physical and health education, psychology, teaching, the ministry and social work.
Purpose: To assist postbaccalaureate study in any relevant professional field.

Eligibility: Open to graduates of Canadian universities who are under 25 years of age. Candidates should have high academic standing with previous experience in the youth field.
Level of Study: Postgraduate.
Type: Fellowship.
Value: Approx. canadian $1,500 per year.
Length of Study: One year.
Frequency: Annual.
Study Establishment: Any appropriate university.
Country of Study: Canada.
No. of awards offered: One.
Application Procedure: Application forms should be accompanied by a transcript of the applicant's university record. Applicants are also responsible for ensuring that three letters of recommendation reach the Committee before the deadline. At least two of the letters should be written by university teachers with whom the applicant has studied.
Closing Date: February 28th.
No. of awards given last year: One.

UNIVERSITY OF WALES, ABERYSTWYTH

Old College
King Street, Aberystwyth, Ceredigion, SY23 2AX, Wales
Tel: (44) 1970 622023
Fax: (44) 1970 622921
Email: pg-admissions@aber.ac.uk
www: http://www.aber.ac.uk
Contact: Dr Rhys Williams, Postgraduate Admissions Officer

Located in beautiful surroundings, the University of Wales provides an ideal learning environment. Information services are among the best in the United Kingdom, and students also enjoy free access to one of the six copyright libraries of Britain, the National Library of Wales, which is adjacent to the University campus.

University of Wales (Aberystwyth) Postgraduate Research Studentships

Subjects: Any full-time research course eg. MPhil, PhD or LLM by research. The university offers a wide range of research opportunities within the faculties of science, social sciences and arts.
Purpose: To enable students to undertake full-time postgraduate research at the University of Wales, Aberystwyth.
Eligibility: Open to United Kingdom and European Union candidates who have obtained at least an Upper Second Class (Honours) Degree or equivalent in their degree examination and who wish to study full-time.
Level of Study: Doctorate, Postgraduate, Research.
Type: Studentship.
Value: United Kingdom fees plus a subsistence allowance based on research council rates.
Length of Study: One year, in the first instance, but usually renewable for up to two additional years subject to satisfactory academic progress.
Frequency: Annual.
Study Establishment: The University of Wales, Aberystwyth.
Country of Study: United Kingdom.
No. of awards offered: Usually 12.
Application Procedure: Applicants must complete an application form, available from the Postgraduate Admissions Office or from the website.
Closing Date: March 1st.
Funding: Private.
Contributor: The University of Wales, Aberystwyth.
No. of awards given last year: 12.
No. of applicants last year: 120.
Additional Information: For all enquiries, please contact the Postgraduate Admissions Office.

UNIVERSITY OF WALES, BANGOR

Academic Registry
College Road, Bangor, Gwynedd, LL57 2DG, Wales
Tel: (44) 1248 382025
Fax: (44) 1248 370451
Email: aos057@bangor.ac.uk
Contact: Dr John C T Perkins, Assistant Registrar

The University of Wales, Bangor is the principal seat of learning, scholarship and research in North Wales. It was established in 1884 and is a constituent institution of the Federal University of Wales. The University attaches considerable importance to research training in all disciplines and offers research studentships of a value similar to those of the British public funding bodies.

Llewellyn and Mary Williams Scholarship

Subjects: All biological sciences, including marine biology.
Purpose: To support doctoral studies and research training in the biological sciences.
Eligibility: Open to First Class (Honours) Degree holders who are classified as home or European Community student for fee purposes.
Level of Study: Doctorate, Postgraduate.
Type: Scholarship.
Value: Equal to that of a British Research Council Studentship.
Length of Study: Three years.
Frequency: Dependent on funds available.
Study Establishment: The University of Wales, Bangor.
Country of Study: United Kingdom.
No. of awards offered: One.
Application Procedure: This scholarship is allocated to the School of Biological Sciences every third year. Applicants must contact the Head of School for details.
Closing Date: May 15th.
Funding: Private.
No. of awards given last year: Two.
No. of applicants last year: 12.

Mr and Mrs David Edward Memorial Award

Subjects: All subjects offered by the university.
Purpose: To support doctoral studies in any subject area.
Eligibility: Open to holders of a relevant First Class (Honours) Degree or, exceptionally, Upper Second Class (Honours) Degree, who are of any nationality classified as a United Kingdom or European Union student for fee purposes.
Level of Study: Doctorate, Postgraduate.
Type: Research studentship.
Value: No less than that of a Research Council or British Academy Research Studentship, including fees.
Length of Study: One year, renewable for a maximum of a further two years if satisfactory progress is maintained.
Frequency: Dependent on funds available.
Study Establishment: The University of Wales, Bangor.
Country of Study: United Kingdom.
No. of awards offered: One.
Application Procedure: Applicants must complete an application form, available from the Postgraduate Admissions Office at the University.
Closing Date: May 15th.
Funding: Private.
No. of awards given last year: One.
No. of applicants last year: 20.

Sir William Roberts Scholarship

Subjects: Agriculture and agricultural science.
Purpose: To fund research training to PhD level.
Eligibility: Open to candidates classified as 'home based' who have attained a First Class (Honours) Degree or Upper Second Class (Honours) Degree. These scholarships are allocated to the School of Agricultural and Forest Sciences and the School of Biological Sciences.

Level of Study: Doctorate, Postgraduate.
Type: Scholarship.
Value: Equal to that of a British Research Council Research Studentship.
Length of Study: One year, renewable for a maximum of two additional years.
Frequency: Annual.
Study Establishment: The University of Wales, Bangor.
Country of Study: United Kingdom.
No. of awards offered: Two.
Application Procedure: Applicants must contact the relevant Head of School.
Closing Date: June 1st.
Funding: Private.
No. of awards given last year: Three.
No. of applicants last year: 20.

University of Wales, Bangor (UWB) Research Studentships

Subjects: All subjects offered by the university.
Purpose: To support students for the duration of a PhD programme.
Eligibility: Open to recent graduates classified at the lower European Union rate, or for payment purposes hold a First Class (Honours) Degree or Upper Second Class (Honours) Degree or equivalent in a relevant subject.
Level of Study: Postgraduate.
Type: Studentship.
Value: Equal to that of a British Research Council Studentship.
Length of Study: Three years.
Frequency: Annual, if funds are available.
Study Establishment: The University of Wales, Bangor.
Country of Study: United Kingdom.
No. of awards offered: 10-14.
Application Procedure: Applicants must contact the Senior Postgraduate Tutor in the department of the proposed research programme.
Closing Date: May 15th. Those interested should make enquiries well before this date.
Funding: Government, Private.
Contributor: The UWB Research Committee and local bequests.
No. of awards given last year: 14.
No. of applicants last year: Approx. 100.
Additional Information: In exceptional circumstances an award may be made to an international student classified for the full cost fee. In such a case the student would be required to pay the difference between the full cost fee and the home or European Union fee.

University of Wales, Bangor Departmental Research Studentships

Subjects: All subjects offered by the university.
Purpose: To fund research training to PhD level.
Eligibility: Open to candidates classified as United Kingdom and European Union students for fee purposes who have attained a First Class (Honours) Degree or, exceptionally, an Upper Second Class Honours Degree or equivalent.
Level of Study: Doctorate, Postgraduate.
Type: Research studentship.
Value: Equal to that of a British Research Council Studentship.
Length of Study: One year, renewable for a maximum of two additional years.
Frequency: Annual.
Study Establishment: The University of Wales, Bangor.
Country of Study: United Kingdom.
No. of awards offered: 12-15.
Application Procedure: Applicants must contact the relevant department of proposed study. The department will nominate the most worthy eligible students.
Closing Date: April 30th.
Funding: Private.
No. of awards given last year: 11.
No. of applicants last year: 90.

UNIVERSITY OF WESTERN AUSTRALIA

Nedlands, Perth, WA, 6009, Australia
Tel: (61) 8 9380 2490
Fax: (61) 8 9380 1919
Email: medwards@admin.uwa.edu.au
www: http://www.uwa.edu.au
Contact: Ms Margaret Edwards, Senior Administrative Officer

Gledden Postgraduate Studentships

Subjects: Applied science, particularly relating to engineering, mining, surveying and cognate subjects.
Purpose: To enable the holder to conduct research in applied science leading to a higher qualification.
Eligibility: Open to postgraduates with a First Class (Honours) Degree, or its equivalent, in an applied science with research experience included in the degree course. Applicants must be graduates of the University of Western Australia of not more than three years.
Level of Study: Postgraduate.
Type: Studentship.
Value: Australian $22,283 per year tax free, and a thesis allowance of australian $420 for Master's candidates or australian $840 for doctoral.
Length of Study: Up to three years.
Frequency: As vacancies occur.
Study Establishment: The University of Western Australia depending on the approved study plan. Permission may exceptionally be given for part of the research to be conducted at another university or recognised institution in Australia.
Country of Study: Australia.
No. of awards offered: One.
Closing Date: October 31st of the year preceding tenure.
Funding: Private.
No. of awards given last year: One.
No. of applicants last year: 10.

Gledden Visiting Senior Fellowships

Subjects: Applied science, particularly relating to surveying, engineering, mining and cognate subjects.
Purpose: To provide travel costs or living expenses, to allow scholars from outside Western Australia to visit the University and contribute to its work and activities in applied science.
Eligibility: Open to graduates from outside Western Australia who have doctoral degrees or qualifications or experience equivalent to doctorate.
Level of Study: Professional development, Research.
Type: Fellowship.
Value: Determined on an individual basis.
Length of Study: From one academic term which is defined as a minimum of three months or up to two years.
Frequency: Annual.
Study Establishment: The University of Western Australia.
Country of Study: Australia.
No. of awards offered: Varies.
Application Procedure: Applications are invited by advertisement as and when directed by the Vice-Chancellor of the University.
Closing Date: March 31st.
Funding: Private.

Richard Walter Gibbon Medical Research Fellowship

Subjects: Research into the causes and treatment of cancer and Parkinson's disease.
Purpose: To promote research by facilitating and encouraging students to pursue postgraduate research in the Faculty of Medicine at the University.
Eligibility: Open to Australian residents who are medical graduates of a recognised tertiary institution.
Level of Study: Postgraduate.
Type: Fellowship.
Value: Australian $23,500 per year.
Length of Study: Up to three years.

Frequency: Varies, depending on the funds available and the standard of the applications.
Study Establishment: The University of Western Australia.
Country of Study: Australia.
No. of awards offered: Varies.
Closing Date: October 31st.
Funding: Private.
Additional Information: Except by permission a Fellow may not engage in any work during tenure of the fellowship other than that for which it was awarded. A full report is required at the end of tenure. Resulting publications must acknowledge that the work was done under the Gibbon Fellowship.

Saw Medical Research Fellowship

Subjects: The cause, prevention and cure of disease, primarily diabetes mellitus.
Purpose: To promote personal research.
Eligibility: Candidates do not need to have medical qualifications.
Level of Study: Doctorate, Predoctorate.
Type: Fellowship.
Value: Up to australian $45,000-50,000 per year depending on qualifications.
Length of Study: One year, renewable for a further year.
Frequency: Annual.
Study Establishment: The University of Western Australia.
Country of Study: Australia.
No. of awards offered: Several, determined annually.
Closing Date: August 1st to September 1st.
Funding: Private.
Additional Information: Except by permission a Fellow may not engage in any work during tenure of the fellowship other than that for which it was awarded. The fellowship may not be held concurrently with other awards.

University of Western Australia Postdoctoral Research Fellowship

Subjects: All areas covered by the University of Western Australia's departments.
Purpose: To provide an appointment to a postdoctoral research Fellow to carry out a research project in a University of Western Australia department, who will bring special new expertise and a high level of relevant experience which is not otherwise available at the University.
Eligibility: Open to all nationalities. Applicants should hold a PhD for all appointments. The appointment of an overseas Fellow is subject to Australian Department of Immigration and Ethnic Affairs' approval of the University's sponsorship for residence, and the Fellow's successful application for appropriate visa.
Level of Study: Postdoctorate.
Type: Fellowship.
Value: Australian $37,345-40,087 per year plus australian $3,500-5,000 per year fellowship grant. A relocation grant is also included.
Length of Study: Two years.
Frequency: Annual.
Study Establishment: The University of Western Australia.
Country of Study: Australia.
No. of awards offered: Three.
Application Procedure: Applicants must apply through the University of Western Australia's departments only.
Closing Date: Approx. March 1st.

University of Western Australia Postgraduate Awards

Subjects: All subjects offered by the university.
Purpose: To enable students to conduct research leading to a Master's or doctoral degree.
Eligibility: Open to Australian citizens who are graduates with a minimum of an Upper Second Class (Honours) Degree, or a small number of overseas graduates who possess a First Class (Honours) Degree, or equivalent.
Level of Study: Postgraduate.
Type: Studentship.

Value: Australian $17,000 per year tax free plus travel costs, relocation allowance within Australia of up to australian $1,345 and thesis allowance of australian $420 for Master's candidates or australian $840 for doctoral.
Length of Study: One year, renewable for a further year for Master's or for a further two years for doctoral.
Frequency: Annual.
Study Establishment: The University of Western Australia.
Country of Study: Australia.
No. of awards offered: Varies.
Application Procedure: Applicants must write for details.
Closing Date: August 31st for overseas applicants, October 31st for Australian applicants.
Funding: Private.
No. of awards given last year: 49.
No. of applicants last year: 450.
Additional Information: Scholarships may not be held concurrently with other awards of a similar nature. Employment is permitted to a maximum of 240 hours in a calendar year and no more than eight hours in any one week.

THE UNIVERSITY OF WESTERN ONTARIO

Centre for Interdisciplinary Studies in Chemical Physics, London, ON, N6A 3K7, Canada
Tel: (1) 519 661 4088
Fax: (1) 519 661 3032
Email: ccp@uwo.ca
www: http://www.uwo.ca/ccp
Contact: Director

The University of Western Ontario is a modern well equipped university offering programmes in all major academic disciplines. With its enrolment of over 25,000 students, Western is the fifth largest Canadian university and the second largest university in Ontario.

The University of Western Ontario Senior Visiting Fellowship

Subjects: Current research programmes are focused on problems in condensed matter, properties of isolated atoms and molecules, surface studies, and biological applications, X-ray spectroscopy, and expert systems.
Purpose: To bring established senior scientists to the Centre for Interdisciplinary Studies in Chemical Physics to work on problems that are interdisciplinary in nature and of interest to Centre members.
Eligibility: Open to senior scientific researchers of established standing. There are no nationality restrictions.
Level of Study: Postdoctorate.
Type: Fellowship.
Value: Estimated living expenses for the period involved, plus travel expenses. Fellowships may be held concurrently with other awards or income.
Length of Study: 3-12 months.
Frequency: Annual.
Study Establishment: The Centre.
Country of Study: Canada.
No. of awards offered: Six.
Application Procedure: Applicants must complete an application form, available on the website.
Closing Date: October of the year preceding tenure.
Funding: Government.
No. of awards given last year: Six.
No. of applicants last year: 158.
Additional Information: Further details are available on request.

UNIVERSITY OF WESTERN SYDNEY

Office of Research Services
Hawkesbury Campus
Building H3
Locked Bag 1797, Penrith South DC, NSW, 1797, Australia
Tel: (61) 2 4570 1463
Fax: (61) 2 4570 1686
Email: h.holmes@nepean.uws.edu.au
www: http://www.uws.edu.au
Contact: Ms Virginia Capel, Research Scholarships Development Officer

University of Western Sydney Postgraduate Research Award (UWSPRA)

Subjects: All subjects offered by the university.
Purpose: To encourage excellence in research and support postgraduate research students enrolled in Doctor of Philosophy or Master's honours courses at UWS.
Eligibility: A student must be enrolled in a full-time postgraduate research degree at the institution. An award holder is not permitted to receive similar funding from another Australian government source or other industry support in the form of a scholarship of equivalent value. Awards are not available to students who already hold a PhD degree or a postgraduate Master's degree in situations where the applicant seeks enrolment in or can only be accepted for a Master's degree.
Level of Study: Doctorate.
Type: Scholarship.
Value: Tax free stipend for each year of the award which will be equivalent to the APRA base rate. The candidate will also receive a thesis allowance.
Length of Study: Three years for PhD candidates and two years for Master's candidates from the commencement of the course.
Frequency: Annual.
Study Establishment: The University of Western Sydney.
Country of Study: Australia.
No. of awards offered: 25.
Application Procedure: Applications must be made on the necessary form and submitted to the Office of Research Services with the required support material.
Closing Date: October 31st.
Funding: Government, Private.
Contributor: The University of Western Sydney.
No. of awards given last year: 25.
No. of applicants last year: 148.

UNIVERSITY OF WOLLONGONG

Northfields Avenue, Wollongong, NSW, 2522, Australia
Tel: (61) 2 4221 3386
Fax: (61) 2 4221 4338
Email: research_office@uow.edu.au
www: http://www.uow.edu.au
Contact: Ms Susan Clare, Postgraduate Research Scholarships Officer

The town of Wollongong sits between the dramatic Illawarra escarpment and the Pacific Ocean just one hour away from Sydney, Australia's largest city. The University of Wollongong enjoys a significant international research profile attracting more Australian Research Council funding per student in 2001 than any other Australian university. Over 850 postgraduate students are enrolled of which 30 per cent are overseas students.

University of Wollongong Postgraduate Awards

Subjects: Any postgraduate research subject offered by the university.
Purpose: To provide financial support for full-time study leading to a Master's or PhD degree.

Eligibility: Open to graduates with at least a First Class (Honours) Degree. Holders of the award must pursue studies on a full-time basis and submit an annual report.
Level of Study: Doctorate, Postgraduate.
Type: Award.
Value: Australian $17,609.
Length of Study: Two years for the Master's or three years for the PhD. Renewals are subject to satisfactory progress.
Frequency: Annual.
Study Establishment: The University of Wollongong.
Country of Study: Australia.
No. of awards offered: Varies.
Application Procedure: Applicants must complete an application form, available from the Office of Research in July and August each year.
Closing Date: October 31st.
Additional Information: Holders of the award must pursue studies on a full-time basis and submit an annual report.

UNIVERSITY OF YORK

Graduate Schools Office
Heslington, York, YO1 5DD, England
Tel: (44) 1904 432143
Fax: (44) 1904 432092
Email: graduate@york.ac.uk
www: http://www.york.ac.uk/admin/gso/gsp
Contact: Mr Philip Simison

The University of York offers postgraduate degree courses in archaeology, art history, biology, biochemistry, chemistry, communication studies, computer science, economics, educational studies, electronics, english, environment, health sciences, health studies, history, language and linguistics, management, mathematics, medieval studies, music, philosophy, physics, politics, psychology, social policy, social work, sociology and women's studies.

University of York Master's Scholarships
Subjects: All subjects.
Purpose: To assist candidates of high academic standards to complete Master's degrees.
Eligibility: Open to full-time candidates for Master's degrees eg. the MA, MSc or Mres.
Level of Study: Postgraduate.
Type: Scholarship.
Value: Fee waiver equivalent to home or European Union fee.
Length of Study: One year.
Frequency: Annual.
Study Establishment: The University of York.
Country of Study: United Kingdom.
No. of awards offered: 15.
Application Procedure: Applicants must complete an application form, available from the Graduate Schools Office.
Closing Date: May 31st.

University of York Postgraduate Student Bursaries
Subjects: Any one year full-time graduate course.
Purpose: To assist home candidates whose access to courses might be limited by shortage of funds.
Eligibility: Open to full-time home students only. Only self-financing students aged 25 years or over are eligible. Students whose fees and maintenance are covered by awards from a Research Council or Local Education Authority are not eligible.
Level of Study: Postgraduate.
Type: Grant.
Value: UK £2,000.
Length of Study: One year, non renewable.
Frequency: Annual.
Study Establishment: The University of York.
Country of Study: United Kingdom.

No. of awards offered: 12.
Application Procedure: Applicants must complete an application form, available from the Graduate Schools Office.
Closing Date: September 15th.

University of York Research Studentships/Scholarships
Subjects: All subjects.
Purpose: To assist candidates of a high academic standard to complete research degrees.
Eligibility: Open to full-time candidates for research degrees eg. the MPhil or Dphil.
Level of Study: Doctorate, Postgraduate.
Type: Scholarship.
Value: Fees at home or European Union rate plus up to UK £6,800.
Length of Study: Up to three years.
Frequency: Annual.
Study Establishment: The University of York.
Country of Study: United Kingdom.
No. of awards offered: 32.
Application Procedure: Applicants must complete an application form, available from Graduate Schools Office.
Closing Date: May 31st.

University of York Scholarships for Overseas Students
Subjects: Any full-time degree, diploma or certificate of the university.
Purpose: To assist overseas candidates of a high academic standard.
Eligibility: Open to students who have been accepted for registration as a full-time student for a degree, diploma or certificate course of the University of York and are liable to pay tuition fees at the full-cost rate for overseas (non European Community) students.
Level of Study: Postgraduate.
Type: Scholarship.
Value: Waiver of up to one-third overseas fee.
Length of Study: Up to three years.
Frequency: Annual.
Study Establishment: The University of York.
Country of Study: United Kingdom.
No. of awards offered: 15.
Application Procedure: Applicants must complete an application form, available from the International Office.
Closing Date: May 1st.

US DEPARTMENT OF EDUCATION

1990 K Street North West, Washington, DC, 20006-8521, United States of America
Tel: (1) 202 502 7635
Fax: (1) 202 502 7859
Email: jose_martinez@ed.gov
www: http://www.ed.gov
Contact: Programme Officer

Indian Fellowship Program
Subjects: Business administration, clinical psychology, education, engineering, law, medicine, natural resources or related fields and psychology.
Purpose: To enable American Indians to pursue a course of study leading to a postbaccalaureate degree.
Eligibility: Open to United States citizens who are Indians, where the definition is that they are a member of a tribe, band or other organised group of Indians, including those terminated since 1940 and those recognised by the state in which they reside, or a descendant in the first or second degree of any individual described above, or considered by the Secretary of the Interior to be an Indian for any purpose, or an Eskimo or Aleut or other Alaska native. In addition, applicants must be full-time degree candidates who have not yet obtained a terminal graduate or post Baccalaureate degree.

Level of Study: Doctorate, Postgraduate.
Value: An amount up to, but not more than, the difference between the student's educational resources and the student's expenses.
Length of Study: Two years for Master's degree or four years for the doctoral degrees.
Frequency: Annual.
Study Establishment: An accredited Institute of Higher Education.
Country of Study: United States of America.
No. of awards offered: Varies.
Application Procedure: Applicants must complete an application available on request during open season, which varies annually.
Closing Date: Please contact the organisation.

US Department of Education International Research and Studies Program

Subjects: Arts and humanities, modern languages and literatures.
Purpose: To allow individuals to conduct research and develop instructional materials in foreign languages, area and international studies, including studies and surveys to assess the use by graduates of programmes supported under Title VI of the Higher Education Act, as amended.
Eligibility: Open to United States citizens or legal residents.
Level of Study: Postdoctorate, Research.
Type: Grant.
Frequency: Dependent on funds available.
Country of Study: Any country.
No. of awards offered: 13-15.
Application Procedure: Applicants must request application forms in August by writing to the organisation.
Closing Date: Late October or early November.
Funding: Government.
Additional Information: Funds awarded by this programme may not be used for the training of teachers or students.

US NAVAL HISTORICAL CENTER

901 M Street South East
Building 57 Washington Navy Yard, Washington, DC, 20374-5060, United States of America
Tel: (1) 202 433 3940
Fax: (1) 202 433 3593
Email: marolda.edward@nhc.navy.mil
www: http://www.history.navy.mil
Contact: Dr Edward J Marolda, Senior Historian

The US Naval Historical Center works to enhance the Navy's effectiveness by preserving, analysing and interpreting its hard earned experience and history for the Navy and the American people.

Rear Admiral John D Hayes Pre-Doctoral Fellowship in US Naval History

Subjects: United States of America naval history.
Purpose: To assist scholars in the research for, or the writing of, doctoral dissertations relating to United States of America naval history.
Eligibility: Applicants must be United States citizens, enrolled in a recognised graduate school, who have completed all the requirements for the PhD except the dissertation, and have an approved topic in the field of United states of America naval history.
Level of Study: Doctorate.
Type: Fellowship.
Value: US$10,000.
Frequency: Annual.
Country of Study: United States of America.
No. of awards offered: One.
Application Procedure: Applicants must submit a completed and signed application with supporting data attached, including a copy of approved dissertation outline.
Closing Date: February 28th.
Funding: Government.

No. of awards given last year: One.
No. of applicants last year: 15.

Vice Admiral Edwin B Hooper Research Grants

Subjects: United States of America naval history.
Purpose: To assist scholars in the research for or the writing of books or articles relating to United States of America naval history.
Eligibility: Applicants must be United States citizens and must hold a PhD from an accredited university, or equivalent attainment as a published author.
Level of Study: Postdoctorate.
Type: Research grant.
Value: US$2,500.
Frequency: Annual.
Country of Study: United States of America.
No. of awards offered: Two.
Application Procedure: Applicants must send a letter stating the purpose and scope of the research project, including a proposed budget, and a completed application. In addition, two letters of recommendation from individuals familiar with the applicant's field of study will be required.
Closing Date: February 28th.
Funding: Government, Private.
Contributor: Non appropriated fund.
No. of awards given last year: Two.
No. of applicants last year: 15.

THE US-UK FULBRIGHT COMMISSION

Fulbright House
62 Doughty Street, London, WC1N 2JZ, England
Tel: (44) 20 7404 6880
Fax: (44) 20 7404 6834
Email: education@fulbright.co.uk
www: http://www.fulbright.co.uk
Contact: Ms H Topel, British Programme Manager

The US-UK Fulbright Commission has a programme of awards offered annually to citizens of the United Kingdom and United States of America. The United States Educational Advisory Service deals with enquiries from the public on all aspects of United States education including sources of funding for study in the United States of America.

Fulbright 2nd Air Division USAAF Librarianship at Memorial Library, Norwich

Subjects: Library science.
Purpose: To assist in the development of the work of the 2nd Air Division Memorial Library in building service links with secondary schools and to develop opportunities for educational work with adults.
Eligibility: Applicants must hold a MLS, MS or MA degree in a relevant field, have a minimum three years of experience of working in a library particularly a public library and have strong communication skills.
Level of Study: Professional development.
Type: Librarianship.
Value: UK £21,800 plus round trip travel for grantee and one dependant.
Length of Study: One year.
Frequency: Annual.
Study Establishment: Memorial Library, Norwich.
Country of Study: United Kingdom.
No. of awards offered: One.
Application Procedure: Applicants must complete an application form.
Closing Date: August 1st
Funding: Private.
No. of awards given last year: One.
No. of applicants last year: Six.

For further information contact:

Grants Management Officer
3007 Tilden Street
Suite 5M, Washington, DC, 20008-3009, United States of America

Fulbright AstraZeneca Research Scholarship

Subjects: Cell biology, molecular biology, bioinformatics, biochemistry or chemistry.
Purpose: To enable a postdoctoral scientist to carry out research at a top centre in the United States of America.
Eligibility: Open to British scientists.
Level of Study: Postdoctorate.
Type: Scholarship.
Value: UK £15,000 plus round trip travel.
Length of Study: A minimum of 10 months.
Frequency: Annual.
Study Establishment: An approved establishment.
Country of Study: United States of America.
No. of awards offered: One.
Application Procedure: Applicants must complete an application form.
Closing Date: Mid March.
Funding: Private.
No. of awards given last year: One.
No. of applicants last year: Three.
Additional Information: Shortlisted candidates will usually be interviewed in April or May.

Fulbright Calvin Klein/Harvey Nichols Award in Fashion Design

Subjects: Fashion design.
Purpose: To enable a graduate student to further knowledge of their subject in the transatlantic country.
Eligibility: Open to citizens normally resident in the United Kingdom. Applicants must hold the minimum of an Upper Second Class (Honours) Degree, have at least two to three years of work experience and be able to demonstrate leadership qualities.
Level of Study: Graduate.
Type: Scholarship.
Value: US$4,000.
Length of Study: A minimum of three months.
Frequency: Offered on alternate years to British or American candidates.
Study Establishment: An approved fashion school of the candidate's own choice.
Country of Study: United Kingdom or the United States of America.
No. of awards offered: One.
Application Procedure: Applicants must complete an application form and attend an interview.
Closing Date: Usually November for British candidates and October for United States of America candidates.
Funding: Commercial.
No. of awards given last year: One.
Additional Information: See the Commission's website for details.

Fulbright Co-Sponsored MBA Awards

Subjects: MBA.
Purpose: To enable MBA candidates to participate in United States of America MBA programmes.
Eligibility: Open to European Union citizens normally resident in the United Kingdom. Applicants must hold the minimum of an Upper Second Class (Honours) Degree, have a minimum of two to three years of work experience and be able to demonstrate leadership qualities.
Level of Study: Postgraduate, MBA.
Type: Scholarship.
Value: Tuition fees and maintenance for the first academic year.
Length of Study: Nine months.
Frequency: Annual.
Country of Study: United States of America.
No. of awards offered: Approx. eight.

Application Procedure: Applicants must complete an application form and submit this with two references.
Closing Date: Late January.
Funding: Government, Private.
No. of awards given last year: Seven.
No. of applicants last year: 50.
Additional Information: Shortlisted candidates will be interviewed in February.

Fulbright Distinguished Scholar Awards

Subjects: All subjects.
Purpose: To allow outstanding academics or professionals who are established or potential leaders in their field to undertake a period of professional development in the United States of America.
Eligibility: Applicants should be European Union citizens normally resident in the United Kingdom, and must be planning a minimum stay of 10 months, normally with an affiliation to one academic institution in the United States. Proof of this affiliation and details of its nature are necessary. Medical doctors intending to work with patients in any capacity while in the United States are not eligible. Awards are not available for peripatetic visits or attendance at conferences only.
Level of Study: Professional development.
Type: Fellowship.
Value: UK £15,000, visa paperwork processed and visa paid by the Commission, and health and accident insurance.
Length of Study: A minimum stay of 10 months.
Frequency: Annual.
Country of Study: United States of America.
No. of awards offered: Three.
Application Procedure: Completed applications should reach the Commission by the deadline and may not be emailed. Applicants must draw up a detailed project outline and provide evidence that a United States institution will agree to act as host and supervisor. Lecturers and researchers must have an invitation from the host institution.
Closing Date: Late March.
No. of awards given last year: Three.

Fulbright Fellowship in Cancer Research

Subjects: Oncology.
Purpose: To enable a scientist or clinician to carry out research into cancer, to enhance mutual understanding and strengthen relations between the two countries.
Eligibility: Open to scientists or clinicians who are British or European Union citizens who are resident in the United Kingdom.
Level of Study: Postdoctorate.
Type: Fellowship.
Value: UK £15,000.
Length of Study: 6-12 months.
Frequency: Annual.
Study Establishment: An approved institution.
Country of Study: United States of America.
No. of awards offered: One.
Application Procedure: Applicants must submit a formal application. Application forms and full details of the Fellowship are available from the website.
Closing Date: Mid April.
Funding: Government, Private.
No. of awards given last year: One.
Additional Information: Shortlisted candidates will be interviewed.

Fulbright Graduate Student Awards

Subjects: All subjects. Some special funding exists for MBA or related studies. Other special funding is available for software or electronic engineering, bioscience, social and cultural studies and geography and the environment.
Purpose: To enable students to follow postgraduate study or research in the United Kingdom.
Eligibility: Open to United States of America citizens, normally resident in the United States of America. Applicants must have a

minimum grade point average of 3.5 and be able to demonstrate evidence of leadership qualities. Applicants should be adventurous and be able to demonstrate that they will maximise academic, social and cultural opportunities available in the United Kingdom. A full profile of the ideal candidate is available from the website.

Level of Study: Postgraduate, MBA.

Value: Maintenance allowance, approved tuition fees and round trip travel are covered.

Length of Study: A minimum of nine months.

Frequency: Annual.

Study Establishment: Any approved Institute of Higher Education.

Country of Study: United Kingdom.

No. of awards offered: Approx. 15.

Application Procedure: Applicants must submit a formal application with four references.

Closing Date: October.

Funding: Commercial, Government, Private.

Contributor: The United States and United Kingdom governments.

No. of awards given last year: 22.

No. of applicants last year: 456.

Additional Information: A telephone interview is required of 48 shortlisted candidates.

For further information contact:

Student Program Division
Institute of International Education
809 United Nations Plaza, New York, NY, 10017, United States of America
Tel: (1) 212 984 5466
Fax: (1) 212 984 5465

Fulbright Louise Buchanan Fellowship in Cancer Research

Subjects: Oncology.

Purpose: To enable a scientist or clinician to carry out research into cancers of the lymph glands.

Eligibility: Open to British scientists or clinicians or European Union citizens who are resident in the United Kingdom.

Level of Study: Postdoctorate.

Type: Fellowship.

Value: UK £4,000 plus round trip travel.

Length of Study: A minimum of four months.

Frequency: Annual.

Study Establishment: An approved Institute of Higher Education.

Country of Study: United States of America.

No. of awards offered: One.

Application Procedure: Applicants must submit a formal application.

Closing Date: Mid April.

Funding: Private.

Contributor: The Louise Buchanan Memorial Trust.

No. of awards given last year: One.

Additional Information: Shortlisted candidates will usually be interviewed in June.

Fulbright Police Studies Fellowships

Subjects: Law enforcement.

Purpose: To enable British police officers to spend time in the United States developing their professional expertise and gaining experience of American policing.

Eligibility: Open to all ranks of police officers and civilian staff. Female and ethnic minority staff are particularly encouraged to apply. Applicants must have a first degree. Candidates will not follow a degree course, but should have some kind of academic affiliation during the award period. It is not necessary for applicants to confirm an affiliation prior to submitting their application.

Level of Study: Professional development.

Type: Fellowship.

Value: UK £5,000 to cover round trip travel and additional expenses.

Length of Study: A minimum of three months.

Frequency: Annual.

Country of Study: United States of America.

No. of awards offered: Two.

Application Procedure: Applicants must contact the Programme Manager.

Closing Date: Late March.

Funding: Government.

Fulbright Postgraduate Student Awards

Subjects: All subjects.

Purpose: To enable students to pursue postgraduate study or research in the United States of America.

Eligibility: Applicants must be European Union citizens normally resident in the United Kingdom, hold a minimum of an Upper Second Class (Honours) Degree and demonstrate outstanding leadership qualities.

Level of Study: Postgraduate.

Value: Tuition and maintenance for nine months and round trip travel.

Length of Study: A minimum of nine months.

Frequency: Annual.

Study Establishment: An approved Institute of Higher Education.

Country of Study: United States of America.

No. of awards offered: 10-15.

Application Procedure: Applicants must submit a formal application with two references.

Closing Date: Usually in early November.

Funding: Government.

No. of awards given last year: 15.

No. of applicants last year: 400.

Additional Information: Shortlisted candidates will be interviewed in mid February.

Fulbright Scholar Grants

Subjects: All subjects, with particular interest in topics which address problems shared by the United States of America and the United Kingdom.

Purpose: To enable Scholars to carry out lecturing and research in the United Kingdom.

Eligibility: Open to United States of America Scholars who took their first degree more than five years ago. Young academics in their twenties and thirties are actively encouraged to apply.

Level of Study: Postdoctorate.

Value: UK £15,000 inclusive of round trip travel.

Length of Study: One full academic year.

Frequency: Annual.

Study Establishment: An approved Institute of Higher Education.

Country of Study: United Kingdom.

No. of awards offered: Three.

Application Procedure: Applicants must submit a formal application with four references.

Closing Date: August 1st.

Funding: Government.

No. of awards given last year: Eight.

No. of applicants last year: 60.

For further information contact:

Grants Management Officer
Council for International Exchange of Scholars
3007 Tilden Street North West
Suite 5M, Washington, DC, 20008-3009, United States of America
Tel: (1) 202 686 6245
Email: we1@ciesnet.cies.org

Fulbright-Chester Schirmer Fellowship in Music Composition

Subjects: Music composition.

Purpose: To enable talented young composers to spend a period of time in the United States extending their artistic expertise and experience and taking an important step in developing an international reputation.

Eligibility: Candidates who are establishing a reputation in the United Kingdom as a professional composer, have completed their

graduate education and show that their work would benefit from exposure to American influences.
Level of Study: Postgraduate, Professional development, Research.
Type: Fellowship.
Value: Up to UK £12,000, pro rata.
Length of Study: A minimum of four months and a maximum of twelve.
Frequency: Annual.
Country of Study: United Kingdom.
No. of awards offered: One.
Application Procedure: The initial application should include six copies of a score and tape of two recent and representative works, a full curriculum vitae plus complete worklist, a list of recent performances and commissions. An outline of reasons for wishing to visit and work in the United States and benefits likely to result to the composer and his or her music should also be included with references from two professional referees.
Closing Date: Mid March.
No. of awards given last year: One.

Fulbright-RCVS Fellowship

Subjects: Animal feeds. The topic changes each time the award is offered.
Purpose: To provide an opportunity for a Scholar to visit the United States of America.
Eligibility: Applicants must be either registered Members of the Royal College of Veterinary Surgeons, food scientists or other individuals working in a discipline related to the issue being investigated. Applicants must have worked professionally for a minimum of 10 years after graduation and must hold a postgraduate academic or professional qualification. They also must be European Union citizens ordinarily resident in the United Kingdom. The successful candidate must have established an affiliation with a host university or research organisation in the United States of America prior to taking up the fellowship. Candidates must satisfactorily pass a medical examination the cost of which must be borne by the Fellow.
Level of Study: Graduate, Postgraduate.
Type: Fellowship.
Value: Up to UK £2,000 per month to cover living and travel expenses within the United States of America. Transatlantic travel costs and limited health and insurance cover will also be provided.
Length of Study: Four-six months.
Frequency: Every two years.
Country of Study: United States of America.
No. of awards offered: One.
Application Procedure: Applicants must complete an application form and ensure that their two referee statement forms are completed and returned before the closing date.
Closing Date: Mid April.
Contributor: RCVS.
Additional Information: Further enquiries concerning applications for the RCVS/Fulbright Fellowship should be directed to the Fulbright Commission's British Programme Manager or the RCVS Trust Manager.

Fulbright-Robertson Visiting Professorship in British History

Subjects: British history.
Purpose: To enable a British Scholar to spend 10 months lecturing in British history at Westminster College, Fulton in Missouri.
Eligibility: Open to Scholars of British history, with one to two years of experience of teaching undergraduates.
Level of Study: Professional development.
Type: Professorship.
Value: Up to US$40,000 plus round trip travel for grantee and up to four accompanying dependants.
Length of Study: 10 months.
Frequency: Annual.
Study Establishment: Westminster College, Fulton, Missouri.
Country of Study: United States of America.
No. of awards offered: One.

Application Procedure: Applicants must submit a formal application with two references.
Closing Date: Usually at the end of January.
No. of awards given last year: One.
No. of applicants last year: Three.
Additional Information: Shortlisted candidates will usually be interviewed in March.

Humphrey-Fulbright Fellowship for Civil Servants

Subjects: Public policy.
Purpose: To enable a British civil servant to spend one year at the Hubert Humphrey Institute of Public Affairs at the University of Minnesota.
Eligibility: Open to British civil servants at Principal Officer level or above.
Level of Study: Professional development.
Type: Fellowship.
Value: US$10,000 plus round trip travel. Confirmation is required that salary will still be paid during the award period.
Length of Study: One year.
Frequency: Annual.
Study Establishment: The Hubert Humphrey Institute of Public Affairs, University of Minnesota.
Country of Study: United States of America.
No. of awards offered: One.
Application Procedure: Applicants must submit a formal application, research proposal and departmental reference.
Closing Date: Usually late November.
Funding: Private.
No. of awards given last year: One.
No. of applicants last year: Four.
Additional Information: Shortlisted candidates will usually be interviewed in January.

US-UK Fulbright Commission Police Studies Grant

Subjects: Criminal law.
Purpose: To enable active domestic police officers and police administrators to extend their professional expertise and experience conducting research into an aspect of policing.
Eligibility: Applicants should ideally hold a Bachelor's degree in criminal justice, police studies or a related discipline within the social sciences.
Level of Study: Professional development.
Value: UK £5,000 plus round trip travel.
Length of Study: Three months.
Frequency: Annual.
Study Establishment: Institutes of Higher Education or a United Kingdom police force.
Country of Study: United Kingdom.
No. of awards offered: Two.
Application Procedure: Applicants must complete an application form available from the organisation.
Closing Date: August 1st.
Funding: Government.
No. of awards given last year: Two.
No. of applicants last year: Six.

For further information contact:

CIES
3007 Tilden Street
Suite 5M, Washington, DC, 2008-3009, United States of America

US-UK Fulbright Commission Postdoctoral Research Scholarship at De Montfort University

Subjects: All subjects offered by the university.
Purpose: To enable a Scholar to undertake postdoctoral research at De Montfort University, Leicester.
Eligibility: Open to United States of America nationals only. Young academics are actively encouraged to apply.
Level of Study: Postdoctorate.
Type: Scholarship.

Value: UK £5,000 plus round trip travel.
Length of Study: One year.
Frequency: Annual.
Study Establishment: De Montfort University, Leicester.
Country of Study: United Kingdom.
No. of awards offered: One.
Application Procedure: Applicants must complete an application form available from the organisation.
Closing Date: August 1st.
Funding: Private.
No. of applicants last year: One.

For further information contact:

CIES
3007 Tilden Street North West
Suite 5M, Washington, DC, 2008-3009, United States of America

VAN SLYKE SOCIETY

2101 L Street North West
Suite 202, Washington, DC, 20037-1558, United States of America
Tel: (1) 202 857 0717
Fax: (1) 202 887 5093
Email: mhorwitz@aacc.org
www: http://www.aacc.org
Contact: Ms Michele Horwitz, Membership Programme Director

The Van Slyke Society is part of a Washington based, non-profit, professional association with a membership of 10,200 clinical chemists, pathologists, medical technologists and others in related fields. Through educational services and publications, the Society works to improve and advance laboratory services to enhance public health and patient care.

Van Slyke Society Research Grant in Clinical Chemistry
Subjects: Clinical laboratory science.
Purpose: To provide support to those clinical laboratory scientists who need limited research funds to explore new ideas in areas where funds are not normally available.
Eligibility: Applicants should be no more than five years past his or her most recently earned degree, or no more than five years past postdoctoral training.
Level of Study: Unrestricted.
Type: Research grant.
Value: US$10,000.
Length of Study: One year.
Frequency: Annual.
Country of Study: Any country.
No. of awards offered: Dependent on funds received.
Application Procedure: Applicants must complete an application form available from the organisation.
Closing Date: March 15th.
Funding: Commercial, Private.
Contributor: Corporate sponsorship.
No. of awards given last year: Two.
No. of applicants last year: Eight.

VATICAN FILM LIBRARY

Pius XII Memorial Library
Saint Louis University
3650 Lindell Boulevard, St Louis, MO, 63108-3302, United States of America
www: http://www.slu.edu/libraries/vfl
Contact: Ms Barbara Channell, Secretary, Fellowship Programme

The Vatican Library is an outstanding library of the world. It is the oldest continuing library in Europe, having been established by Pope Nicholas V (1447-1455). Broadly speaking, its holdings are of two types, either printed books or manuscripts. The Vatican Film Library collection contains manuscripts of the Greek, Latin and Western European vernacular.

Vatican Film Library - Andrew W Mellon Fellowship Program
Subjects: Classical languages and literature, palaeography, scriptural and patristic studies, history, philosophy and sciences in the Middle Ages and the Renaissance, and early Romance literature. There are also opportunities for supported research in the history of music, manuscript illumination, mathematics and technology, theology, liturgy, Roman and canon law or political theory.
Purpose: To assist scholars wishing to conduct research in the manuscript collections in the Vatican Film Library at Saint Louis University.
Eligibility: Applicants must be at the postdoctoral level or be a graduate student formally admitted to PhD candidacy and working on their dissertation.
Level of Study: Graduate, Postdoctorate.
Type: Fellowship.
Value: Travel expenses and a reasonable yearly stipend.
Length of Study: Two-eight weeks.
Study Establishment: The Vatican Film Library.
Country of Study: United States of America.
Application Procedure: Applicants must write, in the first instance, to describe the topic of the planned research and to indicate the exact dates during which support is desired.
Additional Information: Fellowship projects can be scheduled only within one of the following periods: January 15th-May 15th, June 1st-July 31st and September 1st-December 22nd. Further information is available on the website.

VERNE CATT MCDOWELL CORPORATION

PO Box 1336, Albany, OR, 97321-0440, United States of America
Tel: (1) 541 926 6829
Contact: Ms Emily Killin, Business Manager

The Verne Catt McDowell Scholarship educates pastoral ministers of the Christian Church (Disciples of Christ) by providing supplementary financial grants to graduate theology students.

Verne Catt McDowell Scholarship
Subjects: Religion, theology or church administration.
Purpose: To provide supplemental financial grants to men and women for graduate theological education for ministry in the Christian Church (Disciples of Christ) denomination.
Eligibility: All scholarship candidates must be ministers ordained or studying to meet the requirements to be ordained as a minister in the Christian Church (Disciples of Christ). Candidates must be members of the Christian Church (Disciples of Christ) denomination. Preference is given to Oregon graduates and United States citizens.
Level of Study: Postgraduate.
Type: Scholarship.
Value: US$350 per school month.
Length of Study: One-three years.
Frequency: Annual.
Study Establishment: A graduate institution of theological education, accredited by the general assembly of the Christian Church (Disciples of Christ).
Country of Study: United States of America.
No. of awards offered: Six-eight.
Application Procedure: Applicants must complete an application form and provide details of qualifications, transcripts, three references and state where they obtained information about the Scholarship. An interview may be requested.
Closing Date: May 1st.
Funding: Private.
Contributor: I A McDowell.

No. of awards given last year: Four.
No. of applicants last year: 12.

VERNON WILLEY TRUST

Guardian Trust
PO Box 9, Christchurch, 8001, New Zealand
Tel: (64) 3 366 6764
Fax: (64) 3 366 7616
Email: ganderson@nzgt.co.nz
www: http://www.nzgt.co.nz
Contact: G Anderson, Trust & Financial Services Manager

Vernon Willey Trust Awards

Subjects: The sheep and wool industry of New Zealand.
Purpose: To assist with research and education into the production, processing and marketing of wool and the general development of the industry for the national benefit of New Zealand.
Eligibility: Open to New Zealand citizens, permanent New Zealand residents or overseas researchers working in New Zealand.
Level of Study: Doctorate, Postdoctorate.
Type: Fellowship.
Value: Varies, usually between new zealand $30,000-35,000.
Length of Study: Up to three years.
Frequency: Dependent on funds available.
Country of Study: New Zealand.
No. of awards offered: One.
Application Procedure: Applicants must complete an application form.
Closing Date: The first week in November.
Funding: Private.
No. of awards given last year: Two.
No. of applicants last year: Seven.
Additional Information: Applicants for financial grants must satisfy the Committee that their activities are of general or public benefit. The results of the research or studies are expected to be covered by material suitable for publication in recognised scientific or technical journals.

VICTORIA UNIVERSITY

Emmanuel College
75 Queen's Park Crescent East, Toronto, ON, M5S 1K7, Canada
Tel: (1) 416 585 4539
Fax: (1) 416 585 4516
Email: ec.office@utoronto.ca
www: http://www.vicu.utoronto.ca
Contact: Ms Margaret Grisdale

Emmanuel College, set within Victoria University and the University of Toronto, is the United Church of Canada's largest theological college. The College offers four basic or first professional degrees and five advanced or graduate degrees. About 210 students are currently enrolled. Emmanuel College is one of seven member schools of the Toronto School of Theology.

Bertram Maura Memorial Entrance Scholarship

Subjects: Theology, specifically in the fields of the Old and New Testament.
Purpose: To provide funding to doctoral students.
Eligibility: Open to outstanding doctoral students.
Level of Study: Doctorate.
Type: Scholarship.
Value: Canadian $10,000.
Length of Study: Two years.
Frequency: Annual.
Study Establishment: Emmanuel College.
Country of Study: Canada.

No. of awards offered: Varies from year to year.
Closing Date: March 31st.
Funding: Private.
No. of awards given last year: One.
No. of applicants last year: One.

Bloor Lands Entrance Scholarship

Subjects: Religion and theology.
Purpose: To assist newly admitted ThD or PhD students with potential for excellence in scholarship demonstrated by high achievement in previous theological studies.
Level of Study: Doctorate.
Type: Scholarship.
Value: Canadian $10,000 for a two year period.
Length of Study: Two years.
Frequency: Annual.
Study Establishment: Emmanuel College.
Country of Study: Canada.
No. of awards offered: Varies from year to year.
Application Procedure: Admission to the Toronto School of Theology/Emmanuel College must first be granted. Application is then made care of the Director of Advanced Degree Studies.
Closing Date: March 31st.
Funding: Private.
No. of awards given last year: Two.
No. of applicants last year: Four.

Finishing Scholarships

Subjects: Religion and theology.
Purpose: To enable a doctoral student to finish his or her dissertation in the year in which the award is made.
Eligibility: Doctoral students at the end of the programme are eligible.
Level of Study: Doctorate.
Type: Scholarship.
Value: Approx. canadian $10,000.
Length of Study: One year.
Frequency: Annual.
Study Establishment: Emmanuel College.
Country of Study: Canada.
No. of awards offered: Three.
Closing Date: March 31st.
Funding: Private.
No. of awards given last year: One.
No. of applicants last year: One.

Frank P Fidler Memorial Award

Subjects: Religion and theology.
Purpose: To assist alumni returning for further study.
Eligibility: Applications from those interested in studying the Church's ministry with various types of families in today's changing world are particularly encouraged. Preference is given to graduates returning to Emmanuel to complete a ThM or second basic degree.
Level of Study: Doctorate.
Type: Scholarship.
Value: Varies.
Length of Study: One year.
Frequency: Annual.
Study Establishment: Emmanuel College.
Country of Study: Canada.
No. of awards offered: One.
Closing Date: March 31st.
Funding: Private.
No. of awards given last year: One.
No. of applicants last year: Two.

In-Course Scholarships

Subjects: Religion and theology.
Eligibility: Open to doctoral students.
Level of Study: Doctorate.
Type: Scholarship.

Value: Varies.
Length of Study: Two-three years.
Frequency: Annual.
Study Establishment: Emmanuel College.
Country of Study: Canada.
No. of awards offered: Varies from year to year.
Closing Date: March 31st.
Funding: Private.
No. of awards given last year: Four.
No. of applicants last year: Eight.
Additional Information: These scholarships are awarded to students who have demonstrated academic excellence to assist them beyond the residency phase of their studies.

Vernon Hope Emory Entrance Scholarship

Subjects: Religion and theology.
Purpose: To support an outstanding newly admitted ThD or PhD student.
Level of Study: Doctorate.
Type: Scholarship.
Value: Canadian $10,000 for a two year period.
Length of Study: Two years.
Frequency: Annual.
Study Establishment: Emmanuel College.
Country of Study: Canada.
No. of awards offered: One.
Application Procedure: Admission to the Toronto School of Theology/Emmanuel College must be first granted. Application is then made care of the Director of Advanced Degree Studies.
Closing Date: March 31st.
Funding: Private.
No. of awards given last year: One.
No. of applicants last year: Four.

Victoria University Graduate Student Assistantships

Subjects: Religion and theology. Graduate students are assigned to work with the Asian Centre and in the fields of Christian education, church and society, ethics, field education, history of Christianity, homiletics, New Testament, Old Testament, pastoral theology, and systematic theology or worship.
Purpose: To provide funding for doctoral students.
Level of Study: Doctorate.
Type: Scholarship.
Value: Canadian $9,300 per year.
Length of Study: Two years.
Frequency: Annual.
Study Establishment: Emmanuel College.
Country of Study: Canada.
No. of awards offered: 13.
Application Procedure: Admission to the Toronto School of Theology/Emmanuel College must first be granted. Application is then made care of the Director of Advance Degree Studies.
Closing Date: February 28th.
Funding: Private.
No. of awards given last year: 13.
No. of applicants last year: 17.

VIRGINIA CENTER FOR THE CREATIVE ARTS

PO Box VCCA, Sweet Briar, VA, 24595, United States of America
Tel: (1) 804 946 7236
Fax: (1) 804 946 7239
Email: vcca@vcca.com
www: http://www.vcca.com
Contact: Ms Suny Monk, Director

The Virginia Center for the Creative Arts is a year round community that provides a supportive environment for superior national and international visual artists, writers and composers, of all cultural and economic backgrounds, to pursue their creative work without distraction in a pastoral residential setting.

Virginia Center for the Creative Arts Fellowships

Subjects: Writing, musical composition, photography or art.
Purpose: To support literary, musical and visual artists during the most crucial creative phase of their work.
Eligibility: Open to artists with professional competence and promise, regardless of age, sex, citizenship or academic background. Writers, visual artists, composers, choreographers, photographers, film makers, interdisciplinary and multimedia artists are all eligible. Admission is through a jury selection process.
Level of Study: Unrestricted.
Type: Fellowship.
Value: Subsidised residence at the Center. No cash stipends or travel allowances are provided.
Length of Study: One-three months each year, renewable.
Study Establishment: The Center.
Country of Study: United States of America.
No. of awards offered: Approx. 300.
Application Procedure: Applicants must submit an application form, work samples and letters of reference.
Closing Date: January 15th, May 15th or September 15th.
Funding: Commercial, Government, Private.
No. of awards given last year: 309.
No. of applicants last year: 850.

VITUKI TRAINING

International Postgraduate Course on Hydrology
Pf 27, Budapest, H-1453, Hungary
Tel: (36) 1 215 3043
Fax: (36) 1 215 3043
Email: training@vituki.hu
www: http://www.vituki.hu/ceg/tanf_hmem/index.htm
Contact: Director

Supported by hydraulic, hydromachinery, hydrochemical, hydrobiological, wastewater technological and soil mechanical laboratories, equipment, instrumentation, computer facilities and library, VITUKI is one of the most complex water oriented organisations in Europe. It contains three institutes and a training centre in the fields of hydrology, hydrogeology, hydraulics, water quality and pollution control.

VITUKI Training Financial Support for Course Participants

Subjects: Hydrology based subjects such as mathematics, hydraulics, geosciences, hydrological studies, hydrological processes, observation processing, analysis, forecasting, application, aquatic environment and water management.
Purpose: To make a contribution towards raising the level of hydrological sciences in developing and transitional countries.
Eligibility: Open to nationals of any country who are under 40 years of age. A degree from a recognised institution is required in applied mathematics, mathematical statistics, systems analysis, hydrology, fluid mechanics, geology or meteorology.
Level of Study: Postgraduate.
Type: Financial support.
Value: US$8,000.
Length of Study: Four months.
Frequency: Annual.
Study Establishment: The premises of VITUKI in Budapest.
Country of Study: Hungary.
No. of awards offered: Four.
Application Procedure: Applicants must write for details.
Closing Date: December 31st.
Funding: Government.
Contributor: The Hungarian government.
No. of awards given last year: Four.

No. of applicants last year: 40.

Additional Information: The course's finances are essentially based on applicants holding fellowships granted by international organisations, by their own government, or on applicants paying for themselves. The course's admission board may be able to propose fellowship applicants to sponsoring national or international agencies, but awards no fellowships of its own.

VOLZHSKY INSTITUTE OF HUMANITIES (VIH)

Volgograd State University (VSU)
40 Let Pobedy Street, Volzhsky, Volgograd, 404132, Russia
Tel: (7) 844 329 1778
Fax: (7) 844 329 1778
Email: vasin@vgumi.vlink.ru
Contact: Director

The Volzhsky Institute of Humanities (VIH) is the leading scientific and cultural centre of the region on the left bank of the Volga with approx. 2,000 students studying at three faculties. Highly qualified specialists lecture at the VIH, among them 15 doctors of sciences. VIH develops relationships with universities abroad and are interested in making new relationships with universities from any English speaking country.

Volzhsky Institute of Humanities Awards

Subjects: Environmental management, management systems and techniques, applied mathematics, ecology, natural resources, statistics, criminal law, philosophy, computer science, econometrics, soil conservation, modern languages and literatures eg. English, French, German, Russian, comparative literature, foreign languages education, education of foreigners, higher education, teacher training, educational technology, modern history or business computing.
Purpose: To allow recipients to acquire new skills and undertake research.
Level of Study: Doctorate, Graduate, Postgraduate, Predoctorate, Professional development.
Type: Fellowship.
Value: Tuition fees.
Length of Study: Two-four months.
Frequency: Annual.
Study Establishment: The VIH.
Country of Study: Russia.
No. of awards offered: Two in each subject area.
Application Procedure: Applicants must contact the VIH for details. Application forms can be completed either in English or in Russian. The Institute would like the award to cover the subject core of modern languages, preferably English and its variants.
Closing Date: November 30th.
Funding: Government.

VON KARMAN INSTITUTE FOR FLUID DYNAMICS (VKI)

Chausse de Waterloo 72, Rhode-Saint-Genese, B-1640, Belgium
Tel: (32) 2 359 9611
Fax: (32) 2 359 9600
Email: secretariat@vki.ac.be
www: http://www.vki.ac.be
Contact: Mr M Carbonaro, Secretariat

The Von Karman Institute for Fluid Dynamics (VKI) is an international postgraduate training and research centre specialising in the fluid dynamic aspects of aircraft, spacecraft, turbomachines, wind flows and industrial processes.

VKI Fellowship

Subjects: Fluid dynamics.
Purpose: To support the living costs of recipients who attend the VKI Diploma Course.
Eligibility: Open to citizens of NATO countries, with the exception of Canada, Denmark, Greece, the Netherlands and the United Kingdom, who have the equivalent of a five year engineering degree. Applicants must have a working knowledge of English.
Level of Study: Postgraduate.
Type: Fellowship.
Value: Approx. US$1,000 per month.
Length of Study: Nine months.
Frequency: Annual.
Study Establishment: The VKI.
Country of Study: Belgium.
No. of awards offered: 25.
Application Procedure: Applicants must submit two application forms, one endorsed by the RTO National Delegate (NATO Research and Technology Organisation). Copies of college transcripts and three references are required.
Closing Date: Applications received before March 1st will be given priority.
Funding: Government.
No. of awards given last year: 25.
No. of applicants last year: 75.

W EUGENE SMITH MEMORIAL FUND, INC.

c/o International Center of Photography
1133 Avenue of the Americas, New York, NY, 10036, United States of America
Tel: (1) 212 860 1777 ext. 186
www: http://www.smithfund.org
Contact: Ms Anna Winand

The W Eugene Smith Memorial Fund, Inc. presents a major grant to a photographer whose past work and proposed project follows in the humanistic tradition of Smith. The Funds' grant programme is financed by Nikon, Inc.

Smith (W Eugene) Grant in Humanistic Photography

Subjects: Photojournalism.
Purpose: To support a photographer working on a project in the humanistic tradition of W Eugene Smith, in order to continue to pursue the work.
Eligibility: Open to outstanding photographers of any nationality.
Level of Study: Professional development.
Type: Grant.
Value: One grant for US$30,000 with a possible second grant for US$5,000.
Frequency: Annual.
Country of Study: Any country.
No. of awards offered: Two.
Application Procedure: Applicants must send a stamped addressed envelope for application information.
Closing Date: July 15th.
Funding: Commercial.
Contributor: Nikon, Inc.
No. of awards given last year: Three.
No. of applicants last year: 182.
Additional Information: A US$5,000 scholarship grant may be awarded.

WACKER FOUNDATION

10848 Strait Lane, Dallas, TX, 75229, United States of America
Tel: (1) 214 368 0150
Fax: (1) 214 373 3308
Email: wackerjohn@aol.com
www: http://www.crime-times.org
Contact: Mr John A Wacker, President

The Wacker Foundation funds research and dissemination of research information which targets the proving, diagnosing or treating of biologically based disordered behaviour. Areas of special interest include nutrition, food and chemical intolerance, neurochemistry and genetics.

Wacker Foundation Research Grant
Subjects: Neurology, paediatrics, psychiatry, mental health, biomedicine, biophysics, molecular biology, genetics, neurosciences, toxicology and cognitive sciences.
Value: Varies.
Frequency: Dependent on funds available.
Application Procedure: Applicants must submit a brief letter giving a description of the proposed project and stating the appropriate cost.
Closing Date: There is no deadline.
Funding: Private.

THE WARBURG INSTITUTE

University of London
Woburn Square, London, WC1H 0AB, England
Tel: (44) 20 7862 8949
Fax: (44) 20 7862 8955
Email: warburg@sas.ac.uk
www: http://www.sas.ac.uk/warburg
Contact: E A Witchell, Administrative Assistant

The Warburg Institute is concerned with the interdisciplinary study of the continuities between the ancient Mediterranean civilisations and the cultural and intellectual history of post classical Europe before 1800 AD. Its collections are arranged to encourage research into the processes by which different fields of thought and art interact.

Albin Salton Fellowship
Subjects: Cultural contacts between Europe, the East and the New World in the late medieval, Renaissance and early modern periods, in order to promote understanding of those elements of cultural and intellectual history leading to the formation of a new world view.
Purpose: To promote research.
Eligibility: Applicants must normally be under 35 years of age on October 1st of the academic year prior to which the fellowship is taken up, and have completed at least one year of research towards a doctorate.
Level of Study: Doctorate, Postdoctorate.
Type: Fellowship.
Value: UK £1,500 for a United Kingdom holder or UK £1,850 for an overseas holder.
Length of Study: Two months.
Frequency: Annual.
Study Establishment: The Warburg Institute.
Country of Study: United Kingdom.
No. of awards offered: One.
Application Procedure: Applicants must contact the Secretary and Registrar for further information.
Closing Date: Early December.
No. of awards given last year: One.

Brian Hewson Crawford Fellowship
Subjects: The classical tradition.
Purpose: To support research.

Eligibility: Fellowships are generally for younger Scholars and preference will normally be given to those under 35 years of age on October 1st 2001. Candidates may be pre or postdoctoral but must have completed at least one year of research on their doctoral dissertation by the time they submit their application. Postdoctoral candidates, if they are over 35, must normally have been awarded their doctorate within the preceding academic year. If their doctorate was awarded before this they should explain the reasons for the interruption in their academic career in a covering letter.
Level of Study: Doctorate, Postdoctorate.
Type: Fellowship.
Value: UK £1,500-1,850.
Length of Study: Two months.
Frequency: Annual.
Study Establishment: The Warburg Institute.
Country of Study: United Kingdom.
No. of awards offered: One.
Application Procedure: Applicants must contact the Secretary and Registrar for further information.
Closing Date: Early December.
No. of awards given last year: One.

Frances A Yates Fellowships
Subjects: Intellectual and cultural history.
Purpose: To promote research.
Eligibility: Fellowships are generally for younger Scholars and preference will normally be given to those under 35 years of age on October 1st 2001. Candidates may be pre or postdoctoral but must have completed at least one year of research on their doctoral dissertation by the time they submit their application. Postdoctoral candidates, if they are over 35, must normally have been awarded their doctorate within the preceding academic year. If their doctorate was awarded before this they should explain the reasons for the interruption in their academic career in a covering letter.
Level of Study: Doctorate, Postdoctorate.
Type: Fellowship.
Value: UK £1,500-3,500.
Length of Study: The long-term fellowship is one-three years, not normally renewable, and short-term fellowships are two-four months, not renewable.
Frequency: Annually.
Study Establishment: The Warburg Institute.
Country of Study: United Kingdom.
No. of awards offered: One long-term fellowship, not awarded every year and 10 short-term fellowships.
Application Procedure: Applicants must contact the Secretary and Registrar for further information.
Closing Date: Early December.
No. of awards given last year: Seven.

Henri Frankfort Fellowship
Subjects: The intellectual and cultural history of the ancient Near and Middle East.
Purpose: To promote research.
Eligibility: Fellowships are generally for younger Scholars and preference will normally be given to those under 35 years of age on October 1st 2001. Candidates may be pre or postdoctoral but must have completed at least one year's research on their doctoral dissertation by the time they submit their application. Postdoctoral candidates, if they are over 35, must normally have been awarded their doctorate within the preceding academic year. If their doctorate was awarded before this they should explain the reasons for the interruption in their academic career in a covering letter.
Level of Study: Doctorate, Postdoctorate.
Type: Fellowship.
Value: UK £1,500-2,700.
Length of Study: Two-three months.
Frequency: Annual.
Study Establishment: The Warburg Institute.
Country of Study: United Kingdom.
No. of awards offered: One.

Application Procedure: Applicants must contact the Secretary and Registrar for further information.
Closing Date: Early December.
No. of awards given last year: One.
Additional Information: This fellowship is not intended to support archaeological excavation.

Mellon Research Fellowships

Subjects: Humanities.
Purpose: To support Eastern European scholars in the study of the humanities.
Eligibility: Open to Bulgarian, Czech, Hungarian, Polish, Romanian and Slovak Scholars. Candidates should not be permanently resident outside these countries. Fellows should have obtained a doctorate or have equivalent experience. The fellowships are intended for younger postdoctoral Scholars. Preference will be given to those under 40 years of age.
Level of Study: Postdoctorate.
Type: Fellowship.
Value: The sterling equivalent of US$11,500.
Length of Study: Three months.
Frequency: Annual.
Study Establishment: The Warburg Institute.
Country of Study: England.
No. of awards offered: Three.
Application Procedure: Applicants must submit a letter of application, a curriculum vitae, an outline of the proposed research, particulars of any grants received for the same subject, the names and addresses of two to three referees and copies of any published work to the Director. Further information is available from the Secretary and Registrar.
Closing Date: April 2nd.
No. of awards given last year: Three.
Additional Information: Fellows will be expected to participate in the life of the Institute and to put their knowledge at the disposal of the Institute by presenting their work in a seminar and by advising the Library and Photographic Collection. Fellows will be required to present a brief written report at the conclusion of their appointment.

Nord/LB Warburg-Wolfenbüttel Research Fellowship

Subjects: Cultural and intellectual history of early modern Europe.
Purpose: To promote research.
Eligibility: Fellowships are generally for younger Scholars and preference will normally be given to those under 35 years of age on October 1st 2001. Candidates may be pre or postdoctoral but must have completed at least one year of research on their doctoral dissertation by the time they submit their application. Postdoctoral candidates, if they are over 35, must normally have been awarded their doctorate within the preceding academic year. If their doctorate was awarded before this they should explain the reasons for the interruption in their academic career in a covering letter.
Level of Study: Doctorate, Postdoctorate.
Type: Fellowship.
Value: Approx. UK £5,000 paid in Euros.
Length of Study: Two months in the United Kingdom and two months in Germany.
Frequency: Annual.
Study Establishment: Warburg Institute and Herzog August Bibliothek Wolfenbüttel.
Country of Study: United Kingdom or Germany.
No. of awards offered: One.
Application Procedure: Applicants must contact the Secretary and Registrar for further information.
Closing Date: Early December.
Funding: Commercial.
No. of awards given last year: One.

Sophia Fellowship

Subjects: The history of astrology.

Purpose: To promote research into the history of astrological theory, practice, iconography and their relation to other arts and sciences in both Western and non-Western societies.
Eligibility: Applicants must normally be 29 years of age or over on October 1st of the academic year prior to which the fellowship is taken up, and must have completed more than one year of postgraduate research when they apply. There is no upper age limit for this fellowship.
Level of Study: Research.
Type: Fellowship.
Value: UK £1,500-3,500 depending on the length of tenure.
Length of Study: Two-four months.
Frequency: Annual.
Study Establishment: The Warburg Institute.
Country of Study: United Kingdom.
No. of awards offered: One.
Application Procedure: Applicants must contact the Secretary and Registrar for further information.
Closing Date: Early December.
Funding: Private.
No. of awards given last year: One.

WARWICK BUSINESS SCHOOL

University of Warwick, Coventry, CV4 7AL, England
Tel: (44) 24 7652 4306
Fax: (44) 24 7652 3719
Email: inquiries@wbs.warwick.ac.uk
www: http://www.wbs.warwick.ac.uk
Contact: Ms Diana Holton, Assistant Communications Manager

With 300 staff and 4,000 students from around 100 countries worldwide, Warwick Business School is an international school and is accredited with management associations in North America, Europe and the United Kingdom. Its high calibre research feeds into top quality teaching on specialist Master's, doctoral and MBA degrees.

Warwick Business School Scholarships

Subjects: MBA.
Purpose: To allow candidates to pursue the full-time MBA course.
Level of Study: MBA.
Type: Scholarship.
Value: Approx. UK £5,000.
Frequency: Annual.
Study Establishment: Warwick Business School.
Country of Study: England.
No. of awards offered: 10.
Application Procedure: Applicants must submit a competitive essay to the Business School.

WASHINGTON UNIVERSITY

Graduate School of Arts & Sciences
Campus Box 1187
1 Brookings Drive, St Louis, MO, 63130, United States of America
Tel: (1) 314 935 6821
Fax: (1) 314 935 4887
Email: sheri_notaro@aismail.wustl.edu
www: http://www.artsci.wustl.edu/gsas
Contact: Ms Sheri Notaro, Assistant Dean

Mr and Mrs Spencer T Olin Fellowships for Women

Subjects: Any graduate discipline or professional school at Washington University in St. Louis.
Purpose: To encourage women of exceptional promise to prepare for professional careers.
Eligibility: Open to female graduates of a Baccalaureate institution in the United States of America who plan to prepare for a career in

higher education or the professions. Applicants must meet the admission requirements of the graduate or professional school of Washington University. Preference will be given to those who wish to study for the highest earned degree in their chosen field, do not already hold an advanced degree, and are not currently enrolled in a graduate or professional degree programme.
Level of Study: Doctorate, Graduate, Postgraduate.
Type: Fellowship.
Value: Full tuition and, in some cases, a living expense stipend.
Length of Study: One year, renewable for up to four years, or until the completion of the degree programme, whichever comes first.
Frequency: Annual.
Study Establishment: Washington University in St. Louis.
Country of Study: United States of America.
No. of awards offered: Approx. 10.
Application Procedure: Applicants must complete an application form. Candidates must be interviewed on campus at the expense of the University. Applications should be addressed to the Dean, Nancy P Pope.
Closing Date: February 1st.
Funding: Private.
Contributor: The Monticello College Foundation.
No. of awards given last year: 11.
No. of applicants last year: 350.
Additional Information: Candidates must also make concurrent application to the department or school of Washington University in which they plan to study.

Washington University Chancellor's Graduate Fellowship Program for African Americans

Subjects: Any of Washington University's PhD or DSc programmes in arts and sciences, business, engineering or social work.
Purpose: To encourage African Americans who are interested in becoming college or university professors.
Eligibility: Open to African-American doctoral candidates.
Level of Study: Doctorate, Graduate.
Type: Fellowship.
Value: Doctoral candidates will receive full tuition plus US$16,000 stipend and allowances.
Length of Study: Five years, subject to satisfactory academic progress.
Frequency: Annual.
Study Establishment: Washington University.
Country of Study: United States of America.
No. of awards offered: Five-six.
Application Procedure: Applicants must complete an application form.
Closing Date: January 25th.
No. of awards given last year: Nine.
No. of applicants last year: 105.
Additional Information: The fellowship includes other Washington University programmes providing final disciplinary training for prospective college professors.

WEIZMANN INSTITUTE OF SCIENCE

Feinberg Graduate School
PO Box 26, Rehovot, 76100, Israel
Tel: (972) 8 934 3840
Fax: (972) 8 934 2924
Email: nfinfo@weizmann.ac.il
www: http://www.weizmann.ac.il/feinberg
Contact: Grants Management Officer

The Weizmann Institute of Science is one of the top ranking multidisciplinary research institutions in the world. Noted for its wide ranging exploration of the sciences and technology, the Institute houses 2,400 scientists, technicians and research students devoted to a better understanding of nature and our place within it.

Weizmann Institute of Science MSc Fellowships

Subjects: Life sciences, including brain research, cell biology, molecular genetics, biochemistry, biophysics, immunology, biological regulation, plant sciences and bioinformatics. Chemistry, including physical, theoretical, organic, biological, environmental sciences and energy research and material sciences. Physics, including theoretical, experimental, applied, semi-conductor and biological. Mathematics, including pure and applied, computer science or science teaching.
Purpose: To enable study at the Feinberg Graduate School of the Weizmann Institute of Science.
Eligibility: Open to holders of a BSc degree from an accredited Institute of Higher Education in Israel or of an equivalent degree from a recognised overseas university.
Level of Study: Postgraduate.
Type: Fellowship.
Value: To cover living expenses.
Frequency: Annual.
Study Establishment: The Institute.
Country of Study: Israel.
Application Procedure: Applicants must write for details.
Closing Date: June 1st.

Weizmann Institute of Science PhD Fellowships

Subjects: Life sciences, including brain research, cell biology, molecular genetics, biochemistry, biophysics, immunology, biological regulation, plant sciences and bioinformatics. Chemistry, including physical, theoretical, organic, biological, environmental sciences and energy research and material sciences. Physics, including theoretical, experimental, applied, semi-conductor and biological. Mathematics, including pure and applied, computer science or science teaching.
Purpose: To enable study at the Feinberg Graduate School of the Weizmann Institute of Science.
Eligibility: Open to holders of an MSc or MD degree.
Level of Study: Doctorate.
Type: Fellowship.
Value: To cover living expenses.
Frequency: Throughout the year.
Study Establishment: The Institute.
Country of Study: Israel.
Application Procedure: Applicants must write for details.
Additional Information: A special programme is offered to students wishing to take a direct BSc to PhD route.

Weizmann Institute of Science Postdoctoral Fellowships Program

Subjects: Life sciences, including brain research, cell biology, molecular genetics, biochemistry, biophysics, immunology, biological regulation, plant sciences and bioinformatics. Chemistry, including physical, theoretical, organic, biological, environmental sciences and energy research and material sciences. Physics, including theoretical, experimental, applied, semi-conductor and biological. Mathematics, including pure and applied, computer science or science teaching.
Eligibility: Open to holders of a PhD degree.
Level of Study: Postdoctorate.
Type: Fellowship.
Value: To cover living expenses.
Frequency: Twice a year.
Study Establishment: The Institute.
Country of Study: Israel.
Application Procedure: Applicants must write for details.
Closing Date: January 1st and May 15th.

WELLBEING

27 Sussex Place, London, NW1 4SP, England
Tel: (44) 20 7772 6338
Fax: (44) 20 7724 7725
Email: jmarshall.wellbeing@rcog.org.uk
www: http://www.wellbeing.org.uk
Contact: Mr John Marshall, Research Manager

WellBeing is the research arm of the Royal College of Obstetricians and Gynaecologists, funding medical and scientific research in hospitals and universities. WellBeing is involved in research all aspects of pregnancy, birth and the care of the newborn, women's cancers, infertility, period problems, incontinence and the menopause.

WellBeing Project Grants

Subjects: Obstetrics, gynaecology and related disciplines, particularly all aspects of pregnancy, birth and the care of newborns, screening procedures, diagnostic techniques and treatments of gynaecological cancers including ovarian, cervical and endometrial cancer, and quality of life issues including infertility, menstruation, incontinence, the menopause and osteoporosis.
Purpose: For research into all matters of women's obstetric and gynaecological health and the health of their babies.
Eligibility: Open to specialists in any obstetrics and gynaecology interrelated field.
Level of Study: Professional development, Research.
Type: Grant.
Value: Maximum of UK £80,000 over three years, with not more than UK £45,000 in the first year.
Length of Study: One-three years.
Frequency: Annual.
Country of Study: United Kingdom.
No. of awards offered: Varies depending on the amount of disposable income.
Application Procedure: Applicants must write for details or access the website.
Funding: Commercial, Private.

THE WELLCOME TRUST

183 Euston Road, London, NW1 2BE, England
Tel: (44) 20 7611 7371
Fax: (44) 20 7611 0604
Email: grantenquiries@wellcome.ac.uk
www: http://www.wellcome.ac.uk
Contact: Ms Rebecca Christou, Grants Information Officer

The Wellcome Trust's mission is to foster and promote research with the aim of improving human and animal health. The Trust funds most areas of biomedical research, although its support for cancer research is limited.

Wellcome Trust Awards, Fellowships and Studentships

Subjects: Biomedical sciences, from the basic sciences related to medicine to the clinical aspects of medicine and veterinary medicine. The Trust also operates a portfolio of schemes to support research in the history of medicine, the public appreciation of sciences or bioethics.
Purpose: To support and maintain the strength of biomedical research by providing individual researchers of the highest quality with the resources they need to pursue their subject.
Eligibility: Open to academic staff in universities, medical and veterinary schools and other Institutes of Higher Education, who are engaged in all types of medical research.
Level of Study: Postdoctorate, Professional development, Research.
Type: Project and programme grants, fellowships, studentships and travel grants.
Value: Varies.
Length of Study: Varies.
Frequency: Differs for each funding scheme.
Country of Study: Mostly the United Kingdom or the Republic of Ireland, but also schemes available for overseas, particularly in the developing or restructuring countries.
No. of awards offered: Varies.
Application Procedure: Applicants must submit a written preliminary outline for all schemes except United Kingdom based project and programme grants consisting of a brief curriculum vitae of the applicant(s) including their source of salary, an outline of the proposed research project and the approximate cost of project. Requests for application forms for United Kingdom based project and programme grants must be directed to the appropriate scientific panel of the Trust. Further information on application procedures is available on the website.
Closing Date: Preliminary applications are accepted at any time. Please visit the website for scheme deadlines.
Contributor: Endowment.
No. of awards given last year: 1,407.
No. of applicants last year: 3,405.
Additional Information: The Wellcome Trust is one of the most richly endowed of all charitable institutions that fund general medical research in the United Kingdom. The Governors review their policy annually in response to proposals from their advisory panels and professional staff.

WENNER-GREN FOUNDATION FOR ANTHROPOLOGICAL RESEARCH

220 Fifth Avenue
16th Floor, New York, NY, 10001, United States of America

Tel: (1) 212 683 5000

Fax: (1) 212 683 9151

Email: info@wennergren.org

www: http://www.wennergren.org

Contact: Fellowships Office

The Wenner-Gren Foundation for Anthropological Research supports research, conferences, training, archiving and collaboration in all branches of anthropology, including cultural and social anthropology, ethnology, biological and physical anthropology, archaeology and anthropological linguistics, and in closely related disciplines concerned with human origins, development and variation.

Anthropological Research Grants

Subjects: Anthropology.

Purpose: To support research, conferences, training, archiving and collaboration.

Eligibility: Contact the Foundation for information.

Level of Study: Postgraduate.

Type: Varies.

Frequency: Varies.

No. of awards offered: Varies.

Application Procedure: Applicants must contact the Foundation directly for current information on all programmes.

WESLEYAN UNIVERSITY

Center for the Humanities
Wesleyan University, Middletown, CT, 06459-0069, United States of America
Tel: (1) 860 685 3044
Fax: (1) 860 685 2171
Email: bkeating@wesleyan.edu
www: http://www.wesleyan.edu
Contact: Ms Brenda Keating, Administrative Assistant

Wesleyan University offers instruction in 41 departments and programmes and 50 major fields of study and awards the Bachelor of Arts and graduate degrees. Master's degrees are awarded in 11 fields of study and doctoral degrees in six. Students may choose from about 960 courses each year and may be asked to devise, with the faculty, some 1,500 individual tutorials and lessons.

Andrew W Mellon Postdoctoral Fellowship

Subjects: Arts, humanities and cultural studies.
Purpose: To promote interdisciplinary interests among younger scholars.
Eligibility: Open to persons who have received their PhD within the last four years.
Level of Study: Postdoctorate.
Type: Fellowship.
Value: US$40,000, plus US$500 reserve.
Frequency: Annual.
Country of Study: Any country.
No. of awards offered: One.
Application Procedure: Applicants must request a brochure detailing the application process. There is no formal application form.
Closing Date: November 15th.
Funding: Private.
No. of awards given last year: One.
No. of applicants last year: 115.
Additional Information: The Fellow must reside in Middletown during the tenure of the fellowship, give one public lecture and teach one course of 20 students.

THE WHARTON SCHOOL

University of Pennsylvania
MBA Admissions & Financial Aid
102 Vance Hill, Philadelphia, PA, 19104-6361, United States of America
Tel: (1) 215 898 6182
Fax: (1) 215 898 0120
Email: mba.admissions@wharton.upenn.edu
www: http://www.wharton.upenn.edu/mba/catalog
Contact: MBA Programme

European Scholarship Fund

Subjects: MBA.
Eligibility: Candidates must be European nationals and must prove academic and professional achievement as well as financial need.
Level of Study: MBA.
Type: Scholarship.
Value: Up to US$10,000.
Frequency: Annual.
Study Establishment: The Wharton School.
Country of Study: United States of America.
Application Procedure: Applicants must apply to the MBA course in the usual way. Eligible students will receive an application form once they have been accepted onto the programme.
Closing Date: Please contact the organisation.

Henry J Kaiser Family Foundation Fellowships in Health Care Management

Subjects: MBA.
Eligibility: Open to students undertaking the health care management programme.
Level of Study: MBA.
Type: Fellowship.
Frequency: Annual.
Study Establishment: The Wharton School.
Country of Study: United States of America.
Application Procedure: Applicants must submit their Wharton School application, as a separate scholarship application is not required.
Closing Date: March 1st.

Mitchell Fellowships

Subjects: MBA.
Purpose: To assist minority students who demonstrate financial need to pursue the MBA.
Eligibility: Selection is based on academic record, work experience and proven leadership.
Level of Study: MBA.
Type: Fellowship.
Study Establishment: The Wharton School.
Country of Study: United States of America.
Application Procedure: Applicants must apply to the MBA course in the usual way. Eligible students will receive an application form once they have been accepted onto the programme.
Additional Information: The fellowships are named in honour of the first tenured African American professor at Wharton, Mr Howard E Mitchell.

WHATCOM MUSEUM OF HISTORY AND ART

121 Prospect Street, Bellingham, WA, 98225, United States of America
Tel: (1) 360 676 6981
Fax: (1) 360 738 7409
Email: ageise@cob.org
www: http://www.cob.org/museum
Contact: Ms Deanna Zipp, Museum Secretary

Jacobs Research Fund

Subjects: Field research in language, social organisation, political organisation, religion, mythology, music, other arts, psychology and folk science.
Purpose: To support anthropological research, sociocultural or linguistic in content of the indigenous peoples of Canada, mainland United States (including Alaska) and Mexico, with a focus on the Pacific Northwest.
Eligibility: Projects in archaeology, physical anthropology, applied anthropology and applied linguistics are not eligible and archival research is not supported.
Level of Study: Unrestricted.
Type: Grant.
Value: Up to US$1,200.
Length of Study: One year.
Frequency: Annual.
Country of Study: Pacific Northwest or other regions of the North American Continent.
No. of awards offered: Usually 16.
Application Procedure: Applicants must complete an application form. Further information and application forms are available on written request or from the website.
Closing Date: Please contact the organisation.
Funding: Private.
Contributor: Melville and Elizabeth Jacobs.

Additional Information: The Jacobs Research Fund is an enduring expression of a commitment to the collection and preservation of data documenting the languages, ethnography and literature of indigenous peoples.

WHITEHALL FOUNDATION, INC.

PO Box 3423, Palm Beach, FL, 33480, United States of America
Tel: (1) 561 655 4474
Fax: (1) 561 659 4978
Email: email@whitehall.org
www: http://www.whitehall.org
Contact: Ms Catherine Thomas, Corporate Secretary

The Whitehall Foundation, through its programme of grants and grants-in-aid, assists scholarly research in the life sciences. It is the Foundation's policy to assist those dynamic areas of basic biological research that are not heavily supported by Federal agencies or other foundations with specialised missions.

Whitehall Foundation Grants-in-Aid

Subjects: Basic research in neurobiology focusing on invertebrate and vertebrate (excluding clinical) neurobiology, specifically investigations of neural mechanisms involved in sensory, motor and other complex functions of the whole organism as these relate to behaviour.
Purpose: To better understand behavioural output or brain mechanisms of behaviour.
Eligibility: Open to researchers at the assistant professor level who have experienced difficulty in competing for research funds as they have not yet become firmly established. Senior scientists may also apply.
Type: Grant.
Value: Up to US$30,000.
Length of Study: One year.
Application Procedure: Applicants must contact the Foundation.
Closing Date: Please contact the organisation.
Additional Information: For up to date policy, application information and important calendar deadlines please refer to the website.

Whitehall Foundation Research Grants

Subjects: Basic research in neurobiology focusing on invertebrate and vertebrate (excluding clinical) neurobiology, specifically investigations of neural mechanisms involved in sensory, motor and other complex functions of the whole organism as these relate to behaviour.
Purpose: To better understand behavioural output or brain mechanisms of behaviour.
Eligibility: Open to established scientists of all ages working at accredited institutions in the United States of America. The principal investigator must hold no less than the position of assistant professor, or the equivalent, in order to make an application. The Foundation does not award funds to investigators who have substantial existing or potential support.
Type: Research grant.
Value: US$30,000-75,000 per year.
Length of Study: Up to three years.
Additional Information: For up to date policy, application information and important calendar deadlines, please refer to the website.

WILLIAM HONYMAN GILLESPIE SCHOLARSHIP TRUST

Messrs Tod Murray WS
66 Queen Street, Edinburgh, EH2 4NE, Scotland
Tel: (44) 131 226 4771
Fax: (44) 131 225 3676
Contact: Trustee

William Honyman Gillespie Scholarships

Subjects: Theology.
Purpose: To allow the recipient to engage in a full-time approved scheme of theological studies or research.
Eligibility: Open to graduates in theology of any Scottish university.
Level of Study: Postgraduate.
Type: Scholarship.
Value: UK £1,000 per year.
Length of Study: Two years.
Frequency: Annual.
Study Establishment: An approved university or similar institution.
Country of Study: Any country.
No. of awards offered: Varies, usually one to two.
Application Procedure: Applicants must submit applications through the Principal of the theological college of the Scottish university of which the applicant is a graduate. Application guidelines are available from the Trust or the candidate's university department.
Closing Date: May 15th.
Funding: Private.

WILSON ORNITHOLOGICAL SOCIETY

Midcontinent Ecological Science Center
4512 McMurray Avenue, Fort Collins, CO, 80525-3400, United States of America
Tel: (1) 970 226 9466
Email: jim_sedgwick@usgs.gov
www: http://www.ummz.lsa.umich.edu/birds/wos.html
Contact: Dr James Sedgewick

Founded in 1888 and named after Alexander Wilson, the father of American ornithology, the Wilson Ornithological Society publishes a scientific journal, the Wilson Bulletin, holds annual meetings, provides research awards and maintains an outstanding research library.

George A Hall/Harold F Manfield Award

Subjects: Any aspect of ornithology.
Purpose: To encourage and stimulate research projects on birds, by amateurs and students.
Eligibility: Open to independent researchers without access to funds and facilities available at colleges, universities or governmental agencies. The award is restricted to non professionals.
Level of Study: Postgraduate.
Type: Award.
Value: US$1,000.
Frequency: Annual.
Country of Study: Any country.
No. of awards offered: One.
Application Procedure: An application form must be completed and submitted with three letters of recommendation and a research proposal. Forms are available from the website.
Closing Date: January 15th.
Funding: Private.

Louis Agassiz Fuertes Award

Subjects: Any aspect of ornithology.
Eligibility: Open to all ornithologists, although graduate students and young professionals are preferred. Any avian research is eligible.
Level of Study: Unrestricted.
Type: Award.
Value: US $2,500.
Frequency: Annual.
No. of awards offered: One.
Application Procedure: Application forms are available from the website.

Paul A Stewart Awards

Subjects: Ornithology, especially studies of bird movements based on banding, analysis of recoveries and returns of banded birds, with an emphasis on economic ornithology.
Purpose: To support research projects on birds.
Eligibility: Open to students, amateurs and professionals without preference.
Level of Study: Unrestricted.
Type: Award.
Value: US$500.
Frequency: Annual.
Country of Study: Any country.
No. of awards offered: Up to four.
Application Procedure: An application form must be completed and submitted with three letters of recommendation and a research proposal. Forms are available from the website.
Closing Date: January 15th.
Funding: Private.
No. of awards given last year: Four.
No. of applicants last year: Seven.

THE WINGATE SCHOLARSHIPS

2nd Floor
20-22 Stukeley Street, London, WC2B 5LR, England
Email: clark@wingate.org.uk
www: http://www.wingate.org.uk
Contact: Ms Faith Clark, Administrator

Wingate Scholarships are awarded to individuals of great potential or proven excellence who need financial support to undertake creative or original work of intellectual, scientific, artistic, social or environmental value, and to outstanding musicians for advanced training.

Wingate Scholarships

Subjects: Almost any subject, except fine arts and taught courses of any kind, including courses of drama, art or business, or courses leading to professional qualifications and electives.
Purpose: To fund creative or original work of intellectual, scientific, artistic, social or environmental value and advanced music study.
Eligibility: Open to British, Commonwealth, Irish or Israeli and European Union country citizens provided that they are, and have been for at least five years, resident in the United Kingdom. Applicants must be over 24 years of age and resident in British Isles when applying. No qualifications are necessary.
Level of Study: Doctorate, Postdoctorate, Postgraduate, Research.
Type: Scholarship.
Value: Costs of a project which may last for up to three years. This is an average of UK £6,500 total to a maximum in any one year of UK £10,000.
Length of Study: One-three years.
Frequency: Annual.
Study Establishment: Any approved institute.
Country of Study: Any country.
No. of awards offered: Approx. 40-45.
Application Procedure: Applicants must complete application forms, available from the administrator or the website. Applicants must be able to satisfy the Scholarship Committee that they need financial support to undertake the work projected, and show why the proposed work (if it takes the form of academic research) is unlikely to attract Research Council, British Academy or major agency funding.
Closing Date: February 1st.
Funding: Private.
Contributor: HHW Foundation.
No. of awards given last year: 49.
No. of applicants last year: 392.
Additional Information: The scholarships are not intended for professional qualifications, taught courses or electives. Musicians are eligible for advanced training, but apart from that all applicants must

have projects which are personal to them and involve either creative or original work.

WINSTON CHURCHILL FOUNDATION OF THE USA

PO Box 1240
Gracie Station, New York, NY, 10028, United States of America
Tel: (1) 212 879 3480
Fax: (1) 212 879 3480
Email: churchillf@aol.com
Contact: Mr Harold Epstein, Executive Director

The Winston Churchill Foundation of the USA provides scholarships for American students to pursue graduate studies in engineering, mathematics and sciences at Churchill College, the University of Cambridge.

Winston Churchill Scholarship

Subjects: Engineering, mathematics, computer science or natural sciences.
Purpose: To encourage the development of American scientific and technological talent and foster Anglo-American ties.
Eligibility: Open to United States of America citizens only. Applicants must be enrolled in one of 67 institutions participating in programme.
Level of Study: Postgraduate.
Type: Scholarship.
Value: Approx. US$27,000.
Length of Study: One year.
Frequency: Annual.
Study Establishment: Churchill College, the University of Cambridge.
Country of Study: United Kingdom.
No. of awards offered: 11.
Application Procedure: Applicants must complete a formal application, available from the liaison person at institutions participating in this programme.
Closing Date: November 15th.
Funding: Private.
No. of awards given last year: 11.
No. of applicants last year: 100.

WINSTON CHURCHILL MEMORIAL TRUST (AUS)

Churchill House
30 Balmain Crescent, Acton, ACT, 2601, Australia
Tel: (61) 2 6247 8333
Fax: (61) 2 6249 8944
Email: trustaccount@bigpond.com.au
www: http://www.churchilltrust.org.au
Contact: Ms Margaret Bell, Senior Executive Officer, Finance & Administration

The principal object of the Winston Churchill Memorial Trust (Aus) is to perpetuate and honour the memory of Sir Winston Churchill by awarding memorial fellowships known as Churchill Fellowships.

Churchill Fellowships

Subjects: All subjects.
Purpose: To enable Australians from all walks of life to undertake an overseas investigation project of a kind that is not fully available in Australia.
Eligibility: Open to all Australian citizens or permanent residents over the age of 18 years. There are no prescribed qualifications academic or otherwise for the award of most Churchill Fellowships. Merit is the primary test, whether based on past achievement or

demonstrated ability for future achievements in any walk of life. Fellowships will not be awarded to enable the applicant to obtain higher academic or formal qualifications. The only criteria for the awarding of a fellowship is that the applicant has gone as far as they can go in Australia and now needs to go overseas to obtain information not available in Australia.

Level of Study: Unrestricted.

Type: Fellowship.

Value: Approx. australian $20,000, return economy air fare to country or countries to be visited, and a living allowance plus fees if necessary.

Length of Study: 4-10 weeks but this may be longer or shorter depending upon the project.

Frequency: Annual.

Country of Study: Any country.

No. of awards offered: Approx. 100.

Application Procedure: Applicants must complete an application form, which should be sent to the appropriate regional office. For an application form contact the national office.

Funding: Private.

No. of awards given last year: 101.

No. of applicants last year: 800.

Additional Information: Further information is available from the website.

For further information contact:

Secretary
Queensland Regional Committee
Watkins Medical Centre
Level 6
225 Wickham Terrace, Brisbane, QLD, 4000, Australia
Tel: (61) 7 3839 6959

Secretary
NT Regional Committee
GPO Box 2147, Darwin, NT, 0801, Australia
Tel: (61) 8 8981 0870
Fax: (61) 8 8981 0870

Secretary
ACT Regional Committee
The Winston Churchill Memorial Trust
PO Box 869, Dickson, ACT, 2602, Australia
Tel: (61) 2 6255 7652

Secretary
Victorian Regional Committee
Marcus Oldham College
Private Bag 116
Geelong Mail Centre, Geelong, VIC, 3221, Australia
Tel: (61) 3 5247 2901

Secretary
Tasmanian Regional Committee
153 Davey Street
GPO Box 1260N, Hobart, TAS, 7001, Australia
Fax: (61) 3 6234 219

Secretary
SA Regional Committee
7 Hillview Avenue, Panorama, SA, 5041, Australia
Tel: (61) 8 8276 1027

Secretary
NSW Regional Committee
UNSW, Sydney, NSW, 2052, Australia
Tel: (61) 2 9662 4945

Secretary
WA Regional Committee
PO Box 357, West Perth, WA, 6872, Australia
Tel: (61) 8 9226 1588

WINSTON CHURCHILL MEMORIAL TRUST (UK)

15 Queen's Gate Terrace, London, SW7 5PR, England
Tel: (44) 20 7584 9315
Fax: (44) 20 7581 0410
Email: wcmt@dial.pipex.com
Contact: Ms S Matthews, Trust Office Manager

Winston Churchill Memorial Trust (UK) Fellowships

Subjects: Approx. 10 categories of occupation, which vary annually and are representative of culture, social and public service, technology, commerce and industry, agriculture and nature, recreation and adventure.

Purpose: To enable men and women from all walks of life and all ages to travel abroad in pursuit of a worthwhile purpose and so to contribute more to their trade or profession, their community and their country.

Eligibility: Open to British citizens, whose purposes must be covered by one of the categories chosen for the year.

Level of Study: Unrestricted.

Type: Travelling fellowship.

Value: By individual assessment, to cover all travel, living and equipment expenses. The average award is UK £5,500.

Length of Study: Six-eight weeks.

Frequency: Annual.

Country of Study: Any country except the United Kingdom.

No. of awards offered: Approx. 100.

Application Procedure: Applicants must complete an application form.

Closing Date: September to October.

Funding: Private.

Contributor: The public.

No. of awards given last year: 100.

No. of applicants last year: 100.

Additional Information: Fellows must undertake to disseminate the information they gain and to remain officially resident in the United Kingdom for three years following the termination of their fellowship. Awards are announced at the beginning of February. Travel expenses of short-listed candidates will be paid within the United Kingdom only.

THE WISCONSIN HISTORICAL SOCIETY

816 State Street, Madison, WI, 53706, United States of America
Tel: (1) 608 264 6464
Fax: (1) 608 264 6486
www: http://www.shsw.wisc.edu
Contact: Mr Michael E Stevens, State Historian

The Wisconsin Historical Society engages the public with the excitement of discovery, inspires people with new perspectives on the past and illuminates the relevance of history in our lives today.

Alice E Smith Fellowship

Subjects: Wisconsin history.

Purpose: To support research and writing for publication in either the Wisconsin Magazine of History or in book form by the Society Press.

Level of Study: Research.

Type: Fellowship.

Value: US$500-3,000.

Length of Study: One year, generally non renewable.

Frequency: Four times per year.

Country of Study: United States of America.

No. of awards offered: Multiple.

Application Procedure: Application forms are available from the website.

Closing Date: Applications are accepted all year round but are evaluated in January, April, July and October.

No. of awards given last year: One.
No. of applicants last year: 35.

Amy Louise Hunter Fellowship

Subjects: Wisconsin history.
Purpose: To support research and writing for publication in either the Wisconsin Magazine of History or in book form by the Society Press.
Level of Study: Research.
Type: Fellowship.
Value: US$500-3,000.
Length of Study: One year, non renewable.
Country of Study: United States of America.
No. of awards offered: Multiple.
Application Procedure: Application forms are available from the website.
Closing Date: Applications are accepted all year round but are evaluated in January, April, July and October.
No. of awards given last year: One.
No. of applicants last year: 20.

John C Geilfuss Fellowship

Subjects: Wisconsin's business and economic history.
Purpose: To support research and writing for publication in either the Wisconsin Magazine of History or in book form by the Society Press.
Level of Study: Research.
Type: Fellowship.
Value: US$500-3,000.
Length of Study: One year, non renewable.
Frequency: Four times per year.
Country of Study: United States of America.
No. of awards offered: Multiple.
Application Procedure: Application forms are available from the website.
Closing Date: Applications are accepted all year round but are evaluated in January, April, July and October.
No. of awards given last year: One.
No. of applicants last year: 20.

WOLF FOUNDATION

39 Hamaapilim Street
PO Box 398, Herzlia Bet, 46103, Israel
Tel: (972) 9 955 7120
Fax: (972) 9 954 1253
Email: wolffund@netvision.net.il
www: http://www.aquanet.co.il/wolf
Contact: Mr Yaron Gruder, Director General

The Wolf Foundation was established in 1976 by Doctor Ricardo Wolf (1887-1981), inventor, diplomat and philanthropist, and his wife Francisca Subirana-Wolf (1900-1981), in order to promote science and art for the benefit of mankind.

Wolf Foundation Prizes

Subjects: In science the fields are agriculture, chemistry, mathematics, medicine or physics. In the arts the fields are architecture, music, painting or sculpture.
Purpose: To recognise the achievements of outstanding scientists and artists in the interest of mankind and friendly relations among people.
Eligibility: There are no eligibility restrictions.
Level of Study: Postgraduate.
Type: Prize or honorarium.
Value: The prize in each field consists of a diploma and US$100,000.
Frequency: Annual.
Country of Study: Any country.
No. of awards offered: Four prizes in sciences and one in arts.

Application Procedure: Applicants must request an application form.
Closing Date: August 31st.
Funding: Private.
Contributor: The founder, Richard Wolf.

THE WOLFSON FOUNDATION

8 Queen Anne Street, London, W1G 9LD, England
Tel: (44) 20 7323 5730
Fax: (44) 20 7323 3241
Contact: Ms Elinor Lord, Assistant to Executive Secretary

The aims of the Wolfson Foundation are the advancement of arts and humanities, health and education. Grants are given to back excellence and talent, and provide support for promising projects which may be under funded, particularly for renovation and equipment. The emphasis is on science and technology, research, education, health and the arts.

Wolfson Foundation Grants

Subjects: Areas supported by the Trustees are: medicine and health care, including the prevention of disease and the care and treatment of the sick, disadvantaged and disabled, research, science, technology and education, particularly where benefits may accrue to the development of industry or commerce in the United Kingdom, arts and the humanities including libraries, museums, galleries, theatres, academies or historic buildings.
Eligibility: Open to registered charities and to exempt charities such as universities. Eligible applications from registered charities for contributions to appeals will normally be considered only when at least 50 per cent of that appeal has already been raised. Grants to universities for research and scholarship are normally made under the umbrella of designated competitive programmes in which vice chancellors and principals are invited to participate from time to time. Applications from university researchers are not considered outside these programmes. Grants are not made to private individuals.
Level of Study: Postgraduate.
Type: Grant.
Value: The Trustees make several types of grant which are not necessarily independent of each other. Capital Project grants may contribute towards the cost of erecting a new building or extension, or of renovating and refurbishing existing buildings. Equipment Grants supply equipment for specific purposes and/or furnishing and fittings. Recurrent costs are not normally provided.
Frequency: The trustees meet twice a year.
Country of Study: Any country.
No. of awards offered: Varies.
Application Procedure: Applicants must submit in writing a brief outline of the project with one copy of the organisation's most recent audited accounts before embarking on a detailed proposal.
Closing Date: March 15th or September 15th.
Funding: Private.
No. of awards given last year: 194.
No. of applicants last year: 1,200.

THE WOLFSONIAN-FLORIDA INTERNATIONAL UNIVERSITY

1001 Washington Avenue, Miami Beach, FL, 33139, United States of America
Tel: (1) 305 535 2613
Fax: (1) 305 531 2133
Email: research@thewolf.fiu.edu
www: http://www.wolfsonian.fiu.edu
Contact: Ms Sheila Thompson, Public Information Officer

The Wolfsonian-Florida International University promotes the collection of art and design from the period 1885-1945. The University supports projects examining the aesthetics, production, use and cultural significance of objects in its collection. Objects include rare books and periodicals, paintings, sculpture, posters, prints, drawings and furniture.

Wolfsonian FIU Fellowship

Subjects: History and philosophy of art.
Purpose: To conduct research on the Wolfsonian's collection of 70,000 objects from the period 1885-1945, including decorative arts, works on paper, books and ephemera.
Eligibility: Wolfsonian Fellowships are granted on the basis of outstanding professional or academic accomplishment and are limited to those with at least a Master's degree. Doctoral candidates may apply for dissertation research related to the Wolfsonian collection.
Level of Study: Doctorate, Postdoctorate, Professional development.
Type: Fellowship.
Value: Approx. US$4,000.
Length of Study: Approx. six weeks.
Frequency: Varies.
Study Establishment: The Wolfsonian, Florida International University.
Country of Study: United States of America.
No. of awards offered: Varies, approx. five.
Application Procedure: Applicants must complete an application form and submit this with three letters of recommendation. Contact the Academic Programs Officer for details and application materials.
Closing Date: December 31st.
No. of awards given last year: Five.
No. of applicants last year: 18.

WOMEN BAND DIRECTORS INTERNATIONAL (WBDI)

292 Band Hall
Louisiana State University, Baton Rouge, LA, 70803, United States of America
Tel: (1) 225 578 2384
Fax: (1) 225 578 4693
Email: moorhouse@lsu.edu
Contact: Ms Linda Moorhouse, Past President WBDI

Women Band Directors International (WBDI) is an organisation in which every woman band director is represented at the international level regardless of the length of her experience or the level at which she works. It is the only international organisation for women band directors.

WBDI Scholarship Awards

Subjects: Music education.
Purpose: To support young college women presently preparing to be band directors.
Eligibility: Open to women band instrumental majors enrolled in a university and working towards a degree in music education.
Level of Study: Unrestricted.
Type: Scholarship.

Value: US$300.
Frequency: Annual.
Country of Study: United States of America.
No. of awards offered: Six.
Application Procedure: Applicants must write for details or download an application form from the website.
Closing Date: December 1st.
No. of awards given last year: Five.
No. of applicants last year: 145.

WOMEN'S INTERNATIONAL LEAGUE FOR PEACE AND FREEDOM (WILPF)

PO Box 28, Geneva, CH-2012, Switzerland
Tel: (41) 22 919 7080
Fax: (41) 22 919 7081
Email: wilpf@iprolink.ch
www: http://www.wilpf.int.ch
Contact: Internships Programme

Founded in 1915 to protest against the war then raging in Europe, the Women's International League for Peace and Freedom (WILPF) aims to bring together women of different political and philosophical conviction, united in their determination to study, make known and help abolish the political, social, economic and psychological causes of war and to work for a constructive peace.

Internship in Disarmament and Economic Justice

Subjects: Disarmament or economic justice, in the context of the United Nations and international organisations.
Purpose: To focus on the work of the UN and NGOs in their promoting and strengthening efforts for disarmament and the peaceful settlement of conflict, as well as their involvement in economic justice and North-South relations.
Eligibility: The internships are reserved for women in recognition of the fact that women remain largely excluded from positions concerned with questions of foreign policy and international relations, although their presence in these crucial areas is much needed. Priority is given to women between the ages of 25-30 and preference is given to WILPF members. Fluency in oral and written English is essential and Spanish and French speaking skills are an advantage for the work of the interns.
Level of Study: Graduate, Postgraduate, Professional development.
Type: Internship.
Value: WILPF pays for the intern's round trip travel from her home to Geneva and pays a small stipend which covers basic living expenses in an expensive city. Accommodation is also provided.
Length of Study: 11 months, from January 15th to December 15th.
Frequency: Annual.
Study Establishment: The Women's International League for Peace and Freedom in Geneva.
Country of Study: Switzerland.
No. of awards offered: One.
Application Procedure: All applications must be submitted in English and should state clearly the internship for which the application is submitted. Applications must include a curriculum vitae, a covering letter giving reasons for wanting to follow the programme, a 1,000-1,500 word essay about a human rights or disarmament issue stating why this is of interest and two recommendations from non family members.
Closing Date: May 15th for the following year's programme.
Funding: Private.
No. of awards given last year: One.
No. of applicants last year: 150.

WILPF Internship in Human Rights

Subjects: Human rights in the context of the United Nations and international organisations.
Purpose: To provide leadership training for young women.

Eligibility: The internships are reserved for women in recognition of the fact that women remain largely excluded from positions concerned with questions of foreign policy and international relations, although their presence in these crucial areas is much needed. Priority is given to women between the ages of 25-30, and preference is given to WILPF members. Fluency in oral and written English is essential and Spanish and French speaking skills are an advantage for the work of the interns.

Level of Study: Graduate, Postgraduate.

Type: Internship.

Value: WILPF pays for the intern's round trip travel from her home to Geneva and pays a small stipend which covers basic living expenses in an expensive city. Accommodation is also provided.

Length of Study: 11 months.

Frequency: Annual.

Study Establishment: The Women's International League for Peace and Freedom in Geneva.

Country of Study: Switzerland.

No. of awards offered: One.

Application Procedure: Applications must be submitted in English and should state clearly for which internship the application is submitted. Applications must include a curriculum vitae, a covering letter giving the applicant's reasons for wanting to follow the programme, a 1,000-1,500 word essay about a human rights or disarmament issue stating why this is of interest and two recommendations from non family members.

Closing Date: May 15th for the following year's programme.

Funding: Private.

No. of awards given last year: One.

No. of applicants last year: 150.

Additional Information: The intern follows the annual session of the UN Commission on Human Rights, its working group, the Committee on Economic Social and Cultural Rights and meetings of UN Agencies, as well as participating in NGO meetings and WILPF activities.

WOMEN'S NATIONAL FARM AND GARDEN ASSOCIATION, INC.

251 West St Clair Street, Romeo, MI, 48065, United States of America
www: http://www.hortla.okstate.edu
Contact: Mrs Ronald L Hudson, Chairman of the Committee

Sarah Bradley Tyson Memorial Fellowship

Subjects: Agriculture, horticulture and related subjects.

Purpose: To recognise leadership in co-operative extension work and initiative in scientific research, and to assist with advanced study.

Eligibility: Open to properly qualified young women who have proven their ability with several years of experience.

Level of Study: Doctorate, Postgraduate.

Type: Fellowship.

Value: US$1,000.

Length of Study: One year.

Frequency: Annual.

Study Establishment: An educational institution of recognised standing approved by the fellowship committee.

Country of Study: United States of America.

No. of awards offered: One.

Application Procedure: Applicants must send a letter of application including an account of their educational training, a statement, in full, of the object in view and the plan of study, and a certificate from the registrar of the school, college or university awarding the degree or degrees received by the applicant. They must also include testimonials as to character, ability, personality and scholarship, theses, papers, reports, investigations published or unpublished if available, a health certificate, and a small recent photograph. These must be sent to the Chairman of the committee with a stamped addressed envelope. Sent items will be returned if postage is sent for that purpose.

Closing Date: April 15th of the year to be awarded.

Funding: Private.

Contributor: The Woman's National Farm and Garden Association and the Sarah Bradley Tyson Memorial Fellowship.

No. of awards given last year: Three.

Additional Information: The acceptance of the fellowship implies an obligation on the part of the student to devote herself unreservedly to study or research as outlined in the application and to submit any proposed change in plans to the chairman for approval. The student must also send to the chairman at least two reports on work done, one at the end of the first semester and another upon the completion of the year's work. The committee regards the acceptance of the fellowship as creating a contract requiring the fulfilment of these conditions.

WOMEN'S STUDIO WORKSHOP (WSW)

PO Box 489, Rosendale, NY, 12472, United States of America
Tel: (1) 914 658 9133
Fax: (1) 914 658 9031
Email: wsw@ulster.net
www: http://www.wsworkshop.org
Contact: Ms Anita Wetzel, Development Director

The Women's Studio Workshop (WSW) is an artist run workshop with facilities for printmaking, papermaking, photography, book arts and ceramics. WSW supports the creation of new work through an annual book arts grant programme and an ongoing subsidised fellowship programme. WSW offers studio based educational programming in the above disciplines through its annual Summer Arts Institute.

Women's Studio Workshop Artists' Book Residencies

Subjects: Art or books.

Purpose: To enable artists to produce a limited edition of a book work at the Women's Studio Workshop.

Level of Study: Unrestricted.

Type: Residency.

Value: A stipend of up to US$1,800, materials of up to US$450 and housing.

Length of Study: Six weeks.

Frequency: Annual.

Study Establishment: Women's Studio Workshop.

Country of Study: United States of America.

No. of awards offered: Varies, usually between three to five.

Application Procedure: Applicants must submit an application including a one page description of the proposed project, the medium or media used to print the book, the number of pages, page size, edition number, a structural dummy, a materials budget, a curriculum vitae, 6-10 slides and a stamped addressed envelope for return of materials. Applications are reviewed by past grant recipients and a WSW staff artist. Applicants should write for an application form.

Closing Date: November 15th.

Funding: Government, Private.

Contributor: Private foundations.

No. of awards given last year: Two.

No. of applicants last year: 150.

For further information contact:

722 Binnewater Lane, Kingston, NY, 12401, United States of America

Women's Studio Workshop Artists' Fellowships

Subjects: Intaglio, water based silkscreen, photography, papermaking or ceramics.

Purpose: To provide a time for artists to explore new ideas in a dynamic and co-operative community of women artists in a rural environment.

Eligibility: Open to women artists only.
Level of Study: Unrestricted.
Type: Fellowship.
Value: US$200 per week, including housing.
Length of Study: Two-four weeks between September and June.
Frequency: Annual.
Study Establishment: Women's Studio Workshop.
Country of Study: United States of America.
No. of awards offered: 10-20.
Application Procedure: Applicants must complete an application form, available on request.
Closing Date: March 15th or November 1st.
Funding: Government, Private.
Contributor: Private foundations.
No. of awards given last year: 25.
No. of applicants last year: 100.

For further information contact:

722 Binnewater Lane, Kingston, NY, 12401, United States of America

Women's Studio Workshop Internships

Subjects: Book arts, papermaking, printmaking, ceramics or photography.
Purpose: To provide opportunities for young artists to continue development of their work in a supportive environment while learning studio skills and responsibilities.
Eligibility: Open to young women artists or students who are aged between 20 and 30.
Level of Study: Unrestricted.
Type: Internship.
Value: US$100 per month plus housing.
Length of Study: Five-six months.
Frequency: Annual.
Study Establishment: Women's Studio Workshop.
Country of Study: United States of America.
No. of awards offered: Six.
Application Procedure: Applicants must submit a curriculum vitae, 10-20 slides, three current letters of reference, a letter of interest which addresses the question of why an internship at WSW would be important and a stamped addressed envelope.
Closing Date: October 15th for the Spring-Summer session which runs from January through to July and April 1st for the Autumn-Winter session which runs from August to December.
Funding: Government, Private.
Contributor: Private foundations.
No. of awards given last year: Six.
No. of applicants last year: 30.

For further information contact:

722 Binnewater Lane, Kingston, NY, 12401, United States of America

Women's Studio Workshop Production Grants

Subjects: Art or books.
Purpose: To assist artists working in their own studios with the creation and publication of a book work.
Eligibility: Open to all artists.
Level of Study: Unrestricted.
Type: Grant.
Value: To cover production costs up to US$1,000.
Frequency: Annual.
Country of Study: Any country.
No. of awards offered: Varies.
Application Procedure: Applicants must submit an application including a one page description of the proposed project, the medium or media used to print the book, the number of pages, page size, edition number, a structural dummy, a materials budget, a curriculum vitae, 6-10 slides and a stamped addressed envelope for return of materials. Applications are reviewed by past grant recipients and a WSW staff artist. Applicants should write for an application form.
Closing Date: November 15th.

Funding: Government, Private.
Contributor: Private foundations.
No. of awards given last year: Two.
No. of applicants last year: 100.

For further information contact:

722 Binnewater Lane, Kingston, NY, 12401, United States of America

THE WOODROW WILSON NATIONAL FELLOWSHIP FOUNDATION

CN 5281, Princeton, NJ, 08543-5281, United States of America
Tel: (1) 609 542 7007
Fax: (1) 609 542 0066
Email: charlotte@wwnff.org
www: http://www.woodrow.org
Contact: Ms Judith L Pinch

The Woodrow Wilson National Fellowship Foundation, an independent, non-profit organisation, attempts to maximise human potential through education. The Foundation seeks to sponsor excellence in education and thus develop a new generation of leaders.

The Andrew W Mellon Fellowships in Humanistic Studies

Subjects: Humanistic studies.
Purpose: To allow exceptionally promising students to prepare for careers of teaching and scholarship in humanistic studies by providing top level, competitive, portable awards, and to contribute to the continuity of teaching and research of the highest order in America's colleges and universities.
Eligibility: Open to college seniors or recent graduates who are United States of America citizens or permanent residents entering into a programme leading to a PhD in the humanities. Applicants must not be enrolled in graduate or professional study, or hold the MA degree.
Level of Study: Doctorate.
Type: Fellowship.
Value: US$15,000 plus tuition and mandated fees.
Length of Study: One year.
Frequency: Annual.
Country of Study: United States of America or Canada.
No. of awards offered: 85.
Application Procedure: Applicants must provide their full name, current address and telephone number, their physical address in March, details of their undergraduate institution, major and year of graduation, the intended discipline in graduate school, details of their mailing address, and United States of America mail or email. These must be provided by mail, phone, fax or email.
Closing Date: Early December.
Funding: Private.
No. of awards given last year: 85.

Charlotte W Newcombe Doctoral Dissertation Fellowships

Subjects: Topics of religious or ethical values in all fields.
Purpose: To encourage new and significant research.
Eligibility: Open to students enrolled in doctoral programmes in the humanities and social sciences at an American university. Students must have completed all predissertation requirements by November 30th.
Level of Study: Doctorate.
Type: Fellowship.
Value: US$16,000.
Frequency: Annual.
Study Establishment: At any appropriate graduate school in the United States of America.
Country of Study: United States of America.

No. of awards offered: 35.
Application Procedure: Applicants must write for details.
Closing Date: Early December.
Funding: Private.
No. of awards given last year: 35.
No. of applicants last year: 450.

Woodrow Wilson Grants in Women's Studies

Subjects: Women's studies, the history, education or psychology of women.
Purpose: To assist those writing doctoral dissertations.
Eligibility: Open to doctoral candidates at American universities who have completed all the requirements for the degree course, except the dissertation.
Level of Study: Doctorate.
Type: Grant.
Value: Approx. US$2,000.
Length of Study: One year.
Frequency: Annual.
Country of Study: United States of America.
No. of awards offered: 15.
Application Procedure: Applicants must write for details.
Closing Date: Early November.
Funding: Private.
No. of awards given last year: 15.
No. of applicants last year: 250.

WOODS HOLE OCEANOGRAPHIC INSTITUTION

Education Office
Clark Laboratory MS #31
360 Woods Hole Road, Woods Hole, MA, 02543-1541, United States of America
Tel: (1) 508 289 2950
Fax: (1) 508 457 2188
Email: postdoc@whoi.edu
www: http://www.whoi.edu/education
Contact: Ms Janet A Fields, Administration Associate & Program Coordinator

The Woods Hole Oceanographic Institution is a private, independent, non-profit corporation dedicated to research and higher education at the frontiers of ocean science. Its primary mission is to develop and effectively communicate a fundamental understanding of the processes and characteristics governing how the oceans function and how they interact with the earth as a whole.

Woods Hole Oceanographic Institution Geophysical Fluid Dynamics Fellowships

Subjects: Classical fluid dynamics, physical oceanography, meteorology, astrophysics, planetary atmospheres, geological fluid dynamics, hydromagnetics, physics and applied mathematics.
Purpose: To bring together graduate students and researchers from a variety of fields who share a common interest in the non-linear dynamics of rotating, stratified fields.
Eligibility: There are no eligibility restrictions.
Level of Study: Graduate.
Type: Fellowship.
Value: A stipend of US$4,275 and an allowance for travel expenses within the United States of America.
Length of Study: Ten weeks.
Frequency: Annual.
Study Establishment: Woods Hole Oceanographic Institution.
Country of Study: United States of America.
No. of awards offered: Up to 10.
Application Procedure: Application forms may be obtained from the GFD section of the education website or by writing directly to the Fellowship Committee.
Closing Date: February 15th.

Funding: Government.
Contributor: The United States office of Naval Research and the United States National Science Foundation.
No. of awards given last year: Eight.
No. of applicants last year: 28.

Woods Hole Oceanographic Institution Postdoctoral Awards in Marine Policy and Ocean Management

Subjects: The scope of research is not rigidly defined. Novel proposals in such fields as political science, international affairs, decision theory, economics, diplomacy, management, geography, law, engineering and anthropology will be considered.
Eligibility: Open to Scholars and practitioners from relevant fields in the social sciences, natural sciences, law and management who are interested in applying their disciplinary training and experience to investigations which require a significant component of marine research. Applicants must have completed their doctorate degree or possess equivalent professional qualifications through career experience.
Level of Study: Postdoctorate.
Value: US$38,500 per year, plus limited support for supplies and travel.
Length of Study: One year.
Frequency: Annual.
Study Establishment: Woods Hole Oceanographic Institution.
Country of Study: United States of America.
No. of awards offered: Varies.
Closing Date: January 15th for notification in March.
Additional Information: Award recipients in the programme have pursued such studies as the implications of oil exploration along the north eastern coast of the United States of America, problems of international law created by new developments in aquaculture and fish farming, economic benefits of some oceanographic research, a perceptual study of New England fishermen, and oceanic waste disposal.

Woods Hole Oceanographic Institution Postdoctoral Fellowships in Ocean Science and Engineering

Subjects: Oceanography and oceanographic engineering.
Purpose: To further the education and training of recent recipients of doctoral degrees in engineering science or with interests in marine science.
Eligibility: Open to United States citizens and foreign nationals who have earned the PhD degree in biology, physics, microbiology, molecular biology, chemistry, geology, geophysics, oceanography, meteorology, engineering or mathematics. Scientists with more than three years of postdoctoral experience are not eligible.
Level of Study: Postdoctorate.
Type: Fellowship.
Value: US$45,250 per year, plus limited additional support for equipment, supplies and travel.
Length of Study: 18 months.
Frequency: Annual.
Study Establishment: Woods Hole Oceanographic Institution.
Country of Study: United States of America.
No. of awards offered: 7-10.
Application Procedure: Applicants must complete and submit an application form with transcripts, reference letters, complete transcripts of undergraduate and graduate records, and a concise statement describing research interests. Further information and application forms may be obtained from the postdoctoral section of the website.
Closing Date: January 15th for notification in March.
Funding: Government, Private.
No. of awards given last year: 12.
No. of applicants last year: 105.
Additional Information: Award holders work in the laboratory under the general supervision of an appropriate member of the staff, but are expected to work independently on research problems of their own choice.

Woods Hole Oceanographic Institution Postdoctoral Fellowships in the Interdisciplinary Institutes

Subjects: The exploration and characterisation of ocean biodiversity, indicators and assessment of the health of marine ecosystems, development of new sensors, instruments and analyses for ocean biology, the role of the Atlantic Ocean in modes of climate variability, monitoring to improve climate forecasts, ocean and atmosphere interactions, thermohaline circulation and abrupt climate change. Other topics of investigation include the dynamics of deep earth, crustal accretion processes, gas hydrates, earth-ocean-life interactions, seafloor observatory science and instrumentation, mechanisms providing nutrients to drive primary productivity and the fate of organic matter from primary productivity.

Purpose: To foster interdisciplinary research addressing critical issues within the Institute and encourage research and understanding of the subject area.

Eligibility: Applicants must be new or recent doctoral graduates with an interest in oceanographic sciences or engineering. Usually, scientists with more than three-four years of postdoctoral experience are not considered eligible for these awards.

Level of Study: Postdoctorate.

Type: Fellowship.

Value: An annual stipend of US$45,250 plus a relocation allowance. Other benefits include health insurance, travel expenses, equipment, supplies and special services.

Length of Study: 18 months.

Frequency: Varies.

Study Establishment: Fellowships are available at the Ocean Life Institute, the Earth and Ocean Exploration Institute, the Coastal Ocean Institute and the Ocean and Climate Change Institute at the Woods Hole Oceanographic Institution.

Country of Study: United States of America.

No. of awards offered: One-two.

Application Procedure: Applicants must contact the Institute directly. In addition to the application form, the application must also include a current curriculum vitae, a minimum of three non Woods Hole Oceanographic Institute recommendations, a concise statement describing research interests, in particular those that the applicant would like to purse at the Woods Hole facility as well as more general career plans, transcripts of the applicant's complete undergraduate and graduate records and a brief synopsis of their doctoral dissertation. Further information and application forms may be obtained through the education section of the WHOI website.

Closing Date: January 15th.

Additional Information: Announcement of awards will be made by March 31st.

Woods Hole Oceanographic Institution Research Fellowships in Marine Policy

Subjects: Oceanography, social and behavioural sciences, political science, international relations, economics and law as related to marine policy.

Purpose: To provide support and experience to scientists interested in marine policy issues, to provide opportunities for interdisciplinary application of social sciences and natural sciences to marine policy problems, and to conduct research and convey information necessary for the development of effective local, national and international ocean policy.

Eligibility: Open to citizens of the United States and foreign nationals with a PhD or equivalent professional experience.

Level of Study: Postdoctorate, Professional development.

Type: Fellowship.

Value: US$45,250.

Length of Study: One year.

Frequency: Annual.

Study Establishment: Woods Hole Oceanographic Institution.

Country of Study: United States of America.

No. of awards offered: One.

Application Procedure: Applicants must complete and submit a formal application form with transcripts, three references and a proposal for a research project to undertake while in Woods Hole.

Closing Date: January 15th.

Funding: Government, Private.

No. of applicants last year: Four.

Woods Hole Oceanographic Institution/NOAA Co-operative Institute for Climate and Ocean Research Postdoctoral Fellowship

Subjects: Coastal ocean and near-shore processes, the ocean's participation in climate and climate variability and marine ecosystem processes analysis.

Purpose: To build ties between WHOI investigators and colleagues at NOAA laboratories and to develop co-operative NOAA-funded research at academic institutions in the northeastern United States of America. The fellowship also aims to further the education and training of recent recipients of doctoral degrees in the marine sciences.

Eligibility: Open to United States citizens and foreign nationals who have earned a PhD degree in biology, physics, microbiology, molecular biology, chemistry, geology, geophysics, oceanography, meteorology, engineering or mathematics. Scientists with more than three years of postdoctoral experience are not eligible.

Level of Study: Postdoctorate.

Type: Fellowship.

Value: US$45,250 per year, plus limited additional support for equipment, supplies and travel.

Length of Study: 18 months.

Frequency: Annual.

Study Establishment: Woods Hole Oceanographic Institution.

Country of Study: United States of America.

No. of awards offered: One.

Application Procedure: Applicants must complete and submit an application form with transcripts, reference letters, complete transcripts of undergraduate and graduate records and a concise statement describing research interests. Further information and application forms may be obtained from the education section of the website.

Closing Date: January 15th for notification in March.

Funding: Government.

Contributor: The NOAA.

No. of awards given last year: One.

No. of applicants last year: 116.

Additional Information: Award holders work in the laboratory under the general supervision of an appropriate member of the staff, but are expected to work independently on research problems of their own choice.

WORLD CANCER RESEARCH FUND INTERNATIONAL (WCRF)

First Floor
19 Harley Street, London, W1G 9QJ, England
Tel: (44) 20 7343 4200
Fax: (44) 20 7343 4220
Email: research@wcrf.org.uk
www: http://www.wcrf.org
Contact: Grant Administrator

The World Cancer Research Fund International (WCRF) is the umbrella association for the WCRF global network, providing leadership, policy and strategic guidance for its national members. It administers the Research Grant Programme in the United Kingdom, the Netherlands, Germany and Hong Kong. The WCRF global network is dedicated to the prevention of cancer through healthy diets and associated lifestyles. It aims to develop and strengthen the scientific knowledge of the links between food, nutrition and cancer, and also to raise awareness that healthy diets and associated lifestyles reduce cancer risk.

WCRF Research Grants

Subjects: Social and preventive medicine, public health, epidemiology, diet and cancer prevention. Preference is given to research on whole body systems and populations, and also to research that is likely to increase scientific and public understanding of how to reduce the risk of cancer through food, nutrition and associated factors. The organisation are also interested in research proposals designed to develop the findings of the expert report entitled Food, Nutrition and the Prevention of Cancer: a global perspective.

Purpose: To fund innovative research science designed to increase knowledge of the effects of diet and nutrition on the origins, causes and prevention of cancer.

Eligibility: Open to qualified researchers of any nationality. Preference is given to applicants from the United Kingdom, Netherlands, Germany, France and China.

Level of Study: Unrestricted.

Type: Research grant.

Value: Up to a maximum of UK £100,000 over three years.

Length of Study: One-three years.

Frequency: Annual.

Study Establishment: Universities, medical schools, research institutions and other centres of academic excellence.

Country of Study: Any country.

No. of awards offered: Varies.

Application Procedure: The programme is advertised in Nature and The Lancet in August and September each year. An application pack is available from WCRF International as well as from the website.

Closing Date: Mid December, as specified in journal advertisements and the application pack.

Funding: Private.

Contributor: Public donations.

No. of awards given last year: 11.

No. of applicants last year: 61.

WORLD LEARNING

School for International Training (SIT)
Kipling Road
PO Box 676, Brattleboro, VT, 05301, United States of America
Tel: (1) 802 257 7751
Fax: (1) 802 258 3500
Email: shonna.thomas@worldlearning.org
www: http://www.worldlearning.org
Contact: Ms Shonna Thomas, Marketing Department

The School for International Training (SIT) at World Learning educates leaders capable of bridging differences between people and nations in an effort to build a more peaceful and sustainable world. Accredited by the New England Association of Schools and Colleges, SIT offers Masters degrees in international and intercultural fields, as well as continuing education opportunities, management development courses, and peace and conflict transformation training.

School for International Training (SIT) Extension

Subjects: Teacher education, organisational management, web-based research and instruction, and conflict transformation.

Purpose: To offer continuing education opportunities for professionals through innovative, high quality courses.

Eligibility: Open to persons of any nationality.

Length of Study: One week to one month.

Study Establishment: School for International Training.

No. of awards offered: Varies.

Application Procedure: Applicants must write for details or visit the website.

Additional Information: Online and on-campus intensive formats allow professionals from around the world to engage in reflective learning and practice while working in their chosen fields. For information on deadlines and other aspects of the awards please visit the website at http://www.sit.edu/extension.

School for International Training Master of Arts in Teaching Program

Subjects: Reflection, observation, self-evaluation, experiential learning and skills development within a strong learning community. Concentrations are available in English to speakers of other languages, Spanish and French, with options for public school certification.

Purpose: To prepare language teachers committed to professional development and service in their field.

Eligibility: Open to persons of any nationality who are preparing for a language teaching career.

Level of Study: Postgraduate.

Type: Scholarship.

Value: Varies.

Length of Study: A period which includes a time of student teaching and homestay. The programme is offered in a one year or two summer format designed for working professionals.

Frequency: Annual.

Study Establishment: The School for International Training.

Country of Study: Any country.

No. of awards offered: A small number.

Application Procedure: Applicants must complete an Institutional Financial Aid application and should contact Michael Ireland for further details, by email on michael.ireland@worldlearning.org.

Closing Date: Rolling admissions.

Additional Information: Students master technical teaching methodologies through language classroom practice, on-campus coursework and a supervised teaching internship. Further information is available on the website http://www.sit.edu/mat.

School for International Training Programmes in Intercultural Service, Leadership and Management

Subjects: International student services, international recruitment, student advising, community education, citizen exchange and educational travel, theory and history of international education, immigration law and practice, advising and management, multicultural organisation development, citizen capacity building, multinational human resource development, and community development and social action. Human resource development and training, diversity leadership, programme planning, proposal writing, policy advocacy and training, community development, social action and development management, cultural, political, economic and environmental context of management, strategic planning, management of human and financial resources, marketing and the theory and practice of sustainable development, conflict and identity or conflict analysis.

Purpose: To provide funding for competency based, professional level training for intercultural managers through the following courses: SIT's Master of Arts in International Education, SIT's Master of Arts in Conflict Transformation, SIT's Master of Arts in Intercultural Relations, SIT's Master of Arts in Sustainable Development, SIT's Master of Science in Organisational Management and SIT's Master of Arts in Intercultural Service, Leadership and Management.

Eligibility: Open to persons of any nationality.

Level of Study: Postgraduate.

Type: Scholarship.

Value: Varies.

Frequency: Annual.

Study Establishment: The School for International Training.

Country of Study: Any country.

No. of awards offered: Varies.

Application Procedure: Applicants must complete an Institutional Financial Aid application and should contact Michael Ireland for further details by email on michael.ireland@worldlearning.org.

Closing Date: Rolling admissions.

Additional Information: Further information is available on the website http://www.sit.edu/degree.html.

WORLD METEOROLOGICAL ORGANIZATION (WMO)

Education & Training Department
7 bis Avenue de la Paix
Case postale No 2300, Geneva, CH-1211, Switzerland
Tel: (41) 22 730 8111
Fax: (41) 22 734 2326
www: http://www.wmo.ch
Telex: 41 41 99 OMM CH
Contact: Director

The World Meteorological Organization (WMO) is an inter-governmental organisation with a membership of 185 member states and territories. It originated from the International Meteorological Organization, which was founded in 1873. Set up in 1950, WMO became the specialised agency of the United Nations for meteorology, weather and climate, operational hydrology and related sciences.

WMO Education and Training Fellowships

Subjects: Atmospheric science, meteorology, operational hydrology and related sciences.
Purpose: To educate and train meteorological personnel on individually tailored or group study training programmes.
Eligibility: Open to nationals from WMO member countries. Potential candidates should meet the requirements for academic qualifications, relevant experience, language proficiency, age limits and other specific requirements, as stipulated by the host training institutions concerned.
Level of Study: Professional development.
Type: Fellowship.
Value: According to UN rates.
Length of Study: Varies.
Frequency: Dependent on funds available.
Study Establishment: Dependent on the required training or education.
Country of Study: Applicant's home country.
No. of awards offered: Approx. 300.
Application Procedure: Applicants must be designated officially through the permanent representative with WMO, which will normally be the Director of the National Meteorological Service in the requesting country concerned.
Funding: Government.
No. of awards given last year: 310.
No. of applicants last year: 590.

THE WORLD PRESS INSTITUTE (WPI)

1635 Summit Avenue, St Paul, MN, 55105, United States of America
Tel: (1) 651 696 6360
Fax: (1) 651 696 6306
Email: wpi@macalester.edu
www: http://www.worldpressinstitute.org
Contact: Mr John Ullmann, Executive Director

The World Press Institute (WPI) makes it possible for qualified international journalists to report on United States government and politics, business, education, communications, social issues, science, technology and culture on the basis of personal experience and knowledge. WPI Fellows travel throughout the United States to meet, interview and live with Americans of all walks of life. WPI gives lectures and training in the role and responsibilities of a free press in a democracy. It also pays all expenses plus a daily per diem.

World Press Institute Fellowship

Subjects: Journalism.
Purpose: To provide the opportunity for international journalists to study the governance, business, communication, education, culture and social issues of the United States and to offer observation and training in the role of a free press in a democracy.

Eligibility: Open to non United States full-time professional journalists with a minimum of five years of experience in print or electronic journalism. Applicants must be fluent in spoken and written English.
Level of Study: Professional development.
Type: Fellowship.
Value: US$25,000.
Length of Study: Four months.
Frequency: Annual.
Study Establishment: Macalester College.
Country of Study: United States of America.
No. of awards offered: 10.
Application Procedure: Applicants must complete application materials available on request or from the website.
Closing Date: December 31st.
Funding: Commercial, Private.
Contributor: Macalester College, the McCormick Tribune Foundation and the Knight Foundation.
No. of awards given last year: 10.
No. of applicants last year: 100-200.
Additional Information: WPI Fellowships are intended for journalists with a strong commitment to long-term careers in print or broadcast journalism. The programme is purposefully difficult and demanding, requiring each participant to work as part of the group.

WORLD WITHOUT WAR COUNCIL, INC. (WWWC)

Fellows Program Coordinator
1730 Martin Luther King Jr Way, Berkeley, CA, 94709-2140, United States of America
Tel: (1) 510 845 1992
Fax: (1) 510 845 5721
Email: pic@wwwc.org
www: http://www.wwwc.org
Contact: Mr Robert Pickus, President

The aim of the World Without War Council (WWWC) is to make the United States a leader in progress towards a world that resolves political conflict without war, in ways which contribute to the well being of America. It works to build a wiser, better linked independent sector effectively at work for peace and freedom because of a thoughtful perspective of what blocks the way to a more humane and peaceful world.

WWWC Americans and World Affairs Fellows Program

Subjects: International law, human rights, religious studies, economics, political science and government, international relations, history of societies, development studies and area or cultural studies, American history and civic education.
Purpose: To give participants a better understanding of the role the American Independent Sector plays in shaping our engagements with the world, and of the competing perspectives in the field. To initiate a more thoughtful, knowledgeable leadership effective in American and world affairs.
Eligibility: Fellows are generally expected to have completed academic work for an MA or its equivalent. Individuals with a Bachelor's degree and demonstrated commitment to the goals and values of the programme will also be considered. Most fellowships require United States citizenship.
Level of Study: Postgraduate, Professional development.
Type: Fellowship.
Value: Fellows who work full-time may receive stipends ranging from US$12,000 to US$15,000 a year. Payments depend on the financial resources of the organisation to which the Fellow applies. Many Fellows receive only a small stipend, or no stipend at all, they have to use their own resources or hold a second, part-time job to support themselves.
Length of Study: Usually one or two years but some may be of a shorter term.
Frequency: Annual.

Study Establishment: Training takes place in Berkeley, California and Chicago, Illinois.
Country of Study: United States of America.
No. of awards offered: Two, but WWWC places 10 with other organisations. All require full-time work with one of its co-operating organisations.
Application Procedure: Applicants must request an application packet.
Closing Date: June 15th, sometimes accepted January or March.
Funding: Private.
Contributor: Individual contributions, private foundations, occasional government funds and a range of United States Foundations both local and national.
No. of awards given last year: Six.
No. of applicants last year: 100.
Additional Information: The programme accomplishes its purposes by providing participating Fellows with work experience, seminars, encounters, individual study and skills training. It is targeted at individuals interested in a vocation not just a job, but also possessing a good liberal education. Some experience with the shortcomings of idealistic enterprises along with a mature commitment to such purposes is required.

For further information contact:

(For Midwest)
WWWC
5441 S Ridgewood Court, Chicago, IL, 60615, United States of America

THE WORSHIPFUL COMPANY OF MUSICIANS

6th Floor
2 London Wall Buildings, London, EC2M 5PP, England
Tel: (44) 20 7496 8980
Fax: (44) 20 7489 1614
Contact: Ms Margaret Alford, Deputy Clerk

The Worshipful Company of Musicians supports young musicians particularly in the 'wilderness' years between graduating and setting out on their musical careers.

Allcard Grants

Subjects: Music.
Purpose: For the advanced training of performers at home or abroad, or for significant projects of a special nature, eg. in the field of musicology.
Eligibility: Open to individuals wishing to undertake a relevant training or research programme. The grants are not available for courses leading either to a first degree at a university or to a diploma at a college of music, and only in exceptional circumstances will assistance towards the cost of a fourth or fifth year at a college of music be considered. Grants are not available towards the purchase of instruments. Applicants must have studied at a British institution for at least three years.
Level of Study: Postgraduate.
Type: Grant.
Value: Up to UK £3,000.
Frequency: Annual.
Country of Study: Any country.
No. of awards offered: A limited number.
Application Procedure: Applicants must be nominated by principals or heads of music departments at the Royal Academy of Music, the Royal College of Music, the Guildhall School of Music, the Royal Northern College of Music, the Royal Scottish Academy of Music and Drama, the Welsh College of Music, the Birmingham Conservatoire, the Trinity College of Music, City University, Huddersfield University, Goldsmiths or other university departments.
Closing Date: Applications are to be made after January 1st and before April 30th.

No. of awards given last year: Four.
No. of applicants last year: 30.

Carnwath Scholarship

Subjects: Music.
Purpose: To support young pianists.
Eligibility: Open to any person of either sex permanently resident in the United Kingdom and 21-25 years of age. The scholarship is intended only for the advanced student who has successfully completed a solo performance course at a college of music.
Level of Study: Postgraduate.
Type: Scholarship.
Value: UK £3,000.
Length of Study: Up to two years.
Frequency: Every two years.
Country of Study: United Kingdom.
No. of awards offered: One.
Application Procedure: Applicants must be nominated by principals of the Royal Academy of Music, the Guildhall School of Music and Drama, the Royal Northern College of Music, the Royal Scottish Academy of Music, Trinity College of Music, London College of Music, the Welsh College of Music and Drama, Birmingham School of Music or the Royal College of Music. No application should be made directly to the Worshipful Company of Musicians.
Closing Date: June 1st in the year of the award.

John Clementi Collard Fellowship

Subjects: Music.
Eligibility: Open to professional musicians of standing and experience who show excellence in one or more of the higher branches of musical activity, such as composition, research and performance including conducting.
Level of Study: Postgraduate.
Type: Fellowship.
Value: UK £10,000 per year.
Length of Study: Up to three years.
Frequency: Approx. every three years.
Country of Study: United Kingdom.
No. of awards offered: One.
Application Procedure: Applicants must be nominated by professors of music at Oxford, Cambridge or London Universities, directors of the Royal College of Music, principals of the Royal Academy of Music, the Guildhall School of Music and Drama or the Royal Northern College of Music. No application should be made directly to the Worshipful Company of Musicians.
Closing Date: October 13th.

Maisie Lewis Young Artists Fund

Subjects: Musical performance.
Purpose: To assist young artists of outstanding ability who wish to acquire experience on the professional soloist concert platform.
Eligibility: Open to instrumentalists including organists up to 25 years of age and to singers of up to 30 years of age.
Level of Study: Postgraduate.
Value: Reimbursement of recitalists' expenses.
Frequency: Annual.
Country of Study: United Kingdom.
No. of awards offered: Six half recitals per year.
Application Procedure: Applicants must complete an application form, available from January 1st.
Closing Date: May 1st.
No. of awards given last year: Six.
No. of applicants last year: 80.
Additional Information: Auditions are normally held in September.

W T Best Memorial Scholarships

Subjects: Music.
Purpose: To encourage organ music.
Eligibility: Open to advanced students of the organ.
Level of Study: Postgraduate.
Type: Scholarship.

Value: UK £3,000 per year.
Length of Study: Up to three years.
Frequency: Every three years.
Country of Study: United Kingdom.
No. of awards offered: One.
Application Procedure: Applicants must be nominated by professors of music at Oxford, Cambridge or London Universities, directors of the Royal College of Music or the Royal College of Organists, principals of the Royal Academy of Music, the Guildhall School of Music and Drama, the Royal Northern College of Music or the Royal Scottish Academy of Music and Drama, and directors of Edinburgh, Cardiff and Belfast universities. No application should be made directly to the Worshipful Company of Musicians.
Closing Date: June 1st in the year of the award.
Funding: Private.
No. of awards given last year: One.
No. of applicants last year: 10.

WRITER'S DIGEST

1507 Dana Avenue, Cincinnati, OH, 45207, United States of America
Tel: (1) 513 531 2690 ext. 328
Fax: (1) 513 531 0798
Email: competitions@fwpubs.com
www: http://www.writersdigest.com
Contact: Promotion Assistant

Writer's Digest is the world's largest magazine for writers, founded in 1920. Writer's Market, the bible for writers seeking to publish their work, was first published in 1921. Together, these publications form the foundation of a wide range of informational, instructional and inspirational offerings for writers.

Writer's Digest Writing Competition
Subjects: Creative writing of genre short stories and mainstream or literary works, feature articles and personal essays, stage plays and television or movie scripts, rhyming poetry, non-rhyming poetry and children's fiction.
Eligibility: Open to authors of any nationality. Works must be written in English.
Level of Study: Unrestricted.
Type: Competition.
Value: Cash prizes for first to tenth place winners.
Frequency: Annual.
Country of Study: Any country.
No. of awards offered: 1,001.
Application Procedure: Contestants may enter as many categories and as many times in each category as they wish. Manuscripts will not be returned and each entry must be made on an official entry form and accompanied by a US$10 entry fee, drawn on a United States bank. Entries must be original and unprinted.
Closing Date: May 15th.

YALE CENTER FOR BRITISH ART

PO Box 208280, New Haven, CT, 06520-8280, United States of America
Tel: (1) 203 432 2850
Fax: (1) 203 432 9628
Email: bacinfo@minerva.cis.yale.edu
www: http://www.yale.edu/ycba
Contact: Ms Mary Beth Graham, Acting Programme Co-ordinator

The Yale Center for British Art houses the most comprehensive collection of English paintings, prints, drawings, rare books, and sculpture outside the United Kingdom. Given to Yale University by Paul Mellon, the Center's resources illustrate British life and culture from the sixteenth-century to the present.

Yale Center for British Art Fellowships
Subjects: British art from the Elizabethan period onwards.
Purpose: To allow scholars of literature, history, the history of art or related fields to study the Center's holdings of paintings, drawings, prints, and rare books, and to make use of its research facilities.
Eligibility: Open to Scholars in postdoctoral or equivalent research related to British art. Applications are also welcomed from museum professionals whose responsibilities and research interests include British art.
Level of Study: Postdoctorate.
Type: Fellowship.
Value: Cost of travel to and from New Haven, plus accommodation and a living allowance.
Length of Study: Usually four weeks.
Frequency: Annual.
Study Establishment: The Yale Center for British Art.
Country of Study: United States of America.
No. of awards offered: 20.
Application Procedure: Applicants must submit their name, address, telephone number, a curriculum vitae listing professional experience, education and publications, a three page outline of a research proposal and two confidential letters of recommendation. There is no application form.
Closing Date: January 15th.
Funding: Private.
No. of awards given last year: 19.
No. of applicants last year: 33.

YALE UNIVERSITY PRESS

PO Box 209040, New Haven, CT, 06520-9040, United States of America
Tel: (1) 203 432 0960
Fax: (1) 203 432 2394
Email: yyp@yalepress3.unipress.yale.edu
www: http://www.yale.edu/yup
Contact: Poetry Editor

Yale Series of Younger Poets
Subjects: Poetry.
Purpose: To select a book length poetry manuscript for publication.
Eligibility: Open to writers who are United States citizens under 40 years of age who have not yet published a book of poetry. Poems must be original, not translations.
Level of Study: Unrestricted.
Type: Publication.
Frequency: Annual.
Country of Study: United States of America.
No. of awards offered: One.
Application Procedure: Applicants must write for more information on entry criteria.
Closing Date: Submissions must be postmarked between January 1st and the January 31st.
Funding: Commercial.
No. of awards given last year: One.
No. of applicants last year: 600-700.

YONSEI UNIVERSITY

Graduate School of International Studies (GSIS)
134 Shinchon-dong, Sodaemoon-ku, Seoul, 120-749, Korea, Republic (South)
Tel: (82) 2 212 33293
Fax: (82) 2 392 3321
Email: gsis@mail.yonsei.ac.kr
www: http://gsis.yonsei.ac.kr
Contact: Jisook Han, Admissions Officer

Yonsei University Dean's Award

Subjects: All subjects.
Purpose: To financially assist three or four new foreign students based on academic performance and financial need.
Eligibility: Not available to Korean nationals.
Level of Study: MBA.
Type: Scholarship.
Length of Study: One semester.
Study Establishment: Graduate School of International Studies (GSIS).
Country of Study: Korea.
No. of awards offered: Three or four.
Application Procedure: Applicants must apply for the academic course as usual and will be automatically considered for the scholarships.
No. of awards given last year: Eight.

ZONTA INTERNATIONAL FOUNDATION

557 West Randolph Street, Chicago, IL, 60661-2206, United States of America
Tel: (1) 312 930 5848
Fax: (1) 312 930 0951
Email: zontafdtn@zonta.org
www: http://www.zonta.org
Telex: 190200 UT
Contact: Ms Ana L Ubides, Foundation Services Associate

The Zonta International Foundation is a worldwide service organisation of executives in business and the professions working together to advance the status of women.

Amelia Earhart Fellowship Awards

Subjects: Aerospace related science and engineering.
Purpose: To enable women to undertake graduate study in aerospace related sciences and aerospace related engineering.
Eligibility: Open to women of any nationality who have a Bachelor's degree in a qualifying area of science or engineering related to advanced studies in aerospace related science or aerospace related engineering. By the time the fellowship grant is awarded, candidates must have completed one year of aerospace related graduate studies. Applicants must demonstrate a superior academic record with evidence of potential at a recognised university or college and provide evidence of a well-defined research programme.
Level of Study: Graduate.
Type: Fellowship.
Value: US$6,000 which may be used for books and fees, tuition or living expenses. Payments are made in equal instalments in September and December.
Frequency: Annual.
Study Establishment: Any institution offering accredited graduate courses and degrees in aerospace studies.
Country of Study: Any country.
No. of awards offered: Approx. 35.
Application Procedure: Applicants must submit an application form, available from the website, including biographical information, a list of schools attended and degrees received, transcripts of grades and verifications form, employment history, plans for intended study, an essay on academic and professional goals, a photograph and three letters of recommendation from teachers. Information other than transcripts and recommendations must be limited to the space provided on the application form as attachments will not be considered.
Closing Date: November 15th.
Funding: Private.
No. of awards given last year: 35.
No. of applicants last year: 152.

SUBJECT AND ELIGIBILITY GUIDE TO AWARDS

AGRICULTURE, FORESTRY AND FISHERY

General

Agronomy

Animal husbandry and animal production
  Sericulture

Horticulture and viticulture

Crop husbandry and crop production

Agriculture and farm management

Agricultural economics

Food science and production
  Meat and poultry
  Dairy
  Fish
  Oenology
  Brewing
  Harvest technology

Soil and water science
  Water management
  Soil conservation

Veterinary medicine

Tropical/Sub-tropical agriculture

Forestry
  Forest soils
  Forest biology
  Forest pathology
  Forest products
  Forest economics
  Forest management

Fishery
  Aquaculture

ARTS AND HUMANITIES

General

Interpretation and translation

Writing (authorship)

Native language and literature

Modern languages and literatures
  English
  French
  Spanish
  Germanic languages
  German
  Swedish
  Danish
  Norwegian
  Italian
  Portuguese
  Romance languages
  Modern Greek
  Dutch
  Baltic languages
  Celtic languages
  Finnish
  Russian
  Slavonic languages (others)
  Hungarian
  Fino Ugrian languages
  European languages (others)
  Altaic languages
  Arabic
  Hebrew
  Chinese
  Korean
  Japanese
  Indian languages
  Iranic languages
  African Languages
  Amerindian languages
  Austronesian and oceanic languages

Classical languages and literatures
  Latin
  Classical Greek
  Sanskrit

Linguistics and philology
  Applied linguistics
  Psycholinguistics
  Grammar
  Semantics and terminology
  Phonetics
  Logopedics

Comparative literature

History
  Prehistory
  Ancient civilisations
  Medieval history
  Modern history
  Contemporary history

Archaeology

Philosophy
  Philosophical schools
  Metaphysics
  Logic
  Ethics

ARCHITECTURE AND TOWN PLANNING

General

Structural architecture

Architectural restoration

Environmental design

Landscape architecture

Town and community planning

Regional planning

BUSINESS ADMINISTRATION AND MANAGEMENT

General

Business studies

International business

Secretarial studies

Business machine operation

Business computing

Management systems and techniques

Accountancy

Real estate

Marketing and sales management

Insurance management

Finance, banking and investment

Personnel management

Labour/industrial relations

Public administration

Institutional administration

MBA

ENGINEERING

General

Surveying and mapping science

Engineering drawing/design

Chemical engineering

Civil, construction and transportation engineering

Environmental and Sanitary Engineering

Safety engineering

Electrical/electronic and telecommunications engineering

Computer engineering

Industrial and management engineering

Metallurgical engineering

Production engineering

Materials engineering

Mining and minerals engineering

Petroleum engineering

Energy engineering

Nuclear engineering

Mechanical/electromechanical engineering

Hydraulic/pneumatic engineering

Sound engineering

Automotive engineering

Measurement/precision engineering

Control engineering (robotics)

Aeronautical and aerospace engineering

Marine engineering and naval architecture

Agricultural engineering

Forestry engineering

Bioengineering and biomedical engineering

EDUCATION AND TEACHER TRAINING

General

Nonvocational subjects education
  Education in native language
  Foreign languages education
  Mathematics education
  Science education
  Humanities and social science education
  Physical education
  Literacy education

Vocational subjects education
  Agricultural education
  Art education
  Commerce/business education
  Computer education
  Technology education
  Health education
  Home economics education
  Industrial arts education
  Music education

Pre-school education

Primary education

Secondary education

Adult education

Special education
  Education of the gifted
  Education of the handicapped
  Education of specific learning disabilities
  Education of foreigners
  Education of natives
  Education of the socially disadvantaged
  Bilingual/bicultural education

Teacher trainers education

Higher education teacher training

Educational science
  International and comparative education
  Philosophy of education

Curriculum

Teaching and learning

Educational research

Educational technology

Educational and student counselling

Educational administration

Educational testing and evaluation

Distance education

FINE AND APPLIED ARTS

General

History and Philosophy of Art
  Aesthetics

Art management

Drawing and painting

Sculpture

Handicrafts

Music
  Musicology
  Music theory and composition
  Conducting
  Singing
  Musical instruments (performance)
  Religious music
  Jazz and popular music
  Opera

Drama

Dancing

Photography

Cinema and television

Design
  Interior design
  Furniture design
  Fashion design
  Textile design
  Graphic design
  Industrial design
  Display and stage design

HOME ECONOMICS

General

Household management

Clothing and sewing

Nutrition

Child care/child development

House arts and environment

LAW

General

History of law

Comparative law

International law

Human rights

Labour law

Maritime law

Law of the air

Notary studies

Civil law

Commercial law

Public law
  Constitutional law
  Administrative law
  Fiscal law

Criminal law

Canon law

Islamic law

European community law

MATHEMATICS AND COMPUTER SCIENCE

General

Statistics
Actuarial science
Applied mathematics
Computer science
Artificial intelligence
Systems analysis

MASS COMMUNICATION AND INFORMATION SCIENCE

General
Journalism
Radio/television broadcasting
Public relations and publicity
Mass communication
Media studies
Communications skills
Library science
Museum studies and
  conservation
Museum management
Restoration of works of art
Documentation techniques and
  archiving

MEDICAL SCIENCES

General
Public health and hygiene
  Social/preventive medicine
  Dietetics
  Sports medicine
Health administration
Medicine and surgery
  Anaesthesiology
  Cardiology
  Dermatology
  Endocrinology
  Epidemiology
  Gastroenterology
  Geriatrics
  Gynaecology and obstetrics
  Haematology
  Hepathology
  Nephrology
  Neurology
  Oncology
  Ophthalmology
  Otorhinolaryngology
  Parasitology
  Pathology
  Paediatrics
  Plastic surgery
  Pneumology
  Psychiatry and mental health
  Rheumatology
  Urology
  Virology
  Tropical medicine
  Venereology
Rehabilitation medicine and
  therapy
Nursing
Medical auxiliaries
Midwifery
Radiology
Treatment techniques
Medical technology
Dentistry and stomatology
  Oral pathology
  Orthodontics
  Periodontics
  Community dentistry
Dental technology

Prosthetic dentistry
Pharmacy
Biomedicine
Optometry
Podiatry
Forensic medicine and dentistry
Acupuncture
Homeopathy
Chiropractic
Osteopathy
Traditional eastern medicine

NATURAL SCIENCES

General
Biological and life sciences
  Anatomy
  Biochemistry
  Biology
  Histology
  Biophysics and molecular biology
  Biotechnology
  Botany
  Plant pathology
  Embryology and reproduction
    biology
  Genetics
  Immunology
  Marine biology
  Limnology
  Microbiology
  Neurosciences
  Parasitology
  Pharmacology
  Physiology
  Toxicology
  Zoology
Chemistry
  Analytical chemistry
  Inorganic chemistry
  Organic chemistry
  Physical chemistry
Earth and geological sciences
  Geochemistry
  Geography (Scientific)
  Geology
  Mineralogy and crystallography
  Petrology
  Geophysics and seismology
  Palaeontology
Physics
  Atomic and molecular physics
  Nuclear physics
  Optics
  Solid state physics
  Thermal physics
Astronomy and astrophysics
Atmosphere
  science/meteorology
  Arctic studies
  Arid land studies
Oceanography

RELIGION AND THEOLOGY

General
Religious studies
  Christian
  Jewish
  Islam
  Asian religious studies
  Agnosticism and Atheism
  Ancient religions
Religious education
Holy writings

Religious practice
Church administration (pastoral
  work)
Theological studies
Comparative religion
Sociology of religion
History of religion
Esoteric practices

RECREATION, WELFARE, PROTECTIVE SERVICES

General
Police and law enforcement
Criminology
Fire protection/control
Military science
Civil security
Peace and disarmament
Social welfare and social work
  Public and community services
Vocational counselling
Environmental studies
  Ecology
  Natural resources
  Environmental management
  Wildlife and pest management
Physical education and sports
  Sports management
  Sociology of sports
Leisure studies
Parks and recreation

SOCIAL AND BEHAVIOURAL SCIENCES

General
  Economics
  Economic history
  Economic and finance policy
  Taxation
  Econometrics
  Industrial and production
    economics
Political science and
  government
  Comparative politics
International relations
Sociology
  History of societies
  Comparative sociology
  Social policy
  Social institutions
  Social communication problems
  Futurology
Demography
Anthropology
  Ethnology
  Folklore
Women's studies
Urban Studies
Rural studies
Cognitive sciences
Psychology
  Experimental psychology
  Social and community psychology
  Clinical psychology
  Personality psychology
  Industrial/organisational
    psychology
  Psychometrics
  Educational psychology
Geography (social and
  economic)
Development studies

Area and cultural studies
  North African
  Subsahara African
  African studies
  African American
  Native American
  Hispanic American
  American
  Canadian
  Asian
  South Asian
  East Asian
  Southeast Asian
  European (EC)
  Eastern European
  Western European
  Nordic
  Caribbean
  Latin American
  Pacific area
  Aboriginal
  Middle Eastern
  Islamic
  Jewish
Preservation of cultural heritage
Ancient civilisations (Egyptology,
  Assyriology)

SERVICE TRADES

General
Hotel and restaurant
Hotel management
Cooking and catering
Retailing
Tourism

TRADE, CRAFT AND INDUSTRIAL TECHNIQUES

General
Food processing techniques
Building trades
Electrical/electronic equipment
  and maintenance techniques
Metal trades techniques
Mechanical equipment and
  maintenance techniques
Wood technology
Heating, air conditioning and
  refrigeration technology
Leather techniques
Textile techniques
Paper and packaging
  technology
Graphic arts techniques
  Printing
  Publishing and book trade
Laboratory techniques
Optical technology

TRANSPORT AND COMMUNICATIONS

General
Air transport
Marine transport and nautical
  science
Railway transport
Road transport
Transport management
Transport economics
Postal services
Telecommunications services

788

ANY SUBJECT

ANY SUBJECT

Any Country

African Nations

Australia

British Commonwealth

Canada

Indian Sub-Continent

St Catherine's College Overseas Graduate Scholarship, 742
Tetley and Lupton Scholarships for Overseas Students, 713
University of Leeds Overseas Research Students Awards Scheme - National Competition, 714
Zimbabwe Cambridge Scholarships For PhD Study, 221
Zimbabwe Cambridge Scholarships For Postgraduate Study, 221

South America

AAUW International Fellowships Program, 4
Adelaide Postgraduate Coursework Scholarships International (APCS), 688
Argentina Cambridge Scholarships for PhD Study, 186
Argentina Cambridge Scholarships for Postgraduate Study, 186
Balliol College Domus Graduate Scholarships, 722
British Chevening Cambridge Scholarship for PhD Study (Mexico), 190
British Chevening Cambridge Scholarships for Postgraduate Study (Chile), 192
British Chevening Cambridge Scholarships for Postgraduate Study (Mexico), 194
British Chevening Cambridge Scholarships for Postgraduate Study (Peru), 194
Cambridge Foundation Scholarships for Postgraduate Study (Chile), 197
Catholic University of Louvain Co-operation Fellowships, 245
Christ Church Hugh Pilkington Scholarship, 724
Clare Hall Foundation Fellowship, 695
Clarendon Fund Bursaries, 724
International Postgraduate Research Scholarships (IPRS) and University of Sydney International Postgraduate Awards (IPA), 751
Lincoln College Keith Murray Senior Scholarship, 730
Merton College Domus Graduate Scholarships A, 731
NFP Netherlands Fellowships Programme of Development Co-operation, 526
Northumbria University International Scholarships, 533
One World Scholarship Program, 12
PEO International Peace Scholarship, 407
Robert S McNamara Fellowships at Cambridge, 215
Royal Holloway, University of London College Overseas Entrance Scholarships, 601
St Anne's College Overseas Scholarship, 739
St Antony's College Ronaldo Falconer Scholarship, 740
St Catherine's College Overseas Graduate Scholarship, 742
Tate and Lyle/FCO Cambridge Scholarships, 218
Tetley and Lupton Scholarships for Overseas Students, 713
University of Leeds Overseas Research Students Awards Scheme - National Competition, 714

United Kingdom

AAUW International Fellowships Program, 4
Adelaide Postgraduate Coursework Scholarships International (APCS), 688
The Anglo-Danish (London) Scholarships, 100
Anning-Morgan Bursary, 706
ASBAH Bursary Fund, 125
Association of Rhodes Scholars in Australia Travel Bursary, 129
Auber Bequest, 613
Australian Bicentennial Scholarships and Fellowships, 471
Balliol College Snell Exhibition, 722
Bourses Scholarships, 301
Brasenose College Senior Germaine Scholarship, 723
BUNAC Educational Scholarship Trust (BEST), 179
Canada Memorial Foundation Scholarships, 128
Canada Memorial Foundation Scholarships, 222
Canon Foundation Research Fellowships, 242
Christ Church Hugh Pilkington Scholarship, 724
CIMO Bilateral Scholarships, 249
The Cross Trust Grants, 276
The Denmark Liberation Scholarships, 101
Department of Education and Science (Ireland) Exchange Scholarships and Postgraduate Scholarships Exchange Scheme, 281
East Lothian Educational Trust General Grant, 290

Friends of Israel Educational Trust Academic Study Bursary, 323
Fulbright Distinguished Scholar Awards, 758
Fulbright Postgraduate Student Awards, 759
Geoff Lockwood Scholarship, 750
Gilchrist Fieldwork Award, 336
Henry Fellowships (Harvard and Yale), 252
Huygens Scholarships Programme, 525
International Postgraduate Research Scholarships (IPRS) and University of Sydney International Postgraduate Awards (IPA), 751
The James Pantyfedwen Foundation Grants and Loans, 420
King Edward VII Scholarships, 433
May and Ward Scholarships British Schools and Universities, 179
Merton College Domus Graduate Scholarships B, 731
Mr and Mrs David Edward Memorial Award, 753
New Zealand Commonwealth Scholarships, 528
Northcote Graduate Scholarship, 471
Oxford University Graduate Studentships, 733
PEO International Peace Scholarship, 407
The Queen's College Hastings Senior Scholarship, 735
Regent's Park College (Permanent Private Hall) Organ Scholarship, 736
The Reid Trust For the Higher Education of Women, 580
Rose Sidgwick Memorial Fellowship, 166
Soroptomist International of Great Britain and Ireland Golden Jubilee Fellowship, 657
St John's College North Senior Scholarships, 744
Thouron Awards, 675
UK Government Grants, 442
University of Sussex/Association of Commonwealth Universities Access Fund Bursaries, 751
University of York Postgraduate Student Bursaries, 756

United States of America

AAUW Career Development Grants, 3
AAUW Community Action Grants, 3
AAUW Educational Foundation American Fellowships, 3
ACB Scholarship Program, 43
Adelaide Postgraduate Coursework Scholarships International (APCS), 688
Alpha Sigma Nu Graduate Scholarship, 459
The America-Norway Heritage Fund Grant, 536
American Friends of the University of Edinburgh Scholarship, 51
The American-Scandinavian Foundation (ASF), 536
American-Scandinavian Foundation Grants and Fellowships for Advanced Study or Research in Denmark, Finland, Iceland, Norway and Sweden, 99
Balliol College Domus Graduate Scholarships, 722
Christ Church American Friends Scholarship, 723
CIMO Bilateral Scholarships, 249
Clarendon Fund Bursaries, 724
DAAD Guest Lectureships, 330
FEAT Loan, 325
Ford Foundation Dissertation Fellowships for Minorities, 489
Ford Foundation Postdoctoral Fellowships for Minorities, 489
Ford Foundation Predoctoral Fellowships for Minorities, 490
Fulbright Commission (Argentina) Awards for US Lecturers and Researchers, 324
Fulbright Commission (Argentina) US Students Research Grant, 325
Fulbright Graduate Student Awards, 758
Fulbright Oxford University Scholarships, 725
Fulbright Scholar Grants, 759
Fulbright Study and Research Grants for US Citizens, 681
International Postgraduate Research Scholarships (IPRS) and University of Sydney International Postgraduate Awards (IPA), 751
The John Dana Archbold Fellowship Program, 537
Kosciuszko Foundation Graduate and Postgraduate Studies and Research in Poland Program, 435
Lincoln College Keith Murray Senior Scholarship, 730
Marshall Scholarships, 459
May and Ward Scholarships British Schools and Universities, 179
Merton College Domus Graduate Scholarships A, 731
North Dakota Indian Scholarship, 535

West European Countries

AGRICULTURE, FORESTRY AND FISHERY

GENERAL

Any Country

The Walsh Fellowships, 671
William John Thomson Scholarship, 623
Wolf Foundation Prizes, 773

African Nations

ABCCF Student Grant, 103
Friends of Peterhouse Bursary, 561
Fulbright Postdoctoral Research and Lecturing Awards for Non-US Citizens, 270
IFS Grant, 402
Merton College Reed Foundation Scholarship, 732
TWAS Grants for Scientific Meetings in Developing Countries, 673
TWAS South-South Fellowship Scheme, 673

Australia

Friends of Peterhouse Bursary, 561
Fulbright Awards, 143
Fulbright Postdoctoral Fellowships, 143
Fulbright Postdoctoral Research and Lecturing Awards for Non-US Citizens, 270
Fulbright Postgraduate Studentships, 144
Grains Industry Research Scholarships, 342
GRDC In-Service Training, 342
GRDC Industry Development Awards, 343
GRDC Senior Fellowships, 343
The Netherlands Ministry of Agriculture, Nature Management and Fisheries Fellowship Programme, 393
Wingate Scholarships, 771

British Commonwealth

ACU Development Fellowships, 127
Friends of Peterhouse Bursary, 561
Merton College Reed Foundation Scholarship, 732
Wingate Scholarships, 771

Canada

Canadian Forestry Foundation Forest Capital of Canada Award, 230
CIC Pestcon Graduate Scholarship, 255
Friends of Peterhouse Bursary, 561
Fulbright Postdoctoral Research and Lecturing Awards for Non-US Citizens, 270
The Netherlands Ministry of Agriculture, Nature Management and Fisheries Fellowship Programme, 393
NSERC Industrial Research Fellowships (IRF), 524
NSERC Postdoctoral Fellowships, 524
NSERC Postgraduate Scholarships, 524
Olin Fellowship, 135
PRA Fellowships, 549
Swiss Federal Institute of Technology Scholarships, 669
Wingate Scholarships, 771

Caribbean Countries

Friends of Peterhouse Bursary, 561
IFS Grant, 402
Merton College Reed Foundation Scholarship, 732
PRA Fellowships, 549
TWAS Grants for Scientific Meetings in Developing Countries, 673
TWAS South-South Fellowship Scheme, 673

East European Countries

Friends of Peterhouse Bursary, 561
Fulbright Postdoctoral Research and Lecturing Awards for Non-US Citizens, 270
Merton College Reed Foundation Scholarship, 732
The Netherlands Ministry of Agriculture, Nature Management and Fisheries Fellowship Programme, 393
Swiss Federal Institute of Technology Scholarships, 669

Far East

COSTED Travel Fellowship, 262
Friends of Peterhouse Bursary, 561

Fulbright Postdoctoral Research and Lecturing Awards for Non-US Citizens, 270
IFS Grant, 402
Japanese American Citizens League Scholarship and Award Program, 422
Merton College Reed Foundation Scholarship, 732
Swiss Federal Institute of Technology Scholarships, 669
TWAS Grants for Scientific Meetings in Developing Countries, 673
TWAS South-South Fellowship Scheme, 673

Indian Sub-Continent

COSTED Travel Fellowship, 262
Friends of Peterhouse Bursary, 561
Fulbright Postdoctoral Research and Lecturing Awards for Non-US Citizens, 270
IFS Grant, 402
Indian Council of Social Science Research Senior Fellowships, 368
Merton College Reed Foundation Scholarship, 732
Sir William Roberts Scholarship, 753
TWAS Grants for Scientific Meetings in Developing Countries, 673
TWAS South-South Fellowship Scheme, 673
Wingate Scholarships, 771

Middle East

ABCCF Student Grant, 103
BARD Postdoctoral Fellowship, 153
BARD Research Grant, 153
Friends of Peterhouse Bursary, 561
Fulbright Postdoctoral Research and Lecturing Awards for Non-US Citizens, 270
IFS Grant, 402
Merton College Reed Foundation Scholarship, 732
TWAS Grants for Scientific Meetings in Developing Countries, 673
TWAS South-South Fellowship Scheme, 673

New Zealand

Friends of Peterhouse Bursary, 561
Fulbright Postdoctoral Research and Lecturing Awards for Non-US Citizens, 270
The Netherlands Ministry of Agriculture, Nature Management and Fisheries Fellowship Programme, 393
Vernon Willey Trust Awards, 762
Wingate Scholarships, 771

South Africa

Friends of Peterhouse Bursary, 561
Fulbright Postdoctoral Research and Lecturing Awards for Non-US Citizens, 270
IFS Grant, 402
Isie Smuts Research Award, 658
The Netherlands Ministry of Agriculture, Nature Management and Fisheries Fellowship Programme, 393
NRF Bursaries for Study towards an Honours Degree, 517
NRF Doctoral Scholarships and Postdoctoral Fellowships for Study Abroad, 517
NRF Fellowships for Postdoctoral Research, 517
NRF Scholarships for Doctoral Study, 517
NRF Scholarships for Master's Study, 518
TWAS Grants for Scientific Meetings in Developing Countries, 673
TWAS South-South Fellowship Scheme, 673
Wingate Scholarships, 771

South America

Friends of Peterhouse Bursary, 561
Fulbright Commission (Argentina) Master's Program, 325
Fulbright Postdoctoral Research and Lecturing Awards for Non-US Citizens, 270
IFS Grant, 402
Merton College Reed Foundation Scholarship, 732
PRA Fellowships, 549
TWAS Grants for Scientific Meetings in Developing Countries, 673
TWAS South-South Fellowship Scheme, 673

United Kingdom

ACU Development Fellowships, 127
BPF Lord Samuel of Wych Cross Memorial Award, 747
British Schools and Universities Foundation May and Ward Scholarships, 179
Canada Memorial Foundation Scholarships, 222
Fulbright Postdoctoral Research and Lecturing Awards for Non-US Citizens, 270
Hilda Martindale Exhibitions, 358
Linacre College A J Hosier Studentship, 728
Neville Shulman Challenge Award, 600
Polish Embassy Short-Term Bursaries, 571
Polish Government Postgraduate Scholarships Scheme, 572
Silsoe Awards, 274
Sir William Roberts Scholarship, 753
St Anne's College Una Goodwin Research Scholarship, 740
Swiss Federal Institute of Technology Scholarships, 669
University of Wales (Aberystwyth) Postgraduate Research Studentships, 752
University of Wales, Bangor (UWB) Research Studentships, 753
University of Wales, Bangor Departmental Research Studentships, 753
Wingate Scholarships, 771

United States of America

AIGC Fellowship, 54
BARD Postdoctoral Fellowship, 153
BARD Research Grant, 153
British Schools and Universities Foundation May and Ward Scholarships, 179
Congress Bundestag Youth Exchange for Young Professionals, 245
Friends of Peterhouse Bursary, 561
Fulbright Distinguished Chairs Program, 270
Fulbright Scholar Awards for Research and Lecturing Abroad for United States Citizens, 271
Fulbright Scholar Program for US Citizens, 271
Ian Axford (New Zealand) Fellowships in Public Policy, 263
Japanese American Citizens League Scholarship and Award Program, 422
The Netherlands Ministry of Agriculture, Nature Management and Fisheries Fellowship Programme, 393
The Norwegian Thanksgiving Fund Scholarship, 538
Olin Fellowship, 135
PRA Fellowships, 549
Swiss Federal Institute of Technology Scholarships, 669

West European Countries

Friends of Peterhouse Bursary, 561
Fulbright Postdoctoral Research and Lecturing Awards for Non-US Citizens, 270
The Netherlands Ministry of Agriculture, Nature Management and Fisheries Fellowship Programme, 393
Royal Society University Research Fellowships, 610
Scholarship Foundation of the League for Finnish-American Societies, 621
Silsoe Awards, 274
Sir William Roberts Scholarship, 753
St Anne's College Una Goodwin Research Scholarship, 740
Swiss Federal Institute of Technology Scholarships, 669
University of Wales, Bangor (UWB) Research Studentships, 753
University of Wales, Bangor Departmental Research Studentships, 753
Wingate Scholarships, 771

AGRONOMY

Any Country

Central Queensland University Postgraduate Research Award, 248
International Crops Research Institute Research Fellowships, 399
International Crops Research Institute Research Scholarships, 399
Massey Doctoral Scholarship, 461

Perry Postgraduate Scholarships and Research Awards, 560
University of New England Research Scholarships, 719
The Walsh Fellowships, 671
William John Thomson Scholarship, 623

Australia

Wingate Scholarships, 771

British Commonwealth

Wingate Scholarships, 771

Canada

Canadian Window on International Development, 399
CIC Montreal Medal, 255
IDRC Doctoral Research Awards, 400
Swiss Federal Institute of Technology Scholarships, 669
Wingate Scholarships, 771

East European Countries

Swiss Federal Institute of Technology Scholarships, 669

Far East

Swiss Federal Institute of Technology Scholarships, 669

Indian Sub-Continent

Sir William Roberts Scholarship, 753
Wingate Scholarships, 771

New Zealand

Wingate Scholarships, 771

South Africa

Wingate Scholarships, 771

United Kingdom

Sir William Roberts Scholarship, 753
Swiss Federal Institute of Technology Scholarships, 669
University of Wales, Bangor (UWB) Research Studentships, 753
University of Wales, Bangor Departmental Research Studentships, 753
Wingate Scholarships, 771

United States of America

Swiss Federal Institute of Technology Scholarships, 669

West European Countries

Sir William Roberts Scholarship, 753
Swiss Federal Institute of Technology Scholarships, 669
University of Wales, Bangor (UWB) Research Studentships, 753
University of Wales, Bangor Departmental Research Studentships, 753
Wingate Scholarships, 771

ANIMAL HUSBANDRY AND ANIMAL PRODUCTION

Any Country

Central Queensland University Postgraduate Research Award, 248
CQU International Student Scholarship, 248
John Hervey, Broadcasters and Smallsreed Awards, 686
Massey Doctoral Scholarship, 461
Perry Postgraduate Scholarships and Research Awards, 560
Underwood Fund, 155
University of Bristol Postgraduate Scholarships, 691
University of New England Research Scholarships, 719
University of Stirling Research Studentships, 750
Wain Fund, 155
The Walsh Fellowships, 671
William John Thomson Scholarship, 623

South Africa

The Joint Japan/World Bank Graduate Scholarship Program (JJ/WBGSP), 395
Use of Fertility Enhancing Food, Forage and Cover Crops in Sustainably Managed Agroecosystems: The Bentley Fellowship, 400
Wingate Scholarships, 771

South America

The Joint Japan/World Bank Graduate Scholarship Program (JJ/WBGSP), 395
Use of Fertility Enhancing Food, Forage and Cover Crops in Sustainably Managed Agroecosystems: The Bentley Fellowship, 400

United Kingdom

Fulbright-RCVS Fellowship, 760
Linacre College A J Hosier Studentship, 728
Martin McLaren Horticultural Scholarship, 382
Sir William Roberts Scholarship, 753
University of Wales (Aberystwyth) Postgraduate Research Studentships, 752
University of Wales, Bangor (UWB) Research Studentships, 753
University of Wales, Bangor Departmental Research Studentships, 753
Wingate Scholarships, 771

West European Countries

Fulbright-RCVS Fellowship, 760
Sir William Roberts Scholarship, 753
University of Wales, Bangor (UWB) Research Studentships, 753
University of Wales, Bangor Departmental Research Studentships, 753
Wingate Scholarships, 771

AGRICULTURE AND FARM MANAGEMENT

Any Country

International Crops Research Institute Research Fellowships, 399
International Crops Research Institute Research Scholarships, 399
Massey Doctoral Scholarship, 461
Perry Postgraduate Scholarships and Research Awards, 560
RICS Education Trust Award, 588
University of Bristol Postgraduate Scholarships, 691
The Walsh Fellowships, 671
William John Thomson Scholarship, 623

African Nations

The Joint Japan/World Bank Graduate Scholarship Program (JJ/WBGSP), 395

Australia

University of Western Sydney Postgraduate Research Award (UWSPRA), 755
Wingate Scholarships, 771

British Commonwealth

The Joint Japan/World Bank Graduate Scholarship Program (JJ/WBGSP), 395
Wingate Scholarships, 771

Canada

Wingate Scholarships, 771

Caribbean Countries

The Joint Japan/World Bank Graduate Scholarship Program (JJ/WBGSP), 395

East European Countries

Evrika Foundation Awards, 308
Fulbright-RCVS Fellowship, 760
The Joint Japan/World Bank Graduate Scholarship Program (JJ/WBGSP), 395

Far East

The Joint Japan/World Bank Graduate Scholarship Program (JJ/WBGSP), 395

Indian Sub-Continent

The Joint Japan/World Bank Graduate Scholarship Program (JJ/WBGSP), 395
Sir William Roberts Scholarship, 753
Wingate Scholarships, 771

Middle East

The Joint Japan/World Bank Graduate Scholarship Program (JJ/WBGSP), 395

New Zealand

University of Western Sydney Postgraduate Research Award (UWSPRA), 755
Wingate Scholarships, 771

South Africa

The Joint Japan/World Bank Graduate Scholarship Program (JJ/WBGSP), 395
Wingate Scholarships, 771

South America

The Joint Japan/World Bank Graduate Scholarship Program (JJ/WBGSP), 395

United Kingdom

BPF Lord Samuel of Wych Cross Memorial Award, 747
Fulbright-RCVS Fellowship, 760
Harry Steele-Bodger Memorial Travelling Scholarship, 180
Sir William Roberts Scholarship, 753
University of Wales (Aberystwyth) Postgraduate Research Studentships, 752
University of Wales, Bangor (UWB) Research Studentships, 753
Wingate Scholarships, 771

West European Countries

Fulbright-RCVS Fellowship, 760
Sir William Roberts Scholarship, 753
University of Wales, Bangor (UWB) Research Studentships, 753
Wingate Scholarships, 771

AGRICULTURAL ECONOMICS

Any Country

Gilbert F White Postdoctoral Fellowship, 584
Hobart Houghton Research Fellowship, 586
International Crops Research Institute Research Fellowships, 399
International Crops Research Institute Research Scholarships, 399
Joseph L Fisher Dissertation Award, 584
Massey Doctoral Scholarship, 461
Perry Postgraduate Scholarships and Research Awards, 560
RICS Education Trust Award, 588
University of Bristol Postgraduate Scholarships, 691
University of New England Research Scholarships, 719
The Walsh Fellowships, 671
William John Thomson Scholarship, 623

African Nations

The Joint Japan/World Bank Graduate Scholarship Program (JJ/WBGSP), 395

Australia

Wingate Scholarships, 771

British Commonwealth

The Joint Japan/World Bank Graduate Scholarship Program (JJ/WBGSP), 395
Wingate Scholarships, 771

Canada

Horticultural Research Institute Grants, 359
Wingate Scholarships, 771

Caribbean Countries

CATIE Scholarships, 677
The Joint Japan/World Bank Graduate Scholarship Program (JJ/WBGSP), 395

East European Countries

The Joint Japan/World Bank Graduate Scholarship Program (JJ/WBGSP), 395

Far East

The Joint Japan/World Bank Graduate Scholarship Program (JJ/WBGSP), 395

Indian Sub-Continent

The Joint Japan/World Bank Graduate Scholarship Program (JJ/WBGSP), 395
Sir William Roberts Scholarship, 753
Wingate Scholarships, 771

Middle East

The Joint Japan/World Bank Graduate Scholarship Program (JJ/WBGSP), 395

New Zealand

Wingate Scholarships, 771

South Africa

The Joint Japan/World Bank Graduate Scholarship Program (JJ/WBGSP), 395
Wingate Scholarships, 771

South America

CATIE Scholarships, 677
The Joint Japan/World Bank Graduate Scholarship Program (JJ/WBGSP), 395

United Kingdom

Linacre College A J Hosier Studentship, 728
Sir William Roberts Scholarship, 753
University of Wales (Aberystwyth) Postgraduate Research Studentships, 752
University of Wales, Bangor (UWB) Research Studentships, 753
Wingate Scholarships, 771

United States of America

Fulbright Senior Specialists Program, 271
Horticultural Research Institute Grants, 359

West European Countries

Sir William Roberts Scholarship, 753
University of Wales, Bangor (UWB) Research Studentships, 753
Wingate Scholarships, 771

FOOD SCIENCE AND PRODUCTION

Any Country

AIATSIS Research Grants, 139
BBSRC Research Fellowships, 154
BBSRC Research Grants, 154
BBSRC Studentships, 155
Massey Doctoral Scholarship, 461
Perry Postgraduate Scholarships and Research Awards, 560
Scholarships for Advanced Study in Baking Science and Technology and/or Maintenance Engineering, 55
Underwood Fund, 155
University of Bristol Postgraduate Scholarships, 691
Wain Fund, 155

The Walsh Fellowships, 671
William John Thomson Scholarship, 623

African Nations

The Joint Japan/World Bank Graduate Scholarship Program (JJ/WBGSP), 395

Australia

University of Western Sydney Postgraduate Research Award (UWSPRA), 755
Wingate Scholarships, 771

British Commonwealth

The Joint Japan/World Bank Graduate Scholarship Program (JJ/WBGSP), 395
Wingate Scholarships, 771

Canada

AAAS Mass Media Science and Engineering Fellowship, 32
Swiss Federal Institute of Technology Scholarships, 669
Wingate Scholarships, 771

Caribbean Countries

The Joint Japan/World Bank Graduate Scholarship Program (JJ/WBGSP), 395

East European Countries

FEMS Fellowship, 310
Fulbright-RCVS Fellowship, 760
The Joint Japan/World Bank Graduate Scholarship Program (JJ/WBGSP), 395
Swiss Federal Institute of Technology Scholarships, 669

Far East

The Joint Japan/World Bank Graduate Scholarship Program (JJ/WBGSP), 395
Swiss Federal Institute of Technology Scholarships, 669

Indian Sub-Continent

The Joint Japan/World Bank Graduate Scholarship Program (JJ/WBGSP), 395
Sir William Roberts Scholarship, 753
Wingate Scholarships, 771

Middle East

The Joint Japan/World Bank Graduate Scholarship Program (JJ/WBGSP), 395

New Zealand

University of Western Sydney Postgraduate Research Award (UWSPRA), 755
Wingate Scholarships, 771

South Africa

The Joint Japan/World Bank Graduate Scholarship Program (JJ/WBGSP), 395
Wingate Scholarships, 771

South America

The Joint Japan/World Bank Graduate Scholarship Program (JJ/WBGSP), 395

United Kingdom

FEMS Fellowship, 310
Fulbright-RCVS Fellowship, 760
Sir William Roberts Scholarship, 753
Swiss Federal Institute of Technology Scholarships, 669
Wingate Scholarships, 771

United States of America

AAAS Mass Media Science and Engineering Fellowship, 32
Swiss Federal Institute of Technology Scholarships, 669

West European Countries

FEMS Fellowship, 310
Fulbright-RCVS Fellowship, 760
Sir William Roberts Scholarship, 753
Swiss Federal Institute of Technology Scholarships, 669
Wingate Scholarships, 771

MEAT AND POULTRY

Any Country

Perry Postgraduate Scholarships and Research Awards, 560
The Walsh Fellowships, 671

African Nations

The Joint Japan/World Bank Graduate Scholarship Program
(JJ/WBGSP), 395

Australia

University of Western Sydney Postgraduate Research Award
(UWSPRA), 755
Wingate Scholarships, 771

British Commonwealth

The Joint Japan/World Bank Graduate Scholarship Program
(JJ/WBGSP), 395
Wingate Scholarships, 771

Canada

Wingate Scholarships, 771

Caribbean Countries

The Joint Japan/World Bank Graduate Scholarship Program
(JJ/WBGSP), 395

East European Countries

The Joint Japan/World Bank Graduate Scholarship Program
(JJ/WBGSP), 395

Far East

The Joint Japan/World Bank Graduate Scholarship Program
(JJ/WBGSP), 395

Indian Sub-Continent

The Joint Japan/World Bank Graduate Scholarship Program
(JJ/WBGSP), 395
Wingate Scholarships, 771

Middle East

The Joint Japan/World Bank Graduate Scholarship Program
(JJ/WBGSP), 395

New Zealand

University of Western Sydney Postgraduate Research Award
(UWSPRA), 755
Vernon Willey Trust Awards, 762
Wingate Scholarships, 771

South Africa

The Joint Japan/World Bank Graduate Scholarship Program
(JJ/WBGSP), 395
Wingate Scholarships, 771

South America

The Joint Japan/World Bank Graduate Scholarship Program
(JJ/WBGSP), 395

United Kingdom

Wingate Scholarships, 771

West European Countries

Wingate Scholarships, 771

DAIRY

Any Country

Massey Doctoral Scholarship, 461
Perry Postgraduate Scholarships and Research Awards, 560
The Walsh Fellowships, 671

African Nations

The Joint Japan/World Bank Graduate Scholarship Program
(JJ/WBGSP), 395

Australia

University of Western Sydney Postgraduate Research Award
(UWSPRA), 755
Wingate Scholarships, 771

British Commonwealth

The Joint Japan/World Bank Graduate Scholarship Program
(JJ/WBGSP), 395
Wingate Scholarships, 771

Canada

Wingate Scholarships, 771

Caribbean Countries

The Joint Japan/World Bank Graduate Scholarship Program
(JJ/WBGSP), 395

East European Countries

The Joint Japan/World Bank Graduate Scholarship Program
(JJ/WBGSP), 395

Far East

The Joint Japan/World Bank Graduate Scholarship Program
(JJ/WBGSP), 395

Indian Sub-Continent

The Joint Japan/World Bank Graduate Scholarship Program
(JJ/WBGSP), 395
Wingate Scholarships, 771

Middle East

The Joint Japan/World Bank Graduate Scholarship Program
(JJ/WBGSP), 395

New Zealand

University of Western Sydney Postgraduate Research Award
(UWSPRA), 755
Wingate Scholarships, 771

South Africa

The Joint Japan/World Bank Graduate Scholarship Program
(JJ/WBGSP), 395
Wingate Scholarships, 771

South America

The Joint Japan/World Bank Graduate Scholarship Program
(JJ/WBGSP), 395

United Kingdom

Wingate Scholarships, 771

West European Countries

Wingate Scholarships, 771

FISH

Any Country

Woods Hole Oceanographic Institution Research Fellowships in Marine Policy, 778

African Nations

The Joint Japan/World Bank Graduate Scholarship Program (JJ/WBGSP), 395

Australia

University of Western Sydney Postgraduate Research Award (UWSPRA), 755
Wingate Scholarships, 771

British Commonwealth

The Joint Japan/World Bank Graduate Scholarship Program (JJ/WBGSP), 395
Wingate Scholarships, 771

Canada

Olin Fellowship, 135
Wingate Scholarships, 771

Caribbean Countries

The Joint Japan/World Bank Graduate Scholarship Program (JJ/WBGSP), 395

East European Countries

The Joint Japan/World Bank Graduate Scholarship Program (JJ/WBGSP), 395

Far East

The Joint Japan/World Bank Graduate Scholarship Program (JJ/WBGSP), 395

Indian Sub-Continent

The Joint Japan/World Bank Graduate Scholarship Program (JJ/WBGSP), 395
Wingate Scholarships, 771

Middle East

The Joint Japan/World Bank Graduate Scholarship Program (JJ/WBGSP), 395

New Zealand

University of Western Sydney Postgraduate Research Award (UWSPRA), 755
Wingate Scholarships, 771

South Africa

The Joint Japan/World Bank Graduate Scholarship Program (JJ/WBGSP), 395
Wingate Scholarships, 771

South America

The Joint Japan/World Bank Graduate Scholarship Program (JJ/WBGSP), 395

United Kingdom

Wingate Scholarships, 771

United States of America

Olin Fellowship, 135

West European Countries

Wingate Scholarships, 771

OENOLOGY

Australia

Wingate Scholarships, 771

British Commonwealth

Wingate Scholarships, 771

Canada

Wingate Scholarships, 771

Indian Sub-Continent

Wingate Scholarships, 771

New Zealand

Wingate Scholarships, 771

South Africa

Wingate Scholarships, 771

United Kingdom

Wingate Scholarships, 771

West European Countries

Wingate Scholarships, 771

BREWING

Australia

Wingate Scholarships, 771

British Commonwealth

Wingate Scholarships, 771

Canada

Wingate Scholarships, 771

Indian Sub-Continent

Wingate Scholarships, 771

New Zealand

Wingate Scholarships, 771

South Africa

Wingate Scholarships, 771

United Kingdom

Wingate Scholarships, 771

West European Countries

Wingate Scholarships, 771

HARVEST TECHNOLOGY

Any Country

Perry Postgraduate Scholarships and Research Awards, 560

African Nations

The Joint Japan/World Bank Graduate Scholarship Program (JJ/WBGSP), 395

Australia

Wingate Scholarships, 771

British Commonwealth

The Joint Japan/World Bank Graduate Scholarship Program (JJ/WBGSP), 395
Wingate Scholarships, 771

Canada

Wingate Scholarships, 771

Caribbean Countries

The Joint Japan/World Bank Graduate Scholarship Program (JJ/WBGSP), 395

East European Countries

The Joint Japan/World Bank Graduate Scholarship Program (JJ/WBGSP), 395

SOIL AND WATER SCIENCE

WATER MANAGEMENT

SOIL CONSERVATION

Use of Fertility Enhancing Food, Forage and Cover Crops in Sustainably Managed Agroecosystems: The Bentley Fellowship, 400

Australia
Wingate Scholarships, 771

British Commonwealth
Postgraduate Studies in Physical Land Resources Scholarship, 397
Wingate Scholarships, 771

Canada
Canadian Window on International Development, 399
Use of Fertility Enhancing Food, Forage and Cover Crops in Sustainably Managed Agroecosystems: The Bentley Fellowship, 400
Volzhsky Institute of Humanities Awards, 764
Wingate Scholarships, 771

Caribbean Countries
CATIE Scholarships, 677
Postgraduate Studies in Physical Land Resources Scholarship, 397
Use of Fertility Enhancing Food, Forage and Cover Crops in Sustainably Managed Agroecosystems: The Bentley Fellowship, 400

East European Countries
Natural History Museum Sys-Resource, 522

Far East
Postgraduate Studies in Physical Land Resources Scholarship, 397
Use of Fertility Enhancing Food, Forage and Cover Crops in Sustainably Managed Agroecosystems: The Bentley Fellowship, 400

Indian Sub-Continent
Postgraduate Studies in Physical Land Resources Scholarship, 397
Use of Fertility Enhancing Food, Forage and Cover Crops in Sustainably Managed Agroecosystems: The Bentley Fellowship, 400
Wingate Scholarships, 771

Middle East
Postgraduate Studies in Physical Land Resources Scholarship, 397
Use of Fertility Enhancing Food, Forage and Cover Crops in Sustainably Managed Agroecosystems: The Bentley Fellowship, 400

New Zealand
Wingate Scholarships, 771

South Africa
Postgraduate Studies in Physical Land Resources Scholarship, 397
Use of Fertility Enhancing Food, Forage and Cover Crops in Sustainably Managed Agroecosystems: The Bentley Fellowship, 400
Wingate Scholarships, 771

South America
CATIE Scholarships, 677
Postgraduate Studies in Physical Land Resources Scholarship, 397
Use of Fertility Enhancing Food, Forage and Cover Crops in Sustainably Managed Agroecosystems: The Bentley Fellowship, 400

United Kingdom
Silsoe Awards, 274
University of Wales, Bangor (UWB) Research Studentships, 753
University of Wales, Bangor Departmental Research Studentships, 753
Volzhsky Institute of Humanities Awards, 764
Wingate Scholarships, 771

United States of America
Earthwatch Education Awards, 290
Volzhsky Institute of Humanities Awards, 764

West European Countries
Natural History Museum Sys-Resource, 522
Silsoe Awards, 274

University of Wales, Bangor (UWB) Research Studentships, 753
University of Wales, Bangor Departmental Research Studentships, 753
Wingate Scholarships, 771

VETERINARY MEDICINE

Any Country
CIHR Fellowship Programme, 234
James Houston Scholarship, 707
James M Harris/Sarah W Sweatt Student Travel Grant, 279
John Crawford Scholarship, 707
Massey Doctoral Scholarship, 461
Perry Postgraduate Scholarships and Research Awards, 560
Sir Richard Stapley Educational Trust Grants, 632
Underwood Fund, 155
University of Bristol Postgraduate Scholarships, 691
University of Glasgow Postgraduate Research Scholarships, 707
University of Stirling Research Studentships, 750
Wellcome Trust Awards, Fellowships and Studentships, 768

African Nations
The Joint Japan/World Bank Graduate Scholarship Program (JJ/WBGSP), 395

Australia
Wingate Scholarships, 771

British Commonwealth
The Joint Japan/World Bank Graduate Scholarship Program (JJ/WBGSP), 395
Wingate Scholarships, 771

Canada
Wingate Scholarships, 771

Caribbean Countries
The Joint Japan/World Bank Graduate Scholarship Program (JJ/WBGSP), 395

East European Countries
FEMS Fellowship, 310
The Joint Japan/World Bank Graduate Scholarship Program (JJ/WBGSP), 395

Far East
The Joint Japan/World Bank Graduate Scholarship Program (JJ/WBGSP), 395

Indian Sub-Continent
The Joint Japan/World Bank Graduate Scholarship Program (JJ/WBGSP), 395
Sir William Roberts Scholarship, 753
Wingate Scholarships, 771

Middle East
The Joint Japan/World Bank Graduate Scholarship Program (JJ/WBGSP), 395

New Zealand
Wingate Scholarships, 771

South Africa
The Joint Japan/World Bank Graduate Scholarship Program (JJ/WBGSP), 395
Wingate Scholarships, 771

South America
The Joint Japan/World Bank Graduate Scholarship Program (JJ/WBGSP), 395

United Kingdom

FEMS Fellowship, 310
Harry Steele-Bodger Memorial Travelling Scholarship, 180
Petsavers Award, 562
Polish Embassy Short-Term Bursaries, 571
Polish Government Postgraduate Scholarships Scheme, 572
Sir William Roberts Scholarship, 753
University of Wales, Bangor Departmental Research Studentships, 753
Wingate Scholarships, 771

West European Countries

FEMS Fellowship, 310
Henry Dryerre Scholarship, 614
Karl-Enigk-Stipendium, 622
Sir William Roberts Scholarship, 753
University of Wales, Bangor Departmental Research Studentships, 753
Wingate Scholarships, 771

TROPICAL/SUB-TROPICAL AGRICULTURE

Any Country

Center for Field Research Grants, 246
Central Queensland University Postgraduate Research Award, 248
CQU International Student Scholarship, 248
Deputy Chancellors Postdoctoral Research, 535
NTU One Year Postdoctoral Fellowship, 535
NTU Senior Research Fellowship, 536
NTU Three Year Postdoctoral Fellowship, 536

African Nations

The Joint Japan/World Bank Graduate Scholarship Program (JJ/WBGSP), 395
Postgraduate Studies in Physical Land Resources Scholarship, 397
TWNSO Grants to Institutions in the South for Joint Research Projects, 674

Australia

Wingate Scholarships, 771

British Commonwealth

The Joint Japan/World Bank Graduate Scholarship Program (JJ/WBGSP), 395
Postgraduate Studies in Physical Land Resources Scholarship, 397
Wingate Scholarships, 771

Canada

Canadian Window on International Development, 399
Wingate Scholarships, 771

Caribbean Countries

CATIE Scholarships, 677
The Joint Japan/World Bank Graduate Scholarship Program (JJ/WBGSP), 395
Postgraduate Studies in Physical Land Resources Scholarship, 397
TWNSO Grants to Institutions in the South for Joint Research Projects, 674

East European Countries

The Joint Japan/World Bank Graduate Scholarship Program (JJ/WBGSP), 395

Far East

The Joint Japan/World Bank Graduate Scholarship Program (JJ/WBGSP), 395
Postgraduate Studies in Physical Land Resources Scholarship, 397
TWNSO Grants to Institutions in the South for Joint Research Projects, 674

Indian Sub-Continent

The Joint Japan/World Bank Graduate Scholarship Program (JJ/WBGSP), 395
Postgraduate Studies in Physical Land Resources Scholarship, 397
Sir William Roberts Scholarship, 753
TWNSO Grants to Institutions in the South for Joint Research Projects, 674
Wingate Scholarships, 771

Middle East

The Joint Japan/World Bank Graduate Scholarship Program (JJ/WBGSP), 395
Postgraduate Studies in Physical Land Resources Scholarship, 397
TWNSO Grants to Institutions in the South for Joint Research Projects, 674

New Zealand

Wingate Scholarships, 771

South Africa

The Joint Japan/World Bank Graduate Scholarship Program (JJ/WBGSP), 395
Postgraduate Studies in Physical Land Resources Scholarship, 397
TWNSO Grants to Institutions in the South for Joint Research Projects, 674
Wingate Scholarships, 771

South America

CATIE Scholarships, 677
The Joint Japan/World Bank Graduate Scholarship Program (JJ/WBGSP), 395
Postgraduate Studies in Physical Land Resources Scholarship, 397
TWNSO Grants to Institutions in the South for Joint Research Projects, 674

United Kingdom

Sir William Roberts Scholarship, 753
University of Wales, Bangor (UWB) Research Studentships, 753
University of Wales, Bangor Departmental Research Studentships, 753
Wingate Scholarships, 771

West European Countries

Sir William Roberts Scholarship, 753
University of Wales, Bangor (UWB) Research Studentships, 753
University of Wales, Bangor Departmental Research Studentships, 753
Wingate Scholarships, 771

FORESTRY

Any Country

Center for Field Research Grants, 246
Edmund Niles Huyck Preserve, Inc. Graduate and Postgraduate Grants, 292
Gilbert F White Postdoctoral Fellowship, 584
The Hyland R Johns Grant Program, 411
The John Z Duling Grant Program, 411
Joseph L Fisher Dissertation Award, 584
Perry Postgraduate Scholarships and Research Awards, 560
University of New England Research Scholarships, 719
University of Stirling Research Studentships, 750
The Walsh Fellowships, 671

African Nations

The Joint Japan/World Bank Graduate Scholarship Program (JJ/WBGSP), 395

Australia

Wingate Scholarships, 771

West European Countries

Natural History Museum Sys-Resource, 522
Sir William Roberts Scholarship, 753
University of Wales, Bangor (UWB) Research Studentships, 753
University of Wales, Bangor Departmental Research Studentships, 753
Wingate Scholarships, 771

FOREST BIOLOGY

Any Country

Edmund Niles Huyck Preserve, Inc. Graduate and Postgraduate Grants, 292
NFR Open Postdoctoral Fellowships, 668
NFR Research Grants, 668
University of Stirling Research Studentships, 750

African Nations

The Joint Japan/World Bank Graduate Scholarship Program (JJ/WBGSP), 395

Australia

Wingate Scholarships, 771

British Commonwealth

The Joint Japan/World Bank Graduate Scholarship Program (JJ/WBGSP), 395
Wingate Scholarships, 771

Canada

Canadian Forest Service Graduate Supplements, 643
Wingate Scholarships, 771

Caribbean Countries

The Joint Japan/World Bank Graduate Scholarship Program (JJ/WBGSP), 395

East European Countries

The Joint Japan/World Bank Graduate Scholarship Program (JJ/WBGSP), 395
Natural History Museum Sys-Resource, 522

Far East

The Joint Japan/World Bank Graduate Scholarship Program (JJ/WBGSP), 395

Indian Sub-Continent

The Joint Japan/World Bank Graduate Scholarship Program (JJ/WBGSP), 395
Sir William Roberts Scholarship, 753
Wingate Scholarships, 771

Middle East

The Joint Japan/World Bank Graduate Scholarship Program (JJ/WBGSP), 395

New Zealand

Wingate Scholarships, 771

South Africa

The Joint Japan/World Bank Graduate Scholarship Program (JJ/WBGSP), 395
Wingate Scholarships, 771

South America

The Joint Japan/World Bank Graduate Scholarship Program (JJ/WBGSP), 395

United Kingdom

Sir William Roberts Scholarship, 753
University of Wales, Bangor (UWB) Research Studentships, 753

University of Wales, Bangor Departmental Research Studentships, 753
Wingate Scholarships, 771

United States of America

Earthwatch Education Awards, 290

West European Countries

Natural History Museum Sys-Resource, 522
Sir William Roberts Scholarship, 753
University of Wales, Bangor (UWB) Research Studentships, 753
University of Wales, Bangor Departmental Research Studentships, 753
Wingate Scholarships, 771

FOREST PATHOLOGY

Any Country

Edmund Niles Huyck Preserve, Inc. Graduate and Postgraduate Grants, 292

African Nations

The Joint Japan/World Bank Graduate Scholarship Program (JJ/WBGSP), 395

Australia

Wingate Scholarships, 771

British Commonwealth

The Joint Japan/World Bank Graduate Scholarship Program (JJ/WBGSP), 395
Wingate Scholarships, 771

Canada

Canadian Forest Service Graduate Supplements, 643
Wingate Scholarships, 771

Caribbean Countries

The Joint Japan/World Bank Graduate Scholarship Program (JJ/WBGSP), 395

East European Countries

The Joint Japan/World Bank Graduate Scholarship Program (JJ/WBGSP), 395

Far East

The Joint Japan/World Bank Graduate Scholarship Program (JJ/WBGSP), 395

Indian Sub-Continent

The Joint Japan/World Bank Graduate Scholarship Program (JJ/WBGSP), 395
Sir William Roberts Scholarship, 753
Wingate Scholarships, 771

Middle East

The Joint Japan/World Bank Graduate Scholarship Program (JJ/WBGSP), 395

New Zealand

Wingate Scholarships, 771

South Africa

The Joint Japan/World Bank Graduate Scholarship Program (JJ/WBGSP), 395
Wingate Scholarships, 771

South America

The Joint Japan/World Bank Graduate Scholarship Program (JJ/WBGSP), 395

Wingate Scholarships, 771

West European Countries

Sir William Roberts Scholarship, 753
University of Wales, Bangor (UWB) Research Studentships, 753
University of Wales, Bangor Departmental Research Studentships, 753
Wingate Scholarships, 771

FOREST MANAGEMENT

Any Country

Conservation and Research Foundation Grants, 267
Edmund Niles Huyck Preserve, Inc. Graduate and Postgraduate Grants, 292
Trinity College Birkett Scholarship in Environmental Studies, 745

African Nations

The Joint Japan/World Bank Graduate Scholarship Program (JJ/WBGSP), 395

Australia

Wingate Scholarships, 771

British Commonwealth

The Joint Japan/World Bank Graduate Scholarship Program (JJ/WBGSP), 395
Wingate Scholarships, 771

Canada

Canadian Forest Service Graduate Supplements, 643
Community Forestry: Trees and People - John G Bene Fellowship, 400
Wingate Scholarships, 771

Caribbean Countries

The Joint Japan/World Bank Graduate Scholarship Program (JJ/WBGSP), 395

East European Countries

The Joint Japan/World Bank Graduate Scholarship Program (JJ/WBGSP), 395

Far East

The Joint Japan/World Bank Graduate Scholarship Program (JJ/WBGSP), 395

Indian Sub-Continent

The Joint Japan/World Bank Graduate Scholarship Program (JJ/WBGSP), 395
Sir William Roberts Scholarship, 753
Wingate Scholarships, 771

Middle East

The Joint Japan/World Bank Graduate Scholarship Program (JJ/WBGSP), 395

New Zealand

Wingate Scholarships, 771

South Africa

The Joint Japan/World Bank Graduate Scholarship Program (JJ/WBGSP), 395
Wingate Scholarships, 771

South America

The Joint Japan/World Bank Graduate Scholarship Program (JJ/WBGSP), 395

United Kingdom

Sir William Roberts Scholarship, 753
University of Wales, Bangor (UWB) Research Studentships, 753

University of Wales, Bangor Departmental Research Studentships, 753
Wingate Scholarships, 771

United States of America

Earthwatch Education Awards, 290

West European Countries

Sir William Roberts Scholarship, 753
University of Wales, Bangor (UWB) Research Studentships, 753
University of Wales, Bangor Departmental Research Studentships, 753
Wingate Scholarships, 771

FISHERY

Any Country

AIATSIS Research Grants, 139
Andrew Mellon Foundation Scholarship, 585
Center for Field Research Grants, 246
Central Queensland University Postgraduate Research Award, 248
CQU International Student Scholarship, 248
Rhodes University Postgraduate Scholarship, 587
University of Stirling Research Studentships, 750
Woods Hole Oceanographic Institution Research Fellowships in Marine Policy, 778
Woods Hole Oceanographic Institution/NOAA Co-operative Institute for Climate and Ocean Research Postdoctoral Fellowship, 778

African Nations

Austrian Academy of Sciences MSc Course in Limnology and Wetlands Ecosystems, 146
Austrian Academy of Sciences Postgraduate Course in Limnology, 146
The Joint Japan/World Bank Graduate Scholarship Program (JJ/WBGSP), 395

Australia

Wingate Scholarships, 771

British Commonwealth

The Joint Japan/World Bank Graduate Scholarship Program (JJ/WBGSP), 395
Wingate Scholarships, 771

Canada

Olin Fellowship, 135
Wingate Scholarships, 771

Caribbean Countries

The Joint Japan/World Bank Graduate Scholarship Program (JJ/WBGSP), 395

East European Countries

The Joint Japan/World Bank Graduate Scholarship Program (JJ/WBGSP), 395

Far East

Austrian Academy of Sciences MSc Course in Limnology and Wetlands Ecosystems, 146
Austrian Academy of Sciences Postgraduate Course in Limnology, 146
The Joint Japan/World Bank Graduate Scholarship Program (JJ/WBGSP), 395

Indian Sub-Continent

Austrian Academy of Sciences MSc Course in Limnology and Wetlands Ecosystems, 146
Austrian Academy of Sciences Postgraduate Course in Limnology, 146
The Joint Japan/World Bank Graduate Scholarship Program (JJ/WBGSP), 395

ARTS AND HUMANITIES

GENERAL

INTERPRETATION AND TRANSLATION

Any Country

WRITING (AUTHORSHIP)

Any Country

NATIVE LANGUAGE AND LITERATURE

MODERN LANGUAGES AND LITERATURES

ENGLISH

British Commonwealth

Wingate Scholarships, 771

Canada

Wingate Scholarships, 771

East European Countries

AHRB Studentships in the Humanities (Competition A), 112
AHRB Studentships in the Humanities (Competition B), 112

Indian Sub-Continent

Wingate Scholarships, 771

New Zealand

Wingate Scholarships, 771

South Africa

Wingate Scholarships, 771

United Kingdom

AHRB Studentships in the Humanities (Competition A), 112
AHRB Studentships in the Humanities (Competition B), 112
Cardiff University Postgraduate Research Studentships, 242
University of Wales (Aberystwyth) Postgraduate Research Studentships, 752
University of Wales, Bangor (UWB) Research Studentships, 753
University of Wales, Bangor Departmental Research Studentships, 753
Wingate Scholarships, 771

United States of America

Fulbright Teacher and Administrator Exchange, 325
Katherine Singer Kovacs Prize, 479

West European Countries

Cardiff University Postgraduate Research Studentships, 242
University of Wales, Bangor (UWB) Research Studentships, 753
University of Wales, Bangor Departmental Research Studentships, 753
Wingate Scholarships, 771

GERMANIC LANGUAGES

Any Country

Ahmanson and Getty Postdoctoral Fellowships, 678
Austro-American Association of Boston Scholarship, 147
Clark Library Short-Term Resident Fellowships, 679
Clark Predoctoral Fellowships, 679
Clark-Huntington Joint Bibliographical Fellowship, 679
Queen Mary Research Studentships, 576
University of Manchester Research Studentships and Scholarships, 715
University of Stirling Research Studentships, 750

Australia

Wingate Scholarships, 771

British Commonwealth

Wingate Scholarships, 771

Canada

Hochschulsommerkurse at German Universities, 331
Wingate Scholarships, 771

East European Countries

AHRB Studentships in the Humanities (Competition A), 112
AHRB Studentships in the Humanities (Competition B), 112

Indian Sub-Continent

Wingate Scholarships, 771

New Zealand

Wingate Scholarships, 771

South Africa

Wingate Scholarships, 771

United Kingdom

AHRB Studentships in the Humanities (Competition A), 112
AHRB Studentships in the Humanities (Competition B), 112
Wingate Scholarships, 771

United States of America

Germanistic Society of America Fellowships, 334
Hochschulsommerkurse at German Universities, 331

West European Countries

Wingate Scholarships, 771

GERMAN

Any Country

Ahmanson and Getty Postdoctoral Fellowships, 678
Alexander S Onassis Programme of Research Grants, 18
Alexander S Onassis Research Grants, 18
Andrew W Mellon Postdoctoral Fellowships in the Humanities, 749
ASECS (American Society for Eighteenth-Century Studies)/Clark Library Fellowships, 679
Austro-American Association of Boston Scholarship, 147
Clark Library Short-Term Resident Fellowships, 679
Clark Predoctoral Fellowships, 679
Clark-Huntington Joint Bibliographical Fellowship, 679
Hugh Le May Fellowship, 586
Learn German in Germany for Faculty, 331
Massey Doctoral Scholarship, 461
Onassis Programme of Postgraduate Research Scholarships, 19
Queen Mary Research Studentships, 576
Rhodes University Postdoctoral Fellowship, 586
Summer Language Courses at Goethe-Instituts, 332
Thomas Holloway Research Studentship, 602
University of Bristol Postgraduate Scholarships, 691
University of Glasgow Postgraduate Research Scholarships, 707
University of Manchester Research Studentships and Scholarships, 715
University of New England Research Scholarships, 719
University of Stirling Research Studentships, 750
Volzhsky Institute of Humanities Awards, 764

Australia

Wingate Scholarships, 771

British Commonwealth

Wingate Scholarships, 771

Canada

DAAD German Studies Research Grant, 330
Hochschulsommerkurse at German Universities, 331
Volzhsky Institute of Humanities Awards, 764
Wingate Scholarships, 771

East European Countries

AHRB Studentships in the Humanities (Competition A), 112
AHRB Studentships in the Humanities (Competition B), 112

Indian Sub-Continent

Wingate Scholarships, 771

New Zealand

Wingate Scholarships, 771

South Africa

Wingate Scholarships, 771

United Kingdom

AHRB Studentships in the Humanities (Competition A), 112
AHRB Studentships in the Humanities (Competition B), 112
Cardiff University Postgraduate Research Studentships, 242
University of Wales (Aberystwyth) Postgraduate Research Studentships, 752
University of Wales, Bangor (UWB) Research Studentships, 753
University of Wales, Bangor Departmental Research Studentships, 753
Volzhsky Institute of Humanities Awards, 764
Wingate Scholarships, 771

United States of America

DAAD German Studies Research Grant, 330
Fulbright Teacher and Administrator Exchange, 325
Germanistic Society of America Fellowships, 334
Hochschulsommerkurse at German Universities, 331
Volzhsky Institute of Humanities Awards, 764

West European Countries

Cardiff University Postgraduate Research Studentships, 242
Eugen and Ilse Seibold Award, 283
University of Wales, Bangor (UWB) Research Studentships, 753
University of Wales, Bangor Departmental Research Studentships, 753
Wingate Scholarships, 771

SWEDISH

Any Country

American-Scandinavian Foundation Translation Prize, 99

Australia

Wingate Scholarships, 771

British Commonwealth

Wingate Scholarships, 771

Canada

Wingate Scholarships, 771

East European Countries

AHRB Studentships in the Humanities (Competition A), 112
AHRB Studentships in the Humanities (Competition B), 112

Indian Sub-Continent

Wingate Scholarships, 771

New Zealand

Wingate Scholarships, 771

South Africa

Wingate Scholarships, 771

United Kingdom

AHRB Studentships in the Humanities (Competition A), 112
AHRB Studentships in the Humanities (Competition B), 112
Wingate Scholarships, 771

United States of America

Bicentennial Swedish-American Exchange Fund Travel Grants, 153
The Swedish Government 'SASS' Travel Grants, 667

West European Countries

Wingate Scholarships, 771

DANISH

Any Country

American-Scandinavian Foundation Translation Prize, 99

Australia

Wingate Scholarships, 771

British Commonwealth

Wingate Scholarships, 771

Canada

Wingate Scholarships, 771

East European Countries

AHRB Studentships in the Humanities (Competition A), 112
AHRB Studentships in the Humanities (Competition B), 112

Indian Sub-Continent

Wingate Scholarships, 771

New Zealand

Wingate Scholarships, 771

South Africa

Wingate Scholarships, 771

United Kingdom

AHRB Studentships in the Humanities (Competition A), 112
AHRB Studentships in the Humanities (Competition B), 112
Wingate Scholarships, 771

West European Countries

Wingate Scholarships, 771

NORWEGIAN

Any Country

American-Scandinavian Foundation Translation Prize, 99

Australia

Wingate Scholarships, 771

British Commonwealth

Wingate Scholarships, 771

Canada

Wingate Scholarships, 771

East European Countries

AHRB Studentships in the Humanities (Competition A), 112
AHRB Studentships in the Humanities (Competition B), 112

Indian Sub-Continent

Wingate Scholarships, 771

New Zealand

Wingate Scholarships, 771

South Africa

Wingate Scholarships, 771

United Kingdom

AHRB Studentships in the Humanities (Competition A), 112
AHRB Studentships in the Humanities (Competition B), 112
Wingate Scholarships, 771

United States of America

Fulbright Teacher and Administrator Exchange, 325
The Norwegian Emigration Fund of 1975, 537

West European Countries

Wingate Scholarships, 771

ITALIAN

Any Country

Ahmanson and Getty Postdoctoral Fellowships, 678
Aldo and Jeanne Scaglione Prize for Italian Studies, 478
Alexander S Onassis Programme of Research Grants, 18
Andrew W Mellon Postdoctoral Fellowships in the Humanities, 749
ASECS (American Society for Eighteenth-Century Studies)/Clark Library Fellowships, 679
Clark Library Short-Term Resident Fellowships, 679
Clark Predoctoral Fellowships, 679
Clark-Huntington Joint Bibliographical Fellowship, 679
Onassis Programme of Postgraduate Research Scholarships, 19
Thomas Holloway Research Studentship, 602
Universita' Per Stranieri Di Siena CILS Grants, 687
University for Foreigners Scholarships, 686
University of Bristol Postgraduate Scholarships, 691
University of Glasgow Postgraduate Research Scholarships, 707
University of Manchester Research Studentships and Scholarships, 715
University of New England Research Scholarships, 719
USC College Dissertation Fellowship, 749
USC College of Letters, Arts and Sciences Merit Award, 749

African Nations

Universita' Per Stranieri Di Siena PVS Grants, 687

Australia

Universita' Per Stranieri Di Siena Unstra Grants, 688
Wingate Scholarships, 771

British Commonwealth

Balsdon Fellowship, 176
Rome Awards in Archaeology, History and Letters, 177
Rome Scholarships in Ancient, Medieval and Later Italian Studies, 177
Universita' Per Stranieri Di Siena Unstra Grants, 688
Wingate Scholarships, 771

Canada

Universita' Per Stranieri Di Siena Unstra Grants, 688
Wingate Scholarships, 771

Caribbean Countries

Universita' Per Stranieri Di Siena PVS Grants, 687

East European Countries

AHRB Studentships in the Humanities (Competition A), 112
AHRB Studentships in the Humanities (Competition B), 112
Universita' Per Stranieri Di Siena PVS Grants, 687
Universita' Per Stranieri Di Siena Unstra Grants, 688

Far East

Universita' Per Stranieri Di Siena Unstra Grants, 688

Indian Sub-Continent

Universita' Per Stranieri Di Siena PVS Grants, 687
Wingate Scholarships, 771

Middle East

Universita' Per Stranieri Di Siena Unstra Grants, 688

New Zealand

Universita' Per Stranieri Di Siena Unstra Grants, 688
Wingate Scholarships, 771

South Africa

Universita' Per Stranieri Di Siena Unstra Grants, 688
Wingate Scholarships, 771

South America

Universita' Per Stranieri Di Siena PVS Grants, 687

United Kingdom

AHRB Studentships in the Humanities (Competition A), 112
AHRB Studentships in the Humanities (Competition B), 112
Balsdon Fellowship, 176
Cardiff University Postgraduate Research Studentships, 242
Rome Awards in Archaeology, History and Letters, 177
Rome Scholarships in Ancient, Medieval and Later Italian Studies, 177
Universita' Per Stranieri Di Siena Socrates Erasmus Students Mobility, 687
Universita' Per Stranieri Di Siena Unstra Grants, 688
University of Wales (Aberystwyth) Postgraduate Research Studentships, 752
Wingate Scholarships, 771

United States of America

Howard R Marraro Prize, 479
Universita' Per Stranieri Di Siena Unstra Grants, 688

West European Countries

Cardiff University Postgraduate Research Studentships, 242
Universita' Per Stranieri Di Siena Socrates Erasmus Students Mobility, 687
Wingate Scholarships, 771

PORTUGUESE

Any Country

University of Bristol Postgraduate Scholarships, 691
University of Manchester Research Studentships and Scholarships, 715

Australia

Wingate Scholarships, 771

British Commonwealth

Wingate Scholarships, 771

Canada

Wingate Scholarships, 771

East European Countries

AHRB Studentships in the Humanities (Competition A), 112
AHRB Studentships in the Humanities (Competition B), 112

Indian Sub-Continent

Wingate Scholarships, 771

New Zealand

Wingate Scholarships, 771

South Africa

Wingate Scholarships, 771

United Kingdom

AHRB Studentships in the Humanities (Competition A), 112
AHRB Studentships in the Humanities (Competition B), 112
Cardiff University Postgraduate Research Studentships, 242
Wingate Scholarships, 771

United States of America

Katherine Singer Kovacs Prize, 479

West European Countries

Cardiff University Postgraduate Research Studentships, 242
Wingate Scholarships, 771

ROMANCE LANGUAGES

Any Country

Ahmanson and Getty Postdoctoral Fellowships, 678

ASECS (American Society for Eighteenth-Century Studies)/Clark Library Fellowships, 679
Camargo Fellowships, 185
Clark Library Short-Term Resident Fellowships, 679
Clark Predoctoral Fellowships, 679
Clark-Huntington Joint Bibliographical Fellowship, 679
Massey Doctoral Scholarship, 461
University of Bristol Postgraduate Scholarships, 691
University of Glasgow Postgraduate Research Scholarships, 707
USC College Dissertation Fellowship, 749
USC College of Letters, Arts and Sciences Merit Award, 749

Australia
Wingate Scholarships, 771

British Commonwealth
Wingate Scholarships, 771

Canada
Wingate Scholarships, 771

East European Countries
AHRB Studentships in the Humanities (Competition A), 112
AHRB Studentships in the Humanities (Competition B), 112

Indian Sub-Continent
Wingate Scholarships, 771

New Zealand
Wingate Scholarships, 771

South Africa
Wingate Scholarships, 771

United Kingdom
AHRB Studentships in the Humanities (Competition A), 112
AHRB Studentships in the Humanities (Competition B), 112
Wingate Scholarships, 771

West European Countries
Wingate Scholarships, 771

MODERN GREEK

Any Country
Alexander S Onassis Programme of Research Grants, 18
Alexander S Onassis Research Grants, 18
Aristotle University of Thessaloniki Scholarships, 105
M Alison Frantz Fellowship in Post-Classical Studies at The Gennadius Library (formerly known as the Gennadeion Fellowship), 81
Mary Isabel Sibley Fellowship, 567
NEH Research Fellowships, 81
Onassis Programme of Postgraduate Research Scholarships, 19
Samuel H Kress Joint Athens-Jerusalem Fellowship, 81
University of Glasgow Postgraduate Research Scholarships, 707

Australia
Wingate Scholarships, 771

British Commonwealth
Hector and Elizabeth Catling Bursary, 175
Macmillan-Rodewald Studentship, School Studentship, Cary Studentship, 175
Wingate Scholarships, 771

Canada
Thompson (Homer and Dorothy) Fellowship, 222
Wingate Scholarships, 771

East European Countries
AHRB Studentships in the Humanities (Competition A), 112

AHRB Studentships in the Humanities (Competition B), 112

Indian Sub-Continent
Wingate Scholarships, 771

New Zealand
Wingate Scholarships, 771

South Africa
Wingate Scholarships, 771

United Kingdom
AHRB Studentships in the Humanities (Competition A), 112
AHRB Studentships in the Humanities (Competition B), 112
Hector and Elizabeth Catling Bursary, 175
Macmillan-Rodewald Studentship, School Studentship, Cary Studentship, 175
Wingate Scholarships, 771

West European Countries
Wingate Scholarships, 771

DUTCH

Any Country
University of Manchester Research Studentships and Scholarships, 715

Australia
Wingate Scholarships, 771

British Commonwealth
Wingate Scholarships, 771

Canada
Wingate Scholarships, 771

East European Countries
AHRB Studentships in the Humanities (Competition A), 112
AHRB Studentships in the Humanities (Competition B), 112

Indian Sub-Continent
Wingate Scholarships, 771

New Zealand
Wingate Scholarships, 771

South Africa
Wingate Scholarships, 771

United Kingdom
AHRB Studentships in the Humanities (Competition A), 112
AHRB Studentships in the Humanities (Competition B), 112
Wingate Scholarships, 771

West European Countries
Wingate Scholarships, 771

BALTIC LANGUAGES

Any Country
M Alison Frantz Fellowship in Post-Classical Studies at The Gennadius Library (formerly known as the Gennadeion Fellowship), 81

Australia
Wingate Scholarships, 771

British Commonwealth
Wingate Scholarships, 771

East European Countries

AHRB Studentships in the Humanities (Competition A), 112
AHRB Studentships in the Humanities (Competition B), 112

Indian Sub-Continent

Wingate Scholarships, 771

New Zealand

Wingate Scholarships, 771

South Africa

Wingate Scholarships, 771

United Kingdom

AHRB Studentships in the Humanities (Competition A), 112
AHRB Studentships in the Humanities (Competition B), 112
Volzhsky Institute of Humanities Awards, 764
Wingate Scholarships, 771

United States of America

IREX Grant Opportunities for US Scholars, 409
Kennan Institute Research Scholarship, 431
Volzhsky Institute of Humanities Awards, 764

West European Countries

Wingate Scholarships, 771

SLAVONIC LANGUAGES (OTHERS)

Any Country

Aldo and Jeanne Scaglione Prize for Studies in Slavic Languages and Literatures, 478
Alexander S Onassis Programme of Research Grants, 18
Alexander S Onassis Research Grants, 18
Canadian Institute of Ukrainian Studies Research Grants, 233
The Helen Darcovich Memorial Doctoral Fellowship, 233
Kennan Institute Short Term Grants, 431
Marusia and Michael Dorosh Master's Fellowship, 233
Neporany Research and Teaching Fellowship, 233
University of Glasgow Postgraduate Research Scholarships, 707

Australia

Wingate Scholarships, 771

British Commonwealth

Wingate Scholarships, 771

Canada

Wingate Scholarships, 771

East European Countries

AHRB Studentships in the Humanities (Competition A), 112
AHRB Studentships in the Humanities (Competition B), 112

Indian Sub-Continent

Wingate Scholarships, 771

New Zealand

Wingate Scholarships, 771

South Africa

Wingate Scholarships, 771

United Kingdom

AHRB Studentships in the Humanities (Competition A), 112
AHRB Studentships in the Humanities (Competition B), 112
Polish Embassy Short-Term Bursaries, 571
Polish Government Postgraduate Scholarships Scheme, 572
Wingate Scholarships, 771

United States of America

IREX Grant Opportunities for US Scholars, 409
Kennan Institute Research Scholarship, 431
The Kosciuszko Foundation Year Abroad Programme at the Jagiellonian University in Krakow, 435

West European Countries

Wingate Scholarships, 771

HUNGARIAN

Australia

Wingate Scholarships, 771

British Commonwealth

Wingate Scholarships, 771

Canada

Wingate Scholarships, 771

East European Countries

AHRB Studentships in the Humanities (Competition A), 112
AHRB Studentships in the Humanities (Competition B), 112

Indian Sub-Continent

Wingate Scholarships, 771

New Zealand

Wingate Scholarships, 771

South Africa

Wingate Scholarships, 771

United Kingdom

AHRB Studentships in the Humanities (Competition A), 112
AHRB Studentships in the Humanities (Competition B), 112
Wingate Scholarships, 771

United States of America

Fulbright Teacher and Administrator Exchange, 325
IREX Grant Opportunities for US Scholars, 409

West European Countries

Wingate Scholarships, 771

FINO UGRIAN LANGUAGES

Any Country

CIMO Scholarships for Advanced Finnish Studies and Research, 250

Australia

Wingate Scholarships, 771

British Commonwealth

Wingate Scholarships, 771

Canada

Wingate Scholarships, 771

East European Countries

AHRB Studentships in the Humanities (Competition A), 112
AHRB Studentships in the Humanities (Competition B), 112

Indian Sub-Continent

Wingate Scholarships, 771

New Zealand

Wingate Scholarships, 771

South Africa

Wingate Scholarships, 771

United Kingdom

AHRB Studentships in the Humanities (Competition A), 112
AHRB Studentships in the Humanities (Competition B), 112
Wingate Scholarships, 771

West European Countries

Wingate Scholarships, 771

EUROPEAN LANGUAGES (OTHERS)

Australia

Wingate Scholarships, 771

British Commonwealth

Wingate Scholarships, 771

Canada

Wingate Scholarships, 771

East European Countries

AHRB Studentships in the Humanities (Competition A), 112
AHRB Studentships in the Humanities (Competition B), 112

Indian Sub-Continent

Wingate Scholarships, 771

New Zealand

Wingate Scholarships, 771

South Africa

Wingate Scholarships, 771

United Kingdom

AHRB Studentships in the Humanities (Competition A), 112
AHRB Studentships in the Humanities (Competition B), 112
Polish Embassy Scholarship for Polonicum, 571
Wingate Scholarships, 771

United States of America

ACLS East European Language Training Grants, 42

West European Countries

Wingate Scholarships, 771

ALTAIC LANGUAGES

Australia

Wingate Scholarships, 771

British Commonwealth

Wingate Scholarships, 771

Canada

Wingate Scholarships, 771

East European Countries

AHRB Studentships in the Humanities (Competition A), 112
AHRB Studentships in the Humanities (Competition B), 112

Indian Sub-Continent

Wingate Scholarships, 771

New Zealand

Wingate Scholarships, 771

South Africa

Wingate Scholarships, 771

United Kingdom

AHRB Studentships in the Humanities (Competition A), 112
AHRB Studentships in the Humanities (Competition B), 112
Wingate Scholarships, 771

United States of America

ARIT - Bosphorus University Language Fellowships, 78
IREX Grant Opportunities for US Scholars, 409

West European Countries

Wingate Scholarships, 771

ARABIC

Any Country

Anthony Parsons Memorial Scholarship, 706
AUC International Graduate Fellowships in Arabic Studies, Middle
East Studies and Sociology-Anthropology, 96
AUC Teaching Arabic as a Foreign Language Fellowships, 97
SOAS Bursary, 622
SOAS Research Student Fellowships, 622
University of Manchester Research Studentships and Scholarships,
715

Australia

Wingate Scholarships, 771

British Commonwealth

Wingate Scholarships, 771

Canada

Wingate Scholarships, 771

East European Countries

AHRB Studentships in the Humanities (Competition A), 112
AHRB Studentships in the Humanities (Competition B), 112

Indian Sub-Continent

Wingate Scholarships, 771

New Zealand

Wingate Scholarships, 771

South Africa

Wingate Scholarships, 771

United Kingdom

AHRB Studentships in the Humanities (Competition A), 112
AHRB Studentships in the Humanities (Competition B), 112
Wingate Scholarships, 771

United States of America

Fulbright Teacher and Administrator Exchange, 325

West European Countries

Wingate Scholarships, 771

HEBREW

Any Country

Jacob Hirsch Fellowship, 80
JCC Association Scholarships, 423
Samuel H Kress Joint Athens-Jerusalem Fellowship, 81
SOAS Bursary, 622
SOAS Research Student Fellowships, 622
University of Glasgow Postgraduate Research Scholarships, 707
University of Manchester Research Studentships and Scholarships,
715

Australia

Wingate Scholarships, 771

AHRB Studentships in the Humanities (Competition B), 112
Wingate Scholarships, 771

West European Countries

Wingate Scholarships, 771

AMERINDIAN LANGUAGES

Any Country

Jacobs Research Fund, 769

Australia

Wingate Scholarships, 771

British Commonwealth

Wingate Scholarships, 771

Canada

Wingate Scholarships, 771

East European Countries

AHRB Studentships in the Humanities (Competition A), 112
AHRB Studentships in the Humanities (Competition B), 112

Indian Sub-Continent

Wingate Scholarships, 771

New Zealand

Wingate Scholarships, 771

South Africa

Wingate Scholarships, 771

United Kingdom

AHRB Studentships in the Humanities (Competition A), 112
AHRB Studentships in the Humanities (Competition B), 112
Molson Research Awards, 159
Wingate Scholarships, 771

United States of America

UCLA IAC Postdoctoral/Visiting Scholar Fellowships, 680

West European Countries

Wingate Scholarships, 771

AUSTRONESIAN AND OCEANIC LANGUAGES

Australia

Wingate Scholarships, 771

British Commonwealth

Wingate Scholarships, 771

Canada

Wingate Scholarships, 771

East European Countries

AHRB Studentships in the Humanities (Competition A), 112
AHRB Studentships in the Humanities (Competition B), 112

Indian Sub-Continent

Wingate Scholarships, 771

New Zealand

Wingate Scholarships, 771

South Africa

Wingate Scholarships, 771

United Kingdom

AHRB Studentships in the Humanities (Competition A), 112

AHRB Studentships in the Humanities (Competition B), 112
Wingate Scholarships, 771

West European Countries

Wingate Scholarships, 771

CLASSICAL LANGUAGES AND LITERATURES

Any Country

Adolfo Omodeo Scholarship, 418
Aldo and Jean Scaglione Prize for a Translation of a Literary Work, 478
Aldo and Jeanne Scaglione Prize for Comparative Literary Studies, 478
Alexander S Onassis Programme of Research Grants, 18
Alexander S Onassis Research Grants, 18
ASCSA Fellowships, 79
ASCSA Summer Sessions, 80
Center for Advanced Study in the Behavioral Sciences Postdoctoral Residential Fellowships, 245
Center for Hellenic Studies Junior Fellowships, 246
Charlotte W Newcombe Doctoral Dissertation Fellowships, 776
Dumbarton Oaks Fellowships and Junior Fellowships, 288
External Faculty Fellowships, 663
FAMSI Research Grant, 317
Foundation Praemium Erasmianum Study Prize, 318
Frederico Chabod Scholarship, 418
Hugh Le May Fellowship, 586
Jacob Hirsch Fellowship, 80
Lois Roth Award for a Translation of Literary Work, 479
M Alison Frantz Fellowship in Post-Classical Studies at The Gennadius Library (formerly known as the Gennadeion Fellowship), 81
Mary Isabel Sibley Fellowship, 567
Massey Doctoral Scholarship, 461
NHC Fellowships, 509
Onassis Foreigners' Fellowship Programme Educational Scholarships Category B, 18
Onassis Programme of Postgraduate Research Scholarships, 19
Rhodes University Postdoctoral Fellowship, 586
Samuel H Kress Fellowship in Classical Art History, 81
Samuel H Kress Joint Athens-Jerusalem Fellowship, 81
St Hugh's College Dorothea Gray Scholarship, 743
University of Bristol Postgraduate Scholarships, 691
University of Glasgow Postgraduate Research Scholarships, 707
University of Manchester Research Studentships and Scholarships, 715
USC College Dissertation Fellowship, 749
USC College of Letters, Arts and Sciences Merit Award, 749

Australia

Pembroke College Australian Graduate Scholarship, 734
Wingate Scholarships, 771

British Commonwealth

Wingate Scholarships, 771

Canada

Thompson (Homer and Dorothy) Fellowship, 222
Vatican Film Library - Andrew W Mellon Fellowship Program, 761
Wingate Scholarships, 771

East European Countries

AHRB Studentships in the Humanities (Competition A), 112
AHRB Studentships in the Humanities (Competition B), 112
Brian Hewson Crawford Fellowship, 765
CRF (Caledonian Research Foundation)/RSE European Visiting Research Fellowships, 613

Far East

Japanese American Citizens League Scholarship and Award Program, 422

British Institute of Archaeology at Ankara Research Grants, 169
British Institute of Archaeology at Ankara Travel Grants, 169
Dover Fund, 649
Hector and Elizabeth Catling Bursary, 175
Macmillan-Rodewald Studentship, School Studentship, Cary
Studentship, 175
Wingate Scholarships, 771

United States of America

Fulbright Teacher and Administrator Exchange, 325

West European Countries

Merton College Leventis Scholarship, 732
Wingate Scholarships, 771

SANSKRIT

Any Country

SOAS Bursary, 622
SOAS Research Student Fellowships, 622

Australia

Wingate Scholarships, 771

British Commonwealth

Wingate Scholarships, 771

Canada

Wingate Scholarships, 771

East European Countries

AHRB Studentships in the Humanities (Competition A), 112
AHRB Studentships in the Humanities (Competition B), 112

Indian Sub-Continent

Wingate Scholarships, 771

New Zealand

Wingate Scholarships, 771

South Africa

Wingate Scholarships, 771

United Kingdom

AHRB Studentships in the Humanities (Competition A), 112
AHRB Studentships in the Humanities (Competition B), 112
Wingate Scholarships, 771

West European Countries

Wingate Scholarships, 771

LINGUISTICS AND PHILOLOGY

Any Country

Aldo and Jeanne Scaglione Prize for French and Francophone Literary Studies, 478
Aldo and Jeanne Scaglione Prize for Studies in Germanic Languages and Literatures, 478
Aldo and Jeanne Scaglione Prize for Studies in Slavic Languages and Literatures, 478
Alexander S Onassis Programme of Research Grants, 18
Alexander S Onassis Research Grants, 18
Andrew W Mellon Postdoctoral Fellowships in the Humanities, 749
ASCSA Fellowships, 79
ASCSA Summer Sessions, 80
Camargo Fellowships, 185
Center for Advanced Study in the Behavioral Sciences Postdoctoral Residential Fellowships, 245
CIMO Scholarships for Advanced Finnish Studies and Research, 250
Deputy Chancellors Postdoctoral Research, 535

External Faculty Fellowships, 663
FAMSI Research Grant, 317
Fondation Fyssen Postdoctoral Study Grants, 312
Hugh Le May Fellowship, 586
Jacob Hirsch Fellowship, 80
M Alison Frantz Fellowship in Post-Classical Studies at The
Gennadius Library (formerly known as the Gennadeion Fellowship),
81
Marusia and Michael Dorosh Master's Fellowship, 233
NEH Research Fellowships, 81
Neporany Research and Teaching Fellowship, 233
NTU One Year Postdoctoral Fellowship, 535
NTU Senior Research Fellowship, 536
NTU Three Year Postdoctoral Fellowship, 536
Onassis Programme of Postgraduate Research Scholarships, 19
Phillips Fund Grants for Native American Research, 72
Queen Mary Research Studentships, 576
Rhodes University Postdoctoral Fellowship, 586
Samuel H Kress Joint Athens-Jerusalem Fellowship, 81
SOAS Bursary, 622
SOAS Research Student Fellowships, 622
University of Glasgow Postgraduate Research Scholarships, 707
University of Manchester Research Studentships and Scholarships,
715
University of New England Research Scholarships, 719
University of Stirling Research Studentships, 750
USC College Dissertation Fellowship, 749
USC College of Letters, Arts and Sciences Merit Award, 749
Volzhsky Institute of Humanities Awards, 764

Australia

Universita' Per Stranieri Di Siena Unstra Grants, 688
University of Western Sydney Postgraduate Research Award
(UWSPRA), 755
Wingate Scholarships, 771

British Commonwealth

Universita' Per Stranieri Di Siena Unstra Grants, 688
Wingate Scholarships, 771

Canada

The Paul Sargent Memorial Linguistic Scholarship Program, 132
Universita' Per Stranieri Di Siena Unstra Grants, 688
Volzhsky Institute of Humanities Awards, 764
Wingate Scholarships, 771

East European Countries

AHRB Studentships in the Humanities (Competition A), 112
AHRB Studentships in the Humanities (Competition B), 112
CRF (Caledonian Research Foundation)/RSE European Visiting Research Fellowships, 613
Universita' Per Stranieri Di Siena Unstra Grants, 688

Far East

Japanese American Citizens League Scholarship and Award Program, 422
Universita' Per Stranieri Di Siena Unstra Grants, 688

Indian Sub-Continent

Wingate Scholarships, 771

Middle East

Universita' Per Stranieri Di Siena Unstra Grants, 688

New Zealand

Universita' Per Stranieri Di Siena Unstra Grants, 688
University of Western Sydney Postgraduate Research Award
(UWSPRA), 755
Wingate Scholarships, 771

South Africa

Universita' Per Stranieri Di Siena Unstra Grants, 688

Wingate Scholarships, 771

United Kingdom

AHRB Studentships in the Humanities (Competition A), 112
AHRB Studentships in the Humanities (Competition B), 112
Cardiff University Postgraduate Research Studentships, 242
CRF (Caledonian Research Foundation)/RSE European Visiting Research Fellowships, 613
ESRC Research Studentships, 292
Regional Agency for the Right to University Study (DSU) Grants, 686
Universita' Per Stranieri Di Siena Socrates Erasmus Students Mobility, 687
Universita' Per Stranieri Di Siena Unstra Grants, 688
University of Wales, Bangor (UWB) Research Studentships, 753
University of Wales, Bangor Departmental Research Studentships, 753
Volzhsky Institute of Humanities Awards, 764
Wingate Scholarships, 771

United States of America

ETS Postdoctoral Fellowships, 294
Fulbright Distinguished Chairs Program, 270
Fulbright Scholar Awards for Research and Lecturing Abroad for United States Citizens, 271
Fulbright Senior Specialists Program, 271
IREX Grant Opportunities for US Scholars, 409
Japanese American Citizens League Scholarship and Award Program, 422
Kenneth W Mildenberger Prize, 479
Mina P Shaughnessy Prize, 479
MLA Prize for a Distinguished Bibliography, 480
NEH Fellowship, 84
The Swedish Government 'SASS' Travel Grants, 667
Universita' Per Stranieri Di Siena Unstra Grants, 688
US Department of Education International Research and Studies Program, 757
Volzhsky Institute of Humanities Awards, 764

West European Countries

Cardiff University Postgraduate Research Studentships, 242
CRF (Caledonian Research Foundation)/RSE European Visiting Research Fellowships, 613
ESRC Research Studentships, 292
Regional Agency for the Right to University Study (DSU) Grants, 686
Scholarship Foundation of the League for Finnish-American Societies, 621
Universita' Per Stranieri Di Siena Socrates Erasmus Students Mobility, 687
University of Wales, Bangor (UWB) Research Studentships, 753
University of Wales, Bangor Departmental Research Studentships, 753
Wingate Scholarships, 771

APPLIED LINGUISTICS

Any Country

Andrew W Mellon Postdoctoral Fellowships in the Humanities, 749
Camargo Fellowships, 185
Deputy Chancellors Postdoctoral Research, 535
Massey Doctoral Scholarship, 461
Michael Ventris Memorial Award, 380
NTU One Year Postdoctoral Fellowship, 535
NTU Senior Research Fellowship, 536
NTU Three Year Postdoctoral Fellowship, 536
Onassis Programme of Postgraduate Research Scholarships, 19
University of Manchester Research Studentships and Scholarships, 715
University of Stirling Research Studentships, 750

Australia

Universita' Per Stranieri Di Siena Unstra Grants, 688
Wingate Scholarships, 771

British Commonwealth

Universita' Per Stranieri Di Siena Unstra Grants, 688
Wingate Scholarships, 771

Canada

Universita' Per Stranieri Di Siena Unstra Grants, 688
Wingate Scholarships, 771

East European Countries

AHRB Studentships in the Humanities (Competition A), 112
Universita' Per Stranieri Di Siena Unstra Grants, 688

Far East

Universita' Per Stranieri Di Siena Unstra Grants, 688

Indian Sub-Continent

Wingate Scholarships, 771

Middle East

Universita' Per Stranieri Di Siena Unstra Grants, 688

New Zealand

Universita' Per Stranieri Di Siena Unstra Grants, 688
Wingate Scholarships, 771

South Africa

Universita' Per Stranieri Di Siena Unstra Grants, 688
Wingate Scholarships, 771

United Kingdom

AHRB Studentships in the Humanities (Competition A), 112
Regional Agency for the Right to University Study (DSU) Grants, 686
Universita' Per Stranieri Di Siena Socrates Erasmus Students Mobility, 687
Universita' Per Stranieri Di Siena Unstra Grants, 688
University of Wales, Bangor (UWB) Research Studentships, 753
University of Wales, Bangor Departmental Research Studentships, 753
Wingate Scholarships, 771

United States of America

Fulbright Distinguished Chairs Program, 270
Fulbright Senior Specialists Program, 271
Kenneth W Mildenberger Prize, 479
Mina P Shaughnessy Prize, 479
UCLA IAC Postdoctoral/Visiting Scholar Fellowships, 680
Universita' Per Stranieri Di Siena Unstra Grants, 688

West European Countries

Regional Agency for the Right to University Study (DSU) Grants, 686
Universita' Per Stranieri Di Siena Socrates Erasmus Students Mobility, 687
University of Wales, Bangor (UWB) Research Studentships, 753
University of Wales, Bangor Departmental Research Studentships, 753
Wingate Scholarships, 771

PSYCHOLINGUISTICS

Any Country

Andrew W Mellon Postdoctoral Fellowships in the Humanities, 749
Fondation Fyssen Postdoctoral Study Grants, 312
Onassis Programme of Postgraduate Research Scholarships, 19
University of Stirling Research Studentships, 750

Australia

Wingate Scholarships, 771

British Commonwealth

Wingate Scholarships, 771

GRAMMAR

SEMANTICS AND TERMINOLOGY

University of Wales, Bangor (UWB) Research Studentships, 753
University of Wales, Bangor Departmental Research Studentships, 753
Wingate Scholarships, 771

PHONETICS

Any Country

Andrew W Mellon Postdoctoral Fellowships in the Humanities, 749
Camargo Fellowships, 185
Onassis Programme of Postgraduate Research Scholarships, 19
University of Manchester Research Studentships and Scholarships, 715

Australia

Universita' Per Stranieri Di Siena Unstra Grants, 688
Wingate Scholarships, 771

British Commonwealth

Universita' Per Stranieri Di Siena Unstra Grants, 688
Wingate Scholarships, 771

Canada

Universita' Per Stranieri Di Siena Unstra Grants, 688
Wingate Scholarships, 771

East European Countries

AHRB Studentships in the Humanities (Competition A), 112
Universita' Per Stranieri Di Siena Unstra Grants, 688

Far East

Universita' Per Stranieri Di Siena Unstra Grants, 688

Indian Sub-Continent

Wingate Scholarships, 771

Middle East

Universita' Per Stranieri Di Siena Unstra Grants, 688

New Zealand

Universita' Per Stranieri Di Siena Unstra Grants, 688
Wingate Scholarships, 771

South Africa

Universita' Per Stranieri Di Siena Unstra Grants, 688
Wingate Scholarships, 771

United Kingdom

AHRB Studentships in the Humanities (Competition A), 112
Universita' Per Stranieri Di Siena Unstra Grants, 688
University of Wales, Bangor (UWB) Research Studentships, 753
University of Wales, Bangor Departmental Research Studentships, 753
Wingate Scholarships, 771

United States of America

Universita' Per Stranieri Di Siena Unstra Grants, 688

West European Countries

University of Wales, Bangor (UWB) Research Studentships, 753
University of Wales, Bangor Departmental Research Studentships, 753
Wingate Scholarships, 771

LOGOPEDICS

Australia

Wingate Scholarships, 771

British Commonwealth

Wingate Scholarships, 771

Canada

Wingate Scholarships, 771

East European Countries

AHRB Studentships in the Humanities (Competition A), 112

Indian Sub-Continent

Wingate Scholarships, 771

New Zealand

Wingate Scholarships, 771

South Africa

Wingate Scholarships, 771

United Kingdom

AHRB Studentships in the Humanities (Competition A), 112
Wingate Scholarships, 771

West European Countries

Wingate Scholarships, 771

COMPARATIVE LITERATURE

Any Country

Adolfo Omodeo Scholarship, 418
Ahmanson and Getty Postdoctoral Fellowships, 678
Aldo and Jeanne Scaglione Prize for Comparative Literary Studies, 478
Aldo and Jeanne Scaglione Prize for French and Francophone Literary Studies, 478
Aldo and Jeanne Scaglione Prize for Studies in Germanic Languages and Literatures, 478
Aldo and Jeanne Scaglione Prize for Studies in Slavic Languages and Literatures, 478
Alexander S Onassis Programme of Research Grants, 18
Alexander S Onassis Research Grants, 18
Andrew W Mellon Postdoctoral Fellowships in the Humanities, 749
ASCSA Fellowships, 79
ASCSA Summer Sessions, 80
ASECS (American Society for Eighteenth-Century Studies)/Clark Library Fellowships, 679
Camargo Fellowships, 185
Center for Advanced Study in the Behavioral Sciences Postdoctoral Residential Fellowships, 245
Central Queensland University Postgraduate Research Award, 248
Charlotte W Newcombe Doctoral Dissertation Fellowships, 776
ChLA Beiter Scholarships for Graduate Students, 256
ChLA Research Fellowships and Scholarships, 256
Clark Library Short-Term Resident Fellowships, 679
Clark Predoctoral Fellowships, 679
Clark-Huntington Joint Bibliographical Fellowship, 679
CMRS Summer Fellowship, 680
CQU International Student Scholarship, 248
External Faculty Fellowships, 663
Fenia and Yaakov Leviant Memorial Prize, 479
Foundation Praemium Erasmianum Study Prize, 318
Frederico Chabod Scholarship, 418
Humane Studies Fellowships, 376
Institute of Irish Studies Senior Visiting Research Fellowship, 383
Jacob Hirsch Fellowship, 80
Kennan Institute Short Term Grants, 431
M Alison Frantz Fellowship in Post-Classical Studies at The Gennadius Library (formerly known as the Gennadeion Fellowship), 81
Mary Isabel Sibley Fellowship, 567
NEH Research Fellowships, 81
NHC Fellowships, 509
Onassis Programme of Postgraduate Research Scholarships, 19
Queen Mary Research Studentships, 576

HISTORY

African Nations

Australia

British Commonwealth

Canada

PREHISTORY

Any Country

AIATSIS Research Grants, 139
Albert J Beveridge Grant, 53
Alexander S Onassis Programme of Research Grants, 18
Alexander S Onassis Research Grants, 18
Andrew W Mellon Postdoctoral Fellowships in the Humanities, 749
ASCSA Fellowships, 79
ASCSA Summer Sessions, 80
Bernadotte E Schmitt Grants, 54
Center for Field Research Grants, 246
The J B Harley Research Fellowships in the History of Cartography, 418
J Franklin Jameson Fellowship, 54
Jacob Hirsch Fellowship, 80
Littleton-Griswold Research Grant, 54
Mary Isabel Sibley Fellowship, 567
Michael Ventris Memorial Award, 380
NEH Research Fellowships, 81
Onassis Programme of Postgraduate Research Scholarships, 19
Prehistoric Society Conference Fund, 573
Prehistoric Society Research Fund Grant, 574
Prehistoric Society Research Grant Conference Award, 574
Samuel H Kress Joint Athens-Jerusalem Fellowship, 81
University of Manchester Research Studentships and Scholarships, 715

Australia

Wingate Scholarships, 771

British Commonwealth

Balsdon Fellowship, 176
British Institute of Archaeology at Ankara Research Grants, 169
British Institute of Archaeology at Ankara Travel Grants, 169
Hector and Elizabeth Catling Bursary, 175
Macmillan-Rodewald Studentship, School Studentship, Cary Studentship, 175
Rome Awards in Archaeology, History and Letters, 177
Rome Scholarships in Ancient, Medieval and Later Italian Studies, 177
Wingate Scholarships, 771

Canada

Wingate Scholarships, 771

East European Countries

AHRB Studentships in the Humanities (Competition A), 112

Indian Sub-Continent

Wingate Scholarships, 771

New Zealand

Wingate Scholarships, 771

South Africa

Wingate Scholarships, 771

United Kingdom

AHRB Studentships in the Humanities (Competition A), 112
Balsdon Fellowship, 176
British Institute of Archaeology at Ankara Research Grants, 169
British Institute of Archaeology at Ankara Travel Grants, 169
Cardiff University Postgraduate Research Studentships, 242
Hector and Elizabeth Catling Bursary, 175
Macmillan-Rodewald Studentship, School Studentship, Cary Studentship, 175
Rome Awards in Archaeology, History and Letters, 177
Rome Scholarships in Ancient, Medieval and Later Italian Studies, 177
Wingate Scholarships, 771

United States of America

UCLA IAC Postdoctoral/Visiting Scholar Fellowships, 680

West European Countries

Cardiff University Postgraduate Research Studentships, 242
Wingate Scholarships, 771

ANCIENT CIVILISATIONS

Any Country

AIAR Annual Professorship, 82
Albert J Beveridge Grant, 53
Alexander S Onassis Programme of Research Grants, 18
Alexander S Onassis Research Grants, 18
Andrew W Mellon Postdoctoral Fellowships in the Humanities, 749
ASCSA Fellowships, 79
ASCSA Summer Sessions, 80
ASOR Mesopotamian Fellowship, 82
Bernadotte E Schmitt Grants, 54
Center for Field Research Grants, 246
Center for Hellenic Studies Junior Fellowships, 246
Dumbarton Oaks Fellowships and Junior Fellowships, 288
FAMSI Research Grant, 317
Henri Frankfort Fellowship, 765
Hugh Last and Donald Atkinson Funds Committee Grants, 649
The J B Harley Research Fellowships in the History of Cartography, 418
J Franklin Jameson Fellowship, 54
Jacob Hirsch Fellowship, 80
Littleton-Griswold Research Grant, 54
Mary Isabel Sibley Fellowship, 567
Michael Ventris Memorial Award, 380
NEH Research Fellowships, 81
Onassis Programme of Postgraduate Research Scholarships, 19
Samuel H Kress Fellowship in Classical Art History, 81
Samuel H Kress Joint Athens-Jerusalem Fellowship, 81
Thomas Holloway Research Studentship, 602
University of Manchester Research Studentships and Scholarships, 715

African Nations

British School of Archaeology in Iraq Grants, 178

Australia

British School of Archaeology in Iraq Grants, 178
Wingate Scholarships, 771

British Commonwealth

Balsdon Fellowship, 176
British Institute of Archaeology at Ankara Research Grants, 169
British Institute of Archaeology at Ankara Travel Grants, 169
British School of Archaeology in Iraq Grants, 178
Hector and Elizabeth Catling Bursary, 175
Hugh Last Fellowship, 176
Macmillan-Rodewald Studentship, School Studentship, Cary Studentship, 175
Rome Awards in Archaeology, History and Letters, 177
Rome Scholarships in Ancient, Medieval and Later Italian Studies, 177
Wingate Scholarships, 771

Canada

British School of Archaeology in Iraq Grants, 178
Wingate Scholarships, 771

East European Countries

AHRB Studentships in the Humanities (Competition A), 112

Far East

British School of Archaeology in Iraq Grants, 178

Indian Sub-Continent

British School of Archaeology in Iraq Grants, 178
Wingate Scholarships, 771

New Zealand

British School of Archaeology in Iraq Grants, 178
Wingate Scholarships, 771

South Africa

British School of Archaeology in Iraq Grants, 178
Wingate Scholarships, 771

United Kingdom

AHRB Studentships in the Humanities (Competition A), 112
Balsdon Fellowship, 176
British Institute of Archaeology at Ankara Research Grants, 169
British Institute of Archaeology at Ankara Travel Grants, 169
British School of Archaeology in Iraq Grants, 178
Cardiff University Postgraduate Research Studentships, 242
Dover Fund, 649
Hector and Elizabeth Catling Bursary, 175
Hugh Last Fellowship, 176
Macmillan-Rodewald Studentship, School Studentship, Cary
Studentship, 175
Regional Agency for the Right to University Study (DSU) Grants, 686
Rome Awards in Archaeology, History and Letters, 177
Rome Scholarships in Ancient, Medieval and Later Italian Studies,
177
Wingate Scholarships, 771

United States of America

Earthwatch Education Awards, 290

West European Countries

Cardiff University Postgraduate Research Studentships, 242
Merton College Leventis Scholarship, 732
Regional Agency for the Right to University Study (DSU) Grants, 686
Wingate Scholarships, 771

MEDIEVAL HISTORY

Any Country

Albert J Beveridge Grant, 53
Alexander S Onassis Programme of Research Grants, 18
Alexander S Onassis Research Grants, 18
Andrew W Mellon Postdoctoral Fellowships in the Humanities, 749
ASCSA Fellowships, 79
ASCSA Summer Sessions, 80
Barbara Thom Postdoctoral Fellowship, 362
Bernadotte E Schmitt Grants, 54
Camargo Fellowships, 185
Clark-Huntington Joint Bibliographical Fellowship, 679
CMRS Summer Fellowship, 680
Council of the Institute Awards, 572
Dumbarton Oaks Fellowships and Junior Fellowships, 288
Institute of Irish Studies Research Fellowships, 383
Institute of Irish Studies Senior Visiting Research Fellowship, 383
Isobel Thornley Research Fellowship, 381
The J B Harley Research Fellowships in the History of Cartography,
418
J Franklin Jameson Fellowship, 54
Jacob Hirsch Fellowship, 80
Littleton-Griswold Research Grant, 54
Mary Isabel Sibley Fellowship, 567
Massey Doctoral Scholarship, 461
Mellon Postdoctoral Research Fellowships, 363
NEH Research Fellowships, 81
Onassis Programme of Postgraduate Research Scholarships, 19
Queen Mary Research Studentships, 576
Royal History Society Fellowship, 382
Samuel H Kress Joint Athens-Jerusalem Fellowship, 81

Scouloudi Fellowships, 382
Thomas Holloway Research Studentship, 602
University of Manchester Research Studentships and Scholarships,
715
University of Stirling Research Studentships, 750
Yorkist History Trust Fellowship, 382

Australia

Wingate Scholarships, 771

British Commonwealth

Balsdon Fellowship, 176
British Institute of Archaeology at Ankara Research Grants, 169
British Institute of Archaeology at Ankara Travel Grants, 169
Hector and Elizabeth Catling Bursary, 175
Macmillan-Rodewald Studentship, School Studentship, Cary
Studentship, 175
Rome Awards in Archaeology, History and Letters, 177
Rome Scholarships in Ancient, Medieval and Later Italian Studies,
177
Wingate Scholarships, 771

Canada

Mary McNeill Scholarship in Irish Studies, 383
Wingate Scholarships, 771

East European Countries

AHRB Studentships in the Humanities (Competition A), 112
Open Society Sofia Central European University Scholarship, 542

Indian Sub-Continent

Wingate Scholarships, 771

New Zealand

Wingate Scholarships, 771

South Africa

Wingate Scholarships, 771

United Kingdom

AHRB Studentships in the Humanities (Competition A), 112
Balsdon Fellowship, 176
British Institute of Archaeology at Ankara Research Grants, 169
British Institute of Archaeology at Ankara Travel Grants, 169
Cardiff University Postgraduate Research Studentships, 242
Hector and Elizabeth Catling Bursary, 175
Macmillan-Rodewald Studentship, School Studentship, Cary
Studentship, 175
Regional Agency for the Right to University Study (DSU) Grants, 686
Rome Awards in Archaeology, History and Letters, 177
Rome Scholarships in Ancient, Medieval and Later Italian Studies,
177
St Anne's College Olwen Rhys Research Scholarship, 739
University of Wales (Aberystwyth) Postgraduate Research Student-
ships, 752
University of Wales, Bangor (UWB) Research Studentships, 753
University of Wales, Bangor Departmental Research Studentships,
753
Wingate Scholarships, 771

United States of America

Earthwatch Education Awards, 290
Mary McNeill Scholarship in Irish Studies, 383
National Endowment for the Humanities Fellowships, 363
William B Schallek Memorial Graduate Fellowship Award, 587

West European Countries

Cardiff University Postgraduate Research Studentships, 242
Regional Agency for the Right to University Study (DSU) Grants, 686
St Anne's College Olwen Rhys Research Scholarship, 739
University of Wales, Bangor (UWB) Research Studentships, 753

University of Wales, Bangor Departmental Research Studentships, 753

Wingate Scholarships, 771

MODERN HISTORY

Any Country

Adelle and Erwin Tomash Fellowship in the History of Information Processing, 252
Ahmanson and Getty Postdoctoral Fellowships, 678
Albert J Beveridge Grant, 53
Alexander S Onassis Programme of Research Grants, 18
Alexander S Onassis Research Grants, 18
Alice E Smith Fellowship, 772
Amy Louise Hunter Fellowship, 773
Andrew W Mellon Postdoctoral Fellowships in the Humanities, 749
ASCSA Fellowships, 79
ASECS (American Society for Eighteenth-Century Studies)/Clark Library Fellowships, 679
Barbara Thom Postdoctoral Fellowship, 362
Bernadotte E Schmitt Grants, 54
C H Currey Memorial Fellowship, 664
Camargo Fellowships, 185
Clark Library Short-Term Resident Fellowships, 679
Clark Predoctoral Fellowships, 679
Clark-Huntington Joint Bibliographical Fellowship, 679
CMRS Summer Fellowship, 680
CQU International Student Scholarship, 248
Dixon Ryan Fox Manuscript Prize of the New York State Historical Association, 528
E Lyman Stewart Fellowship, 704
Fellowships in the University of Delaware Hagley Program, 704
Hagley/Winterthur Arts and Industries Fellowship, 346
Herbert Hoover Presidential Library Association Travel Grants, 357
IEEE Fellowship in Electrical History, 365
Institute of European History Fellowships, 381
Institute of Irish Studies Research Fellowships, 383
Institute of Irish Studies Senior Visiting Research Fellowship, 383
Isobel Thornley Research Fellowship, 381
The J B Harley Research Fellowships in the History of Cartography, 418
J Franklin Jameson Fellowship, 54
Jacob Hirsch Fellowship, 80
Jean Monnet Fellowships, 307
John C Geilfuss Fellowship, 773
Joyce A Tracy Fellowship, 29
La Pietra Dissertation Travel Fellowship in Transnational History, 547
Lewis Walpole Library Fellowship, 447
Library Company of Philadelphia Program in Early American Economy and Society, 447
Library Company of Philadelphia Research Fellowships in American History and Culture, 447
Littleton-Griswold Research Grant, 54
Mary Isabel Sibley Fellowship, 567
Massey Doctoral Scholarship, 461
Mellon Postdoctoral Research Fellowships, 30
Mellon Postdoctoral Research Fellowships, 363
Minnesota Historical Society Research Grant, 476
NEH Research Fellowships, 81
Neville Chamberlain Scholarship, 690
Onassis Programme of Postgraduate Research Scholarships, 19
Paul H Nitze School of Advanced International Studies (SAIS) Financial Aid and Fellowships, 156
Queen Mary Research Studentships, 576
Queen's University of Belfast Research and Senior Visiting Research Fellowships, 576
Rockefeller Archive Center Research Grant Program, 590
Roosevelt Institute Grant-in-Aid, 319
Royal History Society Fellowship, 382
Samuel H Kress Joint Athens-Jerusalem Fellowship, 81
Scouloudi Fellowships, 382

Thomas Holloway Research Studentship, 602
University of Dundee Research Awards, 704
University of Manchester Research Studentships and Scholarships, 715
University of Stirling Research Studentships, 750
Volzhsky Institute of Humanities Awards, 764
William Randolph Hearst Foundation Fellowship, 482
Wolfsonian FIU Fellowship, 774

Australia

Wingate Scholarships, 771

British Commonwealth

Balsdon Fellowship, 176
Hector and Elizabeth Catling Bursary, 175
Macmillan-Rodewald Studentship, School Studentship, Cary Studentship, 175
Rome Awards in Archaeology, History and Letters, 177
Rome Scholarships in Ancient, Medieval and Later Italian Studies, 177
Wingate Scholarships, 771

Canada

Mary McNeill Scholarship in Irish Studies, 383
Volzhsky Institute of Humanities Awards, 764
Wingate Scholarships, 771

East European Countries

AHRB Studentships in the Humanities (Competition A), 112
Open Society Sofia Central European University Scholarship, 542

Indian Sub-Continent

Wingate Scholarships, 771

New Zealand

J M Sherrard Award, 242
Wingate Scholarships, 771

South Africa

Wingate Scholarships, 771

United Kingdom

AHRB Studentships in the Humanities (Competition A), 112
Balsdon Fellowship, 176
Cardiff University Postgraduate Research Studentships, 242
Hector and Elizabeth Catling Bursary, 175
Macmillan-Rodewald Studentship, School Studentship, Cary Studentship, 175
Polish Embassy Short-Term Bursaries, 571
Polish Government Postgraduate Scholarships Scheme, 572
Rome Awards in Archaeology, History and Letters, 177
Rome Scholarships in Ancient, Medieval and Later Italian Studies, 177
St Antony's College Fay and Geoffrey Elliott Graduate Studentship in Russian and East European Studies, 740
University of Wales (Aberystwyth) Postgraduate Research Studentships, 752
University of Wales, Bangor (UWB) Research Studentships, 753
University of Wales, Bangor Departmental Research Studentships, 753
Volzhsky Institute of Humanities Awards, 764
Wingate Scholarships, 771

United States of America

Earthwatch Education Awards, 290
Fulbright Distinguished Chairs Program, 270
Fulbright Senior Specialists Program, 271
German Historical Institute Dissertation Scholarships, 333
Jamestown Scholars: New Dissertation Fellowships from the National Park Service and OAH, 547
Marine Corps Historical Center Research Grants, 458
Mary McNeill Scholarship in Irish Studies, 383

CONTEMPORARY HISTORY

ARCHAEOLOGY

West European Countries

PHILOSOPHY

Any Country

Australia

British Commonwealth

Canada

East European Countries

Indian Sub-Continent

New Zealand

South Africa

United Kingdom

United States of America

West European Countries

Cardiff University Postgraduate Research Studentships, 242
Wingate Scholarships, 771

ETHICS

Any Country

AIATSIS Research Grants, 139
Andrew W Mellon Postdoctoral Fellowships in the Humanities, 749
Camargo Fellowships, 185
Charlotte W Newcombe Doctoral Dissertation Fellowships, 776
Massey Doctoral Scholarship, 461
NEH Research Fellowships, 81
University of Dundee Research Awards, 704
University of Manchester Research Studentships and Scholarships, 715

Australia

Wingate Scholarships, 771

British Commonwealth

Wingate Scholarships, 771

Canada

Wingate Scholarships, 771

East European Countries

AHRB Studentships in the Humanities (Competition A), 112
AHRB Studentships in the Humanities (Competition B), 112

Indian Sub-Continent

Wingate Scholarships, 771

New Zealand

Wingate Scholarships, 771

South Africa

Wingate Scholarships, 771

United Kingdom

AHRB Studentships in the Humanities (Competition A), 112
AHRB Studentships in the Humanities (Competition B), 112
Cardiff University Postgraduate Research Studentships, 242
English Speaking Union Chautauqua Scholarships, 300
Wingate Scholarships, 771

United States of America

NEH Postdoctoral Research Award, 84
WWWC Americans and World Affairs Fellows Program, 780

West European Countries

Cardiff University Postgraduate Research Studentships, 242
Wingate Scholarships, 771

ARCHITECTURE AND TOWN PLANNING

GENERAL

Any Country

Alexander S Onassis Programme of Research Grants, 18
Alexander S Onassis Research Grants, 18
Architecture Travelling Fellowship, 633
ASCSA Fellowships, 79
Board of Architects of New South Wales Research Grant, 155
Canadian Department of Foreign Affairs Faculty Enrichment Program, 231
Canadian Department of Foreign Affairs Faculty Research Program, 231

Canadian Department of Foreign Affairs Institutional Research Program, 231
Carroll LV Meeks Fellowship, 652
Center for Advanced Study in the Behavioral Sciences Postdoctoral Residential Fellowships, 245
Chicago Institute for Architecture and Urbanism Award, 633
Cotton Research Fellowships, 287
FAMSI Research Grant, 317
Foundation Praemium Erasmianum Study Prize, 318
George Pepler International Award, 617
Humanitarian Trust Awards, 362
Indian Council of Social Science Research General Fellowships, 367
Interior Architecture Travelling Fellowship, 633
M H Joseph Prize, 165
Matsumae International Foundation Research Fellowship, 461
Neville Chamberlain Scholarship, 690
NUS Postgraduate Research Scholarship, 520
Onassis Programme of Postgraduate Research Scholarships, 19
Paul Mellon Centre Grants, 558
Ramsden Bursaries, 653
RIAS Award for Measured Drawing, 603
RIAS John Maclaren Travelling Fellowship, 603
RIAS/Whitehouse Studios Award for Architectural Photography, 604
Rosann Berry Fellowship, 653
RSA Annual Student Competition, 607
RSA Art for Architecture, 611
The Sir John Burnet Memorial Award, 604
The Sir Robert Lorimer Memorial Award, 604
The Sir Rowand Anderson Silver Medal, 604
Stiftelsen Lars Hiertas Minne Scientific Research Award, 665
Stroud Bursaries, 654
The Thomas Ross Award, 604
University of Dundee Research Awards, 704
University of Glasgow Postgraduate Research Scholarships, 707
University of Manchester Research Studentships and Scholarships, 715
University of Stirling Research Studentships, 750
William Randolph Hearst Foundation Fellowship, 482
Wolf Foundation Prizes, 773

African Nations

ABCCF Student Grant, 103
Friends of Peterhouse Bursary, 561
Fulbright Postdoctoral Research and Lecturing Awards for Non-US Citizens, 270
Merton College Reed Foundation Scholarship, 732

Australia

Byera Hadley Travelling Scholarship, Postgraduate Scholarship, Student Scholarship, 156
Friends of Peterhouse Bursary, 561
Fulbright Awards, 143
Fulbright Postdoctoral Fellowships, 143
Fulbright Postdoctoral Research and Lecturing Awards for Non-US Citizens, 270
Fulbright Postgraduate Studentships, 144
The Marten Bequest Travelling Scholarships, 560
University of Western Sydney Postgraduate Research Award (UWSPRA), 755
Wingate Scholarships, 771

British Commonwealth

Friends of Peterhouse Bursary, 561
Merton College Reed Foundation Scholarship, 732
Rome Scholarship in Architecture, 177
Sargant Fellowship, 178
Wingate Scholarships, 771

Canada

Friends of Peterhouse Bursary, 561
Fulbright Postdoctoral Research and Lecturing Awards for Non-US Citizens, 270

STRUCTURAL ARCHITECTURE

Any Country

Structural Engineering Travelling Fellowship, 633
William Randolph Hearst Foundation Fellowship, 482

Australia
Wingate Scholarships, 771

British Commonwealth
Wingate Scholarships, 771

Canada
Swiss Federal Institute of Technology Scholarships, 669
Wingate Scholarships, 771

East European Countries
Swiss Federal Institute of Technology Scholarships, 669

Far East
Swiss Federal Institute of Technology Scholarships, 669

Indian Sub-Continent
Wingate Scholarships, 771

New Zealand
Wingate Scholarships, 771

South Africa
Wingate Scholarships, 771

United Kingdom
Swiss Federal Institute of Technology Scholarships, 669
Wingate Scholarships, 771

United States of America
The Minorities and Women Educational Scholarship Program, 102
Swiss Federal Institute of Technology Scholarships, 669

West European Countries
The Arts Council of Ireland Architecture Publications Assistance Scheme, 113
Swiss Federal Institute of Technology Scholarships, 669
Wingate Scholarships, 771

ARCHITECTURAL RESTORATION

Any Country
Alexander S Onassis Programme of Research Grants, 18
Alexander S Onassis Research Grants, 18
Carroll LV Meeks Fellowship, 652
Center for Field Research Grants, 246
FAMSI Research Grant, 317
Keepers Preservation Education Fund Fellowship, 653
NEH Research Fellowships, 81
Onassis Programme of Postgraduate Research Scholarships, 19
Sir John Soane's Museum Foundation Travelling Fellowship, 631
University of Dundee Research Awards, 704
William Randolph Hearst Foundation Fellowship, 482

Australia
Wingate Scholarships, 771

British Commonwealth
Wingate Scholarships, 771

Canada
Wingate Scholarships, 771

Far East
Asian Cultural Council Fellowship Grants Program, 123

Indian Sub-Continent
Wingate Scholarships, 771

New Zealand
Wingate Scholarships, 771

South Africa
Wingate Scholarships, 771

United Kingdom
Wingate Scholarships, 771

United States of America
Asian Cultural Council Fellowship Grants Program, 123
Sally Kress Tompkins Fellowship, 653

West European Countries
The Arts Council of Ireland Architecture Publications Assistance Scheme, 113
Wingate Scholarships, 771

ENVIRONMENTAL DESIGN

Any Country
Alexander S Onassis Programme of Research Grants, 18
Alexander S Onassis Research Grants, 18
Deputy Chancellors Postdoctoral Research, 535
Interior Architecture Travelling Fellowship, 633
NTU One Year Postdoctoral Fellowship, 535
NTU Senior Research Fellowship, 536
NTU Three Year Postdoctoral Fellowship, 536
Stanley Smith (UK) Horticultural Trust Awards, 663

Australia
Wingate Scholarships, 771

British Commonwealth
Wingate Scholarships, 771

Canada
Horticultural Research Institute Grants, 359
The Jim Bourque Scholarship, 105
Swiss Federal Institute of Technology Scholarships, 669
Wingate Scholarships, 771

East European Countries
Swiss Federal Institute of Technology Scholarships, 669

Far East
Swiss Federal Institute of Technology Scholarships, 669

Indian Sub-Continent
Wingate Scholarships, 771

New Zealand
Wingate Scholarships, 771

South Africa
Wingate Scholarships, 771

United Kingdom
Cardiff University Postgraduate Research Studentships, 242
RSA Student Design Awards, 611
Sheffield Hallam University Research Studentships, 625
Swiss Federal Institute of Technology Scholarships, 669
Wingate Scholarships, 771

United States of America
Horticultural Research Institute Grants, 359
Swiss Federal Institute of Technology Scholarships, 669

West European Countries
The Arts Council of Ireland Architecture Publications Assistance Scheme, 113

Cardiff University Postgraduate Research Studentships, 242
RSA Student Design Awards, 611
Sheffield Hallam University Research Studentships, 625
Swiss Federal Institute of Technology Scholarships, 669
Wingate Scholarships, 771

LANDSCAPE ARCHITECTURE

Any Country

AILA/Yamagani/Hope Fellowship, 441
Alexander S Onassis Programme of Research Grants, 18
Alexander S Onassis Research Grants, 18
Chicago Institute for Architecture and Urbanism Award, 633
The Douglas Dockery Thomas Fellowship In Garden History and Design, 441
Dumbarton Oaks Fellowships and Junior Fellowships, 288
Onassis Programme of Postgraduate Research Scholarships, 19
Stanley Smith (UK) Horticultural Trust Awards, 663
Urban Design Travelling Fellowship, 634
William Randolph Hearst Foundation Fellowship, 482

Australia

Wingate Scholarships, 771

British Commonwealth

Wingate Scholarships, 771

Canada

Horticultural Research Institute Grants, 359
Wingate Scholarships, 771

East European Countries

European Gardens Horticulture Scholarships, 304

Indian Sub-Continent

Wingate Scholarships, 771

New Zealand

Wingate Scholarships, 771

South Africa

Wingate Scholarships, 771

United Kingdom

European Gardens Horticulture Scholarships, 304
Martin McLaren Horticultural Scholarship, 382
Wingate Scholarships, 771

United States of America

Edith H Henderson Scholarship, 441
Hawaii Chapter/David T Woolsey Scholarship, 441
Horticultural Research Institute Grants, 359

West European Countries

The Arts Council of Ireland Architecture Publications Assistance Scheme, 113
European Gardens Horticulture Scholarships, 304
Wingate Scholarships, 771

TOWN AND COMMUNITY PLANNING

Any Country

Alexander S Onassis Programme of Research Grants, 18
Alexander S Onassis Research Grants, 18
Anglo-German Foundation for the Study of Industrial Society Research Grant, 101
Chicago Institute for Architecture and Urbanism Award, 633
George Pepler International Award, 617
Massey Doctoral Scholarship, 461
RICS Education Trust Award, 588
University of Dundee Research Awards, 704

University of New England Research Scholarships, 719
University of Stirling Research Studentships, 750
Urban Design Travelling Fellowship, 634

African Nations

Institute for Housing and Urban Development Studies Fellowships for Courses, 376

Australia

Wingate Scholarships, 771

British Commonwealth

Wingate Scholarships, 771

Canada

Office of Critical Infrastructure Protection and Emergency Preparedness (EPC) Research Fellowship in Honour of Stuart Nesbitt White, 131
Swiss Federal Institute of Technology Scholarships, 669
TAC Scholarships, 677
Wingate Scholarships, 771

Caribbean Countries

Institute for Housing and Urban Development Studies Fellowships for Courses, 376

East European Countries

Institute for Housing and Urban Development Studies Fellowships for Courses, 376
Swiss Federal Institute of Technology Scholarships, 669

Far East

Institute for Housing and Urban Development Studies Fellowships for Courses, 376
Swiss Federal Institute of Technology Scholarships, 669

Indian Sub-Continent

Institute for Housing and Urban Development Studies Fellowships for Courses, 376
Wingate Scholarships, 771

Middle East

Institute for Housing and Urban Development Studies Fellowships for Courses, 376

New Zealand

Wingate Scholarships, 771

South Africa

Institute for Housing and Urban Development Studies Fellowships for Courses, 376
Wingate Scholarships, 771

South America

Institute for Housing and Urban Development Studies Fellowships for Courses, 376

United Kingdom

Cardiff University Postgraduate Research Studentships, 242
Polish Embassy Short-Term Bursaries, 571
Polish Government Postgraduate Scholarships Scheme, 572
Sheffield Hallam University Research Studentships, 625
Swiss Federal Institute of Technology Scholarships, 669
Wingate Scholarships, 771

United States of America

Swiss Federal Institute of Technology Scholarships, 669

West European Countries

Cardiff University Postgraduate Research Studentships, 242
Sheffield Hallam University Research Studentships, 625
Swiss Federal Institute of Technology Scholarships, 669

BUSINESS ADMINISTRATION AND MANAGEMENT

GENERAL

Fulbright Postdoctoral Research and Lecturing Awards for Non-US Citizens, 270
IATF Aviation MBA Scholarship, 394
International Postgraduate Research Scholarships (IPRS), 438
Merton College Reed Foundation Scholarship, 732
PRA Fellowships, 549
Shell Centenary Chevening Scholarships for Postgraduate Study, 216

United Kingdom

ACU Development Fellowships, 127
Canada Memorial Foundation Scholarships, 222
Cardiff University Postgraduate Research Studentships, 242
ESRC Research Studentships, 292
Fulbright Co-Sponsored MBA Awards, 758
Fulbright Postdoctoral Research and Lecturing Awards for Non-US Citizens, 270
Hilda Martindale Exhibitions, 358
International Postgraduate Research Scholarships (IPRS), 438
Sheffield Hallam University Research Studentships, 625
Silsoe Awards, 274
University of Wales (Aberystwyth) Postgraduate Research Studentships, 752
University of Wales, Bangor (UWB) Research Studentships, 753
University of Wales, Bangor Departmental Research Studentships, 753
Wingate Scholarships, 771

United States of America

AAUW Selected Professions Fellowships, 4
AIGC Fellowship, 54
Alfred D Chandler Jr Travelling Fellowships in Business History and Institutional Economic History, 349
Bicentennial Swedish-American Exchange Fund, 667
Bicentennial Swedish-American Exchange Fund Travel Grants, 153
Catching The Dream, 244
CBCF Congressional Fellows Program, 267
Congress Bundestag Youth Exchange for Young Professionals, 245
Consortium for Graduate Study in Management Fellowships for Minorities, 267
Doctoral Dissertation Award, 664
Dow Jones Editing Intern Program, 286
Federal Chancellor Scholarship, 20
Friends of Peterhouse Bursary, 561
Fulbright Distinguished Chairs Program, 270
Fulbright Scholar Awards for Research and Lecturing Abroad for United States Citizens, 271
Fulbright Scholar Program for US Citizens, 271
Fulbright Senior Specialists Program, 271
Indian Fellowship Program, 756
International Postgraduate Research Scholarships (IPRS), 438
ISM Doctoral Grants, 377
ISM Senior Research Fellowship Program, 377
Japanese American Citizens League Scholarship and Award Program, 422
Kennan Institute Research Scholarship, 431
National Restaurant Association Teacher Work-Study Grants, 293
North Dakota Indian Scholarship, 535
PRA Fellowships, 549
Robert Bosch Foundation Fellowship Program, 589
Robert Bosch Foundation Fellowships, 589
Washington University Chancellor's Graduate Fellowship Program for African Americans, 767

West European Countries

Cardiff University Postgraduate Research Studentships, 242
ESRC Research Studentships, 292
Eugen and Ilse Seibold Award, 283
Friends of Peterhouse Bursary, 561
Fulbright Co-Sponsored MBA Awards, 758
Fulbright Postdoctoral Research and Lecturing Awards for Non-US Citizens, 270

International Postgraduate Research Scholarships (IPRS), 438
Janson Johan Helmich Scholarships and Travel Grants, 421
Scholarship Foundation of the League for Finnish-American Societies, 621
Sheffield Hallam University Research Studentships, 625
Silsoe Awards, 274
University of Wales, Bangor (UWB) Research Studentships, 753
University of Wales, Bangor Departmental Research Studentships, 753
Wingate Scholarships, 771

BUSINESS STUDIES

Any Country

Alexander S Onassis Programme of Research Grants, 18
Alexander S Onassis Research Grants, 18
Central Queensland University Postgraduate Research Award, 248
CQU International Student Scholarship, 248
ETS Summer Program in Research for Graduate Students, 294
Golden Key National Honor Society Business Achievement Awards, 338
IEE Management Scholarship, 386
Kennan Institute Short Term Grants, 431
La Trobe University Postgraduate Scholarship, 439
LCCIEB Examinations Board Scholarships, 452
Massey Doctoral Scholarship, 461
NSERC Chairs in the Management of Technological Change, 523
University of Glasgow Postgraduate Research Scholarships, 707
University of Stirling Research Studentships, 750
Volzhsky Institute of Humanities Awards, 764

African Nations

Golda Meir Mount Carmel International Training Centre Assistance for Courses, 337
Golda Meir Mount Carmel International Training Centre Tuition and Maintenance Scholarships, 337

Australia

University of Western Sydney Postgraduate Research Award (UWSPRA), 755

Canada

Volzhsky Institute of Humanities Awards, 764

Caribbean Countries

Golda Meir Mount Carmel International Training Centre Assistance for Courses, 337
Golda Meir Mount Carmel International Training Centre Tuition and Maintenance Scholarships, 337

East European Countries

Golda Meir Mount Carmel International Training Centre Assistance for Courses, 337
Golda Meir Mount Carmel International Training Centre Tuition and Maintenance Scholarships, 337

Far East

Golda Meir Mount Carmel International Training Centre Assistance for Courses, 337
Golda Meir Mount Carmel International Training Centre Tuition and Maintenance Scholarships, 337

Indian Sub-Continent

Golda Meir Mount Carmel International Training Centre Assistance for Courses, 337
Golda Meir Mount Carmel International Training Centre Tuition and Maintenance Scholarships, 337

Middle East

Golda Meir Mount Carmel International Training Centre Assistance for Courses, 337

Golda Meir Mount Carmel International Training Centre Tuition and Maintenance Scholarships, 337

New Zealand

University of Western Sydney Postgraduate Research Award (UWSPRA), 755

South Africa

Golda Meir Mount Carmel International Training Centre Assistance for Courses, 337
Golda Meir Mount Carmel International Training Centre Tuition and Maintenance Scholarships, 337

South America

Golda Meir Mount Carmel International Training Centre Assistance for Courses, 337
Golda Meir Mount Carmel International Training Centre Tuition and Maintenance Scholarships, 337

United Kingdom

Cardiff University Postgraduate Research Studentships, 242
ESRC Research Studentships, 292
Polish Embassy Short-Term Bursaries, 571
Polish Government Postgraduate Scholarships Scheme, 572
Sheffield Hallam University Research Studentships, 625
University of Wales, Bangor (UWB) Research Studentships, 753
University of Wales, Bangor Departmental Research Studentships, 753
Volzhsky Institute of Humanities Awards, 764

United States of America

Fulbright Senior Specialists Program, 271
ISM Doctoral Grants, 377
ISM Senior Research Fellowship Program, 377
Volzhsky Institute of Humanities Awards, 764

West European Countries

Cardiff University Postgraduate Research Studentships, 242
ESRC Research Studentships, 292
Eugen and Ilse Seibold Award, 283
Sheffield Hallam University Research Studentships, 625
University of Wales, Bangor (UWB) Research Studentships, 753
University of Wales, Bangor Departmental Research Studentships, 753

INTERNATIONAL BUSINESS

Any Country

Alexander S Onassis Programme of Research Grants, 18
Alexander S Onassis Research Grants, 18
Central Queensland University Postgraduate Research Award, 248
CQU International Student Scholarship, 248
Deputy Chancellors Postdoctoral Research, 535
Kennan Institute Short Term Grants, 431
LCCIEB Examinations Board Scholarships, 452
Massey Doctoral Scholarship, 461
NTU Senior Research Fellowship, 536
Rhodes University Postdoctoral Fellowship, 586
Thomas Holloway Research Studentship, 602
University of Dundee Research Awards, 704
University of Glasgow Postgraduate Research Scholarships, 707
University of Stirling Research Studentships, 750

Australia

University of Western Sydney Postgraduate Research Award (UWSPRA), 755
Wingate Scholarships, 771

British Commonwealth

Wingate Scholarships, 771

Canada

Wingate Scholarships, 771

Indian Sub-Continent

Wingate Scholarships, 771

Middle East

Derek Fatchett Memorial Scholarships (Palestine), 712

New Zealand

University of Western Sydney Postgraduate Research Award (UWSPRA), 755
Wingate Scholarships, 771

South Africa

Wingate Scholarships, 771

United Kingdom

British Schools and Universities Foundation May and Ward Scholarships, 179
Cardiff University Postgraduate Research Studentships, 242
ESRC Research Studentships, 292
John Speak Trust Scholarships, 157
Polish Embassy Short-Term Bursaries, 571
Polish Government Postgraduate Scholarships Scheme, 572
University of Wales, Bangor (UWB) Research Studentships, 753
Wingate Scholarships, 771

United States of America

British Schools and Universities Foundation May and Ward Scholarships, 179
Fulbright Distinguished Chairs Program, 270
Fulbright Senior Specialists Program, 271
ISM Doctoral Grants, 377
ISM Senior Research Fellowship Program, 377
Kennan Institute Research Scholarship, 431
US Department of Education International Research and Studies Program, 757

West European Countries

Cardiff University Postgraduate Research Studentships, 242
ESRC Research Studentships, 292
Eugen and Ilse Seibold Award, 283
Scholarship Foundation of the League for Finnish-American Societies, 621
University of Wales, Bangor (UWB) Research Studentships, 753
Wingate Scholarships, 771

SECRETARIAL STUDIES

Any Country

Alexander S Onassis Programme of Research Grants, 18
LCCIEB Examinations Board Scholarships, 452
Volzhsky Institute of Humanities Awards, 764

Canada

Volzhsky Institute of Humanities Awards, 764

United Kingdom

Volzhsky Institute of Humanities Awards, 764

United States of America

Volzhsky Institute of Humanities Awards, 764

BUSINESS COMPUTING

Any Country

Central Queensland University Postgraduate Research Award, 248
CQU International Student Scholarship, 248
Massey Doctoral Scholarship, 461
Rhodes University Postdoctoral Fellowship, 586

University of Manchester Research Studentships and Scholarships, 715
Volzhsky Institute of Humanities Awards, 764

Australia

University of Western Sydney Postgraduate Research Award (UWSPRA), 755

Canada

Volzhsky Institute of Humanities Awards, 764

New Zealand

University of Western Sydney Postgraduate Research Award (UWSPRA), 755

United Kingdom

Volzhsky Institute of Humanities Awards, 764

United States of America

Volzhsky Institute of Humanities Awards, 764

MANAGEMENT SYSTEMS AND TECHNIQUES

Any Country

Central Queensland University Postgraduate Research Award, 248
CQU International Student Scholarship, 248
Deputy Chancellors Postdoctoral Research, 535
IEE Management Scholarship, 386
LCCIEB Examinations Board Scholarships, 452
Massey Doctoral Scholarship, 461
NTU One Year Postdoctoral Fellowship, 535
NTU Senior Research Fellowship, 536
NTU Three Year Postdoctoral Fellowship, 536
Rhodes University Postdoctoral Fellowship, 586
Thomas Holloway Research Studentship, 602
University of Stirling Research Studentships, 750
Volzhsky Institute of Humanities Awards, 764

African Nations

Golda Meir Mount Carmel International Training Centre Assistance for Courses, 337
Golda Meir Mount Carmel International Training Centre Tuition and Maintenance Scholarships, 337

Australia

University of Western Sydney Postgraduate Research Award (UWSPRA), 755

Canada

UNBF Atkinson Prize in Accounting, 718
UNBF Brydone Deblois Millidge Memorial Scholarship, 718
UNBF E D Maher Graduate Student Prize, 718
UNBF Frank H Sobey Fund for Excellence Scholarship, 718
UNBF Graduate Research Assistantships, 718
UNBF Research Assistantships from Research Grant-Holders, 719
UNBF Singer Graduate Bursary, 719
UNBF Summer Internships, 719
UNBF Teaching Assistantships (Markers), 719
Volzhsky Institute of Humanities Awards, 764

Caribbean Countries

Golda Meir Mount Carmel International Training Centre Assistance for Courses, 337
Golda Meir Mount Carmel International Training Centre Tuition and Maintenance Scholarships, 337

East European Countries

Evrika Foundation Awards, 308
Golda Meir Mount Carmel International Training Centre Assistance for Courses, 337
Golda Meir Mount Carmel International Training Centre Tuition and Maintenance Scholarships, 337

Far East

Golda Meir Mount Carmel International Training Centre Assistance for Courses, 337
Golda Meir Mount Carmel International Training Centre Tuition and Maintenance Scholarships, 337

Indian Sub-Continent

Golda Meir Mount Carmel International Training Centre Assistance for Courses, 337
Golda Meir Mount Carmel International Training Centre Tuition and Maintenance Scholarships, 337

Middle East

Golda Meir Mount Carmel International Training Centre Assistance for Courses, 337
Golda Meir Mount Carmel International Training Centre Tuition and Maintenance Scholarships, 337

New Zealand

University of Western Sydney Postgraduate Research Award (UWSPRA), 755

South Africa

Golda Meir Mount Carmel International Training Centre Assistance for Courses, 337
Golda Meir Mount Carmel International Training Centre Tuition and Maintenance Scholarships, 337

South America

Golda Meir Mount Carmel International Training Centre Assistance for Courses, 337
Golda Meir Mount Carmel International Training Centre Tuition and Maintenance Scholarships, 337

United Kingdom

British Schools and Universities Foundation May and Ward Scholarships, 179
Cardiff University Postgraduate Research Studentships, 242
Polish Embassy Short-Term Bursaries, 571
Polish Government Postgraduate Scholarships Scheme, 572
Volzhsky Institute of Humanities Awards, 764

United States of America

British Schools and Universities Foundation May and Ward Scholarships, 179
ISM Doctoral Grants, 377
ISM Senior Research Fellowship Program, 377
Minority Accounting and Information Systems Doctoral Scholarship Program, 436
Volzhsky Institute of Humanities Awards, 764

West European Countries

Cardiff University Postgraduate Research Studentships, 242

ACCOUNTANCY

Any Country

Alexander S Onassis Programme of Research Grants, 18
Alexander S Onassis Research Grants, 18
Central Queensland University Postgraduate Research Award, 248
CQU International Student Scholarship, 248
La Trobe University Postgraduate Scholarship, 439
LCCIEB Examinations Board Scholarships, 452
Massey Doctoral Scholarship, 461
Rhodes University Postdoctoral Fellowship, 586
University of Dundee Research Awards, 704
University of Glasgow Postgraduate Research Scholarships, 707
University of Manchester Research Studentships and Scholarships, 715
University of New England Research Scholarships, 719
University of Stirling Research Studentships, 750

IATF IATA Aviation Training and Development Institute (ATDI) Scholarships, 394

Middle East

Golda Meir Mount Carmel International Training Centre Assistance for Courses, 337
Golda Meir Mount Carmel International Training Centre Tuition and Maintenance Scholarships, 337
IATF IATA Aviation Training and Development Institute (ATDI) Scholarships, 394

New Zealand

University of Western Sydney Postgraduate Research Award (UWSPRA), 755

South Africa

Golda Meir Mount Carmel International Training Centre Assistance for Courses, 337
Golda Meir Mount Carmel International Training Centre Tuition and Maintenance Scholarships, 337
IATF IATA Aviation Training and Development Institute (ATDI) Scholarships, 394

South America

Golda Meir Mount Carmel International Training Centre Assistance for Courses, 337
Golda Meir Mount Carmel International Training Centre Tuition and Maintenance Scholarships, 337
IATF IATA Aviation Training and Development Institute (ATDI) Scholarships, 394

United Kingdom

British Schools and Universities Foundation May and Ward Scholarships, 179
Cardiff University Postgraduate Research Studentships, 242
ESRC Research Studentships, 292

United States of America

British Schools and Universities Foundation May and Ward Scholarships, 179
Fulbright Distinguished Chairs Program, 270
Fulbright Senior Specialists Program, 271
Horticultural Research Institute Grants, 359

West European Countries

Cardiff University Postgraduate Research Studentships, 242
ESRC Research Studentships, 292

INSURANCE MANAGEMENT

Any Country

Ernst Meyer Prize, 394
Geneva Association, 395
International Association for the Study of Insurance Economics Research Grants, 395
Massey Doctoral Scholarship, 461

Australia

Fulbright Tim Matthews Memorial Postgraduate Student Award in Statistics and Related Disciplines, 145

Canada

S S Huebner Foundation for Insurance Education Predoctoral Fellowships, 618

United Kingdom

Cardiff University Postgraduate Research Studentships, 242
University of Wales, Bangor (UWB) Research Studentships, 753
University of Wales, Bangor Departmental Research Studentships, 753

United States of America

S S Huebner Foundation for Insurance Education Predoctoral Fellowships, 618

West European Countries

Cardiff University Postgraduate Research Studentships, 242
University of Wales, Bangor (UWB) Research Studentships, 753
University of Wales, Bangor Departmental Research Studentships, 753

FINANCE, BANKING AND INVESTMENT

Any Country

Anglo-German Foundation for the Study of Industrial Society Research Grant, 101
ISMA Centre Doctoral Scholarship, 417
LCCIEB Examinations Board Scholarships, 452
Massey Doctoral Scholarship, 461
University of Dundee Research Awards, 704
University of Glasgow Postgraduate Research Scholarships, 707
University of Manchester Research Studentships and Scholarships, 715
University of Stirling Research Studentships, 750

Australia

Citibank Cambridge Scholarships, 199
Fulbright Tim Matthews Memorial Postgraduate Student Award in Statistics and Related Disciplines, 145
University of Western Sydney Postgraduate Research Award (UWSPRA), 755

Canada

UNBF Atkinson Prize in Accounting, 718
UNBF Brydone Deblois Millidge Memorial Scholarship, 718
UNBF E D Maher Graduate Student Prize, 718
UNBF Frank H Sobey Fund for Excellence Scholarship, 718
UNBF Graduate Research Assistantships, 718
UNBF Research Assistantships from Research Grant-Holders, 719
UNBF Singer Graduate Bursary, 719
UNBF Summer Internships, 719
UNBF Teaching Assistantships (Markers), 719

Caribbean Countries

Prince of Wales (Cable and Wireless) Chevening Cambridge Scholarships for PhD Study, 214
Prince of Wales (Cable and Wireless) Chevening Cambridge Scholarships for Postgraduate Study, 214

East European Countries

Citibank Cambridge Scholarships for Postgraduate Study (Czech Republic, Hungary, Poland and Slovakia), 199
Summer University of The Central European University Scholarship, 544

Far East

Citibank Cambridge Scholarships, 199
Prince of Wales (Cable and Wireless) Chevening Cambridge Scholarships for Postgraduate Study, 214
University of Leeds International Fee Bursary (Vietnam), 714

Indian Sub-Continent

Citibank Cambridge Scholarships, 199

New Zealand

Citibank Cambridge Scholarships, 199
University of Western Sydney Postgraduate Research Award (UWSPRA), 755

United Kingdom

British Schools and Universities Foundation May and Ward Scholarships, 179

PERSONNEL MANAGEMENT

LABOUR/INDUSTRIAL RELATIONS

East European Countries

The Joint Japan/World Bank Graduate Scholarship Program (JJ/WBGSP), 395

Far East

The Joint Japan/World Bank Graduate Scholarship Program (JJ/WBGSP), 395

Indian Sub-Continent

The Joint Japan/World Bank Graduate Scholarship Program (JJ/WBGSP), 395

Middle East

The Joint Japan/World Bank Graduate Scholarship Program (JJ/WBGSP), 395

New Zealand

University of Western Sydney Postgraduate Research Award (UWSPRA), 755

South Africa

The Joint Japan/World Bank Graduate Scholarship Program (JJ/WBGSP), 395

South America

The Joint Japan/World Bank Graduate Scholarship Program (JJ/WBGSP), 395

United Kingdom

British Schools and Universities Foundation May and Ward Scholarships, 179
Cardiff University Postgraduate Research Studentships, 242
University of Wales, Bangor (UWB) Research Studentships, 753
University of Wales, Bangor Departmental Research Studentships, 753

United States of America

British Schools and Universities Foundation May and Ward Scholarships, 179
Fulbright Distinguished Chairs Program, 270
Fulbright Senior Specialists Program, 271

West European Countries

Cardiff University Postgraduate Research Studentships, 242
University of Wales, Bangor (UWB) Research Studentships, 753
University of Wales, Bangor Departmental Research Studentships, 753

PUBLIC ADMINISTRATION

Any Country

Alexander S Onassis Programme of Research Grants, 18
Alexander S Onassis Research Grants, 18
Anglo-German Foundation for the Study of Industrial Society Research Grant, 101
Central Queensland University Postgraduate Research Award, 248
CQU International Student Scholarship, 248
Equiano Memorial Award, 666
Jane Addams/Andrew Carnegie Fellowships in Philanthropy, 368
Massey Doctoral Scholarship, 461
University of Manchester Research Studentships and Scholarships, 715
University of New England Research Scholarships, 719

African Nations

Golda Meir Mount Carmel International Training Centre Assistance for Courses, 337
Golda Meir Mount Carmel International Training Centre Tuition and Maintenance Scholarships, 337
Institute for Housing and Urban Development Studies Fellowships for Courses, 376

The Joint Japan/World Bank Graduate Scholarship Program (JJ/WBGSP), 395

Australia

University of Western Sydney Postgraduate Research Award (UWSPRA), 755
Wingate Scholarships, 771

British Commonwealth

The Joint Japan/World Bank Graduate Scholarship Program (JJ/WBGSP), 395
Wingate Scholarships, 771

Canada

Frank Knox Memorial Fellowships at Harvard University, 131
Wingate Scholarships, 771

Caribbean Countries

Golda Meir Mount Carmel International Training Centre Assistance for Courses, 337
Golda Meir Mount Carmel International Training Centre Tuition and Maintenance Scholarships, 337
Institute for Housing and Urban Development Studies Fellowships for Courses, 376
The Joint Japan/World Bank Graduate Scholarship Program (JJ/WBGSP), 395

East European Countries

Golda Meir Mount Carmel International Training Centre Assistance for Courses, 337
Golda Meir Mount Carmel International Training Centre Tuition and Maintenance Scholarships, 337
Institute for Housing and Urban Development Studies Fellowships for Courses, 376
The Joint Japan/World Bank Graduate Scholarship Program (JJ/WBGSP), 395
Summer University of The Central European University Scholarship, 544

Far East

Golda Meir Mount Carmel International Training Centre Assistance for Courses, 337
Golda Meir Mount Carmel International Training Centre Tuition and Maintenance Scholarships, 337
Institute for Housing and Urban Development Studies Fellowships for Courses, 376
The Joint Japan/World Bank Graduate Scholarship Program (JJ/WBGSP), 395

Indian Sub-Continent

Golda Meir Mount Carmel International Training Centre Assistance for Courses, 337
Golda Meir Mount Carmel International Training Centre Tuition and Maintenance Scholarships, 337
Hubert H Humphrey Fellowships, 682
Institute for Housing and Urban Development Studies Fellowships for Courses, 376
The Joint Japan/World Bank Graduate Scholarship Program (JJ/WBGSP), 395
Wingate Scholarships, 771

Middle East

Golda Meir Mount Carmel International Training Centre Assistance for Courses, 337
Golda Meir Mount Carmel International Training Centre Tuition and Maintenance Scholarships, 337
Institute for Housing and Urban Development Studies Fellowships for Courses, 376
The Joint Japan/World Bank Graduate Scholarship Program (JJ/WBGSP), 395

INSTITUTIONAL ADMINISTRATION

MBA

ENGINEERING

GENERAL

African Nations

Australia

British Commonwealth

Canada

Caribbean Countries

East European Countries

St Anne's College Una Goodwin Research Scholarship, 740
Swiss Federal Institute of Technology Scholarships, 669
Wingate Scholarships, 771
Wolfson Foundation Grants, 773
The Worshipful Company of Weavers' Scholarships, 672

United States of America

AAAS Mass Media Science and Engineering Fellowship, 32
AAUW Selected Professions Fellowships, 4
AIGC Fellowship, 54
Army Research Laboratory Postdoctoral Fellowship Program, 85
BK Krenzer Memorial Re-entry Scholarship, 656
BPW Career Advancement Scholarship Program, 184
British Schools and Universities Foundation May and Ward Scholarships, 179
Catching The Dream, 244
Congress Bundestag Youth Exchange for Young Professionals, 245
The Elisabeth M and Winchell M Parsons Scholarship, 124
Everitt P Blizard Scholarship, 66
Fannie and John Hertz Foundation Fellowships, 309
Friends of Peterhouse Bursary, 561
Fulbright Scholar Awards for Research and Lecturing Abroad for United States Citizens, 271
Fulbright Scholar Program for US Citizens, 271
Fulbright Senior Specialists Program, 271
Indian Fellowship Program, 756
International Postgraduate Research Scholarships (IPRS), 438
James F Schumar Scholarship, 66
Japanese American Citizens League Scholarship and Award Program, 422
John Randall Scholarship, 67
The Marjorie Roy Rothermel Scholarship, 124
NDSEG Fellowship Program, 13
North Dakota Indian Scholarship, 535
NSF(National Science Foundation)-DAAD Grants for the Natural, Engineering and Social Sciences, 332
Olive Lynn Salembier Scholarship, 656
ONR/ASEE Postdoctoral Fellowship Program, 85
Paralyzed Veterans of America Research Grants, 552
Past Presidents Scholarships, 656
PRA Fellowships, 549
Renate W Chasman Scholarship, 183
Robert A Dannels Scholarship, 67
SME Education Foundation Grants Program, 634
SWE General Motors Foundation Graduate Scholarship, 657
Swiss Federal Institute of Technology Scholarships, 669
USAF/NRC Summer Faculty Research Program (SFFP), 14
USAF/NRC-RRA Postdoctoral Research Associateships, 14
Verne R Dapp Scholarship, 67
Walter Meyer Scholarship, 67
Washington University Chancellor's Graduate Fellowship Program for African Americans, 767
Winston Churchill Scholarship, 771

West European Countries

Cardiff University Postgraduate Research Studentships, 242
CERN Doctoral Student Programme, 251
CERN Fellowships, 251
CERN Technical Student Programme, 251
EPSRC Doctoral Training Grants, 298
EPSRC Masters Training Packages (MTP), 298
Eugen and Ilse Seibold Award, 283
Friends of Peterhouse Bursary, 561
Fulbright Postdoctoral Research and Lecturing Awards for Non-US Citizens, 270
HRB Research Project Grants Inter-Disciplinary, 354
International Postgraduate Research Scholarships (IPRS), 438
Janson Johan Helmich Scholarships and Travel Grants, 421
Royal Society University Research Fellowships, 610
RSA Student Design Awards, 611
Scholarship Foundation of the League for Finnish-American Societies, 621

Sheffield Hallam University Research Studentships, 625
St Anne's College Una Goodwin Research Scholarship, 740
Swiss Federal Institute of Technology Scholarships, 669
Wingate Scholarships, 771

SURVEYING AND MAPPING SCIENCE

Any Country

DEED Scholarship, 77
John Moyes Lessells Scholarships, 614
RICS Education Trust Award, 588

Australia

Fulbright Postgraduate Student Award for Engineering, 144
Fulbright Postgraduate Student Award for Science and Engineering, 144
Wingate Scholarships, 771

British Commonwealth

Wingate Scholarships, 771

Canada

Canadian Window on International Development, 399
Wingate Scholarships, 771

Indian Sub-Continent

Wingate Scholarships, 771

New Zealand

Wingate Scholarships, 771

South Africa

Wingate Scholarships, 771

United Kingdom

Wingate Scholarships, 771

West European Countries

Wingate Scholarships, 771

ENGINEERING DRAWING/DESIGN

Any Country

Central Queensland University Postgraduate Research Award, 248
CQU International Student Scholarship, 248
DEED Scholarship, 77
John Moyes Lessells Scholarships, 614

Australia

Fulbright Postgraduate Student Award for Engineering, 144
Fulbright Postgraduate Student Award for Science and Engineering, 144
Wingate Scholarships, 771

British Commonwealth

Wingate Scholarships, 771

Canada

TAC Scholarships, 677
Wingate Scholarships, 771

Indian Sub-Continent

Wingate Scholarships, 771

New Zealand

Wingate Scholarships, 771

South Africa

Wingate Scholarships, 771

United Kingdom

Wingate Scholarships, 771

United States of America

American Society of Naval Engineers Scholarships, 93
Winston Churchill Scholarship, 771

West European Countries

Wingate Scholarships, 771

CHEMICAL ENGINEERING

Any Country

ACS/PRF Scientific Education Grants, 38
ACS/PRF Type AC Grants, 38
ACS/PRF Type B Grants, 38
BP/RSE Research Fellowships, 613
DEED Scholarship, 77
Exxon Mobil Engineering Teaching Fellowships, 592
J E Zajic Postgraduate Scholarship, 237
John Moyes Lessells Scholarships, 614
Massey Doctoral Scholarship, 461
University of Bristol Postgraduate Scholarships, 691
Welch Foundation Scholarship, 416

Australia

C T Taylor Studentship for PhD Study, 196
Fulbright Postgraduate Student Award for Engineering, 144
Fulbright Postgraduate Student Award for Science and Engineering, 144
Wingate Scholarships, 771

British Commonwealth

Wingate Scholarships, 771

Canada

AAAS Mass Media Science and Engineering Fellowship, 32
C T Taylor Studentship for PhD Study, 196
CIC Medal, 254
CIC Montreal Medal, 255
CIC Union Carbide Award for Chemical Education, 255
CSCT Norman and Marion Bright Memorial Award, 238
CSCT NOVA Chemicals Limited Award for Chemistry teaching in Community and Technical Colleges, 238
Swiss Federal Institute of Technology Scholarships, 669
Wingate Scholarships, 771

East European Countries

Swiss Federal Institute of Technology Scholarships, 669
VKI Fellowship, 764

Far East

Huntsman Tioxide Cambridge Scholarship for Postgraduate Study, 204
Swiss Federal Institute of Technology Scholarships, 669

Indian Sub-Continent

Wingate Scholarships, 771

Malaysia

Huntsman Tioxide Cambridge Scholarship for Postgraduate Study, 204

New Zealand

C T Taylor Studentship for PhD Study, 196
Wingate Scholarships, 771

South Africa

Huntsman Tioxide Cambridge Scholarship for Postgraduate Study, 204
Wingate Scholarships, 771

United Kingdom

Polish Embassy Short-Term Bursaries, 571
Polish Government Postgraduate Scholarships Scheme, 572
Swiss Federal Institute of Technology Scholarships, 669
Wingate Scholarships, 771

United States of America

AAAS Mass Media Science and Engineering Fellowship, 32
ACS/PRF Type G 'Starter' Grants, 39
Army Research Laboratory Postdoctoral Fellowship Program, 85
ONR Postdoctoral Fellowship, 539
ONR/ASEE Postdoctoral Fellowship Program, 85
SRC Graduate Fellowship Program, 624
SRC Master's Scholarship Program, 625
SWE General Motors Foundation Graduate Scholarship, 657
Swiss Federal Institute of Technology Scholarships, 669
VKI Fellowship, 764
Winston Churchill Scholarship, 771

West European Countries

Swiss Federal Institute of Technology Scholarships, 669
VKI Fellowship, 764
Wingate Scholarships, 771

CIVIL, CONSTRUCTION AND TRANSPORTATION ENGINEERING

Any Country

Arthur S Tuttle Memorial National Scholarship Fund, 90
Central Queensland University Postgraduate Research Award, 248
Conservation and Research Foundation Grants, 267
CQU International Student Scholarship, 248
DEED Scholarship, 77
Gustave Willems Award, 406
IREF Fellowship, 410
Jack E Leisch Scholarship, 91
John Moyes Lessells Scholarships, 614
Johnson's Wax Research Fellowship, 459
National Research Council Laboratories Research Associateships, 516
O H Ammann Research Fellowship in Structural Engineering, 91
QUEST Institution of Civil Engineers Continuing Education Award, 385
QUEST Institution of Civil Engineers Overseas Travel Awards, 385
Rees Jeffreys Road Fund Bursaries, 580
RICS Education Trust Award, 588
Structural Engineering Travelling Fellowship, 633
University of Bristol Postgraduate Scholarships, 691
University of Dundee Research Awards, 704
University of Glasgow Postgraduate Research Scholarships, 707
University of Manchester Research Studentships and Scholarships, 715

Australia

Fulbright Postgraduate Student Award for Engineering, 144
Fulbright Postgraduate Student Award for Science and Engineering, 144
University of Western Sydney Postgraduate Research Award (UWSPRA), 755
Wingate Scholarships, 771

British Commonwealth

Wingate Scholarships, 771

Canada

Swiss Federal Institute of Technology Scholarships, 669
TAC Scholarships, 677
Wingate Scholarships, 771

East European Countries

CERN Doctoral Student Programme, 251

CERN Fellowships, 251
CERN Technical Student Programme, 251
Swiss Federal Institute of Technology Scholarships, 669

Far East

Swiss Federal Institute of Technology Scholarships, 669

Indian Sub-Continent

Wingate Scholarships, 771

New Zealand

University of Western Sydney Postgraduate Research Award
(UWSPRA), 755
Wingate Scholarships, 771

South Africa

Wingate Scholarships, 771

United Kingdom

Cardiff University Postgraduate Research Studentships, 242
CERN Doctoral Student Programme, 251
CERN Fellowships, 251
CERN Technical Student Programme, 251
QUEST C H Roberts Bequest, 385
Sheffield Hallam University Research Studentships, 625
Swiss Federal Institute of Technology Scholarships, 669
Wingate Scholarships, 771
Young Consulting Engineer of the Year, 128

United States of America

American Society of Naval Engineers Scholarships, 93
ONR Postdoctoral Fellowship, 539
ONR/ASEE Postdoctoral Fellowship Program, 85
Swiss Federal Institute of Technology Scholarships, 669
Winston Churchill Scholarship, 771

West European Countries

Cardiff University Postgraduate Research Studentships, 242
CERN Doctoral Student Programme, 251
CERN Fellowships, 251
CERN Technical Student Programme, 251
QUEST C H Roberts Bequest, 385
Sheffield Hallam University Research Studentships, 625
Swiss Federal Institute of Technology Scholarships, 669
Wingate Scholarships, 771

ENVIRONMENTAL AND SANITARY ENGINEERING

Any Country

Anglo-German Foundation for the Study of Industrial Society Research Grant, 101
AWWA Academic Achievement Award, 98
AWWA Thomas R Camp Scholarship, 99
Chrysalis Scholarship, 126
DEED Scholarship, 77
John Moyes Lessells Scholarships, 614
John Stanley Scholarship, 366
Massey Doctoral Scholarship, 461
NSERC Strategic Project Grants (SPG), 525
QUEST Institution of Civil Engineers Overseas Travel Awards, 385
Solids Handling Award, 390
University of Dundee Research Awards, 704
University of New England Research Scholarships, 719
VITUKI Training Financial Support for Course Participants, 763

African Nations

The Joint Japan/World Bank Graduate Scholarship Program
(JJ/WBGSP), 395

Australia

Fulbright Postgraduate Student Award for Engineering, 144
Fulbright Postgraduate Student Award for Science and Engineering, 144
University of Western Sydney Postgraduate Research Award
(UWSPRA), 755
Wingate Scholarships, 771

British Commonwealth

The Joint Japan/World Bank Graduate Scholarship Program
(JJ/WBGSP), 395
Wingate Scholarships, 771

Canada

AWWA Abel Wolman Doctoral Fellowship, 98
AWWA Larson Aquatic Research Support Scholarships, 98
Canadian Window on International Development, 399
Horticultural Research Institute Grants, 359
TAC Scholarships, 677
Wingate Scholarships, 771

Caribbean Countries

The Joint Japan/World Bank Graduate Scholarship Program
(JJ/WBGSP), 395

East European Countries

CERN Doctoral Student Programme, 251
CERN Fellowships, 251
CERN Technical Student Programme, 251
The Joint Japan/World Bank Graduate Scholarship Program
(JJ/WBGSP), 395
VKI Fellowship, 764

Far East

BPAmoco-Leeds University-FCO Chevening Scholarship, 712
The Joint Japan/World Bank Graduate Scholarship Program
(JJ/WBGSP), 395

Indian Sub-Continent

The Joint Japan/World Bank Graduate Scholarship Program
(JJ/WBGSP), 395
Wingate Scholarships, 771

Middle East

The Joint Japan/World Bank Graduate Scholarship Program
(JJ/WBGSP), 395

New Zealand

University of Western Sydney Postgraduate Research Award
(UWSPRA), 755
Wingate Scholarships, 771

South Africa

The Joint Japan/World Bank Graduate Scholarship Program
(JJ/WBGSP), 395
Wingate Scholarships, 771

South America

AWWA Abel Wolman Doctoral Fellowship, 98
AWWA Larson Aquatic Research Support Scholarships, 98
The Joint Japan/World Bank Graduate Scholarship Program
(JJ/WBGSP), 395

United Kingdom

CERN Doctoral Student Programme, 251
CERN Fellowships, 251
CERN Technical Student Programme, 251
Polish Embassy Short-Term Bursaries, 571
Polish Government Postgraduate Scholarships Scheme, 572
Silsoe Awards, 274
Wingate Scholarships, 771

United States of America

American Society of Naval Engineers Scholarships, 93
Army Research Laboratory Postdoctoral Fellowship Program, 85
AWWA Abel Wolman Doctoral Fellowship, 98
AWWA Holly A Cornell Scholarship, 98
AWWA Larson Aquatic Research Support Scholarships, 98
Horticultural Research Institute Grants, 359
ONR Postdoctoral Fellowship, 539
ONR/ASEE Postdoctoral Fellowship Program, 85
VKI Fellowship, 764
Winston Churchill Scholarship, 771

West European Countries

CERN Doctoral Student Programme, 251
CERN Fellowships, 251
CERN Technical Student Programme, 251
Silsoe Awards, 274
VKI Fellowship, 764
Wingate Scholarships, 771

SAFETY ENGINEERING

Any Country

DEED Scholarship, 77
John Moyes Lessells Scholarships, 614
University of Manchester Research Studentships and Scholarships, 715

African Nations

The Joint Japan/World Bank Graduate Scholarship Program (JJ/WBGSP), 395

Australia

Fulbright Postgraduate Student Award for Engineering, 144
Fulbright Postgraduate Student Award for Science and Engineering, 144
Wingate Scholarships, 771

British Commonwealth

The Joint Japan/World Bank Graduate Scholarship Program (JJ/WBGSP), 395
Wingate Scholarships, 771

Canada

Wingate Scholarships, 771

Caribbean Countries

The Joint Japan/World Bank Graduate Scholarship Program (JJ/WBGSP), 395

East European Countries

CERN Doctoral Student Programme, 251
CERN Fellowships, 251
CERN Technical Student Programme, 251
The Joint Japan/World Bank Graduate Scholarship Program (JJ/WBGSP), 395

Far East

The Joint Japan/World Bank Graduate Scholarship Program (JJ/WBGSP), 395

Indian Sub-Continent

The Joint Japan/World Bank Graduate Scholarship Program (JJ/WBGSP), 395
Wingate Scholarships, 771

Middle East

The Joint Japan/World Bank Graduate Scholarship Program (JJ/WBGSP), 395

New Zealand

Wingate Scholarships, 771

South Africa

The Joint Japan/World Bank Graduate Scholarship Program (JJ/WBGSP), 395
Wingate Scholarships, 771

South America

The Joint Japan/World Bank Graduate Scholarship Program (JJ/WBGSP), 395

United Kingdom

CERN Doctoral Student Programme, 251
CERN Fellowships, 251
CERN Technical Student Programme, 251
University of Wales (Aberystwyth) Postgraduate Research Studentships, 752
Wingate Scholarships, 771

United States of America

American Society of Naval Engineers Scholarships, 93
Winston Churchill Scholarship, 771

West European Countries

CERN Doctoral Student Programme, 251
CERN Fellowships, 251
CERN Technical Student Programme, 251
Wingate Scholarships, 771

ELECTRICAL/ELECTRONIC AND TELECOMMUNICATIONS ENGINEERING

Any Country

Central Queensland University Postgraduate Research Award, 248
CQU International Student Scholarship, 248
The D H Thomas Travel Bursary, 385
DEED Scholarship, 77
Hudswell Bequest Travelling Fellowships, 386
Hudswell International Research Scholarships, 386
IEE Master's Degree Research Scholarship, 386
IEE Postgraduate Scholarships, 386
IEE Younger Members Conference Bursary, 386
J R Beard Travelling Fund Awards, 387
John Moyes Lessells Scholarships, 614
Johnson's Wax Research Fellowship, 459
The Leonard Research Grant, 387
Leslie H Paddle Fellowship, 387
Massey Doctoral Scholarship, 461
Mechanical/Electrical Building Systems Travelling Fellowship, 633
Milwaukee Foundation's Frank Rogers Bacon Research Assistantship, 459
National Research Council Laboratories Research Associateships, 516
The Princess Royal Scholarship, 387
Queen Mary Research Studentships, 576
Robinson Research Scholarship, 387
TUCS Postgraduate Grant, 678
University of Bristol Postgraduate Scholarships, 691
University of Dundee Research Awards, 704
University of Glasgow Postgraduate Research Scholarships, 707

Australia

Fulbright Postgraduate Student Award for Engineering, 144
Fulbright Postgraduate Student Award for Science and Engineering, 144
University of Western Sydney Postgraduate Research Award (UWSPRA), 755
Wingate Scholarships, 771

British Commonwealth

Wingate Scholarships, 771

Canada

Swiss Federal Institute of Technology Scholarships, 669
Wingate Scholarships, 771

East European Countries

CERN Doctoral Student Programme, 251
CERN Fellowships, 251
CERN Technical Student Programme, 251
Swiss Federal Institute of Technology Scholarships, 669

Far East

Swiss Federal Institute of Technology Scholarships, 669

Indian Sub-Continent

Wingate Scholarships, 771

New Zealand

University of Western Sydney Postgraduate Research Award
(UWSPRA), 755
Wingate Scholarships, 771

South Africa

Wingate Scholarships, 771

United Kingdom

Cardiff University Postgraduate Research Studentships, 242
CERN Doctoral Student Programme, 251
CERN Fellowships, 251
CERN Technical Student Programme, 251
The Lord Lloyd of Kilgerran Memorial Prize (Postgraduate Award),
387
NTU AEH Exchange Studentships, 487
Swiss Federal Institute of Technology Scholarships, 669
The University of Kent at Canterbury Department of Electronics Studentships, 710
University of Wales, Bangor (UWB) Research Studentships, 753
University of Wales, Bangor Departmental Research Studentships,
753
Wingate Scholarships, 771

United States of America

American Society of Naval Engineers Scholarships, 93
Army Research Laboratory Postdoctoral Fellowship Program, 85
ONR Postdoctoral Fellowship, 539
ONR/ASEE Postdoctoral Fellowship Program, 85
SRC Graduate Fellowship Program, 624
SRC Master's Scholarship Program, 625
Swiss Federal Institute of Technology Scholarships, 669
Winston Churchill Scholarship, 771

West European Countries

Cardiff University Postgraduate Research Studentships, 242
CERN Doctoral Student Programme, 251
CERN Fellowships, 251
CERN Technical Student Programme, 251
NTU AEH Exchange Studentships, 487
Swiss Federal Institute of Technology Scholarships, 669
The University of Kent at Canterbury Department of Electronics Studentships, 710
University of Wales, Bangor (UWB) Research Studentships, 753
University of Wales, Bangor Departmental Research Studentships,
753
Wingate Scholarships, 771

COMPUTER ENGINEERING

Any Country

CDI Internship, 246

Central Queensland University Postgraduate Research Award, 248
CQU International Student Scholarship, 248
DEED Scholarship, 77
ESRF Postdoctoral Fellowships, 306
Golden Key National Honor Society Information Systems Achievement Awards, 339
John Moyes Lessells Scholarships, 614
Massey Doctoral Scholarship, 461
Queen Mary Research Studentships, 576
TUCS Postgraduate Grant, 678
University of Bristol Postgraduate Scholarships, 691
University of New England Research Scholarships, 719

Australia

Fulbright Postgraduate Student Award for Engineering, 144
Fulbright Postgraduate Student Award for Science and Engineering,
144
University of Western Sydney Postgraduate Research Award
(UWSPRA), 755
Wingate Scholarships, 771

British Commonwealth

Wingate Scholarships, 771

Canada

Swiss Federal Institute of Technology Scholarships, 669
Wingate Scholarships, 771

East European Countries

CERN Doctoral Student Programme, 251
CERN Fellowships, 251
CERN Technical Student Programme, 251
Swiss Federal Institute of Technology Scholarships, 669

Far East

Swiss Federal Institute of Technology Scholarships, 669

Indian Sub-Continent

Wingate Scholarships, 771

New Zealand

University of Western Sydney Postgraduate Research Award
(UWSPRA), 755
Wingate Scholarships, 771

South Africa

Wingate Scholarships, 771

United Kingdom

Cardiff University Postgraduate Research Studentships, 242
CERN Doctoral Student Programme, 251
CERN Fellowships, 251
CERN Technical Student Programme, 251
ESRF Thesis Studentships, 306
NTU AEH Exchange Studentships, 487
The Royal Academy of Engineering International Travel Grants, 593
Swiss Federal Institute of Technology Scholarships, 669
The University of Kent at Canterbury Department of Electronics Studentships, 710
University of Wales (Aberystwyth) Postgraduate Research Studentships, 752
University of Wales, Bangor (UWB) Research Studentships, 753
University of Wales, Bangor Departmental Research Studentships,
753
Wingate Scholarships, 771

United States of America

American Society of Naval Engineers Scholarships, 93
Army Research Laboratory Postdoctoral Fellowship Program, 85
ONR Postdoctoral Fellowship, 539
ONR/ASEE Postdoctoral Fellowship Program, 85
SRC Graduate Fellowship Program, 624

SRC Master's Scholarship Program, 625
Swiss Federal Institute of Technology Scholarships, 669
Winston Churchill Scholarship, 771

West European Countries

Cardiff University Postgraduate Research Studentships, 242
CERN Doctoral Student Programme, 251
CERN Fellowships, 251
CERN Technical Student Programme, 251
ESRF Thesis Studentships, 306
NTU AEH Exchange Studentships, 487
Swiss Federal Institute of Technology Scholarships, 669
The University of Kent at Canterbury Department of Electronics Studentships, 710
University of Wales, Bangor (UWB) Research Studentships, 753
University of Wales, Bangor Departmental Research Studentships, 753
Wingate Scholarships, 771

INDUSTRIAL AND MANAGEMENT ENGINEERING

Any Country

Anglo-German Foundation for the Study of Industrial Society Research Grant, 101
DEED Scholarship, 77
John Moyes Lessells Scholarships, 614
Johnson's Wax Research Fellowship, 459
Kenward Memorial Fellowship, 690
Massey Doctoral Scholarship, 461
University of Bristol Postgraduate Scholarships, 691

African Nations

The Joint Japan/World Bank Graduate Scholarship Program (JJ/WBGSP), 395

Australia

Fulbright Postgraduate Student Award for Engineering, 144
Fulbright Postgraduate Student Award for Science and Engineering, 144
Wingate Scholarships, 771

British Commonwealth

The Joint Japan/World Bank Graduate Scholarship Program (JJ/WBGSP), 395
Wingate Scholarships, 771

Canada

Swiss Federal Institute of Technology Scholarships, 669
Wingate Scholarships, 771

Caribbean Countries

The Joint Japan/World Bank Graduate Scholarship Program (JJ/WBGSP), 395

East European Countries

The Joint Japan/World Bank Graduate Scholarship Program (JJ/WBGSP), 395
Swiss Federal Institute of Technology Scholarships, 669

Far East

The Joint Japan/World Bank Graduate Scholarship Program (JJ/WBGSP), 395
Swiss Federal Institute of Technology Scholarships, 669

Indian Sub-Continent

The Joint Japan/World Bank Graduate Scholarship Program (JJ/WBGSP), 395
Wingate Scholarships, 771

Middle East

The Joint Japan/World Bank Graduate Scholarship Program (JJ/WBGSP), 395

New Zealand

Wingate Scholarships, 771

South Africa

The Joint Japan/World Bank Graduate Scholarship Program (JJ/WBGSP), 395
Wingate Scholarships, 771

South America

The Joint Japan/World Bank Graduate Scholarship Program (JJ/WBGSP), 395

United Kingdom

Cardiff University Postgraduate Research Studentships, 242
Royal Commission Industrial Fellowships, 599
Swiss Federal Institute of Technology Scholarships, 669
Wingate Scholarships, 771

United States of America

American Society of Naval Engineers Scholarships, 93
ONR Postdoctoral Fellowship, 539
SWE General Motors Foundation Graduate Scholarship, 657
Swiss Federal Institute of Technology Scholarships, 669
Winston Churchill Scholarship, 771

West European Countries

Cardiff University Postgraduate Research Studentships, 242
Swiss Federal Institute of Technology Scholarships, 669
Wingate Scholarships, 771

METALLURGICAL ENGINEERING

Any Country

DEED Scholarship, 77
John Moyes Lessells Scholarships, 614
University of Manchester Research Studentships and Scholarships, 715
Welch Foundation Scholarship, 416

Australia

Fulbright Postgraduate Student Award for Engineering, 144
Fulbright Postgraduate Student Award for Science and Engineering, 144
Wingate Scholarships, 771

British Commonwealth

Wingate Scholarships, 771

Canada

Wingate Scholarships, 771

Indian Sub-Continent

Wingate Scholarships, 771

New Zealand

Wingate Scholarships, 771

South Africa

Wingate Scholarships, 771

United Kingdom

Cardiff University Postgraduate Research Studentships, 242
Sheffield Hallam University Research Studentships, 625
Wingate Scholarships, 771

United States of America

American Society of Naval Engineers Scholarships, 93

Army Research Laboratory Postdoctoral Fellowship Program, 85
ONR Postdoctoral Fellowship, 539
ONR/ASEE Postdoctoral Fellowship Program, 85
Winston Churchill Scholarship, 771

West European Countries

Cardiff University Postgraduate Research Studentships, 242
Sheffield Hallam University Research Studentships, 625
Wingate Scholarships, 771

PRODUCTION ENGINEERING

Any Country

DEED Scholarship, 77
John Moyes Lessells Scholarships, 614
Kenward Memorial Fellowship, 690
Massey Doctoral Scholarship, 461
University of Manchester Research Studentships and Scholarships, 715

Australia

Fulbright Postgraduate Student Award for Engineering, 144
Fulbright Postgraduate Student Award for Science and Engineering, 144
Wingate Scholarships, 771

British Commonwealth

Wingate Scholarships, 771

Canada

SME Education Foundation Grants Program, 634
Swiss Federal Institute of Technology Scholarships, 669
Wingate Scholarships, 771

East European Countries

Swiss Federal Institute of Technology Scholarships, 669

Far East

Swiss Federal Institute of Technology Scholarships, 669

Indian Sub-Continent

Wingate Scholarships, 771

New Zealand

Wingate Scholarships, 771

South Africa

Wingate Scholarships, 771

United Kingdom

Cardiff University Postgraduate Research Studentships, 242
Swiss Federal Institute of Technology Scholarships, 669
Wingate Scholarships, 771

United States of America

SME Education Foundation Grants Program, 634
Swiss Federal Institute of Technology Scholarships, 669
Winston Churchill Scholarship, 771

West European Countries

Cardiff University Postgraduate Research Studentships, 242
Swiss Federal Institute of Technology Scholarships, 669
Wingate Scholarships, 771

MATERIALS ENGINEERING

Any Country

Central Queensland University Postgraduate Research Award, 248
CQU International Student Scholarship, 248
DEED Scholarship, 77
ESRF Postdoctoral Fellowships, 306

John Moyes Lessells Scholarships, 614
Johnson's Wax Research Fellowship, 459
Kenward Memorial Fellowship, 690
Linacre College Applied Materials Scholarships, 729
Queen Mary Research Studentships, 576
Trinity College Kandiah Thirunavukkarasu Graduate Scholarship, 745
The University of Western Ontario Senior Visiting Fellowship, 755
Welch Foundation Scholarship, 416

Australia

Fulbright Postgraduate Student Award for Engineering, 144
Fulbright Postgraduate Student Award for Science and Engineering, 144
University of Western Sydney Postgraduate Research Award (UWSPRA), 755
Wingate Scholarships, 771

British Commonwealth

Wingate Scholarships, 771

Canada

Swiss Federal Institute of Technology Scholarships, 669
Wingate Scholarships, 771

East European Countries

CERN Doctoral Student Programme, 251
CERN Fellowships, 251
CERN Technical Student Programme, 251
Swiss Federal Institute of Technology Scholarships, 669

Far East

Swiss Federal Institute of Technology Scholarships, 669

Indian Sub-Continent

Wingate Scholarships, 771

New Zealand

University of Western Sydney Postgraduate Research Award (UWSPRA), 755
Wingate Scholarships, 771

South Africa

Wingate Scholarships, 771

United Kingdom

Cardiff University Postgraduate Research Studentships, 242
CERN Doctoral Student Programme, 251
CERN Fellowships, 251
CERN Technical Student Programme, 251
The Royal Academy of Engineering International Travel Grants, 593
Swiss Federal Institute of Technology Scholarships, 669
Wingate Scholarships, 771

United States of America

American Society of Naval Engineers Scholarships, 93
Army Research Laboratory Postdoctoral Fellowship Program, 85
ONR Postdoctoral Fellowship, 539
ONR/ASEE Postdoctoral Fellowship Program, 85
SRC Graduate Fellowship Program, 624
SRC Master's Scholarship Program, 625
SWE General Motors Foundation Graduate Scholarship, 657
Swiss Federal Institute of Technology Scholarships, 669
Winston Churchill Scholarship, 771

West European Countries

Cardiff University Postgraduate Research Studentships, 242
CERN Doctoral Student Programme, 251
CERN Fellowships, 251
CERN Technical Student Programme, 251
Swiss Federal Institute of Technology Scholarships, 669
Wingate Scholarships, 771

MINING AND MINERALS ENGINEERING

Any Country

Bosworth Smith Trust Fund, 390
Chrysalis Scholarship, 126
DEED Scholarship, 77
G Vernon Hobson Bequest, 391
John Moyes Lessells Scholarships, 614
Stanley Elmore Fellowships, 391

Australia

Edgar Pam Fellowship, 391
Fulbright Postgraduate Student Award for Engineering, 144
Fulbright Postgraduate Student Award for Science and Engineering, 144
Wingate Scholarships, 771

British Commonwealth

Wingate Scholarships, 771

Canada

Edgar Pam Fellowship, 391
Wingate Scholarships, 771

East European Countries

Natural History Museum Sys-Resource, 522

Far East

Stephen and Anna Hui Fellowship, 366

Indian Sub-Continent

Wingate Scholarships, 771

New Zealand

Edgar Pam Fellowship, 391
Wingate Scholarships, 771

South Africa

Edgar Pam Fellowship, 391
Wingate Scholarships, 771

United Kingdom

Cardiff University Postgraduate Research Studentships, 242
Edgar Pam Fellowship, 391
Mining Club Award, 391
Polish Embassy Short-Term Bursaries, 571
Polish Government Postgraduate Scholarships Scheme, 572
Wingate Scholarships, 771

United States of America

Winston Churchill Scholarship, 771

West European Countries

Cardiff University Postgraduate Research Studentships, 242
Natural History Museum Sys-Resource, 522
Wingate Scholarships, 771

PETROLEUM ENGINEERING

Any Country

ACS/PRF Scientific Education Grants, 38
ACS/PRF Type AC Grants, 38
ACS/PRF Type B Grants, 38
Chrysalis Scholarship, 126
DEED Scholarship, 77
Exxon Mobil Engineering Teaching Fellowships, 592
John Moyes Lessells Scholarships, 614

Australia

Fulbright Postgraduate Student Award for Engineering, 144

Fulbright Postgraduate Student Award for Science and Engineering, 144
Wingate Scholarships, 771

British Commonwealth

Wingate Scholarships, 771

Canada

Wingate Scholarships, 771

Far East

Stephen and Anna Hui Fellowship, 366

Indian Sub-Continent

Wingate Scholarships, 771

New Zealand

Wingate Scholarships, 771

South Africa

Wingate Scholarships, 771

United Kingdom

Wingate Scholarships, 771

United States of America

Winston Churchill Scholarship, 771

West European Countries

Wingate Scholarships, 771

ENERGY ENGINEERING

Any Country

The Alberta Research Council Scholarship, 692
ASHRAE Grants-in-Aid for Graduate Students, 92
Center for Field Research Grants, 246
Chrysalis Scholarship, 126
Conservation and Research Foundation Grants, 267
DEED Scholarship, 77
Deputy Chancellors Postdoctoral Research, 535
John Moyes Lessells Scholarships, 614
Kenward Memorial Fellowship, 690
Mechanical/Electrical Building Systems Travelling Fellowship, 633
NSERC Strategic Project Grants (SPG), 525
NTU One Year Postdoctoral Fellowship, 535
NTU Senior Research Fellowship, 536
NTU Three Year Postdoctoral Fellowship, 536
University of Manchester Research Studentships and Scholarships, 715

African Nations

The Joint Japan/World Bank Graduate Scholarship Program (JJ/WBGSP), 395

Australia

Fulbright Postgraduate Student Award for Engineering, 144
Fulbright Postgraduate Student Award for Science and Engineering, 144
Wingate Scholarships, 771

British Commonwealth

The Joint Japan/World Bank Graduate Scholarship Program (JJ/WBGSP), 395
Wingate Scholarships, 771

Canada

Wingate Scholarships, 771

Caribbean Countries

The Joint Japan/World Bank Graduate Scholarship Program (JJ/WBGSP), 395

East European Countries

The Joint Japan/World Bank Graduate Scholarship Program (JJ/WBGSP), 395
VKI Fellowship, 764

Far East

The Joint Japan/World Bank Graduate Scholarship Program (JJ/WBGSP), 395

Indian Sub-Continent

The Joint Japan/World Bank Graduate Scholarship Program (JJ/WBGSP), 395
Wingate Scholarships, 771

Middle East

The Joint Japan/World Bank Graduate Scholarship Program (JJ/WBGSP), 395

New Zealand

Wingate Scholarships, 771

South Africa

The Joint Japan/World Bank Graduate Scholarship Program (JJ/WBGSP), 395
Wingate Scholarships, 771

South America

The Joint Japan/World Bank Graduate Scholarship Program (JJ/WBGSP), 395

United Kingdom

Cardiff University Postgraduate Research Studentships, 242
Wingate Scholarships, 771

United States of America

VKI Fellowship, 764
Winston Churchill Scholarship, 771

West European Countries

Cardiff University Postgraduate Research Studentships, 242
VKI Fellowship, 764
Wingate Scholarships, 771

NUCLEAR ENGINEERING

Any Country

AINSE Grants, 140
DEED Scholarship, 77
John Moyes Lessells Scholarships, 614
University of Manchester Research Studentships and Scholarships, 715

Australia

Fulbright Postgraduate Student Award for Engineering, 144
Fulbright Postgraduate Student Award for Science and Engineering, 144
Wingate Scholarships, 771

British Commonwealth

Wingate Scholarships, 771

Canada

Wingate Scholarships, 771

East European Countries

CERN Doctoral Student Programme, 251
CERN Fellowships, 251
CERN Technical Student Programme, 251

Indian Sub-Continent

Wingate Scholarships, 771

New Zealand

Wingate Scholarships, 771

South Africa

Wingate Scholarships, 771

United Kingdom

CERN Doctoral Student Programme, 251
CERN Fellowships, 251
CERN Technical Student Programme, 251
Wingate Scholarships, 771

United States of America

American Society of Naval Engineers Scholarships, 93
ONR Postdoctoral Fellowship, 539
Winston Churchill Scholarship, 771

West European Countries

CERN Doctoral Student Programme, 251
CERN Fellowships, 251
CERN Technical Student Programme, 251
Wingate Scholarships, 771

MECHANICAL/ELECTROMECHANICAL ENGINEERING

Any Country

ASHRAE Grants-in-Aid for Graduate Students, 92
BP/RSE Research Fellowships, 613
Central Queensland University Postgraduate Research Award, 248
CQU International Student Scholarship, 248
DEED Scholarship, 77
ESRF Postdoctoral Fellowships, 306
Exxon Mobil Engineering Teaching Fellowships, 592
Flatman Grants, 388
James Clayton Awards, 389
James Clayton Lectures, 389
James Clayton Overseas Conference Travel for Senior Engineers, 389
James Clayton Postgraduate Hardship Award, 389
James Watt International Medal, 389
John Moyes Lessells Scholarships, 614
Kenward Memorial Fellowship, 690
Labrow Grants, 390
Massey Doctoral Scholarship, 461
Mechanical/Electrical Building Systems Travelling Fellowship, 633
Neil Watson Grants, 390
Queen Mary Research Studentships, 576
Thomas Andrew Common Grants, 390
University of Bristol Postgraduate Scholarships, 691
University of Dundee Research Awards, 704
University of Edinburgh Faculty of Science and Engineering Scholarship, 705
University of Glasgow Postgraduate Research Scholarships, 707
University of Manchester Research Studentships and Scholarships, 715

Australia

Fulbright Postgraduate Student Award for Engineering, 144
Fulbright Postgraduate Student Award for Science and Engineering, 144
Wingate Scholarships, 771

British Commonwealth

Wingate Scholarships, 771

Canada

Horticultural Research Institute Grants, 359
Paralyzed Veterans of America Research Grants, 552
Wingate Scholarships, 771

HYDRAULIC/PNEUMATIC ENGINEERING

SOUND ENGINEERING

Indian Sub-Continent

Wingate Scholarships, 771

New Zealand

Wingate Scholarships, 771

South Africa

Wingate Scholarships, 771

United Kingdom

Wingate Scholarships, 771

United States of America

American Society of Naval Engineers Scholarships, 93
Winston Churchill Scholarship, 771

West European Countries

Wingate Scholarships, 771

AUTOMOTIVE ENGINEERING

Any Country

Conservation and Research Foundation Grants, 267
John Moyes Lessells Scholarships, 614
Kenward Memorial Fellowship, 690
Massey Doctoral Scholarship, 461
University of Bristol Postgraduate Scholarships, 691

Australia

Fulbright Postgraduate Student Award for Engineering, 144
Fulbright Postgraduate Student Award for Science and Engineering, 144
Wingate Scholarships, 771

British Commonwealth

Wingate Scholarships, 771

Canada

Wingate Scholarships, 771

Indian Sub-Continent

Wingate Scholarships, 771

New Zealand

Wingate Scholarships, 771

South Africa

Wingate Scholarships, 771

United Kingdom

University of Wales (Aberystwyth) Postgraduate Research Studentships, 752
Wingate Scholarships, 771

United States of America

Winston Churchill Scholarship, 771

West European Countries

Wingate Scholarships, 771

MEASUREMENT/PRECISION ENGINEERING

Any Country

ESRF Postdoctoral Fellowships, 306
John Moyes Lessells Scholarships, 614
Kenward Memorial Fellowship, 690

Australia

Fulbright Postgraduate Student Award for Engineering, 144
Fulbright Postgraduate Student Award for Science and Engineering, 144

Wingate Scholarships, 771

British Commonwealth

Wingate Scholarships, 771

Canada

Wingate Scholarships, 771

Indian Sub-Continent

Wingate Scholarships, 771

New Zealand

Wingate Scholarships, 771

South Africa

Wingate Scholarships, 771

United Kingdom

ESRF Thesis Studentships, 306
Wingate Scholarships, 771

United States of America

American Society of Naval Engineers Scholarships, 93
Winston Churchill Scholarship, 771

West European Countries

ESRF Thesis Studentships, 306
Wingate Scholarships, 771

CONTROL ENGINEERING (ROBOTICS)

Any Country

BP/RSE Research Fellowships, 613
Central Queensland University Postgraduate Research Award, 248
CQU International Student Scholarship, 248
John Moyes Lessells Scholarships, 614
Kenward Memorial Fellowship, 690

Australia

Fulbright Postgraduate Student Award for Engineering, 144
Fulbright Postgraduate Student Award for Science and Engineering, 144
University of Western Sydney Postgraduate Research Award (UWSPRA), 755
Wingate Scholarships, 771

British Commonwealth

Wingate Scholarships, 771

Canada

Horticultural Research Institute Grants, 359
Wingate Scholarships, 771

Indian Sub-Continent

Wingate Scholarships, 771

New Zealand

University of Western Sydney Postgraduate Research Award (UWSPRA), 755
Wingate Scholarships, 771

South Africa

Wingate Scholarships, 771

United Kingdom

Cardiff University Postgraduate Research Studentships, 242
University of Wales (Aberystwyth) Postgraduate Research Studentships, 752
Wingate Scholarships, 771

United States of America

American Society of Naval Engineers Scholarships, 93

Army Research Laboratory Postdoctoral Fellowship Program, 85
Horticultural Research Institute Grants, 359
Winston Churchill Scholarship, 771

West European Countries

Cardiff University Postgraduate Research Studentships, 242
Wingate Scholarships, 771

AERONAUTICAL AND AEROSPACE ENGINEERING

Any Country

A Verville Fellowship, 636
Amelia Earhart Fellowship Awards, 783
The Guggenheim Fellowships, 636
John Moyes Lessells Scholarships, 614
Kenward Memorial Fellowship, 690
National Air and Space Museum Aviation/Space Writers Award, 637
Queen Mary Research Studentships, 576
Ramsay Fellowship in Naval Aviation History, 637
University of Bristol Postgraduate Scholarships, 691
University of Glasgow Postgraduate Research Scholarships, 707
University of Manchester Research Studentships and Scholarships, 715

Australia

Fulbright Postgraduate Student Award for Engineering, 144
Fulbright Postgraduate Student Award for Science and Engineering, 144
Wingate Scholarships, 771

British Commonwealth

Handley Page Award, 595
Wingate Scholarships, 771

Canada

Wingate Scholarships, 771

East European Countries

VKI Fellowship, 764

Indian Sub-Continent

Wingate Scholarships, 771

New Zealand

Wingate Scholarships, 771

South Africa

Wingate Scholarships, 771

United Kingdom

Handley Page Award, 595
Wingate Scholarships, 771

United States of America

American Society of Naval Engineers Scholarships, 93
ONR Postdoctoral Fellowship, 539
ONR/ASEE Postdoctoral Fellowship Program, 85
VKI Fellowship, 764
Winston Churchill Scholarship, 771

West European Countries

VKI Fellowship, 764
Wingate Scholarships, 771

MARINE ENGINEERING AND NAVAL ARCHITECTURE

Any Country

Froude Research Scholarship in Naval Architecture, 604

Gustave Willems Award, 406
John Moyes Lessells Scholarships, 614
Sir William White Postgraduate Scholarship in Naval Architecture, 605
Society of Naval Architects and Marine Engineers Graduate Scholarships, 656
University of Glasgow Postgraduate Research Scholarships, 707
Woods Hole Oceanographic Institution Postdoctoral Fellowships in Ocean Science and Engineering, 777
Woods Hole Oceanographic Institution/NOAA Co-operative Institute for Climate and Ocean Research Postdoctoral Fellowship, 778

Australia

Fulbright Postgraduate Student Award for Engineering, 144
Fulbright Postgraduate Student Award for Science and Engineering, 144
Wingate Scholarships, 771

British Commonwealth

Wingate Scholarships, 771

Canada

Wingate Scholarships, 771

Indian Sub-Continent

Wingate Scholarships, 771

New Zealand

Wingate Scholarships, 771

South Africa

Wingate Scholarships, 771

United Kingdom

Wingate Scholarships, 771

United States of America

American Society of Naval Engineers Scholarships, 93
ONR/ASEE Postdoctoral Fellowship Program, 85

West European Countries

Wingate Scholarships, 771

AGRICULTURAL ENGINEERING

Any Country

BBSRC Research Fellowships, 154
BBSRC Research Grants, 154
BBSRC Studentships, 155
DEED Scholarship, 77
John Moyes Lessells Scholarships, 614
Massey Doctoral Scholarship, 461
QUEST Institution of Civil Engineers Overseas Travel Awards, 385
The Walsh Fellowships, 671

African Nations

The Joint Japan/World Bank Graduate Scholarship Program (JJ/WBGSP), 395

Australia

Fulbright Postgraduate Student Award for Engineering, 144
Fulbright Postgraduate Student Award for Science and Engineering, 144
Wingate Scholarships, 771

British Commonwealth

The Joint Japan/World Bank Graduate Scholarship Program (JJ/WBGSP), 395
Wingate Scholarships, 771

Canada

Canadian Window on International Development, 399

EDUCATION AND TEACHER TRAINING

GENERAL

Fulbright Postdoctoral Fellowships, 143
Fulbright Postdoctoral Research and Lecturing Awards for Non-US Citizens, 270
Fulbright Postgraduate Studentships, 144
Fulbright Professional Award for Vocational Education and Training, 145
University of Western Sydney Postgraduate Research Award (UWSPRA), 755
Wingate Scholarships, 771

British Commonwealth

Friends of Peterhouse Bursary, 561
Merton College Reed Foundation Scholarship, 732
Wingate Scholarships, 771
Wolfson Foundation Grants, 773

Canada

Friends of Peterhouse Bursary, 561
Fulbright Postdoctoral Research and Lecturing Awards for Non-US Citizens, 270
J W McConnell Memorial Fellowships, 266
The Jim Bourque Scholarship, 105
PRA Fellowships, 549
SSHRC Doctoral Fellowships, 646
SSHRC Major Collaborative Research Initiatives (MCRI), 646
SSHRC Research Development Initiatives, 647
SSHRC Standard Research Grants, 647
UNBF Teaching Assistantships (Markers), 719
Wingate Scholarships, 771

Caribbean Countries

Friends of Peterhouse Bursary, 561
Merton College Reed Foundation Scholarship, 732
PRA Fellowships, 549

East European Countries

Friends of Peterhouse Bursary, 561
Fulbright Postdoctoral Research and Lecturing Awards for Non-US Citizens, 270
Merton College Reed Foundation Scholarship, 732

Far East

COSTED Travel Fellowship, 262
Friends of Peterhouse Bursary, 561
Fulbright Postdoctoral Research and Lecturing Awards for Non-US Citizens, 270
Japanese American Citizens League Scholarship and Award Program, 422
Merton College Reed Foundation Scholarship, 732

Indian Sub-Continent

COSTED Travel Fellowship, 262
Friends of Peterhouse Bursary, 561
Fulbright Postdoctoral Research and Lecturing Awards for Non-US Citizens, 270
Merton College Reed Foundation Scholarship, 732
Wingate Scholarships, 771

Middle East

ABCCF Student Grant, 103
Friends of Peterhouse Bursary, 561
Fulbright Postdoctoral Research and Lecturing Awards for Non-US Citizens, 270
Merton College Reed Foundation Scholarship, 732

New Zealand

Friends of Peterhouse Bursary, 561
Fulbright Postdoctoral Research and Lecturing Awards for Non-US Citizens, 270
University of Western Sydney Postgraduate Research Award (UWSPRA), 755
Wingate Scholarships, 771

South Africa

Allan Gray Senior Scholarship, 585
Friends of Peterhouse Bursary, 561
Fulbright Postdoctoral Research and Lecturing Awards for Non-US Citizens, 270
Isie Smuts Research Award, 658
Norah Taylor Bursary, 659
NRF Bursaries for Study towards an Honours Degree, 517
NRF Doctoral Scholarships and Postdoctoral Fellowships for Study Abroad, 517
NRF Fellowships for Postdoctoral Research, 517
NRF Scholarships for Doctoral Study, 517
NRF Scholarships for Master's Study, 518
South African Council for English Education (EX-PCE Bursary), 659
Wingate Scholarships, 771
Wolfson Foundation Grants, 773

South America

Friends of Peterhouse Bursary, 561
Fulbright Commission (Argentina) Master's Program, 325
Fulbright Postdoctoral Research and Lecturing Awards for Non-US Citizens, 270
Merton College Reed Foundation Scholarship, 732
PRA Fellowships, 549

United Kingdom

British Schools and Universities Foundation May and Ward Scholarships, 179
Canada Memorial Foundation Scholarships, 222
Cardiff University Postgraduate Research Studentships, 242
Frank Knox Fellowships at Harvard University, 319
Fulbright Postdoctoral Research and Lecturing Awards for Non-US Citizens, 270
Sheffield Hallam University Research Studentships, 625
University of Wales (Aberystwyth) Postgraduate Research Studentships, 752
University of Wales, Bangor (UWB) Research Studentships, 753
University of Wales, Bangor Departmental Research Studentships, 753
Walter Hines Page Scholarships, 130
Wingate Scholarships, 771
Winston Churchill Memorial Trust (UK) Fellowships, 772
Wolfson Foundation Grants, 773

United States of America

AIGC Fellowship, 54
ASME Graduate Teaching Fellowship Program, 123
Bicentennial Swedish-American Exchange Fund, 667
Bicentennial Swedish-American Exchange Fund Travel Grants, 153
British Schools and Universities Foundation May and Ward Scholarships, 179
Catching The Dream, 244
Dow Jones Teacher Fellowship Program, 286
ETS Postdoctoral Fellowships, 294
Federal Chancellor Scholarship, 20
Friends of Peterhouse Bursary, 561
Fulbright Scholar Awards for Research and Lecturing Abroad for United States Citizens, 271
Fulbright Scholar Program for US Citizens, 271
Fulbright Senior Specialists Program, 271
Fulbright Teacher and Administrator Exchange, 325
Ian Axford (New Zealand) Fellowships in Public Policy, 263
Japanese American Citizens League Scholarship and Award Program, 422
Kennan Institute Research Scholarship, 431
NEA Foundation Innovation Grants, 525
North Dakota Indian Scholarship, 535
PRA Fellowships, 549
Robert H Michel Civic Education Grants, 286
UCLA IAC Postdoctoral/Visiting Scholar Fellowships, 680

West European Countries

Cardiff University Postgraduate Research Studentships, 242

Friends of Peterhouse Bursary, 561

Fulbright Postdoctoral Research and Lecturing Awards for Non-US Citizens, 270

Scholarship Foundation of the League for Finnish-American Societies, 621

Sheffield Hallam University Research Studentships, 625

University of Wales, Bangor (UWB) Research Studentships, 753

University of Wales, Bangor Departmental Research Studentships, 753

Wingate Scholarships, 771

NONVOCATIONAL SUBJECTS EDUCATION

Any Country

Alexander S Onassis Programme of Research Grants, 18

Alexander S Onassis Research Grants, 18

Camargo Fellowships, 185

Central Queensland University Postgraduate Research Award, 248

Equiano Memorial Award, 666

National Academy of Education Spencer Postdoctoral Fellowships, 489

University of Stirling Research Studentships, 750

African Nations

The Joint Japan/World Bank Graduate Scholarship Program (JJ/WBGSP), 395

Australia

University of Western Sydney Postgraduate Research Award (UWSPRA), 755

British Commonwealth

The Joint Japan/World Bank Graduate Scholarship Program (JJ/WBGSP), 395

Caribbean Countries

The Joint Japan/World Bank Graduate Scholarship Program (JJ/WBGSP), 395

East European Countries

The Joint Japan/World Bank Graduate Scholarship Program (JJ/WBGSP), 395

Far East

The Joint Japan/World Bank Graduate Scholarship Program (JJ/WBGSP), 395

Indian Sub-Continent

The Joint Japan/World Bank Graduate Scholarship Program (JJ/WBGSP), 395

Middle East

The Joint Japan/World Bank Graduate Scholarship Program (JJ/WBGSP), 395

New Zealand

University of Western Sydney Postgraduate Research Award (UWSPRA), 755

South Africa

The Joint Japan/World Bank Graduate Scholarship Program (JJ/WBGSP), 395

South America

The Joint Japan/World Bank Graduate Scholarship Program (JJ/WBGSP), 395

EDUCATION IN NATIVE LANGUAGE

Any Country

Alexander S Onassis Programme of Research Grants, 18

Alexander S Onassis Research Grants, 18

AUC Writing Center Graduate Fellowships, 97

ETS Summer Program in Research for Graduate Students, 294

Massey Doctoral Scholarship, 461

National Academy of Education Spencer Postdoctoral Fellowships, 489

Onassis Programme of Postgraduate Research Scholarships, 19

Onassis Programme of Scholarships for Post-Educational Training for Teachers of the Greek Language, 19

Canada

Horticultural Research Institute Grants, 359

East European Countries

Soros Supplementary Grants Programme (SSGP), 544

South Africa

Norah Taylor Bursary, 659

United Kingdom

UK Government Grants, 442

Universita' Per Stranieri Di Siena Doctorate in Italian Language and Culture (with an intertextual approach), 687

Universita' Per Stranieri Di Siena Doctorate in the Teaching of Italian to Foreigners, 687

University of Wales (Aberystwyth) Postgraduate Research Studentships, 752

University of Wales, Bangor (UWB) Research Studentships, 753

University of Wales, Bangor Departmental Research Studentships, 753

United States of America

Fulbright Teacher and Administrator Exchange, 325

Horticultural Research Institute Grants, 359

West European Countries

Universita' Per Stranieri Di Siena Doctorate in Italian Language and Culture (with an intertextual approach), 687

Universita' Per Stranieri Di Siena Doctorate in the Teaching of Italian to Foreigners, 687

University of Wales, Bangor (UWB) Research Studentships, 753

University of Wales, Bangor Departmental Research Studentships, 753

FOREIGN LANGUAGES EDUCATION

Any Country

Alexander S Onassis Programme of Research Grants, 18

Alexander S Onassis Research Grants, 18

Camargo Fellowships, 185

Equiano Memorial Award, 666

ETS Summer Program in Research for Graduate Students, 294

LCCIEB Examinations Board Scholarships, 452

National Academy of Education Spencer Postdoctoral Fellowships, 489

Onassis Programme of Postgraduate Research Scholarships, 19

Onassis Programme of Scholarships for Post-Educational Training for Teachers of the Greek Language, 19

School for International Training Master of Arts in Teaching Program, 779

University of Stirling Research Studentships, 750

Volzhsky Institute of Humanities Awards, 764

African Nations

Universita' Per Stranieri Di Siena PVS Grants, 687

Australia

Ministry of Foreign Affairs (France) International Teaching Fellowships, 321
Ministry of Foreign Affairs (France) Stage de la Réunion (One Month Scholarships), 322
Ministry of Foreign Affairs (France) Stage de Nouméa (Three Week Course), 322
Ministry of Foreign Affairs (France) Stage de Paris/Toulon, 322
Universita' Per Stranieri Di Siena Unstra Grants, 688

British Commonwealth

Universita' Per Stranieri Di Siena Unstra Grants, 688

Canada

Universita' Per Stranieri Di Siena Unstra Grants, 688
Volzhsky Institute of Humanities Awards, 764

Caribbean Countries

Universita' Per Stranieri Di Siena PVS Grants, 687

East European Countries

Soros Supplementary Grants Programme (SSGP), 544
Universita' Per Stranieri Di Siena PVS Grants, 687
Universita' Per Stranieri Di Siena Unstra Grants, 688

Far East

Universita' Per Stranieri Di Siena Unstra Grants, 688

Indian Sub-Continent

Universita' Per Stranieri Di Siena PVS Grants, 687

Middle East

Universita' Per Stranieri Di Siena Unstra Grants, 688

New Zealand

Universita' Per Stranieri Di Siena Unstra Grants, 688

South Africa

Norah Taylor Bursary, 659
Universita' Per Stranieri Di Siena Unstra Grants, 688

South America

Universita' Per Stranieri Di Siena PVS Grants, 687

United Kingdom

Prix du Québec, 159
Regional Agency for the Right to University Study (DSU) Grants, 686
Universita' Per Stranieri Di Siena Unstra Grants, 688
University of Wales (Aberystwyth) Postgraduate Research Studentships, 752
Volzhsky Institute of Humanities Awards, 764

United States of America

ETS Postdoctoral Fellowships, 294
Fulbright Teacher and Administrator Exchange, 325
The Swedish Government 'SASS' Travel Grants, 667
Universita' Per Stranieri Di Siena Unstra Grants, 688
US Department of Education International Research and Studies Program, 757
Volzhsky Institute of Humanities Awards, 764

West European Countries

Regional Agency for the Right to University Study (DSU) Grants, 686

MATHEMATICS EDUCATION

Any Country

ETS Summer Program in Research for Graduate Students, 294
Massey Doctoral Scholarship, 461
National Academy of Education Spencer Postdoctoral Fellowships, 489

University of Manchester Research Studentships and Scholarships, 715
University of Stirling Research Studentships, 750

United Kingdom

Sheffield Hallam University Research Studentships, 625
UK Government Grants, 442
University of Wales, Bangor (UWB) Research Studentships, 753
University of Wales, Bangor Departmental Research Studentships, 753

United States of America

ETS Postdoctoral Fellowships, 294

West European Countries

Sheffield Hallam University Research Studentships, 625
University of Wales, Bangor (UWB) Research Studentships, 753
University of Wales, Bangor Departmental Research Studentships, 753

SCIENCE EDUCATION

Any Country

Carski Foundation Distinguished Teaching Award, 87
Conservation and Research Foundation Grants, 267
Crohn's and Colitis Foundation Career Development Awards, 275
Crohn's and Colitis Foundation First Award, 276
Crohn's and Colitis Foundation Research Fellowship Awards, 276
Crohn's and Colitis Foundation Research Grant Program, 276
ETS Summer Program in Research for Graduate Students, 294
Lord Dowding Fund for Humane Research, 453
Massey Doctoral Scholarship, 461
Nathalie Rose Barr PhD Studentship, 413
National Academy of Education Spencer Postdoctoral Fellowships, 489
University of Glasgow Postgraduate Research Scholarships, 707
University of Stirling Research Studentships, 750

African Nations

Golda Meir Mount Carmel International Training Centre Assistance for Courses, 337
Golda Meir Mount Carmel International Training Centre Tuition and Maintenance Scholarships, 337

Canada

CIC The Bayer, Inc. Award for High School Chemistry Teachers, 255
CIC Union Carbide Award for Chemical Education, 255

Caribbean Countries

Golda Meir Mount Carmel International Training Centre Assistance for Courses, 337
Golda Meir Mount Carmel International Training Centre Tuition and Maintenance Scholarships, 337

East European Countries

Canon Foundation Award, 242
Golda Meir Mount Carmel International Training Centre Assistance for Courses, 337
Golda Meir Mount Carmel International Training Centre Tuition and Maintenance Scholarships, 337

Far East

Golda Meir Mount Carmel International Training Centre Assistance for Courses, 337
Golda Meir Mount Carmel International Training Centre Tuition and Maintenance Scholarships, 337

Indian Sub-Continent

Golda Meir Mount Carmel International Training Centre Assistance for Courses, 337
Golda Meir Mount Carmel International Training Centre Tuition and Maintenance Scholarships, 337

Middle East

Golda Meir Mount Carmel International Training Centre Assistance for Courses, 337
Golda Meir Mount Carmel International Training Centre Tuition and Maintenance Scholarships, 337

South Africa

Golda Meir Mount Carmel International Training Centre Assistance for Courses, 337
Golda Meir Mount Carmel International Training Centre Tuition and Maintenance Scholarships, 337

South America

Golda Meir Mount Carmel International Training Centre Assistance for Courses, 337
Golda Meir Mount Carmel International Training Centre Tuition and Maintenance Scholarships, 337

United Kingdom

Canon Foundation Award, 242
Sheffield Hallam University Research Studentships, 625
UK Government Grants, 442
University of Wales (Aberystwyth) Postgraduate Research Studentships, 752
University of Wales, Bangor (UWB) Research Studentships, 753
University of Wales, Bangor Departmental Research Studentships, 753

United States of America

Earthwatch Education Awards, 290
ETS Postdoctoral Fellowships, 294
NIH Research Grants, 511

West European Countries

Canon Foundation Award, 242
Sheffield Hallam University Research Studentships, 625
University of Wales, Bangor (UWB) Research Studentships, 753
University of Wales, Bangor Departmental Research Studentships, 753

HUMANITIES AND SOCIAL SCIENCE EDUCATION

Any Country

Alexander S Onassis Programme of Research Grants, 18
Alexander S Onassis Research Grants, 18
All Saints Educational Trust Personal Awards, 22
Bernadotte E Schmitt Grants, 54
Equiano Memorial Award, 666
ETS Summer Program in Research for Graduate Students, 294
J Franklin Jameson Fellowship, 54
Jane Addams/Andrew Carnegie Fellowships in Philanthropy, 368
National Academy of Education Spencer Postdoctoral Fellowships, 489
Onassis Programme of Postgraduate Research Scholarships, 19
Onassis Programme of Scholarships for Post-Educational Training for Teachers of the Greek Language, 19
University of Stirling Research Studentships, 750
William Randolph Hearst Foundation Fellowship, 482

Canada

Canadian Window on International Development, 399

East European Countries

Soros Supplementary Grants Programme (SSGP), 544

United Kingdom

UK Government Grants, 442
University of Wales, Bangor (UWB) Research Studentships, 753
University of Wales, Bangor Departmental Research Studentships, 753

United States of America

Earthwatch Education Awards, 290
ETS Postdoctoral Fellowships, 294
James Madison Fellowship Program, 420
WWWC Americans and World Affairs Fellows Program, 780

West European Countries

University of Wales, Bangor (UWB) Research Studentships, 753
University of Wales, Bangor Departmental Research Studentships, 753

PHYSICAL EDUCATION

Any Country

JCC Association Scholarships, 423
Massey Doctoral Scholarship, 461
National Academy of Education Spencer Postdoctoral Fellowships, 489
NSCA Challenge Scholarship, 518
NSCA Student Grant Research Grant, 519
Power Systems Professional Scholarship, 519
University of Glasgow Postgraduate Research Scholarships, 707
University of Manchester Research Studentships and Scholarships, 715
University of Stirling Research Studentships, 750

United Kingdom

UK Government Grants, 442
University of Wales, Bangor (UWB) Research Studentships, 753
University of Wales, Bangor Departmental Research Studentships, 753

United States of America

ETS Postdoctoral Fellowships, 294

West European Countries

University of Wales, Bangor (UWB) Research Studentships, 753
University of Wales, Bangor Departmental Research Studentships, 753

LITERACY EDUCATION

Any Country

Albert J Harris Award, 407
AUC Writing Center Graduate Fellowships, 97
Dina Feitelson Research Award, 407
Elva Knight Research Grant, 407
ETS Summer Program in Research for Graduate Students, 294
Helen M Robinson Award, 408
International Reading Association Outstanding Dissertation of the Year Award, 408
International Reading Association Teacher as Researcher Grant, 408
Jeanne S Chall Research Fellowship, 408
National Academy of Education Spencer Postdoctoral Fellowships, 489

African Nations

Reading/Literacy Research Fellowship, 408

Australia

Reading/Literacy Research Fellowship, 408

British Commonwealth

Reading/Literacy Research Fellowship, 408

Canada

SSHRC Valuing Literacy in Canada Doctoral and Postdoctoral Fellowship Supplements, 648
SSHRC Valuing Literacy in Canada Strategic Partnership Development Grants, 648

SSHRC Valuing Literacy in Canada Strategic Research Grants, 648

Caribbean Countries

Reading/Literacy Research Fellowship, 408

East European Countries

Reading/Literacy Research Fellowship, 408
Soros Supplementary Grants Programme (SSGP), 544

Far East

Reading/Literacy Research Fellowship, 408

Indian Sub-Continent

Reading/Literacy Research Fellowship, 408

Middle East

Reading/Literacy Research Fellowship, 408

New Zealand

Reading/Literacy Research Fellowship, 408

South Africa

Reading/Literacy Research Fellowship, 408

South America

Reading/Literacy Research Fellowship, 408

United Kingdom

Reading/Literacy Research Fellowship, 408
UK Government Grants, 442

United States of America

ETS Postdoctoral Fellowships, 294
WWWC Americans and World Affairs Fellows Program, 780

West European Countries

Reading/Literacy Research Fellowship, 408

VOCATIONAL SUBJECTS EDUCATION

Any Country

Anglo-German Foundation for the Study of Industrial Society Research Grant, 101
LCCIEB Examinations Board Scholarships, 452
Lincoln College Erich and Rochelle Endowed Prize in Music, 730
National Academy of Education Spencer Postdoctoral Fellowships, 489

African Nations

The Joint Japan/World Bank Graduate Scholarship Program (JJ/WBGSP), 395

Australia

Fulbright Professional Award for Vocational Education and Training, 145
University of Western Sydney Postgraduate Research Award (UWSPRA), 755

British Commonwealth

The Joint Japan/World Bank Graduate Scholarship Program (JJ/WBGSP), 395

Caribbean Countries

The Joint Japan/World Bank Graduate Scholarship Program (JJ/WBGSP), 395

East European Countries

The Joint Japan/World Bank Graduate Scholarship Program (JJ/WBGSP), 395

Far East

The Joint Japan/World Bank Graduate Scholarship Program (JJ/WBGSP), 395

Indian Sub-Continent

The Joint Japan/World Bank Graduate Scholarship Program (JJ/WBGSP), 395

Middle East

The Joint Japan/World Bank Graduate Scholarship Program (JJ/WBGSP), 395

New Zealand

University of Western Sydney Postgraduate Research Award (UWSPRA), 755

South Africa

The Joint Japan/World Bank Graduate Scholarship Program (JJ/WBGSP), 395
South African Council for English Education (EX-PCE Bursary), 659

South America

The Joint Japan/World Bank Graduate Scholarship Program (JJ/WBGSP), 395

United Kingdom

Hilda Martindale Exhibitions, 358
Smith and Nephew Foundation Postdoctoral Nursing Research Fellowship, 635

AGRICULTURAL EDUCATION

Any Country

National Academy of Education Spencer Postdoctoral Fellowships, 489

African Nations

The Joint Japan/World Bank Graduate Scholarship Program (JJ/WBGSP), 395

British Commonwealth

The Joint Japan/World Bank Graduate Scholarship Program (JJ/WBGSP), 395

Canada

Horticultural Research Institute Grants, 359

Caribbean Countries

The Joint Japan/World Bank Graduate Scholarship Program (JJ/WBGSP), 395

East European Countries

The Joint Japan/World Bank Graduate Scholarship Program (JJ/WBGSP), 395

Far East

The Joint Japan/World Bank Graduate Scholarship Program (JJ/WBGSP), 395

Indian Sub-Continent

The Joint Japan/World Bank Graduate Scholarship Program (JJ/WBGSP), 395

Middle East

The Joint Japan/World Bank Graduate Scholarship Program (JJ/WBGSP), 395

South Africa

The Joint Japan/World Bank Graduate Scholarship Program (JJ/WBGSP), 395

South America

The Joint Japan/World Bank Graduate Scholarship Program (JJ/WBGSP), 395

United Kingdom

UK Government Grants, 442

United States of America

Horticultural Research Institute Grants, 359

ART EDUCATION

Any Country

Massey Doctoral Scholarship, 461
MICA Fellowship, 460
National Academy of Education Spencer Postdoctoral Fellowships, 489
University of Manchester Research Studentships and Scholarships, 715

East European Countries

Soros Supplementary Grants Programme (SSGP), 544

United Kingdom

UK Government Grants, 442

COMMERCE/BUSINESS EDUCATION

Any Country

National Academy of Education Spencer Postdoctoral Fellowships, 489

African Nations

The Joint Japan/World Bank Graduate Scholarship Program (JJ/WBGSP), 395

British Commonwealth

The Joint Japan/World Bank Graduate Scholarship Program (JJ/WBGSP), 395

Caribbean Countries

The Joint Japan/World Bank Graduate Scholarship Program (JJ/WBGSP), 395

East European Countries

The Joint Japan/World Bank Graduate Scholarship Program (JJ/WBGSP), 395

Far East

The Joint Japan/World Bank Graduate Scholarship Program (JJ/WBGSP), 395

Indian Sub-Continent

The Joint Japan/World Bank Graduate Scholarship Program (JJ/WBGSP), 395

Middle East

The Joint Japan/World Bank Graduate Scholarship Program (JJ/WBGSP), 395

South Africa

The Joint Japan/World Bank Graduate Scholarship Program (JJ/WBGSP), 395

South America

The Joint Japan/World Bank Graduate Scholarship Program (JJ/WBGSP), 395

United Kingdom

UK Government Grants, 442

COMPUTER EDUCATION

Any Country

ETS Summer Program in Research for Graduate Students, 294
Massey Doctoral Scholarship, 461
National Academy of Education Spencer Postdoctoral Fellowships, 489

United Kingdom

UK Government Grants, 442

TECHNOLOGY EDUCATION

Any Country

DEED Scholarship, 77
Exxon Mobil Engineering Teaching Fellowships, 592
Massey Doctoral Scholarship, 461
National Academy of Education Spencer Postdoctoral Fellowships, 489
University of Manchester Research Studentships and Scholarships, 715
University of Stirling Research Studentships, 750

African Nations

The Joint Japan/World Bank Graduate Scholarship Program (JJ/WBGSP), 395

British Commonwealth

The Joint Japan/World Bank Graduate Scholarship Program (JJ/WBGSP), 395

Caribbean Countries

The Joint Japan/World Bank Graduate Scholarship Program (JJ/WBGSP), 395

East European Countries

The Joint Japan/World Bank Graduate Scholarship Program (JJ/WBGSP), 395

Far East

The Joint Japan/World Bank Graduate Scholarship Program (JJ/WBGSP), 395

Indian Sub-Continent

The Joint Japan/World Bank Graduate Scholarship Program (JJ/WBGSP), 395

Middle East

The Joint Japan/World Bank Graduate Scholarship Program (JJ/WBGSP), 395

South Africa

The Joint Japan/World Bank Graduate Scholarship Program (JJ/WBGSP), 395

South America

The Joint Japan/World Bank Graduate Scholarship Program (JJ/WBGSP), 395

United Kingdom

UK Government Grants, 442

United States of America

Earthwatch Education Awards, 290
ETS Postdoctoral Fellowships, 294

HEALTH EDUCATION

Any Country

ASBAH Research Grant, 125

Australia

University of Western Sydney Postgraduate Research Award (UWSPRA), 755

British Commonwealth

The Joint Japan/World Bank Graduate Scholarship Program (JJ/WBGSP), 395

Caribbean Countries

Golda Meir Mount Carmel International Training Centre Assistance for Courses, 337
Golda Meir Mount Carmel International Training Centre Tuition and Maintenance Scholarships, 337
The Joint Japan/World Bank Graduate Scholarship Program (JJ/WBGSP), 395

East European Countries

Golda Meir Mount Carmel International Training Centre Assistance for Courses, 337
Golda Meir Mount Carmel International Training Centre Tuition and Maintenance Scholarships, 337
The Joint Japan/World Bank Graduate Scholarship Program (JJ/WBGSP), 395
Soros Supplementary Grants Programme (SSGP), 544

Far East

Golda Meir Mount Carmel International Training Centre Assistance for Courses, 337
Golda Meir Mount Carmel International Training Centre Tuition and Maintenance Scholarships, 337
The Joint Japan/World Bank Graduate Scholarship Program (JJ/WBGSP), 395

Indian Sub-Continent

Golda Meir Mount Carmel International Training Centre Assistance for Courses, 337
Golda Meir Mount Carmel International Training Centre Tuition and Maintenance Scholarships, 337
The Joint Japan/World Bank Graduate Scholarship Program (JJ/WBGSP), 395

Middle East

Golda Meir Mount Carmel International Training Centre Assistance for Courses, 337
Golda Meir Mount Carmel International Training Centre Tuition and Maintenance Scholarships, 337
The Joint Japan/World Bank Graduate Scholarship Program (JJ/WBGSP), 395

New Zealand

University of Western Sydney Postgraduate Research Award (UWSPRA), 755

South Africa

Golda Meir Mount Carmel International Training Centre Assistance for Courses, 337
Golda Meir Mount Carmel International Training Centre Tuition and Maintenance Scholarships, 337
The Joint Japan/World Bank Graduate Scholarship Program (JJ/WBGSP), 395

South America

Golda Meir Mount Carmel International Training Centre Assistance for Courses, 337
Golda Meir Mount Carmel International Training Centre Tuition and Maintenance Scholarships, 337
The Joint Japan/World Bank Graduate Scholarship Program (JJ/WBGSP), 395

United States of America

ETS Postdoctoral Fellowships, 294

PRIMARY EDUCATION

Any Country

Alexander S Onassis Programme of Research Grants, 18
Alexander S Onassis Research Grants, 18
All Saints Educational Trust Personal Awards, 22
Central Queensland University Postgraduate Research Award, 248
CQU International Student Scholarship, 248
Equiano Memorial Award, 666
ETS Summer Program in Research for Graduate Students, 294
Massey Doctoral Scholarship, 461
National Academy of Education Spencer Postdoctoral Fellowships, 489
Onassis Programme of Postgraduate Research Scholarships, 19
Onassis Programme of Scholarships for Post-Educational Training for Teachers of the Greek Language, 19
University of Glasgow Postgraduate Research Scholarships, 707
University of Manchester Research Studentships and Scholarships, 715
University of Stirling Research Studentships, 750

African Nations

The Joint Japan/World Bank Graduate Scholarship Program (JJ/WBGSP), 395

Australia

University of Western Sydney Postgraduate Research Award (UWSPRA), 755

British Commonwealth

The Joint Japan/World Bank Graduate Scholarship Program (JJ/WBGSP), 395

Caribbean Countries

The Joint Japan/World Bank Graduate Scholarship Program (JJ/WBGSP), 395

East European Countries

The Joint Japan/World Bank Graduate Scholarship Program (JJ/WBGSP), 395
Soros Supplementary Grants Programme (SSGP), 544

Far East

The Joint Japan/World Bank Graduate Scholarship Program (JJ/WBGSP), 395

Indian Sub-Continent

The Joint Japan/World Bank Graduate Scholarship Program (JJ/WBGSP), 395

Middle East

The Joint Japan/World Bank Graduate Scholarship Program (JJ/WBGSP), 395

New Zealand

University of Western Sydney Postgraduate Research Award (UWSPRA), 755

South Africa

The Joint Japan/World Bank Graduate Scholarship Program (JJ/WBGSP), 395

South America

The Joint Japan/World Bank Graduate Scholarship Program (JJ/WBGSP), 395

United Kingdom

UK Government Grants, 442
University of Wales (Aberystwyth) Postgraduate Research Studentships, 752
University of Wales, Bangor (UWB) Research Studentships, 753

University of Wales, Bangor Departmental Research Studentships, 753

United States of America

ETS Postdoctoral Fellowships, 294
WWWC Americans and World Affairs Fellows Program, 780

West European Countries

University of Wales, Bangor (UWB) Research Studentships, 753
University of Wales, Bangor Departmental Research Studentships, 753

SECONDARY EDUCATION

Any Country

Alexander S Onassis Programme of Research Grants, 18
Alexander S Onassis Research Grants, 18
All Saints Educational Trust Personal Awards, 22
Central Queensland University Postgraduate Research Award, 248
CQU International Student Scholarship, 248
Equiano Memorial Award, 666
ETS Summer Program in Research for Graduate Students, 294
Massey Doctoral Scholarship, 461
National Academy of Education Spencer Postdoctoral Fellowships, 489
Onassis Programme of Postgraduate Research Scholarships, 19
Onassis Programme of Scholarships for Post-Educational Training for Teachers of the Greek Language, 19
University of Glasgow Postgraduate Research Scholarships, 707
University of Manchester Research Studentships and Scholarships, 715
University of Stirling Research Studentships, 750

African Nations

The Joint Japan/World Bank Graduate Scholarship Program (JJ/WBGSP), 395

Australia

University of Western Sydney Postgraduate Research Award (UWSPRA), 755

British Commonwealth

The Joint Japan/World Bank Graduate Scholarship Program (JJ/WBGSP), 395

Caribbean Countries

The Joint Japan/World Bank Graduate Scholarship Program (JJ/WBGSP), 395

East European Countries

FEMS Fellowship, 310
The Joint Japan/World Bank Graduate Scholarship Program (JJ/WBGSP), 395
Soros Supplementary Grants Programme (SSGP), 544

Far East

The Joint Japan/World Bank Graduate Scholarship Program (JJ/WBGSP), 395

Indian Sub-Continent

The Joint Japan/World Bank Graduate Scholarship Program (JJ/WBGSP), 395

Middle East

The Joint Japan/World Bank Graduate Scholarship Program (JJ/WBGSP), 395

New Zealand

University of Western Sydney Postgraduate Research Award (UWSPRA), 755

South Africa

The Joint Japan/World Bank Graduate Scholarship Program (JJ/WBGSP), 395

South America

The Joint Japan/World Bank Graduate Scholarship Program (JJ/WBGSP), 395

United Kingdom

FEMS Fellowship, 310
UK Government Grants, 442
University of Wales (Aberystwyth) Postgraduate Research Studentships, 752
University of Wales, Bangor (UWB) Research Studentships, 753
University of Wales, Bangor Departmental Research Studentships, 753

United States of America

ETS Postdoctoral Fellowships, 294
WWWC Americans and World Affairs Fellows Program, 780

West European Countries

FEMS Fellowship, 310
University of Wales, Bangor (UWB) Research Studentships, 753
University of Wales, Bangor Departmental Research Studentships, 753

ADULT EDUCATION

Any Country

Central Queensland University Postgraduate Research Award, 248
CQU International Student Scholarship, 248
Equiano Memorial Award, 666
ETS Summer Program in Research for Graduate Students, 294
Massey Doctoral Scholarship, 461
National Academy of Education Spencer Postdoctoral Fellowships, 489
OISE/UT Graduate Assistantships, 541
OISE/UT Local Support, 541
University of Glasgow Postgraduate Research Scholarships, 707
University of Stirling Research Studentships, 750
Volzhsky Institute of Humanities Awards, 764

African Nations

The Joint Japan/World Bank Graduate Scholarship Program (JJ/WBGSP), 395

Australia

University of Western Sydney Postgraduate Research Award (UWSPRA), 755

British Commonwealth

The Joint Japan/World Bank Graduate Scholarship Program (JJ/WBGSP), 395

Canada

Volzhsky Institute of Humanities Awards, 764

Caribbean Countries

The Joint Japan/World Bank Graduate Scholarship Program (JJ/WBGSP), 395

East European Countries

The Joint Japan/World Bank Graduate Scholarship Program (JJ/WBGSP), 395
Soros Supplementary Grants Programme (SSGP), 544

Far East

The Joint Japan/World Bank Graduate Scholarship Program (JJ/WBGSP), 395

Indian Sub-Continent

The Joint Japan/World Bank Graduate Scholarship Program (JJ/WBGSP), 395

Middle East

The Joint Japan/World Bank Graduate Scholarship Program (JJ/WBGSP), 395

New Zealand

University of Western Sydney Postgraduate Research Award (UWSPRA), 755

South Africa

The Joint Japan/World Bank Graduate Scholarship Program (JJ/WBGSP), 395

South America

The Joint Japan/World Bank Graduate Scholarship Program (JJ/WBGSP), 395

United Kingdom

Regional Agency for the Right to University Study (DSU) Grants, 686
UK Government Grants, 442
Volzhsky Institute of Humanities Awards, 764

United States of America

ETS Postdoctoral Fellowships, 294
The Swedish Government 'SASS' Travel Grants, 667
Volzhsky Institute of Humanities Awards, 764
WWWC Americans and World Affairs Fellows Program, 780

West European Countries

Regional Agency for the Right to University Study (DSU) Grants, 686

SPECIAL EDUCATION

Any Country

Deputy Chancellors Postdoctoral Research, 535
Equiano Memorial Award, 666
ETS Summer Program in Research for Graduate Students, 294
JCC Association Scholarships, 423
Massey Doctoral Scholarship, 461
National Academy of Education Spencer Postdoctoral Fellowships, 489
NTU One Year Postdoctoral Fellowship, 535
NTU Senior Research Fellowship, 536
NTU Three Year Postdoctoral Fellowship, 536
OISE/UT Graduate Assistantships, 541
OISE/UT Local Support, 541
University of Manchester Research Studentships and Scholarships, 715
University of Stirling Research Studentships, 750

African Nations

The Joint Japan/World Bank Graduate Scholarship Program (JJ/WBGSP), 395

Australia

University of Western Sydney Postgraduate Research Award (UWSPRA), 755

British Commonwealth

The Joint Japan/World Bank Graduate Scholarship Program (JJ/WBGSP), 395

Caribbean Countries

The Joint Japan/World Bank Graduate Scholarship Program (JJ/WBGSP), 395

East European Countries

The Joint Japan/World Bank Graduate Scholarship Program (JJ/WBGSP), 395
Soros Supplementary Grants Programme (SSGP), 544

Far East

The Joint Japan/World Bank Graduate Scholarship Program (JJ/WBGSP), 395

Indian Sub-Continent

The Joint Japan/World Bank Graduate Scholarship Program (JJ/WBGSP), 395

Middle East

The Joint Japan/World Bank Graduate Scholarship Program (JJ/WBGSP), 395

New Zealand

University of Western Sydney Postgraduate Research Award (UWSPRA), 755

South Africa

The Joint Japan/World Bank Graduate Scholarship Program (JJ/WBGSP), 395

South America

The Joint Japan/World Bank Graduate Scholarship Program (JJ/WBGSP), 395

United Kingdom

Sheffield Hallam University Research Studentships, 625
UK Government Grants, 442

United States of America

ACRES Scholarship, 44
ETS Postdoctoral Fellowships, 294

West European Countries

Sheffield Hallam University Research Studentships, 625

EDUCATION OF THE GIFTED

Any Country

Massey Doctoral Scholarship, 461
National Academy of Education Spencer Postdoctoral Fellowships, 489

African Nations

The Joint Japan/World Bank Graduate Scholarship Program (JJ/WBGSP), 395

British Commonwealth

The Joint Japan/World Bank Graduate Scholarship Program (JJ/WBGSP), 395

Caribbean Countries

The Joint Japan/World Bank Graduate Scholarship Program (JJ/WBGSP), 395

East European Countries

The Joint Japan/World Bank Graduate Scholarship Program (JJ/WBGSP), 395

Far East

The Joint Japan/World Bank Graduate Scholarship Program (JJ/WBGSP), 395

Indian Sub-Continent

The Joint Japan/World Bank Graduate Scholarship Program (JJ/WBGSP), 395

Middle East

The Joint Japan/World Bank Graduate Scholarship Program (JJ/WBGSP), 395

South Africa

The Joint Japan/World Bank Graduate Scholarship Program (JJ/WBGSP), 395

South America

The Joint Japan/World Bank Graduate Scholarship Program (JJ/WBGSP), 395

United Kingdom

UK Government Grants, 442

EDUCATION OF THE HANDICAPPED

Any Country

Apex Foundation Annual Research Grants, 102
ASBAH Research Grant, 125
ETS Summer Program in Research for Graduate Students, 294
Massey Doctoral Scholarship, 461
National Academy of Education Spencer Postdoctoral Fellowships, 489
University of Manchester Research Studentships and Scholarships, 715

African Nations

The Joint Japan/World Bank Graduate Scholarship Program (JJ/WBGSP), 395

British Commonwealth

The Joint Japan/World Bank Graduate Scholarship Program (JJ/WBGSP), 395

Caribbean Countries

The Joint Japan/World Bank Graduate Scholarship Program (JJ/WBGSP), 395

East European Countries

The Joint Japan/World Bank Graduate Scholarship Program (JJ/WBGSP), 395

Far East

The Joint Japan/World Bank Graduate Scholarship Program (JJ/WBGSP), 395

Indian Sub-Continent

The Joint Japan/World Bank Graduate Scholarship Program (JJ/WBGSP), 395

Middle East

The Joint Japan/World Bank Graduate Scholarship Program (JJ/WBGSP), 395

South Africa

The Joint Japan/World Bank Graduate Scholarship Program (JJ/WBGSP), 395

South America

The Joint Japan/World Bank Graduate Scholarship Program (JJ/WBGSP), 395

United Kingdom

UK Government Grants, 442

United States of America

ACRES Scholarship, 44
Emblem Club Scholarship Foundation Grant, 296
ETS Postdoctoral Fellowships, 294

EDUCATION OF SPECIFIC LEARNING DISABILITIES

Any Country

ASBAH Research Grant, 125
ETS Summer Program in Research for Graduate Students, 294
Massey Doctoral Scholarship, 461
National Academy of Education Spencer Postdoctoral Fellowships, 489
University of Manchester Research Studentships and Scholarships, 715

African Nations

Golda Meir Mount Carmel International Training Centre Assistance for Courses, 337
Golda Meir Mount Carmel International Training Centre Tuition and Maintenance Scholarships, 337
The Joint Japan/World Bank Graduate Scholarship Program (JJ/WBGSP), 395

British Commonwealth

The Joint Japan/World Bank Graduate Scholarship Program (JJ/WBGSP), 395

Caribbean Countries

Golda Meir Mount Carmel International Training Centre Assistance for Courses, 337
Golda Meir Mount Carmel International Training Centre Tuition and Maintenance Scholarships, 337
The Joint Japan/World Bank Graduate Scholarship Program (JJ/WBGSP), 395

East European Countries

Golda Meir Mount Carmel International Training Centre Assistance for Courses, 337
Golda Meir Mount Carmel International Training Centre Tuition and Maintenance Scholarships, 337
The Joint Japan/World Bank Graduate Scholarship Program (JJ/WBGSP), 395
Soros Supplementary Grants Programme (SSGP), 544

Far East

Golda Meir Mount Carmel International Training Centre Assistance for Courses, 337
Golda Meir Mount Carmel International Training Centre Tuition and Maintenance Scholarships, 337
The Joint Japan/World Bank Graduate Scholarship Program (JJ/WBGSP), 395

Indian Sub-Continent

Golda Meir Mount Carmel International Training Centre Assistance for Courses, 337
Golda Meir Mount Carmel International Training Centre Tuition and Maintenance Scholarships, 337
The Joint Japan/World Bank Graduate Scholarship Program (JJ/WBGSP), 395

Middle East

Golda Meir Mount Carmel International Training Centre Assistance for Courses, 337
Golda Meir Mount Carmel International Training Centre Tuition and Maintenance Scholarships, 337
The Joint Japan/World Bank Graduate Scholarship Program (JJ/WBGSP), 395

South Africa

Golda Meir Mount Carmel International Training Centre Assistance for Courses, 337
Golda Meir Mount Carmel International Training Centre Tuition and Maintenance Scholarships, 337
The Joint Japan/World Bank Graduate Scholarship Program (JJ/WBGSP), 395

BILINGUAL/BICULTURAL EDUCATION

Any Country

Deputy Chancellors Postdoctoral Research, 535
Equiano Memorial Award, 666
National Academy of Education Spencer Postdoctoral Fellowships, 489
Neporany Research and Teaching Fellowship, 233
NTU One Year Postdoctoral Fellowship, 535
NTU Senior Research Fellowship, 536
NTU Three Year Postdoctoral Fellowship, 536

East European Countries

Soros Supplementary Grants Programme (SSGP), 544

United Kingdom

University of Wales, Bangor (UWB) Research Studentships, 753
University of Wales, Bangor Departmental Research Studentships, 753

United States of America

Fulbright Teacher and Administrator Exchange, 325

West European Countries

University of Wales, Bangor (UWB) Research Studentships, 753
University of Wales, Bangor Departmental Research Studentships, 753

TEACHER TRAINERS EDUCATION

Any Country

Alexander S Onassis Programme of Research Grants, 18
Alexander S Onassis Research Grants, 18
Central Queensland University Postgraduate Research Award, 248
CQU International Student Scholarship, 248
Equiano Memorial Award, 666
ETS Summer Program in Research for Graduate Students, 294
Massey Doctoral Scholarship, 461
National Academy of Education Spencer Postdoctoral Fellowships, 489
University of Glasgow Postgraduate Research Scholarships, 707
University of Stirling Research Studentships, 750
Weizmann Institute of Science MSc Fellowships, 767

African Nations

Golda Meir Mount Carmel International Training Centre Assistance for Courses, 337
Golda Meir Mount Carmel International Training Centre Tuition and Maintenance Scholarships, 337
Institute for Housing and Urban Development Studies Fellowships for Courses, 376

Australia

Japanese Government (Monbukagakusho) Scholarships In-Service Training for Teachers Category, 422
University of Western Sydney Postgraduate Research Award (UWSPRA), 755

Caribbean Countries

Golda Meir Mount Carmel International Training Centre Assistance for Courses, 337
Golda Meir Mount Carmel International Training Centre Tuition and Maintenance Scholarships, 337
Institute for Housing and Urban Development Studies Fellowships for Courses, 376

East European Countries

Golda Meir Mount Carmel International Training Centre Assistance for Courses, 337
Golda Meir Mount Carmel International Training Centre Tuition and Maintenance Scholarships, 337

Institute for Housing and Urban Development Studies Fellowships for Courses, 376
Soros Supplementary Grants Programme (SSGP), 544

Far East

Golda Meir Mount Carmel International Training Centre Assistance for Courses, 337
Golda Meir Mount Carmel International Training Centre Tuition and Maintenance Scholarships, 337
Institute for Housing and Urban Development Studies Fellowships for Courses, 376

Indian Sub-Continent

Golda Meir Mount Carmel International Training Centre Assistance for Courses, 337
Golda Meir Mount Carmel International Training Centre Tuition and Maintenance Scholarships, 337
Institute for Housing and Urban Development Studies Fellowships for Courses, 376

Middle East

Golda Meir Mount Carmel International Training Centre Assistance for Courses, 337
Golda Meir Mount Carmel International Training Centre Tuition and Maintenance Scholarships, 337
Institute for Housing and Urban Development Studies Fellowships for Courses, 376

New Zealand

University of Western Sydney Postgraduate Research Award (UWSPRA), 755

South Africa

Golda Meir Mount Carmel International Training Centre Assistance for Courses, 337
Golda Meir Mount Carmel International Training Centre Tuition and Maintenance Scholarships, 337
Institute for Housing and Urban Development Studies Fellowships for Courses, 376
South African Council for English Education (EX-PCE Bursary), 659

South America

Golda Meir Mount Carmel International Training Centre Assistance for Courses, 337
Golda Meir Mount Carmel International Training Centre Tuition and Maintenance Scholarships, 337
Institute for Housing and Urban Development Studies Fellowships for Courses, 376

United Kingdom

University of Wales, Bangor (UWB) Research Studentships, 753
University of Wales, Bangor Departmental Research Studentships, 753

United States of America

Bicentennial Swedish-American Exchange Fund Travel Grants, 153
BPW Career Advancement Scholarship Program, 184
Dow Jones Teacher Fellowship Program, 286
ETS Postdoctoral Fellowships, 294

West European Countries

University of Wales, Bangor (UWB) Research Studentships, 753
University of Wales, Bangor Departmental Research Studentships, 753

HIGHER EDUCATION TEACHER TRAINING

Any Country

Episcopal Church Foundation Graduate Fellowship Program, 303
Equiano Memorial Award, 666
Massey Doctoral Scholarship, 461

National Academy of Education Spencer Postdoctoral Fellowships, 489
OISE/UT Graduate Assistantships, 541
OISE/UT Local Support, 541
Onassis Programme of Postgraduate Research Scholarships, 19
University of Bristol Postgraduate Scholarships, 691
University of Glasgow Postgraduate Research Scholarships, 707
Volzhsky Institute of Humanities Awards, 764

Canada

Volzhsky Institute of Humanities Awards, 764

East European Countries

Soros Supplementary Grants Programme (SSGP), 544

South Africa

South African Council for English Education (EX-PCE Bursary), 659

United Kingdom

University of Wales, Bangor (UWB) Research Studentships, 753
University of Wales, Bangor Departmental Research Studentships, 753
Volzhsky Institute of Humanities Awards, 764

United States of America

Bicentennial Swedish-American Exchange Fund Travel Grants, 153
ETS Postdoctoral Fellowships, 294
Volzhsky Institute of Humanities Awards, 764

West European Countries

Scholarship Foundation of the League for Finnish-American Societies, 621
University of Wales, Bangor (UWB) Research Studentships, 753
University of Wales, Bangor Departmental Research Studentships, 753

EDUCATIONAL SCIENCE

Any Country

Alexander S Onassis Programme of Research Grants, 18
Alexander S Onassis Research Grants, 18
Camargo Fellowships, 185
Central Queensland University Postgraduate Research Award, 248
CQU International Student Scholarship, 248
Equiano Memorial Award, 666
Esther A and Joseph Klingenstein Fellowship Awards, 304
ETS National Assessment of Educational Progress (NAEP) Visiting Scholar Program, 294
Klingenstein Summer Institute, 304
National Academy of Education Spencer Postdoctoral Fellowships, 489
University of Bristol Postgraduate Scholarships, 691
University of Glasgow Postgraduate Research Scholarships, 707
University of Sussex Overseas Research Studentships, 750
Weizmann Institute of Science MSc Fellowships, 767

African Nations

The Joint Japan/World Bank Graduate Scholarship Program (JJ/WBGSP), 395

Australia

University of Western Sydney Postgraduate Research Award (UWSPRA), 755

British Commonwealth

The Joint Japan/World Bank Graduate Scholarship Program (JJ/WBGSP), 395

Caribbean Countries

The Joint Japan/World Bank Graduate Scholarship Program (JJ/WBGSP), 395

East European Countries

The Joint Japan/World Bank Graduate Scholarship Program (JJ/WBGSP), 395
Summer University of The Central European University Scholarship, 544

Far East

The Joint Japan/World Bank Graduate Scholarship Program (JJ/WBGSP), 395

Indian Sub-Continent

The Joint Japan/World Bank Graduate Scholarship Program (JJ/WBGSP), 395

Middle East

The Joint Japan/World Bank Graduate Scholarship Program (JJ/WBGSP), 395

New Zealand

University of Western Sydney Postgraduate Research Award (UWSPRA), 755

South Africa

The Joint Japan/World Bank Graduate Scholarship Program (JJ/WBGSP), 395

South America

The Joint Japan/World Bank Graduate Scholarship Program (JJ/WBGSP), 395

United Kingdom

ESRC Research Studentships, 292
Sheffield Hallam University Research Studentships, 625

United States of America

ETS Postdoctoral Fellowships, 294

West European Countries

ESRC Research Studentships, 292
Scholarship Foundation of the League for Finnish-American Societies, 621
Sheffield Hallam University Research Studentships, 625

INTERNATIONAL AND COMPARATIVE EDUCATION

Any Country

Alexander S Onassis Programme of Research Grants, 18
Alexander S Onassis Research Grants, 18
Camargo Fellowships, 185
CQU International Student Scholarship, 248
National Academy of Education Spencer Postdoctoral Fellowships, 489
Volzhsky Institute of Humanities Awards, 764

African Nations

Institute for Housing and Urban Development Studies Fellowships for Courses, 376
University of Sussex Overseas Development Administration Shared Scholarship Scheme, 750

Australia

Wingate Scholarships, 771

British Commonwealth

Wingate Scholarships, 771

Canada

Volzhsky Institute of Humanities Awards, 764
Wingate Scholarships, 771

New Zealand

Reading/Literacy Research Fellowship, 408
Wingate Scholarships, 771

South Africa

The Joint Japan/World Bank Graduate Scholarship Program (JJ/WBGSP), 395
Reading/Literacy Research Fellowship, 408
Wingate Scholarships, 771

South America

The Joint Japan/World Bank Graduate Scholarship Program (JJ/WBGSP), 395
Reading/Literacy Research Fellowship, 408

United Kingdom

Polish Embassy Short Visits Grants, 571
Polish Embassy Short-Term Bursaries, 571
Polish Government Postgraduate Scholarships Scheme, 572
Reading/Literacy Research Fellowship, 408
Sheffield Hallam University Research Studentships, 625
University of Wales, Bangor (UWB) Research Studentships, 753
University of Wales, Bangor Departmental Research Studentships, 753
Volzhsky Institute of Humanities Awards, 764
Wingate Scholarships, 771

United States of America

ETS Postdoctoral Fellowships, 294
Volzhsky Institute of Humanities Awards, 764

West European Countries

Reading/Literacy Research Fellowship, 408
Sheffield Hallam University Research Studentships, 625
University of Wales, Bangor (UWB) Research Studentships, 753
University of Wales, Bangor Departmental Research Studentships, 753
Wingate Scholarships, 771

EDUCATIONAL TECHNOLOGY

Any Country

ETS National Assessment of Educational Progress (NAEP) Visiting Scholar Program, 294
Massey Doctoral Scholarship, 461
National Academy of Education Spencer Postdoctoral Fellowships, 489
University of Stirling Research Studentships, 750
Volzhsky Institute of Humanities Awards, 764

African Nations

The Joint Japan/World Bank Graduate Scholarship Program (JJ/WBGSP), 395

British Commonwealth

The Joint Japan/World Bank Graduate Scholarship Program (JJ/WBGSP), 395

Canada

Volzhsky Institute of Humanities Awards, 764

Caribbean Countries

The Joint Japan/World Bank Graduate Scholarship Program (JJ/WBGSP), 395

East European Countries

The Joint Japan/World Bank Graduate Scholarship Program (JJ/WBGSP), 395

Far East

The Joint Japan/World Bank Graduate Scholarship Program (JJ/WBGSP), 395

Indian Sub-Continent

The Joint Japan/World Bank Graduate Scholarship Program (JJ/WBGSP), 395

Middle East

The Joint Japan/World Bank Graduate Scholarship Program (JJ/WBGSP), 395

South Africa

The Joint Japan/World Bank Graduate Scholarship Program (JJ/WBGSP), 395

South America

The Joint Japan/World Bank Graduate Scholarship Program (JJ/WBGSP), 395

United Kingdom

Volzhsky Institute of Humanities Awards, 764

United States of America

Earthwatch Education Awards, 290
ETS Postdoctoral Fellowships, 294
Volzhsky Institute of Humanities Awards, 764

EDUCATIONAL AND STUDENT COUNSELLING

Any Country

ETS National Assessment of Educational Progress (NAEP) Visiting Scholar Program, 294
Massey Doctoral Scholarship, 461
National Academy of Education Spencer Postdoctoral Fellowships, 489
University of Manchester Research Studentships and Scholarships, 715

African Nations

The Joint Japan/World Bank Graduate Scholarship Program (JJ/WBGSP), 395

British Commonwealth

The Joint Japan/World Bank Graduate Scholarship Program (JJ/WBGSP), 395

Caribbean Countries

The Joint Japan/World Bank Graduate Scholarship Program (JJ/WBGSP), 395

East European Countries

The Joint Japan/World Bank Graduate Scholarship Program (JJ/WBGSP), 395

Far East

The Joint Japan/World Bank Graduate Scholarship Program (JJ/WBGSP), 395

Indian Sub-Continent

The Joint Japan/World Bank Graduate Scholarship Program (JJ/WBGSP), 395

Middle East

The Joint Japan/World Bank Graduate Scholarship Program (JJ/WBGSP), 395

South Africa

The Joint Japan/World Bank Graduate Scholarship Program (JJ/WBGSP), 395

FINE AND APPLIED ARTS

GENERAL

HISTORY AND PHILOSOPHY OF ART

AESTHETICS

ART MANAGEMENT

DRAWING AND PAINTING

SCULPTURE

United Kingdom

United States of America

West European Countries

HANDICRAFTS

Any Country

Australia

British Commonwealth

Canada

Far East

Indian Sub-Continent

New Zealand

South Africa

United Kingdom

United States of America

West European Countries

MUSIC

Any Country

Royal College of Music Scholarships, 595
Ryan Davies Memorial Fund Scholarship Grants, 618
Sir Henry Richardson Awards, 631
Sir James McNeill Foundation Postgraduate Scholarship, 481
SOAS Bursary, 622
SOAS Research Student Fellowships, 622
Sybil Tutton Awards, 669
Thomas Holloway Research Studentship, 602
University of Bristol Postgraduate Scholarships, 691
University of Glasgow Postgraduate Research Scholarships, 707
University of Manchester Research Studentships and Scholarships, 715
University of New England Research Scholarships, 719
University of Stirling Research Studentships, 750
W T Best Memorial Scholarships, 781

African Nations

Royal Over-Seas League Annual Music Competition, 590

Australia

AMF Award, 141
The Countess of Munster Musical Trust Awards, 274
Fulbright Postgraduate Student Award for the Visual and Performing Arts, 144
The Marten Bequest Travelling Scholarships, 560
Royal Over-Seas League Annual Music Competition, 590
University of Western Sydney Postgraduate Research Award (UWSPRA), 755
Wingate Scholarships, 771

British Commonwealth

The Countess of Munster Musical Trust Awards, 274
Royal Over-Seas League Annual Music Competition, 590
Wingate Scholarships, 771

Canada

Alfred Einstein Award, 64
The Countess of Munster Musical Trust Awards, 274
Inuit Cultural Grants Program, 442
The Otto Kinkeldey Award, 65
Royal Over-Seas League Annual Music Competition, 590
Thompson (Homer and Dorothy) Fellowship, 222
Vatican Film Library - Andrew W Mellon Fellowship Program, 761
Wingate Scholarships, 771

Caribbean Countries

Royal Over-Seas League Annual Music Competition, 590

East European Countries

AHRB Studentships in the Humanities (Competition A), 112
AHRB Studentships in the Humanities (Competition B), 112

Far East

Asian Cultural Council Fellowship Grants Program, 123
Hong Kong Arts Development Council FCO Chevening-Leeds University Scholarships, 712
Royal Over-Seas League Annual Music Competition, 590

Indian Sub-Continent

The Countess of Munster Musical Trust Awards, 274
Royal Over-Seas League Annual Music Competition, 590
USEFI Professional Fellowships in Plastics and Performing Arts, Museum Studies and Arts/Culture Management, 684
Wingate Scholarships, 771

Middle East

Sharett Scholarship Program, 25

New Zealand

The Countess of Munster Musical Trust Awards, 274
Royal Over-Seas League Annual Music Competition, 590

South Africa

The Countess of Munster Musical Trust Awards, 274
Royal Over-Seas League Annual Music Competition, 590
SAMRO Intermediate Bursaries for Composition Study In Southern Africa, 619
SAMRO Overseas Scholarship, 619
SAMRO Postgraduate Bursaries for Indigenous African Music Study, 619
Wingate Scholarships, 771

United Kingdom

ACW Awards for Advanced Study in Music, 120
ACW Performing Arts Projects, 121
AHRB Doctoral Awards in the Creative and Performing Arts (Competition C), 112
AHRB Studentships in the Humanities (Competition A), 112
AHRB Studentships in the Humanities (Competition B), 112
Carnwath Scholarship, 781
The Countess of Munster Musical Trust Awards, 274
English Speaking Union Chautauqua Scholarships, 300
Francis Chagrin Award, 318
John Clementi Collard Fellowship, 781
Polish Embassy Short-Term Bursaries, 571
Polish Government Postgraduate Scholarships Scheme, 572
Royal Over-Seas League Annual Music Competition, 590
University of Wales, Bangor (UWB) Research Studentships, 753
University of Wales, Bangor Departmental Research Studentships, 753
Wingate Scholarships, 771

United States of America

Alfred Einstein Award, 64
Artists Exploration Fund, 121
ASCAP Foundation Morton Gould Young Composer Awards, 122
Asian Cultural Council Fellowship Grants Program, 123
Bush Artist Fellows Program, 184
Fulbright Senior Specialists Program, 271
The Fund for US Artists at International Festivals and Exhibitions, 122
Harriet Hale Woolley Scholarships, 684
Margaret Fairbank Jory Copying Assistance Program, 64
Meet The Composer Fund, 468
Music Alive, 468
National League of American Pen Women Grants for Mature Women, 512
The Otto Kinkeldey Award, 65
UCLA IAC Postdoctoral/Visiting Scholar Fellowships, 680
Vatican Film Library - Andrew W Mellon Fellowship Program, 761

West European Countries

AHRB Doctoral Awards in the Creative and Performing Arts (Competition C), 112
The Arts Council of Ireland and Arts Council of Northern Ireland Skidmore Jazz Award, 113
The Arts Council of Ireland Critical Reflection Award, 115
The Arts Council of Ireland Margaret Arnold Scholarship, 115
The Arts Council of Ireland Music Publications and Recording Scheme, 116
Maisie Lewis Young Artists Fund, 781
Scholarship Foundation of the League for Finnish-American Societies, 621
University of Wales, Bangor (UWB) Research Studentships, 753
University of Wales, Bangor Departmental Research Studentships, 753
Wingate Scholarships, 771

MUSICOLOGY

Any Country

Ahmanson and Getty Postdoctoral Fellowships, 678
Alexander S Onassis Programme of Research Grants, 18
Alexander S Onassis Research Grants, 18
AMS Subventions for Publications, 65
ARIT Humanities and Social Science Fellowships, 78
ASECS (American Society for Eighteenth-Century Studies)/Clark Library Fellowships, 679
Camargo Fellowships, 185
Center for Advanced Study in the Behavioral Sciences Postdoctoral Residential Fellowships, 245
Center for Field Research Grants, 246
Clark Library Short-Term Resident Fellowships, 679
Clark Predoctoral Fellowships, 679
Clark-Huntington Joint Bibliographical Fellowship, 679
Eastman School of Music Graduate Awards, 291
External Faculty Fellowships, 663
Kurt Weill Foundation for Music Grants Program, 436
NHC Fellowships, 509
The Noah Greenberg Award, 65
Onassis Programme of Postgraduate Research Scholarships, 19
The Paul A Pisk Prize, 65
Royal College of Music Scholarships, 595
Thomas Holloway Research Studentship, 602

Australia

Wingate Scholarships, 771

British Commonwealth

British Institute of Archaeology at Ankara Research Grants, 169
British Institute of Archaeology at Ankara Travel Grants, 169
Gladys Krieble Delmas Foundation Grants, 336
Wingate Scholarships, 771

Canada

Wingate Scholarships, 771

East European Countries

AHRB Studentships in the Humanities (Competition A), 112
AHRB Studentships in the Humanities (Competition B), 112
Mellon Research Fellowship, 79

Far East

Asian Cultural Council Fellowship Grants Program, 123

Indian Sub-Continent

Wingate Scholarships, 771

New Zealand

Wingate Scholarships, 771

South Africa

SAMRO Postgraduate Bursaries for Indigenous African Music Study, 619
Wingate Scholarships, 771

United Kingdom

AHRB Studentships in the Humanities (Competition A), 112
AHRB Studentships in the Humanities (Competition B), 112
British Institute of Archaeology at Ankara Research Grants, 169
British Institute of Archaeology at Ankara Travel Grants, 169
Cardiff University Postgraduate Research Studentships, 242
Frank Knox Fellowships at Harvard University, 319
Kennedy Scholarships, 432
University of Wales, Bangor (UWB) Research Studentships, 753
University of Wales, Bangor Departmental Research Studentships, 753
Wingate Scholarships, 771

United States of America

Asian Cultural Council Fellowship Grants Program, 123
Fulbright Distinguished Chairs Program, 270
Fulbright Senior Specialists Program, 271
Gladys Krieble Delmas Foundation Grants, 336
IREX Grant Opportunities for US Scholars, 409

West European Countries

Cardiff University Postgraduate Research Studentships, 242
University of Wales, Bangor (UWB) Research Studentships, 753
University of Wales, Bangor Departmental Research Studentships, 753
Wingate Scholarships, 771

MUSIC THEORY AND COMPOSITION

Any Country

Alexander S Onassis Programme of Research Grants, 18
Alexander S Onassis Research Grants, 18
American Accordion Musicological Society Music Competition, 27
Camargo Fellowships, 185
Cleveland Institute of Music Scholarships and Accompanying Fellowships, 261
Eastman School of Music Graduate Awards, 291
Golden Key National Honor Society Performing Arts Showcase, 340
Hambidge Center Residency Program Scholarships, 347
International Jeunesses Musicales Competition, 423
Massey Doctoral Scholarship, 461
Mendelssohn Scholarship, 469
National Association of Composers Young Composers Competition, 492
Omaha Symphony Guild International New Music Competition, 540
Onassis Programme of Postgraduate Research Scholarships, 19
Peter Whittingham Award, 561
Queen Marie José Prize International Prize for Musical Composition, 575
Ragdale Foundation Residencies, 579
Royal College of Music Scholarships, 595
Royal Philharmonic Society Composition Prize, 607
Ryan Davies Memorial Fund Scholarship Grants, 618
San Francisco Conservatory Performance Scholarships in Music, 620
Thomas Holloway Research Studentship, 602
Virginia Center for the Creative Arts Fellowships, 763
Yaddo Residency, 269

Australia

Paul Lowin Prizes - Orchestral Prize, 557
Paul Lowin Prizes - Song Cycle Prize, 557
Wingate Scholarships, 771

British Commonwealth

Wingate Scholarships, 771

Canada

Ruth Watson Henderson Choral Composition Competition, 257
Sigma Alpha Iota Inter-American Music Awards, 626
Wingate Scholarships, 771

East European Countries

AHRB Studentships in the Humanities (Competition A), 112
AHRB Studentships in the Humanities (Competition B), 112

Far East

Asian Cultural Council Fellowship Grants Program, 123
Hong Kong Arts Development Council FCO Chevening-Leeds University Scholarships, 712

Indian Sub-Continent

Wingate Scholarships, 771

Middle East

Sharett Scholarship Program, 25

New Zealand

Wingate Scholarships, 771

South Africa

SAMRO Intermediate Bursaries for Composition Study In Southern
Africa, 619
SAMRO Overseas Scholarship, 619
Wingate Scholarships, 771

South America

Sigma Alpha Iota Inter-American Music Awards, 626

United Kingdom

AHRB Studentships in the Humanities (Competition A), 112
AHRB Studentships in the Humanities (Competition B), 112
Cardiff University Postgraduate Research Studentships, 242
Francis Chagrin Award, 318
Francis Chagrin Fund Awards, 319
Frank Knox Fellowships at Harvard University, 319
Fulbright-Chester Schirmer Fellowship in Music Composition, 759
Kennedy Scholarships, 432
University of Wales, Bangor (UWB) Research Studentships, 753
University of Wales, Bangor Departmental Research Studentships,
753
Wingate Scholarships, 771

United States of America

ASCAP Foundation Morton Gould Young Composer Awards, 122
Asian Cultural Council Fellowship Grants Program, 123
Bush Artist Fellows Program, 184
Commissioning Music/USA, 467
Harvey Garl Composition Contest, 570
Joseph H Bearns Prize in Music, 262
Margaret Fairbank Jory Copying Assistance Program, 64
National League of American Pen Women Grants for Mature
Women, 512
Sigma Alpha Iota Inter-American Music Awards, 626

West European Countries

Cardiff University Postgraduate Research Studentships, 242
University of Wales, Bangor (UWB) Research Studentships, 753
University of Wales, Bangor Departmental Research Studentships,
753
Wingate Scholarships, 771

CONDUCTING

Any Country

Alexander S Onassis Programme of Research Grants, 18
Alexander S Onassis Research Grants, 18
Chautauqua Institution Awards, 253
Cleveland Institute of Music Scholarships and Accompanying Fel-
lowships, 261
Eastman School of Music Graduate Awards, 291
Hungarian Television, Interart Festival Center International Conduc-
tors' Competition, 392
Onassis Programme of Postgraduate Research Scholarships, 19
Prague Spring International Music Competition, 573
Royal College of Music Scholarships, 595
Ryan Davies Memorial Fund Scholarship Grants, 618
San Francisco Conservatory Performance Scholarships in Music,
620

Australia

Wingate Scholarships, 771

British Commonwealth

Wingate Scholarships, 771

Canada

Leslie Bell Prize, 257
Ruth Watson Henderson Choral Composition Competition, 257
Wingate Scholarships, 771

Far East

Asian Cultural Council Fellowship Grants Program, 123

Indian Sub-Continent

Wingate Scholarships, 771

Middle East

Sharett Scholarship Program, 25

New Zealand

Wingate Scholarships, 771

South Africa

Wingate Scholarships, 771

United Kingdom

AHRB Doctoral Awards in the Creative and Performing Arts (Compe-
tition C), 112
University of Wales, Bangor (UWB) Research Studentships, 753
University of Wales, Bangor Departmental Research Studentships,
753
Wingate Scholarships, 771

United States of America

Asian Cultural Council Fellowship Grants Program, 123

West European Countries

AHRB Doctoral Awards in the Creative and Performing Arts (Compe-
tition C), 112
University of Wales, Bangor (UWB) Research Studentships, 753
University of Wales, Bangor Departmental Research Studentships,
753
Wingate Scholarships, 771

SINGING

Any Country

Alexander S Onassis Programme of Research Grants, 18
Alexander S Onassis Research Grants, 18
Associated Board of the Royal Schools of Music Scholarships, 124
The Banff Centre Financial Assistance, 148
Boise Foundation Scholarships, 156
Chautauqua Institution Awards, 253
Cleveland Institute of Music Scholarships and Accompanying Fel-
lowships, 261
Eastman School of Music Graduate Awards, 291
Golden Key National Honor Society Performing Arts Showcase, 340
Hambidge Center Residency Program Scholarships, 347
International Jeunesses Musicales Competition, 423
International Music Competition of the ARD, 182
International Robert Schumann Competition, 416
Maria Callas Grand Prix, 134
Maria Callas International Music Competition, 135
Miriam Licette Scholarship, 477
Onassis Programme of Postgraduate Research Scholarships, 19
Paris International Singing Competition, 397
Prize Winner of the International Music Competition of the ARD, 183
Queen Elisabeth International Music Competition of Belgium, 575
Royal College of Music Scholarships, 595
Ryan Davies Memorial Fund Scholarship Grants, 618
San Francisco Conservatory Performance Scholarships in Music,
620
Sorantin Young Artist Award, 620
Thomas Holloway Research Studentship, 602

Australia

AMF Award, 141
The Marten Bequest Travelling Scholarships, 560
Sir Robert Askin Operatic Travelling Scholarship, 560
Wingate Scholarships, 771

British Commonwealth

Making Music Award for Young Concert Artists, 456
Wingate Scholarships, 771

Canada

Loren L Zachary Society National Vocal Competition for Young Opera Singers, 453
Orchestre Symphonique de Montréal Competitions, 545
Wingate Scholarships, 771

Far East

Asian Cultural Council Fellowship Grants Program, 123

Indian Sub-Continent

USEFI Professional Fellowships in Plastics and Performing Arts, Museum Studies and Arts/Culture Management, 684
Wingate Scholarships, 771

Middle East

Sharett Scholarship Program, 25

New Zealand

Wingate Scholarships, 771

South Africa

SAMRO Overseas Scholarship, 619
Wingate Scholarships, 771

South America

Loren L Zachary Society National Vocal Competition for Young Opera Singers, 453

United Kingdom

ACW Awards for Advanced Study in Music, 120
AHRB Doctoral Awards in the Creative and Performing Arts (Competition C), 112
Making Music Award for Young Concert Artists, 456
Richard Tauber Prize, 100
Wingate Scholarships, 771

United States of America

Asian Cultural Council Fellowship Grants Program, 123
Loren L Zachary Society National Vocal Competition for Young Opera Singers, 453

West European Countries

AHRB Doctoral Awards in the Creative and Performing Arts (Competition C), 112
The Arts Council of Ireland Margaret Arnold Scholarship, 115
Richard Tauber Prize, 100
Wingate Scholarships, 771

MUSICAL INSTRUMENTS (PERFORMANCE)

Any Country

Adeline Rosenberg Memorial Prize Competition, 314
AMSA World Piano Competition, 64
Arthur Rubinstein International Piano Master Competition, 111
Associated Board of the Royal Schools of Music Scholarships, 124
The Banff Centre Financial Assistance, 148
Boise Foundation Scholarships, 156
Brandon University Graduate Assistantships, 158
Budapest International Music Competition, 183
Chautauqua Institution Awards, 253
Chopin Piano Competition, 435

Clara Haskil Competition, 260
Cleveland Institute of Music Scholarships and Accompanying Fellowships, 261
Eastman School of Music Graduate Awards, 291
Elizabeth Harper Vaughn Concerto Competition, 670
Emily English Scholarship, 297
Eric Thompson Trust Grants-in-Aid, 303
F Busoni International Piano Competition, 309
Gillian Sinclair Music Trust, 568
Golden Key National Honor Society Performing Arts Showcase, 340
Hambidge Center Residency Program Scholarships, 347
Hattori Foundation Awards, 352
Ian Fleming Charitable Trust Music Education Awards, 364
International Beethoven Piano Competition Vienna, 396
International Chamber Music Competition, 397
International Frederic Chopin Piano Competition, 403
International Géza Anda Piano Competition, 335
International Harp Contest in Israel, 403
International Jeunesses Musicales Competition, 423
International Music Competition of the ARD, 182
International Organ Competition 'Grand Prix de Chartres', 406
International Paulo Cello Competition, 558
International Robert Schumann Competition, 416
Jean Sibelius International Violin Competition, 422
John E Mortimer Foundation Awards, 568
The June Allison Award, 568
KPMG Scholarship, 568
The LDF Casbolt Memorial Award, 568
Leeds International Pianoforte Competition, 443
London International String Quartet Competition, 452
Manoug Parikian Award, 456
Maria Callas Grand Prix, 134
Maria Callas Grand Prix for Pianists, 135
Maria Callas International Music Competition, 135
Martin Musical Scholarships, 568
Miriam Licette Scholarship, 477
Muriel Taylor Cello Scholarship, 484
Myra Hess Trust, 486
National Orchestral Institute Scholarships, 514
Nicolo Paganini International Violin Competition, 534
The Noah Greenberg Award, 65
Paloma O'Shea Santander International Piano Competition, 551
Peter Whittingham Award, 561
Prague Spring International Music Competition, 573
Premier Grand Prix Marguerite Long, Premier Grand Prix Jacques Thibaud, 405
Prize Winner of the International Music Competition of the ARD, 183
Professor Charles Leggett Trust, 574
Queen Elisabeth International Music Competition of Belgium, 575
RCO Grants and Travel Scholarships, 598
RCO Scholarships and Awards, 598
The Reginald Conway Memorial Award for String Performers, 568
Royal College of Music Scholarships, 595
Ryan Davies Memorial Fund Scholarship Grants, 618
San Francisco Conservatory Performance Scholarships in Music, 620
Sidney Perry Scholarship, 568
Sir Henry Richardson Awards, 631
Sorantin Young Artist Award, 620
Sybil Tutton Awards, 669
Thomas Holloway Research Studentship, 602
Tibor Varga International Competition for Violin, 676
TotalFinaElf Ensemble Award, 569
TotalFinaElf in Association with Arts & Business New Partners, Outreach and Access Ensemble Award, 569
TotalFinaElf Recital Series, 569
Trevor Snoad Memorial Trust, 569

African Nations

Royal Over-Seas League Annual Music Competition, 590

Australia

AMF Award, 141
The Marten Bequest Travelling Scholarships, 560
Royal Over-Seas League Annual Music Competition, 590
Wingate Scholarships, 771

British Commonwealth

Making Music Award for Young Concert Artists, 456
Royal Over-Seas League Annual Music Competition, 590
Wingate Scholarships, 771

Canada

Orchestre Symphonique de Montréal Competitions, 545
Royal Over-Seas League Annual Music Competition, 590
Wingate Scholarships, 771

Caribbean Countries

Royal Over-Seas League Annual Music Competition, 590

Far East

Asian Cultural Council Fellowship Grants Program, 123
Royal Over-Seas League Annual Music Competition, 590

Indian Sub-Continent

Royal Over-Seas League Annual Music Competition, 590
USEFI Professional Fellowships in Plastics and Performing Arts, Museum Studies and Arts/Culture Management, 684
Wingate Scholarships, 771

Middle East

Sharett Scholarship Program, 25

New Zealand

Royal Over-Seas League Annual Music Competition, 590
Wingate Scholarships, 771

South Africa

Royal Over-Seas League Annual Music Competition, 590
SAMRO Overseas Scholarship, 619
Wingate Scholarships, 771

United Kingdom

ACW Awards for Advanced Study in Music, 120
AHRB Doctoral Awards in the Creative and Performing Arts (Competition C), 112
Cardiff University Postgraduate Research Studentships, 242
The Emanual Hurwitz Award for Violinists of British Nationality, 568
LSO Music Scholarship, 453
Making Music Award for Young Concert Artists, 456
Royal Over-Seas League Annual Music Competition, 590
University of Wales, Bangor (UWB) Research Studentships, 753
University of Wales, Bangor Departmental Research Studentships, 753
Wingate Scholarships, 771

United States of America

Asian Cultural Council Fellowship Grants Program, 123
JP Morgan Chase Fund for Small Ensembles, 467
Meet The Composer American Symphony Orchestra League, 468
Meet The Composer Fund, 468
Music Alive, 468

West European Countries

AHRB Doctoral Awards in the Creative and Performing Arts (Competition C), 112
The Arts Council of Ireland Margaret Arnold Scholarship, 115
The Arts Council of Ireland Music Publications and Recording Scheme, 116
Cardiff University Postgraduate Research Studentships, 242
Maisie Lewis Young Artists Fund, 781
University of Wales, Bangor (UWB) Research Studentships, 753

University of Wales, Bangor Departmental Research Studentships, 753
Wingate Scholarships, 771

RELIGIOUS MUSIC

Any Country

ASCSA Summer Sessions, 80
Jacob Hirsch Fellowship, 80
Royal College of Music Scholarships, 595
Ryan Davies Memorial Fund Scholarship Grants, 618

Australia

Wingate Scholarships, 771

British Commonwealth

Wingate Scholarships, 771

Canada

Wingate Scholarships, 771

East European Countries

AHRB Studentships in the Humanities (Competition A), 112
AHRB Studentships in the Humanities (Competition B), 112

Far East

Asian Cultural Council Fellowship Grants Program, 123

Indian Sub-Continent

Wingate Scholarships, 771

New Zealand

Wingate Scholarships, 771

South Africa

Wingate Scholarships, 771

United Kingdom

AHRB Studentships in the Humanities (Competition A), 112
AHRB Studentships in the Humanities (Competition B), 112
Wingate Scholarships, 771

United States of America

Asian Cultural Council Fellowship Grants Program, 123

West European Countries

Wingate Scholarships, 771

JAZZ AND POPULAR MUSIC

Any Country

The Banff Centre Financial Assistance, 148
Eastman School of Music Graduate Awards, 291
Kurt Weill Foundation for Music Grants Program, 436
Massey Doctoral Scholarship, 461
Peter Whittingham Award, 561
Ryan Davies Memorial Fund Scholarship Grants, 618

Australia

Wingate Scholarships, 771

British Commonwealth

Wingate Scholarships, 771

Canada

Wingate Scholarships, 771

East European Countries

AHRB Studentships in the Humanities (Competition A), 112
AHRB Studentships in the Humanities (Competition B), 112

British Commonwealth

Canada

East European Countries

Far East

Indian Sub-Continent

Middle East

New Zealand

South Africa

United Kingdom

United States of America

West European Countries

DANCING

Any Country

Australia

British Commonwealth

Canada

East European Countries

Far East

Indian Sub-Continent

Middle East

New Zealand

South Africa

United Kingdom

United States of America

West European Countries

AHRB Doctoral Awards in the Creative and Performing Arts (Competition C), 112
AHRB Professional and Vocational Awards (Competition P), 112
Scholarship Foundation of the League for Finnish-American Societies, 621
Wingate Scholarships, 771

PHOTOGRAPHY

Any Country

Alberta Art Foundation Graduate Scholarships in The Department of Art, 692
Alexander S Onassis Programme of Research Grants, 18
Alexander S Onassis Research Grants, 18
The Banff Centre Financial Assistance, 148
Camargo Fellowships, 185
Hambidge Center Residency Program Scholarships, 347
John Hervey, Broadcasters and Smallsreed Awards, 686
Library Company of Philadelphia Program in Early American Economy and Society, 447
Library Company of Philadelphia Research Fellowships in American History and Culture, 447
Light Work Artist-in-Residence Program, 448
Massey Doctoral Scholarship, 461
The Metropolitan Museum of Art Andrew W Mellon Foundation Fellowships in Conservation, 471
The Metropolitan Museum of Art Sherman Fairchild Foundation, 474
MICA Fellowship, 460
Rhodes University Postdoctoral Fellowship, 586
Roswell Artist-in-Residence Program, 591
Smith (W Eugene) Grant in Humanistic Photography, 764
Virginia Center for the Creative Arts Fellowships, 763
Women's Studio Workshop Artists' Fellowships, 775
Yaddo Residency, 269

Australia

Fulbright Postgraduate Student Award for the Visual and Performing Arts, 144
Wingate Scholarships, 771

British Commonwealth

Sargant Fellowship, 178
Wingate Rome Scholarship in the Fine Arts, 178
Wingate Scholarships, 771

Canada

Wingate Scholarships, 771

Far East

Asian Cultural Council Fellowship Grants Program, 123

Indian Sub-Continent

Wingate Scholarships, 771

Middle East

Sharett Scholarship Program, 25

New Zealand

Wingate Scholarships, 771

South Africa

Wingate Scholarships, 771

United Kingdom

AHRB Professional and Vocational Awards (Competition P), 112
Polish Embassy Short-Term Bursaries, 571
Sargant Fellowship, 178
Wingate Rome Scholarship in the Fine Arts, 178
Wingate Scholarships, 771

United States of America

Asian Cultural Council Fellowship Grants Program, 123
Bush Artist Fellows Program, 184
Fulbright Senior Specialists Program, 271
UCLA IAC Postdoctoral/Visiting Scholar Fellowships, 680

West European Countries

AHRB Professional and Vocational Awards (Competition P), 112
Janson Johan Helmich Scholarships and Travel Grants, 421
Scholarship Foundation of the League for Finnish-American Societies, 621
Wingate Scholarships, 771

CINEMA AND TELEVISION

Any Country

Alexander S Onassis Programme of Research Grants, 18
Alexander S Onassis Research Grants, 18
Austro-American Association of Boston Scholarship, 147
The Banff Centre Financial Assistance, 148
CDI Internship, 246
Don and Gee Nicholl Fellowships in Screenwriting, 6
Golden Key National Honor Society Performing Arts Showcase, 340
Onassis Programme of Postgraduate Research Scholarships, 19
Queen Mary Research Studentships, 576
Ragdale Foundation Residencies, 579
Rhodes University Postdoctoral Fellowship, 586
Thomas Holloway Research Studentship, 602
University of Bristol Postgraduate Scholarships, 691
University of Dundee Research Awards, 704
University of Glasgow Postgraduate Research Scholarships, 707
University of Manchester Research Studentships and Scholarships, 715
University of Stirling Research Studentships, 750
Yaddo Residency, 269

Australia

Fulbright Postgraduate Student Award for the Visual and Performing Arts, 144
Wingate Scholarships, 771

British Commonwealth

Wingate Scholarships, 771

Canada

Wingate Scholarships, 771

East European Countries

AHRB Studentships in the Humanities (Competition A), 112

Far East

Asian Cultural Council Fellowship Grants Program, 123
Hong Kong Arts Development Council FCO Chevening-Leeds University Scholarships, 712

Indian Sub-Continent

Wingate Scholarships, 771

Middle East

Sharett Scholarship Program, 25

New Zealand

Wingate Scholarships, 771

South Africa

Wingate Scholarships, 771

United Kingdom

AHRB Professional and Vocational Awards (Competition P), 112
AHRB Studentships in the Humanities (Competition A), 112
Polish Embassy Short-Term Bursaries, 571

HOME ECONOMICS

NUTRITION

Any Country

The Bio-Serv Award in Experimental Animal Nutrition, 89
The Cenrium Center for Nutritional Science Award, 90
Center for Field Research Grants, 246
The Conrad A Elvehjem Award for Public Service in Nutrition, 90
The E L R Stokstad Award, 90
Indian Council of Social Science Research General Fellowships, 367
The Mead Johnson Award, 90
The Osborne and Mendel Award, 90

African Nations

The Joint Japan/World Bank Graduate Scholarship Program
(JJ/WBGSP), 395

British Commonwealth

The Joint Japan/World Bank Graduate Scholarship Program
(JJ/WBGSP), 395

Canada

Robin Hood Multifoods Scholarship, 232

Caribbean Countries

The Joint Japan/World Bank Graduate Scholarship Program
(JJ/WBGSP), 395

East European Countries

The Joint Japan/World Bank Graduate Scholarship Program
(JJ/WBGSP), 395

Far East

The Joint Japan/World Bank Graduate Scholarship Program
(JJ/WBGSP), 395

Indian Sub-Continent

Indian Council of Social Science Research Senior Fellowships, 368
The Joint Japan/World Bank Graduate Scholarship Program
(JJ/WBGSP), 395

Middle East

The Joint Japan/World Bank Graduate Scholarship Program
(JJ/WBGSP), 395

South Africa

The Joint Japan/World Bank Graduate Scholarship Program
(JJ/WBGSP), 395

South America

The Joint Japan/World Bank Graduate Scholarship Program
(JJ/WBGSP), 395

CHILD CARE/CHILD DEVELOPMENT

Any Country

Center for Field Research Grants, 246
Equiano Memorial Award, 666
Indian Council of Social Science Research General Fellowships, 367
University of Stirling Research Studentships, 750

African Nations

The Joint Japan/World Bank Graduate Scholarship Program
(JJ/WBGSP), 395

British Commonwealth

The Joint Japan/World Bank Graduate Scholarship Program
(JJ/WBGSP), 395

Caribbean Countries

The Joint Japan/World Bank Graduate Scholarship Program
(JJ/WBGSP), 395

East European Countries

The Joint Japan/World Bank Graduate Scholarship Program
(JJ/WBGSP), 395

Far East

The Joint Japan/World Bank Graduate Scholarship Program
(JJ/WBGSP), 395

Indian Sub-Continent

Indian Council of Social Science Research Senior Fellowships, 368
The Joint Japan/World Bank Graduate Scholarship Program
(JJ/WBGSP), 395

Middle East

The Joint Japan/World Bank Graduate Scholarship Program
(JJ/WBGSP), 395

South Africa

The Joint Japan/World Bank Graduate Scholarship Program
(JJ/WBGSP), 395

South America

The Joint Japan/World Bank Graduate Scholarship Program
(JJ/WBGSP), 395

HOUSE ARTS AND ENVIRONMENT

Any Country

Indian Council of Social Science Research General Fellowships, 367

African Nations

The Joint Japan/World Bank Graduate Scholarship Program
(JJ/WBGSP), 395

British Commonwealth

The Joint Japan/World Bank Graduate Scholarship Program
(JJ/WBGSP), 395

Caribbean Countries

The Joint Japan/World Bank Graduate Scholarship Program
(JJ/WBGSP), 395

East European Countries

The Joint Japan/World Bank Graduate Scholarship Program
(JJ/WBGSP), 395

Far East

The Joint Japan/World Bank Graduate Scholarship Program
(JJ/WBGSP), 395

Indian Sub-Continent

Indian Council of Social Science Research Senior Fellowships, 368
The Joint Japan/World Bank Graduate Scholarship Program
(JJ/WBGSP), 395

Middle East

The Joint Japan/World Bank Graduate Scholarship Program
(JJ/WBGSP), 395

South Africa

The Joint Japan/World Bank Graduate Scholarship Program
(JJ/WBGSP), 395

South America

The Joint Japan/World Bank Graduate Scholarship Program
(JJ/WBGSP), 395

LAW

GENERAL

Any Country

ABF Fellowships in Law and Social Science, 38
AIATSIS Research Grants, 139
The Alberta Law Foundation Graduate Scholarship, 692
Alexander S Onassis Programme of Research Grants, 18
Alexander S Onassis Research Grants, 18
American Association of Law Libraries George A Strait Minority Stipend, 36
Andrew Mellon Foundation Scholarship, 585
Bank of Sweden Tercentenary Foundation Grants, 149
Canadian Department of Foreign Affairs Faculty Enrichment Program, 231
Canadian Department of Foreign Affairs Faculty Research Program, 231
Canadian Department of Foreign Affairs Institutional Research Program, 231
Canadian Institute of Ukrainian Studies Research Grants, 233
Center for Advanced Study in the Behavioral Sciences Postdoctoral Residential Fellowships, 245
Central Queensland University Postgraduate Research Award, 248
CQU International Student Scholarship, 248
Downing College Research Fellowships, 696
Equiano Memorial Award, 666
Evan Lewis Thomas Law Studentships, 626
Field Psych Trust Grant, 310
Fitzwilliam College J R W Alexander Studentship in Law, 697
Gonville and Caius College W M Tapp Studentship in Law, 699
H Thomas Austern Memorial Writing Competition - Food and Drug Law, 313
Harvard Law School Liberal Arts Fellowship, 350
The Helen Darcovich Memorial Doctoral Fellowship, 233
The Honourable N D McDermid Graduate Scholarship in Law, 693
Howard Brown Rickard Scholarship, 500
Howard Drake Memorial Fund, 378
Hugh Le May Fellowship, 586
Humane Studies Fellowships, 376
Humanitarian Trust Awards, 362
IALS Visiting Fellowship in Law Librarianship, 379
IALS Visiting Fellowship in Legislative Studies, 379
IALS Visiting Fellowships, 379
IHS Summer Graduate Research Fellowship, 377
Indian Council of Social Science Research General Fellowships, 367
Inns of Court Fellowship, 379
Institute for Advanced Studies in the Humanities Visiting Research Fellowships, 375
International Lawyers: Study and Training Program, 331
Jane Addams/Andrew Carnegie Fellowships in Philanthropy, 368
Kennan Institute Short Term Grants, 431
Law Librarians in Continuing Education Courses (Type V), 36
Library Degree for Law School Graduates (Type I), 36
Library Degree for Non-Law School Graduates (Type III), 36
Library School Graduates Attending Law School (Type II), 36
Linacre College Heselton Legal Research Scholarship, 729
Lincoln College Erich and Rochelle Endowed Prize in Music, 730
Lincoln College Supperstone Law Scholarship, 731
Mackenzie King Open Scholarship, 455
Mackenzie King Travelling Scholarships, 455
Maxwell Boulton QC Fellowship, 461
Monash University International Postgraduate Research Scholarship (MIPRS), 480
Monash University Silver Jubilee Postgraduate Scholarship, 481
Neporany Research and Teaching Fellowship, 233
NHC Fellowships, 509
NUS Postgraduate Research Scholarship, 520
Onassis Programme of Postgraduate Research Scholarships, 19
Queen Mary Research Studentships, 576
Rhodes University Postdoctoral Fellowship, 586

Rhodes University Postgraduate Scholarship, 587
Royal Irish Academy European Exchange Fellowship, 606
Shell Centenary Scholarships and Shell Centenary Chevening Scholarships, 738
Shirtcliffe Fellowship, 529
Sir Allan Sewell Visiting Fellowship, 344
SOAS Bursary, 622
SOAS Research Student Fellowships, 622
Southern Cross University Postgraduate Research Scholarships, 660
Stiftelsen Lars Hiertas Minne Scientific Research Award, 665
University of Bristol Postgraduate Scholarships, 691
University of Calgary Faculty of Law Graduate Scholarship, 694
University of Dundee Research Awards, 704
University of Glasgow Postgraduate Research Scholarships, 707
University of Manchester Research Studentships and Scholarships, 715
University of New England Research Scholarships, 719
University of Stirling Research Studentships, 750
University of Sussex Overseas Research Studentships, 750
Vera Moore International Postgraduate Research Scholarships, 481
Woods Hole Oceanographic Institution Postdoctoral Awards in Marine Policy and Ocean Management, 777
Woods Hole Oceanographic Institution Research Fellowships in Marine Policy, 778
World Universities Network (WUN) Scholarship Scheme, 749

African Nations

Friends of Peterhouse Bursary, 561
Fulbright Postdoctoral Research and Lecturing Awards for Non-US Citizens, 270
International Postgraduate Research Scholarships (IPRS), 438
The Joint Japan/World Bank Graduate Scholarship Program (JJ/WBGSP), 395
Merton College Reed Foundation Scholarship, 732
Pegasus Cambridge Scholarships for Postgraduate Study, 212

Australia

Australian Postgraduate Awards, 438
Chevening Oxford-Australia Scholarships, 723
Friends of Peterhouse Bursary, 561
Fulbright Awards, 143
Fulbright Postdoctoral Fellowships, 143
Fulbright Postdoctoral Research and Lecturing Awards for Non-US Citizens, 270
Fulbright Postgraduate Studentships, 144
International Postgraduate Research Scholarships (IPRS), 438
Law and Justice Foundation of New South Wales Grants Program, 442
Pegasus Cambridge Scholarships for Postgraduate Study, 212
Pembroke College Australian Graduate Scholarship, 734
The Sir Robert Menzies Scholarships in Law, 632
University of Western Sydney Postgraduate Research Award (UWSPRA), 755
W A Frank Downing Studentship in Law, 219
Wingate Scholarships, 771

British Commonwealth

Friends of Peterhouse Bursary, 561
International Postgraduate Research Scholarships (IPRS), 438
The Joint Japan/World Bank Graduate Scholarship Program (JJ/WBGSP), 395
Merton College Reed Foundation Scholarship, 732
Pegasus Cambridge Scholarships for Postgraduate Study, 212
Wingate Scholarships, 771

Canada

CIALS Cambridge Scholarships, 199
Frank Knox Memorial Fellowships at Harvard University, 131
Friends of Peterhouse Bursary, 561
Fulbright Postdoctoral Research and Lecturing Awards for Non-US Citizens, 270

HISTORY OF LAW

COMPARATIVE LAW

INTERNATIONAL LAW

HUMAN RIGHTS

LABOUR LAW

British Commonwealth

The Joint Japan/World Bank Graduate Scholarship Program (JJ/WBGSP), 395
Wingate Scholarships, 771

Canada

Viscount Bennett Fellowship, 223
Wingate Scholarships, 771

Caribbean Countries

The Joint Japan/World Bank Graduate Scholarship Program (JJ/WBGSP), 395

East European Countries

The Joint Japan/World Bank Graduate Scholarship Program (JJ/WBGSP), 395

Far East

The Joint Japan/World Bank Graduate Scholarship Program (JJ/WBGSP), 395

Indian Sub-Continent

The Joint Japan/World Bank Graduate Scholarship Program (JJ/WBGSP), 395
Wingate Scholarships, 771

Middle East

The Joint Japan/World Bank Graduate Scholarship Program (JJ/WBGSP), 395

New Zealand

Wingate Scholarships, 771

South Africa

The Joint Japan/World Bank Graduate Scholarship Program (JJ/WBGSP), 395
Wingate Scholarships, 771

South America

The Joint Japan/World Bank Graduate Scholarship Program (JJ/WBGSP), 395

United Kingdom

Cardiff University Postgraduate Research Studentships, 242
Wingate Scholarships, 771

United States of America

Fulbright Senior Specialists Program, 271

West European Countries

Cardiff University Postgraduate Research Studentships, 242
European University Institute Postgraduate Scholarships, 306
Wingate Scholarships, 771

MARITIME LAW

Any Country

Center for Advanced Study in the Behavioral Sciences Postdoctoral Residential Fellowships, 245
Onassis Programme of Postgraduate Research Scholarships, 19
Woods Hole Oceanographic Institution Research Fellowships in Marine Policy, 778

Australia

Wingate Scholarships, 771

British Commonwealth

Wingate Scholarships, 771

Canada

Viscount Bennett Fellowship, 223

Wingate Scholarships, 771

East European Countries

AHRB Studentships in the Humanities (Competition A), 112
AHRB Studentships in the Humanities (Competition B), 112

Indian Sub-Continent

Wingate Scholarships, 771

New Zealand

Wingate Scholarships, 771

South Africa

Wingate Scholarships, 771

United Kingdom

AHRB Studentships in the Humanities (Competition A), 112
AHRB Studentships in the Humanities (Competition B), 112
Cardiff University Postgraduate Research Studentships, 242
Wingate Scholarships, 771

West European Countries

Cardiff University Postgraduate Research Studentships, 242
Wingate Scholarships, 771

LAW OF THE AIR

Any Country

Center for Advanced Study in the Behavioral Sciences Postdoctoral Residential Fellowships, 245

African Nations

IATF Aviation MBA Scholarship, 394
IATF IATA Aviation Training and Development Institute (ATDI) Scholarships, 394

Australia

Wingate Scholarships, 771

British Commonwealth

Wingate Scholarships, 771

Canada

Viscount Bennett Fellowship, 223
Wingate Scholarships, 771

Caribbean Countries

IATF Aviation MBA Scholarship, 394
IATF IATA Aviation Training and Development Institute (ATDI) Scholarships, 394

East European Countries

AHRB Studentships in the Humanities (Competition A), 112
AHRB Studentships in the Humanities (Competition B), 112
IATF Aviation MBA Scholarship, 394
IATF IATA Aviation Training and Development Institute (ATDI) Scholarships, 394

Far East

IATF Aviation MBA Scholarship, 394
IATF IATA Aviation Training and Development Institute (ATDI) Scholarships, 394

Indian Sub-Continent

IATF Aviation MBA Scholarship, 394
IATF IATA Aviation Training and Development Institute (ATDI) Scholarships, 394
Wingate Scholarships, 771

Middle East

IATF Aviation MBA Scholarship, 394

IATF IATA Aviation Training and Development Institute (ATDI) Scholarships, 394

New Zealand

Wingate Scholarships, 771

South Africa

IATF Aviation MBA Scholarship, 394
IATF IATA Aviation Training and Development Institute (ATDI) Scholarships, 394
Wingate Scholarships, 771

South America

IATF Aviation MBA Scholarship, 394
IATF IATA Aviation Training and Development Institute (ATDI) Scholarships, 394

United Kingdom

AHRB Studentships in the Humanities (Competition A), 112
AHRB Studentships in the Humanities (Competition B), 112
Wingate Scholarships, 771

West European Countries

Wingate Scholarships, 771

NOTARY STUDIES

Any Country

Center for Advanced Study in the Behavioral Sciences Postdoctoral Residential Fellowships, 245

Canada

Viscount Bennett Fellowship, 223

CIVIL LAW

Any Country

Center for Advanced Study in the Behavioral Sciences Postdoctoral Residential Fellowships, 245
H Thomas Austern Memorial Writing Competition - Food and Drug Law, 313
Onassis Programme of Postgraduate Research Scholarships, 19
University of Bristol Postgraduate Scholarships, 691
Volzhsky Institute of Humanities Awards, 764

African Nations

The Joint Japan/World Bank Graduate Scholarship Program (JJ/WBGSP), 395

Australia

Wingate Scholarships, 771

British Commonwealth

The Joint Japan/World Bank Graduate Scholarship Program (JJ/WBGSP), 395
Wingate Scholarships, 771

Canada

Viscount Bennett Fellowship, 223
Volzhsky Institute of Humanities Awards, 764
Wingate Scholarships, 771

Caribbean Countries

The Joint Japan/World Bank Graduate Scholarship Program (JJ/WBGSP), 395

East European Countries

The Joint Japan/World Bank Graduate Scholarship Program (JJ/WBGSP), 395

Far East

The Joint Japan/World Bank Graduate Scholarship Program (JJ/WBGSP), 395

Indian Sub-Continent

The Joint Japan/World Bank Graduate Scholarship Program (JJ/WBGSP), 395
Wingate Scholarships, 771

Middle East

The Joint Japan/World Bank Graduate Scholarship Program (JJ/WBGSP), 395

New Zealand

Wingate Scholarships, 771

South Africa

The Joint Japan/World Bank Graduate Scholarship Program (JJ/WBGSP), 395
Wingate Scholarships, 771

South America

The Joint Japan/World Bank Graduate Scholarship Program (JJ/WBGSP), 395

United Kingdom

Volzhsky Institute of Humanities Awards, 764
Wingate Scholarships, 771

United States of America

Fulbright Senior Specialists Program, 271
Volzhsky Institute of Humanities Awards, 764

West European Countries

Wingate Scholarships, 771

COMMERCIAL LAW

Any Country

Anglo-German Foundation for the Study of Industrial Society Research Grant, 101
Center for Advanced Study in the Behavioral Sciences Postdoctoral Residential Fellowships, 245
H Thomas Austern Memorial Writing Competition - Food and Drug Law, 313
Massey Doctoral Scholarship, 461
Onassis Programme of Postgraduate Research Scholarships, 19
University Institute of European Studies Postgraduate Scholarships, 688
University of Bristol Postgraduate Scholarships, 691
University of Dundee Research Awards, 704
University of Stirling Research Studentships, 750

African Nations

University of Sussex Overseas Development Administration Shared Scholarship Scheme, 750

Canada

Viscount Bennett Fellowship, 223

East European Countries

Open Society Sofia Central European University Scholarship, 542

Far East

University of Sussex Overseas Development Administration Shared Scholarship Scheme, 750

Indian Sub-Continent

University of Sussex Overseas Development Administration Shared Scholarship Scheme, 750

United Kingdom

Cardiff University Postgraduate Research Studentships, 242
Polish Embassy Short-Term Bursaries, 571
Polish Government Postgraduate Scholarships Scheme, 572

West European Countries

Cardiff University Postgraduate Research Studentships, 242

PUBLIC LAW

Any Country

Alexander S Onassis Programme of Research Grants, 18
Alexander S Onassis Research Grants, 18
Center for Advanced Study in the Behavioral Sciences Postdoctoral
Residential Fellowships, 245
Jack Nelson Legal Fellowship, 581
Jean Monnet Fellowships, 307
Lincoln College Supperstone Law Scholarship, 731
NHC Fellowships, 509
Onassis Programme of Postgraduate Research Scholarships, 19
The Reporters Committee Legal Fellowship, 581
Robert R McCormick Tribune Foundation Journalism Fellowship,
581
Robert R McCormick Tribune Foundation Legal Fellowship, 582
University of Bristol Postgraduate Scholarships, 691
University of Dundee Research Awards, 704

Canada

Viscount Bennett Fellowship, 223

East European Countries

Open Society Sofia Central European University Scholarship, 542

United Kingdom

Cardiff University Postgraduate Research Studentships, 242

United States of America

Fulbright Senior Specialists Program, 271

West European Countries

Cardiff University Postgraduate Research Studentships, 242
European University Institute Postgraduate Scholarships, 306

CONSTITUTIONAL LAW

Any Country

Alexander S Onassis Programme of Research Grants, 18
Alexander S Onassis Research Grants, 18
Center for Advanced Study in the Behavioral Sciences Postdoctoral
Residential Fellowships, 245
H Thomas Austern Memorial Writing Competition - Food and Drug
Law, 313
Jack Nelson Legal Fellowship, 581
John Philip Immroth Award for Intellectual Freedom, 60
Onassis Programme of Postgraduate Research Scholarships, 19
The Reporters Committee Legal Fellowship, 581
Robert R McCormick Tribune Foundation Journalism Fellowship,
581
Robert R McCormick Tribune Foundation Legal Fellowship, 582
Volzhsky Institute of Humanities Awards, 764

Canada

Volzhsky Institute of Humanities Awards, 764

East European Countries

Open Society Sofia Central European University Scholarship, 542

United Kingdom

Cardiff University Postgraduate Research Studentships, 242
Molson Research Awards, 159
Volzhsky Institute of Humanities Awards, 764

United States of America

Fulbright Senior Specialists Program, 271
Volzhsky Institute of Humanities Awards, 764

West European Countries

Cardiff University Postgraduate Research Studentships, 242

ADMINISTRATIVE LAW

Any Country

Alexander S Onassis Programme of Research Grants, 18
Alexander S Onassis Research Grants, 18
Center for Advanced Study in the Behavioral Sciences Postdoctoral
Residential Fellowships, 245
Conservation and Research Foundation Grants, 267
H Thomas Austern Memorial Writing Competition - Food and Drug
Law, 313
Onassis Programme of Postgraduate Research Scholarships, 19

East European Countries

Open Society Sofia Central European University Scholarship, 542

United Kingdom

Cardiff University Postgraduate Research Studentships, 242

West European Countries

Cardiff University Postgraduate Research Studentships, 242

FISCAL LAW

Any Country

Center for Advanced Study in the Behavioral Sciences Postdoctoral
Residential Fellowships, 245

East European Countries

Open Society Sofia Central European University Scholarship, 542

CRIMINAL LAW

Any Country

Alexander S Onassis Programme of Research Grants, 18
Alexander S Onassis Research Grants, 18
Center for Advanced Study in the Behavioral Sciences Postdoctoral
Residential Fellowships, 245
Onassis Programme of Postgraduate Research Scholarships, 19
University of Bristol Postgraduate Scholarships, 691
University of Dundee Research Awards, 704
Volzhsky Institute of Humanities Awards, 764

African Nations

University of Sussex Overseas Development Administration Shared
Scholarship Scheme, 750

Canada

Viscount Bennett Fellowship, 223
Volzhsky Institute of Humanities Awards, 764

East European Countries

Sasakawa Scholarship, 750

Far East

The Asia Crime Prevention Foundation Fellowship, 123
Sasakawa Scholarship, 750
University of Sussex Overseas Development Administration Shared
Scholarship Scheme, 750

Indian Sub-Continent

University of Sussex Overseas Development Administration Shared
Scholarship Scheme, 750

United Kingdom

Cardiff University Postgraduate Research Studentships, 242
Sasakawa Scholarship, 750
Volzhsky Institute of Humanities Awards, 764

United States of America

Fulbright Senior Specialists Program, 271
US-UK Fulbright Commission Police Studies Grant, 760
Volzhsky Institute of Humanities Awards, 764

West European Countries

Cardiff University Postgraduate Research Studentships, 242

CANON LAW

Any Country

Center for Advanced Study in the Behavioral Sciences Postdoctoral Residential Fellowships, 245

United Kingdom

Cardiff University Postgraduate Research Studentships, 242

West European Countries

Cardiff University Postgraduate Research Studentships, 242

ISLAMIC LAW

Any Country

Center for Advanced Study in the Behavioral Sciences Postdoctoral Residential Fellowships, 245
Deputy Chancellors Postdoctoral Research, 535
NTU One Year Postdoctoral Fellowship, 535
NTU Three Year Postdoctoral Fellowship, 536

United States of America

US Department of Education International Research and Studies Program, 757

EUROPEAN COMMUNITY LAW

Any Country

Alexander S Onassis Programme of Research Grants, 18
Alexander S Onassis Research Grants, 18
Center for Advanced Study in the Behavioral Sciences Postdoctoral Residential Fellowships, 245
Jean Monnet Fellowships, 307
Lincoln College Supperstone Law Scholarship, 731
Onassis Programme of Postgraduate Research Scholarships, 19
Paul H Nitze School of Advanced International Studies (SAIS) Financial Aid and Fellowships, 156
Volzhsky Institute of Humanities Awards, 764

Canada

Volzhsky Institute of Humanities Awards, 764

East European Countries

AHRB Studentships in the Humanities (Competition A), 112
AHRB Studentships in the Humanities (Competition B), 112
Open Society Sofia Central European University Scholarship, 542

United Kingdom

AHRB Studentships in the Humanities (Competition A), 112
AHRB Studentships in the Humanities (Competition B), 112
Cardiff University Postgraduate Research Studentships, 242
Volzhsky Institute of Humanities Awards, 764

United States of America

US Department of Education International Research and Studies Program, 757
Volzhsky Institute of Humanities Awards, 764

West European Countries

Cardiff University Postgraduate Research Studentships, 242
European University Institute Postgraduate Scholarships, 306

MATHEMATICS AND COMPUTER SCIENCE

GENERAL

Any Country

The Abdus Salam ICTP Fellowships, 5
AIATSIS Research Grants, 139
Airey Neave Trust Award, 14
Andrew Mellon Foundation Scholarship, 585
AUC Assistantships, 96
AUC University Fellowships, 97
AWU Postgraduate Fellowships, 125
Beit Fellowship For Scientific Research, 366
Center for Advanced Study in the Behavioral Sciences Postdoctoral Residential Fellowships, 245
Central Queensland University Postgraduate Research Award, 248
CLM George A Gecowets Graduate Scholarship Program, 271
Computer Laboratory ORS Equivalent Awards, 200
Concordia University Graduate Fellowships, 266
CQU International Student Scholarship, 248
Daphne Jackson Fellowship, 278
David J Azrieli Graduate Fellowship, 266
DEED Scholarship, 77
Dorothy Hodgkin Fellowships, 608
EPSRC Advanced Fellowships, 297
EPSRC Senior Research Fellowships, 299
Foundation for Science and Disability Student Grant Fund, 316
Golden Key National Honor Society Information Systems Achievement Awards, 339
HSS Travel Grant, 359
Humanitarian Trust Awards, 362
IMU Fields Medals, 406
Institute for Advanced Study Postdoctoral Residential Fellowships, 375
Institute Mittag-Leffler Grants, 378
La Trobe University Postgraduate Scholarship, 439
Leverhulme Trust Senior Research Fellowships, 608
Lloyds Fellowship, 449
Massey Doctoral Scholarship, 461
Matsumae International Foundation Research Fellowship, 461
Monash University International Postgraduate Research Scholarship (MIPRS), 480
Nancy Goodhue Lynch Scholarship, 279
The NASA Administrator's Fellowship Program, 490
National Academy of Education Spencer Postdoctoral Fellowships, 489
NFR Junior Research Fellowships, 668
NFR Open Postdoctoral Fellowships, 668
NFR Research Grants, 668
NFR Senior Research Positions, 668
NFR Travel Grants, 669
Queen Mary Research Studentships, 576
Rhodes University Postdoctoral Fellowship, 586
Rhodes University Postgraduate Scholarship, 587
Royal Irish Academy European Exchange Fellowship, 606
Royal Irish Academy Senior Visiting Fellowships, 606
Royal Society Industry Fellowships Scheme, 610
Royal Society Research Grants Scheme, 610
SEELLD Personal Research Fellowships, 614
SEELLD/RSE Support Research Fellowships, 615
Sigma Xi Grants-in-Aid of Research, 629
Solomon Lefschetz Instructorships, 250
Southern Cross University Postgraduate Research Scholarships, 660

African Nations

Australia

British Commonwealth

Canada

Caribbean Countries

East European Countries

Far East

Indian Sub-Continent

Swiss Federal Institute of Technology Scholarships, 669
University of Wales, Bangor (UWB) Research Studentships, 753
University of Wales, Bangor Departmental Research Studentships, 753
Wingate Scholarships, 771

STATISTICS

Any Country

Center for Advanced Study in the Behavioral Sciences Postdoctoral Residential Fellowships, 245
Central Queensland University Postgraduate Research Award, 248
CQU International Student Scholarship, 248
Hugh Kelly Fellowship, 586
Massey Doctoral Scholarship, 461
Pierre Robillard Award, 665
Rhodes University Postdoctoral Fellowship, 586
Shell Centenary Scholarships and Shell Centenary Chevening Scholarships, 738
Sir James McNeill Foundation Postgraduate Scholarship, 481
Solomon Lefschetz Instructorships, 250
Thomas Holloway Research Studentship, 602
University of Bristol Postgraduate Scholarships, 691
University of Glasgow Postgraduate Research Scholarships, 707
The University of Kent IMS Studentships, 711
University of Manchester Research Studentships and Scholarships, 715
University of New England Research Scholarships, 719
University of Stirling Research Studentships, 750
Volzhsky Institute of Humanities Awards, 764

Australia

Fulbright Tim Matthews Memorial Postgraduate Student Award in Statistics and Related Disciplines, 145
Wingate Scholarships, 771

British Commonwealth

Wingate Scholarships, 771

Canada

Volzhsky Institute of Humanities Awards, 764
Wingate Scholarships, 771

Indian Sub-Continent

Wingate Scholarships, 771

New Zealand

Wingate Scholarships, 771

South Africa

Wingate Scholarships, 771

United Kingdom

Cardiff University Postgraduate Research Studentships, 242
ESRC Research Studentships, 292
Sheffield Hallam University Research Studentships, 625
University of Wales, Bangor (UWB) Research Studentships, 753
University of Wales, Bangor Departmental Research Studentships, 753
Volzhsky Institute of Humanities Awards, 764
Wingate Scholarships, 771

United States of America

AAUW Selected Professions Fellowships, 4
COBASE Collaboration in Basic Science and Engineering, 516
ETS Postdoctoral Fellowships, 294
Fulbright Senior Specialists Program, 271
NRC Twinning Program, 516
Volzhsky Institute of Humanities Awards, 764
Winston Churchill Scholarship, 771

West European Countries

Cardiff University Postgraduate Research Studentships, 242
ESRC Research Studentships, 292
Sheffield Hallam University Research Studentships, 625
University of Wales, Bangor (UWB) Research Studentships, 753
University of Wales, Bangor Departmental Research Studentships, 753
Wingate Scholarships, 771

ACTUARIAL SCIENCE

Any Country

AERF Individual Grants Competition, 8
Center for Advanced Study in the Behavioral Sciences Postdoctoral Residential Fellowships, 245
Sir James McNeill Foundation Postgraduate Scholarship, 481

Australia

Fulbright Tim Matthews Memorial Postgraduate Student Award in Statistics and Related Disciplines, 145

United States of America

ETS Postdoctoral Fellowships, 294
Fulbright Senior Specialists Program, 271
Winston Churchill Scholarship, 771

APPLIED MATHEMATICS

Any Country

Center for Advanced Study in the Behavioral Sciences Postdoctoral Residential Fellowships, 245
Central Queensland University Postgraduate Research Award, 248
CQU International Student Scholarship, 248
Hugh Kelly Fellowship, 586
Massey Doctoral Scholarship, 461
NERC Postdoctoral Research Fellowships, 521
Rhodes University Postdoctoral Fellowship, 586
Sir James McNeill Foundation Postgraduate Scholarship, 481
SISSA Fellowship, 410
Slater Fellowship in the History of Twentieth-Century Physical Sciences, 73
Solomon Lefschetz Instructorships, 250
University of Bristol Postgraduate Scholarships, 691
University of Dundee Research Awards, 704
University of Glasgow Postgraduate Research Scholarships, 707
The University of Kent IMS Studentships, 711
University of Manchester Research Studentships and Scholarships, 715
University of Stirling Research Studentships, 750
The University of Western Ontario Senior Visiting Fellowship, 755
Weizmann Institute of Science MSc Fellowships, 767
Woods Hole Oceanographic Institution Postdoctoral Fellowships in Ocean Science and Engineering, 777
Woods Hole Oceanographic Institution/NOAA Co-operative Institute for Climate and Ocean Research Postdoctoral Fellowship, 778

Australia

Fulbright Tim Matthews Memorial Postgraduate Student Award in Statistics and Related Disciplines, 145
University of Western Sydney Postgraduate Research Award (UWSPRA), 755
Wingate Scholarships, 771

British Commonwealth

Wingate Scholarships, 771

Canada

AAAS Mass Media Science and Engineering Fellowship, 32
Wingate Scholarships, 771

COMPUTER SCIENCE

American Society of Naval Engineers Scholarships, 93
Army Research Laboratory Postdoctoral Fellowship Program, 85
BPW Career Advancement Scholarship Program, 184
COBASE Collaboration in Basic Science and Engineering, 516
ETS Postdoctoral Fellowships, 294
Fannie and John Hertz Foundation Fellowships, 309
Fulbright Distinguished Chairs Program, 270
Fulbright Senior Specialists Program, 271
Microsoft Corporation Scholarships, 656
NRC Twinning Program, 516
Olive Lynn Salembier Scholarship, 656
ONR Postdoctoral Fellowship, 539
ONR/ASEE Postdoctoral Fellowship Program, 85
PhRMA Postdoctoral Fellowships in Informatics, 563
PhRMA Research Starter Grants in Informatics, 565
PhRMA Sabbatical Fellowships in Informatics, 566
Volzhsky Institute of Humanities Awards, 764
Winston Churchill Scholarship, 771

West European Countries

Cardiff University Postgraduate Research Studentships, 242
CERN Doctoral Student Programme, 251
CERN Fellowships, 251
CERN Technical Student Programme, 251
EPSRC Quota, 708
NTU AEH Exchange Studentships, 487
Sheffield Hallam University Research Studentships, 625
University of Wales, Bangor Departmental Research Studentships, 753
Wingate Scholarships, 771

ARTIFICIAL INTELLIGENCE

Any Country

BP/RSE Research Fellowships, 613
Center for Advanced Study in the Behavioral Sciences Postdoctoral Residential Fellowships, 245
Central Queensland University Postgraduate Research Award, 248
CQU International Student Scholarship, 248
International School of Crystallography Grants, 411
Keble College Ian Palmer Graduate Scholarship in Information Technology, 727
Thomas Holloway Research Studentship, 602
University of Bristol Postgraduate Scholarships, 691
University of Manchester Research Studentships and Scholarships, 715
University of New England Research Scholarships, 719
University of Sussex Overseas Research Studentships, 750

Australia

University of Western Sydney Postgraduate Research Award (UWSPRA), 755
Wingate Scholarships, 771

British Commonwealth

Wingate Scholarships, 771

Canada

Wingate Scholarships, 771

East European Countries

CERN Fellowships, 251

Indian Sub-Continent

Wingate Scholarships, 771

New Zealand

University of Western Sydney Postgraduate Research Award (UWSPRA), 755
Wingate Scholarships, 771

South Africa

Wingate Scholarships, 771

United Kingdom

Cardiff University Postgraduate Research Studentships, 242
CERN Fellowships, 251
Sheffield Hallam University Research Studentships, 625
University of Wales (Aberystwyth) Postgraduate Research Studentships, 752
Wingate Scholarships, 771

United States of America

American Society of Naval Engineers Scholarships, 93
Army Research Laboratory Postdoctoral Fellowship Program, 85
COBASE Collaboration in Basic Science and Engineering, 516
NRC Twinning Program, 516
ONR Postdoctoral Fellowship, 539
ONR/ASEE Postdoctoral Fellowship Program, 85
Winston Churchill Scholarship, 771

West European Countries

Cardiff University Postgraduate Research Studentships, 242
CERN Fellowships, 251
Sheffield Hallam University Research Studentships, 625
Wingate Scholarships, 771

SYSTEMS ANALYSIS

Any Country

Center for Advanced Study in the Behavioral Sciences Postdoctoral Residential Fellowships, 245
Central Queensland University Postgraduate Research Award, 248
CQU International Student Scholarship, 248
Keble College Ian Palmer Graduate Scholarship in Information Technology, 727
Massey Doctoral Scholarship, 461
University of Bristol Postgraduate Scholarships, 691
University of Manchester Research Studentships and Scholarships, 715
University of Stirling Research Studentships, 750

Australia

University of Western Sydney Postgraduate Research Award (UWSPRA), 755

East European Countries

CERN Doctoral Student Programme, 251
CERN Fellowships, 251
CERN Technical Student Programme, 251
Open Society Sofia Central European University Scholarship, 542

New Zealand

University of Western Sydney Postgraduate Research Award (UWSPRA), 755

United Kingdom

CERN Doctoral Student Programme, 251
CERN Fellowships, 251
CERN Technical Student Programme, 251
Sheffield Hallam University Research Studentships, 625

United States of America

American Society of Naval Engineers Scholarships, 93
COBASE Collaboration in Basic Science and Engineering, 516
NRC Twinning Program, 516
PhRMA Postdoctoral Fellowships in Informatics, 563
PhRMA Research Starter Grants in Informatics, 565
PhRMA Sabbatical Fellowships in Informatics, 566
Physician Research Development Award, 63
Winston Churchill Scholarship, 771

West European Countries

CERN Doctoral Student Programme, 251
CERN Fellowships, 251
CERN Technical Student Programme, 251
Sheffield Hallam University Research Studentships, 625

MASS COMMUNICATION AND INFORMATION SCIENCE

GENERAL

Any Country

Adelle and Erwin Tomash Fellowship in the History of Information Processing, 252
AIATSIS Research Grants, 139
Alexander S Onassis Research Grants, 18
Andrew Mellon Foundation Scholarship, 585
AUC Graduate Merit Fellowships, 96
AUC University Fellowships, 97
Bank of Sweden Tercentenary Foundation Grants, 149
Canadian Department of Foreign Affairs Faculty Enrichment Program, 231
Canadian Department of Foreign Affairs Faculty Research Program, 231
Canadian Department of Foreign Affairs Institutional Research Program, 231
Center for Advanced Study in the Behavioral Sciences Postdoctoral Residential Fellowships, 245
Central Queensland University Postgraduate Research Award, 248
Concordia University Graduate Fellowships, 266
CQU International Student Scholarship, 248
David J Azrieli Graduate Fellowship, 266
Equiano Memorial Award, 666
ETS Summer Program in Research for Graduate Students, 294
Field Psych Trust Grant, 310
HSS Travel Grant, 359
Humane Studies Fellowships, 376
Indian Council of Social Science Research General Fellowships, 367
INE Collaborative Research Initiatives, 644
John and Mary R Markle Foundation Grants, 424
Korea Foundation Advanced Research Grant, 433
Korea Foundation Fellowship for Field Research, 434
Korea Foundation Fellowship for Graduate Studies, 434
Korea Foundation Postdoctoral Fellowship, 434
Lindbergh Grants, 252
Monash University International Postgraduate Research Scholarship (MIPRS), 480
NAB Grants for Research in Broadcasting, 491
Onassis Programme of Postgraduate Research Scholarships, 19
Rhodes University Postgraduate Scholarship, 587
Rolf Nevanlinna Prize, 406
SEELLD Personal Research Fellowships, 614
SEELLD/RSE Support Research Fellowships, 615
Southern Cross University Postgraduate Research Scholarships, 660
Stanley G French Graduate Fellowship, 267
University of Calgary Cogeco Inc Graduate Scholarship, 693
University of Glasgow Postgraduate Research Scholarships, 707
University of Manchester Research Studentships and Scholarships, 715
University of Stirling Research Studentships, 750
Vera Moore International Postgraduate Research Scholarships, 481

African Nations

ABCCF Student Grant, 103
AUC African Graduate Fellowship, 95
Friends of Peterhouse Bursary, 561

Fulbright Postdoctoral Research and Lecturing Awards for Non-US Citizens, 270
The Joint Japan/World Bank Graduate Scholarship Program (JJ/WBGSP), 395
Merton College Reed Foundation Scholarship, 732

Australia

Coral Sea Scholarship, 143
Friends of Peterhouse Bursary, 561
Fulbright Awards, 143
Fulbright Postdoctoral Fellowships, 143
Fulbright Postdoctoral Research and Lecturing Awards for Non-US Citizens, 270
Fulbright Postgraduate Studentships, 144
University of Western Sydney Postgraduate Research Award (UWSPRA), 755
Wingate Scholarships, 771

British Commonwealth

Friends of Peterhouse Bursary, 561
The Joint Japan/World Bank Graduate Scholarship Program (JJ/WBGSP), 395
Merton College Reed Foundation Scholarship, 732
Wingate Scholarships, 771
Wolfson Foundation Grants, 773

Canada

CFUW Memorial/Professional Fellowship, 229
Friends of Peterhouse Bursary, 561
Fulbright Postdoctoral Research and Lecturing Awards for Non-US Citizens, 270
J W McConnell Memorial Fellowships, 266
PRA Fellowships, 549
SSHRC Doctoral Fellowships, 646
SSHRC Major Collaborative Research Initiatives (MCRI), 646
SSHRC Standard Research Grants, 647
Wingate Scholarships, 771

Caribbean Countries

Friends of Peterhouse Bursary, 561
The Joint Japan/World Bank Graduate Scholarship Program (JJ/WBGSP), 395
Merton College Reed Foundation Scholarship, 732
PRA Fellowships, 549

East European Countries

AHRB Studentships in the Humanities (Competition A), 112
AHRB Studentships in the Humanities (Competition B), 112
Friends of Peterhouse Bursary, 561
Fulbright Postdoctoral Research and Lecturing Awards for Non-US Citizens, 270
The Joint Japan/World Bank Graduate Scholarship Program (JJ/WBGSP), 395
Merton College Reed Foundation Scholarship, 732

Far East

COSTED Travel Fellowship, 262
Friends of Peterhouse Bursary, 561
Fulbright Postdoctoral Research and Lecturing Awards for Non-US Citizens, 270
Japanese American Citizens League Scholarship and Award Program, 422
The Joint Japan/World Bank Graduate Scholarship Program (JJ/WBGSP), 395
Merton College Reed Foundation Scholarship, 732

Indian Sub-Continent

COSTED Travel Fellowship, 262
Friends of Peterhouse Bursary, 561
Fulbright Postdoctoral Research and Lecturing Awards for Non-US Citizens, 270
Indian Council of Social Science Research Senior Fellowships, 368

JOURNALISM

Caribbean Countries

East European Countries

Far East

Indian Sub-Continent

Middle East

New Zealand

South Africa

South America

United Kingdom

United States of America

West European Countries

RADIO/TELEVISION BROADCASTING

Any Country

African Nations

Canada

Caribbean Countries

East European Countries

Far East

Indian Sub-Continent

Middle East

South Africa

South America

United Kingdom

United States of America

Fulbright Senior Specialists Program, 271
Ian Axford (New Zealand) Fellowships in Public Policy, 263

West European Countries

AHRB Professional and Vocational Awards (Competition P), 112
Cardiff University Postgraduate Research Studentships, 242
Scholarship Foundation of the League for Finnish-American Societies, 621

PUBLIC RELATIONS AND PUBLICITY

Any Country

Alexander S Onassis Programme of Research Grants, 18
Alexander S Onassis Research Grants, 18
Anglo-German Foundation for the Study of Industrial Society Research Grant, 101
Central Queensland University Postgraduate Research Award, 248
CQU International Student Scholarship, 248
Equiano Memorial Award, 666
John Hervey, Broadcasters and Smallsreed Awards, 686
Onassis Programme of Postgraduate Research Scholarships, 19
Volzhsky Institute of Humanities Awards, 764

Canada

Volzhsky Institute of Humanities Awards, 764

East European Countries

Soros Supplementary Grants Programme (SSGP), 544

United Kingdom

Cardiff University Postgraduate Research Studentships, 242
Volzhsky Institute of Humanities Awards, 764

United States of America

Fulbright Senior Specialists Program, 271
Volzhsky Institute of Humanities Awards, 764

West European Countries

Cardiff University Postgraduate Research Studentships, 242

MASS COMMUNICATION

Any Country

Central Queensland University Postgraduate Research Award, 248
CQU International Student Scholarship, 248
Equiano Memorial Award, 666
John Hervey, Broadcasters and Smallsreed Awards, 686
NAB Grants for Research in Broadcasting, 491
Onassis Programme of Postgraduate Research Scholarships, 19
University of Stirling Research Studentships, 750
William B Ruggles Right to Work Award, 518

African Nations

Golda Meir Mount Carmel International Training Centre Assistance for Courses, 337
Golda Meir Mount Carmel International Training Centre Tuition and Maintenance Scholarships, 337

Australia

University of Western Sydney Postgraduate Research Award (UWSPRA), 755

Canada

The BBM Scholarship, 222
Canadian Window on International Development, 399
Frederick T Metcalf Award Program, 131
The Jim Bourque Scholarship, 105

Caribbean Countries

Golda Meir Mount Carmel International Training Centre Assistance for Courses, 337

Golda Meir Mount Carmel International Training Centre Tuition and Maintenance Scholarships, 337

East European Countries

Golda Meir Mount Carmel International Training Centre Assistance for Courses, 337
Golda Meir Mount Carmel International Training Centre Tuition and Maintenance Scholarships, 337
Soros Supplementary Grants Programme (SSGP), 544

Far East

Golda Meir Mount Carmel International Training Centre Assistance for Courses, 337
Golda Meir Mount Carmel International Training Centre Tuition and Maintenance Scholarships, 337

Indian Sub-Continent

Golda Meir Mount Carmel International Training Centre Assistance for Courses, 337
Golda Meir Mount Carmel International Training Centre Tuition and Maintenance Scholarships, 337

Middle East

Golda Meir Mount Carmel International Training Centre Assistance for Courses, 337
Golda Meir Mount Carmel International Training Centre Tuition and Maintenance Scholarships, 337

New Zealand

University of Western Sydney Postgraduate Research Award (UWSPRA), 755

South Africa

Golda Meir Mount Carmel International Training Centre Assistance for Courses, 337
Golda Meir Mount Carmel International Training Centre Tuition and Maintenance Scholarships, 337

South America

Golda Meir Mount Carmel International Training Centre Assistance for Courses, 337
Golda Meir Mount Carmel International Training Centre Tuition and Maintenance Scholarships, 337

United Kingdom

Cardiff University Postgraduate Research Studentships, 242
Sheffield Hallam University Research Studentships, 625

United States of America

Dow Jones Editing Intern Program, 286
Fulbright Distinguished Chairs Program, 270
Fulbright Senior Specialists Program, 271
Ian Axford (New Zealand) Fellowships in Public Policy, 263
Robert Bosch Foundation Fellowship Program, 589
Robert Bosch Foundation Fellowships, 589

West European Countries

Cardiff University Postgraduate Research Studentships, 242
Scholarship Foundation of the League for Finnish-American Societies, 621
Sheffield Hallam University Research Studentships, 625

MEDIA STUDIES

Any Country

Alexander S Onassis Programme of Research Grants, 18
Alexander S Onassis Research Grants, 18
Anglo-German Foundation for the Study of Industrial Society Research Grant, 101
Central Queensland University Postgraduate Research Award, 248
CQU International Student Scholarship, 248
Joyce A Tracy Fellowship, 29

Massey Doctoral Scholarship, 461
NAB Grants for Research in Broadcasting, 491
NHC Fellowships, 509
Onassis Programme of Postgraduate Research Scholarships, 19
Rhodes University Postdoctoral Fellowship, 586
Thomas Holloway Research Studentship, 602
University of Stirling Research Studentships, 750
University of Sussex Overseas Research Studentships, 750

African Nations

Golda Meir Mount Carmel International Training Centre Assistance for Courses, 337
Golda Meir Mount Carmel International Training Centre Tuition and Maintenance Scholarships, 337

Australia

University of Western Sydney Postgraduate Research Award (UWSPRA), 755

British Commonwealth

ACU Development Fellowships, 127

Caribbean Countries

Golda Meir Mount Carmel International Training Centre Assistance for Courses, 337
Golda Meir Mount Carmel International Training Centre Tuition and Maintenance Scholarships, 337

East European Countries

AHRB Studentships in the Humanities (Competition A), 112
AHRB Studentships in the Humanities (Competition B), 112
Golda Meir Mount Carmel International Training Centre Assistance for Courses, 337
Golda Meir Mount Carmel International Training Centre Tuition and Maintenance Scholarships, 337
Soros Supplementary Grants Programme (SSGP), 544

Far East

Golda Meir Mount Carmel International Training Centre Assistance for Courses, 337
Golda Meir Mount Carmel International Training Centre Tuition and Maintenance Scholarships, 337

Indian Sub-Continent

Golda Meir Mount Carmel International Training Centre Assistance for Courses, 337
Golda Meir Mount Carmel International Training Centre Tuition and Maintenance Scholarships, 337

Middle East

Golda Meir Mount Carmel International Training Centre Assistance for Courses, 337
Golda Meir Mount Carmel International Training Centre Tuition and Maintenance Scholarships, 337

New Zealand

University of Western Sydney Postgraduate Research Award (UWSPRA), 755

South Africa

Golda Meir Mount Carmel International Training Centre Assistance for Courses, 337
Golda Meir Mount Carmel International Training Centre Tuition and Maintenance Scholarships, 337
South African Council for English Education (EX-PCE Bursary), 659

South America

Golda Meir Mount Carmel International Training Centre Assistance for Courses, 337
Golda Meir Mount Carmel International Training Centre Tuition and Maintenance Scholarships, 337

United Kingdom

ACU Development Fellowships, 127
AHRB Studentships in the Humanities (Competition A), 112
AHRB Studentships in the Humanities (Competition B), 112
Cardiff University Postgraduate Research Studentships, 242
ESRC Research Studentships, 292
Polish Embassy Short-Term Bursaries, 571
Polish Government Postgraduate Scholarships Scheme, 572
University of Wales (Aberystwyth) Postgraduate Research Studentships, 752

United States of America

Bicentennial Swedish-American Exchange Fund Travel Grants, 153
Fulbright Distinguished Chairs Program, 270
Fulbright Senior Specialists Program, 271
Ian Axford (New Zealand) Fellowships in Public Policy, 263

West European Countries

Cardiff University Postgraduate Research Studentships, 242
ESRC Research Studentships, 292
Scholarship Foundation of the League for Finnish-American Societies, 621

COMMUNICATIONS SKILLS

Any Country

Central Queensland University Postgraduate Research Award, 248
CQU International Student Scholarship, 248
Humane Studies Fellowships, 376
University of Stirling Research Studentships, 750
Volzhsky Institute of Humanities Awards, 764

Canada

The BBM Scholarship, 222
Volzhsky Institute of Humanities Awards, 764

East European Countries

Soros Supplementary Grants Programme (SSGP), 544

South Africa

South African Council for English Education (EX-PCE Bursary), 659

United Kingdom

ESRC Research Studentships, 292
Volzhsky Institute of Humanities Awards, 764

United States of America

Fulbright Senior Specialists Program, 271
Volzhsky Institute of Humanities Awards, 764

West European Countries

ESRC Research Studentships, 292

LIBRARY SCIENCE

Any Country

3M/NMRT Professional Development Grant, 57
AASL Frances Henne Award, 58
AASL Highsmith Research Grant, 58
AASL Information Technology Pathfinder Award, 58
ALA/Information Today Library of the Future Award, 58
Beta Phi Mu Award, 58
bill boyd Literary Award, 58
Blanche E Woolls Scholarship for School Library Media Service, 150
Bogle-Pratt International Library Travel Fund, 58
Bound to Stay Bound Book Scholarships, 58
Canadian Institute of Ukrainian Studies Research Grants, 233
Carroll Preston Baber Research Grant, 58
Christopher J Hoy/ERT Scholarship, 59
Cunningham Memorial International Fellowship, 462
David Rozkuszka Scholarship, 59

MUSEUM STUDIES AND CONSERVATION

New Zealand

Wingate Scholarships, 771

South Africa

Wingate Scholarships, 771

United Kingdom

AHRB Professional and Vocational Awards (Competition P), 112
Cardiff University Postgraduate Research Studentships, 242
June Baker Trust Awards, 430
Wingate Scholarships, 771

United States of America

Fulbright Senior Specialists Program, 271

West European Countries

AHRB Professional and Vocational Awards (Competition P), 112
Cardiff University Postgraduate Research Studentships, 242
Natural History Museum Sys-Resource, 522
Wingate Scholarships, 771

MUSEUM MANAGEMENT

Any Country

ASCSA Fellowships, 79
J Franklin Jameson Fellowship, 54
Massey Doctoral Scholarship, 461
Samuel H Kress Fellowship in Classical Art History, 81

East European Countries

Natural History Museum Sys-Resource, 522
Soros Supplementary Grants Programme (SSGP), 544

Far East

Hong Kong Arts Development Council FCO Chevening-Leeds University Scholarships, 712

United Kingdom

AHRB Professional and Vocational Awards (Competition P), 112

United States of America

Fulbright Senior Specialists Program, 271
NHPRC Fellowship in Archival Administration, 508

West European Countries

AHRB Professional and Vocational Awards (Competition P), 112
Natural History Museum Sys-Resource, 522

RESTORATION OF WORKS OF ART

Any Country

ASCSA Fellowships, 79
ASCSA Summer Sessions, 80
Jacob Hirsch Fellowship, 80
M Alison Frantz Fellowship in Post-Classical Studies at The Gennadius Library (formerly known as the Gennadeion Fellowship), 81
NEH Research Fellowships, 81
Onassis Programme of Postgraduate Research Scholarships, 19
Samuel H Kress Fellowship in Classical Art History, 81
Samuel H Kress Joint Athens-Jerusalem Fellowship, 81

Australia

Wingate Scholarships, 771

British Commonwealth

Wingate Scholarships, 771

Canada

Wingate Scholarships, 771

East European Countries

Soros Supplementary Grants Programme (SSGP), 544

Far East

Hong Kong Arts Development Council FCO Chevening-Leeds University Scholarships, 712

Indian Sub-Continent

Wingate Scholarships, 771

New Zealand

Wingate Scholarships, 771

South Africa

Wingate Scholarships, 771

United Kingdom

AHRB Professional and Vocational Awards (Competition P), 112
June Baker Trust Awards, 430
Polish Embassy Short-Term Bursaries, 571
Polish Government Postgraduate Scholarships Scheme, 572
Wingate Scholarships, 771

United States of America

Fulbright Senior Specialists Program, 271

West European Countries

AHRB Professional and Vocational Awards (Competition P), 112
Wingate Scholarships, 771

DOCUMENTATION TECHNIQUES AND ARCHIVING

Any Country

Albert J Beveridge Grant, 53
ASCSA Fellowships, 79
Bernadotte E Schmitt Grants, 54
J Franklin Jameson Fellowship, 54
Lester J Cappon Fellowship in Documentary Editing, 531
Littleton-Griswold Research Grant, 54
NEH Research Fellowships, 81
Samuel H Kress Fellowship in Classical Art History, 81

Australia

Wingate Scholarships, 771

British Commonwealth

Wingate Scholarships, 771

Canada

Wingate Scholarships, 771

East European Countries

AHRB Studentships in the Humanities (Competition B), 112
Open Society Sofia Central European University Scholarship, 542
Soros Supplementary Grants Programme (SSGP), 544

Indian Sub-Continent

Wingate Scholarships, 771

New Zealand

Wingate Scholarships, 771

South Africa

Wingate Scholarships, 771

United Kingdom

AHRB Professional and Vocational Awards (Competition P), 112
AHRB Studentships in the Humanities (Competition B), 112
University of Wales (Aberystwyth) Postgraduate Research Studentships, 752

MEDICAL SCIENCES

GENERAL

Any Country

African Nations

Australia

British Commonwealth

Canada

Caribbean Countries

East European Countries

Far East

Indian Sub-Continent

Middle East

New Zealand

North Dakota Indian Scholarship, 535
Parker B Francis Fellowship Program, 554
PhRMA Center of Excellence in Clinical Pharmacology, 562
PhRMA Postdoctoral Fellowships in Health Outcomes Research, 563
PhRMA Predoctoral Fellowships in Health Outcomes Research, 564
PhRMA Research Starter Grants in Health Outcomes Research, 565
PhRMA Sabbatical Fellowships in Health Outcomes Research, 566
Postdoctoral Training Programme in Addiction and Mental Health, 249
Promotion of Doctoral Studies (PODS), 316
RCOG USA/British Isles Visiting Fellowship, 597
RSNA Research Fellow Program, 578
RSNA Scholars Program, 579
Scholarships for Émigrés in the Health Professions, 424
The Steven J Bryant Research Grant, 494

West European Countries

ASHF Graduate Scholarship for International or Minority Student, 94
BHF Research Awards, 167
BIAL Award in Clinical Medicine, 152
DHFETE Postgraduate Studentships and Bursaries for Study in Northern Ireland, 281
Eugen and Ilse Seibold Award, 283
Fulbright Postdoctoral Research and Lecturing Awards for Non-US Citizens, 270
The Hastings Center International Visiting Scholars Program, 352
Health Services Research Fellowships, 353
Henry Dryerre Scholarship, 614
HRB Project Grants-General, 354
HRB Research Project Grants Inter-Disciplinary, 354
HRB Summer Student Grants, 354
International Fellowships in Medical Education, 293
International Postgraduate Research Scholarships (IPRS), 438
ISN Visiting Scholars Program, 412
John Fyffe Memorial Fellowship, 168
MRC Masters Studentships, 464
NORD Clinical Research Grants, 515
The Queen's College Florey EPA Scholarship, 735
Rink Research Fellowship Scheme, 609
Royal Society University Research Fellowships, 610
Scholarship Foundation of the League for Finnish-American Societies, 621
Silsoe Awards, 274
Wingate Scholarships, 771

PUBLIC HEALTH AND HYGIENE

Any Country

AACR Scholar-in-Training Awards, 31
BIAL Merit Award in Medical Sciences, 152
Canadian Blood Services Transfusion Medicine Fellowship Awards, 224
Center for Advanced Study in the Behavioral Sciences Postdoctoral Residential Fellowships, 245
CIHR Fellowship Programme, 234
Colt Foundation PhD Fellowship, 262
Fight for Sight Postdoctoral Research Fellowships, 311
Fight for Sight Student Research Fellowships, 311
IARC Postdoctoral Fellowships for Research Training in Cancer, 393
Indian Council of Social Science Research General Fellowships, 367
Meningitis Research Foundation Project Grant, 469
Meningitis Research Foundation Small Project Grant, 470
Meningitis Trust Research Award, 470
Population Council Fellowships in Population and Social Sciences, 573
Postdoctoral Fellowship in Breast Cancer Research, Public Health or Epidemiology, 667
Roche Research Foundation, 589
Sigma Xi Grants-in-Aid of Research, 629
Sir Allan Sewell Visiting Fellowship, 344

The Susan G Komen Breast Cancer Foundation Dissertation Research Award, 667
University of Bristol Postgraduate Scholarships, 691
University of Glasgow Postgraduate Research Scholarships, 707
University of Manchester Research Studentships and Scholarships, 715
WCRF Research Grants, 778

African Nations

ABCCF Student Grant, 103
The Joint Japan/World Bank Graduate Scholarship Program (JJ/WBGSP), 395

Australia

Asthma Foundation of New South Wales Medical Research Project Grant, 133
Biomedical and Medical Postgraduate Research Scholarships, 133
Dora Lush (Biomedical) and Public Health Postgraduate Scholarships, 504
New South Wales Cancer Council Research Programme Grant, 528
New South Wales Cancer Council Research Project Grants, 528
NHMRC Medical and Dental and Public Health Postgraduate Research Scholarships, 505
Wingate Scholarships, 771

British Commonwealth

ACU Development Fellowships, 127
The Joint Japan/World Bank Graduate Scholarship Program (JJ/WBGSP), 395
Wingate Scholarships, 771

Canada

Alcohol Beverage Medical Research Foundation Research Project Grant, 17
Canada Tobacco Research Initiative Fellowship Doctoral Fellowship Supplements, 642
Canadian Blood Services Postdoctoral Fellowhip (PDF), 223
Canadian Blood Services Research and Development Program Individual Grants, 223
Canadian Blood Services Research and Development Program Major Equipment Grants, 224
Canadian Tobacco Control Research Initiative Planning Grants, 643
Canadian Tobacco Control Research Initiative: Best Practices in Tobacco Control Grants, 643
Canadian Window on International Development, 399
Dr Sydney Segal Research Grants, 231
Frank Knox Memorial Fellowships at Harvard University, 131
PAHO Grants, 552
Wingate Scholarships, 771

Caribbean Countries

The Joint Japan/World Bank Graduate Scholarship Program (JJ/WBGSP), 395
PAHO Grants, 552

East European Countries

The Joint Japan/World Bank Graduate Scholarship Program (JJ/WBGSP), 395
OSI (Open Society Institute) Chevening Scholarships, 733

Far East

The Joint Japan/World Bank Graduate Scholarship Program (JJ/WBGSP), 395

Indian Sub-Continent

Indian Council of Social Science Research Senior Fellowships, 368
The Joint Japan/World Bank Graduate Scholarship Program (JJ/WBGSP), 395
Wingate Scholarships, 771

Middle East

ABCCF Student Grant, 103

SOCIAL/PREVENTIVE MEDICINE

SPORTS MEDICINE

Any Country

Colt Foundation PhD Fellowship, 262
NSCA Challenge Scholarship, 518
NSCA Student Grant Research Grant, 519
OREF Career Development Award, 550
OREF Prospective Clinical Research, 550
OREF Research Grants, 551
OREF Resident Research Award, 551
Queen Elizabeth the Queen Mother Fellowship Award, 583
Research into Ageing Prize Studentships, 583
Research into Ageing Programme Grants, 584
University of Bristol Postgraduate Scholarships, 691
University of Glasgow Postgraduate Research Scholarships, 707

African Nations

The Joint Japan/World Bank Graduate Scholarship Program (JJ/WBGSP), 395

Australia

Wingate Scholarships, 771

British Commonwealth

The Joint Japan/World Bank Graduate Scholarship Program (JJ/WBGSP), 395
Wingate Scholarships, 771

Canada

AAOS/OREF Fellowship in Health Services Research, 550
OREF Clinical Research Award, 550
Wingate Scholarships, 771

Caribbean Countries

The Joint Japan/World Bank Graduate Scholarship Program (JJ/WBGSP), 395

East European Countries

The Joint Japan/World Bank Graduate Scholarship Program (JJ/WBGSP), 395

Far East

The Joint Japan/World Bank Graduate Scholarship Program (JJ/WBGSP), 395

Indian Sub-Continent

The Joint Japan/World Bank Graduate Scholarship Program (JJ/WBGSP), 395
Wingate Scholarships, 771

Middle East

The Joint Japan/World Bank Graduate Scholarship Program (JJ/WBGSP), 395

New Zealand

Wingate Scholarships, 771

South Africa

The Joint Japan/World Bank Graduate Scholarship Program (JJ/WBGSP), 395
Wingate Scholarships, 771

South America

The Joint Japan/World Bank Graduate Scholarship Program (JJ/WBGSP), 395

United Kingdom

Duke of Edinburgh Prize for Sports Medicine, 384
The Robert Atkins Award, 384
Wingate Scholarships, 771

United States of America

AAOS/OREF Fellowship in Health Services Research, 550
Arthritis Foundation New Investigator Grant, 106
Arthritis Investigator Award, 107
New Investigator Fellowships Training Initiative (NIFTI), 316
OREF Clinical Research Award, 550
Promotion of Doctoral Studies (PODS), 316

West European Countries

Wingate Scholarships, 771

HEALTH ADMINISTRATION

Any Country

Anglo-German Foundation for the Study of Industrial Society Research Grant, 101
Center for Advanced Study in the Behavioral Sciences Postdoctoral Residential Fellowships, 245
La Trobe University Postgraduate Scholarship, 439
Massey Doctoral Scholarship, 461
Population Council Fellowships in Population and Social Sciences, 573
Roche Research Foundation, 589
Savoy Foundation Post Doctoral and Clinical Research Fellowships, 621
Savoy Foundation Research Grants, 621
Savoy Foundation Studentships, 621
Sir Allan Sewell Visiting Fellowship, 344
University of Bristol Postgraduate Scholarships, 691
University of Glasgow Postgraduate Research Scholarships, 707
University of New England Research Scholarships, 719

African Nations

ABCCF Student Grant, 103
The Hastings Center International Visiting Scholars Program, 352
The Joint Japan/World Bank Graduate Scholarship Program (JJ/WBGSP), 395

Australia

Fulbright Awards, 143
Harkness Fellowships in Health Care Policy, 263
The Hastings Center International Visiting Scholars Program, 352
New South Wales Cancer Council Research Project Grants, 528
Wingate Scholarships, 771

British Commonwealth

The Hastings Center International Visiting Scholars Program, 352
The Joint Japan/World Bank Graduate Scholarship Program (JJ/WBGSP), 395
Wingate Scholarships, 771

Canada

Albert W Dent Student Scholarships, 318
Foster G McGaw Student Scholarships, 318
Office of Critical Infrastructure Protection and Emergency Preparedness (EPC) Research Fellowship in Honour of Stuart Nesbitt White, 131
PAHO Grants, 552
Wingate Scholarships, 771

Caribbean Countries

The Hastings Center International Visiting Scholars Program, 352
The Joint Japan/World Bank Graduate Scholarship Program (JJ/WBGSP), 395
PAHO Grants, 552

East European Countries

The Hastings Center International Visiting Scholars Program, 352
The Joint Japan/World Bank Graduate Scholarship Program (JJ/WBGSP), 395
OSI (Open Society Institute) Chevening Scholarships, 733

Far East

The Hastings Center International Visiting Scholars Program, 352
The Joint Japan/World Bank Graduate Scholarship Program (JJ/WBGSP), 395

Indian Sub-Continent

The Hastings Center International Visiting Scholars Program, 352
The Joint Japan/World Bank Graduate Scholarship Program (JJ/WBGSP), 395
Wingate Scholarships, 771

Middle East

ABCCF Student Grant, 103
The Hastings Center International Visiting Scholars Program, 352
The Joint Japan/World Bank Graduate Scholarship Program (JJ/WBGSP), 395

New Zealand

Harkness Fellowships in Health Care Policy, 263
The Hastings Center International Visiting Scholars Program, 352
Wingate Scholarships, 771

South Africa

The Hastings Center International Visiting Scholars Program, 352
The Joint Japan/World Bank Graduate Scholarship Program (JJ/WBGSP), 395
Wingate Scholarships, 771

South America

The Hastings Center International Visiting Scholars Program, 352
The Joint Japan/World Bank Graduate Scholarship Program (JJ/WBGSP), 395

United Kingdom

Harkness Fellowships in Health Care Policy, 263
The Hastings Center International Visiting Scholars Program, 352
Wingate Scholarships, 771

United States of America

Albert W Dent Student Scholarships, 318
Arthritis Foundation New Investigator Grant, 106
Arthritis Investigator Award, 107
BPW Career Advancement Scholarship Program, 184
Congress Bundestag Youth Exchange for Young Professionals, 245
Foster G McGaw Student Scholarships, 318
Ian Axford (New Zealand) Fellowships in Public Policy, 263
PAHO Grants, 552
Wyeth Ayerst Scholarship for Women in Graduate Medical and Health Business Programs, 184

West European Countries

The Hastings Center International Visiting Scholars Program, 352
Scholarship Foundation of the League for Finnish-American Societies, 621
Wingate Scholarships, 771

MEDICINE AND SURGERY

Any Country

AAFPRS Investigator Development Grant, 26
BackCare Research Grants, 148
BIAL Merit Award in Medical Sciences, 152
British Journal of Surgery Research Bursaries, 170
CAMS Scholarship, 257
Canadian Cystic Fibrosis Foundation Scholarships, 226
Canadian Cystic Fibrosis Foundation Studentships, 227
Canadian Cystic Fibrosis Foundation Visiting Scientist Awards, 227
CIHR Fellowship Programme, 234
Daland Fellowships in Clinical Investigation, 71
Ethicon Foundation Fund, 598
Fight for Sight Postdoctoral Research Fellowships, 311

Fight for Sight Student Research Fellowships, 311
FRAXA Grants and Fellowships, 320
Glenn/AFAR Scholarships for Research in the Biology of Aging, 49
Humanitarian Trust Awards, 362
Hypertension Trust Studentship, 364
ICS Scholarship, 398
Inflammatory Bowel Disease Grants, 180
The Institute for the Study of Aging Grants Program, 378
ISH Postdoctoral Fellowship, 315
Islamic Organisation for Medical Sciences Prize, 437
John of Arderne Medal, 615
Lionel Colledge Memorial Fellowship in Otolaryngology, 598
Lister Institute Senior Research Fellowships, 449
Medical Insurance Agency Prize, 616
Meningitis Research Foundation Project Grant, 469
Meningitis Research Foundation Small Project Grant, 470
Meningitis Trust Research Award, 470
Michael Geisman Memorial Fellowship Fund, 551
MRC Royal College of Physicians and Pathologists Training Fellowships, 465
National Marfan Foundation Clinical Fellowship Grant, 513
National Marfan Foundation Research Grant, 513
Norman Capener Travelling Fellowships, 599
Norman Tanner Medal and Prize, 616
Novartis Foundation Symposium Bursaries, 539
OREF Career Development Award, 550
OREF Prospective Clinical Research, 550
OREF Research Grants, 551
OREF Resident Research Award, 551
Osteogenesis Imperfecta Foundation Seed Research Grant, 551
Roche Research Foundation, 589
Savoy Foundation Post Doctoral and Clinical Research Fellowships, 621
Savoy Foundation Research Grants, 621
Savoy Foundation Studentships, 621
Sigma Theta Tau International Association of Perioperative Registered Nurses Foundation Grant, 627
Sigma Xi Grants-in-Aid of Research, 629
Sir Richard Stapley Educational Trust Grants, 632
UICC International Fellowships for Beginning Investigators (ACSBI), 414
University of Bristol Postgraduate Scholarships, 691
University of Glasgow Postgraduate Research Scholarships, 707
University of Manchester Research Studentships and Scholarships, 715
WellBeing Project Grants, 768
Wellcome Trust Awards, Fellowships and Studentships, 768

Australia

Asthma Foundation of New South Wales Medical Research Project Grant, 133
Biomedical and Medical Postgraduate Research Scholarships, 133
Foundation for High Blood Pressure Research Postdoctoral Fellowship, 315
NHMRC Medical and Dental and Public Health Postgraduate Research Scholarships, 505
Wingate Scholarships, 771

British Commonwealth

Wingate Scholarships, 771

Canada

AAFPRS Resident Research Grants, 26
AAOS/OREF Fellowship in Health Services Research, 550
Bernstein Grant, 26
Canadian Cystic Fibrosis Foundation Fellowships, 226
Canadian Cystic Fibrosis Foundation Research Grants, 226
Canadian Thoracic Society Fellowships, 239
Canadian Thoracic Society Scholarships, 239
NORD Clinical Research Grants, 515
OREF Clinical Research Award, 550

ANAESTHESIOLOGY

CARDIOLOGY

British Commonwealth

Wingate Scholarships, 771

Canada

Alcohol Beverage Medical Research Foundation Research Project Grant, 17
NORD Clinical Research Grants, 515
Wingate Scholarships, 771

East European Countries

BHF Clinical Science Fellowships, 167
BHF Intermediate Research Fellowships, 167
BHF Junior Research Fellowships, 167
BHF PhD Studentships, 167
BHF Senior Research Fellowships, 168
BHF Travelling Fellowships, 168
Salzburg Medical Seminars, 543

Indian Sub-Continent

Wingate Scholarships, 771

New Zealand

National Heart Foundation of New Zealand Fellowships, 507
National Heart Foundation of New Zealand Limited Budget Grants, 507
National Heart Foundation of New Zealand Project Grants, 508
National Heart Foundation of New Zealand Travel Grants, 508
Wingate Scholarships, 771

South Africa

Wingate Scholarships, 771

United Kingdom

BHF Clinical Science Fellowships, 167
BHF Intermediate Research Fellowships, 167
BHF Junior Research Fellowships, 167
BHF PhD Studentships, 167
BHF Senior Research Fellowships, 168
BHF Travelling Fellowships, 168
Geoffrey Holt, Ivy Powell and Edith Walsh Awards, 172
Hypertension Trust Fellowship, 364
NORD Clinical Research Grants, 515
Sue McCarthy Travelling Scholarship, 168
Wingate Scholarships, 771

United States of America

AFAR Research Grants, 48
AHA National Established Investigator Grant, 52
AHA National Scientist Development Grant, 53
Alcohol Beverage Medical Research Foundation Research Project Grant, 17
NORD Clinical Research Grants, 515
Paul Beeson Physician/Faculty Scholars in Aging Research Programme, 49
RSNA Institutional Clinical Fellowship in Cardiovascular Imaging, 578

West European Countries

BHF Clinical Science Fellowships, 167
BHF Intermediate Research Fellowships, 167
BHF Junior Research Fellowships, 167
BHF PhD Studentships, 167
BHF Senior Research Fellowships, 168
BHF Travelling Fellowships, 168
NORD Clinical Research Grants, 515
Wingate Scholarships, 771

DERMATOLOGY

Any Country

CERIES Research Award, 250

DEBRA Medical Research Grant Scheme, 289
LEPRA Grants, 171
Lister Institute Senior Research Fellowships, 449
OFAS Grants, 545
University of Bristol Postgraduate Scholarships, 691

Australia

New South Wales Cancer Council Research Programme Grant, 528
New South Wales Cancer Council Research Project Grants, 528
Wingate Scholarships, 771

British Commonwealth

Wingate Scholarships, 771

Canada

NORD Clinical Research Grants, 515
Wingate Scholarships, 771

Indian Sub-Continent

Wingate Scholarships, 771

New Zealand

Wingate Scholarships, 771

South Africa

Wingate Scholarships, 771

United Kingdom

NORD Clinical Research Grants, 515
Wingate Scholarships, 771

United States of America

AFAR Research Grants, 48
NORD Clinical Research Grants, 515
Paul Beeson Physician/Faculty Scholars in Aging Research Programme, 49

West European Countries

NORD Clinical Research Grants, 515
Wingate Scholarships, 771

ENDOCRINOLOGY

Any Country

Diabetes UK Equipment Grant, 285
Diabetes UK Project Grants, 285
Diabetes UK Research Fellowships, 285
Diabetes UK Research Studentships, 285
Diabetes UK Small Grant Scheme, 285
GlaxoSmithKline Collaborative Research Projects, 337
LCIF Clinical Research Grant Program, 45
LCIF Equipment Grant Program, 46
LCIF Training Grant Program, 46
Lister Institute Senior Research Fellowships, 449
OFAS Grants, 545
Services to Academia, 337
UICC International Cancer Research Technology Transfer Project (ICRETT), 414
UICC International Fellowships for Beginning Investigators (ACSBI), 414
University of Bristol Postgraduate Scholarships, 691
University of Manchester Research Studentships and Scholarships, 715
WellBeing Project Grants, 768

Australia

New South Wales Cancer Council Research Programme Grant, 528
New South Wales Cancer Council Research Project Grants, 528
Wingate Scholarships, 771

British Commonwealth

Wingate Scholarships, 771

Canada

Alcohol Beverage Medical Research Foundation Research Project Grant, 17
NORD Clinical Research Grants, 515
Wingate Scholarships, 771

Indian Sub-Continent

Wingate Scholarships, 771

New Zealand

Wingate Scholarships, 771

South Africa

Wingate Scholarships, 771

United Kingdom

DRWF Research Fellowship, 284
NORD Clinical Research Grants, 515
Wingate Scholarships, 771

United States of America

ADA Career Development Awards, 44
ADA Clinical Research Grants, 44
ADA Junior Faculty Awards, 45
ADA Medical Scholars Program, 45
ADA Mentor-Based Postdoctoral Fellowship Program, 45
ADA Physician/Scientist Training, 45
ADA Research Awards, 45
AFAR Research Grants, 48
Alcohol Beverage Medical Research Foundation Research Project Grant, 17
NIH Research Grants, 511
NORD Clinical Research Grants, 515
Paul Beeson Physician/Faculty Scholars in Aging Research Programme, 49

West European Countries

NORD Clinical Research Grants, 515
Wingate Scholarships, 771

EPIDEMIOLOGY

Any Country

AHAF Alzheimer's Disease Research Grant, 52
AHAF National Heart Foundation, 52
Ataxia UK Research Studentships, 133
Ataxia UK Travel Award, 134
BackCare Research Grants, 148
Basic Clinical and Translational Breast Cancer Research, 666
Canadian Blood Services Transfusion Medicine Fellowship Awards, 224
GlaxoSmithKline Collaborative Research Projects, 337
Health Research Board and British Council Research Visits Scheme, 353
IARC Postdoctoral Fellowships for Research Training in Cancer, 393
ICR Research Studentships, 380
Imaging Technology, 666
LCIF Clinical Research Grant Program, 45
Lister Institute Senior Research Fellowships, 449
Meningitis Research Foundation Project Grant, 469
Meningitis Research Foundation Small Project Grant, 470
Meningitis Trust Research Award, 470
NARSAD Distinguished Investigator Awards, 491
NARSAD Independent Investigator Awards, 491
NARSAD Young Investigator Awards, 491
National Heart Foundation of New Zealand Maori Cardiovascular Research Fellowship, 508
OFAS Grants, 545
Percy Sladen Memorial Fund Grants, 559
Population Council Fellowships in Population and Social Sciences, 573

Population Specific Research Project, 666
Postdoctoral Fellowship in Breast Cancer Research, Public Health or Epidemiology, 667
Project Grant, 134
Queen Elizabeth the Queen Mother Fellowship Award, 583
Research into Ageing Prize Studentships, 583
Research into Ageing Programme Grants, 584
Satellite Meeting at Major Symposium on Related Disorders, 134
Savoy Foundation Post Doctoral and Clinical Research Fellowships, 621
Savoy Foundation Studentships, 621
Services to Academia, 337
Short Project Grant, 134
The Susan G Komen Breast Cancer Foundation Dissertation Research Award, 667
UICC International Cancer Research Technology Transfer Project (ICRETT), 414
UICC International Fellowships for Beginning Investigators (ACSBI), 414
University of Bristol Postgraduate Scholarships, 691
University of Dundee Research Awards, 704
University of Manchester Research Studentships and Scholarships, 715
WCRF Research Grants, 778

African Nations

AHRI African Fellowship, 105

Australia

Asthma Victoria Research Grants, 133
New South Wales Cancer Council Research Programme Grant, 528
New South Wales Cancer Council Research Project Grants, 528
Wingate Scholarships, 771

British Commonwealth

Wingate Scholarships, 771

Canada

Alcohol Beverage Medical Research Foundation Research Project Grant, 17
American Institute for Cancer Research Investigator Initiator Grants, 54
Canadian Blood Services Postdoctoral Fellowhip (PDF), 223
Canadian Blood Services Research and Development Program Individual Grants, 223
Canadian Blood Services Research and Development Program Major Equipment Grants, 224
Canadian Thoracic Society Fellowships, 239
CNF Scholarships and Fellowships, 236
Dr Sydney Segal Research Grants, 231
Heritage Health Research Career Renewal Awards, 17
NORD Clinical Research Grants, 515
Wingate Scholarships, 771

East European Countries

FEMS Fellowship, 310
Salzburg Medical Seminars, 543

Far East

UICC International Cancer Technology Transfer Fellowships (ICRETT) for Bilateral Exchanges Between Indonesia and the Netherlands, 414

Indian Sub-Continent

Wingate Scholarships, 771

New Zealand

National Heart Foundation of New Zealand Fellowships, 507
National Heart Foundation of New Zealand Limited Budget Grants, 507
National Heart Foundation of New Zealand Project Grants, 508
National Heart Foundation of New Zealand Travel Grants, 508

Wingate Scholarships, 771

South Africa

Wingate Scholarships, 771

United Kingdom

Alzheimer's Society Research Grants, 24
British Lung Foundation Project Grants, 171
FEMS Fellowship, 310
NORD Clinical Research Grants, 515
Wingate Scholarships, 771

United States of America

AFAR Research Grants, 48
AHA National Established Investigator Grant, 52
Alcohol Beverage Medical Research Foundation Research Project Grant, 17
American Institute for Cancer Research Investigator Initiator Grants, 54
NFID Postdoctoral Fellowship in Emerging Infectious Diseases, 502
NORD Clinical Research Grants, 515
Paul Beeson Physician/Faculty Scholars in Aging Research Programme, 49

West European Countries

FEMS Fellowship, 310
Health Services Research Fellowships, 353
HRB Project Grants-General, 354
NORD Clinical Research Grants, 515
Wingate Scholarships, 771

GASTROENTEROLOGY

Any Country

AGA Elsevier Research Initiative Award, 46
AGA June and Donald O Castell, MD Esophageal Clinical Research Award, 47
AGA Merck Clinical Research Career Development Award, 47
AGA Miles and Shirley Fiterman Foundation Basic Research Awards, 47
AGA Miles and Shirley Fiterman Foundation Clinical Research in Gastroenterology or Hepatology/Nutrition Awards, 47
AGA R Robert and Sally D Funderburg Research Scholar Award in Gastric Biology Related to Cancer, 47
AGA Research Scholar Awards, 48
AGA Student Research Fellowship Awards, 48
GlaxoSmithKline Collaborative Research Projects, 337
Inflammatory Bowel Disease Grants, 180
Lister Institute Senior Research Fellowships, 449
Queen Elizabeth the Queen Mother Fellowship Award, 583
Research into Ageing Prize Studentships, 583
Research into Ageing Programme Grants, 584
Services to Academia, 337
University of Bristol Postgraduate Scholarships, 691
University of Manchester Research Studentships and Scholarships, 715

Australia

New South Wales Cancer Council Research Programme Grant, 528
New South Wales Cancer Council Research Project Grants, 528
Wingate Scholarships, 771

British Commonwealth

Wingate Scholarships, 771

Canada

Alcohol Beverage Medical Research Foundation Research Project Grant, 17
NORD Clinical Research Grants, 515
Wingate Scholarships, 771

East European Countries

Salzburg Medical Seminars, 543

Indian Sub-Continent

Wingate Scholarships, 771

New Zealand

Wingate Scholarships, 771

South Africa

Wingate Scholarships, 771

United Kingdom

Digestive Disorders Foundation Fellowships and Grants, 285
NORD Clinical Research Grants, 515
Wingate Scholarships, 771

United States of America

AFAR Research Grants, 48
AGA Astra Zeneca Fellowship/Faculty Transition Awards, 46
AGA Sponsored Research Symposium Awards, 48
Alcohol Beverage Medical Research Foundation Research Project Grant, 17
NORD Clinical Research Grants, 515
Paul Beeson Physician/Faculty Scholars in Aging Research Programme, 49

West European Countries

NORD Clinical Research Grants, 515
Wingate Scholarships, 771

GERIATRICS

Any Country

Alzheimer's Research Trust Research Programme Grant, 24
The Institute for the Study of Aging Grants Program, 378
Lister Institute Senior Research Fellowships, 449
Queen Elizabeth the Queen Mother Fellowship Award, 583
Research into Ageing Prize Studentships, 583
Research into Ageing Programme Grants, 584
Stroke Research Awards, 665
University of Bristol Postgraduate Scholarships, 691
Wilson-Fulton and Robertson Awards in Aging Research, Cecille Gould Memorial Fund Award in Cancer Research, Richard Shepherd Fellowship, 50

Australia

Wingate Scholarships, 771

British Commonwealth

Wingate Scholarships, 771

Canada

Alcohol Beverage Medical Research Foundation Research Project Grant, 17
NORD Clinical Research Grants, 515
Wingate Scholarships, 771

Indian Sub-Continent

Wingate Scholarships, 771

New Zealand

Wingate Scholarships, 771

South Africa

Wingate Scholarships, 771
Zerilda Steyn Memorial Trust, 12

United Kingdom

Alzheimer's Society Research Grants, 24
NORD Clinical Research Grants, 515

Wingate Scholarships, 771

United States of America

AFAR Research Grants, 48
Alcohol Beverage Medical Research Foundation Research Project Grant, 17
Ian Axford (New Zealand) Fellowships in Public Policy, 263
The John A Hartford Foundation/AFAR Medical Student Geriatric Scholars Program, 49
Merck/AFAR Junior Investigator Award in Geriatric Clinical Pharmacology, 49
Merck/AFAR Research Scholarships for Medical and Pharmacy Students in Geriatric Pharmacology, 49
NIH Research Grants, 511
NORD Clinical Research Grants, 515
Paul Beeson Physician/Faculty Scholars in Aging Research Programme, 49
The John A Hartford Foundation/AFAR Academic Fellowship Program in Geriatric Medicine and Geriatric Psychiatry, 50

West European Countries

NORD Clinical Research Grants, 515
Wingate Scholarships, 771

GYNAECOLOGY AND OBSTETRICS

Any Country

BackCare Research Grants, 148
Lalor Foundation Postdoctoral Fellowships, 440
Lister Institute Senior Research Fellowships, 449
Meningitis Research Foundation Project Grant, 469
Meningitis Research Foundation Small Project Grant, 470
Michael Geisman Memorial Fellowship Fund, 551
MRC Royal College of Obstetricians and Gynaecologists Training Fellowship, 465
Osteogenesis Imperfecta Foundation Seed Research Grant, 551
RCOG Edgar Gentilli Prize, 596
RCOG Ethicon Foundation Fund Travel, 596
RCOG Harold Malkin Prize, 597
RCOG Overseas Fund (Founded by the Aileen Dickens Bequest), 597
UICC International Cancer Research Technology Transfer Project (ICRETT), 414
University of Bristol Postgraduate Scholarships, 691
University of Dundee Research Awards, 704
University of Manchester Research Studentships and Scholarships, 715
WellBeing Project Grants, 768

Australia

New South Wales Cancer Council Research Programme Grant, 528
New South Wales Cancer Council Research Project Grants, 528
Wingate Scholarships, 771

British Commonwealth

Wingate Scholarships, 771

Canada

ACOG/3M Pharmaceuticals Research Awards in Lower Genital Infections, 39
ACOG/Cytyc Corporation Research Award for the Prevention of Cervical Cancer, 39
ACOG/Organon, Inc. Research Award in Contraception, 40
ACOG/Ortho-McNeil Academic Training Fellowships in Obstetrics and Gynecology, 40
ACOG/Pharmacia Corporation Research Award on Overactive Bladder, 40
ACOG/Solvay Pharmaceuticals Research Award in Menopause, 40
NORD Clinical Research Grants, 515
Warren H Pearse/Wyeth-Ayerst Women's Health Policy Research Award, 40
Wingate Scholarships, 771

East European Countries

Salzburg Medical Seminars, 543

Indian Sub-Continent

Wingate Scholarships, 771

New Zealand

Wingate Scholarships, 771

South Africa

Wingate Scholarships, 771

United Kingdom

Endometriosis Millennium Fund Award, 596
Katherine Bishop Harman Award, 173
Nichols Fellowship, 616
NORD Clinical Research Grants, 515
RCOG Medical Student Prizes, 597
RCOG USA/British Isles Visiting Fellowship, 597
RCOG William Blair-Bell Memorial Lectureships in Obstetrics and Gynaecology, 597
RCOG/Wyeth Historical Lecture, 597
Wingate Scholarships, 771

United States of America

ACOG/3M Pharmaceuticals Research Awards in Lower Genital Infections, 39
ACOG/Cytyc Corporation Research Award for the Prevention of Cervical Cancer, 39
ACOG/Organon, Inc. Research Award in Contraception, 40
ACOG/Ortho-McNeil Academic Training Fellowships in Obstetrics and Gynecology, 40
ACOG/Pharmacia Corporation Research Award on Overactive Bladder, 40
ACOG/Solvay Pharmaceuticals Research Award in Menopause, 40
AFAR Research Grants, 48
NORD Clinical Research Grants, 515
Paul Beeson Physician/Faculty Scholars in Aging Research Programme, 49
RCOG USA/British Isles Visiting Fellowship, 597
Warren H Pearse/Wyeth-Ayerst Women's Health Policy Research Award, 40

West European Countries

NORD Clinical Research Grants, 515
Wingate Scholarships, 771

HAEMATOLOGY

Any Country

Canadian Blood Services Graduate Fellowship Program, 223
Canadian Blood Services Transfusion Medicine Fellowship Awards, 224
Cooley's Anemia Foundation Research Fellowship Grant, 268
E D Thomas Fellowship, 324
Gordon Piller Studentships, 444
ICR Research Studentships, 380
Leukaemia Research Fund Clinical Research Fellowship, 445
Leukaemia Research Fund Clinical Training Fellowship, 445
Leukaemia Research Fund Grant Programme, 445
Leukaemia Research Fund Grant Project, 445
Leukemia and Lymphoma Society Translational Research Award, 446
Leukemia Research Fund Awards, 446
Lister Institute Senior Research Fellowships, 449
Meningitis Research Foundation Project Grant, 469
Meningitis Research Foundation Small Project Grant, 470
Queen Elizabeth the Queen Mother Fellowship Award, 583
Research into Ageing Prize Studentships, 583
Research into Ageing Programme Grants, 584

UICC International Cancer Research Technology Transfer Project (ICRETT), 414
University of Bristol Postgraduate Scholarships, 691
University of Dundee Research Awards, 704

Australia

New South Wales Cancer Council Research Programme Grant, 528
New South Wales Cancer Council Research Project Grants, 528
Wingate Scholarships, 771

British Commonwealth

Wingate Scholarships, 771

Canada

Alcohol Beverage Medical Research Foundation Research Project Grant, 17
The Aventis Behring Canada Research and Education Fund, 148
Canadian Blood Services Postdoctoral Fellowhip (PDF), 223
Canadian Blood Services Research and Development Program Individual Grants, 223
Canadian Blood Services Research and Development Program Major Equipment Grants, 224
Canadian Blood Services Small Projects Fund, 224
CBS Research Fellowship In Hemostasis (RFH), 224
NORD Clinical Research Grants, 515
Wingate Scholarships, 771

East European Countries

Salzburg Medical Seminars, 543

Indian Sub-Continent

Wingate Scholarships, 771

New Zealand

Wingate Scholarships, 771

South Africa

Wingate Scholarships, 771

United Kingdom

NORD Clinical Research Grants, 515
Wingate Scholarships, 771

United States of America

AFAR Research Grants, 48
Alcohol Beverage Medical Research Foundation Research Project Grant, 17
NORD Clinical Research Grants, 515
Paul Beeson Physician/Faculty Scholars in Aging Research Programme, 49

West European Countries

NORD Clinical Research Grants, 515
Wingate Scholarships, 771

HEPATHOLOGY

Any Country

AGA Elsevier Research Initiative Award, 46
AGA June and Donald O Castell, MD Esophageal Clinical Research Award, 47
AGA Merck Clinical Research Career Development Award, 47
AGA Miles and Shirley Fiterman Foundation Basic Research Awards, 47
AGA Miles and Shirley Fiterman Foundation Clinical Research in Gastroenterology or Hepatology/Nutrition Awards, 47
AGA R Robert and Sally D Funderburg Research Scholar Award in Gastric Biology Related to Cancer, 47
AGA Research Scholar Awards, 48
AGA Student Research Fellowship Awards, 48
Lister Institute Senior Research Fellowships, 449

Australia

Wingate Scholarships, 771

British Commonwealth

Wingate Scholarships, 771

Canada

Alcohol Beverage Medical Research Foundation Research Project Grant, 17
Canadian Liver Foundation Graduate Studentships, 235
Canadian Liver Foundation Operating Grant, 235
NORD Clinical Research Grants, 515
Wingate Scholarships, 771

Indian Sub-Continent

Wingate Scholarships, 771

New Zealand

Wingate Scholarships, 771

South Africa

Wingate Scholarships, 771

United Kingdom

NORD Clinical Research Grants, 515
Wingate Scholarships, 771

United States of America

AFAR Research Grants, 48
AGA Astra Zeneca Fellowship/Faculty Transition Awards, 46
AGA Sponsored Research Symposium Awards, 48
Alcohol Beverage Medical Research Foundation Research Project Grant, 17
ALF Liver Scholar Award, 62
ALF Postdoctoral Research Fellowship, 62
ALF Student Research Fellowship, 62
NORD Clinical Research Grants, 515
Paul Beeson Physician/Faculty Scholars in Aging Research Programme, 49

West European Countries

NORD Clinical Research Grants, 515
Wingate Scholarships, 771

NEPHROLOGY

Any Country

ISN Travel Grants, 412
Lister Institute Senior Research Fellowships, 449
LSA Medical Research Grant, 454
NKRF Research Project Grants, 511
NKRF Senior Fellowships, 511
NKRF Training Fellowships, 512

African Nations

ISN Fellowship Awards, 412

Australia

Australian Kidney Foundation Medical Research Scholarships, 140
Australian Kidney Foundation Seeding and Equipment Grants, 140
ISN Visiting Scholars Program, 412
Wingate Scholarships, 771

British Commonwealth

ISN Fellowship Awards, 412
Wingate Scholarships, 771

Canada

ISN Visiting Scholars Program, 412
The Kidney Foundation of Canada Allied Health Doctoral Fellowship, 432

NEUROLOGY

Any Country

Australia

British Commonwealth

Canada

NORD Clinical Research Grants, 515
Paralyzed Veterans of America Research Grants, 552
Wingate Scholarships, 771

East European Countries

Salzburg Medical Seminars, 543

Indian Sub-Continent

Wingate Scholarships, 771

New Zealand

Wingate Scholarships, 771

South Africa

Wingate Scholarships, 771

United Kingdom

Alzheimer's Research Trust PhD Studentship, 24
Alzheimer's Society Research Grants, 24
Doris Hillier Award, 172
Guillain-Barré Syndrome Support Group Research Fellowship, 345
MND PhD Studentship Award, 482
NORD Clinical Research Grants, 515
Parkinson's Disease Society Research Project Grant, 555
Parkinson's Disease Society Studentships and Junior/Senior Fellows, 555
REMEDI Research Grants, 581
Vera Down Award, 174
Wingate Scholarships, 771

United States of America

AFAR Research Grants, 48
Alcohol Beverage Medical Research Foundation Research Project Grant, 17
Alfred P Sloan Foundation Research Fellowships, 21
American Association of Neurological Surgeons Research Fellowship, 36
MFP in Neuroscience Postdoctoral Fellowship, 76
MFP in Neuroscience Predoctoral Fellowship, 76
National Multiple Sclerosis Society Junior Faculty Awards, 513
NIH Research Grants, 511
NORD Clinical Research Grants, 515
Paralyzed Veterans of America Research Grants, 552
Paul Beeson Physician/Faculty Scholars in Aging Research Programme, 49
Young Clinician Investigator Award, 37

West European Countries

NORD Clinical Research Grants, 515
Wingate Scholarships, 771

ONCOLOGY

Any Country

AACR Career Development Awards in Cancer Research, 30
AACR Gertrude B Elion Cancer Research Award, 31
AACR Research Fellowships, 31
AACR Scholar-in-Training Awards, 31
Action Cancer Research Grants, 7
Action Cancer Research Studentship, 8
Anti-Cancer Foundation Research Grants, 102
Breast Cancer Campaign Project Grants, 158
Cancer Association of South Africa Research Grants, 240
Cancer Research Society, Inc. (Canada) Research Grants, 241
CBCRI Feasibility Grants, 225
CBCRI Research Grants Competition, 225
CBCRI Special Programs/Idea Grants, 225
CBCRI Special Programs/Streams of Excellence Grants, 225
Charles B Wilson Brain Tumor Research Excellence Grant, 493
CRC Studentship, 557
CTCRI Planning Grants, 240
GlaxoSmithKline Collaborative Research Projects, 337

Gordon Piller Studentships, 444
IARC Postdoctoral Fellowships for Research Training in Cancer, 393
ICR Research Studentships, 380
Imperial Cancer Research Fund Clinical Research Fellowships, 365
Imperial Cancer Research Fund Graduate Studentships, 365
Imperial Cancer Research Fund Research Fellowships, 366
Jane Coffin Childs Memorial Fund for Medical Research Fellowships, 420
Leukaemia Research Fund Clinical Research Fellowship, 445
Leukaemia Research Fund Clinical Training Fellowship, 445
Leukaemia Research Fund Grant Programme, 445
Leukaemia Research Fund Grant Project, 445
Leukemia and Lymphoma Society Scholarships, Special Fellowships and Fellowships, 445
Leukemia and Lymphoma Society Translational Research Award, 446
Leukemia Research Fund Awards, 446
Lister Institute Senior Research Fellowships, 449
NABTC/NABTT Research Grant, 493
NCIC Research Grants to Individuals, 495
NCIC Research Scientist Awards, 495
OFAS Grants, 545
ONS Foundation Research Awards, 541
Postdoctoral Fellowship in Breast Cancer Research, Public Health or Epidemiology, 667
Richard Anthony Hollow, Jr Memorial Grant for NABTC Institutions, 494
Ruth Estrin Goldberg Memorial for Cancer Research, 617
Services to Academia, 337
Sylvia Lawler Prize, 617
UICC International Cancer Research Technology Transfer Project (ICRETT), 414
UICC International Fellowships for Beginning Investigators (ACSBI), 414
UICC Translational Cancer Research Fellowships (TCRF), 415
UICC Yamagiwa-Yoshida Memorial International Cancer Study Grants, 415
University of Bristol Postgraduate Scholarships, 691
University of Dundee Research Awards, 704
University of Manchester Research Studentships and Scholarships, 715
WCRF Research Grants, 778
WellBeing Project Grants, 768
Wilson-Fulton and Robertson Awards in Aging Research, Cecille Gould Memorial Fund Award in Cancer Research, Richard Shepherd Fellowship, 50

African Nations

UICC Trish Greene International Oncology Nursing Fellowships, 415

Australia

New South Wales Cancer Council Research Programme Grant, 528
New South Wales Cancer Council Research Project Grants, 528
Richard Walter Gibbon Medical Research Fellowship, 754
Wingate Scholarships, 771

British Commonwealth

UICC Trish Greene International Oncology Nursing Fellowships, 415
Wingate Scholarships, 771

Canada

Alcohol Beverage Medical Research Foundation Research Project Grant, 17
American Institute for Cancer Research Investigator Initiator Grants, 54
CCS Feasibility Grants, 494
CNF Scholarships and Fellowships, 236
Equipment Grants for New Investigators, 494
NCIC Clinical Research Fellowships, 494
NCIC Research Grants for New Investigators, 495
NCIC Research Studentships, 495
NCIC Travel Award for Senior Level PhD Students, 496

NORD Clinical Research Grants, 515
Post-PhD and Post-MD Research Fellowships, 496
Wingate Scholarships, 771

Caribbean Countries

UICC Trish Greene International Oncology Nursing Fellowships, 415

East European Countries

Fulbright Fellowship in Cancer Research, 758
Fulbright Louise Buchanan Fellowship in Cancer Research, 759
Salzburg Medical Seminars, 543
UICC Trish Greene International Oncology Nursing Fellowships, 415

Far East

UICC Asia-Pacific Cancer Society Training Grants (APCASOT), 413
UICC International Cancer Technology Transfer Fellowships (ICRETT) for Bilateral Exchanges Between Indonesia and the Netherlands, 414
UICC Trish Greene International Oncology Nursing Fellowships, 415

Indian Sub-Continent

UICC Trish Greene International Oncology Nursing Fellowships, 415
Wingate Scholarships, 771

Middle East

UICC Trish Greene International Oncology Nursing Fellowships, 415

New Zealand

Wingate Scholarships, 771

South Africa

Cancer Association of South Africa Travel and Subsistence (Study) Grants, 240
Lady Cade Memorial Fellowship, 241
UICC Trish Greene International Oncology Nursing Fellowships, 415
Wingate Scholarships, 771

South America

UICC Latin America COPES Training and Education Fellowships (LACTEF), 414
UICC Trish Greene International Oncology Nursing Fellowships, 415

United Kingdom

British Lung Foundation Project Grants, 171
Fulbright Fellowship in Cancer Research, 758
Fulbright Louise Buchanan Fellowship in Cancer Research, 759
Helen Tomkinson and Albert McMaster Research Awards, 172
NORD Clinical Research Grants, 515
T P Gunton Award, 174
Wingate Scholarships, 771

United States of America

AFAR Research Grants, 48
Alcohol Beverage Medical Research Foundation Research Project Grant, 17
American Institute for Cancer Research Investigator Initiator Grants, 54
NORD Clinical Research Grants, 515
Paul Beeson Physician/Faculty Scholars in Aging Research Programme, 49

West European Countries

Fulbright Fellowship in Cancer Research, 758
Fulbright Louise Buchanan Fellowship in Cancer Research, 759
NORD Clinical Research Grants, 515
Wingate Scholarships, 771

OPHTHALMOLOGY

Any Country

AHAF Macular Degeneration Research, 52
AHAF National Glaucoma Research, 52

Fight for Sight Grants-in-Aid, 311
Fight for Sight Postdoctoral Research Fellowships, 311
Fight for Sight Student Research Fellowships, 311
International Eye Foundation (Colombia) Fellowship, 400
Lister Institute Senior Research Fellowships, 449
LSA Medical Research Grant, 454
MRC Patient Oriented Clinician Scientist Fellowship, 464
MRC Royal College of Surgeons of Edinburgh Training Fellowship, 465
National Marfan Foundation Clinical Fellowship Grant, 513
National Marfan Foundation Research Grant, 513
Ophthalmology Travelling Fellowship, 616
Pilot Project Grants Program, 336
Queen Elizabeth the Queen Mother Fellowship Award, 583
Research into Ageing Prize Studentships, 583
Research into Ageing Programme Grants, 584
Sigma Xi Grants-in-Aid of Research, 629
University of Bristol Postgraduate Scholarships, 691
University of Manchester Research Studentships and Scholarships, 715

Australia

Wingate Scholarships, 771

British Commonwealth

Wingate Scholarships, 771

Canada

Alcohol Beverage Medical Research Foundation Research Project Grant, 17
E A Baker Fellowship/Grant, 236
NORD Clinical Research Grants, 515
Wingate Scholarships, 771

Indian Sub-Continent

Wingate Scholarships, 771

New Zealand

Wingate Scholarships, 771

South Africa

Wingate Scholarships, 771

United Kingdom

Guide Dogs Opthalmic Research Fellowship Grant, 345
Guide Dogs Opthalmic Research Grant, 345
Iris Fund Award, 416
Iris Fund Grants for Research and Equipment (Ophthalmology), 417
John William Clark Award, 173
Middlemore Award, 173
NORD Clinical Research Grants, 515
Wingate Scholarships, 771

United States of America

AFAR Research Grants, 48
Alcohol Beverage Medical Research Foundation Research Project Grant, 17
Heed Award, 355
NORD Clinical Research Grants, 515
Paul Beeson Physician/Faculty Scholars in Aging Research Programme, 49

West European Countries

NORD Clinical Research Grants, 515
Wingate Scholarships, 771

OTORHINOLARYNGOLOGY

Any Country

ATA Scientific and Medical Research Grants, 95
Karl Storz Travelling Scholarship, 615
Lister Institute Senior Research Fellowships, 449

University of Bristol Postgraduate Scholarships, 691
University of Dundee Research Awards, 704
University of Manchester Research Studentships and Scholarships, 715
Wacker Foundation Research Grant, 765

African Nations

Heinz Visiting and Travelling Fellowships, 598
Sally Mugabe Memorial Cambridge DFID Scholarship for Postgraduate Study, 215

Australia

Heinz Visiting and Travelling Fellowships, 598
New South Wales Cancer Council Research Programme Grant, 528
New South Wales Cancer Council Research Project Grants, 528

Canada

Canadian Thoracic Society Fellowships, 239
Dr Sydney Segal Research Grants, 231
Duncan L Gordon Fellowships, 360
Heinz Visiting and Travelling Fellowships, 598
Hospital for Sick Children Foundation External Research Grants, 360
NORD Clinical Research Grants, 515
Physician Scientist Development Award, 107

East European Countries

Salzburg Medical Seminars, 543

Indian Sub-Continent

Heinz Visiting and Travelling Fellowships, 598

New Zealand

Heinz Visiting and Travelling Fellowships, 598

South Africa

Heinz Visiting and Travelling Fellowships, 598

United Kingdom

British Lung Foundation Project Grants, 171
Heinz Visiting and Travelling Fellowships, 598
NORD Clinical Research Grants, 515

United States of America

Arthritis Investigator Award, 107
New Investigator Fellowships Training Initiative (NIFTI), 316
NORD Clinical Research Grants, 515
Paul Beeson Physician/Faculty Scholars in Aging Research Programme, 49
Physician Scientist Development Award, 107
Promotion of Doctoral Studies (PODS), 316

West European Countries

NORD Clinical Research Grants, 515

PLASTIC SURGERY

Any Country

AAFPRS Investigator Development Grant, 26
BAPS European Travelling Scholarship, 160
BAPS Travelling Bursary, 160
Meningitis Research Foundation Project Grant, 469
Meningitis Research Foundation Small Project Grant, 470
Paton/Maser Memorial Fund, 160
Plastic Surgery Basic Research Grant, 570
Plastic Surgery Educational Foundation Scientific Essay Contest, 570
Plastic Surgery Research Fellowship Award, 570

Canada

AAFPRS Resident Research Grants, 26
Bernstein Grant, 26

United Kingdom

NORD Clinical Research Grants, 515

United States of America

AAFPRS Resident Research Grants, 26
Bernstein Grant, 26
NORD Clinical Research Grants, 515
Paul Beeson Physician/Faculty Scholars in Aging Research Programme, 49

West European Countries

NORD Clinical Research Grants, 515

PNEUMOLOGY

Any Country

Fungal Research Trust Travel Grants, 327

Australia

Asthma Victoria Research Grants, 133

Canada

Alcohol Beverage Medical Research Foundation Research Project Grant, 17
Canadian Thoracic Society Fellowships, 239
NORD Clinical Research Grants, 515
Parker B Francis Fellowship Program, 554

East European Countries

Salzburg Medical Seminars, 543

United Kingdom

British Lung Foundation Project Grants, 171
H C Roscoe Fellowship, 172
NORD Clinical Research Grants, 515
T V James Fellowship, 174

United States of America

Alcohol Beverage Medical Research Foundation Research Project Grant, 17
NORD Clinical Research Grants, 515
Parker B Francis Fellowship Program, 554
Paul Beeson Physician/Faculty Scholars in Aging Research Programme, 49

West European Countries

NORD Clinical Research Grants, 515

PSYCHIATRY AND MENTAL HEALTH

Any Country

BackCare Research Grants, 148
Distinguished Research Award, 103
FRAXA Grants and Fellowships, 320
GlaxoSmithKline Collaborative Research Projects, 337
HDSA Fellowships, 363
HDSA Research Grants, 364
HDSA Research Initiative Grants, 364
The Institute for the Study of Aging Grants Program, 378
LSA Medical Research Grant, 454
Meningitis Research Foundation Project Grant, 469
Mental Health Foundation Essay Prize, 616
NARSAD Distinguished Investigator Awards, 491
NARSAD Independent Investigator Awards, 491
NARSAD Young Investigator Awards, 491
Queen Elizabeth the Queen Mother Fellowship Award, 583
Research into Ageing Prize Studentships, 583
Research into Ageing Programme Grants, 584

RHEUMATOLOGY

United Kingdom

ARC Clinical Research Fellowships, 108
ARC Clinician Scientist Fellowship, 108
ARC Educational Project Grants, 108
ARC Educational Research Fellowships, 108
ARC Educational Travel/Training Bursaries, 109
ARC PhD Studentships, 109
ARC Postgraduate Training Bursaries, 109
ARC Project Grants, 109
ARC Travelling Fellowships, 109
CDRF Project Grants, 258
CDRF Research Fellowship, 258
Doris Hillier Award, 172
NORD Clinical Research Grants, 515
REMEDI Research Grants, 581
Senior ARC Fellowships, 110

United States of America

AAOS/OREF Fellowship in Health Services Research, 550
AFAR Research Grants, 48
Alcohol Beverage Medical Research Foundation Research Project Grant, 17
Arthritis Foundation New Investigator Grant, 106
Arthritis Investigator Award, 107
CDRF Project Grants, 258
CDRF Research Fellowship, 258
NORD Clinical Research Grants, 515
OREF Clinical Research Award, 550
Paul Beeson Physician/Faculty Scholars in Aging Research Programme, 49
Physician Scientist Development Award, 107

West European Countries

CDRF Project Grants, 258
CDRF Research Fellowship, 258
Metro A Ogryzlo International Fellowship, 111
NORD Clinical Research Grants, 515

UROLOGY

Any Country

ASBAH Research Grant, 125
CRPF Research Grant, 258
ICR Research Studentships, 380
Lalor Foundation Postdoctoral Fellowships, 440
Lister Institute Senior Research Fellowships, 449
Queen Elizabeth the Queen Mother Fellowship Award, 583
Research into Ageing Prize Studentships, 583
Research into Ageing Programme Grants, 584
Royal Society of Medicine Travelling Fellowship, 616
WellBeing Project Grants, 768

Australia

Australian Kidney Foundation Medical Research Scholarships, 140
Australian Kidney Foundation Seeding and Equipment Grants, 140

Canada

The Kidney Foundation of Canada Allied Health Doctoral Fellowship, 432
The Kidney Foundation of Canada Allied Health Research Grant, 432
The Kidney Foundation of Canada Allied Health Scholarship, 432
The Kidney Foundation of Canada Biomedical Fellowship, 433
The Kidney Foundation of Canada Biomedical Research (Operating) Grant, 433
The Kidney Foundation of Canada Biomedical Scholarship, 433
NORD Clinical Research Grants, 515
Paralyzed Veterans of America Research Grants, 552

East European Countries

Salzburg Medical Seminars, 543

United Kingdom

NORD Clinical Research Grants, 515

United States of America

AFAR Research Grants, 48
NORD Clinical Research Grants, 515
Paralyzed Veterans of America Research Grants, 552
Paul Beeson Physician/Faculty Scholars in Aging Research Programme, 49

West European Countries

NORD Clinical Research Grants, 515

VIROLOGY

Any Country

Canadian Blood Services Transfusion Medicine Fellowship Awards, 224
GlaxoSmithKline Collaborative Research Projects, 337
Lister Institute Senior Research Fellowships, 449
NARSAD Distinguished Investigator Awards, 491
NARSAD Independent Investigator Awards, 491
NARSAD Young Investigator Awards, 491
Queen Elizabeth the Queen Mother Fellowship Award, 583
Research into Ageing Programme Grants, 584
Services to Academia, 337
University of Dundee Research Awards, 704
Wilson-Fulton and Robertson Awards in Aging Research, Cecille Gould Memorial Fund Award in Cancer Research, Richard Shepherd Fellowship, 50

Australia

Wingate Scholarships, 771

British Commonwealth

Wingate Scholarships, 771

Canada

Canadian Blood Services Postdoctoral Fellowhip (PDF), 223
Canadian Blood Services Research and Development Program Individual Grants, 223
Canadian Blood Services Research and Development Program Major Equipment Grants, 224
NORD Clinical Research Grants, 515
Wingate Scholarships, 771

East European Countries

FEMS Fellowship, 310
Salzburg Medical Seminars, 543

Indian Sub-Continent

Wingate Scholarships, 771

New Zealand

Wingate Scholarships, 771

South Africa

Wingate Scholarships, 771

United Kingdom

British Lung Foundation Project Grants, 171
FEMS Fellowship, 310
H C Roscoe Fellowship, 172
NORD Clinical Research Grants, 515
Wingate Scholarships, 771

United States of America

NORD Clinical Research Grants, 515
Paul Beeson Physician/Faculty Scholars in Aging Research Programme, 49

West European Countries

TROPICAL MEDICINE

Any Country

African Nations

Australia

British Commonwealth

Canada

Indian Sub-Continent

New Zealand

South Africa

United Kingdom

United States of America

West European Countries

VENEREOLOGY

Any Country

Australia

British Commonwealth

Canada

East European Countries

Indian Sub-Continent

New Zealand

South Africa

United Kingdom

United States of America

West European Countries

REHABILITATION MEDICINE AND THERAPY

Any Country

Australia

NURSING

Wingate Scholarships, 771

Indian Sub-Continent

Wingate Scholarships, 771

Middle East

ABCCF Student Grant, 103

New Zealand

University of Western Sydney Postgraduate Research Award (UWSPRA), 755
Wingate Scholarships, 771

South Africa

DENOSA Bursaries, Scholarships and Grants, 280
Wingate Scholarships, 771

United Kingdom

Alzheimer's Society Research Grants, 24
British Lung Foundation Project Grants, 171
MND PhD Studentship Award, 482
Parkinson's Disease Society Research Project Grant, 555
Parkinson's Disease Society Studentships and Junior/Senior Fellows, 555
Smith and Nephew Foundation Nursing Research Fellowships, 634
Smith and Nephew Foundation Postdoctoral Nursing Research Fellowship, 635
University of Wales, Bangor (UWB) Research Studentships, 753
University of Wales, Bangor Departmental Research Studentships, 753
Wingate Scholarships, 771

United States of America

Arthritis Foundation Doctoral Dissertation Award, 106
Arthritis Foundation New Investigator Grant, 106
Arthritis Investigator Award, 107
BPW Career Advancement Scholarship Program, 184
Fulbright Scholar Awards for Research and Lecturing Abroad for United States Citizens, 271
Ian Axford (New Zealand) Fellowships in Public Policy, 263
Nurses' Educational Funds Fellowships and Scholarships, 539
Scholarships for Émigrés in the Health Professions, 424
Sigma Theta Tau International Small Research Grants, 627
Sigma Theta Tau International/Association of Operating room Nurses Foundation Grant, 628

West European Countries

University of Wales, Bangor (UWB) Research Studentships, 753
University of Wales, Bangor Departmental Research Studentships, 753
Wingate Scholarships, 771

MEDICAL AUXILIARIES

Any Country

Roche Research Foundation, 589

Australia

Wingate Scholarships, 771

British Commonwealth

Wingate Scholarships, 771

Canada

Wingate Scholarships, 771

Indian Sub-Continent

Wingate Scholarships, 771

New Zealand

Wingate Scholarships, 771

South Africa

Wingate Scholarships, 771

United Kingdom

Wingate Scholarships, 771

West European Countries

Wingate Scholarships, 771

MIDWIFERY

Any Country

Central Queensland University Postgraduate Research Award, 248
CQU International Student Scholarship, 248
Massey Doctoral Scholarship, 461
Roche Research Foundation, 589
University of Dundee Research Awards, 704
University of Glasgow Postgraduate Research Scholarships, 707
University of Manchester Research Studentships and Scholarships, 715
University of Stirling Research Studentships, 750

Australia

University of Western Sydney Postgraduate Research Award (UWSPRA), 755
Wingate Scholarships, 771

British Commonwealth

Wingate Scholarships, 771

Canada

Dr Sydney Segal Research Grants, 231
Wingate Scholarships, 771

Indian Sub-Continent

Wingate Scholarships, 771

New Zealand

University of Western Sydney Postgraduate Research Award (UWSPRA), 755
Wingate Scholarships, 771

South Africa

Wingate Scholarships, 771

United Kingdom

Smith and Nephew Foundation Nursing Research Fellowships, 634
Smith and Nephew Foundation Postdoctoral Nursing Research Fellowship, 635
University of Wales, Bangor (UWB) Research Studentships, 753
University of Wales, Bangor Departmental Research Studentships, 753
Wingate Scholarships, 771

West European Countries

University of Wales, Bangor (UWB) Research Studentships, 753
University of Wales, Bangor Departmental Research Studentships, 753
Wingate Scholarships, 771

RADIOLOGY

Any Country

Alice Ettinger Distinguished Achievement Award, 33
BackCare Research Grants, 148
British Institute of Radiology Travel Bursary, 170
Eleanor Montague Distinguished Resident Award in Radiation Oncology, 33
Fight for Sight Grants-in-Aid, 311
Fight for Sight Postdoctoral Research Fellowships, 311
Fight for Sight Student Research Fellowships, 311

TREATMENT TECHNIQUES

Arthritis Foundation New Investigator Grant, 106
National Headache Foundation Research Grant, 503
OREF Clinical Research Award, 550
Paralyzed Veterans of America Research Grants, 552

West European Countries

Wingate Scholarships, 771

MEDICAL TECHNOLOGY

Any Country

BRPS Research Grants, 175
Fight for Sight Grants-in-Aid, 311
Fight for Sight Postdoctoral Research Fellowships, 311
Fight for Sight Student Research Fellowships, 311
GlaxoSmithKline Collaborative Research Projects, 337
Meningitis Research Foundation Project Grant, 469
Meningitis Research Foundation Small Project Grant, 470
Meningitis Trust Research Award, 470
MND Research Project Grant, 482
Queen Elizabeth the Queen Mother Fellowship Award, 583
Research into Ageing Prize Studentships, 583
Research into Ageing Programme Grants, 584
Roche Research Foundation, 589
Savoy Foundation Post Doctoral and Clinical Research Fellowships, 621
Savoy Foundation Studentships, 621
Services to Academia, 337
UICC International Fellowships for Beginning Investigators (ACSBI), 414

African Nations

The Hastings Center International Visiting Scholars Program, 352

Australia

The Hastings Center International Visiting Scholars Program, 352
Wingate Scholarships, 771

British Commonwealth

The Hastings Center International Visiting Scholars Program, 352
Wingate Scholarships, 771

Canada

Quebec CE Fund Grants, 239
Wingate Scholarships, 771

Caribbean Countries

The Hastings Center International Visiting Scholars Program, 352

East European Countries

The Hastings Center International Visiting Scholars Program, 352

Far East

The Hastings Center International Visiting Scholars Program, 352
UICC International Cancer Technology Transfer Fellowships (ICRETT) for Bilateral Exchanges Between Indonesia and the Netherlands, 414

Indian Sub-Continent

The Hastings Center International Visiting Scholars Program, 352
Wingate Scholarships, 771

Middle East

The Hastings Center International Visiting Scholars Program, 352

New Zealand

The Hastings Center International Visiting Scholars Program, 352
Wingate Scholarships, 771

South Africa

The Hastings Center International Visiting Scholars Program, 352
Wingate Scholarships, 771

South America

The Hastings Center International Visiting Scholars Program, 352

United Kingdom

Alzheimer's Society Research Grants, 24
British Lung Foundation Project Grants, 171
The Hastings Center International Visiting Scholars Program, 352
MND PhD Studentship Award, 482
Wingate Scholarships, 771

United States of America

Ian Axford (New Zealand) Fellowships in Public Policy, 263

West European Countries

The Hastings Center International Visiting Scholars Program, 352
Wingate Scholarships, 771

DENTISTRY AND STOMATOLOGY

Any Country

AADR Student Research Fellowships, 32
CAMS Scholarship, 257
CIHR Fellowship Programme, 234
Colyer Prize, 615
DCF Biennial Research Award, 280
The DDF Scholarship for the Development of a Research Technique for Dentistry/Dental Research, 659
Dentsply Scholarship Fund, 161
Eastman Dental Center Clinical Fellowships, 290
Health Research Board and British Council Research Visits Scheme, 353
Lever Pond's Postgraduate Fellowship, 660
Michael Geisman Memorial Fellowship Fund, 551
National Association of Dental Assistants Annual Scholarship Award, 492
Osteogenesis Imperfecta Foundation Seed Research Grant, 551
Queen Mary Research Studentships, 576
Roche Research Foundation, 589
Sir Richard Stapley Educational Trust Grants, 632
University of Bristol Postgraduate Scholarships, 691
University of Dundee Research Awards, 704
University of Glasgow Postgraduate Research Scholarships, 707
University of Manchester Research Studentships and Scholarships, 715
The Winifred E Preedy Postgraduate Bursary, 139

Australia

NHMRC Medical and Dental and Public Health Postgraduate Research Scholarships, 505
Wingate Scholarships, 771

British Commonwealth

Wingate Scholarships, 771

Canada

DCF Fellowships for Teacher/Researcher Training, 280
DCF/Wrigley Dental Student Research Awards, 281
Frank Knox Memorial Fellowships at Harvard University, 131
Tylman Research Program, 27
Wingate Scholarships, 771

Indian Sub-Continent

Wingate Scholarships, 771

New Zealand

Wingate Scholarships, 771

South Africa

Wingate Scholarships, 771

United Kingdom

Royal College of Surgeons, New York Travelling Fellowships, 599
Wingate Scholarships, 771

United States of America

The ADA Endowment and Assistance Fund, Inc. Dental Student Scholarship, 9
The ADA Endowment and Assistance Fund, Inc. Minority Dental Student Scholarship, 9
ADHA Institute Minority Scholarship, 10
ADHA Institute Scholarship Program, 10
Colgate 'Bright Smiles, Bright Futures' Minority Scholarships, 10
Dr Alfred C Fones Scholarship, 10
Dr Harold Hillenbrand Scholarship, 10
Irene E Newman Scholarship, 11
Margaret E Swanson Scholarship, 11
Scholarships for Émigrés in the Health Professions, 424
Sigma Phi Alpha Graduate Scholarship, 11
Tylman Research Program, 27

West European Countries

Scholarship Foundation of the League for Finnish-American Societies, 621
Wingate Scholarships, 771

ORAL PATHOLOGY

Any Country

Colyer Prize, 615
University of Manchester Research Studentships and Scholarships, 715

Australia

Wingate Scholarships, 771

British Commonwealth

Wingate Scholarships, 771

Canada

Wingate Scholarships, 771

Indian Sub-Continent

Wingate Scholarships, 771

New Zealand

Wingate Scholarships, 771

South Africa

Wingate Scholarships, 771

United Kingdom

Wingate Scholarships, 771

West European Countries

Wingate Scholarships, 771

ORTHODONTICS

Any Country

Eastman Dental Center Clinical Fellowships, 290
Michael Geisman Memorial Fellowship Fund, 551
Osteogenesis Imperfecta Foundation Seed Research Grant, 551
University of Bristol Postgraduate Scholarships, 691
University of Dundee Research Awards, 704
University of Manchester Research Studentships and Scholarships, 715

Australia

Wingate Scholarships, 771

British Commonwealth

Wingate Scholarships, 771

Canada

Wingate Scholarships, 771

Indian Sub-Continent

Wingate Scholarships, 771

New Zealand

Wingate Scholarships, 771

South Africa

Wingate Scholarships, 771

United Kingdom

Wingate Scholarships, 771

West European Countries

Wingate Scholarships, 771

PERIODONTICS

Any Country

Eastman Dental Center Clinical Fellowships, 290
University of Bristol Postgraduate Scholarships, 691
University of Dundee Research Awards, 704
University of Manchester Research Studentships and Scholarships, 715

Australia

Wingate Scholarships, 771

British Commonwealth

Wingate Scholarships, 771

Canada

Wingate Scholarships, 771

Indian Sub-Continent

Wingate Scholarships, 771

New Zealand

Wingate Scholarships, 771

South Africa

Wingate Scholarships, 771

United Kingdom

Wingate Scholarships, 771

West European Countries

Wingate Scholarships, 771

COMMUNITY DENTISTRY

Any Country

University of Dundee Research Awards, 704
University of Manchester Research Studentships and Scholarships, 715

Australia

Wingate Scholarships, 771

British Commonwealth

Wingate Scholarships, 771

Canada

Wingate Scholarships, 771

Indian Sub-Continent

Wingate Scholarships, 771

New Zealand

Wingate Scholarships, 771

South Africa

Wingate Scholarships, 771

United Kingdom

Wingate Scholarships, 771

West European Countries

Wingate Scholarships, 771

DENTAL TECHNOLOGY

Any Country

Colyer Prize, 615
Roche Research Foundation, 589
University of Dundee Research Awards, 704
University of Glasgow Postgraduate Research Scholarships, 707

United States of America

The ADA Endowment and Assistance Fund, Inc. Allied Dental Health Scholarship (Dental Hygiene, Dental Assisting, Dental Laboratory Technology), 9

PROSTHETIC DENTISTRY

Any Country

Eastman Dental Center Clinical Fellowships, 290
University of Bristol Postgraduate Scholarships, 691
University of Dundee Research Awards, 704

Australia

Wingate Scholarships, 771

British Commonwealth

Wingate Scholarships, 771

Canada

Wingate Scholarships, 771

Indian Sub-Continent

Wingate Scholarships, 771

New Zealand

Wingate Scholarships, 771

South Africa

Wingate Scholarships, 771

United Kingdom

Wingate Scholarships, 771

West European Countries

Wingate Scholarships, 771

PHARMACY

Any Country

Alzheimer's Research Trust Research Programme Grant, 24
Andrew Mellon Foundation Scholarship, 585
BIAL Merit Award in Medical Sciences, 152
CIHR Fellowship Programme, 234
GlaxoSmithKline Collaborative Research Projects, 337
HDSA Fellowships, 363
HDSA Research Grants, 364
HDSA Research Initiative Grants, 364

Hugh Kelly Fellowship, 586
The Institute for the Study of Aging Grants Program, 378
Leukemia and Lymphoma Society Translational Research Award, 446
Michael Geisman Memorial Fellowship Fund, 551
Osteogenesis Imperfecta Foundation Seed Research Grant, 551
Rhodes University Postdoctoral Fellowship, 586
Rhodes University Postgraduate Scholarship, 587
Roche Research Foundation, 589
Savoy Foundation Post Doctoral and Clinical Research Fellowships, 621
Savoy Foundation Studentships, 621
Services to Academia, 337
University of Manchester Research Studentships and Scholarships, 715

Australia

Asthma Foundation of New South Wales Medical Research Project Grant, 133
Biomedical and Medical Postgraduate Research Scholarships, 133
Wingate Scholarships, 771

British Commonwealth

Wingate Scholarships, 771

Canada

Wingate Scholarships, 771

Indian Sub-Continent

Wingate Scholarships, 771

New Zealand

Wingate Scholarships, 771

South Africa

Allan Gray Senior Scholarship, 585
Wingate Scholarships, 771

United Kingdom

Parkinson's Disease Society Research Project Grant, 555
Parkinson's Disease Society Studentships and Junior/Senior Fellows, 555
Wingate Scholarships, 771

United States of America

Ian Axford (New Zealand) Fellowships in Public Policy, 263
Merck/AFAR Research Scholarships for Medical and Pharmacy Students in Geriatric Pharmacology, 49
PhRMA Postdoctoral Fellowships in Pharmacology/Toxicology, 564
Scholarships for Émigrés in the Health Professions, 424

West European Countries

BIAL Award in Clinical Medicine, 152
Wingate Scholarships, 771

BIOMEDICINE

Any Country

AHAF Alzheimer's Disease Research Grant, 52
AHAF Macular Degeneration Research, 52
AHAF National Glaucoma Research, 52
AHAF National Heart Foundation, 52
AIDS International Training and Research Programme (AITRP), 428
Alzheimer's Research Trust Research Programme Grant, 24
Arthritis Foundation Postdoctoral Fellowship, 106
Batten Disease Support and Research Association Research Grant Awards, 149
BIAL Merit Award in Medical Sciences, 152
Diabetes UK Project Grants, 285
Diabetes UK Research Fellowships, 285
Diabetes UK Research Studentships, 285
Diabetes UK Small Grant Scheme, 285

FEMS Fellowship, 310
Fogarty International Research Collaboration Award (FIRCA), 428
The Hastings Center International Visiting Scholars Program, 352
MRC Collaborative/Industrial Collaborative Studentships, 463
MRC Research Studentships, 464
Wingate Scholarships, 771

OPTOMETRY

Any Country

CIHR Fellowship Programme, 234
Fight for Sight Grants-in-Aid, 311
Fight for Sight Postdoctoral Research Fellowships, 311
Fight for Sight Student Research Fellowships, 311
Roche Research Foundation, 589
University of Bristol Postgraduate Scholarships, 691

Australia

The Sir Robert Menzies Memorial Research Scholarships in the
Allied Health Sciences, 632
Wingate Scholarships, 771

British Commonwealth

Wingate Scholarships, 771

Canada

Wingate Scholarships, 771

Indian Sub-Continent

Wingate Scholarships, 771

New Zealand

Wingate Scholarships, 771

South Africa

Wingate Scholarships, 771

United Kingdom

Wingate Scholarships, 771

West European Countries

Wingate Scholarships, 771

PODIATRY

Any Country

BackCare Research Grants, 148
Roche Research Foundation, 589

Australia

University of Western Sydney Postgraduate Research Award
(UWSPRA), 755
Wingate Scholarships, 771

British Commonwealth

Wingate Scholarships, 771

Canada

Wingate Scholarships, 771

Indian Sub-Continent

Wingate Scholarships, 771

New Zealand

University of Western Sydney Postgraduate Research Award
(UWSPRA), 755
Wingate Scholarships, 771

South Africa

Wingate Scholarships, 771

United Kingdom

Wingate Scholarships, 771

West European Countries

Wingate Scholarships, 771

FORENSIC MEDICINE AND DENTISTRY

Any Country

Roche Research Foundation, 589
University of Dundee Research Awards, 704
University of Glasgow Postgraduate Research Scholarships, 707

Australia

Wingate Scholarships, 771

British Commonwealth

Wingate Scholarships, 771

Canada

Wingate Scholarships, 771

Indian Sub-Continent

Wingate Scholarships, 771

New Zealand

Wingate Scholarships, 771

South Africa

Wingate Scholarships, 771

United Kingdom

C H Milburn Research Award, 172
Wingate Scholarships, 771

West European Countries

Wingate Scholarships, 771

ACUPUNCTURE

Any Country

BackCare Research Grants, 148
Roche Research Foundation, 589

HOMEOPATHY

Any Country

Roche Research Foundation, 589

CHIROPRACTIC

Any Country

BackCare Research Grants, 148
CIHR Fellowship Programme, 234
CRPF Research Grant, 258
Roche Research Foundation, 589

OSTEOPATHY

Any Country

BackCare Research Grants, 148
Roche Research Foundation, 589

Canada

Alcohol Beverage Medical Research Foundation Research Project
Grant, 17

United States of America

Alcohol Beverage Medical Research Foundation Research Project Grant, 17
AOA Research Grants, 70

TRADITIONAL EASTERN MEDICINE

Any Country

Roche Research Foundation, 589

Australia

University of Western Sydney Postgraduate Research Award (UWSPRA), 755

New Zealand

University of Western Sydney Postgraduate Research Award (UWSPRA), 755

United Kingdom

Alzheimer's Society Research Grants, 24

NATURAL SCIENCES

GENERAL

Any Country

AHA National Grant-in-Aid, 53
AIATSIS Research Grants, 139
Airey Neave Trust Award, 14
Andrew Mellon Foundation Scholarship, 585
Andrew Stratton Scholarship, 705
ASCSA Research Fellow in Faunal Studies, 79
ASCSA Research Fellow in Geoarchaeology, 80
Australian Research Council Discovery Projects Australian Research Fellow/Queen Elizabeth II Fellow (ARF/QEII), 142
Australian Research Council Discovery Projects Postdoctoral Fellow (APD), 142
Australian Research Discovery Projects - Professional Fellow (APF), 143
AWU Postgraduate Fellowships, 125
Balliol College Dervorguilla Scholarship, 722
Beit Fellowship For Scientific Research, 366
BIAL Merit Award in Medical Sciences, 152
Biochemical Society General Travel Fund, 154
Canadian Cystic Fibrosis Foundation Scholarships, 226
Canadian Cystic Fibrosis Foundation Studentships, 227
Canadian Cystic Fibrosis Foundation Visiting Scientist Awards, 227
Carnegie Institution of Washington Fellowships, 243
Center for Field Research Grants, 246
Claude McCarthy Fellowships, 529
Colt Foundation PhD Fellowship, 262
Concordia University Graduate Fellowships, 266
CQU International Student Scholarship, 248
CRPF Research Grant, 258
Danish Cancer Society Scientific Award, 278
Daphne Jackson Fellowship, 278
David J Azrieli Graduate Fellowship, 266
Dorothy Hodgkin Fellowships, 608
Downing College Research Fellowships, 696
Edmund Niles Huyck Preserve, Inc. Graduate and Postgraduate Grants, 292
Foulkes Foundation Fellowship, 314
Foundation for Science and Disability Student Grant Fund, 316
Franklin Research Grant Program, 71
Fund for UFO Research Grants, 327
G M McKinley Research Fund, 575
Girton College Research Fellowships, 698
GlaxoSmithKline Collaborative Research Projects, 337

GSA Research Grants, 328
Heinrich Wieland Prize, 156
Honda Prize, 359
Howard Brown Rickard Scholarship, 500
HSS Travel Grant, 359
Hugh Kelly Fellowship, 586
Humanitarian Trust Awards, 362
ICGEB Long-Term Postdoctoral Fellowship Programme, 396
ICGEB Short-Term Postdoctoral Fellowship Programme, 396
IFT Freshman/Sophomore Scholarships, 381
IFT Graduate Fellowships, 381
International Crops Research Institute Research Fellowships, 399
International Crops Research Institute Research Scholarships, 399
International Human Frontier Science Programme Organization Long-Term Fellowships, 403
International Human Frontier Science Programme Organization Research Grants, 404
International Human Frontier Science Programme Organization Short Term Fellowships, 404
J Lawrence Angel Fellowship in Human Skeletal Studies, 80
Leverhulme Trust Senior Research Fellowships, 608
Lincoln College Erich and Rochelle Endowed Prize in Music, 730
Lindbergh Grants, 252
Lord Dowding Fund for Humane Research, 453
Matsumae International Foundation Research Fellowship, 461
Monash University International Postgraduate Research Scholarship (MIPRS), 480
Monash University Silver Jubilee Postgraduate Scholarship, 481
The NASA Administrator's Fellowship Program, 490
National Marfan Foundation Clinical Fellowship Grant, 513
National Marfan Foundation Research Grant, 513
National Research Council Laboratories Research Associateships, 516
NEH Research Fellowships, 81
NERC Advanced Course Studentships, 520
NERC Advanced Research Fellowships, 521
NERC Postdoctoral Research Fellowships, 521
NERC Research Grants, 521
NERC Senior Research Fellowships, 522
NFR Open Postdoctoral Fellowships, 668
NFR Senior Research Positions, 668
NFR Travel Grants, 669
Novartis Foundation Symposium Bursaries, 539
NSERC Equipment Grants, 523
NSERC Industrial Research Chairs, 523
NSERC International Opportunity Fund, 524
NSERC NATO Science Fellowships, 524
NSERC Project Research Grants, 524
NSERC Strategic Project Grants (SPG), 525
NUS Postgraduate Research Scholarship, 520
Oliver Gatty Studentship, 699
Oriel College Graduate Scholarships, 732
Perry Postgraduate Scholarships and Research Awards, 560
Predoctoral Fellowship Programme ICGEB JNU PhD Course in Molecular Biology, 396
Predoctoral Fellowship Programme ICGEB SISSA PhD Course in Molecular Genetics, 397
Queen Mary Research Studentships, 576
Ralph Brown Expedition Award, 600
Rhodes University Postgraduate Scholarship, 587
Roche Research Foundation, 589
Royal Irish Academy European Exchange Fellowship, 606
Royal Irish Academy Senior Visiting Fellowships, 606
Royal Society Conference Grants, 609
Royal Society EPSRC BBSRC PPARC and Rolls Royce PLC Industry Fellowships, 300
Royal Society Industry Fellowships Scheme, 610
Royal Society Research Grants Scheme, 610
The Royal Society-Wolfson Foundation Laboratory Refurbishment Scheme, 610
SEELLD Personal Research Fellowships, 614
SEELLD/RSE Support Research Fellowships, 615

West European Countries

BIOLOGICAL AND LIFE SCIENCES

Any Country

BIOLOGY

African Nations

Australia

Canada

East European Countries

Far East

Indian Sub-Continent

New Zealand

South America

United Kingdom

United States of America

West European Countries

HISTOLOGY

Any Country

Canada

United Kingdom

United States of America

West European Countries

BIOPHYSICS AND MOLECULAR BIOLOGY

Any Country

African Nations

Australia

Canada

BIOTECHNOLOGY

Grants for Innovative Methods for Control of Tick-Borne Diseases, 63

Washington University Chancellor's Graduate Fellowship Program for African Americans, 767

West European Countries

Cardiff University Postgraduate Research Studentships, 242
Llewellyn and Mary Williams Scholarship, 753
Natural History Museum Sys-Resource, 522
University of Wales, Bangor (UWB) Research Studentships, 753
University of Wales, Bangor Departmental Research Studentships, 753

PLANT PATHOLOGY

Any Country

BBSRC Research Fellowships, 154
BBSRC Research Grants, 154
BBSRC Studentships, 155
Center for Field Research Grants, 246
Central Queensland University Postgraduate Research Award, 248
Deputy Chancellors Postdoctoral Research, 535
ICGEB Long-Term Postdoctoral Fellowship Programme, 396
ICGEB Short-Term Postdoctoral Fellowship Programme, 396
International Crops Research Institute Research Fellowships, 399
International Crops Research Institute Research Scholarships, 399
Joyce W Vickery Scientific Research Fund, 449
Linnean Macleay Fellowship, 449
LSRF Three Year Postdoctoral Fellowships, 448
Massey Doctoral Scholarship, 461
NERC Advanced Course Studentships, 520
NERC Advanced Research Fellowships, 521
NERC Postdoctoral Research Fellowships, 521
NERC Research Grants, 521
NERC Senior Research Fellowships, 522
NTU One Year Postdoctoral Fellowship, 535
NTU Senior Research Fellowship, 536
NTU Three Year Postdoctoral Fellowship, 536
Perry Postgraduate Scholarships and Research Awards, 560
Predoctoral Fellowship Programme ICGEB JNU PhD Course in Molecular Biology, 396
Predoctoral Fellowship Programme ICGEB SISSA PhD Course in Molecular Genetics, 397
Sigma Xi Grants-in-Aid of Research, 629
Thomas Holloway Research Studentship, 602
Underwood Fund, 155
University of Dundee Research Awards, 704
University of New England Research Scholarships, 719
University of Stirling Research Studentships, 750
Wain Fund, 155
The Walsh Fellowships, 671
Weizmann Institute of Science MSc Fellowships, 767

Australia

Ebbe Nielsen Regional Scholarship, 264
University of Western Sydney Postgraduate Research Award (UWSPRA), 755

Canada

IDRC Doctoral Research Awards, 400

New Zealand

University of Western Sydney Postgraduate Research Award (UWSPRA), 755

United Kingdom

Cardiff University Postgraduate Research Studentships, 242
Llewellyn and Mary Williams Scholarship, 753
Martin McLaren Horticultural Scholarship, 382
NERC Research Studentships, 521
The University of Kent at Canterbury Department of Biosciences, 709

University of Wales (Aberystwyth) Postgraduate Research Studentships, 752
University of Wales, Bangor (UWB) Research Studentships, 753
University of Wales, Bangor Departmental Research Studentships, 753

United States of America

Earthwatch Education Awards, 290

West European Countries

Cardiff University Postgraduate Research Studentships, 242
Llewellyn and Mary Williams Scholarship, 753
The University of Kent at Canterbury Department of Biosciences, 709
University of Wales, Bangor (UWB) Research Studentships, 753
University of Wales, Bangor Departmental Research Studentships, 753

EMBRYOLOGY AND REPRODUCTION BIOLOGY

Any Country

BackCare Research Grants, 148
BBSRC Research Fellowships, 154
BBSRC Research Grants, 154
BBSRC Studentships, 155
Children's Medical Research Institute Graduate Scholarships and Postgraduate Fellowships, 256
Children's Medical Research Institute Postdoctoral Fellowship, 256
Foulkes Foundation Fellowship, 314
Lalor Foundation Postdoctoral Fellowships, 440
Lister Institute Senior Research Fellowships, 449
LSRF Three Year Postdoctoral Fellowships, 448
Massey Doctoral Scholarship, 461
Rhodes University Postdoctoral Fellowship, 586
Sigma Xi Grants-in-Aid of Research, 629
University of Stirling Research Studentships, 750
Weizmann Institute of Science MSc Fellowships, 767
WellBeing Project Grants, 768
Wellcome Trust Awards, Fellowships and Studentships, 768

African Nations

The Hastings Center International Visiting Scholars Program, 352

Australia

Children's Medical Research Institute Postgraduate Scholarship, 257
The Hastings Center International Visiting Scholars Program, 352

British Commonwealth

The Hastings Center International Visiting Scholars Program, 352

Caribbean Countries

The Hastings Center International Visiting Scholars Program, 352

East European Countries

The Hastings Center International Visiting Scholars Program, 352

Far East

The Hastings Center International Visiting Scholars Program, 352

Indian Sub-Continent

The Hastings Center International Visiting Scholars Program, 352

Middle East

The Hastings Center International Visiting Scholars Program, 352

New Zealand

The Hastings Center International Visiting Scholars Program, 352

South Africa

The Hastings Center International Visiting Scholars Program, 352

GENETICS

Postdoctoral Training Programme in Addiction and Mental Health, 249

Caribbean Countries

The Hastings Center International Visiting Scholars Program, 352

East European Countries

FEMS Fellowship, 310
The Hastings Center International Visiting Scholars Program, 352
UNESCO-ROSTE Long-term Postgraduate Training Course, 7

Far East

The Hastings Center International Visiting Scholars Program, 352
UNESCO-ROSTE Long-term Postgraduate Training Course, 7

Indian Sub-Continent

The Hastings Center International Visiting Scholars Program, 352
UNESCO-ROSTE Long-term Postgraduate Training Course, 7

Middle East

The Hastings Center International Visiting Scholars Program, 352
UNESCO-ROSTE Long-term Postgraduate Training Course, 7

New Zealand

The Hastings Center International Visiting Scholars Program, 352
University of Western Sydney Postgraduate Research Award (UWSPRA), 755

South Africa

The Hastings Center International Visiting Scholars Program, 352

South America

The Hastings Center International Visiting Scholars Program, 352

United Kingdom

Alzheimer's Research Trust PhD Studentship, 24
Alzheimer's Society Research Grants, 24
British Lung Foundation Project Grants, 171
Cardiff University Postgraduate Research Studentships, 242
FEMS Fellowship, 310
The Hastings Center International Visiting Scholars Program, 352
Llewellyn and Mary Williams Scholarship, 753
MND PhD Studentship Award, 482
Muscular Dystrophy Programme Grant, 485
Muscular Dystrophy Project Grant, 485
Muscular Dystrophy Research Grants, 485
NERC Research Studentships, 521
NORD Clinical Research Grants, 515
Parkinson's Disease Society Research Project Grant, 555
Parkinson's Disease Society Studentships and Junior/Senior Fellows, 555
University of Wales (Aberystwyth) Postgraduate Research Studentships, 752
University of Wales, Bangor (UWB) Research Studentships, 753
University of Wales, Bangor Departmental Research Studentships, 753

United States of America

AFAR Research Grants, 48
AHA National Established Investigator Grant, 52
Alcohol Beverage Medical Research Foundation Research Project Grant, 17
Arthritis Investigator Award, 107
Fulbright Senior Specialists Program, 271
MARC Faculty Predoctoral Fellowships, 509
NIGMS Fellowship Awards for Minority Students, 509
NIGMS Fellowship Awards for Students With Disabilities, 509
NIGMS Postdoctoral Awards, 510
NIGMS Research Project Grants, 510
NIGMS Research Supplements for Underrepresented Minorities, 510
NIH Research Grants, 511

NORD Clinical Research Grants, 515
Paul Beeson Physician/Faculty Scholars in Aging Research Programme, 49
PhRMA Postdoctoral Fellowships in Informatics, 563
PhRMA Research Starter Grants in Informatics, 565
PhRMA Sabbatical Fellowships in Informatics, 566
Physician Scientist Development Award, 107
Postdoctoral Training Programme in Addiction and Mental Health, 249
Washington University Chancellor's Graduate Fellowship Program for African Americans, 767

West European Countries

Cardiff University Postgraduate Research Studentships, 242
FEMS Fellowship, 310
The Hastings Center International Visiting Scholars Program, 352
Llewellyn and Mary Williams Scholarship, 753
NORD Clinical Research Grants, 515
UNESCO-ROSTE Long-term Postgraduate Training Course, 7
University of Wales, Bangor (UWB) Research Studentships, 753
University of Wales, Bangor Departmental Research Studentships, 753

IMMUNOLOGY

Any Country

AACR Scholar-in-Training Awards, 31
Abbott Laboratories Award in Clinical and Diagnostic Immunology, 86
AHAF Macular Degeneration Research, 52
Arthritis Foundation Postdoctoral Fellowship, 106
BBSRC Research Fellowships, 154
BBSRC Research Grants, 154
BBSRC Studentships, 155
CGD Research Trust Grants, 258
CRPF Research Grant, 258
Foulkes Foundation Fellowship, 314
Fungal Research Trust Travel Grants, 327
Gordon Piller Studentships, 444
ICGEB Long-Term Postdoctoral Fellowship Programme, 396
Imperial Cancer Research Fund Clinical Research Fellowships, 365
Imperial Cancer Research Fund Graduate Studentships, 365
Inflammatory Bowel Disease Grants, 180
The Institute for the Study of Aging Grants Program, 378
Leukaemia Research Fund Clinical Research Fellowship, 445
Leukaemia Research Fund Clinical Training Fellowship, 445
Leukaemia Research Fund Grant Programme, 445
Leukaemia Research Fund Grant Project, 445
Leukemia and Lymphoma Society Translational Research Award, 446
Lister Institute Senior Research Fellowships, 449
LSRF Three Year Postdoctoral Fellowships, 448
Meningitis Research Foundation Project Grant, 469
Meningitis Research Foundation Small Project Grant, 470
National Multiple Sclerosis Society Research Grants, 514
NORD/ROSCOE BRADY Lysosomal Storage Diseases Fellowship, 515
Predoctoral Fellowship Programme ICGEB JNU PhD Course in Molecular Biology, 396
Predoctoral Fellowship Programme ICGEB SISSA PhD Course in Molecular Genetics, 397
Queen Elizabeth the Queen Mother Fellowship Award, 583
Research into Ageing Prize Studentships, 583
Research into Ageing Programme Grants, 584
Rhodes University Postdoctoral Fellowship, 586
Savoy Foundation Post Doctoral and Clinical Research Fellowships, 621
Savoy Foundation Studentships, 621
Sigma Xi Grants-in-Aid of Research, 629
University of Dundee Research Awards, 704
University of Manchester Research Studentships and Scholarships, 715

University of Stirling Research Studentships, 750
Weizmann Institute of Science MSc Fellowships, 767
WellBeing Project Grants, 768
Wellcome Trust Awards, Fellowships and Studentships, 768
Wilson-Fulton and Robertson Awards in Aging Research, Cecille
Gould Memorial Fund Award in Cancer Research, Richard Shepherd
Fellowship, 50

Australia

New South Wales Cancer Council Research Programme Grant, 528
New South Wales Cancer Council Research Project Grants, 528
University of Western Sydney Postgraduate Research Award
(UWSPRA), 755

Canada

Eli Lilly and Company Research Award, 88
NORD Clinical Research Grants, 515
Physician Scientist Development Award, 107

East European Countries

FEMS Fellowship, 310

New Zealand

University of Western Sydney Postgraduate Research Award
(UWSPRA), 755

United Kingdom

Alzheimer's Society Research Grants, 24
FEMS Fellowship, 310
Llewellyn and Mary Williams Scholarship, 753
NORD Clinical Research Grants, 515
University of Wales (Aberystwyth) Postgraduate Research Student-
ships, 752
University of Wales, Bangor (UWB) Research Studentships, 753
University of Wales, Bangor Departmental Research Studentships,
753

United States of America

AFAR Research Grants, 48
AFAR/Pfizer Research Grants in Immunology and Aging, 49
Arthritis Investigator Award, 107
Eli Lilly and Company Research Award, 88
MARC Faculty Predoctoral Fellowships, 509
NIGMS Fellowship Awards for Minority Students, 509
NIGMS Fellowship Awards for Students With Disabilities, 509
NIGMS Postdoctoral Awards, 510
NIGMS Research Project Grants, 510
NIGMS Research Supplements for Underrepresented Minorities,
510
NIH Research Grants, 511
NORD Clinical Research Grants, 515
Paul Beeson Physician/Faculty Scholars in Aging Research
Programme, 49
Physician Scientist Development Award, 107
Washington University Chancellor's Graduate Fellowship Program
for African Americans, 767

West European Countries

FEMS Fellowship, 310
Llewellyn and Mary Williams Scholarship, 753
NORD Clinical Research Grants, 515
University of Wales, Bangor (UWB) Research Studentships, 753
University of Wales, Bangor Departmental Research Studentships,
753

MARINE BIOLOGY

Any Country

BBSRC Research Fellowships, 154
BBSRC Research Grants, 154
BBSRC Studentships, 155
Bermuda Biological Station for Research Grant In Aid, 150

Center for Field Research Grants, 246
Hugh Kelly Fellowship, 586
Joyce W Vickery Scientific Research Fund, 449
NERC Advanced Course Studentships, 520
NERC Advanced Research Fellowships, 521
NERC Postdoctoral Research Fellowships, 521
NERC Research Grants, 521
NERC Senior Research Fellowships, 522
Rhodes University Postdoctoral Fellowship, 586
Sigma Xi Grants-in-Aid of Research, 629
Tibor T Polgar Fellowship, 361
University of Dundee Research Awards, 704
University of Manchester Research Studentships and Scholarships,
715
University of Stirling Research Studentships, 750
Woods Hole Oceanographic Institution Research Fellowships in Ma-
rine Policy, 778
Woods Hole Oceanographic Institution/NOAA Co-operative Institute
for Climate and Ocean Research Postdoctoral Fellowship, 778

Australia

Noel and Kate Monkman Postgraduate Award, 420

British Commonwealth

ACU Development Fellowships, 127

Canada

IDRC Doctoral Research Awards, 400

East European Countries

FEMS Fellowship, 310
Natural History Museum Sys-Resource, 522

South Africa

Henderson Postgraduate Scholarships, 585

United Kingdom

ACU Development Fellowships, 127
FEMS Fellowship, 310
Llewellyn and Mary Williams Scholarship, 753
NERC Research Studentships, 521
Polish Embassy Short-Term Bursaries, 571
Polish Government Postgraduate Scholarships Scheme, 572
University of Wales, Bangor (UWB) Research Studentships, 753
University of Wales, Bangor Departmental Research Studentships,
753

United States of America

Earthwatch Education Awards, 290
ONR Postdoctoral Fellowship, 539
Woods Hole Oceanographic Institution Postdoctoral Fellowships in
the Interdisciplinary Institutes, 778

West European Countries

FEMS Fellowship, 310
Llewellyn and Mary Williams Scholarship, 753
Natural History Museum Sys-Resource, 522
University of Wales, Bangor (UWB) Research Studentships, 753
University of Wales, Bangor Departmental Research Studentships,
753

LIMNOLOGY

Any Country

BBSRC Research Grants, 154
BBSRC Studentships, 155
Center for Field Research Grants, 246
Edmund Niles Huyck Preserve, Inc. Graduate and Postgraduate
Grants, 292
Massey Doctoral Scholarship, 461
NERC Advanced Course Studentships, 520
NERC Advanced Research Fellowships, 521

MICROBIOLOGY

East European Countries

FEMS Fellowship, 310
Morrison Rogosa Award, 88
Natural History Museum Sys-Resource, 522
UNESCO-ROSTE Long-term Postgraduate Training Course, 7

Far East

UNESCO-ROSTE Long-term Postgraduate Training Course, 7

Indian Sub-Continent

UNESCO-ROSTE Long-term Postgraduate Training Course, 7

Middle East

UNESCO-ROSTE Long-term Postgraduate Training Course, 7

New Zealand

University of Western Sydney Postgraduate Research Award
(UWSPRA), 755

South Africa

Henderson Postgraduate Scholarships, 585

South America

ASM International Fellowship for Latin America, 86
ASM International Professorship for Latin America, 86

United Kingdom

Cardiff University Postgraduate Research Studentships, 242
ESRF Thesis Studentships, 306
FEMS Fellowship, 310
Llewellyn and Mary Williams Scholarship, 753
NERC Research Studentships, 521
The University of Kent at Canterbury Department of Biosciences,
709
University of Wales (Aberystwyth) Postgraduate Research Student-
ships, 752
University of Wales, Bangor (UWB) Research Studentships, 753
University of Wales, Bangor Departmental Research Studentships,
753

United States of America

AFAR Research Grants, 48
Eli Lilly and Company Research Award, 88
ICAAC Young Investigator Award, 88
MARC Faculty Predoctoral Fellowships, 509
NIGMS Fellowship Awards for Minority Students, 509
NIGMS Fellowship Awards for Students With Disabilities, 509
NIGMS Postdoctoral Awards, 510
NIGMS Research Project Grants, 510
NIGMS Research Supplements for Underrepresented Minorities,
510
Paul Beeson Physician/Faculty Scholars in Aging Research
Programme, 49
Physician Scientist Development Award, 107
Washington University Chancellor's Graduate Fellowship Program
for African Americans, 767

West European Countries

Cardiff University Postgraduate Research Studentships, 242
ESRF Thesis Studentships, 306
FEMS Fellowship, 310
Llewellyn and Mary Williams Scholarship, 753
Natural History Museum Sys-Resource, 522
UNESCO-ROSTE Long-term Postgraduate Training Course, 7
The University of Kent at Canterbury Department of Biosciences,
709
University of Wales, Bangor (UWB) Research Studentships, 753
University of Wales, Bangor Departmental Research Studentships,
753

NEUROSCIENCES

Any Country

AHA National Grant-in-Aid, 53
AHAF Alzheimer's Disease Research Grant, 52
AHAF National Glaucoma Research, 52
ASBAH Research Grant, 125
Ataxia UK Research Studentships, 133
Ataxia UK Travel Award, 134
BBSRC Research Fellowships, 154
BBSRC Research Grants, 154
BBSRC Studentships, 155
Children's Medical Research Institute Graduate Scholarships and
Postgraduate Fellowships, 256
Children's Medical Research Institute Postdoctoral Fellowship, 256
CRPF Research Grant, 258
Direct Research on Ataxia-Telangiectasia, 3
Epilepsy Research Foundation Research Grant, 302
Foulkes Foundation Fellowship, 314
FRAXA Grants and Fellowships, 320
GlaxoSmithKline Collaborative Research Projects, 337
HDSA Fellowships, 363
HDSA Research Grants, 364
HDSA Research Initiative Grants, 364
Herbert H Jasper Fellowship, 248
The Institute for the Study of Aging Grants Program, 378
ISRT Project Grant, 413
Lister Institute Senior Research Fellowships, 449
LSA Medical Research Grant, 454
LSRF Three Year Postdoctoral Fellowships, 448
Migraine Trust Grants, 475
MND Research Project Grant, 482
Muscular Dystrophy Association Grant Programs, 485
Muscular Dystrophy Programme Grant, 485
Muscular Dystrophy Project Grant, 485
NARSAD Distinguished Investigator Awards, 491
NARSAD Independent Investigator Awards, 491
NARSAD Young Investigator Awards, 491
Nathalie Rose Barr PhD Studentship, 413
National Multiple Sclerosis Society Research Grants, 514
Project Grant, 134
Queen Elizabeth the Queen Mother Fellowship Award, 583
Research into Ageing Prize Studentships, 583
Research into Ageing Programme Grants, 584
Rhodes University Postdoctoral Fellowship, 586
Satellite Meeting at Major Symposium on Related Disorders, 134
Savoy Foundation Post Doctoral and Clinical Research Fellowships,
621
Savoy Foundation Research Grants, 621
Savoy Foundation Studentships, 621
Services to Academia, 337
Short Project Grant, 134
Sigma Xi Grants-in-Aid of Research, 629
Tourette Syndrome Association Research Grants, 677
Underwood Fund, 155
University of Dundee Research Awards, 704
University of Manchester Research Studentships and Scholarships,
715
Wacker Foundation Research Grant, 765
Wain Fund, 155
Weizmann Institute of Science MSc Fellowships, 767
Wellcome Trust Awards, Fellowships and Studentships, 768
Wilson-Fulton and Robertson Awards in Aging Research, Cecille
Gould Memorial Fund Award in Cancer Research, Richard Shepherd
Fellowship, 50

Australia

Children's Medical Research Institute Postgraduate Scholarship, 257
University of Western Sydney Postgraduate Research Award
(UWSPRA), 755

Canada

Alcohol Beverage Medical Research Foundation Research Project Grant, 17
JP Cordeau Fellowship, 248
Paralyzed Veterans of America Research Grants, 552
Postdoctoral Training Programme in Addiction and Mental Health, 249

East European Countries

Linacre College European Blaschko Visiting Research Scholarship, 729

New Zealand

University of Western Sydney Postgraduate Research Award (UWSPRA), 755

United Kingdom

Alzheimer's Research Trust PhD Studentship, 24
Alzheimer's Society Research Grants, 24
Cardiff University Postgraduate Research Studentships, 242
MND PhD Studentship Award, 482
Muscular Dystrophy Programme Grant, 485
Muscular Dystrophy Project Grant, 485
Muscular Dystrophy Research Grants, 485
Parkinson's Disease Society Research Project Grant, 555
Parkinson's Disease Society Studentships and Junior/Senior Fellows, 555
Sheffield Hallam University Research Studentships, 625
University of Wales, Bangor (UWB) Research Studentships, 753
University of Wales, Bangor Departmental Research Studentships, 753

United States of America

AFAR Research Grants, 48
Alcohol Beverage Medical Research Foundation Research Project Grant, 17
American Association of Neurological Surgeons Research Fellowship, 36
MFP Neurosciences Training Fellowship, 77
NIH Research Grants, 511
Paralyzed Veterans of America Research Grants, 552
Paul Beeson Physician/Faculty Scholars in Aging Research Programme, 49
Postdoctoral Training Programme in Addiction and Mental Health, 249
Promotion of Doctoral Studies (PODS), 316
Washington University Chancellor's Graduate Fellowship Program for African Americans, 767
Young Clinician Investigator Award, 37

West European Countries

Cardiff University Postgraduate Research Studentships, 242
Linacre College European Blaschko Visiting Research Scholarship, 729
Sheffield Hallam University Research Studentships, 625
University of Wales, Bangor (UWB) Research Studentships, 753
University of Wales, Bangor Departmental Research Studentships, 753

PARASITOLOGY

Any Country

The ABRS Research Grants Scheme, 264
BBSRC Research Fellowships, 154
BBSRC Research Grants, 154
BBSRC Studentships, 155
Edmund Niles Huyck Preserve, Inc. Graduate and Postgraduate Grants, 292
ICGEB Long-Term Postdoctoral Fellowship Programme, 396
Inflammatory Bowel Disease Grants, 180
Lister Institute Senior Research Fellowships, 449

Massey Doctoral Scholarship, 461
NERC Advanced Course Studentships, 520
NERC Advanced Research Fellowships, 521
NERC Postdoctoral Research Fellowships, 521
NERC Research Grants, 521
NERC Senior Research Fellowships, 522
Predoctoral Fellowship Programme ICGEB JNU PhD Course in Molecular Biology, 396
Predoctoral Fellowship Programme ICGEB SISSA PhD Course in Molecular Genetics, 397
Sigma Xi Grants-in-Aid of Research, 629
Underwood Fund, 155
University of Dundee Research Awards, 704
University of Stirling Research Studentships, 750
Wellcome Trust Awards, Fellowships and Studentships, 768

Canada

IDRC Doctoral Research Awards, 400

East European Countries

FEMS Fellowship, 310
Natural History Museum Sys-Resource, 522

United Kingdom

FEMS Fellowship, 310
Llewellyn and Mary Williams Scholarship, 753
NERC Research Studentships, 521
University of Wales (Aberystwyth) Postgraduate Research Studentships, 752
University of Wales, Bangor (UWB) Research Studentships, 753
University of Wales, Bangor Departmental Research Studentships, 753

United States of America

Grants for Innovative Methods for Control of Tick-Borne Diseases, 63

West European Countries

FEMS Fellowship, 310
Karl-Enigk-Stipendium, 622
Llewellyn and Mary Williams Scholarship, 753
Natural History Museum Sys-Resource, 522
University of Wales, Bangor (UWB) Research Studentships, 753
University of Wales, Bangor Departmental Research Studentships, 753

PHARMACOLOGY

Any Country

A J Clark Studentship, 174
AACR Scholar-in-Training Awards, 31
AAPS/AFPE Gateway Scholarships, 50
AHA National Grant-in-Aid, 53
AHAF Alzheimer's Disease Research Grant, 52
AHAF Macular Degeneration Research, 52
AHAF National Glaucoma Research, 52
AHAF National Heart Foundation, 52
BBSRC Research Fellowships, 154
BBSRC Research Grants, 154
BBSRC Studentships, 155
CAAT Research Grants, 430
FRAXA Grants and Fellowships, 320
Fungal Research Trust Travel Grants, 327
GlaxoSmithKline Collaborative Research Projects, 337
ICR Research Studentships, 380
Inflammatory Bowel Disease Grants, 180
The Institute for the Study of Aging Grants Program, 378
International School of Crystallography Grants, 411
Leukemia and Lymphoma Society Translational Research Award, 446
Lister Institute Senior Research Fellowships, 449
MND Research Project Grant, 482

PHYSIOLOGY

TOXICOLOGY

ZOOLOGY

Australia

Canada

East European Countries

New Zealand

South Africa

United Kingdom

United States of America

West European Countries

CHEMISTRY

Any Country

World Universities Network (WUN) Scholarship Scheme, 749

African Nations

ABCCF Student Grant, 103
Corday-Morgan Memorial Fund, 611
Lindemann Trust Fellowships, 301
TWAS Awards in Basic Sciences, 672
TWAS Prizes to Young Scientists in Developing Countries, 673
TWAS Research Grants, 673

Australia

Corday-Morgan Memorial Fund, 611
Fulbright Postgraduate Student Award for Science and Engineering, 144
Lindemann Trust Fellowships, 301
University of Western Sydney Postgraduate Research Award (UWSPRA), 755
Wingate Scholarships, 771

British Commonwealth

British (General) Fellowship, 580
Corday-Morgan Memorial Fund, 611
Lindemann Trust Fellowships, 301
Wingate Scholarships, 771

Canada

AAAS Mass Media Science and Engineering Fellowship, 32
Alfred P Sloan Foundation Research Fellowships, 21
AWWA Larson Aquatic Research Support Scholarships, 98
CIC Medal, 254
CIC Pestcon Graduate Scholarship, 255
Corday-Morgan Memorial Fund, 611
Cottrell College Science Awards, 582
CSCT NOVA Chemicals Limited Award for Chemistry teaching in Community and Technical Colleges, 238
Lindemann Trust Fellowships, 301
Swiss Federal Institute of Technology Scholarships, 669
Wingate Scholarships, 771

Caribbean Countries

TWAS Awards in Basic Sciences, 672
TWAS Prizes to Young Scientists in Developing Countries, 673
TWAS Research Grants, 673

East European Countries

EPSRC Doctoral Training Grants, 298
EPSRC Masters Training Packages (MTP), 298
ICI Cambridge Bursaries, 204
Swiss Federal Institute of Technology Scholarships, 669

Far East

Corday-Morgan Memorial Fund, 611
Lindemann Trust Fellowships, 301
Swiss Federal Institute of Technology Scholarships, 669
TWAS Awards in Basic Sciences, 672
TWAS Prizes to Young Scientists in Developing Countries, 673
TWAS Research Grants, 673

Indian Sub-Continent

Corday-Morgan Memorial Fund, 611
Lindemann Trust Fellowships, 301
TWAS Awards in Basic Sciences, 672
TWAS Prizes to Young Scientists in Developing Countries, 673
TWAS Research Grants, 673
Wingate Scholarships, 771

Middle East

ABCCF Student Grant, 103
TWAS Awards in Basic Sciences, 672
TWAS Prizes to Young Scientists in Developing Countries, 673
TWAS Research Grants, 673

New Zealand

Corday-Morgan Memorial Fund, 611
Lindemann Trust Fellowships, 301
University of Western Sydney Postgraduate Research Award (UWSPRA), 755
Wingate Scholarships, 771

South Africa

Corday-Morgan Memorial Fund, 611
Henderson Postgraduate Scholarships, 585
Lindemann Trust Fellowships, 301
TWAS Awards in Basic Sciences, 672
TWAS Prizes to Young Scientists in Developing Countries, 673
TWAS Research Grants, 673
Wingate Scholarships, 771

South America

AWWA Larson Aquatic Research Support Scholarships, 98
TWAS Awards in Basic Sciences, 672
TWAS Prizes to Young Scientists in Developing Countries, 673
TWAS Research Grants, 673

United Kingdom

Alzheimer's Society Research Grants, 24
British (General) Fellowship, 580
Cardiff University Postgraduate Research Studentships, 242
Corday-Morgan Memorial Fund, 611
EPSRC Doctoral Training Grants, 298
EPSRC Grant, 708
EPSRC Masters Training Packages (MTP), 298
ESRF Thesis Studentships, 306
Lindemann Trust Fellowships, 301
Musgrave Research Studentships, 576
Sheffield Hallam University Research Studentships, 625
Swiss Federal Institute of Technology Scholarships, 669
University of Wales, Bangor Departmental Research Studentships, 753
Wingate Scholarships, 771

United States of America

AAAS Mass Media Science and Engineering Fellowship, 32
ACS/PRF Type G 'Starter' Grants, 39
AFAR Research Grants, 48
Alfred P Sloan Foundation Research Fellowships, 21
Army Research Laboratory Postdoctoral Fellowship Program, 85
AWWA Larson Aquatic Research Support Scholarships, 98
COBASE Collaboration in Basic Science and Engineering, 516
Cottrell College Science Awards, 582
Fannie and John Hertz Foundation Fellowships, 309
Fulbright Senior Specialists Program, 271
MARC Faculty Predoctoral Fellowships, 509
NIGMS Fellowship Awards for Minority Students, 509
NIGMS Fellowship Awards for Students With Disabilities, 509
NIGMS Postdoctoral Awards, 510
NIGMS Research Project Grants, 510
NIGMS Research Supplements for Underrepresented Minorities, 510
NRC Twinning Program, 516
ONR Postdoctoral Fellowship, 539
ONR/ASEE Postdoctoral Fellowship Program, 85
Swiss Federal Institute of Technology Scholarships, 669
Washington University Chancellor's Graduate Fellowship Program for African Americans, 767
Winston Churchill Scholarship, 771

West European Countries

Cardiff University Postgraduate Research Studentships, 242
EPSRC Doctoral Training Grants, 298
EPSRC Grant, 708
EPSRC Masters Training Packages (MTP), 298
ESRF Thesis Studentships, 306
Janson Johan Helmich Scholarships and Travel Grants, 421

The Queen's College Florey EPA Scholarship, 735
Scholarship Foundation of the League for Finnish-American Societies, 621
Sheffield Hallam University Research Studentships, 625
Swiss Federal Institute of Technology Scholarships, 669
University of Wales, Bangor Departmental Research Studentships, 753
Wingate Scholarships, 771

ANALYTICAL CHEMISTRY

Any Country

BP/RSE Research Fellowships, 613
CIC Catalysis Award, 254
GlaxoSmithKline Collaborative Research Projects, 337
JILA Postdoctoral Research Associateship and Visiting Fellowships, 424
Massey Doctoral Scholarship, 461
Rhodes University Postdoctoral Fellowship, 586
Services to Academia, 337
Sigma Xi Grants-in-Aid of Research, 629
University of Bristol Postgraduate Scholarships, 691
University of Manchester Research Studentships and Scholarships, 715
University of New England Research Scholarships, 719
The Walsh Fellowships, 671

African Nations

IFS Grant, 402

Australia

Fulbright Postgraduate Student Award for Science and Engineering, 144
University of Western Sydney Postgraduate Research Award (UWSPRA), 755

British Commonwealth

Hector and Elizabeth Catling Bursary, 175
Macmillan-Rodewald Studentship, School Studentship, Cary Studentship, 175

Canada

AWWA Larson Aquatic Research Support Scholarships, 98
CSCT Norman and Marion Bright Memorial Award, 238

Caribbean Countries

IFS Grant, 402

Far East

IFS Grant, 402

Indian Sub-Continent

IFS Grant, 402

Middle East

IFS Grant, 402

New Zealand

University of Western Sydney Postgraduate Research Award (UWSPRA), 755

South Africa

IFS Grant, 402

South America

AWWA Larson Aquatic Research Support Scholarships, 98
IFS Grant, 402

United Kingdom

Alzheimer's Society Research Grants, 24
Hector and Elizabeth Catling Bursary, 175

Macmillan-Rodewald Studentship, School Studentship, Cary Studentship, 175
University of Wales, Bangor (UWB) Research Studentships, 753
University of Wales, Bangor Departmental Research Studentships, 753

United States of America

AWWA Larson Aquatic Research Support Scholarships, 98
ONR Postdoctoral Fellowship, 539
Washington University Chancellor's Graduate Fellowship Program for African Americans, 767

West European Countries

University of Wales, Bangor (UWB) Research Studentships, 753
University of Wales, Bangor Departmental Research Studentships, 753

INORGANIC CHEMISTRY

Any Country

ACS/PRF Type AC Grants, 38
ACS/PRF Type B Grants, 38
BP/RSE Research Fellowships, 613
GlaxoSmithKline Collaborative Research Projects, 337
JILA Postdoctoral Research Associateship and Visiting Fellowships, 424
Massey Doctoral Scholarship, 461
Rhodes University Postdoctoral Fellowship, 586
Services to Academia, 337
Sigma Xi Grants-in-Aid of Research, 629
University of Bristol Postgraduate Scholarships, 691
University of Dundee Research Awards, 704
University of Manchester Research Studentships and Scholarships, 715
University of New England Research Scholarships, 719
Weizmann Institute of Science MSc Fellowships, 767

Australia

Fulbright Postgraduate Student Award for Science and Engineering, 144

British Commonwealth

Hector and Elizabeth Catling Bursary, 175
Macmillan-Rodewald Studentship, School Studentship, Cary Studentship, 175

United Kingdom

Alzheimer's Society Research Grants, 24
Hector and Elizabeth Catling Bursary, 175
Macmillan-Rodewald Studentship, School Studentship, Cary Studentship, 175
University of Wales, Bangor (UWB) Research Studentships, 753
University of Wales, Bangor Departmental Research Studentships, 753

United States of America

ACS/PRF Type G 'Starter' Grants, 39
ONR Postdoctoral Fellowship, 539
Washington University Chancellor's Graduate Fellowship Program for African Americans, 767

West European Countries

University of Wales, Bangor (UWB) Research Studentships, 753
University of Wales, Bangor Departmental Research Studentships, 753

ORGANIC CHEMISTRY

Any Country

ACS/PRF Type AC Grants, 38
ACS/PRF Type B Grants, 38

PHYSICAL CHEMISTRY

EARTH AND GEOLOGICAL SCIENCES

West European Countries

ESRF Thesis Studentships, 306
Janson Johan Helmich Scholarships and Travel Grants, 421
Natural History Museum Sys-Resource, 522
Silsoe Awards, 274
Swiss Federal Institute of Technology Scholarships, 669
University of Wales, Bangor Departmental Research Studentships, 753
Wingate Scholarships, 771

GEOCHEMISTRY

Any Country

ACS/PRF Scientific Education Grants, 38
ACS/PRF Type AC Grants, 38
ACS/PRF Type B Grants, 38
American Association of Petroleum Geologists Foundation Grants-in-Aid, 37
Anne U White Fund, 127
BP/RSE Research Fellowships, 613
Center for Field Research Grants, 246
GSA Research Grants, 328
NERC Advanced Course Studentships, 520
NERC Advanced Research Fellowships, 521
NERC Postdoctoral Research Fellowships, 521
NERC Research Grants, 521
NERC Senior Research Fellowships, 522
Sigma Xi Grants-in-Aid of Research, 629
Thomas Holloway Research Studentship, 602
University of Bristol Postgraduate Scholarships, 691
University of Manchester Research Studentships and Scholarships, 715
Weizmann Institute of Science MSc Fellowships, 767

Australia

Fulbright Postgraduate Student Award for Science and Engineering, 144

British Commonwealth

Hector and Elizabeth Catling Bursary, 175
Macmillan-Rodewald Studentship, School Studentship, Cary Studentship, 175

East European Countries

Natural History Museum Sys-Resource, 522

Far East

BPAmoco-Leeds University-FCO Chevening Scholarship, 712
Stephen and Anna Hui Fellowship, 366

United Kingdom

Hector and Elizabeth Catling Bursary, 175
Macmillan-Rodewald Studentship, School Studentship, Cary Studentship, 175
NERC Research Studentships, 521
University of Wales, Bangor (UWB) Research Studentships, 753
University of Wales, Bangor Departmental Research Studentships, 753

United States of America

ACS/PRF Type G 'Starter' Grants, 39
Fannie and John Hertz Foundation Fellowships, 309
Washington University Chancellor's Graduate Fellowship Program for African Americans, 767

West European Countries

Albert Maucher Prize, 282
Natural History Museum Sys-Resource, 522
University of Wales, Bangor (UWB) Research Studentships, 753
University of Wales, Bangor Departmental Research Studentships, 753

GEOGRAPHY (SCIENTIFIC)

Any Country

AAG Dissertation Research Grants, 126
AAG General Research Fund, 126
Center for Field Research Grants, 246
CEPS Fellowship, 490
GSA Research Grants, 328
Hugh Kelly Fellowship, 586
Linnean Macleay Fellowship, 449
Massey Doctoral Scholarship, 461
Monica Cole Research Grant, 600
NERC Advanced Course Studentships, 520
NERC Advanced Research Fellowships, 521
NERC Postdoctoral Research Fellowships, 521
NERC Research Grants, 521
NERC Senior Research Fellowships, 522
Sigma Xi Grants-in-Aid of Research, 629
Thomas Holloway Research Studentship, 602
University of Bristol Postgraduate Scholarships, 691
University of Dundee Research Awards, 704
University of Edinburgh Faculty of Science and Engineering Scholarship, 705
University of Manchester Research Studentships and Scholarships, 715
University of New England Research Scholarships, 719
Violet Cressey-Marcks Fisher Travel Scholarship, 601
Warren Nystrom Fund Awards, 127

African Nations

Postgraduate Studies in Physical Land Resources Scholarship, 397

Australia

Fulbright Postgraduate Student Award for Science and Engineering, 144

British Commonwealth

Postgraduate Studies in Physical Land Resources Scholarship, 397

Canada

IDRC Doctoral Research Awards, 400

Caribbean Countries

Postgraduate Studies in Physical Land Resources Scholarship, 397

East European Countries

Natural History Museum Sys-Resource, 522

Far East

Postgraduate Studies in Physical Land Resources Scholarship, 397

Indian Sub-Continent

Postgraduate Studies in Physical Land Resources Scholarship, 397

Middle East

Postgraduate Studies in Physical Land Resources Scholarship, 397

South Africa

Postgraduate Studies in Physical Land Resources Scholarship, 397

South America

Postgraduate Studies in Physical Land Resources Scholarship, 397

United Kingdom

NERC Research Studentships, 521
Polish Embassy Short-Term Bursaries, 571
Polish Government Postgraduate Scholarships Scheme, 572
University of Wales (Aberystwyth) Postgraduate Research Studentships, 752

West European Countries

Natural History Museum Sys-Resource, 522

GEOLOGY

Any Country

Acadia Graduate Teaching Assistantships, 7
ACS/PRF Scientific Education Grants, 38
ACS/PRF Type AC Grants, 38
The Alberta Research Council Scholarship, 692
American Association of Petroleum Geologists Foundation Grants-in-Aid, 37
Betty Mayne Scientific Research Fund, 448
BP/RSE Research Fellowships, 613
Center for Field Research Grants, 246
CEPS Fellowship, 490
Claude Harris Leon Foundation Postdoctoral Fellowship Award, 260
G Vernon Hobson Bequest, 391
Gladys W Cole Memorial Research Award, 328
GSA Research Grants, 328
Hugh Kelly Fellowship, 586
L S B Leakey Foundation General Research Grant, 437
Linnean Macleay Fellowship, 449
NERC Advanced Course Studentships, 520
NERC Advanced Research Fellowships, 521
NERC Postdoctoral Research Fellowships, 521
NERC Research Grants, 521
NERC Senior Research Fellowships, 522
Percy Sladen Memorial Fund Grants, 559
Rhodes University Postdoctoral Fellowship, 586
Sigma Xi Grants-in-Aid of Research, 629
Thomas Holloway Research Studentship, 602
University of Bristol Postgraduate Scholarships, 691
University of Edinburgh Faculty of Science and Engineering Scholarship, 705
University of Manchester Research Studentships and Scholarships, 715
University of New England Research Scholarships, 719

African Nations

Lindemann Trust Fellowships, 301
Postgraduate Studies in Physical Land Resources Scholarship, 397

Australia

Edgar Pam Fellowship, 391
Fulbright Postgraduate Student Award for Science and Engineering, 144
Lindemann Trust Fellowships, 301

British Commonwealth

Hector and Elizabeth Catling Bursary, 175
Lindemann Trust Fellowships, 301
Macmillan-Rodewald Studentship, School Studentship, Cary Studentship, 175
Postgraduate Studies in Physical Land Resources Scholarship, 397

Canada

Edgar Pam Fellowship, 391
IDRC Doctoral Research Awards, 400
Lindemann Trust Fellowships, 301

Caribbean Countries

Postgraduate Studies in Physical Land Resources Scholarship, 397

East European Countries

Natural History Museum Sys-Resource, 522

Far East

Lindemann Trust Fellowships, 301
Postgraduate Studies in Physical Land Resources Scholarship, 397
Stephen and Anna Hui Fellowship, 366

Indian Sub-Continent

Lindemann Trust Fellowships, 301
Postgraduate Studies in Physical Land Resources Scholarship, 397

Middle East

Postgraduate Studies in Physical Land Resources Scholarship, 397

New Zealand

Edgar Pam Fellowship, 391
Lindemann Trust Fellowships, 301

South Africa

Edgar Pam Fellowship, 391
Lindemann Trust Fellowships, 301
Postgraduate Studies in Physical Land Resources Scholarship, 397

South America

Postgraduate Studies in Physical Land Resources Scholarship, 397

United Kingdom

Edgar Pam Fellowship, 391
Hector and Elizabeth Catling Bursary, 175
Lindemann Trust Fellowships, 301
Macmillan-Rodewald Studentship, School Studentship, Cary Studentship, 175
NERC Research Studentships, 521
Polish Embassy Short-Term Bursaries, 571
Polish Government Postgraduate Scholarships Scheme, 572
University of Wales (Aberystwyth) Postgraduate Research Studentships, 752

United States of America

ACS/PRF Type G 'Starter' Grants, 39
Fannie and John Hertz Foundation Fellowships, 309
The Norwegian Thanksgiving Fund Scholarship, 538
ONR Postdoctoral Fellowship, 539
Washington University Chancellor's Graduate Fellowship Program for African Americans, 767

West European Countries

Albert Maucher Prize, 282
Natural History Museum Sys-Resource, 522

MINERALOGY AND CRYSTALLOGRAPHY

Any Country

BP/RSE Research Fellowships, 613
ESRF Postdoctoral Fellowships, 306
GSA Research Grants, 328
International School of Crystallography Grants, 411
L S B Leakey Foundation General Research Grant, 437
Rhodes University Postdoctoral Fellowship, 586
Sigma Xi Grants-in-Aid of Research, 629
University of Bristol Postgraduate Scholarships, 691
University of Manchester Research Studentships and Scholarships, 715
University of New England Research Scholarships, 719
Weizmann Institute of Science MSc Fellowships, 767

Australia

Fulbright Postgraduate Student Award for Science and Engineering, 144
University of Western Sydney Postgraduate Research Award (UWSPRA), 755

British Commonwealth

Hector and Elizabeth Catling Bursary, 175
Macmillan-Rodewald Studentship, School Studentship, Cary Studentship, 175

East European Countries

Natural History Museum Sys-Resource, 522

Far East

Stephen and Anna Hui Fellowship, 366

New Zealand

University of Western Sydney Postgraduate Research Award (UWSPRA), 755

United Kingdom

ESRF Thesis Studentships, 306
Hector and Elizabeth Catling Bursary, 175
Macmillan-Rodewald Studentship, School Studentship, Cary Studentship, 175
Polish Embassy Short-Term Bursaries, 571
Polish Government Postgraduate Scholarships Scheme, 572

United States of America

Fannie and John Hertz Foundation Fellowships, 309

West European Countries

ESRF Thesis Studentships, 306
Natural History Museum Sys-Resource, 522

PETROLOGY

Any Country

American Association of Petroleum Geologists Foundation Grants-in-Aid, 37
BP/RSE Research Fellowships, 613
GSA Research Grants, 328
NERC Advanced Course Studentships, 520
NERC Advanced Research Fellowships, 521
NERC Postdoctoral Research Fellowships, 521
NERC Research Grants, 521
NERC Senior Research Fellowships, 522
Rhodes University Postdoctoral Fellowship, 586
Sigma Xi Grants-in-Aid of Research, 629
University of Manchester Research Studentships and Scholarships, 715
University of New England Research Scholarships, 719

Australia

Fulbright Postgraduate Student Award for Science and Engineering, 144

British Commonwealth

Hector and Elizabeth Catling Bursary, 175
Macmillan-Rodewald Studentship, School Studentship, Cary Studentship, 175

East European Countries

Natural History Museum Sys-Resource, 522

Far East

Stephen and Anna Hui Fellowship, 366

United Kingdom

Hector and Elizabeth Catling Bursary, 175
Macmillan-Rodewald Studentship, School Studentship, Cary Studentship, 175
NERC Research Studentships, 521

West European Countries

Natural History Museum Sys-Resource, 522

GEOPHYSICS AND SEISMOLOGY

Any Country

The Abdus Salam ICTP Fellowships, 5
ACS/PRF Scientific Education Grants, 38
ACS/PRF Type AC Grants, 38
ACS/PRF Type B Grants, 38
American Association of Petroleum Geologists Foundation Grants-in-Aid, 37
BP/RSE Research Fellowships, 613

Center for Field Research Grants, 246
CEPS Fellowship, 490
Dublin Institute for Advanced Studies Scholarship in Astronomy, Astrophysics and Geophysics, 288
GSA Research Grants, 328
JILA Postdoctoral Research Associateship and Visiting Fellowships, 424
NERC Advanced Course Studentships, 520
NERC Advanced Research Fellowships, 521
NERC Postdoctoral Research Fellowships, 521
NERC Research Grants, 521
NERC Senior Research Fellowships, 522
Rhodes University Postdoctoral Fellowship, 586
SEG Scholarships, 655
University of Bristol Postgraduate Scholarships, 691
University of Edinburgh Faculty of Science and Engineering Scholarship, 705
University of Manchester Research Studentships and Scholarships, 715
Weizmann Institute of Science MSc Fellowships, 767

African Nations

Lindemann Trust Fellowships, 301

Australia

Fulbright Postgraduate Student Award for Science and Engineering, 144
Lindemann Trust Fellowships, 301

British Commonwealth

Hector and Elizabeth Catling Bursary, 175
Lindemann Trust Fellowships, 301
Macmillan-Rodewald Studentship, School Studentship, Cary Studentship, 175

Canada

Lindemann Trust Fellowships, 301

East European Countries

Natural History Museum Sys-Resource, 522

Far East

BPAmoco-Leeds University-FCO Chevening Scholarship, 712
Lindemann Trust Fellowships, 301
Stephen and Anna Hui Fellowship, 366

Indian Sub-Continent

Lindemann Trust Fellowships, 301

New Zealand

Lindemann Trust Fellowships, 301

South Africa

Lindemann Trust Fellowships, 301

United Kingdom

Hector and Elizabeth Catling Bursary, 175
Lindemann Trust Fellowships, 301
Macmillan-Rodewald Studentship, School Studentship, Cary Studentship, 175
NERC Research Studentships, 521
University of Wales, Bangor (UWB) Research Studentships, 753
University of Wales, Bangor Departmental Research Studentships, 753

United States of America

ACS/PRF Type G 'Starter' Grants, 39
Fannie and John Hertz Foundation Fellowships, 309
ONR Postdoctoral Fellowship, 539
Washington University Chancellor's Graduate Fellowship Program for African Americans, 767

West European Countries

PALAEONTOLOGY

Any Country

Australia

British Commonwealth

East European Countries

United Kingdom

United States of America

West European Countries

PHYSICS

Any Country

African Nations

Australia

British Commonwealth

John and Muriel Landis Scholarship Awards, 66
Mark Mills Award, 67
Student Design Competition, 67
University of Manchester Research Studentships and Scholarships, 715
Weizmann Institute of Science MSc Fellowships, 767

East European Countries

CERN Doctoral Student Programme, 251
CERN Fellowships, 251
CERN Technical Student Programme, 251

United Kingdom

CERN Doctoral Student Programme, 251
CERN Fellowships, 251
CERN Technical Student Programme, 251

United States of America

American Society of Naval Engineers Scholarships, 93
Everitt P Blizard Scholarship, 66
James F Schumar Scholarship, 66
John Randall Scholarship, 67
ONR Postdoctoral Fellowship, 539
Robert A Dannels Scholarship, 67
Verne R Dapp Scholarship, 67
Walter Meyer Scholarship, 67

West European Countries

CERN Doctoral Student Programme, 251
CERN Fellowships, 251
CERN Technical Student Programme, 251

OPTICS

Any Country

The Abdus Salam ICTP Fellowships, 5
Berthold Leibinger Innovationspreis, 150
BP/RSE Research Fellowships, 613
ESRF Postdoctoral Fellowships, 306
JILA Postdoctoral Research Associateship and Visiting Fellowships, 424
University of New England Research Scholarships, 719
Weizmann Institute of Science MSc Fellowships, 767

East European Countries

CERN Doctoral Student Programme, 251
CERN Fellowships, 251
CERN Technical Student Programme, 251

United Kingdom

CERN Doctoral Student Programme, 251
CERN Fellowships, 251
CERN Technical Student Programme, 251
ESRF Thesis Studentships, 306

United States of America

American Society of Naval Engineers Scholarships, 93
ONR Postdoctoral Fellowship, 539

West European Countries

CERN Doctoral Student Programme, 251
CERN Fellowships, 251
CERN Technical Student Programme, 251
ESRF Thesis Studentships, 306

SOLID STATE PHYSICS

Any Country

The Abdus Salam ICTP Fellowships, 5
Berthold Leibinger Innovationspreis, 150
BP/RSE Research Fellowships, 613

ESRF Postdoctoral Fellowships, 306
International School of Crystallography Grants, 411
JILA Postdoctoral Research Associateship and Visiting Fellowships, 424
SISSA Fellowship, 410
Thomas Holloway Research Studentship, 602
University of New England Research Scholarships, 719
Weizmann Institute of Science MSc Fellowships, 767
Welch Foundation Scholarship, 416

East European Countries

CERN Doctoral Student Programme, 251
CERN Fellowships, 251
CERN Technical Student Programme, 251

United Kingdom

CERN Doctoral Student Programme, 251
CERN Fellowships, 251
CERN Technical Student Programme, 251
ESRF Thesis Studentships, 306
University of Wales (Aberystwyth) Postgraduate Research Studentships, 752

United States of America

American Society of Naval Engineers Scholarships, 93

West European Countries

CERN Doctoral Student Programme, 251
CERN Fellowships, 251
CERN Technical Student Programme, 251
ESRF Thesis Studentships, 306

THERMAL PHYSICS

Any Country

JILA Postdoctoral Research Associateship and Visiting Fellowships, 424
Weizmann Institute of Science MSc Fellowships, 767

East European Countries

CERN Fellowships, 251

United Kingdom

CERN Fellowships, 251

United States of America

American Society of Naval Engineers Scholarships, 93

West European Countries

CERN Fellowships, 251

ASTRONOMY AND ASTROPHYSICS

Any Country

The Abdus Salam ICTP Fellowships, 5
Arthur J Dyer Observatory Research Assistantship, 111
Carnegie Institution of Washington Fellowships, 243
Cottrell Scholars Awards, 582
Daphne Jackson Fellowship, 278
Dublin Institute for Advanced Studies Scholarship in Astronomy, Astrophysics and Geophysics, 288
Fund for UFO Research Grants, 327
Institute for Advanced Study Postdoctoral Residential Fellowships, 375
International Astronomical Union Travel Grant, 395
Isaac Newton Studentship, 699
Jansky Postdoctorals, 515
JILA Postdoctoral Research Associateship and Visiting Fellowships, 424
NCAR Postdoctoral Appointments in the Advanced Study Program, 496

ATMOSPHERE SCIENCE/METEOROLOGY

INM Short-term Fellowship, 391
TWAS South-South Fellowship Scheme, 673

Australia

Wingate Scholarships, 771

British Commonwealth

Wingate Scholarships, 771

Canada

AAAS Mass Media Science and Engineering Fellowship, 32
Wingate Scholarships, 771

Caribbean Countries

TWAS South-South Fellowship Scheme, 673

East European Countries

INM Fellowship for Curso Internacional de Meteorologia Clase II OMM, 391
INM Short-term Fellowship, 391

Far East

TWAS South-South Fellowship Scheme, 673

Indian Sub-Continent

TWAS South-South Fellowship Scheme, 673
Wingate Scholarships, 771

Middle East

INM Fellowship for Curso Internacional de Meteorologia Clase II OMM, 391
INM Short-term Fellowship, 391
TWAS South-South Fellowship Scheme, 673

New Zealand

Wingate Scholarships, 771

South Africa

Henderson Postgraduate Scholarships, 585
TWAS South-South Fellowship Scheme, 673
Wingate Scholarships, 771

South America

INM Fellowship for Curso Internacional de Meteorologia Clase II OMM, 391
INM Short-term Fellowship, 391
TWAS South-South Fellowship Scheme, 673

United Kingdom

NERC Research Studentships, 521
University of Wales (Aberystwyth) Postgraduate Research Studentships, 752
Wingate Scholarships, 771

United States of America

AAAS Mass Media Science and Engineering Fellowship, 32
Fannie and John Hertz Foundation Fellowships, 309
NRC Twinning Program, 516
ONR Postdoctoral Fellowship, 539
Winston Churchill Scholarship, 771

West European Countries

Janson Johan Helmich Scholarships and Travel Grants, 421
Wingate Scholarships, 771

ARCTIC STUDIES

Any Country

AAC Research Grant, 28
Center for Field Research Grants, 246
NERC Advanced Course Studentships, 520
NERC Advanced Research Fellowships, 521

NERC Postdoctoral Research Fellowships, 521
NERC Research Grants, 521
NERC Senior Research Fellowships, 522
University of Stirling Research Studentships, 750

United Kingdom

NERC Research Studentships, 521
University of Wales (Aberystwyth) Postgraduate Research Studentships, 752

United States of America

The Norwegian Thanksgiving Fund Scholarship, 538

ARID LAND STUDIES

Any Country

Center for Field Research Grants, 246
NERC Advanced Course Studentships, 520
NERC Advanced Research Fellowships, 521
NERC Postdoctoral Research Fellowships, 521
NERC Research Grants, 521
NERC Senior Research Fellowships, 522
University of Stirling Research Studentships, 750
W Frank Blair Award, 255

United Kingdom

NERC Research Studentships, 521

OCEANOGRAPHY

Any Country

Bermuda Biological Station for Research Grant In Aid, 150
Center for Field Research Grants, 246
Daphne Jackson Fellowship, 278
GSA Research Grants, 328
Horton (Hydrology) Research Grant, 51
NCAR Postdoctoral Appointments in the Advanced Study Program, 496
NERC Advanced Course Studentships, 520
NERC Advanced Research Fellowships, 521
NERC Postdoctoral Research Fellowships, 521
NERC Research Grants, 521
NFR Research Grants, 668
Queen Mary Research Studentships, 576
Rhodes University Postdoctoral Fellowship, 586
Weizmann Institute of Science MSc Fellowships, 767
Woods Hole Oceanographic Institution Geophysical Fluid Dynamics Fellowships, 777
Woods Hole Oceanographic Institution Postdoctoral Awards in Marine Policy and Ocean Management, 777
Woods Hole Oceanographic Institution Postdoctoral Fellowships in Ocean Science and Engineering, 777
Woods Hole Oceanographic Institution Research Fellowships in Marine Policy, 778
Woods Hole Oceanographic Institution/NOAA Co-operative Institute for Climate and Ocean Research Postdoctoral Fellowship, 778

African Nations

TWAS South-South Fellowship Scheme, 673

Australia

Wingate Scholarships, 771

British Commonwealth

ACU Development Fellowships, 127
Wingate Scholarships, 771

Canada

AAAS Mass Media Science and Engineering Fellowship, 32
Wingate Scholarships, 771

RELIGION AND THEOLOGY

GENERAL

British Commonwealth

Friends of Peterhouse Bursary, 561
The Hastings Center International Visiting Scholars Program, 352
Merton College Reed Foundation Scholarship, 732
Wingate Scholarships, 771

Canada

Friends of Peterhouse Bursary, 561
Fulbright Postdoctoral Research and Lecturing Awards for Non-US Citizens, 270
J W McConnell Memorial Fellowships, 266
Killam Research Fellowships, 221
Ministry Fellowship, 326
North American Doctoral Fellowship, 326
PRA Fellowships, 549
SSHRC Doctoral Fellowships, 646
SSHRC Standard Research Grants, 647
Wingate Scholarships, 771

Caribbean Countries

Friends of Peterhouse Bursary, 561
The Hastings Center International Visiting Scholars Program, 352
Merton College Reed Foundation Scholarship, 732
PRA Fellowships, 549

East European Countries

AHRB Studentships in the Humanities (Competition A), 112
AHRB Studentships in the Humanities (Competition B), 112
Andrew W Mellon Foundation Fellowships in the Humanities, 374
Friends of Peterhouse Bursary, 561
Fulbright Postdoctoral Research and Lecturing Awards for Non-US Citizens, 270
The Hastings Center International Visiting Scholars Program, 352
Mellon Research Fellowship, 79
Merton College Reed Foundation Scholarship, 732
Regent's Park College (Permanent Private Hall) Eastern European Scholarship, 736
Soros Supplementary Grants Programme (SSGP), 544

Far East

Friends of Peterhouse Bursary, 561
Fulbright Postdoctoral Research and Lecturing Awards for Non-US Citizens, 270
The Hastings Center International Visiting Scholars Program, 352
Japanese American Citizens League Scholarship and Award Program, 422
Merton College Reed Foundation Scholarship, 732

Indian Sub-Continent

Friends of Peterhouse Bursary, 561
Fulbright Postdoctoral Research and Lecturing Awards for Non-US Citizens, 270
The Hastings Center International Visiting Scholars Program, 352
Indian Council of Social Science Research Senior Fellowships, 368
Jawaharial Nehru Memorial Fund Cambridge Scholarship for PhD Study, 204
Merton College Reed Foundation Scholarship, 732
Wingate Scholarships, 771

Middle East

Friends of Peterhouse Bursary, 561
Fulbright Postdoctoral Research and Lecturing Awards for Non-US Citizens, 270
The Hastings Center International Visiting Scholars Program, 352
Merton College Reed Foundation Scholarship, 732

New Zealand

Friends of Peterhouse Bursary, 561
Fulbright Postdoctoral Research and Lecturing Awards for Non-US Citizens, 270
The Hastings Center International Visiting Scholars Program, 352
Wingate Scholarships, 771

South Africa

Friends of Peterhouse Bursary, 561
Fulbright Postdoctoral Research and Lecturing Awards for Non-US Citizens, 270
The Hastings Center International Visiting Scholars Program, 352
Isie Smuts Research Award, 658
Wingate Scholarships, 771

South America

Friends of Peterhouse Bursary, 561
Fulbright Commission (Argentina) Master's Program, 325
Fulbright Postdoctoral Research and Lecturing Awards for Non-US Citizens, 270
The Hastings Center International Visiting Scholars Program, 352
Merton College Reed Foundation Scholarship, 732
PRA Fellowships, 549

United Kingdom

AHRB Studentships in the Humanities (Competition A), 112
AHRB Studentships in the Humanities (Competition B), 112
Canada Memorial Foundation Scholarships, 222
Frank Knox Fellowships at Harvard University, 319
Fulbright Postdoctoral Research and Lecturing Awards for Non-US Citizens, 270
The Hastings Center International Visiting Scholars Program, 352
Kennedy Scholarships, 432
Regent's Park College (Permanent Private Hall) Ernest Payne Scholarship, 736
Regent's Park College (Permanent Private Hall) J W Lord Scholarship, 736
University of Wales, Bangor (UWB) Research Studentships, 753
University of Wales, Bangor Departmental Research Studentships, 753
Wingate Scholarships, 771

United States of America

AIGC Fellowship, 54
ARIT - National Endowment for the Humanities for Advanced Fellowships for Research in Turkey, 78
Expanding Horizons - Dissertation Fellowship for African Americans, 326
Expanding Horizons - Doctoral Fellowship for African Americans, 326
Federal Chancellor Scholarship, 20
Friends of Peterhouse Bursary, 561
Fulbright Scholar Awards for Research and Lecturing Abroad for United States Citizens, 271
Fulbright Scholar Program for US Citizens, 271
Fulbright Senior Specialists Program, 271
Japanese American Citizens League Scholarship and Award Program, 422
Kennan Institute Research Scholarship, 431
Ministry Fellowship, 326
NEH Fellowship, 84
North American Doctoral Fellowship, 326
PRA Fellowships, 549
Regent's Park College (Permanent Private Hall) Asheville Scholarship, 736
UCLA IAC Postdoctoral/Visiting Scholar Fellowships, 680
WWWC Americans and World Affairs Fellows Program, 780

West European Countries

Friends of Peterhouse Bursary, 561
Fulbright Postdoctoral Research and Lecturing Awards for Non-US Citizens, 270
The Hastings Center International Visiting Scholars Program, 352
Scholarship Foundation of the League for Finnish-American Societies, 621
University of Wales, Bangor (UWB) Research Studentships, 753
University of Wales, Bangor Departmental Research Studentships, 753
Wingate Scholarships, 771

RELIGIOUS STUDIES

Any Country

Ahmanson and Getty Postdoctoral Fellowships, 678
Alexander S Onassis Programme of Research Grants, 18
Alexander S Onassis Research Grants, 18
Andrew W Mellon Postdoctoral Fellowships in the Humanities, 749
ASECS (American Society for Eighteenth-Century Studies)/Clark Library Fellowships, 679
Clark Library Short-Term Resident Fellowships, 679
Clark Predoctoral Fellowships, 679
Clark-Huntington Joint Bibliographical Fellowship, 679
CMRS Summer Fellowship, 680
Council of the Institute Awards, 572
External Faculty Fellowships, 663
Foundation Praemium Erasmianum Study Prize, 318
Harvard University, Center for the Study of World Religions, Senior Fellowship, 352
Institute for Ecumenical and Cultural Research Resident Scholars Program, 375
Institute of European History Fellowships, 381
M Alison Frantz Fellowship in Post-Classical Studies at The Gennadius Library (formerly known as the Gennadeion Fellowship), 81
Massey Doctoral Scholarship, 461
Onassis Programme of Postgraduate Research Scholarships, 19
Regent's Park College (Permanent Private Hall) Henman Scholarship, 736
SOAS Research Student Fellowships, 622
University of Glasgow Postgraduate Research Scholarships, 707
University of Stirling Research Studentships, 750
USC College Dissertation Fellowship, 749
USC College of Letters, Arts and Sciences Merit Award, 749

Australia

Wingate Scholarships, 771

British Commonwealth

British Institute of Archaeology at Ankara Research Grants, 169
British Institute of Archaeology at Ankara Travel Grants, 169
Wingate Scholarships, 771

Canada

Ministry Fellowship, 326
Wingate Scholarships, 771

East European Countries

AHRB Studentships in the Humanities (Competition A), 112
AHRB Studentships in the Humanities (Competition B), 112
CRF (Caledonian Research Foundation)/RSE European Visiting Research Fellowships, 613

Indian Sub-Continent

Wingate Scholarships, 771

New Zealand

Wingate Scholarships, 771

South Africa

Wingate Scholarships, 771

United Kingdom

AHRB Studentships in the Humanities (Competition A), 112
AHRB Studentships in the Humanities (Competition B), 112
British Institute of Archaeology at Ankara Research Grants, 169
British Institute of Archaeology at Ankara Travel Grants, 169
CRF (Caledonian Research Foundation)/RSE European Visiting Research Fellowships, 613
University of Wales, Bangor (UWB) Research Studentships, 753
University of Wales, Bangor Departmental Research Studentships, 753
Wingate Scholarships, 771

United States of America

Fellowship Programme for Émigrés Pursuing Careers in Jewish Education, 424
Fulbright Senior Specialists Program, 271
Ministry Fellowship, 326
WWWC Americans and World Affairs Fellows Program, 780

West European Countries

CRF (Caledonian Research Foundation)/RSE European Visiting Research Fellowships, 613
University of Wales, Bangor (UWB) Research Studentships, 753
University of Wales, Bangor Departmental Research Studentships, 753
Wingate Scholarships, 771

CHRISTIAN

Any Country

Ahmanson and Getty Postdoctoral Fellowships, 678
Andrew W Mellon Postdoctoral Fellowships in the Humanities, 749
ASECS (American Society for Eighteenth-Century Studies)/Clark Library Fellowships, 679
The Bross Prize, 183
Clark Library Short-Term Resident Fellowships, 679
Clark Predoctoral Fellowships, 679
Clark-Huntington Joint Bibliographical Fellowship, 679
George A Barton Fellowship, 83
Harvard University, Center for the Study of World Religions, Senior Fellowship, 352
Onassis Programme of Postgraduate Research Scholarships, 19
University of Stirling Research Studentships, 750

East European Countries

AHRB Studentships in the Humanities (Competition A), 112
AHRB Studentships in the Humanities (Competition B), 112

United Kingdom

AHRB Studentships in the Humanities (Competition A), 112
AHRB Studentships in the Humanities (Competition B), 112
University of Wales, Bangor (UWB) Research Studentships, 753
University of Wales, Bangor Departmental Research Studentships, 753

West European Countries

University of Wales, Bangor (UWB) Research Studentships, 753
University of Wales, Bangor Departmental Research Studentships, 753

JEWISH

Any Country

Ahmanson and Getty Postdoctoral Fellowships, 678
Andrew W Mellon Postdoctoral Fellowships in the Humanities, 749
ASECS (American Society for Eighteenth-Century Studies)/Clark Library Fellowships, 679
Clark Library Short-Term Resident Fellowships, 679
Clark Predoctoral Fellowships, 679
Clark-Huntington Joint Bibliographical Fellowship, 679
George A Barton Fellowship, 83
Harvard University, Center for the Study of World Religions, Senior Fellowship, 352
International Fellowships in Jewish Studies, 468
International Scholarship Programme for Community Service, 468
Jacob Hirsch Fellowship, 80
JCC Association Scholarships, 423
Memorial Foundation for Jewish Culture International Doctoral Scholarships, 469
Moritz and Charlotte Warburg Prizes, 355
Onassis Programme of Postgraduate Research Scholarships, 19
Samuel H Kress Joint Athens-Jerusalem Fellowship, 81
Scholarships for Post-Rabbinical Students, 469

SOAS Bursary, 622

University of Manchester Research Studentships and Scholarships, 715

University of Stirling Research Studentships, 750

Australia

Wingate Scholarships, 771

British Commonwealth

Wingate Scholarships, 771

Canada

Wingate Scholarships, 771

East European Countries

AHRB Studentships in the Humanities (Competition A), 112

AHRB Studentships in the Humanities (Competition B), 112

Indian Sub-Continent

Wingate Scholarships, 771

New Zealand

Wingate Scholarships, 771

South Africa

Wingate Scholarships, 771

United Kingdom

AHRB Studentships in the Humanities (Competition A), 112

AHRB Studentships in the Humanities (Competition B), 112

Polish Embassy Short-Term Bursaries, 571

Polish Government Postgraduate Scholarships Scheme, 572

University of Wales, Bangor (UWB) Research Studentships, 753

University of Wales, Bangor Departmental Research Studentships, 753

Wingate Scholarships, 771

United States of America

Fellowship Programme for Émigrés Pursuing Careers in Jewish Education, 424

West European Countries

University of Wales, Bangor (UWB) Research Studentships, 753

University of Wales, Bangor Departmental Research Studentships, 753

Wingate Scholarships, 771

ISLAM

Any Country

Ahmanson and Getty Postdoctoral Fellowships, 678

Andrew W Mellon Postdoctoral Fellowships in the Humanities, 749

Harvard University, Center for the Study of World Religions, Senior Fellowship, 352

Onassis Programme of Postgraduate Research Scholarships, 19

SOAS Bursary, 622

University of Manchester Research Studentships and Scholarships, 715

University of Stirling Research Studentships, 750

East European Countries

AHRB Studentships in the Humanities (Competition A), 112

AHRB Studentships in the Humanities (Competition B), 112

United Kingdom

AHRB Studentships in the Humanities (Competition A), 112

AHRB Studentships in the Humanities (Competition B), 112

ASIAN RELIGIOUS STUDIES

Any Country

Ahmanson and Getty Postdoctoral Fellowships, 678

Andrew W Mellon Postdoctoral Fellowships in the Humanities, 749

Harvard University, Center for the Study of World Religions, Senior Fellowship, 352

Onassis Programme of Postgraduate Research Scholarships, 19

SOAS Bursary, 622

University of Manchester Research Studentships and Scholarships, 715

University of Stirling Research Studentships, 750

East European Countries

AHRB Studentships in the Humanities (Competition A), 112

AHRB Studentships in the Humanities (Competition B), 112

United Kingdom

AHRB Studentships in the Humanities (Competition A), 112

AHRB Studentships in the Humanities (Competition B), 112

AGNOSTICISM AND ATHEISM

Any Country

Andrew W Mellon Postdoctoral Fellowships in the Humanities, 749

Harvard University, Center for the Study of World Religions, Senior Fellowship, 352

East European Countries

AHRB Studentships in the Humanities (Competition A), 112

AHRB Studentships in the Humanities (Competition B), 112

United Kingdom

AHRB Studentships in the Humanities (Competition A), 112

AHRB Studentships in the Humanities (Competition B), 112

ANCIENT RELIGIONS

Any Country

Andrew W Mellon Postdoctoral Fellowships in the Humanities, 749

ASCSA Fellowships, 79

ASCSA Summer Sessions, 80

FAMSI Research Grant, 317

Harvard University, Center for the Study of World Religions, Senior Fellowship, 352

Jacob Hirsch Fellowship, 80

Mary Isabel Sibley Fellowship, 567

Onassis Programme of Postgraduate Research Scholarships, 19

Samuel H Kress Joint Athens-Jerusalem Fellowship, 81

SOAS Bursary, 622

Australia

Wingate Scholarships, 771

British Commonwealth

Hector and Elizabeth Catling Bursary, 175

Macmillan-Rodewald Studentship, School Studentship, Cary Studentship, 175

Wingate Scholarships, 771

Canada

Wingate Scholarships, 771

East European Countries

AHRB Studentships in the Humanities (Competition B), 112

Indian Sub-Continent

Wingate Scholarships, 771

New Zealand
Wingate Scholarships, 771

South Africa
Wingate Scholarships, 771

United Kingdom
AHRB Studentships in the Humanities (Competition B), 112
Hector and Elizabeth Catling Bursary, 175
Macmillan-Rodewald Studentship, School Studentship, Cary Studentship, 175
Wingate Scholarships, 771

West European Countries
Wingate Scholarships, 771

RELIGIOUS EDUCATION

Any Country
Alexander S Onassis Programme of Research Grants, 18
Alexander S Onassis Research Grants, 18
All Saints Educational Trust Personal Awards, 22
Dempster Fellowship, 328
Equiano Memorial Award, 666
Onassis Programme of Postgraduate Research Scholarships, 19

Canada
Ministry Fellowship, 326

United Kingdom
University of Wales, Bangor (UWB) Research Studentships, 753
University of Wales, Bangor Departmental Research Studentships, 753

United States of America
Fellowship Programme for Émigrés Pursuing Careers in Jewish Education, 424
Ministry Fellowship, 326
WWWC Americans and World Affairs Fellows Program, 780

West European Countries
University of Wales, Bangor (UWB) Research Studentships, 753
University of Wales, Bangor Departmental Research Studentships, 753

HOLY WRITINGS

Any Country
Alexander S Onassis Programme of Research Grants, 18
Alexander S Onassis Research Grants, 18
Council of the Institute Awards, 572
SOAS Bursary, 622
SOAS Research Student Fellowships, 622

RELIGIOUS PRACTICE

Any Country
Alexander S Onassis Programme of Research Grants, 18
Alexander S Onassis Research Grants, 18
SOAS Bursary, 622
SOAS Research Student Fellowships, 622
Spalding Trusts Grants-in-Aid of Research, 661

Canada
Ministry Fellowship, 326

United Kingdom
University of Wales, Bangor (UWB) Research Studentships, 753
University of Wales, Bangor Departmental Research Studentships, 753

United States of America
Fellowship Programme for Émigrés Pursuing Careers in Jewish Education, 424
Ministry Fellowship, 326

West European Countries
University of Wales, Bangor (UWB) Research Studentships, 753
University of Wales, Bangor Departmental Research Studentships, 753

CHURCH ADMINISTRATION (PASTORAL WORK)

Any Country
Alexander S Onassis Programme of Research Grants, 18
Alexander S Onassis Research Grants, 18

Canada
Ministry Fellowship, 326

United Kingdom
Hilda Martindale Exhibitions, 358
University of Wales, Bangor (UWB) Research Studentships, 753
University of Wales, Bangor Departmental Research Studentships, 753

United States of America
Ministry Fellowship, 326
Verne Catt McDowell Scholarship, 761

West European Countries
University of Wales, Bangor (UWB) Research Studentships, 753
University of Wales, Bangor Departmental Research Studentships, 753

THEOLOGICAL STUDIES

Any Country
Alexander S Onassis Programme of Research Grants, 18
Alexander S Onassis Research Grants, 18
Andrew W Mellon Postdoctoral Fellowships in the Humanities, 749
External Faculty Fellowships, 663
Foundation Praemium Erasmianum Study Prize, 318
Institute of European History Fellowships, 381
M Alison Frantz Fellowship in Post-Classical Studies at The Gennadius Library (formerly known as the Gennadeion Fellowship), 81
Onassis Programme of Postgraduate Research Scholarships, 19
University of Bristol Postgraduate Scholarships, 691

African Nations
The Evelyn Hilchie Betts Memorial Fellowship, 135

British Commonwealth
Hector and Elizabeth Catling Bursary, 175
Macmillan-Rodewald Studentship, School Studentship, Cary Studentship, 175

Canada
Ministry Fellowship, 326

East European Countries
AHRB Studentships in the Humanities (Competition A), 112
AHRB Studentships in the Humanities (Competition B), 112

Indian Sub-Continent
The Evelyn Hilchie Betts Memorial Fellowship, 135

Middle East
The Evelyn Hilchie Betts Memorial Fellowship, 135

COMPARATIVE RELIGION

SOCIOLOGY OF RELIGION

West European Countries

University of Wales, Bangor (UWB) Research Studentships, 753
University of Wales, Bangor Departmental Research Studentships, 753

HISTORY OF RELIGION

Any Country

Ahmanson and Getty Postdoctoral Fellowships, 678
Albert J Beveridge Grant, 53
Alexander S Onassis Programme of Research Grants, 18
Alexander S Onassis Research Grants, 18
Andrew W Mellon Postdoctoral Fellowships in the Humanities, 749
ASCSA Fellowships, 79
ASECS (American Society for Eighteenth-Century Studies)/Clark Library Fellowships, 679
Bernadotte E Schmitt Grants, 54
Camargo Fellowships, 185
Center for Field Research Grants, 246
Clark Library Short-Term Resident Fellowships, 679
Clark-Huntington Joint Bibliographical Fellowship, 679
Council of the Institute Awards, 572
External Faculty Fellowships, 663
Foundation Praemium Erasmianum Study Prize, 318
Harvard University, Center for the Study of World Religions, Senior Fellowship, 352
Institute of European History Fellowships, 381
NEH Research Fellowships, 81
Onassis Programme of Postgraduate Research Scholarships, 19
Samuel H Kress Joint Athens-Jerusalem Fellowship, 81
SOAS Bursary, 622
SOAS Research Student Fellowships, 622
University of Bristol Postgraduate Scholarships, 691

Australia

Wingate Scholarships, 771

British Commonwealth

British Institute of Archaeology at Ankara Research Grants, 169
British Institute of Archaeology at Ankara Travel Grants, 169
Wingate Scholarships, 771

Canada

Wingate Scholarships, 771

East European Countries

AHRB Studentships in the Humanities (Competition A), 112
AHRB Studentships in the Humanities (Competition B), 112
Open Society Sofia Central European University Scholarship, 542

Indian Sub-Continent

Wingate Scholarships, 771

New Zealand

Wingate Scholarships, 771

South Africa

Wingate Scholarships, 771

United Kingdom

AHRB Studentships in the Humanities (Competition A), 112
AHRB Studentships in the Humanities (Competition B), 112
British Institute of Archaeology at Ankara Research Grants, 169
British Institute of Archaeology at Ankara Travel Grants, 169
Regent's Park College Studentships of the Centre for the Study of Christianity and Culture, 737
University of Wales, Bangor (UWB) Research Studentships, 753
University of Wales, Bangor Departmental Research Studentships, 753
Wingate Scholarships, 771

West European Countries

University of Wales, Bangor (UWB) Research Studentships, 753
University of Wales, Bangor Departmental Research Studentships, 753
Wingate Scholarships, 771

ESOTERIC PRACTICES

East European Countries

CRF (Caledonian Research Foundation)/RSE European Visiting Research Fellowships, 613

United Kingdom

CRF (Caledonian Research Foundation)/RSE European Visiting Research Fellowships, 613

West European Countries

CRF (Caledonian Research Foundation)/RSE European Visiting Research Fellowships, 613

RECREATION, WELFARE, PROTECTIVE SERVICES

GENERAL

Any Country

AIATSIS Research Grants, 139
Anglo-German Foundation for the Study of Industrial Society Research Grant, 101
Canadian Department of Foreign Affairs Faculty Enrichment Program, 231
Canadian Department of Foreign Affairs Faculty Research Program, 231
Canadian Department of Foreign Affairs Institutional Research Program, 231
Central Queensland University Postgraduate Research Award, 248
CQU International Student Scholarship, 248
Equiano Memorial Award, 666
Field Psych Trust Grant, 310
Indian Council of Social Science Research General Fellowships, 367
Jane Addams/Andrew Carnegie Fellowships in Philanthropy, 368
Jennings Randolph Program for International Peace Senior Fellowships, 685
John M Olin Institute for Strategic Studies Predoctoral and Postdoctoral Fellowships in National Security, 350
La Trobe University Postgraduate Scholarship, 439
Lincoln College Erich and Rochelle Endowed Prize in Music, 730
Monash University International Postgraduate Research Scholarship (MIPRS), 480
Monash University Silver Jubilee Postgraduate Scholarship, 481
Southern Cross University Postgraduate Research Scholarships, 660
University of Glasgow Postgraduate Research Scholarships, 707
University of Manchester Research Studentships and Scholarships, 715
Vera Moore International Postgraduate Research Scholarships, 481

African Nations

Friends of Peterhouse Bursary, 561
Fulbright Postdoctoral Research and Lecturing Awards for Non-US Citizens, 270
Merton College Reed Foundation Scholarship, 732

Australia

Friends of Peterhouse Bursary, 561
Fulbright Postdoctoral Fellowships, 143

Fulbright Postdoctoral Research and Lecturing Awards for Non-US Citizens, 270
Fulbright Postgraduate Studentships, 144
Wingate Scholarships, 771

British Commonwealth

Friends of Peterhouse Bursary, 561
Merton College Reed Foundation Scholarship, 732
Wingate Scholarships, 771

Canada

Friends of Peterhouse Bursary, 561
Fulbright Postdoctoral Research and Lecturing Awards for Non-US Citizens, 270
PRA Fellowships, 549
Wingate Scholarships, 771

Caribbean Countries

Friends of Peterhouse Bursary, 561
Merton College Reed Foundation Scholarship, 732
PRA Fellowships, 549

East European Countries

Friends of Peterhouse Bursary, 561
Fulbright Postdoctoral Research and Lecturing Awards for Non-US Citizens, 270
Merton College Reed Foundation Scholarship, 732

Far East

Friends of Peterhouse Bursary, 561
Fulbright Postdoctoral Research and Lecturing Awards for Non-US Citizens, 270
Japanese American Citizens League Scholarship and Award Program, 422
Merton College Reed Foundation Scholarship, 732

Indian Sub-Continent

Friends of Peterhouse Bursary, 561
Fulbright Postdoctoral Research and Lecturing Awards for Non-US Citizens, 270
Indian Council of Social Science Research Senior Fellowships, 368
Merton College Reed Foundation Scholarship, 732
Wingate Scholarships, 771

Middle East

Friends of Peterhouse Bursary, 561
Fulbright Postdoctoral Research and Lecturing Awards for Non-US Citizens, 270
Merton College Reed Foundation Scholarship, 732

New Zealand

Friends of Peterhouse Bursary, 561
Fulbright Postdoctoral Research and Lecturing Awards for Non-US Citizens, 270
Wingate Scholarships, 771

South Africa

Friends of Peterhouse Bursary, 561
Fulbright Postdoctoral Research and Lecturing Awards for Non-US Citizens, 270
Isie Smuts Research Award, 658
Wingate Scholarships, 771

South America

Friends of Peterhouse Bursary, 561
Fulbright Commission (Argentina) Master's Program, 325
Fulbright Postdoctoral Research and Lecturing Awards for Non-US Citizens, 270
Merton College Reed Foundation Scholarship, 732
PRA Fellowships, 549

United Kingdom

British Schools and Universities Foundation May and Ward Scholarships, 179
Canada Memorial Foundation Scholarships, 222
Fulbright Postdoctoral Research and Lecturing Awards for Non-US Citizens, 270
Hilda Martindale Exhibitions, 358
University of Wales, Bangor (UWB) Research Studentships, 753
University of Wales, Bangor Departmental Research Studentships, 753
Wingate Scholarships, 771

United States of America

AIGC Fellowship, 54
Bicentennial Swedish-American Exchange Fund Travel Grants, 153
British Schools and Universities Foundation May and Ward Scholarships, 179
Federal Chancellor Scholarship, 20
Friends of Peterhouse Bursary, 561
Fulbright Scholar Awards for Research and Lecturing Abroad for United States Citizens, 271
Fulbright Scholar Program for US Citizens, 271
Japanese American Citizens League Scholarship and Award Program, 422
North Dakota Indian Scholarship, 535
PRA Fellowships, 549
UCLA IAC Postdoctoral/Visiting Scholar Fellowships, 680

West European Countries

Friends of Peterhouse Bursary, 561
Fulbright Postdoctoral Research and Lecturing Awards for Non-US Citizens, 270
University of Wales, Bangor (UWB) Research Studentships, 753
University of Wales, Bangor Departmental Research Studentships, 753
Wingate Scholarships, 771

POLICE AND LAW ENFORCEMENT

Any Country

Equiano Memorial Award, 666

East European Countries

Soros Supplementary Grants Programme (SSGP), 544

Far East

The Asia Crime Prevention Foundation Fellowship, 123

United Kingdom

Fulbright Police Studies Fellowships, 759

United States of America

Fulbright Senior Specialists Program, 271

CRIMINOLOGY

Any Country

Center for Advanced Study in the Behavioral Sciences Postdoctoral Residential Fellowships, 245
Equiano Memorial Award, 666
Humanitarian Trust Awards, 362
Onassis Programme of Postgraduate Research Scholarships, 19
University of Glasgow Postgraduate Research Scholarships, 707
University of Manchester Research Studentships and Scholarships, 715

Australia

Criminology Research Council (CRC) Grants, 275
University of Western Sydney Postgraduate Research Award (UWSPRA), 755
Wingate Scholarships, 771

British Commonwealth

Wingate Scholarships, 771

Canada

SSHRC Doctoral Fellowships, 646
SSHRC Standard Research Grants, 647
Wingate Scholarships, 771

East European Countries

Soros Supplementary Grants Programme (SSGP), 544

Far East

The Asia Crime Prevention Foundation Fellowship, 123

Indian Sub-Continent

Wingate Scholarships, 771

New Zealand

University of Western Sydney Postgraduate Research Award
(UWSPRA), 755
Wingate Scholarships, 771

South Africa

Wingate Scholarships, 771

United Kingdom

ESRC Research Studentships, 292
University of Wales (Aberystwyth) Postgraduate Research Student-
ships, 752
University of Wales, Bangor (UWB) Research Studentships, 753
University of Wales, Bangor Departmental Research Studentships,
753
Wingate Scholarships, 771

United States of America

Ian Axford (New Zealand) Fellowships in Public Policy, 263

West European Countries

ESRC Research Studentships, 292
University of Wales, Bangor (UWB) Research Studentships, 753
University of Wales, Bangor Departmental Research Studentships,
753
Wingate Scholarships, 771

FIRE PROTECTION/CONTROL

United Kingdom

University of Wales (Aberystwyth) Postgraduate Research Studentships, 752

MILITARY SCIENCE

Any Country

CDI Internship, 246
Massey Doctoral Scholarship, 461

United Kingdom

University of Wales (Aberystwyth) Postgraduate Research Studentships, 752

CIVIL SECURITY

Any Country

CDI Internship, 246
Equiano Memorial Award, 666

Canada

SSHRC Standard Research Grants, 647

East European Countries

Soros Supplementary Grants Programme (SSGP), 544

United Kingdom

University of Wales (Aberystwyth) Postgraduate Research Studentships, 752

United States of America

Kennan Institute Research Scholarship, 431
WWWC Americans and World Affairs Fellows Program, 780

PEACE AND DISARMAMENT

Any Country

CDI Internship, 246
Center for Advanced Study in the Behavioral Sciences Postdoctoral
Residential Fellowships, 245
Internship in Disarmament and Economic Justice, 774

Canada

Canadian Window on International Development, 399
IDRC Doctoral Research Awards, 400
SSHRC Doctoral Fellowships, 646
SSHRC Standard Research Grants, 647

East European Countries

Soros Supplementary Grants Programme (SSGP), 544

United Kingdom

University of Wales (Aberystwyth) Postgraduate Research Studentships, 752

United States of America

Fulbright Senior Specialists Program, 271
Hubert H Humphrey Doctoral Fellowships in Arms Control, Non-pro-
liferation and Disarmament, 681
Ian Axford (New Zealand) Fellowships in Public Policy, 263
Kennan Institute Research Scholarship, 431
WWWC Americans and World Affairs Fellows Program, 780

SOCIAL WELFARE AND SOCIAL WORK

Any Country

BackCare Research Grants, 148
Center for Advanced Study in the Behavioral Sciences Postdoctoral
Residential Fellowships, 245
Central Queensland University Postgraduate Research Award, 248
CQU International Student Scholarship, 248
Equiano Memorial Award, 666
International Scholarship Programme for Community Service, 468
JCC Association Scholarships, 423
Massey Doctoral Scholarship, 461
University of Bristol Postgraduate Scholarships, 691
University of Glasgow Postgraduate Research Scholarships, 707
University of Manchester Research Studentships and Scholarships,
715
University of New England Research Scholarships, 719

African Nations

Golda Meir Mount Carmel International Training Centre Assistance
for Courses, 337
Golda Meir Mount Carmel International Training Centre Tuition and
Maintenance Scholarships, 337
Institute for Housing and Urban Development Studies Fellowships
for Courses, 376

Australia

University of Western Sydney Postgraduate Research Award
(UWSPRA), 755
Wingate Scholarships, 771

British Commonwealth

Wingate Scholarships, 771

Canada

Sheriff Willoughby King Memorial Scholarship, 693
SSHRC Doctoral Fellowships, 646
SSHRC Standard Research Grants, 647
Wingate Scholarships, 771

Caribbean Countries

Golda Meir Mount Carmel International Training Centre Assistance for Courses, 337
Golda Meir Mount Carmel International Training Centre Tuition and Maintenance Scholarships, 337
Institute for Housing and Urban Development Studies Fellowships for Courses, 376

East European Countries

Golda Meir Mount Carmel International Training Centre Assistance for Courses, 337
Golda Meir Mount Carmel International Training Centre Tuition and Maintenance Scholarships, 337
Institute for Housing and Urban Development Studies Fellowships for Courses, 376
Soros Supplementary Grants Programme (SSGP), 544

Far East

Golda Meir Mount Carmel International Training Centre Assistance for Courses, 337
Golda Meir Mount Carmel International Training Centre Tuition and Maintenance Scholarships, 337
Institute for Housing and Urban Development Studies Fellowships for Courses, 376

Indian Sub-Continent

Golda Meir Mount Carmel International Training Centre Assistance for Courses, 337
Golda Meir Mount Carmel International Training Centre Tuition and Maintenance Scholarships, 337
Institute for Housing and Urban Development Studies Fellowships for Courses, 376
Wingate Scholarships, 771

Middle East

Golda Meir Mount Carmel International Training Centre Assistance for Courses, 337
Golda Meir Mount Carmel International Training Centre Tuition and Maintenance Scholarships, 337
Institute for Housing and Urban Development Studies Fellowships for Courses, 376

New Zealand

University of Western Sydney Postgraduate Research Award (UWSPRA), 755
Wingate Scholarships, 771

South Africa

Golda Meir Mount Carmel International Training Centre Assistance for Courses, 337
Golda Meir Mount Carmel International Training Centre Tuition and Maintenance Scholarships, 337
Institute for Housing and Urban Development Studies Fellowships for Courses, 376
Wingate Scholarships, 771
Zerilda Steyn Memorial Trust, 12

South America

Golda Meir Mount Carmel International Training Centre Assistance for Courses, 337
Golda Meir Mount Carmel International Training Centre Tuition and Maintenance Scholarships, 337

Institute for Housing and Urban Development Studies Fellowships for Courses, 376

United Kingdom

ESRC Research Studentships, 292
General Social Care Council Postgraduate Bursary, 328
Sheffield Hallam University Research Studentships, 625
University of Wales (Aberystwyth) Postgraduate Research Studentships, 752
University of Wales, Bangor (UWB) Research Studentships, 753
Wingate Scholarships, 771

United States of America

Congress Bundestag Youth Exchange for Young Professionals, 245
CSWE Doctoral Fellowships in Social Work for Ethnic Minority Students Preparing for Leadership Roles in Mental Health and/or Substance Abuse, 273
CSWE Doctoral Fellowships in Social Work for Ethnic Minority Students Specialising in Mental Health, 273
CSWE Minority Fellowship Program, 274
Fulbright Senior Specialists Program, 271
Ian Axford (New Zealand) Fellowships in Public Policy, 263
Washington University Chancellor's Graduate Fellowship Program for African Americans, 767
Whitney Young Fellowships, 670

West European Countries

ESRC Research Studentships, 292
General Social Care Council Postgraduate Bursary, 328
Sheffield Hallam University Research Studentships, 625
University of Wales, Bangor (UWB) Research Studentships, 753
Wingate Scholarships, 771

PUBLIC AND COMMUNITY SERVICES

Any Country

ASBAH Research Grant, 125
Central Queensland University Postgraduate Research Award, 248
CQU International Student Scholarship, 248
International Scholarship Programme for Community Service, 468
JCC Association Scholarships, 423

African Nations

Golda Meir Mount Carmel International Training Centre Assistance for Courses, 337
Golda Meir Mount Carmel International Training Centre Tuition and Maintenance Scholarships, 337

Canada

SSHRC Doctoral Fellowships, 646

Caribbean Countries

Golda Meir Mount Carmel International Training Centre Assistance for Courses, 337
Golda Meir Mount Carmel International Training Centre Tuition and Maintenance Scholarships, 337

East European Countries

Golda Meir Mount Carmel International Training Centre Assistance for Courses, 337
Golda Meir Mount Carmel International Training Centre Tuition and Maintenance Scholarships, 337
Soros Supplementary Grants Programme (SSGP), 544

Far East

Golda Meir Mount Carmel International Training Centre Assistance for Courses, 337
Golda Meir Mount Carmel International Training Centre Tuition and Maintenance Scholarships, 337

Indian Sub-Continent

Golda Meir Mount Carmel International Training Centre Assistance for Courses, 337
Golda Meir Mount Carmel International Training Centre Tuition and Maintenance Scholarships, 337

Middle East

Golda Meir Mount Carmel International Training Centre Assistance for Courses, 337
Golda Meir Mount Carmel International Training Centre Tuition and Maintenance Scholarships, 337

South Africa

Golda Meir Mount Carmel International Training Centre Assistance for Courses, 337
Golda Meir Mount Carmel International Training Centre Tuition and Maintenance Scholarships, 337

South America

Golda Meir Mount Carmel International Training Centre Assistance for Courses, 337
Golda Meir Mount Carmel International Training Centre Tuition and Maintenance Scholarships, 337

United States of America

Congress Bundestag Youth Exchange for Young Professionals, 245

VOCATIONAL COUNSELLING

Any Country

Equiano Memorial Award, 666

United States of America

Ian Axford (New Zealand) Fellowships in Public Policy, 263

ENVIRONMENTAL STUDIES

Any Country

The Alberta Law Foundation Graduate Scholarship, 692
American Association of Petroleum Geologists Foundation Grants-in-Aid, 37
Anglo-German Foundation for the Study of Industrial Society Research Grant, 101
Center for Advanced Study in the Behavioral Sciences Postdoctoral Residential Fellowships, 245
Center for Field Research Grants, 246
Conservation and Research Foundation Grants, 267
Deputy Chancellors Postdoctoral Research, 535
Edmund Niles Huyck Preserve, Inc. Graduate and Postgraduate Grants, 292
George A Hall/Harold F Manfield Award, 770
Gilbert F White Postdoctoral Fellowship, 584
Honda Prize, 359
Joseph L Fisher Dissertation Award, 584
Lindbergh Grants, 252
Louis Agassiz Fuertes Award, 770
NERC Advanced Course Studentships, 520
NERC Advanced Research Fellowships, 521
NERC Postdoctoral Research Fellowships, 521
NERC Research Grants, 521
NERC Senior Research Fellowships, 522
NTU One Year Postdoctoral Fellowship, 535
NTU Senior Research Fellowship, 536
NTU Three Year Postdoctoral Fellowship, 536
Paul A Stewart Awards, 771
Percy Sladen Memorial Fund Grants, 559
RFF Fellowships in Environmental Regulatory Implementation, 584
Rhodes University Postdoctoral Fellowship, 586
Sigma Xi Grants-in-Aid of Research, 629
Tibor T Polgar Fellowship, 361
University of Bristol Postgraduate Scholarships, 691

University of Dundee Research Awards, 704
University of Glasgow Postgraduate Research Scholarships, 707
University of Manchester Research Studentships and Scholarships, 715
University of New England Research Scholarships, 719
University of Stirling Research Studentships, 750
University of Sussex Overseas Research Studentships, 750
Woods Hole Oceanographic Institution Research Fellowships in Marine Policy, 778

African Nations

Corpus Christi ACE Scholarship for Postgraduate Study, 200
The Hastings Center International Visiting Scholars Program, 352
IFS Grant, 402
Shell Centenary Scholarships (Developing Countries of the Commonwealth), 216

Australia

Fulbright Postgraduate Student Award for Science and Engineering, 144
The Hastings Center International Visiting Scholars Program, 352
Wingate Scholarships, 771

British Commonwealth

British Institute of Archaeology at Ankara Research Grants, 169
British Institute of Archaeology at Ankara Travel Grants, 169
The Hastings Center International Visiting Scholars Program, 352
Wingate Scholarships, 771

Canada

Canadian Window on International Development, 399
Horticultural Research Institute Grants, 359
IDRC Doctoral Research Awards, 400
Wingate Scholarships, 771

Caribbean Countries

The Hastings Center International Visiting Scholars Program, 352
IFS Grant, 402

East European Countries

Corpus Christi ACE Scholarship for Postgraduate Study, 200
The Hastings Center International Visiting Scholars Program, 352
Natural History Museum Sys-Resource, 522
Open Society Sofia Central European University Scholarship, 542
OSI (Open Society Institute) Chevening Scholarships, 733
Shell Centenary Scholarships (Countries outside of the Commonwealth), 216
Shell Centenary Scholarships (Developing Countries of the Commonwealth), 216
Soros Supplementary Grants Programme (SSGP), 544
Summer University of The Central European University Scholarship, 544

Far East

Croucher Foundation Fellowships and Scholarships, 277
The Hastings Center International Visiting Scholars Program, 352
IFS Grant, 402
Shell Centenary Scholarships (Countries outside of the Commonwealth), 216
Shell Centenary Scholarships (Developing Countries of the Commonwealth), 216

Indian Sub-Continent

Corpus Christi ACE Scholarship for Postgraduate Study, 200
The Hastings Center International Visiting Scholars Program, 352
IFS Grant, 402
Shell Centenary Scholarships (Developing Countries of the Commonwealth), 216
Wingate Scholarships, 771

Middle East

The Hastings Center International Visiting Scholars Program, 352

IFS Grant, 402
Shell Centenary Scholarships (Countries outside of the Commonwealth), 216

New Zealand

The Hastings Center International Visiting Scholars Program, 352
Wingate Scholarships, 771

South Africa

The Hastings Center International Visiting Scholars Program, 352
IFS Grant, 402
Wingate Scholarships, 771

South America

The Hastings Center International Visiting Scholars Program, 352
IFS Grant, 402
Shell Centenary Scholarships (Countries outside of the Commonwealth), 216

United Kingdom

British Institute of Archaeology at Ankara Research Grants, 169
British Institute of Archaeology at Ankara Travel Grants, 169
The Hastings Center International Visiting Scholars Program, 352
NERC Research Studentships, 521
Polish Embassy Short-Term Bursaries, 571
Polish Government Postgraduate Scholarships Scheme, 572
Sheffield Hallam University Research Studentships, 625
University of Wales (Aberystwyth) Postgraduate Research Studentships, 752
University of Wales, Bangor (UWB) Research Studentships, 753
Wingate Scholarships, 771

United States of America

COBASE Collaboration in Basic Science and Engineering, 516
Congress Bundestag Youth Exchange for Young Professionals, 245
Earthwatch Education Awards, 290
Fulbright Senior Specialists Program, 271
Horticultural Research Institute Grants, 359
Ian Axford (New Zealand) Fellowships in Public Policy, 263
NRC Twinning Program, 516
Woods Hole Oceanographic Institution Postdoctoral Fellowships in the Interdisciplinary Institutes, 778

West European Countries

The Hastings Center International Visiting Scholars Program, 352
Janson Johan Helmich Scholarships and Travel Grants, 421
Natural History Museum Sys-Resource, 522
Sheffield Hallam University Research Studentships, 625
University of Wales, Bangor (UWB) Research Studentships, 753
Wingate Scholarships, 771

ECOLOGY

Any Country

AAC Research Grant, 28
The Anne Keymer Prize, 161
Attendance at Conferences Run by Other Organisations, 161
Attendance at Courses and Workshops Co-sponsored by the BES, 161
Award for the Best Paper by a Young Author, 161
BES Early Career Project Grants, 161
BES Education Innovation and Research Grants, 162
BES Small Ecological Project Grants, 162
BES Specialist Course Grants, 162
BES/Nordecol Student Support for Attendance at the Society's Winter Meeting, 162
Center for Field Research Grants, 246
Conservation and Research Foundation Grants, 267
Darbaker Botany Prize, 575
Edmund Niles Huyck Preserve, Inc. Graduate and Postgraduate Grants, 292
The Founders' Prize, 162

G M McKinley Research Fund, 575
George A Hall/Harold F Manfield Award, 770
Honda Prize, 359
Honorary Membership of the Society, 162
L S B Leakey Foundation Fellowship for Great Ape Research, 437
Louis Agassiz Fuertes Award, 770
The Marsh Award for Ecology, 162
NERC Advanced Course Studentships, 520
NERC Advanced Research Fellowships, 521
NERC Postdoctoral Research Fellowships, 521
NERC Research Grants, 521
NERC Senior Research Fellowships, 522
Paul A Stewart Awards, 771
Prize for the Best Poster at the Winter Meeting, 162
Rhodes University Postdoctoral Fellowship, 586
Sigma Xi Grants-in-Aid of Research, 629
Smithsonian Institution Graduate Student Fellowships, 635
Smithsonian Institution Senior Fellowships, 636
Student Support for Attendance at BES Meetings, 163
Teacher Attendance at BES Meetings, 163
Tibor T Polgar Fellowship, 361
University of Stirling Research Studentships, 750
Volzhsky Institute of Humanities Awards, 764

African Nations

Corpus Christi ACE Scholarship for Postgraduate Study, 200

Australia

Fulbright Postgraduate Student Award for Science and Engineering, 144
Wingate Scholarships, 771

British Commonwealth

Wingate Scholarships, 771

Canada

IDRC Doctoral Research Awards, 400
Volzhsky Institute of Humanities Awards, 764
Wingate Scholarships, 771

East European Countries

Corpus Christi ACE Scholarship for Postgraduate Study, 200
Natural History Museum Sys-Resource, 522
Open Society Sofia Central European University Scholarship, 542

Indian Sub-Continent

Corpus Christi ACE Scholarship for Postgraduate Study, 200
Wingate Scholarships, 771

New Zealand

Wingate Scholarships, 771

South Africa

Wingate Scholarships, 771

United Kingdom

NERC Research Studentships, 521
University of Wales, Bangor (UWB) Research Studentships, 753
Volzhsky Institute of Humanities Awards, 764
Wingate Scholarships, 771

United States of America

Congress Bundestag Youth Exchange for Young Professionals, 245
Earthwatch Education Awards, 290
Fulbright Senior Specialists Program, 271
Volzhsky Institute of Humanities Awards, 764
Welder Wildlife Foundation Fellowship, 588
Woods Hole Oceanographic Institution Postdoctoral Fellowships in the Interdisciplinary Institutes, 778

West European Countries

Natural History Museum Sys-Resource, 522

University of Wales, Bangor (UWB) Research Studentships, 753
Wingate Scholarships, 771

NATURAL RESOURCES

Any Country

The Alberta Law Foundation Graduate Scholarship, 692
American Association of Petroleum Geologists Foundation Grants-in-Aid, 37
AWWA Thomas R Camp Scholarship, 99
Canadian Embassy (USA) Faculty Enrichment Program, 228
Center for Field Research Grants, 246
Conservation and Research Foundation Grants, 267
Edmund Niles Huyck Preserve, Inc. Graduate and Postgraduate Grants, 292
Rhodes University Postdoctoral Fellowship, 586
Sigma Xi Grants-in-Aid of Research, 629
Tibor T Polgar Fellowship, 361
University of Calgary Faculty of Law Graduate Scholarship, 694
University of Stirling Research Studentships, 750
Volzhsky Institute of Humanities Awards, 764

Australia

Fulbright Postgraduate Student Award for Science and Engineering, 144
Wingate Scholarships, 771

British Commonwealth

Wingate Scholarships, 771

Canada

AWWA Abel Wolman Doctoral Fellowship, 98
IDRC Doctoral Research Awards, 400
Volzhsky Institute of Humanities Awards, 764
Wingate Scholarships, 771

East European Countries

Natural History Museum Sys-Resource, 522

Indian Sub-Continent

Wingate Scholarships, 771

New Zealand

Wingate Scholarships, 771

South Africa

Wingate Scholarships, 771

South America

AWWA Abel Wolman Doctoral Fellowship, 98

United Kingdom

University of Wales, Bangor (UWB) Research Studentships, 753
Volzhsky Institute of Humanities Awards, 764
Wingate Scholarships, 771

United States of America

AWWA Abel Wolman Doctoral Fellowship, 98
Congress Bundestag Youth Exchange for Young Professionals, 245
Earthwatch Education Awards, 290
Fulbright Senior Specialists Program, 271
Volzhsky Institute of Humanities Awards, 764

West European Countries

Natural History Museum Sys-Resource, 522
University of Wales, Bangor (UWB) Research Studentships, 753
Wingate Scholarships, 771

ENVIRONMENTAL MANAGEMENT

Any Country

AWWA Academic Achievement Award, 98
Center for Field Research Grants, 246
Central Queensland University Postgraduate Research Award, 248
Conservation and Research Foundation Grants, 267
CQU International Student Scholarship, 248
March of Dimes Research Grants, 457
NERC Advanced Course Studentships, 520
NERC Advanced Research Fellowships, 521
NERC Postdoctoral Research Fellowships, 521
NERC Research Grants, 521
NERC Senior Research Fellowships, 522
Rhodes University Postdoctoral Fellowship, 586
Sigma Xi Grants-in-Aid of Research, 629
Stanley Smith (UK) Horticultural Trust Awards, 663
Tibor T Polgar Fellowship, 361
University of Calgary Faculty of Law Graduate Scholarship, 694
The University of Kent at Canterbury Anthropology Bursaries, 709
University of Stirling Research Studentships, 750
Volzhsky Institute of Humanities Awards, 764

African Nations

Corpus Christi ACE Scholarship for Postgraduate Study, 200

Australia

Fulbright Postgraduate Student Award for Science and Engineering, 144
University of Western Sydney Postgraduate Research Award (UWSPRA), 755
Wingate Scholarships, 771

British Commonwealth

ACU Quality of Life Awards, 127
Wingate Scholarships, 771

Canada

AWWA Abel Wolman Doctoral Fellowship, 98
CIC Award for Environmental Improvement, 254
Horticultural Research Institute Grants, 359
IDRC Doctoral Research Awards, 400
Volzhsky Institute of Humanities Awards, 764
Wingate Scholarships, 771

East European Countries

Corpus Christi ACE Scholarship for Postgraduate Study, 200
Natural History Museum Sys-Resource, 522
Open Society Sofia Central European University Scholarship, 542

Indian Sub-Continent

Corpus Christi ACE Scholarship for Postgraduate Study, 200
Wingate Scholarships, 771

New Zealand

University of Western Sydney Postgraduate Research Award (UWSPRA), 755
Wingate Scholarships, 771

South Africa

Wingate Scholarships, 771

South America

AWWA Abel Wolman Doctoral Fellowship, 98

United Kingdom

NERC Research Studentships, 521
University of Wales (Aberystwyth) Postgraduate Research Studentships, 752
University of Wales, Bangor (UWB) Research Studentships, 753
Volzhsky Institute of Humanities Awards, 764
Wingate Scholarships, 771

United States of America

AWWA Abel Wolman Doctoral Fellowship, 98
AWWA Holly A Cornell Scholarship, 98
Congress Bundestag Youth Exchange for Young Professionals, 245
Earthwatch Education Awards, 290
Fulbright Senior Specialists Program, 271
Horticultural Research Institute Grants, 359
Volzhsky Institute of Humanities Awards, 764

West European Countries

Natural History Museum Sys-Resource, 522
University of Wales, Bangor (UWB) Research Studentships, 753
Wingate Scholarships, 771

WILDLIFE AND PEST MANAGEMENT

Any Country

Center for Field Research Grants, 246
Conservation and Research Foundation Grants, 267
Paul A Stewart Awards, 771
Sigma Xi Grants-in-Aid of Research, 629
Tibor T Polgar Fellowship, 361
University of Stirling Research Studentships, 750

Australia

Wingate Scholarships, 771

British Commonwealth

Wingate Scholarships, 771

Canada

IDRC Doctoral Research Awards, 400
Wingate Scholarships, 771

East European Countries

Open Society Sofia Central European University Scholarship, 542

Indian Sub-Continent

Wingate Scholarships, 771

New Zealand

Wingate Scholarships, 771

South Africa

Wingate Scholarships, 771

United Kingdom

University of Wales, Bangor (UWB) Research Studentships, 753
Wingate Scholarships, 771

United States of America

Congress Bundestag Youth Exchange for Young Professionals, 245
Earthwatch Education Awards, 290
Fulbright Senior Specialists Program, 271
Welder Wildlife Foundation Fellowship, 588

West European Countries

University of Wales, Bangor (UWB) Research Studentships, 753
Wingate Scholarships, 771

PHYSICAL EDUCATION AND SPORTS

Any Country

Acadia Graduate Teaching Assistantships, 7
Central Queensland University Postgraduate Research Award, 248
CQU International Student Scholarship, 248
JCC Association Scholarships, 423
John Hervey, Broadcasters and Smallsreed Awards, 686
Rhodes University Postdoctoral Fellowship, 586
University of Bristol Postgraduate Scholarships, 691
University of Exeter Sports Scholarships, 707

University of Glasgow Postgraduate Research Scholarships, 707
University of Manchester Research Studentships and Scholarships, 715
University of Stirling Research Studentships, 750

United Kingdom

Sheffield Hallam University Research Studentships, 625
University of Wales, Bangor (UWB) Research Studentships, 753

United States of America

AAC Mountaineering Fellowship Fund Grants, 28

West European Countries

Sheffield Hallam University Research Studentships, 625
University of Wales, Bangor (UWB) Research Studentships, 753

SPORTS MANAGEMENT

Any Country

Central Queensland University Postgraduate Research Award, 248
CQU International Student Scholarship, 248
JCC Association Scholarships, 423
Massey Doctoral Scholarship, 461
University of Bristol Postgraduate Scholarships, 691
University of Stirling Research Studentships, 750

United Kingdom

University of Wales, Bangor (UWB) Research Studentships, 753

West European Countries

University of Wales, Bangor (UWB) Research Studentships, 753

SOCIOLOGY OF SPORTS

Any Country

Central Queensland University Postgraduate Research Award, 248
CQU International Student Scholarship, 248
JCC Association Scholarships, 423
University of Stirling Research Studentships, 750

United Kingdom

ESRC Research Studentships, 292

West European Countries

ESRC Research Studentships, 292

LEISURE STUDIES

Any Country

JCC Association Scholarships, 423
NARSAD Independent Investigator Awards, 491

PARKS AND RECREATION

Any Country

JCC Association Scholarships, 423
Stanley Smith (UK) Horticultural Trust Awards, 663

East European Countries

European Gardens Horticulture Scholarships, 304

United Kingdom

European Gardens Horticulture Scholarships, 304
Polish Embassy Short-Term Bursaries, 571
Polish Government Postgraduate Scholarships Scheme, 572

United States of America

Ian Axford (New Zealand) Fellowships in Public Policy, 263

African Nations

Australia

British Commonwealth

Canada

Caribbean Countries

East European Countries

West European Countries

ECONOMICS

Any Country

WWWC Americans and World Affairs Fellows Program, 780

West European Countries

Balliol College Marvin Bower Scholarship, 722
CRF (Caledonian Research Foundation)/RSE European Visiting Research Fellowships, 613
The ESRC 1+3 Awards, 291
ESRC Research Studentships, 292
European University Institute Postgraduate Scholarships, 306
University of Wales, Bangor (UWB) Research Studentships, 753
University of Wales, Bangor Departmental Research Studentships, 753
Wingate Scholarships, 771

ECONOMIC HISTORY

Any Country

AIER Summer Fellowship, 55
Arthur H Cole Grants-in-Aid, 292
Camargo Fellowships, 185
Center for Advanced Study in the Behavioral Sciences Postdoctoral Residential Fellowships, 245
CMRS Summer Fellowship, 680
Harry S Truman Library Institute Dissertation Year Fellowships, 348
Harry S Truman Library Institute Research Grants, 348
Harry S Truman Library Institute Scholar's Award, 348
Harvard-Newcomen Fellowship in Business History, 349
Harvard/Newcomen Postdoctoral Award, 533
Herbert Hoover Presidential Library Association Travel Grants, 357
IHS Summer Graduate Research Fellowship, 377
John C Geilfuss Fellowship, 773
Library Company of Philadelphia Program in Early American Economy and Society, 447
Library Company of Philadelphia Research Fellowships in American History and Culture, 447
Minnesota Historical Society Research Grant, 476
NHC Fellowships, 509
Onassis Programme of Postgraduate Research Scholarships, 19
Paul H Nitze School of Advanced International Studies (SAIS) Financial Aid and Fellowships, 156
Queen's University of Belfast Research and Senior Visiting Research Fellowships, 576
Rhodes University Postdoctoral Fellowship, 586
Roosevelt Institute Grant-in-Aid, 319
Russell Sage Foundation Visiting Fellowships, 617
University of Bristol Postgraduate Scholarships, 691
University of Manchester Research Studentships and Scholarships, 715
University of New England Research Scholarships, 719

Australia

Wingate Scholarships, 771

British Commonwealth

Wingate Scholarships, 771

Canada

Alfred D Chandler Jr Travelling Fellowships in Business History and Institutional Economic History, 349
Wingate Scholarships, 771

East European Countries

CRF (Caledonian Research Foundation)/RSE European Visiting Research Fellowships, 613

Far East

University of Leeds International Fee Bursaries (Vietnam), 713

Indian Sub-Continent

Wingate Scholarships, 771

New Zealand

Wingate Scholarships, 771

South Africa

Wingate Scholarships, 771

United Kingdom

CRF (Caledonian Research Foundation)/RSE European Visiting Research Fellowships, 613
ESRC Research Studentships, 292
Molson Research Awards, 159
Prix du Québec, 159
University of Wales (Aberystwyth) Postgraduate Research Studentships, 752
University of Wales, Bangor (UWB) Research Studentships, 753
University of Wales, Bangor Departmental Research Studentships, 753
Wingate Scholarships, 771

United States of America

Alfred D Chandler Jr Travelling Fellowships in Business History and Institutional Economic History, 349
Fulbright Distinguished Chairs Program, 270
Fulbright Senior Specialists Program, 271
Newcomen Society Dissertation Fellowship in Business and American Culture, 534

West European Countries

CRF (Caledonian Research Foundation)/RSE European Visiting Research Fellowships, 613
ESRC Research Studentships, 292
University of Wales, Bangor (UWB) Research Studentships, 753
University of Wales, Bangor Departmental Research Studentships, 753
Wingate Scholarships, 771

ECONOMIC AND FINANCE POLICY

Any Country

Anglo-German Foundation for the Study of Industrial Society Research Grant, 101
Center for Advanced Study in the Behavioral Sciences Postdoctoral Residential Fellowships, 245
Harry S Truman Library Institute Dissertation Year Fellowships, 348
Harry S Truman Library Institute Research Grants, 348
Harry S Truman Library Institute Scholar's Award, 348
Jean Monnet Fellowships, 307
Massey Doctoral Scholarship, 461
Paul H Nitze School of Advanced International Studies (SAIS) Financial Aid and Fellowships, 156
Thomas Holloway Research Studentship, 602
University of Bristol Postgraduate Scholarships, 691
University of Dundee Research Awards, 704
University of Manchester Research Studentships and Scholarships, 715
University of New England Research Scholarships, 719
University of Stirling Research Studentships, 750

Australia

Fulbright Tim Matthews Memorial Postgraduate Student Award in Statistics and Related Disciplines, 145
Wingate Scholarships, 771

British Commonwealth

Wingate Scholarships, 771

Canada

S S Huebner Foundation for Insurance Education Predoctoral Fellowships, 618
Wingate Scholarships, 771

Far East

University of Leeds International Fee Bursaries (Vietnam), 713
University of Leeds International Fee Bursary (Vietnam), 714

Indian Sub-Continent

Wingate Scholarships, 771

New Zealand

Wingate Scholarships, 771

South Africa

Wingate Scholarships, 771

United Kingdom

ESRC Research Studentships, 292
Molson Research Awards, 159
University of Wales, Bangor (UWB) Research Studentships, 753
University of Wales, Bangor Departmental Research Studentships, 753
Wingate Scholarships, 771

United States of America

Fulbright Distinguished Chairs Program, 270
Fulbright Senior Specialists Program, 271
S S Huebner Foundation for Insurance Education Predoctoral Fellowships, 618

West European Countries

ESRC Research Studentships, 292
European University Institute Postgraduate Scholarships, 306
University of Wales, Bangor (UWB) Research Studentships, 753
University of Wales, Bangor Departmental Research Studentships, 753
Wingate Scholarships, 771

TAXATION

Any Country

AIER Summer Fellowship, 55
AIER Summer Programme for Visiting Research Fellows, 55
Anglo-German Foundation for the Study of Industrial Society Research Grant, 101
Center for Advanced Study in the Behavioral Sciences Postdoctoral Residential Fellowships, 245
Harry S Truman Library Institute Dissertation Year Fellowships, 348
Harry S Truman Library Institute Research Grants, 348
Harry S Truman Library Institute Scholar's Award, 348
Rhodes University Postdoctoral Fellowship, 586
University of Bristol Postgraduate Scholarships, 691
University of Stirling Research Studentships, 750

Australia

Wingate Scholarships, 771

British Commonwealth

Wingate Scholarships, 771

Canada

Alcohol Beverage Medical Research Foundation Research Project Grant, 17
Wingate Scholarships, 771

Indian Sub-Continent

Wingate Scholarships, 771

New Zealand

Wingate Scholarships, 771

South Africa

Wingate Scholarships, 771

United Kingdom

University of Wales (Aberystwyth) Postgraduate Research Studentships, 752
University of Wales, Bangor (UWB) Research Studentships, 753
University of Wales, Bangor Departmental Research Studentships, 753
Wingate Scholarships, 771

United States of America

Alcohol Beverage Medical Research Foundation Research Project Grant, 17

West European Countries

University of Wales, Bangor (UWB) Research Studentships, 753
University of Wales, Bangor Departmental Research Studentships, 753
Wingate Scholarships, 771

ECONOMETRICS

Any Country

Center for Advanced Study in the Behavioral Sciences Postdoctoral Residential Fellowships, 245
Harry S Truman Library Institute Dissertation Year Fellowships, 348
Harry S Truman Library Institute Research Grants, 348
Harry S Truman Library Institute Scholar's Award, 348
Jean Monnet Fellowships, 307
Paul H Nitze School of Advanced International Studies (SAIS) Financial Aid and Fellowships, 156
Queen Mary Research Studentships, 576
University of Bristol Postgraduate Scholarships, 691
University of Dundee Research Awards, 704
University of Manchester Research Studentships and Scholarships, 715
University of New England Research Scholarships, 719
University of Stirling Research Studentships, 750
Volzhsky Institute of Humanities Awards, 764

Australia

Fulbright Tim Matthews Memorial Postgraduate Student Award in Statistics and Related Disciplines, 145
University of Western Sydney Postgraduate Research Award (UWSPRA), 755
Wingate Scholarships, 771

British Commonwealth

Wingate Scholarships, 771

Canada

Alcohol Beverage Medical Research Foundation Research Project Grant, 17
Volzhsky Institute of Humanities Awards, 764
Wingate Scholarships, 771

Indian Sub-Continent

Wingate Scholarships, 771

New Zealand

University of Western Sydney Postgraduate Research Award (UWSPRA), 755
Wingate Scholarships, 771

South Africa

Wingate Scholarships, 771

United Kingdom

Alzheimer's Society Research Grants, 24
University of Wales, Bangor (UWB) Research Studentships, 753
University of Wales, Bangor Departmental Research Studentships, 753
Volzhsky Institute of Humanities Awards, 764

Wingate Scholarships, 771

United States of America

Alcohol Beverage Medical Research Foundation Research Project Grant, 17
COBASE Collaboration in Basic Science and Engineering, 516
Volzhsky Institute of Humanities Awards, 764

West European Countries

European University Institute Postgraduate Scholarships, 306
University of Wales, Bangor (UWB) Research Studentships, 753
University of Wales, Bangor Departmental Research Studentships, 753
Wingate Scholarships, 771

INDUSTRIAL AND PRODUCTION ECONOMICS

Any Country

Anglo-German Foundation for the Study of Industrial Society Research Grant, 101
Center for Advanced Study in the Behavioral Sciences Postdoctoral Residential Fellowships, 245
Harry S Truman Library Institute Dissertation Year Fellowships, 348
Harry S Truman Library Institute Research Grants, 348
Harry S Truman Library Institute Scholar's Award, 348
Houblon-Norman Fellowships, 360
Thomas Holloway Research Studentship, 602

Australia

Wingate Scholarships, 771

British Commonwealth

Wingate Scholarships, 771

Canada

S S Huebner Foundation for Insurance Education Predoctoral Fellowships, 618
Wingate Scholarships, 771

Indian Sub-Continent

Wingate Scholarships, 771

New Zealand

Wingate Scholarships, 771

South Africa

Wingate Scholarships, 771

United Kingdom

University of Wales (Aberystwyth) Postgraduate Research Studentships, 752
University of Wales, Bangor (UWB) Research Studentships, 753
University of Wales, Bangor Departmental Research Studentships, 753
Wingate Scholarships, 771

United States of America

NRC Twinning Program, 516
S S Huebner Foundation for Insurance Education Predoctoral Fellowships, 618

West European Countries

University of Wales, Bangor (UWB) Research Studentships, 753
University of Wales, Bangor Departmental Research Studentships, 753
Wingate Scholarships, 771

POLITICAL SCIENCE AND GOVERNMENT

Any Country

ABF Fellowships in Law and Social Science, 38

Acadia Graduate Teaching Assistantships, 7
Ahmanson and Getty Postdoctoral Fellowships, 678
AIATSIS Research Grants, 139
Alexander S Onassis Programme of Research Grants, 18
Alexander S Onassis Research Grants, 18
Anglo-German Foundation for the Study of Industrial Society Research Grant, 101
ASECS (American Society for Eighteenth-Century Studies)/Clark Library Fellowships, 679
Camargo Fellowships, 185
Canadian Embassy (USA) Senior Fellowship Program, 228
CDI Internship, 246
The Celso Furtado Award, 674
Center for Advanced Study in the Behavioral Sciences Postdoctoral Residential Fellowships, 245
Clark Predoctoral Fellowships, 679
Clark-Huntington Joint Bibliographical Fellowship, 679
Emigré Memorial German Internship Programs, 297
Equiano Memorial Award, 666
Foundation Praemium Erasmianum Study Prize, 318
Gilbert F White Postdoctoral Fellowship, 584
Graduate Institute of International Studies (Geneva) Scholarships, 342
Grant Notley Memorial Postdoctoral Fellowship, 689
Harry Frank Guggenheim Dissertation Fellowship, 348
Harry Frank Guggenheim Research Program, 348
Harry S Truman Library Institute Dissertation Year Fellowships, 348
Harry S Truman Library Institute Research Grants, 348
Harry S Truman Library Institute Scholar's Award, 348
Herbert Hoover Presidential Library Association Travel Grants, 357
IHS Summer Graduate Research Fellowship, 377
Institute of Irish Studies Research Fellowships, 383
Institute of Irish Studies Senior Visiting Research Fellowship, 383
Jane Addams/Andrew Carnegie Fellowships in Philanthropy, 368
Joseph L Fisher Dissertation Award, 584
Kennan Institute Short Term Grants, 431
Lyndon Baines Johnson Foundation Grants-in-Aid of Research, 454
M Alison Frantz Fellowship in Post-Classical Studies at The Gennadius Library (formerly known as the Gennadeion Fellowship), 81
Mansfield College Elfan Rees Scholarship, 731
Marusia and Michael Dorosh Master's Fellowship, 233
NHC Fellowships, 509
Onassis Programme of Postgraduate Research Scholarships, 19
Paul H Nitze School of Advanced International Studies (SAIS) Financial Aid and Fellowships, 156
Queen Mary Research Studentships, 576
Rhodes University Postdoctoral Fellowship, 586
Rockefeller Archive Center Research Grant Program, 590
Roosevelt Institute Grant-in-Aid, 319
Russell Sage Foundation Visiting Fellowships, 617
Shelby Cullom Davis Center Research Projects, Research Fellowships, 625
SOAS Bursary, 622
SOAS Research Student Fellowships, 622
University of Bristol Postgraduate Scholarships, 691
University of Dundee Research Awards, 704
University of Glasgow Postgraduate Research Scholarships, 707
The University of Kent at Canterbury Department of Politics and International Relations Bursary, 710
University of Manchester Research Studentships and Scholarships, 715
University of Stirling Research Studentships, 750
USC College Dissertation Fellowship, 749
USC College of Letters, Arts and Sciences Merit Award, 749
Woods Hole Oceanographic Institution Postdoctoral Awards in Marine Policy and Ocean Management, 777
Woods Hole Oceanographic Institution Research Fellowships in Marine Policy, 778
World Universities Network (WUN) Scholarship Scheme, 749

INTERNATIONAL RELATIONS

SOCIOLOGY

Wingate Scholarships, 771

United States of America

AAAS Mass Media Science and Engineering Fellowship, 32
AAUW University Scholar-in-Residence, 5
AINA Grants-in-Aid, 104
American Sociological Association Minority Fellowship Program, 93
Bicentennial Swedish-American Exchange Fund Travel Grants, 153
COBASE Collaboration in Basic Science and Engineering, 516
Fulbright Distinguished Chairs Program, 270
Fulbright Scholar Awards for Research and Lecturing Abroad for United States Citizens, 271
Fulbright Senior Specialists Program, 271
GMF Research Fellowships Program, 333
Ian Axford (New Zealand) Fellowships in Public Policy, 263
IREX Grant Opportunities for US Scholars, 409
Kennan Institute Research Scholarship, 431
Marine Corps Historical Center Research Grants, 458
National Research Service Award Mental Health and Adjustment in the Life Course, 717
NRC Twinning Program, 516
ONR Postdoctoral Fellowship, 539
UCLA IAC Postdoctoral/Visiting Scholar Fellowships, 680
University of New Hampshire Postdoctoral Fellowships For Research on Family Violence, 720

West European Countries

ESRC Research Studentships, 292
European University Institute Postgraduate Scholarships, 306
The University of Kent at Canterbury Sociology Studentship, 711
University of Wales, Bangor (UWB) Research Studentships, 753
University of Wales, Bangor Departmental Research Studentships, 753
Wingate Scholarships, 771

HISTORY OF SOCIETIES

Any Country

Ahmanson and Getty Postdoctoral Fellowships, 678
Albert J Beveridge Grant, 53
Bernadotte E Schmitt Grants, 54
Camargo Fellowships, 185
Canadian Institute of Ukrainian Studies Research Grants, 233
Center for Advanced Study in the Behavioral Sciences Postdoctoral Residential Fellowships, 245
Center for Field Research Grants, 246
Clark-Huntington Joint Bibliographical Fellowship, 679
CMRS Summer Fellowship, 680
The CSA Adele Filene Travel Award, 269
Equiano Memorial Award, 666
External Faculty Fellowships, 663
FAMSI Research Grant, 317
Library Company of Philadelphia Research Fellowships in American History and Culture, 447
Littleton-Griswold Research Grant, 54
M Alison Frantz Fellowship in Post-Classical Studies at The Gennadius Library (formerly known as the Gennadeion Fellowship), 81
NEH Research Fellowships, 81
NHC Fellowships, 509
Onassis Programme of Postgraduate Research Scholarships, 19

Australia

Wingate Scholarships, 771

British Commonwealth

Wingate Scholarships, 771

Canada

Wingate Scholarships, 771

East European Countries

Open Society Sofia Central European University Scholarship, 542

Indian Sub-Continent

Wingate Scholarships, 771

New Zealand

Wingate Scholarships, 771

South Africa

Wingate Scholarships, 771

United Kingdom

University of Wales, Bangor (UWB) Research Studentships, 753
University of Wales, Bangor Departmental Research Studentships, 753
Wingate Scholarships, 771

United States of America

ACLS Dissertation Fellowships in East European Studies, 41
ACLS Fellowships for Postdoctoral Research in East European Studies, 42
ACLS/SSRC/NEH International and Area Studies Fellowships, 637
Earthwatch Education Awards, 290
Fulbright Senior Specialists Program, 271
WWWC Americans and World Affairs Fellows Program, 780

West European Countries

University of Wales, Bangor (UWB) Research Studentships, 753
University of Wales, Bangor Departmental Research Studentships, 753
Wingate Scholarships, 771

COMPARATIVE SOCIOLOGY

Any Country

Anglo-German Foundation for the Study of Industrial Society Research Grant, 101
Camargo Fellowships, 185
Center for Advanced Study in the Behavioral Sciences Postdoctoral Residential Fellowships, 245
Center for Field Research Grants, 246
Central Queensland University Postgraduate Research Award, 248
CQU International Student Scholarship, 248
External Faculty Fellowships, 663
M Alison Frantz Fellowship in Post-Classical Studies at The Gennadius Library (formerly known as the Gennadeion Fellowship), 81
Onassis Programme of Postgraduate Research Scholarships, 19
University of Bristol Postgraduate Scholarships, 691
University of Manchester Research Studentships and Scholarships, 715
University of Stirling Research Studentships, 750

Australia

Wingate Scholarships, 771

British Commonwealth

ACU Development Fellowships, 127
Wingate Scholarships, 771

Canada

Alcohol Beverage Medical Research Foundation Research Project Grant, 17
Wingate Scholarships, 771

East European Countries

Open Society Sofia Central European University Scholarship, 542

Indian Sub-Continent

Wingate Scholarships, 771

New Zealand

Wingate Scholarships, 771

South Africa

Wingate Scholarships, 771

United Kingdom

ACU Development Fellowships, 127
Polish Embassy Short-Term Bursaries, 571
University of Wales, Bangor (UWB) Research Studentships, 753
University of Wales, Bangor Departmental Research Studentships, 753
Wingate Scholarships, 771

United States of America

Alcohol Beverage Medical Research Foundation Research Project Grant, 17
Fulbright Senior Specialists Program, 271

West European Countries

University of Wales, Bangor (UWB) Research Studentships, 753
University of Wales, Bangor Departmental Research Studentships, 753
Wingate Scholarships, 771

SOCIAL POLICY

Any Country

Anglo-German Foundation for the Study of Industrial Society Research Grant, 101
Center for Advanced Study in the Behavioral Sciences Postdoctoral Residential Fellowships, 245
Equiano Memorial Award, 666
Internship in Disarmament and Economic Justice, 774
Jean Monnet Fellowships, 307
M Alison Frantz Fellowship in Post-Classical Studies at The Gennadius Library (formerly known as the Gennadeion Fellowship), 81
NSERC Chairs in the Management of Technological Change, 523
Onassis Programme of Postgraduate Research Scholarships, 19
Paul H Nitze School of Advanced International Studies (SAIS) Financial Aid and Fellowships, 156
Rockefeller Archive Center Research Grant Program, 590
Sir Halley Stewart Trust Grants, 631
SPSSI Sponsored Research Workshop, 651
Thomas Holloway Research Studentship, 602
University of Bristol Postgraduate Scholarships, 691
The University of Kent at Canterbury Social and Public Policy Studentships, 711
University of Manchester Research Studentships and Scholarships, 715
University of Stirling Research Studentships, 750
WILPF Internship in Human Rights, 774

African Nations

The Hastings Center International Visiting Scholars Program, 352
University of Sussex Overseas Development Administration Shared Scholarship Scheme, 750

Australia

The Hastings Center International Visiting Scholars Program, 352
Wingate Scholarships, 771

British Commonwealth

The Hastings Center International Visiting Scholars Program, 352
Wingate Scholarships, 771

Canada

Alcohol Beverage Medical Research Foundation Research Project Grant, 17
Canadian Tobacco Control Research Initiative Planning Grants, 643

Canadian Tobacco Control Research Initiative: Policy Research Grants, 643
IDRC Doctoral Research Awards, 400
Wingate Scholarships, 771

Caribbean Countries

The Hastings Center International Visiting Scholars Program, 352

East European Countries

The Hastings Center International Visiting Scholars Program, 352
Open Society Sofia Central European University Scholarship, 542

Far East

The Hastings Center International Visiting Scholars Program, 352
University of Sussex Overseas Development Administration Shared Scholarship Scheme, 750

Indian Sub-Continent

The Hastings Center International Visiting Scholars Program, 352
University of Sussex Overseas Development Administration Shared Scholarship Scheme, 750
Wingate Scholarships, 771

Middle East

The Hastings Center International Visiting Scholars Program, 352

New Zealand

The Hastings Center International Visiting Scholars Program, 352
Wingate Scholarships, 771

South Africa

The Hastings Center International Visiting Scholars Program, 352
Wingate Scholarships, 771

South America

The Hastings Center International Visiting Scholars Program, 352

United Kingdom

ESRC Research Studentships, 292
The Hastings Center International Visiting Scholars Program, 352
Humphrey-Fulbright Fellowship for Civil Servants, 760
Molson Research Awards, 159
Parkinson's Disease Society Research Project Grant, 555
Parkinson's Disease Society Studentships and Junior/Senior Fellows, 555
Prix du Québec, 159
University of Wales (Aberystwyth) Postgraduate Research Studentships, 752
University of Wales, Bangor (UWB) Research Studentships, 753
University of Wales, Bangor Departmental Research Studentships, 753
Wingate Scholarships, 771

United States of America

Alcohol Beverage Medical Research Foundation Research Project Grant, 17
Fulbright Senior Specialists Program, 271
National Research Service Award Mental Health and Adjustment in the Life Course, 717
NIH Research Grants, 511

West European Countries

ESRC Research Studentships, 292
European University Institute Postgraduate Scholarships, 306
The Hastings Center International Visiting Scholars Program, 352
University of Wales, Bangor (UWB) Research Studentships, 753
University of Wales, Bangor Departmental Research Studentships, 753
Wingate Scholarships, 771

SOCIAL INSTITUTIONS

Any Country

Anglo-German Foundation for the Study of Industrial Society Research Grant, 101
Center for Advanced Study in the Behavioral Sciences Postdoctoral Residential Fellowships, 245
FAMSI Research Grant, 317
M Alison Frantz Fellowship in Post-Classical Studies at The Gennadius Library (formerly known as the Gennadeion Fellowship), 81
Onassis Programme of Postgraduate Research Scholarships, 19
University of Bristol Postgraduate Scholarships, 691
University of Manchester Research Studentships and Scholarships, 715
University of Stirling Research Studentships, 750

Australia

Wingate Scholarships, 771

British Commonwealth

Wingate Scholarships, 771

Canada

Alcohol Beverage Medical Research Foundation Research Project Grant, 17
Wingate Scholarships, 771

East European Countries

Open Society Sofia Central European University Scholarship, 542

Indian Sub-Continent

Wingate Scholarships, 771

New Zealand

Wingate Scholarships, 771

South Africa

Wingate Scholarships, 771

United Kingdom

University of Wales, Bangor (UWB) Research Studentships, 753
University of Wales, Bangor Departmental Research Studentships, 753
Wingate Scholarships, 771

United States of America

Alcohol Beverage Medical Research Foundation Research Project Grant, 17
Fulbright Senior Specialists Program, 271
NIH Research Grants, 511

West European Countries

University of Wales, Bangor (UWB) Research Studentships, 753
University of Wales, Bangor Departmental Research Studentships, 753
Wingate Scholarships, 771

SOCIAL COMMUNICATION PROBLEMS

Any Country

BackCare Research Grants, 148
Center for Advanced Study in the Behavioral Sciences Postdoctoral Residential Fellowships, 245
Onassis Programme of Postgraduate Research Scholarships, 19
University of Bristol Postgraduate Scholarships, 691
University of Manchester Research Studentships and Scholarships, 715
University of Stirling Research Studentships, 750

Australia

Wingate Scholarships, 771

British Commonwealth

Wingate Scholarships, 771

Canada

Alcohol Beverage Medical Research Foundation Research Project Grant, 17
Wingate Scholarships, 771

East European Countries

Open Society Sofia Central European University Scholarship, 542

Indian Sub-Continent

Wingate Scholarships, 771

New Zealand

Wingate Scholarships, 771

South Africa

Wingate Scholarships, 771

United Kingdom

University of Wales, Bangor (UWB) Research Studentships, 753
University of Wales, Bangor Departmental Research Studentships, 753
Wingate Scholarships, 771

United States of America

Alcohol Beverage Medical Research Foundation Research Project Grant, 17
Fulbright Senior Specialists Program, 271
NIH Research Grants, 511

West European Countries

University of Wales, Bangor (UWB) Research Studentships, 753
University of Wales, Bangor Departmental Research Studentships, 753
Wingate Scholarships, 771

FUTUROLOGY

Any Country

Dublin Institute for Advanced Studies Scholarship in Celtic Studies, 288
Equiano Memorial Award, 666

Australia

Wingate Scholarships, 771

British Commonwealth

Wingate Scholarships, 771

Canada

Wingate Scholarships, 771

Indian Sub-Continent

Wingate Scholarships, 771

New Zealand

Wingate Scholarships, 771

South Africa

Wingate Scholarships, 771

United Kingdom

Molson Research Awards, 159
University of Wales, Bangor (UWB) Research Studentships, 753
Wingate Scholarships, 771

ESRC Research Studentships, 292
The Hastings Center International Visiting Scholars Program, 352
Hector and Elizabeth Catling Bursary, 175
Macmillan-Rodewald Studentship, School Studentship, Cary
Studentship, 175
Sasakawa Scholarship, 750
University of Wales, Bangor (UWB) Research Studentships, 753
University of Wales, Bangor Departmental Research Studentships,
753
Wingate Scholarships, 771

United States of America

AAUW Eleanor Roosevelt Teacher Fellowships, 4
AAUW University Scholar-in-Residence, 5
Alcohol Beverage Medical Research Foundation Research Project
Grant, 17
Bicentennial Swedish-American Exchange Fund Travel Grants, 153
Fulbright Distinguished Chairs Program, 270
Fulbright Senior Specialists Program, 271
Ian Axford (New Zealand) Fellowships in Public Policy, 263
IREX Grant Opportunities for US Scholars, 409
Kennan Institute Research Scholarship, 431
Postdoctoral Training Programme in Addiction and Mental Health,
249
University of New Hampshire Postdoctoral Fellowships For Re-
search on Family Violence, 720

West European Countries

ESRC Research Studentships, 292
The Hastings Center International Visiting Scholars Program, 352
University of Wales, Bangor (UWB) Research Studentships, 753
University of Wales, Bangor Departmental Research Studentships,
753
Wingate Scholarships, 771

URBAN STUDIES

Any Country

AIATSIS Research Grants, 139
ASCSA Fellowships, 79
Center for Advanced Study in the Behavioral Sciences Postdoctoral
Residential Fellowships, 245
Equiano Memorial Award, 666
External Faculty Fellowships, 663
Frederick Soddy Trust Grants, 321
Harry Frank Guggenheim Dissertation Fellowship, 348
Harry Frank Guggenheim Research Program, 348
The J B Harley Research Fellowships in the History of Cartography,
418
Jane Addams/Andrew Carnegie Fellowships in Philanthropy, 368
Joseph L Fisher Dissertation Award, 584
Kennan Institute Short Term Grants, 431
M Alison Frantz Fellowship in Post-Classical Studies at The
Gennadius Library (formerly known as the Gennadeion Fellowship),
81
Minnesota Historical Society Research Grant, 476
Queen Mary Research Studentships, 576
Rockefeller Archive Center Research Grant Program, 590
Russell Sage Foundation Visiting Fellowships, 617
University of Bristol Postgraduate Scholarships, 691
University of Glasgow Postgraduate Research Scholarships, 707
University of Manchester Research Studentships and Scholarships,
715

Australia

Wingate Scholarships, 771

British Commonwealth

British Institute of Archaeology at Ankara Research Grants, 169
British Institute of Archaeology at Ankara Travel Grants, 169
Wingate Scholarships, 771

Canada

Alcohol Beverage Medical Research Foundation Research Project
Grant, 17
Konrad Adenauer Research Award, 20
Wingate Scholarships, 771

East European Countries

Soros Supplementary Grants Programme (SSGP), 544

Indian Sub-Continent

Wingate Scholarships, 771

New Zealand

Wingate Scholarships, 771

South Africa

Wingate Scholarships, 771

United Kingdom

British Institute of Archaeology at Ankara Research Grants, 169
British Institute of Archaeology at Ankara Travel Grants, 169
ESRC Research Studentships, 292
Wingate Scholarships, 771

United States of America

Alcohol Beverage Medical Research Foundation Research Project
Grant, 17
Fulbright Senior Specialists Program, 271
Ian Axford (New Zealand) Fellowships in Public Policy, 263
IREX Grant Opportunities for US Scholars, 409
Kennan Institute Research Scholarship, 431

West European Countries

ESRC Research Studentships, 292
Wingate Scholarships, 771

RURAL STUDIES

Any Country

AIATSIS Research Grants, 139
ASCSA Fellowships, 79
Center for Advanced Study in the Behavioral Sciences Postdoctoral
Residential Fellowships, 245
Center for Field Research Grants, 246
Central Queensland University Postgraduate Research Award, 248
CQU International Student Scholarship, 248
Frederick Soddy Trust Grants, 321
Jane Addams/Andrew Carnegie Fellowships in Philanthropy, 368
Joseph L Fisher Dissertation Award, 584
Kennan Institute Short Term Grants, 431
M Alison Frantz Fellowship in Post-Classical Studies at The
Gennadius Library (formerly known as the Gennadeion Fellowship),
81
Minnesota Historical Society Research Grant, 476
University of Glasgow Postgraduate Research Scholarships, 707
University of Manchester Research Studentships and Scholarships,
715
University of New England Research Scholarships, 719

African Nations

Institute for Housing and Urban Development Studies Fellowships
for Courses, 376
University of Sussex Overseas Development Administration Shared
Scholarship Scheme, 750

Australia

Wingate Scholarships, 771

British Commonwealth

British Institute of Archaeology at Ankara Research Grants, 169
British Institute of Archaeology at Ankara Travel Grants, 169

COGNITIVE SCIENCES

Wingate Scholarships, 771

United States of America

AAAS Mass Media Science and Engineering Fellowship, 32
Alcohol Beverage Medical Research Foundation Research Project Grant, 17
Fulbright Senior Specialists Program, 271
Kennan Institute Research Scholarship, 431
NIH Research Grants, 511
Postdoctoral Training Programme in Addiction and Mental Health, 249

West European Countries

ESRC Research Studentships, 292
Wingate Scholarships, 771

PSYCHOLOGY

Any Country

Acadia Graduate Teaching Assistantships, 7
Adolescent and Youth Research Award, 355
AIATSIS Research Grants, 139
Albert Ellis Institute Clinical Fellowship, 15
Alberta Heritage Clinical Fellowships, 15
Alberta Heritage Clinical Investigatorships, 15
Alberta Heritage Full-Time Fellowships, 15
Alberta Heritage Full-Time Studentship, 16
Alberta Heritage Medical Scholarships, 16
Alberta Heritage Medical Scientist Awards, 16
Alberta Heritage Part-Time Fellowships, 16
Alberta Heritage Part-Time Studentship, 16
Alexander S Onassis Programme of Research Grants, 18
Alexander S Onassis Research Grants, 18
BackCare Research Grants, 148
Center for Advanced Study in the Behavioral Sciences Postdoctoral Residential Fellowships, 245
Central Queensland University Postgraduate Research Award, 248
CQU International Student Scholarship, 248
D Scott Rogo Award for Parapsychological Literature, 553
Danish Cancer Society Psychosocial Research Award, 278
Eileen J Garrett Scholarship, 553
ETS National Assessment of Educational Progress (NAEP) Visiting Scholar Program, 294
ETS Summer Program in Research for Graduate Students, 294
Fondation Fyssen Postdoctoral Study Grants, 312
Harry Frank Guggenheim Dissertation Fellowship, 348
Harry Frank Guggenheim Research Program, 348
Health Research Board and British Council Research Visits Scheme, 353
Henry A Murray Dissertation Award Program, 356
Jane Addams/Andrew Carnegie Fellowships in Philanthropy, 368
Jeanne Humphrey Block Dissertation Award, 356
La Trobe University Postgraduate Scholarship, 439
Massey Doctoral Scholarship, 461
MRC Career Development Award, 463
MRC Clinical Research Training Fellowships, 463
MRC Clinician Scientist Fellowship, 463
MRC Patient Oriented Clinician Scientist Fellowship, 464
MRC Research Training Fellowship, 465
MRC Royal College of Surgeons of Edinburgh Training Fellowship, 465
MRC Royal College of Surgeons of England Training Fellowship, 466
MRC Senior Non-Clinical Fellowship, 466
MRC Special Training Fellowships in Health Services and Health of the Public Research, 466
MRC/Academy of Medical Sciences Tenure Track Clinician Scientist Fellowship, 467
MRC/PPARC Research Training Fellowship, 467
National Academy of Education Spencer Postdoctoral Fellowships, 489
Novartis Foundation Symposium Bursaries, 539

OISE/UT Graduate Assistantships, 541
OISE/UT Local Support, 541
Onassis Programme of Postgraduate Research Scholarships, 19
Parapsychology Foundation Grant, 553
Queen Elizabeth the Queen Mother Fellowship Award, 583
Research into Ageing Prize Studentships, 583
Research into Ageing Programme Grants, 584
Rhodes University Postdoctoral Fellowship, 586
Russell Sage Foundation Visiting Fellowships, 617
Sir James McNeill Foundation Postgraduate Scholarship, 481
Somerville College Margaret Pelly Scholarship, 739
SSSS Student Research Grant Award, 651
Thomas Holloway Research Studentship, 602
Tourette Syndrome Association Research Grants, 677
University of Bristol Postgraduate Scholarships, 691
University of Dundee Research Awards, 704
University of Glasgow Postgraduate Research Scholarships, 707
The University of Kent at Canterbury Department of Psychology Studentships, 710
University of Manchester Research Studentships and Scholarships, 715
University of New England Research Scholarships, 719
University of New Hampshire Postdoctoral Fellowships For Research on Family Violence, 720
University of Stirling Research Studentships, 750
USC College Dissertation Fellowship, 749
USC College of Letters, Arts and Sciences Merit Award, 749

Australia

University of Western Sydney Postgraduate Research Award (UWSPRA), 755
Wingate Scholarships, 771

British Commonwealth

Wingate Scholarships, 771

Canada

AAAS Mass Media Science and Engineering Fellowship, 32
Alberta Heritage Health Research Studentship, 16
Alcohol Beverage Medical Research Foundation Research Project Grant, 17
Heritage Health Research Career Renewal Awards, 17
Postdoctoral Training Programme in Addiction and Mental Health, 249
Wingate Scholarships, 771

East European Countries

Soros Supplementary Grants Programme (SSGP), 544

Indian Sub-Continent

Wingate Scholarships, 771

New Zealand

University of Western Sydney Postgraduate Research Award (UWSPRA), 755
Wingate Scholarships, 771

South Africa

Wingate Scholarships, 771

United Kingdom

Alzheimer's Society Research Grants, 24
ESRC Research Studentships, 292
Mental Health Foundation Project Grant, 470
Parkinson's Disease Society Research Project Grant, 555
Parkinson's Disease Society Studentships and Junior/Senior Fellows, 555
Sheffield Hallam University Research Studentships, 625
Tizard Centre Departmental Scholarships, 709
University of Wales, Bangor (UWB) Research Studentships, 753
University of Wales, Bangor Departmental Research Studentships, 753

Wingate Scholarships, 771

United States of America

AAAS Mass Media Science and Engineering Fellowship, 32
Alcohol Beverage Medical Research Foundation Research Project Grant, 17
ETS Postdoctoral Fellowships, 294
Fulbright Distinguished Chairs Program, 270
Fulbright Senior Specialists Program, 271
IREX Grant Opportunities for US Scholars, 409
Kennan Institute Research Scholarship, 431
National Research Service Award Mental Health and Adjustment in the Life Course, 717
NIH Research Grants, 511
NRC Twinning Program, 516
ONR Postdoctoral Fellowship, 539
Postdoctoral Training Programme in Addiction and Mental Health, 249
UCLA IAC Postdoctoral/Visiting Scholar Fellowships, 680
University of New Hampshire Postdoctoral Fellowships For Research on Family Violence, 720
Washington University Chancellor's Graduate Fellowship Program for African Americans, 767

West European Countries

ESRC Research Studentships, 292
Scholarship Foundation of the League for Finnish-American Societies, 621
Sheffield Hallam University Research Studentships, 625
Tizard Centre Departmental Scholarships, 709
University of Wales, Bangor (UWB) Research Studentships, 753
University of Wales, Bangor Departmental Research Studentships, 753
Wingate Scholarships, 771

EXPERIMENTAL PSYCHOLOGY

Any Country

Center for Advanced Study in the Behavioral Sciences Postdoctoral Residential Fellowships, 245
D Scott Rogo Award for Parapsychological Literature, 553
Eileen J Garrett Scholarship, 553
NARSAD Distinguished Investigator Awards, 491
NARSAD Independent Investigator Awards, 491
NARSAD Young Investigator Awards, 491
Onassis Programme of Postgraduate Research Scholarships, 19
Parapsychology Foundation Grant, 553
Somerville College Margaret Pelly Scholarship, 739
University of Bristol Postgraduate Scholarships, 691
University of Dundee Research Awards, 704

Australia

Wingate Scholarships, 771

British Commonwealth

Wingate Scholarships, 771

Canada

Wingate Scholarships, 771

Indian Sub-Continent

Wingate Scholarships, 771

New Zealand

Wingate Scholarships, 771

South Africa

Wingate Scholarships, 771

United Kingdom

Alzheimer's Society Research Grants, 24
University of Wales, Bangor (UWB) Research Studentships, 753

University of Wales, Bangor Departmental Research Studentships, 753
Wingate Scholarships, 771

United States of America

MFP HIV/AIDS Research Training Fellowship, 76
MFP Research Training Fellowship, 77
NIH Research Grants, 511
Washington University Chancellor's Graduate Fellowship Program for African Americans, 767

West European Countries

University of Wales, Bangor (UWB) Research Studentships, 753
University of Wales, Bangor Departmental Research Studentships, 753
Wingate Scholarships, 771

SOCIAL AND COMMUNITY PSYCHOLOGY

Any Country

ABF Fellowships in Law and Social Science, 38
BackCare Research Grants, 148
Center for Advanced Study in the Behavioral Sciences Postdoctoral Residential Fellowships, 245
D Scott Rogo Award for Parapsychological Literature, 553
Eileen J Garrett Scholarship, 553
Louise Kidder Early Career Award, 650
OISE/UT Graduate Assistantships, 541
OISE/UT Local Support, 541
Onassis Programme of Postgraduate Research Scholarships, 19
Parapsychology Foundation Grant, 553
Shelby Cullom Davis Center Research Projects, Research Fellowships, 625
SPSSI Applied Social Issues Internship Program, 650
SPSSI Grants-in-Aid Program, 650
SPSSI Social Issues Dissertation Award, 650
University of Manchester Research Studentships and Scholarships, 715
University of Stirling Research Studentships, 750

African Nations

Golda Meir Mount Carmel International Training Centre Assistance for Courses, 337
Golda Meir Mount Carmel International Training Centre Tuition and Maintenance Scholarships, 337

Australia

New South Wales Cancer Council Research Programme Grant, 528
New South Wales Cancer Council Research Project Grants, 528

Caribbean Countries

Golda Meir Mount Carmel International Training Centre Assistance for Courses, 337
Golda Meir Mount Carmel International Training Centre Tuition and Maintenance Scholarships, 337

East European Countries

Golda Meir Mount Carmel International Training Centre Assistance for Courses, 337
Golda Meir Mount Carmel International Training Centre Tuition and Maintenance Scholarships, 337

Far East

Golda Meir Mount Carmel International Training Centre Assistance for Courses, 337
Golda Meir Mount Carmel International Training Centre Tuition and Maintenance Scholarships, 337

Indian Sub-Continent

Golda Meir Mount Carmel International Training Centre Assistance for Courses, 337

Golda Meir Mount Carmel International Training Centre Tuition and Maintenance Scholarships, 337

Middle East

Golda Meir Mount Carmel International Training Centre Assistance for Courses, 337
Golda Meir Mount Carmel International Training Centre Tuition and Maintenance Scholarships, 337

South Africa

Golda Meir Mount Carmel International Training Centre Assistance for Courses, 337
Golda Meir Mount Carmel International Training Centre Tuition and Maintenance Scholarships, 337

South America

Golda Meir Mount Carmel International Training Centre Assistance for Courses, 337
Golda Meir Mount Carmel International Training Centre Tuition and Maintenance Scholarships, 337

United Kingdom

Alzheimer's Society Research Grants, 24
ESRC Research Studentships, 292
Mental Health Foundation Project Grant, 470
Parkinson's Disease Society Research Project Grant, 555
Parkinson's Disease Society Studentships and Junior/Senior Fellows, 555
University of Wales, Bangor (UWB) Research Studentships, 753
University of Wales, Bangor Departmental Research Studentships, 753

United States of America

COBASE Collaboration in Basic Science and Engineering, 516
MFP HIV/AIDS Research Training Fellowship, 76
MFP Research Training Fellowship, 77
National Research Service Award Mental Health and Adjustment in the Life Course, 717
NIH Research Grants, 511
ONR Postdoctoral Fellowship, 539
Washington University Chancellor's Graduate Fellowship Program for African Americans, 767

West European Countries

ESRC Research Studentships, 292
University of Wales, Bangor (UWB) Research Studentships, 753
University of Wales, Bangor Departmental Research Studentships, 753

CLINICAL PSYCHOLOGY

Any Country

Albert Ellis Institute Clinical Fellowship, 15
BackCare Research Grants, 148
Center for Advanced Study in the Behavioral Sciences Postdoctoral Residential Fellowships, 245
OISE/UT Graduate Assistantships, 541
OISE/UT Local Support, 541
Queen Elizabeth the Queen Mother Fellowship Award, 583
Research into Ageing Prize Studentships, 583
Research into Ageing Programme Grants, 584
Thomas Holloway Research Studentship, 602
University of Dundee Research Awards, 704
University of Manchester Research Studentships and Scholarships, 715
University of New Hampshire Postdoctoral Fellowships For Research on Family Violence, 720

Australia

New South Wales Cancer Council Research Programme Grant, 528
New South Wales Cancer Council Research Project Grants, 528

University of Western Sydney Postgraduate Research Award (UWSPRA), 755

New Zealand

University of Western Sydney Postgraduate Research Award (UWSPRA), 755

United Kingdom

Alzheimer's Society Research Grants, 24
Mental Health Foundation Project Grant, 470
Parkinson's Disease Society Research Project Grant, 555
Parkinson's Disease Society Studentships and Junior/Senior Fellows, 555
University of Wales, Bangor (UWB) Research Studentships, 753
University of Wales, Bangor Departmental Research Studentships, 753

United States of America

Indian Fellowship Program, 756
MFP Clinical Training Fellowship, 75
MFP Research Training Fellowship, 77
NIH Research Grants, 511
University of New Hampshire Postdoctoral Fellowships For Research on Family Violence, 720
Washington University Chancellor's Graduate Fellowship Program for African Americans, 767

West European Countries

University of Wales, Bangor (UWB) Research Studentships, 753
University of Wales, Bangor Departmental Research Studentships, 753

PERSONALITY PSYCHOLOGY

Any Country

BackCare Research Grants, 148
Center for Advanced Study in the Behavioral Sciences Postdoctoral Residential Fellowships, 245
University of Stirling Research Studentships, 750

United Kingdom

Alzheimer's Society Research Grants, 24
Mental Health Foundation Project Grant, 470
University of Wales, Bangor (UWB) Research Studentships, 753
University of Wales, Bangor Departmental Research Studentships, 753

United States of America

MFP HIV/AIDS Research Training Fellowship, 76
MFP Research Training Fellowship, 77
NIH Research Grants, 511

West European Countries

University of Wales, Bangor (UWB) Research Studentships, 753
University of Wales, Bangor Departmental Research Studentships, 753

INDUSTRIAL/ORGANISATIONAL PSYCHOLOGY

Any Country

BackCare Research Grants, 148
Center for Advanced Study in the Behavioral Sciences Postdoctoral Residential Fellowships, 245

United Kingdom

University of Wales, Bangor (UWB) Research Studentships, 753
University of Wales, Bangor Departmental Research Studentships, 753

United States of America

MFP HIV/AIDS Research Training Fellowship, 76

MFP Research Training Fellowship, 77
National Research Service Award Mental Health and Adjustment in the Life Course, 717

West European Countries

University of Wales, Bangor (UWB) Research Studentships, 753
University of Wales, Bangor Departmental Research Studentships, 753

PSYCHOMETRICS

Any Country

Center for Advanced Study in the Behavioral Sciences Postdoctoral Residential Fellowships, 245
ETS National Assessment of Educational Progress (NAEP) Visiting Scholar Program, 294
ETS Summer Program in Research for Graduate Students, 294
University of New Hampshire Postdoctoral Fellowships For Research on Family Violence, 720

United Kingdom

Alzheimer's Society Research Grants, 24
Mental Health Foundation Project Grant, 470
University of Wales, Bangor (UWB) Research Studentships, 753
University of Wales, Bangor Departmental Research Studentships, 753

United States of America

MFP HIV/AIDS Research Training Fellowship, 76
MFP Research Training Fellowship, 77
NIH Research Grants, 511
University of New Hampshire Postdoctoral Fellowships For Research on Family Violence, 720

West European Countries

University of Wales, Bangor (UWB) Research Studentships, 753
University of Wales, Bangor Departmental Research Studentships, 753

EDUCATIONAL PSYCHOLOGY

Any Country

BackCare Research Grants, 148
Center for Advanced Study in the Behavioral Sciences Postdoctoral Residential Fellowships, 245
Equiano Memorial Award, 666
OISE/UT Graduate Assistantships, 541
OISE/UT Local Support, 541
Onassis Programme of Postgraduate Research Scholarships, 19
University of Bristol Postgraduate Scholarships, 691
University of Dundee Research Awards, 704
University of Stirling Research Studentships, 750

United Kingdom

ESRC Research Studentships, 292
Mental Health Foundation Project Grant, 470
University of Wales, Bangor (UWB) Research Studentships, 753
University of Wales, Bangor Departmental Research Studentships, 753

United States of America

MFP HIV/AIDS Research Training Fellowship, 76
MFP Research Training Fellowship, 77
ONR Postdoctoral Fellowship, 539

West European Countries

ESRC Research Studentships, 292
University of Wales, Bangor (UWB) Research Studentships, 753
University of Wales, Bangor Departmental Research Studentships, 753

GEOGRAPHY (SOCIAL AND ECONOMIC)

Any Country

AAG General Research Fund, 126
ABF Fellowships in Law and Social Science, 38
Ahmanson and Getty Postdoctoral Fellowships, 678
AIAR Annual Professorship, 82
AIATSIS Research Grants, 139
Alexander S Onassis Programme of Research Grants, 18
Alexander S Onassis Research Grants, 18
ASCSA Fellowships, 79
ASCSA Summer Sessions, 80
Center for Advanced Study in the Behavioral Sciences Postdoctoral Residential Fellowships, 245
Center for Field Research Grants, 246
Central Queensland University Postgraduate Research Award, 248
CQU International Student Scholarship, 248
The J B Harley Research Fellowships in the History of Cartography, 418
Jane Addams/Andrew Carnegie Fellowships in Philanthropy, 368
Joseph L Fisher Dissertation Award, 584
Kennan Institute Short Term Grants, 431
M Alison Frantz Fellowship in Post-Classical Studies at The Gennadius Library (formerly known as the Gennadeion Fellowship), 81
Minnesota Historical Society Research Grant, 476
Onassis Programme of Postgraduate Research Scholarships, 19
Population Council Fellowships in Population and Social Sciences, 573
Queen Mary Research Studentships, 576
Queen's University of Belfast Research and Senior Visiting Research Fellowships, 576
Rhodes University Postdoctoral Fellowship, 586
SOAS Bursary, 622
SOAS Research Student Fellowships, 622
University of Bristol Postgraduate Scholarships, 691
University of Dundee Research Awards, 704
University of Glasgow Postgraduate Research Scholarships, 707
University of Manchester Research Studentships and Scholarships, 715
University of New England Research Scholarships, 719
UNPFA Diploma Course in Population Studies, 405
USC College Dissertation Fellowship, 749
USC College of Letters, Arts and Sciences Merit Award, 749
Violet Cressey-Marcks Fisher Travel Scholarship, 601
Warren Nystrom Fund Awards, 127
Woods Hole Oceanographic Institution Postdoctoral Awards in Marine Policy and Ocean Management, 777
Woods Hole Oceanographic Institution Research Fellowships in Marine Policy, 778
World Universities Network (WUN) Scholarship Scheme, 749

African Nations

University of Sussex Overseas Development Administration Shared Scholarship Scheme, 750

Australia

Wingate Scholarships, 771

British Commonwealth

British Institute of Archaeology at Ankara Research Grants, 169
British Institute of Archaeology at Ankara Travel Grants, 169
Wingate Scholarships, 771

Canada

IDRC Doctoral Research Awards, 400
Konrad Adenauer Research Award, 20
Wingate Scholarships, 771

East European Countries

CRF (Caledonian Research Foundation)/RSE European Visiting Research Fellowships, 613

Far East

University of Sussex Overseas Development Administration Shared Scholarship Scheme, 750

Indian Sub-Continent

University of Sussex Overseas Development Administration Shared Scholarship Scheme, 750
Wingate Scholarships, 771

New Zealand

Wingate Scholarships, 771

South Africa

Wingate Scholarships, 771

United Kingdom

British Institute of Archaeology at Ankara Research Grants, 169
British Institute of Archaeology at Ankara Travel Grants, 169
CRF (Caledonian Research Foundation)/RSE European Visiting Research Fellowships, 613
ESRC Research Studentships, 292
Grundy Educational Trust, 344
Polish Embassy Short-Term Bursaries, 571
Polish Government Postgraduate Scholarships Scheme, 572
Royal Geographical Society Expedition Research Grants, 600
University of Wales (Aberystwyth) Postgraduate Research Studentships, 752
Wingate Scholarships, 771

United States of America

COBASE Collaboration in Basic Science and Engineering, 516
Fulbright Distinguished Chairs Program, 270
Fulbright Senior Specialists Program, 271
IREX Grant Opportunities for US Scholars, 409
Kennan Institute Research Scholarship, 431
WWWC Americans and World Affairs Fellows Program, 780

West European Countries

CRF (Caledonian Research Foundation)/RSE European Visiting Research Fellowships, 613
ESRC Research Studentships, 292
Scholarship Foundation of the League for Finnish-American Societies, 621
Wingate Scholarships, 771

DEVELOPMENT STUDIES

Any Country

Center for Advanced Study in the Behavioral Sciences Postdoctoral Residential Fellowships, 245
Center for Field Research Grants, 246
Equiano Memorial Award, 666
Gilbert F White Postdoctoral Fellowship, 584
Gilbert Murray Trust Junior Awards, 335
Henry A Murray Dissertation Award Program, 356
Internship in Disarmament and Economic Justice, 774
Jane Addams/Andrew Carnegie Fellowships in Philanthropy, 368
Jeanne Humphrey Block Dissertation Award, 356
Joseph L Fisher Dissertation Award, 584
Kennan Institute Short Term Grants, 431
M Alison Frantz Fellowship in Post-Classical Studies at The Gennadius Library (formerly known as the Gennadeion Fellowship), 81
Paul H Nitze School of Advanced International Studies (SAIS) Financial Aid and Fellowships, 156
Queen's University of Belfast Research and Senior Visiting Research Fellowships, 576
Rhodes University Postdoctoral Fellowship, 586
Shell Centenary Scholarships and Shell Centenary Chevening Scholarships, 738
SOAS Bursary, 622

SOAS Research Student Fellowships, 622
University of Bristol Postgraduate Scholarships, 691
University of Glasgow Postgraduate Research Scholarships, 707
University of Manchester Research Studentships and Scholarships, 715
World Bank Cambridge Scholarships for Postgraduate Study, 220

African Nations

The Hastings Center International Visiting Scholars Program, 352
Institute for Housing and Urban Development Studies Fellowships for Courses, 376
University of Sussex Overseas Development Administration Shared Scholarship Scheme, 750

Australia

The Hastings Center International Visiting Scholars Program, 352
Wingate Scholarships, 771

British Commonwealth

ACU Development Fellowships, 127
The Hastings Center International Visiting Scholars Program, 352
Wingate Scholarships, 771

Canada

Alcohol Beverage Medical Research Foundation Research Project Grant, 17
Canadian Window on International Development, 399
CIDA Awards Program for Canadians, 225
IDRC Doctoral Research Awards, 400
India Studies Fellowship Competition, 625
Konrad Adenauer Research Award, 20
Wingate Scholarships, 771

Caribbean Countries

British Prize Scholarships for Postgraduate Study, 195
The Hastings Center International Visiting Scholars Program, 352
Institute for Housing and Urban Development Studies Fellowships for Courses, 376
Prince of Wales (Cable and Wireless) Chevening Cambridge Scholarships for PhD Study, 214
Prince of Wales (Cable and Wireless) Chevening Cambridge Scholarships for Postgraduate Study, 214

East European Countries

The Hastings Center International Visiting Scholars Program, 352
Institute for Housing and Urban Development Studies Fellowships for Courses, 376
Sasakawa Scholarship, 750
Soros Supplementary Grants Programme (SSGP), 544

Far East

The Hastings Center International Visiting Scholars Program, 352
Institute for Housing and Urban Development Studies Fellowships for Courses, 376
Prince of Wales (Cable and Wireless) Chevening Cambridge Scholarships for Postgraduate Study, 214
Sasakawa Scholarship, 750
University of Leeds International Fee Bursaries (Vietnam), 713
University of Sussex Overseas Development Administration Shared Scholarship Scheme, 750

Indian Sub-Continent

The Hastings Center International Visiting Scholars Program, 352
Institute for Housing and Urban Development Studies Fellowships for Courses, 376
Jawaharial Nehru Memorial Fund Cambridge Scholarship for PhD Study, 204
University of Sussex Overseas Development Administration Shared Scholarship Scheme, 750
Wingate Scholarships, 771

Middle East

The Hastings Center International Visiting Scholars Program, 352
Institute for Housing and Urban Development Studies Fellowships for Courses, 376

New Zealand

The Hastings Center International Visiting Scholars Program, 352
Wingate Scholarships, 771

South Africa

The Hastings Center International Visiting Scholars Program, 352
Institute for Housing and Urban Development Studies Fellowships for Courses, 376
Wingate Scholarships, 771

South America

The Hastings Center International Visiting Scholars Program, 352
Institute for Housing and Urban Development Studies Fellowships for Courses, 376

United Kingdom

ACU Development Fellowships, 127
ESRC Research Studentships, 292
The Hastings Center International Visiting Scholars Program, 352
Sasakawa Scholarship, 750
Wingate Scholarships, 771

United States of America

Alcohol Beverage Medical Research Foundation Research Project Grant, 17
IREX Grant Opportunities for US Scholars, 409
Kennan Institute Research Scholarship, 431
WWWC Americans and World Affairs Fellows Program, 780

West European Countries

ESRC Research Studentships, 292
The Hastings Center International Visiting Scholars Program, 352
Wingate Scholarships, 771

AREA AND CULTURAL STUDIES

Any Country

AIATSIS Research Grants, 139
Albert J Beveridge Grant, 53
Albin Salton Fellowship, 765
Andrew W Mellon Postdoctoral Fellowship, 769
ASCSA Fellowships, 79
ASCSA Summer Sessions, 80
Austro-American Association of Boston Scholarship, 147
Bernadotte E Schmitt Grants, 54
Bernard and Audre Rapoport Fellowships, 56
Camargo Fellowships, 185
Canadian Embassy (USA) Senior Fellowship Program, 228
CDI Internship, 246
Center for Advanced Study in the Behavioral Sciences Postdoctoral Residential Fellowships, 245
Center for Field Research Grants, 246
Central Queensland University Postgraduate Research Award, 248
CMRS Summer Fellowship, 680
CQU International Student Scholarship, 248
The CSA Adele Filene Travel Award, 269
The CSA Stella Blum Research Grant, 269
The CSA Travel Research Grant, 269
Deputy Chancellors Postdoctoral Research, 535
Equiano Memorial Award, 666
Ethel Marcus Memorial Fellowship, 57
External Faculty Fellowships, 663
Foundation Praemium Erasmianum Study Prize, 318
George A Barton Fellowship, 83
Harry Frank Guggenheim Dissertation Fellowship, 348
Harry Frank Guggenheim Research Program, 348

The Harvard Academy Program for International and Area Studies Predoctoral and Postdoctoral Fellowships, 350
Henry A Murray Dissertation Award Program, 356
Irish Research Funds, 417
The J B Harley Research Fellowships in the History of Cartography, 418
Jane Addams/Andrew Carnegie Fellowships in Philanthropy, 368
Jeanne Humphrey Block Dissertation Award, 356
Joyce A Tracy Fellowship, 29
Kennan Institute Short Term Grants, 431
La Trobe University Postgraduate Scholarship, 439
Loewenstein-Wiener Fellowship Awards, 57
M Alison Frantz Fellowship in Post-Classical Studies at The Gennadius Library (formerly known as the Gennadeion Fellowship), 81
Marguerite R Jacobs Memorial Award, 57
NEH Research Fellowships, 81
NHC Fellowships, 509
NTU One Year Postdoctoral Fellowship, 535
NTU Senior Research Fellowship, 536
NTU Three Year Postdoctoral Fellowship, 536
Paul H Nitze School of Advanced International Studies (SAIS) Financial Aid and Fellowships, 156
Paul Mellon Centre Rome Fellowship, 176
Queen Mary Research Studentships, 576
Queen's University of Belfast Research and Senior Visiting Research Fellowships, 576
Rabbi Frederic A Doppelt Memorial Fellowship, 57
Rabbi Levi A Olan Memorial Fellowship, 57
Rabbi Theodore S Levy Tribute Fellowship, 57
Rockefeller Archive Center Research Grant Program, 590
SAIIA Bradlow Fellowship, 660
Samuel H Kress Joint Athens-Jerusalem Fellowship, 81
Smithsonian Institution Predoctoral Fellowships, 636
Starkoff Fellowship, 57
University of Glasgow Postgraduate Research Scholarships, 707

Australia

University of Western Sydney Postgraduate Research Award (UWSPRA), 755
Wingate Scholarships, 771

British Commonwealth

ACU Development Fellowships, 127
Wingate Scholarships, 771

Canada

Alcohol Beverage Medical Research Foundation Research Project Grant, 17
IDRC Doctoral Research Awards, 400
India Studies Fellowship Competition, 625
Inuit Cultural Grants Program, 442
The Lorraine Allison Scholarship, 105
Wingate Scholarships, 771

East European Countries

AHRB Studentships in the Humanities (Competition A), 112
AHRB Studentships in the Humanities (Competition B), 112
Andrew W Mellon Foundation Fellowships, 82
Canon Foundation Award, 242
Kosciuszko Foundation Tuition Scholarships, 435
Open Society Sofia Central European University Scholarship, 542
Soros Supplementary Grants Programme (SSGP), 544

Far East

Daiwa Anglo-Japanese Foundation General Grants, 278

Indian Sub-Continent

Wingate Scholarships, 771

ASIAN

SOUTH ASIAN

EAST ASIAN

SOUTHEAST ASIAN

NORDIC

Any Country

Bernadotte E Schmitt Grants, 54
Center for Advanced Study in the Behavioral Sciences Postdoctoral Residential Fellowships, 245

Canada

Scholarships in Icelandic Studies, 476

East European Countries

AHRB Studentships in the Humanities (Competition A), 112
AHRB Studentships in the Humanities (Competition B), 112
Scholarships in Icelandic Studies, 476

United Kingdom

AHRB Studentships in the Humanities (Competition A), 112
AHRB Studentships in the Humanities (Competition B), 112
Scholarships in Icelandic Studies, 476

United States of America

The Norwegian Thanksgiving Fund Scholarship, 538
Scholarships in Icelandic Studies, 476
US Department of Education International Research and Studies Program, 757

West European Countries

Scholarships in Icelandic Studies, 476

CARIBBEAN

Any Country

Albert J Beveridge Grant, 53
Center for Advanced Study in the Behavioral Sciences Postdoctoral Residential Fellowships, 245
Equiano Memorial Award, 666
Huggins-Quarles Awards, 547

Canada

Canadian Window on International Development, 399

East European Countries

AHRB Studentships in the Humanities (Competition A), 112
AHRB Studentships in the Humanities (Competition B), 112

United Kingdom

AHRB Studentships in the Humanities (Competition A), 112
AHRB Studentships in the Humanities (Competition B), 112

United States of America

US Department of Education International Research and Studies Program, 757

LATIN AMERICAN

Any Country

Albert J Beveridge Grant, 53
Center for Advanced Study in the Behavioral Sciences Postdoctoral Residential Fellowships, 245
FAMSI Research Grant, 317
Paul H Nitze School of Advanced International Studies (SAIS) Financial Aid and Fellowships, 156
SAIIA Bradlow Fellowship, 660
Shell Centenary Scholarships and Shell Centenary Chevening Scholarships, 738

Canada

Canadian Window on International Development, 399

East European Countries

AHRB Studentships in the Humanities (Competition B), 112

United Kingdom

AHRB Studentships in the Humanities (Competition B), 112
Anglo-Brazilian Society Scholarship, 100

United States of America

US Department of Education International Research and Studies Program, 757
WWWC Americans and World Affairs Fellows Program, 780

PACIFIC AREA

Any Country

Center for Advanced Study in the Behavioral Sciences Postdoctoral Residential Fellowships, 245

East European Countries

AHRB Studentships in the Humanities (Competition A), 112
AHRB Studentships in the Humanities (Competition B), 112

United Kingdom

AHRB Studentships in the Humanities (Competition A), 112
AHRB Studentships in the Humanities (Competition B), 112

United States of America

CFR International Affairs Fellowship Programme in Japan, 272
US Department of Education International Research and Studies Program, 757

ABORIGINAL

Any Country

AIATSIS Research Grants, 139
Center for Advanced Study in the Behavioral Sciences Postdoctoral Residential Fellowships, 245
Deputy Chancellors Postdoctoral Research, 535
Harold White Fellowships, 512
NTU One Year Postdoctoral Fellowship, 535
NTU Senior Research Fellowship, 536
NTU Three Year Postdoctoral Fellowship, 536

East European Countries

AHRB Studentships in the Humanities (Competition A), 112
AHRB Studentships in the Humanities (Competition B), 112

United Kingdom

AHRB Studentships in the Humanities (Competition A), 112
AHRB Studentships in the Humanities (Competition B), 112

MIDDLE EASTERN

Any Country

AIAR Annual Professorship, 82
ASCSA Summer Sessions, 80
AUC International Graduate Fellowships in Arabic Studies, Middle East Studies and Sociology-Anthropology, 96
Bernadotte E Schmitt Grants, 54
Center for Advanced Study in the Behavioral Sciences Postdoctoral Residential Fellowships, 245
Equiano Memorial Award, 666
George A Barton Fellowship, 83
Henri Frankfort Fellowship, 765
Jacob Hirsch Fellowship, 80
M Alison Frantz Fellowship in Post-Classical Studies at The Gennadius Library (forme ly known as the Gennadeion Fellowship), 81
NEH Research Fellowships, 81
Samuel H Kress Joint Athens-Jerusalem Fellowship, 81

British Commonwealth

British Institute of Archaeology at Ankara Research Grants, 169
British Institute of Archaeology at Ankara Travel Grants, 169
Wingate Scholarships, 771

Canada

Konrad Adenauer Research Award, 20
Wingate Scholarships, 771

Caribbean Countries

Institute for Housing and Urban Development Studies Fellowships for Courses, 376

East European Countries

European Gardens Horticulture Scholarships, 304
Institute for Housing and Urban Development Studies Fellowships for Courses, 376
Natural History Museum Sys-Resource, 522
Soros Supplementary Grants Programme (SSGP), 544

Far East

Asian Cultural Council Fellowship Grants Program, 123
Institute for Housing and Urban Development Studies Fellowships for Courses, 376

Indian Sub-Continent

Institute for Housing and Urban Development Studies Fellowships for Courses, 376
Wingate Scholarships, 771

Middle East

Institute for Housing and Urban Development Studies Fellowships for Courses, 376

New Zealand

Wingate Scholarships, 771

South Africa

Institute for Housing and Urban Development Studies Fellowships for Courses, 376
Wingate Scholarships, 771

South America

Institute for Housing and Urban Development Studies Fellowships for Courses, 376

United Kingdom

British Institute of Archaeology at Ankara Research Grants, 169
British Institute of Archaeology at Ankara Travel Grants, 169
European Gardens Horticulture Scholarships, 304
University of Wales, Bangor (UWB) Research Studentships, 753
Wingate Scholarships, 771

United States of America

Asian Cultural Council Fellowship Grants Program, 123
David Baumgardt Memorial Fellowship, 443
Earthwatch Education Awards, 290
Fulbright Senior Specialists Program, 271
Ian Axford (New Zealand) Fellowships in Public Policy, 263
IREX Grant Opportunities for US Scholars, 409
Norwegian Ministry of Foreign Affairs Travel Grants, 538

West European Countries

David Baumgardt Memorial Fellowship, 443
European Gardens Horticulture Scholarships, 304
Fritz Halbers Fellowship, 444
Natural History Museum Sys-Resource, 522
University of Wales, Bangor (UWB) Research Studentships, 753
Wingate Scholarships, 771

ANCIENT CIVILISATIONS (EGYPTOLOGY, ASSYRIOLOGY)

Any Country

ANS Graduate Fellowship, 68
ASCSA Fellowships, 79
ASCSA Research Fellow in Faunal Studies, 79
ASCSA Summer Sessions, 80
ASOR Mesopotamian Fellowship, 82
External Faculty Fellowships, 663
FAMSI Research Grant, 317
Frances M Schwartz Fellowship, 68
Grants for ANS Summer Seminar in Numismatics, 68
J Lawrence Angel Fellowship in Human Skeletal Studies, 80
NEH Research Fellowships, 81
NHC Fellowships, 509
Onassis Programme of Postgraduate Research Scholarships, 19
Samuel H Kress Joint Athens-Jerusalem Fellowship, 81
Shaykh Hamad Fellowship in Islamic Numismatics, 68
SOAS Research Student Fellowships, 622

African Nations

British School of Archaeology in Iraq Grants, 178

Australia

British School of Archaeology in Iraq Grants, 178
Wingate Scholarships, 771

British Commonwealth

British Institute of Archaeology at Ankara Research Grants, 169
British Institute of Archaeology at Ankara Travel Grants, 169
British School of Archaeology in Iraq Grants, 178
Wingate Scholarships, 771

Canada

British School of Archaeology in Iraq Grants, 178
Wingate Scholarships, 771

East European Countries

AHRB Studentships in the Humanities (Competition A), 112
AHRB Studentships in the Humanities (Competition B), 112
Soros Supplementary Grants Programme (SSGP), 544

Far East

British School of Archaeology in Iraq Grants, 178

Indian Sub-Continent

British School of Archaeology in Iraq Grants, 178
Wingate Scholarships, 771

New Zealand

British School of Archaeology in Iraq Grants, 178
Wingate Scholarships, 771

South Africa

British School of Archaeology in Iraq Grants, 178
Wingate Scholarships, 771

United Kingdom

AHRB Studentships in the Humanities (Competition A), 112
AHRB Studentships in the Humanities (Competition B), 112
British Institute of Archaeology at Ankara Research Grants, 169
British Institute of Archaeology at Ankara Travel Grants, 169
British School of Archaeology in Iraq Grants, 178
Wingate Scholarships, 771

United States of America

IREX Grant Opportunities for US Scholars, 409

West European Countries

Wingate Scholarships, 771

SERVICE TRADES

GENERAL

Any Country

AIATSIS Research Grants, 139
Central Queensland University Postgraduate Research Award, 248
CQU International Student Scholarship, 248
Deputy Chancellors Postdoctoral Research, 535
Field Psych Trust Grant, 310
Massey Doctoral Scholarship, 461
NTU One Year Postdoctoral Fellowship, 535
NTU Three Year Postdoctoral Fellowship, 536
Southern Cross University Postgraduate Research Scholarships, 660
University of Dundee Research Awards, 704

African Nations

Friends of Peterhouse Bursary, 561
Fulbright Postdoctoral Research and Lecturing Awards for Non-US Citizens, 270
Merton College Reed Foundation Scholarship, 732

Australia

Friends of Peterhouse Bursary, 561
Fulbright Awards, 143
Fulbright Postdoctoral Fellowships, 143
Fulbright Postdoctoral Research and Lecturing Awards for Non-US Citizens, 270

British Commonwealth

Friends of Peterhouse Bursary, 561
Merton College Reed Foundation Scholarship, 732

Canada

Friends of Peterhouse Bursary, 561
Fulbright Postdoctoral Research and Lecturing Awards for Non-US Citizens, 270
PRA Fellowships, 549

Caribbean Countries

Friends of Peterhouse Bursary, 561
Merton College Reed Foundation Scholarship, 732
PRA Fellowships, 549

East European Countries

Friends of Peterhouse Bursary, 561
Fulbright Postdoctoral Research and Lecturing Awards for Non-US Citizens, 270
Merton College Reed Foundation Scholarship, 732

Far East

Friends of Peterhouse Bursary, 561
Fulbright Postdoctoral Research and Lecturing Awards for Non-US Citizens, 270
Merton College Reed Foundation Scholarship, 732

Indian Sub-Continent

Friends of Peterhouse Bursary, 561
Fulbright Postdoctoral Research and Lecturing Awards for Non-US Citizens, 270
Merton College Reed Foundation Scholarship, 732

Middle East

Friends of Peterhouse Bursary, 561
Fulbright Postdoctoral Research and Lecturing Awards for Non-US Citizens, 270
Merton College Reed Foundation Scholarship, 732

New Zealand

Friends of Peterhouse Bursary, 561

South Africa

Friends of Peterhouse Bursary, 561
Fulbright Postdoctoral Research and Lecturing Awards for Non-US Citizens, 270
Isie Smuts Research Award, 658

South America

Friends of Peterhouse Bursary, 561
Fulbright Commission (Argentina) Master's Program, 325
Fulbright Postdoctoral Research and Lecturing Awards for Non-US Citizens, 270
Merton College Reed Foundation Scholarship, 732
PRA Fellowships, 549

United Kingdom

Canada Memorial Foundation Scholarships, 222
Fulbright Postdoctoral Research and Lecturing Awards for Non-US Citizens, 270
Hilda Martindale Exhibitions, 358
Sheffield Hallam University Research Studentships, 625

United States of America

Congress Bundestag Youth Exchange for Young Professionals, 245
Friends of Peterhouse Bursary, 561
Fulbright Scholar Program for US Citizens, 271
PRA Fellowships, 549

West European Countries

Friends of Peterhouse Bursary, 561
Fulbright Postdoctoral Research and Lecturing Awards for Non-US Citizens, 270
Janson Johan Helmich Scholarships and Travel Grants, 421
Sheffield Hallam University Research Studentships, 625

HOTEL AND RESTAURANT

Any Country

University of Dundee Research Awards, 704

United States of America

Congress Bundestag Youth Exchange for Young Professionals, 245
National Restaurant Association Teacher Work-Study Grants, 293

HOTEL MANAGEMENT

Any Country

University of Dundee Research Awards, 704

United States of America

Congress Bundestag Youth Exchange for Young Professionals, 245
National Restaurant Association Teacher Work-Study Grants, 293

COOKING AND CATERING

United States of America

Congress Bundestag Youth Exchange for Young Professionals, 245

RETAILING

United States of America

Congress Bundestag Youth Exchange for Young Professionals, 245

TOURISM

Any Country

AIATSIS Research Grants, 139

TRADE, CRAFT AND INDUSTRIAL TECHNIQUES

GENERAL

United Kingdom

British Schools and Universities Foundation May and Ward Scholarships, 179
Canada Memorial Foundation Scholarships, 222
Hilda Martindale Exhibitions, 358

United States of America

British Schools and Universities Foundation May and Ward Scholarships, 179
Congress Bundestag Youth Exchange for Young Professionals, 245
Early American Industries Association Research Grants Program, 290
Friends of Peterhouse Bursary, 561
Japanese American Citizens League Scholarship and Award Program, 422
North Dakota Indian Scholarship, 535
PRA Fellowships, 549

West European Countries

Friends of Peterhouse Bursary, 561
Janson Johan Helmich Scholarships and Travel Grants, 421
Royal Society University Research Fellowships, 610

BUILDING TRADES

United States of America

Congress Bundestag Youth Exchange for Young Professionals, 245
Early American Industries Association Research Grants Program, 290

ELECTRICAL/ELECTRONIC EQUIPMENT AND MAINTENANCE TECHNIQUES

Any Country

Scholarships for Advanced Study in Baking Science and Technology and/or Maintenance Engineering, 55

United States of America

AIB Scholarships for Study in Maintenance Engineering, 55
Congress Bundestag Youth Exchange for Young Professionals, 245

METAL TRADES TECHNIQUES

United States of America

Congress Bundestag Youth Exchange for Young Professionals, 245
Early American Industries Association Research Grants Program, 290

MECHANICAL EQUIPMENT AND MAINTENANCE TECHNIQUES

Any Country

Scholarships for Advanced Study in Baking Science and Technology and/or Maintenance Engineering, 55

United States of America

AIB Scholarships for Study in Maintenance Engineering, 55
Congress Bundestag Youth Exchange for Young Professionals, 245
Early American Industries Association Research Grants Program, 290

WOOD TECHNOLOGY

United Kingdom

University of Wales, Bangor (UWB) Research Studentships, 753

United States of America

Congress Bundestag Youth Exchange for Young Professionals, 245

Early American Industries Association Research Grants Program, 290

West European Countries

University of Wales, Bangor (UWB) Research Studentships, 753

HEATING, AIR CONDITIONING AND REFRIGERATION TECHNOLOGY

Any Country

ASHRAE Grants-in-Aid for Graduate Students, 92
Scholarships for Advanced Study in Baking Science and Technology and/or Maintenance Engineering, 55

United States of America

AIB Scholarships for Study in Maintenance Engineering, 55
Congress Bundestag Youth Exchange for Young Professionals, 245

LEATHER TECHNIQUES

Any Country

Rhodes University Postdoctoral Fellowship, 586

United States of America

Early American Industries Association Research Grants Program, 290

TEXTILE TECHNIQUES

Any Country

Center for Field Research Grants, 246
The CSA Adele Filene Travel Award, 269
The CSA Stella Blum Research Grant, 269
The CSA Travel Research Grant, 269
Textile Institute Scholarship, 672

United States of America

Early American Industries Association Research Grants Program, 290

PAPER AND PACKAGING TECHNOLOGY

Any Country

Women's Studio Workshop Artists' Fellowships, 775
Women's Studio Workshop Internships, 776

United States of America

Congress Bundestag Youth Exchange for Young Professionals, 245
Early American Industries Association Research Grants Program, 290

GRAPHIC ARTS TECHNIQUES

Any Country

The J B Harley Research Fellowships in the History of Cartography, 418
Women's Studio Workshop Internships, 776

United States of America

Early American Industries Association Research Grants Program, 290

PRINTING

Any Country

Munby Fellowship in Bibliography, 221
Women's Studio Workshop Artists' Book Residencies, 775
Women's Studio Workshop Artists' Fellowships, 775

Women's Studio Workshop Production Grants, 776

East European Countries
FEMS Fellowship, 310

United Kingdom
FEMS Fellowship, 310

United States of America
Early American Industries Association Research Grants Program, 290

West European Countries
FEMS Fellowship, 310

PUBLISHING AND BOOK TRADE

Any Country
Munby Fellowship in Bibliography, 221

East European Countries
FEMS Fellowship, 310

United Kingdom
FEMS Fellowship, 310

United States of America
Early American Industries Association Research Grants Program, 290

West European Countries
FEMS Fellowship, 310

LABORATORY TECHNIQUES

United States of America
Congress Bundestag Youth Exchange for Young Professionals, 245

OPTICAL TECHNOLOGY

Any Country
Berthold Leibinger Innovationspreis, 150

United States of America
Congress Bundestag Youth Exchange for Young Professionals, 245

TRANSPORT AND COMMUNICATIONS

GENERAL

Any Country
AIATSIS Research Grants, 139
The Alberta Research Council Scholarship, 692
Canadian Department of Foreign Affairs Faculty Enrichment Program, 231
Canadian Department of Foreign Affairs Faculty Research Program, 231
Canadian Department of Foreign Affairs Institutional Research Program, 231
Concordia University Graduate Fellowships, 266
David J Azrieli Graduate Fellowship, 266
Indian Council of Social Science Research General Fellowships, 367
John F Hooper Bursary Scheme, 383
Matsumae International Foundation Research Fellowship, 461
National Port Employers' Fund, 384
Rees Jeffreys Road Fund Bursaries, 580

Rees Jeffreys Road Fund Research Grants, 580
Stanley G French Graduate Fellowship, 267

African Nations
ABCCF Student Grant, 103
Friends of Peterhouse Bursary, 561
Fulbright Postdoctoral Research and Lecturing Awards for Non-US Citizens, 270
Merton College Reed Foundation Scholarship, 732

Australia
Coral Sea Scholarship, 143
Friends of Peterhouse Bursary, 561
Fulbright Awards, 143
Fulbright Postdoctoral Fellowships, 143
Fulbright Postdoctoral Research and Lecturing Awards for Non-US Citizens, 270
Fulbright Postgraduate Studentships, 144

British Commonwealth
Friends of Peterhouse Bursary, 561
Merton College Reed Foundation Scholarship, 732

Canada
Friends of Peterhouse Bursary, 561
Fulbright Postdoctoral Research and Lecturing Awards for Non-US Citizens, 270
J W McConnell Memorial Fellowships, 266
NSERC Postdoctoral Fellowships, 524
NSERC Postgraduate Scholarships, 524
PRA Fellowships, 549
TAC Scholarships, 677

Caribbean Countries
Friends of Peterhouse Bursary, 561
Merton College Reed Foundation Scholarship, 732
PRA Fellowships, 549

East European Countries
Friends of Peterhouse Bursary, 561
Fulbright Postdoctoral Research and Lecturing Awards for Non-US Citizens, 270
Merton College Reed Foundation Scholarship, 732

Far East
Friends of Peterhouse Bursary, 561
Fulbright Postdoctoral Research and Lecturing Awards for Non-US Citizens, 270
Merton College Reed Foundation Scholarship, 732

Indian Sub-Continent
Friends of Peterhouse Bursary, 561
Fulbright Postdoctoral Research and Lecturing Awards for Non-US Citizens, 270
Indian Council of Social Science Research Senior Fellowships, 368
Merton College Reed Foundation Scholarship, 732

Middle East
ABCCF Student Grant, 103
Friends of Peterhouse Bursary, 561
Fulbright Postdoctoral Research and Lecturing Awards for Non-US Citizens, 270
Merton College Reed Foundation Scholarship, 732

New Zealand
Friends of Peterhouse Bursary, 561
Fulbright Postdoctoral Research and Lecturing Awards for Non-US Citizens, 270

South Africa
Friends of Peterhouse Bursary, 561

INDEX OF AWARDS

INDEX OF DISCONTINUED
AWARDS

Alberta Heritage Foundation for Medical Research (AHFMR), *Canada*
Alberta Heritage Dental Fellowships

American Academy of Child and Adolescent Psychiatry, *United States of America*
James Comer Minority Research Fellowship for Medical Students

American Accounting Association (AAA), *United States of America*
AAA Fellowship Programme in Accounting

American Antiquarian Society (AAS), *United States of America*
The Richard F and Virginia P Morgan Fellowship

American Association for Cancer Research (AACR), *United States of America*
AACR Bruce F Cain Memorial Award
AACR American Cancer Society Award for Research Excellence in Cancer Epidemiology and Prevention
AACR G H A Clowes Memorial Award
AACR Joseph H Burchenal AACR Clinical Research Award
AACR Richard and Hinda Rosenthal Foundation Award
AACR Peczoller International Award for Cancer Research
AACR Susan G Komen Breast Cancer Foundation Career Development Award
AACR Gerald B Grindley Memorial Scholar-in-Training

American College of Obstetricians and Gynecologists (ACOG), *United States of America*
ACOG/Ethicon Research Award for Innovations in Gynecological Surgery

American Council of Learned Societies (ACLS), *United States of America*
The Abe Fellowship Program

American Digestive Health Foundation (ADHF), *United States of America*
AGA Student Abstract Prizes
Wilson-Cook Endoscopic Research Career Development Awards
ASGE Endoscopic Research and Outcomes and Effectiveness Awards
ADHF TAP Pharmaceuticals, Inc. Outcomes Research Awards

American Library Association (ALA), *United States of America*
ASCLA Research Grant
Herbert and Virginia White Award for Promoting Librarianship

American Nuclear Society (ANS), *United States of America*
Alvin M Weinberg Medal

American Numismatic Society (ANS), *United States of America*
ANS Fellowship in Roman Studies

American Psychiatric Association, *United States of America*
APA/Glaxo Wellcome Fellowship

American Research Center in Egypt (ARCE), *United States of America*
Egyptian Development Fellowships

American Schools of Oriental Research (ASOR), *United States of America*
NEH Postdoctoral Fellowships
USIA Junior Fellowships

American Society of Hypertension, *United States of America*
American Society of Hypertension/Hoechst Marion Roussel Clinical Fellowship in Hypertension

The Arc of the United States, *United States of America*
The Arc of the United States Research Grant

Arthritis Foundation, *United States of America*
Arthritis Foundation Biomedical Science Grant
Arthritis Foundation Clinical Science Grant

The Arts Council of Ireland, *Ireland*
Arts Council of Ireland Choreographers Bursary
Arts Council of Ireland Postgraduate Scholarships for Architecture
Arts Council of Ireland Bursary in Contemporary Architectural Criticism
Arts Council of Ireland Architectural Research Bursary
Arts Council of Ireland Artists in Residence (Schools)
Arts Council of Ireland Artists in Residence (Youthwork)
Arts Council of Ireland Play Directors in Residence
Arts Council of Ireland Dance Commission Scheme
Arts Council of Ireland Opera Commissioning Scheme
Arts Council of Ireland Playwrights Commissioning Scheme
Arts Council of Ireland Materials/Equipment Grants and Documentation Grants
Arts Council of Ireland Studio Rental Assistance Grants
Arts Council of Ireland Dance Project Scheme
Arts Council of Ireland Opera Training Awards
Arts Council of Ireland Visual Arts Bursaries
Arts Council of Ireland Apprentice/Assistant Scheme for Visual Artists
Arts Council of Ireland Bursaries for Advanced Instrumentalists and Singers
Arts Council of Ireland Composers' Bursaries
Arts Council of Ireland Conductors Study Awards
Arts Council of Ireland Studio Rental Assistance Grant
Arts Council of Ireland Film and Video Awards
Arts Council of Ireland Bursaries in Literature
Arts Council of Ireland Awards to Professional Dance Teachers
Arts Council of Ireland Awards to Designers for the Stage
Arts Council of Ireland Awards for Play Directors
Arts Council of Ireland Visual Arts Postgraduate Scholarships
Arts Council of Ireland Awards to Choreographers
Arts Council of Ireland Awards to Professional Dancers
Arts Council of Ireland Composers Commission Scheme
Arts Council of Ireland Travel Awards to Creative Artists
Arts Council of Ireland Arts Educators' Awards

Arts Council of Wales, *Wales*
ACW Awards for Individual Visual Artists and Craftspeople
ACW Awards for Career Development of Individual Visual Artists and Craftspeople
ACW Music Projects Grants
ACW Barclays Stage Partners
ACW Pilot Training Grants Scheme
ACW Dance and Drama Group Sponsored Training Initiatives
ACW Playwright's Bursaries
ACW Playwrighting Commissions and Writers On Attachment
ACW Visiting Arts Fund
ACW Dance and Drama Development and Training Awards
ACW Director Training
ACW Writers on Tour and Literature Residencies
ACW Capital Grants
ACW Individual Craftspeople Awards
ACW New Music Commission Support
ACW Inter-link
ACW Grants to Periodicals, The Franchise Scheme

Arts International, *United States of America*
Cintas Fellowships
INROADS

Association of Universities and Colleges of Canada (AUCC), *Canada*
CIBC Youthvision Graduate Research Award Program

Asthma Society of Canada, *Canada*
Asthma Society of Canada Research Grants

Asthma Victoria, *Australia*
Lilian Roxon Memorial Research Trust Travel Grant

The British Council, *United States of America*
British Marshall Scholarships

British Institute of Radiology (BIR), *England*
Flude Memorial Prize

The British School at Rome (BSR), *England*
Henry Moore Sculpture Fellowship at the BSR

Broadcast Education Association (BEA) Scholarship Committee, *United States of America*
The Broadcasters' Association Shane Media Scholarships

Cambridge Commonwealth Trust, Cambridge Overseas Trust and Associated Trusts, *England*
Charles Wallace Pakistan Trust Bursaries
Lady Noon Bursary
Citibank Cambridge Scholarship for the MPhil degree in Management Studies
Nedbank and Old Mutual Cambridge Scholarships
President Aylwin Studentship
Monash Scholarship
Charles Wallace Bangladesh and Pakistan Trusts DFID Scholarships
CEU Soros Cambridge Scholarships

Canadian Cystic Fibrosis Foundation (CCFF), *Canada*
Canadian Cystic Fibrosis Foundation/Canadian Institutes of Health Research (CIHR) Fellowships

Canadian Forestry Foundation, *Canada*
Canadian Forestry Foundation Forest Education Scholarship
Canadian Forestry Foundation Trees and People (TAP) Award

Canadian Home Economics Association (CHEA), *Canada*
Nestlé Canada, Inc. Scholarship

The Cancer Research Society, Inc., *Canada*
Cancer Research Society, Inc. (Canada) Predoctoral Fellowships

Clive and Vera Ramaciotti Foundations, *Australia*
Ramaciotto Travel Awards

College of Occupational Therapists, *England*
Lord Byers Memorial Fund

Council for International Exchange of Scholars (CIES), *United States of America*
NATO Advanced Research Fellowships and Institutional Grants

Cranfield University, School of Management, *England*
McKinsey MBA Scholarship

Department of Education and Science (Ireland), *Ireland*
Irish Government Scholarship

Engineering and Physical Sciences Research Council (EPSRC), *England*
EPSRC Standard Research Studentships
EPSRC Advanced Course and Research Master Studentships
EPSRC Studentships

Epilepsy Foundation, *United States of America*
EF International Clinical Research Fellowship

German Academic Exchange Service (DAAD), *United States of America*
Berlin - European Metropolis of the Third Millennium
DAAD Grants for Canadians
DAAD Fulbright Grants
DAAD Program for International Lawyers

Glaucoma Research Foundation, *United States of America*
Clinician-Scientist Fellowship

Grimsby International Singers Competition, *England*
Alec Redshaw Memorial Awards

The Grundy Educational Trust, *England*
Grundy Educational Trust Award

Harvard University, *United States of America*
MacArthur Fellowships on Transnational Security Issues

Health Research Council of New Zealand (HRC), *New Zealand*
HRC Postdoctoral Fellowship

Henry A Murray Research Center, *United States of America*
Radcliffe Institute Fellowships

Horserace Betting Levy Board (HBLB), *England*
Horserace Betting Levy Board Senior Equine Clinical Scholarships
Horserace Betting Levy Board Veterinary Research Training Scholarship

IMC Graduate School of Management, *Hungary*
Demján Scholarship

Imperial College of Science, Technology and Medicine, *England*
Concrete Structures Bursaries

Indiana Historical Society, *United States of America*
Indiana Historical Society Graduate Fellowships in History

INSEAD, *France*
The Minute Maid Company Scholarship
The Estée Lauder INSEAD Scholarship
Eric Salmon & Partners Scholarship
INSEAD Alumni Fund (IAF) Scholarships for Central and Eastern European Countries
Danone MBA Scholarship
IAF Diversity Scholarship for Africa

Institute for Humane Studies (IHS), *United States of America*
IHS Young Communicators Fellowship

The Institution of Electrical Engineers (IEE), *England*
IEE Conference International Bursary

International Centre for Diarrhoeal Disease Research (ICDDR), *Bangladesh*
ICDDR Health Research Training Fellowship

International Development Research Centre (IDRC), *Canada*
Ecosystem Approaches to Human Health Training Award with a Particular Focus on Gender

International Foundation of Employee Benefit Plans (IFEBP), *United States of America*
IFEBP Grants for Research

International Institute for Management Development (IMD), *Switzerland*
President's Scholarship

International Institute for Population Sciences (IIPS), *India*
IIPS Diploma in Population Studies

International Mathematical Union (IMU), *United States of America*
International Mathematical Union Fellowship
IMU Visiting Mathematician Programme

International Research and Exchange Board (IREX), *United States of America*
IREX Mongolia Research Fellowship Program

International Telecommunication Union (ITU), *Switzerland*
International Telecommunication Union Fellowship

Kosciuszko Foundation, *United States of America*
The Kosciuszko Foundation Sembrich Voice Competition
Kosciuszko Foundation Fellowships and Grants for Polish Citizens
Summer Study Abroad Programs in Polish Language and Culture

Marcel Hicter Foundation, *Belgium*
Council of Europe Travel Bursary Scheme

Meet The Composer, Inc., *United States of America*
Meet The Composer New Residencies

Menzies Centre for Australian Studies, *England*
Visual Arts Fellowship

The Metropolitan Museum of Art, *United States of America*
MMA Summer Internships for Graduate Students
MMA Roswell L Gilpatric Internship
The Metropolitan Museum of Art Lifchez/Stronach Curatorial Internship
MMA Six Month Internship
MMA Summer Internships for College Students

Monash University, *Australia*
Logan Research Fellowships

National Cancer Institute of Canada (NCIC), *Canada*
Terry Fox New Frontiers Initiative

National Federation of the Blind (NFB), *United States of America*
Frank Walton Horn Memorial Scholarship
Melva T Owen Memorial Scholarship

National Heart Foundation of Australia, *Australia*
Warren McDonald International Fellowship

National Historical Publications and Records Commission (NHPRC), *United States of America*
NHPRC Documentary Editing and Archival and Records Management Grants

National Kidney Research Fund (NKRF), *England*
NKRF Special Project Grants

National University of Singapore (NUS), *Singapore*
Lee Foundation and Tan Sri Dr Runme Shaw Foundation Fellowships in Orthopaedic Surgery
Mobil-NUS Postgraduate Medical Research Scholarship

Natural Sciences and Engineering Research Council of Canada (NSERC), *Canada*
NSERC New Faculty Support Grants

New Energy and Industrial Technology Development Organisation (NEDO), *Japan*
International Joint Research Grant Programme (NEDO Grant)

North Atlantic Treaty Organization (NATO), *Belgium*
NATO Euro-Atlantic Partnership Council Fellowships Programme (NATO-EPAC)

Philadelphia Museum of Art, *United States of America*
Arts Education Development Project (Program Advancement Grants)

Purina Mills, Inc., *United States of America*
Purina Mills Research Fellowships

The Radcliffe Institute for Advanced Study, *United States of America*
Bunting Institute Biomedical Research Fellowship
Marian Cabot Putnam Fellowship
Bunting Institute Science Scholars Fellowship
Bunting Institute Affiliation
Berkshire Summer Fellowship
Bunting Institute Peace Fellowship

Radio and Television News Directors Foundation (RTNDF), *United States of America*
RTNDF Scholarships

The Reid Trust for the Higher Education of Women, *England*
Reid Trust Awards

Royal College of Obstetricians and Gynaecologists (RCOG), *England*
RCOG Green-Armytage Anglo American Lectureship

Royal Holloway, University of London, *England*
University of London Awards

Royal Irish Academy, *Ireland*
Royal Irish Academy National Committee for Biochemistry Travel Bursary Scheme

Scottish Opera, *Scotland*
John Noble Bursary Award

Shastri Indo-Canadian Institute (SICI), *Canada*
Shastri Indo-Canadian Institute Women and Development Fellowships
Shastri Indo-Canadian Institute Summer Programme
Shastri Indo-Canadian Institute Language Training Fellowship

Sigma Theta Tau International, *United States of America*
Sigma Theta Tau International/Glaxo Wellcome Prescriptive Practice Grant
Sigma Theta Tau International/Glaxo Wellcome New Investigator Mentor Grant
Sigma Theta Tau International/Mead Johnson Nutritionals Perinatal Grant

The Smith and Nephew Foundation, *England*
Smith and Nephew Foundation Medical Research Fellowships
Smith and Nephew Nursing Research Scholarships

Social Science Research Council (SSRC), *United States of America*
The SSRC International Predissertation Field Research Fellowships

Social Sciences and Humanities Research Council of Canada (SSHRC), *Canada*
Ocean Management National Research Network Initiative

Stanford Humanities Center, *United States of America*
Shared Research Group Fellowships for Senior Scholars
Shared Research Group Fellowships for Postdoctoral Scholars

The Textile Institute, *England*
Lee 400 Educational Trust

United States Educational Foundation in India (USEFI), *India*
USEFI Fellowships in Educational Administration

University of Cambridge, *England*
Frazer Studentship in Social Anthropology
Cambridge Overseas Bursaries in Social Anthropology

The University of Kent at Canterbury, *England*
The University of Kent at Canterbury School of Drama, Film and Visual Arts Scholarships

The University of Leeds, *England*
International Fee Bursaries (Indonesia)
Unilever Thai Holdings - Leeds University - FCO Chevening Scholarships
International Fee Bursaries (Brazil)
International Fee Bursaries (Malaysia)

University of Maryland, *United States of America*
International Music Competitions

University of Oxford, *England*
Trinity College Sarnia Scholarship
Oxford Overseas Bursaries
Peter Jenks Vietnam Scholarship
St Antony's College Rothschild Scholarship in Economics
Wolfson College The Hargreaves-Mawdsley Studentship
Somerville College Levick Sisters Senior Scholarship
Korea Foundation Scholarship in Korean Studies
Museveni Scholarship
Linacre College Unipart Scholarship
St Hugh's College Rawnsley Studentship
Somerville College Ruth Adler Scholarship

The University of Reading, *England*
Otway Cave Scholarship

University of Regina, *Canada*
Regina Graduate Scholarships
Regina Teaching Assistantships

The US-UK Fulbright Commission, *England*
Royal Society Fulbright Scholarships
Royal Society-Fulbright Postdoctoral Science Fellowship Programme to the USA

INDEX OF AWARDING
ORGANISATIONS

British Association for Canadian Studies (BACS), *Scotland*, 159
British Association of Plastic Surgeons (BAPS), *England*, 160
The British Council, *United States of America*, 160
British Dental Association, *England*, 161
British Ecological Society (BES), *England*, 161
British Federation of Women Graduates (BFWG), *England*, 163
British Heart Foundation (BHF), *England*, 166
British Hyperlipidaemia Association, *England*, 168
British Institute in Eastern Africa, *Kenya*, 169
British Institute in Paris, *France*, 169
British Institute of Archaeology at Ankara, *England*, 169
British Institute of Radiology (BIR), *England*, 170
British Journal of Surgery, *England*, 170
The British Leprosy Relief Association (LEPRA), *England*, 171
The British Library - Map Library, *England*, 171
British Lung Foundation, *England*, 171
British Medical Association (BMA), *England*, 171
British Pharmacological Society, *England*, 174
British Retinitis Pigmentosa Society (BRPS), *England*, 174
British School at Athens, *Greece*, 175
The British School at Rome (BSR), *England*, 175
British School of Archaeology in Iraq, *England*, 178
The British Schools and Universities Foundation, Inc. (BSUF), *England*, 178
British Sociological Association (BSA), *England*, 179
The British Universities North America Club (BUNAC), *England*, 179
British Vascular Foundation, *England*, 180
British Veterinary Association, *England*, 180
Broad Medical Research Program (BMRP), *United States of America*, 180
Broadcast Education Association (BEA) Scholarship Committee, *United States of America*, 181
The Broadcasting Corporations of the Federal Republic of Germany, *Germany*, 182
Brookhaven National Laboratory, *United States of America*, 183
The Bross Foundation, Lake Forest College, *United States of America*, 183
Budapest International Music Competition, *Hungary*, 183
The Bush Foundation, *United States of America*, 184
Business and Professional Women's Foundation, *United States of America*, 184
Cairo University, *Egypt*, 185
The Caledonian Research Foundation, *Scotland*, 185
The Camargo Foundation, *France*, 185
Cambridge Commonwealth Trust, Cambridge Overseas Trust and Associated Trusts, *England*, 186
Cambridge University Library, *England*, 221
The Canada Council for the Arts, *Canada*, 221
Canada Memorial Foundation, *England*, 222
Canadian Academic Institute in Athens/Canadian Archaeological Institute in Athens (CAIA), *Canada*, 222
Canadian Association of Broadcasters, *Canada*, 222
Canadian Bar Association (CBA), *Canada*, 223
Canadian Blood Services (CBS), *Canada*, 223
Canadian Breast Cancer Research Initiative (CBCRI), *Canada*, 225
Canadian Bureau for International Education (CBIE), *Canada*, 225
Canadian Cystic Fibrosis Foundation (CCFF), *Canada*, 226
Canadian Embassy (USA), *United States of America*, 228
Canadian Federation of University Women (CFUW), *Canada*, 229
Canadian Forestry Foundation, *Canada*, 230
Canadian Foundation for the Study of Infant Deaths, *Canada*, 231
Canadian High Commission, *England*, 231
Canadian Home Economics Association (CHEA), *Canada*, 232
Canadian Institute for Advanced Legal Studies, *Canada*, 232
Canadian Institute of Ukrainian Studies (CIUS), *Canada*, 233
Canadian Institutes of Health Research (CIHR), *Canada*, 233
Canadian Library Association, *Canada*, 234
Canadian Liver Foundation, *Canada*, 235
The Canadian National Institute for the Blind (CNIB), *Canada*, 235
Canadian Nurses Foundation (CNF), *Canada*, 236
Canadian Nurses' Respiratory Society (CNRS), *Canada*, 236
Canadian Physiotherapy Cardio-Respiratory Society (CPCRS), *Canada*, 237

Canadian Society for Chemical Engineering (CSChE), *Canada*, 237
Canadian Society for Chemical Technology, *Canada*, 237
Canadian Society for Chemistry (CSC), *Canada*, 238
Canadian Society for Medical Laboratory Science, *Canada*, 238
Canadian Thoracic Society (CTS), *Canada*, 239
Canadian Tobacco Control Research Initiative (CTCRI), *Canada*, 240
Canadian/Scandinavian Foundation (CSF), *Canada*, 240
Cancer Association of South Africa, *South Africa*, 240
The Cancer Research Society, Inc., *Canada*, 241
The Canon Foundation in Europe, *Netherlands*, 242
Canterbury Historical Association, *New Zealand*, 242
Cardiff University, *Wales*, 242
Carnegie Institution of Washington, *United States of America*, 243
Carnegie Trust for the Universities of Scotland, *Scotland*, 243
Catching The Dream, *United States of America*, 243
Catherine McCaig's Trust, *Scotland*, 244
Catholic Library Association (CLA), *United States of America*, 244
The Catholic University of Louvain (UCL), *Belgium*, 245
CDS International, Inc., *United States of America*, 245
Center for Advanced Study in the Behavioral Sciences, *United States of America*, 245
Center for Defense Information (CDI), *United States of America*, 246
The Center for Field Research (CFR), *United States of America*, 246
Center for Hellenic Studies, *United States of America*, 246
Center for International Studies, University of Missouri-St Louis, *United States of America*, 247
Center for Mental Health Services, *United States of America*, 247
Central Queensland University (CQU), *Australia*, 248
Centre de Recherche en Sciences Neurologiques, *Canada*, 248
Centre for Addiction and Mental Health, *Canada*, 249
Centre for International Mobility (CIMO), *Finland*, 249
Centro de Investigación y Estudios Avanzados Del IPN (CINVESTAV-IPN), *Mexico*, 250
CERIES (Centre de Recherche ed d'Investigations Epidermiques et Sensorielles), *France*, 250
CERN European Laboratory for Particle Physics, *Switzerland*, 251
The Charles A and Anne Morrow Lindbergh Foundation, *United States of America*, 252
Charles and Julia Henry Fund, *England*, 252
Charles Babbage Institute (CBI), *United States of America*, 252
Charles H Hood Foundation, *United States of America*, 252
Chautauqua Institution, *United States of America*, 253
Chemical Heritage Foundation (CHF), *United States of America*, 253
Chemical Institute of Canada, *Canada*, 254
Chihuahuan Desert Research Institute, *United States of America*, 255
Children's Literature Association (ChLA), *United States of America*, 255
Children's Medical Research Institute, *Australia*, 256
Chinese American Medical Society (CAMS), *United States of America*, 257
Choirs Ontario, *Canada*, 257
Christopher Reeve Paralysis Foundation (CRPF), *United States of America*, 257
Chronic Disease Research Foundation (CDRF), *England*, 258
Chronic Granulomatous Disorder Research Trust (CGD), *England*, 258
CIIT - Centers for Health Research, *United States of America*, 259
City University Business School (CUBS), *England*, 259
Clara Haskil Competition, *Switzerland*, 260
Claude Harris Leon Foundation, *South Africa*, 260
Clemson University, *United States of America*, 260
Cleveland Institute of Music, *United States of America*, 260
College of Occupational Therapists, *England*, 261
Colt Foundation, *England*, 262
Columbia University, *United States of America*, 262
Committee on Science and Technology in Developing Countries (COSTED), *India*, 262
The Commonwealth Department of Education, Science and Training (DEST), *Australia*, 263
The Commonwealth Fund of New York, *United States of America*, 263